OFFICIAL Major League BASEBALL FACT BOOK 2003 EDITION

OFFICIAL Major League BASEBALL FACT BOOK 2003 EDITION

Sporting News BOOKS

Historical statistics from *Total Baseball,* the official encyclopedia of Major League Baseball.

ISBN: 0-89204-701-1

10 9 8 7 6 5 4 3 2 1

Contents

INTRODUCTION

Of baseball's many attractive qualities, the one that's perhaps most endearing to us is the game's timelessness.

The game is timeless in the very nature of the way it's played. There's no clock signalling a beginning or an end. A baseball game can go on forever, inning upon inning; you never know beforehand precisely when it might end.

The game is timeless over history. The game today is very much like the game that was played 100 years ago, before the modern era was ushered in. It likely will be roughly the same 100 years from now as well.

That sense of timelessness is a quality we want to bring you in this book, the Official Major League Baseball Fact Book. Whether you're picking up this book during spring training, during the All-Star break or during the World Series, you'll find timely—and timeless—information that you might need.

In a navigable and useful form, the Fact Book presents fans with the details, numbers and pictures of baseball's long and distinguished history. This all-inclusive book looks both to the season ahead and back at the seasons and players that have brought us to 2003.

There are images of the past: Mickey Mantle's 1956 Triple Crown season, Bucky Dent's unlikely homer in 1978, Pete Rose's all-time hits title. We offer a season-by-season review of each team and some of the great players who have played for them, including those players—like Nolan Ryan or Hank Aaron—who sit at the top of the statistical ladders. For a baseball historian, this is a must-have book.

We also offer an extended glimpse back at the 2002 season, including playoff stories and boxes, all the statistics a baseball fan could want and plenty of analysis that the Sporting News has been known for for over 100 years.

And finally, we'll prepare you for the 2003 season ahead and keep you informed throughout the season. We offer player information and projections, team directories, schedules, stadium diagrams, and ticket and broadcast information.

We hope The Fact Book will be a constant reference point for the 2003 season, as well as seasons past.

—THE SPORTING NEWS

2003 Preview

David Eckstein helped lead the Angels to a World Series title in 2002. He will be key for the Angels as they try to repeat.

INTRODUCTION

Baseball changed late last season. And the changes were good. First there was a labor deal, then the Yankees lost again.

Now we can begin a season knowing there will be no threats of a work stoppage. We can begin a season knowing that even though the Yankees could win the World Series, they aren't the overwhelming favorite. Nothing against the Yankees, but dynasties can be boring.

Baseball in 2003 should be anything but boring. There are teams that have a better chance of losing 100 games than reaching the playoffs. But there are a dozen clubs that have a legitimate shot at winning the World Series, including the world champion Angels, who showed us last October how exciting baseball can be.

READY TO RISE?

A year ago, hardly anyone predicted the Angels would reach the postseason, much less win the World Series. It seems unlikely an upstart team will go as far this season, but if one does, chances are it will be one of these five.

Phillies. They have the best chance to break through. Jim Thome, David Bell and Kevin Millwood bring postseason savvy to a team with a talented nucleus. But the rotation beyond Millwood is inexperienced, and the bullpen is questionable. Manager Larry Bowa can't blame his former scapegoat, Scott Rolen, if things go wrong.

Cubs. General manager Jim Hendry spent the winter assembling veteran pieces for new manager Dusty Baker. The Cubs' rotation is among the game's most promising, and their bench and bullpen are improved. But their hitters need to cut down on strikeouts and improve their on-base percentage.

Dodgers. Fred McGriff should help the team improve its anemic offense. The middle-infield combination of Cesar Izturis and Joe Thurston is young, but look out if pitchers Kevin Brown and Darren Dreifort make successful comebacks.

Blue Jays. No one expects them to overtake the Yankees and Red Sox. The Jays reached 78 wins last season only after going 19-8 in September. Still, Cory Lidle joins a rotation fronted by Roy Halladay, and the Jays' young position talent offers considerable promise.

White Sox. It all depends upon how quickly their young talent develops and whether their shaky infield defense compromises their pitching. The addition of closer Billy Koch is a plus, and if Frank Thomas rebounds with a big season, the team could contend in the weak A.L. Central.

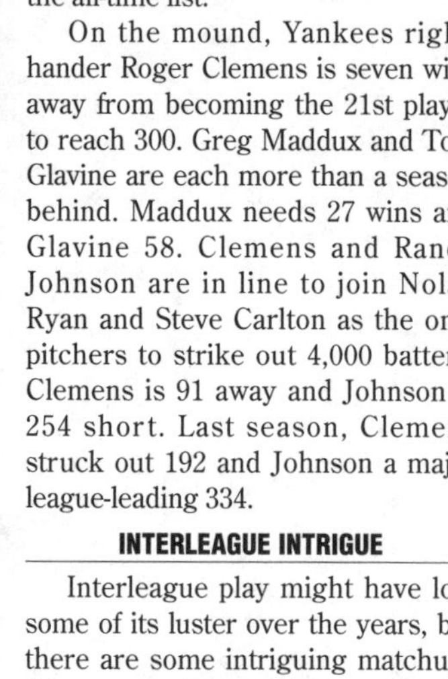

If the Astros keep developing good young pitchers like Roy Oswalt and Wilfredo Rodriguez (pictured), they could be the team to beat in the N.L. Central.

IS .400 NEXT?

Five MVPs, 73 homers, 198 walks, post-season bugaboo dispatched. What can Barry Bonds do for his next encore? How about hit .400? He has a real chance of doing so. His average dropped to .262 in 1999 but since then has jumped 44, 22 and 42 points, an average of 36 each season. He hit .370 in 2002, so assuming he keeps his average increase, he'll hit .406 this season.

Bonds had 403 at-bats and 149 hits last season. If he had picked up just 13 more hits (162-for-403), he would have hit .402. Twelve more hits would have put him at .3995, which MLB considers to be .400.

Bonds will turn 39 in July, but there's no evidence he understands what that is supposed to mean. On the contrary, anecdotal and statistical evidence suggest the gap between his skills and pitchers' attempts to get him out is growing. His hand-eye coordination is unmatched, and his patience at the plate would make Job seem jittery.

MARCHING TOWARD 500

Never before have more than two players reached 500 home runs for a career in the same season. This season, there could be four. Sammy Sosa might do it on opening day. He needs just one. Rafael Palmeiro is 10 away, Fred McGriff needs 22, and Ken Griffey Jr. is 32 short of the mark reached by only 17 players.

Though there will be a rush for 500 homers, it would take a miracle for anyone to join the 3,000-hit club this season. Can you guess which active player has the second-most career hits after Rickey Henderson, 44, who reached 3,000 in 2001 and has 3,040 entering his 25th season in the majors? Give up? It's Palmeiro. He has had a rather unheralded career, yet he could finish as the fourth player with 500 home runs and 3,000 hits. He is 366 hits away from 3,000. Behind Palmeiro is Roberto Alomar, who needs 454 hits. Barry Bonds needs 538 hits for 3,000, but he could reach a different milestone this season. Bonds needs 47 home runs to catch his godfather, Willie Mays, at 660 for third place on the all-time list.

On the mound, Yankees right-hander Roger Clemens is seven wins away from becoming the 21st player to reach 300. Greg Maddux and Tom Glavine are each more than a season behind. Maddux needs 27 wins and Glavine 58. Clemens and Randy Johnson are in line to join Nolan Ryan and Steve Carlton as the only pitchers to strike out 4,000 batters. Clemens is 91 away and Johnson is 254 short. Last season, Clemens struck out 192 and Johnson a major league-leading 334.

INTERLEAGUE INTRIGUE

Interleague play might have lost some of its luster over the years, but there are some intriguing matchups this season. Along with the geographical rivalries, the N.L. Central plays the A.L. East, the N.L. West faces the A.L. Central, and the N.L. East squares off against the A.L. West.

A few series to watch:

Twins at Giants, June 3-5. The young and talented Twins get their shot at Barry & Co. These teams could hook up again in October.

A's at Phillies, June 6-8. The powerful Phillies lineup, which now includes Thome, faces one of the top pitching staffs in baseball.

Mets at Rangers, June 10-12. This is the battle of the most overpaid teams in baseball. Don't expect great baseball to be played, but there will be some potent bats on display.

Cardinals at Yankees, June 13-15. Two of the most storied franchises in baseball hook up for the first time since 1964, when the Cardinals beat the Yankees in the World Series in seven games. Between them, they have won more Fall Classics than any other teams in baseball.

Astros at Red Sox, June 13-15. Jeff Bagwell gets his shot at the team that let him go, and Pedro Martinez gets another chance at N.L. hitters.

Angels at Dodgers, June 20-22; Dodgers at Angels, June 27-29. The defending world champs face their local rivals. If healthy, the Dodgers pitching staff could give the hard-hitting Angels some good games. This should be a fun series to watch twice.

—BY KEN ROSENTHAL AND JEFF PAUR

MAJOR LEAGUE BASEBALL DIRECTORY

Commissioner Bud Selig

President & COO Robert DuPuy

Address ....245 Park Avenue, New York, NY 10167
Telephone ....212-931-7800; 212-949-5654 (FAX)
Website ....www.mlb.com
Commissioner of Baseball ....Allan H. "Bud" Selig
President and chief operating officer....Robert DuPuy
Executive vice president., baseball operations ....Richard "Sandy" Alderson
Executive vice president, business ....Timothy J. Brosnan
Executive vice president, labor relations and human resources ....Robert D. Manfred
Executive vice president, administration ....John McHale
Senior vice president, international business operations ....Paul Archey
Senior vice president, security and facilities ....Kevin Hallinan
Senior vice president, public relations ....Rich Levin
Senior vice president and chief financial officer....Jonathan Mariner
Senior vice president, special events ....Marla Miller
Senior vice president and general counsel ....Ethan Orlinsky
Senior vice president and general counsel ....Tom Ostertag
Senior vice president, licensing ....Howard Smith
Senior vice president, baseball operations ....Jimmie Lee Solomon
Senior vice president, business affairs domestic & international ....Chris Tully
Vice president, domestic licensing ....Steve Armus
Vice president, community affairs....Tom Brasuell
Vice president, baseball operations and administration ....Ed Burns
Vice president, management information systems ....Julio Carbonell
Vice president, accounting and treasurer....Bob Clark
Vice president and general counsel, labor relations ....Frank Coonelly
Vice president, club relations and scheduling....Katy Feeney
Vice president,productions ....Dave Gavant
Vice president, domestic licensing-Cooperstown ....Colin Hagen
Vice president, publishing and photographs ....Don Hintz
Vice president, corporate sales ....Justin Johnson
Vice president, international licensing....Shawn Lawson-Cummings
Vice president, strategic planning, recruiting and diversity ....Wendy L. Lewis
Vice president, broadcast operations....Bernadette McDonald
Vice president, international baseball operations....Lou Melendez
Vice president, club relations ....Phyllis Merhige
Vice president, umpiring ....Ralph Nelson
Vice president, marketing and advertising ....Jacqueline Parks
Vice president, educational programming ....Sharon Robinson
Vice president, human resources....Ray Scott
Vice president, on-field operations....Bob Watson

LABOR RELATIONS COMMITTEE

Address ....245 Park Avenue, New York, NY 10167
Telephone....212-931-7401, 212-949-5690 (FAX)
Executive V.P., labor and human resources ....Robert D. Manfred Jr.
Vice president and general labor counsel ....Francis X. Coonelly
Associate counsels ....Derek Jackson, Paul Mifsud
Deputy general counsel....Jennifer Gefsky
System administration....John Ricco

NATIONAL BASEBALL HALL OF FAME AND MUSEUM

Address ....P.O. Box 590, Cooperstown, NY 13326
Telephone ....607-547-7200, 607-547-2044 (FAX)
Hall of Fame board of directors chairman ....Jane Forbes Clark
President ....Dale Petroskey
Vice president of business and administration....Bill Haase
Vice president and chief curator ....William T. Spencer Jr.
Curator of collections ....Peter P. Clark
Executive director of retail marketing ....Barbara Shinn
Controller....Frances L. Althiser
Librarian ....James L. Gates
Vice president of communications and education....Jeff Idelson

MINOR LEAGUE BASEBALL
NATIONAL ASSOCIATION OF PROFESSIONAL BASEBALL LEAGUES

Address....P.O. Box A, St. Petersburg, FL 33731
Telephone....727-822-6937; 727-821-5819 (FAX)
President/CEO....Mike Moore
Vice President ....Stan Brand
Vice president, administration/COO ....Pat O'Conner
General counsel....Scott Poley
General counsel ....George Yund
Executive director/business operations....Misann Ellmaker
Executive director/Professional Baseball Umpire Corporation ....Mike Fitzpatrick
Director/media relations....Jim Ferguson
Director of baseball operations ....Tim Brunswick
Director of Professional Baseball Employment Opportunities ....Ann Perkins

MAJOR LEAGUE BASEBALL PLAYERS ASSOCIATION

Address....12 E. 49th St., 24th Floor, New York, NY 10017
Telephone....212-826-0808, 212-752-3649 (FAX)
Executive director and general counsel ....Donald M. Fehr
Special assistants ....Tony Bernazard, Phil Bradley, Steve Rogers
Associate general counsel....Eugene D. Orza
Assistant general counsel....Jeff Fannell, Doyle R. Pryor, Michael Weiner
Counsel ....Robert Leneghan
Director of licensing ....Judy Heeter
Director of communications ....Greg Bouris

MAJOR LEAGUE BASEBALL PLAYERS ALUMNI ASSOCIATION

Address ....1631 Mesa Avenue, Suite B, Colorado Springs, Colo. 80906
Telephone....719-477-1870, 719-477-1875 (FAX)
President ....Brooks Robinson
Vice presidents ....Bob Boone, George Brett, Mike Hegan
Chuck Hinton, Al Kaline, Carl Erskine
Rusty Staub, Robin Yount
Vice chairman ....Fred Valentine

MAJOR LEAGUE SCOUTING BUREAU

Address ....3500 Porsche Way, Suite 100, Ontario, CA 91764
Telephone....909-980-1881, 909-980-7794 (FAX)
Director ....Frank Marcos

BASEBALL ASSISTANCE TEAM INC.

Address ....245 Park Avenue, New York, NY 10167
Telephone 212-931-7821
Chairman....Bobby Murcer
President ....Earl Wilson
Vice presidents ....Steve Garvey, Bob Gibson, Lou Gorman, Ed Stack
Executive director....James J. Martin
Secretary ....Tom Ostertag
Treasurer ....Jonathan Mariner

ASSOCIATION OF PROFESSIONAL BASEBALL PLAYERS OF AMERICA

Address ....1820 W. Orangewood Ave., Suite 206, Orange, CA 92868
Telephone....714-935-9993, 714-935-0431 (FAX)
President....John J. McHale
Vice presidents ....Roland Hemond, Robert Kennedy
Secretary/treasurer ....Dick Beverage

BASEBALL WRITERS' ASSOCIATION OF AMERICA

President ....Paul Hagen, Philadelphia Daily News
Vice president ....Drew Olson, Milwaukee Journal Sentinel
Secretary/treasurer ....Jack O'Connell, Hartford Courant

WORLD UMPIRES ASSOCIATION

Address....P.O. Box 760, Cocoa, FL 32923-0760
Telephone....321-637-3471; 321-633-7018 (FAX)
President....John Hirschbeck
Vice president ....Joe Brinkman
Secretary/treasurer ....Tim Welke
Labor counsel....Joel Smith

ELIAS SPORTS BUREAU

Address....500 Fifth Ave., New York, NY 10110
Telephone....212-869-1530, 212-354-0980 (FAX)
General manager ....Seymour Siwoff

SPORTSTICKER ENTERPRISES, L.P.

Address ....Harborside Financial Center, 800 Plaza Two, Jersey City, NJ 07311
Boston office ....Boston Fish Pier, West Building No. 1, Suite 302, Boston, MA 02210
Telephone....201-309-1200; 201-860-9742 (FAX)
Boston office ....617-951-1379; 617-737-9960 (FAX)
General manager ....Jim Morganthaler
Director, minor league operations ....Jim Keller
Assistant director, minor league operations ....Michael Walczak

ANAHEIM ANGELS

AMERICAN LEAGUE WEST DIVISION

2003 SEASON

Angels Schedule

Home games shaded; D—Day game (games starting before 5 p.m.); *—All-Star Game at Comiskey Park, Chicago. Subject to changes. †Game played in Puerto Rico.

March/April

SUN	MON	TUE	WED	THU	FRI	SAT
30 TEX	31	1 TEX	2 D TEX	3	4 OAK	5 D OAK
6 OAK	7	8 D SEA	9 SEA	10 SEA	11 OAK	12 OAK
13 D OAK	14 TEX	15 TEX	16 TEX	17 D TEX	18 SEA	19 SEA
20 D SEA	21	22 NYY	23 NYY	24 NYY	25 BOS	26 BOS
27 BOS	28	29 CLE	30 CLE			

May

SUN	MON	TUE	WED	THU	FRI	SAT
				1 CLE	2 TOR	3 D TOR
4 D TOR	5	6 CLE	7 CLE	8 CLE	9 TOR	10 TOR
11 D TOR	12	13 NYY	14 NYY	15 NYY	16 BOS	17 D BOS
18 D BOS	19	20 BAL	21 BAL	22 BAL	23 TB	24 D TB
25 D TB	26	27 BAL	28 BAL	29 TB	30 TB	31 TB

June

SUN	MON	TUE	WED	THU	FRI	SAT
1 D TB	2	3 † MON	4 † MON	5 † MON	6 FLA	7 FLA
8 D FLA	9 PHI	10 PHI	11 PHI	12	13 NYM	14 NYM
15 D NYM	16 SEA	17 SEA	18 SEA	19 D SEA	20 LA	21 D LA
22 LA	23	24 SEA	25 SEA	26 SEA	27 LA	28 LA
29 D LA	30 TEX					

July

SUN	MON	TUE	WED	THU	FRI	SAT
		1 TEX	2 TEX	3 TEX	4 OAK	5 OAK
6 D OAK	7	8 KC	9 KC	10 D KC	11 MIN	12 D MIN
13 D MIN	14	15 *	16	17 BAL	18 BAL	19 BAL
20 D BAL	21 TB	22 D TB	23 TEX	24 TEX	25 OAK	26 D OAK
27 D OAK	28 OAK	29 NYY	30 NYY	31 NYY		

August

SUN	MON	TUE	WED	THU	FRI	SAT
					1 TOR	2 TOR
3 D TOR	4	5 BOS	6 BOS	7 BOS	8 CLE	9 D CLE
10 D CLE	11 CWS	12 CWS	13 CWS	14 CWS	15 DET	16 DET
17 D DET	18 CWS	19 CWS	20 CWS	21 DET	22 DET	23 D DET
24 D DET	25	26 MIN	27 MIN	28 D MIN	29 KC	30 KC
31 D KC						

September

SUN	MON	TUE	WED	THU	FRI	SAT
	1 D MIN	2 MIN	3 D MIN	4	5 KC	6 KC
7 D KC	8 OAK	9 OAK	10 OAK	11 D OAK	12 SEA	13 SEA
14 D SEA	15 OAK	16 OAK	17 D OAK	18	19 TEX	20 TEX
21 D TEX	22 SEA	23 SEA	24 D SEA	25	26 TEX	27 D TEX
28 D TEX						

FRONT-OFFICE DIRECTORY

Owner .... The Walt Disney Company
Chairman and CEO, The Walt Disney Company .... Michael Eisner
President, Walt Disney Parks and Resorts .... Jay Rasulo
Senior vice president, business operations .... Kevin Uhlich
Vice president and general manager .... Bill Stoneman
Vice president, finance/administration .... Andy Roundtree
Vice president, communications .... Tim Mead
Administrative assistant, general manager .... Laura Fazioli
Administrative assistant, operations, sales and marketing .... Leslie Flammini
Administrative assistant, finance/Administration .... Meta Maynard
Administrative assistant, communications .... Trish Pene
Assistant general manager .... Ken Forsch
Special assistants to the general manager .... Preston Gomez, Gary Sutherland
Director, scouting .... Donny Rowland
Director, player development .... Tony Reagins
Manager, baseball operations .... Abe Flores
Administrative assistant, player development .... Maria Arellano
Clubhouse manager .... Ken Higdon
Assistant equipment manager .... Keith Tarter
Visiting clubhouse manager .... Brian Harkins
Clubhouse staff .... Geoff Bennett, Michael Martinez, Raymond Martinez, Corey Morbeck, Steve Rivera, Scott Smith, Hector Vasquez
Senior video coordinator .... Diego Lopez
Video coordinator .... Ruben Montano
Mesa operations .... Eric Blum
Manager, baseball information .... Larry Babcock
Manager, media services .... Nancy Mazmanian
Manager, community development .... Matt Bennett
Publications manager .... Doug Ward
Traveling secretary .... Tom Taylor
Media relations representatives .... Eric Kay, Marty Sewell
Speakers' bureau .... Clyde Wright, Bobby Grich
Club photographers .... VJ Lovero, John Cordes, Debora Robinson, Bob Binder

MINOR LEAGUE AFFILIATES

Class	Team	League	Manager
AAA	Salt Lake	Pacific Coast	Mike Brumley
AA	Arkansas	Texas	Tyrone Boykin
A	Cedar Rapids	Midwest	Todd Claus
A	Rancho Cucamonga	California	Bobby Meacham
Rookie	Provo	Pioneer	Tom Kotchman
Rookie	Mesa Angels	Arizona	Brian Harper

ASSISTANCE STAFF

Medical director
Dr. Lewis Yocum

Team physician
Dr. Craig Milhouse

Head athletic trainer
Ned Bergert

International supervisor
Clay Daniel

Eastern supervisor
Marc Russo

Western supervisor
Tom Davis

Midwestern supervisor
Ron Marigny

National cross-checkers
Guy Mader Hank Sargent

Major league scouts
Jay Hankins, Jon Niederer, Rich Schlenker, Moose Stubing, Dale Sutherland, Gary Sutherland, John Van Ornum

Scouts
George Biron, Brian Bridges, John Burden, Tom Burns, Arnold Cochran, Tim Corcoran, Jeff Crane, David Crowson, Bobby Dejardin, Kevin Ham, Tom Kotchman, Dan Lynch, Chad MacDonald, Chris McAlpin, Scott Richardson, Jeff Scholzen, Mike Silvestri, Jack Uhey

International scouts
Amador Arias, Felipe Gutierrez, Tak Kawamoto, Charlie Kim, Alex Messier, Leo Perez, Carlos Porte, Dennys Suarez, Takanori Takeuchi, Ramon Valenzuela, Grant Weir

BROADCAST INFORMATION

Radio: ESPN-AM (710).
TV: KCAL-TV (Channel 9).
Cable TV: Fox Sports West.

SPRING TRAINING

Ballpark (city): Tempe Diablo Stadium (Tempe, Ariz.).
Ticket information: 714-940-2000.

BALLPARK INFORMATION

Ballpark (capacity, surface)
Edison International Field of Anaheim
(45,050, grass)

Address
2000 Gene Autry Way
Anaheim, CA 92806

Official website
www.angelsbaseball.com

Business phones
714-940-2000

Ticket information
714-634-2000

Ticket prices
$70 (diamond club), $45 (club MVP)
$44 (field MVP), $32 (terrace MVP)
$30 (club loge), $27 (field box)
$25 (terrace box), $20 (lower view MVP)
$15 (lower view)
$12 (upper view value)
$10 (RF pavilion-adult)
$9 (LF pavilion-adult)
$7 (RF pavilion-child)
$5 (LF pavilion-child)

Field dimensions (from home plate)
To left field at foul line, 330 feet
To center field, 400 feet
To right field at foul line, 330 feet

First game played
April 19, 1966 (White Sox 3, Angels 1)

Follow the Angels all season at: www.sportingnews.com/baseball/teams/angels/

ANGELS SPRING ROSTER

No.	PITCHERS	B/T	Ht./Wt.	Born	2002 clubs	Projection
27	Appier, Kevin	R/R	6-2/200	12-6-67	Anaheim	Won 14 games and had a sub-4.00 ERA as No. 2 starter. Expect the same.
51	Callaway, Mickey	R/R	6-2/200	5-13-75	Salt Lake, Anaheim	Could catch on as the club's No. 5 starter.
53	Donnelly, Brendan	R/R	6-3/205	7-4-71	Salt Lake, Anaheim	Tough on righties, he'll be back in the bullpen for 2003.
	Fischer, Rich	R/R	6-3/180	10-21-80	Arkansas, Rancho Cucamonga	Won eight games between Class A and Class AA. Will be back in minors.
	Green, Steve	R/R	6-2/195	1-26-78	DID NOT PLAY	Starter looking to rebound from injuries that kept off the mound last season.
	Jenks, Bobby	R/R	6-3/240	3-14-81	Arkansas, Rancho Cucamonga	Top prospect just learning how to pitch. Give him one more year.
41	Lackey, John	R/R	6-6/205	10-23-78	Salt Lake, Anaheim	He's tough on lefties, and will be the club's No. 4 starter.
47	Lukasiewicz, Mark	L/L	6-5/240	3-8-73	Anaheim, Salt Lake	Could make the team as a lefty out of the bullpen.
52	Miadich, Bart	R/R	6-4/205	2-3-76	Salt Lake	Had 14 saves in Class AAA. Looks to be ready for the majors.
36	Ortiz, Ramon	R/R	6-0/170	3-23-73	Anaheim	Won 15 games with 3.77 ERA. Gives team solid top of the rotation performance.
40	Percival, Troy	R/R	6-3/235	8-9-69	Anaheim	Still an elite closer, you can count on another 40-save season.
58	Pote, Lou	R/R	6-3/208	8-21-71	Anaheim, Salt Lake	Still trying to find a place with the Angels. Can start or relieve.
57	Rodriguez, Francisco	R/R	6-0/175	1-7-82	Arkansas, Salt Lake, Anaheim	Claimed a spot in the bullpen with his postseason performance.
60	Schoeneweis, Scott	L/L	6-0/185	10-2-73	Anaheim	Went from starter to reliever with tremendous success.
34	Sele, Aaron	R/R	6-5/220	6-25-70	Anaheim	Could be a question mark for 2003 after bypassing shoulder surgery.
62	Shields, Scot	R/R	6-1/175	7-22-75	Salt Lake, Anaheim	Another solid pitcher out of the bullpen, might have to battle to keep his job.
54	Turnbow, Derrick	R/R	6-3/180	1-25-78	Arizona Angels, Rancho Cuca.	Injuries limited him to only 16 games, another season in the minors is on tap.
56	Washburn, Jarrod	L/L	6-1/190	8-13-74	Anaheim	Became the club's staff ace. He is tough on lefties.
77	Weber, Ben	R/R	6-4/210	11-17-69	Anaheim	His delivery keeps hitters off balance. Won seven games and had seven saves, too.
32	Wise, Matt	R/R	6-4/195	11-18-75	Salt Lake, Anaheim	Could make the team, could be back in the minors. Depends on how he pitches.

No.	CATCHERS	B/T	Ht./Wt.	Born	2002 clubs	Projection
1	Molina, Bengie	R/R	5-11/210	7-20-74	Anaheim, Rancho Cucamonga	As long as he stays healthy, he could win another Gold Glove.
28	Molina, Jose	R/R	6-1/215	6-3-75	Salt Lake, Anaheim	In a brief audition, he hit .271; should be the backup.
	Nieves, Wil	R/R	5-11/190	9-25-77	Portland, San Diego	Gives the Angels depth at catcher after being claimed off waivers from the Padres.

No.	INFIELDERS	B/T	Ht./Wt.	Born	2002 clubs	Projection
5	Amezaga, Alfredo	B/R	5-10/165	1-16-78	Salt Lake, Anaheim	Solid defensive player, still needs a little work at the plate.
22	Eckstein, David	R/R	5-8/170	1-20-75	Anaheim	Just keeps getting better and better, in the field and at the plate.
6	Figgins, Chone	B/R	5-9/155	1-22-78	Salt Lake, Anaheim	Showed he can be a key player off the bench in the playoffs.
	Fullmer, Brad	L/R	6-0/220	1-17-75	Anaheim	Hit .289 with 15 homers in limited at-bats in 2002.
10	Gil, Benji	R/R	6-2/210	10-6-72	Anaheim, Salt Lake	Part-time player hit .285 last season, don't expect more.
25	Glaus, Troy	R/R	6-5/245	8-3-76	Anaheim	Drove in 111 runs last season, could have more if he cuts down on strikeouts.
2	Kennedy, Adam	L/R	6-1/192	1-10-76	Anaheim	Looks like he'll get the job at second, now that he's shown he can hit lefties.
	Quinlan, Robb	R/R	6-1/200	3-17-77	Salt Lake	Batted .333 in Class AAA with 20 homers and 112 RBIs.
23	Spiezio, Scott	B/R	6-2/225	9-21-72	Anaheim	Not your traditional power-hitting first baseman, but he gets the job done.

No.	OUTFIELDERS	B/T	Ht./Wt.	Born	2002 clubs	Projection
16	Anderson, Garret	L/L	6-3/228	6-30-72	Anaheim	Led the league in doubles, should continue to tear apart opposing pitchers.
33	DaVanon, Jeff	B/R	6-0/185	12-8-73	Anaheim, Salt Lake, Ariz. Angels	Good minor league hitter has yet to bring that success to the majors.
17	Erstad, Darin	L/L	6-2/220	6-4-74	Anaheim	Sacrificed numbers for good of the team. 2003 should be similar.
38	Haynes, Nathan	L/L	5-9/170	9-7-79	Rancho Cucamonga, Salt Lake	Likely to spend another year in minors. Doesn't walk a lot or hit for high average.
16	Owens, Eric	R/R	6-0/208	2-3-71	Florida	Will replace Alex Ochoa as fourth outfielder/designated hitter.
15	Salmon, Tim	R/R	6-3/225	8-24-68	Anaheim	Things could get interesting in '03 if Salmon stays healthy.
	Wesson, Barry	R/R	6-2/212	4-6-77	Houston, New Orleans	Strikes out too much, but will provide depth in the minors.

THE COACHING STAFF

Mike Scioscia, manager.

Bud Black, pitching coach.

Alfredo Griffin, first base coach.

Mickey Hatcher, hitting coach.

Joe Maddon, bench coach.

Bobby Ramos, bullpen coach.

Ron Roenicke, third base coach.

THE TOP NEWCOMERS

Eric Owens: Will provide the Angels with a versatile bat and a defensive replacement for Tim Salmon in the late innings.

THE TOP PROSPECTS

Robb Quinlan: Has won two Most Valuable Player awards in the minors. If anyone in the Angels lineup is hurt, Quinlan is likely to get the first call up from the minors.

Bobby Jenks: Has harnessed a fastball that reaches 100 mph. It's just a matter of time before he makes his mark in the majors.

BALTIMORE ORIOLES

AMERICAN LEAGUE EAST DIVISION

2003 SEASON

Orioles Schedule

Home games shaded; D—Day game (games starting before 5 p.m.); *—All-Star Game at Comiskey Park, Chicago. Subject to changes.

March/April

SUN	MON	TUE	WED	THU	FRI	SAT
30	31 D CLE	1	2 CLE	3 CLE	4 BOS	5 D BOS
6 D BOS	7	8 TB	9 TB	10 TB	11 D BOS	12 BOS
13 D BOS	14	15 CLE	16 CLE	17 CLE	18 TB	19 D TB
20 D TB	21 TB	22 CWS	23 CWS	24 CWS	25 TB	26 TB
27 D TB	28	29 DET	30 DET			

May

SUN	MON	TUE	WED	THU	FRI	SAT
				1 D DET	2 KC	3 D KC
4 D KC	5 DET	6 DET	7 D DET	8 KC	9 KC	10 KC
11 D KC	12	13 CWS	14 CWS	15 CWS	16 TB	17 TB
18 D TB	19	20 ANA	21 ANA	22 ANA	23 TEX	24 TEX
25 D TEX	26	27 ANA	28 ANA	29 TEX	30 TEX	31 TEX

June

SUN	MON	TUE	WED	THU	FRI	SAT
1 D TEX	2	3 HOU	4 HOU	5 HOU	6 STL	7 D STL
8 D STL	9	10 CUB	11 CUB	12 CUB	13 MIL	14 MIL
15 D MIL	16	17 TOR	18 TOR	19 D TOR	20 ATL	21 ATL
22 D ATL	23 TOR	24 TOR	25 TOR	26 TOR	27 PHI	28 PHI
29 D PHI	30 NYY					

July

SUN	MON	TUE	WED	THU	FRI	SAT
		1 NYY	2 D NYY	3	4 TOR	5 TOR
6 D TOR	7	8 SEA	9 SEA	10 SEA	11 OAK	12 D OAK
13 D OAK	14	15 *	16	17 ANA	18 ANA	19 ANA
20 D ANA	21 TEX	22 D TEX	23 NYY	24 D NYY	25 TOR	26 D TOR
27 D TOR	28	29 MIN	30 MIN	31 MIN		

August

SUN	MON	TUE	WED	THU	FRI	SAT
					1 BOS	2 BOS
3 D BOS	4 MIN	5 MIN	6 MIN	7 D MIN	8 BOS	9 BOS
10 D BOS	11 TB	12 TB	13 D TB	14	15 NYY	16 NYY
17 D NYY	18	19 TB	20 TB	21 TB	22 NYY	23 D NYY
24 D NYY	25 NYY	26 OAK	27 OAK	28 D OAK	29 SEA	30 D SEA
31 D SEA						

September

SUN	MON	TUE	WED	THU	FRI	SAT
	1	2 OAK	3 OAK	4 OAK	5 SEA	6 SEA
7 D SEA	8 BOS	9 BOS	10 D BOS	11	12 TOR	13 D TOR
14 D TOR	15 NYY	16 NYY	17 NYY	18 NYY	19 TOR	20 TOR
21 D TOR	22 BOS	23 BOS	24 BOS	25 BOS	26 NYY	27 D NYY
28 D NYY						

FRONT-OFFICE DIRECTORY

Chairman of the board/chief executive officer .... Peter G. Angelos
Vice chairman/chief operating officer .... Joseph E. Foss
Executive vice president .... John P. Angelos
Vice president/chief financial officer .... Robert A. Ames, CPA
Executive vice president/baseball operations .... Jim Beattie
Vice president/baseball operations .... Mike Flanagan
Special assistant to the v.p., baseball operations .... Ed Kenney Jr.,
Director/scouting .... Tony DeMacio
Director/minor league operations .... To be announced
Assistant director/minor league operations .... Tripp Norton
Traveling secretary .... Philip E. Itzoe
Executive director/communications .... Spiro Alafassos
Director/public relations .... Bill Stetka
Manager/baseball information .... Kevin Behan
Manager/communications .... Monica Pence
Director/ballpark operations .... Roger Hayden
Director/community relations .... Julie Wagner
Director/publishing & creative media .... Jessica Fisher
Director/fan & ticket services .... Don Grove
Director/sales .... Matt Dryer
Director/information systems .... James L. Kline
Director/corporate sponsorship & sales .... Ron Brown

MINOR LEAGUE AFFILIATES

Class	Team	League	Manager
AAA	Ottawa	International	To be announced
AA	Bowie	Eastern	To be announced
A	Frederick	Carolina	To be announced
A	Delmarva	South Atlantic	To be announced
A	Aberdeen	New York-Pennsylvania	To be announced
Rookie	Bluefield	Appalachian	To be announced
Rookie	Gulf Coast Orioles	Gulf Coast	To be announced

BROADCAST INFORMATION

Radio: WBAL-AM (1090).
TV: WJZ (Channel 13), WNUV (Channel 54), WFTY (Channel 50, Washington, D.C.).
Cable TV: Comcast SportsNet.

SPRING TRAINING

Ballpark (city): Fort Lauderdale Stadium (Fort Lauderdale, Fla.).
Ticket information: 954-776-1921.

ASSISTANCE STAFF

Head athletic trainer
Richie Bancells

Assistant athletic trainer
Brian Ebel

Strength and conditioning coach
Tim Bishop

Advance scout
Deacon Jones

Professional scouts
Larry Himes, Bruce Kison, Curt Motton, Tim Thompson, Fred Uhlman Sr.

National cross-checker
Shawn Pender

Regional cross-checkers
Dave Blume, Deron Rombach

Full-time scouts
Joe Almaraz, Bill Bliss, Ralph Garr Jr., John Gillette, Troy Hoerner, Jim Howard, Dave Jennings, Ray Krawczyk, Gil Kubski, Lamar North, Nick Presto, Harry Shelton, Ed Sprague, Marc Tramuta, Mike Tullier, Dominic Viola, Marc Ziegler

Director, Latin American scouting
Carlos Bernhardt

Caribbean & South Amer. supervisor
Jesus Halabi

International scouts
Rob Derkson, Ubaldo Heredia, Salvador Ramirez, Arturo Sanchez, Brett Ward

BALLPARK INFORMATION

Ballpark (capacity, surface)
Oriole Park at Camden Yards (48,190, grass)

Address
333 W. Camden St.
Baltimore, MD 21201

Official website
www.theorioles.com

Business phone
410-685-9800

Ticket information
410-481-SEAT

Ticket prices
$40 (club box), $35 (field box sec. 20-54)
$32 (field box sec. 14-18, 56-58)
$27 (terrace box sec. 17-55)
$25 (LF club sec. 272-288; lower box sec. 6-12, 60-64)
$23 (terrace box sec. 1-15, 59-65)
$20 (upper box sec. 316-356)
$18 (LF lower box sec. 66-86 & 67-75; upper box sec. 306-312 & 358-372; lower res. sec. 17-55)
$15 (LF upper box sec. 374-388; lower res. sec. 4, 7-15, 59-75, 77-87; upper res. sec. 316-356)
$13 (upper res., sec. 306-312 & 360-364; Eutaw St. res. sec. 90-98)
$9 (upper res. sec. 368-372; LF upper res., sec. 374-388)
$8 (standing room)

Field dimensions (from home plate)
To left field at foul line, 333 feet
To center field, 400 feet
To right field at foul line, 318 feet

First game played
April 6, 1992 (Orioles 2, Indians 0)

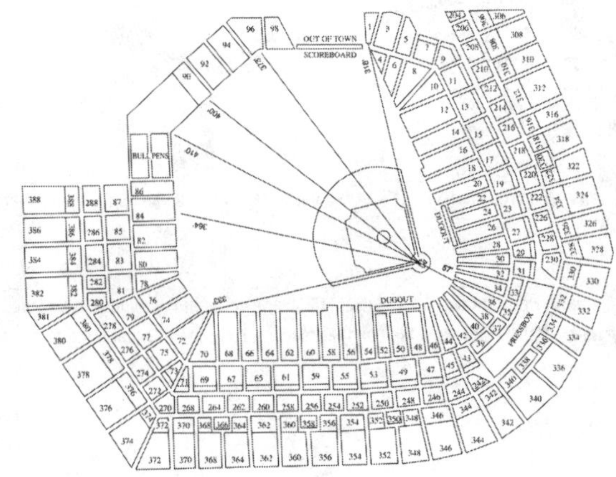

Follow the Orioles all season at: www.sportingnews.com/baseball/teams/orioles/

ORIOLES SPRING ROSTER

No.	PITCHERS	B/T	Ht./Wt.	Born	2002 clubs	Projection
30	Bauer, Rick	R/R	6-6/215	1-10-77	Baltimore, Rochester	Will be back in the bullpen for 2003. Won six games there last season.
51	Bechler, Steve	R/R	6-2/210	11-18-79	Bowie, Rochester, Baltimore	Pitched just over four innings in September. Will likely need a year in Class AAA.
	Bedard, Erik	L/L	6-1/180	3-6-79	Bowie, Baltimore	Had excellent start in Bowie, but then was hurt for the last half of the season.
	Cabrera, Daniel	R/R	6-7/210	5-28-81	Bluefield	Improved control has put this prospect on the radar. Still a year or two away.
	Daal, Omar	L/L	6-3/204	3-1-72	Los Angeles	Will be a valuable innings eater for Orioles staff.
47	Douglass, Sean	R/R	6-6/200	4-28-79	Rochester, Baltimore	Only 23, he's started 12 games in the majors over the last two years.
49	Driskill, Travis	R/R	6-0/225	8-1-71	Rochester, Baltimore	Average stuff, he started getting knocked around after hitters got a look.
57	DuBose, Eric	L/L	6-3/231	5-15-76	Rochester, Bowie, Baltimore	Has yet to dominate in the minors, pitched decently in September call up.
19	Erickson, Scott	R/R	6-4/230	2-2-68	Baltimore	Returned from injuries and still struggling to regain velocity. 2003 will be better.
27	Groom, Buddy	L/L	6-2/207	7-10-65	Baltimore	Solid lefty out of the bullpen. Dominates lefthanded hitters.
41	Hentgen, Pat	R/R	6-2/195	11-13-68	GCOr., Del., Abe., Bow., Fre., Bal.	Returned from elbow surgery and should continue to improve as season goes on.
16	Johnson, Jason	R/R	6-6/235	10-27-73	Baltimore, Bowie	Showed better command, but trips to the disabled list derailed his season.
50	Julio, Jorge	R/R	6-1/190	3-3-79	Baltimore	Had 25 saves for the Orioles, he'll become more valuable if the O's can win more.
	Ligtenberg, Kerry	R/R	6-2/215	5-11-71	Atlanta	Will be used in variety of roles in Orioles bullpen.
13	Lopez, Rodrigo	R/R	6-1/180	12-14-75	Baltimore	15-game winner was the best starting pitcher the Orioles had last season.
	Paradis, Mike	R/R	6-3/190	5-3-78	Bowie	Lost 13 games and had ERA over 5.00. Will be back in minors.
43	Ponson, Sidney	R/R	6-1/225	11-2-76	Baltimore	Shoulder problems led to the disabled list. Will need to overcome injuries.
	Riley, Matt	L/L	6-1/201	8-2-79	Bowie	Started 22 games in first season back from injuries.
37	Roberts, Willis	R/R	6-3/175	6-19-75	Baltimore	A bad September has cast some doubt about whether he'll stay in the bullpen.
52	Ryan, B.J.	L/L	6-6/230	12-28-75	Baltimore	Until he learns to retire righties, he'll remain the Orioles' specialist.
28	Stephens, John	R/R	6-1/204	11-15-79	Rochester, Baltimore	Allowed 13 homers in just 65 innings. Will need more seasoning.

No.	CATCHERS	B/T	Ht./Wt.	Born	2002 clubs	Projection
26	Fordyce, Brook	R/R	6-0/190	5-7-70	Baltimore	Will be out of a job if the Orioles sign Ivan Rodriguez.
17	Gil, Geronimo	R/R	6-2/195	8-7-75	Baltimore	Wore down in his first full major league season. He is the Orioles' No .1 catcher.

No.	INFIELDERS	B/T	Ht./Wt.	Born	2002 clubs	Projection
10	Batista, Tony	R/R	6-0/205	12-9-73	Baltimore	Hit only three of his 31 homers against lefties. Will still be starter at third.
18	Conine, Jeff	R/R	6-1/220	6-27-66	Baltimore	Injuries continue to limit his production. Should be good for 130 games in 2003.
8	Cruz, Deivi	R/R	6-0/184	11-6-72	San Diego	Needing a shortstop the Orioles signed Cruz. Expect similar numbers to 2002.
15	Hairston, Jerry	R/R	5-10/175	5-29-76	Baltimore	Will continue to be a bottom-of-the-order guy until his OBP improves.
31	Leon, Jose	R/R	6-0/175	12-8-76	Rochester, Baltimore	Hits lefties well, but doesn't show enough power to play first or third full-time.
1	Roberts, Brian	B/R	5-9/170	10-9-77	Rochester, Baltimore	Could be the team's starting shortstop if Cruz falters.
11	Rogers, Eddie	R/R	6-1/172	8-29-78	Bowie, Baltimore	Is going to need more time in the minors to improve his plate discipline.
23	Segui, David	B/L	6-1/202	7-19-66	Baltimore	Injuries continue to sideline veteran first baseman. Might be limited to DH duties.

No.	OUTFIELDERS	B/T	Ht./Wt.	Born	2002 clubs	Projection
3	Bigbie, Larry	L/L	6-4/190	11-4-77	Rochester, Baltimore	Good hitter will need to show more power to stick in the majors as an outfielder.
40	Cordova, Marty	R/R	6-0/206	7-10-69	Baltimore	Tied a career high with 111 strikeouts last season. Should be better in 2003.
25	Gibbons, Jay	L/L	6-0/200	3-2-77	Baltimore	Showed good power, but needs to hit better this season.
32	Matos, Luis	R/R	6-0/179	10-30-78	Frederick, Bowie, Baltimore	A broken hand slowed his progress, could be ready for breakout year.
36	Matthews, Gary	B/R	6-3/210	8-25-74	New York N.L., Baltimore	Won the starting center field job with his 2002 performance.
	McDonald, Darnell	R/R	5-11/201	11-17-78	Bowie, Rochester	Starting to come around at the plate, but likely needs another year at Class AAA.
6	Mora, Melvin	R/R	5-10/180	2-2-72	Baltimore	For a guy who can play all positions, he certainly hits for a low average.
63	Raines, Tim	R/R	5-10/185	8-31-79	Bowie	Needs to cut down on strikeouts before he'll win a major league spot.
38	Richard, Chris	L/L	6-2/190	6-7-74	GC Or., Bow., Aber., Roch., Balt.	Shoulder surgery sidelined him for the majority of 2002. He'll bounce back.

THE COACHING STAFF

Mike Hargrove, manager.
Terry Crowley, hitting coach.
Rick Dempsey, first base coach.
Elrod Hendricks, bullpen coach.
Sam Perlozzo, bench coach.
Tom Trebelhorn, third base coach.
Mark Wiley, pitching coach.

THE TOP NEWCOMERS

Deivi Cruz: Some think he's too old and slow to play shortstop every day in the majors. If that's the case, the Orioles might have use for him as the designated hitter.

Omar Daal: He can still start, even though Dodgers used him in the bullpen for part of last season. Had a 3.90 ERA.

THE TOP PROSPECTS

Darnell McDonald: Better strike zone judgment has improved his standing as a prospect. Will likely need another season in Class AAA, but should be called up if the Orioles suffer any injuries to their starting outfielders.

Daniel Cabrera: A 6-7 righthander, he has improved his control and velocity. He struck out 69 batters in 60 innings.

Boston Red Sox

American League East Division

2003 SEASON

Red Sox Schedule

Home games shaded; D—Day game (games starting before 5 p.m.); *—All-Star Game at Comiskey Park, Chicago. Subject to changes.

March/April

SUN	MON	TUE	WED	THU	FRI	SAT
30	31 TB	1 TB	2 TB	3 D TB	4 BAL	5 D BAL
6 D BAL	7	8 TOR	9 TOR	10 TOR	11 D BAL	12 BAL
13 D BAL	14	15 TB	16 TB	17 TB	18 TOR	19 D TOR
20 D TOR	21 D TOR	22 TEX	23 TEX	24 D TEX	25 ANA	26 ANA
27 ANA	28	29 KC	30 KC			

May

SUN	MON	TUE	WED	THU	FRI	SAT
				1 KC	2 MIN	3 D MIN
4 D MIN	5 KC	6 KC	7 D KC	8	9 MIN	10 MIN
11 MIN	12	13 TEX	14 TEX	15 TEX	16 ANA	17 D ANA
18 D ANA	19 NYY	20 NYY	21 NYY	22	23 CLE	24 D CLE
25 D CLE	26 D NYY	27 NYY	28 NYY	29	30 TOR	31 D TOR

June

SUN	MON	TUE	WED	THU	FRI	SAT
1 D TOR	2	3 PIT	4 PIT	5 PIT	6 MIL	7 MIL
8 D MIL	9	10 STL	11 STL	12 STL	13 HOU	14 HOU
15 D HOU	16 CWS	17 CWS	18 CWS	19 D CWS	20 PHI	21 D PHI
22 D PHI	23 DET	24 DET	25 DET	26 D DET	27 FLA	28 FLA
29 D FLA	30					

July

SUN	MON	TUE	WED	THU	FRI	SAT
		1 TB	2 TB	3 TB	4 D NYY	5 D NYY
6 D NYY	7 NYY	8 TOR	9 TOR	10 TOR	11 DET	12 DET
13 D DET	14	15 *	16	17 TOR	18 TOR	19 TOR
20 D TOR	21 DET	22 DET	23 TB	24 D TB	25 NYY	26 D NYY
27 D NYY	28	29 TEX	30 TEX	31 TEX		

August

SUN	MON	TUE	WED	THU	FRI	SAT
					1 BAL	2 BAL
3 D BAL	4	5 ANA	6 ANA	7 ANA	8 BAL	9 BAL
10 D BAL	11 OAK	12 OAK	13 OAK	14 D OAK	15 SEA	16 D SEA
17 D SEA	18	19 OAK	20 OAK	21 OAK	22 SEA	23 D SEA
24 D SEA	25 D SEA	26 TOR	27 TOR	28	29 NYY	30 D NYY
31 D NYY						

September

SUN	MON	TUE	WED	THU	FRI	SAT
	1	2 CWS	3 CWS	4	5 NYY	6 D NYY
7 D NYY	8 BAL	9 BAL	10 D BAL	11	12 CWS	13 CWS
14 D CWS	15 TB	16 TB	17 TB	18 TB	19 CLE	20 CLE
21 D CLE	22 BAL	23 BAL	24 BAL	25 BAL	26 TB	27 TB
28 D TB						

FRONT-OFFICE DIRECTORY

Prinicipal owner .... John W. Henry
Chairman .... Thomas C. Werner
President/chief executive officer .... Larry Lucchino
Vice chairman .... David I. Ginsberg
Vice chairman .... Leslie B. Otten
Director .... George J. Mitchell
Chief legal officer .... Lucinda K. Treat
Senior vice president/general manager .... Theo Epstein
Vice president/baseball operations .... Michael D. Port
Vice president and legal counsel .... Elaine W. Steward
Assistant general manager .... Josh Byrnes
Special assistant to the general manager .... Lee Thomas
Special assistant to the general manager/scouting .... Bill Lajoie
Special assistant to the general manager/player development .... Craig Shipley
Director of baseball operations .... Benjamin P. Cherington
Traveling secretary .... John F. McCormick
Senior baseball operations advisor .... Bill James
Video/advance scouting coordinator .... William Broadbent
Field coordinator .... Rob Leary
Coordinator of Florida operations .... Ryan Richeal
Coordinator, Sarasota .... M. Todd Stephenson
Director of minor league administration .... Raquel S. Ferreira
Director of amateur scouting .... David Chadd
Assistant director of amateur scouting .... James Orr
Director of international scouting .... Louie Eljaua
Assistant scouting director .... Thomas L. Moore
Advance scouting administrator .... Galen Carr
Executive vice president/business affairs .... Mike Dee
Vice president and chief financial officer .... Robert C. Furbush
Controller .... Stanley H. Tran
Director of human resources and office management .... Michele Julian
Executive vice president/public affairs .... Dr. Charles S. Steinberg
Executive consultant of public affairs .... James "Lou" Gorman
Publications manager .... Debra A. Matson
Customer relations manager .... Ann Marie C. Starzyk
Director of media relations .... Kevin J. Shea
Vice president/sales and marketing .... Lawrence C. Cancro
Vice president/corporate partnerships .... Sam Kennedy
Director of advertising and sponsorships .... Jeffrey E. Goldenberg
Promotions and special events manager .... Marcita E. Thompson
Director of sales .... Michael D. Schetzel
Vice president/stadium operations .... Joseph F. McDermott
Superintendent of Park and maintenance .... Joseph P. Mooney
Director of grounds .... David R. Mellor
Director of information technology .... Stephen P. Conley
Information technology manager .... Clay N. Rendon

MINOR LEAGUE AFFILIATES

Class	Team	League	Manager
AAA	Pawtucket	International	Buddy Bailey
AA	Portland	Eastern	Ron Johnson
A	Sarasota	Florida State	Russ Morman
A	Augusta	South Atlantic	John Deeble
A	Lowell	New York-Pennsylvania	Tim Leiper
Rookie	Gulf Coast Red Sox	Gulf Coast	Ralph Treuel

ASSISTANCE STAFF

Medical director/team physician
William J. Morgan, M.D.
Head trainer
James W. Rowe Jr.
Asst. trainer/rehabilitation coordinator
Christopher T. Correnti
Assistant trainer
Chang-Ho Lee
Equipment mgr. and clubhouse ops.
Joseph Cochran
Instructors
Carl M. Yastrzemski, James E. Rice
Special assignment instructors
John M. Pesky, Charles T. Wagner
Major league scout
Frank J. Malzone
Major league special assignment scout
G. Edwin Haas
Scouts
Walter "Chet" Atkins, Raymond Boone, Buzz Bowers, Kevin Burrell, Ben Cherington, Edwin Correa, Ray Crone Jr., George Digby, Johnny DiPuglia, Danny Doyle, Rob English, William Enos, Ray Fagnant, Steve Flores, Danny Haas, Eddie Haas, Matt Haas, Ernie Jacobs, Wally Komatsubara, Chuck Koney, Kenneth "Jack" Lee, Don Lenhardt, Frank Malzone, Joe Mason, Tom Mooney, Gary Rajsich, Eddie Robinson, Jim Robinson, Ed Roebuck, Edward Scott, Mathew Sczesny, Harry Smith, Dick Sorkin, Jerry Stephenson, Joseph Stephenson, Lee Thomas, Fay Thompson, Charles T. Wagner, Jeffrey Zona, Mark Garcia, Jun Kodama, Ray Poitevint, Lee Sigman, Robinson Garcia, Sebastian Martinez, Jose Maza, Carlos Ramirez, Derek Valenzuela, Michael Victoria

BROADCAST INFORMATION

Radio: WEEI-AM (680).
TV: WBZ (Channel 4).
Cable TV: New England Sports Network.

SPRING TRAINING

Ballpark (city): City of Palms Park (Fort Myers, Fla.).
Ticket information: 941-334-4700.

BALLPARK INFORMATION

Ballpark (capacity, surface)
Fenway Park (33,991, grass)
Address
4 Yawkey Way
Boston, MA 02215-3496
Official website
www.redsox.com
Business phone
617-267-9440
Ticket information
617-267-1700, 617-482-4769
Ticket prices
$55 (field box, loge box and infield roof)
$40 (reserved grandstand)
$30 (right-field boxes and right-field roof)
$25 (outfield grandstand)
$20 (lower bleachers)
$18 (upper bleachers)
Field dimensions (from home plate)
To left field at foul line, 310 feet
To center field, 420 feet
To right field at foul line, 302 feet
First game played
April 20, 1912 (Red Sox 7, New York Highlanders 6)

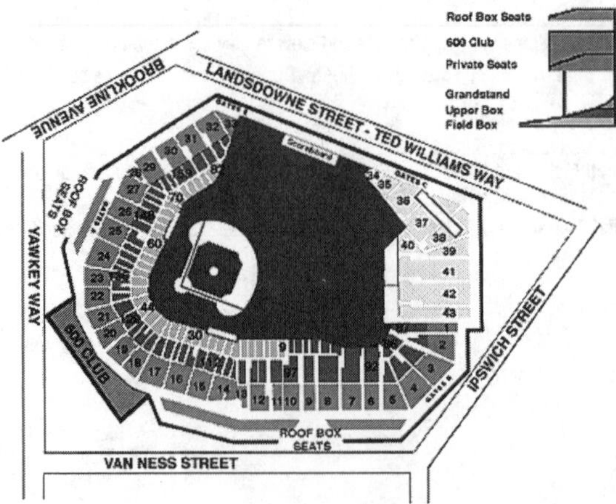

Follow the Red Sox all season at: www.sportingnews.com/baseball/teams/redsox/

RED SOX SPRING ROSTER

No.	PITCHERS	B/T	Ht./Wt.	Born	2002 clubs	Projection
17	Banks, Willie	R/R	6-1/200	2-27-69	Boston, Pawtucket	Emerged as good reliever for the Red Sox. Should hold same role again.
19	Burkett, John	R/R	6-3/215	11-28-64	Pawtucket, Boston	Won 13 games, but faltered as the season went on. Should bounce back in 2003.
37	Castillo, Frank	R/R	6-1/198	4-1-69	Boston	Might be a starer, might be a reliever. It all depends on how he pitches in spring.
74	de la Rosa, Jorge	L/L	6-1/190	11-5-81	Sarasota, Trenton	Won seven games in Class A. Needs more seasoning.
43	Embree, Alan	L/L	6-2/190	1-23-70	San Diego, Boston	Red Sox traded for this lefty in 2002. Will work out of bullpen in 2003
15	Fossum, Casey	B/L	6-1/165	1-6-78	Boston, Pawtucket	Bounced back and forth between the rotation and bullpen. Better as a starter.
	Fox, Chad	R/R	6-3/206	9-3-70	Huntsville, Milwaukee	When healthy, one of the two setup guys in baseball.
61	Gomes, Wayne	R/R	6-2/225	1-15-73	Nashville, Pawtucket, Boston	Has a chance to earn a spot in the bullpen if he's consistent.
46	Howry, Bobby	L/R	6-5/220	8-4-73	Chicago A.L., Boston	Could be the Red Sox closer if his velocity is back up to par.
	Lopez, Javier	L/L	5-10/165	2-22-83	El Paso	Lefty saved six games in Class AA, and struck out a batter per inning.
32	Lowe, Derek	R/R	6-6/214	6-1-73	Boston	Made a seemless transition to starter. Will be No. 2 starter behind Pedro.
	Lyon, Brandon	R/R	6-1/185	8-10-79	Toronto, Syracuse	Control pitcher didn't pitch well in 2002. Red Sox are hoping to turn him around.
73	Martinez, Anastacio	R/R	6-2/180	11-3-80	Trenton	Needs to refine his control after leading Eastern League with 75 walks.
45	Martinez, Pedro	R/R	5-11/180	10-25-71	Boston	Bounced back from shoulder problems and became the best starter in the A.L.
	Mendoza, Ramiro	R/R	6-2/195	6-15-72	New York A.L.	Red Sox will likely give him a chance to start this year.
57	Pena, Juan	R/R	6-5/215	6-27-77	Pawtucket	Injuries shortened this prospect's 2002 season; will be back in Class AAA.
	Rupe, Ryan	R/R	6-5/248	3-31-75	Tampa Bay	Won five games despite playing for the Devil Rays. Should be better in Boston.
	Shibilo, Andy	R/R	6-7/220	9-16-76	Mobile, Trenton, Pawtucket	Reliever will need a few more Class AAA games before making it to the majors.
	Timlin, Mike	R/R	6-4/210	3-10-66	St. Louis, Philadelphia	Veteran reliever will be counted on to provide leadership in bullpen.
49	Wakefield, Tim	R/R	6-2/214	8-2-66	Boston	Finally the Red Sox will make him a starter. He should post good numbers.
	White, Matt	R/L	6-1/180	8-19-77	Akron, Buffalo	Won six games in Class AA. Will have to show pinpoint control to stick around.

No.	CATCHERS	B/T	Ht./Wt.	Born	2002 clubs	Projection
28	Mirabelli, Doug	R/R	6-1/227	10-18-70	Boston	Didn't commit one error behind the plate. But didn't hit all that well, either.
33	Varitek, Jason	B/R	6-2/237	4-11-72	Boston	Hits pretty good for a catcher and is solid behind the plate.

No.	INFIELDERS	B/T	Ht./Wt.	Born	2002 clubs	Projection
2	Crespo, Cesar	B/R	5-11/170	5-23-79	Portland, San Diego	Can play any infield position. Versatility will keep him on the team.
5	Garciaparra, Nomar	R/R	6-0/190	7-23-73	Boston	It wouldn't be a surprise to see his batting average rise to former levels.
7	Giambi, Jeremy	L/L	5-11/216	9-30-74	Oakland, Philadelphia	Could be the answer at first base. But needs to sit on base a lot.
29	Hillenbrand, Shea	R/R	6-1/211	7-27-75	Boston	Hit .293, but didn't walk much. Could be traded if right deal comes along.
2	Jackson, Damian	R/R	5-11/185	8-16-73	Detroit	His speed and versatility in the field will keep him with the Red Sox.
26	Merloni, Lou	R/R	5-10/201	4-6-71	Boston, Pawtucket	His job could be in jeopardy with Crespo and Jackson aboard.
	Mueller, Bill	B/R	5-10/180	3-17-71	Iowa, Chic. N.L., San Fran.	Brings consistency and good defense to third base.
52	Sanchez, Freddy	R/R	5-11/185	12-21-77	Trenton, Pawtucket, Boston	Youngster will have chance to win third base job. Likely a year away.
53	Santos, Angel	B/R	5-11/180	8-14-79	Pawtucket	Will be given another year or two in minors to improve strike zone judgement.
12	Walker, Todd	L/R	6-0/190	5-25-73	Cincinnati	Acquired from Reds to solidify second base. Good hitter will succeed in lineup.

No.	OUTFIELDERS	B/T	Ht./Wt.	Born	2002 clubs	Projection
50	Agbayani, Benny	R/R	6-0/225	12-28-71	Colo., Colo. Sprg.,Pawt., Bos.	Could win a job as DH or bench role, but he'll have to hit better.
13	Brown, Adrian	B/R	6-0/200	2-7-74	Pittsburgh, Nashville	Hit well in the minors, hasn't done it yet in the majors.
18	Damon, Johnny	L/L	6-2/190	11-5-73	Boston	Played through injuries in first season in Boston. Numbers will be better in 2003.
7	Nixon, Trot	L/L	6-2/211	4-11-74	Boston	Pencil him in for 20+ homers and 90+ RBIs.
24	Ramirez, Manny	R/R	6-0/213	5-30-72	Boston, Pawtucket	If he stays healthy, he's the most dangerous hitter in the A.L.
67	Stenson, Dernell	L/L	6-1/230	6-17-78	Pawtucket	Has regressed in recent years in Class AAA. He could stick around if he hits.

THE COACHING STAFF

Grady Little, manager.

Tony Cloninger, pitching coach.

Mike Cubbage, third base coach.

Jerry Narron, bench coach.

Euclides Rojas, bullpen coach.

THE TOP NEWCOMERS

Todd Walker: Traded by the Reds to the Red Sox, Walker will provide the Sox a No. 2 hitter, fitting in nicely between Damon and Garciaparra. His defense isn't too bad either.

Jeremy Giambi: If he can play some defense at first, the job is his. He's a good hitter who'll fit in well with the Red Sox philosophy.

THE TOP PROSPECTS

Freddy Sanchez: He's a good contract hitter who's likely a year away. The Red Sox will be patient with him.

Jorge de la Rose: He wore down as the 2002 season wore on. But he pitched well in Class A, striking out 95 in just over 120 innings.

Chicago White Sox

American League Central Division

2003 SEASON

White Sox Schedule

Home games shaded; D—Day game (games starting before 5 p.m.); *—All-Star Game at Comiskey Park, Chicago. Subject to changes.

March/April

SUN	MON	TUE	WED	THU	FRI	SAT
30	31 D KC	1	2 D KC	3 D KC	4 D DET	5 D DET
6 D DET	7 D CLE	8	9 CLE	10 CLE	11 DET	12 D DET
13 D DET	14	15 KC	16 KC	17 D KC	18 CLE	19 D CLE
20 D CLE	21 D CLE	22 BAL	23 BAL	24 BAL	25 MIN	26 MIN
27 D MIN	28	29 OAK	30 OAK			

May

SUN	MON	TUE	WED	THU	FRI	SAT
				1 OAK	2 SEA	3 SEA
4 SEA	5	6 OAK	7 OAK	8 D OAK	9 SEA	10 SEA
11 D SEA	12	13 BAL	14 BAL	15 BAL	16 MIN	17 MIN
18 D MIN	19 TOR	20 TOR	21 TOR	22	23 DET	24 DET
25 D DET	26 TOR	27 TOR	28 TOR	29 TOR	30 CLE	31 D CLE

June

SUN	MON	TUE	WED	THU	FRI	SAT
1 D CLE	2 D CLE	3 ARI	4 ARI	5 ARI	6 LA	7 LA
8 D LA	9	10 SF	11 SF	12 SF	13 SD	14 SD
15 D SD	16 BOS	17 BOS	18 BOS	19 D BOS	20 D CUB	21 D CUB
22 D CUB	23	24 MIN	25 MIN	26 D MIN	27 D CUB	28 D CUB
29 D CUB	30 MIN					

July

SUN	MON	TUE	WED	THU	FRI	SAT
		1 MIN	2 MIN	3	4 TB	5 TB
6 D TB	7	8 DET	9 DET	10 D DET	11 CLE	12 CLE
13 D CLE	14	15 *	16	17 DET	18 DET	19 DET
20 D DET	21 CLE	22 D CLE	23 TOR	24 TOR	25 TB	26 TB
27 D TB	28	29 KC	30 KC	31 KC		

August

SUN	MON	TUE	WED	THU	FRI	SAT
					1 SEA	2 SEA
3 D SEA	4 KC	5 KC	6 D KC	7	8 OAK	9 OAK
10 D OAK	11 ANA	12 ANA	13 ANA	14 ANA	15 TEX	16 TEX
17 TEX	18 ANA	19 ANA	20 ANA	21 TEX	22 TEX	23 TEX
24 D TEX	25	26 NYY	27 NYY	28 D NYY	29 DET	30 DET
31 D DET						

September

SUN	MON	TUE	WED	THU	FRI	SAT
	1	2 BOS	3 BOS	4	5 CLE	6 D CLE
7 D CLE	8 MIN	9 MIN	10 MIN	11 D MIN	12 BOS	13 BOS
14 D BOS	15	16 MIN	17 MIN	18 MIN	19 KC	20 KC
21 D KC	22 NYY	23 NYY	24 D NYY	25 KC	26 KC	27 KC
28 D KC						

FRONT-OFFICE DIRECTORY

Chairman....................Jerry Reinsdorf
Vice chairman....................Eddie Einhorn
Executive vice president....................Howard Pizer
Senior vice president, general manager....................Ken Williams
Senior vice president, marketing and broadcasting....................Rob Gallas
Vice president, administration and finance....................Tim Buzard
Vice president, stadium operations....................Terry Savarise
Vice president, free agent and major league scouting....................Larry Monroe
Special assistant to Jerry Reinsdorf....................Dennis Gilbert
Special assistant to Ken Williams....................Dave Yoakum
Executive advisor to Ken Williams....................Roland Hemond
Assistant general manager....................Rick Hahn
Special assignment....................Bryan Little
Senior director of scouting....................Duane Shaffer
Director of scouting....................Doug Laumann
Director of player development....................Bob Fontaine Jr.
Director of minor league administration....................Grace Guerrero Zwit
Director of baseball operations systems....................Dan Fabian
Director of minor league instruction....................Jim Snyder
Manager of team travel....................Ed Cassin
Assistant director of baseball operations systems....................Andrew Pinter
Director of broadcasting and marketing....................Bob Grim
Director of community relations....................Christine O'Reilly
Director of sales....................Jim Muno
Director of ticket operations....................Bob DeVoy
Director of management information services....................Don Brown
Director of human resources....................Moira Foy
Controller....................Bill Waters
Director of public relations....................Scott Reifert

MINOR LEAGUE AFFILIATES

Class	Team	League	Manager
AAA	Charlotte	International	Nick Capra
AA	Birmingham	Southern	Wally Backman
A	Winston-Salem	Carolina	Razor Shines
A	Kannapolis	South Atlantic	John Orton
Rookie	Bristol	Appalachian	Jerry Hairston
Rookie	Great Falls	Pioneer	Chris Cron

BROADCAST INFORMATION

Radio: ESPN-AM (1000).
TV: WGN-TV (Channel 9).
Cable TV: Fox Sports Chicago.

SPRING TRAINING

Ballpark (city): Tucson Electric Park (Tucson, Ariz.).
Ticket information: 520-434-1111.

ASSISTANCE STAFF

Senior team physician
Dr. James Boscardin

Head trainer
Herm Schneider

Assistant trainer
Brian Ball

Director of strength & conditioning
Steve Odgers

Scouting national cross-checker
Ed Pebley

Professional scouts
Joe Butler, Larry Maxie, Gary Pellant, Billy Scheerer, Daraka Shaheed, Bill Young

Regional supervisors
Rick Ingalls, Paul Provas, Tumminia, Derek Valenzuela

Full-time area scouts
Rico Cortes, Alex Cosmidis, Curt Daniels, Nathan Durst, Chuck Fox, Larry Grefer, Matt Hattabaugh, Nick Hostetler, Warren Hughes, George Kachigian, John Kazanas, Jose Ortega, Alex Slattery, Keith Staab, Adam Virchis

Part-time scouts
Tom Butler, Javier Centeno, E.J. Chavez, John Doldoorian, James Ellison, Jack Jolly, Reggie Lewis, Glen Murdock, Howard Nakagama, Al Otto, Mike Paris, Ralph Reyes, Mike Shirley, Larry Silveira

Latin-American coordinator
Miguel Ibarra

International scouts
Roberto Espinoza, Denny Gonzalez

BALLPARK INFORMATION

Ballpark (capacity, surface)
Comiskey Park (47,098, grass)
Address
333 W. 35th St.
Chicago, IL 60616
Official website
www.whitesox.com
Business phone
312-674-1000
Ticket information
312-674-1000
Ticket prices
$29 (lower deck box, club level)
$24 (lower deck reserved)
$20 (upper deck box, bleacher reserved)
$14 (upper deck reserved)
Field dimensions (from home plate)
To left field at foul line, 330 feet
To center field, 400 feet
To right field at foul line, 335 feet
First game played
April 18, 1991 (Tigers 16, White Sox 0)

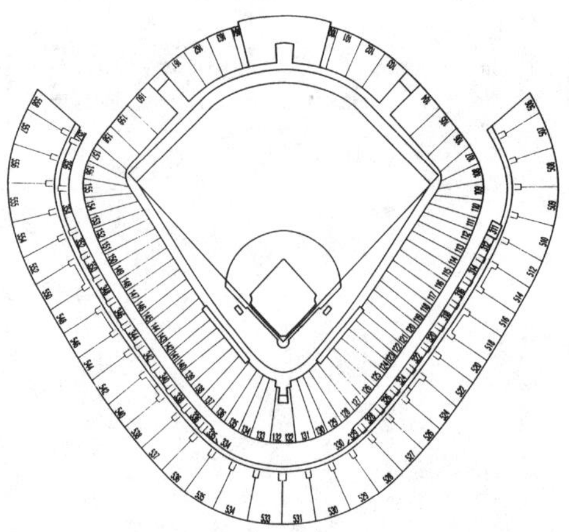

Follow the White Sox all season at: www.sportingnews.com/baseball/teams/whitesox/

WHITE SOX SPRING ROSTER

No.	PITCHERS	B/T	Ht./Wt.	Born	2002 clubs	Projection
	Adkins, Jon	L/R	6-0/200	8-30-77	Modesto, Sacramento, Charlotte	Acquired from the A's, this potential starter will help rotation soon .
55	Almonte, Edwin	R/R	6-3/200	12-17-76	Charlotte	Had 26 saves in Class AAA in 2002. Will be in White Sox bullpen.
56	Buehrle, Mark	L/L	6-2/200	3-23-79	Chicago A.L.	Combines with Colon to give Sox a nice 1-2 punch in rotation.
	Colon, Bartolo	R/R	6-0/240	5-24-73	Cleveland, Montreal	Gives team bona fide No. 1 starter.
	Diaz, Felix	R/R	6-1/180	7-27-81	Shreveport, Birmingham	Went 4-0 in Class AA with the White Sox organization.
52	Garland, Jon	R/R	6-6/205	9-27-79	Chicago A.L.	Won 12 games in first full season in rotation. Coudl duplicate that in 2003.
58	Ginter, Matt	R/R	6-1/220	12-24-77	Charlotte, Chicago A.L.	Didn't lose one game in 46 outings between majors and minors.
38	Glover, Gary	R/R	6-5/205	12-3-76	Chicago A.L.	Better suited to a relief role, he'll be in the bullpen at the start of 2003.
	Gordon, Tom	R/R	5-10/190	11-18-67	Dayt., Iowa, Chi. N.L., Houston	Gives a powerful arm out of bullpen. Needs to stay healthy.
43	Marte, Damaso	L/L	6-2/200	2-14-75	Chicago A.L.	Could become the closer for the Sox, or one of many.
41	Porzio, Mike	L/L	6-3/190	8-20-72	Chicago A.L., Charlotte	Will be hard pressed to make the club with the bullpen depth available.
51	Rauch, Jon	R/R	6-10/230	9-27-78	Chicago A.L., Charlotte	Pitched well in September. White Sox need to get him more work.
36	Wright, Dan	R/R	6-5/225	12-14-77	Chicago A.L.	Slowly but surely becoming a better pitcher in the rotation.
65	Wunsch, Kelly	L/L	6-5/225	7-12-72	Charlotte, Chicago A.L.	Pitched well for guy coming off shoulder surgery. Should be better this year.
	Wylie, Mitch	R/R	6-3/190	1-14-77	Charlotte	Control pitcher's season was shortened by injuries. Needs another year in minors.

No.	CATCHERS	B/T	Ht./Wt.	Born	2002 clubs	Projection
15	Alomar, Sandy	R/R	6-5/235	6-18-66	Chicago A.L., Charlotte, Colorado	Will provide the club catching depth, in case prospects aren't ready.
61	Olivo, Miguel	R/R	6-0/180	7-15-78	Birmingham, Chicago A.L.	Hit .306 in Class AA, but didn't hit well in the majors. May need another year.
27	Paul, Josh	R/R	6-1/200	5-19-75	Charlotte, Chicago A.L.	Only hit .240 and isn't the best defender. Olivo may put him out of job.

No.	INFIELDERS	B/T	Ht./Wt.	Born	2002 clubs	Projection
24	Crede, Joe	R/R	6-2/195	4-26-78	Charlotte, Chicago A.L.	Is ready for the full-time third base job. Hit .285 last season, should do the same.
17	Graffanino, Tony	R/R	6-1/190	6-6-72	Chicago A.L.	A knee injury in 2002 may have cost him any hope of returning to the lineup.
12	Harris, Willie	L/R	5-9/175	6-22-78	Charlotte, Chicago A.L.	Could be the answer at second. Has to hit major league pitching better first.
28	Jimenez, D'Angelo	B/R	6-0/194	12-21-77	San Diego, Char., Chicago A.L.	Won second base job after Ray Durham was traded.
14	Konerko, Paul	R/R	6-2/215	3-5-76	Chicago A.L.	Emerged as power threat and will certainly duplicate 2002 numbers.
35	Thomas, Frank	R/R	6-5/275	5-27-68	Chicago A.L.	Hit only .252, but did hit 28 homers.
22	Valentin, Jose	B/R	5-10/185	10-12-69	Chicago A.L.	Will need to hit and play decent defense as team's only shortstop.

No.	OUTFIELDERS	B/T	Ht./Wt.	Born	2002 clubs	Projection
25	Borchard, Joe	B/R	6-5/220	11-25-78	Win.-Salem, Char.,Chi. A.L.	Top prospect still needs one more season in the minors.
45	Lee, Carlos	R/R	6-2/235	6-20-76	Chicago A.L.	Better plate discipline has made Lee a tougher out.
30	Ordonez, Magglio	R/R	6-0/210	1-28-74	Chicago A.L.	Has developed into one of the better players in the A.L.
	Rios, Armando	L/L	5-9/185	9-13-71	Pitts., Altoona, Nash.	Has chance to win a spot as outfielder or lefthanded pinch hitter.
44	Rowand, Aaron	R/R	6-1/200	8-29-77	Chicago A.L.	An offseason injury could limit his production this season.

THE COACHING STAFF

Jerry Manuel, manager.

Don Cooper, pitching coach.

Bruce Kimm, third base coach.

Art Kusnyer, bullpen coach.

Joe Nossek, bench coach.

Rafael Santana, first base coach.

Gary Ward, hitting coach.

THE TOP NEWCOMERS

Sandy Alomar Jr.: After being traded away by the White Sox during 2002, Alomar returns to anchor a young catching staff. He will provide depth until Miguel Olivo is ready for the majors.

Bartolo Colon: While some expected Colon to slow down last year due to the amount of innings he throws, he just keeps plugging along. He gives the White Sox a power righthanded arm to go along with crafty, young lefty Mark Buerhle.

THE TOP PROSPECTS

Jon Adkins: Acquired by the White Sox in the Ray Durham trade, he showed he may be more than ready for a spot in the rotation in Class AAA.

Joe Borchard: He showed his power at Class AAA, but walked only 49 times while striking out 139. He needs another year of seasoning.

CLEVELAND INDIANS

AMERICAN LEAGUE CENTRAL DIVISION

2003 SEASON

Indians Schedule

Home games shaded; D—Day game (games starting before 5 p.m.); *—All-Star Game at Comiskey Park, Chicago. Subject to changes.

March/April

SUN	MON	TUE	WED	THU	FRI	SAT
30	31 D BAL	1	2 BAL	3 BAL	4 KC	5 D KC
6 D KC	7 D CWS	8	9 CWS	10 CWS	11 KC	12 D KC
13 D KC	14 KC	15 BAL	16 BAL	17 BAL	18 CWS	19 D CWS
20 D CWS	21 D CWS	22 SEA	23 SEA	24 SEA	25 OAK	26 D OAK
27 D OAK	28	29 ANA	30 ANA			

May

SUN	MON	TUE	WED	THU	FRI	SAT
				1 ANA	2 TEX	3 D TEX
4 D TEX	5	6 ANA	7 ANA	8 ANA	9 TEX	10 TEX
11 D TEX	12	13 SEA	14 SEA	15 SEA	16 OAK	17 D OAK
18 D OAK	19 DET	20 DET	21 DET	22 DET	23 BOS	24 D BOS
25 D BOS	26 D DET	27 DET	28 DET	29	30 CWS	31 D CWS

June

SUN	MON	TUE	WED	THU	FRI	SAT
1 D CWS	2 D CWS	3 COL	4 COL	5 D COL	6 ARI	7 D ARI
8 D ARI	9	10 SD	11 SD	12 SD	13 LA	14 D LA
15 D LA	16	17 DET	18 DET	19 D DET	20 PIT	21 PIT
22 D PIT	23	24 KC	25 KC	26 KC	27 CIN	28 D CIN
29 D CIN	30 KC					

July

SUN	MON	TUE	WED	THU	FRI	SAT
		1 KC	2 KC	3 MIN	4 MIN	5 MIN
6 D MIN	7	8 NYY	9 NYY	10 NYY	11 CWS	12 CWS
13 D CWS	14	15 *	16	17 NYY	18 NYY	19 D NYY
20 D NYY	21 CWS	22 D CWS	23 DET	24 DET	25 MIN	26 MIN
27 D MIN	28	29 OAK	30 OAK	31 D OAK		

August

SUN	MON	TUE	WED	THU	FRI	SAT
					1 TEX	2 TEX
3 TEX	4	5 SEA	6 SEA	7 SEA	8 ANA	9 D ANA
10 D ANA	11 MIN	12 MIN	13 MIN	14 D MIN	15 TB	16 TB
17 D TB	18 TB	19 MIN	20 MIN	21	22 TB	23 TB
24 D TB	25	26 DET	27 DET	28 DET	29 TOR	30 TOR
31 D TOR						

September

SUN	MON	TUE	WED	THU	FRI	SAT
	1 D DET	2 DET	3 DET	4 D DET	5 CWS	6 D CWS
7 D CWS	8	9 KC	10 KC	11 D KC	12 MIN	13 MIN
14 D MIN	15 MIN	16 KC	17 KC	18 KC	19 BOS	20 BOS
21 D BOS	22	23 MIN	24 MIN	25	26 TOR	27 D TOR
28 D TOR						

FRONT-OFFICE DIRECTORY

President and chief executive officer .... Lawrence J. Dolan
Executive vice president, general manager .... Mark Shapiro
Executive vice president, business .... Dennis Lehman
Senior vice president, finance & chief financial officer .... Ken Stefanov
Vice president and general counsel .... Paul J. Dolan
Vice president, public relations .... Bob DiBiasio
Vice president, marketing and broadcasting .... Valerie Arcuri
Vice president, sales .... Jon Starrett
Vice president, ballpark operations .... Jim Folk
Vice president, merchandising & licensing .... Jayne Churchmack
Assistant general manager, scouting operations .... John Mirabelli
Assistant general manager .... Neal Huntington
Assistant general manager .... Chris Antonetti
Director of player development .... John Farrell
Director of player personnel .... Steve Lubratich
Assistant director, scouting .... Brad Grant
Director of media relations .... Bart Swain
Manager of media relations, administration & credentials .... Susie Giuliano
Manager, media relations .... Curtis Danburg
Coordinator, media relations .... Jeff Sibel
Director of team travel .... Mike Seghi

MINOR LEAGUE AFFILIATES

Class	Team	League	Manager
AAA	Buffalo	International	Marty Brown
AA	Akron	Eastern	Brad Komminsk
A	Kinston	Carolina	Torey Lovullo
A	Lake County	South Atlantic	Luis Rivera
A	Mahoning Valley	New York-Pennsylvania	Ted Kubiak
Rookie	Burlington	Appalachian	Rouglas Odor

BROADCAST INFORMATION

Radio: WTAM (1100 AM).
Cable TV: Fox Sports Net Ohio.

SPRING TRAINING

Ballpark (city): Chain Of Lakes (Winter Haven, Fla.).
Ticket information: 863-293-3900.

ASSISTANCE STAFF

Head trainer
Paul Spicuzza

Assistant trainer
Rick Jameyson

Clubhouse manager
Tony Amato

Visiting clubhouse
Cy Buynak

Groundskeeper
Brandon Koehnke

West Coast supervisor
Paul Cogan

Southeast supervisor
Jerry Jordan

Northeast supervisor
Chuck Ricci

Midwest supervisor
Ken Stauffer

Full-time scouts
Doug Baker, Keith Boeck, Mike Daly, Rene Gayo, Don Lyle, Scott Meaney, Les Pajari, Matt Ruebel, Jason Smith, Scott Barnsby, Henry Cruz, Jim Gabella, Chris Jefts, Bob Mayer, Tim Moore, Phil Rossi, Bill Schudlich, Shawn Whalen

BALLPARK INFORMATION

Ballpark (capacity, surface)
Jacobs Field (43,368, grass)

Address
2401 Ontario St.
Cleveland, OH 44115

Official website
www.indians.com

Business phone
216-420-4200

Ticket information
216-420-4200

Ticket prices
$50 (diamond box, row 1)
$45 (diamond box, rows 2-6)
$40 (field box)
$27 (baseline box, IF lower box, view box)
$25 (lower box), $21 (IF upper box)
$20 (lower reserved, mezzanine)
$19 (upper box), $12 (bleachers)
$10 (upper reserved)
$7 (upper reserved/general admission)
$6 (corner reserved/general admission)

Field dimensions (from home plate)
To left field at foul line, 325 feet
To center field, 405 feet
To right field at foul line, 325 feet

First game played
April 4, 1994 (Indians 4, Mariners 3, 11 innings)

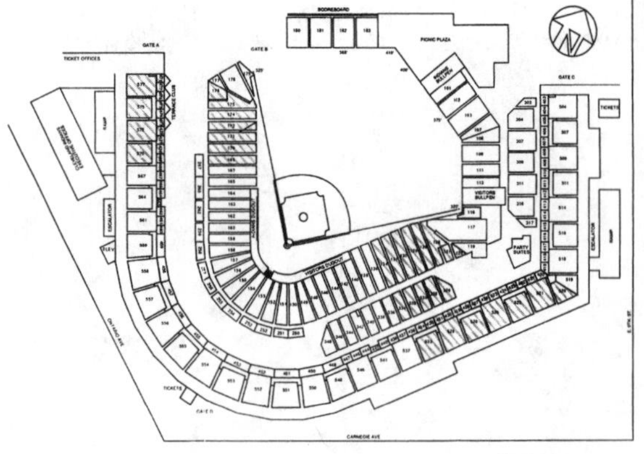

Follow the Indians all season at: www.sportingnews.com/baseball/teams/indians/

INDIANS SPRING ROSTER

No.	PITCHERS	B/T	Ht./Wt.	Born	2002 clubs	Projection
34	Anderson, Brian	R/L	6-1/183	4-26-72	Arizona	Crafty lefthander will bring veteran leadership to a young rotation.
55	Baez, Danys	R/R	6-3/225	9-10-77	Cleveland	Worked as starter and reliever last season. Will be the closer in 2003.
	Bere, Jason	R/R	6-3/225	5-26-71	Chicago N.L., Iowa	Needs to duplicate 2001 numbers for the Indians to have a chance in the division.
	Cressend, Jack	R/R	6-1/185	5-13-75	Minnesota, GC Twins, Ft. Myers	Relief pitcher looking to rebound after injury plagued season.
64	Davis, Jason	R/R	6-6/195	5-8-80	Kinston, Akron, Cleveland	Pitched well in brief audition with Indians. Could make the rotation.
	Guthrie, Jeremy	R/R	6-1/195	4-8-79	DID NOT PLAY	2002 draft pick is another in the long line of Stanford pitchers.
49	Herrera, Alex	L/L	5-11/175	11-5-76	Akron, Cleveland, Buffalo	Reliever slowly moving through the system. Might be ready at the end of '03.
65	Lee, Cliff	L/L	6-3/190	8-30-78	Harris., Akron, Buff., Clev.	Showed he could be ready for the majors with two good outings in September.
45	Mulholland, Terry	R/L	6-3/220	3/9/63	Los Angeles, Cleveland	Re-signed by Indians to bolster bullpen depth.
	Myette, Aaron	R/R	6-4/210	9-26-77	Oklahoma, Texas	Youngster never found groove in Texas system. Change of scenery could help.
16	Paronto, Chad	R/R	6-5/250	7-28-75	Buffalo, Cleveland, Akron	2002 was a learning year for him. Ready for a full-time job in the bullpen.
51	Riggan, Jerrod	R/R	6-3/197	5-16-74	Cleveland, Buffalo	Had trouble adjusting to the majors. Might be ready this year.
54	Riske, Dave	R/R	6-2/175	10-23-76	Cleveland, Akron, Buffalo	Still trying to replicate the success he had in the minors.
46	Rodriguez, Ricardo	R/R	6-3/165	5-21-78	Jacksonville, L.Vegas, Buf., Clev.	Top prospect could be ready this year. Started seven games for Cleveland in '03.
52	Sabathia, C.C.	L/L	6-7/270	7-21-80	Cleveland	Maturing into the staff ace.
53	Sadler, Carl	L/L	6-2/180	10-11-76	Akron, Buffalo, Cleveland	Lefty reliever just needs more major league experience.
60	Tallet, Brian	L/L	6-7/208	9-21-77	Akron, Buffalo, Cleveland	Is in line for a spot in rotation, but needs a strong spring.
37	Westbrook, Jake	R/R	6-3/185	9-29-77	Cleveland, Akron, Buffalo	Injuries limited his effectiveness last season.
26	Wickman, Bob	R/R	6-1/240	2-6-69	Cleveland	Will be sidelined for entire 2003 season after elbow surgery.
39	Wohlers, Mark	R/R	6-4/207	1-23-70	Cleveland	Will be counted on as top set-up man in bullpen. Might save a few games.

No.	CATCHERS	B/T	Ht./Wt.	Born	2002 clubs	Projection
44	Bard, Josh	B/R	6-3/215	3-30-78	Buffalo, Cleveland	Will have to battle for playing time this season.
23	Hinch, A.J.	R/R	6-1/205	5-15-74	Kansas City	Has two young players in front of him. If one isn't ready, he gets a job.
63	Martinez, Victor	B/R	6-2/170	12-23-78	Akron, Cleveland	Catcher of the future hit .336 in Class AA.

No.	INFIELDERS	B/T	Ht./Wt.	Born	2002 clubs	Projection
17	Fryman, Travis	R/R	6-1/195	3-25-69	Cleveland	Veteran looking to rebound after hitting .217 in 2002.
	Garcia, Luis	R/R	6-4/185	11-5-78	New Haven, Akron	Power hitting prospect likely a year away.
12	Gutierrez, Ricky	R/R	6-1/190	5-23-70	Cleveland	Neck injuries sidelined him last year. It's unclear if he'll be able to play again.
	Hafner, Travis	L/R	6-3/240	6-3-77	Oklahoma, Texas	Will be the first baseman for the Tribe as long as he can hit.
8	McDonald, John	R/R	5-11/175	9-24-74	Cleveland	Utility player hit .250 in first full major league season.
61	Phillips, Brandon	R/R	5-11/185	6-28-81	Harrisburg, Ott., Buf., Clev.	Will have every chance to win the second base job. Just might do it, too.
13	Vizquel, Omar	B/R	5-9/175	4-24-67	Cleveland	Picked up his offense last season. Defense didn't slip a bit.

No.	OUTFIELDERS	B/T	Ht./Wt.	Born	2002 clubs	Projection
24	Bradley, Milton	B/R	6-0/190	4-15-78	Cleveland, Buffalo, Akron	Only hit .249 last season and was injured. Should bounce back in 2003.
28	Broussard, Ben	L/L	6-2/220	9-24-76	Louisville, Buffalo, Cleveland	Provides power and versatility off the bench.
10	Crisp, Coco	B/R	6-0/185	11-1-79	New Haven, Akron, Clev., Buf.	May force the Indians to trade one of their outfielders if he continues to play well.
46	Escobar, Alex	R/R	6-1/180	9-6-78	DID NOT PLAY	Knee injury sidelined him for entire season. Indians will take their time with him.
20	Garcia, Karim	L/L	6-0/195	10-29-75	Columbus, N.Y. A.L., Buf., Clev.	If he walked more, he'd be the Indians' best outfielder.
11	Lawton, Matt	L/R	5-10/186	11-3-71	Cleveland, Akron	Shoulder injury wrecked his 2002 season. Should rebound in 2003.
	Spencer, Shane	R/R	6-0/225	2-20-72	New York A.L.	Gives the Indians some veteran outfield depth.

No.	DESIGNATED HITTERS	B/T	Ht./Wt.	Born	2002 clubs	
23	Burks, Ellis	R/R	6-2/205	9-11-64	Cleveland	Veteran who puts up great numbers annually.

THE COACHING STAFF

Eric Wedge, manager.
Buddy Bell, bench coach.
Mike Brown, pitching coach.
Jeff Datz, first base and organizational coach.
Luis Isaac, bullpen coach.
Eddie Murray, batting coach.
Joel Skinner, third base coach.

THE TOP NEWCOMERS

Brian Anderson: Veteran pitcher will bring some stability to a young rotation. Although he has struggled in recent years, Anderson will be a good mentor for young pitchers like C.C. Sabathia.

THE TOP PROSPECTS

Brandon Phillips: The one player the Indians really wanted from the Expos when they traded Bartolo Colon. Can win the second base job as long as he hits well. Hit .258 in his September call up with the Indians.

Travis Hafner: The Rangers had no place to put this first base prospect, so the Indians were glad to get their hands on him. He's a .300 hitter with good power. He has the inside track to replace Jim Thome at first.

DETROIT TIGERS

AMERICAN LEAGUE CENTRAL DIVISION

2003 SEASON

Tigers Schedule

Home games shaded; D—Day game (games starting before 5 p.m.); *—All-Star Game at Comiskey Park, Chicago. Subject to changes.

March/April

SUN	MON	TUE	WED	THU	FRI	SAT
30	31 D MIN	1	2 MIN	3 D MIN	4 D CWS	5 D CWS
6 D CWS	7	8 KC	9 D KC	10 D KC	11 CWS	12 D CWS
13 D CWS	14	15 MIN	16 MIN	17 MIN	18 KC	19 D KC
20 D KC	21	22 OAK	23 OAK	24 D OAK	25 SEA	26 SEA
27 D SEA	28	29 BAL	30 BAL			

May

SUN	MON	TUE	WED	THU	FRI	SAT
				1 D BAL	2 TB	3 D TB
4 D TB	5 BAL	6 BAL	7 D BAL	8	9 TB	10 TB
11 D TB	12	13 OAK	14 OAK	15 OAK	16 SEA	17 D SEA
18 D SEA	19 CLE	20 CLE	21 CLE	22 CLE	23 CWS	24 CWS
25 D CWS	26 D CLE	27 CLE	28 CLE	29	30 NYY	31 D NYY

June

SUN	MON	TUE	WED	THU	FRI	SAT
1 D NYY	2	3 SD	4 SD	5 D SD	6 SF	7 D SF
8 D SF	9	10 LA	11 LA	12 LA	13 COL	14 COL
15 D COL	16	17 CLE	18 CLE	19 D CLE	20 COL	21 COL
22 D COL	23 BOS	24 BOS	25 BOS	26 D BOS	27 ARI	28 ARI
29 D ARI	30 TOR					

July

SUN	MON	TUE	WED	THU	FRI	SAT
		1 TOR	2 TOR	3 KC	4 KC	5 KC
6 D KC	7	8 CWS	9 CWS	10 D CWS	11 BOS	12 BOS
13 D BOS	14	15 *	16	17 CWS	18 CWS	19 CWS
20 D CWS	21 BOS	22 BOS	23 CLE	24 CLE	25 KC	26 KC
27 D KC	28	29 SEA	30 SEA	31 D SEA		

August

SUN	MON	TUE	WED	THU	FRI	SAT
					1 MIN	2 MIN
3 D MIN	4	5 OAK	6 OAK	7 D OAK	8 MIN	9 MIN
10 D MIN	11 TEX	12 TEX	13 TEX	14 TEX	15 ANA	16 ANA
17 D ANA	18 TEX	19 TEX	20 TEX	21 ANA	22 ANA	23 D ANA
24 D ANA	25	26 CLE	27 CLE	28 CLE	29 CWS	30 CWS
31 D CWS						

September

SUN	MON	TUE	WED	THU	FRI	SAT
	1 D CLE	2 CLE	3 CLE	4 D CLE	5 TOR	6 D TOR
7 D TOR	8	9 NYY	10 NYY	11 NYY	12 KC	13 KC
14 D KC	15	16 TOR	17 TOR	18 TOR	19 MIN	20 D MIN
21 D MIN	22 KC	23 KC	24 KC	25 MIN	26 MIN	27 MIN
28 D MIN						

FRONT-OFFICE DIRECTORY

Owner ..... Mike Ilitch
President, chief executive officer, general manager ..... David Dombrowski
Special assistants to the president ..... Al Kaline, Willie Horton
Senior vice president ..... Jim Devellano
Senior vice president of business affairs ..... Jim Stapleton
Senior vice president of marketing and communications ..... Mike Veeck
Vice president of player personnel ..... Scott Reid
Vice president, baseball legal counsel ..... John Westhoff
Vice president, assistant general manager ..... Al Avila
Vice president of sales and service ..... Michael Dietz
Vice president of park operations ..... John Pettit
Vice president of finance and CFO ..... Stephen Quinn
Vice president of planning and research ..... Elaine Lewis
Vice president of suite sales and service ..... Charles P. Jones
Vice president of ticket sales and service ..... Bob Raymond
Special assistant to the general manager ..... Al Hargesheimer
Director of scouting ..... Greg Smith
Director of player development ..... Steve Boros
Director of minor league operations ..... Ricky Bennett
Director of baseball administration ..... Dave Miller
International liaison/instructor ..... Joe Alvarez
Minor league field coordinator ..... Glenn Ezell
Assistant, baseball operations, foreign affairs ..... Ramon Pena
Assistant, baseball operations ..... Mike Smith
Traveling secretary ..... Bill Brown
Senior director of information technology ..... Cole Stewart
Senior director of ticket services ..... Ken Marchetti
Senior director of communications ..... Cliff Russell
Manager, media relations ..... Jim Anderson
Coordinator, media relations ..... Brian Britten
Assistant, media relations ..... Rick Thompson
Manager, broadcasting and media relations ..... Molly Light
Director, marketing ..... Ellen Hill-Zeringue
Director, community relations ..... Celia Bobrowsky
Director, human resources ..... Lara Juras
Director, fantasy camps ..... Jerry Lewis
Director, finance ..... Jennifer Orow
Director, promotions ..... Joel Scott

MINOR LEAGUE AFFILIATES

Class	Team	League	Manager
AAA	Toledo	International	Larry Parrish
AA	Erie	Southern	Kevin Bradshaw
A	Lakeland	Florida State	Gary Green
A	West Michigan	Midwest	Phil Regan
A	Oneonta	New York-Pennsylvania	Randy Ready
Rookie	Gulf Coast Tigers	Gulf Coast	Howard Bushong

ASSISTANCE STAFF

Manager, home clubhouse
Jim Schmakel

Assistant manager, visiting clubhouse
John Nelson

Team physicians
Kyle Anderson, M.D., David J. Collon, M.D., Louis Saco, M.D., Michael Workings, M.D.

Medical director/head athletic trainer
Kevin Rand

Assistant athletic trainer
Steve Carter

Strength and conditioning coach
Dennie Taft

Scouts

Scott Bream, Jerome Cochran, Dick Egan, Rob Guzik, Mike Herbert, Joe Hodges, Jeff Malinoff, Pat Murtaugh, Frank Paine, Derrick Ross, Rueben Smiley, Clyde Weir, Rob Wilfong, Gary York, Bill Buck, Bob Cummings, Tim Grieve, Jack Hays, Tom Hinkle, Lou Laslo, Mark Monahan, Steve Nichols, Brian Reid, Mike Russell, Steve Taylor, Jeff Wetherby, Steve Williams, Harold Zonder

BROADCAST INFORMATION

Radio: WXYT-AM (1270).
TV: WKBD (Channel 50).
Cable TV: Fox Sports Net Detroit.

SPRING TRAINING

Ballpark (city): Joker Marchant Stadium (Lakeland, Fla.).
Ticket information: 863-686-8075.

BALLPARK INFORMATION

Ballpark (capacity, surface)
Comerica Park (40,120)

Address
2100 Woodward
Detroit, MI 48201

Official website
www.detroittigers.com

Business phone
313-471-2000

Ticket information
313-471-BALL

Ticket prices
$60 (On-Deck Circle, Tiger Den)
$35 (terrace), $30 (infield box)
$25 (outfield box, club seats)
$20 (upper box), $15 (mezzanine)
$14 (pavilion), $12 (upper reserved)
$8 (bleachers), $5 (Skyline)

Field dimensions (from home plate)
To left field at foul line, 345 feet
To center field, 420 feet
To right field at foul line, 330 feet

First game played
April 11, 2000 (Tigers 5, Mariners 2)

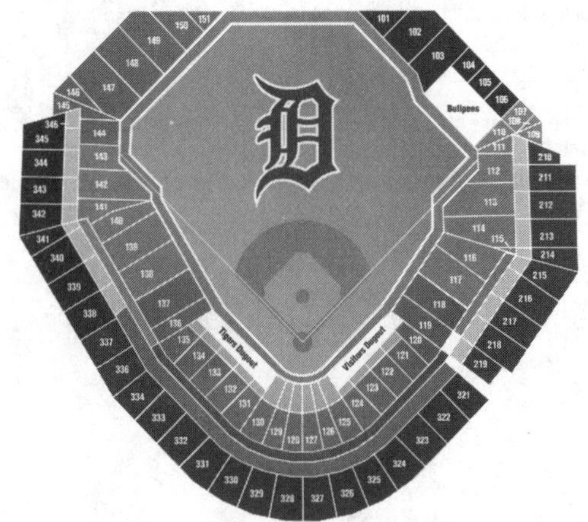

Follow the Tigers all season at: www.sportingnews.com/baseball/teams/tigers/

TIGERS SPRING ROSTER

No.	PITCHERS	B/T	Ht./Wt.	Born	2002 clubs	Projection
14	Anderson, Matt	R/R	6-4/200	8-17-76	Detroit	Closer spent the majority of 2002 injured. Might have to battle to get job back.
24	Bernero, Adam	R/R	6-4/205	11-28-76	Toledo, Detroit	Dominant in the minors, but hasn't translated that into major league success.
	Burnside, Adrian	R/L	6-3/168	3-15-77	Altoona	Has pitched well in the minors, but isn't quite ready for the majors.
	Cordova, Jorge	R/R	6-0/190	1-13-78	Stockton, Chatt., Louisville	Has potential to be a closer. If not, he'll be quite good in long relief.
34	Cornejo, Nate	R/R	6-5/240	9-24-79	Toledo, Detroit	Will likely get a spot in the rotation. Still young and learning how to pitch.
61	Eckenstahler, Eric	L/L	6-7/220	12-17-76	Toledo, Detroit	Had 13 strikeouts in eight major league innings. Needs one more year in minors.
62	German, Franklyn	R/R	6-4/170	1-20-80	Midland, Toledo, Detroit	Can claim the closer job if Matt Anderson falters.
41	Henriquez, Oscar	R/R	6-6/220	1-28-74	Toledo, Detroit	Must stay healthy in order to have a job in the bullpen.
70	Kalita, Tim	R/L	6-2/220	11-21-78	Toledo	Won only one game before succumbing to injuries in Class AAA.
	Knotts, Gary	R/R	6-3/230	2-12-77	Florida, Calgary	Will help to rebuild Tigers pitching depth.
	Ledezma, Wil	L/L	6-3/152	1-21-81	Augusta, Gulf Coast Red Sox	Lefty had 38 strikeouts in 23 innings. Might be too young for the majors.
58	Loux, Shane	R/R	6-2/205	8-31-79	Toledo, Detroit	Still struggling to regain his velocity, but he's only 23, so time is on his side.
46	Maroth, Mike	L/L	6-0/180	8-17-77	Toledo, Detroit	Won six games in only 21 starts. Will be in the Tigers rotation.
28	Patterson, Danny	R/R	6-0/185	2-17-71	Detroit, Toledo	Elbow injury sidelined him last season, he'll be out for almost all of 2003.
	Robertson, Nate	R/L	6-2/215	9-3-77	Portland, Florida	Young lefty could battle for rotation spot this year.
56	Rodney, Fernando	R/R	5-11/170	3-18-77	Erie, Detroit, Toledo	No longer a starter, he'll be battling for a job in the bullpen.
	Roney, Matt	R/R	6-4/225	1-10-80	Asheville, Carolina	Struggled in 13 starts in Class AA. Needs more time in the minors.
37	Sparks, Steve	R/R	6-0/195	7-2-65	Detroit	Knuckleballer was knocked around pretty hard last year. He's still durable.
50	Van Hekken, Andy	R/L	6-3/175	7-31-79	Erie, Toledo, Detroit	Relies on pinpont control. Will be in the Tigers rotation for years to come.
32	Walker, Jamie	L/L	6-2/190	7-1-71	Toledo, Detroit	Doesn't walk very many batters, but is susceptible to the long ball.

No.	CATCHERS	B/T	Ht./Wt.	Born	2002 clubs	Projection
15	Inge, Brandon	R/R	5-11/189	5-19-77	Toledo, Detroit	Great defensive catcher, but only a so-so hitter (.202).

No.	INFIELDERS	B/T	Ht./Wt.	Born	2002 clubs	Projection
22	Bocachica, Hiram	R/R	5-11/165	3-4-76	Los Angeles, Detroit	Will need to hit for average or walk more to have a regular job with the Tigers.
	Chapman, Travis	R/R	6-2/185	6-5-78	Reading	Rule 5 draftee hit .301 with 15 home runs in Class AA.
9	Easley, Damion	R/R	5-11/187	11-11-69	Detroit, Toledo	Might find himself on the bench if the younger kids show they can play.
	Espinosa, David	B/R	6-1/170	12-16-81	Stockton	Hit only .245, but he's only 21. Will need another year or two at least.
17	Halter, Shane	R/R	6-0/180	11-8-69	Detroit	Overachieved in '01 only to underachieve in '02. He's best suited as a utility man.
20	Infante, Omar	R/R	5-9/150	12-26-81	Toledo, Detroit	May be moved to second base if he's ready for the majors.
33	Munson, Eric	L/R	6-3/228	10-3-77	Toledo, Detroit	Power hitter is just starting to hit a groove. Tigers will make a spot for him.
8	Paquette, Craig	R/R	6-0/190	3-28-69	Detroit	Hit under .200 last season. Will have to fight for his job in spring.
43	Pena, Carlos	L/L	6-2/210	5-17-78	Oakland, Sacramento, Detroit	Should start hitting consistently with more playing time.
39	Santiago, Ramon	B/R	5-11/150	8-31-79	Erie, Toledo, Detroit	He'll be the man at short for 2003 and for many years after.

No.	OUTFIELDERS	B/T	Ht./Wt.	Born	2002 clubs	Projection
4	Higginson, Bobby	L/R	5-11/202	8-18-70	Detroit	Injuries have taken their toll, but he's still the Tigers' best option in left.
	Kingsale, Gene	B/R	6-3/190	8-20-76	Tacoma, Seattle, San Diego	Can win a job if he can hit and show his speed on the basepaths.
30	Lombard, George	L/R	6-0/212	9-14-75	Greenville, Richmond, Detroit	Also competing for a job, he'll have to show September slump was just a fluke.
31	Monroe, Craig	R/R	6-1/195	2-27-77	Toledo, Detroit	Hits well in the minors, but time is running out to show he can hit in the majors.
	Ross, Cody	R/L	5-11/180	12-23-80	Erie	Hit .280 with 19 homers in Class AA. At least one year away.
20	Torres, Andres	B/R	5-10/175	1-26-78	Toledo, Detroit	Speedy outfielder might be back in Class AAA for some seasoning.
26	Young, Dmitri	B/R	6-2/235	10-11-73	Detroit	Tigers will have to find an everyday spot for him, so he's comfortable at the plate.

No.	DESIGNATED HITTERS	B/T	Ht./Wt.	Born	2002 clubs	
7	Palmer, Dean	R/R	6-1/219	12-27-68	Detroit	Injuries have sapped his production. Managed only 12 at-bats last season.

THE COACHING STAFF

Alan Trammell, manager.
Bob Cluck, pitching coach.
Bruce Fields, hitting coach.
Kirk Gibson, bench coach.
Mick Kelleher, first base and infield coach.
Lance Parrish, bullpen coach.
Juan Samuel. third base coach.

THE TOP NEWCOMERS

Travis Chapman: Third baseman showed good power and decent defense last season. Tigers either have to keep him on the roster or return him to the Phillies.

Gene Kingsale: While his batting average isn't that high, he still manages to get on base, something the Tigers didn't do very often in 2002.

THE TOP PROSPECTS

Omar Infante: Could possibly be the shortstop of the future. He'll be battling Ramon Santiago for the job. And if Santiago wins, Infante could be moved to second base.

Eric Munson: Hit 24 homers in Class AAA Toledo. He also batted .262 and walked 77 times, chances are he's ready for the big leagues.

Kansas City Royals

American League Central Division

2003 SEASON

Royals Schedule

Home games shaded; D—Day game (games starting before 5 p.m.); *—All-Star Game at Comiskey Park, Chicago. Subject to changes.

March/April

SUN	MON	TUE	WED	THU	FRI	SAT
30	31 D CWS	1	2 D CWS	3 D CWS	4 CLE	5 D CLE
6 D CLE	7	8 DET	9 D DET	10 D DET	11 CLE	12 D CLE
13 D CLE	14 CLE	15 CWS	16 CWS	17 D CWS	18 DET	19 D DET
20 D DET	21	22 MIN	23 MIN	24 D MIN	25 TOR	26 D TOR
27 D TOR	28	29 BOS	30 BOS			

May

SUN	MON	TUE	WED	THU	FRI	SAT
				1 BOS	2 BAL	3 D BAL
4 D BAL	5 BOS	6 BOS	7 D BOS	8 BAL	9 BAL	10 BAL
11 D BAL	12 MIN	13 MIN	14 MIN	15 D MIN	16 TOR	17 TOR
18 D TOR	19	20 SEA	21 SEA	22 D SEA	23 OAK	24 D OAK
25 D OAK	26	27 SEA	28 D SEA	29 OAK	30 OAK	31 D OAK

June

SUN	MON	TUE	WED	THU	FRI	SAT
1 D OAK	2	3 LA	4 LA	5 LA	6 COL	7 COL
8 D COL	9	10 ARI	11 ARI	12 ARI	13 SF	14 SF
15 D SF	16	17 MIN	18 MIN	19 D MIN	20 STL	21 STL
22 D STL	23	24 CLE	25 CLE	26 CLE	27 STL	28 STL
29 D STL	30 CLE					

July

SUN	MON	TUE	WED	THU	FRI	SAT
		1 CLE	2 CLE	3 DET	4 DET	5 DET
6 D DET	7	8 ANA	9 ANA	10 D ANA	11 TEX	12 TEX
13 TEX	14	15 *	16	17 SEA	18 SEA	19 SEA
20 SEA	21 OAK	22 OAK	23 MIN	24 D MIN	25 DET	26 DET
27 D DET	28	29 CWS	30 CWS	31 CWS		

August

SUN	MON	TUE	WED	THU	FRI	SAT
					1 TB	2 TB
3 D TB	4 CWS	5 CWS	6 D CWS	7 TB	8 TB	9 TB
10 D TB	11 NYY	12 NYY	13 NYY	14	15 MIN	16 D MIN
17 D MIN	18 NYY	19 NYY	20 D NYY	21 MIN	22 MIN	23 MIN
24 D MIN	25	26 TEX	27 TEX	28 TEX	29 ANA	30 ANA
31 D ANA						

September

SUN	MON	TUE	WED	THU	FRI	SAT
	1 D TEX	2 TEX	3 TEX	4	5 ANA	6 ANA
7 D ANA	8	9 CLE	10 CLE	11 D CLE	12 DET	13 DET
14 D DET	15	16 CLE	17 CLE	18 CLE	19 CWS	20 CWS
21 D CWS	22 DET	23 DET	24 DET	25 CWS	26 CWS	27 CWS
28 D CWS						

FRONT-OFFICE DIRECTORY

Board of directors	David Glass, Dan Glass, Don Glass, Ruth Glass, Dayna Martz, Julia Irene Kauffman, Herk Robinson
Chairman/owner	David Glass
President	Dan Glass
Executive vice president & chief operating officer	Herk Robinson
Senior vice president & general manager	Allard Baird
Senior vice president, business operations	Mark Gorris
Vice president, baseball operations	George Brett
Vice president, finance & administration	Dale Rohr
Vice president, sales & marketing	Charlie Seraphin
Assistant general manager, player personnel	Muzzy Jackson
Senior advisor to the general manager	Art Stewart
Assistant to the general manager	Brian Murphy
Special assistants to the general manager	Pat Jones, Frank White Jr.
Manager of Major League operations	Karol Kyte
Senior director, scouting	Deric Ladnier
Manager, baseball operations	Jim Wong
Manager, scouting administration	Linda Smith
Manager, minor league operations	Shaun McGinn
Manager, team travel	Jeff Davenport
Director, community relations	Shani Tate
Senior director, broadcasting & public relations	David Witty
Director, broadcast services & Royals alumni	Fred White
Manager, media relations	Aaron Babcock
Manager, media services	Chris Stathos
Senior director/controller	John Luther
Senior director, payroll & benefits accounting	Tom Pfannenstiel
Senior director, information systems	Jim Edwards
Senior director, ticket operations	Lance Buckley
Director, ticket services	Chris Darr
Director, season ticket services	Joe Grigoli
Director, event operations & guest relations	Chris Richardson
Director, groundskeeping & landscaping	Trevor Vance
Manager, stadium engineering	Chris Frank
Director, stadium operations	Rodney Lewallen
Director, season & group ticket sales	Rick Amos
Director of promotions	Kim Hillix
Senior director, sales development	Mike Phillips
Director, corporate sponsorship sales	Michele Kammerer

MINOR LEAGUE AFFILIATES

Class	Team	League	Manager
AAA	Omaha	Pacific Coast	Mike Jirschele
AA	Wichita	Texas	Keith Bodie
A	Wilmington	Carolina	Bill Gardner Jr.
A	Burlington	Midwest	Joe Szekely
Rookie	Arizona Royals	Arizona	Lloyd Simmons

ASSISTANCE STAFF

Team physician
Dr. Steve Joyce

Athletic trainer
Nick Swartz

Assistant athletic trainer
Frank Kyte

Strength and conditioning coordinator
Chris Mihlfeld

Equipment manager
Mike Burkhalter

Visiting clubhouse manager
Chuck Hawke

Professional scouts
Brannon Bonifay, Louie Medina, John Wathan, Earl Winn

Special assignment scout
Carlos Pascual

Regional cross-checkers
Jeff McKay, Junior Vizcaino, Dennis Woody

Latin American scouting coordinator
Albert Gonzalez

Dominican scouting coordinator
Luis Silverio

Territorial scouts
Bob Bishop, Mike Brown, Jason Bryans, Steve Connolly, Albert Gonzalez, Spencer Graham, Phil Huttman, Gary Johnson, Cliff Pastornicky, Johnny Ramos, Max Semler, Chet Sergo, Greg Smith, Keith Snider, Gerald Turner, Brad Vaughn, Jon Weil, Mark Willoughby

BROADCAST INFORMATION

Radio: KMBZ-AM (980).
Cable TV: Royals Television Network, LLC.

SPRING TRAINING

Ballpark (city): Surprise Stadium (Surprise, Ariz.).
Ticket information: 623-594-5600.

BALLPARK INFORMATION

Ballpark (capacity, surface)
Kauffman Stadium (40,793, grass)

Address
P.O. Box 419969
Kansas City, MO 64141-6969

Official website
www.kcroyals.com

Business phone
816-921-8000

Ticket information
816-504-4040, 800-6-ROYALS

Ticket prices
$22 (club box)
$21 (dugout box)
$18 (field box, dugout plaza)
$16 (field plaza)
$12 (view box)
$10 (OF plaza, view level IF)
$5 (view level)

Field dimensions (from home plate)
To left field at foul line, 330 feet
To center field, 400 feet
To right field at foul line, 330 feet

First game played
April 10, 1973 (Royals 12, Rangers 1)

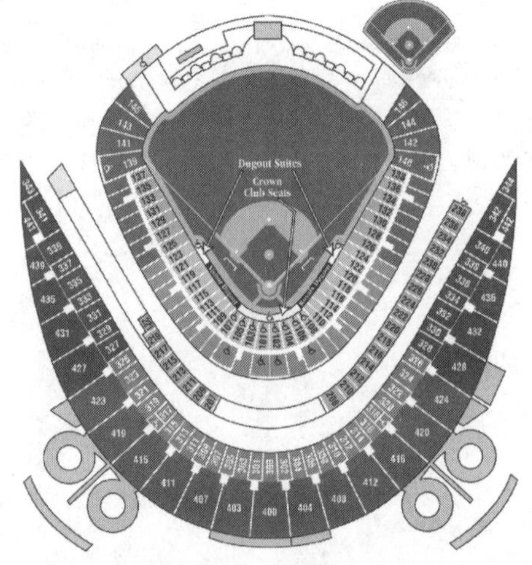

Follow the Royals all season at: www.sportingnews.com/baseball/teams/royals/

ROYALS SPRING ROSTER

No.	PITCHERS	B/T	Ht./Wt.	Born	2002 clubs	Projection
48	Affeldt, Jeremy	L/L	6-4/215	6-6-79	Kansas City, Wichita	Whether he starts or relieves, he pitched himself onto the team last year.
53	Asencio, Miguel	R/R	6-2/190	9-29-80	Kansas City	He may end up in Class AAA to build up arm strength.
26	Austin, Jeff	R/R	6-0/185	10-19-76	Kansas City, Omaha	Only pitched 10 games with the Royals, but showed he could be a good reliever.
35	Bukvich, Ryan	R/R	6-3/235	5-13-78	Wichita, Omaha, Kansas City	Could be potential closer if he can keep control of his fastball.
	Carrasco, Dan	R/R	6-2/191	4-12-77	Lynchburg	Rule 5 closer had 29 saves last season.
	Ferguson, Ian	R/R	6-4/220	8-23-79	Wilmington, Wichita	Went 18-3 in 28 starts in the minors.
32	George, Chris	L/L	6-2/200	9-16-79	Omaha, Kansas City	Compared to Tom Glavine, he relies on control and working the corners.
	Gobble, Jimmy	L/L	6-3/175	7-19-81	Wichita	Will get his fair share of strikeouts, but needs one more minor league season.
38	Grimsley, Jason	R/R	6-3/205	8-7-67	Kansas City, Wichita	Had success as setup man in the bullpen; expect more of the same.
40	Hernandez, Runelvys	R/R	6-1/205	4-27-78	Wilmington, Wichita, Kansas City	Won four games with Kansas City. Expected to be a big part of the rotation.
52	Hill, Jeremy	R/R	5-10/185	8-8-77	Wichita, Kansas City	Had 19 saves in Class AA. Might be one season away.
	Lopez. Albie	R/R	6-2/240	8-18-71	Atlanta, Greenville	Will be given every chance to make the rotation after subpar 2002 season.
54	MacDougal, Mike	B/R	6-4/195	3-5-77	Oma., Wich., GCRoy., Wil., K.C.	Potential closer of the future. The Royals aren't going to rush him.
31	May, Darrell	L/L	6-2/184	6-13-72	Omaha, Kansas City, Wichita	Slowed by injuries, he pitched well as a starter and reliever.
57	Mullen, Scott	R/L	6-2/195	1-17-75	Omaha, Kansas City	Had decent numbers in his 40 games with the Royals. Could be full-time reliever.
43	Obermueller, Wes	R/R	6-2/195	12-22-76	Wilmington, Wichita, Kansas City	Didn't fare well in two starts with the Royals, ticketed for Class AAA.
56	Sedlacek, Shawn	R/R	6-4/200	6-29-77	Wichita, Kansas City, Omaha	Could use another season in the minors, but the Royals might need his arm.
59	Snyder, Kyle	B/R	6-8/220	9-9-77	Wilmington, Wichita	Bouncing back from elbow surgery, he'll be in the minors for one more year.
46	Voyles, Brad	R/R	6-0/195	12-30-76	Omaha, Kansas City	If he can harness his pitches, he could become an effective reliever.
51	Wilson, Kris	R/R	6-4/225	8-6-76	Omaha, Wichita, Kansas City	Will earn a job if he can pitch well during spring training.

No.	CATCHERS	B/T	Ht./Wt.	Born	2002 clubs	Projection
2	Mayne, Brent	L/R	6-1/190	4-19-68	Kansas City, Wichita	His defense and poise behind the plate will keep him as the No. 1 catcher.
	Paulino, Ron	R/R	6-1/194	4-21-81	Lynchburg	Prospect hit .262 last season; also led the league in errors.
	Tonis, Mike	R/R	6-3/215	2-9-79	Gulf Coast Royals	Rebounding from an injury, he's the Royals' catcher of the future.

No.	INFIELDERS	B/T	Ht./Wt.	Born	2002 clubs	Projection
4	Berroa, Angel	R/R	6-0/175	1-27-78	Omaha, Kansas City	Has potential to be the Royals' starting shortstop. But he must hit better.
3	Febles, Carlos	R/R	5-11/185	5-24-76	Kansas City, Omaha	Must show consistency at the plate in order to be the everyday second baseman.
28	Harvey, Ken	R/R	6-2/240	3-1-78	Omaha	A pure hitter, he'll be with the Royals all season long.
	Machado, Alejandro	R/R	6-0/160	4-26-82	Wilmington	Stole 20 bases in Class A. Second baseman of the future.
16	Randa, Joe	R/R	5-11/190	12-18-69	Kansas City	Will be manning the hot corner again. Expect a season similar to 2002.
	Relaford, Desi	B/R	5-9/174	9-16-73	Seattle	Royals can use his consistent bat and glove in their lineup.
29	Sweeney, Mike	R/R	6-3/225	7-22-73	Kansas City, Omaha	If he can stay healthy, he'll be among the league leaders in batting average.

No.	OUTFIELDERS	B/T	Ht./Wt.	Born	2002 clubs	Projection
15	Beltran, Carlos	B/R	6-1/190	4-24-77	Kansas City	Five-tool player is delivering on all fronts.
30	Berger, Brandon	R/R	5-11/205	2-21-75	Omaha, Kansas City	He'll be a platoon player when he recovers from shoulder surgery.
27	Brown, Dee	L/R	6-0/225	3-27-78	Omaha, Kansas City	If he can harness his swing, he'll make it as a designated hitter.
9	Gomez, Alexis	L/L	6-2/180	8-6-80	Wichita, Kansas City	Can hit and steal bases. Will need a year at Class AAA.
45	Guiel, Aaron	L/R	5-10/200	10-5-72	Omaha, Kansas City	Could be a lefty off the bench if he shows he can hit consistently.
18	Ibanez, Raul	L/R	6-2/200	6-2-72	Kansas City	Had six triples in 2002. Pitchers will be ready for him in 2003.
14	Quinn, Mark	R/R	6-1/195	5-21-74	Omaha, Wichita, Kansas City	He'll be a good player whenever he decides to put it all together.
24	Tucker, Michael	L/R	6-2/195	6-25-71	Kansas City	Hits righties well and has a good arm in the outfield.

THE COACHING STAFF

Tony Pena, manager.
John Cumberland, pitching coach.
Tom Gamboa, to be determined.
John Mizerock, to be determined.
Jeff Pentland, hitting coach.
Bob Schaefer, bench coach.

THE TOP NEWCOMERS

Albie Lopez: Will be counted on to bring veteran leadership to a young pitching staff. But he'll need to stay healthy to be of any use to the Royals.

THE TOP PROSPECTS

Alexis Gomez: Hits for power, average and has speed to burn. Could contend for an outfield spot this year, but the Royals would be wise not to rush him.

Ken Harvey: The Royals' top minor league first baseman continues to produce. He hit well in Class AAA (.277, 20 homers, 75 RBIs) and should be in line for a designated hitter spot.

Minnesota Twins

American League Central Division

2003 SEASON

Twins Schedule
Home games shaded; D—Day game (games starting before 5 p.m.); *—All-Star Game at Comiskey Park, Chicago. Subject to changes.

March/April

SUN	MON	TUE	WED	THU	FRI	SAT
30	31 D DET	1	2 DET	3 D DET	4 TOR	5 TOR
6 D TOR	7 D NYY	8	9 NYY	10 D NYY	11 TOR	12 D TOR
13 D TOR	14	15 DET	16 DET	17 DET	18 NYY	19 NYY
20 D NYY	21 D NYY	22 KC	23 KC	24 D KC	25 CWS	26 CWS
27 D CWS	28	29 TB	30 TB			

May

SUN	MON	TUE	WED	THU	FRI	SAT
				1 D TB	2 BOS	3 D BOS
4 D BOS	5	6 TB	7 TB	8 TB	9 BOS	10 BOS
11 BOS	12 KC	13 KC	14 KC	15 D KC	16 CWS	17 CWS
18 D CWS	19	20 OAK	21 D OAK	22 D OAK	23 SEA	24 SEA
25 SEA	26	27 OAK	28 D OAK	29 SEA	30 SEA	31 D SEA

June

SUN	MON	TUE	WED	THU	FRI	SAT
1 D SEA	2	3 SF	4 SF	5 SF	6 SD	7 SD
8 D SD	9	10 COL	11 COL	12 COL	13 ARI	14 ARI
15 D ARI	16	17 KC	18 KC	19 D KC	20 MIL	21 MIL
22 D MIL	23	24 CWS	25 CWS	26 D CWS	27 MIL	28 MIL
29 D MIL	30 CWS					

July

SUN	MON	TUE	WED	THU	FRI	SAT
		1 CWS	2 CWS	3 CLE	4 CLE	5 CLE
6 D CLE	7	8 TEX	9 TEX	10 TEX	11 ANA	12 D ANA
13 D ANA	14	15 *	16	17 OAK	18 OAK	19 D OAK
20 D OAK	21 SEA	22 SEA	23 KC	24 D KC	25 CLE	26 CLE
27 D CLE	28	29 BAL	30 BAL	31 BAL		

August

SUN	MON	TUE	WED	THU	FRI	SAT
					1 DET	2 DET
3 D DET	4 BAL	5 BAL	6 BAL	7 D BAL	8 DET	9 DET
10 D DET	11 CLE	12 CLE	13 CLE	14 D CLE	15 KC	16 D KC
17 D KC	18	19 CLE	20 CLE	21 KC	22 KC	23 KC
24 D KC	25	26 ANA	27 ANA	28 D ANA	29 TEX	30 TEX
31 D TEX						

September

SUN	MON	TUE	WED	THU	FRI	SAT
	1 D ANA	2 ANA	3 D ANA	4	5 TEX	6 D TEX
7 D TEX	8 CWS	9 CWS	10 CWS	11 D CWS	12 CLE	13 CLE
14 D CLE	15 CLE	16 CWS	17 CWS	18 CWS	19 DET	20 D DET
21 D DET	22	23 CLE	24 CLE	25 DET	26 DET	27 DET
28 D DET						

FRONT-OFFICE DIRECTORY

Owner .... Carl R. Pohlad
President, Twins Sports Inc. .... T. Geron Bell
President, Minnesota Twins .... Dave St. Peter
Vice president/general manager .... Terry Ryan
Vice president/assistant general manager .... Bill Smith
Chief financial officer .... Kip Elliott
Vice president, operations .... Matt Hoy
Vice president, human resources and diversity .... Raenell Dorn
Vice president, marketing .... Patrick Klinger
Vice president, corporate partnerships .... Eric Curry
Assistant general manager .... Wayne Krivsky
Director of minor leagues .... Jim Rantz
Director of baseball operations .... Rob Antony
Director of scouting .... Mike Radcliff
Traveling secretary .... Remzi Kiratli
Director of communications .... Brad Ruiter
Media relations manager .... Sean Harlin
Assistant media relations manager .... Mike Herman
Baseball information coordinator .... Kristian Connolly

MINOR LEAGUE AFFILIATES

Class	Team	League	Manager
AAA	Rochester	International	Phil Roof
AA	New Britain	Eastern	Stan Cliburn
A	Fort Myers	Florida State	Jose Marzan
A	Quad City	Midwest	Jeff Carter
Rookie	Elizabethton	Appalachian	Ray Smith
Rookie	Gulf Coast Twins	Gulf Coast	Rudy Hernandez

BROADCAST INFORMATION

Radio: WCCO-AM (830).
TV: KMSP-TV (Channel 9).
Cable TV: Fox Sports Net North.

SPRING TRAINING

Ballpark (city): Lee County Sports Complex (Fort Myers, Fla.).
Ticket information: 800-33-TWINS.

ASSISTANCE STAFF

Team physicians
Dr. Dan Buss
Dr. Tom Jetzer
Dr. VeeJay Eyunni
Dr. John Steubs

Equipment manager
Jim Dunn

Head trainer
Jim Kahmann

Assistant trainer
Rick McWane

Strength and conditioning coach
Randy Popple

Visitor's clubhouse manager
Troy Matchan

Scouts
Vern Followell (Pro Scouting Supervisor)
Deron Johnson (West Supervisor)
Earl Frishman (East Supervisor)
Mike Ruth (Midwest Supervisor)
Joel Lepel (Midwest Supervisor)
Kevin Bootay, Ellsworth Brown, Larry Corrigan, Cal Ermer, Marty Esposito, Bill Harford, Sean Johnson, John Leavitt, Bill Lohr, Bill Mele, Gregg Miller, Bill Milos, Tim O'Neil, Hector Otero, Mark Quimuyog, Ricky Taylor, Brad Weitzel, Jay Weitzel, John Wilson, Mark Wilson

International scouts
Gene Grimaldi
Jose Leon
Yoshi Okamoto
Johnny Sierra
David Kim
Howard Norsetter
Jim Ridley

BALLPARK INFORMATION

Ballpark (capacity, surface)
Hubert H. Humphrey Metrodome
(48,678, artificial)

Address
34 Kirby Puckett Place
Minneapolis, MN 55415

Official website
www.twinsbaseball.com

Business phone
612-375-1366

Ticket information
1-800-33-TWINS

Ticket prices
$31 (lower deck club level)
$29 (Diamond View level)
$21 (lower deck reserved)
$14 (upper deck club level; g.a., lower LF)
$6 (g.a., upper deck)

Field dimensions (from home plate)
To left field at foul line, 343 feet
To center field, 408 feet
To right field at foul line, 327 feet

First game played
April 6, 1982 (Mariners 11, Twins 7)

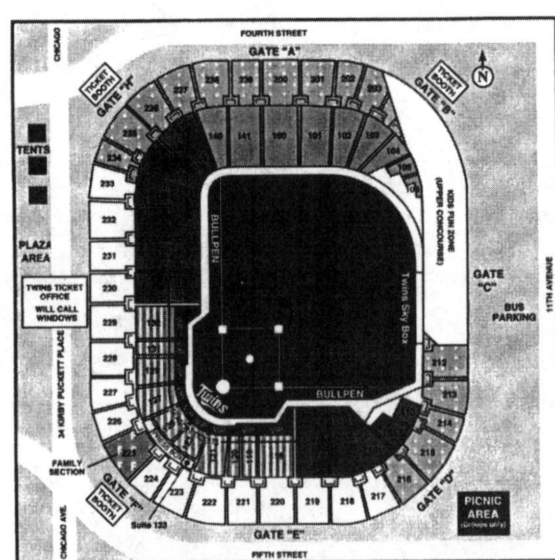

Follow the Twins all season at: www.sportingnews.com/baseball/teams/twins/

TWINS SPRING ROSTER

No.	PITCHERS	B/T	Ht./Wt.	Born	2002 clubs	Projection
19	Balfour, Grant	R/R	6-2/190	12-30-77	Edmonton	Could be ready for a spot in the Twins bullpen. Had 88 strikeouts in 71 innings.
	Eyre, Willie	R/R	6-1/200	7-21-78	Fort Myers, New Britain	Long reliever is capable of saving games.
52	Fiore, Tony	R/R	6-4/210	10-12-71	Edmonton, Minnesota	Won nine games and had a sub-3.00 ERA in 28 games out of the bullpen.
50	Frederick, Kevin	L/R	6-1/208	11-4-76	Edmonton, Minnesota	Allows too many hits, but could land a job in the bullpen.
18	Guardado, Eddie	R/L	6-0/194	10-2-70	Minnesota	Should continue to save games as long as Twins keep winning.
32	Hawkins, LaTroy	R/R	6-5/204	12-21-72	Minnesota	Won six games and posted an ERA under 2.25.
	Hoard, Brent	R/L	6-4/210	11-3-76	New Britain	Won 11 games in Class AA. Will need one more year in the minors.
37	Johnson, Adam	R/R	6-2/210	7-12-79	Edmonton	Shows good pitches as a starter, but could be converted to a closer if needs be.
	Kemp, Beau	R/R	6-0/182	10-31-80	Fort Myers	Had 29 saves and an 0.66 ERA in Class A.
49	Lohse, Kyle	R/R	6-2/190	10-4-78	Minnesota	Still walks too many batters, but those numbers will decline as he pitches more.
25	Mays, Joe	B/R	6-1/185	12-10-75	Minn., Fort Myers, New Britain	An elbow injury limited his effectiveness in 2002. Will be better in 2003.
21	Milton, Eric	L/L	6-3/220	8-4-75	Minnesota	Still gets in trouble against lefties. But a top pitcher nonetheless.
	Pridie, Jon	R/R	6-4/205	12-7-79	Fort Myers, New Britain	Won nine games, but still needs time in the minors.
22	Radke, Brad	R/R	6-2/188	10-27-72	Minnesota, GC Twins, Ft. Myers	Injuries slowed his 2002 season, but he'll rebound to reclaim job as staff ace.
31	Reed, Rick	R/R	6-1/195	8-16-65	Minnesota	Walked only 26 batters all season. Is valuable as trade bait.
39	Rincon, Juan	R/R	5-11/190	1-23-79	Edmonton, Minnesota	He needs just a little more time before he's ready for the majors.
33	Romero, J.C.	B/L	5-11/195	6-4-76	Minnesota	Quite possibly the best setup man in the A.L (1.89 ERA in 81 innings).
57	Santana, Johan	L/L	6-0/195	3-13-79	Edmonton, Minnesota	Has pitched well enough to earn a rotation spot.
56	Thomas, Brad	L/L	6-3/205	10-22-77	Edmonton	Needs one more season in Class AAA before he's ready for the majors.

No.	CATCHERS	B/T	Ht./Wt.	Born	2002 clubs	Projection
	Bowen, Rob	B/R	6-2/206	2-24-81	Fort Myers, Quad City	Switch-hitting catcher still a few years away from the majors.
24	LeCroy, Matt	R/R	6-2/225	12-13-75	Edmonton, Minnesota	Could be the club's DH against lefties after hitting .289 against them in 2002.
26	Pierzynski, A.J.	L/R	6-3/220	12-30-76	Minnesota	Hit .300, but walked only 13 times. Committed only three errors behind the plate.
12	Prince, Tom	R/R	5-11/206	8-13-64	Minnesota	Defensively sound backup. Can't be counted on for more.

No.	INFIELDERS	B/T	Ht./Wt.	Born	2002 clubs	Projection
15	Guzman, Cristian	B/R	6-0/195	3-21-78	Minnesota	Hit .273, but his on-base percentage was a paltry .292.
7	Hocking, Denny	B/R	5-10/183	4-2-70	Minnesota	Can play every position, but his numbers declined last season.
47	Koskie, Corey	L/R	6-3/217	6-28-73	Minnesota	Nagging injuries robbed him of his power. It should return in 2003.
16	Mientkiewicz, Doug	L/R	6-2/200	6-19-74	Minnesota	Not a power hitter, but he'll hit for average and provide good defense at first.
	Morban, Jose	R/R	6-1/170	12-2-79	Charlotte	Stole 21 bases, could be ready in a year or two.
	Morneau, Justin	L/R	6-4/205	5-15-81	New Britain	Hit .298 with 16 homers in Class AA. Twins' first baseman of the future.
2	Rivas, Luis	R/R	5-11/175	8-30-79	Minnesota, Fort Myers	Might be the year he develops into the .300 hitter the Twins have been waiting for.
58	Sears, Todd	L/R	6-5/215	10-23-75	Edmonton, Minnesota	100 RBIs in Class AAA may have earned him a spot on the big club.

No.	OUTFIELDERS	B/T	Ht./Wt.	Born	2002 clubs	Projection
5	Cuddyer, Mike	R/R	6-2/215	3-27-79	Edmonton, Minnesota	Converted third baseman expected to be starting right fielder.
	Ford, Lew	R/R	6-0/190	8-12-76	New Britain, Edmonton	Hit over .300 in both Class AA and AAA. Can steal some bases, too.
	Garbe, B.J.	R/R	6-2/195	2-3-81	Fort Myers	Former first-round pick needs to hit for average before he'll make it in the bigs.
48	Hunter, Torii	R/R	6-2/205	7-18-75	Minnesota	Gold Glove center fielder may be on track to hit .300 this season.
11	Jones, Jacque	L/L	5-10/176	4-25-75	Minnesota	Still has trouble hitting lefties and that'll keep him out of everyday lineup.
23	Kielty, Bobby	B/R	6-1/215	8-5-76	Edmonton, Minnesota	Will battle for right field job; .405 OBP works in his favor.
17	Mohr, Dustan	R/R	6-0/210	6-19-76	Minnesota	Has an uphill battle to get his right-field job back.
41	Restovich, Michael	R/R	6-4/233	1-3-79	Edmonton, Minnesota	Needs better strike zone judgement, but he's well on his way to the majors.
54	Ryan, Michael	L/R	6-0/185	7-6-77	Edmonton, Minnesota	Could be a lefthanded bat off the bench. Can supply power when he needs to.

THE COACHING STAFF

Ron Gardenhire, manager.
Steve Liddle, bench coach.
Al Newman, third-base coach.
Rick Stelmaszek, bullpen coach.
Rick Anderson, pitching coach.
Scott Ullger, hitting coach.

THE TOP PROSPECTS

Justin Morneau: This big lefthanded bat will be aiming for the first-base job in a couple of years. Can hit for power (16 homers) and average (.298).

Lew Ford: Hit .311 with a .401 OBP in Class AA, followed that with a .332 average with a .390 OBP in Class AAA. He also stole 26 bases between the two stops.

NEW YORK YANKEES

AMERICAN LEAGUE EAST DIVISION

2003 SEASON

Yankees Schedule

Home games shaded; D—Day game (games starting before 5 p.m.); *—All-Star Game at Comiskey Park, Chicago. Subject to changes.

March/April

SUN	MON	TUE	WED	THU	FRI	SAT
30	31 TOR	1 D TOR	2 TOR	3	4 TB	5 TB
6 D TB	7 D MIN	8	9 MIN	10 D MIN	11 TB	12 D TB
13 D TB	14 TOR	15 TOR	16 TOR	17 D TOR	18 MIN	19 MIN
20 D MIN	21 D MIN	22 ANA	23 ANA	24 ANA	25 TEX	26 TEX
27 D TEX	28	29 SEA	30 SEA			

May

SUN	MON	TUE	WED	THU	FRI	SAT
				1 SEA	2 OAK	3 D OAK
4 D OAK	5	6 SEA	7 SEA	8 SEA	9 OAK	10 D OAK
11 D OAK	12	13 ANA	14 ANA	15 ANA	16 TEX	17 D TEX
18 D TEX	19 BOS	20 BOS	21 BOS	22 TOR	23 TOR	24 D TOR
25 D TOR	26 D BOS	27 BOS	28 BOS	29	30 DET	31 D DET

June

SUN	MON	TUE	WED	THU	FRI	SAT
1 D DET	2	3 CIN	4 CIN	5 CIN	6 D CUB	7 D CUB
8 CUB	9	10 HOU	11 HOU	12 D HOU	13 STL	14 D STL
15 D STL	16	17 TB	18 TB	19 D TB	20 NYM	21 D NYM
22 NYM	23 TB	24 TB	25 TB	26 D TB	27 NYM	28 D NYM
29 NYM	30 BAL					

July

SUN	MON	TUE	WED	THU	FRI	SAT
		1 BAL	2 D BAL	3	4 D BOS	5 D BOS
6 D BOS	7 BOS	8 CLE	9 CLE	10 CLE	11 TOR	12 D TOR
13 D TOR	14	15 *	16	17 CLE	18 CLE	19 D CLE
20 D CLE	21 TOR	22 TOR	23 BAL	24 D BAL	25 BOS	26 D BOS
27 D BOS	28	29 ANA	30 ANA	31 ANA		

August

SUN	MON	TUE	WED	THU	FRI	SAT
					1 OAK	2 D OAK
3 D OAK	4	5 TEX	6 TEX	7 D TEX	8 SEA	9 D SEA
10 D SEA	11 KC	12 KC	13 KC	14	15 BAL	16 BAL
17 D BAL	18 KC	19 KC	20 D KC	21	22 BAL	23 D BAL
24 D BAL	25 BAL	26 CWS	27 CWS	28 D CWS	29 BOS	30 D BOS
31 D BOS						

September

SUN	MON	TUE	WED	THU	FRI	SAT
	1 D TOR	2	3 TOR	4 TOR	5 BOS	6 D BOS
7 D BOS	8	9 DET	10 DET	11 DET	12 TB	13 D TB
14 D TB	15 BAL	16 BAL	17 BAL	18 BAL	19 TB	20 TB
21 D TB	22 CWS	23 CWS	24 D CWS	25	26 BAL	27 D BAL
28 D BAL						

FRONT-OFFICE DIRECTORY

Principal owner ..... George M. Steinbrenner III
General partners ..... Harold Z. Steinbrenner, Henry G. Steinbrenner, Stephen W. Swindal
President ..... Randy Levine
Chief operating officer ..... Lonn A. Trost
Vice president, chief financial officer ..... Martin Greenspun
Vice president, ticket operations ..... Frank Swaine
Vice president, marketing ..... Deborah A. Tymon
Vice president, corporate & community relations ..... Brian Smith
Vice president, administration ..... Sonny Hight
Vice president ..... Richard Smith
Special advisors ..... Yogi Berra, Reggie Jackson, Clyde King, Don Mattingly
Senior vice president, general manager ..... Brian Cashman
Senior vice president, baseball operations ..... Mark Newman
Vice president, major league scouting ..... Gene Michael
Assistant general manager ..... Jean Afterman
Vice president, international & professional scouting ..... Gordon Blakeley
Vice president, scouting ..... Lin Garrett
Vice president, player personnel ..... Billy Connors
Traveling secretary ..... David Szen
Director, player personnel ..... Damon Oppenheimer
Director, player development ..... Rob Thomson
Baseball operations ..... Anthony Flynn
Assistant directors, baseball operations ..... John Coppolella, Brian Werner, Trevor Schaffer
Director, video operations ..... Charlie Wonsowicz
Manager, equipment ..... Rob Cucuzza
Manager, visiting clubhouse ..... Lou Cucuzza Jr.
Counsel ..... Alan Chang
Team physician, New York ..... Stuart Hershon, M.D.
Team physician, Tampa ..... Andrew Boyer, M.D.
Team orthopedist, Tampa ..... Allen Miller, M.D.
Head trainer ..... Gene Monahan
Assistant trainer ..... Steve Donohue
Coach, strength & conditioning ..... Jeff Mangold
Trainer, player development ..... Mark Littlefield
Coordinator, strength & conditioning ..... Russ Orr
Team chiropractor ..... Scott Hegseth, D.C.
Controller ..... Robert Brown
Senior director, ticket operations ..... Irfan Kirimca
Director, stadium operations ..... Kirk Randazzo
Assistant director, stadium operations ..... Doug Behar
Stadium superintendent ..... Pete Pullara
Head groundskeeper ..... Dan Cunningham
Director, media relations & publicity ..... Rick Cerrone
Assistant director, media relations & publicity ..... Jason Zillo
Senior advisor ..... Arthur Richman
Assistant, media relations ..... Ben Tuliebitz
Director, concessions & hospitality ..... Joel White
Director, publications & multimedia ..... Mark Mandrake
Director, corporate sales & sponsorship ..... Michael Tusiani
Director, scoreboard & broadcasting ..... Michael Bonner

MINOR LEAGUE AFFILIATES

Class	Team	League	Manager
AAA	Columbus	International	Bucky Dent
AA	Trenton	Eastern	Stump Merrill
A	Tampa	Florida State	To be announced
A	Battle Creek	Midwest	To be announced
A	Staten Island	New York-Pennsylvania	To be announced
Rookie	Gulf Coast Yankees	Gulf Coast	To be announced

ASSISTANCE STAFF

Regional cross-checkers
Joe Arnold, Tim Kelly, Greg Orr

Pro scouts
Jim Benedict, Ron Brand, Joe Caro, Bill Emslie

Scouts
Mike Baker, Brian Barber, Mark Batchko, Steve Boros, Wayne Britton, Mike Gibbons, Steve Lemke, Steve McIntosh, Jeff Patterson, Scott Pleis, Cesar Presbott, Gus Quattlebaum, Dan Radison, D.J. Svihlik, Steve Swail

Coordinator of Pacific rim scouting
John Cox

Coordinator of Latin American scouting
Carlos Rios

Foreign scouts
Manuel Duran, Ricardo Finol, Karl Heron, Ricardo Heron, Rudy Jabalera, Abraham Martinez, Victor Mata, Jim Patterson, Jose Quintero, Hector Rincones, Edgar Rodriguez, Arquimedes Rojas, Cesar Suarez, Freddy Tiburcio

BROADCAST INFORMATION

Radio: WCBS (880-AM).
TV: WCBS-TV (Channel 2).
Cable TV: Yankee Entertainment and Sports Network.

SPRING TRAINING

Ballpark (city): Legends Field (Tampa, Fla.).
Ticket information: 813-879-2244, 813-287-8844.

BALLPARK INFORMATION

Ballpark (capacity, surface)
Yankee Stadium (57,478, grass)

Address
Yankee Stadium
E. 161 St. and River Ave., Bronx, NY 10451

Official website
www.yankees.com

Business phone
718-293-4300

Ticket information
212-307-1212, 718-293-6013

Ticket prices
$65 (Championship Seat, loge)
$55 (Championship Seat, main box)
$47 (main box MVP), $42 (field box & loge box MVP)
$37 (main reserved MVP), $37 (main & loge box)
$33 (tier box), $33 (main reserved),
$17 (tier reserved), $15 (tier reserved value)
$8 (bleachers)

Field dimensions (from home plate)
To left field at foul line, 318 feet
To center field, 408 feet
To right field at foul line, 314 feet

First game played
April 18, 1923 (Yankees 4, Red Sox 1)

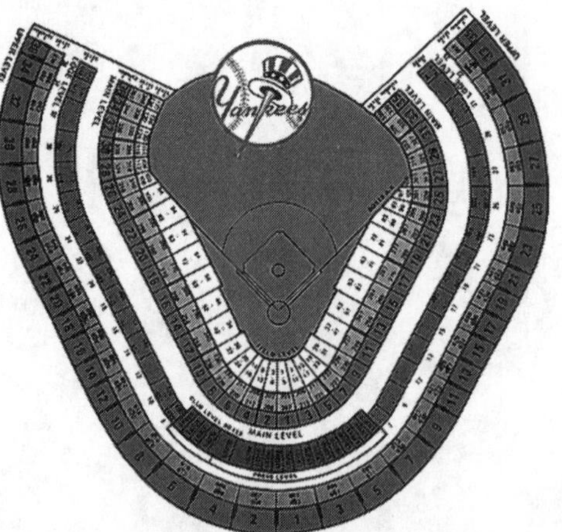

Follow the Yankees all season at: www.sportingnews.com/baseball/teams/yankees/

YANKEES SPRING ROSTER

No.	PITCHERS	B/T	Ht./Wt.	Born	2002 clubs	Projection
38	Choate, Randy	L/L	6-1/180	9-5-75	Columbus, New York A.L.	Is tough on lefties, but has to improve against righties.
77	Claussen, Brandon	L/L	6-2/175	5-1-79	Columbus	Injuries sidelined him after June. Still a year away.
22	Clemens, Roger	R/R	6-4/235	8-4-62	New York A.L., Tampa, Norwich	His ERA rose a bit last season, but he's still an elite pitcher.
	Contreras, Jose	R/R	6-4/225	12-6-71	DID NOT PLAY	Considered to be best pitcher not in Major League Baseball.
	Field, Nate	R/R	6-2/200	12-11-75	Omaha, Kansas City, Columbus	Trying to regain minor league form. Will provide depth if nothing else.
76	Graman, Alex	L/L	6-4/200	11-17-77	Norwich, Columbus	Likely to get a start or two by the end of the 2003 season.
32	Hammond, Chris	L/L	6-1/195	1-21-66	Atlanta	Replaces Mike Stanton as the lefty specialist out of the bullpen.
65	Hernandez, Adrian	R/R	6-1/185	3-25-75	Columbus, New York A.L.	Hasn't fared well in Class AAA. Time is running out.
41	Hitchcock, Sterling	L/L	6-0/205	4-29-71	Tam., Col., N.Y. A.L., GC Yank.	Yanks are paying him a lot of money and not using him a whole lot.
31	Karsay, Steve	R/R	6-3/215	3-24-72	New York A.L.	He injured his back, so '03 might not be as good '02.
62	Keisler, Randy	L/L	6-3/190	2-24-76	DID NOT PLAY	He'll have to bounce back from a season missed due to injuries.
48	Knight, Brandon	L/R	6-0/170	10-1-75	Columbus, New York A.L.	Still trying to figure out how to pitch in the majors. He better do it quickly.
35	Mussina, Mike	L/R	6-2/185	12-8-68	New York A.L.	Had an off year and still won 18 games. He'll turn it around in 2003.
	Osuna, Antonio	R/R	5-11/205	4-12-73	Chicago A.L.	Provides depth. Can close or be a setup man.
46	Pettitte, Andy	L/L	6-5/225	6-15-72	New York A.L., Tampa, Norwich	Still one of the Yankees' best pitchers.
42	Rivera, Mariano	R/R	6-2/185	11-29-69	New York A.L., GC Yankees	It's hard to say if injuries have caught up to him or if the hitters have.
18	Weaver, Jeff	R/R	6-5/200	8-22-76	Detroit, New York A.L.	Pitched himself into the bullpen; one of many starters.
33	Wells, David	L/L	6-4/240	5-20-63	New York A.L.	Fan favorite pitched 200-plus innings in 2002. 2003 shouldn't be any different.

No.	CATCHERS	B/T	Ht./Wt.	Born	2002 clubs	Projection
20	Posada, Jorge	B/R	6-2/205	8-17-71	New York A.L.	Shoulder problems and fatigue affected his 2002 campaign.
11	Widger, Chris	R/R	6-2/215	5-21-71	Columbus, New York A.L.	Provides a solid backup to Posada. Might get more playing time this season.

No.	INFIELDERS	B/T	Ht./Wt.	Born	2002 clubs	Projection
58	Almonte, Erick	R/R	6-2/180	2-1-78	Columbus, Norwich	With Jeter and Soriano blocking his path, he could be traded.
25	Giambi, Jason	L/R	6-3/235	1-8-71	New York A.L.	First season in New York was a success; did everything that was asked of him.
57	Henson, Drew	R/R	6-5/222	2-13-80	Columbus, New York A.L.	Still a work in progress; Class AAA numbers weren't that good.
2	Jeter, Derek	R/R	6-3/195	6-26-74	New York A.L.	His batting average took a dip in '02, but he's still one of the best.
36	Johnson, Nick	L/L	6-3/224	9-19-78	New York A.L., Columbus	Only hit .243, last season. Needs to improve against lefties.
12	Soriano, Alfonso	R/R	6-1/180	1-7-78	New York A.L.	Broke out in a big way last season. Came within whisker of 40-40 season.
19	Ventura, Robin	L/R	6-1/198	7-14-67	New York A.L.	He's keeping third base warm until Henson is ready. He'll split time with Zeile.
14	Wilson, Enrique	B/R	5-11/195	7-27-73	New York A.L.	Will be the utility man, and can play for extended periods if someone is injured.
	Zeile, Todd	R/R	6-1/200	9-9-65	Colorado	He'll be sharing duties with Ventura at third and help out as a designated hitter.

No.	OUTFIELDERS	B/T	Ht./Wt.	Born	2002 clubs	Projection
55	Matsui, Hideki	L/R	6-1/210	12-6-74	Yomiuri	Japanese slugger had 50 homers last season. Also hit .334.
43	Mondesi, Raul	R/R	5-11/230	3-12-71	Toronto, New York A.L.	Yankees are looking to trade him since they have plenty of outfielders.
59	Rivera, Juan	R/R	6-2/170	7-3-78	Col., N.Y.A.L., GC Yankees	He's in a battle for the right-field job. He's almost ready for full-time duty.
18	Thames, Marcus	R/R	6-2/205	3-6-77	Columbus, New York A.L.	Hard to tell which guy will show, his numbers have been up and down since '01.
27	White, Rondell	R/R	6-1/225	2-23-72	New York A.L.	Hit .240 in first season with the Yankees; he'll need to improve to stick around.
51	Williams, Bernie	B/R	6-2/205	9-13-68	New York A.L.	Battled a shoulder injury and still hit .333. Pencil him in for center field.

THE COACHING STAFF

Joe Torre, manager.

Willie Randolph, third base coach.

Lee Mazzilli, first base and outfield coach.

Mel Stottlemyre, pitching coach.

Don Zimmer, bench coach.

Rich Monteleone, bullpen coach.

Rick Down, hitting coach.

THE TOP NEWCOMERS

Hideki Matsui: The Yankees felt they needed more power and consistency from the outfield. So they signed 'Godzilla' out of Japan. The Yankees are hoping he'll make a monster-size splash in the Bronx.

THE TOP PROSPECTS

Drew Henson: Former quarterback is running out of time to show he'll be able to hit in the majors. Hit only .240 with 151 strikeouts in Class AAA last season.

Juan Rivera: He's been a .300 hitter in Class AAA for the past two seasons, and he has a strong arm in the outfield. He could win a job if he hits better than Raul Mondesi and Rondell White in spring training.

OAKLAND ATHLETICS

AMERICAN LEAGUE WEST DIVISION

2003 SEASON

Athletics Schedule

Home games shaded; D—Day game (games starting before 5 p.m.); *—All-Star Game at Comiskey Park, Chicago. Subject to changes. ‡Game played in Tokyo, Japan.

March/April

SUN	MON	TUE	WED	THU	FRI	SAT
23	24	25 ‡ SEA	26 ‡ SEA	27	28	29
30	31	1 SEA	2 SEA	3	4 ANA	5 D ANA
6 ANA	7	8 TEX	9 TEX	10 D TEX	11 ANA	12 ANA
13 D ANA	14 SEA	15 SEA	16 SEA	17 D SEA	18 TEX	19 D TEX
20 TEX	21	22 DET	23 DET	24 D DET	25 CLE	26 D CLE
27 D CLE	28	29 CWS	30 CWS			

May

SUN	MON	TUE	WED	THU	FRI	SAT
				1 CWS	2 NYY	3 D NYY
4 D NYY	5	6 CWS	7 CWS	8 D CWS	9 NYY	10 D NYY
11 D NYY	12	13 DET	14 DET	15 DET	16 CLE	17 D CLE
18 D CLE	19	20 MIN	21 D MIN	22 D MIN	23 KC	24 D KC
25 D KC	26	27 MIN	28 D MIN	29 KC	30 KC	31 D KC

June

SUN	MON	TUE	WED	THU	FRI	SAT
1 D KC	2	3 FLA	4 FLA	5 FLA	6 PHI	7 D PHI
8 D PHI	9	10 ATL	11 ATL	12 D ATL	13 MON	14 D MON
15 D MON	16	17 TEX	18 TEX	19 D TEX	20 SF	21 D SF
22 D SF	23 TEX	24 TEX	25 TEX	26 TEX	27 SF	28 D SF
29 D SF	30					

July

SUN	MON	TUE	WED	THU	FRI	SAT
		1 SEA	2 SEA	3 D SEA	4 ANA	5 ANA
6 D ANA	7	8 TB	9 D TB	10 D TB	11 BAL	12 D BAL
13 D BAL	14	15 *	16	17 MIN	18 MIN	19 D MIN
20 D MIN	21 KC	22 KC	23 SEA	24 SEA	25 ANA	26 D ANA
27 D ANA	28 ANA	29 CLE	30 CLE	31 D CLE		

August

SUN	MON	TUE	WED	THU	FRI	SAT
					1 NYY	2 D NYY
3 D NYY	4	5 DET	6 DET	7 D DET	8 CWS	9 CWS
10 D CWS	11 BOS	12 BOS	13 BOS	14 D BOS	15 TOR	16 D TOR
17 D TOR	18	19 BOS	20 BOS	21 BOS	22 TOR	23 D TOR
24 D TOR	25 TOR	26 BAL	27 BAL	28 D BAL	29 TB	30 TB
31 D TB						

September

SUN	MON	TUE	WED	THU	FRI	SAT
	1	2 BAL	3 BAL	4 BAL	5 TB	6 TB
7 D TB	8 ANA	9 ANA	10 ANA	11 D ANA	12 TEX	13 TEX
14 D TEX	15 ANA	16 ANA	17 D ANA	18	19 SEA	20 D SEA
21 D SEA	22 TEX	23 TEX	24 D TEX	25	26 SEA	27 D SEA
28 D SEA						

FRONT-OFFICE DIRECTORY

Owners ....Stephen C. Schott, Ken Hofmann
President ....Michael P. Crowley
Vice president and general manager....Billy Beane
Assistant general manager ....Paul DePodesta
Special assistants to general manager ....Randy Johnson, Matt Keough
Director of player development ....Keith Lieppman
Director of scouting....Eric Kubota
Director of minor league operations ....Ted Polakowski
Director of baseball administration....Pam Pitts
Traveling secretary ....Mickey Morabito
Scouting and player development coordinator....Danny McCormack
Baseball operations assistant ....Dave Forst
Vice president, broadcasting and communications....Ken Pries
Director of public relations ....Jim Young
Baseball information manager ....Mike Selleck
Media services/credentials....Debbie Gallas
Vice president, stadium operations ....David Rinetti
Vice president, sales and marketing ....David Alioto
Director of corporate sales....Franklin Lowe
Director of ticket operations....Steve Fanelli
Executive assistant ....Carolyn Jones
Executive assistant, baseball operations ....Betty Shinoda

MINOR LEAGUE AFFILIATES

Class	Team	League	Manager
AAA	Sacramento	Pacific Coast	Tony DeFrancesco
AA	Midland	Texas	Greg Sparks
A	Modesto	California	Rich Rodriguez
A	Kane County	Midwest	Webster Garrison
A	Vancouver	Northwest	To be announced
Rookie	Scotttsdale A's	Arizona	Ruben Escalera

BROADCAST INFORMATION

Radio: KFRC-AM (610).
TV: KICU-TV (Channel 36).
Cable TV: Fox Sports Bay Area.

SPRING TRAINING

Ballpark (city): Phoenix Stadium (Phoenix, Ariz.).
Ticket information: 602-392-0074.

ASSISTANCE STAFF

Team physician
Dr. Allan Pont

Team orthopedist
Dr. Jerrald Goldman

Trainers
Larry Davis
Steven Sayles

Equipment manager
Steve Vucinich

Visiting clubhouse manager
Mike Thalblum

National field coordinator
Chris Pittaro

Major League advance scout
Bob Johnson

Scouts
Steve Barningham
Tom Clark
Carl Fraticelli
Tim Holt
Rick Magnante
Billy Owens
Jeremy Scheid
Rich Sparks
Steve Bowden
Ruben Escalera
Kelly Heath
John Kuehl
Kelsey Mucker
Jim Pransky
Will Shock
Ron Vaughn

BALLPARK INFORMATION

Ballpark (capacity, surface)
Network Associates Coliseum (43,662, grass)

Address
Oakland Athletics
7000 Coliseum Way
Oakland, CA 94621

Official website
www.oaklandathletics.com

Business phone
510-638-4900

Ticket information
510-638-4627

Ticket prices
$32 (plaza club)
$30 (MVP infield)
$24 (field level)
$22 (plaza-infield)
$16 (plaza-outfield)
$8 (upper reserved, bleachers)

Field dimensions (from home plate)
To left field at foul line, 330 feet
To center field, 400 feet
To right field at foul line, 330 feet

First game played
April 17, 1968 (Orioles 4, Athletics 1)

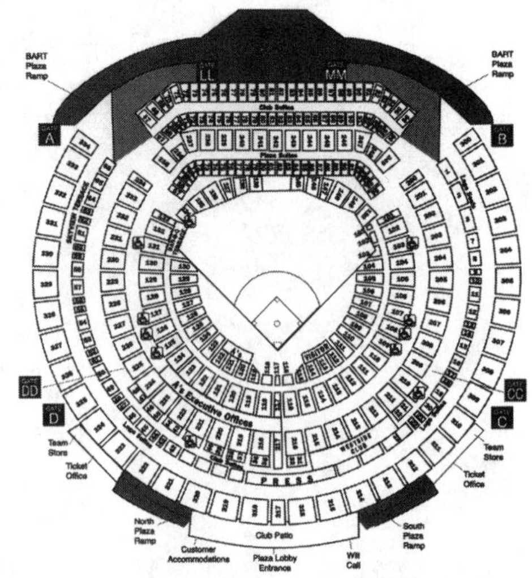

Follow the Athletics all season at: www.sportingnews.com/baseball/teams/athletics/

ATHLETICS SPRING ROSTER

No.	PITCHERS	B/T	Ht./Wt.	Born	2002 clubs	Projection
	Bazzell, Shane	L/R	6-2/180	3-22-79	Midland	Needs at least one more season in the minors working as a reliever.
57	Bowie, Micah	L/L	6-4/210	11-10-74	Sacramento, Oakland	Could claim a job in the bullpen as a lefty specialist.
53	Bradford, Chad	R/R	6-5/203	9-14-74	Oakland	Became one of the better setup men in the A.L. last season.
	Duchscherer, Justin	R/R	6-3/165	11-19-77	Sacramento	Control pitcher needs one more year in Class AAA.
	Fikac, Jeremy	R/R	6-2/185	4-8-75	San Diego, Mobile	Will give the A's more flexibility in the bullpen.
29	Foulke, Keith	R/R	6-0/210	10-19-72	Chicago A.L.	Acquired for Billy Koch, he's the A's new closer.
	Halama, John	L/L	6-5/210	2-22-72	Seattle, Tacoma	A's will be able to use his arm in rotation or bullpen.
56	Harang, Aaron	R/R	6-7/240	5-9-78	Midland, Sacramento, Oakland	Just needs more innings at the major league level.
32	Harville, Chad	R/R	5-9/180	9-16-76	Sacramento	Needs to stay healthy before he'll get another shot with the A's.
	Hernandez, Buddy	R/R	5-9/170	3-3-79	Greenville	Rule 5 lefty could find his niche in the bullpen.
37	Hiljus, Erik	R/R	6-6/222	12-25-72	Oakland, Sacramento	Gives the team depth as a starter.
15	Hudson, Tim	R/R	6-1/164	7-14-75	Oakland	Should win more than the 15 games he won in 2002.
31	Lilly, Ted	L/L	6-0/185	1-4-76	New York A.L., Oakland	Gives the A's another young, formidable starter.
45	Mecir, Jim	B/R	6-1/230	5-16-70	Oakland	Had a bit of an off year, but still an important part of bullpen.
20	Mulder, Mark	L/L	6-6/215	8-5-77	Oakland	Only a strained forearm slowed him down last season.
	Neu, Michael	B/R	5-10/190	3-9-78	Chattanooga, Louisville	Has potential to be closer in the future. Will be at Class AAA.
73	Rincon, Ricky	L/L	5-9/187	4-13-70	Cleveland, Oakland	Another good arm to face tough lefthanded batters.
	Smith, Roy	R/R	6-6/235	5-18-76	Buffalo, Cleveland	Power pitcher able to close out games when necessary.
40	Snow, Bert	R/R	6-1/190	3-23-77	Visalia, Midland	Injuries have slowed his development. Still has good potential for bullpen work.
	Valentine, Joe	R/R	6-2/195	12-24-79	Birmingham	Could be Oakland's closer as soon as 2004.
75	Zito, Barry	L/L	6-4/215	5-13-78	Oakland	Cy Young winner could repeat his phenomenal '02 success..

No.	CATCHERS	B/T	Ht./Wt.	Born	2002 clubs	Projection
55	Hernandez, Ramon	R/R	6-0/210	5-20-76	Oakland	Keeps improving at the plate, and is strong behind it.
8	Johnson, Mark	L/R	6-0/185	9-12-75	Chicago A.L.	Gives the A's a lefthanded option at the plate and another solid receiver.

No.	INFIELDERS	B/T	Ht./Wt.	Born	2002 clubs	Projection
	Bynum, Freddie	L/R	6-1/180	3-15-80	Visalia	Second baseman is .300 hitter with plenty of speed. Defense needs a little work.
3	Chavez, Eric	L/R	6-1/206	12-7-77	Oakland	Pencil him in for 30+ homers and a .275 average.
44	Durazo, Erubiel	L/L	6-3/240	1-23-74	Tucson, Arizona, El Paso	If he stays healthy, he'll have a huge season in this lineup.
14	Ellis, Mark	R/R	5-11/180	6-6-77	Sacramento, Oakland	With a solid 2002 campaign, Ellis stakes a claim to the second-base job.
40	German, Esteban	R/R	5-9/165	1-26-78	Sacramento, Oakland	If he shows consistency at the plate, the A's will have to make room for him.
2	Grabowski, Jason	L/R	6-3/200	5-24-76	Sacramento, Oakland	Will be battling for job as the A's utility man.
10	Hatteberg, Scott	L/R	6-1/210	12-14-69	Oakland	Proved he can play first base and provide veteran leadership.
11	Menechino, Frank	R/R	5-8/198	1-7-71	Oakland, Sacramento	Lost the job at second to Ellis, now has to prove he can hit to stay with team.
	Morrissey, Adam	R/R	5-11/170	6-8-81	Modesto, Midland	Needs at least one year in Class AAA before he'll see the majors.
4	Tejada, Miguel	R/R	5-9/200	5-25-76	Oakland	Had over 200 hits and only 19 errors at short. Don't forget about his MVP award.

No.	OUTFIELDERS	B/T	Ht./Wt.	Born	2002 clubs	Projection
22	Byrnes, Eric	R/R	6-2/210	2-16-76	Sacramento, Oakland	Will have to show more patience at the plate to stick in the majors.
24	Dye, Jermaine	R/R	6-5/220	1-28-74	Sacramento, Modesto, Oakland	Recovering from a broken leg, but should be back to normal in '03.
	Johnson, Rontrez	R/R	5-10/165	12-8-76	Omaha	Rule 5 drafter could be the fourth outfielder, if he shows he can hit.
12	Long, Terrence	L/L	6-1/202	2-29-76	Oakland	Will move back to left field with Singleton on the roster.
6	Piatt, Adam	R/R	6-2/205	2-8-76	Sacramento, Oakland	Streaky hitter needs to show consistent bat to make the team.
29	Singleton, Chris	L/L	6-2/210	8-15-72	Baltimore	Will provide steady defense in center and a solid bat at the plate.

THE COACHING STAFF

Ken Macha, manager.

Thad Bosley, hitting coach.

Brad Fischer, bullpen coach.

Rick Peterson, pitching coach.

Mike Quade, first-base coach.

Ron Washington, third base coach.

THE TOP NEWCOMERS

Keith Foulke: Gives the A's a less-expensive option at closer. Should have the same kind of success with team that Billy Koch did.

Erubiel Durazo: Has suffered through injuries since becoming a major leaguer in 1999. If he stays healthy he'll give the A's the production in the middle of the lineup they've been missing since Jason Giambi left for the Yankees.

THE TOP PROSPECTS

Freddie Bynum: Mark Ellis has the second-base job right now, but Bynum hit .306 with 41 steals in Class A Visalia. Probably still a year or two away.

Rontrez Johnson: Speedy outfielder hit .300 with 31 stolen bases in Class AAA. He posted a good strikeout to walk ratio (51-50), so he fits right in with the A's get-on-base philosophy.

Seattle Mariners

American League West Division

2003 SEASON

Mariners Schedule

Home games shaded; D—Day game (games starting before 5 p.m.); *—All-Star Game at Comiskey Park, Chicago. Subject to changes. ‡Game played in Tokyo, Japan.

March/April

SUN	MON	TUE	WED	THU	FRI	SAT
23	24	25 ‡ OAK	26 ‡ OAK	27	28	29
30	31	1 OAK	2 OAK	3	4 D TEX	5 TEX
6 D TEX	7	8 D ANA	9 ANA	10 ANA	11 TEX	12 TEX
13 D TEX	14 OAK	15 OAK	16 OAK	17 D OAK	18 ANA	19 ANA
20 D ANA	21	22 CLE	23 CLE	24 CLE	25 DET	26 DET
27 D DET	28	29 NYY	30 NYY			

May

SUN	MON	TUE	WED	THU	FRI	SAT
				1 NYY	2 CWS	3 CWS
4 CWS	5	6 NYY	7 NYY	8 NYY	9 CWS	10 CWS
11 D CWS	12	13 CLE	14 CLE	15 CLE	16 DET	17 D DET
18 D DET	19	20 KC	21 KC	22 D KC	23 MIN	24 MIN
25 MIN	26	27 KC	28 D KC	29 MIN	30 MIN	31 D MIN

June

SUN	MON	TUE	WED	THU	FRI	SAT
1 D MIN	2	3 PHI	4 PHI	5 PHI	6 NYM	7 NYM
8 D NYM	9	10 MON	11 MON	12 MON	13 ATL	14 D ATL
15 ATL	16 ANA	17 ANA	18 ANA	19 D ANA	20 SD	21 SD
22 D SD	23	24 ANA	25 ANA	26 ANA	27 SD	28 SD
29 D SD	30					

July

SUN	MON	TUE	WED	THU	FRI	SAT
		1 OAK	2 OAK	3 D OAK	4 TEX	5 TEX
6 TEX	7	8 BAL	9 BAL	10 BAL	11 TB	12 TB
13 D TB	14	15 *	16	17 KC	18 KC	19 KC
20 KC	21 MIN	22 MIN	23 OAK	24 OAK	25 TEX	26 D TEX
27 D TEX	28 TEX	29 DET	30 DET	31 D DET		

August

SUN	MON	TUE	WED	THU	FRI	SAT
					1 CWS	2 CWS
3 D CWS	4	5 CLE	6 CLE	7 CLE	8 NYY	9 D NYY
10 D NYY	11 TOR	12 TOR	13 TOR	14 TOR	15 BOS	16 D BOS
17 D BOS	18	19 TOR	20 TOR	21 TOR	22 BOS	23 D BOS
24 D BOS	25 D BOS	26 TB	27 TB	28 D TB	29 BAL	30 D BAL
31 D BAL						

September

SUN	MON	TUE	WED	THU	FRI	SAT
	1	2 TB	3 TB	4 TB	5 BAL	6 BAL
7 D BAL	8	9 TEX	10 TEX	11 TEX	12 ANA	13 ANA
14 D ANA	15 TEX	16 TEX	17 TEX	18 D TEX	19 OAK	20 D OAK
21 D OAK	22 ANA	23 ANA	24 D ANA	25	26 OAK	27 D OAK
28 D OAK						

FRONT-OFFICE DIRECTORY

Chairman & CEO .... Howard Lincoln
Board of directors .... Howard Lincoln, chairman; John Ellis, chairman emeritus; Minoru Arakawa; Chris Larson; Wayne Perry; Frank Shrontz, Craig Watjen
President & COO .... Chuck Armstrong
Executive vice president, baseball operations .... Pat Gillick
Executive vice president, business operations .... Bob Aylward
Executive vice president, finance & ballpark operations .... Kevin Mather
Executive vice president, legal & governmental affiars & general counsel ...... Clyde MacIver
Vice president, baseball administration .... Lee Pelekoudas
Vice president, scouting and player development .... Roger Jongewaard
Vice president, player development .... Benny Looper
Vice president, corporate business & community relations .... Joe Chard
Vice president, communications .... Randy Adamack
Vice president, marketing .... Kevin Martinez
Vice president, human resources .... Marianne Short
Vice president, ballpark operations .... Neil Campbell
Vice president, technology services .... Larry Witherspoon
Director, professional scouting .... Ken Compton
Director, scouting .... Frank Mattox
Director, team travel .... Ron Spellecy
Director, minor league administration .... Greg Hunter
Director, Pacific Rim operations .... Ted Heid
Director, baseball information .... Tim Hevly
Director, public information .... Rebecca Hale
Special assignment .... Woody Woodward
Home clubhouse manager .... Ted Walsh
Visiting clubhouse manager .... Henry Genzale

MINOR LEAGUE AFFILIATES

Class	Team	League	Manager
AAA	Tacoma	Pacific Coast	Dan Rohn
AA	San Antonio	Texas	Dave Brundage
A	San Bernardino	California	Steve Roadcap
A	Wisconsin	Midwest	Daren Brown
A	Everett	Northwest	To be announced
Rookie	Peoria Mariners	Arizona	Scott Steinmann

BROADCAST INFORMATION

Radio: KIRO-AM (710).
TV: KIRO-TV (Channel 7).
Cable TV: Fox Sports Net Northwest.

SPRING TRAINING

Ballpark: Peoria Stadium (Peoria, Ariz.).
Ticket information: 602-784-4444.

ASSISTANCE STAFF

Medical director
Dr. Larry Pedegana
Trainers
Rick Griffin
Assistant trainers
Tom Newberg, Kiyoshi Egawa
Strength and conditioning coach
Allen Wirtala
Team physicians
Dr. Mitchel Storey
Team dentist
Dr. Robert Hughes
Video coordinator
Carl Hamilton
Head groundskeeper
Bob Christopherson
Assistant groundskeepers
Leo Liebert, Tim Wilson
Senior advisor
Bob Engle
Advance scout
Stan Williams
National cross-checker
Steve Jongewaard
Major league scouts
Bob Harrison, Bill Kearns, Steve Pope
Scouting supervisors
Curtis Dishman, John McMichen, Wayne Norton, Carroll Sembera.
Scouts
Dave Alexander, Pedro Avila, Craig Bell, Tom Burgess, Emiliano Carrasquel, Rodney Davis, Stan Eldridge, Luis Fuenmayor, Phil Geisler, Dennis Gonsalves, Pedro Grifol, Patrick Guerrero, Rolando Gutierrez, Ron Hafner, Ron Kaintz, Mark Leavitt, Jae Lee, Jay Lee, Mark Lummus, Les McTavish, Diego Markwell, David May, Mauro Mazziotti, Luis Molina, Robert Mummau, Omer Munoz Sr., Dana Papasedero, Stacey Pettis, Pat Phelan, Myron Pines, Harry Porter, Phil Pote, Carlos Ramirez, Steve Rath, Tim Reynolds, Eric Robinson, Jesus Salazar, Rafael Santo Domingo, Bob Smyth, Fernando Soto, Dennis Springenatic, Jamey Storvick, Kyle Van Hooke, Ray Vince, Curtis Wallace, Karel Williams, Rob Williams

BALLPARK INFORMATION

Ballpark (capacity, surface)
Safeco Field (47,772, grass)
Address
1st Ave. S. & Atlantic
Seattle, WA 98104
Official website
www.seattlemariners.com
Business phone
206-346-4000
Ticket information
206-346-4001
Ticket prices
$45 (terrace club infield; lower box)
$35 (terrace club outfield)
$32 (field)
$23 (view box, lower outfield reserved)
$16 (view reserved)
$12 (left field bleachers)
$6 (center field bleachers)
Field dimensions (from home plate)
To left field at foul line, 331 feet
To center field, 405 feet
To right field at foul line, 326 feet
First game played
July 15, 1999 (Padres 3, Mariners 2)

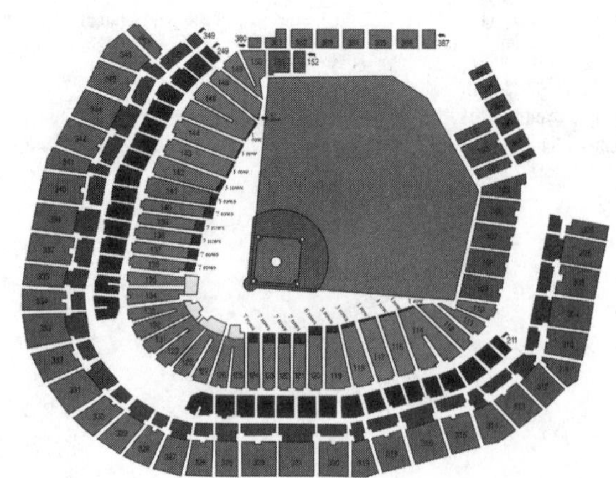

Follow the Mariners all season at: www.sportingnews.com/baseball/teams/mariners/

MARINERS SPRING ROSTER

No.	PITCHERS	B/T	Ht./Wt.	Born	2002 clubs	Projection
6	Anderson, Ryan	L/L	6-10/225	7-12-79	DID NOT PLAY	Top prospect was sidelined with injury for the entire season.
7	Charlton, Norm	B/L	6-3/205	1-6-63	DID NOT PLAY	Mariners are hoping his 40-year-old arm had one good season left.
5	Franklin, Ryan	R/R	6-3/165	3-5-73	Seattle, Everett	Starter or reliever, he pitched well in both roles.
4	Garcia, Freddy	R/R	6-4/235	6-10-76	Seattle	HIs ERA jumped over 4.00 last season. Mariners are hoping it was a fluke.
7	Hasegawa, Shigetoshi	R/R	5-11/178	8-1-68	Seattle	Won eight games in long relief role. Should be as effective in 2003.
8	Heaverlo, Jeff	R/R	6-1/215	1-13-78	DID NOT PLAY	Will be at Class AAA for season after missing 2002 with an injury.
	Johnson, Rett	L/R	6-2/211	7-6-79	San Bernardino, San Antonio	Went 13-5 between two minor league stops.
	Kent, Steve	B/L	5-11/170	10-3-78	Tampa Bay	Could fill lefty role in the bullpen, but likely ticketed for Class AAA.
	Looper, Aaron	R/R	6-2/185	9-7-76	San Antonio	Long reliever won six games, pitched 90 innings.
	Madritsch, Bobby	L/L	6-2/190	2-28-76	Winnipeg	Signed straight from independent leagues, he could contend for a rotation spot.
0	Mateo, Julio	R/R	6-0/177	8-2-77	San Antonio, Tacoma, Seattle	Will find a spot in the bullpen because he can pick the corners.
5	Meche, Gil	R/R	6-3/200	9-8-78	San Antonio	Slowly but surely coming back from an arm injury. Might be back in form for '03.
0	Moyer, Jamie	L/L	6-0/175	11-18-62	Seattle	Veteran shunned free-agent offers elsewhere to stay in Seattle.
3	Nelson, Jeff	R/R	6-8/235	11-17-66	Seattle, Everett	Continues to be a reliable setup man.
8	Pineiro, Joel	R/R	6-1/180	9-25-78	Seattle	Rookie made a big splash by winning 14 games.
1	Putz, J.J.	R/R	6-5/220	2-22-77	San Antonio, Tacoma	Could use one more season in Class AAA. Pitched well, but won only five games.
3	Rhodes, Arthur	L/L	6-2/205	10-24-69	Seattle	Can dominate hitters from either side of the plate.
2	Sasaki, Kazuhiro	R/R	6-4/220	2-22-68	Seattle	Only a sore elbow slowed him up in 2002. He'll bounce back in 2003.
0	Simpson, Allan	R/R	6-4/185	8-26-77	San Antonio	Had 99 strikeouts in 82 innings. Will get a job as a long reliever soon.
9	Soriano, Rafael	R/R	6-1/175	12-19-79	San Antonio, Seattle	Another young arm for the Seattle rotation.
2	Taylor, Aaron	R/R	6-7/230	8-20-77	San Antonio, Seattle	Could be closer of the future. Had 24 saves in Class AA.
5	Thornton, Matt	L/L	6-6/220	9-15-76	San Antonio	Former first-round pick was sidelined by injuries. At least a year away.

No.	CATCHERS	B/T	Ht./Wt.	Born	2002 clubs	Projection
	Christianson, Ryan	R/R	6-2/210	4-21-81	San Bernardino, San Antonio	Being groomed for duty when Dan Wilson's playing days are over.
3	Davis, Ben	B/R	6-4/214	3-10-77	Seattle	Committed only one error behind the plate. Seems to be progressing nicely.
6	Wilson, Dan	R/R	6-3/214	3-25-69	Seattle	Hit .295 last season, showing the Mariners he still can play.

No.	INFIELDERS	B/T	Ht./Wt.	Born	2002 clubs	Projection
29	Boone, Bret	R/R	5-10/190	4-6-69	Seattle	Drove in over 100 runs for the second straight year. Finally found his groove.
9	Cirillo, Jeff	R/R	6-1/190	9-23-69	Seattle	Some wonder if he's on the downside of his career. Still provides good defense.
	Colbrunn, Greg	R/R	6-0/212	7-26-69	Tucson, Arizona	Hit .333 with 10 homers in only 172 at-bats with D-backs last year.
8	Guillen, Carlos	B/R	6-1/202	9-30-75	Seattle	Took a huge step forward last season by hitting .261.
	Mabry, John	L/R	6-4/210	10-17-70	Philadelphia, Oakland	Gives Mariners plenty of depth and lefthanded bat off the bench.
5	Olerud, John	L/L	6-5/220	8-5-68	Seattle	Like Moyer, he too shunned the free agent market. Hit .300 with 22 homers in '02.
23	Ugueto, Luis	B/R	5-11/170	2-15-79	Seattle, Tacoma	Former Rule 5 player will probably spend 2003 in Class AAA.

No.	OUTFIELDERS	B/T	Ht./Wt.	Born	2002 clubs	Projection
16	Bloomquist, Willie	R/R	5-11/180	11-27-77	Tacoma, Seattle	Hit .455 in brief audition with Mariners. Could be on the team this year.
44	Cameron, Mike	R/R	6-2/195	1-8-73	Seattle	Needs to cut down on league-leading 176 strikeouts.
59	Kelly, Kenny	R/R	6-2/180	1-26-79	Tacoma	Needs to improve patience at the plate to claim an outfield job.
4	McLemore, Mark	B/R	5-11/207	10-4-64	Seattle	McLemore will be used more in a DH role to keep his legs fresh.
	Strong, Jamal	R/R	5-10/180	8-5-78	San Antonio	Had 46 steals in Class AA. Mariners might need his speed at top of lineup.
51	Suzuki, Ichiro	L/R	5-9/160	10-22-73	Seattle	Hit .321 and more importantly, walked 68 times.
	Winn, Randy	B/R	6-2/197	6-9-74	Tampa Bay	Will give Mariners the leftfielder they've been missing.

No.	DESIGNATED HITTERS	B/T	Ht./Wt.	Born	2002 clubs	Projection
11	Martinez, Edgar	R/R	5-11/210	1-2-63	Seattle	If healthy, he's still a dangerous hitter.

THE COACHING STAFF

ob Melvin, manager.

ave Myers, third base coach.

ryan Price, pitching coach.

THE TOP NEWCOMERS

reg Colbrunn: His addition will allow Mark McLemore to return to role of giving team's everyday players a day off here and there throughout the season. Expect McLemore to have a season like e did in 2001, and expect Colbrunn to hit at least .300 but with a little less power.

andy Winn: Acquired from Tampa Bay as part of the compensation package for manager Lou Piniella, Winn will be the Mariners' everyday left fielder. Winn hit .298 and stole 27 bases last year nd could easily slide into the lineup in the No. 2 spot in seattle lineup.

THE TOP PROSPECTS

yan Anderson: Mariners' top prospect will have to show he can regain his velocity after arm troubles.

amal Strong: Outfield prospect has hit near or over .300 in every stop in the minors. He knows how to draw walks to get on base and then steal his way into scoring position. He's only a year way from joining the big club.

Tampa Bay Devil Rays

American League East Division

2003 SEASON

Devil Rays Schedule

Home games shaded; D—Day game (games starting before 5 p.m.); *—All-Star Game at Comiskey Park, Chicago. Subject to changes.

March/April

SUN	MON	TUE	WED	THU	FRI	SAT
30	31 BOS	1 BOS	2 BOS	3 D BOS	4 NYY	5 NYY
6 D NYY	7	8 BAL	9 BAL	10 BAL	11 NYY	12 D NYY
13 D NYY	14	15 BOS	16 BOS	17 BOS	18 BAL	19 D BAL
20 D BAL	21 BAL	22 TOR	23 TOR	24 TOR	25 BAL	26 BAL
27 D BAL	28	29 MIN	30 MIN			

May

SUN	MON	TUE	WED	THU	FRI	SAT
				1 D MIN	2 DET	3 D DET
4 D DET	5	6 MIN	7 MIN	8 MIN	9 DET	10 DET
11 D DET	12	13 TOR	14 TOR	15 D TOR	16 BAL	17 BAL
18 D BAL	19	20 TEX	21 TEX	22 D TEX	23 ANA	24 D ANA
25 D ANA	26	27 TEX	28 TEX	29 ANA	30 ANA	31 ANA

June

SUN	MON	TUE	WED	THU	FRI	SAT
1 D ANA	2	3 CUB	4 CUB	5 D CUB	6 HOU	7 HOU
8 D HOU	9	10 CIN	11 CIN	12 CIN	13 PIT	14 PIT
15 D PIT	16	17 NYY	18 NYY	19 D NYY	20 FLA	21 FLA
22 D FLA	23 NYY	24 NYY	25 NYY	26 D NYY	27 ATL	28 ATL
29 D ATL	30					

July

SUN	MON	TUE	WED	THU	FRI	SAT
		1 BOS	2 BOS	3 BOS	4 CWS	5 CWS
6 D CWS	7	8 OAK	9 D OAK	10 D OAK	11 SEA	12 SEA
13 D SEA	14	15 *	16	17 TEX	18 TEX	19 TEX
20 D TEX	21 ANA	22 D ANA	23 BOS	24 D BOS	25 CWS	26 CWS
27 D CWS	28	29 TOR	30 TOR	31 D TOR		

August

SUN	MON	TUE	WED	THU	FRI	SAT
					1 KC	2 KC
3 D KC	4 TOR	5 TOR	6 D TOR	7 KC	8 KC	9 KC
10 D KC	11 BAL	12 BAL	13 D BAL	14	15 CLE	16 CLE
17 D CLE	18 CLE	19 BAL	20 BAL	21 BAL	22 CLE	23 CLE
24 D CLE	25	26 SEA	27 SEA	28 D SEA	29 OAK	30 OAK
31 D OAK						

September

SUN	MON	TUE	WED	THU	FRI	SAT
	1	2 SEA	3 SEA	4 SEA	5 OAK	6 OAK
7 D OAK	8	9 TOR	10 TOR	11 D TOR	12 NYY	13 D NYY
14 D NYY	15 BOS	16 BOS	17 BOS	18 BOS	19 NYY	20 NYY
21 D NYY	22 TOR	23 TOR	24 TOR	25 TOR	26 BOS	27 BOS
28 D BOS						

FRONT-OFFICE DIRECTORY

Managing general partner/CEO .... Vincent J. Naimoli
Sr. v.p. baseball operations/general manager .... Chuck LaMar
Sr. v.p.-admin/CFO& general counsel .... John P. Higgins
Vice president of sales/marketing .... John Browne
Vice president of public relations .... Rick Vaughn
Vice president of stadium operations .... Rick Nafe
Vice president of employee and guest relations .... Jose Tavarez
Assistant general manager .... Bart Braun
Assistant general manager .... Scott Proefrock
Special assistant to general manager .... Eddie Bane
Special assistant to general manager .... Hal McRae
Director of scouting and player personnel .... Cam Bonifay
Assistant to player development .... Mitch Lukevics
Director of team travel .... Jeff Ziegler
Controller .... Patrick Smith
Director of business administration .... Bill Wiener Jr.
Senior director of corporate sales and broadcasting .... Larry McCabe
Director of promotions and special events .... Allen Jernigan
Managers of sponsorship coordination .... Kelly Davis, Lauren Miller
Manager of broadcast operations .... Kevin Daigle
Coordinator of amateur baseball events .... Brian Killingsworth
Director of ticket operations .... Robert Bennett
Assistant director of ticket operations .... Ken Mallory
Assistant to the v.p. of public relations .... Carmen Molina
Director of media relations .... Chris Costello
Assistant media relations manager .... Greg Landy
Manager of print & graphic production .... Charles Parker
Manager of community relations .... Liz-Beth Lauck
Mascot Coordinator .... Shawn Christopherson
Director of event productions .... John Franzone
Manager of Video & graphic production .... Jason Rundle
Video coordinator .... Chris Fernandez

MINOR LEAGUE AFFILIATES

Class	Team	League	Manager
AAA	Durham	International	Bill Evers
AA	Orlando	Southern	To be announced
A	Bakersfield	California	To be announced
A	Charleston (S.C.)	South Atlantic	To be announced
A	Hudson Valley	New York-Pennsylvania	To be announced
Rookie	Princeton	Appalachian	To be announced

ASSISTANCE STAFF

Head trainer
Ken Crenshaw

Strength & conditioning coordinator
Kevin Barr

Medical team physician
Dr. Michael Reilly

Orthopedic team physician
Dr. Koco Eaton

Head groundskeeper
Dan Moeller

Clubhouse operations-home
Chris Westmoreland

Clubhouse operations-visitor
Guy Gallagher

Advance scout
Bart Johnson

Major League scout
Don Williams

Major League consultants
Jerry Gardner, George Zuraw

Crosscheckers
R.J. Harrison, Dave W. Roberts, Mac Seibert III

Area scouts
Rich Aude, Jonathan Bonifay, James Bonnici, Skip Bundy, Rickey Drexler, Kevin Elfering, Milt Hill, Hank King Jr., Paul Kirsch, Benny Latino, Frederick Repke, Dale Tilleman, Craig Weissmann, Doug Witt, Michael Zimmerman

Director of Latin-American operations
Rudy Santin

International staff
Junior Domingo Ramirez

BROADCAST INFORMATION

Radio: WFLA-AM (970).
Cable TV: Fox Sports Net.

SPRING TRAINING

Ballpark (city): Progress Energy Park Home of Al Lang Field (St. Petersburg, Fla.).
Ticket information: 727-825-3250.

BALLPARK INFORMATION

Ballpark (capacity, surface)
Tropicana Field (44,445, artificial)

Address
One Tropicana Drive, St. Petersburg, FL 33705

Official website
www.devilrays.com

Business phone
727-825-3137

Ticket information
727-825-3250

Ticket prices
$140-$195 (catcher's club); $65-$85 (field box)
$35-$45 (lower club box); $25-$40 (diamond club box)
$18-$32 (lower box); $14-$23 (terrace box)
$9-$16 (outfield); $5-$10 (upper reserve)
$1-$7 (the beach-adults); $1-$3 (the beach-children/seniors)
Note: Ticket prices differ from game-to-game depending on whether they are considered "regular" (55 games), "prime" (13 games) or "value" (13 games). Prices indicated are price ranges of those seats.

Field dimensions (from home plate)
To left field at foul line, 315 feet
To center field, 404 feet
To right field at foul line, 322 feet

First game played
March 31, 1998 (Tigers 11, Devil Rays 6)

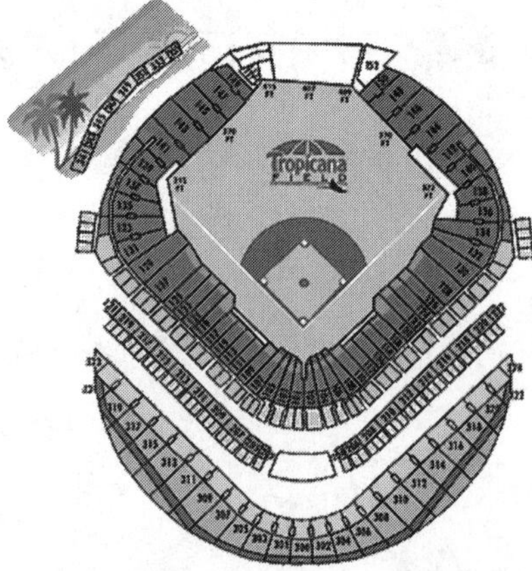

Follow the Devil Rays all season at: www.sportingnews.com/baseball/teams/devilrays/

DEVIL RAYS SPRING ROSTER

No.	PITCHERS	B/T	Ht./Wt.	Born	2002 clubs	Projection
37	Backe, Brandon	R/R	6-0/182	4-5-78	Orlando, Tampa Bay	Young pitcher could use one more year in Class AAA.
32	Bierbrodt, Nick	L/L	6-5/185	5-16-78	DID NOT PLAY	Didn't have a good spring training and missed the year because of injuries.
65	Brazelton, Dewon	R/R	6-4/214	6-16-80	Orlando, Durham, Tampa Bay	He started two games last season and needs another year in minors.
38	Carter, Lance	R/R	6-1/190	12-18-74	Durham, Tampa Bay	Had two saves and a sub-2.00 ERA. Could be the Rays' closer.
46	Colome, Jesus	R/R	6-4/205	12-23-77	Tampa Bay, Durham	Looking to rebound from a horrible year on the mound. Had 8.27 ERA.
36	De Los Santos, Luis	R/R	6-2/216	11-1-77	Durham, Tampa Bay	Pitched well enough in Class AAA, but got hammered in the majors.
	Garcia, Geraldo	R/R	6-0/160	2-13-80	Orlando, Durham	Former Mexican League pitcher will get chance to make rotation.
58	Harper, Travis	R/R	6-4/192	5-21-76	Durham, Tampa Bay	Proved to be more effective coming out of the bullpen.
48	James, Delvin	R/R	6-4/240	1-3-78	Durham, Tampa Bay, Orlando	He was inconsistent in the majors and probably will be at Class AAA in '03.
17	Kennedy, Joe	R/L	6-4/237	5-24-79	Tampa Bay	Won eight games last season and enters 2003 as the Rays' best starter.
	McClung, Seth	R/R	6-6/235	2-7-81	Bakersfield, Orlando	Young pitcher will spend time in minors learning how to pitch.
61	Phelps, Travis	R/R	6-2/166	7-25-77	Tampa Bay, Durham	Showed he can be a contributor out of the bullpen.
34	Reichert, Dan	R/R	6-3/175	7-12-76	Kansas City, Omaha, Wichita	Rays are hoping he can regain form of 2000 when he won eight games.
27	Seay, Bobby	L/L	6-2/221	6-20-78	Orlando, Durham	Spent much of 2002 on disabled list. Likely to spend 2003 in Class AAA.
	Smith, Hans	L/L	6-9/265	8-3-78	Orlando	Big lefty could challenge for a bullpen spot with good spring training.
59	Sosa, Jorge	B/R	6-2/177	4-28-77	Tampa Bay, Orlando	Walked more batters than he struck out; needs to work on his control.
53	Standridge, Jason	R/R	6-4/230	11-9-78	Durham, Tampa Bay	Will be ready for the majors after two years in Class AAA.
	Stokes, Brian	R/R	6-1/203	9-7-79	Bakersfield	Won 10 games and averaged almost a strikeout per inning.
	Waechter, Doug	R/R	6-4/210	1-28-81	Charl., S.C., Bakersfield, Orlando	Strikeout pitcher won 10 games in the minors last season.
21	White, Matt	R/R	6-5/230	8-13-78	Charleston, S.C., Orlando	His progress has been slow; still at least two years away.
60	Zambrano, Victor	R/R	6-0/203	8-6-75	Tampa Bay, Durham	Went 4-4 in 11 starts after moving to the rotation.

No.	CATCHERS	B/T	Ht./Wt.	Born	2002 clubs	Projection
44	Hall, Toby	R/R	6-3/240	10-21-75	Tampa Bay, Durham	As soon as he learns to hit lefties, he'll be the everyday catcher.
	LaForest, Pete	L/R	6-2/208	1-27-78	Orlando, Durham	Hit .270 with 20 homers in Class AA, but defense could use a little work.

No.	INFIELDERS	B/T	Ht./Wt.	Born	2002 clubs	Projection
3	Abernathy, Brent	R/R	6-1/191	9-23-77	Tampa Bay	Needs to show consistency or else it's back to the minors.
	Anderson, Marlon	L/R	5-11/200	1-6-74	Philadelphia	Can become Rays' second baseman if he shows consistent bat.
5	Escalona, Felix	R/R	6-0/196	3-12-79	Tampa Bay	Former Rule 5 shortstop could be in Class AAA for entire season.
19	Huff, Aubrey	L/R	6-4/231	12-20-76	Durham, Tampa Bay	Hit .313 with 23 homers, Devil Rays need to find a place in the field for him.
	Luna, Hector	R/R	6-1/170	2-1-82	Kinston	Rule 5 shortstop with power either makes team or goes back to Indians.
10	Ordonez, Rey	R/R	5-9/159	1-11-71	New York N.L.	Will provide some defense up the middle, something the Rays need.
	Perez, Antonio	R/R	5-11/175	7-28-81	San Antonio, Arizona Mariners	Will be groomed to take over shortstop role; hits better than Ordonez.
33	Rolls, Damian	R/R	6-2/215	9-15-77	Orlando, Durham, Tampa Bay	Hits well enough to be in the majors, just needs a spot in the field.
10	Sandberg, Jared	R/R	6-3/226	3-2-78	Durham, Tampa Bay	Ryne's nephew slugged 18 homers, but struck 139 times. Has potential.

No.	OUTFIELDERS	B/T	Ht./Wt.	Born	2002 clubs	Projection
	Baldelli, Rocco	R/R	6-4/187	9-25-81	Bakersfield, Orlando, Durham	Athletic outfielder could have opening day job if he hits well.
4	Conti, Jason	L/R	5-11/175	1-27-75	Tampa Bay	Hits lefties better than righties, and that will keep him with the big club.
6	Crawford, Carl	L/L	6-2/219	8-5-81	Durham, Tampa Bay	Provided a glimpse of things to come last season; great prospect.
18	Grieve, Ben	L/R	6-4/216	5-4-76	Tampa Bay	His average is in steady decline, a definite cause for concern.
31	Hamilton, Josh	L/L	6-4/200	5-21-81	Bakersfield	Top prospect has struggled with injuries, still has all the tools.
14	Tyner, Jason	L/L	6-1/168	4-23-77	Tampa Bay, Durham	Has to get his batting average back up to stick around in majors.
23	Vaughn, Greg	R/R	6-0/206	7-3-65	Tampa Bay	Hit a paltry .163 last season, maybe new manager Lou Piniella can wake him up.

THE COACHING STAFF

Lou Piniella, manager.
Chris Bosio, pitching coach.
Lee Elia, hitting coach.
Tom Foley, third base coach.
Billy Hatcher, first base coach.
John McLaren, bench coach.
Matt Sinataro, bullpen coach.

THE TOP NEWCOMERS

Rey Ordonez: The Devil Rays brought him over from the Mets to improve the defense up the middle, and while he won't hit all that well, his defense outweighs his offense.

THE TOP PROSPECTS

Seth McClung: Has the build of a power pitcher, but he struggled after reaching Class AA. He's young and learning how to pitch. The Devil Rays will take their time with him.

Rocco Baldelli: By improving his patience at the plate, Baldelli has put himself in line for a job in the Devil Rays outfield. If he can learn to walk a bit more he'll be the team's starting center fielder in 2003 and for years to come.

Josh Hamilton: Injuries to his back, elbow and legs have cost him valuable playing time in the Rays' minor league system. But don't let that fool you. Hamilton still has the five tools he did when the Devil Rays made him the first overall pick in the 1999 draft.

TEXAS RANGERS

AMERICAN LEAGUE WEST DIVISION

2003 SEASON

Rangers Schedule

Home games shaded; D—Day game (games starting before 5 p.m.); *—All-Star Game at Comiskey Park, Chicago. Subject to changes. †Game played in Puerto Rico.

March/April

SUN	MON	TUE	WED	THU	FRI	SAT
30 ANA	31	1 ANA	2 D ANA	3	4 D SEA	5 SEA
6 D SEA	7	8 OAK	9 OAK	10 D OAK	11 SEA	12 SEA
13 D SEA	14 ANA	15 ANA	16 ANA	17 D ANA	18 OAK	19 D OAK
20 OAK	21	22 BOS	23 BOS	24 D BOS	25 NYY	26 NYY
27 D NYY	28	29 TOR	30 TOR			

May

SUN	MON	TUE	WED	THU	FRI	SAT
				1 TOR	2 CLE	3 D CLE
4 D CLE	5	6 TOR	7 TOR	8 D TOR	9 CLE	10 CLE
11 D CLE	12	13 BOS	14 BOS	15 BOS	16 NYY	17 D NYY
18 D NYY	19	20 TB	21 TB	22 D TB	23 BAL	24 BAL
25 D BAL	26	27 TB	28 TB	29 BAL	30 BAL	31 BAL

June

SUN	MON	TUE	WED	THU	FRI	SAT
1 D BAL	2	3 ATL	4 ATL	5 D ATL	6 † MON	7 † MON
8 D† MON	9	10 NYM	11 NYM	12 NYM	13 FLA	14 FLA
15 FLA	16	17 OAK	18 OAK	19 D OAK	20 HOU	21 HOU
22 HOU	23 OAK	24 OAK	25 OAK	26 OAK	27 HOU	28 D HOU
29 D HOU	30 ANA					

July

SUN	MON	TUE	WED	THU	FRI	SAT
		1 ANA	2 ANA	3 ANA	4 SEA	5 SEA
6 SEA	7	8 MIN	9 MIN	10 MIN	11 KC	12 KC
13 KC	14	15 *	16	17 TB	18 TB	19 TB
20 D TB	21 BAL	22 D BAL	23 ANA	24 ANA	25 SEA	26 D SEA
27 D SEA	28 SEA	29 BOS	30 BOS	31 BOS		

August

SUN	MON	TUE	WED	THU	FRI	SAT
					1 CLE	2 CLE
3 CLE	4	5 NYY	6 NYY	7 D NYY	8 TOR	9 D TOR
10 D TOR	11 DET	12 DET	13 DET	14 DET	15 CWS	16 CWS
17 CWS	18 DET	19 DET	20 DET	21 CWS	22 CWS	23 CWS
24 D CWS	25	26 KC	27 KC	28 KC	29 MIN	30 MIN
31 D MIN						

September

SUN	MON	TUE	WED	THU	FRI	SAT
	1 D KC	2 KC	3 KC	4	5 MIN	6 D MIN
7 D MIN	8	9 SEA	10 SEA	11 SEA	12 OAK	13 OAK
14 D OAK	15 SEA	16 SEA	17 SEA	18 D SEA	19 ANA	20 ANA
21 D ANA	22 OAK	23 OAK	24 D OAK	25	26 ANA	27 D ANA
28 D ANA						

FRONT-OFFICE DIRECTORY

Position	Name
Chairman of the board/chief executive officer	Thomas O. Hicks
President/chief operating officer	Michael J. Cramer
Executive vice president, general manager	John Hart
Executive vice president/chief financial officer	Joe Armes
Executive vice president, business operations	Rick McLaughlin
Executive vice president & chief marketing officer	Greg McElroy
Senior vice president, communications	John Blake
Vice president, legal and general counsel	Casey Coffman
Vice president, sponsorship sales	Brad Alberts
Vice president, ticket sales	Kerry Bubolz
Vice president, advertising sales	Tom Comerford
Vice president, finance	Kellie Fischer
Vice president, event operations & security	John Hardin
Vice president, community development	Norm Lyons
Vice president, information technology	Steve McNeill
Vice president, marketing & entertainment	Chuck Morgan
Assistant vice president, luxury suite sales	Paige Jackson
Assistant vice president, facilities operations	Gib Searight
Assistant vice president, human resources	Terry Turner
Assistant general manager, player development & scouting	Grady Fuson
Assistant general manager, baseball operations	Dan O'Brien
Coordinator, player development	Bob Miscik
Coordinator, scouting	Ron Hopkins
Director, minor league operations	John Lombardo
Director, major league administration	Judy Johns
Director, travel	Chris Lyngos
Assistant, scouting operations	Russ Ardolina
Assistant, baseball operations	Jon Daniels
Assistant, professional scouting operations	Jeff Wood
Sr. director, marketing	Kelly Calvert
Sr. director, customer service	Donnie Pordash
Sr. director, graphic design	Rainier Uhlir
Sr. director, ticket operations	Michael Wood
Director, benefits and compensation	Janine Airhart
Director, grounds	Tom Burns
Director, corporate Sales	Jim Cochrane
Director, publications	Kurt Daniels
Director, events	Sherry Flow
Director, merchandising	Todd Grizzle
Director, graphic design	Michelle Hays
Director, facilities & special events	Kevin Jimison
Director, ticket services	Mike Lentz
Director, media	Heidi Leonards
Creative director, media	Rush Olson
Director, Legends of the Game Museum & Learning Center	Amy Polley
Director, advertising sales	Grady Raskin
Director of baseball programs & youth ballpark	Chris Shabay
Director, application systems	Russell Smutzer
Director, community relations	Taunee Paur Taylor
Assistant controllers	Melissa Embry, Starr Pritchard, Christie Steblein
Manager, media relations	Rich Rice

MINOR LEAGUE AFFILIATES

Class	Team	League	Manager
AAA	Oklahoma	Pacific Coast	Bobby Jones
AA	Frisco	Texas	Tim Ireland
A	Stockton	California	Arnie Beyeler
A	Clinton	Midwest	Carlos Subero
A	Spokane	Northwest	Darryl Kennedy
Rookie	Arizona Rangers	Arizona	Pedro Lopez

ASSISTANCE STAFF

Medical director & head trainer
Jamie Reed

Team orthopedist
Dr. John Conway

Team internist
Dr. David Hunter

Assistant trainers
Ray Ramirez, Greg Harrel

Strength & conditioning coach
Fernando Montes

Professional scouts
Dick Bogard, Dom Chiti, Mel Didier, Tom Giordano, Toney Howell, Les Parker, Jay Robertson, Ross Sapp, Rudy Terrasas, Bill Wood

Regional scouting crosscheckers
Manny Batista (Latin Coordinator), Kip Fagg (West), Doug Harris (East), Dave Klipstein (Central)

Amateur scouts
John Castleberry, Jay Eddings, Steve Flores, Tim Fortugno, Mark Giegler, Mike Grouse, Todd Guggiana, Mark Harris, Derek Lee, Gary McGraw, John Poloni, Rick Schroeder, Doug Simons, Tommy Tanous, Randy Taylor, Frankie Thon, Aris Tirado, Ron Toenjes

BROADCAST INFORMATION

Radio: KRLD-AM (1080); KESS-AM (1270), Spanish.
TV: KDFW (Channel 4); KDFI (Channel 27).
Cable TV: Fox Sports Southwest.

SPRING TRAINING

Ballpark (city): Surprise Stadium (Surprise, Ariz.).
Ticket information: 623-594-5600.

BALLPARK INFORMATION

Ballpark (capacity, surface)
The Ballpark in Arlington (49,115, grass)

Address
1000 Ballpark Way, Arlington, TX 76011

Official website
www.texasrangers.com

Business phone
817-273-5222

Ticket information
817-273-5100

Ticket prices
$42 (lowerinfield), $40 (lower box, club box)
$25 (corner box)
$20 (terrace box, lower reserved, lower home run porch)
$16 (upper box), $13 (upper home run porch)
$12 (upper reserved, bleachers)
$5 (grandstand reserved)

Field dimensions (from home plate)
To left field at foul line, 332 feet
To center field, 400 feet
To right field at foul line, 325 feet

First game played
April 11, 1994 (Brewers 4, Rangers 3)

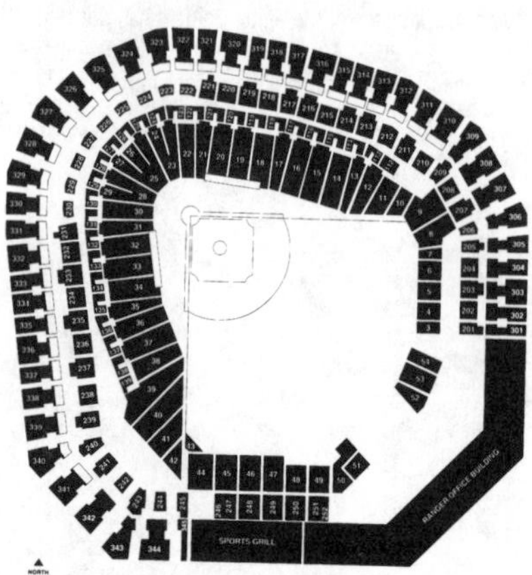

Follow the Rangers all season at: www.sportingnews.com/baseball/teams/rangers/

RANGERS SPRING ROSTER

No.	PITCHERS	B/T	Ht./Wt.	Born	2002 clubs	Projection
30	Bell, Rob	R/R	6-5/225	1-17-77	Oklahoma, Texas, Tulsa	Has pitched well in minors, but hasn't translated that into major league success.
53	Benoit, Joaquin	R/R	6-3/205	7-26-77	Oklahoma, Texas, Charlotte	If he can harnass his stuff, he'll be a good top-of-the-rotation guy for the Rangers.
56	Cedeno, Jovanny	R/R	6-0/170	10-25-79	Gulf Coast Rangers	Has thrown only 14.2 innings the last two seasons; has good promise though.
31	Cordero, Francisco	R/R	6-2/200	5-11-75	Texas, Oklahoma	Had 10 saves in 12 chances, could be Rangers closer if Zimmerman isn't ready.
17	Davis, Doug	R/L	6-4/190	9-21-75	Texas, Oklahoma	If he can find a pitch to use on righties, he'll find a home in the rotation.
	Drese, Ryan	R/R	6-3/220	4-5-76	Cleveland, Buffalo	Won 10 games in 26 starts with Indians, will bolster rotation depth.
38	Fultz, Aaron	L/L	6-0/200	9-4-73	San Francisco, Fresno	Will provide a solid lefthanded option out of the bullpen.
21	Garcia, Reynaldo	R/R	6-3/170	4-15-74	Tulsa, Oklahoma, Texas	Can win a bullpen job with a solid spring performance.
73	Hughes, Travis	R/R	6-5/215	5-25-78	Tulsa	Converted into a starter, he went 10-9 in Class AA.
52	Kolb, Danny	R/R	6-4/215	3-29-75	Charlotte, Tulsa, Texas	Will have to find a pitch to use against lefties in order to stick in the bullpen.
	Koronka, John	L/R	6-1/180	6-3-80	Stockton, Chattanooga	Rule 5 guy who relies on control; either he makes the team or goes back to Cincy.
56	Kozlowski, Ben	L/L	6-6/220	8-16-80	M. Beach, Charl., Tulsa, Texas	Needs more seasoning, but had an ERA just over 2.00 in two stops in the minors.
48	Lewis, Colby	R/R	6-4/215	8-2-79	Texas, Oklahoma	Rangers will use him only as a starter; he should make the 2003 rotation.
61	Park, Chan Ho	R/R	6-2/204	6-30-73	Texas, Oklahoma	Hasn't quite found his groove in the A.L., Rangers are hoping he does quickly.
39	Powell, Jay	R/R	6-4/225	1-9-72	Tulsa, Oklahoma, Texas	Consistent in the bullpen; Rangers will entrust their leads to him in the eighth.
	Ramos, Mario	L/L	6-0/180	10-19-77	Oklahoma	Had a rough first season in Rangers organization; still loads of talent though.
	Thomson, John	R/R	6-3/190	10-1-73	Colorado, New York N.L.	Gives the Rangers some much-needed help with their rotation.
41	Urbina, Ugueth	R/R	6-0/205	2-15-74	Boston	Had 40 saves with Boston, will provide bullpen depth for Texas.
	Valdes, Ismael	R/R	6-4/225	8-21-73	Texas, Seattle	Gives the Rangers one more solid starter for 2003.
47	Van Poppel, Todd	R/R	6-5/240	12-9-71	Texas	Had 85 strikeouts, but also had a 5.45 ERA last season.
43	Yan, Esteban	R/R	6-4/255	6-22-75	Tampa Bay	Like Urbina, he was signed to help bolster a thin bullpen.
59	Zimmerman, Jeff	R/R	6-1/200	8-9-72	Charlotte, Tulsa	Rangers are hoping he'll bounce back from injuries.

No.	CATCHERS	B/T	Ht./Wt.	Born	2002 clubs	Projection
2	Diaz, Einar	R/R	5-10/190	12-28-72	Cleveland	Rangers are hoping he can replace Ivan Rodriguez as club's No. 1 catcher.
27	Greene, Todd	R/R	5-10/208	5-8-71	Las Vegas, Texas, Oklahoma	He'll likely be a designated hitter, as his arm isn't suited for catching anymore.
	Laird, Gerald	R/R	6-2/195	11-13-79	Tulsa	Rangers think he could be a good backup, but probably not this year.

No.	INFIELDERS	B/T	Ht./Wt.	Born	2002 clubs	Projection
12	Blalock, Hank	L/R	6-1/192	11-21-80	Texas, Oklahoma	Rangers will have to find a spot in the infield for his bat.
16	Hart, Jason	R/R	6-4/240	9-5-77	Oklahoma, Texas	This slugger might find time in the outfield or as the designated hitter.
13	Lamb, Mike	L/R	6-1/195	8-9-75	Oklahoma, Texas	He could play every day as the club's utility man.
	McDougall, Marshall	R/R	6-1/200	12-19-78	Midland, M. Valley, Akron	Rule 5 guy is .300 hitter, but may have to learn another position besides third.
25	Palmeiro, Rafael	L/L	6-0/190	9-24-64	Texas	Averaged dropped while homers rose; this trend should continue.
35	Perry, Herbert	R/R	6-2/225	9-15-69	Texas	Either he's the third baseman or designated hitter in 2003.
3	Rodriguez, Alex	R/R	6-3/210	7-27-75	Texas	Hit only .300 but slugged 57 homers in '02. He'll be around those numbers again.
23	Teixeira, Mark	B/R	6-3/225	4-11-80	Charlotte, Tulsa	Being groomed as the third baseman, but might move to first.
10	Young, Mike	R/R	6-1/190	10-19-76	Texas	If he can cut down on strikeouts, the second-base job is his.

No.	OUTFIELDERS	B/T	Ht./Wt.	Born	2002 clubs	Projection
2	Everett, Carl	B/R	6-0/215	6-3-71	Texas, Charlotte	Still has trouble hitting lefties, but should be better now that he's healthy.
	Glanville, Doug	R/R	6-2/174	8-25-70	Philadelphia	Signed to provide center-field depth. Should get plenty of at-bats.
19	Gonzalez, Juan	R/R	6-3/220	10-16-69	Texas	If his thumb is healthy, he'll be back to his usual Juan Gone numbers.
29	Greer, Rusty	L/L	6-0/195	1-21-69	Texas, Tulsa	Expected to miss entire 2003 season with injuries.
15	Ludwick, Ryan	R/L	6-3/203	7-13-78	Oklahoma, Texas	Will need to hit better to stick in the majors this year.
28	Mench, Kevin	R/R	6-0/215	1-7-78	Oklahoma, Texas	He'll get plenty of at-bats and time in left field this season.
	Nix, Laynce	L/L	6-0/190	10-30-80	Charlotte	Florida State League MVP likely a year away.

THE COACHING STAFF

Buck Showalter, manager.

Mark Conner, bullpen coach.

DeMarlo Hale, first base and outfield coach.

Rudy Jaramillo, batting coach.

Steve Smith, third base and infield coach.

Don Wakamatsu, bench coach.

THE TOP NEWCOMERS

John Thomson: Won nine games in season split between Rockies and Mets last year. Has been consistent throughout his career despite pitching half of his games at Coors Field. More importantly, he's been healthy for a few years now.

Ugueth Urbina: Saved 40 games with the Red Sox last season. He will provide the Rangers with some much-needed depth at closer. Finding a consistent closer was a chore for the Rangers last season, John Rocker was a bust and Hideki Irabu got injured. Urbina, along with Esteban Yan, will give the Rangers many options to finish out games.

Einar Diaz: Had an off year in Cleveland. Didn't hit the ball too well and certainly was subpar defensively. The Rangers just need some solid, consistent production this year.

THE TOP PROSPECTS

Laynce Nix: Hit 21 homers and led the Florida State League in RBIs with 110. He also stole 17 bases while only getting caught once. He should be ready for the majors in 2004.

Mark Teixeira: Will probably spend part of the season in Class AAA just to make sure he's ready for the majors. Still, he managed a .320 average in Class A and .316 in Class AA. Just needs a few more at-bats in the minors.

TORONTO BLUE JAYS

AMERICAN LEAGUE EAST DIVISION

2003 SEASON

Blue Jays Schedule

Home games shaded; D—Day game (games starting before 5 p.m.); *—All-Star Game at Comiskey Park, Chicago. Subject to changes.

March/April

SUN	MON	TUE	WED	THU	FRI	SAT
30	31 NYY	1 D NYY	2 NYY	3	4 MIN	5 MIN
6 D MIN	7	8 BOS	9 BOS	10 BOS	11 MIN	12 D MIN
13 D MIN	14 NYY	15 NYY	16 NYY	17 D NYY	18 BOS	19 D BOS
20 D BOS	21 D BOS	22 TB	23 TB	24 TB	25 KC	26 D KC
27 D KC	28	29 TEX	30 TEX			

May

SUN	MON	TUE	WED	THU	FRI	SAT
				1 TEX	2 ANA	3 D ANA
4 D ANA	5	6 TEX	7 TEX	8 D TEX	9 ANA	10 ANA
11 D ANA	12	13 TB	14 TB	15 D TB	16 KC	17 KC
18 D KC	19 CWS	20 CWS	21 CWS	22 NYY	23 NYY	24 D NYY
25 D NYY	26 CWS	27 CWS	28 CWS	29 CWS	30 BOS	31 D BOS

June

SUN	MON	TUE	WED	THU	FRI	SAT
1 D BOS	2	3 STL	4 STL	5 STL	6 CIN	7 CIN
8 D CIN	9	10 PIT	11 PIT	12 PIT	13 CUB	14 D CUB
15 D CUB	16	17 BAL	18 BAL	19 D BAL	20 MON	21 MON
22 D MON	23 BAL	24 BAL	25 BAL	26 BAL	27 MON	28 D MON
29 D MON	30 DET					

July

SUN	MON	TUE	WED	THU	FRI	SAT
		1 DET	2 DET	3	4 BAL	5 BAL
6 D BAL	7	8 BOS	9 BOS	10 BOS	11 NYY	12 D NYY
13 D NYY	14	15 *	16	17 BOS	18 BOS	19 BOS
20 D BOS	21 NYY	22 NYY	23 CWS	24 CWS	25 BAL	26 D BAL
27 D BAL	28	29 TB	30 TB	31 D TB		

August

SUN	MON	TUE	WED	THU	FRI	SAT
					1 ANA	2 ANA
3 D ANA	4 TB	5 TB	6 D TB	7	8 TEX	9 D TEX
10 D TEX	11 SEA	12 SEA	13 SEA	14 SEA	15 OAK	16 D OAK
17 D OAK	18	19 SEA	20 SEA	21 SEA	22 OAK	23 D OAK
24 D OAK	25 OAK	26 BOS	27 BOS	28	29 CLE	30 CLE
31 D CLE						

September

SUN	MON	TUE	WED	THU	FRI	SAT
	1 D NYY	2	3 NYY	4 NYY	5 DET	6 D DET
7 D DET	8	9 TB	10 TB	11 D TB	12 BAL	13 D BAL
14 D BAL	15	16 DET	17 DET	18 DET	19 BAL	20 BAL
21 D BAL	22 TB	23 TB	24 TB	25 TB	26 CLE	27 D CLE
28 D CLE						

FRONT-OFFICE DIRECTORY

President & CEO .... Paul Godfrey
Senior v.p., baseball & general manager .... J.P. Ricciardi
Sr. vice president, sales and marketing .... Paul Allamby
Senior v.p., communications and external relations .... Paul Godfrey
Senior v.p., administration and business .... Lisa Novak
Senior vice president, finance .... Richard Wong
Vice president, baseball .... Bob Mattick
Vice president, baseball .... Tim Wilken
V.p., baseball operations & assistant general manager .... Tim McCleary
Special assistant to general manager .... Bill Livesey
Assistant to the general manager .... Tony LaCava
Special asst. to president, baseball & g.m./director, int'l scouting .... Wayne Morgan
Vice president, special projects .... Howard Starkman
Vice president, ticket sales and service .... Steve Smith
V.p., finance and administration .... Susan Brioux
V.p., corp. partnerships & business dev. .... Mark Lemmon
Director, consumer marketing .... Jim Bloom
Director, scouting .... Chris Buckley
Assistant director, scouting .... Mark Snipp
Director, player development .... Dick Scott
Director, minor leagues .... Bob Nelson
Director, Florida operations .... Ken Carson
Director, communications .... Jay Stenhouse
Director, community, player and alumni relations .... Laurel Lindsay
Director, operations .... Mario Coutinho
Director, merchandising .... Michael Andrejek
Manager, team travel .... Bart Given

MINOR LEAGUE AFFILIATES

Class	Team	League	Manager
AAA	Syracuse	International	Omar Malave
AA	New Haven	Eastern	Marty Pevey
A	Dunedin	Florida State	Mike Basso
A	Charleston (W.Va.)	South Atlantic	Mark Meleski
A	Auburn	New York-Penn	Dennis Holmberg
Rookie	Pulaski	Appalachian	Paul Elliott

BROADCAST INFORMATION

Radio: The Fan (590).
Cable TV: Rogers SportsNet (RSN).

SPRING TRAINING

Ballpark (city): Dunedin Stadium at Grant Field (Dunedin, Fla.).
Ticket information: 800-707-8269; 727-733-0429.

ASSISTANCE STAFF

Trainers
Scott Shannon, George Poulis

Strength and conditioning coordinators
Jeff Krushell, Donovan Santas

Advance scout
Sal Butera

Special assigment scouts
Ted Lekas, Jeff Taylor

National crosschecker
Mike Mangan

Scouting supervisors
Charles Aliano, Jaymie Bane, Andy Beene, Bill Byckowski, John Ceprini, Don Cowan, Joey Davis, Joel Grampietro, Ed Heather, Tim Huff, Walt Jeffries, Marty Miller, Ty Nichols, Demerius Pittman, Jorge Rivera, Jim Rooney, Andrew Tinnish

Director, Latin America operations
Tony Arias

Scouting supervisor, Australia
Greg Wade

BALLPARK INFORMATION

Ballpark (capacity, surface)
SkyDome (45,100, artificial)

Address
One Blue Jays Way
Suite 3200
Toronto, Ontario M5V 1J1

Official website
www.bluejays.com

Business phone
416-341-1000

Ticket information
416-341-1234 and 1-888-OK GO JAY

Ticket prices
$180-$186 ("In the Action"); $49-$57 (premium dugout)
$46-$52 (field level-IF); $27-$40 (field level-bases)
$15-$26 (100 level OF); $7-$24 (200 level OF)
$24 (lower SkyDeck); $7 (family zone; upper SkyDeck)
Note: Ticket prices differ from game-to-game depending on whether they are considered "regular" (48 games), "premium" (7 games) or "value" (26 games). Prices indicated are price ranges of those seats.

Field dimensions (from home plate)
To left field at foul line, 330 feet
To center field, 400 feet
To right field at foul line, 330 feet

First game played
June 5, 1989 (Brewers 5, Blue Jays 3)

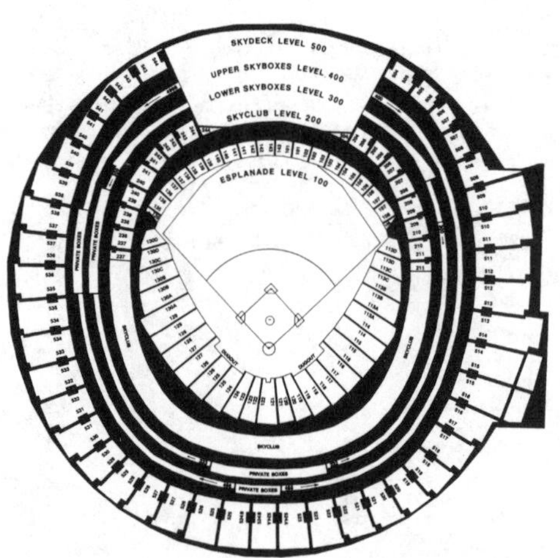

Follow the Blue Jays all season at: www.sportingnews.com/baseball/teams/bluejays/

BLUE JAYS SPRING ROSTER

No.	PITCHERS	B/T	Ht./Wt.	Born	2002 clubs	Projection
	Baker, Chris	R/R	6-1/195	8-24-77	Syracuse	Injuries slowed him in 2002; will probably spend one more year in minors.
37	Bowles, Brian	R/R	6-5/220	8-18-76	Syracuse, Toronto	Showed he can be a quality reliever for the Jays in 2003.
	Chulk, Vinny	R/R	6-2/185	12-19-78	Tennessee, Syracuse	Most Outstanding Pitcher in Southern League posted 13 wins and 2.96 ERA.
38	Coco, Pasqual	R/R	6-1/180	9-24-77	Syracuse, Toronto	Might be running low on chances to make team as a starter or reliever.
	Creek, Doug	L/L	6-0/227	3-1-69	Tampa Bay, Seattle	Was signed to help solidify the lefty situation in the bullpen.
45	Escobar, Kelvim	R/R	6-1/210	4-11-76	Toronto	Earned 38 saves in '02. Should keep his job as closer and improve in 2003.
36	File, Bob	R/R	6-4/215	1-28-77	Dunedin, Toronto, Syracuse	Injuries really affected his performance in 2002. He should get back on track.
32	Halladay, Roy	R/R	6-6/230	5-14-77	Toronto	Became the staff ace last seasonwith 19 wins and a sub-3.00 ERA.
43	Hendrickson, Mark	L/L	6-9/230	6-23-74	Syracuse, Toronto	Former NBA player decided to try his hand as pitcher. One of Jays top prospects.
	Lidle, Cory	R/R	5-11/192	3-22-72	Oakland, Sacramento	Acquired to give Jays a good No. 2 starter behind Halladay.
	Lopez, Aquilino	R/R	6-3/165	7-30-80	Tacoma	Can start or relieve. Either way, he struck out 103 in 109 innings.
	Majewski, Gary	R/R	6-2/200	2-26-80	Birmingham	Could fill a middle relief role if he has a strong spring.
	Markwell, Diegomar	L/L	6-2/197	8-8-80	Tennessee	Won 13 games in Class AA. Could get a look if he pitches well.
34	Miller, Justin	R/R	6-2/195	8-27-77	Syracuse, Toronto	Won nine games between rotation and bullpen. Will get shot at rotation this year.
[illegible]9	Politte, Cliff	R/R	5-11/185	2-27-74	Philadelphia, Toronto	Became the Jays setup man. Should continue to thrive in that role again.
	Rosario, Francisco	R/R	6-0/160	9-28-80	Charleston, W.Va., Dunedin	With improved command, he'll be ready for a spot in the rotation in 2004.
53	Smith, Mike	R/R	5-11/195	9-19-77	Syracuse, Toronto	Needs to harness his stuff before he'll make it in the majors.
49	Sturtze, Tanyon	R/R	6-5/221	10-12-70	Tampa Bay	Lost 18 games with Tampa. Jays expect him to rebound to 2001 form.
	Tam, Jeff	R/R	6-1/219	8-19-70	Oakland, Sacramento	Another pitcher Jays are hoping can get back to his old form.
35	Thurman, Corey	R/R	6-1/215	11-5-78	Toronto	Will likely head to Class AAA for more seasoning. Will be a starter in the future.
41	Walker, Pete	R/R	6-2/195	4-8-69	Norfolk, New York N.L., Toronto	Can start or relieve, probably will start until youngsters are ready.

No.	CATCHERS	B/T	Ht./Wt.	Born	2002 clubs	Projection
29	Cash, Kevin	R/R	6-0/185	12-6-77	Tennessee, Syracuse, Toronto	Likely needs one more season in Class AAA, Arm is ready, bat is not.
20	Huckaby, Ken	R/R	6-1/205	1-27-71	Syracuse, Toronto	Inherits the No.1 catcher job until Cash is ready.
37	Myers, Greg	L/R	6-2/225	4-14-66	Oakland	Hit .222, but knows how to handle a young pitching staff.
17	Phelps, Josh	R/R	6-3/220	5-12-78	Syracuse, Toronto	Doesn't walk a lot, but the Jays like his power. Will see time as designated hitter.
	Quiroz, Guillermo	R/R	6-1/202	11-29-81	Dunedin, Syracuse	Will be a quality backup catcher in a year or two.
15	Wilson, Tom	R/R	6-3/220	12-19-70	Toronto	He'll see time at first, catcher and designated hitter.

No.	INFIELDERS	B/T	Ht./Wt.	Born	2002 clubs	Projection
2	Berg, David	R/R	5-11/196	9-3-70	Toronto	Hit .270 while playing five different positions. Role shouldn't change this year.
14	Bordick, Mike	R/R	5-11/175	7-21-65	Baltimore	Was pondering retirement until Blue Jays came calling. Great defense.
25	Delgado, Carlos	L/R	6-3/230	6-25-72	Toronto	Found his swing near the end of last season, should get back near .300 mark.
11	Hinske, Eric	L/R	6-2/225	8-5-77	Toronto	A.L. Rookie of the Year should be able to top 2002 numbers.
3	Hudson, Orlando	B/R	6-0/185	12-12-77	Syracuse, Toronto	Won the second-base job last year; will improve with more experience.
	Rich, Dominic	L/R	5-10/190	8-22-79	Dunedin, Tennessee	Hit .345 in Class A. Moving up rapidly in the system.
5	Woodward, Chris	R/R	6-0/185	6-27-76	Dunedin, Toronto	Has surprising power for a shortstop, 13 homers in 90 games last season.

No.	OUTFIELDERS	B/T	Ht./Wt.	Born	2002 clubs	Projection
	Catalanotto, Frank	L/R	5-11/195	4-27-74	Texas, Tulsa	Gives the Jays plenty of options with his bat and glove.
	Dubois, Jason	R/R	6-5/225	3-26-79	Daytona	Hit .321 with 20 homers. Another in long line of Toronto outfield prospects.
	Johnson, Reed	R/R	5-10/180	12-8-76	Dunedin, Syracuse	Injuries sidelined him last season. A .300 hitter with great speed.
	Rios, Alexis	R/R	6-5/185	2-18-81	Dunedin	Hit .305 and stole 14 bases in Class A. Progressing nicely.
24	Stewart, Shannon	R/R	6-1/210	2-25-74	Toronto	Leadoff hitter hits for power, average and has speed to burn.
10	Wells, Vernon	R/R	6-1/225	12-8-78	Toronto	Drove in 100 runs at age 23. Just beginning to scratch surface on his potential.
54	Werth, Jayson	R/R	6-5/190	5-20-79	Syracuse, Toronto	Power hitter might be in line for an outfield job.
16	Wise, DeWayne	L/L	6-1/180	2-24-78	Toronto, Tennessee	Has all the tools, but needs more patience at the plate.

THE COACHING STAFF

Carlos Tosca, manager.

Mike Barnett, hitting coach.

Brian Butterfield, third base coach.

John Gibbons, first base coach.

Gil Patterson, pitching coach.

Bruce Walton, bullpen coach.

THE TOP NEWCOMERS

Cory Lidle: Won eight games with the A's in 2002. Certainly doesn't walk a lot of batters (39 in 192 innings) and should be just as good on the turf at the SkyDome with a solid defense behind him.

Frank Catalanotto: Is capable of playing the outfield or infield. Gets on base a lot, something that will fit in well with the Blue Jays philosophy.

THE TOP PROSPECTS

Vinny Chulk: Former 12th-round draft pick had one of the better seasons of any minor league player last season, going 13-5 in 24 starts at Class AA Tennessee. His ERA was under 3.00. But he won't strike out many batters at the major league level—he's a control pitcher who makes his living on the corners.

Kevin Cash: Blue Jays' catcher of the future had a tough season in Class AAA. His defense is major-league, but his bat isn't. He'll need more patience in Syracuse before the Blue Jays will be ready to call him up.

Arizona Diamondbacks

National League West Division

2003 SEASON

Diamondbacks Schedule

Home games shaded; D—Day game (games starting before 5 p.m.); *—All-Star Game at Comiskey Park, Chicago. Subject to changes.

March/April

SUN	MON	TUE	WED	THU	FRI	SAT
30	31 D LA	1 LA	2 LA	3	4 COL	5 D COL
6 D COL	7 D LA	8 LA	9 D LA	10	11 MIL	12 MIL
13 D MIL	14 COL	15 COL	16 COL	17 D COL	18 STL	19 D STL
20 D STL	21	22 MON	23 MON	24 MON	25 NYM	26 D NYM
27 D NYM	28 FLA	29 FLA	30 FLA			

May

SUN	MON	TUE	WED	THU	FRI	SAT
				1 FLA	2 ATL	3 ATL
4 D ATL	5 PHI	6 PHI	7 D PHI	8	9 PIT	10 PIT
11 D PIT	12	13 PHI	14 PHI	15 D PHI	16 PIT	17 PIT
18 D PIT	19 SF	20 SF	21 SF	22	23 SD	24 SD
25 D SD	26 D SD	27 SF	28 SF	29	30 SD	31 SD

June

SUN	MON	TUE	WED	THU	FRI	SAT
1 D SD	2 SD	3 CWS	4 CWS	5 CWS	6 CLE	7 D CLE
8 D CLE	9	10 KC	11 KC	12 KC	13 MIN	14 MIN
15 D MIN	16	17 HOU	18 HOU	19 HOU	20 CIN	21 CIN
22 D CIN	23 HOU	24 HOU	25 D HOU	26	27 DET	28 DET
29 D DET	30 COL					

July

SUN	MON	TUE	WED	THU	FRI	SAT
		1 COL	2 COL	3 COL	4 LA	5 D LA
6 LA	7 COL	8 COL	9 SD	10 D SD	11 SF	12 D SF
13 D SF	14	15 *	16	17 D SD	18 SD	19 SD
20 D SD	21 SF	22 SF	23 SF	24 D SF	25 LA	26 D LA
27 D LA	28 FLA	29 FLA	30 FLA	31		

August

SUN	MON	TUE	WED	THU	FRI	SAT
					1 D CUB	2 D CUB
3 D CUB	4	5 MON	6 MON	7 MON	8 NYM	9 NYM
10 D NYM	11	12 CIN	13 CIN	14 CIN	15 ATL	16 ATL
17 D ATL	18 D ATL	19 CIN	20 CIN	21 CIN	22 CUB	23 D CUB
24 D CUB	25 SD	26 SD	27 SD	28	29 SF	30 D SF
31 SF						

September

SUN	MON	TUE	WED	THU	FRI	SAT
	1 D SF	2 SD	3 SD	4	5 SF	6 D SF
7 D SF	8 LA	9 LA	10 LA	11 LA	12 COL	13 COL
14 D COL	15	16 LA	17 LA	18 LA	19 MIL	20 MIL
21 D MIL	22	23 COL	24 COL	25 D COL	26 STL	27 D STL
28 D STL						

FRONT-OFFICE DIRECTORY

Managing general partner .... Jerry Colangelo
President .... Richard Dozer
Senior vice president and general manager .... Joe Garagiola Jr.
Senior vice president, sales and marketing .... Scott Brubaker
Senior vice president, finance .... Thomas Harris
Vice president, tickets and special services .... Dianne Aguilar
Vice president, corporate sales .... Mark Fernandez
Vice president, event services .... Russ Amaral
Assistant general manager .... Sandy Johnson
Director of Hispanic marketing .... Richard Saenz
Director of public relations .... Mike Swanson
Director of suite services .... Diney Ransford
Director of team travel .... Roger Riley
Director of player development .... Tommy Jones
Director of Pacific Rim operations .... Jim Marshall
Director of scouting .... Mike Rizzo
Director of baseball operations .... Bob Miller

MINOR LEAGUE AFFILIATES

Class	Team	League	Manager
AAA	Tucson	Pacific Coast	Al Pedrique
AA	El Paso	Texas	Scott Coolbaugh
A	Lancaster	California	Mike Aldrete
A	South Bend	Midwest	Von Hayes
A	Yakima	Northwest	Bill Plummer
Rookie	Missoula	Pioneer	Tony Perezchica

BROADCAST INFORMATION

Radio: KTAR-AM (620).
TV: KTVK (Channel 3)
Cable TV: Fox Sports Net Arizona.

SPRING TRAINING

Ballpark (city): Tuscon Electric Park (Tucson, Ariz.).
Ticket information: 520-434-1111.

ASSISTANCE STAFF

Trainer
Paul Lessard

Assistant trainer
Dave Edwards

Club physician
Dr. Michael Lee

National scouting supervisor
Kendall Carter

Regional supervisors
Ed Durkin, Kris Kline
Charles Scott

Latin America supervisor
Junior Noboa

Professional scouts
Bill Earnhart, Doug Gassaway
Mike Sgobba

Major League and advance scouts
Mack Babitt, Bryan Lambe
Jim Marshall, Mike Piatnik

Special assignment scout
Phil Rizzo

Scouts
Mark Baca, Ray Blanco
Fred Costello, Trip Couch
Mike Daughtry, Ed Gustafson
Scott Jaster, Steve Kmetko
Hal Kurtzman, Greg Lonigro
Steve McAllister, Howard McCullough
Matt Merullo, Mike Valarezo
Luke Wrenn

BALLPARK INFORMATION

Ballpark (capacity, surface)
Bank One Ballpark (49,033, grass)

Address
401 East Jefferson
Phoenix, AZ 85004

Official website
www.azdiamondbacks.com

Business phone
602-462-6500

Ticket information
602-514-8400

Ticket prices
$12.50 to $29.50 (lower level)
$1 to $20 (upper level)
$49 to $78 (lower level premium seats)
$30 and $40 (Infiniti Diamond level)

Field dimensions (from home plate)
To left field at foul line, 330 feet
To center field, 407 feet
To right field at foul line, 334 feet

First game played
March 31, 1998 (Rockies 9, Diamondbacks 2)

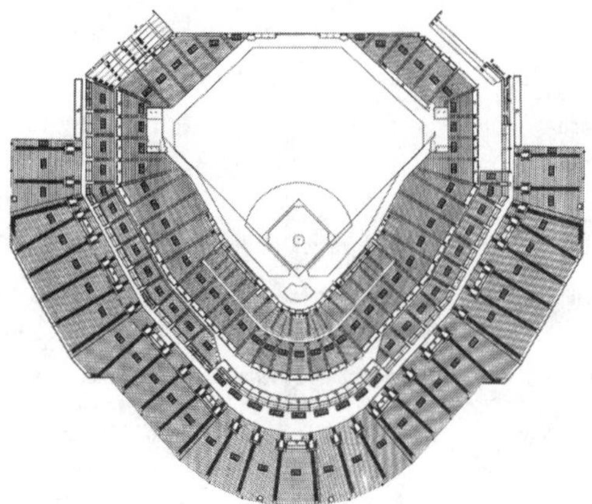

Follow the Diamondbacks all season at:
www.sportingnews.com/baseball/teams/diamondbacks/

DIAMONDBACKS SPRING ROSTER

No.	PITCHERS	B/T	Ht./Wt.	Born	2002 clubs	Projection
43	Batista, Miguel	R/R	6-2/195	2-19-71	Arizona	He's a bona fide starter, just needs to have better command of his pitches.
51	Johnson, Randy	R/L	6-10/232	9-10-63	Arizona	Lost only five games last season. Expect another Cy Young performance this year.
45	Dessens, Elmer	R/R	6-0/187	1-13-72	Cincinnati	Former Red should improve win total with Diamondbacks.
49	Kim, Byung-Hyun	R/R	5-11/177	1-19-79	Arizona	His closer job might be up for grabs now that Mantei is healthy.
58	Koplove, Mike	R/R	6-0/170	8-30-76	Tucson, Arizona	Won six games in relief, he'll be counted on in a variety of roles out of the 'pen.
31	Mantei, Matt	R/R	6-1/200	7-7-73	El Paso, Tucson, Arizona	Finally rounding into form after injuries, he could reclaim closer's job.
35	Myers, Mike	L/L	6-4/212	6-26-69	Arizona	He'll stick as long as he continues to be tough on lefties.
47	Oropesa, Eddie	L/L	6-3/215	11-23-71	Arizona, Tucson	Gives the D-backs another lefthanded option out of the bullpen.
24	Patterson, John	R/R	6-5/183	1-30-78	Tucson, Arizona	Will get a spot in the rotation after his late-season showing.
41	Prinz, Bret	R/R	6-3/185	6-15-77	Arizona, Tucson, Lancaster	Will have to pitch well in spring training in order to earn a job.
68	Randolph, Steve	L/L	6-3/185	5-1-74	Tucson	Won 15 games, but also led league in walks. Will get a look as starter.
38	Schilling, Curt	R/R	6-4/231	11-14-66	Arizona	Lost only seven games last season. He'll battle Johnson for N.L. Cy Young.
22	Swindell, Greg	R/L	6-3/239	1-2-65	Tucson, Arizona	Will get chance to win a bullpen job, but he might be out of gas at age 38.
45	Valverde, Jose	R/R	6-4/220	7-24-79	Tucson	Needs more seasoning at Class AAA, where he had 5.85 ERA in 49 games.
46	Ward, Jeremy	R/R	6-3/220	2-24-78	Tucson	Could be a cheaper alternative to current bullpen members.

No.	CATCHERS	B/T	Ht./Wt.	Born	2002 clubs	Projection
48	Barajas, Rod	R/R	6-2/229	9-5-75	Arizona, Tucson	Will split job with Chad Moeller. Hit .234 in 70 games in 2002.
16	Moeller, Chad	R/R	6-3/210	2-18-75	Tucson, Arizona	He's Randy Johnson's personal catcher, but he can hit (.286) too.

No.	INFIELDERS	B/T	Ht./Wt.	Born	2002 clubs	Projection
10	Cintron, Alex	B/R	6-2/185	12-17-78	Tucson, Arizona	Will probably become club's utility player now that Greg Colbrunn is gone.
4	Counsell, Craig	L/R	6-0/175	8-21-70	Arizona	Neck injury sidelined him for much of 2002, should be ready for 2003.
18	Donnels, Chris	L/R	6-0/185	4-21-66	Arizona, Tucson	Provides the D-backs with a good lefthanded bat off the bench.
23	Overbay, Lyle	L/L	6-2/215	1-28-77	Tucson, Arizona	First baseman of the future, just needs major league experience.
37	Spivey, Junior	R/R	6-0/185	1-28-75	Arizona	HIt .301 in first full season. Expect him to build on that this year.
9	Williams, Matt	R/R	6-2/219	11-28-65	Arizona, Tucson, Lancaster	Needs to stay healthy for the Diamondbacks to win consistently.
5	Womack, Tony	L/R	5-9/170	9-25-69	Arizona	He's the best option at shortstop, but could be traded, too.

No.	OUTFIELDERS	B/T	Ht./Wt.	Born	2002 clubs	Projection
29	Bautista, Danny	R/R	5-11/204	5-24-72	Arizona	If he stays healthy, he should have a career year in right field.
25	Dellucci, David	L/L	5-11/198	10-31-73	Arizona, Tucson	Most likely the top pinch-hitter this year.
62	Devore, Doug	L/L	6-4/200	12-14-77	Tucson	Needs to show more patience at the plate before he'll play in the majors.
12	Finley, Steve	L/L	6-2/195	3-12-65	Arizona	Team's starting centerfielder continues to defy age (38).
20	Gonzalez, Luis	L/R	6-2/195	9-3-67	Arizona	Team is hoping shoulder injury won't affect his 2003 performance.
8	Jose, Felix	B/R	6-1/220	5-8-65	Mexico City Red Devils, Arizona	Showed he can still hit, might just stick around in bench role.
65	Terrero, Luis	B/R	6-2/185	5-18-80	El Paso	Speedy outfielder needs more time in the minors.

THE COACHING STAFF

Bob Brenly, manager.
Chuck Kniffin, pitching coach.
Dwayne Murphy, hitting coach.
Eddie Rodriguez, third base coach.
Glenn Sherlock, bullpen coach.
Robin Yount, first base coach.

THE TOP NEWCOMERS

Elmer Dessens: Had a sterling 3.03 ERA in 30 starts with the Reds last season. Now that he'll be pitching in Arizona, you can expect those numbers to improve as he'll get more run support, be backed by a better defense and have the luxury of being the No. 3 starter behind Johnson and Schilling.

THE TOP PROSPECTS

John Patterson: Started five games for the Diamondbacks in 2002, winning only two. But more importantly, he'll give the Diamondbacks another strikeout pitcher in the rotation. He had 31 strikeouts in 30 innings in the majors. But he also allowed seven home runs in those 30 innings.

Lyle Overbay: Followed a stellar season in Class AA in 2001, with an even better campaign in Class AAA Tucson last year. Hit .343 with 19 homers and 109 RBIs and led the league with 40 doubles. Should get plenty of playing time in Arizona.

ATLANTA BRAVES

NATIONAL LEAGUE EAST DIVISION

2003 SEASON

Braves Schedule

Home games shaded; D—Day game (games starting before 5 p.m.); *—All-Star Game at Comiskey Park, Chicago. Subject to changes. †Game played in Puerto Rico.

March/April

SUN	MON	TUE	WED	THU	FRI	SAT
30	31 MON	1	2 MON	3 MON	4 FLA	5 FLA
6 D FLA	7 D FLA	8 PHI	9 PHI	10 PHI	11 FLA	12 FLA
13 D FLA	14	15 † MON	16 † MON	17 D† MON	18 PHI	19 PHI
20 D PHI	21	22 STL	23 STL	24 STL	25 MIL	26 MIL
27 D MIL	28	29 HOU	30 HOU			

May

SUN	MON	TUE	WED	THU	FRI	SAT
				1 HOU	2 ARI	3 ARI
4 D ARI	5	6 COL	7 COL	8 COL	9 SF	10 SF
11 D SF	12 LA	13 LA	14 LA	15 D SD	16 SD	17 SD
18 D SD	19	20 CIN	21 CIN	22 CIN	23 NYM	24 D NYM
25 D NYM	26 D CIN	27 CIN	28 CIN	29	30 NYM	31 D NYM

June

SUN	MON	TUE	WED	THU	FRI	SAT
1 NYM	2	3 TEX	4 TEX	5 D TEX	6 PIT	7 PIT
8 D PIT	9	10 OAK	11 OAK	12 D OAK	13 SEA	14 D SEA
15 SEA	16	17 PHI	18 PHI	19 D PHI	20 BAL	21 BAL
22 D BAL	23	24 PHI	25 PHI	26 PHI	27 TB	28 TB
29 D TB	30 FLA					

July

SUN	MON	TUE	WED	THU	FRI	SAT
		1 FLA	2 FLA	3 MON	4 MON	5 MON
6 D MON	7 NYM	8 NYM	9 D NYM	10 D CUB	11 D CUB	12 D CUB
13 D CUB	14	15 *	16	17 NYM	18 NYM	19 D NYM
20 D NYM	21 CUB	22 CUB	23 FLA	24 D FLA	25 MON	26 MON
27 D MON	28 MON	29 HOU	30 HOU	31 HOU		

August

SUN	MON	TUE	WED	THU	FRI	SAT
					1 LA	2 D LA
3 D LA	4	5 MIL	6 MIL	7 D MIL	8 STL	9 D STL
10 D STL	11	12 SD	13 SD	14 SD	15 ARI	16 ARI
17 D ARI	18 D ARI	19 SF	20 SF	21 SF	22 COL	23 COL
24 D COL	25	26 NYM	27 NYM	28 NYM	29 PIT	30 D PIT
31 D PIT						

September

SUN	MON	TUE	WED	THU	FRI	SAT
	1 D NYM	2 NYM	3 D NYM	4	5 PIT	6 PIT
7 D PIT	8 PHI	9 PHI	10 PHI	11 PHI	12 FLA	13 FLA
14 D FLA	15 MON	16 MON	17 D MON	18	19 FLA	20 FLA
21 D FLA	22 FLA	23 MON	24 MON	25	26 PHI	27 D PHI
28 D PHI						

FRONT-OFFICE DIRECTORY

Chairman of the board of directors .... William C. Bartholomay
President .... Stanley H. Kasten
Executive vice president and general manager .... John Schuerholz
Senior v.p. and assistant to the president .... Henry L. Aaron
Senior vice president, administration .... Bob Wolfe
Vice president, assistant general manager .... Frank Wren
Vice president .... Lee Douglas
Special assistants to g.m. .... Dick Balderson, Jim Fregosi, Chuck McMichael, Scott Nethery, Paul Snyder
Special assistant to g.m./player development .... Jose Martinez
Director of team travel, equipment manager .... Bill Acree
Director of scouting .... Roy Clark
Director of player personnel .... Dayton Moore
Senior director of promotions and civic affairs .... Miles McRea
Vice president/controller .... Chip Moore
Director of ticket sales .... Paul Adams
Director of minor league business operations .... Bruce Baldwin
Director of stadium operations and security .... Larry Bowman
Field director .... Ed Mangan
Director of ticket operations .... Ed Newman
Team counsel .... John Cooper
Director of community relations .... Cara Maglione
Director of audio video operations .... Jennifer Berger
Director of corporate sales .... Jim Allen
Director of public relations .... Jim Schultz
Director of strategic development, Turner Sports Teams and Venues .... David Lee
Director of human resources .... Michele Golden
Director of advertising and publicity .... Joe Clemente
Director of special events .... Sabrina Jenkins
Director of customer service, Turner Sports Teams and Venues .... Jason Parker
Media relations manager .... Glen Serra
Public relations assistants .... Adam Liberman, Anne, McAlister, Meagan Swingle

MINOR LEAGUE AFFILIATES

Class	Team	League	Manager
AAA	Richmond	International	Pat Kelly
AA	Greenville	Southern	Brian Snitker
A	Myrtle Beach	Carolina	Randy Ingle
A	Rome	South Atlantic	Rocket Wheeler
Rookie	Danville	Appalachian	Ralph Henriquez
Rookie	Gulf Coast Braves	Gulf Coast	Rick Albert

BROADCAST INFORMATION

Radio: WSB-AM (750).
TV: TBS-TV (Channel 17).
Cable TV: FOX Sports Net South, Turner South.

SPRING TRAINING

Ballpark (city): Disney's Wide World Sports Baseball Stadium (Kissimmee, Fla.).
Ticket information: 407-839-3900; 407-939-4263.

ASSISTANCE STAFF

Head trainer
Jeff Porter

Assistant trainer
Jim Lovell

Director of medical services
Dr. Joe Chandler

Associate physicians
Dr. William Barber, Dr. John Cantwell, Dr. Xavier Duralde, Dr. Norman Elliott, Dr. Marvin Royster

Advance scout
Bobby Wine

National supervisors
Tim Conroy, John Flannery

Regional supervisors
Harold Cronin, Paul Faulk, "J" Harrison, Kurt Kemp

Area supervisors
Mike Baker, Daniel Bates, Billy Best, Stu Cann, Sherrod Clinkscales, Ralph Garr, Al Goetz, Robert Lucas, Darryl Monroe, Alex Morales, J.J. Picollo, John Ramey, John Stewart, Don Thomas, Terry Tripp

Scouts
Nez Balelo, Joe Caputo, Matt Dodd, Wayne Kitts, Al Kubski, Charlie Smith, Rip Tutor

International supervisors
Phil Dale, Rene Francisco, Julian Perez

International scouts
Roberto Aquino, Neil Burke, Richard Castro, Jeremy Chou, Edgar Fernandez, Jose Figueroa, Pedro Flores, Bill Froberg, Carlos Garcia, Ruben Garcia, Courtland Hall, Diego Herrera, Rafael Jozela, David Latham, Jason Lee, Jose Leon, Andres Lopez, Hiroyuki Oya, Rolando Petit, Elvis Pineda, Manuel Samaniego, Miguel Teran, Raymond Tew, Marvin Throneberry, Carlos Torres

Professional scouts
Rod Gilbreath, Chet Montgomery, Bob Wadsworth, Gene Watson

BALLPARK INFORMATION

Ballpark (capacity, surface)
Turner Field (50,091, grass)
Address
P.O. Box 4064, Atlanta, GA 30302
Official website
www.atlantabraves.com
Business phone
404-522-7630
Ticket information
404-249-6400 or 800-326-4000
Ticket prices
$45* (dugout level), $32*/$27* (Lexus level)
$27*/$22* (field level, terrace level)
$18* (field pavilion, terrace pavilion)
$12* (upper level box), $8* (upper level reserved)
$5 (upper pavilion), $1 (skyline)
*Tickets to all Fri. & Sat. games from May-Aug. will be charged an additional $3 premium in all sections except upper pavilion and skyline.
Field dimensions (from home plate)
To left field at foul line, 335 feet
To center field, 401 feet
To right field at foul line, 330 feet
First game played
April 4, 1997 (Braves 5, Cubs 4)

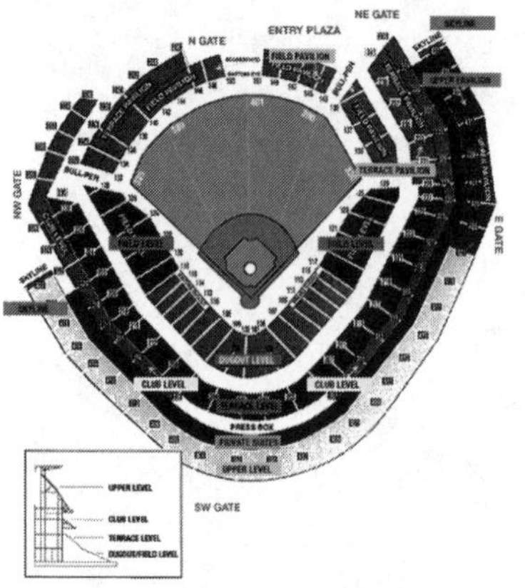

Follow the Braves all season at: www.sportingnews.com/baseball/teams/braves/

BRAVES SPRING ROSTER

No.	PITCHERS	B/T	Ht./Wt.	Born	2002 clubs	Projection
	Belisle, Matt	B/R	6-3/195	6-6-80	Greenville	Bouncing back from injury in 2001, he was able to pitch 150 innings last year.
30	Bong, Jung	L/L	6-3/175	7-15-80	Greenville, Atlanta	Looks to be just a year away from helping the rotation. Still a good prospect.
34	Byrd, Paul	R/R	6-1/185	12-3-70	Kansas City	Won 17 games for a woeful Kansas City team. Should win more with Braves.
33	Dawley, Joey	R/R	6-4/205	9-19-71	Richmond, Atlanta	Had a 2.63 ERA in 140 innings in Class AAA. Might get a job in bullpen.
56	Ennis, John	R/R	6-5/220	10-17-79	Greenville, Atlanta	Still working on command, probably ticketed for Class AAA this year.
	Evert, Brett	L/L	6-6/200	10-23-80	Greenville, Myrtle Beach	Still learning how to pitch; is at least two years away from majors.
49	Gryboski, Kevin	R/R	6-5/235	11-15-73	Richmond, Atlanta, Macon	Struggled with his control, but will probably have a job in the bullpen.
32	Hampton, Mike	R/L	5-10/180	9-9-72	Colorado	Escaping Coors Field for Atlanta will rejuvenate his career.
45	Hodges, Trey	R/R	6-3/187	6-29-78	Richmond, Atlanta	Led International League with 15 wins, likely to get bullpen work.
46	King, Ray	L/L	6-1/242	1-15-74	Milwaukee, Indianapolis	Expected to be No. 1 left reliever in Braves' 2003 bullpen.
31	Maddux, Greg	R/R	6-0/185	4-14-66	Atlanta	Still can give 200 innings and a sub-3.00 ERA.
38	Marquis, Jason	L/R	6-1/210	8-21-78	Atlanta	A better No. 5 starter than you'll see on most teams.
48	Ortiz, Russ	R/R	6-1/208	6-5-74	San Francisco	You can plug him in anywhere in the rotation and he'll be fine.
26	Pratt, Andy	L/L	5-11/160	8-27-79	Greenville, Richmond, Atlanta	Former Rangers prospect, had good start with Braves organization.
51	Ramirez, Horacio	L/L	6-1/170	11-24-79	Macon, Greenville	Likely a year away, could become a solid lefthanded starter in the majors.
29	Smoltz, John	R/R	6-3/220	5-15-67	Atlanta	His first seaso as a closer was better than anyone could have imagined.
50	Spurling, Chris	R/R	6-6/240	6-28-77	Altoona	Rule 5 closer candidate either sticks with team or goes back to Pirates.
66	Sylvester, Billy	R/R	6-5/220	10-1-76	Richmond, Greenville	Held opponents to a .181 average in Class AA.
	Venafro, Mike	L/L	5-10/180	8-2-73	Oakland, Sacramento	Has chance to take Chris Hammond's place in bullpen.
	Waters, Chris	L/L	6-0/170	8-17-80	Myrtle Beach	Crafty lefthander won 13 games and posted a 2.76 ERA.

No.	CATCHERS	B/T	Ht./Wt.	Born	2002 clubs	Projection
20	Blanco, Henry	R/R	5-11/220	8-29-71	Atlanta	Hit only .204, but still a good defensive catcher.
39	Estrada, Johnny	B/R	5-11/209	6-27-76	Scranton/Wilkes-Barre, Phila.	Acquired in Kevin Millwood deal, he's shown a good bat in the minors.
8	Lopez, Javy	R/R	6-3/225	11-5-70	Atlanta	Trying to return to form after injury-plagued 2002 season.

No.	INFIELDERS	B/T	Ht./Wt.	Born	2002 clubs	Projection
24	Betemit, Wilson	B/R	6-2/155	11-2-81	Gulf Coast Braves, Richmond	Only hit .245 in Class AAA but still has loads of talent.
19	Castilla, Vinny	R/R	6-1/205	7-4-67	Atlanta	Hit only .232 with 12 home runs, and the Braves need much more.
16	DeRosa, Mark	R/R	6-1/205	2-26-75	Atlanta, Richmond, Myrtle Beach	Could supplant Castilla as starting third baseman.
23	Franco, Julio	R/R	6-1/188	8-23-58	Atlanta	Will have utility role if he can stay healthy and produce.
4	Franco, Matt	L/R	6-1/210	8-19-69	Richmond, Atlanta	Utility man will probably get loads of playing time.
1	Furcal, Rafael	B/R	5-10/165	8-24-78	Atlanta	Hit .275, but Braves would like to see him get on base a little more.
22	Giles, Marcus	R/R	5-8/180	5-18-78	Atlanta, Richmond	Second base job is his to lose this season.
70	Green, Nick	R/R	6-0/178	9-10-78	Greenville	Braves will give this second-base prospect a good look.
	LaRoche, Adam	L/L	6-3/180	11-6-79	Myrtle Beach, Greenville	First baseman of the future, is still a year away.

No.	OUTFIELDERS	B/T	Ht./Wt.	Born	2002 clubs	Projection
28	Aldridge, Cory	L/R	6-0/210	6-13-79	Gulf Coast Braves	Slugger looking to rebound from injuries. Likely headed back to minors.
	Fick, Robert	L/R	6-1/200	3-15-74	Detroit	Likely to win the job at first base. Outfield is too crowded in Atlanta.
25	Jones, Andruw	R/R	6-1/210	4-23-77	Atlanta	Gold Glover returns to center, Braves are hoping he can raise his average.
10	Jones, Chipper	B/R	6-4/210	4-24-72	Atlanta	First season in left was a success. But 26 homers was low total.
73	Langerhans, Ryan	L/L	6-3/195	2-20-80	Greenville, Atlanta	After hitting .413 in 2001, he came back to earth and hit .251 in Class AA.
11	Sheffield, Gary	R/R	6-0/205	11-18-68	Atlanta	Hit .307 with 25 homers in first season in Atlanta, expect those numbers to go up.

THE COACHING STAFF

Bobby Cox, manager.

Pat Corrales, dugout coach.

Bobby Dews, bullpen coach.

Freddi Gonzalez, third base coach.

Glenn Hubbard, first base coach.

Leo Mazzone, pitching coach.

Otis Nixon, baserunning and batting coach.

Terry Pendleton, hitting coach.

THE TOP NEWCOMERS

Paul Byrd: While many thought he might re-sign with the Royals, Byrd decided to fly south for Atlanta. He'll join a rotation with Greg Maddux, Russ Ortiz and Mike Hampton. Hard to say which spot in the rotation he'll fill, but he'll win plenty not having to be a No. 1 starter on a bad team.

Mike Hampton: After two years of Coors Field abuse, Hampton is moving on. The Braves are sure they can get him back on track and pitching like the Mike Hampton who led the Mets to the World Series in 2000.

Russ Ortiz: Another 200-plus innings workhorse, he won 14 games with the Giants in 2002 and helped them reach the World Series. He still walks too many batters and might have a harder time keeping the ball in the park at Turner Field than he did at Pac Bell Park.

THE TOP PROSPECTS

Jung Bong: His is the one name most often mentioned in trade rumors surrounding the Braves. But the Braves aren't all that willing to let him go. He pitched well in Class AA, bouncing between starting and relieving. Braves believe he's best suited to starting.

Joe Dawley: This major league veteran appears to be getting better with age. Won nine games with 136 strikeouts in 140 innings in Class AAA, and his 2.63 ERA is not to be ignored.

CHICAGO CUBS

NATIONAL LEAGUE CENTRAL DIVISION

2003 SEASON

Cubs Schedule

Home games shaded; D—Day game (games starting before 5 p.m.); *—All-Star Game at Comiskey Park, Chicago. Subject to changes. †Game played in Puerto Rico.

March/April

SUN	MON	TUE	WED	THU	FRI	SAT
30	31 D NYM	1	2 NYM	3 D NYM	4 CIN	5 D CIN
6 D CIN	7 D MON	8	9 D MON	10 D MON	11 D PIT	12 D PIT
13 D PIT	14 CIN	15 D CIN	16 D CIN	17 D CIN	18 PIT	19 PIT
20 D PIT	21	22 SD	23 D SD	24 D SD	25 COL	26 D COL
27 D COL	28	29 SF	30 SF			

May

SUN	MON	TUE	WED	THU	FRI	SAT
				1 D SF	2 D COL	3 D COL
4 D COL	5 MIL	6 MIL	7 D MIL	8	9 D STL	10 D STL
11 D STL	12 MIL	13 MIL	14 MIL	15 D MIL	16 STL	17 D STL
18 D STL	19 D STL	20 PIT	21 PIT	22 PIT	23 HOU	24 HOU
25 D HOU	26 D PIT	27 PIT	28 D PIT	29	30 D HOU	31 D HOU

June

SUN	MON	TUE	WED	THU	FRI	SAT
1 D HOU	2	3 TB	4 TB	5 D TB	6 D NYY	7 D NYY
8 NYY	9	10 BAL	11 BAL	12 BAL	13 TOR	14 D TOR
15 D TOR	16 CIN	17 CIN	18 CIN	19 D CIN	20 D CWS	21 D CWS
22 D CWS	23	24 MIL	25 D MIL	26 D MIL	27 D CWS	28 D CWS
29 D CWS	30 PHI					

July

SUN	MON	TUE	WED	THU	FRI	SAT
		1 PHI	2 PHI	3 PHI	4 D STL	5 D STL
6 D STL	7 FLA	8 D FLA	9 D FLA	10 D ATL	11 D ATL	12 D ATL
13 D ATL	14	15 *	16	17	18 FLA	19 FLA
20 D FLA	21 ATL	22 ATL	23 PHI	24 D PHI	25 HOU	26 D HOU
27 D HOU	28	29 SF	30 D SF	31 D SF		

August

SUN	MON	TUE	WED	THU	FRI	SAT
					1 D ARI	2 D ARI
3 D ARI	4	5 SD	6 SD	7 D SD	8 LA	9 LA
10 D LA	11 HOU	12 HOU	13 D HOU	14 D HOU	15 D LA	16 D LA
17 D LA	18	19 HOU	20 HOU	21 HOU	22 ARI	23 D ARI
24 D ARI	25	26 STL	27 STL	28 STL	29 D MIL	30 D MIL
31 D MIL						

September

SUN	MON	TUE	WED	THU	FRI	SAT
	1 D STL	2 STL	3 D STL	4 D STL	5 MIL	6 MIL
7 D MIL	8	9 † MON	10 † MON	11 D† MON	12 D CIN	13 D CIN
14 D CIN	15 NYM	16 NYM	17 D NYM	18	19 PIT	20 PIT
21 D PIT	22	23 CIN	24 CIN	25 CIN	26 D PIT	27 D PIT
28 D PIT						

FRONT-OFFICE DIRECTORY

Board of directors .... Dennis FitzSimons, Andrew B. MacPhail, Andrew McKenna
President and chief executive officer .... Andrew B. MacPhail
Vice president/general manager .... Jim Hendry
Director, baseball operations .... Scott Nelson
Special assistants to the general manageer .... Keith Champion, Ken Kravec, Ed Lynch, Billy Williams
Director of scouting .... John Stockstill
Director of player development/Latin American operations .... Oneri Fleita
Traveling secretary .... Jimmy Bank
Executive v.p., business operations .... Mark McGuire
Director, information services & special projects .... Carl Rice
Senior legal counsel/corporate secretary .... Crane Kenney
Controller .... Jodi Reischl
Director, human resources .... Jenifer Surma
Vice president, marketing and broadcasting .... John McDonough
Director, promotions and advertising .... Jay Blunk
Director, publications .... Lena McDonagh
Manager, publications .... Jim McArdle
Director, stadium operations .... Paul Rathje
Manager, event operations/security .... Mike Hill
Head groundskeeper .... Roger Baird
Director, ticket operations .... Frank Maloney
Director, media relations .... Sharon Pannozzo
Manager, media information .... Chuck Wasserstrom

MINOR LEAGUE AFFILIATES

Class	Team	League	Manager
AAA	Iowa	Pacific Coast	Mike Quade
AA	West Tenn	Southern	Bobby Dickerson
A	Daytona	Florida State	Rick Kranitz
A	Lansing	Midwest	Julio Garcia
A	Boise	Northwest	Steve McFarland
Rookie	Mesa Cubs	Arizona	Carmelo Martinez

BROADCAST INFORMATION

Radio: WGN-AM (720).
TV: WGN-TV (Channel 9); WCIU-TV (Channel 26).
Cable TV: Fox Sports Net Chicago.

SPRING TRAINING

Ballpark (city): HoHoKam Park (Mesa, Ariz.).
Ticket information: 800-638-4253.

ASSISTANCE STAFF

Team physician
Michael Schafer, M.D.

Head athletic trainer
David Tumbas

Assistant athletic trainer
Sandy Krum

Strength and conditioning coordinator
Tim Buss

Home clubhouse manager, emeritus
Yosh Kawano

Home clubhouse manager
Tom Hellman

Visiting clubhouse manager
Dana Noeltner

Cross-checkers
Mark Adair, Brad Kelley, Mike Soper

Special assignment scouts
Gene Handley, Spider Jorgensen, Glen Van Proyen

Scouts
Billy Blitzer, Jim Crawford, Steve Fuller, Al Geddes, Steve Hinton, Sam Hughes, Brian Milner, Hector Ortega, Fred Peterson, Rolando Pina, Pat Portugal, Tad Powers, Steve Riha, Jose Serra, Tom Shafer, Mitch Sokol, Billy Swoope, Jose Trujillo, Stan Zielinski

BALLPARK INFORMATION

Ballpark (capacity, surface)
Wrigley Field (39,241, grass)

Address
1060 W. Addison St.
Chicago, IL 60613-4397

Official website
www.cubs.com

Business phone
773-404-2827

Ticket information
773-404-2827

Ticket prices
$45 (club box-infield)
$40 (club box-outfield, field box-infield)
$36 (field box-outfield)
$32 (upper deck box, terrace box)
$30 (bleachers)
$25 (terrace reserved)
$15 (upper deck reserved)

Field dimensions (from home plate)
To left field at foul line, 355 feet
To center field, 400 feet
To right field at foul line, 353 feet

First game played
April 20, 1916 (Cubs 7, Reds 6)

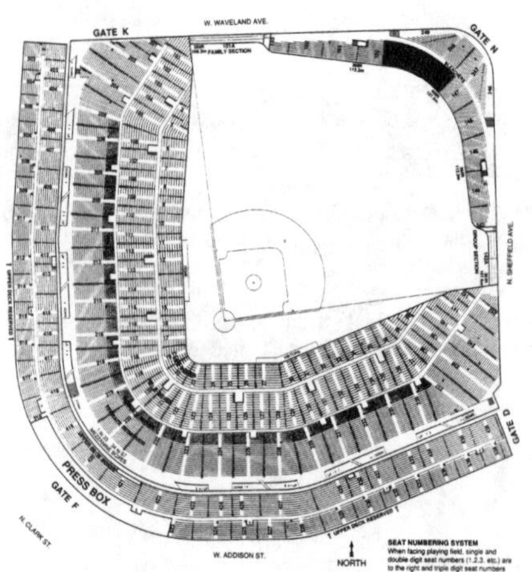

Follow the Cubs all season at: www.sportingnews.com/baseball/teams/cubs/

CUBS SPRING ROSTER

No.	PITCHERS	B/T	Ht./Wt.	Born	2002 clubs	Projection
57	Alfonseca, Antonio	R/R	6-5/250	4-16-72	Chicago N.L.	He's dropping weight this offseason, which should help him keep his job as closer.
53	Beltran, Francis	R/R	6-5/220	11-29-79	West Tenn, Chicago N.L.	Future closer had 23 saves in Class AA. Likely one year away.
35	Benes, Alan	R/R	6-5/235	1-21-72	Iowa, Chicago N.L.	Showed Cubs he can be a solid starter after shoulder surgeries.
48	Borowski, Joe	R/R	6-2/240	5-4-71	Chicago N.L.	Long reliever had sub-3.00 ERA. Expect much of the same in 2003.
	Bruback, Matt	R/R	6-/215	1-12-79	West Tenn	Won nine games and pitched 174 innings. Still a year away.
37	Chiasson, Scott	R/R	6-3/200	8-14-77	Iowa, Chicago N.L., West Tenn	Reliever had troubles adjusting to majors. Will get another shot this year.
30	Clement, Matt	R/R	6-3/213	8-12-74	Chicago N.L.	Found his control in Chicago and struck out 215 batters.
51	Cruz, Juan	R/R	6-2/165	10-15-78	Chicago N.L.	Needs to refine his control before he'll be a full-time starter.
55	Estes, Shawn	R/L	6-2/200	2-18-73	New York N.L., Cincinnati	Only won five games last season, but should rebound under his former manager.
44	Farnsworth, Kyle	R/R	6-4/235	4-14-76	Chicago N.L., Iowa	Many wonder what happened to his stuff after he posted a 7.33 ERA in 2002.
	Leicester, Jon	R/R	6-2/210	2-7-79	Daytona, West Tenn	Moving through the system at a good pace, but still two years away.
91	Ohman, Will	L/L	6-2/195	8-13-77	DID NOT PLAY	Starter missed entire season due to injury. Likely to begin year in minors.
22	Prior, Mark	R/R	6-5/225	9-7-80	West Tenn, Iowa, Chicago N.L.	Future staff ace combines with Kerry Wood to give Cubs scary 1-2 punch.
37	Remlinger, Mike	L/L	6-1/210	3-23-66	Atlanta	Signed to solidify bullpen, might close out a few games here and there.
	Sanchez, Felix	R/R	6-0/160	10-14-79	Lansing	Starter pitched well but only won five games in 21 starts in Class A.
33	Sirotka, Mike	L/L	6-1/200	5-13-71	DID NOT PLAY	Shoulder injuries have sidelined former White Sox pitcher last two seasons.
39	Smyth, Steve	L/L	6-1/195	6-3-78	West Tenn, Iowa, Chicago N.L.	Still needs one more year in Class AAA before he's ready.
	Veres, Dave	R/R	6-2/220	10-19-66	St. Louis	Workhorse brought in to provide bullpen depth. Will give Cubs 70 quality outings.
	Webb, John	R/R	6-3/190	5-23-79	Daytona, West Tenn	Starter went 9-8 in two stops in minors. Still a year or two away.
34	Wood, Kerry	R/R	6-5/230	6-16-77	Chicago N.L.	If he can keep his walks down, he'll join the elite pitchers.
38	Zambrano, Carlos	R/R	6-5/250	6-1-81	Iowa, Chicago N.L.	Has electric stuff, but still learning how to pitch.

No.	CATCHERS	B/T	Ht./Wt.	Born	2002 clubs	Projection
	Bako, Paul	L/R	6-2/205	6-20-72	Milwaukee	Brought in to provide a solid defensive presence when Miller needs a day off.
	Miller, Damian	R/R	6-2/218	10-13-69	Arizona, Tucson	All-Star catcher hit just .249 in 2002, but committed only two errors.

No.	INFIELDERS	B/T	Ht./Wt.	Born	2002 clubs	Projection
28	Bellhorn, Mark	B/R	6-1/205	8-23-74	Chicago N.L.	Hit 24 doubles and 27 homers, should be starting either at third or second.
19	Choi, Hee Seop	L/L	6-5/235	3-16-79	Iowa, Chicago N.L.	Top prospect finally gets chance to shine at first. It's his job to lose.
56	Frese, Nate	R/R	6-3/200	7-10-77	West Tenn	Injuries slowed his development; he's likely going to Class AAA for season.
8	Gonzalez, Alex	R/R	6-0/200	4-8-73	Chicago N.L.	Hit .248 and committed 21 errors in first N.L. season.
	Grudzielanek, Mark	R/R	6-1/185	6-30-70	Los Angeles	Acquired just in case Bobby Hill isn't ready for full-time second base job.
17	Hill, Bobby	B/R	5-10/190	4-3-78	Iowa, Chicago N.L.	Second base job is his to lose in spring training.
	Karros, Eric	R/R	6-4/226	11-4-67	Los Angeles	Will provide veteran option at first if Choi hits a rough stretch in first season.
	Kelton, Dave	R/R	6-3/205	12-17-79	West Tenn	Belted 20 homers in Class AA. Could be third baseman of future.
	Martinez, Ramon	R/R	6-1/183	10-10-72	San Francisco	Might get a lot of playing under former manager Dusty Baker.
1	Ojeda, Augie	B/R	5-8/170	12-20-74	Chicago N.L., Iowa	Hit only .230 in Class AAA. Days might be numbered due to infield depth.
15	Orie, Kevin	R/R	6-4/215	9-1-72	Iowa, Chicago N.L.	Will be in battle for infield spot. Hit .281 in brief cameo last season.

No.	OUTFIELDERS	B/T	Ht./Wt.	Born	2002 clubs	Projection
18	Alou, Moises	R/R	6-3/220	7-3-66	Daytona, Chicago N.L.	Cubs are hoping his second year with team is much more productive than the first.
	Jackson, Nic	L/R	6-3/205	9-25-79	West Tenn	Played in only 32 games before injury ended season. Was hitting .290.
76	Melian, Jackson	R/R	6-2/190	1-7-80	Huntsville, West Tenn	Hit .308 in Class AA, but will need to have better patience at the plate.
	O'Leary, Troy	L/L	6-0/208	8-4-69	Ottawa, Montreal	Provides the Cubs with good outfield depth in case of injury or inconsistency.
20	Patterson, Corey	L/R	5-9/175	8-13-79	Chicago N.L.	His first season was good, Cubs are hoping second will be better.
21	Sosa, Sammy	R/R	6-0/220	11-12-68	Chicago N.L.	Might have monster year with healthy lineup around him.

THE COACHING STAFF

Dusty Baker, manager.
Gene Clines, first base coach.
Wendell Kim, third base coach.
Juan Lopez, bullpen coach.
Gary Matthews, hitting coach.
Dick Pole, bench coach.
Larry Rothschild, pitching coach.

THE TOP NEWCOMERS

Shawn Estes: Gives the Cubs a solid option for a No. 3 starter. It's hoped that Estes can rebound from a subpar 2002 under former manager Dusty Baker. Having Estes also gives the Cubs a solid lefthanded starter in the N.L. Central, something very few teams in the division have.

Mike Remlinger: Has pitched in at least 70 games in each of the last four seasons. Cubs are hoping he'll be able to pitch that many out of the bullpen again in 2003. He also will get his fair share of saves if Alfonseca can't find his form.

Eric Karros: Rebounded from back injuries in 2001 to post some decent numbers in 2002, hitting .271 with 13 home runs and 73 RBIs. He's still pretty good defensively and gives the Cubs a good power hitter off the bench and a stop-gap measure in case Choi isn't ready for full-time duty.

THE TOP PROSPECTS

Hee Seop Choi: Returning Choi to Class AAA last season was the right move. He showed improved patience at the plate and ended up leading the league with 95 walks. And while his brief callup didn't amount to a whole lot, he now has a taste of the major leagues.

Dave Kelton: He's a power hitter who can hit for a decent average. He also showed decent speed by stealing 12 bases in Class AA. He's still a year away, but worth keeping an eye on.

Steve Smyth: Strikeout pitcher has moved through system swiftly and could make the Cubs rotation this season. If not he's likely headed back to Class AAA to keep his arm ready for a starting spot. A good spring training might land him a starting job at beginning of season.

Cincinnati Reds

National League Central Division

2003 SEASON

Reds Schedule

Home games shaded; D—Day game (games starting before 5 p.m.); *—All-Star Game at Comiskey Park, Chicago. Subject to changes. †Game played in Puerto Rico.

March/April

SUN	MON	TUE	WED	THU	FRI	SAT
30	31 D PIT	1	2 PIT	3 D PIT	4 CUB	5 D CUB
6 D CUB	7	8 HOU	9 HOU	10 HOU	11 PHI	12 D PHI
13 D PHI	14 CUB	15 D CUB	16 D CUB	17 D CUB	18 † MON	19 † MON
20 D† MON	21	22 LA	23 LA	24 LA	25 SD	26 D SD
27 D SD	28	29 COL	30 COL			

May

SUN	MON	TUE	WED	THU	FRI	SAT
				1 D COL	2 SF	3 D SF
4 D SF	5 STL	6 STL	7 STL	8 D STL	9 MIL	10 MIL
11 D MIL	12	13 STL	14 STL	15 D STL	16 MIL	17 D MIL
18 D MIL	19	20 ATL	21 ATL	22 ATL	23 FLA	24 FLA
25 D FLA	26 D ATL	27 ATL	28 ATL	29	30 FLA	31 FLA

June

SUN	MON	TUE	WED	THU	FRI	SAT
1 D FLA	2	3 NYY	4 NYY	5 NYY	6 TOR	7 TOR
8 D TOR	9	10 TB	11 TB	12 TB	13 PHI	14 PHI
15 D PHI	16 CUB	17 CUB	18 CUB	19 D CUB	20 ARI	21 ARI
22 D ARI	23	24 STL	25 STL	26 STL	27 CLE	28 D CLE
29 D CLE	30					

July

SUN	MON	TUE	WED	THU	FRI	SAT
		1 PIT	2 PIT	3 PIT	4 D NYM	5 NYM
6 D NYM	7 HOU	8 HOU	9 HOU	10 HOU	11 MIL	12 MIL
13 D MIL	14	15 *	16	17 HOU	18 HOU	19 D HOU
20 D HOU	21 MIL	22 MIL	23 PIT	24 D PIT	25 NYM	26 NYM
27 D NYM	28	29 COL	30 COL	31 COL		

August

SUN	MON	TUE	WED	THU	FRI	SAT
					1 SF	2 D SF
3 D SF	4	5 LA	6 LA	7 LA	8 SD	9 SD
10 D SD	11	12 ARI	13 ARI	14 ARI	15 HOU	16 D HOU
17 D HOU	18	19 ARI	20 ARI	21 ARI	22 HOU	23 HOU
24 D HOU	25 MIL	26 MIL	27 MIL	28 D MIL	29 STL	30 STL
31 D STL						

September

SUN	MON	TUE	WED	THU	FRI	SAT
	1 D MIL	2 MIL	3 MIL	4	5 STL	6 STL
7 D STL	8 PIT	9 PIT	10 PIT	11 D PIT	12 D CUB	13 D CUB
14 D CUB	15 PIT	16 PIT	17 PIT	18 PIT	19 PHI	20 PHI
21 D PHI	22	23 CUB	24 CUB	25 CUB	26 MON	27 D MON
28 D MON						

FRONT-OFFICE DIRECTORY

General manager....Jim Bowden
Assistant general manager....Brad Kullman
Assistant general manager/director of scouting....Leland Maddox
Special assistant to the g.m. and senior advisor/player development....Johnny Almaraz
Senior special assistant to the g.m. and advance scout....Gene Bennett
Special assistants to the g.m. ....Larry Barton Jr., Al Goldis, Darrell "Doc" Rodgers
Special consultants to the general manager....Johnny Bench, Ken Griffey Sr.
Special consultant....Jon Niednagel
Special consultant to the g.m. and scouting....Bob Zuk
Assistant director of baseball....Geoff Silver
Director of player development....Tim Naehring
Senior advisor/player development....Chief Bender
Director of media relations....Rob Butcher
Assistant director of media relations....Michael Vassallo
Media relations coordinator....Larry Herms
Traveling secretary....Gary Wahoff
Senior director of finance and administration/controller....Anthony Ward
Director of communications and community relations....Michael Ringering
Assistant director of communications....Ralph Mitchell
Community relations manager....Lorrie Platt
Merchandise manager....Amy Hafer
Director of human resources and diversity....Stephanie Dicks
Director of season and group operations....Pat McCaffrey
Season tickets operations manager....Cyndi Strzynski
Group tickets operations manager....Brad Callahan
Director of sales....Jenny Gardner
Suite and premium service manager....Libbie Williams
Riverfront club and sales coordinator....Maya Wadleigh
Director of ticket operations....John O'Brien
Business and broadcasting administrator....Ginny Kamp
Director of marketing....Cal Levy
Media and advertising manager....Jen Black
Corporate service manager....Molly Mott
Director of corporate marketing....Brad Blettner
Director of promotions and entertainment....Amy Schneider
Senior director of ball park operations....Declan Mullin
Guest relations manager....Jennifer Green
Ball park operations superintendant....Bob Harrison
Ball park operations assistant....Colleen Brown
Head Groundskeeper....Doug Gallant
Director of scouting administration....Wilma Mann

MINOR LEAGUE AFFILIATES

Class	Team	League	Manager
AAA	Louisville	International	Dave Miley
AA	Chattanooga	Southern	Phil Wellman
A	Potomac	South Atlantic	Jayhawk Owens
A	Dayton	Midwest	Donnie Scott
Rookie	Billings	Pioneer	Rick Burleson
Rookie	Gulf Coast Reds	Gulf Coast	Edgar Caceres

BROADCAST INFORMATION

Radio: WLW-AM (700).
Cable TV: Fox Sports Net.

SPRING TRAINING

Ballpark (city): Ed Smith Stadium (Sarasota, Fla.).
Ticket information: 941-954-4101.

ASSISTANCE STAFF

Head trainer
Mark Mann

Assistant trainer and physical therapist
Lonnie Soloff

Medical director
Dr. Timothy Kremchek

Senior consultant/orthopaedics
Dr. James Andrews

Director of sports science
Bill Harrison

Strength and conditioning coach
Carlo Alvarez

Video coordinator
Joe Harkins

National cross-checkers
Butch Baccala, Jeff Barton, Jimmy Gonzales, Jim Thrift

Director of international scouting
Jorge Oquendo

International scouts
Oswaldo Alvarez, Kevin Carcamo, Orlando Granda, Mike Hartman, Min Lee, Victor Mateo, Rafael Nava, Juan Rodriguez

Scouting supervisors
Terry Abbott, Butch Baccala, Jeff Barton, Larry Barton, Howard Bowens, John Brickley, Rex De La Nuez, Jerry Flowers, Jimmy Gonzales, Mike Keenan, Craig Kornfield, Steve Kring, Steve Mondile, Perry Smith, Brian Wilson, Greg Zunino

Professional scouts
Jason Angel, Greg McClain, Dan Reynolds, Bip Roberts, Mike Williams, Van Schley

Scouts
George Blackburn, Fred Blair, Keith Chapman, Edwin Daub, Jim Grief,
Don Gust, Denny Nagel, Paul Pierson, Glenn Serviente, Tom Severtson, Marlon Styles, Marc Suarez, Mike Wallace, John Walsh, Roger Weberg, Michael Wilder

BALLPARK INFORMATION

Ballpark (capacity, surface)
Great American Ball Park (42,000, grass)

Address
100 Main St.
Cincinnati, OH 45202

Official website
www.cincinnatireds.com

Business phone
513-765-7000

Ticket information
513-765-7400

Ticket prices
$50 (Terrace Dugout), $30 (Terrace IF Box)
$25 (Terrace Box), $20 (Terrace Line)
$16 (View Level IF Box, Mezzanine)
$15 (Terrace OF), $14 (View Level Box, Mezzanine)
$11 (View Level IF), $10 (Bleachers)
$9 (View Level), $5 (Outer View Level)

Field dimensions (from home plate)
To left field at foul line, 328 feet
To center field, 404 feet
To right field at foul line, 325 feet

First game played
Scheduled for March 31, 2003 vs. Pittsburgh

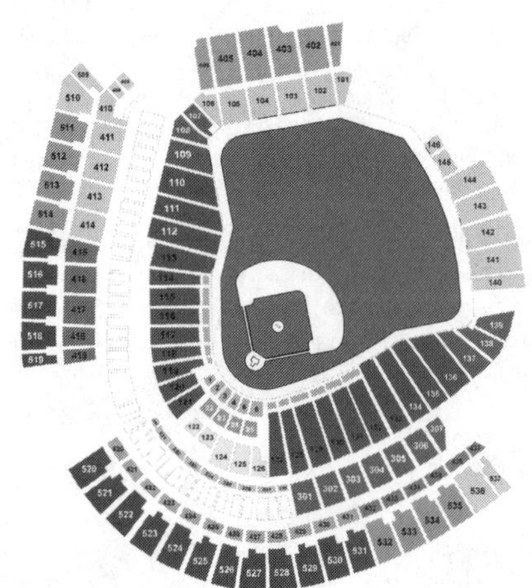

Follow the Reds all season at: www.sportingnews.com/baseball/teams/reds/

REDS SPRING ROSTER

No.	PITCHERS	B/T	Ht./Wt.	Born	2002 clubs	Projection
29	Acevedo, Jose	R/R	6-0/185	12-18-77	Cincinnati, Louisville	In line for a spot in the rotation, he showed good consistency in minors last year.
87	Aramboles, Ricardo	R/R	6-2/170	12-4-81	Chattanooga	Pitched well in four starts before injuries cost him the rest of the season.
52	Chen, Bruce	L/L	6-2/210	6-19-77	N.Y. N.L., Montreal, Cincinnati	Reds think he may have found his role as a reliever.
40	Dempster, Ryan	R/R	6-3/215	5-3-77	Florida, Cincinnati	Didn't pitch nearly as well in Cincinnati as he did in Florida, but that will change.
	Etherton, Seth	R/R	6-1/200	10-17-76	Dayton, Chatt., Louis., Norwich	Team is hoping to coax a healthy season out of him in 2003.
	Gamble, Jerome	R/R	6-2/202	4-5-80	Augusta	Had a 1.82 ERA, but as a Rule 5 guy, he could end up back with Red Sox.
32	Graves, Danny	R/R	6-0/185	8-7-73	Cincinnati	Reds think he's better suited for rotation than as closer.
	Hall, Josh	R/R	6-2/175	12-16-80	Stockton, Chattanooga	Should spend this year in Class AAA before making debut in 2004.
43	Haynes, Jimmy	R/R	6-4/219	9-5-72	Cincinnati	Won 15 games, will assume No. 1 starter role with Elmer Dessens gone.
54	Hudson, Luke	R/R	6-3/195	5-2-77	Louisville, Cincinnati	Reds will give him a chance to start or relieve.
	Prokopec, Luke	L/R	5-11/175	2-23-78	Toronto, Syracuse	Reds are hoping they can turn him around after subpar 2002.
41	Reitsma, Chris	R/R	6-5/215	12-31-77	Cincinnati, Louisville	Had a 3.64 ERA in 32 games with Reds.
46	Riedling, John	R/R	5-11/190	8-29-75	Chatt., Louisville, Cincinnati	Provided solid relief out of the bullpen, expect much of the same.
56	Sullivan, Scott	R/R	6-3/210	3-13-71	Cincinnati	Pitched in over 70 games for fourth straight season, but needs to lower ERA.
36	White, Gabe	L/L	6-2/204	11-20-71	Cincinnati	Another sterling performace out of the bullpen—2.98 ERA over 62 games.
	Williams, Blake	R/R	6-5/210	2-22-79	New Jersey	Team hopes former first rounder is healthy.
48	Williamson, Scott	R/R	6-0/185	2-17-76	Cincinnati	Will battle Sullivan for closer's role, likely to get job.
	Wilson, Paul	R/R	6-5/214	3-28-73	Tampa Bay	Won six games for a woeful Devil Rays team, should win more with Reds.

No.	CATCHERS	B/T	Ht./Wt.	Born	2002 clubs	Projection
23	LaRue, Jason	R/R	5-11/200	3-19-74	Cincinnati	Hit .249 in first full season as catcher, but needs more patience at plate.
37	Miller, Corky	R/R	6-1/225	3-18-76	Louisville, Cincinnati	Will have to show better defense before he'll get regular major league work.
70	Sardinha, Dane	R/R	5-11/205	4-8-79	Chattanooga	Catcher of the future flashes good glove but bat needs a lot of work.
31	Stinnett, Kelly	R/R	5-11/225	2-4-70	Cincinnati, Louisville	Could lose back-up job to Corky Miller if he's not careful.

No.	INFIELDERS	B/T	Ht./Wt.	Born	2002 clubs	Projection
17	Boone, Aaron	R/R	6-2/200	3-9-73	Cincinnati	Coming into his own as power hitter, might switch positions.
33	Branyan, Russell	L/R	6-3/195	12-19-75	Cleveland, Cincinnati	Showed steady improvement in plate discipline. Will get more at-bats in '03.
21	Casey, Sean	L/R	6-4/225	7-2-74	Cincinnati, Louisville	Needs to stay healthy for Reds to contend, also might be traded.
7	Castro, Juan	R/R	5-11/195	6-20-72	Louisville, Cincinnati	Utility man needs to hit better to stick around.
3	Dawkins, Gookie	R/R	6-1/180	5-12-79	Cincinnati, Chatt., Louisville	Still needs one more year in Class AAA.
11	Larkin, Barry	R/R	6-0/185	4-28-64	Cincinnati	Age appears to be catching up with this 17-year major league vet.
16	Larson, Brandon	R/R	6-0/210	5-24-76	Louisville, Cincinnati	Could be team's full-time third baseman with good spring.
	Lopez, Felipe	B/R	6-0/185	5-12-80	Toronto, Syracuse	Top prospect likely to challenge for starting shortstop job.
	Olmedo, Ranier	R/R	5-11/155	5-31-81	Chattanooga	Needs to hit for higher average before he gets to the majors.

No.	OUTFIELDERS	B/T	Ht./Wt.	Born	2002 clubs	Projection
44	Dunn, Adam	L/R	6-6/240	11-9-79	Cincinnati	Average should improve with more protection around him in lineup.
30	Griffey, Ken	L/L	6-3/205	11-21-69	Cincinnati	Reportedly working out hard this offseason to return to All-Star form.
6	Guillen, Jose	R/R	5-11/195	5-17-76	Ariz., Colo. Springs, Louis., Cin.	Has chance to make team as fourth outfielder.
28	Kearns, Austin	R/R	6-3/220	5-20-80	Chatt., Cincinnati, Louisville	Will be in the Reds outfield for years to come.
15	Mateo, Ruben	R/R	6-0/185	2-10-78	Louisville, Cincinnati	Hit pretty well in brief audition with Reds last season.
26	Pena, Wily	R/R	6-3/215	1-23-82	Chattanooga, Cincinnati	Still strikes out too much in minors, likely a year away.
	Smitherman, Steve	R/R	6-4/230	9-1-78	Stockton	Late round pick (23rd) is showing good power and surprising speed.
19	Taylor, Reggie	L/R	6-1/178	1-12-77	Cincinnati	Former first round pick coming off decent first season in majors.

THE COACHING STAFF

Bob Boone, manager.
Jose Cardenal, first base coach.
Tim Foli, third base coach.
Don Gullett, pitching coach.
Tom Hume, bullpen coach.
Ray Knight, bench coach.
Jim Lefebvre, hitting coach.

THE TOP NEWCOMERS

Luke Prokopec: Reds are hoping he can return to 2001 form, when he won eight games and had an ERA under 5.00. He really struggled in Toronto last season.

Paul Wilson: After trading Elmer Dessens, the Reds needed another quality starter. Enter Wilson, who pitched well in Tampa Bay last season. While he won't match Dessens' numbers, he's a good addition.

Felipe Lopez: Tabbed as the shortstop of the future in Toronto, he's shown he can hit for average and power in the minor leagues. It hasn't translated into major league success yet, but he'll get plenty of time to develop in Cincinnati, where expectations will be lower.

THE TOP NEWCOMERS

Ricardo Aramboles: Was having a stellar season in Class AA last year before injuries sidelined him after only four starts.

Dane Sardinha: If his bat can catch up to his glove, there'll be no stopping this guy.

Steve Smitherman: Had 19 home runs, 99 RBIs and 17 steals in the California League. Once he learns to be a bit more patient at the plate, the sky's the limit.

COLORADO ROCKIES

NATIONAL LEAGUE WEST DIVISION

2003 SEASON

Rockies Schedule

Home games shaded; D—Day game (games starting before 5 p.m.); *—All-Star Game at Comiskey Park, Chicago. Subject to changes.

March/April

SUN	MON	TUE	WED	THU	FRI	SAT
30	31	1 HOU	2 HOU	3 D HOU	4 ARI	5 D ARI
6 D ARI	7	8 STL	9 STL	10 D STL	11 SD	12 SD
13 D SD	14 ARI	15 ARI	16 ARI	17 D ARI	18 SD	19 D SD
20 D SD	21	22 PHI	23 PHI	24 D PHI	25 CUB	26 D CUB
27 D CUB	28	29 CIN	30 CIN			

May

SUN	MON	TUE	WED	THU	FRI	SAT
				1 D CIN	2 D CUB	3 D CUB
4 D CUB	5	6 ATL	7 ATL	8 ATL	9 FLA	10 FLA
11 D FLA	12 NYM	13 NYM	14 D NYM	15 MON	16 MON	17 D MON
18 D MON	19	20 LA	21 LA	22 D LA	23 SF	24 D SF
25 D SF	26 D SF	27 LA	28 LA	29 D LA	30 SF	31 D SF

June

SUN	MON	TUE	WED	THU	FRI	SAT
1 D SF	2 SF	3 CLE	4 CLE	5 D CLE	6 KC	7 KC
8 D KC	9	10 MIN	11 MIN	12 MIN	13 DET	14 DET
15 D DET	16 SD	17 SD	18 SD	19 SD	20 DET	21 DET
22 D DET	23 SD	24 SD	25 SD	26	27 PIT	28 PIT
29 D PIT	30 ARI					

July

SUN	MON	TUE	WED	THU	FRI	SAT
		1 ARI	2 ARI	3 ARI	4 D MIL	5 MIL
6 D MIL	7 ARI	8 ARI	9 SF	10 SF	11 LA	12 LA
13 D LA	14	15 *	16	17 SF	18 SF	19 D SF
20 D SF	21 LA	22 LA	23 LA	24 D LA	25 MIL	26 MIL
27 D MIL	28	29 CIN	30 CIN	31 CIN		

August

SUN	MON	TUE	WED	THU	FRI	SAT
					1 PIT	2 PIT
3 D PIT	4	5 PHI	6 PHI	7 D PHI	8 PIT	9 PIT
10 D PIT	11 MON	12 MON	13 MON	14	15 NYM	16 NYM
17 D NYM	18 D NYM	19 FLA	20 FLA	21 FLA	22 ATL	23 ATL
24 D ATL	25	26 SF	27 SF	28 D SF	29 LA	30 LA
31 LA						

September

SUN	MON	TUE	WED	THU	FRI	SAT
	1	2 SF	3 D SF	4	5 LA	6 D LA
7 D LA	8	9 STL	10 STL	11 D STL	12 ARI	13 ARI
14 D ARI	15	16 HOU	17 HOU	18 D HOU	19 SD	20 D SD
21 D SD	22	23 ARI	24 ARI	25 D ARI	26 SD	27 SD
28 D SD						

FRONT-OFFICE DIRECTORY

Chairman and chief executive officer .... Jerry D. McMorris
Vice chairman .... Charles K. Monfort
Vice chairman .... Richard L. Monfort
President .... Keli S. McGregor
Executive vice president, general manager .... Daniel J. O'Dowd
Senior vice president, business operations .... Gregory D. Feasel
Senior vice president, chief financial officer .... Harold R. Roth
Vice president, ballpark operations .... Kevin Kahn
Vice president, finance .... Michael J. Kent
Vice president, ticket operations and sales .... Sue Ann McClaren
Senior director, communications/public relations .... Jay Alves
Senior director, ticket operations & development .... Kevin G. Fenton
Senior director, corporate sales .... Marcy English Glasser
Senior director, personnel & administration .... Elizabeth Stecklein
Senior director, community & retail operations .... Jim Kellogg
Senior director, promotions & broadcasting .... Alan Bossart
Director, player personnel .... Bill Geivett
Director, major league operations .... Paul Egins
Director, scouting .... Bill Schmidt
Director, information systems .... Bill Stephani
Director, season tickets .... Jeff Benner
Director, ticket operations & finances .... Kent Hakes
Director, ticket services & spring training business operations .... Chuck Javernick
Senior director, ticket sales & advertising .... Jill Roberts

MINOR LEAGUE AFFILIATES

Class	Team	League	Manager
AAA	Colorado Springs	Pacific Coast	Rick Sofield
AA	Tulsa	Texas	Marv Foley
A	Visalia	California	Stu Cole
A	Asheville	South Atlantic	Joe Mikulik
A	Tri-City	Northwest	Ron Gideon
Rookie	Casper	Pioneer	P.J. Carey

BROADCAST INFORMATION

Radio: KOA-AM (850), KCUV-AM (1150).
TV: KWGN-TV (Channel 2).
Cable TV: Fox Sports Rocky Mountain.

SPRING TRAINING

Ballpark (city): Hi Corbett Field (Tucson, Ariz.).
Ticket information: 1-800-388-ROCK.

ASSISTANCE STAFF

Head groundskeeper
Mark Razum

Special assignment scout
Dave Holliday, Terry Wetzel

Regional supervisors
Ty Coslow, Bo Hughes, Danny Montgomery

Major League scouts
Pat Daugherty, Will George

Professional scouts
Mike Berger, Joe McDonald, Art Pontarelli, Tom Wheeler

Scouts
Todd Blyleven, John Cedarburg, Scott Corman, Dar Cox, Mike Day, Jeff Edwards, Billy Eppler, Mike Ericson, Mike Garlatti, Orsino Hill, Bert Holt, Greg Hopkins, Damon Iannelli, Jay Matthews, Sean O'Connor, Jorge Posada, Ed Santa, Gary Wilson

Latin-American coordinator
Rolando Fernandez

International scouts
Phil Allen, Kent Blasingame, Francisco Cartaya, Felix Feliz, Cristobal A. Giron, Carlos Gomez, Orlando Medina, Frank Roa

BALLPARK INFORMATION

Ballpark (capacity, surface)
Coors Field (50,449, grass)
Address
2001 Blake St., Denver, CO 80205-2000
Official website
www.coloradorockies.com
Business phone
303-292-0200
Ticket information
800-388-7625
Ticket prices
$32 (club level, infield)
$30 (club level, outfield
$27 (infield box)
$21.50 (midfield box)
$20 (outfield box)
$16/13 (lower reserved, infield/outfield)
$12 (upper reserved infield, RF box)
$11 (lower reserved corner)
$10 (RF mezzanine)
$9 (upper reserved, outfield; pavilion)
$7 (upper reserved corner)
$6/5 (lower/upper RF reserved)
$4/1 (rockpile)
Field dimensions (from home plate)
To left field at foul line, 347 feet
To center field, 415 feet
To right field at foul line, 350
First game played
April 26, 1995 (Rockies 11, Mets 9, 14 innings)

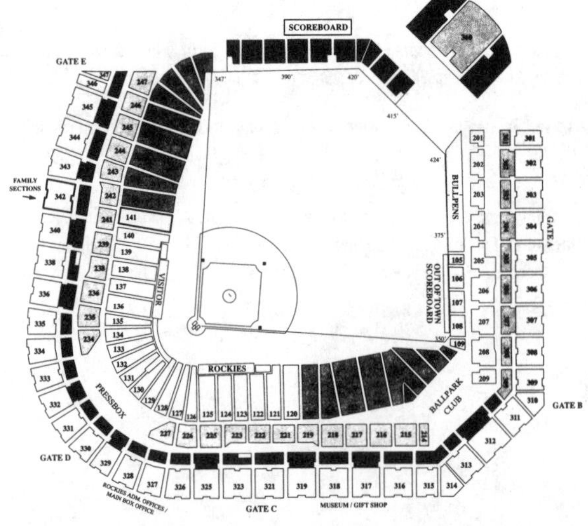

Follow the Rockies all season at: www.sportingnews.com/baseball/teams/rockies/

ROCKIES SPRING ROSTER

No.	PITCHERS	B/T	Ht./Wt.	Born	2002 clubs	Projection
34	Chacon, Shawn	R/R	6-3/212	12-23-77	Colorado, Colorado Springs	Got his feet wet in the majors last season, should have a spot in rotation in '03.
35	Cook, Aaron	R/R	6-3/175	2-8-79	Carolina, Colo. Springs, Colo.	Had five good starts for Colorado late in the season.
41	Cruz, Nelson	R/R	6-1/185	9-13-72	Houston, New Orleans	Long reliever can be counted on for at least 50 good outings each season.
50	Elarton, Scott	R/R	6-7/240	2-23-76	DID NOT PLAY	Injuries kept him sidelined last season, Rockies are hoping he can bounce back.
57	Esslinger, Cam	R/R	5-11/170	12-28-76	Colorado Springs, Carolina	Injuries have hampered his development in recent years, needs a year in minors.
51	Flores, Randy	L/L	6-0/180	7-31-75	Okla., Texas, Colo. Springs, Colo.	Rockies think he can be a solid contributor in 2003.
39	Fuentes, Brian	L/L	6-4/220	8-9-75	Colorado Springs, Colorado	Needed a brief layover in minors last season, he's ready for bullpen job this year.
32	Jennings, Jason	L/R	6-2/242	7-17-78	Colorado	N.L. Rookie of the Year will anchor the rotation for 2003 and years to come.
16	Jimenez, Jose	R/R	6-3/228	7-7-73	Colorado	Showed he can be a consistent closer on road as well as at home.
59	Jones, Todd	B/R	6-3/230	4-24-68	Colorado	Gives bullpen some veteran stability. Pitched in 79 games last year.
15	Neagle, Denny	L/L	6-3/225	9-13-68	Colorado	Rockies are trying to trade him after 8-11 season.
30	Speier, Justin	R/R	6-4/205	11-6-73	Colorado Springs, Colorado	Another solid option out of the bullpen. Five wins and only 19 walks.
41	Stark, Dennis	R/R	6-2/210	10-27-74	Colorado Springs, Colorado	Won 11 games in 2002, will have to cut down on his walks to have same success.
53	Vance, Cory	L/L	6-1/195	6-20-79	Carolina, Colorado	Young lefty is still one year away from helping the rotation.
62	Young, Colin	L/L	6-0/185	8-1-77	Carolina	Future closer suffered through injuries last season.

No.	CATCHERS	B/T	Ht./Wt.	Born	2002 clubs	Projection
8	Estalella, Bobby	R/R	6-1/213	8-23-74	Colorado Springs, Colorado	Hit only .205 in 38 games. Will have to improve if he's going to stick around.
	Johnson, Charles	R/R	6-3/250	7-20-71	Florida	Hit a career-low .217, but often is the perfect panacea in Coors Field.

No.	INFIELDERS	B/T	Ht./Wt.	Born	2002 clubs	Projection
5	Butler, Brent	R/R	6-0/180	2-11-78	Colorado, Colorado Springs	Can play any infield position with success, hit .259 in 113 games.
	Eberwein, Kevin	R/R	6-4/200	3-30-77	Lake Elsinore, Portland	Will need to stay healthy, likely to spend time at Class AAA this year.
23	Gload, Ross	L/L	6-0/185	4-5-76	Colorado Springs, Colorado	Can play first or outfield, has potential to be good hitter.
17	Helton, Todd	L/L	6-2/204	8-20-73	Colorado	Numbers were down a bit last season, but still an offensive/defensive force.
	Hernandez, Jose	R/R	6-1/190	7-14-69	Milwaukee	Free swinger will get plenty of hacks in Colorado's thin air.
14	Norton, Greg	B/R	6-1/200	7-6-72	Colorado, Colorado Springs	Will stick with team as a switch-hitter off the bench.
	Ozuna, Pablo	R/R	6-0/160	8-25-74	Calgary, Florida	Has potential to be second baseman and leadoff hitter.
3	Romano, Jason	R/R	6-0/185	6-24-79	Okla., Texas, Colo. Springs, Colo.	Hit .324 with Rockies, but likely a position player without a home.
	Stynes, Chris	R/R	5-10/205	1-19-73	Chicago N.L.	Will get a shot to be Rockies' full-time third baseman.
4	Uribe, Juan	R/R	5-11/173	7-22-79	Colorado	Struck out 120 times last season, team is hoping he shows some patience in '03.

No.	OUTFIELDERS	B/T	Ht./Wt.	Born	2002 clubs	Projection
21	Cust, Jack	L/R	6-1/205	1-16-79	Colorado Springs, Colorado	Power hitter struggled in first major league action.
27	Payton, Jay	R/R	5-10/185	11-22-72	New York N.L., Colorado	Played errorless center field after trade from Mets. Has to stay healthy.
6	Petrick, Ben	R/R	6-0/200	4-7-77	Colorado, Colorado Springs	Might have found a home in the outfield after failing to nail down catching job.
	Reyes, Rene	B/R	5-11/215	2-21-78	Carolina	Hit .292 in Class AA, he needs to cut down on his errors.
33	Walker, Larry	L/R	6-3/233	12-1-66	Colorado	Must stay healthy to produce. Has never played all 162 games
44	Wilson, Preston	R/R	6-2/213	7-19-74	Florida	Strikeouts increased by 33 last year. He'll hit a ton of homers this year though.

THE COACHING STAFF

Clint Hurdle, manager.

Sandy Alomar Sr., third base coach.

Bob Apodaca, pitching coach.

Dave Collins, first base coach.

Duane Espy, batting coach.

Rick Mathews, bullpen coach.

Jamie Quirk, bench coach.

THE TOP NEWCOMERS

Nelson Cruz: Rockies traded to get him from the Astros. He's capable of pitching in 50-plus gams and should help to bridge the gap between the starters and setup man Todd Jones.

Charles Johnson: Some wonder if Johnson has slowed down so much in recent seasons because of overuse. The Rockies are hoping he's got something left. His bat should rebound with Johnson playing half his games at Coors Field.

Preston Wilson: Strikeouts increased from 107 2001 to 140 in 2002, coincidentally his batting average dropped by 30 points. He managed to increase his walk totals, however, so the Rockies are willing to take the good with the bad.

THE TOP PROSPECTS

Pablo Ozuna: Has the skills to play every day at either shortstop or second base. The Rockies will have a tough decision on their hands come spring training if all of their young players are hitting and fielding well.

Rene Reyes: Outfield prospect has hit well at every step in the minor leagues but he'll need to walk a bit more to make a big splash in the majors.

Florida Marlins

National League East Division

2003 SEASON

Marlins Schedule

Home games shaded; D—Day game (games starting before 5 p.m.); *—All-Star Game at Comiskey Park, Chicago. Subject to changes. †Game played in Puerto Rico.

March/April

SUN	MON	TUE	WED	THU	FRI	SAT
30	31 D PHI	1	2 PHI	3 D PHI	4 ATL	5 ATL
6 D ATL	7 D ATL	8 NYM	9 NYM	10 NYM	11 ATL	12 ATL
13 D ATL	14 PHI	15 PHI	16 PHI	17 D PHI	18 NYM	19 D NYM
20 D NYM	21	22 MIL	23 MIL	24 MIL	25 STL	26 STL
27 D STL	28 ARI	29 ARI	30 ARI			

May

SUN	MON	TUE	WED	THU	FRI	SAT
				1 ARI	2 HOU	3 HOU
4 D HOU	5	6 SF	7 SF	8 SF	9 COL	10 COL
11 D COL	12 SD	13 SD	14 SD	15	16 LA	17 LA
18 D LA	19	20 MON	21 MON	22 MON	23 CIN	24 CIN
25 D CIN	26 D MON	27 MON	28 MON	29 MON	30 CIN	31 CIN

June

SUN	MON	TUE	WED	THU	FRI	SAT
1 D CIN	2	3 OAK	4 OAK	5 OAK	6 ANA	7 ANA
8 D ANA	9	10 MIL	11 MIL	12 D MIL	13 TEX	14 TEX
15 TEX	16 NYM	17 NYM	18 NYM	19 NYM	20 TB	21 TB
22 D TB	23	24 NYM	25 NYM	26 NYM	27 BOS	28 BOS
29 D BOS	30 ATL					

July

SUN	MON	TUE	WED	THU	FRI	SAT
		1 ATL	2 ATL	3	4 D PHI	5 PHI
6 D PHI	7 CUB	8 D CUB	9 D CUB	10	11 MON	12 MON
13 D MON	14	15 *	16	17	18 CUB	19 CUB
20 D CUB	21 MON	22 MON	23 ATL	24 D ATL	25 PHI	26 PHI
27 D PHI	28 ARI	29 ARI	30 ARI	31		

August

SUN	MON	TUE	WED	THU	FRI	SAT
					1 HOU	2 HOU
3 D HOU	4	5 STL	6 STL	7 STL	8 MIL	9 MIL
10 D MIL	11 LA	12 LA	13 LA	14 D LA	15 SD	16 SD
17 D SD	18	19 COL	20 COL	21 COL	22 SF	23 D SF
24 D SF	25	26 PIT	27 PIT	28 PIT	29 MON	30 MON
31 D MON						

September

SUN	MON	TUE	WED	THU	FRI	SAT
	1 D MON	2 PIT	3 PIT	4 D PIT	5 † MON	6 † MON
7 D† MON	8 NYM	9 NYM	10 D NYM	11	12 ATL	13 ATL
14 D ATL	15	16 PHI	17 PHI	18 PHI	19 ATL	20 ATL
21 D ATL	22 ATL	23 PHI	24 PHI	25 PHI	26 NYM	27 NYM
28 D NYM						

FRONT-OFFICE DIRECTORY

Chairman, chief executive officer and managing general partner................Jeffrey H. Loria
President.........David P. Samson
Vice chairman.........Joel A. Mael
Senior vice president/chief financial officer ....Michel Bussiere
Special assistants to the president ....Andre Dawson, Tony Perez
Senior vice president and general manager.........Larry Beinfest
Vice president/assistant general manager.........Michael Hill
Vice president, player personnel ....Dan Jennings
Director, team travel.........Bill Beck
Special assistant to the general manager/pro scout ....Orrin Freeman
Manager, baseball information systems.........David Kuan
Video coordinator ....Cullen McRae
Senior vice president/director of international operations ....Fred Ferreira
Vice president, player development and scouting.........Jim Fleming
Director of player development.........Marc DelPiano
Director of minor league operations......... Cheryl Evans
Assistant director, scouting ....Gregg Leonard
Assistant director, international operations.........Randy Kierce
Vice president, communications and broadcasting .........P.J. Loyello
Director, media relations.........Steve Copses
Manager, media relations ....Andrew Fierstein
Director, broadcast services ....Suzanne Rayson
Broadcasting coordinator.........Alex Bentley
Manager, executive affairs.........Michelle Azel
Manager, community affairs.........Angela Smith
Director, creative services and in-game entertainment ....Leslie Riguero
Director, advertising ....Marla Meilan
Promotions and merchandising manager ....Denise Isaac
Vice president, sales ....Dale Hendricks
Director, corporate sales ....Brendan Cunningham
Executive director/Florida Marlins Community Foundation ....Nancy Olson
Director, season and group sales ....Pat McNamara
Manager, season and group sales.........Marty Mulford
Vice president, finance ....Susan Jaison
Accounting manager.........Barry LaChance
Manager, business information systems ....Ken Strand
Director, human resources.........Ana Hernandez

ASSISTANCE STAFF

Team physician
Daniel Kanell, M.D.

Trainer
Sean Cunningham

Assistant trainer
Mike Kozak

Strength and conditioning director
Dale Torborg

Equipment manager
John Silverman

Visiting clubhouse manager
Bryan Greenberg

Scouting director
Stan Meek

Professional scouts
Orrin Freeman, Joe Moeller, Tommy Thompson

Cross-checkers and supervisors
Mike Cadahia, Dennis Cardoza, Scott Goldby, Joe Jordan

Scouts
Alex Agostino, Matt Anderson, Carlos Berroa, Darrell Brown, John Cole, Robby Corsaro, David Crowson, Dave Dangler, Hal Deberry, Scott Engler, John Hughes, John Martin, Joel Matthews, Bob Oldis, Steve Payne, Joel Smith, Scott Stanley

International scouting supervisors
Carlos Acosta, Jesus Campos, A.B. Jesurun

International scouts
Wilmer Adrian, Evelio Areas, Greg Burrows, Aristides Bustamonte, Nelson Castro, Terry Chinnery, Enrique Constante, Scott Davis, Nathan Davison, Rene Garcia, Carlos Guzman, Ton Hofstede, Go Ikeda, Brian Lombard, Roberto Marquez, Willie Marrugo, Pedro Martinez, Spencer Mills, Romulo Oliveros, Rene Picota, Carlos Rivero, Carlos Sanchez, Craig Stoves, Jamie Torres, Francis Wanga

MINOR LEAGUE AFFILIATES

Class	Team	League	Manager
AAA	Albuquerque	Pacific Coast	Dean Treanor
AA	Carolina	Southern	Tracy Woodson
A	Jupiter	Florida State	Luis Dorante
A	Greensboro	South Atlantic	Steve Phillips
A	Jamestown	New York-Pennsylvania	Benny Castillo
Rookie	Gulf Coast Marlins	Gulf Coast	Timothy Cossins

BROADCAST INFORMATION

Radio: WQAM (560 AM); WQBA-AM (1140 AM, Spanish language).
TV: PAX-TV.
Cable TV: Fox Sports Net.

SPRING TRAINING

Ballpark (city): Roger Dean Stadium (Jupiter, Fla.).
Ticket information: 561-775-1818.

BALLPARK INFORMATION

Ballpark (capacity, surface)
Pro Player Stadium (36,331 grass)

Address
2267 Dan Marino Blvd., Miami, FL 33056

Official website
www.floridamarlins.com

Business phone
305-626-7400

Ticket information
877-MARLINS

Ticket prices
$55 (founders club), $32 (club zone A)
$25 (infield box), $24 (club zone B)
$18 (power alley section C)
$15 (terrace box)
$10 (outfield reserved, adult), $9 (upper deck, adult)
$5 (outfield reserved, children), $4 (fish tank-sec. 127-125, adult)
$3 (mezzanine reserved, children), $2 (fish tank, children)

Field dimensions (from home plate)
To left field at foul line, 330 feet
To center field, 434 feet
To right field at foul line, 345 feet

First game played
April 5, 1993 (Marlins 6, Dodgers 3)

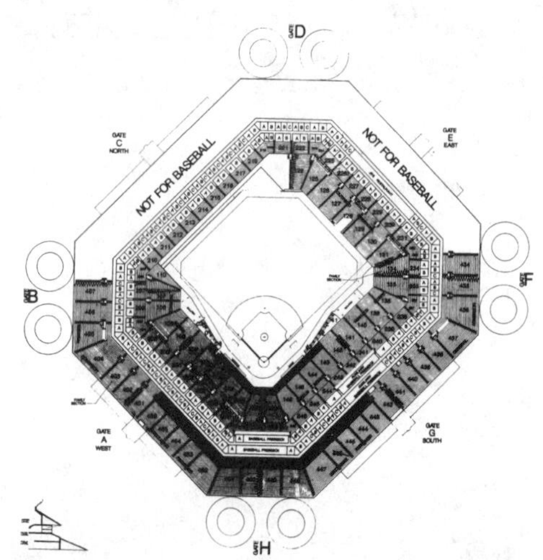

Follow the Marlins all season at: www.sportingnews.com/baseball/teams/marlins/

MARLINS SPRING ROSTER

No.	PITCHERS	B/T	Ht./Wt.	Born	2002 clubs	Projection
55	Almanza, Armando	L/L	6-3/240	10-26-72	Jupiter, Florida	Provides the Marlins with a consistent lefthanded option out of the bullpen.
64	Anderson, Wes	R/R	6-4/175	9-10-79	Gulf Coast Marlins	Marlins are hoping he can get back on track after injuries slowed him down.
61	Beckett, Josh	R/R	6-5/216	5-15-80	Florida, GC Marlins, Jupiter	Decent first big-league season, but needs to stay healthy.
	Bump, Nate	R/R	6-2/185	7-24-76	Portland	Former first-round pick is starting to fulfill his top prospect billing.
43	Burnett, A.J.	R/R	6-4/229	1-3-77	Florida	Has become workhorse and staff ace in last two years.
	Cueto, Jose	R/R	6-2/175	9-13-78	Portland	Strikeout pitcher was sidelined by injury just nine starts into last season.
59	Goetz, Geoff	L/L	5-11/165	3-3-79	Portland	Injuries have kept him in Class AA for three straight years.
41	Looper, Braden	R/R	6-3/220	10-28-74	Florida	Stepped into closer's role when Nunez faltered and recorded 13 saves.
46	Mairena, Oswaldo	L/L	5-11/165	6-30-74	Calgary, Florida, GC Marlins	Lefty is still learning how to pitch; might earn job in bullpen this spring.
54	Neal, Blaine	L/R	6-5/240	4-6-78	Calgary, Florida	Pitched well in 32 games with Marlins, posting a 2.73 ERA.
36	Nunez, Vladimir	R/R	6-4/240	3-15-75	Florida	Struggled with the closer's job for brief while but still saved 20 games.
56	Olsen, Kevin	R/R	6-2/196	7-26-76	Florida, Calgary	Might need one more season in minors before he'll be ready for rotation.
45	Pavano, Carl	R/R	6-5/230	1-8-76	Montreal, Ottawa, Florida	Finally rounding back into form after shoulder surgeries.
31	Penny, Brad	R/R	6-4/247	5-24-78	Florida, Jupiter	Might still be traded but there are concerns about his arm.
	Redman, Mark	L/L	6-5/245	1-5-74	Detroit	Provides a solid lefthanded presence in rotation; pitched pretty well in Detroit in '02.
	Snare, Ryan	L/L	6-0/190	2-8-79	Stockton, Chattanooga, Portland	Won 12 games between Class A and AA, but still a year away from majors.
	Spooneybarger, Tim	R/R	6-3/190	10-21-79	Atlanta, Richmond	Former Brave should provide solid relief for Marlins.
58	Tejera, Michael	L/L	5-9/175	10-18-76	Florida	Bounced between rotation and relief, performed well in both.
48	Wayne, Justin	R/R	6-3/200	4-16-79	Harris., Fla., Portland, Calgary	Former first-round pick needs one more season in Class AAA.

No.	CATCHERS	B/T	Ht./Wt.	Born	2002 clubs	Projection
17	Castro, Ramon	R/R	6-3/235	3-1-76	Florida	Enters the year as the Marlins' backup catcher. Committed no errors in 37 games.
52	Redmond, Mike	R/R	5-11/208	5-5-71	Florida	Hit .305 and Marlins think he is ready for full-time job behind the plate.

No.	INFIELDERS	B/T	Ht./Wt.	Born	2002 clubs	Projection
1	Castillo, Luis	B/R	5-11/190	9-12-75	Florida	Bounced back after subpar '01 season, and had a 35-game hitting streak.
6	Fox, Andy	L/R	6-4/202	1-12-71	Florida	Filled in at shortstop after Gonzalez was hurt, should be back in utility role.
11	Gonzalez, Alex	R/R	6-0/200	2-15-77	Florida, Gulf Coast Marlins	Hasn't produced and has been injury prone. He needs to reverse both trends.
	Hooper, Kevin	R/R	5-10/160	12-7-76	Calgary	1999 draft pick might get a chance to win starting job at shortstop.
25	Lee, Derrek	R/R	6-5/248	9-6-75	Florida	Keeps improving each year, but he still strikes out a bit too often.
19	Lowell, Mike	R/R	6-3/217	2-24-74	Florida	Had All-Star year in 2002, will be hard pressed to top that.
	Medrano, Jesus	R/R	6-0/185	9-11-78	Portland	Had .411 OBP percentage in Class AA, will spend some time Class AAA this year.
12	Mordecai, Mike	R/R	5-10/185	12-13-67	Montreal, Florida	Gives the Marlins another utility man. He's a good pinch hitter too.
	Valdez, Wilson	R/R	5-11/160	5-20-80	Portland	Shortstop needs a little more patience at the plate.
	Willingham, Josh	R/R	6-1/200	2-17-79	Jupiter	Another in long line of power hitting first basemen Marlins have in system.
	Wilson, Josh	R/R	6-1/165	3-26-81	Jupiter, Portland	Shortstop showed he had some pop in his bat with 11 homers in Class A.

No.	OUTFIELDERS	B/T	Ht./Wt.	Born	2002 clubs	Projection
62	Ambres, Chip	R/R	6-1/190	12-19-78	Jupiter	Speedster had tough season in Florida State League.
4	Banks, Brian	B/R	6-3/210	9-28-70	Calgary, Florida	Marlins feel he's ready for the majors as fourth outfielder.
43	Encarnacion, Juan	R/R	6-3/215	3-8-76	Cincinnati, Florida	Might have finally found a home in Florida.
	Hollandsworth, Todd	L/L	6-2/207	4-20-73	Colorado, Texas	Will give the Marlins a dangerous lefthanded bat in their lineup.
27	Nunez, Abraham	B/R	6-2/186	2-5-77	Calgary, Florida	Will have to show the power he showed in minors to stick around.
	Pierre, Juan	L/L	6-0/180	8-14-77	Colorado	With him and Castillo at top of lineup, there will be a lot of stolen bases and runs.
	Williams, Gerald	R/R	6-2/187	8-10-66	N.Y. A.L., Memphis, Louisivlle	Signed in case of injuries and if others aren't ready for outfield job.

THE COACHING STAFF

Jeff Torborg, manager.
Brad Arnsberg, pitching coach.
Pierre Arsenault, bullpen coach.
Jeff Cox, bench coach.
Ozzie Guillen, third base coach.
Perry Hill, first base and infield coach.
Bill Robinson, hitting coach.

THE TOP NEWCOMERS

Mark Redman: The Marlins traded three younger pitchers to get Redman and another minor leaguer. Redman won eight games and posted a 4.21 ERA with Detroit last season. Don't forget that Redman went 12-9 with a 4.76 ERA in Minnesota in 2000, so success in Florida wouldn't be that surprising.

Tim Spooneybarger: The Braves sent him over in the Mike Hampton trade. He'll be a good reliever and help bridge the gap between the starters and the closer.

Todd Hollandsworth: The team was thin on lefthanded bats with power potential, so they signed Hollandsworth. The only concern will be keeping him healthy for the entire season.

Juan Pierre: He'll take over in center field after being acquired for Preston Wilson. He and Luis Castillo could form one of the best top-of-the-order combos in all of baseball. The speed and ability to get on base will no doubt help the Marlins score more runs this season.

THE TOP PROSPECTS

Nate Bump: Acquired from the Giants in the 1999 Livan Hernandez deal, he's been slow to develop in the minors. But he showed why he was a first-round pick a few years back and why the Marlins wanted him in the trade. Still a year away from the starting rotation though.

Jesus Medrano: This second base prospect is blocked by Luis Castillo, but he'll certainly make his case for a starting job soon enough. He hit .297 in Class AA with 39 steaks. He walked 79 times and only struck out 82 times.

HOUSTON ASTROS

NATIONAL LEAGUE CENTRAL DIVISION

2003 SEASON

Astros Schedule

Home games shaded; D—Day game (games starting before 5 p.m.); *—All-Star Game at Comiskey Park, Chicago. Subject to changes.

March/April

SUN	MON	TUE	WED	THU	FRI	SAT
30	31	1 COL	2 COL	3 D COL	4 STL	5 D STL
6 D STL	7	8 CIN	9 CIN	10 CIN	11 STL	12 STL
13 D STL	14 SF	15 SF	16 SF	17 MIL	18 MIL	19 D MIL
20 D MIL	21	22 NYM	23 NYM	24 NYM	25 MON	26 D MON
27 D MON	28	29 ATL	30 ATL			

May

SUN	MON	TUE	WED	THU	FRI	SAT
				1 ATL	2 FLA	3 FLA
4 D FLA	5 PIT	6 PIT	7 PIT	8 D PIT	9 PHI	10 PHI
11 D PHI	12 PIT	13 PIT	14 PIT	15 D PIT	16 PHI	17 D PHI
18 PHI	19	20 STL	21 STL	22 STL	23 CUB	24 CUB
25 D CUB	26 D STL	27 STL	28 STL	29	30 D CUB	31 D CUB

June

SUN	MON	TUE	WED	THU	FRI	SAT
1 D CUB	2	3 BAL	4 BAL	5 BAL	6 TB	7 TB
8 D TB	9	10 NYY	11 NYY	12 D NYY	13 BOS	14 BOS
15 D BOS	16	17 ARI	18 ARI	19 ARI	20 TEX	21 TEX
22 TEX	23 ARI	24 ARI	25 D ARI	26	27 TEX	28 D TEX
29 D TEX	30					

July

SUN	MON	TUE	WED	THU	FRI	SAT
		1 MIL	2 MIL	3 MIL	4 D PIT	5 PIT
6 D PIT	7 CIN	8 CIN	9 CIN	10 CIN	11 PIT	12 PIT
13 D PIT	14	15 *	16	17 CIN	18 CIN	19 D CIN
20 D CIN	21 PIT	22 PIT	23 MIL	24 MIL	25 CUB	26 D CUB
27 D CUB	28	29 ATL	30 ATL	31 ATL		

August

SUN	MON	TUE	WED	THU	FRI	SAT
					1 FLA	2 FLA
3 D FLA	4	5 NYM	6 NYM	7 NYM	8 MON	9 MON
10 D MON	11 CUB	12 CUB	13 D CUB	14 D CUB	15 CIN	16 D CIN
17 D CIN	18	19 CUB	20 CUB	21 CUB	22 CIN	23 CIN
24 D CIN	25	26 LA	27 LA	28 LA	29 SD	30 SD
31 D SD						

September

SUN	MON	TUE	WED	THU	FRI	SAT
	1 LA	2 LA	3 LA	4	5 SD	6 SD
7 D SD	8 MIL	9 MIL	10 MIL	11 D MIL	12 STL	13 STL
14 D STL	15	16 COL	17 COL	18 D COL	19 STL	20 D STL
21 D STL	22 SF	23 SF	24 D SF	25 MIL	26 MIL	27 MIL
28 D MIL						

FRONT-OFFICE DIRECTORY

Chairman and chief executive officer ....Drayton McLane Jr.
President, baseball operations ....Tal Smith
President, business operations ....Pam Gardner
General manager ....Gerry Hunsicker
Assistant general manager ....Tim Purpura
Director of baseball administration ....Barry Waters
Director of scouting ....David Lakey
Special asst. to the g.m. for international scouting and development ....Andres Reiner
Senior vice president, operations and communications ....Rob Matwick
Senior vice president, finance and administration ....Teresa Pelanne
Vice president, community development ....Marian Harper
Vice president, market development ....Rosi Hernandez
Vice president, sales and broadcasting ....Jamie Hildreth
Vice president, engineering ....Bert Pope
Vice president, marketing ....Andrew Huang
Vice president, special events ....Kala Sorenson
Vice president, ticket sales and services ....John Sorrentino
Director of media relations ....Warren Miller
Assistant directors of media relations ....Lisa Ramsperger, Jimmy Stanton

MINOR LEAGUE AFFILIATES

Class	Team	League	Manager
AAA	New Orleans	Pacific Coast	Chris Maloney
AA	Round Rock	Texas	Jackie Moore
A	Salem	Carolina	John Massarelli
A	Lexington	South Atlantic	Russ Nixon
A	Tri-City	New York-Pennsylvania	Ivan DeJesus
Rookie	Martinsville	Appalachian	Jorge Orta

BROADCAST INFORMATION

Radio: KTRH-AM (740); To be announced (Spanish language).
TV: To be announced.
Cable TV: Fox Sports Southwest.

SPRING TRAINING

Ballpark (city): Osceola County Stadium (Kissimmee, Fla.).
Ticket information: 407-839-3900.

ASSISTANCE STAFF

Coordinator of professional scouting
Paul Ricciarini

Dir. of Dominican Republic operations
Julio Linares

Assistant director of scouting
Pat Murphy

Major league scouts
Stan Benjamin, Walt Matthews, Gordy McKenzie, Paul Weaver

Advance scout
Fred Nelson

Professional scouts
Kimball Crossley, Brandy Davis, Gene DeBoer, Joe Pittman, Tom Romenesko, Scipio Spinks

Special assignment scout
Bob Skinner

National supervisors
Joe Robinson, Tad Slowik

Regional supervisors
Ralph Bratton, Kevin Burrell, Gerry Craft

Amateur scouts
Chuck Carlson, Doug Deutsch, Ellis Dungan, James Farrar, David Henderson, Brian Keegan, Bob King, Mike Maggart, Jerry Marik, Tom McCormack, Mel Nelson, Rusty Pendergrass, Bob Poole, Mike Rosamond, Mark Ross, Nick Venuto, Gene Wellman

International scouts
Ricardo Aponte, Jesus Aristimuno, Sergio Beltre, Rafael Cariel, Arnold Elles, Orlando Fernandez, Mario Gonzalez, Julio Linares, Rodney Linares, Omar Lopez, Carlos Maldonado, Ramon Morales, Oscar Padron, Guillermo Ramirez, Rafael Ramirez, Dr. Lester Storey, Pablo Torrealba

BALLPARK INFORMATION

Ballpark (capacity, surface)
Minute Maid Park (40,950, grass)
Address
P.O. Box 288
Houston, TX 77001-0288
Official website
www.astros.com
Business phone
713-259-8000
Ticket information
713-259-8500 or 877-9-ASTROS
Ticket prices
$39 (club I)
$36 (dugout)
$33 (club II)
$30 (field box)
$24 (Crawford box)
$20 (bullpen box)
$15 (mezzanine, terrace deck)
$12 (view deck)
$5-$1 (outfield deck)
Field dimensions (from home plate)
To left field at foul line, 315 feet
To center field, 435 feet
To right field at foul line, 326 feet
First game played
April 7, 2000 (Phillies 4, Astros 1)

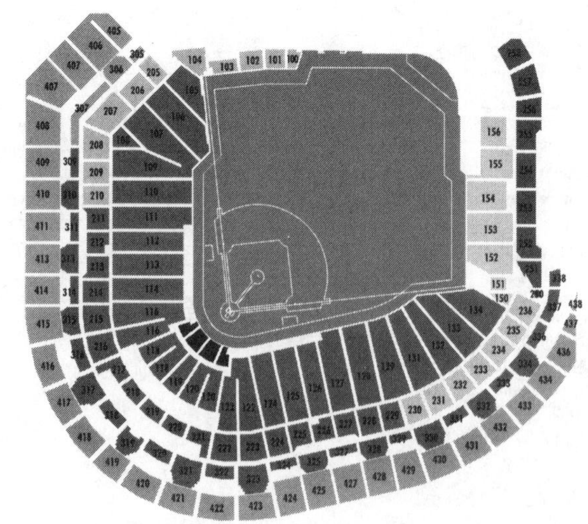

Follow the Astros all season at: www.sportingnews.com/baseball/teams/astros/

ASTROS SPRING ROSTER

No.	PITCHERS	B/T	Ht./Wt.	Born	2002 clubs	Projection
	Barrett, Jimmy	R/R	6-2/190	6-7-81	Lexington	Strikeout pitcher had 2.81 ERA in 22 starts in Class A.
29	Dotel, Octavio	R/R	6-0/200	11-25-73	Houston	Great setup man is key to Astros bullpen.
55	Hernandez, Carlos	B/L	5-10/185	4-22-80	Houston, N. Orl., Round Rock	Needs to stay healthy in order to fulfill expectations.
54	Lidge, Brad	R/R	6-5/200	12-23-76	Round Rock, Houston, N. Orl.	Being groomed as a starter, he could make the rotation in 2003.
52	Miller, Wade	R/R	6-2/210	9-13-76	Houston, New Orleans	Only lost four games last season. Expect another 15 wins this year.
	Mueller, Brian	R/R	6-3/235	12-31-71	Lake., Tal., Detr., Cinc.	Gives Astros insurance in case young arms aren't ready for rotation.
53	Munro, Peter	R/R	6-3/210	6-14-75	New Orleans, Houston	Went 5-5 and started 14 games. Could win rotation spot.
44	Oswalt, Roy	R/R	6-0/175	8-29-77	Houston	Won 19 games en route to establishing himself as staff ace.
59	Puffer, Brandon	R/R	6-3/190	10-5-75	New Orleans, Houston	Another in long line of young arms coming up through Astros system.
	Ramirez, Santiago	R/R	5-11/160	8-15-80	Round Rock, New Orleans	Long reliever will need one more year in Class AAA.
51	Redding, Tim	R/R	6-0/195	2-12-78	New Orleans, Houston	Young starter just needs more experience.
37	Reynolds, Shane	R/R	6-3/215	3-26-68	Houston	Despite injuries, Astros are bringing him back for one more year.
60	Robertson, Jeriome	L/L	6-1/190	3-30-77	New Orleans, Houston	Led Pacific Coast League in ERA, still adjusting to majors though.
68	Rosario, Rodrigo	R/R	6-2/165	12-14-79	Round Rock	Control pitcher is probably still a year away.
50	Saarloos, Kirk	R/R	6-0/185	5-23-79	Round Rock, N. Orl., Houston	Just needs a little more time in minors, but not much more.
	Saladin, Miguel	R/R	5-11/165	5-22-78	Round Rock, New Orleans	Possible closer candidate when Billy Wagner is no longer around.
20	Stone, Ricky	R/R	6-1/190	2-28-75	Houston	Tied rookie record for most games pitched in 2002.
13	Wagner, Billy	L/L	5-11/195	7-25-71	Houston	Almost untouchable at times when Astros bring him in.

No.	CATCHERS	B/T	Ht./Wt.	Born	2002 clubs	Projection
11	Ausmus, Brad	R/R	5-11/200	4-14-69	Houston	Gold Glover behind the plate, shows decent bat at it.
67	Buck, John	R/R	6-3/210	7-7-80	Round Rock	Catcher of the future needs one more year.
46	Chavez, Raul	R/R	5-11/210	3-18-73	New Orleans, Houston	Will be battling for backup job with Zaun.
2	Zaun, Gregg	B/R	5-10/190	4-14-71	Houston	Has advantage over Chavez because he's a switch-hitter.

No.	INFIELDERS	B/T	Ht./Wt.	Born	2002 clubs	Projection
5	Bagwell, Jeff	R/R	6-0/215	5-27-68	Houston	Still one of the most dangerous hitters in the N.L.
7	Biggio, Craig	R/R	5-11/185	12-14-65	Houston	Might be switching positions now that Jeff Kent is in town.
27	Blum, Geoff	B/R	6-3/200	4-26-73	Houston	Was able to provide some stability at third, might be out of job though.
14	Ensberg, Morgan	R/R	6-2/210	8-26-75	Houston, New Orleans	Proved he could hit in minors, but needs more major league experience.
28	Everett, Adam	R/R	6-0/160	2-2-77	Houston, New Orleans	Might be in line for shortstop job this year, after rushed last season.
	Kent, Jeff	R/R	6-1/220	3-7-68	San Francisco	Expected to provide some needed protection for big boppers Bagwell and Berkman.
4	Lugo, Julio	R/R	6-1/170	11-16-75	Houston	Inconsistent defensively, but he made some progress last season.
10	Vizcaino, Jose	B/R	6-1/185	3-26-68	Houston	Hit .303 last season in 125 games.
	Whiteman, Tommy	R/R	6-3/175	7-14-79	Round Rock, Lexington	Hit .303 with 10 homers in Class A; Astros could use a shortstop with power.

No.	OUTFIELDERS	B/T	Ht./Wt.	Born	2002 clubs	Projection
17	Berkman, Lance	B/L	6-1/220	2-10-76	Houston	Wore down a little as 2002 progressed. Should post better numbers in '03.
	Hall, Victor	L/L	6-0/170	9-16-80	Lancaster, El Paso	Potential leadoff hitter might just stick with team.
15	Hidalgo, Richard	R/R	6-3/220	7-2-75	Houston	Astros are hoping he will return to 2000-2001 form.
21	Hunter, Brian	R/R	6-3/180	3-25-71	Houston, New Orleans	Was able to provide some relief when regulars needed a day off.
24	Lane, Jason	R/L	6-2/215	12-22-76	New Orleans, Houston	Astros soon will have to make room for this power hitter.
16	Merced, Orlando	L/R	6-1/195	11-2-66	Houston	His lefthanded bat is what keeps him around. Hit .287 last year.
	Stanley, Henri	L/L	5-10/190	12-15-77	Round Rock	Can hit for power, average and has good speed. Likely one year away.
31	Ward, Daryle	L/L	6-2/240	6-27-75	Houston	Astros have a glut of outfielders, so a trade is possible.

THE COACHING STAFF

Jimy Williams, manager.
Mark Bailey, bullpen coach.
Jose Cruz, first base coach.
Burt Hooton, pitching coach.
Gene Lamont, third base coach.
Harry Spilman, hitting coach.
John Tamargo, bench coach.

THE TOP NEWCOMERS

Jeff Kent: The 2000 N.L. MVP is likely to be Houston's opening-day second baseman. If so, Craig Biggio will move to center field and Lance Berkman will move to left. Kent should be a much more productive hitter in Minute Maid Park than he was at Pac Bell.

THE TOP PROSPECTS

Miguel Saladin: Collected 24 saves in 53 appearances in Class AA last season. While he's likely headed to Class AAA for the start of the season, he might be with the Astros sooner rather than later.

John Buck: Catching prospect hit .263 with 12 homers and 89 RBIs at Class AA Round Rock. He's sound defensively committing only eight errors in almost 800 chances.

Henri Stanley: The Astros seem to develop one good outfielder per year, and he could be the next one. Stanley hit .314 with 16 homers, 72 RBIs and 14 steals in Class AA. Still a year or two away, but his patience at the plate works in his favor.

Los Angeles Dodgers

National League West Division

2003 SEASON

Dodgers Schedule

Home games shaded; D—Day game (games starting before 5 p.m.); *—All-Star Game at Comiskey Park, Chicago. Subject to changes.

March/April

SUN	MON	TUE	WED	THU	FRI	SAT
30	31 D ARI	1 ARI	2 ARI	3 D SD	4 SD	5 SD
6 D SD	7 D ARI	8 ARI	9 D ARI	10 SF	11 SF	12 D SF
13 SF	14	15 SD	16 SD	17 SD	18 SF	19 SF
20 SF	21	22 CIN	23 CIN	24 CIN	25 PIT	26 PIT
27 D PIT	28 PHI	29 PHI	30 PHI			

May

SUN	MON	TUE	WED	THU	FRI	SAT
				1 PHI	2 PIT	3 PIT
4 D PIT	5	6 NYM	7 NYM	8 NYM	9 MON	10 D MON
11 D MON	12 ATL	13 ATL	14 ATL	15	16 FLA	17 FLA
18 D FLA	19	20 COL	21 COL	22 D COL	23 MIL	24 MIL
25 D MIL	26	27 COL	28 COL	29 D COL	30 MIL	31 MIL

June

SUN	MON	TUE	WED	THU	FRI	SAT
1 D MIL	2	3 KC	4 KC	5 KC	6 CWS	7 CWS
8 D CWS	9	10 DET	11 DET	12 DET	13 CLE	14 D CLE
15 D CLE	16	17 SF	18 SF	19 SF	20 ANA	21 D ANA
22 ANA	23 SF	24 SF	25 SF	26	27 ANA	28 ANA
29 D ANA	30					

July

SUN	MON	TUE	WED	THU	FRI	SAT
		1 SD	2 SD	3 SD	4 ARI	5 D ARI
6 ARI	7 SD	8 SD	9 STL	10 STL	11 COL	12 COL
13 D COL	14	15 *	16	17 STL	18 STL	19 D STL
20 STL	21 COL	22 COL	23 COL	24 D COL	25 ARI	26 D ARI
27 D ARI	28	29 PHI	30 PHI	31 PHI		

August

SUN	MON	TUE	WED	THU	FRI	SAT
					1 ATL	2 D ATL
3 D ATL	4	5 CIN	6 CIN	7 CIN	8 CUB	9 CUB
10 D CUB	11 FLA	12 FLA	13 FLA	14 D FLA	15 D CUB	16 D CUB
17 D CUB	18	19 MON	20 MON	21 D MON	22 NYM	23 NYM
24 NYM	25	26 HOU	27 HOU	28 HOU	29 COL	30 COL
31 COL						

September

SUN	MON	TUE	WED	THU	FRI	SAT
	1 HOU	2 HOU	3 HOU	4	5 COL	6 D COL
7 D COL	8 ARI	9 ARI	10 ARI	11 ARI	12 SD	13 SD
14 D SD	15	16 ARI	17 ARI	18 ARI	19 SF	20 SF
21 D SF	22 SD	23 SD	24 SD	25 SD	26 SF	27 D SF
28 D SF						

FRONT-OFFICE DIRECTORY

Managing partner, chairman and CEO ....Robert Daly
President and COO ....Bob Graziano
Board of directors ....Robert Daly, Bob Graziano, Gary Ehrlich, Sam Fernandez
Executive vice president and general manager ....Dan Evans
Vice president, assistant general manager ....Kim Ng
Executive vice president of business operations ....Kris Rone
Senior vice president, communications ....Derrick Hall
Senior vice president, baseball operations ....Dave Wallace
Senior vice president ....Tommy Lasorda
Vice president, external affairs ....Tommy Hawkins
Advisor, team travel ....Billy DeLury
Sr. vice president and general counsel ....Sam Fernandez
Vice president, human resources & administration ....David Walkley
Vice president, spring training/minor league facilities ....Craig Callan
Director of player development ....Bill Bavasi
Vice president and CFO ....Cristine Hurley
Director, chief information officer ....Mike Mularky
Vice president of sales ....Sergio Del Prado
Director, public relations ....John Olguin
Director, team travel ....Shaun Rachau
Director, community affairs ....Erikk Aldridge
Assistant to the president & director, Asian operations ....Acey Kohrogi
Director, Dominican operations ....Pablo Peguero
Director, community relations ....Don Newcombe
Vice president, stadium operations ....Doug Duennes
Director, ticket operations ....Billy Hunter
Director, professional scouting ....Matt Slater
Director, amateur scouting ....Logan White
Director, international scouting ....Rene Francisco
Administrator of security ....Tim Kelly
Scouting coordinator ....Bill McLaughlin

MINOR LEAGUE AFFILIATES

Class	Team	League	Manager
AAA	Las Vegas	Pacific Coast	John Shoemaker
AA	Jacksonville	Southern	Dino Ebel
A	Vero Beach	Florida State	Scott Little
A	South Georgia	South Atlantic	Dann Bilardello
Rookie	Ogden	Pioneer	Travis Barbary
Rookie	Gulf Coast Dodgers	Gulf Coast	Luis Salazar

BROADCAST INFORMATION

Radio: KFWB-AM (1150); KWKW-AM (1330, Spanish language).
TV: KCOP-TV (Channel 13).
Cable TV: Fox Sports Net 2.

SPRING TRAINING

Ballpark (city): Holman Stadium (Vero Beach, Fla.).
Ticket information: 772-569-4900.
General number: 772-569-4900.

ASSISTANCE STAFF

Head athletic trainer
Stan Johnston
Assistant athletic trainer
Matt Wilson
Physical therapist
Pat Screnar
Strength and conditioning coach
Todd Clausen
Club physicians
Dr. Ralph Gambardella, Dr. Herndon Harding, Dr. Frank Jobe, Dr. Michael Mellman
Senior advisor, baseball operations
John Boles
Senior advisor, baseball operations
Joe Amalfitano
Special asst. to the general manager
Jeff Schugal
Senior scouting advisor
Don Welke
Minor league field coordinator
Terry Collins
Advance scout
Mark Weidemaier
Major league scouts
Al LaMacchia, Carl Loewenstine
Coordinator, minor league scouting
Terry Reynolds
Professional scouts
Dan Freed, Vance Lovelace, Ron Rizzi
National crosscheckers
Gib Bodet, Tim Hallgren
Regional supervisors
John Barr, Gary Nickels, Tom Thomas
Area scouts
Doug Carpenter, Jim Chapman, Bobby Darwin, Scott Groot, Mike Hankins, Clarence Johns, Calvin Jones, Hank Jones, Lon Joyce, John Kosciak, Marty Lamb, Mike Leuzinger, James Merriweather, Bill Pleis, Clair Rierson, Mark Sheehy, Chris Smith, Brian Stephenson, Mitch Webster
International scouts
Mike Brito, Pat Kelly, Camilo Pascual

BALLPARK INFORMATION

Ballpark (capacity, surface)
Dodger Stadium (56,000, grass)
Address
1000 Elysian Park Ave.
Los Angeles, CA 90012
Official website
www.dodgers.com
Business phone
323-224-1500
Ticket information
323-224-1448
Ticket prices
$35 (middle field)
$25 (middle loge)
$22 (outer field)
$17 (outer loge, inner reserve)
$10 (outer reserve)
$6 (top deck, left & right pavilion)
Field dimensions (from home plate)
To left field at foul line, 330 feet
To center field, 395 feet
To right field at foul line, 330 feet
First game played
April 10, 1962 (Reds 6, Dodgers 3)

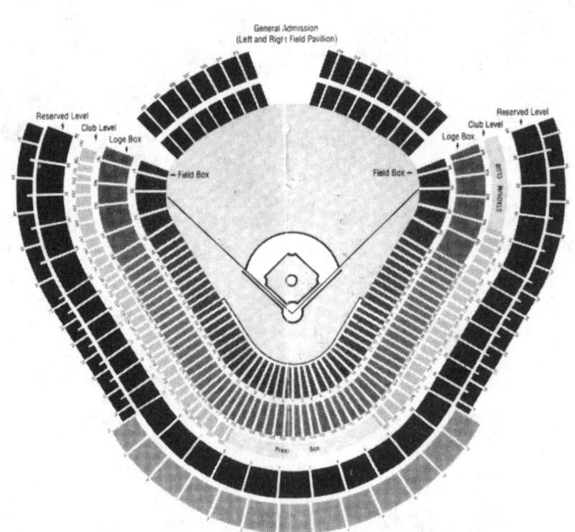

Follow the Dodgers all season at: www.sportingnews.com/baseball/teams/dodgers/

DODGERS SPRING ROSTER

No.	PITCHERS	B/T	Ht./Wt.	Born	2002 clubs	Projection
57	Alvarez, Victor	L/L	5-10/150	11-8-76	Las Vegas, Los Angeles	Looks like he's ready for a shot in the rotation.
43	Ashby, Andy	R/R	6-1/202	7-11-67	Los Angeles	Still pitches well for his age, but won only nine games last season.
	Brown, Andrew	R/R	6-6/230	2-17-81	Vero Beach	Big righthander was acquired as part of Gary Sheffield deal, won 10 games.
27	Brown, Kevin	R/R	6-4/200	3-14-65	Los Angeles, Las Vegas	It's been three years since his last 200-inning season; is he finally healthy?
55	Carrara, Giovanni	R/R	6-2/235	3-4-68	Los Angeles	Long reliever pitched in 63 games and posted a very respectable 3.28 ERA.
	Colyer, Steve	L/L	6-4/205	2-22-79	Jacksonville	Became a closer in Class AA, but Eric Gagne blocks his major league path.
	Diaz, Jose	R/R	6-4/230	2-27-84	South Georgia	Pitched in only 19 games due to injury.
37	Dreifort, Darren	R/R	6-2/211	5-3-72	DID NOT PLAY	Hasn't pitched since June 2001 because of injuries.
38	Gagne, Eric	R/R	6-2/195	1-7-76	Los Angeles	Had ERA under 2.00 in first season as closer.
	Gonzalez, Alfredo	R/R	6-2/181	9-17-79	V. Beach, Jacksonville, L.Vegas	Reliever didn't record ERA over 2.00 until he reached Class AAA.
17	Ishii, Kaz	L/L	6-0/190	9-9-73	Los Angeles	Expected to make a full recovery after taking a shot off his head in game last year.
	Kuo, Hong-Chih	L/L	6-0/200	7-23-81	Gulf Coast Dodgers, Vero Beach	Lefty could move quickly through minor league system.
	Mallette, Brian	R/R	6-0/185	1-19-75	Indianapolis, Milwaukee	Minor league closer will get chance to earn spot in big-league bullpen.
58	Mota, Guillermo	R/R	6-4/205	7-25-73	Las Vegas, Los Angeles	Long reliever should post similar numbers this year.
10	Nomo, Hideo	R/R	6-2/210	8-31-68	Los Angeles	His return to L.A. was successful—16 wins and a 3.39 ERA.
45	Perez, Odalis	L/L	6-0/150	6-11-77	Los Angeles	Seemed to wear down at end of season, but he'll be just as good in 2003.
46	Quantrill, Paul	L/R	6-1/195	11-3-68	Los Angeles	Is good at getting the tough outs. Didn't allow many runs to score.
	Roberts, Rick	L/L	6-1/200	5-20-79	Jacksonville	Won eight, saved two in relief in Class AA.
44	Shuey, Paul	R/R	6-3/215	9-16-70	Cleveland, Akron, Los Angeles	Gives Dodgers another reliable setup man for 2003.
	Thompson, Derek	L/L	6-2/180	1-8-81	Columbia, Kinston	Pitched better than last year's numbers might indicate.

No.	CATCHERS	B/T	Ht./Wt.	Born	2002 clubs	Projection
	Hill, Koyie	B/R	6-0/190	3-9-79	Jacksonville	Will have to improve defensively before he'll play regularly in majors.
9	Hundley, Todd	B/R	5-11/200	5-27-69	Chicago N.L., Iowa	Dodgers are hoping he can return to form he displayed with Mets in 1996-97.
16	LoDuca, Paul	R/R	5-10/185	4-12-72	Los Angeles	While his average and power dipped some in 2002, he's still a good hitter.
40	Ross, Dave	R/R	6-2/205	3-19-77	Las Vegas, Los Angeles	Hard to say if he'll play in majors at all this year.

No.	INFIELDERS	B/T	Ht./Wt.	Born	2002 clubs	Projection
29	Beltre, Adrian	R/R	5-11/170	4-7-79	Los Angeles	Still doesn't walk as much as he should, but he has star potential.
50	Cabrera, Jolbert	R/R	6-1/190	12-8-72	Buf., Cleve., L. Vegas, L.A.	Will probably spend year as a utility man for both infield and outfield.
13	Cora, Alex	L/R	6-0/180	10-18-75	Los Angeles	Shortstop hit .291, likely to platoon with Izturis.
3	Izturis, Cesar	B/R	5-9/175	2-10-80	Los Angeles	Likely to platoon untill either he or Cora show they can handle full-time job.
7	Kinkade, Mike	R/R	6-1/210	5-6-73	Las Vegas, Los Angeles	Hit .380 in just 37 games last season, likely the team's top pinch hitter.
29	McGriff, Fred	L/L	6-3/225	10-31-63	Chicago N.L.	Still going strong after all these years, expect another 25-30 homers.
41	Thurston, Joe	L/R	5-11/175	9-29-79	Las Vegas, Los Angeles	Top prospect will be given every chance to win second-base job.

No.	OUTFIELDERS	B/T	Ht./Wt.	Born	2002 clubs	Projection
49	Allen, Luke	L/R	6-2/208	8-4-78	Las Vegas, Los Angeles	Will have to cut down on errors to get playing time in majors.
52	Chen, Chin-Feng	R/R	6-1/189	10-28-77	Las Vegas, Los Angeles	Power hitter needs little more patience at plate.
15	Green, Shawn	L/L	6-4/200	11-10-72	Los Angeles	Expect another 40-home-run season, with an average close to .300.
	Hermansen, Chad	R/R	6-2/192	9-10-77	Nashville, Pitts., Chicago N.L.	Hasn't hit all that well in recent seasons, could platoon in center with Roberts.
33	Jordan, Brian	R/R	6-1/205	3-29-67	Los Angeles	Was one of team's best players in September; provides veteran leadership.
30	Roberts, Dave	L/L	5-10/180	5-31-72	Los Angeles	Got playing time in center and made most of it.
26	Ruan, Wilkin	R/R	6-0/170	9-18-78	Jacksonville, Las Vegas, L.A.	Will need to walk more before he'll be a full-time player in majors.

THE COACHING STAFF

Jim Tracy, manager.

Jack Clark, hitting coach.

Jim Colburn, pitching coach.

Glenn Hoffman, third base coach.

Jim Lett, bullpen coach.

Manny Mota, coach.

Jim Riggleman, bench coach.

John Shelby, first base coach.

THE TOP NEWCOMERS

Todd Hundley: Catcher returns to Los Angeles after brief stop in Chicago. He's a switch hitter who will likely get some starts at catcher and first base.

Fred McGriff: After trading Eric Karros, the Dodgers made sure they signed McGriff to provide some leadership and experience at first base. He'll get plenty of opportunities to drive in runs in this stacked lineup.

THE TOP PROSPECTS

Alfredo Gonzalez: Reliever amassed over 70 innings through three minor league stops in 2002. His ERA didn't rise above 2.00 until he reached Class AAA, and even then it was only 2.91. Walked only 22 batters.

Joe Thurston: Former fourth-round pick led Pacific Coast League with 196 hits and 106 runs last year. He hit .334 with 12 homers and 22 stolen bases and .462 in a brief audition with the Dodgers. If he hits well during spring training, the second base job should be his.

MILWAUKEE BREWERS

NATIONAL LEAGUE CENTRAL DIVISION

2003 SEASON

Brewers Schedule

Home games shaded; D—Day game (games starting before 5 p.m.); *—All-Star Game at Comiskey Park, Chicago. Subject to changes.

March/April

SUN	MON	TUE	WED	THU	FRI	SAT
30	31 D STL	1	2 STL	3 D STL	4 D SF	5 D SF
6 D SF	7 PIT	8	9 PIT	10 D PIT	11 ARI	12 ARI
13 D ARI	14 STL	15 STL	16 D STL	17 HOU	18 HOU	19 D HOU
20 D HOU	21	22 FLA	23 FLA	24 FLA	25 ATL	26 ATL
27 D ATL	28	29 MON	30 MON			

May

SUN	MON	TUE	WED	THU	FRI	SAT
				1 D MON	2 NYM	3 NYM
4 D NYM	5 CUB	6 CUB	7 D CUB	8	9 CIN	10 CIN
11 D CIN	12 CUB	13 CUB	14 CUB	15 D CUB	16 CIN	17 D CIN
18 D CIN	19 SD	20 SD	21 D SD	22	23 LA	24 LA
25 D LA	26	27 SD	28 SD	29 D SD	30 LA	31 LA

June

SUN	MON	TUE	WED	THU	FRI	SAT
1 D LA	2	3 NYM	4 NYM	5 NYM	6 BOS	7 BOS
8 D BOS	9	10 FLA	11 FLA	12 D FLA	13 BAL	14 BAL
15 D BAL	16 STL	17 STL	18 STL	19 D STL	20 MIN	21 MIN
22 D MIN	23	24 CUB	25 D CUB	26 D CUB	27 MIN	28 MIN
29 D MIN	30					

July

SUN	MON	TUE	WED	THU	FRI	SAT
		1 HOU	2 HOU	3 HOU	4 D COL	5 COL
6 D COL	7 PIT	8 PIT	9 PIT	10 D PIT	11 CIN	12 CIN
13 D CIN	14	15 *	16	17 PIT	18 PIT	19 PIT
20 D PIT	21 CIN	22 CIN	23 HOU	24 HOU	25 COL	26 COL
27 D COL	28	29 NYM	30 NYM	31 D NYM		

August

SUN	MON	TUE	WED	THU	FRI	SAT
					1 MON	2 MON
3 D MON	4	5 ATL	6 ATL	7 D ATL	8 FLA	9 FLA
10 D FLA	11	12 PHI	13 PHI	14 PHI	15 PIT	16 D PIT
17 D PIT	18	19 PHI	20 PHI	21 D PHI	22 PIT	23 PIT
24 D PIT	25 CIN	26 CIN	27 CIN	28 D CIN	29 D CUB	30 D CUB
31 D CUB						

September

SUN	MON	TUE	WED	THU	FRI	SAT
	1 D CIN	2 CIN	3 CIN	4	5 CUB	6 CUB
7 D CUB	8 HOU	9 HOU	10 HOU	11 D HOU	12 SF	13 D SF
14 D SF	15 STL	16 STL	17 STL	18 STL	19 ARI	20 ARI
21 D ARI	22	23 STL	24 STL	25 HOU	26 HOU	27 HOU
28 D HOU						

FRONT-OFFICE DIRECTORY

President and chief executive officer .... Ulice Payne Jr.
Senior vice president and general manager .... Doug Melvin
Vice president and general counsel .... Tom Gausden
Assistant general counsel .... Eugene "Pepi" Randolph
Assistant general manager .... Gord Ash
Vice president, community and governmental affairs .... Lynn Sprangers
Vice president, tickets and advertising .... Dean Rennicke
Vice president, finance .... Paul Baniel
Vice president, marketing .... Laurel Prieb
Vice president, stadium operations .... Scott Jenkins
Director, community relations .... Leonard Peace
Director, event services .... Steve Ethier
Director, grounds .... Gary Vanden Berg
Director, media relations .... Jon Greenberg
Director, Brewers Gold Club & Baseball for Wisconsin .... Mike Harlan
Director, publications .... Mario Ziino
Director, ticket operations .... John Barnes
Director, scouting .... Jack Zduriencik
Director, clubhouse operations .... Tony Migliaccio
Director of team travel .... Dan Larrea
Special assistant to the general manager/player development .... Reid Nichols
Special assistant to the general manager/scouting .... Dick Groch

MINOR LEAGUE AFFILIATES

Class	Team	League	Manager
AAA	Indianapolis	International	Cecil Cooper
AA	Huntsville	Southern	Frank Kremblas
A	High Desert	California	Tim Blackwell
A	Beloit	Midwest	Don Money
Rookie	Helena	Pioneer	Ed Sedar
Rookie	Maryvale	Arizona	Hector Torres

BROADCAST INFORMATION

Radio: WTMJ-AM (620).
TV: WCGV-TV (Channel 24).
Cable TV: Fox Sports North.

SPRING TRAINING

Ballpark (city): Maryvale Baseball Park (Phoenix, Ariz.).
Ticket information: 623-245-5500.

ASSISTANCE STAFF

Trainers
Paul Anderson, Roger Caplinger

Assistant trainer/strength and conditioning coach
Dan Wright

Team physician
Dr. William Raasch

National cross-checker
Larry Doughty

West Coast supervisor
Ric Wilson

Midwest supervisor
Tom Allison

Latin America supervisor
Epy Guerrero

East Coast supervisor
Bobby Heck

Professional scouts
Larry Aaron, Hank Allen, Carl Blando, Dick Hager, Alan Regier, David Wilder

Major League scouts
Russ Bove, Ken Califano, Larry Haney, Elanis Westbrooks

Scouts
Tony Blengino, Jeff Brookens, Jeff Cornwell, Mike Farrell, Manolo Hernandez, Brian Johnson, Harvey Kuenn Jr., Justin McCray, Tom McNamara, Chris Miller, Ray Montgomery, Brandon Newell, Larry Pardo, Douglas Reynolds, Corey Rodriguez, Bruce Seid, Jim Stevenson, George Swain, John Viney

BALLPARK INFORMATION

Ballpark (capacity, surface)
Miller Park (41,900, grass)

Address
One Brewers Way
Milwaukee, WI 53214-3652

Official website
www.milwaukeebrewers.com

Business phone
414-902-4400

Ticket information
414-902-4000, 1-800-933-7890

Ticket prices
$35 (field IF box, club IF box)
$28 (field OF box), $30 (loge diamond box)
$26 (club OF box), $26 (loge IF box)
$20 (loge OF box), $17 (terrace box)
$12 (terrace reserved), $10 (field bleachers)
$6 (loge bleachers)
$5 (Bernie's Terrace)
$1 (Uecker seats)

Field dimensions (from home plate)
To left field at foul line, 342 feet
To center field, 400 feet
To right field at foul line, 345 feet

First game played
April 6, 2001 (Brewers 5, Reds 4)

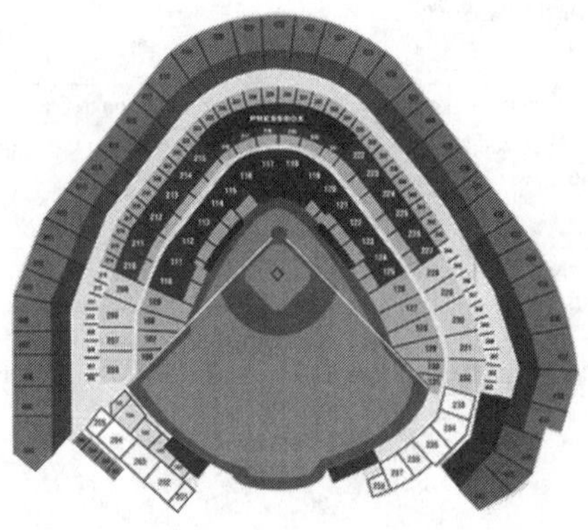

Follow the Brewers all season at: www.sportingnews.com/baseball/teams/brewers/

BREWERS SPRING ROSTER

No.	PITCHERS	B/T	Ht./Wt.	Born	2002 clubs	Projection
31	Campos, Francisco	R/R	6-0/165	8-12-72	Campeche, Indianapolis	Mexican League star is well on his way to becoming a major league pitcher.
43	Childers, Matt	R/R	6-5/195	12-3-78	Huntsville, Milw., Indianapolis	Can start or relieve. Brewers aren't sure where his future lies yet.
28	De Los Santos, Valerio	L/L	6-2/206	10-6-72	Indianapolis, Milwaukee	Held opponents to a .211 batting average over 51 games.
48	DeJean, Mike	R/R	6-4/219	9-28-70	Milwaukee	Filled in as closer while Leskanic was injured, saved 27 games.
53	Diggins, Ben	R/R	6-7/230	6-13-79	Vero Beach, Huntsville, Milw.	Big righthander needs a little more command before he'll be dominant starter.
56	Durocher, Jayson	R/R	6-3/195	8-18-74	Indianapolis, Milwaukee	Posted 1.88 ERA in 39 games out of bullpen.
	Ford, Matthew	B/L	6-1/175	4-8-81	Dunedin	Crafty lefthander won nine games and had 2.37 ERA in Florida State League.
48	Foster, John	L/L	6-0/200	5-17-78	Richmond, Atlanta	Acquired in Ray King trade, he'll help bolster the bullpen.
26	Franklin, Wayne	L/L	6-2/205	3-9-74	New Orleans, Milwaukee	Pitched well in four starts after being acquired from Astros.
55	Gold, J.M.	R/R	6-5/220	4-18-80	High Desert	Injuries limited him to only seven starts in 2002.
50	Kinney, Matt	R/R	6-5/220	12-16-76	Edm., Min., GCTw., F.M., N.B.	Has been a good pitcher at every stop in minors, now has to prove it in majors.
33	Leskanic, Curtis	R/R	6-0/196	4-2-68	Indianapolis, Huntsville	Didn't pitch in majors at all last season due to injury.
64	Liriano, Pedro	R/R	6-2/160	10-23-80	Rancho Cucamonga	Strikeout pitcher was acquired from Angels as part of Alex Ochoa deal.
59	Martinez, Luis	R/R	6-1/185	1-20-80	Huntsville	Can start or relieve, but will need more time in minors.
30	Matthews, Mike	L/L	6-2/175	10-24-73	St. Louis, Milwaukee	Gives the Brewers a lefthanded option out of bullpen.
	Mlicki, Dave	R/R	6-4/200	6-8-68	Houston, N.Orleans, Round Rock	Brewers would like to see a 14-win season out of him. He won 14 in 1999.
47	Nance, Shane	L/L	5-8/180	9-7-77	Las Vegas, Indianapolis, Milw.	Will help bridge the gap between the starters and setup men this season.
32	Neugebauer, Nick	R/R	6-3/235	7-15-80	Milwaukee, Indianapolis	Shoulder injuries slowed his progress in the majors last season.
13	Pember, Dave	R/R	6-5/225	5-24-78	Huntsville, Milwaukee	Pitched well in Class AA, likely to spend this year in Class AAA.
37	Quevedo, Ruben	R/R	6-1/245	1-5-79	Milwaukee, Indianapolis	Brewers are losing patience with Quevedo, who needs to get in better shape.
31	Rigdon, Paul	R/R	6-5/242	11-2-75	Indianapolis	Missed last season with injuries; Brewers will take whatever he can give this year.
	Ritchie, Todd	R/R	6-3/210	11-7-71	Chicago A.L.	Should find success being back in N.L. after faltering with White Sox in 2002.
39	Rusch, Glendon	L/L	6-1/200	11-7-74	Milwaukee	Won 10 games last season, Brewers are counting on him being innings eater.
15	Sheets, Ben	R/R	6-1/203	7-18-78	Milwaukee	Staff ace started 34 games last year but won only 11 of them.
51	Vizcaino, Luis	R/R	5-11/174	8-6-74	Milwaukee	Pitched well in short relief, posting a 2.99 ERA and walking only 30.

No.	CATCHERS	B/T	Ht./Wt.	Born	2002 clubs	Projection
72	Machado, Robert	R/R	6-1/210	6-3-73	Chicago N.L., Milwaukee	Hit .255 as backup catcher with Brewers last season.
58	McKay, Cody	L/R	6-0/208	1-11-74	Sacramento, Oakland	Will provide depth in minor leagues, unless he hits better than Machado.
8	Valentin, Javier	B/R	5-10/192	9-19-75	Edmonton, Minnesota	Has hit 38 homers in last two seasons in Class AAA. Will get chance to start.

No.	INFIELDERS	B/T	Ht./Wt.	Born	2002 clubs	Projection
	Clayton, Royce	R/R	6-0/185	1-2-70	Chicago A.L.	Hit .251 for White Sox, but Brewers signed him for his glove.
	Cruz, Enrique	R/R	6-1/175	11-21-81	St. Lucie	Rule 5 third baseman has speed and can hit for average.
1	Ginter, Keith	R/R	5-10/190	5-5-76	New Orleans, Houston, Milw.	Brewers will give him chance to win job at third, had .363 OBP in 21 games.
2	Hall, Bill	R/R	6-0/175	12-28-79	Indianapolis, Milwaukee	Could use another season in Class AAA, where he hit just .228 last season.
18	Helms, Wes	R/R	6-4/230	5-12-76	Atlanta	If ex-Brave can't win a regular job, he can always pinch hit.
11	Sexson, Richie	R/R	6-8/227	12-29-74	Milwaukee	Power numbers dropped because of nagging injuries, but strikeouts dropped too.
7	Young, Eric	R/R	5-8/180	5-18-67	Milwaukee	Hit .280 and stole 31 bases. Brewers are hoping for more of the same this year.

No.	OUTFIELDERS	B/T	Ht./Wt.	Born	2002 clubs	Projection
15	Clark, Brady	R/R	6-2/195	4-18-73	Cincinnati, Louisville, N.Y. N.L.	Could be full time outfielder with good spring showing.
57	Guerrero, Cristian	R/R	6-5/175	4-12-81	Huntsville	His average fell to .223 in Class AA. He'll probably be there for one more season.
41	Hammonds, Jeffrey	R/R	6-0/200	3-5-71	Milwaukee	Brewers are hoping to get one full injury-free season from him.
5	Jenkins, Geoff	L/R	6-1/213	7-21-74	Milwaukee	An ankle injury ended his season early, Brewers are hoping he's fully recovered.
20	Podsednik, Scott	L/L	6-0/170	3-18-76	Tacoma, Seattle	Has chance to make team as lefthanded bat off bench; if not, it's back to AAA.
22	Sanchez, Alex	L/L	5-10/159	8-26-76	Milwaukee	Will have to show that his 2002 season (.289 average) was no fluke.

THE COACHING STAFF

Ned Yost, manager.

Bill Castro, bullpen coach.

Rich Dauer, bench coach.

Rich Donnelly, third base coach.

Mike Maddux, pitching coach.

Dave Nelson, first base coach.

Butch Wynegar, batting coach.

THE TOP NEWCOMERS

Todd Ritchie: Big things were expected out of Ritchie after the White Sox traded three pitchers for him. Unfortunately he flopped, and Chicago released him after last season. The Brewers are hoping they can get the former Pirate back on the right track.

Javier Valentin: Was rushed to the majors by Twins in the 90s and struggled. Since then he's been developing in minors, where he has shown a good bat while maintaining good defense.

THE TOP PROSPECTS

Francisco Campos: Mexican League veteran was signed b Brewers to bolster their rotation. Went 3-0 with 14 strikeouts in 22 innings.

Pedro Liriano: This tall righthander pitched pretty well in the California League last season while in the Angels system. Traded to the Brewers to complete the Alex Ochoa deal, he rung up 176 strikeouts in 167 innings.

MONTREAL EXPOS

NATIONAL LEAGUE EAST DIVISION

2003 SEASON

Expos Schedule

Home games shaded; D—Day game (games starting before 5 p.m.); *—All-Star Game at Comiskey Park, Chicago. Subject to changes. †Game played in Puerto Rico.

March/April

SUN	MON	TUE	WED	THU	FRI	SAT
30	31 ATL	1	2 ATL	3 ATL	4 NYM	5 D NYM
6 D NYM	7 D CUB	8	9 D CUB	10 D CUB	11 † NYM	12 † NYM
13 D† NYM	14 D† NYM	15 † ATL	16 † ATL	17 D† ATL	18 † CIN	19 † CIN
20 D† CIN	21	22 ARI	23 ARI	24 ARI	25 HOU	26 D HOU
27 D HOU	28	29 MIL	30 MIL			

May

SUN	MON	TUE	WED	THU	FRI	SAT
				1 D MIL	2 STL	3 D STL
4 D STL	5	6 SD	7 SD	8 SD	9 LA	10 D LA
11 D LA	12 SF	13 SF	14 D SF	15 COL	16 COL	17 D COL
18 D COL	19	20 FLA	21 FLA	22 FLA	23 PHI	24 PHI
25 D PHI	26 D FLA	27 FLA	28 FLA	29 FLA	30 PHI	31 PHI

June

SUN	MON	TUE	WED	THU	FRI	SAT
1 D PHI	2	3 † ANA	4 † ANA	5 † ANA	6 † TEX	7 † TEX
8 D† TEX	9	10 SEA	11 SEA	12 SEA	13 OAK	14 D OAK
15 D OAK	16	17 PIT	18 PIT	19 D PIT	20 TOR	21 TOR
22 D TOR	23 PIT	24 D PIT	25 D PIT	26	27 TOR	28 D TOR
29 D TOR	30 NYM					

July

SUN	MON	TUE	WED	THU	FRI	SAT
		1 NYM	2 NYM	3 ATL	4 ATL	5 ATL
6 D ATL	7 PHI	8 PHI	9 PHI	10	11 FLA	12 FLA
13 D FLA	14	15 *	16	17 PHI	18 PHI	19 PHI
20 D PHI	21 FLA	22 FLA	23 NYM	24 NYM	25 ATL	26 ATL
27 D ATL	28 ATL	29 STL	30 STL	31 STL		

August

SUN	MON	TUE	WED	THU	FRI	SAT
					1 MIL	2 MIL
3 D MIL	4	5 ARI	6 ARI	7 ARI	8 HOU	9 HOU
10 D HOU	11 COL	12 COL	13 COL	14	15 SF	16 SF
17 D SF	18 D SF	19 LA	20 LA	21 D LA	22 SD	23 SD
24 D SD	25 PHI	26 PHI	27 PHI	28 D PHI	29 FLA	30 FLA
31 D FLA						

September

SUN	MON	TUE	WED	THU	FRI	SAT
	1 D FLA	2 PHI	3 D PHI	4	5 † FLA	6 † FLA
7 D† FLA	8	9 † CUB	10 † CUB	11 D† CUB	12 NYM	13 NYM
14 D NYM	15 ATL	16 ATL	17 D ATL	18 NYM	19 NYM	20 D NYM
21 D NYM	22	23 ATL	24 ATL	25	26 CIN	27 D CIN
28 D CIN						

FRONT-OFFICE DIRECTORY

President....Tony Tavares
Vice president & general manager....Omar Minaya
Assistant general manager....Tony Siegle
Executive vice president, business affairs....Claude Delorme
Chief financial officer....Bob Nicholson
Special assistant to the general manager....Dan Lunetta
Director, player development....Adam Wogan
Assistant director, player development....Glenn Wilpon
Director, pro scouting....Lee MacPhail
Director, amateur scouting....Dana Brown
Coordinator, scouting operations....Alex Anthopoulos
Director, Latin American development....Ismael Cruz
Director, media services....Monique Giroux
Manager, media relations....Matt Charbonneau
Director, team travel....Rob McDonald
Director, promotions & special events....Gina Hackl
Director, ticket sales....John Di Terlizzi
Director, administration, sales & marketing....Chantal Dalpe
Director, management information systems....Yves Poulin

MINOR LEAGUE AFFILIATES

Class	Team	League	Manager
AAA	Edmonton	Pacific Coast	Dave Huppert
AA	Harrisburg	Eastern	Dave Machemer
A	Brevard County	Florida State	Doug Sisson
A	Savannah	South Atlantic	Joey Cora
A	Vermont	New York-Pennsylvania	To be announced
Rookie	Gulf Coast Expos	Gulf Coast	To be announced

ASSISTANCE STAFF

Team orthopedist
Dr. Larry Coughlin

Team physician
Dr. Mike Thomassin

Minor league rehab coordinator
Mike McGowan

Major League advance scout
Jerry Terrell

Scouts
Jack Bloomfield, Chris Bourjos, Manny Estrada, Rick Williams, Ray Corbett, Zack Hoyrst, Larry Izzo, Ray Jackson, Doug McMillan, Lance Nichols, Delvy Santiago, Alex Smith, Paul Tinnell

BROADCAST INFORMATION

Radio: To be announced.
TV: To be announced.
Cable TV: To be announced.

SPRING TRAINING

Ballpark (city): Space Coast Stadium (Melbourne, Fla.).
Ticket information: 321-633-8119.

BALLPARK INFORMATION

Ballpark (capacity, surface)
Olympic Stadium (46,620, artificial)

Address
P.O. Box 500, Station M
Montreal, Que. H1V 3P2

Official website
www.montrealexpos.com

Business phone
514-253-3434

Ticket information
800-GO-EXPOS

Ticket prices
$36 (VIP box seats)
$26 (box seats)
$16 (terrace)
$8 (general admission)

Field dimensions (from home plate)
To left field at foul line, 325 feet
To center field, 404 feet
To right field at foul line, 325 feet

First game played
April 15, 1977 (Phillies 7, Expos 2)

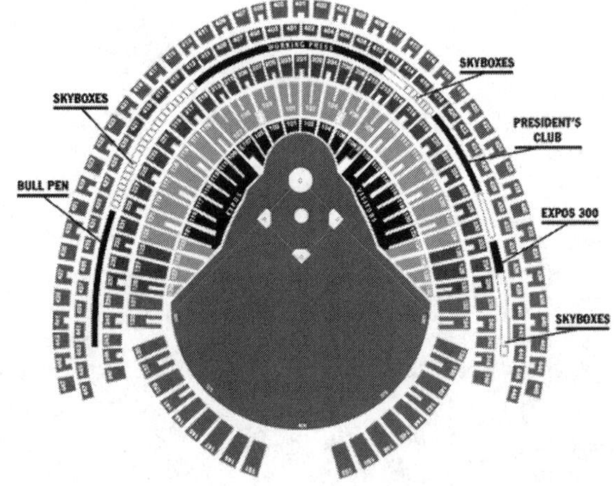

Follow the Expos all season at: www.sportingnews.com/baseball/teams/expos/

EXPOS SPRING ROSTER

No.	PITCHERS	B/T	Ht./Wt.	Born	2002 clubs	Projection
36	Armas, Tony	R/R	6-4/215	4-29-78	Montreal	Slowly but surely developing into the great starter Expos thought he could be.
	Ayala, Luis	R/R	6-2/175	1-12-78	Saltillo, Ottawa	Had 23 saves in Mexican League; Expos would like to see him win spot in bullpen.
	Biddle, Rocky	R/R	6-3/230	5-21-76	Charlotte, Chicago A.L.	Will likely be thrust into Montreal rotation out of need.
32	Brower, Jim	R/R	6-3/215	12-29-72	Cincinnati, Montreal	He'll help the team by giving quality short relief outings.
57	Chiaviacci, Ron	R/R	6-2/220	9-5-77	Harrisburg	Spent another year in Class AA. He's likely to spend 2003 in Class AAA.
54	Day, Zach	R/R	6-4/185	6-15-78	Ottawa, Montreal	Pitched well in 19 games with Expos; can start or relieve.
37	Downs, Scott	L/L	6-2/190	3-17-76	Brevard County, Ottawa	He's coming back from injuries, so Expos will take their time with him.
47	Drew, Tim	R/R	6-1/195	8-31-78	Buffalo, Ottawa, Montreal	Expos think he could be closer; if not, he'll get chance in rotation.
58	Eischen, Joey	L/L	6-0/210	5-25-70	Ottawa, Montreal	Veteran had 1.34 ERA in 59 appearances last season.
	Gonzalez, Dicky	R/R	5-11/170	10-21-78	Norfolk, Ottawa	Could get chance in rotation, but another year in Class AAA is better bet.
	Hernandez, Orlando	R/R	6-2/220	10-11-69	New York A.L., Columbus	Becomes the No. 2 pitcher in rotation behind Javier Vazquez.
31	Kim, Sun-Woo	R/R	6-2/188	9-4-77	Pawtucket, Boston, Ottawa, Mon.	Former Red Sox prospect had 0.89 ERA in 20 innings with Expos.
44	Manon, Julio	L/R	6-0/200	6-10-73	Ottawa, Harrisburg	Struck out 51 batters in 39 innings in Class AA. But still a year away.
24	Ohka, Tomo	R/R	6-1/180	3-18-76	Montreal	Went 13-8 with a 3.18 ERA in 2002; Expos would take repeat performance.
34	Reames, Britt	R/R	5-11/175	8-19-73	Montreal, Ottawa	Failed starter might be better fit for setup role.
43	Smith, Dan	R/R	6-3/210	9-15-75	Ottawa, Montreal	Held opponents to a .210 batting average out of bullpen.
	Song, Seung	R/R	6-1/192	6-29-80	Trenton, Harrisburg	Injuries sidelined him almost upon his arrival from Red Sox in Cliff Floyd deal.
51	Stewart, Scott	R/L	6-2/225	8-14-75	Montreal	Expos will likely give him first crack at closer's job after 17-save season.
52	Tucker, T.J.	R/R	6-3/245	8-20-78	Montreal	Needs to keep batters off base to be successful.
	Vargas, Claudio	R/R	6-3/210	5-19-79	Calgary, Harrisburg	Strikeout pitcher is still a year or two away.
23	Vazquez, Javier	R/R	6-2/195	7-25-76	Montreal	Struggled through middle of last season, but turned the corner in September.

No.	CATCHERS	B/T	Ht./Wt.	Born	2002 clubs	Projection
5	Barrett, Michael	R/R	6-2/200	10-22-76	Montreal	Cooled down after torrid start but showed he can be everyday catcher.
39	Schneider, Brian	L/R	6-1/200	11-26-76	Montreal	Hit .275 while backing up Barrett, might make push for more playing time.

No.	INFIELDERS	B/T	Ht./Wt.	Born	2002 clubs	Projection
18	Cabrera, Orlando	R/R	5-10/185	11-2-74	Montreal	Led league with 29 errors in 2002, a far cry from his 11-error season of 2001.
2	Carroll, Jamey	R/R	5-10/175	2-18-74	Harrisburg, Ottawa, Montreal	Second baseman in waiting with Jose Vidro firmly entrenched as starter.
58	Hodges, Scott	L/R	6-0/185	12-26-78	Harrisburg	Will need to show more power to play third base in majors.
	Liefer, Jeff	L/R	6-3/210	8-17-74	Chicago A.L.	Provides good lefthanded bat off bench, but many wonder where his power went.
12	Mateo, Henry	B/R	5-11/180	10-14-76	Ottawa, Montreal	Will most likely be a utility middle infielder.
21	Tatis, Fernando	R/R	5-10/180	1-1-75	Brevard County, Montreal	It's no secret the Expos will trade him if right deal comes along.
3	Vidro, Jose	B/R	5-11/195	8-27-74	Montreal	Shrugged off injury-prone label by playing in 152 games.

No.	OUTFIELDERS	B/T	Ht./Wt.	Born	2002 clubs	Projection
11	Bergeron, Peter	L/R	6-0/190	11-9-77	Montreal, Ottawa	Still has yet to show he can hit major league pitching consistently.
53	Calloway, Ron	L/L	6-0/190	9-4-76	Ottawa	Will be battling for an outfield spot after two years in Class AAA.
29	Cepicky, Matt	L/R	6-2/215	11-10-77	Harrisburg, Montreal	Likely to spend this season in Class AAA for seasoning.
19	Chavez, Endy	L/L	6-0/165	2-7-78	Ottawa, Montreal	Can win center field job if he hits like he did in 35-game stint with Expos last year.
26	Cordero, Wil	R/R	6-2/200	10-3-71	Cleveland, Montreal	Provides veteran leadership and is a tough out at the plate.
27	Guerrero, Vladimir	R/R	6-3/210	2-9-76	Montreal	Fell one homer short of becoming latest 40-homer, 40-steal guy.
1	Macias, Jose	B/R	5-10/189	1-25-72	Detroit, Montreal	He'll be the Expos utility player for 2003. Hits and runs well.
66	Pascucci, Val	R/R	6-6/235	11-17-78	Harrisburg	Power hitter led Eastern League with 27 homers.
	Sledge, Terrmel	L/L	6-0/185	3-18-77	Harrisburg, Ottawa	Hits for average and knows how to get on base. Likely one year away though.
6	Wilkerson, Brad	L/L	6-0/200	6-1-77	Montreal	Hit 20 homers as a rookie, will having starting job in left or center.

THE COACHING STAFF

Frank Robinson, manager.
Manny Acta, third base coach.
Tim McCraw, hitting coach.
Jerry Morales, first base coach.
Bob Natal, bullpen coach.
Claude Reymond, roving coach.

THE TOP NEWCOMERS

Orlando Hernandez: Former 17-game winner won only eight games with Yankees last season. Injuries were a factor, and Expos hope age (33) and overwork haven't caught up with him.

THE TOP NEWCOMERS

Luis Ayala: Young pitcher (25) saved 23 games and had a 1.68 ERA last season in the Mexican League. He didn't seem to miss a beat in six Class AAA games after the Expos signed him.

Sun-Woo Kim: One of the key acquitisions in the Cliff Floyd deal, he started three games for the Expos and allowed only two runs to score.

Jamey Carroll: Has the makings of a solid but unspectacular second baseman, but with Jose Vidro blocking his path playing time could be sparse.

NEW YORK METS

NATIONAL LEAGUE EAST DIVISION

2003 SEASON

Mets Schedule

Home games shaded; D—Day game (games starting before 5 p.m.); *—All-Star Game at Comiskey Park, Chicago. Subject to changes. †Game played in Puerto Rico.

March/April

SUN	MON	TUE	WED	THU	FRI	SAT
30	31 D CUB	1	2 CUB	3 D CUB	4 MON	5 D MON
6 D MON	7	8 FLA	9 FLA	10 FLA	11 † MON	12 † MON
13 D† MON	14 D† MON	15 PIT	16 PIT	17 PIT	18 FLA	19 D FLA
20 D FLA	21	22 HOU	23 HOU	24 HOU	25 ARI	26 D ARI
27 D ARI	28	29 STL	30 STL			

May

SUN	MON	TUE	WED	THU	FRI	SAT
				1 D STL	2 MIL	3 MIL
4 D MIL	5	6 LA	7 LA	8 LA	9 SD	10 D SD
11 D SD	12 COL	13 COL	14 D COL	15 SF	16 SF	17 D SF
18 D SF	19	20 PHI	21 PHI	22 D PHI	23 ATL	24 D ATL
25 D ATL	26	27 PHI	28 PHI	29 PHI	30 ATL	31 D ATL

June

SUN	MON	TUE	WED	THU	FRI	SAT
1 ATL	2	3 MIL	4 MIL	5 MIL	6 SEA	7 SEA
8 D SEA	9	10 TEX	11 TEX	12 TEX	13 ANA	14 ANA
15 D ANA	16 FLA	17 FLA	18 FLA	19 FLA	20 NYY	21 D NYY
22 NYY	23	24 FLA	25 FLA	26 FLA	27 NYY	28 D NYY
29 NYY	30 MON					

July

SUN	MON	TUE	WED	THU	FRI	SAT
		1 MON	2 MON	3	4 D CIN	5 CIN
6 D CIN	7 ATL	8 ATL	9 D ATL	10 PHI	11 PHI	12 D PHI
13 D PHI	14	15 *	16	17 ATL	18 ATL	19 D ATL
20 D ATL	21 PHI	22 D PHI	23 MON	24 MON	25 CIN	26 CIN
27 D CIN	28	29 MIL	30 MIL	31 D MIL		

August

SUN	MON	TUE	WED	THU	FRI	SAT
					1 STL	2 D STL
3 D STL	4	5 HOU	6 HOU	7 HOU	8 ARI	9 ARI
10 D ARI	11	12 SF	13 SF	14 SF	15 COL	16 COL
17 D COL	18 D COL	19 SD	20 SD	21 D SD	22 LA	23 LA
24 LA	25	26 ATL	27 ATL	28 ATL	29 PHI	30 PHI
31 D PHI						

September

SUN	MON	TUE	WED	THU	FRI	SAT
	1 D ATL	2 ATL	3 D ATL	4 PHI	5 PHI	6 PHI
7 D PHI	8 FLA	9 FLA	10 D FLA	11	12 MON	13 MON
14 D MON	15 CUB	16 CUB	17 D CUB	18 MON	19 MON	20 D MON
21 D MON	22	23 PIT	24 PIT	25 PIT	26 FLA	27 FLA
28 D FLA						

FRONT-OFFICE DIRECTORY

Chairman & chief executive officer ... Fred Wilpon
President ... Saul B. Katz
Executive vice president & chief operating officer ... Jeffrey S. Wilpon
Directors ... Fred Wilpon, Saul B. Katz, Jeffrey S. Wilpon, Marvin Tepper, Steve Phillips, Michael Katz, Richard A. Wilpon, L. Thomas Osterman, David Katz, Arthur Friedman
Special advisor to the board of directors ... Richard Cummins
Senior vice president & general manager ... Stephen F. Phillips
Special assistant to the general manager ... Fred Wright
Senior assistant general manager/player personnel ... Jim Duquette
Assistant general manager/director of scouting operations ... Gary Larocque
Assistant general manager/scouting development ... Carmen Fusco
Director, amateur scouting ... Jack Bowen
Director, minor league operations ... Kevin Morgan
Senior vice president, business and legal affairs ... Dave Howard
Vice president, facilities ... Karl Smolarz
Vice president and consultant ... Bob Mandt
Vice president, ticket sales and services ... Bill Ianniciello
Vice president and consultant ... J. Frank Cashen
Director, marketing ... Tina Bucciarelli
Director, marketing production ... Tim Gunkel
Director, human resources ... To be announced
Vice president, general counsel ... David Cohen
Director, information services ... Dorothy Pope
Director, community outreach ... Jill Knee
Vice president, corporate sales ... Paul Danforth
Controller ... Lennie Labita
Vice president, media relations ... Jay Horwitz
Director, ticket operations ... Dan DeMato
Manager, customer relations ... Joann Galardy
Director, stadium operations ... Kevin McCarthy

MINOR LEAGUE AFFILIATES

Class	Team	League	Manager
AAA	Norfolk	International	Bobby Floyd
AA	Binghamton	Eastern	John Stearns
A	St. Lucie	Florida State	Ken Oberkfell
A	Capital City	South Atlantic	Tony Tijerina
A	Brooklyn	New York-Pennsylvania	Tim Teufel
Rookie	Kingsport	Appalachian	Dave Howard

ASSISTANCE STAFF

Club physician
Dr. Andrew Rokito

Club psychologist/Employee Assistance Program
Dr. Allan Lans

Team trainers
Michael Herbst   Scott Lawrenson

Amateur scouting nat. cross-checkers
Paul Fryer, Terry Tripp

Amateur scouting regional supervisors
Joe DelliCarri, Gene Kerns, Bob Minor

Amateur scouting area supervisors
Dave Birecki, Quincy Boyd, Ty Brown, Erwin Bryant, Joe Bunnell, Larry Chase, Rodney Henderson, Chuck Hensley Jr., Brian Hunter, Steve Leavitt, Lave Lottsfeldt, Marlin McPhail, Greg Morhardt, Joe Nigro, Claude Pelleher, Jim Reeves, Junior Roman, Bob Rossi, Joe Salermo

Major league advance scout
Bruce Benedict

Professional scouts
Dave Engle, Howie Freiling, Carmen Fusco, Roland Johnson, Harry Minor, Fred Wright

International area supervisors
Gregorio Machado, Isao O'Jimi, Eddy Toledo

International part-time scouts
Modesto Abreu, Robert Alfonzo, Wilfredo Blanco, Juan Mercado, Kevin Park, James Waddell

BROADCAST INFORMATION

Radio: WFAN-AM (660).
TV: WPIX (Channel 11).
Cable TV: Fox Sports New York, MSG Network.

SPRING TRAINING

Ballpark (city): Thomas J. White Stadium (Port St. Lucie, Fla.).
Ticket information: 772-871-2115.

BALLPARK INFORMATION

Ballpark (capacity, surface)
Shea Stadium (56,749, grass)

Address
123-01 Roosevelt Ave.
Flushing, NY 11368

Official website
www.mets.com

Business phone
718-507-METS

Ticket information
718-507-TIXX

Ticket prices
$38-53 (inner field box, inner loge box)
$30-39 (outer field box, outer loge box, mezz. box)
$27-33 (loge reserved)
$19-27 (mezzanine reserved, upper box)
$8-16 (upper reserved, loge reserved-back rows, mezzanine-reserved back rows)

Note: Ticket prices differ from game-to-game depending on whether they are considered "gold" (17 games), "silver" (21 games), "bronze" (27 games) or "value" (16 games). Prices indicated are price ranges of those seats.

Field dimensions (from home plate)
To left field at foul line, 338 feet
To center field, 410 feet
To right field at foul line, 338 feet

First game played
April 17, 1964 (Pirates 4, Mets 3)

Follow the Mets all season at: www.sportingnews.com/baseball/teams/mets/

METS SPRING ROSTER

No.	PITCHERS	B/T	Ht./Wt.	Born	2002 clubs	Projection
34	Astacio, Pedro	R/R	6-2/210	11-28-69	New York N.L.	Pitched well out of Coors Field. Will be pitching from the back end of the rotation.
33	Bacsik, Mike	L/L	6-3/190	11-11-77	Norfolk, New York N.L.	Might see time as No. 5 starter in rotation. Had nine starts with Mets last season.
49	Benitez, Armando	R/R	6-4/229	11-3-72	New York N.L.	Lowered his ERA to 2.27 in 2002. Should continue to be dominant closer.
	Bevis, P. J.	R/R	6-3/180	7-28-80	El Paso, Binghamton	Pitched well in four games in Eastern League after trade from D-backs.
43	Cerda, Jaime	L/L	6-0/175	10-26-78	Binghamton, Norfolk, N.Y. N.L.	Lefty specialist helped replace John Franco's production last season.
45	Franco, John	L/L	5-10/185	9-17-60	DID NOT PLAY	Arm injury sidelined veteran for entire season.
47	Glavine, Tom	L/L	6-0/185	3-25-66	Atlanta	Lefty leaves Atlanta and brings 2.96 ERA in 2002 to the Big Apple.
22	Leiter, Al	L/L	6-3/220	10-23-65	New York N.L.	Gives the Mets two tough lefthanded pitchers in the rotation.
27	Middlebrook, Jason	R/R	6-3/215	6-26-75	Portland, S.D., Norfolk, N.Y. N.L.	Was starter late last season, might be reliever due to amount of starters on roster.
	Nunez, Franklin	R/R	6-0/175	1-18-77	Scranton/W.-B., GC Phillies	Spent majority of last season on disabled list, Mets think he can contribute.
	Orloski, Joe	R/R	6-3/180	5-17-79	Tennessee	Spent time closing out games in Toronto's system, likely headed for Class AAA.
36	Roberts, Grant	R/R	6-3/205	9-13-77	New York N.L., Binghamton	Injuries hampered an otherwise productive season in majors.
	Seo, Jae	R/R	6-1/215	5-24-77	Binghamton, Norfolk, N.Y. N.L.	Team thinks he's ready to make jump to majors, will need to find a spot for him.
29	Stanton, Mike	L/L	6-1/215	6-2-67	New York A.L.	Will be counted on as setup man for Benitez.
38	Strange, Pat	R/R	6-5/243	8-23-80	Norfolk, New York N.L.	Might have a bullpen job, pitched in five games with Mets last season.
25	Strickland, Scott	R/R	5-11/180	4-26-76	Montreal, New York N.L.	Mets traded to get him from Expos, he was brought in to get the tough outs.
29	Trachsel, Steve	R/R	6-4/205	10-31-70	New York N.L., Binghamton	Won 11 games and posted 3.37 ERA last season. Gives Mets plenty of innings.
46	Walker, Tyler	R/R	6-3/255	5-15-76	Norfolk, New York N.L.	Probably will spend one more year in Class AAA.
35	Weathers, Dave	R/R	6-3/230	9-25-69	New York N.L.	Posted a 2.91 ERA in 71 appearances.
32	Yates, Tyler	R/R	6-4/220	8-7-77	Norfolk	Saved six games and had 1.32 ERA before injuries interrupted his season.

No.	CATCHERS	B/T	Ht./Wt.	Born	2002 clubs	Projection
7	Phillips, Jason	R/R	6-1/177	9-27-76	Norfolk, New York N.L.	Will either back up Piazza or spend another season in Class AAA.
31	Piazza, Mike	R/R	6-3/215	9-4-68	New York N.L.	Numbers dipped as Mets season didn't go as planned, will be better this year.
3	Wilson, Vance	R/R	5-11/190	3-17-73	New York N.L.	Will have to hit better than Phillips to keep his backup job.

No.	INFIELDERS	B/T	Ht./Wt.	Born	2002 clubs	Projection
12	Alomar, Roberto	B/R	6-0/185	2-5-68	New York N.L.	First season in New York didn't go as planned. Average should bounce back.
	Reyes, Jose	B/R	6-0/160	6-11-83	St. Lucie, Binghamton	Mets won't rush their shortstop of the future.
13	Sanchez, Rey	R/R	5-9/175	10-5-67	Boston	Hit .286 in Boston last season, he'll fill in at short until Reyes is ready.
26	Scutaro, Marcos	R/R	5-10/170	10-30-75	Norfolk, New York N.L.	Utility man might have hard time finding job under Art Howe.
42	Vaughn, Mo	L/R	6-1/275	12-15-67	New York N.L.	First half of season was forgettable. Second half was a little better.
9	Wigginton, Ty	R/R	6-0/200	10-11-77	Norfolk, New York N.L.	Can win third base job if he hits like he did last season.

No.	OUTFIELDERS	B/T	Ht./Wt.	Born	2002 clubs	Projection
20	Burnitz, Jeromy	L/R	6-0/213	4-15-69	New York N.L.	Hit .215 with only 19 homers, Mets are hoping he can find his groove again.
19	Cedeno, Roger	B/R	6-1/205	8-16-74	New York N.L.	Getting paid a lot of money for little production.
30	Floyd, Cliff	L/R	6-4/260	12-5-72	Florida, Montreal, Boston	Will patrol left field, brings good credentials to New York.
21	Gonzalez, Raul	R/R	5-9/190	12-27-73	Louisville, Cincinnati, N.Y. N.L.	Likely a fourth or fifth outfielder, or back to minors.
47	McEwing, Joe	R/R	5-11/170	10-19-72	N.Y. N.L., Brooklyn, Binghamton	Fan favorite, he can play anywhere, and that's why he has a job.
6	Perez, Timo	L/L	5-9/167	4-8-75	Norfolk, New York N.L.	It's still up in the air if he's a full time player or not.
	Shinjo, Tsuyoshi	R/R	6-1/185	1-28-72	San Francisco, Fresno	Only hit .238 with Giants, but played excellent defense in the outfield.
23	Snead, Esix	B/R	5-10/175	6-7-76	Binghamton, New York N.L.	Keeps improving in minors, likely to spend some time in Class AAA this year.
43	Tarasco, Tony	L/R	6-0/205	12-9-70	Norfolk, New York N.L.	Will be battling for outfield and bench spot, might win because he's a lefty.

THE COACHING STAFF

Art Howe, manager.

Chris Chambliss, hitting coach.

Matt Galante, third base coach.

Randy Niemann, bullpen coach.

Mookie Wilson, first base coach.

THE TOP NEWCOMERS

Tom Glavine: Won 18 games last season with Atlanta and then decided to move on and signed with the Mets. In the last three years he has 21, 16 and 18 wins respectively, the Mets will gladly take this kind of production from the top of their rotation.

Mike Stanton: Brings championship credentials with him after winning three World Series rings with Yankees. Will be the top setup man in the bullpen.

Cliff Floyd: Is capable of hitting .300+, with 30+ home runs; numbers he should easily eclipse playing in a stacked Mets lineup.

THE TOP PROSPECTS

Tyler Yates: Only pitched in 24 games with Norfolk before injuries ended his season early. He did have six saves and averaged a strikeout-per-inning when he was healthy.

Jose Reyes: There no doubting he'll be the Mets shortstop someday. The Mets traded Rey Ordonez to make room for this promising rookie. Reyes needs a little more patience at the plate, but otherwise he's as good as ready for the majors.

PHILADELPHIA PHILLIES

NATIONAL LEAGUE EAST DIVISION

2003 SEASON

Phillies Schedule

Home games shaded; D—Day game (games starting before 5 p.m.); *—All-Star Game at Comiskey Park, Chicago. Subject to changes.

March/April

SUN	MON	TUE	WED	THU	FRI	SAT
30	31 D FLA	1	2 FLA	3 D FLA	4 D PIT	5 D PIT
6 D PIT	7	8 ATL	9 ATL	10 ATL	11 CIN	12 D CIN
13 D CIN	14 FLA	15 FLA	16 FLA	17 D FLA	18 ATL	19 ATL
20 D ATL	21	22 COL	23 COL	24 D COL	25 SF	26 SF
27 D SF	28 LA	29 LA	30 LA			

May

SUN	MON	TUE	WED	THU	FRI	SAT
				1 LA	2 SD	3 SD
4 D SD	5 ARI	6 ARI	7 D ARI	8	9 HOU	10 HOU
11 D HOU	12	13 ARI	14 ARI	15 D ARI	16 HOU	17 D HOU
18 HOU	19	20 NYM	21 NYM	22 D NYM	23 MON	24 MON
25 D MON	26	27 NYM	28 NYM	29 NYM	30 MON	31 MON

June

SUN	MON	TUE	WED	THU	FRI	SAT
1 D MON	2	3 SEA	4 SEA	5 SEA	6 OAK	7 D OAK
8 D OAK	9 ANA	10 ANA	11 ANA	12	13 CIN	14 CIN
15 D CIN	16	17 ATL	18 ATL	19 D ATL	20 BOS	21 D BOS
22 D BOS	23	24 ATL	25 ATL	26 ATL	27 BAL	28 BAL
29 D BAL	30 CUB					

July

SUN	MON	TUE	WED	THU	FRI	SAT
		1 CUB	2 CUB	3 CUB	4 D FLA	5 FLA
6 D FLA	7 MON	8 MON	9 MON	10 NYM	11 NYM	12 D NYM
13 D NYM	14	15 *	16	17 MON	18 MON	19 MON
20 D MON	21 NYM	22 D NYM	23 CUB	24 D CUB	25 FLA	26 FLA
27 D FLA	28	29 LA	30 LA	31 LA		

August

SUN	MON	TUE	WED	THU	FRI	SAT
					1 SD	2 SD
3 D SD	4 D SD	5 COL	6 COL	7 D COL	8 SF	9 D SF
10 D SF	11	12 MIL	13 MIL	14 MIL	15 STL	16 STL
17 D STL	18	19 MIL	20 MIL	21 D MIL	22 STL	23 D STL
24 D STL	25 MON	26 MON	27 MON	28 D MON	29 NYM	30 NYM
31 D NYM						

September

SUN	MON	TUE	WED	THU	FRI	SAT
	1	2 MON	3 D MON	4 NYM	5 NYM	6 NYM
7 D NYM	8 ATL	9 ATL	10 ATL	11 ATL	12 PIT	13 PIT
14 D PIT	15	16 FLA	17 FLA	18 FLA	19 CIN	20 CIN
21 D CIN	22	23 FLA	24 FLA	25 FLA	26 ATL	27 D ATL
28 D ATL						

FRONT-OFFICE DIRECTORY

General partner, president and chief executive officer .... David Montgomery
Chairman .... Bill Giles
Senior vice president, CFO .... Jerry Clothier
Vice president & general manager .... Ed Wade
Vice president, public relations .... Larry Shenk
Vice president, ticket operations .... Richard Deats
Vice president, advertising sales .... David Buck
Vice president, general counsel and secretary .... Bill Webb
Vice president, operations and administration .... Michael Stiles
Assistant general manager .... Ruben Amaro Jr.
Assistant general manager, scouting & player development .... Mike Arbuckle
Chief communications officer, new ballpark .... Sharon Swainson
Director, business development .... Joe Giles
Director, baseball administration .... Susan Ingersoll
Director, minor league operations .... Steve Noworyta
Controller .... John Fusco
Director, information systems .... Brian Lamoreaux
Director, media relations .... Leigh Tobin
Director, community relations .... Gene Dias
Director, events .... Kurt Funk
Director, entertainment .... Chris Long
Director, broadcasting & video services .... Rory McNeil
Director, ticket department .... Dan Goroff
Director, sales .... John Weber
Director, group sales .... Kathy Killian
Director, facility management .... Mike DiMuzio
Director, event operations .... Eric Tobin

MINOR LEAGUE AFFILIATES

Class	Team	League	Manager
AAA	Scranton/Wilkes-Barre	International	Marc Bombard
AA	Reading	Eastern	Greg Legg
A	Clearwater	Florida State	Roly de Armas
A	Lakewood	South Atlantic	Buddy Biancalana
A	Batavia	New York-Pennsylvania	To be announced
Rookie	Gulf Coast Phillies	Gulf Coast	Ruben Amaro Sr.

BROADCAST INFORMATION

Radio: WPEN 950 AM.
TV: UPN (Channel 57).
Cable TV: Comcast SportsNet.

SPRING TRAINING

Ballpark (city): Jack Russell Memorial Stadium (Clearwater, Fla.).
Ticket information: 215-463-1000, 727-442-8496.

ASSISTANCE STAFF

Club physician
Dr. Michael Ciccotti

Club trainers
Jeff Cooper   Mark Andersen

Mgr., equipment and team travel
Frank Coppenbarger

Manager, visiting clubhouse
Kevin Steinhour

Director, scouting
Marti Wolever

Coordinator, scouting
Jim Fregosi, Jr.   Mike Ledna

Director, Florida operations
John Timberlake

Director, Latin American operations
Sal Artiaga

Director, Major League scouts
Gordon Lakey

Major League scout
Jimmy Stewart

Advance scout, Major Leagues
Hank King

Coordinator, professional coverage
Ron Hansen

Professional coverage
Sonny Bowers, Dean Jongewaard, Larry Rojas, Del Unser

Regional supervisors
Dean Decillis, Brian Kohlscheen, Bill Moore

Area supervisors
Sal Agostinelli, Therron Brockish, Darrell Connor, Tim Kissner, Jerry Lafferty, Chip Lawrence, Matt Lundin, Miguel Machado, Paul Murphy, Dave Owen, Scott Ramsay, Gene Schall, Paul Scott, Mike Stauffer, Bob Szymkowski, Roy Tanner

International supervisor
Sal Agostinelli

International supervisor
Wil Tejada, Tomas Herrera, Jesus Mendez, Allan Lewis

BALLPARK INFORMATION

Ballpark (capacity, surface)
Veterans Stadium (62,418, artificial)

Address
P.O. Box 7575
Philadelphia, PA 19101

Official website
www.phillies.com

Business phone
215-463-6000

Ticket information
215-463-1000

Ticket prices
$28 (field box)
$24 (sections 201, 258-273, terrace box)
$22 (loge box)
$16 (reserved, 600 level)
$10 (reserved, 700 level, adult gen. admission)
$6 (children's general admission)

Field dimensions (from home plate)
To left field at foul line, 330 feet
To center field, 408 feet
To right field at foul line, 330 feet

First game played
April 10, 1971 (Phillies 4, Expos 1)

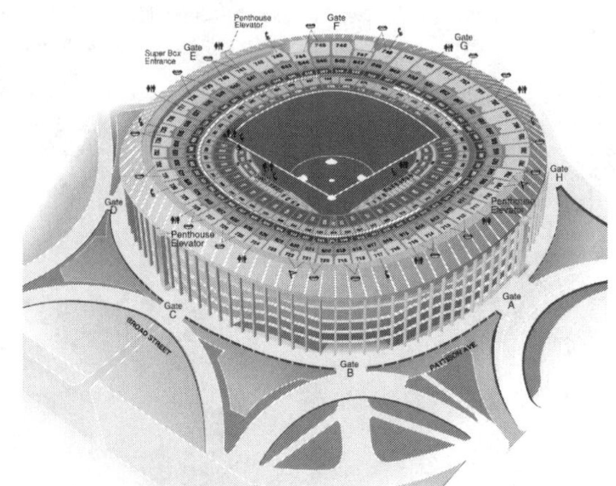

Follow the Phillies all season at: www.sportingnews.com/baseball/teams/phillies/

PHILLIES SPRING ROSTER

No.	PITCHERS	B/T	Ht./Wt.	Born	2002 clubs	Projection
62	Baisley, Brad	R/R	6-9/205	8-24-79	Reading	Tall righty has yet to stay healthy in the last four seasons.
48	Coggin, Dave	R/R	6-4/205	10-30-76	Philadelphia	Phillies think he's better suited to relief pitching as opposed to starting.
37	Cormier, Rheal	L/L	5-10/187	4-23-67	Philadelphia	He was hit hard all season long, he needs to show he can still produce.
56	Duckworth, Brandon	R/R	6-2/185	1-23-76	Philadelphia	Should fare better in his second full season in rotation.
	Hancock, Josh	R/R	6-3/217	4-11-78	Trenton, Pawtucket, Boston	Acquired for Jeremy Giambi, Hancock could be ready for rotation by midseason.
28	Junge, Eric	R/R	6-5/215	1-5-77	Scranton/Wilkes-Barre, Phila.	Pitched well in his four games with Phillies, might be in line for bullpen job.
	Madson, Ryan	L/R	6-6/180	8-28-80	Reading	Led Eastern League with 16 wins last season, likely to spend '03 in Class AAA.
54	Mercado, Hector	L/L	6-3/235	4-29-74	Scranton/Wilkes-Barre, Phila.	Brings depth to the Phillies bullpen, had 40 strikeouts in 39 innings.
49	Mesa, Jose	R/R	6-3/225	5-22-66	Philadelphia	Had 45 saves last season, gives Phils some stability in late innings.
34	Millwood, Kevin	R/R	6-4/220	12-24-74	Atlanta	Rebounded from dreadful 2001, with 18 and a 3.24 ERA.
41	Myers, Brett	R/R	6-4/215	8-17-80	Scranton/Wilkes-Barre, Phila.	Future staff ace is well on his way to being No. 1 starter.
44	Padilla, Vicente	R/R	6-2/200	9-27-77	Philadelphia	Everyone thought he'd be good, no one thought he'd be this good.
	Perez, Franklin	R/R	6-2/175	6-10-81	Reading	Can start or relieve, will spend a year in Class AAA.
19	Plesac, Dan	L/L	6-5/217	2-4-62	Toronto, Philadelphia	Gives team a solid lefthanded option out of bullpen.
35	Roa, Joe	R/R	6-1/194	10-11-71	Scranton/Wilkes-Barre, Phila.	Veteran went undefeated in minors, won four with 4.04 ERA in Philly.
67	Serrano, Elio	R/R	6-3/215	12-4-78	Scranton/Wilkes-Barre	Long reliever posted a 2.92 ERA in 71 innings in Class AAA.
52	Silva, Carlos	R/R	6-4/225	4-23-79	Philadelphia, Reading	Can contribute a lot of innings out of the bullpen.
	Smith, Bud	L/L	6-0/170	10-23-79	Mem., St.L., Scranton/W.-B.	Part of Scott Rolen deal, Phils are hoping he can round back into form.
	Wedel, Jeremy	R/R	6-0/195	11-27-76	Scranton/Wilkes-Barre	Won seven games, saved one in 43 appearances in Class AAA.
99	Wendell, Turk	L/R	6-2/205	5-19-67	DID NOT PLAY	Coming back from injury, he'll give Phillies another veteran option in bullpen.
43	Wolf, Randy	L/L	6-0/194	8-22-76	Clearwater, Philadelphia	Underrated, won 11 games with a 3.20 ERA last season.

No.	CATCHERS	B/T	Ht./Wt.	Born	2002 clubs	Projection
24	Lieberthal, Mike	R/R	6-0/190	1-18-72	Philadelphia	Came back from knee surgery to play 129 games. Phils hope he can stay healthy.
7	Pratt, Todd	R/R	6-3/230	2-9-67	Philadelphia	Provides a solid option at catcher when Lieberthal needs a day off.

No.	INFIELDERS	B/T	Ht./Wt.	Born	2002 clubs	Projection
28	Bell, David	R/R	5-10/195	9-14-72	San Francisco	He's not flashy, but he'll fill in at third nicely for Phillies.
	Houston, Tyler	L/R	6-1/218	1-17-71	Milwaukee, Los Angeles	It's unclear where he'll play, but he can still hit.
65	Machado, Anderson	B/R	5-11/165	1-25-81	Reading	Hit .251 with 40 steals in first full season in Class AA.
9	Perez, Tomas	B/R	5-11/177	12-29-73	Reading, Philadelphia	Will get plenty of at-bats as utility man, can play any infield position.
23	Polanco, Placido	R/R	5-10/168	10-10-75	St. Louis, Philadelphia	Hit .296 with Phillies, he likely becomes the everyday second baseman.
34	Punto, Nick	B/R	5-9/170	11-8-77	Phila., Scranton/Wilkes-Barre	Another middle infield prospect with speed, Phillies have a logjam.
	Richardson, Juan	R/R	6-1/175	1-10-81	Clearwater	Power hitting third baseman slugged 18 homers in Florida State League.
11	Rollins, Jimmy	B/R	5-8/165	11-27-78	Philadelphia	Batting average slipped a bit, but he still led league with 10 triples.
25	Thome, Jim	L/R	6-4/220	8-27-70	Cleveland	Led A.L. in walks, Phils are hoping he doesn't take long to adjust to N.L. pitching.
	Utley, Chase	L/R	6-1/185	12-17-78	Scranton/Wilkes-Barre	In line for job at second or third, whichever Phils need him at.

No.	OUTFIELDERS	B/T	Ht./Wt.	Born	2002 clubs	Projection
53	Abreu, Bobby	L/R	6-0/195	3-11-74	Philadelphia	50 doubles, 20 homers and 31 steals. Phils love his production.
5	Burrell, Pat	R/R	6-4/222	10-10-76	Philadelphia	Posted career highs in homers, RBIs and batting average. He's still getting better.
29	Byrd, Marlon	R/R	6-0/225	8-30-77	Scranton/Wilkes-Barre, Phila.	Starting job in center field is his to lose.
33	Ledee, Ricky	L/L	6-1/190	11-22-73	Philadelphia	Found job as fourth outfielder, only hit .227 though.
22	Michaels, Jason	R/R	6-0/204	5-4-76	Scranton/Wilkes-Barre, Phila.	Gives the team another option in outfield. Hit .267 last season.
66	Padilla, Jorge	R/R	6-2/200	8-11-79	Reading	Still needs a year or two in the minors before he's ready.
12	Valent, Eric	L/L	6-0/191	4-4-77	Scranton/Wilkes-Barre, Phila.	Hasn't been able to put it all together at major league level yet.

THE COACHING STAFF

Larry Bowa, manager.
Greg Gross, hitting coach.
Ramon Henderson, bullpen coach.
Joe Kerrigan, pitching coach.
Tony Scott, first base coach.
Gary Varsho, bench coach.
John Vukovich, third base coach.

THE TOP NEWCOMERS

Kevin Millwood: The Braves traded Millwood after a successful 2002 season and only received a prospect catcher. Phillies will be reaping the rewards with Millwood all season.

David Bell: Helped lead San Francisco to the World Series last year, he'll provide steady play, a decent bat and veteran leadership.

Jim Thome: Hit 52 home runs last season with Cleveland. Phillies are hoping his back doesn't cause him to miss any time.

THE TOP PROSPECTS

Ryan Madson: Went 16-4 in 26 starts in the Eastern League. And while he didn't strike out many batters, he knows how to pitch and get hitters out. More importantly, he doesn't walk many batters either.

Anderson Machado: Showed decent power in Class AA with 12 homers and 24 doubles. He stole 40 bases but will have to cut down on his error total if he's going to make it as a shortstop in the majors.

Chase Utley: He led the International League with 39 doubles. Chances are he'll be moving to second base from third this season, which means he'll spend more time at Class AAA while Polanco patrols second for the Phillies.

PITTSBURGH PIRATES

NATIONAL LEAGUE CENTRAL DIVISION

2003 SEASON

Pirates Schedule

Home games shaded; D—Day game (games starting before 5 p.m.); *—All-Star Game at Comiskey Park, Chicago. Subject to changes.

March/April

SUN	MON	TUE	WED	THU	FRI	SAT
30	31 D CIN	1	2 CIN	3 D CIN	4 D PHI	5 D PHI
6 D PHI	7 MIL	8	9 MIL	10 D MIL	11 D CUB	12 D CUB
13 D CUB	14	15 NYM	16 NYM	17 NYM	18 CUB	19 CUB
20 D CUB	21	22 SF	23 SF	24 D SF	25 LA	26 LA
27 D LA	28	29 SD	30 SD			

May

SUN	MON	TUE	WED	THU	FRI	SAT
				1 D SD	2 LA	3 LA
4 D LA	5 HOU	6 HOU	7 HOU	8 D HOU	9 ARI	10 ARI
11 D ARI	12 HOU	13 HOU	14 HOU	15 D HOU	16 ARI	17 ARI
18 D ARI	19	20 CUB	21 CUB	22 CUB	23 STL	24 STL
25 D STL	26 D CUB	27 CUB	28 D CUB	29	30 STL	31 D STL

June

SUN	MON	TUE	WED	THU	FRI	SAT
1 D STL	2	3 BOS	4 BOS	5 BOS	6 ATL	7 ATL
8 D ATL	9	10 TOR	11 TOR	12 TOR	13 TB	14 TB
15 D TB	16	17 MON	18 MON	19 D MON	20 CLE	21 CLE
22 D CLE	23 MON	24 D MON	25 D MON	26	27 COL	28 COL
29 D COL	30					

July

SUN	MON	TUE	WED	THU	FRI	SAT
		1 CIN	2 CIN	3 CIN	4 D HOU	5 HOU
6 D HOU	7 MIL	8 MIL	9 MIL	10 D MIL	11 HOU	12 HOU
13 D HOU	14	15 *	16	17 MIL	18 MIL	19 MIL
20 D MIL	21 HOU	22 HOU	23 CIN	24 D CIN	25 STL	26 D STL
27 D STL	28 D STL	29 SD	30 SD	31 D SD		

August

SUN	MON	TUE	WED	THU	FRI	SAT
					1 COL	2 COL
3 D COL	4	5 SF	6 SF	7 D SF	8 COL	9 COL
10 D COL	11 STL	12 STL	13 STL	14 D STL	15 MIL	16 D MIL
17 D MIL	18	19 STL	20 STL	21 STL	22 MIL	23 MIL
24 D MIL	25	26 FLA	27 FLA	28 FLA	29 ATL	30 D ATL
31 D ATL						

September

SUN	MON	TUE	WED	THU	FRI	SAT
	1	2 FLA	3 FLA	4 D FLA	5 ATL	6 ATL
7 D ATL	8 CIN	9 CIN	10 CIN	11 D CIN	12 PHI	13 PHI
14 D PHI	15 CIN	16 CIN	17 CIN	18 CIN	19 CUB	20 CUB
21 D CUB	22	23 NYM	24 NYM	25 NYM	26 D CUB	27 D CUB
28 D CUB						

FRONT-OFFICE DIRECTORY

General partner .... Kevin S. McClatchy
Board of directors .... William B. Allen, Donald Beaver, Frank Brenner, Chip Ganassi, Kevin S. McClatchy, Mayor Tom Murphy, G. Ogden Nutting
Chief operating officer .... Dick Freeman
Senior vice president and general manager .... Dave Littlefield
Vice president and baseball legal counsel .... Larry Silverman
Assistant general manager/player personnel .... Roy Smith
Special assistants to the general manager .... Jesse Flores, Jax Robertson, Bill Singer, Pete Vuckovich
Vice president, finance and administration .... Jim Plake
Vice president, human resources .... To be announced
Vice president, broadcasting and marketing .... Vic Gregovits
Vice president, communications and ballpark development .... Patty Paytas
Vice president, operations .... Dennis DaPra
Vice president, corporate projects .... Nellie Briles
Controller .... David Bowman
Director of office services .... Patti Mistick
Traveling secretary .... Greg Johnson
Coordinator of baseball operations .... Jon Mercurio
Director of corporate sales .... Mike Berry
Director of Florida baseball operations .... Mike Kennedy
Director of community development .... Winifred Torbert
Director of information systems .... Terry Zeigler
Director of media relations .... Jim Trdinich
Director of merchandising .... Joe Billetdeaux
Director of operations .... Chris Hunter
Director of player development .... Brian Graham
Director of community and player relations .... Kathy Guy
Director of promotions and advertising .... Rick Orienza
Director of sales .... Jim Alexander
Director of security & contract services .... Jeff Podobnik
Director of ticket operations .... To be announced
Director of guest relations .... Brenda Thompson

MINOR LEAGUE AFFILIATES

Class	Team	League	Manager
AAA	Nashville	Pacific Coast	Trent Jewett
AA	Altoona	Eastern	Dale Sveum
A	Lynchburg	Carolina	Dave Clark
A	Hickory	South Atlantic	Tony Beasley
A	Williamsport	New York-Pennsylvania	Andy Stewart
Rookie	Gulf Coast Pirates	Gulf Coast	Woody Huyke

ASSISTANCE STAFF

Head trainer
Brad Henderson

Assistant trainers
Mark Rogow, Mike Sandoval

Equipment manager
Roger Wilson

Director of scouting
Ed Creech

Regional scouting supervisors
John Green, Jim Lester, Scott Littlefield, Mark McKnight

Major league advance scout
Chris Lein

Professional scout
Doug Strange

Latin America coordinator
Ramon Perez

Area supervisors

Tom Barnard	Kevin Clouser
Joe Ferrone	Steve Fleming
Mark Germann	Duane Gustavson
Mike Kendall	Jaron Madison
Jack Powell	Jim Rough
Everett Russell	Scott Sharp
Rob Sidwell	Charlie Sullivan
Ted Williams	

BROADCAST INFORMATION

Radio: KDKA-AM (1020).
Cable TV: Fox Sports Pittsburgh.

SPRING TRAINING

Ballpark (city): McKechnie Field (Bradenton, Fla.).
Ticket information: 941-748-4610.

BALLPARK INFORMATION

Ballpark (capacity, surface)
PNC Park (37,898, grass)

Address
PNC Park at North Shore
115 Federal Street
Pittsburgh, PA 15212

Official website
www.pittsburghpirates.com

Business phone
412-323-5000

Ticket information
800-BUY-BUCS

Ticket prices
$35 (dugout boxes)
$27 (IF boxes)
$26 (baseline boxes)
$24 (LF/RF boxes)
$18 (OF reserved)
$16 (deck seating, grandstand)
$14 (bleachers)
$11 (LF/RF grandstand)
$9 (LF terrace)

Field dimensions (from home plate)
To left field at foul line, 325 feet
To center field, 399 feet
To right field at foul line, 320 feet

First game played
April 9, 2001 (Reds 8, Pirates 2)

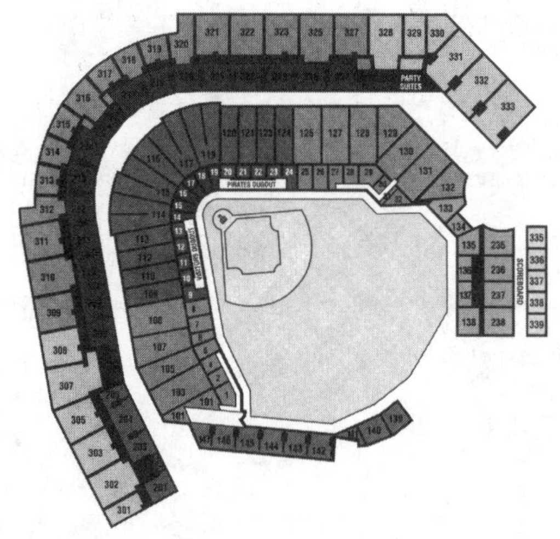

Follow the Pirates all season at: www.sportingnews.com/baseball/teams/pirates/

PIRATES SPRING ROSTER

o.	PITCHERS	B/T	Ht./Wt.	Born	2002 clubs	Projection
9	Arroyo, Bronson	R/R	6-5/194	2-24-77	Nashville, Pittsburgh	Appears he's ready for a spot in the rotation.
3	Beimel, Joe	L/L	6-3/215	4-19-77	Pittsburgh	Was solid in relief role last season. Needs to work on his control.
4	Benson, Kris	R/R	6-4/200	11-7-74	Nashville, Altoona, Pittsburgh	First season back from elbow surgery was a good one.
1	Boehringer, Brian	B/R	6-2/190	1-8-70	Pittsburgh	Workhorse pitched in 70 games for team last season.
	Bradley, Bobby	R/R	6-1/164	12-15-80	DID NOT PLAY	Former first-round pick was hurt for entire season. Pirates will be careful with him.
7	Fogg, Josh	R/R	6-0/202	12-13-76	Pittsburgh	Went 12-12 in first full major league season.
1	Gonzalez, Mike	R/L	6-2/215	5-23-78	Gulf Coast Pirates, Altoona	Strikeout pitcher is likely a year away from joining the Pirates.
	Guerrier, Matt	R/R	6-3/185	8-2-78	Nashville	Could be in line for a rotation spot this year, if not he'll be back in Class AAA.
9	Herges, Matt	L/R	6-0/200	4-1-70	Montreal	He'll give the Pirates plenty of late inning relief in close games.
7	Lincoln, Mike	R/R	6-2/203	4-10-75	Pittsburgh, Nashville	Long reliever posted a 3.11 ERA.
	Mann, Jim	R/R	6-3/225	11-17-74	New Orleans, Hou., Round Rock	Brought in to provide bullpen depth, he might end up in Class AAA.
6	Meadows, Brian	R/R	6-4/220	11-21-75	Nashville, Pittsburgh	Only won once in 11 starts with Pirates, but his numbers say he pitched better.
9	Reyes, Al	R/R	6-1/206	4-10-71	Nashville, Pittsburgh	Showed team he could be reliable out of the bullpen.
5	Sanchez, Duaner	R/R	6-0/190	10-14-79	El Paso, Ari., Tuc., Nash., Pitts.	Has potential to be closer in a few years. Likely to spend 2003 in Class AAA.
7	Sauerbeck, Scott	R/L	6-3/197	11-9-71	Pittsburgh	Is the Pirates top lefthanded option out of the bullpen.
1	Torres, Salomon	R/R	5-11/165	3-11-72	Nashville, Pittsburgh	He'll get every chance to prove he can be a solid starter for Pirates this year.
2	Vogelsong, Ryan	R/R	6-3/195	7-22-77	Lynchburg, Altoona	Injuries limited him to 12 games in 2002.
2	Wells, Kip	R/R	6-3/205	4-21-77	Pittsburgh	Won 12 games and posted a 3.58 ERA, this year should be even better.
8	Williams, David	L/L	6-2/213	3-12-79	Pittsburgh	Injuries limited him to nine starts, team hopes he can contribute more this year.
3	Williams, Mike	R/R	6-2/200	7-29-68	Pittsburgh	Had a career year with 46 saves and a 2.93 ERA.

o.	CATCHERS	B/T	Ht./Wt.	Born	2002 clubs	Projection
1	Cota, Humberto	R/R	6-0/205	2-7-79	Nashville, Pittsburgh	Might be the backup catcher to Kendall this year. Hit .267 in Class AAA.
	Doumit, Ryan	B/R	6-0/180	4-3-81	Hickory	Good hitting catcher needs to work on his defense, he committed seven errors.
25	House, J.R.	R/R	6-1/202	11-11-79	Altoona, Gulf Coast Pirates	Injuries slowed this power hitting prospect's development last season.
18	Kendall, Jason	R/R	6-0/195	6-26-74	Pittsburgh	Power numbers dipped and team would like to see him move to outfield.

o.	INFIELDERS	B/T	Ht./Wt.	Born	2002 clubs	Projection
	Castillo, Jose	R/R	5-11/185	3-19-81	Lynchburg	Power-hitting shortstop slugged 16 homers, hit .300 in Class A.
2	Meares, Pat	R/R	6-0/187	9-6-68	DID NOT PLAY	He's been injured in three of his four seasons with Pirates.
10	Nunez, Abraham	B/R	5-11/190	3-16-76	Pittsburgh, Nashville	Switch hitting utility man, needs to hit better in order to stick with team.
16	Ramirez, Aramis	R/R	6-1/211	6-25-78	Pittsburgh	Had significant drops in each offensive category. Team hopes he can rebound.
3	Reese, Pokey	R/R	5-11/188	6-10-73	Pittsburgh	Provides solid defense at second, Pirates think offense will come back around.
	Rivera, Carlos	L/L	5-11/230	6-10-78	Altoona	First baseman of the future slugged 22 homers in Class AA.
	Simon, Randall	L/L	6-0/230	5-26-75	Detroit	Hit .301 with Tigers last season, only struck out 30 times. First base job is his.
12	Wilson, Jack	R/R	6-0/195	12-29-77	Pittsburgh	Improved offense in second full season, team loves his defense.
29	Young, Kevin	R/R	6-3/225	6-16-69	Pittsburgh	Will be a veteran leader on a young team, likely to play in spot duty at first.
	Young, Walter	L/R	6-5/295	2-18-80	Hickory	Hit .333 with 25 homers, his defense still needs some work.

o.	OUTFIELDERS	B/T	Ht./Wt.	Born	2002 clubs	Projection
56	Alvarez, Tony	R/R	6-1/200	5-10-79	Altoona, Pittsburgh	Could win job with solid spring, but he could use a year in Class AAA.
26	Davis, J.J.	R/R	6-5/250	10-25-78	Altoona, Pittsburgh	Power-hitting outfielder needs one more year of seasoning.
24	Giles, Brian	L/L	5-10/202	1-20-71	Pittsburgh	Walked 135 times last season. Numbers have been steady for last four seasons.
38	Hyzdu, Adam	R/R	6-2/220	12-6-71	Nashville, Pittsburgh	Pirates are waiting for his bat to come around. Might happen this season.
59	Mackowiak, Rob	L/R	5-10/190	6-20-76	Pittsburgh	Could see action in 100 games again this season.
36	Wilson, Craig	R/R	6-2/225	11-30-76	Pittsburgh	Average took a dip last season, can fill in at first or in outfield.

THE COACHING STAFF

loyd McClendon, manager.

lvaro Espinoza, coach.

usty Kuntz, first base coach.

ete Mackanin, bench coach.

erald Perry, hitting coach.

ohn Russell, third base coach.

ruce Tanner, bullpen coach.

pin Williams, pitching coach.

THE TOP NEWCOMERS

Randall Simon: While his OBP won't impress you (.320), he only struck out 30 times while walking 13. He still managed to hit .301 and slug 19 homers while playing half of his games in Comerica Park.

THE TOP PROSPECTS

Jose Castillo: The Pirates don't have many middle infield prospects in the minors right now. But Castillo more than makes up for that. He hits for power, average and was able to steal 27 bases ast season. His defense at short should improve a little, if not, a move to second base isn't out of the question.

Carlos Rivera: Could be ready to take over first base as soon as 2004. After hitting .302 with 22 homers in Class AA, he's likely headed to Class AAA for 2003.

Walter Young: Only played 77 of 132 games at first in Class A, which means he'll have to cut down on his 15 errors at first before he'll make it in the majors. Still, the Pirates will keep him on the radar screen after hitting .333 in 2002.

St. Louis Cardinals

National League Central Division

2003 SEASON

Cardinals Schedule

Home games shaded; D—Day game (games starting before 5 p.m.); *—All-Star Game at Comiskey Park, Chicago. Subject to changes.

March/April

SUN	MON	TUE	WED	THU	FRI	SAT
30	31 D MIL	1	2 MIL	3 D MIL	4 HOU	5 D HOU
6 D HOU	7	8 COL	9 COL	10 D COL	11 HOU	12 HOU
13 D HOU	14 MIL	15 MIL	16 D MIL	17	18 ARI	19 D ARI
20 D ARI	21	22 ATL	23 ATL	24 ATL	25 FLA	26 FLA
27 D FLA	28	29 NYM	30 NYM			

May

SUN	MON	TUE	WED	THU	FRI	SAT
				1 D NYM	2 MON	3 D MON
4 D MON	5 CIN	6 CIN	7 CIN	8 D CIN	9 D CUB	10 D CUB
11 D CUB	12	13 CIN	14 CIN	15 D CIN	16 CUB	17 D CUB
18 D CUB	19 D CUB	20 HOU	21 HOU	22 HOU	23 PIT	24 PIT
25 D PIT	26 D HOU	27 HOU	28 HOU	29	30 PIT	31 D PIT

June

SUN	MON	TUE	WED	THU	FRI	SAT
1 D PIT	2	3 TOR	4 TOR	5 TOR	6 BAL	7 D BAL
8 D BAL	9	10 BOS	11 BOS	12 BOS	13 NYY	14 D NYY
15 D NYY	16 MIL	17 MIL	18 MIL	19 D MIL	20 KC	21 KC
22 D KC	23	24 CIN	25 CIN	26 CIN	27 KC	28 KC
29 D KC	30 SF					

July

SUN	MON	TUE	WED	THU	FRI	SAT
		1 SF	2 SF	3 D SF	4 D CUB	5 D CUB
6 D CUB	7 SF	8 D SF	9 LA	10 LA	11 SD	12 SD
13 D SD	14	15 *	16	17 LA	18 LA	19 D LA
20 LA	21 SD	22 SD	23 D SD	24	25 PIT	26 D PIT
27 D PIT	28 D PIT	29 MON	30 MON	31 MON		

August

SUN	MON	TUE	WED	THU	FRI	SAT
					1 NYM	2 D NYM
3 D NYM	4	5 FLA	6 FLA	7 FLA	8 ATL	9 D ATL
10 D ATL	11 PIT	12 PIT	13 PIT	14 D PIT	15 PHI	16 PHI
17 D PHI	18	19 PIT	20 PIT	21 PIT	22 PHI	23 D PHI
24 D PHI	25	26 CUB	27 CUB	28 CUB	29 CIN	30 CIN
31 D CIN						

September

SUN	MON	TUE	WED	THU	FRI	SAT
	1 D CUB	2 CUB	3 D CUB	4 D CUB	5 CIN	6 CIN
7 D CIN	8	9 COL	10 COL	11 D COL	12 HOU	13 HOU
14 D HOU	15 MIL	16 MIL	17 MIL	18 MIL	19 HOU	20 D HOU
21 D HOU	22	23 MIL	24 MIL	25	26 ARI	27 D ARI
28 D ARI						

FRONT-OFFICE DIRECTORY

Chairman of the board/general partner .... William O. DeWitt Jr.
Vice chairman .... Frederick O. Hanser
Secretary-treasurer .... Andrew N. Baur
President .... Mark C. Lamping
Vice president, general manager .... Walt Jocketty
Admin. assistant to the president .... Julie Laningham
Senior executive assistant to vice president, general manager .... Judy Carpenter-Barada
Vice president/player personnel .... Jerry Walker
Vice president, special assistant to the general manager .... Bob Gebhard
Special assistant to the general manager .... Mike Jorgensen
Senior vice president, sales and marketing .... Dan Farrell
Vice president, controller .... Brad Wood
Vice president, community relations .... Marty Hendin
Vice president and group director, community outreach/ Cardinals Care .... Tim Hanser
Vice president, business development .... Bill DeWitt III
Vice president, stadium operations .... Joe Abernathy
Vice president, ticket operations .... Josie Arnold
Senior director, ticket sales .... Joe Strohm
Director, season and premium ticket sales .... Mark Murray
Director, group sales .... Michael Hall
Director, corporate sales/marketing .... Thane van Breusegen
Director, target marketing .... Ted Savage
Director, media relations .... Brian Bartow
Assistant to director, media relations .... Brad Hainje
Director, publications .... Steve Zesch
Traveling secretary .... C.J. Cherre
Director, player development .... Bruce Manno
Director, baseball operations .... John Mozeliak
Director, professional scouting .... Marteese Robinson
Director, amateur scouting .... Marty Maier
Director, minor league operations .... Scott Smulczenski
Manager, baseball information/player development .... John Vuch

MINOR LEAGUE AFFILIATES

Class	Team	League	Manager
AAA	Memphis	Pacific Coast	Tom Spencer
AA	Tennessee	Southern	Mark DeJohn
A	Palm Beach	Florida State	Tom Nieto
A	Peoria	Midwest	Joe Cunningham
A	New Jersey	New York-Pennsylvania	Tommy Shields
Rookie	Johnson City	Appalachian	Danny Sheaffer

BROADCAST INFORMATION

Radio: KMOX-AM (1120).
TV: KPLR-TV (Channel 11).
Cable TV: Fox Sports Midwest.

SPRING TRAINING

Ballpark (city): Roger Dean Stadium (Jupiter, Fla.).
Ticket information: 561-966-3309.

ASSISTANCE STAFF

Major league trainer
Barry Weinberg

Assistant major league trainer
Mark O'Neal

Equipment manager
Rip Rowan

Assistant equipment manager
Buddy Bates

Video coordinator
Chad Blair

Special assignment scouts
Bing Devine, Jim Leyland, Joe Sparks, Mike Squires

Special assistant, baseball operations
Chuck Fick

Special instructor
Boots Day

Professional scouts
Clark Crist, Marty Keough, Jeff Scott

Cross-checkers
Fred McAlister, Mike Roberts, Roger Smith

Scouts
Randy Benson, Ben Galante, Steve Gossett, Manny Guerra, Nakia Hill, Dave Karaff, Scott Melvin, Scott Nichols, Jay North, Dan Ontiveros, Joe Rigoli, Tommy Shields, Steve Turco, Dane Walker

International scouts
Jorge Brito, Domingo Carrasquel, Bobby Diaz

BALLPARK INFORMATION

Ballpark (capacity, surface)
Busch Stadium (50,354, grass)
Address
250 Stadium Plaza
St. Louis, MO 63102
Official website
www.stlcardinals.com
Business phone
314-421-3060
Ticket information
314-421-2400
Ticket prices
$43 (field boxes-infield), $40 (loge boxes-infield)
$35 (field boxes-outfield), $31 (loge boxes-outfield)
$29 (loge reserved-infield), $25 (terrace boxes-infield)
$23 (loge reserved-outfield), $22 (terrace boxes-outfield)
$18 (terrace reserved-adults), $12 (bleachers)
$9 (upper terrace-outfield-adults, terrace reserved-children)
$5 (upper terrace reserved-children)
Field dimensions (from home plate)
To left field at foul line, 330 feet
To center field, 402 feet
To right field at foul line, 330 feet
First game played
May 12, 1966 (Cardinals 4, Braves 3)

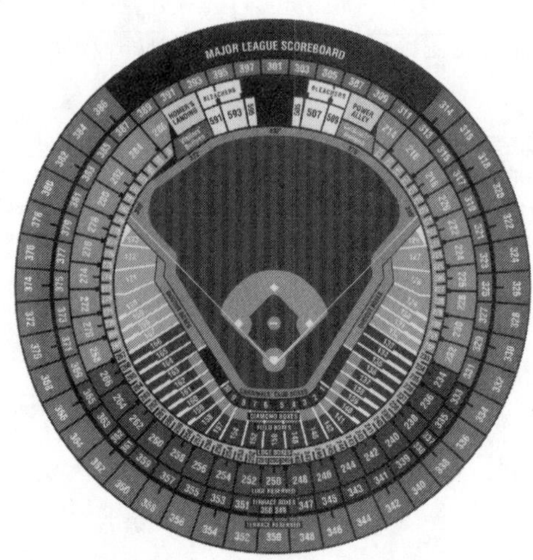

Follow the Cardinals all season at: www.sportingnews.com/baseball/teams/cardinals/

CARDINALS SPRING ROSTER

No.	PITCHERS	B/T	Ht./Wt.	Born	2002 clubs	Projection
66	Ankiel, Rick	L/L	6-1/210	7-19-79	DID NOT PLAY	Club is holding out hope he can pitch out of the bullpen this year.
70	Caple, Chance	R/R	6-6/215	8-9-78	Peoria	Struggling to rebound from injuries that have sidelined him the last two seasons.
	Carpenter, Chris	R/R	6-6/215	4-27-75	Toronto, Tennessee, Syracuse	Out until mid-season recovering from shoulder surgery, team willing to wait.
54	Crudale, Mike	R/R	6-0/205	1-3-77	Memphis, St. Louis	Had a sterling 1.88 ERA out of bullpen last season.
52	Duff, Matt	R/R	6-1/192	10-6-74	Poto., N.Haven, St.L., Memphis	Came out of nowhere last season, Cards think he can contribute to bullpen soon.
13	Fassero, Jeff	L/L	6-1/200	1-5-63	Chicago N.L., St. Louis	Gives the team another lefthanded option out of the pen.
	Hamilton, Joey	R/R	6-4/240	9-9-70	Cincinnati, Louisville	He will replace Dave Veres in the bullpen, could start if club needs him to.
	Hermanson, Dustin	R/R	6-2/200	12-21-72	Boston, Pawtucket, GC Red Sox	Team is hoping he can stay healthy and pitch in rotation.
44	Isringhausen, Jason	R/R	6-3/230	9-7-72	St. Louis	Team is worried about his shoulder, still had 32 saves last season.
73	Journell, Jimmy	R/R	6-4/205	12-29-77	New Haven, Memphis	Could make the rotation this year.
49	Kline, Steve	B/L	6-1/215	8-22-72	St. Louis, Peoria, New Haven	Can close in a pinch, can be used almost every day.
71	Lambert, Jeremy	R/R	6-1/195	1-10-79	New Haven	Potential closer struggled through injuries last season.
79	Layfield, Scotty	R/R	6-2/205	9-13-76	New Haven	Had 24 saves in Class AA. Likely ticketed for Class AAA this year.
	Levine, Al	L/R	6-3/190	5-22-68	Anaheim, Salt Lake	Can eat a lot of innings out of the bullpen.
56	Molina, Gabe	R/R	6-1/220	5-3-75	Memphis, St. Louis	Had success in his 12 appearances last season.
35	Morris, Matt	R/R	6-5/210	8-9-74	St. Louis	Came on late in the season to nail down role as staff ace.
60	Pearce, Josh	R/R	6-3/215	8-20-77	Memphis, St. Louis	Injuries limited him to eight starts last season.
46	Simontacchi, Jason	R/R	6-2/185	11-13-73	Memphis, St. Louis	Rookie came out of nowhere to win 11 games and start 24 games.
36	Stechschulte, Gene	R/R	6-5/210	8-12-73	St. Louis, Memphis	Shoulder injury hampered him all season.
55	Stephenson, Garrett	R/R	6-5/208	1-2-72	St. Louis, Peoria, Memphis	Cards are hoping he can bounce back and find 2000 form.
40	Tomko, Brett	R/R	6-4/215	4-7-73	San Diego	Will eat a lot of innnings as club's No. 3 starter.
54	Walrond, Les	L/L	6-0/195	11-7-76	New Haven, Memphis	Starter needs one more year in Class AAA.
19	Williams, Woody	R/R	6-0/195	8-19-66	St. Louis, Memphis	Ribcage injury really slowed him down in 2002, still had 2.53 ERA in 17 starts.

No.	CATCHERS	B/T	Ht./Wt.	Born	2002 clubs	Projection
22	Matheny, Mike	R/R	6-3/205	9-22-70	St. Louis	Hit better in 2002, but he's looked upon for his defense more than offense.
	Torrealba, Steve	R/R	6-0/175	2-24-78	Richmond, Atlanta	Likely to be in Class AAA, and called up if either catcher gets hurt.
	Girard, Joe	R/R	5-10/200	10-14-64	Chicago N.L.	Cardinals hope he can be a good veteran leader when Matheny isn't catching.

No.	INFIELDERS	B/T	Ht./Wt.	Born	2002 clubs	Projection
41	Cairo, Miguel	R/R	6-1/200	5-4-74	St. Louis	Hit .250 last season and is able to play any position in the field.
30	Delgado, Wilson	B/R	5-11/165	7-15-72	Memphis, St. Louis	Middle infielder is likely to spend this year in Class AAA, again.
21	Martinez, Tino	L/R	6-2/210	12-7-67	St. Louis	Team is hoping last year was just a fluke.
33	Perez, Eduardo	R/R	6-4/215	9-11-69	St. Louis	Provides some righthanded power off the bench.
5	Pujols, Albert	R/R	6-3/210	1-16-80	St. Louis	Followed 2001 campaign with another 30 homer, 100 RBI performance.
3	Renteria, Edgar	R/R	6-1/180	8-7-75	St. Louis	Hit .305, drove in 83 runs and stole 22 bases. Provides solid defense up middle.
27	Rolen, Scott	R/R	6-4/226	4-4-75	Philadelphia, St. Louis	Provides some protection for Pujols and Edmonds in lineup.
4	Vina, Fernando	L/R	5-9/174	4-16-69	St. Louis	Gold Glove defense at second, and gets on base 33% of the time.

No.	OUTFIELDERS	B/T	Ht./Wt.	Born	2002 clubs	Projection
7	Drew, J.D.	L/R	6-1/195	11-20-75	St. Louis	Cards keep waiting for a breakout season.
15	Edmonds, Jim	L/L	6-1/212	6-27-70	St. Louis	Still one of the best all-around centerfielders in the game.
26	Marrero, Eli	R/R	6-1/180	11-17-73	St. Louis	Showed enough improvement in outfield, he'll get plenty of at-bats this season.
0	Robinson, Kerry	L/L	6-0/175	10-3-73	St. Louis	Provides good speed and solid lefthanded bat off bench.
99	Taguchi, So	R/R	5-10/163	7-2-69	Memphis, St. Louis, New Haven	Could win job as defensive replacement and pinch runner.

THE COACHING STAFF

Tony La Russa, manager.

Dave Duncan, pitching coach.

Marty Mason, bullpen coach.

Dave McKay, first base coach.

Mitchell Page, hitting coach.

Joe Pettini, bench coach.

Jose Oquendo, third base coach.

THE TOP NEWCOMERS

Brett Tomko: Went 10-10 with the Padres last season and pitched over 200 innings. Cardinals are counting on him to pitch another 200 this season.

Joey Hamilton: Former starter is willing to take a spot in the bullpen. The team thinks he can handle Dave Veres old role as setup man and a guy who can pitch one or two innings if needed.

THE TOP PROSPECTS

Jimmy Journell: Still a top prospect, the team is taking time developing him in the minors. This could be the year he makes the big club as a starter.

Scotty Layfield: If for some reason Isringhausen's shoulder isn't ready for the 2003 season, the Cardinals might slip him into the closer role. He had 24 saves and a 2.35 ERA in 58 games in Class AA.

San Diego Padres

National League West Division

2003 SEASON

Padres Schedule

Home games shaded; D—Day game (games starting before 5 p.m.); *—All-Star Game at Comiskey Park, Chicago. Subject to changes.

March/April

SUN	MON	TUE	WED	THU	FRI	SAT
30	31 D SF	1 SF	2 SF	3 D LA	4 LA	5 LA
6 D LA	7 D SF	8 SF	9 D SF	10	11 COL	12 COL
13 D COL	14	15 LA	16 LA	17 LA	18 COL	19 D COL
20 D COL	21	22 CUB	23 D CUB	24 D CUB	25 CIN	26 D CIN
27 D CIN	28	29 PIT	30 PIT			

May

SUN	MON	TUE	WED	THU	FRI	SAT
				1 D PIT	2 PHI	3 PHI
4 D PHI	5	6 MON	7 MON	8 MON	9 NYM	10 D NYM
11 D NYM	12 FLA	13 FLA	14 FLA	15 D ATL	16 ATL	17 ATL
18 D ATL	19 MIL	20 MIL	21 D MIL	22	23 ARI	24 ARI
25 D ARI	26 D ARI	27 MIL	28 MIL	29 D MIL	30 ARI	31 ARI

June

SUN	MON	TUE	WED	THU	FRI	SAT
1 D ARI	2 ARI	3 DET	4 DET	5 D DET	6 MIN	7 MIN
8 D MIN	9	10 CLE	11 CLE	12 CLE	13 CWS	14 CWS
15 D CWS	16 COL	17 COL	18 COL	19 COL	20 SEA	21 SEA
22 D SEA	23 COL	24 COL	25 COL	26	27 SEA	28 SEA
29 D SEA	30					

July

SUN	MON	TUE	WED	THU	FRI	SAT
		1 LA	2 LA	3 LA	4 SF	5 SF
6 D SF	7 LA	8 LA	9 ARI	10 D ARI	11 STL	12 STL
13 D STL	14	15 *	16	17 D ARI	18 ARI	19 ARI
20 D ARI	21 STL	22 STL	23 D STL	24	25 SF	26 D SF
27 D SF	28	29 PIT	30 PIT	31 D PIT		

August

SUN	MON	TUE	WED	THU	FRI	SAT
					1 PHI	2 PHI
3 D PHI	4 D PHI	5 CUB	6 CUB	7 D CUB	8 CIN	9 CIN
10 D CIN	11	12 ATL	13 ATL	14 ATL	15 FLA	16 FLA
17 D FLA	18	19 NYM	20 NYM	21 D NYM	22 MON	23 MON
24 D MON	25 ARI	26 ARI	27 ARI	28	29 HOU	30 HOU
31 D HOU						

September

SUN	MON	TUE	WED	THU	FRI	SAT
	1	2 ARI	3 ARI	4	5 HOU	6 HOU
7 D HOU	8	9 SF	10 SF	11 SF	12 LA	13 LA
14 D LA	15 SF	16 SF	17 SF	18 D SF	19 COL	20 D COL
21 D COL	22 LA	23 LA	24 LA	25 LA	26 COL	27 COL
28 D COL						

FRONT-OFFICE DIRECTORY

Chairman .... John Moores
Vice chairman .... Bob Vizas
President and chief operating officer .... Dick Freeman
Exec. v.p., baseball operations and general manager .... Kevin Towers
Executive vice president/business operations .... Steve Violetta
Senior vice president/chief financial officer .... Fred Gerson
Vice president, community relations .... Michele Anderson
Vice president, stadium operations .... Mark Guglielmo
Vice president/development .... Erik Judson
Vice presient/senior advisor .... David Winfield
Assistant general manager .... Fred Uhlman Jr.
Executive director, merchandising .... Michael Babida
Executive director, finance .... Steve Fitch
Exec. director, human resources/admin. .... Lucy Freeman
Executive director, Friartix .... Chandra George
Executive director, new ballpark ticketing .... Dave Gilmore
Executive director, ticket sales .... Mark Tilson
Director, Padres Foundation .... Sue Botos
Director, Padres Productions .... Tom Catlin
Director, military marketing .... Captain Jack Ensch (Ret.)
Director, scouting .... Bill "Chief" Gayton
Director, stadium operations .... Ken Kawachi
Director, corporate communications .... Tim Katzman
Director, ticketing .... Jim Kiersnowski
Director, information systems .... Joe Lewis
Director, minor league operations .... Priscilla Oppenheimer
Director, team travel .... Brian Prilaman
Director, player development .... Tye Waller
Manager, baseball information .... John Dever

MINOR LEAGUE AFFILIATES

Class	Team	League	Manager
AAA	Portland	Pacific Coast	Rick Sweet
AA	Mobile	Southern	Craig Colbert
A	Lake Elsinore	California	Jeff Gardner
A	Fort Wayne	Midwest	George Hendrick
A	Eugene	Northwest	Roy Howell
Rookie	Idaho Falls	Pioneer	Carlos Lezcano

BROADCAST INFORMATION

Radio: KOGO-AM (600), KURS-AM (1040, Spanish).
TV: KUSI (Channel 9/51).
Cable TV: Channel 4 Padres.

SPRING TRAINING

Ballpark (city): Peoria Stadium (Peoria, Ariz.).
Ticket information: 623-878-4337, 800-409-1511.

ASSISTANCE STAFF

Trainer
Todd Hutcheson

Assistant trainer
Jim Daniel

Strength and conditioning coordinator
Bill Henry

Club physicians
Cliff Colwell, Jan Fronek, Paul Hirshman, Blaine Phillips

Major league scouts
Ken Bracey, Ted Simmons, Brad Sloan, Randy Smith

Director of international scouting
Bill Clark

National cross-checker
Jay Darnell

Regional cross-checkers
Tim McWilliam, Scott Trcka

Professional scouts
Steve Demeter, Jimmy Dreyer, Gail Henley, Ben McLure, Tom McNamara, Van Smith

Full-time scouts
Joe Bochy, Rich Bordi, Jim Bretz, Lane Decker, Bob Filotei, Chris Gwynn, Dan Huston, Don "Trip" Keister, Jason McLeod, Billy Merkel, Mike Rickard, Jeff Stewart, Gene Thompson, Scott Trcka, Mark Wasinger, Jake Wilson

BALLPARK INFORMATION

Ballpark (capacity, surface)
Qualcomm Stadium (63,890, grass)
Address
P.O. Box 2000
San Diego, CA 92112-2000
Official website
www.padres.com
Business phone
619-881-6500
Ticket information
888-697-2373
Ticket prices
$32 (field level/IF), $28 (club level/IF)
$27 (field level/OF, plaza level/IF)
$24 (club level/OF, plaza level/OF, loge level/IF)
$17 (loge level/OF), $15 (press level)
$10 (grandstand/plaza level, view level/lower IF, grandstand/club level)
$9 (view/IF)
$8 (view level/OF), $6 (outfield bleachers)
Field dimensions (from home plate)
To left field at foul line, 327 feet
To center field, 405 feet
To right field at foul line, 330 feet
First game played
April 8, 1969 (Padres 2, Astros 1)

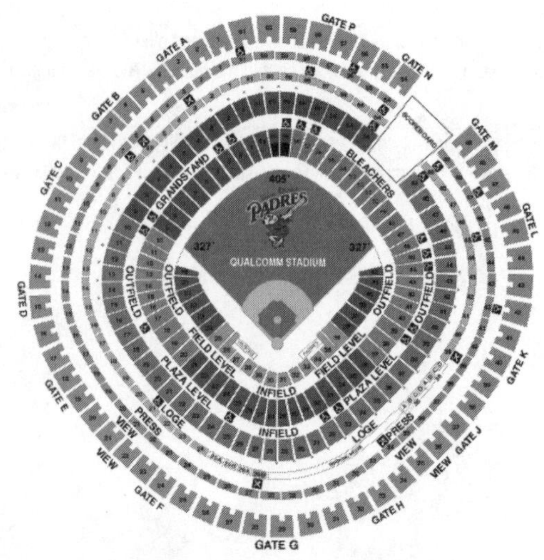

Follow the Padres all season at: www.sportingnews.com/baseball/teams/padres/

PADRES SPRING ROSTER

No.	PITCHERS	B/T	Ht./Wt.	Born	2002 clubs	Projection
65	Bartosh, Cliff	L/L	6-2/175	9-5-79	Mobile	Former starter might have found niche as closer.
54	Bynum, Mike	L/L	6-4/200	3-20-78	Mobile, Portland, San Diego	Lefty had trouble with his command in his 14 games with Padres.
41	Condrey, Clay	R/R	6-3/195	11-19-75	Portland, San Diego	Will battle for a spot in the rotation this year. Had 1.69 ERA in 27 innings in '02.
32	Cordova, Francisco	R/R	6-1/204	4-26-72	DID NOT PLAY	Hasn't pitched a full season since 2000. Team will take whatever he can give.
49	Cyr, Eric	R/L	6-4/200	2-11-79	Mobile, San Diego, Portland	Will need a season in Class AAA. Could be in majors by end of season.
53	Eaton, Adam	R/R	6-2/190	11-23-77	Lake Elsinore, Portland, S.Diego	Came back at end of season after recovering from elbow surgery.
	Garcia, Carlos	R/R	6-3/232	9-23-78	GC Dodgers, South Ga., F.Wayne	Padres have high hopes for this former Dodgers prospect.
	Hackman, Luther	R/R	6-4/195	10-10-74	St. Louis	Padres believe he can be a full time starter.
51	Hoffman, Trevor	R/R	6-0/205	10-13-67	San Diego	Still an elite closer, he'll be closing out games for Padres for awhile to come.
36	Howard, Ben	R/R	6-2/190	1-15-79	Mobile, San Diego, Portland	Earned midseason promotion, but still needs time in minors.
32	Jarvis, Kevin	L/R	6-2/200	8-1-69	San Diego, Mobile, Lake Elsinore	Started only seven games for Padres due to injuries.
50	Lawrence, Brian	R/R	6-0/195	5-14-76	San Diego	Carried the load as the staff ace last season, posted a 3.69 ERA.
	Orosco, Jesse	R/L	6-2/205	4-21-57	Los Angeles	Still around and can still get lefthanded batters out.
44	Peavy, Jake	R/R	6-1/180	5-31-81	Mobile, San Diego	Earned a spot in rotation with performance in San Diego last season.
59	Perez, Oliver	L/L	6-3/160	8-15-81	Lake Elsinore, Mobile, San Diego	Gives the Padres a bona fide lefthanded starter. Average one strikeout-per-inning.
45	Tankersley, Dennis	R/R	6-2/185	2-24-79	Mobile, San Diego, Portland	Another young arm, he struggled in brief promotion last season.
55	Tollberg, Brian	R/R	6-3/195	9-16-72	San Diego	Injuries robbed him of a productive 2002. Expect him to rebound in 2003.
47	Villafuerte, Brandon	R/R	5-11/165	12-17-75	Portland, San Diego	Had miniscule 1.41 ERA in 31 games out of bullpen.
56	Walker, Kevin	L/L	6-4/190	9-20-76	Lake Elsinore, Portland, S. Diego	Lefty has been injured each of last two seasons, will be back in the pen this year.
27	Wright, Jaret	R/R	6-2/230	12-29-75	Buffalo, Cleveland	Padres will give him every chance to win a spot in the rotation.

No.	CATCHERS	B/T	Ht./Wt.	Born	2002 clubs	Projection
29	Bennett, Gary	R/R	6-0/208	4-17-72	Colorado	Only committed four errors in 90 games behind the plate.
7	Gonzalez, Wiki	R/R	5-11/203	5-17-74	San Diego, Lake Elsinore	Hit .220, but had an OBP of .330. Comes into 2003 as backup catcher.
	Rivera, Mike	R/R	6-0/210	9-8-76	Detroit, Toledo	Catcher can hit homers, but needs a little more patience at plate.

No.	INFIELDERS	B/T	Ht./Wt.	Born	2002 clubs	Projection
21	Burroughs, Sean	L/R	6-2/200	9-12-80	San Diego, Portland	Hit .271 in 63 games last season, he'll probably inherit third base job.
	Bush, Homer	R/R	5-10/185	11-12-72	Toronto, Florida	Speedy utility guy hoping to regain form. Provides infield depth.
30	Flores, Jose	R/R	5-11/180	6-28-73	Sacramento, Oakland	Can play short or outfield, hits for average and has good speed.
	Hansen, Dave	L/R	6-0/195	11-24-68	Los Angeles	Gives Padres a nice lefthanded bat off the bench. Hit .292 last season.
30	Klesko, Ryan	L/L	6-3/220	6-12-71	San Diego	Will probably move to the outfield to make room for Burroughs on the infield.
8	Loretta, Mark	R/R	6-0/186	8-14-71	Milwaukee, Houston	He'll get the nod to start at second base. Provides steady defense, decent bat.
17	Mendez, Donaldo	R/R	6-1/155	6-7-78	Mobile, Portland	Provides infield depth in minors, likely to spend 2003 in Class AAA.
23	Nevin, Phil	R/R	6-2/231	1-19-71	San Diego, Lake Elsinore	Moves to first base to make room for Burroughs.
1	Vazquez, Ramon	L/R	5-11/170	8-21-76	San Diego	Padres are hoping he can build on his first successful season in majors.

No.	OUTFIELDERS	B/T	Ht./Wt.	Born	2002 clubs	Projection
	Anderson, Brady	L/L	6-1/202	1-18-64	Cleveland	Will be given a chance to make team as fourth outfielder.
34	Buchanan, Brian	R/R	6-4/230	7-21-73	Minn., Edmonton, San Diego	Hit .293 with Padres after trade from Minnesota.
60	Donovan, Todd	R/R	6-1/175	8-12-78	Mobile, Lake Elsinore	Future leadoff man knows how to get on base and steal a few.
14	Kotsay, Mark	L/L	6-0/201	12-2-75	San Diego	Has taken over center field job, can hit anywhere in lineup.
22	Nady, Xavier	R/R	6-2/205	11-14-78	Lake Elsinore, Portland	Top power hitter could battle for a corner outfield spot.
27	Trammell, Bubba	R/R	6-2/220	11-6-71	San Diego	Numbers dropped a little, he could be odd-man out.
	Victorino, Shane	R/R	5-9/160	11-30-80	Jacksonville	Padres will give this former sixth round pick a chance to make team.

THE COACHING STAFF

Bruce Bochy, manager.

Darrell Akerfelds, bullpen coach.

Greg Booker, pitching coach.

Dave Magadan, hitting coach.

Tony Muser, bench coach.

Rob Picciolo, third base coach.

THE TOP NEWCOMERS

Jaret Wright: After injuries have disrupted his career in the majors, Wright will be given a chance to regain his form in San Diego. Remember this is a guy who helped pitch Cleveland into the World Series in 1997.

Gary Bennett: Will provide veteran leadership behind the plate, and he'll be able to hit .250.

Mark Loretta: He hit .424 in 21 games in Houston after being traded from Milwaukee. While the Padres don't expect those kinds of numbers again this year, his usual .280 and solid defense at second base would be appreciated.

THE TOP PROSPECTS

Carlos Garcia: Former Dodgers prospect has been injured in each of the last two seasons. In his last full season in the minors, he led the league in innings pitched and won 14 games while posting a 2.57 ERA.

Xavier Nady: If he shows he can hit major league pitching during spring training, the Padres might have to make a trade to keep him up with the team for the entire season.

San Francisco Giants

National League West Division

2003 SEASON

Giants Schedule

Home games shaded; D—Day game (games starting before 5 p.m.); *—All-Star Game at Comiskey Park, Chicago. Subject to changes.

March/April

SUN	MON	TUE	WED	THU	FRI	SAT
30	31 D SD	1 SD	2 SD	3	4 D MIL	5 D MIL
6 D MIL	7 D SD	8 SD	9 D SD	10 LA	11 LA	12 D LA
13 LA	14 HOU	15 HOU	16 HOU	17	18 LA	19 LA
20 LA	21	22 PIT	23 PIT	24 D PIT	25 PHI	26 PHI
27 D PHI	28	29 CUB	30 CUB			

May

SUN	MON	TUE	WED	THU	FRI	SAT
				1 D CUB	2 CIN	3 D CIN
4 D CIN	5	6 FLA	7 FLA	8 FLA	9 ATL	10 ATL
11 D ATL	12 MON	13 MON	14 D MON	15 NYM	16 NYM	17 D NYM
18 D NYM	19 ARI	20 ARI	21 ARI	22	23 COL	24 D COL
25 D COL	26 D COL	27 ARI	28 ARI	29	30 COL	31 D COL

June

SUN	MON	TUE	WED	THU	FRI	SAT
1 D COL	2 COL	3 MIN	4 MIN	5 MIN	6 DET	7 D DET
8 D DET	9	10 CWS	11 CWS	12 CWS	13 KC	14 KC
15 D KC	16	17 LA	18 LA	19 LA	20 OAK	21 D OAK
22 D OAK	23 LA	24 LA	25 LA	26	27 OAK	28 D OAK
29 D OAK	30 STL					

July

SUN	MON	TUE	WED	THU	FRI	SAT
		1 STL	2 STL	3 D STL	4 SD	5 SD
6 D SD	7 STL	8 D STL	9 COL	10 COL	11 ARI	12 D ARI
13 D ARI	14	15 *	16	17 COL	18 COL	19 D COL
20 D COL	21 ARI	22 ARI	23 ARI	24 D ARI	25 SD	26 D SD
27 D SD	28	29 CUB	30 D CUB	31 D CUB		

August

SUN	MON	TUE	WED	THU	FRI	SAT
					1 CIN	2 D CIN
3 D CIN	4	5 PIT	6 PIT	7 D PIT	8 PHI	9 D PHI
10 D PHI	11	12 NYM	13 NYM	14 NYM	15 MON	16 MON
17 D MON	18 D MON	19 ATL	20 ATL	21 ATL	22 FLA	23 D FLA
24 D FLA	25	26 COL	27 COL	28 D COL	29 ARI	30 D ARI
31 ARI						

September

SUN	MON	TUE	WED	THU	FRI	SAT
	1 D ARI	2 COL	3 D COL	4	5 ARI	6 D ARI
7 D ARI	8	9 SD	10 SD	11 SD	12 MIL	13 D MIL
14 D MIL	15 SD	16 SD	17 SD	18 D SD	19 LA	20 LA
21 D LA	22 HOU	23 HOU	24 D HOU	25	26 LA	27 D LA
28 D LA						

FRONT-OFFICE DIRECTORY

President and managing general partner ....Peter A. Magowan
Executive vice president/COO ....Larry Baer
Senior vice president and general manager ....Brian Sabean
Vice president and assistant general manager....Ned Colletti
Vice president of player personnel ....Dick Tidrow
Special assistant to the general manager ....Ron Perranoski
Director of player development ....Jack Hiatt
Coordinator of international operations ....Rick Ragazzo
Senior vice president and chief financial officer....John Yee
Senior vice president, ballpark operations/security....Jorge Costa
Senior vice president, corporate marketing ....Mario Alioto
Senior vice president, consumer marketing ....Tom McDonald
Vice president and general manager, retail ....Connie Kullberg
Director of ballpark operations....Gene Telucci
Vice president, ticket services....Russ Stanley
Director of travel ....Reggie Younger Jr.
Senior vice president and general counsel ....Jack Bair
Media relations manager....Jim Moorehead
Baseball information manager ....Blake Rhodes
Manager, media services and broadcasting ....Maria Jacinto

MINOR LEAGUE AFFILIATES

Class	Team	League	Manager
AAA	Fresno	Pacific Coast	Fred Stanley
AA	Norwich	Eastern	Shane Turner
A	San Jose	California	Bill Hayes
A	Hagerstown	South Atlantic	Mike Ramsey
A	Salem-Keizer	Northwest	Jack Lind
Rookie	Arizona Giants	Arizona	Bert Hunter

BROADCAST INFORMATION

Radio: KNBR-AM (680).
TV: KTVU-TV (Channel 2).
Cable TV: Fox Sports Net.

SPRING TRAINING

Ballpark (city): Scottsdale Stadium (Scottsdale, Ariz.).
Ticket information: 602-990-7972.

ASSISTANCE STAFF

National cross-checker
Doug Mapson

Eastern regional cross-checker
Alan Marr

West Coast cross-checker
Darren Wittcke

East Coast cross-checker
Bobby Myrick

Canadian cross-checker -
Steve Arnieri

Major league scouts
Joe DiCarlo, Stan Saleski, Paul Turco, Ted Uhlaender, Randy Waddill, Tom Zimmer

Major league advance scout
Pat Dobson

Special assignment scouts
Dick Cole; Larry "Bo" Osborne

Scouts
John DiCarlo, Lee Elder, Charlie Gonzalez, Tom Korenek, John Shafer, Joe Strain, Todd Thomas, Glenn Tufts, Paul Turco Jr., Matt Woodward, Billy Castell

BALLPARK INFORMATION

Ballpark (capacity, surface)
Pacific Bell Park (41,341, grass)

Address
24 Willie Mays Plaza
San Francisco, CA 94107

Official website
www.sfgiants.com

Business phone
415-972-2000

Ticket information
415-972-2000

Ticket prices
$26 (lower box)
$20 (view box, arcade)
$16 (view reserved)
$10 (bleachers)

Field dimensions (from home plate)
To left field at foul line, 339 feet
To center field, 399 feet
To right field at foul line, 309 feet

First game played
April 11, 2000 (Dodgers 6, Giants 5)

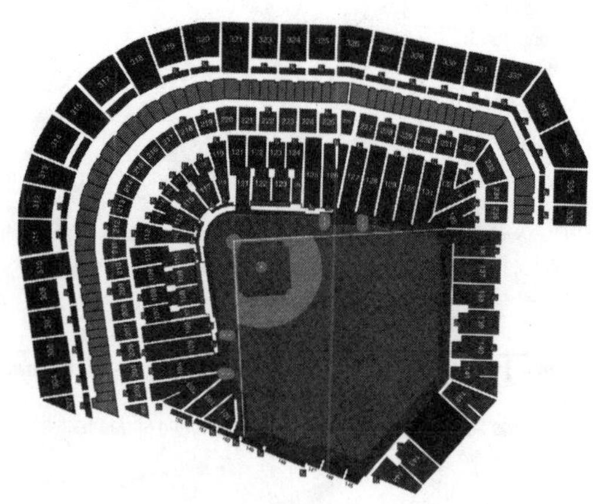

Follow the Giants all season at: www.sportingnews.com/baseball/teams/giants/

GIANTS SPRING ROSTER

No.	PITCHERS	B/T	Ht./Wt.	Born	2002 clubs	Projection
22	Ainsworth, Kurt	R/R	6-3/192	9-9-78	Fresno, San Francisco	Trading Russ Ortiz sends a signal that he's ready for rotation.
	Bonser, Boof	R/R	6-4/230	10-14-81	Shreveport, San Jose	Could be in starting rotation this year, if not next year for sure.
40	Christiansen, Jason	R/L	6-5/241	9-21-69	San Francisco	Only pitched five innings because of injury.
49	Eyre, Scott	L/L	6-1/210	5-30-72	Toronto, San Francisco	Showed team he could be the lefty specialist. Posted 1.59 ERA in 21 appearances.
	Foppert, Jesse	R/R	6-6/210	7-10-80	Shreveport, Fresno	He'll be in the Giants rotation at the start of the season.
61	Hernandez, Livan	R/R	6-2/240	2-20-75	San Francisco	Struggled, only winning 12 games last season. Giants hope he can rebound.
43	Jensen, Ryan	R/R	6-0/205	9-17-75	San Francisco	Went 13-8 in first full season in rotation.
27	Moss, Damian	R/L	6-0/187	11-24-76	Atlanta	Gives the Giants a quality lefty in the rotation.
36	Nathan, Joe	R/R	6-4/195	11-22-74	Fresno, San Francisco	Needs more time in Class AAA this season. Not quite ready for the majors.
31	Nen, Robb	R/R	6-5/222	11-28-69	San Francisco	Showed signs of slowing down in playoffs, but still the guy to close out games.
47	Rodriguez, Felix	R/R	6-1/198	9-9-72	San Francisco	Has pitched over 70 games in each of the last two seasons.
46	Rueter, Kirk	L/L	6-3/212	12-1-70	San Francisco	Only struck out 76 in 203 innings, but still won 14 games.
29	Schmidt, Jason	R/R	6-5/205	1-29-73	Fresno, San Francisco	Showed he can be the staff ace during postseason play.
	Williams, Jerome	R/R	6-3/190	12-4-81	Fresno	Lost 11 games despite a 3.59 ERA in 28 starts in Class AAA.
45	Worrell, Tim	R/R	6-4/230	7-5-67	San Francisco	Pitched in 80 games last season, the Giants' primary setup man.
41	Zerbe, Chad	L/L	6-0/200	4-27-72	Fresno, San Francisco	Can provide one good inning per outing.

No.	CATCHERS	B/T	Ht./Wt.	Born	2002 clubs	Projection
52	Lunsford, Trey	R/R	6-1/195	5-25-79	San Jose, Shreve., Fresno, S.F.	Will need one more season in minors before he's ready to contribute.
33	Santiago, Benito	R/R	6-1/200	3-9-65	San Francisco	Hit .278 and caught 125 games last season. Only committed four errors.
9	Torrealba, Yorvit	R/R	5-11/180	7-19-78	San Francisco	Will back up Santiago again this season, hit .279 last year in 53 games.

No.	INFIELDERS	B/T	Ht./Wt.	Born	2002 clubs	Projection
	Alfonzo, Edgardo	R/R	5-11/187	11-8-73	New York N.L.	Will either play second or third, depending on where Ray Durham ends up.
35	Aurilia, Rich	R/R	6-1/185	9-2-71	San Francisco	Had off season last year, Giants are hoping for a return to 2001 form.
	Durham, Ray	B/R	5-8/180	11-30-71	Chicago A.L., Oakland	Will either be starting second baseman or centerfielder.
39	Feliz, Pedro	R/R	6-1/205	4-27-77	San Francisco	Might get chance to play full time under new manager Felipe Alou.
13	Guzman, Edwards	L/R	5-11/205	9-11-76	Fresno	Spent time in minors last year working on playing different positions.
37	Minor, Damon	L/L	6-7/230	1-5-74	San Francisco, Fresno	Filled in at first when J.T. Snow needed a break. Only hit .237, though.
	Niekro, Lance	R/R	6-3/210	1-29-79	Shreveport	First baseman still a couple of years away from majors.
	Perez, Neifi	B/R	6-0/175	6-2-73	Kansas City	Giants will have to find a place for him in the infield.
2	Ransom, Cody	R/R	6-2/196	2-17-76	Fresno, San Francisco	Light hitting shortstop only had 15 errors in 135 games in Class AAA.
50	Santos, Deivis	L/L	6-1/175	2-9-80	Shreveport, Fresno	Can play outfield or first base, needs a little more patience at plate.
6	Snow, J.T.	L/L	6-2/209	2-26-68	San Francisco	Hit only six homers in 2002, Giants would like to see more power from first base.

No.	OUTFIELDERS	B/T	Ht./Wt.	Born	2002 clubs	Projection
7	Benard, Marvin	L/L	5-9/191	1-20-70	San Francisco	Played sparingly last season, will have uphill battle to reclaim job.
25	Bonds, Barry	L/L	6-2/228	7-24-64	San Francisco	It will be hard to top his .370 average and 198 walks.
	Ellison, Jason	R/R	5-10/180	4-4-78	San Jose, Fresno	Speedy outfielder stole 16 bases in only 49 games in Class AAA.
	Grissom, Marquis	R/R	5-11/188	4-17-67	Los Angeles	Doesn't walk a lot, but still has surprising power. He'll likely platoon in center.
14	Torcato, Tony	L/R	6-1/195	10-25-79	Fresno, San Francisco	Former first round pick finally showed some power in minors. Could win job.
54	Valderrama, Carlos	R/R	6-3/186	11-30-77	Shreveport, San Jose	Has yet to play above Class AA for any length of time.

THE COACHING STAFF

Felipe Alou, manager.
Mark Gardner, bullpen coach.
Gene Glynn, third base coach.
Joe Lefebvre, hitting coach.
Luis Pujols, first base coach.
Dave Righetti, pitching coach.
Ron Wotus, bench coach.

THE TOP NEWCOMERS

Damian Moss: Acquired in trade that sent Russ Ortiz to Atlanta, Moss will provide the Giants with another lefty in the rotation. He'll give opposing teams a different look than Kirk Rueter will.

Edgardo Alfonzo: It's unclear whether he'll play third base or second, but the Giants do know he can produce over a full season after back injuries troubled him in 2001.

Ray Durham: He looked like a new player while playing in Oakland after his trade from the White Sox. Giants are hoping he can make a smooth transition to center field. Or he may wind up at second base.

THE TOP PROSPECTS

Boof Bonser: He was the 21st overall pick in the 2000 draft and has been quickly climbing through the Giants system. It's won't be a surprise if he makes the starting rotation out of spring training. But in all likelihood, he'll spend most, if not all, of the season in the minors.

Jesse Fopprt: Former second round pick has moved all the way up to Class AAA in just two seasons in the minors. He struck out 109 batters in just 79 innings at Fresno last season. Next stop will likely be the Giants rotation.

INFORMATION AND COMPUTATIONS

RULES AND INFORMATION

SUSPENDED GAMES

A game may be suspended and completed at a future date for any of the following reasons:

1. A legally imposed curfew

2. The game is still tied at 1 a.m., local time. No inning may begin after 1 a.m., though an inning already in progress may be completed.

3. Any other mechanical difficulties that make continuing play overly difficult or dangerous.

4. Darkness falls and law prevents the use of lights.

5. Weather conditions make playing overly difficult or dangerous.

DISABLED LISTS

15-day: The player must remain off the active roster for a minimum of 15 calendar days, starting on the day following the player's last game.

60-day: Same rules apply, however, this may only be used when the team's 40-man roster is full. Any player placed on the 60-day disabled list after August 1 may not play for the remaider of the season, including any postseason games.

MAJOR LEAGUE SERVICE

A player gets service time:

1. For every day spent on an active roster, a Major League disabled list or a suspended list.

2. The day he physically reports to the team upon being called up from the minor leagues.

3. For however long it takes him, within reason, to report to his new team following a trade.

4. Up to and including the day he is sent down to the minors.

5. Up to and including the day he was notified of his unconditional release.

6. At the rate of 172 days per season, even though the regular season spans 183 days.

QUALIFICATIONS FOR INDIVIDUAL CHAMPIONSHIPS

Batting championship: It is awarded to the player with the highest batting average and at least 502 plate appearances. A player who falls short of the required 502 plate appearances can still win the title if the difference between his plate appearance total and 502 can be added as hitless at-bats and he still has the highest average.

Pitching championship: Awarded to the pitcher with the lowest ERA and at least 162 innings pitched.

Fielding championship: Awarded to each position player with the highest fielding average. Pitchers need a minimum of 162 innings, catchers 82 games and all other positions 108 games.

Night games: Night games are defined as any game beginning at or after 5 p.m. local time.

Streaks: A consecutive-game hitting streak will continue if the player fails to get a hit, but his at-bats result in a combination of any of the following: a walk, being hit by a pitch, defensive interference or a sacrifice bunt. The streak is terminated if the player's at-bats result only in a sacrifice fly.

A consecutive-games played streak is extended by a half inning of defensive play or a single at-bat, but pinch running will not extend the streak. The player's streak also continues if he is ejected from the game before he can satisfy any of the above requirements.

HOW TO COMPUTE:

Batting average: Divide at-bats into hits.

ERA: Multiply earned runs by 9 and divide the total by innings pitched.

Slugging percentage: Divide total bases by total times at bat (not including walks, hit by pitcher, sacrifices or interference).

On-base percentage: Divide the on-base total (hits, walks and hit by pitcher) by total plate appearances (at-bats, walks, hit by pitcher, sacrifices).

Fielding average: Add putouts and assists, divide the sum by total chances (putouts, assists, and errors).

Winning percentage: Divide the number of games won by the total games played.

Magic number: Determine the number of games yet to be played and add one. Then subtract the number of games the second-place team trails the first-place team in the loss column.

2002 Review

Catcher Bengie Molina leaps into pitcher Troy Percival's arms, celebrating the Angels' first World Series title.

Statistics courtesy of Major League Baseball.

INTRODUCTION

A shortstop put up numbers never before seen at his position. "Pedro, Lowe and pray for snow" became the rallying cry in Beantown. The 40/40 club just missed seeing its membership increase, while a Giant was again spectacular at the plate. Baseball lost some great men in 2002, while fans in Minnesota and Anaheim saw their clubs play into October for the first time in more than a decade. All in all, it was a year to remember.

BAY BASHER

After a 2001 season in which he did miraculous things, Barry Bonds continued to chase down some of baseball's most hallowed records. On August 9 he hit his 600th career home run, joining the likes of Hank Aaron, Babe Ruth and Willie Mays. Bonds hit at least 30 home runs for the 11th straight year, the first National League player to achieve the feat. What the 38-year-old lost in power he made up for in average, hitting .370 to win his first batting title. Bonds also walked 198 times, including a record 68 intentional passes. And his on-base percentage was an outrageous .582, breaking Ted Williams' 61-year-old record of .553. Bonds also stole nine bases, leaving him just seven shy of becoming baseball's first 500/500 man.

SAYING GOODBYE

A number of baseball luminaries passed away in 2002, including Williams, a player considered by many to be the greatest hitter who ever lived, and longtime Cardinals announcer Jack Buck. Four days after Buck's death on June 18, St. Louis was shocked by the death of 33-year-old Cardinals pitcher Darryl Kile. The team's losses continued with the passing of Hall of Fame outfielder Enos Slaughter and Darrell Porter, a key member of St. Louis' last World Series championship team, in 1982. Knuckleballer Hoyt Wilhelm, who pitched briefly for the Cardinals in 1957, was the third Hall of Fame player to die last year.

APRIL

After tossing a one-hitter in his first start of 2002, Boston righthander Derek Lowe went a step further in his next start, throwing a no-hitter against Tampa Bay on April 27. Just a week earlier, fellow Red Sox Pedro Martinez notched his 2,000th career strikeout, reaching the feat faster than any pitcher in baseball history. The Pedro-Lowe duo led the Red Sox to a 40-17 start. ... Japanese pitchers have won games in the major leagues before. And Japanese pitchers have saved games. But, until 2002, never had a Japanese pitcher saved the win for a countryman. On April 8 Seattle closer Kazuhiro Sasaki nailed down a victory for Shigetoshi Hasegawa. ... When Al Leiter beat the Diamondbacks, 10-1, on April 30, the Mets ace became the first pitcher to record a victory against all 30 major league teams.

MAY

When Seattle center fielder Mike Cameron hit four home runs against the White Sox on May 2, he became the first player in nine years to accomplish the four-homer feat. Accordingly, he probably thought it would be awhile before someone else did it. But Los Angeles outfielder Shawn Green did it just three weeks later, clubbing four homers in a May 23 game vs. Milwaukee. Green went 6-for-6 with 19 total bases, eclipsing the record of 18 set by Joe Adcock in 1954. Green then hit three more homers in the Dodgers' next two games to set a record with seven dingers in a three-game span. ... His team trailing 12-9 with the bases loaded in the bottom of the 14th inning in a May 17 game against Minnesota, Jason Giambi did what only one other Yankee had ever done: he hit a walk-off, grand slam. That other Yankee? Babe Ruth, in 1925.

JUNE

Florida's Luis Castillo put together the season's longest hitting streak, a 35-gamer that stretched from May 8 to June 21. It was the longest ever by a second baseman, surpassing Rogers Hornsby's 80-year-old record of 33, and the longest ever by a Latino player, surpassing Benito Santiago's 34-game stretch in 1987. ... When Atlanta's Tom Glavine won his 10th game of the season, pushing his career record to 234-134, he and Greg Maddux (263-148 at the time) became the first pair of teammates in 94 years to each have career records at least 100 games over .500 at the same time. Hall of Famers Joe McGinnity and Christy Mathewson did the same thing as New York Giants in 1908. ... Bartolo Colon became just the second pitcher in history to record double-digit victory totals in both leagues in the same season. After winning 10 with Cleveland, Colon was traded to Montreal on June 27 and subsequently picked up another 10 victories, equalling a feat first achieved by Hank Borowy (Yankees, Cubs) in 1945. ... Phillies pitcher Robert Person took matters into his own hands on June 2, clubbing a grand slam and a three-run homer to help himself to a 18-3 win over Montreal. Person's seven RBIs were the most in one game by a pitcher in 36 years. ... Bryan Bullington, a righthanded pitcher from Ball State, was taken by the Pittsburgh Pirates with the first overall selection of the 2002 first-year player draft.

At age 38, Barry Bonds became the oldest first-time batting title winner in 2002, as he hit .370, 75 points above his career average.

JULY

Indians first baseman Jim Thome homered in seven straight games from June 25 to July 3, falling one game short of tying a big-league record shared by Ken Griffey Jr., Don Mattingly and Dale Long. ... On July 23, his 29th birthday, Boston's Nomar Garciaparra hit three home runs and drove in eight runs in a 22-4 rout of Tampa Bay. Just four days later, Texas' Alex Rodriguez celebrated his 27th birthday by clubbing two home runs, including a walk-off grand slam, against the Oakland A's. ... On July 2, a record 62 homers were hit in the majors, breaking the old mark of 57 set on April 7, 2000. ... For the first time in 41 years, the All-Star Game ended in a tie. With the score 7-7 in the 11th inning, the game was called because both managers had run out of pitchers.

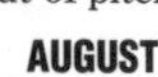

AUGUST

On August 10 at Coors Field, Cubs outfielder Sammy Sosa blasted three, three-run homers off Rockies pitching, all before the sixth inning. The next day Sosa whacked a grand slam in another Cubs victory at Coors. The following day against Houston, Sosa became just the third player in National League history (after Ralph Kiner and Duke Snider) to put together five straight 40-homer seasons. ... Yankees outfielder Bernie Williams smoked 11 straight hits over the course of four games in August and hit .402 for the month. ... Alfonso Soriano became the first second baseman and just the second Yankee ever to record a 30-home run/30-stolen base season. With 39 homers and 41 steals, Soriano narrowly missed 40-40. ... Vladimir Guerrero of the Montreal Expos became just the fifth player in history to compile back-to-back 30-30 seasons.

SEPTEMBER

The Oakland A's began the month on a 17-game winning streak and extended it to 20 before finally losing, 6-0, to the Twins on September 6. It was the longest winning streak in the majors in 67 years and the third longest since 1900. ... The Rangers set a record by homering in 27 straight games from August 11 to September 9. ... Arizona's Randy Johnson (334) and Curt Schilling (316) became the first pair of teammates to strike out at least 300 batters in the same season. ... After making an error on April 10, Orioles shortstop Mike Bordick didn't make another, setting records for highest fielding percentage (.998), fewest errors (1), consecutive errorless games (110) and consecutive errorless chances (543).

—BY MLB.COM

Final Standings, Leaders, Awards

AMERICAN LEAGUE

STANDINGS

EAST DIVISION

Team	W	L	Pct.	GB	Home	Road	vs. A.L. East	vs.A.L. Central	vs. A.L. West	vs. N.L.
New York	103	58	.640	..	52-28	51-30	46-29	29-7	17-15	11-7
Boston	93	69	.574	10.5	42-39	51-30	51-25	19-17	18-14	5-13
Toronto	78	84	.481	25.5	42-39	36-45	41-35	16-16	12-24	9-9
Baltimore	67	95	.414	36.5	34-47	33-48	26-50	18-14	14-22	9-9
Tampa Bay	55	106	.342	48.0	30-51	25-55	25-50	13-19	10-26	7-11

CENTRAL DIVISION

Team	W	L	Pct.	GB	Home	Road	vs. A.L. East	vs.A.L. Central	vs. A.L. West	vs. N.L.
Minnesota	94	67	.584	..	54-27	40-40	15-17	50-25	19-17	10-8
Chicago	81	81	.500	13.5	47-34	34-47	18-14	40-36	15-21	8-10
Cleveland	74	88	.457	20.5	39-42	35-46	19-17	37-39	12-20	6-12
Kansas City	62	100	.383	32.5	37-44	25-56	10-22	33-43	14-22	5-13
Detroit	55	106	.342	39.0	33-47	22-59	11-25	29-46	9-23	6-12

WEST DIVISION

Team	W	L	Pct.	GB	Home	Road	vs. A.L. East	vs.A.L. Central	vs. A.L. West	vs. N.L.
Oakland	103	59	.636	..	54-27	49-32	23-22	32-9	32-26	16-2
Anaheim	99	63	.611	4.0	54-27	45-36	28-13	30-15	30-28	11-7
Seattle	93	69	.574	10.0	48-33	45-36	25-20	23-18	34-24	11-7
Texas	72	90	.444	31.0	42-39	30-51	25-16	18-27	20-38	9-9

MISCELLANEOUS STANDINGS

Team	vs. Lefthanded Starters	vs. Righthanded Starters	Grass	Artificial	Day	Night	One-Run Games	Extra-Inning Games	Doubleheaders W-L-S
Anaheim	30-16	69-47	89-58	10-5	23-12	76-51	31-22	10-5	0-1-0
Baltimore	16-28	51-67	56-81	11-14	14-30	53-65	22-25	9-5	0-0-0
Boston	24-12	69-57	76-64	17-5	30-20	63-49	13-23	3-5	1-0-0
Chicago	17-24	64-57	72-70	9-11	30-28	51-53	15-21	3-2	0-0-0
Cleveland	23-23	51-65	66-78	8-10	25-20	49-68	16-17	4-4	0-0-1
Detroit	12-22	43-84	54-91	1-15	15-37	40-69	23-23	5-6	0-0-0
Kansas City	15-23	47-77	55-89	7-11	21-31	41-69	14-27	7-12	2-1-1
Minnesota	23-29	71-38	34-36	60-31	25-24	69-43	29-16	10-4	0-0-0
New York	25-11	78-47	90-49	13-9	32-26	71-32	21-21	6-7	0-0-0
Oakland	20-14	83-45	96-54	7-5	35-16	68-43	32-14	5-6	0-0-0
Seattle	27-18	66-51	84-63	9-6	25-20	68-49	24-25	11-6	0-0-0
Tampa Bay	8-21	47-85	22-44	33-62	14-27	41-79	17-28	9-10	0-0-0
Texas	15-31	57-59	65-85	7-5	15-21	57-69	18-26	6-12	1-2-0
Toronto	16-24	62-60	32-34	46-50	33-25	45-59	23-21	4-8	0-0-0

MONTHLY

Through April 30

Team	W	L	GB
East			
Boston	16	7	—
New York	17	10	1.0
Baltimore	12	14	5.5
Tampa Bay	9	15	7.5
Toronto	8	16	8.5
Central			
Chicago	16	10	—
Minnesota	16	11	0.5
Cleveland	13	13	3.0
Kansas City	8	16	7.0
Detroit	8	17	7.5
West			
Seattle	18	8	—
Oakland	15	11	3.0
Anaheim	11	14	6.5
Texas	10	15	7.5

Through May 31

Team	W	L	GB
East			
Boston	36	15	—
New York	36	19	2.0
Baltimore	24	28	12.5
Toronto	18	33	18.0
Tampa Bay	18	34	18.5
Central			
Minnesota	31	24	—
Chicago	28	26	2.5
Cleveland	26	28	4.5
Kansas City	21	30	8.0
Detroit	20	32	9.5
West			
Seattle	34	19	—
Anaheim	30	21	3.0
Oakland	25	28	9.0
Texas	21	31	12.5

Through June 30

Team	W	L	GB
East			
New York	50	31	—
Boston	46	31	2.0
Baltimore	38	41	11.0
Toronto	33	45	15.5
Tampa Bay	28	51	21.0
Central			
Minnesota	46	36	—
Chicago	40	42	6.0
Cleveland	37	43	8.0
Kansas City	31	47	13.0
Detroit	27	52	17.5
West			
Seattle	51	30	—
Anaheim	47	33	3.5
Oakland	46	35	5.0
Texas	35	45	15.5

Through July 31

Team	W	L	GB
East			
New York	67	39	—
Boston	63	43	4.0
Baltimore	49	55	17.0
Toronto	46	59	20.5
Tampa Bay	35	71	32.0
Central			
Minnesota	65	43	—
Chicago	51	57	14.0
Cleveland	47	59	17.0
Kansas City	44	63	20.5
Detroit	40	66	24.0
West			
Seattle	66	42	—
Anaheim	63	43	2.0
Oakland	61	47	5.0
Texas	45	62	20.5

Through August 31

Team	W	L	GB
East			
New York	84	50	—
Boston	75	58	8.5
Baltimore	63	71	21.0
Toronto	59	76	25.5
Tampa Bay	46	89	38.5
Central			
Minnesota	80	57	—
Chicago	65	70	14.0
Cleveland	59	75	19.5
Kansas City	55	81	24.5
Detroit	50	85	29.0
West			
Oakland	85	51	—
Anaheim	81	54	3.5
Seattle	79	57	6.0
Texas	60	74	24.0

Through Sept. 29 (Final)

Team	W	L	GB
East			
New York	103	58	—
Boston	93	69	10.5
Toronto	78	84	25.5
Baltimore	67	95	36.5
Tampa Bay	55	106	48.0
Central			
Minnesota	94	67	—
Chicago	81	81	13.5
Cleveland	74	88	20.5
Kansas City	62	100	32.5
Detroit	55	106	39.0
West			
Oakland	103	59	—
Anaheim	99	63	4.0
Seattle	93	69	10.0
Texas	72	90	31.0

NATIONAL LEAGUE

STANDINGS

EAST DIVISION

Team	W	L	Pct.	GB	Home	Road	vs. N.L. East	vs.N.L. Central	vs. N.L. West	vs. A.L.
Atlanta	101	59	.631	..	52-28	49-31	47-28	24-12	15-16	15-3
Montreal	83	79	.512	19.0	49-32	34-47	37-39	21-15	13-19	12-6
Philadelphia	80	81	.497	21.5	40-40	40-41	34-41	22-14	14-18	10-8
Florida	79	83	.488	23.0	46-35	33-48	36-40	18-18	15-17	10-8
New York	75	86	.466	26.5	38-43	37-43	35-41	20-15	10-22	10-8

CENTRAL DIVISION

Team	W	L	Pct.	GB	Home	Road	vs. N.L. East	vs.N.L. Central	vs. N.L. West	vs. A.L.
St. Louis	97	65	.599	..	52-29	45-36	11-19	57-33	21-9	8-4
Houston	84	78	.519	13.0	47-34	37-44	16-14	49-41	14-16	5-7
Cincinnati	78	84	.481	19.0	38-43	40-41	12-18	50-40	14-16	2-10
Pittsburgh	72	89	.447	24.5	38-42	34-47	16-13	43-47	10-20	3-9
Chicago	67	95	.414	30.0	36-45	31-50	12-18	36-54	13-17	6-6
Milwaukee	56	106	.346	41.0	31-50	25-56	7-23	35-55	12-18	2-10

WEST DIVISION

Team	W	L	Pct.	GB	Home	Road	vs. N.L. East	vs.N.L. Central	vs. N.L. West	vs. A.L.
Arizona	98	64	.605	..	55-26	43-38	21-11	23-13	43-33	11-7
San Francisco	95	66	.590	2.5	50-31	45-35	17-14	23-13	47-29	8-10
Los Angeles	92	70	.568	6.0	46-35	46-35	20-12	20-16	40-36	12-6
Colorado	73	89	.451	25.0	47-34	26-55	18-14	17-19	31-45	7-11
San Diego	66	96	.407	32.0	41-40	25-56	16-16	13-23	29-47	8-10

MISCELLANEOUS STANDINGS

Team	vs. Lefthanded Starters	vs. Righthanded Starters	Grass	Artificial	Day	Night	One-Run Games	Extra-Inning Games	Doubleheaders W-L-S
Arizona	28-22	70-42	96-60	2-4	36-21	62-43	23-20	9-3	1-0-0
Atlanta	14-9	87-50	87-52	14-7	33-17	68-42	28-17	7-8	1-0-0
Chicago	15-24	52-71	65-92	2-3	38-49	29-46	18-36	5-9	0-1-2
Cincinnati	17-21	61-63	76-80	2-4	30-28	48-56	26-23	12-6	0-0-1
Colorado	16-26	57-63	71-82	2-7	28-28	45-61	18-19	5-5	0-0-0
Florida	19-23	60-60	66-71	13-12	21-25	58-58	24-20	5-12	1-0-1
Houston	21-16	63-62	82-74	2-4	35-26	49-52	18-25	5-8	0-0-0
Los Angeles	24-15	68-55	86-66	6-4	29-18	63-52	33-15	7-4	1-0-0
Milwaukee	9-23	47-83	55-98	1-8	17-37	39-69	14-28	3-10	0-0-1
Montreal	18-18	65-61	28-40	55-39	22-21	61-58	30-22	13-6	0-0-0
New York	18-21	57-65	66-75	9-11	21-33	54-53	27-26	5-9	0-2-1
Philadelphia	16-20	64-61	37-35	43-46	24-29	56-52	22-24	11-7	0-1-0
Pittsburgh	19-16	53-73	70-85	2-4	22-27	50-62	27-24	4-4	0-0-2
St. Louis	21-16	76-49	93-63	4-2	33-26	64-39	22-19	5-5	0-0-1
San Diego	19-25	47-71	61-91	5-5	22-31	44-65	18-25	4-11	0-0-1
San Francisco	21-18	74-48	91-61	4-5	35-30	60-36	28-22	8-1	0-0-0

MONTHLY

Through April 30

East

Team	W	L	GB
Montreal	16	10	—
New York	16	10	—
Florida	13	13	3.0
Atlanta	12	15	4.5
Philadelphia	9	18	7.5

Central

Team	W	L	GB
Cincinnati	16	9	—
Pittsburgh	14	10	1.5
St. Louis	12	14	4.5
Houston	11	14	5.0
Chicago	8	16	7.5
Milwaukee	8	18	8.5

West

Team	W	L	GB
Arizona	16	10	—
Los Angeles	16	10	—
San Fran.	15	11	1.0
San Diego	14	12	2.0
Colorado	10	16	6.0

Through May 31

East

Team	W	L	GB
Atlanta	30	25	—
New York	29	25	0.5
Montreal	27	27	2.5
Florida	26	29	4.0
Philadelphia	21	32	8.0

Central

Team	W	L	GB
Cincinnati	32	22	—
St. Louis	30	24	2.0
Pittsburgh	25	29	7.0
Houston	24	29	7.5
Chicago	21	32	10.5
Milwaukee	18	36	14.0

West

Team	W	L	GB
Arizona	34	20	—
Los Angeles	31	23	3.0
San Fran.	30	23	3.5
Colorado	29	26	5.5
San Diego	25	30	9.5

Through June 30

East

Team	W	L	GB
Atlanta	51	30	—
Montreal	42	38	8.5
Florida	41	40	10.0
New York	40	40	10.5
Philadelphia	36	43	14.0

Central

Team	W	L	GB
Cincinnati	43	37	—
St. Louis	42	36	—
Houston	36	43	6.5
Pittsburgh	36	44	7.0
Chicago	33	46	9.5
Milwaukee	29	52	14.5

West

Team	W	L	GB
Los Angeles	50	31	—
Arizona	48	32	1.5
San Fran.	45	35	4.5
Colorado	39	43	11.5
San Diego	34	48	16.5

Through July 31

East

Team	W	L	GB
Atlanta	69	38	—
New York	55	51	13.5
Montreal	53	54	16.0
Florida	52	55	17.0
Philadelphia	50	56	18.5

Central

Team	W	L	GB
St. Louis	59	45	—
Cincinnati	55	51	5.0
Houston	54	52	6.0
Pittsburgh	49	58	11.5
Chicago	44	61	15.5
Milwaukee	38	69	22.5

West

Team	W	L	GB
Arizona	65	42	—
Los Angeles	60	47	5.0
San Fran.	59	48	6.0
Colorado	48	59	17.0
San Diego	45	62	20.0

Through August 31

East

Team	W	L	GB
Atlanta	85	49	—
Philadelphia	68	66	17.0
Florida	66	68	19.0
Montreal	66	69	19.5
New York	61	72	23.5

Central

Team	W	L	GB
St. Louis	76	59	—
Houston	72	63	4.0
Cincinnati	66	69	10.0
Pittsburgh	60	76	16.5
Chicago	56	79	20.0
Milwaukee	48	87	28.0

West

Team	W	L	GB
Arizona	84	51	—
Los Angeles	78	57	6.0
San Fran.	77	58	7.0
Colorado	61	75	23.5
San Diego	58	77	26.0

Through Sept. 29 (Final)

East

Team	W	L	GB
Atlanta	101	59	—
Montreal	83	79	19.0
Philadelphia	80	81	21.5
Florida	79	83	23.0
New York	75	86	26.5

Central

Team	W	L	GB
St. Louis	97	65	—
Houston	84	78	13.0
Cincinnati	78	84	19.0
Pittsburgh	72	89	24.5
Chicago	67	95	30.0
Milwaukee	56	106	41.0

West

Team	W	L	GB
Arizona	98	64	—
San Fran.	95	66	2.5
Los Angeles	92	70	6.0
Colorado	73	89	25.0
San Diego	66	96	32.0

AMERICAN LEAGUE LEADERS

TOP 15 QUALIFIERS FOR BATTING CHAMPIONSHIP

(502 or more plate appearances)

Batter	Team	BA	G	PA	AB	R	H	TB	2B	3B	HR	RBI	SH	SF	HBP	BB	IBB	SO	SB	CS	GI DP	SLG	OBP
Manny Ramirez	Bos.	.349	120	518	436	84	152	282	31	0	33	107	0	1	8	73	14	85	0	0	13	.647	.450
Mike Sweeney	K.C.	.340	126	545	471	81	160	265	31	1	24	86	0	7	6	61	10	46	9	7	9	.563	.417
Bernie Williams	N.Y.	.333	154	699	612	102	204	302	37	2	19	102	0	1	3	83	7	97	8	4	19	.493	.415
Ichiro Suzuki	Sea.	.321	157	728	647	111	208	275	27	8	8	51	3	5	5	68	27	62	31	15	8	.425	.388
Magglio Ordonez	Chi.	.320	153	653	590	116	189	352	47	1	38	135	0	3	7	53	2	77	7	5	21	.597	.381
Jason Giambi	N.Y.	.314	155	689	560	120	176	335	34	1	41	122	0	5	15	109	4	112	2	2	18	.598	.435
Adam Kennedy	Ana.	.312	144	509	474	65	148	213	32	6	7	52	5	4	7	19	1	80	17	4	5	.449	.345
Nomar Garciaparra	Bos.	.310	156	693	635	101	197	335	56	5	24	120	0	11	6	41	4	63	5	2	17	.528	.352
Miguel Tejada	Oak.	.308	162	715	662	108	204	336	30	0	34	131	0	4	11	38	3	84	7	2	21	.508	.354
Garret Anderson	Ana.	.306	158	678	638	93	195	344	56	3	29	123	0	10	0	30	11	80	6	4	11	.539	.332
Jim Thome	Cle.	.304	147	613	480	101	146	325	19	2	52	118	0	6	5	122	18	139	1	2	5	.677	.445
Paul Konerko	Chi.	.304	151	630	570	81	173	284	30	0	27	104	0	7	9	44	2	72	0	0	17	.498	.359
Shannon Stewart	Tor.	.303	141	641	577	103	175	255	38	6	10	45	0	1	9	54	2	60	14	2	17	.442	.371
Ellis Burks	Cle.	.301	138	570	518	92	156	280	28	0	32	91	1	1	6	44	3	108	2	3	13	.541	.362
Randall Simon	Det.	.301	130	506	482	51	145	221	17	1	19	82	0	7	4	13	5	30	0	1	13	.459	.320

TOP 15 QUALIFIERS FOR EARNED-RUN AVERAGE CHAMPIONSHIP

(162 or more innings pitched)

Pitcher	Team	W	L	WP	ERA	G	GS	CG	SHO	GF	SV	IP	H	BFP	R	ER	HR	SH	SF	HBP	BB	IBB	SO	WP	BK
Pedro Martinez	Bos.	20	4	.833	2.26	30	30	2	0	0	0	199.1	144	787	62	50	13	2	4	15	40	1	239	3	0
Derek Lowe	Bos.	21	8	.724	2.58	32	32	1	1	0	0	219.2	166	854	65	63	12	5	2	12	48	0	127	5	0
Barry Zito	Oak.	23	5	.821	2.75	35	35	1	0	0	0	229.1	182	939	79	70	24	9	7	9	78	2	182	2	1
Tim Wakefield	Bos.	11	5	.688	2.81	45	15	0	0	10	3	163.1	121	657	57	51	15	1	4	9	51	2	134	5	2
Roy Halladay	Tor.	19	7	.731	2.93	34	34	2	1	0	0	239.1	223	993	93	78	10	9	2	7	62	6	168	4	1
Tim Hudson	Oak.	15	9	.625	2.98	34	34	4	2	0	0	238.1	237	983	87	79	19	6	5	8	62	9	152	7	1
Jarrod Washburn	Ana.	18	6	.750	3.15	32	32	1	0	0	0	206.0	183	852	75	72	19	4	7	3	59	1	139	5	1
Joel Pineiro	Sea.	14	7	.667	3.24	37	28	2	1	4	0	194.1	189	812	75	70	24	5	7	7	54	1	136	8	0
Jamie Moyer	Sea.	13	8	.619	3.32	34	34	4	2	0	0	230.2	198	931	89	85	28	5	7	9	50	4	147	3	0
Mark Mulder	Oak.	19	7	.731	3.47	30	30	2	1	0	0	207.1	182	862	88	80	21	6	4	11	55	3	159	7	1
Jeff Weaver	Det.-N.Y.	11	11	.500	3.52	32	25	3	3	3	2	199.2	193	840	88	78	16	6	3	11	48	4	132	6	0
Rodrigo Lopez	Bal.	15	9	.625	3.57	33	28	1	0	0	0	196.2	172	809	83	78	23	2	4	5	62	4	136	2	1
Mark Buehrle	Chi.	19	12	.613	3.58	34	34	5	2	0	0	239.0	236	984	102	95	25	9	3	3	61	7	134	6	1
David Wells	N.Y.	19	7	.731	3.75	31	31	2	1	0	0	206.1	210	873	100	86	21	6	5	5	45	2	137	4	0
Ramon Ortiz	Ana.	15	9	.625	3.77	32	32	4	1	0	0	217.1	188	896	97	91	40	2	5	5	68	0	162	7	3

BATTING

Runs
128 Alfonso Soriano, N.Y.
125 Alex Rodriguez, Tex.
124 Derek Jeter, N.Y.
120 Jason Giambi, N.Y.
118 Johnny Damon, Bos.
116 Magglio Ordonez, Chi.
114 Carlos Beltran, K.C.
114 Ray Durham, Chi.-Oak.
111 Ichiro Suzuki, Sea.
108 Miguel Tejada, Oak.

Hits
209 Alfonso Soriano, N.Y.
208 Ichiro Suzuki, Sea.
204 Miguel Tejada, Oak.
204 Bernie Williams, N.Y.
197 Nomar Garciaparra, Bos.
195 Garret Anderson, Ana.
191 Derek Jeter, N.Y.
189 Magglio Ordonez, Chi.
187 Alex Rodriguez, Tex.
186 Shea Hillenbrand, Bos.

RBIs
142 Alex Rodriguez, Tex.
135 Magglio Ordonez, Chi.
131 Miguel Tejada, Oak.
123 Garret Anderson, Ana.
122 Jason Giambi, N.Y.
120 Nomar Garciaparra, Bos.
118 Jim Thome, Cle.
111 Troy Glaus, Ana.
109 Eric Chavez, Oak.
108 Carlos Delgado, Tor.

Total bases
389 Alex Rodriguez, Tex.
381 Alfonso Soriano, N.Y.
352 Magglio Ordonez, Chi.
344 Garret Anderson, Ana.
336 Miguel Tejada, Oak.
335 Jason Giambi, N.Y.
335 Nomar Garciaparra, Bos.
325 Jim Thome, Cle.
319 Carlos Beltran, K.C.
312 Rafael Palmeiro, Tex.

Doubles
56 Garret Anderson, Ana.
56 Nomar Garciaparra, Bos.
51 Alfonso Soriano, N.Y.
47 Magglio Ordonez, Chi.
44 Carlos Beltran, K.C.
43 Shea Hillenbrand, Bos.
40 Jorge Posada, N.Y.
39 Randy Winn, T.B.
39 John Olerud, Sea.
38 Eric Hinske, Tor.
38 Shannon Stewart, Tor.

Triples
11 Johnny Damon, Bos.
9 Randy Winn, T.B.
8 Ichiro Suzuki, Sea.
8 Michael Young, Tex.
7 Carlos Beltran, K.C.
6 Shannon Stewart, Tor.
6 Raul Ibanez, K.C.
6 Brad Fullmer, Ana.
6 Ray Durham, Chi.-Oak.
6 Adam Kennedy, Ana.
6 Cristian Guzman, Min.
6 A.J. Pierzynski, Min.
6 Chris Singleton, Bal.
6 Michael Tucker, K.C.
6 Carlos Guillen, Sea.
6 David Eckstein, Ana.
6 Shane Halter, Det.
6 Kenny Lofton, Chi.
6 Frank Catalanotto, Tex.
6 Carl Crawford, T.B.

Home runs
57 Alex Rodriguez, Tex.
52 Jim Thome, Cle.
43 Rafael Palmeiro, Tex.
41 Jason Giambi, N.Y.
39 Alfonso Soriano, N.Y.
38 Magglio Ordonez, Chi.
34 Eric Chavez, Oak.
34 Miguel Tejada, Oak.
33 Carlos Delgado, Tor.
33 Manny Ramirez, Bos.

Walks
122 Jim Thome, Cle.
109 Jason Giambi, N.Y.
104 Rafael Palmeiro, Tex.
102 Carlos Delgado, Tor.
98 John Olerud, Sea.
90 Robin Ventura, N.Y.
88 Troy Glaus, Ana.
88 Frank Thomas, Chi.
87 Alex Rodriguez, Tex.
83 Bernie Williams, N.Y.

Strikeouts
176 Mike Cameron, Sea.
157 Alfonso Soriano, N.Y.
144 Troy Glaus, Ana.
143 Jorge Posada, N.Y.
139 Jim Thome, Cle.
139 Jared Sandberg, T.B.
138 Eric Hinske, Tor.
135 Carlos Beltran, K.C.
129 Jacque Jones, Min.
127 Corey Koskie, Min.

On-base percentage
.450 Manny Ramirez, Bos.
.445 Jim Thome, Cle.
.435 Jason Giambi, N.Y.
.417 Mike Sweeney, K.C.
.415 Bernie Williams, N.Y.
.406 Carlos Delgado, Tor.
.403 John Olerud, Sea.
.392 Alex Rodriguez, Tex.
.391 Rafael Palmeiro, Tex.
.388 Ichiro Suzuki, Sea.

Slugging percentage
.677 Jim Thome, Cle.
.647 Manny Ramirez, Bos.
.623 Alex Rodriguez, Tex.
.598 Jason Giambi, N.Y.
.597 Magglio Ordonez, Chi.
.571 Rafael Palmeiro, Tex.
.563 Mike Sweeney, K.C.
.549 Carlos Delgado, Tor.
.547 Alfonso Soriano, N.Y.
.541 Ellis Burks, Cle.

Stolen bases
41 Alfonso Soriano, N.Y.
35 Carlos Beltran, K.C.
32 Derek Jeter, N.Y.
31 Johnny Damon, Bos.
31 Mike Cameron, Sea.
31 Ichiro Suzuki, Sea.
27 Randy Winn, T.B.
26 Ray Durham, Chi.-Oak.
23 Torii Hunter, Min.
23 Michael Tucker, K.C.
23 Darin Erstad, Ana.

PITCHING

Wins
23 Barry Zito, Oak.
21 Derek Lowe, Bos.
20 Pedro Martinez, Bos.
19 Mark Mulder, Oak.
19 Roy Halladay, Tor.
19 David Wells, N.Y.
19 Mark Buehrle, Chi.
18 Jarrod Washburn, Ana.
18 Mike Mussina, N.Y.
17 Paul Byrd, K.C.

Saves
45 Eddie Guardado, Min.
44 Billy Koch, Oak.
40 Troy Percival, Ana.
40 Ugueth Urbina, Bos.
38 Kelvim Escobar, Tor.
37 Kazuhiro Sasaki, Sea.
28 Juan Acevedo, Det.
28 Mariano Rivera, N.Y.
26 Roberto Hernandez, K.C.
25 Jorge Julio, Bal.

Innings pitched
239.1 Roy Halladay, Tor.
239.0 Mark Buehrle, Chi.
238.1 Tim Hudson, Oak.
230.2 Jamie Moyer, Sea.
229.1 Barry Zito, Oak.
228.1 Paul Byrd, K.C.
224.0 Tanyon Sturtze, T.B.
223.2 Freddy Garcia, Sea.
219.2 Derek Lowe, Bos.
217.1 Ramon Ortiz, Ana.

Hits allowed
271 Tanyon Sturtze, T.B.
238 Steve W. Sparks, Det.
237 Tim Hudson, Oak.
236 Mark Buehrle, Chi.
229 Jeff Suppan, K.C.
227 Freddy Garcia, Sea.
224 Paul Byrd, K.C.
223 Roy Halladay, Tor.
219 Paul Wilson, T.B.
212 Kenny Rogers, Tex.

Home runs allowed
40 Ramon Ortiz, Ana.
36 Paul Byrd, K.C.
33 Tanyon Sturtze, T.B.
32 Jeff Suppan, K.C.
32 Dan Wright, Chi.
32 Rick Reed, Min.
30 Freddy Garcia, Sea.
29 Paul Wilson, T.B.
28 Darrell May, K.C.
28 Jamie Moyer, Sea.

Batting average yielded
.198 Pedro Martinez, Bos.
.204 Tim Wakefield, Bos.
.211 Derek Lowe, Bos.
.218 Barry Zito, Oak.
.230 Jamie Moyer, Sea.
.230 Ramon Ortiz, Ana.
.232 Mark Mulder, Oak.
.234 Rodrigo Lopez, Bal.
.235 Jarrod Washburn, Ana.
.244 Roy Halladay, Tor.

Walks
89 Tanyon Sturtze, T.B.
88 C.C. Sabathia, Cle.
83 Jon Garland, Chi.
82 Danys Baez, Cle.
78 Barry Zito, Oak.
78 Chan Ho Park, Tex.
71 Dan Wright, Chi.
70 Kyle Lohse, Min.
70 Kenny Rogers, Tex.
68 Ramon Ortiz, Ana.
68 Jeff Suppan, K.C.
68 Scott Erickson, Bal.
68 Victor Zambrano, T.B.

Strikeouts
239 Pedro Martinez, Bos.
192 Roger Clemens, N.Y.
182 Barry Zito, Oak.
182 Mike Mussina, N.Y.
181 Freddy Garcia, Sea.
168 Roy Halladay, Tor.
162 Ramon Ortiz, Ana.
159 Mark Mulder, Oak.
152 Tim Hudson, Oak.
149 C.C. Sabathia, Cle.

NATIONAL LEAGUE LEADERS

TOP 15 QUALIFIERS FOR BATTING CHAMPIONSHIP

(502 or more plate appearances)

Batter	Team	BA	G	PA	AB	R	H	TB	2B	3B	HR	RBI	SH	SF	HBP	BB	IBB	SO	SB	CS	GIDP	SLG	OBP
Barry Bonds	S.F.	.370	143	612	403	117	149	322	31	2	46	110	0	2	9	198	68	47	9	2	4	.799	.582
Larry Walker	Col.	.338	136	553	477	95	161	287	40	4	26	104	0	4	7	65	6	73	6	5	8	.602	.421
Vladimir Guerrero	Mon.	.336	161	709	614	106	206	364	37	2	39	111	0	5	6	84	32	70	40	20	20	.593	.417
Todd Helton	Col.	.329	156	667	553	107	182	319	39	4	30	109	0	10	5	99	21	91	5	1	10	.577	.429
Chipper Jones	Atl.	.327	158	662	548	90	179	294	35	1	26	100	0	5	2	107	23	89	8	2	18	.536	.435
Jose Vidro	Mon.	.315	152	681	604	103	190	296	43	3	19	96	11	3	3	60	1	70	2	1	12	.490	.378
Albert Pujols	St.L	.314	157	675	590	118	185	331	40	2	34	127	0	4	9	72	13	69	2	4	20	.561	.394
Jeff Kent	S.F.	.313	152	682	623	102	195	352	42	2	37	108	0	3	4	52	3	101	5	1	20	.565	.368
Jim Edmonds	St.L	.311	144	576	476	96	148	267	31	2	28	83	0	6	8	86	14	134	4	3	9	.561	.420
Edgardo Alfonzo	N.Y.	.308	135	562	490	78	151	225	26	0	16	56	0	3	7	62	8	55	6	0	5	.459	.391
Bobby Abreu	Phi.	.308	157	685	572	102	176	298	50	6	20	85	0	6	3	104	9	117	31	12	11	.521	.413
Gary Sheffield	Atl.	.307	135	579	492	82	151	252	26	0	25	84	0	4	11	72	2	53	12	2	16	.512	.404
Luis Castillo	Fla.	.305	146	668	606	86	185	219	18	5	2	39	4	1	2	55	4	76	48	15	7	.361	.364
Edgar Renteria	St.L	.305	152	609	544	77	166	239	36	2	11	83	7	5	4	49	7	57	22	7	17	.439	.364
Junior Spivey	Ari.	.301	143	626	538	103	162	256	34	6	16	78	1	6	16	65	5	100	11	6	10	.476	.389

TOP 15 QUALIFIERS FOR EARNED-RUN AVERAGE CHAMPIONSHIP

(162 or more innings pitched)

Pitcher	Team	W	L	WP	ERA	G	GS	CG	SHO	GF	SV	IP	H	BFP	R	ER	HR	SH	SF	HBP	BB	IBB	SO	WP	BK
Randy Johnson	Ari.	24	5	.828	2.32	35	35	8	4	0	0	260.0	197	1035	78	67	26	4	2	13	71	1	334	3	2
Greg Maddux	Atl.	16	6	.727	2.62	34	34	0	0	0	0	199.1	194	820	67	58	14	13	4	4	45	7	118	1	0
Tom Glavine	Atl.	18	11	.621	2.96	36	36	2	1	0	0	224.2	210	936	85	74	21	12	6	8	78	8	127	2	0
Odalis Perez	L.A.	15	10	.600	3.00	32	32	4	2	0	0	222.1	182	869	76	74	21	13	7	4	38	5	155	2	3
Roy Oswalt	Hou.	19	9	.679	3.01	35	34	0	0	0	0	233.0	215	956	86	78	17	12	7	5	62	4	208	3	0
Elmer Dessens	Cin.	7	8	.467	3.03	30	30	0	0	0	0	178.0	173	737	70	60	24	7	1	7	49	8	93	3	1
Tomo Ohka	Mon.	13	8	.619	3.18	32	31	2	0	1	0	192.2	194	806	83	68	19	13	6	7	45	7	118	2	1
Randy Wolf	Phi.	11	9	.550	3.20	31	31	3	2	0	0	210.2	172	855	77	75	23	7	6	7	63	5	172	4	0
Kirk Rueter	S.F.	14	8	.636	3.23	33	33	0	0	0	0	203.2	204	846	83	73	22	6	6	1	54	7	76	3	0
Curt Schilling	Ari.	23	7	.767	3.23	36	35	5	1	0	0	259.1	218	1017	95	93	29	5	2	3	33	1	316	6	0
Kevin Millwood	Atl.	18	8	.692	3.24	35	34	1	1	0	0	217.0	186	895	83	78	16	9	4	8	65	7	178	4	0
Vicente Padilla	Phi.	14	11	.560	3.28	32	32	1	1	0	0	206.0	198	862	83	75	16	10	3	15	53	5	128	6	2
Wade Miller	Hou.	15	4	.789	3.28	26	26	1	1	0	0	164.2	151	688	63	60	14	8	5	6	62	9	144	4	0
A.J. Burnett	Fla.	12	9	.571	3.30	31	29	7	5	0	0	204.1	153	844	84	75	12	9	4	9	90	5	203	14	0
Steve Trachsel	N.Y.	11	11	.500	3.37	30	30	1	1	0	0	173.2	170	741	80	65	16	9	3	0	69	4	105	4	0

BATTING

Runs
122 Sammy Sosa, Chi.
118 Albert Pujols, St.L.
117 Barry Bonds, S.F.
110 Shawn Green, L.A.
107 Todd Helton, Col.
106 Vladimir Guerrero, Mon.
106 Lance Berkman, Hou.
103 Jose Vidro, Mon.
103 Junior Spivey, Ari.
102 Bobby Abreu, Phi.
102 Jeff Kent, S.F.

Hits
206 Vladimir Guerrero, Mon.
195 Jeff Kent, S.F.
190 Jose Vidro, Mon.
185 Albert Pujols, St.L.
185 Luis Castillo, Fla.
183 Todd Walker, Cin.
182 Todd Helton, Col.
179 Chipper Jones, Atl.
176 Bobby Abreu, Phi.
175 Rafael Furcal, Atl.

RBIs
128 Lance Berkman, Hou.
127 Albert Pujols, St.L.
116 Pat Burrell, Phi.
114 Shawn Green, L.A.
111 Vladimir Guerrero, Mon.
110 Scott Rolen, Phi.-St.L.
110 Barry Bonds, S.F.
109 Todd Helton, Col.
108 Jeff Kent, S.F.
108 Sammy Sosa, Chi.

Total bases
364 Vladimir Guerrero, Mon.
352 Jeff Kent, S.F.
334 Lance Berkman, Hou.
331 Albert Pujols, St.L.
330 Sammy Sosa, Chi.
325 Shawn Green, L.A.
322 Barry Bonds, S.F.
319 Pat Burrell, Phi.
319 Todd Helton, Col.
309 Brian Giles, Pit.

Doubles
50 Bobby Abreu, Phi.
44 Mike Lowell, Fla.
43 Jose Vidro, Mon.
43 Orlando Cabrera, Mon.
42 Jeff Kent, S.F.
42 Todd Walker, Cin.
41 Kevin Millar, Fla.
40 Albert Pujols, St.L.
40 Larry Walker, Col.
39 Pat Burrell, Phi.
39 Todd Helton, Col.
39 Ryan Klesko, S.D.

Triples
10 Jimmy Rollins, Phi.
8 Rafael Furcal, Atl.
8 Scott Rolen, Phi.-St.L.
8 Brad Wilkerson, Mon.
8 Quinton McCracken, Ari.
7 Derrek Lee, Fla.
7 Mark Kotsay, S.D.
7 Juan Uribe, Col.
7 Jay Payton, N.Y.-Col.
7 Dave Roberts, L.A.
7 Alex Sanchez, Mil.

Home runs
49 Sammy Sosa, Chi.
46 Barry Bonds, S.F.
42 Lance Berkman, Hou.
42 Shawn Green, L.A.
39 Vladimir Guerrero, Mon.
38 Brian Giles, Pit.
37 Jeff Kent, S.F.
37 Pat Burrell, Phi.
35 Andruw Jones, Atl.
34 Albert Pujols, St.L.

Walks
198 Barry Bonds, S.F.
135 Brian Giles, Pit.
128 Adam Dunn, Cin.
107 Lance Berkman, Hou.
107 Chipper Jones, Atl.
104 Bobby Abreu, Phi.
103 Sammy Sosa, Chi.
101 Jeff Bagwell, Hou.
99 Todd Helton, Col.
98 Derrek Lee, Fla.

Strikeouts
188 Jose Hernandez, Mil.
170 Adam Dunn, Cin.
164 Derrek Lee, Fla.
161 Brad Wilkerson, Mon.
153 Pat Burrell, Phi.
145 Mo Vaughn, N.Y.
144 Sammy Sosa, Chi.
144 Mark Bellhorn, Chi.
142 Corey Patterson, Chi.
140 Preston Wilson, Fla.

On-base percentage
.582 Barry Bonds, S.F.
.450 Brian Giles, Pit.
.435 Chipper Jones, Atl.
.429 Todd Helton, Col.
.421 Larry Walker, Col.
.420 Jim Edmonds, St.L.
.417 V. Guerrero, Mon.
.413 Bobby Abreu, Phi.
.405 Lance Berkman, Hou.
.404 Gary Sheffield, Atl.

Slugging percentage
.799 Barry Bonds, S.F.
.622 Brian Giles, Pit.
.602 Larry Walker, Col.
.594 Sammy Sosa, Chi.
.593 V. Guerrero, Mon.
.578 Lance Berkman, Hou.
.577 Todd Helton, Col.
.565 Jeff Kent, S.F.
.561 Albert Pujols, St.L.
.561 Jim Edmonds, St.L.

Stolen bases
48 Luis Castillo, Fla.
47 Juan Pierre, Col.
45 Dave Roberts, L.A.
40 Vladimir Guerrero, Mon.
37 Alex Sanchez, Mil.
32 Aaron Boone, Cin.
31 Bobby Abreu, Phi.
31 Jimmy Rollins, Phi.
31 Eric Young, Mil.
31 Andy Fox, Fla.

PITCHING

Wins
24 Randy Johnson, Ari.
23 Curt Schilling, Ari.
19 Roy Oswalt, Hou.
18 Kevin Millwood, Atl.
18 Tom Glavine, Atl.
17 Matt Morris, St.L.
16 Hideo Nomo, L.A.
16 Greg Maddux, Atl.
16 Jason Jennings, Col.
15 Odalis Perez, L.A.
15 Wade Miller, Hou.
15 Jimmy Haynes, Cin.

Saves
55 John Smoltz, Atl.
52 Eric Gagne, L.A.
46 Mike Williams, Pit.
45 Jose Mesa, Phi.
43 Robb Nen, S.F.
41 Jose Jimenez, Col.
38 Trevor Hoffman, S.D.
36 Byung-Hyun Kim, Ari.
35 Billy Wagner, Hou.
33 Armando Benitez, N.Y.

Innings pitched
260.0 Randy Johnson, Ari.
259.1 Curt Schilling, Ari.
233.0 Roy Oswalt, Hou.
230.1 Javier Vazquez, Mon.
224.2 Tom Glavine, Atl.
222.1 Odalis Perez, L.A.
220.1 Hideo Nomo, L.A.
217.0 Kevin Millwood, Atl.
216.2 Ben Sheets, Mil.
216.0 Livan Hernandez, S.F.

Hits allowed
243 Javier Vazquez, Mon.
237 Ben Sheets, Mil.
233 Livan Hernandez, S.F.
230 Brian Lawrence, S.D.
228 Ryan Dempster, Fla.-Cin.
228 Mike Hampton, Col.
227 Glendon Rusch, Mil.
218 Curt Schilling, Ari.
215 Roy Oswalt, Hou.
212 Brett Tomko, S.D.

Home runs allowed
32 Pedro Astacio, N.Y.
31 Brett Tomko, S.D.
31 Rick Helling, Ari.
30 Glendon Rusch, Mil.
29 Curt Schilling, Ari.
28 Javier Vazquez, Mon.
28 Ryan Dempster, Fla.-Cin.
28 John Thomson, Col.-N.Y.
28 Josh Fogg, Pit.
28 Ruben Quevedo, Mil.

Batting average yielded
.208 Randy Johnson, Ari.
.209 A.J. Burnett, Fla.
.215 Matt Clement, Chi.
.218 Jason Schmidt, S.F.
.221 Kerry Wood, Chi.
.221 Damian Moss, Atl.
.223 Randy Wolf, Phi.
.224 Curt Schilling, Ari.
.226 Odalis Perez, L.A.
.230 Kevin Millwood, Atl.

Walks
106 Kazuhisa Ishii, L.A.
101 Hideo Nomo, L.A.
97 Kerry Wood, Chi.
94 Russ Ortiz, S.F.
93 R. Dempster, Fla.-Cin.
91 Mike Hampton, Col.
90 A.J. Burnett, Fla.
89 Damian Moss, Atl.
85 Matt Clement, Chi.
83 Shawn Estes, N.Y.-Cin.

Strikeouts
334 Randy Johnson, Ari.
316 Curt Schilling, Ari.
217 Kerry Wood, Chi.
215 Matt Clement, Chi.
208 Roy Oswalt, Hou.
203 A.J. Burnett, Fla.
196 Jason Schmidt, S.F.
193 Hideo Nomo, L.A.
179 Javier Vazquez, Mon.
178 Kevin Millwood, Atl.

AMERICAN LEAGUE MVP

Player, Team	1	2	3	4	5	6	7	8	9	10	Pts.
Miguel Tejada, Oakland	21	6	1	-	-	-	-	-	-	-	356
Alex Rodriguez, Texas	5	7	11	4	-	1	-	-	-	-	254
Alfonso Soriano, New York	2	11	9	4	1	-	-	-	-	1	234
Garret Anderson, Anaheim	-	4	5	7	7	1	2	-	2	-	184
Jason Giambi, New York	-	-	2	8	10	4	1	1	1	1	162
Torii Hunter, Minnesota	-	-	-	5	5	8	1	5	4	-	132
Jim Thome, Cleveland	-	-	-	-	2	3	3	8	1	4	69
Magglio Ordonez, Chicago	-	-	-	-	1	4	5	3	-	4	59
Manny Ramirez, Boston	-	-	-	-	-	2	5	1	2	2	39
Bernie Williams, New York	-	-	-	-	1	-	3	2	3	2	32
David Eckstein, Anaheim	-	-	-	-	1	1	-	1	4	2	24
Nomar Garciaparra, Boston	-	-	-	-	-	2	1	1	2	3	24
Barry Zito, Oakland	-	-	-	-	-	1	2	1	2	2	22
Eric Chavez, Oakland	-	-	-	-	-	-	-	2	3	2	14
Troy Percival, Anaheim	-	-	-	-	-	1	1	1	-	-	12
Eddie Guardado, Minnesota	-	-	-	-	-	-	2	1	-	1	12
Ichiro Suzuki, Seattle	-	-	-	-	-	-	-	1	3	1	10
Billy Koch, Oakland	-	-	-	-	-	-	2	-	-	-	8
Derek Lowe, Boston	-	-	-	-	-	-	-	-	1	1	3
Pedro Martinez, Boston	-	-	-	-	-	-	-	-	-	1	1
Mike Sweeney, Kansas City	-	-	-	-	-	-	-	-	-	1	1

Fourteen points awarded for a first-place vote, nine for second and down to one for 10th.

NATIONAL LEAGUE MVP

Player, Team	1	2	3	4	5	6	7	8	9	10	Pts.
Barry Bonds, San Francisco	32	-	-	-	-	-	-	-	-	-	448
Albert Pujols, St. Louis	-	26	4	-	1	-	1	-	-	-	276
Lance Berkman, Houston	-	1	7	5	6	5	2	3	1	1	181
Vladimir Guerrero, Montreal	-	4	5	3	3	5	2	3	5	1	168
Shawn Green, Los Angeles	-	-	3	8	4	3	2	3	3	4	146
Jeff Kent, San Francisco	-	-	3	2	4	8	5	2	3	1	135
Randy Johnson, Arizona	-	-	5	3	4	4	2	4	1	-	127
John Smoltz, Atlanta	-	1	3	5	2	1	6	2	3	3	124
Sammy Sosa, Chicago	-	-	-	2	3	1	1	4	4	2	63
Curt Schilling, Arizona	-	-	-	1	2	3	2	1	3	2	53
Chipper Jones, Atlanta	-	-	2	2	-	-	4	-	1	2	50
Eric Gagne, Los Angeles	-	-	-	1	2	1	1	4	1	2	44
Brian Giles, Pittsburgh	-	-	-	-	-	-	2	4	2	3	27
Junior Spivey, Arizona	-	-	-	-	-	-	2	-	-	-	8
Pat Burrell, Philadelphia	-	-	-	-	-	-	-	1	2	1	8
Andruw Jones, Atlanta	-	-	-	-	-	1	-	-	1	-	7
Gary Sheffield, Atlanta	-	-	-	-	1	-	-	-	-	-	6
Jim Edmonds, St. Louis	-	-	-	-	-	-	-	1	1	1	6
Todd Helton, Colorado	-	-	-	-	-	-	-	-	-	3	3
Benito Santiago, San Francisco	-	-	-	-	-	-	-	-	1	-	2
Edgar Renteria, St. Louis	-	-	-	-	-	-	-	-	-	2	2
Larry Walker, Colorado	-	-	-	-	-	-	-	-	-	2	2
Roy Oswalt, Houston	-	-	-	-	-	-	-	-	-	1	1
Jose Vidro, Montreal	-	-	-	-	-	-	-	-	-	1	1

14 points awarded for a first-place vote, 9 for a second, 8 for a third, 7 for a fourth, etc.

A.L. CY YOUNG

Player, Team	1	2	3	Pts.
Barry Zito, Oakland	17	9	2	114
Pedro Martinez, Boston	11	12	5	96
Derek Lowe, Boston	-	7	20	41
Jarrod Washburn, Anaheim	-	-	1	1

5 points awarded for a first-place vote, 3 for a second, 1 for a third.

A.L. ROOKIE OF THE YEAR

Player, Team	1	2	3	Pts.
Eric Hinske, Toronto	19	9	-	122
Rodrigo Lopez, Baltimore	9	17	1	97
Jorge Julio, Baltimore	-	1	11	14
Bobby Kielty, Minnesota	-	1	2	5
John Lackey, Anaheim	-	-	5	5
Josh Phelps, Toronto	-	-	3	3
Kevin Mench, Texas	-	-	2	2
Mark Ellis, Oakland	-	-	1	1
Tony Fiore, Minnesota	-	-	1	1
Dustan Mohr, Minnesota	-	-	1	1
Carlos Pena, Detroit	-	-	1	1

5 points awarded for a first-place vote, 3 for a second, 1 for a third.

A.L. MANAGER OF THE YEAR

Manager, Team	1	2	3	Pts.
Mike Scioscia, Anaheim	17	10	1	116
Art Howe, Oakland	9	5	14	74
Ron Gardenhire, Minnesota	2	13	10	59
Joe Torre, New York	-	-	3	3

5 points awarded for a first-place vote, 3 for a second, 1 for a third.

Most Valuable Player Miguel Tejada.

N.L. Cy Young Award winner Randy Johnson.

N.L. CY YOUNG

Player, Team	1	2	3	Pts.
Randy Johnson, Arizona	32	-	-	160
Curt Schilling, Arizona	-	29	3	90
John Smoltz, Atlanta	-	1	18	21
Eric Gagne, Los Angeles	-	2	2	8
Roy Oswalt, Houston	-	-	8	8
Bartolo Colon, Montreal	-	-	1	1

5 points awarded for a first-place vote, 3 for a second, 1 for a third.

N.L. ROOKIE OF THE YEAR

Player, Team	1	2	3	Pts.
Jason Jennings, Colorado	27	5	-	150
Brad Wilkerson, Montreal	2	14	5	57
Austin Kearns, Cincinnati	2	8	6	40
Kazuhisa Ishii, Los Angeles	1	2	5	16
Damian Moss, Atlanta	-	2	6	12
Ryan Jensen, San Francisco	-	-	4	4
Mark Prior, Chicago	-	1	-	3
Josh Fogg, Pittsburgh	-	-	3	3
Alex Sanchez, Milwaukee	-	-	1	1
Jason Simontacchi, St. Louis	-	-	1	1
Dennis Stark, Colorado	-	-	1	1

5 points awarded for a first-place vote, 3 for a second, 1 for a third.

N.L. MANAGER OF THE YEAR

Manager, Team	1	2	3	Pts.
Tony La Russa, St. Louis	22	6	1	129
Bobby Cox, Atlanta	9	14	6	93
Frank Robinson, Montreal	-	6	5	23
Jim Tracy, Los Angeles	-	4	10	22
Dusty Baker, San Francisco	1	2	7	18
Bob Brenly, Arizona	-	-	2	2
Bob Boone, Cincinnati	-	-	1	1

5 points awarded for a first-place vote, 3 for a second, 1 for a third.

GOLD GLOVE WINNERS

First basemen	PO	A	E	Pct.
A.L.: John Olerud, Mariners	1169	101	5	.996
N.L.: Todd Helton, Rockies	1357	113	7	.995
Second basemen				
A.L.: Bret Boone, Mariners	251	387	7	.989
N.L.: Fernando Vina, Cardinals	287	401	13	.981
Shortstops				
A.L.: Alex Rodriguez, Rangers	259	472	10	.987
N.L.: Edgar Renteria, Cardinals	202	410	19	.970
Third basemen				
A.L.: Eric Chavez, Athletics	120	301	17	.961
N.L.: Scott Rolen, Phillies-Cards	133	335	16	.967
Outfielders				
A.L.: Darin Erstand, Angels	452	11	1	.998
A.L.: Torii Hunter, Twins	365	7	3	.992
A.L.: Ichiro Suzuki, Mariners	333	8	3	.991
N.L.: Jim Edmonds, Cardinals	347	11	5	.986
N.L.: Andruw Jones, Braves	404	5	3	.993
N.L.: Larry Walker, Rockies	229	14	4	.984
Catchers				
A.L.: Bengie Molina, Angels	707	60	1	.999
N.L.: Brad Ausmus, Astros	942	65	3	.997
Pitchers				
A.L.: Kenny Rogers, Rangers	22	40	3	.954
N.L.: Greg Maddux, Braves	21	48	1	.986

Note: Voting by Major League players and managers is conducted by THE SPORTING NEWS.

SILVER SLUGGERS

First basemen	Avg.	H	HR	RBI
A.L.: Jason Giambi, Yankees	.314	176	41	122
N.L.: Todd Helton, Rockies	.329	182	30	109
Second basemen				
A.L.: Alfonso Soriano, Yankees	.300	209	39	102
N.L.: Jeff Kent, Giants	.313	195	37	108
Shortstops				
A.L.: Alex Rodriguez, Rangers	.300	187	57	142
N.L.: Edgar Renteria, Cardinals	.305	166	11	83
Third basemen				
A.L.: Eric Chavez, Athletics	.275	161	34	109
N.L.: Scott Rolen, Phillies-Cards	.266	154	31	110
Outfielders				
A.L.: Garret Anderson, Angels	.306	195	29	123
A.L.: Magglio Ordonez, White Sox	.320	189	38	135
A.L.: Bernie Williams, Yankees	.333	204	19	102
N.L.: Barry Bonds, Giants	.370	149	46	110
N.L.: Vladimir Guerrero, Expos	.336	206	39	111
N.L.: Sammy Sosa, Cubs	.288	160	49	108
Catchers				
A.L.: Jorge Posada, Yankees	.268	137	20	99
N.L.: Mike Piazza, Mets	.280	134	33	98
Pitcher				
N.L.: Mike Hampton, Rockies	.344	22	3	5
Designated Hitter				
A.L.: Manny Ramirez, Red Sox	.349	152	33	107

Note: Voting by Major League players and managers is conducted by THE SPORTING NEWS.

PLAYERS OF THE WEEK

March 31-April 7	position
A.L.: David Justice, Athletics	outfield
N.L.: Barry Bonds, Giants	outfield
April 8-14	
A.L.:Jim Thome, Indians	first base
N.L.: Michael Barrett, Expos	catcher
April 15-21	
A.L.: Manny Ramirez, Red Sox	designated hitter
N.L.: Brian Lawrence, Padres	pitcher
April 22-28	
A.L.: Derek Lowe, Red Sox	pitcher
N.L.: Vladimir Guerrero, Expos	outfield

Scott Rolen won a Gold Glove and was named third baseman on the N.L. Silver Slugger team in 2002.

April 29-May 5	
A.L.: Mike Cameron, Mariners	outfield
Omar Vizquel, Indians	shortstop
N.L.: Lance Berkman, Astros	outfield
May 6-12	
A.L.: Magglio Ordonez, White Sox	outfield
N.L.: Adam Dunn, Reds	outfield
May 13-19	
A.L.: Roger Clemens, Yankees	pitcher
N.L.: Barry Bonds, Giants	outfield
May 20-26	
A.L.: Mike Sweeney, Royals	first base
N.L.: Shawn Green, Dodgers	outfield
May 27-June 2	
A.L.: Jeff Conine, Orioles	first base
N.L.: Matt Clement, Cubs	pitcher
June 3-9	
A.L.: Jacque Jones, Twins	outfield
N.L.: Andruw Jones, Braves	outfield
June 10-16	
A.L.: Robert Fick, Tigers	outfield
Michael Young, Rangers	second base
N.L.: Craig Wilson, Pirates	outfield
June 17-23	
A.L.: Alfonso Soriano, Yankees	second base
N.L.: Luis Castillo, Marlins	second base
June 24-30	
A.L.: Mike Sweeney, Royals	first base
N.L.: Jeff Kent, Giants	second base
July 1-7	
A.L.: Pedro Martinez, Red Sox	pitcher
Trot Nixon, Red Sox	outfield
N.L.: Albert Pujols, Cardinals	outfield
July 8-14	
A.L.: Alex Rodriguez, Rangers	shortstop
N.L.: Byung-Hyun Kim, Diamondbacks	pitcher
July 15-21	
A.L.: Carlos Beltran, Royals	outfield
Raul Ibanez, Royals	outfield
N.L.: Adam Hyzdu, Pirates	outfield
July 22-28	
A.L.: Randall Simon, Tigers	first base
N.L.: Richie Sexson, Brewers	first base
July 29-August 4	
A.L.: Edgar Martinez, Mariners	designated hitter
N.L.: Chipper Jones, Braves	outfield
August 5-11	
A.L.: Magglio Ordonez, White Sox	outfield
N.L.: Randy Johnson, Diamondbacks	pitcher
Sammy Sosa, Cubs	outfield
August 12-18	
A.L.: Alex Rodriguez, Rangers	shortstop
Bernie Williams, Yankees	outfield
N.L.: A.J. Burnett, Marlins	pitcher
August 19-25	
A.L.: Eric Chavez, Athletics	third base
N.L.: Jay Payton, Rockies	outfield
Jason Schmidt, Giants	pitcher
August 26-September 1	
A.L.: Joe Crede, White Sox	third base
N.L.: Barry Bonds, Giants	outfield
September 2-8	
A.L.: Karim Garcia, Indians	outfield
N.L.: Moises Alou, Cubs	outfield
September 9-15	
A.L.: Tim Hudson, Athletics	pitcher
Manny Ramirez, Red Sox	designated hitter
N.L.: Mike Piazza, Mets	catcher
September 16-22	
A.L.: Magglio Ordonez, White Sox	outfield
N.L.: Scott Rolen, Cardinals	third base
September 23-30	
A.L.: Carlos Delgado, Blue Jays	first base
N.L.: Mike Lowell, Marlins	third base

PLAYERS OF THE MONTH

April	Avg.	R	HR	RBI
A.L.: Torii Hunter, Twins	.371	23	9	20
N.L.: Vladimir Guerrero, Expos	.379	22	7	28
May				
A.L.: Jason Giambi, Yankees	.340	26	10	24
N.L.: Todd Helton, Rockies	.347	24	10	28
June				
A.L.: Paul Konerko, White Sox	.340	18	12	22
N.L.: Jeff Kent, Giants	.414	18	6	28
July				
A.L.: Alex Rodriguez, Rangers	.349	21	12	27
N.L.: Larry Walker, Rockies	.438	18	5	17
August				
A.L.: Alex Rodriguez, Rangers	.339	24	12	27
N.L.: Barry Bonds, Giants	.447	24	11	25
September				
A.L.: Manny Ramirez, Red Sox	.396	20	10	30
N.L.: Brian Jordan, Dodgers	.347	10	5	30

PITCHER OF THE MONTH

April	W	L	ERA
A.L.: Derek Lowe, Red Sox	4	1	2.04
N.L.: Randy Johnson, Diamondbacks	6	0	1.37
May			
A.L.: Bartolo Colon, Indians	4	0	1.13
N.L.: Curt Schilling, Diamondbacks	5	0	2.80
June			
A.L.: Mark Mulder, Athletics	6	0	2.51
N.L.: Eric Gagne, Dodgers	0	0	0.63
July			
A.L.: Pedro Martinez, Red Sox	5	0	0.64
N.L.: Curt Schilling, Diamondbacks	5	0	1.64
August			
A.L.: Cory Lidle, Athletics	5	0	0.20
N.L.: Roy Oswalt, Astros	6	0	1.22
September			
A.L.: Andy Pettitte, Yankees	5	0	2.23
N.L.: Randy Johnson, Diamondbacks	5	0	0.66

American League Statistics

TEAM STATISTICS

BATTING

Team	Avg.	G	AB	R	OR	H	TB	2B	3B	HR	GS	RBI	SH	SF	HP	BB	IBB	SO	SB	CS	GDP	LOB	SHO	SLG	OBP
Anaheim	.282	162	5678	851	644	1603	2456	333	32	152	5	811	49	64	74	462	42	805	117	51	105	1165	8	.433	.341
Boston	.277	162	5640	859	665	1560	2505	348	33	177	6	810	22	53	72	545	39	944	80	28	139	1175	7	.444	.345
New York	.275	161	5601	897	697	1540	2547	314	12	223	6	857	23	41	72	640	48	1171	100	38	150	1191	3	.455	.354
Seattle	.275	162	5569	814	699	1531	2334	285	31	152	7	771	41	72	51	629	62	1003	137	58	123	1239	7	.419	.350
Minnesota	.272	161	5582	768	712	1518	2439	348	36	167	3	731	34	52	56	472	30	1089	79	62	121	1124	8	.437	.332
Texas	.269	162	5618	843	882	1510	2558	304	27	230	4	806	48	50	62	554	45	1055	62	34	129	1155	6	.455	.338
Chicago	.268	162	5502	856	798	1475	2473	289	29	217	8	819	48	53	49	555	17	952	75	31	111	1085	7	.449	.338
Toronto	.261	162	5581	813	828	1457	2399	305	38	187	0	771	17	57	53	522	30	1142	71	18	130	1104	6	.430	.327
Oakland	.261	162	5558	800	654	1450	2400	279	28	205	2	772	20	36	68	609	37	1008	46	20	128	1197	6	.432	.339
Kansas City	.256	162	5535	737	891	1415	2204	285	42	140	4	695	44	51	52	524	27	921	140	65	106	1092	13	.398	.323
Tampa Bay	.253	161	5604	673	918	1418	2184	297	35	133	3	640	44	36	58	456	29	1115	102	45	116	1132	14	.390	.314
Cleveland	.249	162	5423	739	837	1349	2232	255	26	192	9	706	39	39	56	542	35	1000	52	37	149	1066	8	.412	.321
Detroit	.248	161	5406	575	864	1340	2051	265	37	124	1	546	30	57	64	363	22	1035	65	44	125	1029	10	.379	.300
Baltimore	.246	162	5491	667	773	1353	2213	311	27	165	2	636	40	49	64	452	25	993	110	48	128	1037	15	.403	.309
Totals	.264	1132	77788	10892	10862	20519	32995	4218	433	2464	60	10371	499	710	851	7325	488	14233	1236	579	1760	15791	118	.424	.331

PITCHING

Team	W	L	ERA	G	CG	SHO	Rel.	Sv.	IP	H	R	ER	HR	HB	BB	IBB	SO	WP	Bk.	Avg.
Oakland	103	59	3.68	162	9	19	408	48	1452.0	1391	654	593	135	62	474	45	1021	40	9	.252
Anaheim	99	63	3.69	162	7	14	400	54	1452.1	1345	644	595	169	49	509	24	999	52	7	.247
Boston	93	69	3.75	162	5	17	338	51	1446.0	1339	665	603	146	84	430	29	1157	31	6	.246
New York	103	58	3.87	161	9	11	334	53	1452.0	1441	697	625	144	48	403	44	1135	59	2	.256
Seattle	93	69	4.07	162	8	12	343	43	1445.1	1422	699	654	178	49	441	34	1063	42	3	.257
Minnesota	94	67	4.12	161	8	9	435	47	1444.2	1454	712	662	184	45	439	24	1026	62	3	.261
Baltimore	67	95	4.46	162	8	3	407	31	1450.2	1491	773	719	208	54	549	34	967	54	1	.266
Chicago	81	81	4.53	162	7	7	423	35	1423.0	1422	798	716	190	60	528	31	945	54	6	.260
Toronto	78	84	4.80	162	6	6	461	41	1438.1	1504	828	767	177	71	590	56	991	57	4	.269
Cleveland	74	88	4.91	162	9	4	421	34	1424.2	1508	837	777	142	57	603	38	1058	52	8	.274
Detroit	55	106	4.92	161	11	7	372	33	1414.0	1593	864	773	163	62	463	34	794	59	8	.285
Texas	72	90	5.15	162	4	4	487	33	1439.2	1528	882	824	194	76	669	32	1030	84	11	.272
Kansas City	62	100	5.21	162	12	6	421	30	1441.0	1587	891	834	212	52	572	48	909	68	6	.281
Tampa Bay	55	106	5.29	161	12	3	306	25	1440.1	1567	918	846	215	94	620	24	925	62	10	.279
Totals	1129	1135	4.46	1132	115	122	5556	558	20164.0	20592	10862	9988	2457	863	7290	497	14020	776	84	.265

FIELDING

Team	Pct.	G	PO	A	E	TC	DP	TP	PB
Minnesota	.987	161	4334	1422	74	5830	124	0	5
Anaheim	.986	162	4357	1575	87	6019	151	0	7
Baltimore	.985	162	4352	1720	91	6163	173	0	22
Seattle	.985	162	4336	1515	88	5939	134	0	7
Texas	.984	162	4319	1683	99	6101	152	1	11
Chicago	.984	162	4269	1595	97	5961	157	0	9
Oakland	.984	162	4356	1798	102	6256	144	0	9
Boston	.983	162	4338	1645	104	6087	140	0	20
Toronto	.982	162	4315	1613	107	6035	159	0	18
Cleveland	.981	162	4274	1662	113	6049	161	0	15
Tampa Bay	.979	161	4321	1567	126	6014	168	1	13
Kansas City	.979	162	4323	1702	130	6155	153	0	8
New York	.979	161	4356	1524	127	6007	117	0	10
Detroit	.977	161	4242	1719	142	6103	148	0	23
Totals	.982	1132	60492	22740	1487	84719	2081	2	177

ATTENDANCE

	2002				2001	
Team	Home	Road	Dates	Avg.	Dates	Avg.
Seattle	3,540,482	2,233,145	81	43,710	81	43,308
New York	3,461,644	2,940,048	80	43,271	80	40,810
Baltimore	2,682,917	2,019,608	81	33,122	80	38,686
Boston	2,650,063	2,474,060	81	32,717	81	32,412
Cleveland	2,616,940	1,924,931	81	32,308	80	39,694
Texas	2,352,447	2,251,033	80	29,406	81	34,647
Anaheim	2,305,565	2,144,024	81	28,464	81	24,703
Oakland	2,169,811	2,416,196	81	26,788	81	26,337
Minnesota	1,924,473	2,144,110	81	23,759	80	22,287
Chicago	1,676,804	2,075,811	81	20,701	80	22,077
Toronto	1,636,904	2,086,535	81	20,209	81	23,647
Detroit	1,503,623	2,033,697	80	18,795	80	24,016
Kansas City	1,323,034	2,166,489	77	17,182	81	18,353
Tampa Bay	1,065,762	2,122,092	81	13,158	81	15,156
Totals	30,910,469	31,031,779	1,127	27,427	1,128	28,997

Anaheim Angels

INDIVIDUAL STATISTICS

BATTING

Batter	Avg.	G	TPA	AB	R	H	TB	2B	3B	HR	RBI	SH	SF	HP	BB	IBB	SO	SB	CS	GDP	Slg.	OBP
Eckstein, David	.293	152	702	608	107	178	236	22	6	8	63	14	8	27	45	0	44	21	13	7	.388	.363
Anderson, Garret*	.306	158	678	638	93	195	344	56	3	29	123	0	10	0	30	11	80	6	4	11	.539	.332
Glaus, Troy	.250	156	671	569	99	142	258	24	1	30	111	0	8	6	88	4	144	10	3	12	.453	.352
Erstad, Darin*	.283	150	663	625	99	177	243	28	4	10	73	5	4	2	27	4	67	23	3	9	.389	.313
Spiezio, Scott†	.285	153	571	491	80	140	214	34	2	12	82	3	6	4	67	7	52	6	7	12	.436	.371
Salmon, Tim	.286	138	568	483	84	138	243	37	1	22	88	0	7	7	71	3	102	6	3	6	.503	.380
Kennedy, Adam*	.312	144	509	474	65	148	213	32	6	7	52	5	4	7	19	1	80	17	4	5	.449	.345
Fullmer, Brad*	.289	130	479	429	75	124	228	35	6	19	59	0	3	15	32	6	44	10	3	7	.531	.357
Molina, Bengie	.245	122	459	428	34	105	138	18	0	5	47	6	6	4	15	3	34	0	0	15	.322	.274
Palmeiro, Orlando*	.300	110	300	263	35	79	93	12	1	0	31	4	3	0	30	1	22	7	2	7	.354	.368
Gil, Benji	.285	61	139	130	11	37	56	8	1	3	20	2	2	0	5	0	33	2	1	0	.431	.307
Wooten, Shawn	.292	49	121	113	13	33	50	8	0	3	19	0	1	1	6	1	24	2	0	3	.442	.331
Nieves, Jose	.289	45	100	97	17	28	30	2	0	0	6	1	0	0	2	0	14	1	1	3	.309	.303
Fabregas, Jorge*	.193	35	96	88	8	17	18	1	0	0	8	2	0	0	6	1	6	0	0	3	.205	.245
Molina, Jose	.271	29	81	70	5	19	22	3	0	0	5	4	2	0	5	0	15	0	2	2	.314	.312
Ochoa, Alex	.277	37	75	65	8	18	31	7	0	2	10	0	0	0	10	0	5	2	2	0	.477	.373
Ramirez, Julio	.281	29	35	32	6	9	14	0	1	1	7	0	0	1	2	0	14	0	2	0	.438	.343
DaVanon, Jeff†	.167	16	33	30	3	5	11	3	0	1	4	1	0	0	2	0	6	1	0	0	.367	.219
Amezaga, Alfredo†	.538	12	13	13	3	7	9	2	0	0	2	0	0	0	0	0	1	1	0	1	.692	.538
Figgins, Chone†	.167	15	12	12	6	2	3	1	0	0	1	0	0	0	0	0	5	2	1	1	.250	.167
Ortiz, Ramon	.000	2	7	7	0	0	0	0	0	0	0	0	0	0	0	0	3	0	0	1	.000	.000
Washburn, Jarrod*	.200	2	5	5	0	1	1	0	0	0	0	0	0	0	0	0	3	0	0	0	.200	.200
Appier, Kevin	.000	2	4	2	0	0	0	0	0	0	0	2	0	0	0	0	2	0	0	0	.000	.000
Schoeneweis, Scott*	.000	2	2	2	0	0	0	0	0	0	0	0	0	0	0	0	2	0	0	0	.000	.000
Sele, Aaron	.500	1	2	2	0	1	1	0	0	0	0	0	0	0	0	0	1	0	0	0	.500	.500
Bellinger, Clay	.000	2	1	1	0	0	0	0	0	0	0	0	0	0	0	0	1	0	0	0	.000	.000
Fasano, Sal	.000	2	1	1	0	0	0	0	0	0	0	0	0	0	0	0	1	0	0	0	.000	.000

* Lefthanded batter. † Switch-hitter.

PITCHING

Pitcher	W	L	ERA	G	GS	CG	GF	SHO	Sv.	IP	H	R	ER	HR	HB	BB	IBB	SO	WP	Bk.
Ortiz, Ramon	15	9	3.77	32	32	4	0	1	0	217.1	188	97	91	40	5	68	0	162	7	3
Washburn, Jarrod*	18	6	3.15	32	32	1	0	0	0	206.0	183	75	72	19	3	59	1	139	5	1
Appier, Kevin	14	12	3.92	32	32	0	0	0	0	188.1	191	89	82	23	7	64	2	132	7	0
Sele, Aaron	8	9	4.89	26	26	1	0	1	0	160.0	190	92	87	21	7	49	2	82	5	0
Schoeneweis, Scott*	9	8	4.88	54	15	0	4	0	1	118.0	119	68	64	17	5	49	4	65	1	1
Lackey, John	9	4	3.66	18	18	1	0	0	0	108.1	113	52	44	10	4	33	0	69	7	2
Weber, Ben	7	2	2.54	63	0	0	16	0	7	78.0	70	25	22	4	3	22	3	43	2	0
Levine, Al	4	4	4.24	52	0	0	21	0	5	63.2	61	35	30	8	2	34	3	40	2	0
Percival, Troy	4	1	1.92	58	0	0	50	0	40	56.1	38	12	12	5	0	25	1	68	5	0
Pote, Lou	0	2	3.22	31	0	0	13	0	0	50.1	33	20	18	7	3	26	2	32	3	0
Donnelly, Brendan	1	1	2.17	46	0	0	11	0	1	49.2	32	13	12	2	2	19	3	54	1	0
Shields, Scot	5	3	2.20	29	1	0	13	0	0	49.0	31	13	12	4	1	21	1	30	3	0
Callaway, Mickey	2	1	4.19	6	6	0	0	0	0	34.1	31	20	16	4	3	11	0	23	2	0
Cook, Dennis*	1	1	3.38	37	0	0	5	0	0	24.0	21	9	9	2	1	10	0	13	0	0
Wall, Donne	0	0	6.43	17	0	0	8	0	0	21.0	17	15	15	3	1	7	1	13	2	0
Lukasiewicz, Mark*	2	0	3.86	17	0	0	4	0	0	14.0	17	6	6	0	0	9	0	15	0	0
Wise, Matt	0	0	3.24	7	0	0	6	0	0	8.1	7	3	3	0	1	1	0	6	0	0
Rodriguez, Francisco	0	0	0.00	5	0	0	4	0	0	5.2	3	0	0	0	1	2	1	13	0	0

* Throws lefthanded.

Baltimore Orioles

INDIVIDUAL STATISTICS

BATTING

Batter	Avg.	G	TPA	AB	R	H	TB	2B	3B	HR	RBI	SH	SF	HP	BB	IBB	SO	SB	CS	GDP	Slg.	OBP
Batista, Tony	.244	161	682	615	90	150	281	36	1	31	87	0	6	11	50	9	107	5	4	13	.457	.309
Mora, Melvin	.233	149	652	557	86	130	225	30	4	19	64	1	4	20	70	2	108	16	10	7	.404	.338
Gibbons, Jay*	.247	136	541	490	71	121	236	29	1	28	69	0	4	2	45	3	66	1	3	9	.482	.311
Cordova, Marty	.253	131	513	458	55	116	199	25	2	18	64	2	3	3	47	3	111	1	6	17	.434	.325
Singleton, Chris*	.262	136	502	466	67	122	191	30	6	9	50	6	5	4	21	0	83	20	2	8	.410	.296
Conine, Jeff	.273	116	488	451	44	123	202	26	4	15	63	0	10	2	25	6	66	8	0	10	.448	.307
Hairston, Jerry	.268	122	479	426	55	114	160	25	3	5	32	8	4	7	34	0	55	21	6	5	.376	.329
Gil, Geronimo	.232	125	450	422	33	98	153	19	0	12	45	5	1	1	21	1	88	2	2	17	.363	.270
Bordick, Mike	.232	117	413	367	37	85	134	19	3	8	36	6	2	3	35	0	63	7	4	9	.365	.302
Matthews, Gary†	.276	109	397	344	54	95	147	25	3	7	38	5	4	1	43	1	69	15	5	4	.427	.355
Richard, Chris*	.232	50	171	155	15	36	59	11	0	4	21	0	2	2	12	0	30	0	3	2	.381	.292
Roberts, Brian†	.227	38	149	128	18	29	38	6	0	1	11	3	2	1	15	0	21	9	2	3	.297	.308
Fordyce, Brook	.231	56	146	130	7	30	41	8	0	1	8	3	0	4	9	0	19	1	0	5	.315	.301
Lopez, Luis†	.211	52	112	109	10	23	35	6	0	2	9	0	0	0	3	0	20	1	0	3	.321	.232
Segui, David†	.263	26	107	95	10	25	35	4	0	2	16	0	1	0	11	0	22	0	0	0	.368	.336
Leon, Jose	.247	36	93	89	8	22	33	2	0	3	10	0	0	1	3	0	20	1	0	2	.371	.280
Clark, Howie*	.302	14	58	53	3	16	21	5	0	0	4	0	0	2	3	0	6	0	0	5	.396	.362
Bigbie, Larry*	.176	16	36	34	1	6	7	1	0	0	3	0	1	0	1	0	11	1	0	1	.206	.194
Matos, Luis	.129	17	33	31	0	4	5	1	0	0	1	1	0	0	1	0	6	1	0	1	.161	.156
McGuire, Ryan*	.077	17	28	26	0	2	3	1	0	0	2	0	0	0	2	0	7	0	0	2	.115	.143
Moriarty, Mike	.188	8	16	16	0	3	4	1	0	0	3	0	0	0	0	0	2	0	1	3	.250	.188
Driskill, Travis	.000	2	4	3	1	0	0	0	0	0	0	0	0	0	1	0	3	0	0	0	.000	.250
Erickson, Scott	.000	2	4	4	0	0	0	0	0	0	0	0	0	0	0	0	2	0	0	0	.000	.000
Garcia, Luis	.333	6	3	3	0	1	1	0	0	0	0	0	0	0	0	0	1	0	0	0	.333	.333
Johnson, Jason	.000	2	3	3	0	0	0	0	0	0	0	0	0	0	0	0	2	0	0	0	.000	.000
Lopez, Rodrigo	.000	1	3	3	0	0	0	0	0	0	0	0	0	0	0	0	2	0	0	1	.000	.000
Molina, Izzy	.333	1	3	3	1	1	1	0	0	0	0	0	0	0	0	0	0	0	0	0	.333	.333
Ponson, Sidney	.333	2	3	3	1	1	2	1	0	0	0	0	0	0	0	0	1	0	0	0	.667	.333
Rogers, Eddie	.000	5	3	3	0	0	0	0	0	0	0	0	0	0	0	0	0	0	0	1	.000	.000
Brock, Chris	.000	2	2	2	0	0	0	0	0	0	0	0	0	0	0	0	1	0	0	0	.000	.000
Casanova, Raul†	.000	2	1	1	0	0	0	0	0	0	0	0	0	0	0	0	1	0	0	0	.000	.000
Ryan, B.J.*	.000	4	1	1	0	0	0	0	0	0	0	0	0	0	0	0	0	0	0	0	.000	.000

* Lefthanded batter. † Switch-hitter.

PITCHING

Pitcher	W	L	ERA	G	GS	CG	GF	SHO	Sv.	IP	H	R	ER	HR	HB	BB	IBB	SO	WP	Bk.
Lopez, Rodrigo	15	9	3.57	33	28	1	0	0	0	196.2	172	83	78	23	5	62	4	136	2	1
Ponson, Sidney	7	9	4.09	28	28	3	0	0	0	176.0	172	84	80	26	2	63	1	120	3	0
Erickson, Scott	5	12	5.55	29	28	3	0	1	0	160.2	192	109	99	20	8	68	2	74	5	0
Driskill, Travis	8	8	4.95	29	19	0	6	0	0	132.2	150	78	73	21	8	48	1	78	6	0
Johnson, Jason	5	14	4.59	22	22	1	0	0	0	131.1	141	68	67	19	6	41	2	97	4	0
Bauer, Rick	6	7	3.98	56	1	0	15	0	1	83.2	84	41	37	12	4	36	4	45	4	0
Roberts, Willis	5	4	3.36	66	0	0	24	0	1	75.0	79	34	28	5	4	32	3	51	7	0
Julio, Jorge	5	6	1.99	67	0	0	61	0	25	68.0	55	22	15	5	2	27	3	55	8	0
Stephens, John	2	5	6.09	12	11	0	0	0	0	65.0	68	44	44	13	3	22	2	56	2	0
Groom, Buddy*	3	2	1.60	70	0	0	17	0	2	62.0	44	11	11	4	2	12	3	48	0	0
Ryan, B.J.*	2	1	4.68	67	0	0	13	0	1	57.2	51	31	30	7	4	33	4	56	4	0
Maduro, Calvin	2	5	5.56	12	10	0	2	0	0	56.2	64	37	35	12	1	22	1	29	1	0
Douglass, Sean	0	5	6.08	15	8	0	2	0	0	53.1	58	41	36	10	2	35	2	44	3	0
Brock, Chris	2	1	4.70	22	0	0	3	0	0	44.0	52	24	23	6	1	14	1	21	0	0
Perez, Yorkis*	0	0	3.29	23	0	0	8	0	1	27.1	21	12	10	4	0	14	1	25	3	0
Towers, Josh	0	3	7.90	5	3	0	1	0	0	27.1	42	24	24	11	0	5	0	13	1	0
Hentgen, Pat	0	4	7.77	4	4	0	0	0	0	22.0	31	20	19	6	0	10	0	11	1	0
DuBose, Eric*	0	0	3.00	4	0	0	2	0	0	6.0	7	2	2	1	1	1	0	4	0	0
Bechler, Steve	0	0	13.50	3	0	0	0	0	0	4.2	6	7	7	3	1	4	0	3	0	0
Bedard, Erik*	0	0	13.50	2	0	0	0	0	0	0.2	2	1	1	0	0	0	0	1	0	0

* Throws lefthanded.

BOSTON RED SOX

INDIVIDUAL STATISTICS

BATTING

Batter	Avg.	G	TPA	AB	R	H	TB	2B	3B	HR	RBI	SH	SF	HP	BB	IBB	SO	SB	CS	GDP	Slg.	OBP
Damon, Johnny*	.286	154	702	623	118	178	276	34	11	14	63	3	5	6	65	5	70	31	6	4	.443	.356
Garciaparra, Nomar	.310	156	693	635	101	197	335	56	5	24	120	0	11	6	41	4	63	5	2	17	.528	.352
Hillenbrand, Shea	.293	156	676	634	94	186	291	43	4	18	83	0	5	12	25	4	95	4	2	18	.459	.330
Nixon, Trot*	.256	152	612	532	81	136	250	36	3	24	94	3	7	5	65	2	109	4	2	7	.470	.338
Varitek, Jason†	.266	132	519	467	58	124	183	27	1	10	61	1	3	7	41	3	95	4	3	13	.392	.332
Ramirez, Manny	.349	120	518	436	84	152	282	31	0	33	107	0	1	8	73	14	85	0	0	13	.647	.450
Daubach, Brian*	.266	137	506	444	62	118	206	24	2	20	78	0	4	7	51	4	126	2	1	10	.464	.348
Sanchez, Rey	.286	107	386	357	46	102	123	12	3	1	38	5	5	2	17	1	31	2	2	9	.345	.318
Clark, Tony†	.207	90	298	275	25	57	80	12	1	3	29	0	1	1	21	0	57	0	0	11	.291	.265
Offerman, Jose†	.232	72	275	237	39	55	77	10	0	4	27	1	3	1	33	0	29	8	5	9	.325	.325
Henderson, Rickey	.223	72	222	179	40	40	63	6	1	5	16	0	1	4	38	0	47	8	2	3	.352	.369
Merloni, Lou	.247	84	222	194	28	48	76	12	2	4	18	2	1	5	20	0	35	1	2	4	.392	.332
Baerga, Carlos†	.286	73	194	182	17	52	69	11	0	2	19	1	2	2	7	1	20	6	0	6	.379	.316
Floyd, Cliff*	.316	47	190	171	30	54	96	21	0	7	18	0	2	2	15	0	28	4	0	6	.561	.374
Mirabelli, Doug	.225	57	173	151	17	34	62	7	0	7	25	0	2	3	17	0	33	0	0	6	.411	.312
Agbayani, Benny	.297	13	43	37	5	11	12	1	0	0	8	0	0	0	6	1	5	0	0	1	.324	.395
Nelson, Bry†	.265	25	39	34	6	9	12	3	0	0	2	1	0	0	4	0	1	1	1	1	.353	.342
Sanchez, Freddy	.188	12	18	16	3	3	3	0	0	0	2	0	0	0	2	0	3	0	0	0	.188	.278
Andrews, Shane	.077	7	15	13	2	1	2	1	0	0	0	0	0	1	1	0	3	0	0	0	.154	.200
Diaz, Juan	.286	4	8	7	2	2	6	1	0	1	2	0	0	0	1	0	2	0	0	0	.857	.375
Martinez, Pedro	.000	2	7	5	1	0	0	0	0	0	0	1	0	0	1	0	3	0	0	0	.000	.167
Lowe, Derek	.333	2	5	3	0	1	1	0	0	0	0	1	0	0	1	0	0	0	0	1	.333	.500
Burkett, John	.000	2	4	3	0	0	0	0	0	0	0	1	0	0	0	0	1	0	0	0	.000	.000
Arrojo, Rolando	.000	2	3	2	0	0	0	0	0	0	0	1	0	0	0	0	2	0	0	0	.000	.000
Castillo, Frank	.000	1	2	1	0	0	0	0	0	0	0	1	0	0	0	0	1	0	0	0	.000	.000
Brown, Kevin L.	.000	2	1	1	0	0	0	0	0	0	0	0	0	0	0	0	0	0	0	0	.000	.000
Oliver, Darren	.000	2	1	1	0	0	0	0	0	0	0	0	0	0	0	0	0	0	0	0	.000	.000

Batters with more than one A.L. team

Batter	Avg.	G	TPA	AB	R	H	TB	2B	3B	HR	RBI	SH	SF	HP	BB	IBB	SO	SB	CS	GDP	Slg.	OBP
Offerman, Bos.-Sea.†	.232	101	326	284	48	66	95	12	1	5	31	1	3	1	37	0	38	9	6	12	.335	.320

* Lefthanded batter. † Switch-hitter.

PITCHING

Pitcher	W	L	ERA	G	GS	CG	GF	SHO	Sv.	IP	H	R	ER	HR	HB	BB	IBB	SO	WP	Bk.
Lowe, Derek	21	8	2.58	32	32	1	0	1	0	219.2	166	65	63	12	12	48	0	127	5	0
Martinez, Pedro	20	4	2.26	30	30	2	0	0	0	199.1	144	62	50	13	15	40	1	239	3	0
Burkett, John	13	8	4.53	29	29	1	0	1	0	173.0	199	93	87	25	8	50	5	124	2	1
Castillo, Frank	6	15	5.07	36	23	0	2	0	1	163.1	174	101	92	19	7	58	6	112	1	2
Wakefield, Tim	11	5	2.81	45	15	0	10	0	3	163.1	121	57	51	15	9	51	2	134	5	2
Fossum, Casey*	5	4	3.46	43	12	0	13	0	1	106.2	113	56	41	12	4	30	0	101	3	0
Arrojo, Rolando	4	3	4.98	29	8	0	4	0	1	81.1	83	47	45	7	6	27	1	51	2	0
Urbina, Ugueth	1	6	3.00	61	0	0	55	0	40	60.0	44	21	20	8	0	20	5	71	3	1
Oliver, Darren*	4	5	4.66	14	9	1	0	1	0	58.0	70	30	30	7	6	27	0	32	1	0
Banks, Willie	2	1	3.23	29	0	0	18	0	1	39.0	32	15	14	5	3	14	0	26	1	0
Embree, Alan*	1	2	2.97	32	0	0	7	0	2	33.1	24	12	11	4	1	11	1	43	0	0
Haney, Chris*	0	0	4.20	24	0	0	11	0	1	30.0	32	14	14	2	4	10	2	15	0	0
Kim, Sun-Woo	2	0	7.45	15	2	0	7	0	0	29.0	34	24	24	5	1	7	0	18	2	0
Hermanson, Dustin	1	1	7.77	12	1	0	4	0	0	22.0	35	19	19	3	0	7	0	13	2	0
Garces, Rich	0	1	7.59	26	0	0	7	0	0	21.1	21	20	18	4	3	12	2	16	0	0
Gomes, Wayne	1	2	4.64	20	0	0	8	0	1	21.1	20	11	11	2	3	12	2	15	0	0
Howry, Bob	1	3	5.00	20	0	0	9	0	0	18.0	22	15	10	2	2	4	2	14	1	0
Hancock, Josh	0	1	3.68	3	1	0	2	0	0	7.1	5	3	3	1	0	2	0	6	0	0

Pitchers with more than one A.L. team

Pitcher	W	L	ERA	G	GS	CG	GF	SHO	Sv.	IP	H	R	ER	HR	HB	BB	IBB	SO	WP	Bk.
Howry, Chi.-Bos.	3	5	4.19	67	0	0	26	0	0	68.2	67	37	32	9	5	21	4	45	2	0

* Throws lefthanded.

CHICAGO WHITE SOX

INDIVIDUAL STATISTICS

BATTING

Batter	Avg.	G	TPA	AB	R	H	TB	2B	3B	HR	RBI	SH	SF	HP	BB	IBB	SO	SB	CS	GDP	Slg.	OBP
Ordonez, Magglio	.320	153	654	590	116	189	352	47	1	38	135	0	3	7	53	2	77	7	5	21	.597	.381
Konerko, Paul	.304	151	630	570	81	173	284	30	0	27	104	0	7	9	44	2	72	0	0	17	.498	.359
Thomas, Frank................	.252	148	628	523	77	132	247	29	1	28	92	0	10	7	88	2	115	3	0	10	.472	.361
Lee, Carlos	.264	140	576	492	82	130	238	26	2	26	80	0	7	2	75	4	73	1	4	5	.484	.359
Valentin, Jose†	.249	135	527	474	70	118	227	26	4	25	75	3	5	2	43	2	99	3	3	9	.479	.311
Durham, Ray†	.299	96	411	345	71	103	154	20	2	9	48	8	4	5	49	0	59	20	5	13	.446	.390
Lofton, Kenny*	.259	93	406	352	68	91	147	20	6	8	42	4	1	0	49	0	51	22	8	0	.418	.348
Clayton, Royce	.251	112	376	342	51	86	125	14	2	7	35	7	4	3	20	0	67	5	1	7	.365	.295
Rowand, Aaron	.258	126	331	302	41	78	119	16	2	7	29	9	2	6	12	1	54	0	1	8	.394	.298
Johnson, Mark L.*	.209	86	302	263	31	55	77	8	1	4	18	6	0	3	30	1	52	0	0	4	.293	.297
Graffanino, Tony	.262	70	259	229	35	60	98	12	4	6	31	4	2	2	22	1	38	2	1	2	.428	.329
Liefer, Jeff*	.230	76	224	204	28	47	76	8	0	7	26	0	1	0	19	2	60	0	0	3	.373	.295
Crede, Joe	.285	53	209	200	28	57	103	10	0	12	35	0	1	0	8	0	40	0	2	1	.515	.311
Harris, Willie*	.233	49	177	163	14	38	48	4	0	2	12	3	2	0	9	0	21	8	0	3	.294	.270
Alomar, Sandy	.287	51	176	167	21	48	81	10	1	7	25	1	2	1	5	0	14	0	0	5	.485	.309
Jimenez, D'Angelo†........	.287	27	125	108	22	31	44	4	3	1	11	0	0	1	16	0	10	2	1	1	.407	.384
Paul, Josh	.240	33	118	104	11	25	29	4	0	0	11	2	2	1	9	0	22	2	0	1	.279	.302
Borchard, Joe†	.222	16	37	36	5	8	14	0	0	2	5	0	0	0	1	0	14	0	0	0	.389	.243
Olivo, Miguel	.211	6	21	19	2	4	8	1	0	1	5	0	0	0	2	0	5	0	0	1	.421	.286
Buehrle, Mark*	.167	2	6	6	1	1	1	0	0	0	0	0	0	0	0	0	4	0	0	0	.167	.167
Ritchie, Todd	.250	3	5	4	1	1	1	0	0	0	0	0	0	0	1	0	1	0	0	0	.250	.400
Wright, Dan	.000	2	4	4	0	0	0	0	0	0	0	0	0	0	0	0	2	0	0	0	.000	.000
Garland, Jon	.000	2	3	2	0	0	0	0	0	0	0	1	0	0	0	0	0	0	0	0	.000	.000
Foulke, Keith	.000	4	1	1	0	0	0	0	0	0	0	0	0	0	0	0	0	0	0	0	.000	.000
Glover, Gary....................	.000	2	1	1	0	0	0	0	0	0	0	0	0	0	0	0	1	0	0	0	.000	.000
Marte, Damaso*	.000	4	1	1	0	0	0	0	0	0	0	0	0	0	0	0	1	0	0	0	.000	.000

Batters with more than one A.L. team

Batter	Avg.	G	TPA	AB	R	H	TB	2B	3B	HR	RBI	SH	SF	HP	BB	IBB	SO	SB	CS	GDP	Slg.	OBP
Durham, Chi.-Oak.†........	.289	150	659	564	114	163	254	34	6	15	70	10	5	7	73	1	93	26	7	15	.450	.374

* Lefthanded batter. † Switch-hitter.

PITCHING

Pitcher	W	L	ERA	G	GS	CG	GF	SHO	Sv.	IP	H	R	ER	HR	HB	BB	IBB	SO	WP	Bk.
Buehrle, Mark*	19	12	3.58	34	34	5	0	2	0	239.0	236	102	95	25	3	61	7	134	6	1
Wright, Dan	14	12	5.18	33	33	1	0	1	0	196.1	200	124	113	32	6	71	1	136	10	1
Garland, Jon	12	12	4.58	33	33	1	0	1	0	192.2	188	109	98	23	9	83	1	112	5	0
Glover, Gary....................	7	8	5.20	41	22	0	10	0	1	138.1	136	86	80	21	7	52	1	70	6	0
Ritchie, Todd	5	15	6.06	26	23	0	1	0	0	133.2	176	104	90	18	5	52	2	77	10	0
Biddle, Rocky	3	4	4.06	44	7	0	9	0	1	77.2	72	42	35	13	5	39	4	64	5	0
Foulke, Keith	2	4	2.90	65	0	0	35	0	11	77.2	65	26	25	7	2	13	2	58	1	0
Osuna, Antonio	8	2	3.86	59	0	0	28	0	11	67.2	64	32	29	1	4	28	4	66	0	1
Marte, Damaso*	1	1	2.83	68	0	0	22	0	10	60.1	44	19	19	5	4	18	2	72	3	1
Ginter, Matt	1	0	4.47	33	0	0	15	0	1	54.1	59	34	27	6	1	21	0	37	2	0
Howry, Bob	2	2	3.91	47	0	0	17	0	0	50.2	45	22	22	7	3	17	2	31	1	0
Porzio, Mike*	2	2	4.81	32	0	0	8	0	0	43.0	40	25	23	10	3	23	2	33	3	1
Wunsch, Kelly*	2	1	3.41	50	0	0	9	0	0	31.2	26	12	12	3	5	19	1	22	1	0
Rauch, Jon	2	1	6.59	8	6	0	1	0	0	28.2	28	26	21	7	2	14	2	19	1	1
Parque, Jim*	1	4	9.95	8	4	0	0	0	0	25.1	34	29	28	11	1	16	0	13	0	0
Barcelo, Lorenzo	0	1	9.00	4	0	0	0	0	0	6.0	9	6	6	1	0	1	0	1	0	0

Pitchers with more than one A.L. team

Pitcher	W	L	ERA	G	GS	CG	GF	SHO	Sv.	IP	H	R	ER	HR	HB	BB	IBB	SO	WP	Bk.
Howry, Chi.-Bos.	3	5	4.19	67	0	0	26	0	0	68.2	67	37	32	9	5	21	4	45	2	0

* Throws lefthanded.

Cleveland Indians

INDIVIDUAL STATISTICS

BATTING

Batter	Avg.	G	TPA	AB	R	H	TB	2B	3B	HR	RBI	SH	SF	HP	BB	IBB	SO	SB	CS	GDP	Slg.	OBP
Vizquel, Omar†	.275	151	663	582	85	160	243	31	5	14	72	7	10	8	56	3	64	18	10	7	.418	.341
Thome, Jim*	.304	147	613	480	101	146	325	19	2	52	118	0	6	5	122	18	139	1	2	5	.677	.445
Burks, Ellis	.301	138	570	518	92	156	280	28	0	32	91	1	1	6	44	3	108	2	3	13	.541	.362
Lawton, Matt*	.236	114	484	416	71	98	166	19	2	15	57	1	0	8	59	0	34	8	9	13	.399	.342
Fryman, Travis	.217	118	439	397	42	86	139	14	3	11	55	0	0	2	40	1	82	0	0	12	.350	.292
Gutierrez, Ricky	.275	94	384	353	38	97	122	13	0	4	38	3	1	7	20	0	48	0	1	14	.346	.325
Bradley, Milton†	.249	98	358	325	48	81	132	18	3	9	38	1	0	0	32	2	58	6	3	12	.406	.317
Diaz, Einar	.206	102	351	320	34	66	91	19	0	2	16	6	2	6	17	1	27	0	1	13	.284	.258
McDonald, John	.250	93	288	264	35	66	86	11	3	1	12	7	2	5	10	0	50	3	0	4	.326	.288
Magruder, Chris†	.217	87	278	258	34	56	91	15	1	6	29	2	2	1	15	2	55	2	0	7	.353	.261
Garcia, Karim*	.299	51	205	197	29	59	115	8	0	16	52	0	2	0	6	0	40	0	3	6	.584	.317
Branyan, Russell*	.205	50	180	161	16	33	61	4	0	8	17	0	2	0	17	0	65	1	2	3	.379	.278
Selby, Bill*	.214	65	176	159	15	34	63	7	2	6	21	0	2	0	15	2	27	0	1	4	.396	.278
Stevens, Lee*	.222	53	172	153	22	34	58	7	1	5	26	0	4	0	15	0	32	0	0	5	.379	.285
Crisp, Coco†	.260	32	143	127	16	33	49	9	2	1	9	3	2	0	11	0	19	4	1	0	.386	.314
Perez, Eddie	.214	42	125	117	6	25	34	9	0	0	4	2	0	1	5	0	25	0	0	6	.291	.252
Broussard, Ben*	.241	39	120	112	10	27	43	4	0	4	9	0	0	1	7	1	25	0	0	3	.384	.292
Anderson, Brady*	.163	34	101	80	4	13	20	4	0	1	5	0	1	2	18	2	23	4	0	5	.250	.327
Bard, Josh†	.222	24	95	90	9	20	34	5	0	3	12	1	0	0	4	0	13	0	0	6	.378	.255
Cabrera, Jolbert	.111	38	79	72	5	8	9	1	0	0	7	0	1	1	5	0	13	1	1	3	.125	.177
Snyder, Earl	.200	18	62	55	5	11	16	2	0	1	4	1	0	0	6	0	21	0	0	1	.291	.279
LaRocca, Greg	.269	21	60	52	12	14	19	3	1	0	4	0	0	2	6	0	6	1	0	1	.365	.367
Martinez, Victor†	.281	12	36	32	2	9	13	1	0	1	5	0	1	0	3	0	2	0	0	1	.406	.333
Phillips, Brandon	.258	11	36	31	5	8	13	3	1	0	4	1	0	1	3	0	6	0	0	0	.419	.343
Aven, Bruce	.118	7	21	17	1	2	2	0	0	0	0	0	0	0	4	0	4	1	0	2	.118	.286
Cordero, Wil	.222	6	18	18	1	4	4	0	0	0	1	0	0	0	0	0	3	0	0	1	.222	.222
Allen, Chad	.100	5	11	10	0	1	2	1	0	0	0	1	0	0	0	0	2	0	0	1	.200	.100
Dunwoody, Todd*	.000	2	7	6	0	0	0	0	0	0	0	1	0	0	0	0	3	0	0	0	.000	.000
Colon, Bartolo	.167	2	6	6	0	1	1	0	0	0	0	0	0	0	0	0	3	0	0	0	.167	.167
Sabathia, C.C.*	.200	2	6	5	0	1	1	0	0	0	0	0	0	0	1	0	1	0	0	0	.200	.333
Drese, Ryan	.000	2	5	3	0	0	0	0	0	0	0	1	0	0	1	0	0	0	0	0	.000	.250
Finley, Chuck*	.000	2	4	4	0	0	0	0	0	0	0	0	0	0	0	0	2	0	0	1	.000	.000
Baez, Danys	.000	1	2	2	0	0	0	0	0	0	0	0	0	0	0	0	0	0	0	0	.000	.000
Rincon, Ricardo*	.000	3	1	1	0	0	0	0	0	0	0	0	0	0	0	0	0	0	0	0	.000	.000
Nagy, Charles*	.000	1	0	0	1	0	0	0	0	0	0	0	0	0	0	0	0	0	0	0	.000	.000

Batters with more than one A.L. team

Batter	Avg.	G	TPA	AB	R	H	TB	2B	3B	HR	RBI	SH	SF	HP	BB	IBB	SO	SB	CS	GDP	Slg.	OBP
Garcia, N.Y.-Cle.*	.297	53	210	202	30	60	116	8	0	16	52	0	2	0	6	0	41	0	3	6	.574	.314

* Lefthanded batter. † Switch-hitter.

PITCHING

Pitcher	W	L	ERA	G	GS	CG	GF	SHO	Sv.	IP	H	R	ER	HR	HB	BB	IBB	SO	WP	Bk.
Sabathia, C.C.*	13	11	4.37	33	33	2	0	0	0	210.0	198	109	102	17	1	88	2	149	6	3
Baez, Danys	10	11	4.41	39	26	1	9	0	6	165.1	160	84	81	14	9	82	5	130	6	1
Drese, Ryan	10	9	6.55	26	26	1	0	0	0	137.1	176	104	100	15	6	62	1	102	11	0
Colon, Bartolo	10	4	2.55	16	16	4	0	2	0	116.1	104	37	33	11	2	31	1	75	3	0
Finley, Chuck*	4	11	4.44	18	18	1	0	0	0	105.1	114	56	52	6	0	48	3	91	1	0
Wohlers, Mark	3	4	4.79	64	0	0	28	0	7	71.1	71	41	38	6	3	26	3	46	7	0
Riske, David	2	2	5.26	51	0	0	17	0	1	51.1	49	32	30	8	4	35	4	65	1	0
Nagy, Charles	1	4	8.88	19	7	0	7	0	0	48.2	76	51	48	10	2	13	1	22	1	0
Mulholland, Terry*	3	2	4.60	16	3	0	5	0	0	47.0	56	27	24	5	4	14	3	21	0	0
Phillips, Jason C.	1	3	4.97	8	6	0	0	0	0	41.2	41	24	23	7	4	20	0	23	0	1
Westbrook, Jake	1	3	5.83	11	4	0	1	0	0	41.2	50	30	27	6	1	12	1	20	1	0
Rodriguez, Ricardo	2	2	5.66	7	7	0	0	0	0	41.1	40	27	26	5	8	18	3	24	1	0
Shuey, Paul	3	0	2.41	39	0	0	12	0	0	37.1	31	11	10	1	0	10	1	39	2	0
Paronto, Chad	0	2	4.04	29	0	0	11	0	0	35.2	34	19	16	3	2	11	1	23	2	0
Rincon, Ricardo*	1	4	4.79	46	0	0	6	0	0	35.2	36	21	19	3	1	8	1	30	0	0
Wickman, Bob	1	3	4.46	36	0	0	30	0	20	34.1	42	22	17	3	1	10	0	36	0	0
Burba, Dave	1	0	4.50	12	3	0	0	0	0	34.0	30	20	17	3	2	17	0	25	0	0
Riggan, Jerrod	2	1	7.64	29	0	0	9	0	0	33.0	53	28	28	3	0	18	4	22	4	1
Elder, Dave	0	2	3.13	15	0	0	3	0	0	23.0	18	10	8	1	1	14	3	23	0	0
Sadler, Carl*	1	2	4.43	24	0	0	5	0	0	20.1	15	10	10	2	0	11	0	23	3	0
Wright, Jaret	2	3	15.71	8	6	0	1	0	0	18.1	40	34	32	3	2	19	0	12	1	0
Davis, Jason	1	0	1.84	3	2	0	0	0	0	14.2	12	3	3	1	0	4	0	11	0	1
Murray, Heath*	0	2	7.50	9	0	0	2	0	0	12.0	12	10	10	3	2	7	0	11	1	0
Tallet, Brian*	1	0	1.50	2	2	0	0	0	0	12.0	9	3	2	0	1	4	0	5	0	0
Lee, Cliff*	0	1	1.74	2	2	0	0	0	0	10.1	6	2	2	0	0	8	1	6	0	1
Beverlin, Jason	0	0	7.36	4	0	0	1	0	0	7.1	9	7	6	1	0	4	0	9	1	0
DePaula, Sean	1	1	12.79	5	0	0	1	0	0	6.1	11	9	9	3	0	3	0	8	0	0
Smith, Roy	0	0	3.00	4	1	0	1	0	0	6.0	9	4	2	1	1	5	0	2	0	0
Herrera, Alex*	0	0	0.00	5	0	0	1	0	0	5.1	3	0	0	0	0	1	0	5	0	0
Maurer, Dave*	0	1	13.50	2	0	0	2	0	0	1.1	3	2	2	1	0	0	0	0	0	0
Rodriguez, Nerio	0	0	0.00	1	0	0	1	0	0	0.1	0	0	0	0	0	0	0	0	0	0

Pitchers with more than one A.L. team

Pitcher	W	L	ERA	G	GS	CG	GF	SHO	Sv.	IP	H	R	ER	HR	HB	BB	IBB	SO	WP	Bk.
Beverlin, Cle.-Det.	0	3	8.69	7	3	0	1	0	0	19.2	27	22	19	3	0	9	0	16	2	0
Burba, Tex.-Cle.	5	5	5.20	35	21	1	2	0	0	145.1	155	91	84	16	9	57	3	95	9	1
Rincon, Cle.-Oak.*	1	4	4.18	71	0	0	9	0	1	56.0	47	28	26	4	1	11	1	49	0	0

* Throws lefthanded.

DETROIT TIGERS

INDIVIDUAL STATISTICS

BATTING

Batter	Avg.	G	TPA	AB	R	H	TB	2B	3B	HR	RBI	SH	SF	HP	BB	IBB	SO	SB	CS	GDP	Slg.	OBP
Fick, Robert*	.270	148	614	556	66	150	241	36	2	17	63	0	5	7	46	4	90	0	1	17	.433	.331
Simon, Randall*	.301	130	506	482	51	145	221	17	1	19	82	0	7	4	13	5	30	0	1	13	.459	.320
Higginson, Bobby*	.282	119	499	444	50	125	185	24	3	10	63	1	7	6	41	3	45	12	5	8	.417	.345
Halter, Shane	.239	122	458	410	46	98	162	22	6	10	39	1	4	4	39	1	92	0	4	12	.395	.309
Magee, Wendell	.271	97	364	347	34	94	133	19	1	6	35	1	5	1	10	0	64	2	4	9	.383	.289
Inge, Brandon	.202	95	351	321	27	65	107	15	3	7	24	1	1	4	24	0	101	1	3	7	.333	.266
Easley, Damion	.224	85	346	304	29	68	108	14	1	8	30	1	3	11	27	3	43	1	3	4	.355	.307
Pena, Carlos*	.253	75	302	273	31	69	126	13	4	12	36	0	1	2	26	0	73	2	2	5	.462	.321
Truby, Chris	.199	89	292	277	23	55	78	13	2	2	15	3	5	2	5	0	71	1	1	5	.282	.215
Jackson, Damian	.257	81	274	245	31	63	88	20	1	1	25	2	3	3	21	0	36	12	3	3	.359	.320
Lombard, George*	.241	72	270	241	34	58	90	11	3	5	13	7	1	1	20	1	78	13	2	0	.373	.300
Paquette, Craig	.194	72	266	252	20	49	77	14	1	4	20	1	3	0	10	0	53	1	0	7	.306	.223
Santiago, Ramon†	.243	65	249	222	33	54	81	5	5	4	20	4	2	8	13	0	48	8	5	2	.365	.306
Young, Dmitri†	.284	54	216	201	25	57	92	14	0	7	27	0	1	2	12	5	39	2	0	12	.458	.329
Rivera, Michael	.227	39	138	132	11	30	43	8	1	1	11	0	1	1	4	0	35	0	0	5	.326	.254
Macias, Jose†	.234	33	121	107	10	25	29	4	0	0	6	4	1	1	8	0	13	3	2	4	.271	.291
Bocachica, Hiram	.223	34	109	103	14	23	39	4	0	4	8	1	0	0	5	0	22	2	2	2	.379	.259
Cruz, Jacob*	.273	35	107	88	12	24	35	3	1	2	6	1	2	3	13	0	20	3	1	2	.398	.377
Walbeck, Matt†	.235	27	89	85	4	20	22	2	0	0	3	0	1	0	3	0	14	0	0	2	.259	.258
Torres, Andres†	.200	19	79	70	7	14	17	1	1	0	3	0	2	1	6	0	16	2	2	2	.243	.266
Infante, Omar	.333	18	75	72	4	24	30	3	0	1	6	0	0	0	3	0	10	0	1	0	.417	.360
Munson, Eric*	.186	18	67	59	3	11	17	0	0	2	5	0	1	1	6	0	11	0	0	1	.288	.269
Meluskey, Mitch†	.222	8	34	27	3	6	6	0	0	0	1	0	1	1	5	0	3	0	0	0	.222	.353
Monroe, Craig	.120	13	26	25	3	3	7	1	0	1	1	0	0	1	0	0	5	0	2	1	.280	.154
Salazar, Oscar	.190	8	23	21	2	4	8	1	0	1	3	1	0	0	1	0	2	0	0	0	.381	.227
Palmer, Dean	.000	4	13	12	0	0	0	0	0	0	0	0	0	0	1	0	5	0	0	1	.000	.077
Jackson, Ryan*	.333	4	7	6	0	2	5	1	1	0	0	0	0	0	1	0	2	0	0	0	.833	.429
Weaver, Jeff	.286	2	7	7	0	2	2	0	0	0	1	0	0	0	0	0	4	0	0	0	.286	.286
Maroth, Mike*	.167	2	6	6	1	1	1	0	0	0	0	0	0	0	0	0	5	0	0	0	.167	.167
Bernero, Adam	.000	2	5	4	0	0	0	0	0	0	0	1	0	0	0	0	4	0	0	0	.000	.000
Redman, Mark*	.200	2	5	5	1	1	1	0	0	0	0	0	0	0	0	0	0	0	0	1	.200	.200
Sparks, Steve	.000	1	2	2	0	0	0	0	0	0	0	0	0	0	0	0	1	0	0	0	.000	.000

Batters with more than one A.L. team

Batter	Avg.	G	TPA	AB	R	H	TB	2B	3B	HR	RBI	SH	SF	HP	BB	IBB	SO	SB	CS	GDP	Slg.	OBP
Pena, Oak.-Det.*	.242	115	443	397	43	96	178	17	4	19	52	0	2	3	41	0	111	2	2	7	.448	.316

* Lefthanded batter. † Switch-hitter.

PITCHING

Pitcher	W	L	ERA	G	GS	CG	GF	SHO	Sv.	IP	H	R	ER	HR	HB	BB	IBB	SO	WP	Bk.
Redman, Mark*	8	15	4.21	30	30	3	0	0	0	203.0	211	107	95	15	6	51	2	109	11	1
Sparks, Steve	8	16	5.52	32	30	3	0	0	0	189.0	238	134	116	23	12	67	3	98	8	2
Maroth, Mike*	6	10	4.48	21	21	0	0	0	0	128.2	136	68	64	7	2	36	1	58	4	0
Weaver, Jeff	6	8	3.18	17	17	3	0	3	0	121.2	112	50	43	4	8	33	1	75	4	0
Bernero, Adam	4	7	6.20	28	11	0	5	0	0	101.2	128	74	70	17	6	31	1	69	5	1
Acevedo, Juan	1	5	2.65	65	0	0	48	0	28	74.2	68	33	22	4	5	23	3	43	2	0
Farnsworth, Jeff	2	3	5.79	44	0	0	15	0	0	70.0	100	47	45	6	2	29	8	28	6	1
Lima, Jose	4	6	7.77	20	12	0	3	0	0	68.1	86	60	59	12	2	21	0	33	2	0
Powell, Brian	1	5	4.84	13	9	0	1	0	0	57.2	64	34	31	11	1	21	0	30	2	0
Santana, Julio	3	5	2.84	38	0	0	8	0	0	57.0	49	19	18	8	2	28	2	38	3	1
Cornejo, Nate	1	5	5.04	9	9	1	0	0	0	50.0	63	33	28	6	2	18	0	23	2	0
Walker, Jamie*	1	1	3.71	57	0	0	16	0	1	43.2	32	19	18	9	4	9	1	40	1	1
Paniagua, Jose	0	1	5.83	41	0	0	15	0	1	41.2	50	30	27	10	3	15	1	34	2	0
Greisinger, Seth	2	2	6.21	8	8	0	0	0	0	37.2	46	26	26	4	1	13	2	14	0	0
Van Hekken, Andy*	1	3	3.00	5	5	1	0	1	0	30.0	38	13	10	2	0	6	0	5	1	0
Henriquez, Oscar	1	1	4.50	30	0	0	12	0	2	28.0	19	14	14	5	1	15	4	23	3	0
Moehler, Brian	1	1	2.29	3	3	0	0	0	0	19.2	17	5	5	3	0	2	0	13	0	0
Rodney, Fernando	1	3	6.00	20	0	0	10	0	0	18.0	25	15	12	2	0	10	2	10	0	1
Loux, Shane	0	3	9.00	3	3	0	0	0	0	14.0	19	16	14	4	1	3	0	7	1	0
Beverlin, Jason	0	3	9.49	3	3	0	0	0	0	12.1	18	15	13	2	0	5	0	7	1	0
Anderson, Matt	2	1	9.00	12	0	0	8	0	0	11.0	17	13	11	1	2	8	1	8	1	0
Perisho, Matt*	0	0	8.71	5	0	0	1	0	0	10.1	16	11	10	2	0	6	0	3	0	0
Eckenstahler, Eric*	1	0	5.63	7	0	0	2	0	0	8.0	14	5	5	1	0	2	0	13	0	0
German, Franklyn	1	0	0.00	7	0	0	1	0	1	6.2	3	0	0	0	1	2	1	6	0	0
Pearson, Terry	0	0	10.50	4	0	0	3	0	0	6.0	8	7	7	2	0	2	1	4	0	0
Patterson, Danny	0	2	15.00	6	0	0	1	0	0	3.0	5	5	5	0	1	2	0	1	0	0
Keller, Kris	0	0	27.00	1	0	0	1	0	0	1.0	2	3	3	1	0	3	0	1	0	0
Jimenez, Jason*	0	0	27.00	1	0	0	0	0	0	0.2	3	4	2	0	0	1	0	0	0	0
Miller, Matt*	0	0	13.50	2	0	0	0	0	0	0.2	4	2	1	1	0	1	0	1	0	0
Sabel, Erik	0	0	0.00	1	0	0	0	0	0	0.0	2	2	2	1	0	0	0	0	0	0

Pitchers with more than one A.L. team

Pitcher	W	L	ERA	G	GS	CG	GF	SHO	Sv.	IP	H	R	ER	HR	HB	BB	IBB	SO	WP	Bk.
Beverlin, Cle.-Det.	0	3	8.69	7	3	0	1	0	0	19.2	27	22	19	3	0	9	0	16	2	0
Jimenez, T.B.-Det.*	0	0	7.36	6	0	0	4	0	0	7.1	12	8	6	2	0	2	0	5	0	0
Weaver, Det.-N.Y.	11	11	3.52	32	25	3	3	3	2	199.2	193	88	78	16	11	48	4	132	6	0

* Throws lefthanded.

KANSAS CITY ROYALS

INDIVIDUAL STATISTICS

BATTING

Batter	Avg.	G	TPA	AB	R	H	TB	2B	3B	HR	RBI	SH	SF	HP	BB	IBB	SO	SB	CS	GDP	Slg.	OBP
Beltran, Carlos†	.273	162	722	637	114	174	319	44	7	29	105	3	7	4	71	1	135	35	7	12	.501	.346
Randa, Joe	.282	151	617	549	63	155	234	36	5	11	80	2	11	9	46	1	69	2	1	13	.426	.341
Perez, Neifi†	.236	145	585	554	65	131	168	20	4	3	37	5	6	0	20	2	53	8	9	11	.303	.260
Sweeney, Mike	.340	126	545	471	81	160	265	31	1	24	86	0	7	6	61	10	46	9	7	9	.563	.417
Ibanez, Raul*	.294	137	544	497	70	146	267	37	6	24	103	1	4	2	40	5	76	5	3	11	.537	.346
Tucker, Michael*	.248	144	543	475	65	118	193	27	6	12	56	7	2	3	56	1	105	23	9	5	.406	.330
Febles, Carlos	.245	119	404	351	44	86	122	16	4	4	26	5	0	7	41	0	63	16	5	8	.348	.336
Mayne, Brent*	.236	101	370	326	35	77	101	8	2	4	30	4	4	2	34	1	54	4	4	8	.310	.309
Knoblauch, Chuck	.210	80	336	300	41	63	90	9	0	6	22	2	2	4	28	1	32	19	3	5	.300	.284
Alicea, Luis†	.228	94	273	237	28	54	69	8	2	1	23	3	0	1	32	1	34	2	3	5	.291	.322
Guiel, Aaron*	.233	70	269	240	30	56	81	13	0	4	38	2	4	4	19	1	61	1	5	3	.338	.296
Hinch, A.J.	.249	72	220	197	25	49	79	7	1	7	27	2	0	3	18	0	35	3	3	2	.401	.321
Berger, Brandon	.201	51	145	134	16	27	52	5	1	6	17	0	1	2	8	2	32	1	0	2	.388	.255
Ordaz, Luis	.223	33	111	94	11	21	23	2	0	0	4	4	1	0	12	0	13	2	3	2	.245	.308
Quinn, Mark	.237	23	84	76	9	18	28	4	0	2	11	1	0	2	5	0	15	2	1	3	.368	.301
Berroa, Angel	.227	20	83	75	8	17	26	7	1	0	5	0	0	1	7	1	10	3	0	1	.347	.301
Pellow, Kit	.238	29	73	63	6	15	19	1	0	1	5	0	0	1	9	0	21	1	1	2	.302	.342
Sadler, Donnie	.191	35	73	68	10	13	16	1	1	0	5	0	1	0	4	0	12	3	1	0	.235	.233
Brown, Dee*	.235	16	55	51	5	12	20	3	1	1	7	0	0	0	4	0	20	0	0	0	.392	.291
McCarty, Dave	.094	13	34	32	3	3	7	1	0	1	2	0	0	0	2	0	10	0	0	1	.219	.147
McDonald, Donzell†	.182	10	27	22	3	4	6	2	0	0	1	0	1	0	4	0	5	1	0	0	.273	.296
Brito, Juan	.304	9	23	23	1	7	9	2	0	0	1	0	0	0	0	0	3	0	0	2	.391	.304
Caruso, Mike*	.100	12	21	20	3	2	2	0	0	0	0	0	0	0	1	0	2	0	0	0	.100	.143
Perry, Chan	.091	5	11	11	0	1	1	0	0	0	3	0	0	0	0	0	1	0	0	1	.091	.091
Gomez, Alexis*	.200	5	10	10	0	2	2	0	0	0	0	0	0	0	0	0	2	0	0	0	.200	.200
Sedlacek, Shawn	.000	2	6	6	0	0	0	0	0	0	0	0	0	0	0	0	4	0	0	0	.000	.000
Wathan, Dusty	.600	3	6	5	1	3	4	1	0	0	1	0	0	1	0	0	1	0	0	0	.800	.667
May, Darrell*	.000	2	5	4	0	0	0	0	0	0	0	0	0	0	1	0	2	0	0	0	.000	.200
Suppan, Jeff	.000	2	5	1	0	0	0	0	0	0	0	3	0	0	1	0	1	0	0	0	.000	.500
Asencio, Miguel	.000	1	2	2	0	0	0	0	0	0	0	0	0	0	0	0	1	0	0	0	.000	.000
Byrd, Paul	.000	1	2	2	0	0	0	0	0	0	0	0	0	0	0	0	2	0	0	0	.000	.000
Suzuki, Mac	.500	2	2	2	0	1	1	0	0	0	0	0	0	0	0	0	1	0	0	0	.500	.500

Batters with more than one A.L. team

Batter	Avg.	G	TPA	AB	R	H	TB	2B	3B	HR	RBI	SH	SF	HP	BB	IBB	SO	SB	CS	GDP	Slg.	OBP
McCarty, K.C.-T.B.	.136	25	74	66	5	9	16	1	0	2	4	0	0	2	6	0	19	0	0	1	.242	.230
Sadler, K.C.-Tex.	.163	73	109	98	16	16	20	2	1	0	7	1	1	2	7	0	19	5	3	1	.204	.231

* Lefthanded batter. † Switch-hitter.

PITCHING

Pitcher	W	L	ERA	G	GS	CG	GF	SHO	Sv.	IP	H	R	ER	HR	HB	BB	IBB	SO	WP	Bk.
Byrd, Paul	17	11	3.90	33	33	7	0	2	0	228.1	224	111	99	36	7	38	1	129	3	1
Suppan, Jeff	9	16	5.32	33	33	3	0	1	0	208.0	229	134	123	32	7	68	3	109	10	1
May, Darrell*	4	10	5.35	30	21	2	3	1	0	131.1	144	83	78	28	1	50	3	95	2	0
Asencio, Miguel	4	7	5.11	31	21	0	7	0	0	123.1	136	73	70	17	3	64	2	58	7	0
Sedlacek, Shawn	3	5	6.72	16	14	0	1	0	0	84.1	99	64	63	16	6	36	2	52	5	0
Affeldt, Jeremy*	3	4	4.64	34	7	0	4	0	0	77.2	85	41	40	8	3	37	4	67	5	2
Hernandez, Runelvys	4	4	4.36	12	12	0	0	0	0	74.1	79	36	36	8	1	22	0	45	2	0
Grimsley, Jason	4	7	3.91	70	0	0	26	0	1	71.1	64	32	31	4	1	37	8	59	8	0
Reichert, Dan	3	5	5.32	30	6	0	3	0	0	66.0	77	48	39	10	4	25	2	36	3	0
Hernandez, Roberto	1	3	4.33	53	0	0	42	0	26	52.0	62	29	25	6	3	12	2	39	3	0
Stein, Blake	0	4	7.91	27	2	0	7	0	1	46.2	59	41	41	6	3	27	1	42	1	0
Bailey, Cory	3	4	4.11	37	0	0	14	0	1	46.0	53	24	21	5	2	31	7	24	1	1
Mullen, Scott*	4	5	3.15	44	0	0	10	0	0	40.0	40	16	14	5	2	13	2	21	1	0
Voyles, Brad	0	2	6.51	22	0	0	6	0	1	27.2	31	21	20	5	2	18	1	26	1	0
George, Chris*	0	4	5.60	6	6	0	0	0	0	27.1	37	17	17	2	1	8	0	13	1	0
Bukvich, Ryan	1	0	6.12	26	0	0	2	0	0	25.0	26	19	17	2	1	19	3	20	1	0
Suzuki, Mac	0	2	9.00	7	1	0	1	0	0	21.0	24	21	21	2	0	17	2	15	6	1
Wilson, Kris	2	0	8.20	12	0	0	4	0	0	18.2	29	18	17	7	2	5	0	10	0	0
Shouse, Brian*	0	0	6.14	23	0	0	7	0	0	14.2	15	10	10	3	2	9	1	11	2	0
Austin, Jeff	0	0	4.91	10	0	0	6	0	0	11.0	14	6	6	0	0	6	1	6	1	0
Hill, Jeremy	0	1	3.86	10	0	0	6	0	0	9.1	8	4	4	1	0	8	1	7	1	0
MacDougal, Mike	0	1	5.00	6	0	0	1	0	0	9.0	5	5	5	0	0	7	1	10	1	0
Durbin, Chad	0	1	11.88	2	2	0	0	0	0	8.1	13	11	11	3	1	4	0	5	0	0
Obermueller, Wes	0	2	11.74	2	2	0	0	0	0	7.2	14	10	10	3	0	2	0	5	0	0
Rekar, Bryan	0	2	15.43	2	2	0	0	0	0	7.0	12	12	12	1	0	6	0	2	1	0
Field, Nate	0	0	9.00	5	0	0	0	0	0	5.0	8	5	5	2	0	3	1	3	2	0

* Throws lefthanded.

MINNESOTA TWINS

INDIVIDUAL STATISTICS

BATTING

Batter	Avg.	G	TPA	AB	R	H	TB	2B	3B	HR	RBI	SH	SF	HP	BB	IBB	SO	SB	CS	GDP	Slg.	OBP
Guzman, Cristian†	.273	148	656	623	80	170	240	31	6	9	59	8	6	2	17	2	79	12	13	12	.385	.292
Jones, Jacque*	.300	149	626	577	96	173	295	37	2	27	85	4	6	2	37	2	129	6	7	8	.511	.341
Hunter, Torii	.289	148	604	561	89	162	294	37	4	29	94	0	3	5	35	3	118	23	8	17	.524	.334
Koskie, Corey*	.267	140	576	490	71	131	219	37	3	15	69	0	5	9	72	4	127	10	11	14	.447	.368
Mientkiewicz, Doug*	.261	143	554	467	60	122	183	29	1	10	64	0	7	6	74	8	69	1	2	7	.392	.365
Pierzynski, A.J.*	.300	130	469	440	54	132	193	31	6	6	49	2	3	11	13	1	61	1	2	14	.439	.334
Ortiz, David*	.272	125	466	412	52	112	206	32	1	20	75	0	8	3	43	0	87	1	2	5	.500	.339
Mohr, Dustan	.269	120	417	383	55	103	166	23	2	12	45	2	0	1	31	3	86	6	3	5	.433	.325
Kielty, Bobby†	.291	112	348	289	49	84	140	14	3	12	46	0	2	5	52	4	66	4	1	4	.484	.405
Rivas, Luis	.256	93	346	316	46	81	124	23	4	4	35	8	0	3	19	2	51	9	4	12	.392	.305
Hocking, Denny†	.250	102	294	260	28	65	84	13	0	2	25	4	5	1	24	0	44	0	2	3	.323	.310
LeCroy, Matthew	.260	63	196	181	19	47	81	11	1	7	27	0	2	0	13	1	38	0	2	5	.448	.306
Prince, Tom	.224	51	148	125	14	28	49	7	1	4	16	3	2	4	14	0	26	1	3	4	.392	.317
Buchanan, Brian	.252	44	143	135	19	34	56	5	1	5	15	0	0	2	6	0	33	2	1	4	.415	.294
Canizaro, Jay	.214	38	126	112	14	24	34	8	1	0	11	1	2	1	10	0	22	0	1	1	.304	.280
Cuddyer, Michael	.259	41	123	112	12	29	48	7	0	4	13	1	1	1	8	0	30	2	0	3	.429	.311
Blake, Casey	.200	9	22	20	2	4	5	1	0	0	1	0	0	0	2	0	7	0	0	0	.250	.273
Restovich, Michael	.308	8	14	13	3	4	7	0	0	1	1	0	0	0	1	0	4	1	0	2	.538	.357
Sears, Todd*	.333	7	12	12	2	4	6	2	0	0	0	0	0	0	0	0	1	0	0	0	.500	.333
Ryan, Michael*	.091	7	11	11	3	1	1	0	0	0	0	0	0	0	0	0	2	0	0	0	.091	.091
Lamb, David†	.100	7	10	10	0	1	1	0	0	0	0	0	0	0	0	0	2	0	0	1	.100	.100
Morris, Warren*	.000	4	7	7	0	0	0	0	0	0	0	0	0	0	0	0	1	0	0	0	.000	.000
Reed, Rick	.250	2	6	4	0	1	1	0	0	0	0	1	0	0	1	0	2	0	0	0	.250	.400
Milton, Eric*	.400	2	5	5	0	2	2	0	0	0	1	0	0	0	0	0	1	0	0	0	.400	.400
Lohse, Kyle	.250	2	4	4	0	1	1	0	0	0	0	0	0	0	0	0	1	0	0	0	.250	.250
Santana, Johan*	.250	2	4	4	0	1	1	0	0	0	0	0	0	0	0	0	0	0	0	0	.250	.250
Valentin, Javier†	.500	4	4	4	0	2	2	0	0	0	0	0	0	0	0	0	0	0	0	0	.500	.500
Fiore, Tony	.000	4	3	3	0	0	0	0	0	0	0	0	0	0	0	0	1	0	0	0	.000	.000
Kinney, Matt	.000	1	2	2	0	0	0	0	0	0	0	0	0	0	0	0	1	0	0	0	.000	.000

* Lefthanded batter. † Switch-hitter.

PITCHING

Pitcher	W	L	ERA	G	GS	CG	GF	SHO	Sv.	IP	H	R	ER	HR	HB	BB	IBB	SO	WP	Bk.
Reed, Rick	15	7	3.78	33	32	2	0	1	0	188.0	192	89	79	32	6	26	0	121	1	1
Lohse, Kyle	13	8	4.23	32	31	1	0	1	0	180.2	181	92	85	26	9	70	2	124	8	0
Milton, Eric*	13	9	4.84	29	29	2	0	1	0	171.0	173	96	92	24	3	30	0	121	4	0
Radke, Brad	9	5	4.72	21	21	2	0	1	0	118.1	124	64	62	12	7	20	0	62	0	0
Santana, Johan*	8	6	2.99	27	14	0	2	0	1	108.1	84	41	36	7	1	49	0	137	15	2
Mays, Joe	4	8	5.38	17	17	1	0	1	0	95.1	113	60	57	14	2	25	0	38	6	0
Fiore, Tony	10	3	3.16	48	2	0	11	0	0	91.0	74	32	32	10	5	43	4	55	2	0
Romero, J.C.*	9	2	1.89	81	0	0	15	0	1	81.0	62	17	17	3	4	36	4	76	9	0
Hawkins, LaTroy	6	0	2.13	65	0	0	15	0	0	80.1	63	23	19	5	0	15	1	63	5	0
Guardado, Eddie*	1	3	2.93	68	0	0	62	0	45	67.2	53	22	22	9	1	18	2	70	0	0
Kinney, Matt	2	7	4.64	14	12	0	1	0	0	66.0	78	39	34	13	1	33	0	45	5	0
Wells, Bob	2	1	5.90	48	0	0	16	0	0	58.0	78	41	38	8	1	16	1	30	0	0
Jackson, Mike	2	3	3.27	58	0	0	17	0	0	55.0	59	20	20	5	4	13	3	29	2	0
Cressend, Jack	0	1	5.91	23	0	0	4	0	0	32.0	40	25	21	6	1	19	4	22	1	0
Rincon, Juan	0	2	6.28	10	3	0	0	0	0	28.2	44	23	20	5	0	9	0	21	2	0
Frederick, Kevin	0	0	10.03	8	0	0	3	0	0	11.2	13	13	13	3	0	10	0	5	2	0
Miller, Travis*	0	0	4.50	5	0	0	3	0	0	4.0	5	2	2	0	0	2	2	3	0	0
Trombley, Mike	0	1	15.75	5	0	0	3	0	0	4.0	10	7	7	2	0	1	0	3	0	0
Rodriguez, Jose*	0	1	14.73	4	0	0	1	0	0	3.2	8	6	6	0	0	4	1	1	0	0

* Throws lefthanded.

NEW YORK YANKEES

INDIVIDUAL STATISTICS

BATTING

Batter	Avg.	G	TPA	AB	R	H	TB	2B	3B	HR	RBI	SH	SF	HP	BB	IBB	SO	SB	CS	GDP	Slg.	OBP
Soriano, Alfonso	.300	156	741	696	128	209	381	51	2	39	102	1	7	14	23	1	157	41	13	8	.547	.332
Jeter, Derek	.297	157	730	644	124	191	271	26	0	18	75	3	3	7	73	2	114	32	3	14	.421	.373
Williams, Bernie†	.333	154	699	612	102	204	302	37	2	19	102	0	1	3	83	7	97	8	4	19	.493	.415
Giambi, Jason*	.314	155	689	560	120	176	335	34	1	41	122	0	5	15	109	4	112	2	2	18	.598	.435
Posada, Jorge†	.268	143	598	511	79	137	239	40	1	20	99	0	3	3	81	9	143	1	0	23	.468	.370
Ventura, Robin*	.247	141	562	465	68	115	213	17	0	27	93	0	5	2	90	9	101	3	1	14	.458	.368
White, Rondell	.240	126	494	455	59	109	172	21	0	14	62	1	5	8	25	1	86	1	2	11	.378	.288
Johnson, Nick*	.243	129	441	378	56	92	152	15	0	15	58	3	0	12	48	5	98	1	3	11	.402	.347
Spencer, Shane	.247	94	329	288	32	71	108	15	2	6	34	2	4	4	31	4	62	0	3	5	.375	.324
Mondesi, Raul	.241	71	302	270	39	65	116	18	0	11	43	0	2	2	28	2	46	6	4	3	.430	.315
Vander Wal, John*	.260	84	245	219	30	57	94	17	1	6	20	0	3	0	23	3	58	1	1	7	.429	.327
Coomer, Ron	.264	55	156	148	14	39	55	7	0	3	17	1	1	0	6	1	23	0	0	8	.372	.290
Wilson, Enrique†	.181	60	119	105	17	19	31	2	2	2	11	6	0	0	8	0	22	1	1	2	.295	.239
Rivera, Juan	.265	28	91	83	9	22	30	5	0	1	6	1	1	0	6	0	10	1	1	4	.361	.311
Widger, Chris	.297	21	68	64	4	19	24	5	0	0	5	0	0	2	2	0	9	0	0	0	.375	.338
Castillo, Alberto	.135	15	41	37	3	5	8	1	1	0	4	3	0	0	1	0	12	0	0	2	.216	.158
Williams, Gerald	.000	33	19	17	6	0	0	0	0	0	0	0	0	0	2	0	4	2	0	1	.000	.105
Thames, Marcus	.231	7	13	13	2	3	7	1	0	1	2	0	0	0	0	0	4	0	0	0	.538	.231
Arias, Alex	.000	6	8	7	0	0	0	0	0	0	0	0	0	0	1	0	2	0	0	0	.000	.125
Mussina, Mike*	.600	2	6	5	2	3	3	0	0	0	0	1	0	0	0	0	0	0	0	0	.600	.600
Wells, David*	.000	2	5	4	0	0	0	0	0	0	0	1	0	0	0	0	3	0	0	0	.000	.000
Garcia, Karim*	.200	2	5	5	1	1	1	0	0	0	0	0	0	0	0	0	1	0	0	0	.200	.200
Clemens, Roger	.667	3	4	3	1	2	3	1	0	0	1	0	1	0	0	0	1	0	0	0	1.000	.500
Lilly, Ted*	.000	2	3	3	0	0	0	0	0	0	0	0	0	0	0	0	2	0	0	0	.000	.000
Pettitte, Andy*	.333	2	3	3	0	1	2	1	0	0	1	0	0	0	0	0	1	0	0	0	.667	.333
Stanton, Mike*	.000	6	2	2	0	0	0	0	0	0	0	0	0	0	0	0	0	0	0	0	.000	.000
Choate, Randy*	.000	3	1	1	0	0	0	0	0	0	0	0	0	0	0	0	0	0	0	0	.000	.000
Henson, Drew	.000	3	1	1	1	0	0	0	0	0	0	0	0	0	0	0	1	0	0	0	.000	.000
Karsay, Steve	.000	4	1	1	0	0	0	0	0	0	0	0	0	0	0	0	1	0	0	0	.000	.000
Mendoza, Ramiro	.000	9	1	1	0	0	0	0	0	0	0	0	0	0	0	0	1	0	0	0	.000	.000

Batters with more than one A.L. team

Batter	Avg.	G	TPA	AB	R	H	TB	2B	3B	HR	RBI	SH	SF	HP	BB	IBB	SO	SB	CS	GDP	Slg.	OBP
Garcia, N.Y.-Cle.*	.297	53	210	202	30	60	116	8	0	16	52	0	2	0	6	0	41	0	3	6	.574	.314
Mondesi, Tor.-N.Y.	.232	146	637	569	90	132	246	34	1	26	88	0	4	5	59	3	103	15	6	11	.432	.308

* Lefthanded batter. † Switch-hitter.

PITCHING

Pitcher	W	L	ERA	G	GS	CG	GF	SHO	Sv.	IP	H	R	ER	HR	HB	BB	IBB	SO	WP	Bk.
Mussina, Mike	18	10	4.05	33	33	2	0	2	0	215.2	208	103	97	27	5	48	1	182	7	0
Wells, David*	19	7	3.75	31	31	2	0	1	0	206.1	210	100	86	21	5	45	2	137	4	0
Clemens, Roger	13	6	4.35	29	29	0	0	0	0	180.0	172	94	87	18	7	63	6	192	14	0
Hernandez, Orlando	8	5	3.64	24	22	0	1	0	1	146.0	131	63	59	17	8	36	2	113	8	0
Pettitte, Andy*	13	5	3.27	22	22	3	0	1	0	134.2	144	58	49	6	4	32	2	97	2	1
Mendoza, Ramiro	8	4	3.44	62	0	0	14	0	4	91.2	102	43	35	8	2	16	2	61	1	0
Karsay, Steve	6	4	3.26	78	0	0	38	0	12	88.1	87	33	32	7	2	30	14	65	4	0
Stanton, Mike*	7	1	3.00	79	0	0	25	0	6	78.0	73	29	26	4	0	28	3	44	4	0
Weaver, Jeff	5	3	4.04	15	8	0	3	0	2	78.0	81	38	35	12	3	15	3	57	2	0
Lilly, Ted*	3	6	3.40	16	11	2	1	1	0	76.2	57	31	29	10	5	24	3	59	6	0
Rivera, Mariano	1	4	2.74	45	0	0	37	0	28	46.0	35	16	14	3	2	11	2	41	1	1
Hitchcock, Sterling*	1	2	5.49	20	2	0	11	0	0	39.1	57	29	24	4	1	15	3	31	1	0
Thurman, Mike	1	0	5.18	12	2	0	6	0	0	33.0	45	21	19	2	1	12	1	23	0	0
Choate, Randy*	0	0	6.04	18	0	0	11	0	0	22.1	18	18	15	1	3	15	0	17	3	0
Knight, Brandon	0	0	11.42	7	0	0	5	0	0	8.2	11	12	11	2	0	5	0	7	1	0
Hernandez, Adrian	0	1	12.00	2	1	0	0	0	0	6.0	10	8	8	2	0	6	0	9	1	0
Tessmer, Jay	0	0	6.75	2	0	0	0	0	0	1.1	0	1	1	0	0	2	0	0	0	0

Pitchers with more than one A.L. team

Pitcher	W	L	ERA	G	GS	CG	GF	SHO	Sv.	IP	H	R	ER	HR	HB	BB	IBB	SO	WP	Bk.
Lilly, N.Y.-Oak.*	5	7	3.69	22	16	2	1	1	0	100.0	80	43	41	15	6	31	3	77	6	1
Weaver, Det.-N.Y.	11	11	3.52	32	25	3	3	3	2	199.2	193	88	78	16	11	48	4	132	6	0

* Throws lefthanded.

OAKLAND ATHLETICS

INDIVIDUAL STATISTICS

BATTING

Batter	Avg.	G	TPA	AB	R	H	TB	2B	3B	HR	RBI	SH	SF	HP	BB	IBB	SO	SB	CS	GDP	Slg.	OBP
Tejada, Miguel	.308	162	715	662	108	204	336	30	0	34	131	0	4	11	38	3	84	7	2	21	.508	.354
Chavez, Eric*	.275	153	653	585	87	161	300	31	3	34	109	0	2	1	65	13	119	8	3	8	.513	.348
Long, Terrence*	.240	162	640	587	71	141	229	32	4	16	67	0	3	2	48	6	96	3	6	17	.390	.298
Hatteberg, Scott*	.280	136	568	492	58	138	213	22	4	15	61	1	1	6	68	1	56	0	0	8	.433	.374
Dye, Jermaine	.252	131	555	488	74	123	224	27	1	24	86	0	5	10	52	2	108	2	0	15	.459	.333
Justice, David*	.266	118	471	398	54	106	163	18	3	11	49	0	2	1	70	3	66	4	1	12	.410	.376
Hernandez, Ramon	.233	136	457	403	51	94	135	20	0	7	42	3	3	5	43	1	64	0	0	11	.335	.313
Ellis, Mark	.272	98	404	345	58	94	136	16	4	6	35	8	3	4	44	1	54	4	2	3	.394	.359
Durham, Ray†	.274	54	248	219	43	60	100	14	4	6	22	2	1	2	24	1	34	6	2	2	.457	.350
Mabry, John*	.275	89	211	193	27	53	101	13	1	11	40	0	3	1	14	1	37	1	1	7	.523	.322
Giambi, Jeremy*	.274	42	187	157	26	43	74	7	0	8	17	0	0	3	27	0	40	0	0	4	.471	.390
Saenz, Olmedo	.276	68	178	156	15	43	73	10	1	6	18	0	2	7	13	1	31	1	1	2	.468	.354
Myers, Greg*	.222	65	170	144	15	32	55	5	0	6	21	0	0	0	26	3	36	0	0	4	.382	.341
Velarde, Randy	.226	56	155	133	22	30	44	8	0	2	8	1	1	5	15	1	32	3	0	4	.331	.325
Menechino, Frank	.205	38	154	132	22	27	43	7	0	3	15	0	1	1	20	0	32	0	0	4	.326	.312
Piatt, Adam	.234	55	152	137	18	32	55	8	0	5	18	0	1	2	12	0	33	2	1	1	.401	.303
Pena, Carlos*	.218	40	141	124	12	27	52	4	0	7	16	0	1	1	15	0	38	0	0	2	.419	.305
Byrnes, Eric	.245	90	104	94	24	23	40	4	2	3	11	1	2	3	4	0	17	3	0	3	.426	.291
German, Esteban	.200	9	40	35	4	7	7	0	0	0	0	0	0	1	4	0	11	1	0	0	.200	.300
Colangelo, Mike	.174	20	26	23	2	4	5	1	0	0	0	1	0	1	1	0	2	0	0	0	.217	.240
Sutton, Larry*	.105	7	20	19	3	2	5	0	0	1	3	0	0	0	1	0	8	0	0	0	.263	.150
Grabowski, Jason*	.375	4	11	8	3	3	6	1	1	0	1	0	0	0	3	0	1	0	0	0	.750	.545
Hudson, Tim	.200	2	6	5	1	1	2	1	0	0	0	0	0	0	1	0	1	0	0	0	.400	.333
Zito, Barry*	.000	2	6	4	0	0	0	0	0	0	0	2	0	0	0	0	3	0	0	0	.000	.000
Flores, Jose	.000	7	5	3	2	0	0	0	0	0	0	0	0	1	1	0	0	1	1	0	.000	.400
Mulder, Mark*	.000	2	5	5	0	0	0	0	0	0	0	0	0	0	0	0	1	0	0	0	.000	.000
McKay, Cody*	.667	2	4	3	0	2	2	0	0	0	2	0	1	0	0	0	1	0	0	0	.667	.500
Harang, Aaron	.000	2	3	3	0	0	0	0	0	0	0	0	0	0	0	0	3	0	0	0	.000	.000
Lidle, Cory	.000	2	2	1	0	0	0	0	0	0	0	1	0	0	0	0	0	0	0	0	.000	.000

Batters with more than one A.L. team

Batter	Avg.	G	TPA	AB	R	H	TB	2B	3B	HR	RBI	SH	SF	HP	BB	IBB	SO	SB	CS	GDP	Slg.	OBP
Durham, Chi.-Oak.†	.289	150	659	564	114	163	254	34	6	15	70	10	5	7	73	1	93	26	7	15	.450	.374
Pena, Oak.-Det.*	.242	115	443	397	43	96	178	17	4	19	52	0	2	3	41	0	111	2	2	7	.448	.316

* Lefthanded batter. † Switch-hitter.

PITCHING

Pitcher	W	L	ERA	G	GS	CG	GF	SHO	Sv.	IP	H	R	ER	HR	HB	BB	IBB	SO	WP	Bk.
Hudson, Tim	15	9	2.98	34	34	4	0	2	0	238.1	237	87	79	19	8	62	9	152	7	1
Zito, Barry*	23	5	2.75	35	35	1	0	0	0	229.1	182	79	70	24	9	78	2	182	2	1
Mulder, Mark*	19	7	3.47	30	30	2	0	1	0	207.1	182	88	80	21	11	55	3	159	7	1
Lidle, Cory	8	10	3.89	31	30	2	0	2	0	192.0	191	90	83	17	6	39	3	111	6	1
Koch, Billy	11	4	3.27	84	0	0	79	0	44	93.2	73	38	34	7	4	46	6	93	5	0
Harang, Aaron	5	4	4.83	16	15	0	0	0	0	78.1	78	44	42	7	3	45	2	64	1	0
Bradford, Chad	4	2	3.11	75	0	0	14	0	2	75.1	73	29	26	2	5	14	5	56	0	1
Mecir, Jim	6	4	4.26	61	0	0	10	0	1	67.2	68	36	32	5	4	29	4	53	4	1
Fyhrie, Mike	2	4	4.44	16	4	0	2	0	0	48.2	46	25	24	3	4	20	1	29	1	1
Hiljus, Erik	3	3	6.50	9	9	0	0	0	0	45.2	52	36	33	11	0	21	1	29	1	0
Tam, Jeff	1	2	5.13	40	0	0	14	0	0	40.1	56	26	23	2	2	13	5	14	3	0
Venafro, Mike*	2	2	4.62	47	0	0	8	0	0	37.0	45	22	19	5	2	14	2	16	1	0
Magnante, Mike*	0	2	5.97	32	0	0	12	0	0	28.2	38	22	19	2	1	11	1	11	2	1
Lilly, Ted*	2	1	4.63	6	5	0	0	0	0	23.1	23	12	12	5	1	7	0	18	0	1
Rincon, Ricardo*	0	0	3.10	25	0	0	3	0	1	20.1	11	7	7	1	0	3	0	19	0	0
Holtz, Mike*	0	0	6.43	16	0	0	7	0	0	14.0	24	11	10	3	1	9	0	7	0	0
Bowie, Micah*	2	0	1.50	13	0	0	4	0	0	12.0	12	2	2	1	1	8	1	8	0	0

Pitchers with more than one A.L. team

Pitcher	W	L	ERA	G	GS	CG	GF	SHO	Sv.	IP	H	R	ER	HR	HB	BB	IBB	SO	WP	Bk.
Lilly, N.Y.-Oak.*	5	7	3.69	22	16	2	1	1	0	100.0	80	43	41	15	6	31	3	77	6	1
Rincon, Cle.-Oak.*	1	4	4.18	71	0	0	9	0	1	56.0	47	28	26	4	1	11	1	49	0	0

* Throws lefthanded.

SEATTLE MARINERS

INDIVIDUAL STATISTICS

BATTING

Batter	Avg.	G	TPA	AB	R	H	TB	2B	3B	HR	RBI	SH	SF	HP	BB	IBB	SO	SB	CS	GDP	Slg.	OBP
Suzuki, Ichiro*	.321	157	728	647	111	208	275	27	8	8	51	3	5	5	68	27	62	31	15	8	.425	.388
Boone, Bret	.278	155	675	608	88	169	281	34	3	24	107	2	6	6	53	4	102	12	5	11	.462	.339
Olerud, John*	.300	154	668	553	85	166	271	39	0	22	102	0	12	5	98	6	66	0	0	19	.490	.403
Cameron, Mike	.239	158	640	545	84	130	241	26	5	25	80	4	5	7	79	3	176	31	8	8	.442	.340
Cirillo, Jeff	.249	146	547	485	51	121	159	20	0	6	54	13	9	9	31	0	67	8	4	12	.328	.301
Guillen, Carlos†	.261	134	528	475	73	124	187	24	6	9	56	3	3	1	46	4	91	4	5	8	.394	.326
Sierra, Ruben†	.270	122	452	419	47	113	175	23	0	13	60	0	2	0	31	5	66	4	0	17	.418	.319
Martinez, Edgar	.277	97	407	328	42	91	159	23	0	15	59	0	6	6	67	8	69	1	1	6	.485	.403
McLemore, Mark†	.270	104	407	337	54	91	133	17	2	7	41	4	4	1	61	1	63	18	10	3	.395	.380
Wilson, Dan	.295	115	394	359	35	106	142	16	1	6	44	7	8	2	18	1	81	1	0	8	.396	.326
Relaford, Desi†	.267	112	376	329	55	88	123	13	2	6	43	1	7	6	33	2	51	10	3	6	.374	.339
Davis, Ben†	.259	80	253	228	24	59	92	10	1	7	43	1	4	2	18	1	58	1	1	6	.404	.313
Gipson, Charles	.236	79	84	72	22	17	26	5	2	0	8	2	0	1	9	0	14	4	0	3	.361	.329
Offerman, Jose†	.234	29	51	47	9	11	18	2	1	1	4	0	0	0	4	0	9	1	1	3	.383	.294
Bloomquist, Willie	.455	12	38	33	11	15	19	4	0	0	7	0	0	0	5	0	2	3	1	0	.576	.526
Snelling, Chris*	.148	8	29	27	2	4	7	0	0	1	3	0	0	0	2	0	4	0	0	2	.259	.207
Podsednik, Scott*	.200	14	25	20	2	4	7	0	0	1	5	0	1	0	4	0	6	0	0	1	.350	.320
Ugueto, Luis†	.217	62	25	23	19	5	8	0	0	1	1	0	0	0	2	0	8	8	4	0	.348	.280
Garcia, Freddy	.333	2	7	6	0	2	3	1	0	0	0	1	0	0	0	0	1	0	0	0	.500	.333
Pineiro, Joel	.143	2	7	7	0	1	1	0	0	0	2	0	0	0	0	0	2	0	0	0	.143	.143
Moyer, Jamie*	.200	2	5	5	0	1	1	0	0	0	0	0	0	0	0	0	2	0	0	0	.200	.200
Borders, Pat	.500	4	4	4	0	2	3	1	0	0	1	0	0	0	0	0	1	0	0	0	.750	.500
Soriano, Rafael	.000	3	4	4	0	0	0	0	0	0	0	0	0	0	0	0	1	0	0	0	.000	.000
Kingsale, Gene†	.667	2	3	3	0	2	2	0	0	0	0	0	0	0	0	0	0	0	0	1	.667	.667
Wright, Ron	.000	1	3	3	0	0	0	0	0	0	0	0	0	0	0	0	1	0	0	1	.000	.000
Baldwin, James	.500	1	2	2	0	1	1	0	0	0	0	0	0	0	0	0	0	0	0	0	.500	.500

Batters with more than one A.L. team

Batter	Avg.	G	TPA	AB	R	H	TB	2B	3B	HR	RBI	SH	SF	HP	BB	IBB	SO	SB	CS	GDP	Slg.	OBP
Offerman, Bos.-Sea.†	.232	101	326	284	48	66	95	12	1	5	31	1	3	1	37	0	38	9	6	12	.335	.320

* Lefthanded batter. † Switch-hitter.

PITCHING

Pitcher	W	L	ERA	G	GS	CG	GF	SHO	Sv.	IP	H	R	ER	HR	HB	BB	IBB	SO	WP	Bk.
Moyer, Jamie*	13	8	3.32	34	34	4	0	2	0	230.2	198	89	85	28	9	50	4	147	3	0
Garcia, Freddy	16	10	4.39	34	34	1	0	0	0	223.2	227	110	109	30	6	63	3	181	7	1
Pineiro, Joel	14	7	3.24	37	28	2	4	1	0	194.1	189	75	70	24	7	54	1	136	8	0
Baldwin, James	7	10	5.28	30	23	0	4	0	0	150.0	179	95	88	26	7	49	2	88	1	0
Franklin, Ryan	7	5	4.02	41	12	0	10	0	0	118.2	117	62	53	14	5	22	1	65	0	0
Halama, John*	6	5	3.56	31	10	0	12	0	0	101.0	112	45	40	9	1	33	5	70	2	1
Hasegawa, Shigetoshi	8	3	3.20	53	0	0	20	0	1	70.1	60	26	25	4	2	30	8	39	0	1
Rhodes, Arthur*	10	4	2.33	66	0	0	9	0	2	69.2	45	18	18	4	0	13	1	81	2	0
Sasaki, Kazuhiro	4	5	2.52	61	0	0	55	0	37	60.2	44	24	17	6	2	20	4	73	6	0
Valdes, Ismael	2	3	4.93	8	8	1	0	0	0	49.1	59	29	27	7	0	11	0	27	0	0
Soriano, Rafael	0	3	4.56	10	8	0	1	0	1	47.1	45	25	24	8	0	16	1	32	2	0
Nelson, Jeff	3	2	3.94	41	0	0	12	0	2	45.2	36	20	20	4	3	27	3	55	5	0
Abbott, Paul	1	3	11.96	7	5	0	1	0	0	26.1	40	36	35	5	1	20	0	22	2	0
Mateo, Julio	0	0	4.29	12	0	0	7	0	0	21.0	20	10	10	2	1	12	0	15	1	0
Creek, Doug*	1	1	4.91	23	0	0	11	0	0	18.1	18	10	10	2	4	14	1	19	2	0
Fitzgerald, Brian*	0	0	8.53	6	0	0	3	0	0	6.1	11	8	6	2	1	2	0	3	0	0
Taylor, Aaron	0	0	9.00	5	0	0	2	0	0	5.0	8	5	5	2	0	0	0	6	0	0
Watson, Mark*	1	0	18.00	3	0	0	1	0	0	4.0	8	8	8	1	0	4	0	1	1	0
Kaye, Justin	0	0	12.00	3	0	0	2	0	0	3.0	6	4	4	0	0	1	0	3	0	0

Pitchers with more than one A.L. team

Pitcher	W	L	ERA	G	GS	CG	GF	SHO	Sv.	IP	H	R	ER	HR	HB	BB	IBB	SO	WP	Bk.
Creek, T.B.-Sea.*	3	2	5.82	52	0	0	17	0	0	55.2	57	37	36	10	7	35	2	56	4	0
Valdes, Tex.-Sea.	8	12	4.18	31	31	1	0	0	0	196.0	194	94	91	26	9	47	1	102	0	2

* Throws lefthanded.

Tampa Bay Devil Rays

INDIVIDUAL STATISTICS

BATTING

Batter	Avg.	G	TPA	AB	R	H	TB	2B	3B	HR	RBI	SH	SF	HP	BB	IBB	SO	SB	CS	GDP	Slg.	OBP
Winn, Randy†	.298	152	674	607	87	181	280	39	9	14	75	1	5	6	55	3	109	27	8	9	.461	.360
Cox, Steve*	.254	148	633	560	65	142	222	30	1	16	72	0	6	7	60	5	116	5	0	15	.396	.330
Grieve, Ben*	.251	136	561	482	62	121	208	30	0	19	64	0	2	8	69	5	121	8	2	15	.432	.353
Abernathy, Brent	.242	117	504	463	46	112	144	18	4	2	40	8	2	6	25	0	46	10	4	8	.311	.288
Gomez, Chris	.265	130	498	461	51	122	189	31	3	10	46	6	3	7	21	0	58	1	3	8	.410	.305
Huff, Aubrey*	.313	113	494	454	67	142	236	25	0	23	59	0	2	1	37	7	55	4	1	17	.520	.364
Sandberg, Jared	.229	102	401	358	55	82	159	21	1	18	54	1	2	1	39	3	139	3	2	7	.444	.305
Hall, Toby	.258	85	353	330	37	85	124	19	1	6	42	2	3	1	17	3	27	0	1	14	.376	.293
Flaherty, John	.260	76	303	281	27	73	105	20	0	4	33	2	4	1	15	0	50	2	2	6	.374	.296
Vaughn, Greg	.163	69	297	251	28	41	79	10	2	8	29	0	2	3	41	1	82	3	2	5	.315	.286
Crawford, Carl*	.259	63	278	259	23	67	96	11	6	2	30	6	1	3	9	0	41	9	5	0	.371	.290
Conti, Jason*	.257	78	245	222	26	57	85	15	2	3	21	4	0	1	18	1	55	4	2	5	.383	.315
Tyner, Jason*	.214	44	180	168	17	36	40	2	1	0	9	3	1	1	7	0	19	7	1	1	.238	.249
Escalona, Felix	.217	59	171	157	17	34	46	8	2	0	9	3	1	7	3	0	44	7	2	2	.293	.262
Sheets, Andy	.248	41	164	149	18	37	53	4	0	4	22	1	2	0	12	0	41	2	3	1	.356	.301
Johnson, Russ	.216	45	130	111	15	24	32	5	0	1	12	2	0	1	16	1	22	5	2	2	.288	.320
Rolls, Damian	.292	21	95	89	15	26	34	6	1	0	6	1	0	2	3	0	16	2	5	1	.382	.330
Smith, Jason*	.200	26	69	65	9	13	21	1	2	1	6	2	0	0	2	0	24	3	0	0	.323	.224
Smith, Bobby	.175	18	66	63	4	11	16	2	0	1	6	0	0	0	3	0	25	0	0	0	.254	.212
McCarty, Dave	.176	12	40	34	2	6	9	0	0	1	2	0	0	2	4	0	9	0	0	0	.265	.300
Hoover, Paul	.176	5	17	17	1	3	3	0	0	0	2	0	0	0	0	0	5	0	0	0	.176	.176
Kennedy, Joe	.429	2	7	7	1	3	3	0	0	0	1	0	0	0	0	0	1	0	0	0	.429	.429
Wilson, Paul	.000	2	6	5	0	0	0	0	0	0	0	1	0	0	0	0	5	0	0	0	.000	.000
Sturtze, Tanyon	.000	2	5	4	0	0	0	0	0	0	0	1	0	0	0	0	1	0	0	0	.000	.000
Alvarez, Wilson*	.000	2	4	4	0	0	0	0	0	0	0	0	0	0	0	0	1	0	0	0	.000	.000
Creek, Doug*	.000	3	1	1	0	0	0	0	0	0	0	0	0	0	0	0	1	0	0	0	.000	.000
Rupe, Ryan	.000	1	1	1	0	0	0	0	0	0	0	0	0	0	0	0	1	0	0	0	.000	.000
Zambrano, Victor	.000	3	1	1	0	0	0	0	0	0	0	0	0	0	0	0	1	0	0	0	.000	.000

Batters with more than one A.L. team

Batter	Avg.	G	TPA	AB	R	H	TB	2B	3B	HR	RBI	SH	SF	HP	BB	IBB	SO	SB	CS	GDP	Slg.	OBP
McCarty, K.C.-T.B.	.136	25	74	66	5	9	16	1	0	2	4	0	0	2	6	0	19	0	0	1	.242	.230

* Lefthanded batter. † Switch-hitter.

PITCHING

Pitcher	W	L	ERA	G	GS	CG	GF	SHO	Sv.	IP	H	R	ER	HR	HB	BB	IBB	SO	WP	Bk.
Sturtze, Tanyon	4	18	5.18	33	33	4	0	0	0	224.0	271	141	129	33	9	89	2	137	7	2
Kennedy, Joe*	8	11	4.53	30	30	5	0	1	0	196.2	204	114	99	23	16	55	0	109	4	0
Wilson, Paul	6	12	4.83	30	30	1	0	0	0	193.2	219	113	104	29	13	67	2	111	4	1
Zambrano, Victor	8	8	5.53	42	11	0	11	0	1	114.0	120	77	70	15	4	68	5	73	10	0
Sosa, Jorge	2	7	5.53	31	14	0	10	0	0	99.1	88	63	61	16	2	54	0	48	5	0
Rupe, Ryan	5	10	5.60	15	15	2	0	0	0	90.0	83	60	56	11	10	25	0	67	6	0
Harper, Travis	5	9	5.46	37	7	0	16	0	1	85.2	101	54	52	14	9	27	3	60	2	0
Alvarez, Wilson*	2	3	5.28	23	10	0	3	0	1	75.0	80	47	44	13	4	36	3	56	2	0
Yan, Esteban	7	8	4.30	55	0	0	47	0	19	69.0	70	35	33	10	3	29	1	53	5	1
Kent, Steve*	0	2	5.65	34	0	0	10	0	1	57.1	67	41	36	6	3	38	0	41	2	3
Colome, Jesus	2	7	8.27	32	0	0	15	0	0	41.1	56	41	38	6	2	33	5	33	5	0
Phelps, Travis	1	2	4.78	26	0	0	9	0	0	37.2	30	20	20	7	5	27	0	36	6	2
Creek, Doug*	2	1	6.27	29	0	0	6	0	0	37.1	39	27	26	8	3	21	1	37	2	0
James, Delvin	0	3	6.55	8	6	0	2	0	0	34.1	40	25	25	5	1	15	1	17	2	1
Carter, Lance	2	0	1.33	8	0	0	7	0	2	20.1	15	3	3	2	0	5	1	14	0	0
de los Santos, Luis	0	3	11.57	3	3	0	0	0	0	14.0	24	19	18	5	3	4	0	7	0	0
Gardner, Lee	1	1	4.05	12	0	0	3	0	0	13.1	12	11	6	3	3	8	0	8	0	0
Backe, Brandon	0	0	6.92	9	0	0	4	0	0	13.0	15	10	10	3	2	7	0	6	0	0
Brazelton, Dewon	0	1	4.85	2	2	0	0	0	0	13.0	12	7	7	3	2	6	0	5	0	0
Jimenez, Jason*	0	0	5.40	5	0	0	4	0	0	6.2	9	4	4	2	0	1	0	5	0	0
Standridge, Jason	0	0	9.00	1	0	0	0	0	0	3.0	7	3	3	1	0	4	0	1	0	0
Martin, Tom*	0	0	16.20	2	0	0	2	0	0	1.2	5	3	3	0	0	1	0	1	0	0

Pitchers with more than one A.L. team

Pitcher	W	L	ERA	G	GS	CG	GF	SHO	Sv.	IP	H	R	ER	HR	HB	BB	IBB	SO	WP	Bk.
Creek, T.B.-Sea.*	3	2	5.82	52	0	0	17	0	0	55.2	57	37	36	10	7	35	2	56	4	0
Jimenez, T.B.-Det.*	0	0	7.36	6	0	0	4	0	0	7.1	12	8	6	2	0	2	0	5	0	0

* Throws lefthanded.

Texas Rangers

INDIVIDUAL STATISTICS

BATTING

Batter	Avg.	G	TPA	AB	R	H	TB	2B	3B	HR	RBI	SH	SF	HP	BB	IBB	SO	SB	CS	GDP	Slg.	OBP
Rodriguez, Alex	.300	162	725	624	125	187	389	27	2	57	142	0	4	10	87	12	122	9	4	14	.623	.392
Palmeiro, Rafael*	.273	155	663	546	99	149	312	34	0	43	105	0	7	6	104	16	94	2	0	10	.571	.391
Young, Michael	.262	156	633	573	77	150	219	26	8	9	62	13	6	0	41	1	112	6	7	14	.382	.308
Perry, Herbert	.276	132	496	450	64	124	216	24	1	22	77	4	2	6	34	1	66	4	2	17	.480	.333
Rodriguez, Ivan	.314	108	440	408	67	128	221	32	2	19	60	1	4	2	25	2	71	5	4	13	.542	.353
Everett, Carl†	.267	105	418	374	47	100	164	16	0	16	62	1	4	6	33	4	77	2	3	7	.439	.333
Mench, Kevin	.260	110	412	366	52	95	164	20	2	15	60	2	5	8	31	0	83	1	1	4	.448	.327
Lamb, Mike*	.283	115	355	314	54	89	129	13	0	9	33	2	3	3	33	5	48	0	0	7	.411	.354
Gonzalez, Juan	.282	70	296	277	38	78	125	21	1	8	35	0	1	1	17	1	56	2	0	11	.451	.324
Catalanotto, Frank*	.269	68	250	212	42	57	94	16	6	3	23	3	2	8	25	0	27	9	5	3	.443	.364
Greer, Rusty*	.296	51	219	199	24	59	75	9	2	1	17	0	1	0	19	0	17	1	0	5	.377	.356
Kapler, Gabe	.260	72	214	196	25	51	65	12	1	0	17	7	3	0	8	0	30	5	2	3	.332	.285
Haselman, Bill	.246	69	193	179	16	44	60	7	0	3	18	1	0	2	11	1	25	0	0	6	.335	.297
Rivera, Ruben	.209	69	186	158	17	33	49	4	0	4	14	4	2	5	17	0	45	4	2	2	.310	.302
Blalock, Hank*	.211	49	172	147	16	31	48	8	0	3	17	2	2	1	20	1	43	0	0	2	.327	.306
Hollandsworth, Todd*	.258	39	149	132	16	34	55	6	0	5	19	2	1	0	14	0	27	1	0	0	.417	.327
Greene, Todd	.268	42	118	112	15	30	65	5	0	10	19	1	2	1	2	0	23	0	0	4	.580	.282
Ludwick, Ryan	.235	23	88	81	10	19	28	6	0	1	9	0	0	0	7	0	24	2	1	4	.346	.295
Murray, Calvin	.169	37	86	77	16	13	20	5	1	0	1	2	0	1	6	0	15	4	0	0	.260	.238
Hafner, Travis*	.242	23	70	62	6	15	24	4	1	1	6	0	0	0	8	1	15	0	1	0	.387	.329
Romano, Jason	.204	29	60	54	8	11	15	4	0	0	4	1	1	0	4	0	13	2	0	0	.278	.254
Sadler, Donnie	.100	38	36	30	6	3	4	1	0	0	2	1	0	2	3	0	7	2	2	1	.133	.229
Hart, Jason	.267	10	17	15	2	4	7	3	0	0	0	0	0	0	2	0	7	0	0	0	.467	.353
Ortiz, Hector	.214	7	15	14	1	3	7	1	0	1	2	0	0	0	1	0	1	0	0	1	.500	.267
Burba, Dave	.200	2	5	5	0	1	1	0	0	0	0	0	0	0	0	0	3	0	0	0	.200	.200
Park, Chan Ho	.000	2	4	4	0	0	0	0	0	0	0	0	0	0	0	0	0	0	0	1	.000	.000
Rogers, Kenny*	.667	3	4	3	0	2	2	0	0	0	1	0	0	0	1	0	0	1	0	0	.667	.750
Valdes, Ismael	.000	2	4	3	0	0	0	0	0	0	1	1	0	0	0	0	2	0	0	0	.000	.000
Bell, Rob	.000	1	2	1	0	0	0	0	0	0	0	0	0	0	1	0	0	0	0	0	.000	.500
Cordero, Francisco	.000	5	1	1	0	0	0	0	0	0	0	0	0	0	0	0	1	0	0	0	.000	.000
Van Poppel, Todd	.000	2	1	1	0	0	0	0	0	0	0	0	0	0	0	0	1	0	0	0	.000	.000

Batters with more than one A.L. team

Batter	Avg.	G	TPA	AB	R	H	TB	2B	3B	HR	RBI	SH	SF	HP	BB	IBB	SO	SB	CS	GDP	Slg.	OBP
Sadler, K.C.-Tex.	.163	73	109	98	16	16	20	2	1	0	7	1	1	2	7	0	19	5	3	1	.204	.231

* Lefthanded batter. † Switch-hitter.

PITCHING

Pitcher	W	L	ERA	G	GS	CG	GF	SHO	Sv.	IP	H	R	ER	HR	HB	BB	IBB	SO	WP	Bk.
Rogers, Kenny*	13	8	3.84	33	33	2	0	1	0	210.2	212	101	90	21	6	70	1	107	5	1
Valdes, Ismael	6	9	3.93	23	23	0	0	0	0	146.2	135	65	64	19	9	36	1	75	0	2
Park, Chan Ho	9	8	5.75	25	25	0	0	0	0	145.2	154	95	93	20	17	78	2	121	9	0
Burba, Dave	4	5	5.42	23	18	1	2	0	0	111.1	125	71	67	13	7	40	3	70	9	1
Bell, Rob	4	3	6.22	17	15	0	0	0	0	94.0	113	69	65	16	1	35	0	70	7	0
Benoit, Joaquin	4	5	5.31	17	13	0	2	0	1	84.2	91	51	50	6	5	58	2	59	7	0
Van Poppel, Todd	3	2	5.45	50	0	0	19	0	1	72.2	80	44	44	14	3	29	1	85	8	0
Davis, Doug*	3	5	4.98	10	10	1	0	1	0	59.2	67	36	33	7	3	22	0	28	2	2
Powell, Jay	3	2	3.44	51	0	0	5	0	0	49.2	50	28	19	5	1	24	4	35	2	0
Myette, Aaron	2	5	10.06	15	12	0	2	0	0	48.1	64	57	54	11	6	41	0	48	5	0
Irabu, Hideki	3	8	5.74	38	2	0	26	0	16	47.0	51	30	30	11	1	16	2	30	3	0
Cordero, Francisco	2	0	1.79	39	0	0	25	0	10	45.1	33	12	9	2	2	13	1	41	1	0
Reyes, Dennys*	4	3	6.38	15	5	0	2	0	0	42.1	55	33	30	9	0	21	1	29	6	1
Alvarez, Juan*	0	4	4.76	52	0	0	12	0	0	39.2	35	22	21	7	3	21	0	30	0	1
Lewis, Colby	1	3	6.29	15	4	0	4	0	0	34.1	42	26	24	4	2	26	2	28	3	1
Seanez, Rudy	1	3	5.73	33	0	0	4	0	0	33.0	28	25	21	5	0	24	1	40	6	0
Kolb, Danny	3	6	4.22	34	0	0	14	0	1	32.0	27	17	15	1	1	22	2	20	6	0
Rocker, John*	2	3	6.66	30	0	0	10	0	1	24.1	29	19	18	5	0	13	1	30	0	0
Telford, Anthony	2	1	6.46	20	0	0	4	0	1	23.2	30	18	17	3	4	15	2	19	0	0
Woodard, Steve	0	0	6.62	14	0	0	4	0	0	17.2	20	13	13	4	2	8	1	14	0	1
Rodriguez, Rich*	3	2	5.40	36	0	0	6	0	1	16.2	14	10	10	1	1	11	1	12	0	0
Michalak, Chris*	0	2	4.40	13	0	0	4	0	0	14.1	20	7	7	1	1	10	2	5	1	0
Nitkowski, C.J.*	0	1	2.63	12	0	0	2	0	0	13.2	11	4	4	0	0	13	0	14	0	0
Flores, Randy*	0	0	4.50	20	0	0	5	0	1	12.0	11	7	6	2	0	8	2	7	3	0
Kozlowski, Ben*	0	0	6.30	2	2	0	0	0	0	10.0	11	7	7	3	1	11	0	6	0	0
Miceli, Dan	0	2	8.64	9	0	0	5	0	0	8.1	13	8	8	1	0	3	0	5	0	1
Garcia, Reynaldo	0	0	31.50	3	0	0	1	0	0	2.0	7	7	7	3	0	1	0	2	1	0

Pitchers with more than one A.L. team

Pitcher	W	L	ERA	G	GS	CG	GF	SHO	Sv.	IP	H	R	ER	HR	HB	BB	IBB	SO	WP	Bk.
Burba, Tex.-Cle.	5	5	5.20	35	21	1	2	0	0	145.1	155	91	84	16	9	57	3	95	9	1
Valdes, Tex.-Sea.	8	12	4.18	31	31	1	0	0	0	196.0	194	94	91	26	9	47	1	102	0	2

* Throws lefthanded.

Toronto Blue Jays

INDIVIDUAL STATISTICS

BATTING

Batter	Avg.	G	TPA	AB	R	H	TB	2B	3B	HR	RBI	SH	SF	HP	BB	IBB	SO	SB	CS	GDP	Slg.	OBP
Hinske, Eric*	.279	151	650	566	99	158	272	38	2	24	84	0	5	2	77	5	138	13	1	12	.481	.365
Wells, Vernon	.275	159	648	608	87	167	278	34	4	23	100	2	8	3	27	0	85	9	4	15	.457	.305
Stewart, Shannon	.303	141	641	577	103	175	255	38	6	10	45	0	1	9	54	2	60	14	2	17	.442	.371
Delgado, Carlos*	.277	143	628	505	103	140	277	34	2	33	108	0	8	13	102	18	126	1	0	8	.549	.406
Cruz, Jose†	.245	124	522	466	64	114	204	26	5	18	70	1	4	0	51	1	106	7	1	8	.438	.317
Berg, Dave	.270	109	414	374	42	101	143	26	2	4	39	4	5	5	26	1	57	0	2	6	.382	.322
Woodward, Chris	.276	90	350	312	48	86	146	13	4	13	45	1	8	3	26	0	72	3	0	8	.468	.330
Mondesi, Raul	.224	75	335	299	51	67	130	16	1	15	45	0	2	3	31	1	57	9	2	8	.435	.301
Lopez, Felipe†	.227	85	309	282	35	64	109	15	3	8	34	2	1	1	23	1	90	5	4	4	.387	.287
Wilson, Tom	.257	96	302	265	33	68	102	10	0	8	37	0	4	5	28	0	79	0	0	6	.385	.334
Phelps, Josh	.309	74	287	265	41	82	149	20	1	15	58	0	0	3	19	0	82	0	0	7	.562	.362
Huckaby, Ken	.245	88	283	273	29	67	84	6	1	3	22	1	0	0	9	1	44	0	0	10	.308	.270
Hudson, Orlando†	.276	54	207	192	20	53	85	10	5	4	23	0	2	2	11	0	27	0	1	6	.443	.319
Lawrence, Joe	.180	55	174	150	16	27	37	4	0	2	15	2	4	2	16	0	38	2	1	1	.247	.262
Fletcher, Darrin*	.220	45	135	127	8	28	43	6	0	3	22	1	3	0	4	0	13	0	0	4	.339	.239
Wise, Dewayne*	.179	42	116	112	14	20	35	4	1	3	13	0	0	0	4	0	15	5	0	0	.313	.207
Bush, Homer	.231	23	83	78	9	18	23	2	0	1	2	1	0	2	2	0	12	2	0	2	.295	.268
Werth, Jayson	.261	15	53	46	4	12	16	2	1	0	6	0	1	0	6	0	11	1	0	4	.348	.340
Lesher, Brian	.132	24	43	38	2	5	6	1	0	0	2	0	1	0	4	0	15	0	0	2	.158	.209
Cash, Kevin	.143	7	15	14	1	2	2	0	0	0	0	0	0	0	1	0	4	0	0	1	.143	.200
Swann, Pedro*	.083	13	13	12	3	1	1	0	0	0	1	0	0	0	1	0	6	0	0	0	.083	.154
Halladay, Roy	.000	2	6	6	0	0	0	0	0	0	0	0	0	0	0	0	1	0	0	1	.000	.000
Loaiza, Esteban	.167	2	6	6	0	1	1	0	0	0	0	0	0	0	0	0	1	0	0	0	.167	.167
Parris, Steve	.000	2	4	4	0	0	0	0	0	0	0	0	0	0	0	0	2	0	0	0	.000	.000
Carpenter, Chris	1.000	1	2	1	1	1	1	0	0	0	0	1	0	0	0	0	0	0	0	0	1.000	1.000
Miller, Justin	.000	2	2	2	0	0	0	0	0	0	0	0	0	0	0	0	1	0	0	0	.000	.000
Thurman, Corey	.000	3	2	1	0	0	0	0	0	0	0	1	0	0	0	0	0	0	0	0	.000	.000

Batters with more than one A.L. team

Batter	Avg.	G	TPA	AB	R	H	TB	2B	3B	HR	RBI	SH	SF	HP	BB	IBB	SO	SB	CS	GDP	Slg.	OBP
Mondesi, Tor.-N.Y.	.232	146	637	569	90	132	246	34	1	26	88	0	4	5	59	3	103	15	6	11	.432	.308

* Lefthanded batter. † Switch-hitter.

PITCHING

Pitcher	W	L	ERA	G	GS	CG	GF	SHO	Sv.	IP	H	R	ER	HR	HB	BB	IBB	SO	WP	Bk.
Halladay, Roy	19	7	2.93	34	34	2	0	1	0	239.1	223	93	78	10	7	62	6	168	4	1
Loaiza, Esteban	9	10	5.71	25	25	3	0	1	0	151.1	192	102	96	18	4	38	3	87	1	0
Walker, Pete	10	5	4.33	37	20	0	4	0	1	139.1	143	72	67	18	3	51	5	80	2	1
Miller, Justin	9	5	5.54	25	18	0	2	0	0	102.1	103	70	63	12	11	66	2	68	6	0
Escobar, Kelvim	5	7	4.27	76	0	0	68	0	38	78.0	75	39	37	10	5	44	6	85	4	0
Parris, Steve	5	5	5.97	14	14	0	0	0	0	75.1	96	50	50	13	3	35	5	48	3	0
Carpenter, Chris	4	5	5.28	13	13	1	0	0	0	73.1	89	45	43	11	4	27	0	45	3	0
Prokopec, Luke	2	9	6.78	22	12	0	4	0	0	71.2	90	57	54	19	7	25	2	41	3	1
Thurman, Corey	2	3	4.37	43	1	0	5	0	0	68.0	65	34	33	11	2	45	2	56	4	0
Cassidy, Scott	1	4	5.73	58	0	0	17	0	0	66.0	52	42	42	12	7	32	3	48	2	0
Eyre, Scott*	2	4	4.97	49	3	0	3	0	0	63.1	69	37	35	4	0	29	7	51	4	0
Lyon, Brandon	1	4	6.53	15	10	0	0	0	0	62.0	78	47	45	14	2	19	2	30	2	0
Politte, Cliff	1	3	3.61	55	0	0	13	0	1	57.1	38	23	23	5	1	19	1	57	1	0
Heredia, Felix*	1	2	3.61	53	0	0	15	0	0	52.1	51	29	21	5	2	26	3	31	5	0
Hendrickson, Mark*	3	0	2.45	16	4	0	0	0	0	36.2	25	11	10	1	2	12	3	21	0	0
Smith, Mike	0	3	6.62	14	6	0	3	0	0	35.1	43	28	26	3	7	20	0	16	2	0
Bowles, Brian	2	1	4.05	17	0	0	7	0	0	20.0	13	11	9	0	3	14	1	19	5	1
Plesac, Dan*	1	2	3.38	19	0	0	3	0	0	13.1	11	5	5	1	0	6	0	14	0	0
Borbon, Pedro*	1	2	4.97	16	0	0	6	0	0	12.2	12	8	7	3	1	6	3	11	1	0
Cooper, Brian	0	1	14.04	2	2	0	0	0	0	8.1	14	13	13	5	0	4	0	3	1	0
Kershner, Jason*	0	0	1.69	10	0	0	2	0	1	5.1	5	2	1	1	0	4	1	7	3	0
File, Bob	0	1	18.90	5	0	0	3	0	0	3.1	8	7	7	0	0	2	0	2	0	0
Wiggins, Scott*	0	0	3.38	3	0	0	0	0	0	2.2	5	1	1	1	0	1	0	3	1	0
Coco, Pasqual	0	1	18.00	2	0	0	1	0	0	1.0	4	2	2	0	0	3	1	0	0	0

* Throws lefthanded.

NATIONAL LEAGUE STATISTICS

TEAM STATISTICS

BATTING

Team	Avg.	G	AB	R	OR	H	TB	2B	3B	HR	GS	RBI	SH	SF	HP	BB	IBB	SO	SB	CS	GDP	LOB	SHO	SLG	OBP
Colorado	.274	162	5512	778	898	1508	2329	283	41	152	5	726	49	50	56	497	40	1043	103	53	133	1094	7	.423	.337
St. Louis	.268	162	5505	787	648	1475	2337	285	26	175	8	758	83	49	67	542	77	927	86	42	123	1160	10	.425	.338
Arizona	.267	162	5508	819	674	1471	2331	283	41	165	2	783	62	53	50	643	58	1016	92	46	130	1211	10	.423	.346
San Francisco	.267	162	5497	783	616	1465	2429	300	35	198	5	751	68	52	65	616	103	961	74	21	136	1241	7	.442	.344
Los Angeles	.264	162	5554	713	643	1464	2273	286	29	155	3	693	67	44	53	428	50	940	96	37	140	1087	13	.409	.320
Houston	.262	162	5503	749	695	1441	2297	291	32	167	3	719	64	37	59	589	57	1120	71	27	144	1177	6	.417	.338
Montreal	.261	162	5479	735	718	1432	2290	300	36	162	4	695	108	42	46	575	85	1104	118	64	123	1158	10	.418	.334
Florida	.261	162	5496	699	763	1433	2215	280	32	146	2	653	59	49	61	595	69	1130	177	73	129	1190	13	.403	.337
Atlanta	.260	161	5495	708	565	1428	2250	280	25	164	6	669	67	49	54	558	68	1028	76	39	147	1185	7	.409	.331
Philadelphia	.259	161	5523	710	724	1428	2330	325	41	165	2	676	67	39	53	640	70	1095	104	43	129	1260	3	.422	.339
New York	.256	161	5496	690	703	1409	2171	238	22	160	2	650	75	30	63	486	46	1044	87	42	142	1111	7	.395	.322
Cincinnati	.253	162	5470	709	774	1386	2232	297	21	169	9	678	95	40	66	583	66	1188	116	52	119	1169	8	.408	.330
Milwaukee	.253	162	5415	627	821	1369	2113	269	29	139	5	597	79	34	55	500	37	1125	94	50	144	1086	15	.390	.320
San Diego	.253	162	5515	662	815	1393	2102	243	29	136	5	627	45	41	30	547	42	1062	71	44	132	1158	16	.381	.321
Chicago	.246	162	5496	706	759	1351	2268	259	29	200	2	676	78	39	44	585	52	1269	63	21	117	1173	10	.413	.321
Pittsburgh	.244	161	5330	641	730	1300	2029	263	20	142	2	610	68	41	73	537	44	1109	86	49	97	1149	15	.381	.319
Totals	.259	1294	87794	11516	11546	22753	35996	4482	488	2595	65	10961	1134	689	895	8921	964	17161	1514	703	2085	18609	157	.410	.331

PITCHING

Team	W	L	ERA	G	CG	SHO	Rel.	Sv.	IP	H	R	ER	HR	HB	BB	IBB	SO	WP	Bk.	Avg.
Atlanta	101	59	3.13	161	3	15	469	57	1467.1	1302	565	511	123	42	554	63	1058	40	4	.240
San Francisco	95	66	3.54	162	10	13	417	43	1437.1	1349	616	566	116	36	523	44	992	36	2	.251
Los Angeles	92	70	3.69	162	4	15	423	56	1457.2	1311	643	598	165	46	555	45	1132	33	3	.242
St. Louis	97	65	3.70	162	4	9	472	42	1446.1	1355	648	595	141	60	547	39	1009	40	2	.251
New York	75	86	3.89	161	9	10	451	36	1442.2	1408	703	624	163	55	543	75	1107	22	7	.256
Arizona	98	64	3.92	162	14	10	422	40	1446.2	1361	674	630	170	54	421	30	1303	48	11	.247
Montreal	83	79	3.97	162	9	3	437	39	1453.0	1475	718	641	165	46	508	80	1088	51	5	.265
Houston	84	78	4.00	162	2	11	480	43	1445.0	1423	695	643	151	55	546	78	1219	38	3	.260
Philadelphia	80	81	4.17	161	5	9	450	47	1449.2	1381	724	671	153	70	570	54	1075	68	5	.252
Pittsburgh	72	89	4.23	161	2	7	458	47	1412.2	1447	730	664	163	55	572	93	920	34	5	.268
Cincinnati	78	84	4.27	162	2	8	462	42	1453.2	1502	774	690	173	56	550	63	980	52	2	.269
Chicago	67	95	4.29	162	11	9	390	23	1441.1	1373	759	687	167	58	606	53	1333	44	2	.253
Florida	79	83	4.36	162	11	12	461	36	1456.1	1449	763	706	151	58	631	46	1104	55	7	.262
San Diego	66	96	4.62	162	5	10	459	40	1436.1	1522	815	737	177	66	582	61	1108	51	4	.274
Milwaukee	56	106	4.73	162	7	4	446	32	1432.1	1468	821	752	199	62	666	82	1026	64	8	.268
Colorado	73	89	5.20	162	1	8	506	43	1426.2	1554	898	825	225	64	582	49	920	42	6	.277
Totals	1296	1290	4.11	1294	99	153	7203	666	23105.0	22680	11546	10540	2602	883	8956	955	17374	718	76	.258

FIELDING

Team	Pct.	G	PO	A	E	TC	DP	TP	PB
Houston	.986	162	4335	1663	83	6081	149	0	5
Philadelphia	.986	161	4349	1700	88	6137	156	0	12
Los Angeles	.985	162	4373	1686	90	6149	134	0	12
San Francisco	.985	162	4312	1630	90	6032	166	0	7
Arizona	.985	162	4340	1506	89	5935	116	0	13
St. Louis	.983	162	4339	1674	103	6116	168	1	9
Milwaukee	.983	162	4297	1633	103	6033	154	0	12
Florida	.983	162	4369	1636	106	6111	163	1	6
Atlanta	.982	161	4402	1822	114	6338	170	0	12
Colorado	.982	162	4280	1701	112	6093	158	0	12
Pittsburgh	.982	161	4238	1899	115	6252	177	0	12
Cincinnati	.981	162	4361	1773	120	6254	169	0	28
Chicago	.981	162	4324	1500	114	5938	144	0	15
San Diego	.979	162	4309	1681	128	6118	162	0	14
Montreal	.978	162	4359	1799	139	6297	160	1	12
New York	.976	161	4328	1628	144	6100	138	1	11
Totals	.982	1294	69315	26931	1738	97984	2484	4	192

ATTENDANCE

	2002				2001	
Team	Home	Road	Dates	Avg.	Dates	Avg.
San Francisco	3,253,205	2,671,331	81	40,163	81	40,460
Arizona	3,200,725	2,689,308	81	39,515	81	33,834
Los Angeles	3,131,077	2,442,648	81	38,655	81	37,253
St. Louis	3,011,756	2,311,490	81	37,182	81	38,433
New York	2,804,838	2,141,748	78	35,959	81	32,314
Colorado	2,737,918	2,372,413	81	33,801	81	39,005
Chicago	2,693,071	2,621,840	78	34,527	79	34,739
Atlanta	2,603,482	2,121,286	81	32,142	81	34,858
Houston	2,517,407	2,237,917	81	31,079	81	35,855
San Diego	2,220,416	2,414,675	81	27,413	80	29,725
Milwaukee	1,969,693	2,111,690	81	24,317	81	34,704
Cincinnati	1,855,973	2,319,051	80	23,200	79	23,832
Pittsburgh	1,784,993	2,146,882	79	22,595	79	30,837
Philadelphia	1,618,141	2,214,598	79	20,483	78	22,852
Florida	813,111	2,028,570	81	10,038	80	15,765
Montreal	732,901	1,981,950	81	9,048	81	7,524
Totals	36,948,707	36,827,397	1,285	28,754	1,285	30,785
M.L. Totals	67,859,176	67,859,176	2,412	28,134	2,413	29,949

Arizona Diamondbacks

INDIVIDUAL STATISTICS

BATTING

Batter	Avg.	G	TPA	AB	R	H	TB	2B	3B	HR	RBI	SH	SF	HP	BB	IBB	SO	SB	CS	GDP	Slg.	OBP
Womack, Tony*	.271	153	652	590	90	160	208	23	5	5	57	6	6	4	46	2	80	29	12	9	.353	.325
Gonzalez, Luis*	.288	148	633	524	90	151	260	19	3	28	103	0	7	5	97	8	76	9	2	12	.496	.400
Spivey, Junior	.301	143	626	538	103	162	256	34	6	16	78	1	6	16	65	5	100	11	6	10	.476	.389
Finley, Steve*	.287	150	577	505	82	145	252	24	4	25	89	1	3	3	65	7	73	16	4	10	.499	.370
Counsell, Craig*	.282	112	491	436	63	123	153	22	1	2	51	4	3	1	45	3	52	7	5	10	.351	.348
McCracken, Quinton†	.309	123	400	349	60	108	160	27	8	3	40	13	4	2	32	0	68	5	4	3	.458	.367
Grace, Mark*	.252	124	348	298	43	75	115	19	0	7	48	0	3	1	46	6	30	2	0	5	.386	.351
Miller, Damian	.249	101	340	297	40	74	129	22	0	11	42	2	0	3	38	5	88	0	0	14	.434	.340
Durazo, Erubiel*	.261	76	276	222	46	58	122	12	2	16	48	0	3	2	49	2	60	0	1	1	.550	.395
Dellucci, David*	.245	97	261	229	34	56	92	11	2	7	29	0	3	1	28	5	55	2	4	7	.402	.326
Williams, Matt	.260	60	238	215	29	56	103	7	2	12	40	0	2	0	21	1	41	3	1	8	.479	.324
Colbrunn, Greg	.333	72	185	171	30	57	107	16	2	10	27	0	1	0	13	1	19	0	0	5	.626	.378
Barajas, Rod	.234	70	172	154	12	36	55	10	0	3	23	2	3	3	10	4	25	1	0	4	.357	.288
Bautista, Danny	.325	40	166	154	22	50	77	5	2	6	23	0	1	0	11	2	21	4	2	4	.500	.367
Guillen, Jose	.229	54	141	131	13	30	46	4	0	4	15	0	1	2	7	1	25	3	4	7	.351	.277
Moeller, Chad	.286	37	123	105	10	30	49	11	1	2	16	1	0	0	17	3	23	0	1	6	.467	.385
Johnson, Randy	.135	34	99	89	4	12	15	3	0	0	8	6	1	0	3	0	40	0	0	3	.169	.161
Schilling, Curt	.174	34	98	86	7	15	15	0	0	0	3	8	0	0	4	0	26	0	0	2	.174	.211
Donnels, Chris*	.238	74	93	80	5	19	34	4	1	3	16	0	3	0	10	1	14	0	0	2	.425	.312
Cintron, Alex†	.213	38	90	75	11	16	22	6	0	0	4	3	0	0	12	2	13	0	0	2	.293	.322
Helling, Rick	.043	29	61	46	3	2	2	0	0	0	1	6	0	1	8	0	16	0	0	1	.043	.200
Batista, Miguel	.157	33	56	51	5	8	13	2	0	1	2	2	0	0	3	0	28	0	0	2	.255	.204
Bell, Jay	.163	32	56	49	3	8	15	1	0	2	11	0	1	1	5	0	9	0	0	2	.306	.250
Anderson, Brian	.116	36	49	43	0	5	8	1	1	0	2	5	0	1	0	0	9	0	0	0	.186	.136
Little, Mark	.273	15	28	22	8	6	8	0	1	0	2	0	0	4	2	0	5	0	0	0	.364	.429
Jose, Felix†	.263	13	25	19	5	5	11	0	0	2	4	0	2	0	4	0	8	0	0	1	.579	.360
Patterson, John	.100	7	12	10	1	1	1	0	0	0	0	1	0	0	1	0	4	0	0	0	.100	.182
Overbay, Lyle*	.100	10	10	10	0	1	1	0	0	0	1	0	0	0	0	0	5	0	0	0	.100	.100
Stottlemyre, Todd*	.000	5	6	4	0	0	0	0	0	0	0	1	0	0	1	0	2	0	0	0	.000	.200
Klassen, Danny	.333	4	3	3	0	1	1	0	0	0	0	0	0	0	0	0	1	0	0	0	.333	.333
Kim, Byung-Hyun	.500	66	2	2	0	1	1	0	0	0	0	0	0	0	0	0	0	0	0	0	.500	.500
Koplove, Mike	.000	53	1	1	0	0	0	0	0	0	0	0	0	0	0	0	0	0	0	0	.000	.000

Batters with more than one N.L. team

Batter	Avg.	G	TPA	AB	R	H	TB	2B	3B	HR	RBI	SH	SF	HP	BB	IBB	SO	SB	CS	GDP	Slg.	OBP
Guillen, Ari.-Cin.	.238	85	259	240	25	57	88	7	0	8	31	1	1	3	14	1	43	4	5	13	.367	.287
Little, Col.-N.Y.-Ari.	.208	79	154	130	28	27	38	5	3	0	7	1	0	8	15	0	34	2	2	1	.292	.327

* Lefthanded batter. † Switch-hitter.

PITCHING

Pitcher	W	L	ERA	G	GS	CG	GF	SHO	Sv.	IP	H	R	ER	HR	HB	BB	IBB	SO	WP	Bk.
Johnson, Randy*	24	5	2.32	35	35	8	0	4	0	260.0	197	78	67	26	13	71	1	334	3	2
Schilling, Curt	23	7	3.23	36	35	5	0	1	0	259.1	218	95	93	29	3	33	1	316	6	0
Batista, Miguel	8	9	4.29	36	29	1	2	0	0	184.2	172	99	88	12	6	70	3	112	9	2
Helling, Rick	10	12	4.51	30	30	0	0	0	0	175.2	180	94	88	31	6	48	6	120	7	1
Anderson, Brian*	6	11	4.79	35	24	0	1	0	0	156.0	174	86	83	23	1	32	3	81	2	5
Kim, Byung-Hyun	8	3	2.04	72	0	0	66	0	36	84.0	64	20	19	5	6	26	2	92	2	0
Koplove, Mike	6	1	3.36	55	0	0	15	0	0	61.2	47	24	23	2	0	23	4	46	1	0
Myers, Mike*	4	3	4.38	69	0	0	15	0	4	37.0	39	18	18	2	8	17	0	31	0	0
Morgan, Mike	1	1	5.29	29	0	0	9	0	0	34.0	41	22	20	7	3	9	1	13	3	0
Swindell, Greg*	0	2	6.27	34	0	0	5	0	0	33.0	38	23	23	9	0	5	1	23	0	0
Patterson, John	2	0	3.23	7	5	0	1	0	0	30.2	27	11	11	7	1	7	0	31	2	0
Mantei, Matt	2	2	4.73	31	0	0	6	0	0	26.2	28	15	14	3	1	12	0	26	1	0
Oropesa, Eddie*	2	0	10.30	32	0	0	5	0	0	25.1	39	30	29	6	2	15	0	18	1	1
Fetters, Mike	2	3	5.11	33	0	0	9	0	0	24.2	28	18	14	1	2	19	5	24	6	0
Stottlemyre, Todd	0	2	7.52	5	4	0	1	0	0	20.1	26	17	17	4	0	7	0	12	0	0
Parra, Jose	0	1	3.21	16	0	0	3	0	0	14.0	13	5	5	0	1	11	2	8	1	0
Prinz, Bret	0	2	9.45	20	0	0	5	0	0	13.1	23	14	14	1	1	10	1	10	3	0
Sanchez, Duaner	0	0	4.91	6	0	0	3	0	0	3.2	3	2	2	1	0	5	0	4	0	0
Reynoso, Armando	0	0	10.80	2	0	0	1	0	0	1.2	3	2	2	0	0	1	0	2	1	0
Grace, Mark*	0	0	9.00	1	0	0	1	0	0	1.0	1	1	1	1	0	0	0	0	0	0

Pitchers with more than one N.L. team

Pitcher	W	L	ERA	G	GS	CG	GF	SHO	Sv.	IP	H	R	ER	HR	HB	BB	IBB	SO	WP	Bk.
Fetters, Pit.-Ari.	3	3	4.09	65	0	0	22	0	0	55.0	53	31	25	4	3	37	6	53	8	0
Sanchez, Ari.-Pit.	0	0	9.00	9	0	0	5	0	0	6.0	6	6	6	2	0	7	0	6	0	0

* Throws lefthanded.

Atlanta Braves

INDIVIDUAL STATISTICS

BATTING

Batter	Avg.	G	TPA	AB	R	H	TB	2B	3B	HR	RBI	SH	SF	HP	BB	IBB	SO	SB	CS	GDP	Slg.	OBP
Furcal, Rafael†	.275	154	693	636	95	175	246	31	8	8	47	9	2	3	43	0	114	27	15	8	.387	.323
Jones, Chipper†	.327	158	662	548	90	179	294	35	1	26	100	0	5	2	107	23	89	8	2	18	.536	.435
Jones, Andruw	.264	154	659	560	91	148	287	34	0	35	94	0	6	10	83	4	135	8	3	14	.513	.366
Sheffield, Gary	.307	135	579	492	82	151	252	26	0	25	84	0	4	11	72	2	53	12	2	16	.512	.404
Castilla, Vinny	.232	143	578	543	56	126	189	23	2	12	61	0	6	7	22	4	69	4	1	22	.348	.268
Lopez, Javy	.233	109	385	347	31	81	129	15	0	11	52	0	4	8	26	8	63	0	1	15	.372	.299
Franco, Julio	.284	125	383	338	51	96	129	13	1	6	30	2	3	1	39	3	75	5	1	13	.382	.357
Lockhart, Keith*	.216	128	331	296	34	64	98	13	3	5	32	5	2	1	27	9	50	0	1	4	.331	.282
Blanco, Henry	.204	81	249	221	17	45	74	9	1	6	22	2	5	1	20	5	51	0	2	5	.335	.267
Giles, Marcus	.230	68	242	213	27	49	85	10	1	8	23	1	1	2	25	3	41	1	1	5	.399	.315
Bragg, Darren*	.269	109	240	212	34	57	85	15	2	3	15	1	1	2	24	0	52	5	2	4	.401	.347
Franco, Matt*	.317	81	233	205	25	65	106	15	4	6	30	0	1	0	27	2	31	1	0	5	.517	.395
DeRosa, Mark	.297	72	232	212	24	63	91	9	2	5	23	2	3	3	12	3	24	2	3	5	.429	.339
Helms, Wes	.243	85	231	210	20	51	85	16	0	6	22	1	6	3	11	2	57	1	1	5	.405	.283
Surhoff, B.J.*	.293	25	85	75	5	22	27	5	0	0	9	1	0	0	9	0	5	1	3	1	.360	.369
Glavine, Tom*	.103	36	84	68	0	7	8	1	0	0	3	13	0	0	3	0	13	0	0	5	.118	.141
Millwood, Kevin	.200	34	82	70	5	14	22	5	0	1	11	11	0	0	0	0	27	0	0	0	.314	.200
Maddux, Greg	.186	33	68	59	6	11	14	3	0	0	2	9	0	0	0	0	8	1	0	0	.237	.186
Garcia, Jesse	.197	39	61	61	6	12	13	1	0	0	5	0	0	0	0	0	14	0	1	1	.213	.197
Moss, Damian	.100	31	60	50	2	5	6	1	0	0	2	6	0	0	4	0	24	0	0	0	.120	.167
Marquis, Jason*	.132	28	41	38	6	5	8	0	0	1	1	3	0	0	0	0	16	0	0	1	.211	.132
Torrealba, Steve	.059	13	21	17	1	1	1	0	0	0	1	1	0	0	3	0	4	0	0	0	.059	.200
Lopez, Albie	.111	28	9	9	0	1	1	0	0	0	0	0	0	0	0	0	6	0	0	0	.111	.111
Hodges, Trey	.000	4	3	3	0	0	0	0	0	0	0	0	0	0	0	0	2	0	0	0	.000	.000
Bong, Jung*	.000	2	2	2	0	0	0	0	0	0	0	0	0	0	0	0	1	0	0	0	.000	.000
Hammond, Chris*	.000	59	2	1	0	0	0	0	0	0	0	0	0	0	1	0	1	0	0	0	.000	.000
Holmes, Darren	.000	51	2	2	0	0	0	0	0	0	0	0	0	0	1	0	1	0	0	0	.000	.500
Remlinger, Mike*	.000	68	2	2	0	0	0	0	0	0	0	0	0	0	0	0	0	0	0	0	.000	.000
Smoltz, John	.000	72	2	2	0	0	0	0	0	0	0	0	0	0	0	0	1	0	0	0	.000	.000
Ennis, John	.000	1	1	1	0	0	0	0	0	0	0	0	0	0	0	0	1	0	0	0	.000	.000
Langerhans, Ryan*	.000	1	1	1	0	0	0	0	0	0	0	0	0	0	0	0	0	0	0	0	.000	.000
Spooneybarger, Tim	.000	50	1	1	0	0	0	0	0	0	0	0	0	0	0	0	1	0	0	0	.000	.000

* Lefthanded batter. † Switch-hitter.

PITCHING

Pitcher	W	L	ERA	G	GS	CG	GF	SHO	Sv.	IP	H	R	ER	HR	HB	BB	IBB	SO	WP	Bk.
Glavine, Tom*	18	11	2.96	36	36	2	0	1	0	224.2	210	85	74	21	8	78	8	127	2	0
Millwood, Kevin	18	8	3.24	35	34	1	0	1	0	217.0	186	83	78	16	8	65	7	178	4	0
Maddux, Greg	16	6	2.62	34	34	0	0	0	0	199.1	194	67	58	14	4	45	7	118	1	0
Moss, Damian*	12	6	3.42	33	29	0	2	0	0	179.0	140	80	68	20	6	89	5	111	13	2
Marquis, Jason	8	9	5.04	22	22	0	0	0	0	114.1	127	66	64	19	3	49	3	84	4	0
Smoltz, John	3	2	3.25	75	0	0	68	0	55	80.1	59	30	29	4	0	24	1	85	1	1
Hammond, Chris*	7	2	0.95	63	0	0	6	0	0	76.0	53	15	8	1	1	31	9	63	1	0
Remlinger, Mike*	7	3	1.99	73	0	0	7	0	0	68.0	48	17	15	3	1	28	3	69	0	0
Ligtenberg, Kerry	3	4	2.97	52	0	0	25	0	0	66.2	52	23	22	6	0	33	3	51	1	1
Lopez, Albie	1	4	4.37	30	4	0	14	0	0	55.2	66	29	27	1	0	18	3	39	5	0
Holmes, Darren	2	2	1.81	55	0	0	10	0	1	54.2	41	12	11	3	2	12	4	47	0	0
Gryboski, Kevin	2	1	3.48	57	0	0	10	0	0	51.2	50	20	20	6	5	37	5	33	2	0
Spooneybarger, Tim	1	0	2.63	51	0	0	14	0	1	51.1	38	16	15	4	2	26	5	33	4	0
Hodges, Trey	2	0	5.40	4	0	0	0	0	0	11.2	16	7	7	2	1	2	0	6	1	0
Bong, Jung*	0	1	7.50	1	1	0	0	0	0	6.0	8	5	5	0	0	2	0	4	0	0
Foster, John*	1	0	10.80	5	0	0	0	0	0	5.0	6	6	6	3	1	6	0	6	0	0
Ennis, John	0	0	4.50	1	1	0	0	0	0	4.0	5	2	2	0	0	3	0	1	0	0
Pratt, Andy*	0	0	6.75	1	0	0	0	0	0	1.1	1	1	1	0	0	4	0	1	0	0
Dawley, Joey	0	0	0.00	1	0	0	1	0	0	0.1	0	0	0	0	0	0	0	1	0	0
Small, Aaron	0	0	27.00	1	0	0	1	0	0	0.1	2	1	1	0	0	2	0	1	1	0

* Throws lefthanded.

CHICAGO CUBS

INDIVIDUAL STATISTICS

BATTING

Batter	Avg.	G	TPA	AB	R	H	TB	2B	3B	HR	RBI	SH	SF	HP	BB	IBB	SO	SB	CS	GDP	Slg.	OBP
Sosa, Sammy	.288	150	666	556	122	160	330	19	2	49	108	0	4	3	103	15	144	2	0	14	.594	.399
Patterson, Corey*	.253	153	628	592	71	150	232	30	5	14	54	4	5	8	19	1	142	18	3	8	.392	.284
McGriff, Fred*	.273	146	595	523	67	143	264	27	2	30	103	0	5	4	63	6	99	1	2	13	.505	.353
Gonzalez, Alex S.	.248	142	568	513	58	127	218	27	5	18	61	4	2	3	46	7	136	5	3	11	.425	.312
Alou, Moises	.275	132	534	484	50	133	203	23	1	15	61	0	3	0	47	4	61	8	0	15	.419	.337
Bellhorn, Mark†	.258	146	529	445	86	115	228	24	4	27	56	2	0	6	76	3	144	7	5	6	.512	.374
Mueller, Bill†	.266	103	413	353	51	94	142	19	4	7	37	4	5	0	51	2	41	0	0	8	.402	.355
Hundley, Todd†	.211	92	303	266	32	56	112	8	0	16	35	1	1	3	32	3	80	0	0	6	.421	.301
Girardi, Joe	.226	90	256	234	19	53	68	10	1	1	13	5	1	0	16	3	35	1	0	10	.291	.275
Brown, Roosevelt*	.211	111	231	204	14	43	64	12	0	3	23	0	1	3	23	0	50	2	2	4	.314	.299
Stynes, Chris	.241	98	225	195	25	47	73	9	1	5	26	5	3	1	21	1	29	1	1	5	.374	.314
Hill, Bobby†	.253	59	215	190	26	48	71	7	2	4	20	4	0	4	17	4	42	6	1	0	.374	.327
DeShields, Delino*	.192	67	174	146	20	28	45	6	1	3	10	6	1	0	21	2	38	10	1	0	.308	.292
Echevarria, Angel	.306	50	111	98	14	30	46	7	0	3	21	0	4	1	8	0	17	0	0	4	.469	.351
Lewis, Darren	.241	58	91	79	7	19	24	3	1	0	7	2	0	3	7	0	11	1	3	0	.304	.326
Ojeda, Augie†	.186	30	81	70	4	13	17	4	0	0	4	4	1	1	5	0	5	1	0	2	.243	.247
Wood, Kerry	.167	32	81	72	5	12	15	0	0	1	5	6	0	0	3	0	28	0	0	0	.208	.200
Clement, Matt	.049	30	75	61	4	3	5	2	0	0	4	10	0	3	1	0	34	0	0	1	.082	.108
Machado, Robert	.276	22	64	58	5	16	23	4	0	1	5	1	0	0	5	0	11	0	0	2	.397	.333
Choi, Hee Seop*	.180	24	57	50	6	9	16	1	0	2	4	0	0	0	7	0	15	0	0	2	.320	.281
Hermansen, Chad	.209	35	49	43	3	9	15	3	0	1	3	1	0	0	5	0	14	0	0	0	.349	.292
Lieber, Jon*	.163	20	48	43	2	7	8	1	0	0	0	4	0	0	1	0	10	0	0	2	.186	.182
Prior, Mark	.171	17	39	35	3	6	10	4	0	0	4	2	0	0	2	0	15	0	0	1	.286	.216
Orie, Kevin	.281	13	36	32	4	9	12	3	0	0	5	0	2	1	1	0	4	0	0	1	.375	.306
Zambrano, Carlos	.033	31	32	30	0	1	2	1	0	0	0	2	0	0	0	0	15	0	0	0	.067	.033
Bere, Jason	.125	16	31	24	1	3	5	2	0	0	0	7	0	0	0	0	11	0	0	0	.208	.125
Mahoney, Mike	.207	16	31	29	2	6	9	3	0	0	3	1	0	0	1	1	10	0	0	1	.310	.233
Cruz, Juan	.143	44	16	14	0	2	2	0	0	0	0	2	0	0	0	0	4	0	0	0	.143	.143
Benes, Alan	.077	7	14	13	0	1	1	0	0	0	0	0	0	0	1	0	8	0	0	0	.077	.143
Smyth, Steve*	.222	8	10	9	1	2	2	0	0	0	1	1	0	0	0	0	1	0	0	1	.222	.222
Encarnacion, Mario	.000	3	9	7	0	0	0	0	0	0	0	0	0	0	2	0	3	0	0	0	.000	.222
Borowski, Joe	.286	72	7	7	1	2	2	0	0	0	0	0	0	0	0	0	5	0	0	0	.286	.286
Cunnane, Will	.250	16	5	4	2	1	1	0	0	0	0	0	0	0	1	0	0	0	0	0	.250	.400
Mahomes, Pat	.000	18	5	5	1	0	0	0	0	0	0	0	0	0	0	0	3	0	0	0	.000	.000
Alfonseca, Antonio	.667	64	3	3	0	2	2	0	0	0	2	0	0	0	0	0	0	0	0	0	.667	.667
Fassero, Jeff*	.333	55	3	3	0	1	1	0	0	0	0	0	0	0	0	0	2	0	0	0	.333	.333
Osborne, Donovan*	.000	11	3	3	0	0	0	0	0	0	0	0	0	0	0	0	1	0	0	0	.000	.000
Farnsworth, Kyle	.000	43	2	1	0	0	0	0	0	0	1	0	1	0	0	0	0	0	0	0	.000	.000
Beltran, Francis	.000	10	1	1	0	0	0	0	0	0	0	0	0	0	0	0	1	0	0	0	.000	.000
Sanchez, Jesus*	.000	8	1	1	0	0	0	0	0	0	0	0	0	0	0	0	0	0	0	0	.000	.000

Batters with more than one N.L. team

Batter	Avg.	G	TPA	AB	R	H	TB	2B	3B	HR	RBI	SH	SF	HP	BB	IBB	SO	SB	CS	GDP	Slg.	OBP
Hermansen, Pit.-Chi.	.207	100	265	237	25	49	89	14	1	8	18	4	1	1	22	0	82	7	5	1	.376	.276
Machado, Chi.-Mil.	.261	73	233	211	19	55	80	14	1	3	22	2	2	1	17	4	41	0	0	7	.379	.316
Mueller, Chi.-S.F.†	.262	111	427	366	51	96	144	19	4	7	38	4	5	0	52	2	42	0	0	9	.393	.350

* Lefthanded batter. † Switch-hitter.

PITCHING

Pitcher	W	L	ERA	G	GS	CG	GF	SHO	Sv.	IP	H	R	ER	HR	HB	BB	IBB	SO	WP	Bk.
Wood, Kerry	12	11	3.66	33	33	4	0	1	0	213.2	169	92	87	22	16	97	5	217	8	1
Clement, Matt	12	11	3.60	32	32	3	0	2	0	205.0	162	84	82	18	6	85	7	215	7	0
Lieber, Jon	6	8	3.70	21	21	3	0	0	0	141.0	153	64	58	15	1	12	2	87	0	0
Prior, Mark	6	6	3.32	19	19	1	0	0	0	116.2	98	45	43	14	7	38	0	147	1	0
Zambrano, Carlos	4	8	3.66	32	16	0	3	0	0	108.1	94	53	44	9	4	63	2	93	6	0
Cruz, Juan	3	11	3.98	45	9	0	14	0	1	97.1	84	56	43	11	8	59	4	81	1	0
Borowski, Joe	4	4	2.73	73	0	0	25	0	2	95.2	84	31	29	10	1	29	6	97	1	0
Bere, Jason	1	10	5.67	16	16	0	0	0	0	85.2	98	63	54	13	3	28	1	65	5	0
Alfonseca, Antonio	2	5	4.00	66	0	0	55	0	19	74.1	73	34	33	5	3	36	3	61	1	0
Fassero, Jeff*	5	6	6.18	57	0	0	17	0	0	51.0	65	37	35	5	3	22	5	44	2	1
Farnsworth, Kyle	4	6	7.33	45	0	0	17	0	1	46.2	53	47	38	9	1	24	7	46	1	0
Benes, Alan	2	2	4.35	7	7	0	0	0	0	39.1	42	22	19	3	0	12	1	32	2	0
Mahomes, Pat	1	1	3.86	16	2	0	2	0	0	32.2	36	15	14	3	1	17	3	23	1	0
Cunnane, Will	1	1	5.47	16	0	0	2	0	0	26.1	27	16	16	5	1	13	1	30	1	0
Smyth, Steve*	1	3	9.35	8	7	0	0	0	0	26.0	34	28	27	9	1	10	0	16	2	0
Gordon, Tom	1	1	3.42	19	0	0	7	0	0	23.2	27	12	9	1	1	10	1	31	0	0
Osborne, Donovan*	0	1	6.19	11	0	0	1	0	0	16.0	19	11	11	1	0	10	2	13	0	0
Mahay, Ron*	2	0	8.59	11	0	0	1	0	0	14.2	13	14	14	6	0	8	0	14	0	0
Beltran, Francis	0	0	7.50	11	0	0	4	0	0	12.0	14	11	10	2	0	16	1	11	2	0
Sanchez, Jesus*	0	0	12.96	8	0	0	2	0	0	8.1	15	12	12	4	1	10	1	6	3	0
Chiasson, Scott	0	0	23.14	4	0	0	0	0	0	4.2	11	12	12	2	0	6	1	3	0	0
Duncan, Courtney	0	0	0.00	2	0	0	1	0	0	2.1	2	0	0	0	0	1	0	1	0	0

Pitchers with more than one N.L. team

Pitcher	W	L	ERA	G	GS	CG	GF	SHO	Sv.	IP	H	R	ER	HR	HB	BB	IBB	SO	WP	Bk.
Fassero, Chi.-St.L.*	8	6	5.35	73	0	0	18	0	0	69.0	81	43	41	9	3	27	5	56	2	1
Gordon, Chi.-Hou.	1	3	3.38	34	0	0	10	0	0	42.2	42	19	16	3	1	16	3	48	0	0

* Throws lefthanded.

CINCINNATI REDS

INDIVIDUAL STATISTICS

BATTING

Batter	Avg.	G	TPA	AB	R	H	TB	2B	3B	HR	RBI	SH	SF	HP	BB	IBB	SO	SB	CS	GDP	Slg.	OBP
Boone, Aaron	.241	162	685	606	83	146	266	38	2	26	87	9	4	10	56	4	111	32	8	9	.439	.314
Dunn, Adam*	.249	158	676	535	84	133	243	28	2	26	71	1	3	9	128	13	170	19	9	8	.454	.400
Walker, Todd*	.299	155	675	612	79	183	264	42	3	11	64	7	3	3	50	7	81	8	5	9	.431	.353
Larkin, Barry	.245	145	567	507	72	124	186	37	2	7	47	6	7	3	44	9	57	13	4	13	.367	.305
Casey, Sean*	.261	120	476	425	56	111	154	25	0	6	42	0	3	5	43	6	47	2	1	11	.362	.334
Kearns, Austin	.315	107	435	372	66	117	186	24	3	13	56	0	3	6	54	3	81	6	3	11	.500	.407
LaRue, Jason	.249	113	397	353	42	88	143	17	1	12	52	2	2	13	27	6	117	1	2	13	.405	.324
Encarnacion, Juan	.277	83	354	321	43	89	152	11	2	16	51	3	3	1	26	0	63	9	4	7	.474	.330
Taylor, Reggie*	.254	135	311	287	41	73	123	15	4	9	38	5	3	2	14	3	79	11	8	6	.429	.291
Branyan, Russell*	.244	84	255	217	34	53	112	9	1	16	39	0	2	2	34	3	86	3	1	2	.516	.349
Griffey, Ken*	.264	70	232	197	17	52	84	8	0	8	23	0	4	3	28	6	39	1	2	6	.426	.358
Miller, Corky	.254	39	129	114	9	29	48	10	0	3	15	1	1	4	9	2	20	0	0	7	.421	.328
Guillen, Jose	.248	31	118	109	12	27	42	3	0	4	16	1	0	1	7	0	18	1	1	6	.385	.299
Stinnett, Kelly	.226	34	108	93	10	21	35	5	0	3	13	0	0	0	15	1	25	2	0	1	.376	.333
Mateo, Ruben	.256	46	94	86	11	22	34	6	0	2	7	0	0	2	6	0	20	0	0	1	.395	.319
Castro, Juan	.220	54	91	82	5	18	27	3	0	2	11	1	1	0	7	0	18	0	0	0	.329	.278
Guerrero, Wilton†	.244	59	89	78	9	19	22	1	1	0	4	5	0	0	6	0	13	2	1	1	.282	.298
Clark, Brady	.152	51	74	66	6	10	13	3	0	0	9	1	0	1	6	2	9	1	2	2	.197	.233
Haynes, Jimmy	.164	35	72	61	5	10	12	2	0	0	6	10	0	0	1	0	12	0	0	1	.197	.177
Larson, Brandon	.275	23	58	51	8	14	28	2	0	4	13	0	0	1	6	1	10	1	0	1	.549	.362
Dessens, Elmer	.200	30	57	45	1	9	9	0	0	0	5	9	0	0	3	0	11	0	0	0	.200	.250
Dawkins, Gookie	.125	31	55	48	2	6	8	2	0	0	0	1	0	0	6	0	21	2	1	1	.167	.222
Reitsma, Chris	.100	30	38	30	0	3	3	0	0	0	2	7	0	0	1	0	12	0	0	1	.100	.129
Dempster, Ryan	.207	17	35	29	2	6	7	1	0	0	1	5	0	0	1	0	8	0	0	0	.241	.233
Hamilton, Joey	.250	38	33	28	3	7	10	3	0	0	1	4	1	0	0	0	7	0	0	0	.357	.241
Gonzalez, Raul	.261	10	25	23	4	6	7	1	0	0	1	0	0	0	2	0	5	2	0	1	.304	.320
Rijo, Jose	.125	31	19	16	0	2	2	0	0	0	0	3	0	0	0	0	7	0	0	1	.125	.125
Pena, Wily Mo	.222	13	18	18	1	4	7	0	0	1	1	0	0	0	0	0	11	0	0	0	.389	.222
Moehler, Brian	.000	10	16	14	0	0	0	0	0	0	0	1	0	0	1	0	4	0	0	0	.000	.067
Fernandez, Jared	.200	14	13	10	2	2	2	0	0	0	1	2	0	0	1	0	7	0	0	0	.200	.273
Acevedo, Jose	.143	6	10	7	1	1	2	1	0	0	2	2	0	0	1	0	6	0	0	0	.286	.250
Estes, Shawn	.000	6	10	8	0	0	0	0	0	0	0	2	0	0	0	0	3	0	0	0	.000	.000
Graves, Danny	.000	65	8	6	1	0	0	0	0	0	0	2	0	0	0	0	2	0	0	0	.000	.000
Brower, Jim	.000	21	5	4	0	0	0	0	0	0	0	1	0	0	0	0	1	0	0	0	.000	.000
Chen, Bruce*	.000	39	4	3	0	0	0	0	0	0	0	1	0	0	0	0	1	0	0	0	.000	.000
Pineda, Luis	.000	26	3	3	0	0	0	0	0	0	0	0	0	0	0	0	2	0	0	0	.000	.000
Sullivan, Scott	.333	68	3	3	0	1	1	0	0	0	0	0	0	0	0	0	1	0	0	0	.333	.333
White, Gabe*	.000	58	3	2	0	0	0	0	0	0	0	1	0	0	0	0	2	0	0	0	.000	.000
Hudson, Luke	.000	3	1	0	0	0	0	0	0	0	0	1	0	0	0	0	0	0	0	0	.000	.000
Riedling, John	.000	33	1	1	0	0	0	0	0	0	0	0	0	0	0	0	1	0	0	0	.000	.000
Silva, Jose	.000	10	1	0	0	0	0	0	0	0	0	1	0	0	0	0	0	0	0	0	.000	.000

Batters with more than one N.L. team

Batter	Avg.	G	TPA	AB	R	H	TB	2B	3B	HR	RBI	SH	SF	HP	BB	IBB	SO	SB	CS	GDP	Slg.	OBP
Brower, Cin.-Mon.	.000	51	10	9	0	0	0	0	0	0	0	1	0	0	0	0	3	0	0	0	.000	.000
Chen, Mon.-Cin.*	.333	53	17	15	3	5	6	1	0	0	1	2	0	0	0	0	4	0	0	0	.400	.333
Clark, Cin.-N.Y.	.192	61	87	78	9	15	19	4	0	0	10	1	0	1	7	2	11	1	2	2	.244	.267
Dempster, Fla.-Cin.	.127	32	75	63	2	8	11	1	1	0	3	9	0	0	2	0	20	0	0	0	.175	.154
Encarnacion, Cin.-Fla.	.271	152	644	584	77	158	262	22	5	24	85	3	7	4	46	0	113	21	9	18	.449	.324
Estes, N.Y.-Cin.	.070	29	50	43	1	3	7	1	0	1	3	7	0	0	0	0	17	0	0	1	.163	.070
Gonzalez, Cin.-N.Y.	.260	40	111	104	13	27	39	3	0	3	12	0	1	0	6	0	22	4	2	3	.375	.297
Guerrero, Cin.-Mon.†	.221	103	156	140	12	31	35	2	1	0	5	9	0	0	7	1	32	7	1	2	.250	.259
Guillen, Ari.-Cin.	.238	85	259	240	25	57	88	7	0	8	31	1	1	3	14	1	43	4	5	13	.367	.287

* Lefthanded batter. † Switch-hitter.

PITCHING

Pitcher	W	L	ERA	G	GS	CG	GF	SHO	Sv.	IP	H	R	ER	HR	HB	BB	IBB	SO	WP	Bk.
Haynes, Jimmy	15	10	4.12	34	34	0	0	0	0	196.2	210	97	90	21	3	81	4	126	6	0
Dessens, Elmer	7	8	3.03	30	30	0	0	0	0	178.0	173	70	60	24	7	49	8	93	3	1
Reitsma, Chris	6	12	3.64	32	21	1	6	1	0	138.1	144	73	56	17	5	45	5	84	4	0
Hamilton, Joey	4	10	5.27	39	17	0	9	0	1	124.2	136	78	73	11	6	50	2	85	5	0
Graves, Danny	7	3	3.19	68	4	0	54	0	32	98.2	99	37	35	7	3	25	9	58	5	0
Dempster, Ryan	5	5	6.19	15	15	1	0	0	0	88.2	102	61	61	16	3	38	1	66	2	0
Sullivan, Scott	6	5	6.06	71	0	0	16	0	1	78.2	93	60	53	15	5	31	11	78	2	0
Rijo, Jose	5	4	5.14	31	9	0	6	0	0	77.0	89	48	44	13	1	20	1	38	1	0
Williamson, Scott	3	4	2.92	63	0	0	23	0	8	74.0	46	27	24	5	2	36	5	84	8	1
White, Gabe*	6	1	2.98	62	0	0	7	0	0	54.1	49	19	18	3	2	10	2	41	0	0
Fernandez, Jared	1	3	4.44	14	8	0	2	0	0	50.2	59	31	25	5	3	24	1	36	3	0
Riedling, John	2	4	2.70	33	0	0	7	0	0	46.2	39	16	14	2	3	26	6	30	1	0
Moehler, Brian	2	4	6.02	10	9	0	0	0	0	43.1	61	34	29	8	1	11	0	18	0	0
Chen, Bruce*	0	2	4.31	39	1	0	5	0	0	39.2	37	24	19	7	1	20	2	37	1	0
Brower, Jim	2	0	3.89	22	0	0	11	0	0	39.1	38	18	17	2	0	10	1	24	0	0
Pineda, Luis	1	3	4.18	26	2	0	9	0	0	32.1	25	16	15	4	2	24	1	31	4	0
Estes, Shawn*	1	3	7.71	6	6	0	0	0	0	28.0	38	24	24	1	4	17	0	17	1	0
Acevedo, Jose	4	2	7.23	6	5	0	0	0	0	23.2	28	21	19	8	2	12	0	14	1	0
Silva, Jose	1	0	4.24	12	0	0	1	0	0	23.1	25	11	11	3	3	10	3	6	2	0
Almanzar, Carlos	0	1	2.31	8	1	0	4	0	0	11.2	6	4	3	0	0	5	1	7	1	0
Hudson, Luke	0	0	4.50	3	0	0	0	0	0	6.0	5	5	3	1	0	6	0	7	2	0

Pitchers with more than one N.L. team

Pitcher	W	L	ERA	G	GS	CG	GF	SHO	Sv.	IP	H	R	ER	HR	HB	BB	IBB	SO	WP	Bk.
Brower, Cin.-Mon.	3	2	4.37	52	0	0	23	0	0	80.1	77	40	39	7	4	32	2	57	1	0
Chen, N.Y.-Mon.-Cin.*	2	5	5.56	55	6	0	9	0	0	77.2	85	53	48	16	2	43	5	80	4	0
Dempster, Fla.-Cin.	10	13	5.38	33	33	4	0	0	0	209.0	228	127	125	28	10	93	2	153	2	0
Estes, N.Y.-Cin.*	5	12	5.10	29	29	1	0	1	0	160.2	171	94	91	13	9	83	9	109	3	1

* Throws lefthanded.

COLORADO ROCKIES

INDIVIDUAL STATISTICS

BATTING

Batter	Avg.	G	TPA	AB	R	H	TB	2B	3B	HR	RBI	SH	SF	HP	BB	IBB	SO	SB	CS	GDP	Slg.	OBP
Helton, Todd*	.329	156	668	553	107	182	319	39	4	30	109	0	10	5	99	21	91	5	1	10	.577	.429
Pierre, Juan*	.287	152	640	592	90	170	203	20	5	1	35	8	0	9	31	0	52	47	12	7	.343	.332
Uribe, Juan	.240	155	618	566	69	136	193	25	7	6	49	7	6	5	34	1	120	9	2	17	.341	.286
Zeile, Todd	.273	144	580	506	61	138	215	23	0	18	87	0	7	1	66	3	92	1	1	27	.425	.353
Walker, Larry*	.338	136	553	477	95	161	287	40	4	26	104	0	4	7	65	6	73	6	5	8	.602	.421
Butler, Brent	.259	113	367	344	55	89	142	18	4	9	42	4	4	5	10	3	40	2	6	6	.413	.287
Hollandsworth, Todd*	.295	95	328	298	39	88	144	21	1	11	48	1	2	1	26	4	71	7	8	8	.483	.352
Bennett, Gary	.265	90	314	291	26	77	103	10	2	4	26	2	0	6	15	2	45	1	3	10	.354	.314
Shumpert, Terry	.235	106	268	234	30	55	87	12	1	6	21	5	4	4	21	0	41	4	1	9	.372	.304
Ortiz, Jose	.250	65	215	192	22	48	60	7	1	1	12	2	2	3	16	0	30	2	0	3	.313	.315
Norton, Greg†	.220	113	195	168	19	37	68	8	1	7	37	1	2	0	24	0	52	2	3	4	.405	.314
Payton, Jay	.335	47	181	170	36	57	103	14	4	8	28	0	0	3	8	0	20	3	3	3	.606	.376
Estalella, Bobby	.205	38	130	112	17	23	55	8	0	8	25	0	4	0	14	0	33	0	1	1	.491	.285
Agbayani, Benny	.205	48	128	117	10	24	41	5	0	4	19	0	1	0	10	0	35	1	0	4	.350	.266
Kapler, Gabe	.311	40	128	119	12	37	53	4	3	2	17	0	0	1	8	0	23	6	2	2	.445	.359
Little, Mark	.200	61	123	105	20	21	30	5	2	0	5	1	0	4	13	0	28	2	1	1	.286	.311
Alomar, Sandy	.267	38	120	116	8	31	35	4	0	0	12	0	0	0	4	0	19	0	0	6	.302	.292
Petrick, Ben	.211	38	106	95	10	20	40	3	1	5	11	0	1	1	9	0	33	0	1	1	.421	.283
Cust, Jack*	.169	35	78	65	8	11	16	2	0	1	8	0	1	0	12	0	32	0	1	3	.246	.295
Jennings, Jason*	.306	30	68	62	6	19	23	4	0	0	11	2	0	1	3	0	13	0	0	0	.371	.348
Hampton, Mike	.344	33	66	64	9	22	33	2	0	3	5	1	0	0	1	0	13	1	1	1	.516	.354
Neagle, Denny*	.267	34	50	45	5	12	16	4	0	0	1	5	0	0	0	0	11	0	0	2	.356	.267
Stark, Denny	.171	31	45	41	4	7	13	3	0	1	4	3	1	0	0	0	19	0	0	0	.317	.167
Romano, Jason	.324	18	41	37	9	12	14	0	1	0	1	1	0	0	3	0	11	4	1	0	.378	.375
Thomson, John	.176	19	40	34	2	6	6	0	0	0	2	3	1	0	2	0	12	0	0	0	.176	.216
Chacon, Shawn	.257	20	37	35	3	9	10	1	0	0	2	2	0	0	0	0	14	0	0	0	.286	.257
Gload, Ross*	.258	26	34	31	4	8	12	1	0	1	4	0	0	0	3	0	7	0	0	0	.387	.324
McKeel, Walt	.308	5	13	13	1	4	4	0	0	0	0	0	0	0	0	0	3	0	0	0	.308	.308
Cook, Aaron	.091	9	12	11	0	1	1	0	0	0	1	1	0	0	0	0	0	0	0	0	.091	.091
Flores, Randy*	.000	8	4	4	0	0	0	0	0	0	0	0	0	0	0	0	3	0	0	0	.000	.000
Jones, Todd†	.000	76	3	3	0	0	0	0	0	0	0	0	0	0	0	0	2	0	0	0	.000	.000
Nichting, Chris	.333	26	3	3	1	1	1	0	0	0	0	0	0	0	0	0	0	0	0	0	.333	.333
Speier, Justin	.333	60	3	3	0	1	1	0	0	0	0	0	0	0	0	0	2	0	0	0	.333	.333
Santos, Victor	.500	24	2	2	0	1	1	0	0	0	0	0	0	0	0	0	0	0	0	0	.500	.500
Mercker, Kent*	.000	58	1	1	0	0	0	0	0	0	0	0	0	0	0	0	0	0	0	0	.000	.000
Vance, Cory*	.000	2	1	1	0	0	0	0	0	0	0	0	0	0	0	0	1	0	0	0	.000	.000
Corey, Mark	.000	14	1	1	0	0	0	0	0	0	0	0	0	0	0	0	1	0	0	0	.000	.000
Lowe, Sean	.000	8	1	1	0	0	0	0	0	0	0	0	0	0	0	0	1	0	0	0	.000	.000

Batters with more than one N.L. team

Batter	Avg.	G	TPA	AB	R	H	TB	2B	3B	HR	RBI	SH	SF	HP	BB	IBB	SO	SB	CS	GDP	Slg.	OBP
Corey, N.Y.-Col.	.000	27	2	2	0	0	0	0	0	0	0	0	0	0	0	0	2	0	0	0	.000	.000
Little, Col.-N.Y.-Ari.	.208	79	154	130	28	27	38	5	3	0	7	1	0	8	15	0	34	2	2	1	.292	.327
Lowe, Pit.-Col.	.071	50	16	14	0	1	1	0	0	0	0	2	0	0	0	0	6	0	0	0	.071	.071
Payton, N.Y.-Col.	.303	134	481	445	69	135	217	20	7	16	59	2	1	4	29	0	54	7	4	11	.488	.351
Thomson, Col.-N.Y.	.212	28	62	52	4	11	11	0	0	0	3	6	1	0	3	0	19	0	0	0	.212	.250

* Lefthanded batter. † Switch-hitter.

PITCHING

Pitcher	W	L	ERA	G	GS	CG	GF	SHO	Sv.	IP	H	R	ER	HR	HB	BB	IBB	SO	WP	Bk.
Jennings, Jason	16	8	4.52	32	32	0	0	0	0	185.1	201	102	93	26	8	70	2	127	10	0
Hampton, Mike*	7	15	6.15	30	30	0	0	0	0	178.2	228	135	122	24	7	91	4	74	9	2
Neagle, Denny*	8	11	5.26	35	28	1	0	0	0	164.1	170	101	96	26	10	63	5	111	4	1
Stark, Denny	11	4	4.00	32	20	0	1	0	0	128.1	108	69	57	25	5	64	4	64	2	0
Thomson, John	7	8	4.88	21	21	0	0	0	0	127.1	136	77	69	21	2	27	6	76	2	0
Chacon, Shawn	5	11	5.73	21	21	0	0	0	0	119.1	122	84	76	25	7	60	3	67	0	1
Jones, Todd	1	4	4.70	79	0	0	20	0	1	82.1	84	43	43	10	3	28	3	73	1	0
Jimenez, Jose	2	10	3.56	74	0	0	69	0	41	73.1	76	34	29	7	3	11	4	47	0	0
Speier, Justin	5	1	4.33	63	0	0	7	0	1	62.1	51	31	30	9	3	19	4	47	1	2
Mercker, Kent*	3	1	6.14	58	0	0	8	0	0	44.0	55	33	30	12	2	22	2	37	1	0
White, Rick	2	6	6.20	41	0	0	8	0	0	40.2	49	30	28	4	1	18	4	27	3	0
Reyes, Dennys*	0	1	4.24	43	0	0	13	0	0	40.1	43	19	19	1	0	24	3	30	4	0
Nichting, Chris	1	1	4.46	29	0	0	5	0	0	36.1	40	18	18	7	1	5	0	25	1	0
Cook, Aaron	2	1	4.54	9	5	0	1	0	0	35.2	41	18	18	4	2	13	0	14	0	0
Fuentes, Brian*	2	0	4.73	31	0	0	9	0	0	26.2	25	14	14	4	3	13	0	38	1	0
Santos, Victor	0	4	10.38	24	2	0	6	0	0	26.0	41	30	30	3	0	22	3	25	2	0
Flores, Randy*	0	2	9.53	8	2	0	4	0	0	17.0	29	19	18	5	3	8	1	7	1	0
Corey, Mark	0	0	12.00	14	0	0	3	0	0	12.0	22	16	16	7	2	8	1	12	0	0
James, Mike	0	0	5.56	13	0	0	6	0	0	11.1	12	9	7	2	1	5	0	10	0	0
Lowe, Sean	1	1	8.71	8	0	0	0	0	0	10.1	16	13	10	1	0	7	0	7	0	0
Vance, Cory*	0	0	6.75	2	1	0	0	0	0	4.0	4	3	3	2	1	4	0	1	0	0
Zeile, Todd	0	0	0.00	1	0	0	1	0	0	1.0	1	0	0	0	0	0	0	1	0	0

Pitchers with more than one N.L. team

Pitcher	W	L	ERA	G	GS	CG	GF	SHO	Sv.	IP	H	R	ER	HR	HB	BB	IBB	SO	WP	Bk.
Corey, N.Y.-Col.	0	3	8.59	26	0	0	8	0	0	22.0	32	23	21	9	3	16	2	21	1	0
Lowe, Pit.-Col.	5	3	5.79	51	1	0	8	0	0	79.1	101	58	51	9	7	41	6	64	1	1
Thomson, Col.-N.Y.	9	14	4.71	30	30	0	0	0	0	181.2	201	116	95	28	2	44	9	107	2	0
White, Col.-St.L.	5	7	4.31	61	0	0	10	0	0	62.2	62	33	30	4	1	21	5	41	3	0

* Throws lefthanded.

FLORIDA MARLINS

INDIVIDUAL STATISTICS

BATTING

Batter	Avg.	G	TPA	AB	R	H	TB	2B	3B	HR	RBI	SH	SF	HP	BB	IBB	SO	SB	CS	GDP	Slg.	OBP
Lee, Derrek	.270	162	688	581	95	157	287	35	7	27	86	0	4	5	98	8	164	19	9	14	.494	.378
Lowell, Mike	.276	160	678	597	88	165	281	44	0	24	92	0	11	4	65	5	92	4	3	16	.471	.346
Castillo, Luis†	.305	146	668	606	86	185	219	18	5	2	39	4	1	2	55	4	76	48	15	7	.361	.364
Wilson, Preston	.243	141	582	510	80	124	219	22	2	23	65	2	3	9	58	3	140	20	11	17	.429	.329
Fox, Andy*	.251	133	502	435	55	109	145	14	5	4	41	5	3	10	49	6	94	31	7	9	.333	.338
Millar, Kevin	.306	126	489	438	58	134	223	41	0	16	57	0	6	5	40	0	74	0	2	15	.509	.366
Owens, Eric	.270	131	426	385	44	104	141	15	5	4	37	8	1	0	31	1	33	26	9	11	.366	.324
Floyd, Cliff*	.287	84	362	296	49	85	159	20	0	18	57	0	1	7	58	18	68	10	5	0	.537	.414
Redmond, Mike	.305	89	290	256	19	78	99	15	0	2	28	2	3	8	21	8	34	0	2	4	.387	.372
Encarnacion, Juan	.262	69	290	263	34	69	110	11	3	8	34	0	4	3	20	0	50	12	5	11	.418	.317
Johnson, Charles	.217	83	280	244	18	53	90	19	0	6	36	1	4	0	31	7	61	0	0	10	.369	.301
Gonzalez, Alex	.225	42	172	151	15	34	49	7	1	2	18	3	2	4	12	1	32	3	1	2	.325	.296
Castro, Ramon	.238	54	119	101	11	24	46	4	0	6	18	1	3	0	14	3	24	0	0	4	.455	.322
Raines, Tim†	.191	98	114	89	9	17	23	3	0	1	7	0	2	1	22	4	19	0	0	3	.258	.351
Mordecai, Mike	.286	38	86	77	10	22	26	4	0	0	7	3	0	1	5	1	13	1	1	1	.338	.337
Burnett, A.J.	.105	29	69	57	1	6	11	2	0	1	3	7	0	0	5	0	28	0	0	1	.193	.177
Bush, Homer	.222	40	58	54	7	12	12	0	0	0	5	1	0	0	3	0	13	2	1	0	.222	.263
Ozuna, Pablo	.277	34	50	47	4	13	19	2	2	0	3	0	1	1	1	0	3	1	1	2	.404	.300
Penny, Brad	.167	24	49	48	1	8	10	2	0	0	1	1	0	0	0	0	14	0	0	0	.208	.167
Tavarez, Julian*	.125	27	47	40	3	5	5	0	0	0	5	5	0	0	2	0	17	0	0	0	.125	.167
Tejera, Michael*	.189	47	41	37	5	7	10	0	0	1	5	2	0	1	1	0	6	0	0	0	.270	.231
Dempster, Ryan	.059	15	40	34	0	2	4	0	1	0	2	4	0	0	1	0	12	0	0	0	.118	.086
Beckett, Josh	.032	23	36	31	0	1	2	1	0	0	0	5	0	0	0	0	21	0	0	0	.065	.032
Banks, Brian†	.321	20	29	28	3	9	13	1	0	1	4	0	0	0	1	0	6	0	0	0	.464	.345
Malloy, Marty*	.120	24	28	25	1	3	3	0	0	0	1	1	0	0	2	0	8	0	0	1	.120	.185
Pavano, Carl	.188	22	18	16	1	3	5	0	1	0	1	2	0	0	0	0	6	0	0	0	.313	.188
Nunez, Abraham†	.118	19	17	17	2	2	2	0	0	0	1	0	0	0	0	0	5	0	1	1	.118	.118
Olsen, Kevin	.083	15	12	12	0	1	1	0	0	0	0	0	0	0	0	0	7	0	0	0	.083	.083
Wayne, Justin	.000	5	8	7	0	0	0	0	0	0	0	1	0	0	0	0	3	0	0	0	.000	.000
Nunez, Vladimir	.200	73	5	5	0	1	1	0	0	0	0	0	0	0	0	0	4	0	0	0	.200	.200
Darensbourg, Vic*	.000	41	2	1	0	0	0	0	0	0	0	1	0	0	0	0	0	0	0	0	.000	.000
Izquierdo, Hansel	.000	19	2	2	0	0	0	0	0	0	0	0	0	0	0	0	0	0	0	0	.000	.000
Robertson, Nate	.000	6	2	2	0	0	0	0	0	0	0	0	0	0	0	0	1	0	0	0	.000	.000
Teut, Nate	.000	2	2	2	0	0	0	0	0	0	0	0	0	0	0	0	2	0	0	0	.000	.000
Knotts, Gary	.000	28	1	1	0	0	0	0	0	0	0	0	0	0	0	0	0	0	0	0	.000	.000
Looper, Braden	.000	73	1	1	0	0	0	0	0	0	0	0	0	0	0	0	0	0	0	0	.000	.000

Batters with more than one N.L. team

Batter	Avg.	G	TPA	AB	R	H	TB	2B	3B	HR	RBI	SH	SF	HP	BB	IBB	SO	SB	CS	GDP	Slg.	OBP
Dempster, Fla.-Cin.	.127	32	75	63	2	8	11	1	1	0	3	9	0	0	2	0	20	0	0	0	.175	.154
Encarnacion, Cin.-Fla.	.271	152	644	584	77	158	262	22	5	24	85	3	7	4	46	0	113	21	9	18	.449	.324
Floyd, Fla.-Mon.*	.275	99	419	349	56	96	181	22	0	21	61	0	1	8	61	19	78	11	5	0	.519	.394
Mordecai, Mon.-Fla.	.245	93	176	151	19	37	45	8	0	0	11	10	0	2	13	4	27	2	2	3	.298	.313
Pavano, Mon.-Fla.	.200	36	45	40	2	8	11	1	1	0	2	5	0	0	0	0	12	0	0	0	.275	.200

* Lefthanded batter. † Switch-hitter.

PITCHING

Pitcher	W	L	ERA	G	GS	CG	GF	SHO	Sv.	IP	H	R	ER	HR	HB	BB	IBB	SO	WP	Bk.
Burnett, A.J.	12	9	3.30	31	29	7	0	5	0	204.1	153	84	75	12	9	90	5	203	14	0
Tavarez, Julian	10	12	5.39	29	27	0	1	0	0	153.2	188	100	92	9	15	74	7	67	7	2
Tejera, Michael*	8	8	4.45	47	18	0	2	0	1	139.2	144	71	69	17	6	60	3	95	3	0
Penny, Brad	8	7	4.66	24	24	1	0	1	0	129.1	148	76	67	18	1	50	7	93	4	0
Dempster, Ryan	5	8	4.79	18	18	3	0	0	0	120.1	126	66	64	12	7	55	1	87	0	0
Beckett, Josh	6	7	4.10	23	21	0	0	0	0	107.2	93	56	49	13	1	44	2	113	5	0
Nunez, Vladimir	6	5	3.41	77	0	0	43	0	20	97.2	80	38	37	8	0	37	1	73	2	0
Looper, Braden	2	5	3.14	78	0	0	40	0	13	86.0	73	31	30	8	1	28	3	55	1	0
Pavano, Carl	3	2	3.79	22	8	0	2	0	0	61.2	76	33	26	5	3	14	3	41	1	1
Olsen, Kevin	0	5	4.53	17	8	0	3	0	0	55.2	57	31	28	5	1	31	1	38	3	1
Darensbourg, Vic*	1	2	6.14	42	0	0	13	0	0	48.1	61	34	33	10	2	26	4	33	0	0
Almanza, Armando*	3	2	4.34	51	0	0	10	0	2	45.2	36	22	22	8	0	23	1	57	2	1
Mairena, Oswaldo*	2	3	5.35	31	0	0	10	0	0	33.2	38	21	20	7	0	12	0	21	3	1
Neal, Blaine	3	0	2.73	32	0	0	6	0	0	33.0	32	12	10	1	0	14	2	33	4	0
Knotts, Gary	3	1	4.40	28	0	0	7	0	0	30.2	21	15	15	6	1	16	0	21	1	0
Izquierdo, Hansel	2	0	4.55	20	2	0	5	0	0	29.2	33	17	15	2	5	21	3	20	0	0
Lloyd, Graeme*	2	2	4.44	25	0	0	5	0	0	26.1	26	13	13	1	1	11	1	20	1	0
Wayne, Justin	2	3	5.32	5	5	0	0	0	0	23.2	22	16	14	3	0	13	0	16	2	1
Borland, Toby	1	0	5.27	15	0	0	3	0	0	13.2	14	8	8	3	3	5	0	11	2	0
Robertson, Nate*	0	1	11.88	6	1	0	1	0	0	8.1	15	11	11	3	2	4	1	3	0	0
Teut, Nate*	0	1	9.82	2	1	0	0	0	0	7.1	13	8	8	0	0	3	1	4	0	0

Pitchers with more than one N.L. team

Pitcher	W	L	ERA	G	GS	CG	GF	SHO	Sv.	IP	H	R	ER	HR	HB	BB	IBB	SO	WP	Bk.
Dempster, Fla.-Cin.	10	13	5.38	33	33	4	0	0	0	209.0	228	127	125	28	10	93	2	153	2	0
Lloyd, Mon.-Fla.*	4	5	5.21	66	0	0	19	0	5	57.0	67	34	33	6	2	19	4	37	2	0
Pavano, Mon.-Fla.	6	10	5.16	37	22	0	2	0	0	136.0	174	88	78	19	10	45	8	92	3	2

* Throws lefthanded.

Houston Astros

INDIVIDUAL STATISTICS

BATTING

Batter	Avg.	G	TPA	AB	R	H	TB	2B	3B	HR	RBI	SH	SF	HP	BB	IBB	SO	SB	CS	GDP	Slg.	OBP
Berkman, Lance†	.292	158	692	578	106	169	334	35	2	42	128	0	3	4	107	20	118	8	4	10	.578	.405
Bagwell, Jeff	.291	158	691	571	94	166	296	33	2	31	98	0	9	10	101	8	130	7	3	16	.518	.401
Biggio, Craig	.253	145	655	577	96	146	233	36	3	15	58	9	2	17	50	2	111	16	2	15	.404	.330
Ausmus, Brad	.257	130	496	447	57	115	158	19	3	6	50	2	3	6	38	3	71	2	3	30	.353	.322
Ward, Daryle*	.276	136	491	453	41	125	192	31	0	12	72	0	4	1	33	5	82	1	3	9	.424	.324
Hidalgo, Richard	.235	114	439	388	54	91	161	17	4	15	48	0	2	6	43	1	85	6	2	13	.415	.319
Vizcaino, Jose†	.303	125	438	406	53	123	161	19	2	5	37	5	2	1	24	2	40	3	5	5	.397	.342
Blum, Geoff†	.283	130	421	368	45	104	162	20	4	10	52	1	2	1	49	5	70	2	0	8	.440	.367
Lugo, Julio	.261	88	358	322	45	84	125	15	1	8	35	4	2	2	28	3	74	9	3	6	.388	.322
Merced, Orlando*	.287	123	281	251	35	72	109	13	3	6	30	1	3	0	26	5	50	4	0	9	.434	.350
Hunter, Brian L.	.269	98	220	201	32	54	85	16	3	3	20	1	0	2	16	0	39	5	0	3	.423	.329
Zaun, Gregg†	.222	76	202	185	18	41	59	7	1	3	24	2	1	2	12	1	36	1	0	4	.319	.275
Ensberg, Morgan	.242	49	153	132	14	32	52	7	2	3	19	0	0	3	18	0	25	2	0	8	.394	.346
Everett, Adam	.193	40	103	88	11	17	20	3	0	0	4	2	0	1	12	1	19	3	0	1	.227	.297
Oswalt, Roy	.130	33	89	77	5	10	12	2	0	0	4	7	0	1	4	0	26	0	0	0	.156	.183
Lane, Jason	.290	44	80	69	12	20	37	3	1	4	10	0	1	0	10	1	12	1	1	0	.536	.375
Loretta, Mark	.424	21	77	66	10	28	38	4	0	2	8	0	2	0	9	0	5	1	1	1	.576	.481
Miller, Wade	.177	26	69	62	7	11	14	3	0	0	4	6	1	0	0	0	21	0	0	2	.226	.175
Zinter, Alan†	.136	39	44	44	5	6	14	2	0	2	3	0	0	0	0	0	19	0	0	0	.318	.136
Hernandez, Carlos†	.171	25	41	35	3	6	6	0	0	0	1	4	0	0	2	0	11	0	0	0	.171	.216
Saarloos, Kirk	.067	16	35	30	0	2	3	1	0	0	2	5	0	0	0	0	11	0	0	0	.100	.067
Reynolds, Shane	.048	12	30	21	0	1	2	1	0	0	3	9	0	0	0	0	12	0	0	0	.095	.048
Mlicki, Dave	.185	22	27	27	2	5	6	1	0	0	1	0	0	0	0	0	9	0	0	0	.222	.185
Munro, Peter	.136	19	24	22	1	3	3	0	0	0	2	1	0	0	1	0	6	0	0	1	.136	.174
Redding, Tim	.100	17	21	20	0	2	2	0	0	0	2	1	0	0	0	0	12	0	0	0	.100	.100
Wesson, Barry	.200	15	21	20	1	4	6	0	1	0	1	0	0	0	1	0	5	0	0	2	.300	.238
Cruz, Nelson	.000	40	16	13	0	0	0	0	0	0	1	2	0	0	1	0	8	0	0	0	.000	.071
Puffer, Brandon	.000	53	8	6	0	0	0	0	0	0	0	1	0	0	1	0	5	0	0	0	.000	.143
Ginter, Keith	.200	7	8	5	1	1	2	1	0	0	0	0	0	1	2	0	1	0	0	0	.400	.500
Chavez, Raul	.250	2	6	4	1	1	2	1	0	0	0	0	0	1	1	0	0	0	0	0	.500	.500
Stone, Ricky	.000	74	5	4	0	0	0	0	0	0	0	1	0	0	0	0	1	0	0	0	.000	.000
Borbon, Pedro*	.000	54	3	3	0	0	0	0	0	0	0	0	0	0	0	0	3	0	0	0	.000	.000
Lidge, Brad	1.000	5	2	2	0	2	3	1	0	0	2	0	0	0	0	0	0	0	0	0	1.500	1.000
Wagner, Billy*	.000	68	2	2	0	0	0	0	0	0	0	0	0	0	0	0	2	0	0	0	.000	.000
Dotel, Octavio	.000	80	1	1	0	0	0	0	0	0	0	0	0	0	0	0	0	0	0	0	.000	.000
Gordon, Tom	.000	15	1	1	0	0	0	0	0	0	0	0	0	0	0	0	0	0	0	0	.000	.000
Mann, Jim	.000	15	1	1	0	0	0	0	0	0	0	0	0	0	0	0	1	0	0	0	.000	.000
Mathews, T.J.	.000	12	1	1	0	0	0	0	0	0	0	0	0	0	0	0	0	0	0	1	.000	.000

Batters with more than one N.L. team

Batter	Avg.	G	TPA	AB	R	H	TB	2B	3B	HR	RBI	SH	SF	HP	BB	IBB	SO	SB	CS	GDP	Slg.	OBP
Ginter, Hou.-Mil.	.235	28	99	81	7	19	31	9	0	1	8	0	0	1	17	0	15	0	0	0	.383	.374
Loretta, Mil.-Hou.	.304	107	329	283	33	86	116	18	0	4	27	6	3	5	32	1	37	1	1	7	.410	.381

* Lefthanded batter. † Switch-hitter.

PITCHING

Pitcher	W	L	ERA	G	GS	CG	GF	SHO	Sv.	IP	H	R	ER	HR	HB	BB	IBB	SO	WP	Bk.
Oswalt, Roy	19	9	3.01	35	34	0	0	0	0	233.0	215	86	78	17	5	62	4	208	3	0
Miller, Wade	15	4	3.28	26	26	1	0	1	0	164.2	151	63	60	14	6	62	9	144	4	0
Hernandez, Carlos*	7	5	4.38	23	21	0	0	0	0	111.0	112	56	54	11	3	61	5	93	1	2
Dotel, Octavio	6	4	1.85	83	0	0	22	0	6	97.1	58	21	20	7	4	27	2	118	2	0
Mlicki, Dave	4	10	5.34	22	16	0	1	0	0	86.0	101	57	51	11	3	34	5	57	3	0
Saarloos, Kirk	6	7	6.01	17	17	1	0	1	0	85.1	100	59	57	12	6	27	5	54	1	0
Munro, Peter	5	5	3.57	19	14	0	0	0	0	80.2	89	37	32	5	3	23	3	45	2	0
Cruz, Nelson	2	6	4.48	43	5	0	11	0	0	78.1	90	44	39	12	6	29	4	61	4	0
Stone, Ricky	3	3	3.61	78	0	0	16	0	1	77.1	78	36	31	9	1	34	3	63	1	0
Wagner, Billy*	4	2	2.52	70	0	0	61	0	35	75.0	51	21	21	7	2	22	5	88	6	0
Reynolds, Shane	3	6	4.86	13	13	0	0	0	0	74.0	80	43	40	13	1	26	2	47	1	0
Redding, Tim	3	6	5.40	18	14	0	1	0	0	73.1	78	49	44	10	0	35	3	63	5	1
Puffer, Brandon	3	3	4.43	55	0	0	19	0	0	69.0	67	37	34	3	5	38	8	48	2	0
Borbon, Pedro*	3	2	5.50	56	0	0	3	0	1	37.2	41	24	23	7	2	19	5	39	0	0
Linebrink, Scott	0	0	7.03	22	0	0	4	0	0	24.1	31	21	19	2	1	13	4	24	0	0
Mann, Jim	0	1	4.09	17	0	0	12	0	0	22.0	19	10	10	3	5	7	1	19	0	0
Gordon, Tom	0	2	3.32	15	0	0	3	0	0	19.0	15	7	7	2	0	6	2	17	0	0
Mathews, T.J.	0	0	3.44	12	0	0	4	0	0	18.1	19	7	7	2	0	5	3	13	0	0
Robertson, Jeriome*	0	2	6.52	11	1	0	1	0	0	9.2	13	8	7	4	0	5	3	6	2	0
Lidge, Brad	1	0	6.23	6	1	0	2	0	0	8.2	12	6	6	0	2	9	1	12	0	0
Pichardo, Hipolito	0	1	81.00	1	0	0	0	0	0	0.1	3	3	3	0	0	2	1	0	1	0

Pitchers with more than one N.L. team

Pitcher	W	L	ERA	G	GS	CG	GF	SHO	Sv.	IP	H	R	ER	HR	HB	BB	IBB	SO	WP	Bk.
Gordon, Chi.-Hou.	1	3	3.38	34	0	0	10	0	0	42.2	42	19	16	3	1	16	3	48	0	0

* Throws lefthanded.

Los Angeles Dodgers

INDIVIDUAL STATISTICS

BATTING

Batter	Avg.	G	TPA	AB	R	H	TB	2B	3B	HR	RBI	SH	SF	HP	BB	IBB	SO	SB	CS	GDP	Slg.	OBP
Green, Shawn*	.285	158	685	582	110	166	325	31	1	42	114	0	5	5	93	22	112	8	5	26	.558	.385
Beltre, Adrian	.257	159	635	587	70	151	250	26	5	21	75	1	6	4	37	4	96	7	5	17	.426	.303
Lo Duca, Paul	.281	149	632	580	74	163	233	38	1	10	64	4	4	10	34	2	31	3	1	20	.402	.330
Karros, Eric	.271	142	573	524	52	142	209	26	1	13	73	0	6	6	37	1	74	4	2	11	.399	.323
Grudzielanek, Mark	.271	150	566	536	56	145	195	23	0	9	50	1	4	3	22	4	89	4	1	17	.364	.301
Jordan, Brian	.285	128	515	471	65	134	221	27	3	18	80	0	4	6	34	3	86	2	2	10	.469	.338
Roberts, Dave*	.277	127	479	422	63	117	154	14	7	3	34	6	1	2	48	0	51	45	10	1	.365	.353
Izturis, Cesar†	.232	135	468	439	43	102	133	24	2	1	31	10	5	0	14	1	39	7	7	12	.303	.253
Grissom, Marquis	.277	111	371	343	57	95	175	21	4	17	60	0	4	2	22	2	68	5	1	6	.510	.321
Cora, Alex*	.291	115	293	258	37	75	112	14	4	5	28	2	0	7	26	4	38	7	2	3	.434	.371
Hansen, Dave*	.292	96	135	120	15	35	47	6	0	2	17	0	1	0	14	3	22	1	0	2	.392	.363
Kreuter, Chad†	.263	41	108	95	8	25	36	5	0	2	12	0	2	1	10	4	31	1	0	3	.379	.333
Perez, Odalis*	.156	30	75	64	5	10	18	5	0	1	4	10	0	0	1	0	13	0	0	0	.281	.169
Nomo, Hideo	.063	33	74	63	3	4	9	2	0	1	3	6	0	0	5	0	32	0	0	1	.143	.132
Bocachica, Hiram	.215	49	70	65	12	14	29	3	0	4	9	0	0	0	5	0	19	1	1	1	.446	.271
Houston, Tyler*	.200	35	67	65	9	13	20	5	1	0	7	0	0	0	2	0	21	0	0	5	.308	.224
Kinkade, Mike	.380	37	60	50	7	19	30	5	0	2	11	0	0	6	4	0	10	1	0	2	.600	.483
Reboulet, Jeff	.208	38	58	48	3	10	13	3	0	0	2	3	1	0	6	0	13	0	0	1	.271	.291
Ashby, Andy	.125	27	56	48	5	6	9	0	0	1	4	6	0	0	2	0	23	0	0	0	.188	.160
Ishii, Kazuhisa*	.100	26	56	50	1	5	5	0	0	0	2	4	0	0	2	0	21	0	0	2	.100	.135
Daal, Omar*	.154	38	48	39	2	6	11	2	0	1	4	8	0	0	1	0	11	0	0	0	.282	.175
Brown, Kevin	.250	17	22	20	2	5	9	1	0	1	2	2	0	0	0	0	11	0	0	0	.450	.250
Cabrera, Jolbert	.333	10	15	12	3	4	5	1	0	0	1	1	0	0	2	0	2	0	0	0	.417	.429
Thurston, Joe*	.462	8	15	13	1	6	7	1	0	0	1	1	1	0	0	0	1	0	0	0	.538	.429
Ross, Dave	.200	8	13	10	2	2	6	1	0	1	2	0	0	1	2	0	4	0	0	0	.600	.385
Ruan, Wilkin	.273	12	11	11	2	3	4	1	0	0	3	0	0	0	0	0	2	0	0	0	.364	.273
Allen, Luke*	.143	6	9	7	2	1	2	1	0	0	0	0	0	0	2	0	3	0	0	0	.286	.333
Carrara, Giovanni	.000	59	8	6	0	0	0	0	0	0	0	1	0	0	1	0	3	0	0	0	.000	.143
Beirne, Kevin*	.400	12	6	5	1	2	2	0	0	0	0	1	0	0	0	0	0	0	0	0	.400	.400
Chen, Chin-Feng	.000	3	6	5	1	0	0	0	0	0	0	0	0	0	1	0	3	0	0	0	.000	.167
Mota, Guillermo	.250	40	4	4	1	1	1	0	0	0	0	0	0	0	0	0	2	0	0	0	.250	.250
Quantrill, Paul*	.333	83	3	3	0	1	1	0	0	0	0	0	0	0	0	0	2	0	0	0	.333	.333
Shuey, Paul	.333	28	3	3	0	1	1	0	0	0	0	0	0	0	0	0	2	0	0	0	.333	.333
Alvarez, Victor*	.000	4	2	2	0	0	0	0	0	0	0	0	0	0	0	0	2	0	0	0	.000	.000
Williams, Jeff	.500	10	2	2	0	1	1	0	0	0	0	0	0	0	0	0	1	0	0	0	.500	.500
Gagne, Eric	.000	73	1	1	0	0	0	0	0	0	0	0	0	0	0	0	1	0	0	0	.000	.000
Mulholland, Terry	.000	19	1	1	0	0	0	0	0	0	0	0	0	0	0	0	1	0	0	0	.000	.000
Orosco, Jesse	.000	53	1	0	1	0	0	0	0	0	0	0	0	0	1	0	0	0	0	0	.000	1.000

Batters with more than one N.L. team

Batter	Avg.	G	TPA	AB	R	H	TB	2B	3B	HR	RBI	SH	SF	HP	BB	IBB	SO	SB	CS	GDP	Slg.	OBP
Houston, Mil.-L.A.*	.281	111	345	320	34	90	137	20	3	7	40	4	1	4	16	3	62	1	0	9	.428	.323

* Lefthanded batter. † Switch-hitter.

PITCHING

Pitcher	W	L	ERA	G	GS	CG	GF	SHO	Sv.	IP	H	R	ER	HR	HB	BB	IBB	SO	WP	Bk.
Perez, Odalis*	15	10	3.00	32	32	4	0	2	0	222.1	182	76	74	21	4	38	5	155	2	3
Nomo, Hideo	16	6	3.39	34	34	0	0	0	0	220.1	189	92	83	26	2	101	5	193	6	0
Ashby, Andy	9	13	3.91	30	30	0	0	0	0	181.2	179	85	79	20	8	65	3	107	2	0
Daal, Omar*	11	9	3.90	39	23	0	3	0	0	161.1	142	73	70	20	4	54	3	105	0	0
Ishii, Kazuhisa*	14	10	4.27	28	28	0	0	0	0	154.0	137	82	73	20	4	106	3	143	7	0
Carrara, Giovanni	6	3	3.28	63	1	0	13	0	1	90.2	83	34	33	14	6	32	4	56	1	0
Gagne, Eric	4	1	1.97	77	0	0	68	0	52	82.1	55	18	18	6	2	16	4	114	1	0
Quantrill, Paul	5	4	2.70	86	0	0	22	0	1	76.2	80	27	23	1	3	25	7	53	0	0
Brown, Kevin	3	4	4.81	17	10	0	0	0	0	63.2	68	36	34	9	5	23	1	58	2	0
Mota, Guillermo	1	3	4.15	43	0	0	11	0	0	60.2	45	30	28	4	2	27	6	49	3	0
Mulholland, Terry*	0	0	7.31	21	0	0	12	0	0	32.0	45	29	26	10	2	7	0	17	1	0
Shuey, Paul	5	2	4.40	28	0	0	6	0	1	30.2	25	18	15	2	1	21	1	24	1	0
Beirne, Kevin	2	0	3.41	12	3	0	5	0	0	29.0	26	11	11	4	2	17	2	17	4	0
Orosco, Jesse*	1	2	3.00	56	0	0	8	0	1	27.0	24	10	9	4	0	12	1	22	2	0
Alvarez, Victor*	0	1	4.35	4	1	0	1	0	0	10.1	9	5	5	1	0	2	0	7	0	0
Williams, Jeff*	0	0	11.70	10	0	0	7	0	0	10.0	15	13	13	2	1	7	0	11	1	0
Ellis, Robert	0	1	10.13	3	0	0	0	0	0	2.2	6	3	3	1	0	0	0	0	0	0
Springer, Dennis	0	1	6.75	1	0	0	1	0	0	1.1	1	1	1	0	0	2	0	1	0	0
Corey, Bryan	0	0	0.00	1	0	0	1	0	0	1.0	0	0	0	0	0	0	0	0	0	0

* Throws lefthanded.

MILWAUKEE BREWERS

INDIVIDUAL STATISTICS

BATTING

Batter	Avg.	G	TPA	AB	R	H	TB	2B	3B	HR	RBI	SH	SF	HP	BB	IBB	SO	SB	CS	GDP	Slg.	OBP
Sexson, Richie	.279	157	652	570	86	159	287	37	2	29	102	0	4	8	70	7	136	0	0	17	.504	.363
Hernandez, Jose	.288	152	582	525	72	151	251	24	2	24	73	0	1	4	52	5	188	3	5	19	.478	.356
Young, Eric	.280	138	553	496	57	139	183	29	3	3	28	8	4	6	39	0	38	31	11	14	.369	.338
Hammonds, Jeffrey	.257	128	510	448	47	115	178	26	5	9	41	1	7	2	52	0	86	4	5	13	.397	.332
Sanchez, Alex*	.289	112	435	394	55	114	141	10	7	1	33	6	2	2	31	0	62	37	14	4	.358	.343
Belliard, Ronnie	.211	104	317	289	30	61	83	13	0	3	26	6	3	1	18	0	46	2	3	9	.287	.257
Stairs, Matt*	.244	107	315	270	41	66	129	15	0	16	41	0	1	8	36	4	50	2	0	7	.478	.349
Houston, Tyler*	.302	76	278	255	25	77	117	15	2	7	33	4	1	4	14	3	41	1	0	4	.459	.347
Jenkins, Geoff*	.243	67	272	243	35	59	108	17	1	10	29	0	1	6	22	1	60	1	2	8	.444	.320
Bako, Paul*	.235	87	257	234	24	55	77	8	1	4	20	3	0	0	20	3	46	0	2	4	.329	.295
Loretta, Mark	.267	86	252	217	23	58	78	14	0	2	19	6	1	5	23	1	32	0	0	6	.359	.350
Ochoa, Alex	.256	85	250	215	32	55	82	9	0	6	21	1	0	2	32	2	30	8	5	7	.381	.357
Harris, Lenny*	.305	122	215	197	23	60	81	8	2	3	17	1	1	2	14	1	17	4	1	4	.411	.355
Machado, Robert	.255	51	169	153	14	39	57	10	1	2	17	1	2	1	12	4	30	0	0	5	.373	.310
Thompson, Ryan	.248	62	146	137	16	34	71	9	2	8	24	0	0	2	7	0	38	1	0	7	.518	.295
Casanova, Raul†	.184	31	99	87	3	16	20	1	0	1	8	0	1	1	10	4	18	0	0	3	.230	.273
Ginter, Keith	.237	21	91	76	6	18	29	8	0	1	8	0	0	0	15	0	14	0	0	0	.382	.363
Rushford, Jim*	.143	23	84	77	8	11	16	2	0	1	6	0	0	1	6	0	9	0	0	3	.208	.214
Rusch, Glendon*	.288	36	81	66	6	19	22	0	0	1	8	14	0	0	1	0	24	0	0	1	.333	.299
Sheets, Ben	.088	32	76	68	2	6	7	1	0	0	3	4	0	0	4	0	39	0	0	0	.103	.139
Fabregas, Jorge*	.164	30	73	67	5	11	23	3	0	3	14	0	4	0	2	0	7	0	0	2	.343	.178
Christenson, Ryan	.155	22	66	58	5	9	16	4	0	1	3	3	0	0	5	0	13	0	0	1	.276	.222
Quevedo, Ruben	.095	25	47	42	2	4	4	0	0	0	3	3	0	0	2	0	21	0	0	3	.095	.136
Jensen, Marcus†	.114	16	40	35	2	4	7	0	0	1	4	0	1	0	4	2	11	0	0	2	.200	.200
Hall, Bill	.194	19	39	36	3	7	13	1	1	1	5	0	0	0	3	0	13	0	1	1	.361	.256
Wright, Jamey	.152	19	39	33	0	5	8	3	0	0	0	6	0	0	0	0	13	0	0	0	.242	.152
Alcantara, Izzy	.250	16	32	32	3	8	15	1	0	2	5	0	0	0	0	0	6	0	1	0	.469	.250
Cabrera, Jose	.105	47	20	19	1	2	2	0	0	0	0	1	0	0	0	0	10	0	0	0	.105	.105
Figueroa, Nelson	.133	29	20	15	0	2	2	0	0	0	3	4	0	0	1	0	6	0	0	0	.133	.188
Neugebauer, Nick	.105	12	20	19	0	2	3	1	0	0	1	1	0	0	0	0	4	0	0	0	.158	.105
Lopez, Luis†	.000	6	10	8	1	0	0	0	0	0	1	0	0	0	2	0	1	0	0	0	.000	.200
Diggins, Ben	.143	5	8	7	0	1	1	0	0	0	0	1	0	0	0	0	1	0	0	0	.143	.143
Franklin, Wayne*	.000	4	8	6	0	0	0	0	0	0	0	0	0	0	2	0	3	0	0	0	.000	.250
de los Santos, Valerio*	.000	49	5	2	0	0	0	0	0	0	0	2	0	0	1	0	1	0	0	0	.000	.333
Osting, Jimmy	.000	3	4	3	0	0	0	0	0	0	0	1	0	0	0	0	1	0	0	0	.000	.000
Nance, Shane*	.333	4	3	3	0	1	1	0	0	0	1	0	0	0	0	0	2	0	0	0	.333	.333
Stull, Everett	.333	2	3	3	0	1	1	0	0	0	0	0	0	0	0	0	1	0	0	0	.333	.333
Buddie, Mike	.000	25	2	2	0	0	0	0	0	0	0	0	0	0	0	0	1	0	0	0	.000	.000
Durocher, Jayson	.000	36	2	2	0	0	0	0	0	0	0	0	0	0	0	0	1	0	0	0	.000	.000
Lorraine, Andrew*	.000	5	2	1	0	0	0	0	0	0	0	1	0	0	0	0	1	0	0	0	.000	.000
Vizcaino, Luis	.000	74	2	2	0	0	0	0	0	0	0	0	0	0	0	0	2	0	0	0	.000	.000
Childers, Matt	.000	8	1	1	0	0	0	0	0	0	0	0	0	0	0	0	0	0	0	0	.000	.000
DeJean, Mike	.000	67	1	1	0	0	0	0	0	0	0	0	0	0	0	0	1	0	0	0	.000	.000
Pember, Dave	.000	4	1	1	0	0	0	0	0	0	0	0	0	0	0	0	1	0	0	0	.000	.000
Matthews, Mike*	.000	4	1	0	0	0	0	0	0	0	0	1	0	0	0	0	0	0	0	0	.000	.000

Batters with more than one N.L. team

Batter	Avg.	G	TPA	AB	R	H	TB	2B	3B	HR	RBI	SH	SF	HP	BB	IBB	SO	SB	CS	GDP	Slg.	OBP
Ginter, Hou.-Mil.	.235	28	99	81	7	19	31	9	0	1	8	0	0	1	17	0	15	0	0	0	.383	.374
Houston, Mil.-L.A.*	.281	111	345	320	34	90	137	20	3	7	40	4	1	4	16	3	62	1	0	9	.428	.323
Loretta, Mil.-Hou.	.304	107	329	283	33	86	116	18	0	4	27	6	3	5	32	1	37	1	1	7	.410	.381
Machado, Chi.-Mil.	.261	73	233	211	19	55	80	14	1	3	22	2	2	1	17	4	41	0	0	7	.379	.316
Matthews, St.L.-Mil.*	.167	45	7	6	0	1	1	0	0	0	0	1	0	0	0	0	4	0	0	0	.167	.167
Wright, Mil.-St.L.	.132	23	45	38	0	5	8	3	0	0	0	7	0	0	0	0	16	0	0	0	.211	.132

* Lefthanded batter. † Switch-hitter.

PITCHING

Pitcher	W	L	ERA	G	GS	CG	GF	SHO	Sv.	IP	H	R	ER	HR	HB	BB	IBB	SO	WP	Bk.
Sheets, Ben	11	16	4.15	34	34	1	0	0	0	216.2	237	105	100	21	10	70	10	170	9	0
Rusch, Glendon*	10	16	4.70	34	34	4	0	1	0	210.2	227	118	110	30	5	76	1	140	6	0
Quevedo, Ruben	6	11	5.76	26	25	1	0	1	0	139.0	159	100	89	28	4	68	3	93	6	0
Wright, Jamey	5	13	5.35	19	19	1	0	1	0	114.1	115	72	68	15	11	63	8	69	8	0
Cabrera, Jose	6	10	6.79	50	11	0	8	0	0	103.1	131	84	78	23	9	36	9	61	3	0
Figueroa, Nelson	1	7	5.03	30	11	0	4	0	0	93.0	96	59	52	18	4	37	6	51	5	0
Vizcaino, Luis	5	3	2.99	76	0	0	30	0	5	81.1	55	27	27	6	3	30	4	79	3	2
DeJean, Mike	1	5	3.12	68	0	0	60	0	27	75.0	66	28	26	7	2	39	8	65	7	0
King, Ray*	3	2	3.05	76	0	0	15	0	0	65.0	61	24	22	5	3	24	6	50	0	1
de los Santos, Valerio*	2	3	3.12	51	0	0	12	0	0	57.2	42	21	20	4	2	26	3	38	1	0
Neugebauer, Nick	1	7	4.72	12	12	0	0	0	0	55.1	56	33	29	10	0	44	3	47	5	2
Durocher, Jayson	1	1	1.88	39	0	0	10	0	0	48.0	27	13	10	3	2	21	2	44	1	0
Buddie, Mike	1	2	4.54	25	0	0	6	0	0	39.2	46	23	20	5	1	21	7	28	3	0
Diggins, Ben	0	4	8.63	5	5	0	0	0	0	24.0	28	24	23	4	1	18	1	15	3	1
Franklin, Wayne*	2	1	2.63	4	4	0	0	0	0	24.0	16	8	7	1	0	17	1	17	0	0
Nomura, Takahito*	0	0	8.56	21	0	0	2	0	0	13.2	11	14	13	2	2	18	4	9	2	1
Lorraine, Andrew*	0	1	11.25	5	1	0	3	0	0	12.0	22	18	15	7	0	6	0	10	0	0
Osting, Jimmy*	0	2	7.50	3	3	0	0	0	0	12.0	18	11	10	3	0	10	0	7	0	0
Stull, Everett	0	1	6.30	2	2	0	0	0	0	10.0	15	7	7	0	1	9	2	7	0	0
Childers, Matt	0	0	12.00	8	0	0	2	0	0	9.0	13	12	12	2	1	8	1	6	0	0
Pember, Dave	0	1	5.19	4	1	0	1	0	0	8.2	7	6	5	1	0	6	0	5	1	0
Nance, Shane*	0	0	4.26	4	0	0	0	0	0	6.1	4	3	3	1	0	4	0	5	0	0
Mallette, Brian	0	0	10.80	5	0	0	2	0	0	5.0	7	6	6	3	1	3	1	5	1	0
Fox, Chad	1	0	5.79	3	0	0	0	0	0	4.2	6	3	3	0	0	5	1	3	0	0
Matthews, Mike*	0	0	4.50	4	0	0	0	0	0	4.0	3	2	2	0	0	7	1	2	0	1

Pitchers with more than one N.L. team

Pitcher	W	L	ERA	G	GS	CG	GF	SHO	Sv.	IP	H	R	ER	HR	HB	BB	IBB	SO	WP	Bk.
Matthews, St.L.-Mil.*	2	1	3.94	47	0	0	10	0	0	45.2	43	23	20	5	2	29	3	34	5	1
Wright, Mil.-St.L.	7	13	5.29	23	22	1	0	1	0	129.1	130	80	76	17	11	75	9	77	9	0

* Throws lefthanded.

MONTREAL EXPOS

INDIVIDUAL STATISTICS

BATTING

Batter	Avg.	G	TPA	AB	R	H	TB	2B	3B	HR	RBI	SH	SF	HP	BB	IBB	SO	SB	CS	GDP	Slg.	OBP
Guerrero, Vladimir	.336	161	709	614	106	206	364	37	2	39	111	0	5	6	84	32	70	40	20	20	.593	.417
Vidro, Jose†	.315	152	681	604	103	190	296	43	3	19	96	11	3	3	60	1	70	2	1	12	.490	.378
Cabrera, Orlando	.263	153	626	563	64	148	214	43	1	7	56	9	4	2	48	4	53	25	7	16	.380	.321
Wilkerson, Brad*	.266	153	603	507	92	135	238	27	8	20	59	6	4	5	81	7	161	7	8	5	.469	.370
Tatis, Fernando	.228	114	430	381	43	87	152	18	1	15	55	1	5	8	35	1	90	2	2	15	.399	.303
Barrett, Michael	.263	117	428	376	41	99	157	20	1	12	49	6	5	1	40	7	65	6	3	14	.418	.332
Galarraga, Andres	.260	104	334	292	30	76	115	12	0	9	40	0	3	9	30	6	81	2	2	8	.394	.344
O'Leary, Troy*	.286	97	314	273	27	78	103	12	2	3	37	4	0	3	34	5	47	1	2	6	.377	.371
Macias, Jose†	.255	90	252	231	33	59	99	17	1	7	33	4	3	1	13	0	44	5	6	2	.429	.294
Stevens, Lee*	.190	63	245	205	28	39	77	6	1	10	31	0	1	0	39	5	57	1	0	4	.376	.318
Schneider, Brian*	.275	73	232	207	21	57	95	19	2	5	29	2	2	0	21	8	41	1	2	7	.459	.339
Cordero, Wil	.273	66	166	143	21	39	66	9	0	6	29	0	4	2	17	0	26	2	0	3	.462	.349
Bergeron, Peter*	.187	31	148	123	24	23	30	3	2	0	7	3	0	0	22	0	44	10	3	0	.244	.310
Chavez, Endy*	.296	36	138	125	20	37	58	8	5	1	9	7	1	0	5	0	16	3	5	0	.464	.321
Truby, Chris	.257	35	112	105	12	27	42	5	2	2	7	1	0	1	5	1	27	1	1	2	.400	.297
Mordecai, Mike	.203	55	90	74	9	15	19	4	0	0	4	7	0	1	8	3	14	1	1	2	.257	.289
Vazquez, Javier	.178	33	86	73	7	13	13	0	0	0	4	10	0	0	3	0	9	0	1	2	.178	.211
Carroll, Jamey	.310	16	79	71	16	22	36	5	3	1	6	4	0	0	4	0	12	1	0	1	.507	.347
Cepicky, Matt*	.216	32	78	74	7	16	28	3	0	3	15	0	0	0	4	1	21	0	0	0	.378	.256
Ohka, Tomokazu	.127	30	67	55	3	7	8	1	0	0	2	8	0	0	4	0	28	0	0	0	.145	.186
Guerrero, Wilton†	.194	44	67	62	3	12	13	1	0	0	1	4	0	0	1	1	19	5	0	1	.210	.206
Floyd, Cliff*	.208	15	57	53	7	11	22	2	0	3	4	0	0	1	3	1	10	1	0	0	.415	.263
Armas, Tony	.100	26	56	50	1	5	7	0	1	0	2	5	0	0	1	0	16	0	0	0	.140	.118
Yoshii, Masato	.057	29	44	35	2	2	3	1	0	0	0	5	0	1	3	0	13	0	0	2	.086	.154
Colon, Bartolo	.128	17	43	39	1	5	5	0	0	0	3	2	1	1	0	0	20	0	0	0	.128	.146
Pavano, Carl	.208	14	27	24	1	5	6	1	0	0	1	3	0	0	0	0	6	0	0	0	.250	.208
Mateo, Henry†	.174	22	25	23	1	4	6	0	1	0	0	0	0	0	2	1	6	2	0	0	.261	.240
Rodriguez, Henry*	.050	20	25	20	1	1	1	0	0	0	3	0	1	0	4	0	8	0	0	0	.050	.200
Collier, Lou	.091	13	14	11	3	1	2	1	0	0	0	1	0	1	1	1	3	0	0	0	.182	.231
Chen, Bruce*	.417	14	13	12	3	5	6	1	0	0	1	1	0	0	0	0	3	0	0	0	.500	.417
Reames, Britt	.111	40	11	9	0	1	1	0	0	0	1	2	0	0	0	0	1	0	0	0	.111	.111
Day, Zach	.167	19	9	6	1	1	1	0	0	0	0	2	0	0	1	0	4	0	0	0	.167	.286
Eischen, Joey*	.125	56	9	8	1	1	2	1	0	0	0	0	0	0	1	0	3	0	0	0	.250	.222
Kim, Sun-Woo	.250	4	8	8	2	2	2	0	0	0	0	0	0	0	0	0	2	0	0	0	.250	.250
Brower, Jim	.000	30	5	5	0	0	0	0	0	0	0	0	0	0	0	0	2	0	0	1	.000	.000
Drew, Tim	.000	7	4	4	0	0	0	0	0	0	0	0	0	0	0	0	4	0	0	0	.000	.000
Lloyd, Graeme*	.000	37	4	4	0	0	0	0	0	0	0	0	0	0	0	0	2	0	0	0	.000	.000
Tucker, T.J.	.750	53	4	4	1	3	3	0	0	0	0	0	0	0	0	0	0	0	0	0	.750	.750
Smith, Dan	.000	32	3	3	0	0	0	0	0	0	0	0	0	0	0	0	3	0	0	0	.000	.000
Herges, Matt*	.000	58	2	1	0	0	0	0	0	0	0	0	0	0	1	0	1	0	0	0	.000	.500
Stewart, Scott	.000	61	2	2	0	0	0	0	0	0	0	0	0	0	0	0	2	0	0	0	.000	.000

Batters with more than one N.L. team

Batter	Avg.	G	TPA	AB	R	H	TB	2B	3B	HR	RBI	SH	SF	HP	BB	IBB	SO	SB	CS	GDP	Slg.	OBP
Brower, Cin.-Mon.	.000	51	10	9	0	0	0	0	0	0	0	1	0	0	0	0	3	0	0	0	.000	.000
Chen, Mon.-Cin.*	.333	53	17	15	3	5	6	1	0	0	1	2	0	0	0	0	4	0	0	0	.400	.333
Floyd, Fla.-Mon.*	.275	99	419	349	56	96	181	22	0	21	61	0	1	8	61	19	78	11	5	0	.519	.394
Guerrero, Cin.-Mon.†	.221	103	156	140	12	31	35	2	1	0	5	9	0	0	7	1	32	7	1	2	.250	.259
Mordecai, Mon.-Fla.	.245	93	176	151	19	37	45	8	0	0	11	10	0	2	13	4	27	2	2	3	.298	.313
Pavano, Mon.-Fla.	.200	36	45	40	2	8	11	1	1	0	2	5	0	0	0	0	12	0	0	0	.275	.200

* Lefthanded batter. † Switch-hitter.

PITCHING

Pitcher	W	L	ERA	G	GS	CG	GF	SHO	Sv.	IP	H	R	ER	HR	HB	BB	IBB	SO	WP	Bk.
Vazquez, Javier	10	13	3.91	34	34	2	0	0	0	230.1	243	111	100	28	4	49	6	179	3	0
Ohka, Tomokazu	13	8	3.18	32	31	2	1	0	0	192.2	194	83	68	19	7	45	7	118	2	1
Armas, Tony	12	12	4.44	29	29	0	0	0	0	164.1	149	87	81	22	7	78	12	131	14	2
Yoshii, Masato	4	9	4.11	31	20	1	4	0	0	131.1	143	66	60	15	4	32	2	74	5	0
Colon, Bartolo	10	4	3.31	17	17	4	0	1	0	117.0	115	48	43	9	0	39	4	74	1	0
Pavano, Carl	3	8	6.30	15	14	0	0	0	0	74.1	98	55	52	14	7	31	5	51	2	1
Reames, Britt	1	4	5.03	42	6	0	7	0	0	68.0	70	42	38	8	3	38	6	76	2	0
Herges, Matt	2	5	4.04	62	0	0	25	0	6	64.2	80	33	29	10	2	26	8	50	3	0
Stewart, Scott*	4	2	3.09	67	0	0	28	0	17	64.0	49	29	22	4	1	22	5	67	1	0
Tucker, T.J.	6	3	4.11	57	0	0	19	0	4	61.1	69	32	28	5	0	31	9	42	4	0
Eischen, Joey*	6	1	1.34	59	0	0	18	0	2	53.2	43	11	8	1	2	18	5	51	6	1
Smith, Dan	1	1	3.47	33	0	0	13	0	2	46.2	34	18	18	6	1	21	0	34	1	0
Brower, Jim	1	2	4.83	30	0	0	12	0	0	41.0	39	22	22	5	4	22	1	33	1	0
Chen, Bruce*	2	3	6.99	15	5	0	4	0	0	37.1	47	29	29	9	1	23	3	43	3	0
Day, Zach	4	1	3.62	19	2	0	5	0	1	37.1	28	18	15	3	1	15	2	25	1	0
Lloyd, Graeme*	2	3	5.87	41	0	0	14	0	5	30.2	41	21	20	5	1	8	3	17	1	0
Kim, Sun-Woo	1	0	0.89	4	3	0	0	0	0	20.1	18	2	2	0	1	7	2	11	0	0
Drew, Tim	1	0	2.81	7	1	0	3	0	2	16.0	12	8	5	1	0	2	0	10	0	0
Strickland, Scott	0	0	0.00	1	0	0	0	0	0	1.0	0	0	0	0	0	0	0	2	0	0
Vosberg, Ed*	0	0	18.00	4	0	0	0	0	0	1.0	3	3	2	1	0	1	0	0	1	0

Pitchers with more than one N.L. team

Pitcher	W	L	ERA	G	GS	CG	GF	SHO	Sv.	IP	H	R	ER	HR	HB	BB	IBB	SO	WP	Bk.
Brower, Cin.-Mon.	3	2	4.37	52	0	0	23	0	0	80.1	77	40	39	7	4	32	2	57	1	0
Chen, N.Y.-Mon.-Cin.*	2	5	5.56	55	6	0	9	0	0	77.2	85	53	48	16	2	43	5	80	4	0
Lloyd, Mon.-Fla.*	4	5	5.21	66	0	0	19	0	5	57.0	67	34	33	6	2	19	4	37	2	0
Pavano, Mon.-Fla.	6	10	5.16	37	22	0	2	0	0	136.0	174	88	78	19	10	45	8	92	3	2
Strickland, Mon.-N.Y.	6	9	3.54	69	0	0	21	0	2	68.2	61	29	27	7	2	33	9	69	3	0

* Throws lefthanded.

NEW YORK METS

INDIVIDUAL STATISTICS

BATTING

Batter	Avg.	G	TPA	AB	R	H	TB	2B	3B	HR	RBI	SH	SF	HP	BB	IBB	SO	SB	CS	GDP	Slg.	OBP
Alomar, Roberto†	.266	149	655	590	73	157	222	24	4	11	53	6	1	1	57	4	83	16	4	12	.376	.331
Alfonzo, Edgardo	.308	135	562	490	78	151	225	26	0	16	56	0	3	7	62	8	55	6	0	5	.459	.391
Cedeno, Roger†	.260	149	562	511	65	133	177	19	2	7	41	5	2	2	42	1	92	25	4	10	.346	.318
Vaughn, Mo*	.259	139	558	487	67	126	222	18	0	26	72	0	2	10	59	6	145	0	1	15	.456	.349
Burnitz, Jeromy*	.215	154	550	479	65	103	175	15	0	19	54	1	2	10	58	5	135	10	7	11	.365	.311
Piazza, Mike	.280	135	541	478	69	134	260	23	2	33	98	0	3	3	57	9	82	0	3	26	.544	.359
Ordonez, Rey	.254	144	499	460	53	117	149	25	2	1	42	9	4	2	24	11	46	2	2	19	.324	.292
Perez, Timo*	.295	136	481	444	52	131	194	27	6	8	47	10	2	2	23	2	36	10	6	10	.437	.331
Payton, Jay	.284	87	300	275	33	78	114	6	3	8	31	2	1	1	21	0	34	4	1	8	.415	.336
Valentin, John	.240	114	242	208	18	50	74	15	0	3	30	0	2	10	22	0	37	0	0	6	.356	.339
McEwing, Joe	.199	105	214	196	22	39	58	8	1	3	26	3	3	3	9	0	50	4	4	0	.296	.242
Wilson, Vance	.245	74	178	163	19	40	62	7	0	5	26	2	0	8	5	0	32	0	1	4	.380	.301
Wigginton, Ty	.302	46	127	116	18	35	61	8	0	6	18	0	1	2	8	0	19	2	1	4	.526	.354
Tarasco, Tony*	.250	60	105	96	15	24	47	5	0	6	15	0	1	0	8	0	13	2	1	2	.490	.305
Gonzalez, Raul	.259	30	86	81	9	21	32	2	0	3	11	0	1	0	4	0	17	2	2	2	.395	.291
Astacio, Pedro	.161	30	69	62	3	10	12	2	0	0	1	6	0	1	0	0	31	0	0	0	.194	.175
Leiter, Al*	.151	30	64	53	3	8	9	1	0	0	2	3	0	0	8	0	28	0	0	2	.170	.262
Johnson, Mark P.*	.137	42	61	51	5	7	14	4	0	1	4	1	0	0	9	0	18	0	0	0	.275	.267
Trachsel, Steve	.109	29	56	46	4	5	7	0	1	0	4	9	0	0	1	0	19	0	0	2	.152	.128
D'Amico, Jeff	.108	27	44	37	2	4	4	0	0	0	0	5	0	0	2	0	22	0	0	1	.108	.154
Estes, Shawn	.086	23	40	35	1	3	7	1	0	1	3	5	0	0	0	0	14	0	0	1	.200	.086
Scutaro, Marco	.222	27	38	36	2	8	13	0	1	1	6	1	1	0	0	0	11	0	1	1	.361	.216
Phillips, Jason	.368	11	22	19	4	7	10	0	0	1	3	0	1	1	1	0	1	0	0	1	.526	.409
Thomson, John	.278	9	22	18	2	5	5	0	0	0	1	3	0	0	1	0	7	0	0	0	.278	.316
Bacsik, Mike*	.111	11	21	18	0	2	3	1	0	0	2	3	0	0	0	0	3	0	0	0	.167	.111
Snead, Esix†	.308	17	14	13	3	4	7	0	0	1	3	0	0	0	1	0	4	4	3	0	.538	.357
Clark, Brady	.417	10	13	12	3	5	6	1	0	0	1	0	0	0	1	0	2	0	0	0	.500	.462
Middlebrook, Jason	.000	3	6	5	0	0	0	0	0	0	0	0	0	0	1	0	2	0	0	0	.000	.167
Christensen, McKay*	.333	4	4	3	1	1	1	0	0	0	0	0	0	0	1	0	1	0	0	0	.333	.500
Komiyama, Satoru	.000	22	3	1	0	0	0	0	0	0	0	1	0	0	1	0	1	0	0	0	.000	.500
Little, Mark	.000	3	3	3	0	0	0	0	0	0	0	0	0	0	0	0	1	0	1	0	.000	.000
Guthrie, Mark	.000	65	2	2	0	0	0	0	0	0	0	0	0	0	0	0	0	0	0	0	.000	.000
Walker, Tyler	.000	5	2	2	0	0	0	0	0	0	0	0	0	0	0	0	1	0	0	0	.000	.000
Cerda, Jaime*	.000	29	1	1	0	0	0	0	0	0	0	0	0	0	0	0	0	0	0	0	.000	.000
Matthews, Gary†	.000	2	1	1	0	0	0	0	0	0	0	0	0	0	0	0	0	0	0	0	.000	.000
Roberts, Grant	1.000	33	1	1	1	1	1	0	0	0	0	0	0	0	0	0	0	0	0	0	1.000	1.000
Weathers, Dave	.000	68	1	1	0	0	0	0	0	0	0	0	0	0	0	0	0	0	0	0	.000	.000
Corey, Mark	.000	13	1	1	0	0	0	0	0	0	0	0	0	0	0	0	1	0	0	0	.000	.000
Reed, Steve	.000	24	1	1	0	0	0	0	0	0	0	0	0	0	0	0	1	0	0	0	.000	.000

Batters with more than one N.L. team

Batter	Avg.	G	TPA	AB	R	H	TB	2B	3B	HR	RBI	SH	SF	HP	BB	IBB	SO	SB	CS	GDP	Slg.	OBP
Clark, Cin.-N.Y.	.192	61	87	78	9	15	19	4	0	0	10	1	0	1	7	2	11	1	2	2	.244	.267
Corey, N.Y.-Col.	.000	27	2	2	0	0	0	0	0	0	0	0	0	0	0	0	2	0	0	0	.000	.000
Estes, N.Y.-Cin.	.070	29	50	43	1	3	7	1	0	1	3	7	0	0	0	0	17	0	0	1	.163	.070
Gonzalez, Cin.-N.Y.	.260	40	111	104	13	27	39	3	0	3	12	0	1	0	6	0	22	4	2	3	.375	.297
Little, Col.-N.Y.-Ari.	.208	79	154	130	28	27	38	5	3	0	7	1	0	8	15	0	34	2	2	1	.292	.327
Middlebrook, S.D.-N.Y.	.182	13	13	11	2	2	2	0	0	0	0	1	0	0	1	0	3	0	0	0	.182	.250
Payton, N.Y.-Col.	.303	134	481	445	69	135	217	20	7	16	59	2	1	4	29	0	54	7	4	11	.488	.351
Reed, S.D.-N.Y.	.000	61	2	2	0	0	0	0	0	0	0	0	0	0	0	0	2	0	0	0	.000	.000
Thomson, Col.-N.Y.	.212	28	62	52	4	11	11	0	0	0	3	6	1	0	3	0	19	0	0	0	.212	.250

* Lefthanded batter. † Switch-hitter.

PITCHING

Pitcher	W	L	ERA	G	GS	CG	GF	SHO	Sv.	IP	H	R	ER	HR	HB	BB	IBB	SO	WP	Bk.
Leiter, Al*	13	13	3.48	33	33	2	0	2	0	204.1	194	99	79	23	8	69	5	172	1	1
Astacio, Pedro	12	11	4.79	31	31	3	0	1	0	191.2	192	106	102	32	16	63	5	152	1	2
Trachsel, Steve	11	11	3.37	30	30	1	0	1	0	173.2	170	80	65	16	0	69	4	105	4	0
D'Amico, Jeff	6	10	4.94	29	22	1	1	1	0	145.2	152	84	80	20	3	37	8	101	0	0
Estes, Shawn*	4	9	4.55	23	23	1	0	1	0	132.2	133	70	67	12	5	66	9	92	2	1
Weathers, Dave	6	3	2.91	71	0	0	12	0	0	77.1	69	30	25	6	3	36	7	61	2	0
Strickland, Scott	6	9	3.59	68	0	0	21	0	2	67.2	61	29	27	7	2	33	9	67	3	0
Benitez, Armando	1	0	2.27	62	0	0	52	0	33	67.1	46	20	17	8	3	25	0	79	1	0
Bacsik, Mike*	3	2	4.37	11	9	1	1	0	0	55.2	63	29	27	8	4	19	3	30	0	0
Thomson, John	2	6	4.31	9	9	0	0	0	0	54.1	65	39	26	7	0	17	3	31	0	0
Guthrie, Mark*	5	3	2.44	68	0	0	13	0	1	48.0	35	13	13	3	1	19	3	44	4	0
Roberts, Grant	3	1	2.20	34	0	0	6	0	0	45.0	43	12	11	3	1	16	7	31	0	0
Komiyama, Satoru	0	3	5.61	25	0	0	13	0	0	43.1	53	29	27	7	3	12	4	33	1	0
Reed, Steve	0	1	2.08	24	0	0	4	0	0	26.0	23	6	6	0	2	4	1	14	1	0
Cerda, Jaime*	0	0	2.45	32	0	0	7	0	0	25.2	22	7	7	0	1	14	0	21	0	1
Jones, Bobby M.*	0	0	5.29	12	0	0	1	0	0	17.0	20	11	10	3	1	11	2	11	0	0
Middlebrook, Jason	1	0	3.94	3	3	0	0	0	0	16.0	13	7	7	1	0	7	0	14	0	1
Davis, Kane	1	1	7.07	16	0	0	5	0	0	14.0	15	11	11	2	1	11	2	24	1	0
Walker, Tyler	1	0	5.91	5	1	0	3	0	0	10.2	11	7	7	3	0	5	1	7	0	0
Corey, Mark	0	3	4.50	12	0	0	5	0	0	10.0	10	7	5	2	1	8	1	9	1	0
Strange, Pat	0	0	1.13	5	0	0	4	0	0	8.0	6	1	1	0	0	1	1	4	0	1
Feliciano, Pedro*	0	0	7.50	6	0	0	3	0	0	6.0	9	5	5	0	0	1	0	4	0	0
Seo, Jae Weong	0	0	0.00	1	0	0	1	0	0	1.0	0	0	0	0	0	0	0	1	0	0
Walker, Pete	0	0	9.00	1	0	0	0	0	0	1.0	2	1	1	0	0	0	0	0	0	0
Chen, Bruce*	0	0	0.00	1	0	0	0	0	0	0.2	1	0	0	0	0	0	0	0	0	0

Pitchers with more than one N.L. team

Pitcher	W	L	ERA	G	GS	CG	GF	SHO	Sv.	IP	H	R	ER	HR	HB	BB	IBB	SO	WP	Bk.
Chen, N.Y.-Mon.-Cin.*	2	5	5.56	55	6	0	9	0	0	77.2	85	53	48	16	2	43	5	80	4	0
Corey, N.Y.-Col.	0	3	8.59	26	0	0	8	0	0	22.0	32	23	21	9	3	16	2	21	1	0
Estes, N.Y.-Cin.*	5	12	5.10	29	29	1	0	1	0	160.2	171	94	91	13	9	83	9	109	3	1
Jones, N.Y.-S.D.*	0	0	5.74	16	2	0	1	0	0	26.2	30	18	17	4	1	18	2	18	0	0
Middlebrook, S.D.-N.Y.	2	3	4.73	15	5	0	5	0	0	51.1	44	27	27	2	1	22	2	42	2	1
Reed, S.D.-N.Y.	2	5	2.01	64	0	0	15	0	1	67.0	56	15	15	2	8	14	3	50	2	0
Strickland, Mon.-N.Y.	6	9	3.54	69	0	0	21	0	2	68.2	61	29	27	7	2	33	9	69	3	0
Thomson, Col.-N.Y.	9	14	4.71	30	30	0	0	0	0	181.2	201	116	95	28	2	44	9	107	2	0

* Throws lefthanded.

Philadelphia Phillies

INDIVIDUAL STATISTICS

BATTING

Batter	Avg.	G	TPA	AB	R	H	TB	2B	3B	HR	RBI	SH	SF	HP	BB	IBB	SO	SB	CS	GDP	Slg.	OBP
Rollins, Jimmy†	.245	154	705	637	82	156	242	33	10	11	60	6	4	4	54	3	103	31	13	14	.380	.306
Abreu, Bobby*	.308	157	685	572	102	176	298	50	6	20	85	0	6	3	104	9	117	31	12	11	.521	.413
Burrell, Pat	.282	157	684	586	96	165	319	39	2	37	116	0	6	3	89	9	153	1	0	16	.544	.376
Anderson, Marlon*	.258	145	592	539	64	139	205	30	6	8	48	2	4	5	42	14	71	5	1	16	.380	.315
Lee, Travis*	.265	153	592	536	55	142	211	26	2	13	70	0	2	0	54	10	104	5	3	12	.394	.331
Lieberthal, Mike	.279	130	530	476	46	133	211	29	2	15	52	0	2	14	38	2	58	0	1	16	.443	.349
Glanville, Doug	.249	138	460	422	49	105	145	16	3	6	29	8	3	2	25	4	57	19	2	5	.344	.292
Rolen, Scott	.259	100	438	375	52	97	177	21	4	17	66	0	3	8	52	2	68	5	2	12	.472	.358
Ledee, Ricky*	.227	96	241	203	33	46	85	13	1	8	23	1	1	1	35	0	50	1	2	3	.419	.342
Perez, Tomas†	.250	92	237	212	22	53	83	13	1	5	20	2	1	1	21	6	40	1	0	5	.392	.319
Polanco, Placido	.296	53	228	206	28	61	88	13	1	4	22	4	0	4	14	0	14	2	2	3	.427	.353
Giambi, Jeremy*	.244	82	211	156	32	38	84	10	0	12	28	1	0	1	52	2	54	0	1	1	.538	.435
Pratt, Todd	.311	39	136	106	14	33	53	11	0	3	16	0	2	4	24	6	28	2	0	3	.500	.449
Michaels, Jason	.267	81	121	105	16	28	50	10	3	2	11	0	2	1	13	1	33	1	1	1	.476	.347
Wolf, Randy*	.136	30	75	59	6	8	15	4	0	1	4	12	0	0	4	0	24	0	0	3	.254	.190
Padilla, Vicente	.052	29	67	58	1	3	4	1	0	0	5	7	1	1	0	0	31	0	0	1	.069	.067
Duckworth, Brandon	.188	29	59	48	3	9	10	1	0	0	4	6	0	0	5	0	11	0	0	3	.208	.264
Byrd, Marlon	.229	10	36	35	2	8	13	2	0	1	1	0	0	0	1	0	8	0	2	0	.371	.250
Adams, Terry	.080	45	34	25	0	2	2	0	0	0	1	6	0	0	3	0	13	0	0	1	.080	.179
Roa, Joe	.240	14	30	25	1	6	7	1	0	0	2	3	1	0	1	0	5	0	0	0	.280	.259
Person, Robert	.083	15	29	24	3	2	8	0	0	2	7	3	0	0	2	0	17	0	0	0	.333	.154
Myers, Brett	.130	12	26	23	0	3	4	1	0	0	1	3	0	0	0	0	9	0	0	2	.174	.130
Mabry, John*	.286	21	23	21	1	6	6	0	0	0	3	0	1	0	1	1	5	0	0	0	.286	.304
Estrada, Johnny†	.118	10	19	17	0	2	3	1	0	0	2	0	0	0	2	1	2	0	0	0	.176	.211
Hollins, Dave†	.118	14	18	17	1	2	2	0	0	0	0	0	0	1	0	0	3	0	1	0	.118	.167
Coggin, Dave	.000	36	11	8	0	0	0	0	0	0	0	2	0	0	1	0	6	0	0	0	.000	.111
Valent, Eric*	.200	7	10	10	1	2	2	0	0	0	0	0	0	0	0	0	3	0	0	1	.200	.200
Punto, Nick†	.167	9	7	6	0	1	1	0	0	0	0	1	0	0	0	0	3	0	0	0	.167	.167
Cormier, Rheal*	.333	53	4	3	0	1	1	0	0	0	0	0	0	0	1	0	0	0	0	0	.333	.500
Mercado, Hector*	.250	31	4	4	0	1	1	0	0	0	0	0	0	0	0	0	2	0	0	0	.250	.250
Junge, Eric	.000	4	3	3	0	0	0	0	0	0	0	0	0	0	0	0	0	0	0	0	.000	.000
Santiago, Jose	.000	38	3	2	0	0	0	0	0	0	0	0	0	0	1	0	1	0	0	0	.000	.333
Silva, Carlos	.000	66	3	2	0	0	0	0	0	0	0	0	0	0	1	0	1	0	0	0	.000	.333
Nickle, Doug	.000	3	1	1	0	0	0	0	0	0	0	0	0	0	0	0	0	0	0	0	.000	.000
Politte, Cliff	.000	13	1	1	0	0	0	0	0	0	0	0	0	0	0	0	1	0	0	0	.000	.000

Batters with more than one N.L. team

Batter	Avg.	G	TPA	AB	R	H	TB	2B	3B	HR	RBI	SH	SF	HP	BB	IBB	SO	SB	CS	GDP	Slg.	OBP
Polanco, St.L.-Phi.	.288	147	595	548	75	158	221	32	2	9	49	13	0	8	26	1	41	5	3	15	.403	.330
Rolen, Phi.-St.L.	.266	155	667	580	89	154	292	29	8	31	110	0	3	12	72	4	102	8	4	22	.503	.357

* Lefthanded batter. † Switch-hitter.

PITCHING

Pitcher	W	L	ERA	G	GS	CG	GF	SHO	Sv.	IP	H	R	ER	HR	HB	BB	IBB	SO	WP	Bk.
Wolf, Randy*	11	9	3.20	31	31	3	0	2	0	210.2	172	77	75	23	7	63	5	172	4	0
Padilla, Vicente	14	11	3.28	32	32	1	0	1	0	206.0	198	83	75	16	15	53	5	128	6	2
Duckworth, Brandon	8	9	5.41	30	29	0	0	0	0	163.0	167	103	98	26	7	69	5	167	10	0
Adams, Terry	7	9	4.35	46	19	0	10	0	0	136.2	132	76	66	9	3	58	5	96	8	0
Person, Robert	4	5	5.44	16	16	0	0	0	0	87.2	79	58	53	13	5	51	0	61	2	0
Silva, Carlos	5	0	3.21	68	0	0	21	0	1	84.0	88	34	30	4	4	22	6	41	3	0
Coggin, Dave	2	5	4.68	38	7	0	7	0	0	77.0	65	42	40	4	4	51	3	64	11	0
Mesa, Jose	4	6	2.97	74	0	0	64	0	45	75.2	65	26	25	5	4	39	7	64	9	0
Myers, Brett	4	5	4.25	12	12	1	0	0	0	72.0	73	38	34	11	6	29	1	34	2	1
Roa, Joe	4	4	4.04	14	11	0	1	0	0	71.1	78	33	32	11	1	13	2	35	0	1
Cormier, Rheal*	5	6	5.25	54	0	0	7	0	0	60.0	61	38	35	6	4	32	6	49	4	0
Santiago, Jose	1	3	6.70	42	0	0	7	0	0	47.0	56	35	35	7	3	15	1	30	1	0
Mercado, Hector*	2	2	4.62	31	3	0	7	0	0	39.0	32	21	20	2	3	25	2	40	3	1
Timlin, Mike	3	3	3.79	30	0	0	7	0	0	35.2	27	16	15	6	1	7	0	15	2	0
Bottalico, Ricky	0	3	4.61	30	0	0	6	0	0	27.1	33	16	14	3	2	13	2	24	2	0
Plesac, Dan*	2	1	4.70	41	0	0	5	0	1	23.0	16	12	12	5	0	12	3	27	0	0
Politte, Cliff	2	0	3.86	13	0	0	7	0	0	16.1	19	10	7	0	1	9	1	15	1	0
Junge, Eric	2	0	1.42	4	1	0	2	0	0	12.2	14	3	2	0	0	5	0	11	0	0
Nickle, Doug	0	0	6.23	4	0	0	4	0	0	4.1	6	3	3	2	0	4	0	2	0	0
Perez, Tomas	0	0	0.00	1	0	0	1	0	0	0.1	0	0	0	0	0	0	0	0	0	0

Pitchers with more than one N.L. team

Pitcher	W	L	ERA	G	GS	CG	GF	SHO	Sv.	IP	H	R	ER	HR	HB	BB	IBB	SO	WP	Bk.
Nickle, Phi.-S.D.	1	0	7.88	14	0	0	6	0	0	16.0	26	16	14	3	1	13	0	9	0	0
Timlin, St.L.-Phi.	4	6	2.98	72	1	0	17	0	0	96.2	75	35	32	15	5	14	2	50	3	0

* Throws lefthanded.

PITTSBURGH PIRATES

INDIVIDUAL STATISTICS

BATTING

Batter	Avg.	G	TPA	AB	R	H	TB	2B	3B	HR	RBI	SH	SF	HP	BB	IBB	SO	SB	CS	GDP	Slg.	OBP
Giles, Brian*	.298	153	644	497	95	148	309	37	5	38	103	0	5	7	135	24	74	15	6	10	.622	.450
Kendall, Jason	.283	145	605	545	59	154	194	25	3	3	44	0	2	9	49	1	29	15	8	11	.356	.350
Wilson, Jack	.252	147	586	527	77	133	175	22	4	4	47	17	1	4	37	2	74	5	2	7	.332	.306
Ramirez, Aramis	.234	142	570	522	51	122	202	26	0	18	71	0	11	8	29	3	95	2	0	17	.387	.279
Young, Kevin	.246	146	525	468	60	115	191	26	1	16	51	0	3	4	50	2	101	4	6	13	.408	.322
Reese, Pokey	.264	119	475	421	46	111	148	25	0	4	50	5	5	3	41	4	81	12	1	4	.352	.330
Mackowiak, Rob*	.244	136	439	385	57	94	164	22	0	16	48	3	2	7	42	5	120	9	3	0	.426	.328
Wilson, Craig A.	.264	131	424	368	48	97	163	16	1	16	57	1	2	21	32	0	116	2	3	10	.443	.355
Nunez, Abraham O.†	.233	112	286	253	28	59	81	14	1	2	15	3	1	2	27	1	44	3	4	2	.320	.311
Brown, Adrian†	.216	91	232	208	20	45	62	10	2	1	21	3	1	1	19	0	34	10	6	5	.298	.284
Rios, Armando*	.264	76	226	208	20	55	69	11	0	1	24	0	1	1	16	1	39	1	1	8	.332	.319
Hermansen, Chad	.206	65	216	194	22	40	74	11	1	7	15	3	1	1	17	0	68	7	5	1	.381	.272
Hyzdu, Adam	.232	59	179	155	24	36	75	6	0	11	34	0	2	1	21	0	44	0	0	1	.484	.324
Benjamin, Mike	.150	108	130	120	7	18	22	2	1	0	3	1	1	1	7	0	31	0	4	5	.183	.202
Osik, Keith	.160	55	111	100	6	16	25	3	0	2	11	2	2	1	6	0	25	0	0	2	.250	.211
Wells, Kip	.190	34	76	63	4	12	17	2	0	1	5	13	0	0	0	0	28	0	0	0	.270	.190
Fogg, Josh	.121	32	62	58	2	7	7	0	0	0	1	2	0	0	2	0	22	0	0	0	.121	.150
Anderson, Jimmy*	.119	27	47	42	1	5	5	0	0	0	1	3	0	0	2	0	12	0	0	0	.119	.159
Benson, Kris	.175	26	44	40	3	7	8	1	0	0	1	4	0	0	0	0	11	0	0	0	.200	.175
Alvarez, Tony	.308	14	30	26	6	8	13	2	0	1	2	1	0	0	3	0	5	1	0	0	.500	.379
Meadows, Brian	.000	11	22	18	0	0	0	0	0	0	1	3	1	0	0	0	10	0	0	0	.000	.000
Cota, Humberto	.294	7	18	17	2	5	6	1	0	0	0	0	0	0	1	1	4	0	0	0	.353	.333
Villone, Ron*	.250	44	16	16	1	4	6	0	1	0	1	0	0	0	0	0	3	0	0	0	.375	.250
Williams, Dave*	.125	10	16	16	1	2	5	0	0	1	3	0	0	0	0	0	12	0	0	0	.313	.125
Lowe, Sean	.077	42	15	13	0	1	1	0	0	0	0	2	0	0	0	0	5	0	0	0	.077	.077
Beimel, Joe*	.300	51	13	10	0	3	4	1	0	0	1	2	0	0	1	0	3	0	0	0	.400	.364
Torres, Salomon	.154	5	13	13	0	2	2	0	0	0	0	0	0	0	0	0	4	0	0	0	.154	.154
Davis, J.J.	.100	9	11	10	1	1	1	0	0	0	0	0	0	1	0	0	4	0	0	1	.100	.182
Arroyo, Bronson	.000	9	6	6	0	0	0	0	0	0	0	0	0	0	0	0	1	0	0	0	.000	.000
Lincoln, Mike	.000	53	5	5	0	0	0	0	0	0	0	0	0	0	0	0	5	0	0	0	.000	.000
Lopez, Mendy	.000	3	3	3	0	0	0	0	0	0	0	0	0	0	0	0	3	0	0	0	.000	.000
Sauerbeck, Scott	.000	75	2	2	0	0	0	0	0	0	0	0	0	0	0	0	1	0	0	0	.000	.000
Williams, Mike	.000	57	2	1	0	0	0	0	0	0	0	0	0	1	0	0	1	0	0	0	.000	.500

Batters with more than one N.L. team

Batter	Avg.	G	TPA	AB	R	H	TB	2B	3B	HR	RBI	SH	SF	HP	BB	IBB	SO	SB	CS	GDP	Slg.	OBP
Hermansen, Pit.-Chi.	.207	100	265	237	25	49	89	14	1	8	18	4	1	1	22	0	82	7	5	1	.376	.276
Lowe, Pit.-Col.	.071	50	16	14	0	1	1	0	0	0	0	2	0	0	0	0	6	0	0	0	.071	.071

* Lefthanded batter. † Switch-hitter.

PITCHING

Pitcher	W	L	ERA	G	GS	CG	GF	SHO	Sv.	IP	H	R	ER	HR	HB	BB	IBB	SO	WP	Bk.
Wells, Kip	12	14	3.58	33	33	1	0	1	0	198.1	197	92	79	21	7	71	11	134	7	0
Fogg, Josh	12	12	4.35	33	33	0	0	0	0	194.1	199	102	94	28	8	69	12	113	2	0
Anderson, Jimmy*	8	13	5.44	28	25	1	1	0	0	140.2	167	91	85	20	5	63	5	47	4	0
Benson, Kris	9	6	4.70	25	25	0	0	0	0	130.1	152	76	68	18	3	50	8	79	3	1
Villone, Ron*	4	6	5.81	45	7	0	6	0	0	93.0	95	63	60	8	5	34	3	55	1	0
Beimel, Joe*	2	5	4.64	53	8	0	8	0	0	85.1	88	49	44	9	4	45	12	53	2	0
Boehringer, Brian	4	4	3.39	70	0	0	20	0	1	79.2	65	30	30	5	2	33	6	65	1	0
Lincoln, Mike	2	4	3.11	55	0	0	9	0	0	72.1	80	28	25	7	0	27	8	50	2	0
Lowe, Sean	4	2	5.35	43	1	0	8	0	0	69.0	85	45	41	8	7	34	6	57	1	1
Meadows, Brian	1	6	3.88	11	11	0	0	0	0	62.2	62	29	27	7	1	14	8	31	2	0
Sauerbeck, Scott*	5	4	2.30	78	0	0	21	0	0	62.2	50	18	16	4	1	27	4	70	2	1
Williams, Mike	2	6	2.93	59	0	0	59	0	46	61.1	54	24	20	6	1	21	3	43	2	0
Williams, Dave*	2	5	4.98	9	9	0	0	0	0	43.1	38	26	24	9	4	24	2	33	2	2
Fetters, Mike	1	0	3.26	32	0	0	13	0	0	30.1	25	13	11	3	1	18	1	29	2	0
Torres, Salomon	2	1	2.70	5	5	0	0	0	0	30.0	28	10	9	2	3	13	1	12	0	0
Arroyo, Bronson	2	1	4.00	9	4	0	1	0	0	27.0	30	14	12	1	0	15	3	22	0	0
Reyes, Al	0	0	2.65	15	0	0	6	0	0	17.0	9	5	5	1	2	7	0	21	1	0
Manzanillo, Josias	0	0	7.62	13	0	0	5	0	0	13.0	20	11	11	5	1	5	0	4	0	0
Sanchez, Duaner	0	0	15.43	3	0	0	2	0	0	2.1	3	4	4	1	0	2	0	2	0	0

Pitchers with more than one N.L. team

Pitcher	W	L	ERA	G	GS	CG	GF	SHO	Sv.	IP	H	R	ER	HR	HB	BB	IBB	SO	WP	Bk.
Fetters, Pit.-Ari.	3	3	4.09	65	0	0	22	0	0	55.0	53	31	25	4	3	37	6	53	8	0
Lowe, Pit.-Col.	5	3	5.79	51	1	0	8	0	0	79.1	101	58	51	9	7	41	6	64	1	1
Sanchez, Ari.-Pit.	0	0	9.00	9	0	0	5	0	0	6.0	6	6	6	2	0	7	0	6	0	0

* Throws lefthanded.

St. Louis Cardinals

INDIVIDUAL STATISTICS

BATTING

Batter	Avg.	G	TPA	AB	R	H	TB	2B	3B	HR	RBI	SH	SF	HP	BB	IBB	SO	SB	CS	GDP	Slg.	OBP
Vina, Fernando*	.270	150	692	622	75	168	210	29	5	1	54	1	7	18	44	2	36	17	11	11	.338	.333
Pujols, Albert	.314	157	675	590	118	185	331	40	2	34	127	0	4	9	72	13	69	2	4	20	.561	.394
Renteria, Edgar	.305	152	609	544	77	166	239	36	2	11	83	7	5	4	49	7	57	22	7	17	.439	.364
Edmonds, Jim*	.311	144	576	476	96	148	267	31	2	28	83	0	6	8	86	14	134	4	3	9	.561	.420
Martinez, Tino*	.262	150	576	511	63	134	224	25	1	21	75	1	4	2	58	9	71	3	2	12	.438	.337
Drew, J.D.*	.252	135	496	424	61	107	182	19	1	18	56	3	4	8	57	4	104	8	2	4	.429	.349
Marrero, Eli	.262	131	446	397	63	104	179	19	1	18	66	5	4	0	40	11	72	14	2	5	.451	.327
Polanco, Placido	.284	94	367	342	47	97	133	19	1	5	27	9	0	4	12	1	27	3	1	12	.389	.316
Matheny, Mike	.244	110	363	315	31	77	100	12	1	3	35	8	6	2	32	6	49	1	3	3	.317	.313
Rolen, Scott	.278	55	229	205	37	57	115	8	4	14	44	0	0	4	20	2	34	3	2	10	.561	.354
Cairo, Miguel	.250	108	208	184	28	46	65	9	2	2	23	6	2	3	13	2	36	1	1	5	.353	.307
DiFelice, Mike	.230	70	197	174	17	40	63	11	0	4	19	2	3	1	17	3	42	0	0	4	.362	.297
Robinson, Kerry*	.260	124	195	181	27	47	65	7	4	1	15	2	1	0	11	3	29	7	4	1	.359	.301
Perez, Eduardo	.201	96	177	154	22	31	70	9	0	10	26	1	2	3	17	0	36	0	0	7	.455	.290
Morris, Matt	.169	31	79	71	4	12	15	3	0	0	3	5	0	0	3	0	23	0	0	0	.211	.203
Simontacchi, Jason	.240	24	56	50	5	12	12	0	0	0	2	4	0	0	2	0	15	0	0	0	.240	.269
Benes, Andy	.206	19	37	34	3	7	11	1	0	1	2	2	0	0	1	0	9	0	0	1	.324	.229
Williams, Woody	.207	17	36	29	3	6	12	3	0	1	3	5	1	1	0	0	9	0	0	0	.414	.226
Finley, Chuck*	.107	14	33	28	2	3	4	1	0	0	1	5	0	0	0	0	12	0	0	0	.143	.107
Kile, Darryl	.091	12	26	22	0	2	2	0	0	0	0	3	0	0	1	0	9	0	0	0	.091	.130
Delgado, Wilson†	.200	12	21	20	2	4	12	2	0	2	5	1	0	0	0	0	6	0	0	0	.600	.200
Smith, Travis	.167	12	20	18	0	3	3	0	0	0	2	2	0	0	0	0	6	0	0	0	.167	.167
Taguchi, So	.400	19	19	15	4	6	6	0	0	0	2	2	0	0	2	0	1	1	0	0	.400	.471
Smith, Bud*	.214	10	18	14	0	3	4	1	0	0	1	3	0	0	1	0	4	0	0	1	.286	.267
Hackman, Luther	.063	41	17	16	0	1	1	0	0	0	0	0	0	0	1	0	6	0	0	0	.063	.118
Cruz, Ivan*	.357	17	15	14	2	5	8	0	0	1	3	0	0	0	1	0	3	0	0	0	.571	.400
Stephenson, Garrett	.000	12	15	12	0	0	0	0	0	0	0	2	0	0	1	0	8	0	0	0	.000	.077
Coolbaugh, Mike	.083	5	14	12	0	1	1	0	0	0	0	1	0	0	1	0	3	0	0	1	.083	.154
Pearce, Josh	.250	3	6	4	0	1	1	0	0	0	1	2	0	0	0	0	0	0	0	0	.250	.250
Timlin, Mike	.000	39	6	6	0	0	0	0	0	0	0	0	0	0	0	0	4	0	0	0	.000	.000
Matthews, Mike*	.167	41	6	6	0	1	1	0	0	0	0	0	0	0	0	0	4	0	0	0	.167	.167
Wright, Jamey	.000	4	6	5	0	0	0	0	0	0	0	1	0	0	0	0	3	0	0	0	.000	.000
Veres, Dave	.333	68	3	3	0	1	1	0	0	0	0	0	0	0	0	0	1	0	0	0	.333	.333
Crudale, Mike	.000	49	2	2	0	0	0	0	0	0	0	0	0	0	0	0	1	0	0	0	.000	.000
Stechschulte, Gene	.000	28	2	2	0	0	0	0	0	0	0	0	0	0	0	0	2	0	0	0	.000	.000
Kline, Steve†	.000	64	1	1	0	0	0	0	0	0	0	0	0	0	0	0	0	0	0	0	.000	.000
Rodriguez, Nerio	.000	2	1	1	0	0	0	0	0	0	0	0	0	0	0	0	1	0	0	0	.000	.000
White, Rick	.000	20	1	1	0	0	0	0	0	0	0	0	0	0	0	0	1	0	0	0	.000	.000

Batters with more than one N.L. team

Batter	Avg.	G	TPA	AB	R	H	TB	2B	3B	HR	RBI	SH	SF	HP	BB	IBB	SO	SB	CS	GDP	Slg.	OBP
Matthews, St.L.-Mil.*	.167	45	7	6	0	1	1	0	0	0	0	1	0	0	0	0	4	0	0	0	.167	.167
Polanco, St.L.-Phi.	.288	147	595	548	75	158	221	32	2	9	49	13	0	8	26	1	41	5	3	15	.403	.330
Rolen, Phi.-St.L.	.266	155	667	580	89	154	292	29	8	31	110	0	3	12	72	4	102	8	4	22	.503	.357
Wright, Mil.-St.L.	.132	23	45	38	0	5	8	3	0	0	0	7	0	0	0	0	16	0	0	0	.211	.132

* Lefthanded batter. † Switch-hitter.

PITCHING

Pitcher	W	L	ERA	G	GS	CG	GF	SHO	Sv.	IP	H	R	ER	HR	HB	BB	IBB	SO	WP	Bk.
Morris, Matt	17	9	3.42	32	32	1	0	1	0	210.1	210	86	80	16	6	64	3	171	3	0
Simontacchi, Jason	11	5	4.02	24	24	0	0	0	0	143.1	134	68	64	18	6	54	4	72	1	0
Williams, Woody	9	4	2.53	17	17	1	0	0	0	103.1	84	30	29	10	4	25	2	76	2	0
Benes, Andy	5	4	2.78	18	17	1	0	0	0	97.0	80	39	30	10	5	51	3	64	0	0
Finley, Chuck*	7	4	3.80	14	14	1	0	1	0	85.1	69	41	36	7	1	30	3	83	2	0
Kile, Darryl	5	4	3.72	14	14	0	0	0	0	84.2	82	36	35	9	8	28	1	50	0	0
Veres, Dave	5	8	3.48	71	0	0	26	0	4	82.2	67	34	32	12	2	39	4	68	7	0
Hackman, Luther	5	4	4.11	43	6	0	9	0	0	81.0	90	42	37	7	4	39	3	46	7	1
Isringhausen, Jason	3	2	2.48	60	0	0	51	0	32	65.1	46	22	18	0	1	18	1	68	0	0
Timlin, Mike	1	3	2.51	42	1	0	10	0	0	61.0	48	19	17	9	4	7	2	35	1	0
Kline, Steve*	2	1	3.39	66	0	0	17	0	6	58.1	54	23	22	3	1	21	2	41	1	0
Smith, Travis	4	2	7.17	12	10	0	0	0	0	54.0	69	44	43	10	3	20	0	32	2	0
Crudale, Mike	3	0	1.88	49	1	0	14	0	0	52.2	43	11	11	3	1	14	2	47	3	0
Smith, Bud*	1	5	6.94	11	10	0	1	0	0	48.0	67	39	37	4	3	22	2	22	0	1
Stephenson, Garrett	2	5	5.40	12	10	0	0	0	0	45.0	48	27	27	4	5	25	0	34	2	0
Matthews, Mike*	2	1	3.89	43	0	0	10	0	0	41.2	40	21	18	5	2	22	2	32	5	0
Stechschulte, Gene	6	2	4.78	29	0	0	5	0	0	32.0	27	19	17	4	1	17	1	21	3	0
White, Rick	3	1	0.82	20	0	0	2	0	0	22.0	13	3	2	0	0	3	1	14	0	0
Fassero, Jeff*	3	0	3.00	16	0	0	1	0	0	18.0	16	6	6	4	0	5	0	12	0	0
Wright, Jamey	2	0	4.80	4	3	0	0	0	0	15.0	15	8	8	2	0	12	1	8	1	0
Pearce, Josh	0	0	7.62	3	3	0	0	0	0	13.0	20	13	11	1	1	8	0	1	0	0
Molina, Gabe	1	0	1.59	12	0	0	3	0	0	11.1	6	2	2	1	0	6	0	4	0	0
Joseph, Kevin	0	1	4.91	11	0	0	6	0	0	11.0	16	7	6	1	2	6	0	2	0	0
Duff, Matt	0	0	4.76	7	0	0	1	0	0	5.2	3	3	3	0	0	8	2	4	0	0
Rodriguez, Nerio	0	0	4.15	2	0	0	2	0	0	4.1	4	3	2	1	0	1	0	2	0	0
Rodriguez, Jose*	0	0	54.00	2	0	0	0	0	0	0.1	4	2	2	0	0	2	0	0	0	0

Pitchers with more than one N.L. team

Pitcher	W	L	ERA	G	GS	CG	GF	SHO	Sv.	IP	H	R	ER	HR	HB	BB	IBB	SO	WP	Bk.
Fassero, Chi.-St.L.*	8	6	5.35	73	0	0	18	0	0	69.0	81	43	41	9	3	27	5	56	2	1
Matthews, St.L.-Mil.*	2	1	3.94	47	0	0	10	0	0	45.2	43	23	20	5	2	29	3	34	5	1
Timlin, St.L.-Phi.	4	6	2.98	72	1	0	17	0	0	96.2	75	35	32	15	5	14	2	50	3	0
White, Col.-St.L.	5	7	4.31	61	0	0	10	0	0	62.2	62	33	30	4	1	21	5	41	3	0
Wright, Mil.-St.L.	7	13	5.29	23	22	1	0	1	0	129.1	130	80	76	17	11	75	9	77	9	0

* Throws lefthanded.

San Diego Padres

INDIVIDUAL STATISTICS

BATTING

Batter	Avg.	G	TPA	AB	R	H	TB	2B	3B	HR	RBI	SH	SF	HP	BB	IBB	SO	SB	CS	GDP	Slg.	OBP
Kotsay, Mark*	.292	153	646	578	82	169	261	27	7	17	61	2	4	3	59	0	89	11	9	10	.452	.359
Klesko, Ryan*	.300	146	625	540	90	162	290	39	1	29	95	1	4	4	76	11	86	6	2	7	.537	.388
Cruz, Deivi	.263	151	547	514	49	135	188	28	2	7	47	3	5	3	22	2	58	2	3	20	.366	.294
Vazquez, Ramon*	.274	128	474	423	50	116	153	21	5	2	32	3	2	1	45	3	79	7	2	6	.362	.344
Trammell, Bubba	.243	133	465	403	54	98	167	16	1	17	56	3	3	3	53	2	71	1	3	6	.414	.333
Nevin, Phil	.285	107	450	407	53	116	168	16	0	12	57	0	4	1	38	4	87	4	0	12	.413	.344
Jimenez, D'Angelo†	.240	87	357	321	39	77	105	11	4	3	33	0	2	0	34	1	63	4	2	10	.327	.311
Gant, Ron	.262	102	353	309	58	81	151	14	1	18	59	1	5	2	36	1	59	4	6	8	.489	.338
Lampkin, Tom*	.217	104	327	281	32	61	103	10	1	10	37	1	4	3	38	7	59	4	2	4	.367	.313
Kingsale, Gene†	.278	89	243	216	27	60	82	10	3	2	28	3	1	3	20	0	47	9	2	5	.380	.346
Lankford, Ray*	.224	81	240	205	20	46	73	7	1	6	26	1	2	2	30	3	61	2	2	3	.356	.326
Burroughs, Sean*	.271	63	206	192	18	52	62	5	1	1	11	1	0	1	12	1	30	2	0	6	.323	.317
Matos, Julius	.238	76	200	185	19	44	53	3	0	2	19	3	1	2	9	0	33	1	1	5	.286	.279
Gonzalez, Wiki	.220	56	194	164	16	36	49	8	1	1	20	0	2	1	27	3	24	0	0	10	.299	.330
Hubbard, Trenidad	.209	89	144	129	16	27	35	5	0	1	7	0	1	0	14	0	28	9	6	3	.271	.285
Buchanan, Brian	.293	48	102	92	12	27	50	5	0	6	13	0	0	1	9	0	26	0	1	2	.543	.363
Nieves, Wil	.181	28	76	72	2	13	18	3	1	0	3	0	0	0	4	4	15	1	0	1	.250	.224
Tomko, Brett	.182	30	74	66	2	12	14	2	0	0	6	7	0	0	1	0	20	0	0	2	.212	.194
Lawrence, Brian	.095	32	71	63	1	6	8	2	0	0	6	3	0	0	5	0	14	0	0	2	.127	.162
Sweeney, Mark*	.169	48	69	65	3	11	17	3	0	1	4	0	0	0	4	0	19	0	0	1	.262	.217
Cardona, Javier	.103	15	42	39	2	4	5	1	0	0	2	0	1	0	2	0	10	0	0	1	.128	.143
Peavy, Jake	.212	16	35	33	4	7	10	3	0	0	2	2	0	0	0	0	13	0	1	0	.303	.212
Jones, Bobby J.	.152	18	34	33	2	5	5	0	0	0	2	1	0	0	0	0	11	0	0	1	.152	.152
Crespo, Cesar†	.172	25	33	29	5	5	7	2	0	0	0	1	0	0	3	0	6	3	2	0	.241	.250
Perez, Oliver*	.133	16	33	30	1	4	4	0	0	0	0	3	0	0	0	0	11	0	0	0	.133	.133
Tollberg, Brian	.158	12	22	19	0	3	4	1	0	0	0	1	0	0	2	0	5	0	0	2	.211	.238
Barker, Kevin*	.158	7	20	19	0	3	3	0	0	0	0	0	0	0	1	0	6	1	0	1	.158	.200
Tankersley, Dennis	.308	16	13	13	2	4	8	1	0	1	1	0	0	0	0	0	2	0	0	1	.615	.308
Jarvis, Kevin*	.333	7	12	9	0	3	3	0	0	0	0	1	0	0	2	0	3	0	0	0	.333	.455
DeHaan, Kory*	.091	12	11	11	1	1	1	0	0	0	0	0	0	0	0	0	6	0	0	0	.091	.091
Eaton, Adam	.111	6	10	9	0	1	1	0	0	0	0	0	0	0	1	0	4	0	0	1	.111	.200
Bynum, Mike*	.000	14	8	8	0	0	0	0	0	0	0	0	0	0	0	0	3	0	0	0	.000	.000
Pelaez, Alex	.250	3	8	8	0	2	2	0	0	0	0	0	0	0	0	0	0	0	0	2	.250	.250
Middlebrook, Jason	.333	10	7	6	2	2	2	0	0	0	0	1	0	0	0	0	1	0	0	0	.333	.333
Condrey, Clay	.000	9	6	6	0	0	0	0	0	0	0	0	0	0	0	0	3	0	0	0	.000	.000
Howard, Ben	.000	3	5	4	0	0	0	0	0	0	0	1	0	0	0	0	2	0	0	0	.000	.000
Pickford, Kevin*	.000	15	5	5	0	0	0	0	0	0	0	0	0	0	0	0	3	0	0	0	.000	.000
Jones, Bobby M.	.000	4	3	2	0	0	0	0	0	0	0	1	0	0	0	0	1	0	0	0	.000	.000
Fikac, Jeremy	.000	61	2	2	0	0	0	0	0	0	0	0	0	0	0	0	1	0	0	0	.000	.000
Holtz, Mike*	.000	33	2	2	0	0	0	0	0	0	0	0	0	0	0	0	1	0	0	0	.000	.000
Cyr, Eric	.000	4	1	1	0	0	0	0	0	0	0	0	0	0	0	0	1	0	0	0	.000	.000
Kershner, Jason*	.000	15	1	0	0	0	0	0	0	0	0	1	0	0	0	0	0	0	0	0	.000	.000
Myers, Rodney	.000	11	1	1	0	0	0	0	0	0	0	0	0	0	0	0	0	0	0	0	.000	.000
Reed, Steve	.000	37	1	1	0	0	0	0	0	0	0	0	0	0	0	0	1	0	0	0	.000	.000

Batters with more than one N.L. team

Batter	Avg.	G	TPA	AB	R	H	TB	2B	3B	HR	RBI	SH	SF	HP	BB	IBB	SO	SB	CS	GDP	Slg.	OBP
Middlebrook, S.D.-N.Y.	.182	13	13	11	2	2	2	0	0	0	0	1	0	0	1	0	3	0	0	0	.182	.250
Reed, S.D.-N.Y.	.000	61	2	2	0	0	0	0	0	0	0	0	0	0	0	0	2	0	0	0	.000	.000

* Lefthanded batter. † Switch-hitter.

PITCHING

Pitcher	W	L	ERA	G	GS	CG	GF	SHO	Sv.	IP	H	R	ER	HR	HB	BB	IBB	SO	WP	Bk.
Lawrence, Brian	12	12	3.69	35	31	2	0	2	0	210.0	230	97	86	16	11	52	6	149	2	1
Tomko, Brett	10	10	4.49	32	32	3	0	0	0	204.1	212	107	102	31	2	60	9	126	3	0
Jones, Bobby J.	7	8	5.50	19	18	0	1	0	0	108.0	134	68	66	20	1	21	1	60	1	0
Peavy, Jake	6	7	4.52	17	17	0	0	0	0	97.2	106	54	49	11	3	33	4	90	4	1
Perez, Oliver*	4	5	3.50	16	15	0	0	0	0	90.0	71	37	35	13	5	48	1	94	3	0
Fikac, Jeremy	4	7	5.48	65	0	0	15	0	0	69.0	74	50	42	13	3	34	8	66	6	1
Tollberg, Brian	1	5	6.13	12	11	0	0	0	0	61.2	88	47	42	11	1	19	2	33	4	0
Hoffman, Trevor	2	5	2.73	61	0	0	52	0	38	59.1	52	20	18	2	1	18	2	69	3	0
Tankersley, Dennis	1	4	8.06	17	9	0	3	0	0	51.1	59	46	46	10	6	40	3	39	3	0
Reed, Steve	2	4	1.98	40	0	0	11	0	1	41.0	33	9	9	2	6	10	2	36	1	0
Middlebrook, Jason	1	3	5.09	12	2	0	5	0	0	35.1	31	20	20	1	1	15	2	28	2	0
Jarvis, Kevin	2	4	4.37	7	7	0	0	0	0	35.0	36	19	17	5	1	10	1	24	2	0
Eaton, Adam	1	1	5.40	6	6	0	0	0	0	33.1	28	20	20	5	2	17	0	25	2	0
Villafuerte, Brandon	1	2	1.41	31	0	0	11	0	1	32.0	29	5	5	2	2	12	2	25	0	0
Pickford, Kevin*	0	2	6.00	16	4	0	3	0	0	30.0	37	23	20	3	3	20	1	18	1	0
Embree, Alan*	3	4	0.94	36	0	0	13	0	0	28.2	23	7	3	2	0	9	2	38	1	0
Boyd, Jason	1	0	7.94	23	0	0	6	0	0	28.1	33	29	25	6	0	15	1	18	3	0
Bynum, Mike*	1	0	5.27	14	3	0	3	0	0	27.1	33	16	16	3	3	15	2	17	2	0
Condrey, Clay	1	2	1.69	9	3	0	2	0	0	26.2	20	7	5	1	2	8	1	16	1	1
Myers, Rodney	1	1	5.91	14	0	0	4	0	0	21.1	29	20	14	1	3	10	0	11	2	0
Davey, Tom	1	0	5.57	19	0	0	2	0	0	21.0	23	14	13	2	3	11	1	21	1	0
Holtz, Mike*	2	2	4.71	33	0	0	5	0	0	21.0	18	14	11	2	1	21	3	19	3	0
Kershner, Jason*	0	1	5.79	15	0	0	2	0	0	18.2	15	14	12	2	2	10	0	11	0	0
Johnson, Jonathan	1	2	4.11	16	0	0	5	0	0	15.1	15	8	7	2	1	5	1	21	0	0
Nickle, Doug	1	0	8.49	10	0	0	2	0	0	11.2	20	13	11	1	1	9	0	7	0	0
Howard, Ben	0	1	9.28	3	2	0	0	0	0	10.2	13	11	11	4	0	14	1	10	0	0
Jones, Bobby M.*	0	0	6.52	4	2	0	0	0	0	9.2	10	7	7	1	0	7	0	7	0	0
Walker, Kevin*	0	1	5.63	11	0	0	1	0	0	8.0	12	6	5	2	0	5	1	11	1	0
DeWitt, Matt	0	1	1.23	5	0	0	4	0	0	7.1	6	2	1	1	0	3	0	5	0	0
Cyr, Eric*	0	1	10.50	5	0	0	0	0	0	6.0	6	7	7	0	0	6	1	4	0	0
Moreno, Juan*	0	0	7.50	4	0	0	1	0	0	6.0	6	6	5	1	0	10	1	3	0	0
Lundquist, David	0	0	16.88	3	0	0	2	0	0	2.2	8	5	5	0	1	5	2	0	0	0
Trujillo, J.J.	0	1	10.13	4	0	0	1	0	0	2.2	4	3	3	1	1	6	0	3	0	0
Pearson, Jason*	0	0	0.00	2	0	0	1	0	0	1.2	1	0	0	0	0	0	0	3	0	0
Jimenez, D'Angelo	0	0	0.00	1	0	0	1	0	0	1.1	0	0	0	0	0	0	0	0	0	0
Shiell, Jason	0	0	27.00	3	0	0	0	0	0	1.1	7	4	4	0	0	3	0	1	0	0
Nunez, Jose Antonio*	0	0	0.00	1	0	0	1	0	0	1.0	0	0	0	0	0	1	0	0	0	0

Pitchers with more than one N.L. team

Pitcher	W	L	ERA	G	GS	CG	GF	SHO	Sv.	IP	H	R	ER	HR	HB	BB	IBB	SO	WP	Bk.
Jones, N.Y.-S.D.*	0	0	5.74	16	2	0	1	0	0	26.2	30	18	17	4	1	18	2	18	0	0
Middlebrook, S.D.-N.Y.	2	3	4.73	15	5	0	5	0	0	51.1	44	27	27	2	1	22	2	42	2	1
Nickle, Phi.-S.D.	1	0	7.88	14	0	0	6	0	0	16.0	26	16	14	3	1	13	0	9	0	0
Reed, S.D.-N.Y.	2	5	2.01	64	0	0	15	0	1	67.0	56	15	15	2	8	14	3	50	2	0

* Throws lefthanded.

San Francisco Giants

INDIVIDUAL STATISTICS

BATTING

Batter	Avg.	G	TPA	AB	R	H	TB	2B	3B	HR	RBI	SH	SF	HP	BB	IBB	SO	SB	CS	GDP	Slg.	OBP
Kent, Jeff	.313	152	682	623	102	195	352	42	2	37	108	0	3	4	52	3	101	5	1	20	.565	.368
Bell, David	.261	154	628	552	82	144	237	29	2	20	73	6	7	9	54	2	80	1	2	18	.429	.333
Bonds, Barry*	.370	143	612	403	117	149	322	31	2	46	110	0	2	9	198	68	47	9	2	4	.799	.582
Aurilia, Rich	.257	133	589	538	76	138	222	35	2	15	61	3	7	4	37	0	90	1	2	15	.413	.305
Sanders, Reggie	.250	140	571	505	75	126	230	23	6	23	85	0	7	12	47	3	121	18	6	10	.455	.324
Santiago, Benito	.278	126	517	478	56	133	215	24	5	16	74	3	7	2	27	8	73	4	2	19	.450	.315
Snow, J.T.*	.246	143	494	422	47	104	152	26	2	6	53	0	6	7	59	5	90	0	0	11	.360	.344
Shinjo, Tsuyoshi	.238	118	398	362	42	86	134	15	3	9	37	3	3	6	24	2	46	5	0	5	.370	.294
Lofton, Kenny*	.267	46	205	180	30	48	73	10	3	3	9	1	0	1	23	0	22	7	3	1	.406	.353
Minor, Damon*	.237	83	201	173	21	41	77	6	0	10	24	0	2	2	24	6	34	0	0	8	.445	.333
Martinez, Ramon E.	.271	72	200	181	26	49	75	10	2	4	25	0	1	4	14	2	26	2	0	1	.414	.335
Goodwin, Tom*	.260	78	171	154	23	40	52	5	2	1	17	3	0	0	14	0	25	16	2	3	.338	.321
Torrealba, Yorvit	.279	53	155	136	17	38	54	10	0	2	14	3	0	2	14	2	20	0	0	11	.397	.355
Dunston, Shawon	.231	72	153	147	7	34	42	5	0	1	9	1	1	1	3	0	33	1	0	0	.286	.250
Feliz, Pedro	.253	67	153	146	14	37	49	4	1	2	13	0	1	0	6	1	27	0	0	2	.336	.281
Benard, Marvin*	.276	65	131	123	16	34	50	9	2	1	13	0	0	1	7	0	26	5	1	3	.407	.321
Ortiz, Russ	.246	31	84	69	11	17	28	5	0	2	9	7	2	0	6	0	17	0	0	1	.406	.299
Rueter, Kirk*	.177	34	79	62	3	11	11	0	0	0	3	13	2	0	2	0	11	0	0	0	.177	.197
Hernandez, Livan	.234	33	75	64	6	15	21	4	1	0	6	10	1	0	0	0	9	0	0	3	.328	.231
Jensen, Ryan	.107	31	66	56	5	6	8	2	0	0	2	9	0	1	0	0	18	0	0	0	.143	.123
Schmidt, Jason	.125	27	62	56	3	7	9	2	0	0	2	4	0	0	2	0	28	0	0	0	.161	.155
Mueller, Bill†	.154	8	14	13	0	2	2	0	0	0	1	0	0	0	1	0	1	0	0	1	.154	.214
Murray, Calvin	.000	11	13	12	0	0	0	0	0	0	0	0	0	0	1	0	2	0	0	0	.000	.077
Torcato, Tony*	.273	5	11	11	0	3	4	1	0	0	0	0	0	0	0	0	2	0	0	0	.364	.273
Ainsworth, Kurt	.167	6	7	6	1	1	2	1	0	0	0	1	0	0	0	0	1	0	0	0	.333	.167
Zerbe, Chad*	.167	47	7	6	0	1	1	0	0	0	1	1	0	0	0	0	2	0	0	0	.167	.167
Witasick, Jay	.000	42	5	5	0	0	0	0	0	0	0	0	0	0	0	0	4	0	0	0	.000	.000
Ransom, Cody	.667	7	4	3	2	2	2	0	0	0	1	0	0	0	1	1	1	0	0	0	.667	.750
Lunsford, Trey	.667	3	3	3	0	2	3	1	0	0	1	0	0	0	0	0	1	0	0	0	1.000	.667
Worrell, Tim	.000	77	3	3	0	0	0	0	0	0	0	0	0	0	0	0	2	0	0	0	.000	.000
Nen, Robb	.500	64	2	2	0	1	1	0	0	0	0	0	0	0	0	0	1	0	0	0	.500	.500
Aybar, Manny	.000	15	1	1	0	0	0	0	0	0	0	0	0	0	0	0	0	0	0	0	.000	.000
Fultz, Aaron*	.000	42	1	1	0	0	0	0	0	0	0	0	0	0	0	0	0	0	0	0	.000	.000
Rodriguez, Felix	1.000	66	1	1	1	1	1	0	0	0	0	0	0	0	0	0	0	0	0	0	1.000	1.000

Batters with more than one N.L. team

Batter	Avg.	G	TPA	AB	R	H	TB	2B	3B	HR	RBI	SH	SF	HP	BB	IBB	SO	SB	CS	GDP	Slg.	OBP
Mueller, Chi.-S.F.†	.262	111	427	366	51	96	144	19	4	7	38	4	5	0	52	2	42	0	0	9	.393	.350

* Lefthanded batter. † Switch-hitter.

PITCHING

Pitcher	W	L	ERA	G	GS	CG	GF	SHO	Sv.	IP	H	R	ER	HR	HB	BB	IBB	SO	WP	Bk.
Hernandez, Livan	12	16	4.38	33	33	5	0	3	0	216.0	233	113	105	19	4	71	5	134	1	1
Ortiz, Russ	14	10	3.61	33	33	2	0	0	0	214.1	191	89	86	15	4	94	5	137	5	0
Rueter, Kirk*	14	8	3.23	33	33	0	0	0	0	203.2	204	83	73	22	1	54	7	76	3	0
Schmidt, Jason	13	8	3.45	29	29	2	0	2	0	185.1	148	78	71	15	2	73	1	196	12	0
Jensen, Ryan	13	8	4.51	32	30	1	0	0	0	171.2	183	93	86	21	5	66	4	105	3	0
Nen, Robb	6	2	2.20	68	0	0	66	0	43	73.2	64	19	18	2	1	20	8	81	1	0
Worrell, Tim	8	2	2.25	80	0	0	23	0	0	72.0	55	21	18	3	0	30	2	55	0	0
Rodriguez, Felix	8	6	4.17	71	0	0	12	0	0	69.0	53	33	32	5	4	29	1	58	4	0
Witasick, Jay	1	0	2.37	44	0	0	9	0	0	68.1	58	19	18	3	4	21	3	54	3	0
Zerbe, Chad*	2	0	3.04	50	0	0	16	0	0	56.1	52	22	19	3	4	21	2	26	1	0
Fultz, Aaron*	2	2	4.79	43	0	0	12	0	0	41.1	47	22	22	4	3	19	3	31	1	0
Ainsworth, Kurt	1	2	2.10	6	4	0	0	0	0	25.2	22	7	6	1	1	12	0	15	1	0
Aybar, Manny	1	0	2.51	15	0	0	4	0	0	14.1	16	6	4	1	1	3	2	11	0	1
Eyre, Scott*	0	0	1.59	21	0	0	3	0	0	11.1	11	4	2	0	0	7	1	7	1	0
Brohawn, Troy*	0	1	6.35	11	0	0	2	0	0	5.2	5	4	4	1	2	1	0	3	0	0
Christiansen, Jason*	0	1	5.40	6	0	0	2	0	0	5.0	6	3	3	1	0	2	0	1	0	0
Nathan, Joe	0	0	0.00	4	0	0	3	0	0	3.2	1	0	0	0	0	0	0	2	0	0

* Throws lefthanded.

TRANSACTIONS

JANUARY 1, 2002–DECEMBER 31, 2002

January 2

Athletics signed LHP Mike Holtz.
Blue Jays acquired C Tom Wilson from Athletics for C Mike Kremblas.
Cubs signed INF Chris Stynes.
Pirates signed RHP Mike Williams.
Padres organization signed C Matt Walbeck.

January 4

Yankees claimed RHP Brett Jodie off waivers from Padres.
Brewers claimed RHP George Perez off waivers from Blue Jays.

January 5

Giants signed OF Reggie Sanders.

January 11

Athletics signed INF Randy Velarde.
Mariners signed RHP Shigetoshi Hasegawa.
Diamondbacks organization signed INF-OF Chris Donnels.
Reds organization signed RHP Jimmy Haynes and LHP Brian Bohanon.
Rockies signed RHP Todd Jones.
Expos organization signed RHP Dan Smith.
Giants signed INF Desi Relaford.

January 12

Blue Jays organization signed INF Dave Berg.

January 14

Twins organization signed INF Kurt Abbott.
Athletics acquired 1B Carlos Pena and LHP Mike Venafro from Rangers for 1B Jason Hart, LHP Mario Ramos, C Gerald Laird and OF Ryan Ludwick.
Rangers organization signed RHP Steve Woodard.
Cubs signed OF Darren Lewis.
Phillies organization signed LHP Pete Schourek.

January 15

Twins organization signed RHP Brian Meadows.
Braves acquired OF Gary Sheffield from **Dodgers** for OF Brian Jordan, LHP Odalis Perez and RHP Andrew Brown.
Rockies organization signed C Carlos Hernandez, RHP Chris Holt and OF Cliff Brumbaugh.
Mets organization signed OF Darren Bragg.
Phillies signed RHP Terry Adams.

January 16

Red Sox signed C Doug Mirabelli.
Cubs organization signed RHP Alan Benes.
Brewers signed 2B Eric Young.
Pirates organization signed RHP Scott Service, SS Luis Garcia, LHP Sean Fesh, 1B Dave Post, 2B Randy Meadows and 2B Victor Rodriguez.
Giants organization signed C Scott Servais.

January 17

White Sox claimed LHP Thomas Jacquez off waivers from Phillies.
Yankees signed INF Enrique Wilson. Released INF-OF Clay Bellinger.
Rangers organization signed OF Patrick Boyd.
Blue Jays acquired RHP Brian Cooper from Angels for 1B-DH Brad Fullmer.
Astros organization signed RHP Jamie Arnold, RHP Mark Guerra, RHP Peter Munro, LHP Jason Jacome, C Frank Charles, C Chris Tremie, C Alan Zinter, INF Tripp Cromer, OF Chris Prieto and OF Scott Pose.

January 18

Braves acquired RHP Kevin Gryboski from Mariners for RHP Elvis Perez.
Padres organization signed OF Ron Gant.
Giants signed RHP Jay Witasick.

January 20

Diamondbacks organization signed RHP Rick Helling.

January 21

Mets acquired RHP Jeff D'Amico, OF Jeromy Burnitz, INF Lou Collier, INF Mark Sweeney and cash from Brewers, and INF-OF Ross Gload and RHP Craig House from Rockies. Sent LHP Glendon Rusch to Brewers, and INF Todd Zeile, OF Benny Agbayani, INF Lenny Harris and cash to Rockies. Brewers also received OF Alex Ochoa from Rockies. Mets organization signed OF Tony Tarasco.

January 23

Twins organization signed RHP Mike Jackson.
Padres organization signed RHP Steve Reed.

January 24

Tigers claimed INF Oscar Salazar off waivers from Athletics.
Devil Rays organization signed LHP Stevenson Agosto, RHP Carlos Chantres, RHP Luis De Los Santos, RHP Jason Dickson, C Kevin Brown, INF Kevin Sefcik and OF Ryan Freel.

January 25

Yankees organization signed INF Ron Coomer.
Mariners traded 3B David Bell to Giants for INF Desi Relaford and cash.
Brewers signed OF Matt Stairs.

January 26

Mets traded OF-1B Ross Gload to **Rockies** for cash.

January 28

Tigers organization signed RHP Bill Simas.
Devil Rays organization signed LHP Tom Martin, RHP Randy Galvez, C Sal Fasano, C Yamid Haad, INF Andy Sheets and OF Emil Brown.
Rangers signed RHP Ismael Valdes and RHP Rudy Seanez.
Braves organization signed RHP Darren Holmes.
Phillies organization signed OF John Mabry.

January 29

White Sox acquired 2B-OF Willie Harris from Orioles for OF Chris Singleton.
Twins organization signed RHP Dave Lee.
Yankees organization signed RHP Mike Thurman.
Devil Rays organization signed OF Troy O'Leary.
Rangers organization signed RHP Dan Miceli.
Brewers signed LHP Takaki Nomura.
Phillies signed OF Ricky Ledee.

January 30

Mariners signed RHP James Baldwin.
Cubs organization signed RHP Pat Mahomes.
Reds signed RHP Ricardo Aramboles.
Rockies organization signed RHP Mike James.
Dodgers organization signed OF Dante Bichette.
Mets organization signed INF John Valentin.
Pirates signed 2B Pokey Reese.
Padres signed INF Deivi Cruz.

January 31

Angels organization signed INF-OF Clay Bellinger and RHP Donne Wall.
Indians organization signed INF Mike Lansing.
Rockies organization signed LHP Kent Mercker and RHP Bobby Chouinard.

February 1

White Sox signed OF Kenny Lofton.
Indians organization signed OF Bruce Aven and OF Brooks Kieschnick.
Tigers claimed OF Craig Monroe off waivers from Rangers.
Yankees organization signed C Chris Widger.
Athletics claimed RHP Allen Levrault off waivers from Brewers.
Braves organization signed LHP Rich Rodriguez.
Mets claimed OF Endy Chavez off waivers from Tigers.

February 2

Rangers organization signed C Pat Borders.

February 4

Orioles organization signed INF Howie Clark, RHP Travis Driskill, LHP Eric DuBose, OF Luis Garcia, C Mike Hubbard, RHP Rodrigo Lopez, RHP Lee Marshall, 1B Domingo Martinez, OF-1B Ryan McGuire, C Izzy Molina, INF Mike Moriarty and LHP Sean Runyan.
Red Sox organization signed INF Quilvio Veras, OF Jeff Abbott and C Henry Mercedes.
Devil Rays signed LHP Doug Creek.

February 5

Indians organization signed RHP Omar Olivares.
Rangers signed OF Juan Gonzalez.
Cubs organization signed LHP Donovan Osborne.
Dodgers claimed RHP Craig House off waivers from Mets.
Padres organization signed RHP Brad Clontz.
Giants signed RHP Manny Aybar.

February 6

Astros organization signed LHP Chuck McElroy.

February 8

Mariners released LHP Norm Charlton.
Brewers organization signed OF Midre Cummings and INF Izzy Alcantara.
Pirates organization signed RHP Pat Rapp.
Cardinals organization signed OF Al Martin and OF Eduardo Perez.

February 10

Indians organization signed RHP Jose Mercedes.

February 11

Rangers organization signed INF Ed Sprague.
Astros signed RHP Hipolito Pichardo.

February 12

Rockies signed RHP Pete Harnisch.
Dodgers signed RHP Tim Crabtree.
Pirates organization signed LHP Ron Villone.

February 13

Red Sox organization signed OF Rickey Henderson.
Rangers released RHP Mark Petkovsek.
Giants announced retirement of RHP Mark Gardner.

February 14

Yankees signed OF Ruben Rivera.
Brewers signed RHP J.M. Gold.

February 15

Red Sox organization signed SS Gary DiSarcina.
Dodgers organization signed P Shigeki Sano.

February 18

Marlins organization signed OF Tim Raines Sr. and OF Mark Smith.

February 19

Yankees organization signed C Jim Leyritz.
Brewers organization signed RHP Francisco Campos.
Expos organization signed OF Jose Canseco and LHP Ed Vosberg.

February 20

Red Sox organization signed 3B Andy Morales.

February 21

Yankees organization signed LHP Allen Watson.
Mets traded RHP Corey Brittan to Rockies for RHP Kane Davis.

February 22

Expos organization signed OF Lance Johnson and RHP Osvaldo Fernandez to minor league contracts. Expos claimed OF Endy Chavez off waivers from Mets.

February 23

Padres organization signed OF Trenidad Hubbard.

February 27

Red Sox organization signed INF Rey Sanchez.
Pirates organization signed RHP Josias Manzanillo.

March 5

Indians released C Tim Laker and signed him to a minor league contract.
Reds released RHP Arnie Gooch.

March 7

Expos organization signed RHP Alan Mills. Agreed to terms with 1B Andres Galarraga.

March 9

Royals released LHP Jose Rosado.

March 11

White Sox released OF Julio Ramirez.
Yankees released OF Ruben Rivera.

March 12

Astros released LHP Chuck McElroy. Acquired INF Geoff Blum from Expos for 3B Chris Truby.

March 13

Yankees released INF Manny Alexander and LHP Eric Gunderson.
Mets released OF Mark Sweeney and OF Danny Peoples.
Pirates released RHP Gregg Olson and 2B Warren Morris.

March 15

Twins organization signed 2B Warren Morris.
Yankees released LHP Allen Watson.

March 17

Yankees released C Jim Leyritz.
Dodgers released OF Roberto Kelly.
Padres organization signed INF-OF Mark Sweeney.

March 18

Athletics traded RHP Luis Vizcaino to Rangers for RHP Justin Duchscherer.
Devil Rays claimed RHP Jorge Sosa off waivers from Brewers.

March 19

Yankees released SS Kevin Elster.

March 20

Braves acquired C Henry Blanco from Brewers for C Paul Bako and RHP Jose Cabrera.

March 21

Indians acquired C Eddie Perez from Braves for a player to be named.

March 23

Tigers traded C Javier Cardona and OF Rich Gomez to Padres for INF Damian Jackson and C Matt Walbeck.
Athletics announced INF-OF Jason Grabowski refused outright assignment to Sacremento and elected free agency.
Rangers traded RHP Luis Vizcaino to Brewers for LHP Jesus Pena.
Rockies released C Tony Eusebio.
Dodgers announced retirement of OF Dante Bichette.
Expos traded RHP Guillermo Mota and OF Wilkin Ruan to Dodgers for RHP Matt Herges and INF Jorge Nunez.
Phillies sold contract of OF Felipe Crespo to Yomiuri of Japanese Central League.

March 25

White Sox waived OF Brian Simmons.
Devil Rays released OF Troy O'Leary.
Rangers acquired LHP Rich Rodriguez from Braves for a player to be named.
Rockies traded RHP Jose Paniagua to Tigers for RHP Victor Santos and INF Ronnie Merrill. Acquired RHP Chuck Smith from Marlins for a player to be named.
Astros released LHP C.J. Nitkowski.
Padres returned RHP Ryan Baerlocher to Royals per major league Rule 5 guidelines.

March 26

Indians waived LHP Scott Radinsky.
Yankees released C Todd Greene.
Devil Rays released INF Felix Martinez.
Mets traded INF Lou Collier to **Expos** for RHP Jimmy Serrano and OF Jason Bay.

March 27

Orioles organization signed LHP Yorkis Perez.
White Sox acquired LHP Damaso Marte and INF Edwin Yan from Pirates for RHP Matt Guerrier.
Indians waived OF Karim Garcia.
Royals organization signed LHP Jose Rosado.
Devil Rays claimed INF Felix Escalona off waivers from Giants.
Diamondbacks released LHP Troy Brohawn and LHP Yorkis Perez.
Cubs acquired RHP Antonio Alfonseca and RHP Matt Clement from Marlins for RHP Julian Tavarez, RHP Jose Cueto, LHP Dontrelle Willis and C Ryan Jorgensen.
Rockies released C Carlos Hernandez.
Expos released OF Jose Canseco.
Mets claimed OF Chris Latham off waivers from Blue Jays and 1B Andy Tracy off waivers from Expos.
Phillies released LHP Pete Schourek.

March 28

Indians traded OF Donzell McDonald to Royals for a player to be named. Released RHP J.D. Brammer.
Astros organization signed LHP C.J. Nitkowski.
Expos organization signed OF Troy O'Leary and OF Henry Rodriguez to minor league contracts. Expos released OF Lance Johnson.
Phillies traded OF Reggie Taylor to Reds for a player to be named.

March 29

Royals released RHP Doug Henry.
Phillies released INF Kevin Jordan.

March 30

Rangers organization signed OF Ruben Rivera.
Marlins claimed SS Wilson Valdez off waivers from Expos.
Phillies acquired LHP Hector Mercado from Reds to complete an earlier trade.
Pirates released OF Derek Bell.

April 2

Dodgers organization signed C Todd Greene, INF Felix Martinez and OF Scott Pose.

April 3

Reds released OF Jermaine Allensworth. Organization signed INF Kevin Jordan.
Brewers claimed RHP Nelson Figueroa off waivers from Phillies.
Mets traded OF Gary Matthews Jr. to Orioles for LHP John Bale. Claimed OF McKay Christensen off waivers from Dodgers.
Padres acquired LHP Juan Moreno from Rangers for SS Jason Moore.

April 4

Indians acquired OF Chris Magruder from Rangers for OF Rashad Eldridge. Traded RHP Jeff D'Amico to Phillies for a player to be named.
Cubs claimed OF Mario Encarnacion off waivers from Rockies.

April 5

Mets acquired RHP Scott Strickland, OF Matt Watson and LHP Philip Seibel from Expos for LHP Bruce Chen, RHP Dicky Gonzalez, INF Luis Figueroa and a player to be named. Claimed INF Marcos Scutaro off waivers from Brewers.

April 8

Mariners organization signed C Pat Borders.
Dodgers waived OF Tom Goodwin and RHP Mike Trombley.

April 13

Indians released RHP Omar Olivares.
Cubs organization signed OF Bernard Gilkey. Cubs acquired RHP Marc Deschenes from Pirates for future considerations.

April 15

Twins organization signed RHP Mike Trombley.
Pirates claimed INF Tomas De La Rosa off waivers from Expos.

April 16

Pirates organization signed INF Kevin Sefcik.

April 17

Yankees organization signed LHP Bill Pulsipher.

April 18

White Sox organization signed OF Jose Canseco.

April 22

Rangers acquired OF Calvin Murray from Giants for cash.

April 23

Padres acquired LHP Andrew Hazlett from Red Sox for LHP Juan Moreno.

April 26

Rangers purchased contract of C Hector Ortiz from Royals.

April 29

Indians released OF-1B Wil Cordero.

May 3

Blue Jays claimed RHP Pete Walker off waivers from Mets.

May 6

Rangers released RHP Dan Miceli.

May 7

Diamondbacks organization signed INF Hanley Frias.

May 8

Devil Rays released INF Bobby Smith.

May 10

Blue Jays released 2B Homer Bush.

May 12

Expos signed OF Wil Cordero.

May 13

White Sox announced retirement of OF Jose Canseco.

May 15

Blue Jays traded LHP Pedro Borbon to Astros for a player to be named.

May 16

White Sox organization signed OF Damon Buford and OF Brooks Kieschnick.
Tigers acquired 3B Chris Truby from Expos for INF-OF Jose Macias.

May 17

Rockies traded RHP Eduardo Villacis to Royals for RHP Bryan Rekar.

May 21

Indians released OF Brady Anderson.

May 22

Athletics traded OF Jeremy Giambi to Phillies for INF-OF John Mabry.

May 23

Mariners claimed INF-OF Nate Rolison off waivers from Marlins. Released RHP Greg Wooten.

May 26

Blue Jays traded LHP Dan Plesac to Phillies for RHP Cliff Politte.

June 3

Rangers released RHP Steve Woodard.

June 4

Phillies organization signed RHP Steve Woodard.

June 6

Cardinals organization signed LHP C.J. Nitkowski and C Alex Andreopoulos.

June 7

Indians traded INF Russell Branyan to Reds for 1B Ben Broussard.

June 9

Cubs traded C Robert Machado to Brewers for OF Jackson Melian.

June 10

Giants claimed LHP Jason Pearson off waivers from Padres.

June 11

Twins traded 2B Warren Morris to Cardinals for a player to be named.

June 12

Yankees claimed RHP Nate Field off waivers from Royals.
Cardinals organization signed OF Gerald Williams.

June 14

Angels released RHP Donne Wall.
Expos organization signed RHP Mike Buddie.
Padres claimed OF Eugene Kingsale off waivers from Mariners.

June 19

Braves traded OF George Lombard to Tigers for RHP Kris Keller.

June 20

Twins acquired SS Seth Davidson from Cardinals to complete an earlier trade.

June 21

Rockies organization signed RHP Donne Wall.

June 25

Indians traded OF Bruce Aven to Phillies for RHP Jeff D'Amico.
Marlins traded OF Brett Roneberg to Expos for RHP Donnie Bridges.

June 26

Twins released LHP Travis Miller unconditionally.

June 27

Indians traded RHP Bartolo Colon and future considerations to Expos for 1B Lee Stevens, SS Brandon Phillips, LHP Cliff Lee and OF Grady Sizemore. Released RHP Martin Vargas.

June 28

Indians sent RHP Tim Drew to Expos to complete a previous trade.

June 30

Cubs organization signed LHP Travis Miller.

July 1

Yankees acquired OF Raul Mondesi from Blue Jays for LHP Scott Wiggins.

July 2

Red Sox waived LHP Darren Oliver.

July 4

Royals organization signed RHP Edwin Hurtado.

July 5

Yankees acquired RHP Jeff Weaver from Tigers. Sent LHP Ted Lilly, OF John-Ford Griffin and RHP Jason Arnold to Athletics.
Athletics sent 1B Carlos Pena, RHP Franklyn German and a player to be named to Tigers.

July 8

Rangers claimed INF Donnie Sadler off waivers from Royals.

July 11

Marlins traded OF Cliff Floyd and RHP Claudio Vargas to Expos for RHP Carl Pavano, LHP Graeme Lloyd and two minor league players. Traded RHP Ryan Dempster to Reds for OF Juan Encarnacion.

July 12

White Sox acquired INF D'Angelo Jimenez from Padres for OF Alex Fernandez and C Humberto Quintero.
Indians traded INF Anthony Medrano to Expos for 1B Nick Dempsey and traded RHP Jeff D'Amico to Reds for a player to be named. Organization signed RHP Jason Rakers.
Twins traded RF Brian Buchanan to Padres for SS Jason Bartlett.
Reds acquired OF Gerald Williams from Cardinals.

July 13

Padres released OF Mark Sweeney and RHP Dave Lundquist.

July 18

Yankees organization signed RHP Jason Rakers and RHP Ryan Bradley.
Rockies claimed LHP Randy Flores on waivers from Rangers and released RHP Chuck Smith.
Mets claimed RHP Ryan Jamison off waivers from Astros.

July 19

Cardinals acquired LHP Chuck Finley from Indians for 1B Luis Garcia and a player to be named.

July 22

Dodgers acquired INF-OF Jolbert Cabrera from Indians for LHP Lance Caraccioli.

July 23

Reds acquired RHP Brian Moehler and INF Matt Boone from Tigers for INF David Espinosa and two players to be named.
Brewers traded INF Tyler Houston and a player to be named to Dodgers for RHP Ben Diggins and LHP Shane Nance.

July 24

Mariners acquired LHP Doug Creek from Devil Rays for cash.

July 25

Tigers acquired INF Hiram Bocachica from Dodgers for RHP Tom Farmer and a player to be named.
Athletics acquired 2B Ray Durham from White Sox for RHP Jon Adkins.

July 26

Blue Jays announced retirement of C Darrin Fletcher.

July 28

Indians traded RHP Paul Shuey to Dodgers for LHP Terry Mulholland, RHP Ricardo Rodriguez and RHP Francisco Cruceta.
Astros released RHP T.J. Mathews.
Giants traded RHP Felix Diaz and LHP Ryan Meaux to White Sox for OF Kenny Lofton.

July 29

White Sox traded C Sandy Alomar Jr. to Rockies for RHP Enemencio Pacheco.
Rangers released RHP Dave Burba and organization signed LHP C.J. Nitkowski.
Phillies traded 3B Scott Rolen, RHP Doug Nickle and cash to Cardinals for INF Placido Polanco, LHP Bud Smith and RHP Mike Timlin.

July 30

Red Sox acquired OF Cliff Floyd from Expos for RHP Seung Jun Song, RHP Sun Woo Kim and a player to be named.
Athletics acquired LHP Ricardo Rincon from Indians for INF Marshall McDougall.

July 31

White Sox traded RHP Bob Howry and cash to Red Sox for RHP Franklin Francisco and LHP Byeong An.
Rockies traded OF Todd Hollandsworth and LHP Dennys Reyes to Rangers for OF Gabe Kapler and 2B-OF Jason Romano.
Brewers traded OF Alex Ochoa and C Sal Fasano to Angels for C Jorge Fabregas and two players to be named.
Mets traded OF Jay Payton, RHP Mark Corey and OF Robert Stratton to Rockies for RHP John Thomson and OF Mark Little. Claimed INF Oscar Salazar off waivers from Tigers.
Pirates traded OF Chad Hermansen to Cubs for OF Darren Lewis.
Padres traded RHP Steve Reed and RHP Jason Middlebrook to Mets for LHP Bobby Jones, RHP Josh Reynolds and OF Jay Bay.

August 2

Athletics released LHP Mike Magnante.
Cubs acquired OF Aron Weston from Pirates for LHP Ricardo Palma, LHP Tim Lavery and cash.

August 5

Marlins acquired RHP Don Levinski from Expos to complete an earler trade.

August 6

Indians acquired OF Covelli Crisp from Cardinals to complete July 19 trade for LHP Chuck Finley.

August 7

Indians organization signed RHP Dave Burba and LHP Travis Miller.

August 8

Mariners acquired INF Jose Offerman from Red Sox for cash.
Giants claimed LHP Scott Eyre off waivers from Blue Jays.

August 9

Cubs waived INF Delino DeShields.

August 12

Rockies claimed LHP Brian Fitzgerald off waivers from Mariners.

August 14

Angels sent INF Johnny Raburn to Brewers to complete July 31 trade for OF Alex Ochoa.
Pirates released RHP Josias Manzanillo.

August 15

Reds acquired LHP Shawn Estes and cash from Mets for LHP Pedro Feliciano, OF Elvin Andujar and two players to be named.

August 16

Tigers claimed RHP Jason Beverlin off waivers from Indians and optioned him to Toledo (IL).
Diamondbacks acquired OF Mark Little from Mets for a player to be named.
Dodgers organization signed LHP Mike Magnante.

August 18

Mariners acquired RHP Ismael Valdes from Rangers for INF Jermaine Clark and LHP Derrick Van Dusen.
Cardinals signed RHP Rick White.

August 20

Reds traded OF Raul Gonzalez to the Mets to complete an earlier trade. Organization signed OF Jose Guillen.
Mets acquired RHP P.J. Bevis from Diamondbacks to complete an earlier trade.

August 22

Athletics sent RHP Jeremy Bonderman to Tigers to complete an earlier trade.
Cubs traded RHP Tom Gordon to Astros for LHP Russ Rohlicek and two players to be named.

August 23

Padres claimed RHP Carlos Garcia off waivers from Dodgers.

August 25

Cardinals acquired LHP Jeff Fassero from Cubs for two minor leaguers to be named and cash.

August 28

Indians announced retirement of 3B Travis Fryman at the end of the season.
Padres claimed RHP Doug Nickle off waivers from Cardinals.

August 29

Brewers traded RHP Jamey Wright and cash to Cardinals for OF Chris Morris and a player to be named.

August 30

Tigers acquired OF Gary Varner from Reds to partially complete an earlier trade.
Blue Jays claimed LHP Jason Kershner off waivers from Padres.

September 1

Marlins released INF Homer Bush.
Brewers traded INF Mark Loretta and cash to Astros for two players to be named.
Padres released LHP Bobby M. Jones.

September 3

Astros sent LHP Wayne Franklin to Brewers as one of two players to be named in the trade for INF Mark Loretta.
Giants acquired INF Bill Mueller and cash considerations from Cubs for RHP Jeff Verplancke.

September 4

Diamondbacks acquired contract of OF Felix Jose from Mexico City Reds of the Mexican League.

September 5

Astros sent INF Keith Ginter to Brewers to complete an earlier trade.

September 7

White Sox released SS Royce Clayton.
Tigers released RHP Jose Lima and RHP Jose Paniagua.
Pirates released RHP Sean Lowe.

September 9

Mets acquired OF Brady Clark from Reds to complete an earlier trade.

September 11

Cubs acquired RHP Travis Anderson and RHP Mike Nannini from Astros to complete an earlier trade.

September 18

Tigers sent RHP Jason Frasor to Dodgers to complete an earlier trade.

September 19

Indians traded OF Jason Fitzgerald to Braves to complete an earlier trade.

September 20

Angels sent RHP Pedro Liriano to Brewers to complete an earlier trade.

September 21

Devil Rays released OF Toe Nash.

September 24

Tigers claimed LHP Jason Jimenez off waivers from Devil Rays.
Cardinals sent RHP Jason Karnuth and RHP Jared Blasdell to Cubs to complete an earlier trade.
Reds sent RHP Jorge Cordova to Tigers to complete an earlier trade.

September 29

Marlins announced retirement of OF Tim Raines Sr.

September 30

Devil Rays released LHP Wilson Alvarez, SS Chris Gomez and LHP Tom Martin.
Rangers granted free agency to OF Ruben Rivera, INF Donnie Sadler and LHP C.J. Nitkowski after they refused outright assignments to Oklahoma (PCL).

October 1

Orioles released RHP Chris Brock, LHP Yorkis Perez, INF Luis Lopez and C Raul Casanova.
Cubs released LHP Jesus Sanchez.

October 2

Red Sox claimed RHP Jason Shiell off waivers from Padres.
Indians released LHP Heath Murray.
Reds released RHP Jose Silva.
Mets claimed RHP Doug Nickle off waivers from Padres.
Padres released LHP Mike Holtz and RHP Matt DeWitt.

October 3

Rangers released LHP John Rocker.
Marlins released RHP Hansel Izquierdo and LHP Benito Baez.

October 7

Orioles released RHP Calvin Maduro.

October 9

Red Sox claimed RHP Brandon Lyon off waivers from Blue Jays.

October 10

Expos released INF-OF Wilton Guerrero.
Mets claimed RHP Joe Orloski off waivers from Blue Jays and RHP Franklin Nunez from Phillies.
Pirates released OF Adrian Brown. Claimed RHP Jim Mann off waivers from Astros.

October 11

Tigers claimed LHP Pedro Feliciano off waivers from Mets.

October 13

Brewers claimed OF Scott Podsednik off waivers from Mariners.

October 16

Dodgers acquired RHP Brian Mallette from Brewers to complete an earlier trade.

October 17

Red Sox organization signed RHP Hansel Izquierdo.
Indians claimed RHP Jack Cressend off waivers from Twins.

October 28

Mariners acquired OF Randy Winn from Devil Rays for INF Antonio Perez as compensation for losing Lou Piniella as manager.

October 29

Blue Jays signed LHP Doug Creek.

October 30

Blue Jays organization signed RHP Doug Linton and LHP Trever Miller.
Cubs organization signed LHP Mike Sirotka.

November 1

Twins released INF David Lamb.
Blue Jays signed RHP Jeff Tam. Organization signed RHP Evan Thomas, LHP Tim Young and INF Mike Moriarty.
Astros organization signed RHP Chris Gissell, RHP Jonathan Johnson, RHP Miguel Saladin and LHP Ken Vining.

November 3

Indians signed RHP Jose Santiago.

November 4

Dodgers organization signed RHP Luke Prokopec.

November 5

Angels released C Sal Fasano.
Red Sox signed LHP Alan Embree.
Blue Jays organization signed INF Howie Clark and OF Rob Ryan.

November 6

Angels released OF Julio Ramirez.
Devil Rays organization signed OF Adrian Brown, OF Chad Mottola, INF Jay Canizaro, RHP Mike James and LHP Matt Perisho.

November 8

Blue Jays organization signed OF Bruce Aven and RHP Josh Towers.

November 13

Athletics acquired RHP Roy Smith from Indians for cash.
Rangers waived RHP Hideki Irabu. Organization signed RHP Robert Ellis, RHP Rosman Garcia, RHP Victor Santos, LHP Ron Mahay, LHP Brian Shouse, C Danny Ardoin, C Fernando Lunar, INF Donnie Sadler and OF Rontrez Johnson.
Cubs acquired C Damian Miller from Diamondbacks for LHP David Noyce and OF Gary Johnson.
Phillies organization signed INF Mike Coolbaugh.

November 15

Twins traded RHP Matt Kinney and C Javier Valentin to Brewers for RHP Matt Yeatman and RHP Gerard Oakes.
Rangers organization signed LHP C.J. Nitkowski and LHP Ray Beasley.
Padres traded OF Gene Kingsale to Tigers for C Michael Rivera.
Giants waived OF Tsuyoshi Shinjo.

November 17

Athletics traded RHP Cory Lidle to Blue Jays for INF Michael Rouse and RHP Christopher Mowday.

November 18

Tigers organization signed C Matt Walbeck.
Royals waived SS Neifi Perez.
Athletics organization signed RHP Jose Silva, C Mitch Meluskey, 1B David McCarty and OF Billy McMillon.
Rangers released LHP Juan Alvarez.
Rockies traded LHP Mike Hampton, OF Juan Pierre and $6.5 million to Marlins for C Charles Johnson, OF Preston Wilson, LHP Vic Darensbourg and 2B Pablo Ozuna.
Marlins traded LHP Mike Hampton and $30 million to Braves for RHP Tim Spooneybarger and RHP Ryan Baker.

November 19

Mariners released RHP Paul Abbott.
Reds organization signed INF Ryan Freel, RHP Sean DePaula, LHP Mark Watson, INF Kelly Dransfeldt, C Reed Secrist, OF Emil Brown, IF Felipe Crespo, LHP Lance Davis, OF Robin Jennings, INF Jason Maxwell, RHP Carlos Almanzar, RHP Shane Hearns, OF Mike Curry, OF Bobby Darula, RHP Kyle Stanton, RHP Scott MacRae and C Creighton Gubanich.
Padres signed LHP Jesse Orosco and RHP Francisco Cordova.

November 20

Tigers released INF Damian Jackson unconditionally.
Devil Rays released RHP Ryan Rupe.
Giants claimed INF Neifi Perez off waivers from Royals.

November 21

Red Sox organization signed RHP Paul Stewart, RHP Justin Kaye, C-INF Chris Coste, C Jeff Smith, INF James Lofton and INF Nelson Castro.
Devil Rays organization signed INF Justin Baughman, C Charlie Greene, C Sandy Martinez, C Angel Pena, OF Ryan Jackson, RHP Leslie Brea, RHP Jeremi Gonzalez and LHP Cedrick Bowers.

November 22

Red Sox organization signed RHP Steve Woodard, RHP Tom Davey, LHP Kevin Tolar, 1B-OF Larry Sutton and INF Julio Zuleta.

November 23

Phillies signed 3B David Bell.

November 25

Marlins organization signed OF Chad Allen, RHP Toby Borland, RHP Rick Croushore, C Paul Hoover, RHP Allen Levrault, OF Robert Stratton, C Matt Treanor and OF Chris Wakeland.
Brewers signed INF Wilton Veras, INF Jed Hansen and OF Mark Budzinski.
Pirates acquired 1B Randall Simon from Tigers for LHP Adrian Burnside and two minor league players to be named.

November 26

Brewers traded C Paul Bako to Cubs for a player to be named.

November 27

Red Sox claimed RHP Ryan Rupe off waivers from Devil Rays.
Mariners claimed LHP Steve Kent off waivers from Devil Rays.

December 2

Orioles organization signed LHP Bill Pulsipher.

December 3

Athletics traded RHP Billy Koch and two minor league players to White Sox for RHP Keith Foulke, C Mark Johnson and RHP Joe Valentine and cash.
Cubs signed LHP Mike Remlinger.
Expos waived RHP Masato Yoshii.
Phillies signed 1B Jim Thome.
Cardinals signed C Steve Torrealba.

December 4

Yankees signed OF Chris Latham.
Cubs traded C Todd Hundley and OF Chad Hermansen to Dodgers for 1B Eric Karros, 2B Mark Grudzielanek and $2 million.
Cubs released INF Chris Stynes.
Padres signed INF-OF Chris Sexton.

December 5

Red Sox signed RHP Willie Banks and RHP Ryan Rupe.
Mets signed LHP Tom Glavine.

December 6

Indians acquired 1B Travis Hafner and RHP Aaron Myette from Rangers for C Einar Diaz and RHP Ryan Drese.
Dodgers sold contract of RHP Kevin Beirne to Osaka of Japanese Pacific League and LHP Jeff Williams to Hanshin of Japanese Central League.
Padres organization signed OF Brady Anderson.

December 8

Yankees signed C Chris Widger.
Giants signed 2B Ray Durham and OF Marquis Grissom.

December 10

Devil Rays reached agreement with Yokohama of Japan Central League that allows Yokohama to purchase services of 1B Steve Cox.
Astros organization signed LHP Jesus Sanchez.
Padres signed INF Dave Hansen and RHP Jaret Wright.

December 11

Blue Jays signed C Greg Myers.
Cubs signed C Damian Miller.
Brewers signed SS Royce Clayton and organization signed C Joe Lawrence.

December 12

Reds traded 2B Todd Walker to Red Sox for two players to be named.
Padres organization signed INF Homer Bush.

December 13

Devil Rays sold rights to INF Andy Sheets to Hiroshima of Japanese Central League.
Cardinals signed RHP Chris Carpenter.

December 14

Orioles signed SS Deivi Cruz.
Red Sox acquired OF Jeremy Giambi from Phillies for RHP Josh Hancock.
Diamondbacks traded 1B Erubiel Durazo to Athletics. Received RHP Elmer Dessens and cash from Reds. Reds acquired SS Felipe Lopez from Blue Jays. Blue Jays received a player to be named from Athletics.
Reds released RHP Jared Fernandez.
Mets traded SS Rey Ordonez to Devil Rays for two players to be named.
Padres traded RHP Brett Tomko to Cardinals for RHP Luther Hackman and a player to be named.
Giants signed 3B Edgardo Alfonzo.

December 16

Red Sox acquired INF Cesar Crespo from Padres for INF Luis Cruz.
White Sox acquired LHP Neal Cotts and OF Daylan Holt from Athletics to complete an earlier trade.
Tigers acquired RHP Matt Roney from Pirates, and 3B Travis Chapman from Indians for cash. Released LHP Pedro Feliciano. Acquired RHP Roberto Novoa from Pirates as part of their Nov. 25 trade.
Twins released DH David Ortiz.
Athletics released RHP Mike Fyhrie.
Blue Jays acquired RHP Jason Arnold from Athletics to complete an earlier trade.
Reds acquired RHP Josh Thigpen and 3B Tony Blanco from Red Sox to complete an earlier trade.
Astros acquired OF Victor Hall from Rockies in exchange for a player to be named or cash. Traded RHP Nelson Cruz to Rockies to complete the earlier trade.
Dodgers acquired LHP Derek Thompson from Cubs for cash.
Brewers acquired 3B Wes Helms and LHP John Foster from Braves for LHP Ray King.
Mets signed LHP Mike Stanton. Claimed LHP Peter Zamora off waivers from Phillies.
Pirates released LHP Jimmy Anderson.
Padres signed 2B Mark Loretta. Acquired INF-OF Jose Flores from Athletics for RHP Buddy Hernandez, and RHP Mike Wodnicki from Cardinals to complete an earlier trade.

December 17

Braves signed RHP Paul Byrd and organization signed LHP Chris Haney.
Cubs signed OF Troy O'Leary.
Cardinals signed C Joe Girardi.
Giants acquired LHP Damian Moss and RHP Manuel Mateo from Braves for RHP Russ Ortiz.

December 18

Angels claimed C Wilbert Nieves off waivers from Padres.
Red Sox signed RHP Mike Timlin and INF Damian Jackson.
Indians organization signed INF Casey Blake and RHP Mike Thurman.
Yankees signed 3B Todd Zeile.
Rangers signed OF Doug Glanville.
Astros signed 2B Jeff Kent.
Cardinals organization signed RHP Cal Eldred and LHP Lance Painter.

December 19

Indians signed RHP Jason Bere and organization signed C Dusty Wathan.
Tigers organization signed 2B Warren Morris, OF Ernie Young, RHP Carlos Alvarado, RHP Fernando De La Cruz, RHP Tim McClaskey, RHP Chris Mears, RHP Brian Schmack, LHP Rafael Roque, LHP Mike Spiegel, C Robinson Cancel, C Luis Taveras and C Bill Haselman.
Yankees signed OF Hideki Matsui.
Devil Rays organization signed LHP Brian Fitzgerald, RHP John Frascatore, RHP Mel Rojas, RHP Eric Sabel, RHP Blake Stein, OF Brian Lesher, SS Gabby Martinez and C Hector Ortiz.

December 20

White Sox signed C Sandy Alomar Jr.
Blue Jays signed INF Mike Bordick.
Braves traded RHP Kevin Millwood to Phillies for C Johnny Estrada.
Cubs signed LHP Shawn Estes.
Astros organization signed RHP Jared Fernandez.
Dodgers signed 1B Fred McGriff.
Expos traded RHP Matt Herges to Pirates for RHP Chris Young and RHP Jon Searles.
Mets signed OF Cliff Floyd.
Padres organization signed RHP Charles Nagy.

December 21

Rangers signed RHP Ugueth Urbina.
Blue Jays signed RHP Tanyon Sturtze.

December 23

Indians signed LHP Brian Anderson and organization signed C A.J. Hinch.
Athletics signed OF Chris Singleton.
Padres signed C Gary Bennett.

December 26

Rangers signed RHP Esteban Yan.

December 27

Mets signed INF Rey Sanchez.

December 30

Angels signed OF Eric Owens.
Yankees re-signed RHP Roger Clemens.
Blue Jays signed OF Frank Catalanotto.

December 31

Rangers signed LHP Aaron Fultz.

All-Star Game

AT MILLER PARK, MILWAUKEE, JULY 9, 2002

When Curt Schiling started the All-Star Game, little did he or anyone else know it would end in a tie.

BY ADAM MCCALVY

The last time Bob Brenly and Joe Torre squared off on a stage so global, Brenly's Diamondbacks scored a World Series win against Torre's Yankees in the bottom of the ninth inning of Game 7 last season.

This was considerably less dramatic, but may be talked about just as long.

With both teams' 30-man rosters already depleted, the All-Star Game managers, umpires and Major League Baseball Commissioner Bud Selig decided the 73rd All-Star Game would end in a tie, 7-7, after 11 innings on July 9.

The decision was made during an impromptu conference between Selig, Brenly and Torre near the National League dugout before the bottom of the 11th. It was decided that if the National League couldn't push across a run in the bottom of the inning, the game would end. Florida's Mike Lowell made it to second base with two outs, but Seattle's Freddy Garcia finished a scoreless frame by striking out pitcher Vicente Padilla and catcher Benito Santiago.

"Obviously, nobody wanted it to end like this, but it really was the right move," said Minnesota Twins reliever Eddie Guardado. "The fans got to see the stars, they got to see good pitching, good hitting, great plays. The only thing they didn't get to see was a winner."

It was hardly satisfying for the sellout crowd of 41,871 at Miller Park who were informed of the decision before the bottom of the 11th. Fans voiced their displeasure throughout the inning and chanted, "Let them play!" The game-ending decision — considered the correct one by the players, the managers and TV broadcasters — was clearly the dominant topic of postgame discussions.

"I tried to think of any alternative out there, but they were out of players," said Selig, the one-time Brewers owner who hosted Milwaukee's last All-Star Game in 1975. "We'll have to review if we expand rosters or something so we avoid this in the future. This is not the ending I had hoped for."

Garcia, who threw 102 pitches in his last start in a 2-1 Mariners win five days earlier, pitched two innings, allowing a pair of hits on 31 pitches. Padilla finished the game for the National League, allowing only a walk on 25 pitches in two innings of work.

The only other All-Star Game to end in a tie was the second of two games in 1961, a 1-1 tie that was interrupted in the ninth inning because of rain and called after a 30-minute delay.

It was the 10th All-Star Game to go extra innings, and the first since the National League beat the American League, 8-7, in 1994. The senior circuit is 9-0-1 in extra-inning games.

Brenly and Torre's use of all 30 players per side was an All-Star Game record.

"Getting everybody in was important to me," Torre said. "It's a treat for the fans, and the players that come really want to play. It's our job to do that."

The unusual ending overshadowed what was an exciting, back-and-forth game, in which no Most Valuable Player was named.

The National League had a three-run lead entering the seventh inning and was poised to snap a five-game, All-Star Game losing streak. Four lead changes later, that streak was technically over.

"I think the fans got a great show, a great game," said Dodgers outfielder Shawn Green. "It was the best All-Star Game, as far as competitiveness, in a long time."

Offense would rule the day, but one of baseball's best defensive outfielders provided the game's biggest thrill when he robbed Giants star Barry Bonds of a home run in the first inning. Bonds skied a high fly ball to center field, where Minnesota's Torii Hunter ranged back and made a leaping grab to pull the ball back into fair territory for the out.

The National Leaguers struck first, in the second inning. Sammy Sosa notched his first All-Star hit with a leadoff single off AL starter Derek Lowe and was thrown out by left fielder Manny Ramirez trying to advance to third on Vladimir Guerrero's base hit. Guerrero went to second on the throw, moved to third when Lowe balked and scored the game's first run on Mike Piazza's groundout.

With a run already across in the third, Bonds got another chance against Roy Halladay, and this time he didn't give Hunter a chance to pull one back. With Todd Helton at first after his one-out RBI single scored Jimmy Rollins, Bonds worked the count to 3-0 against the Toronto Blue Jays' righthander.

Bonds pounced on the next pitch and lined it 385 feet off the facade of the second deck in right field, smashing a row of advertisements and giving the NL a 4-0 lead. It was Bonds' second All-Star home run and his first since 1998.

The AL got on the board in the fourth. Home Run Derby champ Jason Giambi of the Yankees shortened his swing for a two-out single off Dodgers lefthander Odalis Perez, moved to second on a passed ball and scored an unearned run when Ramirez singled into the right-field corner.

The teams traded runs in the fifth. The Yanks' Alfonso Soriano hit a solo home run for the American League off Dodgers closer Eric Gagne, and Wisconsin native and National Leaguer Damian Miller of the Diamondbacks drove in a run with an RBI double in the bottom of the inning.

In the seventh, the AL broke through. Red Sox outfielder Johnny Damon, the last player added to the AL squad in the 30th Man voting, created a run in the seventh and kick-started a four-run rally. He glanced a line drive off pitcher Mike Remlinger, stole second base and moved to third on a flyout to right. The Angels' Garret Anderson scored Damon with an RBI groundout to second base.

Pinch-hitter Tony Batista of the Orioles singled in a run to cut the deficit to a run, and Chicago's Paul Konerko, fresh off a third-place finish in the Home Run Derby, hit his second double of the game to score two more runs and give the American League a 6-5 lead.

But back came the National League, getting two runs and a one-run lead of its own on Lance Berkman's two-run single off Seattle closer Kaz Sasaki.

"Obviously, I didn't expect this many runs to be scored in the game, period," Berkman said. "At that point, I felt I had a pretty good shot and then they came back and tied it."

In the eighth, the American League tied the game for good. Tigers outfielder Robert Fick hit a pinch-hit single and scored when Cleveland's Omar Vizquel tripled into the right-field corner.

Vizquel thought the decision to end the game was the right one. "You can't ask for Freddie Garcia to pitch five or six innings when he was coming in on short rest," the Indians veteran said. "You don't want to risk a guy getting hurt."

Rollins singled twice and scored twice in two at-bats for the National League, and Konerko and Miller each tied an All-Star Game record with two doubles. The last player to hit two doubles in an All-Star Game was Bonds, in 1993.

National League starter Curt Schilling, in his second All-Star start and third appearance, struck out three and allowed one hit in two scoreless innings. Only four of his 28 pitches missed the strike zone, and many of them were pushing 100 mph.

"I threw the ball as hard as I could throw the ball for two innings. That's what I was planning on going out there and trying to do today," Schilling said. "That was everything I had."

The game followed an hour-long pregame celebration, which included a presentation of the 30 greatest moments in Major League history, foul-line introductions and ceremonial first pitches by Milwaukee baseball legends Warren Spahn, Hank Aaron, Paul Molitor and Robin Yount. Former New York City Mayor Rudy Guiliani was a special guest in the AL dugout.

BOX SCORE

American League	AB	R	H	RBI	PO	A
Suzuki, rf (Mariners)	2	0	0	0	0	0
Winn, rf (Devil Rays)	2	1	1	0	1	0
Urbina, p (Red Sox)	0	0	0	0	0	0
Rivera, p (Yankees)	0	0	0	0	0	0
Garcia, p (Mariners)	1	0	0	0	0	0
Hillenbrand, 3b (Red Sox)	2	0	0	0	1	0

American League	AB	R	H	RBI	PO	A
Ventura, 3b (Yankees)	1	0	0	0	0	1
∞Batista, ph-3b (Orioles)	3	1	1	1	0	4
Rodriguez, ss (Rangers)	2	0	0	0	0	2
Tejada, ss (Athletics)	2	1	1	0	0	1
■Garciaparra, ph-ss (R. Sox)	1	0	0	0	0	0
Giambi, 1b (Yankees)	2	1	1	0	4	0
Konerko, 1b (White Sox)	2	0	2	2	5	0
Sweeney, 1b (Royals)	1	0	0	0	3	0
Ramirez, lf (Red Sox)	2	0	2	1	1	1
Buehrle, p (White Sox)	0	0	0	0	0	0
‡Pierzynski, ph-c (Twins)	3	0	0	0	7	1
Posada, c (Yankees)	3	0	0	0	3	0
Zito, p (Athletics)	0	0	0	0	0	0
Guardado, p (Twins)	0	0	0	0	0	0
Sasaki, p (Mariners)	0	0	0	0	0	0
◆Fick, ph-rf (Tigers)	2	1	1	0	1	0
Hunter, cf (Twins)	2	0	0	0	2	0
Damon, cf (Red Sox)	3	1	1	0	3	0
Soriano, 2b (Yankees)	2	1	1	1	1	1
Vizquel, 2b (Indians)	2	0	1	1	1	1
Lowe, p (Red Sox)	0	0	0	0	0	0
*Jeter, ph (Yankees)	1	0	0	0	0	0
Halladay, p (Blue Jays)	0	0	0	0	0	0
Anderson, lf (Angels)	4	0	0	1	0	0
Totals	45	7	12	7	33	12

National League	AB	R	H	RBI	PO	A
Vidro, 2b (Expos)	2	0	0	0	0	2
Spivey, 2b (Diamondbacks)	2	0	0	0	0	2
Nen, p (Giants)	0	0	0	0	0	0
Smoltz, p (Braves)	0	0	0	0	0	0
▼Santiago, ph-c (Giants)	2	0	1	0	0	0
Helton, 1b (Rockies)	2	1	1	1	4	0
Berkman, lf-1b (Astros)	3	0	1	2	8	1
Bonds, lf (Giants)	2	1	1	2	0	0
Sexson, 1b (Brewers)	1	0	0	0	2	0
Dunn, lf (Reds)	1	0	0	0	0	0
Sosa, rf (Cubs)	2	0	1	0	0	0
Green, rf (Dodgers)	3	0	1	0	4	0
Guerrero, cf (Expos)	2	1	1	0	0	0
§A. Jones, ph-cf (Braves)	3	0	0	0	1	0
Piazza, c (Mets)	2	0	0	1	7	0
Gagne, p (Dodgers)	0	0	0	0	0	0
Hernandez, ss (Brewers)	3	0	0	0	0	2
Rolen, 3b (Phillies)	3	0	0	0	0	0
Castillo, 2b (Marlins)	2	0	0	0	0	3
Rollins, ss (Phillies)	2	2	2	0	1	0
Hoffman, p (Padres)	0	0	0	0	0	0
Remlinger, p (Braves)	0	0	0	0	0	0
Kim, p (Diamondbacks)	0	0	0	0	0	0
▲Lowell, ph-3b (Marlins)	3	1	2	0	0	0
Schilling, p (D'backs)	0	0	0	0	0	0
Williams, p (Pirates)	0	0	0	0	0	0
†Gonzalez, ph (D'backs)	1	0	0	0	0	0
Perez, p (Dodgers)	0	0	0	0	0	0
Miller, c (Diamondbacks)	3	1	2	1	5	0
Padilla, p (Phillies)	1	0	0	0	1	0
Totals	45	7	13	7	33	10

American League	0	0	0	1	1	0	4	1	0	0	0	—7
National League	0	1	3	0	1	0	2	0	0	0	0	—7

American League	IP	H	R	ER	BB	SO
Lowe (Red Sox)	2.0	2	1	1	0	0
Halladay (Blue Jays)	1.0	3	3	3	0	1
Buehrle (White Sox)	2.0	2	1	1	0	2
Zito (Athletics)	0.1	0	0	0	0	0
Guardado (Twins)	0.2	0	0	0	0	2
Sasaki (Mariners)	1.0	3	2	2	1	2
Urbina (Red Sox)	1.0	0	0	0	0	1
Rivera (Yankees)	1.0	1	0	0	0	0
Garcia (Mariners)	2.0	2	0	0	0	3

National League	IP	H	R	ER	BB	SO
Schilling (Diamondbacks)	2.0	1	0	0	0	3
Williams (Pirates)	1.0	0	0	0	0	2
Perez (Dodgers)	1.0	2	1	0	0	2
Gagne (Dodgers)	1.0	2	1	1	0	1
Hoffman (Padres)	1.0	1	0	0	0	1
Remlinger (Braves)	0.2	1	2	2	1	0
Kim (Diamondbacks)	0.1	3	2	2	0	0
Nen (Giants)	1.0	2	1	1	0	2
Smoltz (Braves)	1.0	0	0	0	0	1
Padilla (Phillies)	2.0	0	0	0	1	0

*Struck out for Lowe in third. †Grounded out for Williams in third. ‡Grounded out for Buehrle in sixth. §Struck out for Guerrero in sixth. ∞Singled for Ventura in seventh. ▲Singled for Kim in seventh. ◆Singled for Sasaki in eighth. ■Grounded out for Tejada in ninth. ▼Singled for Smoltz in ninth.

LOB—A.L. 7, N.L. 6. 2B—Winn, Konerko 2, Miller 2. 3B—Vizquel. HR—Bonds, Soriano. SB—Damon, Winn, Fick, Berkman, Green. PB—Piazza. WP—Garcia. Balk—Lowe. T—3:29. A—41,871. U—Davis, plate; Tschida, first; Meriwether, second; Meals, third; Foster, left field; Emmel, right field. Official scorers—Tim O'Driscoll, Bill Center and Drew Olson.

Players listed on rosters but not used: None.

PLAY BY PLAY

First Inning

A.L.—Suzuki grounded to Helton. Hillenbrand and Rodriguez struck out.

N.L.—Vidro and Helton grounded out, Rodriguez to Giambi. Bonds flied to Hunter.

Johnny Damon of the Red Sox slides safely past Brewers shortstop Jose Hernandez on a seventh-inning steal of second base.

Second Inning

A.L.—Giambi struck out. Ramirez singled to center. Posada grounded to Helton as Ramirez advanced to second. Hunter grounded out, Vidro to Helton.

N.L.—Sosa singled to center. Guerrero singled to left, but Ramirez threw to Hillebrand to retire Sosa trying for third as Guerrero advanced to second on the play. Guerrero advanced to third on a balk by Lowe. Piazza grounded out, Soriano to Giambi, as Guerrero scored. Rolen flied to Hunter. One run. N.L. 1, A.L. 0.

Third Inning

A.L.—Williams now pitching. Soriano struck out. Jeter, pinch-hitting for Lowe, struck out. Suzuki grounded out, Vidro to Helton.

N.L.—Halladay now pitching. Rollins singled to center. Gonzalez, pinch-hitting for Williams, grounded to Giambi as Rollins advanced to second. Vidro flied to Ramirez. Helton singled to center, scoring Rollins. Bonds homered to right, scoring Helton. Sosa struck out. Three runs. N.L. 4, A.L. 0.

Fourth Inning

A.L.—Sexson now at first, Spivey at second, Berkman in left, Green in right and Perez pitching. Hillenbrand flied to Berkman. Rodriguez struck out. Giambi singled to center. Giambi advanced to second on a passed ball. Ramirez singled to right, scoring Giambi. Posada struck out. One run. N.L. 4, A.L. 1.

N.L.—Konerko now at first, Ventura at third, Anderson in left, Winn in right and Buehrle pitching. Guerrero struck out. Piazza flied to Winn. Rolen popped to Soriano.

Fifth Inning

A.L.—Miller now catching and Gagne pitching. Hunter popped to Rollins. Soriano homered to left-center. Anderson grounded to Sexson. Winn doubled to left. Ventura struck out. One run. N.L. 4, A.L. 2.

N.L.—Vizquel now at second, Tejada at shortstop and Damon in center. Rollins singled to center. Miller doubled to center, scoring Rollins. Spivey struck out. Berkman grounded out, Vizquel to Konerko, as Miller advanced to third. Sexson grounded out, Ventura to Konerko. One run. N.L. 5, A.L. 2.

Sixth Inning

A.L.—Hernandez now at shortstop and Hoffman pitching. Tejada flied to Green. Konerko doubled to right-center. Pierzynski, pinch-hitting for Buehrle, grounded to Sexson as Konerko advanced to third. Posada struck out.

N.L.—Pierzynski now catching and Zito pitching. Green grounded out, Tejada to Konerko. Jones now pinch-hitting for Guerrero. Guardado now pitching. Jones struck out. Hernandez struck out and was thrown out at first, Pierzynski to Konerko, on the dropped third strike.

Seventh Inning

A.L.—Berkman now at first, Dunn in left, Jones in center and Remlinger pitching. Damon singled to first. Damon stole second. Vizquel flied to Green as Damon advanced to third. Anderson grounded out, Spivey to Berkman, as Damon scored. Winn walked. Batista now pinch-hitting for Ventura. Kim now pitching. Winn stole second. Batista singled to left, scoring Winn. Tejada singled to center as Batista advanced to second. Konerko doubled to left-center, scoring Batista and Tejada. Pierzynski grounded out, Spivey to Berkman. Four runs. A.L. 6, N.L. 5.

N.L.—Batista now at third and Sasaki pitching. Rolen struck out. Lowell, pinch-hitting for Kim, singled to left. Miller doubled to left as Lowell advanced to third. Spivey grounded out, Batista to Konerko. Berkman singled to center, scoring Lowell and Miller. Berkman stole second. Dunn walked. Green struck out. Two runs. N.L. 7, A.L. 6.

Eighth Inning

A.L.—Castillo now at second, Lowell at third and Nen pitching. Fick, pinch-hitting for Sasaki, singled to right-center. Damon struck out as Fick stole second. Vizquel tripled to right, scoring Fick. Anderson grounded out, Castillo to Berkman. Winn struck out. One run. N.L. 7, A.L. 7.

N.L.—Sweeney now at first, Fick in right and Urbina pitching. Jones grounded out, Batista to Sweeney. Hernandez struck out. Castillo flied to Damon.

Ninth Inning

A.L.—Smoltz now pitching. Batista struck out. Garciaparra, pinch-hitting for Tejada, grounded out, Hernandez to Berkman. Sweeney flied to Green.

N.L.—Garciaparra now at shortstop and Rivera pitching. Lowell flied to Fick. Miller grounded out, Batista to Sweeney. Santiago, pinch-hitting for Smoltz, singled to center. Berkman popped to Vizquel.

10th Inning

A.L.—Santiago now catching and Padilla pitching. Pierzynski flied to Jones. Fick grounded out, Castillo to Berkman. Damon grounded out, Berkman to Padilla.

N.L.—Garcia now pitching. Dunn flied to Damon. Green singled to center. Jones struck out as Green stole second. Hernandez grounded out, Batista to Sweeney.

11th Inning

A.L.—Vizquel walked. Anderson grounded out, Castillo to Berkman, as Vizquel advanced to second. Garcia grounded out, Hernandez to Berkman, as Vizquel advanced to third. Batista flied to Green.

N.L.—Castillo flied to Damon. Lowell singled to left. Lowell advanced to second on a wild pitch. Padilla and Santiago struck out. **Game called due to league decision.** Final score: A.L. 7, N.L. 7.

A.L. Division Series

MINNESOTA VS. OAKLAND

By Mark Sheldon

In a deciding Game 5 playoff battle, neither fate nor destiny favors either team. If you want to win the series, you simply have to take it.

The Twins, once threatened with contraction, were headed for the American League Championship Series after beating the heavily favored Oakland A's in Game 5 of the American League Division Series.

The Twins moved on to play the Anaheim Angels, who defeated the defending AL champion Yankees, three games to one, in the other ALDS.

"You can't get rid of the Twins," left fielder Jacque Jones said. "[Contraction proponents] tried it. Then the strike situation. The Oakland A's were up 2-1 [in the series]. We just never quit."

The resilient Twins were used to taking what they believe is rightfully theirs. They hadn't been given much of a chance all season—and even less respect, even as they continued to win games and widen their lead in the AL Central through several obstacles.

"Everybody wanted to eliminate us, even during the offseason," center fielder Torii Hunter said. "We proved everybody wrong. We got to the playoffs, and now we're going to the second round."

The Twins had a 5-1 lead entering the ninth inning behind closer Eddie Guardado, but putting the A's away proved difficult. Oakland rallied with two hits before Mark Ellis smacked a three-run homer to left field to narrow the lead to one. Guardado surrendered another hit before getting Ray Durham to pop out to second baseman Denny Hocking in foul territory to end the game.

At that point, Minnesota's dugout cleared, and players swarmed Guardado in celebration near the mound.

"Watching my players jump around there and hug each other, that's as good as it gets for me," Twins first-year manager Ron Gardenhire said. "My coaching staff—being able to shake their hands and tell them how good they've done—that's what [managing] is all about, for me."

Minnesota was able to absorb the late rally by scoring three runs in the top of the ninth. With one on and the Twins leading 2-1, A.J. Pierzynski hit a two-run home run to right field off A's reliever Billy Koch to provide some insurance.

"I said to myself, 'A.J., I don't care if you hit another home run the rest of your career, but please get him,'" first baseman Doug Mientkiewicz said. "And he hits a home run."

David Ortiz added an RBI double for a fifth run in the game, which proved to be the difference. For the first time in the series, Minnesota was also able to get on the scoreboard before Oakland. Denny Hocking's second-inning RBI single to center field plated the first run of the game, and Matthew LeCroy stretched the lead to 2-0 in the third with his second single of the day.

A's southpaw Mark Mulder paralyzed Minnesota's lefthanded hitters, who went 0-for-14 in Game 5. But the Twins righthanders picked up the slack in a big way by going 9-for-15 during Mulder's seven innings.

"We kept hearing how we can't hit lefties; we can't do this, we can't do that," Mientkiewicz said. "All of a sudden, we're [moving] on."

One big key to the Twins' advancement was starter Brad Radke. The long-time ace righthander delivered in the biggest game of his career, going $6^2/_3$ innings and allowing one run on six hits with no walks and four strikeouts.

"He has been our man for a long time here," Gardenhire said. "And he did it again today. He picked up our baseball team again, and it was vintage Brad Radke—[he] used all his pitches [and] got us through the seventh inning."

After losing Game 3 at the Metrodome, the Twins' situation appeared particularly dire. They had to defeat tough Oakland starters Tim Hudson and Mulder in order to advance.

"It was real grueling," Jones said. "We just beat an outstanding team. I can't say it enough."

Gardenhire was quick to point out that the Twins have usually gotten respect from their opponents. But he understands why people can sometimes underestimate his team.

"They know we never go away," Gardenhire said. "When you start looking at numbers in print, that's when we don't get enough credit. Our numbers don't jump out like a lot of other teams. We don't have a 130-RBI or 40-homer guy. We pitch and catch the ball.

"When you start looking inside the clubhouse and looking at the heart of this baseball team, that's what the other baseball teams always pick up."

After the game, a champagne celebration commenced in the Twins' clubhouse. They already experienced the highs of clinching the division, but the bubbly tastes much better this time around.

"It tastes a lot better, because we're one step from the World Series," Jones said. "We were just clinching to get to this point. Now, we're one step away from the big dance."

Game 1 at Oakland

Tuesday, October 1

MINNESOTA 7, OAKLAND 5

HOW THEY SCORED

First Inning

Athletics—Durham struck out and was tagged out by Pierzynski after a dropped third strike. Hatteberg walked. Tejada reached first on a fielder's choice and Hatteberg reached second on Guzman's throwing error. Chavez singled to right, scoring Hatteberg. Tejada also scored and Chavez advanced to second on the play when Pierzynski dropped a throw to the plate. Dye grounded out, Koskie to Mientkiewicz. Justice singled to center, scoring Chavez. Ellis struck out. Three runs. Athletics 3, Twins 0.

Second Inning

Twins—Hunter doubled to right-center. Mientkiewicz flied to Long as Hunter advanced to third. Cuddyer doubled to left, scoring Hunter. Pierzynski singled to left as Cuddyer advanced to third. Rivas grounded into a double play, Chavez to Ellis to Hatteberg. One run. Athletics 3, Twins 1.

Athletics—Long flied to Cuddyer. Hernandez struck out. Durham doubled to left. Hatteberg singled to the mound, scoring Durham. Tejada reached first on a throwing error by Koskie as Hatteberg advanced to third. Chavez singled to right-center, scoring Hatteberg as Tejada advanced to third. Dye popped to Mientkiewicz. Two runs. Athletics 5, Twins 1.

Third Inning

Twins—Jones struck out. Guzman singled to center. Koskie homered to right, scoring Guzman. Ortiz lined to Dye. Hunter walked. Mientkiewicz grounded out, Ellis to Hatteberg. Two runs. Athletics 5, Twins 3.

Sixth Inning

Twins—Mientkiewicz homered to right. Cuddyer grounded out, Chavez to Hatteberg. Lilly now pitching. Pierzynski singled to left. Rivas singled to left as Pierzynski advanced to second. Jones doubled to left, scoring Pierzynski as Rivas advanced to third. Guzman walked. Koskie grounded out to Hatteberg, scoring Rivas as Jones advanced to third and Guzman to second. Ortiz struck out. Three runs. Twins 6, Athletics 5.

Seventh Inning

Twins—Saenz now at first and Lidle pitching. Hunter grounded out, Chavez to Saenz. Mientkiewicz grounded out to Saenz. Cuddyer singled to third. Pierzynski tripled to right-center, scoring Cuddyer. Rivas flied to Long. One run. Twins 7, Athletics 5.

BOX SCORE

Minnesota	AB	R	H	RBI	PO	A
Jones, lf	5	0	1	1	5	0
Guzman, ss	4	1	2	0	2	0
Koskie, 3b	5	1	1	3	0	2
Ortiz, dh	5	0	0	0	0	0
Hunter, cf	4	1	1	0	2	0
Mientkiewicz, 1b	5	1	1	1	8	0
Cuddyer, rf	3	1	2	1	2	0
Mohr, rf	0	0	0	0	0	0
Pierzynski, c	4	1	4	1	7	0
Rivas, 2b	3	1	1	0	1	1
Radke, p	0	0	0	0	0	1
Santana, p	0	0	0	0	0	1
Romero, p	0	0	0	0	0	2
Guardado, p	0	0	0	0	0	0
Totals	38	7	13	7	27	7

Oakland	AB	R	H	RBI	PO	A
Durham, dh	5	1	2	0	0	0
Hatteberg, 1b	2	2	1	1	7	0
Saenz, ph-1b	0	0	0	0	3	0
Velarde, ph-1b	1	0	1	0	1	0
Tejada, ss	5	1	1	0	0	2
Chavez, 3b	5	1	2	2	1	3
Dye, rf	5	0	2	0	2	0
Justice, lf	5	0	2	1	0	0
Ellis, 2b	4	0	1	0	3	4
Long, cf	4	0	0	0	3	0
Piatt, ph	1	0	0	0	0	0
Hernandez, c	4	0	0	0	7	0
Hudson, p	0	0	0	0	0	1
Lilly, p	0	0	0	0	0	0
Lidle, p	0	0	0	0	0	0
Rincon, p	0	0	0	0	0	0
Mecir, p	0	0	0	0	0	0
Totals	41	5	12	4	27	10

Minnesota	0	1	2	0	0	3	1	0	0—7
Oakland	3	2	0	0	0	0	0	0	0—5

Minnesota	IP	H	R	ER	BB	SO
Radke (W)	5.0	8	5	1	1	3
Santana	1.2	2	0	0	1	2
Romero	1.1	1	0	0	0	1
Guardado (S)	1.0	1	0	0	1	1

Oakland	IP	H	R	ER	BB	SO
Hudson	5.1	8	4	4	2	4
Lilly (L)	0.2	3	2	2	1	1
Lidle	1.0	2	1	1	0	0
Rincon	1.0	0	0	0	0	0
Mecir	1.0	0	0	0	0	2

E—Pierzynski, Koskie, C.Guzman. DP—Oakland 1. LOB—Minnesota 8, Oakland 12. 2B—Jones, Hunter, Cuddyer, Durham 2, Ellis. 3B—Pierzynski. HR—Koskie, Mientkiewicz. SH—Rivas. T—3:44. A—34,853. U—Davis, plate; Meriwether, first; Marquez, second; Cousins, third; West, left field; Diaz, right field.

Game 2 at Oakland

Wednesday, October 2

OAKLAND 9, MINNESOTA 1

HOW THEY SCORED

First Inning

Athletics—Durham walked. Hatteberg doubled to right as Durham advanced to third. Tejada grounded out, Koskie to Mientkiewicz. Chavez homered to right, scoring Durham and Hatteberg. Dye doubled to left. Justice lined into a double play, Mays to Mientkiewicz to Koskie. Three runs. Athletics 3, Twins 0.

Fourth Inning

Athletics—Hernandez grounded out, Rivas to Mientkiewicz. Durham was hit by a pitch. Hatteberg flied to Hunter. Tejada doubled to left-center, scoring Durham. Chavez was walked intentionally. Fiore now pitching. Dye walked. Justice tripled to right, scoring Tejada, Chavez and Dye. Ellis doubled to right, scoring Justice. Long grounded out, Guzman to Mientkiewicz. Five runs. Athletics 8, Twins 0.

Fifth Inning

Athletics—Hernandez grounded out, Koskie to Mientkiewicz. Durham doubled to right-center. Durham advanced to third on a wild pitch. Hatteberg singled to first, scoring Durham. Tejada walked. Chavez fouled to Jones. Dye popped to Rivas. One run. Athletics 9, Twins 0.

Sixth Inning

Twins—Guzman homered to left. Koskie grounded out, Mulder to Hatteberg. LeCroy singled to right. Hunter struck out. Mientkiewicz grounded out to Hatteberg. One run. Athletics 9, Twins 1.

BOX SCORE

Minnesota	AB	R	H	RBI	PO	A
Jones, lf	3	0	1	0	4	0
Mohr, lf	1	0	1	0	0	0
Guzman, ss	3	1	1	1	1	2
Koskie, 3b	3	0	0	0	2	2
LeCroy, dh	4	0	2	0	0	0
Hunter, cf	3	0	0	0	1	0
Hocking, rf	1	0	1	0	0	0
Mientkiewicz, 1b	4	0	0	0	8	1
Cuddyer, rf	1	0	0	0	2	0
Kielty, ph-rf-cf	2	0	0	0	0	0
Pierzynski, c	2	0	0	0	1	0
Prince, c	2	0	0	0	4	0
Rivas, 2b	2	0	1	0	1	2
Mays, p	0	0	0	0	0	1
Fiore, p	0	0	0	0	0	0
Lohse, p	0	0	0	0	0	0
Hawkins, p	0	0	0	0	0	0
Totals	31	1	7	1	24	8

Oakland	AB	R	H	RBI	PO	A
Durham, dh	3	3	1	0	0	0
Hatteberg, 1b	4	1	2	1	10	0
Mabry, ph-1b	1	0	0	0	2	0
Tejada, ss	4	1	1	1	2	1
Chavez, 3b	4	2	2	3	0	1

Oakland	AB	R	H	RBI	PO	A
Dye, rf	4	1	1	0	0	0
Justice, lf	5	1	2	3	1	0
Byrnes, lf	0	0	0	0	1	0
Ellis, 2b	4	0	3	1	2	6
Long, cf	4	0	2	0	4	0
Hernandez, c	4	0	0	0	5	0
Mulder, p	0	0	0	0	0	4
Bradford, p	0	0	0	0	0	1
Koch, p	0	0	0	0	0	0
Totals	37	9	14	9	27	13

Minnesota	0	0	0	0	0	1	0	0	0—1
Oakland	3	0	0	5	1	0	0	0	x—9

Minnesota	IP	H	R	ER	BB	SO
Mays (L)	3.2	9	6	6	2	1
Fiore	1.1	4	3	3	2	0
Lohse	2.0	1	0	0	0	2
Hawkins	1.0	0	0	0	0	2

Oakland	IP	H	R	ER	BB	SO
Mulder (W)	6.0	5	1	1	2	3
Bradford	2.0	1	0	0	0	1
Koch	1.0	1	0	0	0	1

E—Jones. DP—Minnesota 1, Oakland 2. LOB—Minnesota 7, Oakland 9. 2B—Mohr, Durham, Hatteberg, Tejada, Dye, Ellis. 3B—Justice. HR—Chavez, Guzman. SH—Guzman. WP—Fiore. HBP—Durham by Mays, Koskie by Bradford. T—3:04. A—31,953. U—Meriwether, plate; Marquez, first; Cousins, second; West, third; Diaz, left field; Davis, right field.

Game 3 at Minnesota

Friday, October 4

OAKLAND 6, MINNESOTA 3

HOW THEY SCORED

First Inning

Athletics—Durham hit an inside-the-park home run. Hatteberg homered to right-center. Tejada struck out. Chavez flied to Jones. Dye struck out. Two runs. Athletics 2, Twins 0.

Fourth Inning

Athletics—Justice struck out. Ellis grounded out, Guzman to Mientkiewicz. Long homered to right. Hernandez struck out. One run. Athletics 3, Twins 0.

Twins—Hunter doubled to left. Mientkiewicz singled to left as Hunter advanced to third. Cuddyer struck out. Pierzynski singled to center, scoring Hunter as Mientkiewicz advanced to second. Rivas grounded into a double play, Chavez to Hatteberg. One run. Athletics 3, Twins 1.

Fifth Inning

Twins—Jones walked. Guzman struck out. Koskie tripled to left, scoring Jones. Ortiz popped to Chavez. Hunter singled to center, scoring Koskie. Mientkiewicz popped to Chavez. Two runs. Athletics 3, Twins 3.

Sixth Inning

Athletics—Dye homered to left. Santana now pitching. Justice grounded out, Rivas to Mientkiewicz. Ellis popped to Rivas. Long flied to Jones. One run. Athletics 4, Twins 3.

Seventh Inning

Athletics—Hernandez grounded out, Rivas to Mientkiewicz. Durham walked. Velarde, pinch-hitting for Hatteberg, doubled to left-center, scoring Durham, and Velarde advanced to third on the throw to the plate. Jackson now pitching. Tejada scored Velarde on a sacrifice fly to Hunter. Chavez singled to left. Dye fouled to Mientkiewicz. Two runs. Athletics 6, Twins 3.

BOX SCORE

Oakland	AB	R	H	RBI	PO	A
Durham, dh	4	2	1	1	0	0
Hatteberg, 1b	2	1	2	1	3	0
Velarde, ph-1b	2	1	1	1	5	0
Tejada, ss	4	0	0	1	0	2
Chavez, 3b	4	0	1	0	4	3
Dye, rf	4	1	1	1	0	0
Justice, lf	4	0	0	0	1	0
Ellis, 2b	4	0	1	0	0	2
Long, cf	3	1	1	1	2	0
Hernandez, c	4	0	1	0	10	0
Zito, p	0	0	0	0	2	0
Rincon, p	0	0	0	0	0	0
Koch, p	0	0	0	0	0	0
Totals	35	6	9	6	27	7

Minnesota	AB	R	H	RBI	PO	A
Jones, lf	4	1	2	0	5	0
Guzman, ss	4	0	0	0	0	2
Koskie, 3b	5	1	1	1	0	1
Ortiz, dh	3	0	0	0	0	0
Kielty, ph-dh	1	0	0	0	0	0
Hunter, cf	4	1	2	1	2	0
Mientkiewicz, 1b	3	0	1	0	9	0
Cuddyer, rf	4	0	1	0	0	0
Pierzynski, c	3	0	1	1	10	0
Rivas, 2b	3	0	0	0	1	4
Hocking, ph	1	0	0	0	0	0
Reed, p	0	0	0	0	0	0
Santana, p	0	0	0	0	0	0
Jackson, p	0	0	0	0	0	0
Romero, p	0	0	0	0	0	0
Hawkins, p	0	0	0	0	0	0
Totals	35	3	8	3	27	7

Oakland	2	0	0	1	0	1	2	0	0—6
Minnesota	0	0	0	1	2	0	0	0	0—3

Oakland	IP	H	R	ER	BB	SO
Zito (W)	6.0	5	3	3	4	8
Rincon	2.0	2	0	0	0	2
Koch (S)	1.0	1	0	0	0	0

Minnesota	IP	H	R	ER	BB	SO
Reed (L)	*5.0	6	4	4	2	8
Santana	1.1	1	2	2	1	0
Jackson	0.2	1	0	0	0	0
Romero	1.0	1	0	0	1	0
Hawkins	1.0	0	0	0	0	2

*Pitched to one batter in sixth.

E—Ellis. DP—Oakland 1. LOB—Oakland 7, Minnesota 9. 2B—Velarde, Jones, Hunter. 3B—Koskie. HR—Durham, Hatteberg, Long, Dye. SB—Guzman. S—Tejada. WP—Zito. T—3:26. A—55,932. U—Joyce, plate; Winters, first; McClelland, second; Culbreth, third; Crawford, left field; Eddings, right field.

Game 4 at Minnesota

Saturday, October 5

MINNESOTA 11, OAKLAND 2

HOW THEY SCORED

Third Inning

Athletics—Hernandez grounded out, Koskie to Mientkiewicz. Durham flied to Hunter. Hatteberg walked. Tejada homered to left, scoring Hatteberg. Chavez flied to Jones. Two runs. Athletics 2, Twins 0.

Twins—Pierzynski singled to left. Rivas struck out. Jones doubled to right as Pierzynski advanced to third. Guzman grounded out, Tejada to Hatteberg, scoring Pierzynski. Koskie walked. Ortiz doubled to left, scoring Jones as Koskie advanced to third. Hunter grounded out, Chavez to Hatteberg. Two runs. Athletics 2, Twins 2.

Fourth Inning

Twins—Mientkiewicz singled to center. Cuddyer struck out. Pierzynski walked. Rivas reached first on a fielder's choice and advanced to second on a wild throw by Tejada, attempting to force Mientkiewicz at third. Mientkiewicz scored and Pierzynski advanced to third on the play. Pierzynski scored and Rivas advanced to third on a wild pitch. Jones was hit by a pitch. Guzman reached first on a fielder's choice and Rivas scored on a throwing error by Hatteberg. Jones advanced to second on the play. Lilly now pitching. Koskie singled to center, scoring Jones as Guzman advanced to third. Ortiz struck out. Guzman scored and Koskie advanced to second on a wild pitch. Hunter doubled to left-center, scoring Koskie. Mientkiewicz singled to center, scoring Hunter. Cuddyer flied to Justice. Seven runs. Twins 9, Athletics 2.

Seventh Inning

Twins—Hunter singled to center. Mientkiewicz homered to right, scoring Hunter. Mohr singled to right. Pierzynski flied to Long. Rivas doubled to left, but Mohr was thrown out at the plate, Justice to Tejada to Hernandez as Rivas advanced to third. Bowie now pitching. Kielty, pinch-hitting for Jones, struck out. Two runs. Twins 11, Athletics 2.

BOX SCORE

Oakland	AB	R	H	RBI	PO	A
Durham, dh	4	0	0	0	0	0
Hatteberg, 1b	3	1	1	0	6	1
Tejada, ss	4	1	1	2	2	3
Chavez, 3b	4	0	1	0	0	1
Dye, rf	3	0	3	0	0	0
Mabry, rf	1	0	0	0	0	0
Justice, lf	3	0	0	0	2	1
Piatt, lf	1	0	1	0	0	0
Ellis, 2b	3	0	0	0	1	1
Myers, c	1	0	0	0	2	0
Long, cf	3	0	0	0	3	0
Byrnes, ph	1	0	0	0	0	0
Hernandez, c	3	0	0	0	8	0
Velarde, 2b	0	0	0	0	0	0
Hudson, p	0	0	0	0	0	0
Lilly, p	0	0	0	0	0	0
Bowie, p	0	0	0	0	0	0
Totals	34	2	7	2	24	7

Minnesota	AB	R	H	RBI	PO	A
Jones, lf	3	2	1	0	4	0
Kielty, ph-rf	1	0	0	0	1	0
Guzman, ss	5	1	0	1	1	1
Koskie, 3b	4	1	1	1	0	2
Ortiz, dh	3	0	2	1	0	0
LeCroy, ph-dh	2	0	0	0	0	0
Hunter, cf	4	2	2	1	5	0
Mientkiewicz, 1b	4	2	3	3	5	1
Cuddyer, rf	3	0	0	0	1	0
Mohr, rf-lf	1	0	1	0	1	0
Pierzynski, c	3	2	1	0	6	0
Rivas, 2b	4	1	1	0	1	0
Milton, p	0	0	0	0	2	0
Lohse, p	0	0	0	0	0	0
Totals	37	11	12	7	27	4

Oakland	0	0	2	0	0	0	0	0	0—2
Minnesota	0	0	2	7	0	0	2	0	x—11

Oakland	IP	H	R	ER	BB	SO
Hudson (L)	3.1	5	7	2	2	4
Lilly	3.1	7	4	4	0	2
Bowie	1.1	0	0	0	0	3

Minnesota	IP	H	R	ER	BB	SO
Milton (W)	7.0	6	2	2	1	3
Lohse	2.0	1	0	0	0	3

E—Hatteberg, Tejada. LOB—Oakland 6, Minnesota 5. 2B—Hatteberg, Dye, Piatt, Jones, Ortiz, Hunter, Rivas. HR—Tejada, Mientkiewicz. WP—Hudson, Lilly. HBP—Jones by Hudson. T—3:20. A—55,960. U—Winters, plate; McClelland, first; Culbreth, second; Crawford, third; Eddings, left field; Joyce, right field.

Game 5 at Oakland

Sunday, October 6

MINNESOTA 5, OAKLAND 4

HOW THEY SCORED

Second Inning

Twins—LeCroy singled to short. Hunter doubled to left as LeCroy advanced to third. Mientkiewicz lined to Tejada. Cuddyer was walked intentionally. Pierzynski popped to Tejada. Hocking singled to center, scoring LeCroy as Hunter advanced to third and Cuddyer to second. Jones struck out. One run. Twins 1, Athletics 0.

Third Inning

Twins—Guzman doubled to left-center. Koskie struck out. LeCroy singled to center, scoring Guzman. Hunter forced LeCroy at second, Tejada to Ellis. Mientkiewicz grounded out to Hatteberg. One run. Twins 2, Athletics 0.

Athletics—Long grounded out, Guzman to Mientkiewicz. Hernandez struck out. Durham homered to center. Hatteberg grounded out, Mientkiewicz to Radke. One run. Twins 2, Athletics 1.

Ninth Inning

Twins—Myers now catching, Velarde at first and Koch pitching. Mohr walked. Pierzynski homered to right, scoring Mohr. Hocking grounded out, Chavez to Velarde. Jones struck out. Guzman singled to second. Guzman stole second. Koskie walked. Ortiz doubled to right-center, scoring Guzman as Koskie advanced to third. Hunter struck out. Three runs. Twins 5, Athletics 1.

Athletics—Guardado now pitching. Chavez singled to second. Dye forced Chavez at second, Koskie to Hocking. Justice doubled to right-center as Dye advanced to third. Ellis homered to left, scoring Dye and Justice. Long flied to Hunter. Velarde singled to right. Durham fouled to Hocking. Three runs. Twins 5, Athletics 4.

BOX SCORE

Minnesota	AB	R	H	RBI	PO	A
Jones, lf	5	0	0	0	2	0
Guzman, ss	5	2	3	0	1	2
Koskie, 3b	4	0	0	0	0	3
LeCroy, dh	3	1	2	1	0	0
Ortiz, ph-dh	2	0	1	1	0	0
Hunter, cf	5	0	1	0	2	0
Mientkiewicz, 1b	4	0	0	0	5	1
Cuddyer, rf	2	0	2	0	2	0
Mohr, rf	0	1	0	0	0	0
Pierzynski, c	4	1	1	2	7	0
Hocking, 2b	4	0	2	1	7	2
Radke, p	0	0	0	0	1	1
Romero, p	0	0	0	0	0	1
Hawkins, p	0	0	0	0	0	0
Guardado, p	0	0	0	0	0	0
Totals	38	5	12	5	27	10

Oakland	AB	R	H	RBI	PO	A
Durham, dh	5	1	3	1	0	0
Hatteberg, 1b	3	0	1	0	8	1
Piatt, ph	1	0	0	0	0	0
Myers, c	0	0	0	0	2	0
Tejada, ss	4	0	0	0	3	3
Chavez, 3b	4	0	2	0	2	1
Dye, rf	4	1	1	0	2	1
Justice, lf	4	1	1	0	0	0
Ellis, 2b	4	1	2	3	1	4
Long, cf	4	0	0	0	0	0
Hernandez, c	2	0	0	0	8	1
Velarde, ph-1b	2	0	1	0	1	0
Mulder, p	0	0	0	0	0	0
Bradford, p	0	0	0	0	0	0
Koch, p	0	0	0	0	0	0
Totals	37	4	11	4	27	11

Minnesota	0	1	1	0	0	0	0	0	3—5
Oakland	0	0	1	0	0	0	0	0	3—4

Minnesota	IP	H	R	ER	BB	SO
Radke (W)	6.2	6	1	1	0	4
Romero	1.0	1	0	0	0	1
Hawkins	0.1	0	0	0	0	1
Guardado	1.0	4	3	3	0	0

Oakland	IP	H	R	ER	BB	SO
Mulder (L)	7.0	9	2	2	1	9
Bradford	1.0	0	0	0	0	0
Koch	1.0	3	3	3	2	2

DP—Minnesota 1. LOB—Minnesota 9, Oakland 6. 2B—Guzman 2, Hunter, Hocking, Ortiz, Justice. HR—Durham, Pierzynski, Ellis. SB—Guzman, Durham. WP—Mulder. T—3:23. A—32,146. U—West, plate; Diaz, first; Davis, second; Meriwether, third; Marquez, left field; Cousins, right field.

COMPOSITE

BATTING AVERAGES

Minnesota Twins

Player, position	G	AB	R	H	2B	3B	HR	RBI	Avg.
Mohr, lf-rf	4	2	1	2	1	0	0	0	1.000
Hocking, 2b-rf-ph	3	6	0	3	1	0	0	1	.500
LeCroy, dh	3	9	1	4	0	0	0	1	.444
Pierzynski, c	5	16	4	7	0	1	1	4	.438
Cuddyer, rf	5	13	1	5	1	0	0	1	.385
Hunter, cf	5	20	4	6	4	0	0	2	.300
Guzman, ss	5	21	5	6	2	0	1	2	.286
Jones, lf	5	20	3	5	3	0	0	1	.250
Mientkiewicz, 1b	5	20	3	5	0	0	2	4	.250
Rivas, 2b	4	12	2	3	1	0	0	0	.250
Ortiz, dh	4	13	0	3	2	0	0	2	.231
Koskie, 3b	5	21	3	3	0	1	1	5	.143
Fiore, p	1	0	0	0	0	0	0	0	.000
Guardado, p	2	0	0	0	0	0	0	0	.000
Hawkins, p	3	0	0	0	0	0	0	0	.000
Jackson, p	1	0	0	0	0	0	0	0	.000
Lohse, p	2	0	0	0	0	0	0	0	.000
Mays, p	1	0	0	0	0	0	0	0	.000
Milton, p	1	0	0	0	0	0	0	0	.000
Radke, p	2	0	0	0	0	0	0	0	.000
Reed, p	1	0	0	0	0	0	0	0	.000
Romero, p	3	0	0	0	0	0	0	0	.000
Santana, p	2	0	0	0	0	0	0	0	.000
Prince, c	1	2	0	0	0	0	0	0	.000
Kielty, cf-rf-dh-ph	3	4	0	0	0	0	0	0	.000
Totals	5	179	27	52	15	2	5	23	.291

Oakland Athletics

Player, position	G	AB	R	H	2B	3B	HR	RBI	Avg.
Velarde, 1b-2b-ph	4	5	1	3	1	0	0	1	.600
Hatteberg, 1b	5	14	5	7	2	0	1	3	.500
Dye, rf	5	20	3	8	2	0	1	1	.400
Chavez, 3b	5	21	3	8	0	0	1	5	.381
Ellis, 2b	5	19	1	7	2	0	1	4	.368
Durham, dh	5	21	7	7	3	0	2	2	.333
Piatt, lf-ph	3	3	0	1	1	0	0	0	.333
Justice, lf	5	21	2	5	1	1	0	4	.238
Long, cf	5	18	1	3	0	0	1	1	.167
Tejada, ss	5	21	3	3	1	0	1	4	.143
Hernandez, c	5	17	0	1	0	0	0	0	.059
Bowie, p	1	0	0	0	0	0	0	0	.000
Bradford, p	2	0	0	0	0	0	0	0	.000
Hudson, p	2	0	0	0	0	0	0	0	.000
Koch, p	3	0	0	0	0	0	0	0	.000
Lidle, p	1	0	0	0	0	0	0	0	.000
Lilly, p	2	0	0	0	0	0	0	0	.000
Mecir, p	1	0	0	0	0	0	0	0	.000
Mulder, p	2	0	0	0	0	0	0	0	.000
Rincon, p	2	0	0	0	0	0	0	0	.000
Saenz, 1b-ph	1	0	0	0	0	0	0	0	.000
Zito, p	1	0	0	0	0	0	0	0	.000
Byrnes, lf-ph	2	1	0	0	0	0	0	0	.000
Myers, c	2	1	0	0	0	0	0	0	.000
Mabry, 1b-rf-ph	2	2	0	0	0	0	0	0	.000
Totals	5	184	26	53	13	1	8	25	.288

PITCHING AVERAGES

Minnesota Twins

Pitcher	G	IP	H	R	ER	BB	SO	W	L	ERA
Lohse	2	4.0	2	0	0	0	5	0	0	0.00
Romero	3	3.1	3	0	0	1	2	0	0	0.00
Hawkins	3	2.1	0	0	0	0	5	0	0	0.00
Jackson	1	0.2	1	0	0	0	0	0	0	0.00
Radke	2	11.2	14	6	2	1	7	2	0	1.54
Milton	1	7.0	6	2	2	1	3	1	0	2.57
Santana	2	3.0	3	2	2	2	2	0	0	6.00
Reed	1	5.0	6	4	4	2	8	0	1	7.20
Guardado	2	2.0	5	3	3	1	1	0	0	13.50
Mays	1	3.2	9	6	6	2	1	0	1	14.73
Fiore	1	1.1	4	3	3	2	0	0	0	20.25
Totals	5	44.0	53	26	22	12	34	3	2	4.50

No shutouts. Save—Guardado.

Oakland Athletics

Pitcher	G	IP	H	R	ER	BB	SO	W	L	ERA
Bradford	2	3.0	1	0	0	0	1	0	0	0.00
Rincon	2	3.0	2	0	0	0	2	0	0	0.00
Bowie	1	1.1	0	0	0	0	3	0	0	0.00
Mecir	1	1.0	0	0	0	0	2	0	0	0.00
Mulder	2	13.0	14	3	3	3	12	1	1	2.08
Zito	1	6.0	5	3	3	4	8	1	0	4.50
Hudson	2	8.2	13	11	6	4	8	0	1	6.23
Koch	3	3.0	5	3	3	2	3	0	0	9.00
Lidle	1	1.0	2	1	1	0	0	0	0	9.00
Lilly	2	4.0	10	6	6	1	3	0	1	13.50
Totals	5	44.0	52	27	22	14	42	2	3	4.50

No shutouts. Save—Koch.

A.L. Division Series

Anaheim vs. New York

By Doug Miller

In a season full of firsts for Anaheim, the Angels got the sweetest one in Game 4 of the American League Division Series.

For the first time in their 41-year history, the Angels won a postseason series.

They did it in come-from-behind fashion, batting around in an eight-run fifth inning to stun the Yankees, 9-5, and win the ALDS, three games to one, in front of 45,067 at Edison Field.

The Angels put a stop to New York's string of four consecutive AL championships to advance to the American League Championship Series for the first time since 1986.

"We're excited," Angels manager Mike Scioscia said. "Those guys (the Yankees) were deep. They wanted it. We beat them. Those guys on the other side, I can't say how much respect I have for them. They never gave up. ... But I'm just proud of our guys. They just beat an incredible baseball club."

The Angels handed the Yankees a beating in a huge fifth inning.

They had fallen behind, 2-1, in the top of the frame, with Yankees starter David Wells seemingly in control.

But Angels designated hitter Shawn Wooten hit a solo home run over the left-center-field wall, which tied the game at 2-2.

That kick-started the Angels' offense, which crushed Yankee pitching throughout the ALDS. The Angels totaled 56 hits and 31 runs in the series.

With one out in the fifth, Benji Gil singled, starting a string of five consecutive base hits that resulted in three more runs, putting Anaheim up 5-2.

Troy Glaus flew out to right field for the second out, but that was just a brief delay before the second wave of the assault.

Scott Spiezio drove in another run with a single, increasing Anaheim's lead to 6-2 and chasing Wells in the process.

Wells finished his $4^2/_3$ innings with eight runs allowed on 10 hits, making the final line on Yankee starters in the series a ghastly 20 earned runs in $17^1/_3$ innings.

New York brought in reliever Ramiro Mendoza, but he didn't last long.

Wooten singled in another run and Bengie Molina drove in two with a double, pushing the Angels' cushion to 9-2 and pushing Mendoza into the dugout in favor of Orlando "El Duque" Hernandez.

Hernandez gave up a single to Gil before finally retiring the side on a David Eckstein flyout, but the damage was done.

"We knew the hitters were focused, but Wells was pitching a great game," Angels general manager Bill Stoneman said. "Then Shawn drove that ball and we start piecing together one hit at a time. That inning really does kind of describe our team. They play so well together. Things just clicked for us in that inning and in the whole series."

Spiezio called the eight-run outburst "indescribable."

"That was something you dream about," Spiezio said. "Every at-bat was huge that inning, and nobody wanted to make outs. It's why we're standing here right now."

The eight runs in an inning set a Division Series record, and the 10 hits tied the postseason record set by the Philadelphia A's in the 1929 World Series.

Angels lefthander Jarrod Washburn got the win with five solid if unspectacular innings. He gave up two runs — one earned — on six hits while striking out two and walking one.

"I was gassed after the first inning," said Washburn, who was pitching on three days' rest for the second time in his big-league career. "I ran on fumes from there. I almost passed out a couple of times from being so tired and having so much adrenalin."

The Yankees added a run in the sixth on a Jorge Posada home run off reliever Brendan Donnelly and another in the seventh on two hits, a walk, and a Francisco Rodriguez wild pitch.

Closer Troy Percival was called on to pitch the ninth, and he surrendered a run on three hits, but, with police and horses circling the field, he got Nick Johnson to pop out to shortstop to end the game.

"I can't speak for everybody, but for me, it's an end to one thing and a start to another," Percival said. "We got somewhere this organization's never been, and we're getting ready to go somewhere that we've never been. ...

"It's real exciting for all of the guys that have been in this organization, for Jackie Autry, Gene Autry. I tell you, there's a lot of people that put in a lot of time to get us where we're at."

Game 1 at New York

Tuesday, October 1

NEW YORK 8, ANAHEIM 5

HOW THEY SCORED

First Inning

Yankees—Soriano popped to Kennedy. Jeter homered to left-center. Giambi singled to right. Williams grounded into a double play, Glaus to Kennedy to Spiezio. One run. Yankees 1, Angels 0.

Third Inning

Angels—Eckstein grounded out, Ventura to Giambi. Erstad singled to right. Erstad stole second and reached third on a throwing error by Posada. Salmon singled to center, scoring Erstad. Anderson grounded into a double play, Soriano to Jeter to Giambi. One run. Yankees 1, Angels 1.

Fourth Inning

Yankees—Jeter walked. Giambi homered to right-center, scoring Jeter. Williams singled to left. Posada grounded into a double play, Eckstein to Kennedy to Spiezio. Mondesi popped to Eckstein. Two runs. Yankees 3, Angels 1.

Fifth Inning

Angels—B. Molina flied to Williams. Kennedy walked. Eckstein singled to left as Kennedy advanced to third. Erstad struck out. Eckstein stole second. Salmon walked. Anderson doubled to left, scoring Kennedy and Eckstein as Salmon advanced to third. Fullmer grounded out to Giambi. Two runs. Yankees 3, Angels 3.

Yankees—Ventura popped to Eckstein. White homered to right-center. J. Rivera flied to Erstad. Soriano grounded out, Glaus to Spiezio. One run. Yankees 4, Angels 3.

Sixth Inning

Angels—Glaus homered to left. Spiezio struck out. B. Molina struck out and was retired at first after a dropped third strike, Posada to Giambi. Kennedy singled to right. Mendoza now pitching. Eckstein popped to Soriano. One run. Yankees 4, Angels 4.

Eighth Inning

Angels—Glaus homered to left. Karsay now pitching. Spiezio popped to Soriano. B. Molina grounded out, Soriano to Giambi. Kennedy struck out. One run. Angels 5, Yankees 4.

Yankees—Weber now pitching. White grounded out, Glaus to Spiezio. Vander Wal, pinch-hitting for J. Rivera, lined to Anderson. Soriano walked. Soriano stole second. Jeter walked. Schoeneweis now pitching. Giambi singled to first, scoring Soriano as Jeter advanced to third. Donnelly now pitching. Williams homered to right, scoring Jeter and Giambi. Posada flied to Anderson. Four runs. Yankees 8, Angels 5.

BOX SCORE

Anaheim	AB	R	H	RBI	PO	A
Eckstein, ss	5	1	2	0	3	2
Erstad, cf	4	1	3	0	4	0
Salmon, rf	4	0	1	1	1	0
Anderson, lf	5	0	2	2	2	0
Fullmer, dh	4	0	0	0	0	0
Glaus, 3b	4	2	2	2	1	4
Spiezio, 1b	3	0	0	0	6	1
B. Molina, c	4	0	1	0	3	0
Kennedy, 2b	3	1	1	0	4	3
Washburn, p	0	0	0	0	0	0
Weber, p	0	0	0	0	0	0
Schoeneweis, p	0	0	0	0	0	0
Donnelly, p	0	0	0	0	0	0
Totals	36	5	12	5	24	10

New York	AB	R	H	RBI	PO	A
Soriano, 2b	3	1	0	0	3	4
Jeter, ss	2	3	2	1	1	3
Giambi, 1b	4	2	3	3	12	0
Williams, cf	4	1	2	3	4	0
Posada, c	4	0	0	0	5	1
Mondesi, rf	3	0	0	0	0	0
Ventura, 3b	3	0	0	0	1	1
White, dh	3	1	1	1	0	0
J. Rivera, lf	1	0	0	0	1	0
Vander Wal, ph	1	0	0	0	0	0
Spencer, lf	0	0	0	0	0	0
Clemens, p	0	0	0	0	0	3
Mendoza, p	0	0	0	0	0	0
Karsay, p	0	0	0	0	0	0
M. Rivera, p	0	0	0	0	0	0
Totals	28	8	8	8	27	12

Anaheim	0	0	1	0	2	1	0	1	0—5
New York	1	0	0	2	1	0	0	4	x—8

Anaheim	IP	H	R	ER	BB	SO
Washburn	7.0	6	4	4	2	2
Weber (L)	0.2	0	2	2	2	0
Schoeneweis	*0.0	1	1	1	0	0
Donnelly	0.1	1	1	1	0	0

New York	IP	H	R	ER	BB	SO
Clemens	5.2	8	4	4	3	5
Mendoza	*1.1	3	1	1	0	0
Karsay (W)	1.0	0	0	0	0	1
M. Rivera (S)	1.0	1	0	0	0	0

*Pitched to one batter in eighth.

E—Posada. DP—Anaheim 4, New York 2. LOB—Anaheim 8. 2B—Anderson, B. Molina. HR—Jeter, Giambi, White, Glaus 2, Williams. SB—Eckstein, Erstad, Soriano. SH—Erstad. T—3:27. A—56,710. U—Crawford, plate; Eddings, first; Joyce, second; Winters, third; McClelland, left field; Culbreth, right field.

Game 2 at New York

Wednesday, October 2

ANAHEIM 8, NEW YORK 6

HOW THEY SCORED

First Inning

Angels—Eckstein flied to J. Rivera. Erstad grounded out, Jeter to Johnson. Salmon homered to left. Anderson struck out. One run. Angels 1, Yankees 0.

Second Inning

Angels—Glaus flied to Mondesi. Spiezio homered to left. Wooten singled to right. B. Molina singled to center as Wooten advanced to third. Gil singled to center, scoring Wooten as B. Molina advanced to second. Eckstein flied to Williams. Erstad fouled to Posada. Two runs. Angels 3, Yankees 0.

Third Inning

Angels—Salmon grounded out, Pettitte to Jeter to Johnson. Anderson singled to left. Glaus flied to J. Rivera as Anderson advanced to second. Spiezio singled to center, scoring Anderson. Wooten singled to right as Spiezio advanced to second. B. Molina forced Wooten at second, Jeter to Soriano. One run. Angels 4, Yankees 0.

Yankees—Soriano struck out. Jeter homered to left. Giambi lined to Spiezio. Williams grounded out, Gil to Spiezio. One run. Angels 4, Yankees 1.

Fourth Inning

Yankees—Ventura singled to center. Posada flied to Salmon. Johnson walked. Mondesi popped to Spiezio. J. Rivera singled to center and advanced to second on the throw home as Ventura and Johnson scored. Soriano grounded out, Eckstein to Spiezio. Two runs. Angels 4, Yankees 3.

Sixth Inning

Yankees—Rodriguez now pitching. Johnson struck out. Mondesi singled to left-center. J. Rivera forced Mondesi at second, Eckstein to Gil, but on the play, J. Rivera advanced to second when Gil threw wildly to first for an error. Soriano homered to left, scoring J. Rivera. Jeter fouled to Salmon. Two runs. Yankees 5, Angels 4.

Eighth Inning

Angels—Anderson homered to right. Glaus homered to center. Karsay now pitching. Spiezio grounded out, Jeter to Johnson. Wooten singled to center. Figgins now running for Wooten. Figgins stole second. B. Molina singled to center as Figgins advanced to third. Stanton now pitching. Kennedy scored Figgins on a sacrifice fly to Mondesi. Eckstein singled to center as B. Molina advanced to second. Erstad flied to Mondesi. Three runs. Angels 7, Yankees 5.

Ninth Inning

Angels—Vander Wal now in left field and Weaver pitching. Salmon grounded out, Soriano to Johnson. Anderson singled to right. Glaus singled to center as Anderson advanced to third. Spiezio doubled to right, scoring Anderson as Glaus advanced to third. Fullmer, pinch-hitting for Figgins, was walked intentionally. B. Molina grounded into a double play, Jeter to Soriano to Johnson. One run. Angels 8, Yankees 5.

Yankees—Ochoa now in right field. Giambi singled to left. Williams struck out. Ventura singled to right as Giambi advanced to third. Posada singled to left, scoring Giambi as Ventura advanced to second. Wilson now running for Posada. Johnson struck out. Mondesi popped to Eckstein. One run. Angels 8, Yankees 6.

BOX SCORE

Anaheim	AB	R	H	RBI	PO	A
Eckstein, ss	5	0	1	0	1	2
Erstad, cf	5	0	1	0	2	0
Salmon, rf	5	1	1	1	3	0
Ochoa, rf	0	0	0	0	0	0

Anaheim	AB	R	H	RBI	PO	A
Anderson, lf	5	3	3	1	0	0
Glaus, 3b	5	1	2	1	0	0
Spiezio, 1b	5	1	3	3	11	0
Wooten, dh	4	1	3	0	0	0
Figgins, pr-dh	0	1	0	0	0	0
Fullmer, ph-dh	0	0	0	0	0	0
B. Molina, c	5	0	2	0	8	0
Gil, 2b	2	0	1	1	2	2
Kennedy, ph-2b	1	0	0	1	0	1
Appier, p	0	0	0	0	0	1
Rodriguez, p	0	0	0	0	0	0
Weber, p	0	0	0	0	0	0
Donnelly, p	0	0	0	0	0	0
Percival, p	0	0	0	0	0	0
Totals	42	8	17	8	27	6

New York	AB	R	H	RBI	PO	A
Soriano, 2b	4	1	1	2	2	3
Jeter, ss	5	1	3	1	0	8
Giambi, dh	3	1	1	0	0	0
Williams, cf	5	0	0	0	3	0
Ventura, 3b	5	1	2	0	0	1
Posada, c	5	0	1	1	6	0
Wilson, pr	0	0	0	0	0	0
Johnson, 1b	4	1	1	0	10	0
Mondesi, rf	4	0	2	0	3	0
J. Rivera, lf	3	1	1	2	3	0
Vander Wal, ph-lf	1	0	0	0	0	0
Pettitte, p	0	0	0	0	0	1
Hernandez, p	0	0	0	0	0	1
Karsay, p	0	0	0	0	0	0
Stanton, p	0	0	0	0	0	0
Weaver, p	0	0	0	0	0	0
Totals	39	6	12	6	27	14

Anaheim	1	2	1	0	0	0	0	3	1—8
New York........................	0	0	1	2	0	2	0	0	1—6

Anaheim	IP	H	R	ER	BB	SO
Appier	5.0	5	3	3	3	3
Rodriguez (W)	2.0	2	2	2	0	1
Weber	0.1	2	0	0	0	0
Donnelly	0.1	0	0	0	0	1
Percival (S)	1.1	3	1	1	0	3

New York	IP	H	R	ER	BB	SO
Pettitte	3.0	8	4	4	0	1
Hernandez (L)	*4.0	3	2	2	0	4
Karsay	0.1	2	1	1	0	0
Stanton	0.2	1	0	0	0	0
Weaver	1.0	3	1	1	1	0

*Pitched to two batters in eighth.

E—Gil, Jeter. DP—New York 1. LOB—Anaheim 9, New York 11. 2B—Spiezio. HR—Salmon, Spiezio, Jeter, Soriano, Anderson, Glaus. SB—Figgins. S—Kennedy. HBP—Mondesi by Appier, Soriano by Percival. T—4:11. A—56,695. U—Eddings, plate; Joyce, first; Winters, second; McClelland, third; Culbreth, left field; Crawford, right field.

Game 3 at Anaheim

Friday, October 4

ANAHEIM 9, NEW YORK 6

HOW THEY SCORED

First Inning

Yankees—Soriano flied to Salmon. Jeter singled to center. Giambi walked. Jeter advanced to third on a fielder's choice. Williams walked. Ventura doubled to right-center, scoring Jeter and Giambi as Williams advanced to third. Posada scored Williams on a sacrifice fly to Salmon as Ventura advanced to third. Mondesi was hit by a pitch. Johnson fouled to Anderson. Three runs. Yankees 3, Angels 0.

Second Inning

Angels—Anderson struck out. Glaus singled to left. Fullmer doubled to right as Glaus advanced to third. Spiezio grounded to Giambi, scoring Glaus as Fullmer advanced to third. B. Molina grounded out, Soriano to Giambi. One run. Yankees 3, Angels 1.

Third Inning

Yankees—Giambi walked. Williams doubled to left as Giambi advanced to third. Ventura scored Giambi on a sacrifice fly to Erstad. Williams advanced to third on a wild pitch. Posada grounded out, Glaus to Spiezio. Mondesi walked. Lackey now pitching. Johnson singled to center, scoring Williams as Mondesi advanced to second. J. Rivera singled to left, scoring Mondesi as Johnson advanced to second. Soriano struck out. Three runs. Yankees 6, Angels 1.

Angels—Kennedy singled to center. Kennedy stole second. Eckstein lined to Giambi. Erstad singled to right as Kennedy advanced to third. Salmon doubled to left, scoring Kennedy and Erstad. Anderson grounded out, Soriano to Giambi, as Salmon advanced to third. Glaus was hit by a pitch. Fullmer struck out. Two runs. Yankees 6, Angels 3.

Fourth Inning

Angels—Spiezio fouled to Mondesi. B. Molina flied to Mondesi. Kennedy homered to right. Eckstein grounded out, Soriano to Giambi. One run. Yankees 6, Angels 4.

Sixth Inning

Angels—Fullmer singled to left. Spiezio walked. B. Molina sacrificed Fullmer to third and Spiezio to second, Giambi, unassisted. Kennedy scored Fullmer on a sacrifice fly to J. Rivera. Eckstein was hit by a pitch. Stanton now pitching. Erstad flied to Williams. One run. Yankees 6, Angels 5.

Seventh Inning

Angels—Salmon struck out. Anderson doubled to right. Glaus was walked intentionally. Wooten, pinch-hitting for Fullmer, popped to Soriano. Spiezio singled to center, scoring Anderson as Glaus advanced to third. B. Molina flied to Williams. One run. Yankees 6, Angels 6.

Eighth Inning

Angels—Kennedy doubled to right. Eckstein sacrificed Kennedy to third, Ventura to Soriano. Erstad doubled to right, scoring Kennedy. Karsay now pitching. Salmon homered to left, scoring Erstad. Anderson grounded out, Soriano to Giambi. Glaus flied to Mondesi. Three runs. Angels 9, Yankees 6.

BOX SCORE

New York	AB	R	H	RBI	PO	A
Soriano, 2b	5	0	0	0	2	4
Jeter, ss	5	1	1	0	0	1
Giambi, 1b	3	2	0	0	8	0
Williams, cf	2	2	1	0	3	0
Ventura, 3b	3	0	1	3	0	1
Posada, c	3	0	0	1	5	0
Mondesi, rf	2	1	0	0	3	0
Johnson, dh	4	0	1	1	0	0
J. Rivera, lf	4	0	2	1	3	0
Mussina, p	0	0	0	0	0	0
Weaver, p	0	0	0	0	0	0
Stanton, p	0	0	0	0	0	0
Karsay, p	0	0	0	0	0	0
Totals	31	6	6	6	24	6

Anaheim	AB	R	H	RBI	PO	A
Eckstein, ss	3	0	0	0	0	2
Erstad, cf	5	2	2	1	2	0
Salmon, rf	5	1	2	4	2	0
Ochoa, rf	0	0	0	0	0	0
Anderson, lf	4	1	1	0	4	0
Glaus, 3b	3	1	1	0	0	3
Fullmer, dh	3	1	2	0	0	0
Wooten, ph-dh	1	0	0	0	0	0
Spiezio, 1b	3	0	1	2	8	1
B. Molina, c	3	0	0	0	8	0
Kennedy, 2b	3	3	3	2	2	3
Ortiz, p	0	0	0	0	0	0
Lackey, p	0	0	0	0	1	0
Schoeneweis, p	0	0	0	0	0	0
Rodriguez, p	0	0	0	0	0	0
Percival, p	0	0	0	0	0	0
Totals	33	9	12	9	27	9

New York........................	3	0	3	0	0	0	0	0	0—6
Anaheim	0	1	2	1	0	1	1	3	x—9

New York	IP	H	R	ER	BB	SO
Mussina	4.0	6	4	4	0	2
Weaver	1.2	1	1	1	2	1
Stanton (L)	1.2	4	3	3	1	1
Karsay	0.2	1	1	1	0	0

Anaheim	IP	H	R	ER	BB	SO
Ra.Ortiz	2.2	3	6	6	4	1
Lackey	3.0	3	0	0	1	3
Schoeneweis	0.1	0	0	0	0	0
Rodriguez (W)	2.0	0	0	0	0	4
Percival (S)	1.0	0	0	0	0	0

LOB—New York 6, Anaheim 8. 2B—Williams, Ventura, Erstad, Salmon, Anderson, Fullmer, Kennedy. HR—Kennedy, Salmon. SB—Kennedy. S—Ventura, Posada, Kennedy. SH—Eckstein, B. Molina. WP—Ortiz. HBP—Mondesi by Ortiz, Glaus by Mussina, Eckstein by Weaver. T—3:52. A—45,072. U—Marquez, plate; Cousins, first; West, second; Diaz, third; Davis, left field; Meriwether, right field.

Game 4 at Anaheim

Saturday, October 5

ANAHEIM 9, NEW YORK 5

HOW THEY SCORED

Second Inning

Yankees—Posada singled to right. Mondesi flied to Erstad. Coomer singled to left as Posada advanced to third. Ventura doubled to center, scoring Posada as Coomer advanced to third. J. Rivera grounded out, Glaus to Spiezio. Soriano flied to Salmon. One run. Yankees 1, Angels 0.

Third Inning

Angels—Wooten singled to center. B. Molina sacrificed Wooten to second, Posada to Soriano. Gil singled to left as Wooten advanced to third. Eckstein reached first on a fielding error by Soriano as Wooten scored and Gil advanced to third. Erstad grounded into a double play, Soriano to Jeter to Giambi. One run. Yankees 1, Angels 1.

Fifth Inning

Yankees—J. Rivera reached first on a throwing error by Glaus. Soriano doubled to left as J. Rivera advanced to third. Jeter scored J. Rivera on a sacrifice fly to Anderson. Giambi flied to Anderson. Williams lined to Glaus. One run. Yankees 2, Angels 1.

Angels—Wooten homered to left-center. B. Molina flied to Mondesi. Gil singled to center. Eckstein singled to right as Gil advanced to third. Erstad singled to center, scoring Gil as Eckstein advanced to second. Salmon singled to left-center, scoring Eckstein as Erstad advanced to third. Anderson singled to right, scoring Erstad as Salmon advanced to third. Glaus flied to Mondesi. Spiezio singled to left, scoring Salmon as Anderson advanced to second. Mendoza now pitching. Wooten singled to center, scoring Anderson as Spiezio advanced to third. B. Molina doubled to left, scoring Spiezio and Wooten. Hernandez now pitching. Gil singled to center as B. Molina advanced to third. Eckstein flied to Williams. Eight runs. Angels 9, Yankees 2.

Sixth Inning

Yankees—Donnelly now pitching. Posada homered to center. Mondesi flied to Erstad. Johnson, pinch-hitting for Coomer, struck out. Ventura walked. J. Rivera grounded out, Glaus to Spiezio. One run. Angels 9, Yankees 3.

Seventh Inning

Yankees—Soriano popped to Gil. Jeter singled to left. Schoeneweis now pitching. Giambi singled to right as Jeter advanced to second. Rodriguez now pitching. Williams walked. Jeter scored on a wild pitch as Giambi advanced to third and Williams to second. Posada struck out. Mondesi walked. Johnson grounded out, Rodriguez to Spiezio. One run. Angels 9, Yankees 4.

Ninth Inning

Yankees—Kennedy now at second, Ochoa in right field and Percival pitching. Jeter struck out. Giambi flied to Erstad. Williams singled to center. Williams advanced to second on defensive indifference. Posada singled to right as Williams advanced to third. Mondesi singled to second, scoring Williams as Posada advanced to second. Johnson popped to Eckstein. One run. Angels 9, Yankees 5.

BOX SCORE

New York	AB	R	H	RBI	PO	A
Soriano, 2b	5	0	1	0	3	2
Jeter, ss	4	1	2	1	2	2
Giambi, 1b	4	0	1	0	6	1
Williams, cf	4	1	2	0	5	0
Posada, c	5	2	3	1	3	1
Mondesi, rf	3	0	1	1	4	0
Coomer, dh	2	0	1	0	0	0
Johnson, ph-dh	3	0	0	0	0	0
Ventura, 3b	3	0	1	1	0	1
J. Rivera, lf	4	1	0	0	1	0
Wells, p	0	0	0	0	0	0
Mendoza, p	0	0	0	0	0	0
Hernandez, p	0	0	0	0	0	0
Karsay, p	0	0	0	0	0	0
Stanton, p	0	0	0	0	0	0
Totals	37	5	12	4	24	7

Anaheim	AB	R	H	RBI	PO	A
Eckstein, ss	5	1	2	1	2	1
Erstad, cf	5	1	2	1	3	0
Salmon, rf	5	1	1	1	2	0
Ochoa, rf	0	0	0	0	0	0
Anderson, lf	4	1	1	1	3	0
Glaus, 3b	4	0	0	0	1	4
Spiezio, 1b	4	1	2	1	7	1
Wooten, dh	4	3	3	2	0	0
B. Molina, c	3	0	1	2	7	0
Gil, 2b	3	1	3	0	2	1
Kennedy, ph-2b	1	0	0	0	0	0
Washburn, p	0	0	0	0	0	0
Donnelly, p	0	0	0	0	0	0
Schoeneweis, p	0	0	0	0	0	0
Rodriguez, p	0	0	0	0	0	1
Percival, p	0	0	0	0	0	0
Totals	38	9	15	9	27	8

New York........................	0	1	0	0	1	1	1	0	1—5
Anaheim	0	0	1	0	8	0	0	0	x—9

New York	IP	H	R	ER	BB	SO
Wells (L)	4.2	10	8	8	0	0
Mendoza	*0.0	2	1	1	0	0
Hernandez	2.1	2	0	0	0	3
Karsay	0.2	0	0	0	0	0
Stanton	0.1	1	0	0	0	0

Anaheim	IP	H	R	ER	BB	SO
Washburn (W)	5.0	6	2	1	1	2
Donnelly	1.1	2	2	2	1	1
Schoeneweis	†0.0	1	0	0	0	0
Rodriguez	1.2	0	0	0	2	3
Percival	1.0	3	1	1	0	1

*Pitched to two batters in fifth.

†Pitched to one batter in seventh.

E—Wells, Soriano, Glaus. DP—New York 2, Anaheim 2. LOB—New York 11, Anaheim 6. 2B—Soriano, Ventura, Erstad, B. Molina. HR—Wooten, Posada. S—Jeter. SH—B. Molina. WP—F. Rodriguez. HBP—Giambi by Washburn. T—3:37. A—45,067. U—Cousins, plate; West, first; Diaz, second; Davis, third; Meriwether, left field; Marquez, right field.

COMPOSITE

BATTING AVERAGES

Anaheim Angels

Player, position	G	AB	R	H	2B	3B	HR	RBI	Avg.
Gil, 2b	2	5	1	4	0	0	0	1	.800
Wooten, dh	3	9	4	6	0	0	1	2	.667
Kennedy, 2b-ph	4	8	4	4	1	0	1	3	.500
Erstad, cf	4	19	4	8	2	0	0	2	.421
Spiezio, 1b	4	15	2	6	1	0	1	6	.400
Anderson, lf	4	18	5	7	2	0	1	4	.389
Glaus, 3b	4	16	4	5	0	0	3	3	.313
Fullmer, dh	3	7	1	2	1	0	0	0	.286
Eckstein, ss	4	18	2	5	0	0	0	1	.278
B. Molina, c	4	15	0	4	2	0	0	2	.267
Salmon, rf	4	19	3	5	1	0	2	7	.263
Appier, p	1	0	0	0	0	0	0	0	.000
Donnelly, p	1	0	1	0	0	0	0	0	.000
Lackey, p	1	0	0	0	0	0	0	0	.000
Ochoa, rf	3	0	0	0	0	0	0	0	.000
Ortiz, p	1	0	0	0	0	0	0	0	.000
Percival, p	3	0	0	0	0	0	0	0	.000
Rodriguez, p	3	0	0	0	0	0	0	0	.000
Schoeneweis, p	3	0	0	0	0	0	0	0	.000
Washburn, p	2	0	0	0	0	0	0	0	.000
Weber, p	2	0	0	0	0	0	0	0	.000
Totals	4	149	31	56	10	0	9	31	.376

New York Yankees

Player, position	G	AB	R	H	2B	3B	HR	RBI	Avg.
Jeter, ss	4	16	6	8	0	0	2	3	.500
Coomer, dh	1	2	0	1	0	0	0	0	.500
Giambi, 1b-dh	4	14	5	5	0	0	1	3	.357
Williams, cf	4	15	4	5	1	0	1	3	.333
White, dh	1	3	1	1	0	0	1	1	.333
Ventura, 3b	4	14	1	4	2	0	0	4	.286
Mondesi, rf	4	12	1	3	0	0	0	1	.250
J. Rivera, lf	4	12	2	3	0	0	0	3	.250
Posada, c	4	17	2	4	0	0	1	3	.235
Johnson, 1b-dh	3	11	1	2	0	0	0	1	.182
Soriano, 2b	4	17	2	2	1	0	1	2	.118
Clemens, p	1	0	0	0	0	0	0	0	.000
Hernandez, p	2	0	0	0	0	0	0	0	.000
Karsay, p	4	0	0	0	0	0	0	0	.000
Mendoza, p	2	0	0	0	0	0	0	0	.000
Mussina, p	1	0	0	0	0	0	0	0	.000
Pettitte, p	1	0	0	0	0	0	0	0	.000
M. Rivera, p	1	0	0	0	0	0	0	0	.000
Spencer, lf	1	0	0	0	0	0	0	0	.000
Stanton, p	3	0	0	0	0	0	0	0	.000
Weaver, p	2	0	0	0	0	0	0	0	.000
Wells, p	1	0	0	0	0	0	0	0	.000
Wilson, pr	1	0	0	0	0	0	0	0	.000
Vander Wal, lf-ph	2	2	0	0	0	0	0	0	.000
Totals	4	135	25	38	4	0	7	24	.281

PITCHING AVERAGES

Anaheim Angels

Pitcher	G	IP	H	R	ER	BB	SO	W	L	ERA
Lackey	1	3.0	3	0	0	1	3	0	0	0.00
Rodriguez	3	5.2	2	2	2	2	8	2	0	3.18
Washburn	2	12.0	12	6	5	3	4	1	0	3.75
Appier	1	5.0	5	3	3	3	3	0	0	5.40
Percival	3	3.1	6	2	2	0	4	0	0	5.40
Donnelly	3	2.0	3	3	3	1	2	0	0	13.50
Weber	2	1.0	2	2	2	2	0	0	1	18.00
Ortiz	1	2.2	3	6	6	4	1	0	0	20.25
Schoeneweis	3	0.1	2	1	1	0	0	0	0	27.00
Totals	4	35.0	38	25	24	16	25	3	1	6.17

No shutouts. Saves—Percival 2.

New York Yankeess

Pitcher	G	IP	H	R	ER	BB	SO	W	L	ERA
M. Rivera	1	1.0	1	0	0	0	0	0	0	0.00
Hernandez	2	6.1	5	2	2	0	7	0	1	2.84
Clemens	1	5.2	8	4	4	3	5	0	0	6.35
Karsay	4	2.2	3	2	2	0	1	1	0	6.75
Weaver	2	2.2	4	2	2	3	1	0	0	6.75
Mussina	1	4.0	6	4	4	0	2	0	0	9.00
Stanton	3	2.2	6	3	3	1	1	0	1	10.13
Pettitte	1	3.0	8	4	4	0	1	0	0	12.00
Mendoza	2	1.1	5	2	2	0	0	0	0	13.50
Wells	1	4.2	10	8	8	0	0	0	1	15.43
Totals	4	34.0	56	31	31	7	18	1	3	8.21

No shutouts. Save—Rivera.

N.L. Division Series

ST. LOUIS VS. ARIZONA

BY MATTHEW LEACH

Down go the champs. Long live the Cardinals?

Behind some sterling defense, a slew of timely hits and a gutsy performance from the bullpen — exactly the elements that have made the Redbirds winners all year long — St. Louis defeated Arizona, 6-3, in Game 3 of the National League Division Series, completing an improbable three-game sweep of the defending World Series champion Diamondbacks. The Cardinals advanced to the National League Championship Series for the second time in three years, where they would play the San Francisco Giants.

Miguel Cairo came up biggest for the Cardinals for the second straight game, driving in a pair of runs after starting in place of injured third baseman Scott Rolen. Cairo, who was no slam dunk to get the start, had three hits and reached base four times, scoring twice. Andy Benes lasted just $4^2/_3$ innings, getting into trouble in the fifth, but the St. Louis bullpen tossed $4^1/_3$ shutout innings.

"We've got a real team," said manager Tony La Russa. "I mean, I feel like we're never at a disadvantage. If the wind's blowing out, if the wind's blowing in, we can do this. We have lefthanders, righthanders. We have a good team."

In Game 2 at Bank One Ballpark, Cairo came in to play third base in a double switch soon after the injured Rolen was removed from the game. His run-scoring single was the difference in a 2-1 win. Two days later he was rewarded with his second career postseason start.

"I was just lucky and blessed that I got a chance to do it," Cairo said. "I gotta say thank you to Tony (La Russa) for giving me a chance to play today."

Early in the game, it looked like the Cardinals were headed for defeat. David Dellucci's two-run homer off of Benes in the second inning put the Diamondbacks on the board and dulled the enthusiasm of the more than 52,000 fans at Busch Stadium. But Benes seemed to settle in after that, retiring the next nine batters.

"The (whole) second half, it's been the same story," staff ace Matt Morris said of Benes. "He's been gutting it out and making pitches. He gave up two hits. They were pretty big hits, but he kept us in the game. We had the lead when he left (and) never relinquished it."

Meanwhile, the Cardinals chipped away at the usually reliable Miguel Batista, who defeated them in the 2001 Division Series. Batista walked Albert Pujols and Tino Martinez to lead off the second, and two batters later, Cairo's RBI single made it a 2-1 game.

"Today I took it like it was one of the regular games," Cairo said. "Tony's been keeping the whole bench real fresh. The whole season he gives a day off to the regular guys, and today he gave me the chance to play. I came through. I was trying to take advantage of the chance they gave me, and I just got lucky today."

Fernando Vina, who tallied nine hits in the series, got another rally going in the third. He singled, moved to second when Jim Edmonds walked and came home on a Pujols single to right.

St. Louis took the lead in dramatic fashion in the fourth. After Batista hit Cairo on his backside with a pitch, Mike Matheny singled him over to third. Benes then executed a splendid squeeze bunt to score a tumbling Cairo.

"We knew the guy needed to throw a strike (on a) 3-1 (count) and he threw a pretty good pitch," Benes said. "I didn't hit it hard, but got it far enough out that Miguel could score."

Vina followed with a run-scoring single to right, but was caught stealing to end the inning. Still, it was 4-2, and with Benes picking up steam, the Cardinals appeared to be in fine shape.

But catcher Rod Barajas, making his first start of the series, made it a 4-3 game with a solo homer off of Benes in the fifth. A pair of walks in the same inning spelled the end for the St. Louis starter, who gave way to Jeff Fassero.

Steve Finley, the first batter to face Fassero, singled to left, but Pujols threw out Chris Donnels trying to score from second with what would have been the tying run.

"I'm coming (into) a situation to get a lefthander out," Fassero said. "Didn't get him out the way I wanted, but everything worked out all right."

From there, the St. Louis bullpen did its usual superb job. Fassero pitched a scoreless sixth, and Rick White and Steve Kline were perfect in the seventh and eighth, respectively. With Jason Isringhausen looming in the ninth, a one-run lead was already daunting.

But thanks again to Cairo, the Cardinals put the game out of reach in the bottom of the eighth. Pujols led off with a walk against D-Backs closer Byung-Hyun Kim, and Martinez reached on a force at second. Cairo doubled home Martinez for the first insurance run, and two batters later, pinch-hitter Kerry Robinson singled Cairo in.

"Our guys that we've got on the bench, all year long they've been coming through," Pujols said. "And Miguel was one of the guys today and Thursday. That's the way it is. He played a good game today. Everybody played a good game."

Isringhausen, who has been bothered by tendinitis in his right shoulder, showed no ill effects in pitching a perfect ninth. It was his second save of the series, and his fifth in five career playoff chances.

"It's one step farther than I've been the last two years," said Isringhausen, who played on Oakland teams that were eliminated in the first round in 2000 and 2001. "But we've got to keep going. We've got two more steps to go, but we'll take them one at a time. And if we get to play in the World Series, it's gonna be great."

Game 1 at Arizona

Tuesday, October 1

ST. LOUIS 12, ARIZONA 2

HOW THEY SCORED

First Inning

Cardinals—Vina reached first on a throwing error by Womack. Marrero flied to Dellucci as Vina advanced to second. Edmonds homered to right, scoring Vina. Pujols flied to Dellucci. Rolen struck out. Two runs. Cardinals 2, Diamondbacks 0.

Diamondbacks—Womack reached first on a fielding error by Renteria. Spivey singled to left as Womack advanced to third. S. Finley scored Womack on a sacrifice fly to Edmonds. Grace singled to center as Spivey advanced to second. Williams singled to left as Spivey advanced to third and Grace to second, but Spivey was thrown out trying to score, Pujols to Matheny. McCracken flied to Pujols. One run. Cardinals 2, Diamondbacks 1.

Third Inning

Diamondbacks—Spivey grounded out, Rolen to Martinez. S. Finley walked. Finley stole second. Grace walked. Williams fouled to Martinez. McCracken singled to left, scoring S. Finley as Grace advanced to second. Dellucci fouled to Rolen. One run. Cardinals 2, Diamondbacks 2.

Fourth Inning

Cardinals—Pujols tripled to right-center. Rolen homered to left-center, scoring Pujols. Renteria singled to center. Renteria stole second. Martinez grounded out, Spivey to Grace, as Renteria advanced to third. Matheny singled to left, scoring Renteria. Morris struck out. Vina singled to center as Matheny advanced to second. Marrero struck out. Three runs. Cardinals 5, Diamondbacks 2.

Sixth Inning

Cardinals—Matheny doubled to left. Morris struck out. Vina singled to center as Matheny advanced to third. Marrero scored Matheny on a sacrifice fly to S. Finley. Edmonds grounded out, Spivey to Grace. One run. Cardinals 6, Diamondbacks 2.

Seventh Inning

Cardinals—Mantei now pitching and Barajas catching. Pujols walked. Rolen fouled to Grace. Renteria singled to center as Pujols advanced to second. Swindell now pitching. Martinez walked. Matheny bunted and was safe at first on a throwing error by Swindell. Pujols and Renteria scored on the play and Martinez advanced to third and Matheny to second. Morris singled to left, scoring Martinez and Matheny. Vina singled to left as Morris advanced to second. Fetters now pitching. Marrero flied to Dellucci. Edmonds walked. Pujols singled to left, scoring Morris and Vina, as Edmonds advanced to second. Rolen struck out and was retired at first after a dropped third strike, Barajas to Grace. Six runs. Cardinals 12, Diamondbacks 2.

BOX SCORE

St. Louis	AB	R	H	RBI	PO	A
Vina, 2b	6	2	3	0	2	2
Marrero, rf	5	0	0	1	2	0
Edmonds, cf	4	1	3	2	3	0
Pujols, lf	4	2	2	2	1	1
Rolen, 3b	5	1	1	2	1	2
Renteria, ss	4	2	2	0	3	3
Martinez, 1b	4	1	0	0	8	1
Matheny, c	3	2	2	2	6	0
M.Morris, p	4	1	1	2	1	1
Fassero, p	0	0	0	0	0	0
Robinson, ph	1	0	0	0	0	0
Crudale, p	0	0	0	0	0	0
Totals	40	12	14	11	27	10

Arizona	AB	R	H	RBI	PO	A
Womack, ss	5	1	1	0	0	3
Spivey, 2b	5	0	1	0	2	7
S. Finley, cf	2	1	0	1	3	0
Grace, 1b	3	0	1	0	13	0
Williams, 3b	4	0	1	0	0	1
Cintron, 3b	0	0	0	0	0	0
McCracken, rf	4	0	2	1	1	0
Dellucci, lf	3	0	1	0	4	0
Little, ph-lf	1	0	0	0	0	0
Moeller, c	3	0	1	0	4	1
Barajas, c	1	0	0	0	0	1
Johnson, p	2	0	0	0	0	0
Mantei, p	0	0	0	0	0	0
Swindell, p	0	0	0	0	0	0
Fetters, p	0	0	0	0	0	0
Donnels, ph	1	0	0	0	0	0
Helling, p	0	0	0	0	0	1
Durazo, ph	0	0	0	0	0	0
Totals	34	2	8	2	27	14

St. Louis	2	0	0	3	0	1	6	0	0	—12
Arizona	1	0	1	0	0	0	0	0	0	— 2

St. Louis	IP	H	R	ER	BB	SO
Morris (W)	7.0	7	2	1	2	3
Fassero	1.0	1	0	0	0	0
Crudale	1.0	0	0	0	1	2

Arizona	IP	H	R	ER	BB	SO
Johnson (L)	6.0	10	6	5	2	4
Mantei	0.1	1	2	2	1	0
Swindell	*0.0	2	4	1	1	0
Fetters	0.2	1	0	0	1	1
Helling	2.0	0	0	0	0	0

*Pitched to four batters in seventh.

E—Renteria, Swindell, Womack. LOB—St. Louis 8, Arizona 9. 2B—Matheny. 3B—Pujols. HR—Edmonds, Rolen. SB—Renteria, S. Finley. CS—Edmonds. S—Marrero, S. Finley. SH—Matheny. T—2:55. A—49,154. U—Froemming, plate; Miller, first; Kulpa, second; Darling, third; Rippley, left field; M. Hirschbeck, right field.

Game 2 at Arizona

Thursday, October 3

ST. LOUIS 2, ARIZONA 1

HOW THEY SCORED

Third Inning

Cardinals—C. Finley struck out. Vina flied to S. Finley. Drew homered to left. Edmonds flied to Little. One run. Cardinals 1, Diamondbacks 0.

Eighth Inning

Diamondbacks—Marrero now in left field and Pujols moves to third. Colbrunn reached first on a fielding error by Pujols. Williams fouled to Martinez. S. Finley popped to Renteria. McCracken doubled to right, scoring Colbrunn. Miller walked. Grace now pinch-hitting for Little. Cairo now at third, Fassero pitching and Pujols moves to first. Grace flied to Drew. One run. Cardinals 1, Diamondbacks 1.

Ninth Inning

Cardinals—Grace now at first and Dellucci in left field. Renteria singled to left. Matheny sacrificed Renteria to second, Grace to Spivey. Cairo singled to center, scoring Renteria, and Cairo advanced to second on the play. Myers now pitching. Cairo was caught trying to steal third, Myers to Williams to Womack. Vina singled to center. Drew popped to Grace. One run. Cardinals 2, Diamondbacks 1.

BOX SCORE

St. Louis	AB	R	H	RBI	PO	A
Vina, 2b	5	0	4	0	2	3
Drew, rf	4	1	1	1	2	0
Edmonds, cf	4	0	0	0	4	0
Pujols, lf-3b-1b	4	0	0	0	1	0
Rolen, 3b	2	0	2	0	1	2
Marrero, ph-lf	1	0	0	0	0	0
Martinez, 1b	4	0	0	0	7	0
Fassero, p	0	0	0	0	0	0
Isringhausen, p	0	0	0	0	0	0
Renteria, ss	4	1	1	0	2	1
Matheny, c	3	0	1	0	8	2
C. Finley, p	3	0	0	0	0	1

St. Louis	AB	R	H	RBI	PO	A
Kline, p	0	0	0	0	0	0
White, p	0	0	0	0	0	0
Cairo, 3b	1	0	1	1	0	0
Totals	35	2	10	2	27	9

Arizona	AB	R	H	RBI	PO	A
Womack, ss	4	0	1	0	3	3
Spivey, 2b	5	0	1	0	4	2
Colbrunn, 1b	3	1	0	0	4	1
Dellucci, lf	0	0	0	0	0	0
Williams, 3b	4	0	0	0	1	1
S. Finley, cf	4	0	1	0	4	0
McCracken, rf	4	0	1	1	0	0
Miller, c	2	0	1	0	8	0
Little, lf	3	0	0	0	1	0
Grace, ph-1b	1	0	0	0	1	1
Schilling, p	2	0	0	0	0	0
Moeller, ph	1	0	1	0	0	0
Cintron, pr	0	0	0	0	0	0
Koplove, p	0	0	0	0	1	0
Myers, p	0	0	0	0	0	1
Donnels, ph	1	0	0	0	0	0
Totals	34	1	6	1	27	9

St. Louis	0	0	1	0	0	0	0	0	1—2
Arizona	0	0	0	0	0	0	0	1	0—1

St. Louis	IP	H	R	ER	BB	SO
C. Finley	6.1	4	0	0	2	7
Kline	0.1	1	0	0	1	0
White	1.0	1	1	0	1	0
Fassero (W)	0.1	0	0	0	0	0
Isringhausen (S)	1.0	0	0	0	0	1

Arizona	IP	H	R	ER	BB	SO
Schilling	7.0	7	1	1	1	7
Koplove (L)	1.1	2	1	1	0	1
Myers	0.2	1	0	0	0	0

E—Pujols. LOB—St. Louis 9, Arizona 10. 2B—McCracken, Miller. HR—Drew. SB—Renteria. CS—Cairo. SH—Matheny. HBP—Rolen by Schilling. T—3:20. A—48,856. U—Miller, plate; Kulpa, first; Darling, second; Rippley, third; M. Hirschbeck, left field; Froemming, right field.

Game 3 at St. Louis

Saturday, October 5

ST. LOUIS 6, ARIZONA 3

HOW THEY SCORED

Second Inning

Diamondbacks—Durazo flied to Drew. McCracken walked. Dellucci homered to right-center, scoring McCracken. Barajas flied to Edmonds. Batista struck out. Two runs. Diamondbacks 2, Cardinals 0.

Cardinals—Pujols and Martinez walked. Renteria grounded into a double play, Spivey to Womack to Durazo, as Pujols advanced to third. Cairo singled to left, scoring Pujols. Matheny grounded out, Womack to Durazo. One run. Diamondbacks 2, Cardinals 1.

Third Inning

Cardinals—Benes grounded out, Womack to Durazo. Vina singled to left. Drew struck out. Edmonds walked. Pujols singled to right, scoring Vina as Edmonds advanced to third. Martinez lined to Williams. One run. Diamondbacks 2, Cardinals 2.

Fourth Inning

Cardinals—Renteria grounded out, Spivey to Durazo. Cairo was hit by a pitch. Matheny singled to right-center as Cairo advanced to third. Benes scored Cairo and advanced Matheny to second with a sacrifice bunt, Barajas to Spivey. Vina singled to right, scoring Matheny. Swindell now pitching. Vina was caught trying to steal second, Swindell to Durazo to Womack. Two runs. Cardinals 4, Diamondbacks 2.

Fifth Inning

Diamondbacks—Dellucci grounded out, Vina to Martinez. Barajas homered to left. Donnels, pinch-hitting for Swindell, walked. Womack fouled to Renteria. Spivey walked. Fassero now pitching. S. Finley singled to left and advanced to second as Donnels advanced to third, but was out trying to score, Pujols to Matheny. One run. Cardinals 4, Diamondbacks 3.

Eighth Inning

Cardinals—Kim now pitching. Pujols walked. Martinez forced Pujols at second, Kim to Womack. Renteria popped to Spivey. Cairo doubled to left-center, scoring Martinez. Matheny was walked intentionally. Robinson, pinch-hitting for Kline, singled to left, scoring Cairo as Matheny advanced to second. Vina walked. Drew flied to S. Finley. Two runs. Cardinals 6, Diamondbacks 3.

BOX SCORE

Arizona	AB	R	H	RBI	PO	A
Womack, ss	4	0	0	0	4	3
Spivey, 2b	3	0	0	0	2	3
S. Finley, cf	3	0	1	0	5	0
Williams, 3b	4	0	0	0	2	0
Durazo, 1b	4	0	0	0	6	2
McCracken, rf	3	1	1	0	0	0
Dellucci, lf	4	1	1	2	0	0
Barajas, c	3	1	1	1	4	1
Batista, p	1	0	0	0	0	0
Swindell, p	0	0	0	0	0	1
Donnels, ph	0	0	0	0	0	0
Helling, p	0	0	0	0	0	0
Moeller, ph	1	0	0	0	0	0
Myers, p	0	0	0	0	1	0
Kim, p	0	0	0	0	0	1
Totals	30	3	4	3	24	11

St. Louis	AB	R	H	RBI	PO	A
Vina, 2b	4	1	2	1	1	3
Drew, rf	5	0	1	0	3	0
Edmonds, cf	3	0	0	0	4	0
Pujols, lf	2	1	1	1	1	1
Martinez, 1b	3	1	0	0	7	0
Renteria, ss	4	0	0	0	1	0
Cairo, 3b	3	2	3	2	0	2
Matheny, c	3	1	1	0	10	1
Benes, p	1	0	0	1	0	0
Fassero, p	0	0	0	0	0	0
White, p	0	0	0	0	0	0
Perez, ph	1	0	0	0	0	0
Kline, p	0	0	0	0	0	0
Robinson, ph	1	0	1	1	0	0
Isringhausen, p	0	0	0	0	0	0
Totals	30	6	9	6	27	7

Arizona	0	2	0	0	1	0	0	0	0—3
St. Louis	0	1	1	2	0	0	0	2	x—6

Arizona	IP	H	R	ER	BB	SO
Batista (L)	3.2	5	4	4	3	1
Swindell	0.1	0	0	0	0	0
Helling	2.0	1	0	0	0	2
Myers	1.0	1	0	0	0	1
Kim	1.0	2	2	2	3	0

St. Louis	IP	H	R	ER	BB	SO
Benes	4.2	2	3	3	4	5
Fassero (W)	1.1	2	0	0	0	2
White	1.0	0	0	0	0	1
Kline	1.0	0	0	0	0	0
Isringhausen (S)	1.0	0	0	0	0	0

DP—Arizona 1. LOB—Arizona 4, St. Louis 8. 2B—Cairo. HR—Dellucci, Barajas. CS—Vina. SH—Benes. BK—Benes. HBP—Cairo by Batista. T—3:14. A—52,189. U—Hernandez, plate; Layne, first; Tschida, second; Barrett, third; Reilly, left field; Emmel, right field.

COMPOSITE

BATTING AVERAGES

St. Louis Cardinals

Player, position	G	AB	R	H	2B	3B	HR	RBI	Avg.
Cairo, 3b	2	4	2	4	1	0	0	3	1.000
Vina, 2b	3	15	3	9	0	0	0	1	.600
Robinson, ph	2	2	0	1	0	0	0	1	.500
Matheny, c	3	9	3	4	1	0	0	2	.444
Rolen, 3b	2	7	1	3	0	0	1	2	.429
Pujols, 1b-3b-lf	3	10	3	3	0	1	0	3	.300
Edmonds, cf	3	11	1	3	0	0	1	2	.273
Renteria, ss	3	12	3	3	0	0	0	0	.250
Morris, p	1	4	1	1	0	0	0	2	.250
Drew, rf	2	9	1	2	0	0	1	1	.222
Crudale, p	1	0	0	0	0	0	0	0	.000
Fassero, p	3	0	0	0	0	0	0	0	.000
Isringhausen, p	2	0	0	0	0	0	0	0	.000
Kline, p	2	0	0	0	0	0	0	0	.000
White, p	2	0	0	0	0	0	0	0	.000
Benes, p	1	1	0	0	0	0	0	1	.000
Perez, ph	1	1	0	0	0	0	0	0	.000
C. Finley, p	1	3	0	0	0	0	0	0	.000
Marrero, lf-rf-ph	2	6	0	0	0	0	0	1	.000
Martinez, 1b	3	11	2	0	0	0	0	0	.000
Totals	3	105	20	33	2	1	3	19	.314

Arizona Diamondbacks

Player, position	G	AB	R	H	2B	3B	HR	RBI	Avg.
Miller, c	1	2	0	1	1	0	0	0	.500
Moeller, c-ph	3	5	0	2	0	0	0	0	.400
McCracken, rf	3	11	1	4	1	0	0	2	.364
Dellucci, lf	3	7	1	2	0	0	1	2	.286
Barajas, c	2	4	1	1	0	0	1	1	.250
Grace, 1b-ph	2	4	0	1	0	0	0	0	.250
S. Finley, cf	3	9	1	2	0	0	0	1	.222
Spivey, 2b	3	13	0	2	0	0	0	0	.154
Womack, ss	3	13	1	2	0	0	0	0	.154
Williams, 3b	3	12	0	1	0	0	0	0	.083
Cintron, 3b-pr	2	0	0	0	0	0	0	0	.000
Fetters, p	1	0	0	0	0	0	0	0	.000
Helling, p	2	0	0	0	0	0	0	0	.000
Kim, p	1	0	0	0	0	0	0	0	.000
Koplove, p	1	0	0	0	0	0	0	0	.000
Mantei, p	1	0	0	0	0	0	0	0	.000
Myers, p	2	0	0	0	0	0	0	0	.000
Swindell, p	2	0	0	0	0	0	0	0	.000
Batista, p	1	1	0	0	0	0	0	0	.000
Donnels, ph	3	2	0	0	0	0	0	0	.000
Johnson, p	1	2	0	0	0	0	0	0	.000
Schilling, p	1	2	0	0	0	0	0	0	.000
Colbrunn, 1b	1	3	1	0	0	0	0	0	.000
Durazo, 1b-ph	2	4	0	0	0	0	0	0	.000
Little, lf-ph	2	4	0	0	0	0	0	0	.000
Totals	3	98	6	18	2	0	2	6	.184

PITCHING AVERAGES

St. Louis Cardinals

Pitcher	G	IP	H	R	ER	BB	SO	W	L	ERA
C. Finley	1	6.1	4	0	0	2	7	0	0	0.00
Fassero	3	2.2	3	0	0	0	2	2	0	0.00
Isringhausen	2	2.0	0	0	0	0	1	0	0	0.00
White	2	2.0	1	1	0	1	1	0	0	0.00
Kline	2	1.1	1	0	0	1	0	0	0	0.00
Crudale	1	1.0	0	0	0	1	2	0	0	0.00
Morris	1	7.0	7	2	1	2	3	1	0	1.29
Benes	1	4.2	2	3	3	4	5	0	0	5.79
Totals	3	27.0	18	6	4	11	21	3	0	1.33

No shutouts. Saves—Isringhausen 2.

Arizona Diamondbacks

Pitcher	G	IP	H	R	ER	BB	SO	W	L	ERA
Helling	2	4.0	1	0	0	0	2	0	0	0.00
Myers	2	1.2	2	0	0	0	1	0	0	0.00
Fetters	1	0.2	1	0	0	1	1	0	0	0.00
Schilling	1	7.0	7	1	1	1	7	0	0	1.29
Koplove	1	1.1	2	1	1	0	1	0	1	6.75
Johnson	1	6.0	10	6	5	2	4	0	1	7.50
Batista	1	3.2	5	4	4	3	1	0	1	9.82
Kim	1	1.0	2	2	2	3	0	0	0	18.00
Swindell	2	0.1	2	4	1	1	0	0	0	27.00
Mantei	1	0.1	1	2	2	1	0	0	0	54.00
Totals	3	26.0	33	20	16	12	17	0	3	5.54

No shutouts or saves.

N.L. Division Series

San Francisco vs. Atlanta

BY JOSH RAWITCH

Five times in his career Barry Bonds had come face to face with postseason elimination, and five times he had come up empty. With two hits and no RBIs in over 16 at-bats in those games, Bonds had become known as a player who could not perform under playoff pressure.

So much for history.

Bonds homered and scored twice, Russ Ortiz pitched another solid game, and the Giants stared down a ninth-inning Braves rally to become the first team in National League Division Series history to wipe out a two-games-to-one deficit, upsetting the Braves 3-1 in Game 5 at Turner Field to advance to the NL Championship Series against the St. Louis Cardinals.

"Right now I'm just a little bit shocked because I've never been past the first round," said Bonds. "I don't know how to respond right now. I don't know [whether] to be happy or to just sit here."

Ortiz (2-0) followed up a gutsy Game 1 performance with yet another solid outing, holding the Braves to four hits and one run over $5^1/_3$ innings while earning a victory for the eighth consecutive start.

"I felt real relaxed, kind of like I did the first game. So I felt like I was going to be able to go out there and hit my spots and I did for basically the first five innings," said Ortiz. "You just can't say enough about this team. A lot of people counted us out but we never did and we ... took care of what we needed to do and we got the job done."

Bonds, who had never before won a postseason series and entered Game 5 of this series with a .198 career playoff average, singled off Kevin Millwood in the second inning and reached second base on a groundout by Benito Santiago. Two batters later, Reggie Sanders ripped a base hit up the middle off Kevin Millwood to give the Giants a 1-0 lead.

Millwood (1-1), who was starting on three days rest, made few mistakes while striking out seven batters in five innings. But one of his biggest was a full-count fastball over the plate that Bonds crushed in the fourth inning, sending the ball deep into the left-center-field pavilion for his third homer of the series, the most by a Giant in a postseason series since Jeffrey Leonard went deep four times in the 1987 NLCS.

"I'll take a big hit for this [but] we're not playing for Barry," said second baseman Jeff Kent. "I'm sorry. This is a whole team effort. There's a lot of guys in here that did a lot of good things for this series. Barry contributed, you bet. But our pitching staff did a phenomenal job."

Atlanta did its part to try to minimize Bonds' production throughout the series, retiring Kent for the last out of an inning seven times in five games, forcing Bonds to lead off the next frame on each occasion. Bonds, who had hit two meaningless homers in the first four games, came through in the clutch in Game 5, finishing the series with a .294 average (5-for-17) and four RBIs.

Against Ortiz, the Braves certainly had their chances. In the fifth inning, a one-out error by third baseman David Bell and two-out walk to Julio Franco put runners on first and second for Gary Sheffield. A wild pitch allowed both runners to advance and Sheffield walked to load the bases. But after a conference on the mound with pitching coach Dave Righetti, Ortiz got Chipper Jones to ground sharply to shortstop Rich Aurilia, who made a nice play on a bad hop to get the force out at second.

"It hit something right before the base and it took a bad hop on me," said Aurilia. "I don't know how it ended up in my glove. I just stuck my glove out and it ended up in there."

Ortiz was not as lucky in the sixth. Andruw Jones led off with a single and after Javy Lopez struck out, Vinny Castilla singled to put runners on first and second. Giants manager Dusty Baker turned to Aaron Fultz, who allowed a single to pinch-hitter Mark DeRosa, cutting the Giants' lead in half.

But Felix Rodriguez got the final two outs of the inning before the Giants loaded the bases with nobody out against All-Star lefthander, and former Giant, Mike Remlinger. Darren Holmes took over and allowed just a sacrifice fly to Kenny Lofton for a key insurance run, but that was enough breathing room.

Tim Worrell pitched just his second two-inning stint of the year, blanking the Braves in the seventh and eighth, before Robb Nen closed things out to earn his second save of the series.

But the save didn't come easy. Kent made a nice pickup of Rafael Furcal's leadoff grounder but threw wide of first base, causing J.T. Snow to come off the bag. Franco followed with a base hit to right, advancing Furcal to third. Sheffield, the potential winning run, struck out swinging at a Nen blazer before Chipper Jones bounced to Snow, who stepped on first base and caught Franco in a rundown between first and second. Snow tossed to Aurilia, Aurilia applied the tag and the Giants began celebrating.

"I think everybody kind of wrote us off but we just went out and battled and played hard," said Nen. "We stayed positive in the clubhouse and always think we can do what we want to do. This is what we're here to do. We've still got a long way to go, but [we'll] enjoy this, and after tonight look forward to the Cardinals."

Catcher Benito Santiago, who predicted before the regular season ended that his team would not only make the playoffs but upset the Braves, made another prediction during the postgame celebration.

"We're going to win," he said. "I know that I've got to respect [the Cardinals] but this (Atlanta) was a hard team to beat. The way we played yesterday and it carried over until tonight, that's great. I think we're going to beat those guys."

Game 1 at Atlanta

Wednesday, October 2

SAN FRANCISCO 8, ATLANTA 5

HOW THEY SCORED

Second Inning

Giants—Bonds grounded out, Lockhart to J. Franco. Santiago singled to right. Sanders singled to center as Santiago advanced to second. Snow doubled to right, scoring Santiago and Sanders. Bell singled to left-center, scoring Snow. Ortiz and Lofton struck out. Three runs. Giants 3, Braves 0.

Braves—C. Jones grounded out, Kent to Snow. A. Jones singled to left. Lopez popped to Bell. Castilla singled to center as A. Jones advanced to second. A. Jones advanced to third and Castilla to second on a wild pitch. Lockhart was walked intentionally. Glavine singled to left, scoring A. Jones and Castilla. A throwing error by Bonds on the play allowed Lockhart to reach third and Glavine second. Furcal flied to Lofton. Two runs. Giants 3, Braves 2.

Fourth Inning

Giants—Sanders grounded out, Castilla to J. Franco. Snow grounded out, Lockhart to J. Franco. Bell singled to center. Ortiz singled to left-center as Bell advanced to third. Lofton singled to center, scoring Bell as Ortiz advanced to second. Aurilia doubled to right-center, scoring Ortiz and Lofton. Kent walked. Bonds flied to A. Jones. Three runs. Giants 6, Braves 2.

Sixth Inning

Giants—Hammond now pitching. Lofton grounded out, Lockhart to J. Franco. Aurilia grounded out, Hammond to J. Franco. Kent doubled to left. Bonds was walked intentionally. Santiago doubled to right-center, scoring Kent and Bonds. Sanders walked. Gryboski now pitching. Snow flied to C. Jones. Two runs. Giants 8, Braves 2.

Eighth Inning

Braves—Worrell now pitching. J. Franco grounded out, Bell to Snow. Sheffield homered to left-center. C. Jones singled to center. A. Jones forced C. Jones at second, Aurilia to Kent. After his at-bat was prolonged by an error by Santiago, Lopez homered to left, scoring A. Jones. Castilla singled to left. M. Franco now pinch-hitting for Moss. Eyre now pitching. Giles, pinch-hitting for M. Franco, fouled to Santiago. Three runs. Giants 8, Braves 5.

BOX SCORE

San Francisco	AB	R	H	RBI	PO	A
Lofton, cf	4	1	1	1	4	0
Aurilia, ss	5	0	1	2	0	4
Kent, 2b	4	1	1	0	6	5
Bonds, lf	4	1	1	0	2	0
Santiago, c	5	1	3	2	4	0
Sanders, rf	4	1	1	0	1	0
Snow, 1b	5	1	1	2	8	0
Bell, 3b	4	1	2	1	2	3
Ortiz, p	4	1	1	0	0	0
Worrell, p	0	0	0	0	0	0
Eyre, p	0	0	0	0	0	0
Nen, p	0	0	0	0	0	0
Totals	39	8	12	8	27	12

Atlanta	AB	R	H	RBI	PO	A
Furcal, ss	5	0	2	0	1	1
J. Franco, 1b	5	0	1	0	8	0
Sheffield, rf	4	1	1	1	1	0
C. Jones, lf	3	0	1	0	2	0
A. Jones, cf	4	2	1	0	3	0
Lopez, c	4	1	1	2	9	0
Castilla, 3b	4	1	2	0	0	2
Lockhart, 2b	1	0	0	0	3	3
Moss, p	0	0	0	0	0	0
M. Franco, ph	0	0	0	0	0	0
Giles, ph	1	0	0	0	0	0
Holmes, p	0	0	0	0	0	0
Glavine, p	1	0	1	2	0	1
Bragg, ph	1	0	0	0	0	0
Hammond, p	0	0	0	0	0	1
Gryboski, p	0	0	0	0	0	0
DeRosa, ph-2b	1	0	0	0	0	1
Totals	34	5	10	5	27	9

San Francisco	0	3	0	3	0	2	0	0	0—8
Atlanta	0	2	0	0	0	0	0	3	0—5

San Francisco	IP	H	R	ER	BB	SO
Ortiz (W)	7.0	5	2	2	4	3
Worrell	0.2	4	3	1	0	0
Eyre	0.1	0	0	0	0	0
Nen (S)	1.0	1	0	0	1	0

Atlanta	IP	H	R	ER	BB	SO
Glavine (L)	5.0	10	6	6	2	3
Hammond	0.2	2	2	2	2	0
Gryboski	1.1	0	0	0	1	2
Moss	1.0	0	0	0	0	2
Holmes	1.0	0	0	0	0	2

E—Santiago, Bonds. DP—San Francisco 3. LOB—San Francisco 9, Atlanta 7. 2B—Aurilia, Kent, Santiago, Snow. HR—Sheffield, Lopez. WP—Ortiz. T—3:24. A—41,903. U—Reilly, plate; Emmel, first; Hernandez, second; Layne, third; Tschida, left field; Barrett, right field.

Game 2 at Atlanta

Thursday, October 3

ATLANTA 7, SAN FRANCISCO 3

HOW THEY SCORED

First Inning

Braves—Furcal grounded out, Snow to Rueter. Franco walked. Sheffield grounded out, Bell to Snow, as Franco advanced to second. C. Jones singled to left, scoring Franco. A. Jones struck out. One run. Braves 1, Giants 0.

Second Inning

Giants—Bonds struck out. Santiago lined to Sheffield. Snow homered to left. Sanders fouled to Sheffield. One run. Braves 1, Giants 1.

Braves—Lopez homered to left-center. Castilla homered to center. DeRosa doubled to right. Millwood sacrificed DeRosa to third, Santiago to Kent. Furcal singled to center, scoring DeRosa. Furcal caught trying to steal second, Santiago to Aurilia to Snow to Kent. Franco grounded out, Bell to Snow. Three runs. Braves 4, Giants 1.

Fourth Inning

Braves—Lopez singled to center. Castilla walked. DeRosa tripled to right, scoring Lopez and Castilla. Aybar now pitching. Millwood grounded out, Bell to Snow. Furcal struck out. DeRosa scored on a passed ball by Santiago. Franco struck out. Three runs. Braves 7, Giants 1.

Sixth Inning

Giants—Feliz, pinch-hitting for Aybar, struck out. Lofton grounded out, Franco to Millwood. Aurilia homered to left-center. Kent grounded out, Furcal to Franco. One run. Braves 7, Giants 2.

Ninth Inning

Giants—Bonds homered to right. Santiago, Snow and Sanders struck out. One run. Braves 7, Giants 3.

BOX SCORE

San Francisco	AB	R	H	RBI	PO	A
Lofton, cf	4	0	1	0	1	0
Aurilia, ss	4	1	1	1	1	3
Kent, 2b	4	0	0	0	3	3
Bonds, lf	4	1	1	1	2	0
Santiago, c	4	0	1	0	4	2
Snow, 1b	4	1	2	1	12	2
Sanders, rf	4	0	1	0	0	0
Bell, 3b	3	0	0	0	0	7
Rueter, p	1	0	0	0	1	0
Aybar, p	0	0	0	0	0	0
Feliz, ph	1	0	0	0	0	0
Witasick, p	0	0	0	0	0	0
Goodwin, ph	1	0	0	0	0	0
Rodriguez, p	0	0	0	0	0	0
Totals	34	3	7	3	24	17

tlanta	AB	R	H	RBI	PO	A
urcal, ss	4	0	1	1	1	2
. Franco, 1b	3	1	0	0	5	1
moltz, p	0	0	0	0	0	0
heffield, rf	4	0	0	0	2	0
. Jones, lf	3	0	1	1	2	0
. Jones, cf	4	0	1	0	1	0
opez, c	4	2	2	1	14	0
astilla, 3b	2	2	1	1	1	2
eRosa, 2b	3	2	2	2	0	0
emlinger, p	0	0	0	0	0	0
olmes, p	0	0	0	0	0	0
elms, 1b	0	0	0	0	0	0
lillwood, p	1	0	0	0	1	0
ockhart, ph-2b	1	0	0	0	0	0
otals	29	7	8	6	27	5

an Francisco .... 0 1 0 0 0 1 0 0 1—3
tlanta .... 1 3 0 3 0 0 0 0 x—7

an Francisco	IP	H	R	ER	BB	SO
ueter (L)	*3.0	7	7	6	2	1
ybar	2.0	0	0	0	1	2
Vitasick	2.0	0	0	0	0	1
odriguez	1.0	1	0	0	0	0

tlanta	IP	H	R	ER	BB	SO
Millwood (W)	6.0	3	2	2	0	7
Remlinger	1.0	2	0	0	0	2
Holmes	0.2	1	0	0	0	1
Smoltz	1.1	1	1	1	0	4

*Pitched to three batters in fourth.

DP—San Francisco 1. LOB—San Francisco 4, Atlanta 2. 2B—DeRosa. 3B—DeRosa. HR—Snow, Lopez, Castilla, Aurilia, Bonds. CS—Furcal. SH—Millwood. PB—Santiago. T—2:58. A—47,167. U—Emmel, plate; Hernandez, first; Layne, second; Tschida, third; Barrett, left field; Reilly, right field.

Game 3 at San Francisco

Saturday, October 5

ATLANTA 10, SAN FRANCISCO 2

HOW THEY SCORED

First Inning

Giants—Lofton bunted safely to third. Aurilia grounded out, Furcal to Franco, as Lofton advanced to second. Kent doubled to left, scoring Lofton. Bonds was walked intentionally. Santiago grounded into a double play, Castilla to Franco. One run. Giants 1, Braves 0.

Third Inning

Braves—Furcal tripled to left. Franco scored Furcal on a groundout, Aurilia to Snow. Sheffield flied to Sanders. C. Jones grounded out to Snow. One run. Giants 1, Braves 1.

Sixth Inning

Braves—Franco struck out. Sheffield, C. Jones and A. Jones walked. Aybar now pitching. Castilla singled to left, scoring Sheffield and C. Jones, as A. Jones advanced to second. Lockhart homered to right, scoring A. Jones and Castilla. Blanco struck out. Maddux grounded out, Aurilia to Snow. Five runs. Braves 6, Giants 1.

Giants—Aurilia grounded out, Furcal to Franco. Kent lined to Furcal. Bonds homered to left. Santiago grounded out, Castilla to Franco. One run. Braves 6, Giants 2.

Ninth Inning

Braves—Worrell now pitching. M. Franco, pinch-hitting for Remlinger, flied to Lofton. Furcal bunted safely to the mound. J. Franco singled to center as Furcal advanced to second. Sheffield walked. Fultz now pitching. C. Jones singled to third, scoring Furcal, as J. Franco advanced to third and Sheffield to second. Nen now pitching. A. Jones singled to center, scoring J. Franco and Sheffield, as C. Jones advanced to second. Castilla flied to Bonds. Lockhart singled to center, scoring C. Jones, as A. Jones advanced to second. Witasick now pitching. Blanco flied to Bonds. Four runs. Braves 10, Giants 2.

BOX SCORE

Atlanta	AB	R	H	RBI	PO	A
Furcal, ss	5	2	2	0	3	4
J. Franco, 1b	5	1	2	1	10	0
Sheffield, rf	2	2	0	0	2	0
C. Jones, lf	3	2	1	1	2	0
Gryboski, p	0	0	0	0	0	0
A. Jones, cf	3	1	1	2	3	0
Castilla, 3b	5	1	1	2	1	3
Lockhart, 2b	5	1	2	4	0	3
Blanco, c	5	0	1	0	6	0
Maddux, p	3	0	0	0	0	0
Hammond, p	0	0	0	0	0	0
Remlinger, p	0	0	0	0	0	0
M. Franco, ph	1	0	0	0	0	0
Bragg, lf	0	0	0	0	0	0
Totals	37	10	10	10	27	10

San Francisco	AB	R	H	RBI	PO	A
Lofton, cf	4	1	2	0	2	0
Aurilia, ss	4	0	0	0	0	5
Kent, 2b	3	0	1	1	1	1
Bonds, lf	3	1	1	1	3	0
Santiago, c	4	0	0	0	9	0
Snow, 1b	3	0	1	0	7	1
Sanders, rf	3	0	0	0	3	0
Bell, 3b	3	0	0	0	0	1
Schmidt, p	2	0	0	0	1	0
Aybar, p	0	0	0	0	0	0
Rodriguez, p	0	0	0	0	0	0
Eyre, p	0	0	0	0	1	0
Dunston, ph	1	0	0	0	0	0
Worrell, p	0	0	0	0	0	0
Fultz, p	0	0	0	0	0	0
Nen, p	0	0	0	0	0	0
Witasick, p	0	0	0	0	0	0
Totals	30	2	5	2	27	8

Atlanta .... 0 0 1 0 0 5 0 0 4—10
San Francisco .... 1 0 0 0 0 1 0 0 0— 2

Atlanta	IP	H	R	ER	BB	SO
Maddux (W)	6.0	5	2	2	1	3
Hammond	1.0	0	0	0	0	1
Remlinger	1.0	0	0	0	0	1
Gryboski	1.0	0	0	0	0	1

San Francisco	IP	H	R	ER	BB	SO
Schmidt (L)	5.1	3	4	4	4	5
Aybar	0.2	2	2	2	0	1
Rodriguez	1.1	0	0	0	2	2
Eyre	0.2	0	0	0	0	0
Worrell	0.1	2	3	3	1	0
Fultz	*0.0	1	1	1	0	0
Nen	0.1	2	0	0	0	0
Witasick	0.1	0	0	0	0	0

*Pitched to one batter in ninth.

DP—Atlanta 2. LOB—Atlanta 7, San Francisco 3. 2B—Kent. 3B—Furcal. HR—Lockhart, Bonds. SB—J. Franco, Lofton. HBP—Kent by Maddux. T—3:23. A—43,043. U—Kulpa, plate; Darling, first; Rippley, second; M. Hirschbeck, third; Froemming, left field; Miller, right field.

Game 4 at San Francisco

Sunday, October 6

SAN FRANCISCO 8, ATLANTA 3

HOW THEY SCORED

First Inning

Giants—Lofton singled to left. Aurilia singled to center as Lofton advanced to second. Kent walked. Bonds scored Lofton on a sacrifice fly to Sheffield as Aurilia advanced to third. Santiago scored Aurilia on a groundout, Castilla to Franco, as Kent advanced to second. Sanders was walked intentionally. Snow struck out. Two runs. Giants 2, Braves 0.

Second Inning

Giants—Bell singled to center. Hernandez sacrificed Bell to second, Lopez to Lockhart. Lofton flied to C. Jones. Aurilia singled to left, scoring Bell. Kent singled to left-center as Aurilia advanced to third. Bonds was walked intentionally. Santiago walked, scoring Aurilia. Sanders popped to Lockhart. Two runs. Giants 4, Braves 0.

Third Inning

Giants—Snow grounded out, Furcal to Franco. Bell walked. Hernandez sacrificed Bell to second, Glavine to Lockhart. Lofton singled to center as Bell advanced to third. Aurilia homered to left, scoring Bell and Lofton. Gryboski now pitching. Kent singled to short. Bonds flied to C. Jones. Three runs. Giants 7, Braves 0.

Fifth Inning

Braves—Castilla singled to third. Lockhart singled to center as Castilla advanced to second. Bragg, pinch-hitting for Gryboski, grounded into a double play, Snow to Aurilia to Hernandez, as Castilla advanced to third. Furcal doubled to right, scoring Castilla. Franco struck out. One run. Giants 7, Braves 1.

Giants—Moss now pitching. Lofton walked. Aurilia struck out. Kent singled to left as Lofton advanced to second. Bonds flied to C. Jones as Lofton advanced to third. Santiago doubled to left, scoring Lofton as Kent advanced to third. Sanders popped to Franco. One run. Giants 8, Braves 1.

Sixth Inning

Braves—Sheffield struck out. C. Jones singled to right. A. Jones flied to Sanders. Lopez doubled to center, scoring C. Jones. Castilla singled to left-center, scoring Lopez. Lockhart grounded out, Aurilia to Snow. Two runs. Giants 8, Braves 3.

BOX SCORE

Atlanta	AB	R	H	RBI	PO	A
Furcal, ss	5	0	1	1	1	2
J. Franco, 1b	5	0	0	0	8	0
Sheffield, rf	4	0	0	0	1	0
C. Jones, lf	4	1	1	0	5	0
A. Jones, cf	4	0	1	0	1	0
Lopez, c	3	1	1	1	3	1
Castilla, 3b	3	1	2	1	0	4
Lockhart, 2b	3	0	2	0	5	1
Glavine, p	1	0	0	0	0	1
Gryboski, p	0	0	0	0	0	0
Bragg, ph	1	0	0	0	0	0
Moss, p	0	0	0	0	0	1
DeRosa, ph	1	0	0	0	0	0
Ligtenberg, p	0	0	0	0	0	0
M. Franco, ph	0	0	0	0	0	0
Giles, ph	1	0	1	0	0	0
Totals	35	3	9	3	24	10

San Francisco	AB	R	H	RBI	PO	A
Lofton, cf	4	3	2	0	0	0
Aurilia, ss	5	3	3	4	1	6
Kent, 2b	4	0	3	0	1	2
Bonds, lf	3	0	0	1	2	0
Santiago, c	4	0	1	3	6	0
Sanders, rf	4	0	1	0	4	0
Snow, 1b	3	0	0	0	11	2
Bell, 3b	3	2	1	0	0	2
Hernandez, p	2	0	0	0	2	1
Eyre, p	0	0	0	0	0	1
Nen, p	0	0	0	0	0	0
Totals	32	8	11	8	27	14

Atlanta .... 0 0 0 0 1 2 0 0 0—3
San Francisco .... 2 2 3 0 1 0 0 0 x—8

Atlanta	IP	H	R	ER	BB	SO
Glavine (L)	2.2	7	7	7	5	1
Gryboski	1.1	2	0	0	1	0
Moss	2.0	2	1	1	1	1
Ligtenberg	2.0	0	0	0	0	1

San Francisco	IP	H	R	ER	BB	SO
Hernandez (W)	8.1	8	3	3	2	6
Eyre	0.1	1	0	0	0	0
Nen	0.1	0	0	0	0	0

DP—San Francisco 1. LOB—Atlanta 8, San Francisco 10. 2B—Furcal, A. Jones, Lopez, Santiago, Sanders. HR—Aurilia. S—Bonds. SH—Hernandez 2. HBP—Lockhart by Hernandez. T—3:03. A—43,070. U—Darling, plate; Rippley, first; M. Hirschbeck, second; Froemming, third; Miller, left field; Kulpa, right field.

Game 5 at Atlanta

Monday, October 7

SAN FRANCISCO 3, ATLANTA 1

HOW THEY SCORED

Second Inning

Giants—Bonds singled to left-center. Santiago grounded out, Castilla to J. Franco as Bonds advanced to second. Snow struck out. Sanders singled to center, scoring Bonds. Sanders advanced to second on a wild pitch. Bell flied to A. Jones. One run. Giants 1, Braves 0.

Fourth Inning

Giants—Bonds homered to left-center. Santiago grounded out, Furcal to J. Franco. Snow grounded out to J. Franco. Sanders struck out. One run. Giants 2, Braves 0.

Sixth Inning

Braves—A. Jones singled to left-center. Lopez struck out. Castilla singled to center as A. Jones advanced to second. Fultz now pitching. DeRosa, pinch-hitting for Lockhart, singled to center, scoring A. Jones as Castilla advanced to second. Giles now pinch-hitting for Hammond. Rodriguez now pitching. M. Franco, pinch-hitting for Giles, popped to Lofton. Furcal lined to Lofton. One run. Giants 2, Braves 1.

Seventh Inning

Giants—DeRosa now at second and Remlinger pitching. Snow doubled to right. Sanders and Bell walked. Dunston now pinch-hitting for Rodriguez. Holmes now pitching. Goodwin, pinch-hitting for Dunston, struck out. Lofton scored Snow on a sacrifice fly to A. Jones as Sanders advanced to third. Aurilia struck out. One run. Giants 3, Braves 1.

BOX SCORE

San Francisco	AB	R	H	RBI	PO	A
Lofton, cf	4	0	1	1	4	0
Aurilia, ss	3	0	0	0	3	0
Kent, 2b	4	0	0	0	2	0
Bonds, lf	3	2	2	1	1	0
Santiago, c	4	0	0	0	9	0
Snow, 1b	4	1	2	0	4	2
Sanders, rf	3	0	1	1	3	0
Bell, 3b	3	0	0	0	1	1
Ortiz, p	2	0	0	0	0	1
Fultz, p	0	0	0	0	0	0
Rodriguez, p	0	0	0	0	0	0
Dunston, ph	0	0	0	0	0	0
Goodwin, ph	1	0	0	0	0	0
Worrell, p	0	0	0	0	0	1
Martinez, ph	0	0	0	0	0	0
Nen, p	0	0	0	0	0	0
Totals	31	3	6	3	27	5

Atlanta	AB	R	H	RBI	PO	A
Furcal, ss	5	0	0	0	0	3
J. Franco, 1b	4	0	1	0	6	0
Sheffield, rf	2	0	0	0	1	0
C. Jones, lf	4	0	1	0	1	0
A. Jones, cf	4	1	2	0	5	0
Lopez, c	4	0	1	0	10	0
Smoltz, p	0	0	0	0	0	0

Atlanta	AB	R	H	RBI	PO	A
Castilla, 3b	4	0	1	0	0	1
Lockhart, 2b	2	0	0	0	0	0
DeRosa, ph-2b	2	0	1	1	2	0
Millwood, p	1	0	0	0	0	0
Bragg, ph	1	0	0	0	0	0
Hammond, p	0	0	0	0	0	0
Giles, ph	0	0	0	0	0	0
M. Franco, ph	1	0	0	0	0	0
Remlinger, p	0	0	0	0	0	0
Holmes, p	0	0	0	0	0	0
Blanco, c	1	0	0	0	2	2
Totals	35	1	7	1	27	6

San Francisco .... 0 1 0 1 0 0 1 0 0—3
Atlanta............................ 0 0 0 0 0 1 0 0 0—1

San Francisco	IP	H	R	ER	BB	SO
Ortiz (W)	5.1	4	1	1	4	5
Fultz	*0.0	1	0	0	0	0
Rodriguez	0.2	0	0	0	0	0
Worrell	2.0	1	0	0	1	3
Nen (S)	1.0	1	0	0	0	1

Atlanta	IP	H	R	ER	BB	SO
Millwood (L)	5.0	4	2	2	0	7
Hammond	1.0	0	0	0	1	1
Remlinger	†0.0	1	1	1	2	0
Holmes	1.0	0	0	0	0	2
Smoltz	2.0	1	0	0	2	3

*Pitched to one batter in sixth.

†Pitched to three batters in seventh.

E—Kent, Bell. DP—San Francisco 1. LOB—San Francisco 7, Atlanta 12. 2B—Lofton, Snow. HR—Bonds. SB—Furcal. CS—Bonds. S—Lofton. WP—Ortiz, Millwood. T—3:47. A—45,203. U—Layne, plate; Tschida, first; Barrett, second; Reilly, third; Emmel, left field; Hernandez, right field.

COMPOSITE

BATTING AVERAGES

San Francisco Giants

Player, position	G	AB	R	H	2B	3B	HR	RBI	Avg.
Lofton, cf	5	20	5	7	1	0	0	2	.350
Snow, 1b	5	19	3	6	2	0	1	3	.316
Bonds, lf	5	17	5	5	0	0	3	4	.294
Kent, 2b	5	19	1	5	2	0	0	1	.263
Aurilia, ss	5	21	4	5	1	0	2	7	.238
Santiago, c	5	21	1	5	2	0	0	5	.238
Sanders, rf	5	18	1	4	1	0	0	1	.222
Bell, 3b	5	16	3	3	0	0	0	1	.188
Ortiz, p	2	6	1	1	0	0	0	0	.167
Aybar, p	2	0	0	0	0	0	0	0	.000
Eyre, p	3	0	0	0	0	0	0	0	.000
Fultz, p	2	0	0	0	0	0	0	0	.000
Martinez, ph	1	0	0	0	0	0	0	0	.000
Nen, p	4	0	0	0	0	0	0	0	.000
Rodriguez, p	3	0	0	0	0	0	0	0	.000
Witasick, p	2	0	0	0	0	0	0	0	.000
Worrell, p	3	0	0	0	0	0	0	0	.000
Dunston, ph	2	1	0	0	0	0	0	0	.000
Feliz, ph	1	1	0	0	0	0	0	0	.000
Rueter, p	1	1	0	0	0	0	0	0	.000
Goodwin, ph	2	2	0	0	0	0	0	0	.000
Hernandez, p	1	2	0	0	0	0	0	0	.000
Schmidt, p	1	2	0	0	0	0	0	0	.000
Totals	5	166	24	41	9	0	6	24	.247

Atlanta Braves

Player, position	G	AB	R	H	2B	3B	HR	RBI	Avg.
Giles, ph	3	2	0	1	0	0	0	0	.500
Glavine, p	2	2	0	1	0	0	0	2	.500
DeRosa, 2b-ph	4	7	2	3	1	1	0	3	.429
Castilla, 3b	5	18	5	7	0	0	1	4	.389
Lopez, c	4	15	4	5	1	0	2	4	.333
Lockhart, 2b-ph	5	12	1	4	0	0	1	4	.333
A. Jones, cf	5	19	4	6	1	0	0	2	.316
C. Jones, lf	5	17	3	5	0	0	0	2	.294
Furcal, ss	5	24	2	6	1	1	0	2	.250
J. Franco, 1b	5	22	2	4	0	0	0	1	.182
Blanco, c	2	6	0	1	0	0	0	0	.167
Sheffield, rf	5	16	3	1	0	0	1	1	.063
Gryboski, p	3	0	0	0	0	0	0	0	.000
Hammond, p	3	0	0	0	0	0	0	0	.000
Helms, 1b	1	0	0	0	0	0	0	0	.000
Holmes, p	3	0	0	0	0	0	0	0	.000
Ligtenberg, p	1	0	0	0	0	0	0	0	.000
Moss, p	2	0	0	0	0	0	0	0	.000
Remlinger, p	3	0	0	0	0	0	0	0	.000
Smoltz, p	2	0	0	0	0	0	0	0	.000
M. Franco, ph	4	2	0	0	0	0	0	0	.000
Millwood, p	2	2	0	0	0	0	0	0	.000
Bragg, lf-ph	4	3	0	0	0	0	0	0	.000
Maddux, p	1	3	0	0	0	0	0	0	.000
Totals	5	170	26	44	4	2	5	25	.259

PITCHING AVERAGES

San Francisco Giants

Pitcher	G	IP	H	R	ER	BB	SO	W	L	ERA
Rodriguez	3	3.0	1	0	0	2	2	0	0	0.00
Nen	4	2.2	4	0	0	1	1	0	0	0.00
Witasick	2	2.1	0	0	0	0	1	0	0	0.00
Eyre	3	1.1	1	0	0	0	0	0	0	0.00
Ortiz	2	12.1	9	3	3	8	8	2	0	2.19
Hernandez	1	8.1	8	3	3	2	6	1	0	3.24
Schmidt	1	5.1	3	4	4	4	5	0	1	6.75
Aybar	2	2.2	2	2	2	1	3	0	0	6.75
Worrell	3	3.0	7	6	4	2	3	0	0	12.00
Rueter	1	3.0	7	7	6	2	1	0	1	18.00
Fultz	2	0.0	2	1	1	0	0	0	0	Inf.
Totals	5	44.0	44	26	23	22	30	3	2	4.70

No shutouts. Save—Nen.

Atlanta Braves

Pitcher	G	IP	H	R	ER	BB	SO	W	L	ERA
Gryboski	3	3.2	2	0	0	2	3	0	0	0.00
Holmes	3	2.2	1	0	0	0	5	0	0	0.00
Ligtenberg	1	2.0	0	0	0	0	1	0	0	0.00
Smoltz	2	3.1	2	1	1	2	7	0	0	2.70
Maddux	1	6.0	5	2	2	1	3	1	0	3.00
Moss	2	3.0	2	1	1	1	3	0	0	3.00
Millwood	2	11.0	7	4	4	0	14	1	1	3.27
Remlinger	3	2.0	3	1	1	2	3	0	0	4.50
Hammond	3	2.2	2	2	2	3	2	0	0	6.75
Glavine	2	7.2	17	13	13	7	4	0	2	15.26
Totals	5	44.0	41	24	24	18	45	2	3	4.91

No shutouts or saves.

A.L. Championship Series

Anaheim vs. Minnesota

By Doug Miller

Jackie Autry poured champagne down Troy Percival's pants. Benji Gil poured tequila down David Eckstein's throat. The Angels poured back onto the field after pouring champagne all over themselves. And emotion poured out of every seat at Edison Field.

For the first time in baseball history, the Angels were going to the World Series.

Adam Kennedy homered in three straight at-bats, the last one a three-run bomb, and Anaheim rolled to a 10-run seventh inning and beat Minnesota, 13-5, in Game 5 of the American League Championship Series before 44,835 frenzied fans at Edison Field.

With the win, the Angels closed out the Twins, 4-1, in the best-of-seven series.

The rudiments of the game were glossed over and discussed only briefly in the celebratory aftermath.

As they did each time they clinched a milestone in 2002—from gaining a playoff berth in late September to knocking off the mighty Yankees in the ALDS—the Angels reflected on their hard work and deflected individual praise to a team cause.

"Today I did what I did, but we got here because 25-30 guys worked at it all year long," Kennedy said.

Manager Mike Scioscia echoed those sentiments as he stood in a corner of the plastic-covered clubhouse, sipping from a bottle of Korbel and reminiscing on the March morning when he and his coaching staff outlined the plan that would bring the franchise unparalleled success.

It involved situational hitting, solid pitching, and intense effort from everyone.

Not only would stars Garret Anderson, Troy Glaus, Tim Salmon and Darin Erstad be counted on to carry the load, Scioscia said.

Francisco Rodriguez collected his fourth postseason win in the Game 5 clincher, becoming only the fifth AL pitcher to win four games in a single postseason.

The new-look, new-attitude Angels would rely on much-needed stability from every other member of the roster: guys like Brendan Donnelly, Ben Weber, Orlando Palmeiro, Scott Schoeneweis and Bengie Molina.

"We're here because of the depth of our club," Scioscia said. "Orlando, (Alex) Ochoa, Benji Gil, (Shawn) Wooten, the list goes on and on. You look at the guys who didn't get the at-bats, the guys that were there in the key situations and delivered when they were called on. ... That's why we're here. Without that depth, we'd never be here."

Many of the Angels never dreamed they'd be here.

Weber, a 30-year-old rookie reliever in 2001, pitched in Taiwan for a season after almost quitting baseball. "Not in a zillion years would I have thought that I'd be on a World Series team," he said, puffing on a Cuban cigar. "The only thing on my mind back then was, 'I gotta find a baseball job to support my family.' "

Donnelly, a 31-year-old rookie reliever in '02, spent 10 years in minor league organizations and was demoted to Class AAA twice before sticking with the Angels in July.

"I'm going day-to-day, brother," he said. "It sounds like a cliche, but I'm having fun just being a part of it."

The 2002 Angels were picked to finish last in the brutal AL West by many members of the media and, according to Weber, it continues to motivate them.

"We're a bunch of vagabonds," Weber said. "We're described as scrappy, gutty, gritty dirtbags. I love it. I love people calling us that stuff. Because they've labeled us as underdogs all year and it seems to be working."

What also seems to be working for this club is a blatant disregard for history of Angels teams past.

It is the first pennant win in the franchise's 42 years of existence, years filled with frustration, fan apathy, and excruciating almosts.

In 1979, the California Angels lost the ALCS, 3-1, to the Baltimore Orioles.

In 1982, the Angels took the first two games of the then best-of-five ALCS against Milwaukee, then lost three straight and were eliminated.

Torii Hunter helped the Twins reach the ALCS for the first time since 1991.

And in 1986, the Angels were one strike away from the World Series when Dave Henderson of the Boston Red Sox hit a two-run homer in the ninth. The Angels lost the game in 11 innings and dropped two more at Fenway Park to miss out yet again.

On Sunday in front of a red-clad throng banging away on red ThunderStix, the Angels put the Twins and any notion of a curse to bed.

"There is Angel immortality for this entire team," Percival said. "I don't believe we're done yet. I don't think anybody in here does."

Game 1 at Minnesota

Tuesday, October 8

MINNESOTA 2, ANAHEIM 1

HOW THEY SCORED

Second Inning

Twins—Hunter doubled to right-center. Hunter advanced to third on a wild pitch. Mientkiewicz fouled to Glaus. Cuddyer walked. Pierzynski scored Hunter on a sacrifice fly to Erstad. Rivas struck out. One run. Twins 1, Angels 0.

Third Inning

Angels—Spiezio fouled to Pierzynski. B. Molina flied to Cuddyer. Kennedy singled to left. Eckstein singled to right as Kennedy advanced to second. Erstad reached first on Guzman's fielding error, scoring Kennedy as Eckstein advanced to third. Salmon flied to Hunter. One run. Twins 1, Angels 1.

Fifth Inning

Twins—Rivas walked. Jones flied to Anderson. Guzman singled to center as Rivas advanced to second. Koskie doubled to right, scoring Rivas as Guzman advanced to third. Ortiz fouled to Spiezio. Hunter struck out and was retired at first after a dropped third strike, B. Molina to Spiezio. One run. Twins 2, Angels 1.

BOX SCORE

Anaheim	AB	R	H	RBI	PO	A
Eckstein, ss	4	0	1	0	1	1
Erstad, cf	4	0	1	0	2	0
Salmon, rf	3	0	0	0	5	0
Figgins, pr	0	0	0	0	0	0
Anderson, lf	4	0	0	0	3	0
Glaus, 3b	4	0	0	0	2	1
Fullmer, dh	3	0	1	0	0	0
Spiezio, 1b	3	0	0	0	7	0
B. Molina, c	2	0	0	0	2	3
Palmeiro, ph	1	0	0	0	0	0
J. Molina, c	0	0	0	0	2	0
Kennedy, 2b	3	1	1	0	0	0
Appier, p	0	0	0	0	0	0
Donnelly, p	0	0	0	0	0	0
Schoeneweis, p	0	0	0	0	0	0
Weber, p	0	0	0	0	0	0
Totals	31	1	4	0	24	5

Minnesota	AB	R	H	RBI	PO	A
Jones, lf	4	0	0	0	3	0
Guzman, ss	3	0	1	0	0	6
Koskie, 3b	4	0	2	1	0	2
D. Ortiz, dh	3	0	1	0	0	0
Kielty, ph-dh	1	0	0	0	0	0
Hunter, cf	3	1	1	0	2	0
Mientkiewicz, 1b	3	0	0	0	13	0
Cuddyer, rf	2	0	0	0	1	0
Mohr, rf	0	0	0	0	1	0
Pierzynski, c	2	0	0	1	6	0
Rivas, 2b	2	1	0	0	1	3
Mays, p	0	0	0	0	0	1
Guardado, p	0	0	0	0	0	0
Totals	27	2	5	2	27	12

Anaheim	0	0	1	0	0	0	0	0	0	—1
Minnesota	0	1	0	0	1	0	0	0	x	—2

Anaheim	IP	H	R	ER	BB	SO
Appier (L)	5.0	5	2	2	3	2
Donnelly	1.2	0	0	0	0	2
Schoeneweis	0.2	0	0	0	0	0
Weber	0.2	0	0	0	0	2

Minnesota	IP	H	R	ER	BB	SO
Mays (W)	8.0	4	1	0	0	3
Guardado (S)	1.0	0	0	0	1	2

E—Guzman. DP—Minnesota 1. LOB—Anaheim 4, Minnesota 7. 2B—Koskie, Hunter. S—Pierzynski. SH—Hunter. WP—Appier. HBP—Guzman by Donnelly. T—2:58. A—55,562. U—Montague, plate; Everitt, first; Gorman, second; Young, third; DeMuth, left field; Rapuano, right field

Game 2 at Minnesota

Wednesday, October 9

ANAHEIM 6, MINNESOTA 3

HOW THEY SCORED

First Inning

Angels—Eckstein grounded out, Reed to Mientkiewicz. Erstad homered to right-center. Salmon flied to Hunter. Anderson grounded out, Rivas to Mientkiewicz. One run. Angels 1, Twins 0.

Second Inning

Angels—Glaus singled to right. Fullmer doubled to right as Glaus advanced to third. Spiezio doubled to right, scoring Glaus as Fullmer advanced to third. B. Molina flied to Cuddyer. Kennedy reached first on a fielder's choice and Spiezio advanced to third as Fullmer was thrown out at the plate, Reed to Pierzynski. Spiezio was caught trying to steal home, but scored on an error by Pierzynski (Reed and Mientkiewicz assisted). Kennedy advanced to third on the play. Eckstein singled to right, scoring Kennedy. Erstad flied to Jones. Three runs. Angels 4, Twins 0.

Sixth Inning

Angels—Anderson grounded out, Rivas to Mientkiewicz. Glaus tripled to right. Fullmer homered to center, scoring Glaus. Santana now pitching.

Troy Glaus (25) hit .316 in the ALCS, helping the Angels advance to the World Series.

Spiezio flied to Cuddyer. B. Molina struck out, but was safe at first on a wild pitch. Kennedy grounded out to Mientkiewicz. Two runs. Angels 6, Twins 0.

Twins—Guzman doubled to right-center. Koskie singled to right, scoring Guzman. Ortiz struck out. Hunter doubled to left as Koskie advanced to third. Mientkiewicz singled to center, scoring Koskie and Hunter. Donnelly now pitching. Cuddyer struck out. Pierzynski popped to Kennedy. Three runs. Angels 6, Twins 3.

BOX SCORE

Anaheim	AB	R	H	RBI	PO	A
Eckstein, ss	5	0	2	1	0	3
Erstad, cf	5	1	2	1	1	0
Salmon, rf	2	0	0	0	2	0
Palmeiro, rf	1	0	0	0	0	0
Ochoa, ph-rf	2	0	0	0	0	0
Anderson, lf	4	0	0	0	1	0
Glaus, 3b	3	2	2	0	0	0
Fullmer, dh	3	1	2	2	0	0
Wooten, ph-dh	1	0	0	0	0	0
Spiezio, 1b	4	1	2	1	10	0
B. Molina, c	4	0	0	0	10	0
Kennedy, 2b	4	1	0	0	3	3
R. Ortiz, p	0	0	0	0	0	1
Donnelly, p	0	0	0	0	0	0
Rodriguez, p	0	0	0	0	0	0
Percival, p	0	0	0	0	0	0
Totals	38	6	10	5	27	7

Minnesota	AB	R	H	RBI	PO	A
Jones, lf	5	0	0	0	3	0
Guzman, ss	4	1	2	0	0	2
Koskie, 3b	3	1	1	1	0	0
D. Ortiz, dh	4	0	1	0	0	0
Hunter, cf	3	1	1	0	4	0
Mientkiewicz, 1b	4	0	3	2	9	0
Cuddyer, rf	3	0	1	0	5	0
Kielty, ph-rf	1	0	0	0	0	0
Pierzynski, c	4	0	1	0	6	0
Rivas, 2b	3	0	1	0	0	3
Mohr, ph	1	0	0	0	0	0
Reed, p	0	0	0	0	0	2
Santana, p	0	0	0	0	0	1
Romero, p	0	0	0	0	0	0
Hawkins, p	0	0	0	0	0	0
Jackson, p	0	0	0	0	0	0
Totals	35	3	11	3	27	8

Anaheim	1	3	0	0	0	2	0	0	0—6
Minnesota	0	0	0	0	0	3	0	0	0—3

Anaheim	IP	H	R	ER	BB	SO
R. Ortiz (W)	5.1	10	3	3	1	3
Donnelly	0.2	0	0	0	0	1
Rodriguez	1.2	1	0	0	1	3
Percival (S)	1.1	0	0	0	0	3

Minnesota	IP	H	R	ER	BB	SO
Reed (L)	5.1	8	6	6	0	0
Santana	1.2	0	0	0	0	3
Romero	0.1	0	0	0	1	0
Hawkins	0.2	0	0	0	0	1
Jackson	1.0	2	0	0	0	2

E—Pierzynski. DP—Anaheim 2. LOB—Anaheim 6, Minnesota 7. 2B—Fullmer, Spiezio, Guzman, Hunter. 3B—Glaus. HR—Erstad, Fullmer. SB—Spiezio, Kennedy. WP—Santana. T—3:13. A—55,990. U—Everitt, plate; Gorman, first; Young, second; DeMuth, third; Rapuano, left field; Montague, right field.

Game 3 at Anaheim

Friday, October 11

ANAHEIM 2, MINNESOTA 1

HOW THEY SCORED

Second Inning

Angels—Anderson homered to right. Glaus struck out. Spiezio walked. Wooten singled to right as Spiezio advanced to third. B. Molina popped to Mientkiewicz. Gil struck out. One run. Angels 1, Twins 0.

Seventh Inning

Twins—Mohr singled to left. Pierzynski flied to Anderson. Rivas flied to Salmon. Jones doubled to left, scoring Mohr. Guzman popped to Gil. One run. Angels 1, Twins 1.

Eighth Inning

Angels—Glaus homered to right. Spiezio and Wooten struck out. J. Molina popped to Mientkiewicz. One run. Angels 2, Twins 1.

BOX SCORE

Minnesota	AB	R	H	RBI	PO	A
Jones, lf	4	0	1	1	4	0
Guzman, ss	4	0	0	0	2	0
Koskie, 3b	4	0	0	0	0	0
LeCroy, dh	3	0	1	0	0	0
D. Ortiz, ph-dh	1	0	0	0	0	0
Hunter, cf	4	0	1	0	3	0
Mientkiewicz, 1b	4	0	0	0	4	0
Mohr, rf	4	1	2	0	4	0
Pierzynski, c	4	0	0	0	7	0
Rivas, 2b	3	0	1	0	0	1
Milton, p	0	0	0	0	0	0
Hawkins, p	0	0	0	0	0	0
Santana, p	0	0	0	0	0	0
Jackson, p	0	0	0	0	0	0
Romero, p	0	0	0	0	0	0
Totals	35	1	6	1	24	1

Anaheim	AB	R	H	RBI	PO	A
Eckstein, ss	4	0	1	0	0	3
Erstad, cf	4	0	1	0	2	0
Salmon, rf	3	0	0	0	2	0
Ochoa, rf	0	0	0	0	2	0
Anderson, lf	4	1	2	1	5	0
Glaus, 3b	3	1	2	1	0	1
Spiezio, 1b	3	0	0	0	5	0
Wooten, dh	4	0	1	0	0	0
B. Molina, c	2	0	0	0	7	0
Figgins, pr	0	0	0	0	0	0
J. Molina, c	1	0	0	0	2	0
Gil, 2b	2	0	0	0	2	1
Washburn, p	0	0	0	0	0	0
Rodriguez, p	0	0	0	0	0	0
Percival, p	0	0	0	0	0	0
Totals	30	2	7	2	27	5

Minnesota	0	0	0	0	0	0	1	0	0—1
Anaheim	0	1	0	0	0	0	0	1	x—2

Minnesota	IP	H	R	ER	BB	SO
Milton	6.0	5	1	1	2	4
Hawkins	0.1	1	0	0	1	0
Santana	0.1	0	0	0	0	0
Jackson	*0.0	0	0	0	1	0
Romero (L)	1.1	1	1	1	0	2

Anaheim	IP	H	R	ER	BB	SO
Washburn	7.0	6	1	1	0	7
Rodriguez (W)	1.0	0	0	0	0	2
Percival (S)	1.0	0	0	0	0	0

*Pitched to one batter in seventh.

E—Gil, Eckstein. LOB—Minnesota 7, Anaheim 9. 2B—Jones, Anderson. HR—Anderson, Glaus. SB—Mohr. SH—Gil. WP—Santana. T—3:13. A—44,234. U—Gorman, plate; Young, first; DeMuth, second; Rapuano, third; Montague, left field; Everitt, right field.

Game 4 at Anaheim

Saturday, October 12

ANAHEIM 7, MINNESOTA 1

HOW THEY SCORED

Seventh Inning

Angels—Erstad singled to center. Erstad stole second and advanced to third on a throwing error by Pierzynski. Salmon walked. Anderson popped to Koskie. Glaus singled to left, scoring Erstad as Salmon advanced to second. Ochoa now running for Salmon. Fullmer struck out. Spiezio doubled to right, scoring Ochoa as Glaus advanced to third. B. Molina was hit by a pitch. Santana now pitching. Kennedy grounded out to Mientkiewicz. Two runs. Angels 2, Twins 0.

Eighth Inning

Angels—Lamb now at second. Eckstein popped to Mientkiewicz. Erstad singled to left. Erstad advanced to second on a wild pickoff throw by Santana. Hawkins now pitching. Ochoa grounded out, Guzman to Mientkiewicz, as Erstad advanced to third. Romero now pitching. Anderson singled to right, scoring Erstad. Jackson now pitching. Glaus singled to left as Anderson advanced to second. Fullmer doubled to right-center, scoring Anderson and Glaus. Spiezio was walked intentionally. B. Molina tripled to center, scoring Fullmer and Spiezio. Wells now pitching. Kennedy struck out. Five runs. Angels 7, Twins 0.

Ninth Inning

Twins—Weber now pitching. Jones lined to Eckstein. Guzman grounded out, Kennedy to Spiezio. Koskie doubled to right-center. Ortiz singled to right, scoring Koskie. Hunter struck out. One run. Angels 7, Twins 1.

BOX SCORE

Minnesota	AB	R	H	RBI	PO	A
Jones, lf	4	0	0	0	1	0
Guzman, ss	4	0	0	0	2	4
Koskie, 3b	4	1	1	0	1	2
D. Ortiz, dh	4	0	2	1	0	0
Hunter, cf	4	0	0	0	1	0
Mientkiewicz, 1b	3	0	1	0	9	0
Mohr, rf	3	0	1	0	1	0
Pierzynski, c	3	0	0	0	5	0
Rivas, 2b	2	0	1	0	4	1
Kielty, ph	1	0	0	0	0	0
Lamb, 2b	0	0	0	0	0	0
Radke, p	0	0	0	0	0	1
Santana, p	0	0	0	0	0	0
Hawkins, p	0	0	0	0	0	0
Romero, p	0	0	0	0	0	0
Jackson, p	0	0	0	0	0	0
Wells, p	0	0	0	0	0	0
Totals	32	1	6	1	24	8

Anaheim	AB	R	H	RBI	PO	A
Eckstein, ss	4	0	1	0	3	3
Erstad, cf	4	2	2	0	0	0
Salmon, rf	2	0	0	0	1	0
Ochoa, pr-rf	1	1	0	0	0	0
Anderson, lf	4	1	1	1	0	0
Glaus, 3b	4	1	2	1	0	0
Fullmer, dh	4	1	1	2	0	0
Spiezio, 1b	3	1	1	1	9	1
B. Molina, c	3	0	2	2	10	1
Kennedy, 2b	3	0	0	0	2	7
Lackey, p	0	0	0	0	2	0
Rodriguez, p	0	0	0	0	0	0
Weber, p	0	0	0	0	0	0
Totals	32	7	10	7	27	12

Minnesota	0	0	0	0	0	0	0	0	1—1
Anaheim	0	0	0	0	0	0	2	5	x—7

Minnesota	IP	H	R	ER	BB	SO
Radke (L)	6.2	5	2	2	1	4
Santana	0.2	1	1	1	0	0
Hawkins	0.1	0	0	0	0	0
Romero	*0.0	1	1	1	0	0
Jackson	†0.0	3	3	3	1	0
Wells	0.1	0	0	0	0	1

Anaheim	IP	H	R	ER	BB	SO
Lackey (W)	7.0	3	0	0	0	7
Rodriguez	1.0	1	0	0	0	2
Weber	1.0	2	1	1	0	1

*Pitched to one batter in eighth.

†Pitched to four batters in eighth.

E—Santana, Pierzynski. DP—Minnesota 1. LOB—Minnesota 4, Anaheim 5. 2B—Koskie, Mientkiewicz, Fullmer, Spiezio. 3B—B. Molina. SB—Erstad. CS—Pierzynski. SH—Kennedy. HBP—B. Molina by Radke. T—2:49. A—44,830. U—Young, plate; DeMuth, first; Rapuano, second; Montague, third; Everitt, left field; Gorman, right field.

Game 5 at Anaheim

Sunday, October 13

ANAHEIM 13, MINNESOTA 5

HOW THEY SCORED

First Inning

Twins—Jones flied to Salmon. Guzman flied to Erstad. Koskie walked. Koskie advanced to second on a wild pitch. Ortiz doubled to right, scoring Koskie. Hunter popped to Spiezio. One run. Twins 1, Angels 0.

Second Inning

Twins—Mientkiewicz flied to Anderson. Mohr doubled to left-center. Pierzynski singled to left, but was out trying for second, Anderson to Glaus to Kennedy. Mohr scored on the play. Rivas struck out. One run. Twins 2, Angels 0.

Third Inning

Angels—Kennedy homered to right. Eckstein grounded out, Rivas to Mientkiewicz. Erstad grounded out, Guzman to Mientkiewicz. Salmon popped to Guzman. One run. Twins 2, Angels 1.

Fifth Inning

Angels—Spiezio homered to right. B. Molina grounded out, Koskie to Mientkiewicz. Kennedy homered to right-center. Eckstein grounded out, Rivas to Mientkiewicz. Erstad grounded out, Guzman to Mientkiewicz. Two runs. Angels 3, Twins 2.

Seventh Inning

Twins—Hunter flied to Salmon. Mientkiewicz singled to center. Mohr singled to center as Mientkiewicz advanced to second. Pierzynski singled to right as Mientkiewicz advanced to third and Mohr to second. Rodriguez now pitching. Kielty, pinch-hitting for Rivas, walked, scoring Mientkiewicz. Mohr scored on a wild pitch as Pierzynski advanced to third and Kielty to second. Jones scored Pierzynski on a sacrifice fly to Erstad. Guzman grounded out, Kennedy to Spiezio. Three runs. Twins 5, Angels 3.

Angels—Lamb now at second. Spiezio singled to right. B. Molina singled to left as Spiezio advanced to second. Figgins now running for B. Molina. Kennedy homered to right-center, scoring Spiezio and Figgins. Hawkins now pitching. Eckstein singled to third. Erstad singled to left as Eckstein advanced to second. Salmon singled to left as Eckstein advanced to third and Erstad to second. Ochoa now running for Salmon. Romero now pitching. Anderson walked, scoring Eckstein. Glaus struck out. Wooten singled to right, scoring Erstad as Ochoa advanced to third and Anderson to second. Ochoa scored on a wild pitch as Anderson advanced to third and Wooten to second. Spiezio singled to left, scoring Anderson and Wooten. Wells now pitching. Figgins singled to left as Spiezio advanced to second. Kennedy singled to left as Spiezio advanced to third and Figgins to second. Eckstein was hit by a pitch, scoring Spiezio. Erstad grounded out to Mientkiewicz, scoring Figgins as Kennedy advanced to third and Eckstein to second. Ochoa struck out. Ten runs. Angels 13, Twins 5.

BOX SCORE

Minnesota	AB	R	H	RBI	PO	A
Jones, lf	3	0	1	1	0	0
Guzman, ss	3	0	0	0	3	6
Koskie, 3b	3	1	1	0	1	3
D. Ortiz, dh	4	0	1	1	0	0
Hunter, cf	4	0	0	0	1	0
Cuddyer, rf	0	0	0	0	0	0
Mientkiewicz, 1b	4	1	1	0	13	0
Mohr, rf-cf	4	2	2	0	0	0
Pierzynski, c	3	1	3	1	5	1
Prince, c	1	0	0	0	1	0
Rivas, 2b	2	0	0	0	0	4
Kielty, ph	0	0	0	1	0	0
Lamb, 2b	0	0	0	0	0	0
Mays, p	0	0	0	0	0	0
Santana, p	0	0	0	0	0	0
Hawkins, p	0	0	0	0	0	0
Romero, p	0	0	0	0	0	0
Wells, p	0	0	0	0	0	0
Lohse, p	0	0	0	0	0	0
Totals	31	5	9	4	24	14

Anaheim	AB	R	H	RBI	PO	A
Eckstein, ss	4	1	1	1	1	2
Erstad, cf	5	1	2	1	9	0
Salmon, rf	4	0	3	0	3	0
Ochoa, pr-rf	1	1	0	0	1	0
Anderson, lf	4	1	2	1	1	1
Glaus, 3b	5	0	0	0	0	1
Fullmer, dh	2	0	0	0	0	0
Wooten, ph-dh	3	1	1	1	0	0
Spiezio, 1b	4	3	3	3	5	1
B. Molina, c	3	0	1	0	3	0
Figgins, pr	1	2	1	0	0	0
J. Molina, c	0	0	0	0	0	0
Kennedy, 2b	4	3	4	5	4	3
Appier, p	0	0	0	0	0	0
Donnelly, p	0	0	0	0	0	0
Rodriguez, p	0	0	0	0	0	0
Weber, p	0	0	0	0	0	1
Percival, p	0	0	0	0	0	0
Totals	40	13	18	12	27	9

Minnesota	1	1	0	0	0	0	3	0	0	—5
Anaheim	0	0	1	0	2	0	10	0	x	—13

Minnesota	IP	H	R	ER	BB	SO
Mays	5.1	8	3	3	0	0
Santana (L)	*0.2	3	3	3	0	1
Hawkins	*0.0	3	3	3	0	0
Romero	0.1	2	3	3	1	1
Wells	0.2	2	1	1	0	1
Lohse	1.0	0	0	0	0	1

Anaheim	IP	H	R	ER	BB	SO
Appier	5.1	5	2	2	1	1
Donnelly	1.0	3	3	3	0	2
Rodriguez (W)	0.2	0	0	0	1	0
Weber	1.0	1	0	0	0	0
Percival	1.0	0	0	0	0	0

*Pitched to three batters in seventh.

DP—Minnesota 2, Anaheim 2. LOB—Minnesota 3, Anaheim 5. 2B—Ortiz, Mohr. HR—Kennedy 3, Spiezio. CS—Anderson. S—Jones. SH—Guzman. WP—Romero, Appier, Donnelly, F. Rodriguez. HBP—Eckstein by Wells. T—3:30. A—44,835. U—DeMuth, plate; Rapuano, first; Montague, second; Everitt, third; Gorman, left field; Young, right field.

COMPOSITE

BATTING AVERAGES

Anaheim Angels

Player, position	G	AB	R	H	2B	3B	HR	RBI	Avg.
Figgins, pr	3	1	2	1	0	0	0	0	1.000
Erstad, cf	5	22	4	8	0	0	1	2	.364
Kennedy, 2b	4	14	5	5	0	0	3	5	.357
Spiezio, 1b	5	17	5	6	2	0	1	5	.353
Fullmer, dh	4	12	2	4	2	0	1	4	.333
Glaus, 3b	5	19	4	6	0	1	1	2	.316
Eckstein, ss	5	21	1	6	0	0	0	2	.286
Anderson, lf	5	20	3	5	1	0	1	3	.250
Wooten, dh	3	8	1	2	0	0	0	1	.250
B. Molina, c	5	14	0	3	0	1	0	2	.214
Salmon, rf	5	14	0	3	0	0	0	0	.214
Appier, p	2	0	0	0	0	0	0	0	.000
Donnelly, p	3	0	0	0	0	0	0	0	.000
Lackey, p	1	0	0	0	0	0	0	0	.000
Ortiz, p	1	0	0	0	0	0	0	0	.000
Percival, p	3	0	0	0	0	0	0	0	.000
Rodriguez, p	4	0	0	0	0	0	0	0	.000
Schoeneweis, p	1	0	0	0	0	0	0	0	.000
Washburn, p	1	0	0	0	0	0	0	0	.000
Weber, p	3	0	0	0	0	0	0	0	.000
J. Molina, c	3	1	0	0	0	0	0	0	.000
Gil, 2b	1	2	0	0	0	0	0	0	.000
Palmeiro, ph-rf	2	2	0	0	0	0	0	0	.000
Ochoa, rf-ph-pr	4	4	2	0	0	0	0	0	.000
Totals	5	171	29	49	5	2	8	26	.287

Minnesota Twins

Player, position	G	AB	R	H	2B	3B	HR	RBI	Avg.
Mohr, rf-ph-cf	5	12	3	5	1	0	0	0	.417
LeCroy, dh	1	3	0	1	0	0	0	0	.333
Ortiz, dh	5	16	0	5	1	0	0	2	.313
Koskie, 3b	5	18	3	5	2	0	0	2	.278
Mientkiewicz, 1b	5	18	1	5	1	0	0	2	.278
Pierzynski, c	5	16	1	4	0	0	0	2	.250
Rivas, 2b	5	12	1	3	0	0	0	0	.250
Cuddyer, rf	3	5	0	1	0	0	0	0	.200
Guzman, ss	5	18	1	3	1	0	0	0	.167
Hunter, cf	5	18	2	3	2	0	0	0	.167
Jones, lf	5	20	0	2	1	0	0	2	.100
Guardado, p	1	0	0	0	0	0	0	0	.000
Hawkins, p	4	0	0	0	0	0	0	0	.000
Jackson, p	3	0	0	0	0	0	0	0	.000
Lamb, 2b	2	0	0	0	0	0	0	0	.000
Lohse, p	1	0	0	0	0	0	0	0	.000
Mays, p	2	0	0	0	0	0	0	0	.000
Milton, p	1	0	0	0	0	0	0	0	.000
Radke, p	1	0	0	0	0	0	0	0	.000
Reed, p	1	0	0	0	0	0	0	0	.000
Romero, p	4	0	0	0	0	0	0	0	.000
Santana, p	4	0	0	0	0	0	0	0	.000
Wells, p	2	0	0	0	0	0	0	0	.000
Prince, c	1	1	0	0	0	0	0	0	.000
Kielty, dh-rf-ph	4	3	0	0	0	0	0	1	.000
Totals	5	160	12	37	9	0	0	11	.231

Troy Percival had two saves for the Angels in the ALCS.

PITCHING AVERAGES

Anaheim Angels

Pitcher	G	IP	H	R	ER	BB	SO	W	L	ERA
Lackey	1	7.0	3	0	0	0	7	1	0	0.00
Rodriguez	4	4.1	2	0	0	2	7	2	0	0.00
Percival	3	3.1	0	0	0	0	3	0	0	0.00
Schoeneweis	1	0.2	0	0	0	0	0	0	0	0.00
Washburn	1	7.0	6	1	1	0	7	0	0	1.29
Weber	3	2.2	3	1	1	0	3	0	0	3.38
Appier	2	10.1	10	4	4	4	3	0	1	3.48
Ortiz	1	5.1	10	3	3	1	3	1	0	5.06
Donnelly	3	3.1	3	3	3	0	5	0	0	8.10
Totals	5	44.0	37	12	12	7	38	4	1	2.45

No shutouts. Saves—Percival 2.

Minnesota Twins

Pitcher	G	IP	H	R	ER	BB	SO	W	L	ERA
Guardado	1	1.0	0	0	0	1	2	0	0	0.00
Lohse	1	1.0	0	0	0	0	1	0	0	0.00
Milton	1	6.0	5	1	1	2	4	0	0	1.50
Mays	2	13.1	12	4	3	0	3	1	0	2.03
Radke	1	6.2	5	2	2	1	4	0	1	2.70
Wells	2	1.0	2	1	1	0	2	0	0	9.00
Reed	1	5.1	8	6	6	0	0	0	1	10.13
Santana	4	3.1	4	4	4	0	4	0	1	10.80
Hawkins	4	1.1	4	3	3	1	1	0	0	20.25
Romero	4	2.0	4	5	5	2	3	0	1	22.50
Jackson	3	1.0	5	3	3	2	2	0	0	27.00
Totals	**5**	**42.0**	**49**	**29**	**28**	**9**	**26**	**1**	**4**	**6.00**

No shutouts. Save—Guardado.

N.L. Championship Series

San Francisco vs. St. Louis

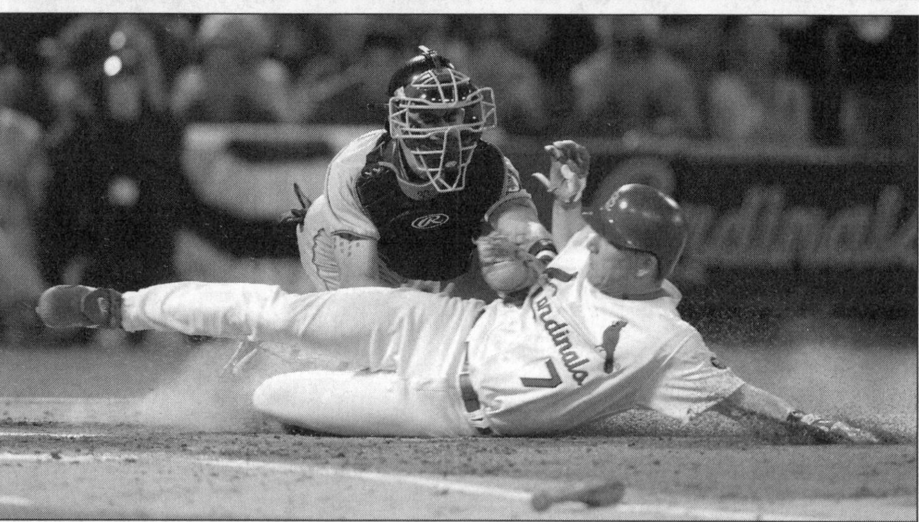

J.D. Drew hit .385 in the NLCS, but it wasn't enough as the Cardinals lost the series to the Giants.

BY JOSH RAWITCH

San Francisco is home to the Golden Gate Bridge and Alcatraz Island. It is home to the world's best sourdough bread and some of the world's luckiest Internet entrepreneurs. On October 14, it officially became home to the 2002 World Series.

After erasing a $4^1/_2$-game deficit in the wild card race, a two-games-to-one deficit in the NL Division Series and an eighth-inning deficit on Oct. 14 against one of the league's top pitchers, the Giants beat St. Louis, 2-1, in Game 5 of the National League Championship Series to win the series 4-1 and advance to their first World Series since 1989.

"I can't even describe it," said David Bell, who dove head-first into home plate with the winning run before being mobbed by his teammates. "I was just hoping I touched the plate because I felt like I was gliding. It's the best feeling I've ever had in this game."

In fitting fashion, it was Kenny Lofton's single off Steve Kline in the ninth inning that clinched it for San Francisco. Lofton, who incited a bench-clearing incident in Game 1 and then went hitless in his next 16 at-bats, had been one of the major differences for a Giants team that entered August an average team but went 43-20 thereafter.

"I knew the team was a good team and they said it needed a leadoff hitter, a guy that can get on base and do some things and that's what I've tried to do," said Lofton, drenched in champagne. "Some things happen for a reason and you can't put your finger on it. ... Maybe it was just meant for me to come through today."

But on this team of veteran players—not one everyday starter was under the age of 30—each day it seemed to be a different player's day to shine.

"It hasn't sunk in yet, to tell you the truth," said J.T. Snow, who came up with several clutch hits in San Francisco's first two postseason series. "It still doesn't feel real. ... You play this game long enough, you realize that the personal things don't really mean as much. It's all about winning and it's all about trying to get a ring and be a champion.

"People are going to remember champions. No one's going to know 10, 15, 20 years down the road what your batting average was or how many home runs you hit, but they're going to remember if you're a champion."

As they had throughout the pennant stretch and playoffs, the contributions came from unexpected sources, including a key two-out hit from Shawon Dunston in the ninth inning that preceded Lofton's game-winner. Dunston batted .231 in the regular season but still called 2002 "the best year of my career because I'm going as a unit to the World Series.

"We don't have the Yankees' payroll but we have the Yankees fire and character," said Dunston. "Like I told everybody, my best position is not shortstop or outfield. My best position is being a good teammate."

That sort of attitude is hard to find on a team of rookies but on a veteran squad like the Giants, it was hard to find anyone willing to take personal credit.

"We've got a bunch of older players, veteran players, but we're playing like a bunch of kids right now," said shortstop Rich Aurilia, who batted .333 in the series. "We've got guys 36 , 37, 38 years old and going out there, jumping around, diving for balls, stealing bases. We're all playing like we're in the Little League World Series right now and it's nice to see."

That includes the series MVP, Benito Santiago, who had six hits, two homers and six runs batted in.

"This is a dream come true and that's why you play," said Santiago, who advanced to the Fall Classic for the first time in his 17-year career. "It's been a long time behind the plate taking the foul tips. It's great, but hey, it can be better. ... Now we just have to go all the way."

Santiago had no problem wearing his heart on his sleeve, unlike some of his teammates. One player who let loose when the game ended but quickly returned to his subdued self while his teammates went ballistic was second baseman Jeff Kent.

"I'm still suppressing a lot of emotion because I want to be able to bottle that and use that for the World Series," he said. "Why get here if you can't win the World Series? For me, this is not the end of the rope."

And then there's Barry Bonds, whose sacrifice fly off Cardinals starter Matt Morris tied Game 5 in the eighth inning. After years of hearing he cannot perform in the playoffs, Bonds silenced his critics with six runs batted in, tying Santiago for the team high.

"I feel I need a day so I can explain to everyone how I'm really feeling," said Bonds.

It's hard to blame him. Bonds has been with this club longer than anyone else on the playoff roster and he and his teammates finally have a chance to win it all.

"I was here when we lost 98 games," said Aurilia. "I was here when we won in '97. ... We've got a bunch of great guys on this team. We had a lot of question marks coming in, a lot of injuries but everybody is healthy now ... and we've got a lot of pieces now to try to pull together for a world championship."

Game 1 at St. Louis

Wednesday, October 9

SAN FRANCISCO 9, ST. LOUIS 6

HOW THEY SCORED

First Inning

Giants—Lofton walked. Aurilia sacrificed Lofton to second, T. Martinez, unassisted. Kent grounded out, Vina to T. Martinez, as Lofton advanced to third. Bonds walked. Santiago singled to third, scoring Lofton as Bonds advanced to second. Snow walked. Sanders grounded out, Vina to T. Martinez. One run. Giants 1, Cardinals 0.

Second Inning

Giants—Bell and Rueter struck out. Lofton singled to center. Lofton stole second. Aurilia singled to right, scoring Lofton. Kent singled to center as Aurilia advanced to second. Bonds tripled to right-center, scoring Aurilia and Kent. Santiago singled to right, scoring Bonds. Snow singled to right as Santiago advanced to third. Sanders flied to Marrero. Four runs. Giants 5, Cardinals 0.

Cardinals—Cairo singled to right. Matheny singled to center as Cairo advanced to second. Morris sacrificed Cairo to third and Matheny to second, Bell to Kent. Vina grounded out, Kent to Snow, scoring Cairo as Matheny advanced to third. Marrero flied out to Sanders. One run. Giants 5, Cardinals 1.

Third Inning

Giants—Bell flied to Marrero. Rueter grounded out, Cairo to T. Martinez. Lofton homered to right. Aurilia flied to Marrero. One run. Giants 6, Cardinals 1.

Fifth Inning

Giants—Sanders lined to Morris. Bell homered to left-center. Crudale now pitching. Rueter grounded out, Crudale to T. Martinez. Lofton flied to Edmonds. One run. Giants 7, Cardinals 1.

Cardinals—Vina grounded out, Kent to Snow. Marrero flied to Sanders. Edmonds doubled to right. Pujols homered to center, scoring Edmonds. Renteria grounded out, Kent to Snow. Two runs. Giants 7, Cardinals 3.

Sixth Inning

Giants—Aurilia flied to Marrero. Kent struck out. Bonds walked. Santiago homered to left-center, scoring Bonds. Snow struck out. Two runs. Giants 9, Cardinals 3.

Cardinals—T. Martinez singled to left. Cairo homered to left, scoring T. Martinez. Rodriguez now pitching. Matheny lined to Aurilia. Robinson, pinch-hitting for Crudale, walked. Vina flied to Bonds. Robinson caught trying to steal second, Santiago to Aurilia. Two runs. Giants 9, Cardinals 5.

Eighth Inning

Cardinals—Worrell now pitching. Cairo struck out. Matheny lined to Aurilia. Drew, pinch-hitting for Veres, homered to right-center. Vina grounded out, Bell to Snow. One run. Giants 9, Cardinals 6.

BOX SCORE

San Francisco	AB	R	H	RBI	PO	A
Lofton, cf	4	3	2	1	3	0
Aurilia, ss	4	1	1	1	4	2
Kent, 2b	5	1	2	0	2	3
Bonds, lf	2	2	1	2	1	0
Santiago, c	5	1	3	4	4	1
Snow, 1b	4	0	1	0	8	1
Sanders, rf	4	0	0	0	4	0
Bell, 3b	4	1	1	1	0	4
Rueter, p	3	0	0	0	1	1
Rodriguez, p	1	0	0	0	0	0
Worrell, p	0	0	0	0	0	0
Nen, p	0	0	0	0	0	1
Totals	36	9	11	9	27	13

St. Louis	AB	R	H	RBI	PO	A
Vina, 2b	5	0	0	1	2	3
Marrero, rf	4	0	1	0	5	0
Edmonds, cf	4	1	2	0	1	0
Pujols, lf	4	1	1	2	0	0
Renteria, ss	4	0	1	0	0	0
T. Martinez, 1b	4	1	1	0	10	0
Cairo, 3b	4	2	3	2	1	2
Matheny, c	4	0	1	0	7	0
Morris, p	1	0	0	0	1	0
Crudale, p	0	0	0	0	0	1
Robinson, ph	0	0	0	0	0	0
Veres, p	0	0	0	0	0	1
Drew, ph	1	1	1	1	0	0
Kline, p	0	0	0	0	0	1
Totals	35	6	11	6	27	8

San Francisco	1	4	1	0	1	2	0	0	0—9
St. Louis	0	1	0	0	2	2	0	1	0—6

San Francisco	IP	H	R	ER	BB	SO
Rueter (W)	*5.0	9	5	5	1	1
Rodriguez	2.0	1	0	0	2	1
Worrell	1.0	1	1	1	0	1
Nen (S)	1.0	0	0	0	1	1

St. Louis	IP	H	R	ER	BB	SO
Morris (L)	4.1	10	7	7	4	2
Crudale	1.2	1	2	2	1	2
Veres	2.0	0	0	0	0	2
Kline	1.0	0	0	0	0	1

*Pitched to two batters in sixth.

DP—San Francisco 1, St. Louis 1. LOB—San Francisco 6, St. Louis 8. 2B—Marrero, Edmonds. 3B—Bonds. HR—Lofton, D.Bell, Pujols, antiago, Cairo, Drew. SB—Lofton. CS—Robinson. SH—Aurilia, Morris. BP—Renteria by Rueter. T—3:31. A—52,175. U—Marsh, plate; elson, first; Scott, second; Kellogg, third; Welke, left field; Reliford, right eld.

Game 2 at St. Louis

Thursday, October 10

SAN FRANCISCO 4, ST. LOUIS 1

HOW THEY SCORED

First Inning

Giants—Lofton flied to Drew. Aurilia homered to left-center. Kent popped to Renteria. Bonds flied to Drew. One run. Giants 1, Cardinals 0.

Fifth Inning

Giants—Bell singled to left. Schmidt sacrificed Bell to second, T. Martinez to Vina. Lofton struck out. Aurilia homered to left-center, scoring Bell. Kent fouled to T. Martinez. Two runs. Giants 3, Cardinals 0.

Eighth Inning

Cardinals—Drew and Matheny struck out. Perez, pinch-hitting for Fassero, homered to left. Eyre now pitching. Vina singled to left. R. Martinez now at shortstop and Nen pitching. Cairo forced Vina at second, R. Martinez, unassisted. One run. Giants 3, Cardinals 1.

Ninth Inning

Giants—Isringhausen now pitching. Snow tripled. Sanders popped to Vina. Bell was walked intentionally. R. Martinez sacrificed Bell to second and scored Snow, Isringhausen to T. Martinez. Lofton was walked intentionally. Nen struck out. One run. Giants 4, Cardinals 1.

BOX SCORE

San Francisco	AB	R	H	RBI	PO	A
Lofton, cf	4	0	0	0	2	1
Aurilia, ss	3	2	2	3	2	3
Nen, p	1	0	0	0	0	0
Kent, 2b	4	0	1	0	1	1
Bonds, lf	3	0	0	0	2	0
Santiago, c	4	0	0	0	9	0
Snow, 1b	4	1	2	0	6	0
Sanders, rf	4	0	0	0	4	0
Bell, 3b	3	1	2	0	0	1
Schmidt, p	2	0	0	0	0	1
Eyre, p	0	0	0	0	0	0
R. Martinez, ss	0	0	0	1	1	1
Totals	32	4	7	4	27	8
St. Louis	**AB**	**R**	**H**	**RBI**	**PO**	**A**
Vina, 2b	4	0	1	0	3	0
Cairo, 3b	4	0	0	0	0	1
Edmonds, cf	4	0	1	0	2	0
Pujols, lf	4	0	1	0	0	0
T. Martinez, 1b	3	0	0	0	4	1
Renteria, ss	4	0	0	0	1	0
Drew, rf	3	0	1	0	5	0
Matheny, c	3	0	1	0	12	0
Williams, p	0	0	0	0	0	0
Robinson, ph	1	0	0	0	0	0
White, p	0	0	0	0	0	0
Fassero, p	0	0	0	0	0	0
Perez, ph	1	1	1	1	0	0
Isringhausen, p	0	0	0	0	0	1
Totals	31	1	6	1	27	3

San Francisco	1	0	0	0	2	0	0	0	1—4
St. Louis	0	0	0	0	0	0	0	1	0—1

San Francisco	IP	H	R	ER	BB	SO
Schmidt (W)	7.2	4	1	1	1	8
Eyre	*0.0	1	0	0	0	0
Nen (S)	1.1	1	0	0	0	0
St. Louis	**IP**	**H**	**R**	**ER**	**BB**	**SO**
Williams (L)	6.0	6	3	3	1	7
White	1.1	0	0	0	1	2
Fassero	0.2	0	0	0	0	1
Isringhausen	1.0	1	1	1	2	1

*Pitched to one batter in eighth.

DP—San Francisco 1. LOB—San Francisco 7, St. Louis 5. 2B—Edmonds. 3B—Snow. HR—Aurilia 2, Perez. SH—Schmidt, R. Martinez, Williams. T—3:17. A—52,195. U—Nelson, plate; Scott, first; Kellogg, second; Welke, third; Reliford, left field; Marsh, right field.

Game 3 at San Francisco

Saturday, October 12

ST. LOUIS 5, SAN FRANCISCO 4

HOW THEY SCORED

Second Inning

Giants—Snow singled to right. Bell singled to right as Snow advanced to second. Ortiz singled to third as Snow advanced to third and Bell to second. Lofton forced Snow at the plate, T. Martinez to Matheny, as Bell advanced to third and Ortiz to second. Aurilia scored Bell on a sacrifice fly to Edmonds. Kent singled to center as Ortiz advanced to third and Lofton to second. Bonds flied to Drew. One run. Giants 1, Cardinals 0.

Third Inning

Cardinals—Finley struck out, but was safe at first on a wild pitch. Vina doubled to center as Finley advanced to third. Renteria scored Finley on a sacrifice fly to Sanders as Vina advanced to third. Edmonds grounded out, Aurilia to Snow, scoring Vina. Pujols and Drew walked. T. Martinez grounded out, Santiago to Snow. Two runs. Cardinals 2, Giants 1.

Fourth Inning

Cardinals—Marrero struck out. Matheny homered to left. Finley flied to Lofton. Vina grounded out, Kent to Snow. One run. Cardinals 3, Giants 1.

Fifth Inning

Cardinals—Renteria flied to Sanders. Edmonds homered to left. Pujols flied to Sanders. Drew singled to right. Fultz now pitching. T. Martinez fouled to Bell. One run. Cardinals 4, Giants 1.

Giants—Aurilia walked. Kent singled to left as Aurilia advanced to second. Bonds homered to right, scoring Aurilia and Kent. Santiago singled to left. Sanders fouled to Pujols. Snow grounded into a double play, T. Martinez to Renteria to T. Martinez. Three runs. Cardinals 4, Giants 4.

Sixth Inning

Cardinals—Witasick now pitching. Marrero homered to left. Matheny grounded out, Aurilia to Snow. DiFelice, pinch-hitting for Finley, grounded out, Bell to Snow. Vina fouled to Bell. One run. Cardinals 5, Giants 4.

BOX SCORE

St. Louis	AB	R	H	RBI	PO	A
Vina, 2b	5	1	1	0	2	1
Renteria, ss	3	0	0	1	2	2
Edmonds, cf	3	1	1	2	4	0
Pujols, 3b	3	0	1	0	1	1
Drew, rf	3	0	1	0	2	0
T. Martinez, 1b	4	0	0	0	8	5
Marrero, lf	4	1	1	1	0	0
Matheny, c	4	1	1	1	7	3
Finley, p	2	1	0	0	1	0
DiFelice, ph	1	0	0	0	0	0
Veres, p	0	0	0	0	0	0
Kline, p	0	0	0	0	0	1
White, p	0	0	0	0	0	0
Perez, ph	1	0	0	0	0	0
Isringhausen, p	0	0	0	0	0	0
Totals	33	5	6	5	27	13
San Francisco	**AB**	**R**	**H**	**RBI**	**PO**	**A**
Lofton, cf	5	0	0	0	4	0
Aurilia, ss	2	1	1	1	0	3
Kent, 2b	5	1	2	0	1	1
Bonds, lf	2	1	1	3	2	0
Santiago, c	5	0	2	0	3	1
Sanders, rf	5	0	0	0	4	0
Snow, 1b	4	0	1	0	11	0
Bell, 3b	3	1	2	0	2	2
Ortiz, p	1	0	1	0	0	0
Fultz, p	0	0	0	0	0	0
Witasick, p	0	0	0	0	0	0
Feliz, ph	1	0	0	0	0	0
Rodriguez, p	0	0	0	0	0	0
Eyre, p	0	0	0	0	0	0
Dunston, ph	0	0	0	0	0	0
Worrell, p	0	0	0	0	0	0
Totals	33	4	10	4	27	7

St. Louis	0	0	2	1	1	1	0	0	0—5
San Francisco	0	1	0	0	3	0	0	0	0—4

St. Louis	IP	H	R	ER	BB	SO
Finley (W)	5.0	7	4	4	3	1
Veres	1.2	2	0	0	1	3
Kline	1.0	1	0	0	0	0
White	0.1	0	0	0	0	0
Isringhausen (S)	1.0	0	0	0	1	2
San Francisco	**IP**	**H**	**R**	**ER**	**BB**	**SO**
Ortiz	4.2	5	4	4	3	3
Fultz	0.1	0	0	0	0	0
Witasick (L)	1.0	1	1	1	0	0
Rodriguez	1.0	0	0	0	0	1
Eyre	1.0	0	0	0	0	0
Worrell	1.0	0	0	0	0	0

E—Renteria. DP—St. Louis 2. LOB—St. Louis 5, San Francisco 11. 2B—Vina, Pujols, Aurilia. HR—Matheny, Edmonds, Bonds, Marrero. S—Renteria, Aurilia. SH—Aurilia, Ortiz, Dunston. WP—Ortiz. T—3:32. A—42,177. U—Scott, plate; Kellogg, first; Welke, second; Reliford, third; Marsh, left field; Nelson, right field.

Game 4 at San Francisco

Sunday, October 13

SAN FRANCISCO 4, ST. LOUIS 3

HOW THEY SCORED

First Inning

Cardinals—Vina doubled to right-center. Renteria flied to Sanders as Vina advanced to third. Edmonds grounded out, Kent to Snow, scoring Vina. Pujols was hit by a pitch. Drew singled to center as Pujols advanced to second. T. Martinez singled to left, scoring Pujols as Drew advanced to third. Marrero grounded out, Bell to Snow. Two runs. Cardinals 2, Giants 0.

Mike Crudale pitched only one game for the Cardinals, and couldn't do much to stop the Giants offense.

Sixth Inning

Giants—Aurilia struck out. Kent and Bonds walked. White now pitching. Santiago struck out. Snow doubled to left-center, scoring Kent and Bonds. Sanders struck out. Two runs. Cardinals 2, Giants 2.

Eighth Inning

Giants—Aurilia flied to Edmonds. Kent grounded out to T. Martinez. Bonds was walked intentionally. Santiago homered to left, scoring Bonds. Robinson now in left field and Kline pitching. Snow grounded out, Renteria to T. Martinez. Two runs. Giants 4, Cardinals 2.

Ninth Inning

Cardinals—Nen now pitching. Robinson struck out, but was safe at first on a wild pitch. Vina singled to right as Robinson advanced to second. Renteria grounded out, Aurilia to Snow, as Robinson advanced to third and Vina to second. Edmonds singled to right, scoring Robinson as Vina advanced to third. Pujols and Drew struck out. One run. Giants 4, Cardinals 3.

BOX SCORE

St. Louis	AB	R	H	RBI	PO	A
Vina, 2b	5	1	3	0	0	2
Renteria, ss	4	0	0	0	1	2
Edmonds, cf	5	0	2	2	3	0
Pujols, 3b	4	1	1	0	1	1
Drew, rf	5	0	2	0	0	0
T. Martinez, 1b	3	0	1	1	10	0
Marrero, lf	4	0	1	0	2	0
Kline, p	0	0	0	0	0	0
Matheny, c	4	0	2	0	7	1
Benes, p	2	0	0	0	0	0
White, p	0	0	0	0	0	0
Robinson, lf	1	1	0	0	0	0
Totals	37	3	12	3	24	6
San Francisco	**AB**	**R**	**H**	**RBI**	**PO**	**A**
Lofton, cf	4	0	0	0	2	0
Worrell, p	0	0	0	0	0	0
Nen, p	0	0	0	0	0	0
Aurilia, ss	4	0	0	0	3	4
Kent, 2b	2	1	0	0	2	4
Bonds, lf	2	2	1	0	1	0
Santiago, c	3	1	1	2	3	0
Snow, 1b	4	0	1	2	12	1
Sanders, rf	3	0	1	0	3	0
Rodriguez, p	0	0	0	0	0	0
Eyre, p	0	0	0	0	0	0
Goodwin, rf	0	0	0	0	0	0
Bell, 3b	3	0	0	0	0	2
Hernandez, p	1	0	0	0	0	2
Shinjo, rf-cf	1	0	0	0	1	0
Totals	27	4	4	4	27	13

St. Louis	2	0	0	0	0	0	0	0	1—3
San Francisco	0	0	0	0	0	2	0	2	x—4

St. Louis	IP	H	R	ER	BB	SO
Benes	5.1	2	2	2	4	5
White (L)	2.1	2	2	2	1	3
Kline	0.1	0	0	0	0	0
San Francisco	**IP**	**H**	**R**	**ER**	**BB**	**SO**
Hernandez	6.1	9	2	2	1	0
Rodriguez	0.2	0	0	0	0	0
Eyre	0.1	1	0	0	0	0
Worrell (W)	0.2	0	0	0	0	0
Nen (S)	1.0	2	1	1	0	3

Cardinals second baseman Fernando Vina had two RBIs and two runs scored in the NLCS.

E—Aurilia. DP—San Francisco 2. LOB—St. Louis 11, San Francisco 5. 2B—Vina, Matheny, Snow. HR—Santiago. SB—T. Martinez. SH—Renteria, Benes, Hernandez. WP—Nen. HBP—Pujols by Hernandez. T—3:26. A—42,676. U—Kellogg, plate; Welke, first; Reliford, second; Marsh, third; Nelson, left field; Scott, right field.

Game 5 at San Francisco

Monday, October 14

SAN FRANCISCO 2, ST. LOUIS 1

HOW THEY SCORED

Seventh Inning

Cardinals—Rodriguez now pitching. Matheny doubled to right-center. Morris sacrificed Matheny to third, but Morris was also safe on a fielder's choice. Vina scored Matheny on a sacrifice fly to Bonds. Cairo singled to center as Morris advanced to second. Edmonds and Pujols flied to Bonds. One run. Cardinals 1, Giants 0.

Eighth Inning

Giants—Dunston struck out. Lofton singled to center. Aurilia singled to left as Lofton advanced to second. Kent was hit by a pitch. Bonds scored Lofton on a sacrifice fly to Marrero as Aurilia advanced to third. Santiago grounded out, Vina to Pujols. One run. Cardinals 1, Giants 1.

Ninth Inning

Giants—R. Martinez, pinch-hitting for Worrell, fouled to Matheny. Snow flied to Marrero. Bell singled to left-center. Dunston singled to center as Bell advanced to second. Kline now pitching. Lofton singled to right-center, scoring Bell as Dunston advanced to second. One run. Giants 2, Cardinals 1.

BOX SCORE

St. Louis	AB	R	H	RBI	PO	A
Vina, 2b	4	0	1	1	3	3
Cairo, 3b	5	0	2	0	2	3
Edmonds, cf	4	0	2	0	1	0
Pujols, 1b	4	0	1	0	9	1
Perez, rf	2	0	0	0	1	0
Drew, rf	1	0	0	0	0	0
Renteria, ss	4	0	2	0	0	1
Marrero, lf	4	0	0	0	5	0
Matheny, c	4	1	1	0	5	0
Morris, p	3	0	0	0	0	2
Kline, p	0	0	0	0	0	0
Totals	35	1	9	1	26	10

San Francisco	AB	R	H	RBI	PO	A
Lofton, cf	4	1	3	1	3	0
Aurilia, ss	2	0	1	0	0	0
Kent, 2b	3	0	0	0	0	5
Bonds, lf	2	0	0	1	5	0
Santiago, c	3	0	0	0	5	0
Goodwin, rf	3	0	0	0	2	0
Eyre, p	0	0	0	0	0	0
Worrell, p	0	0	0	0	0	0
R. Martinez, ph	1	0	0	0	0	0
Snow, 1b	4	0	0	0	11	0
Bell, 3b	4	1	2	0	0	1
Rueter, p	2	0	0	0	1	2
Rodriguez, p	0	0	0	0	0	0
Dunston, rf	2	0	1	0	0	0
Totals	30	2	7	2	27	8

St. Louis	0	0	0	0	0	0	1	0	0	—1
San Francisco	0	0	0	0	0	0	0	1	1	—2

St. Louis	IP	H	R	ER	BB	SO
Morris (L)	8.2	6	2	2	2	4
Kline	*0.0	1	0	0	0	0

San Francisco	IP	H	R	ER	BB	SO
Rueter	6.0	6	0	0	1	2
Rodriguez	1.0	2	1	1	0	0
Eyre	0.1	0	0	0	0	0
Worrell (W)	1.2	1	0	0	0	2

*Pitched to one batter in ninth.

DP—St. Louis 1. LOB—St. Louis 10, San Francisco 9. 2B—Matheny, Bell. S—Vina, Bonds. SH—Morris, Aurilia. HBP—Lofton by Morris, Kent by Morris, Aurilia by Morris. T—3:01. A—42,673. U—Welke, plate; Reliford, first; Marsh, second; Nelson, third; Scott, left field; Kellogg, right field.

COMPOSITE

BATTING AVERAGES

San Francisco Giants

Player, position	G	AB	R	H	2B	3B	HR	RBI	Avg.
Ortiz, p	1	1	0	1	0	0	0	0	1.000
Dunston, ph-rf	2	2	0	1	0	0	0	0	.500
Bell, 3b	5	17	4	7	1	0	1	1	.412
Aurilia, ss	5	15	4	5	1	0	2	5	.333
Santiago, c	5	20	2	6	0	0	2	6	.300
Bonds, lf	5	11	5	3	0	1	1	6	.273
Kent, 2b	5	19	3	5	0	0	0	0	.263
Snow, 1b	5	20	1	5	1	1	0	2	.250
Lofton, cf	5	21	4	5	0	0	1	2	.238
Sanders, rf	4	16	0	1	0	0	0	0	.063
Eyre, p	4	0	0	0	0	0	0	0	.000
Fultz, p	1	0	0	0	0	0	0	0	.000
Witasick, p	1	0	0	0	0	0	0	0	.000
Worrell, p	4	0	0	0	0	0	0	0	.000
Feliz, ph	1	1	0	0	0	0	0	0	.000
Hernandez, p	1	1	0	0	0	0	0	0	.000
R. Martinez, ss-ph	2	1	0	0	0	0	0	1	.000
Nen, p	3	1	0	0	0	0	0	0	.000
Rodriguez, p	4	1	0	0	0	0	0	0	.000
Shinjo, cf-rf	1	1	0	0	0	0	0	0	.000
Schmidt, p	1	2	0	0	0	0	0	0	.000
Goodwin, rf	2	3	0	0	0	0	0	0	.000
Rueter, p	2	5	0	0	0	0	0	0	.000
Totals	5	158	23	39	3	2	7	23	.247

St. Louis Cardinals

Player, position	G	AB	R	H	2B	3B	HR	RBI	Avg.
Edmonds, cf	5	20	2	8	2	0	1	4	.400
Cairo, 3b	3	13	2	5	0	0	1	2	.385
Drew, ph-rf	5	13	1	5	0	0	1	1	.385
Matheny, c	5	19	2	6	2	0	1	1	.316
Pujols, lf-3b-1b	5	19	2	5	1	0	1	2	.263
Vina, 2b	5	23	2	6	2	0	0	2	.261
Perez, ph-rf	3	4	1	1	0	0	1	1	.250
Marrero, rf-lf	4	16	1	3	1	0	1	1	.188
Renteria, ss	5	19	0	3	0	0	0	1	.158
T. Martinez, 1b	4	14	1	2	0	0	0	1	.143
Crudale, p	1	0	0	0	0	0	0	0	.000
Fassero, p	1	0	0	0	0	0	0	0	.000
Isringhausen, p	2	0	0	0	0	0	0	0	.000
Kline, p	4	0	0	0	0	0	0	0	.000
Veres, p	2	0	0	0	0	0	0	0	.000
White, p	3	0	0	0	0	0	0	0	.000
Williams, p	1	0	0	0	0	0	0	0	.000
DiFelice, ph	1	1	0	0	0	0	0	0	.000
Benes, p	1	2	0	0	0	0	0	0	.000
Finley, p	1	2	1	0	0	0	0	0	.000
Robinson, ph-lf	3	2	1	0	0	0	0	0	.000
Morris, p	2	4	0	0	0	0	0	0	.000
Totals	5	171	16	44	8	0	7	16	.257

PITCHING AVERAGES

San Francisco Giants

Pitcher	G	IP	H	R	ER	BB	SO	W	L	ERA
Eyre	4	1.2	2	0	0	0	0	0	0	0.00
Fultz	1	0.1	0	0	0	0	0	0	0	0.00
Schmidt	1	7.2	4	1	1	1	8	1	0	1.17
Rodriguez	4	4.2	3	1	1	2	2	0	0	1.93
Worrell	4	4.1	2	1	1	0	3	2	0	2.08
Nen	3	3.1	3	1	1	1	4	0	0	2.70
Hernandez	1	6.1	9	2	2	1	0	0	0	2.84
Rueter	2	11.0	15	5	5	2	3	1	0	4.09
Ortiz	1	4.2	5	4	4	3	3	0	0	7.71
Witasick	1	1.0	1	1	1	0	0	0	1	9.00
Totals	5	45.0	44	16	16	10	23	4	1	3.20

No shutouts. Saves—Nen 3.

St. Louis Cardinals

Pitcher	G	IP	H	R	ER	BB	SO	W	L	ERA
Veres	2	3.2	2	0	0	1	5	0	0	0.00
Kline	4	2.1	2	0	0	0	1	0	0	0.00
Fassero	1	0.2	0	0	0	0	1	0	0	0.00
Benes	1	5.1	2	2	2	4	5	0	0	3.38
Williams	1	6.0	6	3	3	1	7	0	1	4.50
White	3	4.0	2	2	2	2	5	0	1	4.50
Isringhausen	2	2.0	1	1	1	3	3	0	0	4.50
Morris	2	13.0	16	9	9	6	6	0	2	6.23
Finley	1	5.0	7	4	4	3	1	1	0	7.20
Crudale	1	1.2	1	2	2	1	2	0	0	10.80
Totals	5	43.2	39	23	23	21	36	1	4	4.74

No shutouts. Save—Isringhausen.

Game 1 at Anaheim

Saturday, October 19

SAN FRANCISCO 4, ANAHEIM 3

Key moment: In his first World Series plate appearance, Barry Bonds homered to set the tone for the evening.

Big hit: With two outs in the sixth inning J.T. Snow—who hit only six home runs during the regular season—delivered a two-run homer to give the Giants a 4-1 lead.

Big pitch: Leading 2-1 in the fourth, Jason Schmidt escaped a two-out, runners on second and third situation by getting Bengie Molina to ground out weakly to third on a 1-2 fastball.

Key move: Giants manager Dusty Baker went back to Reggie Sanders in the sixth spot, after using Tom Goodwin there in Game 5 of the NLCS. Sanders contributed two hits, including a homer, and scored two runs.

Costly mistake: The Angels were 1-for-8 with runners in scoring position and stranded nine base runners.

Key stat: The first three combined hits by the Giants and Angels were home runs, the first time that has ever happened to start a World Series.

BOX SCORE

San Francisco	AB	R	H	RBI	PO	A
Lofton, cf	3	0	0	0	3	0
Aurilia, ss	4	0	0	0	1	0
Kent, 2b	4	0	0	0	1	3
Bonds, lf	3	1	1	1	3	0
Santiago, c	4	0	1	0	9	0
Sanders, rf	3	2	2	1	3	0
Snow, 1b	3	1	1	2	6	0
Bell, 3b	4	0	0	0	1	2
Shinjo, dh	3	0	1	0	0	0
§Goodwin, ph-dh	1	0	0	0	0	0
Schmidt, p	0	0	0	0	0	0
Fe. Rodriguez, p	0	0	0	0	0	0
Worrell, p	0	0	0	0	0	0
Nen, p	0	0	0	0	0	0
Totals	32	4	6	4	27	5

Anaheim	AB	R	H	RBI	PO	A
Eckstein, ss	5	0	1	0	0	6
Erstad, cf	5	0	1	0	1	0
Salmon, rf	4	0	0	0	1	0
Anderson, lf	4	0	1	0	4	0
Glaus, 3b	4	2	2	2	1	4
Fullmer, dh	3	1	1	0	0	0
Spiezio, 1b	3	0	1	0	11	1
†Figgins, pr	0	0	0	0	0	0
Wooten, 1b	0	0	0	0	1	0
B. Molina, c	3	0	0	0	6	0
‡Palmeiro, ph	1	0	0	0	0	0
J. Molina, c	0	0	0	0	1	0
Kennedy, 2b	4	0	2	1	0	1
Washburn, p	0	0	0	0	1	1
Donnelly, p	0	0	0	0	0	0
Schoeneweis, p	0	0	0	0	0	0
Weber, p	0	0	0	0	0	0
Totals	36	3	9	3	27	13

San Francisco	0	2	0	0	0	2	0	0	0	—4
Anaheim	0	1	0	0	0	2	0	0	0	—3

San Francisco	IP	H	R	ER	BB	SO
Schmidt (W)	5.2	9	3	3	1	6
Fe. Rodriguez	1.1	0	0	0	0	1
Worrell	1.0	0	0	0	1	1
Nen (S)	1.0	0	0	0	0	1

Anaheim	IP	H	R	ER	BB	SO
Washburn (L)	5.2	6	4	4	2	5
Donnelly	1.2	0	0	0	0	0
Schoeneweis	*0.0	0	0	0	1	0
Weber	1.2	0	0	0	0	2

*Pitched to one batter in eighth.

†Pinch-ran for Spiezio in eighth. ‡Fouled out for B. Molina in eighth. §Grounded out for Shinjo in ninth.

LOB—San Francisco 5, Anaheim 8. 2B—Spiezio, Kennedy. HR—Bonds, Sanders, Glaus 2, Snow. SB—Fullmer. SH—Lofton. T—3:44. A—44,603. U—Crawford, plate; Hernandez, first; Tschida, second; Winters, third; Reilly, left field; McClelland, right field.

PLAY BY PLAY

First Inning

Giants—Lofton struck out. Aurilia fouled to Glaus. Kent struck out.

Angels—Eckstein and Erstad flied to Bonds. Salmon struck out.

Second Inning

Giants—Bonds homered to right. Santiago grounded out, Glaus to Spiezio. Sanders homered to right. Snow grounded out, Kennedy to Spiezio. Bell grounded out, Glaus to Spiezio. Two runs. Giants 2, Angels 0.

Angels—Anderson struck out. Glaus homered to left. Fullmer singled to right. Spiezio flied to Lofton. Fullmer stole second. B. Molina flied to Bonds. One run. Giants 2, Angels 1.

Third Inning

Giants—Shinjo struck out. Lofton flied to Erstad. Aurilia grounded out, Eckstein to Spiezio.

Angels—Kennedy doubled to right. Eckstein grounded out, Kent to Snow. Erstad struck out. Salmon flied to Lofton.

Fourth Inning

Giants—Kent grounded out, Eckstein to Spiezio. Bonds struck out. Santiago singled to center. Sanders and Snow walked. Bell flied to Salmon.

Angels—Anderson singled to right. Glaus popped to Kent. Fullmer struck out. Spiezio doubled to right as Anderson advanced to third. B. Molina grounded out, Bell to Snow.

Fifth Inning

Giants—Shinjo singled to center. Lofton sacrificed Shinjo to second, Washburn to Spiezio. Aurilia flied to Anderson. Kent grounded out, Eckstein to Spiezio.

Angels—Kennedy struck out. Eckstein singled to second. Erstad singled to center as Eckstein advanced to third. Salmon fouled to Snow. Anderson struck out.

Sixth Inning

Giants—Bonds grounded out, Spiezio to Washburn. Santiago struck out. Sanders singled to left. Snow homered to left, scoring Sanders. Donnelly now pitching. Bell fouled to Anderson. Two runs. Giants 4, Angels 1.

Angels—Glaus homered to left. Fullmer walked. Spiezio flied to Sanders. B. Molina grounded out, Bell to Snow, as Fullmer advanced to second. Kennedy singled to right as Fullmer scored. Fe. Rodriguez now pitching. Eckstein lined to Aurilia. Two runs. Giants 4, Angels 3.

Seventh Inning

Giants—Shinjo grounded out, Glaus to Spiezio. Lofton flied to Anderson. Aurilia grounded out, Glaus to Spiezio.

Angels—Erstad struck out. Salmon flied to Sanders. Anderson grounded out, Kent to Snow.

Eighth Inning

Giants—Kent grounded out, Eckstein to Spiezio. Schoeneweis now pitching. Bonds walked. Weber now pitching. Santiago grounded out, Eckstein to Spiezio, as Bonds advanced to second. Sanders struck out.

Angels—Worrell now pitching. Glaus struck out. Fullmer grounded out, Kent to Snow. Spiezio walked. Figgins now running for Spiezio. Palmeiro, pinch-hitting for B. Molina, fouled to Bell.

Ninth Inning

Giants—Wooten now at first and J. Molina catching. Snow flied to Anderson. Bell grounded out, Eckstein to Wooten. Goodwin, pinch-hitting for Shinjo, grounded out, Eckstein to Wooten.

Angels—Nen now pitching. Kennedy flied to Sanders. Eckstein struck out. Erstad flied to Lofton. Final score: Giants 4, Angels 3.

Game 2 at Anaheim

Sunday, October 20

ANAHEIM 11, SAN FRANCISCO 10

Key moment: Tim Salmon snaps a 9-9 tie with a two-out, two-run homer off Felix Rodriguez in the eighth.

Big hit: David Eckstein's single in the eighth ahead of Salmon's shot proved to be crucial when Barry Bonds hit a towering home run in the ninth inning.

Big pitch: Felix Rodriguez tried to get ahead of Salmon with a fastball in the eighth inning. It didn't work.

Key move: Francisco Rodriguez came on in the sixth inning with Anaheim trailing 9-8 and pitched three scoreless innings for his fifth win of postseason.

Costly mistake: Dusty Baker stayed too long with starter Russ Ortiz, who gave up seven runs on nine hits in 1 $^{2}/_{3}$ innings.

Key stat: It was the first time both starters pitched two innings or less in a World Series game since Oct. 5, 1957, when the Braves' Bob Buhl and the Yankees' Bob Turley exited before the third inning of Game 3.

It was a hard-fought series between the Angels and Giants. Close plays at every turn.

BOX SCORE

San Francisco	AB	R	H	RBI	PO	A
Lofton, cf	5	0	1	0	5	0
Aurilia, ss	5	1	1	0	2	2
Kent, 2b	5	1	1	1	2	3
Bonds, lf	2	3	1	1	1	0
Santiago, c	5	1	1	0	0	0
Snow, 1b	4	2	2	2	11	2
Sanders, rf	4	1	2	3	2	1
Bell, 3b	4	1	2	2	0	4
Dunston, dh	4	0	1	1	0	0
Ru. Ortiz, p	0	0	0	0	0	1
Zerbe, p	0	0	0	0	1	1
Witasick, p	0	0	0	0	0	0
Fultz, p	0	0	0	0	0	0
Fe. Rodriguez, p	0	0	0	0	0	0
Worrell, p	0	0	0	0	0	0
Totals	38	10	12	10	24	14

Anaheim	AB	R	H	RBI	PO	A
Eckstein, ss	5	3	3	0	1	3
Erstad, cf	5	2	2	1	4	0
Salmon, rf	4	3	4	4	0	0
Ochoa, rf	0	0	0	0	0	0
Anderson, lf	5	1	2	2	2	0
Glaus, 3b	4	1	2	0	1	0
Fullmer, dh	3	1	2	1	0	0
Spiezio, 1b	3	0	1	2	10	0
B. Molina, c	4	0	0	0	8	0
Kennedy, 2b	4	0	0	0	1	3
Appier, p	0	0	0	0	0	1
Lackey, p	0	0	0	0	0	1
Weber, p	0	0	0	0	0	0
Fr. Rodriguez, p	0	0	0	0	0	1
Percival, p	0	0	0	0	0	0
Totals	37	11	16	10	27	9

San Francisco	0	4	1	0	4	0	0	0	1	—10
Anaheim	5	2	0	0	1	1	0	2	x	—11

San Francisco	IP	H	R	ER	BB	SO
Ru. Ortiz	1.2	9	7	7	0	0
Zerbe	4.0	4	2	1	0	0
Witasick	†0.0	0	0	0	1	0
Fultz	0.1	1	0	0	0	0
Fe. Rodriguez (L)	1.2	2	2	2	1	0
Worrell	0.1	0	0	0	0	0

Anaheim	IP	H	R	ER	BB	SO
Appier	*2.0	5	5	5	2	2
Lackey	2.1	2	2	2	1	1
Weber	0.2	4	2	2	0	1
Fr. Rodriguez (W)	3.0	0	0	0	0	4
Percival (S)	1.0	1	1	1	0	0

Francisco Rodriguez pitched only five games for the Angels in the regular season, but handled a key bullpen role during the postseason.

*Pitched to two batters in third.

†Pitched to one batter in sixth.

E—Lofton, Anderson. DP—San Francisco 1, Anaheim 1. LOB—San Francisco 4, Anaheim 5. 2B—Aurilia, Erstad 2, Glaus. HR—Sanders, Bell, Salmon 2, Kent, Bonds. SB—Sanders, Fullmer, Spiezio. S—Spiezio. PB—Santiago. T—3:57. A—44,584. U—Hernandez, plate; Tschida, first; Winters, second; Reilly, third; McClelland, left field; Crawford, right field.

PLAY BY PLAY

First Inning

Giants—Lofton struck out. Aurilia grounded out, Eckstein to Spiezio. Kent grounded out, Appier to Spiezio.

Angels—Eckstein singled to right. Erstad doubled to right, scoring Eckstein. Salmon singled to right as Erstad advanced to third. Anderson singled to right, scoring Erstad as Salmon advanced to second. Glaus flied to Lofton as Salmon advanced to third. Fullmer singled to center, scoring Salmon as Anderson advanced to third. Spiezio singled to right, scoring Anderson as Fullmer advanced to third. Fullmer stole home as Spiezio stole second. B. Molina flied to Sanders as Spiezio advanced to third. Kennedy grounded out, Ortiz to Snow. Five runs. Angels 5, Giants 0.

Second Inning

Giants—Bonds walked. Santiago flied to Erstad. Snow singled to right as Bonds advanced to third. Sanders homered to left, scoring Bonds and Snow. Bell homered to center. Dunston grounded out, Kennedy to Spiezio. Lofton singled to center. Aurilia struck out. Four runs. Angels 5, Giants 4.

Angels—Eckstein bunted safely to the pitcher. Erstad flied to Lofton. Salmon homered to left, scoring Eckstein. Anderson popped to Snow. Glaus doubled to center. Zerbe now pitching. Glaus advanced to third on a passed ball by Santiago. Fullmer grounded out, Snow to Zerbe. Two runs. Angels 7, Giants 4.

Third Inning

Giants—Kent homered to left. Bonds walked. Lackey now pitching. Santiago lined into a double play, Eckstein to Spiezio. Snow flied to Erstad. One run. Angels 7, Giants 5.

Angels—Spiezio grounded out, Kent to Snow. B. Molina grounded out, Aurilia to Snow. Kennedy grounded out, Zerbe to Snow.

Fourth Inning

Giants—Sanders singled to left. Sanders stole second. Bell grounded out, Lackey to Spiezio. Dunston reached first on a fielder's choice as Sanders was retired, Eckstein to Kennedy to Glaus. Lofton flied to Erstad.

Angels—Eckstein grounded out, Bell to Snow. Erstad grounded out, Bell to Snow. Salmon singled to left. Anderson grounded out, Kent to Snow.

Fifth Inning

Giants—Aurilia doubled to center. Kent struck out. Bonds was walked intentionally. Weber now pitching. Santiago singled to left as Aurilia advanced to third and Bonds to second. Snow singled to right, scoring Aurilia and Bonds as Santiago advanced to third. Sanders struck out. Bell singled to second, scoring Santiago as Snow advanced to second. Dunston singled to left and advanced to second on a throwing error by Anderson as Snow scored and Bell advanced to third. Lofton grounded out, Kennedy to Spiezio. Four runs. Giants 9, Angels 7.

Angels—Glaus singled to center. Fullmer singled to center and Glaus advanced to third when Lofton bobbled the ball. Spiezio hit a sacrifice fly to Lofton, scoring Glaus. B. Molina grounded into a double play, Bell to Kent to Snow. One run. Giants 9, Angels 8.

Sixth Inning

Giants—Fr. Rodriguez now pitching. Aurilia and Kent struck out. Bonds grounded to Spiezio.

Angels—Kennedy grounded to Snow. Eckstein grounded out, Aurilia to Snow. Erstad doubled to right. Witasick now pitching. Salmon walked. Fultz now pitching. Anderson singled to right, scoring Erstad, but Salmon was thrown out, Sanders to Snow to Bell to Aurilia. One run. Giants 9, Angels 9.

Seventh Inning

Giants—Santiago struck out. Snow grounded to Spiezio. Sanders struck out.

Angels—Fe. Rodriguez now pitching. Glaus popped to Kent. Fullmer walked. Spiezio flied to Lofton. B. Molina flied to Sanders.

Eighth Inning

Giants—Bell flied to Erstad. Dunston fouled to Spiezio. Lofton grounded out, Fr. Rodriguez to Spiezio.

Angels—Kennedy flied to Lofton. Eckstein singled to right. Erstad flied to Bonds. Salmon homered to left, scoring Eckstein. Worrell now pitching. Anderson popped to Aurilia. Two runs. Angels 11, Giants 9.

Ninth Inning

Giants—Percival now pitching and Ochoa in right field. Aurilia and Kent flied to Anderson. Bonds homered to right. Santiago popped to Kennedy. One run. Final score: Angels 11, Giants 10.

Game 3 at San Francisco

Tuesday, October 22

ANAHEIM 10, SAN FRANCISCO 4

Key moment: A first in World Series history, the Angels batted around in two consecutive innings. By the time they did so in the fourth, the Halos led 8-1 and had Game 3 in the bag.

Big hit: Scott Spiezio drilled a two-run triple off Livan Hernandez to give Anaheim a 4-1 lead in the third inning.

Big pitch: With Anaheim leading 4-1 in the third, Ramon Ortiz strikes out Barry Bonds on a sinking fastball with a runner on base.

Key move: Mike Scioscia orders Bonds walked intentionally in the first with runners at first and third and one out. Benito Santiago's bases-loaded grounder scores one run, but that's all the Giants would get in the inning.

Costly mistake: David Bell's fielding error allowed Tim Salmon to reach in the third inning and proved costly when Salmon later scord on Spiezio's triple.

Key stat: 6—The number of times the Angels had batted around in the 2002 playoffs.

BOX SCORE

Anaheim	AB	R	H	RBI	PO	A
Eckstein, ss	5	1	2	1	2	2
Erstad, cf	6	2	3	0	3	0
Salmon, rf	4	2	1	1	2	0
Schoeneweis, p	0	0	0	0	0	0
Anderson, lf	6	0	1	1	3	0
Glaus, 3b	5	2	2	1	0	1
Spiezio, 1b	5	1	2	3	10	0
Kennedy, 2b	5	1	2	1	2	2
B. Molina, c	2	1	2	1	5	0
Ra. Ortiz, p	3	0	0	0	0	1
‡Wooten, ph	1	0	0	0	0	0
Donnelly, p	0	0	0	0	0	0
∞Gil, ph	1	0	1	0	0	0
Ochoa, rf	0	0	0	0	0	0
Totals	43	10	16	9	27	6

San Francisco	AB	R	H	RBI	PO	A
Lofton, cf	4	1	0	0	5	0
Aurilia, ss	5	1	2	1	1	4
Kent, 2b	4	1	2	0	1	1
Bonds, lf	2	1	1	2	3	0
Santiago, c	4	0	0	1	6	1
Snow, 1b	4	0	1	0	8	1
Sanders, rf	4	0	0	0	1	0
Bell, 3b	1	0	0	0	0	2
Hernandez, p	0	0	0	0	2	1
Witasick, p	0	0	0	0	0	0
†Feliz, ph	1	0	0	0	0	0
Fultz, p	0	0	0	0	0	0
§Dunston, ph	1	0	0	0	0	0
Fe. Rodriguez, p	0	0	0	0	0	0
Eyre, p	0	0	0	0	0	1
▲Martinez, ph	1	0	0	0	0	0
Totals	31	4	6	4	27	11

Anaheim	0	0	4	4	0	1	0	1	0	—10
San Francisco	1	0	0	0	3	0	0	0	0	— 4

Anaheim	IP	H	R	ER	BB	SO
Ra. Ortiz (W)	5.0	5	4	4	4	3
Donnelly	2.0	0	0	0	2	0
Schoeneweis	2.0	1	0	0	0	2

San Francisco	IP	H	R	ER	BB	SO
Hernandez (L)	3.2	5	6	5	5	3
Witasick	0.1	3	2	2	1	1
Fultz	2.0	3	1	1	1	0
Fe. Rodriguez	1.0	1	0	0	0	0
Eyre	2.0	4	1	0	1	1

†Flied out for Witasick in fourth. ‡Fouled out for Ra. Ortiz in sixth. §Flied out for Fultz in sixth. ∞Singled for Donnelly in eighth. ▲Struck out for Eyre in ninth.

E—Santiago, Bell. DP—Anaheim 1, San Francisco 1. LOB—Anaheim 15, San Francisco 7. 2B—Erstad, Salmon, Kennedy. 3B—Spiezio. HR—Aurilia, Bonds. SB—Erstad, Salmon, Lofton. SH—Hernandez. HBP—Kennedy by Fultz. T—3:37. A—42,707. U—Tschida, plate; Winters, first; Reilly, second; McClelland, third; Crawford, left field; Hernandez, right field.

PLAY BY PLAY

First Inning

Angels—Eckstein lined to Hernandez. Erstad grounded out, Bell to Snow. Salmon struck out.

Giants—Lofton walked. Aurilia struck out. Lofton stole second. Kent singled to the pitcher as Lofton advanced to third. Bonds was walked intentionally. Santiago grounded out, Kennedy to Spiezio, as Lofton scored, Kent advanced to third and Bonds to second. Snow grounded out, Ra. Ortiz to Spiezio. One run. Giants 1, Angels 0.

Second Inning

Angels—Anderson grounded out, Snow to Hernandez. Glaus flied to Lofton. Spiezio walked. Kennedy doubled to left as Spiezio advanced to third. B. Molina was walked intentionally. Ra. Ortiz struck out.

Giants—Sanders struck out. Bell walked. Hernandez sacrificed Bell to second, Spiezio, unassisted. Lofton grounded to Spiezio.

Third Inning

Angels—Eckstein walked. Erstad doubled to right as Eckstein advanced to third. Salmon reached base on a fielding error by Bell, scoring Eckstein. Anderson flied to Bonds. Glaus singled to left-center, scoring Erstad as Salmon advanced to third. Spiezio tripled to right-center, scoring Salmon and Glaus. Kennedy struck out. B. Molina was walked intentionally. Ra. Ortiz grounded out, Hernandez to Snow. Four runs. Angels 4, Giants 1.

Giants—Aurilia singled to left. Kent fouled to Spiezio. Bonds struck out. Santiago grounded out, Glaus to Spiezio.

Fourth Inning

Angels—Eckstein grounded out, Aurilia to Snow. Erstad singled to center. Salmon walked. Erstad stole third and Salmon stole second. Anderson grounded to Snow, scoring Erstad as Salmon advanced to third. Witasick now pitching. Glaus walked. Spiezio singled to right, scoring Salmon as Glaus advanced to second. Kennedy singled to center, scoring Glaus as Spiezio advanced to second. B. Molina singled to right-center, scoring Spiezio as Kennedy advanced to third. Ra. Ortiz struck out. Four runs. Angels 8, Giants 1.

Giants—Snow grounded to Spiezio. Sanders fouled to Spiezio. Bell walked. Feliz, pinch-hitting for Witasick, flied to Anderson.

Fifth Inning

Angels—Fultz now pitching. Eckstein grounded out, Aurilia to Snow. Erstad singled to left-center. Salmon flied to Bonds. Anderson singled to right as Erstad advanced to third. Glaus flied to Sanders.

Giants—Lofton flied to Salmon. Aurilia homered to left. Kent singled to left. Bonds homered to center, scoring Kent. Santiago grounded out, Eckstein to Spiezio. Snow flied to Anderson. Three runs. Angels 8, Giants 4.

Sixth Inning

Angels—Spiezio grounded out, Aurilia to Snow. Kennedy was hit by a pitch. B. Molina walked. Wooten, pinch-hitting for Ra. Ortiz, fouled to Snow. Eckstein singled to center, scoring Kennedy as B. Molina advanced to second. Erstad popped to Aurilia. One run. Angels 9, Giants 4.

Giants—Donnelly now pitching. Sanders flied to Salmon. Bell walked. Dunston, pinch-hitting for Fultz, flied to Anderson. Lofton popped to Eckstein.

Seventh Inning

Angels—Fe. Rodriguez now pitching. Salmon doubled to left. Anderson, Glaus and Spiezio flied to Lofton.

Giants—Aurilia and Kent flied to Erstad. Bonds walked. Santiago popped to Eckstein.

Eighth Inning

Angels—Eyre now pitching. Kennedy flied to Bonds. B. Molina singled to center. Gil, pinch-hitting for Donnelly, singled to left as B. Molina advanced to second. Eckstein singled to first as B. Molina advanced to third and Gil to second. Erstad reached first on a fielder's choice and advanced to second on a throwing error by Santiago as B. Molina scored. On the play, Gil advanced to third, but was out trying to score, Santiago to Bell to Santiago, as Eckstein advanced to third. Salmon was walked intentionally. Anderson flied to Lofton. One run. Angels 10, Giants 4.

Giants—Schoeneweis now pitching and Ochoa in right field. Snow singled to left. Sanders popped to Kennedy. Bell grounded into a double play, Eckstein to Kennedy to Spiezio.

Ninth Inning

Angels—Glaus singled to right-center. Spiezio grounded into a double play, Aurilia to Kent to Snow. Kennedy struck out.

Giants—Martinez, pinch-hitting for Eyre, struck out. Lofton flied to Erstad. Aurilia struck out. Final score: Angels 10, Giants 4.

Game 4 at San Francisco

Wednesday, October 23

SAN FRANCISCO 4, ANAHEIM 3

Big hit: David Bell delivers big time with a game-winning RBI single off Francisco Rodriguez in the eighth inning.

Big pitch: Robb Nen gets Brad Fullmer to hit into a game-ending double play.

Key move: The Angels walk Bonds to load the bases in the first and third innings, but the Giants are unable to break the game open as Benito Santiago hits into two inning-ending double plays.

Costly mistake: Troy Glaus was too late in grabbing Kenny Lofton's third-base-line-hugging bunt in the fifth inning. The bunt had briefly rolled into foul territory, but returned to the line by the time Glaus had it in hand. Lofton is safe and the Giants go on to score three times to tie the game.

Key stat: 5, 0—The number of Angels to reach second base during the first three innings, and after the third inning.

BOX SCORE

Anaheim	AB	R	H	RBI	PO	A
Eckstein, ss	3	0	0	1	1	3
Erstad, cf	4	0	0	0	1	0
Salmon, rf	4	0	1	0	3	0
Anderson, lf	4	1	2	0	2	1
Glaus, 3b	4	1	1	2	1	0
Spiezio, 1b	4	0	1	0	7	1
Gil, 2b	3	1	2	0	3	3
∞Kennedy, ph	1	0	1	0	0	0
B. Molina, c	3	0	1	0	4	1
▲Fullmer, ph	1	0	0	0	0	0
Lackey, p	2	0	1	0	2	0
Weber, p	0	0	0	0	0	0
‡Palmeiro, ph	1	0	0	0	0	0
Fr. Rodriguez, p	0	0	0	0	0	0
Totals	34	3	10	3	24	9

San Francisco	AB	R	H	RBI	PO	A
Lofton, cf	4	1	3	0	3	0
Aurilia, ss	4	1	3	1	4	5
Kent, 2b	3	0	0	1	2	5
Bonds, lf	1	0	0	0	1	0
Santiago, c	4	0	1	1	3	0
Snow, 1b	4	1	1	0	10	2
Sanders, rf	4	0	1	0	1	0
Bell, 3b	4	0	2	1	1	1
Rueter, p	2	1	1	0	1	2
†Goodwin, ph	0	0	0	0	0	0
Fe. Rodriguez, p	0	0	0	0	1	0
Worrell, p	0	0	0	0	0	0
§Martinez, ph	1	0	0	0	0	0
Nen, p	0	0	0	0	0	0
Totals	31	4	12	4	27	15

Anaheim	0	1	2	0	0	0	0	0	0—3
San Francisco	0	0	0	0	3	0	0	1	x—4

Anaheim	IP	H	R	ER	BB	SO
Lackey	5.0	9	3	3	3	2
Weber	1.0	1	0	0	1	0
Fr. Rodriguez (L)	2.0	2	1	0	0	2

San Francisco	IP	H	R	ER	BB	SO
Rueter	6.0	9	3	3	0	2
Fe. Rodriguez	1.0	0	0	0	0	1
Worrell (W)	1.0	0	0	0	0	0
Nen (S)	1.0	1	0	0	0	0

†Walked for Rueter in sixth. ‡Struck out for Weber in seventh. §Struck out into a double play for Worrell in eighth. ∞Singled for Gil in ninth. ▲Grounded into double play for B. Molina in ninth.

E—Salmon, Bell. DP—Anaheim 3, San Francisco 2. LOB—Anaheim 5, San Francisco 8. 2B—Aurilia. HR—Glaus. SB—Goodwin. CS—Bell. S—Eckstein, Kent. PB—B. Molina. T—3:02. A—42,703. U—Winters, plate; Reilly, first; McClelland, second; Crawford, third; Hernandez, left field; Tschida, right field.

PLAY BY PLAY

First Inning

Angels—Eckstein grounded out, Aurilia to Snow. Erstad grounded out, Kent to Snow. Salmon reached first on Bell's throwing error. Anderson singled to center as Salmon advanced to third. Glaus forced Anderson at second, Kent to Aurilia.

Giants—Lofton singled to center. Aurilia singled to right as Lofton advanced to third. Kent struck out. Bonds was walked intentionally. Santiago grounded into a double play, Eckstein to Spiezio.

Second Inning

Angels—Spiezio grounded out, Aurilia to Snow. Gil singled to right. B. Molina singled to center as Gil advanced to second. Lackey singled to right as Gil advanced to third and B. Molina to second. Eckstein scored Gil on a sacrifice fly to Lofton. Erstad grounded out, Kent to Snow. One run. Angels 1, Giants 0.

Giants—Snow grounded out, Spiezio to Lackey. Sanders singled to center. Bell grounded out, Eckstein to Spiezio as Sanders advanced to second. Rueter grounded out, Gil to Spiezio.

Third Inning

Angels—Salmon singled to center. Anderson forced Salmon at second, Aurilia to Kent. Glaus homered to center, scoring Anderson. Spiezio lined to Lofton. Gil singled to center. B. Molina flied to Sanders. Two runs. Angels 3, Giants 0.

Giants—Lofton singled to right. Aurilia doubled to center as Lofton advanced to third. Kent lined to Lackey. Bonds was walked intentionally. Santiago grounded into a double play, Eckstein to Gil to Spiezio.

Fourth Inning

Angels—Lackey grounded out, Rueter to Snow. Eckstein grounded out, Bell to Snow. Erstad grounded out, Kent to Snow.

Giants—Snow grounded out, Gil to Spiezio. Sanders flied to Salmon. Bell flied to Anderson.

Fifth Inning

Angels—Salmon struck out. Anderson singled to left. Glaus grounded into a double play, Aurilia to Kent to Snow.

Giants—Rueter singled to the pitcher. Lofton hit a bunt single to third as Rueter advanced to second. Aurilia singled to right, scoring Rueter as Lofton advanced to third. Kent scored Lofton on a sacrifice fly to Salmon and Aurilia advanced to second on Salmon's throwing error. Bonds was walked intentionally. Santiago singled to center, scoring Aurilia as Bonds advanced to second. Snow flied to Salmon. Sanders struck out. Three runs. Angels 3, Giants 3.

Sixth Inning

Angels—Spiezio singled to center. Gil struck out. B. Molina grounded into a double play, Snow to Aurilia to Rueter.

Giants—Weber now pitching. Bell singled to left, but was out trying for second, Anderson to Gil. Goodwin, pinch-hitting for Rueter, walked. Goodwin stole second. Lofton flied to Erstad as Goodwin advanced to third. Aurilia lined to Glaus.

Seventh Inning

Angels—Fe. Rodriguez now pitching. Palmeiro, pinch-hitting for Weber, struck out. Eckstein popped to Kent. Erstad grounded out, Snow to Fe. Rodriguez.

Giants—Fr. Rodriguez now pitching. Kent struck out. Bonds grounded to Spiezio. Santiago flied to Anderson.

Eighth Inning

Angels—Worrell now pitching. Salmon flied to Lofton. Anderson grounded to Snow. Glaus flied to Bonds.

Giants—Snow singled to right. Snow advanced to second on B. Molina's passed ball. Sanders fouled to Spiezio. Bell singled to center, scoring Snow. Martinez, pinch-hitting for Worrell, struck out as Bell was caught trying to steal second, B. Molina to Gil, for a double play. One run. Giants 4, Angels 3.

Ninth Inning

Angels—Nen now pitching. Spiezio fouled to Bell. Kennedy, pinch-hitting for Gil, singled to right. Fullmer, pinch-hitting for B. Molina, grounded into a double play, Aurilia to Snow. Final score: Giants 4, Angels 3.

Game 5 at San Francisco

Thursday, October 24

SAN FRANCISCO 16, ANAHEIM 4

Key moment: With a runner on third and the tying run at the plate in the sixth, Felix Rodriguez gets Tim Salmon to ground out to third to end the inning.

Big hit: Jeff Kent's two-run homer off Ben Weber in the sixth gives the Giants a four-run lead again after Anaheim had rallied from a 6-0 deficit to cut it to 6-4.

Big pitch: After walking Barry Bonds intentionally, Jarrod Washburn tries to get a fastball past Benito Santiago and the catcher drills it into center for a two-run single and a 5-0 lead in the second.

Key move: Dusty Baker goes to his bullpen after Anaheim sends eight men to the plate and scores three times in the fifth. The pen allows one run in $4^1/_3$ innings.

Costly mistake: Mike Scioscia decides to stay with Jarrod Washburn even after Washburn walks four in the first inning. Washburn gives up six runs on six hits and five walks during the first two innings.

Key stat: 12—Number of home runs hit by San Francisco in the World Series, tying the Major League record set by the 1956 New York Yankees.

BOX SCORE

Anaheim	AB	R	H	RBI	PO	A
Eckstein, ss	4	1	2	1	0	1
Erstad, cf	4	0	1	1	5	0
Salmon, rf	4	1	1	0	1	0
Ochoa, rf	1	0	0	0	1	0
Anderson, lf	5	0	1	0	3	0
Glaus, 3b	4	0	1	1	0	1
Spiezio, 1b	2	0	0	0	4	0
Shields, p	0	0	0	0	0	0
Kennedy, 2b	4	0	0	0	2	3
B. Molina, c	4	1	1	0	6	0
J. Molina, c	0	0	0	0	0	0
Washburn, p	1	0	0	0	0	1
†Palmeiro, ph	1	1	1	0	0	0
Donnelly, p	0	0	0	0	0	0
‡Gil, ph	1	0	1	0	0	0
Weber, p	0	0	0	0	0	1
Wooten, 1b	1	0	1	0	2	0
Totals	36	4	10	3	24	7

San Francisco	AB	R	H	RBI	PO	A
Lofton, cf	6	3	3	2	1	0
Eyre, p	0	0	0	0	0	0
Aurilia, ss	6	2	2	3	1	2
Kent, 2b	5	4	3	4	1	2
Bonds, lf	4	2	3	1	0	0
Santiago, c	3	0	1	3	11	0
Sanders, rf	1	0	0	1	2	0
Fe. Rodriguez, p	0	0	0	0	0	0
§Dunston, ph	1	0	0	0	0	0
Worrell, p	0	0	0	0	0	0
∞Feliz, ph	1	0	0	0	0	0
Goodwin, rf	0	0	0	0	1	0
Snow, 1b	4	2	2	0	7	0
Bell, 3b	3	2	2	1	1	1
Schmidt, p	1	0	0	0	0	0
Zerbe, p	0	0	0	0	1	0
Shinjo, rf-cf	2	1	0	0	1	0
Totals	37	16	16	15	27	5

Anaheim	0	0	0	0	3	1	0	0	0— 4
San Francisco	3	3	0	0	0	2	4	4	x—16

Anaheim	IP	H	R	ER	BB	SO
Washburn (L)	4.0	6	6	6	5	1
Donnelly	1.0	0	0	0	0	2
Weber	1.1	5	5	5	1	2
Shields	1.2	5	5	1	0	1

San Francisco	IP	H	R	ER	BB	SO
Schmidt	4.2	7	3	3	3	8
Zerbe (W)	1.0	2	1	1	0	0
Fe. Rodriguez	0.1	0	0	0	0	0
Worrell	2.0	1	0	0	0	2
Eyre	1.0	0	0	0	0	1

†Doubled for Washburn in fifth. ‡Doubled for Donnelly in sixth. §Struck out for Fe. Rodriguez in sixth. ∞Flied out for Worrell in eighth.

E—Glaus, Erstad. LOB—Anaheim 9, San Francisco 8. 2B—Glaus, Palmeiro, Gil, Kent, Bonds 2. 3B—Lofton. HR—Kent 2, Aurilia. SB—Eckstein. S—Erstad, Santiago, Sanders. SH—Schmidt, Shinjo. WP—Schmidt. HBP—D. Bell by Weber. T—3:53. A—42,713. U—Reilly, plate; McClelland, first; Crawford, second; Hernandez, third; Tschida, left field; Winters, right field.

PLAY BY PLAY

First Inning

Angels—Eckstein singled to center. Erstad forced Eckstein at second, Kent to Aurilia. Salmon struck out. Anderson singled to left as Erstad advanced to second. Glaus struck out.

Giants—Lofton singled to left. Aurilia flied to Erstad. Kent walked. Bonds doubled to right, scoring Lofton as Kent advanced to third. Santiago scored Kent on a sacrifice fly to Anderson. Sanders was walked intentionally. Snow walked. Bell walked, scoring Bonds. Schmidt struck out. Three runs. Giants 3, Angels 0.

Second Inning

Angels—Spiezio struck out. Kennedy grounded to Snow. B. Molina struck out.

Giants—Lofton singled to center. Aurilia lined to Erstad. Kent doubled to right as Lofton advanced to third. Bonds was walked intentionally. Santiago singled to center and advanced to second on Erstad's throwing error as Lofton and Kent scored and Bonds advanced to third. Sanders scored Bonds on a sacrifice fly to Erstad as Santiago advanced to third. Snow flied to Erstad. Three runs. Giants 6, Angels 0.

Third Inning

Angels—Washburn grounded out, Aurilia to Snow. Eckstein walked. Eckstein stole second. Erstad singled to left as Eckstein advanced to third. Salmon struck out. Anderson lined to Sanders.

Giants—Bell singled to short. Schmidt sacrificed Bell to second, Washburn to Kennedy. Lofton grounded out, Kennedy to Spiezio as Bell advanced to third. Aurilia flied to Erstad.

Barry Bonds followed his amazing 2002 season with four home runs in the World Series.

Fourth Inning

Angels—Glaus struck out. Spiezio walked. Kennedy struck out. B. Molina popped to Kent.

Giants—Kent flied to Salmon. Bonds flied to Anderson. Santiago grounded out, Glaus to Spiezio.

Fifth Inning

Angels—Palmeiro, pinch-hitting for Washburn, doubled to right. Eckstein singled to left as Palmeiro advanced to third. Erstad scored Palmeiro on a sacrifice fly to Sanders. Salmon singled to center as Eckstein advanced to third. Eckstein scored and Salmon advanced to second on a wild pitch by Schmidt. Anderson struck out. Glaus doubled to left, scoring Salmon. Spiezio walked. Zerbe now pitching. Kennedy flied to Lofton. Three runs. Giants 6, Angels 3.

Giants—Donnelly now pitching. Sanders and Snow struck out. Bell fouled to Spiezio.

Sixth Inning

Angels—B. Molina singled to center, Gil, pinch-hitting for Donnelly, doubled to center as B. Molina advanced to third. Eckstein grounded out, Aurilia to Snow, scoring B. Molina as Gil advanced to third. Erstad grounded to Zerbe. Fe. Rodriguez now pitching and Shinjo in right field. Salmon grounded out, Bell to Snow. One run. Giants 6, Angels 4.

Giants—Weber now pitching. Shinjo struck out. Lofton grounded out, Kennedy to Spiezio. Aurilia singled to left. Kent homered to left, scoring Aurilia. Bonds doubled to left. Santiago was walked intentionally. Dunston, pinch-hitting for Fe. Rodriguez, struck out. Two runs. Giants 8, Angels 4.

Seventh Inning

Angels—Worrell now pitching. Anderson fouled to Bell. Glaus struck out. Spiezio grounded to Snow.

Giants—Snow singled to center. Bell was hit by a pitch. Shinjo sacrificed Snow to third and Bell to second, Weber to Kennedy. Lofton tripled to right, scoring Snow and Bell. Shields now pitching and Wooten at first base. Aurilia struck out. Kent homered to left, scoring Lofton. Bonds singled to center. Santiago grounded out, Eckstein to Wooten. Four runs. Giants 12, Angels 4.

Eighth Inning

Angels—Kennedy grounded to Snow. B. Molina flied to Shinjo. Wooten singled to center. Eckstein struck out.

Giants—J. Molina now catching and Ochoa in right field. Feliz, pinch-hitting for Worrell, flied to Ochoa. Snow singled to right. Bell singled to center as Snow advanced to second. Shinjo reached first on a fielding error by Glaus as Snow scored and Bell advanced to second. Lofton grounded out, Kennedy to Wooten as Bell advanced to third and Shinjo to second. Aurilia homered to left, scoring Bell and Shinjo. Kent flied to Anderson. Four runs. Giants 16, Angels 4.

Ninth Inning

Angels—Eyre now pitching and Goodwin in right field as Shinjo moves to left field. Erstad struck out. Ochoa flied to Goodwin. Anderson grounded out, Kent to Snow. Final score: Giants 16, Angels 4.

Game 6 at Anaheim

Saturday, October 26

ANAHEIM 6, SAN FRANCISCO 5

Key moment: Troy Glaus' two-run double off Robb Nen in the eighth inning gives the Angels a 6-5 lead after they had trailed 5-0 in the seventh, making this the largest come-from-behind win of any team facing elimination in World Series history.

Big hit: Trailing 5-0 with one out in the seventh, Anaheim's Scott Spiezio belts a 3-2 pitch from Felix Rodriguez for a three-run homer to get the Angels back in the game.

Big pitch: Troy Percival strikes out Rich Aurilia with Jeff Kent on deck and Barry Bonds in the hole to end the game and give the Angels the victory and tie the series at three games apiece.

Key move: Mike Scioscia goes with Brendan Donnelly in the eighth inning, saving closer Troy Percival. Donnelly allows just one base runner, leaving Percival to get the save in the ninth without sluggers Kent and Bonds getting a chance to bat.

Key stat: .615—Anaheim's batting average (8-for-13) in the final two innings. The Angels had only three hits in their previous 32 at-bats, an .094 clip, before their late rally.

BOX SCORE

San Francisco	AB	R	H	RBI	PO	A
Lofton, cf	5	2	2	0	3	0
Aurilia, ss	4	0	0	0	2	3
Kent, 2b	4	0	2	1	0	4
Bonds, lf	2	1	1	1	1	0
Santiago, c	3	0	0	0	5	0
Snow, 1b	4	0	1	0	8	1
Sanders, rf	4	0	0	0	4	0
Bell, 3b	4	1	1	0	0	1
Dunston, dh	3	1	1	2	0	0
∞Goodwin, ph	1	0	0	0	0	0
Ru. Ortiz, p	0	0	0	0	1	0
Fe. Rodriguez, p	0	0	0	0	0	0
Eyre, p	0	0	0	0	0	0
Worrell, p	0	0	0	0	0	0
Nen, p	0	0	0	0	0	1
Totals	**34**	**5**	**8**	**4**	**24**	**10**

Anaheim	AB	R	H	RBI	PO	A
Eckstein, ss	4	0	0	0	4	1
Erstad, cf	3	1	1	1	3	0
Salmon, rf	4	0	2	0	1	0
§Figgins, pr	0	1	0	0	0	0
Ochoa, rf	0	0	0	0	0	0
Anderson, lf	4	1	1	0	0	0
Glaus, 3b	3	1	2	2	1	3
Fullmer, dh	4	1	1	0	0	0
Spiezio, 1b	3	1	1	3	7	0
B. Molina, c	2	0	0	0	6	0
‡Palmeiro, ph	1	0	0	0	0	0
J. Molina, c	0	0	0	0	4	0
Kennedy, 2b	4	0	2	0	1	2
Appier, p	0	0	0	0	0	0
Fr. Rodriguez, p	0	0	0	0	0	0
Donnelly, p	0	0	0	0	0	0
Percival, p	0	0	0	0	0	0
Totals	**32**	**6**	**10**	**6**	**27**	**6**

San Francisco	0	0	0	0	3	1	1	0	0—5
Anaheim	0	0	0	0	0	0	3	3	x—6

San Francisco	IP	H	R	ER	BB	SO
Ru. Ortiz	6.1	4	2	2	2	2
Fe. Rodriguez	0.1	1	1	1	0	1
Eyre	*0.0	1	0	0	0	0
Worrell (L)	†0.1	3	3	2	0	0
Nen	1.0	1	0	0	1	2

Anaheim	IP	H	R	ER	BB	SO
Appier	4.1	4	3	3	3	2
Fr. Rodriguez	2.2	4	2	2	0	4
Donnelly (W)	1.0	0	0	0	1	2
Percival (S)	1.0	0	0	0	0	2

*Pitched to one batter in the seventh.

†Pitched to three batters in eighth.

‡Struck out for B. Molina in seventh. §Pinch-ran for Salmon in eighth. ∞Struck out for Dunston in ninth.

E—Bonds, B. Molina. DP—San Francisco 1, Anaheim 1. LOB—San Francisco 6, Anaheim 6. 2B—Lofton, Glaus. HR—Dunston, Bonds, Spiezio, Erstad. SB—Lofton 2. SH—J. Molina. WP—Fr. Rodriguez. T—3:48. A—44,506. U—McClelland, plate; Crawford, first; Hernandez, second; Tschida, third; Winters, left field; Reilly, right field.

PLAY BY PLAY

First Inning

Giants—Lofton popped to Eckstein. Aurilia flied to Erstad. Kent singled to center. Bonds was walked intentionally. Santiago fouled to Spiezio.

Angels—Eckstein flied to Bonds. Erstad grounded out, Kent to Snow. Salmon grounded out, Bell to Snow.

Second Inning

Giants—Snow flied to Erstad. Sanders and Bell struck out.

Angels—Anderson flied to Lofton. Glaus walked. Fullmer popped to Aurilia. Spiezio flied to Lofton.

Third Inning

Giants—Dunston flied to Salmon. Lofton grounded out, Glaus to Spiezio. Aurilia walked. Kent popped to Eckstein.

Angels—B. Molina flied to Sanders. Kennedy struck out. Eckstein grounded out, Aurilia to Snow.

Fourth Inning

Giants—Bonds walked. Santiago grounded into a double play, Glaus to Kennedy to Spiezio. Snow grounded out, Kennedy to Spiezio.

Angels—Erstad grounded out, Kent to Snow. Salmon singled to short. Anderson grounded into a double play, Kent to Aurilia to Snow.

Fifth Inning

Giants—Sanders popped to Eckstein. Bell singled to short. Dunston homered to left, scoring Bell. Lofton doubled to right-center. Fr. Rodriguez now pitching. Lofton stole third. Aurilia grounded out, Eckstein to Spiezio. Lofton scored on Fr. Rodriguez's wild pitch. Kent grounded out, Glaus to Spiezio. Three runs. Giants 3, Angels 0.

Angels—Glaus flied to Lofton. Fullmer flied to Sanders. Spiezio grounded out, Snow to Ru. Ortiz.

Sixth Inning

Giants—Bonds homered to right. Santiago struck out. Snow singled to left. Sanders struck out. Bell fouled to Spiezio. One run. Giants 4, Angels 0.

Angels—B. Molina flied to Sanders. Kennedy singled to center. Eckstein grounded out, Aurilia to Snow, as Kennedy advanced to second. Erstad walked. Salmon struck out.

Seventh Inning

Giants—Dunston popped to Eckstein. Lofton singled to right. Lofton stole second and advanced to third on B. Molina's throwing error. Aurilia struck out. Kent singled to center, scoring Lofton. Bonds struck out. One run. Giants 5, Angels 0.

Angels—Anderson grounded out, Kent to Snow. Glaus singled to left. Fullmer singled to right as Glaus advanced to second. Fe. Rodriguez now pitching. Spiezio homered to right, scoring Glaus and Fullmer. Palmeiro, pinch-hitting for B. Molina, struck out. Eyre now pitching. Kennedy singled to left. Worrell now pitching. Eckstein flied to Sanders. Three runs. Giants 5, Angels 3.

Eighth Inning

Giants—Donnelly now pitching and J. Molina catching. Santiago walked. Snow flied to Erstad. Sanders and Bell struck out.

Angels—Erstad homered to right. Salmon singled to center. Figgins now running for Salmon. Anderson singled to left and reached second on Bonds' bobble as Figgins advanced to third. Nen now pitching. Glaus doubled to left-center, scoring Figgins and Anderson. Fullmer struck out. Spiezio was walked intentionally. J. Molina sacrificed Glaus to third and Spiezio to second, Nen to Snow. Kennedy struck out. Three runs. Angels 6, Giants 5.

Ninth Inning

Giants—Percival now pitching and Ochoa in right field. Goodwin, pinch-hitting for Dunston, struck out. Lofton fouled to Glaus. Aurilia struck out. Final score: Angels 6, Giants 5.

Game 7 at Anaheim

Sunday, October 27

ANAHEIM 4, SAN FRANCISCO 1

Key moment: Kenny Lofton lofts a fly ball to center field with two on and two out in the ninth inning and Darin Erstad hauls it in to end the game and give the Angels their first world championship in the 42-year history of the franchise.

Big hit: Garret Anderson lines a 1-1 pitch from Livan Hernandez to the right-field corner for a three-run double in the third to give Anaheim a 4-1 lead.

Big pitch: With the Giants trailing 4-1 with runners on second and third and two outs in the sixth, Anaheim's Brendan Donnelly strikes out pinch-hitter Tom Goodwin to end a San Francisco scoring threat.

Key move: The decision to start John Lackey, though a rookie pitcher hadn't won a Game 7 of the World Series in 93 years, was absolutely the right move as Lackey was outstanding with five strong innings and earned the victory.

Costly mistake: Dusty Baker decides to go with Livan Hernandez as his Game 7 starter instead of Kirk Rueter. Hernandez allowed four runs and is tagged with the loss; Rueter followed an inning later with four scoreless innings.

Key stat: 7-for-7—Troy Percival in save situations during the postseason.

BOX SCORE

San Francisco	AB	R	H	RBI	PO	A
Lofton, cf	4	0	0	0	4	1
Aurilia, ss	4	0	0	0	0	2
Kent, 2b	4	0	0	0	3	3
Bonds, lf	3	0	1	0	1	0
Santiago, c	3	1	2	0	6	0
Snow, 1b	4	0	3	0	7	1
Sanders, rf	1	0	0	1	0	0
†Goodwin, ph-rf	2	0	0	0	1	0
Bell, 3b	3	0	0	0	1	1
Feliz, dh	3	0	0	0	0	0
‡Shinjo, ph	1	0	0	0	0	0
Hernandez, p	0	0	0	0	0	1
Zerbe, p	0	0	0	0	0	0
Rueter, p	0	0	0	0	0	1
Worrell, p	0	0	0	0	1	0
Totals	32	1	6	1	24	10

Anaheim	AB	R	H	RBI	PO	A
Eckstein, ss	3	1	1	0	3	0
Erstad, cf	3	1	1	0	4	0
Salmon, rf	2	1	0	0	3	0
Ochoa, rf	0	0	0	0	0	0
Anderson, lf	4	0	1	3	3	0
Glaus, 3b	2	0	0	0	0	2
Fullmer, dh	4	0	0	0	0	0
Spiezio, 1b	3	1	0	0	5	0
B. Molina, c	3	0	2	1	9	1
Kennedy, 2b	3	0	0	0	0	2
Lackey, p	0	0	0	0	0	1
Donnelly, p	0	0	0	0	0	0
Fr. Rodriguez, p	0	0	0	0	0	0
Percival, p	0	0	0	0	0	0
Totals	27	4	5	4	27	6

San Francisco	0	1	0	0	0	0	0	0	0	—1
Anaheim	0	1	3	0	0	0	0	0	x	—4

San Francisco	IP	H	R	ER	BB	SO
Hernandez (L)	*2.0	4	4	4	4	1
Zerbe	1.0	0	0	0	0	0
Rueter	4.0	1	0	0	1	3
Worrell	1.0	0	0	0	0	1

Anaheim	IP	H	R	ER	BB	SO
Lackey (W)	5.0	4	1	1	1	4
Donnelly	2.0	1	0	0	1	2
Fr. Rodriguez	1.0	0	0	0	1	3
Percival (S)	1.0	1	0	0	1	1

*Pitched to five batters in third.

†Struck out for Sanders in sixth. ‡Struck out for Feliz in ninth.

DP—San Francisco 1. LOB—San Francisco 9, Anaheim 6. 2B—Snow, Anderson, B. Molina 2. S—Sanders. SH—Erstad. HBP—Salmon by Hernandez. T—3:16. A—44,598. U—Crawford, plate; Hernandez, first; Tschida, second; Winters, third; Reilly, left field; McClelland, right field.

PLAY BY PLAY

First Inning

Giants—Lofton grounded out, Lackey to Kennedy to Spiezio. Aurilia struck out and was thrown out on the dropped third strike, B. Molina to Spiezio. Kent flied to Salmon.

Angels—Eckstein walked. Erstad sacrificed Eckstein to second, Hernandez to Snow. Salmon walked. Anderson flied to Lofton, who threw to Kent to double Eckstein off second.

Second Inning

Giants—Bonds lined to Eckstein. Santiago singled to center. Snow singled to right-center as Santiago advanced to third. Sanders scored Santiago on a sacrifice fly to Anderson. Bell struck out. One run. Giants 1, Angels 0.

Angels—Glaus struck out. Fullmer flied to Lofton. Spiezio walked. B. Molina doubled to left-center, scoring Spiezio. Kennedy flied to Lofton. One run. Giants 1, Angels 1.

Third Inning

Giants—Feliz grounded out, Glaus to Spiezio. Lofton grounded to Spiezio. Aurilia flied to Anderson.

Angels—Eckstein singled to left. Erstad singled to left as Eckstein advanced to second. Salmon was hit by a pitch. Anderson doubled to right, scoring Eckstein, Erstad and Salmon. Glaus was walked intentionally. Zerbe now pitching. Fullmer forced Glaus at second, Aurilia to Kent, as Anderson advanced to third. Spiezio reached first on a fielder's choice as Anderson was thrown out at home, Bell to Santiago. Fullmer advanced to second on the play. B. Molina grounded out, Kent to Snow. Three runs. Angels 4, Giants 1.

Fourth Inning

Giants—Kent struck out. Bonds singled to short. Santiago singled to center as Bonds advanced to second. Snow flied to Erstad. Sanders flied to Salmon.

Angels—Rueter now pitching. Kennedy struck out. Eckstein flied to Bonds. Erstad struck out.

Fifth Inning

Giants—Bell lined to Erstad. Feliz struck out. Lofton walked. Aurilia flied to Salmon.

Angels—Salmon grounded out, Aurilia to Snow. Anderson grounded to Snow. Glaus walked. Fullmer grounded out, Rueter to Snow.

Sixth Inning

Giants—Donnelly now pitching. Kent grounded out, Glaus to Spiezio. Bonds popped to Eckstein. Santiago walked. Snow doubled to right as Santiago advanced to third. Goodwin, pinch-hitting for Sanders, struck out.

Angels—Goodwin now in right field. Spiezio flied to Goodwin. B. Molina doubled to right-center. Kennedy grounded out, Kent to Snow, as B. Molina advanced to third. Eckstein lined to Kent.

Seventh Inning

Giants—Bell flied to Anderson. Feliz struck out. Lofton flied to Erstad.

Angels—Erstad grounded out, Kent to Snow. Salmon struck out. Anderson flied to Lofton.

Eighth Inning

Giants—Fr. Rodriguez now pitching and Ochoa in right field. Aurilia and Kent struck out. Bonds walked. Santiago struck out.

Angels—Worrell now pitching. Glaus struck out. Fullmer grounded out, Snow to Worrell. Spiezio popped to Bell.

Ninth Inning

Giants—Percival now pitching. Snow singled to right. Goodwin forced Snow at second, Kennedy to Eckstein. Goodwin advanced to second on defensive indifference. Bell walked. Shinjo, pinch-hitting for Feliz, struck out. Lofton flied to Erstad. Final score: Angels 4, Giants 1.

For the first time ever, the Angels won a World Series championship.

COMPOSITE

BATTING AVERAGES

Anaheim Angels

Player, position	G	AB	R	H	2B	3B	HR	RBI	Avg.
Gil, ph-2b	3	5	1	4	1	0	0	0	.800
Lackey, p	3	2	0	1	0	0	0	0	.500
Wooten, 1b-ph	3	2	0	1	0	0	0	0	.500
Glaus, 3b	7	26	7	10	3	0	3	8	.385
Salmon, rf	7	26	7	9	1	0	2	5	.346
Eckstein, ss	7	29	6	9	0	0	0	3	.310
Erstad, cf	7	30	6	9	3	0	1	3	.300
B. Molina, c	7	21	2	6	2	0	0	2	.286
Anderson, lf	7	32	3	9	1	0	0	6	.281
Kennedy, 2b-ph	7	25	1	7	2	0	0	2	.280
Fullmer, dh-ph	5	15	3	4	0	0	0	1	.267
Spiezio, 1b	7	23	3	6	1	1	1	8	.261
Palmeiro, ph	4	4	1	1	1	0	0	0	.250
Appier, p	2	0	0	0	0	0	0	0	.000
Donnelly, p	5	0	0	0	0	0	0	0	.000
Figgins, pr	2	0	1	0	0	0	0	0	.000
J. Molina, c	3	0	0	0	0	0	0	0	.000
Percival, p	3	0	0	0	0	0	0	0	.000
Fr. Rodriguez, p	4	0	0	0	0	0	0	0	.000
Schoeneweis, p	2	0	0	0	0	0	0	0	.000
Shields, p	1	0	0	0	0	0	0	0	.000
Weber, p	4	0	0	0	0	0	0	0	.000
Ochoa, rf	5	1	0	0	0	0	0	0	.000
Washburn, p	2	1	0	0	0	0	0	0	.000
Ortiz, p	1	3	0	0	0	0	0	0	.000
Totals	7	245	41	76	15	1	7	38	.310

San Francisco Giants

Player, position	G	AB	R	H	2B	3B	HR	RBI	Avg.
Rueter, p	2	2	1	1	0	0	0	0	.500
Bonds, lf	7	17	8	8	2	0	4	6	.471
Snow, 1b	7	27	6	11	1	0	1	4	.407
Bell, 3b	7	23	4	7	0	0	1	4	.304
Lofton, cf	7	31	7	9	1	1	0	2	.290
Kent, 2b	7	29	6	8	1	0	3	7	.276
Aurilia, ss	7	32	5	8	2	0	2	5	.250
Sanders, rf	7	21	3	5	0	0	2	6	.238
Santiago, c	7	26	2	6	0	0	0	5	.231
Dunston, dh-ph	4	9	1	2	0	0	1	3	.222
Shinjo, dh-cf-rf	3	6	1	1	0	0	0	0	.167
Eyre, p	3	0	0	0	0	0	0	0	.000
Fultz, p	2	0	0	0	0	0	0	0	.000
Hernandez, p	2	0	0	0	0	0	0	0	.000
Nen, p	3	0	0	0	0	0	0	0	.000
Ortiz, p	2	0	0	0	0	0	0	0	.000
Fe. Rodriguez, p	6	0	0	0	0	0	0	0	.000
Witasick, p	2	0	0	0	0	0	0	0	.000
Worrell, p	6	0	0	0	0	0	0	0	.000
Zerbe, p	3	0	0	0	0	0	0	0	.000
Schmidt, p	2	1	0	0	0	0	0	0	.000
Martinez, ph	2	2	0	0	0	0	0	0	.000
Goodwin, dh-ph-rf	5	4	0	0	0	0	0	0	.000
Feliz, ph-dh	3	5	0	0	0	0	0	0	.000
Totals	7	235	44	66	7	1	14	42	.281

PITCHING AVERAGES

Anaheim Angels

Pitcher	G	IP	H	R	ER	BB	SO	W	L	ERA
Donnelly	5	7.2	1	0	0	4	6	1	0	0.00
Schoeneweis	2	2.0	1	0	0	1	2	0	0	0.00
Fr. Rodriguez	4	8.2	6	3	2	1	13	1	1	2.08
Percival	3	3.0	2	1	1	1	3	0	0	3.00
Lackey	3	12.1	15	6	6	5	7	1	0	4.38
Shields	1	1.2	5	5	1	0	1	0	0	5.40
Ortiz	1	5.0	5	4	4	4	3	1	0	7.20
Washburn	2	9.2	12	10	10	7	6	0	2	9.31
Appier	2	6.1	9	8	8	5	4	0	0	11.37
Weber	4	4.2	10	7	7	2	5	0	0	13.50
Totals	7	61.0	66	44	39	30	50	4	3	5.75

No shutouts. Saves—Percival 3.

San Francisco Giants

Pitcher	G	IP	H	R	ER	BB	SO	W	L	ERA
Eyre	3	3.0	5	1	0	1	2	0	0	0.00
Nen	3	3.0	2	0	0	1	3	0	0	0.00
Rueter	2	10.0	10	3	3	1	5	0	0	2.70
Zerbe	3	6.0	6	3	2	0	0	1	0	3.00
Worrell	6	5.2	4	3	2	1	4	1	1	3.18
Fultz	2	2.1	4	1	1	1	0	0	0	3.86
Fe. Rodriguez	6	5.2	4	3	3	1	3	0	1	4.76
Schmidt	2	10.1	16	6	6	4	14	1	0	5.23
Ortiz	2	8.0	13	9	9	2	2	0	0	10.13
Hernandez	2	5.2	9	10	9	9	4	0	2	14.29
Witasick	2	0.1	3	2	2	2	1	0	0	54.00
Totals	7	60.0	76	41	37	23	38	3	4	5.55

No shutouts. Saves—Nen 2.

Who's Who

This Hall of Fame gathering at the 1939 Cooperstown induction ceremonies included (front row from left) Eddie Collins, Babe Ruth, Connie Mack, Cy Young and (back row) Honus Wagner, Grover Alexander, Tris Speaker, Nap Lajoie, George Sisler and Walter Johnson.

Introduction

MURRAY ELECTED ON FIRST TRY

Perhaps in July, when Eddie Murray steps to that podium in Cooperstown, officially joining baseball's immortal legends, he will transform from the reserved man with eye-popping numbers to another thrilled and enthusiastic Hall of Famer.

Murray etched his way to Cooperstown in his own style, not by wowing the media and other outsiders with his witty and warm personality, as did some of his counterparts. Murray paved his Hall of Fame trail with a bat in one hand and glove in another, and little coming from his mouth besides grunts from his vicious swings that produced 504 homers and 3,255 hits.

On January 13, the longtime Oriole became the 38th player elected to Baseball's Hall of Fame on the first ballot as he collected 423 votes, 85.3 percent of the tally. Former Expos, Mets, Dodgers and Giants catcher Gary Carter also was elected, receiving 78 percent of the vote.

Murray was scheduled for a press conference with the Baseball Writers' Association of America on the day his election was announced, but he was in Los Angeles attending the funeral of his sister, Tanya, 38, who passed away on Jan. 2 from kidney failure.

He obviously was joyful about the announcement, but his emotions were tempered by his personal tragedy.

"I am thrilled by the tremendous honor of being elected to the Baseball Hall of Fame and joining the other greats of the game," Murray said in a statement. "For those with whom I shared space on the playing field and in the clubhouse, I share this honor with you.

"Although I dedicated my professional career to the game, I have dedicated my life to my family. The elation I feel by being recognized for my achievements on the field is overshadowed by the anguish of losing someone so dear to me."

This election year spotlighted Murray's outstanding but under-recognized career. Despite his icy relationship with the media and his quiet demeanor, Murray was a no-doubt Hall of Famer, one of only three players—Willie Mays and Hank Aaron being the others—to amass at least 500 homers and 3,000 hits, a testament to his versatility.

Although he was never a league MVP and no favorite of the media, Murray's 504 homers and 3,255 hits over 21 seasons made him a virtual lock for the Hall of Fame in his first year of eligibility.

Murray won the 1977 American League Rookie of the Year award, was an eight-time All-Star and a three-time Gold Glove winner, and finished in the top 10 in MVP voting eight times, including two second-place finishes.

A native of Los Angeles, Murray emerged as one of the greatest switch-hitters in history and possessed the ability to hit for average and power while being a clutch hitter and clubhouse leader.

"He was the greatest clutch hitter I have ever seen," former teammate and current Orioles Vice President of Baseball Operations Mike Flanagan said. "There were so many things he could do, but he never liked to talk about himself or reveal his secrets. But I never saw anyone work harder."

Murray signed with the Orioles out of Locke High School (Los Angeles) and spent four years in the farm system before manager Earl Weaver named Murray his first baseman for the 1977 season. Murray flourished as one of the team's power hitters, hitting .283 with 27 homers and 88 RBIs, edging Oakland's Mitchell Page for the AL Rookie of the Year.

He quickly emerged as a mainstay in the lineup at first base and designated hitter, helping lead the Orioles to the 1979 World Series, which they lost in seven games to the Pittsburgh Pirates. Murray hit .417 in the Series with one homer and five RBIs.

By the time a young shortstop named Cal Ripken arrived in Baltimore, Murray was already an established superstar. In 1982, Ripken's rookie season, Murray put up MVP-type numbers, batting .316 with 32 homers and 110 RBIs. He finished second in MVP voting to Milwaukee's Robin Yount.

While Ripken and Murray were close teammates, they battled fiercely for the title of the league's top player. The 1983 season highlighted this competition, as Ripken and Murray put up career seasons and the Orioles overtook the Brewers and won the American League East.

Ripken won the MVP award that year, beating Murray by just 18 points. But Murray's overall numbers were better that year. Ripken hit .318 with 27 homers, 102 RBIs and a .371 on-base percentage, while Murray hit .333 with 32 homers, 111 RBIs and a .393 on-base percentage.

The Orioles beat the Phillies to win the 1983 World Series, their first title in 13 years.

Ripken became Baltimore's darling because of his talents, good looks and warmth with the media, while Murray quietly continued to be one of the league's most dangerous hitters.

His best season was 1985, when he hit 31 homers with 124 RBIs. Murray's first Orioles era ended in 1988, when he was traded to the Dodgers. The Orioles retired Murray's No. 33 after the trade.

Murray spent the next five years in the National League, three with the Dodgers and two with the Mets.

Carter, who was glowing with excitement and relief after making the Hall on his sixth try, was Murray's teammate with the Dodgers in 1991.

"He really just wanted to go about his business," Carter said. "I would put Eddie Murray in the same category as Andre Dawson. He would like to kid around with the press and [be surly], but he was a total professional. I see why he is a Hall of Famer. I am just glad I had the pleasure of playing with Eddie for one year."

Murray signed with the Cleveland Indians, with whom he collected his 3,000th hit in 1995. Meanwhile, rumors were swirling that the Orioles were interested in reuniting with Murray.

He returned to Baltimore for the Orioles' pennant run in 1996 and belted his 500th homer on Sept. 6, 1996, a year to the day after Ripken broke Lou Gehrig's consecutive-games streak.

"Eddie was not only a great teammate but he was a great friend as well," Ripken said. "When I first came to the big leagues, he really helped me out and showed me the way. His professionalism and the way he was there for his team and ready to play really made an impact on me as a young player.

"It makes me sad to see how Eddie is misunderstood by some of the fans and members of the media. The Eddie that I know always put his team ahead of everything else and went about his business in a manner that all players should follow. On the field, he was dangerous both offensively and defensively, and he was one of the greatest clutch hitters that I ever saw. I am very happy for him and his family today and I am grateful for all that he gave me during our careers."

Murray signed with Anaheim before the 1997 season and finished his career with 1,917 RBIs, eighth on the all-time list.

He was a coach for the Orioles for four seasons before being named the Indians' hitting coach in 2002. In 13 seasons with Baltimore, Murray hit .294 with 343 home runs and 1,224 RBIs.

—Gary Washburn

CARTER MAKES IT TO COOPERSTOWN ON SIXTH TRY

Gary Carter, the boisterous catcher whose infectious enthusiasm defined his 19-year career, achieved baseball's version of immortality on January 13 when it was announced that he had been voted into the Hall of Fame by the Baseball Writers' Association of America. Carter, who spent the majority of his career with the Expos and Mets, joins slugging first baseman Eddie Murray in the Class of 2003.

And in typical Carter fashion, No. 8 bubbled over, exuding the joy and passion that was his trademark for the better part of two decades. He got the news early Tuesday afternoon, fittingly at 12:08 p.m. ET, shortly after picking up a birdie on, you guessed it, the eighth hole at the Ibis Golf and Country Club in Florida.

The Hartford Courant's Jack O'Connell made the call for the BBWAA, giving Carter the news he had waited so long to hear.

"My wife [Sandy] had the phone and she handed it to me and it was Jack's voice," said Carter, who was playing golf with former player-turned-broadcaster Tommy Hutton at the time. "I know his voice and when he said, 'I know this is the call you've been waiting for,' that's when my fist went up in the air. Obviously, I got excited and screamed. ... I'm going to savor every moment."

There was much for Carter to savor on Tuesday. The 11-time All-Star was named on 78 percent of the ballots cast (75 percent is needed for entry), garnering 387 of the 496 ballots cast. Murray, who spent two seasons with the Mets, received 423 votes (85.3 percent). The pair will be inducted on July 27.

Carter's election into Cooperstown ends a six-year wait; one that brought him oh so close to induction in 2002. He earned 72.67 percent of the votes that year, leaving him, at the time, as the only person to have received more than 70 percent of the votes yet not get enshrined.

"I don't think I was ever at a point where I didn't think I wasn't going to make it," Carter said. "I think my second year on the ballot, with Nolan Ryan and George Brett and Robin Yount, when I actually lost some votes, that was the most discouraging.

"Overall, I wasn't so much impatient as I was discouraged. It was a process, more of a buildup. Questions were being asked and each year I was coming closer and closer. Last year, Sandy had put together a party for a few friends and when it didn't happen I never broke down, but she did. What I learned is that good things happen to those who wait. I thank God for letting me be more patient because this is a great thrill now. Those five years feel like they went by in a day."

Carter's infectious enthusiasm for the game and his all-out playing style were as much a part of his Hall of Fame portfolio as his impressive career numbers.

Now Carter can rest easy, safe with the knowledge that he is forever linked to the game's greatest players. He is the 13th catcher elected to the Hall after a career in which many feel he was the best backstop of his generation. Carter, along with fellow Hall of Famer Carlton Fisk, bridged the gap between Johnny Bench and Mike Piazza/Ivan Rodriguez.

He was dominant for more than a decade in leading the Expos to their only playoff berth in 1981 and then helping guide the Mets to a World Series title in 1986. He won three Gold Gloves and his 298 homers as a catcher is sixth best for the position. Carter holds the Major League record for most career putouts (11,785) and total chances accepted (12,988) by a catcher. He won the All-Star Game MVP twice (1981 and 1984) and was runner-up to Mike Schmidt in 1980 in the National League's MVP voting. Carter finished with 324 homers, 1,225 RBIs and a .262 batting average. He scored 1,025 runs and had 2,092 hits.

"My first year in the big leagues I divided time between catching with Barry Foote and playing the outfield," Carter said. "It wasn't until my breakthrough year in 1977, when I had the opportunity to catch every day under Dick Williams, that I hit 31 home runs. It was then that I said maybe if I keep putting some of these years together, maybe I can dream of the Hall of Fame. I'm just very proud the day became a reality."

While the numbers are certainly impressive, he brought more than just statistics to the table. His hustle and determination, combined with a will to excel, were just two of the intangibles that separated him not only from other backstops but almost every other player. Playing on a pair of knees that were cut often by the surgeon's blade, Carter never once stopped hustling. The sight of his brown curly hair bouncing out from underneath his helmet as he legged out a hit or attempted to throw out a runner remains as vivid in New York and Montreal as his million-dollar smile.

"It's an honor to be part of the Hall with the 12 other catchers," said Carter, who is currently a roving catching instructor for the Mets. "It's a grueling position. I had nine knee surgeries and a couple of broken thumbs. Now, though, even with all the injuries, I can look back and say it's OK. It was worth it to be enshrined in Cooperstown. To be part of that fraternity; I don't feel any pain in my knees now.

"Johnny Bench befriended me my first year in the big leagues. He took me under his wing during my first All-Star Game and we've been friends ever since. He's one guy I've tried to emulate and I'll always compare myself to Johnny."

—Kevin Czerwinski

HALL OF FAMERS

CLASS BY CLASS

1936

TY COBB — **OF**
6-1, 175. **B:** L. **T:** R.
Born: Dec. 18, 1886. **Died:** July 17, 1961.
Career: .366 avg., 1st on all-time list; 117 HR; 1,937 RBIs; 4,189 hits; 891 SB.
Teams: Tigers 1905-26; Athletics 1927-28.
How elected: 98.2 percent of vote.

WALTER JOHNSON — **P**
6-1, 200. **B:** R. **T:** R.
Born: Nov. 6, 1887. **Died:** Dec. 10, 1946.
Career: 417-279; 2.16 ERA; 3,509 SO.
Team: Senators 1907-27.
How elected: 83.6 percent of vote.

CHRISTY MATHEWSON — **P**
6-1, 195. **B:** R. **T:** R.
Born: Aug. 12, 1880. **Died:** Oct. 7, 1925.
Career: 373-188; 2.13 ERA; 2,502 SO.
Teams: Giants 1900-16; Reds 1916.
How elected: 90.7 percent of vote.

BABE RUTH — **OF**
6-2, 215. **B:** L. **T:** L.
Born: Feb. 6, 1895. **Died:** Aug. 16, 1948.
Career: .342 avg.; 714 HR; 2,213 RBIs.
Teams: Red Sox 1914-19; Yankees 1920-34; Braves 1935.
How elected: 95.1 percent of vote.

HONUS WAGNER — **SS**
5-11, 200. **B:** R. **T:** R.
Born: Feb. 24, 1874. **Died:** Dec. 6, 1955.
Career: .327 avg.; 101 HR; 1,732 RBIs; 3,415 hits.
Teams: Louisville (Nat.) 1897-99; Pirates 1900-17.
How elected: 95.1 percent of vote.

1937

MORGAN BULKELEY — **EXECUTIVE**
First president of N.L.
Born: Dec. 26, 1837. **Died:** Nov. 6, 1922.
Career: Former Connecticut governor and U.S. senator; helped N.L. organize its first league.
How elected: Centennial Commission.

BAN JOHNSON — **EXECUTIVE**
A.L. founder/president.
Born: Jan. 5, 1864. **Died:** March 28, 1931.
Career: A former sportswriter who revived the old Western League and later renamed it the American League; A.L. president 1901-27.
How elected: Centennial Commission.

NAPOLEON LAJOIE — **2B**
6-1, 195. **B:** R. **T:** R.
Born: Sept. 5, 1874. **Died:** Feb. 7, 1959.
Career: .338 avg.; 83 HR; 1,599 RBIs; 3,242 hits.
Teams: Phillies 1896-1900; Athletics 1901-02, 1915-16; Indians 1902-14.
How elected: 83.6 percent of vote.

CONNIE MACK — **C, MAN.**
6-1, 150. **B:** R. **T:** R.
Born: Dec. 22, 1862. **Died:** Feb. 8, 1956.
Managing career: 3,731-3,948, 53 years; 3 World Series championships.
Teams: Pirates 1894-96; Athletics 1901-50.
How elected: Centennial Commission.

JOHN MCGRAW — **IF, MAN.**
5-7, 155 **B:** L. **T:** R.
Born: April 7, 1873. **Died:** Feb. 25, 1934.
Playing career: .334 avg.; 13 HR; 462 RBIs.
Managing career: 2,784-1,959, 33 years; 3 World Series championships.
Teams (player): Baltimore (A.A.) 1891; Baltimore (Nat.) 1892-99; St. Louis (Nat.) 1900; Baltimore (Amer.) 1901-02; Giants 1902-06.
Teams (manager): Baltimore (Nat.) 1899; Baltimore (Amer.) 1901-02; Giants 1902-32.
How elected: Centennial Commission.

TRIS SPEAKER — **OF**
5-11, 193. **B:** L. **T:** L.
Born: April 4, 1888. **Died:** Dec. 8, 1958.
Career: .345 avg.; 117 HR; 1,529 RBIs; 3,514 hits.
Teams: Red Sox 1907-15; Indians 1916-26; Senators 1927; Athletics 1928.
How elected: 82.1 percent of vote.

GEORGE WRIGHT — **SS**
5-9, 150. **B:** R. **T:** R.
Born: Jan. 28, 1847. **Died:** Aug. 21, 1937.
Career: .256 avg.; 2 HR; 132 RBIs.
Teams: Boston (Nat.) 1876-78, 1880-81; Providence (Nat.) 1879, 1882.
How elected: Centennial Commission.

CY YOUNG — **P**
6-2, 210. **B:** R. **T:** R.
Born: March 29, 1867. **Died:** Nov. 4, 1955.
Career: 511-316, 1st on all-time win list; 2.63 ERA; 2,800 SO.
Teams: Cleveland (Nat.) 1890-98; St. Louis (Nat.) 1899-1900; Red Sox 1901-08; Indians 1909-11; Braves 1911.
How elected: 76.1 percent of vote.

1938

GROVER CLEVELAND ALEXANDER — **P**
6-1, 185. **B:** R. **T:** R.
Born: Feb. 26, 1887. **Died:** Nov. 4, 1950.
Career: 373-208; 2.56 ERA; 2,198 SO.
Teams: Phillies 1911-17, 1930; Cubs 1918-26; Cardinals 1926-29.
How elected: 80.9 percent of vote.

ALEXANDER CARTWRIGHT — **ORGANIZER**
Organized 1st baseball club in 1845.
Born: April 17, 1820. **Died:** July 12, 1892.
Career: Formed the Knickerbocker Ball Club in 1845 and taught the new game to Americans from coast to coast; served as unofficial ambassador for the game until his death.
How elected: Centennial Commission.

HENRY CHADWICK — **ORGANIZER**
Known as "Father of Baseball."
Born: Oct. 5, 1824. **Died:** April 29, 1908.
Career: A longtime New York baseball writer and contributor to numerous statistical publications dealing with the game; longtime chairman of baseball's committee on rules and author of many significant rules changes during the game's formative years.
How elected: Centennial Commission.

Pirates shortstop Honus Wagner was a member of baseball's first Hall of Fame class.

1939

Cap Anson 1B
6-1, 227. **B:** R. **T:** R.
Born: April 17, 1852. **Died:** April 14, 1922.
Career: .329 avg.; 97 HR; 1,879 RBIs.
Team: Chicago (Nat.) 1876-97.
How elected: Committee old-time players and writers.

Eddie Collins 2B
5-9, 175. **B:** L. **T:** R.
Born: May 2, 1887. **Died:** March 25, 1951.
Career: .333 avg.; 47 HR; 1,300 RBIs; 3,312 hits.
Teams: Athletics 1906-14; White Sox 1915-26; Athletics 1927-30.
How elected: 77.7 percent of vote.

Charles Comiskey 1B, Man., Exec.
Founder/owner of Chicago White Sox.
6-0, 180. **B:** R. **T:** R.
Born: Aug. 15, 1859. **Died:** Oct. 26, 1931.
Playing career: .264 avg.; 29 HR; revolutionized art of playing first base by playing off the bag.
Managing career: 839-542, 12 years.
Teams: St. Louis (A.A.) 1882-89, 1891; Chicago (P.L.) 1890; Cincinnati (Nat.) 1892-94.
How elected: Committee old-time players and writers.

Candy Cummings P
5-9, 120. **B:** R. **T:** R.
Born: Oct. 17, 1848. **Died:** May 17, 1924.
Career: 21-22; 2.78 ERA; credited with throwing the first curveball.
Teams: Hartford (Nat.) 1876; Cincinnati (Nat.) 1877.
How elected: Committee old-time players and writers.

Buck Ewing C, IF, Man.
5-10, 188. **B:** R. **T:** R.
Born: Oct. 27, 1859. **Died:** Oct. 20, 1906.
Playing career: .303 avg.; 71 HR; 883 RBIs.
Managing career: 489-395, 7 years.
Teams (player): Troy (Nat.) 1880-82; New York (Nat.) 1883-89, 1891-92; New York (P.L.) 1890; Cleveland (Nat.) 1893-94; Cincinnati (Nat.) 1895-97.
Teams (manager): New York (P.L.) 1890; Cincinnati (Nat.) 1895-99; New York (Nat.) 1900.
How elected: Committee old-time players and writers.

Lou Gehrig 1B
6-1, 200. **B:** L. **T:** L.
Born: June 19, 1903. **Died:** June 2, 1941.
Career: .340 avg.; 493 HR; 1,995 RBIs.
Team: Yankees 1923-39.
How elected: Special election Baseball Writers.

Willie Keeler OF
5-4, 140. **B:** L. **T:** L.
Born: March 3, 1872. **Died:** Jan. 1, 1923.
Career: .341 avg.; 33 HR; 810 RBIs; 495 SB.
Teams: New York (Nat.) 1892-93, 1910; Brooklyn (Nat.) 1893, 1899-1902; Baltimore (Nat.) 1894-98; Yankees 1903-09.
How elected: 75.5 percent of vote.

Hoss Radbourn P
5-9, 168. **B:** R. **T:** R.
Born: Dec. 9, 1853. **Died:** Feb. 5, 1897.
Career: 309-195; 2.67 ERA; 1,830 SO.
Teams: Providence (Nat.) 1881-85; Boston (Nat.) 1886-90; Cincinnati (Nat.) 1891.
How elected: Committee old-time players and writers.

George Sisler 1B
5-11, 170. **B:** L. **T:** L.
Born: March 24, 1893. **Died:** March 26, 1973.
Career: .340 avg.; 102 HR; 1,175 RBIs.
Teams: Browns 1915-27; Senators 1928; Braves 1928-30.
How elected: 85.8 percent of vote.

Al Spalding P, Man., Owner
Founder A.G. Spalding & Bros. sporting goods.
6-1, 170. **B:** R. **T:** R.
Born: Sept. 2, 1850. **Died:** Sept. 9, 1915.
Career: 48-12; 1.78 ERA.
Team (player): Chicago (Nat.) 1876-77.
Team (manager): Chicago (Nat.) 1876-78.
Team (owner): Chicago (Nat.) 1882-91.
How elected: Committee old-time players and writers.

1942

Rogers Hornsby 2B
5-11, 200. **B:** R. **T:** R.
Born: April 27, 1896. **Died:** Jan. 5, 1963.
Career: .358 avg.; 301 HR; 1,584 RBIs.
Teams: Cardinals 1915-26, 1933; Giants 1927; Braves 1928; Cubs 1929-32; Browns 1933-37.
How elected: 78.1 percent of vote.

1944

Kenesaw Mountain Landis Exec.
First baseball commissioner.
Born: Nov. 20, 1866. **Died:** Nov. 25, 1944.
Career: Former U.S. District judge; became baseball's first commissioner in 1921 and served until his death.
How elected: Committee on Old-Timers.

1945

Roger Bresnahan C
5-9, 190. **B:** R. **T:** R.
Born: June 11, 1879. **Died:** Dec. 4, 1944.
Career: .279 avg.; 26 HR; 530 RBIs; credited with introducing shinguards for catchers.
Teams: Washington (Nat.) 1897; Chicago (Nat.) 1900; Orioles 1901-02; Giants 1902-08; Cardinals 1909-12; Cubs 1913-15.
How elected: Committee on Old-Timers.

Dan Brouthers 1B
6-2, 200. **B:** L. **T:** L.
Born: May 8, 1858. **Died:** Aug. 3, 1932.
Career: .342 avg.; 106 HR; 1,296 RBIs.
Teams: Troy (Nat.) 1879-80; Buffalo (Nat.) 1881-85; Detroit (Nat.) 1886-88; Boston (Nat.) 1889; Boston (P.L.) 1890; Boston (A.A.) 1891; Brooklyn (Nat.) 1892-93; Baltimore (Nat.) 1894-95; Louisville (Nat.) 1895; Philadelphia (Nat.) 1896; Giants 1904.
How elected: Committee on Old-Timers.

Fred Clarke OF, Man.
5-10, 165. **B:** L. **T:** R.
Born: Oct. 3, 1872. **Died:** Aug. 14, 1960.
Playing career: .312 avg.; 67 HR; 1,015 RBIs.
Managing career: 1,602-1,181, 19 years.
Teams (player): Louisville (Nat.) 1894-99; Pirates 1900-15.
Teams (manager): Louisville (Nat.) 1897-99; Pirates 1900-15.
How elected: Committee on Old-Timers.

Jimmy Collins 3B
5-9, 178. **B:** R. **T:** R.
Born: Jan. 16, 1873. **Died:** March 6, 1943.
Career: .294 avg.; 65 HR; 983 RBIs.
Teams: Boston (Nat.) 1895, 1896-1900; Louisville 1895; Red Sox 1901-07; Athletics 1907-08.
How elected: Committee on Old-Timers.

Ed Delahanty 1B, OF
6-1, 170. **B:** R. **T:** R.
Born: Oct. 30, 1867. **Died:** July 2, 1903.
Career: .346 avg.; 101 HR; 1,464 RBIs.
Teams: Philadelphia (Nat.) 1888-89, 1891-1901; Cleveland (P.L) 1890; Senators 1902-03.
How elected: Committee on Old-Timers.

Hugh Duffy OF
5-7, 168. **B:** R. **T:** R.
Born: Nov. 26, 1866. **Died:** Oct. 19, 1954.
Career: .324 avg.; 106 HR; 1,302 RBIs.
Teams: Chicago (Nat.) 1888-89; Chicago (P.L.) 1890; Boston (A.A.) 1891; Boston (Nat.) 1892-1900; Milwaukee (Amer.) 1901; Phillies 1904-06.
How elected: Committee on Old-Timers.

Hugh Jennings IF
5-8, 165. **B:** R. **T:** R.
Born: April 2, 1869. **Died:** Feb. 1, 1928.
Career: .311 avg.; 18 HR; 840 RBIs.

Lou Gehrig was the original "Iron Man," playing in 2,131 consecutive games.

Teams: Louisville (A.A.) 1891; Louisville (Nat.) 1892-93; Baltimore (Nat.) 1893-99; Brooklyn (Nat.) 1899-1900, 1903; Phillies 1901-02; Tigers 1907-1909, 1912, 1918.
How elected: Committee on Old-Timers.

Mike (King) Kelly C, IF
5-10, 180. **B:** R. **T:** R.
Born: Dec. 31, 1857. **Died:** Nov. 8, 1894.
Career: .308 avg.; 69 HR; 950 RBIs.
Teams: Cincinnati (Nat.) 1878-79; Chicago (Nat.) 1880-86; Boston (Nat.) 1887-90, 1891-92; Cincinnati (A.A.) 1891; New York (Nat.) 1893.
How elected: Committee on Old-Timers.

Jim O'Rourke OF, IF
5-8, 185. **B:** R. **T:** R.
Born: Aug. 24, 1852. **Died:** Jan. 8, 1919.
Career: .310 avg.; 50 HR; 1,010 RBIs.
Teams: Boston (Nat.) 1876-78, 1880; Providence (Nat.) 1879; Buffalo (Nat.) 1881-84; New York (Nat.) 1885-89, 1891-92, 1904; New York (P.L.) 1890; Washington (Nat.) 1893.
How elected: Committee on Old-Timers.

Wilbert Robinson C, Man.
5-8, 215. **B:** R. **T:** R.
Born: June 2, 1864. **Died:** Aug. 8, 1934.
Playing career: .273 avg.; 18 HR; 622 RBIs.
Managing career: 1,399-1,398, 19 years.
Teams (player): Philadelphia (A.A.) 1886-90; Baltimore (A.A.) 1890-91; Baltimore (Nat.) 1892-99; St. Louis (Nat.) 1900; Baltimore (Amer.) 1901-02.
Teams (manager): Baltimore (Amer.) 1902; Dodgers 1914-31.
How elected: Committee on Old-Timers.

1946

Jesse Burkett OF
5-8, 155. **B:** L. **T:** L.
Born: Dec. 4, 1868. **Died:** May 27, 1953.
Career: .338 avg.; 75 HR; 952 RBIs.
Teams: New York (Nat.) 1890; Cleveland (Nat.) 1891-98; St. Louis (Nat.) 1899-1901; Browns 1902-04; Red Sox 1905.
How elected: Committee on Old-Timers.

Frank Chance 1B, Man.
6-0, 190. **B:** R. **T:** R.
Born: Sept. 9, 1877. **Died:** Sept. 15, 1924.
Playing career: .296 avg.; 20 HR; 596 RBIs.

Athletics slugger Jimmie Foxx was the second player to reach the 500-home run plateau.

Managing career: 946-648, 11 years.
Teams (player): Cubs 1898-1912; Yankees 1913-14.
Teams (manager): Cubs 1905-12; Yankees 1913-14; Red Sox 1923.
How elected: Committee on Old-Timers.

JACK CHESBRO — P
5-9, 180. **B:** R. **T:** R.
Born: June 5, 1874. **Died:** Nov. 6, 1931.
Career: 198-132; 2.68 ERA; 1,265 SO.
Teams: Pirates 1899-1902; Yankees 1903-09; Red Sox 1909.
How elected: Committee on Old-Timers.

JOHNNY EVERS — 2B
5-9, 130. **B:** R. **T:** R.
Born: July 21, 1881. **Died:** March 28, 1947.
Career: .270 avg.; 12 HR; 538 RBIs.
Teams: Cubs 1902-13; Braves 1914-17, 1929; Phillies 1917; White Sox 1922.
How elected: Committee on Old-Timers.

CLARK GRIFFITH — P, MAN., EXEC.
5-7, 156. **B:** R. **T:** R.
Born: Nov. 20, 1869. **Died:** Oct. 27, 1955.
Playing career: 237-146; 3.31 ERA; 955 SO.
Managing career: 1,491-1,367, 20 years.
Teams (player): St. Louis (A.A.) 1891; Boston (A.A.) 1891; Chicago (Nat.) 1893-1900; White Sox 1901-02; Yankees 1903-07; Reds 1909-10; Senators 1912-14.
Teams (manager): White Sox 1901-02; Yankees 1903-08; Reds 1909-11; Senators 1912-20.
How elected: Committee on Old-Timers.

TOMMY MCCARTHY — OF, IF
5-7, 170. **B:** R. **T:** R.
Born: July 24, 1864 **Died:** Aug. 5, 1922.
Career: .292 avg.; 44 HR, 666 RBIs.
Teams: Boston (U.A.) 1884; Boston (Nat.) 1885; Philadelphia (Nat.) 1886-87; St. Louis (A.A.) 1888-91; Boston (Nat.) 1892-95; Brooklyn (Nat.) 1896.
How elected: Committee on Old-Timers.

JOE MCGINNITY — P
5-11, 206. **B:** R. **T:** R.
Born: March 19, 1871. **Died:** Nov. 14, 1929.
Career: 246-142; 2.66 ERA; 1,068 SO.
Teams: Baltimore (Nat.) 1899; Brooklyn (Nat.) 1900; Orioles 1901-02; Giants 1902-08.
How elected: Committee on Old-Timers.

EDDIE PLANK — P
5-11, 175. **B:** L. **T:** L.
Born: Aug. 31, 1875. **Died:** Feb. 24, 1926.
Career: 326-194; 2.35 ERA; 2,246 SO.
Teams: Athletics 1901-14; St. Louis (Fed.) 1915; Browns 1916-17.
How elected: Committee on Old-Timers.

JOE TINKER — SS
5-9, 175. **B:** R. **T:** R.
Born: July 27, 1880. **Died:** July 27, 1948.
Career: .262 avg.; 31 HR; 782 RBIs.
Teams: Cubs 1902-13, 1916; Chicago (Fed.) 1914-15.
How elected: Committee on Old-Timers.

RUBE WADDELL — P
6-1, 196. **B:** L. **T:** L.
Born: Oct. 13, 1876. **Died:** April 1, 1914.
Career: 193-143; 2.16 ERA; 2,316 SO.
Teams: Louisville (Nat.) 1897, 1899; Pirates 1900-01; Cubs 1901; Athletics 1902-07; Browns 1908-10.
How elected: Committee on Old-Timers.

ED WALSH — P
6-1, 193. **B:** R. **T:** R.
Born: May 14, 1881. **Died:** May 26, 1959.
Career: 195-126; 1.82 ERA; 1,736 SO.
Teams: White Sox 1904-16; Braves 1917.
How elected: Committee on Old-Timers.

1947

MICKEY COCHRANE — C
5-10, 180. **B:** L. **T:** R.
Born: April 6, 1903. **Died:** June 28, 1962.
Career: .320 avg.; 119 HR; 832 RBIs.
Teams: Athletics 1925-33; Tigers 1934-37.
How elected: 79.5 percent of vote.

FRANK FRISCH — 2B, MAN.
5-11, 165. **B:** B. **T:** R.
Born: Sept. 9, 1898. **Died:** March 12, 1973.
Playing career: .316 avg.; 105 HR; 1,244 RBIs.
Managing career: 1,138-1,078, 16 years.
Teams (player): Giants 1919-26; Cardinals 1927-37.
Teams (manager): Cardinals 1933-38; Pirates 1940-46; Cubs 1949-51.
How elected: 84.5 percent of vote.

LEFTY GROVE — P
6-3, 200. **B:** L. **T:** L.
Born: March 6, 1900. **Died:** May 22, 1975.
Career: 300-141; 3.06 ERA; 2,266 SO.
Teams: Athletics 1925-33; Red Sox 1934-41.
How elected: 76.4 percent of vote.

CARL HUBBELL — P
6-0, 170. **B:** R. **T:** L.
Born: June 22, 1903. **Died:** Nov. 21, 1988.
Career: 253-154; 2.98 ERA; 1,677 SO.
Teams: Giants 1928-43.
How elected: 87 percent of vote.

1948

HERB PENNOCK — P
6-0, 160. **B:** B. **T:** L.
Born: Feb. 10, 1894. **Died:** Jan. 30, 1948.
Career: 240-162; 3.60 ERA; 1,227 SO.
Teams: Athletics 1912-15; Red Sox 1915-22; Yankees 1923-33; Red Sox 1934.
How elected: 77.7 percent of vote.

PIE TRAYNOR — 3B
6-0, 170. **B:** R. **T:** R.
Born: Nov. 11, 1899. **Died:** March 16, 1972.
Career: .320 avg.; 58 HR; 1,273 RBIs.
Team: Pirates 1920-37.
How elected: 76.9 percent of vote.

1949

MORDECAI (THREE FINGER) BROWN — P
5-10, 175. **B:** B. **T:** R.
Born: Oct. 19, 1876. **Died:** Feb. 14, 1948.
Career: 239-130; 2.06 ERA; 1,375 SO.
Teams: Cardinals 1903; Cubs 1904-12, 1916; Reds 1913; St. Louis (Fed.) 1914; Brooklyn (Fed.) 1914; Chicago (Fed.) 1915.
How elected: Committee on Old-Timers.

CHARLEY GEHRINGER — 2B
5-11, 180. **B:** L. **T:** R.
Born: May 11, 1903. **Died:** Jan. 21, 1993.
Career: .320 avg.; 184 HR; 1,427 RBIs.
Team: Tigers 1924-42.
How elected: 85 percent of vote.

KID NICHOLS — P
5-10, 175. **B:** R. **T:** R.
Born: Sept. 14, 1869. **Died:** April 11, 1953.
Career: 361-208; 2.95 ERA; 1,868 SO.
Teams: Boston (Nat.) 1890-1901; Cardinals 1904-05; Phillies 1905-06.
How elected: Committee on Old-Timers.

1951

JIMMIE FOXX — C, 3B, 1B
6-0, 195. **B:** R. **T:** R.
Born: Oct. 22, 1907. **Died:** July 21, 1967.
Career: .325 avg.; 534 HR; 1,922 RBIs.
Teams: Athletics 1925-35; Red Sox 1936-42; Cubs 1942, 1944; Phillies 1945.
How elected: 79.2 percent of vote.

MEL OTT — OF
5-9, 170. **B:** L. **T:** R.
Born: March 2, 1909. **Died:** Nov. 21, 1958.
Career: .304 avg.; 511 HR; 1,860 RBIs.
Team: Giants 1926-47.
How elected: 87.2 percent of vote.

1952

HARRY HEILMANN — OF, 1B
6-1, 195. **B:** R. **T:** R.
Born: Aug. 3, 1894. **Died:** July 9, 1951.
Career: .342 avg.; 183 HR; 1,539 RBIs.
Teams: Tigers 1914-29; Reds 1930-32.
How elected: 86.8 percent of vote.

PAUL WANER — OF
5-8, 153. **B:** L. **T:** L.
Born: April 16, 1903. **Died:** Aug. 29, 1965.
Career: .333 avg.; 113 HR; 1,309 RBIs; 3,152 hits.
Teams: Pirates 1926-40; Dodgers 1941, 1943-44; Braves 1941-42; Yankees 1944-45.
How elected: 83.3 percent of vote.

1953

ED BARROW — MAN., EXEC.
Born: May 10, 1868. **Died:** Dec. 15, 1953.
Managing career: 310-320, 5 years.
Executive career: Architect of Yankees dynasty that produced 14 A.L. pennants and 10 World Series championships as business manager and president from 1921-45; managed Red Sox to 1918 World Series title and started conversion of Babe Ruth from a pitcher to an outfielder.
How elected: Committee on Veterans.

CHIEF BENDER — P
6-2, 185. **B:** R. **T:** R.
Born: May 5, 1884. **Died:** May 22, 1954.
Career: 212-127; 2.46 ERA; 1,711 SO.
Teams: Athletics 1903-14; Baltimore (Fed.) 1915; Phillies 1916-17; White Sox 1925.
How elected: Committee on Veterans.

TOMMY CONNOLLY — UMPIRE
Born: Dec. 31, 1870. **Died:** April 28, 1961.
Career: Umpired from 1901, the A.L.'s first season, until 1931; served as A.L. umpires' chief of staff until retirement in 1954; an influential member of baseball's rules committee for many years.
How elected: Committee on Veterans.

Dizzy Dean — P
6-2, 200. **B:** R. **T:** R.
Born: Jan. 16, 1911. **Died:** July 17, 1974.
Career: 150-83; 3.03 ERA; 1,155 SO.
Teams: Cardinals 1930, 1932-37; Cubs 1938-41; Browns 1947.
How elected: 79.2 percent of vote.

Bill Klem — Umpire
Born: Feb. 22, 1874. **Died:** Sept. 1, 1951.
Career: Joined N.L. as an umpire in 1905 and served with distinction until 1941; called 18 World Series, more than any other umpire; served as N.L. umpires' chief of staff from 1941 until death; responsible for many umpiring innovations; generally considered the greatest arbiter of all time.
How elected: Committee on Veterans.

Al Simmons — OF
5-11, 190. **B:** R. **T:** R.
Born: May 22, 1902. **Died:** May 26, 1956.
Career: .334 avg.; 307 HR; 1,827 RBIs.
Teams: Athletics 1924-32, 1940-41, 1944; White Sox 1933-35; Tigers 1936; Senators 1937-38; Braves 1939; Reds 1939; Red Sox 1943.
How elected: 75.4 percent of vote.

Bobby Wallace — SS
5-8, 170. **B:** R. **T:** R.
Born: Nov. 4, 1874. **Died:** Nov. 3, 1960.
Career: .268 avg.; 34 HR; 1,121 RBIs.
Teams: Cleveland (Nat.) 1894-98; St. Louis (Nat.) 1899-1901, 1917-18; Browns 1902-16;
How elected: Committee on Veterans.

Harry Wright — Manager
Born: Jan. 10, 1835. **Died:** Oct. 3, 1895.
Career: 933-660, 18 years.
Teams: Boston (Nat.) 1876-81; Providence (Nat.) 1882-83; Philadelphia (Nat.) 1884-93.
How elected: Committee on Veterans.

1954

Bill Dickey — C
6-1, 185. **B:** L. **T:** R.
Born: June 6, 1907. **Died:** Nov. 12, 1993.
Career: .313 avg.; 202 HR; 1,210 RBIs.
Teams: Yankees 1928-43, 1946.
How elected: 80.2 percent of vote.

Rabbit Maranville — SS
5-5, 155. **B:** R. **T:** R.
Born: Nov. 11, 1891. **Died:** Jan. 5, 1954.
Career: .258 avg.; 28 HR; 884 RBIs.
Teams: Braves 1912-20, 1929-35; Pirates 1921-24; Cubs 1925; Dodgers 1926; Cardinals 1927-28.
How elected: 82.9 percent of vote.

Bill Terry — 1B, Man.
6-1, 200. **B:** L. **T:** L.
Born: Oct. 30, 1898. **Died:** Jan. 9, 1989.
Playing career: .341 avg.; 154 HR; 1,078 RBIs.
Managing career: 823-661, 10 years.
Team (player): Giants 1923-36.
Team (manager): Giants 1932-41.
How elected: 77.4 percent of vote.

1955

Frank (Home Run) Baker — 3B
5-11, 173. **B:** L. **T:** R.
Born: March 13, 1886. **Died:** June 28, 1963.
Career: .307 avg.; 96 HR; 987 RBIs.
Teams: Athletics 1908-14; Yankees 1916-19, 1921-22.
How elected: Committee on Veterans.

Joe DiMaggio — OF
6-2, 193. **B:** R. **T:** R.
Born: Nov. 25, 1914. **Died:** March 8, 1999.
Career: .325 avg.; 361 HR; 1,537 RBIs.
Team: Yankees 1936-42, 1946-51.
How elected: 88.8 percent of vote.

Gabby Hartnett — C
6-1, 200. **B:** R. **T:** R.
Born: Dec. 20, 1900. **Died:** Dec. 20, 1972.
Career: .297 avg.; 236 HR; 1,179 RBIs.
Teams: Cubs 1922-40; Giants 1941.
How elected: 77.7 percent of vote.

Ted Lyons — P
5-11, 200. **B:** B. **T:** R.
Born: Dec. 28, 1900. **Died:** July 25, 1986.
Career: 260-230; 3.67 ERA; 1,073 SO.
Team: White Sox 1923-42, 1946.
How elected: 86.5 percent of vote.

Ray Schalk — C
5-9, 165. **B:** R. **T:** R.
Born: Aug. 12, 1892. **Died:** May 19, 1970.
Career: .253 avg.; 11 HR; 594 RBIs.
Teams: White Sox 1912-28; Giants 1929.
How elected: Committee on Veterans.

Dazzy Vance — P
6-2, 200. **B:** R. **T:** R.
Born: March 4, 1891. **Died:** Feb. 16, 1961.
Career: 197-140; 3.24 ERA; 2,045 SO.
Teams: Pirates 1915; Yankees 1915, 1918; Dodgers 1922-32, 1935; Cardinals 1933, 1934; Reds 1934.
How elected: 81.7 percent of vote.

1956

Joe Cronin — IF, Man., Exec.
6-0, 180. **B:** R. **T:** R.
Born: Oct. 12, 1906. **Died:** Sept. 7, 1984.
Playing career: .301 avg.; 170 HR; 1,424 RBIs.
Managing career: 1,236-1,055, 15 years.
Teams (player): Pirates 1926-27; Senators 1928-34; Red Sox 1935-45.
Teams (manager): Senators 1933-34; Red Sox 1935-47.
Executive career: President of A.L. 1959-73.
How elected: 78.8 percent of vote.

Hank Greenberg — 1B, OF
6-3, 210. **B:** R. **T:** R.
Born: Jan. 1, 1911. **Died:** Sept. 4, 1986.
Career: .313 avg.; 331 HR; 1,276 RBIs.
Teams: Tigers 1930, 1933-41, 1945-46; Pirates 1947.
How elected: 85.0 percent of vote.

1957

Sam Crawford — OF
6-0, 190. **B:** L. **T:** L.
Born: April 18, 1880. **Died:** June 15, 1968.
Career: .309 avg.; 98 HR; 1,525 RBIs.
Teams: Reds 1899-1902; Tigers 1903-17.
How elected: Committee on Veterans.

Joe McCarthy — Manager
Born: April 21, 1887. **Died:** Jan. 13, 1978.
Career: 2,125-1,333, 24 years; 7 World Series championships.
Teams: Cubs 1926-30; Yankees 1931-46; Red Sox 1948-50.
How elected: Committee on Veterans.

1959

Zack Wheat — OF
5-10, 170. **B:** L. **T:** R.
Born: May 23, 1888. **Died:** March 11, 1972.
Career: .317 avg.; 132 HR; 1,248 RBIs.
Teams: Dodgers 1909-26; Athletics 1927.
How elected: Committee on Veterans.

1961

Max Carey — OF
5-11, 170. **B:** B. **T:** R.
Born: Jan. 11, 1890. **Died:** May 30, 1976.
Career: .285 avg.; 69 HR; 800 RBIs.
Teams: Pirates 1910-26; Dodgers 1926-29.
How elected: Committee on Veterans.

Frank "Home Run" Baker earned his nickname by hitting two dramatic homers in the 1911 World Series.

Billy Hamilton — OF
5-6, 165. **B:** L. **T:** R.
Born: Feb. 16, 1866. **Died:** Dec. 16, 1940.
Career: .344 avg.; 40 HR; 736 RBIs; 912 SB.
Teams: Kansas City (A.A.) 1888-89; Philadelphia (Nat.) 1890-95; Boston (Nat.) 1896-1901.
How elected: Committee on Veterans.

1962

Bob Feller — P
6-0, 185. **B:** R. **T:** R.
Born: Nov. 3, 1918.
Career: 266-162; 3.25 ERA; 2,581 SO.
Team: Indians 1936-41, 1945-56.
How elected: 93.8 percent of vote.

Bill McKechnie — Manager
Born: Aug. 7, 1887. **Died:** Oct. 29, 1965.
Career: 1,896-1,723, 25 years; 2 World Series championships.
Teams: Newark (Fed.) 1915; Pirates 1922-26; Cardinals 1928-29; Braves 1930-37; Reds 1938-46.
How elected: Committee on Veterans.

Jackie Robinson — IF
5-11, 195. **B:** R. **T:** R.
Born: Jan. 31, 1919. **Died:** Oct. 24, 1972.
Career: .311 avg.; 137 HR; 734 RBIs.
Team: Dodgers 1947-56.
How elected: 77.5 percent of vote.

Edd Roush — OF
5-11, 170. **B:** L. **T:** L.
Born: May 8, 1893. **Died:** March 21, 1988.
Career: .323 avg.; 67 HR; 981 RBIs.
Teams: White Sox 1913; Indianapolis (Fed.) 1914; Newark (Fed.) 1915; Giants 1916, 1927-29; Reds 1916-26, 1931.
How elected: Committee on Veterans.

1963

John Clarkson — P
5-10, 165. **B:** R. **T:** R.
Born: July 1, 1861. **Died:** Feb. 4, 1909.
Career: 328-178; 2.81 ERA; 1,978 SO.
Teams: Worcester (Nat.) 1882; Chicago (Nat.) 1884-87; Boston (Nat.) 1888-92; Cleveland (Nat.) 1892-94.
How elected: Committee on Veterans.

Red Sox left fielder Ted Williams compiled a lofty .344 career batting average.

Elmer Flick — OF
5-9, 168. **B:** L. **T:** R.
Born: Jan. 11, 1876. **Died:** Jan. 9, 1971.
Career: .313 avg.; 48 HR; 756 RBIs.
Teams: Philadelphia (Nat.) 1898-1902; Indians 1902-10.
How elected: Committee on Veterans.

Sam Rice — OF
5-9, 150. **B:** L. **T:** L.
Born: Feb. 20, 1890. **Died:** Oct. 13, 1974.
Career: .322 avg.; 34 HR; 1,078 RBIs.
Teams: Senators 1915-33; Indians 1934.
How elected: Committee on Veterans.

Eppa Rixey — P
6-5, 210. **B:** R: **T:** L.
Born: May 3, 1891. **Died:** Feb. 28, 1963.
Career: 266-251; 3.15 ERA; 1,350 SO.
Teams: Phillies 1912-1917, 1919-20; Reds 1921-33.
How elected: Committee on Veterans.

1964

Luke Appling — SS
5-10, 183. **B:** R. **T:** R.
Born: April 2, 1907. **Died:** Jan. 3, 1991.
Career: .310 avg.; 45 HR; 1,116 RBIs.
Team: White Sox 1930-43, 1945-50.
How elected: 84 percent of vote.

Red Faber — P
6-2, 180. **B:** B. **T:** R.
Born: Sept. 6, 1888. **Died:** Sept. 25, 1976.
Career: 254-213; 3.15 ERA; 1,471 SO.
Team: White Sox 1914-33.
How elected: Committee on Veterans.

Burleigh Grimes — P
5-10, 175. **B:** R. **T:** R.
Born: Aug. 18, 1893. **Died:** Dec. 6, 1985.
Career: 270-212; 3.53 ERA; 1,512 SO.
Teams: Pirates 1916-17, 1928-29, 1934; Dodgers 1918-26; Giants 1927; Braves 1930; Cardinals 1930-31, 1933-34; Cubs 1932-33; Yankees 1934.
How elected: Committee on Veterans.

Miller Huggins — Manager
Born: March 27, 1880. **Died:** Sept. 25, 1929.
Career: 1,413-1,134, 17 years.
Teams: Cardinals 1913-17; Yankees 1918-29.
How elected: Committee on Veterans.

Tim Keefe — P
5-10, 185. **B:** R. **T:** R.
Born: Jan. 1, 1857. **Died:** April 23, 1933.
Career: 342-225; 2.62 ERA; 2,527 SO.
Teams: Troy (Nat.) 1880-82; Metropolitan (A.A.) 1883-84; New York (Nat.) 1885-91; Philadelphia (Nat.) 1891-93.
How elected: Committee on Veterans.

Heinie Manush — OF
6-1, 200. **B:** L. **T:** L.
Born: July 20, 1901. **Died:** May 12, 1971.
Career: .330 avg.; 110 HR; 1,183 RBIs.
Teams: Tigers 1923-27; Browns 1928-30; Senators 1930-35; Red Sox 1936; Dodgers 1937-38; Pirates 1938-39.
How elected: Committee on Veterans.

John Montgomery Ward — IF, P
5-9, 165. **B:** L. **T:** R.
Born: March 3, 1860. **Died:** March 4, 1925.
Playing career: .275 avg.; 26 HR; 867 RBIs.
Pitching career: 164-102; 2.10 ERA; 920 SO.
Teams: Providence (Nat.) 1878-82; New York (Nat.) 1883-89, 1893-94; Brooklyn 1890-92.
How elected: Committee on Veterans.

1965

Pud Galvin — P
5-8, 190. **B:** R. **T:** R.
Born: Dec. 25, 1856. **Died:** March 7, 1902.
Career: 360-308; 2.87 ERA; 1,799 SO.
Teams: Buffalo (Nat.) 1879-85; Allegheny (A.A.) 1885-86; Pittsburgh (Nat.) 1887-89, 1891-92; Pittsburgh (P.L.) 1890; St. Louis (Nat.) 1892.
How elected: Committee on Veterans.

1966

Casey Stengel — OF, Man.
5-11, 175. **B:** L. **T:** L.
Born: July 30, 1890. **Died:** Sept. 29, 1975.
Playing career: .284 avg.; 60 HR; 535 RBIs.
Managing career: 1,905-1,842, 25 years; 7 World Series championships.
Teams (player): Dodgers 1912-17; Pirates 1918-19; Phillies 1920-21; Giants 1921-23; Braves 1924-25.
Teams (manager): Dodgers 1934-36; Braves 1938-43; Yankees 1949-60; Mets 1962-65.
How elected: Committee on Veterans.

Ted Williams — OF
6-3, 205. **B:** L. **T:** R.
Born: Aug. 30, 1918. **Died:** July 5, 2002.
Career: .344 avg.; 521 HR; 1,839 RBIs.
Team: Red Sox 1939-42, 1946-60.
How elected: 93.4 percent of vote.

1967

Branch Rickey — Executive
Born: Dec. 20, 1881. **Died:** Dec. 9, 1965.
Career: Began baseball association as a minor league catcher in 1903 and played briefly for the Cardinals in three seasons; advanced through the chains of the Browns, Cardinals, Dodgers and Pirates in various front-office positions; introduced concept of a farm system as a member of Cardinals organization; broke baseball's color barrier when he brought Jackie Robinson to the Dodgers in 1947.
How elected: Committee on Veterans.

Red Ruffing — P
6-1, 205. **B:** R. **T:** R.
Born: May 5, 1905. **Died:** Feb. 17, 1986.
Career: 273-225; 3.80 ERA; 1,987 SO.
Teams: Red Sox 1924-30; Yankees 1930-42, 1945-46; White Sox 1947.
How elected: 86.9 percent of vote.

Lloyd Waner — OF
5-9, 150. **B:** L. **T:** R.
Born: March 16, 1906. **Died:** July 22, 1982.
Career: .316 avg.; 27 HR; 598 RBIs.
Teams: Pirates 1927-41, 1944-45; Braves 1941; Reds 1941; Phillies 1942; Dodgers 1944.
How elected: Committee on Veterans.

1968

Kiki Cuyler — OF
5-10, 180. **B:** R. **T:** R.
Born: Aug. 30, 1899. **Died:** Feb. 11, 1950.
Career: .321 avg.; 128 HR; 1,065 RBIs.
Teams: Pirates 1921-27; Cubs 1928-35; Reds 1935-37; Dodgers 1938.
How elected: Committee on Veterans.

Goose Goslin — OF
5-11, 185. **B:** L. **T:** R.
Born: Oct. 16, 1900. **Died:** May 15, 1971.
Career: .316 avg.; 248 HR; 1,609 RBIs.
Teams: Senators 1921-30, 1933, 1938; Browns 1930-32; Tigers 1934-37.
How elected: Committee on Veterans.

Joe Medwick — OF
5-10, 187. **B:** R. **T:** R.
Born: Nov. 24, 1911. **Died:** March 21, 1975.
Career: .324 avg.; 205 HR; 1,383 RBIs.
Teams: Cardinals 1932-40, 1947-48; Dodgers 1940-43, 1946; Giants 1943-45; Braves 1945.
How elected: 84.8 percent of vote.

1969

Roy Campanella — C
5-9, 200. **B:** R. **T:** R.
Born: Nov. 19, 1921. **Died:** June 26, 1993.
Career: .276 avg.; 242 HR; 856 RBIs.
Team: Dodgers 1948-57.
How elected: 79.4 percent of vote.

Stan Coveleski — P
5-11, 166. **B:** R. **T:** R.
Born: July 13, 1890. **Died:** March 20, 1984.
Career: 215-142; 2.89 ERA; 981 SO.
Teams: Athletics 1912; Indians 1916-24; Senators 1925-27; Yankees 1928.
How elected: Committee on Veterans.

Waite Hoyt — P
6-0, 180. **B:** R. **T:** R.
Born: Sept. 9, 1899. **Died:** Aug. 25, 1984.
Career: 237-182; 3.59 ERA; 1,206 SO.
Teams: Giants 1918, 1932; Red Sox 1919-20; Yankees 1921-30; Tigers 1930-31; Athletics 1931; Dodgers 1932, 1937-38; Pirates 1933-37.
How elected: Committee on Veterans.

Stan Musial — OF, 1B
6-0, 175. **B:** L. **T:** L.
Born: Nov. 21, 1920.
Career: .331 avg.; 475 HR; 1,951 RBIs; 3,630 hits.
Team: Cardinals 1941-44, 1946-63.
How elected: 93.2 percent of vote.

1970

Lou Boudreau — SS, Man.
5-11, 185. **B:** R. **T:** R.
Born: July 17, 1917. **Died:** Aug. 10, 2001.
Playing career: .295 avg.; 68 HR; 789 RBIs.
Managing career: 1,162-1,224, 16 years.
Teams (player): Indians 1938-50; Red Sox 1951-52.
Teams (manager): Indians 1942-50; Red Sox 1952-54; Athletics 1955-57; Cubs 1960.
How elected: 77.3 percent of vote.

Earle Combs — OF
6-0, 185. **B:** L. **T:** R.
Born: May 14, 1899. **Died:** July 21, 1976.
Career: .325 avg.; 58 HR; 632 RBIs.
Team: Yankees 1924-35.
How elected: Committee on Veterans.

Ford Frick — Executive
Baseball's third commissioner.
Born: Dec. 19, 1894. **Died:** April 8, 1978.

Career: Newspaper reporter and sportswriter; N.L. president from 1934-51; elected as baseball's third commissioner following resignation of Happy Chandler in 1951; served until retirement Dec. 14, 1965.
How elected: Committee on Veterans.

JESSE HAINES — P
6-0, 190. **B:** R. **T:** R.
Born: July 22, 1893. **Died:** Aug. 5, 1978.
Career: 210-158; 3.64 ERA; 981 SO.
Teams: Reds 1918; Cardinals 1920-37.
How elected: Committee on Veterans.

1971

DAVE BANCROFT — SS
5-9, 160. **B:** B. **T:** R.
Born: April 20, 1892. **Died:** Oct. 9, 1972.
Career: .279 avg.; 32 HR; 591 RBIs.
Teams: Phillies 1915-20; Giants 1920-23, 1930; Braves 1924-27; Dodgers 1928-29.
How elected: Committee on Veterans.

JAKE BECKLEY — 1B
5-10, 200. **B:** L. **T:** L.
Born: Aug. 4, 1867. **Died:** June 25, 1918.
Career: .308 avg.; 86 HR; 1,575 RBIs.
Teams: Pittsburgh (Nat.) 1888-89, 1891-96; Pittsburgh (P.L.) 1890; New York (Nat.) 1896-97; Cincinnati (Nat.) 1897-1903; Cardinals 1904-07.
How elected: Committee on Veterans.

CHICK HAFEY — OF
6-0, 185. **B:** R. **T:** R.
Born: Feb. 12, 1903. **Died:** July 2, 1973.
Career: .317 avg.; 164 HR; 833 RBIs.
Teams: Cardinals 1924-31; Reds 1932-35, 1937.
How elected: Committee on Veterans.

HARRY HOOPER — OF
5-10, 168. **B:** L. **T:** R.
Born: Aug. 24, 1887. **Died:** Dec. 18, 1974.
Career: .281 avg.; 75 HR; 817 RBIs.
Teams: Red Sox 1909-20; White Sox 1921-25.
How elected: Committee on Veterans.

JOE KELLEY — OF
5-11, 190. **B:** R. **T:** R.
Born: Dec. 9, 1871. **Died:** Aug. 14, 1943.
Career: .317 avg.; 65 HR; 1,194 RBIs.
Teams: Boston (Nat.) 1891; Pittsburgh (Nat.) 1891-92; Baltimore (Nat.) 1892-98; Brooklyn (Nat.) 1899-1901; Orioles 1902; Reds 1902-06; Braves 1908.
How elected: Committee on Veterans.

RUBE MARQUARD — P
6-3, 180. **B:** B. **T:** L.
Born: Oct. 9, 1889. **Died:** June 1, 1980.
Career: 201-177; 3.08 ERA; 1,593 SO.
Teams: Giants 1908-15; Dodgers 1915-20; Reds 1921; Braves 1922-25.
How elected: Committee on Veterans.

SATCHEL PAIGE — P
6-3, 180. **B:** R. **T:** R.
Born: July 7, 1906. **Died:** June 8, 1982.
Career: 28-31; 3.29 ERA; 290 SO.
Teams: Indians 1948-49; Browns 1951-53; Athletics 1965.
How elected: Special Committee on Negro Leagues.

GEORGE WEISS — EXECUTIVE
Born: June 23, 1895. **Died:** Aug. 13, 1972.
Career: Joined Yankees as farm director in 1932 after impressive career as minor league executive; built Yankees farm system that stocked pennant-winning machines of the 1930s, '40s and '50s; became general manager in 1948 and led Yankees to 10 pennants and seven World Series championships in 13 seasons; the man who hired Casey Stengel as manager; president of the expansion Mets from 1961-66.
How elected: Committee on Veterans.

1972

YOGI BERRA — C
5-8, 194. **B:** L. **T:** R.
Born: May 12, 1925.
Career: .285 avg.; 358 HR; 1,430 RBIs.
Teams: Yankees 1946-63; Mets 1965.
How elected: 85.6 percent of vote.

JOSH GIBSON — C
6-1, 215. **B:** R. **T:** R.
Born: Dec. 21, 1911. **Died:** Jan. 20, 1947.
Career: Negro League star; statistics not available.
How elected: Special Committee on Negro Leagues.

LEFTY GOMEZ — P
6-2, 173. **B:** L. **T:** L.
Born: Nov. 26, 1910. **Died:** Feb. 17, 1989.
Career: 189-102; 3.34 ERA; 1,468 SO.
Teams: Yankees 1930-42; Senators 1943.
How elected: Committee on Veterans.

WILL HARRIDGE — EXECUTIVE
Born: Oct. 16, 1883. **Died:** April 9, 1971.
Career: Private secretary to A.L. President Ban Johnson; A.L. secretary after Johnson's retirement; became A.L. president when Ernest Barnard died suddenly in 1931; served with distinction until retirement in 1958.
How elected: Committee on Veterans.

SANDY KOUFAX — P
6-2, 210. **B:** R. **T:** L.
Born: Dec. 30, 1935.
Career: 165-87; 2.76 ERA; 2,396 SO.
Team: Dodgers 1955-66.
How elected: 86.9 percent of vote.

WALTER (BUCK) LEONARD — 1B
5-10, 185 **B:** L. **T:** L.
Born: Sept. 8, 1907. **Died:** Nov. 27, 1997.
Career: Negro League star; statistics not available.
How elected: Special Committee on Negro Leagues.

EARLY WYNN — P
6-0, 200. **B:** B. **T:** R.
Born: Jan. 6, 1920. **Died:** April 4, 1999.
Career: 300-244; 3.54 ERA; 2,334 SO.
Teams: Senators 1939, 1941-44, 1946-48; Indians 1949-57, 1963; White Sox 1958-62.
How elected: 76.0 percent of vote.

ROSS YOUNGS — OF
5-8, 162. **B:** B. **T:** R.
Born: April 10, 1897. **Died:** Oct. 22, 1927.
Career: .322 avg.; 42 HR; 592 RBIs.
Team: Giants 1917-26.
How elected: Committee on Veterans.

1973

ROBERTO CLEMENTE — OF
5-11, 175. **B:** R. **T:** R.
Born: Aug. 18, 1934. **Died:** Dec. 31, 1972.
Career: .317 avg.; 240 HR; 1,305 RBIs; 3,000 hits.
Team: Pirates 1955-72.
How elected: 92.7 percent of vote.

BILLY EVANS — UMPIRE
Born: Feb. 10, 1884. **Died:** Jan. 23, 1956.
Career: A.L. umpire from 1906-27; considered a master of the rules book and an expert at rules applications on tricky plays; front-office executive for the Indians, Red Sox and Tigers; president of Southern League from 1942-46.
How elected: Committee on Veterans.

MONTE IRVIN — OF
6-1, 195. **B:** R. **T:** R.
Born: Feb. 25, 1919.
Career: .293 avg.; 99 HR; 443 RBIs; Negro League statistics not available.
Teams: Giants 1949-55; Cubs 1956.
How elected: Special Committee on Negro Leagues.

Satchel Paige pitched in his last game at the age of 59.

GEORGE KELLY — 1B
6-4, 190. **B:** R. **T:** R.
Born: Sept. 10, 1895. **Died:** Oct. 13, 1984.
Career: .297 avg.; 148 HR; 1,020 RBIs.
Teams: Giants 1915-17, 1919-26; Pirates 1917; Reds 1927-30; Cubs 1930; Dodgers 1932.
How elected: Committee on Veterans.

WARREN SPAHN — P
6-0, 175. **B:** L. **T:** L.
Born: April 23, 1921.
Career: 363-245; 3.09 ERA; 2,583 SO.
Teams: Braves 1942, 1946-64; Mets 1965; Giants 1965.
How elected: 83.2 percent of vote.

MICKEY WELCH — P
5-8, 160. **B:** R. **T:** R.
Born: July 4, 1859. **Died:** July 30, 1941.
Career: 307-210; 2.71 ERA; 1,850 SO.
Teams: Troy (Nat.) 1880-82; New York (Nat.) 1883-92.
How elected: Committee on Veterans.

1974

COOL PAPA BELL — OF
6-0, 143. **B:** B. **T:** L.
Born: May 17, 1903. **Died:** March 7, 1991.
Career: Negro League star; statistics not available.
How elected: Special Committee on Negro Leagues.

JIM BOTTOMLEY — 1B
6-0, 180. **B:** L. **T:** L.
Born: April 23, 1900. **Died:** Dec. 11, 1959.
Career: .310 avg.; 219 HR; 1,422 RBIs.
Teams: Cardinals 1922-32; Reds 1933-35; Browns 1936-37.
How elected: Committee on Veterans.

JOCKO CONLAN — UMPIRE
Born: Dec. 6, 1899. **Died:** April 1, 1989.
Career: N.L. umpire from 1941-64; worked 5 World Series and 6 All-Star Games; a master of the rules book known for fair and impartial decisions.
How elected: Committee on Veterans.

WHITEY FORD — P
5-10, 181. **B:** L. **T:** L.
Born: Oct. 21, 1928.
Career: 236-106; 2.75 ERA; 1,956 SO.
Team: Yankees 1950, 1953-67.
How elected: 77.8 percent of vote.

Hank Aaron's Hall of Fame credentials include record totals of 755 home runs and 2,297 RBIs.

MICKEY MANTLE **OF**
6-0, 198. **B:** B. **T:** R.
Born: Oct. 20, 1931. **Died:** Aug. 13, 1995.
Career: .298 avg.; 536 HR; 1,509 RBIs.
Team: Yankees 1951-68.
How elected: 88.2 percent of vote.

SAM THOMPSON **OF**
6-2, 207. **B:** L. **T:** L.
Born: March 5, 1860. **Died:** Nov. 7, 1922.
Career: .331 avg.; 127 HR; 1,299 RBIs.
Teams: Detroit (Nat.) 1885-88; Philadelphia (Nat.) 1889-98; Tigers 1906.
How elected: Committee on Veterans.

1975

EARL AVERILL **OF**
5-9, 172. **B:** L. **T:** R.
Born: May 21, 1902. **Died:** Aug. 16, 1983.
Career: .318 avg.; 238 HR; 1,164 RBIs.
Teams: Indians 1929-39; Tigers 1939-40; Braves 1941.
How elected: Committee on Veterans.

BUCKY HARRIS **2B, MAN.**
5-9, 156. **B:** R. **T:** R.
Born: Nov. 8, 1896. **Died:** Nov. 8, 1977.
Playing career: .274 avg.; 9 HR; 506 RBIs.
Managing career: 2,157-2,218, 29 years; 2 World Series championships.
Teams (player): Senators 1919-28; Tigers 1929, 1931.
Teams (manager): Senators 1924-28, 1935-42, 1950-54; Tigers 1929-33, 1955-56; Red Sox 1934; Phillies 1943; Yankees 1947-48.
How elected: Committee on Veterans.

BILLY HERMAN **2B**
5-11, 180. **B:** R. **T:** R.
Born: July 7, 1909. **Died:** Sept. 5, 1992.
Career: .304 avg.; 47 HR; 839 RBIs.
Teams: Cubs 1931-41; Dodgers 1941-43, 1946; Braves 1946; Pirates 1947.
How elected: Committee on Veterans.

JUDY JOHNSON **3B**
5-11, 150. **B:** R. **T:** R.
Born: Oct. 26, 1899. **Died:** June 14, 1989.
Career: Negro League star; statistics not available.
How elected: Special Committee on Negro Leagues.

RALPH KINER **OF**
6-2, 195. **B:** R. **T:** R.
Born: Oct. 27, 1922.
Career: .279 avg.; 369 HR; 1,015 RBIs.
Teams: Pirates 1946-53; Cubs 1953-54; Indians 1955.
How elected: 75.4 percent of vote.

1976

OSCAR CHARLESTON **OF**
5-11, 190. **B:** L. **T:** L.
Born: Oct. 14, 1896. **Died:** Oct. 5, 1954.
Career: Negro League star; statistics not available.
How elected: Special Committee on Negro Leagues.

ROGER CONNOR **1B**
6-3, 220. **B:** L. **T:** L.
Born: July 1, 1857. **Died:** Jan. 4, 1931.
Career: .317 avg.; 138 HR; 1,322 RBIs.
Teams: Troy (Nat.) 1880-82; New York (Nat.) 1883-89, 1891, 1893-94; New York (P.L.) 1890; Philadelphia (Nat.) 1892; St. Louis (Nat.) 1894-97.
How elected: Committee on Veterans.

CAL HUBBARD **UMPIRE**
Born: Oct. 31, 1900. **Died:** Oct. 17, 1977.
Career: A.L. umpire from 1936-50; assistant to A.L. supervisor of umpires 1952-53; supervisor of umpires 1954-69; a former pro football player and a member of the National Football League Hall of Fame.
How elected: Committee on Veterans.

BOB LEMON **P**
6-0, 185. **B:** L. **T:** R.
Born: Sept. 22, 1920. **Died:** Jan. 11, 2000.
Career: 207-128; 3.23 ERA; 1,277 SO.
Team: Indians 1946-58.
How elected: 78.6 percent of vote.

FRED LINDSTROM **3B**
5-11, 170. **B:** R. **T:** R.
Born: Nov. 21, 1905. **Died:** Oct. 4, 1981.
Career: .311 avg.; 103 HR; 779 RBIs.
Teams: Giants 1924-32; Pirates 1933-34; Cubs 1935; Dodgers 1936.
How elected: Committee on Veterans.

ROBIN ROBERTS **P**
6-0, 190. **B:** B. **T:** R.
Born: Sept. 30, 1926.
Career: 286-245; 3.41 ERA; 2,357 SO.
Teams: Phillies 1948-61; Orioles 1962-65; Astros 1965-66; Cubs 1966.
How elected: 86.9 percent of vote.

1977

ERNIE BANKS **SS**
6-1, 180. **B:** R. **T:** R.
Born: Jan. 31, 1931.
Career: .274 avg.; 512 HR; 1,636 RBIs.
Team: Cubs 1953-71.
How elected: 83.8 percent of vote.

MARTIN DIHIGO **P, IF, OF**
6-3, 225. **B:** R. **T:** R.
Born: May 24, 1905. **Died:** May 20, 1971.
Career: Negro League star; statistics not available.
How elected: Special Committee on Negro Leagues.

JOHN HENRY LLOYD **SS**
5-11, 180. **B:** L. **T:** R.
Born: April 25, 1884. **Died:** March 19, 1965.
Career: Negro League star; statistics not available.
How elected: Special Committee on Negro Leagues.

AL LOPEZ **C, MAN.**
5-11, 165. **B:** R. **T:** R.
Born: Aug. 20, 1908.
Playing career: .261 avg.; 51 HR; 652 RBIs.
Managing career: 1,410-1,004, 17 years.
Teams (player): Dodgers 1928, 1930-35; Braves 1936-40; Pirates 1940-46; Indians 1947.
Teams (manager): Indians 1951-56; White Sox 1957-65, 1968-69.
How elected: Committee on Veterans.

AMOS RUSIE **P**
6-1, 200. **B:** R. **T:** R.
Born: May 30, 1871. **Died:** Dec. 6, 1942.
Career: 245-174; 3.07 ERA; 1,934 SO.
Teams: Indianapolis (Nat.) 1889; New York (Nat.) 1890-95, 1897-98; Reds 1901.
How elected: Committee on Veterans.

JOE SEWELL **SS, 3B**
5-7, 155. **B:** L. **T:** R.
Born: Oct. 9, 1898. **Died:** March 6, 1990.
Career: .312 avg.; 49 HR; 1,055 RBIs.
Teams: Indians 1920-30; Yankees 1931-33.
How elected: Committee on Veterans.

1978

ADDIE JOSS **P**
6-3, 185. **B:** R. **T:** R.
Born: April 12, 1880. **Died:** April 14, 1911.
Career: 160-97; 1.89 ERA; 920 SO.
Team: Indians 1902-10.
How elected: Committee on Veterans.

LARRY MACPHAIL **EXECUTIVE**
Born: Feb. 3, 1890. **Died:** Oct. 1, 1975.
Career: A franchise builder and innovator; built championship teams for the Reds, Dodgers and Yankees; introduced night baseball in 1935 at Cincinnati; first to use radio broadcasts to increase revenues for his teams.
How elected: Committee on Veterans.

EDDIE MATHEWS **3B**
6-1, 200. **B:** L. **T:** R.
Born: Oct. 13, 1931. **Died:** Feb. 18, 2001.
Career: .271 avg.; 512 HR; 1,453 RBIs.
Teams: Braves 1952-66; Astros 1967; Tigers 1967-68.
How elected: 79.4 percent of vote.

1979

WARREN GILES **EXECUTIVE**
Born: May 28, 1896. **Died:** Feb. 7, 1979.
Career: Reds general manager from 1937-47; Reds president from 1947-52; N.L. president from 1952-69.
How elected: Committee on Veterans.

WILLIE MAYS **OF**
5-11, 180. **B:** R. **T:** R.
Born: May 6, 1931.
Career: .302 avg.; 660 HR; 1,903 RBIs; 3,283 hits.
Teams: Giants 1951-52, 1954-72; Mets 1972-73.
How elected: 94.7 percent of vote.

HACK WILSON **OF**
5-6, 190. **B:** R. **T:** R.
Born: April 26, 1900. **Died:** Nov. 23, 1948.
Career: .307 avg.; 244 HR; 1,062 RBIs.
Teams: Giants 1923-25; Cubs 1926-31; Dodgers 1932-34; Phillies 1934.
How elected: Committee on Veterans.

1980

AL KALINE **OF**
6-2, 180. **B:** R. **T:** R.
Born: Dec. 19, 1934.
Career: .297 avg.; 399 HR; 1,583 RBIs; 3,007 hits.
Team: Tigers 1953-74.
How elected: 88.3 percent of vote.

CHUCK KLEIN **OF**
6-0, 185. **B:** L. **T:** R.
Born: Oct. 7, 1905. **Died:** March 28, 1958.
Career: .320 avg.; 300 HR; 1,201 RBIs.
Teams: Phillies 1928-33, 1936-39, 1940-44; Cubs 1934-36; Pirates 1939.
How elected: Committee on Veterans.

DUKE SNIDER **OF**
6-0, 190. **B:** L. **T:** R.
Born: Sept. 19, 1926.

Career: .295 avg.; 407 HR; 1,333 RBIs.
Teams: Dodgers 1947-62; Mets 1963; Giants 1964.
How elected: 86.5 percent of vote

TOM YAWKEY — EXECUTIVE
Born: Feb. 21, 1903. **Died:** July 9, 1976.
Career: Owner of Red Sox franchise from 1933 until death; longtime champion of the A.L. and one of the most respected figures in the game.
How elected: Committee on Veterans.

1981

RUBE FOSTER — P, MAN., EXEC.
6-4, 240.
Born: Sept. 17, 1879. **Died:** Dec. 9, 1930.
Playing career: Negro League star; statistics not available.
Executive career: Founder of Negro American and Negro National leagues; owner of Chicago-based American Giants, the model from which all other Negro clubs were built.
How elected: Committee on Veterans.

BOB GIBSON — P
6-1, 195. **B:** R. **T:** R.
Born: Nov. 9, 1935.
Career: 251-174; 2.91 ERA; 3,117 SO.
Team: Cardinals 1959-75.
How elected: 84 percent of vote.

JOHNNY MIZE — 1B
6-2, 215. **B:** L. **T:** R.
Born: Jan. 7, 1913. **Died:** June 2, 1993.
Career: .312 avg.; 359 HR; 1,337 RBIs.
Teams: Cardinals 1936-41; Giants 1942, 1946-49; Yankees 1949-53.
How elected: Committee on Veterans.

1982

HANK AARON — OF
6-0, 180. **B:** R. **T:** R.
Born: Feb. 5, 1934.
Career: .305 avg.; 755 HR, 1st on all-time list; 2,297 RBIs, 1st on all-time list; 3,771 hits.
Teams: Braves 1954-74; Brewers 1975-76.
How elected: 97.8 percent of vote.

HAPPY CHANDLER — EXECUTIVE
Second commissioner of baseball.
Born: July 14, 1898. **Died:** June 15, 1991.
Career: Former U.S. senator from Kentucky; was elected commissioner in 1945 after the death of Kenesaw Mountain Landis; served until his forced retirement in 1950; returned to Kentucky and won two terms as the state's governor.
How elected: Committee on Veterans.

TRAVIS JACKSON — SS
5-11, 160. **B:** R. **T:** R.
Born: Nov. 2, 1903. **Died:** July 17, 1987.
Career: .291 avg.; 135 HR; 929 RBIs.
Team: Giants 1922-36.
How elected: Committee on Veterans.

FRANK ROBINSON — OF
6-1, 195. **B:** R. **T:** R.
Born: Aug. 31, 1935.
Career: .294 avg.; 586 HR; 1,812 RBIs.
Teams: Reds 1956-65; Orioles 1966-71; Dodgers 1972; Angels 1973-74; Indians 1974-76.
How elected: 89.2 percent of vote.

1983

WALTER ALSTON — MANAGER
Born: Dec. 1, 1911. **Died:** Oct. 1, 1984.
Career: 2,040-1,613, 23 years; 4 World Series championships.
Team: Dodgers 1954-76.
How elected: Committee on Veterans.

GEORGE KELL — 3B
5-9, 175. **B:** R. **T:** R.
Born: Aug. 23, 1922.
Career: .306 avg.; 78 HR; 870 RBIs.
Teams: Athletics 1943-46; Tigers 1946-52; Red Sox 1952-54; White Sox 1954-56; Orioles 1956-57.
How elected: Committee on Veterans.

JUAN MARICHAL — P
6-0, 185. **B:** R. **T:** R.
Born: Oct. 20, 1938.
Career: 243-142; 2.89 ERA; 2,303 SO.
Teams: Giants 1960-73; Red Sox 1974; Dodgers 1975.
How elected: 83.7 percent of vote.

BROOKS ROBINSON — 3B
6-1, 190. **B:** R. **T:** R.
Born: May 18, 1937.
Career: .267 avg.; 268 HR; 1,357 RBIs.
Team: Orioles 1955-77.
How elected: 92 percent of vote

1984

LUIS APARICIO — SS
5-9, 160. **B:** R. **T:** R.
Born: April 29, 1934.
Career: .262 avg.; 83 HR; 791 RBIs.
Teams: White Sox 1956-62, 1968-70; Orioles 1963-67; Red Sox 1971-73.
How elected: 84.6 percent of vote.

DON DRYSDALE — P
6-6, 216. **B:** R. **T:** R.
Born: July 23, 1936. **Died:** July 3, 1993.
Career: 209-166; 2.95 ERA; 2,486 SO.
Team: Dodgers 1956-69.
How elected: 78.4 percent of vote.

RICK FERRELL — C
5-10, 160. **B:** R. **T:** R.
Born: Oct. 12, 1906. **Died:** July 27, 1995.
Career: .281 avg.; 28 HR; 734 RBIs.
Teams: Browns 1929-33, 1941-43; Red Sox 1933-37; Senators 1937-41, 1944-45, 1947.
How elected: Committee on Veterans.

HARMON KILLEBREW — 3B, 1B
5-11, 213. **B:** R. **T:** R.
Born: June 29, 1936.
Career: .256 avg.; 573 HR; 1,584 RBIs.
Teams: Senators 1954-60; Twins 1961-74; Royals 1975.
How elected: 83.1 percent of vote.

PEE WEE REESE — SS
5-10, 175. **B:** R. **T:** R.
Born: July 23, 1918. **Died:** August 14, 1999.
Career: .269 avg.; 126 HR; 885 RBIs.
Teams: Dodgers 1940-42, 1946-58.
How elected: Committee on Veterans.

1985

LOU BROCK — OF
5-11, 170. **B:** L. **T:** L.
Born: June 18, 1939.
Career: .293 avg.; 149 HR; 900 RBIs; 3,023 hits; 938 SB.
Teams: Cubs 1961-64; Cardinals 1964-79.
How elected: 79.7 percent of vote.

ENOS SLAUGHTER — OF
5-9, 192. **B:** L. **T:** R.
Born: April 27, 1916. **Died:** Aug. 12, 2002.
Career: .300 avg.; 169 HR; 1,304 RBIs.
Teams: Cardinals 1938-42, 1946-53; Yankees 1954-55, 1956-59; Athletics 1955-56; Braves 1959.
How elected: Committee on Veterans.

ARKY VAUGHAN — IF
5-11, 175. **B:** L. **T:** R.
Born: March 9, 1912. **Died:** Aug. 30, 1952.
Career: .318 avg.; 96 HR; 926 RBIs.
Teams: Pirates 1932-41; Dodgers 1942-43, 1947-48.
How elected: Committee on Veterans.

Shortstop Pee Wee Reese anchored the Dodgers infield through two glorious decades.

HOYT WILHELM — P
6-0, 195. **B:** R. **T:** R.
Born: July 26, 1923. **Died:** Aug. 23, 2002.
Career: 143-122; 2.52 ERA; 1,610 SO; 1,070 games, 1st on all-time list; 227 saves.
Teams: Giants 1952-56; Cardinals 1957; Indians 1957-58; Orioles 1958-62; White Sox 1963-68; Angels 1969; Braves 1969-70, 1971; Cubs 1970; Dodgers 1971-72.
How elected: 83.8 percent of vote.

1986

BOBBY DOERR — 2B
5-11, 175. **B:** R. **T:** R.
Born: April 7, 1918.
Career: .288 avg.; 223 HR; 1,247 RBIs.
Team: Red Sox 1937-44, 1946-51.
How elected: Committee on Veterans.

ERNIE LOMBARDI — C
6-3, 230. **B:** R. **T:** R.
Born: April 6, 1908. **Died:** Sept. 26, 1977.
Career: .306 avg.; 190 HR; 990 RBIs.
Teams: Dodgers 1931; Reds 1932-41; Braves 1942; Giants 1943-47.
How elected: Committee on Veterans.

WILLIE MCCOVEY — 1B
6-4, 210. **B:** L. **T:** L.
Born: Jan. 10, 1938.
Career: .270 avg.; 521 HR; 1,555 RBIs.
Teams: Giants 1959-73, 1977-80; Padres 1974-76; Athletics 1976.
How elected: 81.4 percent of vote.

1987

RAY DANDRIDGE — 3B
5-7, 175. **B:** R. **T:** R.
Born: Aug. 31, 1913. **Died:** Feb. 12, 1994.
Career: Negro League star; statistics not available.
How elected: Committee on Veterans.

JIM (CATFISH) HUNTER — P
6-0, 195. **B:** R. **T:** R.
Born: April 8, 1946. **Died:** September 9, 1999.
Career: 224-166; 3.26 ERA; 2,012 SO.
Teams: Athletics 1965-74; Yankees 1975-79.
How elected: 76.3 percent of vote.

BILLY WILLIAMS — OF
6-1, 175. **B:** L. **T:** R.

More than a decade of Tom Seaver's outstanding career was spent in New York.

Born: June 15, 1938.
Career: .290 avg.; 426 HR; 1,475 RBIs.
Teams: Cubs 1959-74; Athletics 1975-76.
How elected: 85.7 percent of vote.

1988

WILLIE STARGELL — OF, 1B
6-2, 225. **B:** L. **T:** L.
Born: March 6, 1940. **Died:** April 9, 2001.
Career: .282 avg.; 475 HR; 1,540 RBIs.
Team: Pirates 1962-82.
How elected: 82.4 percent of vote.

1989

AL BARLICK — UMPIRE
Born: April 2, 1915. **Died:** December 27, 1995.
Career: N.L. umpire from 1940-1971; worked as N.L. umpire supervisor after retirement.
How elected: Committee on Veterans.

JOHNNY BENCH — C
6-1, 208. **B:** R. **T:** R.
Born: Dec. 7, 1947.
Career: .267 avg.; 389 HR; 1,376 RBIs.
Team: Reds 1967-83.
How elected: 96.4 percent of vote.

RED SCHOENDIENST — 2B
6-0, 170. **B:** B. **T:** R.
Born: Feb. 2, 1923.
Career: .289 avg.; 84 HR; 773 RBIs.
Teams: Cardinals 1945-56, 1961-63; Giants 1956-57; Braves 1957-60.
How elected: Committee on Veterans.

CARL YASTRZEMSKI — OF
5-11, 182. **B:** L. **T:** R.
Born: Aug. 22, 1939.
Career: .285 avg.; 452 HR; 1,844 RBIs; 3,419 hits.
Team: Red Sox 1961-83.
How elected: 94.6 percent of vote.

1990

JOE MORGAN — 2B
5-7, 160. **B:** L. **T:** R.
Born: Sept. 19, 1943.
Career: .271 avg.; 268 HR; 1,133 RBIs.
Teams: Astros 1963-71, 1980; Reds 1972-79; Giants 1981-82; Phillies 1983; Athletics 1984.
How elected: 81.8 percent of vote.

JIM PALMER — P
6-3, 196. **B:** R. **T:** R.
Born: Oct. 15, 1945.
Career: 268-152; 2.86 ERA; 2,212 SO.
Team: Orioles 1965-67; 1969-84.
How elected: 92.6 percent of vote.

1991

ROD CAREW — 2B, 1B
6-0, 182. **B:** L. **T:** R.
Born: Oct. 1, 1945.
Career: .328 avg.; 92 HR; 1,015 RBIs; 3,053 hits.
Teams: Twins 1967-78; Angels 1979-85.
How elected: 89.7 percent of vote.

FERGUSON JENKINS — P
6-5, 210. **B:** R. **T:** R.
Born: Dec. 13, 1943.
Career: 284-226; 3.34 ERA; 3,192 SO.
Teams: Phillies 1965-66; Cubs 1966-73, 1982-83; Rangers 1974-75, 1978-81; Red Sox 1976-77.
How elected: 74.7 percent of vote.

TONY LAZZERI — 2B
6-0, 170. **B:** R. **T:** R.
Born: Dec. 6, 1903. **Died:** Aug. 6, 1946.
Career: .292 avg.; 178 HR; 1,191 RBIs.
Teams: Yankees 1926-37; Cubs 1938; Dodgers 1939; Giants 1939.
How elected: Committee on Veterans.

GAYLORD PERRY — P
6-4, 215. **B:** R. **T:** R.
Born: Sept. 15, 1938.
Career: 314-265; 3.11 ERA; 3,534 SO.
Teams: Giants 1962-71; Indians 1972-75; Rangers 1975-77, 1980; Padres 1978-79; Yankees 1980; Braves 1981; Mariners 1982-83; Royals 1983.
How elected: 76.5 percent of vote.

BILL VEECK — EXECUTIVE
Born: Feb. 9, 1914. **Died:** Jan. 2, 1986.
Career: A three-time major league owner best known for his showmanship and promotional stunts; owned Indians, Browns and White Sox franchises; broke A.L. color barrier in 1947 by signing Larry Doby to an Indians contract; remembered as the man who sent a midget to the plate for the Browns in a 1951 promotional stunt.
How elected: Committee on Veterans.

1992

ROLLIE FINGERS — P
6-4, 195. **B:** R. **T:** R.
Born: Aug. 25, 1946.
Career: 114-118; 2.90 ERA; 1,299 SO; 341 saves.
Teams: Athletics 1968-76; Padres 1977-80; Brewers 1981-82, 1984-85.
How elected: 81.2 percent of vote.

BILL McGOWAN — UMPIRE
Born: Jan. 18, 1896. **Died:** Dec. 9, 1954.
Career: Served as an A.L. umpire from 1925-53; worked 8 World Series and 4 All-Star Games; worked 2,541 consecutive games over a 16½-year period.
How elected: Committee on Veterans.

HAL NEWHOUSER — P
6-2, 192. **B:** L. **T:** L.
Born: May 20, 1921. **Died:** November 10, 1998.
Career: 207-150; 3.06 ERA; 1,796 SO.
Teams: Tigers 1939-53; Indians 1954-55.
How elected: Committee on Veterans.

TOM SEAVER — P
6-1, 206. **B:** R. **T:** R.
Born: Nov. 17, 1944.
Career: 311-205; 2.86 ERA; 3,640 SO.
Teams: Mets 1967-77, 1983; Reds 1977-82; White Sox 1984-86; Red Sox 1986.
How elected: 98.8 percent of vote.

1993

REGGIE JACKSON — OF
6-0, 200. **B:** L. **T:** L.
Born: May 18, 1946.
Career: .262 avg.; 563 HR; 1,702 RBIs.
Teams: Athletics 1967-75, 1987; Orioles 1976; Yankees 1977-81; Angels 1982-86.
How elected: 93.6 percent of vote.

1994

STEVE CARLTON — P
6-4, 210. **B:** L. **T:** L.
Born: Dec. 22, 1944.
Career: 329-244; 3.22 ERA; 4,136 SO.
Teams: Cardinals 1965-71; Phillies 1972-86; Giants 1986; White Sox 1986; Indians 1987; Twins 1987-88.
How elected: 95.8 percent of vote.

Leo Durocher — SS, Man.
5-10, 160. **B:** R. **T:** R.
Born: July 27, 1905. **Died:** Oct. 7, 1991.
Playing career: .247 avg.; 24 HR; 567 RBIs.
Managing career: 2,008-1,709, 24 years; 1 World Series championship.
Teams (player): Yankees 1925, 1928-29; Reds 1930-33; Cardinals 1933-37; Dodgers 1938-41, 1943, 1945.
Teams (manager): Dodgers 1939-46, 1948; Giants 1948-55; Cubs 1966-72; Astros 1972-73.
How elected: Committee on Veterans.

Phil Rizzuto — SS
5-6, 160. **B:** R. **T:** R.
Born: Sept. 25, 1917.
Career: .273 avg.; 38 HR; 563 RBIs.
Team: Yankees 1941-42, 1946-56.
How elected: Committee on Veterans.

1995

Richie Ashburn — OF
5-10, 170 **B:** L. **T:** R.
Born: March 19, 1927. **Died:** September 9, 1997.
Career: .308 avg.; 29 HR; 586 RBIs.
Teams: Phillies 1948-59; Cubs 1960-61; Mets 1962.
How elected: Committee on Veterans.

Leon Day — P
5-10, 180. **B:** R. **T:** R.
Born: Oct. 30, 1916. **Died:** March 13, 1995.
Career: Negro League star; statistics not available.
How elected: Committee on Veterans.

William Hulbert — Executive
Born: Oct. 23, 1832. **Died:** April 10, 1882.
Career: A former National Association executive and founder of the National League in 1876; served as second president of the new circuit when Morgan Bulkeley left the job after 10 months; he also is credited with hiring baseball's first umpiring staff.
How elected: Committee on Veterans.

Mike Schmidt — 3B
6-2, 203. **B:** R. **T:** R.
Born: Sept. 27, 1949.
Career: .267 avg.; 548 HR; 1,595 RBIs.
Team: Phillies 1972-89.
How elected: 96.5 percent of vote.

Vic Willis — P
6-2, 185. **B:** R. **T:** R.
Born: April 12, 1876. **Died:** Aug. 3, 1947.
Career: 249-205; 2.63 ERA; 1,651 SO.
Teams: Braves 1898-1905; Pirates 1906-09; Cardinals 1910.
How elected: Committee on Veterans.

1996

Jim Bunning — P
6-3, 195. **B:** R. **T:** R.
Born: Oct. 23, 1931.
Career: 224-184; 3.27 ERA; 2,855 SO.
Teams: Tigers 1955-63; Phillies 1964-67, 1970-71; Pirates 1968-69; Dodgers 1969.
How elected: Committee on Veterans.

Bill Foster — P
6-1, 196. **B:** B. **T:** L.
Born: June 12, 1904. **Died:** Sept. 16, 1978.
Career: Negro League star; statistics not available.
How elected: Committee on Veterans.

Ned Hanlon — OF, Man.
5-10, 170. **B:** L. **T:** R.
Born: Aug. 22, 1857. **Died:** April 14, 1937.
Playing career: .260 avg.; 30 HR; 517 RBIs.
Managing career: 1,313-1,164, 19 years; 5 championships.

Larry Doby, baseball's second black player, began his career in 1947 under Hall of Fame Cleveland player-manager Lou Boudreau (left).

Teams (player): Cleveland 1880; Detroit 1881-88; Pittsburgh (N.L.) 1889, 1891; Pittsburgh (P.L.) 1890; Baltimore (N.L.) 1892.
Teams (manager): Pittsburgh (N.L.) 1889, 1891; Pittsburgh (P.L.) 1890; Baltimore (N.L.) 1892-98; Dodgers 1899-1905; Reds 1906-07.
How elected: Committee on Veterans.

Earl Weaver — Manager
Born: Aug. 14, 1930.
Career: 1,480-1,060, 17 years; 1 World Series championship.
Team: Orioles 1968-82, 1985-86.
How elected: Committee on Veterans.

1997

Nellie Fox — 2B
5-9,150. **B:** L. **T:** R
Born: Dec. 25, 1927. **Died:** Dec. 1, 1975.
Career: .288 avg.; 35 HR; 790 RBIs.
Teams: Athletics 1947-49; White Sox 1950-63; Astros 1964-65.
How elected: Committee on Veterans.

Tom Lasorda — Manager
Born: September 22, 1927.
Career: 1,599-1,439, 21 years; 2 World Series championships.
Team: Dodgers 1976-96.
How elected: Committee on Veterans.

Phil Niekro — P
6-1,180. **B:** R. **T:** R
Born: April 1, 1939.
Career: 318-274; 3.35 ERA; 3,342 strikeouts.
Teams: Braves 1964-83, 1987; Yankees 1984-85; Indians 1986, 1987; Blue Jays 1987.
How elected: 80.3 percent of vote.

Willie Wells — SS, 3B, 2B, P
5-8, 160. **B:** R. **T:** R.
Born: Aug. 10, 1905. **Died:** Jan. 22, 1989.
Career: Negro League star; statistics not available.
How elected: Committee on Veterans.

1998

George Davis — 3B, OF, SS
5-9, 180. **B:** B. **T:** R.
Born: Aug. 23, 1870. **Died:** Oct. 17, 1940.
Career: .295 avg.; 73 HR; 1,437 RBIs.
Teams: Cleveland N.L. 1890-92; Giants 1893-1901, 1903; White Sox 1902, 1904-09.
How elected: Committee on Veterans.

Larry Doby — OF
6-1, 182. **B:** L. **T:** R.
Born: Dec. 13, 1924.
Career: .283 avg.; 253 HR; 970 RBIs.
Teams: Indians 1947-55, 1958; White Sox 1956-57, 1959; Tigers 1959.
How elected: Committee on Veterans.

Lee MacPhail — Executive
Born: Oct. 25, 1917.
Career: A former minor league executive, major league executive and president of the American League (1974-83); as director of player personnel for the New York Yankees, he helped build the farm system that fueled seven World Series titles in 10 years; as general manager of the Baltimore Orioles, he helped build another championship organization; the son of Larry MacPhail, a Hall of Fame executive and innovator who paved the way for his son's career.
How elected: Committee on Veterans.

Joe Rogan — P, OF, IF
5-7, 180. **B:** R. **T:** R.
Born: July 28, 1889. **Died:** March 4, 1967.
Career: Negro League star; statistics not available.
How elected: Committee on Veterans.

Kirby Puckett's career was cut short due to vision problems.

DON SUTTON **P**
6-1, 185. **B:** R. **T:** R.
Born: April 2, 1945.
Career: 324-256; 3.26 ERA; 3,574 strikeouts.
Teams: Dodgers 1966-80, 1988; Astros 1981-82; Brewers 1982-84; Athletics 1985; Angels 1985-87.
How elected: 81.6 percent of vote.

1999

GEORGE BRETT **3B**
6-0, 200. **B:** L. **T:** R.
Born: May 15, 1953.
Career: .305 avg.; 317 HR; 1,595 RBIs.
Teams: Royals 1973-93.
How elected: 98.2 percent of vote.

ORLANDO CEPEDA **1B, OF**
6-2, 210. **B:** R. **T:** R.
Born: September 17, 1937.
Career: .297 avg.; 379 HR; 1,365 RBIs.
Teams: Giants 1958-66, Cardinals 1966-68, Braves 1969-72, Athletics 1972, Red Sox 1973, Royals 1974.
How elected: Committee on Veterans.

NESTOR CHYLAK **UMPIRE**
Born: May 11, 1922. **Died:** February 17, 1982.
Career: Served as an A.L. umpire from 1954-78; worked 5 World Series and 6 All-Star Games; known as an excellent teacher of umpires.
How elected: Committee on Veterans.

NOLAN RYAN **P**
6-2, 195 **B:** R. **T:** R.
Born: January 31, 1947.
Career: 324-292; 3.19 ERA; 5,714 strikeouts.
Teams: Mets 1966-71, Angels 1972-79, Astros 1980-88; Rangers 1989-93.
How elected: 98.8 percent of vote.

FRANK SELEE **MANAGER**
Born: Oct. 26, 1859. **Died:** July 5, 1909.
Career: 1,284-862, 16 years.
Teams: Braves 1890-1901, Cubs 1902-1905.
How elected: Committee on Veterans.

SMOKEY JOE WILLIAMS **P, OF, 1B, MAN.**
6-4, 200. **B:** R. **T:** R.
Born: April 6, 1885. **Died:** March 12, 1946.
Career: Negro League star; statistics not available.
How elected: Committee on Veterans.

ROBIN YOUNT **SS, OF**
6-0, 170. **B:** R. **T:** R.
Born: September 16, 1955.
Career: .285 avg.; 251 HR; 1,406 RBIs.
Teams: Brewers 1974-93.
How elected: 77.5 percent of vote.

2000

SPARKY ANDERSON **MANAGER**
Born: February 22, 1934.
Career: 2,194-1,834, 26 years; 3 World Series championships.
Team: Reds 1970-78; Tigers 1979-95.
How elected: Committee on Veterans.

CARLTON FISK **C**
6-2, 220. **B:** R. **T:** R.
Born: December 26, 1947.
Career: .269 avg.; 376 HR; 1,330 RBIs.
Teams: Red Sox 1969-80; White Sox 1982-93.
How elected: 79.6 percent of vote.

JOHN (BID) MCPHEE **2B**
5-8, 152. **B:** R. **T:** R.
Born: Nov. 1, 1859. **Died:** Jan. 3, 1943.
Career: .271 avg.; 53 HR; 1,067 RBIs.
Teams: Cincinnati (A.A.) 1882-89; Cincinnati (Nat.) 1890-99.
How elected: Committee on Veterans.

TONY PEREZ **3B, 1B**
6-2, 190. **B:** R. **T:** R.
Born: May 14, 1942.
Career: .279 avg.; 379 HR; 1,652 RBIs.
Teams: Reds 1964-76, 1984-86; Expos 1977-79; Red Sox 1980-82; Phillies 1983.
How elected: 77.15 percent of vote.

NORMAN (TURKEY) STEARNES **OF, 1B**
6-0, 175. **B:** L. **T:** L.
Born: May 8, 1901. **Died:** Sept. 4, 1979.
Career: Negro League star; statistics not available.
How elected: Committee on Veterans.

2001

BILL MAZEROSKI **2B**
6-0, 183. **B:** R. **T:** R.
Born: September 5, 1936.
Career: .260 avg.; 138 HR; 853 RBIs.
Teams: Pirates 1956-72.
How elected: Committee on Veterans.

KIRBY PUCKETT **OF**
5-8, 210. **B:** R. **T:** R.
Born: March 14, 1961.
Career: .318 avg.; 207 HR; 1,085 RBIs.
Teams: Twins 1984-95.
How elected: 82.1 percent of vote.

HILTON SMITH **P, OF, 1B**
6-2, 180. **B:** R. **T:** R.
Born: Feb. 27, 1912. **Died:** Nov. 18, 1983.
Career: Negro League star; statistics not available.
How elected: Committee on Veterans.

DAVE WINFIELD **OF**
6-6, 220. **B:** R. **T:** R.
Born: October 3, 1951.
Career: .283 avg.; 465 HR; 1,833 RBIs.
Teams: Padres 1973-80; Yankees 1981-90; Angels 1990-91; Blue Jays 1992; Twins 1993-94; Indians 1995.
How elected: 84.5 percent of vote.

2002

OZZIE SMITH **SS**
5-10, 180. **B:** B. **T:** R.
Born: December 26, 1954.
Career: .262 avg.; 28 HR; 793 RBIs.
Teams: Padres 1978-81; Cardinals 1982-96.
How elected: 91.7 percent of vote.

2003

GARY CARTER **C**
6-2, 215. **B:** R. **T:** R.
Born: April 8, 1954.
Career: .262 avg.; 324 HR; 1225 RBIs.
Teams: Expos 1974-84, 1992; Mets 1985-89; Giants 1990; Dodgers 1991.
How elected: 78.0 percent of vote.

EDDIE MURRAY **1B**
6-2, 200. **B:** B. **T:** R.
Born: February 24, 1956.
Career: .287 avg.; 504 HR; 1917 RBIs.
Teams: Orioles 1977-88, 1996; Dodgers 1989-91, 1997; Mets 1992-93; Indians 1994-96; Angels 1997.
How elected: 85.3 percent of vote.

Award Winners

Baseball Writers' Association of America

1931

Lefty Grove — A.L. MVP
Team: Athletics. **Position:** Pitcher.
Season: 31-4; 2.06 ERA; 175 SO.
(See Hall of Fame section, 1947.)

Frank Frisch — N.L. MVP
Team: Cardinals. **Position:** Second base.
Season: .311 avg.; 4 HR; 82 RBIs; 28 SB.
(See Hall of Fame section, 1947.)

1932

Jimmie Foxx — A.L. MVP
Team: Athletics. **Position:** First base.
Season: .364 avg.; 58 HR; 169 RBIs.
(See Hall of Fame section, 1951.)

Chuck Klein — N.L. MVP
Team: Phillies. **Position:** Outfield.
Season: .348 avg.; 38 HR; 137 RBIs.
(See Hall of Fame section, 1980.)

1933

Jimmie Foxx — A.L. MVP
Team: Athletics. **Position:** First base.
Season: .356 avg.; 48 HR; 163 RBIs.
(See Hall of Fame section, 1951.)

Carl Hubbell — N.L. MVP
Team: Giants. **Position:** Pitcher.
Season: 23-12; 1.66 ERA; 156 SO.
(See Hall of Fame section, 1947.)

1934

Mickey Cochrane — A.L. MVP
Team: Tigers. **Position:** Catcher.
Season: .320 avg.; 2 HR; 76 RBIs.
(See Hall of Fame section, 1947.)

Dizzy Dean — N.L. MVP
Team: Cardinals. **Position:** Pitcher.
Season: 30-7; 2.66 ERA; 195 SO.
(See Hall of Fame section, 1953.)

1935

Hank Greenberg — A.L. MVP
Team: Tigers. **Position:** First base.
Season: .328 avg.; 36 HR; 170 RBIs.
(See Hall of Fame section, 1956.)

Gabby Hartnett — N.L. MVP
Team: Cubs. **Position:** Catcher.
Season: .344 avg.; 13 HR; 91 RBIs.
(See Hall of Fame section, 1955.)

1936

Lou Gehrig — A.L. MVP
Team: Yankees. **Position:** First base.
Season: .354 avg.; 49 HR; 152 RBIs.
(See Hall of Fame section, 1939.)

Carl Hubbell — N.L. MVP
Team: Giants. **Position:** Pitcher.
Season: 26-6; 2.31 ERA; 123 SO.
(See Hall of Fame section, 1947.)

Hank Greenberg (left) and Charley Gehringer were Tigers teammates for 10 seasons.

1937

Charley Gehringer — A.L. MVP
Team: Tigers. **Position:** Second base.
Season: .371 avg.; 14 HR; 96 RBIs.
(See Hall of Fame section, 1949.)

Joe Medwick — N.L. MVP
Team: Cardinals. **Position:** Outfield.
Season: .374 avg.; 31 HR; 154 RBIs; Triple Crown winner.
(See Hall of Fame section, 1968.)

1938

Jimmie Foxx — A.L. MVP
Team: Red Sox. **Position:** First base.
Season: .349 avg.; 50 HR; 175 RBIs.
(See Hall of Fame section, 1951.)

Ernie Lombardi — N.L. MVP
Team: Reds. **Position:** Catcher.
Season: .342 avg.; 19 HR; 95 RBIs.
(See Hall of Fame section, 1986.)

1939

Joe DiMaggio — A.L. MVP
Team: Yankees. **Position:** Outfield.
Season: .381 avg.; 30 HR; 126 RBIs.
(See Hall of Fame section, 1955.)

Bucky Walters — N.L. MVP
Team: Reds. **Position:** Pitcher.
6-1, 180. **B:** R. **T:** R.
Born: April 19, 1909. **Died:** April 20, 1991.
Season: 27-11; 2.29 ERA; 137 SO.
Career: 198-160; 3.30 ERA; 1,107 SO.
Teams: Phillies 1934-38; Reds 1938-48; Braves 1950.

1940

Hank Greenberg — A.L. MVP
Team: Tigers. **Position:** Outfield.
Season: .340 avg.; 41 HR; 150 RBIs.
(See Hall of Fame section, 1956.)

Frank McCormick — N.L. MVP
Team: Reds. **Position:** First base.
6-4, 205. **B:** R. **T:** R.
Born: June 9, 1911. **Died:** Nov. 21, 1982.
Season: .309 avg.; 19 HR; 127 RBIs.
Career: .299 avg.; 128 HR; 951 RBIs.
Teams: Reds 1934, 1937-45; Phillies 1946-47; Braves 1947-48.

1941

Joe DiMaggio — A.L. MVP
Team: Yankees. **Position:** Outfield.
Season: .357 avg.; 30 HR; 125 RBIs.
(See Hall of Fame section, 1955.)

Dolph Camilli — N.L. MVP
Team: Dodgers. **Position:** First base.
5-10, 185. **B:** L. **T:** L.
Born: April 23, 1907. **Died:** Oct. 21, 1997.
Season: .285 avg.; 34 HR; 120 RBIs.
Career: .277 avg.; 239 HR; 950 RBIs.
Teams: Cubs 1933-34; Phillies 1934-37; Dodgers 1938-43; Red Sox 1945.

Jackie Robinson was the first Rookie of the Year after his barrier-breaking 1947 season.

1942

JOE GORDON — A.L. MVP
Team: Yankees. **Position:** Second base.
5-10, 180. **B:** R. **T:** R.
Born: Feb. 18, 1915. **Died:** April 14, 1978.
Season: .322 avg.; 18 HR; 103 RBIs.
Career: .268 avg.; 253 HR; 975 RBIs.
Teams: Yankees 1938-43, 1946; Indians 1947-50.

MORT COOPER — N.L. MVP
Team: Cardinals. **Position:** Pitcher.
6-2, 210. **B:** R. **T:** R.
Born: March 2, 1913. **Died:** Nov. 17, 1958.
Season: 22-7; 1.78 ERA; 152 SO.
Career: 128-75; 2.97 ERA; 913 SO.
Teams: Cardinals 1938-45; Braves 1945-47; Giants 1947; Cubs 1949.

1943

SPUD CHANDLER — A.L. MVP
Team: Yankees. **Position:** Pitcher.
6-0, 181. **B:** R. **T:** R.
Born: Sept. 12, 1907. **Died:** Jan. 9, 1990.
Season: 20-4; 1.64 ERA; 134 SO.
Career: 109-43; 2.84 ERA; 614 SO.
Team: Yankees 1937-47.

STAN MUSIAL — N.L. MVP
Team: Cardinals. **Position:** Outfield.
Season: .357 avg.; 13 HR; 81 RBIs.
(See Hall of Fame section, 1969.)

1944

HAL NEWHOUSER — A.L. MVP
Team: Tigers. **Position:** Pitcher.
Season: 29-9; 2.22 ERA; 187 SO.
(See Hall of Fame section, 1992.)

MARTY MARION — N.L. MVP
Team: Cardinals. **Position:** Shortstop.
6-2, 170. **B:** R. **T:** R.
Born: Dec. 1, 1917.
Season: .267 avg.; 6 HR; 63 RBIs.
Career: .263 avg.; 36 HR; 624 RBIs.
Team: Cardinals 1940-50, 1952-53.

1945

HAL NEWHOUSER — A.L. MVP
Team: Tigers. **Position:** Pitcher.
Season: 25-9; 1.81 ERA; 212 SO.
(See Hall of Fame section, 1992.)

PHIL CAVARRETTA — N.L. MVP
Team: Cubs. **Position:** First base.
5-11, 175. **B:** L. **T:** L.
Born: July 19, 1916.
Season: .355 avg.; 6 HR; 97 RBIs.
Career: .293 avg.; 95 HR; 920 RBIs.
Team: Cubs 1934-55.

1946

TED WILLIAMS — A.L. MVP
Team: Red Sox. **Position:** Outfield.
Season: .342 avg.; 38 HR; 123 RBIs.
(See Hall of Fame section, 1966.)

STAN MUSIAL — N.L. MVP
Team: Cardinals. **Position:** First base.
Season: .365 avg.; 16 HR; 103 RBIs.
(See Hall of Fame section, 1969.)

1947

JOE DIMAGGIO — A.L. MVP
Team: Yankees. **Position:** Outfield.
Season: .315 avg.; 20 HR; 97 RBIs.
(See Hall of Fame section, 1955.)

BOB ELLIOTT — N.L. MVP
Team: Braves. **Position:** Third base.
6-0, 185. **B:** R. **T:** R.
Born: Nov. 26, 1916. **Died:** May 4, 1966.
Season: .317 avg.; 22 HR; 113 RBIs.
Career: .289 avg.; 170 HR; 1,195 RBIs.
Teams: Pirates 1939-46; Braves 1947-51; Giants 1952; Browns 1953; White Sox 1953.

JACKIE ROBINSON — ROOKIE
Team: Dodgers. **Position:** First base.
Season: .297 avg.; 12 HR; 48 RBIs; 29 SB.
(See Hall of Fame section, 1962.)

1948

LOU BOUDREAU — A.L. MVP
Team: Indians. **Position:** Shortstop.
Season: .355 avg.; 18 HR; 106 RBIs.
(See Hall of Fame section, 1970.)

STAN MUSIAL — N.L. MVP
Team: Cardinals. **Position:** Outfield.
Season: .376 avg.; 39 HR; 131 RBIs.
(See Hall of Fame section, 1969.)

ALVIN DARK — ROOKIE
Team: Braves. **Position:** Shortstop.
5-11, 185. **B:** R. **T:** R.
Born: Jan. 7, 1922.
Season: .322 avg.; 3 HR; 48 RBIs.
Career: .289 avg.; 126 HR; 757 RBIs.
Teams: Braves 1946, 1948-49, 1960; Giants 1950-56; Cardinals 1956-58; Cubs 1958-59; Phillies 1960.

1949

TED WILLIAMS — A.L. MVP
Team: Red Sox. **Position:** Outfield.
Season: .343 avg.; 43 HR; 159 RBIs.
(See Hall of Fame section, 1966.)

JACKIE ROBINSON — N.L. MVP
Team: Dodgers. **Position:** Second base.
Season: .342 avg.; 16 HR; 124 RBIs; 37 SB.
(See Hall of Fame section, 1962.)

ROY SIEVERS — A.L. ROOKIE
Team: Browns. **Position:** Outfield.
6-1, 195. **B:** R. **T:** R.
Born: Nov. 18, 1926.
Season: .306 avg.; 16 HR; 91 RBIs.
Career: .267 avg.; 318 HR; 1,147 RBIs.
Teams: Browns 1949-53; Senators 1954-59, 1964-65; White Sox 1960-61; Phillies 1962-64.

DON NEWCOMBE — N.L. ROOKIE
Team: Dodgers. **Position:** Pitcher.
6-4, 225. **B:** L. **T:** R.
Born: June 14, 1926.
Season: 17-8; 3.17 ERA; 149 SO.
Career: 149-90; 3.56 ERA; 1,129 SO.
Teams: Dodgers 1949-51, 1954-58; Reds 1958-60; Indians 1960.

1950

PHIL RIZZUTO — A.L. MVP
Team: Yankees. **Position:** Shortstop.
Season: .324 avg.; 7 HR; 66 RBIs.
(See Hall of Fame section, 1994.)

JIM KONSTANTY — N.L. MVP
Team: Phillies. **Position:** Pitcher.
6-2, 202. **B:** R. **T:** R.
Born: March 2, 1917. **Died:** June 11, 1976.
Season: 16-7; 2.66 ERA; 56 SO.
Career: 66-48; 3.46 ERA; 268 SO.
Teams: Reds 1944; Braves 1946; Phillies 1948-54; Yankees 1954-56; Cardinals 1956.

WALT DROPO — A.L. ROOKIE
Team: Red Sox. **Position:** First base.
6-5, 220. **B:** R. **T:** R.
Born: Jan. 30, 1923.
Season: .322 avg.; 34 HR; 144 RBIs.
Career: .270 avg.; 152 HR; 704 RBIs.
Teams: Red Sox 1949-52; Tigers 1952-54; White Sox 1955-58; Reds 1958-59; Orioles 1959-61.

SAM JETHROE — N.L. ROOKIE
Team: Braves. **Position:** Outfield.
6-1, 178. **B:** B. **T:** R.
Born: Jan. 20, 1922. **Died:** June 16, 2001.
Season: .273 avg.; 18 HR; 58 RBIs.
Career: .261 avg.; 49 HR; 181 RBIs.
Teams: Braves 1950-52; Pirates 1954.

1951

YOGI BERRA — A.L. MVP
Team: Yankees. **Position:** Catcher.
Season: .294 avg.; 27 HR; 88 RBIs.
(See Hall of Fame section, 1972.)

ROY CAMPANELLA — N.L. MVP
Team: Dodgers. **Position:** Catcher.
Season: .325 avg.; 33 HR; 108 RBIs.
(See Hall of Fame section, 1969.)

GIL MCDOUGALD — A.L. ROOKIE
Team: Yankees. **Position:** Third base.
6-1, 180. **B:** R. **T:** R.
Born: May 19, 1928.
Season: .306 avg.; 14 HR; 63 RBIs.
Career: .276 avg.; 112 HR; 576 RBIs.
Team: Yankees 1951-60.

WILLIE MAYS — N.L. ROOKIE
Team: Giants. **Position:** Outfield.
Season: .274 avg.; 20 HR; 68 RBIs.
(See Hall of Fame section, 1979.)

1952

BOBBY SHANTZ — A.L. MVP
Team: Athletics. **Position:** Pitcher.
5-6, 142. **B:** R. **T:** L.
Born: Sept. 26, 1925.
Season: 24-7; 2.48 ERA; 152 SO.
Career: 119-99; 3.38 ERA; 1,072 SO.
Teams: Athletics 1949-56; Yankees 1957-60; Pirates 1961; Colt .45s 1962; Cardinals 1962-64; Cubs 1964; Phillies 1964.

Hank Sauer N.L. MVP
Team: Cubs. **Position:** Outfield.
6-4, 199. **B:** R. **T:** R.
Born: March 17, 1919. **Died:** Aug. 24, 2001.
Season: .270 avg.; 37 HR; 121 RBIs.
Career: .266 avg.; 288 HR; 876 RBIs.
Teams: Reds 1941-42, 1945, 1948-49; Cubs 1949-55; Cardinals 1956; Giants 1957-59.

Harry Byrd A.L. Rookie
Team: Athletics. **Position:** Pitcher.
6-1, 188. **B:** R. **T:** R.
Born: Feb. 3, 1925. **Died:** May 14, 1985.
Season: 15-15; 3.31 ERA; 116 SO.
Career: 46-54; 4.35 ERA; 381 SO.
Teams: Athletics 1950, 1952-53; Yankees 1954; Orioles 1955; White Sox 1955-56; Tigers 1957.

Joe Black N.L. Rookie
Team: Dodgers. **Position:** Pitcher.
6-2, 220. **B:** R. **T:** R.
Born: Feb. 8, 1924.
Season: 15-4; 2.15 ERA; 85 SO.
Career: 30-12; 3.91 ERA; 222 SO.
Teams: Dodgers 1952-55; Reds 1955-56; Senators 1957.

1953

Al Rosen A.L. MVP
Team: Indians. **Position:** Third base.
5-11, 180. **B:** R. **T:** R.
Born: Feb. 29, 1924.
Season: .336 avg.; 43 HR; 145 RBIs.
Career: .285 avg.; 192 HR; 717 RBIs.
Team: Indians 1947-56.

Roy Campanella N.L. MVP
Team: Dodgers. **Position:** Catcher.
Season: .312 avg.; 41 HR; 142 RBIs.
(See Hall of Fame section, 1969.)

Harvey Kuenn A.L. Rookie
Team: Tigers. **Position:** Shortstop.
6-2, 190. **B:** R. **T:** R.
Born: Dec. 4, 1930. **Died:** Feb. 28, 1988.
Season: .308 avg.; 2 HR; 48 RBIs.
Career: .303 avg.; 87 HR; 671 RBIs.
Teams: Tigers 1952-59; Indians 1960; Giants 1961-65; Cubs 1965-66; Phillies 1966.

Jim Gilliam N.L. Rookie
Team: Dodgers. **Position:** Second base.
5-11, 175. **B:** B. **T:** R.
Born: Oct. 17, 1928. **Died:** Oct. 8, 1978.
Season: .278 avg.; 6 HR; 63 RBIs; 21 SB.
Career: .265 avg.; 65 HR; 558 RBIs; 203 SB.
Team: Dodgers 1953-66.

1954

Yogi Berra A.L. MVP
Team: Yankees. **Position:** Catcher.
Season: .307 avg.; 22 HR; 125 RBIs.
(See Hall of Fame section, 1972.)

Willie Mays N.L. MVP
Team: Giants. **Position:** Outfield.
Season: .345 avg.; 41 HR; 110 RBIs.
(See Hall of Fame section, 1979.)

Bob Grim A.L. Rookie
Team: Yankees. **Position:** Pitcher.
6-1, 185. **B:** R. **T:** R.
Born: March 8, 1930.
Season: 20-6; 3.26 ERA; 108 SO.
Career: 61-41; 3.61 ERA; 443 SO.
Teams: Yankees 1954-58; Athletics 1958-59, 1962; Indians 1960; Reds 1960; Cardinals 1960.

Wally Moon N.L. Rookie
Team: Cardinals. **Position:** Outfield.
6-0, 175. **B:** L. **T:** R.
Born: April 3, 1930.
Season: .304 avg.; 12 HR; 76 RBIs.
Career: .289 avg.; 142 HR; 661 RBIs.
Teams: Cardinals 1954-58; Dodgers 1959-65.

1955

Yogi Berra A.L. MVP
Team: Yankees. **Position:** Catcher.
Season: .272 avg.; 27 HR; 108 RBIs.
(See Hall of Fame section, 1972.)

Roy Campanella N.L. MVP
Team: Dodgers. **Position:** Catcher.
Season: .318 avg.; 32 HR; 107 RBIs.
(See Hall of Fame section, 1969.)

Herb Score A.L. Rookie
Team: Indians. **Position:** Pitcher.
6-2, 185. **B:** L. **T:** L.
Born: June 7, 1933.
Season: 16-10; 2.85 ERA; 245 SO.
Career: 55-46; 3.36 ERA; 837 SO.
Teams: Indians 1955-59; White Sox 1960-62.

Bill Virdon N.L. Rookie
Team: Cardinals. **Position:** Outfield.
6-0, 175. **B:** L. **T:** R.
Born: June 9, 1931.
Season: .281 avg.; 17 HR; 68 RBIs.
Career: .267 avg.; 91 HR; 502 RBIs.
Teams: Cardinals 1955-56; Pirates 1956-65, 1968.

1956

Mickey Mantle A.L. MVP
Team: Yankees. **Position:** Outfield.
Season: .353 avg.; 52 HR; 130 RBIs; Triple Crown winner.
(See Hall of Fame section, 1974.)

Don Newcombe N.L. MVP, Cy Young
Team: Dodgers. **Position:** Pitcher.
Season: 27-7; 3.06 ERA; 139 SO.
(See 1949 N.L. Rookie of Year.)

Luis Aparicio A.L. Rookie
Team: White Sox. **Position:** Shortstop.
Season: .266 avg.; 3 HR; 56 RBIs; 21 SB.
(See Hall of Fame section, 1984.)

Frank Robinson N.L. Rookie
Team: Reds. **Position:** Outfield.
Season: .290 avg.; 38 HR; 83 RBIs.
(See Hall of Fame section, 1982.)

1957

Mickey Mantle A.L. MVP
Team: Yankees. **Position:** Outfield.
Season: .365 avg.; 34 HR; 94 RBIs.
(See Hall of Fame section, 1974.)

Hank Aaron N.L. MVP
Team: Braves. **Position:** Outfield.
Season: .322 avg.; 44 HR; 132 RBIs.
(See Hall of Fame section, 1982.)

Warren Spahn Cy Young
Team: Braves.
Season: 21-11; 2.69 ERA; 111 SO.
(See Hall of Fame section, 1973.)

Tony Kubek A.L. Rookie
Team: Yankees. **Position:** Infield, outfield.
6-3, 190. **B:** L. **T:** R.
Born: Oct. 12, 1936.
Season: .297 avg.; 3 HR; 39 RBIs.
Career: .266 avg.; 57 HR; 373 RBIs.
Team: Yankees 1957-65.

Giants star Willie Mays was named N.L. MVP after his second full Major League season.

Jack Sanford N.L. Rookie
Team: Phillies. **Position:** Pitcher.
6-0, 190. **B:** R. **T:** R.
Born: May 18, 1929. **Died:** March 7, 2000.
Season: 19-8; 3.08 ERA; 188 SO.
Career: 137-101; 3.69 ERA; 1,182 SO.
Teams: Phillies 1956-58; Giants 1959-65; Angels 1965-67; Athletics 1967.

1958

Jackie Jensen A.L. MVP
Team: Red Sox. **Position:** Outfield.
5-11, 190. **B:** R. **T:** R.
Born: March 9, 1927. **Died:** July 14, 1982.
Season: .286 avg.; 35 HR; 122 RBIs.
Career: .279 avg.; 199 HR; 929 RBIs.
Teams: Yankees 1950-52; Senators 1952-53; Red Sox 1954-59, 1961.

Ernie Banks N.L. MVP
Team: Cubs. **Position:** Shortstop.
Season: .313 avg.; 47 HR; 129 RBIs.
(See Hall of Fame section, 1977.)

Bob Turley Cy Young
Team: Yankees.
6-2, 215. **B:** R. **T:** R.
Born: Sept. 19, 1930.
Season: 21-7; 2.97 ERA; 168 SO.
Career: 101-85; 3.64 ERA; 1,265 SO.
Teams: Browns 1951, 1953; Orioles 1954; Yankees 1955-62; Angels 1963; Red Sox 1963.

Albie Pearson A.L. Rookie
Team: Senators. **Position:** Outfield.
5-5, 140. **B:** L. **T:** L.
Born: Sept. 12, 1934.
Season: .275 avg.; 3 HR; 33 RBIs.
Career: .270 avg.; 28 HR; 214 RBIs.
Teams: Senators 1958-59; Orioles 1959-60; Angels 1961-66.

Orlando Cepeda N.L. Rookie
Team: Giants. **Position:** First base.
Season: .312 avg.; 25 HR; 96 RBIs.
(See Hall of Fame section, 1999.)

Dodgers ace Sandy Koufax swept N.L. Cy Young and MVP honors in 1963.

1959

NELLIE FOX — **A.L. MVP**
Team: White Sox. **Position:** Second base.
Season: .306 avg.; 2 HR; 70 RBIs.
(See Hall of Fame section, 1999.)

ERNIE BANKS — **N.L. MVP**
Team: Cubs. **Position:** Shortstop.
Season: .304 avg.; 45 HR; 143 RBIs.
(See Hall of Fame section, 1977.)

EARLY WYNN — **CY YOUNG**
Team: White Sox.
Season: 22-10; 3.17 ERA; 179 SO.
(See Hall of Fame section, 1972.)

BOB ALLISON — **A.L. ROOKIE**
Team: Senators. **Position:** Outfield.
6-4, 215. **B:** R. **T:** R.
Born: July 11, 1934. **Died:** April 9, 1995.
Season: .261 avg.; 30 HR; 85 RBIs.
Career: .255 avg.; 256 HR; 796 RBIs.
Teams: Senators 1958-60; Twins 1961-70.

WILLIE McCOVEY — **N.L. ROOKIE**
Team: Giants. **Position:** First base.
Season: .354 avg.; 13 HR; 38 RBIs.
(See Hall of Fame section, 1986.)

1960

ROGER MARIS — **A.L. MVP**
Team: Yankees. **Position:** Outfield.
6-0, 203. **B:** L. **T:** R.
Born: Sept. 10, 1934. **Died:** Dec. 14, 1985.
Season: .283 avg.; 39 HR; 112 RBIs.
Career: .260 avg.; 275 HR; 851 RBIs.
Teams: Indians 1957-58; Athletics 1958-59; Yankees 1960-66; Cardinals 1967-68.

DICK GROAT — **N.L. MVP**
Team: Pirates. **Position:** Shortstop.
6-0, 180. **B:** R. **T:** R.
Born: Nov. 4, 1930.
Season: .325 avg.; 2 HR; 50 RBIs.
Career: .286 avg.; 39 HR; 707 RBIs.
Teams: Pirates 1952, 1955-62; Cardinals 1963-65; Phillies 1966-67; Giants 1967.

VERNON LAW — **CY YOUNG**
Team: Pirates.
6-2, 195. **B:** R. **T:** R.
Born: March 12, 1930.
Season: 20-9; 3.08 ERA; 120 SO.
Career: 162-147; 3.77 ERA; 1,092 SO.
Team: Pirates 1950-51, 1954-67.

RON HANSEN — **A.L. ROOKIE**
Team: Orioles. **Position:** Shortstop.
6-3, 200. **B:** R. **T:** R.
Born: April 5, 1938.
Season: .255 avg.; 22 HR; 86 RBIs.
Career: .234 avg.; 106 HR; 501 RBIs.
Teams: Orioles 1958-62; White Sox 1963-67, 1968-69; Senators 1968; Yankees 1970-71; Royals 1972.

FRANK HOWARD — **N.L. ROOKIE**
Team: Dodgers. **Position:** Outfield.
6-7, 255. **B:** R. **T:** R.
Born: Aug. 8, 1936.
Season: .268 avg.; 23 HR; 77 RBIs.
Career: .273 avg.; 382 HR; 1,119 RBIs.
Teams: Dodgers 1958-64; Senators 1965-71; Rangers 1972; Tigers 1972-73.

1961

ROGER MARIS — **A.L. MVP**
Team: Yankees. **Position:** Outfield.
Season: .269 avg.; 61 HR; 142 RBIs.
(See 1960 A.L. MVP.)

FRANK ROBINSON — **N.L. MVP**
Team: Reds. **Position:** Outfield.
Season: .323 avg.; 37 HR; 124 RBIs.
(See Hall of Fame section, 1982.)

WHITEY FORD — **CY YOUNG**
Team: Yankees.
Season: 25-4; 3.21 ERA; 209 SO.
(See Hall of Fame section, 1974.)

DON SCHWALL — **A.L. ROOKIE**
Team: Red Sox. **Position:** Pitcher.
6-6, 200. **B:** R. **T:** R.
Born: March 2, 1936.
Season: 15-7; 3.22 ERA; 91 SO.
Career: 49-48; 3.72 ERA; 408 SO.
Teams: Red Sox 1961-62; Pirates 1963-66; Braves 1966-67.

BILLY WILLIAMS — **N.L. ROOKIE**
Team: Cubs. **Position:** Outfield.
Season: .278 avg.; 25 HR; 86 RBIs.
(See Hall of Fame section, 1987.)

1962

MICKEY MANTLE — **A.L. MVP**
Team: Yankees. **Position:** Outfield.
Season: .321 avg.; 30 HR; 89 RBIs.
(See Hall of Fame section, 1974.)

MAURY WILLS — **N.L. MVP**
Team: Dodgers. **Position:** Shortstop.
5-11, 170. **B:** B. **T:** R.
Born: Oct. 2, 1932.
Season: .299 avg.; 6 HR; 48 RBIs; 104 SB.
Career: .281 avg.; 20 HR; 458 RBIs; 586 SB.
Teams: Dodgers 1959-66, 1969-72; Pirates 1967-68; Expos 1969.

DON DRYSDALE — **CY YOUNG**
Team: Dodgers.
Season: 25-9; 2.83 ERA; 232 SO.
(See Hall of Fame section, 1984.)

TOM TRESH — **A.L. ROOKIE**
Team: Yankees. **Position:** Shortstop, Outfield.
6-1, 190. **B:** B. **T:** R.
Born: Sept. 20, 1937.
Season: .286 avg.; 20 HR; 93 RBIs.
Career: .245 avg.; 153 HR; 530 RBIs.
Teams: Yankees 1961-69; Tigers 1969.

KEN HUBBS — **N.L. ROOKIE**
Team: Cubs. **Position:** Second base.
6-2, 175. **B:** R. **T:** R.
Born: Dec. 23, 1941. **Died:** Feb. 13, 1964.
Season: .260 avg.; 5 HR; 49 RBIs.
Career: .247 avg.; 14 HR; 98 RBIs.
Team: Cubs 1961-63.

1963

ELSTON HOWARD — **A.L. MVP**
Team: Yankees. **Position:** Catcher.
6-2, 200. **B:** R. **T:** R.
Born: Feb. 23, 1929. **Died:** Dec. 14, 1980.
Season: .287 avg.; 28 HR; 85 RBIs.
Career: .274 avg.; 167 HR; 762 RBIs.
Teams: Yankees 1955-67; Red Sox 1967-68.

SANDY KOUFAX — **N.L. MVP, CY YOUNG**
Team: Dodgers. **Position:** Pitcher.
Season: 25-5; 1.88 ERA; 306 SO.
(See Hall of Fame section, 1972.)

GARY PETERS — **A.L. ROOKIE**
Team: White Sox. **Position:** Pitcher.
6-2, 200. **B:** L. **T:** L.
Born: April 21, 1937.
Season: 19-8; 2.33 ERA; 189 SO.
Career: 124-103; 3.25 ERA; 1,420 SO.
Teams: White Sox 1959-69; Red Sox 1970-72.

PETE ROSE — **N.L. ROOKIE**
Team: Reds. **Position:** Second base.
5-11, 200. **B:** B. **T:** R.
Born: April 14, 1941.
Season: .273 avg.; 6 HR; 41 RBIs.
Career: .303 avg.; 160 HR; 1,314 RBIs; 4,256 hits, 1st on all-time list.
Teams: Reds 1963-78, 1984-86; Phillies 1979-83; Expos 1984.

1964

BROOKS ROBINSON — **A.L. MVP**
Team: Orioles. **Position:** Third base.
Season: .317 avg.; 28 HR; 118 RBIs.
(See Hall of Fame section, 1983.)

KEN BOYER — **N.L. MVP**
Team: Cardinals. **Position:** Third base.
6-2, 200. **B:** R. **T:** R.
Born: May 20, 1931. **Died:** Sept. 7, 1982.
Season: .295 avg.; 24 HR; 119 RBIs.
Career: .287 avg.; 282 HR; 1,141 RBIs.
Teams: Cardinals 1955-65; Mets 1966-67; Cubs 1967-68; Dodgers 1968-69.

DEAN CHANCE — **CY YOUNG**
Team: Angels.
6-3, 200. **B:** R. **T:** R.
Born: June 1, 1941.
Season: 20-9; 1.65 ERA; 207 SO.
Career: 128-115; 2.92 ERA; 1,534 SO.
Teams: Angels 1961-66; Twins 1967-69; Indians 1970; Mets 1970; Tigers 1971.

TONY OLIVA — **A.L. ROOKIE**
Team: Twins. **Position:** Outfield.
6-2, 190. **B:** L. **T:** R.
Born: July 20, 1940.
Season: .323 avg.; 32 HR; 94 RBIs; 217 hits.
Career: .304 avg.; 220 HR; 947 RBIs.
Team: Twins 1962-76.

DICK ALLEN — **N.L. ROOKIE**
Team: Phillies. **Position:** Third base.
5-11, 190. **B:** R. **T:** R.
Born: March 8, 1942.

eason: .318 avg.; 29 HR; 91 RBIs.
areer: .292 avg.; 351 HR; 1,119 RBIs.
eams: Phillies 1963-69, 1975-76; Cardinals 1970; odgers 1971; White Sox 1972-74; Athletics 1977.

1965

oilo Versalles — A.L. MVP
eam: Twins. **Position:** Shortstop.
-10, 150. **B:** R. **T:** R.
orn: Dec. 18, 1939.
eason: .273 avg.; 19 HR; 77 RBIs; 27 SB.
areer: .242 avg.; 95 HR; 471 RBIs.
eams: Senators 1959-60, 1969; Twins 1961-67; odgers 1968; Indians 1969; Braves 1971.

Villie Mays — N.L. MVP
eam: Giants. **Position:** Outfield.
eason: .317 avg.; 52 HR; 112 RBIs.
See Hall of Fame section, 1979.)

Sandy Koufax — Cy Young
eam: Dodgers.
eason: 26-8; 2.04 ERA; 382 SO.
See Hall of Fame section, 1972.)

Curt Blefary — A.L. Rookie
eam: Orioles. **Position:** Outfield.
-2, 195. **B:** L. **T:** R.
orn: July 5, 1943. **Died:** Jan. 28, 2001.
eason: .260 avg.; 22 HR; 70 RBIs.
areer: .237 avg.; 112 HR; 382 RBIs.
eams: Orioles 1965-68; Astros 1969; Yankees 1970-71; thletics 1971-72; Padres 1972.

Jim Lefebvre — N.L. Rookie
eam: Dodgers. **Position:** Second base.
-0, 185. **B:** B. **T:** R.
orn: Jan. 7, 1942.
eason: .250 avg.; 12 HR; 69 RBIs.
areer: .251 avg.; 74 HR; 404 RBIs.
eam: Dodgers 1965-72.

1966

Frank Robinson — A.L. MVP
Team: Orioles. **Position:** Outfield.
Season: .316 avg.; 49 HR; 122 RBIs.
(See Hall of Fame section, 1982.)

Roberto Clemente — N.L. MVP
Team: Pirates. **Position:** Outfield.
Season: .317 avg.; 29 HR; 119 RBIs.
(See Hall of Fame section, 1973.)

Sandy Koufax — Cy Young
Team: Dodgers.
Season: 27-9; 1.73 ERA; 317 SO.
(See Hall of Fame section, 1972.)

Tommie Agee — A.L. Rookie
Team: White Sox. **Position:** Outfield.
5-11, 195. **B:** R. **T:** R.
Born: Aug. 9, 1942. **Died:** Jan. 22, 2001.
Season: .273 avg.; 22 HR; 86 RBIs.
Career: .255 avg.; 130 HR; 433 RBIs.
Teams: Indians 1962-64; White Sox 1965-67; Mets 1968-72; Astros 1973; Cardinals 1973.

Tommy Helms — N.L. Rookie
Team: Reds. **Position:** Third base.
5-10, 175. **B:** R. **T:** R.
Born: May 5, 1941.
Season: .284 avg.; 9 HR; 49 RBIs.
Career: .269 avg.; 34 HR; 477 RBIs.
Teams: Reds 1964-71; Astros 1972-75; Pirates 1976-77; Red Sox 1977.

1967

Carl Yastrzemski — A.L. MVP
Team: Red Sox. **Position:** Outfield.
Season: .326 avg.; 44 HR; 121 RBIs; Triple Crown winner.
(See Hall of Fame section, 1989.)

Orlando Cepeda — N.L. MVP
Team: Cardinals. **Position:** First base.
Season: .325 avg.; 25 HR; 111 RBIs.
(See Hall of Fame section, 1999.)

Jim Lonborg — A.L. Cy Young
Team: Red Sox.
6-5, 210. **B:** R. **T:** R.
Born: April 16, 1942.
Season: 22-9; 3.16 ERA; 246 SO.
Career: 157-137; 3.86 ERA; 1,475 SO.
Teams: Red Sox 1965-71; Brewers 1972; Phillies 1973-79.

Mike McCormick — N.L. Cy Young
Team: Giants.
6-2, 195. **B:** L. **T:** L.
Born: Sept. 29, 1938.
Season: 22-10; 2.85 ERA; 150 SO.
Career: 134-128; 3.73 ERA; 1.321 SO.
Teams: Giants 1956-62, 1967-70; Orioles 1963-64; Senators 1965-66; Yankees 1970; Royals 1971.

Rod Carew — A.L. Rookie
Team: Twins. **Position:** Second base.
Season: .292 avg.; 8 HR; 51 RBIs.
(See Hall of Fame section, 1991.)

Tom Seaver — N.L. Rookie
Team: Mets. **Position:** Pitcher.
Season: 16-13; 2.76 ERA; 170 SO.
(See Hall of Fame section, 1992.)

1968

Denny McLain — A.L. MVP, Cy Young
Team: Tigers. **Position:** Pitcher.
6-1, 185. **B:** R. **T:** R.
Born: March 29, 1944.
Season: 31-6; 1.96 ERA; 280 SO.
Career: 131-91; 3.39 ERA; 1,282 SO.
Teams: Tigers 1963-70; Senators 1971; Athletics 1972; Braves 1972.

Bob Gibson — N.L. MVP, Cy Young
Team: Cardinals. **Position:** Pitcher.
Season: 22-9; 1.12 ERA; 268 SO.
(See Hall of Fame section, 1981.)

Stan Bahnsen — A.L. Rookie
Team: Yankees. **Position:** Pitcher.
6-2, 203. **B:** R. **T:** R.
Born: Dec. 15, 1944.
Season: 17-12; 2.05 ERA; 162 SO.
Career: 146-149; 3.60 ERA; 1,359 SO.
Teams: Yankees 1966, 1968-71; White Sox 1972-75; Athletics 1975-77; Expos 1977-81; Angels 1982; Phillies 1982.

Johnny Bench — N.L. Rookie
Team: Reds. **Position:** Catcher.
Season: .275 avg.; 15 HR; 82 RBIs.
(See Hall of Fame section, 1989.)

1969

Harmon Killebrew — A.L. MVP
Team: Twins. **Position:** First base, third base.
Season: .276 avg.; 49 HR; 140 RBIs.
(See Hall of Fame section, 1984.)

Willie McCovey — N.L. MVP
Team: Giants. **Position:** First base.
Season: .320 avg.; 45 HR; 126 RBIs.
(See Hall of Fame section, 1986.)

Denny McLain — A.L. co-Cy Young
Team: Tigers.
Season: 24-9; 2.80 ERA; 181 SO.
(See 1968 A.L. MVP.)

Mike Cuellar — A.L. co-Cy Young
Team: Orioles.
5-11, 175. **B:** L. **T:** L.
Born: May 8, 1937.
Season: 23-11; 2.38 ERA; 182 SO.
Career: 185-130; 3.14 ERA; 1,632 SO.
Teams: Reds 1959; Cardinals 1964; Astros 1965-68; Orioles 1969-76; Angels 1977.

Tom Seaver — N.L. Cy Young
Team: Mets.
Season: 25-7; 2.21 ERA; 208 SO.
(See Hall of Fame section, 1992.)

Lou Piniella — A.L. Rookie
Team: Royals. **Position:** Outfield.
6-2, 198. **B:** R. **T:** R.
Born: Aug. 28, 1943.
Season: .282 avg.; 11 HR; 68 RBIs.
Career: .291 avg.; 102 HR; 766 RBIs.
Teams: Orioles 1964; Indians 1968; Royals 1969-73; Yankees 1974-84.

Ted Sizemore — N.L. Rookie
Team: Dodgers. **Position:** Second base.
5-10, 165. **B:** R. **T:** R.
Born: April 15, 1945.
Season: .271 avg.; 4 HR; 46 RBIs.
Career: .262 avg.; 23 HR; 430 RBIs.
Teams: Dodgers 1969-70, 1976; Cardinals 1971-75; Phillies 1977-78; Cubs 1979; Red Sox 1979-80.

1970

Boog Powell — A.L. MVP
Team: Orioles. **Position:** First base.
6-4, 240. **B:** L. **T:** R.
Born: Aug. 17, 1941.
Season: .297 avg.; 35 HR; 114 RBIs.
Career: .266 avg.; 339 HR; 1,187 RBIs.
Teams: Orioles 1961-74; Indians 1975-76; Dodgers 1977.

Johnny Bench — N.L. MVP
Team: Reds. **Position:** Catcher.
Season: .293 avg.; 45 HR; 148 RBIs.
(See Hall of Fame section, 1989.)

Jim Perry — A.L. Cy Young
Team: Twins.
6-4, 200. **B:** B. **T:** R.
Born: Oct. 30, 1936.
Season: 24-12; 3.04 ERA; 168 SO.
Career: 215-174; 3.45 ERA; 1,576.
Teams: Indians 1959-63, 1974-75; Twins 1963-72; Tigers 1973; Athletics 1975.

Bob Gibson — N.L. Cy Young
Team: Cardinals.
Season: 23-7; 3.12 ERA; 274 SO.
(See Hall of Fame section, 1981.)

Thurman Munson — A.L. Rookie
Team: Yankees. **Position:** Catcher.
5-11, 190. **B:** R. **T:** R.
Born: June 7, 1947. **Died:** Aug. 2, 1979.
Season: .302 avg.; 6 HR; 53 RBIs.
Career: .292 avg.; 113 HR; 701 RBIs.
Team: Yankees 1969-79.

Cincinnati catcher Johnny Bench won the first of two N.L. MVP awards in 1970.

Carl Morton N.L. Rookie
Team: Expos. **Position:** Pitcher.
6-0, 200. **B:** R. **T:** R.
Born: Jan. 18, 1944. **Died:** April 12, 1983.
Season: 18-11; 3.60 ERA; 154 SO.
Career: 87-92; 3.73 ERA; 650 SO.
Teams: Expos 1969-72; Braves 1973-76.

1971

Vida Blue A.L. MVP, Cy Young
Team: Athletics. **Position:** Pitcher.
6-0, 189. **B:** B. **T:** L.
Born: July 28, 1949.
Season: 24-8; 1.82 ERA; 301 SO.
Career: 209-161; 3.27 ERA; 2,175 SO.
Teams: Athletics 1969-77; Giants 1978-81, 1985-86; Royals 1982-83.

Joe Torre N.L. MVP
Team: Cardinals. **Position:** Third base.
6-2, 212. **B:** R. **T:** R.
Born: July 18, 1940.
Season: .363 avg.; 24 HR; 137 RBIs.
Career: .297 avg.; 252 HR; 1,185 RBIs.
Teams: Braves 1960-68; Cardinals 1969-74; Mets 1975-77.

Ferguson Jenkins N.L. Cy Young
Team: Cubs.
Season: 24-13; 2.77 ERA; 263 SO.
(See Hall of Fame section, 1991.)

Chris Chambliss A.L. Rookie
Team: Indians. **Position:** First base.
6-1, 215. **B:** L. **T:** R.
Born: Dec. 26, 1948.
Season: .275 avg.; 9 HR; 48 RBIs.
Career: .279 avg.; 185 HR; 972 RBIs.
Teams: Indians 1971-74; Yankees 1974-79, 1988; Braves 1980-86.

Earl Williams N.L. Rookie
Team: Braves. **Position:** Catcher.
6-3, 220. **B:** R. **T:** R.
Born: July 14, 1948.
Season: .260 avg.; 33 HR; 87 RBIs.
Career: .247 avg.; 138 HR; 457 RBIs.
Teams: Braves 1970-72, 1975-76; Orioles 1973-74; Expos 1976; Athletics 1977.

1972

Dick Allen A.L. MVP
Team: White Sox. **Position:** First base.
Season: .308 avg.; 37 HR; 113 RBIs.
(See 1964 N.L. Rookie of Year.)

Johnny Bench N.L. MVP
Team: Reds. **Position:** Catcher.
Season: .270 avg.; 40 HR; 125 RBIs.
(See Hall of Fame section, 1989.)

Gaylord Perry A.L. Cy Young
Team: Indians.
Season: 24-16; 1.92 ERA; 234 SO.
(See Hall of Fame section, 1991.)

Steve Carlton N.L. Cy Young
Team: Phillies.
Season: 27-10; 1.97 ERA; 310 SO.
(See Hall of Fame section, 1994.)

Carlton Fisk A.L. Rookie
Team: Red Sox. **Position:** Catcher.
6-2, 220. **B:** R. **T:** R.
Born: Dec. 26, 1947.
Season: .293 avg.; 22 HR; 61 RBIs.
Career: .269 avg.; 376 HR; 1,330 RBIs.
Teams: Red Sox 1969, 1971-80; White Sox 1981-93.

Jon Matlack N.L. Rookie
Team: Mets. **Position:** Pitcher.
6-3, 205. **B:** L. **T:** L.
Born: Jan. 19, 1950.
Season: 15-10; 2.32 ERA; 169 SO.
Career: 125-126; 3.18 ERA; 1,516 SO.
Teams: Mets 1971-77; Rangers 1978-83.

1973

Reggie Jackson A.L. MVP
Team: Athletics. **Position:** Outfield.
Season: .293 avg.; 32 HR; 117 RBIs.
(See Hall of Fame section, 1993.)

Pete Rose N.L. MVP
Team: Reds. **Position:** Outfield.
Season: .338 avg.; 5 HR; 64 RBIs; 230 hits.
(See 1963 N.L. Rookie of Year.)

Jim Palmer A.L. Cy Young
Team: Orioles.
Season: 22-9; 2.40 ERA; 158 SO.
(See Hall of Fame section, 1990.)

Tom Seaver N.L. Cy Young
Team: Mets.
Season: 19-10; 2.08 ERA; 251 SO.
(See Hall of Fame section, 1992.)

Al Bumbry A.L. Rookie
Team: Orioles. **Position:** Outfield.
5-8, 175. **B:** L. **T:** R.
Born: April 21, 1947.
Season: .337 avg.; 7 HR; 34 RBIs; 23 SB.
Career: .281 avg.; 54 HR; 402 RBIs; 254 SB.
Teams: Orioles 1972-84; Padres 1985.

Gary Matthews N.L. Rookie
Team: Giants. **Position:** Outfield.
6-3, 190. **B:** R. **T:** R.
Born: July 5, 1950.
Season: .300 avg.; 12 HR; 58 RBIs.
Career: .281 avg.; 234 HR; 978 RBIs.
Teams: Giants 1972-76; Braves 1977-80; Phillies 1981-83; Cubs 1984-87; Mariners 1987.

1974

Jeff Burroughs A.L. MVP
Team: Rangers. **Position:** Outfield.
6-1, 200. **B:** R. **T:** R.
Born: March 7, 1951.
Season: .301 avg.; 25 HR; 118 RBIs.
Career: .261 avg.; 240 HR; 882 RBIs.
Teams: Senators 1970-71; Rangers 1972-76; Braves 1977-80; Mariners 1981; Athletics 1982-84; Blue Jays 1985.

Steve Garvey N.L. MVP
Team: Dodgers. **Position:** First base.
5-10, 192. **B:** R. **T:** R.
Born: Dec. 22, 1948.
Season: .312 avg.; 21 HR; 111 RBIs.
Career: .294 avg.; 272 HR; 1,308 RBIs.
Teams: Dodgers 1969-82; Padres 1983-87.

Jim (Catfish) Hunter A.L. Cy Young
Team: Athletics.
Season: 25-12; 2.49 ERA; 143 SO.
(See Hall of Fame section, 1987.)

Mike Marshall N.L. Cy Young
Team: Dodgers.
5-10, 180. **B:** R. **T:** R.
Born: Jan. 15, 1943.
Season: 15-12; 2.42 ERA; 143 SO; 21 saves; 106 games.
Career: 97-112; 3.14 ERA; 880 SO; 188 saves.
Teams: Tigers 1967; Mariners 1969; Astros 1970; Expos 1970-73; Dodgers 1974-76; Braves 1976-77; Rangers 1977; Twins 1978-80; Mets 1981.

Mike Hargrove A.L. Rookie
Team: Rangers. **Position:** First base.
6-0, 195. **B:** L. **T:** L.
Born: Oct. 26, 1949.
Season: .323 avg.; 4 HR; 66 RBIs.
Career: .290 avg.; 80 HR; 686 RBIs.
Teams: Rangers 1974-78; Padres 1979; Indians 1979-85.

Bake McBride N.L. Rookie
Team: Cardinals. **Position:** Outfield.
6-2, 190. **B:** L. **T:** R.
Born: Feb. 3, 1949.
Season: .309 avg.; 6 HR; 56 RBIs.
Career: .299 avg.; 63 HR; 430 RBIs.
Teams: Cardinals 1973-77; Phillies 1977-81; Indians 1982-83.

1975

Fred Lynn A.L. MVP, Rookie
Team: Red Sox. **Position:** Outfield.
6-1, 190. **B:** L. **T:** L.
Born: Feb. 3, 1952.
Season: .331 avg.; 21 HR; 105 RBIs.
Career: .283 avg.; 306 HR; 1,111 RBIs.
Teams: Red Sox 1974-80; Angels 1981-84; Orioles 1985-88; Tigers 1988-89; Padres 1990.

Joe Morgan N.L. MVP
Team: Reds. **Position:** Second base.
Season: .327 avg.; 17 HR; 94 RBIs; 67 SB.
(See Hall of Fame section, 1990.)

Jim Palmer A.L. Cy Young
Team: Orioles.
Season: 23-11; 2.09 ERA; 193 SO.
(See Hall of Fame section, 1990.)

Tom Seaver N.L. Cy Young
Team: Mets.
Season: 22-9; 2.38 ERA; 243 SO.
(See Hall of Fame section, 1992.)

John Montefusco N.L. Rookie
Team: Giants. **Position:** Pitcher.
6-1, 180. **B:** R. **T:** R.
Born: May 25, 1950.

Season: 15-9; 2.88 ERA; 215 SO.
Career: 90-83; 3.54 ERA; 1,081 SO.
Teams: Giants 1974-80; Braves 1981; Padres 1982-83; Yankees 1983-86.

1976

THURMAN MUNSON — **A.L. MVP**
Team: Yankees. **Position:** Catcher.
Season: .302 avg.; 17 HR; 105 RBIs.
(See 1970 A.L. Rookie of Year.)

JOE MORGAN — **N.L. MVP**
Team: Reds. **Position:** Second base.
Season: .320 avg.; 27 HR; 111 RBIs; 60 SB.
(See Hall of Fame section, 1990.)

JIM PALMER — **A.L. CY YOUNG**
Team: Orioles.
Season: 22-13; 2.51 ERA; 159 SO.
(See Hall of Fame section, 1990.)

RANDY JONES — **N.L. CY YOUNG**
Team: Padres.
6-0, 178. **B:** R. **T:** L.
Born: Jan. 12, 1950.
Season: 22-14; 2.74 ERA; 93 SO.
Career: 100-123; 3.42 ERA; 735 SO.
Teams: Padres 1973-80; Mets 1981-82.

MARK FIDRYCH — **A.L. ROOKIE**
Team: Tigers. **Position:** Pitcher.
6-3, 175. **B:** R. **T:** R.
Born: Aug. 14, 1954.
Season: 19-9; 2.34 ERA; 97 SO.
Career: 29-19; 3.10 ERA; 170 SO.
Team: Tigers 1976-80.

BUTCH METZGER — **N.L. CO-ROOKIE**
Team: Padres. **Position:** Pitcher.
6-1, 185. **B:** R. **T:** R.
Born: May 23, 1952.
Season: 11-4; 2.92 ERA; 89 SO.
Career: 18-9; 3.74 ERA; 175 SO.
Teams: Giants 1974; Padres 1975-77; Cardinals 1977; Mets 1978.

PAT ZACHRY — **N.L. CO-ROOKIE**
Team: Reds. **Position:** Pitcher.
6-5, 180. **B:** R. **T:** R.
Born: April 24, 1952.
Season: 14-7; 2.74 ERA; 143 SO.
Career: 69-67; 3.52 ERA; 669 SO.
Teams: Reds 1976-77; Mets 1977-82; Dodgers 1983-84; Phillies 1985.

1977

ROD CAREW — **A.L. MVP**
Team: Twins. **Position:** First base.
Season: .388 avg.; 14 HR; 100 RBIs; 239 hits.
(See Hall of Fame section, 1991.)

GEORGE FOSTER — **N.L. MVP**
Team: Reds. **Position:** Outfield.
6-1, 185. **B:** R. **T:** R.
Born: Dec. 1, 1948.
Season: .320 avg.; 52 HR; 149 RBIs.
Career: .274 avg.; 348 HR; 1,239 RBIs.
Teams: Giants 1969-71; Reds 1971-81; Mets 1982-86; White Sox 1986.

SPARKY LYLE — **A.L. CY YOUNG**
Team: Yankees.
6-1, 192. **B:** L. **T:** L.
Born: July 22, 1944.
Season: 13-5; 2.17 ERA; 68 SO; 26 saves.
Career: 99-76; 2.88 ERA; 873 SO; 238 saves.
Teams: Red Sox 1967-71; Yankees 1972-78; Rangers 1979-80; Phillies 1980-82; White Sox 1982.

STEVE CARLTON — **N.L. CY YOUNG**
Team: Phillies.
Season: 23-10; 2.64 ERA; 198 SO.
(See Hall of Fame section, 1994.)

EDDIE MURRAY — **A.L. ROOKIE**
Team: Orioles. **Position:** First base.
6-2, 200. **B:** B. **T:** R.
Born: Feb. 24, 1956.
Season: .283 avg.; 27 HR; 88 RBIs.
Career: .287 avg.; 504 HR; 1,917 RBIs.
Teams: Orioles 1977-88, 1996; Dodgers 1989-91, 1997; Mets 1992-93; Indians 1994-96; Angels 1997.

ANDRE DAWSON — **N.L. ROOKIE**
Team: Expos. **Position:** Outfield.
6-3, 195. **B:** R. **T:** R.
Born: July 10, 1954.
Season: .282 avg.; 19 HR; 65 RBIs.
Career: .279 avg.; 438 HR; 1,591 RBIs; still active.
Teams: Expos 1976-86; Cubs 1987-92; Red Sox 1993-94; Marlins 1995-96.

1978

JIM RICE — **A.L. MVP**
Team: Red Sox. **Position:** Outfield.
6-2, 205. **B:** R. **T:** R.
Born: March 8, 1953.
Season: .315 avg.; 46 HR; 139 RBIs.
Career: .298 avg.; 382 HR; 1,451 RBIs.
Team: Red Sox 1974-89.

DAVE PARKER — **N.L. MVP**
Team: Pirates. **Position:** Outfield.
6-5, 230. **B:** L. **T:** R.
Born: June 9, 1951.
Season: .334 avg.; 30 HR; 117 RBIs.
Career: .290 avg.; 339 HR; 1,493 RBIs.
Teams: Pirates 1973-83; Reds 1984-87; Athletics 1988-89; Brewers 1990; Angels 1991; Blue Jays 1991.

RON GUIDRY — **A.L. CY YOUNG**
Team: Yankees.
5-11, 161. **B:** L. **T:** L.
Born: Aug. 28, 1950.
Season: 25-3; 1.74 ERA; 248 SO.
Career: 170-91; 3.29 ERA; 1,778 SO.
Team: Yankees 1975-88.

GAYLORD PERRY — **N.L. CY YOUNG**
Team: Padres.
Season: 21-6; 2.73 ERA; 154 SO.
(See Hall of Fame section, 1991.)

LOU WHITAKER — **A.L. ROOKIE**
Team: Tigers. **Position:** Second base.
5-11, 160. **B:** L. **T:** R.
Born: May 12, 1957.
Season: .285 avg.; 3 HR; 58 RBIs.
Career: .276 avg.; 244 HR; 1,084 RBIs.
Team: Tigers 1977-95.

BOB HORNER — **N.L. ROOKIE**
Team: Braves. **Position:** Third base.
6-1, 210. **B:** R. **T:** R.
Born: Aug. 6, 1957.
Season: .266 avg.; 23 HR; 63 RBIs.
Career: .277 avg.; 218 HR; 685 RBIs.
Teams: Braves 1978-86; Cardinals 1988.

1979

DON BAYLOR — **A.L. MVP**
Team: Angels. **Position:** Outfield.
6-1, 200. **B:** R. **T:** R.
Born: June 28, 1949.
Season: .296 avg.; 36 HR; 139 RBIs.
Career: .260 avg.; 338 HR; 1,276 RBIs.

Pittsburgh first baseman Willie Stargell had to share N.L. MVP honors in 1979.

Teams: Orioles 1970-75; Athletics 1976, 1988; Angels 1977-82; Yankees 1983-85; Red Sox 1986-87; Twins 1987.

WILLIE STARGELL — **N.L. CO-MVP**
Team: Pirates. **Position:** First base.
Season: .281 avg.; 32 HR; 82 RBIs.
(See Hall of Fame section, 1988.)

KEITH HERNANDEZ — **N.L. CO-MVP**
Team: Cardinals. **Position:** First base.
6-0, 195. **B:** L. **T:** L.
Born: Oct. 20, 1953.
Season: .344 avg.; 11 HR; 105 RBIs.
Career: .296 avg.; 162 HR; 1,071 RBIs.
Teams: Cardinals 1974-83; Mets 1983-89; Indians 1990.

MIKE FLANAGAN — **A.L. CY YOUNG**
Team: Orioles.
6-0, 195. **B:** L. **T:** L.
Born: Dec. 16, 1951.
Season: 23-9; 3.08 ERA; 190 SO.
Career: 167-143; 3.90 ERA; 1,491 SO.
Teams: Orioles 1975-87, 1991-92; Blue Jays 1987-90.

BRUCE SUTTER — **N.L. CY YOUNG**
Team: Cubs.
6-2, 190. **B:** R. **T:** R.
Born: Jan. 8, 1953.
Season: 6-6; 2.22 ERA; 110 SO; 37 saves.
Career: 68-71; 2.83 ERA; 861 SO; 300 saves.
Teams: Cubs 1976-80; Cardinals 1981-84; Braves 1985-88.

JOHN CASTINO — **A.L. CO-ROOKIE**
Team: Twins. **Position:** Third base.
5-11, 175. **B:** R. **T:** R.
Born: Oct. 23, 1954.
Season: .285 avg.; 5 HR; 52 RBIs.
Career: .278 avg.; 41 HR; 249 RBIs.
Team: Twins 1979-84.

ALFREDO GRIFFIN — **A.L. CO-ROOKIE**
Team: Blue Jays. **Position:** Shortstop.
5-11, 165. **B:** B. **T:** R.
Born: Oct. 6, 1957.
Season: .287 avg.; 2 HR; 31 RBIs; 21 SB.
Career: .249 avg.; 24 HR; 527 RBIs.
Teams: Indians 1976-78; Blue Jays 1979-84, 1992-93; Athletics 1985-87; Dodgers 1988-91.

RICK SUTCLIFFE — **N.L. ROOKIE**
Team: Dodgers. **Position:** Pitcher.
6-7, 220. **B:** L. **T:** R.

Atlanta outfielder Dale Murphy won consecutive MVP awards in 1982 and '83.

Born: June 21, 1956.
Season: 17-10; 3.46 ERA; 117 SO.
Career: 171-139; 4.08 ERA; 1,679 SO.
Teams: Dodgers 1976, 1978-81; Indians 1982-84; Cubs 1984-91; Orioles 1992-93; Cardinals 1994.

WHO'S WHO

1980

George Brett — A.L. MVP
Team: Royals. **Position:** Third base.
Season: .390 avg.; 24 HR; 118 RBIs.
(See Hall of Fame section, 1999.)

Mike Schmidt — N.L. MVP
Team: Phillies. **Position:** Third base.
Season: .286 avg.; 48 HR; 121 RBIs.
(See Hall of Fame section, 1995.)

Steve Stone — A.L. Cy Young
Team: Orioles.
5-10, 175. **B:** R. **T:** R.
Born: July 14, 1947.
Season: 25-7; 3.23 ERA; 149 SO.
Career: 107-93; 3.97 ERA; 1,065 SO.
Teams: Giants 1971-72; White Sox 1973, 1977-78; Cubs 1974-76; Orioles 1979-81.

Steve Carlton — N.L. Cy Young
Team: Phillies.
Season: 24-9; 2.34 ERA; 286 SO.
(See Hall of Fame section, 1994.)

Joe Charboneau — A.L. Rookie
Team: Indians. **Position:** Outfield.
6-2, 205. **B:** R. **T:** R.
Born: June 17, 1955.
Season: .289 avg.; 23 HR; 87 RBIs.
Career: .266 avg.; 29 HR; 114 RBIs.
Team: Indians 1980-82.

Steve Howe — N.L. Rookie
Team: Dodgers. **Position:** Pitcher.
6-1, 180. **B:** L. **T:** L.
Born: March 10, 1958.
Season: 7-9; 2.66 ERA; 39 SO; 17 saves.
Career: 47-41; 3.03 ERA; 328 SO; 91 saves.
Teams: Dodgers 1980-83, 1985; Twins 1985; Rangers 1987; Yankees 1991-95.

1981

Rollie Fingers — A.L. MVP, Cy Young
Team: Brewers. **Position:** Pitcher.
Season: 6-3; 1.04 ERA; 61 SO; 28 saves.
(See Hall of Fame section, 1992.)

Mike Schmidt — N.L. MVP
Team: Phillies. **Position:** Third base.
Season: .316 avg.; 31 HR; 91 RBIs.
(See Hall of Fame section, 1995.)

Fernando Valenzuela — N.L. Rookie, Cy Young
Team: Dodgers.
5-11, 195. **B:** L. **T:** L.
Born: Nov. 1, 1960.
Season: 13-7; 2.48 ERA; 180 SO.
Career: 173-153; 3.54 ERA; 2,074 SO.
Teams: Dodgers 1980-90; Angels 1991; Orioles 1993; Phillies 1994; Padres 1995-97; Cardinals 1997.

Dave Righetti — A.L. Rookie
Team: Yankees. **Position:** Pitcher.
6-3, 205. **B:** L. **T:** L.
Born: Nov. 28, 1958.
Season: 8-4; 2.05 ERA; 89 SO.
Career: 82-79; 3.46 ERA; 1,112 SO.
Teams: Yankees 1979, 1981-90; Giants 1991-93; Athletics 1994; White Sox 1995.

1982

Robin Yount — A.L. MVP
Team: Brewers. **Position:** Shortstop.
Season: .331 avg.; 29 HR; 114 RBIs.
(See Hall of Fame section, 1999.)

Dale Murphy — N.L. MVP
Team: Braves. **Position:** Outfield.
6-4, 215. **B:** R. **T:** R.
Born: March 12, 1956.
Season: .281 avg; 36 HR; 109 RBIs.
Career: .265 avg.; 398 HR; 1,266 RBIs.
Teams: Braves 1976-90; Phillies 1990-92; Rockies 1993.

Pete Vuckovich — A.L. Cy Young
Team: Brewers.
6-4, 220. **B:** R. **T:** R.
Born: Oct. 27, 1952.
Season: 18-6; 3.34 ERA; 105 SO.
Career: 93-69; 3.66 ERA; 882 SO.
Teams: White Sox 1975-76; Blue Jays 1977; Cardinals 1978-80; Brewers 1981-83, 1985-86.

Steve Carlton — N.L. Cy Young
Team: Phillies.
Season: 23-11; 3.10 ERA; 286 SO.
(See Hall of Fame section, 1994.)

Cal Ripken — A.L. Rookie
Team: Orioles. **Position:** Shortstop, third base.
6-4, 220. **B:** R. **T:** R.
Born: Aug. 24, 1960.
Season: .264 avg.; 28 HR; 93 RBIs.
Career: .276 avg.; 431 HR; 1,695 RBI.
Team: Orioles 1981-2001.

Steve Sax — N.L. Rookie
Team: Dodgers. **Position:** Second base.
5-11, 185. **B:** R. **T:** R.
Born: Jan. 29, 1960.
Season: .282 avg.; 4 HR; 47 RBIs; 49 SB.
Career: .281 avg.; 54 HR; 550 RBIs; 444 SB.
Teams: Dodgers 1981-88; Yankees 1989-91; White Sox 1992-93; Athletics 1994.

1983

Cal Ripken — A.L. MVP
Team: Orioles. **Position:** Shortstop.
Season: .318 avg.; 27 HR; 102 RBIs.
(See 1982 A.L. Rookie.)

Dale Murphy — N.L. MVP
Team: Braves. **Position:** Outfield.
Season: .302 avg.; 36 HR; 121 RBIs.
(See 1982 N.L. MVP.)

LaMarr Hoyt — A.L. Cy Young
Team: White Sox.
6-1, 222. **B:** R. **T:** R.
Born: Jan. 1, 1955.
Season: 24-10; 3.66 ERA; 148 SO.
Career: 98-68; 3.99 ERA; 681 SO.
Teams: White Sox 1979-84; Padres 1985-86.

John Denny — N.L. Cy Young
Team: Phillies.
6-3, 190. **B:** R. **T:** R.
Born: Nov. 8, 1952.
Season: 19-6; 2.37 ERA; 139 SO.
Career: 123-108; 3.59 ERA; 1,146 SO.
Teams: Cardinals 1974-79; Indians 1980-82; Phillies 1982-85; Reds 1986.

Ron Kittle — A.L. Rookie
Team: White Sox. **Position:** Outfield.
6-4, 220. **B:** R. **T:** R.
Born: Jan. 5, 1958.
Season: .254 avg.; 35 HR; 100 RBIs.
Career: .239 avg.; 176 HR; 460 RBIs.
Teams: White Sox 1982-86, 1989-91; Yankees 1986-87; Indians 1988; Orioles 1990.

Darryl Strawberry — N.L. Rookie
Team: Mets. **Position:** Outfield.
6-6, 200. **B:** L. **T:** L.
Born: March 12, 1962.
Season: .257 avg.; 26 HR; 74 RBIs.
Career: .259 avg.; 335 HR; 1,000 RBIs.
Teams: Mets 1983-90; Dodgers 1991-93; Giants 1994; Yankees 1995-99.

1984

Willie Hernandez — **A.L. MVP, Cy Young**

Team: Tigers. **Position:** Pitcher.
6-3, 180. **B:** L. **T:** L.
Born: Nov. 14, 1954.
Season: 9-3; 1.92 ERA; 112 SO; 32 saves.
Career: 70-63; 3.38 ERA; 788 SO; 147 saves.
Teams: Cubs 1977-83; Phillies 1983; Tigers 1984-89.

Ryne Sandberg — **N.L. MVP**

Team: Cubs. **Position:** Second base.
6-2, 180. **B:** R. **T:** R.
Born: Sept. 18, 1959.
Season: .314 avg.; 19 HR; 84 RBIs.
Career: .285 avg.; 282 HR; 1,061 RBIs.
Teams: Phillies 1981; Cubs 1982-94, 1996-97.

Rick Sutcliffe — **N.L. Cy Young**

Team: Cubs.
Season: 16-1; 2.69 ERA; 155 SO.
(See 1979 N.L. Rookie of Year.)

Alvin Davis — **A.L. Rookie**

Team: Mariners. **Position:** First base.
6-1, 195. **B:** L. **T:** R.
Born: Sept. 9, 1960.
Season: .284 avg.; 27 HR; 116 RBIs.
Career: .280 avg.; 160 HR; 683 RBIs.
Team: Mariners 1984-91; Angels 1992.

Dwight Gooden — **N.L. Rookie**

Team: Mets. **Position:** Pitcher.
6-3, 210. **B:** R. **T:** R.
Born: Nov. 16, 1964.
Season: 17-9; 2.60 ERA; 276 SO.
Career: 188-107; 3.46 ERA; 2,238 SO.
Team: Mets 1984-94; Yankees 1996-97, 2000; Indians 1998-99, Astros 2000, Devil Rays 2000.

1985

Don Mattingly — **A.L. MVP**

Team: Yankees. **Position:** First base.
6-0, 185. **B:** L. **T:** L.
Born: April 20, 1961.
Season: .324 avg.; 35 HR; 145 RBIs.
Career: .307 avg.; 222 HR; 1,099 RBIs.
Team: Yankees 1982-95.

Willie McGee — **N.L. MVP**

Team: Cardinals. **Position:** Outfield.
6-1, 185. **B:** B. **T:** R.
Born: Nov. 2, 1958.
Season: .353 avg.; 10 HR; 82 RBIs; 216 hits; 56 SB.
Career: .295 avg.; 79 HR; 856 RBIs; 352 SB.
Teams: Cardinals 1982-90, 1996-99; Athletics 1990; Giants 1991-94; Red Sox 1995.

Bret Saberhagen — **A.L. Cy Young**

Team: Royals.
6-1, 200. **B:** R. **T:** R.
Born: April 11, 1964.
Season: 20-6; 2.87 ERA; 158 SO.
Career: 167-1175; 3.34 ERA; 1,715 SO.
Teams: Royals 1984-91; Mets 1992-95; Rockies 1995-96; Red Sox 1997-99, 2001.

Dwight Gooden — **N.L. Cy Young**

Team: Mets.
Season: 24-4; 1.53 ERA; 268 SO.
(See 1984 N.L. Rookie of Year.)

Ozzie Guillen — **A.L. Rookie**

Team: White Sox. **Position:** Shortstop.
5-11, 160. **B:** L. **T:** R.
Born: Jan. 20, 1964.
Season: .273 avg.; 1 HR; 33 RBIs.
Career: .264 avg.; 28 HR; 619 RBIs.
Team: White Sox 1985-97; Orioles 1998; Braves 1998-99, Devil Rays 2000.

Willie McGee's .353 average, 56 stolen bases and outstanding defense in center field for the '85 pennant-winning Cardinals won him the N.L. MVP award.

Vince Coleman — **N.L. Rookie**

Team: Cardinals. **Position:** Outfield
6-0, 170. **B:** B. **T:** R.
Born: Sept. 22, 1961.
Season: .267 avg.; 1 HR; 40 RBIs; 110 SB.
Career: .264 avg.; 28 HR; 346 RBIs; 752 SB.
Teams: Cardinals 1985-90; Mets 1991-93; Royals 1994-95; Mariners 1995; Reds 1996; Tigers 1997.

1986

Roger Clemens — **A.L. MVP, Cy Young**

Team: Red Sox. **Position:** Pitcher.
6-4, 235. **B:** R. **T:** R.
Born: Aug. 4, 1962.
Season: 24-4; 2.48 ERA; 238 SO.
Career: 293-151; 3.15 ERA; 3,909 SO; still active.
Team: Red Sox 1984-96; Blue Jays 1997-98; Yankees 1999-2002.

Mike Schmidt — **N.L. MVP**

Team: Phillies. **Position:** Third base.
Season: .290 avg.; 37 HR; 119 RBIs.
(See Hall of Fame section, 1995.)

Mike Scott — **N.L. Cy Young**

Team: Astros.
6-3, 215. **B:** R. **T:** R.
Born: April 26, 1955.
Season: 18-10; 2.22 ERA; 306 SO.
Career: 124-108; 3.54 ERA; 1,469 SO.
Teams: Mets 1979-82; Astros 1983-91.

Jose Canseco — **A.L. Rookie**

Team: Athletics. **Position:** Outfield.
6-4, 240. **B:** R. **T:** R.
Born: July 2, 1964.
Season: .240 avg.; 33 HR; 117 RBIs.
Career: .266 avg.; 462 HR; 1,407 RBIs.
Teams: Athletics 1985-92, 1997; Rangers 1992-94; Red Sox 1995-96; Blue Jays 1998; Devil Rays 1999-2000, Yankees 2000, White Sox 2001.

Todd Worrell — **N.L. Rookie**

Team: Cardinals. **Position:** Pitcher.
6-5, 215. **B:** R. **T:** R.
Born: Sept. 28, 1959.
Season: 9-10; 2.08 ERA; 73 SO; 36 saves.
Career: 50-52; 3.09 ERA; 628 SO; 256 saves.
Teams: Cardinals 1985-89, 1992; Dodgers 1993-97.

1987

George Bell — **A.L. MVP**

Team: Blue Jays. **Position:** Outfield.
6-1, 200. **B:** R. **T:** R.
Born: Oct. 21, 1959.
Season: .308 avg.; 47 HR; 134 RBIs.
Career: .278 avg.; 265 HR; 1,002 RBIs.
Teams: Blue Jays 1981, 1983-90; Cubs 1991; White Sox 1992-93.

Andre Dawson — **N.L. MVP**

Team: Cubs. **Position:** Outfield.
Season: .287 avg.; 49 HR; 137 RBIs.
(See 1977 N.L. Rookie of Year.)

Roger Clemens — **A.L. Cy Young**

Team: Red Sox.
Season: 20-9; 2.97 ERA; 256 SO.
(See 1986 A.L. MVP.)

Steve Bedrosian — **N.L. Cy Young**

Team: Phillies.

Red Sox ace Roger Clemens won the first of six Cy Youngs in 1986.

6-3, 200. **B:** R. **T:** R.
Born: Dec. 6, 1957.
Season: 5-3; 2.83 ERA; 74 SO; 40 saves.
Career: 76-79; 3.38 ERA; 921 SO; 184 saves.
Teams: Braves 1981-85, 1993-95; Phillies 1986-89; Giants 1989-90; Twins 1991.

MARK MCGWIRE A.L. ROOKIE
Team: Athletics. **Position:** First base.
6-5, 250. **B:** R. **T:** R.
Born: Oct. 1, 1963.
Season: .289 avg.; 49 HR; 118 RBIs.
Career: .263 avg.; 583 HR; 1,414 RBIs.
Team: Athletics 1986-97; Cardinals 1997-2001.

BENITO SANTIAGO N.L. ROOKIE
Team: Padres. **Position:** Catcher.
6-1, 200. **B:** R. **T:** R.
Born: March 9, 1965.
Season: .300 avg.; 18 HR; 79 RBIs.
Career: .262 avg.; 200 HR; 841 RBIs; still active.
Teams: Padres 1986-92; Marlins 1993-94; Reds 1995, 2000; Phillies 1996; Blue Jays 1997-98; Cubs 1999, Giants 2001-02.

1988

JOSE CANSECO A.L. MVP
Team: Athletics. **Position:** Outfield.
Season: .307 avg.; 42 HR; 124 RBIs; 40 SB.
(See 1986 A.L. Rookie of Year.)

KIRK GIBSON N.L. MVP
Team: Dodgers. **Position:** Outfield.
6-3, 215. **B:** L. **T:** L.
Born: May 28, 1957.
Season: .290 avg.; 25 HR; 76 RBIs; 31 SB.
Career: .268 avg.; 255 HR; 870 RBIs.
Teams: Tigers 1979-87, 1993-95; Dodgers 1988-90; Royals 1991; Pirates 1992.

FRANK VIOLA A.L. CY YOUNG
Team: Twins.
6-4, 210. **B:** L. **T:** L.
Born: April 19, 1960.
Season: 24-7; 2.64 ERA; 193 SO.
Career: 176-150; 3.73 ERA; 1,844 SO.
Teams: Twins 1982-89; Mets 1989-91; Red Sox 1992-94; Reds 1995; Blue Jays 1996.

OREL HERSHISER N.L. CY YOUNG
Team: Dodgers.
6-3, 195. **B:** R. **T:** R.
Born: Sept. 16, 1958.
Season: 23-8; 2.26 ERA; 178 SO.
Career: 204-150; 3.48 ERA; 2,014 SO.
Team: Dodgers 1983-94, 2000; Indians 1995-97; Giants 1998; Mets 1999.

WALT WEISS A.L. ROOKIE
Team: Athletics. **Position:** Shortstop.
6-0, 188. **B:** B. **T:** R.
Born: Nov. 28, 1963.
Season: .250 avg.; 3 HR; 39 RBIs.
Career: .258 avg.; 25 HR; 386 RBIs.
Teams: Athletics 1987-92; Marlins 1993; Rockies 1994-97, Braves 1998-2000.

CHRIS SABO N.L. ROOKIE
Team: Reds. **Position:** Third base.
5-11, 185. **B:** R. **T:** R.
Born: Jan. 19, 1962.
Season: .271 avg.; 11 HR; 44 RBIs; 46 SB.
Career: .268 avg.; 116 HR; 426 RBIs; 120 SB.
Teams: Reds 1988-93, 1996; Orioles 1994; White Sox 1995; Cardinals 1995.

1989

ROBIN YOUNT A.L. MVP
Team: Brewers. **Position:** Outfield.
Season: .318 avg.; 21 HR; 103 RBIs.
(See Hall of Fame section, 1999.)

KEVIN MITCHELL N.L. MVP
Team: Giants. **Position:** Outfield.
5-11, 220. **B:** R. **T:** R.
Born: Jan. 13, 1962.
Season: .291 avg.; 47 HR; 125 RBIs.
Career: .284 avg.; 234 HR; 760 RBIs.
Teams: Mets 1984, 1986; Padres 1987; Giants 1987-91; Mariners 1992; Reds 1993-94, 1996; Red Sox 1996; Indians 1997; Athletics 1998.

BRET SABERHAGEN A.L. CY YOUNG
Team: Royals.
Season: 23-6, 2.16 ERA; 193 SO.
(See 1985 A.L. Cy Young.)

MARK DAVIS N.L. CY YOUNG
Team: Padres.
6-4, 205. **B:** L. **T:** L.
Born: Oct. 19, 1960.
Season: 4-3; 1.85 ERA; 92 SO; 44 saves.
Career: 51-84; 4.15 ERA; 993 SO; 96 saves.
Teams: Phillies 1980-81; Giants 1983-87; Padres 1987-89, 1993-94; Royals 1990-92; Braves 1992; Phillies 1993.

GREGG OLSON A.L. ROOKIE
Team: Orioles. **Position:** Pitcher.
6-4, 208. **B:** R. **T:** R.
Born: Oct. 11, 1966.
Season: 5-2; 1.69 ERA; 90 SO; 27 saves.
Career: 40-38; 3.28 ERA; 564 SO; 217 saves.
Teams: Orioles 1988-93; Braves 1994; Indians 1995; Royals 1995, 1997; Tigers 1996; Astros 1996; Twins 1997; Diamondbacks 1998-99, Dodgers 2000.

JEROME WALTON N.L. ROOKIE
Team: Cubs. **Position:** Outfield.
6-1, 200. **B:** R. **T:** R.
Born: July 8, 1965.
Season: .293 avg.; 5 HR; 46 RBIs; 24 SB.
Career: .269 avg.; 25 HR; 132 RBIs.
Teams: Cubs 1989-92; Angels 1993; Reds 1994-95; Braves 1996; Orioles 1997, Devil Rays 1998.

1990

RICKEY HENDERSON A.L. MVP
Team: Athletics. **Position:** Outfield.
5-10, 190. **B:** R. **T:** L.
Born: Dec. 25, 1958.
Season: .325 avg.; 28 HR; 61 RBIs; 65 SB.
Career: .279 avg.; 295 HR; 1,110 RBIs; 1,403 SB; still active.
Teams: Athletics 1979-84, 1989-93, 1994-95, 1998; Yankees 1985-89; Blue Jays 1993; Padres 1996-97, 2001; Angels 1997; Mets 1999-2000, Mariners 2000, Red Sox 2002.

BARRY BONDS N.L. MVP
Team: Pirates. **Position:** Outfield.
6-2, 228. **B:** L. **T:** L.
Born: July 24, 1964.
Season: .301 avg.; 33 HR; 114 RBIs; 52 SB.
Career: .295 avg.; 613 HR; 1,652 RBIs; 493 SB; still active.
Teams: Pirates 1986-92; Giants 1993-2002.

BOB WELCH A.L. CY YOUNG
Team: Athletics.
6-3, 190. **B:** R. **T:** R.
Born: Nov. 3, 1956.
Season: 27-6; 2.95 ERA; 127 SO.
Career: 211-146; 3.47 ERA; 1,969 SO.
Teams: Dodgers 1978-87; Athletics 1988-94.

DOUG DRABEK N.L. CY YOUNG
Team: Pirates.
6-1, 185. **B:** R. **T:** R.
Born: July 25, 1962.
Season: 22-6; 2.76 ERA; 131 SO.
Career: 155-134; 3.73 ERA; 1,594 SO.
Teams: Yankees 1986; Pirates 1987-92; Astros 1993-96; White Sox 1997; Orioles 1998.

SANDY ALOMAR JR. A.L. ROOKIE
Team: Indians. **Position:** Catcher.
6-5, 235. **B:** R. **T:** R.
Born: June 18, 1966.
Season: .290 avg.; 9 HR; 66 RBIs.
Career: .275 avg.; 104 HR; 517 RBIs; still active.
Teams: Padres 1988-89; Indians 1990-2000, White Sox 2001-02, Rockies 2002.

DAVID JUSTICE N.L. ROOKIE
Team: Braves. **Position:** Outfield.
6-3, 215. **B:** L. **T:** L.
Born: April 14, 1966.
Season: .282 avg.; 28 HR; 78 RBIs.
Career: .279 avg.; 305 HR; 1,017 RBIs; still active.
Team: Braves 1989-96; Indians 1997-2000, Yankees 2000-01, Athletics 2002.

1991

CAL RIPKEN A.L. MVP
Team: Orioles. **Position:** Shortstop.
Season: .323 avg.; 34 HR; 114 RBIs.
(See 1982 A.L. Rookie of Year.)

TERRY PENDLETON N.L. MVP
Team: Braves. **Position:** Third base.
5-9, 190. **B:** B. **T:** R.
Born: July 16, 1960.
Season: .319 avg.; 22 HR; 86 RBIs.
Career: .270 avg.; 140 HR; 946 RBIs.
Teams: Cardinals 1984-90; Braves 1991-94, 1996; Marlins 1995-96; Reds 1997; Royals 1998.

ROGER CLEMENS A.L. CY YOUNG
Team: Red Sox.
Season: 18-10; 2.62 ERA; 241 SO.
(See 1986 A.L. MVP.)

Tom Glavine **N.L. Cy Young**
Team: Braves.
6-0, 185. **B:** L. **T:** L.
Born: March 25, 1966.
Season: 20-11; 2.55 ERA; 192 SO.
Career: 242-143; 3.37 ERA; 2,054 SO; still active.
Team: Braves 1987-2002.

Chuck Knoblauch **A.L. Rookie**
Team: Twins. **Position:** Second base.
5-9, 175. **B:** R. **T:** R.
Born: July 7, 1968.
Season: .281 avg.; 1 HR; 50 RBIs; 25 SB.
Career: .289 avg.; 98 HR; 615 RBIs; 407 SB; still active.
Team: Twins 1991-97; Yankees 1998-2001, Royals 2002.

Jeff Bagwell **N.L. Rookie**
Team: Astros. **Position:** First base.
6-0, 215. **B:** R. **T:** R.
Born: May 27, 1968.
Season: .294 avg.; 15 HR; 82 RBIs.
Career: .302 avg.; 380 HR; 1,321 RBIs; still active.
Team: Astros 1991-2002.

1992

Dennis Eckersley **A.L. MVP, Cy Young**
Team: Athletics. **Position:** Pitcher.
6-2, 195. **B:** R. **T:** R.
Born: Oct. 3, 1954.
Season: 7-1; 1.91 ERA; 93 SO; 51 saves.
Career: 197-171; 3.50 ERA; 2,401 SO; 390 saves.
Teams: Indians 1975-77; Red Sox 1978-84, 1998; Cubs 1984-86; Athletics 1987-95; Cardinals 1996-97.

Barry Bonds **N.L. MVP**
Team: Pirates. **Position:** Outfield.
Season: .311 avg.; 34 HR; 103 RBIs; 39 SB.
(See 1990 N.L. MVP.)

Greg Maddux **N.L. Cy Young**
Team: Cubs.
6-0, 185. **B:** R. **T:** R.
Born: April 14, 1966.
Season: 20-11; 2.18 ERA; 199 SO.
Career: 273-152; 2.83 ERA; 2,641 SO; still active.
Teams: Cubs 1986-92; Braves 1993-2002.

Pat Listach **A.L. Rookie**
Team: Brewers. **Position:** Shortstop.
5-9, 180. **B:** B. **T:** R.
Born: Sept. 12, 1967.
Season: .290 avg.; 1 HR; 47 RBIs; 54 SB.
Career: .251 avg.; 5 HR; 143 RBIs; 116 SB.
Team: Brewers 1992-96; Astros 1997.

Eric Karros **N.L. Rookie**
Team: Dodgers. **Position:** First base.
6-4, 226. **B:** R. **T:** R.
Born: Nov. 4, 1967.
Season: .257 avg.; 20 HR; 88 RBIs.
Career: .268 avg.; 270 HR; 976 RBIs; still active.
Team: Dodgers 1991-2002.

1993

Frank Thomas **A.L. MVP**
Team: White Sox. **Position:** First base.
6-5, 275. **B:** R. **T:** R.
Born: May 27, 1968.
Season: .317 avg.; 41 HR; 128 RBIs.
Career: .314 avg.; 376 HR; 1,285 RBIs; still active.
Team: White Sox 1990-2002.

Arizona's Randy Johnson overpowered hitters in his first full season in the National League. He struck out 364 hitters, recorded a 2.48 ERA and brought home his second Cy Young Award in 1999.

Barry Bonds **N.L. MVP**
Team: Giants. **Position:** Outfield.
Season: .336 avg.; 46 HR; 123 RBIs; 29 SB.
(See 1990 N.L. MVP.)

Jack McDowell **A.L. Cy Young**
Team: White Sox.
6-5, 190. **B:** R. **T:** R.
Born: Jan. 16, 1966.
Season: 22-10; 3.37 ERA; 158 SO.
Career: 127-87; 3.85 ERA; 1,311 SO.
Teams: White Sox 1987-88, 1990-94; Yankees 1995; Indians 1996-97; Angels 1998-99.

Greg Maddux **N.L. Cy Young**
Team: Braves.
Season: 20-10; 2.36 ERA; 197 SO.
(See 1992 N.L. Cy Young.)

Tim Salmon **A.L. Rookie**
Team: Angels. **Position:** Outfield.
6-3, 225. **B:** R. **T:** R.
Born: Aug. 24, 1968.
Season: .283 avg.; 31 HR; 95 RBIs.
Career: .285 avg.; 269 HR; 894 RBIs; still active.
Team: Angels 1992-2002.

Mike Piazza **N.L. Rookie**
Team: Dodgers. **Position:** Catcher.
6-3, 215. **B:** R. **T:** R.
Born: Sept. 4, 1968.
Season: .318 avg.; 35 HR; 112 RBIs.
Career: .321 avg.; 347 HR; 1,073 RBIs; still active.
Team: Dodgers 1992-98; Marlins 1998; Mets 1998-2002.

1994

Frank Thomas **A.L. MVP**
Team: White Sox. **Position:** First base.
Season: .353 avg.; 38 HR; 101 RBIs.
(See 1993 A.L. MVP.)

Jeff Bagwell **N.L. MVP**
Team: Astros. **Position:** First base.
Season: .368 avg.; 39 HR; 116 RBIs.
(See 1991 N.L. Rookie of Year.)

David Cone **A.L. Cy Young**
Team: Royals.
6-1, 200. **B:** L. **T:** R.
Born: Jan. 2, 1963.
Season: 16-5; 2.94 ERA; 132 SO.
Career: 193-123; 3.44 ERA; 2,655 SO.
Teams: Royals 1986, 1993-94; Mets 1987-92; Blue Jays 1992, 1995; Yankees 1995-2000, Red Sox 2001.

Greg Maddux **N.L. Cy Young**
Team: Braves.
Season: 16-6; 1.56 ERA; 156 SO.
(See 1992 N.L. Cy Young.)

Bob Hamelin **A.L. Rookie**
Team: Royals. **Position:** Designated hitter.
6-0, 235. **B:** L. **T:** L.
Born: Nov. 29, 1967.
Season: .282 avg.; 24 HR; 65 RBIs.
Career: .246 avg.; 67 HR; 209 RBIs.
Team: Royals 1993-96; Tigers 1997; Brewers 1998.

Raul Mondesi **N.L. Rookie**
Team: Dodgers. **Position:** Outfield.
5-11, 230. **B:** R. **T:** R.
Born: March 12, 1971.
Season: .306 avg.; 16 HR; 56 RBIs.
Career: .276 avg.; 240 HR; 757 RBIs; still active.
Team: Dodgers 1993-99, Blue Jays 2000-02, Yankees 2002.

1995

Mo Vaughn **A.L. MVP**
Team: Red Sox. **Position:** First base.
6-1, 275. **B:** L. **T:** R.

Boston Red Sox shortstop Nomar Garciaparra.

Born: Dec. 15, 1967.
Season: .300 avg.; 39 HR; 126 RBIs.
Career: .294 avg.; 325 HR; 1,049 RBIs; still active.
Team: Red Sox 1991-98; Angels 1999-2001, Mets 2002.

BARRY LARKIN N.L. MVP
Team: Reds. **Position:** Shortstop.
6-0, 185. **B:** R. **T:** R.
Born: April 28, 1964.
Season: .319 avg.; 15 HR; 66 RBIs; 51 SBs.
Career: .296 avg.; 188 HR; 898 RBIs; 375 SBs; still active.
Team: Reds 1986-2002.

RANDY JOHNSON A.L. CY YOUNG
Team: Mariners.
6-10, 232. **B:** R. **T:** L.
Born: Sept. 10, 1963
Season: 18-2; 2.48 ERA; 294 SO.
Career: 224-106; 3.06 ERA; 3,746 SO; still active.
Teams: Expos 1988-89; Mariners 1989-98; Astros 1998; Diamondbacks 1999-2002.

GREG MADDUX N.L. CY YOUNG
Team: Braves.
Season: 19-2; 1.63 ERA; 181 SO.
(See 1992 N.L. Cy Young.)

MARTY CORDOVA A.L. ROOKIE
Team: Twins. **Position:** Outfield.
6-0, 206. **B:** R. **T:** R.
Born: July 10, 1969.
Season: .277 avg.; 24 HR; 84 RBIs.
Career: .276 avg.; 105 HR; 487 RBIs; still active.
Team: Twins 1995-99, Blue Jays 2000, Indians 2001, Orioles 2002.

HIDEO NOMO N.L. ROOKIE
Team: Dodgers. **Position:** Pitcher.
6-2, 210. **B:** R. **T:** R.
Born: Aug. 31, 1968.
Season: 13-6; 2.54 ERA; 236 SO.
Career: 61-49; 3.82 ERA; 1,031 SO; still active.
Team: Dodgers 1995-98, 2002; Mets 1998; Brewers 1999, Tigers 2000, Red Sox 2001.

1996

JUAN GONZALEZ A.L. MVP
Team: Rangers. **Position:** Outfield.
6-3, 220 **B:** R. **T:** R.
Born: Oct. 16, 1969.
1996 season: .314 avg.; 47 HR; 144 RBIs.
Career: .296 avg.; 405 HR; 1,317 RBIs; still active.
Teams: Rangers 1989-99, 2002, Tigers 2000, Indians 2001.

KEN CAMINITI N.L. MVP
Team: Padres. **Position:** Third base.
6-0, 200. **B:** B. **T:** R.
Born: April 21, 1963.
Season: .326 avg.; 40 HR; 130 RBIs.
Career: .272 avg.; 239 HR; 983 RBIs; still active.
Teams: Astros 1987-94, 1999-2000; Padres 1995-98, Rangers 2001, Braves 2001.

PAT HENTGEN A.L. CY YOUNG
Team: Blue Jays.
6-2, 195. **B:** R. **T:** R.
Born: Nov. 13, 1968
Season: 20-10; 3.22 ERA; 177 SO.
Career: 122-95; 4.22 ERA; 1,157 SO; still active.
Teams: Blue Jays 1991-99, Cardinals 2000, Orioles 2001-02.

JOHN SMOLTZ N.L. CY YOUNG
Team: Braves.
6-3, 220. **B:** R. **T:** R.
Born: May 15, 1967.
Season: 24-8; 2.94 ERA; 276 SO.
Career: 163-118; 3.34 ERA; 2,240 SO; still active.
Teams: Braves 1988-2002.

DEREK JETER A.L. ROOKIE
Team: Yankees. **Position:** Shortstop.
6-3, 195. **B:** R. **T:** R.
Born: June 26, 1974.
Season: .314 avg.; 10 HR; 78 RBIs.
Career: .317 avg.; 117 HR; 563 RBIs; still active.
Team: Yankees 1995-2002.

TODD HOLLANDSWORTH N.L. ROOKIE
Team: Dodgers. **Position:** Outfield.
6-2, 207. **B:** L. **T:** L.
Born: April 20, 1973.
Season: .291 avg.; 12 HR; 59 RBIs.
Career: .278 avg.; 74 HR; 288 RBIs; still active.
Team: Dodgers 1995-2000, Rockies 2000-02, Rangers 2002.

1997

KEN GRIFFEY JR. A.L. MVP
Team: Mariners. **Position:** Outfield.
6-3, 205. **B:** L. **T:** L.
Born: November 21, 1969.
Season: .304 avg.; 56 HR; 147 RBIs.
Career: .295 avg.; 468 HR; 1,358 RBIs; still active.
Team: Mariners 1989-99, Reds 2000-02.

LARRY WALKER N.L. MVP
Team: Rockies. **Position:** Outfield.
6-3, 233. **B:** L. **T:** R.
Born: December 1, 1966.
Season: .366 avg.; 49 HR; 130 RBIs; 33 SBs.
Career: .317 avg.; 335 HR; 1,133 RBIs; still active.
Team: Expos 1989-94; Rockies 1995-2002.

ROGER CLEMENS A.L. CY YOUNG
Team: Blue Jays.
Season: 21-7; 2.05 ERA; 292 SO.
(See 1986 A.L. MVP.)

PEDRO MARTINEZ N.L. CY YOUNG
Team: Expos.
5-11, 180. **B:** R. **T:** R.
Born: October 25, 1971.
Season: 17-8; 1.90 ERA; 305 SO.
Career: 152-63; 2.62 ERA; 2,220 SO; still active.
Team: Dodgers 1992-93; Expos 1994-97; Red Sox 1998-2002.

NOMAR GARCIAPARRA A.L. ROOKIE
Team: Red Sox. **Position:** Shortstop.
6-0, 190. **B:** R. **T:** R.
Born: July 23, 1973.
Season: .306 avg.; 30 HR; 98 RBIs; 22 SB.
Career: .328 avg.; 145 HR; 564 RBIs; 63 SB; still active.
Team: Red Sox 1996-2002.

SCOTT ROLEN N.L. ROOKIE
Team: Phillies. **Position:** Third base.
6-4, 226. **B:** R. **T:** R.
Born: April 4, 1975.
Season: .283 avg.; 21 HR; 92 RBIs.
Career: .281 avg.; 164 HR; 603 RBIs; still active.
Team: Phillies 1996-2002, Cardinals 2002.

1998

JUAN GONZALEZ A.L. MVP
Team: Rangers. **Position:** Outfield.
Season: .318 avg.; 45 HR; 157 RBIs.
(See 1997 A.L. MVP.)

SAMMY SOSA N.L. MVP
Team: Cubs. **Position:** Outfield.
6-0, 220. **B:** R. **T:** R.
Born: November 12, 1968.
Season: .307 avg.; 66 HR; 158 RBIs.
Career: .278 avg.; 499 HR; 1,347 RBIs; still active.
Team: Rangers 1989; White Sox 1989-91; Cubs 1992-2002.

ROGER CLEMENS A.L. CY YOUNG
Team: Blue Jays.
Season: 20-6; 2.65 ERA; 271 SO.
(See 1986 A.L. MVP.)

TOM GLAVINE N.L. CY YOUNG
Team: Braves.
Season: 20-6; 2.47 ERA; 157 SO.
(See 1991 N.L. Cy Young.)

BEN GRIEVE A.L. ROOKIE
Team: Athletics. **Position:** Outfield.
6-4, 216. **B:** L. **T:** R.
Born: May 4, 1976.
Season: .288 avg.; 18 HR; 89 RBIs.
Career: .272 avg.; 106 HR; 439 RBIs; still active
Team: Athletics 1997-2000, Devil Rays 2001-02.

KERRY WOOD N.L. ROOKIE
Team: Cubs. **Position:** Pitcher.
6-5, 230. **B:** R. **T:** R.
Born: June 16, 1977.
Season: 13-6; 3.40 ERA; 233 SO.
Career: 445-30; 3.75 ERA; 799 SO; still active.
Team: Cubs 1998-2002.

1999

Ivan Rodriguez — **A.L. MVP**

Team: Rangers. **Position:** Catcher.
5-9, 205. **B:** R. **T:** R.
Born: November 30, 1971.
Season: .332 avg.; 35 HR; 113 RBIs; 25 SBs.
Career: .305 avg.; 215 HR; 829 RBIs; 60 SBs; still active.
Team: Rangers 1991-2002.

Chipper Jones — **N.L. MVP**

Team: Braves. **Position:** Third base.
6-4, 210. **B:** B. **T:** R.
Born: April 24, 1972.
Season: .319 avg.; 45 HR; 110 RBIs; 25 SBs.
Career: .309 avg.; 253 HR; 837 RBIs; 114 SBs; still active.
Team: Braves 1993-2002.

Pedro Martinez — **A.L. Cy Young**

Team: Red Sox.
Season: 23-4; 2.07 ERA; 313 SO.
(See 1997 N.L. Cy Young.)

Randy Johnson — **N.L. Cy Young**

Team: Diamondbacks.
Season: 17-9; 2.48 ERA; 364 SO.
(See 1995 A.L. Cy Young.)

Carlos Beltran — **A.L. Rookie**

Team: Royals. **Position:** Outfield.
6-1, 190. **B:** B. **T:** R.
Born: April 24, 1977.
Season: .293 avg.; 22 HR; 108 RBIs; 27 SBs.
Career: .283 avg.; 82 HR; 365 RBIs; 109 SBs; still active
Team: Royals 1998-2002.

Scott Williamson — **N.L. Rookie**

Team: Reds. **Position:** Pitcher.
6-0, 185. **B:** R. **T:** R.
Born: February 17, 1976.
Season: .12-7, 2.41 ERA, 107 SO; 19 saves.
Career: .20-19; 2.89 ERA; 327 SO, 33 saves; still active.
Team: Reds 1999-2002.

2000

Jason Giambi — **A.L. MVP**

6-3, 235 **B:** L. **T:** R.
Position: First base.
Born: January 8, 1971.
Season: .333 avg.; 43 HR; 137 RBIs.
Career: .309 avg.; 228 HRs; 797 RBIs; still active.
Teams: Athletics 1995-2001, Yankees 2002.

Jeff Kent — **N.L. MVP**

6-1, 220 **B:** R. **T:** R.
Position: Second base.
Born: March 7, 1968.
Season: .334 avg.; 33 HR; 125 RBIs.
Career: .289 avg.; 253 HRs; 1,007 RBIs; still active.
Teams: Blue Jays 1992; Mets 1992-96; Indians 1996; Giants 1997-2002.

Pedro Martinez — **A.L. Cy Young**

Team: Red Sox.
Season: 18-6; 1.74 ERA; 284 SO.
(See 1997 N.L. Cy Young.)

Randy Johnson — **N.L. Cy Young**

Team: Diamondbacks.
Season: 19-7; 2.64 ERA; 347 SO.
(See 1995 A.L. Cy Young.)

Kazuhiro Sasaki — **A.L. Rookie**

Team: Mariners. **Position:** Pitcher.
6-4, 220 **B:** R. **T:** R.

Ichiro Suzuki was both A.L. MVP and A.L. Rookie of the Year in 2001.

Born: February 22, 1968.
Season: 2-5; 3.16 ERA; 37 saves.
Career: 6-14; 2.98 ERA; 119 saves; still active.
Team: Mariners 2000-2002.

Rafael Furcal — **N.L. Rookie**

Team: Braves. **Position:** Second base, shortstop.
5-10, 165 **B:** B. **T:** R.
Born: August 24, 1980.
Season: .294 avg.; 4 HR; 37 RBIs; 40 SB.
Career: .281 avg.; 16 HR; 114 RBIs; 89 SB; still active.
Team: Braves 2000-2002.

2001

Ichiro Suzuki — **A.L. MVP, Rookie**

5-9, 160. **B:** L.**T:** R.
Team: Mariners.
Born: October 22, 1973.
Season: .350 avg.; 8 HR; 69 RBIs; 56 SB.
Career: .336 avg.; 16 HR; 120 RBIs; 87 SB; still active.
Team: Mariners 2001-02.

Barry Bonds — **N.L. MVP**

Team: Giants.
Season: .328 avg.; 73 HR; 137 RBIs
(See 1990 N.L. MVP.)

Roger Clemens — **A.L. Cy Young**

Team: Yankees.
Season: 20-3; 3.51 ERA; 213 SO.
(See 1986 A.L. MVP.)

Randy Johnson — **N.L. Cy Young**

Team: Diamondbacks.
Season: 21-6; 2.49 ERA; 372 SO.
(See 1995 A.L. Cy Young.)

Albert Pujols — **N.L. Rookie**

6-3, 210. **B:** R. **T:** R.
Team: Cardinals.
Born: January 16, 1980.
Season: .329 avg.; 37 HR; 130 RBIs.
Career: .321 avg.; 71 HR; 257 RBIs; still active.
Team: Cardinals 2001-02.

2002

Ichiro Suzuki — **A.L. MVP**

Team: Mariners.
Season: .350 avg.; 8 HR; 69 RBIs; 56 SB.
(See 2001 A.L. MVP, Rookie)

Barry Bonds — **N.L. MVP**

Team: Giants.
Season: .370 avg.; 46 HR; 110 RBIs.
(See 1990 N.L. MVP.)

Barry Zito — **A.L. Cy Young**

6-4, 215. **B:** L. **T:** L.
Team: Athletics.
Season: 23-5; 2.75 ERA; 182 SO.
Career: .47-14, 3.04 ERA, 465 SO; still active.
Team: Athletics 2000-02.

Randy Johnson — **N.L. Cy Young**

Team: Diamondbacks.
Season: 24-5; 2.32 ERA; 334 SO.
(See 1995 A.L. Cy Young.)

Eric Hinske — **A.L. Rookie**

6-2, 225. **B:** L. **T:** R.
Team: Blue Jays.
Season: .279 avg.; 24 HR; 84 RBIs.
Career: .279 avg.; 24 HR; 84 RBIs; still active.
Team: Blue Jays.

Jason Jennings — **N.L. Rookie**

6-2, 242. **B:** L. **T:** R.
Team: Rockies.
Season: 16-8; 4.52 ERA; 127 SO.
Career: 20-9; 4.53 ERA; 153 SO; still active.
Team: Rockies.

History

The year before Jackie Robinson became the first black player in modern baseball history, he performed his magic for the Montreal Royals, Brooklyn's Class AAA farm team.

INTRODUCTION

IN THE BEGINNING

When Chicago businessman William Ambrose Hulbert set out to cure the ills that had afflicted his favorite sport in its formative years, he called a meeting in New York.

And what a meeting it turned out to be. When all was said and done, Major League Baseball—in the form of the National League—had become a part of the American sports landscape.

It all happened at the Grand Central Hotel on February 2, 1876. Hulbert, a baseball fan of the first rank, was determined to end the rowdyism, alcohol abuse and gambling that had troubled baseball. What he ended up with was the founding of the National League of Professional Baseball Clubs, with franchises awarded to Chicago, Cincinnati, St. Louis, Louisville, New York, Hartford, Boston and Philadelphia.

Hulbert, who had headed the Chicago club in baseball's first professional league, the wild and woolly National Association (1871-75), wanted the new league to exhibit a higher caliber of play and, just as important, be beyond reproach in terms of integrity and orderliness. To help achieve his goals, Hulbert named prominent businessman Morgan Bulkeley—the son of the founder of the Aetna Insurance Co.—as the National League's first president.

Bulkeley indicated his reign would be brief, and it was. His one year on the job was long enough, though, to get the National League off on a firm footing. And this new league, with strong leadership and outstanding talent, won billing as baseball's first major league.

Franchises came and went in the National League's first 24 years, but the alignment in place for 1900—Brooklyn, Boston, New York, Philadelphia, Pittsburgh, Chicago, Cincinnati and St. Louis—remained intact through the 1952 season.

Rivals to the N.L. came and went, too, with only the American League surviving. The A.L., with Ban Johnson as its first president, was founded in 1901. And, from 1903 through 1953, the American League was another model of stability, with its membership (New York, Boston, Washington, Cleveland, Detroit, Chicago, Philadelphia and St. Louis) holding firm.

Spurred by franchise shifts and expansion, the major league landscape has changed dramatically since '52. The leagues have grown from two entities of eight teams each to two of 16 and 14 clubs, and the majors have moved into Milwaukee, Baltimore, Kansas City, Los Angeles, San Francisco, Minneapolis-St. Paul, Houston, Anaheim, Atlanta, Oakland, Seattle, Montreal, San Diego, Arlington, Toronto, Miami, Denver, Tampa-St. Petersburg and Phoenix. The latter two areas were new to the big-league map in 1998.

Major League Baseball's growth since that 1876 meeting in New York has mirrored that of the nation. It has been an exhilarating and frenetic 125 years in America's ballparks—and as season No. 126 unfolds in 2001, fans are expecting more of the same.

Commissioner Kenesaw Mountain Landis, pictured with American League president Will Harridge (left), brought order to the game after the Black Sox scandal.

THE WAY IT WAS ... AND IS

When the first pitch in major league history was thrown on April 22, 1876 (in a game matching the Boston and Philadelphia teams in the fledgling National League), Ulysses S. Grant was serving as the 18th president of the United States, the Union consisted of 37 states, George Armstrong Custer and his troops had yet to meet their fate at the Battle of the Little Bighorn, the Statue of Liberty was eight years away from completion in France and aviation's Wright brothers were 9 and 4 years old. In that first game, another Wright—Harry, known as the "father of professional baseball" because he organized the first pro team, the 1869 Cincinnati Red Stockings—managed Boston to a 6-5 victory. ... The Boston franchise, later to be known as the Braves, lives on today in Atlanta and is one of only two big-league clubs to have been in continuous operation since the start of major league ball. Of course, the franchise has bounced from Beantown to Milwaukee to Atlanta, leaving Chicago's N.L. team as the only franchise to be operated continuously in one city from Day One of the majors' inception. ... Other "big leagues" sprung up in 1882 (the American Association, which lasted through 1891), 1884 (the Union Association), 1890 (the Players League, like the UA, a one-season operation), 1901 (the American League) and 1914 (the Federal League, which lasted two years). ... Although the Cubs and Red Sox will be among teams hoping to end long World Series droughts in 2001, those clubs were among the scourges of baseball in the early part of the 20th century. The Cubs, who haven't even played in a Series since 1945 and last won one in 1908, took two consecutive Series crowns while making four fall classic appearances in five years (1906-1910). The Red Sox, who haven't claimed a Series title since 1918, won the first-ever fall classic in 1903 and were champions in their first five Series ('03, 1912, 1915, 1916, 1918). Boston has lost in its last four Series. The Red Sox qualified for the playoffs for the second consecutive year in 1999 (the first time they had made back-to-back postseason appearances since '15-'16), but New England fans were disappointed once more when the Sox were eliminated in the League Championship Series by the Yankees. ... The Yankees, who won their 37th A.L. pennant in 2000, won their first flag in the club's pre-Bronx Bombers days. Yes, the Yanks had Babe Ruth and other robust hitters when they copped their first pennant in 1921, but the club was still playing at the Polo Grounds—in the borough of Manhattan—in those days. The move to the Bronx and Yankee Stadium came in 1923, the year the Yankees won their first of 26 World Series championships. ... The Athletics and Giants also fielded powerhouse teams in the century's first three decades. Connie Mack's A's were World Series champions three times in a four-year span (1910-13) and ruled again in 1929 and 1930. John McGraw's Giants won it all in 1905, 1921 and 1922 and appeared in six other Series. ... Commissioner Kenesaw Mountain Landis' unyielding stewardship, Ruth's slugging (and accompanying gate appeal) and the presence of great Yankees teams helped baseball overcome the Black Sox mess of 1919. Starting in '23, the Yanks won eight Series titles in 17 years. ... In the 18 seasons from 1947 through 1964, the Yankees rolled to 15 pennants in a run that included a record-setting five consecutive Series championships (1949-53). ... Since '64, the Oakland A's (three straight Series crowns in the early 1970s) and Cincinnati's Big Red Machine (1975 and 1976 Series championships and strong clubs before and after) have been in the spotlight, joined in recent years by the Series-winning Toronto Blue Jays of 1992 and 1993 and the Yankees, whose 2000 Series title was their fourth in five years. Also rating mention are the Atlanta Braves, who have won divisional crowns in the last 10 non-strike seasons; the Florida Marlins won the World Series in only the fifth season in franchise history, 1997; and the Arizona Diamondbacks won the World Series in only their fourth year of existence.

—JOE HOPPEL

1876

FINAL STANDINGS

National League

Team	W	L	Pct.	GB
Chicago	52	14	.788	...
St. Louis	45	19	.703	6
Hartford	47	21	.691	6
Boston	39	31	.557	15
Louisville	30	36	.455	22
New York	21	35	.375	26
Philadelphia	14	45	.237	34.5
Cincinnati	9	56	.138	42.5

SIGNIFICANT EVENTS

■ William Hulbert, president of the National Association's Chicago franchise, presided over a February meeting that signaled the official beginning of a new National League. Morgan Bulkeley was selected as the new circuit's first president.

■ The New York Mutuals, following the lead of the Philadelphia Athletics, announced they would not make their season-ending Western trip, forcing cancellation of a major chunk of the N.L.'s September schedule.

■ During a December meeting in Cleveland, the Athletics and Mutuals were expelled from the N.L. lineup and William Hulbert was elected president.

MEMORABLE MOMENTS

■ Boston 6, Philadelphia 5 in the first N.L. game. Jim O'Rourke entered the record books as the first player to get a hit in the April 22 battle at Athletic Park.

■ Chicago's Ross Barnes became the first N.L. player to hit a home run—an inside-the-park drive in a game at Cincinnati.

■ St. Louis' George Bradley pitched the first no-hitter in N.L. history, defeating Hartford, 2-0.

■ Hartford 14-8, Cincinnati 4-1 in baseball's first doubleheader.

■ Chicago clinched the N.L.'s first pennant with a victory over Hartford.

LEADERS

BA: Ross Barnes, Chi., .403.
Runs: Ross Barnes, Chi., 126.
Hits: Ross Barnes, Chi., 138.
TB: Ross Barnes, Chi., 190.
HR: George Hall, Phil., 5.
RBI: Deacon White, Chi., 60.
Wins: Al Spalding, Chi., 47.
ERA: George Bradley, St.L., 1.23.
CG: Jim Devlin, Lou., 66.
IP: Jim Devlin, Lou., 622.
SO: Jim Devlin, Lou., 122.

20-game winners

Al Spalding, Chi., 47-12
George Bradley, St.L., 45-19
Tommy Bond, Hart., 31-13
Jim Devlin, Lou., 30-35
Bobby Mathews, N.Y., 21-34

THE RULES

■ The new National League adopted a detailed rule book that included these interesting variations to the rules we use today:

■ The Strike Zone: The batter, upon stepping into position, had to call for a high or low pitch and the umpire notified the pitcher to deliver the ball as requested, making his calls accordingly.

■ The Strikeout: When a batter with two strikes failed to swing at the next good pitch, the umpire warned him by calling "good ball." If the batter swung and missed or failed to swing at the next "good ball", the umpire called "three strikes" and the batter was expected to run to first as if he had hit a fair ball.

■ Substitutions: No player could be replaced after the fourth inning, except those giving way temporarily for a pinch runner.

■ Batter/Position: When batters stepped outside the box while striking at the ball, the umpire would call "foul balk and out," allowing all runners to return to their bases.

■ Pitchers threw underhanded from a box with a front line that was 45 feet from the center of home base.

1877

FINAL STANDINGS

National League

Team	W	L	Pct.	GB
Boston	42	18	.700	...
Louisville	35	25	.583	7
Hartford	31	27	.534	10
St. Louis	28	32	.467	14
Chicago	26	33	.441	15.5
Cincinnati	15	42	.263	25.5

SIGNIFICANT EVENTS

■ The Hartford club announced in March that it would play its 1877 "home games" in Brooklyn while retaining its "home base" of Hartford.

■ Without enough money to finance a mid-season trip, the Cincinnati club disbanded. It was reorganized three days later under new ownership.

■ The Louisville team expelled players George Hall, Jim Devlin, Al Nichols and Bill Craver for fixing games, a move that later would be supported by league officials.

■ At its December meeting, the N.L. dropped franchises in Hartford and St. Louis and admitted teams in Indianapolis and Milwaukee.

MEMORABLE MOMENTS

■ Boston and Hartford opened the N.L.'s second season with an 11-inning 1-1 tie at Brooklyn.

■ Boston clinched the N.L. pennant with a victory over Hartford.

LEADERS

BA: Deacon White, Bos., .387.
Runs: Jim O'Rourke, Bos., 68.
Hits: Deacon White, Bos., 103.
TB: Deacon White, Bos., 145.
HR: Lip Pike, Cin., 4.
RBI: Deacon White, Bos., 49.
Wins: Tommy Bond, Bos., 40.
ERA: Tommy Bond, Bos., 2.11.
CG: Jim Devlin, Lou., 61.
IP: Jim Devlin, Lou., 559.
SO: Tommy Bond, Bos., 170.

20-game winners

Tommy Bond, Bos., 40-17
Jim Devlin, Lou., 35-25
Terry Larkin, Hart., 29-25

MAJOR RULES CHANGES

■ Any batted ball that bounced into foul territory before passing first or third base became a "foul" ball instead of a "fair" ball.

■ Home base was repositioned entirely in fair territory, two sides laying flush with the foul lines. The 17-inch move forward forced a corresponding move back of the pitcher's box.

■ The batter's box was changed to 6 feet in length—3 feet in front and 3 feet in back of the home-base line.

■ The size of bases was enlarged to 15 square inches, with their sides positioned parallel to the base lines.

■ An at-bat was not charged when a batter drew a base on balls.

1878

FINAL STANDINGS

National League

Team	W	L	Pct.	GB
Boston	41	19	.683	...
Cincinnati	37	23	.617	4
Providence	33	27	.550	8
Chicago	30	30	.500	11
Indianapolis	24	36	.400	17
Milwaukee	15	45	.250	26

SIGNIFICANT EVENTS

■ The N.L. increased its membership to seven with the addition of the Grays, a new franchise in Providence, R.I., but the field was reduced back to six when Louisville, unable to put together a competitive roster, resigned from the league.

■ At its winter meetings, the N.L. admitted new members Syracuse, Buffalo and Cleveland while dropping Indianapolis and Milwaukee.

MEMORABLE MOMENTS

■ Defending-champion Boston spoiled the Major League debut of the Grays, 1-0, in an opening day game at Providence's new Messer Street Park.

■ Tommy Bond defeated Providence for his 40th victory and brought Boston within range of its second consecutive pennant.

LEADERS

BA: Abner Dalrymple, Mil., .354.
Runs: Dick Higham, Pro., 60.
Hits: Joe Start, Chi., 100.
TB: Paul Hines, Pro.; Joe Start, Chi.; Tom York, Pro., 125.
HR: Paul Hines, Pro., 4.
RBI: Paul Hines, Pro., 50.
Wins: Tommy Bond, Bos., 40.
ERA: Monte Ward, Pro., 1.51.
CG: Tommy Bond, Bos., 57.
IP: Tommy Bond, Bos., 532.2.
SO: Tommy Bond, Bos., 182.

20-game winners

Tommy Bond, Bos., 40-19
Will White, Cin., 30-21
Terry Larkin, Chi. 29-26
Monte Ward, Pro., 22-13

MAJOR RULES CHANGES

■ Captains were required to position their players and after one at-bat, the batting order could no longer be changed.

■ Pinch runners were not allowed except in cases of illness or injury. The emergency substitute could enter the game only after the original player had reached base.

1879

FINAL STANDINGS

National League

Team	W	L	Pct.	GB
Providence	59	25	.702	...
Boston	54	30	.643	5
Buffalo	46	32	.590	10
Chicago	46	33	.582	10.5
Cincinnati	43	37	.538	14
Cleveland	27	55	.329	31
Syracuse	22	48	.314	30
Troy	19	56	.253	35.5

SIGNIFICANT EVENTS

■ The N.L. beefed up its preseason roster by admitting a new Troy franchise.

■ The Syracuse Stars, facing bankruptcy in mid-September, resigned from the N.L., leaving the league with an incomplete schedule.

■ The financially strapped Cincinnati club ended the season and folded operation, refusing to pay its players their final month's salary.

■ A new Cincinnati club gained quick N.L. acceptance during the annual winter meetings.

MEMORABLE MOMENTS

■ John Montgomery Ward's streak of having pitched every inning of 73 consecutive Providence games ended in mid-July when he was relieved in the fourth inning of a 9-0 loss to Cincinnati.

■ The Providence Grays scored a ninth-inning run and claimed a pennant-clinching victory over Boston.

■ Cincinnati pitcher Will White completed the season with 75 complete games and 680 innings—still-standing Major League records.

LEADERS

BA: Cap Anson, Chi., .317.
Runs: Charley Jones, Bos., 85.
Hits: Paul Hines, Pro., 146.
TB: Paul Hines, Pro., 197.
HR: Charley Jones, Bos., 9.
RBI: Charley Jones, Bos.; Jim O'Rourke, Bos., 62.
Wins: Monte Ward, Pro., 47.
ERA: Tommy Bond, Bos., 1.96.
CG: Will White, Cin., 75.
IP: Will White, Cin., 680.
SO: Monte Ward, Pro., 239.

20-game winners

Monte Ward, Pro., 47-19
Tommy Bond, Bos., 43-19
Will White, Cin., 43-31
Pud Galvin, Buf., 37-27
Terry Larkin, Chi., 31-23
Jim McCormick, Cle., 20-40

MAJOR RULES CHANGES

■ The size of the pitcher's box was enlarged to 4-by-6 feet.

■ A batter was declared out after three strikes if the pitch was caught before touching the ground.

■ Any pitcher who, in the opinion of the umpire, intentionally hit a batter with a pitch was fined from $10 to $50.

■ The "Spalding League Ball" was adopted as the official ball.

1880

FINAL STANDINGS

National League

Team	W	L	Pct.	GB
Chicago	67	17	.798	...
Providence	52	32	.619	15
Cleveland	47	37	.560	20
Troy	41	42	.494	25.5
Worcester	40	43	.482	26.5
Boston	40	44	.476	27
Buffalo	24	58	.293	42
Cincinnati	21	59	.263	44

SIGNIFICANT EVENTS

■ The preseason addition of a team in Worcester brought the N.L. field back to eight.

■ After kicking Cincinnati out of the league for rules violations, the N.L. admitted a new franchise from Detroit.

MEMORABLE MOMENTS

■ A Major League first—Worcester's Lee Richmond was perfect in a 1-0 victory over Cleveland.

■ Providence ace John Montgomery Ward matched the perfect-game feat of Lee Richmond five days earlier, retiring all 27 Buffalo batters he faced in a 5-0 victory.

■ Fred Dunlap's ninth-inning home run broke a scoreless tie and gave Cleveland a victory over Chicago, snapping the White Stockings' record 21-game inning streak.

■ Chicago completed its season with a 67-17 record and a 15-game bulge over second-place Providence.

LEADERS

BA: George Gore, Chi., .360.
Runs: Abner Dalrymple, Chi., 91.
Hits: Abner Dalrymple, Chi., 126.
TB: Abner Dalrymple, Chi., 175.
HR: Jim O'Rourke, Bos.; Harry Stovey, Wor., 6.
RBI: Cap Anson, Chi., 74.
Wins: Jim McCormick, Cle., 45.
ERA: Tim Keefe, Troy, 0.86.
CG: Jim McCormick, Cle., 72.
IP: Jim McCormick, Cle., 657.2.
SO: Larry Corcoran, Chi., 268.

20-game winners

Jim McCormick, Cle., 45-28
Larry Corcoran, Chi., 43-14
Monte Ward, Pro., 39-24
Mickey Welch, Troy, 34-30
Lee Richmond, Wor., 32-32
Tommy Bond, Bos., 26-29
Fred Goldsmith, Chi., 21-3
Pud Galvin, Buf., 20-35

MAJOR RULES CHANGES

■ A walk was awarded after eight balls instead of nine.

■ A runner was declared out if hit by a batted ball, and no run was allowed to score on the play.

■ The batter was required to run for first base immediately after "strike three" was called by the umpire.

1881

FINAL STANDINGS

National League

Team	W	L	Pct.	GB
Chicago	56	28	.667	...
Providence	47	37	.560	9
Buffalo	45	38	.542	10.5
Detroit	41	43	.488	15
Troy	39	45	.464	17
Boston	38	45	.458	17.5
Cleveland	36	48	.429	20
Worcester	32	50	.390	23

SIGNIFICANT EVENTS

■ One month after the 1881 season had ended, officials announced the formation of the American Association, a rival Major League with franchises in St. Louis, Cincinnati, Louisville, Philadelphia, Pittsburgh and Brooklyn.

■ American Association officials voted to ignore N.L. rules against Sunday games, liquor sales and 25-cent ticket prices. They also announced their decision not to abide by the N.L.'s restrictive reserve clause in player contracts.

MEMORABLE MOMENTS

■ Troy's Roger Connor hit the first grand slam in N.L. history—a bottom-of-the-ninth blow that handed Worcester an 8-7 defeat.

■ Chicago clinched its second straight pennant with a victory over Boston and White Stockings star Cap Anson put the finishing touches on his league-leading .399 average.

LEADERS

BA: Cap Anson, Chi., .399.
Runs: George Gore, Chi., 86.
Hits: Cap Anson, Chi., 137.
TB: Cap Anson, Chi., 175.
HR: Dan Brouthers, Buf., 8.
RBI: Cap Anson, Chi., 82.
Wins: Larry Corcoran, Chi.; Jim Whitney, Bos., 31.
ERA: Stump Weidman, Det., 1.80.
CG: Jim McCormick, Cle.; Jim Whitney, Bos., 57.
IP: Jim Whitney, Bos., 552.1.
SO: George Derby, Det., 212.

20-game winners

Larry Corcoran, Chi., 31-14
Jim Whitney, Bos., 31-33
George Derby, Det., 29-26
Pud Galvin, Buf., 28-24
Jim McCormick, Cle., 26-30
Hoss Radbourn, Pro., 25-11
Lee Richmond, Wor., 25-26
Fred Goldsmith, Chi., 24-13
Mickey Welch, Troy, 21-18

MAJOR RULES CHANGES

■ The front line of the pitcher's box was moved from 45 to 50 feet from the center of home base.

■ A batter was awarded first base after seven balls.

■ No substitutes were permitted except in the cases of illness or injury.

■ Umpires no longer gave players the "good ball" warning on called third strikes.

1882

FINAL STANDINGS

American Association

Team	W	L	Pct.	GB
Cincinnati	55	25	.688	...
Philadelphia	41	34	.547	11.5
Louisville	42	38	.525	13
Pittsburgh	39	39	.500	15
St. Louis	37	43	.463	18
Baltimore	19	54	.260	32.5

SIGNIFICANT EVENTS

■ After completing its first season as a six-team circuit, the American Association added franchises in Columbus and New York.

■ A baseball first: The Association formed the first permanent staff of umpires.

MEMORABLE MOMENTS

■ Opening day for the new American Association: St. Louis 9, Louisville 7; Philadelphia 10, Baltimore 7; Allegheny 10, Cincinnati 9.

■ Louisville ace Tony Mullane recorded the league's first no-hitter, beating the Red Stockings 2-0 at Cincinnati.

■ Cincinnati clinched the first A.A. pennant with a 6-1 mid-September victory over Louisville as the second-place Athletics dropped a game at Pittsburgh.

■ In the first post-season matchup of Major League champions, the Red Stockings split a two-game series with N.L. pennant winner Chicago.

LEADERS

BA: Pete Browning, Lou., .378.
Runs: Ed Swartwood, Pit., 86.
Hits: Hick Carpenter, Cin., 120.
TB: Ed Swartwood, Pit., 159.
HR: Oscar Walker, St.L., 7.
Wins: Will White, Cin., 40.
ERA: Denny Driscoll, Pit., 1.21.
CG: Will White, Cin., 52.
IP: Will White, Cin., 480.
SO: Tony Mullane, Lou., 170.

20-game winners

Will White, Cin., 40-12
Tony Mullane, Lou., 30-24
Sam Weaver, Phil., 26-15
George McGinnis, St.L., 25-18
Harry Salisbury, Pit., 20-18

THE RULES

■ The new American Association began its first season with several modifications to the existing rules book. Among the variations:

■ Sunday games were allowed.

■ Teams could charge 25 cents for admission rather than the N.L. price of 50 cents.

■ Liquor could be sold at the ballparks.

■ Pitchers judged to be intentionally throwing at batters were not subject to immediate fines.

FINAL STANDINGS

National League

Team	W	L	Pct.	GB
Chicago	55	29	.655	...
Providence	52	32	.619	3
Boston	45	39	.536	10
Buffalo	45	39	.536	10
Cleveland	42	40	.512	12
Detroit	42	41	.506	12.5
Troy	35	48	.422	19.5
Worcester	18	66	.214	37

SIGNIFICANT EVENTS

■ When N.L. President William Hulbert died of a heart attack in April, Boston team president A.H. Soden was named as his replacement.

■ At the winter meetings, N.L. officials replaced the Troy and Worcester franchises with teams from New York and Philadelphia, keeping the league roster at eight.

MEMORABLE MOMENTS

■ Chicago 35, Cleveland 4: a record rout in which seven White Stockings got four or more hits.

■ Chicago ace Larry Corcoran pitched his second career no-hitter, beating Worcester, 5-0.

■ Chicago finished with a 55-29 record and claimed its third straight N.L. pennant by three games over Providence.

LEADERS

BA: Dan Brouthers, Buf., .368.
Runs: George Gore, Chi., 99.
Hits: Dan Brouthers, Buf., 129.
TB: Dan Brouthers, Buf., 192.
HR: George Wood, Det., 7.
RBI: Cap Anson, Chi., 83.
Wins: Jim McCormick, Cle., 36.
ERA: Larry Corcoran, Chi., 1.95.
CG: Jim McCormick, Cle., 65.
IP: Jim McCormick, Cle., 595.2.
SO: Hoss Radbourn, Pro., 201.

20-game winners

Jim McCormick, Cle., 36-30
Hoss Radbourn, Pro., 33-20
Fred Goldsmith, Chi., 28-17
Pud Galvin, Buf., 28-23
Larry Corcoran, Chi., 27-12
George Weidman, Det., 25-20
Jim Whitney, Bos., 24-21

MAJOR RULES CHANGES

■ Umpires could call for a new ball at the end of even innings, provided the old ball was unfit for fair use.

■ The home team was required to provide a players' bench, 12 feet in length and fastened to the ground. Racks that held at least 20 bats became mandatory.

■ A baserunner obstructing a player attempting to field a batted ball was called out for interference.

■ Spectators caught hissing or hooting at the umpire were ejected from the park.

1883

FINAL STANDINGS

American Association

Team	W	L	Pct.	GB
Philadelphia	66	32	.673	...
St. Louis	65	33	.663	1
Cincinnati	61	37	.622	5
New York	54	42	.563	11
Louisville	52	45	.536	13.5
Columbus	32	65	.330	33.5
Pittsburgh	31	67	.316	35
Baltimore	28	68	.292	37

SIGNIFICANT EVENTS

■ In a significant February meeting, baseball officials drafted the first National Agreement, ensuring peaceful co-existence and respect for player contracts between the N.L. and American Association. Both leagues embraced the controversial reserve clause.

■ The Association announced post-season plans to expand to 12 teams with new franchises in Brooklyn, Washington, Indianapolis and Toledo.

MEMORABLE MOMENTS

■ New York's Tim Keefe celebrated Independence Day by winning both ends of a doubleheader against Columbus. Keefe allowed only three total hits.

■ The Athletics posted a late-September victory over Louisville and claimed the American Association's second pennant.

LEADERS

BA: Ed Swartwood, Pit., .357.
Runs: Harry Stovey, Phil., 110.
Hits: Ed Swartwood, Pit., 147.
TB: Harry Stovey, Phil., 213.
HR: Harry Stovey, Phil., 14.
Wins: Will White, Cin., 43.
ERA: Will White, Cin., 2.09.
CG: Tim Keefe, N.Y., 68.
IP: Tim Keefe, N.Y., 619.
SO: Tim Keefe, N.Y., 359.

20-game winners

Will White, Cin., 43-22
Tim Keefe, N.Y., 41-27
Tony Mullane, St.L., 35-15
Bobby Mathews, Phil., 30-13
George McGinnis, St.L., 28-16
Sam Weaver, Lou., 26-22
Guy Hecker, Lou., 26-23
Frank Mountain, Col., 26-33

MAJOR RULES CHANGES

■ Pitchers were allowed to deliver the ball from a shoulder-length position instead of the former below-the-waist position.

■ A runner touching and overrunning first base put himself at risk of being tagged out if he turned to his left while returning to the bag.

■ Pinch runners were allowed in cases of illness and injury.

FINAL STANDINGS

National League

Team	W	L	Pct.	GB
Boston	63	35	.643	...
Chicago	59	39	.602	4
Providence	58	40	.592	5
Cleveland	55	42	.567	7.5
Buffalo	52	45	.536	10.5
New York	46	50	.479	16
Detroit	40	58	.408	23
Philadelphia	17	81	.173	46

SIGNIFICANT EVENTS

■ Peace prevails: The N.L. and American Association signed a new National Agreement, ensuring respect for player contracts under the controversial reserve system.

MEMORABLE MOMENTS

■ Philadelphia 28, Providence 0—the most lopsided shutout in Major League history.

■ The White Stockings exploded for a record 18 runs in the seventh inning of a victory over Detroit.

■ Boston broke Chicago's three-year stranglehold on the N.L. pennant with a clinching victory over Cleveland.

LEADERS

BA: Dan Brouthers, Buf., .374.
Runs: Joe Hornung, Bos., 107.
Hits: Dan Brouthers, Buf., 159.
TB: Dan Brouthers, Buf., 243.
HR: Buck Ewing, N.Y., 10.
RBI: Dan Brouthers, Buf., 97.
Wins: Hoss Radbourn, Pro., 48.
ERA: Jim McCormick, Cle., 1.84.
CG: Pud Galvin, Buf., 72.
IP: Pud Galvin, Buf., 656.1.
SO: Jim Whitney, Bos., 345.

20-game winners

Hoss Radbourn, Pro., 48-25
Pud Galvin, Buf., 46-29
Jim Whitney, Bos., 37-21
Larry Corcoran, Chi., 34-20
Jim McCormick, Cle., 28-12
Charlie Buffinton, Bos., 25-14
Fred Goldsmith, Chi., 25-19
Mickey Welch, N.Y., 25-23
Hugh Daily, Cle., 23-19

MAJOR RULES CHANGES

■ Pitchers working within the confines of the box and facing the batter could deliver the ball with more forceful motion. The ball, on delivery, had to pass below the line of the pitcher's shoulder instead of below his waist.

■ A batted ball caught in foul territory was declared an out. Previously, balls caught on one bounce in foul territory were outs.

■ A player batting out of order was declared out.

■ Umpires became salaried employees.

1884

FINAL STANDINGS

Union Association

Team	W	L	Pct.	GB
St. Louis	94	19	.832	...
Milwaukee	8	4	.667	35.5
Cincinnati	69	36	.657	21
Baltimore	58	47	.552	32
Boston	58	51	.532	34
Chicago-Pitt.	41	50	.451	42
Washington	47	65	.420	46.5
Philadelphia	21	46	.313	50
St. Paul	2	6	.250	39.5
Altoona	6	19	.240	44
Kansas City	16	63	.203	61
Wilmington	2	16	.111	44.5

SIGNIFICANT EVENTS

■ The new Union Association, organized the previous September as a third Major League, added a Boston team to its roster while preparing for its first season.

■ U.A. casualties: Altoona (6-19) ceased operations in May, Philadelphia (21-46) disbanded in August and Chicago transferred operations in late August to Pittsburgh. Wilmington and Pittsburgh later were replaced by Milwaukee and Omaha—a franchise that lasted eight days and was replaced by St. Paul.

■ Only five teams attended the U.A.'s winter meetings, setting the stage for the league to disband in January.

MEMORABLE MOMENTS

■ Boston defeated St. Louis and ended the Maroons' 20-game winning streak

■ Boston's Fred Shaw held St. Louis to one hit and struck out 18, but he still lost a 1-0 decision to the pennant-bound Maroons.

LEADERS

BA: Fred Dunlap, St.L., .412.
Runs: Fred Dunlap, St.L., 160.
Hits: Fred Dunlap, St.L., 185.
TB: Fred Dunlap, St.L., 279.
HR: Fred Dunlap, St.L., 13.
Wins: Bill Sweeney, Bal., 40.
ERA: Jim McCormick, Cin., 1.54.
CG: Bill Sweeney, Bal., 58.
IP: Bill Sweeney, Bal., 538.
SO: Hugh Daily, CP-Wash., 483.

20-game winners

Bill Sweeney, Bal., 40-21
Hugh Daily, C-W-P, 28-28
Billy Taylor, St.L., 25-4
George Bradley, Cin., 25-15
Charlie Sweeney, St.L., 24-7
Dick Burns, Cin., 23-15
Bill Wise, Wash., 23-18
Jim McCormick, Cin., 21-3
Fred Shaw, Bos., 21-15

THE RULES

■ The Union Association, in its only Major League season, adopted the American Association rules book, which still included the shoulder-length restriction on pitching deliveries and seven-ball walks. The U.A., however, did adopt the N.L. rule on foul flies. The A.A.'s new hit-by-pitch rule was not adopted by the U.A.

FINAL STANDINGS

American Association

Team	W	L	Pct.	GB
New York	75	32	.701	...
Columbus	69	39	.639	6.5
Louisville	68	40	.630	7.5
St. Louis	67	40	.626	8
Cincinnati	68	41	.624	8
Baltimore	63	43	.594	11.5
Philadelphia	61	46	.570	14
Toledo	46	58	.442	27.5
Brooklyn	40	64	.385	33.5
Richmond	12	30	.286	30.5
Pittsburgh	30	78	.278	45.5
Indianapolis	29	78	.271	46
Washington	12	51	.190	41

SIGNIFICANT EVENTS

■ Toledo's Fleetwood Walker became the Major League's first black player when he went 0-for-3 in an opening day loss to Louisville.

■ Columbus, a second-place finisher in its only season, sold its players and dropped out of the league.

MEMORABLE MOMENTS

■ Louisville ace Guy Hecker, en route to Association season-high totals of 52 wins and 72 complete games, pitched both ends of a Fourth of July doubleheader sweep of Brooklyn.

■ The Metropolitans captured their first A.A. pennant with a 4-1 victory over Columbus.

■ The N.L.'s Providence Grays posted a 6-0 victory over New York in a post-season matchup of pennant winners. The Grays would go on to win three straight games and an unofficial world championship.

LEADERS

BA: Dude Esterbrook, N.Y., .314.
Runs: Harry Stovey, Phil., 124.
Hits: Dave Orr, N.Y., 162.
TB: Dave Orr, N.Y.; John Reilly, Cin., 247.
HR: John Reilly, Cin., 11.
Wins: Guy Hecker, Lou., 52.
ERA: Guy Hecker, Lou., 1.80.
CG: Guy Hecker, Lou., 72.
IP: Guy Hecker, Lou., 670.2.
SO: Guy Hecker, Lou., 385.

20-game winners

Guy Hecker, Lou., 52-20
Jack Lynch, N.Y., 37-15
Tim Keefe, N.Y., 37-17
Tony Mullane, Tol., 36-26
Ed Morris, Col., 34-13
Will White, Cin., 34-18
Bob Emslie, Bal., 32-17
Bobby Mathews, Phil., 30-18
Hardie Henderson, Bal., 27-23
George McGinnis, St.L., 24-16
Frank Mountain, Col., 23-17

MAJOR RULES CHANGES

■ Any batter hit by a pitch after trying to avoid the ball was awarded first base.

■ Each team was allowed an extra person on the field to take charge of bats—the equivalent of a modern-day bat boy.

1884

FINAL STANDINGS

National League

Team	W	L	Pct.	GB
Providence	84	28	.750	...
Boston	73	38	.658	10.5
Buffalo	64	47	.577	19.5
Chicago	62	50	.554	22
New York	62	50	.554	22
Philadelphia	39	73	.348	45
Cleveland	35	77	.313	49
Detroit	28	84	.250	56

SIGNIFICANT EVENTS

■ N.L. officials legalized overhand pitching, stipulating that pitchers must keep both feet on the ground through their delivery.

MEMORABLE MOMENTS

■ Providence pitcher Charlie Sweeney struck out a record 19 Boston batters in a 2-1 victory over the Red Stockings.
■ Chicago ace Larry Corcoran pitched his record third career no-hitter, ending a 10-game Providence winning streak with a 6-0 victory.
■ New York's Mickey Welch opened a game against Philadelphia with a record nine consecutive strikeouts.
■ September 11: Hoss Radbourn, who would finish the season with a record 59 wins, pitched pennant-bound Providence to a victory over Cleveland—the Grays' 20th consecutive triumph.
■ Providence completed a three-game sweep of the American Association's New York Metropolitans with an 12-2 victory, punctuating baseball's second post-season matchup between pennant winners.

LEADERS

BA: Jim O'Rourke, Buf., .347.
Runs: King Kelly, Chi., 120.
Hits: Jim O'Rourke, Buf.; Ezra Sutton, Bos., 162.
TB: Abner Dalrymple, Chi., 263.
HR: Ned Williamson, Chi., 27.
RBI: Cap Anson, Chi., 102.
Wins: Hoss Radbourn, Pro., 59.
ERA: Hoss Radbourn, Pro., 1.38.
CG: Hoss Radbourn, Pro., 73.
IP: Hoss Radbourn, Pro., 678.2.
SO: Hoss Radbourn, Pro., 441.

20-game winners

Hoss Radbourn, Pro., 59-12
Charlie Buffinton, Bos., 48-16
Pud Galvin, Buf., 46-22
Mickey Welch, N.Y., 39-21
Larry Corcoran, Chi., 35-23
Jim Whitney, Bos., 23-14
Charlie Ferguson, Phil., 21-25

POST-SEASON PLAYOFF

(Providence N.L. 3, New York A.A. 0)

Game 1—Providence 6, New York 0

Game 2—Providence 3, New York 1

Game 3—Providence 12, New York 2 (6 innings, darkness)

MAJOR RULES CHANGES

■ All restrictions against pitching deliveries were lifted, meaning pitchers could throw overhand for the first time.

■ Batters were awarded first base after six balls.

■ Any ball leaving the park was declared either fair or foul, depending on its position within the foul lines.

1885

FINAL STANDINGS

American Association

Team	W	L	Pct.	GB
St. Louis	79	33	.705	...
Cincinnati	63	49	.563	16
Pittsburgh	56	55	.505	22.5
Philadelphia	55	57	.491	24
Louisville	53	59	.473	26
Brooklyn	53	59	.473	26
New York	44	64	.407	33
Baltimore	41	68	.376	36.5

SIGNIFICANT EVENTS

■ The reorganized American Association began play with teams located in St. Louis, Philadelphia, Cincinnati, Pittsburgh, Brooklyn, Louisville, New York and Baltimore.

MEMORABLE MOMENTS

■ St. Louis jumped into first place with an early May victory over Philadelphia—a position the Browns would hold the remainder of the season.
■ Baltimore snapped St. Louis' A.A.-record 17-game winning streak with a 7-1 victory.
■ The Browns, refusing to acknowledge a controversial Game 2 forfeit loss to N.L.-champion Chicago, "claimed" status as baseball world champions after beating the White Stockings and knotting the post-season series at three games apiece.

LEADERS

BA: Pete Browning, Lou., .362.
Runs: Harry Stovey, Phil., 130.
Hits: Pete Browning, Phil., 174.
TB: Pete Browning, Lou., 255.
HR: Harry Stovey, Phil., 13.
Wins: Bob Caruthers, St.L., 40.
ERA: Bob Caruthers, St.L., 2.07.
CG: Ed Morris, Pit., 63.
IP: Ed Morris, Pit., 581.
SO: Ed Morris, Pit., 298.

20-game winners

Bob Caruthers, St.L., 40-13
Ed Morris, Pit., 39-24
Dave Foutz, St.L., 33-14
Henry Porter, Brk., 33-21
Bobby Mathews, Phil., 30-17
Guy Hecker, Lou., 30-23
Hardie Henderson, Bal., 25-35
Jack Lynch, N.Y., 23-21
Larry McKeon, Cin., 20-13

MAJOR RULES CHANGES

■ The one-bounce rule was dropped and fielders were required to catch foul balls on the fly to record an out.

■ Home-team captains were given the option of batting first or second.

■ The overhand delivery was permitted, bringing league pitchers in line with their N.L. counterparts.

■ Every team was required to wear a neat and attractive uniform.

FINAL STANDINGS

National League

Team	W	L	Pct.	GB
Chicago	87	25	.777	...
New York	85	27	.759	2
Philadelphia	56	54	.509	30
Providence	53	57	.482	33
Boston	46	66	.411	41
Detroit	41	67	.380	44
Buffalo	38	74	.339	49
St. Louis	36	72	.333	49

SIGNIFICANT EVENTS

■ Providence ace Hoss Radbourn, the N.L.'s highest paid player, was suspended for poor pitching after a lopsided loss to New York.
■ The Washington Nationals were accepted into the league, replacing Providence.

MEMORABLE MOMENTS

■ Philadelphia snapped Chicago's 18-game winning streak—the White Stockings' first loss at new West Side Park.
■ John Clarkson, en route to a Major League-high 53 wins, held Providence hitless in an 4-0 victory.
■ Game 2 of a post-season "World's Series" between Chicago and American Association-champion St. Louis ended in controversy when the Browns refused to continue the game in the sixth inning because of umpiring decisions. The White Stockings were declared forfeit winners.
■ The Browns defeated the White Stockings 13-4 in the championship finale, tying the series at 3-3. The Browns claimed victory, refusing to accept the forfeit decision.

LEADERS

BA: Roger Connor, N.Y., .371.
Runs: King Kelly, Chi., 124.
Hits: Roger Connor, N.Y., 169.
TB: Roger Connor, N.Y., 225.
HR: Abner Dalrymple, Chi., 11.
RBI: Cap Anson, Chi., 108.
Wins: John Clarkson, Chi., 53.
ERA: Tim Keefe, N.Y., 1.58.
CG: John Clarkson, Chi., 68.
IP: John Clarkson, Chi., 623.
SO: John Clarkson, Chi., 308.

20-game winners

John Clarkson, Chi., 53-16
Mickey Welch, N.Y., 44-11
Tim Keefe, N.Y., 32-13
Hoss Radbourn, Pro., 28-21
Charlie Ferguson, Phil., 26-20
Ed Daily, Phil., 26-23
Fred Shaw, Pro., 23-26
Charlie Buffinton, Bos., 22-27
Jim McCormick, Pro.-Chi., 21-7

POST-SEASON PLAYOFF

(Chicago N.L. 3, St. Louis A.A. 3; 1 tie)

Game 1—Chicago 5, St. Louis 5 (8 innings, darkness)

Game 2—Chicago awarded 5-4 forfeit victory

Game 3—St. Louis 7, Chicago 4

Game 4—St. Louis 3, Chicago 2

Game 5—Chicago 9, St. Louis 2 (7 innings, darkness)

Game 6—Chicago 9, St. Louis 2

Game 7—St. Louis 13, Chicago 4 (8 innings, darkness)

MAJOR RULES CHANGES

■ The batter's box was resized to 4 feet wide by 6 feet long and moved a foot closer to home base.

■ Pitchers were required to keep both feet in contact with the ground during delivery. Batters were awarded first base after two "foul balks," a rule that was eliminated at midseason.

■ Players were permitted to use bats with one flat side.

■ Any ball leaving the park at a distance of less than 210 feet was declared an automatic double.

1886

FINAL STANDINGS

American Association

Team	W	L	Pct.	GB
St. Louis	93	46	.669	...
Pittsburgh	80	57	.584	12
Brooklyn	76	61	.555	16
Louisville	66	70	.485	25.5
Cincinnati	65	73	.471	27.5
Philadelphia	63	72	.467	28
New York	53	82	.393	38
Baltimore	48	83	.366	41

SIGNIFICANT EVENTS

■ When Pittsburgh defected to the rival N.L. in November, the American Association filled the void with a new Cleveland franchise.

MEMORABLE MOMENTS

■ Louisville pitcher Guy Hecker belted a record-tying three home runs and scored a Major League-record seven times in a victory over Brooklyn.
■ The St. Louis Browns posted a 4-3 victory over the N.L.'s Chicago White Stockings in Game 6 of the "World's Series," staking their undisputed claim as king of baseball.

LEADERS

BA: Dave Orr, N.Y., .338.
Runs: Arlie Latham, St.L., 152.
Hits: Dave Orr, N.Y., 193.
TB: Dave Orr, N.Y., 301.
HR: Bid McPhee, Cin., 8.
SB: Harry Stovey, Phil., 68.
Wins: Dave Foutz, St.L.; Ed Morris, Pit., 41.
ERA: Dave Foutz, St.L., 2.11.
CG: Matt Kilroy, Bal.; Toad Ramsey, Lou., 66.
IP: Toad Ramsey, Lou., 588.2.
SO: Matt Kilroy, Bal., 513.

20-game winners

Dave Foutz, St.L., 41-16
Ed Morris, Pit., 41-20
Tom Ramsey, Lou., 38-27
Tony Mullane, Cin., 33-27
Bob Caruthers, St.L., 30-14
Pud Galvin, Pit., 29-21
Matt Kilroy, Bal., 29-34
Henry Porter, Brk., 27-19
Guy Hecker, Lou., 26-23
Al Atkinson, Phil., 25-17
Jack Lynch, N.Y., 20-30

MAJOR RULES CHANGES

■ A 4-by-1 foot smooth stone slab was placed at the front end of the pitcher's box, helping umpires determine if the pitcher had stepped beyond the front line.

■ The number of balls required for a walk was decreased from seven to six.

■ The A.A. adopted the reshaped 6-by-3 foot batter's box and 4-by-7 foot pitcher's box.

■ Stolen bases were credited for any base a runner was able to gain on his own volition, such as a first-to-third dash on a single.

1886

FINAL STANDINGS

National League

Team	W	L	Pct.	GB
Chicago	90	34	.726	...
Detroit	87	36	.707	2.5
New York	75	44	.630	12.5
Philadelphia	71	43	.623	14
Boston	56	61	.479	30.5
St. Louis	43	79	.352	46
Kansas City	30	91	.248	58.5
Washington	28	92	.233	60

SIGNIFICANT EVENTS

- The N.L. increased its preseason roster to eight with the addition of a Kansas City team on a one-year trial basis.
- The N.L. adopted the stolen base as an official statistic and reshaped the pitcher's box to 4-by-7 feet.
- New rules: 4 strikes for an out; 5 balls for a walk; a standardized strike zone from the knees to the shoulders, and a 55½-foot pitching distance.
- Pittsburgh made a November jump from the American Association to the N.L., replacing Kansas City.

MEMORABLE MOMENTS

- The White Stockings clinched another N.L. pennant with a final-day victory over Boston. The final lead was 2½ games over Detroit.
- Chicago dropped a 4-3 decision to the American Association-champion Browns and lost the best-of-seven "World's Series" in six games.

LEADERS

BA: King Kelly, Chi., .388.
Runs: King Kelly, Chi., 155.
Hits: Hardy Richardson, Det., 189.
TB: Dan Brouthers, Det., 284.
HR: Dan Brouthers, Det.;
Hardy Richardson, Det., 11.
RBI: Cap Anson, Chi., 147.
SB: Ed Andrews, Phil., 56.
Wins: Lady Baldwin, Det.; Tim Keefe, N.Y., 42.
ERA: Henry Boyle, St.L., 1.76.
CG: Tim Keefe, N.Y., 62.
IP: Tim Keefe, N.Y., 535.
SO: Lady Baldwin, Det., 323.

20-game winners

Lady Baldwin, Det., 42-13
Tim Keefe, N.Y., 42-20
John Clarkson, Chi., 36-17]
Mickey Welch, N.Y., 33-22
Charlie Ferguson, Phil., 30-9
Charlie Getzien, Det., 30-11
Jim McCormick, Chi., 31-11
Hoss Radbourn, Bos., 27-31
Dan Casey, Phil., 24-18
Jocko Flynn, Chi., 23-6
Bill Stemmeyer, Bos., 22-18

POST-SEASON PLAYOFF

(St. Louis A.A. 4, Chicago N.L. 2)
Game 1—Chicago 6, St. Louis 0
Game 2—St. Louis 12, Chicago 0 (8 innings, darkness)
Game 3—Chicago 11, St. Louis 4 (8 innings, darkness)
Game 4—St. Louis 8, Chicago 5 (7 innings, darkness)
Game 5—St. Louis 10, Chicago 3 (8 innings, darkness)
Game 6—St. Louis 4, Chicago 3 (10 innings)

MAJOR RULES CHANGES

- The number of balls required for a walk was increased from six to seven.
- The shape of the pitcher's box was changed from 6-by-6 to 4-by-7 feet.
- Pitchers no longer were required to keep both feet on the ground during delivery. "Foul balks" were eliminated.
- The batter's box was reshaped to its 6-by-3 shape, 12 inches from home base.
- Stolen bases were credited for any base a runner was able to gain on his own volition, such as a first-to-third dash on a single.

1887

FINAL STANDINGS

American Association

Team	W	L	Pct.	GB
St. Louis	95	40	.704	...
Cincinnati	81	54	.600	14
Baltimore	77	58	.570	18
Louisville	76	60	.559	19.5
Philadelphia	64	69	.481	30
Brooklyn	60	74	.448	34.5
New York	44	89	.331	50
Cleveland	39	92	.298	54

SIGNIFICANT EVENTS

- The 4-strike rule was eliminated in a November meeting and officials reversed their preseason decision to count walks as "hits."

MEMORABLE MOMENTS

- St. Louis, en route to 95 victories and its third straight A.A. pennant, defeated the Athletics for its 15th consecutive victory.
- The 52-game hitting streak of Athletics star Denny Lyons came to an end in late August. Lyons' streak included two games in which he managed only walks, which were counted as hits in the 1887 season.
- The Browns defeated New York for their 12th straight victory and increased their lead over second-place Cincinnati to a whopping 19½ games.
- The Browns closed their best-of-15 "World's Series" battle against Detroit with a 9-2 victory, but they still lost the war, 10 games to 5.

LEADERS

BA: Tip O'Neill, St.L., .485.
Runs: Tip O'Neill, St.L., 167.
Hits: Tip O'Neill, St.L., 275.
TB: Tip O'Neill, St.L., 407.
HR: Tip O'Neill, St.L., 14.
SB: Hugh Nicol, Cin., 138.
Wins: Matt Kilroy, Bal., 46.
ERA: Elmer Smith, Cin., 2.94.
CG: Matt Kilroy, Bal., 66.
IP: Matt Kilroy, Bal., 589.1.
SO: Toad Ramsey, Lou., 355.

20-game winners

Matt Kilroy, Bal., 46-19
Toad Ramsey, Lou., 37-27
Silver King, St.L., 32-12
Elmer Smith, Cin., 34-17
Tony Mullane, Cin., 31-17
Bob Caruthers, St.L., 29-9
John Smith, Bal., 25-30
Gus Weyhing, Phil., 26-28
Ed Seward, Phil., 25-25
Dave Foutz, St.L., 25-12

MAJOR RULES CHANGES

- The National League and American Association agreed to abide by a uniform rules book and several rules were rewritten. Here are some of the more significant changes:
- Batters no longer were allowed to call for high or low pitches and the strike zone was defined as the area between the top of the shoulder and the bottom of the knees.
- The pitcher's box was reshaped to 4-by-5½ feet.
- Batters hit by a pitch were awarded first base and not charged with an at-bat.
- The number of balls required for a walk was dropped to five.
- The batter was declared out after four strikes.
- Batters drawing a base on balls were credited with a hit and charged with a time at-bat.

FINAL STANDINGS

National League

Team	W	L	Pct.	GB
Detroit	79	45	.637	...
Philadelphia	75	48	.610	3.5
Chicago	71	50	.587	6.5
New York	68	55	.553	10.5
Boston	61	60	.504	16.5
Pittsburgh	55	69	.444	24
Washington	46	76	.377	32
Indianapolis	37	89	.294	43

SIGNIFICANT EVENTS

- The N.L.'s St. Louis franchise was sold to Indianapolis interests.
- The Phillies christened their new ballpark, which would remain in use as the "Baker Bowl" until 1938.
- N.L. officials held a November meeting with the Brotherhood of Professional Base Ball Players, an organization set up to protect players' contract interests.

MEMORABLE MOMENTS

- Detroit posted a doubleheader sweep of Chicago, increasing its N.L. lead to seven games and putting the city on the verge of its first pennant.
- The best-of-15 "World's Series" opened with the Browns posting a 6-1 victory over Detroit.
- The post-season title series ended with Detroit holding a commanding 10 games to 5 advantage.

LEADERS

BA: Cap Anson, Chi., .421.
Runs: Dan Brouthers, Det., 153.
Hits: Sam Thompson, Det., 235.
TB: Sam Thompson, Det., 340.
HR: Billy O'Brien, Wash., 19.
RBI: Sam Thompson, Det., 166.
SB: Monte Ward, N.Y., 111.
Wins: John Clarkson, Chi., 38.
ERA: Dan Casey, Phil., 2.86.
CG: John Clarkson, Chi., 56.
IP: John Clarkson, Chi., 523.
SO: John Clarkson, Chi., 237.

20-game winners

John Clarkson, Chi., 38-21
Tim Keefe, N.Y., 35-19
Charlie Getzien, Det., 29-13
Dan Casey, Phil., 28-13
Pud Galvin, Pit., 28-21
Jim Whitney, Wash., 24-21
Hoss Radbourn, Bos., 24-23
Charlie Ferguson, Phil., 22-10
Mickey Welch, N.Y., 22-15
Kid Madden, Bos., 21-14
Charlie Buffinton, Phil., 21-17

POST-SEASON PLAYOFF

(Detroit N.L. 10, St. Louis A.A. 5)
Game 1—St. Louis 6, Detroit 1
Game 2—Detroit 5, St. Louis 3
Game 3—Detroit 2, St. Louis 1(13 innings)
Game 4—Detroit 8, St. Louis 0
Game 5—St. Louis 5, Detroit 2
Game 6—Detroit 9, St. Louis 0
Game 7—Detroit 3, St. Louis 1
Game 8—Detroit 9, St. Louis 2
Game 9—Detroit 4, St. Louis 2
Game 10—St. Louis 11, Detroit 4
Game 11—Detroit 13, St. Louis 3
Game 12—St. Louis 5, Detroit 1 (7 innings, darkness)
Game 13—Detroit 6, St. Louis 3
Game 14—Detroit 4, St. Louis 3
Game 15—St. Louis 9, Detroit 2 (6 innings, cold)

MAJOR RULES CHANGES

- The National League and American Association agreed to abide by a uniform rules book and several rules were rewritten. Here are some of the more significant changes:
- Batters no longer were allowed to call for high or low pitches and the strike zone was defined as the area between the top of the shoulder and the bottom of the knees.
- The pitcher's box was reshaped to 4-by-5½ feet.
- Batters hit by a pitch were awarded first base and not charged with an at-bat.
- The number of balls required for a walk was dropped to five.
- The batter was declared out after four strikes.
- Batters drawing a base on balls were credited with a hit and charged with a time at-bat.

1888

FINAL STANDINGS

American Association

Team	W	L	Pct.	GB
St. Louis	92	43	.681	...
Brooklyn	88	52	.629	6.5
Philadelphia	81	52	.609	10
Cincinnati	80	54	.597	11.5
Baltimore	57	80	.416	36
Cleveland	50	82	.379	40.5
Louisville	48	87	.356	44
Kansas City	43	89	.326	47.5

SIGNIFICANT EVENTS

- Columbus became a member of the American Association roster in December, replacing Cleveland.

MEMORABLE MOMENTS

- The St. Louis Browns, seeking their fourth straight A.A. pennant, moved into first place with a mid-July victory over Kansas City—a position they would not relinquish the rest of the season.
- St. Louis ace Silver King posted his 45th victory and raised his league-leading totals in games (66), innings (585⅔), complete games (64) and ERA (1.64).
- The Browns fell to N.L.-champion New York in a best-of-10 "World's Series," despite winning the finale, 18-7.

LEADERS

BA: Tip O'Neill, St.L., .335.
Runs: George Pinkney, Brk., 134.
Hits: Tip O'Neill, St.L., 177.
TB: John Reilly, Cin., 264.
HR: John Reilly, Cin., 13.
RBI: John Reilly, Cin., 103.
SB: Arlie Latham, St.L., 109.
Wins: Silver King, St.L., 45.
ERA: Silver King, St.L., 1.64.
CG: Silver King, St.L., 64.
IP: Silver King, St.L., 585.2.
SO: Ed Seward, Phil., 272.

20-game winners

Silver King, St.L., 45-21
Ed Seward, Phil., 35-19
Bob Caruthers, Brk., 29-15
Gus Weyhing, Phil., 28-18
Lee Viau, Cin., 27-14
Tony Mullane, Cin., 26-16
Nat Hudson, St.L., 25-10
Elton Chamberlain, Lou.-St.L., 25-11
Mickey Hughes, Brk., 25-13
Ed Bakely, Cle., 25-33
Elmer Smith, Cin., 22-17
Bert Cunningham, Bal., 22-29

MAJOR RULES CHANGES

- The rule awarding the batter a hit on a base on balls was reversed.
- The batter was credited with a "hit" on any batted ball that struck a baserunner, even though the runner was declared out.
- The number of strikes required for a strikeout was reduced to three.
- Pitchers were charged with an error for walks, wild pitches, hit batters and balks.

1888

FINAL STANDINGS

National League

Team	W	L	Pct.	GB
New York	84	47	.641	...
Chicago	77	58	.570	9
Philadelphia	69	61	.531	14.5
Boston	70	64	.522	15.5
Detroit	68	63	.519	16
Pittsburgh	66	68	.493	19.5
Indianapolis	50	85	.370	36
Washington	48	86	.358	37.5

SIGNIFICANT EVENTS

■ Rules changes: 4 balls for a walk and 3 strikes for a strikeout—standards that would hold up for more than a century.

■ Cleveland, a former American Association franchise, was admitted to the N.L., replacing Detroit.

MEMORABLE MOMENTS

■ With more than 10,000 fans watching at New York's Polo Grounds, Giants pitcher Tim Keefe dropped a 4-2 decision to Pittsburgh, snapping his record 19-game winning streak.

■ Pittsburgh ace Ed Morris pitched his record fourth consecutive shutout—a 1-0 victory over New York.

■ The Giants clinched the first of many N.L. pennants.

■ The Giants clinched their best-of-10 "World's Series" against St. Louis in Game 8 with an 11-3 victory.

LEADERS

BA: Cap Anson, Chi., .344.
Runs: Dan Brouthers, Det., 118.
Hits: Jimmy Ryan, Chi., 182.
TB: Jimmy Ryan, Chi., 283.
HR: Jimmy Ryan, Chi., 16.
RBI: Cap Anson, Chi., 84.
SB: Dummy Hoy, Wash., 82.
Wins: Tim Keefe, N.Y., 35.
ERA: Tim Keefe, N.Y., 1.74.
CG: Ed Morris, Pit., 54.
IP: John Clarkson, Bos., 483.1.
SO: Tim Keefe, N.Y., 333.

20-game winners

Tim Keefe, N.Y., 35-12
John Clarkson, Bos., 33-20
Pete Conway, Det., 30-14
Ed Morris, Pit., 29-23
Charlie Buffinton, Phil., 28-17
Mickey Welch, N.Y., 26-19
Gus Krock, Chi., 25-14
Pud Galvin, Pit., 23-25

POST-SEASON PLAYOFF

(New York N.L. 6, St. Louis A.A. 4)

Game 1—New York 2, St. Louis 1
Game 2—St. Louis 3, New York 0
Game 3—New York 4, St. Louis 2
Game 4—New York 6, St. Louis 3
Game 5—St. Louis 6, New York 4 (8 innings, darkness)
Game 6—New York 12, St. Louis 5 (8 innings, darkness)
Game 7—St. Louis 7, New York 5 (8 innings, darkness)
Game 8—New York 11, St. Louis 3
Game 9—St. Louis 14, New York 11 (10 innings)
Game 10—St. Louis 18, New York 7

MAJOR RULES CHANGES

■ The rule awarding the batter a hit on a base on balls was reversed.

■ The batter was credited with a "hit" on any batted ball that struck a baserunner, even though the runner was declared out.

■ Pitchers were charged with an error for walks, wild pitches, hit batters and balks.

1889

FINAL STANDINGS

American Association

Team	W	L	Pct.	GB
Brooklyn	93	44	.679	...
St. Louis	90	45	.667	2
Philadelphia	75	58	.564	16
Cincinnati	76	63	.547	18
Baltimore	70	65	.519	22
Columbus	60	78	.435	33.5
Kansas City	55	82	.401	38
Louisville	27	111	.196	66.5

SIGNIFICANT EVENTS

■ A record Association crowd of 22,122 showed up for a May 30 game in Brooklyn to watch the Bridegrooms play the Browns.

■ Baltimore, following the lead of Brooklyn, Cincinnati and Kansas City, dropped out of the American Association.

MEMORABLE MOMENTS

■ Toad Ramsey pitched Louisville to a victory over St. Louis, snapping the Colonels' Major League-record losing streak at 26 games.

■ The Browns, leading 4-2 in the ninth inning of a September 7 game, walked off the field in Brooklyn, claiming it was too dark to continue. The Bridegrooms were declared forfeit winners, a ruling that later would be reversed.

■ The Browns, claiming they feared for the personal safety amid unruly Brooklyn fans, forfeited their September 8 game to the Bridegrooms—a defeat that would help Brooklyn claim the A.A. pennant.

■ The Bridegrooms dropped a 3-2 decision to the N.L.-champion Giants in the decisive Game 9 of the "World's Series."

LEADERS

BA: Tommy Tucker, Bal., .372.
Runs: Mike Griffin, Bal.; Harry Stovey, Phil., 152.
Hits: Tommy Tucker, Bal., 196.
TB: Harry Stovey, Phil., 292.
HR: Bug Holliday, Cin.; Harry Stovey, Phil., 19.
RBI: Harry Stovey, Phil., 119.
SB: Billy Hamilton, K.C., 111.
Wins: Bob Caruthers, Brk., 40.
ERA: Jack Stivetts, St.L., 2.25.
CG: Matt Kilroy, Bal., 55.
IP: Mark Baldwin, Col., 513.2.
SO: Mark Baldwin, Col., 368.

20-game winners

Bob Caruthers, Brk., 40-11
Silver King, St.L., 35-16
Elton Chamberlain, St.L., 32-15
Jesse Duryea, Cin., 32-19
Gus Weyhing, Phil., 30-21
Matt Kilroy, Bal., 29-25
Mark Baldwin, Col., 27-34
Frank Foreman, Bal., 23-21
Adonis Terry, Brk., 22-15
Lee Viau, Cin., 22-20
Ed Seward, Phil., 21-15

MAJOR RULES CHANGES

■ The number of balls required for a walk was reduced to four.

■ A foul tip was defined as a foul hit that did not rise above the batter's head and was caught within 10 feet of home base. Batters could not be declared out on a caught foul tip and runners were permitted to return safely to their bases.

■ Pitchers were required to get into pitching position by placing one foot on the back line of the pitching box and only one step was allowed during delivery.

■ One "extra player" could be substituted at the end of any complete inning, but the player leaving the game could not return. Substitutions could be made at any time for a disabled player.

■ Pitchers no longer were charged with errors for walks, wild pitches, hit batsmen and balks.

■ The sacrifice bunt was recognized for the first time, although the hitter still was charged with an at-bat.

FINAL STANDINGS

National League

Team	W	L	Pct.	GB
New York	83	43	.659	...
Boston	83	45	.648	1
Chicago	67	65	.508	19
Philadelphia	63	64	.496	20.5
Pittsburgh	61	71	.462	25
Cleveland	61	72	.459	25.5
Indianapolis	59	75	.440	28
Washington	41	83	.331	41

SIGNIFICANT EVENTS

■ Brooklyn and Cincinnati made a November jump from the American Association to the N.L., creating a 10-team circuit.

■ A threat becomes official: The Brotherhood of Professional Base Ball Players formally organized the Players League, a third major circuit partially operated by the players themselves.

MEMORABLE MOMENTS

■ The Giants christened their new Polo Grounds with a victory over Pittsburgh.

■ The New York Giants captured their second straight pennant on the final day of the season, beating Cleveland while Boston was losing to Pittsburgh.

■ The Giants reigned as world champions again, thanks to a 6 games to 3 post-season victory over the American Association's Brooklyn Bridegrooms. New York won Game 9, 3-2.

LEADERS

BA: Dan Brouthers, Bos., .373.
Runs: Mike Tiernan, N.Y., 147.
Hits: Jack Glasscock, Ind., 205.
TB: Jimmy Ryan, Chi., 287.
HR: Sam Thompson, Phil., 20.
RBI: Roger Connor, N.Y., 130.
SB: Jim Fogarty, Phil., 99.
Wins: John Clarkson, Bos., 49.
ERA: John Clarkson, Bos., 2.73.
CG: John Clarkson, Bos., 68.
IP: John Clarkson, Bos., 620.
SO: John Clarkson, Bos., 284.

20-game winners

John Clarkson, Bos., 49-19
Tim Keefe, N.Y., 28-13
Charlie Buffinton, Phil., 28-16
Mickey Welch, N.Y., 27-12
Pud Galvin, Pit., 23-16
Darby O'Brien, Cle., 22-17
Henry Boyle, Ind., 21-23
Harry Staley, Pit., 21-26
Hoss Radbourn, Bos., 20-11
Ed Beatin, Cle., 20-15

POST-SEASON PLAYOFF

(New York N.L. 6, Brooklyn A.A. 3)

Game 1—Brooklyn 12, New York 10 (8 innings, darkness)
Game 2—New York 6, Brooklyn 2
Game 3—Brooklyn 8, New York 7 (8 innings, darkness)
Game 4—Brooklyn 10, New York 7 (6 innings, darkness)
Game 5—New York 11, Brooklyn 3
Game 6—New York 2, Brooklyn 1 (11 innings)
Game 7—New York 11, Brooklyn 7
Game 8—New York 16, Brooklyn 7
Game 9—New York 3, Brooklyn 2

MAJOR RULES CHANGES

■ The number of balls required for a walk was reduced to four.

■ A foul tip was defined as a foul hit that did not rise above the batter's head and was caught within 10 feet of home base. Batters could not be declared out on a caught foul tip and runners were permitted to return safely to their bases.

■ Pitchers were required to get into pitching position by placing one foot on the back line of the pitching box and only one step was allowed during delivery.

■ One "extra player" could be substituted at the end of any complete inning, but the player leaving the game could not return. Substitutions could be made at any time for a disabled player.

■ Pitchers no longer were charged with errors for walks, wild pitches, hit batsmen and balks.

■ The sacrifice bunt was recognized for the first time, although the hitter still was charged with an at-bat.

1890

FINAL STANDINGS

Players League

Team	W	L	Pct.	GB
Boston	81	48	.628	...
Brooklyn	76	56	.576	6.5
New York	74	57	.565	8
Chicago	75	62	.547	10
Philadelphia	68	63	.519	14
Pittsburgh	60	68	.469	20.5
Cleveland	55	75	.423	26.5
Buffalo	36	96	.273	46.5

SIGNIFICANT EVENTS

■ The new Players League won the first of many lawsuits it would have to endure when a judge refused to grant a January injunction against Brotherhood president John Montgomery Ward.

■ The Players League began its inaugural season in a war-like atmosphere, thanks to the league-jumping antics of many big-name stars from the National League and American Association.

■ The New York and Pittsburgh teams combined with the same-city franchises from the N.L., pronouncing last rites for the one-year circuit. The December defections would prompt Players League backers to seek their own deals in a scramble to remain solvent.

MEMORABLE MOMENTS

■ Willie McGill, a 16-year-old Cleveland hurler, became the youngest Major League pitcher to throw a complete game when he defeated Buffalo.

■ Boston closed out the first and last Players League season with an 81-48 record, capturing the pennant by 6½ games over Brooklyn.

LEADERS

BA: Pete Browning, Cle., .373.
Runs: Hugh Duffy, Chi., 161.
Hits: Hugh Duffy, Chi., 191.
TB: Billy Shindle, Phil., 281.
HR: Roger Connor, N.Y., 14.
RBI: Hardy Richardson, Bos., 146.
SB: Harry Stovey, Bos., 97.
Wins: Mark Baldwin, Chi., 34.
ERA: Silver King, Chi., 2.69.
CG: Mark Baldwin, Chi., 54.
IP: Mark Baldwin, Chi., 501.
SO: Mark Baldwin, Chi., 211.

20-game winners

Mark Baldwin, Chi., 34-24
Gus Weyhing, Brk., 30-16
Silver King, Chi., 30-22
Hoss Radbourn, Bos., 27-12
Addison Gumbert, Bos., 23-12
Phil Knell, Phil., 22-11
Hank O'Day, N.Y., 22-13
Henry Gruber, Cle., 22-23
Harry Staley, Pit., 21-25

THE RULES

■ The one-season Players League adopted its own rules book with only slight variations to the ones used by the American Association and National League. The most significant was a resized pitcher's box that reverted to the 6-by-4 foot rectangle last used in 1885 with a front line 51 feet from the center of home base. Other key variations:

■ If a team failed to begin play within one minute after the umpire called "play" at the start of a game, a forfeit was declared.

■ Each corner of the reshaped pitcher's box was marked by a wooden peg, a variation from the flat rubber plates used by the other leagues.

■ Two umpires were required for each championship game, one behind the plate and the other standing in the field.

1890

FINAL STANDINGS

American Association

Team	W	L	Pct.	GB
Louisville	88	44	.667	...
Columbus	79	55	.590	10
St. Louis	78	58	.574	12
Toledo	68	64	.515	20
Rochester	63	63	.500	22
Baltimore	15	19	.441	24
Syracuse	55	72	.433	30.5
Philadelphia	54	78	.409	34
Brooklyn	26	73	.263	45.5

SIGNIFICANT EVENTS

■ Brooklyn joined Syracuse, Rochester and Toledo as new American Association cities.

■ The bankrupt Athletics disbanded, releasing and selling their players. A patchwork Philadelphia club would close the season with 22 consecutive losses.

■ The Athletics were expelled, a new Philadelphia franchise was admitted and new teams from Boston, Washington and Chicago replaced Syracuse, Rochester and Toledo in action at the winter meetings.

MEMORABLE MOMENT

■ Louisville defeated N.L.-champion Brooklyn 6-2 to salvage a "World's Series" split. Each team won three games and one ended in a tie.

LEADERS

BA: Jimmy Wolf, Lou., .363.
Runs: Jim McTamany, Col., 140.
Hits: Jimmy Wolf, Lou., 197.
TB: Jimmy Wolf, Lou., 260.
HR: Count Campau, St.L., 9.
SB: Tommy McCarthy, St.L., 83.
Wins: Sadie McMahon, Phil.-Bal., 36.
ERA: Scott Stratton, Lou., 2.36.
CG: Sadie McMahon, Phil.-Bal., 55.
IP: Sadie McMahon, Phil.-Bal., 509.
SO: Sadie McMahon, Phil.-Bal., 291.

20-game winners

Sadie McMahon, Phil.-Bal., 36-21
Scott Stratton, Lou., 34-14
Hank Gastright, Col., 30-14
Bob Barr, Rch., 28-24
Jack Stivetts, St.L., 27-21
Red Ehret, Lou., 25-14
Toad Ramsey, St.L., 24-17
John Healy, Tol., 22-21

MAJOR RULES CHANGES

■ Pitchers and other players were no longer allowed to discolor the ball by rubbing it with soil or other foreign substances.

■ Each team was allowed a second "extra player" and substitutions could be made at any time with retiring players unable to return.

FINAL STANDINGS

National League

Team	W	L	Pct.	GB
Brooklyn	86	43	.667	...
Chicago	84	53	.613	6
Philadelphia	78	54	.591	9.5
Cincinnati	77	55	.583	10.5
Boston	76	57	.571	12
New York	63	68	.481	24
Cleveland	44	88	.333	43.5
Pittsburgh	23	113	.169	66.5

SIGNIFICANT EVENTS

■ Committees from the three rival Major Leagues began October peace negotiations that eventually would signal the end of the Players League.

MEMORABLE MOMENTS

■ N.L. newcomer Brooklyn moved into first place with a victory over Cincinnati. The Bridegrooms would win the pennant with a six-game edge over Chicago.

■ Brooklyn swept a tripleheader from hapless Pittsburgh and stretched its losing streak to 22 games. Pittsburgh would finish the season with a record 113 losses.

■ Brooklyn (N.L.) and Louisville (A.A.) began play in a "World's Series" that did not include Players League champion Boston. The Bridegrooms won the opener, 9-0, but the series would end in a 3-3 deadlock with one tie.

LEADERS

BA: Jack Glasscock, N.Y., .336.
Runs: Hub Collins, Brk., 148.
Hits: Jack Glasscock, N.Y.; Sam Thompson, Phil., 172.
TB: Mike Tiernan, N.Y., 274.
HR: Oyster Burns, Brk.; Mike Tiernan, N.Y.; Walt Wilmot, Chi., 13.
RBI: Oyster Burns, Brk., 128.
SB: Billy Hamilton, Phil., 102.
Wins: Bill Hutchinson, Chi., 42.
ERA: Billy Rhines, Cin., 1.95.
CG: Bill Hutchinson, Chi., 65.
IP: Bill Hutchinson, Chi., 603.
SO: Amos Rusie, N.Y., 341.

20-game winners

Bill Hutchison, Chi., 42-25
Kid Gleason, Phil., 38-17
Tom Lovett, Brk., 30-11
Amos Rusie, N.Y., 29-34
Billy Rhines, Cin., 28-17
Kid Nichols, Bos., 27-19
Adonis Terry, Brk., 26-16
John Clarkson, Bos., 26-18
Tom Vickery, Phil., 24-22
Bob Caruthers, Brk., 23-11
Charlie Getzien, Bos., 23-17
Ed Beatin, Cle., 22-30
Pat Luby, Chi., 20-9

POST-SEASON PLAYOFF

(Brooklyn N.L. 3, Louisville A.A. 3; 1 tie)

Game 1—Brooklyn 9, Louisville 0 (8 innings, darkness)

Game 2—Brooklyn 5, Louisville 3

Game 3—Brooklyn 7, Louisville 7 (8 innings, darkness)

Game 4—Louisville 5, Brooklyn 4

Game 5—Brooklyn 7, Louisville 2

Game 6—Louisville 9, Brooklyn 8

Game 7—Louisville 6, Brooklyn 2

MAJOR RULES CHANGES

■ Pitchers and other players were no longer allowed to discolor the ball by rubbing it with soil or other foreign substances.

■ Each team was allowed a second "extra player" and substitutions could be made at any time with retiring players unable to return.

1891

FINAL STANDINGS

American Association

Team	W	L	Pct.	GB
Boston	93	42	.689	...
St. Louis	86	52	.623	8.5
Milwaukee	21	15	.583	22.5
Baltimore	71	64	.526	22
Philadelphia	73	66	.525	22
Columbus	61	76	.445	33
Cincinnati	43	57	.430	32.5
Louisville	55	84	.396	40
Washington	44	91	.326	49

SIGNIFICANT EVENTS

■ In a February declaration of war, the American Association withdrew from the National Agreement and moved its Chicago franchise to Cincinnati to compete with the N.L.'s Reds.

■ The Association's Cincinnati franchise folded in mid-August and was replaced by the Western Association's Milwaukee Brewers.

■ The Boston Reds, en route to the A.A. pennant, were shocked by the August defection of star King Kelly to their Boston N.L. rival.

■ A "World's Series" challenge by Reds owners was turned down by the the N.L.-champion Boston team. N.L. officials cited the A.A.'s withdrawal from the National Agreement.

■ After 10 Major League seasons, the Association died when four of its eight teams joined the N.L. and the other four accepted buyouts.

MEMORABLE MOMENTS

■ The Boston Reds defeated Baltimore and clinched the final A.A. pennant.

■ Browns rookie Ted Breitenstein, making his first Major League start on the final day of the season, pitched an 8-0 no-hitter against Louisville.

LEADERS

BA: Dan Brouthers, Bos., .350.
Runs: Tom Brown, Bos., 177.
Hits: Tom Brown, Bos., 189.
TB: Tom Brown, Bos., 276.
HR: Duke Farrell, Bos., 12.
RBI: Hugh Duffy, Bos.; Duke Farrell, Bos., 110.
SB: Tom Brown, Bos., 106.
Wins: Sadie McMahon, Bal., 35.
ERA: Ed Crane, Cin., 2.45.
CG: Sadie McMahon, Bal., 53.
IP: Sadie McMahon, Bal., 503.
SO: Jack Stivetts, St.L., 259.

20-game winners

Sadie McMahon, Bal., 35-24
George Haddock, Bos., 34-11
Jack Stivetts, St.L., 33-22
Gus Weyhing, Phil., 31-20
Charlie Buffinton, Bos., 29-9
Phil Knell, Col., 28-27
Elton Chamberlain, Phil., 22-23
Willie McGill, Cin.-St.L., 21-15

MAJOR RULES CHANGE

■ All teams were required to have one or more substitutes available for each game.

FINAL STANDINGS

National League

Team	W	L	Pct.	GB
Boston	87	51	.630	...
Chicago	82	53	.607	3.5
New York	71	61	.538	13
Philadelphia	68	69	.496	18.5
Cleveland	65	74	.468	22.5
Brooklyn	61	76	.445	25.5
Cincinnati	56	81	.409	30.5
Pittsburgh	55	80	.407	30.5

SIGNIFICANT EVENTS

■ The American Association withdrew from the National Agreement in February and declared war, moving its Chicago franchise to Cincinnati to compete with the N.L.'s Reds.

■ Pittsburgh secured its nickname as "Pirates" when it lured stars Pete Browning and Scott Stratton away from the A.A.'s Louisville team.

■ With August peace talks between the National League and American Association in progress, the N.L. Boston team shattered the calm by pirating King Kelly away from its A.A. Boston rival.

■ The American Association ceased operations in December when four A.A. clubs (St. Louis, Louisville, Washington and Baltimore) joined the N.L., creating "The National League and American Association of Professional Base Ball Clubs."

MEMORABLE MOMENTS

■ Cy Young christened Cleveland's new League Park, pitching the Spiders to an easy victory over the Reds.

■ Chicago's Wild Bill Hutchison defeated Boston for his 40th victory en route to a Major League-high 44.

■ Boston clinched the N.L. pennant with a victory over Philadelphia—its 17th in a row.

LEADERS

BA: Billy Hamilton, Phil., .340.
Runs: Billy Hamilton, Phil., 141.
Hits: Billy Hamilton, Phil., 179.
TB: Harry Stovey, Bos., 271.
HR: Harry Stovey, Bos.; Mike Tiernan, N.Y., 16.
RBI: Cap Anson, Chi., 120.
SB: Billy Hamilton, Phil., 111.
Wins: Bill Hutchinson, Chi., 44.
ERA: John Ewing, N.Y., 2.27.
CG: Bill Hutchinson, Chi., 56.
IP: Bill Hutchinson, Chi., 561.
SO: Amos Rusie, N.Y., 337.

20-game winners

Bill Hutchison, Chi., 44-19
John Clarkson, Bos., 33-19
Amos Rusie, N.Y., 33-20
Kid Nichols, Bos., 30-17
Cy Young, Cle., 27-22
Harry Staley, Pit.-Bos., 24-13
Kid Gleason, Phil., 24-22
Tom Lovett, Brk., 23-19
Tony Mullane, Cin., 23-26
Mark Baldwin, Pit., 22-28
John Ewing, N.Y., 21-8
Duke Esper, Phil., 20-15

MAJOR RULES CHANGE

■ All teams were required to have one or more substitutes available for each game.

1892

FINAL STANDINGS

National League

Team	W	L	Pct.	GB
Boston	102	48	.680	...
Cleveland	93	56	.624	8.5
Brooklyn	95	59	.617	9
Philadelphia	87	66	.569	16.5
Cincinnati	82	68	.547	20
Pittsburgh	80	73	.523	23.5
Chicago	70	76	.479	30
New York	71	80	.470	31.5
Louisville	63	89	.414	40
Washington	58	93	.384	44.5
St. Louis	56	94	.373	46
Baltimore	46	101	.313	54.5

SIGNIFICANT EVENTS

■ The new 12-team N.L. adopted a 154-game split schedule featuring first-half and second-half champions.
■ Cincinnati, playing host to the first Sunday game in N.L. history, defeated the Browns, 5-1.
■ N.L. owners, holding a mid-November meeting in Chicago, shortened the 1893 schedule to 132 games and dropped the split-season format.

MEMORABLE MOMENTS

■ Baltimore catcher Wilbert Robinson collected a record seven hits during a 25-7 victory over the Browns.
■ Cincinnati's Bumpus Jones made his Major League debut a spectacular one, holding Pittsburgh hitless in a 7-1 victory.
■ First-half champion Boston swept aside second-half champion Cleveland in a post-season playoff. The Beaneaters won five of the six games and the other ended in a tie.

LEADERS

BA: Dan Brouthers, Brk., .335.
Runs: Cupid Childs, Cle., 136.
Hits: Dan Brouthers, Brk., 197.
TB: Dan Brouthers, Brk., 282.
HR: Bug Holliday, Cin., 13.
RBI: Dan Brouthers, Brk., 124.
SB: Monte Ward, Brk., 88.
Wins: Bill Hutchinson, Chi.; Cy Young, Cle., 36.
ERA: Cy Young, Cle., 1.93.
CG: Bill Hutchinson, Chi., 67.
IP: Bill Hutchinson, Chi., 627.
SO: Bill Hutchinson, Chi., 316.

20-game winners

Bill Hutchinson, Chi., 36-36
Cy Young, Cle., 36-12
Kid Nichols, Bos., 35-16
Jack Stivetts, Bos., 35-16
Gus Weyhing, Phil., 32-21
Amos Rusie, N.Y., 31-31
George Haddock, Brk., 29-13
Frank Killen, Wash., 29-26
George Cuppy, Cle., 28-13
Ed Stein, Brk., 27-16
Mark Baldwin, Pit., 26-27
John Clarkson, Bos.-Cle., 25-16
Silver King, N.Y., 23-24
Harry Staley, Bos., 22-10
Ad Gumbert, Chi., 22-19
Tony Mullane, Cin., 21-13
Frank Dwyer, St.L.-Cin., 21-18
Scott Stratton, Lou., 21-19
Kid Gleason, St.L., 20-24

POST-SEASON PLAYOFF

(Boston 5, Cleveland 0; 1 tie)
Game 1—Boston 0, Cleveland 0 (11 innings, darkness)
Game 2—Boston 4, Cleveland 3
Game 3—Boston 3, Cleveland 2
Game 4—Boston 4, Cleveland 0
Game 5—Boston 12, Cleveland 7
Game 6—Boston 8, Cleveland 3

MAJOR RULES CHANGES

■ Games were declared "official" after five full innings or 4½ if the home team was leading.

■ An umpire was given authority to declare a forfeit when he believed players were using delay tactics to gain suspension of a game.

■ Any ball hit over an outfield fence was declared a home run, except in cases where the distance was less than 235 feet from home base. Such drives were called ground-rule doubles.

■ Any batter obstructing or interfering with a catcher's throw was declared out.

1893

FINAL STANDINGS

National League

Team	W	L	Pct.	GB
Boston	86	43	.667	...
Pittsburgh	81	48	.628	5
Cleveland	73	55	.570	12.5
Philadelphia	72	57	.558	14
New York	68	64	.515	19.5
Brooklyn	65	63	.508	20.5
Cincinnati	65	63	.508	20.5
Baltimore	60	70	.462	26.5
Chicago	56	71	.441	29
St. Louis	57	75	.432	30.5
Louisville	50	75	.400	34
Washington	40	89	.310	46

SIGNIFICANT EVENT

■ A revolutionary rules change: The pitching box was eliminated and a pitcher's rubber was placed 5 feet behind the back line of the box—60 feet, 6 inches from home plate.

MEMORABLE MOMENTS

■ Boston defeated Baltimore 6-2 in a late July game and took over permanent posession of first place en route to its third consecutive pennant.
■ Cleveland ended the 33-game hitting streak of George Davis during an 8-6 victory over the Giants.

LEADERS

BA: Hugh Duffy, Bos., .363.
Runs: Herman Long, Bos., 149.
Hits: Sam Thompson, Phil., 222.
TB: Ed Delahanty, Phil., 347.
HR: Ed Delahanty, Phil., 19.
RBI: Ed Delahanty, Phil., 146.
SB: Tom Brown, Lou., 66.
Wins: Frank Killen, Pit., 36.
ERA: Ted Breitenstein, St.L., 3.18.
CG: Amos Rusie, N.Y., 50.
IP: Amos Rusie, N.Y., 482.
SO: Amos Rusie, N.Y., 208.

20-game winners

Frank Killen, Pit., 36-14
Kid Nichols, Bos., 34-14
Cy Young, Cle., 34-16
Amos Rusie, N.Y., 33-21
Brickyard Kennedy, Brk., 25-20
Gus Weyhing, Phil., 23-16
Sadie McMahon, Bal., 23-18
Kid Gleason, St.L., 21-22
Jack Stivetts, Bos., 20-12

MAJOR RULES CHANGES

■ The pitcher's box was eliminated and the pitching distance was lengthened to 60 feet, 6 inches from the outer corner of home base. The distance was marked by a rubber slab (a pitching rubber) 12 inches long and 4 inches wide.

■ Pitchers were required to deliver the ball with one foot remaining in contact with the rubber.

■ Bats with a flat surface were outlawed. Bats were required to be completely round.

■ Lineups were submitted before each game and the batting order was followed throughout the contest. Each new inning started with the batter whose name followed the man who had made the final out of the previous inning.

1894

FINAL STANDINGS

National League

Team	W	L	Pct.	GB
Baltimore	89	39	.695	...
New York	88	44	.667	3
Boston	83	49	.629	8
Philadelphia	71	57	.555	18
Brooklyn	70	61	.534	20.5
Cleveland	68	61	.527	21.5
Pittsburgh	65	65	.500	25
Chicago	57	75	.432	34
St. Louis	56	76	.424	35
Cincinnati	55	75	.423	35
Washington	45	87	.341	46
Louisville	36	94	.277	54

SIGNIFICANT EVENT

■ Rules changes: Foul bunts became strikes and the infield fly rule was entered into the books.

MEMORABLE MOMENTS

■ Boston second baseman Bobby Lowe became baseball's first four-homer man when he connected in consecutive at-bats during a rout of Cincinnati.
■ Chicago shortstop Bill Dahlen failed to get a hit in six at-bats against Cincinnati, ending his 42-game hitting streak.
■ Philadelphia star Billy Hamilton tied a Major League record with seven stolen bases in a victory over Washington.
■ The Orioles clinched the first of three consecutive pennants with a victory over Cleveland.
■ Second-place New York defeated regular-season champion Baltimore 16-3 and concluded its sweep of the best-of-seven Temple Cup series—a new post-season playoff.

LEADERS

BA: Hugh Duffy, Bos., .440.
Runs: Billy Hamilton, Phil., 192.
Hits: Hugh Duffy, Bos., 237.
TB: Hugh Duffy, Bos., 374.
HR: Hugh Duffy, Bos., 18.
RBI: Hugh Duffy, Bos., 145.
SB: Billy Hamilton, Phil., 98.
Wins: Amos Rusie, N.Y., 36.
ERA: Amos Rusie, N.Y., 2.78.
CG: Ted Breitenstein, St.L., 46.
IP: Ted Breitenstein, St.L., 447.1.
SO: Amos Rusie, N.Y., 195.

20-game winners

Amos Rusie, N.Y., 36-13
Jouett Meekin, N.Y., 33-9
Kid Nichols, Bos., 32-13
Ted Breitenstein, St.L., 27-23
Ed Stein, Brk., 26-14
Jack Stivetts, Bos., 26-14
Cy Young, Cle., 26-21
Sadie McMahon, Bal., 25-8
George Cuppy, Cle., 24-15
Brickyard Kennedy, Brk., 24-20
Jack Taylor, Phil., 23-13
Clark Griffith, Chi., 21-14

TEMPLE CUP

(New York 4, Baltimore 0)
Game 1—New York 4, Baltimore 1
Game 2—New York 9, Baltimore 6
Game 3—New York 4, Baltimore 1
Game 4—New York 16, Baltimore 3

MAJOR RULES CHANGES

■ Batters were charged with a strike when bunting the ball into foul territory.

■ Batters who advanced a runner with a bunt while being put out were credited with a sacrifice and not charged with an at-bat.

1895

FINAL STANDINGS

National League

Team	W	L	Pct.	GB
Baltimore	87	43	.669	...
Cleveland	84	46	.646	3
Philadelphia	78	53	.595	9.5
Chicago	72	58	.554	15
Boston	71	60	.542	16.5
Brooklyn	71	60	.542	16.5
Pittsburgh	71	61	.538	17
Cincinnati	66	64	.508	21
New York	66	65	.504	21.5
Washington	43	85	.336	43
St. Louis	39	92	.298	48.5
Louisville	35	96	.267	52.5

SIGNIFICANT EVENT

■ N.L. officials, reacting to player complaints, restricted the size of gloves for everybody but first basemen and catchers to 10 ounces and 14 inches in circumference around the palm.

MEMORABLE MOMENTS

■ Louisville defeated Washington, but Colonels star Fred Clarke saw his 35-game hitting streak come to an end.
■ Baltimore clinched its second straight pennant with a victory over New York—two days before the regular season ended.
■ Cleveland captured the Temple Cup with a fifth-game, 5-2 victory over Baltimore.

LEADERS

BA: Jesse Burkett, Cle., .409.
Runs: Billy Hamilton, Phil., 166.
Hits: Jesse Burkett, Cle., 225.
TB: Sam Thompson, Phil., 352.
HR: Sam Thompson, Phil., 18.
RBI: Sam Thompson, Phil., 165.
SB: Billy Hamilton, Phil., 97.
Wins: Cy Young, Cle., 35.
ERA: Al Maul, Wash., 2.45.
CG: Ted Breitenstein, St.L., 46.
IP: Pink Hawley, Pit., 444.1.
SO: Amos Rusie, N.Y., 201.

20-game winners

Cy Young, Cle., 35-10
Bill Hoffer, Bal., 31-6
Pink Hawley, Pit., 31-22
George Cuppy, Cle., 26-14
Clark Griffith, Chi., 26-14
Jack Taylor, Phil., 26-14
Kid Nichols, Bos., 26-16
Kid Carsey, Phil., 24-16
Amos Rusie, N.Y., 23-23
Adonis Terry, Chi., 21-14
George Hemming, Bal., 20-13

TEMPLE CUP

(Cleveland 4, Baltimore 1)
Game 1—Cleveland 5, Baltimore 4
Game 2—Cleveland 7, Baltimore 2
Game 3—Cleveland 7, Baltimore 1
Game 4—Baltimore 5, Cleveland 0
Game 5—Cleveland 5, Baltimore 2

MAJOR RULES CHANGES

■ The pitching rubber was enlarged to 24-by-6 inches, its current size.

■ A foul tip caught by the catcher became a strike.

■ The infield fly rule became official.

■ Bats were limited to 2¾ inches in diameter.

■ Catchers and first basemen were given permission to use oversized gloves. Other fielders still were restricted to gloves weighing 10 ounces with a hand size not more than 14 inches.

1896

FINAL STANDINGS

National League

Team	W	L	Pct.	GB
Baltimore	90	39	.698	...
Cleveland	80	48	.625	9.5
Cincinnati	77	50	.606	12
Boston	74	57	.565	17
Chicago	71	57	.555	18.5
Pittsburgh	66	63	.512	24
New York	64	67	.489	27
Philadelphia	62	68	.477	28.5
Brooklyn	58	73	.443	33
Washington	58	73	.443	33
St. Louis	40	90	.308	50.5
Louisville	38	93	.290	53

SIGNIFICANT EVENT

■ Cleveland's Jesse Burkett collected three final-day hits and finished with a league-leading .410 average—his record second consecutive .400 season.

MEMORABLE MOMENTS

■ Philadelphia star Ed Delahanty matched Bobby Lowe's 1894 record of four home runs in a game—all inside-the-park shots in a loss to Chicago.
■ Baltimore clinched its third straight pennant with a victory over Brooklyn.
■ Regular-season champion Baltimore defeated Cleveland 5-0 and capped its four-game sweep of the Temple Cup series.

LEADERS

BA: Jesse Burkett, Cle., .410.
Runs: Jesse Burkett, Cle., 160.
Hits: Jesse Burkett, Cle., 240.
TB: Jesse Burkett, Cle., 317.
HR: Ed Delahanty, Phil.;
Bill Joyce, Wash.-N.Y., 13.
RBI: Ed Delahanty, Phil., 126.
SB: Joe Kelley, Bal., 87.
Wins: Frank Killen, Pit.; Kid Nichols, Bos., 30.
ERA: Billy Rhines, Cin., 2.45.
CG: Frank Killen, Pit., 44.
IP: Frank Killen, Pit., 432.1.
SO: Cy Young, Cle., 140.

20-game winners

Kid Nichols, Bos., 30-14
Frank Killen, Pit., 30-18
Cy Young, Cle., 28-15
Jouett Meekin, N.Y., 26-14
Bill Hoffer, Bal., 25-7
George Cuppy, Cle., 25-14
George Mercer, Wash., 25-18
Frank Dwyer, Cin., 24-11
Clark Griffith, Chi., 23-11
Jack Stivetts, Bos., 22-14
Pink Hawley, Pit., 22-21
Jack Taylor, Phil., 20-21

TEMPLE CUP

(Baltimore 4, Cleveland 0)
Game 1—Baltimore 7, Cleveland 1
Game 2—Baltimore 7, Cleveland 2 (8 innings, darkness)
Game 3—Baltimore 6, Cleveland 2
Game 4—Baltimore 5, Cleveland 0

MAJOR RULES CHANGES

■ Pitchers were no longer required to hold the ball in full sight of the umpire up to delivery.
■ Umpires were given authority to eject players using vulgar language and fine them $25. Umpires also were allowed to fine players $5 to $10 for specified misconduct.
■ Home teams were required to have at least 12 regulation balls available for each game.

1897

FINAL STANDINGS

National League

Team	W	L	Pct.	GB
Boston	93	39	.705	...
Baltimore	90	40	.692	2
New York	83	48	.634	9.5
Cincinnati	76	56	.576	17
Cleveland	69	62	.527	23.5
Brooklyn	61	71	.462	32
Washington	61	71	.462	32
Pittsburgh	60	71	.458	32.5
Chicago	59	73	.447	34
Philadelphia	55	77	.417	38
Louisville	52	78	.400	40
St. Louis	29	102	.221	63.5

SIGNIFICANT EVENT

■ The 4-year-old Temple Cup series, which failed to attract fan interest, died a quiet death after regular-season champion Boston lost a five-game series to second-place Baltimore.

MEMORABLE MOMENTS

■ Pittsburgh pitcher Frank Killen defeated Baltimore and ended Willie Keeler's 44-game hitting streak.
■ Chicago set an N.L. single-game scoring record during a 36-7 demolition of Louisville.
■ Boston's victory over Brooklyn, coupled with Baltimore's same-day loss to Washington, gave the Beaneaters the N.L. pennant.

LEADERS

BA: Willie Keeler, Bal., .424.
Runs: Billy Hamilton, Bos., 152.
Hits: Willie Keeler, Bal., 239.
TB: Nap Lajoie, Phil., 310.
HR: Hugh Duffy, Bos., 11.
RBI: George Davis, N.Y., 136.
SB: Bill Lange, Chi., 73.
Wins: Kid Nichols, Bos., 31.
ERA: Amos Rusie, N.Y., 2.54.
CG: Red Donahue, St.L.; Clark Griffith, Chi.;
Frank Killen, Pit., 38.
IP: Kid Nichols, Bos., 368.
SO: Doc McJames, Wash., 156.

20-game winners

Kid Nichols, Bos., 31-11
Amos Rusie, N.Y., 28-10
Fred Klobedanz, Bos., 26-7
Joe Corbett, Bal., 24-8
Ted Breitenstein, Cin., 23-12
Bill Hoffer, Bal., 22-11
Ted Lewis, Bos., 21-12
Bill Rhines, Cin., 21-15
Clark Griffith, Chi., 21-18
Cy Young, Cle., 21-19
Jerry Nops, Bal., 20-6
Jouett Meekin, N.Y., 20-11
George Mercer, Wash., 20-20

TEMPLE CUP

(Baltimore 4, Boston 1)
Game 1—Boston 13, Baltimore 12
Game 2—Baltimore 13, Boston 11
Game 3—Baltimore 8, Boston 3 (7 innings, rain)
Game 4—Baltimore 12, Boston 11
Game 5—Baltimore 9, Boston 3

MAJOR RULES CHANGES

■ Runners who were held or obstructed by fielders without the ball were given the base they were trying to reach. Any fielder stopping a ball in any way other than with his hands was guilty of obstruction and runners were allowed to advance.
■ Runners returning to their original base after a caught fly ball were required to retouch all bases they had passed in reverse order.
■ Any judgement call by the umpire was final and could not be reversed.
■ Earned runs were defined as runs scored without the aid of errors.

1898

FINAL STANDINGS

National League

Team	W	L	Pct.	GB
Boston	102	47	.685	...
Baltimore	96	53	.644	6
Cincinnati	92	60	.605	11.5
Chicago	85	65	.567	17.5
Cleveland	81	68	.544	21
Philadelphia	78	71	.523	24
New York	77	73	.513	25.5
Pittsburgh	72	76	.486	29.5
Louisville	70	81	.464	33
Brooklyn	54	91	.372	46
Washington	51	101	.336	52.5
St. Louis	39	111	.260	63.5

SIGNIFICANT EVENT

■ Cap Anson, who compiled a 1,293-932 record over 19 seasons as a Chicago manager, was fired.

MEMORABLE MOMENTS

■ A Major League first: Baltimore's Jim Hughes and Cincinnati's Ted Breitenstein pitched nine-inning no-hitters on the same day.
■ Philadelphia pitcher Bill Duggleby hit a grand slam in his first Major League at-bat—a feat never since duplicated.
■ Boston, en route to a record-tying 102 wins, clinched its second straight pennant with a victory over Washington.

LEADERS

BA: Willie Keeler, Bal., .385.
Runs: John McGraw, Bal., 143.
Hits: Willie Keeler, Bal., 216.
TB: Jimmy Collins, Bos., 286.
HR: Jimmy Collins, Bos., 15.
RBI: Nap Lajoie, Phil., 127.
SB: Ed Delahanty, Phil., 58.
Wins: Kid Nichols, Bos., 31.
ERA: Clark Griffith, Chi., 1.88.
CG: Jack Taylor, St.L., 42.
IP: Jack Taylor, St.L., 397.1.
SO: Cy Seymour, N.Y., 239.

20-game winners

Kid Nichols, Bos., 31-12
Bert Cunningham, Lou., 28-15
Pink Hawley, Cin., 27-11
Doc McJames, Bal., 27-15
Ted Lewis, Bos., 26-8
Jesse Tannehill, Pit., 25-13
Vic Willis, Bos., 25-13
Cy Young, Cle., 25-13
Cy Seymour, N.Y., 25-19
Clark Griffith, Chi., 24-10
Wiley Piatt, Phil., 24-14
Jim Hughes, Bal., 23-12
Jack Powell, Cle., 23-15
Al Maul, Bal., 20-7
Jim Callahan, Chi., 20-10
Amos Rusie, N.Y., 20-11
Ted Breitenstein, Cin., 20-14

MAJOR RULES CHANGES

■ Penalties were specified for teams batting out of order.
■ Detailed definitions were provided for pitchers committing balks, including illegal motions to home base and to the bases.
■ Stolen bases were awarded for bases attained without the aid of batted balls or errors.

1899

FINAL STANDINGS

National League

Team	W	L	Pct.	GB
Brooklyn	101	47	.682	...
Boston	95	57	.625	8
Philadelphia	94	58	.618	9
Baltimore	86	62	.581	15
St. Louis	84	67	.556	18.5
Cincinnati	83	67	.553	19
Pittsburgh	76	73	.510	25.5
Chicago	75	73	.507	26
Louisville	75	77	.493	28
New York	60	90	.400	42
Washington	54	98	.355	49
Cleveland	20	134	.130	84

SIGNIFICANT EVENTS

■ John McGraw made his managerial debut a successful one, leading Baltimore to a victory over New York.
■ The Western League changed its name to the American Baseball League, setting the stage for Ban Johnson's circuit to gain "Major League" credibility.

MEMORABLE MOMENTS

■ Cleveland defeated Washington and snapped its 24-game losing streak.
■ The Brooklyn Superbas, en route to 101 victories, clinched the pennant with a win over New York.
■ Cincinnati posted a season-closing sweep of Cleveland, handing the Spiders their 133rd and 134th losses.

LEADERS

BA: Ed Delahanty, Phil., .410.
Runs: Willie Keeler, Brk.;
John McGraw, Bal., 140.
Hits: Ed Delahanty, Phil., 238.
TB: Ed Delahanty, Phil., 338.
HR: Buck Freeman, Wash., 25.
RBI: Ed Delahanty, Phil., 137.
SB: Jimmy Sheckard, Bal., 77.
Wins: Jim Hughes, Brk.; Joe McGinnity, Bal., 28.
ERA: Vic Willis, Bos., 2.50.
CG: Bill Carrick, N.Y.; Jack Powell, St.L.;
Cy Young, St.L., 40.
IP: Sam Leever, Pit., 379.
SO: Noodles Hahn, Cin., 145.

20-game winners

Jim Hughes, Brk., 28-6
Joe McGinnity, Bal., 28-16
Vic Willis, Bos., 27-8
Cy Young, St.L., 26-16
Jesse Tannehill, Pit., 24-14
Noodles Hahn, Cin., 23-8
Jack Dunn, Brk., 23-13
Wiley Piatt, Phil., 23-15
Jack Powell, St.L., 23-19
Brickyard Kennedy, Brk., 22-9
Clark Griffith, Chi., 22-14
Frank Kitson, Bal., 22-16
Red Donahue, Phil., 21-8
Jim Callahan, Chi., 21-12
Chick Fraser, Phil., 21-12
Deacon Phillippe, Lou., 21-17
Kid Nichols, Bos., 21-19
Sam Leever, Pit., 21-23

MAJOR RULES CHANGES

■ The score of any game suspended or called before the full nine innings had been played reverted back to the last full inning completed.
■ Batters were awarded first base for catcher's interference.
■ The 1898 balk rules were further defined.
■ Each team was required to wear uniforms that conformed in color and style.

1900

FINAL STANDINGS

National League

Team	W	L	Pct.	GB
Brooklyn	82	54	.603	...
Pittsburgh	79	60	.568	4.5
Philadelphia	75	63	.543	8
Boston	66	72	.478	17
Chicago	65	75	.464	19
St. Louis	65	75	.464	19
Cincinnati	62	77	.446	21.5
New York	60	78	.435	23

SIGNIFICANT EVENTS

■ **March 8:** The National League streamlined its product, reducing from 12 to eight teams.

■ **March 9:** N.L. officials expanded the strike zone by reshaping home plate from a 12-inch square to a 17-inch-wide, five-sided figure.

■ **March 16:** Ban Johnson announced formation of a franchise in Chicago, giving his young American League teams in eight cities. The others were Kansas City, Minneapolis, Milwaukee, Indianapolis, Detroit, Cleveland and Buffalo.

■ **October 11:** Ban Johnson's new American League, claiming status as an equal to the National League, announced plans to locate franchises in Baltimore and Washington.

■ **November 14:** The N.L. declared war when it rejected the A.L. as an equal and pronounced it an "outlaw league" outside the National Agreement.

■ **December 15:** The Giants traded aging Amos Rusie to the Reds for a young pitcher named Christy Mathewson.

MEMORABLE MOMENTS

■ **April 19:** Ban Johnson's new American League opened with a bang when Buffalo's Doc Amole pitched an 8-0 no-hitter against the Tigers.

■ **July 7:** Boston's Kid Nichols defeated the Cubs 11-4 for his 300th career victory.

■ **October 3:** Brooklyn clinched the N.L. pennant with a 6-4, 5-4 sweep at Boston, giving manager Ned Hanlon his fifth championship in seven years.

LEADERS

BA: Honus Wagner, Pit., .381.
Runs: Roy Thomas, Phil., 132.
Hits: Willie Keeler, Brk., 204.
TB: Honus Wagner, Pit., 302.
HR: Herman Long, Bos., 12.
RBI: Elmer Flick, Phil., 110.
SB: Patsy Donovan, St.L.; George Van Haltren, N.Y., 45.
Wins: Joe McGinnity, Brk., 28.
ERA: Rube Waddell, Pit., 2.37.
CG: Pink Hawley, N.Y., 34.
IP: Joe McGinnity, Brk., 343.
SO: Noodles Hahn, Cin., 132.

20-game winners

Joe McGinnity, Brk., 28-8
Jesse Tannehill, Pit., 20-6
Brickyard Kennedy, Brk., 20-13
Deacon Phillippe, Pit., 20-13
Bill Dinneen, Bos., 20-14

100 RBIs

Elmer Flick, Phil., 110
Ed Delahanty, Phil., 109
Honus Wagner, Pit., 100

CHRONICLE-TELEGRAPH CUP

(Brooklyn 3, Pittsburgh 1)

Game 1—Brooklyn 5, Pittsburgh 2
Game 2—Brooklyn 4, Pittsburgh 2
Game 3—Pittsburgh 10, Brooklyn 0
Game 4—Brooklyn 6, Pittsburgh 1

MAJOR RULES CHANGES

■ Home "base" became home "plate" when its shape was changed from a 12-inch square to a five-sided flat surface 17 inches wide.

■ A batter was not awarded first base on a pitcher's balk.

1901

FINAL STANDINGS

American League

Team	W	L	Pct.	GB
Chicago	83	53	.610	...
Boston	79	57	.581	4
Detroit	74	61	.548	8.5
Philadelphia	74	62	.544	9
Baltimore	68	65	.511	13.5
Washington	61	72	.459	20.5
Cleveland	54	82	.397	29
Milwaukee	48	89	.350	35.5

National League

Team	W	L	Pct.	GB
Pittsburgh	90	49	.647	...
Philadelphia	83	57	.593	7.5
Brooklyn	79	57	.581	9.5
St. Louis	76	64	.543	14.5
Boston	69	69	.500	20.5
Chicago	53	86	.381	37
New York	52	85	.380	37
Cincinnati	52	87	.374	38

SIGNIFICANT EVENTS

■ **January 28:** When the A.L. formally organized as an eight-team "Major League," it placed franchises in Chicago, Philadelphia and Boston—N.L. strongholds.

■ **February 27:** Among a series of N.L. rules changes was the declaration that all foul balls will count as strikes, except when the batter already has two.

■ **March 28:** In a move to keep Napoleon Lajoie from jumping to the A.L.'s Athletics, the Phillies filed for an injunction to keep him from playing for any other team.

■ **September 19:** The baseball schedule was canceled because of the funeral of President William McKinley, who was killed by an assassin's bullet.

■ **October 20:** Seven Cardinals, including top hitters Jesse Burkett and Bobby Wallace, jumped to the American League's new St. Louis franchise.

■ **November 20:** A.L. President Ban Johnson shifted his Milwaukee franchise to St. Louis for a head-to-head battle with the N.L.'s Cardinals.

MEMORABLE MOMENTS

■ **April 24:** Chicago played host to the A.L.'s first Major League game, defeating Cleveland, 8-2.

■ **April 25:** Detroit celebrated its A.L. debut by scoring 10 ninth-inning runs and beating Milwaukee, 14-13.

■ **July 15:** Christy Mathewson, the Giants' 21-year-old rookie righthander, held the Cardinals hitless in a 5-0 New York victory at St. Louis.

■ **September 29:** The White Stockings captured the first A.L. pennant, but Philadelphia's Napoleon Lajoie compiled Triple Crown totals of .426, 14 homers and 125 RBI.

LEADERS

American League

BA: Nap Lajoie, Phil., .426.
Runs: Nap Lajoie, Phil., 145.
Hits: Lajoie, Phil., 232.
TB: Nap Lajoie, Phil., 350.
HR: Nap Lajoie, Phil., 14.
RBI: Nap Lajoie, Phil., 125.
SB: Frank Isbell, Chi., 52.
Wins: Cy Young, Bos., 33
ERA: Cy Young, Bos., 1.62
CG: Joe McGinnity, Balt., 39.
IP: Joe McGinnity, Balt., 382.
SO: Cy Young, Bos., 158.

National League

BA: Jesse Burkett, St.L., .376.
Runs: Jesse Burkett, St.L., 142.
Hits: Jesse Burkett, St.L., 226.
TB: Jesse Burkett, St.L., 306.
HR: Sam Crawford, Cin., 16.
RBI: Honus Wagner, Pit., 126.
SB: Honus Wagner, Pit., 49.
Wins: Bill Donovan, Brk., 25.
ERA: Jesse Tannehill, Pit., 2.18.
CG: Noodles Hahn, Cin., 41.
IP: Noodles Hahn, Cin., 375.1.
SO: Noodles Hahn, Cin., 239.

A.L. 20-game winners

Cy Young, Bos., 33-10
Joe McGinnity, Bal., 26-20
Clark Griffith, Chi., 24-7
Roscoe Miller, Det., 23-13
Chick Fraser, Phil., 22-16
Roy Patterson, Chi., 20-15
Red Donahue, Phil., 21-13
Al Orth, Phil., 20-12
Christy Mathewson, N.Y., 20-17
Vic Willis, Bos., 20-17

N.L. 20-game winners

Bill Donovan, Brk., 25-15
Jack Harper, St.L., 23-13
Deacon Phillippe, Pit., 22-12
Noodles Hahn, Cin., 22-19
Jack Chesbro, Pit., 21-10

A.L. 100 RBIs

Nap Lajoie, Phil., 125
Buck Freeman, Bos., 114

N.L. 100 RBIs

Honus Wagner, Pit., 126
Ed Delahanty, Phil., 108
Jimmy Sheckard, Brk., 104
Sam Crawford, Cin., 104

1902

FINAL STANDINGS

American League

Team	W	L	Pct.	GB
Philadelphia	83	53	.610	..
St. Louis	78	58	.574	5
Boston	77	60	.562	6.5
Chicago	74	60	.552	8
Cleveland	69	67	.507	14
Washington	61	75	.449	22
Detroit	52	83	.385	30.5
Baltimore	50	88	.362	34

National League

Team	W	L	Pct.	GB
Pittsburgh	103	36	.741	..
Brooklyn	75	63	.543	27.5
Boston	73	64	.533	29
Cincinnati	70	70	.500	33.5
Chicago	68	69	.496	34
St. Louis	56	78	.418	44.5
Philadelphia	56	81	.409	46
New York	48	88	.353	53.5

SIGNIFICANT EVENTS

■ **April 21:** The Pennsylvania Supreme Court granted an injunction barring league-jumper Napoleon Lajoie from playing for any team but the Phillies.

■ **May 27:** To keep Lajoie from returning to the N.L., A.L. president Ban Johnson shifted his contract from the Athletics to the Indians, getting him out of Pennsylvania.

■ **July 8:** The A.L. lost Baltimore manager John McGraw, who jumped to the N.L. as manager of the Giants and took five players with him.

■ **September 28:** Philadelphia Athletics star Socks Seybold completed the American League season with a Major League single-season record 16 home runs.

■ **December 9:** The A.L. announced plans to locate a franchise in New York for the 1903 season.

■ **December 12:** Owners elected Harry Pulliam as N.L. president.

MEMORABLE MOMENTS

■ **April 26:** In a stirring Major League debut, Cleveland's Addie Joss fired a one-hitter and beat the Browns, 3-0.

■ **July 19:** The New York Giants, en route to a last-place finish in the N.L., dropped a 5-3 decision to Philadelphia in the managerial debut of John McGraw.

■ **October 4:** The Pirates completed their 103-36 season with a 27½-game lead over second-place Brooklyn in the N.L.

LEADERS

American League

BA: Nap Lajoie, Phil-Cle., .378.
Runs: Dave Fultz, Phil.; Topsy Hartsel, Phil., 109.
Hits: Charlie Hickman, Bos.-Cle., 193.
TB: Charlie Hickman, Bos.-Cle., 288.
HR: Socks Seybold, Phil., 16.
RBI: Buck Freeman, Bos., 121.
SB: Topsy Hartsel, Phil., 47.
Wins: Cy Young, Bos., 32.
ERA: Ed Siever, Det., 1.91.
CG: Cy Young, Bos., 41.
IP: Cy Young, Bos., 384.2
SO: Rube Waddell, Phil., 210.

National League

BA: Ginger Beaumont, Pit., .357.
Runs: Honus Wagner, Pit., 105.
Hits: Ginger Beaumont, Pit., 193.
TB: Sam Crawford, Cin., 256.
HR: Tommy Leach, Pit., 6.
RBI: Honus Wagner, Pit., 91.
SB: Honus Wagner, Pit., 42.
Wins: Jack Chesbro, Pit., 28.
ERA: Jack Taylor, Chi., 1.33.
CG: Vic Willis, Bos., 45
IP: Vic Willis, Bos., 410.
SO: Vic Willis, Bos., 225.

A.L. 20-game winners

Cy Young, Bos., 32-11
Rube Waddell, Phil., 24-7
Red Donahue, St.L., 22-11
Jack Powell, St.L., 22-17
Bill Dinneen, Bos., 21-21
Eddie Plank, Phil., 20-15

N.L. 20-game winners

Jack Chesbro, Pit., 28-6
Togie Pittinger, Bos., 27-16
Vic Willis, Bos., 27-20
Jack Taylor, Chi., 23-11
Noodles Hahn, Cin., 23-12
Jesse Tannehill, Pit., 20-6
Deacon Phillippe, Pit., 20-9

A.L./N.L. 20-game winner

Joe McGinnity, Bal.-Pit., 21

A.L. 100 RBIs

Buck Freeman, Bos., 121
Charlie Hickman, Bos.-Cle., 110
Lave Cross, Phil., 108

1903

FINAL STANDINGS

American League

Team	W	L	Pct.	GB
Boston	91	47	.659	...
Philadelphia	75	60	.556	14.5
Cleveland	77	63	.550	15
New York	72	62	.537	17
Detroit	65	71	.478	25
St. Louis	65	74	.468	26.5
Chicago	60	77	.438	30.5
Washington	43	94	.314	47.5

National League

Team	W	L	Pct.	GB
Pittsburgh	91	49	.650	...
New York	84	55	.604	6.5
Chicago	82	56	.594	8
Cincinnati	74	65	.532	16.5
Brooklyn	70	66	.515	19
Boston	58	80	.420	32
Philadelphia	49	86	.363	39.5
St. Louis	43	94	.314	46.5

SIGNIFICANT EVENTS

- **January 9:** A peace treaty was signed with the N.L. agreeing to recognize the A.L. as a Major League and both parties agreeing to honor the reserve clause in player contracts.
- **July 2:** Washington star Ed Delahanty died when he fell off a railroad bridge spanning the Niagara River at Fort Erie, Ontario.
- **August 8:** A bleacher overhang at Philadelphia's N.L. park collapsed, killing 12 and injuring 282.
- **September 16:** The presidents of the A.L. Boston and N.L. Pittsburgh teams agreed to a best-of-nine championship playoff—baseball's first World Series.

MEMORABLE MOMENTS

- **April 22:** The A.L.'s new New York team officially opened play, but the Highlanders dropped a 3-1 decision at Washington.
- **April 30:** The A.L.'s New York team opened new Hilltop Park with a 6-2 victory over Washington.
- **September 17:** Boston clinched the A.L. pennant with a victory over Cleveland and set up a championship showdown with N.L.-winner Pittsburgh.

LEADERS

American League

BA: Nap Lajoie, Cle., .344.
Runs: Patsy Dougherty, Bos., 107.
Hiis: Patsy Dougherty, Bos., 195.
TB: Buck Freeman, Bos., 281.
HR: Buck Freeman, Bos., 13.
RBI: Buck Freeman, Bos., 104.
SB: Harry Bay, Cle., 45.
Wins: Cy Young, Bos., 28.
ERA: Earl Moore, Cle., 1.74.
CG: Bill Donovan, Det.; Rube Waddell, Phil.; Cy Young, Bos., 34.
IP: Cy Young, Bos., 341.2.
SO: Rube Waddell, Phil., 302.

National League

BA: Honus Wagner, Pit., .355.
Runs: Ginger Beaumont, Pit., 137.
Hits: Ginger Beaumont, Pit., 209.
TB: Ginger Beaumont, Pit., 272.
HR: Jimmy Sheckard, Brk., 9.
RBI: Sam Mertes, N.Y., 104.
SB: Frank Chance, Chi.; Jimmy Sheckard, Brk., 67.
Wins: Joe McGinnity, N.Y., 31.
ERA: Sam Leever, Pit., 2.06.
CG: Joe McGinnity, N.Y., 44.
IP: Joe McGinnity, N.Y., 434.
SO: Christy Mathewson, N.Y., 267.

A.L. 20-game winners

Cy Young, Bos., 28-9
Eddie Plank, Phil., 23-16
Bill Dinneen, Bos., 21-13
Jack Chesbro, N.Y., 21-15
Willie Sudhoff, St.L., 21-15
Rube Waddell, Phil., 21-16
Tom Hughes, Bos., 20-7
Earl Moore, Cle., 20-8

N.L. 20-game winners

Joe McGinnity, N.Y., 31-20
Christy Mathewson, N.Y., 30-13
Sam Leever, Pit., 25-7
Deacon Phillippe, Pit., 25-9
Noodles Hahn, Cin., 22-12
Henry Schmidt, Brk., 22-13
Jack Taylor, Chi., 21-14
Jake Weimer, Chi., 20-8
Bob Wicker, St.L.-Chi., 20-9

A.L. 100 RBIs

Buck Freeman, Bos., 104

N.L. 100 RBIs

Sam Mertes, N.Y., 104
Honus Wagner, Pit., 101

WORLD SERIES

- **Winner:** The Red Sox captured the first modern World Series with a five-games-to-three victory over the N.L.-champion Pirates.
- **Turning point:** A 7-3 Game 7 victory in which the Red Sox claimed a 4-3 Series lead and finally showed they could beat Pirates starter Deacon Phillippe.
- **Memorable moments:** Pirates right fielder Jimmy Sebring's Game 1 home run—the first in World Series history.
- **Top guns:** Bill Dinneen (35 IP, 3-1, 2.06 ERA), Cy Young (34 IP, 2-1, 1.59), Red Sox; Phillippe (44 IP, 3-2), Pirates.

Linescores

Game 1—October 1, at Boston
Pittsburgh...... 4 0 1 1 0 0 1 0 0 — 7 12 2
Boston............ 0 0 0 0 0 0 2 0 1 — 3 6 4
Phillippe; Young. W—Phillippe. L—Young.
HR—Sebring (Pit.).

Game 2—October 2, at Boston
Pittsburgh...... 0 0 0 0 0 0 0 0 0 — 0 3 2
Boston............ 2 0 0 0 0 1 0 0 x — 3 9 0
Leever, Veil (2); Dinneen. W—Dinneen. L—Leever.
HR—Dougherty 2 (Bos.).

Game 3—October 3, at Boston
Pittsburgh...... 0 1 2 0 0 0 0 1 0 — 4 7 0
Boston............ 0 0 0 1 0 0 0 1 0 — 2 4 2
Phillippe; Hughes, Young (3). W—Phillippe.
L—Hughes.

Game 4—October 6, at Pittsburgh
Boston............ 0 0 0 0 1 0 0 0 3 — 4 9 1
Pittsburgh...... 1 0 0 0 1 0 3 0 x — 5 12 1
Dinneen; Phillippe. W—Phillippe. L—Dinneen.

Game 5—October 7, at Pittsburgh
Boston............ 0 0 0 0 0 6 4 1 0 — 11 14 2
Pittsburgh...... 0 0 0 0 0 0 0 2 0 — 2 6 4
Young; Kennedy, Thompson (8). W—Young.
L—Kennedy.

Game 6—October 8, at Pittsburgh
Boston............ 0 0 3 0 2 0 1 0 0 — 6 10 1
Pittsburgh...... 0 0 0 0 0 0 3 0 0 — 3 10 3
Dinneen; Leever. W—Dinneen. L—Leever.

Game 7—October 10, at Pittsburgh
Boston............ 2 0 0 2 0 2 0 1 0 — 7 11 4
Pittsburgh...... 0 0 0 1 0 1 0 0 1 — 3 10 3
Young; Phillippe. W—Young. L—Phillippe.

Game 8—October 13, at Boston
Pittsburgh...... 0 0 0 0 0 0 0 0 0 — 0 4 3
Boston............ 0 0 0 2 0 1 0 0 x — 3 8 0
Phillippe; Dinneen. W—Dinneen. L—Phillippe.

1904

FINAL STANDINGS

American League

Team	W	L	Pct.	GB
Boston	95	59	.617	...
New York	92	59	.609	1.5
Chicago	89	65	.578	6
Cleveland	86	65	.570	7.5
Philadelphia	81	70	.536	12.5
St. Louis	65	87	.428	29
Detroit	62	90	.408	32
Washington	38	113	.252	55.5

National League

Team	W	L	Pct.	GB
New York	106	47	.693	...
Chicago	93	60	.608	13
Cincinnati	88	65	.575	18
Pittsburgh	87	66	.569	19
St. Louis	75	79	.487	31.5
Brooklyn	56	97	.366	50
Boston	55	98	.359	51
Philadelphia	52	100	.342	53.5

SIGNIFICANT EVENT

- **October 10:** Chastising the A.L. as a "minor circuit," Giants owner John T. Brush and manager John McGraw refused to meet the A.L.-champion Red Sox in a second "World Series."

MEMORABLE MOMENTS

- **May 5:** Boston great Cy Young pitched the century's first perfect game, retiring all 27 Athletics he faced in a 3-0 victory.
- **July 5:** The Phillies defeated the Giants 6-5 in 10 innings, ending New York's winning streak at 18 games.
- **October 6:** Cardinals pitcher Jack Taylor pitched his Major League-record 39th consecutive complete game, but dropped a 6-3 decision to Pittsburgh.
- **October 10:** The Red Sox captured their second straight A.L. pennant when New York's Jack Chesbro uncorked a final-day wild pitch that allowed the winning run to score in a 3-2 victory.

LEADERS

American League

BA: Nap Lajoie, Cle., .376.
Runs: Patsy Dougherty, Bos.-N.Y., 113.
Hits: Nap Lajoie, Cle., 208.
TB: Nap Lajoie, Cle., 305.
HR: Harry Davis, Phil., 10.
RBI: Nap Lajoie, Cle., 102.
SB: Harry Bay, Cle.; Elmer Flick, Cle., 38.
Wins: Jack Chesbro, N.Y., 41.
ERA: Addie Joss, Cle., 1.59.
CG: Jack Chesbro, N.Y., 48.
IP: Jack Chesbro, N.Y., 454.2.
SO: Rube Waddell, Phil., 349.

National League

BA: Honus Wagner, Pit., .349.
Runs: George Browne, N.Y., 99.
Hits: Ginger Beaumont, Pit., 185.
TB: Honus Wagner, Pit., 255.
HR: Harry Lumley, Brk., 9.
RBI: Bill Dahlen, N.Y., 80.
SB: Honus Wagner, Pit., 53.
Wins: Joe McGinnity, N.Y., 35.
ERA: Joe McGinnity, N.Y., 1.61.
CG: Jack Taylor, St.L.; Vic Willis, Bos., 39.
IP: Joe McGinnity, N.Y., 408.
SO: Christy Mathewson, N.Y., 212.

A.L. 20-game winners

Jack Chesbro, N.Y., 41-12
Cy Young, Bos., 26-16
Eddie Plank, Phil., 26-17
Rube Waddell, Phil., 25-19
Bill Bernhard, Cle., 23-13
Bill Dinneen, Bos., 23-14
Jack Powell, N.Y., 23-19
Jesse Tannehill, Bos., 21-11
Frank Owen, Chi., 21-15

N.L. 20-game winners

Joe McGinnity, N.Y., 35-8
Christy Mathewson, N.Y., 33-12
Jack Harper, Cin., 23-9
Kid Nichols, St.L., 21-13
Dummy Taylor, N.Y., 21-15
Jake Weimer, Chi., 20-14
Jack Taylor, St.L., 20-19

A.L./N.L. 20-game winner

Patsy Flaherty, Chi.-Pit., 20

A.L. 100 RBIs

Nap Lajoie, Cle., 102

No World Series in 1904.

Cleveland's Nap Lajoie won his fourth consecutive A.L. batting championship in 1904.

HISTORY

1905

FINAL STANDINGS

American League

Team	W	L	Pct.	GB
Philadelphia	92	56	.622	...
Chicago	92	60	.605	2
Detroit	79	74	.516	15.5
Boston	78	74	.513	16
Cleveland	76	78	.494	19
New York	71	78	.477	21.5
Washington	64	87	.424	29.5
St. Louis	54	99	.353	40.5

National League

Team	W	L	Pct.	GB
New York	105	48	.686	...
Pittsburgh	96	57	.627	9
Chicago	92	61	.601	13
Philadelphia	83	69	.546	21.5
Cincinnati	79	74	.516	26
St. Louis	58	96	.377	47.5
Boston	51	103	.331	54.5
Brooklyn	48	104	.316	56.5

SIGNIFICANT EVENTS

■ **October 3:** The National Commission adopted the John T. Brush rules for World Series play: a seven-game format, four umpires, two from each league, to work the Series and a revenue-sharing formula for the teams involved.

MEMORABLE MOMENTS

■ **June 13:** New York's Christy Mathewson pitched his second career no-hitter, but the Giants needed a ninth-inning run off Chicago's Mordecai Brown to post a 1-0 victory.

■ **August 30:** Detroit's Ty Cobb made his Major League debut, doubling off New York's Jack Chesbro in a 5-3 Tigers victory.

■ **September 27:** Boston's Bill Dinneen pitched the fourth no-hitter of the season, beating Chicago 2-0 in the first game of a doubleheader.

■ **October 6:** Despite losing to Washington 10-4, the Athletics clinched the A.L. pennant when the Browns defeated the White Sox 6-2 on the next-to-last day of the season.

LEADERS

American League

BA: Elmer Flick, Cle., .308
Runs: Harry Davis, Phil., 93.
Hits: George Stone, St.L., 187.
TB: George Stone, St.L., 259.
HR: Harry Davis, Phil., 8.
RBI: Harry Davis, Phil., 83.
SB: Danny Hoffman, Phil., 46.
Wins: Rube Waddell, Phil., 27.
ERA: Rube Waddell, Phil., 1.48.
CG: Harry Howell, St.L.; George Mullin, Det.; Eddie Plank, Phil., 35.
IP: George Mullin, Det., 347.2.
SO: Rube Waddell, Phil., 287.

National League

BA: Cy Seymour, Cin., .377.
Runs: Mike Donlin, N.Y., 124.
Hits: Cy Seymour, Cin., 219.
TB: Cy Seymour, Cin., 325.
HR: Fred Odwell, Cin., 9.
RBI: Cy Seymour, Cin., 121.
SB: Art Devlin, N.Y.; Billy Maloney, Chi., 59.
Wins: Christy Mathewson, N.Y., 31.
ERA: Christy Mathewson, N.Y., 1.28.
CG: Irv Young, Bos., 41.
IP: Irv Young, Bos., 378.
SO: Christy Mathewson, N.Y., 206.

A.L. 20-game winners

Rube Waddell, Phil., 27-10
Eddie Plank, Phil., 24-12
Nick Altrock, Chi., 23-12
Ed Killian, Det., 23-14
Jesse Tannehill, Bos., 22-9
Frank Owen, Chi., 21-13
George Mullin, Det., 21-21
Addie Joss, Cle., 20-12
Frank Smith, Chi., 20-14

N.L. 20-game winners

Christy Mathewson, N.Y., 31-9
Togie Pittinger, Phil., 23-14
Red Ames, N.Y., 22-8
Joe McGinnity, N.Y., 21-15
Sam Leever, Pit., 20-5
Bob Ewing, Cin., 20-11
Deacon Phillippe, Pit., 20-13
Irv Young, Bos., 20-21

N.L. 100 RBIs

Cy Seymour, Cin., 121
Sam Mertes, N.Y., 108
Honus Wagner, Pit., 101

WORLD SERIES

■ **Winner:** The Giants prevailed over the Athletics in an all-shutout fall classic.

■ **Turning point:** Joe McGinnity's five-hit, 1-0 victory over Athletics lefthander Eddie Plank in Game 4. Plank allowed only four hits.

■ **Memorable moment:** New York's John McGraw and Philadelphia's Connie Mack exchanging lineups before Game 1. The two managers would dominate baseball for more than three decades.

■ **Top guns:** Christy Mathewson (3 shutouts, 0.00 ERA), Joe McGinnity, (17 IP, 0.00), Giants; Chief Bender (17 IP, 1.06), Athletics.

Linescores

Game 1—October 9, at Philadelphia

New York........ 0 0 0 0 2 0 0 0 1 — 3 10 1
Philadelphia.... 0 0 0 0 0 0 0 0 0 — 0 4 0
Mathewson; Plank. W—Mathewson. L—Plank.

Game 2—October 10, at New York

Philadelphia.... 0 0 1 0 0 0 0 2 0 — 3 6 2
New York........ 0 0 0 0 0 0 0 0 0 — 0 4 2
Bender; McGinnity, Ames (9). W—Bender. L—McGinnity.

Game 3—October 12, at Philadelphia

New York........ 2 0 0 0 5 0 0 0 2 — 9 9 1
Philadelphia.... 0 0 0 0 0 0 0 0 0 — 0 4 5
Mathewson; Coakley. W—Mathewson. L—Coakley.

Game 4—October 13, at New York

Philadelphia.... 0 0 0 0 0 0 0 0 0 — 0 5 2
New York........ 0 0 0 1 0 0 0 0 x — 1 4 1
Plank; McGinnity. W—McGinnity. L—Plank.

Game 5—October 14, at New York

Philadelphia.... 0 0 0 0 0 0 0 0 0 — 0 6 0
New York........ 0 0 0 0 1 0 0 1 x — 2 5 1
Bender; Mathewson. W—Mathewson. L—Bender.

1906

FINAL STANDINGS

American League

Team	W	L	Pct.	GB
Chicago	93	58	.616	...
New York	90	61	.596	3
Cleveland	89	64	.582	5
Philadelphia	78	67	.538	12
St. Louis	76	73	.510	16
Detroit	71	78	.477	21
Washington	55	95	.367	37.5
Boston	49	105	.318	45.5

National League

Team	W	L	Pct.	GB
Chicago	116	36	.763	...
New York	96	56	.632	20
Pittsburgh	93	60	.608	23.5
Philadelphia	71	82	.464	45.5
Brooklyn	66	86	.434	50
Cincinnati	64	87	.424	51.5
St. Louis	52	98	.347	63
Boston	49	102	.325	66.5

SIGNIFICANT EVENTS

■ **August 13:** When Chicago's Jack Taylor failed to last through the third inning of a game against Brooklyn, it ended his record complete-game streak at 187.

■ **October 7:** The Cubs ended an amazing regular season with a Major League-record 116 victories and a team ERA of 1.76.

MEMORABLE MOMENTS

■ **May 25:** Jesse Tannehill snapped Boston's A.L.-record 20-game losing streak with a 3-0 victory over the White Sox.

■ **June 9:** The Boston Beaneaters ended their 19-game losing streak with a 6-3 victory over the Cardinals.

■ **August 23:** Washington ended the Chicago White Stockings' A.L.-record winning streak at 19 games.

■ **September 1:** The Athletics scored three times in the top of the 24th inning and claimed a 4-1 victory over Boston in the longest game in Major League history.

■ **October 3:** Chicago's "Hitless Wonders" clinched the A.L. pennant when the Athletics posted a 3-0 victory over New York in the second game of a doubleheader.

LEADERS

American League

BA: George Stone, St.L.,.358.
Runs: Elmer Flick, Cle., 98.
Hits: Nap Lajoie, Cle., 214.
TB: George Stone, St.L., 291.
HR: Harry Davis, Phil., 12.
RBI: Harry Davis, Phil., 96.
SB: John Anderson, Wash.; Elmer Flick, Cle., 39.
Wins: Al Orth, N.Y., 27.
ERA: Doc White, Chi., 1.52.
CG: Al Orth, N.Y., 36.
IP: Al Orth, N.Y., 338.2.
SO: Rube Waddell, Phil., 196.

National League

BA: Honus Wagner, Pit., .339.
Runs: Frank Chance, Chi.; Honus Wagner, Pit., 103.
Hits: Harry Steinfeldt, Chi., 176.
TB: Honus Wagner, Pit., 237.
HR: Tim Jordan, Brk., 12.
RBI: Jim Nealon, Pit.; Harry Steinfeldt, Chi., 83.
SB: Frank Chance, Chi., 57.
Wins: Joe McGinnity, N.Y., 27.
ERA: Mordecai Brown, Chi., 1.04.
CG: Irv Young, Bos., 37.
IP: Irv Young, Bos., 358.1.
SO: Fred Beebe, Chi.-St.L., 171.

A.L. 20-game winners

Al Orth, N.Y., 27-17
Jack Chesbro, N.Y., 23-17
Bob Rhoades, Cle., 22-10
Frank Owen, Chi., 22-13
Addie Joss, Cle., 21-9
George Mullin, Det., 21-18
Nick Altrock, Chi., 20-13
Otto Hess, Cle., 20-17

N.L. 20-game winners

Joe McGinnity, N.Y., 27-12
Mordecai Brown, Chi., 26-6
Vic Willis, Pit., 23-13
Sam Leever, Pit., 22-7
Christy Mathewson, N.Y., 22-12
Jack Pfiester, Chi., 20-8
Jack Taylor, St.L.-Chi., 20-12
Jake Weimer, Cin., 20-14

WORLD SERIES

■ **Winner:** Chicago's "Hitless Wonders" pulled an intra-city shocker with a six-game victory over the powerful Cubs.

■ **Turning point:** An eight-run Game 5 explosion by the light-hitting White Sox, which was spiced by Frank Isbell's four doubles and two RBIs.

■ **Memorable moment:** Big Ed Walsh's two-hit Game 3 shutout. The Cubs were held hitless after getting a first-inning single and double.

■ **Top guns:** Walsh (2-0, 1.80 ERA), George Rohe (.333, 4 RBIs), White Sox; Ed Reulbach (Game 2 1-hitter), Cubs.

Linescores

Game 1—October 9, at Chicago Cubs

White Sox....... 0 0 0 0 1 1 0 0 0 — 2 4 1
Cubs.............. 0 0 0 0 0 1 0 0 0 — 1 4 2
Altrock; Brown. W—Altrock. L—Brown.

Game 2—October 10, at Chicago White Sox

Cubs.............. 0 3 1 0 0 1 0 2 0 — 7 10 2
White Sox....... 0 0 0 0 1 0 0 0 0 — 1 1 2
Reulbach; White, Owen (4). W—Reulbach. L—White.

Game 3—October 11, at Chicago Cubs

White Sox....... 0 0 0 0 0 3 0 0 0 — 3 4 1
Cubs.............. 0 0 0 0 0 0 0 0 0 — 0 2 2
Walsh; Pfiester. W—Walsh. L—Pfiester.

Game 4—October 12, at Chicago White Sox

Cubs.............. 0 0 0 0 0 0 1 0 0 — 1 7 1
White Sox....... 0 0 0 0 0 0 0 0 0 — 0 2 1
Brown; Altrock. W—Brown. L—Altrock.

Game 5—October 13, at Chicago Cubs

White Sox....... 1 0 2 4 0 1 0 0 0 — 8 12 6
Cubs.............. 3 0 0 1 0 2 0 0 0 — 6 6 0
Walsh, White (7); Reulbach, Pfiester (3), Overall (4). W—Walsh. L—Pfiester.

Game 6—October 14, at Chicago White Sox

Cubs.............. 1 0 0 0 1 0 0 0 1 — 3 7 0
White Sox....... 3 4 0 0 0 0 0 1 x — 8 14 3
Brown, Overall (2); White. W—White. L—Brown.

1907

FINAL STANDINGS

American League

Team	W	L	Pct.	GB
Detroit	92	58	.613	...
Philadelphia	88	57	.607	1.5
Chicago	87	64	.576	5.5
Cleveland	85	67	.559	8
New York	70	78	.473	21
St. Louis	69	83	.454	24
Boston	59	90	.396	32.5
Washington	49	102	.325	43.5

National League

Team	W	L	Pct.	GB
Chicago	107	45	.704	...
Pittsburgh	91	63	.591	17
Philadelphia	83	64	.565	21.5
New York	82	71	.536	25.5
Brooklyn	65	83	.439	40
Cincinnati	66	87	.431	41.5
Boston	58	90	.392	47
St. Louis	52	101	.340	55.5

SIGNIFICANT EVENTS

■ **April 11:** Giants catcher Roger Bresnahan introduced his newest innovation in a game against the Phillies: wooden shinguards to protect his legs and knees.

■ **August 2:** Washington fireballer Walter Johnson dropped a 3-2 decision to Detroit in his Major League debut.

MEMORABLE MOMENTS

■ **May 20:** The Cardinals ended New York's 17-game winning streak with a 6-4 victory at the Polo Grounds.

■ **October 3:** The seventh-place Boston Red Sox edged sixth-place St. Louis 1-0 and ended their 16-game losing streak.

■ **October 5:** The Tigers, locked in a tight A.L. pennant race with Philadelphia, clinched the title with a 10-2 victory over St. Louis.

LEADERS

American League

BA: Ty Cobb, Det., .350.
Runs: Sam Crawford, Det., 102.
Hits: Ty Cobb, Det., 212.
TB: Ty Cobb, Det., 283.
HR: Harry Davis, Phil., 8.
RBI: Ty Cobb, Det., 119.
SB: Ty Cobb, Det., 49.
Wins: Addie Joss, Cle.; Doc White, Chi., 27.
ERA: Ed Walsh, Chi., 1.60.
CG: Ed Walsh, Chi., 37.
IP: Ed Walsh, Chi., 422.1.
SO: Rube Waddell, Phil., 232.

National League

BA: Honus Wagner, Pit., .350.
Runs: Spike Shannon, N.Y., 104.
Hits: Ginger Beaumont, Bos., 187.
TB: Honus Wagner, Pit., 264.
HR: Dave Brain, Bos., 10.
RBI: Sherry Magee, Phil., 85.
SB: Honus Wagner, Pit., 61.
Wins: Christy Mathewson, N.Y., 24.
ERA: Jack Pfiester, Chi., 1.15.
CG: Stoney McGlynn, St.L., 33.
IP: Stoney McGlynn, St.L., 352.1.
SO: Christy Mathewson, N.Y., 178.

A.L. 20-game winners

Addie Joss, Cle., 27-11
Doc White, Chi., 27-13
Bill Donovan, Det., 25-4
Ed Killian, Det., 25-13
Eddie Plank, Phil., 24-16
Ed Walsh, Chi., 24-18
Frank Smith, Chi., 23-10
Jimmy Dygert, Phil., 21-8
Cy Young, Bos., 21-15
George Mullin, Det., 20-20

N.L. 20-game winners

Christy Mathewson, N.Y., 24-12
Orval Overall, Chi., 23-7
Tully Sparks, Phil., 22-8
Vic Willis, Pit., 21-11
Mordecai Brown, Chi., 20-6
Lefty Leifield, Pit., 20-16

A.L. 100 RBIs

Ty Cobb, Det., 119

WORLD SERIES

■ **Winner:** The powerful Cubs, atoning for their shocking loss to the White Sox in 1906, made short work of the A.L.-champion Tigers.

■ **Turning point:** A ninth-inning passed ball by Tigers catcher Charlie Schmidt that allowed the Cubs to score the tying run in a Game 1 battle that would end in a 3-3 deadlock.

■ **Memorable moment:** Schmidt's passed ball, which awoke the Cubs and set the stage for their sweeping finish.

■ **Top guns:** Harry Steinfeldt (.471), Johnny Evers (.350), Cubs; Claude Rossman (.400), Tigers.

Linescores

Game 1—October 8, at Chicago
Detroit...0 0 0 0 0 0 0 3 0 0 0 0 — 3 9 3
Chicago.0 0 0 1 0 0 0 0 2 0 0 0 — 3 10 5
Donovan; Overall, Reulbach (10). Game called after 12 innings because of darkness.

Game 2—October 9, at Chicago
Detroit............ 0 1 0 0 0 0 0 0 0 — 1 9 1
Chicago.......... 0 1 0 2 0 0 0 0 x — 3 9 1
Mullin; Pfiester. W—Pfiester. L—Mullin.

Game 3—October 10, at Chicago
Detroit............ 0 0 0 0 0 1 0 0 0 — 1 6 1
Chicago.......... 0 1 0 3 1 0 0 0 x — 5 10 1
Siever, Killian (5); Reulbach. W—Reulbach. L—Siever.

Game 4—October 11, at Detroit
Chicago.......... 0 0 0 0 2 0 3 0 1 — 6 7 2
Detroit............ 0 0 0 1 0 0 0 0 0 — 1 5 2
Overall; Donovan. W—Overall. L—Donovan.

Game 5—October 12, at Detroit
Chicago.......... 1 1 0 0 0 0 0 0 0 — 2 7 1
Detroit............ 0 0 0 0 0 0 0 0 0 — 0 7 2
Brown; Mullin. W—Brown. L—Mullin.

1908

FINAL STANDINGS

American League

Team	W	L	Pct.	GB
Detroit	90	63	.588	...
Cleveland	90	64	.584	.5
Chicago	88	64	.579	1.5
St. Louis	83	69	.546	6.5
Boston	75	79	.487	15.5
Philadelphia	68	85	.444	22
Washington	67	85	.441	22.5
New York	51	103	.331	39.5

National League

Team	W	L	Pct.	GB
Chicago	99	55	.643	...
New York	98	56	.636	1
Pittsburgh	98	56	.636	1
Philadelphia	83	71	.539	16
Cincinnati	73	81	.474	26
Boston	63	91	.409	36
Brooklyn	53	101	.344	46
St. Louis	49	105	.318	50

SIGNIFICANT EVENTS

■ **February 27:** Baseball adopted the sacrifice fly rule, stating that a batter will not be charged with an at-bat if a runner tags up and scores after the catch of his fly ball.

MEMORABLE MOMENTS

■ **June 30:** Boston's 41-year-old Cy Young became the first pitcher to notch three career no-hitters when he defeated New York, 8-0.

■ **September 23:** The outcome of an important Giants-Cubs game was thrown into confusion when New York baserunner Fred Merkle failed to touch second base on an apparent game-ending hit, prompting the Cubs' claims of a game-prolonging forceout.

■ **September 24:** N.L. President Harry Pulliam declared the September 23 Cubs-Giants game a tie.

■ **September 26:** Chicago's Ed Reulbach made baseball history when he shut out Brooklyn twice—5-0 and 3-0—on the same day.

■ **October 2:** Cleveland's Addie Joss became the second modern-era pitcher to throw a perfect game, retiring all 27 Chicago batters he faced in a 1-0 victory.

■ **October 6:** The Tigers defeated the White Sox, 7-0, and claimed the A.L. pennant on the season's final day.

■ **October 8:** In an N.L. pennant-deciding matchup dictated by the controversial September 23 tie game, Chicago defeated the Giants, 4-2.

LEADERS

American League

BA: Ty Cobb, Det., .324.
Runs: Matty McIntyre, Det., 105.
Hits: Ty Cobb, Det., 188.
TB: Ty Cobb, Det., 276.
HR: Sam Crawford, Det., 7.
RBI: Ty Cobb, Det., 108.
SB: Patsy Dougherty, Chi., 47.
Wins: Ed Walsh, Chi., 40.
ERA: Addie Joss, Cle., 1.16.
CG: Ed Walsh, Chi., 42.
IP: Ed Walsh, Chi., 464.
SO: Ed Walsh, Chi., 269.

National League

BA: Honus Wagner, Pit., .354.
Runs: Fred Tenney, N.Y., 101.
Hits: Honus Wagner, Pit., 201.
TB: Honus Wagner, Pit., 308.
HR: Tim Jordan, Brk., 12.
RBI: Honus Wagner, Pit., 109.
SB: Honus Wagner, Pit., 53.
Wins: Christy Mathewson, N.Y., 37.
ERA: Christy Mathewson, N.Y., 1.43.
CG: Christy Mathewson, N.Y., 34.
IP: Christy Mathewson, N.Y., 390.2.
SO: Christy Mathewson, N.Y., 259.

A.L. 20-game winners

Ed Walsh, Chi., 40-15
Addie Joss, Cle., 24-11
Ed Summers, Det., 24-12
Cy Young, Bos., 21-11

N.L. 20-game winners

Christy Mathewson, N.Y., 37-11
Mordecai Brown, Chi., 29-9
Ed Reulbach, Chi., 24-7
Nick Maddox, Pit., 23-8
Vic Willis, Pit. 23-11
Hooks Wiltse, N.Y., 23-14
George McQuillan, Phil., 23-17

A.L. 100 RBIs

Ty Cobb, Det., 108

N.L. 100 RBIs

Honus Wagner, Pit., 109
Mike Donlin, N.Y., 106

WORLD SERIES

■ **Winner:** The Cubs became the first two-time Series champs by defeating Detroit for the second consecutive year.

■ **Turning point:** A five-run ninth-inning rally that turned a 6-5 Game 1 deficit into a 10-6 Cubs victory.

■ **Memorable moment:** A two-run eighth-inning home run by Chicago's Joe Tinker that broke up a scoreless Game 2 pitching duel and gave Orval Overall a 6-1 victory over Bill Donovan.

■ **Top guns:** Overall (2-0, 0.98 ERA), Frank Chance (.421), Cubs; Ty Cobb (.368), Tigers.

Linescores

Game 1—October 10, at Detroit
Chicago.......... 0 0 4 0 0 0 1 0 5 —10 14 2
Detroit............ 1 0 0 0 0 0 3 2 0 — 6 10 4
Reulbach, Overall (7), Brown (8); Killian, Summers (3). W—Brown. L—Summers.

Game 2—October 11, at Chicago
Detroit............ 0 0 0 0 0 0 0 0 1 — 1 4 1
Chicago.......... 0 0 0 0 0 0 0 6 x — 6 7 1
Donovan; Overall. W—Overall. L—Donovan. HR—Tinker (Chi.).

Game 3—October 12, at Chicago
Detroit............ 1 0 0 0 0 5 0 2 0 — 8 11 4
Chicago.......... 0 0 0 3 0 0 0 0 0 — 3 7 2
Mullin; Pfiester, Reulbach (9). W—Mullin. L—Pfiester.

Game 4—October 13, at Detroit
Chicago.......... 0 0 2 0 0 0 0 0 1 — 3 10 0
Detroit............ 0 0 0 0 0 0 0 0 0 — 0 4 1
Brown; Summers, Winter (9). W—Brown. L—Summers.

Game 5—October 14, at Detroit
Chicago.......... 1 0 0 0 1 0 0 0 0 — 2 10 0
Detroit............ 0 0 0 0 0 0 0 0 0 — 0 3 0
Overall; Donovan. W—Overall. L—Donovan.

1909

FINAL STANDINGS

American League

Team	W	L	Pct.	GB
Detroit	98	54	.645	...
Philadelphia	95	58	.621	3.5
Boston	88	63	.583	9.5
Chicago	78	74	.513	20
New York	74	77	.490	23.5
Cleveland	71	82	.464	27.5
St. Louis	61	89	.407	36
Washington	42	110	.276	56

National League

Team	W	L	Pct.	GB
Pittsburgh	110	42	.724	...
Chicago	104	49	.680	6.5
New York	92	61	.601	18.5
Cincinnati	77	76	.503	33.5
Philadelphia	74	79	.484	36.5
Brooklyn	55	98	.359	55.5
St. Louis	54	98	.355	56
Boston	45	108	.294	65.5

SIGNIFICANT EVENTS

- **April 12:** The Athletics and pitcher Eddie Plank christened Philadelphia's new Shibe Park with an 8-1 victory over Boston.
- **June 30:** The Cubs spoiled Pittsburgh's opening of new Forbes Field, posting a 3-2 victory over the Pirates.
- **July 29:** N.L. President Harry Pulliam shocked the baseball world when he shot himself to death.
- **October 5:** Detroit's Ty Cobb finished his Triple Crown season with a .377 average, 9 home runs and 107 RBIs.

MEMORABLE MOMENTS

- **April 15:** New York's Red Ames lost his Opening Day no-hit bid in the 10th inning and the game in the 13th when Brooklyn scored a 3-0 victory.
- **July 16:** A Detroit-Washington game ended 0-0 after 18 innings—the longest scoreless tie in A.L. history.
- **July 19:** Cleveland shortstop Neal Ball pulled off the first unassisted triple play of the century in a game against the Red Sox.

LEADERS

American League

BA: Ty Cobb, Det., .377.
Runs: Ty Cobb, Det., 116.
Hits: Ty Cobb, Det., 216.
TB: Ty Cobb, Det., 296.
HR: Ty Cobb, Det., 9.
RBI: Ty Cobb, Det., 107.
SB: Ty Cobb, Det., 76.
Wins: George Mullin, Det., 29.
ERA: Harry Krause, Phil., 1.39.
CG: Frank Smith, Chi., 37.
IP: Frank Smith, Chi., 365.
SO: Frank Smith, Chi., 177.

National League

BA: Honus Wagner, Pit., .339.
Runs: Tommy Leach, Pit., 126.
Hits: Larry Doyle, N.Y., 172.
TB: Honus Wagner, Pit., 242.
HR: Red Murray, N.Y., 7.
RBI: Honus Wagner, Pit., 100.
SB: Bob Bescher, Cin., 54.
Wins: Mordecai Brown, Chi., 27.
ERA: Christy Mathewson, N.Y., 1.14.
CG: Mordecai Brown, Chi., 32.
IP: Mordecai Brown, Chi., 342.2.
SO: Orval Overall, Chi., 205.

A.L. 20-game winners

George Mullin, Det., 29-8
Frank Smith, Chi., 25-17
Ed Willett, Det., 21-10

N.L. 20-game winners

Mordecai Brown, Chi., 27-9
Howie Camnitz, Pit., 25-6
Christy Mathewson, N.Y., 25-6
Vic Willis, Pit., 22-11
Orval Overall, Chi., 20-11
Hooks Wiltse, N.Y., 20-11

A.L. 100 RBIs

Ty Cobb, Det., 107

N.L. 100 RBIs

Honus Wagner, Pit., 100

WORLD SERIES

- **Winner:** The Pirates, losers in baseball's first World Series, bounced back to hand the Tigers their third straight post-season loss.
- **Turning point:** A tie-breaking three-run homer by Pirates player/manager Fred Clarke that keyed an 8-4 victory in the pivotal fifth game.
- **Memorable moment:** When Pirates pitcher Babe Adams retired the final Tiger in Game 7 and ended the first Series to go the distance.
- **Top guns:** Adams (3-0, 1.33 ERA), Honus Wagner (.333, 7 RBIs, 6 SB), Pirates; Jim Delahanty (.346), Tigers.

Linescores

Game 1—October 8, at Pittsburgh

Detroit........... 1 0 0 0 0 0 0 0 0 — 1 6 4
Pittsburgh...... 0 0 0 1 2 1 0 0 x — 4 5 0
Mullin; Adams. W—Adams. L—Mullin. HR—Clarke (Pit.).

Game 2—October 9, at Pittsburgh

Detroit........... 0 2 3 0 2 0 0 0 0 — 7 9 3
Pittsburgh...... 2 0 0 0 0 0 0 0 0 — 2 5 1
Donovan; Camnitz, Willis (3). W—Donovan. L—Camnitz.

Game 3—October 11, at Detroit

Pittsburgh...... 5 1 0 0 0 0 0 0 2 — 8 10 3
Detroit........... 0 0 0 0 0 0 4 0 2 — 6 10 5
Maddox; Summers, Willett (1), Works (8). W—Maddox. L—Summers.

Game 4—October 12, at Detroit

Pittsburgh...... 0 0 0 0 0 0 0 0 0 — 0 5 6
Detroit........... 0 2 0 3 0 0 0 0 x — 5 8 0
Leifield, Phillippe (5); Mullin. W—Mullin. L—Leifield.

Game 5—October 13, at Pittsburgh

Detroit........... 1 0 0 0 0 2 0 1 0 — 4 6 1
Pittsburgh...... 1 1 1 0 0 0 4 1 x — 8 10 1
Summers, Willett (8); Adams. W—Adams. L—Summers. HR—D. Jones, Crawford (Det.); Clarke (Pit.).

Game 6—October 14, at Detroit

Pittsburgh...... 3 0 0 0 0 0 0 0 1 — 4 7 3
Detroit........... 1 0 0 2 1 1 0 0 x — 5 10 3
Willis, Camnitz (6), Phillippe (7); Mullin. W—Mullin. L—Willis.

Game 7—October 16, at Detroit

Pittsburgh...... 0 2 0 2 0 3 0 1 0 — 8 7 0
Detroit........... 0 0 0 0 0 0 0 0 0 — 0 6 3
Adams; Donovan, Mullin (4). W—Adams. L—Donovan.

1910

FINAL STANDINGS

American League

Team	W	L	Pct.	GB
Philadelphia	102	48	.680	...
New York	88	63	.583	14.5
Detroit	86	68	.558	18
Boston	81	72	.529	22.5
Cleveland	71	81	.467	32
Chicago	68	85	.444	35.5
Washington	66	85	.437	36.5
St. Louis	47	107	.305	57

National League

Team	W	L	Pct.	GB
Chicago	104	50	.675	...
New York	91	63	.591	13
Pittsburgh	86	67	.562	17.5
Philadelphia	78	75	.510	25.5
Cincinnati	75	79	.487	29
Brooklyn	64	90	.416	40
St. Louis	63	90	.412	40.5
Boston	53	100	.346	50.5

SIGNIFICANT EVENTS

- **February 18:** The N.L. approved a 154-game schedule, a plan already adopted by the A.L.
- **April 14:** William Howard Taft became the first U.S. President to throw out the first ball at a season opener in Washington.
- **April 21:** Detroit spoiled the opening of Cleveland's League Park with a 5-0 victory over the Indians.
- **July 1:** Chicago unveiled White Sox Park (Comiskey Park), but the Browns spoiled the occasion with a 2-0 victory.

MEMORABLE MOMENTS

- **July 19:** The incredible Cy Young earned his 500th career victory when he pitched Cleveland to an 11-inning, 5-2 win over Washington.
- **August 30:** The Highlanders' Tom Hughes lost his no-hit bid against Cleveland with one out in the 10th and lost the game, 5-0, in the 11th.
- **September 25:** The scoreless streak of Philadelphia's Jack Coombs ended at 53 innings in a darkness-shortened 5-2 loss to Chicago in the second game of a doubleheader.
- **October 9:** Cleveland's Napoleon Lajoie collected eight final-day hits, seven of them bunt singles, in a doubleheader against the Browns and lifted his final average to .384—one point ahead of Detroit's Ty Cobb.
- **October 15:** A.L. President Ban Johnson adjusted Cobb's final average to .385 and declared him winner of the A.L. batting title.

LEADERS

American League

BA: Ty Cobb, Det., .383.
Runs: Ty Cobb, Det., 106.
Hits: Nap Lajoie, Cle., 227.
TB: Nap Lajoie, Cle., 304.
HR: Jake Stahl, Bos., 10.
RBI: Sam Crawford, Det., 120.
SB: Eddie Collins, Phil., 81.
Wins: Jack Coombs, Phil., 31.
ERA: Ed Walsh, Chi., 1.27.
CG: Walter Johnson, Wash., 38.
IP: Walter Johnson, Wash., 370.
SO: Walter Johnson, Wash., 313.

National League

BA: Sherry Magee, Phil., .331.
Runs: Sherry Magee, Phil., 110.
Hits: Bobby Byrne, Pit.; Honus Wagner, Pit., 178.
TB: Sherry Magee, Phil., 263.
HR: Fred Beck, Bos.; Frank Schulte, Chi., 10.
RBI: Sherry Magee, Phil., 123.
SB: Bob Bescher, Cin., 70.
Wins: Christy Mathewson, N.Y., 27.
ERA: King Cole, Chi., 1.80.
CG: Mordecai Brown, Chi.; Christy Mathewson, N.Y.; Nap Rucker, Brk., 27
IP: Nap Rucker, Brk., 320.1.
SO: Earl Moore, Phil., 185.

A.L. 20-game winners

Jack Coombs, Phil., 31-9
Russ Ford, N.Y., 26-6
Walter Johnson, Wash., 25-17
Chief Bender, Phil., 23-5
George Mullin, Det., 21-12

N.L. 20-game winners

Christy Mathewson, N.Y., 27-9
Mordecai Brown, Chi., 25-14
Earl Moore, Phil., 22-15
King Cole, Chi., 20-4
George Suggs, Cin., 20-12

A.L. 100 RBIs

Sam Crawford, Det., 120

N.L. 100 RBIs

Sherry Magee, Phil., 123

WORLD SERIES

- **Winner:** Philadelphia won their first Series championship and thwarted the Cubs' bid to become a three-time winner.
- **Turning point:** The Cubs' failure to take advantage of the less-than-artistic Jack Coombs in Game 2. Coombs allowed eight hits and nine walks but still won, 9-3.
- **Memorable moment:** A three-run homer by Danny Murphy that broke up a tight Game 3 and helped Philadelphia to a 12-5 victory.
- **Top guns:** Eddie Collins (.429), Murphy (.350, 8 RBIs), Frank Baker (.409), Athletics; Frank Chance (.353), Frank Schulte (.353), Cubs.

Linescores

Game 1—October 17, at Philadelphia

Chicago.......... 0 0 0 0 0 0 0 0 1 — 1 3 1
Philadelphia.... 0 2 1 0 0 0 0 1 x — 4 7 2
Overall, McIntire (4); Bender. W—Bender. L—Overall.

Game 2—October 18, at Philadelphia

Chicago.......... 1 0 0 0 0 0 1 0 1 — 3 8 3
Philadelphia.... 0 0 2 0 1 0 6 0 x — 9 14 4
Brown, Richie (8); Coombs. W—Coombs. L—Brown.

Game 3—October 20, at Chicago

Philadelphia.... 1 2 5 0 0 0 4 0 0 — 12 15 1
Chicago.......... 1 2 0 0 0 0 0 2 0 — 5 6 5
Coombs; Reulbach, McIntire (3), Pfiester (3). W—Coombs. L—McIntire. HR—Murphy (Phil.).

Game 4—October 22, at Chicago

Philadelphia 0 0 1 2 0 0 0 0 0 0 — 3 11 3
Chicago 1 0 0 1 0 0 0 0 1 1 — 4 9 1
Bender; Cole, Brown (9). W—Brown. L—Bender.

Game 5—October 23, at Chicago

Philadelphia.... 1 0 0 0 1 0 0 5 0 — 7 9 1
Chicago.......... 0 1 0 0 0 0 0 1 0 — 2 9 2
Coombs; Brown. W—Coombs. L—Brown.

1911

FINAL STANDINGS

American League

Team	W	L	Pct.	GB
Philadelphia	101	50	.669	...
Detroit	89	65	.578	13.5
Cleveland	80	73	.523	22
Chicago	77	74	.510	24
Boston	78	75	.510	24
New York	76	76	.500	25.5
Washington	64	90	.416	38.5
St. Louis	45	107	.296	56.5

National League

Team	W	L	Pct.	GB
New York	99	54	.647	...
Chicago	92	62	.597	7.5
Pittsburgh	85	69	.552	14.5
Philadelphia	79	73	.520	19.5
St. Louis	75	74	.503	22
Cincinnati	70	83	.458	29
Brooklyn	64	86	.427	33.5
Boston	44	107	.291	54

SIGNIFICANT EVENTS

- **April 14:** New York's Polo Grounds burned down, forcing the Giants to play a big stretch of their schedule at the Highlanders' Hilltop Park.
- **June 28:** The Giants defeated the Braves, 3-0, in the first game at the new Polo Grounds.
- **October 11:** Chalmers automobile recipients as baseball's first MVPs: Detroit's Ty Cobb in the A.L. and Chicago's Frank Schulte in the N.L.

MEMORABLE MOMENTS

- **May 13:** The Giants exploded for a record 13 first-inning runs, 10 before the first out was recorded, in a 19-5 victory over St. Louis.
- **July 4:** Chicago ace Ed Walsh stopped Detroit, 7-3, and ended Ty Cobb's hitting streak at 40 games.
- **September 29:** Phillies righthander Grover Cleveland Alexander defeated Pittsburgh 7-4 and claimed his rookie-record 28th victory.
- **September 22:** Cy Young, ending his career with the Braves, won his 511th and final game, beating Pittsburgh 1-0.

LEADERS

American League

BA: Ty Cobb, Det., .420.
Runs: Ty Cobb, Det., 147.
Hits: Ty Cobb, Det., 248.
TB: Ty Cobb, Det., 367.
HR: Frank Baker, Phil., 11.
RBI: Ty Cobb, Det., 127.
SB: Ty Cobb, Det., 83.
Wins: Jack Coombs, Phil., 28.
ERA: Vean Gregg, Cle., 1.80.
CG: Walter Johnson, Wash., 36.
IP: Ed Walsh, Chi., 368.2.
SO: Ed Walsh, Chi., 255.

National League

BA: Honus Wagner, Pit., .334.
Runs: Jimmy Sheckard, Chi., 121.
Hits: Doc Miller, Bos., 192.
TB: Frank Schulte, Chi., 308.
HR: Frank Schulte, Chi., 21.
RBI: Frank Schulte, Chi.; Chief Wilson, Pit., 107.
SB: Bob Bescher, Cin., 80.
Wins: Grover Alexander, Phil., 28.
ERA: Christy Mathewson, N.Y., 1.99.
CG: Grover Alexander, Phil., 31.
IP: Grover Alexander, Phil., 367.
SO: Rube Marquard, N.Y., 237.

A.L. 20-game winners

Jack Coombs, Phil., 28-12
Ed Walsh, Chi., 27-18
Walter Johnson, Wash., 25-13
Vean Gregg, Cle., 23-7
Eddie Plank, Phil., 23-8
Joe Wood, Bos., 23-17
Russ Ford, N.Y., 22-11

N.L. 20-game winners

Grover Alexander, Phil., 28-13
Christy Mathewson, N.Y., 26-13
Rube Marquard, N.Y., 24-7
Bob Harmon, St.L., 23-16
Babe Adams, Pit., 22-12
Nap Rucker, Brk., 22-18
Mordecai Brown, Chi., 21-11
Howie Camnitz, Pit., 20-15

A.L. 100 RBIs

Ty Cobb, Det., 127
Frank Baker, Phil., 115
Sam Crawford, Det., 115

N.L. 100 RBIs

Frank Schulte, Chi., 107
Chief Wilson, Pit., 107

Chalmers MVP

A.L.: Ty Cobb, OF, Det.
N.L.: Frank Schulte, OF, Chi.

WORLD SERIES

- **Winner:** The Athletics became baseball's second back-to-back winners and gained revenge for their 1905 loss to the Giants.
- **Turning point:** A ninth-inning Game 3 homer by Frank Baker off Christy Mathewson. The solo shot tied the game at 1-1 and the A's won in 11 innings, 3-2.
- **Memorable moment:** Baker's homer off Mathewson.
- **Top guns:** Chief Bender (2-1, 1.04 ERA), Baker (.375, 2 HR), Jack Barry (.368), Athletics; Mathewson (27 IP, 2.00), Giants.

Linescores

Game 1—October 14, at New York
Philadelphia.... 0 1 0 0 0 0 0 0 0 — 1 6 2
New York........ 0 0 0 1 0 0 1 0 x — 2 5 0
Bender; Mathewson. W—Mathewson. L—Bender.

Game 2—October 16, at Philadelphia
New York........ 0 1 0 0 0 0 0 0 0 — 1 5 3
Philadelphia.... 1 0 0 0 0 2 0 0 x — 3 4 0
Marquard, Crandall (8); Plank. W—Plank. L—Marquard. HR—Baker (Phil.).

Game 3—October 17, at New York
Philadelphia ....0 0 0 0 0 0 0 0 1 0 2—3 9 2
New York ....0 0 1 0 0 0 0 0 0 0 1—2 3 5
Coombs; Mathewson. W—Coombs. L—Mathewson. HR—Baker (Phil.).

Game 4—October 24, at Philadelphia
New York........ 2 0 0 0 0 0 0 0 0 — 2 7 3
Philadelphia.... 0 0 0 3 1 0 0 0 x — 4 1 1
Mathewson, Wiltse (8); Bender. W—Bender. L—Mathewson.

Game 5—October 25, at New York
Philadelphia.... 0 0 3 0 0 0 0 0 0 0 — 3 7 1
New York........ 0 0 0 0 0 0 1 0 2 1 — 4 9 2
Coombs, Plank (10); Marquard, Ames (4), Crandall (8). W—Crandall. L—Plank. HR—Oldring (Phil.).

Game 6—October 26, at Philadelphia
New York........ 1 0 0 0 0 0 0 0 1 — 2 4 3
Philadelphia.... 0 0 1 4 0 1 7 0 x — 13 3 5
Ames, Wiltse (5), Marquard (7); Bender. W—Bender. L—Ames.

1912

FINAL STANDINGS

American League

Team	W	L	Pct.	GB
Boston	105	47	.691	...
Washington	91	61	.599	14
Philadelphia	90	62	.592	15
Chicago	78	76	.506	28
Cleveland	75	78	.490	30.5
Detroit	69	84	.451	36.5
St. Louis	53	101	.344	53
New York	50	102	.329	55

National League

Team	W	L	Pct.	GB
New York	103	48	.682	...
Pittsburgh	93	58	.616	10
Chicago	91	59	.607	11.5
Cincinnati	75	78	.490	29
Philadelphia	73	79	.480	30.5
St. Louis	63	90	.412	41
Brooklyn	58	95	.379	46
Boston	52	101	.340	52

SIGNIFICANT EVENTS

- **April 11**: Cincinnati celebrated the opening of new Redland Field with a 10-6 victory over the Cubs.
- **April 20:** The Red Sox christened Fenway Park with an 11-inning 7-6 victory over New York and the Tigers opened Navin Field with an 11-inning 6-5 victory over Cleveland.
- **May 16:** A.L. President Ban Johnson handed Detroit's Ty Cobb an indefinite suspension after Cobb entered the stands at New York's Hilltop Park to fight a heckler.
- **May 18:** A team of amateur Tigers dropped a 24-2 decision to the Athletics when the regular Tigers went on strike to protest Cobb's suspension.
- **May 20:** The Tigers, facing the threat of lifetime suspensions from Johnson, returned to uniform.

MEMORABLE MOMENTS

- **June 13:** New York's Christy Mathewson earned his 300th career victory and 20th win of the season when he defeated the Cubs, 3-2.
- **July 3:** Giants lefty Rube Marquard earned his record 19th consecutive victory of the season and 21st straight over two years, stopping Brooklyn, 2-1.
- **August 26:** The Browns handed Washington's Walter Johnson a 3-2 loss and ended his A.L.-record winning streak at 16 games.
- **September 20:** Joe Wood's record-tying 16-game winning streak ended when Detroit handed Boston a 6-4 loss.
- **September 22:** For the second time in 11 days, Athletics star Eddie Collins stole a modern-record six bases in a game—an 8-2 victory over the Browns.

LEADERS

American League

BA: Ty Cobb, Det., .409.
Runs: Eddie Collins, Phil., 137.
Hits: Ty Cobb, Det.; Joe Jackson, Cle., 226.
TB: Joe Jackson, Cle., 331.
HR: Frank Baker, Phil.; Tris Speaker, Bos., 10.
RBI: Frank Baker, Phil., 130.
SB: Clyde Milan, Wash., 88.
Wins: Joe Wood, Bos., 34.
ERA: Walter Johnson, Wash., 1.39.
CG: Joe Wood, Bos., 35.
IP: Ed Walsh, Chi., 393.
SO: Walter Johnson, Wash., 303.

National League

BA: Heinie Zimmerman, Chi., .372.
Runs: Bob Bescher, Cin., 120.
Hits: Heinie Zimmerman, Chi., 207.
TB: Heinie Zimmerman, Chi., 318.
HR: Heinie Zimmerman, Chi., 14.
RBI: Honus Wagner, Pit., 102.
SB: Bob Bescher, Cin., 67.
Wins: Larry Cheney, Chi.; Rube Marquard, N.Y., 26.
ERA: Jeff Tesreau, N.Y., 1.96.
CG: Larry Cheney, Chi., 28.
IP: Grover Alexander, Phil., 310.1.
SO: Grover Alexander, Phil., 195.

A.L. 20-game winners

Joe Wood, Bos., 34-5
Walter Johnson, Wash., 33-12
Ed Walsh, Chi., 27-17
Eddie Plank, Phil., 26-6
Bob Groom, Wash., 24-13
Jack Coombs, Phil., 21-10
Hugh Bedient, Bos., 20-9
Vean Gregg, Cle., 20-13
Buck O'Brien, Bos., 20-13

N.L. 20-game winners

Larry Cheney, Chi., 26-10
Rube Marquard, N.Y., 26-11
Claude Hendrix, Pit., 24-9
Christy Mathewson, N.Y., 23-12
Howie Camnitz, Pit., 22-12

A.L. 100 RBIs

Frank Baker, Phil., 130
Sam Crawford, Det., 109
Duffy Lewis, Bos., 109
Stuffy McInnis, Phil., 101

N.L. 100 RBIs

Honus Wagner, Pit., 102
Bill Sweeney, Bos., 100

Chalmers MVP

A.L.: Tris Speaker, OF, Bos.
N.L.: Larry Doyle, 2B, N.Y.

WORLD SERIES

- **Winners:** The Red Sox, who had not made a Series appearance since beating Pittsburgh in the 1903 inaugural, made it two for two with a victory over the Giants.
- **Turning point:** A dropped fly ball by Giants center fielder Fred Snodgrass in the Series-deciding eighth game. The Red Sox wiped out a 2-1 deficit against Christy Mathewson and claimed a 3-2 victory.
- **Memorable moment:** Snodgrass' muff and the failure of catcher Chief Meyers and first baseman Fred Merkle to catch a foul pop in the same inning.
- **Top guns:** Joe Wood (3-1), Red Sox; Buck Herzog (.400), Meyers (.357), Giants.

Linescores

Game 1—October 8, at New York
Boston....................0 0 0 0 0 1 3 0 0 — 4 6 1
New York................0 0 2 0 0 0 0 0 1 — 3 8 1
Wood; Tesreau, Crandall (8). W—Wood. L—Tesreau.

Game 2—October 9, at Boston
New York......0 1 0 1 0 0 0 3 0 1 0 — 6 11 5
Boston..........3 0 0 0 1 0 0 1 0 1 0 — 6 10 1
Mathewson; Collins, Hall (8), Bedient (11). Game called after 11 innings because of darkness.

Game 3—October 10, at Boston
New York................0 1 0 0 1 0 0 0 0 — 2 7 1
Boston....................0 0 0 0 0 0 0 0 1 — 1 7 0
Marquard; O'Brien, Bedient (9). W—Marquard. L—O'Brien.

Game 4—October 11, at New York
Boston....................0 1 0 1 0 0 0 0 1 — 3 8 1
New York................0 0 0 0 0 0 1 0 0 — 1 9 1
Wood; Tesreau, Ames (8). W—Wood. L—Tesreau.

Game 5—October 12, at Boston
New York.............0 0 0 0 0 0 1 0 0 — 1 3 11
Boston..................0 0 2 0 0 0 0 0 x — 2 5 1
Mathewson; Bedient. W—Bedient. L—Mathewson.

Game 6—October 14, at New York
Boston..................0 2 0 0 0 0 0 0 0 — 2 7 2
New York.............5 0 0 0 0 0 0 0 x — 5 11 2
O'Brien, Collins (2); Marquard. W—Marquard. L—O'Brien.

Game 7—October 15, at Boston
New York............6 1 0 0 0 2 1 0 1 — 11 16 4
Boston................0 1 0 0 0 0 2 1 0 — 4 9 3
Tesreau; Wood, Hall (2). W—Tesreau. L—Wood. HR—Doyle (N.Y.); Gardner (Bos.).

Game 8—October 16, at Boston
New York...........0 0 1 0 0 0 0 0 0 1 — 2 9 2
Boston.............0 0 0 0 0 0 1 0 0 2 — 3 8 5
Mathewson; Bedient, Wood (8). W—Wood. L—Mathewson.

HISTORY

1913

FINAL STANDINGS

American League

Team	W	L	Pct.	GB
Philadelphia	96	57	.627	...
Washington	90	64	.584	6.5
Cleveland	86	66	.566	9.5
Boston	79	71	.527	15.5
Chicago	78	74	.513	17.5
Detroit	66	87	.431	30
New York	57	94	.377	38
St. Louis	57	96	.373	39

National League

Team	W	L	Pct.	GB
New York	101	51	.664	...
Philadelphia	88	63	.583	12.5
Chicago	88	65	.575	13.5
Pittsburgh	78	71	.523	21.5
Boston	69	82	.457	31.5
Brooklyn	65	84	.436	34.5
Cincinnati	64	89	.418	37.5
St. Louis	51	99	.340	49

SIGNIFICANT EVENTS

■ **January 22:** The Yankees, no longer tenants of Hilltop Park, received permission from the New York Giants to use the Polo Grounds as co-tenants.
■ **April 9:** The Dodgers lost their Ebbets Field debut to the Phillies, 1-0.
■ **April 10:** The A.L.'s New York team began life anew as the "Yankees," losing to Washington, 2-1, in the season opener.
■ **November 2:** The outlaw Federal League began its challenge as a third Major League when its Kansas City entry enticed Browns manager George Stovall to jump.
■ **December 9:** N.L. owners elected Pennsylvania Governor John K. Tener as their new president.

MEMORABLE MOMENTS

■ **May 14:** Walter Johnson's Major League-record 56-inning scoreless streak ended when the Washington righthander yielded a fourth-inning run to the Browns.
■ **August 28:** Johnson's 14-game winning streak came to an end when the Senators fell to Boston, 1-0, in 11 innings.
■ **September 29:** Johnson defeated the Athletics, 1-0, and closed his incredible season with a 36-7 record, 11 shutouts and a 1.14 ERA.

LEADERS

American League

BA: Ty Cobb, Det., .390.
Runs: Eddie Collins, Phil., 125.
Hits: Joe Jackson, Cle., 197.
TB: Sam Crawford, Det., 298.
HR: Frank Baker, Phil., 12.
RBI: Frank Baker, Phil., 117.
SB: Clyde Milan, Wash., 75.
Wins: Walter Johnson, Wash., 36.
ERA: Walter Johnson, Wash., 1.14.
CG: Walter Johnson, Wash., 29.
IP: Walter Johnson, Wash., 346.
SO: Walter Johnson, Wash., 243.

National League

BA: Jake Daubert, Brk., .350.
Runs: Max Carey, Pit.; Tommy Leach, Chi., 99.
Hits: Gavvy Cravath, Phil., 179.
TB: Gavvy Cravath, Phil., 298.
HR: Gavvy Cravath, Phil., 19.
RBI: Gavvy Cravath, Phil., 128.
SB: Max Carey, Pit., 61.
Wins: Tom Seaton, Phil., 27.
ERA: Christy Mathewson, N.Y., 2.06.
CG: Lefty Tyler, Bos., 28.
IP: Tom Seaton, Phil., 322.1.
SO: Tom Seaton, Phil., 168.

A.L. 20-game winners

Walter Johnson, Wash., 36-7
Cy Falkenberg, Cle., 23-10
Reb Russell, Chi., 22-16
Chief Bender, Phil., 21-10
Vean Gregg, Cle., 20-13
Jim Scott, Chi., 20-21

N.L. 20-game winners

Tom Seaton, Phil., 27-12
Christy Mathewson, N.Y., 25-11
Rube Marquard, N.Y., 23-10
Grover Alexander, Phil., 22-8
Jeff Tesreau, N.Y., 22-13
Babe Adams, Pit., 21-10
Larry Cheney, Chi., 21-14

A.L. 100 RBIs

Frank Baker, Phil., 117

N.L. 100 RBIs

Gavvy Cravath, Phil., 128

Chalmers MVP

A.L.: Walter Johnson, P, Wash.
N.L.: Jake Daubert, 1B, Brk.

WORLD SERIES

■ **Winner:** The Athletics needed only five games to win their third Series in four years and hand the Giants their third straight loss.

■ **Turning point:** Complete-game victories by A's pitchers Joe Bush and Chief Bender in Games 3 and 4, setting up Eddie Plank for the kill.

■ **Memorable moment:** A Game 2 pitching duel between Plank and Christy Mathewson. The Giants scored three runs in the 10th for a 3-0 win.

■ **Top guns:** Frank Baker (.450, 7 RBIs), Eddie Collins (.421), Athletics; Mathewson (19 IP, 0.95 ERA), Giants.

Linescores

Game 1—October 7, at New York
Philadelphia........ 0 0 0 3 2 0 0 1 0 — 6 11 1
New York........... 0 0 1 0 3 0 0 0 0 — 4 11 0
Bender; Marquard, Crandall (6), Tesreau (8). W—Bender. L—Marquard. HR—Baker (Phil.).

Game 2—October 8, at Philadelphia
New York.......... 0 0 0 0 0 0 0 0 0 3 — 3 7 2
Philadelphia...... 0 0 0 0 0 0 0 0 0 0 — 0 8 2
Mathewson; Plank. W—Mathewson. L—Plank.

Game 3—October 9, at New York
Philadelphia........ 3 2 0 0 0 0 2 1 0 — 8 12 1
New York............ 0 0 0 0 1 0 1 0 0 — 2 5 1
Bush; Tesreau, Crandall (7). W—Bush. L—Tesreau. HR—Schang (Phil.).

Game 4—October 10, at Philadelphia
New York............. 0 0 0 0 0 0 3 2 0 — 5 8 2
Philadelphia.......... 0 1 0 3 2 0 0 0 x — 6 9 0
Demaree, Marquard (5); Bender. W—Bender. L—Demaree. HR—Merkle (N.Y.).

Game 5—October 11, at New York
Philadelphia.......... 1 0 2 0 0 0 0 0 0 — 3 6 1
New York............. 0 0 0 0 1 0 0 0 0 — 1 2 2
Plank; Mathewson. W—Plank. L—Mathewson.

1914

FINAL STANDINGS

American League

Team	W	L	Pct.	GB
Philadelphia	99	53	.651	...
Boston	91	62	.595	8.5
Washington	81	73	.526	19
Detroit	80	73	.523	19.5
St. Louis	71	82	.464	28.5
Chicago	70	84	.455	30
New York	70	84	.455	30
Cleveland	51	102	.333	48.5

National League

Team	W	L	Pct.	GB
Boston	94	59	.614	...
New York	84	70	.545	10.5
St. Louis	81	72	.529	13
Chicago	78	76	.506	16.5
Brooklyn	75	79	.487	19.5
Philadelphia	74	80	.481	20.5
Pittsburgh	69	85	.448	25.5
Cincinnati	60	94	.390	34.5

SIGNIFICANT EVENTS

■ **April 13:** The outlaw Federal League, claiming to be a Major League equal, opened play with Baltimore defeating Buffalo, 3-2.
■ **November 1:** Philadelphia's Connie Mack began dismantling his powerful Athletics team by asking waivers on Jack Coombs, Eddie Plank and Chief Bender.
■ **December 8:** Connie Mack continued his housecleaning by selling star second baseman Eddie Collins to the White Sox for $50,000.

MEMORABLE MOMENTS

■ **May 14:** Chicago's Jim Scott lost his no-hit bid and the game when the Senators scored on two 10th-inning hits for a 1-0 victory.
■ **July 11:** Young Babe Ruth pitched the Red Sox to a 4-3 victory over Cleveland in his Major League debut.
■ **July 17:** Giants 3, Pirates 1 as Rube Marquard outpitched Babe Adams in a 21-inning marathon.
■ **September 23:** The Reds snapped their team-record 19-game losing streak with a 3-0 victory over the Braves.
■ **September 27:** Cleveland's Napoleon Lajoie collected career hit No. 3,000, a double, and the Indians defeated the Yankees, 5-3.
■ **September 29:** The Miracle Braves, who would finish with an incredible 68-19 rush, clinched their first N.L. pennant with a 3-2 victory over the Cubs.
■ **October 7:** The Indianapolis Hoosiers defeated St. Louis, 4-0, and claimed the Federal League pennant.

LEADERS

American League

BA: Ty Cobb, Det., .368.
Runs: Eddie Collins, Phil., 122.
Hits: Tris Speaker, Bos., 193.
TB: Tris Speaker, Bos., 287.
HR: Frank Baker, Phil., 9.
RBI: Sam Crawford, Det., 104.
SB: Fritz Maisel, N.Y., 74.
Wins: Walter Johnson, Wash., 28.
ERA: Dutch Leonard, Bos., 0.96.
CG: Walter Johnson, Wash., 33.
IP: Walter Johnson, Wash., 371.2.
SO: Walter Johnson, Wash., 225.

National League

BA: Jake Daubert, Brk., .329.
Runs: George Burns, N.Y., 100.
Hits: Sherry Magee, Phil., 171.
TB: Sherry Magee, Phil., 277.
HR: Gavvy Cravath, Phil., 19.
RBI: Sherry Magee, Phil., 103.
SB: George Burns, N.Y., 62.
Wins: Grover Alexander, Phil., 27.
ERA: Bill Doak, St.L., 1.72.
CG: Grover Alexander, Phil., 32.
IP: Grover Alexander, Phil., 355.
SO: Grover Alexander, Phil., 214.

A.L. 20-game winners

Walter Johnson, Wash., 28-18
Harry Coveleski, Det., 22-12
Ray Collins, Bos., 20-13

N.L. 20-game winners

Grover Alexander, Phil., 27-15
Bill James, Bos., 26-7
Dick Rudolph, Bos., 26-10
Jeff Tesreau, N.Y., 26-10
Christy Mathewson, N.Y., 24-13
Jeff Pfeffer, Brk., 23-12
Hippo Vaughn, Chi., 21-13
Erskine Mayer, Phil., 21-19
Larry Cheney, Chi., 20-18

A.L. 100 RBIs

Sam Crawford, Det., 104

N.L. 100 RBIs

Sherry Magee, Phil., 103
Gavvy Cravath, Phil., 100

Chalmers MVP

A.L.: Eddie Collins, 2B, Phil.
N.L.: Johnny Evers, 2B, Bos.

WORLD SERIES

■ **Winner:** The Braves, playing their Series home games in Fenway Park because it was deemed a more attractive facility than their South End Grounds venue, punctuated their miracle pennant run with a shocking four-game sweep of the powerful Athletics.

■ **Turning point:** Boston's come-from-behind effort in Game 3 that produced a 5-4 victory in 12 innings. The Braves stayed alive by scoring two 10th-inning runs after falling behind in the top of the inning.

■ **Memorable moment:** A dramatic Game 2 pitching duel between Boston's Bill James and Eddie Plank. James won 1-0 on Les Mann's ninth-inning single.

■ **Top guns:** James (2-0, 0.00 ERA), Dick Rudolph (2-0, 0-50), Hank Gowdy (.545), Johnny Evers (.438), Braves.

Linescores

Game 1—October 9, at Philadelphia
Boston............ 0 2 0 0 1 3 0 1 0 — 7 11 2
Phil................ 0 1 0 0 0 0 0 0 0 — 1 5 0
Rudolph; Bender, Wyckoff (6). W—Rudolph. L—Bender.

Game 2—October 10, at Philadelphia
Boston............ 0 0 0 0 0 0 0 0 1 — 1 7 1
Phil................ 0 0 0 0 0 0 0 0 0 — 0 2 1
James; Plank. W—James. L—Plank.

Game 3—October 12, at Boston
Phil..........1 0 0 1 0 0 0 0 0 2 0 0 — 4 8 2
Boston......0 1 0 1 0 0 0 0 0 2 0 1 — 5 9 1
Bush; Tyler, James (11). W—James. L—Bush. HR—Gowdy (Bos.).

Game 4—October 13, at Boston
Phil. ....0 0 0 0 1 0 0 0 0 — 1 7 0
Boston ....0 0 0 1 2 0 0 0 x — 3 6 0
Shawkey, Pennock (6); Rudolph. W—Rudolph. L—Shawkey.

1914—Federal League

FINAL STANDINGS

Team	W	L	Pct.	GB
Indianapolis	88	65	.575	...
Chicago	87	67	.565	1.5
Baltimore	84	70	.545	4.5
Buffalo	80	71	.530	7
Brooklyn	77	77	.500	11.5
Kansas City	67	84	.444	20
Pittsburgh	64	86	.427	22.5
St. Louis	62	89	.411	25

SIGNIFICANT EVENT

■ **November 1:** After being released by A's boss Connie Mack, pitchers Eddie Plank (St. Louis) and Chief Bender (Baltimore) signed contracts to play in the second-year Federal League.

MEMORABLE MOMENTS

■ **April 13:** Baltimore pitcher Jack Quinn, working before an estimated crowd of 28,000 at new Terrapin Park, posted a 3-2 victory over Buffalo in the Federal League inaugural.

■ **April 23:** The Chicago Whales christened new Weeghman Park—the future Wrigley Field—with a 9-1 victory over the Kansas City Packers.

■ **September 19:** Brooklyn's Ed Lafitte pitched the Federal League's first no-hitter, beating the Packers 6-2.

■ **October 6:** An Indianapolis victory over St. Louis combined with a Chicago loss to Kansas City clinched the first Federal League pennant for the Hoosiers, who finished with an 88-65 record.

LEADERS

BA: Benny Kauff, Ind., .370
Runs: Benny Kauff, Ind., 120
Hits: Benny Kauff, Ind., 211
TB: Benny Kauff, Ind., 305
HR: Dutch Zwilling, Chi., 16
RBI: Frank LaPorte, Ind., 107
SB: Benny Kauff, Ind., 75
Wins: Claude Hendrix, Chi., 29
ERA: Claude Hendrix, Chi., 1.69
CG: Claude Hendrix, Chi., 34
IP: Cy Falkenberg, Ind., 377.1
SO: Cy Falkenberg, Ind., 236

20-game winners
Claude Hendrix, Chi., 29-10
Jack Quinn, Bal., 26-14
Tom Seaton, Brk., 25-14
Cy Falkenberg, Ind., 25-16
George Suggs, Bal., 24-14
Russ Ford, Buf., 21-6
Elmer Knetzer, Pit., 20-12
Gene Packard, K.C., 20-14

100 RBIs
Frank LaPorte, Ind., 107

1915—Federal League

FINAL STANDINGS

Team	W	L	Pct.	GB
Chicago	86	66	.566	...
St. Louis	87	67	.565	...
Pittsburgh	86	67	.562	0.5
Kansas City	81	72	.529	5.5
Newark	80	72	.526	6
Buffalo	74	78	.487	12
Brooklyn	70	82	.461	16
Baltimore	47	107	.305	40

SIGNIFICANT EVENTS

■ **January 5:** The Federal League filed a lawsuit challenging Organized Baseball as an illegal trust that should be dissolved.
■ **December 22:** Organized Baseball's costly two-year battle against the Federal League ended when a peace treaty was arranged and the outlaw circuit was disbanded.

MEMORABLE MOMENTS

■ **April 24:** Pittsburgh's Frank Allen held St. Louis hitless in the Rebels' 2-0 victory.
■ **May 15:** Chicago's Claude Hendrix pitched a Whale of a game—a 10-0 no-hitter against Pittsburgh.
■ **July 31:** St. Louis' Dave Davenport pitched a pair of 1-0 games on the same day against Buffalo, winning the opener and dropping the nightcap.
■ **August 16, September 7:** Kansas City's Miles Main and St. Louis' Dave Davenport joined the no-hit fraternity. Main stopped Buffalo 5-0 and Davenport beat Chicago 3-0.
■ **October 3:** Chicago's season-ending victory over Pittsburgh clinched the second Federal League pennant—by an incredible .001 over St. Louis and a half game over the Rebels.

LEADERS

BA: Benny Kauff, Brk., .342
Runs: Babe Borton, St.L., 97
Hits: Jack Tobin, St.L., 184
TB: Ed Konetchy, Pit., 278
HR: Hal Chase, Buf., 17
RBI: Dutch Zwilling, Chi., 94
SB: Benny Kauff, Brk., 55
Wins: George McConnell, Chi., 25
ERA: Earl Moseley, New., 1.91
CG: Dave Davenport, St.L., 30
IP: Dave Davenport, St.L., 392.2
SO: Dave Davenport, St.L., 229

20-game winners
George McConnell, Chi., 25-10
Frank Allen, Pit., 23-13
Nick Cullop, K.C., 22-11
Dave Davenport, St.L., 22-18
Ed Reulbach, New., 21-10
Eddie Plank, St.L., 21-11
Al Schulz, Buf., 21-14
Doc Crandall, St.L., 21-15
Gene Packard, K.C., 20-12

1915

FINAL STANDINGS

American League

Team	W	L	Pct.	GB
Boston	101	50	.669	...
Detroit	100	54	.649	2.5
Chicago	93	61	.604	9.5
Washington	85	68	.556	17
New York	69	83	.454	32.5
St. Louis	63	91	.409	39.5
Cleveland	57	95	.375	44.5
Philadelphia	43	109	.283	58.5

National League

Team	W	L	Pct.	GB
Philadelphia	90	62	.592	...
Boston	83	69	.546	7
Brooklyn	80	72	.526	10
Chicago	73	80	.477	17.5
Pittsburgh	73	81	.474	18
St. Louis	72	81	.471	18.5
Cincinnati	71	83	.461	20
New York	69	83	.454	21

SIGNIFICANT EVENTS

■ **August 18:** Boston defeated St. Louis, 3-1, in the first game at new Braves Field.
■ **December 22:** Organized Baseball's costly two-year battle against the Federal League ended when a peace treaty was arranged and the outlaw circuit was disbanded.

MEMORABLE MOMENTS

■ **September 29:** Grover Cleveland Alexander pitched a one-hitter and his 12th shutout of the season as the Phillies clinched their first N.L. pennant with a 5-0 victory over the Braves.
■ **September 30:** The Red Sox clinched the A.L. pennant when the St. Louis Browns handed the Tigers an 8-2 loss in a game at Detroit.
■ **October 3:** Detroit's Ty Cobb, on his way to a record ninth consecutive A.L. batting title, stole his record 96th base in a 6-5 victory over Cleveland.

LEADERS

American League
BA: Ty Cobb, Det., .369.
Runs: Ty Cobb, Det., 144.
Hits: Ty Cobb, Det., 208.
TB: Ty Cobb, Det., 274.
HR: Braggo Roth, Chi.-Cle., 7.
RBI: Sam Crawford, Det.; Bobby Veach, Det., 112.
SB: Ty Cobb, Det., 96.
Wins: Walter Johnson, Wash., 27.
ERA: Joe Wood, Bos., 1.49.
CG: Walter Johnson, Wash., 35.
IP: Walter Johnson, Wash., 336.2.
SO: Walter Johnson, Wash., 203.

National League
BA: Larry Doyle, N.Y., .320.
Runs: Gavvy Cravath, Phil., 89.
Hits: Larry Doyle, N.Y., 189.
TB: Gavvy Cravath, Phil., 266.
HR: Gavvy Cravath, Phil., 24.
RBI: Gavvy Cravath, Phil., 115.
SB: Max Carey, Pit., 36.
Wins: Grover Alexander, Phil., 31.
ERA: Grover Alexander, Phil., 1.22.
CG: Grover Alexander, Phil., 36.
IP: Grover Alexander, Phil, 376.1
SO: Grover Alexander, Phil., 241.

A.L. 20-game winners
Walter Johnson, Wash., 27-13
Jim Scott, Chi., 24-11
Hooks Dauss, Det., 24-13
Red Faber, Chi., 24-14
Harry Coveleski, Det., 22-13

N.L. 20-game winners
Grover Alexander, Phil., 31-10
Dick Rudolph, Bos., 22-19
Al Mamaux, Pit., 21-8
Erskine Mayer, Phil., 21-15
Hippo Vaughn, Chi., 20-12

A.L. 100 RBIs
Sam Crawford, Det., 112
Bobby Veach, Det., 112

N.L. 100 RBIs
Gavvy Cravath, Phil., 115

WORLD SERIES

■ **Winner:** The Red Sox, playing their Series home games in new Braves Field because of its large capacity, matched the Athletics as three-time Series winners with a five-game romp past another Philadelphia team — the Phillies.

■ **Turning point:** Dutch Leonard's 2-1 Game 3 victory over Phillies ace Grover Cleveland Alexander. The game was decided in the ninth inning on Duffy Lewis' RBI single.

■ **Memorable moment:** Harry Hooper's Series-deciding ninth-inning home run in Game 5 off Philadelphia reliever Eppa Rixey.

■ **Top guns:** Rube Foster (2-0, 2.00 ERA), Lewis (.444), Red Sox; Fred Luderus (.438), Phillies.

Linescores

Game 1—October 8, at Philadelphia
Boston........... 0 0 0 0 0 0 0 1 0 — 1 8 1
Philadelphia... 0 0 0 1 0 0 0 2 x — 3 5 1
Shore; Alexander. W—Alexander. L—Shore.

Game 2—October 9, at Philadelphia
Boston........... 1 0 0 0 0 0 0 0 1 — 2 10 0
Philadelphia... 0 0 0 0 1 0 0 0 0 — 1 3 1
Foster; Mayer. W—Foster. L—Mayer.

Game 3—October 11, at Boston
Philadelphia... 0 0 1 0 0 0 0 0 0 — 1 3 0
Boston........... 0 0 0 1 0 0 0 0 1 — 2 6 1
Alexander; Leonard. W—Leonard. L—Alexander.

Game 4—October 12, at Boston
Philadelphia... 0 0 0 0 0 0 0 1 0 — 1 7 0
Boston........... 0 0 1 0 0 1 0 0 x — 2 8 1
Chalmers; Shore. W—Shore. L—Chalmers.

Game 5—October 13, at Philadelphia
Boston........... 0 1 1 0 0 0 0 2 1 — 5 10 1
Philadelphia... 2 0 0 2 0 0 0 0 0 — 4 9 1
Foster; Mayer, Rixey (3). W—Foster. L—Rixey. HR—Hooper 2, Lewis (Bos.); Luderus (Phil.).

1916

FINAL STANDINGS

American League

Team	W	L	Pct.	GB
Boston	91	63	.591	...
Chicago	89	65	.578	2
Detroit	87	67	.565	4
New York	80	74	.519	11
St. Louis	79	75	.513	12
Cleveland	77	77	.500	14
Washington	76	77	.497	14.5
Philadelphia	36	117	.235	54.5

National League

Team	W	L	Pct.	GB
Brooklyn	94	60	.610	...
Philadelphia	91	62	.595	2.5
Boston	89	63	.586	4
New York	86	66	.566	7
Chicago	67	86	.438	26.5
Pittsburgh	65	89	.422	29
Cincinnati	60	93	.392	33.5
St. Louis	60	93	.392	33.5

SIGNIFICANT EVENTS

■ **July 20:** Giants great Christy Mathewson was traded to Cincinnati in a career-prolonging deal that allowed him to become manager of the Reds.
■ **November 1:** Harry Frazee, a New York theater owner and producer, bought the Red Sox for $675,000.

MEMORABLE MOMENTS

■ **August 9:** The Athletics' 20-game losing streak came to a merciful end when they defeated the Tigers, 7-1.
■ **September 30:** The Braves ended New York's winning streak at a Major League-record 26 games with an 8-3 victory in the second game of a doubleheader.
■ **October 2:** Grover Cleveland Alexander pitched the Phillies to a 2-0 victory over the Braves—his modern record 16th shutout of the season.

LEADERS

American League
BA: Tris Speaker, Cle., .386.
Runs: Ty Cobb, Det., 113.
Hits: Tris Speaker, Cle., 211.
TB: Joe Jackson, Chi., 293.
HR: Wally Pipp, N.Y., 12.
RBI: Del Pratt, St L., 103.
SB: Ty Cobb, Det., 68.
Wins: Walter Johnson, Wash., 25.
ERA: Babe Ruth, Bos., 1.75.
CG: Walter Johnson, Wash., 36.
IP: Walter Johnson, Wash., 369.2.
SO: Walter Johnson, Wash., 228.

National League
BA: Hal Chase, Cin., .339.
Runs: George Burns, N.Y., 105.
Hits: Hal Chase, Cin., 184.
TB: Zack Wheat, Brk., 262.
HR: Dave Robertson, N.Y.; Cy Williams, Chi., 12.
RBI: Heinie Zimmerman, Chi.-N.Y., 83.
SB: Max Carey, Pit., 63.
Wins: Grover Alexander, Phil., 33.
ERA: Grover Alexander, Phil., 1.55.
CG: Grover Alexander, Phil., 38.
IP: Grover Alexander, Phil., 389.
SO: Grover Alexander, Phil., 167.

A.L. 20-game winners
Walter Johnson, Wash., 25-20
Bob Shawkey, N.Y., 24-14
Babe Ruth, Bos., 23-12
Harry Coveleski, Det., 21-11

N.L. 20-game winners
Grover Alexander, Phil., 33-12
Jeff Pfeffer, Brk., 25-11
Eppa Rixey, Phil., 22-10
Al Mamaux, Pit., 21-15

A.L. 100 RBIs
Del Pratt, St.L., 103

WORLD SERIES

■ **Winner:** Stingy Boston pitchers allowed only eight earned runs and the Red Sox closed down the Dodgers to become the first four-time Series winners.

■ **Turning point:** Larry Gardner's three-run Game 4 homer propelled Dutch Leonard to a 6-2 victory and the Red Sox to a 3-1 Series advantage.

■ **Memorable moment:** A 14-inning Game 2 pitching duel between Boston's Babe Ruth and Brooklyn's Sherry Smith. Ruth won 2-1 on Del Gainor's pinch-hit single.

■ **Top guns:** Ernie Shore (2-0, 1.53 ERA), Duffy Lewis (.353), Red Sox; Casey Stengel (.364), Dodgers.

Linescores

Game 1—October 7, at Boston
Brooklyn ....0 0 0 1 0 0 0 0 4 — 5 10 4
Boston ....0 0 1 0 1 0 3 1 x — 6 8 1
Marquard, Pfeffer (8); Shore, Mays (9). W—Shore. L—Marquard.

Game 2—October 9, at Boston
Brooklyn........1 0 0 0 0 0 0 0 0 0 0 0 0 0 — 1 6 2
Boston...........0 0 1 0 0 0 0 0 0 0 0 0 0 1 — 2 7 1
Smith; Ruth. W—Ruth. L—Smith. HR—Myers (Brk.).

Game 3—October 10, at Brooklyn
Boston ....0 0 0 0 0 2 1 0 0 — 3 7 1
Brooklyn...........................0 0 1 1 2 0 0 0 x — 4 10 0
Mays, Foster (6); Coombs, Pfeffer (7). W—Coombs. L—Mays. HR—Gardner (Bos.).

Game 4—October 11, at Brooklyn
Boston ....0 3 0 1 1 0 1 0 0 — 6 10 1
Brooklyn ....2 0 0 0 0 0 0 0 0 — 2 5 4
Leonard; Marquard, Cheney (5), Rucker (8). W—Leonard. L—Marquard. HR—Gardner (Bos.).

Game 5—October 12, at Boston
Brooklyn ....0 1 0 0 0 0 0 0 0 — 1 3 3
Boston ....0 1 2 0 1 0 0 0 x — 4 7 2
Pfeffer, Dell (8); Shore. W—Shore. L—Pfeffer.

1917

FINAL STANDINGS

American League

Team	W	L	Pct.	GB
Chicago	100	54	.649	...
Boston	90	62	.592	9
Cleveland	88	66	.571	12
Detroit	78	75	.510	21.5
Washington	74	79	.484	25.5
New York	71	82	.464	28.5
St. Louis	57	97	.370	43
Philadelphia	55	98	.359	44.5

National League

Team	W	L	Pct.	GB
New York	98	56	.636	...
Philadelphia	87	65	.572	10
St. Louis	82	70	.539	15
Cincinnati	78	76	.506	20
Chicago	74	80	.481	24
Boston	72	81	.471	25.5
Brooklyn	70	81	.464	26.5
Pittsburgh	51	103	.331	47

SIGNIFICANT EVENTS

■ **October 26:** New York owner Jacob Ruppert took a dynastic step when he signed former Cardinals manager Miller Huggins to manage the Yankees.

MEMORABLE MOMENTS

■ **April 14:** Chicago ace Eddie Cicotte kicked off the season's no-hitter parade with an 11-0 victory over St. Louis. Cicotte's no-hitter was the first of five in the American League.

■ **May 2:** Cincinnati's Fred Toney and Chicago's Hippo Vaughn matched no-hitters for an unprecedented nine innings before Vaughn wilted in the 10th and the Reds scored a 1-0 victory.

■ **May 6:** Browns pitcher Bob Groom pitched a 3-0 no-hitter against the White Sox, matching the previous-day feat of teammate Ernie Koob in a 1-0 victory over Chicago.

■ **June 23:** Boston's Ernie Shore retired 27 consecutive Senators after replacing starter Babe Ruth, who was ejected after walking the first batter of the game. The runner was thrown out trying to steal and Shore went on to claim a 4-0 victory.

■ **September 3:** Grover Alexander, en route to a Major League-leading 30 victories, pitched both ends of the Phillies' 6-0 and 9-3 doubleheader sweep of Brooklyn.

LEADERS

American League

BA: Ty Cobb, Det., .383.
Runs: Donie Bush, Det., 112.
Hits: Ty Cobb, Det., 225.
TB: Ty Cobb, Det., 335.
HR: Wally Pipp, N.Y., 9.
RBI: Bobby Veach, Det., 103.
SB: Ty Cobb, Det., 55.
Wins: Eddie Cicotte, Chi., 28.
ERA: Eddie Cicotte, Chi., 1.53.
CG: Babe Ruth, Bos., 35.
IP: Eddie Cicotte, Chi., 346.2.
SO: Walter Johnson, Wash., 188.

National League

BA: Edd Roush, Cin., .341.
Runs: George Burns, N.Y., 103.
Hits: Heinie Groh, Cin., 182.
TB: Rogers Hornsby, St.L., 253.
HR: Gavvy Cravath, Phil.; Dave Robertson, N.Y., 12.
RBI: Heinie Zimmerman, N.Y., 102.
SB: Max Carey, Pit., 46.
Wins: Grover Alexander, Phil., 30.
ERA: Fred Anderson, N.Y., 1.44.
CG: Grover Alexander, Phil., 34.
IP: Grover Alexander, Phil., 388.
SO: Grover Alexander, Phil., 200.

A.L. 20-game winners

Ed Cicotte, Chi., 28-12
Babe Ruth, Bos., 24-13
Jim Bagby, Cle., 23-13
Walter Johnson, Wash., 23-16
Carl Mays, Bos., 22-9

N.L. 20-game winners

Grover Alexander, Phil., 30-13
Fred Toney, Cin., 24-16
Hippo Vaughn, Chi., 23-13
Ferdie Schupp, N.Y., 21-7
Pete Schneider, Cin., 20-19

A.L. 100 RBIs

Bobby Veach, Det., 103
Ty Cobb, Det., 102
Happy Felsch, Chi., 102

N.L. 100 RBIs

Heinie Zimmerman, N.Y., 102

WORLD SERIES

■ **Winner:** The White Sox, making their first Series appearance since 1906, took advantage of the Giants' sloppy play for a six-game victory.

■ **Turning point:** The White Sox rallied for six seventh and eighth-inning runs to claim an 8-5 victory in the pivotal fifth game.

■ **Memorable moment:** Third baseman Heinie Zimmerman giving futile chase to Chicago's Eddie Collins as he bolted toward the uncovered plate on one of several Game 6 fielding gaffes by the Giants. The White Sox closed out the Series with a 4-2 victory.

■ **Top guns:** Red Faber (3-1), Collins (.409), White Sox; Dave Robertson (.500), Giants.

Linescores

Game 1—October 6, at Chicago
New York........ 0 0 0 0 1 0 0 0 0 — 1 7 1
Chicago.......... 0 0 1 1 0 0 0 0 x — 2 7 1
Sallee; Cicotte. W—Cicotte. L—Sallee. HR—Felsch (Chi.).

Game 2—October 7, at Chicago
New York........ 0 2 0 0 0 0 0 0 0 — 2 8 1
Chicago.......... 0 2 0 5 0 0 0 0 x — 7 14 1
Schupp, Anderson (2), Perritt (4), Tesreau (8); Faber. W—Faber. L—Anderson.

Game 3—October 10, at New York
Chicago.......... 0 0 0 0 0 0 0 0 0 — 0 5 3
New York........ 0 0 0 2 0 0 0 0 x — 2 8 2
Cicotte; Benton. W—Benton. L—Cicotte.

Game 4—October 11, at New York
Chicago.......... 0 0 0 0 0 0 0 0 0 — 0 7 0
New York........ 0 0 0 1 1 0 1 2 x — 5 10 1
Faber, Danforth (8); Schupp. W—Schupp. L—Faber. HR—Kauff 2 (N.Y.).

Game 5—October 13, at Chicago
New York........ 2 0 0 2 0 0 1 0 0 — 5 12 3
Chicago.......... 0 0 1 0 0 1 3 3 x — 8 14 6
Sallee, Perritt (8); Russell, Cicotte (1), Williams (7), Faber (8). W—Faber. L—Sallee.

Game 6—October 15, at New York
Chicago.......... 0 0 0 3 0 0 0 0 1 — 4 7 1
New York........ 0 0 0 0 2 0 0 0 0 — 2 6 3
Faber; Benton, Perritt (6). W—Faber. L—Benton.

1918

FINAL STANDINGS

American League

Team	W	L	Pct.	GB
Boston	75	51	.595	...
Cleveland	73	54	.575	2.5
Washington	72	56	.563	4
New York	60	63	.488	13.5
St. Louis	58	64	.475	15
Chicago	57	67	.460	17
Detroit	55	71	.437	20
Philadelphia	52	76	.406	24

National League

Team	W	L	Pct.	GB
Chicago	84	45	.651	...
New York	71	53	.573	10.5
Cincinnati	68	60	.531	15.5
Pittsburgh	65	60	.520	17
Brooklyn	57	69	.452	25.5
Philadelphia	55	68	.447	26
Boston	53	71	.427	28.5
St. Louis	51	78	.395	33

SIGNIFICANT EVENTS

■ **April 30:** Cubs great Grover Cleveland Alexander answered the draft call and reported for World War I duty with the Army.

■ **May 14:** Washington D.C. officials repealed the ban against night baseball in the nation's capital, citing the need for more wartime recreational outlets.

■ **July 19:** U.S. Secretary of War Newton Baker issued a "Work or Fight" order forcing all able-bodied Americans into jobs considered essential to the war.

■ **August 2:** A.L. and N.L. officials voted to close down the regular season by September 2 (Labor Day) with the World Series to follow immediately.

■ **October 5:** Infielder Eddie Grant became baseball's first war casualty when he was killed during action in France.

■ **December 10:** N.L. secretary John Heydler was selected to replace John K. Tener as the league's new president.

MEMORABLE MOMENTS

■ **April 15:** Babe Ruth got the Red Sox' s season off to a rousing start with an opening day 7-1 victory over the A's.

■ **June 3:** Boston's Dutch Leonard pitched the season's only no-hitter, beating the Tigers 5-0 with the aide of a Babe Ruth home run.

■ **August 31:** Babe Ruth pitched the Red Sox to an A.L. pennant-clinching 6-1 victory over the Athletics.

LEADERS

American League

BA: Ty Cobb, Det., .382.
Runs: Ray Chapman, Cle., 84.
Hits: George Burns, Phil., 178.
TB: George Burns, Phil., 236.
HR: Babe Ruth, Bos.; Tilly Walker, Phil., 11.
RBI: Bobby Veach, Det., 78.
SB: George Sisler, St.L., 45.
Wins: Walter Johnson, Wash., 23.
ERA: Walter Johnson, Wash., 1.27.
CG: Carl Mays, Bos.; Scott Perry, Phil., 30.
IP: Scott Perry, Phil., 332.1.
SO: Walter Johnson, Wash., 162.

National League

BA: Zack Wheat, Brk., .335.
Runs: Heinie Groh, Cin., 86.
Hits: Charlie Hollocher, Chi., 161.
TB: Charlie Hollocher, Chi., 202.
HR: Gavvy Cravath, Phil., 8.
RBI: Sherry Magee, Cin., 76.
SB: Max Carey, Pit., 58.
Wins: Hippo Vaughn, Chi., 22.
ERA: Hippo Vaughn, Chi., 1.74.
CG: Art Nehf, Bos., 28.
IP: Hippo Vaughn, Chi., 290.1.
SO: Hippo Vaughn, Chi., 148.

A.L. 20-game winners

Walter Johnson, Wash., 23-13
Stan Coveleski, Cle., 22-13
Carl Mays, Bos., 21-13
Scott Perry, Phil., 20-19

N.L. 20-game winners

Hippo Vaughn, Chi., 22-10
Claude Hendrix, Chi., 20-7

WORLD SERIES

■ **Winner:** The Red Sox ended baseball's war-depleted season by defeating the Cubs and winning their fifth Series in as many tries.

■ **Turning point:** Babe Ruth's second victory, a 3-2 Game 4 decision that gave the Red Sox a three games to one advantage.

■ **Memorable moment:** A Game 6 delay while players haggled with the owners over gate receipts. The Red Sox closed out the Cubs with a 2-1 victory.

■ **Top guns:** Carl Mays (2-0, 1.00 ERA), Ruth (2-0, 1.06), Red Sox; Charlie Pick (.389), Cubs.

Linescores

Game 1—September 5, at Chicago
Boston ....0 0 0 1 0 0 0 0 0 — 1 5 0
Chicago..........0 0 0 0 0 0 0 0 0 — 0 6 0
Ruth; Vaughn. W—Ruth. L—Vaughn.

Game 2—September 6, at Chicago
Boston ....0 0 0 0 0 0 0 0 1 — 1 6 1
Chicago..........0 3 0 0 0 0 0 0 x — 3 7 1
Bush; Tyler. W—Tyler. L—Bush.

Game 3—September 7, at Chicago
Boston ....0 0 0 2 0 0 0 0 0 — 2 7 0
Chicago..........0 0 0 0 1 0 0 0 0 — 1 7 1
Mays; Vaughn. W—Mays. L—Vaughn.

Game 4—September 9, at Boston
Chicago..........0 0 0 0 0 0 0 2 0 — 2 7 1
Boston............0 0 0 2 0 0 0 1 x — 3 4 0
Tyler, Douglas (8); Ruth, Bush (9). W—Ruth. L—Douglas.

Game 5—September 10, at Boston
Chicago..........0 0 1 0 0 0 0 2 0 — 3 7 0
Boston ....0 0 0 0 0 0 0 0 0 — 0 5 0
Vaughn; Jones. W—Vaughn. L—Jones.

Game 6—September 11, at Boston
Chicago..........0 0 0 1 0 0 0 0 0 — 1 3 2
Boston............0 0 2 0 0 0 0 0 x — 2 5 0
Tyler, Hendrix (8); Mays. W—Mays. L—Tyler.

1919

FINAL STANDINGS

American League

Team	W	L	Pct.	GB
Chicago	88	52	.629	...
Cleveland	84	55	.604	3.5
New York	80	59	.576	7.5
Detroit	80	60	.571	8
St. Louis	67	72	.482	20.5
Boston	66	71	.482	20.5
Washington	56	84	.400	32
Philadelphia	36	104	.257	52

National League

Team	W	L	Pct.	GB
Cincinnati	96	44	.686	...
New York	87	53	.621	9
Chicago	75	65	.536	21
Pittsburgh	71	68	.511	24.5
Brooklyn	69	71	.493	27
Boston	57	82	.410	38.5
St. Louis	54	83	.394	40.5
Philadelphia	47	90	.343	47.5

SIGNIFICANT EVENTS

- **April 19:** New York Governor Al Smith signed a bill permitting Sunday baseball throughout the state.
- **April 23:** The slimmed-down 140-game Major League schedule opened in Washington, where Walter Johnson shut out the A's, 1-0.
- **September 2:** Major League officials approved a best-of-nine World Series format, replacing the long-running seven-game format.

MEMORABLE MOMENTS

- **September 16:** The Reds defeated the Giants, 4-3, and clinched their first N.L. pennant of the century.
- **September 24:** The White Sox captured their second A.L. pennant in three years when they defeated St. Louis, 6-5.
- **September 27:** Boston's Babe Ruth stretched his one-season home run record to 29 in a game at Washington.

LEADERS

American League

BA: Ty Cobb, Det., .384.
Runs: Babe Ruth, Bos., 103.
Hits: Ty Cobb, Det.; Bobby Veach, Det., 191.
TB: Babe Ruth, Bos., 284.
HR: Babe Ruth, Bos., 29.
RBI: Babe Ruth, Bos., 114.
SB: Eddie Collins, Chi., 33.
Wins: Eddie Cicotte, Chi., 29.
ERA: Walter Johnson, Wash., 1.49.
CG: Eddie Cicotte, Chi., 30.
IP: Eddie Cicotte, Chi.; Jim Shaw, Wash., 306.2.
SO: Walter Johnson, Wash., 147.

National League

BA: Gavvy Cravath, Phil., .341.
Runs: George Burns, N.Y., 86.
Hits: Ivy Olson, Brk., 164.
TB: Hy Myers, Brk., 223.
HR: Gavvy Cravath, Phil., 12.
RBI: Hy Myers, Brk., 73.
SB: George Burns, N.Y., 40.
Wins: Jesse Barnes, N.Y., 25.
ERA: Grover Alexander, Chi., 1.72.
CG: Wilbur Cooper, Pit., 27.
IP: Hippo Vaughn, Chi., 306.2.
SO: Hippo Vaughn, Chi., 141.

A.L. 20-game winners

Ed Cicotte, Chi., 29-7
Stan Coveleski, Cle., 24-12
Lefty Williams, Chi., 23-11
Hooks Dauss, Det., 21-9
Allen Sothoron, St.L., 20-12
Bob Shawkey, N.Y., 20-11
Walter Johnson, Wash., 20-14

N.L. 20-game winners

Jess Barnes, N.Y., 25-9
Slim Sallee, Cin., 21-7
Hippo Vaughn, Chi., 21-14

A.L. 100 RBIs

Babe Ruth, Bos., 114
Bobby Veach, Det., 101

WORLD SERIES

- **Winner:** The Reds earned their first Series victory amid suspicions the White Sox were consorting with gamblers in a fall classic fix.
- **Turning point:** The Series' first pitch, when Chicago starter Eddie Cicotte hit Cincinnati leadoff man Morrie Rath, reportedly signaling to bettors the fix was on.
- **Memorable moment:** White Sox lefthander Dickey Kerr, suspecting something was brewing among his teammates, fired a heroic three-hit shutout in Game 3.
- **Top guns:** Hod Eller (2-0, 2.00 ERA), Greasy Neale (.357), Reds; Kerr (2-0, 1.42), White Sox.

Linescores

Game 1—October 1, at Cincinnati

Chicago.......... 0 1 0 0 0 0 0 0 0 — 1 6 1
Cincinnati....... 1 0 0 5 0 0 2 1 x — 9 14 1

Cicotte, Wilkinson (4), Lowdermilk (8); Ruether. W—Ruether. L—Cicotte.

Game 2—October 2, at Cincinnati

Chicago.......... 0 0 0 0 0 0 2 0 0 — 2 10 1
Cincinnati....... 0 0 0 3 0 1 0 0 x — 4 4 2

Williams; Sallee. W—Sallee. L—Williams.

Game 3—October 3, at Chicago

Cincinnati....... 0 0 0 0 0 0 0 0 0 — 0 3 1
Chicago.......... 0 2 0 1 0 0 0 0 x — 3 7 0

Fisher, Luque (8); Kerr. W—Kerr. L—Fisher.

Game 4—October 4, at Chicago

Cincinnati....... 0 0 0 0 2 0 0 0 0—2 5 2
Chicago.......... 0 0 0 0 0 0 0 0 0—0 3 2

Ring; Cicotte. W—Ring. L—Cicotte.

Game 5—October 6, at Chicago

Cincinnati....... 0 0 0 0 0 4 0 0 1 — 5 4 0
Chicago.......... 0 0 0 0 0 0 0 0 0 — 0 3 3

Eller; Williams, Mayer (9). W—Eller. L—Williams.

Game 6—October 7, at Cincinnati

Chicago.......... 0 0 0 0 1 3 0 0 0 1—5 10 3
Cincinnati....... 0 0 2 2 0 0 0 0 0 0—4 11 0

Kerr; Ruether, Ring (6). W—Kerr. L—Ring.

Game 7—October 8, at Cincinnati

Chicago.......... 1 0 1 0 2 0 0 0 0 — 4 10 1
Cincinnati....... 0 0 0 0 0 1 0 0 0 — 1 7 4

Cicotte; Sallee, Fisher (5), Luque (6). W—Cicotte. L—Sallee.

Game 8—October 9, at Chicago

Cincinnati....... 4 1 0 0 1 3 0 1 0 — 10 16 2
Chicago.......... 0 0 1 0 0 0 0 4 0 — 5 10 1

Eller; Williams, James (1), Wilkinson (6). W—Eller. L—Williams. HR—Jackson (Chi.).

1920

FINAL STANDINGS

American League

Team	W	L	Pct.	GB
Cleveland	98	56	.636	...
Chicago	96	58	.623	2
New York	95	59	.617	3
St. Louis	76	77	.497	21.5
Boston	72	81	.471	25.5
Washington	68	84	.447	29
Detroit	61	93	.396	37
Philadelphia	48	106	.312	50

National League

Team	W	L	Pct.	GB
Brooklyn	93	61	.604	...
New York	86	68	.558	7
Cincinnati	82	71	.536	10.5
Pittsburgh	79	75	.513	14
Chicago	75	79	.487	18
St. Louis	75	79	.487	18
Boston	62	90	.408	30
Philadelphia	62	91	.405	30.5

SIGNIFICANT EVENTS

- **January 5:** The New York Yankees acquired pitcher-outfielder Babe Ruth from Boston Red Sox owner Harry Frazee for the incredible price of $125,000.
- **February 9:** Baseball's joint rules committee banned the use of all foreign substances and ball-doctoring methods used by pitchers.
- **September 28:** A Chicago grand jury indicted eight White Sox players, including star center fielder Joe Jackson, for conspiring to fix the 1919 World Series. All eight were immediately suspended by Chicago owner Charles Comiskey.

MEMORABLE MOMENTS

- **May 1:** Boston's Joe Oeschger and Brooklyn's Leon Cadore traded pitches for a Major League-record 26 innings in a game that ended in a 1-1 tie at Braves Field.
- **May 14:** Washington great Walter Johnson defeated Detroit for his 300th career victory.
- **August 17:** Cleveland shortstop Ray Chapman died a day after he was hit on the head by a pitch from Yankee righthander Carl Mays.
- **October 2:** Pittsburgh and Cincinnati played the century's only tripleheader.
- **October 3:** Browns first baseman George Sisler collected his record-setting 257th hit of the season.

LEADERS

American League

BA: George Sisler, St.L., .407.
Runs: Babe Ruth, N.Y., 158.
Hits: George Sisler, St.L., 257.
TB: George Sisler, St.L., 399.
HR: Babe Ruth, N.Y., 54.
RBI: Babe Ruth, N.Y., 137.
SB: Sam Rice, Wash., 63.
Wins: Jim Bagby, Cle., 31.
ERA: Bob Shawkey, N.Y., 2.45.
CG: Jim Bagby, Cle., 30.
IP: Jim Bagby, Cle., 339.2.
SO: Stan Coveleski, Cle., 133.

National League

BA: Rogers Hornsby, St.L., .370.
Runs: George Burns, N.Y., 115.
Hits: Rogers Hornsby, St.L., 218.
TB: Rogers Hornsby, St.L., 329.
HR: Cy Williams, Phil., 15.
RBI: Rogers Hornsby, St.L.; George Kelly, N.Y., 94.
SB: Max Carey, Pit., 52.
Wins: Grover Alexander, Chi., 27.
ERA: Grover Alexander, Chi., 1.91.
CG: Grover Alexander, Chi., 33.
IP: Grover Alexander, Chi., 363.1.
SO: Grover Alexander, Chi., 173.

A.L. 20-game winners

Jim Bagby, Cle., 31-12
Carl Mays, N.Y., 26-11
Stan Coveleski, Cle., 24-14
Red Faber, Chi., 23-13
Lefty Williams, Chi., 22-14
Dickie Kerr, Chi., 21-9
Ed Cicotte, Chi., 21-10
Ray Caldwell, Cle., 20-10
Urban Shocker, St.L., 20-10
Bob Shawkey, N.Y., 20-13

N.L. 20-game winners

Grover Alexander, Chi., 27-14
Wilbur Cooper, Pit., 24-15
Burleigh Grimes, Brk., 23-11
Fred Toney, N.Y., 21-11
Art Nehf, N.Y., 21-12
Bill Doak, St.L., 20-12
Jess Barnes, N.Y., 20-15

A.L. 100 RBIs

Babe Ruth, N.Y., 137
Bill Jacobson, St.L., 122
George Sisler, St.L., 122
Joe Jackson, Chi., 121
Larry Gardner, Cle., 118
Happy Felsch, Chi., 115
Bobby Veach, Det., 113
Tris Speaker, Cle., 107
Elmer Smith, Cle., 103

A.L. 40 homers

Babe Ruth, N.Y., 54

WORLD SERIES

- **Winner:** The Indians, Series newcomers, held off the Dodgers in a seven-game fall classic filled with memorable firsts.
- **Turning point:** Stan Coveleski's second win, a 5-1 Game 4 decision, that knotted the Series at two and set up a dramatic Game 5.
- **Memorable moments:** There were several for the Indians in Game 5. Elmer Smith hit the first grand slam in Series history, Jim Bagby became the first pitcher to hit a Series homer and second baseman Bill Wambsganss pulled off the first Series triple play — unassisted.
- **Top guns:** Coveleski (3-0, 0.67 ERA), Smith (.308, 5 RBIs), Indians; Zack Wheat (.333), Dodgers.

Linescores

Game 1—October 5, at Brooklyn

Cleveland........ 0 2 0 1 0 0 0 0 0 — 3 5 0
Brooklyn......... 0 0 0 0 0 0 1 0 0 — 1 5 1

Coveleski; Marquard, Mamaux (7), Cadore (9). W—Coveleski. L—Marquard.

Game 2—October 6, at Brooklyn

Cleveland........ 0 0 0 0 0 0 0 0 0 — 0 7 1
Brooklyn......... 1 0 1 0 1 0 0 0 x — 3 7 0

Bagby, Uhle (7); Grimes. W—Grimes. L—Bagby.

Game 3—October 7, at Brooklyn

Cleveland........ 0 0 0 1 0 0 0 0 0 — 1 3 1
Brooklyn......... 2 0 0 0 0 0 0 0 x — 2 6 1

Caldwell, Mails (1), Uhle (8); S. Smith. W—S. Smith. L—Caldwell.

Game 4—October 9, at Cleveland

Brooklyn......... 0 0 0 1 0 0 0 0 0 — 1 5 1
Cleveland........ 2 0 2 0 0 1 0 0 x — 5 12 2

Cadore, Mamaux (2), Marquard (3), Pfeffer (6); Coveleski. W—Coveleski. L—Cadore.

Game 5—October 10, at Cleveland

Brooklyn......... 0 0 0 0 0 0 0 0 1 — 1 13 1
Cleveland........ 4 0 0 3 1 0 0 0 x — 8 12 2

Grimes, Mitchell (4); Bagby. W—Bagby. L—Grimes. HR—E. Smith, Bagby (Cle.).

Game 6—October 11, at Cleveland

Brooklyn......... 0 0 0 0 0 0 0 0 0 — 0 3 0
Cleveland........ 0 0 0 0 0 1 0 0 x — 1 7 3

S. Smith; Mails. W—Mails. L—S. Smith.

Game 7—October 12, at Cleveland

Brooklyn......... 0 0 0 0 0 0 0 0 0 — 0 5 2
Cleveland........ 0 0 0 1 1 0 1 0 x — 3 7 3

Grimes, Mamaux (8); Coveleski. W—Coveleski. L—Grimes.

1921

FINAL STANDINGS

American League

Team	W	L	Pct.	GB
New York	98	55	.641	...
Cleveland	94	60	.610	4.5
St. Louis	81	73	.526	17.5
Washington	80	73	.523	18
Boston	75	79	.487	23.5
Detroit	71	82	.464	27
Chicago	62	92	.403	36.5
Philadelphia	53	100	.346	45

National League

Team	W	L	Pct.	GB
New York	94	59	.614	...
Pittsburgh	90	63	.588	4
St. Louis	87	66	.569	7
Boston	79	74	.516	15
Brooklyn	77	75	.507	16.5
Cincinnati	70	83	.458	24
Chicago	64	89	.418	30
Philadelphia	51	103	.331	43.5

SIGNIFICANT EVENTS

■ **January 21:** Federal Judge Kenesaw Mountain Landis began his seven-year contract as baseball's first commissioner.

■ **August 3:** Commissioner Landis banned eight Chicago White Sox players from baseball for life, even though a Chicago jury had cleared them of charges that they conspired to fix the 1919 World Series.

■ **August 5:** Pittsburgh radio station KDKA did the first Major League baseball broadcast—a Pirates-Phillies game at Forbes Field.

■ **October 5:** Pittsburgh radio station KDKA broadcast the opening game of the Yankees-Giants World Series.

■ **October 21:** Commissioner Landis suspended Babe Ruth and Yankee teammates Bob Meusel and Bill Piercy for their illegal barnstorming tour after the 1921 World Series.

MEMORABLE MOMENTS

■ **August 19:** Detroit's Ty Cobb collected career hit No. 3,000 off Boston pitcher Elmer Myers.

■ **October 2:** Babe Ruth connected for record home run No. 59 off Boston's Curt Fullerton.

LEADERS

American League

BA: Harry Heilmann, Det., .394.
Runs: Babe Ruth, N.Y., 177.
Hits: Harry Heilmann, Det., 237.
TB: Babe Ruth, N.Y., 457.
HR: Babe Ruth, N.Y., 59.
RBI: Babe Ruth, N.Y., 171.
SB: George Sisler, St.L., 35.
Wins: Carl Mays, N.Y.; Urban Shocker, St.L., 27.
ERA: Red Faber, Chi., 2.48.
CG: Red Faber, Chi., 32.
IP: Carl Mays, N.Y., 336.2.
SO: Walter Johnson, Wash., 143.

National League

BA: Rogers Hornsby, St.L., .397.
Runs: Rogers Hornsby, St.L., 131.
Hits: Rogers Hornsby, St.L., 235.
TB: Rogers Hornsby, St.L., 378.
HR: George Kelly, N.Y., 23.
RBI: Rogers Hornsby, St.L., 126.
SB: Frank Frisch, N.Y., 49.
Wins: Wilbur Cooper, Pit.; Burleigh Grimes, Brk., 22.
ERA: Bill Doak, St.L., 2.59.
CG: Burleigh Grimes, Brk., 30.
IP: Wilbur Cooper, Pit., 327.
SO: Burleigh Grimes, Brk., 136.

A.L. 20-game winners

Carl Mays, N.Y., 27-9
Urban Shocker, St.L., 27-12
Red Faber, Chi., 25-15
Stan Coveleski, Cle., 23-13
Sam Jones, Bos., 23-16

N.L. 20-game winners

Burleigh Grimes, Brk., 22-13
Wilbur Cooper, Pit., 22-14
Art Nehf, N.Y., 20-10
Joe Oeschger, Bos., 20-14

A.L. 100 RBIs

Babe Ruth, N.Y., 170
Harry Heilmann, Det., 139
Bob Meusel, N.Y., 135
Bobby Veach, Det., 128
Ken Williams, St.L., 117
Larry Gardner, Cle., 115
George Sisler, St.L., 104
Ty Cobb, Det., 101
Tilly Walker, Phil., 101
Del Pratt, Bos., 100

N.L. 100 RBIs

Rogers Hornsby, St.L., 126
George Kelly, N.Y., 122
Austin McHenry, St.L., 102
Ross Youngs, N.Y., 102
Frank Frisch, N.Y., 100

A.L. 40 homers

Babe Ruth, N.Y., 59

WORLD SERIES

■ **Winner:** The Giants shook the ghosts of Series past and rallied for an eight-game victory in the battle of New York.

■ **Turning point:** Down two games to none and trailing 4-0 in the third inning of Game 3, the Giants rallied for a 13-5 victory.

■ **Memorable moment:** An unusual 4-3-5 double play that finished off Art Nehf's 1-0 Game 8 victory over Yankee Waite Hoyt and provided a dramatic conclusion to the Series.

■ **Top guns:** Jesse Barnes (2-0, 1.65 ERA), Frank Snyder (.364), Irish Meusel (.345, 7 RBIs), Giants; Hoyt (2-1, 0.00), Yankees.

Linescores

Game 1—October 5, at Polo Grounds
Yankees.......... 1 0 0 0 1 1 0 0 0 — 3 7 0
Giants............ 0 0 0 0 0 0 0 0 0 — 0 5 0
Mays; Douglas, Barnes (9). W—Mays. L—Douglas.

Game 2—October 6, at Polo Grounds
Giants............ 0 0 0 0 0 0 0 0 0 — 0 2 3
Yankees.......... 0 0 0 1 0 0 0 2 x — 3 3 0
Nehf; Hoyt. W—Hoyt. L—Nehf.

Game 3—October 7, at Polo Grounds
Yankees.......... 0 0 4 0 0 0 0 1 0 — 5 8 0
Giants............ 0 0 4 0 0 0 8 1 x — 13 20 0
Shawkey, Quinn (3), Collins (7), Rogers (7); Toney, Barnes (3). W—Barnes. L—Quinn.

Game 4—October 9, at Polo Grounds
Giants............ 0 0 0 0 0 0 0 3 1 — 4 9 1
Yankees.......... 0 0 0 0 1 0 0 0 1 — 2 7 1
Douglas; Mays. W—Douglas. L—Mays. HR—Ruth (NYY).

Game 5—October 10, at Polo Grounds
Yankees.......... 0 0 1 2 0 0 0 0 0 — 3 6 1
Giants............ 1 0 0 0 0 0 0 0 0 — 1 10 1
Hoyt; Nehf. W—Hoyt. L—Nehf.

Game 6—October 11, at Polo Grounds
Giants............ 0 3 0 4 0 1 0 0 0 — 8 13 0
Yankees.......... 3 2 0 0 0 0 0 0 0 — 5 7 2
Toney, Barnes (1); Harper, Shawkey (2), Piercy (9). W—Barnes. L—Shawkey. HR—E. Meusel, Snyder (NYG); Fewster (NYY).

Game 7—October 12, at Polo Grounds
Yankees.......... 0 1 0 0 0 0 0 0 0 — 1 8 1
Giants............ 0 0 0 1 0 0 1 0 x — 2 6 0
Mays; Douglas. W—Douglas. L—Mays.

Game 8—October 13, at Polo Grounds
Giants............ 1 0 0 0 0 0 0 0 0 — 1 6 0
Yankees.......... 0 0 0 0 0 0 0 0 0 — 0 4 1
Nehf; Hoyt. W—Nehf. L—Hoyt.

1922

FINAL STANDINGS

American League

Team	W	L	Pct.	GB
New York	94	60	.610	...
St. Louis	93	61	.604	1
Detroit	79	75	.513	15
Cleveland	78	76	.506	16
Chicago	77	77	.500	17
Washington	69	85	.448	25
Philadelphia	65	89	.422	29
Boston	61	93	.396	33

National League

Team	W	L	Pct.	GB
New York	93	61	.604	...
Cincinnati	86	68	.558	7
Pittsburgh	85	69	.552	8
St. Louis	85	69	.552	8
Chicago	80	74	.519	13
Brooklyn	76	78	.494	17
Philadelphia	57	96	.373	35.5
Boston	53	100	.346	39.5

SIGNIFICANT EVENTS

■ **March 5:** Babe Ruth signed a three-year Yankee contract for a record $52,000 per season.

■ **September 21:** Browns first baseman George Sisler, a .420 hitter, was the choice of A.L. baseball writers for the first MVP award presented since 1914.

■ **October:** The World Series returned to a best-of-seven format and the entire Series was broadcast over the radio.

MEMORABLE MOMENTS

■ **April 30:** Chicago rookie Charlie Robertson became the third modern-era pitcher to throw a perfect game, retiring all 27 Tigers he faced in a 2-0 victory at Detroit.

■ **May 7:** Giants righthander Jesse Barnes pitched a 6-0 no-hitter against Philadelphia, an effort blemished only by a fifth-inning walk.

■ **June 28:** Washington fireballer Walter Johnson outdueled New York ace Waite Hoyt and recorded his 95th career shutout with a 1-0 victory at Griffith Stadium.

■ **August 25:** Chicago and Philadelphia combined for a record 49 runs and 51 hits in the Cubs' 26-23 victory at Wrigley Field.

■ **September 18:** The New York Yankees ended George Sisler's modern-era record hitting streak at 41 games during a 3-2 victory over the Browns.

■ **October 1:** Cardinals second baseman Rogers Hornsby became baseball's third Triple Crown winner when he finished the season at .401 with 42 homers and 152 RBI.

LEADERS

American League

BA: George Sisler, St.L., .420.
Runs: George Sisler, St.L., 134.
Hits: George Sisler, St.L., 246.
TB: Ken Williams, St.L., 367.
HR: Ken Williams, St.L., 39.
RBI: Ken Williams, St.L., 155.
SB: George Sisler, St.L., 51.
Wins: Eddie Rommel, Phil., 27.
ERA: Red Faber, Chi., 2.81.
CG: Red Faber, Chi., 31.
IP: Red Faber, Chi., 352.
SO: Urban Shocker, St.L., 149.

National League

BA: Rogers Hornsby, St.L., .401.
Runs: Rogers Hornsby, St.L., 141.
Hits: Rogers Hornsby, St.L., 250.
TB: Rogers Hornsby, St.L., 450.
HR: Rogers Hornsby, St.L., 42.
RBI: Rogers Hornsby, St.L., 152.
SB: Max Carey, Pit., 51.
Wins: Eppa Rixey, Cin., 25.
ERA: Phil Douglas, N.Y., 2.63.
CG: Wilbur Cooper, Pit., 27.
IP: Eppa Rixey, Cin., 313.1.
SO: Dazzy Vance, Brk., 134.

A.L. 20-game winners

Eddie Rommel, Phil., 27-13
Joe Bush, N.Y., 26-7
Urban Shocker, St.L., 24-17
George Uhle, Cle., 22-16
Red Faber, Chi., 21-17
Bob Shawkey, N.Y., 20-12

N.L. 20-game winners

Eppa Rixey, Cin., 25-13
Wilbur Cooper, Pit., 23-14
Dutch Ruether, Brk., 21-12

A.L. 100 RBIs

Ken Williams, St.L., 155
Bobby Veach, Det., 126
Marty McManus, St.L., 109
George Sisler, St.L., 105
Bill Jacobson, St.L., 102

N.L. 100 RBIs

Rogers Hornsby, St.L., 152
Irish Meusel, N.Y., 132
Zack Wheat, Brk., 112
George Kelly, N.Y., 107

N.L 40 homers

Rogers Hornsby, St.L., 42

League MVP

A.L.: George Sisler, 1B, St.L.
N.L.: No selection.

WORLD SERIES

■ **Winner:** The all-New York rematch had the same result, the Giants winning this time in five games.

■ **Turning point:** A 3-3 Game 2 tie that took away the Yankees' best hope for a victory.

■ **Memorable moment:** Giants lefthander Art Nehf closing out the Yankees in the Series finale for the second straight year.

■ **Top guns:** Heinie Groh (.474), Frankie Frisch (.471), Irish Meusel (7 RBIs), Giants.

Linescores

Game 1—October 4, at Polo Grounds
Yankees.......... 0 0 0 0 0 1 1 0 0 — 2 7 0
Giants............ 0 0 0 0 0 0 0 3 x — 3 11 3
Bush, Hoyt (8); Nehf, Ryan (8). W—Ryan. L—Bush.

Game 2—October 5, at Polo Grounds
Giants............ 3 0 0 0 0 00 0 0 0 — 3 8 1
Yankees.......... 1 0 0 1 0 00 1 0 0 — 3 8 0
J. Barnes; Shawkey. HR—E. Meusel (NYG); Ward (NYY). Game called after 10 innings because of darkness.

Game 3—October 6, at Polo Grounds
Yankees.......... 0 0 0 0 0 0 0 0 0 — 0 4 1
Giants............ 0 0 2 0 0 0 1 0 x — 3 12 1
Hoyt, Jones (8); J. Scott. W—J. Scott. L—Hoyt.

Game 4—October 7, at Polo Grounds
Giants............ 0 0 0 0 4 0 0 0 0 — 4 9 1
Yankees.......... 2 0 0 0 0 0 1 0 0 — 3 8 0
McQuillan; Mays, Jones (9). W—McQuillan. L—Mays. HR—Ward (NYY).

Game 5—October 8, at Polo Grounds
Yankees.......... 1 0 0 0 1 0 1 0 0 — 3 5 0
Giants............ 0 2 0 0 0 0 0 3 x — 5 10 0
Bush; Nehf. W—Nehf. L—Bush.

1923

FINAL STANDINGS

American League

Team	W	L	Pct.	GB
New York	98	54	.645	...
Detroit	83	71	.539	16
Cleveland	82	71	.536	16.5
Washington	75	78	.490	23.5
St. Louis	74	78	.487	24
Philadelphia	69	83	.454	29
Chicago	69	85	.448	30
Boston	61	91	.401	37

National League

Team	W	L	Pct.	GB
New York	95	58	.621	...
Cincinnati	91	63	.591	4.5
Pittsburgh	87	67	.565	8.5
Chicago	83	71	.539	12.5
St. Louis	79	74	.516	16
Brooklyn	76	78	.494	19.5
Boston	54	100	.351	41.5
Philadelphia	50	104	.325	45.5

SIGNIFICANT EVENTS

■ **April 18:** A Major League-record 74,217 fans watched Babe Ruth christen new Yankee Stadium with a three-run homer that sparked a 4-1 victory over Boston.

MEMORABLE MOMENTS

■ **May 2:** New York Yankee shortstop Everett Scott was honored when his ironman streak reached 1,000 games.
■ **May 11:** The Phillies defeated the Cardinals 20-14 in a game that featured 10 homers—three by Philadelphia's Cy Williams.
■ **July 7:** Cleveland, scoring in each of its eight at-bats, set an A.L. record for runs in a 27-3 victory over Boston.
■ **July 22:** Washington's Walter Johnson fanned five Indians and became the first pitcher to record 3,000 career strikeouts.
■ **September 7:** Boston's Howard Ehmke, duplicating the no-hit feat of New York Yankee Sam Jones three days earlier in the same stadium, stopped the Athletics 4-0 at Philadelphia.
■ **October 7:** St. Louis ended the regular season with a doubleheader split against the Cubs and Cardinals star Rogers Hornsby captured his fourth straight batting title with a .384 average.

LEADERS

American League
BA: Harry Heilmann, Det., .403.
Runs: Babe Ruth, N.Y., 151.
Hits: Charlie Jamieson, Cle., 222.
TB: Babe Ruth, N.Y., 399.
HR: Babe Ruth, N.Y., 41.
RBI: Babe Ruth, N.Y., 131.
SB: Eddie Collins, Chi., 49.
Wins: George Uhle, Cle., 26.
ERA: Stan Coveleski, Cle., 2.76.
CG: George Uhle, Cle., 29.
IP: George Uhle, Cle., 357.2.
SO: Walter Johnson, Wash., 130.

National League
BA: Rogers Hornsby, St.L., .384.
Runs: Ross Youngs, N.Y., 121.
Hits: Frank Frisch, N.Y., 223.
TB: Frank Frisch, N.Y., 311.
HR: Cy Williams, Phil., 41.
RBI: Irish Meusel, N.Y., 125.
SB: Max Carey, Pit., 51.
Wins: Dolf Luque, Cin., 27.
ERA: Dolf Luque, Cin., 1.93.
CG: Burleigh Grimes, Brk., 33.
IP: Burleigh Grimes, Brk., 327.
SO: Dazzy Vance, Brk., 197.

A.L. 20-game winners
George Uhle, Cle., 26-16
Sam Jones, N.Y., 21-8
Hooks Dauss, Det., 21-13
Urban Shocker, St.L., 20-12
Howard Ehmke, Bos., 20-17

N.L. 20-game winners
Dolf Luque, Cin., 27-8
Johnny Morrison, Pit., 25-13
Grover Alexander, Chi., 22-12
Pete Donohue, Cin., 21-15
Burleigh Grimes, Brk., 21-18
Jesse Haines, St.L., 20-13
Eppa Rixey, Cin., 20-15

A.L. 100 RBIs
Babe Ruth, N.Y., 130
Tris Speaker, Cle., 130
Harry Heilmann, Det., 115
Joe Sewell, Cle., 109
Wally Pipp, N.Y., 108

N.L. 100 RBIs
Irish Meusel, N.Y., 125
Cy Williams, Phil., 114
Frank Frisch, N.Y., 111
George Kelly, N.Y., 103
Jack Fournier, Brk., 102
Pie Traynor, Pit., 101

A.L. 40 homers
Babe Ruth, N.Y., 41

N.L. 40 homers
Cy Williams, Phil., 41

League MVP
A.L.: Babe Ruth, OF, N.Y.
N.L.: No selection.

WORLD SERIES

■ **Winner:** The third Series was a charm for the Yankees, who ascended to baseball's throne with a six-game victory over the Giants.

■ **Turning point:** A three-hit Game 5 performance by Joe Bush that helped the Yankees claim an 8-1 victory and a 3-2 Series lead.

■ **Memorable moment:** Veteran Casey Stengel chugging around the bases on a ninth-inning inside-the-park home run that gave the Giants a 5-4 Game 1 victory in the first Series contest at new Yankee Stadium.

■ **Top guns:** Aaron Ward (.417), Babe Ruth (.368, 3 HR), Yankees; Stengel (.417, 2 HR), Giants.

Linescores

Game 1—October 10, at Yankee Stadium
Giants............ 0 0 4 0 0 0 0 0 1 — 5 8 0
Yankees.......... 1 2 0 0 0 0 1 0 0 — 4 12 1
Watson, Ryan (3); Hoyt, Bush (3). W—Ryan. L—Bush. HR—Stengel (NYG).

Game 2—October 11, at Polo Grounds
Yankees.......... 0 1 0 2 1 0 0 0 0 — 4 10 0
Giants............ 0 1 0 0 0 1 0 0 0 — 2 9 2
Pennock; McQuillan, Bentley (4). W—Pennock. L—McQuillan. HR—Ward, Ruth 2 (NYY); E. Meusel (NYG).

Game 3—October 12, at Yankee Stadium
Giants............ 0 0 0 0 0 0 1 0 0 — 1 4 0
Yankees.......... 0 0 0 0 0 0 0 0 0 — 0 6 1
Nehf; Jones, Bush (9). W—Nehf. L—Jones. HR—Stengel (NYG).

Game 4—October 13, at Polo Grounds
Yankees.......... 0 6 1 1 0 0 0 0 0 — 8 13 1
Giants............ 0 0 0 0 0 0 0 3 1 — 4 13 1
Shawkey, Pennock (8); J. Scott, Ryan (2), McQuillan (2), Jonnard (8), Barnes (9). W—Shawkey. L—J. Scott. HR—Youngs (NYG).

Game 5—October 14, at Yankee Stadium
Giants............ 0 1 0 0 0 0 0 0 0 — 1 3 2
Yankees.......... 3 4 0 1 0 0 0 0 x — 8 14 0
Bentley, J. Scott (2), Barnes (4), Jonnard (8); Bush. W—Bush. L—Bentley. HR—Dugan (NYY).

Game 6—October 15, at Polo Grounds
Yankees.......... 1 0 0 0 0 0 0 5 0 — 6 5 0
Giants............ 1 0 0 1 1 1 0 0 0 — 4 10 1
Pennock, Jones (8); Nehf, Ryan (8). W—Pennock. L—Nehf. HR—Ruth (NYY); Snyder (NYG).

1924

FINAL STANDINGS

American League

Team	W	L	Pct.	GB
Washington	92	62	.597	...
New York	89	63	.586	2
Detroit	86	68	.558	6
St. Louis	74	78	.487	17
Philadelphia	71	81	.467	20
Cleveland	67	86	.438	24.5
Boston	67	87	.435	25
Chicago	66	87	.431	25.5

National League

Team	W	L	Pct.	GB
New York	93	60	.608	...
Brooklyn	92	62	.597	1.5
Pittsburgh	90	63	.588	3
Cincinnati	83	70	.542	10
Chicago	81	72	.529	12
St. Louis	65	89	.422	28.5
Philadelphia	55	96	.364	37
Boston	53	100	.346	40

SIGNIFICANT EVENTS

■ **March 7:** Reds manager Pat Moran died of Bright's disease at a hospital in Orlando, Fla., the team's spring training home.
■ **December 10:** National League owners accepted a proposal to go to a 2-3-2 World Series format.

MEMORABLE MOMENTS

■ **June 13:** The Yankees were awarded a 9-0 forfeit victory over the Tigers when a ninth-inning players' fight escalated into a full-scale fan riot at Detroit's Navin Field, creating a life-threatening situation for players, umpires and police.
■ **July 16:** Giants first baseman George Kelly set a Major League record when he homered in his sixth consecutive game—an 8-7 victory over the Pirates.
■ **September 16:** Jim Bottomley collected six hits, belted two homers and drove in a single-game record 12 runs in St. Louis' 17-3 victory over Brooklyn.
■ **September 28:** Cardinals second baseman Rogers Hornsby finished the season with the highest average in baseball history—.424.

LEADERS

American League
BA: Babe Ruth, N.Y., .378.
Runs: Babe Ruth, N.Y., 143.
Hits: Sam Rice, Wash., 216.
TB: Babe Ruth, N.Y., 391.
HR: Babe Ruth, N.Y., 46.
RBI: Goose Goslin, Wash., 129.
SB: Eddie Collins, Chi., 42.
Wins: Walter Johnson, Wash., 23.
ERA: Walter Johnson, Wash., 2.72.
CG: Sloppy Thurston, Chi., 28.
IP: Howard Ehmke, Bos., 315.
SO: Walter Johnson, Wash., 158.

National League
BA: Rogers Hornsby, St.L., .424.
Runs: Frank Frisch, N.Y.; Rogers Hornsby, St.L., 121.
Hits: Rogers Hornsby, St.L., 227.
TB: Rogers Hornsby, St.L., 373.
HR: Jack Fournier, Brk., 27.
RBI: George Kelly, N.Y., 136.
SB: Max Carey, Pit., 49.
Wins: Dazzy Vance, Brk., 28.
ERA: Dazzy Vance, Brk., 2.16.
CG: Burleigh Grimes, Brk.; Dazzy Vance, Brk., 30.
IP: Burleigh Grimes, Brk., 310.2.
SO: Dazzy Vance, Brk., 262.

A.L. 20-game winners
Walter Johnson, Wash., 23-7
Herb Pennock, N.Y., 21-9
Sloppy Thurston, Chi., 20-14
Joe Shaute, Cle., 20-17

N.L. 20-game winners
Dazzy Vance, Brk., 28-6
Burleigh Grimes, Brk., 22-13
Carl Mays, Cin., 20-9
Wilbur Cooper, Pit., 20-14

A.L. 100 RBIs
Goose Goslin, Wash., 129
Babe Ruth, N.Y., 121
Bob Meusel, N.Y., 120
Joe Hauser, Phil., 115
Harry Heilmann, Det., 113
Wally Pipp, N.Y., 113
Joe Sewell, Cle., 104
Earl Sheely, Chi., 103
Al Simmons, Phil., 102

N.L. 100 RBIs
George Kelly, N.Y., 136
Jack Fournier, Brk., 116
Jim Bottomley, St.L., 111
Glenn Wright, Pit., 111
Irish Meusel, N.Y., 102

A.L. 40 homers
Babe Ruth, N.Y., 46

League MVP
A.L.: Walter Johnson, P, Wash.
N.L.: Dazzy Vance, P, Brk.

WORLD SERIES

■ **Winner:** The Senators made their first appearance in baseball's fall classic a successful one.

■ **Turning point:** A dramatic 2-1 Game 6 victory that kept Washington's hopes alive. Tom Zachary allowed seven hits and player/manager Bucky Harris drove in both runs with a fifth-inning single.

■ **Memorable moment:** Earl McNeely's 12th-inning Game 7 ground ball that took an inexplicable hop over third baseman Fred Lindstrom's head and gave the Senators a Series-ending 4-3 victory.

■ **Top guns:** Zachary (2-0, 2.04 ERA), Goose Goslin (.344, 3 HR, 7 RBIs), Harris (.333, 7 RBIs), Senators; Bill Terry (.429), Giants.

Linescores

Game 1—October 4, at Washington
N,Y,........0 1 0 1 0 0 0 0 0 0 0 2 — 4 14 1
Wash.....0 0 0 0 0 1 0 0 1 0 0 1 — 3 10 1
Nehf; Johnson. W—Nehf. L—Johnson. HR—Kelly, Terry (N.Y.).

Game 2—October 5, at Washington
N.Y. .... 0 0 0 0 0 0 1 0 2 — 3 6 0
Wash............. 2 0 0 0 1 0 0 0 1 — 4 6 1
Bentley; Zachary, Marberry (9). W—Zachary. L—Bentley. HR—Goslin, Harris (Wash.).

Game 3—October 6, at New York
Wash............. 0 0 0 2 0 0 0 1 1 — 4 9 2
N.Y. .... 0 2 1 1 0 1 0 1 x — 6 12 0
Marberry, Russell (4), Martina (7), Speece (8); McQuillan, Ryan (4), Jonnard (9), Watson (9). W—McQuillan. L—Marberry. HR—Ryan (N.Y.).

Game 4—October 7, at New York
Wash............. 0 0 3 0 2 0 0 2 0 — 7 13 3
N.Y. .... 1 0 0 0 0 1 0 1 1 — 4 6 1
Mogridge, Marberry (8); Barnes, Baldwin (6), Dean (8). W—Mogridge. L—Barnes. HR—Goslin (Wash.).

Game 5—October 8, at New York
Wash............. 0 0 0 1 0 0 0 1 0 — 2 9 1
N.Y. .... 0 0 1 0 2 0 0 3 x — 6 13 0
Johnson; Bentley, McQuillan (8). W—Bentley. L—Johnson. HR—Bentley (N.Y.); Goslin (Wash.).

Game 6—October 9, at Washington
N.Y. .... 1 0 0 0 0 0 0 0 0 — 1 7 1
Wash............. 0 0 0 0 2 0 0 0 x — 2 4 0
Nehf, Ryan (8); Zachary. W—Zachary. L—Nehf.

Game 7—October 10, at Washington
N.Y.........0 0 0 0 0 3 0 0 0 0 0 0 — 3 8 3
Wash.....0 0 0 1 0 0 0 2 0 0 0 1 — 4 10 4
Barnes, Nehf (8), McQuillan (9), Bentley (11); Ogden, Mogridge (1), Marberry (6), Johnson (9). W—Johnson. L—Bentley. HR—Harris (Wash.).

1925

FINAL STANDINGS

American League

Team	W	L	Pct.	GB
Washington	96	55	.636	...
Philadelphia	88	64	.579	8.5
St. Louis	82	71	.536	15
Detroit	81	73	.526	16.5
Chicago	79	75	.513	18.5
Cleveland	70	84	.455	27.5
New York	69	85	.448	28.5
Boston	47	105	.309	49.5

National League

Team	W	L	Pct.	GB
Pittsburgh	95	58	.621	...
New York	86	66	.566	8.5
Cincinnati	80	73	.523	15
St. Louis	77	76	.503	18
Boston	70	83	.458	25
Brooklyn	68	85	.444	27
Philadelphia	68	85	.444	27
Chicago	68	86	.442	27.5

SIGNIFICANT EVENTS

■ **April 17:** Yankee slugger Babe Ruth underwent surgery for an intestinal abscess, an injury that would sideline him until June 1.

■ **April 18:** Brooklyn owner Charles Ebbets died on the morning of his Dodgers' home opener against the Giants at Ebbets Field.

■ **October 7:** Christy Mathewson, considered by many the greatest pitcher in history, died after a five-year bout with tuberculosis at age 45.

MEMORABLE MOMENTS

■ **May 5:** Detroit's Ty Cobb enjoyed a six-hit, three-homer game against the Browns, setting a modern Major League record with 16 total bases.

■ **May 6:** Yankee manager Miller Huggins benched shortstop Everett Scott, ending his record consecutive-games streak at 1,307.

■ **May 17:** Cleveland's Tris Speaker collected career hit No. 3,000 off Washington lefthander Tom Zachary.

■ **June 3:** White Sox manager Eddie Collins joined baseball's select 3,000-hit circle in a game against Detroit.

■ **June 15:** The Philadelphia Athletics, trailing 15-4 in the eighth inning, exploded for 13 runs and a 17-15 victory over the Indians.

■ **October 4:** St. Louis manager Rogers Hornsby matched his 1922 Triple Crown feat when he finished with a .403 average, 39 home runs and 143 RBIs.

LEADERS

American League

BA: Harry Heilmann, Det., .393.
Runs: Johnny Mostil, Chi., 135.
Hits: Al Simmons, Phil., 253.
TB: Al Simmons, Phil., 392.
HR: Bob Meusel, N.Y., 33.
RBI: Bob Meusel, N.Y., 138.
SB: Johnny Mostil, Chi., 43.
Wins: Ted Lyons, Chi.; Eddie Rommel, Phil., 21.
ERA: Stan Coveleski, Wash., 2.84.
CG: Howard Ehmke, Bos.; Sherry Smith, Cle., 22.
IP: Herb Pennock, N.Y., 277.
SO: Lefty Grove, Phil., 116.

National League

BA: Rogers Hornsby, St.L., .403.
Runs: Kiki Cuyler, Pit., 144.
Hits: Jim Bottomley, St.L., 227.
TB: Rogers Hornsby, St.L., 381.
HR: Rogers Hornsby, St.L., 39.
RBI: Rogers Hornsby, St.L., 143.
SB: Max Carey, Pit., 46.
Wins: Dazzy Vance, Brk., 22.
ERA: Dolf Luque, Cin., 2.63.
CG: Pete Donohue, Cin., 27.
IP: Pete Donohue, Cin., 301.
SO: Dazzy Vance, Brk., 221.

A.L. 20-game winners

Eddie Rommel, Phil., 21-10
Ted Lyons, Chi., 21-11
Stan Coveleski, Wash., 20-5
Walter Johnson, Wash., 20-7

N.L. 20-game winners

Dazzy Vance, Brk., 22-9
Eppa Rixey, Cin., 21-11
Pete Donohue, Cin., 21-14

A.L. 100 RBIs

Bob Meusel, N.Y., 138
Harry Heilmann, Det., 133
Al Simmons, Phil., 129
Goose Goslin, Wash., 113
Earl Sheely, Chi., 111
George Sisler, St.L., 105
Ken Williams, St.L., 105
Ty Cobb, Det., 102

N.L. 100 RBIs

Rogers Hornsby, St.L., 143
Jack Fournier, Brk., 130
Jim Bottomley, St.L., 128
Glenn Wright, Pit., 121
Clyde Barnhart, Pit., 114
Irish Meusel, N.Y., 111
Pie Traynor, Pit., 106
Zack Wheat, Brk., 103
Kiki Cuyler, Pit., 102

League MVP

A.L.: Roger Peckinpaugh, SS, Wash.
N.L.: Rogers Hornsby, 2B, St.L.

WORLD SERIES

■ **Winner:** The Pirates became the first team to rally from a three-games-to-one Series deficit and ruined Washington's hopes for a repeat victory.

■ **Turning point:** A Game 6 home run by Eddie Moore that gave Pittsburgh a 3-2 victory and knotted the Series at three games apiece.

■ **Memorable moment:** Washington's 37-year-old Walter Johnson battling valiantly but coming up short in Pittsburgh's 9-7 Game 7 victory.

■ **Top guns:** Max Carey (.458), Pirates; Joe Harris (.440, 3 HR, 6 RBIs), Goose Goslin (3 HR, 6 RBIs), Senators.

Linescores

Game 1—October 7, at Pittsburgh
Washington.... 0 1 0 0 2 0 0 0 1 — 4 8 1
Pittsburgh...... 0 0 0 0 1 0 0 0 0 — 1 5 0
Johnson; Meadows, Morrison (9). W—Johnson. L—Meadows. HR—J. Harris (Wash.); Traynor (Pit.).

Game 2—October 8, at Pittsburgh
Washington.... 0 1 0 0 0 0 0 0 1 — 2 8 2
Pittsburgh...... 0 0 0 1 0 0 0 2 x — 3 7 0
Coveleski; Aldridge. W—Aldridge. L—Coveleski. HR—Judge (Wash.); Wright, Cuyler (Pit.).

Game 3—October 10, at Washington
Pittsburgh...... 0 1 0 1 0 1 0 0 0 — 3 8 3
Washington.... 0 0 1 0 0 1 2 0 x — 4 10 1
Kremer; Ferguson, Marberry (8). W—Ferguson. L—Kremer. HR—Goslin (Wash.).

Game 4—October 11, at Washington
Pittsburgh...... 0 0 0 0 0 0 0 0 0 — 0 6 1
Washington.... 0 0 4 0 0 0 0 0 x — 4 12 0
Yde, Morrison (3), C. Adams (8); Johnson. W—Johnson. L—Yde. HR—Goslin, J. Harris (Wash.).

Game 5—October 12, at Washington
Pittsburgh...... 0 0 2 0 0 0 2 1 1 — 6 13 0
Washington.... 1 0 0 1 0 0 1 0 0 — 3 8 1
Aldridge; Coveleski, Ballou (7), Zachary (8), Marberry (9). W—Aldridge. L—Coveleski. HR—J. Harris (Wash.).

Game 6—October 13, at Pittsburgh
Washington.... 1 1 0 0 0 0 0 0 0 — 2 6 2
Pittsburgh...... 0 0 2 0 1 0 0 0 x — 3 7 1
Ferguson, Ballou (8); Kremer. W—Kremer. L—Ferguson. HR—Goslin (Wash.); Moore (Pit.).

Game 7—October 15, at Pittsburgh
Washington.... 4 0 0 2 0 0 0 1 0 — 7 7 2
Pittsburgh...... 0 0 3 0 1 0 2 3 x — 9 15 2
Johnson; Aldridge, Morrison (1), Kremer (5), Oldham (9). W—Kremer. L—Johnson. HR—Peckinpaugh (Wash.).

1926

FINAL STANDINGS

American League

Team	W	L	Pct.	GB
New York	91	63	.591	...
Cleveland	88	66	.571	3
Philadelphia	83	67	.553	6
Washington	81	69	.540	8
Chicago	81	72	.529	9.5
Detroit	79	75	.513	12
St. Louis	62	92	.403	29
Boston	46	107	.301	44.5

National League

Team	W	L	Pct.	GB
St. Louis	89	65	.578	...
Cincinnati	87	67	.565	2
Pittsburgh	84	69	.549	4.5
Chicago	82	72	.532	7
New York	74	77	.490	13.5
Brooklyn	71	82	.464	17.5
Boston	66	86	.434	22
Philadelphia	58	93	.384	29.5

SIGNIFICANT EVENTS

■ **January 30:** The Major League rules committee granted pitchers permission to use a resin bag during the course of games.

■ **October 13:** Cleveland first baseman George Burns, who batted .358 with a record 64 doubles, captured A.L. MVP honors, even though the Yankees' Babe Ruth batted .372 with 47 homers and 146 RBIs.

■ **December 16:** Commissioner Kenesaw Mountain Landis was elected to a second seven-year term.

■ **December 20:** In a trade billed as the biggest in baseball history, Cardinals manager Rogers Hornsby was dealt to the Giants for second baseman Frank Frisch and pitcher Jimmy Ring.

■ **December 22:** Baseball greats Ty Cobb and Tris Speaker denied accusations by former Detroit pitcher Dutch Leonard that they had conspired to throw 1919 Tigers-Indians games and had bet on their outcome. The charges would be investigated by Commissioner Kenesaw Mountain Landis and later dismissed for lack of evidence.

MEMORABLE MOMENTS

■ **May 12:** Washington fireballer Walter Johnson defeated St. Louis, 7-4, and became baseball's second 400-game winner.

■ **May 21:** Chicago's Earl Sheely belted a home run and three doubles in a game against Boston, giving him a record seven consecutive extra-base hits.

LEADERS

American League

BA: Heinie Manush, Det., .378.
Runs: Babe Ruth, N.Y., 139.
Hits: George Burns, Cle.; Sam Rice, Wash., 216.
TB: Babe Ruth, N.Y., 365.
HR: Babe Ruth, N.Y., 47.
RBI: Babe Ruth, N.Y., 146.
SB: Johnny Mostil, Chi., 35.
Wins: George Uhle, Cle., 27.
ERA: Lefty Grove, Phil., 2.51.
CG: George Uhle, Cle., 32.
IP: George Uhle, Cle., 318.1.
SO: Lefty Grove, Phil., 194.

National League

BA: Bubbles Hargrave, Cin., .353.
Runs: Kiki Cuyler, Pit., 113.
Hits: Eddie Brown, Bos., 201.
TB: Jim Bottomley, St.L., 305.
HR: Hack Wilson, Chi., 21.
RBI: Jim Bottomley, St.L., 120.
SB: Kiki Cuyler, Pit., 35.
Wins: Pete Donohue, Cin.; Ray Kremer, Pit.; Lee Meadows, Pit.; Flint Rhem, St.L., 20.
ERA: Ray Kremer, Pit., 2.61.
CG: Carl Mays, Cin., 24.
IP: Pete Donohue, Cin., 285.2.
SO: Dazzy Vance, Brk., 140.

A.L. 20-game winners

George Uhle, Cle., 27-11
Herb Pennock, N.Y., 23-11

N.L. 20-game winners

Remy Kremer, Pit., 20-6
Flint Rhem, St.L., 20-7
Lee Meadows, Pit., 20-9
Pete Donohue, Cin., 20-14

A.L. 100 RBIs

Babe Ruth, N.Y., 146
George Burns, Cle., 114
Tony Lazzeri, N.Y., 114
Al Simmons, Phil., 109
Bibb Falk, Chi., 108
Goose Goslin, Wash., 108
Lou Gehrig, N.Y., 107
Harry Heilmann, Det., 103

N.L. 100 RBIs

Jim Bottomley, St.L., 120
Hack Wilson, Chi., 109
Les Bell, St.L., 100

A.L. 40 homers

Babe Ruth, N.Y., 47

League MVP

A.L.: George Burns, 1B, Cle.
N.L.: Bob O'Farrell, C, St.L.

WORLD SERIES

■ **Winner:** The Cardinals, making their first Series appearance, outlasted the Yankees in a seven-game classic.

■ **Turning point:** A Series-squaring 10-2 Cardinals victory in Game 6. Lester Bell homered and drove in four runs.

■ **Memorable moment:** The aging Grover Cleveland Alexander striking out Yankee slugger Tony Lazzeri with the bases loaded in the seventh inning of Game 7, saving the Cardinals.

■ **Top guns:** Jesse Haines (2-0, 1.08 ERA), Alexander (2-0, 1.33), Tommy Thevenow (.417), Cardinals; Babe Ruth (4 HR), Yankees.

Linescores

Game 1—October 2, at New York
St. Louis......... 1 0 0 0 0 0 0 0 0 — 1 3 1
New York........ 1 0 0 0 0 1 0 0 x — 2 6 0
Sherdel, Haines (8); Pennock. W—Pennock. L—Sherdel.

Game 2—October 3, at New York
St. Louis......... 0 0 2 0 0 0 3 0 1 — 6 12 1
New York........ 0 2 0 0 0 0 0 0 0 — 2 4 0
Alexander; Shocker, Shawkey (8), Jones (9). W—Alexander. L—Shawkey. HR—Southworth, Thevenow (St.L.).

Game 3—October 5, at St. Louis
New York........ 0 0 0 0 0 0 0 0 0 — 0 5 1
St. Louis......... 0 0 0 3 1 0 0 0 x — 4 8 0
Ruether, Shawkey (5), Thomas (8); Haines. W—Haines. L—Ruether. HR—Haines (St.L.).

Game 4—October 6, at St. Louis
New York........ 1 0 1 1 4 2 1 0 0 — 10 14 1
St. Louis......... 1 0 0 3 0 0 0 0 1 — 5 14 0
Hoyt; Rhem, Reinhart (5), H. Bell (5), Hallahan (7), Keen (9). W—Hoyt. L—Reinhart. HR—Ruth 3 (N.Y.).

Game 5—October 7, at St. Louis
New York........ 0 0 0 0 0 10 0 1 1—3 9 1
St. Louis......... 0 0 0 1 0 01 0 0 0—2 7 1
Pennock; Sherdel. W—Pennock. L—Sherdel.

Game 6—October 9, at New York
St. Louis......... 3 0 0 0 1 0 5 0 1 — 10 13 2
New York........ 0 0 0 1 0 0 1 0 0 — 2 8 1
Alexander; Shawkey, Shocker (7), Thomas (8). W—Alexander. L—Shawkey. HR—L. Bell (St.L.).

Game 7—October 10, at New York
St. Louis......... 0 0 0 3 0 0 0 0 0 — 3 8 0
New York........ 0 0 1 0 0 1 0 0 0 — 2 8 3
Haines, Alexander (7); Hoyt, Pennock (7). W—Haines. L—Hoyt. HR—Ruth (N.Y.).

1927

FINAL STANDINGS

American League

Team	W	L	Pct.	GB
New York	110	44	.714	...
Philadelphia	91	63	.591	19
Washington	85	69	.552	25
Detroit	82	71	.536	27.5
Chicago	70	83	.458	39.5
Cleveland	66	87	.431	43.5
St. Louis	59	94	.386	50.5
Boston	51	103	.331	59

National League

Team	W	L	Pct.	GB
Pittsburgh	94	60	.610	...
St. Louis	92	61	.601	1.5
New York	92	62	.597	2
Chicago	85	68	.556	8.5
Cincinnati	75	78	.490	18.5
Brooklyn	65	88	.425	28.5
Boston	60	94	.390	34
Philadelphia	51	103	.331	43

SIGNIFICANT EVENTS

- **March 3:** The Yankees made slugger Babe Ruth the highest paid player in baseball history, signing him for three years at a reported $70,000 per season.
- **October 17:** A.L. founder and 28-year president Ban Johnson retired, three days after 416-game winner Walter Johnson called it quits after 21 seasons with Washington.
- **October 22:** Ross Youngs, a .322 hitter over 10 seasons with the Giants, died of Bright's disease at age 30.
- **November 2:** E.S. Barnard was named new A.L. president, replacing Ban Johnson.

MEMORABLE MOMENTS

- **May 30-31:** Cubs shortstop Jimmy Cooney and Detroit first baseman Johnny Neun pulled off rare unassisted triple plays on consecutive days.
- **July 18:** Philadelphia's Ty Cobb opened a new club when he doubled against his former Detroit teammates for hit No. 4,000.
- **July 19:** The Cubs spoiled John McGraw Day at the Polo Grounds by beating the Giants. But fans enjoyed festivities honoring McGraw for his 25 years as New York manager.
- **September 30:** Yankee slugger Babe Ruth broke his own one-season record when he blasted home run No. 60 off Washington lefty Tom Zachary.

LEADERS

American League

BA: Harry Heilmann, Det., .398.
Runs: Babe Ruth, N.Y., 158.
Hits: Earle Combs, N.Y., 231.
TB: Lou Gehrig, N.Y., 447.
HR: Babe Ruth, N.Y., 60.
RBI: Lou Gehrig, N.Y., 175.
SB: George Sisler, St.L., 27.
Wins: Waite Hoyt, N.Y.; Ted Lyons, Chi., 22.
ERA: Wilcy Moore, N.Y., 2.28.
CG: Ted Lyons, Chi., 30.
IP: Ted Lyons, Chi.; Tommy Thomas, Chi., 307.2
SO: Lefty Grove, Phil., 174.

National League

BA: Paul Waner, Pit., .380.
Runs: Rogers Hornsby, N.Y.; Lloyd Waner, Pit., 133.
Hits: Paul Waner, Pit., 237.
TB: Paul Waner, Pit., 342.
HR: Cy Williams, Phil.; Hack Wilson, Chi., 30.
RBI: Paul Waner, Pit., 131.
SB: Frank Frisch, St.L., 48.
Wins: Charlie Root, Chi., 26.
ERA: Ray Kremer, Pit., 2.47.
CG: Jesse Haines, St.L.; Lee Meadows, Pit.; Dazzy Vance, Brk., 25.
IP: Charlie Root, Chi., 309.
SO: Dazzy Vance, Brk., 184.

A.L. 20-game winners
Waite Hoyt, N.Y., 22-7
Ted Lyons, Chi., 22-14
Lefty Grove, Phil., 20-13

N.L. 20-game winners
Charlie Root, Chi., 26-15
Jesse Haines, St.L., 24-10
Carmen Hill, Pit., 22-11
Grover Alexander, St.L., 21-10

A.L. 100 RBIs
Lou Gehrig, N.Y., 175
Babe Ruth, N.Y., 164
Goose Goslin, Wash., 120
Harry Heilmann, Det., 120
Bob Fothergill, Det., 114
Al Simmons, Phil., 108
Bob Meusel, N.Y., 103
Tony Lazzeri, N.Y., 102

N.L. 100 RBIs
Paul Waner, Pit., 131
Hack Wilson, Chi., 129
Rogers Hornsby, N.Y., 125
Jim Bottomley, St.L., 124
Bill Terry, N.Y., 121
Pie Traynor, Pit., 106
Glenn Wright, Pit., 105

A.L. 40 homers
Babe Ruth, N.Y., 60
Lou Gehrig, N.Y., 47

League MVP
A.L.: Lou Gehrig, 1B, N.Y.
N.L.: Paul Waner, OF, Pit.

WORLD SERIES

- **Winner:** The powerful Yankees made short work of the overmatched Pirates.
- **Turning point:** When the Pirates watched the Yankees take batting practice before Game 1.
- **Memorable moment:** Yankee Earle Combs dancing across the plate with the Series-ending run after a John Miljus wild pitch.
- **Top guns:** Wilcy Moore (1-0, 0.84 ERA), Herb Pennock (1-0, 1.00), Mark Koenig (.500), Babe Ruth (.400, 2 HR, 7 RBIs), Yankees; Lloyd Waner (.400), Pirates.

Linescores

Game 1—October 5, at Pittsburgh
New York........ 1 0 3 0 1 0 0 0 0 — 5 6 1
Pittsburgh...... 1 0 1 0 1 0 0 1 0 — 4 9 2
Hoyt, Moore (8); Kremer, Miljus (6). W—Hoyt. L—Kremer.

Game 2—October 6, at Pittsburgh
New York........ 0 0 3 0 0 0 0 3 0 — 6 11 0
Pittsburgh...... 1 0 0 0 0 0 0 1 0 — 2 7 2
Pipgras; Aldridge, Cvengros (8), Dawson (9). W—Pipgras. L—Aldridge.

Game 3—October 7, at New York
Pittsburgh...... 0 0 0 0 0 0 0 1 0 — 1 3 1
New York........ 2 0 0 0 0 0 6 0 x — 8 9 0
Meadows, Cvengros (7); Pennock. W—Pennock. L—Meadows. HR—Ruth (N.Y.).

Game 4—October 8, at New York
Pittsburgh...... 1 0 0 0 0 0 2 0 0 — 3 10 1
New York........ 1 0 0 0 2 0 0 0 1 — 4 12 2
Hill, Miljus (7); Moore. W—Moore. L—Miljus. HR—Ruth (N.Y.).

1928

FINAL STANDINGS

American League

Team	W	L	Pct.	GB
New York	101	53	.656	...
Philadelphia	98	55	.641	2.5
St. Louis	82	72	.532	19
Washington	75	79	.487	26
Chicago	72	82	.468	29
Detroit	68	86	.442	33
Cleveland	62	92	.403	39
Boston	57	96	.373	43.5

National League

Team	W	L	Pct.	GB
St. Louis	95	59	.617	...
New York	93	61	.604	2
Chicago	91	63	.591	4
Pittsburgh	85	67	.559	9
Cincinnati	78	74	.513	16
Brooklyn	77	76	.503	17.5
Boston	50	103	.327	44.5
Philadelphia	43	109	.283	51

SIGNIFICANT EVENTS

- **May 14:** Giants manager John McGraw was hit by a car while crossing a street outside Chicago's Wrigley Field, an injury that would sideline him for six weeks.
- **September 9:** Urban Shocker, a 187-game winner for the Yankees and Browns, died of pneumonia at age 38.
- **November 7:** Massachusetts voters cleared the way for Sunday baseball in Boston, leaving Pennsylvania as the only state still enforcing the blue law.
- **December 13:** National League President John Heydler, contending fans were tired of watching weak-hitting pitchers try to bat, proposed a designated hitter rule that was voted down at the annual winter meetings.

MEMORABLE MOMENTS

- **July 21:** Philadelphia's Jimmie Foxx became the first player to hit a ball over the double-decked left-field stands of Shibe Park during a game against St. Louis.
- **September 3:** Athletics pinch-hitter Ty Cobb stroked his 724th career double and final career hit—No. 4,191—in a game against Washington.
- **September 28-29:** The New York Yankees clinched the A.L. pennant with a victory over the Tigers and the Cardinals closed out a tight N.L. race with a next-day win over the Braves.

LEADERS

American League

BA: Goose Goslin, Wash., .379.
Runs: Babe Ruth, N.Y., 163.
Hits: Heinie Manush, St.L., 241.
TB: Babe Ruth, N.Y., 380.
HR: Babe Ruth, N.Y., 54.
RBI: Lou Gehrig, N.Y.; Babe Ruth, N.Y., 142.
SB: Buddy Myer, Bos., 30.
Wins: Lefty Grove, Phil.; George Pipgras, N.Y., 24.
ERA: Garland Braxton, Wash., 2.51.
CG: Red Ruffing, Bos., 25.
IP: George Pipgras, N.Y., 300.2.
SO: Lefty Grove, Phil., 183.

National League

BA: Rogers Hornsby, Bos., .387.
Runs: Paul Waner, Pit., 142.
Hits: Fred Lindstrom, N.Y., 231.
TB: Jim Bottomley, St.L., 362.
HR: Jim Bottomley, St.L.; Hack Wilson, Chi., 31.
RBI: Jim Bottomley, St.L., 136.
SB: Kiki Cuyler, Chi., 37.
Wins: Larry Benton, N.Y.; Burleigh Grimes, Pit., 25.
ERA: Dazzy Vance, Brk., 2.09.
CG: Larry Benton, N.Y.; Burleigh Grimes, Pit., 28.
IP: Burleigh Grimes, Pit., 330.2.
SO: Dazzy Vance, Brk., 200.

A.L. 20-game winners
Lefty Grove, Phil., 24-8
George Pipgras, N.Y., 24-13
Waite Hoyt, N.Y., 23-7
General Crowder, St.L., 21-5
Sam Gray, St.L., 20-12

N.L. 20-game winners
Larry Benton, N.Y., 25-9
Burleigh Grimes, Pit., 25-14
Dazzy Vance, Brk., 22-10
Bill Sherdel, St.L., 21-10
Jesse Haines, St.L., 20-8
Fred Fitzsimmons, N.Y., 20-9

A.L. 100 RBIs
Lou Gehrig, N.Y., 142
Babe Ruth, N.Y., 142
Bob Meusel, N.Y., 113
Heinie Manush, St.L., 108
Harry Heilmann, Det., 107
Al Simmons, Phil., 107
Goose Goslin, Wash., 102

N.L. 100 RBIs
Jim Bottomley, St.L., 136
Pie Traynor, Pit., 124
Hack Wilson, Chi., 120
Chick Hafey, St.L., 111
Fred Lindstrom, N.Y., 107
Del Bissonette, Brk., 106
Pinky Whitney, Phil., 103
Bill Terry, N.Y., 101

A.L. 40 homers
Babe Ruth, N.Y., 54

League MVP
A.L.: Mickey Cochrane, C, Phil.
N.L.: Jim Bottomley, 1B, St.L.

WORLD SERIES

- **Winner:** The muscular Yankees swept aside St. Louis for their third Series victory of the decade.
- **Turning point:** A 9-3 second-game romp that made it clear the Cardinals were overmatched.
- **Memorable moment:** Babe Ruth's show-stealing three-home run performance in Game 4 at St. Louis' Sportsman's Park.
- **Top guns:** Waite Hoyt (2-0, 1.50 ERA), Ruth (.625, 3 HR), Lou Gehrig, (.545, 4 HR, 9 RBIs).

Linescores

Game 1—October 4, at New York
St. Louis......... 0 0 0 0 0 0 1 0 0 — 1 3 1
New York........ 1 0 0 2 0 0 0 1 x — 4 7 0
Sherdel, Johnson (8); Hoyt. W—Hoyt. L—Sherdel. HR—Meusel (N.Y.); Bottomley (St.L.).

Game 2—October 5, at New York
St. Louis......... 0 3 0 0 0 0 0 0 0 — 3 4 1
New York........ 3 1 4 0 0 0 1 0 x — 9 8 2
Alexander, Mitchell (3); Pipgras. W—Pipgras. L—Alexander. HR—Gehrig (N.Y.).

Game 3—October 7, at St. Louis
New York........ 0 1 0 2 0 3 1 0 0 — 7 7 2
St. Louis......... 2 0 0 0 1 0 0 0 0 — 3 9 3
Zachary; Haines, Johnson (7), Rhem (8). W—Zachary. L—Haines. HR—Gehrig 2 (N.Y.).

Game 4—October 9, at St. Louis
New York........ 0 0 0 1 0 0 4 2 0 — 7 15 2
St. Louis......... 0 0 1 1 0 0 0 0 1 — 3 11 0
Hoyt; Sherdel, Alexander (7). W—Hoyt. L—Sherdel. HR—Ruth 3, Durst, Gehrig (N.Y.).

1929

FINAL STANDINGS

American League

Team	W	L	Pct.	GB
Philadelphia	104	46	.693	...
New York	88	66	.571	18
Cleveland	81	71	.533	24
St. Louis	79	73	.520	26
Washington	71	81	.467	34
Detroit	70	84	.455	36
Chicago	59	93	.388	46
Boston	58	96	.377	48

National League

Team	W	L	Pct.	GB
Chicago	98	54	.645	...
Pittsburgh	88	65	.575	10.5
New York	84	67	.556	13.5
St. Louis	78	74	.513	20
Philadelphia	71	82	.464	27.5
Brooklyn	70	83	.458	28.5
Cincinnati	66	88	.429	33
Boston	56	98	.364	43

SIGNIFICANT EVENTS

■ **January 22:** The Yankees announced an innovation: permanent numbers on the backs of uniforms corresponding to players' positions in the batting order.

■ **September 25:** New York manager Miller Huggins, who led the Yankees to six pennants and three World Series championships in 12 seasons, died suddenly of blood poisoning at age 49.

MEMORABLE MOMENTS

■ **July 6:** The Cardinals set a modern Major League record for runs and an N.L. record for hits (28) when they pounded the Phillies, 28-6.

■ **August 10:** Cardinals great Grover Cleveland Alexander shut out Philadelphia in four innings of relief and was credited with an 11-9 victory—the 373rd and last of his career.

■ **August 11:** Yankee Babe Ruth drove a Willis Hudlin pitch out of Cleveland's League Park for career homer No. 500.

■ **October 5:** Philadelphia slugger Chuck Klein hit home run No. 43 in a final-day doubleheader against New York, setting a one-season N.L. record and edging Giants outfielder Mel Ott by one.

■ **October 6:** Cleveland third baseman Joe Sewell finished the season with an amazing four strikeouts in 578 official at-bats.

LEADERS

American League

BA: Lew Fonseca, Cle., .369.
Runs: Charley Gehringer, Det., 131.
Hits: Dale Alexander, Det.; Charley Gehringer, Det., 215.
TB: Al Simmons, Phil., 373.
HR: Babe Ruth, N.Y., 46.
RBI: Al Simmons, Phil., 157.
SB: Charley Gehringer, Det., 27.
Wins: George Earnshaw, Phil., 24.
ERA: Lefty Grove, Phil., 2.81.
CG: Tommy Thomas, Chi., 24.
IP: Sam Gray, St.L., 305.
SO: Lefty Grove, Phil., 170.

National League

BA: Lefty O'Doul, Phil., .398.
Runs: Rogers Hornsby, Chi., 156.
Hits: Lefty O'Doul, Phil., 254.
TB: Rogers Hornsby, Chi., 409.
HR: Chuck Klein, Phil., 43.
RBI: Hack Wilson, Chi., 159.
SB: Kiki Cuyler, Chi., 43.
Wins: Pat Malone, Chi., 22.
ERA: Bill Walker, N.Y., 3.09.
CG: Red Lucas, Cin., 28.
IP: Watty Clark, Brk., 279.
SO: Pat Malone, Chi., 166.

A.L. 20-game winners
George Earnshaw, Phil., 24-8
Wes Ferrell, Cle., 21-10
Lefty Grove, Phil., 20-6

N.L. 20-game winners
Pat Malone, Chi., 22-10

A.L. 100 RBIs
Al Simmons, Phil., 157
Babe Ruth, N.Y., 154
Dale Alexander, Det., 137
Lou Gehrig, N.Y., 126
Harry Heilmann, Det., 120
Jimmie Foxx, Phil., 117
Red Kress, St.L., 107
Charlie Gehringer, Det., 106
Tony Lazzeri, N.Y., 106
Lew Fonseca, Cle., 103

N.L. 100 RBIs
Hack Wilson, Chi., 159
Mel Ott, N.Y., 151
Rogers Hornsby, Chi., 149
Chuck Klein, Phil., 145
Jim Bottomley, St.L., 137
Chick Hafey, St.L., 125
Don Hurst, Phil., 125
Lefty O'Doul, Phil., 122
Bill Terry, N.Y., 117
Pinky Whitney, Phil., 115
Babe Herman, Brk., 113
Riggs Stephenson, Chi., 110
Pie Traynor, Pit., 108
George Kelly, Cin., 103
Kiki Cuyler, Chi., 102
Paul Waner, Pit., 100

A.L. 40 homers
Babe Ruth, N.Y., 46

N.L. 40 homers
Chuck Klein, Phil., 43
Mel Ott, N.Y., 42

League MVP
A.L.: No selection.
N.L.: Rogers Hornsby, 2B, Chi.

WORLD SERIES

■ **Winner:** The Athletics, an A.L. doormat since their last Series appearance in 1914, re-emerged as baseball's dominant team.

■ **Turning point:** The seventh inning of Game 4. Leading the Series two games to one but trailing the Cubs 8-0, the A's exploded for an incredible 10 runs.

■ **Memorable moments:** Mule Haas' three-run inside-the-park home run in the 10-run seventh inning and his ninth-inning game-tying homer in the Series-ending fifth game; surprise starter Howard Ehmke's record 13 strikeouts in Game 1.

■ **Top guns:** Jimmie Dykes (.421), Jimmie Foxx (.350, 2 HR, 5 RBIs), Haas (2 HR, 6 RBIs), Athletics; Hack Wilson (.471), Cubs.

Linescores

Game 1—October 8, at Chicago
Philadelphia.... 0 0 0 0 0 0 1 0 2 — 3 6 1
Chicago.......... 0 0 0 0 0 0 0 0 1 — 1 8 2
Ehmke; Root, Bush (8). W—Ehmke. L—Root. HR—Foxx (Phil.).

Game 2—October 9, at Chicago
Philadelphia.... 0 0 3 3 0 0 1 2 0 — 9 12 0
Chicago.......... 0 0 0 0 3 0 0 0 0 — 3 11 1
Earnshaw, Grove (5); Malone, Blake (4), Carlson (6), Nehf (9). W—Earnshaw. L—Malone. HR—Simmons, Foxx (Phil.).

Game 3—October 11, at Philadelphia
Chicago.......... 0 0 0 0 0 3 0 0 0 — 3 6 1
Philadelphia.... 0 0 0 0 1 0 0 0 0 — 1 9 1
Bush; Earnshaw. W—Bush. L—Earnshaw.

Game 4—October 12, at Philadelphia
Chicago.......... 0 0 0 2 0 5 1 0 0 — 8 10 2
Philadelphia.... 0 0 0 0 0 0 10 0 x — 10 15 2
Root, Nehf (7), Blake (7), Malone (7), Carlson (8); Quinn, Walberg (6), Rommel (7), Grove (8). W—Rommel. L—Blake. HR—Grimm (Chi.); Haas, Simmons (Phil.).

Game 5—October 14, at Philadelphia
Chicago.......... 0 0 0 2 0 0 0 0 0 — 2 8 1
Philadelphia.... 0 0 0 0 0 0 0 0 3 — 3 6 0
Malone; Ehmke, Walberg (4). W—Walberg. L—Malone. HR—Haas (Phil.).

1930

FINAL STANDINGS

American League

Team	W	L	Pct.	GB
Philadelphia	102	52	.662	...
Washington	94	60	.610	8
New York	86	68	.558	16
Cleveland	81	73	.526	21
Detroit	75	79	.487	27
St. Louis	64	90	.416	38
Chicago	62	92	.403	40
Boston	52	102	.338	50

National League

Team	W	L	Pct.	GB
St. Louis	92	62	.597	...
Chicago	90	64	.584	2
New York	87	67	.565	5
Brooklyn	86	68	.558	6
Pittsburgh	80	74	.519	12
Boston	70	84	.455	22
Cincinnati	59	95	.383	33
Philadelphia	52	102	.338	40

SIGNIFICANT EVENTS

■ **March 8:** Yankee slugger Babe Ruth signed a record two-year contract at $80,000 per season.

■ **December 11:** Major League officials granted the Baseball Writers Association of America permission to conduct future MVP balloting—a practice that would continue without interruption.

■ **December 12:** Rules changes: The sacrifice fly was eliminated and balls bouncing into the stands were classified as ground-rule doubles instead of home runs.

MEMORABLE MOMENTS

■ **May 2:** Commissioner Kenesaw Mountain Landis attended Organized Baseball's first game under permanently installed lights at Des Moines (Iowa) of the Western League.

■ **September 27:** Chicago's Hack Wilson hit home runs 55 and 56—an N.L. record—in a game against the Reds.

■ **September 28:** Wilson drove in his Major League-record 190th and 191st runs in Chicago's season-finale victory over the Reds.

■ **September 28:** New York's Bill Terry finished with a .401 average and N.L. hitters closed with a composite .303 mark.

LEADERS

American League

BA: Al Simmons, Phil., .381.
Runs: Al Simmons, Phil., 152.
Hits: Johnny Hodapp, Cle., 225.
TB: Lou Gehrig, N.Y., 419.
HR: Babe Ruth, N.Y., 49.
RBI: Lou Gehrig, N.Y., 174.
SB: Marty McManus, Det., 23.
Wins: Lefty Grove, Phil., 28.
ERA: Lefty Grove, Phil., 2.54.
CG: Ted Lyons, Chi., 29.
IP: Lyons, Chi., 297.2.
SO: Lefty Grove, Phil., 209.

National League

BA: Bill Terry, N.Y., .401.
Runs: Chuck Klein, Phil., 158.
Hits: Bill Terry, N.Y., 254.
TB: Chuck Klein, Phil., 445.
HR: Hack Wilson, Chi., 56.
RBI: Hack Wilson, Chi., 191.
SB: Kiki Cuyler, Chi., 37.
Wins: Ray Kremer, Pit.; Pat Malone, Chi., 20.
ERA: Dazzy Vance, Brk., 2.61.
CG: Erv Brame, Pit.; Pat Malone, Chi., 22.
IP: Ray Kremer, Pit., 276.
SO: Bill Hallahan, St.L., 177.

A.L. 20-game winners
Lefty Grove, Phil., 28-5
Wes Ferrell, Cle., 25-13
George Earnshaw, Phil., 22-13
Ted Lyons, Chi., 22-15
Lefty Stewart, St.L., 20-12

N.L. 20-game winners
Pat Malone, Chi., 20-9
Remy Kremer, Pit., 20-12

A.L. 100 RBIs
Lou Gehrig, N.Y., 174
Al Simmons, Phil., 165
Jimmie Foxx, Phil., 156
Babe Ruth, N.Y., 153
Goose Goslin, Wash.-St.L., 138
Ed Morgan, Cle., 136
Dale Alexander, Det., 135
Joe Cronin, Wash., 126
Johnny Hodapp, Cle., 121
Tony Lazzeri, N.Y., 121
Earl Averill, Cle., 119
Smead Jolley, Chi., 114
Red Kress, St.L., 112
Carl Reynolds, Chi., 104
Bing Miller, Phil., 100

N.L. 100 RBIs
Hack Wilson, Chi., 190
Chuck Klein, Phil., 170
Kiki Cuyler, Chi., 134
Babe Herman, Brk., 130
Bill Terry, N.Y., 129
Glenn Wright, Brk., 126
Gabby Hartnett, Chi., 122
Wally Berger, Bos., 119
Adam Comorosky, Pit., 119
Mel Ott, N.Y., 119
Pie Traynor, Pit., 119
Pinky Whitney, Phil., 117
Frank Frisch, St.L., 114
Del Bissonette, Brk., 113
Chick Hafey, St.L., 107
Gus Suhr, Pit., 107
Fred Lindstrom, N.Y., 106

A.L. 40 homers
Babe Ruth, N.Y., 49
Lou Gehrig, N.Y., 41

N.L. 40 homers
Hack Wilson, Chi., 56
Chuck Klein, Phil., 40

WORLD SERIES

■ **Winner:** The Athletics became the first team to win back-to-back Series twice.

■ **Turning point:** Jimmie Foxx's two-run ninth-inning home run off Burleigh Grimes, which broke open a scoreless Game 5 and put Philadelphia in the driver's seat.

■ **Memorable moment:** Foxx's Game 5-winning home run.

■ **Top guns:** George Earnshaw (2-0, 0.72 ERA), Al Simmons (.364, 2 HR, 4 RBIs), Athletics; Jesse Haines (1-0, 1.00), Cardinals.

Linescores

Game 1—October 1, at Philadelphia
St. Louis ....0 0 2 0 0 0 0 0 0—2 9 0
Philadelphia........0 1 0 1 0 1 1 1 x—5 5 0
Grimes; Grove. W—Grove. L—Grimes. HR—Cochrane, Simmons (Phil.).

Game 2—October 2, at Philadelphia
St. Louis ....0 1 0 0 0 0 0 0 0—1 6 2
Philadelphia........2 0 2 2 0 0 0 0 x—6 7 2
Rhem, Lindsey (4), Johnson (7); Earnshaw. W—Earnshaw. L—Rhem. HR—Cochrane (Phil.); Watkins (St.L.).

Game 3—October 4, at St. Louis
Philadelphia......0 0 0 0 0 0 0 0 0—0 7 0
St. Louis ....0 0 0 1 1 0 2 1 x—5 10 0
Walberg, Shores (5), Quinn (7); Hallahan. W—Hallahan. L—Walberg. HR—Douthit (St.L.).

Game 4—October 5, at St. Louis
Philadelphia........1 0 0 0 0 0 0 0 0—1 4 1
St. Louis ....0 0 1 2 0 0 0 0 x—3 5 1
Grove; Haines. W—Haines. L—Grove.

Game 5—October 6, at St. Louis
Philadelphia........0 0 0 0 0 0 0 0 2—2 5 0
St. Louis ....0 0 0 0 0 0 0 0 0—0 3 1
Earnshaw, Grove (8); Grimes. W—Grove. L—Grimes. HR—Foxx (Phil.).

Game 6—October 8, at Philadelphia
St. Louis ....0 0 0 0 0 0 0 0 1—1 5 1
Philadelphia........2 0 1 2 1 1 0 0 x—7 7 0
Hallahan, Johnson (3), Lindsey (6), Bell (8); Earnshaw. W—Earnshaw. L—Hallahan. HR—Dykes, Simmons (Phil.).

1931

FINAL STANDINGS

American League

Team	W	L	Pct.	GB
Philadelphia	107	45	.704	...
New York	94	59	.614	13.5
Washington	92	62	.597	16
Cleveland	78	76	.506	30
St. Louis	63	91	.409	45
Boston	62	90	.408	45
Detroit	61	93	.396	47
Chicago	56	97	.366	51.5

National League

Team	W	L	Pct.	GB
St. Louis	101	53	.656	...
New York	87	65	.572	13
Chicago	84	70	.545	17
Brooklyn	79	73	.520	21
Pittsburgh	75	79	.487	26
Philadelphia	66	88	.429	35
Boston	64	90	.416	37
Cincinnati	58	96	.377	43

SIGNIFICANT EVENTS

■ **March 27-28:** Former A.L. president and founder Ban Johnson died at age 67, 16 hours after E.S. Barnard, the man who succeeded him, died of a heart attack at age 56.
■ **October 20, 28:** The Baseball Writers Association of America named its first MVPs: Cardinals infielder Frank Frisch and Athletics 31-game winner Lefty Grove.
■ **October 26:** Charles Comiskey, one of the A.L.'s founding fathers and longtime owner of the White Sox, died at age 72.

MEMORABLE MOMENTS

■ **May 26:** The Yankees ended Philadelphia's winning streak at 17 games with a 6-2 victory.
■ **August 21:** Yankee Babe Ruth belted his historic 600th career home run off Browns righthander George Blaeholder.
■ **August 23:** Philadelphia's Lefty Grove, bidding to break the A.L. record of 16 straight victories, dropped a 1-0 decision to the Browns.
■ **September 1:** Yankee Lou Gehrig, en route to an A.L.-record 184 RBIs, became the third player to hit home runs in six straight games —a streak that included three grand slams in five days.

LEADERS

American League

BA: Al Simmons, Phil., .390.
Runs: Lou Gehrig, N.Y., 163.
Hits: Lou Gehrig, N.Y., 211.
TB: Lou Gehrig, N.Y., 410.
HR: Lou Gehrig, N.Y.; Babe Ruth, N.Y., 46.
RBI: Lou Gehrig, N.Y., 184.
SB: Ben Chapman, N.Y., 61.
Wins: Lefty Grove, Phil., 31.
ERA: Lefty Grove, Phil., 2.06.
CG: Wes Ferrell, Cle.; Lefty Grove, Phil., 27.
IP: Rube Walberg, Phil., 291.
SO: Lefty Grove, Phil., 175.

National League

BA: Chick Hafey, St.L., .349.
Runs: Chuck Klein, Phil.; Bill Terry, N.Y., 121.
Hits: Lloyd Waner, Pit., 214.
TB: Chuck Klein, Phil., 347.
HR: Chuck Klein, Phil., 31.
RBI: Chuck Klein, Phil., 121.
SB: Frank Frisch, St.L., 28.
Wins: Jumbo Elliott, Phil.; Bill Hallahan, St.L.; Heinie Meine, Pit., 19.
ERA: Bill Walker, N.Y., 2.26.
CG: Red Lucas, Cin., 24.
IP: Heinie Meine, Pit., 284.
SO: Bill Hallahan, St.L., 159.

A.L. 20-game winners
Lefty Grove, Phil., 31-4
Wes Ferrell, Cle., 22-12
George Earnshaw, Phil., 21-7
Lefty Gomez, N.Y., 21-9
Rube Walberg, Phil., 20-12

A.L. 100 RBIs
Lou Gehrig, N.Y., 184
Babe Ruth, N.Y., 163
Earl Averill, Cle., 143
Al Simmons, Phil., 128
Joe Cronin, Wash., 126
Ben Chapman, N.Y., 122
Jimmie Foxx, Phil., 120
Joe Vosmik, Cle., 117
Red Kress, St.L., 114
Lyn Lary, N.Y., 107
Goose Goslin, St.L., 105
Earl Webb, Bos., 103

N.L. 100 RBIs
Chuck Klein, Phil., 121
Mel Ott, N.Y., 115
Bill Terry, N.Y., 112
Pie Traynor, Pit., 103

A.L. 40 homers
Lou Gehrig, N.Y., 46
Babe Ruth, N.Y., 46

Most Valuable Player
A.L.: Lefty Grove, P, Phil.
N.L.: Frank Frisch, 2B, St.L.

WORLD SERIES

■ **Winner:** The Cardinals spoiled Philadelphia's bid to win a record third consecutive Series.

■ **Turning point:** A pair of two-run innings that staked Cardinals spitballer Burleigh Grimes to a 4-0 lead in Game 7.

■ **Memorable moment:** The Series-long do-everything performance of exciting Cardinals center fielder Pepper Martin.

■ **Top guns:** Grimes (2-0, 2.04 ERA), Bill Hallahan (2-0, 0.49), Martin (.500, 12 hits, 5 RBIs, 5 SB), Cardinals; Al Simmons (.333, 2 HR, 8 RBIs), Athletics.

Linescores

Game 1—October 1, at St. Louis
Philadelphia......0 0 4 0 0 0 2 0 0—6 11 0
St. Louis ....2 0 0 0 0 0 0 0 0—2 12 0
Grove; Derringer, Johnson (8). W—Grove. L—Derringer. HR—Simmons (Phil.).

Game 2—October 2, at St. Louis
Philadelphia........0 0 0 0 0 0 0 0 0—0 3 0
St. Louis ....0 1 0 0 0 0 1 0 x—2 6 1
Earnshaw; Hallahan. W—Hallahan. L—Earnshaw.

Game 3—October 5, at Philadelphia
St. Louis ....0 2 0 2 0 0 0 0 1—5 12 0
Philadelphia......0 0 0 0 0 0 0 0 2—2 2 0
Grimes; Grove, Mahaffey (9). W—Grimes. L—Grove. HR—Simmons (Phil).

Game 4—October 6, at Philadelphia
St. Louis ....0 0 0 0 0 0 0 0 0—0 2 1
Philadelphia......1 0 0 0 0 2 0 0 x—3 10 0
Johnson, Lindsey (6), Derringer (8); Earnshaw. W—Earnshaw. L—Johnson. HR—Foxx (Phil.).

Game 5—October 7, at Philadelphia
St. Louis ....1 0 0 0 0 2 0 1 1—5 12 0
Philadelphia......0 0 0 0 0 0 1 0 0—1 9 0
Hallahan; Hoyt, Walberg (7), Rommel (9). W—Hallahan. L—Hoyt. HR—Martin (St.L.).

Game 6—October 9, at St. Louis
Philadelphia........0 0 0 0 4 0 4 0 0—8 8 1
St. Louis ....0 0 0 0 0 1 0 0 0—1 5 2
Grove; Derringer, Johnson (5), Lindsey (7), Rhem (9). W—Grove. L—Derringer.

Game 7—October 10, at St. Louis
Philadelphia........0 0 0 0 0 0 0 0 2—2 7 1
St. Louis ....2 0 2 0 0 0 0 0 x—4 5 0
Earnshaw, Walberg (8); Grimes, Hallahan (9). W—Grimes. L—Earnshaw. HR—Watkins (St.L.).

1932

FINAL STANDINGS

American League

Team	W	L	Pct.	GB
New York	107	47	.695	...
Philadelphia	94	60	.610	13
Washington	93	61	.604	14
Cleveland	87	65	.572	19
Detroit	76	75	.503	29.5
St. Louis	63	91	.409	44
Chicago	49	102	.325	56.5
Boston	43	111	.279	64

National League

Team	W	L	Pct.	GB
Chicago	90	64	.584	...
Pittsburgh	86	68	.558	4
Brooklyn	81	73	.526	9
Philadelphia	78	76	.506	12
Boston	77	77	.500	13
New York	72	82	.468	18
St. Louis	72	82	.468	18
Cincinnati	60	94	.390	30

SIGNIFICANT EVENTS

■ **June 22:** N.L. officials, after a long holdout, approved the use of numbers to identify their players.
■ **July 31:** The 76,979 fans who turned out for Cleveland's unveiling of Municipal Stadium watched the Indians lose a 1-0 decision to the Athletics and Lefty Grove.
■ **September 28:** Connie Mack began dismantling his powerful Athletics with the sale of Al Simmons, Jimmie Dykes and Mule Haas to the White Sox for $150,000.
■ **October 19:** A Philadelphia double: Athletics slugger Jimmie Foxx earned A.L. MVP honors and Phillies slugger Chuck Klein captured the N.L. award.

MEMORABLE MOMENTS

■ **June 3:** An historic day: Yankee Lou Gehrig belted four home runs in a game at Philadelphia and John McGraw retired after 31 seasons as manager of the Giants.
■ **July 4:** In a Fourth of July battle between the Yankees and Senators, New York catcher Bill Dickey punched Washington outfielder Carl Reynolds and broke his jaw, a tantrum that would cost him a 30-day suspension and $1,000.
■ **September 25:** Athletics slugger Jimmie Foxx hit home run No. 58 in the season finale against Washington, falling two short of Babe Ruth's single-season record.

LEADERS

American League

BA: Dale Alexander, Det.-Bos., .367.
Runs: Jimmie Foxx, Phil., 151.
Hits: Al Simmons, Phil., 216.
TB: Jimmie Foxx, Phil., 438.
HR: Jimmie Foxx, Phil., 58.
RBI: Jimmie Foxx, Phil., 169.
SB: Ben Chapman, N.Y., 38.
Wins: General Crowder, Wash., 26.
ERA: Lefty Grove, Phil., 2.84.
CG: Lefty Grove, Phil., 27.
IP: General Crowder, Wash., 327.
SO: Red Ruffing, N.Y., 190.

National League

BA: Lefty O'Doul, Brk., .368.
Runs: Chuck Klein, Phil., 152.
Hits: Chuck Klein, Phil., 226.
TB: Chuck Klein, Phil., 420.
HR: Chuck Klein, Phil.; Mel Ott, N.Y., 38.
RBI: Don Hurst, Phil., 143.
SB: Chuck Klein, Phil., 20.
Wins: Lon Warneke, Chi., 22.
ERA: Lon Warneke, Chi., 2.37.
CG: Red Lucas, Cin., 28.
IP: Dizzy Dean, St.L., 286.
SO: Dizzy Dean, St.L., 191.

A.L. 20-game winners
General Crowder, Wash., 26-13
Lefty Grove, Phil., 25-10
Lefty Gomez, N.Y., 24-7
Wes Ferrell, Cle., 23-13
Monte Weaver, Wash., 22-10

N.L. 20-game winners
Lon Warneke, Chi., 22-6
Watty Clark, Brk., 20-12

A.L. 100 RBIs
Jimmie Foxx, Phil., 169
Lou Gehrig, N.Y., 151
Al Simmons, Phil., 151
Babe Ruth, N.Y., 137
Earl Averill, Cle., 124
Joe Cronin, Wash., 116
Heinie Manush, Wash., 116
Tony Lazzeri, N.Y., 113
Mickey Cochrane, Phil., 112
John Stone, Det., 108
Ben Chapman, N.Y., 107
Charlie Gehringer, Det., 107
Smead Jolley, Chi.-St.L., 106
Goose Goslin, St.L., 104

N.L. 100 RBIs
Don Hurst, Phil., 143
Chuck Klein, Phil., 137
Pinky Whitney, Phil., 124
Mel Ott, N.Y., 123
Hack Wilson, Brk., 123
Bill Terry, N.Y., 117

A.L. 40 homers
Jimmie Foxx, Phil., 58
Babe Ruth, N.Y., 41

Most Valuable Player
A.L.: Jimmie Foxx, 1B, Phil.
N.L.: Chuck Klein, OF, Phil.

WORLD SERIES

■ **Winner:** The Yankees played long ball in their sweep of the Cubs.

■ **Turning point:** A fourth-inning Game 1 homer by Lou Gehrig that gave the Yankees a 3-2 lead and propelled them to their sweep.

■ **Memorable moment:** Babe Ruth's second homer in Game 3 off Cubs righthander Charlie Root — whether it was a "called shot" or not.

■ **Top guns:** Gehrig (.529, 3 HR, 8 RBIs), Ruth (.333, 2 HR, 6 RBIs), Yankees; Riggs Stephenson (.444), Cubs.

Linescores

Game 1—September 28, at New York
Chicago..........2 0 0 0 0 0 2 2 0— 6 10 1
New York........0 0 0 3 0 5 3 1 x—12 8 2
Bush, Grimes (6), Smith (8); Ruffing. W—Ruffing. L—Bush. HR—Gehrig (N.Y.).

Game 2—September 29, at New York
Chicago............1 0 1 0 0 0 0 0 0—2 9 0
New York.........2 0 2 0 1 0 0 0 x—5 10 1
Warneke; Gomez. W—Gomez. L—Warneke.

Game 3—October 1, at Chicago
New York ....3 0 1 0 2 0 0 0 1—7 8 1
Chicago..............1 0 2 1 0 0 0 0 1—5 9 4
Pipgras, Pennock (9); Root, Malone (5), May (8), Tinning (9). W—Pipgras. L—Root. HR—Ruth 2, Gehrig 2 (N.Y.); Cuyler, Hartnett (Chi.).

Game 4—October 2, at Chicago
New York ......1 0 2 0 0 2 4 0 4—13 19 4
Chicago..........4 0 0 0 0 1 0 0 1— 6 9 1
Allen, W. Moore (1), Pennock (7); Bush, Warneke (1), May (4), Tinning (7), Grimes (9). W—W. Moore. L—May. HR—Demaree (Chi.); Lazzeri 2, Combs (N.Y.).

1933

FINAL STANDINGS

American League

Team	W	L	Pct.	GB
Washington	99	53	.651	...
New York	91	59	.607	7
Philadelphia	79	72	.523	19.5
Cleveland	75	76	.497	23.5
Detroit	75	79	.487	25
Chicago	67	83	.447	31
Boston	63	86	.423	34.5
St. Louis	55	96	.364	43.5

National League

Team	W	L	Pct.	GB
New York	91	61	.599	...
Pittsburgh	87	67	.565	5
Chicago	86	68	.558	6
Boston	83	71	.539	9
St. Louis	82	71	.536	9.5
Brooklyn	65	88	.425	26.5
Philadelphia	60	92	.395	31
Cincinnati	58	94	.382	33

SIGNIFICANT EVENTS

■ **January 7:** Commissioner Kenesaw Mountain Landis, sending a Depression-era message to owners and players, took a voluntary $25,000 cut in salary.

■ **November 7:** A referendum was passed by Pennsylvania voters legalizing Sunday baseball for Pittsburgh and Philadelphia — the only Major League cities still observing the blue law.

MEMORABLE MOMENTS

■ **July 30:** Cardinals ace Dizzy Dean set a modern record with 17 strikeouts in an 8-2 victory over Chicago.

■ **July 2:** Giants pitchers Carl Hubbell (18) and Roy Parmelee (9) combined for 27 scoreless innings in a doubleheader shutout of the St. Louis Cardinals. Both games ended 1-0.

■ **August 1:** Giants lefty Carl Hubbell extended his N.L.-record scoreless-innings streak to 45 in a game eventually won by Boston, 3-1.

■ **August 17:** Yankee Lou Gehrig broke Everett Scott's Major League record when he played in his 1,308th consecutive game — a 7-6 loss at St. Louis.

■ **October 1:** Philadelphia stars Jimmie Foxx (.356, 48 homers, 163 RBIs) and Chuck Klein (.368, 28, 120) completed an unprecedented one-season double, becoming the fifth and sixth Triple Crown winners of the century.

LEADERS

American League

BA: Jimmie Foxx, Phil., .356.
Runs: Lou Gehrig, N.Y., 138.
Hits: Heinie Manush, Wash., 221.
TB: Jimmie Foxx, Phil., 403.
HR: Jimmie Foxx, Phil., 48.
RBI: Jimmie Foxx, Phil., 163.
SB: Ben Chapman, N.Y., 27.
Wins: General Crowder, Wash.; Lefty Grove, Phil., 24.
ERA: Mel Harder, Cle., 2.95.
CG: Lefty Grove, Phil., 21.
IP: Bump Hadley, St.L., 316.2.
SO: Lefty Gomez, N.Y., 163.

National League

BA: Chuck Klein, Phil., .368.
Runs: Pepper Martin, St.L., 122.
Hits: Chuck Klein, Phil., 223.
TB: Chuck Klein, Phil., 365.
HR: Chuck Klein, Phil., 28.
RBI: Chuck Klein, Phil., 120.
SB: Pepper Martin, St.L., 26.
Wins: Carl Hubbell, N.Y., 23.
ERA: Carl Hubbell, N.Y., 1.66.
CG: Dizzy Dean, St.L.; Lon Warneke, Chi., 26.
IP: Carl Hubbell, N.Y., 308.2.
SO: Dizzy Dean, St.L., 199.

A.L. 20-game winners
Lefty Grove, Phil., 24-8
General Crowder, Wash., 24-15
Earl Whitehill, Wash., 22-8

N.L. 20-game winners
Carl Hubbell, N.Y., 23-12
Ben Cantwell, Bos., 20-10
Guy Bush, Chi., 20-12
Dizzy Dean, St.L., 20-18

A.L. 100 RBIs
Jimmie Foxx, Phil., 163
Lou Gehrig, N.Y., 139
Al Simmons, Chi., 119
Joe Cronin, Wash., 118
Joe Kuhel, Wash., 107
Bruce Campbell, St.L., 106
Charlie Gehringer, Det., 105
Tony Lazzeri, N.Y., 104
Babe Ruth, N.Y., 103

N.L. 100 RBIs
Chuck Klein, Phil., 120
Wally Berger, Bos., 106
Mel Ott, N.Y., 103

A.L. 40 homers
Jimmie Foxx, Phil., 48

Most Valuable Player
A.L.: Jimmie Foxx, 1B, Phil.
N.L.: Carl Hubbell, P, N.Y.

ALL-STAR GAME

■ **Winner:** The American League prevailed 4-2 in baseball's "Game of the Century," which gathered the biggest stars from both leagues for an unprecedented meeting at Chicago's Comiskey Park.

■ **Key inning:** The third, when Yankee slugger Babe Ruth poured a two-run homer and gave the A.L. a 3-0 lead.

■ **Memorable moment:** The star-studded pregame introductions for baseball's first All-Star classic.

■ **Top guns:** Lefty Gomez (Yankees), Ruth (Yankees), Jimmie Dykes (White Sox), A.L.; Frank Frisch (Cardinals), Bill Terry (Giants), N.L.

■ **MVP:** Ruth.

Linescore

July 6, at Chicago's Comiskey Park
N.L. ....0 0 0 0 0 2 0 0 0—2 8 0
A.L. ....0 1 2 0 0 1 0 0 x—4 9 1
Hallahan (Cardinals), Warneke (Cubs) 3, Hubbell (Giants) 7; Gomez (Yankees), Crowder (Senators) 4, Grove (Athletics) 7. W—Gomez. L—Hallahan. HR—Ruth, A.L.; Frisch (N.L.).

WORLD SERIES

■ **Winner:** The pitching-rich Giants, now under the direction of player/manager Bill Terry, captured their first Series without John McGraw at the helm.

■ **Turning point:** Carl Hubbell's 2-1, 11-inning victory that gave the Giants a three-games-to-one edge.

■ **Memorable moment:** A 10th-inning home run by Mel Ott that gave the Giants a Series-ending 4-3 victory.

■ **Top guns:** Hubbell (2-0, 0.00 ERA), Ott (.389, 2 HR, 4 RBIs), Giants; Fred Schulte (.333), Senators.

Linescores

Game 1—October 3, at New York
Washington.............0 0 0 1 0 0 0 0 1—2 5 3
New York.................2 0 2 0 0 0 0 0 x—4 10 2
Stewart, Russell (3), Thomas (8); Hubbell. W—Hubbell. L—Stewart. HR—Ott (N.Y.).

Game 2—October 4, at New York
Washington.............0 0 1 0 0 0 0 0 0—1 5 0
New York.................0 0 0 0 0 6 0 0 x—6 10 0
Crowder, Thomas (6), McColl (7); Schumacher. W—Schumacher. L—Crowder. HR—Goslin (Wash.).

Game 3—October 5, at Washington
New York...................0 0 0 0 0 0 0 0 0—0 5 0
Washington...............2 1 0 0 0 0 1 0 x—4 9 1
Fitzsimmons, Bell (8); Whitehill. W—Whitehill. L—Fitzsimmons.

Game 4—October 6, at Washington
New York........0 0 0 1 0 0 0 0 0 0 1—2 11 1
Washington....0 0 0 0 0 0 1 0 0 0 0—1 8 0
Hubbell; Weaver, Russell (11). W—Hubbell. L—Weaver. HR—Terry (N.Y.).

Game 5—October 7, at Washington
New York...........0 2 0 0 0 1 0 0 0 1—4 11 1
Washington........0 0 0 0 0 3 0 0 0 0—3 10 0
Schumacher, Luque (6); Crowder, Russell (6). W—Luque. L—Russell. HR—Schulte (Wash.); Ott (N.Y.).

1934

FINAL STANDINGS

American League

Team	W	L	Pct.	GB
Detroit	101	53	.656	...
New York	94	60	.610	7
Cleveland	85	69	.552	16
Boston	76	76	.500	24
Philadelphia	68	82	.453	31
St. Louis	67	85	.441	33
Washington	66	86	.434	34
Chicago	53	99	.349	47

National League

Team	W	L	Pct.	GB
St. Louis	95	58	.621	...
New York	93	60	.608	2
Chicago	86	65	.570	8
Boston	78	73	.517	16
Pittsburgh	74	76	.493	19.5
Brooklyn	71	81	.467	23.5
Philadelphia	56	93	.376	37
Cincinnati	52	99	.344	42

SIGNIFICANT EVENTS

■ **February 25:** John McGraw, considered by many the greatest manager of all time, died of cancer at age 60.

■ **November 9:** N.L. officials selected Ford Frick as league president, six days after John Heydler resigned for health reasons.

■ **December 12:** The N.L., acting independently of the A.L., voted to allow night baseball on a limited basis.

MEMORABLE MOMENTS

■ **July 13:** Yankee outfielder Babe Ruth opened the 700-homer club when he connected off righthander Tommy Bridges in a game at Detroit.

■ **August 25:** Detroit rookie Schoolboy Rowe defeated Washington 4-2 for his A.L. record-tying 16th consecutive victory.

■ **September 21:** Cardinals ace Dizzy Dean shut out Brooklyn on three hits in the first game of a doubleheader and brother Paul pitched a no-hitter against the Dodgers in the nightcap.

LEADERS

American League

BA: Lou Gehrig, N.Y., .363.
Runs: Charley Gehringer, Det., 134.
Hits: Charley Gehringer, Det., 214.
TB: Lou Gehrig, N.Y., 409.
HR: Lou Gehrig, N.Y., 49.
RBI: Lou Gehrig, N.Y., 165.
SB: Billy Werber, Bos., 40.
Wins: Lefty Gomez, N.Y., 26.
ERA: Lefty Gomez, N.Y., 2.33.
CG: Lefty Gomez, N.Y., 25.
IP: Lefty Gomez, N.Y., 281.2.
SO: Lefty Gomez, N.Y., 158.

National League

BA: Paul Waner, Pit., .362.
Runs: Paul Waner, Pit., 122.
Hits: Paul Waner, Pit., 217.
TB: Ripper Collins, St.L., 369.
HR: Ripper Collins, St.L.; Mel Ott, N.Y., 35.
RBI: Mel Ott, N.Y., 135.
SB: Pepper Martin, St.L., 23.
Wins: Dizzy Dean, St.L., 30.
ERA: Carl Hubbell, N.Y., 2.30.
CG: Carl Hubbell, N.Y., 25.
IP: Van Lingle Mungo, Brk., 315.1.
SO: Dizzy Dean, St.L., 195.

A.L. 20-game winners
Lefty Gomez, N.Y., 26-5
Schoolboy Rowe, Det., 24-8
Tommy Bridges, Det., 22-11
Mel Harder, Cle., 20-12

N.L. 20-game winners
Dizzy Dean, St.L., 30-7
Hal Schumacher, N.Y., 23-10
Lon Warneke, Chi., 22-10
Carl Hubbell, N.Y., 21-12

A.L. 100 RBIs
Lou Gehrig, N.Y., 165
Hal Trosky, Cle., 142
Hank Greenberg, Det., 139
Jimmie Foxx, Phil., 130
Charlie Gehringer, Det., 127
Roy Johnson, Bos., 119
Earl Averill, Cle., 113
Zeke Bonura, Chi., 110
Al Simmons, Chi., 104
Joe Cronin, Wash., 101
Odell Hale, Cle., 101
Roy Pepper, St.L., 101
Goose Goslin, Det., 100
Billy Rogell, Det., 100

N.L. 100 RBIs
Mel Ott, N.Y., 135
Ripper Collins, St.L., 128
Wally Berger, Bos., 121
Joe Medwick, St.L., 106
Gus Suhr, Pit., 103
Sam Leslie, Brk., 102
Travis Jackson, N.Y., 101

A.L. 40 homers
Lou Gehrig, N.Y., 49
Jimmie Foxx, Phil., 44

Most Valuable Player
A.L.: Mickey Cochrane, C, Det.
N.L.: Dizzy Dean, P, St.L.

ALL-STAR GAME

■ **Winner:** The A.L. made it two in a row by roaring back from a 4-0 deficit for a 9-7 victory.

■ **Key inning:** The fifth, when the A.L. scored six times to take command. Cleveland's Earl Averill doubled home two runs and Yankee pitcher Red Ruffing singled in two more.

■ **Memorable moment:** The first- and second-inning performance of Giants lefthander Carl Hubbell, who struck out A.L. bashers Babe Ruth (Yankees), Lou Gehrig (Yankees), Jimmie Foxx (Athletics), Al Simmons (White Sox) and Joe Cronin (Senators) consecutively.

■ **Top guns:** Mel Harder (Indians), Averill (Indians), Cronin (Senators), Simmons (White Sox), A.L.; Hubbell (Giants), Joe Medwick (Cardinals), Frank Frisch (Cardinals), N.L.

■ **MVP:** Averill.

Linescore

July 10, at New York's Polo Grounds
A.L. ....0 0 0 2 6 1 0 0 0—9 14 1
N.L. ....1 0 3 0 3 0 0 0 0—7 8 1
Gomez (Yankees), Ruffing (Yankees) 4, Harder (Indians) 5, A.L.; Hubbell (Giants), Warneke (Cubs) 4, Mungo (Dodgers) 5, Dean (Cardinals) 6, Frankhouse (Braves) 9. W—Harder. L—Mungo. HR—Frisch, Medwick, N.L.

WORLD SERIES

■ **Winner:** St. Louis' Gas House Gang defeated the Tigers in the infamous "Garbage" World Series.

■ **Turning point:** Paul Dean's pitching and hitting gave the Cardinals a 4-3 Game 6 victory that set up a winner-take-all seventh game.

■ **Memorable moment:** A seventh-game outburst by frustrated Tigers fans who pelted Cardinals left fielder Joe Medwick with garbage and other debris, forcing a long delay. The Cardinals were leading 9-0 en route to an 11-0 victory.

■ **Top guns:** Paul Dean (2-0, 1.00 ERA), Dizzy Dean (2-1, 1.73), Medwick (.379, 5 RBIs), Cardinals; Charley Gehringer (.379), Tigers.

Linescores

Game 1—October 3, at Detroit
St. Louis ....0 2 1 0 1 4 0 0 0—8 13 2
Detroit.......................0 0 1 0 0 1 0 1 0—3 8 5
D. Dean; Crowder, Marberry (6), Hogsett (6). W—D. Dean. L—Crowder. HR—Medwick (St.L.); Greenberg (Det.).

Game 2—October 4, at Detroit
St. Louis ......0 1 1 0 0 0 0 0 0 0 0 0—2 7 3
Detroit..........0 0 0 1 0 0 0 0 1 0 0 1—3 7 0
Hallahan, W. Walker (9); Rowe. W—Rowe. L—W. Walker.

Game 3—October 5, at St. Louis
Detroit........................0 0 0 0 0 0 0 0 1—1 8 2
St. Louis ....1 1 0 0 2 0 0 0 x—4 9 1
Bridges, Hogsett (5); P. Dean. W—P. Dean. L—Bridges.

Game 4—October 6, at St. Louis
Detroit....................0 0 3 1 0 0 1 5 0—10 13 1
St. Louis ....0 1 1 2 0 0 0 0 0— 4 10 5
Auker; Carleton, Vance (3), W. Walker (5), Haines (8), Mooney (9). W—Auker. L—W. Walker.

Game 5—October 7, at St. Louis
Detroit........................0 1 0 0 0 2 0 0 0—3 7 0
St. Louis ....0 0 0 0 0 0 1 0 0—1 7 1
Bridges; D. Dean, Carleton (9). W—Bridges. L—D. Dean. HR—Gehringer (Det.); DeLancey (St.L.).

Game 6—October 8, at Detroit
St. Louis ....1 0 0 0 2 0 1 0 0—4 10 2
Detroit......................0 0 1 0 0 2 0 0 0—3 7 1
P. Dean; Rowe. W—P. Dean. L—Rowe.

Game 7—October 9, at Detroit
St. Louis ....0 0 7 0 0 2 2 0 0—11 17 1
Detroit....................0 0 0 0 0 0 0 0 0— 0 6 3
D. Dean; Auker, Rowe (3), Hogsett (3), Bridges (3), Marberry (8), Crowder (9). W—D. Dean. L—Auker.

1935

FINAL STANDINGS

American League

Team	W	L	Pct.	GB
Detroit	93	58	.616	...
New York	89	60	.597	3
Cleveland	82	71	.536	12
Boston	78	75	.510	16
Chicago	74	78	.487	19.5
Washington	67	86	.438	27
St. Louis	65	87	.428	28.5
Philadelphia	58	91	.389	34

National League

Team	W	L	Pct.	GB
Chicago	100	54	.649	...
St. Louis	96	58	.623	4
New York	91	62	.595	8.5
Pittsburgh	86	67	.562	13.5
Brooklyn	70	83	.458	29.5
Cincinnati	68	85	.444	31.5
Philadelphia	64	89	.418	35.5
Boston	38	115	.248	61.5

SIGNIFICANT EVENTS

■ **February 26:** Babe Ruth ended his long love affair with New York fans when the Yankees granted him a release to sign with the Braves.

■ **December 10:** A.L. owners attending the winter meetings voted not to sanction night baseball.

MEMORABLE MOMENTS

■ **May 24:** Larry MacPhail's Reds staged the first night game in Major League history and defeated the Phillies, 2-1, at Crosley Field.

■ **June 2:** Braves slugger Babe Ruth retired, eight days after a three-homer game at Pittsburgh had raised his career total to 714.

■ **August 31:** Chicago pitcher Vern Kennedy pitched the first no-hitter in Comiskey Park history and punctuated his 5-0 victory over Cleveland with a bases-loaded triple.

■ **September 22:** The lowly Braves lost their Major League-record 110th game en route to 115 losses.

■ **September 27:** The Cubs clinched the N.L. pennant with a 6-2 victory over St. Louis — their 20th straight win in a streak that would end at 21.

LEADERS

American League

BA: Buddy Myer, Wash., .349.
Runs: Lou Gehrig, N.Y., 125.
Hits: Joe Vosmik, Cle., 216.
TB: Hank Greenberg, Det., 389.
HR: Jimmie Foxx, Phil.; Hank Greenberg, Det., 36.
RBI: Hank Greenberg, Det., 170.
SB: Billy Werber, Bos., 29.
Wins: Wes Ferrell, Bos., 25.
ERA: Lefty Grove, Bos., 2.70.
CG: Wes Ferrell, Bos., 31.
IP: Wes Ferrell, Bos., 322.1.
SO: Tommy Bridges, Det., 163.

National League

BA: Arky Vaughan, Pit., .385.
Runs: Augie Galan, Chi., 133.
Hits: Billy Herman, Chi., 227.
TB: Joe Medwick, St.L., 365.
HR: Wally Berger, Bos., 34.
RBI: Wally Berger, Bos., 130.
SB: Augie Galan, Chi., 22.
Wins: Dizzy Dean, St.L., 28.
ERA: Cy Blanton, Pit., 2.58.
CG: Dizzy Dean, St.L., 29.
IP: Dizzy Dean, St.L., 325.1
SO: Dizzy Dean, St.L., 190.

A.L. 20-game winners

Wes Ferrell, Bos., 25-14
Mel Harder, Cle., 22-11
Tommy Bridges, Det., 21-10
Lefty Grove, Bos., 20-12

N.L. 20-game winners

Dizzy Dean, St.L., 28-12
Carl Hubbell, N.Y., 23-12
Paul Derringer, Cin., 22-13
Bill Lee, Chi., 20-6
Lon Warneke, Chi., 20-13

A.L. 100 RBIs

Hank Greenberg, Det., 170
Lou Gehrig, N.Y., 119
Jimmie Foxx, Phil., 115
Hal Trosky, Cle., 113
Moose Solters, Bos.-St.L., 112
Joe Vosmik, Cle., 110
Goose Goslin, Det., 109
Bob Johnson, Phil., 109
Charlie Gehringer, Det., 108
Odell Hale, Cle., 101
Buddy Myer, Wash., 100

N.L. 100 RBIs

Wally Berger, Bos., 130
Joe Medwick, St.L., 126
Ripper Collins, St.L., 122
Mel Ott, N.Y., 114
Hank Leiber, N.Y., 107

Most Valuable Player

A.L.: Hank Greenberg, 1B, Det.
N.L.: Gabby Hartnett, C, Chi.

ALL-STAR GAME

■ **Winner:** New York's Lefty Gomez and Cleveland's Mel Harder combined on a four-hitter and the A.L. recorded its third straight All-Star victory, 4-1.

■ **Key inning:** The first, when Athletics slugger Jimmie Foxx belted a two-run homer off Bill Walker, giving Gomez and Harder all the runs they would need.

■ **Memorable moment:** The ovation for hometown favorite Harder after his three-inning, one-hit pitching to close out the N.L.

■ **Top guns:** Gomez (Yankees), Harder (Indians), Foxx (Athletics), Charley Gehringer (Tigers), A.L.; Bill Terry (Giants), N.L.

■ **MVP:** Foxx.

Linescore

July 8, at Cleveland Stadium
N.L. ....0 0 0 1 0 0 0 0 0—1 4 1
A.L. ....2 1 0 0 1 0 0 0 x—4 8 0
Walker (Cardinals), Schumacher (Giants) 3, Derringer (Reds) 7, Dean (Cardinals) 8; Gomez (Yankees), Harder (Indians) 7. W—Gomez. L—Walker. HR—Foxx, A.L.

WORLD SERIES

■ **Winner:** The Tigers, four-time Series losers, won their first in a six-game battle with the Cubs.

■ **Turning point:** Detroit's 6-5 Game 3 victory. Jo Jo White drove in the game-winner with an 11th-inning single, giving the Tigers a two-games-to-one edge.

■ **Memorable moment:** Detroit pitcher Tommy Bridges' dramatic ninth-inning escape in Game 7 after giving up a leadoff triple to Stan Hack with the game tied, 3-3. The Tigers ended the Series in the bottom of the inning.

■ **Top guns:** Bridges (2-0, 2.50 ERA), Pete Fox (.385), Tigers; Lon Warneke (2-0, 0.54), Billy Herman (.333, 6 RBIs), Cubs.

Linescores

Game 1—October 2, at Detroit
Chicago........................2 0 0 0 0 0 0 0 1—3 7 0
Detroit........................0 0 0 0 0 0 0 0 0—0 4 3
Warneke; Rowe. W—Warneke. L—Rowe. HR—Demaree (Chi.).

Game 2—October 3, at Detroit
Chicago........................0 0 0 0 1 0 2 0 0—3 6 1
Detroit........................4 0 0 3 0 0 1 0 x—8 9 2
Root, Henshaw (1), Kowalik (4); Bridges. W—Bridges. L—Root. HR—Greenberg (Det.).

Game 3—October 4, at Chicago
Detroit...........0 0 0 0 0 1 0 4 0 0 1—6 12 2
Chicago..........0 2 0 0 1 0 0 0 2 0 0—5 10 3
Auker, Hogsett (7), Rowe (8); Lee, Warneke (8), French (10). W—Rowe. L—French. HR—Demaree (Chi.).

Game 4—October 5, at Chicago
Detroit........................0 0 1 0 0 1 0 0 0—2 7 0
Chicago........................0 1 0 0 0 0 0 0 0—1 5 2
Crowder; Carleton, Root (8). W—Crowder. L—Carleton. HR—Hartnett (Chi.).

Game 5—October 6, at Chicago
Detroit........................0 0 0 0 0 0 0 0 1—1 7 1
Chicago........................0 0 2 0 0 0 1 0 x—3 8 0
Rowe; Warneke, Lee (7). W—Warneke. L—Rowe. HR—Klein (Chi.).

Game 6—October 7, at Detroit
Chicago....................0 0 1 0 2 0 0 0 0—3 12 0
Detroit....................1 0 0 1 0 1 0 0 1—4 12 1
French; Bridges. W—Bridges. L—French. HR—Herman (Chi.).

1936

FINAL STANDINGS

American League

Team	W	L	Pct.	GB
New York	102	51	.667	...
Detroit	83	71	.539	19.5
Chicago	81	70	.536	20
Washington	82	71	.536	20
Cleveland	80	74	.519	22.5
Boston	74	80	.481	28.5
St. Louis	57	95	.375	44.5
Philadelphia	53	100	.346	49

National League

Team	W	L	Pct.	GB
New York	92	62	.597	...
Chicago	87	67	.565	5
St. Louis	87	67	.565	5
Pittsburgh	84	70	.545	8
Cincinnati	74	80	.481	18
Boston	71	83	.461	21
Brooklyn	67	87	.435	25
Philadelphia	54	100	.351	38

SIGNIFICANT EVENTS

■ **February 2:** Ty Cobb, Babe Ruth, Honus Wagner, Walter Johnson and Christy Mathewson were named charter members of baseball's new Hall of Fame.

■ **June 4:** Detroit player/manager Mickey Cochrane collapsed in a Shibe Park dugout and was hospitalized on the threshhold of a career-threatening nervous breakdown.

■ **December 9:** A.L. owners granted the Browns permission to play night baseball in St. Louis and ruled that players must have at least 400 at-bats to qualify for a batting championship.

MEMORABLE MOMENTS

■ **May 24:** Tony Lazzeri drilled three home runs, including a single-game record two grand slams, and drove in an A.L.-record 11 runs in the Yankees' 25-2 pounding of the Athletics.

■ **July 10:** Philadelphia's Chuck Klein became the fourth Major Leaguer to hit four homers in one game, completing his big day with a solo blast leading off the 10th inning of a 9-6 victory over Pittsburgh.

■ **September 13:** Cleveland 17-year-old Bob Feller tied a Major League record when he struck out 17 Athletics in a 5-2 victory.

LEADERS

American League

BA: Luke Appling, Chi., .388.
Runs: Lou Gehrig, N.Y., 167.
Hits: Earl Averill, Cle., 232.
TB: Hal Trosky, Cle., 405.
HR: Lou Gehrig, N.Y., 49.
RBI: Hal Trosky, Cle., 162.
SB: Lyn Lary, St.L., 37.
Wins: Tommy Bridges, Det., 23.
ERA: Lefty Grove, Bos., 2.81.
CG: Wes Ferrell, Bos., 28.
IP: Wes Ferrell, Bos., 301.
SO: Tommy Bridges, Det., 175.

National League

BA: Paul Waner, Pit., .373.
Runs: Arky Vaughan, Pit., 122.
Hits: Joe Medwick, St.L., 223.
TB: Joe Medwick, St.L., 367.
HR: Mel Ott, N.Y., 33.
RBI: Joe Medwick, St.L., 138.
SB: Pepper Martin, St.L., 23.
Wins: Carl Hubbell, N.Y., 26.
ERA: Carl Hubbell, N.Y., 2.31.
CG: Dizzy Dean, St.L., 28.
IP: Dizzy Dean, St.L., 315.
SO: Van Lingle Mungo, Brk., 238.

A.L. 20-game winners

Tommy Bridges, Det., 23-11
Vern Kennedy, Chi., 21-9
Johnny Allen, Cle., 20-10
Red Ruffing, N.Y., 20-12
Wes Ferrell, Bos., 20-15

N.L. 20-game winners

Carl Hubbell, N.Y., 26-6
Dizzy Dean, St.L., 24-13

A.L. 100 RBIs

Hal Trosky, Cle., 162
Lou Gehrig, N.Y., 152
Jimmie Foxx, Bos., 143
Zeke Bonura, Chi., 138
Moose Solters, St.L., 134
Luke Appling, Chi., 128
Earl Averill, Cle., 126
Joe DiMaggio, N.Y., 125
Goose Goslin, Det., 125
Beau Bell, St.L., 123
Bob Johnson, Phil., 121
Joe Kuhel, Wash., 118
Charlie Gehringer, Det., 116
Al Simmons, Det., 112
Tony Lazzeri, N.Y., 109
Bill Dickey, N.Y., 107
George Selkirk, N.Y., 107
Marv Owen, Det., 105

N.L. 100 RBIs

Joe Medwick, St.L., 138
Mel Ott, N.Y., 135
Gus Suhr, Pit., 118
Chuck Klein, Chi.-Phil.,, 104
Bill Brubaker, Pit., 102
Dolph Camilli, Phil., 102

A.L. 40 homers

Lou Gehrig, N.Y., 49
Hal Trosky, Cle., 42
Jimmie Foxx, Bos., 41

Most Valuable Player

A.L.: Lou Gehrig, 1B, N.Y.
N.L.: Carl Hubbell, P, N.Y.

Hall of Fame additions

Charter Class

Ty Cobb, OF, 1905-28
Walter Johnson, P, 1907-27
Christy Mathewson, P, 1900-16
Babe Ruth, P/OF, 1914-35
Honus Wagner, SS, 1897-1917

ALL-STAR GAME

■ **Winner:** The N.L. recorded its first All-Star victory, thanks to the work of three Cubs — Gabby Hartnett (a run-scoring triple), Augie Galan (a solo home run) and pitcher Lon Warneke.

■ **Key inning:** After the A.L. had cut its deficit to 4-3 in the seventh, Warneke retired Yankee slugger Joe DiMaggio on a line drive with the bases loaded.

■ **Memorable moment:** Galan's fifth-inning blast into the right-field bleachers. It drew a vehement protest from A.L. manager Joe McCarthy, who thought it was foul.

■ **Top guns:** Dizzy Dean (Cardinals), Warneke (Cubs), Galan (Cubs), Hartnett (Cubs), N.L.; Lou Gehrig (Yankees), Luke Appling (White Sox), A.L.

■ **MVP:** Warneke.

Linescore

July 7, at Boston's Braves Field
A.L. ....0 0 0 0 0 0 3 0 0—3 7 1
N.L. ....0 2 0 0 2 0 0 0 x—4 9 0
Grove (Red Sox), Rowe (Tigers) 4, Harder (Indians) 7; D. Dean (Cardinals), Hubbell (Giants) 4, Davis (Cubs) 7, Warneke (Cubs) 7. W—D. Dean. L—Grove. HR—Galan, N.L.; Gehrig, A.L.

WORLD SERIES

■ **Winner:** Renewing an old New York rivalry, the Yankees prevailed in their first Series without Babe Ruth.

■ **Turning point:** Lou Gehrig's two-run Game 4 homer off Giants ace Carl Hubbell propelled the Yankees to a 5-2 victory and a three-games-to-one Series lead.

■ **Memorable moment:** Yankee slugger Tony Lazzeri's Game 2 grand slam, only the second in Series history.

■ **Top guns:** Jake Powell (.455), Gehrig (2 HR, 7 RBIs), Red Rolfe (.400), Yankees; Dick Bartell (.381), Giants.

Linescores

Game 1—September 30, at Polo Grounds
Yankees......................0 0 1 0 0 0 0 0 0—1 7 2
Giants ....0 0 0 0 1 1 0 4 x—6 9 1
Ruffing; Hubbell. W—Hubbell. L—Ruffing. HR—Bartell (NYG); Selkirk (NYY).

Game 2—October 2, at Polo Grounds
Yankees.................2 0 7 0 0 1 2 0 6—18 17 0
Giants ....0 1 0 3 0 0 0 0 0— 4 6 1
Gomez; Schumacher, Smith (3), Coffman (3), Gabler (5), Gumbert (9). W—Gomez. L—Schumacher. HR—Dickey, Lazzeri (NYY).

Game 3—October 3, at Yankee Stadium
Giants ....0 0 0 0 1 0 0 0 0—1 11 0
Yankees...................0 1 0 0 0 0 0 1 x—2 4 0
Fitzsimmons; Hadley, Malone (9). W—Hadley. L—Fitzsimmons. HR—Gehrig (NYY); Ripple (NYG).

Game 4—October 4, at Yankee Stadium
Giants ....0 0 0 1 0 0 0 1 0—2 7 1
Yankees...................0 1 3 0 0 0 0 1 x—5 10 1
Hubbell, Gabler (8); Pearson. W—Pearson. L—Hubbell. HR—Gehrig (NYY).

Game 5—October 5, at Yankee Stadium
Giants ....3 0 0 0 0 1 0 0 0 1—5 8 3
Yankees...............0 1 1 0 0 2 0 0 0 0—4 10 1
Schumacher; Ruffing, Malone (7). W—Schumacher. L—Malone. HR—Selkirk (NYY).

Game 6—October 6, at Polo Grounds
Yankees.................0 2 1 2 0 0 0 1 7—13 17 2
Giants ....2 0 0 0 1 0 1 1 0— 5 9 1
Gomez, Murphy (7); Fitzsimmons, Castleman (4), Coffman (9), Gumbert (9). W—Gomez. L—Fitzsimmons. HR—Moore, Ott (NYG); Powell (NYY).

1937

FINAL STANDINGS

American League

Team	W	L	Pct.	GB
New York	102	52	.662	...
Detroit	89	65	.578	13
Chicago	86	68	.558	16
Cleveland	83	71	.539	19
Boston	80	72	.526	21
Washington	73	80	.477	28.5
Philadelphia	54	97	.358	46.5
St. Louis	46	108	.299	56

National League

Team	W	L	Pct.	GB
New York	95	57	.625	...
Chicago	93	61	.604	3
Pittsburgh	86	68	.558	10
St. Louis	81	73	.526	15
Boston	79	73	.520	16
Brooklyn	62	91	.405	33.5
Philadelphia	61	92	.399	34.5
Cincinnati	56	98	.364	40

SIGNIFICANT EVENTS

■ **May 25:** Detroit player/manager Mickey Cochrane suffered a career-ending skull fracture when he was struck by a pitch from Yankee Bump Hadley.

■ **May 26:** Commissioner Kenesaw Mountain Landis took the All-Star vote away from the fans and decreed that the two managers would select future teams.

MEMORABLE MOMENTS

■ **April 20:** Detroit outfielder Gee Walker carved out his own piece of the Major League record book when he hit a single, double, triple and home run in a season-opening victory over Cleveland—the first player to hit for the cycle on Opening Day.

■ **May 27:** Giants lefty Carl Hubbell, asked to make a rare relief appearance, pitched two scoreless innings and earned a 3-2 victory over the Reds, his record 24th straight over two seasons.

■ **August 31:** Detroit rookie Rudy York hit two home runs against Washington, capping the biggest home run-hitting month in baseball history with 18.

■ **October 3:** Cleveland's Johnny Allen, 15-0 and one win from tying the A.L. record for consecutive victories, dropped a 1-0 final-day decision to Detroit.

■ **October 3:** St. Louis' Joe Medwick captured an N.L. Triple Crown, batting .374, driving in 154 runs and tying New York's Mel Ott with 31 homers.

LEADERS

American League

BA: Charley Gehringer, Det., .371.
Runs: Joe DiMaggio, N.Y., 151.
Hits: Beau Bell, St.L., 218.
TB: Joe DiMaggio, N.Y., 418.
HR: Joe DiMaggio, N.Y., 46.
RBI: Hank Greenberg, Det., 183.
SB: Ben Chapman, Wash.-Bos.; Billy Werber, Phil., 35.
Wins: Lefty Gomez, N.Y., 21.
ERA: Lefty Gomez, N.Y., 2.33.
CG: Wes Ferrell, Wash.-Bos., 26.
IP: Wes Ferrell, Wash.-Bos., 281.
SO: Lefty Gomez, N.Y., 194.

National League

BA: Joe Medwick, St.L., .374.
Runs: Joe Medwick, St.L., 111.
Hits: Joe Medwick, St.L., 237.
TB: Joe Medwick, St.L., 406.
HR: Joe Medwick, St.L.; Mel Ott, N.Y., 31.
RBI: Joe Medwick, St.L., 154.
SB: Augie Galan, Chi., 23.
Wins: Carl Hubbell, N.Y., 22.
ERA: Jim Turner, Bos., 2.38.
CG: Jim Turner, Bos., 24.
IP: Claude Passeau, Phil., 292.1.
SO: Carl Hubbell, N.Y., 159.

A.L. 20-game winners

Lefty Gomez, N.Y., 21-11
Red Ruffing, N.Y., 20-7

N.L. 20-game winners

Carl Hubbell, N.Y., 22-8
Cliff Melton, N.Y., 20-9
Lou Fette, Bos., 20-10
Jim Turner, Bos., 20-11

A.L. 100 RBIs

Hank Greenberg, Det., 183
Joe DiMaggio, N.Y., 167
Lou Gehrig, N.Y., 159
Bill Dickey, N.Y., 133
Hal Trosky, Cle., 128
Jimmie Foxx, Bos., 127
Harlond Clift, St.L., 118
Beau Bell, St.L., 117
Gee Walker, Det., 113
Joe Cronin, Bos., 110
Moose Solters, Cle., 109
Bob Johnson, Phil., 108
Pinky Higgins, Bos., 106
Rudy York, Det., 103
Zeke Bonura, Chi., 100

N.L. 100 RBIs

Joe Medwick, St.L., 154
Frank Demaree, Chi., 115
Johnny Mize, St.L., 113

A.L. 40 homers

Joe DiMaggio, N.Y., 46
Hank Greenberg, Det., 40

Most Valuable Player

A.L.: Charley Gehringer, 2B, Det.
N.L.: Joe Medwick, OF, St.L.

Hall of Fame additions

Morgan Bulkeley, executive
Ban Johnson, executive
Napoleon Lajoie, 2B, 1896-1916
Connie Mack, manager/owner
John McGraw, manager
Tris Speaker, OF, 1907-28
George Wright, player/manager
Cy Young, P, 1890-1911

ALL-STAR GAME

■ **Winner:** Yankees Lou Gehrig, Red Rolfe and Bill Dickey combined for seven RBIs and teammate Lefty Gomez claimed his third All-Star victory as the A.L. won for the fourth time in five years.

■ **Key inning:** The third, when Gehrig blasted a Dizzy Dean pitch for a two-run homer. The Yankee first baseman later added a two-run double.

■ **Memorable moment:** A third-inning Earl Averill line drive that deflected off the foot of Dean. The Cardinals' righthander suffered a broken toe that would begin to unravel his outstanding career.

■ **Top guns:** Gomez (Yankees), Gehrig (Yankees), Rolfe (Yankees), Dickey (Yankees), Charley Gehringer (Tigers), A.L.; Joe Medwick (Cardinals), Billy Herman (Cubs), N.L.

■ **MVP:** Gehrig.

Linescore

July 7, at Washington's Griffith Stadium
N.L. ....0 0 0 1 1 1 0 0—3 13 0
A.L. ....0 0 2 3 1 2 0 0 x—8 13 2
D. Dean (Cardinals), Hubbell (Giants) 4, Blanton (Pirates) 4, Grissom (Reds) 5, Mungo (Dodgers) 6, Walters (Phillies) 8; Gomez (Yankees), Bridges (Tigers) 4, Harder (Indians) 7. W—Gomez. L—D. Dean. HR—Gehrig, A.L.

WORLD SERIES

■ **Winner:** Two in a row. The first of several big Yankee World Series runs began to take shape.

■ **Turning point:** The Yankees' 8-1 pounding of Giants ace Carl Hubbell in Game 1.

■ **Memorable moment:** Yankee pitcher Lefty Gomez, a notoriously poor hitter, driving in the Game 5 winner with a fifth-inning single.

■ **Top guns:** Gomez (2-0, 1.50 ERA), Tony Lazzeri (.400), Yankees; Joe Moore (.391), Giants.

Linescores

Game 1—October 6, at Yankee Stadium
Giants ....0 0 0 0 1 0 0 0 0—1 6 2
Yankees ....0 0 0 0 0 7 0 1 x—8 7 0
Hubbell, Gumbert (6), Coffman (6), Smith (8); Gomez. W—Gomez. L—Hubbell. HR—Lazzeri (NYY).

Game 2—October 7, at Yankee Stadium
Giants ....1 0 0 0 0 0 0 0 0—1 7 0
Yankees ....0 0 0 0 2 4 2 0 x—8 12 0
Melton, Gumbert (5), Coffman (6); Ruffing. W—Ruffing. L—Melton.

Game 3—October 8, at Polo Grounds
Yankees ....0 1 2 1 1 0 0 0 0—5 9 0
Giants ....0 0 0 0 0 0 1 0 0—1 5 4
Pearson, Murphy (9); Schumacher, Melton (7), Brennan (9). W—Pearson. L—Schumacher.

Game 4—October 9, at Polo Grounds
Yankees ....1 0 1 0 0 0 0 0 1—3 6 0
Giants ....0 6 0 0 0 0 1 0 x—7 12 3
Hadley, Andrews (2), Wicker (8); Hubbell. W—Hubbell. L—Hadley. HR—Gehrig (NYY).

Game 5—October 10, at Polo Grounds
Yankees ....0 1 1 0 2 0 0 0 0—4 8 0
Giants ....0 0 2 0 0 0 0 0 0—2 10 0
Gomez; Melton, Smith (6), Brennan (8). W—Gomez. L—Melton. HR—DiMaggio, Hoag (NYY); Ott (NYG).

1938

FINAL STANDINGS

American League

Team	W	L	Pct.	GB
New York	99	53	.651	...
Boston	88	61	.591	9.5
Cleveland	86	66	.566	13
Detroit	84	70	.545	16
Washington	75	76	.497	23.5
Chicago	65	83	.439	32
St. Louis	55	97	.362	44
Philadelphia	53	99	.349	46

National League

Team	W	L	Pct.	GB
Chicago	89	63	.586	...
Pittsburgh	86	64	.573	2
New York	83	67	.553	5
Cincinnati	82	68	.547	6
Boston	77	75	.507	12
St. Louis	71	80	.470	17.5
Brooklyn	69	80	.463	18.5
Philadelphia	45	105	.300	43

SIGNIFICANT EVENTS

■ **April 16:** The Cardinals sent shockwaves through baseball when they traded ace Dizzy Dean to the Cubs for two pitchers and an outfielder.

■ **May 31:** Yankee Lou Gehrig stretched his ironman streak to an incredible 2,000 games during a victory over Boston.

■ **December 14:** The N.L. granted Cincinnati, baseball's first professional team, permission to play its traditional season opener.

MEMORABLE MOMENTS

■ **June 15:** Cincinnati's Johnny Vander Meer pitched his record second consecutive no-hitter, a 6-0 victory that stole the spotlight from the Dodgers in the first night game at Brooklyn's Ebbets Field.

■ **June 21:** Boston third baseman Pinky Higgins etched his name in the record books when he collected 12 consecutive hits over a two-day, four-game stretch against Chicago and Detroit.

■ **September 28:** Moments away from a suspended game, Chicago catcher Gabby Hartnett stroked a ninth-inning homer into the thickening darkness of Wrigley Field, giving the Cubs a crucial 6-5 victory over Pittsburgh and half-game lead in the tense N.L. pennant race.

■ **October 2:** Cleveland's Bob Feller struck out a Major League-record 18 batters while losing a 4-1 decision to the Tigers.

LEADERS

American League

BA: Jimmie Foxx, Bos., .349.
Runs: Hank Greenberg, Det., 144.
Hits: Joe Vosmik, Bos., 201.
TB: Jimmie Foxx, Bos., 398.
HR: Hank Greenberg, Det., 58.
RBI: Jimmie Foxx, Bos., 175.
SB: Frank Crosetti, N.Y., 27.
Wins: Red Ruffing, N.Y., 21.
ERA: Lefty Grove, Bos., 3.08.
CG: Bobo Newsom, St.L., 31.
IP: Bobo Newsom, St.L., 329.2.
SO: Bob Feller, Cle., 240.

National League

BA: Ernie Lombardi, Cin., .342.
Runs: Mel Ott, N.Y., 116.
Hits: Frank McCormick, Cin., 209.
TB: Johnny Mize, St.L., 326.
HR: Mel Ott, N.Y., 36.
RBI: Joe Medwick, St.L., 122.
SB: Stan Hack, Chi., 16.
Wins: Bill Lee, Chi., 22.
ERA: Bill Lee, Chi., 2.66.
CG: Paul Derringer, Cin., 26.
IP: Paul Derringer, Cin., 307.
SO: Clay Bryant, Chi., 135.

A.L. 20-game winners

Red Ruffing, N.Y., 21-7
Bobo Newsom, St.L., 20-16

N.L. 20-game winners

Bill Lee, Chi., 22-9
Paul Derringer, Cin., 21-14

A.L. 100 RBIs

Jimmie Foxx, Bos., 175
Hank Greenberg, Det., 146
Joe DiMaggio, N.Y., 140
Rudy York, Det., 127
Harlond Clift, St.L., 118
Bill Dickey, N.Y., 115
Zeke Bonura, Wash., 114
Lou Gehrig, N.Y., 114
Bob Johnson, Phil., 113
Ken Keltner, Cle., 113
Jeff Heath, Cle., 112
Hal Trosky, Cle., 110
Charlie Gehringer, Det., 107
Pinky Higgins, Bos., 106

N.L. 100 RBIs

Joe Medwick, St.L., 122
Mel Ott, N.Y., 116
Johnny Rizzo, Pit., 111
Frank McCormick, Cin., 106
Johnny Mize, St.L., 102
Dolph Camilli, Brk., 100

A.L. 40 homers

Hank Greenberg, Det., 58
Jimmie Foxx, Bos., 50

Most Valuable Player

A.L.: Jimmie Foxx, 1B, Bos.
N.L.: Ernie Lombardi, C, Cin.

Hall of Fame additions

Grover Alexander, P, 1911-30
Alexander Cartwright, executive
Henry Chadwick, historian, executive

ALL-STAR GAME

■ **Winner:** Cincinnati's Johnny Vander Meer, Chicago's Bill Lee and Pittsburgh's Mace Brown held the A.L. to seven hits as the N.L. claimed its second All-Star victory.

■ **Key inning:** The first, when the N.L. took a lead it never surrendered on Red Sox shortstop Joe Cronin's error.

■ **Memorable moment:** A seventh-inning sacrifice bunt by Brooklyn's Leo Durocher that resulted in two N.L. runs. Durocher circled the bases when third baseman Jimmie Foxx and right fielder Joe DiMaggio made wild throws on the play.

■ **Top guns:** Vander Meer (Reds), Lee (Cubs), Ernie Lombardi (Reds), N.L.; Cronin (Red Sox), A.L.

■ **MVP:** Vander Meer.

Linescore

July 6, at Cincinnati's Crosley Field
A.L. ....0 0 0 0 0 0 0 0 1—1 7 4
N.L. ....1 0 0 1 0 0 2 0 x—4 8 0
Gomez (Yankees), Allen (Indians) 4, Grove (Red Sox) 7; Vander Meer (Reds), Lee (Cubs) 4, Brown (Pirates) 7. W—Vander Meer. L—Gomez.

WORLD SERIES

■ **Winner:** Three in a row. Another Series first for the vaunted Yankee machine of Joe McCarthy.

■ **Turning point:** Light-hitting Frankie Crosetti hit an eighth-inning Game 2 homer, helping the Yankees rally to a 6-3 victory over Chicago veteran Dizzy Dean.

■ **Memorable moment:** Lou Gehrig's fourth-game single — his last hit in World Series competition.

■ **Top guns:** Red Ruffing (2-0, 1.50 ERA), Bill Dickey (.400), Joe Gordon (.400, 6 RBIs), Crosetti (6 RBIs), Yankees; Stan Hack (.471), Cubs.

Linescores

Game 1—October 5, at Chicago
New York ....0 2 0 0 0 0 1 0 0—3 12 1
Chicago ....0 0 1 0 0 0 0 0 0—1 9 1
Ruffing; Lee, Russell (9). W—Ruffing. L—Lee.

Game 2—October 6, at Chicago
New York ....0 2 0 0 0 0 0 2 2—6 7 2
Chicago ....1 0 2 0 0 0 0 0 0—3 11 0
Gomez, Murphy (8); Dean, French (9). W—Gomez. L—Dean. HR—Crosetti, DiMaggio (N.Y.).

Game 3—October 8, at New York
Chicago ....0 0 0 0 1 0 0 1 0—2 5 1
New York ....0 0 0 0 2 2 0 1 x—5 7 2
Bryant, Russell (6), French (7); Pearson. W—Pearson. L—Bryant. HR—Dickey, Gordon (N.Y.); Marty (Chi.).

Game 4—October 9, at New York
Chicago ....0 0 0 1 0 0 0 2 0—3 8 1
New York ....0 3 0 0 0 1 0 4 x—8 11 1
Lee, Root (4), Page (7), French (8), Carleton (8), Dean (8); Ruffing. W—Ruffing. L—Lee. HR—Henrich (N.Y.); O'Dea (Chi.).

1939

FINAL STANDINGS

American League

Team	W	L	Pct.	GB
New York	106	45	.702	...
Boston	89	62	.589	17
Cleveland	87	67	.565	20.5
Chicago	85	69	.552	22.5
Detroit	81	73	.526	26.5
Washington	65	87	.428	41.5
Philadelphia	55	97	.362	51.5
St. Louis	43	111	.279	64.5

National League

Team	W	L	Pct.	GB
Cincinnati	97	57	.630	...
St. Louis	92	61	.601	4.5
Brooklyn	84	69	.549	12.5
Chicago	84	70	.545	13
New York	77	74	.510	18.5
Pittsburgh	68	85	.444	28.5
Boston	63	88	.417	32.5
Philadelphia	45	106	.298	50.5

SIGNIFICANT EVENTS

■ **June 12:** Baseball dignitaries, gathering in Cooperstown, N.Y., for a centennial celebration, dedicated the sport's new Hall of Fame museum and inducted its first four classes of Hall of Famers.

■ **August 26:** Red Barber handled the play-by-play as experimental station W2XBS presented Major League baseball's first telecast, a game between the Dodgers and Reds at Ebbets Field.

MEMORABLE MOMENTS

■ **May 16:** The visiting Indians recorded a 10-inning 8-3 victory in the A.L.'s first night game at Philadelphia's Shibe Park.

■ **June 27:** Brooklyn and Boston battled for 23 innings and more than five hours before settling for a 2-2 tie in a marathon game at Braves Field.

■ **June 28:** The New York Yankees rocketed a doubleheader-record 13 home runs out of Shibe Park in a 23-2 and 10-0 sweep of the Athletics.

■ **July 4:** Lou Gehrig, forced to end his incredible ironman streak at 2,130 games and retire because of a life-threatening disease, was honored in an emotional farewell at Yankee Stadium.

■ **July 4:** Boston's Jim Tabor tied a Major League record with two grand slams during an 18-12 victory over the Athletics.

LEADERS

American League

BA: Joe DiMaggio, N.Y., .381.
Runs: Red Rolfe, N.Y., 139.
Hits: Red Rolfe, N.Y., 213.
TB: Ted Williams, Bos., 344.
HR: Jimmie Foxx, Bos., 35.
RBI: Ted Williams, Bos., 145.
SB: George Case, Wash., 51.
Wins: Bob Feller, Cle., 24.
ERA: Lefty Grove, Bos., 2.54.
CG: Bob Feller, Cle.; Bobo Newsom, St.L.-Det., 24.
IP: Bob Feller, Cle., 296.2.
SO: Bob Feller, Cle., 246.

National League

BA: Johnny Mize, St.L., .349.
Runs: Billy Werber, Cin., 115.
Hits: Frank McCormick, Cin., 209.
TB: Johnny Mize, St.L., 353.
HR: Johnny Mize, St.L., 28.
RBI: Frank McCormick, Cin., 128.
SB: Stan Hack, Chi.; Lee Handley, Pit., 17.
Wins: Bucky Walters, Cin., 27.
ERA: Bucky Walters, Cin., 2.29.
CG: Bucky Walters, Cin., 31.
IP: Bucky Walters, Cin., 319.
SO: Claude Passeau, Phil.-Chi.; Bucky Walters, Cin., 137.

A.L. 20-game winners
Bob Feller, Cle., 24-9
Red Ruffing, N.Y., 21-7
Dutch Leonard, Wash., 20-8
Bobo Newsom, St.L.-Det., 20-11

N.L. 20-game winners
Bucky Walters, Cin., 27-11
Paul Derringer, Cin., 25-7
Curt Davis, St.L., 22-16
Luke Hamlin, Brk., 20-13

A.L. 100 RBIs
Ted Williams, Bos., 145
Joe DiMaggio, N.Y., 126
Bob Johnson, Phil., 114
Hank Greenberg, Det., 112
Joe Gordon, N.Y., 111
Gee Walker, Chi., 111
Joe Cronin, Bos., 107
Bill Dickey, N.Y., 105
Jimmie Foxx, Bos., 105
Hal Trosky, Cle., 104
George Selkirk, N.Y., 101

N.L. 100 RBIs
Frank McCormick, Cin., 128
Joe Medwick, St.L., 117
Johnny Mize, St.L., 108
Dolph Camilli, Brk., 104

Most Valuable Player
A.L.: Joe DiMaggio, OF, N.Y.
N.L.: Bucky Walters, P, Cin.

Hall of Fame additions
Cap Anson, 1B, 1876-97
Eddie Collins, 2B, 1906-30
Charles Comiskey, manager/exec.
Candy Cummings, P, 1872-77
Buck Ewing, C, 1880-97
Lou Gehrig, 1B, 1923-39
Willie Keeler, OF, 1892-1910
Hoss Radbourn, P, 1880-91
George Sisler, 1B, 1915-30
Al Spalding, pitcher/executive

ALL-STAR GAME

■ **Winner:** The A.L.'s Yankee-studded lineup posted a ho-hum 3-1 victory before 62,892 fans at Yankee Stadium.

■ **Key inning:** The sixth, when the N.L. loaded the bases with one out. Indians fireballer Bob Feller was summoned and got Pittsburgh's Arky Vaughan to hit into a first-pitch double play. Feller allowed one hit the rest of the way.

■ **Memorable moment:** Joe DiMaggio's fifth-inning home run, which touched off a celebration among ecstatic Yankee fans.

■ **Top guns:** Tommy Bridges (Tigers), Feller (Indians), George Selkirk (Yankees), DiMaggio (Yankees), A.L.; Paul Derringer (Reds), Lonny Frey (Reds), N.L.

■ **MVP:** Feller.

Linescore

July 11, at New York's Yankee Stadium
N.L. ....0 0 1 0 0 0 0 0 0 — 1 7 1
A.L. ....0 0 0 2 1 0 0 0 x — 3 6 1
Derringer (Reds), Lee (Cubs) 4, Fette (Braves) 7; Ruffing (Yankees), Bridges (Tigers) 4, Feller (Indians) 6. W—Bridges. L—Lee. HR—DiMaggio, A.L.

WORLD SERIES

■ **Winner:** Four in a row. The Yankees recorded their second straight sweep and 13th victory in 14 Series games.

■ **Turning point:** Bill Dickey's ninth-inning single gave New York a 2-1 victory in Game 1 and momentum the Reds could not stop.

■ **Memorable moment:** A strange Game 4 play that helped produce three 10th-inning Yankee runs. Joe DiMaggio singled to right with two runners aboard and circled the bases when Reds catcher Ernie Lombardi lay dazed after a home-plate collision with Yankee runner Charlie Keller. "Lombardi's Snooze."

■ **Top guns:** Keller (.438, 3 HR, 6 RBIs), Dickey (2 HR, 5 RBIs), Yankees; Frank McCormick (.400), Reds.

Linescores

Game 1—October 4, at New York
Cincinnati 0 0 0 1 0 0 0 0 0 — 1 4 0
New York 0 0 0 0 1 0 0 0 1 — 2 6 0
Derringer; Ruffing. W—Ruffing. L—Derringer.

Game 2—October 5, at New York
Cincinnati 0 0 0 0 0 0 0 0 0 — 0 2 0
New York 0 0 3 1 0 0 0 0 x — 4 9 0
Walters; Pearson. W—Pearson. L—Walters. HR—Dahlgren (N.Y.).

Game 3—October 7, at Cincinnati
New York 2 0 2 0 3 0 0 0 0 — 7 5 1
Cincinnati 1 2 0 0 0 0 0 0 0 — 3 10 0
Gomez, Hadley (2); Thompson, Grissom (5), Moore (7). W—Hadley. L—Thompson. HR—Keller 2, DiMaggio, Dickey (N.Y.).

Game 4—October 8, at Cincinnati
New York 0 0 0 0 0 0 2 0 2 3—7 7 1
Cincinnati 0 0 0 0 0 0 3 1 0 0—4 11 4
Hildebrand, Sundra (5), Murphy (7); Derringer, Walters (8). W—Murphy. L—Walters. HR—Keller, Dickey (N.Y.).

1940

FINAL STANDINGS

American League

Team	W	L	Pct.	GB
Detroit	90	64	.584	...
Cleveland	89	65	.578	1
New York	88	66	.571	2
Boston	82	72	.532	8
Chicago	82	72	.532	8
St. Louis	67	87	.435	23
Washington	64	90	.416	26
Philadelphia	54	100	.351	36

National League

Team	W	L	Pct.	GB
Cincinnati	100	53	.654	...
Brooklyn	88	65	.575	12
St. Louis	84	69	.549	16
Pittsburgh	78	76	.506	22.5
Chicago	75	79	.487	25.5
New York	72	80	.474	27.5
Boston	65	87	.428	34.5
Philadelphia	50	103	.327	50

SIGNIFICANT EVENTS

■ **January 14:** In the biggest free-agency ruling ever handed down, Commissioner Kenesaw Mountain Landis freed 91 members of the Tigers organization, citing player-movement coverup.

■ **May 7:** The Dodgers became the first N.L. team to travel by air, flying in two planes from St. Louis to Chicago.

■ **May 24, June 4:** The first night games were played at New York's Polo Grounds, St. Louis' Sportsman's Park and Pittsburgh's Forbes Field.

■ **August 3:** Reds catcher Willard Hershberger, despondent over what he considered inadequate play, committed suicide in his Boston hotel room.

MEMORABLE MOMENTS

■ **April 16:** Cleveland's Bob Feller fired the first Opening Day no-hitter in baseball history, beating the White Sox, 1-0, at Chicago's Comiskey Park.

■ **September 24:** Jimmie Foxx became baseball's second 500-homer man when he hit one of Boston's four sixth-inning blasts in a 16-8 victory over the Athletics.

■ **September 27:** Detroit rookie Floyd Giebell ignored near-riotous Cleveland fans and outpitched Bob Feller in an A.L. pennant-clinching 2-0 Tigers victory.

LEADERS

American League

BA: Joe DiMaggio, N.Y., .352.
Runs: Ted Williams, Bos., 134.
Hits: Doc Cramer, Bos.; Barney McCosky, Det.; Rip Radcliff, St.L., 200.
TB: Hank Greenberg, Det., 384.
HR: Hank Greenberg, Det., 41.
RBI: Hank Greenberg, Det., 150.
SB: George Case, Wash., 35.
Wins: Bob Feller, Cle., 27.
ERA: Bob Feller, Cle., 2.61.
CG: Bob Feller, Cle., 31.
IP: Bob Feller, Cle., 320.1.
SO: Bob Feller, Cle., 261.

National League

BA: Debs Garms, Pit., .355.
Runs: Arky Vaughan, Pit., 113.
Hits: Stan Hack, Chi.; Frank McCormick, Cin., 191.
TB: Johnny Mize, St.L., 368.
HR: Johnny Mize, St.L., 43.
RBI: Johnny Mize, St.L., 137.
SB: Lonny Frey, Cin., 22.
Wins: Bucky Walters, Cin., 22.
ERA: Bucky Walters, Cin., 2.48.
CG: Bucky Walters, Cin., 29.
IP: Bucky Walters, Cin., 305.
SO: Kirby Higbe, Phil., 137.

A.L. 20-game winners
Bob Feller, Cle., 27-11
Bobo Newsom, Det., 21-5

N.L. 20-game winners
Bucky Walters, Cin., 22-10
Paul Derringer, Cin., 20-12
Claude Passeau, Chi., 20-13

A.L. 100 RBIs
Hank Greenberg, Det., 150
Rudy York, Det., 134
Joe DiMaggio, N.Y., 133
Jimmie Foxx, Bos., 119
Ted Williams, Bos., 113
Joe Cronin, Bos, 111
Bobby Doerr, Bos., 105
Joe Gordon, N.Y., 103
Bob Johnson, Phil., 103
Lou Boudreau, Cle., 101

N.L. 100 RBIs
Johnny Mize, St.L., 137
Frank McCormick, Cin., 127
Maurice Van Robays, Pit., 116
Elbie Fletcher, Pit., 104
Babe Young, N.Y., 101

A.L. 40 homers
Hank Greenberg, Det., 41

N.L. 40 homers
Johnny Mize, St.L., 43

Most Valuable Player
A.L.: Hank Greenberg, OF, Det.
N.L.: Frank McCormick, 1B, Cin.

ALL-STAR GAME

■ **Winner:** Five N.L. pitchers shut down the A.L. on three hits and recorded the first shutout in All-Star Game history.

■ **Key inning:** The first, when Boston's Max West connected with a Red Ruffing delivery for a three-run homer.

■ **Memorable moment:** An inning after his home run, West crashed into the outfield wall while chasing a fly ball and had to be helped off the field.

■ **Top guns:** Paul Derringer (Reds), Bucky Walters (Reds), Whitlow Wyatt (Dodgers), Larry French (Cubs), Carl Hubbell (Giants), West (Braves), Billy Herman (Cubs), N.L.; Luke Appling (White Sox), A.L.

■ **MVP:** West.

Linescore

July 9, at St. Louis' Sportsman's Park
A.L. ....0 0 0 0 0 0 0 0 0—0 3 1
N.L. ....3 0 0 0 0 0 0 1 x—4 7 0
Ruffing (Yankees), Newsom (Tigers) 4, Feller (Indians) 7; Derringer (Reds), Walters (Reds) 3, Wyatt (Dodgers) 5, French (Cubs) 7, Hubbell (Giants) 9. W—Derringer. L—Ruffing. HR—West, N.L.

WORLD SERIES

■ **Winner:** The Reds needed seven games to dispatch the Tigers and capture their first non-tainted World Series.

■ **Turning point:** The Reds' Game 6 victory in which Bucky Walters pitched a 4-0 shutout and also hit a home run.

■ **Memorable moment:** Reds pitcher Paul Derringer retiring Detroit in order in a tense ninth inning of Game 7.

■ **Top guns:** Walters (2-0, 1.50 ERA), Jimmy Ripple (.333, 6 RBIs), Reds; Hank Greenberg (.357, 6 RBIs), Pinky Higgins (.333, 6 RBIs), Tigers.

Linescores

Game 1—October 2, at Cincinnati
Detroit ....0 5 0 0 2 0 0 0 0—7 10 1
Cincinnati.................0 0 0 1 0 0 0 1 0—2 8 3
Newsom; Derringer, Moore (2), Riddle (9). W—Newsom. L—Derringer. HR—Campbell (Det.).

Game 2—October 3, at Cincinnati
Detroit ....2 0 0 0 0 1 0 0 0—3 3 1
Cincinnati.................0 2 2 1 0 0 0 0 x—5 9 0
Rowe, Gorsica (4); Walters. W—Walters. L—Rowe. HR—Ripple (Cin.).

Game 3—October 4, at Detroit
Cincinnati.................1 0 0 0 0 0 0 1 2—4 10 1
Detroit ....0 0 0 1 0 0 4 2 x—7 13 1
Turner, Moore (7), Beggs (8); Bridges. W—Bridges. L—Turner. HR—York, Higgins (Det.).

Game 4—October 5, at Detroit
Cincinnati.................2 0 1 1 0 0 0 1 0—5 11 1
Detroit ....0 0 1 0 0 1 0 0 0—2 5 1
Derringer; Trout, Smith (3), McKain (7). W—Derringer. L—Trout.

Game 5—October 6, at Detroit
Cincinnati.................0 0 0 0 0 0 0 0 0—0 3 0
Detroit ....0 0 3 4 0 0 0 1 x—8 13 0
Thompson, Moore (4), Vander Meer (5), Hutchings (8); Newsom. W—Newsom. L—Thompson. HR—Greenberg (Det.).

Game 6—October 7, at Cincinnati
Detroit ....0 0 0 0 0 0 0 0 0—0 5 0
Cincinnati.................2 0 0 0 0 1 0 1 x—4 10 2
Rowe, Gorsica (1), Hutchinson (8); Walters. W—Walters. L—Rowe. HR—Walters (Cin.).

Game 7—October 8, at Cincinnati
Detroit ....0 0 1 0 0 0 0 0 0—1 7 0
Cincinnati.................0 0 0 0 0 0 2 0 x—2 7 1
Newsom; Derringer. W—Derringer. L—Newsom.

HISTORY

1941

FINAL STANDINGS

American League

Team	W	L	Pct.	GB
New York	101	53	.656	...
Boston	84	70	.545	17
Chicago	77	77	.500	24
Cleveland	75	79	.487	26
Detroit	75	79	.487	26
St. Louis	70	84	.455	31
Washington	70	84	.455	31
Philadelphia	64	90	.416	37

National League

Team	W	L	Pct.	GB
Brooklyn	100	54	.649	...
St. Louis	97	56	.634	2.5
Cincinnati	88	66	.571	12
Pittsburgh	81	73	.526	19
New York	74	79	.484	25.5
Chicago	70	84	.455	30
Boston	62	92	.403	38
Philadelphia	43	111	.279	57

SIGNIFICANT EVENTS

■ **May 1:** Dodgers President Larry MacPhail submitted a patent application on the "Brooklyn Safety Cap," a hat lined with plastic to protect players from bean balls.

■ **May 7:** Detroit slugger Hank Greenberg reported for duty in the U.S. Army—one of many Major Leaguers who would leave baseball to fight in World War II.

■ **June 2:** Former Yankee great Lou Gehrig died at age 37 from the incurable disease that had forced his retirement two years earlier.

■ **May 28:** The Senators dropped a 6-5 decision to the Yankees in the first night game at Washington's Griffith Stadium.

MEMORABLE MOMENTS

■ **July 17:** Yankee center fielder Joe DiMaggio's record 56-game hitting streak was stopped by pitchers Al Smith and Jim Bagby Jr. at Cleveland Stadium.

■ **July 25:** Boston's Lefty Grove joined the 300-victory club when he staggered to a 10-6 victory over Cleveland at Fenway Park.

■ **September 4:** The Yankees recorded the earliest pennant-clinching date in history when they defeated Boston, 6-3.

■ **November 27:** Yankee Joe DiMaggio won the A.L. MVP by a slim 37-point margin over Boston's Ted Williams, baseball's first .400 hitter (.406) since 1930.

LEADERS

American League

BA: Ted Williams, Bos., .406.
Runs: Ted Williams, Bos., 135.
Hits: Cecil Travis, Wash., 218.
TB: Joe DiMaggio, N.Y., 348.
HR: Ted Williams, Bos., 37.
RBI: Joe DiMaggio, N.Y., 125.
SB: George Case, Wash., 33.
Wins: Bob Feller, Cle., 25.
ERA: Thornton Lee, Chi., 2.37.
CG: Thornton Lee, Chi., 30.
IP: Bob Feller, Cle., 343.
SO: Bob Feller, Cle., 260.

National League

BA: Pete Reiser, Brk., .343.
Runs: Pete Reiser, Brk., 117.
Hits: Stan Hack, Chi., 186.
TB: Pete Reiser, Brk., 299.
HR: Dolph Camilli, Brk., 34.
RBI: Dolph Camilli, Brk., 120.
SB: Danny Murtaugh, Phil., 18.
Wins: Kirby Higbe, Brk.; Whitlow Wyatt, Brk., 22.
ERA: Elmer Riddle, Cin., 2.24.
CG: Bucky Walters, Cin., 27.
IP: Bucky Walters, Cin., 302.
SO: Johnny Vander Meer, Cin., 202.

A.L. 20-game winners
Bob Feller, Cle., 25-13
Thornton Lee, Chi., 22-11

N.L. 20-game winners
Kirby Higbe, Brk., 22-9
Whitlow Wyatt, Brk., 22-10

A.L. 100 RBIs
Joe DiMaggio, N.Y., 125
Jeff Heath, Cle., 123
Charlie Keller, N.Y., 122
Ted Williams, Bos., 120
Rudy York, Det., 111
Bob Johnson, Phil., 107
Sam Chapman, Phil., 106
Jimmie Foxx, Bos., 105
Jim Tabor, Bos., 101
Cecil Travis, Wash., 101

N.L. 100 RBIs
Dolph Camilli, Brk., 120
Babe Young, N.Y., 104
Vince DiMaggio, Pit., 100
Johnny Mize, St.L., 100

Most Valuable Player
A.L.: Joe DiMaggio, OF, N.Y.
N.L.: Dolf Camilli, 1B, Brk.

ALL-STAR GAME

■ **Winner:** The A.L. scored four ninth-inning runs and overcame a pair of home runs by Pittsburgh's Arky Vaughan for a 7-5 victory in the most exciting All-Star Game in the classic's nine-year history.

■ **Key inning:** The ninth, when the A.L. overcame a 5-3 deficit to claim its sixth victory in nine All-Star Games.

■ **Memorable moment:** A dramatic game-ending, three-run homer by Boston slugger Ted Williams with two out in the ninth. Williams connected off Chicago's Claude Passeau after the N.L. had botched what could have been a game-ending double play.

■ **Top guns:** Bob Feller (Indians), Williams (Red Sox), Lou Boudreau (Indians), A.L.; Vaughan (Pirates), N.L.

■ **MVP:** Williams.

Linescore

July 8, at Detroit's Briggs Stadium
N.L. ....0 0 0 0 0 1 2 2 0—5 10 2
A.L. ....0 0 0 1 0 1 0 1 4—7 11 3
Wyatt (Dodgers), Derringer (Reds) 3, Walters (Reds) 5, Passeau (Cubs) 7; Feller (Indians), Lee (White Sox) 4, Hudson (Senators) 7, Smith (White Sox) 8. W—Smith. L—Passeau. HR—Vaughan 2, N.L.; Williams, A.L.

WORLD SERIES

■ **Winner:** The Yankees returned to the top and won the first of many memorable meetings with the Dodgers.

■ **Turning point:** A two-out, ninth-inning passed ball by Dodgers catcher Mickey Owen that could have finished off a 4-3 Brooklyn victory in Game 4. Given new life, the Yanks scored four times and took a three-games-to-one Series lead.

■ **Memorable moment:** Owen's passed ball.

■ **Top guns:** Joe Gordon (.500, 5 RBIs), Charlie Keller (.389, 5 RBIs), Yankees.

Linescores

Game 1—October 1, at New York
Brooklyn ....0 0 0 0 1 0 1 0 0—2 6 0
New York....................0 1 0 1 0 1 0 0 x—3 6 1
Davis, Casey (6), Allen (7); Ruffing. W—Ruffing. L—Davis. HR—Gordon (N.Y.).

Game 2—October 2, at New York
Brooklyn ....0 0 0 0 2 1 0 0 0—3 6 2
New York....................0 1 1 0 0 0 0 0 0—2 9 1
Wyatt; Chandler, Murphy (6). W—Wyatt. L—Chandler.

Game 3—October 4, at Brooklyn
New York....................0 0 0 0 0 0 0 2 0—2 8 0
Brooklyn ....0 0 0 0 0 0 0 1 0—1 4 0
Russo; Fitzsimmons, Casey (8), French (8), Allen (9). W—Russo. L—Casey.

Game 4—October 5, at Brooklyn
New York..................1 0 0 2 0 0 0 0 4—7 12 0
Brooklyn ....0 0 0 2 2 0 0 0 0—4 9 1
Donald, Breuer (5), Murphy (8); Higbe, French (4), Allen (5), Casey (5). W—Murphy. L—Casey. HR—Reiser (Brk.).

Game 5—October 6, at Brooklyn
New York....................0 2 0 0 1 0 0 0 0—3 6 0
Brooklyn ....0 0 1 0 0 0 0 0 0—1 4 1
Bonham; Wyatt. W—Bonham. L—Wyatt. HR—Henrich (N.Y.).

1942

FINAL STANDINGS

American League

Team	W	L	Pct.	GB
New York	103	51	.669	...
Boston	93	59	.612	9
St. Louis	82	69	.543	19.5
Cleveland	75	79	.487	28
Detroit	73	81	.474	30
Chicago	66	82	.446	34
Washington	62	89	.411	39.5
Philadelphia	55	99	.357	48

National League

Team	W	L	Pct.	GB
St. Louis	106	48	.688	...
Brooklyn	104	50	.675	2
New York	85	67	.559	20
Cincinnati	76	76	.500	29
Pittsburgh	66	81	.449	36.5
Chicago	68	86	.442	38
Boston	59	89	.399	44
Philadelphia	42	109	.278	62.5

SIGNIFICANT EVENTS

■ **January 6:** Cleveland ace Bob Feller became the second high-profile star to leave baseball for the armed services when he enlisted in the Navy and reported for duty.

■ **January 16:** U.S. President Franklin D. Roosevelt gave baseball the "green light" to continue wartime play as a needed diversion for hard-working Americans.

■ **February 3:** In response to President Roosevelt's request for more night games, baseball owners softened restrictions and more than doubled the nocturnal schedule.

■ **October 29:** Cardinals Vice-President Branch Rickey resigned to become president of the Dodgers.

■ **November 4:** Yankee second baseman Joe Gordon edged out Boston Triple Crown winner Ted Williams by 21 votes for A.L. MVP.

MEMORABLE MOMENTS

■ **June 19:** Boston's Paul Waner became baseball's seventh 3,000-hit man when he singled off Pittsburgh's Rip Sewell.

■ **July 7:** One day after defeating the N.L. in the annual All-Star Game, the A.L. beat Mickey Cochrane's Armed Service All-Stars, 5-0, in a game to raise money for the war effort.

■ **September 27:** The Cardinals recorded a final-day sweep of the Cubs and finished with 106 victories, two more than the Dodgers in an amazing N.L. pennant battle.

LEADERS

American League

BA: Ted Williams, Bos., .356.
Runs: Ted Williams, Bos., 141.
Hits: Johnny Pesky, Bos., 205.
TB: Ted Williams, Bos., 338.
HR: Ted Williams, Bos., 36.
RBI: Ted Williams, Bos., 137.
SB: George Case, Wash., 44.
Wins: Tex Hughson, Bos., 22.
ERA: Ted Lyons, Chi., 2.10.
CG: Tiny Bonham, N.Y.; Tex Hughson, Bos., 22.
IP: Tex Hughson, Bos., 281.
SO: Tex Hughson, Bos.;
Bobo Newsom, Wash., 113.

National League

BA: Ernie Lombardi, Cin., .330.
Runs: Mel Ott, N.Y., 118.
Hits: Enos Slaughter, St.L., 188.
TB: Enos Slaughter, St.L., 292.
HR: Mel Ott, N.Y., 30.
RBI: Johnny Mize, N.Y., 110.
SB: Pete Reiser, Brk., 20.
Wins: Mort Cooper, St.L., 22.
ERA: Mort Cooper, St.L., 1.78.
CG: Jim Tobin, Bos., 28.
IP: Jim Tobin, Bos., 287.2.
SO: Johnny Vander Meer, Cin., 186.

A.L. 20-game winners
Tex Hughson, Bos., 22-6
Tiny Bonham, N.Y., 21-5

N.L. 20-game winners
Mort Cooper, St.L., 22-7
Johnny Beazley, St.L., 21-6

A.L. 100 RBIs
Ted Williams, Bos., 137
Joe DiMaggio, N.Y., 114
Charlie Keller, N.Y., 108
Joe Gordon, N.Y., 103
Bobby Doerr, Bos., 102

N.L. 100 RBIs
Johnny Mize, N.Y., 110
Dolph Camilli, Brk., 109

Most Valuable Player
A.L.: Joe Gordon, 2B, N.Y.
N.L.: Mort Cooper, P, St.L.

Hall of Fame addition
Rogers Hornsby, 2B, 1915-37

ALL-STAR GAME

■ **Winner:** Spud Chandler and Al Benton combined on a six-hitter and the A.L. made it 7 for 10 with a rainy-day victory in an All-Star Game played with war-depleted rosters.

■ **Key inning:** The first, when the A.L. scored all of its runs, one coming on a leadoff home run by Cleveland's Lou Boudreau.

■ **Memorable moment:** After New York's Tommy Henrich had followed Boudreau's home run with a double, Detroit slugger Rudy York lined an opposite-field shot that settled into the right-field bleachers for a two-run homer.

■ **Top guns:** Chandler (Yankees), Benton (Tigers), Boudreau (Indians), York (Tigers), A.L.; Johnny Vander Meer (Reds), Mickey Owen (Dodgers), N.L.

■ **MVP:** York.

Linescore

July 7, at New York's Polo Grounds
A.L. ....3 0 0 0 0 0 0 0 0—3 7 0
N.L. ....0 0 0 0 0 0 0 1 0—1 6 1
Chandler (Yankees), Benton (Tigers) 5; M. Cooper (Cardinals), Vander Meer (Reds) 4, Passeau (Cubs) 7, Walters (Reds) 9. W—Chandler. L—M. Cooper. HR—Boudreau, York, A.L.; Owen, N.L.

WORLD SERIES

■ **Winner:** After losing the opener, the Cardinals tamed the powerful Yankees with four consecutive victories.

■ **Turning point:** The ninth inning of Game 1. Although the Cardinals' four-run rally fell short in a 7-4 Yankee victory, they delivered a message that would become more clear as the Series progressed.

■ **Memorable moment:** A two-run, ninth-inning home run by Whitey Kurowski that gave St. Louis a Series-ending 4-2 victory.

■ **Top guns:** Johnny Beazley (2-0, 2.50 ERA), Kurowski (5 RBIs), Cardinals; Phil Rizzuto (.381), Yankees.

Linescores

Game 1—September 30, at St. Louis
New York.................0 0 0 1 1 0 0 3 2—7 11 0
St. Louis ....0 0 0 0 0 0 0 0 4—4 7 4
Ruffing, Chandler (9); M. Cooper, Gumbert (8), Lanier (9). W—Ruffing. L—M. Cooper.

Game 2—October 1, at St. Louis
New York.................0 0 0 0 0 0 0 3 0—3 10 2
St. Louis ....2 0 0 0 0 0 1 1 x—4 6 0
Bonham; Beazley. W—Beazley. L—Bonham. HR—Keller (N.Y.).

Game 3—October 3, at New York
St. Louis ....0 0 1 0 0 0 0 0 1—2 5 1
New York...................0 0 0 0 0 0 0 0 0—0 6 1
White; Chandler, Breuer (9), Turner (9). W—White. L—Chandler.

Game 4—October 4, at New York
St. Louis ....0 0 0 6 0 0 2 0 1—9 12 1
New York.................1 0 0 0 0 5 0 0 0—6 10 1
M. Cooper, Gumbert (6), Pollet (6), Lanier (7); Borowy, Donald (4), Bonham (7). W—Lanier. L—Donald. HR—Keller (N.Y.).

Game 5—October 5, at New York
St. Louis ....0 0 0 1 0 1 0 0 2—4 9 4
New York...................1 0 0 1 0 0 0 0 0—2 7 1
Beazley; Ruffing. W—Beazley. L—Ruffing. HR—Rizzuto (N.Y.); Slaughter, Kurowski (St.L.).

1943

FINAL STANDINGS

American League

Team	W	L	Pct.	GB
New York	98	56	.636	...
Washington	84	69	.549	13.5
Cleveland	82	71	.536	15.5
Chicago	82	72	.532	16
Detroit	78	76	.506	20
St. Louis	72	80	.474	25
Boston	68	84	.447	29
Philadelphia	49	105	.318	49

National League

Team	W	L	Pct.	GB
St. Louis	105	49	.682	...
Cincinnati	87	67	.565	18
Brooklyn	81	72	.529	23.5
Pittsburgh	80	74	.519	25
Chicago	74	79	.484	30.5
Boston	68	85	.444	36.5
Philadelphia	64	90	.416	41
New York	55	98	.359	49.5

SIGNIFICANT EVENTS

■ **January 5:** In concessions to the war and travel restrictions, Major League owners agreed to open the season a week late and to conduct spring training in northern cities.

■ **February 28:** The Texas League suspended operations, cutting the minor league ranks to nine circuits—down from the 41 that operated in 1941.

■ **April 20:** Boston Braves manager Casey Stengel suffered a broken leg when he was hit by a Boston taxicab—an injury that would sideline him for much of the season.

■ **May 8:** Baseball's two-week "dead ball" era came to an end when A.G. Spalding's "war ball" was replaced with a more lively ball.

MEMORABLE MOMENTS

■ **June 4:** Cardinals ace Mort Cooper stopped Philadelphia 5-0 at Sportsman's Park—his second consecutive one-hit shutout.

■ **June 17:** Boston player-manager Joe Cronin made history when he blasted three-run pinch-hit homers in both ends of a doubleheader against Philadelphia at Fenway Park.

■ **August 24:** The Athletics ended their A.L. record-tying losing streak at 20 with an 8-1 victory in the second game of a doubleheader at Chicago.

LEADERS

American League

BA: Luke Appling, Chi., .328.
Runs: George Case, Wash., 102.
Hits: Dick Wakefield, Det., 200.
TB: Rudy York, Det., 301.
HR: Rudy York, Det., 34.
RBI: Rudy York, Det., 118.
SB: George Case, Wash., 61.
Wins: Spud Chandler, N.Y.; Dizzy Trout, Det., 20.
ERA: Spud Chandler, N.Y., 1.64.
CG: Spud Chandler, N.Y.; Tex Hughson, Bos., 20.
IP: Jim Bagby, Cle., 273.
SO: Allie Reynolds, Cle., 151.

National League

BA: Stan Musial, St.L., .357.
Runs: Arky Vaughan, Brk., 112.
Hits: Stan Musial, St.L., 220.
TB: Stan Musial, St.L., 347.
HR: Bill Nicholson, Chi., 29.
RBI: Bill Nicholson, Chi., 128.
SB: Arky Vaughan, Brk., 20.
Wins: Mort Cooper, St.L.; Elmer Riddle, Cin.; Rip Sewell, Pit., 21.
ERA: Max Lanier, St.L., 1.90.
CG: Rip Sewell, Pit., 25.
IP: Al Javery, Bos., 303.
SO: Johnny Vander Meer, Cin., 174.

A.L. 20-game winners
Spud Chandler, N.Y., 20-4
Dizzy Trout, Det., 20-12

N.L. 20-game winners
Mort Cooper, St.L., 21-8
Rip Sewell, Pit., 21-9
Elmer Riddle, Cin., 21-11

A.L. 100 RBIs
Rudy York, Det., 118
Nick Etten, N.Y., 107

N.L. 100 RBIs
Bill Nicholson, Chi., 128
Bob Elliott, Pit., 101
Billy Herman, Brk., 100

Most Valuable Player
A.L.: Spud Chandler, P, N.Y.
N.L.: Stan Musial, OF, St.L.

ALL-STAR GAME

■ **Winner:** A.L. manager Joe McCarthy, tired of complaints that he favored his own Yankee players in All-Star competition, guided his team to a Yankeeless victory.

■ **Key inning:** The second, when Boston's Bobby Doerr belted a three-run homer that gave the A.L. a lead it never relinquished.

■ **Memorable moments:** A seventh-inning run-scoring triple and a ninth-inning home run by Pittsburgh's Vince DiMaggio, brother of Yankee great Joe DiMaggio.

■ **Top guns:** Hal Newhouser (Tigers), Doerr (Red Sox), Dick Wakefield (Tigers), A.L.; V. DiMaggio (Pirates), Stan Hack (Cubs), N.L.

■ **MVP:** Doerr.

Linescore

July 13, at Philadelphia's Shibe Park
N.L. ....1 0 0 0 0 0 1 0 1—3 10 3
A.L.........................0 3 1 0 1 0 0 0 x—5 8 1
M. Cooper (Cardinals), Vander Meer (Reds) 3, Sewell (Pirates) 6, Javery (Braves) 7; Leonard (Senators), Newhouser (Tigers) 4, Hughson (Red Sox) 7. W—Leonard. L—M. Cooper. HR—Doerr, A.L.; DiMaggio, N.L.

WORLD SERIES

■ **Winner:** Joe McCarthy managed his seventh and final Series champion as the Yankees avenged their 1942 loss to the Cardinals.

■ **Turning point:** Billy Johnson's bases-loaded triple that keyed a five-run eighth inning and helped the Yankees to a 6-2 victory in Game 3.

■ **Memorable moment:** Bill Dickey's two-run, sixth-inning home run in New York's 2-0 Series-ending victory.

■ **Top guns:** Spud Chandler (2-0, 0.50 ERA), Dickey (4 RBIs), Yankees; Marty Marion (.357), Cardinals.

Linescores

Game 1—October 5, at New York
St. Louis....................0 1 0 0 1 0 0 0 0—2 7 2
New York ....0 0 0 2 0 2 0 0 x—4 8 2
Lanier, Brecheen (8); Chandler. W—Chandler. L—Lanier. HR—Gordon (N.Y.).

Game 2—October 6, at New York
St. Louis....................0 0 1 3 0 0 0 0 0—4 7 2
New York ....0 0 0 1 0 0 0 0 2—3 6 0
M. Cooper; Bonham, Murphy (9). W—M. Cooper. L—Bonham. HR—Marion, Sanders (St.L.).

Game 3—October 7, at New York
St. Louis....................0 0 0 2 0 0 0 0 0—2 6 4
New York ....0 0 0 0 0 1 0 5 x—6 8 0
Brazle, Krist (8), Brecheen (8); Borowy, Murphy (9). W—Borowy. L—Brazle.

Game 4—October 10, at St. Louis
New York ....0 0 0 1 0 0 0 1 0—2 6 2
St. Louis....................0 0 0 0 0 0 1 0 0—1 7 1
Russo; Lanier, Brecheen (8). W—Russo. L—Brecheen.

Game 5—October 11, at St. Louis
New York ....0 0 0 0 0 2 0 0 0—2 7 1
St. Louis.................0 0 0 0 0 0 0 0 0—0 10 1
Chandler; M. Cooper, Lanier (8), Dickson (9). W—Chandler. L—M. Cooper. HR—Dickey (N.Y.).

1944

FINAL STANDINGS

American League

Team	W	L	Pct.	GB
St. Louis	89	65	.578	...
Detroit	88	66	.571	1
New York	83	71	.539	6
Boston	77	77	.500	12
Cleveland	72	82	.468	17
Philadelphia	72	82	.468	17
Chicago	71	83	.461	18
Washington	64	90	.416	25

National League

Team	W	L	Pct.	GB
St. Louis	105	49	.682	...
Pittsburgh	90	63	.588	14.5
Cincinnati	89	65	.578	16
Chicago	75	79	.487	30
New York	67	87	.435	38
Boston	65	89	.422	40
Brooklyn	63	91	.409	42
Philadelphia	61	92	.399	43.5

SIGNIFICANT EVENTS

■ **June 6:** Baseball canceled its schedule as Americans braced for D-day—the invasion of Europe on the beaches of Normandy, France.

■ **October:** Major League baseball raised $329,555 for the National War Fund Inc. and the American Red Cross through its 16 war relief games.

■ **November 25:** Kenesaw Mountain Landis, baseball's first commissioner, died of a heart attack at age 78.

MEMORABLE MOMENTS

■ **April 30:** Giants first baseman Phil Weintraub drove in 11 runs, one short of the Major League record, in a 26-8 victory over the Dodgers.

■ **June 10:** Reds pitcher Joe Nuxhall, at 15 years and 10 months, became the youngest player to compete in a Major League game when he worked 2/3 of an inning against the Cardinals.

■ **August 10:** Braves righthander Red Barrett threw a record-low 58 pitches in a 2-0 victory over the Reds.

■ **October 1:** The Browns recorded a final-day 5-2 victory over the Yankees and clinched the first pennant of their frustrating 44-year history.

LEADERS

American League

BA: Lou Boudreau, Cle., .327.
Runs: Snuffy Stirnweiss, N.Y., 125.
Hits: Snuffy Stirnweiss, N.Y., 205.
TB: Johnny Lindell, N.Y., 297.
HR: Nick Etten, N.Y., 22.
RBI: Vern Stephens, St.L., 109.
SB: Snuffy Stirnweiss, N.Y., 55.
Wins: Hal Newhouser, Det., 29.
ERA: Dizzy Trout, Det., 2.12.
CG: Dizzy Trout, Det., 33.
IP: Dizzy Trout, Det., 352.1.
SO: Hal Newhouser, Det., 187.

National League

BA: Dixie Walker, Brk., .357.
Runs: Bill Nicholson, Chi., 116.
Hits: Phil Cavarretta, Chi.; Stan Musial, St.L., 197.
TB: Bill Nicholson, Chi., 317.
HR: Bill Nicholson, Chi., 33.
RBI: Bill Nicholson, Chi., 122.
SB: Johnny Barrett, Pit., 28.
Wins: Bucky Walters, Cin., 23.
ERA: Ed Heusser, Cin., 2.38.
CG: Jim Tobin, Bos., 28.
IP: Bill Voiselle, N.Y., 312.2.
SO: Bill Voiselle, N.Y., 161.

A.L. 20-game winners
Hal Newhouser, Det., 29-9
Dizzy Trout, Det., 27-14

N.L. 20-game winners
Bucky Walters, Cin., 23-8
Mort Cooper, St.L., 22-7
Rip Sewell, Pit., 21-12
Bill Voiselle, N.Y., 21-16

A.L. 100 RBIs
Vern Stephens, St.L., 109
Bob Johnson, Bos., 106
Johnny Lindell, N.Y., 103
Stan Spence, Wash., 100

N.L. 100 RBIs
Bill Nicholson, Chi., 122
Bob Elliott, Pit., 108
Ron Northey, Phil., 104
Frank McCormick, Cin., 102
Ray Sanders, St.L., 102
Babe Dahlgren, Pit., 101

Most Valuable Player
A.L.: Hal Newhouser, P, Det.
N.L.: Marty Marion, SS, St.L.

Hall of Fame addition
Kenesaw M. Landis, commissioner

ALL-STAR GAME

■ **Winner:** With many of baseball's stars serving their country in World War II, four pitchers held the A.L. to six hits and the N.L. claimed a 7-1 victory.

■ **Key inning:** The fifth, when the N.L. scored four times on RBI hits by Chicago's Bill Nicholson, St. Louis' Walker Cooper and Dodgers' Augie Galan and Dixie Walker.

■ **Memorable moment:** Pittsburgh's Rip Sewell threw two "ephus pitches" to Browns first baseman George McQuinn, who took one for a called strike and bunted the other for an out.

■ **Top guns:** Sewell (Pirates), Phil Cavarretta (Cubs), Cooper (Cardinals), Walker (Dodgers), Whitey Kurowski (Cardinals), Nicholson (Cubs), N.L.; Hank Borowy (Yankees), A.L.

■ **MVP:** Sewell.

Linescore

July 11, at Pittsburgh's Forbes Field
A.L..........................0 1 0 0 0 0 0 0 0—1 6 3
N.L..........................0 0 0 0 4 0 2 1 x—7 12 1
Borowy (Yankees), Hughson (Red Sox) 4, Muncrief (Browns) 5, Newhouser (Tigers) 7, Newsom (Athletics) 8; Walters (Reds), Raffensberger (Phillies) 4, Sewell (Pirates) 6, Tobin (Braves) 9. W—Raffensberger. L—Hughson.

WORLD SERIES

■ **Winner:** Playing with a war-depleted roster, the Cardinals won the all-Sportsman's Park Series and the Battle of St. Louis.

■ **Turning point:** Game 5 homers by Ray Sanders and Danny Litwhiler that gave the Cardinals a 2-0 victory and a three-games-to-two edge.

■ **Memorable moment:** A two-run George McQuinn homer that gave the long-suffering Browns a 2-1 victory in their first-ever Series game.

■ **Top guns:** Emil Verban (.412), Walker Cooper (.318), Cardinals; McQuinn (.438, 5 RBIs), Browns.

Linescores

Game 1—October 4, at St. Louis
Browns......................0 0 0 2 0 0 0 0 0—2 2 0
Cardinals...................0 0 0 0 0 0 0 0 1—1 7 0
Galehouse; M. Cooper, Donnelly (8). W—Galehouse. L—M. Cooper. HR—McQuinn (Browns).

Game 2—October 5, at St. Louis
Browns............0 0 0 0 0 0 2 0 0 0 0—2 7 4
Cardinals..........0 0 1 1 0 0 0 0 0 0 1—3 7 0
Potter, Muncrief (7); Lanier, Donnelly (8). W—Donnelly. L—Muncrief.

Game 3—October 6, at St. Louis
Cardinals...................1 0 0 0 0 0 1 0 0—2 7 0
Browns ....0 0 4 0 0 0 2 0 x—6 8 2
Wilks, Schmidt (3), Jurisich (7), Byerly (7); Kramer. W—Kramer. L—Wilks.

Game 4—October 7, at St. Louis
Cardinals.................2 0 2 0 0 1 0 0 0—5 12 0
Browns ....0 0 0 0 0 0 0 1 0—1 9 1
Brecheen; Jakucki, Hollingsworth (4), Shirley (8). W—Brecheen. L—Jakucki. HR—Musial (Cardinals).

Game 5—October 8, at St. Louis
Cardinals...................0 0 0 0 0 1 0 1 0—2 6 1
Browns ....0 0 0 0 0 0 0 0 0—0 7 1
M. Cooper; Galehouse. W—M. Cooper. L—Galehouse. HR—Sanders, Litwhiler (Cardinals).

Game 6—October 9, at St. Louis
Browns ....0 1 0 0 0 0 0 0 0—1 3 2
Cardinals..................0 0 0 3 0 0 0 0 0—3 10 0
Potter, Muncrief (4), Kramer (7); Lanier, Wilks (6). W—Lanier. L—Potter.

1945

FINAL STANDINGS

American League

Team	W	L	Pct.	GB
Detroit	88	65	.575	...
Washington	87	67	.565	1.5
St. Louis	81	70	.536	6
New York	81	71	.533	6.5
Cleveland	73	72	.503	11
Chicago	71	78	.477	15
Boston	71	83	.461	17.5
Philadelphia	52	98	.347	34.5

National League

Team	W	L	Pct.	GB
Chicago	98	56	.636	...
St. Louis	95	59	.617	3
Brooklyn	87	67	.565	11
Pittsburgh	82	72	.532	16
New York	78	74	.513	19
Boston	67	85	.441	30
Cincinnati	61	93	.396	37
Philadelphia	46	108	.299	52

SIGNIFICANT EVENTS

■ **January 26:** The Yankees were sold to the triumvirate of Larry MacPhail, Dan Topping and Del Webb for $2.8 million.

■ **April 24:** Kentucky Senator Albert B. (Happy) Chandler was the unanimous selection as baseball's second commissioner.

■ **July 10:** The All-Star Game, a baseball fixture since 1933, was not played because of wartime travel restrictions.

■ **October 23:** Brooklyn President Branch Rickey signed Jackie Robinson to a minor league contract, giving Organized Baseball its first black player since the turn of the century.

MEMORABLE MOMENTS

■ **April 18:** One-armed St. Louis outfielder Pete Gray collected one hit in his Major League debut—a 7-1 Browns victory over Detroit.

■ **July 12:** Boston's Tommy Holmes failed to get a hit during a 6-1 loss to the Cubs, ending his modern-era N.L.-record 37-game hitting streak.

■ **August 1:** Giants slugger Mel Ott became baseball's third 500-homer man when he connected off Boston's Johnny Hutchings.

■ **September 9:** Philadelphia's Dick Fowler, released from military duty nine days earlier, pitched a 1-0 no-hitter against the Browns in his first post-war appearance.

LEADERS

American League

BA: Snuffy Stirnweiss, N.Y., .309.
Runs: Snuffy Stirnweiss, N.Y., 107.
Hits: Snuffy Stirnweiss, N.Y., 195.
TB: Snuffy Stirnweiss, N.Y., 301.
HR: Vern Stephens, St.L., 24.
RBI: Nick Etten, N.Y., 111.
SB: Snuffy Stirnweiss, N.Y., 33.
Wins: Hal Newhouser, Det., 25.
ERA: Hal Newhouser, Det., 1.81.
CG: Hal Newhouser, Det., 29.
IP: Hal Newhouser, Det., 313.1.
SO: Hal Newhouser, Det., 212.

National League

BA: Phil Cavarretta, Chi., .355.
Runs: Eddie Stanky, Brk., 128.
Hits: Tommy Holmes, Bos., 224.
TB: Tommy Holmes, Bos., 367.
HR: Tommy Holmes, Bos., 28.
RBI: Dixie Walker, Brk., 124.
SB: Red Schoendienst, St.L., 26.
Wins: Red Barrett, Bos.-St.L., 23.
ERA: Ray Prim, Chi., 2.40.
CG: Red Barrett, Bos.-St.L., 24.
IP: Red Barrett, Bos.-St.L., 284.2.
SO: Preacher Roe, Pit., 148.

A.L. 20-game winners

Hal Newhouser, Det., 25-9
Boo Ferriss, Bos., 21-10
Roger Wolff, Wash., 20-10

N.L. 20-game winners

Red Barrett, Bos.-St.L., 23-12
Hank Wyse, Chi., 22-10

A.L./N.L. 20-game winner

Hank Borowy, N.Y.-Chi., 21

A.L. 100 RBIs

Nick Etten, N.Y., 111

N.L. 100 RBIs

Dixie Walker, Brk., 124
Tommy Holmes, Bos., 117
Luis Olmo, Brk., 110
Andy Pafko, Chi., 110
Buster Adams, Phil.-St.L., 109
Bob Elliott, Pit., 108
Whitey Kurowski, St.L., 102

Most Valuable Player

A.L.: Hal Newhouser, P, Det.
N.L.: Phil Cavarretta, 1B, Chi.

Hall of Fame additions

Roger Bresnahan, C, 1897-1915
Dan Brouthers, 1B, 1879-1904
Fred Clarke, OF, 1894-1915
Jimmy Collins, 3B, 1895-1908
Ed Delahanty, OF, 1888-1903
Hugh Duffy, OF, 1888-1906
Hugh Jennings, SS, 1891-1918
Mike (King) Kelly, C, 1878-93
Jim O'Rourke, OF, 1876-1904
Wilbert Robinson, manager

ALL-STAR GAME

The scheduled 13th All-Star Game was called off because of wartime travel restrictions.

WORLD SERIES

■ **Winner:** The Tigers won only their second Series and the Cubs lost their seventh straight in the last of the wartime fall classics.

■ **Turning point:** A four-run, sixth-inning explosion that broke a 1-1 tie and helped the Tigers to an 8-4 victory in the pivotal fifth game.

■ **Memorable moment:** Stan Hack's 12th-inning bad-hop double that gave the Cubs an 8-7 victory in a must-win sixth game.

■ **Top guns:** Roger Cramer (.379), Hank Greenberg (.304, 2 HR, 7 RBIs), Tigers; Phil Cavarretta (.423, 5 RBIs), Cubs.

Linescores

Game 1—October 3, at Detroit
Chicago....................4 0 3 0 0 0 2 0 0—9 13 0
Detroit.....................0 0 0 0 0 0 0 0 0—0 6 0
Borowy; Newhouser, Benton (3), Tobin (5), Mueller (8). W—Borowy. L—Newhouser. HR—Cavarretta (Chi.).

Game 2—October 4, at Detroit
Chicago......................0 0 0 1 0 0 0 0 0—1 7 0
Detroit.......................0 0 0 0 4 0 0 0 x—4 7 0
Wyse, Erickson (7); Trucks. W—Trucks. L—Wyse. HR—Greenberg (Det.).

Game 3—October 5, at Detroit
Chicago.....................0 0 0 2 0 0 1 0 0—3 8 0
Detroit.......................0 0 0 0 0 0 0 0 0—0 1 2
Passeau; Overmire, Benton (7). W—Passeau. L—Overmire.

Game 4—October 6, at Chicago
Detroit.......................0 0 0 4 0 0 0 0 0—4 7 1
Chicago.....................0 0 0 0 0 1 0 0 0—1 5 1
Trout; Prim, Derringer (4), Vandenberg (6), Erickson (8). W—Trout. L—Prim.

Game 5—October 7, at Chicago
Detroit.....................0 0 1 0 0 4 1 0 2—8 11 0
Chicago...................0 0 1 0 0 0 2 0 1—4 7 2
Newhouser; Borowy, Vandenberg (6), Chipman (6), Derringer (7), Erickson (9). W—Newhouser. L—Borowy.

Game 6—October 8, at Chicago
Detroit........0 1 0 0 0 0 2 4 0 0 0 0—7 13 1
Chicago......0 0 0 0 4 1 2 0 0 0 0 1—8 15 3
Trucks, Caster (5), Bridges (6), Benton (7), Trout (8); Passeau, Wyse (7), Prim (8), Borowy (9). W—Borowy. L—Trout. HR—Greenberg (Det.).

Game 7—October 10, at Chicago
Detroit.....................5 1 0 0 0 0 1 2 0—9 9 1
Chicago...................1 0 0 1 0 0 0 1 0—3 10 0
Newhouser; Borowy, Derringer (1), Vandenberg (2), Erickson (6), Passeau (8), Wyse (9). W—Newhouser. L—Borowy.

1946

FINAL STANDINGS

American League

Team	W	L	Pct.	GB
Boston	104	50	.675	...
Detroit	92	62	.597	12
New York	87	67	.565	17
Washington	76	78	.494	28
Chicago	74	80	.481	30
Cleveland	68	86	.442	36
St. Louis	66	88	.429	38
Philadelphia	49	105	.318	55

National League

Team	W	L	Pct.	GB
*St. Louis	98	58	.628	...
Brooklyn	96	60	.615	2
Chicago	82	71	.536	14.5
Boston	81	72	.529	15.5
Philadelphia	69	85	.448	28
Cincinnati	67	87	.435	30
Pittsburgh	63	91	.409	34
New York	61	93	.396	36

*Defeated Brooklyn 2-0 in pennant playoff.

SIGNIFICANT EVENTS

■ **February 19:** Giants outfielder Danny Gardella jumped to the outlaw Mexican League, the first in a group of Major Leaguers who would fall victim to big-money inducements.

■ **April 18:** Jackie Robinson broke Organized Baseball's color barrier with a four-hit debut for the International League's Montreal Royals.

■ **September 16:** Among the benefits awarded players in a history-making New York meeting were a $5,000 minimum salary, upgraded hospital and medical expenses and salary-cut guarantees.

■ **December 6:** Baseball owners decided to return the All-Star vote to the fans.

MEMORABLE MOMENTS

■ **July 27:** Boston's Rudy York belted a record-tying two grand slams and drove in 10 runs in a 13-6 victory over the Browns.

■ **October 3:** The Cardinals capped their two-game sweep of the Dodgers with an 8-4 victory in baseball's first pennant playoff.

LEADERS

American League

BA: Mickey Vernon, Wash., .353.
Runs: Ted Williams, Bos., 142.
Hits: Johnny Pesky, Bos., 208.
TB: Ted Williams, Bos., 343.
HR: Hank Greenberg, Det., 44.
RBI: Hank Greenberg, Det., 127.
SB: George Case, Cle., 28.
Wins: Bob Feller, Cle.; Hal Newhouser, Det., 26.
ERA: Hal Newhouser, Det., 1.94.
CG: Bob Feller, Cle., 36.
IP: Bob Feller, Cle., 371.1.
SO: Bob Feller, Cle., 348.

National League

BA: Stan Musial, St.L., .365.
Runs: Stan Musial, St.L., 124.
Hits: Stan Musial, St.L., 228.
TB: Stan Musial, St.L., 366.
HR: Ralph Kiner, Pit., 23.
RBI: Enos Slaughter, St.L., 130.
SB: Pete Reiser, Brk., 34.
Wins: Howie Pollet, St.L., 21.
ERA: Howie Pollet, St.L., 2.10.
CG: Johnny Sain, Bos., 24.
IP: Howie Pollet, St.L., 266.
SO: Johnny Schmitz, Chi., 135.

A.L. 20-game winners

Hal Newhouser, Det., 26-9
Bob Feller, Cle., 26-15
Boo Ferriss, Bos., 25-6
Spud Chandler, N.Y., 20-8
Tex Hughson, Bos., 20-11

N.L. 20-game winners

Howie Pollet, St.L., 21-10
Johnny Sain, Bos., 20-14

A.L. 100 RBIs

Hank Greenberg, Det., 127
Ted Williams, Bos., 123
Rudy York, Bos., 119
Bobby Doerr, Bos., 116
Charlie Keller, N.Y., 101

N.L. 100 RBIs

Enos Slaughter, St.L., 130
Dixie Walker, Brk., 116
Stan Musial, St.L., 103

A.L. 40 homers

Hank Greenberg, Det., 44

Most Valuable Player

A.L.: Ted Williams, OF, Bos.
N.L.: Stan Musial, 1B, St.L.

Hall of Fame additions

Jesse Burkett, OF, 1890-1905
Frank Chance, 1B, 1898-1914
Jack Chesbro, P, 1899-1909
Johnny Evers, 2B, 1902-29
Clark Griffith, P/Man./Exec.
Tommy McCarthy, OF, 1884-96
Joe McGinnity, P, 1899-1908
Eddie Plank, P, 1901-17
Joe Tinker, SS, 1902-16
Rube Waddell, P, 1897-1910
Ed Walsh, P, 1904-17

ALL-STAR GAME

■ **Winner:** War hero Ted Williams rewarded his home fans with a four-hit, two-homer, five-RBI performance and three pitchers — Cleveland's Bob Feller, Detroit's Hal Newhouser and St. Louis' Jack Kramer — combined on a three-hitter that produced a 12-0 victory.

■ **Key inning:** The first, when Yankee Charlie Keller hit a two-run homer that ignited the A.L. charge.

■ **Memorable moment:** Williams' three-run, eighth-inning homer off Rip Sewell's famed "ephus pitch"—one of the All-Star Game's classic moments.

■ **Top guns:** Feller (Indians), Newhouser (Tigers), Kramer (Browns), Williams (Red Sox), Keller (Yankees), Vern Stephens (Browns), A.L.

■ **MVP:** Williams.

Linescore

July 9, at Boston's Fenway Park
N.L.........................0 0 0 0 0 0 0 0 0— 0 3 0
A.L.........................2 0 0 1 3 0 2 4 x—12 14 1
Passeau (Cubs), Higbe (Dodgers) 4, Blackwell (Reds) 5, Sewell (Pirates) 8; Feller (Indians), Newhouser (Tigers) 4, Kramer (Browns) 7. W—Feller. L—Passeau. HR—Keller, Williams 2, A.L.

WORLD SERIES

■ **Winner:** The Cardinals celebrated the end of wartime baseball with seven-game victory over the Red Sox.

■ **Turning point:** Harry Brecheen's seven-hit pitching gave the Cardinals a 4-1 victory in a must-win sixth game.

■ **Memorable moments:** The eighth inning of Game 7, when Enos Slaughter made his game-winning "Mad Dash" around the bases on Harry Walker's double. The ninth inning of Game 7, when Brecheen pitched out of a two-on, nobody out jam to secure the victory.

■ **Top guns:** Brecheen (3-0, 0.45 ERA), Slaughter (.320), Walker (.412, 6 RBIs), Cardinals; Bobby Doerr (.409), Rudy York (2 HR, 5 RBIs), Red Sox.

Linescores

Game 1—October 6, at St. Louis
Boston ....0 1 0 0 0 0 0 0 1 1—3 9 2
St. Louis ....0 0 0 0 0 1 0 1 0 0—2 7 0
Hughson, Johnson (9); Pollet. W—Johnson. L—Pollet. HR—York (Bos.).

Game 2—October 7, at St. Louis
Boston ....0 0 0 0 0 0 0 0 0—0 4 1
St. Louis ....0 0 1 0 2 0 0 0 x—3 6 0
Harris, Dobson (8); Brecheen. W—Brecheen. L—Harris.

Game 3—October 9, at Boston
St. Louis ....0 0 0 0 0 0 0 0 0—0 6 1
Boston.........................3 0 0 0 0 0 0 1 x—4 8 0
Dickson, Wilks (8); Ferriss. W—Ferriss. L—Dickson. HR—York (Bos.).

Game 4—Ocotber 10, at Boston
St. Louis ....0 3 3 0 1 0 1 0 4—12 20 1
Boston ....0 0 0 1 0 0 0 2 0— 3 9 4
Munger; Hughson, Bagby (3), Zuber (6), Brown (8), Ryba (9), Driesewerd (9). W—Munger. L—Hughson. HR—Slaughter (St.L.); Doerr (Bos.).

Game 5—October 11, at Boston
St. Louis ....0 1 0 0 0 0 0 0 2—3 4 1
Boston......................1 1 0 0 0 1 3 0 x—6 11 3
Pollet, Brazle (1), Beazley (8); Dobson. W—Dobson. L—Brazle. HR—Culberson (Bos.).

Game 6—October 13, at St. Louis
Boston ....0 0 0 0 0 0 1 0 0—1 7 0
St. Louis ....0 0 3 0 0 0 0 1 x—4 8 0
Harris, Hughson (3), Johnson (8); Brecheen. W—Brecheen. L—Harris.

Game 7—October 15, at St. Louis
Boston ....1 0 0 0 0 0 0 2 0—3 8 0
St. Louis ....0 1 0 0 2 0 0 1 x—4 9 1
Ferriss, Dobson (5), Klinger (8), Johnson (8); Dickson, Brecheen (8). W—Brecheen. L—Klinger.

1947

FINAL STANDINGS

American League

Team	W	L	Pct.	GB
New York	97	57	.630	...
Detroit	85	69	.552	12
Boston	83	71	.539	14
Cleveland	80	74	.519	17
Philadelphia	78	76	.506	19
Chicago	70	84	.455	27
Washington	64	90	.416	33
St. Louis	59	95	.383	38

National League

Team	W	L	Pct.	GB
Brooklyn	94	60	.610	...
St. Louis	89	65	.578	5
Boston	86	68	.558	8
New York	81	73	.526	13
Cincinnati	73	81	.474	21
Chicago	69	85	.448	25
Philadelphia	62	92	.403	32
Pittsburgh	62	92	.403	32

SIGNIFICANT EVENTS

■ **April 9:** Brooklyn manager Leo Durocher was suspended by Commissioner Happy Chandler for the entire 1947 season for "conduct detrimental to baseball."

■ **April 15:** The Major League color barrier came tumbling down when Jackie Robinson went hitless in the Dodgers' 5-3 Opening Day victory over the Braves at Ebbets Field.

■ **April 27:** Cancer-stricken Babe Ruth was honored throughout baseball on "Babe Ruth Day" and in special ceremonies at Yankee Stadium.

■ **July 5:** Cleveland's Larry Doby became the A.L.'s first black player when he struck out as a pinch-hitter in a 6-5 loss at Chicago.

■ **November 12:** Dodgers first baseman Jackie Robinson capped his historic season by capturing the first Rookie of the Year award.

MEMORABLE MOMENTS

■ **June 22:** Cincinnati's Ewell Blackwell fell two outs short of matching Johnny Vander Meer's back-to-back no-hitter feat when Brooklyn's Eddie Stanky stroked a ninth-inning single.

■ **September 28:** The greatest home run battle in history ended with neither Pittsburgh's Ralph Kiner nor New York's Johnny Mize adding to their 51-homer totals.

LEADERS

American League

BA: Ted Williams, Bos., .343.
Runs: Ted Williams, Bos., 125.
Hits: Johnny Pesky, Bos., 207.
TB: Ted Williams, Bos., 335.
HR: Ted Williams, Bos., 32.
RBI: Ted Williams, Bos., 114.
SB: Bob Dillinger, St.L., 34.
Wins: Bob Feller, Cle., 20.
ERA: Joe Haynes, Chi., 2.42.
CG: Hal Newhouser, Det., 24.
IP: Bob Feller, Cle., 299.
SO: Bob Feller, Cle., 196.

National League

BA: Harry Walker, St.L.-Phil., .363.
Runs: Johnny Mize, N.Y., 137.
Hits: Tommy Holmes, Bos., 191.
TB: Ralph Kiner, Pit., 361.
HR: Ralph Kiner, Pit.; Johnny Mize, N.Y., 51.
RBI: Johnny Mize, N.Y., 138.
SB: Jackie Robinson, Brk., 29.
Wins: Ewell Blackwell, Cin., 22.
ERA: Warren Spahn, Bos., 2.33.
CG: Ewell Blackwell, Cin., 23.
IP: Warren Spahn, Bos., 289.2.
SO: Ewell Blackwell, Cin., 193.

A.L. 20-game winners

Bob Feller, Cle., 20-11

N.L. 20-game winners

Ewell Blackwell, Cin., 22-8
Larry Jansen, N.Y., 21-5
Warren Spahn, Bos., 21-10
Ralph Branca, Brk., 21-12
Johnny Sain, Bos., 21-12

A.L. 100 RBIs

Ted Williams, Bos., 114

N.L. 100 RBIs

Johnny Mize, N.Y., 138
Ralph Kiner, Pit., 127
Walker Cooper, N.Y., 122
Bob Elliott, Bos., 113
Willard Marshall, N.Y., 107
Whitey Kurowski, St.L., 104

N.L. 40 homers

Ralph Kiner, Pit., 51
Johnny Mize, N.Y., 51

Most Valuable Player

A.L.: Joe DiMaggio, OF, N.Y.
N.L.: Bob Elliott, 3B, Bos.

Rookie of the Year

A.L.-N.L.: Jackie Robinson, 1B, Brk.

Hall of Fame additions

Mickey Cochrane, C, 1925-37
Frank Frisch, 2B, 1919-37
Lefty Grove, P, 1925-41
Carl Hubbell, P, 1928-43

ALL-STAR GAME

■ **Winner:** The A.L. won its 10th All-Star Game in 14 tries with a 2-1 decision at windswept Wrigley Field.

■ **Key inning:** The seventh, when Washington pinch-hitter Stan Spence singled home Boston's Bobby Doerr with the eventual winning run.

■ **Memorable moment:** A game-saving defensive play by Cleveland shortstop Lou Boudreau in the eighth inning on a ball hit by St. Louis' Enos Slaughter with two men on base.

■ **Top guns:** Hal Newhouser (Tigers), Spec Shea (Yankees), Ted Williams (Red Sox), Spence (Senators), A.L.; Ewell Blackwell (Reds), Johnny Mize (Giants), N.L.

■ **MVP:** Spence.

Linescore

July 8, at Chicago's Wrigley Field
A.L. ....0 0 0 0 0 1 1 0 0—2 8 0
N.L. ....0 0 0 1 0 0 0 0 0—1 5 1
Newhouser (Tigers), Shea (Yankees) 4, Masterson (Senators) 7, Page (Yankees) 8; Blackwell (Reds), Brecheen (Cardinals) 4, Sain (Braves) 7, Spahn (Braves) 8. W—Shea. L—Sain. HR—Mize, N.L.

WORLD SERIES

■ **Winner:** After a three-year drought, the Yankees returned to the top in a memorable seven-game battle against the Dodgers.

■ **Turning point:** Spec Shea's 2-1 Game 5 victory — the day after teammate Bill Bevens, one out away from victory and the first no-hitter in Series history, had surrendered a game-deciding two-run double to Dodgers pinch-hitter Cookie Lavagetto.

■ **Memorable moments:** Lavagetto's Game 4 hit and a spectacular Game 6 catch by Dodgers left fielder Al Gionfriddo that robbed Joe DiMaggio of a home run and helped secure an 8-6 must victory for Brooklyn.

■ **Top guns:** Shea (2-0, 2.35 ERA), Johnny Lindell (.500, 7 RBIs), Yankees; Hugh Casey (2-0, 0.87), Carl Furillo (.353), Dodgers.

Linescores

Game 1—September 30, at New York
Brooklyn ....1 0 0 0 0 1 1 0 0—3 6 0
New York...................0 0 0 0 5 0 0 0 x—5 4 0
Branca, Behrman (5), Casey (7); Shea, Page (6). W—Shea. L—Branca.

Game 2—October 1, at New York
Brooklyn ....0 0 1 1 0 0 0 0 1— 3 9 2
New York................1 0 1 1 2 1 4 0 x—10 15 1
Lombardi, Gregg (5), Behrman (7), Barney (7); Reynolds. W—Reynolds. L—Lombardi. HR—Walker (Brk.); Henrich (N.Y.).

Game 3—October 2, at Brooklyn
New York.................0 0 2 2 2 1 1 0 0—8 13 0
Brooklyn ....0 6 1 2 0 0 0 0 x—9 13 1
Newsom, Raschi (2), Drews (3), Chandler (4), Page (6); Hatten, Branca (5), Casey (7). W—Casey. L—Newsom. HR—DiMaggio, Berra (N.Y.).

Game 4—October 3, at Brooklyn
New York...................1 0 0 1 0 0 0 0 0—2 8 1
Brooklyn ....0 0 0 0 1 0 0 0 2—3 1 3
Bevens; Taylor, Gregg (1), Behrman (8), Casey (9). W—Casey. L—Bevens.

Game 5—October 4, at Brooklyn
New York...................0 0 0 1 1 0 0 0 0—2 5 0
Brooklyn ....0 0 0 0 0 1 0 0 0—1 4 1
Shea; Barney, Hatten (5), Behrman (7), Casey (8). W—Shea. L—Barney. HR—DiMaggio (N.Y.).

Game 6—October 5, at New York
Brooklyn ....2 0 2 0 0 4 0 0 0—8 12 1
New York.................0 0 4 1 0 0 0 0 1—6 15 2
Lombardi, Branca (3), Hatten (6), Casey (9); Reynolds, Drews (3), Page (5), Newsom (6), Raschi (7), Wensloff (8). W—Branca. L—Page.

Game 7—October 6, at New York
Brooklyn ....0 2 0 0 0 0 0 0 0—2 7 0
New York...................0 1 0 2 0 1 1 0 x—5 7 0
Gregg, Behrman (4), Hatten (6), Barney (6), Casey (7); Shea, Bevens (2), Page (5). W—Page. L—Gregg.

1948

FINAL STANDINGS

American League

Team	W	L	Pct.	GB
*Cleveland	97	58	.626	...
Boston	96	59	.619	1
New York	94	60	.610	2.5
Philadelphia	84	70	.545	12.5
Detroit	78	76	.506	18.5
St. Louis	59	94	.386	37
Washington	56	97	.366	40
Chicago	51	101	.336	44.5

*Defeated Boston in one-game pennant playoff.

National League

Team	W	L	Pct.	GB
Boston	91	62	.595	...
St. Louis	85	69	.552	6.5
Brooklyn	84	70	.545	7.5
Pittsburgh	83	71	.539	8.5
New York	78	76	.506	13.5
Philadelphia	66	88	.429	25.5
Cincinnati	64	89	.418	27
Chicago	64	90	.416	27.5

SIGNIFICANT EVENTS

■ **June 15:** The Tigers became the final A.L. team to host a night game when they posted a 4-1 victory over the Athletics at Briggs Stadium.

■ **August 16:** Babe Ruth, whose uniform No. 3 had been retired by the Yankees two months earlier, died of throat cancer at age 53.

■ **October 3:** The Indians finished the season with a record attendance of 2,620,627.

■ **October 12:** Casey Stengel brought his colorful antics to New York when he signed a two-year contract to manage the Yankees.

MEMORABLE MOMENTS

■ **July 18:** Chicago's Pat Seerey joined a select club when he pounded an 11th-inning home run, his fourth of the game, to give the White Sox a 12-11 victory over the Athletics.

■ **October 4:** Player-manager Lou Boudreau belted two home runs and the Indians posted an 8-3 victory over Boston in a one-game playoff to decide the A.L. pennant.

LEADERS

American League

BA: Ted Williams, Bos., .369.
Runs: Tommy Henrich, N.Y., 138.
Hits: Bob Dillinger, St.L., 207.
TB: Joe DiMaggio, N.Y., 355.
HR: Joe DiMaggio, N.Y., 39.
RBI: Joe DiMaggio, N.Y., 155.
SB: Bob Dillinger, St.L., 28.
Wins: Hal Newhouser, Det., 21.
ERA: Gene Bearden, Cle., 2.43.
CG: Bob Lemon, Cle., 20.
IP: Bob Lemon, Cle., 293.2.
SO: Bob Feller, Cle., 164.

National League

BA: Stan Musial, St.L., .376.
Runs: Stan Musial, St.L., 135.
Hits: Stan Musial, St.L., 230.
TB: Stan Musial, St.L., 429.
HR: Ralph Kiner, Pit.; Johnny Mize, N.Y., 40.
RBI: Stan Musial, St.L., 131.
SB: Richie Ashburn, Phil., 32.
Wins: Johnny Sain, Bos., 24.
ERA: Harry Brecheen, St.L., 2.24.
CG: Johnny Sain, Bos., 28.
IP: Johnny Sain, Bos., 314.2.
SO: Harry Brecheen, St.L., 149.

A.L. 20-game winners

Hal Newhouser, Det., 21-12
Gene Bearden, Cle., 20-7
Bob Lemon, Cle., 20-14

N.L. 20-game winners

Johnny Sain, Bos., 24-15
Harry Brecheen, St.L., 20-7

A.L. 100 RBIs

Joe DiMaggio, N.Y., 155
Vern Stephens, Bos., 137
Ted Williams, Bos., 127
Joe Gordon, Cle., 124
Hank Majeski, Phil., 120
Ken Keltner, Cle., 119
Bobby Doerr, Bos., 111
Lou Boudreau, Cle., 106
Hoot Evers, Det., 103
Tommy Henrich, N.Y., 100

N.L. 100 RBIs

Stan Musial, St.L., 131
Johnny Mize, N.Y., 125
Ralph Kiner, Pit., 123
Sid Gordon, N.Y., 107
Andy Pafko, Chi., 101
Bob Elliott, Bos., 100

N.L. 40 homers

Ralph Kiner, Pit., 40
Johnny Mize, N.Y., 40

Most Valuable Player

A.L.: Lou Boudreau, SS, Cle.
N.L.: Stan Musial, OF, St.L.

Rookie of the Year

A.L.-N.L.: Alvin Dark, SS, Bos. (N.L.).

Hall of Fame additions

Herb Pennock, P, 1912-34
Pie Traynor, 3B, 1920-37

ALL-STAR GAME

■ **Winner:** Yankee Vic Raschi and Philadelphia's Joe Coleman pitched six innings of shutout relief and the A.L. won for the 11th time in 15 All-Star classics.

■ **Key inning:** The fourth, when the A.L. broke a 2-2 tie with three runs. Two scored on a bases-loaded single by pitcher Raschi.

■ **Memorable moment:** A first-inning home run by hometown favorite Stan Musial — the first of a record six All-Star homers he would hit.

■ **Top guns:** Raschi (Yankees), Coleman (Athletics), Hoot Evers (Tigers), A.L.; Musial (Cardinals), Richie Ashburn (Phillies).

■ **MVP:** Raschi.

Linescore

July 13, at St. Louis' Sportsman's Park
N.L. ....2 0 0 0 0 0 0 0 0—2 8 0
A.L. ....0 1 1 3 0 0 0 0 x—5 6 0
Branca (Dodgers), Schmitz (Cubs) 4, Sain (Braves) 4, Blackwell (Reds) 6; Masterson (Senators), Raschi (Yankees) 4, Coleman (Athletics) 7. W—Raschi. L—Schmitz. HR—Musial, N.L.; Evers, A.L.

WORLD SERIES

■ **Winner:** The Indians, survivors of a pennant playoff against the Red Sox, needed six games to dispatch Boston's other team in the Series.

■ **Turning point:** Gene Bearden's 2-0 Game 3 shutout, which put the Indians in the driver's seat.

■ **Memorable moment:** The Game 5 appearance of Indians pitcher Satchel Paige, the 42-year-old former Negro Leagues legend. Paige became the first black pitcher in Series history.

■ **Top guns:** Bob Lemon (2-0, 1.65 ERA), Larry Doby (.318), Indians; Bob Elliott (.333, 2 HR, 5 RBIs), Braves.

Linescores

Game 1—October 6, at Boston
Cleveland ....0 0 0 0 0 0 0 0 0—0 4 0
Boston.......................0 0 0 0 0 0 0 1 x—1 2 2
Feller; Sain. W—Sain. L—Feller.

Game 2—October 7, at Boston
Cleveland ....0 0 0 2 1 0 0 0 1—4 8 1
Boston ....1 0 0 0 0 0 0 0 0—1 8 3
Lemon; Spahn, Barrett (5), Potter (8). W—Lemon. L—Spahn.

Game 3—October 8, at Cleveland
Boston ....0 0 0 0 0 0 0 0 0—0 5 1
Cleveland...................0 0 1 1 0 0 0 0 x—2 5 0
Bickford, Voiselle (4), Barrett (8); Bearden. W—Bearden. L—Bickford.

Game 4—October 9, at Cleveland
Boston ....0 0 0 0 0 0 1 0 0—1 7 0
Cleveland...................1 0 1 0 0 0 0 0 x—2 5 0
Sain; Gromek. W—Gromek. L—Sain. HR—Doby (Cle.); Rickert (Bos.).

Game 5—October 10, at Cleveland
Boston ....3 0 1 0 0 1 6 0 0—11 12 0
Cleveland ....1 0 0 4 0 0 0 0 0— 5 6 2
Potter, Spahn (4); Feller, Klieman (7), Christopher (7), Paige (7), Muncrief (8). W—Spahn. L—Feller. HR—Elliott 2, Salkeld (Bos.); Mitchell, Hegan (Cle.).

Game 6—October 11, at Boston
Cleveland ....0 0 1 0 0 2 0 1 0—4 10 0
Boston ....0 0 0 1 0 0 0 2 0—3 9 0
Lemon, Bearden (8); Voiselle, Spahn (8). W—Lemon. L—Voiselle. HR—Gordon (Cle.).

1949

FINAL STANDINGS

American League

Team	W	L	Pct.	GB
New York	97	57	.630	...
Boston	96	58	.623	1
Cleveland	89	65	.578	8
Detroit	87	67	.565	10
Philadelphia	81	73	.526	16
Chicago	63	91	.409	34
St. Louis	53	101	.344	44
Washington	50	104	.325	47

National League

Team	W	L	Pct.	GB
Brooklyn	97	57	.630	...
St. Louis	96	58	.623	1
Philadelphia	81	73	.526	16
Boston	75	79	.487	22
New York	73	81	.474	24
Pittsburgh	71	83	.461	26
Cincinnati	62	92	.403	35
Chicago	61	93	.396	36

SIGNIFICANT EVENTS

■ **February 7:** Yankee star Joe DiMaggio signed baseball's first $100,000 contract.

■ **April 19:** In ceremonies at Yankee Stadium, the Yankees unveiled center-field granite monuments honoring Babe Ruth, Lou Gehrig and Miller Huggins.

■ **June 5:** Commissioner Happy Chandler lifted the five-year suspensions of the 18 players who jumped to the outlaw Mexican League in 1946.

■ **June 15:** Phillies star Eddie Waitkus was shot and seriously wounded in a Chicago hotel room by a 19-year-old woman who professed to having a secret crush on him.

■ **December 12:** Baseball's Rules Committee redefined the strike zone as the area over home plate between the batter's armpits and the top of his knees.

MEMORABLE MOMENTS

■ **September 30:** Pittsburgh's Ralph Kiner, the first N.L. player to top the 50-homer plateau twice, blasted No. 54 in a 3-2 victory over the Reds.

■ **October 2:** The Yankees posted a 5-3 final-day victory over Boston in a pennant-deciding battle at Yankee Stadium.

■ **October 2:** The Dodgers held off the Cardinals and claimed the N.L. pennant with a 10-inning, 9-7 final-day victory over Philadelphia.

LEADERS

American League

BA: George Kell, Det., .343.
Runs: Ted Williams, Bos., 150.
Hits: Dale Mitchell, Cle., 203.
TB: Ted Williams, Bos., 368.
HR: Ted Williams, Bos., 43.
RBI: Vern Stephens, Bos,; Ted Williams, Bos., 159.
SB: Bob Dillinger, St.L., 20.
Wins: Mel Parnell, Bos., 25.
ERA: Mike Garcia, Cle., 2.36.
CG: Mel Parnell, Bos., 27.
IP: Mel Parnell, Bos., 295.1.
SO: Virgil Trucks, Det., 153.

National League

BA: Jackie Robinson, Brk., .342.
Runs: Pee Wee Reese, Brk., 132.
Hits: Stan Musial, St.L., 207.
TB: Stan Musial, St.L., 382.
HR: Ralph Kiner, Pit., 54.
RBI: Ralph Kiner, Pit., 127.
SB: Jackie Robinson, Brk., 37.
Wins: Warren Spahn, Bos., 21.
ERA: Dave Koslo, N.Y., 2.50.
CG: Warren Spahn, Bos., 25.
IP: Warren Spahn, Bos., 302.1.
SO: Warren Spahn, Bos., 151.

A.L. 20-game winners
Mel Parnell, Bos., 25-7
Ellis Kinder, Bos., 23-6
Bob Lemon, Cle., 22-10
Vic Raschi, N.Y., 21-10
Alex Kellner, Phil., 20-12

N.L. 20-game winners
Warren Spahn, Bos., 21-14
Howie Pollet, St.L., 20-9

A.L. 100 RBIs
Vern Stephens, Bos., 159
Ted Williams, Bos., 159
Vic Wertz, Det., 133
Bobby Doerr, Bos., 109
Sam Chapman, Phil., 108

N.L. 100 RBIs
Ralph Kiner, Pit., 127
Jackie Robinson, Brk., 124
Stan Musial, St.L., 123
Gil Hodges, Brk., 115
Del Ennis, Phil., 110
Bobby Thomson, N.Y., 109
Carl Furillo, Brk., 106
Wally Westlake, Pit., 104

A.L. 40 homers
Ted Williams, Bos., 43

N.L. 40 homers
Ralph Kiner, Pit., 54

Most Valuable Player
A.L.: Ted Williams, OF, Bos.
N.L.: Jackie Robinson, 2B, Brk.

Rookie of the Year
A.L.: Roy Sievers, OF, St.L.
N.L.: Don Newcombe, P, Brk.

Hall of Fame additions
Three Finger Brown, P, 1903-16
Charley Gehringer, 2B, 1924-42
Kid Nichols, P, 1890-1906

ALL-STAR GAME

■ **Winner:** The DiMaggios, Boston's Dom and New York's Joe, combined for four RBIs and Yankee pitcher Vic Raschi shut down the N.L. over the last three innings as the A.L. prevailed in a sloppy game at Brooklyn.

■ **Key inning:** The seventh, when the A.L. broke open a close game with a three-run rally.

■ **Memorable moment:** Jackie Robinson's first-inning double — the first hit by a black player in the first integrated All-Star Game.

■ **Top guns:** Raschi (Yankees), D. DiMaggio (Red Sox), J. DiMaggio (Yankees), George Kell (Tigers), A.L.; Stan Musial (Cardinals), Ralph Kiner (Pirates), N.L.

■ **MVP:** Joe DiMaggio.

Linescore

July 12, at Brooklyn's Ebbets Field
A.L. ....4 0 0 2 0 2 3 0 0—1 13 1
N.L. ....2 1 2 0 0 2 0 0 0—7 12 5
Parnell (Red Sox), Trucks (Tigers) 2, Brissie (Athletics) 4, Raschi (Yankees) 7; Spahn (Braves), Newcombe (Dodgers) 2, Munger (Cardinals) 5, Bickford (Braves) 6, Pollet (Cardinals) 7, Blackwell (Reds) 8, Roe (Dodgers) 9. W—Trucks. L—Newcombe. HR—Musial, Kiner, N.L.

WORLD SERIES

■ **Winner:** The Yankee machine was back, this time with a new driver. Casey Stengel made his Series managerial debut a successful one.

■ **Turning point:** A three-run ninth inning that produced a 4-3 Yankee victory in Game 3.

■ **Memorable moment:** Tommy Henrich's leadoff ninth-inning home run that decided a 1-0 pitching duel between Dodgers ace Don Newcombe and Yankee righthander Allie Reynolds in Game 1.

■ **Top guns:** Reynolds (12⅓ IP, 0.00 ERA), Bobby Brown (.500, 5 RBIs), Yankees; Pee Wee Reese (.316), Dodgers.

Linescores

Game 1—Oct. 5, at New York
Brooklyn ....0 0 0 0 0 0 0 0 0—0 2 0
New York....................0 0 0 0 0 0 0 0 1—1 5 1
Newcombe; Reynolds. W—Reynolds. L—Newcombe. HR—Henrich (N.Y.).

Game 2—October 6, at New York
Brooklyn ....0 1 0 0 0 0 0 0 0—1 7 2
New York....................0 0 0 0 0 0 0 0 0—0 6 1
Roe; Raschi, Page (9). W—Roe. L—Raschi.

Game 3—October 7, at Brooklyn
New York....................0 0 1 0 0 0 0 0 3—4 5 0
Brooklyn ....0 0 0 1 0 0 0 0 2—3 5 0
Byrne, Page (4); Branca, Banta (9). W—Page. L—Branca. HR—Reese, Olmo, Campanella (Brk.).

Game 4—October 8, at Brooklyn
New York..................0 0 0 3 3 0 0 0 0—6 10 0
Brooklyn ....0 0 0 0 0 4 0 0 0—4 9 1
Lopat, Reynolds (6); Newcombe, Hatten (4), Erskine (6), Banta (7). W—Lopat. L—Newcombe.

Game 5—October 9, at Brooklyn
New York................2 0 3 1 1 3 0 0 0—10 11 1
Brooklyn ....0 0 1 0 0 1 4 0 0— 6 11 2
Raschi, Page (7); Barney, Banta (3), Erskine (6), Hatten (6), Palica (7), Minner (9). W—Raschi. L—Barney. HR—DiMaggio (N.Y.); Hodges (Brk.).

1950

FINAL STANDINGS

American League

Team	W	L	Pct.	GB
New York	98	56	.636	...
Detroit	95	59	.617	3
Boston	94	60	.610	4
Cleveland	92	62	.597	6
Washington	67	87	.435	31
Chicago	60	94	.390	38
St. Louis	58	96	.377	40
Philadelphia	52	102	.338	46

National League

Team	W	L	Pct.	GB
Philadelphia	91	63	.591	...
Brooklyn	89	65	.578	2
New York	86	68	.558	5
Boston	83	71	.539	8
St. Louis	78	75	.510	12.5
Cincinnati	66	87	.431	24.5
Chicago	64	89	.418	26.5
Pittsburgh	57	96	.373	33.5

SIGNIFICANT EVENTS

■ **January 31:** Pittsburgh made 18-year-old pitcher Paul Pettit baseball's first $100,000 bonus baby.

■ **October 18:** Connie Mack retired after 50 years as manager and owner of the Athletics, the team he built in 1901 when the American League was organized.

■ **December 11:** Major League owners pulled a shocker when they voted not to renew the contract of Commissioner Happy Chandler.

■ **December 26:** Chandler announced that the Gillette Safety Razor Company had agreed to pay a six-year fee of $6 million for rights to the World Series and All-Star Game.

MEMORABLE MOMENTS

■ **June 8:** The Red Sox, in the biggest single-game explosion in history, defeated the Browns 29-4 at Boston's Fenway Park.

■ **August 31:** Brooklyn's Gil Hodges became the sixth player to hit four home runs in a game during a 19-3 rout of the Braves at Ebbets Field. Hodges also singled and tied the single-game record of 17 total bases.

■ **October 1:** Dick Sisler crashed a three-run 10th-inning home run to give the Phillies a 4-1 victory over the Dodgers and their first N.L. pennant in 35 years.

LEADERS

American League

BA: Billy Goodman, Bos., .354.
Runs: Dom DiMaggio, Bos., 131.
Hits: George Kell, Det., 218.
TB: Walt Dropo, Bos., 326.
HR: Al Rosen, Cle., 37.
RBI: Walt Dropo, Bos.; Vern Stephens, Bos., 144.
SB: Dom DiMaggio, Bos., 15.
Wins: Bob Lemon, Cle., 23.
ERA: Early Wynn, Cle., 3.20.
CG: Ned Garver, St.L.; Bob Lemon, Cle., 22.
IP: Bob Lemon, Cle., 288.
SO: Bob Lemon, Cle., 170.

National League

BA: Stan Musial, St.L., .346.
Runs: Earl Torgeson, Bos., 120.
Hits: Duke Snider, Brk., 199.
TB: Duke Snider, Brk., 343.
HR: Ralph Kiner, Pit., 47.
RBI: Del Ennis, Phil., 126.
SB: Sam Jethroe, Bos., 35.
Wins: Warren Spahn, Bos., 21.
ERA: Sal Maglie, N.Y., 2.71.
CG: Vern Bickford, Bos., 27.
IP: Vern Bickford, Bos., 311.2.
SO: Warren Spahn, Bos., 191.

A.L. 20-game winners
Bob Lemon, Cle., 23-11
Vic Raschi, N.Y., 21-8

N.L. 20-game winners
Warren Spahn, Bos., 21-17
Robin Roberts, Phil., 20-11
Johnny Sain, Bos., 20-13

A.L. 100 RBIs
Walt Dropo, Bos., 144
Vern Stephens, Bos., 144
Yogi Berra, N.Y., 124
Vic Wertz, Det., 123
Joe DiMaggio, N.Y., 122
Bobby Doerr, Bos., 120
Al Rosen, Cle., 116
Luke Easter, Cle., 107
Hoot Evers, Det., 103
Larry Doby, Cle., 102
George Kell, Det., 101

N.L. 100 RBIs
Del Ennis, Phil., 126
Ralph Kiner, Pit., 118
Gil Hodges, Brk., 113
Ted Kluszewski, Cin., 111
Stan Musial, St.L., 109
Bob Elliott, Bos., 107
Duke Snider, Brk., 107
Carl Furillo, Brk., 106
Sid Gordon, Bos., 103
Hank Sauer, Chi., 103
Enos Slaughter, St.L., 101

N.L. 40 homers
Ralph Kiner, Pit., 47

Most Valuable Player
A.L.: Phil Rizzuto, SS, N.Y.
N.L.: Jim Konstanty, P, Phil.

Rookie of the Year
A.L.: Walt Dropo, 1B, Bos.
N.L.: Sam Jethroe, OF, Bos.

ALL-STAR GAME

■ **Winner:** The N.L. broke a four-game losing streak with a 4-3 victory in the first extra-inning All-Star Game.

■ **Key inning:** The ninth, when Tigers pitcher Art Houtteman, trying to close out a 3-2 A.L. victory, surrendered a game-tying home run to Pirates slugger Ralph Kiner.

■ **Memorable moment:** A dramatic 14th-inning home run by Cardinals second baseman Red Schoendienst that gave the N.L. its first win since 1944. Schoendienst was an 11th-inning defensive replacement.

■ **Top guns:** Larry Jansen (Giants), Ewell Blackwell (Reds), Kiner (Pirates), Schoendienst (Cardinals), N.L.; Bob Lemon (Indians), Larry Doby (Indians), A.L.

■ **MVP:** Schoendienst.

Linescore

July 11, at Chicago's Comiskey Park
N.L.......0 2 0 0 0 0 0 0 1 0 0 0 0 1—4 10 0
A.L.......0 0 1 0 2 0 0 0 0 0 0 0 0 0—3 8 1
Roberts (Phillies), Newcombe (Dodgers) 4, Konstanty (Phillies) 6, Jansen (Giants) 7, Blackwell (Reds) 12; Raschi (Yankees), Lemon (Indians) 4, Houtteman (Tigers) 7, Reynolds (Yankees) 10, Gray (Tigers) 13, Feller (Indians) 14. W—Blackwell. L—Gray. HR—Kiner, Schoendienst, N.L.

WORLD SERIES

■ **Winner:** Rekindling memories of New York's 1936-39 machine, the Bronx Bombers captured their second straight Series with a sweep of the Phillies.

■ **Turning point:** Joe DiMaggio's 10th-inning homer that gave the Yankees and Allie Reynolds a 2-1 victory in Game 2.

■ **Memorable moment:** Rookie Whitey Ford's first Series victory — a 5-2 Game 4 decision.

■ **Top guns:** Gene Woodling (.429), Bobby Brown (.333), Yankees; Granny Hamner (.429), Phillies.

Linescores

Game 1—October 4, at Philadelphia
New York ....0 0 0 1 0 0 0 0 0—1 5 0
Philadelphia ....0 0 0 0 0 0 0 0 0—0 2 1
Raschi; Konstanty, Meyer (9). W—Raschi. L—Konstanty.

Game 2—October 5, at Philadelphia
New York ....0 1 0 0 0 0 0 0 0 1—2 10 0
Philadelphia ....0 0 0 0 1 0 0 0 0 0—1 7 0
Reynolds; Roberts. W—Reynolds. L—Roberts. HR—DiMaggio (N.Y.).

Game 3—October 6, at New York
Philadelphia ....0 0 0 0 0 1 1 0 0—2 10 2
New York ....0 0 1 0 0 0 0 1 1—3 7 0
Heintzelman, Konstanty (8), Meyer (9); Lopat, Ferrick (9). W—Ferrick. L—Meyer.

Game 4—October 7, at New York
Philadelphia ....0 0 0 0 0 0 0 0 2—2 7 1
New York ....2 0 0 0 0 3 0 0 x—5 8 2
Miller, Konstanty (1), Roberts (8); Ford, Reynolds (9). W—Ford. L—Miller. HR—Berra (N.Y.).

1951

FINAL STANDINGS

American League

Team	W	L	Pct.	GB
New York	98	56	.636	...
Cleveland	93	61	.604	5
Boston	87	67	.565	11
Chicago	81	73	.526	17
Detroit	73	81	.474	25
Philadelphia	70	84	.455	28
Washington	62	92	.403	36
St. Louis	52	102	.338	46

National League

Team	W	L	Pct.	GB
*New York	98	59	.624	...
Brooklyn	97	60	.618	1
St. Louis	81	73	.526	15.5
Boston	76	78	.494	20.5
Philadelphia	73	81	.474	23.5
Cincinnati	68	86	.442	28.5
Pittsburgh	64	90	.416	32.5
Chicago	62	92	.403	34.5

*Defeated Brooklyn 2-1 in pennant playoff.

SIGNIFICANT EVENTS

■ **August 19:** Browns owner Bill Veeck pulled off a wild promotional stunt when he sent midget Eddie Gaedel to the plate as a surprise pinch-hitter in a Sportsman's Park game against the Tigers.

■ **September 20:** N.L. President Ford Frick was selected as baseball's third commissioner during a marathon meeting in Chicago.

■ **December 11:** Yankee center fielder Joe DiMaggio, a three-time A.L. MVP, announced his retirement.

MEMORABLE MOMENTS

■ **September 14:** Browns outfielder Bob Nieman became the first player to hit home runs in his first two big-league at-bats. Both came off Mickey McDermott in a game at Boston.

■ **September 28:** New York's Allie Reynolds fired his record-tying second no-hitter of the season in the opener of a doubleheader against Boston, earning an 8-0 decision and clinching at least a tie for the A.L. pennant. The Yankees clinched their third straight flag with an 11-3 win in the nightcap.

■ **October 3:** Bobby Thomson smashed a three-run, ninth-inning homer—giving the Giants a dramatic 5-4 victory over the Dodgers in the decisive third game of an N.L. pennant playoff.

LEADERS

American League

BA: Ferris Fain, Phil., .344.
Runs: Dom DiMaggio, Bos., 113.
Hits: George Kell, Det., 191.
TB: Ted Williams, Bos., 295.
HR: Gus Zernial, Chi.-Phil., 33.
RBI: Gus Zernial, Chi.-Phil., 129.
SB: Minnie Minoso, Cle.-Chi., 31.
Wins: Bob Feller, Cle., 22.
ERA: Saul Rogovin, Det.-Chi., 2.78.
CG: Ned Garver, St.L., 24.
IP: Early Wynn, Cle., 274.1.
SO: Vic Raschi, N.Y., 164.

National League

BA: Stan Musial, St.L., .355.
Runs: Ralph Kiner, Pit.; Stan Musial, St.L., 124.
Hits: Richie Ashburn, Phil., 221.
TB: Stan Musial, St.L., 355.
HR: Ralph Kiner, Pit., 42.
RBI: Monte Irvin, N.Y., 121.
SB: Sam Jethroe, Bos., 35.
Wins: Larry Jansen, N.Y.; Sal Maglie, N.Y., 23.
ERA: Chet Nichols, Bos., 2.88.
CG: Warren Spahn, Bos., 26.
IP: Robin Roberts, Phil., 315.
SO: Don Newcombe, Brk.; Warren Spahn, Bos., 164.

A.L. 20-game winners

Bob Feller, Cle., 22-8
Eddie Lopat, N.Y., 21-9
Vic Raschi, N.Y., 21-10
Ned Garver, St.L., 20-12
Mike Garcia, Cle., 20-13
Early Wynn, Cle., 20-13

N.L. 20-game winners

Sal Maglie, N.Y., 23-6
Larry Jansen, N.Y., 23-11
Preacher Roe, Brk., 22-3
Warren Spahn, Bos., 22-14
Robin Roberts, Phil., 21-15
Don Newcombe, Brk., 20-9
Murry Dickson, Pit., 20-16

A.L. 100 RBIs

Gus Zernial, Chi.-Phil., 129
Ted Williams, Bos., 126
Eddie Robinson, Chi., 117
Luke Easter, Cle., 103
Al Rosen, Cle., 102

N.L. 100 RBIs

Monte Irvin, N.Y., 121
Sid Gordon, Bos., 109
Ralph Kiner, Pit., 109
Roy Campanella, Brk., 108
Stan Musial, St.L., 108
Gil Hodges, Brk., 103
Duke Snider, Brk., 101
Bobby Thomson, N.Y., 101

N.L. 40 homers

Ralph Kiner, Pit., 42
Gil Hodges, Brk., 40

Most Valuable Player

A.L.: Yogi Berra, C, N.Y.
N.L.: Roy Campanella, C, Brk.

Rookie of the Year

A.L.: Gil McDougald, 3B, N.Y.
N.L.: Willie Mays, OF, N.Y.

Hall of Fame additions

Jimmie Foxx, 1B, 1925-45
Mel Ott, OF, 1926-47

ALL-STAR GAME

■ **Winner:** The N.L. hit an All-Star Game-record four home runs in an 8-3 victory. It marked the first time the senior circuit had recorded back-to-back wins.

■ **Key inning:** A three-run fourth, when St. Louis' Stan Musial and Boston's Bob Elliott connected off Yankee lefty Eddie Lopat.

■ **Memorable moments:** A.L. home runs by Vic Wertz and George Kell before their home fans at Detroit's Briggs Stadium.

■ **Top guns:** Don Newcombe (Dodgers), Musial (Cardinals), Elliott (Braves), Jackie Robinson (Dodgers), Ralph Kiner (Pirates), Gil Hodges (Dodgers), N.L.; Wertz (Tigers), Kell (Tigers), A.L.

■ **MVP:** Elliott.

Linescore

July 10, at Detroit's Briggs Stadium
N.L. ....1 0 0 3 0 2 1 1 0—8 12 1
A.L. ....0 1 0 1 1 0 0 0 0—3 10 2
Roberts (Phillies), Maglie (Giant) 3, Newcombe (Dodgers) 6, Blackwell (Reds) 9; Garver (Browns), Lopat (Yankees) 4, Hutchinson (Tigers) 5, Parnell (Red Sox) 8, Lemon (Indians) 9. W—Maglie. L—Lopat. HR—Musial, Elliott, Hodges, Kiner, N.L.; Wertz, Kell, A.L.

WORLD SERIES

■ **Winner:** The Yankees' third straight Series victory came at the expense of the torrid Giants, who had beaten Brooklyn in a memorable pennant playoff series.

■ **Turning point:** Infielder Gil McDougald's Game 5 grand slam, which sparked a momentum-turning 13-1 Yankee victory.

■ **Memorable moment:** Yankee right fielder Hank Bauer's Game 6 heroics: a bases-loaded triple and a spectacular Series-ending catch in a 4-3 victory.

■ **Top guns:** Eddie Lopat (2-0, 0.50 ERA), Bobby Brown (.357), McDougald (7 RBIs), Yankees; Monte Irvin (.458), Alvin Dark (.417), Giants.

Linescores

Game 1—October 4, at Yankee Stadium
Giants ....2 0 0 0 0 3 0 0 0—5 10 1
Yankees ....0 1 0 0 0 0 0 0 0—1 7 1
Koslo; Reynolds, Hogue (7), Morgan (8). W—Koslo. L—Reynolds. HR—Dark (Giants).

Game 2—October 5, at Yankee Stadium
Giants ....0 0 0 0 0 0 1 0 0—1 5 1
Yankees ....1 1 0 0 0 0 0 1 x—3 6 0
Jansen, Spencer (7); Lopat. W—Lopat. L—Jansen. HR—Collins (Yankees).

Game 3—October 6, at Polo Grounds
Yankees ....0 0 0 0 0 0 0 1 1—2 5 2
Giants ....0 1 0 0 5 0 0 0 x—6 7 2
Raschi, Hogue (5), Ostrowski (8); Hearn, Jones (8). W—Hearn. L—Raschi. HR—Lockman (Giants); Woodling (Yankees).

Game 4—October 8, at Polo Grounds
Yankees ....0 1 0 1 2 0 2 0 0—6 12 0
Giants ....1 0 0 0 0 0 0 0 1—2 8 2
Reynolds; Maglie, Jones (6), Kennedy (9). W—Reynolds. L—Maglie. HR—DiMaggio (Yankees).

Game 5—October 9, at Polo Grounds
Yankees ....0 0 5 2 0 2 4 0 0—13 12 1
Giants ....1 0 0 0 0 0 0 0 0— 1 5 3
Lopat; Jansen, Kennedy (4), Spencer (6), Corwin (7), Konikowski (9). W—Lopat. L—Jansen. HR—McDougald, Rizzuto (Yankees).

Game 6—October 10, at Yankee Stadium
Giants ....0 0 0 0 1 0 0 0 2—3 11 1
Yankees ....1 0 0 0 0 3 0 0 x—4 7 0
Koslo, Hearn (7), Jansen (8); Raschi, Sain (7), Kuzava (9). W—Raschi. L—Koslo.

1952

FINAL STANDINGS

American League

Team	W	L	Pct.	GB
New York	95	59	.617	...
Cleveland	93	61	.604	2
Chicago	81	73	.526	14
Philadelphia	79	75	.513	16
Washington	78	76	.506	17
Boston	76	78	.494	19
St. Louis	64	90	.416	31
Detroit	50	104	.325	45

National League

Team	W	L	Pct.	GB
Brooklyn	96	57	.627	...
New York	92	62	.597	4.5
St. Louis	88	66	.571	8.5
Philadelphia	87	67	.565	9.5
Chicago	77	77	.500	19.5
Cincinnati	69	85	.448	27.5
Boston	64	89	.418	32
Pittsburgh	42	112	.273	54.5

SIGNIFICANT EVENTS

■ **May 2:** Boston's Ted Williams, who lost three years to military service in World War II, returned to a 17-month tour of duty with the U.S. Marines as a fighter pilot in Korea.

■ **May-June-July:** Joining Williams on the Korean front were such name players as Don Newcombe, Willie Mays, Jerry Coleman, Bob Kennedy, Bobby Brown and Tom Morgan.

MEMORABLE MOMENTS

■ **April 23:** Browns lefty Bob Cain outdueled Cleveland ace Bob Feller, 1-0, in a record-tying battle of one-hitters at St. Louis' Sportsman's Park.

■ **May 21:** The Dodgers exploded for a Major League-record 15 first-inning runs and coasted to a 19-1 victory over the Reds at Ebbets Field.

■ **July 15:** Detroit first baseman Walt Dropo doubled in the second game of a doubleheader against Washington for his 12th consecutive hit, tying the 1938 record set by Boston's Pinky Higgins.

■ **August 25:** Detroit's Virgil Trucks became the third pitcher to throw two no-hitters in one season when he stopped New York, 1-0, at Yankee Stadium.

LEADERS

American League

BA: Ferris Fain, Phil., .327.
Runs: Larry Doby, Cle., 104.
Hits: Nellie Fox, Chi., 192.
TB: Al Rosen, Cle., 297.
HR: Larry Doby, Cle., 32.
RBI: Al Rosen, Cle., 105.
SB: Minnie Minoso, Chi., 22.
Wins: Bobby Shantz, Phil., 24.
ERA: Allie Reynolds, N.Y., 2.06.
CG: Bob Lemon, Cle., 28.
IP: Bob Lemon, Cle., 309.2.
SO: Allie Reynolds, N.Y., 160.

National League

BA: Stan Musial, St.L., .336.
Runs: Solly Hemus, St.L.; Stan Musial, St.L., 105.
Hits: Stan Musial, St.L., 194.
TB: Stan Musial, St.L., 311.
HR: Ralph Kiner, Pit.; Hank Sauer, Chi., 37.
RBI: Hank Sauer, Chi., 121.
SB: Pee Wee Reese, Brk., 30.
Wins: Robin Roberts, Phil., 28.
ERA: Hoyt Wilhelm, N.Y., 2.43.
CG: Robin Roberts, Phil., 30.
IP: Robin Roberts, Phil., 330.
SO: Warren Spahn, Bos., 183.

A.L. 20-game winners

Bobby Shantz, Phil., 24-7
Early Wynn, Cle., 23-12
Mike Garcia, Cle., 22-11
Bob Lemon, Cle., 22-11
Allie Reynolds, N.Y., 20-8

N.L. 20-Game Winner

Robin Roberts, Phil., 28-7

A.L. 100 RBIs

Al Rosen, Cle., 105
Larry Doby, Cle., 104
Eddie Robinson, Chi., 104
Gus Zernial, Phil., 100

N.L. 100 RBIs

Hank Sauer, Chi., 121
Bobby Thomson, N.Y., 108
Del Ennis, Phil., 107
Gil Hodges, Brk., 102
Enos Slaughter, St.L., 101

Most Valuable Player

A.L.: Bobby Shantz, P, Phil.
N.L.: Hank Sauer, OF, Chi.

Rookie of the Year

A.L.: Harry Byrd, P, Phil.
N.L.: Joe Black, P, Brk.

Hall of Fame additions

Harry Heilmann, OF/1B, 1914-32
Paul Waner, OF, 1926-45

ALL-STAR GAME

■ **Winner:** The N.L. recorded a rain-shortened 3-2 victory and closed its All-Star deficit to 12-7.

■ **Key inning:** The fourth, when the A.L. scored twice for a 2-1 lead and the N.L. answered with a two-run homer by the Cubs' Hank Sauer.

■ **Memorable moments:** The pitching of Philadelphia stars Curt Simmons (Phillies) and Bobby Shantz (Athletics) before their home fans. Simmons pitched three scoreless innings for the N.L. and Shantz struck out all three batters he faced in a scoreless fifth.

■ **Top guns:** Simmons (Phillies), Jackie Robinson (Dodgers), Sauer (Cubs), N.L.; Shantz (Athletics), Bobby Avila (Indians), A.L.

■ **MVP:** Sauer.

Linescore

July 8, at Philadelphia's Shibe Park
A.L. ....0 0 0 2 0—2 5 0
N.L. ....1 0 0 2 0—3 3 0
Raschi (Yankees), Lemon (Indians) 3, Shantz (Athletics) 5; Simmons (Phillies), Rush (Cubs) 4. W—Rush. L—Lemon. HR—J. Robinson, Sauer, N.L.

WORLD SERIES

■ **Winner:** The Yankees tied their own previous best run of four consecutive Series championships with a seven-game thriller against the Dodgers.

■ **Turning point:** Game 6 home runs by Yogi Berra and Mickey Mantle that keyed a 3-2 victory and tied the Series at three games apiece.

■ **Memorable moment:** Yankee second baseman Billy Martin's Series-saving shoetop catch of Jackie Robinson's bases-loaded infield popup, which appeared destined to fall untouched. Martin's mad-dash catch saved a 4-2 victory.

■ **Top guns:** Vic Raschi (2-0, 1.59 ERA), Johnny Mize (.400, 3 HR, 6 RBIs), Mantle (.345, 2 HR), Yankees; Duke Snider (.345, 4 HR, 8 RBIs), Pee Wee Reese (.345), Dodgers.

Linescores

Game 1—October 1, at Brooklyn
New York....................0 0 1 0 0 0 0 1 0—2 6 2
Brooklyn ....0 1 0 0 0 2 0 1 x—4 6 0
Reynolds, Scarborough (8); Black. W—Black. L—Reynolds. HR—Robinson, Snider, Reese (Brk.); McDougald (N.Y.).

Game 2—October 2, at Brooklyn
New York..................0 0 0 1 1 5 0 0 0—7 10 0
Brooklyn ....0 0 1 0 0 0 0 0 0—1 3 1
Raschi; Erskine, Loes (6), Lehman (8). W—Raschi. L—Erskine. HR—Martin (N.Y.).

Game 3—October 3, at New York
Brooklyn ....0 0 1 0 1 0 0 1 2—5 11 0
New York..................0 1 0 0 0 0 0 1 1—3 6 2
Roe; Lopat, Gorman (9). W—Roe. L—Lopat. HR—Berra, Mize (N.Y.).

Game 4—October 4, at New York
Brooklyn ....0 0 0 0 0 0 0 0 0—0 4 1
New York....................0 0 0 1 0 0 0 1 x—2 4 1
Black, Rutherford (8); Reynolds. W—Reynolds. L—Black. HR—Mize (N.Y.).

Game 5—October 5, at New York
Brooklyn ....0 1 0 0 3 0 1 0 0 0 1—6 10 0
New York........0 0 0 0 5 0 0 0 0 0 0—5 5 1
Erskine; Blackwell, Sain (6). W—Erskine. L—Sain. HR—Snider (Brk.); Mize (N.Y.).

Game 6—October 6, at Brooklyn
New York....................0 0 0 0 0 0 2 1 0—3 9 0
Brooklyn ....0 0 0 0 0 1 0 1 0—2 8 1
Raschi, Reynolds (8); Loes, Roe (9). W—Raschi. L—Loes. HR—Mantle, Berra (N.Y.); Snider 2 (Brk.).

Game 7—October 7, at Brooklyn
New York..................0 0 0 1 1 1 1 0 0—4 10 4
Brooklyn ....0 0 0 1 1 0 0 0 0—2 8 1
Lopat, Reynolds (4), Raschi (7), Kuzava (7); Black, Roe (6), Erskine (8). W—Reynolds. L—Black. HR—Woodling, Mantle (N.Y.).

1953

FINAL STANDINGS

American League

Team	W	L	Pct.	GB
New York	99	52	.656	...
Cleveland	92	62	.597	8.5
Chicago	89	65	.578	11.5
Boston	84	69	.549	16
Washington	76	76	.500	23.5
Detroit	60	94	.390	40.5
Philadelphia	59	95	.383	41.5
St. Louis	54	100	.351	46.5

National League

Team	W	L	Pct.	GB
Brooklyn	105	49	.682	...
Milwaukee	92	62	.597	13
Philadelphia	83	71	.539	22
St. Louis	83	71	.539	22
New York	70	84	.455	35
Cincinnati	68	86	.442	37
Chicago	65	89	.422	40
Pittsburgh	50	104	.325	55

SIGNIFICANT EVENTS

■ **March 18:** The Braves, a fixture in Boston for 77 years, received unanimous approval for a move to Milwaukee—baseball's first franchise shift since 1903.

■ **September 29:** Bill Veeck sold his St. Louis Browns to a syndicate that received quick approval to move the franchise to Baltimore.

■ **November 9:** Baseball won a major victory when the U.S. Supreme Court ruled that it is a sport, not an interstate business, and therefore not subject to federal antitrust laws.

MEMORABLE MOMENTS

■ **May 6:** Browns rookie Bobo Holloman made baseball history when he pitched a 6-0 no-hitter against Philadelphia in his first Major League start.

■ **May 25:** Milwaukee's Max Surkont struck out a modern-record eight consecutive Reds en route to a 10-3 victory.

■ **June 18:** The Red Sox scored a record 17 runs in the seventh inning of a 23-3 victory over the Tigers.

LEADERS

American League

BA: Mickey Vernon, Wash., .337.
Runs: Al Rosen, Cle., 115.
Hits: Harvey Kuenn, Det., 209.
TB: Al Rosen, Cle., 367.
HR: Al Rosen, Cle., 43.
RBI: Al Rosen, Cle., 145.
SB: Minnie Minoso, Chi., 25.
Wins: Bob Porterfield, Wash., 22.
ERA: Eddie Lopat, N.Y., 2.42.
CG: Bob Porterfield, Wash., 24.
IP: Bob Lemon, Cle., 286.2.
SO: Billy Pierce, Chi., 186.

National League

BA: Carl Furillo, Brk., .344.
Runs: Duke Snider, Brk., 132.
Hits: Richie Ashburn, Phil., 205.
TB: Duke Snider, Brk., 370.
HR: Eddie Mathews, Mil., 47.
RBI: Roy Campanella, Brk., 142.
SB: Bill Bruton, Mil., 26.
Wins: Robin Roberts, Phil.; Warren Spahn, Mil., 23.
ERA: Warren Spahn, Mil., 2.10.
CG: Robin Roberts, Phil., 33.
IP: Robin Roberts, Phil., 346.2.
SO: Robin Roberts, Phil., 198.

A.L. 20-game winners
Bob Porterfield, Wash., 22-10
Mel Parnell, Bos., 21-8
Bob Lemon, Cle., 21-15
Virgil Trucks, St.L.-Chi., 20-10

N.L. 20-game winners
Warren Spahn, Mil., 23-7
Robin Roberts, Phil., 23-16
Carl Erskine, Brk., 20-6
Harvey Haddix, St.L., 20-9

A.L. 100 RBIs
Al Rosen, Cle., 145
Mickey Vernon, Wash., 115
Ray Boone, Cle.-Det., 114
Yogi Berra, N.Y., 108
Gus Zernial, Phil., 108
Minnie Minoso, Chi., 104
Larry Doby, Cle., 102
Eddie Robinson, Phil., 102

N.L. 100 RBIs
Roy Campanella, Brk., 142
Eddie Mathews, Mil., 135
Duke Snider, Brk., 126
Del Ennis, Phil., 125
Gil Hodges, Brk., 122
Ralph Kiner, Pit.-Chi., 116
Stan Musial, St.L., 113
Ray Jablonski, St.L., 112
Ted Kluszewski, Cin., 108
Bobby Thomson, N.Y., 106
Gus Bell, Cin., 105
Frank Thomas, Pit., 102
Jim Greengrass, Cin., 100

A.L. 40 homers
Al Rosen, Cle., 43
Gus Zernial, Phil., 42

N.L. 40 homers
Eddie Mathews, Mil., 47
Duke Snider, Brk., 42
Roy Campanella, Brk., 41
Ted Kluszewski, Cin., 40

Most Valuable Player
A.L.: Al Rosen, 3B, Cle.
N.L.: Roy Campanella, C, Brk.

Rookie of the Year
A.L.: Harvey Kuenn, SS, Det.
N.L.: Jim Gilliam, 2B, Brk.

Hall of Fame additions
Ed Barrow, manager/executive
Chief Bender, P, 1903-25
Tommy Connolly, umpire
Dizzy Dean, P, 1930-47
Bill Klem, umpire
Al Simmons, OF, 1924-44
Bobby Wallace, SS, 1894-1918
Harry Wright, manager

ALL-STAR GAME

■ **Winner:** Robin Roberts (Phillies), Warren Spahn (Braves), Curt Simmons (Phillies) and Murry Dickson (Pirates) combined on a six-hitter and the N.L. rolled to its fourth consecutive victory.

■ **Key inning:** The N.L.'s two-run fifth, when Philadelphia's Richie Ashburn and Brooklyn's Pee Wee Reese singled home runs.

■ **Memorable moment:** The eighth-inning appearance of Browns righthander Satchel Paige, a former Negro League legend and the oldest man (47) ever to play in an All-Star Game.

■ **Top guns:** Roberts (Phillies), Spahn (Braves), Simmons (Phillies), Reese (Dodgers), N.L.; Billy Pierce (White Sox), Minnie Minoso (White Sox), A.L.

■ **MVP:** Reese.

Linescore

July 14, at Cincinnati's Crosley Field
A.L. ....0 0 0 0 0 0 0 0 1—1 5 0
N.L. ....0 0 0 0 2 0 1 2 x—5 10 0
Pierce (White Sox), Reynolds (Yankees) 4, Garcia (Indians) 6, Paige (Browns) 8; Roberts (Phillies), Spahn (Braves) 4, Simmons (Phillies) 6, Dickson (Pirates) 8. W—Spahn. L—Reynolds.

WORLD SERIES

■ **Winner:** The Yankees earned their record fifth consecutive Series victory and remained perfect in post-season play under manager Casey Stengel.

■ **Turning point:** Billy Martin's two-run homer and Mickey Mantle's grand slam in the Yankees' 11-7 fifth-game Series-turning triumph.

■ **Memorable moment:** Martin's ninth-inning Series-ending single in Game 6 — his record-tying 12th hit of the fall classic.

■ **Top guns:** Martin (.500, 12 hits, 2 HR, 8 RBIs), Mantle (2 HR, 7 RBIs), Yankees; Gil Hodges (.364), Carl Furillo (.333), Dodgers.

Linescores

Game 1—September 30, at New York
Brooklyn ....0 0 0 0 1 3 1 0 0—5 12 2
New York ....4 0 0 0 1 0 1 3 x—9 12 0
Erskine, Hughes (2), Labine (6), Wade (7); Reynolds, Sain (6). W—Sain. L—Labine. HR—Berra, Collins (N.Y.); Gilliam, Hodges, Shuba (Brk.).

Game 2—October 1, at New York
Brooklyn ....0 0 0 2 0 0 0 0 0—2 9 1
New York ....1 0 0 0 0 0 1 2 x—4 5 0
Roe; Lopat. W—Lopat. L—Roe. HR—Martin, Mantle (N.Y.).

Game 3—October 2, at Brooklyn
New York....................0 0 0 0 1 0 0 1 0—2 6 0
Brooklyn ....0 0 0 0 1 1 0 1 x—3 9 0
Raschi; Erskine. W—Erskine. L—Raschi. HR—Campanella (Brk.).

Game 4—October 3, at Brooklyn
New York..................0 0 0 0 2 0 0 0 1—3 9 0
Brooklyn ....3 0 0 1 0 2 1 0 x—7 12 0
Ford, Gorman (2), Sain (5), Schallock (7); Loes, Labine (9). W—Loes. L—Ford. HR—McDougald (N.Y.); Snider (Brk.).

Game 5—October 4, at Brooklyn
New York.................1 0 5 0 0 0 3 1 1—11 11 1
Brooklyn ....0 1 0 0 1 0 0 4 1— 7 14 1
McDonald, Kuzava (8), Reynolds (9); Podres, Meyer (3), Wade (8), Black (9). W—McDonald. L—Podres. HR—Woodling, Mantle, Martin, McDougald (N.Y.); Cox, Gilliam (Brk.).

Game 6—October 5, at New York
Brooklyn ....0 0 0 0 0 1 0 0 2—3 8 3
New York..................2 1 0 0 0 0 0 0 1—4 13 0
Erskine, Milliken (5), Labine (7); Ford, Reynolds (8). W—Reynolds. L—Labine. HR—Furillo (Brk.).

1954

FINAL STANDINGS

American League

Team	W	L	Pct.	GB
Cleveland	111	43	.721	...
New York	103	51	.669	8
Chicago	94	60	.610	17
Boston	69	85	.448	42
Detroit	68	86	.442	43
Washington	66	88	.429	45
Baltimore	54	100	.351	57
Philadelphia	51	103	.331	60

National League

Team	W	L	Pct.	GB
New York	97	57	.630	...
Brooklyn	92	62	.597	5
Milwaukee	89	65	.578	8
Philadelphia	75	79	.487	22
Cincinnati	74	80	.481	23
St. Louis	72	82	.468	25
Chicago	64	90	.416	33
Pittsburgh	53	101	.344	44

SIGNIFICANT EVENTS

■ **July 12:** Big league players organized into a group called the Major League Baseball Players Association and hired J. Norman Lewis to represent it in negotiations with owners.

■ **November 8:** A.L. owners approved the sale of the Athletics to Chicago industrialist Arnold Johnson and transfer of the team to Kansas City.

■ **December 1:** The finishing touches were put on a record 17-player trade between the Orioles and Yankees.

MEMORABLE MOMENTS

■ **April 15:** Baltimore welcomed its new Orioles with a huge celebration and the team responded with a 3-1 victory over Chicago at Memorial Stadium.

■ **May 2:** Cardinals slugger Stan Musial hit a doubleheader-record five home runs in a split with the Giants at Busch Stadium.

■ **July 31:** Milwaukee's Joe Adcock joined the exclusive four-homer club in a 15-7 victory over Brooklyn and set a record for total bases (18) when he added a double to his offensive explosion.

■ **September 25:** Early Wynn fired a two-hitter and the Indians defeated Detroit, 11-1, for their A.L.-record 111th victory of the season.

LEADERS

American League

BA: Bobby Avila, Cle., .341.
Runs: Mickey Mantle, N.Y., 129.
Hits: Nellie Fox, Chi.; Harvey Kuenn, Det., 201.
TB: Minnie Minoso, Chi., 304.
HR: Larry Doby, Cle., 32.
RBI: Larry Doby, Cle., 126.
SB: Jackie Jensen, Bos., 22.
Wins: Bob Lemon, Cle.; Early Wynn, Cle., 23.
ERA: Mike Garcia, Cle., 2.64.
CG: Bob Lemon, Cle.; Bob Porterfield, Wash., 21.
IP: Early Wynn, Cle., 270.2.
SO: Bob Turley, Bal., 185.

National League

BA: Willie Mays, N.Y., .345.
Runs: Stan Musial, St.L.; Duke Snider, Brk., 120.
Hits: Don Mueller, N.Y., 212.
TB: Duke Snider, Brk., 378.
HR: Ted Kluszewski, Cin., 49.
RBI: Ted Kluszewski, Cin., 141.
SB: Bill Bruton, Mil., 34.
Wins: Robin Roberts, Phil., 23.
ERA: Johnny Antonelli, N.Y., 2.30.
CG: Robin Roberts, Phil., 29.
IP: Robin Roberts, Phil., 336.2.
SO: Robin Roberts, Phil., 185.

A.L. 20-game winners
Bob Lemon, Cle., 23-7
Early Wynn, Cle., 23-11
Bob Grim, N.Y., 20-6

N.L. 20-game winners
Robin Roberts, Phil., 23-15
Johnny Antonelli, N.Y., 21-7
Warren Spahn, Mil., 21-12

A.L. 100 RBIs
Larry Doby, Cle., 126
Yogi Berra, N.Y., 125
Jackie Jensen, Bos., 117
Minnie Minoso, Chi., 116
Mickey Mantle, N.Y., 102
Al Rosen, Cle., 102
Roy Sievers, Wash., 102

N.L. 100 RBIs
Ted Kluszewski, Cin., 141
Gil Hodges, Brk., 130
Duke Snider, Brk., 130
Stan Musial, St.L., 126
Del Ennis, Phil., 119
Willie Mays, N.Y., 110
Ray Jablonski, St.L., 104
Eddie Mathews, Mil., 103
Hank Sauer, Chi., 103
Gus Bell, Cin., 101

N.L. 40 homers
Ted Kluszewski, Cin., 49
Gil Hodges, Brk., 42
Willie Mays, N.Y., 41
Hank Sauer, Chi., 41
Eddie Mathews, Mil., 40
Duke Snider, Brk., 40

Most Valuable Player
A.L.: Yogi Berra, C, N.Y.
N.L.: Willie Mays, OF, N.Y.

Rookie of the Year
A.L.: Bob Grim, P, N.Y.
N.L.: Wally Moon, OF, St.L.

Hall of Fame additions
Bill Dickey, C, 1928-46
Rabbit Maranville, SS, 1912-35
Bill Terry, 1B, 1923-36

ALL-STAR GAME

■ **Winner:** Chicago's Nellie Fox looped a two-run eighth-inning single to spark the A.L. in a game that featured two home runs and five RBIs by Cleveland fan favorite Al Rosen.

■ **Key inning:** The eighth. Before Fox's game-winning single, Cleveland's Larry Doby excited the home fans with a game-tying home run.

■ **Memorable moment:** Senators lefthander Dean Stone's no-pitch victory. Stone entered the game with two out in the eighth and retired St. Louis' Red Schoendienst trying to steal home.

■ **Top guns:** Rosen (Indians), Bobby Avila (Indians), Doby (Indians), Ray Boone (Tigers), Fox (White Sox), Yogi Berra (Yankees), A.L.; Duke Snider (Dodgers), Ted Kluszewski (Reds), Gus Bell (Reds), N.L.

■ **MVP:** Rosen.

Linescore

July 13, at Cleveland Stadium
N.L. ....0 0 0 5 2 0 0 2 0— 9 14 0
A.L. ....0 0 4 1 2 1 0 3 x—11 17 1
Roberts (Phillies), Antonelli (Giants) 4, Spahn (Braves) 6, Grissom (Giants) 6, Conley (Braves) 8, Erskine (Dodgers) 8; Ford (Yankees), Consuegra (White Sox) 4, Lemon (Indians) 4, Porterfield (Senators) 5, Keegan (White Sox) 8, Stone (Senators) 8, Trucks (White Sox) 9. W—Stone. L—Conley. HR—Rosen 2, Boone, Doby, A.L.; Kluszewski, Bell, N.L.

WORLD SERIES

■ **Winner:** The Giants pulled off a surprising sweep of the Indians, who had won an A.L.-record 111 games.

■ **Turning point:** A three-run 10th-inning home run by pinch-hitter Dusty Rhodes that decided Game 1. Rhodes' pop-fly homer traveled 260 feet.

■ **Memorable moment:** Center fielder Willie Mays' over-the-shoulder catch of a Game 1 blast by Cleveland's Vic Wertz — perhaps the greatest defensive play in Series history.

■ **Top guns:** Rhodes (.667, 2 HR, 7 RBIs), Alvin Dark (.412), Don Mueller (.389), Giants; Wertz (.500), Indians.

Linescores

Game 1—September 29, at New York
Cleveland ....2 0 0 0 0 0 0 0 0 0—2 8 0
New York..............0 0 2 0 0 0 0 0 0 3—5 9 3
Lemon; Maglie, Liddle (8), Grissom (8). W—Grissom. L—Lemon. HR—Rhodes (N.Y.).

Game 2—September 30, at New York
Cleveland ....1 0 0 0 0 0 0 0 0—1 8 0
New York....................0 0 0 0 2 0 1 0 x—3 4 0
Wynn, Mossi (8); Antonelli. W—Antonelli. L—Wynn. HR—Smith (Cle.); Rhodes (N.Y.).

Game 3—October 1, at Cleveland
New York..................1 0 3 0 1 1 0 0 0—6 10 1
Cleveland ....0 0 0 0 0 0 1 1 0—2 4 2
Gomez, Wilhelm (8); Garcia, Houtteman (4), Narleski (6), Mossi (9). W—Gomez. L—Garcia. HR—Wertz (Cle.).

Game 4—October 2, at Cleveland
New York..................0 2 1 0 4 0 0 0 0—7 10 3
Cleveland ....0 0 0 0 3 0 1 0 0—4 6 2
Liddle, Wilhelm (7), Antonelli (8); Lemon, Newhouser (5), Narleski (5), Mossi (6), Garcia (8). W—Liddle. L—Lemon. HR—Majeski (Cle.).

1955

FINAL STANDINGS

American League

Team	W	L	Pct.	GB
New York	96	58	.623	...
Cleveland	93	61	.604	3
Chicago	91	63	.591	5
Boston	84	70	.545	12
Detroit	79	75	.513	17
Kansas City	63	91	.409	33
Baltimore	57	97	.370	39
Washington	53	101	.344	43

National League

Team	W	L	Pct.	GB
Brooklyn	98	55	.641	...
Milwaukee	85	69	.552	13.5
New York	80	74	.519	18.5
Philadelphia	77	77	.500	21.5
Cincinnati	75	79	.487	23.5
Chicago	72	81	.471	26
St. Louis	68	86	.442	30.5
Pittsburgh	60	94	.390	38.5

SIGNIFICANT EVENT

■ **April 14:** The New York Yankees, one of four non-integrated teams, broke the color barrier when Elston Howard singled in his first big-league at-bat in a game at Boston.

MEMORABLE MOMENTS

■ **April 12:** The Athletics made their Kansas City debut with a 6-2 victory over the Tigers.

■ **April 23:** The White Sox hit seven home runs and tied a modern run-scoring record with a 29-6 victory at Kansas City.

■ **September 25:** Giants slugger Willie Mays, baseball's seventh 50-homer man, belted No. 51 in a 5-2 victory over the Phillies.

■ **September 25:** 20-year-old Tigers outfielder Al Kaline became baseball's youngest batting champ when he finished with an A.L.-best .340 average.

LEADERS

American League

BA: Al Kaline, Det., .340.
Runs: Al Smith, Cle., 123.
Hits: Al Kaline, Det., 200.
TB: Al Kaline, Det., 321.
HR: Mickey Mantle, N.Y., 37.
RBI: Ray Boone, Det.; Jackie Jensen, Bos., 116.
SB: Jim Rivera, Chi., 25.
Wins: Whitey Ford, N.Y.; Bob Lemon, Cle.; Frank Sullivan, Bos., 18.
ERA: Billy Pierce, Chi., 1.97.
CG: Whitey Ford, N.Y., 18.
IP: Frank Sullivan, Bos., 260.
SO: Herb Score, Cle., 245.

National League

BA: Richie Ashburn, Phil., .338.
Runs: Duke Snider, Brk., 126.
Hits: Ted Kluszewski, Cin., 192.
TB: Willie Mays, N.Y., 382.
HR: Willie Mays, N.Y., 51.
RBI: Duke Snider, Brk., 136.
SB: Bill Bruton, Mil., 25.
Wins: Robin Roberts, Phil., 23.
ERA: Bob Friend, Pit., 2.83.
CG: Robin Roberts, Phil., 26.
IP: Robin Roberts, Phil., 305.
SO: Sam Jones, Chi., 198.

N.L. 20-game winners
Robin Roberts, Phil., 23-14
Don Newcombe, Brk., 20-5

A.L. 100 RBIs
Ray Boone, Det., 116
Jackie Jensen, Bos., 116
Yogi Berra, N.Y., 108
Roy Sievers, Wash., 106
Al Kaline, Det., 102

N.L. 100 RBIs
Duke Snider, Brk., 136
Willie Mays, N.Y., 127
Del Ennis, Phil., 120
Ernie Banks, Chi., 117
Ted Kluszewski, Cin., 113
Wally Post, Cin., 109
Stan Musial, St.L., 108
Roy Campanella, Brk., 107
Hank Aaron, Mil., 106
Gus Bell, Cin., 104
Gil Hodges, Brk., 102
Eddie Mathews, Mil., 101

N.L. 40 homers
Willie Mays, N.Y., 51
Ted Kluszewski, Cin., 47
Ernie Banks, Chi., 44
Duke Snider, Brk., 42
Eddie Mathews, Mil., 41
Wally Post, Cin., 40

Most Valuable Player
A.L.: Yogi Berra, C, N.Y.
N.L.: Roy Campanella, C, Brk.

Rookie of the Year
A.L.: Herb Score, P, Cle.
N.L.: Bill Virdon, OF, St.L.

Hall of Fame additions
Home Run Baker, 3B, 1908-22
Joe DiMaggio, OF, 1936-51
Gabby Hartnett, C, 1922-41
Ted Lyons, P, 1923-46
Ray Schalk, C, 1912-29
Dazzy Vance, P, 1915-35

ALL-STAR GAME

■ **Winner:** The N.L., down 5-0 entering the seventh inning, rallied for a 6-5 victory in 12 innings — the second longest All-Star Game.

■ **Key inning:** The N.L.'s three-run eighth, which tied the score and forced extra innings. The tying run scored on right fielder Al Kaline's wild throw.

■ **Memorable moment:** Stan Musial's first-pitch home run in the 12th off Boston's Frank Sullivan. It was Musial's record fourth All-Star homer.

■ **Top guns:** Joe Nuxhall (Reds), Gene Conley (Braves), Willie Mays (Giants), Hank Aaron (Braves), Musial (Cardinals), N.L.; Billy Pierce (White Sox), Chico Carrasquel (White Sox), Mickey Mantle (Yankees), A.L.

■ **MVP:** Musial.

Linescore

July 12, at Milwaukee's County Stadium
A.L. ....4 0 0 0 0 1 0 0 0 0 0 0—5 10 2
N.L. ....0 0 0 0 0 0 2 3 0 0 0 1—6 13 1
Pierce (White Sox), Wynn (Indians) 4, Ford (Yankees) 7, Sullivan (Red Sox) 8; Roberts (Phillies), Haddix (Cardinals) 4, Newcombe (Dodgers) 7, Jones (Cubs) 8, Nuxhall (Reds) 8, Conley (Braves) 12. W—Conley. L—Sullivan. HR—Mantle, A.L.; Musial, N.L.

WORLD SERIES

■ **Winner:** Brooklyn's long wait finally ended as the Dodgers won a Series on their eighth try — beating the hated Yankees in the process.
Turning point: Hot-hitting Duke Snider's two home runs powered the Dodgers to within a game of their first championship in a 5-3 Game 5 victory.

■ **Memorable moment:** A spectacular Series-saving catch by Dodgers outfielder Sandy Amoros in the sixth inning of Game 7. The two-on, nobody-out catch of Yogi Berra's line drive resulted in a double play and preserved Johnny Podres' 2-0 shutout.

■ **Top guns:** Podres (2-0, 1.00 ERA), Snider (.320, 4 HR, 7 RBIs), Dodgers; Whitey Ford (2-0, 2.12), Hank Bauer (.429), Berra (.417), Yankees.

■ **MVP:** Podres.

Linescores

Game 1—September 28, at New York
Brooklyn ....0 2 1 0 0 0 0 2 0—5 10 0
New York..................0 2 1 1 0 2 0 0 x—6 9 1
Newcombe, Bessent (6), Labine (8); Ford, Grim (9). W—Ford. L—Newcombe. HR—Collins 2, Howard (N.Y.); Furillo, Snider (Brk.).

Game 2—September 29, at New York
Brooklyn ....0 0 0 1 1 0 0 0 0—2 5 2
New York....................0 0 0 4 0 0 0 0 x—4 8 0
Loes, Bessent (4), Spooner (5), Labine (8); Byrne. W—Byrne. L—Loes.

Game 3—September 30, at Brooklyn
New York..................0 2 0 0 0 0 1 0 0—3 7 0
Brooklyn ....2 2 0 2 0 0 2 0 x—8 11 1
Turley, Morgan (2), Kucks (5), Sturdivant (7); Podres. W—Podres. L—Turley. HR—Campanella (Brk.); Mantle (N.Y.).

Game 4—October 1, at Brooklyn
New York..................1 1 0 1 0 2 0 0 0—5 9 0
Brooklyn ....0 0 1 3 3 0 1 0 x—8 14 0
Larsen, Kucks (5), R. Coleman (6), Morgan (7), Sturdivant (8); Erskine, Bessent (4), Labine (5). W—Labine. L—Larsen. HR—McDougald (N.Y.); Campanella, Hodges, Snider (Brk).

Game 5—October 2, at Brooklyn
New York....................0 0 0 1 0 0 1 1 0—3 6 0
Brooklyn ....0 2 1 0 1 0 0 1 x—5 9 2
Grim, Turley (7); Craig, Labine (7). W—Craig. L—Grim. HR—Snider 2, Amoros (Brk.); Cerv, Berra (N.Y.).

Game 6—October 3, at New York
Brooklyn ....0 0 0 1 0 0 0 0 0—1 4 1
New York....................5 0 0 0 0 0 0 0 x—5 8 0
Spooner, Meyer (1), Roebuck (7); Ford. W—Ford. L—Spooner. HR—Skowron (N.Y.).

Game 7—October 4, at New York
Brooklyn ....0 0 0 1 0 1 0 0 0—2 5 0
New York....................0 0 0 0 0 0 0 0 0—0 8 1
Podres; Byrne, Grim (6), Turley (8). W—Podres. L—Byrne.

1956

FINAL STANDINGS

American League

Team	W	L	Pct.	GB
New York	97	57	.630	...
Cleveland	88	66	.571	9
Chicago	85	69	.552	12
Boston	84	70	.545	13
Detroit	82	72	.532	15
Baltimore	69	85	.448	28
Washington	59	95	.383	38
Kansas City	52	102	.338	45

National League

Team	W	L	Pct.	GB
Brooklyn	93	61	.604	...
Milwaukee	92	62	.597	1
Cincinnati	91	63	.591	2
St. Louis	76	78	.494	17
Philadelphia	71	83	.461	22
New York	67	87	.435	26
Pittsburgh	66	88	.429	27
Chicago	60	94	.390	33

SIGNIFICANT EVENTS

■ **April 19:** The Dodgers played the first of seven "home-away-from-home" games at Jersey City's Roosevelt Stadium and posted a 10-inning, 5-4 victory over the Phillies.

■ **September 30:** Yankee slugger Mickey Mantle finished his Triple Crown journey with a .353 average, 52 home runs and 130 RBIs.

■ **November 21:** N.L. MVP Don Newcombe, who finished 27-7 for the Dodgers, captured the inaugural Cy Young Award as baseball's top pitcher.

MEMORABLE MOMENTS

■ **May 28:** Pittsburgh first baseman Dale Long hit a home run in his record eighth consecutive game as the Pirates defeated Brooklyn, 3-2.

■ **September 11:** Cincinnati's Frank Robinson tied the rookie home run record when he hit No. 38 in an 11-5 victory over the Giants.

■ **September 30:** The Dodgers posted a final-day 8-6 victory over Pittsburgh and captured their second straight N.L. pennant by one game over Milwaukee.

LEADERS

American League

BA: Mickey Mantle, N.Y., .353.
Runs: Mickey Mantle, N.Y., 132.
Hits: Harvey Kuenn, Det., 196.
TB: Mickey Mantle, N.Y., 376.
HR: Mickey Mantle, N.Y., 52.
RBI: Mickey Mantle, N.Y., 130.
SB: Luis Aparicio, Chi., 21.
Wins: Frank Lary, Det., 21.
ERA: Whitey Ford, N.Y., 2.47.
CG: Bob Lemon, Cle.; Billy Pierce, Chi., 21.
IP: Frank Lary, Det., 294.
SO: Herb Score, Cle., 263.

National League

BA: Hank Aaron, Mil., .328.
Runs: Frank Robinson, Cin., 122.
Hits: Hank Aaron, Mil., 200.
TB: Hank Aaron, Mil., 340.
HR: Duke Snider, Brk., 43.
RBI: Stan Musial, St.L., 109.
SB: Willie Mays, N.Y., 40.
Wins: Don Newcombe, Brk., 27.
ERA: Lew Burdette, Mil., 2.70.
CG: Robin Roberts, Phil., 22.
IP: Bob Friend, Pit., 314.1
SO: Sam Jones, Chi., 176.

A.L. 20-game winners
Frank Lary, Det., 21-13
Herb Score, Cle., 20-9
Early Wynn, Cle., 20-9
Billy Pierce, Chi., 20-9
Bob Lemon, Cle., 20-14
Billy Hoeft, Det., 20-14

N.L. 20-game winners
Don Newcombe, Brk., 27-7
Warren Spahn, Mil., 20-11
Johnny Antonelli, N.Y., 20-13

A.L. 100 RBIs
Mickey Mantle, N.Y., 130
Al Kaline, Det., 128
Vic Wertz, Cle., 106
Yogi Berra, N.Y., 105
Harry Simpson, K.C., 105
Larry Doby, Chi., 102

N.L. 100 RBIs
Stan Musial, St.L., 109
Joe Adcock, Mil., 103
Ted Kluszewski, Cin., 102
Duke Snider, Brk., 101

A.L. 40 homers
Mickey Mantle, N.Y., 52

N.L. 40 homers
Duke Snider, Brk., 43

Most Valuable Player
A.L.: Mickey Mantle, OF, N.Y.
N.L.: Don Newcombe, P, Brk.

Cy Young Award
A.L.-N.L.: Don Newcombe, Brk.

Rookie of the Year
A.L.: Luis Aparicio, SS, Chi.
N.L.: Frank Robinson, OF, Cin.

Hall of Fame additions
Joe Cronin, SS/Man./Exec.
Hank Greenberg, 1B, 1930-47

ALL-STAR GAME

■ **Winner:** Third baseman Ken Boyer singled three times and made three outstanding defensive plays to lead the N.L. to victory — its sixth in seven years.

■ **Key inning:** The fourth, when the N.L. stretched its 1-0 lead on a two-run pinch-hit homer by Willie Mays.

■ **Memorable moment:** Stan Musial's fifth All-Star home run, a seventh-inning shot that offset sixth-inning blasts by A.L. stars Ted Williams and Mickey Mantle.

■ **Top guns:** Bob Friend (Pirates), Boyer (Cardinals), Mays (Giants), Ted Kluszewski (Reds), Musial (Cardinals), N.L.; Williams (Red Sox), Mantle (Yankees), Yogi Berra (Yankees), A.L.

■ **MVP:** Boyer.

Linescore

July 10, at Washington's Griffith Stadium
N.L. ....0 0 1 2 1 1 2 0 0—7 11 0
A.L. ....0 0 0 0 0 3 0 0 0—3 11 0
Friend (Pirates), Spahn (Braves) 4, Antonelli (Giants) 6; Pierce (White Sox), Ford (Yankees) 4, Wilson (White Sox) 5, Brewer (Red Sox) 6, Score (Indians) 8, Wynn (Indians) 9. W—Friend. L—Pierce. HR—Mays, Musial, N.L.; Williams, Mantle, A.L.

WORLD SERIES

■ **Winner:** The Yankees turned the tables on the Dodgers in a Series featuring one of baseball's most incredible pitching performances.

■ **Turning point:** 5-3 and 6-2 Yankee victories in Games 3 and 4 after the Dodgers had won the first two games.

■ **Memorable moment:** The final pitch of Yankee righthander Don Larsen's Game 5 perfect game — the first no-hitter in Series history. Larsen struck out pinch-hitter Dale Mitchell to complete his 2-0 shutout.

■ **Top guns:** Larsen (1-0, 0.00 ERA), Yogi Berra (.360, 3 HR, 10 RBIs), Enos Slaughter (.350), Yankees; Gil Hodges (.304, 8 RBIs), Dodgers.

■ **MVP:** Larsen.

Linescores

Game 1—October 3, at Brooklyn
New York....................2 0 0 1 0 0 0 0 0—3 9 1
Brooklyn ....0 2 3 1 0 0 0 0 x—6 9 0
Ford, Kucks (4), Morgan (6), Turley (8); Maglie. W—Maglie. L—Ford. HR—Mantle, Martin (N.Y.); Robinson, Hodges (Brk.).

Game 2—October 5, at Brooklyn
New York................1 5 0 1 0 0 0 0 1— 8 12 2
Brooklyn ....0 6 1 2 2 0 0 2 x—13 12 0
Larsen, Kucks (2), Byrne (2), Sturdivant (3), Morgan (3), Turley (5), McDermott (6); Newcombe, Roebuck (2), Bessent (3). W—Bessent. L—Morgan. HR—Berra (N.Y.); Snider (Brk.).

Game 3—October 6, at New York
Brooklyn ....0 1 0 0 0 1 1 0 0—3 8 1
New York....................0 1 0 0 0 3 0 1 x—5 8 1
Craig, Labine (7); Ford. W—Ford. L—Craig. HR—Martin, Slaughter (N.Y.).

Game 4—October 7, at New York
Brooklyn ....0 0 0 1 0 0 0 0 1—2 6 0
New York....................1 0 0 2 0 1 2 0 x—6 7 2
Erskine, Roebuck (5), Drysdale (7); Sturdivant. W—Sturdivant. L—Erskine. HR—Mantle, Bauer (N.Y.).

Game 5—October 8, at New York
Brooklyn ....0 0 0 0 0 0 0 0 0—0 0 0
New York....................0 0 0 1 0 1 0 0 x—2 5 0
Maglie; Larsen. W—Larsen. L—Maglie. HR—Mantle (N.Y.).

Game 6—October 9, at Brooklyn
New York.............0 0 0 0 0 0 0 0 0 0—0 7 0
Brooklyn ....0 0 0 0 0 0 0 0 0 1—1 4 0
Turley; Labine. W—Labine. L—Turley.

Game 7—October 10, at Brooklyn
New York.................2 0 2 1 0 0 4 0 0—9 10 0
Brooklyn ....0 0 0 0 0 0 0 0 0—0 3 1
Kucks; Newcombe, Bessent (4), Craig (7), Roebuck (7), Erskine (9). W—Kucks. L—Newcombe. HR—Berra 2, Howard, Skowron (N.Y.).

1957

FINAL STANDINGS

American League

Team	W	L	Pct.	GB
New York	98	56	.636	...
Chicago	90	64	.584	8
Boston	82	72	.532	16
Detroit	78	76	.506	20
Baltimore	76	76	.500	21
Cleveland	76	77	.497	21.5
Kansas City	59	94	.386	38.5
Washington	55	99	.357	43

National League

Team	W	L	Pct.	GB
Milwaukee	95	59	.617	...
St. Louis	87	67	.565	8
Brooklyn	84	70	.545	11
Cincinnati	80	74	.519	15
Philadelphia	77	77	.500	18
New York	69	85	.448	26
Chicago	62	92	.403	33
Pittsburgh	62	92	.403	33

SIGNIFICANT EVENTS

■ **February 2:** Baseball owners approved a five-year pension plan offering more liberal benefits to players, coaches and trainers.
■ **April 22:** The Phillies became the final N.L. team to break the color barrier when John Kennedy was inserted as a pinch-runner in a 5-1 loss to Brooklyn.
■ **May 28:** N.L. owners approved the proposed moves of the Dodgers and Giants to the West Coast, opening the door for relocations that would become official in the fall.
■ **June 28:** Commissioner Ford Frick infuriated ballot-stuffing Cincinnati fans when he replaced three members of an all-Reds starting lineup for the All-Star Game.

MEMORABLE MOMENTS

■ **May 7:** Young Cleveland ace Herb Score suffered a career-threatening injury when he was hit in the eye by Yankee Gil McDougald's line drive.
■ **September 23:** Hank Aaron belted a two-run, 11th-inning homer to give the Braves a 4-2 victory over St. Louis and their first pennant since moving to Milwaukee.

LEADERS

American League
BA: Ted Williams, Bos., .388.
Runs: Mickey Mantle, N.Y., 121.
Hits: Nellie Fox, Chi., 196.
TB: Roy Sievers, Wash., 331.
HR: Roy Sievers, Wash., 42.
RBI: Roy Sievers, Wash., 114.
SB: Luis Aparicio, Chi., 28.
Wins: Jim Bunning, Det.; Billy Pierce, Chi., 20.
ERA: Bobby Shantz, N.Y., 2.45.
CG: Dick Donovan, Chi.; Billy Pierce, Chi., 16.
IP: Jim Bunning, Det., 267.1.
SO: Early Wynn, Cle., 184.

National League
BA: Stan Musial, St.L., .351.
Runs: Hank Aaron, Mil., 118.
Hits: Red Schoendienst, N.Y.-Mil., 200.
TB: Hank Aaron, Mil., 369.
HR: Hank Aaron, Mil., 44.
RBI: Hank Aaron, Mil., 132.
SB: Willie Mays, N.Y., 38.
Wins: Warren Spahn, Mil., 21.
ERA: Johnny Podres, Brk., 2.66.
CG: Warren Spahn, Mil., 18.
IP: Bob Friend, Pit., 277.
SO: Jack Sanford, Phil., 188.

A.L. 20-game winners
Jim Bunning, Det., 20-8
Billy Pierce, Chi., 20-12

N.L. 20-game winners
Warren Spahn, Mil., 21-11

A.L. 100 RBIs
Roy Sievers, Wash., 114
Vic Wertz, Cle., 105
Jackie Jensen, Bos., 103
Frank Malzone, Bos., 103
Minnie Minoso, Chi., 103

N.L. 100 RBIs
Hank Aaron, Mil., 132
Del Ennis, St.L., 105
Ernie Banks, Chi., 102
Stan Musial, St.L., 102

A.L. 40 homers
Roy Sievers, Wash., 42

N.L. 40 homers
Hank Aaron, Mil., 44
Ernie Banks, Chi., 43
Duke Snider, Brk., 40

Most Valuable Player
A.L.: Mickey Mantle, OF, N.Y.
N.L.: Hank Aaron, OF, Mil.

Cy Young Award
A.L.-N.L.: Warren Spahn, Mil.

Rookie of the Year
A.L.: Tony Kubek, IF/OF, N.Y.
N.L.: Jack Sanford, P, Phil.

Hall of Fame additions
Sam Crawford, OF, 1899-1917
Joe McCarthy, manager

ALL-STAR GAME

■ **Winner:** Minnie Minoso, who had doubled home a run in the top of the ninth, made two outstanding defensive plays in the bottom of the inning to preserve the A.L.'s victory.

■ **Key inning:** The ninth. After the A.L. had scored three times in the top of the frame for a 6-2 lead, the N.L. answered with three runs and had the tying run on second when the game ended.

■ **Memorable moment:** Left fielder Minoso, who had just thrown out a runner trying to advance to third, made an outstanding game-ending catch of a Gil Hodges drive into left-center field.

■ **Top guns:** Jim Bunning (Tigers), Al Kaline (Tigers), Bill Skowron (Yankees), Minoso (White Sox), A.L.; Lew Burdette (Braves), Willie Mays (Giants), Gus Bell (Reds), N.L.

■ **MVP:** Minoso.

Linescore

July 9, at St. Louis' Busch Stadium
A.L. ....0 2 0 0 0 1 0 0 3—6 10 0
N.L. ....0 0 0 0 0 0 2 0 3—5 9 1
Bunning (Tigers), Loes (Orioles) 4, Wynn (Indians) 7, Pierce (White Sox) 7, Mossi (Indians) 9, Grim (Yankees) 9; Simmons (Phillies), Burdette (Braves) 2, Sanford (Phillies) 6, Jackson (Cardinals) 7, Labine (Dodgers) 9. W—Bunning. L—Simmons.

WORLD SERIES

■ **Winner:** The Braves' fifth Milwaukee season produced the franchise's first Series winner since the miracle of 1914.

■ **Turning point:** A two-run 10th-inning home run by Eddie Mathews that gave Milwaukee a 7-5 victory in Game 4 and evened the Series at two games apiece.

■ **Memorable moment:** The final pitch of Milwaukee righthander Lew Burdette's 5-0 seventh-game shutout, giving Milwaukee its first Series championship.

■ **Top guns:** Burdette (3-0, 0-67 ERA), Hank Aaron (.393, 3 HR, 7 RBIs), Frank Torre (.300, 2 HR), Braves; Jerry Coleman (.364), Yankees.

■ **MVP:** Burdette.

Linescores

Game 1—October 2, at New York
Milwaukee.................0 0 0 0 0 0 1 0 0—1 5 0
New York...................0 0 0 0 1 2 0 0 x—3 9 1
Spahn, Johnson (6), McMahon (7); Ford. W—Ford. L—Spahn.

Game 2—October 3, at New York
Milwaukee.................0 1 1 2 0 0 0 0 0—4 8 0
New York...................0 1 1 0 0 0 0 0 0—2 7 2
Burdette; Shantz, Ditmar (4), Grim (8). W—Burdette. L—Shantz. HR—Logan (Mil.); Bauer (N.Y.).

Game 3—October 5, at Milwaukee
New York.................3 0 2 2 0 0 5 0 0—12 9 0
Milwaukee................0 1 0 0 2 0 0 0 0— 3 8 1
Turley, Larsen (2); Buhl, Pizarro (1), Conley (3), Johnson (5), Trowbridge (7), McMahon (8). W—Larsen. L—Buhl. HR—Kubek 2, Mantle (N.Y.); Aaron (Mil.).

Game 4—October 6, at Milwaukee
New York...........1 0 0 0 0 0 0 0 3 1—5 11 0
Milwaukee.........0 0 0 4 0 0 0 0 0 3—7 7 0
Sturdivant, Shantz (5), Kucks (8), Byrne (8), Grim (10); Spahn. W—Spahn. L—Grim. HR—Aaron, Torre, Mathews (Mil.); Howard (N.Y.).

Game 5—October 7, at Milwaukee
New York...................0 0 0 0 0 0 0 0 0—0 7 0
Milwaukee ....0 0 0 0 0 1 0 0 x—1 6 1
Ford, Turley (8); Burdette. W—Burdette. L—Ford.

Game 6—October 9, at New York
Milwaukee.................0 0 0 0 1 0 1 0 0—2 4 0
New York...................0 0 2 0 0 0 1 0 x—3 7 0
Buhl, Johnson (3), McMahon (8); Turley. W—Turley. L—Johnson. HR—Berra, Bauer (N.Y.); Torre, Aaron (Mil.).

Game 7—October 10, at New York
Milwaukee.................0 0 4 0 0 0 0 1 0—5 9 1
New York...................0 0 0 0 0 0 0 0 0—0 7 3
Burdette; Larsen, Shantz (3), Ditmar (4), Sturdivant (6), Byrne (8). W—Burdette. L—Larsen. HR—Crandall (Mil.).

1958

FINAL STANDINGS

American League

Team	W	L	Pct.	GB
New York	92	62	.597	...
Chicago	82	72	.532	10
Boston	79	75	.513	13
Cleveland	77	76	.503	14.5
Detroit	77	77	.500	15
Baltimore	74	79	.484	17.5
Kansas City	73	81	.474	19
Washington	61	93	.396	31

National League

Team	W	L	Pct.	GB
Milwaukee	92	62	.597	...
Pittsburgh	84	70	.545	8
San Francisco	80	74	.519	12
Cincinnati	76	78	.494	16
Chicago	72	82	.468	20
St. Louis	72	82	.468	20
Los Angeles	71	83	.461	21
Philadelphia	69	85	.448	23

SIGNIFICANT EVENTS

■ **January 28:** Dodgers catcher Roy Campanella suffered a broken neck and paralysis from his shoulders down when the car he was driving overturned on a slippery road in Glen Cove, N.Y.
■ **January 29:** Stan Musial became the N.L.'s first six-figure star when he signed with the Cardinals for $100,000.
■ **January 30:** Commissioner Ford Frick took the All-Star vote away from the fans, handing it back to the players, coaches and managers.
■ **September 28:** Boston's 40-year-old Ted Williams used a 7-for-11 closing surge to win his sixth A.L. batting title with a .328 average.
■ **December 3:** Will Harridge, who served as A.L. president for more than 27 years, retired at age 72.

MEMORABLE MOMENTS

■ **April 15:** The Giants rolled to an 8-0 victory over the Dodgers in the first West Coast game at San Francisco's Seals Stadium.
■ **April 18:** The Dodgers rewarded a record Los Angeles Coliseum crowd of 78,672 with a 6-5 victory over the Giants in their West Coast home debut.
■ **May 13:** Stan Musial became the eighth member of baseball's 3,000-hit club when he stroked a pinch-hit double off Moe Drabowsky in a 5-3 Cardinals' victory at Chicago.

LEADERS

American League
BA: Ted Williams, Bos., .328.
Runs: Mickey Mantle, N.Y., 127.
Hits: Nellie Fox, Chi., 187.
TB: Mickey Mantle, N.Y., 307.
HR: Mickey Mantle, N.Y., 42.
RBI: Jackie Jensen, Bos., 122.
SB: Luis Aparicio, Chi., 29.
Wins: Bob Turley, N.Y., 21.
ERA: Whitey Ford, N.Y., 2.01.
CG: Frank Lary, Det.; Billy Pierce, Chi.; Bob Turley, N.Y., 19.
IP: Frank Lary, Det., 260.1.
SO: Early Wynn, Chi., 179.

National League
BA: Richie Ashburn, Phil., .350.
Runs: Willie Mays, S.F., 121.
Hits: Richie Ashburn, Phil., 215.
TB: Ernie Banks, Chi., 379.
HR: Ernie Banks, Chi., 47.
RBI: Ernie Banks, Chi., 129.
SB: Willie Mays, S.F., 31.
Wins: Bob Friend, Pit.; Warren Spahn, Mil., 22.
ERA: Stu Miller, S.F., 2.47.
CG: Warren Spahn, Mil., 23.
IP: Warren Spahn, Mil., 290.
SO: Sam Jones, St.L., 225.

A.L. 20-game winners
Bob Turley, N.Y., 21-7

N.L. 20-game winners
Warren Spahn, Mil., 22-11
Bob Friend, Pit., 22-14
Lew Burdette, Mil., 20-10

A.L. 100 RBIs
Jackie Jensen, Bos., 122
Rocky Colavito, Cle., 113
Roy Sievers, Wash., 108
Bob Cerv, K.C., 104

N.L. 100 RBIs
Ernie Banks, Chi., 129
Frank Thomas, Pit., 109

A.L. 40 homers
Mickey Mantle, N.Y., 42
Rocky Colavito, Cle., 41

N.L. 40 homers
Ernie Banks, Chi., 47

Most Valuable Player
A.L.: Jackie Jensen, OF, Bos.
N.L.: Ernie Banks, SS, Chi.

Cy Young Award
A.L.-N.L.: Bob Turley, N.Y. (AL).

Rookie of the Year
A.L.: Albie Pearson, OF, Wash.
N.L.: Orlando Cepeda, 1B, S.F.

ALL-STAR GAME

■ **Winner:** After spotting the N.L. a 3-1 lead, the A.L. rallied for a 4-3 victory in the first All-Star Game without an extra-base hit. Ray Narleski, Early Wynn and Billy O'Dell allowed one hit over the final 7 1/3 innings.

■ **Key inning:** The sixth, when the A.L. scored the go-ahead run on a single by Gil McDougald.

■ **Memorable moment:** The last out of the game — the ninth consecutive batter retired by hometown favorite O'Dell.

■ **Top guns:** Narleski (Indians), Wynn (White Sox), O'Dell (Orioles), Nellie Fox (White Sox), McDougald (Yankees), A.L.; Willie Mays (Giants), N.L.

■ **MVP:** O'Dell.

Linescore

July 8, at Baltimore's Memorial Stadium
N.L. ....2 1 0 0 0 0 0 0 0—3 4 2
A.L. ....1 1 0 0 1 1 0 0 x—4 9 2
Spahn (Braves), Friend (Pirates) 4, Jackson (Cardinals) 6, Farrell (Phillies) 7; Turley (Yankees), Narleski (Indians) 2, Wynn (White Sox) 6, O'Dell (Orioles) 7. W—Wynn. L—Friend.

WORLD SERIES

■ **Winner:** The Yankees became only the second team to recover from a three-games-to-one deficit en route to their seventh Series victory in 10 years under manager Casey Stengel.

■ **Turning point:** Bob Turley's five-hit 7-0 victory in Game 5 with his Yankees on the brink of elimination.

■ **Memorable moment:** A 10th-inning Game 6 home run by Gil McDougald that lifted the Yankees to a 4-3 victory and forced a seventh game.

■ **Top guns:** Turley (2-1, 2.76 ERA), Hank Bauer (.323, 4 HR, 8 RBIs), McDougald (.321, 2 HR, 4 RBIs), Yankees; Bill Bruton (.412), Braves.

■ **MVP:** Turley.

Linescores

Game 1—October 1, at Milwaukee
New York............0 0 0 1 2 0 0 0 0 0—3 8 1
Milwaukee..........0 0 0 2 0 0 0 1 0 1—4 10 0
Ford, Duren (8); Spahn. W—Spahn. L—Duren. HR—Skowron, Bauer (N.Y.).

Game 2—October 2, at Milwaukee
New York................1 0 0 1 0 0 0 0 3— 5 7 0
Milwaukee ....7 1 0 0 0 0 2 3 x—13 15 1
Turley, Maas (1), Kucks (1), Dickson (5), Monroe (8); Burdette. W—Burdette. L—Turley. HR—Bruton, Burdette (Mil.); Mantle 2, Bauer (N.Y.).

Game 3—October 4, at New York
Milwaukee..................0 0 0 0 0 0 0 0 0—0 6 0
New York....................0 0 0 0 2 0 2 0 x—4 4 0
Rush, McMahon (7); Larsen, Duren (8). W—Larsen. L—Rush. HR—Bauer (N.Y.).

Game 4—October 5, at New York
Milwaukee..................0 0 0 0 0 1 1 1 0—3 9 0
New York....................0 0 0 0 0 0 0 0 0—0 2 1
Spahn; Ford, Kucks (8), Dickson (9). W—Spahn. L—Ford.

Game 5—October 6, at New York
Milwaukee................0 0 0 0 0 0 0 0 0—0 5 0
New York..................0 0 1 0 0 6 0 0 x—7 10 0
Burdette, Pizarro (6), Willey (8); Turley. W—Turley. L—Burdette. HR—McDougald (N.Y.).

Game 6——October 8, at Milwaukee
New York............1 0 0 0 0 1 0 0 0 2—4 10 1
Milwaukee..........1 1 0 0 0 0 0 0 0 1—3 10 4
Ford, Ditmar (2), Duren (6), Turley (10); Spahn, McMahon (10). W—Duren. L—Spahn. HR—Bauer, McDougald (N.Y.).

Game 7—October 9, at Milwaukee
New York....................0 2 0 0 0 0 0 4 0—6 8 0
Milwaukee..................1 0 0 0 0 1 0 0 0—2 5 2
Larsen, Turley (3); Burdette, McMahon (9). W—Turley. L—Burdette. HR—Crandall (Mil.); Skowron (N.Y.).

1959

FINAL STANDINGS

American League

Team	W	L	Pct.	GB
Chicago	94	60	.610	...
Cleveland	89	65	.578	5
New York	79	75	.513	15
Detroit	76	78	.494	18
Boston	75	79	.487	19
Baltimore	74	80	.481	20
Kansas City	66	88	.429	28
Washington	63	91	.409	31

National League

Team	W	L	Pct.	GB
*Los Angeles	88	68	.564	...
Milwaukee	86	70	.551	2
San Francisco	83	71	.539	4
Pittsburgh	78	76	.506	9
Chicago	74	80	.481	13
Cincinnati	74	80	.481	13
St. Louis	71	83	.461	16
Philadelphia	64	90	.416	23

*Defeated Milwaukee 2-0 in pennant playoff.

SIGNIFICANT EVENT

■ **July 21:** The Red Sox became the last Major League team to break the color barrier when infielder Pumpsie Green played briefly in a game at Chicago.

MEMORABLE MOMENTS

■ **May 26:** In an amazing pitching exhibition, Pittsburgh's Harvey Haddix worked 12 perfect innings before losing to the Braves, 1-0, in the 13th.

■ **June 10:** Cleveland's Rocky Colavito became the eighth member of an exclusive club when he belted four home runs during the Indians' 11-8 victory over Baltimore.

■ **September 11:** The Dodgers ended the two-year, 22-game winning streak of Pittsburgh reliever Elroy Face when they scored two ninth-inning runs for a 5-4 victory.

■ **September 29:** The Dodgers completed their two-game sweep of a pennant-playoff series against Milwaukee with a 12-inning, 6-5 victory at Los Angeles.

LEADERS

American League

BA: Harvey Kuenn, Det., .353.
Runs: Eddie Yost, Det., 115.
Hits: Harvey Kuenn, Det., 198.
TB: Rocky Colavito, Cle., 301.
HR: Rocky Colavito, Cle.; Harmon Killebrew, Wash., 42.
RBI: Jackie Jensen, Bos., 112.
SB: Luis Aparicio, Chi., 56.
Wins: Early Wynn, Chi., 22.
ERA: Hoyt Wilhelm, Bal., 2.19.
CG: Camilo Pascual, Wash., 17.
IP: Early Wynn, Chi., 255.2.
SO: Jim Bunning, Det., 201.

National League

BA: Hank Aaron, Mil., .355.
Runs: Vada Pinson, Cin., 131.
Hits: Hank Aaron, Mil., 223.
TB: Hank Aaron, Mil., 400.
HR: Eddie Mathews, Mil., 46.
RBI: Ernie Banks, Chi., 143.
SB: Willie Mays, S.F., 27.
Wins: Lew Burdette, Mil.; Sam Jones, S.F.; Warren Spahn, Mil., 21.
ERA: Sam Jones, S.F., 2.83.
CG: Warren Spahn, Mil., 21.
IP: Warren Spahn, Mil., 292.
SO: Don Drysdale, L.A., 242.

A.L. 20-game winners

Early Wynn, Chi., 22-10

N.L. 20-game winners

Lew Burdette, Mil., 21-15
Warren Spahn, Mil., 21-15
Sam Jones, S.F., 21-15

A.L. 100 RBIs

Jackie Jensen, Bos., 112
Rocky Colavito, Cle., 111
Harmon Killebrew, Wash., 105
Jim Lemon, Wash., 100

N.L. 100 RBIs

Ernie Banks, Chi., 143
Frank Robinson, Cin., 125
Hank Aaron, Mil., 123
Gus Bell, Cin., 115
Eddie Mathews, Mil., 114
Orlando Cepeda, S.F., 105
Willie Mays, S.F., 104

A.L. 40 homers

Rocky Colavito, Cle., 42
Harmon Killebrew, Wash., 42

N.L. 40 homers

Eddie Mathews, Mil., 46
Ernie Banks, Chi., 45

Most Valuable Player

A.L.: Nellie Fox, 2B, Chi.
N.L.: Ernie Banks, SS, Chi.

Cy Young Award

A.L.-N.L.: Early Wynn, Chi. (AL)

Rookie of the Year

A.L.: Bob Allison, OF, Wash.
N.L.: Willie McCovey, 1B, S.F.

Hall of Fame addition

Zack Wheat, OF, 1909-27

ALL-STAR GAMES

■ **Winner:** Home runs by Frank Malzone, Yogi Berra and Rocky Colavito helped the A.L. to a 5-3 victory and a split of the first All-Star doubleheader. The N.L. had won the first game four weeks earlier, 5-4.

■ **Key Innings:** The eighth in Game 1, when San Francisco's Willie Mays tripled home the winning run. The third in Game 2, when Berra pounded a two-run homer to give the A.L. a lead it never relinquished.

■ **Memorable moment:** The final out of Game 2. With hometown favorite Jim Gilliam at bat and the potential tying runs on second and third, Los Angeles fans roared. But Gilliam grounded out.

■ **Top guns:** Game 1: Don Drysdale (Dodgers), Eddie Mathews (Braves), Hank Aaron (Braves), N.L.; Al Kaline (Tigers), Gus Triandos (Orioles), A.L.; Game 2: Berra (Yankees), Malzone (Red Sox), Colavito (Indians), A.L.; Frank Robinson (Reds), Gilliam (Dodgers), N.L.

■ **MVPs:** Game 1: Drysdale. Game 2: Berra.

Linescores

Game 1, July 7, at Pittsburgh's Forbes Field
A.L. ....0 0 0 1 0 0 0 3 0—4 8 0
N.L. ....1 0 0 0 0 0 2 2 x—5 9 1
Wynn (White Sox), Duren (Yankees) 4, Bunning (Tigers) 7, Ford (Yankees) 8, Daley (Athletics) 8; Drysdale (Dodgers), Burdette (Braves) 4, Face (Pirates) 7, Antonelli (Giants) 8, Elston (Cubs) 9. W—Antonelli. L—Ford. HR—Mathews, N.L.; Kaline, A.L.

Game 2, August 3, at Los Angeles Coliseum
A.L. ....0 1 2 0 0 0 1 1 0—5 6 0
N.L. ....1 0 0 0 1 0 1 0 0—3 6 3
Walker (Orioles), Wynn (White Sox) 4, Wilhelm (Orioles) 6, O'Dell (Orioles) 7, McLish (Indians) 8; Drysdale (Dodgers), Conley (Phillies) 4, Jones (Giants) 6, Face (Pirates) 8. W—Walker. L—Drysdale. HR—Malzone, Berra, Colavito, A.L.; Robinson, Gilliam, N.L.

WORLD SERIES

■ **Winner:** The Dodgers, winners of a pennant playoff against Milwaukee, defeated the "Go-Go" White Sox for their first Series victory in Los Angeles.

■ **Turning point:** The Dodgers' 5-4 fourth-game victory, which was decided by Gil Hodges' home run.

■ **Memorable moment:** The first West Coast World Series contest — a 3-1 Dodger victory in Game 3.

■ **Top guns:** Larry Sherry (2-0, 0.71 ERA), Charlie Neal (.370, 2 HR, 6 RBIs), Chuck Essegian (2 PH HR), Dodgers; Ted Kluszewski (.391, 3 HR, 10 RBIs), Nellie Fox (.375), White Sox.

■ **MVP:** Sherry.

Linescores

Game 1—October 1, at Chicago
Los Angeles ....0 0 0 0 0 0 0 0 0— 0 8 3
Chicago..................2 0 7 2 0 0 0 0 x—11 11 0
Craig, Churn (3), Labine (4), Koufax (5), Klippstein (7); Wynn, Staley (8). W—Wynn. L—Craig. HR—Kluszewski 2 (Chi.).

Game 2—October 2, at Chicago
Los Angeles ....0 0 0 0 1 0 3 0 0—4 9 1
Chicago......................2 0 0 0 0 0 0 1 0—3 8 0
Podres, Sherry (7); Shaw, Lown (7). W—Podres. L—Shaw. HR—Neal 2, Essegian (L.A.).

Game 3—October 4, at Los Angeles.
Chicago....................0 0 0 0 0 0 0 1 0—1 12 0
Los Angeles ....0 0 0 0 0 0 2 1 x—3 5 0
Donovan, Staley (7); Drysdale, Sherry (8). W—Drysdale. L—Donovan.

Game 4—October 5, at Los Angeles
Chicago....................0 0 0 0 0 0 4 0 0—4 10 3
Los Angeles ....0 0 4 0 0 0 0 1 x—5 9 0
Wynn, Lown (3), Pierce (4), Staley (7); Craig, Sherry (8). W—Sherry. L—Staley. HR—Lollar (Chi.); Hodges (L.A.).

Game 5—October 6, at Los Angels
Chicago......................0 0 0 1 0 0 0 0 0—1 5 0
Los Angeles ....0 0 0 0 0 0 0 0 0—0 9 0
Shaw, Pierce (8), Donovan (8); Koufax, Williams (8). W—Shaw. L—Koufax.

Game 6—October 8, at Chicago
Los Angeles ....0 0 2 6 0 0 0 0 1—9 13 0
Chicago....................0 0 0 3 0 0 0 0 0—3 6 1
Podres, Sherry (4); Wynn, Donovan (4), Lown (4), Staley (5), Pierce (8), Moore (9). W—Sherry. L—Wynn. HR—Snider, Moon, Essegian (L.A.); Kluszewski (Chi.).

1960

FINAL STANDINGS

American League

Team	W	L	Pct.	GB
New York	97	57	.630	...
Baltimore	89	65	.578	8
Chicago	87	67	.565	10
Cleveland	76	78	.494	21
Washington	73	81	.474	24
Detroit	71	83	.461	26
Boston	65	89	.422	32
Kansas City	58	96	.377	39

National League

Team	W	L	Pct.	GB
Pittsburgh	95	59	.617	...
Milwaukee	88	66	.571	7
St. Louis	86	68	.558	9
Los Angeles	82	72	.532	13
San Francisco	79	75	.513	16
Cincinnati	67	87	.435	28
Chicago	60	94	.390	35
Philadelphia	59	95	.383	36

SIGNIFICANT EVENTS

■ **August 3:** In baseball's most bizarre trade, the Indians swapped manager Joe Gordon to Detroit for manager Jimmie Dykes.

■ **October 18:** Casey Stengel, who managed the Yankees to 10 pennants and seven World Series titles in 12 years, was fired.

■ **October 26:** The A.L. announced relocation of the Senators to Minneapolis-St. Paul and 1961 expansion to Los Angeles and Washington.

MEMORABLE MOMENTS

■ **June 17:** Ted Williams became the fourth member of the 500-homer fraternity when he connected off Cleveland's Wynn Hawkins in a 3-1 Boston victory.

■ **September 28:** Williams belted career homer No. 521 in Boston's 5-4 victory over Baltimore and promptly retired.

LEADERS

American League

BA: Pete Runnels, Bos., .320.
Runs: Mickey Mantle, N.Y., 119.
Hits: Minnie Minoso, Chi., 184.
TB: Mickey Mantle, N.Y., 294.
HR: Mickey Mantle, N.Y., 40.
RBI: Roger Maris, N.Y., 112.
SB: Luis Aparicio, Chi., 51.
Wins: Chuck Estrada, Bal.; Jim Perry, Cle., 18.
ERA: Frank Baumann, Chi., 2.67.
CG: Frank Lary, Det., 15.
IP: Frank Lary, Det., 274.1.
SO: Jim Bunning, Det., 201.

National League

BA: Dick Groat, Pit., .325.
Runs: Bill Bruton, Mil., 112.
Hits: Willie Mays, S.F., 190.
TB: Hank Aaron, Mil., 334.
HR: Ernie Banks, Chi., 41.
RBI: Hank Aaron, Mil., 126.
SB: Maury Wills, L.A., 50.
Wins: Ernie Broglio, St.L.; Warren Spahn, Mil., 21.
ERA: Mike McCormick, S.F., 2.70.
CG: Lew Burdette, Mil.; Vernon Law, Pit.; Warren Spahn, Mil., 18.
IP: Larry Jackson, St.L., 282.
SO: Don Drysdale, L.A., 246.

N.L. 20-game winners

Ernie Broglio, St.L., 21-9
Warren Spahn, Mil., 21-10
Vernon Law, Pit., 20-9

A.L. 100 RBIs

Roger Maris, N.Y., 112
Minnie Minoso, Chi., 105
Vic Wertz, Bos., 103
Jim Lemon, Wash., 100

N.L. 100 RBIs

Hank Aaron, Mil., 126
Eddie Mathews, Mil., 124
Ernie Banks, Chi., 117
Willie Mays, S.F., 103

A.L. 40 homers

Mickey Mantle, N.Y., 40

N.L. 40 homers

Ernie Banks, Chi., 41
Hank Aaron, Mil., 40

Most Valuable Player

A.L.: Roger Maris, OF, N.Y.
N.L.: Dick Groat, SS, Pit.

Cy Young Award

A.L.-N.L.: Vernon Law, Pit.

Rookie of the Year

A.L.: Ron Hansen, SS, Bal.
N.L.: Frank Howard, OF, L.A.

ALL-STAR GAMES

■ **Winner:** In a three-day All-Star doubleheader, the N.L. pulled off a 5-3 and 6-0 sweep and narrowed its once-embarrassing overall deficit to 16-13.

■ **Key Innings:** The first in Game 1, when a Willie Mays triple and an Ernie Banks homer sparked the N.L. to a 3-0 lead; the second in Game 2, when Eddie Mathews opened the N.L. scoring with a two-run homer.

■ **Memorable moment:** A third-inning Game 2 home run by Mays, who was 6 for 8 in the two games. The homer gave Mays a perfect 6-for-6 All-Star ledger against Yankee great Ford.

■ **Top guns:** Game 1: Bob Friend (Pirates), Mays (Giants), Banks (Cubs), N.L.; Al Kaline (Tigers), A.L.; Game 2: Vernon Law (Pirates), Mays (Giants), Mathews (Braves), Ken Boyer (Cardinals), N.L.

■ **MVPs:** Games 1 and 2 : Mays.

Linescores

Game 1, July 11, at Kansas City's Municipal Stadium
N.L. ....3 1 1 0 0 0 0 0 0—5 12 4
A.L. ....0 0 0 0 0 1 0 2 0—3 6 1
Friend (Pirates), McCormick (Giants) 4, Face (Pirates) 6, Buhl (Braves) 8, Law (Pirates) 9; Monbouquette (Red Sox), Estrada (Orioles) 3, Coates (Yankees) 4, Bell (Indians) 6, Lary (Tigers) 8, Daley (Athletics) 9. W—Friend. L—Monbouquette. HR—Banks, Crandall, N.L.; Kaline, A.L.

Game 2, July 13, at New York's Yankee Stadium
N.L. ....0 2 1 0 0 0 1 0 2—6 10 0
A.L. ....0 0 0 0 0 0 0 0 0—0 8 0
Law (Pirates), Podres (Dodgers) 3, S. Williams (Dodgers) 5, Jackson (Cardinals) 7, Henry (Reds) 8, McDaniel (Cardinals) 9; Ford (Yankees), Wynn (White Sox) 4, Staley (White Sox) 6, Lary (Tigers) 8, Bell (Indians) 9. W—Law. L—Ford. HR—Mathews, Mays, Musial, Boyer, N.L.

WORLD SERIES

■ **Winner:** Despite being outscored 55-27, the Pirates edged the Yankees in a seven-game Series that will be long remembered for its classic ending.

■ **Turning point:** The Pirates' 3-2 fourth-game victory after suffering successive 16-3 and 10-0 losses to the hard-hitting Yankees.

■ **Memorable moment:** Bill Mazeroski's Series-ending ninth-inning home run that broke a 9-9 tie after the Yankees had rallied for two runs in the top of the frame. One of the classic moments in Series history.

■ **Top guns:** Vernon Law (2-0), Mazeroski (.320, 2 HR, 5 RBIs), Pirates; Whitey Ford (2-0, 0.00 ERA), Mickey Mantle (.400, 3 HR, 11 RBIs), Bobby Richardson (.367, 12 RBIs), Yankees.

■ **MVP:** Richardson.

Linescores

Game 1—October 5, at Pittsburgh
New York..................1 0 0 1 0 0 0 0 2—4 13 2
Pittsburgh ....3 0 0 2 0 1 0 0 x—6 8 0
Ditmar, Coates (1), Maas (5), Duren (7); Law, Face (8). W—Law. L—Ditmar. HR—Maris, Howard (N.Y.); Mazeroski (Pit.).

Game 2—October 6, at Pittsburgh
New York................0 0 2 1 2 7 3 0 1—16 19 1
Pittsburgh ....0 0 0 1 0 0 0 0 2— 3 13 1
Turley, Shantz (9); Friend, Green (5), Labine (6), Witt (6), Gibbon (7), Cheney (9). W—Turley. L—Friend. HR—Mantle 2 (N.Y.).

Game 3—October 8, at New York
Pittsburgh ....0 0 0 0 0 0 0 0 0— 0 4 0
New York................6 0 0 4 0 0 0 0 x—10 16 1
Mizell, Labine (1), Green (1), Witt (4), Cheney (6), Gibbon (8); Ford. W—Ford. L—Mizell. HR—Richardson, Mantle (N.Y.).

Game 4—October 9, at New York
Pittsburgh ....0 0 0 0 3 0 0 0 0—3 7 0
New York....................0 0 0 1 0 0 1 0 0—2 8 0
Law, Face (7); Terry, Shantz (7), Coates (8). W—Law. L—Terry. HR—Skowron (N.Y.).

Game 5—October 10, at New York
Pittsburgh ....0 3 1 0 0 0 0 0 1—5 10 2
New York..................0 1 1 0 0 0 0 0 0—2 5 2
Haddix, Face (7); Ditmar, Arroyo (2), Stafford (3), Duren (8). W—Haddix. L—Ditmar. HR—Maris (N.Y.).

Game 6—October 12, at Pittsburgh
New York...............0 1 5 0 0 2 2 2 0—12 17 1
Pittsburgh ....0 0 0 0 0 0 0 0 0— 0 7 1
Ford; Friend, Cheney (3), Mizell (4), Green (6), Labine (6), Witt (9). W—Ford. L—Friend.

Game 7—October 13, at Pittsburgh
New York...............0 0 0 0 1 4 0 2 2— 9 13 1
Pittsburgh ....2 2 0 0 0 0 0 5 1—10 11 0
Turley, Stafford (2), Shantz (3), Coates (8), Terry (8); Law, Face (6), Friend (9), Haddix (9). W—Haddix. L—Terry. HR—Skowron, Berra (N.Y.); Nelson, Smith, Mazeroski (Pit.).

1961

FINAL STANDINGS

American League

Team	W	L	Pct.	GB
New York	109	53	.673	...
Detroit	101	61	.623	8
Baltimore	95	67	.586	14
Chicago	86	76	.531	23
Cleveland	78	83	.484	30.5
Boston	76	86	.469	33
Minnesota	70	90	.438	38
Los Angeles	70	91	.435	38.5
Kansas City	61	100	.379	47.5
Washington	61	100	.379	47.5

National League

Team	W	L	Pct.	GB
Cincinnati	93	61	.604	...
Los Angeles	89	65	.578	4
San Francisco	85	69	.552	8
Milwaukee	83	71	.539	10
St. Louis	80	74	.519	13
Pittsburgh	75	79	.487	18
Chicago	64	90	.416	29
Philadelphia	47	107	.305	46

SIGNIFICANT EVENTS

■ **April 6:** The Cubs designated Vedie Himsl as the first of nine coaches who would rotate as the team's manager during the season.

■ **July 17:** Commissioner Ford Frick ruled that nobody could be credited with breaking Babe Ruth's 60-homer record unless he did it in the first 154 games of a season.

■ **October 10:** The Mets and Colt .45s combined to pick 45 players in the N.L.'s first expansion draft.

MEMORABLE MOMENTS

■ **April 30:** Willie Mays became the ninth player to hit four homers in a game during the Giants' 14-4 victory at Milwaukee.

■ **August 11:** Warren Spahn pitched Milwaukee to a 2-1 victory over Chicago and claimed his 300th career victory.

■ **August 20:** The Phillies defeated Milwaukee, 7-4, and ended their modern-era record losing streak at 23.

■ **October 1:** Roger Maris drove a pitch from Boston's Tracy Stallard for his record-setting 61st home run, giving New York a 1-0 victory at Yankee Stadium.

LEADERS

American League

BA: Norm Cash, Det., .361.
Runs: Mickey Mantle, N.Y.; Roger Maris, N.Y., 132.
Hits: Norm Cash, Det., 193.
TB: Roger Maris, N.Y., 366.
HR: Roger Maris, N.Y., 61.
RBI: Roger Maris, N.Y., 142.
SB: Luis Aparicio, Chi., 53.
Wins: Whitey Ford, N.Y., 25.
ERA: Dick Donovan, Wash., 2.40.
CG: Frank Lary, Det., 22.
IP: Whitey Ford, N.Y., 283.
SO: Camilo Pascual, Min., 221.

National League

BA: Roberto Clemente, Pit., .351.
Runs: Willie Mays, S.F., 129.
Hits: Vada Pinson, Cin., 208.
TB: Hank Aaron, Mil., 358.
HR: Orlando Cepeda, S.F., 46.
RBI: Orlando Cepeda, S.F., 142.
SB: Maury Wills, L.A., 35.
Wins: Joey Jay, Cin.; Warren Spahn, Mil., 21.
ERA: Warren Spahn, Mil., 3.02.
CG: Warren Spahn, Mil., 21.
IP: Lew Burdette, Mil., 272.1.
SO: Sandy Koufax, L.A., 269.

A.L. 20-game winners
Whitey Ford, N.Y., 25-4
Frank Lary, Det., 23-9

N.L. 20-game winners
Joey Jay, Cin., 21-10
Warren Spahn, Mil., 21-13

A.L. 100 RBIs
Roger Maris, N.Y., 142
Jim Gentile, Bal., 141
Rocky Colavito, Det., 140
Norm Cash, Det., 132
Mickey Mantle, N.Y., 128
Harmon Killebrew, Min., 122
Bob Allison, Min., 105

N.L. 100 RBIs
Orlando Cepeda, S.F., 142
Frank Robinson, Cin., 124
Willie Mays, S.F., 123
Hank Aaron, Mil., 120
Dick Stuart, Pit., 117
Joe Adcock, Mil., 108

A.L. 40 homers
Roger Maris, N.Y., 61
Mickey Mantle, N.Y., 54
Jim Gentile, Bal., 46
Harmon Killebrew, Min., 46
Rocky Colavito, Det., 45
Norm Cash, Det., 41

N.L. 40 homers
Orlando Cepeda, S.F., 46
Willie Mays, S.F., 40

Most Valuable Player
A.L.: Roger Maris, OF, N.Y.
N.L.: Frank Robinson, OF, Cin.

Cy Young Award
A.L.-N.L.: Whitey Ford, N.Y. (AL)

Rookie of the Year
A.L.: Don Schwall, P, Bos.
N.L.: Billy Williams, OF, Chi.

Hall of Fame additions
Max Carey, OF, 1910-29
Billy Hamilton, OF, 1888-1901

ALL-STAR GAMES

■ **Winner:** The N.L. captured a wind-blown 5-4 victory in the All-Star opener at Candlestick Park and played to a 1-1 tie in a second game that was halted by a Boston rainstorm after nine innings.

■ **Key inning:** The 10th in Game 1, when the A.L. took a 4-3 lead and the N.L. answered with two runs. The winner was driven home by a Roberto Clemente single.

■ **Memorable moment:** The ninth inning of Game 1 when the A.L.'s two-run, game-tying rally received a big assist from a gust of wind that blew Giants reliever Stu Miller off the mound in mid delivery for a balk.

■ **Top guns:** Game 1: Warren Spahn (Braves), Willie Mays (Giants), Clemente (Pirates), N.L.; Harmon Killebrew (Twins), A.L.; Game 2: Jim Bunning (Tigers), Camilo Pascual (Twins), Rocky Colavito (Tigers), A.L.; Miller (Giants), Bill White (Cardinals), N.L.

■ **MVPs:** Game 1: Clemente; Game 2: Bunning.

Linescores

Game 1, July 11, at San Francisco's Candlestick Park
A.L. ....0 0 0 0 0 1 0 0 2 1—4 4 2
N.L. ....0 1 0 1 0 0 0 1 0 2—5 11 5
Ford (Yankees), Lary (Tigers) 4, Donovan (Senators) 4, Bunning (Tigers) 6, Fornieles (Red Sox) 8, Wilhelm (Orioles) 8; Spahn (Braves), Purkey (Reds) 4, McCormick (Giants) 6, Face (Pirates) 9, Koufax (Dodgers) 9, Miller (Giants) 9. W—Miller. L—Wilhelm. HR—Killebrew, A.L.; Altman, N.L.

Game 2, July 31, at Boston's Fenway Park
N.L. ....0 0 0 0 0 1 0 0 0—1 5 1
A.L. ....1 0 0 0 0 0 0 0 0—1 4 0
Purkey (Reds), Mahaffey (Phillies) 3, Koufax (Dodgers) 5, Miller (Giants) 7; Bunning (Tigers), Schwall (Red Sox) 4, Pascual (Twins) 7. HR—Colavito, A.L.

WORLD SERIES

■ **Winner:** The Yankee machine, powered by 61-homer man Roger Maris, earned its first Series championship since 1947 without Casey Stengel at the helm.

■ **Turning point:** A ninth-inning Maris home run that lifted the Yankees to a 3-2 victory in Game 3.

■ **Memorable moment:** Yankee lefthander Whitey Ford's five shutout innings in Game 4, which lifted his consecutive-inning scoreless streak to a Series-record 32.

■ **Top guns:** Ford (2-0, 0.00 ERA), John Blanchard (.400, 2 HR), Bill Skowron (.353, 5 RBIs), Hector Lopez (.333, 7 RBIs), Yankees; Wally Post (.333), Reds.

■ **MVP:** Ford.

Linescores

Game 1—October 4, at New York
Cincinnati ....0 0 0 0 0 0 0 0 0—0 2 0
New York.....................0 0 0 1 0 1 0 0 x—2 6 0
O'Toole, Brosnan (8); Ford. W—Ford. L—O'Toole. HR—Howard, Skowron (N.Y.).

Game 2—October 5, at New York
Cincinnati ....0 0 0 2 1 1 0 2 0—6 9 0
New York.....................0 0 0 2 0 0 0 0 0—2 4 3
Jay; Terry, Arroyo (8). W—Jay. L—Terry. HR—Coleman (Cin.); Berra (N.Y.).

Game 3—October 7, at Cincinnati
New York.....................0 0 0 0 0 0 1 1 1—3 6 1
Cincinnati ....0 0 1 0 0 0 1 0 0—2 8 0
Stafford, Daley (7), Arroyo (8); Purkey. W—Arroyo. L—Purkey. HR—Blanchard, Maris (N.Y.).

Game 4—October 8, at Cincinnati
New York..................0 0 0 1 1 2 3 0 0—7 11 0
Cincinnati ....0 0 0 0 0 0 0 0 0—0 5 1
Ford, Coates (6); O'Toole, Brosnan (6), Henry (9). W—Ford. L—O'Toole.

Game 5—October 9, at Cincinnati
New York................5 1 0 5 0 2 0 0 0—13 15 1
Cincinnati ....0 0 3 0 2 0 0 0 0— 5 11 3
Terry, Daley (3); Jay, Maloney (1), K. Johnson (2), Henry (3), Jones (4), Purkey (5), Brosnan (7), Hunt (9). W—Daley. L—Jay. HR—Blanchard, Lopez (N.Y.); Robinson, Post (Cin.).

1962

FINAL STANDINGS

American League

Team	W	L	Pct.	GB
New York	96	66	.593	...
Minnesota	91	71	.562	5
Los Angeles	86	76	.531	10
Detroit	85	76	.528	10.5
Chicago	85	77	.525	11
Cleveland	80	82	.494	16
Baltimore	77	85	.475	19
Boston	76	84	.475	19
Kansas City	72	90	.444	24
Washington	60	101	.373	35.5

National League

Team	W	L	Pct.	GB
*San Francisco	103	62	.624	...
Los Angeles	102	63	.618	1
Cincinnati	98	64	.605	3.5
Pittsburgh	93	68	.578	8
Milwaukee	86	76	.531	15.5
St. Louis	84	78	.519	17.5
Philadelphia	81	80	.503	20
Houston	64	96	.400	36.5
Chicago	59	103	.364	42.5
New York	40	120	.250	60.5

*Defeated Los Angeles 2-1 in pennant playoff.

SIGNIFICANT EVENTS

■ **April 9-10:** The Senators christened their $20-million D.C. Stadium with a 4-1 victory over Detroit, but Cincinnati beat Los Angeles 6-3 in the first game at Dodger Stadium.

■ **November 23:** Dodgers shortstop Maury Wills, who ran his way to a record 104 stolen bases, walked away with the N.L. MVP.

MEMORABLE MOMENTS

■ **September 12:** Washington's Tom Cheney set a single-game record when he struck out 21 batters in a 16-inning 2-1 victory over the Orioles.

■ **October 3:** The Giants captured the N.L. pennant with a 6-4 victory over the Dodgers in the third game of a three-game playoff.

LEADERS

American League

BA: Pete Runnels, Bos., .326.
Runs: Albie Pearson, L.A., 115.
Hits: Bobby Richardson, N.Y., 209.
TB: Rocky Colavito, Det., 309.
HR: Harmon Killebrew, Min., 48.
RBI: Harmon Killebrew, Min., 126.
SB: Luis Aparicio, Chi., 31.
Wins: Ralph Terry, N.Y., 23.
ERA: Hank Aguirre, Det., 2.21.
CG: Camilo Pascual, Min., 18.
IP: Ralph Terry, N.Y., 298.2.
SO: Camilo Pascual, Min., 206.

National League

BA: Tommy Davis, L.A., .346.
Runs: Frank Robinson, Cin., 134.
Hits: Tommy Davis, L.A., 230.
TB: Willie Mays, S.F., 382.
HR: Willie Mays, S.F., 49.
RBI: Tommy Davis, L.A., 153.
SB: Maury Wills, L.A., 104.
Wins: Don Drysdale, L.A., 25.
ERA: Sandy Koufax, L.A., 2.54.
CG: Warren Spahn, Mil., 22.
IP: Don Drysdale, L.A., 314.1.
SO: Don Drysdale, L.A., 232.

A.L. 20-game winners
Ralph Terry, N.Y., 23-12
Ray Herbert, Chi., 20-9
Dick Donovan, Cle., 20-10
Camilo Pascual, Min., 20-11

N.L. 20-game winners
Don Drysdale, L.A., 25-9
Jack Sanford, S.F., 24-7
Bob Purkey, Cin., 23-5
Joey Jay, Cin., 21-14

A.L. 100 RBIs
Harmon Killebrew, Min., 126
Norm Siebern, K.C., 117
Rocky Colavito, Det., 112
Floyd Robinson, Chi., 109
Leon Wagner, L.A., 107
Lee Thomas, L.A., 104
Bob Allison, Min., 102
Roger Maris, N.Y., 100

N.L. 100 RBIs
Tommy Davis, L.A., 153
Willie Mays, S.F., 141
Frank Robinson, Cin., 136
Hank Aaron, Mil., 128
Frank Howard, L.A., 119
Orlando Cepeda, S.F., 114
Don Demeter, Phil., 107
Ernie Banks, Chi., 104
Bill White, St.L., 102
Vada Pinson, Cin., 100

N.L. 40 homers
Willie Mays, S.F., 49
Hank Aaron, Mil., 45

A.L. 40 homers
Harmon Killebrew, Min., 48

Most Valuable Player
A.L.: Mickey Mantle, OF, N.Y.
N.L.: Maury Wills, SS, L.A.

Cy Young Award
A.L.-N.L.: Don Drysdale, L.A. (NL)

Rookie of the Year
A.L.: Tom Tresh, SS, N.Y.
N.L.: Ken Hubbs, 2B, Chi.

Hall of Fame additions
Bob Feller, P, 1936-56
Bill McKechnie, manager
Jackie Robinson, 2B, 1947-56
Edd Roush, OF, 1913-31

ALL-STAR GAMES

■ **Winner:** The N.L. narrowed its series deficit to 16-15 with a 3-1 victory in the All-Star opener, but the A.L. pulled out its heavy artillery in a 9-4 second-game rout.

■ **Key Innings:** The sixth in Game 1, when pinch-runner Maury Wills sparked a two-run rally with a stolen base; the seventh in Game 2, when Rocky Colavito belted a three-run homer.

■ **Memorable moment:** The final out of the second game. The A.L. would not win again in the 1960s.

■ **Top guns:** Game 1: Don Drysdale (Dodgers), Juan Marichal (Giants), Roberto Clemente (Pirates), Wills (Dodgers), N.L.; Game 2: Leon Wagner (Angels), Pete Runnels (Red Sox), Colavito (Tigers), A.L.

■ **MVPs:** Game 1: Wills; Game 2: Wagner.

Linescores

Game 1, July 10, at Washington's D.C. Stadium
N.L. ....0 0 0 0 0 2 0 1 0—3 8 0
A.L. ....0 0 0 0 0 1 0 0 0—1 4 0
Drysdale (Dodgers), Marichal (Giants) 4, Purkey (Reds) 6, Shaw (Braves) 8; Bunning (Tigers), Pascual (Twins) 4, Donovan (Indians) 7, Pappas (Orioles) 9. W—Marichal. L—Pascual.

Game 2, July 30, at Chicago's Wrigley Field
A.L. ....0 0 1 2 0 1 3 0 2—9 10 0
N.L. ....0 1 0 0 0 0 1 1 1—4 10 4
Stenhouse (Senators), Herbert (White Sox) 3, Aguirre (Tigers) 6, Pappas (Orioles) 9; Podres (Dodgers), Mahaffey (Phillies) 3, Gibson (Cardinals) 5, Farrell (Colts) 7, Marichal (Giants) 8. W—Herbert. L—Mahaffey. HR—Runnels, Wagner, Colavito, A.L.; Roseboro, N.L.

WORLD SERIES

■ **Winner:** The Yankees prevailed over the Giants, who were making their first Series appearance since moving from New York to San Francisco.

■ **Turning point:** A three-run eighth-inning homer by rookie Tom Tresh that lifted Ralph Terry and the Yankees to a 5-3 Game 5 victory.

■ **Memorable moment:** Yankee second baseman Bobby Richardson snagging Willie McCovey's vicious seventh-game line drive with runners on second and third base, preserving Terry's 1-0 shutout and ending the Series. A slight variation in the path of McCovey's shot would have given the Giants a championship.

■ **Top guns:** Terry (2-1, 1.80 ERA), Tresh (.321, 4 RBIs), Yankees; Jose Pagan (.368), Giants.

■ **MVP:** Terry.

Linescores

Game 1—October 4, at San Francisco
New York..................2 0 0 0 0 0 1 2 1—6 11 0
San Francisco ....0 1 1 0 0 0 0 0 0—2 10 0
Ford; O'Dell, Larsen (8), Miller (9). W—Ford. L—O'Dell. HR—Boyer (N.Y.).

Game 2—October 5, at San Francisco
New York.....................0 0 0 0 0 0 0 0 0—0 3 1
San Francisco ....1 0 0 0 0 0 1 0 x—2 6 0
Terry, Daley (8); Sanford. W—Sanford. L—Terry. HR—McCovey (S.F.).

Game 3—October 7, at New York
San Francisco ....0 0 0 0 0 0 0 0 2—2 4 3
New York.....................0 0 0 0 0 0 3 0 x—3 5 1
Pierce, Larsen (7), Bolin (8); Stafford. W—Stafford. L—Pierce. HR—Bailey (S.F.).

Game 4—October 8, at New York
San Francisco ....0 2 0 0 0 0 4 0 1—7 9 1
New York.....................0 0 0 0 0 2 0 0 1—3 9 1
Marichal, Bolin (5), Larsen (6), O'Dell (7); Ford, Coates (7), Bridges (7). W—Larsen. L—Coates. HR—Haller, Hiller (S.F.).

Game 5—October 10, at New York
San Francisco ....0 0 1 0 1 0 0 0 1—3 8 2
New York.....................0 0 0 1 0 1 0 3 x—5 6 0
Sanford, Miller (8); Terry. W—Terry. L—Sanford. HR—Pagan (S.F.); Tresh (N.Y.).

Game 6—October 15, at San Francisco
New York..................0 0 0 0 1 0 0 1 0—2 3 2
San Francisco ....0 0 0 3 2 0 0 0 x—5 10 1
Ford, Coates (5), Bridges (8); Pierce. W—Pierce. L—Ford. HR—Maris (N.Y.).

Game 7—October 16, at San Francisco
New York.....................0 0 0 0 1 0 0 0 0—1 7 0
San Francisco ....0 0 0 0 0 0 0 0 0—0 4 1
Terry; Sanford, O'Dell (8). W—Terry. L—Sanford.

1963

FINAL STANDINGS

American League

Team	W	L	Pct.	GB
New York	104	57	.646	...
Chicago	94	68	.580	10.5
Minnesota	91	70	.565	13
Baltimore	86	76	.531	18.5
Cleveland	79	83	.488	25.5
Detroit	79	83	.488	25.5
Boston	76	85	.472	28
Kansas City	73	89	.451	31.5
Los Angeles	70	91	.435	34
Washington	56	106	.346	48.5

National League

Team	W	L	Pct.	GB
Los Angeles	99	63	.611	...
St. Louis	93	69	.574	6
San Francisco	88	74	.543	11
Philadelphia	87	75	.537	12
Cincinnati	86	76	.531	13
Milwaukee	84	78	.519	15
Chicago	82	80	.506	17
Pittsburgh	74	88	.457	25
Houston	66	96	.407	33
New York	51	111	.315	48

SIGNIFICANT EVENTS

■ **January 26:** Baseball's Rules Committee expanded the strike zone—from the top of the shoulders to the bottom of the knees.

■ **September 29:** Cardinals great Stan Musial retired with N.L. records for hits (3,630) and RBIs (1,951).

■ **November 7:** Yankee catcher Elston Howard became the first black MVP in A.L. history.

MEMORABLE MOMENTS

■ **July 13:** Cleveland's Early Wynn struggled through five rocky innings but still won his 300th career game, a 7-4 victory over Kansas City.

■ **August 21:** Pittsburgh's Jerry Lynch hit his record-setting 15th career pinch-hit homer in a 7-6 victory at Chicago.

■ **September 8:** 42-year-old Braves lefty Warren Spahn tied the N.L. record when he stopped Philadelphia 3-2, becoming a 20-game winner for the 13th time.

LEADERS

American League

BA: Carl Yastrzemski, Bos., .321.
Runs: Bob Allison, Min., 99.
Hits: Carl Yastrzemski, Bos., 183.
TB: Dick Stuart, Bos., 319.
HR: Harmon Killebrew, Min., 45.
RBI: Dick Stuart, Bos., 118.
SB: Luis Aparicio, Bal., 40.
Wins: Whitey Ford, N.Y., 24.
ERA: Gary Peters, Chi., 2.33.
CG: Camilo Pascual, Min.; Ralph Terry, N.Y., 18.
IP: Whitey Ford, N.Y., 269.1.
SO: Camilo Pascual, Min., 202.

National League

BA: Tommy Davis, L.A., .326.
Runs: Hank Aaron, Mil., 121.
Hits: Vada Pinson, Cin., 204.
TB: Hank Aaron, Mil., 370.
HR: Hank Aaron, Mil.; Willie McCovey, S.F., 44.
RBI: Hank Aaron, Mil., 130.
SB: Maury Wills, L.A., 40.
Wins: Sandy Koufax, L.A.; Juan Marichal, S.F., 25.
ERA: Sandy Koufax, L.A., 1.88.
CG: Warren Spahn, Mil., 22.
IP: Juan Marichal, S.F., 321.1.
SO: Sandy Koufax, L.A., 306.

A.L. 20-game winners

Whitey Ford, N.Y., 24-7
Jim Bouton, N.Y., 21-7
Camilo Pascual, Min., 21-9
Bill Monbouquette, Bos., 20-10
Steve Barber, Bal., 20-13

N.L. 20-game winners

Sandy Koufax, L.A., 25-5
Juan Marichal, S.F., 25-8
Jim Maloney, Cin., 23-7
Warren Spahn, Mil., 23-7
Dick Ellsworth, Chi., 22-10

A.L. 100 RBIs

Dick Stuart, Bos., 118
Al Kaline, Det., 101

N.L. 100 RBIs

Hank Aaron, Mil., 130
Ken Boyer, St.L., 111
Bill White, St.L., 109
Vada Pinson, Cin., 106
Willie Mays, S.F., 103
Willie McCovey, S.F., 102

A.L. 40 homers

Harmon Killebrew, Min., 45
Dick Stuart, Bos., 42

N.L. 40 homers

Hank Aaron, Mil., 44
Willie McCovey, S.F., 44

Most Valuable Player

A.L.: Elston Howard, C, N.Y.
N.L.: Sandy Koufax, P, L.A.

Cy Young Award

A.L.-N.L.: Sandy Koufax, L.A. (NL)

Rookie of the Year

A.L.: Gary Peters, P, Chi.
N.L.: Pete Rose, 2B, Cin.

Hall of Fame additions

John Clarkson, P, 1882-94
Elmer Flick, OF, 1898-1910
Sam Rice, OF, 1915-35
Eppa Rixey, P, 1912-33

ALL-STAR GAME

■ **Winner:** The N.L. unleashed secret weapon Willie Mays on the A.L. again and claimed a 5-3 victory in a return to the single All-Star Game format.

■ **Key inning:** The third, when Mays singled home a run, stole his second base and scored on a single by Dick Groat. Mays scored two runs, drove in two and made an outstanding catch.

■ **Memorable moment:** Pinch-hitter Stan Musial lining out to right field in his 24th, and last, All-Star appearance. Musial batted .317 and hit a record six home runs.

■ **Top guns:** Mays (Giants), Ron Santo (Cubs), N.L.; Albie Pearson (Angels), Leon Wagner (Angels), A.L.

■ **MVP:** Mays.

Linescore

July 9, at Cleveland Stadium
N.L. ....0 1 2 0 1 0 0 1 0—5 6 0
A.L. ....0 1 2 0 0 0 0 0 0—3 11 1
O'Toole (Reds), Jackson (Cubs) 3, Culp (Phillies) 5, Woodeshick (Colts) 6, Drysdale (Dodgers) 8; McBride (Angels), Bunning (Tigers) 4, Bouton (Yankees) 6, Pizarro (White Sox) 7, Radatz (Red Sox) 8. W—Jackson. L—Bunning.

WORLD SERIES

■ **Winner:** The Dodgers cut down their old nemesis in an impressive pitching-dominated sweep.

■ **Turning point:** The first two innings of Game 1. Dodgers lefthander Sandy Koufax set the tone for the Series when he struck out the first five Yankees he faced en route to a record-setting 15-strikeout performance.

■ **Memorable moment:** The first World Series game at new Dodger Stadium — a three-hit 1-0 victory for Los Angeles righthander Don Drysdale in Game 3.

■ **Top guns:** Koufax (2-0, 1.50 ERA), Tommy Davis (.400), Bill Skowron (.385), Dodgers; Elston Howard (.333), Yankees.

■ **MVP:** Koufax.

Linescores

Game 1—October 2, at New York
Los Angeles ....0 4 1 0 0 0 0 0 0—5 9 0
New York....................0 0 0 0 0 0 0 2 0—2 6 0
Koufax; Ford, Williams (6), Hamilton (9). W—Koufax. L—Ford. HR—Roseboro (L.A.); Tresh (N.Y.).

Game 2—October 3, at New York
Los Angeles ....2 0 0 1 0 0 0 1 0—4 10 1
New York..................0 0 0 0 0 0 0 0 1—1 7 0
Podres, Perranoski (9); Downing, Terry (6), Reniff (9). W—Podres. L—Downing. HR—Skowron (L.A.).

Game 3—October 5, at Los Angeles
New York....................0 0 0 0 0 0 0 0 0—0 3 0
Los Angeles ....1 0 0 0 0 0 0 0 0—1 4 1
Bouton, Reniff (8); Drysdale. W—Drysdale. L—Bouton.

Game 4—October 6, at Los Angeles
New York....................0 0 0 0 0 0 1 0 0—1 6 1
Los Angeles................0 0 0 0 1 0 1 0 x—2 2 1
Ford, Reniff (8); Koufax. W—Koufax. L—Ford. HR—F. Howard (L.A.); Mantle (N.Y.).

1964

FINAL STANDINGS

American League

Team	W	L	Pct.	GB
New York	99	63	.611	...
Chicago	98	64	.605	1
Baltimore	97	65	.599	2
Detroit	85	77	.525	14
Los Angeles	82	80	.506	17
Cleveland	79	83	.488	20
Minnesota	79	83	.488	20
Boston	72	90	.444	27
Washington	62	100	.383	37
Kansas City	57	105	.352	42

National League

Team	W	L	Pct.	GB
St. Louis	93	69	.574	...
Cincinnati	92	70	.568	1
Philadelphia	92	70	.568	1
San Francisco	90	72	.556	3
Milwaukee	88	74	.543	5
Los Angeles	80	82	.494	13
Pittsburgh	80	82	.494	13
Chicago	76	86	.469	17
Houston	66	96	.407	27
New York	53	109	.327	40

SIGNIFICANT EVENTS

■ **February 13:** Ken Hubbs, the Cubs' 22-year-old second baseman, died when the single-engine plane he was flying crashed near Provo, Utah.

■ **April 17:** The Mets opened $25-million Shea Stadium with a 4-3 loss to the Pirates.

■ **November 7:** The Braves received N.L. permission to move their sagging franchise from Milwaukee to Atlanta after the 1965 season.

MEMORABLE MOMENTS

■ **April 23:** Houston's Ken Johnson became the first pitcher to lose a game in which he had thrown a complete-game no-hitter. Johnson dropped a 1-0 decision to the Reds.

■ **June 4:** Dodgers lefty Sandy Koufax joined Bob Feller as the only three-time no-hit pitchers of the 20th Century when he stopped the Phillies, 3-0.

■ **June 21:** Philadelphia's Jim Bunning fired baseball's first regular-season perfect game in 42 years, beating the Mets, 6-0.

LEADERS

American League

BA: Tony Oliva, Min., .323.
Runs: Tony Oliva, Min., 109.
Hits: Tony Oliva, Min., 217.
TB: Tony Oliva, Min., 374.
HR: Harmon Killebrew, Min., 49.
RBI: Brooks Robinson, Bal., 118.
SB: Luis Aparicio, Bal., 57.
Wins: Dean Chance, L.A.; Gary Peters, Chi., 20.
ERA: Dean Chance, L.A., 1.65.
CG: Dean Chance, L.A., 15.
IP: Dean Chance, L.A., 278.1.
SO: Al Downing, N.Y., 217.

National League

BA: Roberto Clemente, Pit., .339.
Runs: Dick Allen, Phil., 125.
Hits: Roberto Clemente, Pit.; Curt Flood, St.L., 211.
TB: Dick Allen, Phil., 352.
HR: Willie Mays, S.F., 47.
RBI: Ken Boyer, St.L., 119.
SB: Maury Wills, L.A., 53.
Wins: Larry Jackson, Chi., 24.
ERA: Sandy Koufax, L.A., 1.74.
CG: Juan Marichal, S.F., 22.
IP: Don Drysdale, L.A., 321.1.
SO: Bob Veale, Pit., 250.

A.L. 20-game winners

Dean Chance, L.A., 20-9
Gary Peters, Chi., 20-8

N.L. 20-game winners

Larry Jackson, Chi., 24-11
Juan Marichal, S.F., 21-8
Ray Sadecki, St.L., 20-11

A.L. 100 RBIs

Brooks Robinson, Bal., 118
Dick Stuart, Bos., 114
Harmon Killebrew, Min., 111
Mickey Mantle, N.Y., 111
Rocky Colavito, K.C., 102
Joe Pepitone, N.Y., 100
Leon Wagner, Cle., 100

N.L. 100 RBIs

Ken Boyer, St.L., 119
Ron Santo, Chi., 114
Willie Mays, S.F., 111
Joe Torre, Mil., 109
Johnny Callison, Phil., 104
Bill White, St.L., 102

A.L. 40 homers

Harmon Killebrew, Min., 49

N.L. 40 homers

Willie Mays, S.F., 47

Most Valuable Player

A.L.: Brooks Robinson, 3B, Bal.
N.L.: Ken Boyer, 3B, St.L.

Cy Young Award

A.L.-N.L.: Dean Chance, L.A. (AL)

Rookie of the Year

A.L.: Tony Oliva, OF, Min.
N.L.: Dick Allen, 3B, Phil.

Hall of Fame additions

Luke Appling, SS, 1930-50
Red Faber, P, 1914-33
Burleigh Grimes, P, 1916-34
Miller Huggins, manager
Tim Keefe, P, 1880-93
Heinie Manush, OF, 1923-39
Monte Ward, IF/P, 1878-94

ALL-STAR GAME

■ **Winner:** In a game that rekindled memories of 1941, the N.L. struck for four ninth-inning runs and escaped with a stunning 7-4 victory.

■ **Key inning:** The ninth, when Willie Mays walked, stole second moved to third on Orlando Cepeda's bloop single and scored the tying run on a wild throw. But the N.L. was far from finished.

■ **Memorable moment:** Johnny Callison's stunning three-run homer that finished off the A.L. in the ninth. The blast was hit off Boston relief ace Dick Radatz.

■ **Top guns:** Billy Williams (Cubs), Ken Boyer (Cardinals), Callison (Phillies), N.L.; Dean Chance (Angels), Harmon Killebrew (Twins), A.L.

■ **MVP:** Callison.

Linescore

July 7, at New York's Shea Stadium
A.L. ....1 0 0 0 0 2 1 0 0—4 9 1
N.L. ....0 0 0 2 1 0 0 0 4—7 8 0
Chance (Angels), Wyatt (Athletics) 4, Pascual (Twins) 5, Radatz (Red Sox) 7; Drysdale (Dodgers), Bunning (Phillies) 4, Short (Phillies) 6, Farrell (Colts) 7, Marichal (Giants) 9. W—Marichal. L—Radatz. HR—Williams, Boyer, Callison, N.L.

WORLD SERIES

■ **Winner:** The Cardinals brought down the curtain on the Yankee dynasty with a seven-game triumph.

■ **Turning point:** Trailing two games to one and 3-0 in the sixth inning of Game 4, the Cardinals rallied to a 4-3 victory when Ken Boyer connected for a grand slam.

■ **Memorable moment:** A dramatic Game 3-ending homer by Mickey Mantle on the first ninth-inning pitch by St. Louis reliever Barney Schultz.

■ **Top guns:** Bob Gibson (2-1, 3.00 ERA), Tim McCarver (.478, 5 RBIs), Boyer (2 HR, 6 RBIs), Lou Brock (.300, 5 RBIs), Cardinals; Bobby Richardson (13 hits, .406), Mantle (.333, 3 HR, 8 RBIs), Yankees.

■ **MVP:** Gibson.

Linescores

Game 1—October 7, at St. Louis
New York..................0 3 0 0 1 0 0 1 0—5 12 2
St. Louis ....1 1 0 0 0 4 0 3 x—9 12 0
Ford, Downing (6), Sheldon (8), Mikkelsen (8); Sadecki, Schultz (7). W—Sadecki. L—Ford. HR—Tresh (N.Y.); Shannon (St.L.).

Game 2—October 8, at St. Louis
New York..................0 0 0 1 0 1 2 0 4—8 12 0
St. Louis ....0 0 1 0 0 0 0 1 1—3 7 0
Stottlemyre; Gibson, Schultz (9); G. Richardson (9); Craig (9). W—Stottlemyre. L—Gibson. HR—Linz (N.Y.).

Game 3—October 10, at New York
St. Louis ....0 0 0 0 1 0 0 0 0—1 6 0
New York...................0 1 0 0 0 0 0 0 1—2 5 2
Simmons, Schultz (9); Bouton. W—Bouton. L—Schultz. HR—Mantle (N.Y.).

Game 4—October 11, at New York
St. Louis ....0 0 0 0 0 4 0 0 0—4 6 1
New York...................3 0 0 0 0 0 0 0 0—3 6 1
Sadecki, Craig (1), Taylor (6); Downing, Mikkelsen (7), Terry (8). W—Craig. L—Downing. HR—K. Boyer (St.L.).

Game 5—October 12, at New York
St. Louis ....0 0 0 0 2 0 0 0 0 3—5 10 1
New York...........0 0 0 0 0 0 0 0 2 0—2 6 2
Gibson; Stottlemyre, Reniff (8), Mikkelsen (8). W—Gibson. L—Mikkelsen. HR—Tresh (N.Y.); McCarver (St.L.).

Game 6—October 14, at St. Louis
New York.................0 0 0 0 1 2 0 5 0—8 10 0
St. Louis ....1 0 0 0 0 0 0 1 1—3 10 1
Bouton, Hamilton (9); Simmons, Taylor (7), Schultz (8), G. Richardson (8), Humphreys (9). W—Bouton. L—Simmons. HR—Maris, Mantle, Pepitone (N.Y.).

Game 7—October 15, at St. Louis
New York.................0 0 0 0 0 3 0 0 2—5 9 2
St. Louis ....0 0 0 3 3 0 1 0 x—7 10 1
Stottlemyre, Downing (5), Sheldon (5), Hamilton (7), Mikkelsen (8); Gibson. W—Gibson. L—Stottlemyre. HR—Brock, K. Boyer (St.L.); Mantle, C. Boyer, Linz (N.Y.).

1965

FINAL STANDINGS

American League

Team	W	L	Pct.	GB
Minnesota	102	60	.630	...
Chicago	95	67	.586	7
Baltimore	94	68	.580	8
Detroit	89	73	.549	13
Cleveland	87	75	.537	15
New York	77	85	.475	25
California	75	87	.463	27
Washington	70	92	.432	32
Boston	62	100	.383	40
Kansas City	59	103	.364	43

National League

Team	W	L	Pct.	GB
Los Angeles	97	65	.599	...
San Francisco	95	67	.586	2
Pittsburgh	90	72	.556	7
Cincinnati	89	73	.549	8
Milwaukee	86	76	.531	11
Philadelphia	85	76	.528	11.5
St. Louis	80	81	.497	16.5
Chicago	72	90	.444	25
Houston	65	97	.401	32
New York	50	112	.309	47

SIGNIFICANT EVENTS

■ **April 9:** The Houston Astrodome, baseball's first domed stadium, was unveiled for an exhibition game between the Astros and Yankees.

■ **August 22:** Giants pitcher Juan Marichal touched off a wild 14-minute brawl when he attacked Dodgers catcher John Roseboro with a bat.

■ **August 29:** Citing poor health, Casey Stengel stepped down as Mets manager and ended his 56-year baseball career.

■ **September 2:** The Los Angeles Angels, preparing to move to Anaheim, changed their name to the California Angels.

MEMORABLE MOMENTS

■ **August 19:** Cincinnati's Jim Maloney, who had no-hit the Mets two months earlier only to lose in the 11th, fired another 10-inning no-hitter and beat the Cubs, 1-0.

■ **September 13:** San Francisco's Willie Mays, en route to his second 50-homer season, became the fifth member of the 500 club when he connected off Houston's Don Nottebart in a game at the Astrodome.

■ **September 29:** Dodgers ace Sandy Koufax reached perfection when he retired all 27 Cubs he faced in a 1-0 victory—his record fourth career no-hitter.

LEADERS

American League

BA: Tony Oliva, Min., .321.
Runs: Zoilo Versalles, Min., 126.
Hits: Tony Oliva, Min., 185.
TB: Zoilo Versalles, Min., 308.
HR: Tony Conigliaro, Bos., 32.
RBI: Rocky Colavito, Cle., 108.
SB: Campy Campaneris, K.C., 51.
Wins: Jim (Mudcat) Grant, Min., 21.
ERA: Sam McDowell, Cle., 2.18.
CG: Mel Stottlemyre, N.Y., 18.
IP: Mel Stottlemyre, N.Y., 291.
SO: Sam McDowell, Cle., 325.

National League

BA: Roberto Clemente, Pit., .329.
Runs: Tommy Harper, Cin., 126.
Hits: Pete Rose, Cin., 209.
TB: Willie Mays, S.F., 360.
HR: Willie Mays, S.F., 52.
RBI: Deron Johnson, Cin., 130.
SB: Maury Wills, L.A., 94.
Wins: Sandy Koufax, L.A., 26.
ERA: Sandy Koufax, L.A., 2.04.
CG: Sandy Koufax, L.A., 27.
IP: Sandy Koufax, L.A., 335.2.
SO: Sandy Koufax, L.A., 382.

A.L. 20-game winners

Jim (Mudcat) Grant, Min., 21-7
Mel Stottlemyre, N.Y., 20-9

N.L. 20-game winners

Sandy Koufax, L.A., 26-8
Tony Cloninger, Mil., 24-11
Don Drysdale, L.A., 23-12
Sammy Ellis, Cin., 22-10
Juan Marichal, S.F., 22-13
Jim Maloney, Cin., 20-9
Bob Gibson, St.L., 20-12

A.L. 100 RBIs

Rocky Colavito, Cle., 108
Willie Horton, Det., 104

N.L. 100 RBIs

Deron Johnson, Cin., 130
Frank Robinson, Cin., 113
Willie Mays, S.F., 112
Billy Williams, Chi., 108
Willie Stargell, Pit., 107
Ernie Banks, Chi., 106
Johnny Callison, Phil., 101
Ron Santo, Chi., 101

N.L. 40 homers

Willie Mays, S.F., 52

Most Valuable Player

A.L: Zoilo Versalles, SS, Min.
N.L.: Willie Mays, OF, S.F.

Cy Young Award

A.L.-N.L.: Sandy Koufax, L.A. (NL)

Rookie of the Year

A.L.: Curt Blefary, OF, Bal.
N.L.: Jim Lefebvre, 2B, L.A.

Hall of Fame addition

Pud Galvin, P, 1879-92

ALL-STAR GAME

■ **Winner:** The N.L. took its first All-Star lead when Ron Santo drove home Willie Mays with a seventh-inning infield single that produced the winning run.

■ **Key Innings:** An N.L. first that featured home runs by Mays and Joe Torre and an A.L. fifth that featured Dick McAuliffe and Harmon Killebrew homers.

■ **Memorable moment:** Bob Gibson striking out Killebrew and New York's Joe Pepitone in the ninth inning with the tying run on second base.

■ **Top guns:** Juan Marichal (Giants), Mays (Giants), Willie Stargell (Pirates), Joe Torre (Braves), N.L.; McAuliffe (Tigers), Killebrew (Twins), A.L.

■ **MVP:** Marichal.

Linescore

July 13, at Minnesota's Metropolitan Stadium
N.L. ....3 2 0 0 0 0 1 0 0—6 11 0
A.L. ....0 0 0 1 4 0 0 0 0—5 8 0
Marichal (Giants), Maloney (Reds) 4, Drysdale (Dodgers) 5, Koufax (Dodgers) 6, Farrell (Astros) 7, Gibson (Cardinals) 8; Pappas (Orioles), Grant (Twins) 2, Richert (Senators) 4, McDowell (Indians) 6, Fisher (White Sox) 8. W—Koufax. L—McDowell. HR—Mays, Torre, Stargell, N.L.; McAuliffe, Killebrew, A.L.

WORLD SERIES

■ **Winner:** The pitching-rich Dodgers prevailed after dropping the first two games to the Twins — Minnesota's first World Series representative.

■ **Turning point:** A 4-0 shutout by Dodgers lefthander Claude Osteen in Game 3, after the Twins had beaten Don Drysdale and Sandy Koufax in Games 1 and 2.

■ **Memorable moment:** A three-hit seventh-game shutout by Koufax, who struck out 10 in his 2-0 victory.

■ **Top guns:** Koufax (2-1, 0.38 ERA), Ron Fairly (2 HR, 6 RBIs), Dodgers; Jim Grant (2-1, 2.74), Twins.

■ **MVP:** Koufax.

Linescores

Game 1—October 6, at Minnesota
Los Angeles ....0 1 0 0 0 0 0 0 1—2 10 1
Minnesota ....0 1 6 0 0 1 0 0 x—8 10 0
Drysdale, Reed (3), Brewer (5), Perranoski (7); Grant. W—Grant. L—Drysdale. HR—Fairly (L.A.); Mincher, Versalles (Min.).

Game 2—October 7, at Minnesota
Los Angeles ....0 0 0 0 0 0 1 0 0—1 7 3
Minnesota ....0 0 0 0 0 2 1 2 x—5 9 0
Koufax, Perranoski (7), Miller (8); Kaat. W—Kaat. L—Koufax.

Game 3—October 9, at Los Angeles
Minnesota................0 0 0 0 0 0 0 0 0—0 5 0
Los Angeles.............0 0 0 2 1 1 0 0 x—4 10 1
Pascual, Merritt (6), Klippstein (8); Osteen. W—Osteen. L—Pascual.

Game 4—October 10, at Los Angeles
Minnesota................0 0 0 1 0 1 0 0 0—2 5 2
Los Angeles.............1 1 0 1 0 3 0 1 x—7 10 0
Grant, Worthington (6), Pleis (8); Drysdale. W—Drysdale. L—Grant. HR—Killebrew, Oliva (Min.); Parker, Johnson (L.A.).

Game 5—October 11, at Los Angeles
Minnesota................0 0 0 0 0 0 0 0 0—0 4 1
Los Angeles.............2 0 2 1 0 0 2 0 x—7 14 0
Kaat, Boswell (3), Perry (6); Koufax. W—Koufax. L—Kaat.

Game 6—October 13, at Minnesota
Los Angeles ....0 0 0 0 0 0 1 0 0—1 6 1
Minnesota ....0 0 0 2 0 3 0 0 x—5 6 1
Osteen, Reed (6), Miller (8); Grant. W—Grant. L—Osteen. HR—Fairly (L.A.); Allison, Grant (Min.).

Game 7—October 14, at Minnesota
Los Angeles ....0 0 0 2 0 0 0 0 0—2 7 0
Minnesota ....0 0 0 0 0 0 0 0 0—0 3 1
Koufax; Kaat, Worthington (4), Klippstein (6), Merritt (7), Perry (9). W—Koufax. L—Kaat. HR—Johnson (L.A.).

1966

FINAL STANDINGS

American League

Team	W	L	Pct.	GB
Baltimore	97	63	.606	...
Minnesota	89	73	.549	9
Detroit	88	74	.543	10
Chicago	83	79	.512	15
Cleveland	81	81	.500	17
California	80	82	.494	18
Kansas City	74	86	.463	23
Washington	71	88	.447	25.5
Boston	72	90	.444	26
New York	70	89	.440	26.5

National League

Team	W	L	Pct.	GB
Los Angeles	95	67	.586	...
San Francisco	93	68	.578	1.5
Pittsburgh	92	70	.568	3
Philadelphia	87	75	.537	8
Atlanta	85	77	.525	10
St. Louis	83	79	.512	12
Cincinnati	76	84	.475	18
Houston	72	90	.444	23
New York	66	95	.410	28.5
Chicago	59	103	.364	36

SIGNIFICANT EVENTS

■ **March 30:** The joint 32-day holdout of Dodger pitchers Sandy Koufax and Don Drysdale ended when they agreed to a combined package worth more than $210,000.

■ **April 11:** Another barrier fell when Emmett Ashford, baseball's first black umpire, worked the season opener at Washington.

■ **April 12:** The Braves dropped a 3-2 verdict to the Pirates in their debut at the new $18-million Atlanta Stadium.

■ **November 18:** Sandy Koufax, baseball's only three-time Cy Young Award winner, stunned the Dodgers when he announced his retirement at age 30 because of an arthritic elbow.

MEMORABLE MOMENTS

■ **June 9:** Rich Rollins, Zoilo Versalles, Tony Oliva, Don Mincher and Harmon Killebrew hit home runs in a seventh-inning explosion against Kansas City, matching a Major League record.

■ **August 17:** San Francisco's Willie Mays belted career homer No. 535 off St. Louis' Ray Washburn and moved into second place on the all-time list.

■ **September 22:** The Orioles clinched their first A.L. pennant with a 6-1 victory over Kansas City.

■ **October 2:** Sandy Koufax, working on two days rest, beat Philadelphia 6-3 for his 27th victory and clinched the Dodgers' third pennant in four years.

■ **November 8:** Baltimore's Frank Robinson, baseball's 13th Triple Crown winner, became the first player to win MVP honors in both leagues.

LEADERS

American League

BA: Frank Robinson, Bal., .316.
Runs: Frank Robinson, Bal., 122.
Hits: Tony Oliva, Min., 191.
TB: Frank Robinson, Bal., 367.
HR: Frank Robinson, Bal., 49.
RBI: Frank Robinson, Bal., 122.
SB: Campy Campaneris, K.C., 52.
Wins: Jim Kaat, Min., 25.
ERA: Gary Peters, Chi., 1.98.
CG: Jim Kaat, Min., 19.
IP: Jim Kaat, Min., 304.2.
SO: Sam McDowell, Cle., 225.

National League

BA: Matty Alou, Pit., .342.
Runs: Felipe Alou, Atl., 122.
Hits: Felipe Alou, Atl., 218.
TB: Felipe Alou, Atl., 355.
HR: Hank Aaron, Atl., 44.
RBI: Hank Aaron, Atl., 127.
SB: Lou Brock, St.L., 74.
Wins: Sandy Koufax, L.A., 27.
ERA: Sandy Koufax, L.A., 1.73.
CG: Sandy Koufax, L.A., 27.
IP: Sandy Koufax, L.A., 323.
SO: Sandy Koufax, L.A., 317.

A.L. 20-game winners

Jim Kaat, Min., 25-13
Denny McLain, Det., 20-14

N.L. 20-game winners

Sandy Koufax, L.A., 27-9
Juan Marichal, S.F., 25-6
Gaylord Perry, S.F., 21-8
Bob Gibson, St.L., 21-12
Chris Short, Phil., 20-10

A.L. 100 RBIs

Frank Robinson, Bal., 122
Harmon Killebrew, Min., 110
Boog Powell, Bal., 109
Willie Horton, Det., 100
Brooks Robinson, Bal., 100

N.L. 100 RBIs

Hank Aaron, Atl., 127
Roberto Clemente, Pit., 119
Dick Allen, Phil., 110
Willie Mays, S.F., 103
Bill White, Phil., 103
Willie Stargell, Pit., 102
Joe Torre, Atl., 101

A.L. 40 homers

Frank Robinson, Bal., 49

N.L. 40 homers

Hank Aaron, Atl., 44
Dick Allen, Phil., 40

Most Valuable Player

A.L.: Frank Robinson, OF, Bal.
N.L.: Roberto Clemente, OF, Pit.

Cy Young Award

A.L.-N.L.: Sandy Koufax, L.A. (NL)

Rookie of the Year

A.L.: Tommie Agee, OF, Chi.
N.L.: Tommy Helms, 3B, Cin.

Hall of Fame additions

Casey Stengel, manager
Ted Williams, OF, 1939-60

ALL-STAR GAME

■ **Winner:** The N.L. needed 10 innings to win its fourth consecutive All-Star Game in the blistering 105-degree heat of St. Louis.

■ **Key inning:** The 10th, when Maury Wills singled home Tim McCarver with the game-ending run.

■ **Memorable moment:** The almost-constant sight of fans being helped in the stands after passing out because of the heat.

■ **Top guns:** Gaylord Perry (Giants), Roberto Clemente (Pirates), Wills (Dodgers), N.L.; Denny McLain (Tigers), Brooks Robinson (Orioles), A.L.

■ **MVP:** Robinson.

Linescore

July 12, at St. Louis' Busch Stadium
A.L. ....0 1 0 0 0 0 0 0 0 0—1 6 0
N.L. ....0 0 0 1 0 0 0 0 0 1—2 6 0
McLain (Tigers), Kaat (Twins) 4, Stottlemyre (Yankees) 6, Siebert (Indians) 8, Richert (Senators) 10; Koufax (Dodgers), Bunning (Phillies) 4, Marichal (Giants) 6, Perry (Giants) 9. W—Perry. L—Richert.

WORLD SERIES

■ **Winner:** The Orioles, making only the second Series appearance in franchise history and first since moving from St. Louis to Baltimore, allowed only two Dodger runs — none after the third inning of Game 1.

■ **Turning point:** Game 1, when Moe Drabowsky relieved Baltimore lefty Dave McNally with the bases loaded in the third inning. Drabowsky worked 6⅔ innings of shutout relief and struck out 11 Dodgers in a 5-2 victory.

■ **Memorable moments:** Series-ending 1-0 victories by Wally Bunker (six-hitter) and McNally (four-hitter).

■ **Top guns:** Boog Powell (.357), Frank Robinson (2 HR, 3 RBIs), Orioles.

■ **MVP:** Frank Robinson.

Linescores

Game 1—October 5, at Los Angeles
Baltimore ....3 1 0 1 0 0 0 0 0—5 9 0
Los Angeles ....0 1 1 0 0 0 0 0 0—2 3 0
McNally, Drabowsky (3); Drysdale, Moeller (3), R. Miller (5), Perranoski (8). W—Drabowsky. L—Drysdale. HR—F. Robinson, B. Robinson (Bal.); Lefebvre (L.A.).

Game 2—October 6, at Los Angeles
Baltimore ....0 0 0 0 3 1 0 2 0—6 8 0
Los Angeles ....0 0 0 0 0 0 0 0 0—0 4 6
Palmer; Koufax, Perranoski (7), Regan (8), Brewer (9). W—Palmer. L—Koufax.

Game 3—October 8, at Baltimore
Los Angeles ....0 0 0 0 0 0 0 0 0—0 6 0
Baltimore....................0 0 0 0 1 0 0 0 x—1 3 0
Osteen, Regan (8); Bunker. W—Bunker. L—Osteen. HR—Blair (Bal.).

Game 4—October 9, at Baltimore
Los Angeles ....0 0 0 0 0 0 0 0 0—0 4 0
Baltimore....................0 0 0 1 0 0 0 0 x—1 4 0
Drysdale; McNally. W—McNally. L—Drysdale. HR—F. Robinson.

1967

FINAL STANDINGS

American League

Team	W	L	Pct.	GB
Boston	92	70	.568	...
Detroit	91	71	.562	1
Minnesota	91	71	.562	1
Chicago	89	73	.549	3
California	84	77	.522	7.5
Baltimore	76	85	.472	15.5
Washington	76	85	.472	15.5
Cleveland	75	87	.463	17
New York	72	90	.444	20
Kansas City	62	99	.385	29.5

National League

Team	W	L	Pct.	GB
St. Louis	101	60	.627	...
San Francisco	91	71	.562	10.5
Chicago	87	74	.540	14
Cincinnati	87	75	.537	14.5
Philadelphia	82	80	.506	19.5
Pittsburgh	81	81	.500	20.5
Atlanta	77	85	.475	24.5
Los Angeles	73	89	.451	28.5
Houston	69	93	.426	32.5
New York	61	101	.377	40.5

SIGNIFICANT EVENT

■ **October 18:** The A.L. approved the Athletics' move to Oakland and 1969 expansion to Kansas City and Seattle.

MEMORABLE MOMENTS

■ **April 14:** Boston lefthander Bill Rohr, making his Major League debut, lost a no-hit bid when Yankee Elston Howard singled with two out in the ninth inning of a 3-0 Red Sox victory.
■ **April 30:** Baltimore's Steve Barber and Stu Miller combined to pitch a no-hitter, but the Orioles lost, 2-1, when Detroit scored two ninth-inning runs.
■ **May 14, July 14:** New York's Mickey Mantle and Houston's Eddie Mathews became the sixth and seventh members of the 500-homer club exactly two months apart.

LEADERS

American League

BA: Carl Yastrzemski, Bos., .326.
Runs: Carl Yastrzemski, Bos., 112.
Hits: Carl Yastrzemski, Bos., 189.
TB: Carl Yastrzemski, Bos., 360.
HR: Harmon Killebrew, Min.; Carl Yastrzemski, Bos., 44.
RBI: Carl Yastrzemski, Bos., 121.
SB: Campy Campaneris, K.C., 55.
Wins: Jim Lonborg, Bos.; Earl Wilson, Det., 22.
ERA: Joel Horlen, Chi., 2.06.
CG: Dean Chance, Min., 18.
IP: Dean Chance, Min., 283.2.
SO: Jim Lonborg, Bos., 246.

National League

BA: Roberto Clemente, Pit., .357.
Runs: Hank Aaron, Atl.; Lou Brock, St.L., 113.
Hits: Roberto Clemente, Pit., 209.
TB: Hank Aaron, Atl., 344.
HR: Hank Aaron, Atl., 39.
RBI: Orlando Cepeda, St.L., 111.
SB: Lou Brock, St.L., 52.
Wins: Mike McCormick, S.F., 22.
ERA: Phil Niekro, Atl., 1.87.
CG: Ferguson Jenkins, Chi., 20.
IP: Jim Bunning, Phil., 302.1.
SO: Jim Bunning, Phil., 253.

A.L. 20-game winners
Jim Lonborg, Bos., 22-9
Earl Wilson, Det., 22-11
Dean Chance, Min., 20-14

N.L. 20-game winners
Mike McCormick, S.F., 22-10
Ferguson Jenkins, Chi., 20-13

A.L. 100 RBIs
Carl Yastrzemski, Bos., 121
Harmon Killebrew, Min., 113

N.L. 100 RBIs
Orlando Cepeda, St.L., 111
Roberto Clemente, Pit., 110
Hank Aaron, Atl., 109
Jim Wynn, Hou., 107
Tony Perez, Cin., 102

A.L. 40 homers
Harmon Killebrew, Min., 44
Carl Yastrzemski, Bos., 44

Most Valuable Player
A.L.: Carl Yastrzemski, OF, Bos.
N.L.: Orlando Cepeda, 1B, St.L.

Cy Young Award
A.L.: Jim Lonborg, Bos.
N.L.: Mike McCormick, S.F.

Rookie of the Year
A.L.: Rod Carew, 2B, Min.
N.L.: Tom Seaver, P, N.Y.

Hall of Fame additions
Branch Rickey, executive
Red Ruffing, P, 1924-47
Lloyd Waner, OF, 1927-45

ALL-STAR GAME

■ **Winner:** The N.L. continued its All-Star hex with a pulsating 15-inning 2-1 victory — the longest game in the classic's 35-year history.

■ **Key inning:** The 15th, when Cincinnati's Tony Perez deposited a Catfish Hunter pitch over the left-field fence, ending the N.L.'s 12-inning scoreless run.

■ **Memorable moment:** The overall performance of 12 pitchers, who gave up only 17 hits and two bases on balls while recording 30 strikeouts.

■ **Top guns:** Juan Marichal (Giants), Don Drysdale (Dodgers), Richie Allen (Phillies), Perez (Reds), N.L.; Gary Peters (White Sox), Hunter (Athletics), Carl Yastrzemski (Red Sox), Brooks Robinson (Orioles), A.L.

■ **MVP:** Perez.

Linescore

July 11, at California's Anaheim Stadium
N.L. ..0 1 0 000 000 000 001—2 9 0
A.L. ..0 0 0 001 000 000 000—1 8 0
Marichal (Giants), Jenkins (Cubs) 4, Gibson (Cardinals) 7, Short (Phillies) 9, Cuellar (Astros) 11, Drysdale (Dodgers) 13, Seaver (Mets) 15; Chance (Twins), McGlothlin (Angels) 4, Peters (White Sox) 6, Downing (Yankees) 9, Hunter (Athletics) 11. W—Drysdale. L—Hunter. HR—Allen, Perez, N.L.; Robinson, A.L.

WORLD SERIES

■ **Winner:** It took seven games for the Cardinals to ruin Boston's "impossible dream" of winning its first Series championship since 1918.

■ **Turning point:** The seventh-game heroics of Bob Gibson, who belted a home run and pitched the Cardinals to a 7-2 victory.

■ **Memorable moment:** A two-out eighth-inning double by St. Louis' Julian Javier in Game 2, ending Boston righthander Jim Lonborg's no-hit bid. Lonborg finished with a one-hit 5-0 victory.

■ **Top guns:** Gibson (3-0, 1.00 ERA), Lou Brock (.414), Roger Maris (.385, 7 RBIs), Cardinals; Lonborg (2-1), Carl Yastrzemski (.400, 3 HR, 5 RBIs), Red Sox.

■ **MVP:** Gibson.

Linescores

Game 1—October 4, at Boston
St. Louis ....0 0 1 0 0 0 1 0 0—2 10 0
Boston ....0 0 1 0 0 0 0 0 0—1 6 0
Gibson; Santiago, Wyatt (8). W—Gibson. L—Santiago. HR—Santiago (Bos.).

Game 2—October 5, at Boston
St. Louis ....0 0 0 0 0 0 0 0 0—0 1 1
Boston.......................0 0 0 1 0 1 3 0 x—5 9 0
Hughes, Willis (6), Hoerner (7), Lamabe (7); Lonborg. W—Lonborg. L—Hughes. HR—Yastrzemski 2 (Bos.).

Game 3—Ocotber 7, at St. Louis
Boston ....0 0 0 0 0 1 1 0 0—2 7 1
St. Louis ....1 2 0 0 0 1 0 1 x—5 10 0
Bell, Waslewski (3), Stange (6), Osinski (8); Briles. W—Briles. L—Bell. HR—Shannon (St.L.); Smith (Bos.).

Game 4—October 8, at St. Louis
Boston ....0 0 0 0 0 0 0 0 0—0 5 0
St. Louis ....4 0 2 0 0 0 0 0 x—6 9 0
Santiago, Bell (1), Stephenson (3), Morehead (5), Brett (8); Gibson. W—Gibson. L—Santiago.

Game 5—October 9, at St. Louis
Boston ....0 0 1 0 0 0 0 0 2—3 6 1
St. Louis ....0 0 0 0 0 0 0 0 1—1 3 2
Lonborg; Carlton, Washburn (7), Willis (9), Lamabe (9). W—Lonborg. L—Carlton. HR—Maris.

Game 6—October 11, at Boston
St. Louis ....0 0 2 0 0 0 2 0 0— 4 8 0
Boston.....................0 1 0 3 0 0 4 0 x—8 12 1
Hughes, Willis (4), Briles (5), Lamabe (7), Hoerner (7), Jaster (7), Washburn (7), Woodeshick (8); Waslewski, Wyatt (6), Bell (8). W—Wyatt. L—Lamabe. HR—Petrocelli 2, Yastrzemski, Smith (Bos.); Brock (St.L.).

Game 7—October 12, at Boston
St. Louis ....0 0 2 0 2 3 0 0 0—7 10 1
Boston ....0 0 0 0 1 0 0 1 0—2 3 1
Gibson; Lonborg, Santiago (7), Morehead (9), Osinski (9), Brett (9). W—Gibson. L—Lonborg. HR—Gibson, Javier (St.L.).

1968

FINAL STANDINGS

American League

Team	W	L	Pct.	GB
Detroit	103	59	.636	...
Baltimore	91	71	.562	12
Cleveland	86	75	.534	16.5
Boston	86	76	.531	17
New York	83	79	.512	20
Oakland	82	80	.506	21
Minnesota	79	83	.488	24
California	67	95	.414	36
Chicago	67	95	.414	36
Washington	65	96	.404	37.5

National League

Team	W	L	Pct.	GB
St. Louis	97	65	.599	...
San Francisco	88	74	.543	9
Chicago	84	78	.519	13
Cincinnati	83	79	.512	14
Atlanta	81	81	.500	16
Pittsburgh	80	82	.494	17
Los Angeles	76	86	.469	21
Philadelphia	76	86	.469	21
New York	73	89	.451	24
Houston	72	90	.444	25

SIGNIFICANT EVENTS

■ **May 27:** The N.L. crossed the Canadian border when it awarded 1969 expansion franchises to Montreal and San Diego.
■ **July 10:** A.L. and N.L. officials agreed to uniformity in their 1969 expansions: two-division formats, 162-game schedules and best-of-five League Championship Series.
■ **December 3:** The Rules Committee lowered the mound, shrunk the strike zone and cracked down on illegal pitches in an effort to increase offense.
■ **December 6:** Baseball owners forced William Eckert to resign as commissioner.

MEMORABLE MOMENTS

■ **May 8:** A's righthander Catfish Hunter fired baseball's ninth perfect game, retiring all 27 Twins he faced in a 4-0 victory at Oakland.
■ **July 30:** Washington shortstop Ron Hansen pulled off baseball's eighth unassisted triple play in the first inning of a 10-1 loss at Cleveland.
■ **September 14:** The Tigers rallied for two ninth-inning runs and defeated Oakland 5-4, allowing Denny McLain to become baseball's first 30-game winner since 1934.

LEADERS

American League

BA: Carl Yastrzemski, Bos., .301.
Runs: Dick McAuliffe, Det., 95.
Hits: Campy Campaneris, Oak., 177.
TB: Frank Howard, Wash., 330.
HR: Frank Howard, Wash., 44.
RBI: Ken Harrelson, Bos., 109.
SB: Campy Campaneris, Oak., 62.
Wins: Denny McLain, Det., 31.
ERA: Luis Tiant, Cle., 1.60.
CG: Denny McLain, Det., 28.
IP: Denny McLain, Det., 336.
SO: Sam McDowell, Cle., 283.

National League

BA: Pete Rose, Cin., .335.
Runs: Glenn Beckert, Chi., 98.
Hits: Felipe Alou, Atl.; Pete Rose, Cin., 210.
TB: Billy Williams, Chi., 321.
HR: Willie McCovey, S.F., 36.
RBI: Willie McCovey, S.F., 105.
SB: Lou Brock, St.L., 62.
Wins: Juan Marichal, S.F., 26.
ERA: Bob Gibson, St.L., 1.12.
CG: Juan Marichal, S.F., 30.
IP: Juan Marichal, S.F., 326.
SO: Bob Gibson, St.L., 268.

A.L. 20-game winners
Denny McLain, Det., 31-6
Dave McNally, Bal., 22-10
Luis Tiant, Cle., 21-9
Mel Stottlemyre, N.Y., 21-12

N.L. 20-game winners
Juan Marichal, S.F., 26-9
Bob Gibson, St.L., 22-9
Ferguson Jenkins, Chi., 20-15

A.L. 100 RBIs
Ken Harrelson, Bos., 109
Frank Howard, Wash., 106

N.L. 100 RBIs
Willie McCovey, S.F., 105

A.L. 40 homers
Frank Howard, Wash., 44

Most Valuable Player
A.L.: Denny McLain, P, Det.
N.L.: Bob Gibson, P, St.L.

Cy Young Award
A.L.: Denny McLain, Det.
N.L.: Bob Gibson, St.L.

Rookie of the Year
A.L.: Stan Bahnsen, P, N.Y.
N.L.: Johnny Bench, C, Cin.

Hall of Fame additions
Kiki Cuyler, OF, 1921-38
Goose Goslin, OF, 1921-38
Joe Medwick, OF, 1932-48

ALL-STAR GAME

■ **Winner:** The N.L. stretched its winning streak to six with the first 1-0 game in All-Star history. It also was the first played indoors and on an artificial surface.

■ **Key inning:** The first, when the N.L. scored the game's only run on a double-play grounder.

■ **Memorable moment:** The performance of a six-man N.L. staff that held the A.L. to three hits.

■ **Top guns:** Don Drysdale (Dodgers), Juan Marichal (Giants), Steve Carlton (Cardinals), Tom Seaver (Mets), Willie Mays (Giants), N.L.; Blue Moon Odom (Athletics), Denny McLain (Tigers), A.L.

■ **MVP:** Mays.

Linescore

July 9, at Houston's Astrodome
A.L. ....0 0 0 0 0 0 0 0 0—0 3 1
N.L. ....1 0 0 0 0 0 0 0 x—1 5 0
Tiant (Indians), Odom (Athletics) 3, McLain (Tigers) 5, McDowell (Indians) 7, Stottlemyre (Yankees) 8, John (White Sox) 8; Drysdale (Dodgers), Marichal (Giants) 4, Carlton (Cardinals) 6, Seaver (Mets) 7, Reed (Braves) 9, Koosman (Mets) 9. W—Drysdale. L—Tiant.

WORLD SERIES

■ **Winner:** The Tigers, down three games to one, rallied to win their first World Series since 1945.

■ **Turning point:** With the Tigers on the brink of elimination entering Game 5, lefthander Mickey Lolich pitched them to a 5-3 victory.

■ **Memorable moments:** Bob Gibson striking out 17 Tigers in Game 1. Cardinals center fielder Curt Flood misjudging Jim Northrup's seventh-game fly ball, which became a Series-deciding two-run triple.

■ **Top guns:** Lolich (3-0, 1.67 ERA), Norm Cash (.385, 5 RBIs); Al Kaline (.379, 2 HR, 8 RBIs), Tigers; Gibson (2-1, 1.67), Lou Brock (.464, 2 HR, 5 RBIs), Cardinals.

■ **MVP:** Lolich.

Linescores

Game 1—October 2, at St. Louis
Detroit.......................0 0 0 0 0 0 0 0 0—0 5 3
St. Louis ....0 0 0 3 0 0 1 0 x—4 6 0
McLain, Dobson (6), McMahon (8); Gibson. W—Gibson. L—McLain. HR—Brock (St.L.).

Game 2—October 3, at St. Louis
Detroit.....................0 1 1 0 0 3 1 0 2—8 13 1
St. Louis ....0 0 0 0 0 1 0 0 0—1 6 1
Lolich; Briles, Carlton (6), Willis (7), Hoerner (9). W—Lolich. L—Briles. HR—Horton, Lolich, Cash (Det.).

Game 3—October 5, at Detroit
St. Louis ....0 0 0 0 4 0 3 0 0—7 13 0
Detroit.....................0 0 2 0 1 0 0 0 0—3 4 0
Washburn, Hoerner (6); Wilson, Dobson (5), McMahon (6), Patterson (7), Hiller (8). W—Washburn. L—Wilson. HR—Kaline, McAuliffe (Det.); McCarver, Cepeda (St.L.).

Game 4—October 6, at Detroit
St. Louis ....2 0 2 2 0 0 0 4 0—10 13 0
Detroit...................0 0 0 1 0 0 0 0 0— 1 5 4
Gibson; McLain, Sparma (3), Patterson (4), Lasher (6), Hiller (8), Dobson (8). W—Gibson. L—McLain. HR—Brock, Gibson (St.L.); Northrup (Det.).

Game 5—October 7, at Detroit
St. Louis ....3 0 0 0 0 0 0 0 0—3 9 0
Detroit.......................0 0 0 2 0 0 3 0 x—5 9 1
Briles, Hoerner (7), Willis (7); Lolich. W—Lolich. L—Hoerner. HR—Cepeda (St.L.).

Game 6—October 9, at St. Louis
Detroit..................0 2 10 0 1 0 0 0 0—13 12 1
St. Louis ....0 0 0 0 0 0 0 0 1— 1 9 1
McLain; Washburn, Jaster (3), Willis (3), Hughes (3), Carlton (4), Granger (7), Nelson (9). W—McLain. L—Washburn. HR—Northrup, Kaline (Det.).

Game 7—October 10, at St. Louis
Detroit.......................0 0 0 0 0 0 3 0 1—4 8 1
St. Louis ....0 0 0 0 0 0 0 0 1—1 5 0
Lolich; Gibson. W—Lolich. L—Gibson. HR—Shannon (St.L.).

FINAL STANDINGS

American League

East Division

Team	Bal.	Det.	Bos.	Wash.	N.Y.	Cle.	Min.	Oak.	Cal.	K.C.	Chi.	Sea.	W	L	Pct.	GB
Baltimore	...	11	10	13	11	13	8	8	6	11	9	9	109	53	.673	...
Detroit	7	...	8	7	10	11	6	7	7	8	9	10	90	72	.556	19
Boston	8	10	...	6	11	12	7	4	8	10	5	6	87	75	.537	22
Washington	5	11	12	...	8	15	6	4	7	5	8	5	86	76	.531	23
New York	7	8	7	10	...	8	2	6	9	7	9	7	80	81	.497	28.5
Cleveland	5	7	6	3	9	...	5	5	4	7	4	7	62	99	.385	46.5

West Division

Team	Min.	Oak.	Cal.	K.C.	Chi.	Sea.	Bal.	Det.	Bos.	Wash.	N.Y.	Cle.	W	L	Pct.	GB
Minnesota	...	13	11	10	13	12	4	6	5	6	10	7	97	65	.599	...
Oakland	5	...	12	10	10	13	4	5	8	8	6	7	88	74	.543	9
California	7	6	...	9	9	9	6	5	4	5	3	8	71	91	.438	26
Kansas City	8	8	9	...	10	10	1	4	2	7	5	5	69	93	.426	28
Chicago	5	8	9	8	...	10	3	3	7	4	3	8	68	94	.420	29
Seattle	6	5	9	8	8	...	3	2	6	7	5	5	64	98	.395	33

National League

East Division

Team	N.Y.	Chi.	Pit.	St.L.	Phi.	Mon.	Atl.	S.F.	Cin.	L.A.	Hou.	S.D.	W	L	Pct.	GB
New York	...	10	10	12	12	13	8	8	6	8	2	11	100	62	.617	...
Chicago	8	...	7	9	12	10	9	6	6	6	8	11	92	70	.568	8
Pittsburgh	8	11	...	9	8	13	4	5	7	4	9	10	88	74	.543	12
St. Louis	6	9	9	...	11	11	6	9	4	9	5	8	87	75	.537	13
Philadelphia	6	6	10	7	...	7	6	3	2	4	4	8	63	99	.389	37
Montreal	5	8	5	7	11	...	4	1	4	2	1	4	52	110	.321	48

West Division

Team	Atl.	S.F.	Cin.	L.A.	Hou.	S.D.	N.Y.	Chi.	Pit.	St.L	Phi.	Mon.	W	L	Pct.	GB
Atlanta	...	9	12	9	15	13	4	3	8	6	6	8	93	69	.574	...
San Fran.	9	...	8	13	8	12	4	6	7	3	9	11	90	72	.556	3
Cincinnati	6	10	...	10	9	11	6	6	5	8	10	8	89	73	.549	4
Los Angeles	9	5	8	...	12	12	4	6	8	3	8	10	85	77	.525	8
Houston	3	10	9	6	...	10	10	4	3	7	8	11	81	81	.500	12
San Diego	5	6	7	6	8	...	1	1	2	4	4	8	52	110	.321	41

SIGNIFICANT EVENTS

■ **February 4:** Bowie Kuhn, a little-known attorney, was handed a one-year term as a compromise choice to succeed William Eckert as commissioner.

■ **February 25:** Baseball owners avoided a strike by increasing player pension plan contributions and granting improvements in other important benefits.

■ **April 8:** The four expansion teams—Kansas City, Seattle, Montreal and San Diego—recorded Opening Day victories.

■ **April 14:** The first Major League game on foreign soil: Montreal defeated the Cardinals, 8-7, at Jarry Park.

■ **December 4:** Chub Feeney was named to succeed Warren Giles as N.L. president.

MEMORABLE MOMENTS

■ **April 30-May 1:** Cincinnati's Jim Maloney and Houston's Don Wilson fired back-to-back no-hitters at Crosley Field, matching the Gaylord Perry-Ray Washburn feat of 1968.

■ **September 15:** Cardinals lefty Steve Carlton struck out a record 19 batters, but the Mets won the game 4-3 on a pair of two-run homers by Ron Swoboda.

■ **September 22:** San Francisco's Willie Mays became the second batter to hit 600 home runs when he connected off Mike Corkins in a 4-2 victory over San Diego.

LEADERS

American League
BA: Rod Carew, Min., .332.
Runs: Reggie Jackson, Oak., 123.
Hits: Tony Oliva, Min., 197.
TB: Frank Howard, Wash., 340.
HR: Harmon Killebrew, Min., 49.
RBI: Harmon Killebrew, Min., 140.
SB: Tommy Harper, Sea., 73.
Wins: Denny McLain, Det., 24.
ERA: Dick Bosman, Wash., 2.19.
CG: Mel Stottlemyre, N.Y., 24.
IP: Denny McLain, Det., 325.
SO: Sam McDowell, Cle., 279.
SV: Ron Perranoski, Min., 31.

National League
BA: Pete Rose, Cin., .348.
Runs: Bobby Bonds, S.F.; Pete Rose, Cin., 120.
Hits: Matty Alou, Pit., 231.
TB: Hank Aaron, Atl., 332.
HR: Willie McCovey, S.F., 45.
RBI: Willie McCovey, S.F., 126.
SB: Lou Brock, St.L., 53.
Wins: Tom Seaver, N.Y., 25.
ERA: Juan Marichal, S.F., 2.10.
CG: Bob Gibson, St.L., 28.
IP: Gaylord Perry, S.F., 325.1.
SO: Ferguson Jenkins, Chi., 273.
SV: Fred Gladding, Hou., 29.

A.L. 20-game winners
Denny McLain, Det., 24-9
Mike Cuellar, Bal., 23-11
Jim Perry, Min., 20-6
Dave McNally, Bal., 20-7
Dave Boswell, Min., 20-12
Mel Stottlemyre, N.Y., 20-14

N.L. 20-game winners
Tom Seaver, N.Y., 25-7
Phil Niekro, Atl., 23-13
Juan Marichal, S.F., 21-11
Ferguson Jenkins, Chi., 21-15
Bill Singer, L.A., 20-12
Larry Dierker, Hou., 20-13
Bob Gibson, St.L., 20-13
Bill Hands, Chi., 20-14
Claude Osteen, L.A., 20-15

A.L. 100 RBIs
Harmon Killebrew, Min., 140
Boog Powell, Bal., 121
Reggie Jackson, Oak., 118
Sal Bando, Oak., 113
Frank Howard, Wash., 111
Carl Yastrzemski, Bos., 111
Tony Oliva, Min., 101
Frank Robinson, Bal., 100

N.L. 100 RBIs
Willie McCovey, S.F., 126
Ron Santo, Chi., 123
Tony Perez, Cin., 122
Lee May, Cin., 110
Ernie Banks, Chi., 106
Joe Torre, St.L., 101

A.L. 40 homers
Harmon Killebrew, Min., 49
Frank Howard, Wash., 48
Reggie Jackson, Oak., 47
Rico Petrocelli, Bos., 40
Carl Yastrzemski, Bos., 40

N.L. 40 homers
Willie McCovey, S.F., 45
Hank Aaron, Atl., 44

Most Valuable Player
A.L.: Harmon Killebrew, 3B, Min.
N.L.: Willie McCovey, 1B, S.F.

Cy Young Award
A.L.: Denny McLain, Det.
Mike Cuellar, Bal.
N.L.: Tom Seaver, N.Y.

Rookie of the Year
A.L.: Lou Piniella, OF, K.C.
N.L.: Ted Sizemore, 2B, L.A.

Hall of Fame additions
Roy Campanella, C, 1948-57
Stan Coveleski, P, 1912-28
Waite Hoyt, P, 1918-38
Stan Musial, OF/1B, 1941-63

ALL-STAR GAME

■ **Winner:** Willie McCovey belted a pair of home runs and Johnny Bench hit another as the N.L. stretched its winning streak to seven.

■ **Key inning:** A five-run N.L. third, fueled by the first of McCovey's two blasts. The explosion broke open a 3-1 contest.

■ **Memorable moment:** A sensational leaping catch by A.L. left fielder Carl Yastrzemski in the sixth inning, robbing Bench of another home run.

■ **Top guns:** McCovey (Giants), Bench (Reds), Cleon Jones (Mets), Felix Millan (Braves), N.L.; Frank Howard (Senators), Bill Freehan (Tigers), A.L.

■ **MVP:** McCovey.

Linescore
July 22, at Washington's RFK Stadium
N.L............1 2 5 1 0 0 0 0 0—9 11 0
A.L............0 1 1 1 0 0 0 0 0—3 6 2
Carlton (Cardinals), Gibson (Cardinals) 4, Singer (Dodgers) 5, Koosman (Mets) 7, Dierker (Astros) 8, Niekro (Braves) 9; Stottlemyre (Yankees), Odom (Athletics) 3, Knowles (Senators) 3, McLain (Tigers) 4, McNally (Orioles) 5, McDowell (Indians) 7, Culp (Red Sox) 9. W—Carlton. L—Stottlemyre. HR—McCovey 2, Bench, N.L.; Howard, Freehan, A.L.

ALCS

■ **Winner:** The Baltimore Orioles, hailed by many as the best A.L. team since the Yankee pennant-winning machines of yesteryear, swept past Minnesota in baseball's first season of League Championship Series play.

■ **Turning point:** Paul Blair's 12th-inning squeeze bunt gave the Orioles a 4-3 Game 1 victory after Boog Powell had tied the contest with a ninth-inning home run.

■ **Memorable moment:** An 11th-inning Curt Motton pinch-hit single that put the capper on a second-game, three-hit, 1-0 shutout by Orioles lefthander Dave McNally.

■ **Top guns:** McNally (1-0, 0.00 ERA), Brooks Robinson (.500), Blair (.400, 6 RBIs), Orioles; Tony Oliva (.385), Twins.

■ **MVP:** McNally.

Linescores

Game 1—October 4, at Baltimore
Minn. 0 0 0 0 1 0 2 0 0 0 0 0—3 4 2
Balt. ..0 0 0 1 1 0 0 0 1 0 0 1—4 10 1
Perry, Perranoski (9); Cuellar, Richert (9), Watt (10), Lopez (12), Hall (12). W—Hall. L—Perranoski. HR—F. Robinson, Belanger, Powell (Bal.); Oliva (Min.).

Game 2—October 5, at Baltimore
Minn. ....0 0 0 0 0 0 0 0 0 0 0—0 3 1
Balt. ......0 0 0 0 0 0 0 0 0 0 1—1 8 0
Boswell, Perranoski (11); McNally. W—McNally. L—Boswell.

Game 3—October 6, at Minnesota
Balt. ....0 3 0 2 0 1 0 2 3—11 18 0
Minn. ......1 0 0 0 1 0 0 0 0— 2 10 2
Palmer; Miller, Woodson (2), Hall (4), Worthington (5), Grzenda (6), Chance (7), Perranoski (9). W—Palmer. L—Miller. HR—Blair (Bal.).

NLCS

■ **Winner:** The Mets completed their stunning pennant run by sweeping the Braves in the N.L.'s first League Championship Series.

■ **Turning point:** A five-run eighth-inning rally that produced a 9-5 Mets victory in Game 1 and set the tone for the rest of the series.

■ **Memorable moment:** Young Nolan Ryan's Game 3 heroics. Ryan took over for starter Gary Gentry in the third inning with runners on second and third, none out and the Braves leading 2-0. He pitched out of the jam and recorded the series-ending victory with seven innings of three-hit pitching.

■ **Top guns:** Art Shamsky (.538), Cleon Jones (.429), Ken Boswell (.333, 2 HR, 5 RBIs), Mets; Orlando Cepeda (.455), Hank Aaron (.357, 3 HR, 7 RBIs), Braves.

■ **MVP:** Boswell.

Linescores

Game 1—October 4, at Atlanta
New York ..0 2 0 2 0 0 0 5 0—9 10 1
Atlanta ......0 1 2 0 1 0 1 0 0—5 10 2
Seaver, Taylor (8); Niekro, Upshaw (9). W—Seaver. L—Niekro. S—Taylor. HR—Gonzalez, H. Aaron (Atl.).

Game 2—October 5, at Atlanta
New York 1 3 2 2 1 0 2 0 0—11 13 1
Atlanta ....0 0 0 1 5 0 0 0 0— 6 9 3
Koosman, Taylor (5), McGraw (7); Reed, Doyle (2), Pappas (3), Britton (6), Upshaw (6), Neibauer (9). W—Taylor. L—Reed. S—McGraw. HR—Agee, Boswell, Jones (N.Y.); H. Aaron (Atl.).

Game 3—October 6, at New York
Atlanta ......2 0 0 0 2 0 0 0 0—4 8 1
New York ..0 0 1 2 3 1 0 0 x—7 14 0
Jarvis, Stone (5), Upshaw (6); Gentry, Ryan (3). W—Ryan. L—Jarvis. HR—H. Aaron, Cepeda (Atl.); Agee, Boswell, Garrett (N.Y.).

WORLD SERIES

■ **Winner:** The Amazing Mets completed their Cinderella season with a shocking five-game victory over the powerful Orioles.

■ **Turning point:** A ninth-inning RBI single by light-hitting Al Weis that gave the Mets and Jerry Koosman a Series-evening 2-1 victory in Game 2.

■ **Memorable moments:** Tommie Agee's Game 3 performance. Center fielder Agee hit a first-inning home run and made two spectacular catches that saved five runs and preserved a 5-0 victory.

■ **Top guns:** Koosman (2-0, 2.04 ERA), Weis (.455), Donn Clendenon (.357, 3 HR, 4 RBIs), Mets.

■ **MVP:** Clendenon.

Linescores

Game 1—October 11, at Baltimore
NY................0 0 0 0 0 0 1 0 0—1 6 1
Balt. ....1 0 0 3 0 0 0 0 x—4 6 0
Seaver, Cardwell (6), Taylor (7); Cuellar. W—Cuellar. L—Seaver. HR—Buford (Bal.).

Game 2—October 12, at Baltimore
NY................0 0 0 1 0 0 0 0 1—2 6 0
Balt. ....0 0 0 0 0 0 1 0 0—1 2 0
Koosman, Taylor (9); McNally. W—Koosman. L—McNally. HR—Clendenon (N.Y.).

Game 3—October 14, at New York
Balt. ....0 0 0 0 0 0 0 0 0—0 4 1
NY................1 2 0 0 0 1 0 1 x—5 6 0
Palmer, Leonhard (7); Gentry, Ryan (7). W—Gentry. L—Palmer. S—Ryan. HR—Agee, Kranepool (N.Y.).

Game 4—Ocotber 15, at New York
Balt. ....0 0 0 0 0 0 0 0 1 0—1 6 1
NY ....0 1 0 0 0 0 0 0 0 1—2 10 1
Cuellar, Watt (8), Hall (10), Richert (10); Seaver. W—Seaver. L—Hall. HR—Clendenon (N.Y.).

Game 5—October 16, at New York
Balt. ....0 0 3 0 0 0 0 0 0—3 5 2
NY................0 0 0 0 0 2 1 2 x—5 7 0
McNally, Watt (8); Koosman. W—Koosman. L—Watt. HR—McNally, F. Robinson (Bal.); Clendenon, Weis (N.Y.).

FINAL STANDINGS

American League

East Division

Team	Bal.	N.Y.	Bos.	Det.	Cle.	Wsh.	Min.	Oak.	Cal.	K.C.	Mil.	Chi.	W	L	Pct.	GB
Baltimore	...	11	13	11	14	12	5	7	7	12	7	9	108	54	.667	...
New York	7	...	8	11	10	10	7	6	7	11	9	7	93	69	.574	15
Boston	5	10	...	9	12	12	7	7	5	7	5	8	87	75	.537	21
Detroit	7	7	9	...	11	9	4	6	6	6	8	6	79	83	.488	29
Cleveland	4	8	6	7	...	11	6	7	6	8	7	6	76	86	.469	32
Washington	6	8	6	9	7	...	6	2	5	6	7	8	70	92	.432	38

West Division

Team	Min.	Oak.	Cal.	K.C.	Mil.	Chi.	Bal.	N.Y.	Bos.	Det.	Cle.	Wsh.	W	L	Pct.	GB
Minnesota	...	13	10	13	13	12	7	5	5	8	6	6	98	64	.605	...
Oakland	5	...	10	11	10	16	5	6	5	6	5	10	89	73	.549	9
California	8	8	...	10	12	12	5	5	7	6	6	7	86	76	.531	12
Kansas City	5	7	8	...	12	11	0	1	5	6	4	6	65	97	.401	33
Milwaukee	5	8	6	6	...	11	5	3	7	4	5	5	65	97	.401	33
Chicago	6	2	6	7	7	...	3	5	4	6	6	4	56	106	.346	42

National League

East Division

Team	Pit.	Chi.	N.Y.	St.L.	Phi.	Mon.	Cin.	L.A.	S.F.	Hou.	Atl.	S.D.	W	L	Pct.	GB
Pittsburgh	...	10	12	12	14	9	4	6	4	6	6	6	89	73	.549	...
Chicago	8	...	7	7	9	13	7	6	7	7	4	9	84	78	.519	5
New York	6	11	...	12	13	8	4	5	6	6	6	6	83	79	.512	6
St. Louis	6	11	6	...	10	11	3	5	5	6	5	8	76	86	.469	13
Philadelphia	4	9	5	8	...	7	5	5	8	8	5	9	73	88	.453	15.5
Montreal	9	5	10	7	11	...	5	4	6	4	6	6	73	89	.451	16

West Division

Team	Cin.	L.A.	S.F.	Hou.	Atl.	S.D.	Pit.	Chi.	N.Y.	St.L.	Phi.	Mon.	W	L	Pct.	GB
Cincinnati	...	13	9	15	13	8	8	5	8	9	7	7	102	60	.630	...
Los Angeles	5	...	9	10	12	11	6	6	7	7	6	8	87	74	.540	14.5
San Fran.	9	9	...	8	11	13	8	5	6	7	4	6	86	76	.531	16
Houston	3	8	10	...	9	14	6	5	6	6	4	8	79	83	.488	23
Atlanta	5	6	7	9	...	9	6	8	6	7	7	6	76	86	.469	26
San Diego	10	7	5	4	9	...	6	3	6	4	3	6	63	99	.389	39

LEADERS

American League
BA: Alex Johnson, Cal., .329.
Runs: Carl Yastrzemski, Bos., 125.
Hits: Tony Oliva, Min., 204.
TB: Carl Yastrzemski, Bos., 335.
HR: Frank Howard, Wash., 44.
RBI: Frank Howard, Wash., 126.
SB: Campy Campaneris, Oak., 42.
Wins: Mike Cuellar, Bal.; Dave McNally, Bal.; Jim Perry, Min., 24.
ERA: Diego Segui, Oak., 2.56.
CG: Mike Cuellar, Bal., 21.
IP: Sam McDowell, Cle.; Jim Palmer, Bal., 305.
SO: Sam McDowell, Cle., 304.
SV: Ron Perranoski, Min., 34.

National League
BA: Rico Carty, Atl., .366.
Runs: Billy Williams, Chi., 137.
Hits: Pete Rose, Cin.; Billy Williams, Chi., 205.
TB: Billy Williams, Chi., 373.
HR: Johnny Bench, Cin., 45.
RBI: Johnny Bench, Cin., 148.
SB: Bobby Tolan, Cin., 57.
Wins: Bob Gibson, St.L.; Gaylord Perry, S.F., 23.
ERA: Tom Seaver, N.Y., 2.82.
CG: Ferguson Jenkins, Chi., 24.
IP: Gaylord Perry, S.F., 328.2.
SO: Tom Seaver, N.Y., 283.
SV: Wayne Granger, Cin., 35.

A.L. 20-game winners
Mike Cuellar, Bal., 24-8
Dave McNally, Bal., 24-9
Jim Perry, Min., 24-12
Clyde Wright, Cal., 22-12
Jim Palmer, Bal., 20-10
Fritz Peterson, N.Y., 20-11
Sam McDowell, Cle., 20-12

N.L. 20-game winners
Bob Gibson, St.L., 23-7
Gaylord Perry, S.F., 23-13
Ferguson Jenkins, Chi., 22-16
Jim Merritt, Cin., 20-12

A.L. 100 RBIs
Frank Howard, Wash., 126
Tony Conigliaro, Bos., 116
Boog Powell, Bal., 114
Harmon Killebrew, Min., 113
Tony Oliva, Min., 107
Rico Petrocelli, Bos., 103
Carl Yastrzemski, Bos., 102

N.L. 100 RBIs
Johnny Bench, Cin., 148
Tony Perez, Cin., 129
Billy Williams, Chi., 129
Willie McCovey, S.F., 126
Hank Aaron, Atl., 118
Jim Hickman, Chi., 115
Ron Santo, Chi., 114
Orlando Cepeda, Atl., 111
Wes Parker, L.A., 111
Dick Dietz, S.F., 107
Dick Allen, St.L., 101
Rico Carty, Atl., 101
Joe Torre, St.L., 100

A.L. 40 homers
Frank Howard, Wash., 44
Harmon Killebrew, Min., 41
Carl Yastrzemski, Bos., 40

N.L. 40 homers
Johnny Bench, Cin., 45
Billy Williams, Chi., 42
Tony Perez, Cin., 40

Most Valuable Player
A.L.: Boog Powell, 1B, Bal.
N.L.: Johnny Bench, C, Cin.

Cy Young Award
A.L.: Jim Perry, Min.
N.L.: Bob Gibson, St.L.

Rookie of the Year
A.L.: Thurman Munson, C, N.Y.
N.L.: Carl Morton, P, Mon.

Hall of Fame additions
Lou Boudreau, SS, 1938-52
Earle Combs, OF, 1924-35
Ford Frick, exec./commissioner
Jesse Haines, P, 1918-37

SIGNIFICANT EVENTS

■ **January 16:** Outfielder Curt Flood, who refused to report to Philadelphia after being traded by the Cardinals, filed a federal lawsuit challenging baseball's reserve clause.

■ **March 28:** Commissioner Bowie Kuhn returned the All-Star selection to the fans, with voting to be done on punch cards and processed by computer.

■ **March 31:** The financially strapped Pilots ended their one-year Seattle existence when the team was sold and moved to Milwaukee.

■ **June 30, July 16:** The Reds lost in their Riverfront Stadium debut to Atlanta, 8-2, but spoiled the Pirates' Three Rivers Stadium inaugural, 3-2.

■ **September 3:** Exhausted Cubs star Billy Williams ended his N.L.-record ironman streak at 1,117 games.

■ **October 4:** Umpires ended their unprecedented one-day strike when they accepted a four-year contract and returned to work for the second games of the League Championship Series.

MEMORABLE MOMENTS

■ **April 22:** Mets righthander Tom Seaver tied the Major League record when he struck out 19 Padres, including a record 10 in succession, during a 2-1 victory at Shea Stadium.

■ **May 10:** Atlanta knuckleballer Hoyt Wilhelm became the first pitcher to appear in 1,000 Major League games.

■ **May 12:** Cubs shortstop Ernie Banks hit his 500th career home run off Atlanta's Pat Jarvis in a 4-3 victory at Wrigley Field.

■ **May 17, July 18:** Two new members of baseball's 3,000-hit club: Atlanta's Hank Aaron and San Francisco's Willie Mays.

■ **June 21:** Detroit's Cesar Gutierrez performed a 20th Century first when he collected seven hits (six singles and a double) in a 12-inning 9-8 victory over Cleveland.

■ **June 26:** Baltimore's Frank Robinson belted a record-tying two grand slams in the Orioles' 12-2 victory over the Senators.

■ **October 1:** California's Alex Johnson collected two final-day hits and edged Boston's Carl Yastrzemski, .3289 to .3286, in the tightest A.L. batting race since 1946.

ALL-STAR GAME

■ **Winner:** Chicago's Jim Hickman singled home Pete Rose in the 12th inning, giving the N.L. a come-from-behind victory that pushed its All-Star winning streak to eight games.
■ **Key inning:** The bottom of the ninth, when a Dick Dietz home run, an RBI single by Willie McCovey and Roberto Clemente's sacrifice fly brought the N.L. back from a 4-1 deficit and forced extra innings.
■ **Memorable moment:** A game-ending collision between Rose and A.L. catcher Ray Fosse. Rose, playing before his home fans, jarred the ball free and sent Fosse sprawling with a nasty body block.
■ **Top guns:** Tom Seaver (Mets), Bud Harrelson (Mets), Dietz (Giants), McCovey (Giants), Rose (Reds), Hickman (Cubs), N.L.; Jim Palmer (Orioles), Sam McDowell (Indians), Carl Yastrzemski (Red Sox), Brooks Robinson (Orioles), A.L.
■ **MVP:** Yastrzemski

Linescore
July 14, at Cincinnati's Riverfront Stadium
A.L....0 0 0 0 0 1 1 2 0 0 0 0—4 12 0
N.L. 0 0 0 0 0 0 1 0 3 0 0 1—5 10 0
Palmer (Orioles), McDowell (Indians) 4, J. Perry (Twins) 7, Hunter (Athletics) 9, Peterson (Yankees) 9, Stottlemyre (Yankees) 9, Wright (Angels) 11; Seaver (Mets), Merritt (Reds) 4, G. Perry (Giants) 6, Gibson (Cardinals) 8, Osteen (Dodgers) 10. W—Osteen. L—Wright. HR—Dietz, N.L.

ALCS

■ **Winner:** Powerful Baltimore made it two straight over the Twins, who were outscored by an average of almost six runs per game.
■ **Turning point:** The fourth inning of Game 1. The Orioles scored seven times and broke the only tie the Twins could manage in the entire series.
■ **Memorable moment:** A fourth-inning Game 1 grand slam homer by light-hitting pitcher Mike Cuellar. He pulled the pitch down the right-field line, clearly foul, but a gusty wind brought the ball back inside the foul pole.
■ **Top guns:** Jim Palmer (1-0, 1.00 ERA), Brooks Robinson (.583), Boog Powell (.429, 6 RBIs), Don Buford (.429), Orioles; Tony Oliva (.500), Twins.
■ **MVP:** Powell.

Linescores
Game 1—October 3, at Minnesota
Balt. ....0 2 0 7 0 1 0 0 0—10 13 0
Minn. ......1 1 0 1 3 0 0 0 0— 6 11 2
Cuellar, Hall (5); Perry, Zepp (4), Woodson (5), Williams (6), Perranoski (9). W—Hall. L—Perry. HR—Cuellar, Buford, Powell (Bal.); Killebrew (Min.).

Game 2—October 4, at Minnesota
Balt. ....1 0 2 1 0 0 0 0 7—11 13 0
Minn. ......0 0 0 3 0 0 0 0 0— 3 6 2
McNally; Hall, Zepp (4), Williams (5), Perranoski (8), Tiant (9). W—McNally. L—Hall. HR—F. Robinson, Johnson (Bal.); Killebrew, Oliva (Min.).

Game 3—October 5, at Baltimore
Minn. ....0 0 0 0 1 0 0 0 0—1 7 2
Balt. ....1 1 3 0 0 0 1 0 x—6 10 0
Kaat, Blyleven (3), Hall (5), Perry (7); Palmer. W—Palmer. L—Kaat. HR—Johnson (Bal.).

NLCS

■ **Winner:** Power-packed Cincinnati's sweep of Pittsburgh was orchestrated by an oft-maligned pitching staff that recorded a 0.96 series ERA.
■ **Turning point:** Don Gullett's 3⅓ innings of hitless relief in Game 2. He secured a 3-1 Cincinnati victory and struck out the side in an impressive seventh inning.
■ **Memorable moment:** Back-to-back Game 3 homers by Tony Perez and Johnny Bench — the Reds' only power display of the series.
■ **Top guns:** Gary Nolan (1-0, 0-00 ERA), Bobby Tolan (.417), Reds; Richie Hebner (.667), Willie Stargell (.500), Pirates.
■ **MVP:** Reds' pitching staff (0.96 ERA).

Linescores
Game 1—October 3, at Pittsburgh
Cin. ....0 0 0 0 0 0 0 0 0 3—3 9 0
Pitt. ....0 0 0 0 0 0 0 0 0 0—0 8 0
Nolan, Carroll (10); Ellis, Gibbon (10). W—Nolan. L—Ellis S—Carroll.

Game 2—October 4, at Pittsburgh
Cincinnati ....0 0 1 0 1 0 0 1 0—3 8 1
Pittsburgh....0 0 0 0 0 1 0 0 0—1 5 2
Merritt, Carroll (6), Gullett (6); Walker, Giusti (8). W—Merritt. L—Walker. HR—Tolan (Cin.).

Game 3—October 5, at Cincinnati
Pittsburgh..1 0 0 0 1 0 0 0 0—2 10 0
Cincinnati ..2 0 0 0 0 0 0 1 x—3 5 0
Moose, Gibbon (8), Giusti (8); Cloninger, Wilcox (6), Granger (9), Gullett (9). W—Wilcox. L—Moose. S—Gullett. HR—Perez, Bench (Cin.).

WORLD SERIES

■ **Winner:** The Orioles, still reeling from their five-game 1969 loss to the Mets, turned the tables on the young Reds.
■ **Turning point:** Game 1. The Orioles, down 3-0 in the first Series game at new Riverfront Stadium, rallied on home runs by Boog Powell, Brooks Robinson and Elrod Hendricks for a 4-3 victory.
■ **Memorable moments:** The incredible fielding artistry of Orioles third baseman Brooks Robinson, who constantly foiled the Reds with big plays, and Baltimore pitcher Dave McNally's third-game grand slam.
■ **Top guns:** Brooks Robinson (.429, 6 RBIs), Paul Blair (.474), Orioles; Hal McRae (.455), Lee May (.389, 2 HR, 8 RBIs), Reds.
■ **MVP:** Brooks Robinson.

Linescores
Game 1—October 10, at Cincinnati
Balt. ....0 0 0 2 1 0 1 0 0—4 7 2
Cin. ....1 0 2 0 0 0 0 0 0—3 5 0
Palmer, Richert (9); Nolan, Carroll (7). W—Palmer. L—Nolan. S—Richert. HR—May (Cin.); Powell, Hendricks, B. Robinson (Bal.).

Game 2—October 11, at Cincinnati
Balt. ....0 0 0 1 5 0 0 0 0—6 10 2
Cin. ....3 0 1 0 0 1 0 0 0—5 7 0
Cuellar, Phoebus (3), Drabowsky (5), Lopez (7), Hall (7); McGlothlin, Wilcox (5), Carroll (5), Gullett (8). W—Phoebus. L—Wilcox. S—Hall. HR—Tolan, Bench (Cin.); Powell (Bal.).

Game 3—October 13, at Baltimore
Cin. ....0 1 0 0 0 0 2 0 0—3 9 0
Balt. ....2 0 1 0 1 4 1 0 x—9 10 1
Cloninger, Granger (6), Gullett (7); McNally. W—McNally. L—Cloninger. HR—F. Robinson, Buford, McNally (Bal.).

Game 4—October 14, at Baltimore
Cin. ....0 1 1 0 1 0 0 3 0—6 8 3
Balt. ....0 1 3 0 0 1 0 0 0—5 8 0
Nolan, Gullett (3), Carroll (6); Palmer, Watt (8), Drabowsky (9). W—Carroll. L—Watt. HR—B. Robinson (Bal.); Rose, May (Cin.).

Game 5—October 15, at Baltimore
Cin. ....3 0 0 0 0 0 0 0 0—3 6 0
Balt. ....2 2 2 0 1 0 0 2 x—9 15 0
Merritt, Granger (2), Wilcox (3), Cloninger (5), Washburn (7), Carroll (8); Cuellar. W—Cuellar. L—Merritt. HR—F. Robinson, Rettenmund (Bal.).

FINAL STANDINGS

American League

East Division

Team	Bal.	Det.	Bos.	N.Y.	Wash.	Cle.	Oak.	K.C.	Chi.	Cal.	Min.	Mil.	W	L	Pct.	GB
Baltimore	...	8	9	11	13	13	7	6	8	7	10	9	101	57	.639	...
Detroit	10	...	6	10	14	12	4	8	5	6	6	10	91	71	.562	12
Boston	9	12	...	7	12	11	3	1	10	6	8	6	85	77	.525	18
New York	7	8	11	...	7	10	5	7	7	6	4	10	82	80	.506	21
Washington	3	4	6	11	...	11	3	3	2	8	6	6	63	96	.396	38.5
Cleveland	5	6	7	8	7	...	4	2	9	4	4	4	60	102	.370	43

West Division

Team	Oak.	K.C.	Chi.	Cal.	Min.	Mil.	Bal.	Det.	Bos.	N.Y.	Wash.	Cle.	W	L	Pct.	GB
Oakland	...	13	7	11	10	15	4	8	9	7	9	8	101	60	.627	...
Kansas City	5	...	9	10	9	8	5	4	11	5	9	10	85	76	.528	16
Chicago	11	9	...	10	7	11	4	7	2	5	10	3	79	83	.488	22.5
California	7	8	8	...	12	6	5	6	6	6	4	8	76	86	.469	25.5
Minnesota	8	9	11	6	...	7	2	6	4	8	5	8	74	86	.463	26.5
Milwaukee	3	10	7	12	10	...	3	2	6	2	6	8	69	92	.429	32

National League

East Division

Team	Pit.	St.L.	Chi.	N.Y.	Mon.	Phi.	S.F.	L.A.	Atl.	Cin.	Hou.	S.D.	W	L	Pct.	GB
Pittsburgh	...	11	12	8	11	12	3	8	8	7	8	9	97	65	.599	...
St. Louis	7	...	9	8	14	11	7	6	6	4	10	8	90	72	.556	7
Chicago	6	9	...	11	8	11	3	8	7	6	5	9	83	79	.512	14
New York	10	10	7	...	9	13	4	7	5	4	7	7	83	79	.512	14
Montreal	7	4	10	9	...	6	7	4	5	5	8	6	71	90	.441	25.5
Philadelphia	6	7	7	5	12	...	6	5	4	7	4	4	67	95	.414	30

West Division

Team	S.F.	L.A.	Atl.	Cin.	Hou.	S.D.	Pit.	St.L.	Chi.	N.Y.	Mon.	Phi.	W	L	Pct.	GB
San Fran.	...	6	11	9	9	13	9	5	9	8	5	6	90	72	.556	...
L.A.	12	...	9	11	10	13	4	6	4	5	8	7	89	73	.549	1
Atlanta	7	9	...	9	9	11	4	6	5	7	7	8	82	80	.506	8
Cincinnati	9	7	9	...	5	10	5	8	6	8	7	5	79	83	.488	11
Houston	9	8	9	13	...	10	4	2	7	5	4	8	79	83	.488	11
San Diego	5	5	7	8	8	...	3	4	3	5	5	8	61	100	.379	28.5

SIGNIFICANT EVENTS

■ **April 10:** The Phillies made their Veterans Stadium debut a successful one, defeating Montreal, 4-1.

■ **May 6:** Commissioner Bowie Kuhn closed a deal with NBC-TV that would net the 24 teams $72 million over four years.

■ **September 21:** Baseball ended its 71-year association with the nation's capital when owners approved the Senators' transfer to the Dallas-Fort Worth area.

MEMORABLE MOMENTS

■ **April 27:** The 600-homer club welcomed its third member when Atlanta's Hank Aaron connected off Gaylord Perry in a 10-inning 6-5 loss to the Giants.

■ **June 23:** Philadelphia's Rick Wise pitched a no-hitter and spiced his 4-0 victory over Cincinnati with two home runs.

■ **August 10, September 13:** Minnesota's Harmon Killebrew and Baltimore's Frank Robinson became the 10th and 11th players to hit 500 career home runs.

■ **September 26:** When Jim Palmer blanked Cleveland 5-0 for his 20th victory, the Orioles joined the 1920 White Sox as the only teams to boast four 20-game winners in one season. Palmer joined Dave McNally, Mike Cuellar and Pat Dobson in the select circle.

■ **September 30:** The Senators had to forfeit their final game in Washington to the Yankees when fans swarmed out of the stands in the ninth inning and began tearing up RFK Stadium.

LEADERS

American League
BA: Tony Oliva, Min., .337.
Runs: Don Buford, Bal., 99.
Hits: Cesar Tovar, Min., 204.
TB: Reggie Smith, Bos., 302.
HR: Bill Melton, Chi., 33.
RBI: Harmon Killebrew, Min., 119.
SB: Amos Otis, K.C., 52.
Wins: Mickey Lolich, Det., 25.
ERA: Vida Blue, Oak., 1.82.
CG: Mickey Lolich, Det., 29.
IP: Mickey Lolich, Det., 376.
SO: Mickey Lolich, Det., 308.
SV: Ken Sanders, Mil., 31.

National League
BA: Joe Torre, St.L., .363.
Runs: Lou Brock, St.L., 126.
Hits: Joe Torre, St.L., 230.
TB: Joe Torre, St.L., 352.
HR: Willie Stargell, Pit., 48.
RBI: Joe Torre, St.L., 137.
SB: Lou Brock, St.L., 64.
Wins: Ferguson Jenkins, Chi., 24.
ERA: Tom Seaver, N.Y., 1.76.
CG: Ferguson Jenkins, Chi., 30.
IP: Ferguson Jenkins, Chi., 325.
SO: Tom Seaver, N.Y., 289.
SV: Dave Giusti, Pit., 30.

A.L. 20-game winners
Mickey Lolich, Det., 25-14
Vida Blue, Oak., 24-8
Wilbur Wood, Chi., 22-13
Dave McNally, Bal., 21-5
Catfish Hunter, Oak., 21-11
Pat Dobson, Bal., 20-8
Jim Palmer, Bal., 20-9
Mike Cuellar, Bal., 20-9
Joe Coleman, Det., 20-9
Andy Messersmith, Cal., 20-13

N.L. 20-game winners
Ferguson Jenkins, Chi., 24-13
Al Downing, L.A., 20-9
Steve Carlton, St.L., 20-9
Tom Seaver, N.Y., 20-10

A.L. 100 RBIs
Harmon Killebrew, Min., 119

N.L. 100 RBIs
Joe Torre, St.L., 137
Willie Stargell, Pit., 125
Hank Aaron, Mil., 118
Bobby Bonds, S.F., 102

N.L. 40 homers
Willie Stargell, Pit., 48
Hank Aaron, Atl., 47

Most Valuable Player
A.L.: Vida Blue, P, Oak.
N.L.: Joe Torre, 3B, St.L.

Cy Young Award
A.L.: Vida Blue, Oak.
N.L.: Ferguson Jenkins, Chi.

Rookie of the Year
A.L.: Chris Chambliss, 1B, Cle.
N.L.: Earl Williams, C, Atl.

Hall of Fame additions
Dave Bancroft, SS, 1915-30
Jake Beckley, 1B, 1888-1907
Chick Hafey, OF, 1924-37
Harry Hooper, OF, 1909-25
Joe Kelley, OF, 1891-1908
Rube Marquard, P, 1908-25
Satchel Paige, P, 1948-65
George Weiss, executive

ALL-STAR GAME

■ **Winner:** The A.L. ended its eight-year All-Star drought with a three-homer barrage that produced a 6-4 victory.

■ **Key inning:** After falling behind 3-0 on Johnny Bench and Hank Aaron home runs, the A.L. struck for four third-inning runs on two-run homers by Reggie Jackson and Frank Robinson.

■ **Memorable moment:** The titanic third-inning blast by Jackson, which struck a light tower on the roof of Tiger Stadium, 520 feet from home plate in right-center field.

■ **Top guns:** Jackson (Athletics), F. Robinson (Orioles), Harmon Killebrew (Twins), A.L.; Bench (Reds), Aaron (Braves), Roberto Clemente (Pirates), N.L.

■ **MVP:** F. Robinson.

Linescore
July 13, at Detroit's Tiger Stadium
N.L...............0 2 1 0 0 0 0 1 0—4 5 0
A.L. ....0 0 4 0 0 2 0 0 x—6 7 0
Ellis (Pirates), Marichal (Giants) 4, Jenkins (Cubs) 6, Wilson (Astros) 7; Blue (Athletics), Palmer (Orioles) 4, Cuellar (Orioles) 6, Lolich (Tigers) 8. W—Blue. L—Ellis. HR—Bench, Aaron, Clemente, N.L.; Jackson, F. Robinson, Killebrew, A.L.

ALCS

■ **Winner:** The Orioles recorded their third consecutive Championship Series sweep, turning aside the up-and-coming Oakland Athletics.

■ **Turning point:** A four-run seventh-inning Game 1 rally that wiped out a 3-1 deficit and marked the last time Baltimore trailed in the series.

■ **Memorable moments:** A four-homer Game 2 salvo and Mike Cuellar's six-hit pitching added up to a 5-1 Orioles' victory.

■ **Top guns:** Cuellar (1-0, 1.00 ERA), Brooks Robinson (.364, 3 RBIs), Boog Powell (2 HR, 3 RBIs), Orioles; Sal Bando (.364), Reggie Jackson (.333, 2 HR), Athletics.

■ **MVP:** Cuellar.

Linescores

Game 1—October 3, at Baltimore
Oakland........0 2 0 1 0 0 0 0 0—3 9 0
Baltimore ....0 0 0 1 0 0 4 0 x—5 7 1
Blue, Fingers (8); McNally, Watt (8). W—McNally. L—Blue. S—Watt.

Game 2—October 4, at Baltimore
Oakland........0 0 0 1 0 0 0 0 0—1 6 0
Baltimore ....0 1 1 0 0 0 1 2 x—5 7 0
Hunter; Cuellar. W—Cuellar. L—Hunter. HR—B. Robinson, Powell 2, Hendricks (Bal.).

Game 3—October 5, at Oakland
Baltimore ..1 0 0 0 2 0 2 0 0—5 12 0
Oakland......0 0 1 0 0 1 0 1 0—3 7 0
Palmer; Segui, Fingers (5), Knowles (7), Locker (7), Grant (8). W—Palmer. L—Segui. HR—Jackson 2, Bando (Oak.).

NLCS

■ **Winner:** Pittsburgh defeated San Francisco to claim its first pennant since 1960. The Pirates needed four games to win the first LCS not decided by a sweep.

■ **Turning point:** Richie Hebner's eighth-inning Game 3 home run, which gave substitute starter Bob Johnson a 2-1 victory and the Pirates a 2-1 series edge.

■ **Memorable moment:** Pittsburgh first baseman Bob Robertson's ninth-inning Game 2 home run — his record-setting third of the game — capping a 9-4 Pirates victory.

■ **Top guns:** Robertson (.438, 4 HR, 6 RBIs), Dave Cash (.421), Hebner (2 HR, 4 RBIs), Pirates; Willie McCovey (.429, 2 HR, 6 RBIs), Chris Speier (.357), Giants.

■ **MVP:** Robertson.

Linescores

Game 1—October 2, at San Francisco
Pitt...............0 0 2 0 0 0 2 0 0—4 9 0
San Fran.......0 0 1 0 4 0 0 0 x—5 7 2
Blass, Moose (6), Giusti (8); Perry. W—Perry. L—Blass. HR—Fuentes, McCovey (S.F.).

Game 2—October 3, at San Francisco
Pitt.............0 1 0 2 1 0 4 0 1—9 15 0
San Fran. ..1 1 0 0 0 0 0 0 2—4 9 0
Ellis, Miller (6), Giusti (9); Cumberland, Barr (4), McMahon (5), Carrithers (7), Bryant (7), Hamilton (9). W—Ellis. L—Cumberland. S—Giusti. HR—Robertson 3, Clines (Pit.); Mays (S.F.).

Game 3—October 5, at Pittsburgh
San Fran. ....0 0 0 0 0 1 0 0 0—1 5 2
Pitt..............0 1 0 0 0 0 0 1 x—2 4 1
Marichal; Johnson, Giusti (9). W—Johnson. L—Marichal. S—Giusti. HR—Robertson, Hebner (Pit.).

Game 4—October 6, at Pittsburgh
San Fran. ..1 4 0 0 0 0 0 0 0—5 10 0
Pitt.............2 3 0 0 0 4 0 0 x—9 11 2
Perry, Johnson (6), McMahon (8); Blass, Kison (3), Giusti (7). W—Kison. L—Perry. S—Giusti. HR—Speier, McCovey (S.F.); Hebner, Oliver (Pit.).

WORLD SERIES

■ **Winner:** The Pirates, absent from Series competition for a decade, rebounded after losing the first two games.

■ **Turning point:** After Pittsburgh starter Luke Walker surrendered three first-inning runs in Game 4, Bruce Kison and Dave Giusti pitched 8⅓ scoreless innings and the Pirates rallied for a 4-3 victory.

■ **Memorable moments:** The Game 7 performances of Roberto Clemente, who homered, and Steve Blass, who shut down the Orioles 2-1 on a gritty four-hitter.

■ **Top guns:** Blass (2-0, 1.00 ERA), Clemente (.414, 12 hits, 2 HR, 4 RBIs), Manny Sanguillen (.379), Pirates; Dave McNally (2-1, 1.98), Orioles.

■ **MVP:** Clemente.

Linescores

Game 1—October 9, at Baltimore
Pitt.............0 3 0 0 0 0 0 0 0—3 3 0
Balt. ....0 1 3 0 1 0 0 0 x—5 10 3
Ellis, Moose (3), Miller (7); McNally. W—McNally. L—Ellis. HR—F. Robinson, Rettenmund, Buford (Bal.).

Game 2—October 11, at Baltimore
Pitt...........0 0 0 0 0 0 0 3 0— 3 8 1
Balt. ....0 1 0 3 6 1 0 0 x—11 14 1
R. Johnson, Kison (4), Moose (4), Veale (5), Miller (6), Giusti (8); Palmer, Hall (9). W—Palmer. L—R. Johnson. S—Hall. HR—Hebner (Pit.).

Game 3—October 12, at Pittsburgh
Balt. ....0 0 0 0 0 0 1 0 0—1 3 3
Pitt..............1 0 0 0 0 1 3 0 x—5 7 0
Cuellar, Dukes (7), Watt (8); Blass. W—Blass. L—Cuellar. HR—F. Robinson (Bal.); Robertson (Pit.).

Game 4—October 13, at Pittsburgh
Balt. ....3 0 0 0 0 0 0 0 0—3 4 1
Pitt............2 0 1 0 0 0 1 0 x—4 14 0
Dobson, Jackson (6), Watt (7), Richert (8); Walker, Kison (1), Giusti (8). W—Kison. L—Watt. S—Giusti.

Game 5—October 14, at Pittsburgh
Balt. ....0 0 0 0 0 0 0 0 0—0 2 1
Pitt..............0 2 1 0 1 0 0 0 x—4 9 0
McNally, Leonhard (5), Dukes (6); Briles. W—Briles. L—McNally. HR—Robertson (Pit.).

Game 6—October 16, at Baltimore
Pitt..........0 1 1 0 0 0 0 0 0 0—2 9 1
Balt. ....0 0 0 0 0 1 1 0 0 1—3 8 0
Moose, R. Johnson (6), Giusti (7), Miller (10); Palmer, Dobson (10), McNally (10). W—McNally. L—Miller. HR—Clemente (Pit.); Buford (Bal.).

Game 7—October 17, at Baltimore
Pitt..............0 0 0 1 0 0 0 1 0—2 6 1
Balt. ....0 0 0 0 0 0 0 1 0—1 4 0
Blass; Cuellar, Dobson (9), McNally (9). W—Blass. L—Cuellar. HR—Clemente (Pit.).

FINAL STANDINGS

American League

East Division

Team	Det.	Bos.	Bal.	N.Y.	Cle.	Mil.	Oak.	Chi.	Min.	K.C.	Cal.	Tex.	W	L	Pct.	GB
Detroit	...	9	8	7	8	10	4	7	9	7	7	10	86	70	.551	...
Boston	5	...	11	9	8	11	9	6	4	6	8	8	85	70	.548	.5
Baltimore	10	7	...	7	8	10	6	8	6	6	6	6	80	74	.519	5
New York	9	9	6	...	11	9	3	5	6	5	8	8	79	76	.510	6.5
Cleveland	10	7	10	7	...	5	2	4	8	6	4	9	72	84	.462	14
Milwaukee	8	7	5	9	10	...	4	3	4	5	5	5	65	91	.417	21

West Division

Team	Oak.	Chi.	Min.	K.C.	Cal.	Tex.	Det.	Bos.	Bal.	N.Y.	Cle.	Mil	W	L	Pct.	GB
Oakland	...	8	9	11	10	11	8	3	6	9	10	8	93	62	.600	...
Chicago	7	...	8	8	11	14	5	6	4	7	8	9	87	67	.565	5.5
Minnesota	8	6	...	9	8	11	3	8	6	6	4	8	77	77	.500	15.5
Kansas City	7	9	9	...	6	8	5	6	6	7	6	7	76	78	.494	16.5
California	8	7	7	9	...	10	5	4	6	4	8	7	75	80	.484	18
Texas	4	4	7	6	7	...	2	4	6	4	3	7	54	100	.351	38.5

National League

East Division

Team	Pit.	Chi.	N.Y.	St.L.	Mon.	Phi.	Cin.	Hou.	L.A.	Atl.	S.F.	S.D.	W	L	Pct.	GB
Pittsburgh	...	12	6	10	12	13	4	9	5	6	9	10	96	59	.619	...
Chicago	3	...	10	10	10	10	8	3	8	7	7	9	85	70	.548	11
New York	8	8	...	7	12	13	4	6	5	5	8	7	83	73	.532	13.5
St. Louis	8	8	9	...	8	7	2	8	4	6	7	8	75	81	.481	21.5
Montreal	6	5	6	9	...	10	4	4	6	8	6	6	70	86	.449	26.5
Philadelphia	5	7	5	8	6	...	2	3	5	6	6	6	59	97	.378	37.5

West Division

Team	Cin.	Hou.	L.A.	Atl.	S.F.	S.D.	Pit.	Chi.	N.Y.	St.L.	Mon.	Phi.	W	L	Pct.	GB
Cincinnati	...	11	9	9	10	8	8	4	8	10	8	10	95	59	.617	...
Houston	6	...	7	7	13	12	3	9	6	4	8	9	84	69	.549	10.5
Los Angeles	5	11	...	8	9	13	7	4	7	8	6	7	85	70	.548	10.5
Atlanta	9	7	7	...	7	6	6	5	7	6	4	6	70	84	.455	25
San Fran.	5	5	9	11	...	10	3	5	4	5	6	6	69	86	.445	26.5
San Diego	10	2	5	11	4	...	2	3	5	4	6	6	58	95	.379	36.5

SIGNIFICANT EVENTS

■ **April 2:** Gil Hodges, completing spring training preparations for his fifth season as Mets manager, died from a heart attack at West Palm Beach, Fla., at age 47.

■ **April 13:** The first players' strike in baseball history was settled after 13 days and 86 cancelled games.

■ **April 21:** The Rangers celebrated their Texas debut with a 7-6 victory over California at Arlington Stadium.

■ **June 19:** The U.S. Supreme Court upheld baseball's antitrust exemption and ended Curt Flood's long, frustrating challenge to the sport's reserve clause.

■ **November 2:** Steve Carlton, who posted 27 of the last-place Phillies' 59 victories, captured the N.L. Cy Young Award.

■ **December 31:** Pirates outfielder Roberto Clemente, the newest member of baseball's 3,000-hit club, died when a cargo plane carrying supplies to Nicaraguan earthquake victims crashed near San Juan, Puerto Rico.

MEMORABLE MOMENTS

■ **May 14:** Willie Mays, returning to New York after more than 14 seasons in San Francisco, belted a game-winning solo home run against the Giants in his first game with the Mets.

■ **June 10:** Atlanta's Hank Aaron hit his N.L. record-tying 14th grand slam in a 15-3 victory over the Phillies and moved into second place on the all-time home run list.

■ **August 1:** San Diego's Nate Colbert belted a record-tying five homers and drove in a doubleheader-record 13 runs in a 9-0 and 11-7 sweep of the Braves.

LEADERS

American League
BA: Rod Carew, Min., .318.
Runs: Bobby Murcer, N.Y., 102.
Hits: Joe Rudi, Oak., 181.
TB: Bobby Murcer, N.Y., 314.
HR: Dick Allen, Chi., 37.
RBI: Dick Allen, Chi., 113.
SB: Campy Campaneris, Oak., 52.
Wins: Gaylord Perry, Cle.; Wilbur Wood, Chi., 24.
ERA: Luis Tiant, Bos., 1.91.
CG: Gaylord Perry, Cle., 29.
IP: Wilbur Wood, Chi., 376.2.
SO: Nolan Ryan, Cal., 329.
SV: Sparky Lyle, N.Y., 35.

National League
BA: Billy Williams, Chi., .333.
Runs: Joe Morgan, Cin., 122.
Hits: Pete Rose, Cin., 198.
TB: Billy Williams, Chi., 348.
HR: Johnny Bench, Cin., 40.
RBI: Johnny Bench, Cin., 125.
SB: Lou Brock, St.L., 63.
Wins: Steve Carlton, Phil., 27.
ERA: Steve Carlton, Phil., 1.97.
CG: Steve Carlton, Phil., 30.
IP: Steve Carlton, Phil., 346.1.
SO: Steve Carlton, Phil., 310.
SV: Clay Carroll, Cin., 37.

A.L. 20-game winners
Gaylord Perry, Cle., 24-16
Wilbur Wood, Chi., 24-17
Mickey Lolich, Det., 22-14
Catfish Hunter, Oak., 21-7
Jim Palmer, Bal., 21-10
Stan Bahnsen, Chi., 21-16

N.L. 20-game winners
Steve Carlton, Phil., 27-10
Tom Seaver, N.Y., 21-12
Claude Osteen, L.A., 20-11
Ferguson Jenkins, Chi., 20-12

A.L. 100 RBIs
Dick Allen, Chi., 113
John Mayberry, K.C., 100

N.L. 100 RBIs
Johnny Bench, Cin., 125
Billy Williams, Chi., 122
Willie Stargell, Pit., 112
Nate Colbert, S.D., 111

N.L. 40 homers
Johnny Bench, Cin., 40

Most Valuable Player
A.L.: Dick Allen, 1B, Chi.
N.L.: Johnny Bench, C, Cin.

Cy Young Award
A.L.: Gaylord Perry, Cle.
N.L.: Steve Carlton, Phil.

Rookie of the Year
A.L.: Carlton Fisk, C, Bos.
N.L.: Jon Matlack, P, N.Y.

Hall of Fame additions
Yogi Berra, C, 1946-65
Josh Gibson, C, Negro Leagues
Lefty Gomez, P, 1930-43
Will Harridge, executive
Sandy Koufax, P, 1955-66
Buck Leonard, 1B, Negro Leagues
Early Wynn, P, 1939-63
Ross Youngs, OF, 1917-26

ALL-STAR GAME

■ **Winner:** Joe Morgan's 10th-inning single capped another N.L. comeback that produced a 4-3 victory — the senior circuit's seventh consecutive extra-inning All-Star decision.
■ **Key inning:** The ninth, when the N.L. tied the game 3-3 on a pair of singles and Lee May's ground-ball out.
■ **Memorable moment:** Hank Aaron, who entered the game with 659 career home runs, sent the Atlanta crowd into a frenzy when he hit a two-run shot in the sixth inning.
■ **Top guns:** Tug McGraw (Mets), Aaron (Braves), Morgan (Reds), N.L.; Jim Palmer (Orioles), Cookie Rojas (Royals), Rod Carew (Twins), A.L.
■ **MVP:** Morgan.

Linescore
July 25, at Atlanta Stadium
A.L...........0 0 1 0 0 0 0 2 0 0—3 6 0
N.L...........0 0 0 0 0 2 0 0 1 1—4 8 0
Palmer (Orioles), Lolich (Tigers) 4, Perry (Indians) 6, Wood (White Sox) 8, McNally (Orioles) 10; Gibson (Cardinals), Blass (Pirates) 3, Sutton (Dodgers) 4, Carlton (Phillies) 6, Stoneman (Expos) 7, McGraw (Mets) 9. W—McGraw. L—McNally. HR—Aaron, N.L.; Rojas, A.L.

ALCS

■ **Winner:** The Athletics claimed their first pennant in 41 years and first since moving to Oakland. The A's victory over Detroit marked the first ALCS to go beyond three games.
■ **Turning point:** The Game 5 pitching of left-hander Vida Blue, who worked four scoreless innings in relief of Blue Moon Odom to secure the A's series-ending 2-1 victory.
■ **Memorable moment:** A seventh-inning melee triggered by A's shortstop Bert Campaneris in Game 2. When Campaneris was hit by a Lerrin LaGrow pitch, he threw his bat at the pitcher and both benches emptied. Campaneris was suspended for the remainder of the series.
■ **Top guns:** Odom (2-0, 0.00 ERA), Blue (0.00), Matty Alou (.381), Athletics; Joe Coleman (1-0, 0-00 ERA), Jim Northrup (.357), Tigers.
■ **MVP:** Odom.

Linescores

Game 1—October 7, at Oakland
Det...0 1 0 0 0 0 0 0 0 0 1—2 6 2
Oak. 0 0 1 0 0 0 0 0 0 0 2—3 10 1
Lolich, Seelbach (11); Hunter, Blue (9), Fingers (9). W—Fingers. L—Lolich. HR—Cash, Kaline (Det.).

Game 2—October 8, at Oakland
Det...............0 0 0 0 0 0 0 0 0—0 3 1
Oak. ....1 0 0 0 4 0 0 0 x—5 8 0
Fryman, Zachary (5), Scherman (5), LaGrow (6), Hiller (7); Odom. W—Odom. L—Fryman.

Game 3—October 10, at Detroit
Oak. ....0 0 0 0 0 0 0 0 0—0 7 0
Det...............0 0 0 2 0 0 0 1 x—3 8 1
Holtzman, Fingers (5), Blue (6), Locker (7); Coleman. W—Coleman. L—Holtzman. HR—Freehan (Det.).

Game 4—October 11, at Detroit
Oak. ......0 0 0 0 0 0 1 0 0 2—3 9 2
Det.........0 0 1 0 0 0 0 0 0 3—4 10 1
Hunter, Fingers (8), Blue (9), Locker (10), Horlen (10), Hamilton (10); Lolich, Seelbach (10), Hiller (10). W—Hiller. L—Horlen. HR—McAuliffe (Det.); Epstein (Oak.).

Game 5—October 12, at Detroit
Oak. ....0 1 0 1 0 0 0 0 0—2 4 0
Det...............1 0 0 0 0 0 0 0 0—1 5 2
Odom, Blue (6); Fryman, Hiller (9). W—Odom. L—Fryman. S—Blue.

NLCS

■ **Winner:** Cincinnati needed an N.L.-record five games to get past Pittsburgh and claim its second pennant in three years.
■ **Turning point:** Down two games to one and facing elimination, the Reds got two-hit pitching from Ross Grimsley and forged a 7-1 victory that forced a decisive fifth game.
■ **Memorable moment:** Cincinnati's George Foster racing across the plate with the series-ending run on a Bob Moose wild pitch with two out in the ninth inning of Game 5. The Reds had tied the game moments earlier on a Johnny Bench home run.
■ **Top guns:** Pete Rose (.450), Bench (.333), Reds; Manny Sanguillen (.313), Pirates.
■ **MVP:** Rose.

Linescores

Game 1—October 7, at Pittsburgh
Cin. ....1 0 0 0 0 0 0 0 0—1 8 0
Pitt. ....3 0 0 0 2 0 0 0 x—5 6 0
Gullett, Borbon (7); Blass, R. Hernandez (9). W—Blass. L—Gullett. S—R. Hernandez. HR—Morgan (Cin.); Oliver (Pit.).

Game 2—October 8, at Pittsburgh
Cin. ....4 0 0 0 0 0 0 1 0—5 8 1
Pitt. ....0 0 0 1 1 1 0 0 0—3 7 1
Billingham, Hall (5); Moose, Johnson (1), Kison (6), R. Hernandez (7), Giusti (9). W—Hall. L—Moose. HR—Morgan (Cin.).

Game 3—October 9, at Cincinnati
Pitt. ....0 0 0 0 1 0 1 1 0—3 7 0
Cin. ....0 0 2 0 0 0 0 0 0—2 8 1
Briles, Kison (7), Giusti (8); Nolan, Borbon (7), Carroll (7), McGlothlin (9). W—Kison. L—Carroll. S—Giusti. HR—Sanguillen (Pit.).

Game 4—October 10, at Cincinnati
Pitt. ....0 0 0 0 0 0 1 0 0—1 2 3
Cin. ....1 0 0 2 0 2 2 0 x—7 11 1
Ellis, Johnson (6), Walker (7), Miller (8); Grimsley. W—Grimsley. L—Ellis. HR—Clemente (Pit.).

Game 5—October 11, at Cincinnati
Pitt. ....0 2 0 1 0 0 0 0 0—3 8 0
Cin. ....0 0 1 0 1 0 0 0 2—4 7 1
Blass, R. Hernandez (8), Giusti (9), Moose (9); Gullett, Borbon (4), Hall (6), Carroll (9). W—Carroll. L—Giusti. HR—Geronimo, Bench (Cin.).

WORLD SERIES

■ **Winner:** The Athletics, who had not played in a World Series since 1931 when the franchise was located in Philadelphia, began a run that would put them in select company.
■ **Turning point:** A Game 4 ninth-inning rally that gave Oakland a three games to one lead. Down 2-1 with one out, the A's scored two runs on four consecutive singles.
■ **Memorable moment:** A's catcher Gene Tenace blasting home runs in his first two Series at-bats — and a record-tying four overall.
■ **Top guns:** Catfish Hunter (2-0, 2.81 ERA), Tenace (.348, 4 HR, 9 RBIs), Athletics; Tony Perez (.435), Bobby Tolan (6 RBIs), Reds.
■ **MVP:** Tenace.

Linescores

Game 1—October 14, at Cincinnati
Oakland........0 2 0 0 1 0 0 0 0—3 4 0
Cincinnati ....0 1 0 1 0 0 0 0 0—2 7 0
Holtzman, Fingers (6), Blue (7); Nolan, Borbon (7), Carroll (8). W—Holtzman. L—Nolan. S—Blue. HR—Tenace 2 (Oak.).

Game 2—October 15, at Cincinnati
Oakland........0 1 1 0 0 0 0 0 0—2 9 2
Cincinnati ....0 0 0 0 0 0 0 0 1—1 6 0
Hunter, Fingers (9); Grimsley, Borbon (6), Hall (8). W—Hunter. L—Grimsley. S—Fingers. HR—Rudi (Oak.).

Game 3—October 18, at Oakland
Cincinnati ....0 0 0 0 0 0 1 0 0—1 4 2
Oakland........0 0 0 0 0 0 0 0 0—0 3 2
Billingham, Carroll (9); Odom, Blue (8), Fingers (8). W—Billingham. L—Odom. S—Carroll.

Game 4—October 19, at Oakland
Cincinnati ..0 0 0 0 0 0 0 2 0—2 7 1
Oakland......0 0 0 0 1 0 0 0 2—3 10 1
Gullett, Borbon (8), Carroll (9); Holtzman, Blue (8), Fingers (9). W—Fingers. L—Carroll. HR—Tenace (Oak.).

Game 5—October 20, at Oakland
Cincinnati ....1 0 0 1 1 0 0 1 1—5 8 0
Oakland........0 3 0 1 0 0 0 0 0—4 7 2
McGlothlin, Borbon (4), Hall (5), Carroll (7), Grimsley (8), Billingham (9); Hunter, Fingers (5), Hamilton (9). W—Grimsley. L—Fingers. S—Billingham. HR—Rose, Menke (Cin.); Tenace (Oak.).

Game 6—October 21, at Cincinnati
Oakland......0 0 0 0 1 0 0 0 0—1 7 1
Cincinnati ..0 0 0 1 1 1 5 0 x—8 10 0
Blue, Locker (6), Hamilton (7), Horlen (7); Nolan, Grimsley (5), Borbon (6), Hall (7). W—Grimsley. L—Blue. S—Hall. HR—Bench (Cin.).

Game 7—October 22, at Cincinnati
Oakland........1 0 0 0 0 2 0 0 0—3 6 1
Cincinnati ....0 0 0 0 1 0 0 1 0—2 4 2
Odom, Hunter (5), Holtzman (8), Fingers (8); Billingham, Borbon (6), Carroll (6), Grimsley (7), Hall (8). W—Hunter. L—Borbon. S—Fingers.

FINAL STANDINGS

American League

East Division

Team	Bal.	Bos.	Det.	N.Y.	Mil.	Cle.	Cal.	Chi.	K.C.	Min.	Oak.	Tex.	W	L	Pct.	GB
Baltimore	...	7	9	9	15	12	6	8	8	8	5	10	97	65	.599	...
Boston	11	...	3	14	12	9	7	6	8	6	4	9	89	73	.549	8
Detroit	9	15	...	7	12	9	5	7	4	5	7	5	85	77	.525	12
New York	9	4	11	...	8	11	6	4	6	9	4	8	80	82	.494	17
Milwaukee	3	6	6	10	...	9	7	9	4	8	4	8	74	88	.457	23
Cleveland	6	9	9	7	9	...	7	5	2	7	3	7	71	91	.438	26

West Division

Team	Oak.	K.C.	Min.	Cal.	Chi.	Tex.	Bal.	Bos.	Cle.	Det.	Mil.	N.Y.	W	L	Pct.	GB
Oakland	...	10	4	12	12	11	7	8	9	5	8	8	94	68	.580	...
Kansas City	8	...	9	8	12	11	4	4	10	8	8	6	88	74	.543	6
Minnesota	14	9	...	8	9	12	4	6	5	7	4	3	81	81	.500	13
California	6	10	10	...	8	11	6	5	5	7	5	6	79	83	.488	15
Chicago	6	6	9	10	...	13	4	6	7	5	3	8	77	85	.475	17
Texas	7	7	6	7	5	...	2	3	5	7	4	4	57	105	.352	37

National League

East Division

Team	N.Y.	St.L.	Pit.	Mon.	Chi.	Phi.	Atl.	Cin.	Hou.	L.A.	S.D.	S.F.	W	L	Pct.	GB
New York	...	10	13	9	7	9	6	4	6	5	8	5	82	79	.509	...
St. Louis	8	...	8	10	9	9	6	6	7	4	8	6	81	81	.500	1.5
Pittsburgh	5	10	...	12	12	10	5	5	6	2	8	5	80	82	.494	2.5
Montreal	9	8	6	...	9	13	6	4	6	5	7	6	79	83	.488	3.5
Chicago	10	9	6	9	...	10	5	8	6	5	7	2	77	84	.478	5
Philadelphia	9	9	8	5	8	...	6	4	5	3	9	5	71	91	.438	11.5

West Division

Team	Cin.	L.A.	S.F.	Hou.	Atl.	S.D.	Chi.	Mon.	N.Y.	Phi.	Pit.	St.L.	W	L	Pct.	GB
Cincinnati	...	11	10	11	13	13	4	8	8	8	7	6	99	63	.611	...
Los Angeles	7	...	9	7	15	9	7	7	7	9	10	8	95	66	.590	3.5
San Fran.	8	9	...	7	10	11	10	6	7	7	7	6	88	74	.543	11
Houston	7	11	11	...	7	10	6	6	6	7	6	5	82	80	.506	17
Atlanta	5	2	8	11	...	12	7	6	6	6	7	6	76	85	.472	22.5
San Diego	5	9	7	8	6	...	5	5	4	3	4	4	60	102	.370	39

SIGNIFICANT EVENTS

■ **January 3:** An investment group headed by shipbuilder George Steinbrenner purchased the Yankees from CBS for $10 million.

■ **February 25:** Owners and players approved a three-year Basic Agreement that included binding arbitration and modifications of the controversial reserve clause.

■ **April 6:** The A.L. began its designated hitter experiment when Yankee Ron Blomberg drew a first-inning walk in a game at Boston's Fenway Park.

■ **April 10:** New Royals Stadium received a rousing welcome when Kansas City pounded Texas, 12-1.

MEMORABLE MOMENTS

■ **July 15:** Angels ace Nolan Ryan held Detroit hitless in a 6-0 victory, becoming the fourth pitcher to throw two no-hitters in one season.

■ **July 21:** Atlanta's Hank Aaron inched closer to Babe Ruth's all-time record when he belted homer No. 700 off Philadelphia's Ken Brett in an 8-4 loss.

■ **September 28:** Ryan struck out 16 Twins in his final start, raising his record season strikeout total to 383.

■ **October 1:** The Mets posted a final-day 6-4 victory over Chicago and clinched the N.L. East championship with an 82-79 record.

LEADERS

American League
BA: Rod Carew, Min., .350.
Runs: Reggie Jackson, Oak., 99.
Hits: Rod Carew, Min., 203.
TB: Sal Bando, Oak.; Dave May, Mil.; George Scott, Mil., 295.
HR: Reggie Jackson, Oak., 32.
RBI: Reggie Jackson, Oak., 117.
SB: Tommy Harper, Bos., 54.
Wins: Wilbur Wood, Chi., 24.
ERA: Jim Palmer, Bal., 2.40.
CG: Gaylord Perry, Cle., 29.
IP: Wilbur Wood, Chi., 359.1.
SO: Nolan Ryan, Cal., 383.
SV: John Hiller, Det., 38.

National League
BA: Pete Rose, Cin., .338.
Runs: Bobby Bonds, S.F., 131.
Hits: Pete Rose, Cin., 230.
TB: Bobby Bonds, S.F., 341.
HR: Willie Stargell, Pit., 44.
RBI: Willie Stargell, Pit., 119.
SB: Lou Brock, St.L., 70.
Wins: Ron Bryant, S.F., 24.
ERA: Tom Seaver, N.Y., 2.08.
CG: Steve Carlton, Phil.; Tom Seaver, N.Y., 18.
IP: Jack Billingham, Cin.; Steve Carlton, Phil., 293.1.
SO: Tom Seaver, N.Y., 251.
SV: Mike Marshall, Mon., 31.

A.L. 20-game winners
Wilbur Wood, Chi., 24-20
Joe Coleman, Det., 23-15
Jim Palmer, Bal., 22-9
Catfish Hunter, Oak., 21-5
Ken Holtzman, Oak., 21-13
Nolan Ryan, Cal., 21-16
Vida Blue, Oak., 20-9
Paul Splittorff, K.C., 20-11
Jim Colborn, Mil., 20-12
Luis Tiant, Bos., 20-13
Bill Singer, Cal., 20-14
Bert Blyleven, Min., 20-17

N.L. 20-game winners
Ron Bryant, S.F., 24-12

A.L. 100 RBIs
Reggie Jackson, Oak., 117
George Scott, Mil., 107
John Mayberry, K.C., 100

N.L. 100 RBIs
Willie Stargell, Pit., 119
Lee May, Hou., 105
Johnny Bench, Cin., 104
Darrell Evans, Atl., 104
Ken Singleton, Mon., 103
Tony Perez, Cin., 101

N.L. 40 homers
Willie Stargell, Pit., 44
Dave Johnson, Atl., 43
Darrell Evans, Atl., 41
Hank Aaron, Atl., 40

Most Valuable Player
A.L.: Reggie Jackson, OF, Oak.
N.L.: Pete Rose, OF, Cin.

Cy Young Award
A.L.: Jim Palmer, Bal.
N.L.: Tom Seaver, N.Y.

Rookie of the Year
A.L.: Al Bumbry, OF, Bal.
N.L.: Gary Matthews, OF, S.F.

Hall of Fame additions
Roberto Clemente, OF, 1955-72
Billy Evans, umpire
Monte Irvin, OF, 1949-56
George Kelly, 1B, 1915-32
Warren Spahn, P, 1942-65
Mickey Welch, P, 1880-92

ALL-STAR GAME

■ **Winners:** Johnny Bench, Bobby Bonds and Willie Davis powered the N.L. to its 10th All-Star victory in 11 years in the 40th anniversary of the midsummer classic.

■ **Key innings:** The fourth, fifth and sixth, when the N.L.'s Big Three hit home runs that accounted for five runs.

■ **Memorable moment:** An eighth-inning strikeout by pinch-hitter Willie Mays, who was making his 24th and final appearance in the baseball classic he had dominated like no other player.

■ **Top guns:** Bonds (Giants), Bench (Reds), Davis (Dodgers), N.L.; Amos Otis (Royals), A.L.

■ **MVP:** Bonds.

Linescore
July 24, at Kansas City's Royals Stadium
N.L.............0 0 2 1 2 2 0 0 0—7 10 0
A.L............0 1 0 0 0 0 0 0 0—1 5 0
Wise (Cardinals), Osteen (Dodgers) 3, Sutton (Dodgers) 5, Twitchell (Phillies) 6, Giusti (Pirates) 7, Seaver (Mets) 8, Brewer (Dodgers) 9; Hunter (Athletics), Holtzman (Athletics) 2, Blyleven (Twins) 3, Singer (Angels) 4, Ryan (Angels) 6, Lyle (Yankees) 8, Fingers (Athletics) 9. W—Wise. L—Blyleven. HR—Bench, Bonds, Davis, N.L.

ALCS

■ **Winner:** The Athletics earned their second consecutive pennant and the Orioles lost their first ALCS after three previous sweeps.

■ **Turning point:** An 11th-inning Game 3 home run by Bert Campaneris that broke up a pitching duel between Oakland's Ken Holtzman and Baltimore's Mike Cuellar. The 2-1 victory gave the A's a 2-1 series advantage.

■ **Memorable moment:** A game-tying three-run seventh-inning home run by catcher Andy Etchebarren that kept Baltimore's hopes alive in Game 4. The Orioles won, 5-4, and forced a fifth game.

■ **Top guns:** Catfish Hunter (2-0, 1.65 ERA), Vic Davalillo (.625), Campaneris (.333, 2 HR), Athletics; Etchebarren (.357, 4 RBIs), Orioles.

■ **MVP:** Hunter.

Linescores

Game 1—October 6, at Baltimore
Oak. ....0 0 0 0 0 0 0 0 0—0 5 1
Balt. ....4 0 0 0 0 0 1 1 x—6 12 0
Blue, Pina (1), Odom (3), Fingers (8); Palmer. W—Palmer. L—Blue.

Game 2—October 7, at Baltimore
Oak. ....1 0 0 0 0 2 0 2 1—6 9 0
Balt. ....1 0 0 0 0 1 0 1 0—3 8 0
Hunter, Fingers (8); McNally, Reynolds (8), G. Jackson (9). W—Hunter. L—McNally. S—Fingers. HR—Campaneris, Rudi, Bando 2 (Oak.).

Game 3—October 9, at Oakland
Balt. ....0 1 0 0 0 0 0 0 0 0 0—1 3 0
Oak. ....0 0 0 0 0 0 0 1 0 0 1—2 4 3
Cuellar; Holtzman. W—Holtzman. L—Cuellar. HR—Williams (Bal.); Campaneris (Oak.).

Game 4—October 10, at Oakland
Balt. ....0 0 0 0 0 0 4 1 0—5 8 0
Oak. ....0 3 0 0 0 1 0 0 0—4 7 0
Palmer, Reynolds (2), Watt (7), G. Jackson (7); Blue, Fingers (7). W—G. Jackson. L—Fingers. HR—Etchebarren, Grich (Bal.).

Game 5—October 11, at Oakland
Balt. ....0 0 0 0 0 0 0 0 0—0 5 2
Oak. ....0 0 1 2 0 0 0 0 x—3 7 0
Alexander, Palmer (4); Hunter. W—Hunter. L—Alexander.

NLCS

■ **Winner:** The New York Mets captured their second pennant in five years and kept Cincinnati from repeating as N.L. champion.

■ **Turning point:** New York's 9-2 Game 3 victory that was spiced by a fifth-inning fight between Mets shortstop Bud Harrelson and Cincinnati leftfielder Pete Rose. Reds manager Sparky Anderson had to temporarily pull his team from the field in the next half inning when fans began pelting Rose with garbage and other debris.

■ **Memorable moment:** Rose's 12th-inning Game 4 home run that kept the Reds alive and forced a fifth game.

■ **Top guns:** Jon Matlack (1-0, 0.00 ERA), Felix Millan (.316), Rusty Staub (3 HR, 5 RBIs), Mets; Rose (.381, 2 HR), Reds.

■ **MVP:** Staub.

Linescores

Game 1—October 6, at Cincinnati
N.Y...............0 1 0 0 0 0 0 0 0—1 3 0
Cin. ....0 0 0 0 0 0 0 1 1—2 6 0
Seaver; Billingham, Hall (9), Borbon (9). W—Borbon. L—Seaver. HR—Rose, Bench (Cin.).

Game 2—October 7, at Cincinnati
N.Y...............0 0 0 1 0 0 0 0 4—5 7 0
Cin. ....0 0 0 0 0 0 0 0 0—0 2 0
Matlack; Gullett, Carroll (6), Hall (9), Borbon (9). W—Matlack. L—Gullett. HR—Staub (N.Y.).

Game 3—October 8, at New York
Cin. ....0 0 2 0 0 0 0 0 0—2 8 1
N.Y. ....1 5 1 2 0 0 0 0 x—9 11 1
Grimsley, Hall (2), Tomlin (3), Nelson (4), Borbon (7); Koosman. W—Koosman. L—Grimsley. HR—Staub 2 (N.Y.); Menke (Cin.).

Game 4—October 9, at New York
Cin.......0 0 0 0 0 0 1 0 0 0 0 1—2 8 0
N.Y.......0 0 1 0 0 0 0 0 0 0 0 0—1 3 2
Norman, Gullett (6), Carroll (10), Borbon (12); Stone, McGraw (7), Parker (12). W—Carroll. L—Parker. S—Borbon. HR—Perez, Rose (Cin.).

Game 5—October 10, at New York
Cin. ....0 0 1 0 1 0 0 0 0—2 7 1
N.Y. ....2 0 0 0 4 1 0 0 x—7 13 1
Billingham, Gullett (5), Carroll (5), Grimsley (7); Seaver, McGraw (9). W—Seaver. L—Billingham. S—McGraw.

WORLD SERIES

■ **Winner:** The Athletics made it two in a row with a seven-game scramble against the resilient Mets.

■ **Turning point:** In a valiant Game 6 performance that staved off elimination, the A's prevailed 3-1 behind Catfish Hunter's pitching and the two-RBI hitting of Reggie Jackson.

■ **Memorable moment:** The "firing" of A's second baseman Mike Andrews by owner Charles O. Finley. Andrews' two 12th-inning errors in Game 2 enabled the Mets to post a 10-7 victory.

■ **Top guns:** Joe Rudi (.333), Jackson (.310, 6 RBIs), Athletics; Rusty Staub (.423, 6 RBIs), Mets.

■ **MVP:** Jackson.

Linescores

Game 1—October 13, at Oakland
N.Y...............0 0 0 1 0 0 0 0 0—1 7 2
Oak. ....0 0 2 0 0 0 0 0 x—2 4 0
Matlack, McGraw (7); Holtzman, Fingers (6), Knowles (9). W—Holtzman. L—Matlack. S—Knowles.

Game 2—October 14, at Oakland
N.Y...........011 004 000 004—10 15 1
Oak. ....210 000 102 001— 7 13 5
Koosman, Sadecki (3), Parker (5), McGraw (6), Stone (12); Blue, Pina (6), Knowles (6), Odom (8), Fingers (10), Lindblad (12). W—McGraw. L—Fingers. S—Stone. HR—Jones, Garrett (N.Y.).

Game 3—October 16, at New York
Oak. ....000 001 010 01—3 10 1
N.Y. ....200 000 000 00—2 10 2
Hunter, Knowles (7), Lindblad (9), Fingers (11); Seaver, Sadecki (9), McGraw (9), Parker (11). W—Lindblad. L—Parker. S—Fingers. HR—Garrett (N.Y.).

Game 4—October 17, at New York
Oak. ....000 100 000—1 5 1
N.Y...................300 300 00x—6 13 1
Holtzman, Odom (1), Knowles (4), Pina (5), Lindblad (8); Matlack, Sadecki (9). W—Matlack. L—Holtzman. S—Sadecki. HR—Staub (N.Y.).

Game 5—October 18, at New York
Oak. ....0 0 0 0 0 0 0 0 0—0 3 1
N.Y. ....0 1 0 0 0 1 0 0 x—2 7 1
Blue, Knowles (6), Fingers (7); Koosman, McGraw (7). W—Koosman. L—Blue. S—McGraw.

Game 6—October 20, at Oakland
N.Y...............0 0 0 0 0 0 0 1 0—1 6 2
Oak. ....1 0 1 0 0 0 0 1 x—3 7 0
Seaver, McGraw (8); Hunter, Knowles (8), Fingers (8). W—Hunter. L—Seaver. S—Fingers.

Game 7—October 21, at Oakland
N.Y...............0 0 0 0 0 1 0 0 1—2 8 1
Oak. ....0 0 4 0 1 0 0 0 x—5 9 1
Matlack, Parker (3), Sadecki (5), Stone (7); Holtzman, Fingers (6), Knowles (9). W—Holtzman. L—Matlack. S—Knowles. HR—Campaneris, Jackson (Oak.).

HISTORY

FINAL STANDINGS

American League

East Division

Team	Bal.	N.Y.	Bos.	Cle.	Mil.	Det.	Cal.	Chi.	K.C.	Min.	Oak.	Tex.	W	L	Pct.	GB
Baltimore	...	11	10	12	8	14	7	5	8	6	6	4	91	71	.562	...
New York	7	...	7	11	9	7	9	8	8	8	7	8	89	73	.549	2
Boston	8	11	...	9	10	11	4	8	4	6	8	5	84	78	.519	7
Cleveland	6	7	9	...	10	9	9	4	8	6	5	4	77	85	.475	14
Milwaukee	10	9	8	8	..	9	9	4	1	6	5	7	76	86	.469	15
Detroit	4	11	7	9	9	...	7	5	7	3	5	5	72	90	.444	19

West Division

Team	Oak.	Tex.	Min.	Chi.	K.C.	Cal.	Bal.	Bos.	Cle.	Det.	Mil.	N.Y.	W	L	Pct.	GB
Oakland	...	8	13	11	10	12	6	4	7	7	7	5	90	72	.556	...
Texas	10	...	9	7	10	9	8	7	8	7	5	4	84	76	.525	5
Minnesota	5	9	...	11	10	10	6	6	6	9	6	4	82	80	.506	8
Chicago	7	9	7	...	11	8	7	4	8	7	8	4	80	80	.500	9
Kansas City	8	8	8	7	...	10	4	8	4	5	11	4	77	85	.475	13
California	6	9	8	10	8	...	5	8	3	5	3	3	68	94	.420	22

National League

East Division

Team	Pit.	St.L.	Phi.	Mon.	N.Y.	Chi.	Atl.	Cin.	Hou.	L.A.	S.D.	S.F.	W	L	Pct.	GB
Pittsburgh	...	7	8	9	11	9	8	4	7	8	9	8	88	74	.543	...
St. Louis	11	...	9	9	12	13	3	6	4	6	7	6	86	75	.534	1.5
Philadelphia	10	9	...	7	11	10	4	4	6	6	5	8	80	82	.494	8
Montreal	9	8	11	...	9	13	3	6	6	4	6	4	79	82	.491	8.5
New York	7	6	7	9	...	10	4	3	6	7	6	6	71	91	.438	17
Chicago	9	5	8	5	8	...	8	5	4	2	6	6	66	96	.407	22

West Division

Team	L.A.	Cin.	Atl.	Hou.	S.F.	S.D.	Chi.	Mon.	N.Y.	Phi.	Pit.	St.L.	W	L	Pct.	GB
Los Angeles	...	12	10	13	12	16	10	8	5	6	4	6	102	60	.630	...
Cincinnati	6	...	11	14	11	12	7	6	9	8	8	6	98	64	.605	4
Atlanta	8	7	...	6	8	17	4	9	8	8	4	9	88	74	.543	14
Houston	5	4	12	...	10	11	8	6	6	6	5	8	81	81	.500	21
San Fran.	6	7	10	8	...	7	6	8	6	4	4	6	72	90	.444	30
San Diego	2	6	1	7	11	...	6	6	6	7	3	5	60	102	.370	42

SIGNIFICANT EVENTS

- **January 1:** Lee MacPhail took the reins as A.L. president, succeeding retiring Joe Cronin.
- **February 11:** Baseball's first arbitration hearing was decided in favor of Twins pitcher Dick Woodson.
- **October 3:** The Indians crossed another color barrier when they named Frank Robinson as baseball's first black manager and the game's first player-manager since 1959.
- **November 2:** The Braves honored the request of home run king Hank Aaron when they traded him to Milwaukee, the city where he started his career in 1954.
- **November 6:** Mike Marshall, who appeared in a record 106 games for the Dodgers, became the first relief pitcher to earn a Cy Young Award.
- **December 31:** The Yankees won the most celebrated free-agent chase in history when they signed former Oakland ace Catfish Hunter to a five-year, $3.75-million contract.

MEMORABLE MOMENTS

- **April 8:** Atlanta's Hank Aaron overtook Babe Ruth as baseball's all-time greatest slugger when he connected off Al Downing for record home run No. 715 in a 7-4 victory over the Dodgers.
- **July 17:** Bob Gibson became the second pitcher to reach 3,000 strikeouts when he fanned Cincinnati's Cesar Geronimo in a game at St. Louis.
- **August 12:** California's Nolan Ryan tied the single-game record when he struck out 19 Red Sox in a 4-2 victory.
- **September 24:** Al Kaline doubled off Baltimore's Dave McNally for hit No. 3,000 in Detroit's 5-4 loss.
- **September 29:** St. Louis speedster Lou Brock swiped his record 118th base in a 7-3 victory over the Cubs.
- **October 1:** The Orioles, who finished the season on a 28-6 run, clinched the A.L. East with a 7-6 victory over the Tigers.

LEADERS

American League
BA: Rod Carew, Min., .364.
Runs: Carl Yastrzemski, Bos., 93.
Hits: Rod Carew, Min., 218.
TB: Joe Rudi, Oak., 287.
HR: Dick Allen, Chi., 32.
RBI: Jeff Burroughs, Tex., 118.
SB: Bill North, Oak., 54.
Wins: Catfish Hunter, Oak.; Ferguson Jenkins, Tex., 25.
ERA: Catfish Hunter, Oak., 2.49.
CG: Ferguson Jenkins, Tex., 29.
IP: Nolan Ryan, Cal., 332.2.
SO: Nolan Ryan, Cal., 367.
SV: Terry Forster, Chi., 24.

National League
BA: Ralph Garr, Atl., .353.
Runs: Pete Rose, Cin., 110.
Hits: Ralph Garr, Atl., 214.
TB: Johnny Bench, Cin., 315.
HR: Mike Schmidt, Phil., 36.
RBI: Johnny Bench, Cin., 129.
SB: Lou Brock, St.L., 118.
Wins: Andy Messersmith, L.A.; Phil Niekro, Atl., 20.
ERA: Buzz Capra, Atl., 2.28.
CG: Phil Niekro, Atl., 18.
IP: Phil Niekro, Atl., 302.1.
SO: Steve Carlton, Phil., 240.
SV: Mike Marshall, L.A., 21.

A.L. 20-game winners
Catfish Hunter, Oak., 25-12
Ferguson Jenkins, Tex., 25-12
Mike Cuellar, Bal., 22-10
Luis Tiant, Bos., 22-13
Steve Busby, K.C., 22-14
Nolan Ryan, Cal., 22-16
Jim Kaat, Chi., 21-13
Gaylord Perry, Cle., 21-13
Wilbur Wood, Chi., 20-19

N.L. 20-game winners
Andy Messersmith, L.A., 20-6
Phil Niekro, Atl., 20-13

A.L. 100 RBIs
Jeff Burroughs, Tex., 118
Sal Bando, Oak., 103

N.L. 100 RBIs
Johnny Bench, Cin., 129
Mike Schmidt, Phil., 116
Steve Garvey, L.A., 111
Jim Wynn, L.A., 108
Ted Simmons, St.L., 103
Cesar Cedeno, Hou., 102
Tony Perez, Cin., 101
Reggie Smith, St.L., 100
Richie Zisk, Pit., 100

Most Valuable Player
A.L.: Jeff Burroughs, OF, Tex.
N.L.: Steve Garvey, 1B, L.A.

Cy Young Award
A.L.: Catfish Hunter, Oak.
N.L.: Mike Marshall, L.A.

Rookie of the Year
A.L.: Mike Hargrove, 1B, Tex.
N.L.: Bake McBride, OF, St.L.

Hall of Fame additions
Cool Papa Bell, OF, Negro Leagues
Jim Bottomley, 1B, 1922-37
Jocko Conlan, umpire
Whitey Ford, P, 1950-67
Mickey Mantle, OF, 1951-68
Sam Thompson, OF, 1885-1906

ALL-STAR GAME

- **Winner:** The N.L. continued its amazing All-Star run with a 7-2 victory fashioned by five pitchers who had never worked in a mid-summer classic.
- **Key inning:** A two-run N.L. fourth, when Steve Garvey doubled home the tying run and the lead run scored on Ron Cey's groundout.
- **Memorable moment:** A third-inning diving stop by N.L. first baseman Garvey on a smash by Bobby Murcer. The play saved at least two A.L. runs and possibly the game.
- **Top guns:** Mike Marshall (Dodgers), Reggie Smith (Cardinals), Garvey (Dodgers), Cey (Dodgers), N.L.; Dick Allen (White Sox), A.L.
- **MVP:** Garvey.

Linescore
July 23, at Pittsburgh's Three Rivers Stadium
A.L. ....0 0 2 0 0 0 0 0 0—2 4 1
N.L. ....0 1 0 2 1 0 1 2 x—7 10 1
Perry (Indians), Tiant (Red Sox) 4, Hunter (Athletics) 6, Fingers (Athletics) 8; Messersmith (Dodgers), Brett (Pirates) 4, Matlack (Mets) 6, McGlothen (Cardinals) 7, Marshall (Dodgers) 8. W—Brett. L—Tiant. HR—Smith, N.L.

ALCS

- **Winner:** The Athletics needed only four games to earn their third consecutive A.L. pennant and second straight ALCS victory over Baltimore.
- **Turning point:** Oakland's 1-0 Game 3 victory, which was decided by a fourth-inning Sal Bando home run. A's lefty Vida Blue allowed only two hits and gave his team a 2-1 series advantage.
- **Memorable moment:** Reggie Jackson's seventh-inning double in Game 4. The A's only hit in a 2-1 series-ending victory drove in the winning run.
- **Top guns:** Blue (1-0, 0-00 ERA), Ken Holtzman (1-0, 0.00), Bando (2 HR), Athletics; Andy Etchebarren (.333), Orioles.
- **MVP:** Blue.

Linescores

Game 1—October 5, at Oakland
Baltimore ..1 0 0 1 4 0 0 0 0—6 10 0
Oakland......0 0 1 0 1 0 0 0 1—3 9 0
Cuellar, Grimsley (9); Hunter, Odom (5), Fingers (9). W—Cuellar. L—Hunter. HR—Blair, Robinson, Grich (Bal.).

Game 2—October 6, at Oakland
Baltimore ....0 0 0 0 0 0 0 0 0—0 5 2
Oakland........0 0 0 1 0 1 0 3 x—5 8 0
McNally, Garland (6), Reynolds (7), G. Jackson (8); Holtzman. W—Holtzman. L—McNally. HR—Bando, Fosse (Oak.).

Game 3—October 8, at Baltimore
Oakland........0 0 0 1 0 0 0 0 0—1 4 2
Baltimore ....0 0 0 0 0 0 0 0 0—0 2 1
Blue; Palmer. W—Blue. L—Palmer. HR—Bando (Oak.).

Game 4—October 9, at Baltimore
Oakland........0 0 0 0 1 0 1 0 0—2 1 0
Baltimore ....0 0 0 0 0 0 0 0 1—1 5 1
Hunter, Fingers (8); Cuellar, Grimsley (5). W—Hunter. L—Cuellar. S—Fingers.

NLCS

- **Winner:** Los Angeles, making its first Championship Series appearance, overpowered Pittsburgh and claimed its first pennant since 1966.
- **Turning point:** Pitchers Don Sutton, Andy Messersmith and Mike Marshall held the Pirates scoreless in 17 of the first 18 innings as the Dodgers forged a 2-0 series advantage.
- **Memorable moment:** The Game 4 performance of Los Angeles first baseman Steve Garvey, who collected four hits, belted two home runs and drove in four runs in a 12-1 series-ending victory.
- **Top guns:** Sutton (2-0, 0.53 ERA), Garvey (.389, 2 HR, 5 RBIs), Bill Russell (.389), Dodgers; Bruce Kison (1-0, 0.00), Willie Stargell (.400, 2 HR, 4 RBIs), Pirates.
- **MVP:** Sutton.

Linescores

Game 1—October 5, at Pittsburgh
L.A. ....0 1 0 0 0 0 0 0 2—3 9 2
Pitt. ....0 0 0 0 0 0 0 0 0—0 4 0
Sutton; Reuss, Giusti (8). W—Sutton. L—Reuss.

Game 2—October 6, at Pittsburgh
L.A. ....1 0 0 1 0 0 0 3 0—5 12 0
Pitt. ....0 0 0 0 0 0 2 0 0—2 8 3
Messersmith, Marshall (8); Rooker, Giusti (8), Demery (8), Hernandez (8). W—Messersmith. L—Giusti. HR—Cey (L.A.).

Game 3—October 8, at Los Angeles
Pitt. ....5 0 2 0 0 0 0 0 0—7 10 0
L.A. ....0 0 0 0 0 0 0 0 0—0 4 5
Kison, Hernandez (7); Rau, Hough (1), Downing (4), Solomon (8). W—Kison. L—Rau. HR—Stargell, Hebner (Pit.).

Game 4—October 9, at Los Angeles
Pitt. ....0 0 0 0 0 0 1 0 0— 1 3 1
L.A. ....1 0 2 0 2 2 2 3 x—12 12 0
Reuss, Brett (3), Demery (6), Giusti (7), Pizarro (8); Sutton, Marshall (9). W—Sutton. L—Reuss. HR—Garvey 2 (L.A.); Stargell (Pit.).

WORLD SERIES

- **Winner:** Manager Alvin Dark's Athletics, who had won the previous two years under Dick Williams, became only the second team to win three consecutive World Series.
- **Turning point:** The A's 5-2 Game 4 victory, which featured a home run by pitcher Ken Holtzman, who had not batted all season because of the A.L.'s designated hitter rule.
- **Memorable moment:** Joe Rudi's tie-breaking solo home run off Dodger ironman reliever Mike Marshall in the seventh inning of Game 5.
- **Top guns:** Rollie Fingers (1-0, 2 saves, 1.93 ERA), Holtzman (1-0, 1.50, 1 HR), Rudi (.333, 4 RBIs), A's; Steve Garvey (.381), Dodgers.
- **MVP:** Fingers.

Linescores

Game 1—October 12, at Los Angeles
Oakland......0 1 0 0 1 0 0 1 0—3 6 2
L.A. ....0 0 0 0 1 0 0 0 1—2 11 1
Holtzman, Fingers (5), Hunter (9); Messersmith, Marshall (9). W—Fingers. L—Messersmith. S—Hunter. HR—Jackson (Oak.); Wynn (L.A.).

Game 2—October 13, at Los Angeles
Oakland........0 0 0 0 0 0 0 0 2—2 6 0
L.A. ....0 1 0 0 0 2 0 0 x—3 6 1
Blue, Odom (8); Sutton, Marshall (9). W—Sutton. L—Blue. S—Marshall. HR—Ferguson (L.A.).

Game 3—October 15, at Oakland
L.A. ....0 0 0 0 0 0 0 1 1—2 7 2
Oakland........0 0 2 1 0 0 0 0 x—3 5 2
Downing, Brewer (4), Hough (5), Marshall (7); Hunter, Fingers (8). W—Hunter. L—Downing. S—Fingers. HR—Buckner, Crawford (L.A.).

Game 4—October 16, at Oakland
L.A. ....0 0 0 2 0 0 0 0 0—2 7 1
Oakland........0 0 1 0 0 4 0 0 x—5 7 0
Messersmith, Marshall (7); Holtzman, Fingers (8). W—Holtzman. L—Messersmith. S—Fingers. HR—Holtzman.

Game 5—October 17, at Oakland
L.A. ....0 0 0 0 0 2 0 0 0—2 5 1
Oakland........1 1 0 0 0 0 1 0 x—3 6 1
Sutton, Marshall (6); Blue, Odom (7), Fingers (8). W—Odom. L—Marshall. S—Fingers. HR—Fosse, Rudi (Oak.).

FINAL STANDINGS

American League

East Division

Team	Bos.	Bal.	N.Y.	Cle.	Mil.	Det.	Cal.	Chi.	K.C.	Min.	Oak.	Tex.	W	L	Pct.	GB
Boston	...	9	11	7	10	13	6	8	7	10	6	8	95	65	.594	...
Baltimore	9	...	8	10	14	12	6	7	7	6	4	7	90	69	.566	4.5
New York	5	10	...	9	9	12	5	6	5	8	6	8	83	77	.519	12
Cleveland	11	8	9	...	9	12	9	5	6	3	2	5	79	80	.497	15.5
Milwaukee	8	4	9	9	...	11	5	4	5	2	5	6	68	94	.420	28
Detroit	5	4	6	6	7	...	5	7	6	4	6	1	57	102	.358	37.5

West Division

Team	Oak.	K.C.	Tex.	Min.	Chi.	Cal.	Bal.	Bos.	Cle.	Det.	Mil.	N.Y.	W	L	Pct.	GB
Oakland	...	11	12	12	9	11	8	6	10	6	7	6	98	64	.605	...
Kansas City	7	...	14	11	9	14	5	5	6	6	7	7	91	71	.562	7
Texas	6	4	...	10	13	9	5	4	7	11	6	4	79	83	.488	19
Minnesota	6	7	8	...	9	10	6	2	6	8	10	4	76	83	.478	20.5
Chicago	9	9	5	9	...	9	4	4	7	5	8	6	75	86	.466	22.5
California	7	4	9	8	9	...	6	6	3	6	7	7	72	89	.447	25.5

National League

East Division

Team	Pit.	Phi.	N.Y.	St.L.	Chi.	Mon.	Atl.	Cin.	Hou.	L.A.	S.D.	S.F.	W	L	Pct.	GB
Pittsburgh	...	7	13	10	12	11	8	6	5	7	8	5	92	69	.571	...
Philadelphia	11	...	11	10	6	11	7	5	6	5	7	7	86	76	.531	6.5
New York	5	7	...	9	11	8	8	4	8	6	8	8	82	80	.506	10.5
St. Louis	8	8	9	...	7	7	9	4	8	7	8	7	82	80	.506	10.5
Chicago	6	12	7	11	...	9	7	1	7	5	5	5	75	87	.463	17.5
Montreal	7	7	10	11	9	...	4	4	4	7	7	5	75	87	.463	17.5

West Division

Team	Cin.	L.A.	S.F.	S.D.	Atl.	Hou.	Chi.	Mon.	N.Y.	Phi.	Pit.	St.L.	W	L	Pct.	GB
Cincinnati	...	8	13	11	15	13	11	8	8	7	6	8	108	54	.667	...
L.A.	10	...	10	11	10	12	7	5	6	7	5	5	88	74	.543	20
San Fran.	5	8	...	10	9	13	7	7	4	5	7	5	80	81	.497	27.5
San Diego	7	7	8	...	11	9	7	5	4	5	4	4	71	91	.438	37
Atlanta	3	8	8	7	...	12	5	8	4	5	4	3	67	94	.416	40.5
Houston	5	6	5	9	6	...	5	8	4	6	6	4	64	97	.398	43.5

SIGNIFICANT EVENTS

■ **January 5:** Houston righthander Don Wilson died of carbon monoxide poisoning in the garage of his Houston home, an apparent suicide victim at age 29.

■ **November 26:** Boston's Fred Lynn became the first rookie MVP winner in baseball history.

■ **December 23:** Baseball's reserve system was shattered when labor arbitrator Peter Seitz handed pitchers Andy Messersmith and Dave McNally their unqualified free agency.

MEMORABLE MOMENTS

■ **April 8:** Frank Robinson belted a dramatic home run and led the Indians to a 5-3 Opening Day victory over the Yankees in his historic debut as baseball's first black manager.

■ **May 1:** Milwaukee's Hank Aaron drove in two runs in a 17-3 victory over Detroit and became baseball's all-time RBI leader with 2,211.

■ **June 1:** California's Nolan Ryan tied Sandy Koufax's record when he pitched his fourth career no-hitter, a 1-0 victory over the Orioles.

■ **June 18:** Boston rookie Fred Lynn drove in 10 runs with three home runs, a triple and a single in a 15-1 victory over the Tigers.

■ **September 16:** Pirates second baseman Rennie Stennett became the first modern-era player to collect seven hits in a nine-inning game—a 22-0 victory over the Cubs.

■ **September 28:** Oakland's Vida Blue, Glenn Abbott, Paul Lindblad and Rollie Fingers combined for the first multi-pitcher no-hitter in baseball history—a final-day 5-0 victory over the Angels.

LEADERS

American League
BA: Rod Carew, Min., .359.
Runs: Fred Lynn, Bos., 103.
Hits: George Brett, K.C., 195.
TB: George Scott, Mil., 318.
HR: Reggie Jackson, Oak.; George Scott, Mil., 36.
RBI: George Scott, Mil., 109.
SB: Mickey Rivers, Cal., 70.
Wins: Catfish Hunter, N.Y.; Jim Palmer, Bal., 23.
ERA: Jim Palmer, Bal., 2.09.
CG: Catfish Hunter, N.Y., 30.
IP: Catfish Hunter, N.Y., 328.
SO: Frank Tanana, Cal., 269.
SV: Goose Gossage, Chi., 26.

National League
BA: Bill Madlock, Chi., .354.
Runs: Pete Rose, Cin., 112.
Hits: Dave Cash, Phil., 213.
TB: Greg Luzinski, Phil., 322.
HR: Mike Schmidt, Phil., 38.
RBI: Greg Luzinski, Phil., 120.
SB: Dave Lopes, L.A., 77.
Wins: Tom Seaver, N.Y., 22.
ERA: Randy Jones, S.D., 2.24.
CG: Andy Messersmith, L.A., 19.
IP: Andy Messersmith, L.A., 321.2.
SO: Tom Seaver, N.Y., 243.
SV: Rawly Eastwick, Cin.; Al Hrabosky, St.L., 22.

A.L. 20-game winners
Jim Palmer, Bal., 23-11
Catfish Hunter, N.Y., 23-14
Vida Blue, Oak., 22-11
Mike Torrez, Bal., 20-9
Jim Kaat, Chi., 20-14

N.L. 20-game winners
Tom Seaver, N.Y., 22-9
Randy Jones, S.D., 20-12

A.L. 100 RBIs
George Scott, Mil., 109
John Mayberry, K.C., 106
Fred Lynn, Bos., 105
Reggie Jackson, Oak., 104
Thurman Munson, N.Y., 102
Jim Rice, Bos., 102

N.L. 100 RBIs
Greg Luzinski, Phil., 120
Johnny Bench, Cin., 110
Tony Perez, Cin., 109
Rusty Staub, N.Y., 105
Ron Cey, L.A., 101
Willie Montanez, Phil.-S.F., 101
Dave Parker, Pit., 101
Ted Simmons, St.L., 100

Most Valuable Player
A.L.: Fred Lynn, OF, Bos.
N.L.: Joe Morgan, 2B, Cin.

Cy Young Award
A.L.: Jim Palmer, Bal.
N.L.: Tom Seaver, N.Y.

Rookie of the Year
A.L.: Fred Lynn, OF, Bos.
N.L.: John Montefusco, P, S.F.

Hall of Fame additions
Earl Averill, OF, 1929-41
Bucky Harris, manager
Billy Herman, 2B, 1931-47
Judy Johnson, 3B, Negro Leagues
Ralph Kiner, OF, 1946-55

ALL-STAR GAME

■ **Winner:** The N.L., having uncharacteristically squandered a 3-0 lead, scored three ninth-inning runs and escaped with a 6-3 victory, its 12th in 13 years.

■ **Key inning:** The ninth, when Bill Madlock delivered the big blow with a two-run single and Pete Rose added an insurance run with a sacrifice fly.

■ **Memorable moment:** A long sixth-inning three-run homer by Carl Yastrzemski that wiped away the 3-0 deficit and gave the A.L. brief hope for a victory.

■ **Top guns:** Steve Garvey (Dodgers), Jim Wynn (Dodgers), Rose (Reds), Madlock (Cubs), N.L.; Yastrzemski (Red Sox), Bert Campaneris (Athletics), A.L.

■ **MVP:** Madlock.

Linescore
July 15, at Milwaukee's County Stadium
N.L. ....0 2 1 0 0 0 0 0 3—6 13 1
A.L. ....0 0 0 0 0 3 0 0 0—3 10 1
Reuss (Pirates), Sutton (Dodgers) 4, Seaver (Mets) 6, Matlack (Mets) 7, Jones (Padres) 9; Blue (Athletics), Busby (Royals) 3, Kaat (White Sox) 5, Hunter (Yankees) 7, Gossage (White Sox) 9. W—Matlack. L—Hunter. HR—Garvey, Wynn, N.L.; Yastrzemski, A.L.

ALCS

■ **Winner:** The Boston Red Sox brought a surprising end to Oakland's three-year championship reign and made it look as easy as 1-2-3.

■ **Turning point:** Oakland's four-error first-game performance that helped Boston to a 7-1 victory and set the tone for the series.

■ **Memorable moment:** Reggie Jackson's first-inning Game 2 home run, which gave Oakland its only lead of the series.

■ **Top guns:** Luis Tiant (1-0, 0.00 ERA), Carl Yastrzemski (.455), Rick Burleson (.444), Carlton Fisk (.417), Red Sox; Sal Bando (.500), Jackson (.417), Athletics.

■ **MVP:** Yastrzemski.

Linescores

Game 1—October 4, at Boston
Oakland........0 0 0 0 0 0 0 1 0—1 3 4
Boston ....2 0 0 0 0 0 5 0 x—7 8 3
Holtzman, Todd (7), Lindblad (7), Bosman (7), Abbott (8); Tiant. W—Tiant. L—Holtzman.

Game 2—October 5, at Boston
Oakland......2 0 0 1 0 0 0 0 0—3 10 0
Boston ......0 0 0 3 0 1 1 1 x—6 12 0
Blue, Todd (4), Fingers (5); Cleveland, Moret (6), Drago (7). W—Moret. L—Fingers. S—Drago. HR—Jackson (Oak.); Yastrzemski, Petrocelli (Bos.)

Game 3—October 7, at Oakland
Boston ......0 0 0 1 3 0 0 1 0—5 11 1
Oakland......0 0 0 0 0 1 0 2 0—3 6 2
Wise, Drago (8); Holtzman, Todd (5), Lindblad (5). W—Wise. L—Holtzman. S—Drago.

NLCS

■ **Winner:** Cincinnati's Big Red Machine rolled over Pittsburgh in a quick and easy Championship Series.

■ **Turning point:** Reds pitcher Don Gullett hit a homer, drove in three runs and pitched an eight-hit, first-game victory.

■ **Memorable moment:** A two-run eighth-inning home run by Cincinnati's Pete Rose erased a 2-1, Game 3 deficit in a contest eventually won by the Reds in 10 innings, 5-3.

■ **Top guns:** Gullett (1-0, 1 HR, 3 RBIs), Dave Concepcion (.455), Tony Perez (.417, 4 RBIs), Reds; Richie Zisk (.500), Pirates.

■ **MVP:** Gullett.

Linescores

Game 1—October 4, at Cincinnati
Pitt............0 2 0 0 0 0 0 0 1—3 8 0
Cin. ....0 1 3 0 4 0 0 0 x—8 11 0
Reuss, Brett (3), Demery (5), Ellis (7); Gullett. W—Gullett. L—Reuss. HR—Gullett (Cin.).

Game 2—October 5, at Cincinnati
Pitt.............0 0 0 1 0 0 0 0 0—1 5 0
Cin. ....2 0 0 2 0 1 1 0 x—6 12 1
Rooker, Tekulve (5), Brett (6), Kison (7); Norman, Eastwick (7). W—Norman. L—Rooker. S—Eastwick. HR—Perez (Cin.).

Game 3—October 7, at Pittsburgh
Cin. ....0 1 0 0 0 0 0 2 0 2—5 6 0
Pitt...........0 0 0 0 0 2 0 0 1 0—3 7 2
Nolan, Carroll (7), McEnaney (8), Eastwick (9), Borbon (10); Candelaria, Giusti (8), Hernandez (10), Tekulve (10). W—Eastwick. L—Hernandez. S—Borbon. HR—Concepcion, Rose (Cin.); Oliver (Pit.).

WORLD SERIES

■ **Winner:** Cincinnati's Big Red Machine held off the gritty Red Sox in one of the most exciting Series in baseball history.

■ **Turning point:** Reds second baseman Joe Morgan's Series-deciding single in the ninth inning of Game 7. The Series was that close.

■ **Memorable moments:** In the Red Sox's 7-6 Game 6 victory: Boston pinch-hitter Bernie Carbo's game-tying, three-run homer in the eighth inning; Boston right fielder Dwight Evans' spectacular, leaping, 11th-inning catch that he turned into a rally-killing double play; Boston catcher Carlton Fisk's dramatic, game-ending, "fair-or-foul" home run in the 12th inning.

■ **Top guns:** Pete Rose (.370), Tony Perez (3 HR, 7 RBIs), Reds; Carbo (2 PH HR), Carl Yastrzemski (.310, 4 RBIs), Rico Petrocelli (.308, 4 RBIs), Red Sox.

■ **MVP:** Rose.

Linescores

Game 1—October 11, at Boston
Cin. ....0 0 0 0 0 0 0 0 0—0 5 0
Bos. ....0 0 0 0 0 0 6 0 x—6 12 0
Gullett, Carroll (7), McEnaney (7); Tiant. W—Tiant. L—Gullett.

Game 2—October 12, at Boston
Cin. ....0 0 0 1 0 0 0 0 2—3 7 1
Bos. ....1 0 0 0 0 1 0 0 0—2 7 0
Billingham, Borbon (6), McEnaney (7), Eastwick (8); Lee, Drago (9). W—Eastwick. L—Drago.

Game 3—October 14, at Cincinnati
Bos. ......0 1 0 0 0 1 1 0 2 0—5 10 2
Cin. ....0 0 0 2 3 0 0 0 0 1—6 7 0
Wise, Burton (5), Cleveland (5), Willoughby (7), Moret (10); Nolan, Darcy (5), Carroll (7), McEnaney (7), Eastwick (9). W—Eastwick. L—Willoughby. HR—Fisk, Carbo, Evans (Bos.); Bench, Concepcion, Geronimo (Cin.).

Game 4—October 15, at Cincinnati
Bos. ....0 0 0 5 0 0 0 0 0—5 11 1
Cin. ....2 0 0 2 0 0 0 0 0—4 9 1
Tiant; Norman, Borbon (4), Carroll (5), Eastwick (7). W—Tiant. L—Norman.

Game 5—October 16, at Cincinnati
Bos. ....1 0 0 0 0 0 0 0 1—2 5 0
Cin. ....0 0 0 1 1 3 0 1 x—6 8 0
Cleveland, Willoughby (6), Pole (8), Segui (8); Gullett, Eastwick (9). W—Gullett. L—Cleveland. S—Eastwick. HR—Perez 2 (Cin.).

Game 6—October 21, at Boston
Cin.....0 0 0 0 3 0 2 1 0 0 0 0—6 14 0
Bos. ..3 0 0 0 0 0 0 3 0 0 0 1—7 10 1
Nolan, Norman (3), Billingham (3), Carroll (5), Borbon (6), Eastwick (8), McEnaney (9), Darcy (10); Tiant, Moret (8), Drago (9), Wise (12). W—Wise. L—Darcy. HR—Lynn, Carbo, Fisk (Bos.); Geronimo (Cin.).

Game 7—October 22, at Boston
Cin. ....0 0 0 0 0 2 1 0 1—4 9 0
Bos. ....0 0 3 0 0 0 0 0 0—3 5 2
Gullett, Billingham (5), Carroll (7), McEnaney (9); Lee, Moret (7), Willoughby (7), Burton (9), Cleveland (9). W—Carroll. L—Burton. S—McEnaney. HR—Perez (Cin.).

FINAL STANDINGS

American League

East Division

Team	N.Y.	Bal.	Bos.	Cle.	Det.	Mil.	Cal.	Chi.	K.C.	Min.	Oak.	Tex.	W	L	Pct.	GB
New York	...	5	11	12	8	13	7	11	5	10	6	9	97	62	.610	...
Baltimore	13	...	7	7	12	11	8	8	6	4	4	8	88	74	.543	10.5
Boston	7	11	...	9	14	12	7	6	3	7	4	3	83	79	.512	15.5
Cleveland	4	11	9	...	6	11	5	9	6	9	4	7	81	78	.509	16
Detroit	9	6	4	12	...	12	6	6	4	4	6	5	74	87	.460	24
Milwaukee	5	7	6	6	6	...	8	5	4	4	5	10	66	95	.410	32

West Division

Team	K.C.	Oak.	Min.	Cal.	Tex.	Chi.	Bal.	Bos.	Cle.	Det.	Mil.	N.Y.	W	L	Pct.	GB
Kansas City	...	9	10	10	7	10	6	9	6	8	8	7	90	72	.556	...
Oakland	9	...	7	12	7	9	8	8	8	6	7	6	87	74	.540	2.5
Minnesota	8	11	...	10	11	11	8	5	3	8	8	2	85	77	.525	5
California	8	6	8	...	12	11	4	5	7	6	4	5	76	86	.469	14
Texas	11	11	7	6	...	11	4	9	5	7	2	3	76	86	.469	14
Chicago	8	8	7	7	7	...	4	6	3	6	7	1	64	97	.398	25.5

National League

East Division

Team	Phi.	Pit.	N.Y.	Chi.	St.L.	Mon.	Atl.	Cin.	Hou.	L.A.	S.D.	S.F.	W	L	Pct.	GB
Philadelphia	...	8	13	10	12	15	7	7	8	7	8	6	101	61	.623	...
Pittsburgh	10	...	8	10	12	10	9	4	10	3	7	9	92	70	.568	9
New York	5	10	...	13	9	10	8	6	6	5	7	7	86	76	.531	15
Chicago	8	8	5	...	12	11	6	3	5	3	6	8	75	87	.463	26
St. Louis	6	6	9	6	...	11	8	6	3	2	8	7	72	90	.444	29
Montreal	3	8	8	7	7	...	4	3	2	2	4	7	55	107	.340	46

West Division

Team	Cin.	L.A.	Hou.	S.F.	S.D.	Atl.	Chi.	Mon.	N.Y.	Phi.	Pit.	St.L.	W	L	Pct.	GB
Cincinnati	...	13	12	9	13	12	9	9	6	5	8	6	102	60	.630	...
L.A.	5	...	13	8	6	10	9	10	7	5	9	10	92	70	.568	10
Houston	6	5	...	10	10	11	7	10	6	4	2	9	80	82	.494	22
San Fran.	9	10	8	...	10	9	4	5	5	6	3	5	74	88	.457	28
San Diego	5	12	8	8	...	8	6	8	5	4	5	4	73	89	.451	29
Atlanta	6	8	7	9	10	...	6	8	4	5	3	4	70	92	.432	32

SIGNIFICANT EVENTS

■ **January 14:** N.L. owners approved the sale of the Braves to Ted Turner, head of Turner Communications, for $12 million.

■ **April 10:** Free-agent pitcher Andy Messersmith signed a "lifetime contract" to pitch for new Braves owner Turner.

■ **April 25:** Cubs center fielder Rick Monday dashed into left field at Dodger Stadium and snatched an American flag away from two protestors who were trying to set it on fire.

■ **June 18:** Commissioner Bowie Kuhn voided Oakland owner Charles O. Finley's sale of Vida Blue to the Yankees and Joe Rudi and Rollie Fingers to the Red Sox.

■ **September 29:** Walter Alston, who compiled 2,040 victories over 23 seasons as manager of the Dodgers, retired at age 64.

■ **November 5:** The A.L. conducted its third expansion draft to fill rosters of new teams in Seattle and Toronto.

■ **November 6:** Reliever Bill Campbell, one of the plums of baseball's first free-agent reentry draft, signed a four-year, $1 million contract with the Red Sox.

MEMORABLE MOMENTS

■ **April 17:** Mike Schmidt's two-run, 10th-inning home run, his record-tying fourth of the game, gave the Phillies an 18-16 victory over the Cubs at Wrigley Field.

■ **October 3:** George Brett collected three final-day hits and edged Kansas City teammate Hal McRae, .3333 to .3326, for the A.L. batting title.

LEADERS

American League
BA: George Brett, K.C., .333.
Runs: Roy White, N.Y., 104.
Hits: George Brett, K.C., 215.
TB: George Brett, K.C., 298.
HR: Graig Nettles, N.Y., 32.
RBI: Lee May, Bal., 109.
SB: Bill North, Oak., 75.
Wins: Jim Palmer, Bal., 22.
ERA: Mark Fidrych, Det., 2.34.
CG: Mark Fidrych, Det., 24.
IP: Jim Palmer, Bal., 315.
SO: Nolan Ryan, Cal., 327.
SV: Sparky Lyle, N.Y., 23.

National League
BA: Bill Madlock, Chi., .339.
Runs: Pete Rose, Cin., 130.
Hits: Pete Rose, Cin., 215.
TB: Mike Schmidt, Phil., 306.
HR: Mike Schmidt, Phil., 38.
RBI: George Foster, Cin., 121.
SB: Dave Lopes, L.A., 63.
Wins: Randy Jones, S.D., 22.
ERA: John Denny, St.L., 2.52.
CG: Randy Jones, S.D., 25.
IP: Randy Jones, S.D., 315.1.
SO: Tom Seaver, N.Y., 235.
SV: Rawly Eastwick, Cin., 26.

A.L. 20-game winners
Jim Palmer, Bal., 22-13
Luis Tiant, Bos., 21-12
Wayne Garland, Bal., 20-7

N.L. 20-game winners
Randy Jones, S.D., 22-14
Jerry Koosman, N.Y., 21-10
Don Sutton, L.A., 21-10
Steve Carlton, Phil., 20-7
J.R. Richard, Hou., 20-15

A.L. 100 RBIs
Lee May, Bal., 109
Thurman Munson, N.Y., 105
Carl Yastrzemski, Bos., 102

N.L. 100 RBIs
George Foster, Cin., 121
Joe Morgan, Cin., 111
Mike Schmidt, Phil., 107
Bob Watson, Hou., 102

Most Valuable Player
A.L.: Thurman Munson, C, N.Y.
N.L.: Joe Morgan, 2B, Cin.

Cy Young Award
A.L.: Jim Palmer, Bal.
N.L.: Randy Jones, S.D.

Rookie of the Year
A.L.: Mark Fidrych, P, Det.
N.L.: Butch Metzger, P, S.D.
Pat Zachry, P, Cin.

Hall of Fame additions
Oscar Charleston, OF, Negro Leagues
Roger Connor, 1B, 1880-97
Cal Hubbard, umpire
Bob Lemon, P, 1946-58
Fred Lindstrom, 3B, 1924-36
Robin Roberts, P, 1948-66

ALL-STAR GAME

■ **Winner:** Baseball celebrated the nation's Bicentennial with another N.L. All-Star victory — a 7-1 rout sparked by George Foster and Cesar Cedeno.

■ **Key innings:** The third, when Foster blasted a two-run homer, and the eighth, when Cedeno secured the outcome with another two-run shot.

■ **Memorable moment:** The five-hit pitching of an N.L. staff that surrendered the A.L.'s lone run on a homer by Fred Lynn.

■ **Top guns:** Randy Jones (Padres), Foster (Reds), Cedeno (Astros), Pete Rose (Reds), N.L.; Lynn (Red Sox), Rusty Staub (Tigers), A.L.

■ **MVP:** Foster.

Linescore
July 13, at Philadelphia's Veterans Stadium
A.L. ....0 0 0 1 0 0 0 0 0—1 5 0
N.L. ....2 0 2 0 0 0 0 3 x—7 10 0
Fidrych (Tigers), Hunter (Yankees) 3, Tiant (Red Sox) 5, Tanana (Angels) 7; Jones (Padres), Seaver (Mets) 4, Montefusco (Giants) 6, Rhoden (Dodgers) 8, Forsch (Astros) 9. W—Jones. L—Fidrych. HR—Foster, Cedeno, N.L.; Lynn, A.L.

ALCS

■ **Winner:** The New York Yankees, absent from post-season play since 1964, qualified for their 30th World Series with a riveting five-game victory over postseason newcomer Kansas City.

■ **Turning point:** The Yankees' 5-3 Game 3 victory, which was fueled by a homer and three RBIs by first baseman Chris Chambliss.

■ **Memorable moment:** Chambliss' dramatic series-ending home run leading off the ninth inning of Game 5. The blast off Royals reliever Mark Littell gave the Yankees a 7-6 victory and touched off a wild mob scene at Yankee Stadium.

■ **Top guns:** Chambliss (.524, 2 HR, 8 RBIs), Thurman Munson (.435), Mickey Rivers (.348), Yankees; Paul Splittorff (1-0, 1.93 ERA), George Brett (.444, 5 RBIs), Royals.

■ **MVP:** Chambliss.

Linescores

Game 1—October 9, at Kansas City
N.Y. ....2 0 0 0 0 0 0 0 2—4 12 0
K.C. ....0 0 0 0 0 0 0 1 0—1 5 2
Hunter; Gura, Littell (9). W—Hunter. L—Gura.

Game 2—October 10, at Kansas City
N.Y ....0 1 2 0 0 0 0 0 0—3 12 5
K.C. ....2 0 0 0 0 2 0 3 x—7 9 0
Figueroa, Tidrow (6); Leonard, Splittorff (3), Mingori (9). W—Splittorff. L—Figueroa.

Game 3—October 12, at New York
K.C. ....3 0 0 0 0 0 0 0 0—3 6 0
N.Y. ....0 0 0 2 0 3 0 0 x—5 9 0
Hassler, Pattin (6), Hall (6), Mingori (6), Littell (6); Ellis, Lyle (9). W—Ellis. L—Hassler. S—Lyle. HR—Chambliss (N.Y.).

Game 4—October 13, at New York
K.C. ....0 3 0 2 0 1 0 1 0—7 9 1
N.Y. ....0 2 0 0 0 0 1 0 1—4 11 0
Gura, Bird (3), Mingori (7); Hunter, Tidrow (4), Jackson (7). W—Bird. L—Hunter. S—Mingori. HR—Nettles 2 (N.Y.).

Game 5—October 14, at New York
K.C. ....2 1 0 0 0 0 0 3 0—6 11 1
N.Y. ....2 0 2 0 0 2 0 0 1—7 11 1
Leonard, Splittorff (1), Pattin (4), Hassler (5), Littell (7); Figueroa, Jackson (8), Tidrow (9). W—Tidrow. L—Littell. HR—Mayberry, Brett (K.C.); Chambliss (N.Y.).

NLCS

■ **Winner:** Philadelphia was no match for the powerful Reds, who were being hailed as one of the great teams in baseball history.

■ **Turning point:** The Reds took quick control with a 6-3 first-game victory over the Phillies and ace lefthander Steve Carlton.

■ **Memorable moment:** The ninth inning of Game 3. After tying the game with consecutive home runs by George Foster and Johnny Bench, the Reds claimed a 7-6 victory when Ken Griffey singled with the bases loaded off reliever Tom Underwood.

■ **Top guns:** Don Gullett (1-0, 1.13 ERA), Pete Rose (.429), Griffey (.385), Foster (2 HR, 4 RBIs), Reds; Jay Johnstone (.778), Phillies.

■ **MVP:** Griffey.

Linescores

Game 1—October 9, at Philadelphia
Cin. ....0 0 1 0 0 2 0 3 0—6 10 0
Phil. ....1 0 0 0 0 0 0 0 2—3 6 1
Gullett, Eastwick (9); Carlton, McGraw (8). W—Gullett. L—Carlton. HR—Foster (Cin.).

Game 2—October 10, at Philadelphia
Cin. ....0 0 0 0 0 4 2 0 0—6 6 0
Phil. ....0 1 0 0 1 0 0 0 0—2 10 1
Zachry, Borbon (6); Lonborg, Garber (6), McGraw (7), Reed (7). W—Zachry. L—Lonborg. S—Borbon. HR—Luzinski (Phil.).

Game 3—October 12, at Cincinnati
Phil. ....0 0 0 1 0 0 2 2 1—6 11 0
Cin. ....0 0 0 0 0 0 4 0 3—7 9 2
Kaat, Reed (7), Garber (9), Underwood (9); Nolan, Sarmiento (6), Borbon (7), Eastwick (8). W—Eastwick. L—Garber. HR—Foster, Bench (Cin.).

WORLD SERIES

■ **Winner:** Cincinnati's Big Red Machine was in full gear as it rolled over the Yankees, who were making their first Series appearance since 1964.

■ **Turning point:** Joe Morgan's first-inning home run in Game 1. The Reds never looked back.

■ **Memorable moment:** Game 3 at refurbished Yankee Stadium. Despite a 6-2 New York loss, the atmosphere was electric and baseball's most revered ballpark was the stately host for its 28th World Series.

■ **Top guns:** Johnny Bench (.533, 2 HR, 6 RBIs), George Foster (.429), Dave Concepcion (.357), Dan Driessen (.357), Reds; Thurman Munson (.529), Yankees.

■ **MVP:** Bench.

Linescores

Game 1—October 16, at Cincinnati
N.Y. ....0 1 0 0 0 0 0 0 0—1 5 1
Cin. ....1 0 1 0 0 1 2 0 x—5 10 1
Alexander, Lyle (7); Gullett, Borbon (8). W—Gullett. L—Alexander. HR—Morgan (Cin.).

Game 2—October 17, at Cincinnati
N.Y. ....0 0 0 1 0 0 2 0 0—3 9 1
Cin. ....0 3 0 0 0 0 0 0 1—4 10 0
Hunter; Norman, Billingham (7). W—Billingham. L—Hunter.

Game 3—October 19, at New York
Cin. ....0 3 0 1 0 0 0 2 0—6 13 2
N.Y. ....0 0 0 1 0 0 1 0 0—2 8 0
Zachry, McEnaney (7); Ellis, Jackson (4), Tidrow (8). W—Zachry. L—Ellis. S—McEnaney. HR—Driessen (Cin.); Mason (N.Y.).

Game 4—October 21, at New York
Cin. ....0 0 0 3 0 0 0 0 4—7 9 2
N.Y. ....1 0 0 0 1 0 0 0 0—2 8 0
Nolan, McEnaney (7); Figueroa, Tidrow (9), Lyle (9). W—Nolan. L—Figueroa. S—McEnaney. HR—Bench 2 (Cin.).

FINAL STANDINGS

American League

East Division

Team	N.Y.	Bos.	Bal.	Det.	Cle.	Mil.	Tor.	Cal.	Chi.	K.C.	Min.	Oak.	Sea.	Tex.	W	L	Pct.	GB
New York	...	7	7	9	12	7	9	7	7	5	8	9	6	7	100	62	.617	...
Boston	8	...	8	9	8	9	12	7	3	5	4	8	10	6	97	64	.602	2.5
Baltimore	8	6	...	12	11	11	10	5	5	4	6	8	7	4	97	64	.602	2.5
Detroit	6	6	3	...	7	10	10	6	6	3	5	5	5	2	74	88	.457	26
Cleveland	3	7	4	8	...	11	9	4	4	3	2	7	7	2	71	90	.441	28.5
Milwaukee	8	6	4	5	4	...	8	5	5	2	3	5	7	5	67	95	.414	33
Toronto	6	3	5	5	5	7	...	4	3	2	1	3	6	4	54	107	.335	45.5

West Division

Team	K.C.	Tex.	Chi.	Min.	Cal.	Sea.	Oak.	Bal.	Bos.	Cle.	Det.	Mil.	N.Y.	Tor.	W	L	Pct.	GB
Kansas City	...	8	7	10	9	11	9	7	5	7	8	8	5	8	102	60	.630	...
Texas	7	...	9	7	10	6	13	6	4	9	8	5	3	7	94	68	.580	8
Chicago	8	6	...	10	7	10	10	5	7	6	4	6	3	8	90	72	.556	12
Minnesota	5	8	5	...	8	7	8	4	6	9	5	8	2	9	84	77	.522	17.5
California	6	5	8	7	...	9	5	6	3	6	4	5	4	6	74	88	.457	28
Seattle	4	9	5	8	6	...	8	3	1	3	6	3	4	4	64	98	.395	38
Oakland	6	2	5	6	10	7	...	2	3	3	5	5	2	7	63	98	.391	38.5

National League

East Division

Team	Phi.	Pit.	St.L.	Chi.	Mon.	N.Y.	Atl.	Cin.	Hou.	L.A.	S.D.	S.F.	W	L	Pct.	GB
Philadelphia	...	8	11	12	11	13	10	4	8	6	9	9	101	61	.623	...
Pittsburgh	10	...	9	11	11	14	9	9	8	3	10	2	96	66	.593	5
St.Louis	7	9	...	11	6	10	11	7	7	6	4	5	83	79	.512	18
Chicago	6	7	7	...	10	9	7	7	6	6	7	9	81	81	.500	20
Montreal	7	7	12	8	...	10	6	5	4	5	5	6	75	87	.463	26
New York	5	4	8	9	8	...	5	2	6	4	6	7	64	98	.395	37

West Division

Team	L.A.	Cin.	Hou.	S.F.	S.D.	Atl.	Chi.	Mon.	N.Y.	Phi.	Pit.	St.L.	W	L	Pct.	GB
Los Angeles	...	8	9	14	12	13	6	7	8	6	9	6	98	64	.605	...
Cincinnati	10	...	5	10	11	14	5	7	10	8	3	5	88	74	.543	10
Houston	9	13	...	9	8	9	6	8	6	4	4	5	81	81	.500	17
San Fran.	4	8	9	..	10	10	3	6	5	3	10	7	75	87	.463	23
San Diego	6	7	10	8	...	7	5	7	6	3	2	8	69	93	.426	29
Atlanta	5	4	9	8	11	...	5	6	7	2	3	1	61	101	.377	37

SIGNIFICANT EVENTS

■ **January 2:** Commissioner Bowie Kuhn suspended Braves owner Ted Turner for a year and fined him $10,000 for "tampering" with free-agent outfielder Gary Matthews.

■ **April 6-7:** The expansion Mariners lost their debut, 7-0, to the Angels, but the Blue Jays won their Toronto inaugural, 9-5, over the White Sox.

■ **April 15:** The Expos opened new Olympic Stadium, but the Phillies spoiled the occasion with a 7-2 victory.

■ **March 28:** Texas second baseman Lenny Randle, frustrated over losing his starting job, sent 50-year-old manager Frank Lucchesi to the hospital with a vicious beating before a spring training game.

■ **October 25:** Yankees lefty Sparky Lyle became the first A.L. reliever to win a Cy Young Award.

■ **November 8:** Cincinnati's George Foster, the first player to top the 50-homer barrier since 1965, earned N.L. MVP honors.

MEMORABLE MOMENTS

■ **June 8:** California's Nolan Ryan struck out 19 Blue Jays in a 10-inning performance, reaching that single-game plateau for the fourth time.

■ **August 29:** St. Louis' Lou Brock swiped two bases in a game against San Diego, lifting his career total to 893 and passing Ty Cobb as baseball's greatest modern-era basestealer.

LEADERS

American League
BA: Rod Carew, Min., .388.
Runs: Rod Carew, Min., 128.
Hits: Rod Carew, Min., 239.
TB: Jim Rice, Bos., 382.
HR: Jim Rice, Bos., 39.
RBI: Larry Hisle, Min., 119.
SB: Fred Patek, K.C., 53.
Wins: Dave Goltz, Min.; Dennis Leonard, K.C.; Jim Palmer, Bal., 20.
ERA: Frank Tanana, Cal., 2.54.
CG: Jim Palmer, Bal.; Nolan Ryan, Cal., 22.
IP: Jim Palmer, Bal., 319.
SO: Nolan Ryan, Cal., 341.
SV: Bill Campbell, Bos., 31.

National League
BA: Dave Parker, Pit., .338.
Runs: George Foster, Cin., 124.
Hits: Dave Parker, Pit., 215.
TB: George Foster, Cin., 388.
HR: George Foster, Cin., 52.
RBI: George Foster, Cin., 149.
SB: Frank Taveras, Pit., 70.
Wins: Steve Carlton, Phil., 23.
ERA: John Candelaria, Pit., 2.34.
CG: Phil Niekro, Atl., 20.
IP: Phil Niekro, Atl., 330.1.
SO: Phil Niekro, Atl., 262.
SV: Rollie Fingers, S.D., 35.

A.L. 20-game winners
Jim Palmer, Bal., 20-11
Dave Goltz, Min., 20-11
Dennis Leonard, K.C., 20-12

N.L. 20-game winners
Steve Carlton, Phil., 23-10
Tom Seaver, N.Y.-Cin., 21-6
John Candelaria, Pit., 20-5
Bob Forsch, St.L., 20-7
Tommy John, L.A., 20-7
Rick Reuschel, Chi., 20-10

A.L. 100 RBIs
Larry Hisle, Min., 119
Bobby Bonds, Cal., 115
Jim Rice, Bos., 114
Al Cowens, K.C., 112
Butch Hobson, Bos., 112
Reggie Jackson, N.Y., 110
Graig Nettles, N.Y., 107
Jason Thompson, Det., 105
Carlton Fisk, Bos., 102
Carl Yastrzemski, Bos., 102
Rusty Staub, Det., 101
Richie Zisk, Chi., 101
Rod Carew, Min., 100
Thurman Munson, N.Y., 100

N.L. 100 RBIs
George Foster, Cin., 149
Greg Luzinski, Phil., 130
Steve Garvey, L.A., 115
Jeff Burroughs, Atl., 114
Ron Cey, L.A., 110
Bob Watson, Hou., 110
Johnny Bench, Cin., 109
Bill Robinson, Pit., 104
Mike Schmidt, Phil., 101

N.L. 40 homers
George Foster, Cin., 52
Jeff Burroughs, Atl., 41

Most Valuable Player
A.L.: Rod Carew, 1B, Min.
N.L.: George Foster, OF, Cin.

Cy Young Award
A.L.: Sparky Lyle, N.Y.
N.L.: Steve Carlton, Phil.

Rookie of the Year
A.L.: Eddie Murray, 1B, Bal.
N.L.: Andre Dawson, OF, Mon.

Hall of Fame additions
Ernie Banks, SS, 1953-71
Martin Dihigo, P/IF, Negro Leagues
John Henry Lloyd, SS, Negro Leagues
Al Lopez, manager
Amos Rusie, P, 1889-1901
Joe Sewell, SS, 1920-33

ALL-STAR GAME

■ **Winner:** The N.L. continued its All-Star mastery with a 7-5 victory — its sixth in a row and 14th in 15 contests.

■ **Key inning:** The first, when the N.L. struck for four quick runs. A leadoff homer by Joe Morgan and a two-run shot by Greg Luzinski were the big blows.

■ **Memorable moment:** Watching the N.L. close out another All-Star victory at venerable Yankee Stadium, where so much A.L. glory had been achieved.

■ **Top guns:** Don Sutton (Dodgers), Morgan (Reds), Luzinski (Phillies), Dave Winfield (Padres), Steve Garvey (Dodgers), N.L.; Dennis Eckersley (Indians), Richie Zisk (White Sox), George Scott (Red Sox), A.L.

■ **MVP:** Sutton.

Linescore
July 19, at New York's Yankee Stadium
N.L..............4 0 1 0 0 0 0 2 0—7 9 1
A.L..............0 0 0 0 0 2 1 0 2—5 8 0
Sutton (Dodgers), Lavelle (Giants) 4, Seaver (Reds) 6, R. Reuschel (Cubs) 8, Gossage (Pirates) 9; Palmer (Orioles), Kern (Indians) 3, Eckersley (Indians) 4, LaRoche (Angels) 6, Campbell (Red Sox) 7, Lyle (Yankees) 8. W—Sutton. L—Palmer. HR—Morgan, Luzinski, Garvey, N.L.; Scott, A.L.

ALCS

■ **Winner:** The Yankees, bidding to return to the World Series for a second consecutive season, needed a three-run ninth-inning rally to defeat Kansas City in the decisive fifth game.

■ **Turning point:** Sparky Lyle's 5⅓ innings of scoreless Game 4 relief after the Royals, bidding to close out the series, had cut a 4-0 Yankee lead to 5-4. The Yanks evened the series with a 6-4 win.

■ **Memorable moment:** A bloop single by light-hitting Yankee Paul Blair leading off the ninth inning of Game 5. Blair's hit off Royals ace Dennis Leonard set up the Yankees' series-winning rally.

■ **Top guns:** Lyle (2-0, 0.96 ERA), Cliff Johnson (.400), Mickey Rivers (.391), Yankees; Hal McRae (.444), Fred Patek (.389), Royals.

■ **MVP:** Lyle.

Linescores

Game 1—October 5, at New York
K.C..............2 2 2 0 0 0 0 1 0—7 9 0
N.Y..............0 0 2 0 0 0 0 0 0—2 9 0
Splittorff, Bird (9); Gullett, Tidrow (3), Lyle (9). W—Splittorff. L—Gullett. HR—McRae, Mayberry, Cowens (K.C.); Munson (N.Y.).

Game 2—October 6, at New York
K.C............0 0 1 0 0 1 0 0 0—2 3 1
N.Y............0 0 0 0 2 3 0 1 x—6 10 1
Hassler, Littell (6), Mingori (8); Guidry. W—Guidry. L—Hassler. HR—Johnson (N.Y.).

Game 3—October 7, at Kansas City
N.Y............0 0 0 0 1 0 0 0 1—2 4 1
K.C............0 1 1 0 1 2 1 0 x—6 12 1
Torrez, Lyle (6); Leonard. W—Leonard. L—Torrez.

Game 4—October 8, at Kansas City
N.Y............1 2 1 1 0 0 0 0 1—6 13 0
K.C............0 0 2 2 0 0 0 0 0—4 8 2
Figueroa, Tidrow (4), Lyle (4); Gura, Pattin (3), Mingori (9), Bird (9). W—Lyle. L—Gura.

Game 5—October 9, at Kansas City
N.Y............0 0 1 0 0 0 0 1 3—5 10 0
K.C............2 0 1 0 0 0 0 0 0—3 10 1
Guidry, Torrez (3), Lyle (8); Splittorff, Bird (8), Mingori (8), Leonard (9), Gura (9), Littell (9). W—Lyle. L—Leonard.

NLCS

■ **Winner:** The Dodgers returned to the World Series for the second time in four years and denied Philadelphia its first pennant since 1950.

■ **Turning point:** The ninth inning of Game 3. With the series tied at a game apiece and the Phillies holding a 5-3 lead with two out and nobody on base in the final inning, the Dodgers collected four straight hits, scored three runs and escaped with a 6-5 victory.

■ **Memorable moment:** Dusty Baker's two-run fourth-game homer that helped Dodgers lefty Tommy John record a 4-1 series-ending victory in a steady rain.

■ **Top guns:** John (1-0, 0.66 ERA), Baker (.357, 2 HR, 8 RBIs), Ron Cey (.308, 4 RBIs), Dodgers; Bob Boone (.400), Richie Hebner (.357), Phillies.

■ **MVP:** Baker.

Linescores

Game 1—October 4, at Los Angeles
Phil. ....2 0 0 0 2 1 0 0 2—7 9 0
L.A..............0 0 0 0 1 0 4 0 0—5 9 2
Carlton, Garber (7), McGraw (9); John, Garman (5), Hough (6), Sosa (8). W—Garber. L—Sosa. S—McGraw. HR—Luzinski (Phil.); Cey (L.A.).

Game 2—October 5, at Los Angeles
Phil. ....0 0 1 0 0 0 0 0 0—1 9 1
L.A..............0 0 1 4 0 1 1 0 x—7 9 1
Lonborg, Reed (5), Brusstar (7); Sutton. W—Sutton. L—Lonborg. HR—McBride (Phil.); Baker (L.A.).

Game 3—October 7, at Philadelphia
L.A............0 2 0 1 0 0 0 0 3—6 12 2
Phil. ....0 3 0 0 0 0 0 2 0—5 6 2
Hooton, Rhoden (2), Rau (7), Sosa (8), Rautzhan (8), Garman (9); Christenson, Brusstar (4), Reed (5), Garber (7). W—Rautzhan. L—Garber. S—Garman.

Game 4—October 8, at Philadelphia
L.A..............0 2 0 0 2 0 0 0 0—4 5 0
Phil. ....0 0 0 1 0 0 0 0 0—1 7 0
John; Carlton, Reed (6), McGraw (7), Garber (9). W—John. L—Carlton. HR—Baker (L.A.).

WORLD SERIES

■ **Winner:** The Yankees won their record 21st World Series — but first since 1962.

■ **Turning point:** Ron Guidry's four-hit pitching in Game 4 — a 4-2 victory that gave the Yankees a three-games-to-one edge.

■ **Memorable moment:** Reggie Jackson's eighth-inning Game 6 blast into the center field bleachers — his record-tying third home run of the contest. The Yankees ended the classic with an 8-4 victory and Jackson finished with a Series-record five homers.

■ **Top guns:** Mike Torrez (2-0, 2.50 ERA), Jackson (.450, 5 HR, 8 RBIs), Yankees; Steve Garvey (.375), Steve Yeager (.316, 2 HR, 5 RBIs), Dodgers.

■ **MVP:** Jackson.

Linescores

Game 1—October 11, at New York
L.A.....2 0 0 0 0 0 0 0 1 0 0 0—3 6 0
N.Y.....1 0 0 0 0 1 0 1 0 0 0 1—4 11 0
Sutton, Rautzhan (8), Sosa (8), Garman (9), Rhoden (12); Gullett, Lyle (9). W—Lyle. L—Rhoden. HR—Randolph (N.Y.).

Game 2—October 12, at New York
L.A..............2 1 2 0 0 0 0 0 1—6 9 0
N.Y..............0 0 0 1 0 0 0 0 0—1 5 0
Hooton; Hunter, Tidrow (3), Clay (6), Lyle (9). W—Hooton. L—Hunter. HR—Cey, Yeager, Smith, Garvey (L.A.).

Game 3——October 14, at Los Angeles
N.Y............3 0 0 1 1 0 0 0 0—5 10 0
L.A............0 0 3 0 0 0 0 0 0—3 7 1
Torrez; John, Hough (7). W—Torrez. L—John. HR—Baker (L.A.).

Game 4—October 15, at Los Angeles
N.Y..............0 3 0 0 0 1 0 0 0—4 7 0
L.A..............0 0 2 0 0 0 0 0 0—2 4 0
Guidry; Rau, Rhoden (2), Garman (9). W—Guidry. L—Rau. HR—Lopes (L.A.); Jackson (N.Y.).

Game 5—October 16, at Los Angeles
N.Y..........0 0 0 0 0 0 2 2 0— 4 9 2
L.A. ....1 0 0 4 3 2 0 0 x—10 13 0
Gullett, Clay (5), Tidrow (6), Hunter (7); Sutton. W—Sutton. L—Gullett. HR—Yeager, Smith (L.A.); Munson, Jackson (N.Y.).

Game 6—October 18, at New York
L.A..............2 0 1 0 0 0 0 0 1—4 9 0
N.Y. ....0 2 0 3 2 0 0 1 x—8 8 1
Hooton, Sosa (4), Rau (5), Hough (7); Torrez. W—Torrez. L—Hooton. HR—Chambliss, Jackson 3 (N.Y.); Smith (L.A.).

FINAL STANDINGS

American League

East Division

Team	N.Y.	Bos.	Mil.	Bal.	Det.	Cle.	Tor.	Cal.	Chi.	K.C.	Min.	Oak.	Sea.	Tex.	W	L	Pct.	GB
New York	...	9	5	9	11	9	11	5	9	5	7	8	6	6	100	63	.613	...
Boston	7	...	10	8	12	7	11	9	7	4	9	5	7	3	99	64	.607	1
Milwaukee	10	5	...	8	8	10	12	5	7	4	4	9	5	6	93	69	.574	6.5
Baltimore	6	7	7	...	7	9	8	4	8	2	5	11	9	7	90	71	.559	9
Detroit	4	3	7	8	...	10	9	7	9	4	4	6	8	7	86	76	.531	13.5
Cleveland	6	8	5	6	5	...	10	4	2	5	5	4	8	1	69	90	.434	29
Toronto	4	4	3	7	6	4	...	3	6	5	4	4	2	7	59	102	.366	40

West Division

Team	K.C.	Cal.	Tex.	Min.	Chi.	Oak.	Sea.	Bal.	Bos.	Cle.	Det.	Mil.	N.Y.	Tor.	W	L	Pct.	GB
Kansas City	...	6	7	7	7	10	12	8	6	6	6	6	6	5	92	70	.568	...
California	9	...	5	12	8	9	9	6	2	6	4	5	5	7	87	75	.537	5
Texas	8	10	...	9	4	9	12	4	7	9	3	4	4	4	87	75	.537	5
Minnesota	8	3	6	...	7	9	6	5	2	5	6	7	3	6	73	89	.451	19
Chicago	8	7	11	8	...	7	7	1	3	8	2	4	1	4	71	90	.441	20.5
Oakland	5	6	6	6	8	...	13	0	5	6	4	1	2	7	69	93	.426	23
Seattle	3	6	3	9	8	2	...	1	3	1	2	5	5	8	56	104	.350	35

National League

East Division

Team	Phi.	Pit.	Chi.	Mon.	St.L.	N.Y.	Atl.	Cin.	Hou.	L.A.	S.D.	S.F.	W	L	Pct.	GB
Philadelphia	...	11	14	9	10	12	4	5	6	5	8	6	90	72	.556	...
Pittsburgh	7	...	11	11	9	11	10	7	8	5	5	4	88	73	.547	1.5
Chicago	4	7	...	7	15	11	7	7	6	4	7	4	79	83	.488	11
Montreal	9	7	11	...	9	8	7	4	6	4	6	5	76	86	.469	14
St. Louis	8	9	3	9	...	11	7	4	5	7	3	3	69	93	.426	21
New York	6	7	7	10	7	...	6	5	5	5	5	3	66	96	.407	24

West Division

Team	L.A.	Cin.	S.F.	S.D.	Hou.	Atl.	Chi.	Mon.	N.Y.	Phi.	Pit.	St.L.	W	L	Pct.	GB
Los Angeles	...	9	11	9	11	13	8	8	7	7	7	5	95	67	.586	...
Cincinnati	9	...	12	9	11	12	5	8	7	7	4	8	92	69	.571	2.5
San Fran.	7	6	...	10	12	7	8	7	9	6	8	9	89	73	.549	6
San Diego	9	9	8	...	10	10	5	6	7	4	7	9	84	78	.519	11
Houston	7	7	6	8	...	10	6	6	7	6	4	7	74	88	.457	21
Atlanta	5	6	11	8	8	...	5	5	6	8	2	5	69	93	.426	26

SIGNIFICANT EVENTS

- **June 31:** Larry Doby, baseball's second black player in 1947, became the game's second black manager when he took the White Sox reins from Bob Lemon.
- **August 26:** Major League umpires were forced back to work by a restraining order after a one-day strike.
- **September 23:** Angels outfielder Lyman Bostock, a .311 career hitter, was killed by an errant shotgun blast while riding in a car in Gary, Ind.
- **October 24:** Padres ace Gaylord Perry became the first pitcher to win a Cy Young Award in both leagues.
- **December 5:** Pete Rose completed his high-profile free-agency showcase by signing with the Phillies for $3.2 million over four years.

MEMORABLE MOMENTS

- **May 5:** Cincinnati's Pete Rose collected career hit No. 3,000 in a 4-3 loss to the Expos.
- **June 30:** Giants first baseman Willie McCovey crashed his 500th career home run off Jamie Easterly in a 10-9 loss to the Braves.
- **August 1:** Atlanta pitchers Larry McWilliams and Gene Garber stopped Rose's N.L. record-tying hitting streak at 44 games in a 16-4 victory over the Reds.
- **October 2:** The Yankees capped their incredible comeback from a 14-game A.L. East Division deficit with a 5-4 victory over Boston in a one-game playoff to decide the A.L. East Division title.

LEADERS

American League
BA: Rod Carew, Min., .333.
Runs: Ron LeFlore, Det., 126.
Hits: Jim Rice, Bos., 213.
TB: Jim Rice, Bos., 406.
HR: Jim Rice, Bos., 46.
RBI: Jim Rice, Bos., 139.
SB: Ron LeFlore, Det., 68.
Wins: Ron Guidry, N.Y., 25.
ERA: Ron Guidry, N.Y., 1.74.
CG: Mike Caldwell, Mil., 23.
IP: Jim Palmer, Bal., 296.
SO: Nolan Ryan, Cal., 260.
SV: Goose Gossage, N.Y., 27.

National League
BA: Dave Parker, Pit., .334.
Runs: Ivan DeJesus, Chi., 104.
Hits: Steve Garvey, L.A., 202.
TB: Dave Parker, Pit., 340.
HR: George Foster, Cin., 40.
RBI: George Foster, Cin., 120.
SB: Omar Moreno, Pit., 71.
Wins: Gaylord Perry, S.D., 21.
ERA: Craig Swan, N.Y., 2.43.
CG: Phil Niekro, Atl., 22.
IP: Phil Niekro, Atl., 334.1.
SO: J.R. Richard, Hou., 303.
SV: Rollie Fingers, S.D., 37.

A.L. 20-game winners
Ron Guidry, N.Y., 25-3
Mike Caldwell, Mil., 22-9
Jim Palmer, Bal., 21-12
Dennis Leonard, K.C., 21-17
Dennis Eckersley, Bos., 20-8
Ed Figueroa, N.Y., 20-9

N.L. 20-game winners
Gaylord Perry, S.D., 21-6
Ross Grimsley, Mon., 20-11

A.L. 100 RBIs
Jim Rice, Bos., 139
Rusty Staub, Det., 121
Larry Hisle, Mil., 115
Andre Thornton, Cle., 105

N.L. 100 RBIs
George Foster, Cin., 120
Dave Parker, Pit., 117
Steve Garvey, L.A., 113
Greg Luzinski, Phil., 101

A.L. 40 homers
Jim Rice, Bos., 46

N.L. 40 homers
George Foster, Cin., 40

Most Valuable Player
A.L.: Jim Rice, OF, Bos.
N.L.: Dave Parker, OF, Pit.

Cy Young Award
A.L.: Ron Guidry, N.Y.
N.L.: Gaylord Perry, S.D.

Rookie of the Year
A.L.: Lou Whitaker, 2B, Det.
N.L.: Bob Horner, 3B, Atl.

Hall of Fame additions
Addie Joss, P, 1902-10
Larry MacPhail, executive
Eddie Mathews, 3B, 1952-68

ALL-STAR GAME

- **Winner:** The N.L. varied its approach, spotting the A.L. a 3-0 lead before roaring to its seventh straight All-Star victory.
- **Key inning:** The eighth, when the N.L. broke a 3-3 deadlock with four runs. The tie-breaker scored on a Goose Gossage wild pitch and two more came home on Bob Boone's single.
- **Memorable moment:** A stunning third-inning collapse by A.L. starting pitcher Jim Palmer, who issued consecutive two-out walks to Joe Morgan, George Foster and Greg Luzinski to force in a run and then gave up a game-tying, two-run single to Steve Garvey.
- **Top guns:** Bruce Sutter (Cubs), Garvey (Dodgers), Boone (Phillies), N.L.; Lary Sorensen (Brewers), George Brett (Royals), Rod Carew (Twins), A.L.
- **MVP:** Garvey.

Linescore
July 11, at San Diego Stadium
A.L. ....2 0 1 0 0 0 0 0 0—3 8 1
N.L. ....0 0 3 0 0 0 0 4 x—7 10 0
Palmer (Orioles), Keough (Athletics) 3, Sorensen (Brewers) 4, Kern (Indians) 7, Guidry (Yankees) 7, Gossage (Yankees) 8; Blue (Giants), Rogers (Expos) 4, Fingers (Padres) 6, Sutter (Cubs) 8, Niekro (Braves) 9. W—Sutter. L—Gossage.

ALCS

- **Winner:** The Yankees, extended to the limit by the Royals in 1976 and '77, needed only four games to claim their third consecutive A.L. pennant.
- **Turning point:** Yankee catcher Thurman Munson's two-run, eighth-inning home run off Royals reliever Doug Bird in Game 3. The shot turned a 5-4 New York deficit into a 6-5 victory.
- **Memorable moment:** The three-home run performance of Kansas City's George Brett in the pivotal third game. Brett's three solo shots off Yankee ace Catfish Hunter were wasted.
- **Top guns:** Reggie Jackson (.462, 2 HR, 6 RBIs), Mickey Rivers (.455), Chris Chambliss (.400), Yankees; Amos Otis (.429), Brett (.389, 3 HR), Royals.
- **MVP:** Munson.

Linescores

Game 1—October 3, at Kansas City
N.Y. ....0 1 1 0 2 0 0 3 0—7 16 0
K.C. ....0 0 0 0 0 1 0 0 0—1 2 2
Beattie, Clay (6); Leonard, Mingori (5), Hrabosky (8), Bird (9). W—Beattie. L—Leonard. S—Clay. HR—Jackson (N.Y.).

Game 2—October 4, at Kansas City
N.Y. ....0 0 0 0 0 0 2 2 0— 4 12 1
K.C. ....1 4 0 0 0 0 3 2 0—10 16 1
Figueroa, Tidrow (2), Lyle (7); Gura, Pattin (7), Hrabosky (8). W—Gura. L—Figueroa. HR—Patek (K.C.).

Game 3—October 6, at New York
K.C. ....1 0 1 0 1 0 0 2 0—5 10 1
N.Y. ....0 1 0 2 0 1 0 2 x—6 10 0
Splittorff, Bird (8), Hrabosky (8); Hunter, Gossage (7). W—Gossage. L—Bird. \HR—Brett 3 (K.C.); Jackson, Munson (N.Y.).

Game 4—October 7, at New York
K.C. ....1 0 0 0 0 0 0 0 0—1 7 0
N.Y. ....0 1 0 0 0 1 0 0 x—2 4 0
Leonard; Guidry, Gossage (9). W—Guidry. L—Leonard. S—Gossage. HR—Nettles, R. White (N.Y.).

NLCS

- **Winner:** Los Angeles earned its second consecutive pennant and handed Philadelphia its third straight NLCS defeat.
- **Turning point:** The first inning of Game 4, when the Phillies loaded the bases against Dodgers starter Doug Rau with nobody out — and failed to score.
- **Memorable moment:** The two-out, 10th-inning line drive that sure-handed Phillies center fielder Garry Maddox dropped. Dodger shortstop Bill Russell followed with a game- and series-winning single.
- **Top guns:** Tommy John (1-0, 0.00 ERA), Dusty Baker (.467), Russell (.412), Steve Garvey (.389, 4 HR, 7 RBIs), Dodgers; Ted Sizemore (.385), Greg Luzinski (.375, 2 HR), Phillies.
- **MVP:** Garvey.

Linescores

Game 1—October 4, at Philadelphia
L.A. ....0 0 4 2 1 1 0 0 1—9 13 1
Phil. ....0 1 0 0 3 0 0 0 1—5 12 1
Hooton, Welch (5); Christenson, Brusstar (5), Eastwick (6), McGraw (7). W—Welch. L—Christenson. HR—Garvey 2, Lopes, Yeager (L.A.); Martin (Phil.).

Game 2—October 5, at Philadelphia
L.A. ....0 0 0 1 2 0 1 0 0—4 8 0
Phil. ....0 0 0 0 0 0 0 0 0—0 4 0
John; Ruthven, Brusstar (5), Reed (7), McGraw (9). W—John. L—Ruthven. HR—Lopes (L.A.).

Game 3—October 6, at Los Angeles
Phil. ....0 4 0 0 0 3 1 0 1—9 11 1
L.A. ....0 1 2 0 0 0 0 1 0—4 8 2
Carlton; Sutton, Rautzhan (6), Hough (8). W—Carlton. L—Sutton. HR—Carlton, Luzinski (Phil.); Garvey (L.A.).

Game 4—October 7, at Los Angeles
Phil. ......0 0 2 0 0 0 1 0 0 0—3 8 2
L.A. ....0 1 0 1 0 1 0 0 0 1—4 13 0
Lerch, Brusstar (6), Reed (7), McGraw (9); Rau, Rhoden (6), Forster (10). W—Forster. L—McGraw. HR—Luzinski, McBride (Phil.); Cey, Garvey (L.A.).

WORLD SERIES

- **Winner:** The Yankees became the first team to win a six-game Series after losing the first two games. The Dodgers became their Series victim for the eighth time.
- **Turning point:** A 10th-inning RBI single by Lou Piniella that gave the Yankees a 4-3 Game 4 victory and tied the Series at two games.
- **Memorable moment:** A Bob Welch-Reggie Jackson battle in Game 2. With the Dodgers leading 4-3 and two out in the ninth, Dodger rookie Welch needed nine pitches to strike out Yankee slugger Jackson in a classic duel with two men on base.
- **Top guns:** Denny Doyle (.438), Bucky Dent (.417, 7 RBIs), Jackson (.391, 2 HR, 8 RBIs), Yankees; Bill Russell (.423), Dave Lopes (3 HR, 7 RBIs), Dodgers.
- **MVP:** Dent.

Linescores

Game 1—October 10, at Los Angeles
N.Y. ....0 0 0 0 0 0 3 2 0— 5 9 1
L.A. ....0 3 0 3 1 0 3 1 x—11 15 2
Figueroa, Clay (2), Lindblad (5), Tidrow (7); John, Forster (8). W—John. L—Figueroa. HR—Jackson (N.Y.); Baker, Lopes 2 (L.A.).

Game 2—October 11, at Los Angeles
N.Y. ....0 0 2 0 0 0 1 0 0—3 11 0
L.A. ....0 0 0 1 0 3 0 0 x—4 7 0
Hunter, Gossage (7); Hooton, Forster (7), Welch (9). W—Hooton. L—Hunter. S—Welch. HR—Cey (L.A.).

Game 3—October 13, at New York
L.A. ....0 0 1 0 0 0 0 0 0—1 8 0
N.Y. ....1 1 0 0 0 0 3 0 x—5 10 1
Sutton, Rautzhan (7), Hough (8); Guidry. W—Guidry. L—Sutton. HR—White (N.Y.).

Game 4—October 14, at New York
L.A. ....0 0 0 0 3 0 0 0 0 0—3 6 1
N.Y. ....0 0 0 0 0 2 0 1 0 1—4 9 0
John, Forster (8), Welch (8); Figueroa, Tidrow (6), Gossage (9). W—Gossage. L—Welch. HR—Smith (L.A.).

Game 5—October 15, at New York
L.A. ....1 0 1 0 0 0 0 0 0— 2 9 3
N.Y. ....0 0 4 3 0 0 4 1 x—12 18 0
Hooton, Rautzhan (3), Hough (4); Beattie. W—Beattie. L—Hooton.

Game 6—October 17, at Los Angeles
N.Y. ....0 3 0 0 0 2 2 0 0—7 11 0
L.A. ....1 0 1 0 0 0 0 0 0—2 7 1
Hunter, Gossage (8); Sutton, Welch (6), Rau (8). W—Hunter. L—Sutton. HR—Lopes (L.A.); Jackson (N.Y.).

1979

FINAL STANDINGS

American League

East Division

Team	Bal.	Mil.	Bos.	N.Y.	Det.	Cle.	Tor.	Cal.	Chi.	K.C.	Min.	Oak.	Sea.	Tex.	W	L	Pct.	GB
Baltimore	...	8	8	5	7	8	11	9	8	6	8	8	10	6	102	57	.642	...
Milwaukee	5	...	4	9	7	9	10	5	7	7	8	6	9	9	95	66	.590	8
Boston	5	8	...	5	8	6	9	5	5	8	9	9	8	6	91	69	.569	11.5
New York	6	4	8	...	6	8	9	5	8	7	5	9	6	8	89	71	.556	13.5
Detroit	6	6	5	7	...	6	9	8	9	5	4	7	7	6	85	76	.528	18
Cleveland	5	4	7	5	6	...	8	6	6	6	8	8	7	5	81	80	.503	22
Toronto	2	3	4	4	4	5	...	5	5	3	1	8	4	5	53	109	.327	50.5

West Division

Team	Cal.	K.C.	Tex.	Min.	Chi.	Sea.	Oak.	Bal.	Bos.	Cle.	Det.	Mil.	N.Y.	Tor.	W	L	Pct.	GB
California	...	7	5	9	9	7	10	3	7	6	4	7	7	7	88	74	.543	...
Kansas City	6	...	6	7	8	7	9	6	4	6	7	5	5	9	85	77	.525	3
Texas	8	7	...	9	2	7	11	6	6	7	6	3	4	7	83	79	.512	5
Minnesota	4	6	4	...	8	10	9	4	3	4	8	4	7	11	82	80	.506	6
Chicago	4	5	11	5	...	5	9	3	6	6	3	5	4	7	73	87	.456	14
Seattle	6	6	6	3	8	...	5	2	4	5	5	3	6	8	67	95	.414	21
Oakland	3	4	2	4	4	8	...	4	3	4	5	6	3	4	54	108	.333	34

National League

East Division

Team	Pit.	Mon.	St.L.	Phi.	Chi.	N.Y.	Atl.	Cin.	Hou.	L.A.	S.D.	S.F.	W	L	Pct.	GB
Pittsburgh	...	11	11	10	12	10	8	4	8	8	7	9	98	64	.605	...
Montreal	7	...	10	11	12	15	9	6	5	6	7	7	95	65	.594	2
St. Louis	7	8	...	11	10	11	8	4	6	6	8	7	86	76	.531	12
Philadelphia	8	7	7	...	9	13	5	4	7	9	9	6	84	78	.519	14
Chicago	6	6	8	9	...	8	8	7	6	5	9	8	80	82	.494	18
New York	8	3	7	5	10	...	8	4	3	3	4	8	63	99	.389	35

West Division

Team	Cin.	Hou.	L.A.	S.F.	S.D.	Atl.	Chi.	Mon.	N.Y.	Phi.	Pit.	St.L.	W	L	Pct.	GB
Cincinnati	...	8	11	6	10	12	5	6	8	8	8	8	90	71	.559	...
Houston	10	...	10	7	14	11	6	7	9	5	4	6	89	73	.549	1.5
Los Angeles	7	8	...	14	9	6	7	6	9	3	4	6	79	83	.488	11.5
San Fran.	12	11	4	...	10	7	4	5	4	6	3	5	71	91	.438	19.5
San Diego	7	4	9	8	...	12	3	5	8	3	5	4	68	93	.422	22
Atlanta	6	7	12	11	6	...	4	1	4	7	4	4	66	94	.413	23.5

SIGNIFICANT EVENTS

■ **May 19:** Major League umpires returned to work after a six-week strike that forced baseball to play its games with amateur and minor league arbiters.

■ **July 12:** Bill Veeck's "Disco Demolition Night" promotion turned into Comiskey Park bedlam when fans refused to leave the field, and the White Sox were forced to forfeit the second game of a doubleheader to Detroit.

■ **August 2:** Yankee catcher Thurman Munson, the 1976 A.L. MVP, died at age 32 when the plane he was flying crashed short of the runway at the Akron-Canton Airport in Ohio.

■ **October 29:** Willie Mays was banned from baseball after accepting a job with a corporation that operates gambling casinos.

■ **November 13:** The N.L. crowned baseball's first co-MVPs—Pittsburgh's Willie Stargell and St. Louis' Keith Hernandez.

MEMORABLE MOMENTS

■ **May 17:** The Phillies beat the Cubs, 23-22, in an 11-homer, 50-hit slugfest at wind-swept Wrigley Field.

■ **August 13, September 12:** St. Louis' Lou Brock and Boston's Carl Yastrzemski became baseball's 14th and 15th 3,000-hit men in games against the Cubs and Yankees.

■ **September 23:** Brock stole his 938th and final base in a 7-4 victory over the Mets, moving past Billy Hamilton into first place on the all-time list.

LEADERS

American League
BA: Fred Lynn, Bos., .333.
Runs: Don Baylor, Cal., 120.
Hits: George Brett, K.C., 212.
TB: Jim Rice, Bos., 369.
HR: Gorman Thomas, Mil., 45.
RBI: Don Baylor, Cal., 139.
SB: Willie Wilson, K.C., 83.
Wins: Mike Flanagan, Bal., 23.
ERA: Ron Guidry, N.Y., 2.78.
CG: Dennis Martinez, Bal., 18.
IP: Dennis Martinez, Bal., 292.1.
SO: Nolan Ryan, Cal., 223.
SV: Mike Marshall, Min., 32.

National League
BA: Keith Hernandez, St.L., .344.
Runs: Keith Hernandez, St.L., 116.
Hits: Garry Templeton, St.L., 211.
TB: Dave Winfield, S.D., 333.
HR: Dave Kingman, Chi., 48.
RBI: Dave Winfield, S.D., 118.
SB: Omar Moreno, Pit., 77.
Wins: Joe Niekro, Hou.; Phil Niekro, Atl., 21.
ERA: J.R. Richard, Hou., 2.71.
CG: Phil Niekro, Atl., 23.
IP: Phil Niekro, Atl., 342.
SO: J.R. Richard, Hou., 313.
SV: Bruce Sutter, Chi., 37.

A.L. 20-game winners
Mike Flanagan, Bal., 23-9
Tommy John, N.Y., 21-9
Jerry Koosman, Min., 20-13

N.L. 20-game winners
Joe Niekro, Hou., 21-11
Phil Niekro, Atl., 21-20

A.L. 100 RBIs
Don Baylor, Cal., 139
Jim Rice, Bos., 130
Gorman Thomas, Mil., 123
Fred Lynn, Bos., 122
Darrell Porter, K.C., 112
Ken Singleton, Bal., 111
George Brett, K.C., 107
Cecil Cooper, Mil., 106
Willie Horton, Sea., 106
Steve Kemp, Det., 105
Buddy Bell, Tex., 101
Dan Ford, Cal., 101
Bobby Grich, Cal., 101
Sixto Lezcano, Mil., 101
Bruce Bochte, Sea., 100

N.L. 100 RBIs
Dave Winfield, S.D., 118
Dave Kingman, Chi., 115
Mike Schmidt, Phil., 114
Steve Garvey, L.A., 110
Keith Hernandez, St.L., 105

A.L. 40 homers
Gorman Thomas, Mil., 45

N.L. 40 homers
Dave Kingman, Chi., 48
Mike Schmidt, Phil., 45

Most Valuable Player
A.L.: Don Baylor, OF, Cal.
N.L.: Willie Stargell, 1B, Pit.
Keith Hernandez, 1B, St.L.

Cy Young Award
A.L.: Mike Flanagan, Bal.
N.L.: Bruce Sutter, Chi.

Rookie of the Year
A.L.: John Castino, 3B, Min.
Alfredo Griffin, SS, Tor.
N.L.: Rick Sutcliffe, P, L.A.

Hall of Fame additions
Warren Giles, executive
Willie Mays, OF, 1951-73
Hack Wilson, OF, 1923-34

ALL-STAR GAME

■ **Winner:** Lee Mazzilli tied the game with an eighth-inning homer and drove in the winner in the ninth with a bases-loaded walk as the N.L. recorded a 7-6 victory in the 50th All-Star Game.

■ **Key innings:** The eighth, when Mazzilli erased a 6-5 deficit with an opposite-field blast, and the ninth, when he drew a base on balls off Ron Guidry after Jim Kern had walked the bases loaded.

■ **Memorable moments:** Game-saving seventh- and eighth-inning throws by right fielder Dave Parker that cut down A.L. runners at third base and home plate.

■ **Top guns:** Steve Rogers (Expos), Mazzilli (Mets), Mike Schmidt (Phillies), Parker (Pirates), N.L.; Fred Lynn (Red Sox), Don Baylor (Angels), Carl Yastrzemski (Red Sox), A.L.

■ **MVP:** Parker.

Linescore
July 17, at Seattle's Kingdome
N.L. ....2 1 1 0 0 1 0 1 1—7 10 1
A.L. ....3 0 2 0 0 1 0 0 0—6 10 0
Carlton (Phillies), Andujar (Astros) 2, Rogers (Expos) 4, Perry (Padres) 6, Sambito (Astros) 6, LaCoss (Reds) 6, Sutter (Cubs) 8; Ryan (Angels), Stanley (Red Sox) 3, Clear (Angels) 5, Kern (Rangers) 7, Guidry (Yankees) 9. W—Sutter. L—Kern. HR—Lynn, A.L.; Mazzilli, N.L.

ALCS

■ **Winner:** Baltimore, winner of the first three A.L. Championship Series, ruined California's first experience in the post-season spotlight.

■ **Turning point:** A dramatic three-run homer by Baltimore pinch-hitter John Lowenstein in the 10th inning of Game 1. Lowenstein's opposite-field shot broke a 3-3 deadlock and propelled the Orioles to their first pennant since 1971.

■ **Memorable moment:** A dramatic defensive play by Orioles third baseman Doug DeCinces. With one out and the bases loaded in the fifth inning of Game 4, DeCinces made a diving stop of Jim Anderson's shot down the third-base line, stepped on third and fired to first for a rally-killing double play that preserved a 3-0 lead.

■ **Top guns:** Scott McGregor (1-0, 0.00 ERA), Eddie Murray (.417, 5 RBIs), Rick Dempsey (.400), Orioles; Rod Carew (.412), Dan Ford (2 HR, 4 RBIs), Angels.

■ **MVP:** Murray.

Linescores

Game 1—October 3, at Baltimore
Cal. ....1 0 1 0 0 1 0 0 0 0—3 7 1
Balt. ....0 0 2 1 0 0 0 0 0 3—6 6 0
Ryan, Montague (8); Palmer, Stanhouse (10). W—Stanhouse. L—Montague. HR—Ford (Cal.); Lowenstein (Bal.).

Game 2—October 4, at Baltimore
Cal. ....1 0 0 0 0 1 1 3 2—8 10 1
Balt. ....4 4 1 0 0 0 0 0 x—9 11 1
Frost, Clear (2), Aase (8); Flanagan, Stanhouse (8). W—Flanagan. L—Frost. HR—Ford (Cal.); Murray (Bal.).

Game 3—October 5, at California
Balt. ....0 0 0 1 0 1 1 0 0—3 8 3
Cal. ....1 0 0 1 0 0 0 0 2—4 9 0
D. Martinez, Stanhouse (9); Tanana, Aase (6). W—Aase. L—Stanhouse. HR—Baylor (Cal.).

Game 4—October 6, at California
Balt. ....0 0 2 1 0 0 5 0 0—8 12 1
Cal. ....0 0 0 0 0 0 0 0 0—0 6 0
McGregor; Knapp, LaRoche (3), Frost (4), Montague (7), Barlow (9). W—McGregor. L—Knapp. HR—Kelly (Bal.).

NLCS

■ **Winner:** Pittsburgh, which had been swept by Cincinnati in the 1970 and '75 NLCS, turned the tables on the Reds and earned its first World Series berth since 1971.

■ **Turning point:** A 10th-inning single by Dave Parker that gave the Pirates a 3-2 victory in Game 2.

■ **Memorable moment:** Willie Stargell's three-run, 11th-inning home run, which gave the Pirates a 5-2 Game 1 victory and all the momentum they needed.

■ **Top guns:** Stargell (.455, 2 HR, 6 RBIs), Phil Garner (.417), Pirates; Dave Concepcion (.429), Reds.

■ **MVP:** Stargell.

Linescores

Game 1—October 2, at Cincinnati
Pitt. ....0 0 2 0 0 0 0 0 0 0 3—5 10 0
Cin. ....0 0 0 2 0 0 0 0 0 0 0—2 7 0
Candelaria, Romo (8), Tekulve (8), Jackson (10), D. Robinson (11); Seaver, Hume (9), Tomlin (11). W—Jackson. L—Hume. S—D. Robinson. HR—Garner, Stargell (Pit); Foster (Cin.).

Game 2—October 3, at Cincinnati
Pitt.........0 0 0 1 1 0 0 0 0 1—3 11 0
Cin. ....0 1 0 0 0 0 0 0 1 0—2 8 0
Bibby, Jackson (8), Romo (8), Tekulve (8), Roberts (9), D. Robinson (9); Pastore, Tomlin (8), Hume (8), Bair (10). W—D. Robinson. L—Bair.

Game 3—October 5, at Pittsburgh
Cin. ....0 0 0 0 0 1 0 0 0—1 8 1
Pitt. ....1 1 2 2 0 0 0 1 x—7 7 0
LaCoss, Norman (2), Leibrandt (4), Soto (5), Tomlin (7), Hume (8); Blyleven. W—Blyleven. L—LaCoss. HR—Stargell, Madlock (Pit.); Bench (Cin.).

WORLD SERIES

■ **Winner:** Pittsburgh's "Family" beat the Orioles and became the fourth team to recover from a three-games-to-one deficit.

■ **Turning point:** After blowing a 6-3, eighth-inning lead in Game 4 to fall within a game of elimination, the Pirates regrouped to win Game 5, 7-1, behind the six-hit pitching of Jim Rooker and Bert Blyleven.

■ **Memorable moment:** Willie Stargell's two-run, sixth-inning homer that put the Pirates ahead to stay in a 4-1 Series-ending victory.

■ **Top guns:** Phil Garner (.500, 12 hits), Stargell (.400, 12 hits, 3 HR, 7 RBIs), Bill Madlock (.375), Pirates; Kiko Garcia (.400, 6 RBIs), Orioles.

■ **MVP:** Stargell.

Linescores

Game 1—October 10, at Baltimore
Pitt.............0 0 0 1 0 2 0 1 0—4 11 3
Balt. ....5 0 0 0 0 0 0 0 x—5 6 3
Kison, Rooker (1), Romo (5), D. Robinson (6), Jackson (8); Flanagan. W—Flanagan. L—Kison. HR—DeCinces (Bal.); Stargell (Pit.).

Game 2—October 11, at Baltimore
Pitt.............0 2 0 0 0 0 0 0 1—3 11 2
Balt. ....0 1 0 0 0 1 0 0 0—2 6 1
Blyleven, D. Robinson (7), Tekulve (9); Palmer, T. Martinez (8), Stanhouse (9). W—D. Robinson. L—Stanhouse. S—Tekulve. HR—Murray (Bal.).

Game 3—October 12, at Pittsburgh
Balt. ....0 0 2 5 0 0 1 0 0—8 13 0
Pitt.............1 2 0 0 0 1 0 0 0—4 9 2
McGregor; Candelaria, Romo (4), Jackson (7), Tekulve (8). W—McGregor. L—Candelaria. HR—Ayala (Bal.).

Game 4—October 13, at Pittsburgh
Balt. ....0 0 3 0 0 0 0 6 0—9 12 0
Pitt.............0 4 0 0 1 1 0 0 0—6 17 1
D. Martinez, Stewart (2), Stone (5), Stoddard (7); Bibby, Jackson (7), D. Robinson (8), Tekulve (8). W—Stoddard. L—Tekulve. HR—Stargell (Pit.).

Game 5—October 14, at Pittsburgh
Balt. ....0 0 0 0 1 0 0 0 0—1 6 2
Pitt.............0 0 0 0 0 2 2 3 x—7 13 1
Flanagan, Stoddard (7), T. Martinez (7), Stanhouse (8); Rooker, Blyleven (6). W—Blyleven. L—Flanagan.

Game 6—October 16, at Baltimore
Pitt.............0 0 0 0 0 0 2 2 0—4 10 0
Balt. ....0 0 0 0 0 0 0 0 0—0 7 1
Candelaria, Tekulve (7); Palmer, Stoddard (9). W—Candelaria. L—Palmer. S—Tekulve.

Game 7—October 17, at Baltimore
Pitt.............0 0 0 0 0 2 0 0 2—4 10 0
Balt. ....0 0 1 0 0 0 0 0 0—1 4 2
Bibby, D. Robinson (5), Jackson (5), Tekulve (8); McGregor, Stoddard (9), Flanagan (9), Stanhouse (9), T. Martinez (9), D. Martinez (9). W—Jackson. L—McGregor. S—Tekulve. HR—Dauer (Bal.); Stargell (Pit.).

FINAL STANDINGS

American League

East Division

Team	N.Y.	Bal.	Mil.	Bos.	Det.	Cle.	Tor.	Cal.	Chi.	K.C.	Min.	Oak.	Sea.	Tex.	W	L	Pct.	GB
New York	...	6	8	10	8	8	10	10	7	4	8	8	9	7	103	59	.636	...
Baltimore	7	...	7	8	10	6	11	10	6	6	10	7	6	6	100	62	.617	3
Milwaukee	5	6	...	7	6	10	5	6	7	6	7	7	9	5	86	76	.531	17
Boston	3	5	6	...	8	7	7	9	6	5	6	9	7	5	83	77	.519	19
Detroit	5	3	7	5	...	10	9	7	10	2	6	6	10	4	84	78	.519	19
Cleveland	5	7	3	6	3	...	8	6	7	5	9	6	8	6	79	81	.494	23
Toronto	3	2	8	6	4	5	...	9	7	3	5	4	6	5	67	95	.414	36

West Division

Team	K.C.	Oak.	Min.	Tex.	Chi.	Cal.	Sea.	Bal.	Bos.	Cle.	Det.	Mil.	N.Y.	Tor.	W	L	Pct.	GB
Kansas City	...	6	5	10	8	8	7	6	7	7	10	6	8	9	97	65	.599	...
Oakland	7	...	7	7	7	10	8	5	3	6	6	5	4	8	83	79	.512	14
Minnesota	8	6	...	9	8	6	7	2	6	3	6	5	4	7	77	84	.478	19.5
Texas	3	6	3	...	7	2	9	6	7	6	8	7	5	7	76	85	.472	20.5
Chicago	5	6	5	6	...	10	6	6	4	5	2	5	5	5	70	90	.438	26
California	5	3	7	11	3	...	11	2	3	4	5	6	2	3	65	95	.406	31
Seattle	6	5	6	4	7	2	...	6	5	4	2	3	3	6	59	103	.364	38

National League

East Division

Team	Phi.	Mon.	Pit.	St.L.	N.Y.	Chi.	Atl.	Cin.	Hou.	L.A.	S.D.	S.F.	W	L	Pct.	GB
Philadelphia	...	9	7	9	12	13	7	5	9	6	8	6	91	71	.562	...
Montreal	9	...	6	12	10	12	7	9	7	1	10	7	90	72	.556	1
Pittsburgh	11	12	...	10	8	10	1	6	5	6	6	8	83	79	.512	8
St. Louis	9	6	8	...	9	9	6	7	5	5	5	5	74	88	.457	17
New York	6	8	10	9	...	8	9	4	4	5	1	3	67	95	.414	24
Chicago	5	6	8	9	10	...	4	7	1	5	4	5	64	98	.395	27

West Division

Team	Hou.	L.A.	Cin.	Atl.	S.F.	S.D.	Chi.	Mon.	N.Y.	Phi.	Pit.	St.L.	W	L	Pct.	GB
Houston	...	9	10	11	11	11	11	5	8	3	7	7	93	70	.571	...
Los Angeles	10	...	9	7	13	9	7	11	7	6	6	7	92	71	.564	1
Cincinnati	8	9	...	16	7	15	5	3	8	7	6	5	89	73	.549	3.5
Atlanta	7	11	2	...	11	12	8	5	3	5	11	6	81	80	.503	11
San Fran.	7	5	11	6	...	8	7	5	9	6	4	7	75	86	.466	17
San Diego	7	9	3	6	10	...	8	2	11	4	6	7	73	89	.451	19.5

SIGNIFICANT EVENTS

■ **January 24:** Nelson Doubleday and Fred Wilpon headed a group that bought the New York Mets for a reported $21.1 million.

■ **May 23:** The owners and players agreed to defer settlement of the free-agent compensation issue, thus avoiding the first player in-season walkout in baseball history.

■ **July 30:** Houston ace J.R. Richard was rushed to the hospital after suffering a career-ending stroke during a light workout at the Astrodome.

■ **November 18:** Kansas City's George Brett, who finished the season with the highest average (.390) since 1941, captured A.L. MVP honors.

MEMORABLE MOMENTS

■ **September 30:** Oakland's Rickey Henderson, en route to the A.L.'s first 100-steal season, passed Ty Cobb's A.L. record of 96 in a 5-1 victory over Chicago.

■ **October 6:** The Astros, who allowed the Dodgers to force a division playoff with a three-game season-closing sweep, rebounded to win their first N.L. West title with a 7-1 victory.

LEADERS

American League
BA: George Brett, K.C., .390.
Runs: Willie Wilson, K.C., 133.
Hits: Willie Wilson, K.C., 230.
TB: Cecil Cooper, Mil., 335.
HR: Reggie Jackson, N.Y.; Ben Oglivie, Mil., 41.
RBI: Cecil Cooper, Mil., 122.
SB: Rickey Henderson, Oak., 100.
Wins: Steve Stone, Bal., 25.
ERA: Rudy May, N.Y., 2.46.
CG: Rick Langford, Oak., 28.
IP: Rick Langford, Oak., 290.
SO: Len Barker, Cle., 187.
SV: Goose Gossage, N.Y.; Dan Quisenberry, K.C., 33.

National League
BA: Bill Buckner, Chi., .324.
Runs: Keith Hernandez, St.L., 111.
Hits: Steve Garvey, L.A., 200.
TB: Mike Schmidt, Phil., 342.
HR: Mike Schmidt, Phil., 48.
RBI: Mike Schmidt, Phil., 121.
SB: Ron LeFlore, Mon., 97.
Wins: Steve Carlton, Phil., 24.
ERA: Don Sutton, L.A., 2.20.
CG: Steve Rogers, Mon., 14.
IP: Steve Carlton, Phil., 304.
SO: Steve Carlton, Phil., 286.
SV: Bruce Sutter, Chi., 28.

A.L. 20-game winners
Steve Stone, Bal., 25-7
Tommy John, N.Y., 22-9
Mike Norris, Oak., 22-9
Scott McGregor, Bal., 20-8
Dennis Leonard, K.C., 20-11

N.L. 20-game winners
Steve Carlton, Phil., 24-9
Joe Niekro, Hou., 20-12

A.L. 100 RBIs
Cecil Cooper, Mil., 122
George Brett, K.C., 118
Ben Oglivie, Mil., 118
Al Oliver, Tex., 117
Eddie Murray, Bal., 116
Reggie Jackson, N.Y., 111
Tony Armas, Oak., 109
Tony Perez, Bos., 105
Gorman Thomas, Mil., 105
Ken Singleton, Bal., 104
Steve Kemp, Det., 101

N.L. 100 RBIs
Mike Schmidt, Phil., 121
George Hendrick, St.L., 109
Steve Garvey, L.A., 106
Gary Carter, Mon., 101

A.L. 40 homers
Reggie Jackson, N.Y., 41
Ben Oglivie, Mil., 41

N.L. 40 homers
Mike Schmidt, Phil., 48

Most Valuable Player
A.L.: George Brett, 3B, K.C.
N.L.: Mike Schmidt, 3B, Phil.

Cy Young Award
A.L.: Steve Stone, Bal.
N.L.: Steve Carlton, Phil.

Rookie of the Year
A.L.: Joe Charboneau, OF, Cle.
N.L.: Steve Howe, P, L.A.

Hall of Fame additions
Al Kaline, OF, 1953-74
Chuck Klein, OF, 1928-44
Duke Snider, OF, 1947-64
Tom Yawkey, executive/owner

ALL-STAR GAME

■ **Winner:** The N.L., held hitless for 4⅔ innings, scored the go-ahead run on a sixth-inning error and started the new decade with a 4-2 victory, its ninth straight in All-Star competition.

■ **Key inning:** The sixth, when the N.L. took a 3-2 lead on George Hendrick's single and second baseman Willie Randolph's error on a smash hit by Dave Winfield.

■ **Memorable moment:** Ken Griffey's two-out homer in the fifth. Before the solo blast, the N.L. had not even managed a baserunner against A.L. hurlers Steve Stone and Tommy John.

■ **Top guns:** J.R. Richard (Astros), Griffey (Reds), Hendrick (Cardinals), N.L.; Stone (Orioles), Rod Carew (Angels), Fred Lynn (Red Sox), A.L.

■ **MVP:** Griffey.

Linescore

July 8, at Los Angeles' Dodger Stadium
A.L. ....0 0 0 0 2 0 0 0 0—2 7 2
N.L. ....0 0 0 0 1 2 1 0 x—4 7 0
Stone (Orioles), John (Yankees) 4, Farmer (White Sox) 6, Stieb (Blue Jays) 7, Gossage (Yankees) 8; Richard (Astros), Welch (Dodgers) 3, Reuss (Dodgers) 6, Bibby (Pirates) 7, Sutter (Cubs) 8. W—Reuss. L—John. S—Sutter. HR—Lynn, A.L.; Griffey, N.L.

ALCS

■ **Winner:** Kansas City, a Championship Series loser to the Yankees in 1976, '77 and '78, qualified for its first World Series with an impressive sweep.

■ **Turning point:** The eighth inning of Game 2, when the Royals threw out Yankee Willie Randolph at the plate, preserving a 3-2 victory. Randolph was trying to score on a two-out double by Bob Watson.

■ **Memorable moment:** A titanic three-run homer by George Brett that produced a 4-2 series-ending victory. Brett's seventh-inning blast off relief ace Goose Gossage landed in the third deck at Yankee Stadium.

■ **Top guns:** Dan Quisenberry (1-0, 1 save, 0.00 ERA), Frank White (.545), Brett (2 HR, 4 RBIs), Royals; Watson (.500), Randolph (.385), Yankees.

■ **MVP:** White.

Linescores

Game 1—October 8, at Kansas City
N.Y. ....0 2 0 0 0 0 0 0 0—2 10 1
K.C. ....0 2 2 0 0 0 1 2 x—7 10 0
Guidry, Davis (4), Underwood (8); Gura. W—Gura. L—Guidry. HR—Cerone, Piniella (N.Y.); Brett (K.C.).

Game 2—October 9, at Kansas City
N.Y. ....0 0 0 0 2 0 0 0 0—2 8 0
K.C. ....0 0 3 0 0 0 0 0 x—3 6 0
May; Leonard, Quisenberry (9). W—Leonard. L—May. S—Quisenberry. HR—Nettles (N.Y.).

Game 3—October 10, at New York
K.C. ....0 0 0 0 1 0 3 0 0—4 12 1
N.Y. ....0 0 0 0 0 2 0 0 0—2 8 0
Splittorff, Quisenberry (6); John, Gossage (7), Underwood (8). W—Quisenberry. L—Gossage. HR—White, Brett (K.C.).

NLCS

■ **Winner:** Philadelphia scored in the 10th inning of Game 5 to dispatch Houston, 8-7, and qualify for its first World Series since 1950.

■ **Turning point:** A Game 4 collision in which Pete Rose bowled over Houston catcher Bruce Bochy. Rose scored the winning run on the 10th-inning play, giving the Phillies a series-tying victory.

■ **Memorable moment:** A fourth-game controversy that wiped out Houston claims of a triple play and sparked protests by both teams. The fourth-inning confusion revolved around the "catch" or "trap" of a line drive by Astros pitcher Vern Ruhle and stopped play for 20 minutes.

■ **Top guns:** Rose (.400), Manny Trillo (.381), Phillies; Joe Niekro (10 IP, 0.00 ERA), Terry Puhl (.526), Jose Cruz (.400), Astros.

■ **MVP:** Trillo.

Linescores

Game 1—October 7, at Philadelphia
Hou. ....0 0 1 0 0 0 0 0 0—1 7 0
Phil. ....0 0 0 0 0 2 1 0 x—3 8 1
Forsch; Carlton, McGraw (8). W—Carlton. L—Forsch. S—McGraw. HR—Luzinski (Phil.).

Game 2—October 8, at Philadelphia
Hou. ......0 0 1 0 0 0 1 1 0 4—7 8 1
Phil. ......0 0 0 2 0 0 0 1 0 1—4 14 2
Ryan, Sambito (7), D. Smith (7), LaCorte (9), Andujar (10); Ruthven, McGraw (8), Reed (9), Saucier (10). W—LaCorte. L—Reed. S—Andujar.

Game 3—October 10, at Houston
Phil. ..0 0 0 0 0 0 0 0 0 0 0—0 7 1
Hou. ..0 0 0 0 0 0 0 0 0 0 1—1 6 1
Christenson, Noles (7), McGraw (8); Niekro, D. Smith (11). W—D. Smith. L—McGraw.

Game 4—October 11, at Houston
Phil. ......0 0 0 0 0 0 0 3 0 2—5 13 0
Hou. ......0 0 0 1 1 0 0 0 1 0—3 5 1
Carlton, Noles (6), Saucier (7), Reed (7), Brusstar (8), McGraw (10); Ruhle, D. Smith (8), Sambito (8). W—Brusstar. L—Sambito. S—McGraw.

Game 5—October 12, at Houston
Phil. ......0 2 0 0 0 0 0 5 0 1—8 13 2
Hou. ......1 0 0 0 0 1 3 2 0 0—7 14 0
Bystrom, Brusstar (6), Christenson (7), Reed (7), McGraw (8), Ruthven (9); Ryan, Sambito (8), Forsch (8), LaCorte (9). W—Ruthven. L—LaCorte.

WORLD SERIES

■ **Winner:** The Phillies, two-time Series qualifiers in their 97-year history, won their first fall classic with a six-game victory over the Royals — first-time Series participants.

■ **Turning point:** A two-run, ninth-inning rally that gave the Phillies a 4-3 victory in Game 5 and a three-games-to-two Series lead.

■ **Memorable moments:** The clutch pitching of Phillies reliever Tug McGraw, who recorded bases-loaded, game-ending strikeouts in Games 5 and 6.

■ **Top guns:** Steve Carlton (2-0, 2.40 ERA), McGraw (2 saves, 1.17), Mike Schmidt (.381, 2 HR, 7 RBIs), Phillies; Amos Otis (.478, 3 HR, 7 RBIs), Willie Aikens (.400, 4 HR, 8 RBIs), Royals.

■ **MVP:** Schmidt.

Linescores

Game 1—October 14, at Philadelphia
K.C. ....0 2 2 0 0 0 0 2 0—6 9 1
Phil. ....0 0 5 1 1 0 0 0 x—7 11 0
Leonard, Martin (4), Quisenberry (8); Walk, McGraw (8). W—Walk. L—Leonard. S—McGraw. HR—Otis, Aikens 2 (K.C.); McBride (Phil.).

Game 2—October 15, at Philadelphia
K.C. ....0 0 0 0 0 1 3 0 0—4 11 0
Phil. ....0 0 0 0 2 0 0 4 x—6 8 1
Gura, Quisenberry (7); Carlton, Reed (9). W—Carlton. L—Quisenberry. S—Reed.

Game 3—October 17, at Kansas City
Phil. ......0 1 0 0 1 0 0 1 0 0—3 14 0
K.C. ......1 0 0 1 0 0 1 0 0 1—4 11 0
Ruthven, McGraw (10); Gale, Martin (5), Quisenberry (8). W—Quisenberry. L—McGraw. HR—Brett, Otis (K.C.); Schmidt (Phil.).

Game 4—October 18, at Kansas City
Phil. ....0 1 0 0 0 0 1 1 0—3 10 1
K.C. ....4 1 0 0 0 0 0 0 x—5 10 2
Christenson, Noles (1), Saucier (6), Brusstar (6); Leonard, Quisenberry (8). W—Leonard. L—Christenson. S—Quisenberry. HR—Aikens 2 (K.C.).

Game 5—October 19, at Kansas City
Phil. ....0 0 0 2 0 0 0 0 2—4 7 0
K.C. ....0 0 0 0 1 2 0 0 0—3 12 2
Bystrom, Reed (6), McGraw (7); Gura, Quisenberry (7). W—McGraw. L—Quisenberry. HR—Schmidt (Phil.); Otis (K.C.).

Game 6—October 21, at Philadelphia
K.C. ....0 0 0 0 0 0 0 1 0—1 7 2
Phil. ....0 0 2 0 1 1 0 0 x—4 9 0
Gale, Martin (3), Splittorff (5), Pattin (7), Quisenberry (8); Carlton, McGraw (8). W—Carlton. L—Gale. S—McGraw.

1981

FINAL STANDINGS

American League

East Division

Team	Mil.	Bal.	N.Y.	Det.	Bos.	Cle.	Tor.	Oak.	Tex.	Chi.	K.C.	Cal.	Sea.	Min.	W	L	Pct.	GB
Milwaukee†	...	4	3	8	7	6	6	4	4	1	5	3	2	9	62	47	.569	...
Baltimore	2	...	7	6	2	4	5	7	2	3	5	6	4	6	59	46	.562	1
New York*	3	6	...	7	3	5	2	4	5	7	10	2	2	3	59	48	.551	2
Detroit	5	7	3	...	1	5	6	1	9	3	3	3	5	9	60	49	.550	2
Boston	6	2	3	6	...	7	4	7	3	5	3	2	9	2	59	49	.546	2.5
Cleveland	3	2	7	1	6	...	4	3	2	5	4	5	8	2	52	51	.505	7
Toronto	4	2	3	4	0	2	...	2	2	5	3	6	3	1	37	69	.349	23.5

West Division

Team	Oak.	Tex.	Chi.	K.C.	Cal.	Sea.	Min.	Mil.	Bal.	N.Y.	Det.	Bos.	Cle.	Tor.	W	L	Pct.	GB
Oakland*	...	4	6	3	8	6	8	2	5	3	2	5	2	10	64	45	.587	...
Texas	2	...	4	4	4	8	8	5	1	4	3	6	2	6	57	48	.543	5
Chicago	7	2	...	2	7	3	2	4	6	5	3	4	2	7	54	52	.509	8.5
Kansas City†	3	3	0	...	6	6	9	4	3	2	2	3	4	5	50	53	.485	11
California	2	2	6	0	...	6	3	4	6	2	3	4	7	6	51	59	.464	13.5
Seattle	1	5	3	7	4	...	6	2	2	3	1	3	4	3	44	65	.404	20
Minnesota	2	5	4	4	3	3	...	3	0	3	3	5	1	5	41	68	.376	23

National League

East Division

Team	St.L.	Mon.	Phi.	Pit.	N.Y.	Chi.	Cin.	L.A.	Hou.	S.F.	Atl.	S.D.	W	L	Pct.	GB
St.Louis	...	9	6	8	5	4	5	5	4	3	3	7	59	43	.578	...
Montreal†	6	...	7	10	9	7	4	2	2	2	7	4	60	48	.556	2
Philadelphia*	7	4	...	7	7	10	2	3	6	4	5	4	59	48	.551	2.5
Pittsburgh	3	3	5	...	6	10	2	1	4	3	3	6	46	56	.451	13
New York	6	3	7	3	...	8	3	1	3	2	3	2	41	62	.398	18.5
Chicago	5	4	2	4	5	...	1	6	1	5	2	3	38	65	.369	21.5

West Division

Team	Cin.	L.A.	Hou.	S.F.	Atl.	S.D.	St.L.	Mon.	Phi.	Pit.	N.Y.	Chi.	W	L	Pct.	GB
Cincinnati	...	8	8	9	5	10	0	5	5	4	7	5	66	42	.611	...
Los Angeles*	8	...	8	7	7	6	5	5	3	5	5	4	63	47	.573	4
Houston†	4	4	...	9	8	11	2	5	4	2	6	6	61	49	.555	6
San Fran.	5	5	6	...	7	7	2	5	3	7	4	5	56	55	.505	11.5
Atlanta	6	7	4	5	...	9	4	3	4	2	3	3	50	56	.472	15
San Diego	2	5	3	6	6	...	3	2	2	4	5	3	41	69	.373	26

* Won first-half division title † Won second-half division title

SIGNIFICANT EVENTS

■ **February 12:** Boston catcher Carlton Fisk was declared a free agent because the Red Sox violated the Basic Agreement by mailing his contract two days beyond the deadline.

■ **July 31:** Baseball's 50-day strike, the longest in American sports history, ended when owners and players reached agreement on the free-agent compensation issue.

■ **November 11:** Dodgers lefty Fernando Valenzuela became the first rookie to win a Cy Young when he outpointed the Reds' Tom Seaver for N.L. honors.

■ **November 25:** Milwaukee's Rollie Fingers, who earlier was named A.L. Cy Young winner, became the first relief pitcher to win an A.L. MVP.

MEMORABLE MOMENTS

■ **May 15:** Cleveland's Len Barker retired 27 consecutive Blue Jays in a 3-0 victory and pitched the first Major League perfect game in 13 years.

■ **August 10:** Philadelphia's Pete Rose collected career hit No. 3,631 in a 6-2 loss to St. Louis and moved into third place on the all-time list.

■ **September 26:** Houston's Nolan Ryan stepped into uncharted territory when he fired his record-setting fifth no-hitter, beating the Dodgers, 5-0.

■ **October 11:** The Dodgers, Expos and Yankees won decisive fifth games of special post-season series set up to determine division champions because of the 50-day baseball strike.

LEADERS

American League
BA: Carney Lansford, Bos., .336.
Runs: Rickey Henderson, Oak., 89.
Hits: Rickey Henderson, Oak., 135.
TB: Dwight Evans, Bos., 215.
HR: Tony Armas, Oak.; Dwight Evans, Bos.; Bobby Grich, Cal.; Eddie Murray, Bal., 22.
RBI: Eddie Murray, Bal., 78.
SB: Rickey Henderson, Oak., 56.
Wins: Dennis Martinez, Bal.; Steve McCatty, Oak.; Jack Morris, Det.; Pete Vuckovich, Mil., 14.
ERA: Dave Righetti, N.Y., 2.05
CG: Rick Langford, Oak., 18.
IP: Dennis Leonard, K.C., 201.2.
SO: Len Barker, Cle., 127.
SV: Rollie Fingers, Mil., 28.

National League
BA: Bill Madlock, Pit., .341.
Runs: Mike Schmidt, Phil., 78.
Hits: Pete Rose, Phil., 140.
TB: Mike Schmidt, Phil., 228.
HR: Mike Schmidt, Phil., 31.
RBI: Mike Schmidt, Phil., 91.
SB: Tim Raines, Mon., 71.
Wins: Tom Seaver, Cin., 14.
ERA: Nolan Ryan, Hou., 1.69.
CG: Fernando Valenzuela, L.A., 11.
IP: Fernando Valenzuela, L.A., 192.1.
SO: Fernando Valenzuela, L.A., 180.
SV: Bruce Sutter, St.L., 25.

Most Valuable Player
A.L.: Rollie Fingers, P, Mil.
N.L.: Mike Schmidt, 3B, Phil.

Cy Young Award
A.L.: Rollie Fingers, Mil.
N.L.: Fernando Valenzuela, L.A.

Rookie of the Year
A.L.: Dave Righetti, P, N.Y.
N.L.: Fernando Valenzuela, P, L.A.

Hall of Fame additions
Rube Foster, manager/executive, Negro Leagues
Bob Gibson, P, 1959-75
Johnny Mize, 1B, 1936-53

ALL-STAR GAME

■ **Winner:** With the All-Star Game serving as the official resumption of the season after a 50-day players' strike, the N.L. continued its winning ways by belting four home runs and stretching its winning streak to 10.

■ **Key inning:** The eighth, when Mike Schmidt drilled a two-run homer off Rollie Fingers, giving the N.L. its tying and winning runs.

■ **Memorable moment:** Gary Carter's solo blast in the seventh inning, his second home run of the game. Carter became the fifth All-Star performer to homer twice.

■ **Top guns:** Schmidt (Phillies), Carter (Expos), Dave Parker (Pirates), N.L.; Len Barker (Indians), Fred Lynn (Angels), Ken Singleton (Orioles), A.L.

■ **MVP:** Carter.

Linescore
August 9, at Cleveland Stadium
N.L.............0 0 0 0 1 1 1 2 0—5 9 1
A.L.............0 1 0 0 0 3 0 0 0—4 11 1
Valenzuela (Dodgers), Seaver (Reds) 2, Knepper (Astros) 3, Hooton (Dodgers) 5, Ruthven (Phillies) 6, Blue (Giants) 7, Ryan (Astros) 8, Sutter (Cardinals) 9; Morris (Tigers), Barker (Indians) 3, Forsch (Angels) 5, Norris (Athletics) 6, Davis (Yankees) 7, Fingers (Brewers) 8, Stieb (Blue Jays) 8. W—Blue. L—Fingers. S—Sutter. HR—Singleton, A.L.; Carter 2, Parker, Schmidt, N.L.

DIVISIONAL PLAYOFFS

Los Angeles defeated Houston, 3 games to 2
Montreal defeated Philadelphia, 3 games to 2
NY Yankees defeated Milwaukee, 3 games to 2
Oakland defeated Kansas City, 3 games to 0

ALCS

■ **Winner:** The New York Yankees captured their 33rd pennant with a 1-2-3 Championship Series victory over Oakland.

■ **Turning point:** The first inning of Game 1, when Yankee third baseman Graig Nettles drilled a three-run double, giving lefty Tommy John and two relievers all the runs they needed for a 3-1 victory.

■ **Memorable moment:** The ninth inning of Game 3, when Nettles drilled another three-run double, putting the wraps on a 4-0 series-ending victory.

■ **Top guns:** Nettles (.500, 1 HR, 9 RBIs), Jerry Mumphrey (.500), Larry Milbourne (.462), Yankees; Rickey Henderson (.364), Athletics.

■ **MVP:** Nettles.

Linescores

Game 1—October 13 at New York
Oakland........0 0 0 0 1 0 0 0 0—1 6 1
N.Y. ....3 0 0 0 0 0 0 0 x—3 7 1
Norris, Underwood (8); John, Davis (7), Gossage (8). W—John. L—Norris. S—Gossage.

Game 2—October 14, at New York
Oakland....0 0 1 2 0 0 0 0 0— 3 11 1
N.Y. ....1 0 0 7 0 1 4 0 x—13 19 0
McCatty, Beard (4), Jones (5), Kingman (7), Owchinko (7); May, Frazier (4). W—Frazier. L—McCatty. HR—Piniella, Nettles (N.Y.).

Game 3—October 15, at Oakland
N.Y. ....0 0 0 0 0 1 0 0 3—4 10 0
Oakland......0 0 0 0 0 0 0 0 0—0 5 2
Righetti, Davis (7), Gossage (9); Keough, Underwood (9). W—Righetti. L—Keough. HR—Randolph (N.Y.).

NLCS

■ **Winner:** The Los Angeles Dodgers ruined Montreal's bid to become the first Canadian qualifier for a World Series with a dramatic ninth-inning home run in the fifth game.

■ **Turning point:** An eighth-inning Game 4 home run by Steve Garvey that broke a 1-1 tie and propelled the Dodgers to an elimination-saving 7-1 victory.

■ **Memorable moment:** A ninth-inning series-winning home run by Dodgers outfielder Rick Monday off Expos ace Steve Rogers in Game 5 at frigid Montreal.

■ **Top guns:** Burt Hooton (2-0, 0.00 ERA), Monday (.333), Dusty Baker (.316), Dodgers; Ray Burris (1-0, 0.53 ERA), Gary Carter (.438), Expos.

■ **MVP:** Hooton.

Linescores

Game 1—October 13, at Los Angeles
Montreal......0 0 0 0 0 0 0 0 1—1 9 0
L.A. ....0 2 0 0 0 0 0 3 x—5 8 0
Gullickson, Reardon (8); Hooton, Welch (8), Howe (9). W—Hooton. L—Gullickson. HR—Guerrero, Scioscia (L.A.).

Game 2—October 14, at Los Angeles
Montreal ....0 2 0 0 0 1 0 0 0—3 10 1
L.A. ....0 0 0 0 0 0 0 0 0—0 5 1
Burris; Valenzuela, Niedenfuer (7), Forster (7), Pena (7), Castillo (9). W—Burris. L—Valenzuela.

Game 3—October 16, at Montreal
L.A. ....0 0 0 1 0 0 0 0 0—1 7 0
Montreal ......0 0 0 0 0 4 0 0 x—4 7 1
Reuss, Pena (8); Rogers. W—Rogers. L—Reuss. HR—White (Mon.).

Game 4—October 17, at Montreal
L.A. ....0 0 1 0 0 0 0 2 4—7 12 1
Montreal ....0 0 0 1 0 0 0 0 0—1 5 1
Hooton, Welch (8), Howe (9); Gullickson, Fryman (8), Sosa (9), Lee (9). W—Hooton. L—Gullickson. HR—Garvey (L.A.).

Game 5—October 19, at Montreal
L.A. ....0 0 0 0 1 0 0 0 1—2 6 0
Montreal ......1 0 0 0 0 0 0 0 0—1 3 1
Valenzuela, Welch (9); Burris, Rogers (9). W—Valenzuela. L—Rogers. S—Welch. HR—Monday (L.A.).

WORLD SERIES

■ **Winner:** The Dodgers brought the strike-shortened season to an end by duplicating the Yankees' 1978 feat against them—four straight victories after two opening losses.

■ **Turning point:** After falling behind 4-0 and 6-3 in Game 4, the Dodgers rallied for an 8-7 victory that squared the Series at two games.

■ **Memorable moment:** Back-to-back, seventh-inning home runs by Pedro Guerrero and Steve Yeager that gave Jerry Reuss a 2-1 victory over Ron Guidry and the Yankees in the pivotal fifth game.

■ **Top guns:** Steve Garvey (.417), Ron Cey (.350, 6 RBIs), Guerrero (.333, 2 HR, 7 RBIs), Dodgers; Bob Watson (.318, 2 HR, 7 RBIs), Yankees.

■ **Co-MVPs:** Guerrero, Yeager, Cey.

Linescores

Game 1—October 20, at New York
L.A. ....0 0 0 0 1 0 0 2 0—3 5 0
N.Y. ....3 0 1 1 0 0 0 0 x—5 6 0
Reuss, Castillo (3), Goltz (4), Niedenfuer (5), Stewart (8); Guidry, Davis (8), Gossage (8). W—Guidry. L—Reuss. S—Gossage. HR—Yeager (L.A.); Watson (N.Y.).

Game 2—October 21, at New York
L.A. ....0 0 0 0 0 0 0 0 0—0 4 2
N.Y. ....0 0 0 0 1 0 0 2 x—3 6 1
Hooton, Forster (7), Howe (8), Stewart (8); John, Gossage (8). W—John. L—Hooton. S—Gossage.

Game 3—October 23, at Los Angeles
N.Y. ....0 2 2 0 0 0 0 0 0—4 9 0
L.A. ....3 0 0 0 2 0 0 0 x—5 11 1
Righetti, Frazier (3), May (5), Davis (8); Valenzuela. W—Valenzuela. L—Frazier. HR—Cey (L.A.); Watson, Cerone (N.Y.).

Game 4—October 24, at Los Angeles
N.Y. ....2 1 1 0 0 2 0 1 0—7 13 1
L.A. ....0 0 2 0 1 3 2 0 x—8 14 2
Reuschel, May (4), Davis (5), Frazier (6), John (7); Welch, Goltz (1), Forster (4), Niedenfuer (5), Howe (7). W—Howe. L—Frazier. HR—Randolph, Jackson (N.Y.); Johnstone (L.A.).

Game 5—October 25, at Los Angeles
N.Y. ....0 1 0 0 0 0 0 0 0—1 5 0
L.A. ....0 0 0 0 0 0 2 0 x—2 4 3
Guidry, Gossage (8); Reuss. W—Reuss. L—Guidry. HR—Guerrero, Yeager (L.A.).

Game 6—October 28, at New York
L.A. ....0 0 0 1 3 4 0 1 0—9 13 1
N.Y. ....0 0 1 0 0 1 0 0 0—2 7 2
Hooton, Howe (6); John, Frazier (5), Davis (6), Reuschel (6), May (7), LaRoche (9). W—Hooton. L—Frazier. S—Howe. HR—Randolph (N.Y.); Guerrero (L.A.).

FINAL STANDINGS

American League

East Division

Team	Mil.	Bal.	Bos.	Det.	N.Y.	Tor.	Cle.	Cal.	Chi.	K.C.	Min.	Oak.	Sea.	Tex.	W	L	Pct.	GB
Milwaukee	...	4	9	10	8	9	6	6	9	5	7	7	8	7	95	67	.586	...
Baltimore	9	...	4	7	11	10	6	7	5	4	8	7	7	9	94	68	.580	1
Boston	4	9	...	8	7	7	6	7	4	6	6	8	7	10	89	73	.549	6
Detroit	3	6	5	...	8	6	7	7	3	6	9	9	6	8	83	79	.512	12
New York	5	2	6	5	...	6	9	5	4	7	10	7	6	7	79	83	.488	16
Toronto	4	3	6	7	7	...	6	4	4	8	7	9	5	8	78	84	.481	17
Cleveland	7	7	7	6	4	7	...	4	6	2	8	4	9	7	78	84	.481	17

West Division

Team	Cal.	K.C.	Chi.	Sea.	Oak.	Tex.	Min.	Bal.	Bos.	Cle.	Det.	Mil.	N.Y.	Tor.	W	L	Pct.	GB
California	...	7	8	10	9	8	7	5	5	8	5	6	7	8	93	69	.574	...
Kansas City	6	...	10	7	7	7	7	8	6	10	6	7	5	4	90	72	.556	3
Chicago	5	3	...	6	9	8	7	7	8	6	9	3	8	8	87	75	.537	6
Seattle	3	6	7	...	7	9	8	5	5	3	6	4	6	7	76	86	.469	17
Oakland	4	6	4	6	...	5	10	5	4	8	3	5	5	3	68	94	.420	25
Texas	5	6	5	4	8	...	8	3	2	5	4	5	5	4	64	98	.395	29
Minnesota	6	6	6	5	3	5	...	4	6	4	3	5	2	5	60	102	.370	33

National League

East Division

Team	St.L.	Phi.	Mon.	Pit.	Chi.	N.Y.	Atl.	Cin.	Hou.	L.A.	S.D.	S.F.	W	L	Pct	.GB
St. Louis	...	11	8	11	12	12	5	7	6	5	8	7	92	70	.568	...
Philadelphia	7	...	10	9	9	11	6	7	5	8	7	10	89	73	.549	3
Montreal	10	8	...	7	12	11	7	8	8	4	7	4	86	76	.531	6
Pittsburgh	7	9	11	...	9	10	8	8	3	7	6	6	84	78	.519	8
Chicago	6	9	6	9	...	9	4	6	9	5	4	6	73	89	.451	19
New York	6	7	7	8	9	...	3	5	4	6	6	4	65	97	.401	27

West Division

Team	Atl.	L.A.	S.F.	S.D.	Hou.	Cin.	Chi.	Mon.	N.Y.	Phi.	Pit.	St.L.	W	L	Pct.	GB
Atlanta	...	7	8	11	10	14	8	5	9	6	4	7	89	73	.549	...
Los Angeles	11	..	9	9	11	11	7	8	6	4	5	7	88	74	.543	1
San Fran.	10	9	...	8	13	12	6	8	8	2	6	5	87	75	.537	2
San Diego	7	9	10	...	9	12	8	5	6	5	6	4	81	81	.500	8
Houston	8	7	5	9	...	11	3	4	8	7	9	6	77	85	.475	12
Cincinnati	4	7	6	6	7	...	6	4	7	5	4	5	61	101	.377	28

SIGNIFICANT EVENTS

■ **April 6:** Seattle spoiled the Metrodome inaugural for Minnesota fans with an 11-7 Opening Day victory over the Twins.

■ **April 22:** The Reds defeated Atlanta, 2-1, handing the Braves their first loss after a season-opening record 13 consecutive victories.

■ **October 3:** The Brewers captured their first A.L. East title when they defeated Baltimore, 10-2, in a winner-take-all final-day battle.

■ **October 3:** The Braves, final-day losers to San Diego, clinched their first division title since 1969 when San Francisco defeated the Dodgers, 5-3, on Joe Morgan's three-run homer.

■ **October 26:** Phillies ace Steve Carlton captured his record fourth N.L. Cy Young Award.

■ **November 1:** Owners ended the 14-year reign of commissioner Bowie Kuhn when they voted not to renew his contract at a meeting in Chicago.

MEMORABLE MOMENTS

■ **May 6:** Gaylord Perry pitched the Mariners to a 7-3 victory over the Yankees and became the 15th member of baseball's 300-win club.

■ **June 22:** Philadelphia's Pete Rose doubled off the Cardinals' John Stuper and moved into second place on the all-time hit list with 3,772.

■ **August 27:** Oakland's Rickey Henderson claimed the one-season basestealing record when he swiped four in a game at Milwaukee, giving him 122 en route to a final total of 130.

LEADERS

American League
BA: Willie Wilson, K.C., .332.
Runs: Paul Molitor, Mil., 136.
Hits: Robin Yount, Mil., 210.
TB: Robin Yount, Mil., 367.
HR: Reggie Jackson, Cal.; Gorman Thomas, Mil., 39.
RBI: Hal McRae, K.C., 133.
SB: Rickey Henderson, Oak., 130.
Wins: LaMarr Hoyt, Chi., 19.
ERA: Rick Sutcliffe, Cle., 2.96.
CG: Dave Stieb, Tor., 19.
IP: Dave Stieb, Tor., 288.1.
SO: Floyd Bannister, Sea., 209.
SV: Dan Quisenberry, K.C., 35.

National League
BA: Al Oliver, Mon., .331.
Runs: Lonnie Smith, St.L., 120.
Hits: Al Oliver, Mon., 204.
TB: Al Oliver, Mon., 317.
HR: Dave Kingman, N.Y., 37.
RBI: Dale Murphy, Atl.; Al Oliver, Mon., 109.
SB: Tim Raines, Mon., 78.
Wins: Steve Carlton, Phil., 23.
ERA: Steve Rogers, Mon., 2.40.
CG: Steve Carlton, Phil., 19.
IP: Steve Carlton, Phil., 295.2.
SO: Steve Carlton, Phil., 286.
SV: Bruce Sutter, St.L., 36.

N.L. 20-game winner
Steve Carlton, Phil., 23-11

A.L. 100 RBIs
Hal McRae, K.C., 133
Cecil Cooper, Mil., 121
Andre Thornton, Cle., 116
Robin Yount, Mil., 114
Gorman Thomas, Mil., 112
Eddie Murray, Bal., 110
Dave Winfield, N.Y., 106
Harold Baines, Chi., 105
Greg Luzinski, Chi., 102
Ben Oglivie, Mil., 102
Reggie Jackson, Cal., 101

N.L. 100 RBIs
Dale Murphy, Atl., 109
Al Oliver, Mon., 109
Bill Buckner, Chi., 105
George Hendrick, St.L., 104
Jack Clark, S.F., 103
Jason Thompson, Pit., 101
Pedro Guerrero, L.A., 100

Most Valuable Player
A.L.: Robin Yount, SS, Mil.
N.L.: Dale Murphy, OF, Atl.

Cy Young Award
A.L.: Pete Vuckovich, Mil.
N.L.: Steve Carlton, Phil.

Rookie of the Year
A.L.: Cal Ripken, SS, Bal.
N.L.: Steve Sax, 2B, L.A.

Hall of Fame additions
Hank Aaron, OF, 1954-76
Happy Chandler, commissioner
Travis Jackson, SS, 1922-36
Frank Robinson, OF, 1956-76

ALL-STAR GAME

■ **Winner:** The N.L. made it 11 in a row and 19 of 20 with a 4-1 victory at Montreal — the first midsummer classic played on foreign soil.

■ **Key inning:** The second, when Dave Concepcion pounded a two-run homer, giving N.L. pitchers all the runs they would need.

■ **Memorable moment:** A sixth-inning run manufactured by a pair of Expos. Al Oliver thrilled the home fans with a double and Gary Carter singled him home.

■ **Top guns:** Steve Carlton (Phillies), Oliver (Expos), Concepcion (Reds), N.L.; Rickey Henderson (Athletics), George Brett (Royals), A.L.

■ **MVP:** Concepcion.

Linescore
July 13, at Montreal's Olympic Stadium
A.L. ....1 0 0 0 0 0 0 0 0—1 8 2
N.L. ....0 2 1 0 0 1 0 0 x—4 8 1
Eckersley (Red Sox), Clancy (Blue Jays) 4, Bannister (Mariners) 5, Quisenberry (Royals) 6, Fingers (Brewers) 8; Rogers (Expos), Carlton (Phillies) 4, Soto (Reds) 6, Valenzuela (Dodgers) 8, Minton (Giants) 8, Howe (Dodgers) 9, Hume (Reds) 9. W—Rogers. L—Eckersley. S—Hume. HR—Concepcion, N.L.

ALCS

■ **Winner:** In a battle of first-time pennant hopefuls, the Milwaukee Brewers defeated California and became the first team to recover from a two-games-to-none deficit in a League Championship Series.

■ **Turning point:** The unexpected Game 4 boost the Brewers received from substitute left fielder Mark Brouhard, who collected three hits, belted a home run and drove in three runs in Milwaukee's elimination-saving 9-5 victory.

■ **Memorable moment:** Cecil Cooper's two-run, seventh-inning single that wiped out a 3-2 Angels lead and gave the Brewers a 4-3 Game 5 victory and the franchise's first World Series berth.

■ **Top guns:** Charlie Moore (.462), Paul Molitor (.316, 2 HR, 5 RBIs), Brouhard (.750), Brewers; Bruce Kison (1-0, 1.93 ERA), Fred Lynn (.611, 5 RBIs), Don Baylor (10 RBIs), Angels.

■ **MVP:** Lynn.

Linescores

Game 1—October 5, at California
Mil. ....0 2 1 0 0 0 0 0 0—3 7 2
Cal. ....1 0 4 2 1 0 0 0 x—8 10 0
Caldwell, Slaton (4), Ladd (7), Bernard (8); John. W—John. L—Caldwell. HR—Thomas (Mil.); Lynn (Cal.).

Game 2—October 6, at California
Mil. ....0 0 0 0 2 0 0 0 0—2 5 0
Cal. ....0 2 1 1 0 0 0 0 x—4 6 0
Vuckovich; Kison. W—Kison. L—Vuckovich. HR—Re. Jackson (Cal.); Molitor (Mil.).

Game 3—October 8, at Milwaukee
Cal. ....0 0 0 0 0 0 0 3 0—3 8 0
Mil. ....0 0 0 3 0 0 2 0 x—5 6 0
Zahn, Witt (4), Hassler (7); Sutton, Ladd (8). W—Sutton. L—Zahn. S—Ladd. HR—Molitor (Mil.); Boone (Cal).

Game 4—October 9, at Milwaukee
Cal. ....0 0 0 0 0 1 0 4 0—5 5 3
Mil. ....0 3 0 3 0 1 0 2 x—9 9 2
John, Goltz (4), Sanchez (8); Haas, Slaton (8). W—Haas. L—John. S—Slaton. HR—Baylor (Cal.); Brouhard (Mil.).

Game 5—October 10, at Milwaukee
Cal. ....1 0 1 1 0 0 0 0 0—3 11 1
Mil. ....1 0 0 1 0 0 2 0 x—4 6 4
Kison, Sanchez (6), Hassler (7); Vuckovich, McClure (7), Ladd (9). W—McClure. L—Sanchez. S—Ladd. HR—Oglivie (Mil.).

NLCS

■ **Winner:** The Atlanta Braves, who were swept by the New York Mets in the first NLCS in 1969, suffered the same fate against St. Louis in the franchise's second post-season appearance.

■ **Turning point:** A Game 1 rainstorm that wiped out a 1-0 Braves lead after 4½ innings and forced Atlanta to bypass ace Phil Niekro in the rescheduled opener.

■ **Memorable moment:** Ken Oberkfell's ninth-inning line drive that eluded Braves center fielder Brett Butler and drove home David Green, giving the Cardinals a 4-3 Game 2 victory.

■ **Top guns:** Bob Forsch (1-0, 0.00 ERA), Darrell Porter (.556), Ozzie Smith (.556), Cardinals; Claudell Washington (.333), Braves.

■ **MVP:** Porter.

Linescores

Game 1—October 7, at St. Louis
Atlanta ....0 0 0 0 0 0 0 0 0—0 3 0
St. Louis ....0 0 1 0 0 5 0 1 x—7 13 1
Perez, Bedrosian (6), Moore (6), Walk (8); Forsch. W—Forsch. L—Perez.

Game 2—October 9, at St. Louis
Atlanta ....0 0 2 0 1 0 0 0 0—3 6 0
St. Louis ......1 0 0 0 0 1 0 1 1—4 9 1
Niekro, Garber (7); Stuper, Bair (7), Sutter (8). W—Sutter. L—Garber.

Game 3—October 10, at Atlanta
St. Louis ....0 4 0 0 1 0 0 0 1—6 12 0
Atlanta ......0 0 0 0 0 0 2 0 0—2 6 1
Andujar, Sutter (7); Camp, Perez (2), Moore (5), Mahler (7), Bedrosian (8), Garber (9). W—Andujar. L—Camp. S—Sutter. HR—McGee (St.L.).

WORLD SERIES

■ **Winner:** The resilient Cardinals tamed "Harvey's Wallbangers" and spoiled the Brewers' first World Series.

■ **Turning point:** A special Game 3 performance by center fielder Willie McGee, who stepped out of character to hit two home runs and added two spectacular catches in a 6-2 victory that gave the Cardinals their first Series lead.

■ **Memorable moment:** A two-run single by Keith Hernandez and a run-scoring single by George Hendrick in a three-run sixth inning that rallied the Cardinals to a seventh-game 6-3 victory.

■ **Top guns:** Joaquin Andujar (2-0, 1.35 ERA), Dane Iorg (.529), Darrell Porter (5 RBIs), Hernandez (8 RBIs), Cardinals; Mike Caldwell (2-0, 2.04), Robin Yount (.414, 12 hits, 6 RBIs), Paul Molitor (.355), Brewers.

■ **MVP:** Porter.

Linescores

Game 1—October 12, at St. Louis
Mil. ....2 0 0 1 1 2 0 0 4—10 17 0
St. Louis ..0 0 0 0 0 0 0 0 0— 0 3 1
Caldwell; Forsch, Kaat (6), LaPoint (8), Lahti (9). W—Caldwell. L—Forsch. HR—Simmons (Mil.).

Game 2—October 13, at St. Louis
Mil. ....0 1 2 0 1 0 0 0 0—4 10 1
St. Louis ....0 0 2 0 0 2 0 1 x—5 8 0
Sutton, McClure (7), Ladd (8); Stuper, Kaat (5), Bair (5), Sutter (7). W—Sutter. L—McClure. HR—Simmons (Mil.).

Game 3—October 15, at Milwaukee
St. Louis ......0 0 0 0 3 0 2 0 1—6 6 1
Mil. ....0 0 0 0 0 0 0 2 0—2 5 3
Andujar, Kaat (7), Bair (7), Sutter (7); Vuckovich, McClure (9). W—Andujar. L—Vuckovich. S—Sutter. HR—McGee 2 (St.L.); Cooper (Mil.).

Game 4—October 16, at Milwaukee
St. Louis ....1 3 0 0 0 1 0 0 0—5 8 1
Mil. ....0 0 0 0 1 0 6 0 x—7 10 2
LaPoint, Bair (7), Kaat (7), Lahti (7); Haas, Slaton (6), McClure (8). W—Slaton. L—Bair. S—McClure.

Game 5—October 17, at Milwaukee
St. Louis ....0 0 1 0 0 0 1 0 2—4 15 2
Mil. ....1 0 1 0 1 0 1 2 x—6 11 1
Forsch, Sutter (8); Caldwell, McClure (9). W—Caldwell. L—Forsch. S—McClure. HR—Yount (Mil.).

Game 6—October 19, at St. Louis
Mil. ....0 0 0 0 0 0 0 0 1— 1 4 4
St. Louis ..0 2 0 3 2 6 0 0 x—13 12 1
Sutton, Slaton (5), Medich (6), Bernard (8); Stuper. W—Stuper. L—Sutton. HR—Porter, Hernandez (St.L.).

Game 7—October 20, at St. Louis
Mil. ....0 0 0 0 1 2 0 0 0—3 7 0
St. Louis ....0 0 0 1 0 3 0 2 x—6 15 1
Vuckovich, McClure (6), Haas (6), Caldwell (8); Andujar, Sutter (8). W—Andujar. L—McClure. S—Sutter. HR—Oglivie (Mil.).

FINAL STANDINGS

American League

East Division

Team	Bal.	Det.	N.Y.	Tor.	Mil.	Bos.	Cle.	Cal.	Chi.	K.C.	Min.	Oak.	Sea.	Tex.	W	L	Pct.	GB
Baltimore	...	5	6	7	11	8	6	7	7	8	8	8	8	9	98	64	.605	...
Detroit	8	...	5	6	6	9	8	8	4	7	9	6	8	8	92	70	.568	6
New York	7	8	...	7	9	6	7	7	4	6	8	8	7	7	91	71	.562	7
Toronto	6	7	6	...	5	6	9	8	7	6	7	6	8	8	89	73	.549	9
Milwaukee	2	7	4	8	...	9	10	6	8	6	8	6	5	8	87	75	.537	11
Boston	5	4	7	7	4	...	7	6	6	5	5	8	7	7	78	84	.481	20
Cleveland	7	5	6	4	3	6	...	4	4	7	6	7	8	3	70	92	.432	28

West Division

Team	Chi.	K.C.	Tex.	Oak.	Cal.	Min.	Sea.	Bal.	Bos.	Cle.	Det.	Mil.	N.Y.	Tor.	W	L	Pct.	GB
Chicago	...	9	8	8	10	8	12	5	6	8	8	4	8	5	99	63	.611	...
Kansas City	4	...	8	7	7	6	8	4	7	5	5	6	6	6	79	83	.488	20
Texas	5	5	...	11	7	8	7	3	5	9	4	4	5	4	77	85	.475	22
Oakland	5	6	2	...	8	9	9	4	4	5	6	6	4	6	74	88	.457	25
California	3	6	6	5	...	6	6	5	6	8	4	6	5	4	70	92	.432	29
Minnesota	5	7	5	4	7	...	9	4	7	6	3	4	4	5	70	92	.432	29
Seattle	1	5	6	4	7	4	...	4	5	4	4	7	5	4	60	102	.370	39

National League

East Division

Team	Phi.	Pit.	Mon.	St.L.	Chi.	N.Y.	Atl.	Cin.	Hou.	L.A.	S.D.	S.F.	W	L	Pct.	GB
Philadelphia	...	11	10	14	13	12	5	6	8	1	5	5	90	72	.556	...
Pittsburgh	7	...	10	10	9	9	6	6	6	6	9	6	84	78	.519	6
Montreal	8	8	...	9	11	8	5	8	4	5	8	8	82	80	.506	8
St. Louis	4	8	9	...	8	12	5	6	10	3	6	8	79	83	.488	11
Chicago	5	9	7	10	...	9	7	4	5	6	5	4	71	91	.438	19
New York	6	9	10	6	9	...	4	5	3	5	6	5	68	94	.420	22

West Division

Team	L.A.	Atl.	Hou.	S.D.	S.F.	Cin.	Chi.	Mon.	N.Y.	Phi.	Pit.	St.L.	W	L	Pct.	GB
Los Angeles	...	11	12	6	5	11	6	7	7	11	6	9	91	71	.562	...
Atlanta	7	...	11	9	9	12	5	7	8	7	6	7	88	74	.543	3
Houston	6	7	...	11	12	13	7	8	9	4	6	2	85	77	.525	6
San Diego	12	9	7	...	11	9	7	4	6	7	3	6	81	81	.500	10
San Fran.	13	9	6	7	...	8	8	4	7	7	6	4	79	83	.488	12
Cincinnati	7	6	5	9	10	...	8	4	7	6	6	6	74	88	.457	17

SIGNIFICANT EVENTS

■ **April 7:** ABC and NBC agreed to share a lucrative six-year television contract that would pay baseball $1.2 billion.

■ **February 8:** Former Yankee great Mickey Mantle was ordered to sever ties with baseball after taking a job with an Atlantic City hotel and casino.

■ **July 29:** The N.L.-record ironman streak of San Diego's Steve Garvey ended at 1,207 games when he dislocated his thumb in a home-plate collision against the Braves.

■ **November 17:** A U.S. magistrate handed three members of the 1983 Royals, Willie Wilson, Willie Aikens and Jerry Martin, three-month prison sentences for attempting to purchase cocaine.

■ **December 8:** Dr. Bobby Brown was elected as the successor to retiring A.L. president Lee MacPhail.

■ **December 19:** Former Cy Young winner Vida Blue became the fourth Kansas City player to receive a three-month prison sentence for attempting to purchase cocaine.

MEMORABLE MOMENTS

■ **July 24:** A two-out, game-winning home run by Kansas City's George Brett off Yankee reliever Goose Gossage was nullified by umpires who said Brett's bat was illegally covered by pine tar—a controversial ruling that later would be overturned.

■ **June 26:** Mets veteran Rusty Staub collected his record-tying eighth consecutive pinch hit in an 8-4 loss to the Phillies.

■ **September 23:** Philadelphia lefty Steve Carlton became baseball's 16th 300-game winner when he defeated St. Louis, 6-2.

LEADERS

American League
BA: Wade Boggs, Bos., .361.
Runs: Cal Ripken, Bal., 121.
Hits: Cal Ripken, Bal., 211.
TB: Jim Rice, Bos., 344.
HR: Jim Rice, Bos., 39.
RBI: Cecil Cooper, Mil.; Jim Rice, Bos., 126.
SB: Rickey Henderson, Oak., 108.
Wins: LaMarr Hoyt, Chi., 24.
ERA: Rick Honeycutt, Tex., 2.42.
CG: Ron Guidry, N.Y., 21.
IP: Jack Morris, Det., 293.2.
SO: Jack Morris, Det., 232.
SV: Dan Quisenberry, K.C., 45.

National League
BA: Bill Madlock, Pit., .323.
Runs: Tim Raines, Mon., 133.
Hits: Jose Cruz, Hou.; Andre Dawson, Mon., 189.
TB: Andre Dawson, Mon., 341.
HR: Mike Schmidt, Phil., 40.
RBI: Dale Murphy, Atl., 121.
SB: Tim Raines, Mon., 90.
Wins: John Denny, Phil., 19.
ERA: Atlee Hammaker, S.F., 2.25.
CG: Mario Soto, Cin., 18.
IP: Steve Carlton, Phil., 283.2.
SO: Steve Carlton, Phil., 275.
SV: Lee Smith, Chi., 29.

A.L. 20-game winners
LaMarr Hoyt, Chi., 24-10
Rich Dotson, Chi., 22-7
Ron Guidry, N.Y., 21-9
Jack Morris, Det., 20-13

A.L. 100 RBIs
Cecil Cooper, Mil., 126
Jim Rice, Bos., 126
Dave Winfield, N.Y., 116
Lance Parrish, Det., 114
Eddie Murray, Bal., 111
Ted Simmons, Mil., 108
Tony Armas, Bos., 107
Willie Upshaw, Tor., 104
Cal Ripken, Bal., 102
Ron Kittle, Chi., 100

N.L. 100 RBIs
Dale Murphy, Atl., 121
Andre Dawson, Mon., 113
Mike Schmidt, Phil., 109
Pedro Guerrero, L.A., 103

N.L. 40 homers
Mike Schmidt, Phil., 40

Most Valuable Player
A.L.: Cal Ripken, SS, Bal.
N.L.: Dale Murphy, OF, Atl.

Cy Young Award
A.L.: LaMarr Hoyt, Chi.
N.L.: John Denny, Phil.

Rookie of the Year
A.L.: Ron Kittle, OF, Chi.
N.L.: Darryl Strawberry, OF, N.Y.

Manager of the Year
A.L.: Tony La Russa, Chi.
N.L.: Tommy Lasorda, L.A.

Hall of Fame additions
Walter Alston, manager
George Kell, 3B, 1943-57
Juan Marichal, P, 1960-75
Brooks Robinson, 3B, 1955-77

ALL-STAR GAME

■ **Winner:** The A.L. snapped its frustrating 11-game All-Star losing streak with a 13-3 rout in a special 50th-anniversary celebration of the midsummer classic at Chicago's Comiskey Park.

■ **Key inning:** A record seven-run third that gave the A.L. a 9-1 lead and set the course for its first victory since 1971.

■ **Memorable moment:** Fred Lynn's third-inning bases-loaded homer off Atlee Hammaker — the first grand slam in 54 All-Star Games.

■ **Top guns:** Dave Stieb (Blue Jays), Lynn (Angels), Jim Rice (Red Sox), George Brett (Royals), Dave Winfield (Yankees), A.L.; Steve Sax (Dodgers), N.L.

■ **MVP:** Lynn.

Linescore
July 6, Chicago's Comiskey Park
N.L. ....1 0 0 1 1 0 0 0 0— 3 8 3
A.L. ....1 1 7 0 0 0 2 2 x—13 15 2
Soto (Reds), Hammaker (Giants) 3, Dawley (Astros) 3, Dravecky (Padres) 5, Perez (Braves) 7, Orosco (Mets) 7, L. Smith (Cubs) 8; Stieb (Blue Jays), Honeycutt (Rangers) 4, Stanley (Red Sox) 6, Young (Mariners) 8, Quisenberry (Royals) 9. W—Stieb. L—Soto. HR—Rice, Lynn, A.L.

ALCS

■ **Winner:** Baltimore, a 2-1 loser to the Chicago White Sox in the opener, roared to three consecutive victories and claimed its fifth pennant since LCS play began in 1969.

■ **Turning point:** Mike Boddicker's five-hit, 4-0 shutout in Game 2. Orioles pitchers would finish the series with a 0.49 ERA.

■ **Memorable moment:** A 10th-inning home run by unlikely Baltimore hero Tito Landrum off Chicago lefty Britt Burns in Game 4. The blast broke up a scoreless battle and propelled the Orioles to a series-ending 3-0 victory.

■ **Top guns:** Boddicker (1-0, 0.00 ERA), Tippy Martinez (1-0, 0.00), Cal Ripken (.400), Orioles; LaMarr Hoyt (1-0, 1.00), Rudy Law (.389), White Sox.

■ **MVP:** Boddicker.

Linescores

Game 1—October 5, at Baltimore
Chi. ....0 0 1 0 0 1 0 0 0—2 7 0
Balt. ....0 0 0 0 0 0 0 0 1—1 5 1
Hoyt; McGregor, Stewart (7), T. Martinez (8). W—Hoyt. L—McGregor.

Game 2—October 6, at Baltimore
Chi. ....0 0 0 0 0 0 0 0 0—0 5 2
Balt. ....0 1 0 1 0 2 0 0 x—4 6 0
Bannister, Barojas (7), Lamp (8); Boddicker. W—Boddicker. L—Bannister. HR—Roenicke (Bal.).

Game 3—October 7, at Chicago
Balt. ....3 1 0 0 2 0 0 1 4—11 8 1
Chi. ....0 1 0 0 0 0 0 0 0— 1 6 1
Flanagan, Stewart (6); Dotson, Tidrow (6), Koosman (9), Lamp (9). W—Flanagan. L—Dotson. S—Stewart. HR—Murray (Bal.).

Game 4—October 8, at Chicago
Balt. ....0 0 0 0 0 0 0 0 0 3—3 9 0
Chi. ......0 0 0 0 0 0 0 0 0 0—0 10 0
Davis, T. Martinez (7); Burns, Barojas (10), Agosto (10), Lamp (10). W—T. Martinez. L—Burns. HR—Landrum (Bal.).

NLCS

■ **Winner:** The Philadelphia Phillies advanced to their second World Series in four years and settled an old NLCS score with the Dodgers, who had defeated them in 1977 and '78.

■ **Turning point:** The Game 3 performance of veteran outfielder Gary Matthews: three hits, a home run and four RBIs in a 7-2 Phillies victory.

■ **Memorable moment:** A three-run, first-inning home run by Matthews in Game 4. Matthews' third homer in as many games propelled the Phillies to a series-ending 7-2 victory.

■ **Top guns:** Steve Carlton (2-0, 0.66 ERA), Mike Schmidt (.467), Matthews (.429, 3 HR, 8 RBIs), Phillies; Fernando Valenzuela (1-0, 1.13), Dusty Baker (.357), Dodgers.

■ **MVP:** Matthews.

Linescores

Game 1—October 4, at Los Angeles
Phil. ....1 0 0 0 0 0 0 0 0—1 5 1
L.A. ....0 0 0 0 0 0 0 0 0—0 7 0
Carlton, Holland (8); Reuss, Niedenfuer (9). W—Carlton. L—Reuss. S—Holland. HR—Schmidt (Phil.).

Game 2—October 5, at Los Angeles
Phil. ....0 1 0 0 0 0 0 0 0—1 7 2
L.A. ....1 0 0 0 2 0 0 1 x—4 6 1
Denny, Reed (7); Valenzuela, Niedenfuer (9). W—Valenzuela. L—Denny. S—Niedenfuer. HR—Matthews (Phil.).

Game 3—October 7, at Philadelphia
L.A. ....0 0 0 2 0 0 0 0 0—2 4 0
Phil. ....0 2 1 1 2 0 1 0 x—7 9 1
Welch, Pena (2), Honeycutt (5), Beckwith (5), Zachry (7); Hudson. W—Hudson. L—Welch. HR—Marshall (L.A.); Matthews (Phil.).

Game 4—October 8, at Philadelphia
L.A. ....0 0 0 1 0 0 0 1 0—2 10 0
Phil. ....3 0 0 0 2 2 0 0 x—7 13 1
Reuss, Beckwith (5), Honeycutt (5), Zachry (7); Carlton, Reed (7), Holland (8). W—Carlton. L—Reuss. HR—Matthews, Lezcano (Phil.); Baker (L.A.).

WORLD SERIES

■ **Winner:** The Orioles lost the opener and then sprinted past the Phillies for their first championship since 1970.

■ **Turning point:** When Phillies manager Paul Owens let starting pitcher Steve Carlton bat with two runners on base in the sixth inning of Game 3. Carlton struck out and then yielded two seventh-inning runs that vaulted the Orioles to a 3-2 victory.

■ **Memorable moment:** Garry Maddox's game-deciding eighth-inning homer in Game 1. Maddox connected on the first pitch from Scott McGregor, who stood on the mound for about five minutes while President Ronald Reagan was being interviewed for television.

■ **Top guns:** Rick Dempsey (.385), John Lowenstein (.385), Orioles; Bo Diaz (.333), Phillies.

■ **MVP:** Dempsey.

Linescores

Game 1—October 11, at Baltimore
Phil. ....0 0 0 0 0 1 0 1 0—2 5 0
Baltimore ....1 0 0 0 0 0 0 0 0—1 5 1
Denny, Holland (8); McGregor, Stewart (9), T. Martinez (9). W—Denny. L—McGregor. S—Holland. HR—Dwyer (Bal.); Morgan, Maddox (Phil.).

Game 2—October 12, at Baltimore
Phil. ....0 0 0 1 0 0 0 0 0—1 3 0
Baltimore ....0 0 0 0 3 0 1 0 x—4 9 1
Hudson, Hernandez (5), Andersen (6), Reed (8); Boddicker. W—Boddicker. L—Hudson. HR—Lowenstein (Bal.).

Game 3—October 14, at Philadelphia
Baltimore ....0 0 0 0 0 1 2 0 0—3 6 1
Phil. ....0 1 1 0 0 0 0 0 0—2 8 2
Flanagan, Palmer (5), Stewart (7), T. Martinez (9); Carlton, Holland (7). W—Palmer. L—Carlton. S—T. Martinez. HR—Matthews, Morgan (Phil.); Ford (Bal.).

Game 4—October 15, at Philadelphia
Baltimore ..0 0 0 2 0 2 1 0 0—5 10 1
Phil. ....0 0 0 1 2 0 0 0 1—4 10 0
Davis, Stewart (6), T. Martinez (8); Denny, Hernandez (6), Reed (6), Andersen (8). W—Davis. L—Denny. S—T. Martinez.

Game 5—October 16, at Philadelphia
Baltimore ....0 1 1 2 1 0 0 0 0—5 5 0
Phil. ....0 0 0 0 0 0 0 0 0—0 5 1
McGregor; Hudson, Bystrom (5), Hernandez (6), Reed (9). W—McGregor. L—Hudson. HR—Murray 2, Dempsey (Bal.).

FINAL STANDINGS

American League

East Division

Team	Det.	Tor.	N.Y.	Bos.	Bal.	Cle.	Mil.	Cal.	Chi.	K.C.	Min.	Oak.	Sea.	Tex.	W	L	Pct.	GB
Detroit	...	8	7	6	6	9	11	8	8	7	9	9	6	10	104	58	.642	...
Toronto	5	...	5	8	9	7	3	5	8	7	11	8	7	6	89	73	.549	15
New York	6	8	...	6	8	11	7	4	5	7	4	8	7	6	87	75	.537	17
Boston	7	5	7	...	7	10	9	9	7	3	6	7	4	5	86	76	.531	18
Baltimore	7	4	5	6	...	7	7	8	7	5	5	6	9	9	85	77	.525	19
Cleveland	4	6	2	3	6	...	9	4	4	6	7	7	8	9	75	87	.463	29
Milwaukee	2	10	6	4	6	4	...	4	5	6	5	4	6	5	67	94	.416	36.5

West Division

Team	K.C.	Cal.	Min.	Oak.	Chi.	Sea.	Tex.	Bal.	Bos.	Cle.	Det.	Mil.	N.Y.	Tor.	W	L	Pct.	GB
Kansas City	...	7	6	5	8	9	6	7	9	6	5	6	5	5	84	78	.519	...
California	6	...	4	7	8	9	5	4	3	8	4	8	8	7	81	81	.500	3
Minnesota	7	9	...	8	5	7	8	7	6	5	3	7	8	1	81	81	.500	3
Oakland	8	6	5	...	7	8	8	6	5	5	3	8	4	4	77	85	.475	7
Chicago	5	5	8	6	...	5	5	5	5	8	4	7	7	4	74	88	.457	10
Seattle	4	4	6	5	8	...	10	3	8	4	6	6	5	5	74	88	.457	10
Texas	7	8	5	5	8	3	...	3	7	3	2	6	6	6	69	92	.429	14.5

National League

East Division

Team	Chi.	N.Y.	St.L.	Phi.	Mon.	Pit.	Atl.	Cin.	Hou.	L.A.	S.D.	S.F.	W	L	Pct.	GB
Chicago	...	12	13	9	10	8	9	7	6	7	6	9	96	65	.596	...
New York	6	...	7	10	11	12	8	9	8	9	6	4	90	72	.556	6.5
St. Louis	5	11	...	10	9	14	7	8	4	6	5	5	84	78	.519	12.5
Philadelphia	9	8	8	...	7	7	5	7	6	9	7	8	81	81	.500	15.5
Montreal	7	7	9	11	...	7	7	5	5	6	7	7	78	83	.484	18
Pittsburgh	10	6	4	11	11	...	4	5	6	8	4	6	75	87	.463	21.5

West Division

Team	S.D.	Atl.	Hou.	L.A.	Cin.	S.F.	Chi.	Mon.	N.Y.	Phi.	Pit.	St.L.	W	L	Pct.	GB
San Diego	...	11	12	8	11	13	6	5	6	5	8	7	92	70	.568	...
Atlanta	7	...	12	6	13	10	3	5	4	7	8	5	80	82	.494	12
Houston	6	6	...	9	10	12	6	7	4	6	6	8	80	82	.494	12
L.A.	10	12	9	...	11	10	5	6	3	3	4	6	79	83	.488	13
Cincinnati	7	5	8	7	...	12	5	7	3	5	7	4	70	92	.432	22
San Fran.	5	8	6	8	6	...	3	5	8	4	6	7	66	96	.407	26

SIGNIFICANT EVENTS

■ **March 3:** Baseball's owners selected businessman Peter V. Ueberroth as the sixth commissioner, succeeding Bowie Kuhn.

■ **August 16:** Pete Rose, who joined the select 4,000-hit circle early in the season as a member of the Expos, returned to his hometown Cincinnati as the Reds' player-manager.

■ **September 20, 24:** The Padres clinched their first-ever division title and the Cubs clinched their first post-season appearance since 1945.

■ **October 7:** Major League umpires, agreeing to let Commissioner Ueberroth arbitrate their dispute over post-season pay, ended a one-week strike and returned for the final game of the NLCS.

■ **November 6:** Detroit reliever Willie Hernandez capped his big season with an A.L. Cy Young-MVP sweep.

MEMORABLE MOMENTS

■ **September 17:** Kansas City posted a 10-1 victory, but the night belonged to Angels slugger Reggie Jackson, who belted his 500th homer off lefty Bud Black.

■ **September 28:** Cardinals reliever Bruce Sutter notched his 45th save in a 4-1 victory over the Cubs, matching the 1-year-old record of Kansas City's Dan Quisenberry.

■ **September 30:** California's Mike Witt brought a dramatic end to the regular season when he fired baseball's 11th perfect game, beating Texas, 1-0.

LEADERS

American League
BA: Don Mattingly, N.Y., .343.
Runs: Dwight Evans, Bos., 121.
Hits: Don Mattingly, N.Y., 207.
TB: Tony Armas, Bos., 339.
HR: Tony Armas, Bos., 43.
RBI: Tony Armas, Bos., 123.
SB: Rickey Henderson, Oak., 66.
Wins: Mike Boddicker, Bal., 20.
ERA: Mike Boddicker, Bal., 2.79.
CG: Charlie Hough, Tex., 17.
IP: Dave Stieb, Tor., 267.
SO: Mark Langston, Sea., 204.
SV: Dan Quisenberry, K.C., 44.

National League
BA: Tony Gwynn, S.D., .351.
Runs: Ryne Sandberg, Chi., 114.
Hits: Tony Gwynn, S.D., 213.
TB: Dale Murphy, Atl., 332.
HR: Dale Murphy, Atl.; Mike Schmidt, Phil., 36.
RBI: Gary Carter, Mon.; Mike Schmidt, Phil., 106.
SB: Tim Raines, Mon., 75.
Wins: Joaquin Andujar, St.L., 20.
ERA: Alejandro Pena, L.A., 2.48.
CG: Mario Soto, Cin., 13.
IP: Joaquin Andujar, St.L., 261.1.
SO: Dwight Gooden, N.Y., 276.
SV: Bruce Sutter, St.L., 45.

A.L. 20-game winner
Mike Boddicker, Bal., 20-11

N.L. 20-game winner
Joaquin Andujar, St.L., 20-14

A.L./N.L. 20-game winner
Rick Sutcliffe, Cle.-Chi., 20

A.L. 100 RBIs
Tony Armas, Bos., 123
Jim Rice, Bos., 122
Dave Kingman, Oak., 118
Alvin Davis, Sea., 116
Don Mattingly, N.Y., 110
Eddie Murray, Bal., 110
Kent Hrbek, Min., 107
Dwight Evans, Bos., 104
Larry Parrish, Tex., 101
Dave Winfield, N.Y., 100

N.L. 100 RBIs
Gary Carter, Mon., 106
Mike Schmidt, Phil., 106
Dale Murphy, Atl., 100

A.L. 40 homers
Tony Armas, Bos., 43

Most Valuable Player
A.L.: Willie Hernandez, P, Det.
N.L.: Ryne Sandberg, 2B, Chi.

Cy Young Award
A.L.: Willie Hernandez, Det.
N.L.: Rick Sutcliffe, Chi.

Rookie of the Year
A.L.: Alvin Davis, 1B, Sea.
N.L.: Dwight Gooden, P, N.Y.

Manager of the Year
A.L.: Sparky Anderson, Det.
N.L.: Jim Frey, Chi.

Hall of Fame additions
Luis Aparicio, SS, 1956-73
Don Drysdale, P, 1956-69
Rick Ferrell, C, 1929-47
Harmon Killebrew, 1B/3B, 1954-75
Pee Wee Reese, SS, 1940-58

ALL-STAR GAME

■ **Winner:** After a one-year lull, it was business as usual for the N.L., which used home runs by Gary Carter and Dale Murphy to post a 3-1 All-Star victory.

■ **Key inning:** The second, when Carter belted a solo shot to give the N.L. a 2-1 lead after the A.L. had tied in the top of the inning on George Brett's home run.

■ **Memorable moment:** A fourth and fifth-inning strikeout flurry by the N.L.'s Fernando Valenzuela and Dwight Gooden. Consecutive victims Dave Winfield, Reggie Jackson, Brett, Lance Parrish, Chet Lemon and Alvin Davis broke the 50-year-old record of five straight.

■ **Top guns:** Valenzuela (Dodgers), Gooden (Mets), Carter (Expos), Murphy (Braves), N.L.; Brett (Royals), Lou Whitaker (Tigers), A.L.

■ **MVP:** Carter.

Linescore
July 10, at San Francisco's Candlestick Park
A.L. ....0 1 0 0 0 0 0 0 0—1 7 2
N.L. ....1 1 0 0 0 0 0 1 x—3 8 0
Stieb (Blue Jays), Morris (Tigers) 3, Dotson (White Sox) 5, Caudill (Athletics) 7, W. Hernandez (Tigers) 8; Lea (Expos), Valenzuela (Dodgers) 3, Gooden (Mets) 5, Soto (Reds) 7, Gossage (Padres) 9. W—Lea. L—Steib. S—Gossage. HR—Brett, A.L.; Carter, Murphy, N.L.

ALCS

■ **Winner:** The Detroit Tigers capped their 104-victory regular season with a sweep of Kansas City and claimed their first pennant since 1968.

■ **Turning point:** The 11th inning of Game 2, when Johnny Grubb's one-out double off Royals relief ace Dan Quisenberry drove in two runs and gave the Tigers a 5-3 victory and a two-games-to-none series edge.

■ **Memorable moment:** The Game 3 pitching performance of Tigers veteran Milt Wilcox, who allowed only two hits in eight innings of a series-clinching 1-0 victory.

■ **Top guns:** Wilcox (1-0, 0.00 ERA), Jack Morris (1-0, 1.29), Kirk Gibson (.417), Alan Trammell (.364), Tigers; Don Slaught (.364), Royals.

■ **MVP:** Gibson.

Linescores
Game 1—October 2, at Kansas City
Det.............2 0 0 1 1 0 1 2 1—8 14 0
K.C.............0 0 0 0 0 0 1 0 0—1 5 1
Morris, Hernandez (8); Black, Huismann (6), M. Jones (8). W—Morris. L—Black. HR—Herndon, Trammell, Parrish (Det.).

Game 2—October 3, at Kansas City
Det...2 0 1 0 0 0 0 0 0 0 2—5 8 1
K.C...0 0 0 1 0 0 1 1 0 0 0—3 10 3
Petry, Hernandez (8), Lopez (9); Saberhagen, Quisenberry (9). W—Lopez. L—Quisenberry. HR—Gibson (Det.).

Game 3—October 5, at Detroit
K.C...............0 0 0 0 0 0 0 0 0—0 3 3
Det. ....0 1 0 0 0 0 0 0 x—1 3 0
Leibrandt; Wilcox, Hernandez (9). W—Wilcox. L—Leibrandt. S—Hernandez.

NLCS

■ **Winner:** The San Diego Padres became the first N.L. team to recover from a two-game deficit and captured their first-ever pennant, denying the Cubs their first World Series appearance since 1945.

■ **Turning point:** The seventh inning of Game 5. The key blows in San Diego's four-run series-deciding rally were an error by Cubs first baseman Leon Durham and a bad-hop double by Tony Gwynn that drove in two runs and broke a 3-3 tie.

■ **Memorable moment:** Steve Garvey's two-run ninth-inning home run that gave the Padres an elimination-saving 7-5 victory in Game 4.

■ **Top guns:** Craig Lefferts (2-0, 0.00 ERA), Garvey (.400, 7 RBIs), Gwynn (.368), Padres; Jody Davis (.389, 2 HR, 6 RBIs), Gary Matthews (2 HR, 5 RBIs), Cubs.

■ **MVP:** Garvey.

Linescores
Game 1—October 2, at Chicago
S.D............0 0 0 0 0 0 0 0 0— 0 6 1
Chicago....2 0 3 0 6 2 0 0 x—13 16 0
Show, Harris (5), Booker (7); Sutcliffe, Brusstar (8). W—Sutcliffe. L—Show. HR—Dernier, Matthews 2, Sutcliffe, Cey (Chi.).

Game 2—October 3, at Chicago
S.D...............0 0 0 1 0 1 0 0 0—2 5 0
Chicago.........1 0 2 1 0 0 0 0 x—4 8 1
Thurmond, Hawkins (4), Dravecky (6), Lefferts (8); Trout, Smith (9). W—Trout. L—Thurmond. S—Smith.

Game 3—October 4, at San Diego
Chicago......0 1 0 0 0 0 0 0 0—1 5 0
S.D.............0 0 0 0 3 4 0 0 x—7 11 0
Eckersley, Frazier (6), Stoddard (8); Whitson, Gossage (9). W—Whitson. L—Eckersley. HR—McReynolds (S.D.).

Game 4—October 6, at San Diego
Chicago......0 0 0 3 0 0 0 2 0—5 8 1
S.D.............0 0 2 0 1 0 2 0 2—7 11 0
Sanderson, Brusstar (5), Stoddard (7), Smith (8); Lollar, Hawkins (5), Dravecky (6), Gossage (8), Lefferts (9). W—Lefferts. L—Smith. HR—Davis, Durham (Chi.); Garvey (S.D.).

Game 5—October 7, at San Diego
Chicago ....2 1 0 0 0 0 0 0 0—3 5 1
S.D...............0 0 0 0 0 2 4 0 x—6 8 0
Sutcliffe, Trout (7), Brusstar (8); Show, Hawkins (2), Dravecky (4), Lefferts (6), Gossage (8). W—Lefferts. L—Sutcliffe. S—Gossage. HR—Durham, Davis (Chi.).

WORLD SERIES

■ **Winner:** The Tigers made short work of first-time Series qualifier San Diego and Sparky Anderson became the first man to manage champions in both leagues.

■ **Turning point:** Jack Morris pitched a five-hitter and Alan Trammell drove in all of Detroit's runs with two homers in a 4-2 Game 4 victory.

■ **Memorable moment:** The ever-intense Kirk Gibson stomping on home plate after an eighth-inning upper-deck home run in the Series finale — his second of the game. Gibson also drove in five runs and scored three times in the Tigers' 8-4 victory.

■ **Top guns:** Morris (2-0, 2.00 ERA), Trammell (.450, 2 HR, 6 RBIs), Gibson (.333, 2 HR, 7 RBIs), Tigers; Kurt Bevacqua (.412), Alan Wiggins (.364), Padres.

■ **MVP:** Trammell.

Linescores
Game 1—October 9, at San Diego
Detroit..........1 0 0 0 2 0 0 0 0—3 8 0
San Diego ....2 0 0 0 0 0 0 0 0—2 8 1
Morris; Thurmond, Hawkins (6), Dravecky (8). W—Morris. L—Thurmond. HR—Herndon (Det.).

Game 2—October 10, at San Diego
Detroit........3 0 0 0 0 0 0 0 0—3 7 3
San Diego ..1 0 0 1 3 0 0 0 x—5 11 0
Petry, Lopez (5), Scherrer (6), Bair (7), Hernandez (8); Whitson, Hawkins (1), Lefferts (7). W—Hawkins. L—Petry. S—Lefferts. HR—Bevacqua (S.D.).

Game 3—October 12, at Detroit
San Diego ..0 0 1 0 0 0 1 0 0—2 10 0
Detroit........0 4 1 0 0 0 0 0 x—5 7 0
Lollar, Booker (2), Harris (3); Wilcox, Scherrer (7), Hernandez (7). W—Wilcox. L—Lollar. S—Hernandez. HR—Castillo (Det.).

Game 4—October 13, at Detroit
San Diego ....0 1 0 0 0 0 0 0 1—2 5 2
Detroit..........2 0 2 0 0 0 0 0 x—4 7 0
Show, Dravecky (3), Lefferts (7), Gossage (8); Morris. W—Morris. L—Show. HR—Trammell 2 (Det.); Kennedy (S.D.).

Game 5—October 14, at Detroit
San Diego ..0 0 1 2 0 0 0 1 0—4 10 1
Detroit........3 0 0 0 1 0 1 3 x—8 11 1
Thurmond, Hawkins (1), Lefferts (5), Gossage (7); Petry, Scherrer (4), Lopez (5), Hernandez (8). W—Lopez. L—Hawkins. S—Hernandez. HR—Gibson 2, Parrish (Det.); Bevacqua (S.D.).

FINAL STANDINGS

American League

East Division

Team	Tor.	N.Y.	Det.	Bal.	Bos.	Mil.	Cle.	K.C.	Cal.	Chi.	Min.	Oak.	Sea.	Tex.	W	L	Pct.	GB
Toronto	...	7	7	8	4	9	9	5	7	9	8	7	10	9	99	62	.615	...
New York	6	...	3	12	8	6	7	7	9	6	9	7	9	8	97	64	.602	2
Detroit	6	9	...	7	7	9	8	5	4	6	3	8	5	7	84	77	.522	15
Baltimore	4	1	6	...	5	9	8	6	7	8	6	7	6	10	83	78	.516	16
Boston	9	5	6	8	...	5	8	5	5	4	7	8	6	5	81	81	.500	18.5
Milwaukee	4	7	4	4	8	...	6	4	3	7	9	3	4	8	71	90	.441	28
Cleveland	4	6	5	5	5	7	...	2	4	2	4	3	6	7	60	102	.370	39.5

West Division

Team	K.C.	Cal.	Chi.	Min.	Oak.	Sea.	Tex.	Tor.	N.Y.	Det.	Bal.	Bos.	Mil.	Cle.	W	L	Pct.	GB
Kansas City	...	9	8	7	8	3	6	7	5	7	6	7	8	10	91	71	.562	...
California	4	...	8	9	6	9	9	5	3	8	5	7	9	8	90	72	.556	1
Chicago	5	5	...	6	8	9	10	3	6	6	4	8	5	10	85	77	.525	6
Minnesota	6	4	7	...	8	6	8	4	3	9	6	5	3	8	77	85	.475	14
Oakland	5	7	5	5	...	8	6	5	5	4	5	4	9	9	77	85	.475	14
Seattle	10	4	4	7	5	...	6	2	3	7	6	6	8	6	74	88	.457	17
Texas	7	4	3	5	7	7	...	3	4	5	2	7	3	5	62	99	.385	28.5

National League

East Division

Team	St.L.	N.Y.	Mon.	Chi.	Phi.	Pit.	L.A.	Cin.	Hou.	S.D.	Atl.	S.F.	W	L	Pct.	GB
St. Louis	...	10	7	14	10	15	5	7	6	8	9	10	101	61	.623	...
New York	8	...	9	14	11	10	5	8	8	7	10	8	98	64	.605	3
Montreal	11	9	...	11	8	9	5	4	6	5	9	7	84	77	.522	16.5
Chicago	4	4	7	...	13	13	5	5	5	8	7	6	77	84	.478	23.5
Philadelphia	8	7	10	5	...	11	8	5	8	5	2	6	75	87	.463	26
Pittsburgh	3	8	8	5	7	...	4	3	6	4	6	3	57	104	.354	43.5

West Division

Team	L.A.	Cin.	Hou.	S.D.	Atl.	S.F.	St.L.	N.Y.	Mon.	Chi.	Phi.	Pit.	W	L	Pct.	GB
Los Angeles	...	11	12	8	13	11	7	7	7	7	4	8	95	67	.586	...
Cincinnati	7	...	11	9	11	12	5	4	8	6	7	9	89	72	.553	5.5
Houston	6	7	...	12	10	15	6	4	6	7	4	6	83	79	.512	12
San Diego	10	9	6	...	11	12	4	5	7	4	7	8	83	79	.512	12
Atlanta	5	7	8	7	...	10	3	2	3	5	10	6	66	96	.407	29
San Fran.	7	6	3	6	8	...	2	4	5	6	6	9	62	100	.383	33

SIGNIFICANT EVENTS

■ **April 25:** Denny McLain, a 31-game winner in 1968, was sentenced to 23 years in prison after his conviction on racketeering, extortion and cocaine-possession charges in Tampa, Fla.
■ **March 18:** The baseball bans against former greats Mickey Mantle and Willie Mays were lifted by Commissioner Peter V. Ueberroth.
■ **April 3:** The owners and players agreed to expand the League Championship Series from a best-of-five to best-of-seven format.
■ **August 7:** Major League players ended their two-day, 25-game strike when owners dropped their demand for an arbitration salary cap.

MEMORABLE MOMENTS

■ **July 11:** Houston's Nolan Ryan became the first pitcher to record 4,000 career strikeouts when he fanned Danny Heep in a 4-3 victory over the Mets.
■ **August 4:** Chicago's Tom Seaver earned career win No. 300 against the Yankees and California's Rod Carew got hit No. 3,000 against the Twins in games played a continent apart on the same day.
■ **September 11:** Reds player-manager Pete Rose overtook all-time hit leader Ty Cobb when he singled off San Diego's Eric Show for career hit No. 4,192.
■ **October 6:** Yankee knuckleballer Phil Niekro fired a final-day 8-0 shutout at the Blue Jays and joined baseball's 300-win club.

ALL-STAR GAME

■ **Winner:** The N.L. made it 21 of 23 and two in a row as five pitchers shut down the A.L. on five hits.
■ **Key inning:** The third, when the N.L. took the lead on a double by Tommy Herr and Steve Garvey's single.
■ **Memorable moment:** The performance of the N.L. pitchers, who did not even allow an extra-base hit.
■ **Top guns:** LaMarr Hoyt (Padres), Nolan Ryan (Astros), Garvey (Dodgers), Willie McGee (Cardinals), Ozzie Virgil (Phillies), N.L.; Rickey Henderson (Yankees), A.L.
■ **MVP:** Hoyt.

Linescore

July 16, at Minnesota's Metrodome
N.L..............0 1 1 0 2 0 0 0 2—6 9 1
A.L...............1 0 0 0 0 0 0 0 0—1 5 0
Hoyt (Padres), Ryan (Astros) 4, Valenzuela (Dodgers) 7, Reardon (Expos) 8, Gossage (Padres) 9; Morris (Tigers), Key (Blue Jays) 3, Blyleven (Indians) 4, Stieb (Blue Jays) 6, Moore (Angels) 7, Petry (Tigers) 9, Hernandez (Tigers) 9. W—Hoyt. L—Morris.

ALCS

■ **Winner:** The Kansas City Royals, taking advantage of baseball's expanded seven-game playoff format, rallied from a three-games-to-one deficit to deny Toronto's bid for a first Canadian pennant.
■ **Turning point:** One day after the Blue Jays had rallied for three ninth-inning runs and a 3-1 series edge, Danny Jackson steadied the Royals with an eight-hit, 2-0 shutout at Royals Stadium.
■ **Memorable moment:** A bases-loaded, opposite-field Jim Sundberg blast that bounded high off the wall and resulted in a three-run, sixth-inning triple — the big blow in Kansas City's seventh-game 6-2 victory.
■ **Top guns:** Jackson (1-0, 0.00 ERA), George Brett (.348, 3 HR, 5 RBIs), Willie Wilson (.310), Royals; Al Oliver (.375), Cliff Johnson (.368), Blue Jays.
■ **MVP:** Brett.

Linescores

Game 1—October 8, at Toronto
K.C..............0 0 0 0 0 0 0 0 1—1 5 1
Tor. ....0 2 3 1 0 0 0 0 x—6 11 0
Leibrandt, Farr (3), Gubicza (5), Jackson (8); Stieb, Henke (9). W—Stieb. L—Leibrandt.

Game 2—October 9, at Toronto
K.C.........0 0 2 1 0 0 0 0 1 1—5 10 3
Tor. ....0 0 0 1 0 2 0 1 0 2—6 10 0
Black, Quisenberry (8); Key, Lamp (4), Lavelle (8), Henke (8). W—Henke. L—Quisenberry. HR—Wilson, Sheridan (K.C.).

Game 3—October 11, at Kansas City
Tor. ....0 0 0 0 5 0 0 0 0—5 13 1
K.C..............1 0 0 1 1 2 0 1 x—6 10 1
Alexander, Lamp (6), Clancy (8); Saberhagen, Black (5), Farr (5). W—Farr. L—Clancy. HR—Brett 2, Sundberg (K.C.); Barfield, Mulliniks (Tor.)

Game 4—October 12, at Kansas City
Tor. ....0 0 0 0 0 0 0 0 3—3 7 0
K.C...............0 0 0 0 0 1 0 0 0—1 2 0
Stieb, Henke (7); Leibrandt, Quisenberry (9). W—Henke. L—Leibrandt.

Game 5—October 13, at Kansas City
Tor. ....0 0 0 0 0 0 0 0 0—0 8 0
K.C...............1 1 0 0 0 0 0 0 x—2 8 0
Key, Acker (6); Jackson. W—Jackson. L—Key.

Game 6—October 15, at Toronto
K.C...............1 0 1 0 1 2 0 0 0—5 8 1
Tor. ....1 0 1 0 0 1 0 0 0—3 8 2
Gubicza, Black (6), Quisenberry (9); Alexander, Lamp (6). W—Gubicza. L—Alexander. S—Quisenberry. HR—Brett (K.C.).

Game 7—October 16, at Toronto
K.C...............0 1 0 1 0 4 0 0 0—6 8 0
Tor. ....0 0 0 0 1 0 0 0 1—2 8 1
Saberhagen, Leibrandt (4), Quisenberry (9); Stieb, Acker (6). W—Leibrandt. L—Stieb. HR—Sheridan (K.C.).

LEADERS

American League
BA: Wade Boggs, Bos., .368.
Runs: Rickey Henderson, N.Y., 146.
Hits: Wade Boggs, Bos., 240.
TB: Don Mattingly, N.Y., 370.
HR: Darrell Evans, Det., 40.
RBI: Don Mattingly, N.Y., 145.
SB: Rickey Henderson, N.Y., 80.
Wins: Ron Guidry, N.Y., 22.
ERA: Dave Stieb, Tor., 2.48.
CG: Bert Blyleven, Cle.-Min., 24.
IP: Bert Blyleven, Cle.-Min., 293.2.
SO: Bert Blyleven, Cle.-Min., 206.
SV: Dan Quisenberry, K.C., 37.

National League
BA: Willie McGee, St.L., .353.
Runs: Dale Murphy, Atl., 118.
Hits: Willie McGee, St.L., 216.
TB: Dave Parker, Cin., 350.
HR: Dale Murphy, Atl., 37.
RBI: Dave Parker, Cin., 125.
SB: Vince Coleman, St.L., 110.
Wins: Dwight Gooden, N.Y., 24.
ERA: Dwight Gooden, N.Y., 1.53.
CG: Dwight Gooden, N.Y., 16.
IP: Dwight Gooden, N.Y., 276.2.
SO: Dwight Gooden, N.Y., 268.
SV: Jeff Reardon, Mon., 41.

A.L. 20-game winners
Ron Guidry, N.Y., 22-6
Bret Saberhagen, K.C., 20-6

N.L. 20-game winners
Dwight Gooden, N.Y., 24-4
John Tudor, St.L., 21-8
Joaquin Andujar, St.L., 21-12
Tom Browning, Cin., 20-9

A.L. 100 RBIs
Don Mattingly, N.Y., 145
Eddie Murray, Bal., 124
Dave Winfield, N.Y., 114
Harold Baines, Chi., 113
George Brett, K.C., 112
Bill Buckner, Bos., 110
Cal Ripken, Bal., 110
Carlton Fisk, Chi., 107
Jim Rice, Bos., 103

N.L. 100 RBIs
Dave Parker, Cin., 125
Dale Murphy, Atl., 111
Tommy Herr, St.L., 110
Keith Moreland, Chi., 106
Glenn Wilson, Phil., 102
Hubie Brooks, Mon., 100
Gary Carter, N.Y., 100

A.L. 40 homers
Darrell Evans, Det., 40

Most Valuable Player
A.L.: Don Mattingly, 1B, N.Y.
N.L.: Willie McGee, OF, St.L.

Cy Young Award
A.L.: Bret Saberhagen, K.C.
N.L.: Dwight Gooden, N.Y.

Rookie of the Year
A.L.: Ozzie Guillen, SS, Chi.
N.L.: Vince Coleman, OF, St.L.

Manager of the Year
A.L.: Bobby Cox, Tor.
N.L.: Whitey Herzog, St.L.

Hall of Fame additions
Lou Brock, OF, 1961-79
Enos Slaughter, OF, 1938-59
Arky Vaughan, IF, 1932-48
Hoyt Wilhelm, P, 1952-72

NLCS

■ **Winner:** The speed-and-pitching oriented St. Louis Cardinals used a new weapon — the dramatic home run — to post a six-game NLCS victory over Los Angeles.
■ **Turning point:** The ninth inning of Game 5 when light-hitting Ozzie Smith, who had hit only 14 career home runs, stunned the Dodgers with a shot down the right-field line against Tom Niedenfuer that produced a 3-2 Cardinals victory and a 3-2 series edge.
■ **Memorable moment:** A three-run, series-clinching home run by Cardinals first baseman Jack Clark in the ninth inning of Game 6. The shot off Niedenfuer gave St. Louis a 7-5 victory — its fourth straight after the Dodgers had won Games 1 and 2.
■ **Top guns:** Ken Dayley (6 IP, 2 saves, 0.00 ERA), Smith (.435), Clark (.381), Cardinals; Fernando Valenzuela (1-0, 1.88), Bill Madlock (.333, 3 HR, 7 RBIs), Dodgers.
■ **MVP:** Smith.

Linescores

Game 1—October 9, at Los Angeles
St. Louis......0 0 0 0 0 0 1 0 0—1 8 1
L.A. ....0 0 0 1 0 3 0 0 x—4 8 0
Tudor, Dayley (6), Campbell (7), Worrell (8); Valenzuela, Niedenfuer (7). W—Valenzuela. L—Tudor. S—Niedenfuer.

Game 2—October 10, at Los Angeles
St. Louis ....0 0 1 0 0 0 0 0 1—2 8 1
L.A. ....0 0 3 2 1 2 0 0 x—8 13 1
Andujar, Horton (5), Campbell (6), Dayley (7), Lahti (8); Hershiser.
W—Hershiser. L—Andujar. HR—Brock (L.A.).

Game 3—October 12, at St. Louis
L.A. ....0 0 0 1 0 0 1 0 0—2 7 2
St. Louis ......2 2 0 0 0 0 0 0 x—4 8 0
Welch, Honeycutt (3), Diaz (5), Howell (7); Cox, Horton (7), Worrell (7), Dayley (9). W—Cox. L—Welch. S—Dayley. HR—Herr (St.L.).

Game 4—October 13, at St. Louis
L.A. ....0 0 0 0 0 0 1 1 0— 2 5 2
St. Louis ..0 9 0 1 1 0 0 1 x—12 15 0
Reuss, Honeycutt (2), Castillo (2), Diaz (8); Tudor, Horton (8), Campbell (9). W—Tudor. L—Reuss. HR—Madlock (L.A.).

Game 5—October 14, at St. Louis
L.A. ....0 0 0 2 0 0 0 0 0—2 5 1
St. Louis ......2 0 0 0 0 0 0 0 1—3 5 1
Valenzuela, Niedenfuer (9); Forsch, Dayley (4), Worrell (7), Lahti (9). W—Lahti. L—Niedenfuer. HR—Madlock (L.A.); Smith (St.L.).

Game 6—October 16, at Los Angeles
St. Louis ....0 0 1 0 0 0 3 0 3—7 12 1
L.A. ....1 1 0 0 2 0 0 1 0—5 8 0
Andujar, Worrell (7), Dayley (9); Hershiser, Niedenfuer (7). W—Worrell. L—Niedenfuer. S—Dayley. HR—Madlock, Marshall (L.A.); Clark (St.L.).

WORLD SERIES

■ **Winner:** The Royals needed three consecutive victories and a controversial sixth-game decision to claim their first Series triumph in an all-Missouri fall classic.
■ **Turning point:** A blown call at first base by umpire Don Denkinger in the Royals' ninth inning of Game 6. After arguing vehemently, the Cardinals unraveled and the Royals scored twice, claiming a 2-1 victory and forcing a seventh game.
■ **Memorable moment:** Royals catcher Jim Sundberg sliding around the tag of Cardinals catcher Darrell Porter with the winning run in Game 6. Sundberg and Onix Concepcion scored on Dane Iorg's one-out single.
■ **Top guns:** Bret Saberhagen (2-0, 0.50 ERA), George Brett (.370), Willie Wilson (.367), Royals; Tito Landrum (.360), Cardinals.
■ **MVP:** Saberhagen.

Linescores

Game 1—October 19, at Kansas City
St. Louis......0 0 1 1 0 0 0 0 1—3 7 1
K.C. ....0 1 0 0 0 0 0 0 0—1 8 0
Tudor, Worrell (7); Jackson, Quisenberry (8), Black (9). W—Tudor. L—Jackson. S—Worrell.

Game 2—October 20, at Kansas City
St. Louis......0 0 0 0 0 0 0 0 4—4 6 0
K.C. ....0 0 0 2 0 0 0 0 0—2 9 0
Cox, Dayley (8), Lahti (9); Leibrandt, Quisenberry (9). W—Dayley. L—Leibrandt. S—Lahti.

Game 3—October 22, at St. Louis
K.C. ....0 0 0 2 2 0 2 0 0—6 11 0
St. Louis ....0 0 0 0 0 1 0 0 0—1 6 0
Saberhagen; Andujar, Campbell (5), Horton (6), Dayley (8). W—Saberhagen. L—Andujar. HR—White (K.C.).

Game 4—October 23, at St. Louis
K.C. ....0 0 0 0 0 0 0 0 0—0 5 1
St. Louis ......0 1 1 0 1 0 0 0 x—3 6 0
Black, Beckwith (6), Quisenberry (8); Tudor. W—Tudor. L—Black. HR—Landrum, McGee (St.L.).

Game 5—October 24, at St. Louis
K.C. ....1 3 0 0 0 0 0 1 1—6 11 2
St. Louis ....1 0 0 0 0 0 0 0 0—1 5 1
Jackson; Forsch, Horton (2), Campbell (4), Worrell (6), Lahti (8). W—Jackson. L—Forsch.

Game 6—October 26, at Kansas City
St. Louis ....0 0 0 0 0 0 0 1 0—1 5 0
K.C. ....0 0 0 0 0 0 0 0 2—2 10 0
Cox, Dayley (8), Worrell (9); Leibrandt, Quisenberry (8). W—Quisenberry. L—Worrell.

Game 7—October 27, at Kansas City
St. Louis ..0 0 0 0 0 0 0 0 0— 0 5 0
K.C. ....0 2 3 0 6 0 0 0 x—11 14 0
Tudor, Campbell (3), Lahti (5), Horton (5), Andujar (5), Forsch (5), Dayley (7); Saberhagen. W—Saberhagen. L—Tudor. HR—Motley (K.C.).

1986

FINAL STANDINGS

American League

East Division

Team	Bos.	N.Y.	Det.	Tor.	Cle.	Mil.	Bal.	Cal.	Tex.	K.C.	Oak.	Chi.	Min.	Sea.	W	L	Pct.	GB
Boston	...	5	7	7	10	6	9	5	8	6	7	7	10	8	95	66	.590	...
New York	8	...	7	7	8	5	8	5	7	8	5	6	8	8	90	72	.556	5.5
Detroit	6	6	...	4	9	8	12	5	7	5	6	6	7	6	87	75	.537	8.5
Toronto	6	6	9	...	10	6	5	6	7	7	4	6	8	6	86	76	.531	9.5
Cleveland	3	5	4	3	...	8	9	6	6	8	10	7	6	9	84	78	.519	11.5
Milwaukee	6	8	5	7	5	...	7	7	4	6	5	7	4	6	77	84	.478	18
Baltimore	4	5	1	8	4	6	...	6	5	6	5	9	8	6	73	89	.451	22.5

West Division

Team	Cal.	Tex.	K.C.	Oak.	Chi.	Min.	Sea.	Bos.	N.Y.	Det.	Tor.	Cle.	Mil.	Bal.	W	L	Pct.	GB
California	...	8	8	10	7	7	8	7	7	7	6	6	5	6	92	70	.568	...
Texas	5	...	5	10	11	7	9	4	5	5	5	6	8	7	87	75	.537	5
Kansas City	5	8	...	8	6	6	5	6	4	7	5	4	6	6	76	86	.469	16
Oakland	3	3	5	...	6	7	10	5	7	6	8	2	7	7	76	86	.469	16
Chicago	6	2	7	7	...	6	8	5	6	6	6	5	5	3	72	90	.444	20
Minnesota	6	6	7	6	7	...	6	2	4	5	4	6	8	4	71	91	.438	21
Seattle	5	4	8	3	5	7	...	4	4	6	6	3	6	6	67	95	.414	25

National League

East Division

Team	N.Y.	Phi.	St.L.	Mon.	Chi.	Pit.	Hou.	Cin.	S.F.	S.D.	L.A.	Atl.	W	L	Pct.	GB
New York	...	8	12	10	12	17	7	8	7	10	9	8	108	54	.667	...
Phil.	10	...	6	10	8	11	6	5	9	6	7	8	86	75	.534	21.5
St. Louis	6	12	...	9	7	11	5	5	7	7	4	6	79	82	.491	28.5
Montreal	8	8	9	...	10	11	4	5	5	4	7	7	78	83	.484	29.5
Chicago	6	9	10	8	...	7	4	5	6	6	6	3	70	90	.438	37
Pittsburgh	1	7	7	7	11	...	6	2	4	8	4	7	64	98	.395	44

West Division

Team	Hou.	Cin.	S.F.	S.D.	L.A.	Atl.	N.Y.	Phi.	St.L.	Mon.	Chi.	Pit.	W	L	Pct.	GB
Houston	...	14	9	10	10	13	5	6	7	8	8	6	96	66	.593	...
Cincinnati	4	...	9	9	10	12	4	7	7	7	7	10	86	76	.531	10
San Fran.	9	9	...	10	10	11	5	3	5	7	6	8	83	79	.512	13
San Diego	8	9	8	...	12	6	2	6	5	8	6	4	74	88	.457	22
Los Angeles	8	8	8	6	...	8	3	5	8	5	6	8	73	89	.451	23
Atlanta	5	6	7	12	10	...	4	4	6	4	9	5	72	89	.447	23.5

LEADERS

American League
BA: Wade Boggs, Bos., .357.
Runs: Rickey Henderson, N.Y., 130.
Hits: Don Mattingly, N.Y., 238.
TB: Don Mattingly, N.Y., 388.
HR: Jesse Barfield, Tor., 40.
RBI: Joe Carter, Cle., 121.
SB: Rickey Henderson, N.Y., 87.
Wins: Roger Clemens, Bos., 24.
ERA: Roger Clemens, Bos., 2.48.
CG: Tom Candiotti, Cle., 17.
IP: Bert Blyleven, Min., 271.2.
SO: Mark Langston, Sea., 245.
SV: Dave Righetti, N.Y., 46.

National League
BA: Tim Raines, Mon., .334.
Runs: Tony Gwynn, S.D.;
Von Hayes, Phil., 107.
Hits: Tony Gwynn, S.D., 211.
TB: Dave Parker, Cin., 304.
HR: Mike Schmidt, Phil., 37.
RBI: Mike Schmidt, Phil., 119.
SB: Vince Coleman, St.L., 107.
Wins: Fernando Valenzuela, L.A., 21.
ERA: Mike Scott, Hou., 2.22.
CG: Fernando Valenzuela, L.A., 20.
IP: Mike Scott, Hou., 275.1.
SO: Mike Scott, Hou., 306.
SV: Todd Worrell, St.L., 36.

A.L. 20-game winners
Roger Clemens, Bos., 24-4
Jack Morris, Det., 21-8
Ted Higuera, Mil., 20-11

N.L. 20-game winners
Fernando Valenzuela, L.A., 21-11
Mike Krukow, S.F., 20-9

A.L. 100 RBIs
Joe Carter, Cle., 121
Jose Canseco, Oak., 117
Don Mattingly, N.Y., 113
Jim Rice, Bos., 110
Jesse Barfield, Tor., 108
George Bell, Tor., 108
Gary Gaetti, Min., 108
Jim Presley, Sea., 107
Dave Winfield, N.Y., 104
Bill Buckner, Bos., 102
Wally Joyner, Cal., 100

N.L. 100 RBIs
Mike Schmidt, Phil., 119
Dave Parker, Cin., 116
Gary Carter, N.Y., 105
Glenn Davis, Hou., 101

A.L. 40 homers
Jesse Barfield, Tor., 40

Most Valuable Player
A.L.: Roger Clemens, P, Bos.
N.L.: Mike Schmidt, 3B, Phil.

Cy Young Award
A.L.: Roger Clemens, Bos.
N.L.: Mike Scott, Hou.

Rookie of the Year
A.L.: Jose Canseco, OF, Oak.
N.L.: Todd Worrell, P, St.L.

Manager of the Year
A.L.: John McNamara, Bos.
N.L.: Hal Lanier, Hou.

Hall of Fame additions
Bobby Doerr, 2B, 1937-51
Ernie Lombardi, C, 1931-47
Willie McCovey, 1B, 1959-80

SIGNIFICANT EVENTS

■ **February 28:** Commissioner Peter V. Ueberroth handed one-year suspensions to players Dave Parker, Keith Hernandez, Lonnie Smith, Dale Berra, Jeffrey Leonard, Enos Cabell and Joaquin Andujar for drug-related activities.

■ **June 20:** Bo Jackson, the 1985 Heisman Trophy winner from Auburn, stunningly signed with the Royals instead of the NFL's Tampa Bay Buccaneers.

MEMORABLE MOMENTS

■ **April 29:** Boston's Roger Clemens broke a long-standing Major League record when he struck out 20 Mariners in a 3-1 victory at Fenway Park.

■ **June 18:** California's Don Sutton became a 300-game winner when he defeated the Rangers, 5-1.

■ **July 6:** Bob Horner became the 11th Major Leaguer to hit four homers in a game, but his Braves still dropped an 11-8 decision to the Expos.

■ **August 5:** Giants lefty Steve Carlton joined Nolan Ryan in the exclusive 4,000-strikeout club, but dropped an 11-6 decision to the Reds.

■ **September 25:** Houston righthander Mike Scott pitched the first pennant-clinching no-hitter in baseball history, beating the Giants, 2-0.

■ **October 4:** Yankee closer Dave Righetti set a one-season record when he recorded his 45th and 46th saves in a doubleheader sweep of the Red Sox.

ALL-STAR GAME

■ **Winner:** The A.L., looking to break its one-win-per-decade streak, got home runs from second basemen Lou Whitaker and Frank White and scored a 3-2 victory — its second of the 1980s.

■ **Key inning:** The second, when Whitaker followed a Dave Winfield double with a two-run shot off Dwight Gooden.

■ **Memorable moment:** Fernando Valenzuela tied Carl Hubbell's 1934 All-Star record when he struck out, consecutively, Don Mattingly, Cal Ripken, Jesse Barfield, Whitaker and Ted Higuera.

■ **Top guns:** Roger Clemens (Red Sox), Higuera (Brewers), Whitaker (Tigers), White (Royals), A.L.; Valenzuela (Dodgers), Steve Sax (Dodgers), N.L.

■ **MVP:** Clemens.

Linescore

July 15, at Houston's Astrodome
A.L. ....0 2 0 0 0 0 1 0 0—3 5 0
N.L. ....0 0 0 0 0 0 0 2 0—2 5 1
Clemens (Red Sox), Higuera (Brewers) 4, Hough (Rangers) 7, Righetti (Yankees) 8, Aase (Orioles) 9; Gooden (Mets), Valenzuela (Dodgers) 4, Scott (Astros) 7, Fernandez (Mets) 8, Krukow (Giants) 9. W—Clemens. L—Gooden. HR—Whitaker, White, A.L.

ALCS

■ **Winner:** Boston, on the verge of elimination in the ninth inning of Game 5, roared back to post a seven-game triumph over the stunned California Angels.

■ **Turning point:** Dave Henderson, one strike away from becoming the final out in the Angels' pennant-clinching victory, stroked a Donnie Moore pitch into the left-field bleachers for a two-run homer. The blast gave the Red Sox a 6-5 lead and they went on to post a series-turning 7-6 victory in 11 innings.

■ **Memorable moment:** Henderson dancing triumphantly around the bases as a crowd of 64,223 watched in stunned silence at Anaheim Stadium.

■ **Top guns:** Spike Owen (.429), Marty Barrett (.367, 5 RBIs), Rich Gedman (.357, 6 RBIs), Jim Rice (2 HR, 6 RBIs), Red Sox; Bob Boone (.455), Wally Joyner (.455), Angels.

■ **MVP:** Barrett.

Linescores

Game 1—October 7, at Boston
Cal. ....0 4 1 0 0 0 0 3 0—8 11 0
Boston ......0 0 0 0 0 1 0 0 0—1 5 1
Witt; Clemens, Sambito (8), Stanley (8). W—Witt. L—Clemens.

Game 2—October 8, at Boston
Cal. ....0 0 0 1 1 0 0 0 0—2 11 3
Boston ......1 1 0 0 1 0 3 3 x—9 13 2
McCaskill, Lucas (8), Corbett (8); Hurst. W—Hurst. L—McCaskill. HR—Joyner (Cal.); Rice (Bos.).

Game 3—October 10, at California
Boston ....0 1 0 0 0 0 0 2 0—3 9 1
Cal. ....0 0 0 0 0 1 3 1 x—5 8 0
Boyd, Sambito (7), Schiraldi (8); Candelaria, Moore (8). W—Candelaria. L—Boyd. S—Moore. HR—Schofield, Pettis (Cal.).

Game 4—October 11, at California
Boston....0 0 0 0 0 1 0 2 0 0 0—3 6 1
Cal. ....0 0 0 0 0 0 0 0 3 0 1—4 11 2
Clemens, Schiraldi (9); Sutton, Lucas (7), Ruhle (7), Finley (8), Corbett (8). W—Corbett. L—Schiraldi. HR—DeCinces (Cal.).

Game 5—October 12, at California
Boston....0 2 0 0 0 0 0 0 4 0 1—7 12 0
Cal. ....0 0 1 0 0 2 2 0 1 0 0—6 13 0
Hurst, Stanley (7), Sambito (9), Crawford (9), Schiraldi (11); Witt, Lucas (9), Moore (9), Finley (11). W—Crawford. L—Moore. S—Schiraldi. HR—Gedman, Baylor, Henderson (Bos.); Boone, Grich (Cal.).

Game 6—October 14, at Boston
Cal. ....2 0 0 0 0 0 1 1 0— 4 11 1
Boston ....2 0 5 0 1 0 2 0 x—10 16 1
McCaskill, Lucas (3), Corbett (4), Finley (7); Boyd, Stanley (8). W—Boyd. L—McCaskill. HR—Downing (Cal.).

Game 7—October 15, at Boston
Cal. ....0 0 0 0 0 0 0 1 0—1 6 2
Boston ....0 3 0 4 0 0 1 0 x—8 8 1
Candelaria, Sutton (4), Moore (8); Clemens, Schiraldi (8). W—Clemens. L—Candelaria. HR—Rice, Evans (Bos.).

NLCS

■ **Winner:** The New York Mets overcame the outstanding pitching of Houston's Mike Scott and denied the Astros their first-ever pennant.

■ **Turning point:** The Mets claimed a 6-5 Game 3 victory when Lenny Dykstra stroked a two-run homer in the bottom of the ninth inning.

■ **Memorable moment:** Mets relief ace Jesse Orosco fired a pennant-winning third strike past Houston's Kevin Bass with two runners on base in the bottom of the 16th inning, preserving New York's 7-6 victory in the longest Championship Series game ever played.

■ **Top guns:** Orosco (3-0), Dykstra (.304), Darryl Strawberry (2 HR, 5 RBIs), Mets; Scott (2-0, 0.50 ERA), Craig Reynolds (.333), Astros.

■ **MVP:** Scott.

Linescores

Game 1—October 8, at Houston
N.Y. ....0 0 0 0 0 0 0 0 0—0 5 0
Hou. ....0 1 0 0 0 0 0 0 x—1 7 1
Gooden, Orosco (8); Scott. W—Scott. L—Gooden. HR—Davis (Hou.).

Game 2—October 9, at Houston
N.Y. ....0 0 0 2 3 0 0 0 0—5 10 0
Hou. ....0 0 0 0 0 0 1 0 0—1 10 2
Ojeda; Ryan, Andersen (6), Lopez (8), Kerfeld (9). W—Ojeda. L—Ryan.

Game 3—October 11, at New York
Hou. ....2 2 0 0 0 0 1 0 0—5 8 1
N.Y. ....0 0 0 0 0 4 0 0 2—6 10 1
Knepper, Kerfeld (8), Smith (9); Darling, Aguilera (6), Orosco (8). W—Orosco. L—Smith. HR—Doran (Hou.); Strawberry, Dykstra (N.Y.).

Game 4—October 12, at New York
Hou. ....0 2 0 0 1 0 0 0 0—3 4 1
N.Y. ....0 0 0 0 0 0 0 1 0—1 3 0
Scott; Fernandez, McDowell (7), Sisk (9). W—Scott. L—Fernandez. HR—Ashby, Thon (Hou.).

Game 5—October 14, at New York
Hou. ......0 0 0 0 1 0 0 0 0 0 0 0—1 9 1
N.Y. ....0 0 0 0 1 0 0 0 0 0 0 1—2 4 0
Ryan, Kerfeld (10); Gooden, Orosco (11). W—Orosco. L—Kerfeld. HR—Strawberry (N.Y.).

Game 6—October 15, at Houston
N.Y. ....0 0 0 0 0 0 0 0 3 0 0 0 0 1 0 3—7 11 0
Hou.....3 0 0 0 0 0 0 0 0 0 0 0 0 1 0 2—6 11 1
Ojeda, Aguilera (6), McDowell (9), Orosco (14); Knepper, Smith (9), Andersen (11), Lopez (14), Calhoun (16). W—Orosco. L—Lopez. HR—Hatcher (Hou.).

WORLD SERIES

■ **Winner:** The Mets, on the brink of elimination, made a wild Game 6 recovery and kept the Red Sox without a Series victory since 1918.

■ **Turning point:** The bottom of the 10th inning of Game 6. One out away from elimination and trailing 5-3 with nobody on base, the Mets amazingly rallied for three runs and a 6-5, Game 7-forcing victory.

■ **Memorable moments:** A tense, 10-pitch battle between Mets batter Mookie Wilson and Boston pitcher Bob Stanley in the fateful 10th inning of Game 6. One Stanley pitch was wild, allowing the tying run to score, and Wilson slapped the final one to first baseman Bill Buckner, who let the ball dribble between his legs for a game-deciding error.

■ **Top guns:** Ray Knight (.391), Gary Carter (2 HR, 9 RBIs), Mets; Bruce Hurst (2-0, 1.96 ERA), Dwight Evans (2 HR, 9 RBIs), Red Sox.

■ **MVP:** Knight.

Linescores

Game 1—October 18, at New York
Boston ....0 0 0 0 0 0 1 0 0—1 5 0
N.Y. ....0 0 0 0 0 0 0 0 0—0 4 1
Hurst, Schiraldi (9); Darling, McDowell (8). W—Hurst. L—Darling. S—Schiraldi.

Game 2—October 19, at New York
Boston ......0 0 3 1 2 0 2 0 1—9 18 0
N.Y. ....0 0 2 0 1 0 0 0 0—3 8 1
Clemens, Crawford (5), Stanley (7); Gooden, Aguilera (6), Orosco (7), Fernandez (9), Sisk (9). W—Crawford. L—Gooden. S—Stanley. HR—Henderson, Evans (Bos.).

Game 3—October 21, at Boston
N.Y. ....4 0 0 0 0 0 2 1 0—7 13 0
Boston ......0 0 1 0 0 0 0 0 0—1 5 0
Ojeda, McDowell (8); Boyd, Sambito (8), Stanley (8). W—Ojeda. L—Boyd. HR—Dykstra (N.Y.).

Game 4—October 22, at Boston
N.Y. ....0 0 0 3 0 0 2 1 0—6 12 0
Boston ......0 0 0 0 0 0 0 2 0—2 7 1
Darling, McDowell (8), Orosco (8); Nipper, Crawford (7), Stanley (9). W—Darling. L—Nipper. S—Orosco. HR—Carter 2, Dykstra (N.Y.).

Game 5—October 23, at Boston
N.Y. ....0 0 0 0 0 0 0 1 1—2 10 1
Boston ......0 1 1 0 2 0 0 0 x—4 12 0
Gooden, Fernandez (5); Hurst. W—Hurst. L—Gooden. HR—Teufel (N.Y.).

Game 6—October 25, at New York
Boston ..1 1 0 0 0 0 1 0 0 2—5 13 3
N.Y. ....0 0 0 0 2 0 0 1 0 3—6 8 2
Clemens, Schiraldi (8), Stanley (10); Ojeda, McDowell (7), Orosco (8), Aguilera (9). W—Aguilera. L—Schiraldi. HR—Henderson (Bos.).

Game 7—October 27, at New York
Boston ......0 3 0 0 0 0 0 2 0—5 9 0
N.Y. ....0 0 0 0 0 3 3 2 x—8 10 0
Hurst, Schiraldi (7), Sambito (7), Stanley (7), Nipper (8), Crawford (8); Darling, Fernandez (4), McDowell (7), Orosco (8). W—McDowell. L—Schiraldi. S—Orosco. HR—Evans, Gedman (Bos.); Knight, Strawberry (N.Y.).

FINAL STANDINGS

American League

East Division

Team	Det.	Tor.	Mil.	N.Y.	Bos.	Bal.	Cle.	Min.	K.C.	Oak.	Sea.	Chi.	Tex.	Cal.	W	L	Pct.	GB
Detroit	...	7	6	5	11	9	9	8	5	5	7	9	8	9	98	64	.605	...
Toronto	6	...	4	7	7	12	8	9	4	5	10	8	9	7	96	66	.593	2
Milwaukee	7	9	...	7	7	11	9	3	8	6	4	6	9	5	91	71	.562	7
New York	8	6	6	...	6	10	7	6	7	5	7	7	5	9	89	73	.549	9
Boston	2	6	6	7	...	12	7	7	6	4	7	3	7	4	78	84	.481	20
Baltimore	4	1	2	3	1	...	7	5	9	7	4	8	7	9	67	95	.414	31
Cleveland	4	5	4	6	6	6	...	3	6	4	5	5	2	5	61	101	.377	37

West Division

Team	Min.	K.C.	Oak.	Sea.	Chi.	Tex.	Cal.	Det.	Tor.	Mil.	N.Y.	Bos.	Bal.	Cle.	W	L	Pct.	GB
Minnesota	...	5	10	9	7	6	5	4	3	9	6	5	7	9	85	77	.525	...
Kansas City	8	...	5	9	7	7	8	7	8	4	5	6	3	6	83	79	.512	2
Oakland	3	8	...	5	4	6	7	7	7	6	7	8	5	8	81	81	.500	4
Seattle	4	4	8	...	7	9	6	5	2	8	5	5	8	7	78	84	.481	7
Chicago	6	6	9	6	...	7	5	3	4	6	5	9	4	7	77	85	.475	8
Texas	7	6	7	4	6	...	8	4	3	3	7	5	5	10	75	87	.463	10
California	8	5	6	7	8	5	...	3	5	7	3	8	3	7	75	87	.463	10

National League

East Division

Team	St.L.	N.Y.	Mon.	Phi.	Pit.	Chi.	S.F.	Cin.	Hou.	L.A.	Atl.	S.D.	W	L	Pct.	GB
St. Louis	...	9	7	10	11	12	5	8	7	9	9	8	95	67	.586	...
New York	9	...	10	13	12	9	9	5	6	6	5	8	92	70	.568	3
Montreal	11	8	...	10	11	8	5	6	5	9	9	9	91	71	.562	4
Philadelphia	8	5	8	...	11	10	2	7	6	10	5	8	80	82	.494	15
Pittsburgh	7	6	7	7	...	14	6	8	6	6	5	8	80	82	.494	15
Chicago	6	9	10	8	4	...	5	6	8	6	5	9	76	85	.472	18.5

West Division

Team	S.F.	Cin.	Hou.	L.A.	Atl.	S.D.	St.L.	N.Y.	Mon.	Phi.	Pit.	Chi.	W	L	Pct.	GB
San Fran.	...	11	8	8	10	13	7	3	7	10	6	7	90	72	.556	...
Cincinnati	7	...	13	10	10	12	4	7	6	5	4	6	84	78	.519	6
Houston	10	5	...	12	10	5	5	6	7	6	6	4	76	86	.469	14
Los Angeles	10	8	6	...	12	11	3	6	3	2	6	6	73	89	.451	17
Atlanta	8	8	8	6	...	6	3	7	3	7	7	6	69	92	.429	20.5
San Diego	5	6	13	7	12	...	4	4	3	4	4	3	65	97	.401	25

SIGNIFICANT EVENTS

■ **April 8:** Dodgers vice president Al Campanis, reeling from criticism he had generated two days earlier with his nationally televised comments about the role of blacks in sports, resigned.

■ **July 14:** Kansas City's Bo Jackson became a two-sport star when he signed a five-year contract to play football for the Los Angeles Raiders.

MEMORABLE MOMENTS

■ **April 18:** Mike Schmidt joined the 500-homer club with a dramatic three-run ninth-inning shot that gave the Phillies an 8-6 victory over the Pirates.

■ **July 18:** Yankee Don Mattingly tied a 31-year-old Major League record when he hit a home run in his eighth consecutive game—a 7-2 loss to the Rangers.

■ **August 26:** Cleveland pitcher John Farrell stopped Paul Molitor's 39-game hitting streak, but Milwaukee won in 10 innings, 1-0.

■ **September 14:** Catcher Ernie Whitt belted three home runs to lead a Toronto assault that produced a record 10 homers and an 18-3 rout of the Orioles.

■ **September 29:** Oakland's Mark McGwire pounded his 49th home run in a 5-4 victory over Cleveland, giving him 11 more than the previous rookie record.

■ **October 3:** Dodgers ace Orel Hershiser ended Padres catcher Benito Santiago's rookie-record 34-game hitting streak.

■ **October 4:** The Tigers defeated Toronto, 1-0, and completed a season-ending, A.L. East-deciding sweep of the Blue Jays.

LEADERS

American League
BA: Wade Boggs, Bos., .363.
Runs: Paul Molitor, Mil., 114.
Hits: Kirby Puckett, Min.; Kevin Seitzer, K.C., 207.
TB: George Bell, Tor., 369.
HR: Mark McGwire, Oak., 49.
RBI: George Bell, Tor., 134.
SB: Harold Reynolds, Sea., 60.
Wins: Roger Clemens, Bos.; Dave Stewart, Oak., 20.
ERA: Jimmy Key, Tor., 2.76.
CG: Roger Clemens, Bos., 18.
IP: Charlie Hough, Tex., 285.1.
SO: Mark Langston, Sea., 262.
SV: Tom Henke, Tor., 34.

National League
BA: Tony Gwynn, S.D., .370.
Runs: Tim Raines, Mon., 123.
Hits: Tony Gwynn, S.D., 218.
TB: Andre Dawson, Chi., 353.
HR: Andre Dawson, Chi., 49.
RBI: Andre Dawson, Chi., 137.
SB: Vince Coleman, St.L., 109.
Wins: Rick Sutcliffe, Chi., 18.
ERA: Nolan Ryan, Hou., 2.76.
CG: Rick Reuschel, Pit.-S.F.; Fernando Valenzuela, L.A., 12.
IP: Orel Hershiser, L.A., 264.2.
SO: Nolan Ryan, Hou., 270.
SV: Steve Bedrosian, Phil., 40.

A.L. 20-game winners
Roger Clemens, Bos., 20-9
Dave Stewart, Oak., 20-13

A.L. 100 RBIs
George Bell, Tor., 134
Dwight Evans, Bos., 123
Mark McGwire, Oak., 118
Wally Joyner, Cal., 117
Don Mattingly, N.Y., 115
Jose Canseco, Oak., 113
Gary Gaetti, Min., 109
Ruben Sierra, Tex., 109
Joe Carter, Cle., 106
Alan Trammell, Det., 105
Robin Yount, Mil., 103
Danny Tartabull, K.C., 101
Alvin Davis, Sea., 100
Larry Parrish, Tex., 100

N.L. 100 RBIs
Andre Dawson, Chi., 137
Tim Wallach, Mon., 123
Mike Schmidt, Phil., 113
Jack Clark, St.L., 106
Willie McGee, St.L., 105
Dale Murphy, Atl., 105
Darryl Strawberry, N.Y., 104
Eric Davis, Cin., 100
Juan Samuel, Phil., 100

A.L. 40 homers
Mark McGwire, Oak., 49
George Bell, Tor., 47

N.L. 40 homers
Andre Dawson, Chi., 49
Dale Murphy, Atl., 44

Most Valuable Player
A.L.: George Bell, OF, Tor.
N.L.: Andre Dawson, OF, Chi.

Cy Young Award
A.L.: Roger Clemens, Bos.
N.L.: Steve Bedrosian, Phil.

Rookie of the Year
A.L.: Mark McGwire, 1B, Oak.
N.L.: Benito Santiago, C, S.D.

Manager of the Year
A.L.: Sparky Anderson, Det.
N.L.: Buck Rodgers, Mon.

Hall of Fame additions
Ray Dandridge, 3B, Negro Leagues
Catfish Hunter, P, 1965-79
Billy Williams, OF, 1959-76

ALL-STAR GAME

■ **Winner:** The N.L. broke a scoreless deadlock in the 13th inning to claim a 2-0 victory.

■ **Key inning:** The 13th, when Tim Raines drilled a two-out Jay Howell pitch for a two-run triple, scoring Ozzie Virgil and Hubie Brooks.

■ **Memorable moment:** A violent collision between Dave Winfield and N.L. catcher Virgil in the ninth. Winfield, trying to score from second on a failed double-play attempt, was called out when Virgil held onto the ball.

■ **Top guns:** Mike Scott (Astros), Rick Sutcliffe (Cubs), Orel Hershiser (Dodgers), Raines (Expos), N.L.; Bret Saberhagen (Royals), Mark Langston (Mariners), A.L.

■ **MVP:** Raines.

Linescore

July 14, at the Oakland Coliseum
N.L. ....000 000 000 0002—2 8 2
A.L. ....000 000 000 0000—0 6 1
Scott (Astros), Sutcliffe (Cubs) 3, Hershiser (Dodgers) 5, Reuschel (Pirates) 7, Franco (Reds) 8, Bedrosian (Phillies) 9, L. Smith (Cubs) 10, S. Fernandez (Mets) 13; Saberhagen (Royals), Morris (Tigers) 4, Langston (Mariners) 6, Plesac (Brewers) 8, Righetti (Yankees) 9, Henke (Blue Jays) 9, Howell (Athletics) 12. W—L. Smith. L—Howell. S—S. Fernandez.

ALCS

■ **Winner:** Minnesota, a loser in the A.L.'s first two LCS in 1969 and '70, surprised the favored Detroit Tigers in a five-game romp.

■ **Turning point:** The sixth inning of Game 4. With the Twins leading the series 2-1 and the game 4-3, Detroit's Darrell Evans let Minnesota catcher Tim Laudner pick him off third base—a mistake that doomed the Tigers' pennant hopes.

■ **Memorable moment:** The Game 5 hitting of Twins right fielder Tom Brunansky, who collected a single, double, homer and three RBIs in Minnesota's series-closing 9-5 victory.

■ **Top guns:** Brunansky (.412, 2 HR, 9 RBIs), Dan Gladden (.350), Gary Gaetti (.300, 2 HR, 5 RBIs), Twins; Johnny Grubb (.571), Chet Lemon (2 HR, 4 RBIs), Tigers.

■ **MVP:** Gaetti.

Linescores

Game 1—October 7, at Minnesota
Detroit.........0 0 1 0 0 1 1 2 0—5 10 0
Minnesota..0 1 0 0 3 0 0 4 x—8 10 0
Alexander, Henneman (8), Hernandez (8), King (8); Viola, Reardon (8). W—Reardon. L—Alexander. HR—Gaetti 2 (Min.); Heath, Gibson (Det.).

Game 2—October 8, at Minnesota
Detroit..........0 2 0 0 0 0 0 1 0—3 7 1
Minnesota....0 3 0 2 1 0 0 0 x—6 6 0
Morris; Blyleven, Berenguer (8). W—Blyleven. L—Morris. S—Berenguer. HR—Lemon, Whitaker (Det.); Hrbek (Min.).

Game 3—October 10, at Detroit
Minnesota....0 0 0 2 0 2 2 0 0—6 8 1
Detroit..........0 0 5 0 0 0 0 2 x—7 7 0
Straker, Schatzeder (3), Berenguer (7), Reardon (8); Terrell, Henneman (7). W—Henneman. L—Reardon. HR—Gagne, Brunansky (Min.); Sheridan (Det.).

Game 4—October 11, at Detroit
Minnesota....0 0 1 1 1 1 0 1 0—5 7 1
Detroit..........1 0 0 0 1 1 0 0 0—3 7 3
Viola, Atherton (6), Berenguer (6), Reardon (9); Tanana, Petry (6), Thurmond (9). W—Viola. L—Tanana. S—Reardon. HR—Puckett, Gagne (Min.).

Game 5—October 12, at Detroit
Minnesota..0 4 0 0 0 0 1 1 3—9 15 1
Detroit.........0 0 0 3 0 0 0 1 1—5 9 1
Blyleven, Schatzeder (7), Berenguer (8), Reardon (8); Alexander, King (2), Henneman (7), Robinson (9). W—Blyleven. L—Alexander. S—Reardon. HR—Nokes, Lemon (Det.); Brunansky (Min.).

NLCS

■ **Winner:** The Cardinals had to overcome the lusty hitting of San Francisco's Jeffrey Leonard to claim their third pennant of the decade.

■ **Turning point:** The combined six-hit pitching of Cardinals John Tudor, Todd Worrell and Ken Dayley in a 1-0 Game 6 victory.

■ **Memorable moment:** Leonard's two-run homer in the fifth inning of Game 4—his record-tying fourth in the series.

■ **Top guns:** Tony Pena (.381), Willie McGee (.308), Cardinals; Dave Dravecky (1-1, 0.60 ERA), Leonard (.417, 4 HR, 5 RBIs), Giants.

■ **MVP:** Leonard.

Linescores

Game 1—October 6, at St. Louis
San Fran. ....1 0 0 1 0 0 0 1 0—3 7 1
St. Louis ......0 0 1 1 0 3 0 0 x—5 10 1
Reuschel, Lefferts (7), Garrelts (8); Mathews, Worrell (8), Dayley (8). W—Mathews. L—Reuschel. S—Dayley. HR—Leonard (S.F.).

Game 2—October 7, at St. Louis
San Fran. ....0 2 0 1 0 0 0 2 0—5 10 0
St. Louis ......0 0 0 0 0 0 0 0 0—0 2 1
Dravecky; Tudor, Forsch (9). W—Dravecky. L—Tudor. HR—W. Clark, Leonard (S.F.).

Game 3—October 9, at San Francisco
St. Louis ......0 0 0 0 0 2 4 0 0—6 11 1
San Fran. ....0 3 1 0 0 0 0 0 1—5 7 1
Magrane, Forsch (5), Worrell (7); Hammaker, D. Robinson (7), Lefferts (7), LaCoss (8). W—Forsch. L—D. Robinson. S—Worrell. HR—Leonard, Spilman (S.F.); Lindeman (St.L.).

Game 4—October 10, at San Francisco
St. Louis ....0 2 0 0 0 0 0 0 0—2 9 0
San Fran.........0 0 0 1 2 0 0 1 x—4 9 2
Cox; Krukow. W—Krukow. L—Cox. HR—Thompson, Leonard, Brenly (S.F.).

Game 5—October 11, at San Francisco
St. Louis ....1 0 1 1 0 0 0 0 0—3 7 0
San Fran. ......1 0 1 4 0 0 0 0 x—6 7 1
Mathews, Forsch (4), Horton (4), Dayley (7); Reuschel, Price (5). W—Price. L—Forsch. HR—Mitchell (S.F.).

Game 6—October 13, at St. Louis
San Fran. ......0 0 0 0 0 0 0 0 0—0 6 0
St. Louis ....0 1 0 0 0 0 0 0 x—1 5 0
Dravecky, D. Robinson (7); Tudor, Worrell (8), Dayley (9). W—Tudor. L—Dravecky. S—Dayley.

Game 7—October 14, at St. Louis
San Fran. ....0 0 0 0 0 0 0 0 0—0 8 1
St. Louis ......0 4 0 0 0 2 0 0 x—6 12 0
Hammaker, Price (3), Downs (3), Garrelts (5), Lefferts (6), LaCoss (6), D. Robinson (8); Cox. W—Cox. L—Hammaker. HR—Oquendo (St.L.).

WORLD SERIES

■ **Winner:** The Twins held off the Cardinals and captured a Series in which the home team won every game.

■ **Turning point:** Don Baylor's two-run fifth-inning homer and Kent Hrbek's grand slam, blows that turned a 5-2 deficit into an 11-5 sixth-game victory for the Twins.

■ **Memorable moment:** Hrbek's arm-pumping jaunt around the bases after his Game 6 slam.

■ **Top guns:** Frank Viola (2-1), Steve Lombardozzi (.412), Twins; Tony Pena (.409), Willie McGee (.370), Cardinals.

■ **MVP:** Viola.

Linescores

Game 1—October 17, at Minnesota
St. Louis ..0 1 0 0 0 0 0 0 0— 1 5 1
Minn. ......0 0 0 7 2 0 1 0 x—10 11 0
Magrane, Forsch (4), Horton (7); Viola, Atherton (9). W—Viola. L—Magrane. HR—Gladden, Lombardozzi (Min.).

Game 2—October 18, at Minnesota
St. Louis ....0 0 0 0 1 0 1 2 0—4 9 0
Minn. ....0 1 0 6 0 1 0 0 x—8 10 0
Cox, Tunnell (4), Dayley (7), Worrell (8); Blyleven, Berenguer (8), Reardon (9). W—Blyleven. L—Cox. HR—Gaetti, Laudner (Min.).

Game 3—October 20, at St. Louis
Minn. ....0 0 0 0 0 1 0 0 0—1 5 1
St. Louis ......0 0 0 0 0 0 3 0 x—3 9 1
Straker, Berenguer (7), Schatzeder (7); Tudor, Worrell (8). W—Tudor. L—Berenguer. S—Worrell.

Game 4—October 21, at St. Louis
Minn. ....0 0 1 0 1 0 0 0 0—2 7 1
St. Louis ....0 0 1 6 0 0 0 0 x—7 10 1
Viola, Schatzeder (4), Niekro (5), Frazier (7); Mathews, Forsch (4), Dayley (7). W—Forsch. L—Viola. S—Dayley. HR—Gagne (Min.); Lawless (St.L.).

Game 5—October 22, at St. Louis
Minn. ....0 0 0 0 0 0 0 2 0—2 6 1
St. Louis ....0 0 0 0 0 3 1 0 x—4 10 0
Blyleven, Atherton (7), Reardon (7); Cox, Dayley (8), Worrell (8). W—Cox. L—Blyleven. S—Worrell.

Game 6—October 24, at Minnesota
St. Louis ..1 1 0 2 1 0 0 0 0— 5 11 2
Minn. ......2 0 0 0 4 4 0 1 x—11 15 0
Tudor, Horton (5), Forsch (6), Dayley (6), Tunnell (7); Straker, Schatzeder (4), Berenguer (6), Reardon (9). W—Schatzeder. L—Tudor. HR—Herr (St.L.); Baylor, Hrbek (Min.).

Game 7—October 25, at Minnesota
St. Louis ....0 2 0 0 0 0 0 0 0—2 6 1
Minn. ....0 1 0 0 1 1 0 1 x—4 10 0
Magrane, Cox (5), Worrell (6); Viola, Reardon (9). W—Viola. L—Cox. S—Reardon.

FINAL STANDINGS

American League

East Division

Team	Bos.	Det.	Mil.	Tor.	N.Y.	Cle.	Bal.	Oak.	Min.	K.C.	Cal.	Chi.	Tex.	Sea.	W	L	Pct.	GB
Boston	...	6	10	2	9	8	9	3	7	6	8	7	8	6	89	73	.549	...
Detroit	7	...	5	5	8	9	8	4	1	8	7	9	8	9	88	74	.543	1
Milwaukee	3	8	...	7	6	4	9	3	7	9	9	6	8	8	87	75	.537	2
Toronto	11	8	6	...	7	7	8	3	5	8	6	5	6	7	87	75	.537	2
New York	4	5	7	6	...	7	10	6	9	6	6	9	5	5	85	76	.528	3.5
Cleveland	5	4	9	6	6	...	9	4	5	6	4	9	6	5	78	84	.481	11
Baltimore	4	5	4	5	3	4	...	4	3	0	5	4	6	7	54	107	.335	34.5

West Division

Team	Oak.	Min.	K.C.	Cal.	Chi.	Tex.	Sea.	Bos.	Det.	Mil.	Tor.	N.Y.	Cle.	Bal.	W	L	Pct.	GB
Oakland	...	8	5	9	8	8	9	9	8	9	9	6	8	8	104	58	.642	...
Minnesota	5	...	6	9	9	7	8	5	11	5	7	3	7	9	91	71	.562	13
Kansas City	8	7	...	8	6	7	7	6	4	3	4	6	6	12	84	77	.522	19.5
California	4	4	5	...	9	8	6	4	5	3	6	6	8	7	75	87	.463	29
Chicago	5	4	7	4	...	8	9	5	3	6	7	3	3	7	71	90	.441	32.5
Texas	5	6	6	5	5	...	7	4	4	4	6	6	6	6	70	91	.435	33.5
Seattle	4	5	5	7	4	6	...	6	3	4	5	7	7	5	68	93	.422	35.5

National League

East Division

Team	N.Y.	Pit.	Mon.	Chi.	St.L.	Phi.	L.A.	Cin.	S.D.	S.F.	Hou.	Atl.	W	L	Pct.	GB
New York	...	12	12	9	14	10	10	7	7	4	7	8	100	60	.625	...
Pittsburgh	6	...	10	11	11	11	6	5	8	8	4	5	85	75	.531	15
Montreal	6	8	...	9	13	9	4	7	4	7	6	8	81	81	.500	20
Chicago	9	7	9	...	7	8	4	6	8	5	7	7	77	85	.475	24
St. Louis	4	7	5	11	...	12	5	6	6	5	6	9	76	86	.469	25
Philadelphia	8	7	9	10	6	...	1	3	4	7	4	6	65	96	.404	35.5

West Division

Team	L.A.	Cin.	S.D.	S.F.	Hou.	Atl.	N.Y.	Pit.	Mon.	Chi.	St.L.	Phi.	W	L	Pct.	GB
Los Angeles	...	11	7	12	9	14	1	6	8	8	7	11	94	67	.584	...
Cincinnati	7	...	10	11	9	13	4	7	5	6	6	9	87	74	.540	7
San Diego	11	8	...	8	12	10	5	4	8	4	6	7	83	78	.516	11
San Fran.	6	7	10	...	11	13	8	4	5	7	7	5	83	79	.512	11.5
Houston	9	9	6	7	...	13	5	8	6	5	6	8	82	80	.506	12.5
Atlanta	4	5	8	5	5	...	4	5	4	5	3	6	54	106	.338	39.5

LEADERS

American League
BA: Wade Boggs, Bos., .366.
Runs: Wade Boggs, Bos., 128.
Hits: Kirby Puckett, Min., 234.
TB: Kirby Puckett, Min., 358.
HR: Jose Canseco, Oak., 42.
RBI: Jose Canseco, Oak., 124.
SB: Rickey Henderson, N.Y., 93.
Wins: Frank Viola, Min., 24.
ERA: Allan Anderson, Min., 2.45.
CG: Roger Clemens, Bos.; Dave Stewart, Oak., 14.
IP: Dave Stewart, Oak., 275.2.
SO: Roger Clemens, Bos., 291.
SV: Dennis Eckersley, Oak., 45.

National League
BA: Tony Gwynn, S.D., .313.
Runs: Brett Butler, S.F., 109.
Hits: Andres Galarraga, Mon., 184.
TB: Andres Galarraga, Mon., 329.
HR: Darryl Strawberry, N.Y., 39.
RBI: Will Clark, S.F., 109.
SB: Vince Coleman, St.L., 81.
Wins: Orel Hershiser, L.A.; Danny Jackson, Cin., 23.
ERA: Joe Magrane, St.L., 2.18.
CG: Orel Hershiser, L.A.; Danny Jackson, Cin., 15.
IP: Orel Hershiser, L.A., 267.
SO: Nolan Ryan, Hou., 228.
SV: John Franco, Cin., 39.

A.L. 20-game winners
Frank Viola, Min., 24-7
Dave Stewart, Oak., 21-12
Mark Gubicza, K.C., 20-8

N.L. 20-game winners
Orel Hershiser, L.A., 23-8
Danny Jackson, Cin., 23-8
David Cone, N.Y., 20-3

A.L. 100 RBIs
Jose Canseco, Oak., 124
Kirby Puckett, Min., 121
Mike Greenwell, Bos., 119
Dwight Evans, Bos., 111
Dave Winfield, N.Y, 107
George Brett, K.C., 103
Danny Tartabull, K.C., 102

N.L. 100 RBIs
Will Clark, S.F., 109
Darryl Strawberry, N.Y., 101
Bobby Bonilla, Pit., 100
Andy Van Slyke, Pit., 100

A.L. 40 homers
Jose Canseco, Oak., 42

Most Valuable Player
A.L.: Jose Canseco, OF, Oak.
N.L.: Kirk Gibson, OF, L.A.

Cy Young Award
A.L.: Frank Viola, Min.
N.L.: Orel Hershiser, L.A.

Rookie of the Year
A.L.: Walt Weiss, SS, Oak.
N.L.: Chris Sabo, 3B, Cin.

Manager of the Year
A.L.: Tony La Russa, Oak.
N.L.: Tommy Lasorda, L.A.

Hall of Fame addition
Willie Stargell, OF/1B, 1962-82

SIGNIFICANT EVENTS

■ **January 22:** Kirk Gibson and Carlton Fisk were among seven players declared free agents by an arbitrator who ruled that owners had acted in collusion against free agents after the 1985 season.
■ **June 23:** Yankee owner George Steinbrenner fired manager Billy Martin for a fifth time and replaced him with the man he had replaced—Lou Piniella.
■ **August 9:** The Cubs defeated the Mets, 6-4, in the first official night game at Chicago's 74-year-old Wrigley Field.
■ **August 31:** Major League owners were stunned when a labor arbitrator found them guilty of collusion for a second time—this time against the 1986 class of free agents.
■ **September 8:** N.L. President A. Bartlett Giamatti was elected to succeed Peter V. Ueberroth as baseball's seventh commissioner.

MEMORABLE MOMENTS

■ **April 29:** The Orioles defeated Chicago, 9-0, and ended their record season-opening losing streak at 21 games.
■ **June 25:** Orioles shortstop Cal Ripken stretched his ironman streak to 1,000 games in a 10-3 loss to Boston.
■ **September 16:** Cincinnati's Tom Browning retired 27 consecutive Dodgers in a 1-0 victory—baseball's 12th perfect game.
■ **September 23:** Oakland's Jose Canseco swiped two bases in a victory over Milwaukee and became the first player to hit 40 homers and record 40 steals in the same season.
■ **September 28:** Dodgers righthander Orel Hershiser worked 10 shutout innings against the Padres in his final regular-season start and stretched his scoreless-innings streak to a record 59.

ALL-STAR GAME

■ **Winner:** A.L. pitchers held the N.L. to five hits and catcher Terry Steinbach supplied all the offense they needed for a 2-1 All-Star Game victory.
■ **Key inning:** The third, when Steinbach drove a Dwight Gooden pitch over the right-field wall, giving the A.L. a lead it never relinquished.
■ **Memorable moment:** Steinbach, maligned by the media as an unworthy starter because of his .217 season average, drove in the winning run with a fourth-inning sacrifice fly and walked away with MVP honors.
■ **Top guns:** Frank Viola (Twins), Dennis Eckersley (Athletics), Steinbach (Athletics), A.L.; Vince Coleman (Cardinals), N.L.
■ **MVP:** Steinbach.

Linescore
July 12, at Cincinnati's Riverfront Stadium
A.L. ....0 0 1 1 0 0 0 0 0—2 6 2
N.L. ....0 0 0 1 0 0 0 0 0—1 5 0
Viola (Twins), Clemens (Red Sox) 3, Gubicza (Royals) 4, Stieb (Blue Jays) 6, Russell (Rangers) 7, Jones (Indians) 8, Plesac (Brewers) 8, Eckersley (Athletics) 9; Gooden (Mets), Knepper (Astros) 4, Cone (Mets) 5, Gross (Dodgers) 6, Davis (Padres) 7, Walk (Phillies) 7, Hershiser (Dodgers) 8, Worrell (Cardinals) 9. W—Viola. L—Gooden. S—Eckersley. HR—Steinbach, A.L.

ALCS

■ **Winner:** The Oakland Athletics, making their first Championship Series appearance since 1975, recorded the first sweep in the best-of-seven format and claimed their first pennant since 1974.
■ **Turning point:** Amid a flurry of Oakland home runs, the Athletics actually took control on a ninth-inning Walt Weiss single that produced a 4-3 Game 2 victory over the Red Sox at Fenway Park.
■ **Memorable moment:** Jose Canseco's first-inning home run in the fourth game, his third of the series and Oakland's seventh. The A's went on to close out the Red Sox with a 4-1 victory.
■ **Top guns:** Dennis Eckersley (4 games, 4 saves, 0.00 ERA), Gene Nelson (2-0, 0.00), Rickey Henderson (.375), Canseco (.313, 3 HR, 4 RBIs), Athletics; Wade Boggs (.385), Rich Gedman (.357), Red Sox.
■ **MVP:** Eckersley.

Linescores

Game 1—October 5, at Boston
Oakland........0 0 0 1 0 0 0 1 0—2 6 0
Boston ....0 0 0 0 0 0 1 0 0—1 6 0
Stewart, Honeycutt (7), Eckersley (8); Hurst. W—Honeycutt. L—Hurst. S—Eckersley. HR—Canseco (Oak.).

Game 2—October 6, at Boston
Oakland......0 0 0 0 0 0 3 0 1—4 10 1
Boston ......0 0 0 0 0 2 1 0 0—3 4 1
Davis, Cadaret (7), Nelson (7), Eckersley (9); Clemens, Stanley (8), Smith (8). W—Nelson. L—Smith. S—Eckersley. HR—Canseco (Oak.); Gedman (Bos.).

Game 3—October 8, at Oakland
Boston ....3 2 0 0 0 0 1 0 0— 6 12 0
Oakland....0 4 2 0 1 0 1 2 x—10 15 1
Boddicker, Gardner (3), Stanley (8); Welch, Nelson (2), Young (6), Plunk (7), Honeycutt (7), Eckersley (8). W—Nelson. L—Boddicker. S—Eckersley. HR—Greenwell (Bos.); McGwire, Lansford, Hassey, Henderson (Oak.).

Game 4—October 9, at Oakland
Boston ......0 0 0 0 0 1 0 0 0—1 4 0
Oakland.....1 0 1 0 0 0 0 2 x—4 10 1
Hurst, Smithson (5), Smith (7); Stewart, Honeycutt (8), Eckersley (9). W—Stewart. L—Hurst. S—Eckersley. HR—Canseco (Oak.).

NLCS

■ **Winner:** Los Angeles ace Orel Hershiser denied New York's bid for its second pennant in three years with a 6-0 shutout in Game 7.
■ **Turning point:** Game 4, when Dodgers catcher Mike Scioscia hit a game-tying two-run homer in the ninth inning and Kirk Gibson settled matters with a solo shot in the 12th, knotting the series at two games apiece.
■ **Memorable moment:** The eighth inning of Game 3, when Dodgers relief ace Jay Howell was thrown out of the game because a foreign substance was found in his glove. The Mets scored five runs in the inning and claimed an 8-4 victory.
■ **Top guns:** Hershiser (1-0, 1.09 ERA), Scioscia (.364), Gibson (2 HR, 6 RBIs), Dodgers; Randy Myers (2-0, 0.00), Lenny Dykstra (.429), Darryl Strawberry (.300, 6 RBIs), Mets.
■ **MVP:** Hershiser.

Linescores

Game 1—October 4, at Los Angeles
N.Y.............0 0 0 0 0 0 0 0 3—3 8 1
L.A..............1 0 0 0 0 0 1 0 0—2 4 0
Gooden, Myers (8); Hershiser, J. Howell (9). W—Myers. L—J. Howell.

Game 2—October 5, at Los Angeles
N.Y.............0 0 0 2 0 0 0 0 1—3 6 0
L.A. ....1 4 0 0 1 0 0 0 x—6 7 0
Cone, Aguilera (3), Leach (6), McDowell (8); Belcher, Orosco (9), Pena (9). W—Belcher. L—Cone. S—Pena. HR—Hernandez (N.Y.).

Game 3—October 8, at New York
L.A. ....0 2 1 0 0 0 0 1 0—4 7 2
N.Y. ....0 0 1 0 0 2 0 5 x—8 9 2
Hershiser, J. Howell (8), Pena (8), Orosco (8), Horton (8); Darling, McDowell (7), Myers (8), Cone (9). W—Myers. L—Pena.

Game 4—October 9, at New York
L.A......2 0 0 0 0 0 0 0 2 0 0 1—5 7 1
N.Y......0 0 0 3 0 1 0 0 0 0 0 0—4 10 2
Tudor, Holton (6), Horton (7), Pena (9), Leary (12), Orosco (12), Hershiser (12); Gooden, Myers (9), McDowell (11). W—Pena. L—McDowell. S—Hershiser. HR—Strawberry, McReynolds (N.Y.); Scioscia, Gibson (L.A.).

Game 5—October 10, at New York
L.A. ....0 0 0 3 3 0 0 0 1—7 12 0
N.Y. ....0 0 0 0 3 0 0 1 0—4 9 1
Belcher, Horton (8), Holton (8); Fernandez, Leach (5), Aguilera (6), McDowell (8). W—Belcher. L—Fernandez. S—Holton. HR—Gibson (L.A.); Dykstra (N.Y.).

Game 6—October 11, at Los Angeles
N.Y. ....1 0 1 0 2 1 0 0 0—5 11 0
L.A. ....0 0 0 0 1 0 0 0 0—1 5 2
Cone; Leary, Holton (5), Horton (6), Orosco (8). W—Cone. L—Leary. HR—McReynolds (N.Y.).

Game 7—October 12, at Los Angeles
N.Y. ....0 0 0 0 0 0 0 0 0—0 5 2
L.A. ....1 5 0 0 0 0 0 0 x—6 10 0
Darling, Gooden (2), Leach (5), Aguilera (7); Hershiser. W—Hershiser. L—Darling.

WORLD SERIES

■ **Winner:** The Cinderella Dodgers pulled off a five-game surprise against the powerful Athletics.
■ **Turning point:** A two-out, ninth-inning, two-run homer by Kirk Gibson that gave the Dodgers a shocking 5-4 victory in Game 1.
■ **Memorable moment:** The gimpy Gibson, wincing in pain with every swing, connecting with a Dennis Eckersley pitch and then limping triumphantly around the bases with the winning run in the Series opener.
■ **Top guns:** Orel Hershiser (2-0, 1.00 ERA), Gibson (1 AB, 1 hit, 1 HR, 2 RBIs), Mickey Hatcher (.368, 5 RBIs), Dodgers; Terry Steinbach (.364), Athletics.
■ **MVP:** Hershiser.

Linescores

Game 1—October 15, at Los Angeles
Oakland........0 4 0 0 0 0 0 0 0—4 7 0
L.A. ....2 0 0 0 0 1 0 0 2—5 7 0
Stewart, Eckersley (9); Belcher, Leary (3), Holton (6), Pena (8). W—Pena. L—Eckersley. HR—Hatcher, Gibson (L.A.); Canseco (Oak.).

Game 2—October 16, at Los Angeles
Oakland......0 0 0 0 0 0 0 0 0—0 3 0
L.A. ....0 0 5 1 0 0 0 0 x—6 10 1
S. Davis, Nelson (4), Young (6), Plunk (7), Honeycutt (8); Hershiser. W—Hershiser. L—S. Davis. HR—Marshall (L.A.).

Game 3—October 18, at Oakland
L.A. ....0 0 0 0 1 0 0 0 0—1 8 1
Oakland.......0 0 1 0 0 0 0 0 1—2 5 0
Tudor, Leary (2), Pena (6), J. Howell (9); Welch, Cadaret (6), Nelson (6), Honeycutt (8). W—Honeycutt. L—J. Howell. HR—McGwire (Oak.).

Game 4—October 19, at Oakland
L.A. ....2 0 1 0 0 0 1 0 0—4 8 1
Oakland........1 0 0 0 0 1 1 0 0—3 9 2
Belcher, J. Howell (7); Stewart, Cadaret (7), Eckersley (9). W—Belcher. L—Stewart. S—J. Howell.

Game 5—October 20, at Oakland
L.A. ....2 0 0 2 0 1 0 0 0—5 8 0
Oakland........0 0 1 0 0 0 0 1 0—2 4 0
Hershiser; S. Davis, Cadaret (5), Nelson (5), Honeycutt (8), Plunk (9), Burns (9). W—Hershiser. L—S. Davis. HR—Hatcher, M. Davis (L.A.).

FINAL STANDINGS

American League

East Division

Team	Tor.	Bal.	Bos.	Mil.	N.Y.	Cle.	Det.	Oak.	K.C.	Cal.	Tex.	Min.	Sea.	Chi.	W	L	Pct.	GB
Toronto	...	6	8	7	6	8	11	5	5	5	7	3	7	11	89	73	.549	...
Baltimore	7	...	6	7	8	7	10	5	6	6	9	4	6	6	87	75	.537	2
Boston	5	7	...	6	7	8	11	7	4	4	6	6	5	7	83	79	.512	6
Milwaukee	6	6	7	...	8	10	7	5	4	5	5	9	7	2	81	81	.500	8
New York	7	5	6	5	...	4	7	3	6	6	5	6	8	6	74	87	.460	14.5
Cleveland	5	6	5	3	9	...	5	2	8	7	7	5	6	5	73	89	.451	16
Detroit	2	3	2	6	6	8	...	4	6	1	4	5	4	8	59	103	.364	30

West Division

Team	Oak.	K.C.	Cal.	Tex.	Min.	Sea.	Chi.	Tor.	Bal.	Bos.	Mil.	N.Y.	Cle.	Det.	W	L	Pct.	GB
Oakland	...	6	8	8	7	9	8	7	7	5	7	9	10	8	99	63	.611	...
Kansas City	7	...	9	8	7	9	7	7	6	8	8	6	4	6	92	70	.568	7
California	5	4	...	6	11	7	8	7	6	8	7	6	5	11	91	71	.562	8
Texas	5	5	7	...	8	7	10	5	3	6	7	7	5	8	83	79	.512	16
Minnesota	6	6	2	5	...	7	8	9	8	6	3	6	7	7	80	82	.494	19
Seattle	4	4	6	6	6	...	6	5	6	7	5	4	6	8	73	89	.451	26
Chicago	5	6	5	3	5	7	...	1	6	5	10	5	7	4	69	92	.429	29.5

National League

East Division

Team	Chi.	N.Y.	St.L.	Mon.	Pit.	Phi.	S.F.	S.D.	Hou.	L.A.	Cin.	Atl.	W	L	Pct.	GB
Chicago	...	10	11	10	12	10	6	8	5	7	7	7	93	69	.574	...
New York	8	...	10	9	9	12	3	5	6	7	8	10	87	75	.537	6
St. Louis	7	8	...	13	5	11	5	10	5	9	4	9	86	76	.531	7
Montreal	8	9	5	...	11	9	7	5	8	5	8	6	81	81	.500	12
Pittsburgh	6	9	13	7	...	8	5	3	5	5	5	8	74	88	.457	19
Philadelphia	8	6	7	9	10	...	4	2	3	6	8	4	67	95	.414	26

West Division

Team	S.F.	S.D.	Hou.	L.A.	Cin.	Atl.	Chi.	N.Y.	St.L.	Mon.	Pit.	Phi.	W	L	Pct.	GB
San Fran.	...	10	10	8	10	12	6	9	7	5	7	8	92	70	.568	...
San Diego	8	...	10	12	9	11	4	7	2	7	9	10	89	73	.549	3
Houston	8	8	...	10	10	10	7	6	7	4	7	9	86	76	.531	6
Los Angeles	10	6	8	...	10	10	5	5	3	7	7	6	77	83	.481	14
Cincinnati	8	9	8	8	...	10	5	4	8	4	7	4	75	87	.463	17
Atlanta	6	7	8	6	8	...	5	2	3	6	4	8	63	97	.394	28

SIGNIFICANT EVENTS

■ **January 5:** Commissioner Peter Ueberroth signed a $400-million cable television package with ESPN, a month after signing a four-year, $1.06-billion contract with CBS-TV.

■ **February 3:** Bill White became the highest ranking black executive in professional sports when he was tabbed to succeed A. Bartlett Giamatti as N.L. president.

■ **June 5:** The Blue Jays opened SkyDome with a 5-3 loss to the Brewers.

■ **August 24:** Commissioner A. Bartlett Giamatti handed all-time hits leader Pete Rose, who had been implicated in a gambling scandal, a lifetime ban from baseball.

■ **September 1:** Giamatti, 51, died of a heart attack at his Massachusetts summer cottage, eight days after handing Rose his lifetime ban.

■ **September 13:** Giamatti assistant Fay Vincent was elected as baseball's eighth commissioner.

■ **December 25:** Former player and manager Billy Martin died when a pickup truck in which he was riding crashed near his home in Binghamton, N.Y.

MEMORABLE MOMENTS

■ **August 15:** Giants lefty Dave Dravecky, on the comeback trail from cancer surgery, broke his arm while throwing a pitch in a game at Montreal.

■ **August 22:** Nolan Ryan fired a fastball past Oakland's Rickey Henderson and became the first Major Leaguer to record 5,000 career strikeouts.

LEADERS

American League
BA: Kirby Puckett, Min., .339.
Runs: Wade Boggs, Bos.; Rickey Henderson, N.Y.-Oak., 113.
Hits: Kirby Puckett, Min., 215.
TB: Ruben Sierra, Tex., 344.
HR: Fred McGriff, Tor., 36.
RBI: Ruben Sierra, Tex., 119.
SB: Rickey Henderson, N.Y.-Oak., 77.
Wins: Bret Saberhagen, K.C., 23.
ERA: Bret Saberhagen, K.C., 2.16.
CG: Bret Saberhagen, K.C., 12.
IP: Bret Saberhagen, K.C., 262.1.
SO: Nolan Ryan, Tex., 301.
SV: Jeff Russell, Tex., 38.

National League
BA: Tony Gwynn, S.D., .336.
Runs: Will Clark, S.F.; Howard Johnson, N.Y.; Ryne Sandberg, Chi., 104.
Hits: Tony Gwynn, S.D., 203.
TB: Kevin Mitchell, S.F., 345.
HR: Kevin Mitchell, S.F., 47.
RBI: Kevin Mitchell, S.F., 125.
SB: Vince Coleman, St.L., 65.
Wins: Mike Scott, Hou., 20.
ERA: Scott Garrelts, S.F., 2.28.
CG: Tim Belcher, L.A.; Bruce Hurst, S.D., 10.
IP: Orel Hershiser, L.A., 256.2.
SO: Jose DeLeon, St.L., 201.
SV: Mark Davis, S.D., 44.

A.L. 20-game winners
Bret Saberhagen, K.C., 23-6
Dave Stewart, Oak., 21-9

N.L. 20-game winner
Mike Scott, Hou., 20-10

A.L. 100 RBIs
Ruben Sierra, Tex., 119
Don Mattingly, N.Y., 113
Nick Esasky, Bos., 108
Joe Carter, Cle., 105
Bo Jackson, K.C., 105
George Bell, Tor., 104
Robin Yount, Mil., 103
Dwight Evans, Bos., 100

N.L. 100 RBIs
Kevin Mitchell, S.F., 125
Pedro Guerrero, St.L., 117
Will Clark, S.F., 111
Eric Davis, Cin., 101
Howard Johnson, N.Y., 101

N.L. 40 homers
Kevin Mitchell, S.F., 47

Most Valuable Player
A.L.: Robin Yount, OF, Mil.
N.L.: Kevin Mitchell, OF, S.F.

Cy Young Award
A.L.: Bret Saberhagen, K.C.
N.L.: Mark Davis, S.D.

Rookie of the Year
A.L.: Gregg Olson, P, Bal.
N.L.: Jerome Walton, OF, Chi.

Manager of the Year
A.L.: Frank Robinson, Bal.
N.L.: Don Zimmer, Chi.

Hall of Fame additions
Al Barlick, umpire
Johnny Bench, C, 1967-83
Red Schoendienst, 2B, 1945-63
Carl Yastrzemski, OF, 1961-83

ALL-STAR GAME

■ **Winner:** The A.L.'s 5-3 victory marked its first back-to-back All-Star wins since 1957-58.
■ **Key inning:** The third, when the A.L. added to its 3-2 advantage with run-scoring singles by Harold Baines and Ruben Sierra.
■ **Memorable moment:** Consecutive home runs by Bo Jackson and Wade Boggs to lead off the A.L. first inning. That was an All-Star first.
■ **Top guns:** Nolan Ryan (Rangers), Jackson (Royals), Boggs (Red Sox), Sierra (Rangers), A.L.; Kevin Mitchell (Giants), Bobby Bonilla (Pirates), N.L.
■ **MVP:** Jackson.

Linescore
July 11, at California's Anaheim Stadium
N.L.............2 0 0 0 0 0 0 1 0—3 9 1
A.L. ....2 1 2 0 0 0 0 0 x—5 12 0
Reuschel (Giants), Smoltz (Braves) 2, Sutcliffe (Cubs) 3, Burke (Expos) 4, M. Davis (Padres) 6, Howell (Dodgers) 7, Williams (Cubs) 8; Stewart (Athletics), Ryan (Rangers) 2, Gubicza (Royals) 4, Moore (Athletics) 5, Swindell (Indians) 6, Russell (Rangers) 7, Plesac (Brewers) 8, Jones (Indians) 8. W—Ryan. L—Smoltz. S—Jones. HR—Jackson, Boggs, A.L.

ALCS

■ **Winner:** The Oakland Athletics ran and muscled their way past Toronto in a series dominated by leadoff hitter Rickey Henderson.
■ **Turning point:** After killing the Blue Jays in Games 1 and 2 with his speed, Henderson muscled up for two home runs in a 6-5 Game 4 victory that gave Oakland a 3-1 series edge.
■ **Memorable moment:** A mammoth Game 4 home run by Oakland slugger Jose Canseco that landed in the fifth tier of the left-field bleachers at SkyDome. The ball officially was measured at 490 feet, but most observers claimed it traveled well beyond 500.
■ **Top guns:** Dennis Eckersley (4 games, 3 saves, 1.59 ERA), Carney Lansford (.455), Henderson (.400, 8 SB, 8 runs, 2 HR, 5 RBIs), Mark McGwire (.389), Athletics; Tony Fernandez (.350), Blue Jays.
■ **MVP:** Henderson.

Linescores

Game 1—October 3, at Oakland
Toronto......0 2 0 1 0 0 0 0 0—3 5 1
Oakland......0 1 0 0 1 3 0 2 x—7 11 0
Stieb, Acker (6), Ward (8); Stewart, Eckersley (9). W—Stewart. L—Stieb. HR—D. Henderson, McGwire (Oak.); Whitt (Tor.).

Game 2—October 4, at Oakland
Toronto........0 0 1 0 0 0 0 2 0—3 5 1
Oakland........0 0 0 2 0 3 1 0 x—6 9 1
Stottlemyre, Acker (6), Wells (6), Henke (7), Cerutti (8); Moore, Honeycutt (8), Eckersley (8). W—Moore. L—Stottlemyre. S—Eckersley. HR—Parker (Oak.).

Game 3—October 6, at Toronto
Oakland........1 0 1 1 0 0 0 0 0—3 8 1
Toronto ....0 0 0 4 0 0 3 0 x—7 8 0
Davis, Honeycutt (7), Nelson (7), M. Young (8); Key, Acker (7), Henke (9). W—Key. L—Davis. HR—Parker (Oak.).

Game 4—October 7, at Toronto
Oakland......0 0 3 0 2 0 1 0 0—6 11 1
Toronto......0 0 0 1 0 1 1 2 0—5 13 0
Welch, Honeycutt (6), Eckersley (8); Flanagan, Ward (5), Cerutti (8), Acker (9). W—Welch. L—Flanagan. S—Eckersley. HR—R. Henderson 2, Canseco (Oak.).

Game 5—October 8, at Toronto
Oakland........1 0 1 0 0 0 2 0 0—4 4 0
Toronto ....0 0 0 0 0 0 0 1 2—3 9 0
Stewart, Eckersley (9); Stieb, Acker (7), Henke (9). W—Stewart. L—Stieb. S—Eckersley. HR—Moseby, Bell (Tor.).

NLCS

■ **Winner:** First basemen Will Clark and Mark Grace took center stage as San Francisco won its first pennant since 1962 and stretched Chicago's pennant drought to 44 years.
■ **Turning point:** The seventh inning of Game 3 when Giants second baseman Robby Thompson belted a two-run homer off reliever Les Lancaster, giving San Francisco a 5-4 victory and a 2-1 series edge.
■ **Memorable moment:** Game 1 at Chicago — the first post-season game played under the lights of Wrigley Field. San Francisco's Clark stole the show with four hits, a grand slam and six RBIs in the Giants' 11-3 victory.
■ **Top guns:** Steve Bedrosian (3 saves), Clark (.650, 13 hits, 2 HR, 8 RBIs), Kevin Mitchell (.353, 2 HR, 7 RBIs), Matt Williams (2 HR, 9 RBIs), Giants; Grace (.647, 8 RBIs), Ryne Sandberg (.400), Cubs.
■ **MVP:** Clark.

Linescores

Game 1—October 4, at Chicago
S.F. ....3 0 1 4 0 0 0 3 0—11 13 0
Chicago....2 0 1 0 0 0 0 0 0— 3 10 1
Garrelts, Brantley (8), Hammaker (9); Maddux, Kilgus (5), Wilson (8). W—Garrelts. L—Maddux. HR—Grace, Sandberg (Chi.); Clark 2, Mitchell (S.F.).

Game 2—October 5, at Chicago
S.F. ....0 0 0 2 0 0 0 2 1—5 10 0
Chicago......6 0 0 0 0 3 0 0 x—9 11 0
Reuschel, Downs (1), Lefferts (6), Brantley (7), Bedrosian (8); Bielecki, Assenmacher (5), Lancaster (6). W—Lancaster. L—Reuschel. HR—Mitchell, Ma. Williams, Thompson (S.F.).

Game 3—October 7, at San Francisco
Chicago......2 0 0 1 0 0 1 0 0—4 10 0
S.F. ....3 0 0 0 0 0 2 0 x—5 8 3
Sutcliffe, Assenmacher (7), Lancaster (7); LaCoss, Brantley (4), Robinson (7), Lefferts (8), Bedrosian (9). W—Robinson. L—Lancaster. S—Bedrosian. HR—Thompson (S.F.).

Game 4—October 8, at San Francisco
Chicago......1 1 0 0 2 0 0 0 0—4 12 1
S.F. ....1 0 2 1 2 0 0 0 x—6 9 1
Maddux, Wilson (4), Sanderson (6), Mi. Williams (8); Garrelts, Downs (5), Bedrosian (9). W—Downs. L—Wilson. S—Bedrosian. HR—Salazar (Chi.); Ma. Williams (S.F.).

Game 5—October 9, at San Francisco
Chicago......0 0 1 0 0 0 0 0 1—2 10 1
S.F. ....0 0 0 0 0 0 1 2 x—3 4 1
Bielecki, Mi. Williams (8), Lancaster (8); Reuschel, Bedrosian (9). W—Reuschel. L—Bielecki. S—Bedrosian.

WORLD SERIES

■ **Winner:** Oakland's four-game sweep of San Francisco in the first Bay Area Series was overshadowed by a massive earthquake that rocked parts of California, causing death and destruction and forcing postponement of the fall classic's final two games for 10 days.
■ **Turning point:** The second inning of Game 1, when Oakland jumped on the Giants for three runs en route to a 5-0 victory. That outburst set the pattern for the rest of the Series.
■ **Memorable moment:** The moments leading up to Game 3, when an earthquake measuring 7.1 on the Richter scale shook San Francisco and Candlestick Park. With the power out and incoming reports of mass destruction, Commissioner Fay Vincent ordered postponement of the game and told officials to clear the park.
■ **Top guns:** Dave Stewart (2-0, 1.69 ERA), Mike Moore (2-0, 2.08), Rickey Henderson (.474), Carney Lansford (.438), Athletics; Kevin Mitchell (.294), Giants.
■ **MVP:** Stewart.

Linescores

Game 1—October 14, at Oakland
S.F. ....0 0 0 0 0 0 0 0 0—0 5 1
Oakland......0 3 1 1 0 0 0 0 x—5 11 1
Garrelts, Hammaker (5), Brantley (6), LaCoss (8); Stewart. W—Stewart. L—Garrelts. HR—Parker, Weiss (Oak.).

Game 2—October 15, at Oakland
S.F. ....0 0 1 0 0 0 0 0 0—1 4 0
Oakland........1 0 0 4 0 0 0 0 x—5 7 0
Reuschel, Downs (5), Lefferts (7), Bedrosian (8); Moore, Honeycutt (8), Eckersley (9). W—Moore. L—Reuschel. HR—Steinbach (Oak.).

Game 3—October 27, at San Francisco
Oakland....2 0 0 2 4 1 0 4 0—13 14 0
S.F. ....0 1 0 2 0 0 0 0 4— 7 10 3
Stewart, Honeycutt (8), Nelson (9), Burns (9); Garrelts, Downs (4), Brantley (5), Hammaker (8), Lefferts (8). W—Stewart. L—Garrelts. HR—Williams, Bathe (S.F.); D. Henderson 2, Phillips, Canseco, Lansford (Oak.).

Game 4—October 28, at San Francisco
Oakland......1 3 0 0 3 1 0 1 0—9 12 0
S.F. ....0 0 0 0 0 2 4 0 0—6 9 0
Moore, Nelson (7), Honeycutt (7), Burns (7), Eckersley (9); Robinson, LaCoss (2), Brantley (6), Downs (6), Lefferts (8), Bedrosian (8). W—Moore. L—Robinson. S—Eckersley. HR—R. Henderson (Oak.); Mitchell, Litton (S.F.).

1990

FINAL STANDINGS

American League

East Division

Team	Bos.	Tor.	Det.	Cle.	Bal.	Mil.	N.Y.	Oak.	Chi.	Tex.	Cal.	Sea.	K.C.	Min.	W	L	Pct.	GB
Boston	...	10	8	9	9	5	9	4	6	5	7	8	4	4	88	74	.543	...
Toronto	3	...	8	9	8	6	8	5	7	5	5	6	7	9	86	76	.531	2
Detroit	5	5	...	8	7	3	7	6	7	6	7	7	5	6	79	83	.488	9
Cleveland	4	4	5	...	7	9	5	4	7	7	5	7	6	7	77	85	.475	11
Baltimore	4	5	6	6	...	7	6	4	6	8	7	3	8	6	76	85	.472	11.5
Milwaukee	8	7	10	4	6	...	6	5	2	5	5	4	8	4	74	88	.457	14
New York	4	5	6	8	7	7	...	0	2	3	6	9	4	6	67	95	.414	21

West Division

Team	Oak.	Chi.	Tex.	Cal.	Sea.	K.C.	Min.	Bos.	Tor.	Det.	Cle.	Bal.	Mil.	N.Y.	W	L	Pct.	GB
Oakland	...	5	8	9	9	9	7	8	7	6	8	8	7	12	103	59	.636	...
Chicago	8	...	7	8	8	9	7	6	5	5	5	6	10	10	94	68	.580	9
Texas	5	6	...	5	6	8	8	7	7	6	5	4	7	9	83	79	.512	20
California	4	5	8	...	5	7	9	5	7	5	7	5	7	6	80	82	.494	23
Seattle	4	5	7	8	...	6	7	4	6	5	5	9	8	3	77	85	.475	26
Kansas City	4	4	5	6	7	...	8	8	5	7	6	3	4	8	75	86	.466	27.5
Minnesota	6	6	5	4	6	5	...	8	3	6	5	6	8	6	74	88	.457	29

National League

East Division

Team	Pit.	N.Y.	Mon.	Chi.	Phi.	St.L.	Cin.	L.A.	S.F.	Hou.	S.D.	Atl.	W	L	Pct.	GB
Pittsburgh	...	8	5	14	12	10	6	8	8	7	10	7	95	67	.586	...
New York	10	...	10	9	10	12	6	7	7	7	5	8	91	71	.562	4
Montreal	13	8	...	7	10	11	3	6	7	7	7	6	85	77	.525	10
Chicago	4	9	11	...	11	8	4	3	7	6	8	6	77	85	.475	18
Philadelphia	6	8	8	7	...	10	5	4	8	7	7	7	77	85	.475	18
St. Louis	8	6	7	10	8	...	3	5	3	6	9	5	70	92	.432	25

West Division

Team	Cin.	L.A.	S.F.	Hou.	S.D.	Atl.	Pit.	N.Y.	Mon.	Chi.	Phi.	St.L.	W	L	Pct.	GB
Cincinnati	...	9	7	11	9	10	6	6	9	8	7	9	91	71	.562	...
Los Angeles	9	...	8	9	9	12	4	5	6	9	8	7	86	76	.531	5
San Fran.	11	10	...	8	11	13	4	5	5	5	4	9	85	77	.525	6
Houston	7	9	10	...	4	13	5	5	5	6	5	6	75	87	.463	16
San Diego	9	9	7	14	...	10	2	7	5	4	5	3	75	87	.463	16
Atlanta	8	6	5	5	8	...	5	4	6	6	5	7	65	97	.401	26

SIGNIFICANT EVENTS

- **March 18:** Players and owners reached agreement on a four-year contract that ended a 32-day lockout and cleared the way for spring training camps to open.
- **June 14:** The N.L. announced plans to expand from 12 to 14 teams for the 1993 season.
- **July 30:** Commissioner Fay Vincent banned George Steinbrenner from involvement with the Yankees for actions "not in the best interests of baseball."
- **August 8:** Former baseball great Pete Rose reported to a federal work camp at Marion, Ill., to begin serving his five-month sentence for income tax evasion.

MEMORABLE MOMENTS

- **June 11:** Rangers ace Nolan Ryan fired his record sixth no-hitter, defeating Oakland 5-0.
- **June 12:** Baltimore's Cal Ripken Jr. moved into second place on the all-time ironman list when he pushed his consecutive-games streak to 1,308 in a 4-3 victory over Milwaukee.
- **June 29:** A baseball first: Oakland's Dave Stewart and Dodgers lefthander Fernando Valenzuela threw no-hitters on the same day.
- **July 1:** Yankees righthander Andy Hawkins became the second Major League pitcher to throw a complete-game no-hitter and lose when the White Sox stumbled to a 4-0 victory.
- **July 31:** Ryan became baseball's 20th 300-game winner when the Rangers pounded the Brewers, 11-3.
- **August 31:** The Griffeys, 20-year-old Ken Jr. and 40-year-old Ken Sr., became baseball's first father-son combination when both played for Seattle in a game against Kansas City.
- **September 2:** Dave Stieb held Cleveland without a hit in a 3-0 victory—the first no-hitter in Blue Jays history and the record ninth of the season in the Major Leagues.
- **October 3:** Detroit's Cecil Fielder became the first player in 13 years to break the 50-homer barrier when he crashed Nos. 50 and 51 in a final-day 10-3 victory over the Yankees.

LEADERS

American League
BA: George Brett, K.C., .329.
Runs: Rickey Henderson, Oak., 119.
Hits: Rafael Palmeiro, Tex., 191.
TB: Cecil Fielder, Det., 339.
HR: Cecil Fielder, Det., 51.
RBI: Cecil Fielder, Det., 132.
SB: Rickey Henderson, Oak., 65.
Wins: Bob Welch, Oak., 27.
ERA: Roger Clemens, Bos., 1.93.
CG: Jack Morris, Det.; Dave Stewart, Oak., 11.
IP: Dave Stewart, Oak., 267.
SO: Nolan Ryan, Tex., 232.
SV: Bobby Thigpen, Chi., 57.

National League
BA: Willie McGee, St.L., .335.
Runs: Ryne Sandberg, Chi., 116.
Hits: Brett Butler, S.F.; Lenny Dykstra, Phil., 192.
TB: Ryne Sandberg, Chi., 344.
HR: Ryne Sandberg, Chi., 40.
RBI: Matt Williams, S.F., 122.
SB: Vince Coleman, St.L., 77.
Wins: Doug Drabek, Pit., 22.
ERA: Danny Darwin, Hou., 2.21.
CG: Ramon Martinez, L.A., 12.
IP: Frank Viola, N.Y., 249.2.
SO: David Cone, N.Y., 233.
SV: John Franco, N.Y., 33.

A.L. 20-game winners
Bob Welch, Oak., 27-6
Dave Stewart, Oak., 22-11
Roger Clemens, Bos., 21-6

N.L. 20-game winners
Doug Drabek, Pit., 22-6
Ramon Martinez, L.A., 20-6
Frank Viola, N.Y., 20-12

A.L. 100 RBIs
Cecil Fielder, Det., 132
Kelly Gruber, Tor., 118
Mark McGwire, Oak., 108
Jose Canseco, Oak., 101

N.L. 100 RBIs
Matt Williams, S.F., 122
Bobby Bonilla, Pit., 120
Joe Carter, S.D., 115
Barry Bonds, Pit., 114
Darryl Strawberry, N.Y., 108
Andre Dawson, Chi., 100
Ryne Sandberg, Chi., 100

A.L. 40 homers
Cecil Fielder, Det., 51

N.L. 40 homers
Ryne Sandberg, Chi., 40

Most Valuable Player
A.L.: Rickey Henderson, OF, Oak.
N.L.: Barry Bonds, OF, Pit.

Cy Young Award
A.L.: Bob Welch, Oak.
N.L.: Doug Drabek, Pit.

Rookie of the Year
A.L.: Sandy Alomar Jr., C, Cle.
N.L.: Dave Justice, OF, Atl.

Manager of the Year
A.L.: Jeff Torborg, Chi.
N.L.: Jim Leyland, Pit.

Hall of Fame additions
Joe Morgan, 2B, 1963-84
Jim Palmer, P, 1965-84

ALL-STAR GAME

- **Winner:** Six pitchers held the N.L. to an All-Star record-low two hits and the A.L. won for the third straight year, 2-0.
- **Key inning:** The seventh, when the A.L. broke a scoreless deadlock on a two-run double by Julio Franco off fireballer Rob Dibble. Franco was the first batter after a 68-minute rain delay.
- **Memorable moment:** The performance of an A.L. staff that allowed only a first-inning single by Will Clark and a ninth-inning single by Lenny Dykstra and retired 16 consecutive batters at one point.
- **Top guns:** Bob Welch (Athletics), Dave Stieb (Blue Jays), Bret Saberhagen (Royals), Franco (Rangers), Wade Boggs (Red Sox), A.L.
- **MVP:** Franco.

Linescore
July 10, at Chicago's Wrigley Field
A.L..............0 0 0 0 0 0 2 0 0—2 7 0
N.L..............0 0 0 0 0 0 0 0 0—0 2 1
Welch (Athletics), Stieb (Blue Jays) 3, Saberhagen (Royals) 5, Thigpen (White Sox) 7, Finley (Angels) 8, Eckersley (Athletics) 9; Armstrong (Reds), R. Martinez (Dodgers) 3, D. Martinez (Expos) 4, Viola (Mets) 5, D. Smith (Astros) 6, Brantley (Giants) 6, Dibble (Reds) 7, Myers (Reds) 8, Jo. Franco (Mets) 9. W—Saberhagen. L—Brantley. S—Eckersley.

ALCS

- **Winner:** The powerful Athletics swept to their third consecutive pennant without benefit of a home run — their trademark offensive weapon.
- **Turning point:** The final three innings of Game 1. Trailing 1-0 when Boston starter Roger Clemens left the game, the A's pounded five Red Sox relievers for nine runs and set the pattern for the series.
- **Memorable moment:** The second inning of Game 4 when Clemens, frustrated by his team's 3-0 series deficit and the calls of umpire Terry Cooney, was ejected during an angry exchange, killing any hopes for a Boston comeback.
- **Top guns:** Dave Stewart (2-0, 1.13 ERA), Terry Steinbach (.455), Carney Lansford (.438), Athletics; Wade Boggs (.438), Red Sox.
- **MVP:** Stewart.

Linescores

Game 1—October 6, at Boston
Oakland......0 0 0 0 0 0 1 1 7—9 13 0
Boston ......0 0 0 1 0 0 0 0 0—1 5 1
Stewart, Eckersley (9); Clemens, Andersen (7), Bolton (8), Gray (8), Lamp (9), Murphy (9). W—Stewart. L—Andersen. HR—Boggs (Bos.).

Game 2—October 7, at Boston
Oakland......0 0 0 1 0 0 1 0 2—4 13 1
Boston ......0 0 1 0 0 0 0 0 0—1 6 0
Welch, Honeycutt (8), Eckersley (8); Kiecker, Harris (6), Andersen (7), Reardon (8). W—Welch. L—Harris. S—Eckersley.

Game 3—October 9, at Oakland
Boston ....0 1 0 0 0 0 0 0 0—1 8 3
Oakland........0 0 0 2 0 2 0 0 x—4 6 0
Boddicker; Moore, Nelson (7), Honeycutt (8), Eckersley (9). W—Moore. L—Boddicker. S—Eckersley.

Game 4—October 10, at Oakland
Boston ....0 0 0 0 0 0 0 0 1—1 4 1
Oakland........0 3 0 0 0 0 0 0 x—3 6 0
Clemens, Bolton (2), Gray (5), Andersen (8); Stewart, Honeycutt (9). W—Stewart. L—Clemens. S—Honeycutt.

NLCS

- **Winner:** Cincinnati prevailed over Pittsburgh in a matchup of teams that dominated in the 1970s and failed to qualify for post-season play in the 1980s.
- **Turning point:** The pivotal third game when the Reds got unlikely home runs from Billy Hatcher and Mariano Duncan and recorded a 6-3 victory.
- **Memorable moment:** Glenn Braggs, a defensive replacement in right field, made a sensational over-the-wall catch in the ninth inning of Game 6, robbing Pittsburgh's Carmelo Martinez of a two-run homer and preserving the Reds' series-ending 2-1 victory.
- **Top guns:** Randy Myers (3 saves, 7 SO, 0.00 ERA), Rob Dibble (1 save, 10 SO, 0.00), Paul O'Neill (.471), Hal Morris (.417), Reds; Doug Drabek (1-1, 1.65), Pirates.
- **MVPs:** Dibble and Myers.

Linescores

Game 1—October 4, at Cincinnati
Pitt...............0 0 1 2 0 0 1 0 0—4 7 1
Cin. ....3 0 0 0 0 0 0 0 0—3 5 0
Walk, Belinda (7), Patterson (9), Power (9); Rijo, Charlton (6), Dibble (9). W—Walk. L—Charlton. S—Power. HR—Bream (Pit.).

Game 2—October 5, at Cincinnati
Pitt...............0 0 0 0 1 0 0 0 0—1 6 0
Cin. ....1 0 0 0 1 0 0 0 x—2 5 0
Drabek; Browning, Dibble (7), Myers (8). W—Browning. L—Drabek. S—Myers. HR—Lind (Pit.).

Game 3—October 8, at Pittsburgh
Cin.............0 2 0 0 3 0 0 0 1—6 13 1
Pitt.............0 0 0 2 0 0 0 1 0—3 8 0
Jackson, Dibble (6), Charlton (8), Myers (9); Smith, Landrum (6), Smiley (7), Belinda (9). W—Jackson. L—Smith. S—Myers. HR—Hatcher, Duncan (Cin.).

Game 4—October 9, at Pittsburgh
Cin.............0 0 0 2 0 0 2 0 1—5 10 1
Pitt.............1 0 0 1 0 0 0 1 0—3 8 0
Rijo, Myers (8), Dibble (9); Walk, Power (8). W—Rijo. L—Walk. S—Dibble. HR—O'Neill, Sabo (Cin.); Bell (Pit.).

Game 5—October 10, at Pittsburgh
Cin. ....1 0 0 0 0 0 0 1 0—2 7 0
Pitt. ....2 0 0 1 0 0 0 0 x—3 6 1
Browning, Mahler (6), Charlton (7), Scudder (8); Drabek, Patterson (9). W—Drabek. L—Browning. S—Patterson.

Game 6—October 12, at Cincinnati
Pitt...............0 0 0 0 1 0 0 0 0—1 1 3
Cin. ....1 0 0 0 0 0 1 0 x—2 9 0
Power, Smith (3), Belinda (7), Landrum (8); Jackson, Charlton (7), Myers (8). W—Charlton. L—Smith. S—Myers.

WORLD SERIES

- **Winner:** The Oakland Athletics' aura of invincibility was shattered by the Cincinnati Reds in a startling sweep. The A's, who were looking for a second straight championship, entered the Series with a 10-game post-season winning streak.
- **Turning point:** Game 1. Eric Davis' first-inning home run and the combined nine-hit pitching of Jose Rijo, Rob Dibble and Randy Myers in a 7-0 victory served notice that the A's had their hands full.
- **Memorable moment:** Relief ace Myers retiring Jose Canseco and Carney Lansford in the ninth inning of Game 4 to preserve a 2-1 victory for Rijo and complete the sweep.
- **Top guns:** Rijo (2-0, 0.59 ERA), Myers (3 games, 0.00), Dibble (1-0, 0.00), Billy Hatcher (.750), Chris Sabo (.563, 2 HR, 5 RBIs), Reds; Rickey Henderson (.333), Athletics.
- **MVP:** Rijo.

Linescores

Game 1—October 16, at Cincinnati
Oak. ....0 0 0 0 0 0 0 0 0—0 9 1
Cin. ....2 0 2 0 3 0 0 0 x—7 10 0
Stewart, Burns (5), Nelson (5), Sanderson (7), Eckersley (8); Rijo, Dibble (8), Myers (9). W—Rijo. L—Stewart. HR—Davis (Cin.).

Game 2—October 17, at Cincinnati
Oak. ......1 0 3 0 0 0 0 0 0 0—4 10 2
Cin.........2 0 0 1 0 0 0 1 0 1—5 14 2
Welch, Honeycutt (8), Eckersley (10); Jackson, Scudder (3), Armstrong (5), Charlton (8), Dibble (9). W—Dibble. L—Eckersley. HR—Canseco (Oak.).

Game 3—October 19, at Oakland
Cin.............0 1 7 0 0 0 0 0 0—8 14 1
Oak. ....0 2 1 0 0 0 0 0 0—3 7 1
Browning, Dibble (7), Myers (8); Moore, Sanderson (3), Klink (4), Nelson (4), Burns (8), Young (9). W—Browning. L—Moore. HR—Sabo 2 (Cin.); Baines, R. Henderson (Oak.).

Game 4—October 20, at Oakland
Cin. ....0 0 0 0 0 0 0 2 0—2 7 1
Oak. ....1 0 0 0 0 0 0 0 0—1 2 1
Rijo, Myers (9); Stewart. W—Rijo. L—Stewart. S—Myers.

FINAL STANDINGS

American League

East Division

Team	Tor.	Det.	Bos.	Mil.	N.Y.	Bal.	Cle.	Min.	Chi.	Tex.	Oak.	Sea.	K.C.	Cal.	W	L	Pct.	GB
Toronto	...	8	4	7	7	8	12	8	5	6	6	7	7	6	91	71	.562	...
Detroit	5	...	8	4	8	8	6	4	8	6	4	8	8	7	84	78	.519	7
Boston	9	5	...	7	6	5	9	3	7	5	8	9	7	4	84	78	.519	7
Milwaukee	6	9	6	...	6	10	8	6	5	7	8	3	3	6	83	79	.512	8
New York	6	5	7	7	...	8	7	2	4	5	6	3	5	6	71	91	.438	20
Baltimore	5	5	8	3	5	...	7	4	4	9	3	4	4	6	67	95	.414	24
Cleveland	1	7	4	5	6	6	...	2	6	4	5	2	4	5	57	105	.352	34

West Division

Team	Min.	Chi.	Tex.	Oak.	Sea.	K.C.	Cal.	Tor.	Det.	Bos.	Mil.	N.Y.	Bal.	Cle.	W	L	Pct.	GB
Minnesota	...	5	6	8	9	7	5	4	8	9	6	10	8	10	95	67	.586	...
Chicago	8	...	8	7	7	7	5	7	4	5	7	8	8	6	87	75	.537	8
Texas	7	5	...	9	8	6	8	6	6	7	5	7	3	8	85	77	.525	10
Oakland	5	6	4	...	6	7	12	6	8	4	4	6	9	7	84	78	.519	11
Seattle	4	6	5	7	...	6	7	5	4	3	9	9	8	10	83	79	.512	12
Kansas City	6	6	7	6	7	...	4	5	4	5	9	7	8	8	82	80	.506	13
California	8	8	5	1	6	9	...	6	5	8	6	6	6	7	81	81	.500	14

National League

East Division

Team	Pit.	St.L.	Phi.	Chi.	N.Y.	Mon.	Atl.	L.A.	S.D.	S.F.	Cin.	Hou.	W	L	Pct.	GB
Pittsburgh	...	11	12	11	12	12	3	5	7	7	10	8	98	64	.605	...
St. Louis	7	...	12	8	11	11	3	6	3	8	8	7	84	78	.519	14
Philadelphia	6	6	...	10	7	14	7	5	9	6	3	5	78	84	.481	20
Chicago	7	10	8	...	11	10	6	2	4	6	4	9	77	83	.481	20
New York	6	7	11	6	...	14	3	5	7	6	7	5	77	84	.478	20.5
Montreal	6	7	4	7	4	...	7	7	6	7	6	10	71	90	.441	26.5

West Division

Team	Atl.	L.A.	S.D.	S.F.	Cin.	Hou.	Pit.	St.L.	Phi.	Chi.	N.Y.	Mon.	W	L	Pct.	GB
Atlanta	...	7	11	9	11	13	9	9	5	6	9	5	94	68	.580	...
Los Angeles	11	...	10	8	12	10	7	6	7	10	7	5	93	69	.574	1
San Diego	7	8	...	11	10	12	5	9	3	8	5	6	84	78	.519	10
San Fran.	9	10	7	...	8	9	5	4	6	6	6	5	75	87	.463	19
Cincinnati	7	6	8	10	...	9	2	4	9	8	5	6	74	88	.457	20
Houston	5	8	6	9	9	...	4	5	7	3	7	2	65	97	.401	29

LEADERS

American League
BA: Julio Franco, Tex., .341.
Runs: Paul Molitor, Mil., 133.
Hits: Paul Molitor, Mil., 216.
TB: Cal Ripken, Bal., 368.
HR: Jose Canseco, Oak.; Cecil Fielder, Det., 44.
RBI: Cecil Fielder, Det., 133.
SB: Rickey Henderson, Oak., 58.
Wins: Scott Erickson, Min.; Bill Gullickson, Det., 20.
ERA: Roger Clemens, Bos., 2.62.
CG: Jack McDowell, Chi., 15.
IP: Roger Clemens, Bos., 271.1.
SO: Roger Clemens, Bos., 241.
SV: Bryan Harvey, Cal., 46.

National League
BA: Terry Pendleton, Atl., .319.
Runs: Brett Butler, L.A., 112.
Hits: Terry Pendleton, Atl., 187.
TB: Will Clark, S.F.; Terry Pendleton, Atl., 303.
HR: Howard Johnson, N.Y., 38.
RBI: Howard Johnson, N.Y., 117.
SB: Marquis Grissom, Mon., 76.
Wins: Tom Glavine, Atl.; John Smiley, Pit., 20.
ERA: Dennis Martinez, Mon., 2.39.
CG: Tom Glavine, Atl.; Dennis Martinez, Mon., 9.
IP: Greg Maddux, Chi., 263.
SO: David Cone, N.Y., 241.
SV: Lee Smith, St.L., 47.

A.L. 20-game winners
Scott Erickson, Min., 20-8
Bill Gullickson, Det., 20-9

N.L. 20-game winners
John Smiley, Pit., 20-8
Tom Glavine, Atl., 20-11

A.L. 100 RBIs
Cecil Fielder, Det., 133
Jose Canseco, Oak., 122
Ruben Sierra, Tex., 116
Cal Ripken, Bal., 114
Frank Thomas, Chi., 109
Joe Carter, Tor., 108
Juan Gonzalez, Tex., 102
Ken Griffey Jr., Sea., 100
Danny Tartabull, K.C., 100
Robin Ventura, Chi., 100

N.L. 100 RBIs
Howard Johnson, N.Y., 117
Barry Bonds, Pit., 116
Will Clark, S.F., 116
Fred McGriff, S.D., 106
Ron Gant, Atl., 105
Andre Dawson, Chi., 104
Ryne Sandberg, Chi., 100
Bobby Bonilla, Pit., 100

A.L. 40 homers
Jose Canseco, Oak., 44
Cecil Fielder, Det., 44

Most Valuable Player
A.L.: Cal Ripken, SS, Bal.
N.L.: Terry Pendleton, 3B, Atl.

Cy Young Award
A.L.: Roger Clemens, Bos.
N.L.: Tom Glavine, Atl.

Rookie of the Year
A.L.: Chuck Knoblauch, 2B, Min.
N.L.: Jeff Bagwell, 1B, Hou.

Manager of the Year
A.L.: Tom Kelly, Min.
N.L.: Bobby Cox, Atl.

Hall of Fame additions
Rod Carew, 2B/1B, 1967-85
Ferguson Jenkins, P, 1965-83
Tony Lazzeri, 2B, 1926-39
Gaylord Perry, P, 1962-83
Bill Veeck, executive/owner

SIGNIFICANT EVENTS

■ **April 18:** The Tigers spoiled the dedication of Chicago's new Comiskey Park when they routed the White Sox, 16-0.
■ **June 10:** Miami and Denver were declared winners by a four-man N.L. expansion committee.

MEMORABLE MOMENTS

■ **May 1:** Oakland's Rickey Henderson swiped his 939th base in a game against the Yankees, passing Lou Brock as baseball's all-time greatest base stealer.
■ **May 1:** Nolan Ryan, stealing the day's headlines from Henderson, fired his seventh career no-hitter, striking out 16 Blue Jays in a 3-0 victory.
■ **July 28:** Montreal's Dennis Martinez became the 14th pitcher to throw a perfect game when he retired all 27 Dodgers he faced in a 2-0 victory.
■ **October 2:** Cardinals closer Lee Smith, who had notched his 300th career save earlier in the year, recorded his single-season N.L.-record 47th in a 6-4 victory over Montreal.
■ **October 6:** Mets righthander David Cone tied the N.L. single-game record when he struck out 19 Phillies in a 7-0 victory.

ALL-STAR GAME

■ **Winner:** The A.L. ran its winning streak to four with a 4-2 victory and the N.L. ran its four-year run total to a paltry six.
■ **Key inning:** The third, when Cal Ripken followed singles by Rickey Henderson and Wade Boggs with a home run.
■ **Memorable moment:** A first-inning line drive by Bobby Bonilla that struck A.L. starter Jack Morris on the ankle, reviving All-Star memories of the 1937 Earl Averill shot that broke Dizzy Dean's toe.
■ **Top guns:** Ripken (Orioles), Ken Griffey Jr. (Mariners), Henderson (Athletics), Boggs (Red Sox), A.L.; Tom Glavine (Braves), Bonilla (Pirates), Andre Dawson (Cubs), N.L.
■ **MVP:** Ripken.

Linescore
July 9, at Toronto's SkyDome
N.L............1 0 0 1 0 0 0 0—2 10 1
A.L. ....0 0 3 0 0 0 1 0 x—4 8 0
Glavine (Braves), De. Martinez (Expos) 3, Viola (Mets) 5, Harnisch (Astros) 6, Smiley (Pirates) 7, Dibble (Reds) 7, Morgan (Dodgers) 8; Morris (Twins), Key (Blue Jays) 3, Clemens (Red Sox) 4, McDowell (White Sox) 5, Reardon (Red Sox) 7, Aguilera (Twins) 7, Eckersley (Athletics) 9. W—Key. L—De. Martinez. S—Eckersley. HR—Ripken, A.L.; Dawson, N.L.

ALCS

■ **Winner:** Minnesota won an LCS-record three road games and its second pennant in five years while handing Toronto its third Championship Series defeat.
■ **Turning point:** The 10th inning of Game 3 when Minnesota's Mike Pagliarulo homered off Toronto reliever Mike Timlin, giving the Twins a 3-2 victory and a 2-1 series advantage.
■ **Memorable moment:** Minnesota first baseman Kent Hrbek delivered a two-run single off David Wells in the eighth inning of Game 5 to cap a series-ending 8-5 victory.
■ **Top guns:** Rick Aguilera (3 saves, 0.00 ERA), Kirby Puckett (.429, 2 HR, 6 RBIs), Twins; Roberto Alomar (.474), Blue Jays.
■ **MVP:** Puckett.

Linescores
Game 1—October 8, at Minnesota
Toronto......0 0 0 1 0 3 0 0 0—4 9 3
Minn. ....2 2 1 0 0 0 0 0 x—5 11 0
Candiotti, Wells (3), Timlin (6); Morris, Willis (6), Aguilera (8). W—Morris. L—Candiotti. S—Aguilera.
Game 2—October 9, at Minnesota
Toronto........1 0 2 0 0 0 2 0 0—5 9 0
Minn. ....0 0 1 0 0 1 0 0 0—2 5 1
Guzman, Henke (6), Ward (8); Tapani, Bedrosian (7), Guthrie (7). W—Guzman. L—Tapani. S—Ward.
Game 3—October 11, at Toronto
Minn. ......0 0 0 0 1 1 0 0 0 1—3 7 0
Tor. ....2 0 0 0 0 0 0 0 0 0—2 5 1
Erickson, West (5), Willis (7), Guthrie (9), Aguilera (10); Key, Wells (7), Henke (8), Timlin (10). W—Guthrie. L—Timlin. S—Aguilera. HR—Carter (Tor.); Pagliarulo (Min.).
Game 4—October 12, at Toronto
Minn. ....0 0 0 4 0 2 1 1 1—9 13 1
Toronto......0 1 0 0 0 1 0 0 1—3 11 2
Morris, Bedrosian (9); Stottlemyre, Wells (4), Acker (6), Timlin (7), MacDonald (9). W—Morris. L—Stottlemyre. HR—Puckett (Min.).
Game 5—October 13, at Toronto
Minn. ....1 1 0 0 0 3 0 3 0—8 14 2
Toronto......0 0 3 2 0 0 0 0 0—5 9 1
Tapani, West (5), Willis (8), Aguilera (9); Candiotti, Timlin (6), Ward (6), Wells (8). W—West. L—Ward. S—Aguilera. HR—Puckett (Min.).

NLCS

■ **Winner:** The young Braves, last-place N.L. West finishers in 1990, defeated the Pirates and won their first Atlanta pennant.
■ **Turning point:** Greg Olson's run-scoring double in the ninth inning of Game 6, which gave Braves lefthander Steve Avery his second 1-0 victory.
■ **Memorable moment:** The final pitch of John Smoltz's 4-0 Game 7 victory. The shutout, the Braves' third, gave Atlanta fans their first World Series qualifier.
■ **Top guns:** Avery (2-0, 0.00 ERA), Smoltz (2-0, 1.76), Olson (.333), Brian Hunter (.333), Braves; Doug Drabek (1-1, 0.60), Zane Smith (1-1, 0.61), Jay Bell (.414), Pirates.
■ **MVP:** Avery.

Linescores
Game 1—October 9, at Pittsburgh
Atlanta ....0 0 0 0 0 0 0 0 1—1 5 1
Pit. ....1 0 2 0 0 1 0 1 x—5 8 1
Glavine, Wohlers (7), Stanton (8); Drabek, Walk (7). W—Drabek. L—Glavine. S—Walk. HR—Van Slyke (Pit.); Justice (Atl.).
Game 2—October 10, at Pittsburgh
Atlanta ....0 0 0 0 0 1 0 0 0—1 8 0
Pit. ....0 0 0 0 0 0 0 0 0—0 6 0
Avery, Pena (9); Z. Smith, Mason (8), Belinda (9). W—Avery. L—Z. Smith. S—Pena.
Game 3—October 12, at Atlanta
Pit. ....1 0 0 1 0 0 1 0 0— 3 10 2
Atlanta......4 1 1 0 0 0 1 3 x—10 11 0
Smiley, Landrum (3), Patterson (4), Kipper (6), Rodriguez (8); Smoltz, Stanton (7), Wohlers (8), Pena (8). W—Smoltz. L—Smiley. S—Pena. HR—Gant, Olson, Bream (Atl.); Merced, Bell (Pit.).
Game 4—October 13, at Atlanta
Pit. ......0 1 0 0 1 0 0 0 0 1—3 11 1
Atlanta 2 0 0 0 0 0 0 0 0 0—2 7 1
Tomlin, Walk (7), Belinda (9); Leibrandt, Clancy (7), Stanton (8), Mercker (10), Wohlers (10). W—Belinda. L—Mercker.
Game 5—October 14, at Atlanta
Pit. ....0 0 0 0 1 0 0 0 0—1 6 2
Atlanta ....0 0 0 0 0 0 0 0 0—0 9 1
Z. Smith, Mason (8); Glavine, Pena (9). W—Z. Smith. L—Glavine. S—Mason.
Game 6—October 16, at Pittsburgh
Atlanta ....0 0 0 0 0 0 0 0 1—1 7 0
Pit. ....0 0 0 0 0 0 0 0 0—0 4 0
Avery, Pena (9); Drabek. W—Avery. L—Drabek. S—Pena.
Game 7—October 17, at Pittsburgh
Atlanta ....3 0 0 0 1 0 0 0 0—4 6 1
Pit. ....0 0 0 0 0 0 0 0 0—0 6 0
Smoltz; Smiley, Walk (1), Mason (6), Belinda (8). W—Smoltz. L—Smiley. HR—Hunter (Atl.).

WORLD SERIES

■ **Winner:** Minnesota defeated Atlanta in the "worst-to-first" World Series, which featured teams that had risen from last-place 1990 finishes to win pennants.
■ **Turning point:** The 11th-inning of Game 6, when Kirby Puckett greeted Braves reliever Charlie Leibrandt with a game-ending home run, squaring the Series. Puckett had made an outstanding leaping catch earlier in the 4-3 victory.
■ **Memorable moment:** A seventh-game baserunning blunder by Atlanta's Lonnie Smith, who failed to score on Terry Pendleton's eighth-inning double. The Twins and Jack Morris went on to post a 1-0 Series-ending victory on Gene Larkin's 12th-inning single.
■ **Top guns:** Morris (2-0, 1.17 ERA), Brian Harper (.381), Puckett (2 HR, 4 RBIs), Twins; David Justice (2 HR, 6 RBIs), Braves.
■ **MVP:** Morris.

Linescores
Game 1—October 19, at Minnesota
Atlanta ....0 0 0 0 0 1 0 1 0—2 6 1
Minn. ....0 0 1 0 3 1 0 0 x—5 9 1
Leibrandt, Clancy (5), Wohlers (7), Stanton (8); Morris, Guthrie (8), Aguilera (8). W—Morris. L—Leibrandt. S—Aguilera. HR—Gagne, Hrbek (Min.).
Game 2—October 20, at Minnesota
Atlanta ....0 1 0 0 1 0 0 0 0—2 8 1
Minn. ....2 0 0 0 0 0 0 1 x—3 4 1
Glavine; Tapani, Aguilera (9). W—Tapani. L—Glavine. S—Aguilera. HR—Davis, Leius (Min.).
Game 3—October 22, at Atlanta
Minn. ....100 000 120 000—4 10 1
Atl. ....010 120 000 001—5 8 2
Erickson, West (5), Leach (5), Bedrosian (6), Willis (8), Guthrie (10), Aguilera (12); Avery, Pena (8), Stanton (10), Wohlers (12), Mercker (12), Clancy (12). W—Clancy. L—Aguilera. HR—Justice, Smith (Atl.); Puckett, Davis (Min.).
Game 4—October 23, at Atlanta
Minn. ....0 1 0 0 0 0 1 0 0—2 7 0
Atlanta ....0 0 1 0 0 0 1 0 1—3 8 0
Morris, Willis (7), Guthrie (8), Bedrosian (9); Smoltz, Wohlers (8), Stanton (8). W—Stanton. L—Guthrie. HR—Pendleton, Smith (Atl.); Pagliarulo (Min.).
Game 5—October 24, at Atlanta
Minn. ......0 0 0 0 0 3 0 1 1— 5 7 1
Atlanta......0 0 0 4 1 0 6 3 x—14 17 1
Tapani, Leach (5), West (7), Bedrosian (7), Willis (8); Glavine, Mercker (6), Clancy (7), St. Claire (9). W—Glavine. L—Tapani. HR—Justice, Smith, Hunter (Atl.).
Game 6—October 26, at Minnesota
Atl. ....0 0 0 0 2 0 1 0 0 0 0—3 9 0
Minn. 2 0 0 0 1 0 0 0 0 0 1—4 9 1
Avery, Stanton (7), Pena (9), Leibrandt (11); Erickson, Guthrie (7), Willis (7), Aguilera (10). W—Aguilera. L—Leibrandt. HR—Pendleton (Atl.); Puckett (Min.).
Game 7—October 27, at Minnesota
Atl. ....0 0 0 0 0 0 0 0 0 0—0 7 0
Minn. ....0 0 0 0 0 0 0 0 0 1—1 10 0
Smoltz, Stanton (8), Pena (9); Morris. W—Morris. L—Pena.

HISTORY

FINAL STANDINGS

American League

East Division

Team	Tor.	Mil.	Bal.	Cle.	N.Y.	Det.	Bos.	Oak.	Min.	Chi.	Tex.	Cal.	K.C.	Sea.	W	L	Pct.	GB
Toronto	...	5	8	7	11	8	6	6	7	7	9	7	7	8	96	66	.593	...
Milwaukee	8	...	7	8	6	8	8	7	6	7	7	7	5	8	92	70	.568	4
Baltimore	5	6	...	7	5	10	8	6	6	6	7	8	8	7	89	73	.549	7
Cleveland	6	5	6	...	7	5	7	6	6	5	5	6	5	7	76	86	.469	20
New York	2	7	8	6	...	8	6	6	5	4	6	5	7	6	76	86	.469	20
Detroit	5	5	3	8	5	...	9	6	3	2	8	5	7	9	75	87	.463	21
Boston	7	5	5	6	7	4	...	5	3	6	4	8	7	6	73	89	.451	23

West Division

Team	Oak.	Min.	Chi.	Tex.	Cal.	K.C.	Sea.	Tor.	Mil.	Bal.	Cle.	N.Y.	Det.	Bos.	W	L	Pct.	GB
Oakland	...	8	8	9	8	9	12	6	5	6	6	6	6	7	96	66	.593	...
Minnesota	5	...	5	6	11	7	8	5	6	6	6	7	9	9	90	72	.556	6
Chicago	5	8	...	5	10	7	4	5	5	6	7	8	10	6	86	76	.531	10
Texas	4	7	8	...	4	7	9	3	5	5	7	6	4	8	77	85	.475	19
California	5	2	3	9	...	8	7	5	5	4	6	7	7	4	72	90	.444	24
Kansas City	4	6	6	6	5	...	7	5	7	4	7	5	5	5	72	90	.444	24
Seattle	1	5	9	4	6	6	...	4	4	5	5	6	3	6	64	98	.395	32

National League

East Division

Team	Pit.	Mon.	St.L.	Chi.	N.Y.	Phi.	Atl.	Cin.	S.D.	Hou.	S.F.	L.A.	W	L	Pct.	GB
Pittsburgh	...	9	15	10	14	13	5	6	5	6	6	7	96	66	.593	...
Montreal	9	...	6	11	12	9	8	7	8	4	5	8	87	75	.537	9
St. Louis	3	12	...	7	9	11	6	5	8	7	7	8	83	79	.512	13
Chicago	8	7	11	...	9	9	2	5	5	8	8	6	78	84	.481	18
New York	4	6	9	9	...	6	5	5	4	7	10	7	72	90	.444	24
Philadelphia	5	9	7	9	12	...	6	5	3	4	3	7	70	92	.432	26

West Division

Team	Atl.	Cin.	S.D.	Hou.	S.F.	L.A.	Pit.	Mon.	St.L.	Chi.	N.Y.	Phi.	W	L	Pct.	GB
Atlanta	...	9	13	13	11	12	7	4	6	10	7	6	98	64	.605	...
CIncinnati	9	...	11	10	10	11	6	5	7	7	7	7	90	72	.556	8
San Diego	5	7	...	11	11	9	7	4	4	7	8	9	82	80	.506	16
Houston	5	8	7	...	12	13	6	8	5	4	5	8	81	81	.500	17
San Fran.	7	8	7	6	...	11	6	7	5	4	2	9	72	90	.444	26
Los Angeles	6	7	9	5	7	...	5	4	4	6	5	5	63	99	.389	35

LEADERS

American League
BA: Edgar Martinez, Sea., .343.
Runs: Tony Phillips, Det., 114.
Hits: Kirby Puckett, Min., 210.
TB: Kirby Puckett, Min., 313.
HR: Juan Gonzalez, Tex., 43.
RBI: Cecil Fielder, Det., 124.
SB: Kenny Lofton, Cle., 66.
Wins: Kevin Brown, Tex.; Jack Morris, Tor., 21.
ERA: Roger Clemens, Bos., 2.41.
CG: Jack McDowell, Chi., 13.
IP: Kevin Brown, Tex., 265.2.
SO: Randy Johnson, Sea., 241.
SV: Dennis Eckersley, Oak., 51.

National League
BA: Gary Sheffield, S.D., .330.
Runs: Barry Bonds, Pit., 109.
Hits: Terry Pendleton, Atl.; Andy Van Slyke, Pit., 199.
TB: Gary Sheffield, S.D., 323.
HR: Fred McGriff, S.D., 35.
RBI: Darren Daulton, Phil., 109.
SB: Marquis Grissom, Mon., 78.
Wins: Tom Glavine, Atl.; Greg Maddux, Chi., 20.
ERA: Bill Swift, S.F., 2.08.
CG: Terry Mulholland, Phil., 12.
IP: Greg Maddux, Chi., 268.
SO: John Smoltz, Atl., 215.
SV: Lee Smith, St.L., 43.

A.L. 20-game winners
Jack Morris, Tor., 21-6
Kevin Brown, Tex., 21-11
Jack McDowell, Chi., 20-10

N.L. 20-game winners
Tom Glavine, Atl., 20-8
Greg Maddux, Chi., 20-11

A.L. 100 RBIs
Cecil Fielder, Det., 124
Joe Carter, Tor., 119
Frank Thomas, Chi., 115
George Bell, Chi., 112
Albert Belle, Cle., 112
Kirby Puckett, Min., 110
Juan Gonzalez, Tex., 109
Dave Winfield, Tor., 108
Mike Devereaux, Bal., 107
Carlos Baerga, Cle., 105
Mark McGwire, Oak., 104
Ken Griffey Jr., Sea., 103

N.L. 100 RBIs
Darren Daulton, Phil., 109
Terry Pendleton, Atl., 105
Fred McGriff, S.D., 104
Barry Bonds, Pit., 103
Gary Sheffield, S.D., 100

A.L. 40 homers
Juan Gonzalez, Tex., 43
Mark McGwire, Oak., 42

Most Valuable Player
A.L.: Dennis Eckersley, P, Oak.
N.L.: Barry Bonds, OF, Pit.

Cy Young Award
A.L.: Dennis Eckersley, Oak.
N.L.: Greg Maddux, Chi.

Rookie of the Year
A.L.: Pat Listach, SS, Mil.
N.L.: Eric Karros, 1B, L.A.

Manager of the Year
A.L.: Tony La Russa, Oak.
N.L.: Jim Leyland, Pit.

Hall of Fame additions
Rollie Fingers, P, 1968-85
Bill McGowan, umpire
Hal Newhouser, P, 1939-55
Tom Seaver, P, 1967-86

SIGNIFICANT EVENTS

■ **April 6:** The Orioles opened their new Camden Yards home with a 2-0 victory over Cleveland.

■ **September 7:** Fay Vincent, reacting to an 18-9 no-confidence vote by the owners, resigned his post as baseball's eighth commissioner.

■ **November 17:** The Florida Marlins and Colorado Rockies selected 36 players apiece in baseball's first expansion draft since 1976.

MEMORABLE MOMENTS

■ **April 12:** Boston's Matt Young became the third pitcher in history to lose a complete-game no-hitter when he dropped a 2-1 decision to Cleveland.

■ **September 9, 30:** Milwaukee's Robin Yount and Kansas City's George Brett became the 17th and 18th members of baseball's 3,000-hit club.

■ **September 20:** Philadelphia second baseman Mickey Morandini pulled off baseball's ninth unassisted triple play and the N.L.'s first since 1927 in the sixth inning of a game against Pittsburgh.

ALL-STAR GAME

■ **Winner:** Ken Griffey Jr. went 3 for 3 as the suddenly dominant A.L. pounded out 19 hits and romped to an easy 13-6 victory.

■ **Key inning:** The A.L. first, when N.L. starter Tom Glavine was touched for four runs on seven consecutive singles.

■ **Memorable moment:** Ruben Sierra's two-run sixth-inning homer, which lifted the A.L.'s lead to 10-0.

■ **Top guns:** Griffey Jr. (Mariners), Sierra (Rangers), Robin Ventura (White Sox), Joe Carter (Blue Jays), Will Clark (Giants), Fred McGriff (Padres), N.L.

■ **MVP:** Griffey Jr.

Linescore

July 14, at San Diego's Jack Murphy Stadium
A.L. ....4 1 1 0 0 4 0 3 0—13 19 1
N.L. ....0 0 0 0 0 1 0 3 2— 6 12 1
Brown (Rangers), McDowell (White Sox) 2, Guzman (Blue Jays) 3, Clemens (Red Sox) 4, Mussina (Orioles) 5, Langston (Angels) 6, Nagy (Indians) 7, Montgomery (Royals) 8, Aguilera (Twins) 8, Eckersley (Athletics) 9; Glavine (Braves), Maddux (Braves) 2, Cone (Mets) 4, Tewksbury (Cardinals) 5, Smoltz (Braves) 6, D. Martinez (Expos) 7, Jones (Astros) 8, Charlton (Reds) 9. W—Brown. L—Glavine. HR—Griffey, Sierra, A.L.; Clark, N.L.

ALCS

■ **Winner:** The Toronto Blue Jays, three-time Championship Series losers, brought Canada its first pennant with a rousing six-game victory over Oakland.

■ **Turning point:** Down 6-1 entering the eighth inning of Game 4, the Blue Jays rallied to tie against A's relief ace Dennis Eckersley and won in the 11th on Pat Borders' sacrifice fly. Instead of a 2-2 series tie, Toronto was up 3-1.

■ **Memorable moment:** Roberto Alomar's stunning game-tying homer off Eckersley in the ninth inning of Game 4. The two-run shot forced extra innings.

■ **Top guns:** Juan Guzman (2-0, 2.08 ERA), Alomar (.423, 2 HR), Candy Maldonado (2 HR, 6 RBIs), Blue Jays; Harold Baines (.440), Ruben Sierra (.333, 7 RBIs), Athletics.

■ **MVP:** Alomar.

Linescores

Game 1—October 7, at Toronto
Oak. ....0 3 0 0 0 0 0 0 1—4 6 1
Tor. ....0 0 0 0 1 1 0 1 0—3 9 0
Stewart, Russell (8), Eckersley (9); Morris. W—Russell. L—Morris. S—Eckersley. HR—McGwire, Steinbach, Baines (Oak.); Borders, Winfield (Tor.).

Game 2—October 8, at Toronto
Oak. ....0 0 0 0 0 0 0 0 1—1 6 0
Tor. ....0 0 0 0 2 0 1 0 x—3 4 0
Moore, Corsi (8), Parrett (8); Cone, Henke (9). W—Cone. L—Moore. S—Henke. HR—Gruber (Tor.).

Game 3—October 10, at Oakland
Tor. ....0 1 0 1 1 0 2 1 1—7 9 1
Oak. ....0 0 0 2 0 0 2 1 0—5 13 3
Guzman, Ward (7), Timlin (8), Henke (8); Darling, Downs (7), Corsi (8), Russell (8), Honeycutt (9), Eckersley (9). W—Guzman. L—Darling. S—Henke. HR—Alomar, Maldonado (Tor.).

Game 4—October 11, at Oakland
Tor. ....0 1 0 0 0 0 0 3 2 0 1—7 17 4
Oak. ....0 0 5 0 0 1 0 0 0 0 0—6 12 2
Morris, Stottlemyre (4), Timlin (8), Ward (9), Henke (11); Welch, Parrett (8), Eckersley (8), Corsi (9), Downs (10). W—Ward. L—Downs. S—Henke. HR—Olerud, Alomar (Tor.).

Game 5—October 12, at Oakland
Tor. ....0 0 0 1 0 0 1 0 0—2 7 3
Oak. ....2 0 1 0 3 0 0 0 x—6 8 0
Cone, Key (5), Eichhorn (8); Stewart. W—Stewart. L—Cone. HR—Sierra (Oak.); Winfield (Tor.).

Game 6—October 14, at Toronto
Oak. ....0 0 0 0 0 1 0 1 0—2 7 1
Tor. ....2 0 4 0 1 0 0 2 x—9 13 0
Moore, Parrett (3), Honeycutt (5), Russell (7), Witt (8); Guzman, Ward (8), Henke (9). W—Guzman. L—Moore. HR—Carter, Maldonado (Tor.).

NLCS

■ **Winner:** Atlanta won its rematch with Pittsburgh and captured its second straight pennant in a stirring Championship Series that was decided on the final pitch.

■ **Turning point:** The incredible ninth inning of Game 7. Down 2-0 to Pirates ace Doug Drabek after eight innings and on the brink of blowing what had once been a three-games- to-one advantage, the Braves rallied for three runs.

■ **Memorable moment:** With two out and the bases loaded in the bottom of the ninth inning of Game 7, pinch-hitter Francisco Cabrera delivered a two-run, pennant-deciding single to left field off Stan Belinda.

■ **Top guns:** John Smoltz (2-0, 2.66 ERA), Mark Lemke (.333), David Justice (2 HR, 6 RBIs), Ron Gant (2 HR, 6 RBIs), Braves; Tim Wakefield (2-0, 3.00), Lloyd McClendon (.727), Gary Redus (.438), Pirates.

■ **MVP:** Smoltz.

Linescores

Game 1—October 6, at Atlanta
Pitt. ....0 0 0 0 0 0 0 1 0—1 5 1
Atlanta..........0 1 0 2 1 0 1 0 x—5 8 0
Drabek, Patterson (5), Neagle (7), Cox (8); Smoltz, Stanton (9). W—Smoltz. L—Drabek. HR—Blauser (Atl.); Lind (Pit.).

Game 2—October 7, at Atlanta
Pitt. ....0 0 0 0 0 0 4 1 0— 5 7 0
Atlanta......0 4 0 0 4 0 5 0 x—13 14 0
Jackson, Mason (2), Walk (3), Tomlin (5), Neagle (7), Patterson (7), Belinda (8); Avery, Freeman (7), Stanton (7), Wohlers (8), Reardon (9). W—Avery. L—Jackson. HR—Gant (Atl.).

Game 3—October 9, at Pittsburgh
Atlanta ....0 0 0 1 0 0 1 0 0—2 5 0
Pitt. ....0 0 0 0 1 1 1 0 x—3 8 1
Glavine, Stanton (7), Wohlers (8); Wakefield. W—Wakefield. L—Glavine. HR—Slaught (Pit.); Bream, Gant (Atl.).

Game 4—October 10, at Pittsburgh
Atlanta ......0 2 0 0 2 2 0 0 0—6 11 1
Pitt. ....0 2 1 0 0 0 1 0 0—4 6 1
Smoltz, Stanton (7), Reardon (9); Drabek, Tomlin (5), Cox (6), Mason (7). W—Smoltz. L—Drabek. S—Reardon.

Game 5—October 11, at Pittsburgh
Atlanta ......0 0 0 0 0 0 0 1 0—1 3 0
Pitt. ....4 0 1 0 0 1 1 0 x—7 13 0
Avery, P. Smith (1), Leibrandt (5), Freeman (6), Mercker (8); Walk. W—Walk. L—Avery.

Game 6—October 13, at Atlanta
Pitt. ....0 8 0 0 4 1 0 0 0—13 13 1
Atlanta ....0 0 0 1 0 0 1 0 2— 4 9 1
Wakefield; Glavine, Leibrandt (2), Freeman (5), Mercker (7), Wohlers (9). W—Wakefield. L—Glavine. HR—Bonds, Bell, McClendon (Pit.); Justice 2 (Atl.).

Game 7—October 14, at Atlanta
Pitt. ....1 0 0 0 0 1 0 0 0—2 7 1
Atlanta ....0 0 0 0 0 0 0 0 3—3 7 0
Drabek, Belinda (9); Smoltz, Stanton (7), P. Smith (7), Avery (7), Reardon (9). W—Reardon. L—Drabek.

WORLD SERIES

■ **Winner:** Toronto brought a baseball championship to Canada and the Braves failed to give Atlanta its long-awaited title for the second year in a row.

■ **Turning point:** The Blue Jays took a three-games-to-one advantage with a 2-1 victory in Game 4, thanks to the combined five-hit pitching of Jimmy Key, Duane Ward and Tom Henke and a home run by Pat Borders.

■ **Memorable moment:** Dave Winfield's two-run double in the 11th inning of Game 6 , which gave Toronto a 4-3 Series-clinching win.

■ **Top guns:** Key (2-0, 1.00 ERA), Borders (.450), Joe Carter (2 HR), Blue Jays; Deion Sanders (.533), Braves.

■ **MVP:** Borders.

Linescores

Game 1—October 17, at Atlanta
Tor. ....0 0 0 1 0 0 0 0 0—1 4 0
Atl. ....0 0 0 0 0 3 0 0 x—3 4 0
Morris, Stottlemyre (7), Wells (8); Glavine. W—Glavine. L—Morris. HR—Carter (Tor.); Berryhill (Atl.).

Game 2—October 18, at Atlanta
Tor. ....0 0 0 0 2 0 0 1 2—5 9 2
Atl. ....0 1 0 1 2 0 0 0 0—4 5 1
Cone, Wells (5), Stottlemyre (7), Ward (8), Henke (9); Smoltz, Stanton (8), Reardon (8). W—Ward. L—Reardon. S—Henke. HR—Sprague (Tor.).

Game 3—October 20, at Toronto
Atl. ....0 0 0 0 0 1 0 1 0—2 9 0
Tor. ....0 0 0 1 0 0 0 1 1—3 6 1
Avery, Wohlers (9), Stanton (9), Reardon (9); Guzman, Ward (9). W—Ward. L—Avery. HR—Carter, Gruber (Tor.).

Game 4—October 21, at Toronto
Atl. ....0 0 0 0 0 0 0 1 0—1 5 0
Tor. ....0 0 1 0 0 0 1 0 x—2 6 0
Glavine; Key, Ward (8), Henke (9). W—Key. L—Glavine. S—Henke. HR—Borders (Tor.).

Game 5—October 22, at Toronto
Atl. ....1 0 0 1 5 0 0 0 0—7 13 0
Tor. ....0 1 0 1 0 0 0 0 0—2 6 0
Smoltz, Stanton (7); Morris, Wells (5), Timlin (7), Eichhorn (8), Stottlemyre (9). W—Smoltz. L—Morris. S—Stanton. HR—Justice, L. Smith (Atl.).

Game 6—October 24, at Atlanta
Tor. ..1 0 0 1 0 0 0 0 0 0 2—4 14 1
Atl. ..0 0 1 0 0 0 0 0 1 0 1—3 8 1
Cone, Stottlemyre (7), Wells (7), Ward (8), Henke (9), Key (10), Timlin (11); Avery, P. Smith (5), Stanton (8), Wohlers (9), Leibrandt (10). W—Key. L—Leibrandt. S—Timlin. HR—Maldonado (Tor.).

FINAL STANDINGS

American League

East Division

Team	Tor.	N.Y.	Det.	Bal.	Bos.	Cle.	Mil.	Chi.	Tex.	K.C.	Sea.	Min.	Cal.	Oak.	W	L	Pct.	GB
Toronto	...	8	7	8	10	9	8	6	5	4	5	10	8	7	95	67	.586	...
New York	5	...	9	7	7	7	9	8	3	6	7	8	6	6	88	74	.543	7
Detroit	6	4	...	8	7	7	8	5	6	5	7	6	8	8	85	77	.525	10
Baltimore	5	6	5	...	6	8	8	4	4	7	7	8	7	10	85	77	.525	10
Boston	3	6	6	7	...	5	5	7	6	5	7	7	7	9	80	82	.494	15
Cleveland	4	6	6	5	8	...	8	3	7	7	3	4	7	8	76	86	.469	19
Milwaukee	5	4	5	5	8	5	...	3	4	7	4	7	5	7	69	93	.426	26

West Division

Team	Chi.	Tex.	K.C.	Sea.	Min.	Cal.	Oak.	Tor.	N.Y.	Det.	Bal.	Bos.	Cle.	Mil.	W	L	Pct.	GB
Chicago	...	8	6	9	10	6	7	6	4	7	8	5	9	9	94	68	.580	...
Texas	5	...	6	5	6	7	8	7	9	6	8	6	5	8	86	76	.531	8
Kansas City	7	7	...	7	7	7	6	8	6	7	5	7	5	5	84	78	.519	10
Seattle	4	8	6	...	9	7	4	7	5	5	5	5	9	8	82	80	.506	12
Minnesota	3	7	6	4	...	9	8	2	4	6	4	5	8	5	71	91	.438	23
California	7	6	6	6	4	...	6	4	6	4	5	5	5	7	71	91	.438	23
Oakland	6	5	7	9	5	7	...	5	6	4	2	3	4	5	68	94	.420	26

National League

East Division

Team	Phi.	Mon.	St.L.	Chi.	Pit.	Fla.	N.Y.	Atl.	S.F.	Hou.	L.A.	Cin.	Col.	S.D.	W	L	Pct.	GB
Philadelphia	...	7	8	6	7	9	10	6	4	7	10	8	9	6	97	65	.599	...
Montreal	6	...	7	8	8	8	9	5	3	7	6	8	9	10	94	68	.580	3
St. Louis	5	6	...	5	9	9	8	6	8	6	6	7	7	5	87	75	.537	10
Chicago	7	5	8	...	5	6	8	5	6	4	7	7	8	8	84	78	.519	13
Pittsburgh	6	5	4	8	...	7	9	5	5	5	4	4	4	9	75	87	.463	22
Florida	4	5	4	7	6	...	4	5	4	3	5	5	5	7	64	98	.395	33
New York	3	4	5	5	4	9	...	3	4	1	4	6	6	5	59	103	.364	38

West Division

Team	Atl.	S.F.	Hou.	L.A.	Cin.	Col.	S.D.	Phi.	Mon.	St.L.	Chi.	Pit.	Fla.	N.Y.	W	L	Pct.	GB
Atlanta	...	7	8	8	10	13	9	6	7	6	7	7	7	9	104	58	.642	...
San Fran.	6	...	10	6	11	10	10	8	9	4	6	7	8	8	103	59	.636	1
Houston	5	3	...	9	7	2	8	5	5	6	8	7	9	11	85	77	.525	19
Los Angeles	5	7	4	...	8	6	9	2	6	6	5	8	7	8	81	81	.500	23
Cincinnati	3	2	6	5	...	9	9	4	4	5	5	8	7	6	73	89	.451	31
Colorado	0	3	11	7	4	...	6	3	3	5	4	8	7	6	67	95	.414	37
San Diego	4	3	5	4	4	7	...	6	2	7	4	3	5	7	61	101	.377	43

LEADERS

American League
BA: John Olerud, Tor., .363.
Runs: Rafael Palmeiro, Tex., 124.
Hits: Paul Molitor, Tor., 211.
TB: Ken Griffey, Jr., Sea., 359.
HR: Juan Gonzalez, Tex., 46.
RBI: Albert Belle, Cle., 129.
SB: Kenny Lofton, Cle., 70.
Wins: Jack McDowell, Chi., 22.
ERA: Kevin Appier, K.C., 2.56.
CG: Chuck Finley, Cal., 13.
IP: Cal Eldred, Mil., 258.
SO: Randy Johnson, Sea., 308.
SV: Jeff Montgomery, K.C.;
Duane Ward, Tor., 45.

National League
BA: Andres Galarraga, Col., .370.
Runs: Lenny Dykstra, Phil., 143.
Hits: Lenny Dykstra, Phil., 194.
HR: Barry Bonds, S.F., 46.
RBI: Barry Bonds, S.F., 123.
SB: Chuck Carr, Fla., 58.
Wins: John Burkett, S.F.;
Tom Glavine, Atl., 22.
ERA: Greg Maddux, Atl., 2.36.
CG: Greg Maddux, Atl., 8.
IP: Greg Maddux, Atl., 267.
SO: Jose Rijo, Cin., 227.
SV: Randy Myers, Chi., 53.

A.L. 20-game winner
Jack McDowell, Chi., 22-10

N.L. 20-game winners
Tom Glavine, Atl., 22-6
John Burkett, S.F., 22-7
Bill Swift, S.F., 21-8
Greg Maddux, Atl., 20-10

A.L. 100 RBIs
Albert Belle, Cle., 129
Frank Thomas, Chi., 128
Joe Carter, Tor., 121
Juan Gonzalez, Tex., 118
Cecil Fielder, Det., 117
Carlos Baerga, Cle., 114
Chili Davis, Cal., 112
Paul Molitor, Tor., 111
Mickey Tettleton, Det., 110
Ken Griffey Jr., Sea., 109
John Olerud, Tor., 107
Rafael Palmeiro, Tex., 105
Danny Tartabull, N.Y., 102
Mo Vaughn, Bos., 101
Ruben Sierra, Oak., 101

N.L. 100 RBIs
Barry Bonds, S.F., 123
David Justice, Atl., 120
Ron Gant, Atl., 117
Mike Piazza, L.A., 112
Matt Williams, S.F., 110
Darren Daulton, Phil., 105
Todd Zeile, St.L., 103
Fred McGriff, S.D.-Atl., 101
Eddie Murray, N.Y., 100
Phil Plantier, S.D., 100

A.L. 40 homers
Juan Gonzalez, Tex., 46
Ken Griffey Jr., Sea., 45
Frank Thomas, Chi., 41

N.L. 40 homers
Barry Bonds, S.F., 46
David Justice, Atl., 40

Most Valuable Player
A.L.: Frank Thomas, 1B, Chi.
N.L.: Barry Bonds, OF, S.F.

Cy Young Award
A.L.: Jack McDowell, Chi.
N.L.: Greg Maddux, Atl.

Rookie of the Year
A.L.: Tim Salmon, OF, Cal.
N.L.: Mike Piazza, C, L.A.

Manager of the Year
A.L.: Gene Lamont, Chi.
N.L.: Dusty Baker, S.F.

Hall of Fame addition
Reggie Jackson, OF, 1967-87

SIGNIFICANT EVENTS

■ **March 22:** Cleveland players Steve Olin and Tim Crews were killed and pitcher Bob Ojeda was seriously injured in a spring training boating accident near Orlando, Fla.
■ **September 9:** Owners and players agreed to split the A.L. and N.L. into three divisions and expand the number of playoff qualifiers from four to eight teams.
■ **October 3:** The Braves clinched the N.L. West Division title with a final-day 5-3 victory over Colorado while the Giants were losing to the Dodgers, 12-1.

MEMORABLE MOMENTS

■ **July 28:** Seattle's Ken Griffey Jr. tied a long-standing record when he homered in his eighth consecutive game—a 5-1 loss to Minnesota.
■ **July 28:** The Mets scored two ninth-inning runs against Florida, handing Anthony Young a 5-4 victory and ending his record 27-game losing streak.
■ **September 7:** St. Louis' Mark Whiten tied a pair of records when he hit four homers and drove in 12 runs in a 15-2 victory over Cincinnati.
■ **September 16:** Minnesota's Dave Winfield joined baseball's exclusive 3,000-hit club in a game against Oakland.

ALL-STAR GAME

■ **Winner:** Kirby Puckett fueled the high-powered A.L. offense to a 9-3 victory — its sixth straight.
■ **Key inning:** The fifth. After hitting a solo home run in the second, Puckett contributed a run-scoring double in a three-run fifth that broke a 2-2 tie.
■ **Memorable moment:** Hard-throwing A.L. lefty Randy Johnson striking out John Kruk, who bailed out on three straight pitches, swinging feebly at the third.
■ **Top guns:** Johnson (Mariners), Puckett (Twins), Roberto Alomar (Blue Jays), Albert Belle (Indians), A.L.; Gary Sheffield (Marlins), Barry Bonds (Giants), N.L.
■ **MVP:** Puckett.

Linescore
July 13, at Baltimore's Camden Yards
N.L. ....2 0 0 0 0 1 0 0 0—3 7 2
A.L. ....0 1 1 0 3 3 1 0 x—9 11 0
Mulholland (Phillies), Benes (Padres) 3, Burkett (Giants) 5, Avery (Braves) 5, Smoltz (Braves) 6, Beck (Giants) 7, Harvey (Marlins) 8; Langston (Angels), Johnson (Mariners) 3, McDowell (White Sox) 5, Key (Yankees) 6, Montgomery (Royals) 7, Aguilera (Twins) 8, Ward (Blue Jays) 9. W—McDowell. L—Burkett. HR—Sheffield, N.L.; Puckett, Alomar, A.L.

ALCS

■ **Winner:** Toronto kept the A.L. pennant on Canadian soil and denied Chicago's bid for its first World Series appearance since 1959.
■ **Turning point:** The Blue Jays defeated the White Sox, 5-3, in the pivotal fifth game, which wasn't decided until reliever Duane Ward struck out Bo Jackson with a man on base in the ninth inning.
■ **Memorable moment:** A 6-3 finale in which Toronto's Dave Stewart lifted his LCS record to 8-0 and pitched his fourth pennant-clinching victory in six seasons.
■ **Top guns:** Stewart (2-0, 2.03 ERA), Juan Guzman (2-0, 2.08), Devon White (.444), Blue Jays; Tim Raines (.444), White Sox.
■ **MVP:** Stewart.

Linescores
Game 1—October 5, at Chicago
Toronto ......0 0 0 2 3 0 2 0 0—7 17 1
Chicago......0 0 0 3 0 0 0 0 0—3 6 1
Guzman, Cox (7), Ward (9); McDowell, DeLeon (7), Radinsky (8), McCaskill (9). W—Guzman. L—McDowell. HR—Molitor (Tor.).
Game 2—October 6, at Chicago
Toronto ....1 0 0 2 0 0 0 0 0—3 8 0
Chicago........1 0 0 0 0 0 0 0 0—1 7 2
Stewart, Leiter (7), Ward (9); A. Fernandez, Hernandez (9). W—Stewart. L—A. Fernandez. S—Ward.
Game 3—October 8, at Toronto
Chicago......0 0 5 1 0 0 0 0 0—6 12 0
Toronto ......0 0 1 0 0 0 0 0 0—1 7 1
Alvarez; Hentgen, Cox (4), Eichhorn (7), Castillo (9). W—Alvarez. L—Hentgen.
Game 4—October 9, at Toronto
Chicago......0 2 0 0 0 3 1 0 1—7 11 0
Toronto ......0 0 3 0 0 1 0 0 0—4 9 0
Bere, Belcher (3), McCaskill (7), Radinsky (8), Hernandez (9); Stottlemyre, Leiter (7), Timlin (7). W—Belcher. L—Stottlemyre. S—Hernandez. HR—Thomas, Johnson (Chi.).
Game 5—October 10, at Toronto
Chicago......0 0 0 0 1 0 0 0 2—3 5 1
Toronto ....1 1 1 1 0 0 1 0 x—5 14 0
McDowell, DeLeon (3), Radinsky (7), Hernandez (7); Guzman, Castillo (8), Ward (9). W—Guzman. L—McDowell. HR—Burks, Ventura (Chi.).
Game 6—October 12, at Chicago
Toronto ......0 2 0 1 0 0 0 0 3—6 10 0
Chicago......0 0 2 0 0 0 0 0 1—3 5 3
Stewart, Ward (8); A. Fernandez, McCaskill (8), Radinsky (9), Hernandez (9). W—Stewart. L—A. Fernandez. S—Ward. HR—White (Tor.); Newson (Chi.).

NLCS

■ **Winner:** Philadelphia needed six games to ruin Atlanta's bid for a third consecutive pennant.
■ **Turning point:** The pivotal fifth game, when Curt Schilling pitched eight innings of four-hit ball and Lenny Dykstra hit a game-winning 10th-inning home run.
■ **Memorable moment:** The ninth inning of Game 6. Phillies lefthander Mitch Williams, also known as "Wild Thing," pulled a shocker when he retired the Braves 1-2-3 for his second series save and a 6-3 pennant-clinching victory.
■ **Top guns:** Schilling (1.69 ERA), Williams (2-0, 2 saves, 1.69), Dykstra (2 HR), Phillies; Fred McGriff (.435), Otis Nixon (.348), Terry Pendleton (.346), Braves.
■ **MVP:** Schilling.

Linescores
Game 1—October 6, at Philadelphia
Atlanta ....0 0 1 1 0 0 0 1 0 0—3 9 0
Phil. ....1 0 0 1 0 1 0 0 0 1—4 9 1
Avery, Mercker (7), McMichael (9); Schilling, Williams (9). W—Williams. L—McMichael. HR—Incaviglia (Phil.).
Game 2—October 7, at Philadelphia
Atlanta ....2 0 6 0 1 0 0 4 1—14 16 0
Phil. ....0 0 0 2 0 0 0 0 1— 3 7 2
Maddux, Stanton (8), Wohlers (9); Greene, Thigpen (3), Rivera (4), Mason (6), West (8), Andersen (9). W—Maddux. L—Greene. HR—McGriff, Blauser, Berryhill, Pendleton (Atl.); Hollins, Dykstra (Phil.).
Game 3—October 9, at Atlanta
Phil. ....0 0 0 1 0 1 0 1 1—4 10 1
Atlanta........0 0 0 0 0 5 4 0 x—9 12 0
Mulholland, Mason (6), Andersen (7), West (7), Thigpen (8); Glavine, Mercker (8), McMichael (9). W—Glavine. L—Mulholland. HR—Kruk (Phil.)
Game 4—October 10, at Atlanta
Phil. ....0 0 0 2 0 0 0 0 0—2 8 1
Atlanta ......0 1 0 0 0 0 0 0 0—1 10 1
Jackson, Williams (8); Smoltz, Mercker (7), Wohlers (8). W—Jackson. L—Smoltz. S—Williams.
Game 5—October 11, at Atlanta
Phil. ....1 0 0 1 0 0 0 0 1 1—4 6 1
Atlanta ....0 0 0 0 0 0 0 0 3 0—3 7 1
Schilling, Williams (9), Andersen (10); Avery, Mercker (8), McMichael (9), Wohlers (10). W—Williams. L—Wohlers. S—Andersen. HR—Daulton, Dykstra (Phil.).
Game 6—October 13, at Philadelphia
Atlanta ....0 0 0 0 1 0 2 0 0—3 5 3
Phil. ....0 0 2 0 2 2 0 0 x—6 7 1
Maddux, Mercker (6), McMichael (7), Wohlers (7); Greene, West (8), Williams (9). W—Greene. L—Maddux. S—Williams. HR—Hollins (Phil.); Blauser (Atl.).

WORLD SERIES

■ **Winner:** Toronto defeated Philadelphia to become the first back-to-back Series winner since the Yankees of 1977-78.
■ **Turning point:** The Blue Jays' six-run, eighth-inning rally that turned a 14-9 Game 4 deficit into a 15-14 victory and a 3-1 Series lead.
■ **Memorable moment:** Joe Carter's three-run, ninth-inning home run that turned a 6-5 Game 6 deficit into one of the most dramatic victories in World Series history.
■ **Top guns:** Paul Molitor (.500, 2 HR, 8 RBIs), Roberto Alomar (.480), Tony Fernandez (.333, 9 RBIs), Carter (2 HR, 8 RBIs), Blue Jays; Lenny Dykstra (.348, 4 HR, 8 RBIs), John Kruk (.348), Phillies.
■ **MVP:** Molitor.

Linescores
Game 1—October 16, at Toronto
Phil. ....2 0 1 0 1 0 0 0 1—5 11 1
Toronto ......0 2 1 0 1 1 3 0 x—8 10 3
Schilling, West (7), Andersen (7), Mason (8); Guzman, Leiter (6), Ward (8). W—Leiter. L—Schilling. S—Ward. HR—White, Olerud (Tor.).
Game 2—October 17, at Toronto
Phil. ....0 0 5 0 0 0 1 0 0—6 12 0
Toronto ......0 0 0 2 0 1 0 1 0—4 8 0
Mulholland, Mason (6), Williams (7); Stewart, Castillo (7), Eichhorn (8), Timlin (8). W—Mulholland. L—Stewart. S—Williams. HR—Carter (Tor.); Dykstra, Eisenreich (Phil.).
Game 3—October 19, at Philadelphia
Toronto ....3 0 1 0 0 1 3 0 2—10 13 1
Phil. ....0 0 0 0 1 0 1 0 1— 3 9 0
Hentgen, Cox (7), Ward (9); Jackson, Rivera (6), Thigpen (7), Andersen (9). W—Hentgen. L—Jackson. HR—Thompson (Phil.); Molitor (Tor.).
Game 4—October 20, at Philadelphia
Toronto ....3 0 4 0 0 2 0 6 0—15 18 0
Phil. ....4 2 0 1 5 1 1 0 0—14 14 0
Stottlemyre, Leiter (3), Castillo (5), Timlin (8), Ward (8); Greene, Mason (3), West (6), Andersen (7), Williams (8), Thigpen (9). W—Castillo. L—Williams. S—Ward. HR—Dykstra 2, Daulton (Phil.).
Game 5—October 21, at Philadelphia
Toronto ....0 0 0 0 0 0 0 0 0—0 5 1
Phil. ....1 1 0 0 0 0 0 0 x—2 5 1
Guzman, Cox (8); Schilling. W—Schilling. L—Guzman.
Game 6—October 23, at Toronto
Phil. ....0 0 0 1 0 0 5 0 0—6 7 0
Toronto ......3 0 0 1 1 0 0 0 3—8 10 2
Mulholland, Mason (6), West (8), Andersen (8), Williams (9); Stewart, Cox (7), Leiter (7), Ward (9). W—Ward. L—Williams. HR—Molitor, Carter (Tor.); Dykstra (Phil.).

FINAL STANDINGS

American League

East Division

Team	N.Y.	Bal.	Tor.	Bos.	Det.	Chi.	Cle.	K.C.	Min.	Mil.	Tex.	Oak.	Sea.	Cal.	W	L	Pct.	GB
New York	...	6	3	7	3	2	9	2	5	7	3	7	8	8	70	43	.619	...
Baltimore	4	...	7	4	3	2	4	4	4	7	3	7	6	8	63	49	.563	6.5
Toronto	4	2	...	3	4	3	4	6	8	3	8	1	5	4	55	60	.478	16
Boston	3	2	7	...	4	2	3	4	1	5	1	9	6	7	54	61	.470	17
Detroit	3	4	5	2	...	4	2	4	3	6	5	5	6	4	53	62	.461	18

Central Division

Team	Chi.	Cle.	K.C.	Min.	Mil.	N.Y.	Bal.	Tor.	Bos.	Det.	Tex.	Oak.	Sea.	Cal.	W	L	Pct.	GB
Chicago	...	7	3	2	9	4	4	2	4	8	4	6	9	5	67	46	.593	...
Cleveland	5	...	1	9	5	0	6	6	7	8	5	6	3	5	66	47	.584	1
Kansas City	7	4	...	6	5	4	1	6	2	8	4	7	6	4	64	51	.557	4
Minnesota	4	3	4	...	6	4	5	4	8	3	4	2	3	3	53	60	.469	14
Milwaukee	3	2	7	6	...	2	3	7	5	4	3	4	4	3	53	62	.461	15

West Division

Team	Tex.	Oak.	Sea.	Cal.	N.Y.	Bal.	Tor.	Bos.	Det.	Chi.	Cle.	K.C.	Min.	Mil.	W	L	Pct.	GB
Texas	...	3	1	4	2	3	4	5	7	5	7	3	5	3	52	62	.456	...
Oakland	7	...	4	6	5	5	5	3	4	3	0	3	5	1	51	63	.447	1
Seattle	9	3	...	7	4	4	1	6	3	1	2	4	3	2	49	63	.438	2
California	6	3	2	...	4	4	3	5	3	5	0	6	3	3	47	68	.409	5.5

National League

East Division

Team	Mon.	Atl.	N.Y.	Phi.	Fla.	Cin.	Hou.	Pit.	St.L.	Chi.	L.A.	S.F.	Col.	S.D.	W	L	Pct.	GB
Montreal	...	5	4	5	7	2	4	8	7	4	9	5	2	12	74	40	.649	...
Atlanta	4	...	5	6	8	5	3	3	5	4	6	5	8	6	68	46	.596	6
New York	3	4	...	4	4	4	3	4	6	4	6	6	1	6	55	58	.487	18.5
Philadelphia	4	3	6	...	6	2	1	5	4	6	5	4	4	4	54	61	.470	20.5
Florida	2	4	6	4	...	5	2	1	3	5	3	2	9	5	51	64	.443	23.5

Central Division

Team	Cin.	Hou.	Pit.	St.L.	Chi.	Mon.	Atl.	N.Y.	Phi.	Fla.	L.A.	S.F.	Col.	S.D.	W	L	Pct.	GB
Cincinnati	...	4	9	2	7	4	5	2	4	7	3	7	4	8	66	48	.579	...
Houston	6	...	8	8	8	2	3	3	5	4	1	8	5	5	66	49	.574	.5
Pittsburgh	3	4	...	5	5	2	9	5	4	6	3	1	3	3	53	61	.465	13
St. Louis	2	4	5	...	5	3	7	3	3	7	4	4	4	2	53	61	.465	13
Chicago	5	4	5	5	...	2	2	1	1	4	3	5	6	6	49	64	.434	16.5

West Division

Team	L.A.	S.F.	Col.	S.D.	Mon.	Atl.	N.Y.	Phi.	Fla.	Cin.	Hou.	Pit.	St.L.	Chi.	W	L	Pct.	GB
Los Angeles	...	5	6	6	3	0	6	7	3	6	8	3	2	3	58	56	.509	...
San Fran.	5	...	7	2	7	1	6	8	4	2	2	5	2	4	55	60	.478	3.5
Colorado	4	3	...	5	4	2	5	2	3	4	5	2	8	6	53	64	.453	6.5
San Diego	4	5	5	...	0	1	6	8	1	2	5	3	4	3	47	70	.402	12.5

SIGNIFICANT EVENTS

■ **March 1, June 7:** The N.L. elected Leonard Coleman as its new president and the A.L. opted for Gene Budig.

■ **April 4, 11:** Two parks were dedicated: The Indians needed 11 innings to beat Seattle, 4-3, in their Jacobs Field opener and the Rangers lost their debut at The Ballpark in Arlington to Milwaukee, 4-3.

■ **August 12:** Major League players brought the season to a skidding halt when they called a general strike—baseball's eighth work stoppage since 1972.

■ **September 14:** Baseball owners announced cancellation of the regular season and Post Season, rubber-stamping the first uncompleted season in the game's long history.

■ **December 28:** The Astros and Padres completed a 12-player trade, baseball's largest since 1957.

Despite the short season and a late injury, hot-hitting Houston first baseman Jeff Bagwell drove in a Major League-leading 116 runs.

Atlanta righthander Greg Maddux claimed the third of his four consecutive Cy Young Awards during the strike-shortened season.

MEMORABLE MOMENTS

■ **April 4:** Tuffy Rhodes became the first player to homer in his first three Opening Day at-bats, but the Cubs still dropped a 12-8 decision to the Mets.

■ **July 8:** Boston shortstop John Valentin pulled off baseball's 10th unassisted triple play and the Red Sox beat Seattle, 4-3.

■ **July 28:** When Kenny Rogers retired all 27 Minnesota hitters in a 4-0 victory, he became the first A.L. lefthander to throw a perfect game.

■ **August 1:** Cal Ripken stretched his ironman streak to 2,000 games and the Orioles celebrated with a 1-0 victory over Minnesota.

■ **August 6:** The Mariners routed Kansas City, 11-2, and ended the Royals' winning streak at 14 games.

LEADERS

American League
BA: Paul O'Neill, N.Y., .359.
Runs: Frank Thomas, Chi., 106.
Hits: Kenny Lofton, Cle., 160.
TB: Albert Belle, Cle., 294.
HR: Ken Griffey, Jr., Sea., 40.
RBI: Kirby Puckett, Min., 112.
SB: Lofton, Cle., 60.
Wins: Jimmy Key, N.Y., 17.
ERA: Steve Ontiveros, Oak., 2.65.
CG: Randy Johnson, Sea., 9.
IP: Chuck Finley, Cal., 183.1.
SO: Randy Johnson, Sea., 204.
SV: Lee Smith, Bal., 33.

National League
BA: Tony Gwynn, S.D., .394.
Runs: Jeff Bagwell, Hou., 104.
Hits: Gwynn, S.D., 165.
TB: Bagwell, Hou., 300.
HR: Matt Williams, S.F., 43.
RBI: Bagwell, Hou., 116.
SB: Craig Biggio, Hou., 39.
Wins: Ken Hill, Mon.; Greg Maddux, Atl., 16.
ERA: Greg Maddux, Atl., 1.56.
CG: Maddux, Atl., 10.
IP: Maddux, Atl., 202.
SO: Andy Benes, S.D., 189.
SV: John Franco, N.Y., 30.

A.L. 100 RBIs
Kirby Puckett, Min., 112
Joe Carter, Tor., 103
Albert Belle, Cle., 101
Frank Thomas, Chi., 101

N.L. 100 RBIs
Jeff Bagwell, Hou., 116

A.L. 40 homers
Ken Griffey Jr., Sea., 40

N.L. 40 homers
Matt Williams, S.F., 43

Most Valuable Player
A.L.: Frank Thomas, 1B, Chi.
N.L.: Jeff Bagwell, 1B, Hou.

Cy Young Award
A.L.: David Cone, K.C.
N.L.: Greg Maddux, Atl.

Rookie of the Year
A.L.: Bob Hamelin, DH, K.C.
N.L.: Raul Mondesi, OF, L.A.

Manager of the Year
A.L.: Buck Showalter, N.Y.
N.L.: Felipe Alou, Mon.

Hall of Fame additions
Steve Carlton, P, 1965-88
Leo Durocher, manager
Phil Rizzuto, SS, 1941-56

ALL-STAR GAME

■ **Winner:** The N.L. scored two runs in the ninth and one in the 10th to snap the A.L.'s six-game All-Star winning streak with an 8-7 victory.

■ **Key inning:** The 10th, when the N.L. scored its winning run on a single by Tony Gwynn and a game-ending double by Moises Alou.

■ **Memorable moment:** Fred McGriff's two-run, game-tying homer in the ninth off relief ace Lee Smith.

■ **Top guns:** Ken Hill (Expos), Gwynn (Padres), Alou (Expos), Marquis Grissom (Expos), McGriff (Braves), Gregg Jefferies (Cardinals), N.L.; Ken Griffey Jr. (Mariners), Kenny Lofton (Indians), Frank Thomas (White Sox), A.L.

■ **MVP:** McGriff.

Linescore

July 12, at Pittsburgh's Three Rivers Stadium
A.L.........1 0 0 0 0 3 3 0 0 0—7 15 0
N.L.........1 0 3 0 0 1 0 0 2 1—8 12 1
Key (Yankees), Cone (Royals) 3, Mussina (Orioles) 5, Johnson (Mariners) 6, Hentgen (Blue Jays) 7, Alvarez (White Sox) 8, L. Smith (Orioles) 9, Bere (White Sox) 10; Maddux (Braves), Hill (Expos) 4, Drabek (Astros) 6, Hudek (Astros) 6, Jackson (Phillies) 7, Beck (Giants) 7, Myers (Cubs) 9, Jones (Phillies) 10. W—Jones. L—Bere. HR—Grissom, McGriff, N.L.

HISTORY

FINAL STANDINGS

American League

East Division

Team	Bos.	N.Y.	Bal.	Det.	Tor.	Cle.	K.C.	Chi.	Mil.	Min.	Sea.	Cal.	Tex.	Oak.	W	L	Pct.	GB
Boston	...	5	9	8	8	6	3	5	8	5	7	11	3	8	86	58	.597	...
New York	8	...	7	8	12	6	7	2	6	4	4	5	6	4	79	65	.549	7
Baltimore	4	6	...	8	7	2	4	6	7	3	6	9	4	5	71	73	.493	15
Detroit	5	5	5	...	7	3	3	4	8	7	5	2	4	2	60	84	.417	26
Toronto	5	1	6	6	...	3	5	5	5	4	4	2	3	7	56	88	.389	30

Central Division

Team	Cle.	K.C.	Chi.	Mil.	Min.	Bos.	N.Y.	Bal.	Det.	Tor.	Sea.	Cal.	Tex.	Oak.	W	L	Pct.	GB
Cleveland	...	11	8	9	9	7	6	10	10	10	5	2	6	7	100	44	.694	...
Kansas City	1	...	5	10	6	2	3	5	4	7	7	7	8	5	70	74	.486	30
Chicago	5	8	...	6	10	3	3	1	8	6	4	2	5	7	68	76	.472	32
Milwaukee	4	2	7	...	9	4	5	5	5	7	3	2	5	7	65	79	.451	35
Minnesota	4	7	3	4	...	4	3	6	5	1	4	5	5	5	56	88	.389	44

West Division

Team	Sea.	Cal.	Tex.	Oak.	Bos.	N.Y.	Bal.	Det.	Tor.	Cle.	K.C.	Chi.	Mil.	Min.	W	L	Pct.	GB
Seattle	...	6	10	6	5	9	7	5	3	4	5	9	2	8	79	66	.545	...
California	7	...	6	6	3	7	4	6	8	3	5	10	5	8	78	67	.538	1
Texas	3	7	...	8	4	3	1	8	9	3	6	7	7	8	74	70	.514	4.5
Oakland	7	7	5	...	4	9	7	3	3	0	8	5	2	7	67	77	.465	11.5

National League

East Division

Team	Atl.	Phi.	N.Y.	Fla.	Mon.	Cin.	Hou.	Chi.	St.L.	Pit.	L.A.	Col.	S.D.	S.F.	W	L	Pct.	GB
Atlanta	...	7	5	10	9	8	6	8	7	4	5	9	5	7	90	54	.625	...
Philadelphia	6	...	6	7	5	3	7	1	5	6	9	2	6	6	69	75	.479	21
New York	8	7	...	6	6	5	6	3	3	4	6	4	6	5	69	75	.479	21
Florida	3	6	7	...	6	6	8	4	4	5	3	7	3	5	67	76	.469	22.5
Montreal	4	8	7	7	...	4	3	5	4	4	5	1	7	7	66	78	.458	24

Central Division

Team	Cin.	Hou.	Chi.	St.L.	Pit.	Atl.	Phi.	N.Y.	Fla.	Mon.	L.A.	Col.	S.D.	S.F.	W	L	Pct.	GB
Cincinnati	...	12	7	8	8	5	9	7	6	8	4	5	3	3	85	59	.590	...
Houston	1	...	8	9	9	6	5	6	4	9	3	4	7	5	76	68	.528	9
Chicago	3	5	...	9	8	4	6	4	8	3	7	6	5	5	73	71	.507	12
St. Louis	5	4	4	...	7	5	4	4	3	3	5	7	5	6	62	81	.434	22.5
Pittsburgh	5	4	5	6	...	2	3	3	8	4	4	4	4	6	58	86	.403	27

West Division

Team	L.A.	Col.	S.D.	S.F.	Atl.	Phi.	N.Y.	Fla.	Mon.	Cin.	Hou.	Chi.	St.L.	Pit.	W	L	Pct.	GB
Los Angeles	...	9	7	8	4	4	6	7	7	3	2	5	7	9	78	66	.542	...
Colorado	4	...	9	8	4	4	5	5	7	7	4	7	5	8	77	67	.535	1
San Diego	6	4	...	6	2	6	7	2	5	6	4	7	7	8	70	74	.486	8
San Fran.	5	5	7	...	1	6	8	3	6	3	3	7	7	6	67	77	.465	11

SIGNIFICANT EVENTS

■ **April 2:** Baseball owners, blocked by an injunction preventing them from imposing new work rules and using replacement players in the 1995 season, invited striking players to return to work, ending the 234-day work stoppage. Opening Day was pushed back to April 25 and the schedule was reduced to 144 games.

■ **April 30:** Major League Baseball agreed to a new contract with its umpires, ending a lockout that had extended a week into the regular season and forced use of replacement arbiters.

■ **March 9:** Major League owners approved expansion franchises for Tampa Bay (Devil Rays) and Phoenix (Arizona Diamondbacks), with play to begin in 1998.

■ **August 13:** Baseball was stung by the loss of former Yankee great Mickey Mantle, who died at age 63 of lung cancer.

■ **October 2:** Sparky Anderson, whose 2,194 managerial victories ranked third all-time to Connie Mack and John McGraw, retired after nine seasons with the Reds and 17 with the Tigers.

■ **November 13:** Atlanta righthander Greg Maddux won his record-setting fourth consecutive N.L. Cy Young after a 19-2, 1.63-ERA season. Maddux joined Steve Carlton as the only four-time Cy Young winners.

MEMORABLE MOMENTS

■ **June 3:** Montreal's Pedro Martinez pitched nine perfect innings before giving up a 10th-inning double to San Diego's Bip Roberts after the Expos had scored in the top of the inning. Martinez did not finish his 1-0 victory.

■ **June 30:** Cleveland's Eddie Murray joined baseball's 3,000-hit club when he singled off Minnesota righthander Mike Trombley.

■ **September 6:** Baltimore shortstop Cal Ripken passed Lou Gehrig's ironman streak when he played in his 2,131st consecutive game — a 4-2 victory over California at Camden Yards.

■ **September 8:** Cleveland defeated Baltimore 3-2 and clinched the team's first title of any kind in 41 years. The Indians' final 30-game A.L. Central Division margin over Kansas City was the largest in modern baseball history.

■ **October 2:** The Mariners defeated California 9-1 in a one-game playoff, giving Seattle its first division title in the franchise's 19-year history.

ALL-STAR GAME

■ **Winner:** The N.L. managed only three hits off seven A.L. pitchers, but all were solo home runs and produced an unlikely 3-2 victory.

■ **Key inning:** The seventh, when Los Angeles catcher Mike Piazza collected the N.L.'s second hit, a game-tying homer off Texas' Kenny Rogers, and Phillies reliever Heathcliff Slocumb pitched the N.L. out of a two-on, one-out jam.

■ **Memorable moment:** Pinch-hitter Jeff Conine's eighth-inning blast off Oakland's Steve Ontiveros, which broke the 2-2 tie and gave the N.L. its first lead. Conine became the 10th player to hit a homer in his first All-Star at-bat.

■ **Top guns:** Randy Johnson (Mariners), Kevin Appier (Royals), Frank Thomas (White Sox), Carlos Baerga (Indians), A.L.; Hideo Nomo (Dodgers), Slocumb (Phillies), Craig Biggio (Astros), Piazza (Dodgers), Conine (Marlins), N.L.

■ **MVP:** Conine.

Linescore

July 11, at Texas' The Ballpark in Arlington
N.L. ....0 0 0 0 0 1 1 1 0—3 3 0
A.L. ....0 0 0 2 0 0 0 0 0—2 8 0
Nomo (Dodgers), Smiley (Reds) 3, Green (Phillies) 5, Neagle (Pirates) 6, C. Perez (Expos) 7, Slocumb (Phillies) 7, Henke (Cardinals) 8, Myers (Cubs) 9; Johnson (Mariners), Appier (Royals) 3, Martinez (Indians) 5, Rogers (Rangers) 7, Ontiveros (A's) 8, Wells (Tigers) 8, Mesa (Indians) 9. W—Slocumb. L—Ontiveros. S—Myers. HR—Thomas, A.L.; Biggio, Piazza, Conine, N.L.

A.L. DIVISION SERIES

■ **Winners:** Cleveland swept past Boston, but Seattle needed five games and extra innings to defeat New York in baseball's inaugural Division Series. The Mariners could not secure victory until the 11th inning of Game 5.

■ **Turning points:** For Cleveland, catcher Tony Pena's Game 1-ending home run in the bottom of the 13th inning. For Seattle, Edgar Martinez's two-homer, seven-RBI Game 4 effort that kept the Mariners' title hopes alive.

■ **Memorable moments:** Martinez's tie-breaking eighth-inning grand slam in Game 4 and his Series-ending two-run double in the 11th inning of Game 5.

■ **Memorable performances:** The playoff-record five-home run effort of Seattle outfielder Ken Griffey and Martinez's 10-RBI effort.

Linescores

Cleveland vs. Boston

Game 1—October 3, at Cleveland
Bos. ....0 0 2 0 0 0 0 1 0 0 1 0 0—4 11 2
Cle. ....0 0 0 0 0 3 0 0 0 0 1 0 1—5 10 2
Clemens, Cormier (8), Belinda (8), Stanton (8), Aguilera (11), Maddux (11), Smith (13); Martinez, Tavarez (7), Assenmacher (8), Plunk (8), Mesa (10), Poole (11), Hill (12). W—Hill. L—Smith. HR—Valentin, Alicea, Naehring (Bos.); Belle, Pena (Cle.).

Game 2—October 4, at Cleveland
Bos. ....0 0 0 0 0 0 0 0 0—0 3 1
Cle. ....0 0 0 0 2 0 0 2 x—4 4 2
Hanson; Hershiser, Tavarez (8), Assenmacher (8), Mesa (9). W—Hershiser. L—Hanson. HR—Murray (Cle.).

Game 3—October 6, at Boston
Cle. ....0 2 1 0 0 5 0 0 0—8 11 2
Bos. ....0 0 0 1 0 0 0 1 0—2 7 1
Nagy, Tavarez (8), Assenmacher (9); Wakefield, Cormier (6), Maddux (6), Hudson (9). W—Nagy. L—Wakefield. HR—Thome (Cle.).

Seattle vs. New York

Game 1—October 3, at New York
Seattle........0 0 0 1 0 1 2 0 2—6 9 0
N.Y. ....0 0 2 0 0 2 4 1 x—9 13 0
Bosio, Nelson (6), Ayala (7), Risley (7), Wells (8); Cone, Wetteland (9). W—Cone. L—Nelson. HR—Griffey 2 (Sea.); Boggs, Sierra (N.Y.).

Game 2—October 4, at New York
Seattle......0 0 1 0 0 1 2 0 0 0 0 1 0 0 0—5 16 2
N.Y. ....0 0 0 0 1 2 1 0 0 0 0 1 0 0 2—7 11 0
Benes, Risley (6), Charlton (7), Nelson (11), Belcher (12); Pettitte, Wickman (8), Wetteland (9), Rivera (12). W—Rivera. L—Belcher. HR—Coleman, Griffey (Sea.); Sierra, Mattingly, O'Neill, Leyritz (N.Y.).

Game 3—October 6, at Seattle
N.Y. ....0 0 0 1 0 0 1 2 0—4 6 2
Seattle..........0 0 0 0 2 4 1 0 x—7 7 0
McDowell, Howe (6), Wickman (6), Hitchcock (7), Rivera (7); Johnson, Risley (8), Charlton (8). W—Johnson. L—McDowell. S—Charlton. HR—B. Williams 2, Stanley (N.Y.); T. Martinez (Sea.).

Game 4—October 7, at Seattle
N.Y. ....3 0 2 0 0 0 0 1 2— 8 14 1
Seattle......0 0 4 0 1 1 0 5 x—11 16 0
Kamieniecki, Hitchcock (6), Wickman (7), Wetteland (8), Howe (8); Bosio, Nelson (3), Belcher (7), Charlton (8), Ayala (9), Risley (9). W—Charlton. L—Wetteland. S—Risley. HR—O'Neill (N.Y.); E. Martinez 2, Griffey, Buhner (Sea.).

Game 5—October 8, at Seattle
N.Y. ......0 0 0 2 0 2 0 0 0 0 1—5 6 0
Seattle 0 0 1 1 0 0 0 2 0 0 2—6 15 0
Cone, Rivera (8), McDowell (9); Benes, Charlton (7), Johnson (9). W—Johnson. L—McDowell. HR—O'Neill (N.Y.); Cora, Griffey (Sea.).

N.L. DIVISION SERIES

■ **Winners:** Atlanta and Cincinnati powered past West Division opponents in the N.L.'s first Division Series.

■ **Turning points:** For the Braves, a four-run ninth-inning Game 2 rally that produced a 7-4 victory and a two-games-to-none edge over the Rockies. For the Reds, a 5-4 Game 2 victory, despite being outhit by the Dodgers, 14-6.

■ **Memorable moment:** Colorado pitcher Lance Painter striking out with the bases loaded in the ninth inning of a 5-4 Game 1 loss to the Braves. Painter was pinch-hitting because Colorado manager Don Baylor had no more position players on his bench.

■ **Top performances:** Atlanta third baseman Chipper Jones belted two Game 1 homers, including the game-winner in the top of the ninth inning; Braves first baseman Fred McGriff broke out of a slump with a two-homer, five-RBI Game 5 effort; Reds infielder Mark Lewis broke open Game 3 against the Dodgers with the first pinch-hit grand slam in playoff history.

Linescores

Atlanta vs. Colorado

Game 1—October 3, at Colorado
Atlanta ......0 0 1 0 0 2 0 1 1—5 12 1
Colorado....0 0 0 3 0 0 0 1 0—4 13 4
Maddux, McMichael (8), Pena (8), Wohlers (9); Ritz, Reed (6), Ruffin (7), Munoz (8), Holmes (8), Leskanic (9). W—Pena. L—Leskanic. S—Wohlers. HR—Jones 2, Grissom (Atl.); Castilla (Col.).

LEADERS

American League

BA: Edgar Martinez, Sea., .356.
Runs: Albert Belle, Cle.;
Edgar Martinez, Sea., 121.
Hits: Lance Johnson, Chi., 186.
TB: Albert Belle, Cle., 377.
HR: Albert Belle, Cle., 50.
RBI: Albert Belle, Cle.;
Mo Vaughn, Bos., 126.
SB: Kenny Lofton, Cle., 54.
Wins: Mike Mussina, Bal., 19.
ERA: Randy Johnson, Sea., 2.48.
CG: Jack McDowell, N.Y., 8.
IP: David Cone, Tor.-N.Y., 229.1.
SO: Randy Johnson, Sea., 294.
SV: Jose Mesa, Cle., 46.

National League

BA: Tony Gwynn, S.D., .368.
Runs: Craig Biggio, Hou., 123.
Hits: Dante Bichette, Col.;
Tony Gwynn, S.D., 197.
TB: Dante Bichette, Col., 359.
HR: Dante Bichette, Col., 40.
RBI: Dante Bichette, Col., 128.
SB: Quilvio Veras, Fla., 56.
Wins: Greg Maddux, Atl., 19.
ERA: Greg Maddux, Atl., 1.63.
CG: Greg Maddux, Atl., 10.
IP: Greg Maddux, Atl.;
Denny Neagle, Pit., 209.2.
SO: Hideo Nomo, L.A., 236.
SV: Randy Myers, Chi., 38.

A.L. 100 RBIs
Albert Belle, Cle., 126
Mo Vaughn, Bos., 126
Jay Buhner, Sea., 121
Edgar Martinez, Sea., 113
Tino Martinez, Sea., 111
Frank Thomas, Chi., 111
Jim Edmonds, Cal., 107
Manny Ramirez, Cle., 107
Tim Salmon, Cal., 105
Rafael Palmeiro, Bal., 104
J.T. Snow, Cal., 102
John Valentin, Bos., 102

N.L. 100 RBIs
Dante Bichette, Col., 128
Sammy Sosa, Chi., 119
Andres Galarraga, Col., 106
Jeff Conine, Fla., 105
Eric Karros, L.A., 105
Barry Bonds, S.F., 104
Larry Walker, Col., 101

A.L. 40 homers
Albert Belle, Cle., 50
Jay Buhner, Sea., 40
Frank Thomas, Chi., 40

N.L. 40 homers
Dante Bichette, Col., 40

Most Valuable Player
A.L.: Mo Vaughn, 1B, Bos.
N.L.: Barry Larkin, SS, Cin.

Cy Young Award
A.L.: Randy Johnson, Sea.
N.L.: Greg Maddux, Atl.

Rookie of the Year
A.L.: Marty Cordova, OF, Min.
N.L.: Hideo Nomo, P, L.A.

Manager of the Year
A.L.: Lou Piniella, Sea.
N.L.: Don Baylor, Col.

Hall of Fame additions
Richie Ashburn, OF, 1948-62
Leon Day, P, Negro Leagues
William Hulbert, Executive
Mike Schmidt, 3B, 1972-89
Vic Willis, P, 1898-1910

Game 2—October 4, at Colorado
Atlanta ......1 0 1 1 0 0 0 0 4—7 13 1
Colorado....0 0 0 0 0 3 0 1 0—4 8 2
Glavine, Avery (8), Pena (8), Wohlers (9); Painter, Reed (6), Ruffin (7), Leskanic (8), Munoz (9), Holmes (9). W—Pena. L—Munoz. S—Wohlers. HR—Grissom 2 (Atl.); Walker (Col.).

Game 3—October 6, at Atlanta
Colorado......1 0 2 0 0 2 0 0 0 2—7 9 0
Atlanta ....0 0 0 3 0 0 1 0 1 0—5 11 0
Swift, Reed (7), Munoz (7), Leskanic (7), Ruffin (8), Holmes (9), Thompson (10); Smoltz, Clontz (6), Borbon (8), McMichael (9), Wohlers (10), Mercker (10). W—Holmes. L—Wohlers. S—Thompson. HR—Young, Castilla (Col.).

Game 4— October 7, at Atlanta
Colorado..........0 0 3 0 0 1 0 0 0— 4 11 1
Atlanta ....0 0 4 2 1 3 0 0 x—10 15 0
Saberhagen, Ritz (5), Munoz (6), Reynoso (7), Ruffin (8); Maddux, Pena (8). W—Maddux. L—Saberhagen. HR—Bichette, Castilla (Col.); McGriff 2 (Atl.).

Cincinnati vs. Los Angeles

Game 1—October 3, at Los Angeles
Cincinnati ....4 0 0 0 3 0 0 0 0—7 12 0
Los Angeles ......0 0 0 0 1 1 0 0 0—2 8 0
Schourek, Jackson (8), Brantley (9); Martinez, Cummings (5), Astacio (6), Guthrie (8), Osuna (9). W—Schourek. L—Martinez. HR—Santiago (Cin.); Piazza (L.A.).

Game 2—October 4, at Los Angeles
Cincinnati ....0 0 0 2 0 0 0 1 2—5 6 0
Los Angeles ......1 0 0 1 0 0 0 0 2—4 14 2
Smiley, Burba (7), Jackson (8), Brantley (9); Valdes, Osuna (8), Tapani (9), Guthrie (9), Astacio (9). W—Burba. L—Osuna. S—Brantley. HR—Sanders (Cin.); Karros 2 (L.A.).

Game 3—October 6, at Cincinnati
Los Angeles ....0 0 0 1 0 0 0 0 0— 1 9 1
Cincinnati ....0 0 2 1 0 4 3 0 x—10 11 2
Nomo, Tapani (6), Guthrie (6), Astacio (6), Cummings (7), Osuna (7); Wells, Jackson (7), Brantley (9). W—Wells. L—Nomo. HR—Gant, Boone, M. Lewis (Cin.).

ALCS

■ **Winner:** The Cleveland Indians needed six games and a hard-fought victory over Seattle ace lefthander Randy Johnson to secure their first World Series berth in 41 years.

■ **Turning point:** With the intimidating Johnson scheduled to pitch Game 6 in Seattle, the Indians won the pivotal fifth game, 3-2, on Jim Thome's two-run sixth-inning homer. The victory gave them a three-games-to-two advantage.

■ **Memorable moment:** A two-run passed ball in the eighth inning of Cleveland's 4-0 pennant-clinching victory. Ruben Amaro scored from third base and speedy Kenny Lofton surprised the Mariners with a mad dash from second, extending the Indians' lead to 3-0.

■ **Top guns:** Orel Hershiser (2-0, 1.29 ERA), Lofton (.458, 5 SB), Carlos Baerga (.400), Thome (2 HR, 5 RBI), Indians; Ken Griffey (.333), Jay Buhner (3 HR, 5 RBI), Norm Charlton (1-0, 0.00, 1 sv), Mariners.

■ **MVP:** Hershiser.

Linescores

Game 1—October 10, at Seattle
Cleveland ....0 0 1 0 0 0 1 0 0—2 10 1
Seattle ....0 2 0 0 0 0 1 0 x—3 7 0
D. Martinez, Tavarez (7), Assenmacher (8), Plunk (8); Wolcott, Nelson (8), Charlton (8). W—Wolcott. L—D. Martinez. S—Charlton. HR—Belle (Cle.); Blowers (Sea.).

Game 2—October 11, at Seattle
Cleveland ....0 0 0 0 2 2 0 1 0—5 12 0
Seattle ....0 0 0 0 0 1 0 0 1—2 6 1
Hershiser, Mesa (9); Belcher, Ayala (6), Risley (9). W—Hershiser. L—Belcher. HR—Ramirez 2 (Cle.); Griffey, Buhner (Sea.).

Game 3—October 13, at Cleveland
Seattle ......0 1 1 0 0 0 0 0 0 0 3—5 9 1
Cleveland ..0 0 0 1 0 0 0 1 0 0 0—2 4 2
Johnson, Charlton (9); Nagy, Mesa (9), Tavarez (10), Assenmacher (11), Plunk (11). W—Charlton. L—Tavarez. HR—Buhner 2 (Sea.).

Game 4—October 14, at Cleveland
Seattle ....0 0 0 0 0 0 0 0 0—0 6 1
Cleveland ....3 1 2 0 0 1 0 0 x—7 9 0
Benes, Wells (3), Ayala (6), Nelson (7), Risley (8); Hill, Poole (8), Ogea (9), Embree (9). W—Hill. L—Benes. HR—Murray, Thome (Cle.).

Game 5—October 15, at Cleveland
Seattle ....0 0 1 0 1 0 0 0 0—2 5 2
Cleveland ....1 0 0 0 0 2 0 0 x—3 10 4
Bosio, Nelson (6), Risley (7); Hershiser, Tavarez (7), Assenmacher (7), Plunk (8), Mesa (9). W—Hershiser. L—Bosio. S—Mesa. HR—Thome (Cle.).

Game 6—October 17, at Seattle
Cleveland ....0 0 0 0 1 0 0 3 0—4 8 0
Seattle ....0 0 0 0 0 0 0 0 0—0 4 1
D. Martinez, Tavarez (8), Mesa (9); Johnson, Charlton (8). W—D. Martinez. L—Johnson. HR—Baerga (Cle.).

NLCS

■ **Winner:** Atlanta pitchers limited Cincinnati to five total runs and the Braves swept past the Reds and claimed their third World Series berth of the decade.

■ **Turning point:** It came early, in the 11th inning of Game 1. Mike Devereaux singled home the winner in a 2-1 victory and the Braves cruised the rest of the way.

■ **Memorable moment:** A three-run, 10th-inning blast off the left-field foul pole by Atlanta catcher Javier Lopez that secured Atlanta's 6-2 victory in Game 2.

■ **Top guns:** Greg Maddux (1-0, 1.13 ERA), Steve Avery (1-0, 0.00), Fred McGriff (.438), Chipper Jones (.438), Lopez (.357), Devereaux (5 RBI), Braves; Barry Larkin (.389), Reds.

■ **MVP:** Devereaux.

Linescores

Game 1—October 10, at Cincinnati
Atlanta ......0 0 0 0 0 0 0 0 1 0 1—2 7 0
Cincinnati ..0 0 0 1 0 0 0 0 0 0 0—1 8 0
Glavine, Pena (8), Wohlers (9), Clontz (11), Avery (11), McMichael (11); Schourek, Brantley (9), Jackson (11). W—Wohlers. L—Jackson. S—McMichael.

Game 2—October 11, at Cincinnati
Atlanta ....1 0 0 1 0 0 0 0 0 4—6 11 1
Cincinnati ....0 0 0 0 2 0 0 0 0 0—2 9 1
Smoltz, Pena (8), McMichael (9), Wohlers (10); Smiley, Burba (6), Jackson (8), Brantley (9), Portugal (10). W—McMichael. L—Portugal. HR—Lopez (Atl.)

Game 3—October 13, at Atlanta
Cincinnati ....0 0 0 0 0 0 0 1 1—2 8 0
Atlanta ....0 0 0 0 0 3 2 0 x—5 12 1
Wells, Hernandez (7), Carrasco (7); Maddux, Wohlers (9). W—Maddux. L—Wells. HR: O'Brien, Jones (Atl.).

Game 4—October 14, at Atlanta
Cincinnati ....0 0 0 0 0 0 0 0 0—0 3 1
Atlanta ....0 0 1 0 0 0 0 5 x—6 12 1
Schourek, Jackson (7), Burba (7); Avery, McMichael (7), Pena (8), Wohlers (9). W—Avery. L—Schourek. HR—Devereaux (Atl.).

WORLD SERIES

■ **Winner:** The Braves needed six games to give Atlanta its first championship in any major sport and the franchise its first World Series title since 1957. The loss extended Cleveland's championship drought to 47 years.

■ **Turning point:** A two-run, sixth-inning homer by Javier Lopez in Game 2. It gave the Braves a 4-3 victory and put the Indians in a two-games-to-none hole.

■ **Memorable moment:** A Series-opening two-hitter by Braves ace Greg Maddux and a Series-closing combined one-hitter by Tom Glavine and Mark Wohlers. The 1-0 finale was decided by a Dave Justice home run.

■ **Top guns:** Glavine (2-0, 1.29 ERA), Wohlers (1.80, 2 sv), Marquis Grissom (.360), Ryan Klesko (.313, 3 HR), Braves; Albert Belle (2 HR), Indians.

■ **MVP:** Glavine.

Linescores

Game 1—October 21, at Atlanta
Cleveland ....1 0 0 0 0 0 0 0 1—2 2 0
Atlanta ....0 1 0 0 0 0 2 0 x—3 3 2
Hershiser, Assenmacher (7), Tavarez (7), Embree (8); Maddux. W—Maddux. L—Hershiser. HR—McGriff (Atl.).

Game 2—October 22, at Atlanta
Cleveland ....0 2 0 0 0 0 1 0 0—3 6 2
Atlanta ....0 0 2 0 0 2 0 0 x—4 8 2
Martinez, Embree (6), Poole (7), Tavarez (8); Glavine, McMichael (7), Pena (7), Wohlers (8). W—Glavine. L—Martinez. S—Wohlers. HR—Murray (Cle.), Lopez (Atl.).

Game 3—October 24, at Cleveland
Atlanta ....1 0 0 0 0 1 1 3 0 0 0—6 12 1
Cleveland ....2 0 2 0 0 0 1 1 0 0 1—7 12 2
Smoltz, Clontz (3), Mercker (5), McMichael (7), Wohlers (8), Pena (11); Nagy, Assenmacher (8), Tavarez (8), Mesa (9). W—Mesa. L—Pena. HR—McGriff, Klesko (Atl.).

Game 4—October 25, at Cleveland
Atlanta ....0 0 0 0 0 1 3 0 1—5 11 1
Cleveland ....0 0 0 0 0 1 0 0 1—2 6 0
Avery, McMichael (7), Wohlers (9), Borbon (9); Hill, Assenmacher (7), Tavarez (8), Embree (8). W—Avery. L—Hill. S—Borbon. HR—Klesko (Atl.); Belle, Ramirez (Cle.).

Game 5—October 26, at Cleveland
Atlanta ....0 0 0 1 1 0 0 0 2—4 7 0
Cleveland ....2 0 0 0 0 2 0 1 x—5 8 1
Maddux, Clontz (8); Hershiser, Mesa (8). W—Hershiser. L—Maddux. S—Mesa. HR—Polonia, Klesko (Atl.); Belle, Thome (Cle.).

Game 6—October 28, at Atlanta
Cleveland......... 0 0 0 0 0 0 0 0 0—0 1 1
Atlanta ....0 0 0 0 0 1 0 0 x—1 6 0
Martinez, Poole (5), Hill (7), Embree (7), Tavarez (8), Assenmacher (8); Glavine, Wohlers (9). W—Glavine. L—Poole. S—Wohlers. HR—Justice (Atl.).

Despite the strike-shortened schedule, Cleveland outfielder Albert Belle became the 12th 50-homer man in Major League history.

HISTORY

1996

FINAL STANDINGS

American League

East Division

Team	N.Y.	Bal.	Bos.	Tor.	Det.	Cle.	Chi.	Mil.	Min.	K.C.	Tex.	Sea.	Oak.	Cal.	W	L	Pct.	GB
New York	—	10	6	8	8	9	7	6	7	8	5	3	9	6	92	70	.568	—
Baltimore	3	—	7	8	11	5	4	9	7	9	3	7	9	6	88	74	.543	4.0
Boston	7	6	—	8	12	1	6	7	6	3	6	7	8	8	85	77	.525	7.0
Toronto	5	5	5	—	7	5	5	7	5	8	2	7	8	5	74	88	.457	18.0
Detroit	5	2	1	6	—	3	4	6	6	0	4	6	4	6	53	109	.327	39.0

Central Division

Team	Cle.	Chi.	Mil.	Min.	K.C.	N.Y.	Bal.	Bos.	Tor.	Det.	Tex.	Sea.	Oak.	Cal.	W	L	Pct.	GB
Cleveland	—	8	7	10	7	3	7	11	7	12	4	8	6	9	99	62	.615	—
Chicago	5	—	6	6	7	6	8	6	7	10	8	5	5	6	85	77	.525	14.5
Milwaukee	6	7	—	9	9	6	3	5	5	8	6	4	7	5	80	82	.494	19.5
Minnesota	3	7	4	—	7	5	5	6	8	6	7	6	6	8	78	84	.481	21.5
Kansas City	6	6	4	6	—	4	3	9	5	6	6	7	5	8	75	86	.466	24

West Division

Team	Tex.	Sea.	Oak.	Cal.	N.Y.	Bal.	Bos.	Tor.	Det.	Cle.	Chi.	Mil.	Min.	K.C.	W	L	Pct.	GB
Texas	—	3	6	9	7	10	6	10	9	8	4	7	5	6	90	72	.556	—
Seattle	10	—	5	8	9	5	6	5	6	4	7	9	6	5	85	76	.528	4.5
Oakland	7	8	—	7	3	4	5	4	8	6	7	5	7	7	78	84	.481	12
California	4	5	6	—	7	6	4	7	6	4	6	7	4	4	70	91	.435	19.5

National League

East Division

Team	Atl.	Mon.	Fla.	N.Y.	Phil.	St.L.	Hou.	Cin.	Chi.	Pit.	S.D.	L.A.	Col.	S.F.	W	L	Pct.	GB
Atlanta	—	10	6	7	9	9	6	7	7	9	9	5	5	7	96	66	.593	—
Montreal	3	—	8	7	6	8	9	9	6	7	4	3	9	9	88	74	.543	8
Florida	7	5	—	7	6	6	7	9	6	5	3	6	8	5	80	82	.494	16
New York	6	6	6	—	7	5	4	6	5	8	3	4	5	6	71	91	.438	25
Philadelphia	4	7	7	6	—	4	2	2	6	7	4	6	6	6	67	95	.414	29

Central Division

Team	St.L.	Hou.	Cin.	Chi.	Pit.	Atl.	Mon.	Fla.	N.Y.	Phil.	S.D.	L.A.	Col.	S.F.	W	L	Pct.	GB
St. Louis	—	11	8	8	10	4	4	6	7	8	8	4	4	6	88	74	.543	—
Houston	2	—	6	8	8	6	4	5	8	10	6	6	5	8	82	80	.506	6
Cincinnati	5	7	—	8	5	5	3	3	6	10	9	4	7	9	81	81	.500	7
Chicago	5	5	5	—	4	5	6	6	7	7	6	8	5	7	76	86	.469	12
Pittsburgh	3	5	8	9	—	3	5	7	5	5	4	6	5	8	73	89	.451	15

West Division

Team	S.D.	L.A.	Col.	S.F.	Atl.	Mon.	Fla.	N.Y.	Phil.	St.L.	Hou.	Cin.	Chi.	Pit.	W	L	Pct.	GB
San Diego	—	8	5	11	4	8	9	10	8	4	6	3	6	9	91	71	.562	—
Los Angeles	5	—	7	7	7	9	7	8	7	8	6	8	5	6	90	72	.556	1
Colorado	8	6	—	5	7	3	5	7	6	8	8	6	7	7	83	79	.512	8
San Fran.	2	6	8	—	5	4	7	6	6	7	4	4	5	4	68	94	.420	23

LEADERS

American League
BA: Alex Rodriguez, Sea., .358.
Runs: Alex Rodriguez, Sea., .358.
Hits: Paul Molitor, Min., 225.
TB: Alex Rodriguez, Sea., 379.
HR: Mark McGwire, Oak., 52.
RBI: Albert Belle, Cle., 148.
SB: Kenny Lofton, Cle., 75.
Wins: Andy Pettitte, N.Y., 21.
ERA: Juan Guzman, Tor., 2.93.
CG: Pat Hentgen, Tor., 10.
IP: Pat Hentgen, Tor., 265.2.
SO: Roger Clemens, Bos., 257.
SV: John Wetteland, N.Y., 43.

National League
BA: Tony Gwynn, S.D., .353.
Runs: Ellis Burks, Col., 142.
Hits: Lance Johnson, N.Y., 227.
TB: Ellis Burks, Col., 392
HR: Andres Galarraga, Col., 47.
RBI: Andres Galarraga, Col., 150
SB: Eric Young, Col., 53.
Wins: John Smoltz, Atl., 24.
ERA: Kevin Brown, Fla., 1.89.
CG: Curt Schilling, Phi., 8.
IP: John Smoltz, Atl., 253.2
SO: John Smoltz, Atl., 276.
SV: Jeff Brantley, Cin.;
Todd Worrell, L.A., 44.

A.L. 20-game winners
Andy Pettitte, N.Y., 21
Pat Hentgen, Tor., 20

N.L. 20-game winner
John Smoltz, Atl., 24

A.L. 100 RBIs
Albert Belle, Cle., 148
Juan Gonzalez, Tex., 144
Mo Vaughn, Bos., 143
Rafael Palmeiro, Bal., 142
Ken Griffey Jr., Sea., 140
Jay Buhner, Sea., 138
Frank Thomas, Chi., 134
Alex Rodriguez, Sea., 123
John Jaha, Mil., 118
Cecil Fielder, Det.-N.Y., 117
Tino Martinez, N.Y., 117
Bobby Bonilla, Bal., 116
Jim Thome, Cle., 116
Mark McGwire, Oak., 113
Paul Molitor, Min., 113
Manny Ramirez, Cle., 112
Marty Cordova, Min., 111
Brady Anderson, Bal., 110
Joe Carter, Tor., 107
Dean Palmer, Tex., 107
Geronimo Berroa, Oak., 106
Robin Ventura, Chi., 105
Edgar Martinez, Sea., 103
Cal Ripken, Bal., 102
Bernie Williams, N.Y., 102
Ed Sprague, Tor., 101
Danny Tartabull, Chi., 101
Travis Fryman, Det., 100
Rusty Greer, Tex., 100
Terry Steinbach, Oak., 100

N.L. 100 RBIs
Andres Galarraga, Col., 150
Dante Bichette, Col., 141
Ken Caminiti, S.D., 130
Barry Bonds, S.F., 129
Ellis Burks, Col., 128
Jeff Bagwell, Hou., 120
Gary Sheffield, Fla., 120
Bernard Gilkey, N.Y., 117
Derek Bell, Hou., 113
Vinny Castilla, Col., 113
Todd Hundley, N.Y., 112
Eric Karros, L.A., 111
Jeff King, Pit., 111
Chipper Jones, Atl., 110
Fred McGriff, Atl., 107
Mike Piazza, L.A., 105
Brian Jordan, St.L., 104
Henry Rodriguez, Mon., 103
Sammy Sosa, Chi., 100

A.L./N.L. 100 RBIs
Greg Vaughn, Mil.-S.D., 117

A.L. 40 homers
Mark McGwire, Oak., 52
Brady Anderson, Bal., 50
Ken Griffey Jr., Sea., 49
Albert Belle, Cle., 48
Juan Gonzalez, Tex., 47
Jay Buhner, Sea., 44
Mo Vaughn, Bos., 44
Frank Thomas, Chi., 40

N.L. 40 homers
Andres Galarraga, Col., 47
Barry Bonds, S.F., 42
Gary Sheffield, Fla., 42
Todd Hundley, N.Y., 41
Ellis Burks, Col., 40
Ken Caminiti, S.D., 40
Vinny Castilla, Col., 40
Sammy Sosa, Chi., 40

A.L./N.L. 40 homers
Greg Vaughn, Mil.-S.D., 41

Most Valuable Player
A.L.: Juan Gonzalez, OF, Tex.
N.L.: Ken Caminiti, 3B, Hou.

Cy Young Award
A.L.: Pat Hentgen, Tor.
N.L.: John Smoltz, Atl.

Rookie of the Year
A.L.: Derek Jeter, SS, N.Y.
N.L.: Todd Hollandsworth, OF, L.A.

Manager of the Year
A.L.: Johnny Oates, Tex.; Joe Torre, N.Y.
N.L.: Bruce Bochy, S.D.

Hall of Fame additions
Jim Bunning, P, 1955-71
Bill Foster, P, Negro Leagues
Ned Hanlon, manager
Earl Weaver, manager

SIGNIFICANT EVENTS

■ **January:** The Official Playing Rules Committee lowered the strike zone from "a line at the top of the knees" to "a line at the hollow beneath the kneecap."

■ **April 1:** Umpire John McSherry collapsed seven pitches into the opening day game between the Expos and Reds at Cincinnati and died about an hour later from a heart problem. The game was postponed.

■ **June 12:** Reds owner Marge Schott agreed to surrender day-to-day control of the team through the 1998 season as discipline for actions and statements detrimental to baseball.

■ **September 27:** In what would develop into one of the most controversial player-umpire disputes in baseball history, Baltimore second baseman Roberto Alomar spat in the face of umpire John Hirshbeck during a called-strike argument.

■ **November 19:** White Sox owner Jerry Reinsdorf signed Cleveland slugger Albert Belle to the richest contract in baseball history—$50 million over five years.

■ **November 26:** After completing the first full-schedule season since 1993, Major League Baseball and the players' association agreed on a contract that would run through October 31, 2000.

MEMORABLE MOMENTS

■ **September 6:** Baltimore's Eddie Murray connected for his 500th career home run against Detroit and joined 14 other players in that exclusive circle.

■ **September 16:** Minnesota's Paul Molitor became the 21st player to record 3,000 career hits when he tripled in the fifth inning of a game at Kansas City.

■ **September 18:** Boston ace Roger Clemens matched his own major league record when he struck out 20 Tigers in a nine-inning game.

■ **September 29:** Giants slugger Barry Bonds completed the season with 42 homers and 40 stolen bases, joining Jose Canseco as the only members of the 40-40 club.

■ **September 29:** The Orioles, led by Brady Anderson's 50 home runs, finished the season with a one-season record 257.

■ **September 29:** San Diego's Tony Gwynn finished the season with a .353 average and won his seventh N.L. batting title.

ALL-STAR GAME

■ **Winner:** Nine N.L. pitchers combined on a seven hitter as the A.L. lost its third consecutive midsummer classic and saw the N.L.'s All-Star domination grow to 40-26-1.

■ **Key inning:** The second, when the A.L. failed to score after putting its leadoff man on second base and the N.L. stretched its lead to 2-0 on Dodgers catcher Mike Piazza's solo home run.

■ **Memorable moment:** Piazza, who drove in two runs with his homer and a double, holding up the MVP trophy for a large hometown contingent at Philadelphia. Piazza was born in nearby Norristown, Pa., and once served as a bat boy at Veterans Stadium.

■ **Top guns:** Piazza (Dodgers), Lance Johnson (Mets), John Smoltz (Braves), Steve Trachsel (Cubs), N.L.; Kenny Lofton (Indians), A.L.

■ **MVP:** Piazza.

Linescore
July 9, at Philadelphia's Veterans Stadium
A.L. ....0 0 0 0 0 0 0 0 0—0 7 0
N.L. ....1 2 1 0 0 2 0 0 x—6 12 1
Smoltz (Braves), Brown (Marlins) 3, Glavine (Braves) 4, Bottalico (Phillies) 5, P. Martinez (Expos) 6, Trachsel (Cubs) 7, Worrell (Dodgers) 8, Wohlers (Braves) 9, Leiter (Marlins) 9; Nagy (Indians), Finley (Angels) 3, Pavlik (Rangers) 5, Percival (Angels) 7, Hernandez (White Sox) 8. W—Smoltz. L—Nagy. HR—Piazza, Caminiti, N.L.

A.L. DIVISION SERIES

■ **Winners:** The Yankees, bidding for their 34th World Series appearance, ruined the Rangers' Post Season debut with a four-game victory; the wild-card Orioles pulled off a surprising four-game upset of the Indians.

■ **Turning points:** Throwing errors turned the tide for both the Yankees and Orioles. New York took control in the 10th inning of Game 2 when the Rangers failed to score after loading the bases in the top of the inning and the Yankees won in the bottom of the frame on third baseman Dean Palmer's wild throw. The Orioles took control when Cleveland catcher Sandy Alomar fired wildly on an eighth-inning home-to-first double-play attempt in Game 2, allowing the winning run to score in an eventual 7-4 victory. The Indians argued that batter B.J. Surhoff ran out of the baseline, causing Alomar's miscue.

■ **Memorable moments:** The final out of Texas' 6-2 Game 1 victory over the Yankees—the first postseason win in Rangers history. The Game 4 heroics of Baltimore second baseman Roberto Alomar, who tied the game with a ninth-inning single and clinched the series victory with a 12th-inning home run. It was sweet vindication for Alomar, who had been the center of controversy since a late-season spitting incident involving umpire John Hirschbeck.

■ **Memorable performances:** Bernie Williams batted .467, hit three home runs, including two in the decisive fourth game, and drove in five runs for the Yankees; Yankee relievers Mariano Rivera, David Weathers, Jeff Nelson and John Wetteland combined for 17⅓ scoreless innings, allowing only five hits; Juan Gonzalez set a record pace for the Rangers, hitting .438 with five home runs and nine RBIs; B.J. Surhoff hit three home runs and Bobby Bonilla hit two, including a grand slam, for the Orioles; Albert Belle hit a Game 3 grand slam for the Indians.

Linescores
Baltimore vs. Cleveland

Game 1—October 1, at Baltimore
Cleveland ..0 1 0 2 0 0 1 0 0— 4 10 0
Baltimore....1 1 2 0 0 5 1 0 x—10 12 1
Nagy, Embree (6), Shuey (6), Tavarez (8); Wells, Orosco (7), Mathews (7), Rhodes (8), Myers (9). W—Wells. L—Nagy. HR—Ramirez (Cle.); Anderson, Bonilla, Surhoff 2 (Bal.).

Game 2—October 2, at Baltimore
Cleveland ......0 0 0 0 0 3 0 1 0—4 8 2
Baltimore........1 0 0 0 3 0 0 3 x—7 9 0
Hershiser, Plunk (6), Assenmacher (8), Tavaraz (8); Erickson, Orosco (7), Benitez (8), Myers (9). W—Benitez. L—Plunk. S—Myers. HR—Belle (Cle.); Anderson (Bal.).

Game 3—October 4, at Cleveland
Baltimore ....0 1 0 3 0 0 0 0 0—4 8 2
Cleveland......1 2 0 1 0 0 4 1 x—9 10 0
Mussina, Orosco (7), Benitez (7), Rhodes (8), Mathews (8); McDowell, Embree (6), Shuey (7), Assenmacher (7), Plunk (8), Mesa (9). W—Assenmacher. L—Orosco. HR—Surhoff (Bal.); Belle, Ramirez (Cle.).

Game 4—October 5, at Cleveland
Bal. 0 2 0 0 0 0 0 0 1 0 0 1—4 14 1
Cle. ..0 0 0 2 1 0 0 0 0 0 0 0—3 7 1
Wells, Mathews (8), Orosco (9), Benitez (10), Myers (12); Nagy, Embree (7), Shuey (7), Assenmacher (7), Plunk (8), Mesa (9), Ogea (12). W—Benitez. L—Mesa. S—Myers. HR—R. Alomar, Palmeiro, Bonilla (Bal.).

New York vs. Texas

Game 1—October 1, at New York
Texas............0 0 0 5 0 1 0 0 0—6 8 0
New York......1 0 0 1 0 0 0 0 0—2 10 0
Burkett; Cone, Lloyd (7), Weathers (8). W—Burkett. L—Cone. HR—Gonzalez, Palmer (Tex.).

Game 2—October 2, at New York
Texas0 1 3 0 0 0 0 0 0 0 0 0—4 8 1
N.Y. ..0 1 0 1 0 0 1 1 0 0 0 1—5 8 0
Hill, Cook (7), Russell (8), Stanton (10), Henneman (12); Pettitte, M. Rivera (7), Wetteland (10), Lloyd (12), Nelson (12), Rogers (12), Boehringer (12). W—Boehringer. L—Stanton. HR—Gonzalez 2 (Tex.); Fielder (N.Y.).

Game 3—October 4, at Texas
New York........1 0 0 0 0 0 0 0 2—3 7 1
Texas..............0 0 0 1 1 0 0 0 0—2 6 1
Key, Nelson (6), Wetteland (9); Oliver, Henneman (9), Stanton (9). W—Nelson. L—Oliver. S–Wetteland. HR—Williams (N.Y.); Gonzalez (Tex.).

Game 4—October 5, at Texas
New York......0 0 0 3 1 0 1 0 1—6 12 1
Texas............0 2 2 0 0 0 0 0 0—4 9 0
Rogers, Boehringer (3), Weathers (4), M. Rivera (7), Wetteland (9); Witt, Patterson (4), Cook (4), Pavlik (5), Vosberg (7), Russell (7), Stanton (8), Henneman (9). W—Weathers. L—Pavlik. S—Wetteland. HR—Williams 2 (N.Y.); Gonzalez (Tex.).

N.L. DIVISION SERIES

■ **Winners:** The Braves continued their quest for back-to-back World Series titles with a sweep of the Dodgers; St. Louis matched that 1-2-3 effort against San Diego.

■ **Turning points:** For the Braves, catcher Javy Lopez's Game 1-winning 10th-inning home run in a 2-1 victory. The Cardinals took control of their series in the opening inning of Game 1 when Gary Gaetti hit a three-run homer, giving pitcher Todd Stottlemyre all the runs he would need for a 3-1 victory.
■ **Memorable moments:** The Braves put the Dodgers away in the seventh inning of Game 2 when Fred McGriff and Jermaine Dye hit solo home runs, wiping out a 2-1 deficit and setting up Greg Maddux for a 3-2 victory. Cardinals right fielder Brian Jordan finished off the Padres in Game 3 with a great run-saving catch in the eighth inning and a game-winning two-run homer in the ninth.
■ **Top performances:** The Braves' pitching staff, with starters John Smoltz, Maddux and Tom Glavine working 22⅔ innings, posted a sparkling 0.96 ERA against the Dodgers.
St. Louis' Ron Gant batted .400, hit a home run and drove in four runs against the Padres and closer Dennis Eckersley saved all three victories.

Linescores

St. Louis vs. San Diego

Game 1—October 1, at St. Louis
San Diego ......0 0 0 0 0 1 0 0 0—1 8 1
St. Louis ....3 0 0 0 0 0 0 0 x—3 6 0
Hamilton, Blair (7); Stottlemyre, Honeycutt (7), Eckersley (8). W—Stottlemyre. L—Hamilton. S—Eckersley. HR—Henderson (S.D.); Gaetti (St.L.).

Game 2—October 3, at St. Louis
San Diego ....0 0 0 0 1 2 0 1 0—4
St. Louis ....0 0 1 0 3 0 0 1 x—5
Sanders, Veras (5), Worrell (6), Bochtler (8), Hoffman (8); An. Benes, Honeycutt (8), Eckersley (9). W—Honeycutt. L—Bochtler. S—Eckersley. HR—Caminiti (S.D.).

Game 3—October 5, at San Diego
St. Louis ....1 0 0 0 0 3 1 0 2—7
San Diego ....0 2 1 1 0 0 0 1 0—5
Osborne, Petkovsek (5), Honeycutt (7), Mathews (8), Eckersley (9); Ashby, Worrell (6), Valenzuela (8), Veras (8), Hoffman (9). W—Mathews. L—Hoffman. S—Eckersley. HR—Gant, Jordan (St.L.); Caminiti 2 (S.D.).

Atlanta vs. Los Angeles

Game 1—October 2, at Los Angeles
Atlanta ....0 0 0 1 0 0 0 0 0 1—2 4 1
Los Angeles...0 0 0 0 1 0 0 0 0 0—1 5 0
Smoltz, Wohlers (10); Martinez, Radinsky (9), Osuna (9). W—Smoltz. L—Osuna. S—Wohlers. HR—Lopez (Atl.).

Game 2—October 3, at Los Angeles
Atlanta...........0 1 0 0 0 0 2 0 0—3 5 2
Los Angeles....1 0 0 1 0 0 0 0 0—2 3 0
Maddux, McMichael (8), Wohlers (9); Valdes, Astacio (7), Worrell (9). W—Maddux. L—Valdes. S—Wohlers. HR—McGriff, Klesko, Dye (Atl.).

Game 3—October 5, at Atlanta
Los Angeles....0 0 0 0 0 0 1 1 0—2 6 1
Atlanta...........1 0 0 4 0 0 0 0 x—5 7 0
Nomo, Guthrie (4), Candiotti (5), Radinsky (7), Osuna (8), Dreifort (8); Glavine, McMichael (7), Bielecki (8), Wohlers (8). W—Glavine. L—Nomo. S—Wohlers. HR—C. Jones (Atl.).

ALCS

■ **Winner:** The Yankees overpowered Baltimore, the most prolific home run team in baseball history, and earned the franchise's 34th pennant. The five-game victory set up the Yankees' first World Series appearance since 1981.
■ **Turning point:** The eighth inning of Game 3, when the Yankees, trailing 2-1, struck for four two-out runs against Orioles ace Mike Mussina. The key plays were Bernie Williams' game-tying single, third baseman Todd Zeile's error and Cecil Fielder's two-run homer.
■ **Memorable moment:** The eighth inning of Game 1, when 12-year-old fan Jeff Maier reached over Yankee Stadium's right field wall and unwittingly set the course for the series. The Orioles held a 4-3 advantage when shortstop Derek Jeter hit a fly ball to deep right that backed Baltimore outfielder Tony Tarasco to the wall. As Tarasco reached up in an attempt to make the catch, Maier stuck his glove over the wall and pulled the ball into the stands. The Orioles argued vehemently for fan interference, but umpire Richie Garcia ruled it a game-tying home run and the Yankees won in the 11th on a Williams home run. Maier became an instant national celebrity.
■ **Top guns:** Williams (.474, 2 HR, 6 RBI), Jeter (.417), Darryl Strawberry (.417, 3 HR), Cecil Fielder (8 RBI), Mariano Rivera (0.00 ERA), Yankees; Zeile (3 HR, 5 RBI), Rafael Palmeiro (2 HR), Orioles.
MVP: Williams.

Linescores

Game 1—October 9, at New York
Bal. ....0 1 1 1 0 1 0 0 0 0 0—4 11 1
N.Y. .....1 1 0 0 0 0 1 1 0 0 1—5 11 0
Erickson, Orosco (7), Benitez (7), Rhodes (8), Mathews (9), Myers (9); Pettitte, Nelson (8), Wetteland (9), M. Rivera (10). W—M. Rivera. L—Myers. HR—Anderson, Palmeiro (Bal.); Jeter, Williams (N.Y.).

Game 2—October 10, at New York
Baltimore......0 0 2 0 0 0 2 1 0—5 10 0
New York......2 0 0 0 0 0 1 0 0—3 11 1
Wells, Mills (7), Orosco (7), Myers (9), Benitez (9); Cone, Nelson (7), Lloyd (8), Weathers (9). W—Wells. L—Nelson. S—Benitez. HR—Zeile, Palmeiro (Bal.).

Game 3—October 11, at Baltimore
New York........0 0 0 1 0 0 0 4 0—5 8 0
Baltimore........2 0 0 0 0 0 0 0 0—2 3 2
Key, Wetteland (9); Mussina, Orosco (8), Mathews (9). W—Key. L—Mussina. S—Wetteland. HR—Fielder (N.Y.); Zeile (Bal.).

Game 4—October 12, at Baltimore
New York......2 1 0 2 0 0 0 3 0—8 9 0
Baltimore......1 0 1 2 0 0 0 0 0—4 11 0
Rogers, Weathers (4), Lloyd (6), M. Rivera (7), Wetteland (9); Coppinger, Rhodes (6), Mills (7), Orosco (8), Benitez (8), Mathews (9). W—Weathers. L—Coppinger. HR—Williams, Strawberry 2, O'Neill (N.Y.); Hoiles (Bal.).

Game 5—October 13, at Baltimore
New York......0 0 6 0 0 0 0 0 0—6 11 0
Baltimore......0 0 0 0 0 1 0 1 2—4 4 1
Pettitte, Wetteland (9); Erickson, Rhodes (6), Mills (7), Myers (8). W—Pettitte. L—Erickson. HR—Fielder, Strawberry, Leyritz (N.Y.); Zeile, Bonilla, Murray (Bal.).

NLCS

■ **Winner:** The Braves, hoping to become the N.L.'s first repeat World Series champion in 20 years, recovered from a three-games-to-one deficit in a tense seven-game victory over the Cardinals. The Braves, on the brink of elimination, outscored St. Louis 32-1 over the final three games to earn their eighth fall classic appearance and fourth of the decade.
■ **Turning point:** The first inning of Game 5, when the Braves scored five runs off Cardinals starter Todd Stottlemyre. That 14-0 victory served notice that rumors of the Braves' demise were premature.
■ **Memorable moment:** An eighth-inning Game 4 home run by St. Louis' Brian Jordan, the blow that gave ecstatic home fans a 4-3 victory and put the Cardinals on the brink of a 16th World Series appearance.
■ **Top guns:** Javier Lopez (.542, 6 RBI), Mark Lemke (.444), Fred McGriff (2 HR, 7 RBI), John Smoltz (2-0, 1.20 ERA), Braves; Royce Clayton (.350), Ron Gant (2 HR, 4 RBI), Cardinals.
■ **MVP:** Lopez.

Linescores

Game 1—October 9, at Atlanta
St. Louis ....0 1 0 0 0 0 1 0 0—2 5 1
Atlanta ....0 0 0 0 2 0 0 2 x—4 9 0
An. Benes, Petkovsek (7), Fossas (8), Mathews (8); Smoltz, Wohlers (9). W—Smoltz. L—Petkovsek. S—Wohlers.

Game 2—October 10, at Atlanta
St. Louis ......1 0 2 0 0 0 5 0 0—8 11 2
Atlanta...........0 0 2 0 0 1 0 0 0—3 5 2
Stottlemyre, Petkovsek (7), Honeycutt (8), Eckersley (8); Maddux, McMichael (7), Neagle (8), Avery (9). W—Stottlemyre. L—Maddux. HR—Gaetti (St.L.); Grissom (Atl.).

Game 3—October 12, at St. Louis
Atlanta...........1 0 0 0 0 0 0 1 0—2 8 1
St. Louis ....2 0 0 0 0 1 0 0 x—3 7 0
Glavine, Bielecki (7), McMichael (8); Osborne, Petkovsek (8), Honeycutt (9), Eckersley (9). W—Osborne. L—Glavine. S—Eckersley. HR—Gant 2 (St.L.).

Game 4—October 13, at St. Louis
Atlanta...........0 1 0 0 0 2 0 1 0—3 9 1
St. Louis ....0 0 0 0 0 0 3 1 x—4 5 0
Neagle, McMichael (7), Wohlers (8); An. Benes, Fossas (6), Mathews (6), Al. Benes (6), Honeycutt (8), Eckersley (8). W—Eckersley. L—McMichael. HR—Lemke, Klesko (Atl.); Jordan (St.L.).

Game 5—October 14, at St. Louis
Atlanta........5 2 0 3 1 0 0 1 2—14 22 0
St. Louis ....0 0 0 0 0 0 0 0 0— 0 7 0
Smoltz, Bielecki (8), Wade (9), Clontz (9); Stottlemyre, Jackson (2), Fossas (5), Petkovsek (7), Honeycutt (9). W—Smoltz. L—Stottlemyre. HR—McGriff, Lopez (Atl.).

Game 6—October16, at Atlanta
St. Louis ....0 0 0 0 0 0 0 1 0—1 6 1
Atlanta ....0 1 0 0 1 0 0 1 x—3 7 0
Al. Benes, Fossas (6), Petkovsek (6), Stottlemyre (8); Maddux, Wohlers (8). W—Maddux. L—Al. Benes. S—Wohlers.

Game 7—October 17, at Atlanta
St. Louis ....0 0 0 0 0 0 0 0 0— 0 4 2
Atlanta........6 0 0 4 0 3 2 0 x—15 17 0
Osborne, An. Benes (1), Petkovsek (6), Honeycutt (6), Fossas (8); Glavine, Bielecki (8), Avery (9). W—Glavine. L—Osborne. HR—McGriff, Lopez, A. Jones (Atl.).

WORLD SERIES

■ **Winner:** The Yankees, missing from the World Series scene since 1981, collected their franchise-record 23rd championship when they spotted Atlanta two wins and stormed back to post an impressive six-game victory. The New York triumph dashed the Braves' hope of becoming the N.L.'s first back-to-back fall classic winner in 20 years.
■ **Turning point:** The eighth inning of Game 4, when catcher Jim Leyritz rocked Braves closer Mark Wohlers for a three-run, game-tying homer that set up an eventual 8-6 Yankees victory. The Braves had led the game 6-0 and appeared on the verge of taking a three games-to-one series lead.
■ **Memorable moment:** Right fielder Paul O'Neill's over-the-shoulder Game 5-ending catch that saved a 1-0 victory for the Yankees and Andy Pettitte. The catch denied Braves pinch-hitter Luis Polonia extra bases with runners on first and third.
■ **Top guns:** Cecil Fielder (.391), Jeff Nelson (3 games, 0.00 ERA), Mariano Rivera (4 games, 1.59 ERA), John Wetteland (4 saves, 2.08 ERA), Yankees; Grissom (.444), A. Jones (.400, 2 HR, 6 RBI), Fred McGriff (2 HR, 6 RBI), John Smoltz (1-1, 0.64 ERA), Braves.
■ **MVP:** Wetteland.

Linescores

Game 1—October 20, at New York
Atlanta........0 2 6 0 1 3 0 0 0—12 13 0
New York....0 0 0 0 1 0 0 0 0— 1 4 1
Smoltz, McMichael (7), Neagle (8), Wade (9), Clontz (9); Pettitte, Boehringer (3), Weathers (6), Nelson (8), Wetteland (9). W—Smoltz. L—Pettitte. HR—McGriff, A. Jones 2 (Atl.).

Game 2—October 21, at New York
Atlanta..........1 0 1 0 1 1 0 0 0—4 10 0
New York......0 0 0 0 0 0 0 0 0—0 7 1
Maddux, Wohlers (9); Key, Lloyd (7), Nelson (7), M. Rivera (9). W—Maddux. L—Key.

Game 3—October 22, at Atlanta
New York........1 0 0 1 0 0 0 3 0—5 8 1
Atlanta............0 0 0 0 0 1 0 1 0—2 6 1
Cone, M. Rivera (7), Lloyd (8), Wetteland (9); Glavine, McMichael (8), Clontz (8), Bielecki (9). W—Cone. L—Glavine. S—Wetteland. HR—Williams (N.Y.).

Game 4—October 23, at Atlanta
N.Y. ....0 0 0 0 0 3 0 3 0 2—8 12 0
Atlanta....0 4 1 0 1 0 0 0 0 0—6 9 2
Rogers, Boehringer (3), Weathers (5), Nelson (6), M. Rivera (8), Lloyd (9), Wetteland (10); Neagle, Wade (6), Bielecki (6), Wohlers (8), Avery (10), Clontz (10). W—Lloyd. L—Avery. S—Wetteland. HR—Leyritz (N.Y.); McGriff (Atl.).

Game 5—October 24, at Atlanta
New York........0 0 0 1 0 0 0 0 0—1 4 1
Atlanta............0 0 0 0 0 0 0 0 0—0 5 1
Pettitte, Wetteland (9); Smoltz, Wohlers (9). W—Pettitte. L—Smoltz. S—Wetteland.

Game 6—October 26, at New York
Atlanta............0 0 0 1 0 0 0 0 1—2 8 0
New York........0 0 3 0 0 0 0 0 x—3 8 1
Maddux, Wohlers (8); Key, Weathers (6), Lloyd (6), M. Rivera (7), Wetteland (9). W—Key. L—Maddux. S—Wetteland.

Talented Yankees lefthander Andy Pettitte won an American League-high 21 games in 1996 and earned a World Series ring to boot.

HISTORY

FINAL STANDINGS

American League

East Division

Team	Bal.	NYY	Det.	Bos.	Tor.	Cle.	ChW	Mil.	Min.	K.C.	Sea.	Ana.	Tex.	Oak.	Atl.	Fla.	NYM	Mtl.	Phi.	W	L	Pct.	GB
Baltimore	—	8	6	5	6	6	5	5	10	7	7	7	10	8	3	0	1	1	3	98	64	.605	—
New York	4	—	10	8	7	6	9	7	8	8	4	7	7	6	1	1	2	1	0	96	66	.593	2
Detroit	6	2	—	7	6	5	7	4	4	6	4	6	7	7	2	1	3	0	2	79	83	.488	19
Boston	7	4	5	—	6	6	3	8	8	3	7	5	3	7	0	1	2	0	3	78	84	.481	20
Toronto	6	5	6	6	—	5	6	4	8	6	3	5	7	5	1	0	0	1	2	76	86	.469	22

Central Division

Team	Bal.	NYY	Det.	Bos.	Tor.	Cle.	ChW	Mil.	Min.	K.C.	Sea.	Ana.	Tex.	Oak.	Hou.	Pit.	Cin.	St.L.	ChC	W	L	Pct.	GB
Cleveland	5	5	6	5	6	—	7	8	8	8	3	4	5	7	2	2	1	2	2	86	75	.534	—
Chicago	6	2	4	8	5	5	—	4	6	11	5	5	3	8	3	0	2	1	2	80	81	.497	6
Milwaukee	6	4	7	3	7	4	7	—	5	6	5	4	7	5	2	2	0	3	1	78	83	.484	8
Minnesota	1	3	7	3	3	4	6	7	—	5	5	7	3	7	2	2	2	0	1	68	94	.420	18½
Kansas City	4	3	5	8	5	3	1	6	7	—	5	5	6	3	2	2	1	1	0	67	94	.416	19

West Division

Team	Bal.	NYY	Det.	Bos.	Tor.	Cle.	ChW	Mil.	Min.	K.C.	Sea.	Ana.	Tex.	Oak.	S.F.	L.A.	Col.	S.D.	W	L	Pct.	GB
Seattle	4	7	7	4	8	8	6	6	6	6	—	6	8	7	1	3	2	1	90	72	.556	—
Anaheim	4	4	5	6	6	7	6	7	4	6	6	—	8	11	1	0	1	2	84	78	.519	6
Texas	1	4	4	8	4	6	8	4	8	5	4	4	—	7	2	3	3	2	77	85	.475	13
Oakland	3	5	4	4	6	4	3	6	4	8	5	1	5	—	2	1	1	3	65	97	.401	25

National League

East Division

Team	Atl.	Fla.	NYM	Mtl.	Phi.	Hou.	Pit.	Cin.	St.L.	ChC	S.F.	L.A.	Col.	S.D.	Bal.	NYY	Det.	Bos.	Tor.	W	L	Pct.	GB
Atlanta	—	4	5	10	10	7	5	9	8	9	7	6	5	8	0	2	1	3	2	101	61	.623	—
Florida	8	—	4	7	6	7	7	6	5	9	5	7	4	5	3	2	2	2	3	92	70	.568	9
New York	7	8	—	7	7	4	7	9	9	5	3	5	5	5	2	1	0	1	3	88	74	.543	13
Montreal	2	5	5	—	6	3	5	5	6	7	6	4	4	8	2	2	3	3	2	78	84	.481	23
Philadelphia	2	6	5	6	—	7	5	3	6	5	3	1	7	7	0	3	1	0	1	68	94	.420	33

Central Division

Team	Atl.	Fla.	NYM	Mtl.	Phi.	Hou.	Pit.	Cin.	St.L.	ChC	S.F.	L.A.	Col.	S.D.	Cle.	ChW	Mil.	Min.	K.C.	W	L	Pct.	GB
Houston	4	4	7	8	4	—	6	7	9	9	3	7	6	6	1	0	1	1	1	84	78	.519	—
Pittsburgh	6	4	4	6	6	6	—	4	9	5	8	2	7	5	1	3	1	1	1	79	83	.488	5
Cincinnati	2	5	2	6	8	5	8	—	6	5	4	6	5	5	2	1	3	1	2	76	86	.469	8
St. Louis	3	6	2	5	5	3	3	6	—	8	8	6	4	6	1	2	0	3	2	73	89	.451	11
Chicago	2	2	6	4	6	3	7	7	4	—	5	5	2	6	1	1	2	2	3	68	94	.420	16

West Division

Team	Atl.	Fla.	NYM	Mtl.	Phi.	Hou.	Pit.	Cin.	St.L.	ChC	S.F.	L.A.	Col.	S.D.	Sea.	Ana.	Tex.	Oak.	W	L	Pct.	GB
San Fran.	4	6	8	5	8	8	3	7	3	6	—	6	8	8	3	3	2	2	90	72	.556	—
Los Angeles	5	4	6	7	10	4	9	5	5	6	6	—	7	5	1	4	1	3	88	74	.543	2
Colorado	6	7	6	7	4	5	4	6	7	9	4	5	—	4	2	3	1	3	83	79	.512	7
San Diego	3	6	6	3	4	5	6	6	5	5	4	7	8	—	3	2	2	1	76	86	.469	14

SIGNIFICANT EVENTS

■ **April 4:** The Atlanta Braves christened new Turner Field with a 5-4 come-from-behind victory over Chicago.

■ **April 15:** Celebrating the 50th anniversary of Jackie Robinson's debut as the first black Major League player of the century, baseball announced every team would retire Robinson's uniform No. 42.

■ **April 19:** St. Louis recorded a 1-0 victory over San Diego in the opener of the three-game Paradise Series—the first Major League regular-season game ever played in Hawaii.

■ **April 20:** The Chicago Cubs defeated the New York Mets in the second game of a doubleheader, ending their season-opening losing streak at 14 games.

■ **June 12:** The San Francisco Giants posted a 4-3 victory at Texas in the first interleague game in baseball history.

■ **November 5:** The Milwaukee Brewers agreed to move from the American League to the National League Central Division, completing a re-alignment that placed Tampa Bay in the A.L. East, moved Detroit to the A.L. Central and positioned Arizona in the N.L. West.

■ **November 18:** Tampa Bay opened the expansion draft by selecting pitcher Tony Saunders off the Florida roster and Arizona followed by grabbing Cleveland pitcher Brian Anderson.

MEMORABLE MOMENTS

■ **June 30:** Texas' Bobby Witt became the first American League pitcher to hit a home run since October 1972 when he connected off Los Angeles' Ismael Valdes in an interleague contest.

■ **August 8:** For the second time in six weeks, Seattle lefthander Randy Johnson struck out 19 batters in a game—the first time a pitcher had reached that plateau twice in a season. Johnson shut out Chicago, 5-0.

■ **September 20:** Colorado's Larry Walker doubled during a victory over Los Angeles, becoming the first National League player to reach 400 total bases in a season since Hank Aaron in 1959.

■ **September 26:** Philadelphia's Curt Schilling struck out six Marlins in a 5-3 victory over Florida, setting a National League record for most strikeouts by a righthander with 319.

■ **September 27:** San Francisco clinched the N.L. West title with a 6-1 victory over San Diego, becoming the fourth last-to-first team of the century.

■ **September 28:** St. Louis' Mark McGwire, the second player in history to record back-to-back 50-homer seasons, connected for No. 58 in a final-day victory over Chicago—matching Jimmie Foxx and Hank Greenberg for the single-season record by a righthanded hitter. The total topped Seattle's Ken Griffey Jr. by two and was the highest in one season since Roger Maris hit his record 61 in 1961.

■ **September 28:** San Diego's Tony Gwynn completed a .372 season and captured his N.L.-record tying eighth batting championship.

ALL-STAR GAME

■ **Winner:** The A.L. snapped a three-year losing streak with a 3-1 victory behind the late-inning heroics of hometown Cleveland catcher Sandy Alomar and the three-hit work of an eight-man pitching parade.

■ **Key inning:** The fourth, when the N.L. ran itself out of a potential big inning that opened with walks to San Francisco's Barry Bonds and Los Angeles' Mike Piazza. After Bonds had advanced to third on a fly ball by Houston's Jeff Bagwell, Piazza was caught trying to advance to second on a ball that momentarily eluded Rangers catcher Ivan Rodriguez. Larry Walker grounded out to end the N.L.'s only serious threat of the game.

■ **Memorable moment:** Alomar, who entered the mid-summer classic with a 30-game hitting streak, broke a 1-1 tie with a seventh-inning two-run homer—in his only at-bat. The blow wiped out a game-tying solo homer in the top of the inning by Atlanta catcher Javy Lopez and earned Alomar home-field MVP honors.

■ **Top guns:** S. Alomar (Indians), Edgar Martinez (Mariners), Brady Anderson (Orioles), Randy Johnson (Mariners), A.L.; Lopez (Braves), Curt Schilling (Phillies), N.L.

■ **MVP:** S. Alomar.

Linescore

July 8 at Cleveland's Jacobs Field

N.L. ....0 0 0 0 0 0 1 0 0—1 3 0
A.L. ....0 1 0 0 0 0 2 0 x—3 7 0

Maddux (Braves), Schilling (Phillies) 3, Brown (Marlins) 5, P. Martinez (Expos) 6, Estes (Giants) 7, B. Jones (Mets) 8; R. Johnson (Mariners), Clemens (Blue Jays) 3, Cone (Yankees) 4, Thompson (Tigers) 5, Hentgen (Blue Jays) 6, Rosado (Royals) 7, Myers (Orioles) 8, Rivera (Yankees) 9. W—Rosado. L—Estes. HR—E. Martinez, S. Alomar, A.L.; Lopez, N.L.

LEADERS

American League
BA: Frank Thomas, Chi., .347.
Runs: Ken Griffey Jr., Sea., 125.
Hits: Nomar Garciaparra, Bos., 209.
TB: Ken Griffey Jr., Sea., 393.
HR: Ken Griffey Jr., Sea., 56.
RBI: Ken Griffey Jr., Sea., 147.
SB: Brian Hunter, Det., 74.
Wins: Roger Clemens, Tor., 21.
ERA: Roger Clemens, Tor., 2.05.
CG: Roger Clemens, Tor.; Pat Hentgen, Tor., 9.
IP: Roger Clemens, Tor.; Pat Hentgen, Tor., 264.0.
SO: Roger Clemens, Tor., 292.
SV: Randy Myers, Bal., 45.

National League
BA: Tony Gwynn, S.D., .372.
Runs: Craig Biggio, Hou., 146.
Hits: Tony Gwynn, S.D., 220.
TB: Larry Walker, Col., 409.
HR: Larry Walker, Col., 49.
RBI: Larry Walker, Col., 140.
SB: Tony Womack, Pit., 60.
Wins: Denny Neagle, Atl., 20.
ERA: Pedro J. Martinez, Mon., 1.90.
CG: Pedro J. Martinez, Mon., 13.
IP: John Smoltz, Atl., 256.0.
SO: Curt Schilling, Phi., 319.
SV: Jeff Shaw, Cin., 42.

A.L. 20-game winners
Roger Clemens, Tor., 21
Randy Johnson, Sea., 20
Brad Radke, Min., 20

N.L. 20-game winner
Denny Neagle, Atl., 20

A.L. 100 RBIs
Ken Griffey Jr., Sea., 147
Tino Martinez, N.Y., 141
Juan Gonzalez, Tex., 131
Tim Salmon, Ana., 129
Frank Thomas, Chi., 125
Tony Clark, Det., 117
Paul O'Neill, N.Y., 117
Albert Belle, Chi., 116
Jeff King, K.C., 112
Rafael Palmeiro, Bal., 110
Jay Buhner, Sea., 109
Edgar Martinez, Sea., 108
Matt Williams, Cle., 105
Joe Carter, Tor., 102
Travis Fryman, Det., 102
Jim Thome, Cle., 102
Bobby Higginson, Det., 101
David Justice, Cle., 101
Bernie Williams, N.Y., 100

N.L. 100 RBIs
Andres Galarraga, Col., 140
Jeff Bagwell, Hou., 135
Larry Walker, Col., 130
Mike Piazza, L.A., 124
Jeff Kent, S.F., 121
Tony Gwynn, S.D., 119
Sammy Sosa, Chi., 119
Dante Bichette, Col., 118
Moises Alou, Fla., 115
Vinny Castilla, Col., 113
Chipper Jones, Atl., 111
Eric Karros, L.A., 104
J.T. Snow, S.F., 104
John Olerud, N.Y., 102
Barry Bonds, S.F., 101

A.L./N.L. 100 RBIs
Mark McGwire, Oak.-St.L., 123

A.L. 40 homers
Ken Griffey Jr., Sea., 56
Tino Martinez, N.Y., 44
Juan Gonzalez, Tex., 42
Jay Buhner, Sea., 40
Jim Thome, Cle., 40

N.L. 40 homers
Larry Walker, Col., 49
Jeff Bagwell, Hou., 43
Andres Galarraga, Col., 41
Barry Bonds, S.F., 40
Vinny Castilla, Col., 40
Mike Piazza, L.A., 40

A.L./N.L. 40 homers
Mark McGwire, Oak.-St.L., 58

Most Valuable Player
A.L.: Ken Griffey Jr., OF, Sea.
N.L.: Larry Walker, OF, Col.

Cy Young Award
A.L.: Roger Clemens, Tor.
N.L.: Pedro Martinez, Mon.

Rookie of the Year
A.L.: Nomar Garciaparra, SS, Bos.
N.L.: Scott Rolen, 3B, Phi.

Manager of the Year
A.L.: Davey Johnson, Bal.
N.L.: Dusty Baker, S.F.

Hall of Fame additions
Nellie Fox, 2B, 1947-65.
Tom Lasorda, manager
Phil Niekro, P, 1964-87.
Willie Wells, IF-P, Negro Leagues

A.L. DIVISION SERIES

■ **Winners:** Baltimore claimed a surprisingly easy four-game victory over Seattle and Cleveland survived a comeback-filled five-game battle against the wild-card New York Yankees. The Indians' victory set up a grudge match with the Orioles, who had eliminated them in a 1996 Division Series.

■ **Turning points:** The Orioles claimed their second straight A.L. Championship Series berth because of their ability to beat Mariners ace Randy Johnson. Baltimore scored five earned runs in Johnson's five Game 1 innings en route to a 9-3 victory and then handed the big left-hander a 3-1 defeat in the Game 4 clincher. The Indians advanced because they finally were able to break the stranglehold of a powerful New York bullpen that had worked 11⅔ scoreless innings entering Game 4. Cleveland scored single runs in the eighth and ninth innings off Mariano Rivera and Ramiro Mendoza to claim a 3-2 Game 4 win and prevailed in a 4-3 clincher behind the pitching of rookie Jaret Wright.

■ **Memorable moments:** The Game 4 home run of light-hitting Baltimore second baseman Jeff Reboulet, who also hit two regular-season homers off the intimidating Johnson. The consecutive Game 1 home runs by Yankees Tim Raines, Derek Jeter and Paul O'Neill, a post-season record that helped the New Yorkers rally for an 8-6 victory. Omar Vizquel's ninth-inning single that completed the Indians' rally for a series-tying Game 4 victory.

■ **Memorable performances:** Geronimo Berroa hit a pair of home runs, including one in the decisive 3-1 series-clinching victory, and batted .385 for the Orioles; Baltimore right-hander Mike Mussina recorded two wins and a 1.93 ERA while outdueling Mariners ace Johnson; Yankees right fielder O'Neill batted .421 with two homers, including a Game 3 grand slam, and seven RBIs against the Indians; catcher Sandy Alomar hit a pair of home runs and the 21-year-old Wright won twice for Cleveland.

Linescores

Baltimore vs. Seattle

Game 1—October 1, at Seattle
Baltimore......0 0 1 0 4 4 0 0 0—9 13 0
Seattle..........0 0 0 1 0 0 1 0 1—3 7 1
Mussina, Orosco (8), Benitez (9); Johnson, Timlin (6), Spoljaric (6), Wells (7), Charlton (8). W—Mussina. L—Johnson. HR—Berroa, Hoiles (Bal.); Martinez, Buhner, Rodriguez (Sea.).

Game 2—October 2, at Seattle
Baltimore......0 1 0 0 2 0 2 4 0—9 14 0
Seattle..........2 0 0 0 0 0 1 0 0—3 9 0
Erickson, Benitez (7), Orosco (8), Myers (9); Moyer, Spoljaric (5), Ayala (7), Charlton (8), Slocumb (9). W—Erickson. L—Moyer. HR—Baines, Anderson (Bal.).

Game 3—October 4, at Baltimore
Seattle..........0 0 1 0 1 0 0 0 2—4 11 0
Baltimore......0 0 0 0 0 0 0 0 2—2 5 0
Fassero, Slocumb (9); Key, Mills (5), Rhodes (6), Mathews (9). W—Fassero. L—Key. HR—Buhner, Sorrento (Sea.).

Game 4—October 5, at Baltimore
Seattle............0 1 0 0 0 0 0 0 0—1 2 0
Baltimore........2 0 0 0 1 0 0 0 x—3 7 0
Johnson; Mussina, Benitez (8), Myers (9). W—Mussina. L—Johnson. S—Myers. HR—Reboulet, Berroa (Bal.); Martinez (Sea.).

Cleveland vs. New York

Game 1—September 30, at New York
Cleveland......5 0 0 1 0 0 0 0 0—6 11 0
New York......0 1 0 1 1 5 0 0 0—8 11 0
Hershiser, Morman (5), Plunk (5), Assenmacher (6), Jackson (7); Cone, Mendoza (4), Stanton (7), Nelson (7), Rivera (8). W—Mendoza. L—Plunk. S—Rivera. HR—Alomar (Cle.); Martinez, Raines, Jeter, O'Neill (N.Y.).

Game 2—October 2, at New York
Cleveland......0 0 0 5 2 0 0 0 0—7 11 1
New York......3 0 0 0 0 0 0 1 1—5 7 2
Wright, Jackson (7), Assenmacher (7), Mesa (8); Pettitte, Boehringer (6), Lloyd (7), Nelson (9). W—Wright. L—Pettitte. HR—M. Williams (Cle.); Jeter (N.Y.).

Game 3—October 4, at Cleveland
New York........1 0 1 4 0 0 0 0 0—6 4 1
Cleveland........0 1 0 0 0 0 0 0 0—1 5 1

HISTORY

Wells; Nagy, Ogea (4). W—Wells. L—Nagy. HR—O'Neill (N.Y.).

Game 4—October 5, at Cleveland
New York........2 0 0 0 0 0 0 0 0—2 9 1
Cleveland........0 1 0 0 0 0 0 1 1—3 9 0
Gooden, Lloyd (6), Nelson (6), Stanton (7), Rivera (8), Mendoza (8); Hershiser, Assenmacher (8), Jackson (8). W—Jackson. L—Mendoza. HR—Justice, Alomar (Cle.).

Game 5—October 6, at Cleveland
New York......0 0 0 0 2 1 0 0 0—3 12 0
Cleveland......0 0 3 1 0 0 0 0 x—4 7 2
Pettitte, Nelson (7), Stanton (8); Wright, Jackson (6), Assenmacher (7), Mesa (8). W—Wright. L—Pettitte. S—Mesa.

N.L. DIVISION SERIES

■ **Winners:** The Atlanta Braves and the wild-card Florida Marlins set up an NLCS showdown of East Division teams with convincing sweeps of the Houston Astros and San Francisco Giants. The Braves earned a record sixth straight LCS appearance behind the outstanding pitching of Greg Maddux, John Smoltz and Tom Glavine. The 5-year-old Marlins became the youngest expansion team to win a playoff series behind the near-perfect combination of clutch hitting and pitching.
■ **Turning points:** Maddux set the tone for Atlanta's victory by throwing a Game 1 seven-hitter and outdueling Houston ace Darryl Kile for a 2-1 victory. Edgar Renteria gave the Marlins a 2-1 Game 1 victory with a bases-loaded, ninth-inning single and Moises Alou singled home the winning run in the ninth inning of a 7-6 Game 2 win—a two-games-to-none hole from which the Giants could not recover.
■ **Memorable moments:** Smoltz took Atlanta honors with an 11-strikeout three-hitter in a 4-1 Game 3 victory that completed the Braves' sweep of Houston. Florida's 6-2 third-game victory over the Giants was keyed by Devon White's sixth-inning grand slam, which erased a 1-0 deficit.
■ **Memorable performances:** Third baseman Chipper Jones batted .500 with a home run and Jeff Blauser had a home run and four RBIs for the Braves, who also got a victory from each of their Big Three—Maddux, Glavine and Smoltz. The Marlins rode the clutch hitting of Renteria, Alou and White and the outstanding pitching of Kevin Brown and Alex Fernandez. The Giants got two home runs from second baseman Jeff Kent and a nice pitching effort from Kirk Rueter, who failed to get a decision.

Linescores

Atlanta vs. Houston

Game 1—September 30, at Atlanta
Houston................0 0 0 0 1 0 0 0 0—1 7 1
Atlanta ....1 1 0 0 0 0 0 0 x—2 2 0
Kile, Springer (8), Martin (8); Maddux. W—Maddux. L—Kile. HR—Klesko (Atl.).

Game 2—October 1, at Atlanta
Houston............0 0 0 3 0 0 0 0 0— 3 6 2
Atlanta ....0 0 3 0 3 5 0 2 x—13 10 1
Hampton, Magnante (5), Garcia (6), Lima (7), Wagner (8); Glavine, Cather (7), Wohlers (9). W—Glavine. L—Hampton. HR—Blauser (Atl.).

Game 3—October 3, at Houston
Atlanta ....1 1 0 0 0 0 1 1 0—4 8 2
Houston.................0 0 0 0 0 0 1 0 0—1 3 1
Smoltz; Reynolds, Springer (7), Martin (8), Garcia (8), Magnante (9). W—Smoltz. L—Reynolds. HR—C. Jones (Atl.), Carr (Hou.).

Florida vs. San Francisco

Game 1—September 30, at Florida
San Francisco ......0 0 0 0 0 0 1 0 0—1 4 0
Florida ....0 0 0 0 0 0 1 0 1—2 7 0
Rueter, Tavarez (8), R. Hernandez (9); Brown, Cook (8). W—Cook. L—Tavarez. HR—Mueller (S.F.), C. Johnson (Fla.).

Game 2—October 1, at Florida
San Francisco ....1 1 1 1 0 0 1 0 1—6 11 0
Florida ....2 0 1 2 0 1 0 0 1—7 10 2
Estes, Henry (3), Tavarez (6), Rodriguez (8), R. Hernandez (9); Leiter, L. Hernandez (5), Nen (9). W—Nen. L—R. Hernandez. HR—Bonilla, Sheffield (Fla.), B. Johnson (S.F.).

Game 3—October 3, at San Francisco
Florida ....0 0 0 0 0 4 0 2 0—6 10 2
San Francisco ....0 0 0 1 0 1 0 0 0—2 7 0
Fernandez, Cook (8), Nen (9); Alvarez, Tavarez (7), R. Hernandez (8), Rodriguez (8), Beck (8). W—Fernandez. L—Alvarez. HR—Kent 2 (S.F.), White (Fla.).

ALCS

■ **Winner:** The Indians, looking for their first championship since 1948, earned their second World Series appearance in three years with a six-game victory over the Orioles. The Indians overcame a .193 team average to claim the franchise's fifth pennant behind clutch pitching and timely hitting that produced four one-run wins over the A.L.'s winningest regular-season team.
■ **Turning point:** The fifth inning of Game 4, when Indians catcher Sandy Alomar took center stage with a baserunning gamble. The bases were loaded and the score was tied when Alomar, stationed at second, alertly raced home after an Arthur Rhodes wild pitch led to a home-plate collision between lead runner Dave Justice and catcher Lenny Webster. The Orioles fought back for a 7-7 tie, but Alomar decided the game with a ninth-inning single off Baltimore closer Armando Benitez to give the Indians a three-games-to-one series advantage.
■ **Memorable moment:** The 11th inning of Game 6 when shortstop Tony Fernandez drove a Benitez pitch into the right field seats at Camden Yards and gave the Indians a 1-0 series-clinching win. The Indians had managed only one hit through eight innings off Orioles starter Mike Mussina and while Baltimore stranded 14 baserunners and was 0-for-12 with men in scoring position against Cleveland starter Charles Nagy and four relievers.
■ **Top guns:** Manny Ramirez (2 HR, 3 RBI), Fernandez (.357, 1 HR, 2 RBI), Marquis Grissom (1 HR, 4 RBI), S. Alomar (1 HR, 4 RBI), Mike Jackson (5 games, 0.00 ERA), Indians; Brady Anderson (.360, 2 HR, 3 RBI), Cal Ripken (.348, 1 HR, 3 RBI), Harold Baines (.353, 1 HR), Mussina (15 IP, 0.60 ERA), Orioles.
■ **MVP:** Marquis Grissom.

Linescores

Game 1—October 8, at Baltimore
Cleveland........0 0 0 0 0 0 0 0 0—0 4 1
Baltimore........1 0 2 0 0 0 0 0 x—3 6 1
Ogea, Bri. Anderson (7); Erickson, Myers (9). W—Erickson. L—Ogea. S—Myers. HR—Bra. Anderson, R. Alomar (Bal.).

Game 2—October 9, at Baltimore
Cleveland........2 0 0 0 0 0 0 3 0—5 6 3
Baltimore........0 2 0 0 0 2 0 0 0—4 8 1
Nagy, Morman (6), Juden (7), Assenmacher (7), Jackson (8), Mesa (9); Key, Kamieniecki (5), Benitez (8), Mills (9). W—Assenmacher. L—Benitez. S—Mesa. HR—Ramirez, Grissom (Cle.); Ripken (Bal.).

Game 3—October 11, at Cleveland
Bal. ....0 0 0 0 0 0 0 0 1 0 0 0—1 8 1
Cle. ....0 0 0 0 0 0 1 0 0 0 0 1—2 6 0
Mussina, Benitez (8), Orosco (9), Mills (9), Rhodes (10), Myers (11); Hershiser, Assenmacher (8), Jackson (8), Mesa (9), Juden (11), Morman (11), Plunk (12). W—Plunk. L—Myers.

Game 4—October 12, at Cleveland
Baltimore ....0 1 4 0 0 0 1 0 1—7 12 2
Cleveland......0 2 0 1 4 0 0 0 1—8 13 0
Erickson, Rhodes (5), Mills (7), Orosco (9), Benitez (9); Wright, Bri. Anderson (4), Juden (7), Assenmacher (7), Jackson (7), Mesa (8). W—Mesa. L—Mills. HR—S. Alomar, Ramirez (Cle.); Bra. Anderson, Baines, Palmeiro (Bal.).

Game 5—October 13, at Cleveland
Baltimore......0 0 2 0 0 0 0 0 2—4 10 0
Cleveland......0 0 0 0 0 0 0 0 2—2 8 1
Kamieniecki, Key (6), Myers (9); Ogea, Assenmacher (9), Jackson (9). W—Kamieniecki. L—Ogea. HR—Davis (Bal.).

Game 6—October 15, at Baltimore
Cle. ....0 0 0 0 0 0 0 0 0 0 1—1 3 0
Bal. ....0 0 0 0 0 0 0 0 0 0 0—0 10 0
Nagy, Assenmacher (8), Jackson (8), Bri. Anderson (10), Mesa (11); Mussina, Myers (9), Benitez (11). W—Bri. Anderson. L—Benitez. S—Mesa. HR—Fernandez (Cle.).

NLCS

■ **Winner:** The Marlins became the first wild-card team to reach the World Series when they upended the defending-N.L. champion Braves in a six-game NLCS. The 5-year-old Marlins also became the youngest expansion team to reach the fall classic while giving the spring training haven of South Florida its first World Series. The Marlins, who finished nine games behind Atlanta in the N.L. East, didn't even exist in 1991 when the Braves began their long playoff run.
■ **Turning point:** After righthander Livan Hernandez surrendered a Game 5-opening triple to Kenny Lofton and a walk to Keith Lockhart, he came back to strike out Chipper Jones, Fred McGriff and Ryan Klesko in a scoreless first inning. Bolstered by that great escape, Hernandez surrendered only two more hits and tied the LCS record with 15 strikeouts while outdueling Greg Maddux in a 2-1 victory at Pro Player Stadium.
■ **Memorable moment:** Kevin Brown's final pitch of Game 6, which extended the Marlins' Cinderella run and gave manager Jim Leyland his first World Series appearance in a career that spanned 33 years. Brown, the Game 1 winner, struggled through an 11-hit, complete-game 7-4 victory while fighting a stomach flu.
■ **Top guns:** Craig Counsell (.429), Bobby Bonilla (4 RBI), Charles Johnson (5 RBI), Jeff Conine (5 RBI), Hernandez (2-0, 0.84 ERA), Brown (2-0), Marlins; Lockhart (.500), Andruw Jones (.444), McGriff (.333, 4 RBI), Chipper Jones (2 HR, 4 RBI), Ryan Klesko (2 HR, 4 RBI), Denny Neagle (12 IP, 1-0, 0.00 ERA), Maddux (13 IP, 0-2, 1.38 ERA), Braves.
■ **MVP:** Hernandez.

Linescores

Game 1—October 7, at Atlanta
Florida............3 0 2 0 0 0 0 0 0—5 6 0
Atlanta............1 0 1 0 0 1 0 0 0—3 5 2
Brown, Cook (7), Powell (8), Nen (9); Maddux, Neagle (7). W—Brown. L—Maddux. S—Nen. HR—C. Jones, Klesko (Atl.).

Game 2—October 8, at Atlanta
Florida..........0 0 0 0 0 0 0 1 0—1 3 1
Atlanta..........3 0 2 0 0 0 2 0 x—7 13 0
Fernandez, Leiter (3), Heredia (6), Vosberg (7); Glavine, Cather (8), Wohlers (9). W—Glavine. L—Fernandez. HR—Klesko, C. Jones (Atl.).

Game 3—October 10, at Florida
Atlanta............0 0 0 1 0 1 0 0 0—2 6 1
Florida ....0 0 0 1 0 4 0 0 x—5 8 1
Smoltz, Cather (7), Ligtenberg (8); Saunders, Hernandez (6), Cook (8), Nen (9). W—Hernandez. L—Smoltz. S—Nen. HR—Sheffield (Fla.).

Game 4—October 11, at Florida
Atlanta..........1 0 1 0 2 0 0 0 0—4 11 0
Florida ....0 0 0 0 0 0 0 0 0—0 4 0
Neagle; Leiter, Heredia (7), Vosberg (9). W—Neagle. L—Leiter. HR—Blauser (Atl.).

Game 5—October 12, at Florida
Atlanta............0 1 0 0 0 0 0 0 0—1 3 0
Florida ....1 0 0 0 0 0 1 0 x—2 5 0
Maddux, Cather (8); Hernandez. W—Hernandez. L—Maddux. HR—Tucker (Atl.).

Game 6—October 14, at Atlanta
Florida..........4 0 0 0 0 3 0 0 0—7 10 1
Atlanta..........1 2 0 0 0 0 0 0 1—4 11 1
Brown; Glavine, Cather (6), Ligtenberg (7), Embree (9). W—Brown. L—Glavine.

WORLD SERIES

■ **Winner:** The expansion Marlins, who had undergone an $89 million offseason facelift, made the investment pay off when they outlasted the Indians in an exciting World Series that was decided in the 11th inning of Game 7 at Pro Player Stadium. The victory gave the 5-year-old Marlins distinction as the youngest team ever to win a fall classic and the only wild-card team to earn a championship. The Indians failed to win their first World Series since 1948 for the second time in three years.
■ **Turning point:** It didn't arrive until the ninth inning of Game 7, when the Indians were leading 2-1 and two outs away from an elusive championship. That's when the Marlins scored the tying run on Craig Counsell's sacrifice fly, setting the stage for a dramatic finish to a closely contested series in which the teams alternated victories.
■ **Memorable moment:** The bases-loaded, 11th-inning single by shortstop Edgar Renteria that gave the Marlins their unlikely victory and sent 67,204 fans at Pro Player Stadium into a frenzy. The two-out hit completed a gutsy comeback after the Marlins had been limited to two hits over eight innings by starter Jaret Wright and three Cleveland relievers. It also made a winner out of Jay Powell, who completed the six-pitcher six-hitter with a scoreless top of the 11th.
■ **Top guns:** Darren Daulton (.389), Charles Johnson (.357), Moises Alou (.321, 3 HR, 9 RBI), Livan Hernandez (2-0), Marlins; Matt Williams (.385), Sandy Alomar (.367, 2 HR, 10 RBI), Manny Ramirez (2 HR, 6 RBI); Chad Ogea (2-0, 1.54 ERA), Wright (1-0, 2.92), Indians.
■ **MVP:** Hernandez.

Linescores

Game 1—October 18, at Florida
Cleveland......1 0 0 0 1 1 0 1 0—4 11 0
Florida ....0 0 1 4 2 0 0 0 x—7 7 1
Hershiser, Juden (5), Plunk (6), Assenmacher (8); Hernandez, Cook (6), Powell (8), Nen (9). W—Hernandez. L—Hershiser. S—Nen. HR—Alou, Johnson (Fla.), Ramirez, Thome (Cle.).

Game 2—October 19, at Florida
Cleveland......1 0 0 0 3 2 0 0 0—6 14 0
Florida..........1 0 0 0 0 0 0 0 0—1 8 0
Ogea, Jackson (7), Mesa (9); Brown, Heredia (7), Alfonseca (8). W—Ogea. L—Brown. HR—Alomar (Cle.).

Game 3—October 21, at Cleveland
Florida........1 0 1 1 0 2 2 0 7—14 16 3
Cleveland....2 0 0 3 2 0 0 0 4—11 10 3
Leiter, Heredia (5), Cook (8), Nen (9); Nagy, Anderson (7), Jackson (7), Assenmacher (8), Plunk (8), Morman (9), Mesa (9). W—Cook. L—Plunk. HR—Sheffield, Daulton, Eisenreich (Fla.), Thome (Cle.).

Game 4—October 22, at Cleveland
Florida........0 0 0 1 0 2 0 0 0— 3 6 2
Cleveland....3 0 3 0 0 1 1 2 x—10 15 0
Saunders, Alfonseca (3), Vosberg (6), Powell (8); Wright, Anderson (7). W—Wright. L—Saunders. S—Anderson. HR—Ramirez, Williams (Cle.), Alou (Fla.).

Game 5—October 23, at Cleveland
Florida..........0 2 0 0 0 4 0 1 1—8 15 2
Cleveland......0 1 3 0 0 0 0 0 3—7 9 0
Hernandez, Nen (9); Hershiser, Morman (6), Plunk (6), Juden (7), Assenmacher (8), Mesa (9). W—Hernandez. L—Hershiser. S—Nen. HR—Alomar (Cle.), Alou (Fla.).

Game 6—October 25, at Florida
Cleveland........0 2 1 0 1 0 0 0 0—4 8 0
Florida ....0 0 0 0 1 0 0 0 0—1 8 0
Ogea, Jackson (6), Assenmacher (8), Mesa (9); Brown, Heredia (6), Powell (8), Vosberg (9). W—Ogea. L—Brown. S—Mesa.

Game 7—October 26, at Florida
Cle. ......0 0 2 0 0 0 0 0 0 0 0—2 6 2
Fla. ......0 0 0 0 0 0 1 0 1 0 1—3 8 0
Wright, Assenmacher (7), Jackson (8), Anderson (8), Mesa (9), Nagy (10); Leiter, Cook (7), Alfonseca (8), Heredia (9), Nen (9), Powell (11). W—Powell. L—Nagy. HR—Bonilla (Fla.).

Padres right fielder Tony Gwynn captured his eighth batting championship in 1997, joining Honus Wagner as the all-time National League leader.

HISTORY

FINAL STANDINGS

American League

East Division

Team	N.Y.	Bos.	Tor.	Bal.	T.B.	Cle.	Chi.	K.C.	Min.	Det.	Tex.	Ana.	Sea.	Oak.	Atl.	NYM	Phi.	Mtl.	Fla.	W	L	Pct.	GB
New York	—	7	6	9	11	7	7	10	7	8	8	5	8	8	3	2	3	2	3	114	48	.704	—
Boston	5	—	5	6	9	8	5	8	5	5	6	5	7	9	2	1	1	3	2	92	70	.568	22
Toronto	6	7	—	7	7	4	6	5	7	6	4	7	7	6	1	2	1	4	1	88	74	.543	26
Baltimore	3	6	5	—	5	5	2	5	7	10	6	6	6	8	1	1	2	0	1	79	83	.488	35
Tampa Bay	1	3	5	7	—	3	6	3	4	6	4	5	5	6	0	1	2	1	1	63	99	.389	51

Central Division

Team	N.Y.	Bos.	Tor.	Bal.	T.B.	Cle.	Chi.	K.C.	Min.	Det.	Tex.	Ana.	Sea.	Oak.	Hou.	ChC	Stl.	Cin.	Mil.	Pit.	W	L	Pct.	GB
Cleveland	4	3	7	6	7	—	6	8	6	9	4	7	9	3	1	2	2	2	2	1	89	73	.549	—
Chicago	4	6	4	9	5	6	—	8	6	6	5	6	4	4	1	0	2	1	1	2	80	82	.494	9
Kansas City	0	3	6	6	8	4	4	—	7	6	3	5	4	7	1	2	2	2	1	1	72	89	.447	16.5
Minnesota	4	6	4	3	7	6	6	5	—	4	7	5	2	4	1	2	2	1	0	1	70	92	.432	19
Detroit	3	5	5	1	5	3	6	6	8	—	3	3	3	7	0	2	1	0	2	2	65	97	.401	24

West Division

Team	N.Y.	Bos.	Tor.	Bal.	T.B.	Cle.	Chi.	K.C.	Min.	Det.	Tex.	Ana.	Sea.	Oak.	S.D.	S.F.	L.A.	Col.	Ari.	W	L	Pct.	GB
Texas	3	5	7	5	7	7	6	8	4	8	—	7	7	6	2	1	0	2	3	88	74	.543	—
Anaheim	6	6	4	5	6	4	5	6	6	8	5	—	9	5	1	1	3	3	2	85	77	.525	3
Seattle	3	4	4	5	6	2	7	6	9	8	5	3	—	7	2	1	1	2	1	76	85	.472	11.5
Oakland	3	2	5	3	5	8	7	4	7	4	6	7	5	—	2	2	1	1	2	74	88	.457	14

National League

East Division

Team	Atl.	N.Y.	Phi.	Mtl.	Fla.	Hou.	Chi.	Stl.	Cin.	Mil.	Pit.	S.D.	S.F.	L.A.	Col.	Ari.	NYY	Bos.	Tor.	Bal.	T.B.	W	L	Pct.	GB
Atlanta	—	9	8	6	7	4	3	6	7	7	7	5	7	8	5	8	1	1	2	2	3	106	56	.654	—
New York	3	—	8	4	7	4	5	6	6	8	4	4	4	5	6	5	1	2	1	3	2	88	74	.543	18
Philadelphia	4	4	—	7	6	2	6	3	5	5	8	1	2	4	4	7	0	3	2	1	1	75	87	.463	31
Montreal	6	8	5	—	7	2	2	3	1	3	2	4	3	4	2	7	1	0	0	3	2	65	97	.401	41
Florida	5	5	6	5	—	3	2	4	0	0	3	4	0	4	3	2	0	1	2	2	3	54	108	.333	52

Central Division

Team	Atl.	N.Y.	Phi.	Mtl.	Fla.	Hou.	Chi.	Stl.	Cin.	Mil.	Pit.	S.D.	S.F.	L.A.	Col.	Ari.	Cle.	ChW	K.C.	Min.	Det.	W	L	Pct.	GB
Houston	5	5	7	7	6	—	7	5	8	9	9	5	6	3	5	5	2	2	2	1	3	102	60	.630	—
Chicago	6	4	3	7	7	4	—	4	6	6	8	5	7	4	7	7	0	3	1	1	0	90	73	.552	12.5
St. Louis	3	3	6	6	5	7	7	—	3	8	5	3	5	5	6	7	0	1	1	1	1	83	79	.512	19
Cincinnati	2	3	4	8	9	3	5	8	—	6	5	1	2	5	4	5	1	1	0	2	3	77	85	.475	25
Milwaukee	2	1	4	6	9	2	6	3	5	—	6	3	5	4	7	3	1	2	2	2	1	74	88	.457	28
Pittsburgh	2	5	1	7	6	2	3	6	7	5	—	5	2	5	4	3	2	0	1	2	1	69	93	.426	33

West Division

Team	Atl.	N.Y.	Phi.	Mtl.	Fla.	Hou.	Chi.	Stl.	Cin.	Mil.	Pit.	S.D.	S.F.	L.A.	Col.	Ari.	Tex.	Ana.	Sea.	Oak.	W	L	Pct.	GB
San Diego	4	5	8	4	5	4	4	6	11	6	4	—	8	7	7	9	1	2	2	1	98	64	.605	—
San Fran.	2	5	6	6	9	3	3	7	7	4	7	4	—	6	5	7	2	2	2	2	89	74	.546	9.5
Los Angeles	1	3	5	5	5	6	5	4	4	5	7	5	6	—	6	8	3	1	2	2	83	79	.512	15
Colorado	3	3	5	7	6	6	2	3	5	4	5	5	7	6	—	6	1	0	1	2	77	85	.475	21
Arizona	1	4	2	2	6	4	5	2	4	6	6	3	5	4	6	—	1	1	2	1	65	97	.401	33

LEADERS

American League
BA: Bernie Williams, N.Y., .339.
Runs: Derek Jeter, N.Y., 127.
Hits: Alex Rodriguez, Sea., 213.
TB: Albert Belle, Chi., 399.
HR: Ken Griffey Jr., Sea., 56.
RBI: Juan Gonzalez, Tex., 157.
SB: Rickey Henderson, Oak., 66.
Wins: Roger Clemens, Tor., David Cone, N.Y., Rick Helling, Tex., 20.
ERA: Roger Clemens, Tor., 2.65.
CG: Scott Erickson, Bal., 11.
IP: Scott Erickson, Bal., 251.1.
SO: Roger Clemens, Tor., 271.
Sv.: Tom Gordon, Bos., 46.

National League
BA: Larry Walker, Col., .363.
Runs: Sammy Sosa, Chi., 134.
Hits: Dante Bichette, Col., 219.
TB: Sammy Sosa, Chi., 416.
HR: Mark McGwire, St.L., 70.
RBI: Sammy Sosa, Chi., 158.
SB: Tony Womack, Pit., 58.
Wins: Tom Glavine, Atl., 20.
ERA: Greg Maddux, Atl., 2.22.
CG: Curt Schilling, Phi., 15.
IP: Curt Schilling, Phi., 268.2.
SO: Curt Schilling, Phi., 300.
Sv.: Trevor Hoffman, S.D., 53.

A.L. 20-game winners
Roger Clemens, Tor., 20
David Cone, N.Y., 20
Rick Helling, Tex., 20

N.L. 20-game winner
Tom Glavine, Atl., 20

A.L. 100 RBIs
Juan Gonzalex, Tex., 157
Albert Belle, Chi., 152
Ken Griffey Jr., Sea., 146
Manny Ramirez, Cle., 145
Alex Rodriguez, Sea., 124
Tino Martinez, N.Y., 123
Nomar Garciaparra, Bos., 122
Rafael Palmeiro, Bal., 121
Dean Palmer, K.C., 119
Paul O'Neill, N.Y., 116
Carlos Delgado, Tor., 115
Mo Vaughn, Bos., 115
Jason Giambi, Oak., 110
Frank Thomas, Chi., 109
Rusty Greer, Tex., 108
Jose Canseco, Tor., 107
Matt Stairs, Oak., 106
Tony Clark, Det., 103
Will Clark, Tex., 102
Edgar Martinez, Sea., 102
Damion Easley, Det., 100
Shawn Green, Tor., 100

N.L. 100 RBIs
Sammy Sosa, Chi., 158
Mark McGwire, St.L., 147
Vinny Castilla, Col., 144
Jeff Kent, S.F., 128
Jeromy Burnitz, Mil., 125
Moises Alou, Hou., 124
Dante Bichette, Col., 122
Barry Bonds, S.F., 122
Andres Galarraga, Atl., 121
Greg Vaughn, S.D., 119
Jeff Bagwell, Hou., 111
Mike Piazza, L.A., Fla., N.Y., 111
Scott Rolen, Phi., 110
Vladimir Guerrero, Mon., 109
Derek Bell, Hou., 108
Kevin Young, Pit., 108
Chipper Jones, Atl., 107
Javy Lopez, Atl., 106
Ray Lankford, St.L., 105
Rico Brogna, Phi., 104

A.L. 40 homers
Ken Griffey Jr., Sea., 56
Albert Belle, Chi., 49
Jose Canseco, Tor., 46
Juan Gonzalez, Tex., 45
Manny Ramirez, Cle., 45
Rafael Palmeiro, Bal., 43
Alex Rodriguez, Sea., 42
Mo Vaughn, Bos., 40

N.L. 40 homers
Mark McGwire, St.L., 70
Sammy Sosa, Chi., 66
Greg Vaughn, S.D., 50
Vinny Castilla, Col., 46
Andres Galarraga, Atl., 44

Most Valuable Player
A.L.: Juan Gonzalez, OF, Tex.
N.L.: Sammy Sosa, OF, Chi.

Cy Young Award
A.L.: Roger Clemens, Tor.
N.L.: Tom Glavine, Atl.

Rookie of the Year
A.L.: Ben Grieve, OF, Oak.
N.L.: Kerry Wood, P, Chi.

Manager of the Year
A.L.: Joe Torre, N.Y.
N.L.: Larry Dierker, Hou.

Hall of Fame additions
George Davis, SS, 1890-1909
Larry Doby, OF, 1947-59.
Lee MacPhail, Executive
Joe Rogan, P, Negro Leagues
Don Sutton, P, 1966-88

SIGNIFICANT EVENTS

■ **March 31:** Two expansion teams made their major league debut, Arizona losing 9-2 to the Colorado Rockies at new Bank One Ballpark in Phoenix and Tampa Bay dropping an 11-6 decision to Detroit at new Tropicana Field.

■ **March 31:** The Milwaukee Brewers, transplanted to the National League because of expansion, lost their first N.L. game, 2-1, at Atlanta. The Brewers became the first modern-era team in baseball history to switch leagues.

■ **April 15:** The New York Yankees, forced to temporarily abandon Yankee Stadium when a steel beam fell from beneath the upper deck to the empty seats below, posted a 6-3 win over the Angels at Shea Stadium, home of the Mets. The Mets came back that night to beat the Cubs 2-1—the first time this century that two regular-season games involving four teams were played in the same stadium on the same day.

■ **July 9:** After serving as chairman of the Executive Committee and interim commissioner for almost six years, Allan (Bud) Selig, the Milwaukee Brewers' president and chief executive officer, accepted a five-year term as baseball's ninth commissioner.

■ **August 9:** Atlanta veteran Dennis Martinez posted his 244th career victory in a relief role against San Francisco, making him the winningest Latin pitcher in major league history.

■ **September 28:** Gary Gaetti's two-run homer lifted Chicago to a 5-3 win over San Francisco in the first-ever playoff to decide a league's wild-card representative.

■ **December 12:** The Los Angeles Dodgers broke new ground when they signed pitcher Kevin Brown to a seven-year contract worth $105 million—the first $100 million deal in baseball history.

MEMORABLE MOMENTS

■ **May 6:** Chicago Cubs rookie Kerry Wood tied Roger Clemens' single-game strikeout record when he fanned 20 Houston batters in a one-hit, 2-0 shutout at Wrigley Field.

■ **May 17:** Lefthander David Wells fired the first regular-season perfect game in New York Yankees history and the 13th perfecto of the modern era when he retired all 27 Minnesota Twins he faced in a 4-0 win before 49,820 fans at Yankee Stadium.

■ **September 8:** St. Louis first baseman Mark McGwire broke Roger Maris' 37-year-old single-season home run record when he drove a pitch from Chicago righthander Steve Trachsel over the left field fence at Busch Stadium for homer No. 62.

■ **September 13:** Chicago right fielder Sammy Sosa, following McGwire's home run lead, hit Nos. 61 and 62 during a Sunday night victory over Milwaukee at Wrigley Field.

■ **September 20:** Baltimore third baseman Cal Ripken ended his record ironman streak at 2,632 consecutive games when he sat out against the New York Yankees in the Orioles' final home contest of the season.

■ **September 25:** The Yankees posted a 6-1 victory over Tampa Bay at Yankee Stadium for their 112th win, topping the American League record of 111 set by the 1954 Cleveland Indians. The Yanks would go on to win 114 times.

■ **September 27:** McGwire, who trailed Sosa briefly on the final Friday of the great 1998 home run race, capped a five-homer final weekend with two final-day shots against Montreal, bringing his record season total to 70.

ALL-STAR GAME

■ **Winner:** The A.L. obliterated the N.L. with a 19-hit, five-stolen base barrage that resulted in a 13-8 victory. The A.L.'s second straight win featured home runs by Alex Rodriguez and Roberto Alomar and a surprising running attack.

■ **Key inning:** The sixth, when the A.L. broke out its ugly game and scored three times for an 8-6 lead. The rally off Montreal righthander Ugueth Urbina featured four stolen bases and runners crossing the plate on a wild pitch and a passed ball. The uprising wiped out a three-run fifth-inning homer by San Francisco's Barry Bonds.

■ **Memorable moment:** A towering two-run double to right by third baseman Cal Ripken in the fourth. The double was Ripken's 11th hit in his 16th All-Star Game.

■ **Top guns:** Rafael Palmeiro (Orioles), Alex Rodriguez (Mariners), Ken Griffey Jr. (Mariners), Roberto Alomar (Indians), Ripken (Orioles), David Wells (Yankees), A.L.; Bonds (Giants), Tony Gwynn (Padres), N.L.

■ **MVP:** Roberto Alomar.

Linescore

July 7 at Colorado's Coors Field
A.L. ....0 0 0 4 1 3 1 1 3—13 19 2
N.L. ....0 0 2 1 3 0 0 2 0— 8 12 1
Wells (Yankees), Clemens (Blue Jays) 3, Radke (Twins) 4, Colon (Indians) 5, Arrojo (Devil Rays) 6, Wetteland (Rangers) 7, Gordon (Red Sox) 8, Percival (Angels) 9 and I. Rodriguez (Rangers), S. Alomar (Indians); Maddux (Braves), Glavine (Braves) 3, Brown (Padres) 4, Ashby (Padres) 5, Urbina (Expos) 6, Hoffman (Padres) 7, Shaw (Dodgers) 8, Nen (Giants) 9 and Piazza (Mets), Lopez (Braves). W—Colon. L—Urbina. HR—A. Rodriguez, R. Alomar, A.L.; Bonds, N.L.

A.L. DIVISION SERIES

■ **Winners:** The New York Yankees, who won an A.L.-record 114 regular-season games, carried that dominance into the postseason with a three-game Division Series sweep of the Texas Rangers, and the Cleveland Indians earned their third ALCS berth in four years with an exciting four-game victory over the wild-card Boston Red Sox. Yankee pitchers shut down the A.L.'s top-hitting team (a .141 average) en route to their second ALCS opportunity in three years and the Indians overcame an 11-3 series-opening loss while extending Boston's 80-year World Series championship drought.

■ **Turning points:** What little offense the Yankees needed in 2-0, 3-1 and 4-0 victories was provided by unlikely sources: Third baseman Scott Brosius singled in the go-ahead run in Game 1 and hit a lead-extending two-run homer in Game 2; backup outfielder Shane Spencer homered in Game 2 and hit a key three-run shot in Game 3. A Game 2 first-inning ejection of Cleveland manager Mike Hargrove and starting pitcher Dwight Gooden seemed to energize the lethargic Indians, who erupted for six runs in the first two innings and went on to a 9-5 series-squaring win.

■ **Memorable moments:** A Game 3 Texas-type downpour that forced a 3-hour, 16-minute rain delay in Game 3, but merely delayed the inevitable for the Rangers. The delay knocked Yankee starter David Cone out of the game, but three relievers came on to complete his shutout and Spencer delivered the big blow. Left fielder David Justice provided the big plays in Game 4 for the Indians, a sixth-inning throw that cut down Boston runner John Valentin at the plate and a two-run, eighth-inning double that secured a 2-1 victory.

■ **Memorable performances:** Brosius and Spencer combined for seven of the Yankees' eight RBIs in the series, but the real heroes were pitchers David Wells, Andy Pettitte, Cone, Mariano Rivera, Jeff Nelson and Graeme Lloyd, who combined for a 0.33 ERA—allowing only one run in three games. Texas starters—Todd Stottlemyre, Rick Helling, Aaron Sele—all pitched well, but got little run support. Kenny Lofton, Manny Ramirez, Jim Thome and Justice provided the bulk of Cleveland's offense and the Indians got good pitching from starters Charles Nagy and Bartolo Colon and three saves from Mike Jackson. First baseman Mo Vaughn (2 homers, 7 RBIs) and shortstop Nomar Garciaparra (3, 11) were prolific offensively for the losing Red Sox.

Linescores

New York vs. Texas

Game 1—September 29, at New York
Texas..............0 0 0 0 0 0 0 0 0—0 5 0
New York........0 2 0 0 0 0 0 0 x—2 6 0
Stottlemyre and Rodriguez; Wells, Rivera (9) and Posada. W—Wells. L—Stottlemyre. S—Rivera.

Game 2—September 30, at New York
Texas..............0 0 0 0 1 0 0 0 0—1 5 0
New York........0 1 0 2 0 0 0 0 x—3 8 0
Helling, Crabtree (7) and Rodriguez; Pettitte, Nelson (8), Rivera (8) and Girardi. W—Pettitte. L—Helling. S—Rivera. HR—Spencer, Brosius (N.Y.).

Game 3—October 2, at Texas
New York........0 0 0 0 0 4 0 0 0—4 9 1
Texas..............0 0 0 0 0 0 0 0 0—0 3 1
Cone, Lloyd (6), Nelson (7), Rivera (9) and Girardi; Sele, Crabtree (7), Wetteland (9) and Rodriguez. W—Cone. L—Sele. HR—O'Neill, Spencer (N.Y.).

Boston vs. Cleveland

Game 1—September 29, at Cleveland
Boston........3 0 0 0 3 2 0 3 0—11 12 0
Cleveland....0 0 0 0 0 2 1 0 0— 3 7 0
Martinez, Corsi (8) and Hatteberg; Wright, Jones (5), Reed (8), Poole (8), Shuey (8), Assenmacher (9) and Alomar. W—Martinez. L—Wright. HR—Vaughn 2, Garciaparra (Bos.); Lofton, Thome (Cle.).

Game 2—September 30, at Cleveland
Boston..........2 0 1 0 0 2 0 0 0—5 10 0
Cleveland......1 5 1 0 0 1 0 1 x—9 9 1
Wakefield, Wasdin (2), Lowe (4), Swindell (6), Gordon (8) and Varitek; Gooden, Burba (1), Shuey (6), Assenmacher (8), Jackson (8) and Alomar. W—Burba. L—Wakefield. S—Jackson. HR—Justice (Cle.).

Game 3—October 2, at Boston
Cleveland........0 0 0 0 1 1 1 0 1—4 5 0
Boston............0 0 0 1 0 0 0 0 2—3 6 0
Nagy, Jackson (9) and Alomar; Saberhagen, Corsi (8), Eckersley (9) and Hatteberg. W—Nagy. L—Saberhagen. S—Jackson. HR—Thome, Lofton, M. Ramirez 2 (Cle.); Garciaparra (Bos.).

Game 4—October 3, at Boston
Cleveland........0 0 0 0 0 0 0 2 0—2 5 0
Boston............0 0 0 1 0 0 0 0 0—1 6 0
Colon, Poole (6), Reed (7), Assenmacher (8), Shuey (8), Jackson (9) and Alomar; Schourek, Lowe (6), Gordon (8) and Hatteberg. W—Reed. L—Gordon. S—Jackson. HR—Garciaparra (Bos.).

N.L. DIVISION SERIES

■ **Winners:** The Atlanta Braves earned their seventh straight N.L. Championship Series berth by sweeping past the wild-card Chicago Cubs, and the San Diego Padres reached the NLCS for the first time since 1984 by throttling the Houston Astros and their N.L.-leading offense. Braves pitchers simply were too much for the overmatched Cubs, who scored only four runs in the three games, and the Padres followed that lead by holding the high-powered Astros to a .182 average in a surprising four-game victory.
■ **Turning points:** The Braves took control of the series in Game 2 when they tied the game at 1-1 in the bottom of the ninth and then won in the 10th on a Chipper Jones single down the left field line. The Padres served notice to the Astros in Game 1 when starter Kevin Brown struck out 16 batters and allowed two hits over eight innings while outdueling Houston ace Randy Johnson, 2-1.
■ **Memorable moments:** The ninth inning of Game 2, when Atlanta catcher Javy Lopez connected off Chicago pitcher Kevin Tapani for a one-out home run that tied the game 1-1. The Padres got a dramatic Game 2-tying home run from Jim Leyritz off Houston closer Billy Wagner in the ninth inning, but the Astros rebounded in the bottom of the ninth to post a 5-4 victory—their only win of the series.
■ **Memorable performances:** Atlanta catchers Lopez and Eddie Perez combined for eight RBIs and Braves pitchers, led by starters John Smoltz, Tom Glavine and Greg Maddux, posted a 1.29 ERA. Tapani and rookie Kerry Wood had outstanding starting efforts for the Cubs, but there was too little offensive support. San Diego's biggest offensive gun was Leyritz, who came off the bench to hit three home runs, while pitchers Brown and Sterling Hitchcock led a staff that compiled a 1.78 ERA. Johnson allowed only three earned runs in two starts covering 14 innings for the Astros, but all he had to show for his efforts were two losses.

Linescores

Chicago vs. Atlanta

Game 1—September 30, at Atlanta
Chicago..........0 0 0 0 0 0 0 1 0—1 5 1
Atlanta ....0 2 0 0 0 1 4 0 x—7 8 0
Clark, Heredia (7), Karchner (7), Morgan (8) and Houston; Smoltz, Rocker (8), Ligtenberg (9) and Lopez. W—Smoltz. L—Clark. HR—Houston (Chi.); Tucker, Klesko (Atl.).

Game 2—October 1, at Atlanta
Chicago....0 0 0 0 0 1 0 0 0 0—1 4 1
Atlanta ....0 0 0 0 0 0 0 0 1 1—2 6 0
Tapani, Mulholland (10) and Servais, Houston; Glavine, Rocker (8), Seanez (9), O. Perez (10) and Lopez. W—O. Perez. L—Mulholland. HR—Lopez (Atl.).

Game 3—October 3, at Chicago
Atlanta............0 0 1 0 0 0 0 5 0—6 9 0
Chicago..........0 0 0 0 0 0 0 2 0—2 8 2
Maddux, Ligtenberg (8) and E. Perez; Wood, Mulholland (6), Beck (8), Morgan (9) and Houston, Martinez. W—Maddux. L—Wood. HR—E. Perez (Atl.).

Houston vs. San Diego

Game 1—September 29, at Houston
San Diego ......0 0 0 0 0 1 0 1 0—2 9 1
Houston ....0 0 0 0 0 0 0 0 1—1 4 0
Brown, Hoffman (9) and Hernandez; Johnson, Powell (9), Henry (9) and Ausmus. W—Brown. L—Johnson. S—Hoffman. HR—Vaughn (S.D.).

Game 2—October 1, at Houston
San Diego ....0 0 0 0 0 2 0 0 2—4 8 1
Houston ......1 0 2 0 0 0 0 1 1—5 11 1
Ashby, Hamilton (5), Wall (8), Miceli (9), Hoffman (9) and Hernandez, Myers; Reynolds, Powell (8), Wagner (9) and Eusebio, Ausmus. W—Wagner. L—Miceli. HR—Leyritz (S.D.); Bell (Hou.).

Game 3—October 3, at San Diego
Houston ....0 0 0 0 0 0 1 0 0—1 4 0
San Diego ......0 0 0 0 0 1 1 0 x—2 3 0
Hampton, Elarton (7) and Ausmus; Brown, Miceli (7), Hoffman (9) and Hernandez. W—Miceli. L—Elarton. S—Hoffman. HR—Leyritz (S.D.).

Game 4—October 4, at San Diego
Houston ....0 0 0 1 0 0 0 0 0—1 3 1
San Diego ......0 1 0 0 0 1 0 4 x—6 7 1
Johnson, Miller (7), Henry (7), Powell (8) and Ausmus; Hitchcock, Hamilton (7), Miceli (7), Hoffman (9) and Leyritz, Hernandez. W—Hitchcock. L—Johnson. HR—Leyritz, Joyner (S.D.).

ALCS

■ **Winner:** The New York Yankees raised their incredible 1998 season record to 121-50 with a surprisingly difficult six-game victory over Cleveland. After watching the Indians jump to a two-games-to-one advantage, the Yankees won three straight times and advanced to the franchise's record 35th World Series.
■ **Turning point:** Down two-games-to-one and in danger of watching an incredible season unravel, the Yankees tied the series at Cleveland's Jacobs Field behind the four-hit pitching of Orlando Hernandez, Mike Stanton and Mariano Rivera, who combined for a 4-0 shutout of the powerful Indians. Paul O'Neill provided all the offense the trio would need with a solo home run in the first inning.
■ **Memorable moment:** The 12th inning of Game 2 at New York, when a sacrifice bunt by Cleveland's Travis Fryman transformed a 1-1 tie into a 4-1 Indians victory. Yankees first baseman Tino Martinez fielded the bunt and fired to second baseman Chuck Knoblauch covering first. But the ball hit Fryman, who appeared to be running illegally inside the line, and caromed about 20 feet away. Instead of chasing the ball, Knoblauch argued the noncall of umpire Ted Hendry as pinch runner Enrique Wilson circled the bases to score the go-ahead run. Kenny Lofton's two-run single finished the Yankees in an ugly and controversial end to what had been a well-played game.
■ **Top guns:** Bernie Williams (.381, 5 RBIs), Scott Brosius (.300, 6 RBIs), Hernandez (1-0, 0.00 ERA), David Wells (2-0, 2.87), Rivera (4 games, 0.00), Yankees; Omar Vizquel (.440), Jim Thome (.304, 4 HRs, 8 RBIs), Manny Ramirez (.333, 2 HRs, 4 RBIs), Bartolo Colon (1-0, 1.00 ERA), Paul Shuey (5 games, 0.00), Indians.
■ **MVP:** Wells.

Linescores

Game 1—October 6, a New York
Cleveland......0 0 0 0 0 0 0 0 2—2 5 0
New York......5 0 0 0 0 1 1 0 x—7 11 0
Wright, Ogea (1), Poole (7), Reed (7), Shuey (8) and Alomar, Diaz; Wells, Nelson (9) and Posada. W—Wells. L—Wright. HR—Ramirez (Cle.); Posada (N.Y.).

Game 2—October 7, at New York
Cleveland0 0 0 1 0 0 0 0 0 0 0 3—4 7 1
New York0 0 0 0 0 0 1 0 0 0 0 0—1 7 1
Nagy, Reed (7), Poole (8), Shuey (8), Assenmacher (10), Burba (11), Jackson (12) and Alomar; Cone, Rivera (9), Stanton (11), Nelson (11), Lloyd (12) and Girardi. W—Burba. L—Nelson. S—Jackson. HR—Justice (Cle.).

Game 3—October 9, at Cleveland
New York.......1 0 0 0 0 0 0 0 0—1 4 0
Cleveland.......0 2 0 0 4 0 0 0 x—6 12 0
Pettitte, Mendoza (5), Stanton (7) and Girardi, Posada; Colon and Alomar. W—Colon. L—Pettitte. HR—Thome 2, Ramirez, Whiten (Cle.).

Game 4—October 10, at Cleveland
New York........1 0 0 2 0 0 0 0 1—4 4 0
Cleveland........0 0 0 0 0 0 0 0 0—0 4 3
Hernandez, Stanton (8), Rivera (9) and Posada; Gooden, Poole (5), Burba (6), Shuey (9) and Alomar, Diaz. W—Hernandez. L—Gooden. HR—O'Neill (N.Y.).

Game 5—October 11, at Cleveland
New York........3 1 0 1 0 0 0 0 0—5 6 0
Cleveland........2 0 0 0 0 1 0 0 0—3 8 0
Wells, Nelson (8), Rivera (8) and Posada; Ogea, Wright (2), Reed (8), Assenmacher (8), Shuey (9) and Diaz. W—Wells. L—Ogea. S—Rivera. HR—Lofton, Thome (Cle.); Davis (N.Y.).

Game 6—October 13, at New York
Cleveland......0 0 0 0 5 0 0 0 0—5 8 3
New York......2 1 3 0 0 3 0 0 x—9 11 1
Nagy, Burba (4), Poole (6), Shuey (6), Assenmacher (8) and Alomar, Diaz; Cone, Mendoza (6), Rivera (9) and Girardi. W—Cone. L—Nagy. HR—Brosius (N.Y.); Thome (Cle.).

NLCS

■ **Winner:** The San Diego Padres, the dark horse in National League playoffs that featured high-powered teams from Houston and Atlanta, claimed the second pennant of their 30-year existence with a six-game victory over the N.L. East Division-champion Braves, who had won a club-record 106 games during the regular season. The Padres, 98-game winners, beat the Braves at their own game—pitching and defense—and gave them the distinction of becoming the winningest team not to reach the World Series.
■ **Turning point:** Game 3, when the Braves loaded the bases three times—twice with less than two out—and failed to score. Starting pitcher Sterling Hitchcock worked out of the first jam, Dan Miceli came out of the bullpen in the sixth to strike out consecutive pinch hitters and Trevor Hoffman came on in the eighth to strike out catcher Javy Lopez, who represented the potential winning run. The Padres' 4-1 win over Greg Maddux gave them a shocking three-games-to-none advantage over an experienced Braves team appearing in its seventh straight NLCS.
■ **Memorable moment:** Michael Tucker's three-run, eighth-inning homer off Padres ace Kevin Brown in Game 5, a blow that temporarily rescued the Braves from elimination and gave them hope of becoming the first baseball team to come back and win a post-season series after losing the first three games. Brown, who was making a surprise relief appearance after throwing a three-hit shutout in Game 2, escaped a seventh-inning jam but coughed up a 4-2 San Diego lead in the eighth when he walked Ryan Klesko, gave up an infield single to Lopez and then surrendered the game-turning homer to Tucker.
■ **Top guns:** Ozzie Guillen (.417), Tucker (.385, 1 HR, 5 RBIs), John Rocker (6 games, 1-0, 0.00 ERA), Braves; John Vander Wal (.429), Steve Finley (.333), Ken Caminiti (2 HRs, 4 RBIs), Brown (1-1, 2.61 ERA), Hitchcock (2-0, 0-90), Padres.
■ **MVP:** Hitchcock.

Game 1—October 7, at Atlanta
San Diego....0 0 0 0 1 0 0 1 0 1—3 7 0
Atlanta ....0 0 1 0 0 0 0 0 1 0—2 8 3
Ashby, R. Myers (8), Miceli (8), Hoffman (8), Wall (10) and Hernandez; Smoltz, Rocker (8), Martinez (8), Ligtenberg (9) and Lopez, E. Perez. W—Hoffman. L—Ligtenberg. S—Wall. HR—A. Jones (Atl.); Caminiti (S.D.).

Game 2—October 8, at Atlanta
San Diego ....0 0 0 0 0 1 0 0 2—3 11 0
Atlanta..........0 0 0 0 0 0 0 0 0—0 3 1
Brown and Hernandez; Glavine, Rocker (7), Seanez (8), O. Perez (9), Ligtenberg (9) and Lopez. W—Brown. L—Glavine.

Game 3—October 10, at San Diego
Atlanta ....0 0 1 0 0 0 0 0 0—1 8 2
San Diego ......0 0 0 0 2 0 0 2 x—4 7 0
Maddux, Martinez (6), Rocker (7), Seanez (8) and E. Perez, Lopez; Hitchcock, Wall (6), Miceli (8) R. Myers (8), Hoffman (8) and Leyritz, Hernandez. W—Hitchcock. L—Maddux. S—Hoffman.

Game 4—October 11, at San Diego
Atlanta..........0 0 0 1 0 1 6 0 0—8 12 0
San Diego ....0 0 2 0 0 1 0 0 0—3 8 0
Neagle, Martinez (6), Rocker (7), O. Perez (8), Seanez (8), Ligtenberg (9) and Lopez; Hamilton, R. Myers (7), Miceli (7), Boehringer (8), Langston (9) and Hernandez. W—Martinez. L—Hamilton. HR—Leyritz (S.D.); Lopez, Galarraga (Atl.).

Game 5—October 12, at San Diego
Atlanta..........0 0 0 1 0 1 0 5 0—7 14 1
San Diego ....2 0 0 0 0 2 0 0 2—6 10 1
Smoltz, Rocker (7), Seanez (8), Ligtenberg (9), Maddux (9) and Lopez, E. Perez; Ashby, Langston (7), Brown (7), Wall (8), Boehringer (9), R. Myers (9) and Hernandez. W—Rocker. L—Brown. S—Maddux. HR—Caminiti, Vander Wal (S.D.); Tucker (Atl.).

Game 6—October 14, at Atlanta
San Diego ....0 0 0 0 0 5 0 0 0—5 10 0
Atlanta..........0 0 0 0 0 0 0 0 0—0 2 1
Hitchcock, Boehringer (6), Langston (7), Hamilton (7), Hoffman (9) and Leyritz, Hernandez; Glavine, Rocker (6), Martinez (6), Neagle (8) and Lopez. W—Hitchcock. L—Glavine.

WORLD SERIES

■ **Winner:** New York closed out its remarkable season with a four-game sweep of San Diego, giving the Yankees a shockingly efficient 125-50 final 1998 record, including regular season and playoffs. The World Series championship was New York's record 24th overall and second in three years. The sweep was the first in Series play since 1990.
■ **Turning point:** A second-inning Chili Davis smash in Game 1 that struck the left shin of Padres righthander Kevin Brown. San Diego's ace went on to pitch 61/3 innings before leaving with a sore leg and the Yankees exploded for seven runs in the seventh inning, turning a 5-2 deficit into a 9-5 advantage. New York's 9-6 win deflated the overmatched Padres.
■ **Memorable moment:** When Scott Brosius, the World Series MVP, hit a three-run, eighth-inning Game 3 home run off San Diego closer Trevor Hoffman, wiping away a 3-2 New York deficit and giving the Yankees a lead they never relinquished. It was Brosius' second homer of the game and he finished the 5-4 victory with four RBIs.
■ **Top guns:** Tony Gwynn (.500, 3 RBIs), Greg Vaughn (2 HR, 4 RBIs), Sterling Hitchcock (1.50 ERA), Padres; Ricky Ledee (.600, 4 RBIs), Brosius (.471, 2 HR, 6 RBIs), Tino Martinez (.385, 1 HR, 4 RBIs), Andy Pettitte (1-0, 0.00 ERA), Orlando Hernandez (1-0, 1.29 ERA), Mariano Rivera (3 games, 0.00 ERA, 3 saves), Yankees.
■ **MVP:** Brosius.

Game 1—October 17, at New York
San Diego ......0 0 2 0 3 0 0 1 0—6 8 1
New York........0 2 0 0 0 0 7 0 x—9 9 1
Brown, Wall (7), Langston (7), Boehringer (8), R. Myers (8) and C. Hernandez; Wells, Nelson (8), Rivera (8) and Posada. W—Wells. L—Wall. S—Rivera. HR—Vaughn 2, Gwynn (S.D.); Knoblauch, Martinez (N.Y.).

Game 2—October 18, at New York
San Diego ....0 0 0 0 1 0 0 2 0—3 10 1
New York......3 3 1 0 2 0 0 0 x—9 16 0
Ashby, Boehringer (3), Wall (5), Miceli (8) and G. Myers; O. Hernandez, Stanton (8), Nelson (8) and Posada. W—O. Hernandez. L—Ashby. HR—Williams, Posada (N.Y.).

Game 3—October 20, at San Diego
New York........0 0 0 0 0 0 2 3 0—5 9 1
San Diego ......0 0 0 0 0 3 0 1 0—4 7 1
Cone, Lloyd (7), Mendoza (7), Rivera (8) and Girardi; Hitchcock, Hamilton (7), R. Myers (8), Hoffman (8) and Leyritz, C. Hernandez. W—Mendoza. L—Hoffman. S—Rivera. HR—Brosius 2 (N.Y.).

Game 4—October 21, at San Diego
New York........0 0 0 0 0 1 0 2 0—3 9 0
San Diego ......0 0 0 0 0 0 0 0 0—0 7 0
Pettitte, Nelson (8), Rivera (8) and Girardi; Brown, Miceli (9), R. Myers (9) and C. Hernandez. W—Pettitte. L—Brown. S—Rivera.

Roger Clemens brought home the Cy Young Award for a record fifth time.

FINAL STANDINGS

American League

East Division

Team	N.Y.	Bos	Tor.	Bal.	T.B.	Cle.	Chi.	Det.	K.C.	Min.	Tex.	Oak.	Sea.	Ana.	Atl.	N.Y.	Phi.	Mon.	Fla.	W	L	Pct.	GB
New York	—	4	10	9	8	7	7	7	4	6	8	6	9	4	1	3	1	2	2	98	64	.605	—
Boston	8	—	9	7	4	8	7	7	8	6	4	4	7	9	2	1	1	0	2	94	68	.580	4
Toronto	2	3	—	11	8	7	4	10	7	6	4	2	2	9	3	0	1	4	1	84	78	.519	14
Baltimore	4	5	1	—	5	1	7	5	6	8	6	5	5	9	3	1	3	3	1	78	84	.481	20
Tampa Bay	4	9	5	7	—	4	4	5	8	5	4	1	4	5	0	1	1	1	1	69	93	.426	29

Central Division

Team	Cle.	Chi.	Det.	K.C.	Min.	N.Y.	Bos.	Tor.	Bal.	T.B.	Tex.	Oak.	Sea.	Ana.	Hou.	Cin.	Pit.	St.L.	Mil.	Chi.	W	L	Pct.	GB
Cleveland	—	9	8	7	9	3	4	5	9	5	3	10	7	9	1	4	1	—	1	2	97	65	.599	—
Chicago	3	—	7	6	8	5	5	6	3	6	5	3	4	5	1	—	2	1	1	4	75	86	.466	21.5
Detroit	5	5	—	7	6	5	5	2	5	4	5	4	3	5	0	2	2	3	1	—	69	92	.429	27.5
Kansas City	5	6	4	—	5	5	2	3	4	2	4	6	7	5	0	0	1	2	1	2	64	97	.398	32.5
Minnesota	3	3	6	8	—	4	4	4	1	5	0	7	4	4	1	2	2	2	2	1	63	97	.394	33

West Division

Team	Tex.	Oak.	Sea.	Ana.	N.Y.	Bos.	Tor.	Bal.	T.B.	Cle.	Chi.	Det.	K.C.	Min.	Ari.	S.F.	L.A.	S.D.	Col.	W	L	PCT	GB
Texas	—	7	8	6	4	5	6	6	8	7	5	5	6	12	3	3	2	1	1	95	67	.586	—
Oakland	5	—	6	4	4	6	8	7	9	2	7	6	6	5	2	3	3	1	3	87	75	.537	8
Seattle	5	6	—	6	1	3	7	5	8	3	8	7	5	8	2	1	0	2	2	79	83	.488	16
Anaheim	6	8	6	—	6	1	3	3	7	1	5	5	7	6	1	1	2	0	2	70	92	.432	25

National League

East Division

Team	Atl.	N.Y.	Phi.	Mon.	Fla.	Hou.	Cin.	Pit.	St.L.	Mil.	Chi.	Ari.	S.F.	L.A.	S.D.	Col.	N.Y.	Bos.	Tor.	Bal.	T.B.	W	L	Pct.	GB
Atlanta	—	9	8	9	9	6	8	6	8	5	2	5	4	5	5	5	2	4	0	0	3	103	59	.636	—
New York	3	—	6	8	10	5	5	7	5	5	6	2	7	4	7	5	3	2	3	2	2	97	66	.595	6.5
Philadelphia	5	6	—	6	11	1	3	3	4	4	7	1	2	3	6	4	2	2	2	3	2	77	85	.475	26
Montreal	4	5	6	—	4	2	3	3	5	4	5	3	4	4	5	3	1	3	2	0	2	68	94	.420	35
Florida	4	3	2	8	—	2	1	3	3	5	3	1	4	7	3	4	1	1	2	2	5	64	98	.395	39

Central Division

Team	Hou.	Cin.	Pit.	St.L.	Mil.	Chi.	Atl.	N.Y.	Phi.	Mon.	Fla.	Ari.	S.F.	L.A.	S.D.	Col.	Cle.	Chi.	Det.	K.C.	Min.	W	L	Pct.	GB
Houston	—	4	5	5	8	9	1	4	6	7	7	4	5	6	8	6	2	2	3	3	2	97	65	.599	—
Cincinnati	9	—	7	8	6	8	1	5	6	4	6	8	4	4	6	7	2	—	1	3	1	96	67	.589	1.5
Pittsburgh	7	6	—	7	4	6	3	2	4	6	4	2	4	6	3	7	2	1	1	2	1	78	83	.484	18.5
St. Louis	7	4	5	—	6	5	1	2	5	4	4	4	3	6	7	5	—	2	3	1	1	75	86	.466	21.5
Milwaukee	5	6	8	7	—	6	2	2	5	5	4	4	4	2	3	3	2	2	2	2	0	74	87	.460	22.5
Chicago	3	5	7	7	6	—	5	3	2	2	6	2	1	2	6	4	1	2	—	1	2	67	95	.414	30

West Division

Team	Ari.	S.F.	L.A.	S.D.	Col.	Atl.	N.Y.	Phi.	Mon.	Fla.	Hou.	Cin.	Pit.	St.L.	Mil.	Chi.	Tex.	Oak.	Sea.	Ana.	W	L	Pct.	GB
Arizona	—	9	7	11	6	4	7	8	6	8	5	1	5	4	5	7	3	1	1	2	100	62	.617	—
San Fran.	3	—	5	7	9	5	2	6	5	5	4	5	5	6	5	7	0	3	2	2	86	76	.531	14
Los Angeles	6	8	—	3	5	4	4	6	5	2	3	3	3	3	7	7	1	0	3	4	77	85	.475	23
San Diego	2	5	9	—	9	4	2	3	3	6	1	3	6	2	5	3	2	2	4	3	74	88	.457	26
Colorado	7	4	8	4	—	4	4	5	6	5	2	2	2	4	6	5	2	0	1	1	72	90	.444	28

SIGNIFICANT EVENTS

■ **March 28:** As part of a U.S. initiative to build ties with Cuba, the Baltimore Orioles played the first game of a two-game exhibition series against the Cuban National Team. The Orioles won the game, played in Havana, 3-2 in 11 innings. The second game was played on May 3 in Baltimore, and this time the Cubans won, 12-6.

■ **April 4:** The San Diego Padres opened their "home" season with a game in Monterrey, Mexico, losing before a capaticy crowd of 27,104 to the Colorado Rockies, 8-2.

■ **July 14:** A 567-foot crane lifting a 400-ton section of Miller Park, the Milwaukee Brewers' new home under construction, collapsed, killing three in the accident. The damage was estimated at $50 to $75 million and postponed the anticipated opening of the park until the 2001 season.

■ **July 14:** Richie Phillips, general counsel of the Major League Umpires Association, announced a mass resignation of umpires, effective September 2. This strategy, designed to force management to the bargaining table before December 31, the expiration date of the contract, backfired. Major League Baseball accepted the resignations of 22 umpires, and the union split in two. On November 30, dissidents won an NLRB election, decertifying the MLUA.

■ **July 15:** The Mariners opened their new park, Safeco Field, with a 3-2 loss to the San Diego Padres. The Mariners had played their final game at the Kingdome on June 27, defeating Texas, 5-2.

■ **September 27:** The Detroit Tigers played their final game at Tiger Stadium, beating Kansas City, 8-2.

■ **September 30:** The San Francisco Giants played their final game at 3Com Park (formerly Candlestick Park), losing a 9-4 contest to the Los Angeles Dodgers.

■ **October 9:** The Astros played their final game at the Houston Astrodome—baseball's first domed stadium—losing the fourth and final game of the N.L. Division Series to the Atlanta Braves, 7-5.

MEMORABLE MOMENTS

■ **April 13:** Fernando Tatis of the St. Louis Cardinals became the first player in major league history to hit two grand slams in the same inning. Both came off Los Angeles Dodgers starter Chan Ho Park during an 11-run third inning in a 12-5 victory over the Dodgers.

■ **May 3:** Creighton Gubanich of the Boston Red Sox became the fourth player to hit a grand slam for his first big-league hit in a game at Oakland.

■ **May 20:** Robin Ventura of the New York Mets became the first player in major league history to belt grand slams in both games of a doubleheader against Milwaukee at Shea Stadium.

■ **July 18:** David Cone of the New York Yankees pitched the second perfect game at Yankee Stadium in two years and only the 14th perfecto of the modern era, when he retired all 27 Montreal Expos batters in a 6-0 victory.

■ **August 5:** Mark McGwire of St. Louis became the 17th member of the 500-home run club, and reached the milestone in his 5,487th career at-bat—the fewest at-bats ever needed to reach 500 homers. McGwire ended the season in 10th place on the all-time list with 522.

■ **August 6:** San Diego's Tony Gwynn singled off the Expos' Dan Smith at Montreal for his 3,000th major league hit.

■ **August 7:** Wade Boggs of the Devil Rays homered off Chris Haney of the Cleveland Indians for his 3,000th big-league hit.

■ **September 18:** Sammy Sosa became the first player to hit 60 homers twice when he hit his 60th at Wrigley Field against Milwaukee. Mark McGwire of the Cardinals joined Sosa eight days later, and hit five more thereafter to edge Sosa for the home run crown, 65-63.

ALL-STAR GAME

■ **Winner:** The A.L. won the contest with pitching and timely hitting, extending its streak to four straight victories over the N.L. American League starting pitcher Pedro Martinez struck out the first four batters and five of the six he retired.

■ **Key inning:** The first, when Cleveland players provided most of the excitement. Kenny Lofton singled and two outs later stole second. Manny Ramirez walked and Jim Thome singled Lofton home with the game's first run. Baltimore's Cal Ripken followed with a single to drive in Ramirez.

■ **Memorable moment:** Mike Mussina struck out Sammy Sosa and Mark McGwire with runners on second and third to end the fifth inning. The strikeouts shut down the N.L.'s last big scoring threat of the game.

■ **Top guns:** Martinez (Red Sox), Lofton (Indians), Thome (Indians), Ripken (Orioles), Rafael Palmeiro (Rangers), A.L.; Jeromy Burnitz (Brewers), Barry Larkin (Reds), N.L.

■ **MVP:** Martinez.

Linescore

July 13 at Boston's Fenway Park

N.L. ....0 0 1 0 0 0 0 0 0—1 7 1
A.L. ....2 0 0 2 0 0 0 0 x—4 6 2

Schilling (Phillies), Johnson (Diamondbacks) 3, Bottenfield (Cardinals) 4, Lima (Astros) 5, Millwood (Braves) 6, Ashby (Padres) 7, Hampton (Astros) 7, Hoffman (Padres) 8, Wagner (Astros) 8 and Piazza (Mets), Lieberthal (Phillies), Nilsson (Brewers); Martinez (Red Sox), Cone (Yankees) 3, Mussina (Orioles) 5, Rosado (Royals) 6, Zimmerman (Rangers) 7, Hernandez (Devil Rays) 8, Wetteland (Rangers) 9 and Rodriguez (Rangers), Ausmus (Tigers). W—Martinez. L—Schilling. S—Wetteland.

A.L. DIVISION SERIES

■ **Winners:** For the second straight year the New York Yankees swept the Texas Rangers and held the Rangers to only one run in the series. The Boston Red Sox came back from a two-game deficit to defeat the Cleveland Indians in a high-scoring five-game series.

■ **Turning points:** The Yankees' Bernie Williams lined a two-run double in the fifth inning of the opener and finished the game with six RBIs in an 8-0 victory. Down 1-0 with runners on second and third and nobody out in the fifth inning of Game 2, Andy Pettitte settled down by striking out Mark McLemore, getting Royce Clayton to ground out and striking out Rusty Greer to end the inning. The Yankees scored three runs over the next four innings to win the game. A pair of 37-year-olds—pitcher Roger Clemens and slugger Darryl Strawberry— were the heroes of Game 3. Clemens pitched seven shutout innings after Strawberry gave the Yankees all their runs with a three-run homer in the first inning.

■ **Memorable moments:** Troy O'Leary, who had hit a grand slam earlier in the game, hit a two-run homer in the seventh inning to break an 8-8 tie in the deciding fifth game. O'Leary collected seven RBIs in the game, matching John Valentin's total a night earlier when the Red Sox tied the series with a 23-7 trouncing of the Indians. Valentin also contributed heavily in the Game 3 victory with a two-run double, and Brian Daubach chipped in a three-run homer in the 9-3 victory.

■ **Memorable performances:** Orlando Hernandez allowed only two hits in his series-opening victory. Clemens was unscored upon in his seven-inning Game 3 stint, and Pettitte allowed only a home run to Juan Gonzalez in his Game 2 victory. Derek Jeter led all batters with five hits, three runs scored and a .455 average during the series. Williams finished with a .364 average, four hits and six RBIs. The Red Sox had many offensive stars in their series. Mike Stanley led all batters with 10 hits, and batted .500. Nomar Garciaparra batted .417 with six runs, two doubles and two homers. Valentin hit three homers and collected 12 RBIs, and Jose Offerman added seven hits, six RBIs and batted .389. Much of the Red Sox's offense was provided in Game 4, when they exploded for 24 hits and slugged four home runs in a 23-7 thrashing of Cleveland. While the Indians were outhit, .318 to .233, they had some offensive stars, led by Jim Thome (four homers, seven runs, .353 average) and Roberto Alomar (four doubles, seven hits, .368 average).

LEADERS

American League
BA: Nomar Garciaparra, Bos., .357.
Runs: Roberto Alomar, Cle., 138.
Hits: Derek Jeter, N.Y., 219.
TB: Shawn Green, Tor., 361.
HR: Ken Griffey Jr., Sea., 48.
RBI: Manny Ramirez, Cle., 165.
SB: Brian L. Hunter, Det.-Sea., 44.
Wins: Pedro Martinez, Bos., 23.
ERA: Pedro Martinez, Bos., 2.07.
CG: David Wells, Tor., 7.
IP: David Wells, Tor., 231.2.
SO: Pedro Martinez, Bos., 313.
Sv.: Mariano Rivera, N.Y., 45.

National League
BA: Larry Walker, Col., .379.
Runs: Jeff Bagwell, Hou., 143.
Hits: Luis Gonzalez, Ari., 206.
TB: Sammy Sosa, Chi., 397.
HR: Mark McGwire, St.L., 65.
RBI: Mark McGwire, St.L., 147.
SB: Tony Womack, Ari., 72.
Wins: Mike Hampton, Hou., 22.
ERA: Randy Johnson, Ari., 2.48.
CG: Randy Johnson, Ari., 12.
IP: Randy Johnson, Ari., 271.2.
SO: Randy Johnson, Ari., 364.
Sv.: Ugueth Urbina, Mon., 41.

A.L. 20-game winner
Pedro Martinez, Bos., 23

N.L. 20-game winners
Mike Hampton, Hou., 22
Jose Lima, Hou., 21

A.L. 100 RBIs
Manny Ramirez, Cle., 165
Rafael Palmeiro, Tex., 148
Ken Griffey Jr., Sea., 134
Carlos Delgado, Tor., 134
Juan Gonzalez, Tex., 128
Jason Giambi, Oak., 123
Shawn Green, Tor., 123
Roberto Alomar, Cle., 120
Jermaine Dye, K.C., 119
Albert Belle, Bal., 117
Magglio Ordonez, Chi., 117
Richie Sexson, Cle., 116
Bernie Williams, N.Y., 115
Ivan Rodriguez, Tex., 113
John Jaha, Oak., 111
Alex Rodriguez, Sea., 111
Paul O'Neill, N.Y., 110
Carlos Beltran, K.C., 108
Jim Thome, Cle., 108
Mo Vaughn, Ana., 108
B.J. Surhoff, Bal., 107
Tino Martinez, N.Y., 105
Nomar Garciaparra, Bos., 104
Fred McGriff, T.B., 104
Harold Baines, Bal.-Cle., 103
Troy O'Leary, Bos., 103
Derek Jeter, N.Y., 102
Matt Stairs, Oak., 102
Mike Sweeney, K.C., 102
Rusty Greer, Tex., 101
Dean Palmer, Det., 100

N.L. 100 RBIs
Mark McGwire, St.L., 147
Matt Williams, Ari., 142
Sammy Sosa, Chi., 141
Dante Bichette, Col, 133
Vladimir Guerrero, Mon., 131
Jeff Bagwell, Hou., 126
Mike Piazza, N.Y., 124
Robin Ventura, N.Y., 120
Greg Vaughn, Cin., 118
Brian Giles, Pit., 115
Brian Jordan, Atl., 115
Larry Walker, Col., 115
Todd Helton, Col., 113
Jay Bell, Ari., 112
Eric Karros, L.A., 112
Luis Gonzalez, Ari., 111
Chipper Jones, Atl., 110
Edgardo Alfonzo, N.Y., 108
Carl Everett, Hou., 108
Fernando Tatis, St.L., 107
Kevin Young, Pit., 106
Jeromy Burnitz, Mil., 103
Steve Finley, Ari., 103
Rico Brogna, Phi., 102
Vinny Castilla, Col., 102
Jeff Kent, S.F., 101
Gary Sheffield, L.A., 101

N.L./A.L. 100 RBIs
Tony Batista, Ari.-Tor., 100

A.L. 40 homers
Ken Griffey Jr., Sea., 48
Rafael Palmeiro, Tex., 47
Carlos Delgado, Tor., 44
Manny Ramirez, Cle., 44
Shawn Green, Tor., 42
Alex Rodriguez, Sea., 42

N.L. 40 homers
Mark McGwire, St.L., 65
Sammy Sosa, Chi., 63
Chipper Jones, Atl., 45
Greg Vaughn, Cin., 45
Jeff Bagwell, Hou., 42
Vladimir Guerrero, Mon., 42
Mike Piazza, N.Y., 40

Most Valuable Player
A.L.: Ivan Rodriguez, C, Tex.
N.L.: Chipper Jones, 3B, Atl.

Cy Young Award
A.L.: Pedro Martinez, Bos.
N.L.: Randy Johnson, Ari.

Rookie of the Year
A.L.: Carlos Beltran, OF, K.C.
N.L.: Scott Williamson, P, Cin.

Manager of the Year
A.L.: Jimy Williams, Bos.
N.L.: Jack McKeon, Cin.

Hall of Fame additions
George Brett, 3B, 1973-93
Orlando Cepeda, OF-1B, 1958-74
Nestor Chylak, umpire
Nolan Ryan, P, 1966-93
Frank Selee, manager
Smokey Joe Williams, P, Negro Leagues
Robin Yount, SS-OF, 1974-93

Linescores

New York vs. Texas

Game 1—October 5, at New York
Texas............0 0 0 0 0 0 0 0 0—0 2 1
New York......0 1 0 0 2 4 0 1 x—8 10 0
Sele, Crabtree (6), Venafro (6), Patterson (7), Fassero (8) and Rodriguez; Hernandez, Nelson (9) and Posada. W—Hernandez. L—Crabtree. HR—Williams (N.Y.).

Game 2—October 7, at New York
Texas..............0 0 0 1 0 0 0 0 0—1 7 0
New York........0 0 0 0 1 0 1 1 x—3 7 2
Helling, Crabtree (7), Venafro (8) and Rodriguez; Pettitte, Nelson (8), Rivera (9) and Girardi. W—Pettitte. L—Helling. S—Rivera. HR—Gonzalez (Tex.).

Game 3—October 9, at Texas
New York........3 0 0 0 0 0 0 0 0—3 6 0
Texas..............0 0 0 0 0 0 0 0 0—0 5 1
Clemens, Nelson (8), Rivera (8) and Girardi; Loaiza, Zimmerman (8), Wetteland (9) and Rodriguez. W—Clemens. L—Loaiza. S—Rivera. HR—Strawberry (N.Y.).

Boston vs. Cleveland

Game 1—October 6, at Cleveland
Boston............0 1 0 1 0 0 0 0 0—2 5 1
Cleveland........0 0 0 0 0 2 0 0 1—3 6 1
P. Martinez, Lowe (5), Cormier (9), Garces (9) and Varitek; Colon, Shuey (9) and S. Alomar. W—Shuey. L—Lowe. HR—Garciaparra (Bos.); Thome (Cle.).

Game 2—October 7, at Cleveland
Boston..........0 0 1 0 0 0 0 0 0— 1 6 0
Cleveland......0 0 6 5 0 0 0 0 x—11 8 0
Saberhagen, Wasdin (3), Wakefield (5), Gordon (7), Beck (8) and Varitek; Nagy, Karsay (8), Jackson (8) and S. Alomar. W—Nagy. L—Saberhagen. HR—Baines, Thome (Cle.).

Game 3—October 9, at Boston
Cleveland......0 0 0 1 0 1 1 0 0—3 9 1
Boston..........0 0 0 0 2 1 6 0 x—9 11 2
Burba, Wright (5), Rincon (7), DePaula (7), Reed (8) and S. Alomar; R. Martinez, Lowe (6), Beck (9) and Varitek. W—Lowe. L—Wright. HR—Valentin, Daubach (Bos.).

Game 4—October 10, at Boston
Cleveland....1 1 0 0 4 0 0 0 1— 7 8 0
Boston........2 5 3 5 3 0 3 2 x—23 24 0
Colon, Karsay (2), Reed (4), DePaula (5), Assenmacher (7), Shuey (8) and S. Alomar, Diaz; Mercker, Garces (2), Wakefield (5), Wasdin (5), Cormier (5), Gordon (9) and Varitek, Hatteberg. W—Garces. L—Colon. HR—Cordero (Cle.); Valentin 2, Offerman, Varitek (Bos.).

Game 5—October 11, at Cleveland
Boston........2 0 5 1 0 0 3 0 1—12 10 0
Cleveland....3 2 3 0 0 0 0 0 0— 8 7 1
Saberhagen, Lowe (2), P. Martinez (4) and Varitek; Nagy, DePaula (4), Shuey (7), Jackson (9) and S. Alomar. W—P. Martinez. L—Shuey. HR—O'Leary 2, Garciaparra (Bos.); Thome 2, Fryman (Cle.).

N.L. DIVISION SERIES

■ **Winners:** Following an opening game loss, the Atlanta Braves earned their eighth straight N.L. Championship Series berth by defeating the Houston Astros in three straight games. The wild-card New York Mets, playing in their first postseason action since 1988, beat the second-year expansion Arizona Diamondbacks in four games.
■ **Turning points:** Atlanta starter Kevin Milwood pitched a one-hitter in Game 2, allowing only a home run to Ken Caminiti. John Rocker escaped a 10th inning jam with the bases loaded and no outs in Game 3. Two innings later, Brian Jordan's two-run double drove home the winning runs. The Braves jumped out to a 7-0 lead and held on to a 7-5 victory in Game 4. The Mets took the first game of their series on a ninth-inning grand slam by Edgardo Alfonzo to win the game, 8-4. A two-run single by John Olerud in the sixth inning helped the Mets win Game 3, 9-2, and Todd Pratt's homer in the 10th inning of Game 4 clinched the series for New York. A costly error by Diamondbacks outfielder Tony Womack in the eighth allowed the Mets to tie the game.
■ **Memorable moments:** After the Astros came back from a 7-0 deficit in Game 4, they were down 7-5 with a runner on and nobody out in the ninth. Rocker struck out Jeff Bagwell and Carl Everett, then retired Ken Caminiti, a .471 hitter during the series, for the final out. Olerud's Game 1 homer off Randy Johnson was the first homer by a lefthander off Johnson since September 23, 1997. The two-run third-inning shot gave the Mets a 3-0 lead in the game.
■ **Memorable performances:** Olerud led all hitters with seven hits and a .438 average. In addition, he collected six RBIs. Alfonzo clubbed three homers and also had six RBIs for the Mets. Bret Boone had nine hits and a .474 average to lead the Braves. Jordan chipped in eight hits and seven RBIs while batting .471 for Atlanta. Millwood pitched 10 innings, allowing only one hit, one run, and struck out nine for the Braves.

Linescores

New York vs. Arizona

Game 1—October 5, at Arizona
New York......1 0 2 1 0 0 0 0 4—8 10 0
Arizona ...... 0 0 1 1 0 2 0 0 0—4 7 0
Yoshii, Cook (6), Wendell (8), Benitez (9) and Piazza; Johnson, Chouinard (9) and Stinnett. W—Wendell. L—Johnson. HR—Alfonzo 2, Olerud (N.Y.); Durazo, Gonzalez (Ari.).

Game 2—October 6, at Arizona
New York........0 0 1 0 0 0 0 0 0—1 5 0
Arizona .... 0 0 3 0 2 0 2 0 x—7 9 1
Rogers, Mahomes (5), Dotel (7), J. Franco (7) and Piazza; Stottlemyre, Olson (7), Swindell (8) and Stinnett. W—Stottlemyre. L—Rogers.

Game 3—October 8, at New York
Arizona ...... 0 0 0 0 2 0 0 0 0—2 5 3
New York......0 1 2 0 0 6 0 0 x—9 11 0
Daal, Holmes (5), Plesac (6), Chouinard (6), Swindell (8) and Stinnett; Reed, Wendell (7), J. Franco (8), Hershiser (9) and Pratt. W—Reed. L—Daal. HR—Ward (Ari.).

Game 4—October 9, at New York
Arizona .... 0 0 0 0 1 0 0 2 0 0—3 5 1
New York ..0 0 0 1 0 1 0 1 0 1—4 8 0
Anderson, Olson (8), Swindell (8), Mantei (8) and Stinnett; Leiter, Benitez (8), J. Franco (9) and Pratt. W—J. Franco. L—Mantei. HR—Colbrunn (Ari.); Alfonzo, Pratt (N.Y.).

Atlanta vs. Houston

Game 1—October 5, at Atlanta
Houston ......0 1 0 0 0 1 0 0 4—6 13 0
Atlanta..........0 0 0 0 1 0 0 0 0—1 7 0
Reynolds, Miller (7), Henry (7), Wagner (9) and Eusebio; Maddux, Remlinger (8) and Perez. W—Reynolds. L—Maddux. HR—Ward, Caminiti (Hou.).

Game 2—October 6, at Atlanta
Houston ....0 1 0 0 0 0 0 0 0—1 1 1
Atlanta ....1 0 0 0 0 1 3 0 x—5 11 1
Lima, Elarton (7), Powell (8) and Eusebio; Millwood and Perez. W—Millwood. L—Lima. HR—Caminiti (Hou.).

Game 3—October 8, at Houston
Atl. ....0 0 0 0 0 3 0 0 0 0 0 2—5 12 0
Hou. ..2 0 0 0 0 0 1 0 0 0 0 0—3 9 2
Glavine, Mulholland (7), Maddux (7), Remlinger (7), Springer (9), Rocker (10), Millwood (12) and Perez; Hampton, Cabrera (8), Henry (10), Powell (12) and Eusebio. W—Rocker. L—Powell. S—Millwood. HR—Jordan (Atl.).

Game 4—October 4, at San Diego
Atlanta ....1 0 1 0 0 5 0 0 0—7 15 1
Houston ....0 0 0 0 0 0 1 4 0—5 8 1
Smoltz, Mulholland (8), McGlinchy (8), Rocker (8) and Perez; Reynolds, Holt (6), Elarton (6), Miller (8), Powell (9) and Eusebio. W—Smoltz. L—Reynolds. S—Rocker. HR—Eusebio, Caminiti (Hou.).

ALCS

■ **Winner:** Despite being outhit, .293 to .239, the New York Yankees used timely hitting to defeat the Boston Red Sox in five games to advance to the franchise's record 36th World Series.
■ **Turning point:** Yankee center fielder Bernie Williams belted a home run in the bottom of the 10th inning to cap a 4-3 comeback win in the opening game. Down, 2-0 and then 3-2 early in the contest, the Yankees tied the score in the seventh when Derek Jeter singled home Scott Brosius.
■ **Memorable moment:** With his team trailing, 3-2 in the bottom of the eighth, Boston's Jose Offerman was declared out on a tag play that umpire Tim Tschida later admitted he called wrong. It was the second time in the series an umpire admitted making an incorrect call against the Red Sox. An inning later, the Red Sox allowed six runs in the top of the ninth and lost, 9-2. In that frame, Offerman made a bad throw on a double-play ball. The error kept the inning alive and Ricky Ledee followed with a grand slam.
■ **Top guns:** Derek Jeter (.350, 7 hits), Hernandez (1-0, 15 IP, 13 SO, 1.80 ERA), Chuck Knoblauch (.333, 6 hits), Scott Brosius (2 HRs), Yankees; Jose Offerman (.458, 11 hits), Nomar Garciaparra (.400, 8 hits, 2 HR, 5 RBIs), Troy O'Leary (.350, 7 hits, 3 doubles), John Valentin (.348, 8 hits, 5 RBIs), P. Martinez (1-0, 7 IP, 12 SO, 0.00 ERA), Red Sox.
■ **MVP:** Hernandez.

Linescores

Game 1—October 13, at New York
Boston ....2 1 0 0 0 0 0 0 0 0—3 8 3
New York ....0 2 0 0 0 0 1 0 0 1—4 10 0
Mercker, Garces (5), Lowe (7), Cormier (9), Beck (10) and Varitek; Hernandez, Rivera (9) and Posada. W—Rivera. L—Beck. HR—Brosius, Williams (N.Y.).

Game 2—October 14, at New York
Boston..........0 0 0 0 2 0 0 0 0—2 10 0
New York......0 0 0 1 0 0 2 0 x—3 7 0
R. Martinez, Gordon (7), Cormier (7) and Varitek; Cone, Stanton (8), Nelson (8), Watson (8), Mendoza (8), Rivera (9) and Girardi. W—Cone. L—R. Martinez. S—Rivera. HR—Garciaparra (Bos.); T. Martinez (N.Y.).

Game 3—October 16, at Boston
New York....0 0 0 0 0 0 0 1 0— 1 3 3
Boston........2 2 2 0 2 1 4 0 x—13 21 1
Clemens, Irabu (3), Stanton (7), Watson (8) and Girardi, Posada; P. Martinez, Gordon (8), Rapp (9) and Varitek, Hatteberg. W—P. Martinez. L—Clemens. HR—Brosius (N.Y.); Valentin, Daubach, Garciaparra (Bos.).

Game 4—October 10, at Boston
New York......0 1 0 2 0 0 0 0 6—9 11 0
Boston..........0 1 1 0 0 0 0 0 0—2 10 4
Pettitte, Rivera (8) and Girardi; Saberhagen, Lowe (7), Cormier (8), Garces (8), Beck (9) and Varitek. W—Pettitte. L—Saberhagen. S—Rivera. HR—Strawberry, Ledee (N.Y.).

Game 5—October 11, at Boston
New York......2 0 0 0 0 0 2 0 2—6 11 1
Boston..........0 0 0 0 0 0 0 1 0—1 5 2
Hernandez, Stanton (8), Nelson (8), Watson (8), Mendoza (8) and Posada; Mercker, Lowe (4), Cormier (7), Gordon (9) and Varitek. W—Hernandez. L—Mercker. S—Mendoza. HR—Jeter, Posada (N.Y.); Varitek (Bos.).

NLCS

■ **Winner:** The Atlanta Braves jumped out to a three-game lead in the series, then held on to win their fifth National League pennant of the '90s in six games. The Braves dominated the Mets during the regular season, winning nine of 12 games. Atlanta compiled a 103-59 record and finished 6 1/2 games ahead of the wild-card Mets. New York, which had a major league low 68 errors during the regular season, didn't field as well in the series, committing eight errors.
■ **Turning point:** Game 2, when Mets manager Bobby Valentine decided to stay with starter Kenny Rogers over reliever Turk Wendell against Eddie Perez in the sixth inning. Rogers had just given up a two-run homer to Brian Jordan and a single to Andruw Jones, and the hot-hitting Perez was coming to bat. Valentine left Rogers in, and Perez belted a two-run homer giving the Braves a 4-2 lead.
■ **Memorable moment:** Robin Ventura belted a game-ending grand slam in the 15th inning in Game 5, but the hit was officially declared a single when he was mobbed by teammates after rounding first base and couldn't complete the trip around the bases. The hit enabled to Mets to win the game, 4-3, and kept New York in the series.
■ **Top guns:** Perez (.500, 10 hits, 2 doubles, 2 HRs, 5 RBIs), Jordan (2 HRs, 5 RBIs), Greg Maddux (1-0, 14 IP, 1.93 ERA), Braves; Roger Cedeno (.500, 6 hits), John Olerud (8 hits, 6 RBIs), Edgardo Alfonzo (4 doubles), Mets.
■ **MVP:** Perez.

Game 1—October 12, at Atlanta
New York..........0 0 0 1 0 0 0 0 1—2 6 2
Atlanta ....1 0 0 0 1 1 0 1 x—4 8 2
Yoshii, Mahomes (5), Cook (7), Wendell (8) and Piazza; Maddux, Remlinger (8), Rocker (8) and Perez. W—Maddux. L—Yoshii. S—Rocker. HR—Perez (Atl.).

Game 2—October 13, at Atlanta
New York........0 1 0 0 1 0 0 1 0—3 5 1
Atlanta............0 0 0 0 0 4 0 0 0—4 9 1
Rogers, Wendell (6), Benitez (8) and Piazza; Millwood, Rocker (8), Smoltz (9) and Perez. W—Millwood. L—Rogers. S—Smoltz. HR—Mora (N.Y.); Jordan, Perez (Atl.).

Game 3—October 15, at New York
Atlanta ....1 0 0 0 0 0 0 0 0—1 3 1
New York........0 0 0 0 0 0 0 0 0—0 7 2
Glavine, Remlinger (8), Rocker (9) and Perez; Leiter, J. Franco (8), Benitez (8) and Piazza. W—Glavine. L—Leiter. S—Rocker.

Game 4—October 16, at New York
Atlanta............0 0 0 0 0 0 0 2 0—2 3 0
New York........0 0 0 0 0 1 0 2 x—3 5 0
Smoltz, Remlinger (8), Rocker (8) and Perez; Reed, Wendell (8), Benitez (9) and Piazza. W—Wendell. L—Remlinger. S—Benitez. HR—Jordan, Klesko (Atl.); Olerud (N.Y.).

Game 5—October 17, at New York
Atl. ..0 0 0 2 0 0 0 0 0 0 0 0 0 0 1—3 13 2
N.Y. ..2 0 0 0 0 0 0 0 0 0 0 0 0 0 2—4 11 1
Maddux, Mulholland (8), Remlinger (10), Springer (12), Rocker (13), McGlinchy (14) and Perez, Myers; Yoshii, Hershiser (4), Wendell (7), Cook (7), Mahomes (7), J. Franco (8), Benitez (10), Rogers (11), Dotel (13) and Piazza, Pratt. W—Dotel. L—McGlinchy. HR—Olerud (N.Y.).

Game 6—October 19, at Atlanta
N.Y. ....0 0 0 0 0 3 4 1 0 1 0— 9 15 2
Atlanta ....5 0 0 0 0 2 0 1 0 1 1—10 10 1
Leiter, Mahomes (1), Wendell (5), Cook (6), Hershiser (7), J. Franco (8), Benitez (9), Rogers (11) and Piazza, Pratt; Millwood, Mulholland (6), Smoltz (7), Remlinger (7), Rocker (9), Springer (11) and Perez, Myers. W—Springer. L—Rogers. HR—Piazza (N.Y.).

WORLD SERIES

■ **Winner:** After sweeping San Diego in the 1999 World Series, the New York Yankees swept their second straight World Series, this time against Atlanta. The World Series championship was New York's record 25th overall and third in four years. The sweep was the eighth by the Yankees.
■ **Turning point:** Two errors by Brian Hunter, inserted into the lineup as a defensive replacement for Ryan Klesko at first base in the eighth inning, allowed the Yankees to turn a 1-0 deficit into a 4-1 victory in the opener. After Scott Brosius singled and Darryl Strawberry walked, Chad Curtis came in to pinch-run for Strawberry. Chuck Knoblauch sacrificed but was safe at first on Hunter's first error, which allowed the other runners to advance to third and second. Derek Jeter singled home Brosius to tie the game, 1-1, and John Rocker replaced starter Greg Maddux on the mound. Paul O'Neill singled and went to second on a wild throw by Hunter—his second error of the inning—as Curtis and Knoblauch scored and Jeter went to third. The Yankees scored one more run in the inning to take a 4-1 lead, which became the final score.
■ **Memorable moment:** When Knoblauch tied Game 3 in the eighth with a two-run homer off Braves starter Tom Glavine. Glavine, who had been pushed back from a Game 1 start because of the flu, had given his club seven strong innings. Atlanta manager Bobby Cox gambled and left Glavine in to pitch the eighth, but the Braves lefthander allowed a leadoff single to Joe Girardi, followed by Knoblauch's shot, which knotted the game, 5-5.
■ **Top guns:** Brosius (.375, 6 hits), Jeter (.353, 4 runs, 6 hits), Curtis (.333, 2 HR), Tino Martinez (5 RBIs), David Cone (1-0, 0.00 ERA), Roger Clemens (1-0, 1.17 ERA), Orlando Hernandez (1-0, 1.29 ERA, 10 SO), Mariano Rivera (1-0, 2 Saves, 0.00 ERA), Yankees; Bret Boone (.538, 7 hits, 4 doubles), Braves.
■ **MVP:** Rivera.

Linescores

Game 1—October 23, at Atlanta
New York........0 0 0 0 0 0 0 4 0—4 6 0
Atlanta............0 0 0 1 0 0 0 0 0—1 2 2
O. Hernandez, Nelson (8), Stanton (8), Rivera (8) and Posada; Maddux, Rocker (8), Remlinger (9) and Perez. W—O. Hernandez. L—Maddux. S—Rivera. HR—C. Jones (Atl.).

Game 2—October 24, at Atlanta
New York......3 0 2 1 1 0 0 0 0—7 14 1
Atlanta..........0 0 0 0 0 0 0 0 2—2 5 1
Cone, Mendoza (8), Nelson (9) and Girardi; Millwood, Mulholland (3), Springer (6), McGlinchy and Myers. W—Cone. L—Millwood.

Game 3—October 26, at New York
Atlanta ....1 0 3 1 0 0 0 0 0 0—5 14 1
New York..1 0 0 0 1 0 1 2 0 1—6 9 0
Glavine, Rocker (8), Remlinger (10) and Perez, Myers; Pettitte, Grimsley (4), Nelson (7), Rivera (9) and Girardi. W—Rivera. L—Remlinger. HR—Curtis 2, Knoblauch, Martinez (N.Y.).

Game 4—October 27, at New York
Atlanta............0 0 0 0 0 0 0 1 0—1 5 0
New York........0 0 3 0 0 0 0 1 x—4 8 0
Smoltz, Mulholland (8), Springer (8) and Perez, Myers; Clemens, Nelson (8), Rivera (8) and Posada. W—Clemens. L—Smoltz. S—Rivera.

FINAL STANDINGS

American League

East Division

Team	N.Y.	Bos.	Tor.	Bal.	T.B.	Chi.	Cle.	Det.	K.C.	Min.	Oak.	Sea.	Ana.	Tex.	Atl.	N.Y.	Fla.	Mon.	Phi.	W	L	Pct.	GB
New York	—	7	5	7	6	4	5	4	8	5	6	4	5	10	2-1	4-2	1-1	2-1	2-1	87	74	.540	—
Boston	6	—	4	7	6	7	6	7	4	8	5	5	4	7	2-4	2-1	2-1	3-0	0-3	85	77	.525	2.5
Toronto	7	8	—	6	7	5	4	9	6	4	3	2	7	6	2-1	1-2	1-2	4-2	1-2	83	79	.512	4.5
Baltimore	5	5	7	—	8	4	5	6	3	6	4	3	5	6	0-3	1-2	2-1	0-3	4-2	74	88	.457	13.5
Tampa Bay	6	6	5	5	—	4	2	5	5	6	2	3	6	5	1-2	1-2	3-3	2-1	2-1	69	92	.429	18.0

Central Division

Team	Chi.	Cle.	Det.	K.C.	Min.	N.Y.	Bos.	Tor.	Bal.	T.B.	Oak.	Sea.	Ana.	Tex.	St.L.	Cin.	Mil.	Hou.	Pit.	Chi.	W	L	Pct.	GB
Chicago	—	8	9	5	7	8	5	5	6	6	6	7	6	5	1-2	3-0	3-0	2-1	—	3-3	95	67	.586	—
Cleveland	5	—	6	5	5	5	6	8	4	8	6	7	6	6	2-1	3-3	3-0	2-1	3-0	—	90	72	.556	5.0
Detroit	3	7	—	5	7	8	5	3	4	4	6	7	5	5	2-1	2-1	1-2	2-1	1-2	2-1	79	83	.488	16.0
Kansas City	7	7	7	—	7	2	6	4	7	5	4	4	6	3	1-2	—	1-2	1-2	4-2	1-2	77	85	.475	18.0
Minnesota	5	8	6	5	—	5	2	5	3	4	5	3	3	8	2-1	0-3	1-2	2-1	1-2	1-2	69	93	.426	26.0

West Division

Team	Oak.	Sea.	Ana.	Tex.	N.Y.	Bos.	Tor.	Bal.	T.B.	Chi.	Cle.	Det.	K.C.	Min.	S.F.	L.A.	Ari.	Col.	S.D.	W	L	Pct.	GB
Oakland	—	9	8	5	3	5	7	8	7	3	6	4	8	7	3-3	2-1	2-1	1-2	3-0	91	70	.565	—
Seattle	4	—	8	7	6	5	8	7	9	5	2	2	8	9	2-1	2-1	2-1	2-1	3-3	91	71	.562	0.5
Anaheim	5	5	—	7	5	5	5	7	6	4	3	5	6	7	2-1	4-2	1-2	3-0	2-1	82	80	.506	9.5
Texas	7	5	5	—	2	3	4	6	7	5	4	5	7	4	0-3	1-2	4-2	0-3	2-1	71	91	.438	20.5

Note: Read across for wins, down for losses.

Clinching dates: New York (East)—September 29; Chicago (Central)—September 24; Oakland (West)—October 1; Seattle (wild card)—October 1.

National League

East Division

Team	Atl.	N.Y.	Fla.	Mon.	Phi.	St.L.	Cin.	Mil.	Hou.	Pit.	Chi.	S.F.	L.A.	Ari.	Col.	S.D.	N.Y.	Bos.	Tor.	Bal.	T.B.	W	L	Pct.	GB
Atlanta	—	7	6	6	8	3	2	6	5	5	4	6	7	6	5	8	1-2	4-2	1-2	3-0	2-1	95	67	.586	—
New York	6	—	6	9	6	6	4	7	5	7	5	3	5	7	6	3	2-4	1-2	2-1	2-1	2-1	94	68	.580	1.0
Florida	6	6	—	7	9	3	6	3	3	5	6	3	2	5	5	2	1-1	1-2	2-1	1-2	3-3	79	82	.491	15.5
Montreal	7	3	6	—	5	2	3	5	5	3	5	3	3	5	2	3	1-2	0-3	2-4	3-0	1-2	67	95	.414	28.0
Philadelphia	5	7	4	7	—	2	4	5	4	3	3	2	4	1	3	2	1-2	3-0	2-1	2-4	1-2	65	97	.401	30.0

Central Division

Team	St.L.	Cin.	Mil.	Hou.	Pit.	Chi.	Atl.	N.Y.	Fla.	Mon.	Phi.	S.F.	L.A.	Ari.	Col.	S.D.	Chi.	Cle.	Det.	K.C.	Min.	W	L	Pct.	GB
St. Louis	—	6	7	6	8	10	4	3	6	5	7	4	6	4	3	9	2-1	1-2	1-2	2-1	1-2	95	67	.586	—
Cincinnati	7	—	5	7	7	8	5	5	3	6	3	3	4	5	6	4	0-3	3-3	1-2	—	3-0	85	77	.525	10.0
Milwaukee	5	8	—	6	7	7	3	2	4	4	2	3	4	5	5	2	0-3	0-3	2-1	2-1	2-1	73	89	.451	22.0
Houston	6	5	7	—	10	7	4	2	5	4	5	1	3	1	4	2	1-2	1-2	1-2	2-1	1-2	72	90	.444	23.0
Pittsburgh	4	6	5	3	—	9	2	2	4	4	6	2	5	2	2	7	—	0-3	2-1	2-4	2-1	69	93	.426	26.0
Chicago	3	4	6	5	3	—	5	2	1	4	6	4	3	4	4	3	3-3	—	1-2	2-1	2-1	65	97	.401	30.0

West Division

Team	S.F.	L.A.	Ari.	Col.	S.D.	Atl.	N.Y.	Fla.	Mon.	Phi.	St.L.	Cin.	Mil.	Hou.	Pit.	Chi.	Oak.	Sea.	Ana.	Tex.	W	L	Pct.	GB
San Fran.	—	5	7	7	7	3	5	6	6	7	5	6	6	8	6	5	3-3	1-2	1-2	3-0	97	65	.599	—
Los Angeles	7	—	6	9	8	2	4	7	5	5	3	5	3	6	4	6	1-2	1-2	2-4	2-1	86	76	.531	11.0
Arizona	6	7	—	7	9	3	2	4	4	8	5	2	4	6	7	5	1-2	1-2	2-1	2-4	85	77	.525	12.0
Colorado	6	4	6	—	7	4	3	4	7	6	5	3	4	5	7	5	2-1	1-2	0-3	3-0	82	80	.506	15.0
San Diego	5	5	4	6	—	1	6	7	6	5	0	5	7	7	2	5	0-3	3-3	1-2	1-2	76	86	.469	21.0

Note: Read across for wins, down for losses.

Tie game—Milwaukee at Cincinnati, April 3 (5 innings).

Clinching dates: Atlanta (East)—September 26; St. Louis (Central)—September 20; San Francisco (West)—September 21; New York (wild card)—September 27.

LEADERS

American League

BA: Nomar Garciaparra, Bos., .372.
Runs: Johnny Damon, K.C., 136.
Hits: Darin Erstad, Ana., 240.
TB: Carlos Delgado, Tor., 378.
HR: Troy Glaus, Ana., 47.
RBI: Edgar Martinez, Sea., 145.
SB: Johnny Damon, K.C., 46.
Wins: Tim Hudson, Oak.; David Wells, Tor., 20.
ERA: Pedro Martinez, Bos., 1.74.
CG: David Wells, Tor., 9.
IP: Mike Mussina, Bal., 237.2.
SO: Pedro Martinez, Bos., 284.
Sv.: Todd Jones, Det.; Derek Lowe, Bos., 42.

National League

BA: Todd Helton, Col., .372.
Runs: Jeff Bagwell, Hou., 152.
Hits: Todd Helton, Col., 216.
TB: Todd Helton, Col., 405.
HR: Sammy Sosa, Chi., 50.
RBI: Todd Helton, Col., 147.
SB: Luis Castillo, Fla., 62.
Wins: Tom Glavine, Atl., 21.
ERA: Kevin Brown, L.A., 2.58.
CG: Randy Johnson, Ari.; Curt Schilling, Phi.-Ari., 8.
IP: Jon Lieber, Chi., 251.0.
SO: Randy Johnson, Ari., 347.
Sv.: Antonio Alfonseca, Fla., 45.

A.L. 20-game winners
Tim Hudson, Oak., 20
David Wells, Tor., 20

N.L. 20-game winners
Tom Glavine, Atl., 21
Darryl Kile, St.L., 20

A.L. 100 RBIs
Edgar Martinez, Sea., 145
Mike Sweeney, K.C., 144
Frank Thomas, Chi., 143
Carlos Delgado, Tor., 137
Jason Giambi, Oak., 137
Alex Rodriguez, Sea., 132
Magglio Ordonez, Chi., 126
Manny Ramirez, Cle., 122
Bernie Williams, N.Y., 121
Rafael Palmeiro, Tex., 120
Jermaine Dye, K.C., 118
David Justice, Cle.-N.Y., 118
Garret Anderson, Ana., 117
Mo Vaughn, Ana., 117
Miguel Tejada, Oak., 115
Tony Batista, Tor., 114
Carl Everett, Bos., 108
Travis Fryman, Cle., 106
Fred McGriff, T.B., 106
Joe Randa, K.C., 106
Jim Thome, Cle., 106
Brad Fullmer, Tor., 104
Ben Grieve, Oak., 104
Albert Belle, Bal., 103
John Olerud, Sea., 103
David Segui, Tex.-Cle., 103
Troy Glaus, Ana., 102
Bobby Higginson, Det., 102
Dean Palmer, Det., 102
Darin Erstad, Ana., 100
Paul O'Neill, N.Y., 100

N.L. 100 RBIs
Todd Helton, Col., 147
Sammy Sosa, Chi., 138
Jeff Bagwell, Hou., 132
Jeff Kent, S.F., 125
Brian Giles, Pit., 123
Vladimir Guerrero, Mon., 123
Richard Hidalgo, Hou., 122
Preston Wilson, Fla., 121
Ken Griffey Jr., Cin., 118
Jeff Cirillo, Col., 115
Moises Alou, Hou., 114
Luis Gonzalez, Ari., 114
Mike Piazza, N.Y., 113
Chipper Jones, Atl., 111
Gary Sheffield, L.A., 109
Jim Edmonds, St.L., 108
Phil Nevin, S.D., 107
Barry Bonds, S.F., 106
Jeffrey Hammonds, Col., 106
Eric Karros, L.A., 106
Andruw Jones, Atl., 104
Andres Galarraga, Atl., 100

A.L. 40 homers
Troy Glaus, Ana., 47
Jason Giambi, Oak., 43
Frank Thomas, Chi., 43
Tony Batista, Tor., 41
Carlos Delgado, Tor., 41
David Justice, Cle.-N.Y., 41
Alex Rodriguez, Sea., 41

N.L. 40 homers
Sammy Sosa, Chi., 50
Barry Bonds, S.F., 49
Jeff Bagwell, Hou., 47
Vladimir Guerrero, Mon., 44
Richard Hidalgo, Hou., 44
Gary Sheffield, L.A., 43
Jim Edmonds, St.L., 42
Todd Helton, Col., 42
Ken Griffey Jr., Cin., 40

Most Valuable Player
A.L.: Jason Giambi, 1B, Oak.
N.L.: Jeff Kent, 2B, S.F.

Cy Young Award
A.L.: Pedro Martinez, Bos.
N.L.: Randy Johnson, Ari.

Rookie of the Year
A.L.: Kazuhiro Sasaki, P, Sea.
N.L.: Rafael Furcal, SS-2B, Atl.

Manager of the Year
A.L.: Jerry Manuel, Chi.
N.L.: Dusty Baker, S.F.

Hall of Fame additions
Sparky Anderson, manager
Carlton Fisk, C, 1969-93
John (Bid) McPhee, 2B, 1882-99
Tony Perez, 3B-1B, 1964-86
Norman (Turkey) Stearnes, OF-1B, Negro Leagues

SIGNIFICANT EVENTS

■ **March 29:** As part of a Major League Baseball's desire to expand its international presence, the Cubs and Mets opened the season in Japan. The Cubs beat the Mets, 5-3 at the Tokyo Dome. The Mets beat the Cubs, 5-1 in 11 innings the next day.

■ **April 7:** The Houston Astros opened their new park, Enron Field, with a 4-1 loss to the Philadelphia Phillies.

■ **April 11:** The Detroit Tigers opened their new park, Comerica Park, by beating the Seattle Mariners, 5-2. The San Francisco Giants also opened their new park, Pacific Bell Park, with a 6-5 loss to the Los Angeles Dodgers. Kevin Elster of the Dodgers belted three home runs in the contest.

■ **September 28:** The Milwaukee Brewers played their final game at County Stadium, losing to Cincinnati, 8-1.

■ **October 1:** The Pirates played their final game at Three Rivers Stadium, losing to the Cubs, 10-9.

MEMORABLE MOMENTS

■ **April 15:** Cal Ripken Jr. of the Baltimore Orioles collected his 3,000th career hit, a single off Twins pitcher Hector Carrasco in the seventh inning of a game at Minnesota.

■ **May 29:** Second baseman Randy Velarde of the Oakland Athletics became the 11th player to turn an unassisted triple play, retiring three New York Yankees on one play in the sixth inning.

■ **July 6:** Keith McDonald of the St. Louis Cardinals becomes only the second player in major league history to homer in his first two major league at-bats. McDonald, who hit his first home run two days earlier, joined Bob Nieman of the St. Louis Browns, who homered in his first two big-league at-bats on September 14, 1951.

■ **September 6:** Scott Sheldon of the Texas Rangers became the third player in big league history to play all nine positions in one game, performing his feat against the Chicago White Sox.

■ **October 1:** Shane Halter of the Detroit Tigers became the fourth player in major league history to play all nine positions in one game. Halter performed his feat on the last day of the regular season against the Minnesota Twins.

ALL-STAR GAME

■ **Winner:** The A.L. used eight pitchers to hold the N.L. to only three runs, and Derek Jeter led the American Leaguers with three hits and two RBIs to pace the offense. It gave the A.L. its fourth straight victory and 10th in its last 13 games.

■ **Key inning:** The fourth, when Jeter singled home Jermaine Dye and Travis Fryman to give the A.L. a 3-1 lead. N.L. shortstop Barry Larkin made a costly error on a forceout attempt of Fryman at second base earlier in the inning.

■ **Memorable moment:** N.L. center fielder Jim Edmonds made a twisting, back-to-the-infield catch on Mike Bordick's drive leading off the third inning. Despite the great play, the A.L. managed to score a run off Kevin Brown, who walked three in the inning, including a bases-loaded walk to Carl Everett.

■ **Top guns:** Jeter (Yankees), Matt Lawton (Twins), Magglio Ordonez (White Sox), A.L.; Chipper Jones (Braves), Andruw Jones (Braves), Steve Finley (Diamondbacks), N.L.

■ **MVP:** Jeter.

Linescore

July 11 at Atlanta's Turner Field
A.L. ....0 0 1 2 0 0 0 0 3—6
N.L. ....0 0 1 0 1 0 0 0 1—3
Wells (Blue Jays), Baldwin (White Sox) 3, Sele (Mariners) 4, Isringhausen (Athletics) 5, Lowe (Red Sox) 6, T. Jones, (Tigers) 7, Hudson (Athletics) 8, Rivera (Yankees) 9; Johnson (Diamondbacks), Graves (Reds) 2, Brown (Dodgers) 3, Leiter (Mets) 4, Glavine (Braves) 5, Kile (Cardinals) 6, Wickman (Brewers) 8, Hoffman (Padres) 9. W—Baldwin. L—Leiter.

A.L. DIVISION SERIES

■ **Winners:** Seattle completed a three-game sweep of Chicago, allowing the White Sox only seven runs. The Yankees edged Oakland in a five-game series victory.

■ **Turning points:** White Sox pitcher Keith Foulke surrendered a single to Mike Cameron leading off the 10th inning of the opener. Cameron proceeded to take long leads off first base and lured Foulke into throwing a number of pickoff attempts. After Cameron finally stole second, Foulke, obviously rattled, surrendered home runs to Edgar Martinez and John Olerud, giving the Mariners a 7-4 victory. In Game 2, the White Sox scored a run in the first and had Jose Valentin on third with none out, but failed to score. Mariners pitcher Paul Abbott retired Frank Thomas, Carlos Lee and Paul Konerko to keep the White Sox from scoring more. It shifted the momentum to the Mariners, who scored two runs the following inning to take the lead. For the White Sox, the first inning represented just one of a number of frustrating innings they endured during the series. Their trio of Thomas, Lee and Konerko hit a combined 1-for-29 during the three games. The Yankees received a big lift from Andy Pettitte in Game 2 of their series. Pettitte and Mariano Rivera combined to shut out Oakland 4-0 to tie the series and end an eight-game losing streak the Yankees had suffered ending the season and going through Game 1. Orlando Hernandez kept the momentum on the Yankees' side in Game 3 as he allowed four hits and combined with Rivera for a 4-2 victory.

■ **Memorable moments:** The Mariners won the series in the ninth inning of Game 3 when pinch-hitter Carlos Guillen squeezed home Rickey Henderson with the winning run. After the Yankees were blown out 11-1 in Game 4, they jumped on A's starter Gil Heredia for six runs in the first inning of the deciding Game 5. Tino Martinez highlighted the frame with a bases-loaded double.

■ **Memorable performances:** David Bell and Edgar Martinez each batted .364 for the Mariners. Game 3 starter Aaron Sele didn't get a decision, but allowed only one run and three hits in 7.1 innings of the Mariners' 2-1 series-clinching victory. A.L. Rookie of the Year Kazuhiro Sasaki struck out five batters and saved two games in his two innings of work during the series. Tino Martinez collected eight hits and four RBIs, and batted .421 for the Yankees. Luis Sojo had only three hits, but drove in a team-high five runs for New York. Rivera was unscored upon in three relief appearances, and saved all three Yankee victories. Catcher Ramon Hernandez led the Athletics with a .375 average, and Eric Chavez batted .350 for the A's in a losing cause.

Linescores

Seattle vs. Chicago

Game 1—October 3, at Chicago
Seattle ....2 1 0 0 0 0 1 0 0 3—7
Chicago ....0 2 2 0 0 0 0 0 0 0—4
Garcia, Tomko (4), Paniagua (7), Rhodes (9), Mesa (9), Sasaki (10) and Oliver, Wilson; Parque, Howry (7), Bradford (7), Wunsch (8), Simas (8), Foulke (9) and Johnson. W—Mesa. L—Foulke. S—Sasaki. HR—Olerud, Martinez, Oliver (Sea.); Durham (Chi.).

Game 2—October 4, at Chicago
Seattle ....0 2 0 1 1 0 0 0 1—5
Chicago ....1 0 1 0 0 0 0 0 0—2
P. Abbott, Rhodes (6), Mesa (6), Sasaki (9) and Oliver, Wilson; Sirotka, Barcelo (6), Wunsch (8),

Simas (8), Buehrle (9) and Johnson. W—P. Abbott, L—Sirotka. S—Sasaki. HR—Buhner (Sea.).

Game 3—October 6, at Seattle
Chicago..................0 1 0 0 0 0 0 0 0—1
Seattle...................0 0 0 1 0 0 0 0 1—2
One out when winning run scored.
Baldwin, Howry (7), Wunsch (9), Foulke (9) and Johnson; Sele, Rhodes (8), Paniagua (9) and Oliver. W—Paniagua. L—Wunsch.

New York vs. Oakland

Game 1—October 3, at Oakland
New York...............0 2 0 0 0 1 0 0 0—3
Oakland..................0 0 0 0 3 1 0 1 x—5
Clemens, Stanton (7), Nelson (8) and Posada; Heredia, Tam (7), Mecir (7), Isringhausen (9) and R. Hernandez. W—Heredia. L—Clemens. S—Isringhausen.

Game 2—October 4, at Oakland
New York...............0 0 0 0 0 3 0 0 1—4
Oakland..................0 0 0 0 0 0 0 0 0—0
Pettitte, Rivera (8) and Posada; Appier, Magnante (7), Tam (9), Jones (9) and R. Hernandez. W—Pettitte. L—Appier. S—Rivera.

Game 3—October 6, at New York
Oakland..................0 1 0 0 1 0 0 0 0—2
New York................0 2 0 1 0 0 0 1 x—4
Hudson and R. Hernandez; O. Hernandez, Rivera (8) and Posada. W—O. Hernandez. L—Hudson. S—Rivera. HR—Long (Oak.).

Game 4—October 7, at New York
Oakland................3 0 0 0 0 3 0 1 4—11
New York.............0 0 0 0 0 1 0 0 0— 1
Zito, Mecir (6), Magnante (7), Jones (9) and R. Hernandez; Clemens, Stanton (6), Choate (7), Gooden (8) and Posada. W—Zito. L—Clemens. HR—Saenz (Oak.).

Game 5—October 8, at Oakland
New York...............6 0 0 1 0 0 0 0 0—7
Oakland..................0 2 1 2 0 0 0 0 0—5
Pettitte, Stanton (4), Nelson (6), O. Hernandez (8), Rivera (8) and Posada; Heredia, Tam (1), Appier (2), Mecir (6), Isringhausen (9) and R. Hernandez, Fasano. HR—Justice (N.Y.).

N.L. DIVISION SERIES

■ **Winners:** The Cardinals rocked the Braves for 24 runs to end the Braves' division series mastery during the '90s with a three-game sweep. Atlanta had been 15-2 in division series games prior to 2000. The wild-card Mets followed an opening game loss with three straight victories to beat the Giants, whose 97 victories represented the best record in baseball during the regular season.

■ **Turning points:** The Cardinals pounded Greg Maddux for six first-inning runs to take the opener, 7-5. The Cardinals' big lead was enough to offset the control troubles of their starter, rookie Rick Ankiel, who threw a record five wild pitches and allowed four runs in the first three innings. St. Louis struck early and often in the second game, too, as they erased a 2-0 deficit with three first-inning runs. They added one in the second and three in the third off Braves 21-game winner Tom Glavine to coast to a 10-4 win. The Mets, after losing the first game, held a 4-1 lead going into the bottom of the ninth inning of Game 2, before J.T. Snow belted a game-tying home run. New York managed to grab the lead and the momentum in the 10th when Darryl Hamilton hit a two-out double and scored when Jay Payton singled him home with the winning run. The Mets took the series lead in Game 3 when Benny Agbayani smacked a 13th-inning home run to win an exhausting game that lasted 5 hours and 22 minutes.

■ **Memorable moments:** Mark McGwire, out of the lineup with a sore knee, thrilled the hometown fans in Game 2 with an eighth-inning pinch home run that gave the Cardinals a 10-4 lead. Fernando Vina started the Cardinals on their way to a 7-1 Game 3 victory with a leadoff home run in the first inning. The Braves tied the game with a run in their first, but St. Louis went ahead to stay in the third on a two-run home run by Jim Edmonds. The Giants had a chance to win Game 3 of their series, but Mets reliever Rick White induced Barry Bonds to pop out with two runners on base in the 13th inning. Agbayani ended the game a short time later with his home run.

■ **Memorable performances:** Edmonds led all hitters with two home runs, four doubles, eight hits , seven RBIs and a .571 batting average. Brian Jordan batted .364 to lead the Braves' meager offense (.189 team batting average). Agbayani led the Mets offense with a .333 average. He joined Edgardo Alfonso and Timo Perez as the Mets' leaders with five hits apiece. Snow led the Giants with a .400 average, while National League MVP Jeff Kent collected six hits and batted .375.

Linescores

New York vs. San Francisco

Game 1—October 4, at San Francisco
New York................0 0 1 0 0 0 0 0 0—1
San Francisco ....1 0 4 0 0 0 0 x—5
Hampton, Wendell (6), Cook (7), White (7), Rusch (8) and Piazza; Hernandez, Rodriguez (8), Nen (9) and Estalella. W—Hernandez. L—Hampton. HR—Burks (S.F.).

Game 2—October 5, at San Francisco
New York..........0 2 0 0 0 0 0 0 2 1—5
San Francisco ..0 1 0 0 0 0 0 0 3 0—4
Leiter, Benitez (9), J. Franco (10) and Piazza; Estes, Rueter (4), Henry (8), Rodriguez (9) and Estalella. W—Benitez. L—Rodriguez. S—J. Franco. HR—Alfonzo (N.Y.); Snow (S.F.).

Game 3—October 7, at New York
S.F. ....0 0 0 2 0 0 0 0 0 0 0 0 0—2
N.Y. ....0 0 0 0 0 1 0 1 0 0 0 0 1—3
One out when winning run scored.
Ortiz, Embree (6), Henry (7), Nen (8), Rodriguez (10), Fultz (12) and Estalella, Mirabelli; Reed, Cook (7), Wendell (7), J. Franco (9), Benitez (10), White (12) and Piazza, Pratt. W—White. L—Fultz. HR—Agbayani (N.Y.).

Game 4—October 8, at New York
San Francisco ....0 0 0 0 0 0 0 0 0—0
New York................2 0 0 0 2 0 0 x—4
Gardner, Henry (5), Embree (7), Del Toro (8) and Mirabelli, Estalella; B.J. Jones and Piazza. W—B.J. Jones. L—Gardner. HR—Ventura (N.Y.).

St. Louis vs. Atlanta

Game 1—October 3, at St. Louis
Atlanta....................0 0 4 0 0 0 0 0 1—5
St. Louis ....6 0 0 1 0 0 0 0 x—7
Maddux, Remlinger (5), Mulholland (6), Rocker (7), Ligtenberg (8) and Bako, Lopez; Ankiel, James (3), Timlin (6), Reames (7), Veres (9) and Hernandez. W—James. L—Maddux. S—Veres. HR—Edmonds (St.L.).

Game 2—October 5, at St. Louis
Atlanta.................2 0 0 0 0 0 0 2 0— 4
St. Louis ....3 1 3 1 0 1 0 1 x—10
Glavine, Ashby (3), Burkett (5), Mulholland (6), Ligtenberg (7), Remlinger (8) and Lopez; Kile, Christiansen (8), Timlin (8), Morris (9) and Hernandez. W—Kile. L—Glavine. HR—McGwire, Hernandez, Clark (St.L.); A. Jones (Atl.).

Game 3—October 7, at Atlanta
St. Louis ....1 0 2 0 1 3 0 0 0—7
Atlanta....................1 0 0 0 0 0 0 0 0—1
Stephenson, Reames (4), James (6), Morris (8), Veres (9) and Hernandez; Millwood, Mulholland (5), Ligtenberg (6), Remlinger (6), Ashby (8) and Lopez, Bako. W—Reames. L—Millwood. HR—Vina, Edmonds (St.L.).

NLCS

■ **Winner:** The Mets' lefthanded pitchers led them to a relatively easy victory over the Cardinals despite the fact that St. Louis outhit New York, .266 to .262. Mike Hampton dominated the Cardinals with 16 innings of scoreless pitching, allowing a total of nine hits and four walks, and striking out 12 in his two victories. Their series victory made the Mets only the second wild-card team (Florida Marlins, 1997) to win a league pennant since the format was begun in 1995.

■ **Turning point:** Hampton shut the Cardinals down on six hits in seven innings in the opener. Mike Piazza's double keyed a two-run first inning, and ninth-inning homers by Todd Zeile and Jay Payton iced the victory. The next night, Payton hit a run-scoring ninth-inning single to give the Mets a 2-0 series lead.

■ **Memorable moments:** Will Clark, normally a sure-handed first baseman, booted a ground ball hit by Robin Ventura leading off the ninth inning of Game 2. Joe McEwing pinch-ran for Ventura later in the inning and scored the winning run on Payton's single. Cardinals rookie Rick Ankiel continued his postseason wildness problems in Game 2. The lefthander started and allowed three walks, two hits, two runs and threw two wild pitches before being relieved in the first inning. The Mets pounded St. Louis with a record five doubles in the first inning of Game 4, and built a 7-2 lead after two innings. The Cardinals fought back to make the score 8-6, but they couldn't catch the Mets.

■ **Top guns:** Edgardo Alfonso (.444, 8 hits), Piazza (.412, 7 runs, 7 hits, 2 HRs), Zeile (.368, 7 hits, 8 RBIs), Agbayani (.353, 6 hits), Perez (.304, 7 hits, 8 runs), Hampton (16 IP, 12 SO, 0.00 ERA), Mets; Clark (.412, 7 hits), J.D. Drew (.333, 4 hits), Ray Lankford (.333, 4 hits), Cardinals.

■ **MVP:** Hampton.

Linescores

Game 1—October 11, at St. Louis
New York....................2 0 0 0 1 0 0 0 3—6
St. Louis ....0 0 0 0 0 0 0 0 2—2
Hampton, J. Franco (8), White (9) and Piazza; Kile, James (8), Christiansen (8) and Hernandez, Marrero. W—Hampton. L—Kile. HR—Zeile, Payton (N.Y.).

Game 2—October 12, at St. Louis
New York................2 0 1 0 0 0 0 2 1—6
St. Louis ....0 1 0 0 2 0 0 2 0—5
Leiter, J. Franco (8), Wendell (8), Benitez (9) and Piazza; Ankiel, Reames (1), Morris (6), Veres (9), Timlin (9) and Marrero, Hernandez. W—Wendell. L—Timlin. S—Benitez. HR—Piazza (N.Y.).

Game 3—October 14, at New York
St. Louis ....2 0 2 1 3 0 0 0 0—8
New York................1 0 0 1 0 0 0 0 0—2
Benes, James (9), Veres (9) and Hernandez; Reed, Rusch (4), White (5), Cook (8), Wendell (9) and Piazza. W—Benes. L—Reed.

Game 4—October 15, at New York
St. Louis ....2 0 0 1 3 0 0 0 0— 6
New York.............4 3 0 1 0 2 0 0 x—10
Kile, James (4), Timlin (5), Morris (7), Christiansen (8) and Hernandez; B.J. Jones, Rusch (5), J. Franco (8), Benitez (9) and Piazza. W—Rusch. L—Kile. HR—Edmonds, Clark (St.L.); Piazza (N.Y.).

Game 5—October 16, at New York
St. Louis ....0 0 0 0 0 0 0 0 0—0
New York...............3 0 0 3 0 0 1 0 x—7
Hentgen, Timlin (4), Reames (5), Ankiel (7), James (7), Veres (8) and Hernandez; Hampton and Piazza. W—Hampton. L—Hentgen.

ALCS

■ **Winner:** The New York Yankees, after losing the first game, allowed Seattle only three runs over the next three games and beat the Mariners in a six-game series. The victory gave the Yankees their third straight A.L. title, making them the first team since the 1988-90 Oakland A's to win three straight pennants.

■ **Turning point:** Game 2, when the Yankees, trailing 1-0, rallied for seven runs in the eighth inning to win 7-1. Starter John Halama and reliever Jose Paniagua had held New York to six hits over the first seven innings. But David Justice greeted reliever Arthur Rhodes with a leadoff double in the eighth. Bernie Williams followed with a single to center and the Yankees went on to collect eight straight hits in the big inning. Williams and Tino Martinez hit back-to-back home runs in the second inning of Game 3 and the Yankees took control of the series, winning Games 3 and 4 by scores of 8-2 and 5-0. In the latter game, Roger Clemens overpowered the Mariners, striking out 15 in a one-hit shutout.

■ **Memorable moment:** Trailing 4-3 in the seventh inning of Game 6, David Justice slugged a dramatic three-run homer, and the Yankees went on to score six runs to win the series with a 9-7 victory.

■ **Top guns:** Williams (.435,10 hits), T. Martinez (.320, 8 hits), Jeter (.318, 6 runs, 7 hits, 2 HRs), Justice (2 HRs, 8 RBIs), Clemens, (9 IP, 1 H, 15 SO), Yankees; Alex Rodriguez (.409, 9 hits, 2 HRs), John Olerud (.350, 7 hits), Mariners.

■ **MVP:** Justice.

Game 1—October 10, at New York
Seattle....................0 0 0 0 1 1 0 0 0—2
New York................0 0 0 0 0 0 0 0 0—0
Garcia, Paniagua (7), Rhodes (8), Sasaki (9) and Oliver; Neagle, Nelson (6), Choate (9), Grimsley (9) and Posada. W—Garcia. L—Neagle. S—Sasaki. HR—Rodriguez (Sea.).

Game 2—October 11, at New York
Seattle....................0 0 1 0 0 0 0 0 0—1
New York................0 0 0 0 0 0 0 7 x—7
Halama, Paniagua (7), Rhodes (8), Mesa (8) and Wilson; Hernandez, Rivera (9) and Posada. W—Hernandez. L—Rhodes. HR—Jeter (N.Y.).

Game 3—October 13, at Seattle
New York...............0 2 1 0 0 1 0 0 4—8
Seattle....................1 0 0 0 1 0 0 0 0—2
Pettitte, Nelson (7), Rivera (8) and Posada; Sele, Tomko (7), Ramsay (9) and Oliver. W—Pettitte. L—Sele. S—Rivera. HR—Williams, T. Martinez (N.Y.).

Game 4—October 14, at Seattle
New York...............0 0 0 0 3 0 0 2 0—5
Seattle....................0 0 0 0 0 0 0 0 0—0
Clemens and Posada; Abbott, Ramsay (6), Mesa (7), Paniagua (9) and Wilson, Oliver. W—Clemens. L—Abbott. HR—Jeter, Justice (N.Y.).

Game 5—October 15, at Seattle
New York...............0 0 0 2 0 0 0 0 0—2
Seattle....................1 0 0 0 5 0 0 0 x—6
Neagle, Nelson (5), Grimsley (5), Gooden (5), Cone (8) and Posada; Garcia, Paniagua (6), Rhodes (7), Sasaki (8) and Wilson. W—Garcia. L—Neagle. HR—E. Martinez, Olerud (Sea.).

Game 6—October 17, at New York
Seattle....................2 0 0 2 0 0 0 3 0—7
New York...............0 0 0 3 0 0 6 0 x—9
Halama, Tomko (4), Paniagua (7), Rhodes (7), Mesa (7) and Wilson, Oliver; Hernandez, Rivera (8) and Posada. W—Hernandez. L—Paniagua. HR—Rodriguez, Guillen (Sea.); Justice (N.Y.).

WORLD SERIES

■ **Winner:** The Yankees won their 26th World Series in 37 tries and won their third in a row, making them the first team since the 1972-74 Oakland A's to win three World Series.

■ **Turning point:** Jose Vizcaino, making his first start of the postseason, went 4-for-6 and drove in the winning run in the 12th inning to win Game 1, 4-3.

■ **Memorable moment:** When Clemens faced Piazza in the first inning of Game 2. Piazza shattered his bat hitting a foul ball and then ran toward first not realizing it was foul. Clemens tossed the barrel of the bat toward the Mets catcher, with the jagged end of the bat coming dangerously close to Piazza. Piazza glared at Clemens and the players exchanged words as the benches cleared. Clemens was later fined $50,000.

■ **Top guns:** O'Neill (.474, 9 hits), Jeter (.409, 6 runs, 9 hits, 2 HRs), Martinez (.364, 8 hits), Clemens (0.00 ERA, 8 IP, 2 hits, 9 SO), Yankees; Zeile (.400, 8 hits), Payton (.333, 7 hits), Piazza (2 HRs), Mets.

■ **MVP:** Jeter.

Linescores

Game 1—October 21, at Yankee Stadium
N.Y. Mets ......0 0 0 0 0 0 3 0 0 0 0 0—3
N.Y. Yankees..0 0 0 0 0 2 0 0 1 0 0 1—4
Leiter, J. Franco (8), Benitez (9), Cook (10), Rusch (10), Wendell (11) and Pratt; Pettitte, Nelson (7), Rivera (9), Stanton (11) and Posada. W—Stanton. L—Wendell.

Game 2—October 22, at Yankee Stadium
New York Mets ......0 0 0 0 0 0 0 0 5—5
New York Yankees..2 1 0 0 1 0 1 1 x—6
Hampton, Rusch (7), White (7), Cook (8) and Piazza; Clemens, Nelson (9), Rivera (9) and Posada. W—Clemens. L—Hampton. HR—Piazza, Payton (Mets); Brosius (Yankees).

Game 3—October 24, at Shea Stadium
New York Yankees..0 0 1 1 0 0 0 0 0—2
New York Mets ......0 1 0 0 0 1 0 2 x—4
Hernandez, Stanton (8) and Posada; Reed, Wendell (7), Cook (7), J. Franco (8), Benitez (9) and Piazza. W—J. Franco. L—Hernandez. S—Benitez. HR—Ventura (Mets).

Game 4—October 25, at Shea Stadium
New York Yankees..1 1 1 0 0 0 0 0 0—3
New York Mets ......0 0 2 0 0 0 0 0 0—2
Neagle, Cone (5), Nelson (6), Stanton (7), Rivera (8) and Posada; B.J. Jones, Rusch (6), J. Franco (8), Benitez (9) and Piazza. W—Nelson. L—B.J. Jones. S—Rivera. HR—Jeter (Yankees); Piazza (Mets).

Game 5—October 26, at Shea Stadium
New York Yankees..0 1 0 0 0 1 0 0 2—4
New York Mets ......0 2 0 0 0 0 0 0 0—2
Pettitte, Stanton (8), Rivera (9) and Posada; Leiter, J. Franco (9) and Piazza. W—Stanton. L—Leiter. S—Rivera. HR—Jeter, Williams (Yankees).

HISTORY

FINAL STANDINGS

American League

East Division

Team	N.Y.	Bos.	Tor.	Bal.	T.B.	Cle.	Min.	Chi.	Det.	K.C.	Sea.	Oak.	Ana.	Tex.	Atl.	Phi.	N.Y.	Fla.	Mon.	W	L	Pct.	GB
New York	—	13	11	13	13	5	2	5	5	6	3	3	3	3	1-2	2-1	4-2	1-2	2-1	95	65	.594	—
Boston	5	—	12	10	14	3	3	3	4	3	3	4	3	5	3-3	2-1	1-2	2-1	2-1	82	79	.509	13.5
Toronto	8	7	—	12	10	4	5	3	4	3	3	3	4	6	2-1	2-1	0-3	1-2	3-3	80	82	.494	16.0
Baltimore	5	9	7	—	10	1	3	3	4	5	1	2	5	2	1-2	2-4	1-2	0-3	2-1	63	98	.391	32.5
Tampa Bay	6	5	9	9	—	1	6	2	2	2	2	2	2	4	2-1	3-0	2-1	2-4	1-2	62	100	.383	34.0

Central Division

Team	Cle.	Min.	Chi.	Det.	K.C.	N.Y.	Bos.	Tor.	Bal.	T.B.	Sea.	Oak.	Ana.	Tex.	Hou.	St.L.	Chi.	Mil.	Cin.	Pit.	Ari.	W	L	Pct.	GB
Cleveland	—	14	9	13	11	4	6	2	5	5	2	4	4	5	1-2	2-1	—	1-2	3-3	0-3	—	91	71	.562	—
Minnesota	5	—	14	15	13	4	3	2	3	1	1	5	6	4	2-1	0-3	0-3	2-1	3-0	2-1	—	85	77	.525	6.0
Chicago	10	5	—	13	14	1	3	3	4	5	2	1	3	7	—	0-3	4-2	3-0	3-0	2-1	—	83	79	.512	8.0
Detroit	6	4	6	—	8	4	5	2	2	4	2	1	4	8	—	2-1	1-2	2-1	2-1	2-1	1-2	66	96	.407	25.0
Kansas City	8	6	5	11	—	0	3	4	2	4	3	3	4	4	0-3	3-0	1-2	2-1	—	1-2	1-2	65	97	.401	26.0

West Division

Team	Sea.	Oak.	Ana.	Tex.	N.Y.	Bos.	Tor.	Bal.	T.B.	Cle.	Min.	Chi.	Det.	K.C.	Ari.	S.F.	L.A.	S.D.	Col.	Hou.	W	L	Pct.	GB
Seattle	—	10	15	15	6	6	6	8	7	5	8	7	5	6	2-1	2-1	2-1	4-2	2-1	—	116	46	.716	—
Oakland	9	—	14	9	6	5	6	7	7	3	4	8	6	6	3-0	2-4	2-1	2-1	3-0	—	102	60	.630	14.0
Anaheim	4	6	—	7	4	4	5	4	7	5	3	6	5	5	1-2	0-3	4-2	2-1	3-0	—	75	87	.463	41.0
Texas	5	10	12	—	4	2	3	7	5	4	5	2	1	5	—	1-2	1-2	1-2	2-1	3-3	73	89	.451	43.0

NOTE: Read across for wins, down for losses; interleague games are shaded.

Tie game—Baltimore at New York, September 30 (15 innings).

Clinching dates: New York (East)—September 25; Cleveland (Central)—September 30; Seattle (West)—September 19; Oakland (wild card)—September 23.

National League

East Division

Team	Atl.	Phi.	N.Y.	Fla.	Mon.	Hou.	St.L.	Chi.	Mil.	Cin.	Pit.	Ari.	S.F.	L.A.	S.D.	Col.	N.Y.	Bos.	Tor.	Bal.	T.B.	W	L	Pct.	GB
Atlanta	—	10	10	9	13	3	3	4	3	4	5	2	4	2	3	4	2-1	3-3	1-2	2-1	1-2	88	74	.543	—
Philadelphia	9	—	8	14	10	3	2	2	3	4	5	4	3	3	5	4	1-2	1-2	1-2	4-2	0-3	86	76	.531	2.0
New York	9	11	—	12	11	3	1	2	3	2	4	3	3	4	1	3	2-4	2-1	3-0	2-1	1-2	82	80	.506	6.0
Florida	10	5	7	—	12	3	3	3	4	2	4	2	2	2	3	2	2-1	1-2	2-1	3-0	4-2	76	86	.469	12.0
Montreal	6	9	8	7	—	0	2	3	2	2	5	3	2	4	3	4	1-2	1-2	3-3	1-2	2-1	68	94	.420	20.0

Central Division

Team	Hou.	St.L.	Chi.	Mil.	Cin.	Pit.	Atl.	Phi.	N.Y.	Fla.	Mon.	Ari.	S.F.	L.A.	S.D.	Col.	Tex.	Cle.	Min.	Chi.	Det.	K.C.	W	L	Pct.	GB
Houston	—	9	9	12	11	9	3	3	3	3	6	4	3	2	3	4	3-3	2-1	1-2	—	—	3-0	93	69	.574	—
St. Louis	7	—	8	10	10	14	3	4	5	3	4	4	2	3	5	3	—	1-2	3-0	3-0	1-2	0-3	93	69	.574	—
Chicago	8	9	—	8	13	10	2	4	4	3	3	3	3	4	2	3	—	—	3-0	2-4	2-1	2-1	88	74	.543	5.0
Milwaukee	5	7	9	—	10	6	3	3	3	2	4	3	5	1	1	1	—	2-1	1-2	0-3	1-2	1-2	68	94	.420	25.0
Cincinnati	6	7	4	6	—	9	2	2	4	4	4	1	4	4	2	3	—	3-3	0-3	0-3	1-2	—	66	96	.407	27.0
Pittsburgh	8	3	6	11	8	—	1	1	2	2	1	2	1	2	2	4	—	3-0	1-2	1-2	1-2	2-1	62	100	.383	31.0

West Division

Team	Ari.	S.F.	L.A.	S.D.	Col.	Atl.	Phi.	N.Y.	Fla.	Mon.	Hou.	St.L.	Chi.	Mil.	Cin.	Pit.	K.C.	Det.	Sea.	Oak.	Ana.	Tex.	W	L	Pct.	GB
Arizona	—	10	10	12	13	5	3	3	4	3	2	2	6	3	5	4	2-1	2-1	1-2	0-3	2-1	—	92	70	.568	—
San Fran.	9	—	8	14	10	2	3	4	4	5	3	4	3	4	2	5	—	—	1-2	4-2	3-0	2-1	90	72	.556	2.0
Los Ang.	9	11	—	9	11	5	3	2	5	2	4	3	2	5	2	7	—	—	1-2	1-2	2-4	2-1	86	76	.531	6.0
San Diego	7	5	10	—	10	3	2	5	4	3	6	1	4	5	4	4	—	—	2-4	1-2	1-2	2-1	79	83	.488	13.0
Colorado	6	9	8	9	—	2	2	4	4	3	2	6	3	5	6	2	—	—	1-2	0-3	0-3	1-2	73	89	.451	19.0

NOTE: Read across for wins, down for losses; interleague games are shaded.

Clinching dates: Atlanta (East)—October 5; Houston (Central)—October 7; Arizona (West)—October 5; St. Louis (wild card)—October 7.

SIGNIFICANT EVENTS

■ **April 1:** As part of Major League Baseball's desire to expand its international presence, the Rangers and Blue Jays opened the season in Puerto Rico. The Blue Jays beat the Rangers, 8-1, at Hiram Bithorn Stadium.

■ **April 6:** The Milwaukee Brewers opened their new park, Miller Park, with a 5-4 victory over the Cincinnati Reds.

■ **April 9:** The Pittsburgh Pirates opened their new park, PNC Park, by losing to the Cincinnati Reds, 8-2.

■ **September 11:** Following terrorist attacks that saw hijacked airplanes crash into New York City's World Trade Center, the Pentagon and a field in western Pennsylvania, baseball cancelled all games—a total of 91—until September 17. The games were made up at the end of the schedule by extending the season one week.

MEMORABLE MOMENTS

■ **April 17:** Barry Bonds of the San Francisco Giants collects his 500th career home run, a two-run shot in the eighth inning off Los Angeles Dodgers reliever Terry Adams.

■ **September 19:** Roger Clemens of the New York Yankees wins his 16th consecutive game to tie an American League record. Clemens' 6-3 victory over the White Sox in Chicago enabled him to join Walter Johnson (Washington, 1912), Joe Wood (Boston, 1912), Lefty Grove (Philadelphia, 1931) and Schoolboy Rowe (Detroit, 1934) as the only pitchers in A.L. history to win 16 straight games.

■ **October 5:** Barry Bonds belts his 71st homer of the season, breaking Mark McGwire's 1998 record. Bonds hit the record home run in the first inning off Los Angeles Dodgers starter Chan Ho Park, and two innings later clubbed another homer off Park. Two days later, Bonds hit his 73rd and final homer of the season off Dodgers starter Dennis Springer.

■ **October 6:** The Seattle Mariners defeat the Texas Rangers, 1-0, to win their 116th game of the season, tying the major league record set by the 1906 Chicago Cubs. The Mariners finished the season the next day with a record of 116-46.

ALL-STAR GAME

■ **Winner:** The A.L. used nine pitchers to hold the N.L. to only three hits and one run, and Derek Jeter, Cal Ripken Jr. and Magglio Ordonez each hit solo home runs to lead the American Leaguers. It gave the A.L. its fourth straight victory and 10th in the last 13 All-Star Games.

■ **Key inning:** The sixth, when leading, 2-1, Jeter and Ordonez homered consecutively to give the A.L. a 4-1 lead.

■ **Memorable moment:** A.L. third baseman Ripken, playing in his 18th and final All-Star Game, led off the third inning with a home run off Chan Ho Park to give the A.L. a 1-0 lead. Ripken, who at age 40 became the oldest player to hit a home run in an All-Star Game, received a thunderous standing ovation and later was named the game's MVP. It was Ripken's second All-Star Game MVP performance, as he joined Ted Williams, Willie Mays, Steve Garvey and Gary Carter as two-time winners.

■ **Top guns:** Jeff Kent (Giants), Randy Johnson (Diamondbacks), N.L.; Ripken (Orioles), Jeter (Yankees), Ordonez (White Sox), Roger Clemens (Yankees), A.L.

■ **MVP:** Ripken.

Linescore

July 10 at Seattle's Safeco Field

N.L. ....0 0 0 0 0 1 0 0 0—1
A.L. ....0 0 1 0 1 2 0 0 x—4

R. Johnson (Diamondbacks), Park (Dodgers) 3, Burkett (Braves) 4, Hampton (Rockies) 5, Lieber (Cubs) 6, Morris (Cardinals) 7, Shaw (Dodgers) 8, Wagner (Astros) 8, Sheets (Brewers) 8; Clemens (Yankees), Garcia (Mariners) 3, Pettitte (Yankees) 4, Mays (Twins) 5, Quantrill (Blue Jays) 6, Stanton (Yankees) 6, Nelson (Mariners) 7, Percival (Angels) 8, Sasaki (Mariners) 9. W—Garcia. L—Park. S—Sasaki.

A.L. DIVISION SERIES

■ **Winners:** Seattle, down 2-1 after the first three games, came back to beat Cleveland two straight. The Yankees came back from a 2-0 deficit with three straight wins to edge Oakland in a five-game series victory.

■ **Turning points:** The tide turned in favor of the Mariners in the seventh inning of Game 4. Bartolo Colon was enjoying a 1-0 lead and the Indians were nine outs away from a series victory when the roof caved in. John Olerud started the inning with a walk and advanced to second on single by Stan Javier. Colon tried to pick Olerud off second, but his throw sailed into center field, allowing the runner to go to third. Colon then walked Mike Cameron to load the bases. Al Martin reached on a forceout at the plate. David Bell followed by hitting a foul ball down the left field line which outfielder Marty Cordova caught, but the ball was hit deep enough to allow Javier to score the tying run after the catch. Ichiro Suzuki and Mark McLemore followed with RBI singles to give the Mariners the lead on their way to a 6-2 victory. The Yankees lost the first two games of their series, but managed to win the third game, 1-0, on a home run by catcher Jorge Posada. Posada was hitless in nine previous career at-bats against lefthander Barry Zito, but he managed to connect in the fifth inning. His hit was one of only two safeties by the Yankees in the game.

■ **Memorable moments:** The Mariners were leading, 2-1, in Game 5, when the Indians loaded the bases in the third inning. The Indians' next batter, switch-hitter Roberto Alomar, had not grounded into a double play from the right side all season. But Mariners lefty Jamie Moyer induced Alomar into hitting into his second double play from the right side in three innings and Seattle survived the threat. The Mariners bullpen, which had been pounded two days earlier in a 17-2 loss, pitched three scoreless innings to secure the victory. Yankees righthander Roger Clemens was trailing 2-0 in the fifth inning of the opener, when he appeared uncomfortable on the mound. After manager Joe Torre went to investigate, Clemens was removed from the game, having suffered a strained hamstring making a play in the field earlier in the game. The Yankee bullpen couldn't keep them in the game, and the A's took the first game. In Game 4, A's right fielder Jermaine Dye suffered a broken leg while fouling off a pitch, ending his participation in the series.

■ **Memorable performances:** American League Rookie of the Year Suzuki collected 12 hits and batted .600, while teammates Bell and Edgar Martinez each batted .313 for the Mariners. Omar Vizquel had nine hits, six RBIs and a .409 batting mark for the Indians. His teammate, Juan Gonzalez, batted .348 with two home runs and five RBIs. Shortstop Derek Jeter and Posada each collected eight hits and batted .444 for the Yankees. A's center fielder Johnny Damon batted .409, first baseman Jason Giambi hit .353 and Terrence Long homered twice while batting .389. Zito allowed only two hits in eight innings of Game 3, but the big blow was Posada's home run that won the game, 1-0. Mike Mussina allowed only four hits in seven innings in winning the game for the Yankees. Tim Hudson hurled eight shutout innings in a 2-0 Game 2 victory.

Linescores

Seattle vs. Cleveland

Game 1—October 9, at Seattle
Cleveland................0 0 0 3 0 1 0 1 0—5
Seattle....................0 0 0 0 0 0 0 0 0—0

LEADERS

American League
BA: Ichiro Suzuki, Sea., .350.
Runs: Alex Rodriguez, Tex., 133.
Hits: Ichiro Suzuki, Sea., 242.
TB: Alex Rodriguez, Tex., 393.
HR: Alex Rodriguez, Tex., 52.
RBI: Bret Boone, Sea., 141.
SB: Ichiro Suzuki, Sea., 56.
Wins: Mark Mulder, Oak., 21.
ERA: Freddy Garcia, Sea., 3.05.
CG: Steve W. Sparks, Det., 8.
IP: Freddy Garcia, Sea., 238.2.
SO: Hideo Nomo, Bos., 220.
Sv.: Mariano Rivera, N.Y., 50.

National League
BA: Larry Walker, Col., .350.
Runs: Sammy Sosa, Chi., 146.
Hits: Rich Aurilia, S.F., 206.
TB: Sammy Sosa, Chi., 425.
HR: Barry Bonds, S.F., 73.
RBI: Sammy Sosa, Chi., 160.
SB: Juan Pierre, Col.; Jimmy Rollins, Phi., 46.
Wins: Matt Morris, St.L.; Curt Schilling, Ari., 22.
ERA: Randy Johnson, Ari., 2.49.
CG: Curt Schilling, Ari., 6.
IP: Curt Schilling, Ari., 256.2.
SO: Randy Johnson, Ari., 372.
Sv.: Robb Nen, S.F., 45.

A.L. 20-game winners
Mark Mulder, Oak., 21
Roger Clemens, N.Y., 20
Jamie Moyer, Sea., 20

N.L. 20-game winners
Matt Morris, St.L., 22
Curt Schilling, Ari., 22
Randy Johnson, Ari., 21
Jon Lieber, Chi., 20

A.L. 100 RBIs
Bret Boone, Sea., 141
Juan Gonzalez, Cle., 140
Alex Rodriguez, Tex., 135
Manny Ramirez, Bos., 125
Jim Thome, Cle., 124
Garret Anderson, Ana., 123
Rafael Palmeiro, Tex., 123
Jason Giambi, Oak., 120
Edgar Martinez, Sea., 116
Eric Chavez, Oak., 114
Tino Martinez, N.Y., 113
Magglio Ordonez, Chi., 113
Miguel Tejada, Oak., 113
Mike Cameron, Sea., 110
Troy Glaus, Ana., 108
Jermaine Dye, K.C.-Oak., 106
Corey Koskie, Min., 103
Carlos Delgado, Tor., 102
Carlos Beltran, K.C., 101
Roberto Alomar, Cle., 100

N.L. 100 RBIs
Sammy Sosa, Chi., 160
Todd Helton, Col., 146
Luis Gonzalez, Ari., 142
Barry Bonds, S.F., 137
Jeff Bagwell, Hou., 130
Albert Pujols, St.L., 130
Lance Berkman, Hou., 126
Phil Nevin, S.D., 126
Shawn Green, L.A., 125
Richie Sexson, Mil., 125
Larry Walker, Col., 123
Ryan Klesko, S.D., 113
Aramis Ramirez, Pit., 112
Bobby Abreu, Phi., 110
Jim Edmonds, St.L., 110
Moises Alou, Hou., 108
Vladimir Guerrero, Mon., 108
Scott Rolen, Phi., 107
Jeff Kent, S.F., 106
Andruw Jones, Atl., 104
Cliff Floyd, Fla., 103
Chipper Jones, Atl., 102
Jeromy Burnitz, Mil., 100
Mike Lowell, Fla., 100
Gary Sheffield, L.A., 100

A.L. 40 homers
Alex Rodriguez, Tex., 52
Jim Thome, Cle., 49
Rafael Palmeiro, Tex., 47
Troy Glaus, Ana., 41
Manny Ramirez, Bos., 41

N.L. 40 homers
Barry Bonds, S.F., 73
Sammy Sosa, Chi., 64
Luis Gonzalez, Ari., 57
Shawn Green, L.A., 49
Todd Helton, Col., 49
Richie Sexson, Mil., 45
Phil Nevin, S.D., 41

Most Valuable Player
A.L.: Ichiro Suzuki, OF, Sea.
N.L.: Barry Bonds, OF, S.F.

Cy Young Award
A.L.: Roger Clemens, N.Y.
N.L.: Randy Johnson, Ari.

Rookie of the Year
A.L.: Ichiro Suzuki, OF, Sea.
N.L.: Albert Pujols, OF-3B-1B, St.L.

Manager of the Year
A.L.: Lou Piniella, Sea.
N.L.: Larry Bowa, Phi.

Hall of Fame additions
Bill Mazeroski, 2B, 1956-72
Kirby Puckett, OF, 1984-95
Hilton Smith, P-OF-1B, Negro Leagues
Dave Winfield, OF, 1973-95

Colon, Wickman (9); Garcia, Charlton (6), Paniagua (8), Halama. W—Colon. L—Garcia. HR—Burks (Cle.).

Game 2—October 11, at Seattle
Cleveland................0 0 0 0 0 0 1 0 0—1
Seattle....................4 0 0 0 1 0 0 0 x—5
Finley, Riske (5), Shuey (7), Baez (8); Moyer, Nelson (7), Rhodes (8), Sasaki (9). W—Moyer. L—Finley. HR—Cameron, Martinez, Bell (Sea.).

Game 3—October 13, at Cleveland
Seattle ....1 0 0 0 0 0 1 0 0— 2
Cleveland.............2 2 4 0 1 3 0 5 x—17
Sele, Abbott (3), Halama (6), Paniagua (8); Sabathia, Riske (7), Rincon (7), Burba (8), Rocker (9). W—Sabathia. L—Sele. HR—Gonzalez, Lofton, Thome (Cle.).

Game 4—October 14, at Cleveland
Seattle....................0 0 0 0 0 0 3 1 2—6
Cleveland................0 1 0 0 0 0 1 0 0—2
Garcia, Nelson (7), Rhodes (7), Sasaki (9); Colon, Baez (7), Rincon (8), Shuey (8). W—Garcia. L—Colon. HR—Martinez (Sea.); Gonzalez (Sea.).

Game 5—October 15, at Seattle
Cleveland................0 0 1 0 0 0 0 0 0—1
Seattle....................0 2 0 0 0 0 1 0 x—3
Finley, Riske (5), Rincon (6), Baez (7); Moyer, Nelson (7), Rhodes (8), Sasaki (9). W—Moyer. L—Finley. S—Sasaki.

New York vs. Oakland

Game 1—October 10, at New York
Oakland..................1 0 0 1 0 0 1 2 0—5
New York................0 0 0 0 1 0 0 2 0—3
Mulder, Mecir (7), Isringhausen (9); Clemens, Hitchcock (5), Witasick (8), Stanton (8). W—Mulder. L—Clemens. S—Isringhausen. HR—Long 2, Ja. Giambi (Oak.); Martinez (N.Y.).

Game 2—October 11, at New York
Oakland..................0 0 0 1 0 0 0 0 1—2
New York................0 0 0 0 0 0 0 0 0—0
Hudson, Isringhausen (9); Pettitte, Mendoza (7), Rivera (9). W—Hudson. L—Pettitte. S—Isringhausen. HR—Gant (Oak.).

Game 3—October 13, at Oakland
New York................0 0 0 0 1 0 0 0 0—1
Oakland..................0 0 0 0 0 0 0 0 0—0
Mussina, Rivera (8); Zito, Guthrie (9). W—Mussina. L—Zito. S—Rivera. HR—Posada (N.Y.).

Game 4—October 14, at Oakland
New York................0 2 2 3 0 0 0 0 2—9
Oakland..................0 0 2 0 0 0 0 0 0—2
O. Hernandez, Stanton (6), Mendoza (8); Lidle, Hiljus (4), Magnante (4), Guthrie (6), Bradford (8), Tam (9). W—O. Hernandez. L—Lidle.

Game 5—October 15, at New York
Oakland..................1 1 0 0 1 0 0 0 0—3
New York................0 2 1 1 0 1 0 0 x—5
Mulder, Hudson (5), Mecir (7); Clemens, Stanton (5), Mendoza (7), Rivera (8). W—Stanton. L—Mulder. S—Rivera. HR—Justice (N.Y.).

N.L. DIVISION SERIES

■ **Winners:** The Braves swept the Astros, outscoring Houston 14-6 in the three games. The Astros batted only .200 during the series and went hitless with runners in scoring position. The Diamondbacks edged the Cardinals in five games in a low-scoring series in which St. Louis actually outscored Arizona, 12-10. Righthander Curt Schilling was the difference in the series, as he twice defeated the Cardinals, holding them to one run on nine hits in 18 innings.

■ **Turning points:** The Braves took control of the series in the eighth inning of Game 1, when Chipper Jones belted a three-run homer off Astros closer Billy Wagner, giving Atlanta a 6-3 lead in an eventual 7-4 win. Shortly after the Cardinals' J.D. Drew homered in the eighth inning of Game 5 to tie the score, 1-1, the Diamondbacks ended the series in dramatic fashion with a ninth-inning rally at home. Matt Williams doubled to lead off the inning. Midre Cummings pinch-ran for Williams and was sacrificed to third by Damian Miller. After the Cardinals brought in reliever Steve Kline, Greg Colbrunn was intentionally walked. The next batter, Tony Womack, missed the pitch trying to bunt and Cummings was tagged out trying to steal home while Colbrunn advanced to second. After Danny Bautista pinch-ran for Colbrunn at second, Womack slapped a single to left field, scoring Bautista with the series-winning run.

■ **Memorable moments:** Craig Counsell of the Diamondbacks, who had hit only four home runs in 458 at-bats during the regular season, connected for a three-run homer in the seventh inning of Game 3, breaking a 2-2 deadlock in a game Arizona would win, 5-3.

■ **Memorable performances:** The Braves' Andruw Jones led all regulars with six hits and a .500 batting average. Chipper Jones smacked two home runs, drove in five runs and batted .444, and Julio Franco batted .308. Tom Glavine pitched eight scoreless innings and John Burkett allowed only two runs in 6.1 innings for Atlanta. Jeff Bagwell batted .429 on three hits for Houston.

Linescores

Atlanta vs. Houston

Game 1—October 9, at Houston
Atlanta....................1 0 0 1 0 0 0 4 1—7
Houston ....0 0 0 0 2 1 0 0 1—4
Maddux, Seanez (7), Smoltz (8); Miller, Jackson (8), Wagner (8), Williams (9). W—Seanez. L—Jackson. S—Smoltz. HR—C. Jones, Jordan, A. Jones, Castilla (Atl.); Ausmus (Hou.).

Game 2—October 10, at Houston
Atlanta....................0 1 0 0 0 0 0 0 0—1
Houston ....0 0 0 0 0 0 0 0 0—0
Glavine, Smoltz (9); Mlicki, Dotel (6), Jackson (8), Cruz (8), Wagner (9). W—Glavine. L—Mlicki. S—Smoltz.

Game 3—October 12, at Atlanta
Houston ....0 0 0 0 0 0 2 0 0—2
Atlanta....................0 2 1 1 0 0 0 2 x—6
Reynolds, Cruz (5), Dotel (7), Villone (8); Burkett, Reed (7), Remlinger (7), Karsay (8), Smoltz (9). W—Burkett. L—Reynolds. HR—Ward (Hou.); Franco, C. Jones, Bako (Atl.).

St. Louis vs. Atlanta

Game 1—October 9, at Arizona
St. Louis ....0 0 0 0 0 0 0 0 0—0
Arizona ....0 0 0 0 1 0 0 0 x—1
Morris, Stechschulte (8), Veres (8); Schilling. W—Schilling. L—Morris.

Game 2—October 10, at Arizona
St. Louis ....2 0 1 0 0 0 0 0 1—4
Arizona ....0 0 0 0 0 0 0 1 0—1
W. Williams, Kline (8); Johnson, Morgan (9), Swindell (9), Batista (9). W—W. Williams. L—Johnson. HR—Pujols (St.L.).

Game 3—October 12, at St. Louis
Arizona ....0 0 0 0 0 1 4 0 0—5
St. Louis ....0 0 0 2 0 0 1 0 0—3
Batista, Anderson (7), Morgan (8), Kim (8); Kile, Matthews (7), Timlin (7), Stechschulte (9), Kline (9). W—Batista. L—Matthews. S—Kim. HR—Counsell, Gonzalez (Ari.); Edmonds, Renteria (St.L.).

Game 4—October 13, at St. Louis
Arizona ....1 0 0 0 0 0 0 0 0—1
St. Louis ....1 1 2 0 0 0 0 0 x—4
Lopez, Anderson (4), Swindell (7), Morgan (8); Smith, Hermanson (6), Kline (9). W—Smith. L—Lopez. S—Kline. HR—Vina, Edmonds (St.L.).

Game 5—October 14, at Arizona
St. Louis ....0 0 0 0 0 0 0 1 0—1
Arizona ....0 0 0 1 0 0 0 0 1—2
Morris, Veres (9), Kline (9); Schilling. W—Schilling. L—Kline. HR—Drew (St.L.); Sanders (Ari.).

NLCS

■ **Winner:** The Diamondbacks, in only their fourth year of existence, became the fastest expansion team in major league history to reach the World Series. Led by dominating pitching performances by aces Randy Johnson and Curt Schilling, and helped by some costly Atlanta errors, Arizona defeated the Braves in five games.

■ **Turning point:** Johnson's three-hit shutout in the opener and Schilling's four-hit win in Game 3 gave the Diamondbacks all the momentum they needed.

■ **Memorable moments:** A pinch-homer by Erubiel Durazo in the fifth inning of Game 5 broke a 1-1 tie and sent the Diamondbacks toward their first World Series. Atlanta second baseman Marcus Giles started the inning by booting a grounder by Craig Counsell. Two outs later, Mark Grace was due to bat, but he left the game with a tight hamstring. Durazo replaced Grace and made the Braves pay for Giles' error with his two-run shot.

■ **Top guns:** Craig Counsell (.381, 8 hits, 5 runs, 3 2Bs), Mark Grace (.375, 6 hits), Randy Johnson (2-0, 16.0 IP, 10 hits, 19 SO, 1.13 ERA), Curt Schilling (1-0, 9 IP, 12 SO, 1.00 ERA), Byung-Hyun Kim (5.0 IP, 2 Sv., 0.00 ERA), Diamondbacks; Tom Glavine (1-1, 12.0 IP, 1.50 ERA), Braves.

■ **MVP:** Counsell.

Linescores

Game 1—October 16, at Arizona
Atlanta....................0 0 0 0 0 0 0 0 0—0
Arizona ....1 0 0 0 1 0 0 0 x—2
Maddux, Remlinger (8), Karsay (8); Johnson. W—Johnson. L—Maddux.

Game 2—October 17, at Arizona
Atlanta....................1 0 0 0 0 0 2 5 0—8
Arizona ....0 0 0 0 0 0 0 0 1—1
Glavine, Karsay (8), Smoltz; Batista, Morgan (8), Swindell (8), Witt (8), Kim (9). W—Glavine. L—Batista. HR—Giles, Surhoff, J. Lopez (Atl.).

Game 3—October 19, at Atlanta
Arizona ....0 0 2 0 3 0 0 0 0—5
Atlanta....................0 0 0 1 0 0 0 0 0—1
Schilling; Burkett, Reed (5), Remlinger (5), Ligtenberg (6), Seanez (7), Millwood (8), Marquis (9). W—Schilling. L—Burkett.

Game 4—October 20, at Atlanta
Arizona ....0 0 4 2 0 0 0 1 4—11
Atlanta..................1 1 0 0 0 0 1 1 0— 4
A. Lopez, Anderson (4), Morgan (7), Swindell (7), Batista (8), Kim (8); Maddux, Remlinger (4), Ligtenberg (5), Seanez (7), Karsay (8), Marquis (9). W—Anderson. L—Maddux. S—Kim. HR—Gonzalez (Ari.); A. Jones (Atl.).

Game 5—October 21, at Atlanta
Arizona ....0 0 0 1 2 0 0 0 0—3
Atlanta....................0 0 0 1 0 0 1 0 0—2
Johnson, Kim (8); Glavine, Karsay (6), Smoltz (8). W—Johnson. L—Glavine. S—Kim. HR—Durazo (Ari.); Franco (Atl.).

ALCS

■ **Winner:** The New York Yankees won their fourth straight pennant by holding the Mariners to a .211 batting average. The Mariners romped, 14-3, in Game 3, but could score only eight runs in their other four games. Seattle's scoring drought represented quite a turnaround for a Seattle team which won a major league record-tying 116 games and led the big leagues with 927 runs scored during the regular season.

■ **Turning point:** The Yankees took control in Game 1, scoring on an RBI single by Chuck Knoblauch in the second and adding two runs in the fourth on a home run by Paul O'Neill. They scored three second-inning runs the next day and held on to a 3-2 victory and a two-game series lead.

■ **Memorable moments:** The Mariners not only trounced the Yankees, 14-3 in Game 3, but they turned in two great defensive plays. In the third inning, Stan Javier robbed Alfonso Soriano of a home run with a leaping catch in left field. The following inning, right fielder Ichiro Suzuki nabbed Bernie Williams' drive to the wall.

■ **Top guns:** Paul O'Neill (.417, 5 hits, 2 HRs), Alfonso Soriano (.400, 6 hits, 5 runs), Chuck Knoblauch (.333, 6 hits), Bernie Williams (3 HRs), Andy Pettitte, (2-0, 14.1 IP, 11 hits, 2.51 ERA), Yankees; Bret Boone (.316, 6 hits, 2 HRs, 6 RBIs), Mariners.

■ **MVP:** Pettitte.

Game 1—October 17, at Seattle
New York...............0 1 0 2 0 0 0 1—4
Seattle....................0 0 0 0 1 0 0 0 1—2
Pettitte, Rivera (9); Sele, Charlton (7), Paniagua (8). W—Pettitte. L—Sele. S—Rivera. HR—O'Neill (N.Y.).

Game 2—October 18, at Seattle
New York...............0 3 0 0 0 0 0 0 0—3
Seattle....................0 0 0 2 0 0 0 0 0—2
Mussina, Mendoza (7), Rivera (8); Garcia, Rhodes (8), Nelson (9). W—Mussina. L—Garcia. S—Rivera. HR—Javier (Sea.).

Game 3—October 20, at New York
Seattle..................0 0 0 0 2 7 2 1 2—14
New York.............2 0 0 0 0 0 0 1 0— 3
Moyer, Paniagua (8), Halama (9); Hernandez, Stanton (6), Wohlers (6), Witasick (7). W—Moyer. L—Hernandez. HR—Boone, Buhner, Olerud (Sea.); Williams (N.Y.).

Game 4—October 21, at New York
Seattle....................0 0 0 0 0 0 0 1 0—1
New York................0 0 0 0 0 0 0 1 2—3
Abbott, Charlton (6), Nelson (6), Rhodes (8), Sasaki (9); Clemens, Mendoza (6), Rivera (9). W—Rivera. L—Sasaki. HR—Boone (Sea.); Williams, Soriano (N.Y.).

Game 5—October 22, at New York
Seattle ....0 0 0 0 0 0 3 0 0— 3
New York..............0 0 4 1 0 4 0 3 x—12
Sele, Halama (5), Pineiro (6), Paniagua (8); Pettitte, Mendoza (7), Stanton (8), Rivera (9). W—Pettitte. L—Sele. HR—Williams, T. Martinez, O'Neill (N.Y.).

WORLD SERIES

■ **Winner:** The Diamondbacks won their first World Series in a drama-filled series. Trailing 3-2 in the series, Arizona enjoyed a 15-2 laugher in Game 6, but had to rally for two runs off Yankee closer Mariano Rivera in the bottom of the ninth in Game 7.

■ **Turning point:** Luis Gonzalez' one-out single in the bottom of the ninth inning of Game 7 drove in Jay Bell with the series-ending run. Trailing 2-1, Arizona opened the inning with a single by Mark Grace. After David Dellucci was sent in to run for Grace, Damian Miller bunted to Rivera, who threw wildly to second, putting runners at first and second. Bell tried bunting the runners over, but forced Dellucci at third. Tony Womack then doubled home the tying run and Craig Counsell was hit by a pitch to load the bases. Gonzalez was the next batter and, with the infield playing in, blooped a single over short that scored Bell.

■ **Memorable moments:** With the Yankees trailing 3-1 with two out in the bottom of the ninth and a runner on first in Game 4, Tino Martinez hit a dramatic home run to tie the game. One inning later, Derek Jeter homered to give New York a 4-3 win in 10 innings. The next night the Yankees were trailing 2-0 with two out in the bottom of the ninth and this time Scott Brosius provided the dramatics with a home run to tie the game. Alfonso Soriano drove in the winning run for New York in the bottom of the 12th.

■ **Top guns:** Johnson (3-0, 17.1 IP, 9 hits, 19 SO, 1.04 ERA), Schilling (1-0, 21.1 IP, 12 hits, 26 SO, 1.69 ERA), Danny Bautista (.583, 7 hits), Steve Finley (.368, 7 hits, 5 runs), Reggie Sanders (.304, 6 runs, 7 hits), Diamondbacks; Paul O'Neill (.333, 5 hits), Roger Clemens (1-0, 13.1 IP, 10 hits, 19 SO, 1.35 ERA), Yankees.

■ **MVPs:** Johnson, Schilling.

Linescores

Game 1—October 27, at Arizona
New York...............1 0 0 0 0 0 0 0 0—1
Arizona ....1 0 4 4 0 0 0 0 x—9
Mussina, Choate (4), Hitchcock (5), Stanton (8); Schilling, Morgan (8), Swindell (9). W—Schilling. L—Mussina. HR—Counsell, Gonzalez (Ari.).

Game 2—October 28, at Arizona
New York...............0 0 0 0 0 0 0 0 0—0
Arizona ....0 1 0 0 0 0 3 0 x—4
Pettitte, Stanton (8); Johnson. W—Johnson. L—Pettitte. HR—M. Williams (Ari.).

Game 3—October 30, at New York
Arizona ....0 0 0 1 0 0 0 0 0—1
New York...............0 1 0 0 0 1 0 0 x—2
Anderson, Morgan (6), Swindell (7); Clemens, Rivera (8). W—Clemens. L—Anderson. S—Rivera. HR—Posada (N.Y.).

Game 4—October 31, at New York
Arizona ....0 0 0 1 0 0 0 2 0 0—3
New York.........0 0 1 0 0 0 0 0 2 1—4
Schilling, Kim (8); Hernandez, Stanton (7), Mendoza (8), Rivera (10). W—Rivera. L—Kim. HR—Grace (Ari.); Martinez, Jeter, Spencer (N.Y.).

Game 5—November 1, at New York
Arizona ....0 0 0 0 2 0 0 0 0 0 0 0—2
New York..0 0 0 0 0 0 0 0 2 0 0 1—3
Batista, Swindell (8), Kim (9), Morgan (9), Lopez (12); Mussina, Mendoza (9), Rivera (10), Hitchcock (12). W—Hitchcock. L—Lopez. HR—Finley, Barajas (Ari.); Brosius (N.Y.).

Game 6—November 3, at Arizona
New York.............0 0 0 0 0 2 0 0 0— 2
Arizona ....1 3 8 3 0 0 0 0 x—15
Pettitte, Witasick (3), Choate (4), Stanton (7); Johnson, Witt (8), Brohawn (9). W—Johnson. L—Pettitte.

Game 7—November 4, at Arizona
New York...............0 0 0 0 0 0 1 1 0—2
Arizona ....0 0 0 0 0 1 0 0 2—3
Clemens, Stanton (7), Rivera (8); Schilling, Batista (8), Johnson (8). W—Johnson. L—Rivera. HR—Soriano (N.Y.).

HISTORY

Franchise Histories

The 1930 Athletics, the consecutive World Series champions managed by the incomparable Connie Mack (center, in suit), rank among the great teams in baseball history.

ANAHEIM ANGELS

FRANCHISE CHRONOLOGY

First season: 1961, as the Los Angeles Angels, with home games played at Los Angeles' Wrigley Field. The Angels, who shared distinction with the second-edition Washington Senators as baseball's first expansion teams, recorded a 7-2 victory at Baltimore in their Major League debut. They went on to post a 70-91 first-season record, good for eighth place in the 10-team A.L.

1962-present: The second-year Angels moved out of tiny Wrigley Field and up in the standings. Sharing new Dodger Stadium with the N.L. Dodgers, they posted a surprising 86-76 record, good for third place behind New York and Minnesota. That success was an illusion. The Angels, who swapped the "Los Angeles" part of their name for "California" in 1965 and moved into new Anaheim Stadium a year later, didn't win their first West Division title until 1979 and failed in their three journeys into the A.L. Championship Series. In 2002, they won a club-record 99 games and as the A.L. wild-card representatives, defeated the New York Yankees, Minnesota Twins and San Francisco Giants in the postseason to win their first world championship. The Angels, under the new ownership flag of Walt Disney Company, changed their name to "Anaheim Angels" after the 1996 season.

First baseman Rod Carew.

ANGELS VS. OPPONENTS BY DECADE

	A's	Indians	Orioles	Red Sox	Tigers	Twins	White Sox	Yankees	Rangers	Brewers	Royals	Blue Jays	Mariners	Devil Rays	Interleague	Decade Recor
1961-69	88-74	82-74	72-83	79-76	60-96	79-82	70-92	61-95	76-80	9-9	9-9					685-770
1970-79	72-97	58-58	52-65	53-64	53-63	89-77	90-79	52-65	77-79	61-67	79-87	20-12	25-18			781-831
1980-89	57-70	69-49	49-71	55-59	55-59	66-57	68-62	49-63	68-55	61-54	50-73	57-63	79-48			783-783
1990-99	55-68	44-59	46-73	47-71	54-53	54-61	60-58	59-58	63-61	47-37	64-56	53-58	59-64	13-10	20-30	738-817
2000-02	20-33	14-13	18-12	12-11	18-10	14-14	16-12	12-12	26-24		17-13	17-13	18-33	21-9	33-21	256-230
Totals	292-342	267-253	237-304	246-281	240-281	302-291	304-303	233-293	310-299	178-167	219-238	147-146	181-163	34-19	53-51	3243-3431

Interleague results: 5-7 vs. Diamondbacks, 2-1 vs. Reds, 12-4 vs. Rockies, 16-16 vs. Dodgers, 3-0 vs. Brewers, 2-1 vs. Pirates, 1-2 vs. Cardinals, 7-9 vs. Padres, 5-11 vs. Giants.

MANAGERS

(Los Angeles Angels, 1961-65; California Angels, 1965-96)

Name	*Years*	*Record*
Bill Rigney	1961-69	625-707
Lefty Phillips	1969-71	222-225
Del Rice	1972	75-80
Bobby Winkles	1973-74	109-127
Whitey Herzog	1974	2-2
Dick Williams	1974-76	147-194
Norm Sherry	1976-77	76-71
Dave Garcia	1977-78	60-66
Jim Fregosi	1978-81	237-249
Gene Mauch	1981-82, 1985-87	379-332
John McNamara	1983-84, 1996	161-191
Cookie Rojas	1988	75-79
Moose Stubing	1988	0-8
Doug Rader	1989-91	232-216
Buck Rodgers	1991-94	140-172
John Wathan	1992	39-50
Marcel Lachemann	1994-96	161-170
Joe Maddon	1996	8-14
Terry Collins	1997-99	220-237
Joe Maddon	1999	19-10
Mike Scioscia	2000-02	256-230

WORLD SERIES CHAMPIONS

Year	*Record*	*Manager*	*MVP*
2002	99-63	Scioscia	Troy Glaus

A.L. PENNANT WINNERS

Year	*Record*	*Manager*	*Series Result*
2002	99-63	Scioscia	Defeated Giants

WEST DIVISION CHAMPIONS

Year	*Record*	*Manager*	*ALCS Result*
1979	88-74	Fregosi	Lost to Orioles
1982	93-69	Mauch	Lost to Brewers
1986	92-70	Mauch	Lost to Red Sox

WILD-CARD QUALIFIERS

Year	*Record*	*Manager*	*Div. Series Result*	*ALCS Result*	*World Series Result*
2002	99-63	Scioscia	Defeated Yankees	Defeated Twins	Defeated Giants

ALL-TIME RECORD OF EXPANSION TEAMS

Team	W	L	Pct.	DT	P	WS
Arizona	440	370	.543	3	1	1
Kansas City	2,675	2,694	.498	6	2	1
Houston	3,229	3,285	.496	7	0	0
Toronto	2,025	2,063	.495	5	2	2
Anaheim	3,243	3,431	.486	3	1	1
Montreal	2,605	2,769	.485	2	0	0
Colorado	740	817	.475	0	0	0
New York	3,091	3,412	.475	4	4	2
Milwaukee	2,545	2,831	.473	2	1	0
Seattle	1,924	2,163	.471	3	0	0
Texas	3,097	3,560	.465	4	0	0
San Diego	2,460	2,921	.457	3	2	0
Florida	706	847	.455	0	1	1
Tampa Bay	318	490	.394	0	0	0

DT—Division Titles. P—Pennants won. WS—World Series won.

ATTENDANCE HIGHS

Total	*Season*	*Park*
2,807,360	1982	Anaheim Stadium
2,696,299	1987	Anaheim Stadium
2,655,892	1986	Anaheim Stadium
2,647,291	1989	Anaheim Stadium
2,567,427	1985	Anaheim Stadium

BALLPARK CHRONOLOGY

Edison International Field of Anaheim, formerly Anaheim Stadium (1966-present)

Capacity: 45,050.
First game: Chicago 3, Angels 1 (April 19, 1966).
First batter: Tommie Agee, White Sox.
First hit: Jim Fregosi, Angels (double).
First run: Rick Reichardt, Angels (2nd inning).
First home run: Rick Reichardt, Angels.
First winning pitcher: Tommy John, White Sox.
First-season attendance: 1,400,321.

Wrigley Field, Los Angeles (1961)

Capacity: 20,457.
First game: Minnesota 4, Angels 2 (April 27, 1961).
First-season attendance: 603,510.

Dodger Stadium (1962-65)

Capacity: 56,000.
First game: Kansas City 5, Angels 3 (April 17, 1962).
First-season attendance: 1,144,063.

A.L. MVP

Don Baylor, OF, 1979

CY YOUNG WINNER

Dean Chance, RH, 1964

ROOKIE OF THE YEAR

Tim Salmon, OF, 1993

MANAGER OF THE YEAR

Mike Scioscia, 2002

RETIRED UNIFORMS

No.	*Name*	*Pos.*
11	Jim Fregosi	SS, Manage
26	Gene Autry	Owner
29	Rod Carew	2B-1B
30	Nolan Ryan	P
50	Jimmie Reese	Coach

Mike Scioscia led the Angels to a franchise-record 99 victories and their first world championship in 2002.

MILESTONE PERFORMANCES

25-plus home runs

47— Troy Glaus 2000
41— Troy Glaus 2001
39— Reggie Jackson 1982
37— Bobby Bonds 1977
Leon Wagner 1962
36— Don Baylor 1979
Mo Vaughn 2000
35— Garret Anderson 2000
34— Wally Joyner 1987
Don Baylor 1978
Tim Salmon 1995, 2000
33— Jim Edmonds 1995
Tim Salmon 1997
Mo Vaughn 1999
31— Tim Salmon 1993
30— Doug DeCinces 1982
Bobby Grich 1979
Frank Robinson 1973
Tim Salmon 1996
Troy Glaus 2002
29— Brian Downing 1987
Troy Glaus 1999
Garret Anderson 2002
28— Leon Wagner 1961
Brian Downing 1982
Dave Winfield 1991
Chili Davis 1996
Garret Anderson 2001
27— Reggie Jackson 1985
Chili Davis 1993
Tony Phillips 1995
Jim Edmonds 1996
26— Lee Thomas 1962
Leon Wagner 1963
Doug DeCinces 1986
Chili Davis 1994
Jim Edmonds 1997
Tim Salmon 1998
25— Ken Hunt 1961
Dan Mincher 1967
Don Baylor 1977
Reggie Jackson 1985
Brian Downing 1988
Jim Edmonds 1998
Darin Erstad 2000

100-plus RBIs

139— Don Baylor 1979
129— Tim Salmon 1997
123— Garret Anderson 2001, 2002
117— Wally Joyner 1987
Mo Vaughn 2000
Garret Anderson 2000
115— Bobby Bonds 1977
112— Chili Davis 1993
111— Troy Glaus 2002
108— Mo Vaughn 1999
Troy Glaus 2001
107— Leon Wagner 1962
Jim Edmonds 1995
105— Tim Salmon 1995
104— Lee Thomas 1962
102— J.T. Snow 1995
Troy Glaus 2000
101— Reggie Jackson 1982
Dan Ford 1979
Bobby Grich 1979
100— Wally Joyner 1986
Darin Erstad 2000

20-plus victories

1964— Dean Chance 20-9
1970— Clyde Wright 22-12
1971— Andy Messersmith 20-13
1973— Nolan Ryan 21-16
Bill Singer 20-14
1974— Nolan Ryan 22-16

A.L. home run champions

1981— Bobby Grich *22
1982— Reggie Jackson *39
2000— Troy Glaus 47

* Tied for league lead

A.L. RBI champions

1979— Don Baylor 139

A.L. batting champions

1970— Alex Johnson .... .329

A.L. ERA champions

1964— Dean Chance 1.65
1977— Frank Tanana 2.54

A.L. strikeout champions

1972— Nolan Ryan 329
1973— Nolan Ryan 383
1974— Nolan Ryan 367
1975— Frank Tanana 269
1976— Nolan Ryan 327
1977— Nolan Ryan 341
1978— Nolan Ryan 260
1979— Nolan Ryan 223

No-hit pitchers

(9 innings or more)

1962— Bo Belinsky .... 2-0 vs. Baltimore
1970— Clyde Wright .... 4-0 vs. Oakland
1973— Nolan Ryan .... 3-0 vs. Kansas City
1973— Nolan Ryan .... 6-0 vs. Detroit
1974— Nolan Ryan .... 4-0 vs. Minnesota
1975— Nolan Ryan .... 1-0 vs. Baltimore
1984— Mike Witt .... 1-0 vs. Texas (Perfect)
1990— Mark Langston-Mike Witt .... 1-0 vs. Seattle

Longest hitting streaks

28— Garret Anderson 1998
25— Rod Carew 1984
23— Jim Edmonds 1995
22— Sandy Alomar 1970
21— Bobby Grich 1981
Randy Velarde 1996
20— Bobby Grich 1979
19— Rod Carew 1982
18— Chad Curtis 1993
Fred Lynn 1982
Rod Carew 1980
Sandy Alomar 1971
Bob Rodgers 1964
17— Ken McMullen 1972
Brian Downing 1987
Garret Anderson 1997
Garret Anderson 1999
Tim Salmon 2000
16— Lee Thomas 1961
Aurelio Rodriguez 1968
Dan Ford 1980
Johnny Ray 1988
Wally Joyner 1991
Garret Anderson 1999
15— Felix Torres 1962
Bobby Knoop 1967
John Stephenson 1971
Leo Cardenas 1972
Dave Collins 1975
Rick Burleson 1981
Brian Downing 1985
Johnny Ray 1989
Dave Gallagher 1991
Chad Curtis 1993
Tim Salmon 1995
Darin Erstad 1998, 2001
Garret Anderson 2002
David Eckstein 2002

Outfielders Leon Wagner (left) and Lee Thomas enjoyed good homer and run-production seasons in the 1960s.

INDIVIDUAL SEASON, GAME RECORDS

Dean Chance, the A.L.'s 1964 ERA champion, holds the team single-season record for shutouts with 11.

SEASON

Batting			
At-bats	689	Sandy Alomar	1971
Runs	121	Darin Erstad	2000
Hits	240	Darin Erstad	2000
Singles	170	Darin Erstad	2000
Doubles	56	Garret Anderson	2002
Triples	13	3 times	
		Last by Devon White	1989
Home runs	47	Troy Glaus	2000
Home runs, rookie	31	Tim Salmon	1993
Grand slams	3	Joe Rudi	1978, 1979
		David Eckstein	2002
Total bases	366	Darin Erstad	2000
RBIs	139	Don Baylor	1979
Walks	113	Tony Phillips	1995
Most strikeouts	181	Mo Vaughn	2000
Fewest strikeouts	29	Gary DiSarcina	1997
Batting average	.355	Darin Erstad	2000
Slugging pct.	.604	Troy Glaus	2000
Stolen bases	70	Mickey Rivers	1975
Pitching			
Games	72	Minnie Rojas	1967
Complete games	26	Nolan Ryan	1973, 1974
Innings	332.2	Nolan Ryan	1974
Wins	22	Clyde Wright	1970
		Nolan Ryan	1974
Losses	19	4 times	
		Last by Kirk McCaskill	1991
Winning pct.	.773 (17-5)	Bert Blyleven	1989
Walks	204	Nolan Ryan	1977
Strikeouts	383	Nolan Ryan	1973
Shutouts	11	Dean Chance	1964
Home runs allowed	40	Shawn Boskie	1996
		Ramon Ortiz	2002
Lowest ERA	1.65	Dean Chance	1964
Saves	46	Bryan Harvey	1991

GAME

Batting			
Runs	5	Last by Tim Salmon	4-12-98
Hits	6	Garret Anderson	9-27-96
Doubles	3	Last by Garret Anderson	8-16-2001
Triples	2	Last by Reggie Williams	6-30-99
Home runs	3	Last by Troy Glaus	9-15-02
RBIs	8	Last by Adam Kennedy	4-18-2000
Total bases	15	Dave Winfield	4-13-91
Stolen bases	4	Last by Chad Curtis	4-17-93

CAREER RECORDS

BATTING

Games

Player	Games
Brian Downing	1,661
Jim Fregosi	1,429
Tim Salmon	1,388
Bobby Grich	1,222
Garret Anderson	1,206
Gary DiSarcina	1,086
Dick Schofield	1,086
Bob Boone	968
Chili Davis	950
Darin Erstad	935

At-bats

Player	At-bats
Brian Downing	5,854
Jim Fregosi	5,244
Tim Salmon	5,009
Garret Anderson	4,817
Bobby Grich	4,100
Darin Erstad	3,801
Gary DiSarcina	3,744
Chili Davis	3,491
Dick Schofield	3,434
Wally Joyner	3,356

Runs

Player	Runs
Brian Downing	889
Tim Salmon	863
Jim Fregosi	691
Garret Anderson	623
Darin Erstad	610
Bobby Grich	601
Chili Davis	520
Don Baylor	481
Rod Carew	474
Wally Joyner	469

Hits

Player	Hits
Brian Downing	1,588
Garret Anderson	1,432
Tim Salmon	1,426
Jim Fregosi	1,408
Darin Erstad	1,107
Bobby Grich	1,103
Chili Davis	973
Rod Carew	968
Gary DiSarcina	966
Wally Joyner	961

Doubles

Player	Doubles
Garret Anderson	300
Tim Salmon	289
Brian Downing	282
Jim Fregosi	219
Darin Erstad	202
Gary DiSarcina	186
Bobby Grich	183
Wally Joyner	175
Chili Davis	167
Jim Edmonds	161

Triples

Player	Triples
Jim Fregosi	70
Mickey Rivers	32
Luis Polonia	27
Dick Schofield	27
Bobby Knoop	25
Darin Erstad	24
Devon White	24
Garret Anderson	23
Gary Pettis	23
Rod Carew	22
Brian Downing	22

Home runs

Player	Home runs
Tim Salmon	269
Brian Downing	222
Garret Anderson	164
Chili Davis	156
Bobby Grich	154
Troy Glaus	148
Don Baylor	141
Doug DeCinces	130
Reggie Jackson	123
Jim Edmonds	121

Total bases

Player	Total bases
Brian Downing	2,580
Tim Salmon	2,558
Garret Anderson	2,270
Jim Fregosi	2,112
Bobby Grich	1,788
Darin Erstad	1,645
Chili Davis	1,620
Wally Joyner	1,511
Don Baylor	1,390
Doug DeCinces	1,334

Runs batted in

Player	RBI
Tim Salmon	894
Brian Downing	846
Garret Anderson	756
Chili Davis	618
Bobby Grich	557
Jim Fregosi	546
Wally Joyner	532
Don Baylor	523
Doug DeCinces	481
Darin Erstad	468

Extra-base hits

Player	Extra-base hits
Tim Salmon	576
Brian Downing	526
Garret Anderson	487
Jim Fregosi	404
Bobby Grich	357
Chili Davis	329
Darin Erstad	322
Wally Joyner	304
Doug DeCinces	294
Jim Edmonds	294

Batting average

(Minimum 500 games)

Player	Average
Rod Carew	.314
Garret Anderson	.297
Luis Polonia	.294
Juan Beniquez	.293
Darin Erstad	.291
Jim Edmonds	.290
Wally Joyner	.286
Tim Salmon	.285
Orlando Palmeiro	.281
Chili Davis	.279

Stolen bases

Player	Stolen bases
Gary Pettis	186
Luis Polonia	174
Sandy Alomar	139
Darin Erstad	134
Mickey Rivers	126
Devon White	123
Chad Curtis	116
Jerry Remy	110
Dick Schofield	99
Don Baylor	89

PITCHING

Earned-run average

(Minimum 500 innings)

Player	ERA
Andy Messersmith	2.78
Dean Chance	2.83
Nolan Ryan	3.07
Frank Tanana	3.08
George Brunet	3.13
Paul Hartzell	3.27
Clyde Wright	3.28
Jim McGlothlin	3.37
Fred Newman	3.41
Geoff Zahn	3.64

Wins

Player	Wins
Chuck Finley	165
Nolan Ryan	138
Mike Witt	109
Frank Tanana	102
Mark Langston	88
Clyde Wright	87
Kirk McCaskill	78
Dean Chance	74
Andy Messersmith	59
Jim Abbott	54
George Brunet	54

Losses

Player	Losses
Chuck Finley	140
Nolan Ryan	121
Mike Witt	107
Clyde Wright	85
Frank Tanana	78
Rudy May	76
Jim Abbott	74
Mark Langston	74
Kirk McCaskill	74
George Brunet	69

Innings pitched

Player	Innings
Chuck Finley	2,675.0
Nolan Ryan	2,181.1
Mike Witt	1,965.1
Frank Tanana	1,615.1
Mark Langston	1,445.1
Clyde Wright	1,403.1
Dean Chance	1,236.2
Kirk McCaskill	1,221.0
Rudy May	1,138.2
Jim Abbott	1,073.2

Strikeouts

Player	Strikeouts
Nolan Ryan	2,416
Chuck Finley	2,151
Mike Witt	1,283
Frank Tanana	1,233
Mark Langston	1,112
Dean Chance	857
Rudy May	844
Andy Messersmith	768
Kirk McCaskill	714
George Brunet	678

Bases on balls

Player	Bases on balls
Nolan Ryan	1,302
Chuck Finley	1,118
Mike Witt	656
Mark Langston	551
Rudy May	484
Dean Chance	462
Clyde Wright	449
Kirk McCaskill	448
Frank Tanana	422
Andy Messersmith	402

Games

Player	Games
Troy Percival	475
Chuck Finley	436
Mike Witt	314
Dave LaRoche	304
Mike Holtz	301
Nolan Ryan	291
Shigetoshi Hasegawa	287
Clyde Wright	266
Andy Hassler	259
Bryan Harvey	250

Shutouts

Player	Shutouts
Nolan Ryan	40
Frank Tanana	24
Dean Chance	21
George Brunet	14
Chuck Finley	14
Geoff Zahn	13
Rudy May	12
Kirk McCaskill	11
Andy Messersmith	11
Mike Witt	10

Saves

Player	Saves
Troy Percival	250
Bryan Harvey	126
Dave LaRoche	65
Donnie Moore	61
Bob Lee	58
Joe Grahe	45
Minnie Rojas	43
Ken Tatum	39
Lee Smith	37
Don Aase	27
Art Fowler	27
Luis Sanchez	27

TEAM SEASON, GAME RECORDS

SEASON

Batting

Record	Total	Year
Most at-bats	5,686	1996
Most runs	866	1979
Fewest runs	454	1972
Most hits	1,603	2002
Most singles	1,114	1979
Most doubles	333	2002
Most triples	54	1966
Most home runs	236	2000
Fewest home runs	55	1975
Most grand slams	8	1979, 1983
Most pinch-hit home runs	9	1987
Most total bases	2,659	2000
Most stolen bases	220	1975
Highest batting average	.282	1979, 2002
Lowest batting average	.227	1968
Highest slugging pct	.472	2000

Pitching

Record	Total	Year
Lowest ERA	2.91	1964
Highest ERA	5.30	1996
Most complete games	72	1973
Most shutouts	28	1964
Most saves	54	2002
Most walks	713	1961
Most strikeouts	1,091	1998

Fielding

Record	Total	Year
Most errors	192	1961
Fewest errors	87	2002
Most double plays	202	1985
Highest fielding average	.986	2002

General

Record	Total	Year
Most games won	99	2002
Most games lost	95	1968, 1980
Highest win pct	.611	2002
Lowest win pct	.406	1980

GAME, INNING

Batting

Record	Total	Date
Most runs, game	24	8-25-79
Most runs, inning	13	9-14-78 5-12-97
Most hits, game	26	8-25-79, 6-20-80
Most home runs, game	6	Last 4-21-2000
Most total bases, game	52	6-20-80

Lefthander Frank Tanana recorded 102 victories in his eight successful seasons with the Angels.

ANGELS YEAR-BY-YEAR

Year	W	L	Place	Games Back	Manager	Leaders: Batting avg.	Hits	Home runs	RBIs	Wins	ERA
1961	70	91	8th	38½	Rigney	Pearson, .288	L. Thomas, 129	Wagner, 28	Hunt, 84	McBride, 12	Morgan, 2.36
1962	86	76	3rd	10	Rigney	L. Thomas, .290	Moran, 186	Wagner, 37	Wagner, 107	Chance, 14	Chance, 2.96
1963	70	91	9th	34	Rigney	Pearson, .304	Pearson, 176	Wagner, 26	Wagner, 90	Chance, McBride, 13	Navarro, 2.89
1964	82	80	5th	17	Rigney	W. Smith, .301	Fregosi, 140	Adcock, 21	Fregosi, 72	Chance, 20	Lee, 1.51
1965	75	87	7th	27	Rigney	Pearson, .278	Fregosi, 167	Fregosi, 15	Fregosi, 64	Chance, 15	Lee, 1.92
1966	80	82	6th	18	Rigney	Cardenal, .276	Cardenal, 155	Adcock, 18	Knoop, 72	Brunet, Sanford 13	Lee, 2.74
1967	84	77	5th	7½	Rigney	Fregosi, .290	Fregosi, 171	Mincher, 25	Mincher, 76	R. Clark, McGlothlin, Rojas, 12	Rojas, 2.52
1968	67	95	8th	36	Rigney	Reichardt, .255	Fregosi, 150	Reichardt, 21	Reichardt, 73	Brunet, 13	Murphy, 2.17
								—WEST DIVISION—			
1969	71	91	3rd	26	Rigney, Phillips	Johnstone, .270	Alomar, 153	Reichardt, 13	Reichardt, 68	Messersmith, 16	Messersmith, 2.52
1970	86	76	3rd	12	Phillips	A. Johnson, .329	A. Johnson, 202	Fregosi, 22	A. Johnson, 86	Wright, 22	Wright, 2.83
1971	76	86	4th	25½	Phillips	Alomar, .260	Alomar, 179	McMullen, 21	McMullen, 68	Messersmith, 20	Allen, 2.49
1972	75	80	5th	18	Rice	Berry, .289	Oliver, 154	Oliver, 20	Oliver, 76	Ryan, 19	Ryan, 2.28
1973	79	83	4th	15	Winkles	Berry, .284	Oliver, 144	Robinson, 30	Robinson, 97	Ryan, 21	Ryan, 2.87
1974	68	94	6th	22	Winkles, D. Williams, Herzog	Rivers, .285	Doyle, Rivers, 133	Robinson, 20	Robinson, 63	Ryan, 22	Hassler, 2.61
1975	72	89	6th	25½	D. Williams	Bochte, .285	Rivers, 175	Stanton, 14	Stanton, 82	Figueroa, Tanana, 16	Tanana, 2.62
1976	76	86	*4th	14	D. Williams, Sherry	Bonds, .265	Remy, 132	Bonds, 10	Bonds, 54	Tanana, 19	Tanana, 2.43
1977	74	88	5th	28	Sherry, Garcia	Chalk, .277	Bonds, 156	Bonds, 37	Bonds, 115	Ryan, 19	Tanana, 2.54
1978	87	75	*2nd	5	Garcia, Fregosi	Ro. Jackson, .297	Bostock, 168	Baylor, 34	Baylor, 99	Tanana, 18	LaRoche, 2.82
1979	88	74	†1st	+3	Fregosi	Downing, .326	Lansford, 188	Baylor, 36	Baylor, 139	Frost, Ryan, 16	Frost, 3.57
1980	65	95	6th	31	Fregosi	Carew, .331	Carew, 179	Thompson, 17	Lansford, 80	Clear, Tanana, 11	Clear, 3.30
1981	51	59	‡4th/7th	—	Fregosi, Mauch	Carew, .305	Burleson, 126	Grich, 22	Baylor, 66	Forsch, 11	Forsch, 2.88
1982	93	69	†1st	+3	Mauch	Carew, .319	Downing, 175	Jackson, 39	Jackson, 101	Zahn, 18	Kison, 3.17
1983	70	92	*5th	29	McNamara	Carew, .339	Carew, 160	Lynn, 22	Lynn, 74	Forsch, John, Kison, 11	Zahn, 3.33
1984	81	81	*2nd	3	McNamara	Beniquez, .336	Downing, 148	Jackson, 25	Downing, 91	Witt, 15	Zahn, 3.12
1985	90	72	2nd	1	Mauch	Beniquez, .304	Downing, 137	Jackson, 27	Downing, Jackson, 85	Witt, 15	Moore, 1.92
1986	92	70	†1st	+5	Mauch	Joyner, .290	Joyner, 172	DeCinces, 26	Joyner, 100	Witt, 18	Candelaria, 2.55
1987	75	87	*6th	10	Mauch	Joyner, .285	White, 168	Joyner, 34	Joyner, 117	Witt, 16	Buice, 3.39
1988	75	87	4th	29	Rojas, Stubing	Ray, .306	Ray, 184	Downing, 25	C. Davis, 93	Witt, 13	Witt, 4.15
1989	91	71	3rd	8	Rader	Ray, .289	Joyner, 167	C. Davis, 22	C. Davis, 90	Blyleven, 17	Minton, 2.20
1990	80	82	4th	23	Rader	Polonia, .336	Polonia, 135	Parrish, 24	Winfield, 78	Finley, 18	Finley, 2.40
1991	81	81	7th	14	Rader, Rodgers	Joyner, .301	Polonia, 179	Winfield, 28	Joyner, 96	Langston, 19	J. Abbott, 2.89
1992	72	90	*5th	24	Rodgers, Wathan	Polonia, .286	Polonia, 165	Gaetti, 12	Felix, 72	Langston, 13	J. Abbott, 2.77
1993	71	91	*5th	23	Rodgers	Curtis, .285	Curtis, 166	Salmon, 31	C. Davis, 112	Finley, Langston, 16	Finley, 3.15
1994	47	68	4th	5½	M. Lachemann	C. Davis, .311	C. Davis, 122	C. Davis, 26	C. Davis, 84	Finley, 10	Finley, 4.32
1995	78	66	§2nd	1	M. Lachemann	Salmon, .330	Salmon, 177	Salmon, 34	Edmonds, 107	Finley, Langston, 15	Finley, 4.21
1996	70	91	4th	18½	M. Lachemann, McNamara	Edmonds, .304	Anderson, 173	Salmon, 30	Salmon, 98	Finley, 15	Finley, 4.16
1997	84	78	2nd	6	Collins	Anderson, .303	Anderson, 189	Salmon, 33	Salmon, 129	Finley, Dickson, 13	Hasegawa, 3.93
1998	85	77	2nd	3	Collins	Edmonds, .307	Edmonds, 184	Salmon, 26	Edmonds, 91	Finley, 11	Hasegawa, 3.14
1999	70	92	4th	25	Collins, Maddon	Velarde, .306	Anderson, 188	Vaughn, 33	Vaughn, 108	Finley, 12	Olivares, 4.05
2000	82	80	3rd	9½	Scioscia	Erstad, .355	Erstad, 240	Glaus, 47	Vaughn, Anderson, 117	Hasegawa, 10	Hasegawa, 3.57
2001	75	87	3rd	41	Scioscia	Anderson, .289	Anderson, 194	Glaus, 41	Anderson, 123	Ortiz, 13	Washburn, 3.77
2002	99	63	2nd	4	Scioscia	Kennedy, .312	Anderson, 195	Glaus, 30	Anderson, 123	Washburn, 18	Washburn, 3.15

* Tied for position. † Lost Championship Series. ‡ First half 31-29; second half 20-30. § Lost division playoff. ∞Won Division Series.

Note: Batting average minimum 350 at-bats; ERA minimum 90 innings pitched.

Eli Grba

THE ANGELS joined an exclusive fraternity in 1960 when actor/singer Gene Autry and partner Bob Reynolds were awarded the Los Angeles franchise in baseball's first expansion. The Angels, based in Los Angeles, joined the new-edition Washington Senators in an American League lineup that increased from eight to 10 teams. The former Washington Senators, owned by Calvin Griffith, were granted permission to transfer operations to Minneapolis-St. Paul.

The Los Angeles Angels participated in baseball's first expansion draft on December 14, 1960, and grabbed righthanded pitcher Eli Grba with their first pick. They went on to select 30 players and opened play on April 11, 1961, with a 7-2 victory over Baltimore.

Expansion draft (December 14, 1960)

Players

Player	From	Position
Ken Aspromonte	Cleveland	second base
Earl Averill	Chicago	catcher
Julio Becquer	Minnesota	infield
Steve Bilko	Detroit	first base
Bob Cerv	New York	outfield
Jim Fregosi	Boston	shortstop
Ken Hamlin	Kansas City	first base
Ken Hunt	New York	outfield
Ted Kluszewski	Chicago	first base
Gene Leek	Cleveland	infield
Jim McAnany	Chicago	outfield
Albie Pearson	Baltimore	outfield
Bob Rodgers	Detroit	catcher
Don Ross	Baltimore	infield
Ed Sadowski	Boston	catcher
Faye Throneberry	Minnesota	outfield
Red Wison	Cleveland	catcher
Eddie Yost	Detroit	third base

Pitchers

Pitcher	From	Throws
Jerry Casale	Boston	righthander
Dean Chance	Baltimore	righthander
Tex Clevenger	Minnesota	righthander
Bob Davis	Kansas City	righthander
Ned Garver	Kansas City	righthander
Aubrey Gatewood	Detroit	righthander
*Eli Grba	New York	righthander
Duke Maas	New York	righthander
Ken McBride	Chicago	righthander
Ron Moeller	Baltimore	lefthander
Fred Newman	Boston	righthander
Bob Sprout	Detroit	lefthander

*First pick

Opening day lineup

April 11, 1961

Eddie Yost, third base
Ken Aspromonte, second base
Albie Pearson, rightfield
Ted Kluszewski, first base
Bob Cerv, left field
Ken Hunt, center field
Fritzie Brickell, shortstop
Del Rice, catcher
Eli Grba, pitcher

Albie Pearson

Angels firsts

First hit: Ted Kluszewski, April 11, 1961, at Baltimore (home run)
First home run: Ted Kluszewski, April 11, 1961, at Baltimore
First RBI: Ted Kluszewski, April 11, 1961, at Baltimore
First win: Eli Grba, April 11, 1961, at Baltimore
First shutout: Ken McBride, May 23, 1961, 9-0 vs. Cleveland

BALTIMORE ORIOLES

FRANCHISE CHRONOLOGY

First season: 1901, in Milwaukee, as a member of the new American League. The team lost its Major League debut when Detroit rallied for 10 ninth-inning runs and a 14-13 victory and finished its first season in last place with a 48-89 record.

1902-1953: The franchise played its second season in St. Louis and remained there for more than half a century. The Browns moved up to second place in the 1902 standings (78-58), but such success would be elusive. The Browns won their only A.L. pennant in 1944 and lost their only World Series to the cross-town Cardinals. When owner Bill Veeck sold out to Baltimore interests in 1953, the team was relocated and renamed the Orioles.

1954-present: The Orioles posted a 3-1 victory over Chicago at Memorial Stadium in their Baltimore debut but went on to finish seventh in the A.L. standings at 54-100. Over the next four-plus decades, they would become an A.L. power, winning six pennants, three World Series, eight East Division titles and one wild-card playoff berth (1996).

Manager Earl Weaver.

ORIOLES VS. OPPONENTS BY DECADE

	A's	Indians	Red Sox	Tigers	Twins	White Sox	Yankees	Angels	Rangers	Brewers	Royals	Blue Jays	Mariners	Devil Rays	Interleague	Decade Record
1901-09	79-105	82-109	76-114	90-101	108-81	74-112	90-99									599-721
1910-19	93-120	81-130	71-142	90-126	96-119	74-132	92-123									597-892
1920-29	105-114	106-112	137-82	111-109	111-108	114-104	78-140									762-769
1930-39	88-127	64-155	103-117	85-135	84-135	90-127	64-155									578-951
1940-49	115-105	95-124	98-120	90-129	110-110	113-102	77-143									698-833
1950-59	110-109	67-151	77-143	106-114	117-103	86-134	69-151									632-905
1960-69	107-69	99-85	105-79	90-94	91-87	95-83	111-73	83-72	110-52	9-3	11-1					911-698
1970-79	66-50	104-65	83-85	102-65	64-52	74-39	89-73	65-52	77-50	100-54	65-51	29-14	26-6			944-656
1980-89	63-57	59-64	48-73	61-69	63-51	63-53	56-74	71-49	72-39	64-59	55-61	62-61	63-51			800-761
1990-99	65-54	51-67	57-63	69-49	63-45	46-59	50-75	73-46	60-46	52-45	62-43	54-69	58-57	10-14	24-25	794-757
2000-02	10-20	7-14	20-30	12-10	14-7	10-14	16-33	12-18	11-19		15-9	18-33	9-19	28-23	22-32	204-281
Totals	901-930	815-1076	875-1048	906-1001	921-898	839-959	792-1139	304-237	330-206	225-161	208-165	163-177	156-133	38-37	46-57	7519-8224

Interleague results: 1-2 vs. Diamondbacks, 8-7 vs. Braves, 4-11 vs. Marlins, 1-2 vs. Dodgers, 6-9 vs. Expos, 5-11 vs. Mets, 17-13 vs. Phillies, 2-1 vs. Padres, 2-1 vs. Giants.

MANAGERS

(Milwaukee Brewers, 1901)
(St. Louis Browns, 1902-53)

Name	*Years*	*Record*
Hugh Duffy	1901	48-89
Jimmy McAleer	1902-09	551-632
Jack O'Connor	1910	47-107
Bobby Wallace	1911-12	57-134
George Stovall	1912-13	91-158
Branch Rickey	1913-15	139-179
Fielder Jones	1916-18	158-196
Jimmy Austin	1913, 1918, 1923	31-44
Jimmy Burke	1918-20	172-180
Lee Fohl	1921-23	226-183
George Sisler	1924-26	218-241
Dan Howley	1927-29	220-239
Bill Killefer	1930-33	224-329
Al Sothoron	1933	2-6
Rogers Hornsby	1933-37, 1952	255-381
Jim Bottomley	1937	21-56
Gabby Street	1938	55-97
Fred Haney	1939-41	125-227
Luke Sewell	1941-46	432-410
Zack Taylor	1946, 1948-51	235-410
Marty Marion	1952-53	96-161
Jimmie Dykes	1954	54-100
Paul Richards	1955-61	517-539
Lum Harris	1961	17-10
Billy Hitchcock	1962-63	163-161
Hank Bauer	1964-68	407-318
Earl Weaver	1968-82, 1985-86	1480-1060
Joe Altobelli	1983-85	212-167
Cal Ripken Sr.	1987-88	68-101
Frank Robinson	1988-91	230-285
Johnny Oates	1991-94	362-343
Phil Regan	1995	71-73
Davey Johnson	1996-97	186-138
Ray Miller	1998-99	157-167
Mike Hargrove	2000-02	204-281

WORLD SERIES CHAMPIONS

Year	*Loser*	*Length*	*MVP*
1966	Los Angeles	4 games	F. Robinson
1970	Cincinnati	5 games	B. Robinson
1983	Philadelphia	5 games	Dempsey

A.L. PENNANT WINNERS

Year	*Record*	*Manager*	*Series Result*
1944	89-65	Sewell	Lost to Cardinals
1966	97-63	Bauer	Defeated Dodgers
1969	109-53	Weaver	Lost to N.Y. Mets
1970	108-54	Weaver	Defeated Reds
1971	101-57	Weaver	Lost to Pirates
1979	102-57	Weaver	Lost to Pirates
1983	98-64	Altobelli	Defeated Phillies

EAST DIVISION CHAMPIONS

Year	*Record*	*Manager*	*ALCS Result*
1969	109-53	Weaver	Defeated Twins
1970	108-54	Weaver	Defeated Twins
1971	101-57	Weaver	Defeated A's
1973	97-65	Weaver	Lost to A's
1974	91-71	Weaver	Lost to A's
1979	102-57	Weaver	Defeated Angels
1983	98-64	Altobelli	Defeated White Sox
1997	98-64	Johnson	Lost to Indians

WILD-CARD QUALIFIERS

Year	*Record*	*Manager*	*Div. Series Result*
1996	88-74	Johnson	Defeated Indians

ALCS Result
Lost to Yankees

ATTENDANCE HIGHS

Total	*Season*	*Park*
3,711,132	1997	Camden Yards
3,685,194	1998	Camden Yards
3,646,950	1996	Camden Yards
3,644,965	1993	Camden Yards
3,567,819	1992	Camden Yards

BALLPARK CHRONOLOGY

Oriole Park at Camden Yards (1992-present)

Capacity: 48,190.
First game: Orioles 2, Cleveland 0 (April 6, 1992).
First batter: Kenny Lofton, Indians.
First hit: Paul Sorrento, Indians (single).
First run: Sam Horn, Orioles (5th inning).
First home run: Paul Sorrento, Indians (April 8).
First winning pitcher: Rick Sutcliffe, Orioles.
First-season attendance: 3,567,819.

Lloyd Street Park, Milwaukee (1901)

Capacity: 10,000.
First game: Chicago 11, Brewers 3 (May 4, 1901).
First-season attendance: 139,034.

Sportsman's Park, St. Louis (1902-53)

Capacity: 30,500
First game: Browns 5, Cleveland 2 (April 23, 1902).
First-season attendance: 272,283.

Memorial Stadium, Baltimore (1954-91)

Capacity: 53,371
First game: Orioles 3, Chicago 1 (April 15, 1954).
First-season attendance: 1,060,910.

A.L. MVPs

Brooks Robinson, 3B, 1964
Frank Robinson, OF, 1966
Boog Powell, 1B, 1970
Cal Ripken, SS, 1983
Cal Ripken, SS, 1991

CY YOUNG WINNERS

*Mike Cuellar, LH, 1969
Jim Palmer, RH, 1973
Jim Palmer, RH, 1975
Jim Palmer, RH, 1976
Mike Flanagan, LH, 1979
Steve Stone, RH, 1980
* Co-winner.

ROOKIES OF THE YEAR

Roy Sievers, OF, 1949
Ron Hansen, SS, 1960
Curt Blefary, OF, 1965
Al Bumbry, OF, 1973
Eddie Murray, 1B, 1977
Cal Ripken, SS, 1982
Gregg Olson, P, 1989

MANAGER OF THE YEAR

Frank Robinson, 1989
Davey Johnson, 1997

RETIRED UNIFORMS

No.	*Name*	*Position*
4	Earl Weaver	Man.
5	Brooks Robinson	3B
20	Frank Robinson	OF
22	Jim Palmer	P
33	Eddie Murray	1B

MILESTONE PERFORMANCES

30-plus home runs

50— Brady Anderson ... 1996
49— Frank Robinson ... 1966
46— Jim Gentile ... 1961
43— Rafael Palmeiro ... 1998
39— Ken Williams ... 1922
Boog Powell ... 1964
Rafael Palmeiro ... 1995
Rafael Palmeiro ... 1996
38— Rafael Palmeiro ... 1997
37— Boog Powell ... 1969
Albert Belle ... 1999
35— Boog Powell ... 1970
Ken Singleton ... 1979
34— Harlond Clift ... 1938
Boog Powell ... 1966
Cal Ripken ... 1991
33— Jim Gentile ... 1962
Eddie Murray ... 1983
32— Frank Robinson ... 1969
Eddie Murray ... 1980, 1982
31— Eddie Murray ... 1985
Larry Sheets ... 1987
Tony Batista ... 2002
30— Goose Goslin ... 1930
Gus Triandos ... 1958
Frank Robinson ... 1967
Eddie Murray ... 1987

100-plus RBIs

155— Ken Williams ... 1922
142— Rafael Palmeiro ... 1996
141— Jim Gentile ... 1961
134— Moose Solters ... 1936
124— Eddie Murray ... 1985
123— Beau Bell ... 1936
122— George Sisler ... 1920
Baby Doll Jacobson ... 1920
Frank Robinson ... 1966
121— Boog Powell ... 1969
Rafael Palmeiro ... 1998
118— Harlond Clift ... 1937, 1938
Brooks Robinson ... 1964
117— Ken Williams ... 1921
Beau Bell ... 1937
Albert Belle ... 1999
116— Eddie Murray ... 1980
Bobby Bonilla ... 1996
114— Red Kress ... 1931
Boog Powell ... 1970
Cal Ripken ... 1991
112— Red Kress ... 1930
111— Ken Singleton ... 1979
Eddie Murray ... 1983
110— Eddie Murray ... 1982, 1984
Cal Ripken ... 1985
Brady Anderson ... 1996
Rafael Palmeiro ... 1997
109— Marty McManus ... 1922
Vern Stephens ... 1944
Boog Powell ... 1966
Lee May ... 1976
108— Heinie Manush ... 1928
107— Red Kress ... 1929
Mike Devereaux ... 1992
B.J. Surhoff ... 1999
106— Bruce Campbell ... 1933
105— George Sisler ... 1922, 1925
Ken Williams ... 1925
Goose Goslin ... 1931
104— George Sisler ... 1921
Goose Goslin ... 1932
Moose Solters ... 1935
Ken Singleton ... 1980
Rafael Palmeiro ... 1995
103— George Sisler ... 1916
Albert Belle ... 2000
102— Baby Doll Jacobson ... 1922
Cal Ripken ... 1983
Cal Ripken ... 1996
101— Ray Pepper ... 1934
100— Goose Goslin ... 1930
Brooks Robinson ... 1966
Frank Robinson ... 1969

20-plus victories

1902— Red Donahue ... 22-11
Jack Powell ... 22-17
1903— Willie Sudhoff ... 21-15
1919— Allen Sothoron ... 20-12
1920— Urban Shocker ... 20-10
1921— Urban Shocker ... 27-12
1922— Urban Shocker ... 24-17
1923— Urban Shocker ... 20-12
1928— General Crowder ... 21-5
Sam Gray ... 20-12
1930— Lefty Stewart ... 20-12
1938— Bobo Newsom ... 20-16
1951— Ned Garver ... 20-12
1963— Steve Barber ... 20-13
1968— Dave McNally ... 22-10
1969— Mike Cuellar ... 23-11
Dave McNally ... 20-7
1970— Mike Cuellar ... 24-8
Dave McNally ... 24-9
Jim Palmer ... 20-10
1971— Dave McNally ... 21-5
Pat Dobson ... 20-8
Jim Palmer ... 20-9
Mike Cuellar ... 20-9
1972— Jim Palmer ... 21-10
1973— Jim Palmer ... 22-9
1974— Mike Cuellar ... 22-10
1975— Jim Palmer ... 23-11
Mike Torrez ... 20-9
1976— Jim Palmer ... 22-13
Wayne Garland ... 20-7
1977— Jim Palmer ... 20-11
1978— Jim Palmer ... 21-12
1979— Mike Flanagan ... 23-9
1980— Steve Stone ... 25-7
Scott McGregor ... 20-8
1984— Mike Boddicker ... 20-11

When slugging outfielder Frank Robinson arrived on the Baltimore scene in 1966, the Orioles took on a championship aura.

INDIVIDUAL SEASON, GAME RECORDS

SEASON

Batting

At-bats	673	B.J. Surhoff	1999
Runs	145	Harlond Clift	1936
Hits	257	George Sisler	1920
Singles	179	Jack Tobin	1921
Doubles	51	Beau Bell	1937
Triples	20	Heinie Manush	1928
Home runs	50	Brady Anderson	1996
Home runs, rookie	28	Cal Ripken	1982
Grand slams	5	Jim Gentile	1961
Total bases	399	George Sisler	1920
RBIs	155	Ken Williams	1922
Walks	126	Lu Blue	1929
Most strikeouts	160	Mickey Tettleton	1990
Fewest strikeouts	13	Jack Tobin	1923
Batting average	.420	George Sisler	1922
Slugging pct.	.646	Jim Gentile	1961
Stolen bases	57	Luis Aparicio	1964

Pitching

Games	76	Tippy Martinez	1982
Complete games	36	Jack Powell	1902
Innings	348	Urban Shocker	1922
Wins	27	Urban Shocker	1922
Losses	25	Fred Glade	1905
Winning pct.	.808	General Crowder	1928
		Dave McNally	1971
Walks	192	Bobo Newsom	1938
Strikeouts	232	Rube Waddell	1908
Shutouts	10	Jim Palmer	1975
Home runs allowed	35	3 times	
		Last by Sidney Ponson	1999
Lowest ERA	1.95	Dave McNally	1968
Saves	45	Randy Myers	1997

GAME

Batting

Runs	5	Last by Cal Ripken	6-13-99
Hits	6	Last by Cal Ripken	6-13-99
Doubles	4	Last by Albert Belle	9-23-99
Triples	3	Last by Al Bumbry	9-22-73
Home runs	3	Last by Albert Belle	7-25-99
RBIs	9	Last by Eddie Murray	8-26-85
Total bases	13	Last by Chris Richard	9-3-2000
Stolen bases	4	Last by Brady Anderson	7-5-98

A.L. home run champions

1922— Ken Williams ... 39
1945— Vern Stephens ... 24
1966— Frank Robinson ... 49
1981— Eddie Murray ... *22

* Tied for league lead

A.L. RBI champions

1916— Del Pratt ... 103
1922— Ken Williams ... 155
1944— Vern Stephens ... 109
1964— Brooks Robinson ... 118
1966— Frank Robinson ... 122
1976— Lee May ... 109
1981— Eddie Murray ... 78

A.L. batting champions

1906— George Stone ... .358
1920— George Sisler ... .407
1922— George Sisler ... .420
1966— Frank Robinson ... .316

A.L. ERA champions

1959— Hoyt Wilhelm ... 2.19
1973— Jim Palmer ... 2.40
1975— Jim Palmer ... 2.09
1984— Mike Boddicker ... 2.79

A.L. strikeout champions

1922— Urban Shocker ... 149
1954— Bob Turley ... 185

No-hit pitchers

1912— Earl Hamilton ... 5-1 vs. Detroit
1917— Ernie Koob ... 1-0 vs. Chicago
1917— Bob Groom ... 3-0 vs. Chicago
1953— Bobo Holloman ... 6-0 vs. Philadelphia
1958— Hoyt Wilhelm ... 1-0 vs. New York
1967— Steve Barber-Stu Miller ... 1-2 vs. Detroit
1968— Tom Phoebus ... 6-0 vs. Boston
1969— Jim Palmer ... 8-0 vs. Oakland
1991— Bob Milacki-Mike Flanagan-Mark Williamson-Gregg Olson ... 2-0 vs. Oakland

Longest hitting streaks

41— George Sisler ... 1922
34— George Sisler ... 1925
George McQuinn ... 1938
30— Eric Davis ... 1998
29— Mel Almada ... 1938
28— Ken Williams ... 1922
27— Bob Dillinger ... 1948
26— Hobe Ferris ... 1908
25— George Sisler ... 1920
24— Rafael Palmeiro ... 1994
22— Red Kress ... 1930
Eddie Murray ... 1984
Roberto Alomar ... 1996
Bobby Bonilla ... *1995-96
21— Jack Tobin ... 1922
Beau Bell ... 1936
Joe Vosmik ... 1937
Johnny Berardino ... 1946
Doug DeCinces ... 1978
Joe Orsulak ... 1991
B.J. Surhoff ... 1999, 2000
20— Jack Burns ... 1932
Harlond Clift ... 1937
Bob Nieman ... 1956
Lee Lacy ... 1985
Bobby Bonilla ... 1995

*20 games in 1995; 2 in 1996

CAREER LEADERS

BATTING

Games

Cal Ripken	3,001
Brooks Robinson	2,896
Mark Belanger	1,962
Eddie Murray	1,884
Boog Powell	1,763
Brady Anderson	1,759
Paul Blair	1,700
George Sisler	1,647
Bobby Wallace	1,569
Ken Singleton	1,446

At-bats

Cal Ripken	11,551
Brooks Robinson	10,654
Eddie Murray	7,075
George Sisler	6,667
Brady Anderson	6,271
Boog Powell	5,912
Mark Belanger	5,734
Paul Blair	5,606
Bobby Wallace	5,529
Harlond Clift	5,281

Runs

Cal Ripken	1,647
Brooks Robinson	1,232
George Sisler	1,091
Eddie Murray	1,084
Brady Anderson	1,044
Harlond Clift	1,013
Boog Powell	796
Al Bumbry	772
Ken Williams	757
Paul Blair	737

Hits

Cal Ripken	3,184
Brooks Robinson	2,848
George Sisler	2,295
Eddie Murray	2,080
Brady Anderson	1,614
Boog Powell	1,574
Baby Doll Jacobson	1,508
Harlond Clift	1,463
Ken Singleton	1,455
Paul Blair	1,426

Doubles

Cal Ripken	603
Brooks Robinson	482
Eddie Murray	363
George Sisler	343
Brady Anderson	329
Harlond Clift	294
Paul Blair	269
Baby Doll Jacobson	269
George McQuinn	254
Boog Powell	243

Triples

George Sisler	145
Baby Doll Jacobson	88
Del Pratt	72
Jack Tobin	72
Ken Williams	70
Brooks Robinson	68
George Stone	68
Jimmy Austin	67
Bobby Wallace	65
Brady Anderson	64

Home runs

Cal Ripken	431
Eddie Murray	343
Boog Powell	303
Brooks Robinson	268
Brady Anderson	209
Ken Williams	185
Rafael Palmeiro	182
Ken Singleton	182
Frank Robinson	179
Harlond Clift	170

Total bases

Cal Ripken	5,168
Brooks Robinson	4,270
Eddie Murray	3,522
George Sisler	3,207
Boog Powell	2,748
Brady Anderson	2,698
Harlond Clift	2,391
Ken Singleton	2,274
Ken Williams	2,239
Baby Doll Jacobson	2,181

Runs batted in

Cal Ripken	1,695
Brooks Robinson	1,357
Eddie Murray	1,224
Boog Powell	1,063
George Sisler	959
Ken Williams	808
Harlond Clift	769
Ken Singleton	766
Brady Anderson	744
Baby Doll Jacobson	704

Extra-base hits

Cal Ripken	1,078
Brooks Robinson	818
Eddie Murray	731
Brady Anderson	602
George Sisler	581
Boog Powell	557
Harlond Clift	526
Ken Williams	491
Paul Blair	446
Ken Singleton	436

Batting average
(Minimum 500 games)

George Sisler	.344
Ken Williams	.326
Jack Tobin	.318
Baby Doll Jacobson	.317
Bob Dillinger	.309
Beau Bell	.309
Sam West	.305
George Stone	.301
Bob Boyd	.301
Bob Nieman	.301

Stolen bases

George Sisler	351
Brady Anderson	307
Al Bumbry	252
Burt Shotton	247
Jimmy Austin	192
Del Pratt	174
Paul Blair	167
Luis Aparicio	166
Mark Belanger	166
Ken Williams	144

PITCHING

Earned-run average
(Minimum 1,000 innings)

Harry Howell	2.06
Fred Glade	2.52
Barney Pelty	2.62
Jack Powell	2.63
Carl Weilman	2.67
Jim Palmer	2.86
Allen Sothoron	2.98
Earl Hamilton	3.00
Steve Barber	3.12
Mike Cuellar	3.18

Wins

Jim Palmer	268
Dave McNally	181
Mike Mussina	147
Mike Cuellar	143
Mike Flanagan	141
Scott McGregor	138
Urban Shocker	126
Jack Powell	117
Milt Pappas	110
Dennis Martinez	108

Losses

Jim Palmer	152
Jack Powell	143
Mike Flanagan	116
Dave McNally	113
Barney Pelty	113
George Blaeholder	111
Scott McGregor	108
Dennis Martinez	93
Carl Weilman	93
Harry Howell	91
Elam Vangilder	91

Innings pitched

Jim Palmer	3,948.0
Dave McNally	2,652.2
Mike Flanagan	2,317.2
Jack Powell	2,229.2
Scott McGregor	2,140.2
Mike Cuellar	2,028.1
Mike Mussina	2,009.2
Barney Pelty	1,864.1
Dennis Martinez	1,775.0
Urban Shocker	1,749.2

Strikeouts

Jim Palmer	2,212
Mike Mussina	1,535
Dave McNally	1,476
Mike Flanagan	1,297
Mike Cuellar	1,011
Milt Pappas	944
Steve Barber	918
Scott McGregor	904
Jack Powell	884
Dennis Martinez	858

Bases on balls

Jim Palmer	1,311
Dave McNally	790
Mike Flanagan	740
Steve Barber	668
Dixie Davis	640
Elam Vangilder	625
Mike Cuellar	601
Dennis Martinez	583
Milt Pappas	531
Barney Pelty	522

Games

Jim Palmer	558
Tippy Martinez	499
Mike Flanagan	450
Dave McNally	412
Mark Williamson	365
Eddie Watt	363
Scott McGregor	356
Alan Mills	346
Dick Hall	342
Jesse Orosco	336

Shutouts

Jim Palmer	53
Dave McNally	33
Mike Cuellar	30
Jack Powell	27
Milt Pappas	26
Scott McGregor	23
Urban Shocker	23
Barney Pelty	22
Steve Barber	19
Mike Flanagan	17

Saves

Gregg Olson	160
Tippy Martinez	105
Stu Miller	100
Randy Myers	76
Eddie Watt	74
Dick Hall	58
Tim Stoddard	57
Don Aase	50
Don Stanhouse	45
Sammy Stewart	42

TEAM SEASON, GAME RECORDS

SEASON

Batting

Most at-bats	5,689	1996
Most runs	949	1996
Fewest runs	441	1909
Most hits	1,693	1922
Most singles	1,239	1920
Most doubles	327	1937
Most triples	106	1921
Most home runs	257	1996
Fewest home runs	9	1906
Most grand slams	11	1996
Most pinch-hit home runs	11	1982
Most total bases	2,685	1996
Most stolen bases	234	1916
Highest batting average	.313	1922
Lowest batting average	.216	1910
Highest slugging pct	.472	1996

Pitching

Lowest ERA	2.15	1908
Highest ERA	6.24	1936
Most complete games	135	1904
Most shutouts	21	1909, 1961
Most saves	59	1997
Most walks	801	1951
Most strikeouts	1,139	1997

Fielding

Most errors	378	1910
Fewest errors	81	1998
Most double plays	190	1948
Highest fielding average	.987	1998

General

Most games won	109	1969
Most games lost	111	1939
Highest win pct.	.673	1969
Lowest win pct.	.279	1939

GAME, INNING

Batting

Most runs, game	23	9-28-2000
Most runs, inning	12	4-11-2002
Most hits, game	26	8-28-80
Most home runs, game	7	Last 8-26-85
Most total bases, game	44	6-13-99

George Sisler (right) was an early franchise star and a contemporary of Babe Ruth.

ORIOLES YEAR-BY-YEAR

Year	W	L	Place	Games Back	Manager	Leaders: Batting avg.	Hits	Home runs	RBIs	Wins	ERA
							MILWAUKEE BREWERS				
1901	48	89	8th	35½	Duffy	Anderson, .330	Anderson, 190	Anderson, 8	Anderson, 99	Reidy, 16	Garvin, 3.46
							ST. LOUIS BROWNS				
1902	78	58	2nd	5	McAleer	Hemphill, .317	Burkett, 169	Hemphill, 6	Anderson, 85	Donahue, Powell, 22	Donahue, 2.76
1903	65	74	6th	26½	McAleer	Burkett, .293	Anderson, 156	Burkett, Hemphill, 3	Anderson, 78	Sudhoff, 21	Sudhoff, 2.27
1904	65	87	6th	29	McAleer	Wallace, .275	T. Jones, 152	4 Tied, 2	Wallace, 69	Glade, 18	Howell, 2.19
1905	54	99	8th	40½	McAleer	Stone, .296	Stone, 187	Stone, 7	Wallace, 59	Howell, 15	Howell, 1.98
1906	76	73	5th	16	McAleer	Stone, .358	Stone, 208	Stone, 6	Stone, 71	Pelty, 16	Pelty, 1.59
1907	69	83	6th	24	McAleer	Stone, .320	Stone, 191	Stone, 4	Wallace, 70	Howell, 16	Howell, 1.93
1908	83	69	4th	6½	McAleer	Stone, .281	Stone, 165	Stone, 5	Ferris, 74	Waddell, 19	Howell, Waddell, 1.89
1909	61	89	7th	36	McAleer	Griggs, .280	Hartzell, 161	Ferris, 3	Ferris, 58	Powell, 12	Powell, 2.11
1910	47	107	8th	57	O'Connor	Wallace, .258	Stone, 144	4 Tied, 2	Stone, 40	Lake, 11	Lake, 2.20
1911	45	107	8th	56½	Wallace	LaPorte, .314	LaPorte, 159	Kutina, Meloan, Murray, 3	LaPorte, 82	Lake, 10	Pelty, 2.97
1912	53	101	7th	53	Wallace, Stovall	Pratt, .302	Pratt, 172	Pratt, 5	Pratt, 69	Baumgardner, Hamilton, 11	E. Brown, 2.99
1913	57	96	8th	39	Stovall, Rickey	Shotton, .297	Pratt, 175	Williams, 5	Pratt, 87	Hamilton, Mitchell, 13	Hamilton, 2.57
1914	71	82	5th	28½	Rickey	T. Walker, .298	Pratt, 165	T. Walker, 6	T. Walker, 78	Weilman, 18	Weilman, 2.08
1915	63	91	6th	39½	Rickey	Pratt, .291	Pratt, 175	T. Walker, 5	Pratt, 78	Weilman, 18	Weilman, 2.34
1916	79	75	5th	12	Jones	Sisler, .305	Sisler, 177	Pratt, 5	Pratt, 103	Weilman, 17	Weilman, 2.15
1917	57	97	7th	43	Jones	Sisler, .353	Sisler, 190	Jacobson, 4	Severeid, 57	Davenport, 17	Plank, 1.79
1918	58	64	5th	15	Jones, Austin, Burke	Sisler, .341	Sisler, 154	Sisler, 2	Demmitt, 61	Sothoron, 12	Shocker, 1.81
1919	67	72	5th	20½	Burke	Sisler, .352	Sisler, 180	Sisler, 10	Sisler, 83	Sothoron, 20	Weilman, 2.07
1920	76	77	4th	21½	Burke	Sisler, .407	Sisler, 257	Sisler, 19	Jacobson, Sisler, 122	Shocker, 20	Shocker, 2.71
1921	81	73	3rd	17½	Fohl	Sisler, .371	Tobin, 236	Williams, 24	Williams, 117	Shocker, 27	Shocker, 3.55
1922	93	61	2nd	1	Fohl	Sisler, .420	Sisler, 246	Williams, 39	Williams, 155	Shocker, 24	Pruett, 2.33
1923	74	78	5th	24	Fohl, Austin	Williams, .357	Tobin, 202	Williams, 29	McManus, 94	Shocker, 20	Vangilder, 3.06
1924	74	78	4th	17	Sisler	McManus, .333	Sisler, 194	Jacobson, 19	Jacobson, 97	Shocker, 16	Wingard, 3.51
1925	82	71	3rd	15	Sisler	Rice, .359	Sisler, 224	Williams, 25	Sisler, Williams, 105	Gaston, 15	Danforth, 4.36
1926	62	92	7th	29	Sisler	B. Miller, .331	Rice, 181	Williams, 17	Williams, 74	Zachary, 14	Wingard, 3.57
1927	59	94	7th	50½	Howley	Sisler, .327	Sisler, 201	Williams, 17	Sisler, 97	Gaston, 13	Stewart, 4.28
1928	82	72	3rd	19	Howley	Manush, .378	Manush, 241	Blue, 14	Manush, 108	Crowder, 21	Gray, 3.19
1929	79	73	4th	26	Howley	Manush, .355	Manush, 204	Kress, 9	Kress, 107	Gray, 18	Stewart, 3.25
1930	64	90	6th	38	Killefer	Goslin, .326	Kress, 192	Goslin, 30	Kress, 112	Stewart, 20	Stewart, 3.45
1931	63	91	5th	45	Killefer	Goslin, .328	Goslin, 194	Goslin, 24	Kress, 114	Stewart, 14	Collins, 3.79
1932	63	91	6th	44	Killefer	Ferrell, .315	Burns, 188	Goslin, 17	Goslin, 104	Stewart, 15	Gray, 4.53
1933	55	96	8th	43½	Killefer, Sothoron, Hornsby	West, .300	Burns, 160	Campbell, 16	Campbell, 106	Blaeholder, Hadley, 15	Hadley, 3.92
1934	67	85	6th	33	Hornsby	West, .326	Pepper, 168	Clift, 14	Pepper, 101	Newsom, 16	Newsom, 4.01
1935	65	87	7th	28½	Hornsby	Solters, .330	Solters, 182	Solters, 18	Solters, 104	Andrews, 13	Andrews, 3.54
1936	57	95	7th	44½	Hornsby	Bell, .344	Bell, 212	Clift, 20	Solters, 134	Hogsett, 13	Andrews, 4.84
1937	46	108	8th	56	Hornsby, Bottomley	Bell, .340	Bell, 218	Clift, 29	Clift, 118	Walkup, 9	Knott, 4.89
1938	55	97	7th	44	Street	Almada, .342	McQuinn, 195	Clift, 34	Clift, 118	Newsom, 20	Newsom, 5.08
1939	43	111	8th	64½	Haney	McQuinn, .316	McQuinn, 195	McQuinn, 20	McQuinn, 94	Kennedy, Kramer, 9	Lawson, 5.32
1940	67	87	6th	23	Haney	Radcliff, .342	Radcliff, 200	Judnich, 24	Judnich, 89	Auker, 16	Trotter, 3.77
1941	70	84	*6th	31	Haney, Sewell	Cullenbine, .317	Cullenbine, 159	McQuinn, 18	Berardino, 89	Auker, 14	Galehouse, 3.64
1942	82	69	3rd	19½	Sewell	Judnich, .313	Stephens, 169	Laabs, 27	Laabs, 99	Niggeling, 15	Niggeling, 2.66
1943	72	80	6th	25	Sewell	Stephens, .289	Stephens, 148	Stephens, 22	Stephens, 91	Sundra, 15	Galehouse, 2.77
1944	89	65	1st	+1	Sewell	Kreevich, .301	Stephens, 164	Stephens, 20	Stephens, 109	Potter, 19	Kramer, 2.49
1945	81	70	3rd	6	Sewell	Stephens, .289	Stephens, 165	Stephens, 24	Stephens, 89	Potter, 15	Potter, 2.47
1946	66	88	7th	38	Sewell, Taylor	Stephens, .307	Berardino, 154	Laabs, 16	Judnich, 72	Kramer, 13	Kramer, 3.19
1947	59	95	8th	38	Ruel	Dillinger, .294	Dillinger, 168	Heath, 27	Heath, 85	Kramer, 11	Zoldak, 3.47
1948	59	94	6th	37	Taylor	Zarilla, .329	Dillinger, 207	Moss, 14	Platt, 82	Sanford, 12	Garver, 3.41
1949	53	101	7th	44	Taylor	Dillinger, .324	Dillinger, 176	Graham, 24	Sievers, 91	Garver, 12	Ferrick, 3.88
1950	58	96	7th	40	Taylor	Lollar, .280	Lenhardt, 131	Lenhardt, 22	Lenhardt, 81	Garver, 13	Garver, 3.39
1951	52	102	8th	46	Taylor	Young, .260	Young, 159	Wood, 15	Coleman, 55	Garver, 20	Garver, 3.73
1952	64	90	7th	31	Hornsby, Marion	Nieman, .289	Young, 142	Nieman, 18	Nieman, 74	Cain, Paige, 12	Paige, 3.07
1953	54	100	8th	46½	Marion	Wertz, .268	Groth, 141	Wertz, 19	Wertz, 70	Stuart, 8	Brecheen, 3.07
							BALTIMORE ORIOLES				
1954	54	100	7th	57	Dykes	Abrams, .293	Abrams, 124	Stephens, 8	Stephens, 46	Turley, 14	Pillette, 3.12
1955	57	97	7th	39	Richards	Triandos, .277	Triandos, 133	Triandos, 12	Triandos, 65	Wilson, 12	Wight, 2.45
1956	69	85	6th	28	Richards	Nieman, .322	Triandos, 126	Triandos, 21	Triandos, 88	Moore, 12	C. Johnson, 3.43
1957	76	76	5th	21	Richards	Boyd, .318	Gardner, 169	Triandos, 19	Triandos, 72	C. Johnson, 14	Zuverink, 2.48
1958	74	79	6th	17½	Richards	Boyd, .309	Gardner, 126	Triandos, 30	Triandos, 79	Portocarrero, 15	Harshman, 2.89
1959	74	80	6th	20	Richards	Woodling, .300	Woodling, 132	Triandos, 25	Woodling, 77	Pappas, Wilhelm, 15	Wilhelm, 2.19
1960	89	65	2nd	8	Richards	B. Robinson, .294	B. Robinson, 175	Hansen, 22	Gentile, 98	Estrada, 18	Brown, 3.06
1961	95	67	3rd	14	Richards, Harris	Gentile, .302	B. Robinson, 192	Gentile, 46	Gentile, 141	Barber, 18	Hoeft, 2.02
1962	77	85	7th	19	Hitchcock	Snyder, .305	B. Robinson, 192	Gentile, 33	Gentile, 87	Pappas, 12	Wilhelm, 1.94
1963	86	76	4th	18½	Hitchcock	Orsino, A. Smith, .272	Aparicio, 150	Powell, 25	Powell, 82	Barber, 20	Miller, 2.24
1964	97	65	3rd	2	Bauer	B. Robinson, .317	B. Robinson, 194	Powell, 39	B. Robinson, 118	Bunker, 19	Haddix, 2.31
1965	94	68	3rd	8	Bauer	B. Robinson, .297	B. Robinson, 166	Blefary, 22	B. Robinson, 80	Barber, 15	Miller, 1.89
1966	97	63	1st	+9	Bauer	F. Robinson, .316	Aparicio, F. Robinson, 182	F. Robinson, 49	F. Robinson, 122	Palmer, 15	Miller, 2.25
1967	76	85	*6th	15½	Bauer	F. Robinson, .311	B. Robinson, 164	F. Robinson, 30	F. Robinson, 94	Phoebus, 14	Drabowsky, 1.60
1968	91	71	2nd	12	Bauer, Weaver	Buford, .282	B. Robinson, 154	B. Robinson, 17	Powell, 85	McNally, 22	McNally, 1.95
							EAST DIVISION				
1969	109	53	†1st	+19	Weaver	F. Robinson, .308	Blair, 178	Powell, 37	Powell, 121	Cuellar, 23	Palmer, 2.34
1970	108	54	†1st	+15	Weaver	F. Robinson, .306	B. Robinson, 168	Powell, 35	Powell, 114	Cuellar, McNally, 24	Palmer, 2.71
1971	101	57	†1st	+12	Weaver	Rettenmund, .318	B. Robinson, 160	F. Robinson, 28	F. Robinson, 99	McNally, 21	Palmer, 2.68
1972	80	74	3rd	5	Weaver	Grich, .278	B. Robinson, 139	Powell, 21	Powell, 81	Palmer, 21	Palmer, 2.07
1973	97	65	‡1st	+8	Weaver	Coggins, .319	T. Davis, 169	Williams, 22	T. Davis, 89	Palmer, 22	Reynolds, 1.95
1974	91	71	‡1st	+2	Weaver	T. Davis, .289	T. Davis, 181	Grich, 19	T. Davis, 84	Cuellar, 22	Garland, 2.97
1975	90	69	2nd	4½	Weaver	Singleton, .300	Singleton, 176	Baylor, 25	L. May, 99	Palmer, 23	Palmer, 2.09
1976	88	74	2nd	10½	Weaver	Singleton, .278	Singleton, 151	R. Jackson, 27	L. May, 109	Palmer, 22	Palmer, 2.51
1977	97	64	*2nd	2½	Weaver	Singleton, .328	Singleton, 176	L. May, Murray, 27	L. May, Singleton, 99	Palmer, 20	Palmer, 2.91
1978	90	71	4th	9	Weaver	Singleton, .293	Murray, 174	DeCinces, 28	Murray, 95	Palmer, 21	Palmer, 2.46
1979	102	57	†1st	+8	Weaver	Murray, .Singleton, .295	Murray, 179	Singleton, 35	Singleton, 111	Flanagan, 23	Flanagan, 3.08
1980	100	62	2nd	3	Weaver	Bumbry, .318	Bumbry, 205	Murray, 32	Murray, 116	Stone, 25	Stone, 3.23
1981	59	46	§2nd/4th	—	Weaver	Murray, .294	Murray, 111	Murray, 22	Murray, 78	D. Martinez, 14	Stewart, 2.32
1982	94	68	2nd	1	Weaver	Murray, .316	Murray, 174	Murray, 32	Murray, 110	D. Martinez, 16	Palmer, 3.13
1983	98	64	†1st	+6	Altobelli	C. Ripken, .318	C. Ripken, 211	Murray, 33	Murray, 111	McGregor, 18	T. Martinez, 2.35
1984	85	77	5th	19	Altobelli	Murray, .306	C. Ripken, 195	Murray, 29	Murray, 110	Boddicker, 20	Boddicker, 2.79
1985	83	78	4th	16	Altobelli, Weaver	Rayford, .306	C. Ripken, 181	Murray, 31	Murray, 124	McGregor, 14	Snell, 2.69
1986	73	89	7th	22½	Weaver	Murray, .305	C. Ripken, 177	C. Ripken, 25	Murray, 84	Boddicker, 14	S. Davis, 3.62
1987	67	95	6th	31	C. Ripken, Sr.	Sheets, .316	Murray, 171	Sheets, 31	C. Ripken, 98	Bell, Boddicker, Schmidt, 10	Schmidt, 3.77
1988	54	107	7th	34½	C. Ripken, Sr., F. Robinson	Orsulak, .288	Murray, 171	Murray, 28	Murray, 84	Ballard, Schmidt, 8	Schmidt, 3.40
1989	87	75	2nd	2	F. Robinson	Orsulak, .285	C. Ripken, 166	Tettleton, 26	C. Ripken, 93	Ballard, 18	Williamson, 2.93
1990	76	85	5th	11½	F. Robinson	B. Ripken, .291	C. Ripken, 150	C. Ripken, 21	C. Ripken, 84	D. Johnson, 13	McDonald, 2.43
1991	67	95	6th	24	F. Robinson, Oates	C. Ripken, .323	C. Ripken, 210	C. Ripken, 34	C. Ripken, 114	Milacki, 10	Frohwirth, 1.87
1992	89	73	3rd	7	Oates	Orsulak, .289	Devereaux, 180	Devereaux, 24	Devereaux, 107	Mussina, 18	Frohwirth, 2.46
1993	85	77	*3rd	10	Oates	Baines, .313	McLemore, 165	Hoiles, 29	C. Ripken, 90	Mussina, 14	Mills, 3.23
1994	63	49	2nd	6½	Oates	Palmeiro, .319	C. Ripken, 140	Palmeiro, 23	Palmeiro, 76	Mussina, 16	Mussina, 3.06
1995	71	73	3rd	15	Regan	Palmeiro, .310	Palmeiro, 172	Palmeiro, 39	Palmeiro, 104	Mussina, 19	Mussina, 3.29
1996	88	74	∞‡2nd	4	Johnson	Alomar, .328	Alomar, 193	Anderson, 50	Palmeiro, 142	Mussina, 19	Mussina, 4.81
1997	98	64	∞1st	+2	Johnson	Alomar, .333	Anderson, 170	Palmeiro, 38	Palmeiro, 110	Key, Erickson, 16	Rhodes, 3.02
1998	79	83	4th	35	Miller	E. Davis, .327	Palmeiro, 183	Palmeiro, 43	Palmeiro, 121	Erickson, 16	Mussina, 3.49
1999	78	84	4th	20	Miller	Surhoff, .308	Surhoff, 207	Belle, 37	Belle, 117	Mussina, 18	Mussina, 3.50
2000	74	88	4th	13½	Hargrove	Bordick, .297	DeShields, 167	Belle, 23	Belle, 103	Mercedes, 14	Mussina, 3.79
2001	63	98	4th	32½	Hargrove	Conine, .311	Conine, 163	Gibbons, Richard, 15	Conine, 97	Johnson, 10	Johnson, 4.09
2002	67	95	4th	36½	Hargrove	Singleton, .262	Batista, 150	Batista, 31	Batista, 87	Lopez, 15	Lopez, 3.57

* Tied for position. † Won Championship Series. ‡ Lost Championship Series. § First half 31-23; second half 28-23. ∞ Won Division Series.

Note: Batting average minimum 350 at-bats; ERA minimum 90 innings pitched.

BOSTON RED SOX

FRANCHISE CHRONOLOGY

First season: 1901, as a member of the new American League. The Red Sox, who also were known in the early years as the Pilgrims, Puritans and Somersets, dropped a 10-6 decision to Baltimore in their Major League debut and went on to finish 79-57, four games behind pennant-winner Chicago.

1902-present: The Red Sox captured their first pennant in 1903 and defeated the National League's Pirates in the first modern World Series. Boston went on to enjoy distinction as baseball's most successful franchise over its first two decades, winning six A.L. pennants and all five World Series appearances. But the Red Sox's 1918 championship marked the beginning of a dry spell that would last the remainder of the century. They failed to win another pennant until 1946 and have lost their four World Series appearances since World War II, all in dramatic seventh games.

Outfielder Ted Williams.

RED SOX VS. OPPONENTS BY DECADE

	A's	Indians	Orioles	Tigers	Twins	White Sox	Yankees	Angels	Rangers	Brewers	Royals	Blue Jays	Mariners	Devil Rays	Interleague	Decade Record
1901-09	88-102	93-96	114-76	92-97	113-76	90-101	101-86									691-634
1910-19	129-84	115-97	142-71	124-88	115-93	117-97	115-94									857-624
1920-29	86-131	90-130	82-137	81-139	82-135	103-117	71-149									595-938
1930-39	116-99	89-131	117-103	99-121	90-128	114-97	80-136									705-815
1940-49	137-83	105-116	120-98	127-93	133-86	134-85	98-122									854-683
1950-59	141-79	98-122	143-77	121-99	120-100	98-122	93-126									814-725
1960-69	96-82	90-94	79-105	88-95	74-104	76-102	83-101	76-79	86-75	6-6	10-2					764-845
1970-79	63-54	86-80	85-83	96-69	70-47	67-48	89-79	64-53	72-56	93-63	53-63	32-11	25-8			895-714
1980-89	68-52	78-52	73-48	65-59	62-53	56-59	60-63	59-55	64-53	62-67	49-65	59-62	66-54			821-742
1990-99	71-46	61-60	63-57	64-54	48-62	54-54	60-64	71-47	43-61	50-47	52-51	72-52	71-46	13-12	21-28	814-741
2000-02	15-13	14-16	30-20	16-14	14-8	12-12	20-30	11-12	16-8		11-11	29-21	12-16	36-14	24-30	260-225
Totals	1010-825	919-994	1048-875	973-928	921-892	921-894	870-1050	281-246	281-253	211-183	175-192	192-146	174-124	49-26	45-58	8070-7686

Interleague results: 0-3 vs. Diamondbacks, 10-20 vs. Braves, 2-1 vs. Rockies, 9-6 vs. Marlins, 0-3 vs. Dodgers, 8-7 vs. Expos, 7-8 vs. Mets, 7-9 vs. Phillies, 2-1 vs. Padres.

MANAGERS

Name	*Years*	*Record*
Jimmy Collins	1901-06	455-376
Chick Stahl	1906	14-26
George Huff	1907	2-6
Bob Unglaub	1907	9-20
Cy Young	1907	3-3
Deacon McGuire	1907-08	98-123
Fred Lake	1908-09	110-80
Patsy Donovan	1910-11	159-147
Jake Stahl	1912-13	144-88
Bill Carrigan	1913-16, 1927-29	489-500
Jack Barry	1917	90-62
Ed Barrow	1918-20	213-203
Hugh Duffy	1921-22	136-172
Frank Chance	1923	61-91
Lee Fohl	1924-26	160-299
Heinie Wagner	1930	52-102
Shano Collins	1931-32	73-134
Marty McManus	1932-33	95-153
Bucky Harris	1934	76-76
Joe Cronin	1935-47	1071-916
Joe McCarthy	1948-50	223-145
Steve O'Neill	1950-51	150-99
Lou Boudreau	1952-54	229-232
Pinky Higgins	1955-59, 1960-62	560-556
Rudy York	1959	0-1
Billy Jurges	1959-60	59-63
Del Baker	1960	2-5
Johnny Pesky	1963-64, 1980	147-179
Billy Herman	1964-66	128-182
Pete Runnels	1966	8-8
Dick Williams	1967-69	260-217
Eddie Popowski	1969, 1973	6-4
Eddie Kasko	1970-73	345-295
Darrell Johnson	1974-76	220-188
Don Zimmer	1976-80	411-304
Ralph Houk	1981-84	312-282
John McNamara	1985-88	297-273
Joe Morgan	1988-91	301-252
Butch Hobson	1992-94	207-232
Kevin Kennedy	1995-96	171-135
Jimy Williams	1997-2001	414-352
Joe Kerrigan	2001	17-26
Grady Little	2002	93-69

WORLD SERIES CHAMPIONS

Year	*Loser*	*Length*	*MVP*
1903	Pittsburgh	8 games	None
1912	N.Y. Giants	7 games	None
1915	Philadelphia	5 games	None
1916	Brooklyn	5 games	None
1918	Chicago	6 games	None

A.L. PENNANT WINNERS

Year	*Record*	*Manager*	*Series Result*
1903	91-47	J. Collins	Defeated Pirates
1904	95-59	J. Collins	No Series
1912	105-47	J. Stahl	Defeated N.Y. Giants
1915	101-50	Carrigan	Defeated Phillies
1916	91-63	Carrigan	Defeated Dodgers
1918	75-51	Barrow	Defeated Cubs
1946	104-50	Cronin	Lost to Cardinals
1967	92-70	Williams	Lost to Cardinals
1975	95-65	Johnson	Lost to Reds
1986	95-66	McNamara	Lost to N.Y. Mets

EAST DIVISION CHAMPIONS

Year	*Record*	*Manager*	*ALCS Result*
1975	95-65	Johnson	Defeated A's
1986	95-66	McNamara	Defeated Angels
1988	89-73	McNamara, Morgan	Lost to A's
1990	88-74	Morgan	Lost to A's
1995	86-58	Kennedy	Lost in Div. Series

WILD-CARD QUALIFIERS

Year	*Record*	*Manager*	*ALCS Result*
1998	92-70	Williams	Lost in Div. Series
1999	94-68	Williams	Lost to Yankees

ATTENDANCE HIGHS

Total	*Season*	*Park*
2,650,063	2002	Fenway Park
2,625,333	2001	Fenway Park
2,586,024	2000	Fenway Park
2,562,435	1991	Fenway Park
2,528,986	1990	Fenway Park

BALLPARK CHRONOLOGY

Fenway Park—(1912-present)

Capacity: 33,991.
First game: Red Sox 7, New York 6, 11 innings (April 20, 1912).
First batter: Guy Zinn, Yankees.
First hit: Harry Wolter, Yankees.
First run: Guy Zinn, Yankees (1st inning).
First home run: Hugh Bradley, Red Sox (April 26).
First winning pitcher: Charley Hall, Red Sox.
First-season attendance: 597,096.

Huntington Avenue Grounds (1901-11)

Capacity: 9,000.
First game: Red Sox 12, Philadelphia 4 (May 8, 1901).
First-season attendance: 289,448.

A.L. MVPs

Jimmie Foxx, 1B, 1938
Ted Williams, OF, 1946
Ted Williams, OF, 1949
Jackie Jensen, OF, 1958
Carl Yastrzemski, OF, 1967
Fred Lynn, OF, 1975
Jim Rice, OF, 1978
Roger Clemens, P, 1986
Mo Vaughn, 1B, 1995

CY YOUNG WINNERS

Jim Lonborg, RH, 1967
Roger Clemens, RH, 1986
Roger Clemens, RH, 1987
Roger Clemens, RH, 1991
Pedro Martinez, RH, 1999
Pedro Martinez, RH, 2000

ROOKIES OF THE YEAR

Walt Dropo, 1B, 1950
Don Schwall, P, 1961
Carlton Fisk, C, 1972
Fred Lynn, OF, 1975
Nomar Garciaparra, SS, 1997

MANAGERS OF THE YEAR

John McNamara, 1986
Jimy Williams, 1999

RETIRED UNIFORMS

No.	*Name*	*Pos.*
1	Bobby Doerr	2B
4	Joe Cronin	SS
8	Carl Yastrzemski	OF
9	Ted Williams	OF

MILESTONE PERFORMANCES

30-plus home runs
50— Jimmie Foxx 1938
46— Jim Rice 1978
44— Carl Yastrzemski 1967
Mo Vaughn 1996
43— Tony Armas 1984
Ted Williams 1949
42— Dick Stuart 1963
41— Jimmie Foxx 1936
Manny Ramirez 2001
40— Carl Yastrzemski 1969, 1970
Rico Petrocelli 1969
Mo Vaughn 1998
39— Vern Stephens 1949
Jim Rice 1977, 1979, 1983
Fred Lynn 1979
Mo Vaughn 1995
38— Ted Williams 1946, 1957
37— Ted Williams 1941
36— Jimmie Foxx 1937, 1940
Ted Williams 1942
Tony Conigliaro 1970
Tony Armas 1983
35— Jimmie Foxx 1939
Jackie Jensen 1958
Ken Harrelson 1968
Mo Vaughn 1997
Nomar Garciaparra 1998
34— Walt Dropo 1950
Dwight Evans 1987
Carl Everett 2000
33— Dick Stuart 1964
George Scott 1977
Manny Ramirez 2002
32— Ted Williams 1947
Tony Conigliaro 1965
Dwight Evans 1982, 1984
31— Ted Williams 1939
Don Baylor 1986
30— Vern Stephens 1950
Ted Williams 1951
Felix Mantilla 1964
Reggie Smith 1971
Butch Hobson 1977
Nick Esasky 1989
Nomar Garciaparra 1997

100-plus RBIs
175— Jimmie Foxx 1938
159— Vern Stephens 1949
Ted Williams 1949
145— Ted Williams 1939
144— Walt Dropo 1950
Vern Stephens 1950
143— Jimmie Foxx 1936
Mo Vaughn 1996
139— Jim Rice 1978
137— Ted Williams 1942
Vern Stephens 1948
130— Jim Rice 1979
127— Jimmie Foxx 1937
Ted Williams 1948
126— Ted Williams 1951
Jim Rice 1983
Mo Vaughn 1995
125— Manny Ramirez 2001
123— Ted Williams 1946
Tony Armas 1984
Dwight Evans 1987
122— Jackie Jensen 1958
Fred Lynn 1979
Jim Rice 1984
Nomar Garciaparra 1998
121— Buck Freeman 1902
Carl Yastrzemski 1967
120— Ted Williams 1941
Bobby Doerr 1950
Nomar Garciaparra 2002
119— Roy Johnson 1934
Jimmie Foxx 1940
Rudy York 1946
Mike Greenwell 1988
118— Dick Stuart 1963
117— Jackie Jensen 1954
116— Bobby Doerr 1946
Jackie Jensen 1955
Tony Conigliaro 1970
115— Mo Vaughn 1998
114— Buck Freeman 1901
Babe Ruth 1919
Ted Williams 1947
Dick Stuart 1964
Jim Rice 1977
113— Ted Williams 1940
112— Jackie Jensen 1959
Butch Hobson 1977
111— Joe Cronin 1940
Bobby Doerr 1948
Carl Yastrzemski 1969
Dwight Evans 1988
110— Joe Cronin 1937
Bill Buckner 1985
Jim Rice 1986
109— Duffy Lewis 1912
Bobby Doerr 1949
Ken Harrelson 1968
108— Nick Esasky 1989
Carl Everett 2000
107— Joe Cronin 1939
Tony Armas 1983
Manny Ramirez 2002
106— Mike Higgins 1937, 1938
Bob Johnson 1944
105— Jimmie Foxx 1939, 1941
Bobby Doerr 1940
Fred Lynn 1975
Tony Perez 1980
104— Buck Freeman 1903
Dwight Evans 1984
Nomar Garciaparra 1999
103— Earl Webb 1931
Frank Malzone 1957
Jackie Jensen 1957
Vic Wertz 1960
Rico Petrocelli 1970
Jim Rice 1985
Troy O'Leary 1999
102— Bobby Doerr 1942
Carl Yastrzemski 1970, 1976, 1977
Jim Rice 1975
Carlton Fisk 1977
Bill Buckner 1986
John Valentin 1995
101— Jim Tabor 1941
Mo Vaughn 1993
100— Del Pratt 1921
Dwight Evans 1989

20-plus victories
1901— Cy Young 33-10
1902— Cy Young 32-11
Bill Dinneen 21-21
1903— Cy Young 28-9
Bill Dinneen 21-13
Tom Hughes 20-7
1904— Cy Young 26-16
Bill Dinneen 23-14
Jesse Tannehill 21-11
1905— Jesse Tannehill 22-9
1907— Cy Young 21-15
1908— Cy Young 21-11
1911— Joe Wood 23-17
1912— Joe Wood 34-5
Hugh Bedient 20-9
Buck O'Brien 20-13
1914— Ray Collins 20-13
1916— Babe Ruth 23-12
1917— Babe Ruth 24-13
Carl Mays 22-9
1918— Carl Mays 21-13
1921— Sam Jones 23-16
1923— Howard Ehmke 20-17
1935— Wes Ferrell 25-14
Lefty Grove 20-12
1936— Wes Ferrell 20-15
1942— Tex Hughson 22-6
1945— Dave Ferriss 21-10
1946— Dave Ferriss 25-6
Tex Hughson 20-11
1949— Mel Parnell 25-7
Ellis Kinder 23-6
1953— Mel Parnell 21-8
1963— Bill Monbouquette 20-10
1967— Jim Lonborg 22-9
1973— Luis Tiant 20-13
1974— Luis Tiant 22-13
1976— Luis Tiant 21-12
1978— Dennis Eckersley 20-8
1986— Roger Clemens 24-4
1987— Roger Clemens 20-9
1990— Roger Clemens 21-6
1999— Pedro Martinez 23-4
2002— Derek Lowe 21-8
Pedro Martinez 20-4

A.L. home run champions
1903— Buck Freeman 13
1910— Jake Stahl 10
1912— Tris Speaker *10
1918— Babe Ruth *11
1919— Babe Ruth 29
1939— Jimmie Foxx 35
1941— Ted Williams 37
1942— Ted Williams 36
1947— Ted Williams 32
1949— Ted Williams 43
1965— Tony Conigliaro 32
1967— Carl Yastrzemski *44
1977— Jim Rice 39
1978— Jim Rice 46
1981— Dwight Evans *22
1983— Jim Rice 39
1984— Tony Armas 43

* Tied for league lead

A.L. RBI champions
1902— Buck Freeman 121
1903— Buck Freeman 104
1919— Babe Ruth 114
1938— Jimmie Foxx 175
1939— Ted Williams 145
1942— Ted Williams 137
1947— Ted Williams 114
1949— Ted Williams *159
Vern Stephens *159
1950— Walt Dropo *144
Vern Stephens *144
1955— Jackie Jensen *116
1958— Jackie Jensen 122
1959— Jackie Jensen 112
1963— Dick Stuart 118
1967— Carl Yastrzemski 121
1968— Ken Harrelson 109
1978— Jim Rice 139
1983— Jim Rice *126
1984— Tony Armas 123
1995— Mo Vaughn *126

* Tied for league lead

INDIVIDUAL SEASON, GAME RECORDS

SEASON

Batting

Record		Player	Year
At-bats	684	Nomar Garciaparra	1997
Runs	150	Ted Williams	1949
Hits	240	Wade Boggs	1985
Singles	187	Wade Boggs	1985
Doubles	67	Earl Webb	1931
Triples	22	Tris Speaker	1913
Home runs	50	Jimmie Foxx	1938
Home runs, rookie	34	Walt Dropo	1950
Grand slams	4	Babe Ruth	1919
Total bases	406	Jim Rice	1978
RBIs	175	Jimmie Foxx	1938
Walks	162	Ted Williams	1947, 1949
Most strikeouts	162	Butch Hobson	1977
Fewest strikeouts	9	Stuffy McInnis	1921
Batting average	.406	Ted Williams	1941
Slugging pct.	.735	Ted Williams	1941
Stolen bases	54	Tommy Harper	1973

Pitching

Record		Player	Year
Games	80	Greg Harris	1993
Complete games	41	Cy Young	1902
Innings	384.2	Cy Young	1902
Wins	34	Joe Wood	1912
Losses	25	Charley Ruffing	1928
Winning pct.	.882 (15-2)	Bob Stanley	1978
Walks	134	Mel Parnell	1949
Strikeouts	313	Pedro Martinez	1999
Shutouts	10	Cy Young	1904
		Joe Wood	1912
Home runs allowed	38	Tim Wakefield	1996
Lowest ERA	0.96	Dutch Leonard	1914
Saves	46	Tom Gordon	1998

GAME

Batting

Record		Player	Date
Runs	6	Last by Spike Owen	8-21-86
Hits	6	Last by Jerry Remy	9-3-81 (20 innings)
Doubles	4	Last by Rick Miller	5-11-81
Triples	3	Patsy Dougherty	9-5-03
Home runs	3	Last by Nomar Garciaparra	7-23-2001 (a.m. game)
RBIs	10	Last by Nomar Garciaparra	5-10-99
Total bases	16	Fred Lynn	6-18-75
Stolen bases	4	Jerry Remy	6-14-80

A.L. batting champions
1932— Dale Alexander .367
1938— Jimmie Foxx .349
1941— Ted Williams .406
1942— Ted Williams .356
1947— Ted Williams .343
1948— Ted Williams .369
1950— Billy Goodman .354
1957— Ted Williams .388
1958— Ted Williams .328
1960— Pete Runnels .320
1962— Pete Runnels .326
1963— Carl Yastrzemski .321
1967— Carl Yastrzemski .326
1968— Carl Yastrzemski .301
1979— Fred Lynn .333
1981— Carney Lansford .336
1983— Wade Boggs .361
1985— Wade Boggs .368
1986— Wade Boggs .357
1987— Wade Boggs .363
1988— Wade Boggs .366
1999— Nomar Garciaparra .357
2000— Nomar Garciaparra .372
2002— Manny Ramirez .349

A.L. ERA champions
1901— Cy Young 1.62
1914— Dutch Leonard 0.96
1915— Joe Wood 1.49
1916— Babe Ruth 1.75
1935— Lefty Grove 2.70
1936— Lefty Grove 2.81
1938— Lefty Grove 3.08
1939— Lefty Grove 2.54
1949— Mel Parnell 2.78
1972— Luis Tiant 1.91
1986— Roger Clemens 2.48
1990— Roger Clemens 1.93
1991— Roger Clemens 2.62
1992— Roger Clemens 2.41
1999— Pedro Martinez 2.07
2000— Pedro Martinez 1.74
2002— Pedro Martinez 2.26

A.L. strikeout champions
1901— Cy Young 158
1942— Tex Hughson 113
1967— Jim Lonborg 246
1988— Roger Clemens 291
1991— Roger Clemens 241
1996— Roger Clemens 257
1999— Pedro Martinez 313
2000— Pedro Martinez 284
2001— Hideo Nomo 220
2002— Pedro Martinez 239

No-hit pitchers
(9 innings or more)
1904— Cy Young 3-0 vs. Philadelphia (Perfect)
Jesse Tannehill 6-0 vs. Chicago
1905— Bill Dinneen 2-0 vs. Chicago
1908— Cy Young 8-0 vs. New York
1911— Joe Wood 5-0 vs. St. Louis
1916— George Foster 2-0 vs. New York
Dutch Leonard 4-0 vs. St. Louis
1917— Ernie Shore 4-0 vs. Washington (Perfect)
1918— Dutch Leonard 5-0 vs. Detroit
1923— Howard Ehmke 4-0 vs. Philadelphia
1956— Mel Parnell 4-0 vs. Chicago
1962— Earl Wilson 2-0 vs. Los Angeles
Bill Monbouquette 1-0 vs. Chicago
1965— Dave Morehead 2-0 vs. Cleveland
1992— †Matt Young 1-2 vs. Cleveland
2001— Hideo Nomo 3-0 vs. Baltimore
2002— Derek Lowe 10-0 vs. Tampa Bay

† Pitched 8 innings

Longest hitting streaks
34— Dom DiMaggio 1949
30— Tris Speaker 1912
Nomar Garciaparra 1997
28— Wade Boggs 1985
27— Dom DiMaggio 1951
26— Buck Freeman 1902
Johnny Pesky 1947
25— George Metkovich 1944
Wade Boggs 1987
24— Nomar Garciaparra 1998
23— Gorge Burns 1922
Del Pratt 1922
Buddy Myer 1928
Ted Williams 1941
22— Tris Speaker 1913
Dom DiMaggio 1942
Denny Doyle 1975
Reggie Jefferson 1997
21— Bobby Doerr 1943
Jim Rice 1980
Mike Greenwell 1989
20— Tris Speaker 1912
Tris Speaker 1912
Babe Ruth 1919
Ike Boone 1925
Smead Jolley 1932
Ed Bressoud 1964
Fred Lynn 1975
Fred Lynn 1979
Mike Easler 1984
Wade Boggs 1986
Nomar Garciaparra 2000

HISTORY

CAREER LEADERS

BATTING

Games	
Carl Yastrzemski	3,308
Dwight Evans	2,505
Ted Williams	2,292
Jim Rice	2,089
Bobby Doerr	1,865
Harry Hooper	1,647
Wade Boggs	1,625
Rico Petrocelli	1,553
Dom DiMaggio	1,399
Frank Malzone	1,359

At-bats	
Carl Yastrzemski	11,988
Dwight Evans	8,726
Jim Rice	8,225
Ted Williams	7,706
Bobby Doerr	7,093
Harry Hooper	6,270
Wade Boggs	6,213
Dom DiMaggio	5,640
Rico Petrocelli	5,390
Frank Malzone	5,273

Runs	
Carl Yastrzemski	1,816
Ted Williams	1,798
Dwight Evans	1,435
Jim Rice	1,249
Bobby Doerr	1,094
Wade Boggs	1,067
Dom DiMaggio	1,046
Harry Hooper	988
Johnny Pesky	776
Jimmie Foxx	721

Hits	
Carl Yastrzemski	3,419
Ted Williams	2,654
Jim Rice	2,452
Dwight Evans	2,373
Wade Boggs	2,098
Bobby Doerr	2,042
Harry Hooper	1,707
Dom DiMaggio	1,680
Frank Malzone	1,454
Mike Greenwell	1,400

Doubles	
Carl Yastrzemski	646
Ted Williams	525
Dwight Evans	474
Wade Boggs	422
Bobby Doerr	381
Jim Rice	373
Dom DiMaggio	308
Mike Greenwell	275
Joe Cronin	270
John Valentin	266

Triples	
Harry Hooper	130
Tris Speaker	106
Buck Freeman	90
Bobby Doerr	89
Larry Gardner	87
Jim Rice	79
Hobe Ferris	77
Dwight Evans	72
Ted Williams	71
Jimmy Collins	65

Home runs	
Ted Williams	521
Carl Yastrzemski	452
Jim Rice	382
Dwight Evans	379
Mo Vaughn	230
Bobby Doerr	223
Jimmie Foxx	222
Rico Petrocelli	210
Jackie Jensen	170
Tony Conigliaro	162
Carlton Fisk	162

Total bases	
Carl Yastrzemski	5,539
Ted Williams	4,884
Jim Rice	4,129
Dwight Evans	4,128
Bobby Doerr	3,270
Wade Boggs	2,869
Dom DiMaggio	2,363
Harry Hooper	2,303
Rico Petrocelli	2,263
Mike Greenwell	2,141

Runs batted in	
Carl Yastrzemski	1,844
Ted Williams	1,839
Jim Rice	1,451
Dwight Evans	1,346
Bobby Doerr	1,247
Jimmie Foxx	788
Rico Petrocelli	773
Mo Vaughn	752
Joe Cronin	737
Jackie Jensen	733

Extra-base hits	
Carl Yastrzemski	1,157
Ted Williams	1,117
Dwight Evans	925
Jim Rice	834
Bobby Doerr	693
Wade Boggs	554
Rico Petrocelli	469
Dom DiMaggio	452
Jimmie Foxx	448
Mike Greenwell	443

Batting average (Minimum 500 games)	
Ted Williams	.344
Wade Boggs	.338
Tris Speaker	.337
Nomar Garciaparra	.328
Pete Runnels	.320
Jimmie Foxx	.320
Roy Johnson	.313
Johnny Pesky	.313
Fred Lynn	.308
Billy Goodman	.306

Stolen bases	
Harry Hooper	300
Tris Speaker	267
Carl Yastrzemski	168
Heinie Wagner	141
Larry Gardner	134
Freddy Parent	129
Tommy Harper	107
Billy Werber	107
Chick Stahl	105
Jimmy Collins	102
Duffy Lewis	102

PITCHING

Earned-run average (Minimum 1,000 innings)	
Joe Wood	1.99
Cy Young	2.00
Dutch Leonard	2.13
Babe Ruth	2.19
Carl Mays	2.21
Ray Collins	2.51
Bill Dinneen	2.81
George Winter	2.91
Tex Hughson	2.94
Roger Clemens	3.06

Wins	
Roger Clemens	192
Cy Young	192
Mel Parnell	123
Luis Tiant	122
Joe Wood	117
Bob Stanley	115
Joe Dobson	106
Lefty Grove	105
Tex Hughson	96
Bill Monbouquette	96

Losses	
Cy Young	112
Roger Clemens	111
Bob Stanley	97
George Winter	97
Red Ruffing	96
Jack Russell	94
Bill Monbouquette	91
Bill Dinneen	85
Tom Brewer	82
Tim Wakefield	82

Innings pitched	
Roger Clemens	2,776.0
Cy Young	2,728.1
Luis Tiant	1,774.2
Mel Parnell	1,752.2
Bob Stanley	1,707.0
Bill Monbouquette	1,622.0
George Winter	1,599.2
Joe Dobson	1,544.0
Lefty Grove	1,539.2
Tom Brewer	1,509.1

Strikeouts	
Roger Clemens	2,590
Cy Young	1,341
Pedro Martinez	1,250
Luis Tiant	1,075
Tim Wakefield	1,044
Bruce Hurst	1,043
Joe Wood	986
Bill Monbouquette	969
Frank Sullivan	821
Ray Culp	794

Bases on balls	
Roger Clemens	856
Mel Parnell	758
Tom Brewer	669
Joe Dobson	604
Tim Wakefield	585
Jack Wilson	564
Willard Nixon	530
Ike Delock	514
Mickey McDermott	504
Luis Tiant	501

Games	
Bob Stanley	637
Roger Clemens	383
Ellis Kinder	365
Cy Young	327
Ike Delock	322
Bill Lee	321
Tim Wakefield	320
Derek Lowe	318
Mel Parnell	289
Greg Harris	287

Shutouts	
Roger Clemens	38
Cy Young	38
Joe Wood	28
Luis Tiant	26
Dutch Leonard	25
Mel Parnell	20
Ray Collins	19
Tex Hughson	19
Sam Jones	18
Joe Dobson	17
Babe Ruth	17

Saves	
Bob Stanley	132
Dick Radatz	104
Ellis Kinder	91
Jeff Reardon	88
Derek Lowe	85
Sparky Lyle	69
Tom Gordon	68
Lee Smith	58
Bill Campbell	51
Ugueth Urbina	49

TEAM SEASON, GAME RECORDS

SEASON

Batting		
Most at-bats	5,781	1997
Most runs	1,027	1950
Fewest runs	463	1906
Most hits	1,684	1997
Most singles	1,156	1905
Most doubles	373	1997
Most triples	112	1903
Most home runs	213	1977
Fewest home runs	12	1906
Most grand slams	9	1941, 1950, 1987, 2001
Most pinch-hit home runs	6	1953
Most total bases	2,676	1997
Most stolen bases	215	1909
Highest batting average	.302	1950
Lowest batting average	.234	1905, 1907
Highest slugging pct	.465	1977

Pitching		
Lowest ERA	2.12	1904
Highest ERA	5.02	1932
Most complete games	148	1904
Most shutouts	26	1918
Most saves	53	1998
Most walks	748	1950
Most strikeouts	1,259	2001

Fielding		
Most errors	373	1901
Fewest errors	93	1988
Most double plays	207	1949
Highest fielding averag	.984	1988

General		
Most games won	105	1912
Most games lost	111	1932
Highest win pct	.691	1912
Lowest win pct	.279	1932

GAME, INNING

Batting		
Most runs, game	29	6-8-50
Most runs, inning	17	6-18-53
Most hits, game	28	6-8-50
Most home runs, game	8	7-4-77
Most total bases, game	60	6-8-50

Jackie Jensen (left) and Ted Williams formed two-thirds of a prolific outfield for six seasons.

RED SOX YEAR-BY-YEAR

Year	W	L	Place	Games Back	Manager	Leaders: Batting avg.	Hits	Home runs	RBIs	Wins	ERA
1901	79	57	2nd	4	J. Collins	Freeman, .339	J. Collins, 187	Freeman, 12	Freeman, 114	Young, 33	Young, 1.62
1902	77	60	3rd	6½	J. Collins	Dougherty, .342	Freeman, 174	Freeman, 11	Freeman, 121	Young, 32	Young, 2.15
1903	91	47	1st	+14½	J. Collins	Dougherty, .331	Dougherty, 195	Freeman, 13	Freeman, 104	Young, 28	Young, 2.08
1904	95	59	1st	+1½	J. Collins	Parent, .291	Parent, 172	Freeman, 7	Freeman, 84	Young, 26	Young, 1.97
1905	78	74	4th	16	J. Collins	J. Collins, .276	Burkett, 147	Ferris, 6	J. Collins, 65	Tannehill, 22	Young, 1.82
1906	49	105	8th	45½	J. Collins, Stahl	Grimshaw, .290	Stahl, 170	Stahl, 4	Stahl, 51	Tannehill, Young, 13	Dinneen, 2.92
1907	59	90	7th	32½	Huff, Unglaub, McGuire	Congalton, .286	Congalton, 142	Ferris, 4	Unglaub, 62	Young, 21	Morgan, 1.97
1908	75	79	5th	15½	McGuire, Lake	Gessler, .308	Lord, 145	Gessler, 3	Gessler, 63	Young, 21	Young, 1.26
1909	88	63	3rd	9½	Lake	Lord, .311	Speaker, 168	Speaker, 7	Speaker, 77	Arellanes, 16	Cicotte, 1.97
1910	81	72	4th	22½	Donovan	Speaker, .340	Speaker, 183	Stahl, 10	Stahl, 77	Cicotte, 15	R. Collins, 1.62
1911	78	75	5th	24	Donovan	Speaker, .334	Speaker, 167	Speaker, 8	Lewis, 86	Wood, 23	Wood, 2.02
1912	105	47	1st	+14	Stahl	Speaker, .383	Speaker, 222	Speaker, 10	Lewis, 109	Wood, 34	Wood, 1.91
1913	79	71	4th	15½	Stahl, Carrigan	Speaker, .363	Speaker, 189	Hooper, 4	Lewis, 90	R. Collins, 19	Wood, 2.29
1914	91	62	2nd	8½	Carrigan	Speaker, .338	Speaker, 193	Speaker, 4	Speaker, 90	R. Collins, 20	Leonard, 0.96
1915	101	50	1st	+2½	Carrigan	Speaker, .322	Speaker, 176	Ruth, 4	Lewis, 76	Foster, Shore, 19	Wood, 1.49
1916	91	63	1st	+2	Carrigan	Gardner, .308	Hooper, 156	Walker, Ruth, Gainor, 3	Gardner, 62	Ruth, 23	Ruth, 1.75
1917	90	62	2nd	9	Barry	Lewis, .302	Lewis, 167	Hooper, 3	Lewis, 65	Ruth, 24	Mays, 1.74
1918	75	51	1st	+1½	Barrow	Hooper, .289	Hooper, 137	Ruth, 11	Ruth, 66	Mays, 21	Bush, 2.11
1919	66	71	6th	20½	Barrow	Ruth, .322	Scott, 141	Ruth, 29	Ruth, 114	Pennock, 16	Mays, 2.47
1920	72	81	5th	25½	Barrow	Hendryx, .328	Hooper, 167	Hooper, 7	Hendryx, 73	Pennock, 16	Myers, 2.13
1921	75	79	5th	23½	Duffy	Pratt, .324	McInnis, 179	Pratt, 5	Pratt, 100	S. Jones, 23	S. Jones, 3.22
1922	61	93	8th	33	Duffy	J. Harris, .316	Pratt, 183	Burns, 12	Pratt, 86	R. Collins, 14	Quinn, 3.48
1923	61	91	8th	37	Chance	J. Harris, .335	Burns, 181	J. Harris, 13	Burns, 82	Ehmke, 20	Piercy, 3.41
1924	67	87	7th	25	Fohl	Boone, .333	Wambsganss, 174	Boone, 13	Veach, 99	Ehmke, 19	Quinn, 3.27
1925	47	105	8th	49½	Fohl	Boone, .330	Flagstead, 160	Todt, 11	Todt, 75	Wingfield, 12	Ehmke, 3.73
1926	46	107	8th	44½	Fohl	Jacobson, .305	Todt, 153	Todt, 7	Jacobson, Todt, 69	Wingfield, 11	Russell, 3.58
1927	51	103	8th	59	Carrigan	Tobin, .310	Myer, 135	Todt, 6	Flagstead, 69	Harriss, 14	Russell, 4.10
1928	57	96	8th	43½	Carrigan	Myer, .313	Myer, 168	Todt, 12	Regan, 75	Morris, 19	Morris, 3.53
1929	58	96	8th	48	Carrigan	Rothrock, .300	Scarritt, 159	Rothrock, 6	Scarritt, 71	Morris, 14	MacFayden, 3.62
1930	52	102	8th	50	Wagner	Webb, .323	Oliver, 189	Webb, 16	Webb, 66	Gaston, 13	Gaston, 3.92
1931	62	90	6th	45	S. Collins	Webb, .333	Webb, 196	Webb, 14	Webb, 103	MacFayden, 16	Moore, 3.88
1932	43	111	8th	64	S. Collins, McManus	Alexander, .372	Jolley, 164	Jolley, 18	Jolley, 99	Kline, 11	Durham, 3.80
1933	63	86	7th	34½	McManus	R. Johnson, .313	R. Johnson, 151	R. Johnson, 10	R. Johnson, 95	Rhodes, 12	Weiland, 3.87
1934	76	76	4th	24	B. Harris	Werber, .321	Werber, 200	Werber, 11	R. Johnson, 119	Ferrell, 14	Ostermueller, 3.49
1935	78	75	4th	16	Cronin	R. Johnson, .315	Almada, 176	Werber, 14	Cronin, 95	Ferrell, 25	Grove, 2.70
1936	74	80	6th	28½	Cronin	Foxx, .338	Foxx, 198	Foxx, 41	Foxx, 143	Ferrell, 20	Grove, 2.81
1937	80	72	5th	21	Cronin	Chapman,.Cronin, .307	Cronin, 175	Foxx, 36	Foxx, 127	Grove, 17	Grove, 3.02
1938	88	61	2nd	9½	Cronin	Foxx, .349	Vosmik, 201	Foxx, 50	Foxx, 175	Bagby, J. Wilson, 15	Grove, 3.08
1939	89	62	2nd	17	Cronin	Foxx, .360	T. Williams, 185	Foxx, 35	T. Williams, 145	Grove, 15	Grove, 2.54
1940	82	72	4th	8	Cronin	T. Williams, .344	Cramer, 200	Foxx, 36	Foxx, 119	Heving, J. Wilson, 12	Grove, 3.99
1941	84	70	2nd	17	Cronin	T. Williams, .406	T. Williams, 185	T. Williams, 37	T. Williams, 120	D. Newsome, 19	Wagner, 3.07
1942	93	59	2nd	9	Cronin	T. Williams, .356	Pesky, 205	T. Williams, 36	T. Williams, 137	Hughson, 22	Butland, 2.51
1943	68	84	7th	29	Cronin	Fox, .288	Doerr, 163	Doerr, 16	Tabor, 85	Hughson, 12	Brown, 2.12
1944	77	77	4th	12	Cronin	Doerr, .325	B. Johnson, 170	B. Johnson, 17	B. Johnson, 106	Hughson, 18	Hughson, 2.26
1945	71	83	7th	17½	Cronin	S. Newsome, .290	B. Johnson, 148	B. Johnson, 12	B. Johnson, 74	Ferriss, 21	Ryba, 2.49
1946	104	50	1st	+12	Cronin	T. Williams, .342	Pesky, 208	T. Williams, 38	T. Williams, 123	Ferriss, 25	Hughson, 2.75
1947	83	71	3rd	14	Cronin	T. Williams, .343	Pesky, 207	T. Williams, 32	T. Williams, 114	Dobson, 18	Dobson, 2.95
1948	96	59	*2nd	1	McCarthy	T. Williams, .369	T. Williams, 188	Stephens, 29	Stephens, 137	Kramer, 18	Parnell, 3.14
1949	96	58	2nd	1	McCarthy	T. Williams, .343	T. Williams, 194	T. Williams, 43	Stephens, Williams, 159	Parnell, 25	Parnell, 2.77
1950	94	60	3rd	4	McCarthy, O'Neill	Goodman, .354	D. DiMaggio, 193	Dropo, 34	Dropo, Stephens, 144	Parnell, 18	Parnell, 3.61
1951	87	67	3rd	11	O'Neill	T. Williams, .318	D. DiMaggio, 189	T. Williams, 30	T. Williams, 126	Parnell, 18	Kinder, 2.55
1952	76	78	6th	19	Boudreau	Goodman, .306	Goodman, 157	Gernert, 19	Gernert, 67	Parnell, 12	Kinder, 2.58
1953	84	69	4th	16	Boudreau	Goodman, .313	Goodman, 161	Gernert, 21	Kell, 73	Parnell, 21	Kinder, 1.85
1954	69	85	4th	42	Boudreau	T. Williams, .345	Jensen, 160	T. Williams, 29	Jensen, 117	Sullivan, 15	Sullivan, 3.14
1955	84	70	4th	12	Higgins	Goodman, .294	Goodman, 176	T. Williams, 28	Jensen, 116	Sullivan, 18	Kiely, 2.80
1956	84	70	4th	13	Higgins	T. Williams, .345	Jensen, 182	T. Williams, 24	Jensen, 97	Brewer, 19	Sullivan, 3.42
1957	82	72	3rd	16	Higgins	T. Williams, .388	Malzone, 185	T. Williams, 38	Jensen, Malzone, 103	Brewer, 16	Sullivan, 2.73
1958	79	75	3rd	13	Higgins	T. Williams, .328	Malzone, 185	Jensen, 35	Jensen, 122	Delock, 14	Delock, 3.37
1959	75	79	5th	19	Higgins, York, Jurges	Runnels, .314	Runnels, 176	Jensen, 28	Jensen, 112	Casale, 13	DeLock, 2.95
1960	65	89	7th	32	Jurges, Baker, Higgins	Runnels, .320	Runnels, 169	T. Williams, 29	Wertz, 103	Monbouquette, 14	Fornieles, 2.64
1961	76	86	6th	33	Higgins	Runnels, .317	Schilling, 167	Geiger, 18	Malzone, 87	Schwall, 15	Schwall, 3.22
1962	76	84	8th	19	Higgins	Runnels, .326	Yastrzemski, 191	Malzone, 21	Malzone, 95	Conley, Monbouquette, 15	Radatz, 2.24
1963	76	85	7th	28	Pesky	Yastrzemski, .321	Yastrzemski, 183	Stuart, 42	Stuart, 118	Monbouquette, 20	Radatz, 1.97
1964	72	90	8th	27	Pesky, Herman	Bressoud, .293	Stuart, 168	Stuart, 33	Stuart, 114	Radatz, 16	Radatz, 2.29
1965	62	100	9th	40	Herman	Yastrzemski, .312	Yastrzemski, 154	Conigliaro, 32	Mantilla, 92	Wilson, 13	Monbouquette, 3.70
1966	72	90	9th	26	Herman, Runnels	Yastrzemski, .278	Yastrzemski, 165	Conigliaro, 28	Conigliaro, 93	Santiago, 12	Brandon, 3.31
1967	92	70	1st	+1	D. Williams	Yastrzemski, .326	Yastrzemski, 189	Yastrzemski, 44	Yastrzemski, 121	Lonborg, 22	Wyatt, 2.60
1968	86	76	4th	17	D. Williams	Yastrzemski, .301	Yastrzemski, 162	Harrelson, 35	Harrelson, 109	Culp, Ellsworth, 16	Santiago, 2.25
								EAST DIVISION			
1969	87	75	3rd	22	D. Williams, Popowski	R. Smith, .309	R. Smith, 168	Petrocelli, Yastrzemski, 40	Yastrzemski, 111	Culp, 17	Lyle, 2.54
1970	87	75	3rd	21	Kasko	Yastrzemski, .329	Yastrzemski, 186	Yastrzemski, 40	Conigliaro, 116	Culp, 17	Culp, 3.04
1971	85	77	3rd	18	Kasko	R. Smith, .283	R. Smith, 175	R. Smith, 30	R. Smith, 96	Siebert, 16	Lee, 2.74
1972	85	70	2nd	½	Kasko	Fisk, .293	Harper, 141	Fisk, 22	Petrocelli, 75	Pattin, 17	Tiant, 1.91
1973	89	73	2nd	8	Kasko, Popowski	R. Smith, .303	Yastrzemski, 160	Fisk, 26	Yastrzemski, 95	Tiant, 20	Lee, 2.75
1974	84	78	3rd	7	D. Johnson	Yastrzemski, .301	Yastrzemski, 155	Petrocelli, Yastrzemski, 15	Yastrzemski, 79	Tiant, 22	Tiant, 2.92
1975	95	65	†1st	+4½	D. Johnson	Lynn, .331	Lynn, 175	Rice, 22	Lynn, 105	Wise, 19	Moret, 3.60
1976	83	79	3rd	15½	D. Johnson, Zimmer	Lynn, .314	Lynn, 164	Rice, 25	Yastrzemski, 102	Tiant, 21	Willoughby, 2.82
1977	97	64	‡2nd	2½	Zimmer	Rice, .320	Rice, 206	Rice, 39	Rice, 114	Campbell, 13	Campbell, 2.96
1978	99	64	§2nd	1	Zimmer	Rice, .315	Rice, 213	Rice, 46	Rice, 139	Eckersley, 20	Stanley, 2.60
1979	91	69	3rd	11½	Zimmer	Lynn, .333	Rice, 201	Lynn, Rice, 39	Rice, 130	Eckersley, 17	Eckersley, 2.99
1980	83	77	4th	19	Zimmer, Pesky	Stapleton, .321	Burleson, 179	Perez, 25	Perez, 105	Eckersley, 12	Burgmeier, 2.00
1981	59	49	∞5th/2nd	—	Houk	Lansford, .336	Lansford, 134	Evans, 22	Evans, 71	Stanley, Torrez, 10	Torrez, 3.68
1982	89	73	3rd	6	Houk	Rice, .309	Evans, Remy, 178	Evans, 32	Evans, 98	Clear, 14	Burgmeier, 2.29
1983	78	84	6th	20	Houk	Boggs, .361	Boggs, 210	Rice, 39	Rice, 126	Tudor, 13	Stanley, 2.85
1984	86	76	4th	18	Houk	Boggs, .325	Boggs, 203	Armas, 43	Armas, 123	Boyd, Hurst, Ojeda, 12	Stanley, 3.54
1985	81	81	5th	18½	McNamara	Boggs, .368	Boggs, 240	Evans, 29	Buckner, 110	Boyd, 15	Clemens, 3.29
1986	95	66	†1st	+5½	McNamara	Boggs, .357	Boggs, 207	Baylor, 31	Rice, 110	Clemens, 24	Clemens, 2.48
1987	78	84	5th	20	McNamara	Boggs, .363	Boggs, 200	Evans, 34	Evans, 123	Clemens, 20	Clemens, 2.97
1988	89	73	▲1st	+1	McNamara, Morgan	Boggs, .366	Boggs, 214	Greenwell, 22	Greenwell, 119	Clemens, Hurst, 18	Clemens, 2.93
1989	83	79	3rd	6	Morgan	Boggs, .330	Boggs, 205	Esasky, 30	Esasky, 108	Clemens, 17	Lamp, 2.32
1990	88	74	▲1st	+2	Morgan	Boggs, .302	Boggs, 187	Burks, 21	Burks, 89	Clemens, 21	Clemens, 1.93
1991	84	78	‡2nd	7	Morgan	Boggs, .332	Boggs, 181	Clark, 28	Clark, 87	Clemens, 18	Clemens, 2.62
1992	73	89	7th	23	Hobson	Zupcic, .276	Reed, 136	Brunansky, 15	Brunansky, 74	Clemens, 18	Clemens, 2.41
1993	80	82	5th	15	Hobson	Greenwell, .315	Greenwell, 170	Vaughn, 29	Vaughn, 101	Darwin, 15	Sele, 2.74
1994	54	61	4th	17	Hobson	Vaughn, .310	Vaughn, 122	Vaughn, 26	Vaughn, 82	Clemens, 9	Clemens, 2.85
1995	86	58	◆1st	+7	Kennedy	O'Leary, .308	Vaughn, 165	Vaughn, 39	Vaughn, 126	Wakefield, 18	Wakefield, 2.95
1996	85	77	3rd	7	Kennedy	Jefferson, .347	Vaughn, 207	Vaughn, 44	Vaughn, 143	Wakefield, 14	Clemens, 3.63
1997	78	84	4th	20	J. Williams	Jefferson, .319	Garciaparra, 209	Vaughn, 35	Garciaparra, 98	Sele, 13	Gordon, 3.74
1998	92	70	◆2nd	22	J. Williams	Vaughn, .337	Vaughn, 205	Vaughn, 40	Garciaparra, 122	P.Martinez, 19	P.Martinez, 2.89
1999	94	68	▲2nd	4	J. Williams	Garciaparra, .357	Garciaparra, 190	O'Leary, 28	Garciaparra, 104	P.Martinez, 23	P.Martinez, 2.07
2000	85	77	2nd	2½	J. Williams	Garciaparra, .372	Garciaparra, 197	Everett, 34	Everett, 108	P. Martinez, 18	P. Martinez, 1.74
2001	82	79	3rd	16	J. Williams, Kerrigan	Ramirez, .306	Ramirez, 162	Ramirez, 41	Ramirez, 125	Nomo, 13	P. Martinez, 2.39
2002	93	69	2nd	10½	Little	Ramirez, .349	Garciaparra, 197	Ramirez, 33	Garciaparra, 120	Lowe, 21	P. Martinez, 2.26

* Lost pennant playoff. † Won Championship Series. ‡ Tied for position. § Lost division playoff. ∞ First half 30-26, second half 29-23. ▲ Lost Championship Series. ◆ Lost Division Series.

Note: Batting average minimum 350 at-bats; ERA minimum 90 innings pitched.

Chicago White Sox

FRANCHISE CHRONOLOGY

First season: 1901, as a member of the new American League. Charles Comiskey's White Sox defeated Cleveland, 8-2, in their Major League debut and proceeded to win the circuit's first pennant. Chicago's 83-53 record was four games better than second-place Boston.

1902-present: The Hitless Wonder White Sox of 1906 won another A.L. pennant and stunned the powerful Cubs in a six-game World Series, and Chicago repeated as Series champion in 1917 with a six-game triumph over the New York Giants. But the franchise would never taste such success again. The team's image was tarnished two years later when the White Sox won another pennant and conspired with gamblers to lose the World Series. In the wake of the infamous "Black Sox" scandal, it would take four decades for the Sox to win another pennant and another 24 to qualify again for postseason play. The "Go Go Sox" of 1959 lost to Los Angeles in the World Series and the 1983, '93 and 2000 Sox won division titles, only to lose in the A.L. Championship Series or Division Series. Chicago, a charter member of the West Division, was one of five teams placed in the Central when the A.L. adopted a three-division format in 1994.

Shortstop Luis Aparicio.

WHITE SOX VS. OPPONENTS BY DECADE

	A's	Indians	Orioles	Red Sox	Tigers	Twins	Yankees	Angels	Rangers	Brewers	Royals	Blue Jays	Mariners	Devil Rays	Interleague	Decade Record
1901-09	92-98	100-89	112-74	101-90	96-93	130-57	113-74									744-575
1910-19	125-90	114-102	132-74	97-117	103-109	109-106	118-94									798-692
1920-29	100-119	105-114	104-114	117-103	124-95	95-125	86-134									731-804
1930-39	102-118	94-125	127-90	97-114	89-129	101-117	68-148									678-841
1940-49	112-108	103-114	102-113	85-134	95-125	124-93	86-133									707-820
1950-59	124-96	116-104	134-86	122-98	122-98	141-79	88-132									847-693
1960-69	118-66	104-74	83-95	102-76	81-97	83-101	76-102	92-70	95-61	10-8	8-10					852-760
1970-79	76-89	62-54	39-74	48-67	50-67	76-89	44-72	79-90	90-65	68-62	79-89	19-14	22-21			752-853
1980-89	70-60	61-54	53-63	59-56	48-66	57-66	58-61	62-68	59-64	55-58	55-64	50-70	71-52			758-802
1990-99	60-57	58-64	59-46	54-54	69-51	71-48	54-52	58-60	58-59	56-41	72-52	53-54	59-62	11-10	24-25	816-735
2000-02	9-18	27-24	14-10	12-12	34-16	20-30	11-13	12-16	17-11		30-20	12-10	14-16	15-9	32-22	259-227
Totals	988-919	944-918	959-839	894-921	911-946	1007-911	802-1015	303-304	319-260	189-169	244-235	134-148	166-151	26-19	56-47	7942-7802

Interleague results: 0-3 vs. Braves, 16-14 vs. Cubs, 9-2 vs. Reds, 7-5 vs. Astros, 8-4 vs. Brewers, 1-2 vs. Expos, 2-1 vs. Mets, 2-1 vs. Phillies, 6-5 vs. Pirates, 5-10 vs. Cardinals.

MANAGERS

Name	*Years*	*Record*
Clark Griffith	1901-02	157-113
Nixey Callahan	1903-04, 1912-14	309-329
Fielder Jones	1904-08	426-293
Billy Sullivan	1909	78-74
Hugh Duffy	1910-11	145-159
Pants Rowland	1915-18	339-247
Kid Gleason	1919-23	392-364
Johnny Evers	1924	66-87
Eddie Collins	1925-26	160-147
Ray Schalk	1927-28	102-125
Lena Blackburne	1928-29	99-133
Donie Bush	1930-31	118-189
Lew Fonseca	1932-34	120-196
Jimmie Dykes	1934-46	899-940
Ted Lyons	1946-48	185-245
Jack Onslow	1949-50	71-113
Red Corriden	1950	52-72
Paul Richards	1951-54, 1976	406-362
Marty Marion	1954-56	179-138
Al Lopez	1957-65, 1968-69	840-650
Eddie Stanky	1966-68	206-197
Don Gutteridge	1969-70	109-172

Nellie Fox was a second-base fixture for more than a decade in Chicago.

MANAGERS—*cont'd.*

Name	*Years*	*Record*
Chuck Tanner	1970-75	401-414
Bob Lemon	1977-78	124-112
Larry Doby	1978	37-50
Don Kessinger	1979	46-60
Tony La Russa	1979-86	522-510
Jim Fregosi	1986-88	193-226
Jeff Torborg	1989-91	250-235
Gene Lamont	1992-95	258-210
Terry Bevington	1995-97	222-214
Jerry Manuel	1998-2002	414-395

WORLD SERIES CHAMPIONS

Year	*Loser*	*Length*	*MVP*
1906	Chicago Cubs	6 games	None
1917	N.Y. Giants	6 games	None

A.L. PENNANT WINNERS

Year	*Record*	*Manager*	*Series Result*
1901	83-53	Griffith	None
1906	93-58	Jones	Defeated Cubs
1917	100-54	Rowland	Defeated Giants
1919	88-52	Gleason	Lost to Reds
1959	94-60	Lopez	Lost to Dodgers

WEST DIVISION CHAMPIONS

Year	*Record*	*Manager*	*ALCS Result*
1983	99-63	La Russa	Lost to Orioles
1993	94-68	Lamont	Lost to Blue Jays
1994	67-46	Lamont	None

CENTRAL DIVISION CHAMPIONS

Year	*Record*	*Manager*	*ALCS Result*
2000	95-67	Manuel	Lost in Div. Series

BALLPARK CHRONOLOGY

New Comiskey Park (1991-present)

Capacity: 44,098.
First game: Detroit 16, White Sox 0 (April 18, 1991).
First batter: Tony Phillips, Tigers.
First hit: Alan Trammell, Tigers (single).
First run: Travis Fryman, Tigers (3rd inning).
First home run: Cecil Fielder, Tigers.
First winning pitcher: Frank Tanana, Tigers.
First-season attendance: 2,934,154.

Southside Park (1901-10)

Capacity: 15,000.
First game: White Sox 8, Cleveland 2 (April 24, 1901).
First-season attendance: 354,350.

Comiskey Park (1910-90)

Capacity: 43,931.
First game: St. Louis 2, White Sox 0 (July 1, 1910).
First-season attendance (1911): 583,208.

ATTENDANCE HIGHS

Total	*Season*	*Park*
2,934,154	1991	New Comiskey Park
2,681,156	1992	New Comiskey Park
2,581,091	1993	New Comiskey Park
2,136,988	1984	Comiskey Park
2,132,821	1983	Comiskey Park

A.L. MVPs

Nellie Fox, 2B, 1959
Dick Allen, 1B, 1972
Frank Thomas, 1B, 1993
Frank Thomas, 1B, 1994

CY YOUNG WINNERS

Early Wynn, RH, 1959
LaMarr Hoyt, RH, 1983
Jack McDowell, RH, 1993

ROOKIES OF THE YEAR

Luis Aparicio, SS, 1956
Gary Peters, P, 1963
Tommie Agee, OF, 1966
Ron Kittle, OF, 1983
Ozzie Guillen, SS, 1985

MANAGERS OF THE YEAR

Tony La Russa, 1983
Jeff Torborg, 1990
Gene Lamont, 1993
Jerry Manuel, 2000

RETIRED UNIFORMS

No.	*Name*	*Pos.*
2	Nellie Fox	2B
3	Harold Baines	OF
4	Luke Appling	SS
9	Minnie Minoso	OF
11	Luis Aparicio	SS
16	Ted Lyons	P
19	Billy Pierce	P
72	Carlton Fisk	C

MILESTONE PERFORMANCES

30-plus home runs

49—Albert Belle 1998
43—Frank Thomas 2000
41—Frank Thomas 1993
40—Frank Thomas 1995
Frank Thomas 1996
38—Frank Thomas 1994
Magglio Ordonez 2002
37—Carlton Fisk 1985
Dick Allen 1972
35—Ron Kittle 1983
Frank Thomas 1997
34—Robin Ventura 1996
33—Bill Melton 1971
Bill Melton 1970
32—Frank Thomas 1991
Ron Kittle 1984
Greg Luzinski 1983
Dick Allen 1974
Magglio Ordonez 2000
Paul Konerko 2001
31—Oscar Gamble 1977
Charles Johnson 2000
Magglio Ordonez 2001
30—Albert Belle 1997
Magglio Ordonez 1999

100-plus RBIs

152—Albert Belle 1998
143—Frank Thomas 2000
138—Zeke Bonura 1936
135—Magglio Ordonez 2002
134—Frank Thomas 1996
128—Frank Thomas 1993
Luke Appling 1936
126—Magglio Ordonez 2000
125—Frank Thomas 1997
121—Joe Jackson 1920
119—Al Simmons 1933
117—Eddie Robinson 1951
Magglio Ordonez 1999
116—Minnie Minoso 1954
Albert Belle 1997
115—Frank Thomas 1992
Happy Felsch 1920
114—Smead Jolley 1930
113—Harold Baines 1985
Dick Allen 1972
Magglio Ordonez 2001
112—George Bell 1992
111—Gee Walker 1939
Earl Sheely 1925
Frank Thomas 1995
110—Zeke Bonura 1934
109—Frank Thomas 1991, 1998
Floyd Robinson 1962
108—Bib Falk 1926
107—Carlton Fisk 1985
105—Harold Baines 1982
Minnie Minoso 1960
Robin Ventura 1996
104—Minnie Minoso 1953
Eddie Robinson 1952
Al Simmons 1934
Carl Reynolds 1930
Paul Konerko 2002
103—Minnie Minoso 1957
Earl Sheely 1924
102—Greg Luzinski 1982
Larry Doby 1956
Happy Felsch 1917
101—Frank Thomas 1994
Richie Zisk 1977
Danny Tartabull 1996
100—Robin Ventura 1991
Ron Kittle 1983
Zeke Bonura 1937

20-plus victories

1901—Clark Griffith 24-7
Roy Patterson 20-15
1904—Frank Owen 21-15
1905—Nick Altrock 23-12
Frank Owen 21-13
1906—Frank Owen 22-13
Nick Altrock 20-13
1907—Guy White 27-13
Ed Walsh 24-18
Frank Smith 23-10
1908—Ed Walsh 40-15
1909—Frank Smith 25-17
1911—Ed Walsh 27-18
1912—Ed Walsh 27-17
1913—Reb Russell 22-16
Jim Scott 20-21
1915—Jim Scott 24-11
Urban Faber 24-14
1917—Ed Cicotte 28-12
1919—Ed Cicotte 29-7
Lefty Williams 23-11
1920—Red Faber 23-13
Lefty Williams 22-14
Dickie Kerr 21-9
Ed Cicotte 21-10
1921—Red Faber 25-15
1922—Red Faber 21-17
1924—Sloppy Thurston 20-14
1925—Ted Lyons 21-11
1927—Ted Lyons 22-14
1930—Ted Lyons 22-15
1936—Vern Kennedy 21-9
1941—Thornton Lee 22-11
1953—Virgil Trucks *20-10
1956—Billy Pierce 20-9
1957—Billy Pierce 20-12
1959—Early Wynn 22-10
1962—Ray Herbert 20-9
1964—Gary Peters 20-8
1971—Wilbur Wood 22-13
1972—Wilbur Wood 24-17
Stan Bahnsen 21-16
1973—Wilbur Wood 24-20
1974—Jim Kaat 21-13
Wilbur Wood 20-19
1975—Jim Kaat 20-14
1983—LaMarr Hoyt 24-10
Rich Dotson 22-7
1992—Jack McDowell 20-10
1993—Jack McDowell 22-10

* 15-6 with White Sox; 5-4 with Browns.

A.L. home run champions

1971—Bill Melton 33
1972—Dick Allen 37
1974—Dick Allen 32

A.L. RBI champions

1972—Dick Allen 113

A.L. batting champions

1936—Luke Appling .388
1943—Luke Appling .328
1997—Frank Thomas .347

A.L. ERA champions

1906—Doc White 1.52
1907—Ed Walsh 1.60
1910—Ed Walsh 1.27
1917—Ed Cicotte 1.53
1921—Red Faber 2.48
1922—Red Faber 2.80
1941—Thornton Lee 2.37
1942—Ted Lyons 2.10
1947—Joe Haynes 2.42
1951—Saul Rogovin *2.48
1955—Billy Pierce 1.97
1960—Frank Baumann 2.67
1963—Gary Peters 2.33
1966—Gary Peters 1.98
1967—Joel Horlen 2.06

*ERA compiled with two teams.

A.L. strikeout champions

1908—Ed Walsh 269
1909—Frank Smith 177
1911—Ed Walsh 255
1953—Billy Pierce 186
1958—Early Wynn 179

No-hit pitchers

(9 innings or more)

1902—Nixey Callahan 3-0 vs. Detroit
1905—Frank Smith 15-0 vs. Detroit
1908—Frank Smith 1-0 vs. Philadelphia
1911—Ed Walsh 5-0 vs. Boston
1914—Joe Benz 6-1 vs. Cleveland
1917—Ed Cicotte 11-0 vs. St. Louis
1922—Charlie Robertson 2-0 vs. Detroit (Perfect)
1926—Ted Lyons 6-0 vs. Boston
1935—Vern Kennedy 5-0 vs. Cleveland
1937—Bill Dietrich 8-0 vs. St. Louis
1957—Bob Keegan 6-0 vs. Washington
1967—Joel Horlen 6-0 vs. Detroit
1976—Blue Moon Odom-Francisco Barrios 2-1 vs. Oakland
1986—Joe Cowley 7-1 vs. California
1991—Wilson Alvarez 7-0 vs. Baltimore

Longest hitting streaks

27—Luke Appling 1936
Albert Belle 1997
26—Guy Curtright 1943
25—Lance Johnson 1992
24—Chico Carrasquel 1950
23—Minnie Minoso 1955
22—Sam Mele 1953
Eddie Collins 1920
21—Roy Sievers 1960
Frank Thomas 1999
20—Ken Berry 1967
Rip Radcliff 1937
Eddie Collins 1916

Shortstop Luke Appling, who spent 20 seasons with the White Sox, batted a hefty .388 in 1936, still a team record.

INDIVIDUAL SEASON, GAME RECORDS

SEASON

Batting

At-bats	649	Nellie Fox	1956
Runs	135	John Mostil	1925
Hits	222	Eddie Collins	1920
Singles	169	Eddie Collins	1920
Doubles	48	Albert Belle	1998
Triples	21	Joe Jackson	1916
Home runs	49	Albert Belle	1998
Home runs, rookie	35	Ron Kittle	1983
Grand slams	4	Albert Belle	1997
Total bases	399	Albert Belle	1998
RBIs	152	Albert Belle	1998
Walks	138	Frank Thomas	1991
Most strikeouts	175	Dave Nicholson	1963
Fewest strikeouts	11	Nellie Fox	1958
Batting average	.388	Luke Appling	1936
Slugging pct.	.729	Frank Thomas	1994
Stolen bases	77	Rudy Law	1983

Pitching

Games	88	Wilbur Wood	1968
Complete games	42	Ed Walsh	1908
Innings	464.0	Ed Walsh	1908
Wins	40	Ed Walsh	1908
Losses	25	Patrick Flaherty	1903
Winning pct.	.857 (12-2)	Jason Bere	1994
Walks	147	Vern Kennedy	1936
Strikeouts	269	Ed Walsh	1908
Shutouts	11	Ed Walsh	1908
Home runs allowed	34	4 times Last by James Baldwin	 2000
Lowest ERA	1.52	Doc White	1906
Saves	57	Bobby Thigpen	1990

GAME

Batting

Runs	5	Last by Walt Williams	5-31-70
Hits	6	Last by Lance Johnson	9-23-95
Doubles	4	Last by Marv Owen	4-23-39
Triples	3	Lance Johnson	9-23-95
Home runs	4	Pat Seerey	7-18-48
RBIs	8	Last by Robin Ventura	9-4-95
Total bases	16	Pat Seerey	7-18-48
Stolen bases	4	Last by Lou Frazier	4-19-98

CAREER LEADERS

BATTING

Games

Player	Games
Luke Appling	2,422
Nellie Fox	2,115
Ray Schalk	1,757
Ozzie Guillen	1,743
Frank Thomas	1,698
Harold Baines	1,670
Eddie Collins	1,670
Luis Aparicio	1,511
Carlton Fisk	1,421
Minnie Minoso	1,373

At-bats

Player	At-bats
Luke Appling	8,856
Nellie Fox	8,486
Harold Baines	6,149
Ozzie Guillen	6,067
Eddie Collins	6,065
Frank Thomas	6,065
Luis Aparicio	5,856
Ray Schalk	5,304
Minnie Minoso	5,011
Carlton Fisk	4,896

Runs

Player	Runs
Luke Appling	1,319
Nellie Fox	1,187
Frank Thomas	1,168
Eddie Collins	1,065
Minnie Minoso	893
Luis Aparicio	791
Harold Baines	786
Ray Durham	784
Ozzie Guillen	693
Fielder Jones	693

Hits

Player	Hits
Luke Appling	2,749
Nellie Fox	2,470
Eddie Collins	2,007
Frank Thomas	1,902
Harold Baines	1,773
Ozzie Guillen	1,608
Luis Aparicio	1,576
Minnie Minoso	1,523
Ray Schalk	1,345
Buck Weaver	1,308

Doubles

Player	Doubles
Luke Appling	440
Frank Thomas	393
Nellie Fox	335
Harold Baines	320
Eddie Collins	266
Minnie Minoso	260
Bibb Falk	245
Willie Kamm	243
Ozzie Guillen	240
Ray Durham	249

Triples

Player	Triples
Shano Collins	104
Nellie Fox	104
Luke Appling	102
Eddie Collins	102
Johnny Mostil	82
Joe Jackson	79
Minnie Minoso	79
Lance Johnson	77
Buck Weaver	69
Ozzie Guillen	68

Home runs

Player	Home runs
Frank Thomas	376
Harold Baines	221
Carlton Fisk	214
Robin Ventura	171
Bill Melton	154
Magglio Ordonez	149
Ron Kittle	140
Minnie Minoso	135
Sherm Lollar	124
Greg Walker	113

Total bases

Player	Total bases
Luke Appling	3,528
Frank Thomas	3,445
Nellie Fox	3,118
Harold Baines	2,844
Eddie Collins	2,570
Minnie Minoso	2,346
Carlton Fisk	2,143
Ozzie Guillen	2,056
Luis Aparicio	2,036
Robin Ventura	2,000

Runs batted in

Player	RBI
Frank Thomas	1,285
Luke Appling	1,116
Harold Baines	981
Minnie Minoso	808
Eddie Collins	804
Carlton Fisk	762
Robin Ventura	741
Nellie Fox	740
Sherm Lollar	631
Bibb Falk	627

Extra-base hits

Player	Extra-base hits
Frank Thomas	780
Luke Appling	587
Harold Baines	585
Nellie Fox	474
Minnie Minoso	474
Carlton Fisk	442
Ray Durham	408
Robin Ventura	402
Eddie Collins	399
Shano Collins	351

Batting average

(Minimum 500 games)

Player	Average
Joe Jackson	.340
Eddie Collins	.331
Zeke Bonura	.317
Bibb Falk	.315
Frank Thomas	.314
Taffy Wright	.312
Luke Appling	.310
Rip Radcliff	.310
Magglio Ordonez	.305
Earl Sheely	.305

Stolen bases

Player	Stolen bases
Eddie Collins	368
Luis Aparicio	318
Frank Isbell	250
Lance Johnson	226
Ray Durham	219
Fielder Jones	206
Shano Collins	192
Luke Appling	179
Ray Schalk	177
Johnny Mostil	176

PITCHING

Earned-run average

(Minimum 1,000 innings)

Player	ERA
Ed Walsh	1.81
Frank Smith	2.18
Eddie Cicotte	2.25
Jim Scott	2.30
Doc White	2.30
Reb Russell	2.33
Nick Altrock	2.40
Joe Benz	2.43
Frank Owen	2.48
Roy Patterson	2.75

Wins

Player	Wins
Ted Lyons	260
Red Faber	254
Ed Walsh	195
Billy Pierce	186
Wilbur Wood	163
Doc White	159
Eddie Cicotte	156
Joe Horlen	113
Frank Smith	108
Jim Scott	107

Losses

Player	Losses
Ted Lyons	230
Red Faber	213
Billy Pierce	152
Wilbur Wood	148
Ed Walsh	125
Doc White	123
Jim Scott	114
Joe Horlen	113
Thornton Lee	104
Eddie Cicotte	101

Innings pitched

Player	Innings
Ted Lyons	4,161.0
Red Faber	4,086.2
Ed Walsh	2,946.1
Billy Pierce	2,931.0
Wilbur Wood	2,524.1
Doc White	2,498.1
Eddie Cicotte	2,322.1
Joe Horlen	1,918.0
Jim Scott	1,892.0
Thornton Lee	1,888.0

Strikeouts

Player	Strikeouts
Billy Pierce	1,796
Ed Walsh	1,732
Red Faber	1,471
Wilbur Wood	1,332
Gary Peters	1,098
Ted Lyons	1,073
Doc White	1,067
Joe Horlen	1,007
Eddie Cicotte	961
Alex Fernandez	951

Bases on balls

Player	Bases on balls
Red Faber	1,213
Ted Lyons	1,121
Billy Pierce	1,052
Wilbur Wood	671
Richard Dotson	637
Thornton Lee	633
Jim Scott	609
Ed Walsh	608
Bill Dietrich	561
Eddie Smith	545

Games

Player	Games
Red Faber	669
Ted Lyons	594
Wilbur Wood	578
Billy Pierce	456
Ed Walsh	426
Bobby Thigpen	424
Hoyt Wilhelm	361
Doc White	360
Eddie Cicotte	353
Keith Foulke	346

Shutouts

Player	Shutouts
Ed Walsh	57
Doc White	42
Billy Pierce	35
Red Faber	29
Eddie Cicotte	28
Ted Lyons	27
Jim Scott	26
Frank Smith	25
Reb Russell	24
Wilbur Wood	24

Saves

Player	Saves
Bobby Thigpen	201
Roberto Hernandez	161
Keith Foulke	100
Hoyt Wilhelm	98
Terry Forster	75
Wilbur Wood	57
Bob James	56
Ed Farmer	54
Clint Brown	53
Bob Howry	49

TEAM SEASON, GAME RECORDS

SEASON

Batting

Record		Year
Most at-bats	5,646	2000
Most runs	978	2000
Fewest runs	447	1910
Most hits	1,615	2000
Most singles	1,199	1936
Most doubles	325	2000
Most triples	102	1915
Most home runs	217	2002
Fewest home runs	3	1908
Most grand slams	8	1996
Most pinch-hit home runs	9	1984
Most total bases	2,654	2000
Most stolen bases	280	1901
Highest batting average	.295	1920
Lowest batting average	.211	1910
Highest slugging pct	.447	1996

Pitching

Record		Year
Lowest ERA	1.99	1905
Highest ERA	5.41	1934
Most complete games	134	1904
Most shutouts	32	1906
Most saves	68	1990
Most walks	734	1950
Most strikeouts	1,039	1996

Fielding

Record		Year
Most errors	345	1901
Fewest errors	97	2002
Most double plays	190	2000
Highest fielding average	.984	2002

General

Record		Year
Most games won	100	1917
Most games lost	106	1970
Highest win pct	.649	1917
Lowest win pct	.325	1932

GAME, INNING

Batting

Record		Date
Most runs, game	29	4-23-55
Most runs, inning	13	9-26-43
Most hits, game	29	4-23-55
Most home runs, game	7	4-23-55
Most total bases, game	55	4-23-55

Durable righthander Ed Walsh recorded a sparkling 1.81 earned-run average over 13 Chicago seasons.

WHITE SOX YEAR-BY-YEAR

Year	W	L	Place	Games Back	Manager	Leaders: Batting avg.	Hits	Home runs	RBIs	Wins	ERA
1901	83	53	1st	+4	Griffith	Jones, .311	Jones, 162	Mertes, 5	Mertes, 98	Griffith, 24	Callahan, 2.42
1902	74	60	4th	8	Griffith	Jones, .321	Jones, 171	Isbell, 4	Davis, 93	Patterson, 19	Garvin, 2.21
1903	60	77	7th	30½	Callahan	Green, .309	Green, 154	Green, 6	Green, 62	White, 17	White, 2.13
1904	89	65	3rd	6	Callahan, Jones	Green, .265	Davis, 143	Jones, 3	Davis, 69	Owen, 21	White, 1.78
1905	92	60	2nd	2	Jones	Donahue, .287	Davis, Donahue, 153	Isbell, Jones, Sullivan, 2	Donahue, 76	Altrock, 23	White, 1.76
1906	93	58	1st	+3	Jones	Isbell, .279	Isbell, 153	Jones, Sullivan, 2	Davis, 80	Altrock, 20	White, 1.52
1907	87	64	3rd	5½	Jones	Dougherty, .270	Donahue, 158	Rohe, 2	Donahue, 68	White, 27	Walsh, 1.60
1908	88	64	3rd	1½	Jones	Dougherty, .278	Dougherty, Jones, 134	Isbell, Jones, Walsh, 1	Jones, 50	Walsh, 40	Walsh, 1.42
1909	78	74	4th	20	Sullivan	Dougherty, .285	Dougherty, 140	4 Tied, 1	Dougherty, 55	Smith, 25	Walsh, 1.41
1910	68	85	6th	35½	Duffy	Dougherty, .248	Dougherty, 110	Gandil, 2	Dougherty, 43	Walsh, 18	Walsh, 1.27
1911	77	74	4th	24	Duffy	McIntyre, .323	McIntyre, 184	Bodie, S. Collins, 4	Bodie, 97	Walsh, 27	Walsh, 2.22
1912	78	76	4th	28	Callahan	Bodie, .294	S. Collins, 168	Bodie, Lord, 5	Collins, 81	Walsh, 27	Walsh, 2.15
1913	78	74	5th	17½	Callahan	Chase, .286	Weaver, 145	Bodie, 8	Weaver, 52	Russell, 22	Cicotte, 1.58
1914	70	84	*6th	30	Callahan	Fournier, .311	S. Collins, 164	Fournier, 6	S. Collins, 65	Benz, Scott, 14	Wolfgang, 1.89
1915	93	61	3rd	9½	Rowland	E. Collins, .332	E. Collins, 173	Fournier, 5	S. Collins, 85	Faber, Scott, 24	Scott, 2.03
1916	89	65	2nd	2	Rowland	Jackson, .341	Jackson, 202	Felsch, 7	Jackson, 78	Russell, 18	Cicotte, 1.78
1917	100	54	1st	+9	Rowland	Felsch, .308	Felsch, 177	Felsch, 6	Felsch, 102	Cicotte, 28	Cicotte, 1.53
1918	57	67	6th	17	Rowland	Weaver, .300	Weaver, 126	E. Collins, 2	S. Collins, 56	Cicotte, 12	Russell, 2.60
1919	88	52	1st	+3½	Gleason	Jackson, .351	Jackson, 181	Felsch, Jackson, 7	Jackson, 96	Cicotte, 29	Cicotte, 1.82
1920	96	58	2nd	2	Gleason	Jackson, .382	E. Collins, 224	Felsch, 14	Jackson, 121	Faber, 23	Faber, 2.99
1921	62	92	7th	36½	Gleason	E. Collins, .337	Johnson, 181	Sheely, 11	Sheely, 95	Faber, 25	Faber, 2.48
1922	77	77	5th	17	Gleason	E. Collins, .324	E. Collins, 194	Falk, 12	Hooper, Sheely, 80	Faber, 21	Faber, 2.81
1923	69	85	7th	30	Gleason	E. Collins, .360	E. Collins, 182	Hooper, 10	Sheely, 88	Faber, 14	Thurston, 3.05
1924	66	87	8th	25½	Evers	Falk, .352	E. Collins, 194	Hooper, 10	Sheely, 103	Thurston, 20	Thurston, 3.80
1925	79	75	5th	18½	E. Collins	E. Collins, .346	Sheely, 189	Sheely, 9	Sheely, 111	Lyons, 21	Blankenship, 3.03
1926	81	72	5th	9½	E. Collins	Falk, .345	Mostil, 197	Falk, 8	Falk, 108	Lyons, 18	Lyons, 3.01
1927	70	83	5th	29½	Schalk	Falk, .327	Falk, 175	Falk, 9	Barrett, Falk, 83	Lyons, 22	Lyons, 2.84
1928	72	82	5th	29	Schalk, Blackburne	Kamm, .308	Kamm, 170	Barrett, Metzler, 3	Kamm, 84	Thomas, 17	Thomas, 3.08
1929	59	93	7th	46	Blackburne	Reynolds, .317	Cissell, 173	Reynolds, 11	Reynolds, 67	Lyons, Thomas, 14	Thomas, 3.19
1930	62	92	7th	40	Bush	Reynolds, .359	Reynolds, 202	Reynolds, 22	Jolley, 114	Lyons, 22	Lyons, 3.78
1931	56	97	8th	51	Bush	Blue, .304	Blue, 179	Reynolds, 6	Reynolds, 77	Frazier, 13	Faber, 3.82
1932	49	102	7th	56½	Fonseca	Seeds, .290	Kress, 147	Kress, 9	Appling, 63	Jones, Lyons, 10	Lyons, 3.28
1933	67	83	6th	31	Fonseca	Simmons, .331	Simmons, 200	Simmons, 14	Simmons, 119	Durham, Jones, Lyons, 10	Heving, 2.67
1934	53	99	8th	47	Fonseca, Dykes	Simmons, .344	Simmons, 192	Bonura, 27	Bonura, 110	Earnshaw, 14	Earnshaw, 4.52
1935	74	78	5th	19½	Dykes	Appling, .307	Radcliff, 178	Bonura, 21	Bonura, 92	Lyons, 15	Lyons, 3.02
1936	81	70	3rd	20	Dykes	Appling, .388	Radcliff, 207	Bonura, 12	Bonura, 138	Kennedy, 21	Kennedy, 4.63
1937	86	68	3rd	16	Dykes	Bonura, .345	Radcliff, 190	Bonura, 19	Bonura, 100	Stratton, 15	Stratton, 2.40
1938	65	83	6th	32	Dykes	Steinbacher, .331	Radcliff, 166	G. Walker, 16	G. Walker, 87	Stratton, 15	Lee, 3.49
1939	85	69	4th	22½	Dykes	McNair, .324	Kreevich, 175	Kuhel, 15	G. Walker, 111	Lee, Rigney, 15	Lyons, 2.76
1940	82	72	*4th	8	Dykes	Appling, .348	Appling, 197	Kuhel, 27	Kuhel, 94	Rigney, Smith, 14	Rigney, 3.11
1941	77	77	3rd	24	Dykes	Wright, .322	Appling, 186	Kuhel, 12	Wright, 97	Lee, 22	Lee, 2.37
1942	66	82	6th	34	Dykes	Kolloway, .273	Kolloway, 164	Moses, 7	Kolloway, 60	Lyons, 14	Lyons, 2.10
1943	82	72	4th	16	Dykes	Appling, .328	Appling, 192	Kuhel, 5	Appling, 80	Grove, 15	Maltzberger, 2.46
1944	71	83	7th	18	Dykes	Hodgin, .295	Moses, 150	Trosky, 10	Trosky, 70	Dietrich, 16	Haynes, 2.57
1945	71	78	6th	15	Dykes	Cuccinello, .308	Moses, 168	Curtright, Dickshot, 4	Schalk, 65	Lee, 15	Lee, 2.44
1946	74	80	5th	30	Dykes	Appling, .309	Appling, 180	Wright, 7	Appling, 55	Caldwell, Lopat, 13	Caldwell, 2.08
1947	70	84	6th	27	Lyons	Wright, .324	Appling, 154	York, 15	York, 64	Lopat, 16	Haynes, 2.42
1948	51	101	8th	44½	Lyons	Appling, .314	Appling, 156	Seerey, 18	Seerey, 64	Haynes, Wight, 9	Gumpert, 3.79
1949	63	91	6th	34	Onslow	Michaels, .308	Michaels, 173	Souchock, 7	Michaels, 83	Wight, 15	Wight, 3.31
1950	60	94	6th	38	Onslow, Corriden	E. Robinson, .314	E. Robinson, 163	Zernial, 29	Zernial, 93	Pierce, 12	Wight, 3.58
1951	81	73	4th	17	Richards	Minoso, .324	Fox, 189	E. Robinson, 29	E. Robinson, 117	Pierce, 15	Rogovin, 2.48
1952	81	73	3rd	14	Richards	Fox, E. Robinson, .296	Fox, 192	E. Robinson, 22	E. Robinson, 104	Pierce, 15	Dorish, 2.47
1953	89	65	3rd	11½	Richards	Minoso, .313	Fox, 178	Minoso, 15	Minoso, 104	Pierce, 18	Consuegra, 2.54
1954	94	60	3rd	17	Richards, Marion	Minoso, .320	Fox, 201	Minoso, 19	Minoso, 116	Trucks, 19	Consuegra, 2.69
1955	91	63	3rd	5	Marion	Kell, .312	Fox, 198	Dropo, 19	Kell, 81	Donovan, Pierce, 15	Pierce, 1.97
1956	85	69	3rd	12	Marion	Minoso, .316	Fox, 192	Doby, 24	Doby, 102	Pierce, 20	Staley, 2.92
1957	90	64	2nd	8	Lopez	Fox, .317	Fox, 196	Doby, Rivera, 14	Minoso, 103	Pierce, 20	Staley, 2.06
1958	82	72	2nd	10	Lopez	Fox, .300	Fox, 187	Lollar, 20	Lollar, 84	Pierce, 17	Pierce, 2.68
1959	94	60	1st	+5	Lopez	Fox, .306	Fox, 191	Lollar, 22	Lollar, 84	Wynn, 22	Staley, 2.24
1960	87	67	3rd	10	Lopez	A. Smith, .315	Minoso, 184	Sievers, 28	Minoso, 105	Pierce, 14	Staley, 2.42
1961	86	76	4th	23	Lopez	F. Robinson, .310	Aparicio, 170	A. Smith, 28	A. Smith, 93	Pizarro, 14	Lown, 2.76
1962	85	77	5th	11	Lopez	F. Robinson, .312	F. Robinson, 187	A. Smith, 16	F. Robinson, 109	Herbert, 20	Fisher, 3.10
1963	94	68	2nd	10½	Lopez	Ward, .295	Ward, 177	Nicholson, Ward, 22	Ward, 84	Peters, 19	Peters, 2.33
1964	98	64	2nd	1	Lopez	F. Robinson, .301	F. Robinson, 158	Ward, 23	Ward, 94	Peters, 20	Horlen, 1.88
1965	95	67	2nd	7	Lopez	Buford, .283	Buford, 166	Romano, Skowron, 18	Skowron, 78	Fisher, 15	Wilhelm, 1.87
1966	83	79	4th	15	Stanky	Agee, .273	Agee, 172	Agee, 22	Agee, 86	John, 14	Peters, 1.98
1967	89	73	4th	3	Stanky	Berry, Buford, .241	Buford, 129	Ward, 18	Ward, 62	Horlen, 19	McMahon, 1.67
1968	67	95	*8th	36	Stanky, Lopez	T. Davis, .268	Aparicio, 164	Ward, 15	T. Davis, Ward, 50	Wood, 13	Wilhelm, 1.73
								WEST DIVISION			
1969	68	94	5th	29	Lopez, Gutteridge	Williams, .304	Aparicio, 168	Melton, 23	Melton, 87	Horlen, 13	Wood, 3.01
1970	56	106	6th	42	Gutteridge, Tanner	Aparicio, .313	Aparicio, 173	Melton, 33	Melton, 96	John, 12	Wood, 2.81
1971	79	83	3rd	22½	Tanner	May, Williams, .294	May, 147	Melton, 33	Melton, 86	Wood, 22	Wood, 1.91
1972	87	67	2nd	5½	Tanner	Allen, May, .308	May, 161	Allen, 37	Allen, 113	Wood, 24	Forster, 2.25
1973	77	85	5th	17	Tanner	Kelly, .280	Melton, 155	May, Melton, 20	May, 96	Wood, 24	Acosta, 2.23
1974	80	80	4th	9	Tanner	Orta, .316	Henderson, 176	Allen, 32	Henderson, 95	Kaat, 21	B. Johnson, 2.74
1975	75	86	5th	22½	Tanner	Orta, .304	Orta, 165	D. Johnson, 18	Orta, 83	Kaat, 20	Gossage, 1.84
1976	64	97	6th	25½	Richards	Garr, .300	Orta, 174	Orta, Spencer, 14	Orta, 72	Brett, 10	Brett, 3.32
1977	90	72	3rd	12	Lemon	L. Johnson, .302	Garr, 163	Gamble, 31	Zisk, 101	Stone, 15	LaGrow, 2.46
1978	71	90	5th	20½	Lemon, Doby	Lemon, .300	Lam. Johnson, 136	Soderholm, 20	Lam. Johnson, 72	Stone, 12	Willoughby, 3.86
1979	73	87	5th	14	Kessinger, La Russa	Lemon, .318	Lemon, 177	Lemon, 17	Lemon, 86	Kravec, 15	Baumgarten, 3.54
1980	70	90	5th	26	La Russa	Lemon, .292	Morrison, 171	Morrison, Nordhagen, 15	Lam. Johnson, 81	Burns, 15	Burns, 2.84
1981	54	52	†3rd/6th	—	La Russa	Bernazard, .276	Bernazard, 106	Luzinski, 21	Luzinski, 62	Burns, 10	Lamp, 2.41
1982	87	75	3rd	6	La Russa	Paciorek, .312	Luzinski, 170	Baines, 25	Baines, 105	Hoyt, 19	Hoyt, 3.53
1983	99	63	‡1st	+20	La Russa	Paciorek, .307	Baines, 167	Kittle, 35	Kittle, 100	Hoyt, 24	Dotson, 3.23
1984	74	88	*5th	10	La Russa	Baines, .304	Baines, 173	Kittle, 32	Baines, 94	Seaver, 15	Dotson, 3.59
1985	85	77	3rd	6	La Russa	Baines, .309	Baines, 196	Fisk, 37	Baines, 113	Burns, 18	James, 2.13
1986	72	90	5th	20	La Russa, Fregosi	Baines, .296	Baines, 169	Baines, 21	Baines, 88	Cowley, 11	Schmidt, 3.31
1987	77	85	5th	8	Fregosi	Baines, Calderon, .293	Calderon, 159	Calderon, 28	Walker, 94	Bannister, 16	Bannister, 3.58
1988	71	90	5th	32½	Fregosi	Baines, .277	Baines, 166	Pasqua, 20	Baines, 81	Reuss, 13	Thigpen, 3.30
1989	69	92	7th	29½	Torborg	Martinez, .300	Calderon, 178	Calderon, 14	Calderon, 87	Perez, 11	Hibbard, 3.21
1990	94	68	2nd	9	Torborg	Fisk, Lan. Johnson, .285	Calderon, 166	Fisk, 18	Calderon, 74	Hibbard, McDowell, 14	Hibbard, 3.16
1991	87	75	2nd	8	Torborg	F. Thomas, .318	F. Thomas, 178	F. Thomas, 32	F. Thomas, 109	McDowell, 17	Perez, 3.12
1992	86	76	3rd	10	Lamont	F. Thomas, .323	F. Thomas, 185	Bell, 25	F. Thomas, 115	McDowell, 20	McDowell, 3.18
1993	94	68	‡1st	+8	Lamont	F. Thomas, .317	F. Thomas, 174	F. Thomas, 41	F. Thomas, 128	McDowell, 22	Alvarez, 2.95
								CENTRAL DIVISION			
1994	67	46	1st	+1	Lamont	F. Thomas, .353	F. Thomas, 141	F. Thomas, 38	F. Thomas, 101	Bere, Alvarez, 12	Alvarez, 3.45
1995	68	76	3rd	32	Lamont, Bevington	F. Thomas, .308	Lan. Johnson, 186	F. Thomas, 40	F. Thomas, 111	Fernandez, 12	Fernandez, 3.80
1996	85	77	∞2nd	14½	Bevington	F. Thomas, .349	F. Thomas, 184	F. Thomas, 40	F. Thomas, 134	Fernandez, 16	Fernandez, 3.45
1997	80	81	2nd	6	Bevington	F. Thomas, .347	F. Thomas, 184	F. Thomas, 35	F. Thomas, 125	Baldwin, Drabek, 12	Alvarez, 3.03
1998	80	82	2nd	9	Manuel	Belle, .328	Belle, 200	Belle, 49	Belle, 152	Sirotka, 14	Sirotka, 5.06
1999	75	86	2nd	21½	Manuel	F. Thomas, .305	Ordonez, 188	Ordonez, 30	Ordonez, 117	Baldwin, 12	Foulke, 2.22
2000	95	67	▲1st	+5	Manuel	F. Thomas, .328	F. Thomas, 191	F. Thomas, 43	F. Thomas, 143	Sirotka, 15	Sirotka, 3.79
2001	83	79	3rd	8	Manuel	Ordonez, .305	Ordonez, 181	Konerko, 32	Ordonez, 113	Buehrle, 16	Buehrle, 3.29
2002	81	81	2nd	13½	Manuel	Ordonez, .320	Ordonez, 189	Ordonez, 38	Ordonez, 135	Buehrle, 19	Buehrle, 3.58

* Tied for position. † First half 31-22, second half 23-30. ‡ Lost Championship Series. ∞ Lost division playoff. ▲ Lost Division Series.

Note: Batting average minimum 350 at-bats, ERA minimum 90 innings pitched.

Cleveland Indians

FRANCHISE CHRONOLOGY

First season: 1901, as a member of the new American League. Cleveland lost its Major League debut at Chicago, 8-2, and struggled through a difficult first season. The Indians won only 54 games and finished seventh in the eight-team A.L. field.

1902-present: The early decade Indians (also known as the Naps after star second baseman Napoleon Lajoie) were annual contenders, but it took almost two decades before they had anything to show for their efforts. And after the 1920 Indians captured the team's first pennant and defeated Brooklyn in an historic World Series, Cleveland fans had to wait 28 years for another. The 1948 championship was followed by an amazing 1954 season in which the Indians won an A.L.-record 111 games—and then fell to the Giants in a shocking four-game Series sweep. That would be it for more than four decades as the Indians languished in the lower reaches of the A.L. standings, posting only 11 winning records. They finally resurfaced in the strike-shortened 1995 season to claim their first of five consecutive Central Division titles with a league-leading 100 victories. But their fourth pennant in 1995 resulted in a six-game World Series loss to Atlanta and a Cinderella World Series run in 1997 came up short in the seventh game against the Florida Marlins.

Righthander Bob Feller.

INDIANS VS. OPPONENTS BY DECADE

	A's	Orioles	Red Sox	Tigers	Twins	White Sox	Yankees	Angels	Rangers	Brewers	Royals	Blue Jays	Mariners	Devil Rays	Interleague	Decade Record
1901-09	86-105	109-82	96-93	95-95	118-72	89-100	104-85									697-632
1910-19	110-105	130-81	97-115	94-114	92-123	102-114	117-95									742-747
1920-29	113-106	112-106	130-90	109-111	113-106	114-105	95-125									786-749
1930-39	114-106	155-64	131-89	101-118	114-104	125-94	84-133									824-708
1940-49	136-80	124-95	116-105	105-115	115-104	114-103	90-129									800-731
1950-59	153-67	151-67	122-98	136-84	141-79	104-116	97-123									904-634
1960-69	92-85	85-99	94-90	83-101	96-82	74-104	83-100	74-82	88-73	7-5	7-5					783-826
1970-79	46-70	65-104	80-86	78-90	58-56	54-62	64-103	58-58	58-71	75-78	52-65	27-14	22-9			737-866
1980-89	50-63	64-59	52-78	41-82	55-56	54-61	56-73	49-69	55-57	56-70	54-62	52-71	72-48			710-849
1990-99	62-45	67-51	60-61	76-47	70-52	64-58	45-72	59-44	50-63	56-41	64-49	56-65	54-52	12-7	28-21	823-728
2000-02	12-14	14-7	16-14	29-22	27-24	24-27	12-16	13-14	15-13		25-25	13-11	12-11	17-5	26-28	255-231
Totals	974-846	1076-815	994-919	947-979	999-858	918-944	847-1054	253-267	266-277	194-194	202-206	148-161	160-120	29-12	54-49	8061-7701

Interleague results: 1-2 vs. Diamondbacks, 6-2 vs. Cubs, 13-11 vs. Reds, 2-1 vs. Rockies, 0-3 vs. Marlins, 7-8 vs. Astros, 7-5 vs. Brewers, 1-2 vs. Expos, 1-2 vs. Mets, 1-2 vs. Phillies, 7-8 vs. Pirates, 8-3 vs. Cardinals.

MANAGERS

Name	*Years*	*Record*
Jimmy McAleer	1901	55-82
Bill Armour	1902-04	232-195
Nap Lajoie	1905-09	377-309
Deacon McGuire	1909-11	91-117
George Stovall	1911	74-62
Harry Davis	1912	54-71
Joe Birmingham	1912-15	170-191
Lee Fohl	1915-19	327-310
Tris Speaker	1919-26	617-520
Jack McCallister	1927	66-87
Roger Peckinpaugh	1928-33, 1941	490-481
Walter Johnson	1933-35	179-168
Steve O'Neill	1935-37	199-168
Oscar Vitt	1938-40	262-198
Lou Boudreau	1942-50	728-649
Al Lopez	1951-56	570-354
Kerby Farrell	1957	76-77
Bobby Bragan	1958	31-36
Joe Gordon	1958-60	184-151
Jimmie Dykes	1960-61	103-115
Mel McGaha	1962	78-82
Birdie Tebbetts	1963-66	278-259
George Strickland	1964, 1966	48-63
Joe Adcock	1967	75-87
Alvin Dark	1968-71	266-321
Johnny Lipon	1971	18-41
Ken Aspromonte	1972-74	220-260
Frank Robinson	1975-77	186-189
Jeff Torborg	1977-79	157-201
Dave Garcia	1979-82	247-244
Mike Ferraro	1983	40-60
Pat Corrales	1983-87	280-355
Doc Edwards	1987-89	173-207
John Hart	1989	8-11
John McNamara	1990-91	102-137
Mike Hargrove	1991-99	721-591
Charlie Manuel	2000-02	220-190
Joel Skinner	2002	35-41

WORLD SERIES CHAMPIONS

Year	*Loser*	*Length*	*MVP*
1920	Brooklyn	7 games	None
1948	Boston	6 games	None

A.L. PENNANT WINNERS

Year	*Record*	*Manager*	*Series Result*
1920	98-56	Speaker	Defeated Dodgers
1948	97-58	Boudreau	Defeated Braves
1954	111-43	Lopez	Lost to Giants
1995	100-44	Hargrove	Lost to Braves
1997	86-75	Hargrove	Lost to Marlins

CENTRAL DIVISION CHAMPIONS

Year	*Record*	*Manager*	*ALCS Result*
1995	100-44	Hargrove	Defeated Mariners
1996	99-62	Hargrove	Lost in Division Series
1997	86-75	Hargrove	Defeated Orioles
1998	89-73	Hargrove	Lost to Yankees
1999	97-65	Hargrove	Lost in Division Series
2001	91-71	Manuel	Lost in Division Series

ATTENDANCE HIGHS

Total	*Season*	*Park*
3,467,299	1998	Jacobs Field
3,456,278	2000	Jacobs Field
3,404,750	1997	Jacobs Field
3,384,788	1999	Jacobs Field
3,318,174	1996	Jacobs Field

BALLPARK CHRONOLOGY

Jacobs Field (1994-present)

Capacity: 43,368.
First game: Indians 4, Seattle 3 (April 4, 1994).
First batter: Rich Amaral, Mariners.
First hit: Eric Anthony, Mariners (home run).
First run: Edgar Martinez, Mariners (1st inning).
First home run: Eric Anthony, Mariners.
First winning pitcher: Eric Plunk, Indians.
First-season attendance: 1,995,174.

League Park I (1901-09)

Capacity: 9,000.
First game: Indians 4, Milwaukee 3 (April 29, 1901).
First-season attendance: 131,380.

League Park II (1910-46)

Capacity: 21,414.
First game: Detroit 5, Indians 0 (April 21, 1910).
First-season attendance: 293,456.

Cleveland (Municipal) Stadium (1932-93)

Capacity: 74,483.
First game: Philadelphia 1, Indians 0 (July 31, 1932).
First-season attendance (1947): 1,521,978.

Note: League Park II was known as Dunn Field from 1920-27; Cleveland Stadium was originally called Municipal Stadium and games were played there on a part-time basis from 1932-46.

A.L. MVPs

Lou Boudreau, SS, 1948
Al Rosen, 3B, 1953

CY YOUNG WINNER

Gaylord Perry, RH, 1972

ROOKIES OF THE YEAR

Herb Score, P, 1955
Chris Chambliss, 1B, 1971
Joe Charboneau, OF, 1980
Sandy Alomar Jr., C, 1990

RETIRED UNIFORMS

No.	*Name*	*Pos.*
3	Earl Averill	OF
5	Lou Boudreau	SS
14	Larry Doby	OF
18	Mel Harder	P
19	Bob Feller	P
21	Bob Lemon	P

MILESTONE PERFORMANCES

30-plus home runs

52— Jim Thome 2002
50— Albert Belle 1995
49— Jim Thome 2001
48— Albert Belle 1996
45— Manny Ramirez 1998
44— Manny Ramirez 1999
43— Al Rosen 1953
42— Hal Trosky 1936
Rocky Colavito 1959
41— Rocky Colavito 1958
40— Jim Thome 1997
38— Albert Belle 1993
Jim Thome 1996
Manny Ramirez 2000
37— Al Rosen 1950
Jim Thome 2000
36— Albert Belle 1994
35— Hal Trosky 1934
Joe Carter 1989
Juan Gonzalez 2001
34— Albert Belle 1992
33— Andre Thornton 1978, 1984
Manny Ramirez 1996
David Justice 1997
Jim Thome 1999
32— Earl Averill 1931, 1932
Hal Trosky 1937
Joe Gordon 1948
Larry Doby 1952, 1954
Vic Wertz 1956
Andre Thornton 1982
Joe Carter 1987
Brook Jacoby 1987
Cory Snyder 1987
Matt Williams 1997
Ellis Burks 2002
31— Earl Averill 1934
Ken Keltner 1948
Luke Easter 1952
Leon Wagner 1964
Manny Ramirez 1995
Richie Sexson 1999
30— Rocky Colavito 1966
Jim Thome 1998

100-plus RBIs

165— Manny Ramirez 1999
162— Hal Trosky 1936
148— Albert Belle 1996
145— Al Rosen 1953
Manny Ramirez 1998
143— Earl Averill 1931
142— Hal Trosky 1934
140— Juan Gonzalez 2001
136— Eddie Morgan 1930
130— Tris Speaker 1923
129— Albert Belle 1993
128— Hal Trosky 1937
126— Earl Averill 1936
Larry Doby 1954
Albert Belle 1995
124— Earl Averill 1932
Joe Gordon 1948
Jim Thome 2001
123— Jeff Heath 1941
122— Manny Ramirez 2000
121— Johnny Hodapp 1930
Joe Carter 1986
120— Roberto Alomar 1999
119— Earl Averill 1930
Ken Keltner 1948
118— Larry Gardner 1920
Jim Thome 2002
117— Joe Vosmik 1931
116— Al Rosen 1950
Andre Thornton 1982
Jim Thome 1996
Richie Sexson 1999
115— Larry Gardner 1921
114— George Burns 1926
Carlos Baerga 1993
113— Earl Averill 1934
Hal Trosky 1935
Ken Keltner 1938
Rocky Colavito 1938
112— Jeff Heath 1938
Albert Belle 1992
Manny Ramirez 1996
111— Rocky Colavito 1959
110— Joe Vosmik 1935
Hal Trosky 1938
109— Joe Sewell 1923
Julius Solters 1937
108— Rocky Colavito 1965
Jim Thome 1999
107— Tris Speaker 1920
Luke Easter 1950
Manny Ramirez 1995
106— Lou Boudreau 1948
Vic Wertz 1956
Joe Carter 1987
Travis Fryman 2000
Jim Thome 2000
105— Al Rosen 1952
Vic Wertz 1957
Andre Thornton 1978
Joe Carter 1989
Carlos Baerga 1992
Matt Williams 1997
104— Joe Sewell 1924
Hal Trosky 1939
Larry Doby 1952
103— Elmer Smith 1920
Lew Fonseca 1929
Luke Easter 1951
Harold Baines *1999
David Segui 2000
102— Nap Lajoie 1904
Al Rosen 1951, 1954
Larry Doby 1950, 1953
Jim Thome 1997
101— Odell Hale 1934, 1935
Lou Boudreau 1940
Albert Belle 1994
David Justice 1997
100— Leon Wagner 1964
Roberto Alomar 2001

*81 with Orioles; 22 with Indians.

20-plus victories

1903— Earl Moore 20-8
1904— William Bernhard 23-13
1905— Addie Joss 20-11
1906— Robert Rhodes 22-10
Addie Joss 21-9
Otto Hess 20-17
1907— Addie Joss 27-10
1908— Addie Joss 24-11
1911— Vean Gregg 23-7
1912— Vean Gregg 20-13
1913— Fred Falkenberg 23-10
Vean Gregg 20-13
1917— Jim Bagby 23-13
1918— Stan Coveleski 22-13
1919— Stan Coveleski 23-17
1920— Jim Bagby 31-12
Stanley Coveleski 24-14
Ray Caldwell 20-10
1921— Stan Coveleski 23-13
1922— George Uhle 22-16
1923— George Uhle 26-16
1924— Joe Shaute 20-17
1926— George Uhle 27-11
1929— Wesley Ferrell 21-10
1930— Wesley Ferrell 25-13
1931— Wesley Ferrell 22-12
1932— Wesley Ferrell 23-13
1934— Mel Harder 20-12
1935— Mel Harder 22-11
1936— Johnny Allen 20-10
1939— Bob Feller 24-9
1940— Bob Feller 27-11
1941— Bob Feller 25-12
1946— Bob Feller 26-15
1947— Bob Feller 20-11
1948— Gene Bearden 20-7
Bob Lemon 20-14
1949— Bob Lemon 22-10
1950— Bob Lemon 23-11
1951— Bob Feller 22-8
Mike Garcia 20-13
Early Wynn 20-13
1952— Early Wynn 23-12
Mike Garcia 22-11
Bob Lemon 22-11
1953— Bob Lemon 21-15
1954— Bob Lemon 23-7
Early Wynn 23-11
1956— Herb Score 20-9
Early Wynn 20-9
Bob Lemon 20-14
1962— Dick Donovan 20-10
1968— Luis Tiant 21-9
1970— Sam McDowell 20-12
1972— Gaylord Perry 24-16
1974— Gaylord Perry 21-13

A.L. home run champions

1915— Bobby Roth 7
1950— Al Rosen 37
1952— Larry Doby 32
1953— Al Rosen 43
1954— Larry Doby 32
1959— Rocky Colavito *42
1995— Albert Belle 50

* Tied for league lead

A.L. RBI champions

1904— Nap Lajoie 102
1936— Hal Trosky 162
1952— Al Rosen 105
1953— Al Rosen 145
1954— Larry Doby 126
1965— Rocky Colavito 108
1986— Joe Carter 121
1993— Albert Belle 129
1995— Albert Belle *126
1996— Albert Belle 148
1999— Manny Ramirez 165

* Tied for league lead

A.L. batting champions

1903— Nap Lajoie .344
1904— Nap Lajoie .376
1905— Elmer Flick .306
1914— Tris Speaker .386
1929— Lew Fonseca .369
1944— Lou Boudreau .327
1954— Bobby Avila .341

A.L. ERA champions

1903— Earl Moore 1.74
1904— Addie Joss 1.59
1908— Addie Joss 1.16
1911— Vean Gregg 1.80
1923— Stan Coveleski 2.76
1933— Monte Pearson 2.33
1940— Bob Feller 2.61
1948— Gene Bearden 2.43
1950— Early Wynn 3.20
1954— Mike Garcia 2.64
1965— Sam McDowell 2.18
1968— Luis Tiant 1.60
1982— Rick Sutcliffe 2.96

A.L. strikeout champions

1920— Stan Coveleski 133
1938— Bob Feller 240
1939— Bob Feller 246
1940— Bob Feller 261
1941— Bob Feller 260
1943— Allie Reynolds 151
1946— Bob Feller 348
1947— Bob Feller 196
1948— Bob Feller 164
1950— Bob Lemon 170
1955— Herb Score 245
1956— Herb Score 263
1957— Early Wynn 184
1965— Sam McDowell 325
1966— Sam McDowell 225
1968— Sam McDowell 283
1969— Sam McDowell 279
1970— Sam McDowell 304
1980— Len Barker 187
1981— Len Barker 127

No-hit pitchers
(9 innings or more)

1908— Robert Rhoads 2-1 vs. Boston
1908— Addie Joss 1-0 vs. Chicago (Perfect)
1910— Addie Joss 1-0 vs. Chicago
1919— Ray Caldwell 3-0 vs. New York
1931— Wesley Ferrell 9-0 vs. St. Louis
1940— Bob Feller 1-0 vs. Chicago
1946— Bob Feller 1-0 vs. New York
1947— Don Black 3-0 vs. Philadelphia
1948— Bob Lemon 2-0 vs. Detroit
1951— Bob Feller 2-1 vs. Detroit
1966— Sonny Siebert 2-0 vs. Washington
1974— Dick Bosman 4-0 vs. Oakland
1977— Dennis Eckersley 1-0 vs. California
1981— Len Barker 3-0 vs. Toronto (Perfect)

Longest hitting streaks

31— Nap Lajoie 1906
30— Sandy Alomar Jr. 1997
29— Bill Bradley 1902
28— Joe Jackson 1911
Hal Trosky 1936
27— Dale Mitchell 1953
26— Harry Bay 1902
24— Matt Williams 1997
23— Charlie Jamieson 1923
Tris Speaker 1923
Dale Mitchell 1951
Ray Fosse 1970
Mike Hargrove 1980
22— John Hodapp 1929
Dale Mitchell 1947
Al Smith 1956
John Romano 1961
Julio Franco 1988
Marty Cordova 2001
21— Nap Lajoie 1904
Odell Hale 1936
Dale Mitchell 1948, 1953
Larry Doby 1951
Joe Carter 1986
Julio Franco 1988
Albert Belle 1996
20— Earl Averill 1936
Roy Weatherly 1936
Joe Vosmik 1936
Al Rosen 1953
Vic Power 1960
Manny Ramirez 2000

Note: Joey Cora hit in 20 straight games for Seattle (16) and Cleveland (4) in 1998.

INDIVIDUAL SEASON, GAME RECORDS

SEASON

Batting			
At-bats	663	Joe Carter	1986
Runs	140	Earl Averill	1931
Hits	233	Joe Jackson	1911
Singles	172	Charley Jamieson	1923
Doubles	64	George Burns	1926
Triples	26	Joe Jackson	1912
Home runs	52	Jim Thome	2002
Home runs, rookie	37	Al Rosen	1950
Grand slams	4	Al Rosen	1951
Total bases	405	Hal Trosky	1936
RBIs	165	Manny Ramirez	1999
Walks	127	Jim Thome	1999
Most strikeouts	185	Jim Thome	2001
Fewest strikeouts	4	Joe Sewell	1925, 1929
Batting average	.408	Joe Jackson	1911
Slugging pct.	.714	Albert Belle	1994
Stolen bases	75	Kenny Lofton	1996
Pitching			
Games	76	Sid Monge	1979
Complete games	36	Bob Feller	1946
Innings	371	Bob Feller	1946
Wins	31	Jim Bagby Sr.	1920
Losses	22	Pete Dowling	1901
Winning pct.	.938 (15-1)	Johnny Allen	1937
Walks	208	Bob Feller	1936
Strikeouts	348	Bob Feller	1946
Shutouts	10	Bob Feller	1946
		Bob Lemon	1948
Home runs allowed	37	Luis Tiant	1969
Lowest ERA	1.16	Addie Joss	1908
Saves	46	Jose Mesa	1995

GAME

Batting			
Runs	5	Last by Joe Carter	9-6-86
Hits	6	Last by Jorge Orta	6-15-80
Doubles	4	Last by Sandy Alomar Jr.	6-6-97
Triples	3	Last by Ben Chapman	7-3-39
Home runs	4	Rocky Colavito	6-10-59
RBIs	9	Chris James	5-4-91
Total bases	16	Rocky Colavito	6-10-59
Stolen bases	5	Last by Kenny Lofton	9-3-2000

HISTORY

CAREER LEADERS

BATTING

Games

Player	Games
Terry Turner	1,619
Nap Lajoie	1,614
Lou Boudreau	1,560
Jim Hegan	1,526
Tris Speaker	1,519
Ken Keltner	1,513
Joe Sewell	1,513
Earl Averill	1,510
Charlie Jamieson	1,483
Jack Graney	1,402

At-bats

Player	At-bats
Nap Lajoie	6,034
Earl Averill	5,909
Terry Turner	5,787
Lou Boudreau	5,754
Ken Keltner	5,655
Joe Sewell	5,621
Charlie Jamieson	5,551
Tris Speaker	5,546
Omar Vizquel	4,891
Kenny Lofton	4,872

Runs

Player	Runs
Earl Averill	1,154
Tris Speaker	1,079
Kenny Lofton	951
Charlie Jamieson	942
Jim Thome	917
Nap Lajoie	865
Joe Sewell	857
Lou Boudreau	823
Larry Doby	808
Omar Vizquel	781

Hits

Player	Hits
Nap Lajoie	2,046
Tris Speaker	1,965
Earl Averill	1,903
Joe Sewell	1,800
Charlie Jamieson	1,753
Lou Boudreau	1,706
Ken Keltner	1,561
Terry Turner	1,472
Kenny Lofton	1,463
Omar Vizquel	1,390

Doubles

Player	Doubles
Tris Speaker	486
Nap Lajoie	424
Earl Averill	377
Joe Sewell	375
Lou Boudreau	367
Ken Keltner	306
Charlie Jamieson	296
Hal Trosky	287
Jim Thome	259
Omar Vizquel	247

Triples

Player	Triples
Earl Averill	121
Tris Speaker	108
Elmer Flick	106
Joe Jackson	89
Jeff Heath	83
Ray Chapman	81
Jack Graney	79
Nap Lajoie	78
Terry Turner	77
Bill Bradley	74
Charlie Jamieson	74

Home runs

Player	Home runs
Jim Thome	334
Albert Belle	242
Manny Ramirez	236
Earl Averill	226
Hal Trosky	216
Larry Doby	215
Andy Thornton	214
Al Rosen	192
Rocky Colavito	190
Ken Keltner	163

Total bases

Player	Total bases
Earl Averill	3,200
Tris Speaker	2,886
Nap Lajoie	2,725
Jim Thome	2,633
Ken Keltner	2,494
Hal Trosky	2,406
Lou Boudreau	2,392
Joe Sewell	2,391
Charlie Jamieson	2,251
Larry Doby	2,159

Runs batted in

Player	RBI
Earl Averill	1,084
Jim Thome	927
Nap Lajoie	919
Hal Trosky	911
Tris Speaker	884
Joe Sewell	869
Ken Keltner	850
Manny Ramirez	804
Larry Doby	776
Albert Belle	751

Extra-base hits

Player	Extra-base hits
Earl Averill	724
Tris Speaker	667
Jim Thome	613
Hal Trosky	556
Ken Keltner	538
Nap Lajoie	535
Lou Boudreau	495
Manny Ramirez	484
Albert Belle	481
Joe Sewell	468

Batting average

(Minimum 500 games)

Player	Average
Joe Jackson	.375
Tris Speaker	.354
Nap Lajoie	.339
George Burns	.327
Ed Morgan	.323
Earl Averill	.322
Joe Sewell	.320
Johnny Hodapp	.318
Charlie Jamieson	.316
Manny Ramirez	.313

Stolen bases

Player	Stolen bases
Kenny Lofton	450
Terry Turner	254
Omar Vizquel	252
Nap Lajoie	240
Ray Chapman	233
Elmer Flick	207
Harry Bay	165
Brett Butler	164
Bill Bradley	157
Tris Speaker	151

PITCHING

Earned-run average

(Minimum 1,000 innings)

Player	ERA
Addie Joss	1.89
Bob Rhoads	2.39
Bill Bernhard	2.45
Earl Moore	2.58
Gaylord Perry	2.71
Stan Coveleski	2.80
Luis Tiant	2.84
Willie Mitchell	2.89
Sam McDowell	2.99
Jim Bagby	3.03

Wins

Player	Wins
Bob Feller	266
Mel Harder	223
Bob Lemon	207
Stan Coveleski	172
Early Wynn	164
Addie Joss	160
Willis Hudlin	157
George Uhle	147
Mike Garcia	142
Charles Nagy	129

Losses

Player	Losses
Mel Harder	186
Bob Feller	162
Willis Hudlin	151
Bob Lemon	128
Stan Coveleski	123
George Uhle	119
Sam McDowell	109
Charles Nagy	103
Early Wynn	102
Addie Joss	97

Innings pitched

Player	Innings
Bob Feller	3,827.0
Mel Harder	3,426.1
Bob Lemon	2,850.0
Willis Hudlin	2,557.2
Stan Coveleski	2,502.1
Addie Joss	2,327.0
Early Wynn	2,286.2
George Uhle	2,200.1
Mike Garcia	2,138.0
Sam McDowell	2,109.2

Strikeouts

Player	Strikeouts
Bob Feller	2,581
Sam McDowell	2,159
Bob Lemon	1,277
Early Wynn	1,277
Charles Nagy	1,235
Mel Harder	1,161
Gary Bell	1,104
Mike Garcia	1,095
Luis Tiant	1,041
Addie Joss	920

Bases on balls

Player	Bases on balls
Bob Feller	1,764
Bob Lemon	1,251
Mel Harder	1,118
Sam McDowell	1,072
Early Wynn	877
Willis Hudlin	832
George Uhle	709
Mike Garcia	696
Gary Bell	670
Stan Coveleski	616

Games

Player	Games
Mel Harder	582
Bob Feller	570
Willis Hudlin	475
Bob Lemon	460
Gary Bell	419
Mike Garcia	397
Eric Plunk	373
Paul Shuey	361
Stan Coveleski	360
George Uhle	357

Shutouts

Player	Shutouts
Addie Joss	45
Bob Feller	44
Stan Coveleski	31
Bob Lemon	31
Mike Garcia	27
Mel Harder	25
Early Wynn	24
Sam McDowell	22
Luis Tiant	21
Guy Morton	19
Bob Rhoads	19

Saves

Player	Saves
Doug Jones	129
Jose Mesa	104
Mike Jackson	94
Bob Wickman	66
Ray Narleski	53
Steve Olin	48
Jim Kern	46
Sid Monge	46
Gary Bell	45
Ernie Camacho	44

TEAM SEASON, GAME RECORDS

SEASON

Batting

Record		Year
Most at-bats	5,702	1986
Most runs	1,009	1999
Fewest runs	472	1972
Most hits	1,715	1936
Most singles	1,218	1925
Most doubles	358	1930
Most triples	95	1920
Most home runs	221	2000
Fewest home runs	8	1910
Most grand slams	12	1999
Most pinch-hit home runs	9	1965, 1970
Most total bases	2,700	1996
Most stolen bases	210	1917
Highest batting average	.308	1921
Lowest batting average	.234	1968, 1972
Highest slugging pct	.484	1994

Pitching

Record		Year
Lowest ERA	2.02	1908
Highest ERA	5.28	1987
Most complete games	141	1904
Most shutouts	27	1906
Most saves	50	1995
Most walks	770	1971
Most strikeouts	1,218	2001

Fielding

Record		Year
Most errors	329	1901
Fewest errors	72	2000
Most double plays	197	1953
Highest fielding average	.988	2000

General

Record		Year
Most games won	111	1954
Most games lost	105	1991
Highest win pct	.721	1954
Lowest win pct	.333	1914

GAME, INNING

Batting

Record		Date
Most runs, game	27	7-7-23
Most runs, inning	14	6-18-50
Most hits, game	33	7-10-32
Most home runs, game	7	7-17-66
Most total bases, game	45	7-10-32

Outfielder Rocky Colavito led the A.L. with 42 home runs in 1959.

INDIANS YEAR-BY-YEAR

Year	W	L	Place	Games Back	Manager	Leaders: Batting avg.	Hits	Home runs	RBIs	Wins	ERA
1901	54	82	7th	29	McAleer	Pickering, .309	Pickering, 169	Beck, 6	Beck, 79	Moore, 16	Moore, 2.90
1902	69	67	5th	14	Armour	Hickman, .379	Bradley, 187	Bradley, 11	Hickman, 94	Bernhard, Joss, Moore, 17	Bernhard, 2.20
1903	77	63	3rd	15	Armour	Lajoie, .344	Bradley, Hickman, 171	Hickman, 12	Hickman, 97	Moore, 19	Moore, 1.74
1904	86	65	4th	7½	Armour	Lajoie, .376	Lajoie, 211	Flick, Lajoie, 6	Lajoie, 102	Bernhard, 23	Joss, 1.59
1905	76	78	5th	19	Lajoie	Flick, .306	Bay, 164	Flick, 4	Flick, 64	Joss, 20	Joss, 2.01
1906	89	64	3rd	5	Lajoie	Lajoie, .355	Lajoie, 214	4 Tied, 2	Lajoie, 91	Rhoads, 22	Joss, 1.72
1907	85	67	4th	8	Lajoie	Flick, .302	Flick, 166	Flick, 3	Lajoie, 63	Joss, 27	Joss, 1.83
1908	90	64	2nd	½	Lajoie	Stovall, .292	Lajoie, 168	Hinchman, 6	Lajoie, 74	Joss, 24	Joss, 1.16
1909	71	82	6th	27½	Lajoie, McGuire	Lajoie, .324	Lajoie, 152	Hinchman, Stovall, 6	Hinchman, 53	Young, 19	Joss, 1.71
1910	71	81	5th	32	McGuire	Lajoie, .384	Lajoie, 227	Lajoie, 4	Lajoie, 76	Falkenberg, 14	Kahler, 1.60
1911	80	73	3rd	22	McGuire, Stovall	Jackson, .408	Jackson, 233	Jackson, 7	Jackson, 83	Gregg, 23	Gregg, 1.80
1912	75	78	5th	30½	Davis, Birmingham	Jackson, .395	Jackson, 226	Jackson, 3	Jackson, Lajoie, 90	Gregg, 20	Gregg, 2.59
1913	86	66	3rd	9½	Birmingham	Jackson, .373	Jackson, 197	Jackson, 7	Jackson, 71	Falkenberg, 23	W. Mitchell, 1.91
1914	51	102	8th	48½	Birmingham	Jackson, .338	Jackson, 153	Jackson, 3	Jackson, 53	W. Mitchell, 12	Steen, 2.60
1915	57	95	7th	44½	Birmingham, Fohl	Chapman, .270	Chapman, 154	Roth, 7	Chapman, E. Smith, 67	Morton, 16	Morton, 2.14
1916	77	77	6th	14	Fohl	Speaker, .386	Speaker, 211	Graney, 5	Speaker, 79	Bagby, 16	Coumbe, 2.02
1917	88	66	3rd	12	Fohl	Speaker, .352	Speaker, 184	Graney, E. Smith, 3	Roth, 72	Bagby, 23	Coveleski, 1.81
1918	73	54	2nd	2½	Fohl	Speaker, .318	Speaker, 150	Wood, 5	Wood, 66	Coveleski, 22	Coveleski, 1.82
1919	84	55	2nd	3½	Fohl, Speaker	Chapman, Gardner, .300	Gardner, 157	E. Smith, 9	Gardner, 79	Coveleski, 24	Coveleski, 2.61
1920	98	56	1st	+2	Speaker	Speaker, .388	Speaker, 214	E. Smith, 12	Gardner, 118	Bagby, 31	Coveleski, 2.49
1921	94	60	2nd	4½	Speaker	Speaker, .362	Gardner, 187	E. Smith, 16	Gardner, 115	Coveleski, 23	Morton, 2.76
1922	78	76	4th	16	Speaker	Speaker, .378	Jamieson, 183	Speaker, 11	Wood, 92	Uhle, 22	Coveleski, 3.32
1923	82	71	3rd	16½	Speaker	Speaker, .380	Jamieson, 222	Speaker, 17	Speaker, 130	Uhle, 26	Coveleski, 2.76
1924	67	86	6th	24½	Speaker	Jamieson, .359	Jamieson, 213	Myatt, Speaker, 8	Sewell, 104	Shaute, 20	S. Smith, 3.01
1925	70	84	6th	27½	Speaker	Speaker, .389	Sewell, 204	Speaker, 12	Sewell, 98	Buckeye, Uhle, 13	Miller, 3.31
1926	88	66	2nd	3	Speaker	Burns, .358	Burns, 216	Speaker, 7	Burns, 114	Uhle, 27	Uhle, 2.83
1927	66	87	6th	43½	McAllister	Burns, .319	Sewell, 180	Hodapp, 5	Sewell, 92	Hudlin, 18	Miller, 3.21
1928	62	92	7th	39	Peckinpaugh	Sewell, Hodapp, .323	Lind, 191	Burns, 5	Hodapp, 73	Hudlin, 14	Hudlin, Shaute, 4.04
1929	81	71	3rd	24	Peckinpaugh	Fonseca, .369	Fonseca, 209	Averill, 18	Fonseca, 103	Ferrell, 21	Holloway, 3.03
1930	81	73	4th	21	Peckinpaugh	Hodapp, .354	Hodapp, 225	Morgan, 26	Morgan, 136	Ferrell, 25	Ferrell, 3.31
1931	78	76	4th	30	Peckinpaugh	Morgan, .351	Averill, 209	Averill, 32	Averill, 143	Ferrell, 22	Ferrell, 3.75
1932	87	65	4th	19	Peckinpaugh	Cissell, .320	Averill, 198	Averill, 32	Averill, 124	Ferrell, 23	Ferrell, 3.66
1933	75	76	4th	23½	Peckinpaugh, Johnson	Averill, .301	Averill, 180	Averill, 11	Averill, 92	Hildebrand, 16	Pearson, 2.33
1934	85	69	3rd	16	Johnson	Vosmik, .341	Trosky, 206	Trosky, 35	Trosky, 142	Harder, 20	Harder, 2.61
1935	82	71	3rd	12	Johnson, O'Neill	Vosmik, .348	Vosmik, 216	Trosky, 26	Trosky, 113	Harder, 22	Harder, 3.29
1936	80	74	5th	22½	O'Neill	Averill, .378	Averill, 232	Trosky, 42	Trosky, 162	Allen, 20	Allen, 3.44
1937	83	71	4th	19	O'Neill	Solters, .323	Solters, 190	Trosky, 32	Trosky, 128	Allen, Harder, 15	Allen, 2.55
1938	86	66	3rd	13	Vitt	Heath, .343	Trosky, 185	Keltner, 26	Keltner, 113	Feller, Harder, 17	Harder, 3.83
1939	87	67	3rd	20½	Vitt	Trosky, .335	Keltner, 191	Trosky, 25	Trosky, 104	Feller, 24	Feller, 2.85
1940	89	65	2nd	1	Vitt	Weatherly, .303	Boudreau, 185	Trosky, 25	Boudreau, 101	Feller, 27	Feller, 2.61
1941	75	79	*4th	26	Peckinpaugh	Heath, .340	Heath, 199	Heath, 24	Heath, 123	Feller, 25	Feller, 3.15
1942	75	79	4th	28	Boudreau	Fleming, .292	Keltner, 179	Fleming, 14	Fleming, 82	Bagby, 17	Bagby, 2.96
1943	82	71	3rd	15½	Boudreau	Cullenbine, .289	Hockett, 166	Heath, 18	Heath, 79	Bagby, A. Smith, 17	Kennedy, 2.45
1944	72	82	*5th	17	Boudreau	Boudreau, .327	Boudreau, 191	Cullenbine, 16	Keltner, 91	Harder, 12	Heving, 1.96
1945	73	72	5th	11	Boudreau	Heath, .305	Meyer, 153	Heath, 15	Heath, 61	Gromek, 19	Gromek, 2.55
1946	68	86	6th	36	Boudreau	Edwards, .301	Boudreau, 151	Seerey, 26	Boudreau, Seerey, 62	Feller, 26	Feller, 2.18
1947	80	74	4th	17	Boudreau	D. Mitchell, .316	Boudreau, 165	Gordon, 29	Gordon, 93	Feller, 20	Feller, 2.68
1948	97	58	†1st	+1	Boudreau	Boudreau, .355	D. Mitchell, 204	Gordon, 32	Gordon, 124	Bearden, Lemon, 20	Bearden, 2.43
1949	89	65	3rd	8	Boudreau	D. Mitchell, .317	D. Mitchell, 203	Doby, 24	Doby, 85	Lemon, 22	Benton, 2.12
1950	92	62	4th	6	Boudreau	Doby, .326	Doby, 164	Rosen, 37	Rosen, 116	Lemon, 23	Wynn, 3.20
1951	93	61	2nd	5	Lopez	Avila, .304	Avila, 165	Easter, 27	Easter, 103	Feller, 22	Gromek, 2.77
1952	93	61	2nd	2	Lopez	D. Mitchell, .323	Avila, 179	Doby, 32	Rosen, 105	Wynn, 23	Garcia, 2.37
1953	92	62	2nd	8½	Lopez	Rosen, .336	Rosen, 201	Rosen, 43	Rosen, 145	Lemon, 21	Garcia, 3.25
1954	111	43	1st	+8	Lopez	Avila, .341	Avila, 189	Doby, 32	Doby, 126	Lemon, Wynn, 23	Mossi, 1.94
1955	93	61	2nd	3	Lopez	A. Smith, .306	A. Smith, 186	Doby, 26	Rosen, 81	Lemon, 18	Wynn, 2.82
1956	88	66	2nd	9	Lopez	A. Smith, .274	A. Smith, 144	Wertz, 32	Wertz, 106	Lemon, Score, Wynn 20	Score, 2.53
1957	76	77	6th	21½	Farrell	Woodling, .321	Wertz, 145	Wertz, 28	Wertz, 105	Wynn, 14	McLish, 2.74
1958	77	76	4th	14½	Bragan, Gordon	Power, .317	Minoso, 168	Colavito, 41	Colavito, 113	McLish, 16	Wilhelm, 2.49
1959	89	65	2nd	5	Gordon	Francona, .363	Minoso, Power, 172	Colavito, 42	Colavito, 111	McLish, 19	J. Perry, 2.65
1960	76	78	4th	21	Gordon, Dykes	Kuenn, .308	Power, 167	Held, 21	Power, 84	J. Perry, 18	Locke, 3.37
1961	78	83	5th	30½	Dykes	Piersall, .322	Francona, 178	Kirkland, 27	Kirkland, 95	Grant, 15	Funk, 3.31
1962	80	82	6th	16	McGaha	Francona, .272	Francona, 169	Romano, 25	Romano, 81	Donovan, 20	Donovan, 3.59
1963	79	83	*5th	25½	Tebbetts	Davalillo, .292	Alvis, 165	Alvis, 22	Alvis, 67	Grant, Kralick 13	Kralick, 2.92
1964	79	83	*6th	20	Tebbetts	B. Chance, .279	Howser, 163	Wagner, 31	Wagner, 100	Kralick, 12	McMahon, 2.41
1965	87	75	5th	15	Tebbetts	Davalillo, .301	Colavito, 170	Wagner, 28	Colavito, 108	McDowell, 17	McDowell, 2.18
1966	81	81	5th	17	Tebbetts, Strickland	Wagner, .279	Wagner, 153	Colavito, 30	Whitfield, 78	Siebert, 16	Hargan, 2.48
1967	75	87	8th	17	Adcock	Davalillo, .287	Alvis, 163	Alvis, 21	Alvis, 70	Hargan, 14	Siebert, 2.38
1968	86	75	3rd	16½	Dark	Azcue, .280	Cardenal, 150	Horton, 14	Horton, 59	Tiant, 21	Tiant, 1.60
							EAST DIVISION				
1969	62	99	6th	46½	Dark	Horton, .278	Horton, 174	Harrelson, Horton 27	Horton, 93	McDowell, 18	McDowell, 2.94
1970	76	86	5th	32	Dark	Fosse, .307	Pinson, 164	Nettles, 26	Pinson, 82	McDowell, 20	Hargan, 2.90
1971	60	102	6th	43	Dark, Lipon	Uhlaender, .288	Nettles, 156	Nettles, 28	Nettles, 86	McDowell, 13	Lamb, 3.35
1972	72	84	5th	14	Aspromonte	Chambliss, .292	Nettles, 141	Nettles, 17	Nettles, 70	G. Perry, 24	G. Perry, 1.92
1973	71	91	6th	26	Aspromonte	Williams, .289	B. Bell, 169	Spikes, 23	Spikes, 73	G. Perry, 19	Hilgendorf, 3.14
1974	77	85	4th	14	Aspromonte	Gamble, .291	Spikes, 154	Spikes, 22	Spikes, 80	G. Perry, 21	G. Perry, 2.51
1975	79	80	4th	15½	Robinson	Carty, .308	B. Bell, 150	Powell, 27	Hendrick, Powell ,86	Peterson, 14	Eckersley, 2.60
1976	81	78	4th	16	Robinson	Carty, .310	Carty, 171	Hendrick, 25	Carty, 83	Dobson, 16	LaRoche, 2.24
1977	71	90	5th	28½	Robinson, Torborg	Bochte, .304	Kuiper, 169	Thornton, 28	Carty, 80	Eckersley, 14	Hood, 3.00
1978	69	90	6th	29	Torborg	Kuiper, Norris .283	B. Bell, 157	Thornton, 33	Thornton, 105	Waits, 13	Kern, 3.08
1979	81	80	6th	22	Torborg, Garcia	Harrah, .279	Bonds, 148	Thornton, 26	Thornton, 93	Waits, 16	Monge, 2.40
1980	79	81	6th	23	Garcia	Dilone, .341	Dilone, 180	Charboneau, 23	Charboneau, 87	Barker, 19	Monge, 3.53
1981	52	51	‡6th/5th	—	Garcia	Hargrove, .317	Harrah, 105	Diaz, 7	Hargrove, 49	Blyleven, 11	Blyleven, 2.88
1982	78	84	*6th	17	Garcia	Harrah, .304	Harrah, 183	Thornton, 32	Thornton, 116	Barker, 15	Sutcliffe, 2.96
1983	70	92	7th	28	Ferraro, Corrales	Tabler, .291	Franco, 153	Thomas, 17	Franco, 80	Sutcliffe, 17	Blyleven, 3.91
1984	75	87	6th	29	Corrales	Vukovich, .304	Franco, 188	Thornton, 33	Thornton, 99	Blyleven, 19	Camacho, 2.43
1985	60	102	7th	39½	Corrales	Butler, .311	Butler, 184	Thornton, 22	Franco, 90	Heaton, 9	Blyleven, 3.26
1986	84	78	5th	11½	Corrales	Tabler, .326	Carter, 200	Carter, 29	Carter, 121	Candiotti, 16	Candiotti, 3.57
1987	61	101	7th	37	Corrales, Edwards	Franco, .319	Tabler, 170	Snyder, 33	Carter, 106	Bailes, Candiotti, Niekro, 7	Jones, 3.15
1988	78	84	6th	11	Edwards	Franco, .303	Franco, 186	Carter, 27	Carter, 98	Swindell, 18	Swindell, 3.20
1989	73	89	6th	16	Edwards, Hart	Browne, .299	Browne, 179	Carter, 35	Carter, 105	Candiotti, Swindell 13	Candiotti, 3.10
1990	77	85	4th	11	McNamara	C. James, .299	Jacoby, 162	Maldonado, 22	Maldonado, 95	Candiotti, 15	Olin, 3.41
1991	57	105	7th	34	McNamara, Hargrove	Cole, .295	Baerga, 171	Belle, 28	Belle, 95	Nagy, 10	Candiotti, 2.24
1992	76	86	*4th	20	Hargrove	Baerga, .312	Baerga, 205	Belle, 34	Belle, 112	Nagy, 17	Power, 2.54
1993	76	86	6th	19	Hargrove	Lofton, .325	Baerga, 200	Belle, 38	Belle, 129	Mesa, 10	Kramer, 4.02
							CENTRAL DIVISION				
1994	66	47	2nd	1	Hargrove	Belle, .357	Lofton, 160	Belle, 36	Belle, 101	M. Clark, Martinez, 11	Nagy, 3.45
1995	100	44	§∞1st	+30	Hargrove	Murray, .323	Baerga, 175	Belle, 50	Belle, 126	Hershiser, Nagy 16	Ogea, 3.05
1996	99	62	▲1st	+14½	Hargrove	Franco, .322	Lofton, 210	Belle, 48	Belle, 148	Nagy, 17	Nagy, 3.41
1997	86	75	§∞1st	+6	Hargrove	Justice, .329	Ramirez, 184	Thome, 40	Williams, 105	Nagy, 15	Nagy, 4.28
1998	89	73	§◆1st	+9	Hargrove	Ramirez, .294	Lofton,169	Ramirez, 45	Ramirez, 145	Burba, Nagy, 15	Colon, 3.71
1999	97	65	▲1st	+21½	Hargrove	Ramirez, .333	R.Alomar,138	Ramirez, 44	Ramirez, 165	Colon, 18	Colon, 3.95
2000	90	72	2nd	5	C. Manuel	Ramirez, .351	R. Alomar, 189	Ramirez, 38	Ramirez, 122	Finley, Burba, 16	Colon, 3.88
2001	91	71	▲1st	+6	C. Manuel	R. Alomar, .336	R. Alomar, 193	Thome, 49	Gonzalez, 140	Sabathia, 17	Colon, 4.09
2002	74	88	3rd	20½	C. Manuel, Skinner	Thome, .304	Vizquel, 160	Thome, 52	Thome, 118	Sabathia, 13	Sabathia, 4.37

* Tied for position. † Won pennant playoff. ‡ First half 26-24; second half 26-27. § Won Division Series. ∞ Won Championship Series. ▲ Lost Division Series. ◆ Lost Championship Series.
Note: Batting average minimum 350 at-bats; ERA minimum 90 innings pitched.

Detroit Tigers

FRANCHISE CHRONOLOGY

First season: 1901, as a member of the new American League. The Tigers made a spectacular Major League debut by rallying for 10 ninth-inning runs in a 14-13 victory over Milwaukee and rode that success to a third-place finish (74-61) behind league-champion Chicago and Boston.

1902-present: The Tigers, who have captured nine A.L. pennants and four World Series, rank behind only the Yankees in sustained A.L. success. After losing three straight fall classics from 1907-09, the Tigers went a quarter of a century before qualifying again. But after a 1934 loss to the Cardinals, they rebounded to defeat the Cubs in 1935 and matched that with another victory over the Cubs in 1945. Their other two championship seasons were 1968 and 1984, an amazing campaign in which they capped their wire-to-wire pennant run with a six-game Series victory over the Padres. After division play began in 1969, the Tigers won three A.L. East titles before moving to the A.L. Central Division in a realignment that sent Milwaukee to the National League.

Right fielder Al Kaline.

TIGERS VS. OPPONENTS BY DECADE

	A's	Indians	Orioles	Red Sox	Twins	White Sox	Yankees	Angels	Rangers	Brewers	Royals	Blue Jays	Mariners	Devil Rays	Interleague	Decade Record
1901-09	80-102	95-95	101-90	97-92	114-72	93-96	103-85									683-632
1910-19	116-99	114-94	126-90	88-124	116-100	109-103	121-94									790-704
1920-29	105-114	111-109	109-111	139-81	107-113	95-124	94-126									760-778
1930-39	111-106	118-101	135-85	121-99	118-102	129-89	86-134									818-716
1940-49	130-90	115-105	129-90	93-127	130-90	125-95	112-108									834-705
1950-59	122-98	84-136	114-106	99-121	121-99	98-122	100-120									738-802
1960-69	109-69	101-83	94-90	95-88	88-90	97-81	90-94	96-60	94-68	10-2	8-4					882-729
1970-79	56-60	90-78	65-102	69-96	48-68	67-50	74-92	63-53	64-64	91-66	54-63	28-15	20-13			789-820
1980-89	58-53	82-41	69-61	59-65	66-54	66-48	62-64	59-55	73-47	66-64	54-59	59-68	66-48			839-727
1990-99	53-53	47-76	49-69	54-64	53-60	51-69	47-72	53-54	54-63	42-56	57-56	52-70	58-53	9-11	23-26	702-852
2000-02	8-16	22-29	10-12	14-16	15-35	16-34	13-17	10-18	18-10		22-28	5-19	11-12	10-11	26-28	200-285
Totals	948-860	979-947	1001-906	928-973	976-883	946-911	902-1006	281-240	303-252	209-188	195-210	144-172	155-126	19-22	49-54	8035-7750

Interleague results: 2-4 vs. Diamondbacks, 3-3 vs. Braves, 5-3 vs. Cubs, 6-6 vs. Reds, 2-4 vs. Marlins, 2-7 vs. Astros, 6-6 vs. Brewers, 2-4 vs. Expos, 3-0 vs. Mets, 2-4 vs. Phillies, 8-7 vs. Pirates, 8-6 vs. Cardinals.

MANAGERS

Name	Years	Record
George Stallings	1901	74-61
Frank Dwyer	1902	52-83
Ed Barrow	1903-04	97-117
Bobby Lowe	1904	30-44
Bill Armour	1905-06	150-152
Hugh Jennings	1907-20	1131-972
Ty Cobb	1921-26	479-444
George Moriarty	1927-28	150-157
Bucky Harris	1929-33, 1955-56	516-557
Del Baker	1933, 1937-42	399-339
Mickey Cochrane	1934-38	366-266
Ralph Perkins	1937	6-9
Steve O'Neill	1943-48	509-414
Red Rolfe	1949-52	278-256
Fred Hutchinson	1952-54	155-235
Jack Tighe	1957-58	99-104
Bill Norman	1958-59	58-64
Jimmie Dykes	1959-60	118-115
Joe Gordon	1960	26-31
Bob Scheffing	1961-63	210-173
Chuck Dressen	1963-65, 1966	221-189
Bob Swift	1965, 1966	56-43
Frank Skaff	1966	40-39
Mayo Smith	1967-70	363-285

Promising first baseman Carlos Pena belted 19 home runs playing for Oakland and Detroit in 2002.

MANAGERS—*cont'd.*

Name	Years	Record
Billy Martin	1971-73	248-204
Joe Schultz	1973	14-14
Ralph Houk	1974-78	363-443
Les Moss	1979	27-26S
Sparky Anderson	1979-95	1331-1248
Buddy Bell	1996-98	184-277
Larry Parrish	1998-99	82-104
Phil Garner	2000-02	145-185
Luis Pujols	2002	55-100

WORLD SERIES CHAMPIONS

Year	Loser	Length	MVP
1935	Chicago	6 games	None
1945	Chicago	7 games	None
1968	St. Louis	7 games	Lolich
1984	San Diego	5 games	Trammell

A.L. PENNANT WINNERS

Year	Record	Manager	Series Result
1907	92-58	Jennings	Lost to Cubs
1908	90-63	Jennings	Lost to Cubs
1909	98-54	Jennings	Lost to Pirates
1934	101-53	Cochrane	Lost to Cardinals
1935	93-58	Cochrane	Defeated Cubs
1940	90-64	Baker	Lost to Reds
1945	88-65	O'Neill	Defeated Cubs
1968	103-59	Smith	Defeated Cardinals
1984	104-58	Anderson	Defeated Padres

EAST DIVISION CHAMPIONS

Year	Record	Manager	ALCS Result
1972	86-70	Martin	Lost to A's
1984	104-58	Anderson	Defeated Royals
1987	98-64	Anderson	Lost to Twins

ATTENDANCE HIGHS

Total	Season	Park
2,704,794	1984	Tiger Stadium
2,533,752	2000	Comerica Park
2,286,609	1985	Tiger Stadium
2,081,162	1988	Tiger Stadium
2,061,830	1987	Tiger Stadium

BALLPARK CHRONOLOGY

Comerica Park (2000-present)

Capacity: 40,120.
First game: Tigers 5, Seattle 2 (April 11, 2000).
First batter: Mark McLemore, Mariners.
First hit: John Olerud, Mariners (double).
First run: Luis Polonia, Tigers (1st inning).
First home run: Juan Gonzalez, Tigers.
First winning pitcher: Brian Moehler, Tigers.
First-season attendance: 2,533,752.

BALLPARK CHRONOLOGY

Tiger Stadium (1912-present)

Capacity: 46,945.
First game: Tigers 6, Cleveland 5, 11 innings (April 20, 1912).
First-season attendance: 402,870.

Bennett Park (1901-11)

Capacity: 8,500.
First game: Tigers 14, Milwaukee 13 (April 25, 1901).
First-season attendance: 259,430.

Note: Tiger Stadium was known as Navin Field from 1912-37 and Briggs Stadium from 1938-60.

A.L. MVPs

Mickey Cochrane, C, 1934
Hank Greenberg, 1B, 1935
Charley Gehringer, 2B, 1937
Hank Greenberg, OF, 1940
Hal Newhouser, P, 1944
Hal Newhouser, P, 1945
Denny McLain, P, 1968
Willie Hernandez, P, 1984

CY YOUNG WINNERS

Denny McLain, RH, 1968
*Denny McLain, RH, 1969
Willie Hernandez, LH, 1984

* Co-winner.

ROOKIES OF THE YEAR

Harvey Kuenn, SS, 1953
Mark Fidrych, P, 1976
Lou Whitaker, 2B, 1978

MANAGERS OF THE YEAR

Sparky Anderson, 1984
Sparky Anderson, 1987

RETIRED UNIFORMS

No.	Name	Pos.
2	Charley Gehringer	2B
5	Hank Greenberg	1B
6	Al Kaline	OF
16	Hal Newhouser	P

MILESTONE PERFORMANCES

30-plus home runs

58— Hank Greenberg 1938
51— Cecil Fielder 1990
45— Rocky Colavito 1961
44— Hank Greenberg 1946
Cecil Fielder 1991
41— Hank Greenberg 1940
Norm Cash 1961
40— Hank Greenberg 1937
Darrell Evans 1985
39— Norm Cash 1962
38— Dean Palmer 1999
37— Rocky Colavito 1962
36— Hank Greenberg 1935
Willie Horton 1968
35— Rudy York 1937
Rocky Colavito 1960
Cecil Fielder 1992
34— Rudy York 1943
Darrell Evans 1987
Tony Clark 1998
33— Rudy York 1938, 1940
Hank Greenberg 1939
Lance Parrish 1984
32— Norm Cash 1966, 1971
Lance Parrish 1982
Matt Nokes 1987
Mickey Tettleton 1992, 1993
Rob Deer 1992
Tony Clark 1997
31— Charlie Maxwell 1959
Jason Thompson 1977
Mickey Tettleton 1991
Cecil Fielder 1995
Tony Clark 1999
30— Norm Cash 1965
Cecil Fielder 1993
Bobby Higginson 2000

100-plus RBIs

183— Hank Greenberg 1937
170— Hank Greenberg 1935
150— Hank Greenberg 1940
146— Hank Greenberg 1938
140— Rocky Colavito 1961
139— Harry Heilmann 1921
Hank Greenberg 1934
137— Dale Alexander 1929
135— Dale Alexander 1930
134— Rudy York 1940
133— Harry Heilmann 1925
Vic Wertz 1949
Cecil Fielder 1991
132— Norm Cash 1961
Cecil Fielder 1990
128— Bobby Veach 1921
Al Kaline 1956
127— Ty Cobb 1911
Charley Gehringer 1934
Rudy York 1938
Hank Greenberg 1946
126— Bobby Veach 1922
125— Goose Goslin 1936
124— Cecil Fielder 1992
123— Vic Wertz 1950
121— Rusty Staub 1978
120— Sam Crawford 1910
Harry Heilmann 1927, 1929
119— Ty Cobb 1907
118— Rudy York 1943
117— Cecil Fielder 1993
Tony Clark 1997
116— Charley Gehringer 1936
Ray Boone 1955
115— Sam Crawford 1911
Harry Heilmann 1923
114— Bob Fothergill 1927
Lance Parrish 1983
113— Bobby Veach 1920
Harry Heilmann 1924
Gee Walker 1937
112— Sam Crawford 1915
Bobby Veach 1915
Al Simmons 1936
Hank Greenberg 1939
Rocky Colavito 1962
111— Rudy York 1941
110— Mickey Tettleton 1993
109— Sam Crawford 1912
Goose Goslin 1935
108— Ty Cobb 1908
John Stone 1932
Charley Gehringer 1935
107— Ty Cobb 1909
Harry Heilmann 1928
Charley Gehringer 1932, 1938
106— Charley Gehringer 1929
105— Charley Gehringer 1933
Marv Owen 1936
Jason Thompson 1977
Steve Kemp 1979
Alan Trammell 1987
104— Sam Crawford 1914
Willie Horton 1965
103— Bobby Veach 1917
Harry Heilmann 1926
Rudy York 1937
Hoot Evers 1948, 1950
Tony Clark 1998
102— Ty Cobb 1917, 1925
Al Kaline 1955
Travis Fryman 1997
Bobby Higginson 2000
Dean Palmer 2000
101— Ty Cobb 1921
Bobby Veach 1919
George Kell 1950
Al Kaline 1963
Rusty Staub 1977
Steve Kemp 1980
Bobby Higginson 1997
100— Goose Goslin 1934
Billy Rogell 1934
Willie Horton 1966
Travis Fryman 1996
Damion Easley 1998
Dean Palmer 1999

20-plus victories

1901— Roscoe Miller 23-13
1905— Ed Killian 23-14
George Mullin 21-21
1906— George Mullin 21-18
1907— Bill Donovan 25-4
Ed Killian 25-13
George Mullin 20-20
1908— Ed Summers 24-12
1909— George Mullin 29-9
Edgar Willett 21-10
1910— George Mullin 21-12
1914— Harry Coveleski 22-12
1915— George Dauss 24-13
Harry Coveleski 22-13
1916— Harry Coveleski 21-11
1919— George Dauss 21-9
1923— George Dauss 21-13
1934— Schoolboy Rowe 24-8
Tommy Bridges 22-11
1935— Tommy Bridges 21-10
1936— Tommy Bridges 23-11
1939— Bobo Newsom *20-11
1940— Bobo Newsom 21-5
1943— Dizzy Trout 20-12
1944— Hal Newhouser 29-9
Dizzy Trout 27-14
1945— Hal Newhouser 25-9
1946— Hal Newhouser 26-9
1948— Hal Newhouser 21-12
1956— Frank Lary 21-13
Billy Hoeft 20-14
1957— Jim Bunning 20-8
1961— Frank Lary 23-9
1966— Denny McLain 20-14
1967— Earl Wilson 22-11
1968— Denny McLain 31-6
1969— Denny McLain 24-9
1971— Mickey Lolich 25-14
Joe Coleman 20-9
1972— Mickey Lolich 22-14
1973— Joe Coleman 23-15
1983— Jack Morris 20-13
1986— Jack Morris 21-8
1991— Bill Gullickson 20-9

*3-1 with St. Louis; 17-10 with Detroit.

A.L. home run champions

1908— Sam Crawford 7
1909— Ty Cobb 9
1935— Hank Greenberg *36
1938— Hank Greenberg 58
1940— Hank Greenberg 41
1943— Rudy York 34
1946— Hank Greenberg 44
1985— Darrell Evans 40
1990— Cecil Fielder 51
1991— Cecil Fielder *44

* Tied for league lead

A.L. RBI champions

1907— Ty Cobb 119
1908— Ty Cobb 108
1909— Ty Cobb 107
1910— Sam Crawford 120
1911— Ty Cobb 127
1914— Sam Crawford 104
1915— Sam Crawford *112
Bobby Veach *112
1917— Bobby Veach 103
1918— Bobby Veach 78
1935— Hank Greenberg 170
1937— Hank Greenberg 183
1940— Hank Greenberg 150
1943— Rudy York 118
1946— Hank Greenberg 127
1955— Ray Boone *116
1990— Cecil Fielder 132
1991— Cecil Fielder 133
1992— Cecil Fielder 124

* Tied for league lead

A.L. batting champions

1907— Ty Cobb .350
1908— Ty Cobb .324
1909— Ty Cobb .377
1910— Ty Cobb .385
1911— Ty Cobb .420
1912— Ty Cobb .410
1913— Ty Cobb .390
1914— Ty Cobb .368
1915— Ty Cobb .369
1917— Ty Cobb .383
1918— Ty Cobb .382
1919— Ty Cobb .384
1921— Harry Heilmann .394
1923— Harry Heilmann .403
1925— Harry Heilmann .393
1926— Heinie Manush .378
1927— Harry Heilmann .398
1937— Charley Gehringer .371
1949— George Kell .343
1955— Al Kaline .340
1959— Harvey Kuenn .353
1961— Norm Cash .361

A.L. ERA champions

1902— Ed Siever 1.91
1944— Dizzy Trout 2.12
1945— Hal Newhouser 1.81
1946— Hal Newhouser 1.94
1962— Hank Aguirre 2.21
1976— Mark Fidrych 2.34

A.L. strikeout champions

1935— Tommy Bridges 163
1936— Tommy Bridges 175
1944— Hal Newhouser 187
1945— Hal Newhouser 212
1949— Virgil Trucks 153
1959— Jim Bunning 201
1960— Jim Bunning 201
1971— Mickey Lolich 308
1983— Jack Morris 232

No-hit pitchers

(9 innings or more)
1912— George Mullin 7-0 vs. St. Louis
1952— Virgil Trucks 1-0 vs. Washington
Virgil Trucks 1-0 vs. New York
1958— Jim Bunning 3-0 vs. Boston
1984— Jack Morris 4-0 vs. Chicago

Longest hitting streaks

40— Ty Cobb 1911
35— Ty Cobb 1917
34— John Stone 1930
30— Goose Goslin 1934
Ron LeFlore 1976
29— Dale Alexander 1930
Pete Fox 1935
27— Gee Walker 1937
Ron LeFlore 1978
25— Kid Gleason 1901
Ty Cobb 1906
23— Sam Crawford 1909
Harry Heilmann 1921
John Stone 1931
22— Harvey Kuenn 1959
Al Kaline 1961
21— Harry Heilmann 1923
Ty Cobb 1926
Charley Gehringer 1927
Dick Wakefield 1943
20— Kid Gleason 1901
Sam Crawford 1903
Charley Gehringer 1937
Alan Trammell 1984

INDIVIDUAL SEASON, GAME RECORDS

SEASON

Batting

Category	Record	Player	Year
At-bats	679	Harvey Kuenn	1953
Runs	147	Ty Cobb	1911
Hits	248	Ty Cobb	1911
Singles	169	Ty Cobb	1911
Doubles	63	Hank Greenberg	1934
Triples	26	Sam Crawford	1926
Home runs	58	Hank Greenberg	1938
Home runs, rookie	35	Rudy York	1937
Grand slams	4	3 times	
		Last by Jim Northrup	1968
Total bases	397	Hank Greenberg	1937
RBIs	183	Hank Greenberg	1937
Walks	137	Roy Cullenbine	1947
Most strikeouts	182	Cecil Fielder	1990
Fewest strikeouts	13	Charley Gehringer	1936
		Harvey Kuenn	1954
Batting average	.420	Ty Cobb	1911
Slugging pct.	.683	Hank Greenberg	1938
Stolen bases	96	Ty Cobb	1915

Pitching

Category	Record	Player	Year
Games	88	Mike Myers	1997
		Sean Runyan	1998
Complete games	42	George Mullin	1904
Innings	382.1	George Mullin	1904
Wins	31	Denny McLain	1968
Losses	23	George Mullin	1904
Winning pct.	.862 (25-4)	Bill Donovan	1907
Walks	158	Joe Coleman	1974
Strikeouts	308	Mickey Lolich	1971
Shutouts	9	Denny McLain	1969
Home runs allowed	42	Denny McLain	1966
Lowest ERA	1.64	Ed Summers	1908
Saves	42	Todd Jones	2000

GAME

Batting

Category	Record	Player	Date
Runs	5	Last by Travis Fryman	4-17-93
Hits	7	Rocky Colavito	6-24-62
		Cesar Gutierrez	6-21-70
Doubles	4	Frank Dillon	4-25-01
		Bill Bruton	5-19-63
Triples	3	Charley Gehringer	8-5-29
Home runs	3	Last by Bobby Higginson	6-24-2000
RBIs	8	Jim Northrup	6-24-68
		Jim Northrup	7-11-73
Total bases	16	Ty Cobb	5-5-25
Stolen bases	5	Johnny Neun	7-9-27

HISTORY

CAREER LEADERS

BATTING

Games

Al Kaline	2,834
Ty Cobb	2,806
Lou Whitaker	2,390
Charlie Gehringer	2,323
Alan Trammell	2,293
Sam Crawford	2,114
Norm Cash	2,018
Harry Heilmann	1,990
Donie Bush	1,872
Bill Freehan	1,774

At-bats

Ty Cobb	10,591
Al Kaline	10,116
Charlie Gehringer	8,860
Lou Whitaker	8,570
Alan Trammell	8,288
Sam Crawford	7,984
Harry Heilmann	7,297
Donie Bush	6,970
Norm Cash	6,593
Bill Freehan	6,073

Runs

Ty Cobb	2,088
Charlie Gehringer	1,774
Al Kaline	1,622
Lou Whitaker	1,386
Donie Bush	1,242
Alan Trammell	1,231
Harry Heilmann	1,209
Sam Crawford	1,115
Norm Cash	1,028
Hank Greenberg	980

Hits

Ty Cobb	3,900
Al Kaline	3,007
Charlie Gehringer	2,839
Harry Heilmann	2,499
Sam Crawford	2,466
Lou Whitaker	2,369
Alan Trammell	2,365
Bobby Veach	1,859
Norm Cash	1,793
Donie Bush	1,745

Doubles

Ty Cobb	665
Charlie Gehringer	574
Al Kaline	498
Harry Heilmann	497
Lou Whitaker	420
Alan Trammell	412
Sam Crawford	402
Hank Greenberg	366
Bobby Veach	345
Harvey Kuenn	244

Triples

Ty Cobb	284
Sam Crawford	249
Charlie Gehringer	146
Harry Heilmann	145
Bobby Veach	136
Al Kaline	75
Donie Bush	73
Dick McAuliffe	70
Hank Greenberg	69
Lu Blue	66

Home runs

Al Kaline	399
Norm Cash	373
Hank Greenberg	306
Willie Horton	262
Cecil Fielder	245
Lou Whitaker	244
Rudy York	239
Lance Parrish	212
Bill Freehan	200
Kirk Gibson	195

Total bases

Ty Cobb	5,466
Al Kaline	4,852
Charlie Gehringer	4,257
Harry Heilmann	3,778
Lou Whitaker	3,651
Sam Crawford	3,576
Alan Trammell	3,442
Norm Cash	3,233
Hank Greenberg	2,950
Bobby Veach	2,653

Runs batted in

Ty Cobb	1,805
Al Kaline	1,583
Harry Heilmann	1,442
Charlie Gehringer	1,427
Sam Crawford	1,264
Hank Greenberg	1,202
Norm Cash	1,087
Lou Whitaker	1,084
Bobby Veach	1,042
Alan Trammell	1,003

Extra-base hits

Ty Cobb	1,060
Al Kaline	972
Charlie Gehringer	904
Harry Heilmann	806
Hank Greenberg	741
Lou Whitaker	729
Sam Crawford	721
Norm Cash	654
Alan Trammell	652
Bobby Veach	540

Batting average
(Minimum 500 games)

Ty Cobb	.368
Harry Heilmann	.342
Bob Fothergill	.337
George Kell	.325
Heinie Manush	.321
Charlie Gehringer	.320
Hank Greenberg	.319
Gee Walker	.317
Harvey Kuenn	.314
Barney McCosky	.312

Stolen bases

Ty Cobb	865
Donie Bush	400
Sam Crawford	317
Ron LeFlore	294
Alan Trammell	236
Kirk Gibson	194
George Moriarty	190
Bobby Veach	189
Charlie Gehringer	181
Lou Whitaker	143

PITCHING

Earned-run average
(Minimum 1,000 innings)

Harry Coveleski	2.34
Ed Killian	2.38
Bill Donovan	2.49
Ed Siever	2.61
George Mullin	2.76
John Hiller	2.83
Ed Willett	2.89
Jean Dubuc	3.06
Hal Newhouser	3.07
Bernie Boland	3.09

Wins

Hooks Dauss	223
George Mullin	209
Mickey Lolich	207
Hal Newhouser	200
Jack Morris	198
Tommy Bridges	194
Dizzy Trout	161
Bill Donovan	140
Earl Whitehill	133
Frank Lary	123

Losses

Hooks Dauss	182
George Mullin	179
Mickey Lolich	175
Dizzy Trout	153
Jack Morris	150
Hal Newhouser	148
Tommy Bridges	138
Earl Whitehill	119
Frank Lary	110
Vic Sorrell	101

Innings pitched

George Mullin	3,394.0
Hooks Dauss	3,390.2
Mickey Lolich	3,361.2
Jack Morris	3,042.2
Hal Newhouser	2,944.0
Tommy Bridges	2,826.1
Dizzy Trout	2,591.2
Earl Whitehill	2,171.1
Bill Donovan	2,137.1
Frank Lary	2,008.2

Strikeouts

Mickey Lolich	2,679
Jack Morris	1,980
Hal Newhouser	1,770
Tommy Bridges	1,674
Jim Bunning	1,406
George Mullin	1,380
Hooks Dauss	1,201
Dizzy Trout	1,199
Denny McLain	1,150
Bill Donovan	1,079

Bases on balls

Hal Newhouser	1,227
Tommy Bridges	1,192
George Mullin	1,106
Jack Morris	1,086
Hooks Dauss	1,067
Mickey Lolich	1,014
Dizzy Trout	978
Earl Whitehill	831
Dan Petry	744
Virgil Trucks	732

Games

John Hiller	545
Hooks Dauss	538
Mickey Lolich	508
Dizzy Trout	493
Mike Henneman	491
Hal Newhouser	460
George Mullin	435
Jack Morris	430
Tommy Bridges	424
Willie Hernandez	358

Shutouts

Mickey Lolich	39
George Mullin	34
Tommy Bridges	33
Hal Newhouser	33
Bill Donovan	29
Dizzy Trout	28
Denny McLain	26
Jack Morris	24
Hooks Dauss	22
Frank Lary	20
Virgil Trucks	20

Saves

Mike Henneman	154
Todd Jones	142
John Hiller	125
Willie Hernandez	120
Aurelio Lopez	85
Terry Fox	55
Al Benton	45
Hooks Dauss	39
Larry Sherry	37
Fred Scherman	34
Dizzy Trout	34

TEAM SEASON, GAME RECORDS

SEASON

Batting

Most at-bats	5,664	1998
Most runs	958	1934
Fewest runs	499	1904
Most hits	1,724	1921
Most singles	1,298	1921
Most doubles	349	1934
Most triples	102	1913
Most home runs	225	1987
Fewest home runs	9	1906
Most grand slams	10	1938
Most pinch-hit home runs	8	1971
Most total bases	2,548	1987
Most stolen bases	280	1909
Highest batting average	.316	1921
Lowest batting average	.230	1904
Highest slugging pct.	.453	1929

Pitching

Lowest ERA	2.26	1909
Highest ERA	6.38	1996
Most complete games	143	1904
Most shutouts	22	1917, 1944, 1969
Most saves	51	1984
Most walks	784	1996
Most strikeouts	1,115	1968

Fielding

Most errors	410	1901
Fewest errors	92	1997
Most double plays	194	1950
Highest fielding average	.985	1997

General

Most games won	104	1984
Most games lost	109	1996
Highest win pct.	.656	1934
Lowest win pct.	.325	1952

GAME, INNING

Batting

Most runs, game	21	Last 7-1-36
Most runs, inning	13	6-17-25, 8-8-2001
Most hits, game	28	9-29-28
Most home runs, game	8	6-20-2000
Most total bases, game	47	6-20-2000

Hal Newhouser claimed A.L. MVP citations during the war seasons of 1944 and '45.

TIGERS YEAR-BY-YEAR

				Games		Leaders					
Year	W	L	Place	Back	Manager	Batting avg.	Hits	Home runs	RBIs	Wins	ERA
1901	74	61	3rd	8½	Stallings	Elberfeld, .310	Barrett, 159	Barrett, Holmes, 4	Elberfeld, 76	Miller, 23	Yeager, 2.61
1902	52	83	7th	30½	Dwyer	Barrett, .303	Barrett, 154	Casey, 3	Elberfeld, 64	Mercer, 15	Siever, 1.91
1903	65	71	5th	25	Barrow	Crawford, .335	Crawford, 184	Crawford, 4	Crawford, 89	Mullin, 19	Mullin, 2.25
1904	62	90	7th	32	Barrow, Lowe	Barrett, .268	Barrett, 167	3 Tied, 2	Crawford, 73	Donovan, Mullin, 17	Mullin, 2.40
1905	79	74	3rd	15½	Armour	Crawford, .297	Crawford, 171	Crawford, 6	Crawford, 75	Killian, 23	Killian, 2.27
1906	71	78	6th	21	Armour	Cobb, .316	Crawford, 166	4 Tied, 2	Crawford, 72	Mullin, 21	Siever, 2.71
1907	92	58	1st	+1½	Jennings	Cobb, .350	Cobb, 212	Cobb, 5	Cobb, 119	Donovan, Killian, 25	Killian, 1.78
1908	90	63	1st	+½	Jennings	Cobb, .324	Cobb, 188	Crawford, 7	Cobb, 108	Summers, 24	Summers, 1.64
1909	98	54	1st	+3½	Jennings	Cobb, .377	Cobb, 216	Cobb, 9	Cobb, 107	Mullin, 29	Killian, 1.71
1910	86	68	3rd	18	Jennings	Cobb, .383	Cobb, 196	Cobb, 8	Crawford, 120	Mullin, 21	Willett, 2.37
1911	89	65	2nd	13½	Jennings	Cobb, .420	Cobb, 248	Cobb, 8	Cobb, 144	Mullin, 18	Mullin, 3.07
1912	69	84	6th	36½	Jennings	Cobb, .410	Cobb, 227	Cobb, 7	Crawford, 109	Dubuc, Willett, 17	Dubuc, 2.77
1913	66	87	6th	30	Jennings	Cobb, .390	Crawford, 193	Crawford, 9	Crawford, 83	Dubuc, 15	Dauss, 2.68
1914	80	73	4th	19½	Jennings	Crawford, .314	Crawford, 183	Crawford, 8	Crawford, 104	Coveleski, 21	Cavet, 2.44
1915	100	54	2nd	2½	Jennings	Cobb, .369	Cobb, 208	Burns, 5	Crawford, Veach, 112	Dauss, 24	Coveleski, 2.45
1916	87	67	3rd	4	Jennings	Cobb, .371	Cobb, 201	Cobb, 5	Veach, 91	Coveleski, 21	Coveleski, 1.97
1917	78	75	4th	21½	Jennings	Cobb, .383	Cobb, 225	Veach, 8	Veach, 103	Dauss, 17	James, 2.09
1918	55	71	7th	20	Jennings	Cobb, .382	Cobb, 161	Heilmann, 5	Veach, 78	Boland, 14	Erickson, 2.48
1919	80	60	4th	8	Jennings	Cobb, .384	Cobb, Veach, 191	Heilmann, 8	Veach, 101	Dauss, 21	Ayers, 2.69
1920	61	93	7th	37	Jennings	Cobb, .334	Veach, 188	Veach, 11	Veach, 113	Ehmke, 15	Ehmke, 3.25
1921	71	82	6th	27	Cobb	Heilmann, .394	Heilmann, 237	Heilmann, 19	Heilmann, 139	Ehmke, 13	Leonard, 3.75
1922	79	75	3rd	15	Cobb	Cobb, .401	Cobb, 211	Heilmann, 21	Veach, 126	Pillette, 19	Pillette, 2.85
1923	83	71	2nd	16	Cobb	Heilmann, .403	Heilmann, 211	Heilmann, 18	Heilmann, 115	Dauss, 21	Dauss, 3.62
1924	86	68	3rd	6	Cobb	Bassler, Heilmann, .346	Cobb, 211	Heilmann, 10	Heilmann, 113	Whitehill, 17	Collins, 3.21
1925	81	73	4th	16½	Cobb	Heilmann, .393	Heilmann, 225	Heilmann, 13	Heilmann, 133	Dauss, 16	Dauss, 3.16
1926	79	75	6th	12	Cobb	Manush, .378	Manush, 188	Manush, 14	Heilmann, 103	Whitehill, 16	Collins, 2.73
1927	82	71	4th	27½	Moriarty	Heilmann, .398	Heilmann, 201	Heilmann, 14	Heilmann, 120	Whitehill, 16	Whitehill, 3.36
1928	68	86	6th	33	Moriarty	Heilmann, .328	Gehringer, 193	Heilmann, 14	Heilmann, 107	Carroll, 16	Carroll, 3.27
1929	70	84	6th	36	Harris	Heilmann, .344	Alexander, Gehringer, 215	Alexander, 25	Alexander, 137	Uhle, 15	Uhle, 4.08
1930	75	79	5th	27	Harris	Gehringer, .330	Gehringer, 201	Alexander, 20	Alexander, 135	Whitehill, 17	Uhle, 3.65
1931	61	93	7th	47	Harris	Stone, .327	Stone, 191	Stone, 10	Alexander, 87	Sorrell, Whitehill, 13	Uhle, 3.50
1932	76	75	5th	29½	Harris	Walker, .323	Gehringer, 184	Gehringer, 19	Stone, 108	Whitehill, 16	Bridges, 3.36
1933	75	79	5th	25	Harris, Baker	Gehringer, .325	Gehringer, 204	Gehringer, Greenberg, 12	Gehringer, 105	Marberry, 16	Bridges, 3.09
1934	101	53	1st	+7	Cochrane	Gehringer, .356	Gehringer, 214	Greenberg, 26	Greenberg, 139	Rowe, 24	Auker, 3.42
1935	93	58	1st	+3	Cochrane	Gehringer, .330	Greenberg, 203	Greenberg, 36	Greenberg, 170	Bridges, 21	Bridges, Sullivan, 3.51
1936	83	71	2nd	19½	Cochrane	Gehringer, .354	Gehringer, 227	Goslin, 24	Goslin, 125	Bridges, 23	Bridges, 3.60
1937	89	65	2nd	13	Cochrane, Perkins	Gehringer, .371	Walker, 213	Greenberg, 40	Greenberg, 183	Lawson, 18	Auker, 3.88
1938	84	70	4th	16	Cochrane, Baker	Greenberg, .315	Fox, 186	Greenberg, 58	Greenberg, 146	Bridges, 13	Benton, 3.30
1939	81	73	5th	26½	Baker	Gehringer, .325	McCosky, 190	Greenberg, 33	Greenberg, 112	Bridges, Newsom, 17	Newsom, 3.37
1940	90	64	1st	+1	Baker	Greenberg, McCosky, .340	McCosky, 200	Greenberg, 41	Greenberg, 150	Newsom, 21	Newsom, 2.83
1941	75	79	*4th	26	Baker	McCosky, .324	Higgins, 161	York, 27	York, 111	Benton, 15	Benton, 2.97
1942	73	81	5th	30	Baker	McCosky, .293	McCosky, 176	York, 21	York, 90	Trucks, 14	Newhouser, 2.45
1943	78	76	5th	20	O'Neill	Wakefield, .316	Wakefield, 200	York, 34	York, 118	Trout, 20	Bridges, 2.39
1944	88	66	2nd	1	O'Neill	Higgins, .297	Cramer, 169	York, 18	York, 98	Newhouser, 29	Trout, 2.12
1945	88	65	1st	+1½	O'Neill	Mayo, .285	York, 157	Cullenbine, York, 18	Cullenbine, 93	Newhouser, 25	Newhouser, 1.81
1946	92	62	2nd	12	O'Neill	Kell, .327	Lake, 149	Greenberg, 44	Greenberg, 127	Newhouser, 26	Newhouser, 1.94
1947	85	69	2nd	12	O'Neill	Kell, .320	Kell, 188	Cullenbine, 24	Kell, 93	Hutchinson, 18	Newhouser, 2.87
1948	78	76	5th	18½	O'Neill	Evers, .314	Evers, 169	Mullin, 23	Evers, 103	Newhouser, 21	Newhouser, 3.01
1949	87	67	4th	10	Rolfe	Kell, .343	Wertz, 185	Wertz, 20	Wertz, 133	Trucks, 19	Trucks, 2.81
1950	95	59	2nd	3	Rolfe	Kell, .340	Kell, 218	Wertz, 27	Wertz, 123	Houtteman, 19	Houtteman, 3.54
1951	73	81	5th	25	Rolfe	Kell, .319	Kell, 191	Wertz, 27	Wertz, 94	Trucks, 13	Hutchinson, 3.68
1952	50	104	8th	45	Rolfe, Hutchinson	Groth, .284	Groth, 149	Dropo, 23	Dropo, 70	Gray, 12	Newhouser, 3.74
1953	60	94	6th	40½	Hutchinson	Boone, .312	Kuenn, 209	Boone, 22	Dropo, 96	Garver, 11	Branca, 4.15
1954	68	86	5th	43	Hutchinson	Kuenn, .306	Kuenn, 201	Boone, 20	Boone, 85	Gromek, 18	Gromek, 2.74
1955	79	75	5th	17	Harris	Kaline, .340	Kaline, 200	Kaline, 27	Boone, 116	Hoeft, 16	Hoeft, 2.99
1956	82	72	5th	15	Harris	Kuenn, .332	Kuenn, 196	Maxwell, 28	Kaline, 128	Lary, 21	Lary, 3.15
1957	78	76	4th	20	Tighe	Kaline, .295	Kuenn, 173	Maxwell, 24	Kaline, 90	Bunning, 20	Bunning, 2.69
1958	77	77	5th	15	Tighe, Norman	Kuenn, .319	Kuenn, 179	Harris, 20	Kaline, 85	Lary, 16	Lary, 2.90
1959	76	78	4th	18	Norman, Dykes	Kuenn, .353	Kuenn, 198	Maxwell, 31	Maxwell, 95	Bunning, Lary, Mossi, 17	Mossi, 3.36
1960	71	83	6th	26	Dykes, Gordon	Kaline, .278	Kaline, 153	Colavito, 35	Colavito, 87	Lary, 15	Bunning, 2.79
1961	101	61	2nd	8	Scheffing	Cash, .361	Cash, 193	Colavito, 45	Colavito, 140	Lary, 23	Mossi, 2.96
1962	85	76	4th	10½	Scheffing	Kaline, .304	Colavito, 164	Cash, 39	Colavito, 112	Bunning, 19	Aguirre, 2.21
1963	79	83	*5th	25½	Scheffing, Dressen	Kaline, .312	Kaline, 172	Kaline, 27	Kaline, 101	Regan, 15	Lary, 3.27
1964	85	77	4th	14	Dressen	Freehan, .300	Lumpe, 160	McAuliffe, 24	Cash, 83	Wickersham, 19	Lolich, 3.26
1965	89	73	4th	13	Dressen, Swift	Kaline, .281	Wert, 159	Cash, 30	Horton, 104	McLain, 16	McLain, 2.61
1966	88	74	3rd	10	Dressen, Swift, Skaff	Kaline, .288	Cash, 168	Cash, 32	Horton, 100	McLain, 20	Wilson, 2.59
1967	91	71	*2nd	1	Smith	Kaline, .308	Freehan, 146	Kaline, 25	Kaline, 78	Wilson, 22	Lolich, 3.04
1968	103	59	1st	+12	Smith	Horton, .285	Northrup, 153	Horton, 36	Northrup, 90	McLain, 31	McLain, 1.96
								—EAST DIVISION—			
1969	90	72	2nd	19	Smith	Northrup, .295	Northrup, 160	Horton, 28	Horton, 91	McLain, 24	McLain, 2.80
1970	79	83	4th	29	Smith	Horton, .305	Stanley, 143	Northrup, 24	Northrup, 80	Lolich, 14	Hiller, 3.03
1971	91	71	2nd	12	Martin	Kaline, .294	Rodriguez, 153	Cash, 32	Cash, 91	Lolich, 25	Scherman, 2.71
1972	86	70	†1st	+½	Martin	Freehan, .262	Rodriguez, 142	Cash, 22	Cash, 61	Lolich, 22	Fryman, 2.06
1973	85	77	3rd	12	Martin, Schultz	Horton, .316	Stanley, 147	Cash, 19	Rodriguez, 58	Coleman, 23	Hiller, 1.44
1974	72	90	6th	19	Houk	Freehan, .297	Sutherland, 157	Freehan, 18	Kaline, 64	Hiller, 17	Hiller, 2.64
1975	57	102	6th	37½	Houk	Horton, .275	Horton, 169	Horton, 25	Horton, 92	Lolich, 12	Lolich, 3.78
1976	74	87	5th	24	Houk	LeFlore, .316	Staub, 176	Thompson, 17	Staub, 96	Fidrych, 19	Fidrych, 2.34
1977	74	88	4th	26	Houk	LeFlore, .325	LeFlore, 212	Thompson, 31	Thompson, 105	Rozema, 15	Rozema, 3.09
1978	86	76	5th	13½	Houk	LeFlore, .297	LeFlore, 198	Thompson, 26	Staub, 121	Slaton, 17	Hiller, 2.34
1979	85	76	5th	18	Moss, Anderson	Kemp, .318	LeFlore, 180	Kemp, 26	Kemp, 105	Morris, 17	Lopez, 2.41
1980	84	78	5th	19	Anderson	Trammell, .300	Trammell, 168	Parrish, 24	Kemp, 101	Morris, 16	P. Underwood, 3.59
1981	60	49	‡4th/2nd	—	Anderson	Gibson, .328	Kemp, 103	Parrish, 10	Kemp, 49	Morris, 14	Petry, 3.00
1982	83	79	4th	12	Anderson	Herndon, .292	Herndon, 179	Parrish, 32	Herndon, 88	Morris, 17	Petry, 3.22
1983	92	70	2nd	6	Anderson	Whitaker, .320	Whitaker, 206	Parrish, 27	Parrish, 114	Morris, 20	Lopez, 2.81
1984	104	58	§1st	+15	Anderson	Trammell, .314	Trammell, 174	Parrish, 33	Parrish, 98	Morris, 19	Hernandez, 1.92
1985	84	77	3rd	15	Anderson	K. Gibson, .287	Whitaker, 170	Evans, 40	Parrish, 98	Morris, 16	Hernandez, 2.70
1986	87	75	3rd	8½	Anderson	Trammell, .277	Trammell, 159	Evans, 29	Coles, Gibson, 86	Morris, 21	Morris, 3.27
1987	98	64	†1st	+2	Anderson	Trammell, .343	Trammell, 205	Evans, 34	Trammell, 105	Morris, 18	Henneman, 2.98
1988	88	74	2nd	1	Anderson	Trammell, .311	Trammell, 145	Evans, 22	Trammell, 69	Morris, 15	Henneman, 1.87
1989	59	103	7th	30	Anderson	Bergman, .268	Whitaker, 128	Whitaker, 28	Whitaker, 85	Henneman, 11	Tanana, 3.58
1990	79	83	3rd	9	Anderson	Trammell, .304	Trammell, 170	Fielder, 51	Fielder, 132	Morris, 15	P. Gibson, Henneman, 3.05
1991	84	78	2nd	7	Anderson	Phillips, .284	Fielder, 163	Fielder, 44	Fielder, 133	Gullickson, 20	Tanana, 3.77
1992	75	87	6th	21	Anderson	Livingstone, .282	Fryman, 175	Fielder, 35	Fielder, 124	Gullickson, 14	Doherty, 3.88
1993	85	77	*3rd	10	Anderson	Trammell, .329	Fryman, 182	Tettleton, 32	Tettleton, 117	Doherty, 14	Wells, 4.19
1994	53	62	5th	18	Anderson	Whitaker, .301	Phillips, 123	Fielder, 28	Fielder, 90	Moore, 11	Wells, 3.96
1995	60	84	4th	26	Anderson	Fryman, .275	Curtis, 157	Fielder, 31	Fielder, 82	Wells, 10	Wells, 3.04
1996	53	109	5th	39	Bell	Higginson, .320	Fryman, 165	Clark, 27	Fryman, 100	Olivares, 7	Olivares, 4.89
1997	79	83	3rd	19	Bell	Higginson, .299	Hunter, 177	Clark, 32	Clark, 117	Blair, 16	Thompson, 3.02
1998	65	97	5th	24	Bell, Parrish	Clark, .291	Clark, 175	Clark, 34	Clark, 103	Moehler, 14	Moehler, 3.90
1999	69	92	3rd	27½	Parrish	D.Cruz, .284	Clark, 150	Palmer, 38	Palmer, 100	Mlicki, 14	Mlicki, 4.60
2000	79	83	3rd	16	Garner	D. Cruz, .302	Higginson, 179	Higginson, 30	Higginson, Palmer, 102	Moehler, 12	Sparks, 4.07
2001	66	96	4th	25	Garner	Cedeno, .293	Cedeno, 153	Fick, 19	T. Clark, 75	Sparks, 14	Sparks, 3.65
2002	55	106	5th	39	Garner, Pujols	Simon, .301	Fick, 150	Simon, 19	Simon, 82	Redman, Sparks, 8	Redman, 4.21

* Tied for position. † Lost Championship Series. ‡ First half 31-26; second half 29-23. § Won Championship Series.

Note: Batting average minimum 350 at-bats; ERA minimum 90 innings pitched.

Kansas City Royals

FRANCHISE CHRONOLOGY

First season: 1969, as one of two expansion teams in the American League. The young Royals excited their home fans with a 12-inning, 4-3 victory over the Minnesota Twins in their Major League debut and went on to carve out a respectable 69-93 first-season record, good for a fourth-place finish in the six-team A.L. West Division.

1970-present: It didn't take long for the Royals to become the model for future expansion franchises as they built an A.L. power through minor league player development and an astute series of trades. In 1976, their eighth major league season, the Royals joined the baseball elite by winning the first of three consecutive West Division championships, all of which were followed by heartbreaking losses to the New York Yankees in the A.L. Championship Series. The Royals turned the tables on the Yankees in 1980 for their first pennant, losing to Philadelphia in the World Series. But they captured their first Series championship in 1985 with a seven-game victory over the cross-state Cardinals. The Royals were one of five teams placed in the Central Division when baseball adopted a three-division format in 1994.

Third baseman George Brett.

ROYALS VS. OPPONENTS BY DECADE

	A's	Indians	Orioles	Red Sox	Tigers	Twins	White Sox	Yankees	Angels	Rangers	Brewers	Blue Jays	Mariners	Devil Rays	Interleague	Decade Record
1969	8-10	5-7	1-11	2-10	4-8	8-10	10-8	5-7	9-9	7-5	10-8					69-93
1970-79	79-90	65-52	51-65	63-53	63-54	85-84	89-79	53-64	87-79	84-69	80-48	22-10	30-13			851-760
1980-89	64-59	62-54	61-55	65-49	59-54	68-62	64-55	52-68	73-50	70-54	58-59	60-56	70-59			826-734
1990-99	53-68	49-64	43-62	51-52	56-57	64-61	52-72	45-61	56-64	56-61	50-47	55-62	64-55	10-11	21-28	725-825
2000-02	8-22	25-25	9-15	11-11	28-22	18-32	20-30	3-19	13-17	14-14		11-13	10-20	13-9	21-33	204-282
Totals	212-249	206-202	165-208	192-175	210-195	243-249	235-244	158-219	238-219	231-203	198-162	148-141	174-147	23-20	42-61	2675-2694

Interleague results: 1-2 vs. Diamondbacks, 6-9 vs. Cubs, 3-5 vs. Reds, 1-2 vs. Marlins, 4-11 vs. Astros, 5-7 vs. Brewers, 0-3 vs. Expos, 1-2 vs. Mets, 9-8 vs. Pirates, 10-11 vs. Cardinals, 2-1 vs. Padres.

MANAGERS

Name	*Years*	*Record*
Joe Gordon	1969	69-93
Charlie Metro	1970	19-33
Bob Lemon	1970-72	207-218
Jack McKeon	1973-75	215-205
Whitey Herzog	1974-79	410-304
Jim Frey	1980-81	127-105
Dick Howser	1981-86	404-365
Mike Ferraro	1986	36-38
Billy Gardner	1987	62-64
John Wathan	1987-91	287-270
Bob Schaefer	1991	1-0

Frank White, an eight-time Gold Glove-winning second baseman, spent his entire 17-year career with the Royals.

MANAGERS—*cont'd.*

Name	*Years*	*Record*
Hal McRae	1991-94	286-277
Bob Boone	1995-97	181-206
Tony Muser	1997-2002	317-431
John Mizerock	2002	5-8
Tony Pena	2002	49-77

WORLD SERIES CHAMPIONS

Year	*Loser*	*Length*	*MVP*
1985	St. Louis	7 games	Saberhagen

A.L. PENNANT WINNERS

Year	*Record*	*Manager*	*Series Result*
1980	97-65	Frey	Lost to Phillies
1985	91-71	Howser	Defeated Cardinals

WEST DIVISION CHAMPIONS

Year	*Record*	*Manager*	*ALCS Result*
1976	90-72	Herzog	Lost to Yankees
1977	102-60	Herzog	Lost to Yankees
1978	92-70	Herzog	Lost to Yankees
1980	97-65	Frey	Defeated Yankees
*1981	50-53	Frey, Howser	None
1984	84-78	Howser	Lost to Tigers
1985	91-71	Howser	Defeated Blue Jays

* Second-half champion; lost division playoff to A's.

ALL-TIME RECORD OF EXPANSION TEAMS

Team	W	L	Pct.	DT	P	WS
Arizona	440	370	.543	3	1	1
Kansas City	2,675	2,694	.498	6	2	1
Houston	3,229	3,285	.496	7	0	0
Toronto	2,025	2,063	.495	5	2	2
Anaheim	3,243	3,431	.486	3	1	1
Montreal	2,605	2,769	.485	2	0	0
Colorado	740	817	.475	0	0	0
New York	3,091	3,412	.475	4	4	2
Milwaukee	2,545	2,831	.473	2	1	0
Seattle	1,924	2,163	.471	3	0	0
Texas	3,097	3,560	.465	4	0	0
San Diego	2,460	2,921	.457	3	2	0
Florida	706	847	.455	0	1	1
Tampa Bay	318	490	.394	0	0	0

DT—Division Titles. P—Pennants won. WS—World Series won.

ATTENDANCE HIGHS

Total	*Season*	*Park*
2,477,700	1989	Royals Stadium
2,392,471	1987	Royals Stadium
2,350,181	1988	Royals Stadium
2,320,764	1986	Royals Stadium
2,288,714	1980	Royals Stadium

BALLPARK CHRONOLOGY

Kauffman Stadium (1973-present)

Capacity: 40,793.
First game: Royals 12, Texas 1 (April 10, 1973).
First batter: Dave Nelson, Rangers.
First hit: Amos Otis, Royals (single).
First run: Fred Patek, Royals (1st inning).
First home run: John Mayberry, Royals.
First winning pitcher: Paul Splittorff, Royals.
First-season attendance: 1,345,341.

Municipal Stadium (1969-72)

Capacity: 35,020.
First game: Royals 4, Minnesota 3, 12 innings (April 8, 1969).
First-season attendance: 902,414.

Note: Kauffman Stadium was known as Royals Stadium from 1973-93.

A.L. MVP

George Brett, 3B, 1980

CY YOUNG WINNERS

Bret Saberhagen, RH, 1985
Bret Saberhagen, RH, 1989
David Cone, RH, 1994

ROOKIES OF THE YEAR

Lou Piniella, OF, 1969
Bob Hamelin, DH, 1994
Carlos Beltran, OF, 1999

RETIRED UNIFORMS

No.	*Name*	*Pos.*
5	George Brett	3B
10	Dick Howser	Man.
20	Frank White	2B

MILESTONE PERFORMANCES

25-plus home runs

36— Steve Balboni 1985
35— Gary Gaetti 1995
34— John Mayberry 1975
Danny Tartabull....................1987
Dean Palmer....................1998
33— Jermaine Dye 2000
32— Bo Jackson....................1989
31— Danny Tartabull....................1991
30— George Brett....................1985
Chili Davis....................1997
29— Steve Balboni 1986
Mike Sweeney 2000, 2001
Carlos Beltran....................2002
28— Steve Balboni 1984
Bo Jackson....................1990
Jeff King....................1997
27— Hal McRae 1982
Bob Oliver....................1970
Jermaine Dye 1999
26— John Mayberry 1973
Amos Otis....................1973
Danny Tartabull....................1988
25— John Mayberry 1972
George Brett....................1983
Bo Jackson....................1988

100-plus RBIs

144— Mike Sweeney....................2000
133— Hal McRae 1982
119— Dean Palmer....................1998
Jermaine Dye 1999
118— George Brett....................1980
Jermaine Dye 2000
112— Al Cowens....................1977
Darrell Porter 1979
George Brett....................1985
Jeff King....................1997
108— Carlos Beltran....................1999
107— George Brett....................1979
106— John Mayberry 1975
Joe Randa....................2000
105— Bo Jackson....................1989
Carlos Beltran....................2002
103— George Brett....................1988
Raul Ibanez....................2002
102— Danny Tartabull....................1988
Mike Sweeney....................1999
101— Danny Tartabull....................1987
Carlos Beltran....................2001
100— John Mayberry 1972, 1973
Danny Tartabull....................1991

20-plus victories

1973— Paul Splittorff 20-11
1974— Steve Busby 22-14
1977— Dennis Leonard....................20-12
1978— Dennis Leonard....................21-17
1980— Dennis Leonard....................20-11
1985— Bret Saberhagen 20-6
1988— Mark Gubicza 20-8
1989— Bret Saberhagen 23-6

A.L. home run champions

None

A.L. RBI champions

1982— Hal McRae 133

A.L. batting champions

1976— George Brett .... .333
1980— George Brett .... .390
1982— Willie Wilson .... .332
1990— George Brett .... .329

A.L. ERA champions

1989— Bret Saberhagen 2.16
1993— Kevin Appier 2.56

A.L. strikeout champions

None

No-hit pitchers

(9 innings or more)

1973— Steve Busby....................3-0 vs. Detroit
1974— Steve Busby....................2-0 vs. Milwaukee
1977— Jim Colborn....................6-0 vs. Texas
1991— Bret Saberhagen ....7-0 vs. Chicago

Longest hitting streaks

30— George Brett....................1980
27— Jose Offerman 1998
25— George Brett....................1983
Mike Sweeney....................1999
22— Brian McRae....................1991
21— Rey Sanchez....................2001
19— Amos Otis....................1974
18— Lou Piniella....................1970
Ed Kirkpatrick....................1973
Willie Wilson....................1984
Gregg Jefferies....................1992
Joe Randa....................1999
17— Hal McRae 1974
Willie Wilson....................1982
Kevin Seitzer....................1990
Kevin McReynolds 1992
Vince Coleman 1995
16— John Mayberry 1975
Al Cowens....................1977
George Brett....................1987
George Brett....................1990
Gregg Jefferies....................1992
Jose Lind 1994
Johnny Damon....................1999, 2000
Mike Sweeney 1999, 2000
15— Willie Wilson....................1981
George Brett....................1985
Kevin Seitzer....................1989
Carlos Febles 2000

Hal McRae was a key contributor to the Royals' 1970s success.

INDIVIDUAL SEASON, GAME RECORDS

Lefthander Paul Splittorff, who spent 15 popular years in Kansas City, holds several career team records.

SEASON

Batting

Record		Player	Year
At-bats	705	Willie Wilson	1980
Runs	136	Johnny Damon	2000
Hits	230	Willie Wilson	1980
Singles	184	Willie Wilson	1980
Doubles	54	Hal McRae	1977
Triples	21	Willie Wilson	1985
Home runs	36	Steve Balboni	1985
Home runs, rookie	24	Bob Hamelin	1994
Grand slams	3	Danny Tartabull	1988
Total bases	363	George Brett	1979
RBIs	144	Mike Sweeney	2000
Walks	122	John Mayberry	1973
Most strikeouts	172	Bo Jackson	1989
Fewest strikeouts	22	George Brett	1980
Batting average	.390	George Brett	1980
Slugging pct.	.664	George Brett	1980
Stolen bases	83	Willie Wilson	1979

Pitching

Record		Player	Year
Games	84	Dan Quisenberry	1985
Complete games	21	Dennis Leonard	1977
Innings	294.2	Dennis Leonard	1978
Wins	23	Bret Saberhagen	1989
Losses	19	Paul Splittorff	1974
Winning pct.	.793 (23-6)	Bret Saberhagen	1989
Walks	120	Mark Gubicza	1987
Strikeouts	244	Dennis Leonard	1977
Shutouts	6	Roger Nelson	1972
Home runs allowed	37	Tim Belcher	1998
Lowest ERA	2.08	Roger Nelson	1972
Saves	45	Dan Quisenberry	1983
		Jeff Montgomery	1993

GAME

Batting

Record		Player	Date
Runs	5	Tony Solaita	6-18-75
		Tom Poquette	6-15-76
Hits	6	Bob Oliver	5-4-69
		Kevin Seitzer	8-2-87
Doubles	4	Johnny Damon	7-18-2000
Triples	2	Last by Johnny Damon	9-8-2000
Home runs	3	Last by Danny Tartabull	7-6-91
RBIs	7	Last by Raul Ibanez	7-14-2002
Total bases	13	George Brett	4-20-83
		Kevin Seitzer	8-2-87
Stolen bases	5	Amos Otis	9-7-71

HISTORY

CAREER LEADERS

BATTING

Games

Player	Games
George Brett	2,707
Frank White	2,324
Amos Otis	1,891
Hal McRae	1,837
Willie Wilson	1,787
Freddie Patek	1,245
John Mayberry	897
Mike Macfarlane	890
Cookie Rojas	880
John Wathan	860

At-bats

Player	At-bats
George Brett	10,349
Frank White	7,859
Amos Otis	7,050
Willie Wilson	6,799
Hal McRae	6,568
Freddie Patek	4,305
John Mayberry	3,131
Cookie Rojas	3,072
Johnny Damon	3,057
Mike Sweeney	2,914

Runs

Player	Runs
George Brett	1,583
Amos Otis	1,074
Willie Wilson	1,060
Frank White	912
Hal McRae	873
Freddie Patek	571
Johnny Damon	504
Mike Sweeney	470
John Mayberry	459
Kevin Seitzer	408

Hits

Player	Hits
George Brett	3,154
Frank White	2,006
Amos Otis	1,977
Willie Wilson	1,968
Hal McRae	1,924
Freddie Patek	1,036
Mike Sweeney	899
Johnny Damon	894
Cookie Rojas	824
John Mayberry	816

Doubles

Player	Doubles
George Brett	665
Hal McRae	449
Frank White	407
Amos Otis	365
Willie Wilson	241
Mike Sweeney	187
Freddie Patek	182
Mike Macfarlane	174
Joe Randa	161
Johnny Damon	156

Triples

Player	Triples
George Brett	137
Willie Wilson	133
Amos Otis	65
Hal McRae	63
Frank White	58
Johnny Damon	47
Al Cowens	44
Freddie Patek	41
Carlos Beltran	33
Brian McRae	32

Home runs

Player	Home runs
George Brett	317
Amos Otis	193
Hal McRae	169
Frank White	160
John Mayberry	143
Danny Tartabull	124
Mike Sweeney	123
Steve Balboni	119
Bo Jackson	109
Mike Macfarlane	103

Total bases

Player	Total bases
George Brett	5,044
Amos Otis	3,051
Frank White	3,009
Hal McRae	3,006
Willie Wilson	2,595
Mike Sweeney	1,461
John Mayberry	1,404
Freddie Patek	1,384
Johnny Damon	1,339
Mike Macfarlane	1,232

Runs batted in

Player	RBI
George Brett	1,595
Hal McRae	1,012
Amos Otis	992
Frank White	886
John Mayberry	552
Mike Sweeney	521
Willie Wilson	509
Danny Tartabull	425
Joe Randa	405
Mike Macfarlane	398

Extra-base hits

Player	Extra-base hits
George Brett	1,119
Hal McRae	681
Frank White	625
Amos Otis	623
Willie Wilson	414
Mike Sweeney	313
Mike Macfarlane	293
John Mayberry	292
Danny Tartabull	274
Johnny Damon	268

Batting average
(Minimum 500 games)

Player	Average
Mike Sweeney	.308
George Brett	.305
Kevin Seitzer	.294
Wally Joyner	.293
Hal McRae	.293
Johnny Damon	.292
Danny Tartabull	.290
Willie Wilson	.289
Joe Randa	.288
Lou Piniella	.286

Stolen bases

Player	Stolen bases
Willie Wilson	612
Amos Otis	340
Freddie Patek	336
George Brett	201
Frank White	178
Johnny Damon	156
Tom Goodwin	150
U.L. Washington	120
Carlos Beltran	109
Hal McRae	105
John Wathan	105

PITCHING

Earned-run average
(Minimum 500 innings)

Player	ERA
Dan Quisenberry	2.55
Steve Farr	3.05
Jeff Montgomery	3.20
Bret Saberhagen	3.21
Kevin Appier	3.46
Al Fitzmorris	3.46
Marty Pattin	3.48
Dick Drago	3.52
Doug Bird	3.56
Charlie Leibrandt	3.60

Wins

Player	Wins
Paul Splittorff	166
Dennis Leonard	144
Mark Gubicza	132
Kevin Appier	114
Larry Gura	111
Bret Saberhagen	110
Tom Gordon	79
Charlie Leibrandt	76
Steve Busby	70
Al Fitzmorris	70

Losses

Player	Losses
Paul Splittorff	143
Mark Gubicza	135
Dennis Leonard	106
Kevin Appier	89
Larry Gura	78
Bret Saberhagen	78
Tom Gordon	71
Dick Drago	70
Charlie Leibrandt	61
Bud Black	57

Innings pitched

Player	Innings
Paul Splittorff	2,554.2
Mark Gubicza	2,218.2
Dennis Leonard	2,187.0
Kevin Appier	1,820.2
Larry Gura	1,701.1
Bret Saberhagen	1,660.1
Charlie Leibrandt	1,257.0
Tom Gordon	1,149.2
Dick Drago	1,134.0
Al Fitzmorris	1,098.0

Strikeouts

Player	Strikeouts
Kevin Appier	1,451
Mark Gubicza	1,366
Dennis Leonard	1,323
Bret Saberhagen	1,093
Paul Splittorff	1,057
Tom Gordon	999
Jeff Montgomery	720
Steve Busby	659
Larry Gura	633
Charlie Leibrandt	618

Bases on balls

Player	Bases on balls
Mark Gubicza	783
Paul Splittorff	780
Kevin Appier	624
Dennis Leonard	622
Tom Gordon	587
Larry Gura	503
Steve Busby	433
Al Fitzmorris	359
Charlie Leibrandt	359
Bret Saberhagen	331

Games

Player	Games
Jeff Montgomery	686
Dan Quisenberry	573
Paul Splittorff	429
Mark Gubicza	382
Dennis Leonard	312
Larry Gura	310
Doug Bird	292
Steve Farr	289
Kevin Appier	281
Hipolito Pichardo	281

Shutouts

Player	Shutouts
Dennis Leonard	23
Paul Splittorff	17
Mark Gubicza	16
Larry Gura	14
Bret Saberhagen	14
Al Fitzmorris	11
Kevin Appier	10
Dick Drago	10
Charlie Leibrandt	10
Steve Busby	7
Roger Nelson	7
Jim Rooker	7

Saves

Player	Saves
Jeff Montgomery	304
Dan Quisenberry	238
Doug Bird	58
Roberto Hernandez	54
Steve Farr	49
Ted Abernathy	40
Al Hrabosky	31
Tom Burgmeier	28
Mark Littell	28
Steve Mingori	27

TEAM SEASON, GAME RECORDS

SEASON

Batting

Record	Total	Year
Most at-bats	5,714	1980
Most runs	879	2000
Fewest runs	586	1969
Most hits	1,644	2000
Most singles	1,193	1980
Most doubles	316	1990
Most triples	79	1979
Most home runs	168	1987
Fewest home runs	65	1976
Most grand slams	7	1991
Most pinch-hit home runs	6	1995
Most total bases	2,440	1977
Most stolen bases	218	1976
Highest batting average	.288	2000
Lowest batting average	.240	1969
Highest slugging pct	.436	1977

Pitching

Record	Total	Year
Lowest ERA	3.21	1976
Highest ERA	5.48	2000
Most complete games	54	1974
Most shutouts	16	1972
Most saves	50	1984
Most walks	693	2000
Most strikeouts	1,006	1990

Fielding

Record	Total	Year
Most errors	167	1973
Fewest errors	91	1997
Most double plays	204	2001
Highest fielding average	.985	1997

General

Record	Total	Year
Most games won	102	1977
Most games lost	100	2002
Highest win pct	.630	1977
Lowest win pct	.383	2002

GAME, INNING

Batting

Record	Total	Date
Most runs, game	23	4-6-74
Most runs, inning	11	8-6-79, 8-2-86
Most hits, game	24	6-15-76
Most home runs, game	6	7-14-91
Most total bases, game	37	9-12-82, 7-18-2000

Center fielder Amos Otis posted career numbers second only to George Brett among Royals players.

HISTORY

ROYALS YEAR-BY-YEAR

Year	W	L	Place	Games Back	Manager	Batting avg.	Hits	Home runs	RBIs	Wins	ERA
						WEST DIVISION					
1969	69	93	4th	28	Gordon	Piniella, .282	Foy, 139	Kirkpatrick, 14	Piniella, 68	Bunker, 12	Drabowsky, 2.94
1970	65	97	*4th	33	Metro, Lemon	Piniella, .301	Otis, 176	Oliver, 27	Oliver, 99	Rooker, 10	Johnson, 3.07
1971	85	76	2nd	16	Lemon	Otis, .301	Otis, 167	Otis, 15	Otis, 79	Drago, 17	Splittorff, 2.68
1972	76	78	4th	16½	Lemon	Piniella, .312	Piniella, 179	Mayberry, 25	Mayberry, 100	Drago, Splittorff, 12	Nelson, 2.08
1973	88	74	2nd	6	McKeon	Otis, .300	Otis, 175	Mayberry, Otis, 26	Mayberry, 100	Splittorff, 20	Bird, 2.99
1974	77	85	5th	13	McKeon	H. McRae, .310	H. McRae, 167	Mayberry, 22	H. McRae, 88	Busby, 22	Bird, 2.73
1975	91	71	2nd	7	McKeon, Herzog	Brett, .308	Brett, 195	Mayberry, 34	Mayberry, 106	Busby, 18	Busby, 3.08
1976	90	72	†1st	+2½	Herzog	Brett, .333	Brett, 215	Otis, 18	Mayberry, 95	Leonard, 17	Littell, 2.08
1977	102	60	†1st	+8	Herzog	Brett, .312	H. McRae, 191	Cowens, Mayberry, 23	Cowens, 112	Leonard, 20	Leonard, 3.04
1978	92	70	†1st	+5	Herzog	Otis, .298	H. McRae, 170	Otis, 22	Otis, 96	Leonard, 21	Gura, 2.72
1979	85	77	2nd	3	Herzog	Brett, .329	Brett, 212	Brett, 23	Porter, 112	Splittorff, 15	Busby, 3.63
1980	97	65	‡1st	+14	Frey	Brett, .390	Wilson, 230	Brett, 24	Brett, 118	Leonard, 20	Gura, 2.95
1981	50	53	§5th/1st	—	Frey, Howser	Brett, .314	Wilson, 133	Aikens, 17	Otis, 57	Leonard, 13	Gura, 2.72
1982	90	72	2nd	3	Howser	Wilson, .332	Wilson, 194	H. McRae, 27	H. McRae, 133	Gura, 18	Quisenberry, 2.57
1983	79	83	2nd	20	Howser	H. McRae, .311	H. McRae, 183	Brett, 25	Brett, 93	Splittorff, 13	Quisenberry, 1.94
1984	84	78	†1st	+3	Howser	Wilson, .301	Wilson, 163	Balboni, 28	Balboni, 77	Black, 17	Quisenberry, 2.64
1985	91	71	‡1st	+1	Howser	Brett, .335	Brett, 184	Balboni, 36	Brett, 112	Saberhagen, 20	Quisenberry, 2.37
1986	76	86	*3rd	16	Howser, Ferraro	Brett, .290	Wilson, 170	Balboni, 29	Balboni, 88	Leibrandt, 14	Farr, 3.13
1987	83	79	2nd	2	Gardner, Wathan	Seitzer, .323	Seitzer, 207	Tartabull, 34	Tartabull, 101	Saberhagen, 18	Saberhagen, 3.36
1988	84	77	3rd	19½	Wathan	Brett, .306	Brett, 180	Tartabull, 26	Brett, 103	Gubicza, 20	Gubicza, 2.70
1989	92	70	2nd	7	Wathan	Eisenreich, .293	Seitzer, 168	Jackson, 32	Jackson 105	Saberhagen, 23	Saberhagen, 2.16
1990	75	86	6th	27½	Wathan	Brett, .329	Brett, 179	Jackson, 28	Brett, 87	Farr, 13	Farr, 1.98
1991	82	80	6th	13	Wathan, Schaefer, H. McRae	Tartabull, .316	B. McRae, 164	Tartabull, 31	Tartabull, 100	Appier, Saberhagen, 13	Montgomery, 2.90
1992	72	90	*5th	24	H. McRae	Brett, Jefferies, .285	Jefferies, 172	Macfarlane, 17	Jefferies, 75	Appier, 15	Appier, 2.46
1993	84	78	3rd	10	H. McRae	Joyner, .292	B. McRae, 177	Macfarlane, 20	Brett, 75	Appier, 18	Appier, 2.56
						CENTRAL DIVISION					
1994	64	51	3rd	4	H. McRae	Joyner, .311	B. McRae, 119	Hamelin, 24	Hamelin, 65	Cone, 16	Cone, 2.94
1995	70	74	2nd	30	Boone	Joyner, .310	Joyner, 144	Gaetti, 35	Gaetti, 96	Appier, 15	Gubicza, 3.75
1996	75	86	5th	24	Boone	Offerman, .303	Offerman, 170	Paquette, 22	Paquette, 67	Belcher, 15	Rosado, 3.21
1997	67	94	5th	19	Boone, Muser	Offerman, .297	Bell, 167	Davis, 30	King, 112	Belcher, 13	Appier, 3.40
1998	72	89	3rd	16½	Muser	Offerman, .315	Offerman, 191	Palmer, 34	Palmer, 119	Belcher, 14	Belcher, 4.27
1999	64	97	4th	32½	Muser	Sweeney, .322	Randa, 197	Dye, 27	Dye, 119	Rosado, Suppan, 10	Rosado, 3.85
2000	77	85	4th	18	Muser	Sweeney, .333	Damon, 214	Dye, 33	Sweeney, 144	Suppan, 10	Suzuki, 4.34
2001	65	97	5th	26	Muser	Beltran, .306	Beltran, 189	Sweeney, 29	Beltran, 101	Suppan, 10	Byrd, 4.05
2002	62	100	4th	32½	Muser, Mizerock, Pena	Sweeney, .340	Beltran, 174	Beltran, 29	Beltran, 105	Byrd, 17	Byrd, 3.90

* Tied for position. † Lost Championship Series. ‡ Won Championship Series. § First half 20-30; second half 30-23.

Note: Batting average minimum 350 at-bats; ERA minimum 90 innings pitched.

Roger Nelson

THE ROYALS were born as part of a four-team 1969 expansion that included the Seattle Pilots in the American League and the San Diego Padres and Montreal Expos in the National League. The franchise came to life on January 11, 1968, when Kansas City businessman Ewing Kauffman was awarded a team that would compete in the A.L.'s newly-created Western Division.

The Royals grabbed righthanded pitcher Roger Nelson with their first pick of the expansion draft and went on to select 30 players, concentrating heavily on youth. The team won its Major League debut on April 8, 1969, when Joe Keough's 12th-inning sacrifice fly produced a 4-3 victory over Minnesota at Kansas City's Municipal Stadium.

Expansion draft (October 15, 1968)

Players

Player	Team	Position
Jerry Adair	Boston	second base
Mike Fiore	Baltimore	first base
Joe Foy	Boston	third base
Bill Harris	Cleveland	second base
Dan Haynes	Chicago	first base
Fran Healy	Cleveland	catcher
Jackie Hernandez	Minnesota	shortstop
Pat Kelly	Minnesota	outfield
Joe Keough	Oakland	outfield
Scott Northey	Chicago	outfield
Bob Oliver	Minnesota	first base
Ellie Rodriguez	New York	catcher
Paul Schaal	California	third base
Steve Whitaker	New York	outfield

Pitchers

Pitcher	Team	Throws
Ike Brookens	Washington	righthander
Wally Bunker	Baltimore	righthander
Tom Burgmeier	California	lefthander
Bill Butler	Detroit	lefthander
Jerry Cram	Minnesota	righthander
Moe Drabowsky	Baltimore	righthander
Dick Drago	Detroit	righthander
Al Fitzmorris	Chicago	righthander
Mike Hedlund	Cleveland	righthander
Steve Jones	Washington	lefthander
Dave Morehead	Boston	righthander
*Roger Nelson	Baltimore	righthander
Don O'Riley	Oakland	righthander
Jim Rooker	New York	lefthander
Jon Warden	Detroit	lefthander
Hoyt Wilhelm	Chicago	righthander

*First pick

Opening day lineup

April 8, 1969

Lou Piniella, center field
Jerry Adair, second base
Ed Kirkpatrick, left field
Joe Foy, third base
Chuck Harrison, first base
Bob Oliver, right field
Ellie Rodriguez, catcher
Jackie Hernandez, shortstop
Wally Bunker, pitcher

Lou Piniella

Royals firsts

First hit: Lou Piniella, April 8, 1969, vs. Minnesota (double)
First home run: Mike Fiore, April 13, 1969, vs. Oakland
First RBI: Jerry Adair, April 8, 1969, vs. Minnesota
First win: Moe Drabowsky, April 8, 1969, vs. Minnesota
First shutout: Roger Nelson, May 21, 1969, 4-0 at Cleveland

Minnesota Twins

FRANCHISE CHRONOLOGY

First season: 1901, in Washington, as a member of the new American League. The Senators recorded a 5-1 victory over Philadelphia in their major league debut and went on to post a 61-72 record, good for sixth place in the eight-team A.L. field.

1902-1960: To say the Senators struggled through their 60-year existence is an understatement. Through the 1911 season, the Senators never finished higher than sixth place and they failed to win their first pennant until 1924. In their six Washington decades, they qualified for the World Series three times, winning once—a 1924 victory over the Giants.

1961-present: The Senators were shifted to Minnesota after the 1960 season as part of a complicated A.L. expansion that brought the Angels and another Washington Senators team into existence. The Twins shut out the Yankees, 6-0, in their first game and went on to compile a 70-90 record. The change of scenery proved agreeable. By 1965, the Twins were consistent contenders who would win three pennants, two World Series and four West Division titles over the next three decades. The Twins were assigned to the Central Division when baseball adopted its three-division format in 1994.

Third baseman Harmon Killebrew.

TWINS VS. OPPONENTS BY DECADE

	A's	Indians	Orioles	Red Sox	Tigers	White Sox	Yankees	Angels	Rangers	Brewers	Royals	Blue Jays	Mariners	Devil Rays	Interleague	Decade Record
1901-09	56-128	72-118	81-108	76-113	72-114	57-130	66-122									480-833
1910-19	101-108	123-92	119-96	93-115	100-116	106-109	113-101									755-737
1920-29	108-105	106-113	108-111	135-82	113-107	125-95	97-122									792-735
1930-39	124-91	104-114	135-84	128-90	102-118	117-101	96-124									806-722
1940-49	125-95	104-115	110-110	86-133	90-130	93-124	69-151									677-858
1950-59	107-113	79-141	103-117	100-120	99-121	79-141	73-145									640-898
1960-69	105-79	82-96	87-91	104-74	90-88	101-83	90-87	82-79	99-56	12-6	10-8					862-747
1970-79	91-76	56-58	52-64	47-70	68-48	89-76	44-72	77-89	80-76	75-54	84-85	26-6	23-20			812-794
1980-89	58-69	56-55	51-63	53-62	54-66	66-57	43-71	57-66	64-65	52-68	62-68	50-64	67-59			733-833
1990-99	58-60	52-70	45-63	62-48	60-53	48-71	50-58	61-54	50-70	46-52	61-64	38-72	51-65	12-9	24-24	718-833
2000-02	13-17	24-27	7-14	8-14	35-15	30-20	9-13	14-14	18-12		32-18	13-10	9-21	10-14	26-28	248-237
Totals	946-941	858-999	898-921	892-921	883-976	911-1007	750-1066	291-302	311-279	185-180	249-243	127-152	150-165	22-23	50-52	7523-8227

Interleague results: 1-2 vs. Braves, 5-10 vs. Cubs, 8-7 vs. Reds, 2-1 vs. Marlins, 8-6 vs. Astros, 9-7 vs. Brewers, 1-2 vs. Mets, 2-1 vs. Phillies, 8-7 vs. Pirates, 6-9 vs. Cardinals.

MANAGERS

(Washington Senators, 1901-1960)

Name	Years	Record
Jimmy Manning	1901	61-72
Tom Loftus	1902-03	104-169
Patsy Donovan	1904	38-113
Jake Stahl	1905-06	119-182
Joe Cantillon	1907-09	158-297
Jimmy McAleer	1910-11	130-175
Clark Griffith	1912-20	693-646
George McBride	1921	80-73
Clyde Milan	1922	69-85
Donie Bush	1923	75-78
Bucky Harris	1924-28, 1935-42, 1950-54	1336-1416
Walter Johnson	1929-32	350-264
Joe Cronin	1933-34	165-139
Ossie Bluege	1943-47	375-394
Joe Kuhel	1948-49	106-201
Chuck Dressen	1955-57	116-212
Cookie Lavagetto	1957-61	271-384
Sam Mele	1961-67	524-436
Cal Ermer	1967-68	145-129
Billy Martin	1969	97-65
Bill Rigney	1970-72	208-184
Frank Quilici	1972-75	280-287
Gene Mauch	1976-80	378-394
Johnny Goryl	1980-81	34-38
Billy Gardner	1981-85	268-353
Ray Miller	1985-86	109-130

The Twins' 1970 staff featured (left to right) Dave Boswell, Jim Perry, Jim Kaat and Luis Tiant.

MANAGERS—*cont'd.*

Name	Years	Record
Tom Kelly	1986-2001	1140-1244
Ron Gardenhire	2002	94-67

WORLD SERIES CHAMPIONS

Year	Loser	Length	MVP
1924	N.Y. Giants	7 games	None
1987	St. Louis	7 games	Viola
1991	Atlanta	7 games	Morris

A.L. PENNANT WINNERS

Year	Record	Manager	Series Result
1924	92-62	Harris	Defeated Giants
1925	96-55	Harris	Lost to Pirates
1933	99-53	Cronin	Lost to Giants
1965	102-60	Mele	Lost to Dodgers
1987	85-77	Kelly	Defeated Cardinals
1991	95-67	Kelly	Defeated Braves

WEST DIVISION CHAMPIONS

Year	Record	Manager	ALCS Result
1969	97-65	Martin	Lost to Orioles
1970	98-64	Rigney	Lost to Orioles
1987	85-77	Kelly	Defeated Tigers
1991	95-67	Kelly	Defeated Blue Jays

CENTRAL DIVISION CHAMPIONS

Year	Record	Manager	Div. Series Result	ALCS Result
2002	94-67	Gardenhire	Defeated A's	Lost to Angels

ATTENDANCE HIGHS

Total	Season	Park
3,030,672	1988	Metrodome
2,482,428	1992	Metrodome
2,293,842	1991	Metrodome
2,277,438	1989	Metrodome
2,081,976	1987	Metrodome

BALLPARK CHRONOLOGY

Hubert H. Humphrey Metrodome (1982-present)

Capacity: 48,678.
First game: Seattle 11, Twins 7 (April 6, 1982).
First batter: Julio Cruz, Mariners.
First hit: Dave Engle, Twins (home run).
First run: Dave Engle, Twins (1st inning).
First home run: Dave Engle, Twins.
First winning pitcher: Floyd Bannister, Mariners.
First-season attendance: 921,186.

American League Park, Washington, D.C. (1901-02)

Capacity: 10,000.
First game: Senators 5, Baltimore 2 (April 29, 1901).
First-season attendance: 161,661.

Griffith Stadium, Washington, D.C. (1903-60)

Capacity: 27,410.
First game: Senators 3, New York 1 (April 22, 1903).
First-season attendance: 128,878.

Metropolitan Stadium, Minnesota (1961-81)

Capacity: 45,919.
First game: Washington 5, Twins 3 (April 21, 1961).
First-season attendance: 1,256,723.

Note: Griffith Stadium was known as National Park from 1901-20.

A.L. MVPs

Zoilo Versalles, SS, 1965
Harmon Killebrew, 1B-3B, 1969
Rod Carew, 1B, 1977

CY YOUNG WINNERS

Jim Perry, RH, 1970
Frank Viola, LH, 1988

ROOKIES OF THE YEAR

Albie Pearson, OF, 1958
Bob Allison, OF, 1959
Tony Oliva, OF, 1964
Rod Carew, 2B, 1967
*John Castino, 3B, 1979
Chuck Knoblauch, 2B, 1991
Marty Cordova, OF, 1995

* Co-winner

MANAGER OF THE YEAR

Tom Kelly, 1991

RETIRED UNIFORMS

No.	Name	Pos.
3	Harmon Killebrew	3B-1B
6	Tony Oliva	OF
14	Kent Hrbek	1B
29	Rod Carew	2B-1B
34	Kirby Puckett	OF

MILESTONE PERFORMANCES

30-plus home runs

49—Harmon Killebrew	1964, 1969
48—Harmon Killebrew	1962
46—Harmon Killebrew	1961
45—Harmon Killebrew	1963
44—Harmon Killebrew	1967
42—Roy Sievers	1957
Harmon Killebrew	1959
41—Harmon Killebrew	1970
39—Roy Sievers	1958
Harmon Killebrew	1966
38—Jim Lemon	1960
35—Bob Allison	1963
34—Gary Gaetti	1986
Kent Hrbek	1987
33—Jim Lemon	1959
Jimmie Hall	1963
32—Bob Allison	1964
Tony Oliva	1964
Tom Brunansky	1984, 1987
31—Harmon Killebrew	1960
Kirby Puckett	1986
Gary Gaetti	1987
30—Bob Allison	1959

100-plus RBIs

140—Harmon Killebrew	1969
129—Goose Goslin	1924
126—Joe Cronin	1930, 1931
Harmon Killebrew	1962
122—Harmon Killebrew	1961
121—Kirby Puckett	1988
120—Goose Goslin	1927
119—Harmon Killebrew	1971
Larry Hisle	1977
118—Joe Cronin	1933
Joe Kuhel	1936
116—Joe Cronin	1932
Heinie Manush	1932
115—Mickey Vernon	1953
114—Zeke Bonura	1938
Roy Sievers	1957
113—Goose Goslin	1925
Harmon Killebrew	1967, 1970
Paul Molitor	1996
112—Kirby Puckett	1994
111—Harmon Killebrew	1964
Marty Cordova	1996
110—Harmon Killebrew	1966
Kirby Puckett	1992
109—Gary Gaetti	1987
108—Goose Goslin	1926
Roy Sievers	1958
Gary Gaetti	1986
107—Joe Kuhel	1933
Tony Oliva	1970
Kent Hrbek	1984
106—Roy Sievers	1955
105—Harmon Killebrew	1959
Bob Allison	1961
103—Corey Koskie	2001
102—Goose Goslin	1928
Roy Sievers	1954
Bob Allison	1962
101—Joe Cronin	1934
Cecil Travis	1941
Tony Oliva	1969
100—Buddy Myer	1935
Stan Spence	1944
Jim Lemon	1959, 1960
Rod Carew	1977

20-plus victories

1910—Walter Johnson	25-17
1911—Walter Johnson	25-13
1912—Walter Johnson	33-12
Bob Groom	24-13
1913—Walter Johnson	36-7
1914—Walter Johnson	28-18
1915—Walter Johnson	27-13
1916—Walter Johnson	25-20
1917—Walter Johnson	23-16
1918—Walter Johnson	23-13
1919—Walter Johnson	20-14
1924—Walter Johnson	23-7
1925—Stan Coveleski	20-5
Walter Johnson	20-7
1932—General Crowder	26-13
Monte Weaver	22-10
1933—General Crowder	24-15
Earl Whitehill	22-8
1939—Dutch Leonard	20-8
1945—Roger Wolff	20-10
1953—Bob Porterfield	22-10
1962—Camilo Pascual	20-11
1963—Camilo Pascual	21-9
1965—Mudcat Grant	21-7
1966—Jim Kaat	25-13
1967—Dean Chance	20-14
1969—Jim Perry	20-6
Dave Boswell	20-12
1970—Jim Perry	24-12
1973—Bert Blyleven	20-17
1977—Dave Goltz	20-11
1979—Jerry Koosman	20-13
1988—Frank Viola	24-7
1991—Scott Erickson	20-8
1997—Brad Radke	20-10

A.L. home run champions

1957—Roy Sievers	42
1959—Harmon Killebrew	*42
1962—Harmon Killebrew	48
1963—Harmon Killebrew	45
1964—Harmon Killebrew	49
1967—Harmon Killebrew	*44
1969—Harmon Killebrew	49

* Tied for league lead

A.L. RBI champions

1924—Goose Goslin	129
1957—Roy Sievers	114
1962—Harmon Killebrew	126
1969—Harmon Killebrew	140
1971—Harmon Killebrew	119
1977—Larry Hisle	119
1994—Kirby Puckett	112

A.L. batting champions

1902—Ed Delahanty	.376
1928—Goose Goslin	.379
1935—Buddy Myer	.349
1946—Mickey Vernon	.353
1953—Mickey Vernon	.337
1964—Tony Oliva	.323
1965—Tony Oliva	.321
1969—Rod Carew	.332
1971—Tony Oliva	.337
1972—Rod Carew	.318
1973—Rod Carew	.350
1974—Rod Carew	.364
1975—Rod Carew	.359
1977—Rod Carew	.388
1978—Rod Carew	.333
1989—Kirby Puckett	.339

A.L. ERA champions

1912—Walter Johnson	1.39
1913—Walter Johnson	1.09
1918—Walter Johnson	1.27
1919—Walter Johnson	1.49
1924—Walter Johnson	2.72
1925—Stan Coveleski	2.84
1928—Garland Braxton	2.51
1988—Allan Anderson	2.45

A.L. strikeout champions

1910—Walter Johnson	313
1912—Walter Johnson	303
1913—Walter Johnson	243
1914—Walter Johnson	225
1915—Walter Johnson	203
1916—Walter Johnson	228
1917—Walter Johnson	188
1918—Walter Johnson	162
1919—Walter Johnson	147
1921—Walter Johnson	143
1923—Walter Johnson	130
1924—Walter Johnson	158
1942—Bobo Newsom	*113
1961—Camilo Pascual	221
1962—Camilo Pascual	206
1963—Camilo Pascual	202
1985—Bert Blyleven	*206

* Tied for league lead

No-hit pitchers

(9 innings or more)

1920—Walter Johnson	1-0 vs. Boston
1931—Bobby Burke	5-0 vs. Boston
1962—Jack Kralick	1-0 vs. Kansas City
1967—Dean Chance	2-1 vs. Cleveland
1994—Scott Erickson	6-0 vs. Milwaukee
1999—Eric Milton	7-0 vs. Anaheim

Longest hitting streaks

33—Heinie Manush	1933
31—Sam Rice	1924
Ken Landreaux	1980
29—Sam Rice	1920
28—Sam Rice	1930
26—Heinie Manush	1933
25—Goose Goslin	1928
Brian Harper	1990
24—Cecil Travis	1941
Lenny Green	1961
23—Kent Hrbek	1982
Marty Cordova	1996
Cristian Guzman	2002
22—Joe Cronin	1932
Heinie Manush	1932
Mickey Vernon	1946
Shane Mack	1992
21—Eddie Foster	1918
Buddy Myer	1935
Taffy Wright	1938
20—Joe Cronin	1930
George Case	1939
Jackie Jensen	1952
Mickey Vernon	1953
Ted Uhlaender	1969
Chuck Knoblauch	1991

INDIVIDUAL SEASON, GAME RECORDS

Longtime ace Walter Johnson (left) delivered his powerful fastball to catcher Gabby Street from 1908-11.

SEASON

Batting			
At-bats	691	Kirby Puckett	1985
Runs	140	Chuck Knoblauch	1996
Hits	239	Rod Carew	1977
Singles	182	Sam Rice	1925
Doubles	51	Mickey Vernon	1946
Triples	20	Goose Goslin	1925
		Cristian Guzman	2000
Home runs	49	Harmon Killebrew	1964, 1969
Home runs, rookie	33	Jimmie Hall	1963
Grand slams	3	4 times	
		Last by Kirby Puckett	1992
Total bases	374	Tony Oliva	1964
RBIs	140	Harmon Killebrew	1969
Walks	151	Eddie Yost	1956
Most strikeouts	145	Bob Darwin	1972
Fewest strikeouts	9	Sam Rice	1929
Batting average	.388	Rod Carew	1977
Slugging pct.	.614	Goose Goslin	1928
Stolen bases	88	Clyde Milan	1912

Pitching			
Games	90	Mike Marshall	1979
Complete games	38	Walter Johnson	1910
Innings	374	Walter Johnson	1910
Wins	36	Walter Johnson	1913
Losses	26	Jack Townsend	1904
		Bob Groom	1909
Winning pct.	.837	Walter Johnson	1913
Walks	146	Bobo Newsom	1936
Strikeouts	313	Walter Johnson	1910
Shutouts	11	Walter Johnson	1913
Home runs allowed	50	Bert Blyleven	1986
Lowest ERA	1.14	Walter Johnson	1913
Saves	45	Eddie Guardado	2002

GAME

Batting			
Runs	5	Last by Paul Molitor	4-26-96
Hits	6	Last by Kirby Puckett	5-23-91
Doubles	4	Kirby Puckett	5-13-89
Triples	3	Last by Ken Landreaux	7-3-80
Home runs	3	Last by Tony Oliva	7-3-73
RBIs	8	Last by Randy Bush	5-20-89
Total bases	14	Kirby Puckett	8-30-87
Stolen bases	5	Clyde Milan	6-14-12

CAREER LEADERS

BATTING

Games

Harmon Killebrew	2,329
Sam Rice	2,307
Joe Judge	2,084
Clyde Milan	1,982
Ossie Bluege	1,867
Mickey Vernon	1,805
Kirby Puckett	1,783
Kent Hrbek	1,747
Eddie Yost	1,690
Tony Oliva	1,676

At-bats

Sam Rice	8,934
Harmon Killebrew	7,835
Joe Judge	7,663
Clyde Milan	7,359
Kirby Puckett	7,244
Mickey Vernon	6,930
Ossie Bluege	6,440
Tony Oliva	6,301
Rod Carew	6,235
Kent Hrbek	6,192

Runs

Sam Rice	1,466
Harmon Killebrew	1,258
Joe Judge	1,154
Kirby Puckett	1,071
Buddy Myer	1,037
Clyde Milan	1,004
Eddie Yost	971
Mickey Vernon	956
Rod Carew	950
Kent Hrbek	903

Hits

Sam Rice	2,889
Kirby Puckett	2,304
Joe Judge	2,291
Clyde Milan	2,100
Rod Carew	2,085
Harmon Killebrew	2,024
Mickey Vernon	1,993
Tony Oliva	1,917
Buddy Myer	1,828
Ossie Bluege	1,751

Doubles

Sam Rice	479
Joe Judge	421
Kirby Puckett	414
Mickey Vernon	391
Tony Oliva	329
Kent Hrbek	312
Rod Carew	305
Buddy Myer	305
Goose Goslin	289
Eddie Yost	282

Triples

Sam Rice	183
Joe Judge	157
Goose Goslin	125
Buddy Myer	113
Mickey Vernon	108
Clyde Milan	105
Buddy Lewis	93
Rod Carew	90
Howie Shanks	87
Cecil Travis	78

Home runs

Harmon Killebrew	559
Kent Hrbek	293
Bob Allison	256
Tony Oliva	220
Kirby Puckett	207
Gary Gaetti	201
Roy Sievers	180
Tom Brunansky	163
Jim Lemon	159
Goose Goslin	127

Total bases

Harmon Killebrew	4,026
Sam Rice	3,833
Kirby Puckett	3,453
Joe Judge	3,239
Tony Oliva	3,002
Kent Hrbek	2,976
Mickey Vernon	2,963
Rod Carew	2,792
Clyde Milan	2,601
Goose Goslin	2,579

Runs batted in

Harmon Killebrew	1,540
Kent Hrbek	1,086
Kirby Puckett	1,085
Sam Rice	1,045
Mickey Vernon	1,026
Joe Judge	1,001
Tony Oliva	947
Goose Goslin	931
Ossie Bluege	848
Bob Allison	796

Extra-base hits

Harmon Killebrew	860
Sam Rice	695
Kirby Puckett	678
Joe Judge	649
Kent Hrbek	623
Mickey Vernon	620
Tony Oliva	597
Goose Goslin	541
Bob Allison	525
Gary Gaetti	478

Batting average
(Minimum 500 games)

Rod Carew	.334
Heinie Manush	.328
Sam Rice	.323
Goose Goslin	.323
Kirby Puckett	.318
John Stone	.317
Cecil Travis	.314
Shane Mack	.309
Brian Harper	.306
Joe Cronin	.304

Stolen bases

Clyde Milan	495
Sam Rice	346
George Case	321
Chuck Knoblauch	276
Rod Carew	271
Joe Judge	210
Cesar Tovar	186
Howie Shanks	177
Eddie Foster	166
Bucky Harris	166

PITCHING

Earned-run average
(Minimum 1,000 innings)

Walter Johnson	2.17
Doc Ayers	2.64
Harry Harper	2.75
Tom Hughes	3.02
Bob Groom	3.04
Jim Shaw	3.07
Jim Perry	3.15
Dutch Leonard	3.27
Bert Blyleven	3.28
Mickey Haefner	3.29

Wins

Walter Johnson	417
Jim Kaat	190
Bert Blyleven	149
Camilo Pascual	145
Jim Perry	128
Dutch Leonard	118
Firpo Marberry	117
Frank Viola	112
Case Patten	106
Alvin Crowder	98

Losses

Walter Johnson	279
Jim Kaat	159
Camilo Pascual	141
Bert Blyleven	138
Sid Hudson	130
Case Patten	127
Tom Hughes	124
Pedro Ramos	112
Tom Zachary	103
Dutch Leonard	101

Innings pitched

Walter Johnson	5,914.2
Jim Kaat	3,014.1
Bert Blyleven	2,566.2
Camilo Pascual	2,465.0
Case Patten	2,059.1
Dutch Leonard	1,899.1
Jim Perry	1,883.1
Sid Hudson	1,819.1
Tom Hughes	1,776.0
Frank Viola	1,772.2

Strikeouts

Walter Johnson	3,509
Bert Blyleven	2,035
Camilo Pascual	1,885
Jim Kaat	1,851
Frank Viola	1,214
Jim Perry	1,025
Brad Radke	1,004
Dave Goltz	887
Tom Hughes	884
Dave Boswell	865

Bases on balls

Walter Johnson	1,363
Camilo Pascual	909
Jim Kaat	729
Sid Hudson	720
Walt Masterson	694
Jim Shaw	688
Bert Blyleven	674
Bump Hadley	572
Firpo Marberry	568
Tom Hughes	567

Games

Walter Johnson	802
Eddie Guardado	573
Rick Aguilera	490
Jim Kaat	484
Firpo Marberry	470
Camilo Pascual	432
Jim Perry	376
Mike Trombley	365
Bert Blyleven	348
Al Worthington	327

Shutouts

Walter Johnson	110
Camilo Pascual	31
Bert Blyleven	29
Jim Kaat	23
Dutch Leonard	23
Bob Porterfield	19
Tom Hughes	17
Case Patten	17
Jim Perry	17
Jim Shaw	17

Saves

Rick Aguilera	254
Ron Davis	108
Jeff Reardon	104
Firpo Marberry	96
Al Worthington	88
Ron Perranoski	76
Mike Marshall	54
Bill Campbell	51
Doug Corbett	43
Eddie Guardado	75

TEAM SEASON, GAME RECORDS

SEASON

Batting

Most at-bats	5,677	1969
Most runs	892	1930
Fewest runs	380	1909
Most hits	1,633	1996
Most singles	1,209	1935
Most doubles	348	2002
Most triples	100	1932
Most home runs	225	1963
Fewest home runs	4	1917
Most grand slams	8	1938, 1961
Most pinch-hit home runs	7	1964, 1967
Most total bases	2,439	2002
Most stolen bases	287	1913
Highest batting average	.303	1925
Lowest batting average	.223	1909
Highest slugging pct	.437	2002

Pitching

Lowest ERA	2.14	1918
Highest ERA	5.76	1995
Most complete games	137	1904
Most shutouts	25	1914
Most saves	58	1970
Most walks	779	1949
Most strikeouts	1,099	1964

Fielding

Most errors	323	1901
Fewest errors	74	2002
Most double plays	203	1979
Highest fielding average	.987	2002

General

Most games won	102	1965
Most games lost	113	1904
Highest win pct	.651	1933
Lowest win pct	.252	1904

GAME, INNING

Batting

Most runs, game	24	4-24-96
Most runs, inning	12	7-10-26
Most hits, game	25	6-4-2002
Most home runs, game	8	8-29-63
Most total bases, game	47	8-29-63

Hard-hitting outfielder Tony Oliva was part of the Twins' offensive wrecking crew in the 1960s.

TWINS YEAR-BY-YEAR

Year	W	L	Place	Games Back	Manager	Leaders: Batting avg.	Hits	Home runs	RBIs	Wins	ERA
								WASHINGTON SENATORS			
1901	61	72	6th	20½	Manning	Waldron, .322	Dungan, 179	Grady, 9	Dungan, 73	Patten, 18	Carrick, 3.75
1902	61	75	6th	22	Loftus	E. Delahanty, .376	E. Delahanty, 178	E. Delahanty, 10	E. Delahanty, 93	Orth, 19	Orth, 3.97
1903	43	94	8th	47½	Loftus	Selbach, .251	Selbach, 134	Ryan, 7	Selbach, 49	Orth, Patten, 10	Lee, 3.08
1904	38	113	8th	55½	Donovan	Stahl, .262	Cassidy, 140	Stahl, 3	Stahl, 50	Patten, 14	Patten, 3.07
1905	64	87	7th	29½	Stahl	Hickman, .311	Cassidy, 124	Stahl, 5	Stahl, 66	Hughes, 17	Hughes, 2.35
1906	55	95	7th	37½	Stahl	Hickman, .284	Anderson, 158	Hickman, 9	Anderson, 70	Patten, 19	Patten, 2.17
1907	49	102	8th	43½	Cantillon	J. Delahanty, .292	Ganley, 167	Altizer, J. Delahanty, 2	J. Delahanty, 54	Patten, 12	Johnson, 1.88
1908	67	85	7th	22½	Cantillon	Clymer, .253	Freeman, 134	Pickering, 2	Freeman, 45	Hughes, 18	Johnson, 1.64
1909	42	110	8th	56	Cantillon	Lelivelt, .292	Unglaub, 127	Unglaub, 3	Unglaub, 41	Johnson, 13	Johnson, 2.21
1910	66	85	7th	36½	McAleer	Milan, .279	Milan, 148	Elberfeld, Gessler, 2	McBride, 55	Johnson, 25	Johnson, 1.35
1911	64	90	7th	38½	McAleer	Schaefer, .334	Milan, 194	Gessler, 4	Gessler, 78	Johnson, 25	Johnson, 1.89
1912	91	61	2nd	14	Griffith	Milan, .306	Milan, 184	Moeller, 6	Gandil, 81	Johnson, 33	Johnson, 1.39
1913	90	64	2nd	6½	Griffith	Gandil, .318	Gandil, 175	Moeller, 5	Gandil, 72	Johnson, 36	Johnson, 1.14
1914	81	73	3rd	19	Griffith	Milan, .295	Foster, 174	Shanks, 4	Gandil, 75	Johnson, 28	Johnson, 1.72
1915	85	68	4th	17	Griffith	Gandil, .291	Foster, 170	Gandil, Milan, Moeller, 2	Milan, 66	Johnson, 27	Johnson, 1.55
1916	76	77	7th	14½	Griffith	Milan, .273	Milan, 154	E. Smith, 2	Shanks, 48	Johnson, 25	Johnson, 1.89
1917	74	79	5th	25½	Griffith	Rice, .302	Rice, 177	Judge, 2	Rice, 69	Johnson, 23	Ayers, 2.17
1918	72	56	3rd	4	Griffith	Milan, .290	Foster, 147	4 Tied, 1	Milan, Shanks, 56	Johnson, 23	Johnson, 1.27
1919	56	84	7th	32	Griffith	Rice, .321	Rice, 179	Menosky, 6	Rice, 71	Johnson, 20	Johnson, 1.49
1920	68	84	6th	29	Griffith	Rice, .338	Rice, 211	Roth, 9	Roth, 92	Zachary, 15	Johnson, 3.13
1921	80	73	4th	18	McBride	Rice, .330	Judge, 187	B. Miller, 9	Rice, 79	Mogridge, Zachary, 18	Mogridge, 3.00
1922	69	85	6th	25	Milan	Goslin, .324	Rice, 187	Judge, 10	Judge, 81	Mogridge, 18	Johnson, 2.99
1923	75	78	4th	23½	Bush	Rice, .316	Rice, 188	Goslin, 9	Goslin, 99	Johnson, 17	A. Russell, 3.03
1924	92	62	1st	+2	Harris	Goslin, .344	Rice, 216	Goslin, 12	Goslin, 129	Johnson, 23	Ogden, 2.58
1925	96	55	1st	+8½	Harris	Rice, .350	Rice, 227	Goslin, 18	Goslin, 113	Coveleski, Johnson, 20	Coveleski, 2.84
1926	81	69	4th	8	Harris	Goslin, .354	Rice, 216	Goslin, 17	Goslin, 108	Johnson, 15	Marberry, 3.00
1927	85	69	3rd	25	Harris	Goslin, .334	Goslin, 194	Goslin, 13	Goslin, 120	Lisenbee, 18	Hadley, 2.85
1928	75	79	4th	26	Harris	Goslin, .379	Rice, 202	Goslin, 17	Goslin, 102	S. Jones, 17	Braxton, 2.51
1929	71	81	5th	34	Johnson	Rice, .323	Rice, 199	Goslin, 18	Goslin, 91	Marberry, 19	Marberry, 3.06
1930	94	60	2nd	8	Johnson	Manush, .362	Rice, 207	Cronin, 13	Cronin, 126	Brown, 16	Liska, 3.29
1931	92	62	3rd	16	Johnson	West, .333	Manush, 189	Cronin, 12	Cronin, 126	Crowder, 18	Hadley, 3.06
1932	93	61	3rd	14	Johnson	Manush, .342	Manush, 214	Manush, 14	Cronin, Manush, 116	Crowder, 26	Crowder, 3.33
1933	99	53	1st	+7	Cronin	Manush, .336	Manush, 221	Kuhel, 11	Cronin, 118	Crowder, 24	J. Russell, 2.69
1934	66	86	7th	34	Cronin	Manush, .349	Manush, 194	Manush, 11	Cronin, 101	Whitehill, 14	Burke, 3.21
1935	67	86	6th	27	Harris	Myer, .349	Myer, 215	Powell, 6	Myer, 100	Whitehill, 14	Whitehill, 4.29
1936	82	71	4th	20	Harris	Stone, .341	Kuhel, 189	Kuhel, 16	Kuhel, 118	DeShong, 18	Appleton, 3.53
1937	73	80	6th	28½	Harris	Travis, .344	Lewis, 210	Lewis, 10	Stone, 88	DeShong, 14	Ferrell, 3.94
1938	75	76	5th	23½	Harris	Myer, .336	Lewis, 194	Bonura, 22	Bonura, 114	Ferrell, 13	Krakauskas, 3.12
1939	65	87	6th	41½	Harris	Lewis, .319	Lewis, 171	Lewis, 10	Wright, 93	Leonard, 20	Leonard, 3.54
1940	64	90	7th	26	Harris	Travis, .322	Case, 192	Walker, 13	Walker, 96	Hudson, 17	Chase, 3.23
1941	70	84	*6th	31	Harris	Travis, .359	Travis, 218	Early, 10	Travis, 101	Leonard, 18	Carrasquel, 3.44
1942	62	89	7th	39½	Harris	Spence, .323	Spence, 203	Vernon, 9	Vernon, 86	Newsom, 11	Masterson, 3.34
1943	84	69	2nd	13½	Bluege	Case, .294	Case, 180	Spence, 12	Spence, 88	Wynn, 18	Haefner, 2.29
1944	64	90	8th	25	Bluege	Spence, .316	Spence, 187	Spence, 18	Spence, 100	Leonard, 14	Niggeling, 2.32
1945	87	67	2nd	1½	Bluege	Myatt, .296	Binks, 153	Clift, 8	Binks, 81	Wolff, 20	Wolff, 2.12
1946	76	78	4th	28	Bluege	Vernon, .353	Vernon, 207	Spence, 16	Spence, 87	Haefner, 14	Wolff, 2.58
1947	64	90	7th	33	Bluege	Spence, .279	Vernon, 159	Spence, 16	Vernon, 85	Wynn, 17	Masterson, 3.13
1948	56	97	7th	40	Kuhel	Stewart, .279	Kozar, 144	Coan, Stewart, 7	Stewart, 69	Scarborough, 15	Scarborough, 2.82
1949	50	104	8th	47	Kuhel	Robinson, .294	Dente, 161	Robinson, 18	Robinson, 78	Scarborough, 13	Hittle, 4.21
1950	67	87	5th	31	Harris	Vernon, .306	Yost, 169	Noren, 14	Noren, 98	Hudson, 14	Kuzava, 3.95
1951	62	92	7th	36	Harris	Coan, .303	Coan, 163	Yost, 12	Mele, 94	Marrero, 11	Porterfield, 3.24
1952	78	76	5th	17	Harris	Jensen, .286	Jensen, 163	Yost, 12	Jensen, Vernon, 80	Porterfield, 13	Porterfield, 2.72
1953	76	76	5th	23½	Harris	Vernon, .337	Vernon, 205	Vernon, 15	Vernon, 115	Porterfield, 22	Marrero, 3.03
1954	66	88	6th	45	Harris	Busby, .298	Busby, 187	Sievers, 24	Sievers, 102	Porterfield, 13	Schmitz, 2.91
1955	53	101	8th	43	Dressen	Vernon, .301	Vernon, 162	Sievers, 25	Sievers, 106	McDermott, Porterfield, 10	Schmitz, 3.71
1956	59	95	7th	38	Dressen	Runnels, .310	Runnels, 179	Sievers, 29	Lemon, 96	Stobbs, 15	Stobbs, 3.60
1957	55	99	8th	43	Dressen, Lavagetto	Sievers, .301	Sievers, 172	Sievers, 42	Sievers, 114	Ramos, 12	Byerly, 3.13
1958	61	93	8th	31	Lavagetto	Sievers, .295	Sievers, 162	Sievers, 39	Sievers, 108	Ramos, 14	Hyde, 1.75
1959	63	91	8th	31	Lavagetto	Lemon, .279	Allison, 149	Killebrew, 42	Killebrew, 105	Pascual, 17	Pascual, 2.64
1960	73	81	5th	24	Lavagetto	Green, .294	Gardner, 152	Lemon, 38	Lemon, 100	Pascual, Stobbs, 12	Pascual, 3.03
								MINNESOTA TWINS			
1961	70	90	7th	38	Lavagetto, Mele	Battey, .302	Green, 171	Killebrew, 46	Killebrew, 122	Pascual, 15	Pascual, 3.46
1962	91	71	2nd	5	Mele	Rollins, .298	Rollins, 186	Killebrew, 48	Killebrew, 126	Pascual, 20	Kaat, 3.14
1963	91	70	3rd	13	Mele	Rollins, .307	Rollins, 163	Killebrew, 45	Killebrew, 96	Pascual, 21	Dailey, 1.98
1964	79	83	*6th	20	Mele	Oliva, .323	Oliva, 217	Killebrew, 49	Killebrew, 111	Kaat, 17	Grant, 2.82
1965	102	60	1st	+7	Mele	Oliva, .321	Oliva, 185	Killebrew, 25	Oliva, 98	Grant, 21	J. Perry, 2.63
1966	89	73	2nd	9	Mele	Oliva, .307	Oliva, 191	Killebrew, 39	Killebrew, 110	Kaat, 25	Worthington, 2.46
1967	91	71	*2nd	1	Mele, Ermer	Carew, .292	Oliva, 161	Killebrew, 44	Killebrew, 113	Chance, 20	Merritt, 2.53
1968	79	83	7th	24	Ermer	Oliva, .289	Tovar, 167	Allison, 22	Oliva, 68	Chance, 16	J. Perry, 2.27
								WEST DIVISION			
1969	97	65	†1st	+9	Martin	Carew, .332	Oliva, 197	Killebrew, 49	Killebrew, 140	Boswell, J. Perry, 20	Perranoski, 2.11
1970	98	64	†1st	+9	Rigney	Oliva, .325	Oliva, 204	Killebrew, 41	Killebrew, 113	J. Perry, 24	Williams, 1.99
1971	74	86	5th	26½	Rigney	Oliva, .337	Tovar, 204	Killebrew, 28	Killebrew, 119	Perry, 17	Blyleven, 2.81
1972	77	77	3rd	15½	Rigney, Quilici	Carew, .318	Carew, 170	Killebrew, 26	Darwin, 80	Blyleven, 17	Kaat, 2.06
1973	81	81	3rd	13	Quilici	Carew, .350	Carew, 203	Darwin, 18	Oliva, 92	Blyleven, 20	Blyleven, 2.52
1974	82	80	3rd	8	Quilici	Carew, .364	Carew, 218	Darwin, 25	Darwin, 94	Blyleven, 17	Campbell, 2.62
1975	76	83	4th	20½	Quilici	Carew, .359	Carew, 192	Ford, 15	Carew, 80	Hughes, 16	Blyleven, 3.00
1976	85	77	3rd	5	Mauch	Carew, .331	Carew, 200	Ford, 20	Hisle, 96	Campbell, 17	Burgmeier, 2.50
1977	84	77	4th	17½	Mauch	Carew, .388	Carew, 239	Hisle, 28	Hisle, 119	Goltz, 20	Johnson, 3.13
1978	73	89	4th	19	Mauch	Carew, .333	Carew, 188	Smalley, 19	Ford, 82	Goltz, 15	Marshall, 2.45
1979	82	80	4th	6	Mauch	Wilfong, .313	Landreaux, 172	Smalley, 24	Smalley, 95	Koosman, 20	Marshall, 2.65
1980	77	84	3rd	19½	Mauch, Goryl	Castino, .302	Castino, 165	Castino, 13	Castino, 64	Koosman, 16	Corbett, 1.98
1981	41	68	‡7th/4th	–	Goryl, Gardner	Castino, .268	Castino, 102	Smalley, 7	Hatcher, 37	Redfern, 9	Erickson, 3.84
1982	60	102	7th	33	Gardner	Hrbek, .301	Ward, 165	Ward, 28	Hrbek, 92	Castillo, 13	Castillo, 3.66
1983	70	92	*5th	29	Gardner	Hatcher, .317	Ward, 173	Brunansky, 28	Ward, 88	Schrom, 15	Lysander, 3.38
1984	81	81	*2nd	3	Gardner	Hrbek, .311	Hatcher, 174	Brunansky, 32	Hrbek, 107	Viola, 18	Viola, 3.21
1985	77	85	*4th	14	Gardner, Miller	Salas, .300	Puckett, 199	Brunansky, 27	Hrbek, 93	Viola, 18	Blyleven, 3.00
1986	71	91	6th	21	Miller, Kelly	Puckett, .328	Puckett, 223	Gaetti, 34	Gaetti, 108	Blyleven, 17	Heaton, 3.98
1987	85	77	§1st	+2	Kelly	Puckett, .332	Puckett, 207	Hrbek, 34	Gaetti, 109	Viola, 17	Viola, 2.90
1988	91	71	2nd	13	Kelly	Puckett, .356	Puckett, 234	Gaetti, 28	Puckett, 121	Viola, 24	Anderson, 2.45
1989	80	82	5th	19	Kelly	Puckett, .339	Puckett, 215	Hrbek, 25	Puckett, 85	Anderson, 17	Berenguer, 3.48
1990	74	88	7th	29	Kelly	Puckett, .298	Puckett, 164	Hrbek, 22	Gaetti, 85	Tapani, 12	Erickson, 2.87
1991	95	67	§1st	+8	Kelly	Puckett, .319	Puckett, 195	Davis, 29	Davis, 93	Erickson, 20	Tapani, 2.99
1992	90	72	2nd	6	Kelly	Puckett, .329	Puckett, 210	Puckett, 19	Puckett, 110	Smiley, Tapani, 16	Smiley, 3.21
1993	71	91	*5th	23	Kelly	Harper, .304	Puckett, 184	Hrbek, 25	Puckett, 89	Tapani, 12	Banks, 4.04
								CENTRAL DIVISION			
1994	53	60	4th	14	Kelly	Puckett, .317	Knoblauch, Puckett, 139	Puckett, 20	Puckett, 112	Tapani, 11	Tapani, 4.62
1995	56	88	5th	44	Kelly	Knoblauch, .333	Knoblauch, 179	Cordova, 24	Puckett, 99	Radke, 11	Tapani, 4.92
1996	78	84	4th	21½	Kelly	Molitor, .3409	Molitor, 225	Cordova, 16	Molitor, 113	Rodriguez, 13	Radke, 4.46
1997	68	94	4th	18½	Kelly	Molitor, .305	Knoblauch, 178	Cordova, 15	Molitor, 89	Radke, 20	Swindell, 3.58
1998	70	92	4th	19	Kelly	Walker, .316	Walker, 167	Lawton, 21	Lawton, 77	Radke, 12	Trombley, 3.63
1999	63	97	5th	33	Kelly	Cordova, .285	Walker, 148	Coomer, 16	Cordova, 70	Radke, 12	Radke, 3.75
2000	69	93	5th	26	Kelly	Lawton, .305	Lawton, 171	J. Jones, 19	Lawton, 88	Milton, 13	Radke, 4.45
2001	85	77	2nd	6	Kelly	Mientkiewicz, .306	Mientkiewicz, 166	Hunter, 27	Koskie, 103	Mays, 17	Mays, 3.16
2002	94	67	∞†1st	+13½	Gardenhire	Jones, .300	Jones, 173	Hunter, 29	Hunter, 94	Reed, 15	Reed, 3.78

* Tied for position. † Lost Championship Series. ‡ First half 17-39; second half 24-29. § Won Championship Series. ∞ Won Division Series.

Note: Batting average minimum 350 at-bats; ERA minimum 90 innings pitched.

HISTORY

NEW YORK YANKEES

Outfielder Babe Ruth.

FRANCHISE CHRONOLOGY

First season: 1901, in Baltimore, as a member of the new American League. The Orioles made their Major League debut with a 10-6 victory over Boston en route to a 68-65 record, but dropped to the bottom of the A.L. in their second and final Baltimore season.
1903-present: The Highlanders/Yankees dropped a 3-1 decision to Washington in their New York debut and spent the next 18 seasons languishing among the A.L. also-rans. That would change. With the arrival of Babe Ruth in 1920, the Yankees rose into prominence as baseball's most dominant franchise and began the most glorious success run in sports history. In a 44-year stretch (1921-64), the Bronx Bombers won 29 pennants and 20 World Series. They won four straight fall classics (1936-39) under Joe McCarthy and five in a row (1949-53) under Casey Stengel. After playing in their first Series in 1921, the Yankees never went three years without playing in another through 1964. Success became more elusive after that 1964 loss to the Cardinals, but the Yankees ended the decade back on top. The Yanks have won four of the last seven World Series, including sweeps in 1998 and 1999, for a record 26 titles.

YANKEES VS. OPPONENTS BY DECADE

	A's	Indians	Orioles	Red Sox	Tigers	Twins	White Sox	Angels	Rangers	Brewers	Royals	Blue Jays	Mariners	Devil Rays	Interleague	Decade Record
1901-09	87-94	85-104	99-90	86-101	85-103	122-66	74-113									638-671
1910-19	100-104	95-117	123-92	94-115	94-121	101-113	94-118									701-780
1920-29	137-81	125-95	140-78	149-71	126-94	122-97	134-86									933-602
1930-39	140-76	133-84	155-64	136-80	134-86	124-96	148-68									970-554
1940-49	143-77	129-90	143-77	122-98	108-112	151-69	133-86									929-609
1950-59	158-62	123-97	151-69	126-93	120-100	145-73	132-88									955-582
1960-69	117-61	100-83	73-111	101-83	94-90	87-90	102-76	95-61	104-55	7-5	7-5					887-720
1970-79	63-54	103-64	73-89	79-89	92-74	72-44	72-44	65-52	79-49	83-74	64-53	29-14	18-15			892-715
1980-89	61-54	73-56	74-56	63-60	64-62	71-43	61-58	63-49	62-54	61-62	68-52	65-57	68-45			854-708
1990-99	58-59	72-45	75-50	64-60	72-47	58-50	52-54	58-59	54-54	56-39	61-45	64-57	61-56	19-5	27-22	851-702
2000-02	14-13	16-12	33-16	30-20	17-13	13-9	13-11	12-12	17-9		19-3	26-24	11-17	32-17	32-21	285-197
Totals	1078-735	1054-847	1139-792	1050-870	1006-902	1066-750	1015-802	293-233	316-221	207-180	219-158	184-152	158-133	51-22	59-43	8895-6840

Interleague results: 2-1 vs. Diamondbacks, 8-8 vs. Braves, 2-1 vs. Rockies, 8-6 vs. Marlins, 9-6 vs. Expos, 18-12 vs. Mets, 8-7 vs. Phillies, 2-1 vs. Padres, 2-1 vs. Giants.

MANAGERS

(Baltimore Orioles, 1901-02)

Name	*Years*	*Record*
John McGraw	1901-02	94-96
Wilbert Robinson	1902	24-57
Clark Griffith	1903-08	419-370
Kid Elberfeld	1908	27-71
George Stallings	1909-10	152-136
Hal Chase	1910-11	86-80
Harry Wolverton	1912	50-102
Frank Chance	1913-14	117-168
Roger Peckinpaugh	1914	10-10
Bill Donovan	1915-17	220-239
Miller Huggins	1918-29	1067-719
Art Fletcher	1929	6-5
Bob Shawkey	1930	86-68
Joe McCarthy	1931-46	1460-867
Bill Dickey	1946	57-48
Johnny Neun	1946	8-6
Bucky Harris	1947-48	191-117
Casey Stengel	1949-60	1149-696
Ralph Houk	1961-63, 1966-73	944-806
Yogi Berra	1964, 1984-85	192-148
Johnny Keane	1965-66	81-101
Bill Virdon	1974-75	142-124
Billy Martin	1975-78, 1979, 1983, 1985, 1988	556-385
Bob Lemon	1978-79, 1981-82	99-73
Dick Howser	1978, 1980	103-60
Gene Michael	1981, 1982	92-76
Clyde King	1982	29-33
Lou Piniella	1986-87, 1988	224-193
Dallas Green	1989	56-65
Bucky Dent	1989-90	36-53
Stump Merrill	1990-91	120-155
Buck Showalter	1992-95	313-268
Joe Torre	1996-2002	685-445

WORLD SERIES CHAMPIONS

Year	*Loser*	*Length*	*MVP*
1923	N.Y. Giants	6 games	None
1927	Pittsburgh	4 games	None
1928	St. Louis	4 games	None
1932	Chicago	4 games	None
1936	N.Y. Giants	6 games	None
1937	N.Y. Giants	5 games	None
1938	Chicago	4 games	None
1939	Cincinnati	4 games	None
1941	Brooklyn	5 games	None
1943	St. Louis	5 games	None
1947	Brooklyn	7 games	None
1949	Brooklyn	5 games	None
1950	Philadelphia	4 games	None
1951	N.Y. Giants	6 games	None
1952	Brooklyn	7 games	None
1953	Brooklyn	6 games	None
1956	Brooklyn	7 games	Larsen

WORLD SERIES CHAMPIONS—*cont'd.*

Year	*Loser*	*Length*	*MVP*
1958	Milwaukee	7 games	Turley
1961	Cincinnati	5 games	Ford
1962	San Francisco	7 games	Terry
1977	Los Angeles	6 games	Jackson
1978	Los Angeles	6 games	Dent
1996	Atlanta	6 games	Wetteland
1998	San Diego	4 games	Brosius
1999	Atlanta	4 games	Rivera
2000	N.Y. Mets	5 games	Jeter

A.L. PENNANT WINNERS

Year	*Record*	*Manager*	*Series Result*
1921	98-55	Huggins	Lost to Giants
1922	94-60	Huggins	Lost to Giants
1923	98-54	Huggins	Defeated Giants
1926	91-63	Huggins	Lost to Cardinals
1927	110-44	Huggins	Defeated Pirates
1928	101-53	Huggins	Defeated Cardinals
1932	107-47	McCarthy	Defeated Cubs
1936	102-51	McCarthy	Defeated Giants
1937	102-52	McCarthy	Defeated Giants
1938	99-53	McCarthy	Defeated Cubs
1939	106-45	McCarthy	Defeated Reds
1941	101-53	McCarthy	Defeated Dodgers
1942	103-51	McCarthy	Lost to Cardinals
1943	98-56	McCarthy	Defeated Cardinals
1947	97-57	Harris	Defeated Dodgers
1949	97-57	Stengel	Defeated Dodgers
1950	98-56	Stengel	Defeated Phillies
1951	98-56	Stengel	Defeated Giants
1952	95-59	Stengel	Defeated Dodgers
1953	99-52	Stengel	Defeated Dodgers
1955	96-58	Stengel	Lost to Dodgers
1956	97-57	Stengel	Defeated Dodgers
1957	98-56	Stengel	Lost to Braves
1958	92-62	Stengel	Defeated Braves
1960	97-57	Stengel	Lost to Pirates
1961	109-53	Houk	Defeated Reds
1962	96-66	Houk	Defeated Giants
1963	104-57	Houk	Lost to Dodgers
1964	99-63	Berra	Lost to Cardinals
1976	97-62	Martin	Lost to Reds
1977	100-62	Martin	Defeated Dodgers
1978	100-63	Martin, Lemon	Defeated Dodgers
*1981	59-48	Michael, Lemon	Lost to Dodgers
1996	92-70	Torre	Defeated Braves
1998	114-48	Torre	Defeated Padres
1999	98-64	Torre	Defeated Braves
2000	87-74	Torre	Defeated Mets
2001	95-65	Torre	Lost to D'backs

EAST DIVISION CHAMPIONS

Year	*Record*	*Manager*	*ALCS Result*
1976	97-62	Martin	Defeated Royals
1977	100-62	Martin	Defeated Royals

EAST DIVISION CHAMPIONS—*cont'd.*

Year	*Record*	*Manager*	*ALCS Result*
1978	100-63	Martin, Lemon	Defeated Royals
1980	103-59	Howser	Lost to Royals
*1981	59-48	Michael, Lemon	Defeated A's
1994	70-43	Showalter	None
1996	92-70	Torre	Defeated Orioles
1998	114-48	Torre	Defeated Indians
1999	98-64	Torre	Defeated Red Sox
2000	87-74	Torre	Defeated Mariners
2001	95-65	Torre	Defeated A's
2002	103-58	Torre	Lost in Div. Series

* First-half champion; won division playoff from Brewers.

WILD-CARD QUALIFIERS

Year	*Record*	*Manager*	*Div. Series Result*
1995	79-65	Showalter	Lost to Mariners
1997	96-66	Torre	Lost to Indians

ATTENDANCE HIGHS

Total	*Season*	*Park*
3,461,644	2002	Yankee Stadium
3,292,629	1999	Yankee Stadium
3,264,777	2001	Yankee Stadium
3,227,657	2000	Yankee Stadium
2,949,734	1998	Yankee Stadium

BALLPARK CHRONOLOGY

Yankee Stadium (1923-present)

Capacity: 57,478.
First game: Yankees 4, Boston 1 (April 18, 1923).
First batter: Chick Fewster, Red Sox.
First hit: George Burns, Red Sox (single).
First run: Bob Shawkey, Yankees (3rd inning).
First home run: Babe Ruth, Yankees.
First winning pitcher: Bob Shawkey, Yankees.
First-season attendance: 1,007,066.

Oriole Park, Baltimore (1901-02)

First game: Orioles 10, Boston 6 (April 26, 1901).
First-season attendance: 141,952.

Hilltop Park, New York (1903-12)

Capacity: 15,000.
First game: Yankees 6, Washington 2 (May 1, 1903).
First-season attendance: 211,808.

Polo Grounds (1913-22)

Capacity: 38,000.
First game: Washington 9, Yankees 3 (April 17, 1913).
First-season attendance: 357,551.

Shea Stadium (1974-75)

Capacity: 55,101.
First game: Yankees 6, Cleveland 1 (April 6, 1974).
First-season attendance: 1,273,075.

Note: The Yankees played two seasons at Shea Stadium while Yankee Stadium was being refurbished. Before its facelift, Yankee Stadium capacity was 67,224.

A.L. MVPs

Lou Gehrig, 1B, 1936
Joe DiMaggio, OF, 1939
Joe DiMaggio, OF, 1941
Joe Gordon, 2B, 1942
Spud Chandler, P, 1943
Joe DiMaggio, OF, 1947
Phil Rizzuto, SS, 1950
Yogi Berra, C, 1951
Yogi Berra, C, 1954
Yogi Berra, C, 1955
Mickey Mantle, OF, 1956
Mickey Mantle, OF, 1957
Roger Maris, OF, 1960
Roger Maris, OF, 1961
Mickey Mantle, OF, 1962
Elston Howard, C, 1963
Thurman Munson, C, 1976
Don Mattingly, 1B, 1985

CY YOUNG WINNERS

Bob Turley, RH, 1958
Whitey Ford, LH, 1961
Sparky Lyle, LH, 1977
Ron Guidry, LH, 1978
Roger Clemens, RH, 2001

ROOKIES OF THE YEAR

Gil McDougald, 3B, 1951
Bob Grim, P, 1954
Tony Kubek, SS/OF, 1957

ROOKIES OF THE YEAR—*cont'd.*

Tom Tresh, SS/OF, 1962
Stan Bahnsen, P, 1968
Thurman Munson, C, 1970
Dave Righetti, P, 1981
Derek Jeter, SS, 1996

MANAGER OF THE YEAR

Buck Showalter, 1994
*Joe Torre, 1996
Joe Torre, 1998
*Co-winner

RETIRED UNIFORMS

No.	*Name*	*Pos.*
1	Billy Martin	2B-Man.
3	Babe Ruth	OF
4	Lou Gehrig	1B
5	Joe DiMaggio	OF
7	Mickey Mantle	OF
8	Bill Dickey	C
	Yogi Berra	C
9	Roger Maris	OF
10	Phil Rizzuto	SS
15	Thurman Munson	C
16	Whitey Ford	P
23	Don Mattingly	1B
32	Elston Howard	C
37	Casey Stengel	Man.
44	Reggie Jackson	OF

INDIVIDUAL SEASON, GAME RECORDS

SEASON

Batting

At-bats	692	Bobby Richardson	1962
Runs	177	Babe Ruth	1921
Hits	238	Don Mattingly	1986
Singles	171	Steve Sax	1989
Doubles	53	Don Mattingly	1986
Triples	23	Earle Combs	1927
Home runs	61	Roger Maris	1961
Home runs, rookie	29	Joe DiMaggio	1936
Grand slams	6	Don Mattingly	1987
Total bases	457	Babe Ruth	1921
RBIs	184	Lou Gehrig	1931
Walks	170	Babe Ruth	1923
Most strikeouts	157	Alfonso Soriano	2002
Fewest strikeouts	3	Joe Sewell	1932
Batting average	.393	Babe Ruth	1923
Slugging pct.	.847	Babe Ruth	1920
Stolen bases	93	Rickey Henderson	1988

Pitching

Games	79	Mike Stanton	2002
Complete games	48	Jack Chesbro	1904
Innings	454.2	Jack Chesbro	1904
Wins	41	Jack Chesbro	1904
Losses	22	Joe Lake	1908
Winning pct.	.893 (25-3)	Ron Guidry	1978
Walks	179	Tommy Byrne	1949
Strikeouts	248	Ron Guidry	1978
Shutouts	9	Ron Guidry	1978
Home runs allowed	40	Ralph Terry	1962
Lowest ERA	1.64	Spud Chandler	1943
Saves	50	Mariano Rivera	2001

GAME

Batting

Runs	5	Last by Tino Martinez	4-2-97
Hits	6	Last by Gerald Williams	5-1-96
Doubles	4	Last by Jim Mason	7-8-74
Triples	3	Last by Joe DiMaggio	8-28-38
Home runs	4	Lou Gehrig	6-3-32
RBIs	11	Tony Lazzeri	5-24-36
Total bases	16	Lou Gehrig	6-3-32
Stolen bases	4	Last by Gerald Williams	6-2-96

MILESTONE PERFORMANCES

30-plus home runs

61—Roger Maris 1961
60—Babe Ruth 1927
59—Babe Ruth 1921
54—Babe Ruth 1920, 1928
Mickey Mantle 1961
52—Mickey Mantle 1956
49—Babe Ruth 1930
Lou Gehrig 1934, 1936
47—Babe Ruth 1926
Lou Gehrig 1927
46—Babe Ruth 1924, 1929, 1931
Lou Gehrig 1931
Joe DiMaggio 1937
44—Tino Martinez 1997
42—Mickey Mantle 1958
41—Babe Ruth 1923, 1932
Lou Gehrig 1930
Reggie Jackson 1980
David Justice *2000
Jason Giambi 2002
40—Mickey Mantle 1960
39—Joe DiMaggio 1948
Roger Maris 1960
Alfonso Soriano 2002
37—Lou Gehrig 1937
Mickey Mantle 1955
Graig Nettles 1977
Dave Winfield 1982
35—Babe Ruth 1922
Mickey Mantle 1964
Don Mattingly 1985
34—Babe Ruth 1933
Mickey Mantle 1957
Tino Martinez 2001
33—Bob Meusel 1925
Charlie Keller 1941
Roger Maris 1962
Bobby Murcer 1972
32—Lou Gehrig 1933
Joe DiMaggio 1938, 1950
Bobby Bonds 1975
Graig Nettles 1976
Reggie Jackson 1977
Dave Winfield 1983
Mike Pagliarulo 1987
31—Joe DiMaggio 1940
Tommy Henrich 1941
Charlie Keller 1943
Mickey Mantle 1959
Joe Pepitone 1966
Don Mattingly 1986
Danny Tartabull 1993
30—Lou Gehrig 1935
Joe DiMaggio 1939, 1941
Joe Gordon 1940
Charlie Keller 1946
Yogi Berra 1952
Mickey Mantle 1962
Don Mattingly 1987
Bernie Williams 2000

*21 with Indians; 20 with Yankees.

100-plus RBIs

184—Lou Gehrig 1931
175—Lou Gehrig 1927
174—Lou Gehrig 1930
171—Babe Ruth 1921
167—Joe DiMaggio 1937
165—Lou Gehrig 1934
164—Babe Ruth 1927
163—Babe Ruth 1931
159—Lou Gehrig 1937
155—Joe DiMaggio 1948
154—Babe Ruth 1929
153—Babe Ruth 1930
152—Lou Gehrig 1936
151—Lou Gehrig 1932
146—Babe Ruth 1926
145—Don Mattingly 1985
142—Lou Gehrig 1928
Babe Ruth 1928
Roger Maris 1961
141—Tino Martinez 1997
140—Joe DiMaggio 1938
139—Lou Gehrig 1933
138—Bob Meusel 1925
137—Babe Ruth 1920, 1932
135—Bob Meusel 1921
133—Bill Dickey 1937
Joe DiMaggio 1940
131—Babe Ruth 1923
130—Mickey Mantle 1956
128—Mickey Mantle 1961
126—Lou Gehrig 1929
Joe DiMaggio 1939
125—Joe DiMaggio 1936, 1941
Yogi Berra 1954
124—Yogi Berra 1950
123—Tino Martinez 1998
122—Ben Chapman 1931
Charlie Keller 1941
Joe DiMaggio 1950
Jason Giambi 2002
121—Babe Ruth 1924
Tony Lazzeri 1930
Bernie Williams 2000
120—Bob Meusel 1924
119—Lou Gehrig 1935
118—David Justice *2000
117—Tino Martinez 1996
Paul O'Neill 1997
116—Dave Winfield 1983
Paul O'Neill 1998
115—Bill Dickey 1938
Don Mattingly 1987
Bernie Williams 1999
114—Tony Lazzeri 1926
Lou Gehrig 1938
Joe DiMaggio 1942
Dave Winfield 1985
113—Wally Pipp 1924
Bob Meusel 1928
Tony Lazzeri 1932
Don Mattingly 1986, 1989
Tino Martinez 2001
112—Lou Gehrig 1926
Roger Maris 1960
111—Joe Gordon 1939
Nick Etten 1945
Mickey Mantle 1964
Reggie Jackson 1980
110—Reggie Jackson 1977
Don Mattingly 1984
Paul O'Neill 1999
109—Tony Lazzeri 1936
108—Wally Pipp 1923
Charlie Keller 1942
Yogi Berra 1953, 1955
107—Lyn Lary 1931
Ben Chapman 1932
Bill Dickey 1936
George Selkirk 1936
Nick Etten 1943
Graig Nettles 1977
Dave Winfield 1988
106—Tony Lazzeri 1929
Dave Winfield 1982
105—Bill Dickey 1939
Yogi Berra 1956
Thurman Munson 1976
Tino Martinez 1999
104—Tony Lazzeri 1933
Dave Winfield 1986
103—Bob Meusel 1927
Babe Ruth 1933
Joe Gordon 1940, 1942
Johnny Lindell 1944
102—Tony Lazzeri 1927
Mickey Mantle 1954
Thurman Munson 1975
Danny Tartabull 1993
Bernie Williams 1996
Derek Jeter 1999
Alfonso Soriano 2002
Bernie Williams 2002
101—George Selkirk 1939
Charlie Keller 1946
100—Tommy Henrich 1948
Roger Maris 1962
Joe Pepitone 1964
Thurman Munson 1977
Dave Winfield 1984
Bernie Williams 1997
Paul O'Neill 2000

*58 with Indians; 60 with Yankees.

20-plus victories

1901—Joe McGinnity 26-20
1903—Jack Chesbro 21-15
1904—Jack Chesbro 41-12
Jack Powell 23-19
1906—Albert Orth 27-17
Jack Chesbro 23-17
1910—Russell Ford 26-6
1911—Russell Ford 22-11
1916—Bob Shawkey 24-14
1919—Bob Shawkey 20-11
1920—Carl Mays 26-11
Bob Shawkey 20-13
1921—Carl Mays 27-9
1922—Joe Bush 26-7
Bob Shawkey 20-12
1923—Sad Sam Jones 21-8
1924—Herb Pennock 21-9
1926—Herb Pennock 23-11
1927—Waite Hoyt 22-7
1928—George Pipgras 24-13
Waite Hoyt 23-7
1931—Lefty Gomez 21-9
1932—Lefty Gomez 24-7
1934—Lefty Gomez 26-5
1936—Red Ruffing 20-12
1937—Lefty Gomez 21-11
Red Ruffing 20-7
1938—Red Ruffing 21-7
1939—Red Ruffing 21-7
1942—Ernie Bonham 21-5
1943—Spud Chandler 20-4
1946—Spud Chandler 20-8
1949—Vic Raschi 21-10
1950—Vic Raschi 21-8
1951—Eddie Lopat 21-9
Vic Raschi 21-10
1952—Allie Reynolds 20-8
1954—Bob Grim 20-6
1958—Bob Turley 21-7
1961—Whitey Ford 25-4
1962—Ralph Terry 23-12
1963—Whitey Ford 24-7
Jim Bouton 21-7
1965—Mel Stottlemyre 20-9
1968—Mel Stottlemyre 21-12
1969—Mel Stottlemyre 20-14
1970—Fritz Peterson 20-11
1975—Catfish Hunter 23-14
1978—Ron Guidry 25-3
Ed Figueroa 20-9
1979—Tommy John 21-9
1980—Tommy John 22-9
1983—Ron Guidry 21-9
1985—Ron Guidry 22-6
1996—Andy Pettitte 21-8

MILESTONE PERFORMANCES

1998— David Cone ... 20-7
2001— Roger Clemens ... 20-3

A.L. home run champions

1916— Wally Pipp ... 12
1917— Wally Pipp ... 9

A.L. home run champions—*cont'd.*

1920— Babe Ruth ... 54
1921— Babe Ruth ... 59
1923— Babe Ruth ... 41
1924— Babe Ruth ... 46
1925— Bob Meusel ... 33
1926— Babe Ruth ... 47
1927— Babe Ruth ... 60
1928— Babe Ruth ... 54
1929— Babe Ruth ... 46
1930— Babe Ruth ... 49
1931— Lou Gehrig ... 46
Babe Ruth ... 46
1934— Lou Gehrig ... 49
1936— Lou Gehrig ... 49
1937— Joe DiMaggio ... 46
1944— Nick Etten ... 22
1948— Joe DiMaggio ... 39
1955— Mickey Mantle ... 37
1956— Mickey Mantle ... 52
1958— Mickey Mantle ... 42
1960— Mickey Mantle ... 40
1961— Roger Maris ... 61
1976— Graig Nettles ... 32
1980— Reggie Jackson ... *41

* Tied for league lead

A.L. RBI champions

1920— Babe Ruth ... 137
1921— Babe Ruth ... 171
1923— Babe Ruth ... 131
1925— Bob Meusel ... 138
1926— Babe Ruth ... 146
1927— Lou Gehrig ... 175
1928— Lou Gehrig ... *142
Babe Ruth ... *142
1930— Lou Gehrig ... 174
1931— Lou Gehrig ... 184
1934— Lou Gehrig ... 165
1941— Joe DiMaggio ... 125
1945— Nick Etten ... 111
1948— Joe DiMaggio ... 155
1956— Mickey Mantle ... 130
1960— Roger Maris ... 112
1961— Roger Maris ... 142
1985— Don Mattingly ... 145

* Tied for league lead

A.L. batting champions

1924— Babe Ruth ... .378
1934— Lou Gehrig ... .363
1939— Joe DiMaggio ... .381
1940— Joe DiMaggio ... .352
1945— Snuffy Stirnweiss ... .309
1956— Mickey Mantle ... .353
1984— Don Mattingly ... .343
1994— Paul O'Neill ... .359
1998— Bernie Williams ... .339

A.L. ERA champions

1920— Bob Shawkey ... 2.45
1927— Wilcy Moore ... 2.28
1934— Lefty Gomez ... 2.33
1937— Lefty Gomez ... 2.33
1943— Spud Chandler ... 1.64
1947— Spud Chandler ... 2.46
1952— Allie Reynolds ... 2.06
1953— Eddie Lopat ... 2.42
1956— Whitey Ford ... 2.47
1957— Bobby Shantz ... 2.45
1958— Whitey Ford ... 2.01
1978— Ron Guidry ... 1.74
1979— Ron Guidry ... 2.78
1980— Rudy May ... 2.46

A.L. strikeout champions

1932— Red Ruffing ... 190
1933— Lefty Gomez ... 163
1934— Lefty Gomez ... 158
1937— Lefty Gomez ... 194
1951— Vic Raschi ... 164
1952— Allie Reynolds ... 160
1964— Al Downing ... 217

No-hit pitchers

(9 innings or more)

1917— George Mogridge ... 2-1 vs. Boston
1923— Sad Sam Jones ... 2-0 vs. Philadelphia
1938— Monte Pearson ... 13-0 vs. Cleveland
1951— Allie Reynolds ... 1-0 vs. Cleveland
Allie Reynolds ... 8-0 vs. Boston
1956— *Don Larsen ... 2-0 vs. Brooklyn (Perfect)
1983— Dave Righetti ... 4-0 vs. Boston
1990— Andy Hawkins ... 0-4 vs. Chicago
1993— Jim Abbott ... 4-0 vs. Cleveland
1996— Dwight Gooden ... 2-0 vs. Seattle
1998— David Wells ... 4-0 vs. Minnesota (Perfect)
1999— David Cone ... 6-0 vs. Montreal (Perfect)

* World Series game

Longest hitting streaks

56— Joe DiMaggio ... 1941
33— Hal Chase ... 1907
29— Roger Peckinpaugh ... 1919
Earle Combs ... 1931
Joe Gordon ... 1942
27— Hal Chase ... 1907
26— Babe Ruth ... 1921
23— Joe DiMaggio ... 1940
22— Joe DiMaggio ... 1937
21— Wally Pipp ... 1923
Joe DiMaggio ... 1937
Bernie Williams ... 1993
20— Buddy Hassett ... 1942
Mickey Rivers ... 1976
Dave Winfield ... 1984
Don Mattingly ... 1985

TEAM SEASON, GAME RECORDS

SEASON

Batting		
Most at-bats	5,710	1997
Most runs	1,067	1931
Fewest runs	459	1908
Most hits	1,683	1930
Most singles	1,237	1988
Most doubles	325	1997
Most triples	111	1901
Most home runs	240	1961
Fewest home runs	8	1913
Most grand slams	10	1987
Most pinch-hit home runs	10	1961
Most total bases	2,703	1936
Most stolen bases	288	1910
Highest batting average	.309	1930
Lowest batting average	.214	1968
Highest slugging pct	.489	1927
Pitching		
Lowest ERA	2.57	1904
Highest ERA	4.88	1930
Most complete games	123	1904
Most shutouts	24	1951
Most saves	58	1986
Most walks	812	1949
Most strikeouts	1,266	2001
Fielding		
Most errors	401	1901
Fewest errors	91	1996
Most double plays	214	1956
Highest fielding average	.986	1995
General		
Most games won	114	1998
Most games lost	103	1908
Highest win pct	.714	1927
Lowest win pct	.329	1912

GAME, INNING

Batting		
Most runs, game	25	5-24-36
Most runs, inning	14	7-6-20
Most hits, game	30	9-28-23
Most home runs, game	8	6-28-39
Most total bases, game	53	6-28-39

Mickey Mantle's 536 career home runs rank only second on the Yankees' career list—thanks to Babe Ruth.

CAREER LEADERS

BATTING

Games	
Mickey Mantle	2,401
Lou Gehrig	2,164
Yogi Berra	2,116
Babe Ruth	2,084
Roy White	1,881
Bill Dickey	1,789
Don Mattingly	1,785
Joe DiMaggio	1,736
Willie Randolph	1,694
Frankie Crosetti	1,683

At-bats	
Mickey Mantle	8,102
Lou Gehrig	8,001
Yogi Berra	7,546
Babe Ruth	7,217
Don Mattingly	7,003
Joe DiMaggio	6,821
Roy White	6,650
Willie Randolph	6,303
Bill Dickey	6,300
Frankie Crosetti	6,277

Runs	
Babe Ruth	1,959
Lou Gehrig	1,888
Mickey Mantle	1,677
Joe DiMaggio	1,390
Earle Combs	1,186
Yogi Berra	1,174
Bernie Williams	1,066
Willie Randolph	1,027
Don Mattingly	1,007
Frankie Crosetti	1,006
Roy White	964

Hits	
Lou Gehrig	2,721
Babe Ruth	2,518
Mickey Mantle	2,415
Joe DiMaggio	2,214
Don Mattingly	2,153
Yogi Berra	2,148
Bill Dickey	1,969
Earle Combs	1,866
Bernie Williams	1,833
Roy White	1,803

Doubles	
Lou Gehrig	534
Don Mattingly	442
Babe Ruth	424
Joe DiMaggio	389
Bernie Williams	353
Mickey Mantle	344
Bill Dickey	343
Bob Meusel	338
Tony Lazzeri	327
Yogi Berra	321

Triples	
Lou Gehrig	163
Earle Combs	154
Joe DiMaggio	131
Wally Pipp	121
Tony Lazzeri	115
Babe Ruth	106
Bob Meusel	87
Tommy Henrich	73
Bill Dickey	72
Mickey Mantle	72

Home runs	
Babe Ruth	659
Mickey Mantle	536
Lou Gehrig	493
Joe DiMaggio	361
Yogi Berra	358
Graig Nettles	250
Bernie Williams	226
Don Mattingly	222
Dave Winfield	205
Roger Maris	203

Total bases	
Babe Ruth	5,131
Lou Gehrig	5,060
Mickey Mantle	4,511
Joe DiMaggio	3,948
Yogi Berra	3,641
Don Mattingly	3,301
Bill Dickey	3,062
Bernie Williams	2,968
Tony Lazzeri	2,848
Roy White	2,685

Runs batted in	
Lou Gehrig	1,995
Babe Ruth	1,971
Joe DiMaggio	1,537
Mickey Mantle	1,509
Yogi Berra	1,430
Bill Dickey	1,209
Tony Lazzeri	1,154
Don Mattingly	1,099
Bob Meusel	1,005
Bernie Williams	998

Extra-base hits	
Lou Gehrig	1,190
Babe Ruth	1,189
Mickey Mantle	952
Joe DiMaggio	881
Yogi Berra	728
Don Mattingly	684
Bernie Williams	631
Bill Dickey	617
Tony Lazzeri	611
Bob Meusel	571

Batting average

(Minimum 500 games)

Player	Avg.
Babe Ruth	.349
Lou Gehrig	.340
Earle Combs	.325
Joe DiMaggio	.325
Derek Jeter	.317
Wade Boggs	.313
Bill Dickey	.313
Bob Meusel	.311
Bernie Williams	.308
Don Mattingly	.307

Stolen bases

Player	SB
Rickey Henderson	326
Willie Randolph	251
Hal Chase	248
Roy White	233
Ben Chapman	184
Wid Conroy	184
Fritz Maisel	183
Derek Jeter	167
Mickey Mantle	153
Horace Clarke	151
Roberto Kelly	151

PITCHING

Earned-run average

(Minimum 1,000 innings)

Player	ERA
Russ Ford	2.54
Jack Chesbro	2.58
Al Orth	2.72
Tiny Bonham	2.73
Whitey Ford	2.75
Spud Chandler	2.84
Ray Fisher	2.91
Mel Stottlemyre	2.97
Ray Caldwell	3.00
Fritz Peterson	3.10

Wins

Player	W
Whitey Ford	236
Red Ruffing	231
Lefty Gomez	189
Ron Guidry	170
Bob Shawkey	168
Mel Stottlemyre	164
Herb Pennock	162
Waite Hoyt	157
Allie Reynolds	131
Jack Chesbro	128
Andy Pettitte	128

Losses

Player	L
Mel Stottlemyre	139
Bob Shawkey	131
Red Ruffing	124
Whitey Ford	106
Fritz Peterson	106
Lefty Gomez	101
Ray Caldwell	99
Waite Hoyt	98
Jack Chesbro	93
Jack Warhop	92

Innings pitched

Player	IP
Whitey Ford	3,170.1
Red Ruffing	3,168.2
Mel Stottlemyre	2,661.1
Lefty Gomez	2,498.1
Bob Shawkey	2,488.2
Ron Guidry	2,392.0
Waite Hoyt	2,272.1
Herb Pennock	2,203.1
Jack Chesbro	1,952.0
Fritz Peterson	1,857.1

Strikeouts

Player	SO
Whitey Ford	1,956
Ron Guidry	1,778
Red Ruffing	1,526
Lefty Gomez	1,468
Mel Stottlemyre	1,257
Bob Shawkey	1,163
Andy Pettitte	1,095
Al Downing	1,028
Allie Reynolds	967
Dave Righetti	940

Bases on balls

Player	BB
Lefty Gomez	1,090
Whitey Ford	1,086
Red Ruffing	1,066
Bob Shawkey	855
Allie Reynolds	819
Mel Stottlemyre	809
Tommy Byrne	763
Bob Turley	761
Ron Guidry	633
Waite Hoyt	631

Games

Player	G
Dave Righetti	522
Whitey Ford	498
Red Ruffing	426
Sparky Lyle	420
Bob Shawkey	415
Mariano Rivera	448
Mike Stanton	428
Johnny Murphy	383
Ron Guidry	368
Lefty Gomez	367

Shutouts

Player	ShO
Whitey Ford	45
Red Ruffing	40
Mel Stottlemyre	40
Lefty Gomez	28
Allie Reynolds	27
Spud Chandler	26
Ron Guidry	26
Bob Shawkey	26
Vic Raschi	24
Bob Turley	21

Saves

Player	SV
Mariano Rivera	243
Dave Righetti	224
Rich Gossage	150
Sparky Lyle	141
Johnny Murphy	104
Steve Farr	78
Joe Page	76
John Wetteland	74
Lindy McDaniel	58
Luis Arroyo	43
Ryne Duren	43

YANKEES YEAR-BY-YEAR

				Games		Leaders					
Year	W	L	Place	Back	Manager	Batting avg.	Hits	Home runs	RBIs	Wins	ERA
							BALTIMORE ORIOLES				
1901	68	65	5th	13½	McGraw	Donlin, .341	Seymour, 167	Williams, 7	Williams, 96	McGinnity, 26	McGinnity, 3.56
1902	50	88	8th	34	McGraw, Robinson	Selbach, .320	Selbach, 161	Williams, 8	Williams, 83	McGinnity, 13	McGinnity, 3.44
							HIGHLANDERS/YANKEES				
1903	72	62	4th	17	Griffith	Keeler, .318	Keeler, 164	McFarland, 5	Williams, 82	Chesbro, 21	Griffith, 2.70
1904	92	59	2nd	1½	Griffith	Keeler, .343	Keeler, 185	Ganzel, 6	Anderson, 82	Chesbro, 41	Chesbro, 1.82
1905	71	78	6th	21½	Griffith	Keeler, .302	Keeler, 169	Williams, 6	Williams, 60	Chesbro, 20	Griffity, 1.68
1906	90	61	2nd	3	Griffith	Chase, .323	Chase, 193	Conroy, 4	Williams, 77	Orth, 27	Clarkson, 2.32
1907	70	78	5th	21	Griffith	Chase, .287	Chase, 143	Hoffman, 5	Chase, 68	Orth, 14	Chesbro, 2.53
1908	51	103	8th	39½	Griffith, Elberfeld	Hemphill, .297	Hemphill, 150	Niles, 4	Hemphill, 44	Chesbro, 14	Chesbro, 2.93
1909	74	77	5th	23½	Stallings	Chase, .283	Engle, 137	Chase, Demmitt, 4	Engle, 71	Lake, 14	Lake, 1.88
1910	88	63	2nd	14½	Stallings, Chase	Knight, .312	Chase, 152	Cree, Wolter, 4	Chase, 73	Ford, 26	Ford, 1.65
1911	76	76	6th	25½	Chase	Cree, .348	Cree, 181	Cree, Wolter, 4	Hartzell, 91	Ford, 22	Ford, 2.28
1912	50	102	8th	55	Wolverton	Chase, Daniels, .274	Chase, 143	Zinn, 6	Chase, 58	Ford, 13	McConnell, 2.75
1913	57	94	7th	38	Chance	Cree, .272	Cree, 145	Sweeney, Wolter, 2	Cree, 63	Fisher, Ford, 11	Caldwell, 2.41
1914	70	84	*6th	30	Chance, Peckinpaugh	Cook, .283	Cook, 133	Peckinpaugh, 3	Peckinpaugh, 51	Caldwell, 17	Caldwell, 1.94
1915	69	83	5th	32½	Donovan	Maisel, .281	Maisel, 149	Peckinpaugh, 5	Pipp, 58	Caldwell, 19	Fisher, 2.11
1916	80	74	4th	11	Donovan	Baker, .269	Pipp, 143	Pipp, 12	Pipp, 99	Shawkey, 23	Cullop, 2.05
1917	71	82	6th	28½	Donovan	Baker, .306	Baker, 154	Baker, 6	Baker, 68	Mogridge, 16	Mogridge, 2.18
1918	60	63	4th	13½	Huggins	Baker, .306	Baker, 154	Baker, 6	Baker, 68	Mogridge, 16	Mogridge, 2.18
1919	80	59	3rd	7½	Huggins	Peckinpaugh, .305	Baker, 166	Baker, 10	Baker, 78	Shawkey, 20	Mays, 1.65
1920	95	59	3rd	3	Huggins	Ruth, .376	Pratt, 180	Ruth, 54	Ruth, 137	Mays, 26	Shawkey, 2.45
1921	98	55	1st	+4½	Huggins	Ruth, .378	Ruth, 204	Ruth, 59	Ruth, 171	Mays, 27	Mays, 3.05
1922	94	60	1st	+1	Huggins	Pipp, .329	Pipp, 190	Ruth, 35	Ruth, 96	Bush, 26	Shawkey, 2.91
1923	98	54	1st	+16	Huggins	Ruth, .393	Ruth, 205	Ruth, 41	Ruth, 131	Jones, 21	Hoyt, 3.02
1924	89	63	2nd	2	Huggins	Ruth, .378	Ruth, 200	Ruth, 46	Ruth, 121	Pennock, 21	Pennock, 2.83
1925	69	85	7th	28½	Huggins	Combs, .342	Combs, 203	Meusel, 33	Meusel, 138	Pennock, 16	Pennock, 2.96
1926	91	63	1st	+3	Huggins	Ruth, .372	Ruth, 184	Ruth, 47	Ruth, 146	Pennock, 23	Shocker, 3.38
1927	110	44	1st	+19	Huggins	Gehrig, .373	Combs, 231	Ruth, 60	Gehrig, 175	Hoyt, 22	W. Moore, 2.28
1928	101	53	1st	+2½	Huggins	Gehrig, .374	Gehrig, 210	Ruth, 54	Gehrig, Ruth, 142	Pipgras, 24	Pennock, 2.56
1929	88	66	2nd	18	Huggins, Fletcher	Lazzeri, .354	Combs, 202	Ruth, 46	Ruth, 154	Pipgras, 18	Zachary, 2.48
1930	86	68	3rd	16	Shawkey	Gehrig, .379	Gehrig, 220	Ruth, 49	Gehrig, 174	Pipgras, Ruffing, 15	Pipgras, 4.11
1931	94	59	2nd	13½	McCarthy	Ruth, .373	Gehrig, 211	Gehrig, Ruth, 46	Gehrig, 184	Gomez, 21	Gomez, 2.67
1932	107	47	1st	+13	McCarthy	Gehrig, .349	Gehrig, 208	Ruth, 41	Gehrig, 151	Gomez, 24	Ruffing, 3.09
1933	91	59	2nd	7	McCarthy	Gehrig, .334	Gehrig, 198	Ruth, 34	Gehrig, 139	Gomez, 16	Gomez, 3.18
1934	94	60	2nd	7	McCarthy	Gehrig, .363	Gehrig, 210	Gehrig, 49	Gehrig, 165	Gomez, 26	Gomez, 2.33
1935	89	60	2nd	3	McCarthy	Gehrig, .329	Rolfe, 192	Gehrig, 30	Gehrig, 119	Ruffing, 16	Ruffing, 3.12
1936	102	51	1st	+19½	McCarthy	Dickey, .362	DiMaggio, 206	Gehrig, 49	Gehrig, 152	Ruffing, 20	Pearson, 3.71
1937	102	52	1st	+13	McCarthy	Gehrig, .351	DiMaggio, 215	DiMaggio, 46	DiMaggio, 167	Gomez, 21	Gomez, 2.33
1938	99	53	1st	+9½	McCarthy	DiMaggio, .324	Rolfe, 196	DiMaggio, 32	DiMaggio, 140	Ruffing, 21	Ruffing, 3.31
1939	106	45	1st	+17	McCarthy	DiMaggio, .381	Rolfe, 213	DiMaggio, 30	DiMaggio, 126	Ruffing, 21	Russo, 2.41
1940	88	66	3rd	2	McCarthy	DiMaggio, .352	DiMaggio, 179	DiMaggio, 31	DiMaggio, 133	Ruffing, 15	Bonham, 1.90
1941	101	53	1st	+17	McCarthy	DiMaggio, .357	DiMaggio, 193	Keller, 33	DiMaggio, 125	Gomez, Ruffing, 15	Bonham, 2.98
1942	103	51	1st	+9	McCarthy	Gordon, .322	DiMaggio, 186	Keller, 26	DiMaggio, 114	Bonham, 21	Bonham, 2.27
1943	98	56	1st	+13½	McCarthy	B. Johnson, .280	B. Johnson, 166	Keller, 31	Etten, 107	Chandler, 20	Chandler, 1.64
1944	83	71	3rd	6	McCarthy	Stirnweiss, .319	Stirnweiss, 205	Etten, 22	Lindell, 103	Borowy, 17	Borowy, 2.64
1945	81	71	4th	6½	McCarthy	Stirnweiss, .309	Stirnweiss, 195	Etten, 18	Etten, 111	Bevens, 13	Page, 2.82
1946	87	67	3rd	17	McCarthy, Dickey, Neun	DiMaggio, .290	Keller, 148	Keller, 30	Keller, 101	Chandler, 20	Chandler, 2.10
1947	97	57	1st	+12	Harris	DiMaggio, .315	DiMaggio, 168	DiMaggio, 20	Henrich, 98	Reynolds, 19	Chandler, 2.46
1948	94	60	3rd	2½	Harris	DiMaggio, .320	DiMaggio, 190	DiMaggio, 39	DiMaggio, 155	Raschi, 19	Byrne, 3.30
1949	97	57	1st	+1	Stengel	Henrich, .287	Rizzuto, 169	Henrich, 24	Berra, 91	Raschi, 21	Page, 2.59
1950	98	56	1st	+3	Stengel	Rizzuto, .324	Rizzuto, 200	DiMaggio, 32	Berra, 124	Raschi, 21	Ford, 2.81
1951	98	56	1st	+5	Stengel	McDougald, .306	Berra, 161	Berra, 27	Berra, 88	Lopat, Raschi, 21	Lopat, 2.91
1952	95	59	1st	+2	Stengel	Mantle, .311	Mantle, 171	Berra, 30	Berra, 98	Reynolds, 20	Reynolds, 2.06
1953	99	52	1st	+8½	Stengel	Woodling, .306	McDougald, 154	Berra, 27	Berra, 108	Ford, 18	Lopat, 2.42
1954	103	51	2nd	8	Stengel	Noren, .319	Berra, 179	Mantle, 27	Berra, 125	Grim, 20	Ford, 2.82
1955	96	58	1st	+3	Stengel	Mantle, .306	Mantle, 158	Mantle, 37	Berra, 108	Ford, 18	Ford, 2.63

YANKEES YEAR-BY-YEAR

Year	W	L	Place	Games Back	Manager	Leaders: Batting avg.	Hits	Home runs	RBIs	Wins	ERA
1956	97	57	1st	+9	Stengel	Mantle, .353	Mantle, 188	Mantle, 52	Mantle, 130	Ford, 19	Ford, 2.47
1957	98	56	1st	+8	Stengel	Mantle, .365	Mantle, 173	Mantle, 34	Mantle, 94	Sturdivant, 16	Shantz, 2.45
1958	92	62	1st	+10	Stengel	Howard, .314	Mantle, 158	Mantle, 42	Mantle, 97	Turley, 21	Ford, 2.01
1959	79	75	3rd	15	Stengel	Richardson, .301	Mantle, 154	Mantle, 31	Lopez, 93	Ford, 16	Shantz, 2.38
1960	97	57	1st	+8	Stengel	Skowron, .309	Skowron, 166	Mantle, 40	Maris, 112	Ditmar, 15	Ditmar, 3.06
1961	109	53	1st	+8	Houk	Howard, .348	Richardson, 173	Maris, 61	Maris, 142	Ford, 25	Arroyo, 2.19
1962	96	66	1st	+5	Houk	Mantle, .321	Richardson, 209	Maris, 33	Maris, 100	Terry, 23	Ford, 2.90
1963	104	57	1st	+10½	Houk	Howard, .287	Richardson, 167	Howard, 28	Pepitone, 89	Ford, 24	Bouton, 2.53
1964	99	63	1st	+1	Berra	Howard, .313	Richardson, 181	Mantle, 35	Mantle, 111	Bouton, 18	Stottlemyre, 2.06
1965	77	85	6th	25	Keane	Tresh, .279	Tresh, 168	Tresh, 26	Tresh, 74	Stottlemyre, 20	Stottlemyre, 2.63
1966	70	89	10th	26½	Keane, Houk	Howard, .256	Richardson, 153	Pepitone, 31	Pepitone, 83	Peterson, Stottlemyre, 12	Bouton, 2.69
1967	72	90	9th	20	Houk	Clarke, .272	Clarke, 160	Mantle, 22	Pepitone, 64	Stottlemyre, 15	Monbouquette, 2.36
1968	83	79	5th	20	Houk	White, .267	White, 154	Mantle, 18	White, 62	Stottlemyre, 21	Bahnsen, 2.05
								EAST DIVISION			
1969	80	81	5th	28½	Houk	White, .290	Clarke, 183	Pepitone, 27	Murcer, 62	Stottlemyre, 20	Peterson, 2.55
1970	93	69	2nd	15	Houk	Munson, .302	White, 180	Murcer, 23	White, 94	Peterson, 20	McDaniel, 2.01
1971	82	80	4th	21	Houk	Murcer, .331	Murcer, 175	Murcer, 25	Murcer, 94	Stottlemyre, 16	Stottlemyre, 2.87
1972	79	76	4th	6½	Houk	Murcer, .292	Murcer, 171	Murcer, 33	Murcer, 96	Peterson, 17	Lyle, 1.92
1973	80	82	4th	17	Houk	Murcer, .304	Murcer, 187	Murcer, Nettles, 22	Murcer, 95	Stottlemyre, 16	Beene, 1.68
1974	89	73	2nd	2	Virdon	Piniella, .305	Murcer, 166	Nettles, 22	Murcer, 88	Dobson, Medich, 19	Lyle, 1.66
1975	83	77	3rd	12	Virdon, Martin	Munson, .318	Munson, 190	Bonds, 32	Munson, 102	Hunter, 23	Hunter, 2.58
1976	97	62	†1st	+10½	Martin	Rivers, .312	Chambliss, 188	Nettles, 32	Munson, 105	Figueroa, 19	Lyle, 2.26
1977	100	62	†1st	+2½	Martin	Rivers, .326	Rivers, 184	Nettles, 37	Jackson, 110	Figueroa, Guidry, 16	Lyle, 2.17
1978	100	63	‡†1st	+1	Martin, Lemon	Piniella, .314	Munson, 183	Jackson, Nettles, 27	Jackson, 97	Guidry, 25	Guidry, 1.74
1979	89	71	4th	13½	Lemon, Martin	Jackson, Piniella, .297	Chambliss, Randolph, 155	Jackson, 29	Jackson, 89	John, 21	Guidry, 2.78
1980	103	59	§1st	+3	Howser	Watson, .307	Jackson, 154	Jackson, 41	Jackson, 111	John, 22	May, 2.46
1981	59	48	∞†1st/6th	—	Michael, Lemon	Winfield, .294	Winfield, 114	Jackson, Nettles, 15	Winfield, 68	Guidry, 11	Righetti, 2.05
1982	79	83	5th	16	Lemon, Michael, King	Mumphrey, .300	Randolph, 155	Winfield, 37	Winfield, 106	Guidry, 14	Gossage, 2.23
1983	91	71	3rd	7	Martin	Griffey, .306	Winfield, 169	Winfield, 32	Winfield, 116	Guidry, 21	Fontenot, 3.33
1984	87	75	3rd	17	Berra	Mattingly, .343	Mattingly, 207	Baylor, 27	Mattingly, 110	Niekro, 16	Righetti, 2.34
1985	97	64	2nd	2	Berra, Martin	Mattingly, .324	Mattingly, 211	Mattingly, 35	Mattingly, 145	Guidry, 22	Fisher, 2.38
1986	90	72	2nd	5½	Piniella	Mattingly, .352	Mattingly, 238	Mattingly, 31	Mattingly, 113	Rasmussen, 18	Righetti, 2.45
1987	89	73	4th	9	Piniella	Mattingly, .327	Mattingly, 186	Pagliarulo, 32	Mattingly, 115	Rhoden, 16	Stoddard, 3.50
1988	85	76	5th	3½	Martin, Piniella	Winfield, .322	Mattingly, 186	Clark, 27	Winfield, 107	Candelaria, 13	Candelaria, 3.38
1989	74	87	5th	14½	Green, Dent	Sax, .315	Sax, 205	Mattingly, 23	Mattingly, 113	Hawkins, 15	Guetterman, 2.45
1990	67	95	7th	21	Dent, Merrill	Kelly, .285	Kelly, 183	Barfield, 25	Barfield, 78	Guetterman, 11	Guetterman, 3.39
1991	71	91	5th	20	Merrill	Sax, .304	Sax, 198	Nokes, 24	Hall, 80	Sanderson, 16	Habyan, 2.30
1992	76	86	*4th	20	Showalter	Mattingly, .288	Mattingly, 184	Tartabull, 25	Mattingly, 86	Perez, 13	Perez, 2.87
1993	88	74	2nd	7	Showalter	O'Neill, .311	Boggs, 169	Tartabull, 31	Tartabull, 102	Key, 18	Key, 3.00
1994	70	43	1st	+6½	Showalter	O'Neill, .359	O'Neill, 132	O'Neill, 21	O'Neill, 83	Key, 17	Key, 3.27
1995	79	65	▲2nd	7	Showalter	Boggs, .324	B. Williams, 173	O'Neill, 22	O'Neill, 96	Cone, 18	Cone, 3.57
1996	92	70	◆†1st	+4	Torre	Duncan, .340	Jeter, 183	B. Williams, 29	Martinez, 117	Pettitte, 21	M. Rivera, 2.09
1997	96	66	▲2nd	2	Torre	B. Williams, .328	Jeter, 190	Martinez, 44	Martinez, 141	Pettitte, 18	Cone, 2.82
1998	114	48	◆†1st	+22	Torre	B. Williams, .339	Jeter, 203	Martinez, 28	Martinez, 123	Cone, 20	O. Hernandez, 3.13
1999	98	64	◆†1st	+4	Torre	Jeter, .349	Jeter, 219	Martinez, 28	B. Williams, 115	O. Hernandez, 17	Cone, 3.44
2000	87	74	◆†1st	+2½	Torre	Jeter, .339	Jeter, 201	B. Williams, 30	B. Williams, 121	Pettitte, 19	Clemens, 3.70
2001	95	65	◆†1st	+6½	Torre	Jeter, .311	Jeter, 191	Martinez, 34	Martinez, 113	Clemens, 20	Mussina, 3.15
2002	103	58	▲1st	+10½	Torre	B. Williams, .333	B. Williams, 204	Giambi, 41	Giambi, 122	Wells, 19	Wells, 3.75

* Tied for position. † Won Championship Series. ‡ Won division playoff. § Lost Championship Series. ∞ First half 34-22; second half 25-26. ▲ Lost Division Series. ◆ Won Division Series.

Note: Batting average minimum 350 at-bats; ERA minimum 90 innings pitched.

OAKLAND ATHLETICS

FRANCHISE CHRONOLOGY

First season: 1901, in Philadelphia, as a member of the new American League. The Athletics lost their big-league debut to Washington, 5-1, and went on to a 74-62 record and fourth-place finish.
1902-54: A team of extremes, Connie Mack's Athletics won nine pennants and five World Series—and finished eighth 18 times. Those first and last-place finishes accounted for 27 of the team's 54 seasons in Philadelphia. The powerful A's won three World Series from 1910 through 1913 and consecutive championships in 1929 and '30. But from 1934 through 1954, the A's never got their heads above fourth place and finished either seventh or eighth 14 times.
1955-1967: The A's defeated Detroit, 6-2, in their Kansas City debut and completed their first season in sixth place with a 63-91 record. That was as good as it got. The A's never finished above seventh place in the remainder of their Kansas City existence and never came closer than 19 games to the A.L. champion.
1968-present: The A's lost their Oakland debut to Baltimore, 3-1, but went on to record their first above-.500 record (82-80) since 1952. Young and talented, they would return to prominence and claim 12 West Division titles, six pennants and four World Series championships, including three straight fall classic titles from 1972 through 1974.

Manager Connie Mack.

A'S VS. OPPONENTS BY DECADE

	Indians	Orioles	Red Sox	Tigers	Twins	White Sox	Yankees	Angels	Rangers	Brewers	Royals	Blue Jays	Mariners	Devil Rays	Interleague	Decade Record
1901-09	105-86	105-79	102-88	102-80	128-56	98-92	94-87									734-568
1910-19	105-110	120-93	84-129	99-116	108-101	90-125	104-100									710-774
1920-29	106-113	114-105	131-86	114-105	105-108	119-100	81-137									770-754
1930-39	106-114	127-88	99-116	106-111	91-124	118-102	76-140									723-795
1940-49	80-136	105-115	83-137	90-130	95-125	108-112	77-143									638-898
1950-59	67-153	109-110	79-141	98-122	113-107	96-124	62-158									624-915
1960-69	85-92	69-107	82-96	69-109	79-105	66-118	61-117	74-88	78-77	13-5	10-8					686-922
1970-79	70-46	50-66	54-63	60-56	76-91	89-76	54-63	97-72	78-76	74-54	90-79	18-15	28-15			838-772
1980-89	63-50	57-63	52-68	53-58	69-58	60-70	54-61	70-57	57-66	64-50	59-64	67-53	78-46			803-764
1990-99	45-62	54-65	46-71	53-53	60-58	57-60	59-58	68-55	61-63	35-50	68-53	55-53	71-50	14-7	27-23	773-781
2000-02	14-12	20-10	13-15	16-8	17-13	18-9	13-14	33-20	27-23		22-8	16-12	26-25	22-5	39-15	296-189
Totals	846-974	930-901	825-1010	860-948	941-946	919-988	735-1078	342-292	301-305	186-159	249-212	156-133	203-136	36-12	66-38	7595-8132

Interleague results: 9-3 vs. Diamondbacks, 3-0 vs. Reds, 9-7 vs. Rockies, 3-0 vs. Astros, 9-7 vs. Dodgers, 3-0 vs. Brewers, 3-0 vs. Pirates, 11-5 vs. Padres, 16-16 vs. Giants.

MANAGERS

(Philadelphia Athletics, 1901-54)
(Kansas City Athletics, 1955-67)

Name	*Years*	*Record*
Connie Mack	1901-50	3582-3814
Jimmie Dykes	1951-53	208-254
Eddie Joost	1954	51-103
Lou Boudreau	1955-57	151-260
Harry Craft	1957-59	162-196
Bob Elliott	1960	58-96
Joe Gordon	1961	26-33
Hank Bauer	1961-62, 1969	187-226
Eddie Lopat	1963-64	90-124
Mel McGaha	1964-65	45-91
Haywood Sullivan	1965	54-82
Alvin Dark	1966-67, 1974-75	314-291
Luke Appling	1967	10-30
Bob Kennedy	1968	82-80
John McNamara	1969-70	97-78
Dick Williams	1971-73	288-190
Chuck Tanner	1976	87-74
Jack McKeon	1977, 1978	71-105
Bobby Winkles	1977-78	61-86
Jim Marshall	1979	54-108
Billy Martin	1980-82	215-218
Steve Boros	1983-84	94-112
Jackie Moore	1984-86	163-190
Tony La Russa	1986-95	798-673
Art Howe	1996-2002	600-533

WORLD SERIES CHAMPIONS

Year	*Loser*	*Length*	*MVP*
1910	Chicago	5 games	None
1911	N.Y. Giants	6 games	None
1913	N.Y. Giants	5 games	None
1929	Chicago	5 games	None
1930	St. Louis	6 games	None
1972	Cincinnati	7 games	Tenace
1973	N.Y. Mets	7 games	Jackson
1974	Los Angeles	5 games	Fingers
1989	San Francisco	4 games	Stewart

A.L. PENNANT WINNERS

Year	*Record*	*Manager*	*Series Result*
1902	83-53	Mack	None
1905	92-56	Mack	Lost to Giants
1910	102-48	Mack	Defeated Cubs
1911	101-50	Mack	Defeated Giants
1913	96-57	Mack	Defeated Giants
1914	99-53	Mack	Lost to Braves
1929	104-46	Mack	Defeated Cubs

A.L. PENNANT WINNERS—*cont'd.*

Year	*Record*	*Manager*	*Series Result*
1930	102-52	Mack	Defeated Cardinals
1931	107-45	Mack	Lost to Cardinals
1972	93-62	Williams	Defeated Reds
1973	94-68	Williams	Defeated Mets
1974	90-72	Dark	Defeated Dodgers
1988	104-58	La Russa	Lost to Dodgers
1989	99-63	La Russa	Defeated Giants
1990	103-59	La Russa	Lost to Reds

WEST DIVISION CHAMPIONS

Year	*Record*	*Manager*	*ALCS Result*
1971	101-60	Williams	Lost to Orioles
1972	93-62	Williams	Defeated Tigers
1973	94-68	Williams	Defeated Orioles
1974	90-72	Dark	Defeated Orioles
1975	98-64	Dark	Lost to Red Sox
1981*	64-45	Martin	Lost to Yankees
1988	104-58	La Russa	Defeated Red Sox
1989	99-63	La Russa	Defeated Blue Jays
1990	103-59	La Russa	Defeated Red Sox
1992	96-66	La Russa	Lost to Blue Jays
2000	91-70	Howe	Lost in Div. Series
2002	103-59	Howe	Lost in Div. Series

* First-half champion; won division playoff from Royals.

WILD-CARD QUALIFIERS

Year	*Record*	*Manager*	*Div. Series Result*
2001	102-60	Howe	Lost to Yankees

ATTENDANCE HIGHS

Total	*Season*	*Park*
2,900,217	1990	Oakland Coliseum
2,713,493	1991	Oakland Coliseum
2,667,255	1989	Oakland Coliseum
2,494,160	1992	Oakland Coliseum
2,287,335	1988	Oakland Coliseum

BALLPARK CHRONOLOGY

Network Associates Coliseum, formerly Oakland Alameda County Coliseum (1968-present)

Capacity: 43,662.
First game: Baltimore 4, A's 1 (April 17, 1968).
First batter: Curt Blefary, Orioles.
First hit: Boog Powell, Orioles (home run).
First run: Boog Powell, Orioles (2nd inning).
First home run: Boog Powell, Orioles.
First winning pitcher: Dave McNally, Orioles.
First-season attendance: 837,466.

Columbia Park, Philadelphia (1901-08)

Capacity: 9,500.
First game: Washington 5, Athletics 1 (April 26, 1901).
First-season attendance: 206,329.

Shibe Park, Philadelphia (1909-54)

Capacity: 33,608.
First game: Athletics 8, Boston 1 (April 12, 1909).
First-season attendance: 517,653.

Municipal Stadium, Kansas City (1955-67)

Capacity: 35,020.
First game: Athletics 6, Detroit 2 (April 12, 1955).
First-season attendance: 1,393,054.

Note: Shibe Park was changed to Connie Mack Stadium in 1953.

A.L. MVPs

Lefty Grove, P, 1931
Jimmie Foxx, 1B, 1932
Jimmie Foxx, 1B, 1933
Bobby Shantz, P, 1952
Vida Blue, P, 1971
Reggie Jackson, OF, 1973
Jose Canseco, OF, 1988
Rickey Henderson, OF, 1990
Dennis Eckersley, P, 1992
Jason Giambi, 1B, 2000
Miguel Tejada, SS, 2002

CY YOUNG WINNERS

Vida Blue, LH, 1971
Catfish Hunter, RH, 1974
Bob Welch, RH, 1990
Dennis Eckersley, RH, 1992
Barry Zito, LH, 2002

ROOKIES OF THE YEAR

Harry Byrd, P, 1952
Jose Canseco, OF, 1986
Mark McGwire, 1B, 1987
Walt Weiss, SS, 1988
Ben Grieve, OF, 1998

MANAGERS OF THE YEAR

Tony La Russa, 1988
Tony La Russa, 1992

RETIRED UNIFORMS

No.	*Name*	*Pos.*
27	Catfish Hunter	P
34	Rollie Fingers	P

MILESTONE PERFORMANCES

30-plus home runs

58—Jimmie Foxx 1932
52—Mark McGwire 1996
49—Mark McGwire 1987
48—Jimmie Foxx 1933
47—Reggie Jackson 1969
44—Jimmie Foxx 1934
Jose Canseco 1991
43—Jason Giambi 2000
42—Gus Zernial 1953
Jose Canseco 1988
Mark McGwire 1992
39—Mark McGwire 1990
Mark McGwire 1995
38—Bob Cerv 1958
Matt Stairs 1999
Jason Giambi 2001
37—Tilly Walker 1922
Jimmie Foxx 1930
Jose Canseco 1990
36—Al Simmons 1930
Jimmie Foxx 1935
Reggie Jackson 1975
Geronimo Berroa 1996
35—Al Simmons 1932
Tony Armas 1980
Dave Kingman 1984, 1986
Terry Steinbach 1996
John Jaha 1999
34—Al Simmons 1929
Bob Johnson 1934
Rocky Colavito 1964
Mark McGwire 1997
Eric Chavez 2002
Miguel Tejada 2002
33—Jimmie Foxx 1929
Gus Zernial 1951
Dwayne Murphy 1984
Jose Canseco 1986
Mark McGwire 1989
Jason Giambi 1999
32—Reggie Jackson 1971, 1973
Mark McGwire 1988
Eric Chavez 2001
31—Bob Johnson 1940
Sal Bando 1969
Jose Canseco 1987
Miguel Tejada 2001
30—Jimmie Foxx 1931
Bob Johnson 1938
Gus Zernial 1955
Dave Kingman 1985
Miguel Tejada 2000

100-plus RBIs

169—Jimmie Foxx 1932
165—Al Simmons 1930
163—Jimmie Foxx 1933
157—Al Simmons 1929
156—Jimmie Foxx 1930
151—Al Simmons 1932
137—Jason Giambi 2000
131—Miguel Tejada 2002
130—Frank Baker 1912
Jimmie Foxx 1934
129—Al Simmons 1925
Gus Zernial *1951
128—Al Simmons 1931
125—Nap Lajoie 1901
124—Jose Canseco 1988
123—Jason Giambi 1999
122—Jose Canseco 1991
121—Bob Johnson 1936
120—Jimmie Foxx 1931
Hank Majeski 1948
Jason Giambi 2001
118—Reggie Jackson 1969
Dave Kingman 1984
Mark McGwire 1987
117—Frank Baker 1913
Jimmie Foxx 1929
Norm Siebern 1962
Reggie Jackson 1973
Jose Canseco 1986
115—Frank Baker 1911
Joe Hauser 1924
Jimmie Foxx 1935
Miguel Tejada 2000
114—Bob Johnson 1939
Eric Chavez 2001
113—Bob Johnson 1938
Sal Bando 1969
Jose Canseco 1987
Mark McGwire 1996
Miguel Tejada 2001
112—Mickey Cochrane 1932
111—John Jaha 1999
110—Jason Giambi 1998
109—Al Simmons 1926
Bob Johnson 1935
Tony Armas 1980
Eric Chavez 2002
108—Lave Cross 1902
Al Simmons 1927
Bob Johnson 1937
Sam Chapman 1949
Gus Zernial 1953
Mark McGwire 1990
107—Al Simmons 1928
Bob Johnson 1941
106—Sam Chapman 1941
Geronimo Berroa 1996
Matt Stairs 1998
105—Harry Simpson 1956
104—Bob Cerv 1958
Reggie Jackson 1975
Mark McGwire 1992
Ben Grieve 2000
103—Bob Johnson 1940
Sal Bando 1974
102—Al Simmons 1924
Eddie Robinson 1953
Rocky Colavito 1964
Matt Stairs 1999
101—Stuffy McInnis 1912
Tilly Walker 1921
Jose Canseco 1990
Ruben Sierra 1993
100—Bing Miller 1930
Gus Zernial 1952
Terry Steinbach 1996

*125 with Athletics; 4 with White Sox.

20-plus victories

1901—Chick Fraser 22-16
1902—Rube Waddell 24-7
Eddie Plank 20-15
1903—Eddie Plank 23-16
Rube Waddell 21-16
1904—Eddie Plank 26-17
Rube Waddell 25-19
1905—Rube Waddell 27-10
Eddie Plank 24-12
1907—Eddie Plank 24-16
Jimmy Dygert 21-8
1910—Jack Coombs 31-9
Chief Bender 23-5
1911—Jack Coombs 28-12
Eddie Plank 23-8
1912—Eddie Plank 26-6
Jack Coombs 21-10
1913—Chief Bender 21-10
1918—Scott Perry 20-19
1922—Eddie Rommel 27-13
1925—Eddie Rommel 21-10
1927—Lefty Grove 20-13
1928—Lefty Grove 24-8
1929—George Earnshaw 24-8
Lefty Grove 20-6
1930—Lefty Grove 28-5
George Earnshaw 22-13
1931—Lefty Grove 31-4
George Earnshaw 21-7
Rube Walberg 20-12
1932—Lefty Grove 25-10
1933—Lefty Grove 24-8
1949—Alex Kellner 20-12
1952—Bobby Shantz 24-7
1971—Vida Blue 24-8
Catfish Hunter 21-11
1972—Catfish Hunter 21-7
1973—Catfish Hunter 21-5
Ken Holtzman 21-13
Vida Blue 20-9
1974—Catfish Hunter 25-12
1975—Vida Blue 22-11
1980—Mike Norris 22-9
1987—Dave Stewart 20-13
1988—Dave Stewart 21-12
1989—Dave Stewart 21-9
1990—Bob Welch 27-6
Dave Stewart 22-11
2000—Tim Hudson 20-6
2001—Mark Mulder 21-8
2002—Barry Zito 23-5

A.L. home run champions

1901—Nap Lajoie 14
1902—Socks Seybold 16
1904—Harry Davis 10
1905—Harry Davis 8
1906—Harry Davis 12
1907—Harry Davis 8
1911—Frank Baker 11
1912—Frank Baker *10
1913—Frank Baker 12
1914—Frank Baker 9
1918—Tilly Walker *11
1932—Jimmie Foxx 58
1933—Jimmie Foxx 48
1935—Jimmie Foxx *36
1951—Gus Zernial 33
1973—Reggie Jackson 32
1975—Reggie Jackson *36
1981—Tony Armas *22
1987—Mark McGwire 49
1988—Jose Canseco 42
1991—Jose Canseco *44
1996—Mark McGwire 52

* Tied for league lead

INDIVIDUAL SEASON, GAME RECORDS

SEASON

Batting

At-bats	670	Al Simmons	1932
Runs	152	Al Simmons	1930
Hits	253	Al Simmons	1925
Singles	174	Al Simmons	1925
Doubles	53	Al Simmons	1926
Triples	21	Frank Baker	1912
Home runs	58	Jimmie Foxx	1932
Home runs, rookie	49	Mark McGwire	1987
Grand slams	4	Jason Giambi	2000
Total bases	438	Jimmie Foxx	1932
RBIs	169	Jimmie Foxx	1932
Walks	149	Ed Joost	1949
Most strikeouts	175	Jose Canseco	1986
Fewest strikeouts	17	Dick Siebert	1942
Batting average	.426	Nap Lajoie	1901
Slugging pct.	.749	Jimmie Foxx	1932
Stolen bases	130	Rickey Henderson	1982

Pitching

Games	84	Billy Koch	2002
Complete games	39	Rube Waddell	1904
Innings	383	Rube Waddell	1904
Wins	31	Jack Coombs	1910
		Lefty Grove	1931
Losses	25	Scott Perry	1920
Winning pct.	.886 (31-4)	Lefty Grove	1931
Walks	168	Elmer Myers	1916
Strikeouts	349	Rube Waddell	1904
Shutouts	13	Jack Coombs	1910
Home runs allowed	40	Orlando Pena	1964
Lowest ERA	1.30	Jack Coombs	1910
Saves	51	Dennis Eckersley	1992

GAME

Batting

Runs	5	Last by Luis Polonia	9-9-88
Hits	6	Last by Joe DeMaestri	7-8-55
Doubles	4	Frankie Hayes	7-25-36
Triples	3	Bert Campaneris	8-29-67
Home runs	3	Last by Miguel Tejada	6-11-99
RBIs	10	Reggie Jackson	6-14-69
Total bases	16	Jimmie Foxx	7-10-32
Stolen bases	6	Eddie Collins	9-11-12, 9-22-12

A.L. RBI champions

1901—Nap Lajoie 125
1905—Harry Davis 83
1906—Harry Davis 96
1912—Frank Baker 130
1913—Frank Baker 117
1929—Al Simmons 157
1932—Jimmie Foxx 169
1933—Jimmie Foxx 163
1951—Gus Zernial *129
1973—Reggie Jackson 117
1988—Jose Canseco 124

*125 with Athletics; 4 with White Sox.

A.L. batting champions

1901—Nap Lajoie .426
1930—Al Simmons .381
1931—Al Simmons .390
1933—Jimmie Foxx .356
1951—Ferris Fain .344
1952—Ferris Fain .327

A.L. ERA champions

1905—Rube Waddell 1.48
1909—Harry Krause 1.39
1926—Lefty Grove 2.51
1929—Lefty Grove 2.81
1930—Lefty Grove 2.54
1931—Lefty Grove 2.06
1932—Lefty Grove 2.84
1970—Diego Segui 2.56
1971—Vida Blue 1.82
1974—Catfish Hunter 2.49
1981—Steve McCatty 2.32
1994—Steve Ontiveros 2.65

A.L. strikeout champions

1902—Rube Waddell 210
1903—Rube Waddell 302
1904—Rube Waddell 349
1905—Rube Waddell 287
1906—Rube Waddell 196
1907—Rube Waddell 232
1925—Lefty Grove 116
1926—Lefty Grove 194
1927—Lefty Grove 174
1928—Lefty Grove 183
1929—Lefty Grove 170
1930—Lefty Grove 209
1931—Lefty Grove 175

No-hit pitchers

(9 innings or more)
1905—Weldon Henley 6-0 vs. St. Louis
1910—Chief Bender 4-0 vs. Cleveland
1916—Joe Bush 5-0 vs. Cleveland
1945—Dick Fowler 1-0 vs. St. Louis
1947—Bill McCahan 3-0 vs. Washington
1968—Catfish Hunter 4-0 vs. Minnesota (Perfect)
1970—Vida Blue 6-0 vs. Minnesota
1975—Vida Blue-Glenn Abbott-Paul Lindblad-Rollie Fingers 5-0 vs. California
1983—Mike Warren 3-0 vs. Chicago
1990—Dave Stewart 5-0 vs. Toronto

Longest hitting streaks

29—Bill Lamar 1925
28—Bing Miller 1929
27—Socks Seybold 1901
Al Simmons 1931
26—Bob Johnson 1938
25—Jason Giambi 1997
24—Jimmie Foxx 1929
Ferris Fain 1952
Carney Lansford 1984
Miguel Tejada 2002
23—Al Simmons 1925
22—Al Simmons 1925
Doc Cramer 1932
Hector Lopez 1957
Vic Power 1958
21—Ty Cobb 1927
20—Wally Schang 1916
Wally Moses 1938
Dave Philley 1953
Hal Smith 1958
Vic Power *1958
Jerry Lumpe 1962

*Two teams

CAREER LEADERS

BATTING

Games
Bert Campaneris	1,795
Rickey Henderson	1,704
Jimmy Dykes	1,702
Sal Bando	1,468
Bob Johnson	1,459
Pete Suder	1,421
Harry Davis	1,413
Danny Murphy	1,412
Bing Miller	1,361
Elmer Valo	1,361

At-bats
Bert Campaneris	7,180
Rickey Henderson	6,140
Jimmy Dykes	6,023
Bob Johnson	5,428
Harry Davis	5,367
Sal Bando	5,145
Danny Murphy	5,138
Al Simmons	5,130
Pete Suder	5,085
Bing Miller	4,762

Runs
Rickey Henderson	1,270
Bob Johnson	997
Bert Campaneris	983
Jimmie Foxx	975
Al Simmons	969
Max Bishop	882
Jimmy Dykes	881
Mickey Cochrane	823
Harry Davis	811
Mark McGwire	773

Hits
Bert Campaneris	1,882
Al Simmons	1,827
Rickey Henderson	1,768
Jimmy Dykes	1,705
Bob Johnson	1,617
Harry Davis	1,500
Jimmie Foxx	1,492
Danny Murphy	1,489
Bing Miller	1,480
Mickey Cochrane	1,317
Carney Lansford	1,317

Doubles
Jimmy Dykes	365
Al Simmons	348
Harry Davis	319
Bob Johnson	307
Bing Miller	292
Rickey Henderson	289
Danny Murphy	279
Wally Moses	274
Bert Campaneris	270
Jimmie Foxx	257

Triples
Danny Murphy	102
Al Simmons	98
Frank Baker	88
Eddie Collins	85
Harry Davis	82
Jimmie Foxx	79
Rube Oldring	75
Topsy Hartsel	74
Bing Miller	74
Jimmy Dykes	73

Home runs
Mark McGwire	363
Jimmie Foxx	302
Reggie Jackson	269
Jose Canseco	254
Bob Johnson	252
Al Simmons	209
Sal Bando	192
Gus Zernial	191
Jason Giambi	187
Sam Chapman	174

Total bases
Al Simmons	2,998
Bob Johnson	2,824
Jimmie Foxx	2,813
Rickey Henderson	2,640
Bert Campaneris	2,502
Jimmy Dykes	2,474
Mark McGwire	2,451
Reggie Jackson	2,323
Bing Miller	2,202
Harry Davis	2,190

Runs batted in
Al Simmons	1,178
Jimmie Foxx	1,075
Bob Johnson	1,040
Mark McGwire	941
Sal Bando	796
Jose Canseco	793
Reggie Jackson	776
Jimmy Dykes	764
Bing Miller	762
Harry Davis	761

Extra-base hits
Al Simmons	655
Jimmie Foxx	638
Bob Johnson	631
Mark McGwire	563
Reggie Jackson	530
Jimmy Dykes	524
Rickey Henderson	497
Harry Davis	470
Bing Miller	460
Jose Canseco	448

Batting average
(Minimum 500 games)

Al Simmons	.356
Jimmie Foxx	.339
Eddie Collins	.337
Mickey Cochrane	.321
Frank Baker	.321
Stuffy McInnis	.313
Bing Miller	.311
Doc Cramer	.308
Jason Giambi	.308
Wally Moses	.307

Stolen bases
Rickey Henderson	867
Bert Campaneris	566
Eddie Collins	377
Billy North	232
Harry Davis	223
Topsy Hartsel	196
Rube Oldring	187
Danny Murphy	185
Frank Baker	172
Carney Lansford	146

PITCHING

Earned-run average
(Minimum 1,000 innings)

Rube Waddell	1.97
Chief Bender	2.32
Eddie Plank	2.39
Jack Coombs	2.60
Lefty Grove	2.88
Rollie Fingers	2.91
Ken Holtzman	2.92
Vida Blue	2.95
Catfish Hunter	3.13
Joe Bush	3.19

Wins
Eddie Plank	284
Lefty Grove	195
Chief Bender	193
Eddie Rommel	171
Catfish Hunter	161
Rube Walberg	134
Rube Waddell	131
Vida Blue	124
Dave Stewart	119
Jack Coombs	115

Losses
Eddie Plank	162
Eddie Rommel	119
Rube Walberg	114
Catfish Hunter	113
Alex Kellner	108
Rick Langford	105
Chief Bender	102
Slim Harriss	93
Vida Blue	86
Rollie Naylor	83

Innings pitched
Eddie Plank	3,860.2
Chief Bender	2,602.0
Eddie Rommel	2,556.1
Catfish Hunter	2,456.1
Lefty Grove	2,401.0
Rube Walberg	2,186.2
Vida Blue	1,945.2
Rube Waddell	1,869.1
Alex Kellner	1,730.1
Dave Stewart	1,717.1

Strikeouts
Eddie Plank	1,985
Rube Waddell	1,576
Chief Bender	1,536
Lefty Grove	1,523
Catfish Hunter	1,520
Vida Blue	1,315
Dave Stewart	1,152
Rube Walberg	907
Jack Coombs	870
Blue Moon Odom	799

Bases on balls
Eddie Plank	913
Rube Walberg	853
Lefty Grove	740
Blue Moon Odom	732
Eddie Rommel	724
Alex Kellner	717
Catfish Hunter	687
Phil Marchildon	682
Dave Stewart	655
Vida Blue	617

Games
Dennis Eckersley	525
Eddie Plank	524
Rollie Fingers	502
Eddie Rommel	500
Paul Lindblad	479
Rube Walberg	412
Lefty Grove	402
Rick Honeycutt	387
Chief Bender	385
Catfish Hunter	363

Shutouts
Eddie Plank	59
Rube Waddell	37
Chief Bender	36
Catfish Hunter	31
Vida Blue	28
Jack Coombs	28
Lefty Grove	20
Eddie Rommel	18
Jimmy Dygert	16
Joe Bush	15
Rube Walberg	15

Saves
Dennis Eckersley	320
Rollie Fingers	136
Billy Taylor	100
Jason Isringhausen	75
John Wyatt	73
Jay Howell	61
Jack Aker	58
Lefty Grove	51
Billy Koch	44
Paul Lindblad	41

TEAM SEASON, GAME RECORDS

SEASON

Batting		
Most at-bats	5,630	1996
Most runs	981	1932
Fewest runs	447	1916
Most hits	1,659	1925
Most singles	1,206	1925
Most doubles	334	2001
Most triples	108	1912
Most home runs	243	1996
Fewest home runs	16	1915, 1917
Most grand slams	14	2000
Most pinch-hit home runs	8	1970
Most total bases	2,546	1996
Most stolen bases	341	1976
Highest batting average	.307	1925
Lowest batting average	.223	1908
Highest slugging pct.	.458	2000
Pitching		
Lowest ERA	1.79	1910
Highest ERA	6.08	1936
Most complete games	136	1904
Most shutouts	27	1907, 1909
Most saves	64	1988, 1990
Most walks	827	1915
Most strikeouts	1,117	2001
Fielding		
Most errors	337	1901
Fewest errors	87	1990
Most double plays	217	1949
Highest fielding average	.986	1990
General		
Most games won	107	1931
Most games lost	117	1916
Highest win pct.	.704	1931
Lowest win pct.	.235	1916

GAME, INNING

Batting		
Most runs, game	24	Last 5-1-29
Most runs, inning	13	Last 7-5-96
Most hits, game	29	5-1-29
Most home runs, game	8	6-27-96
Most total bases, game	44	5-1-29, 6-27-96

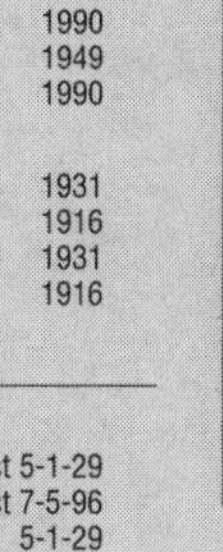

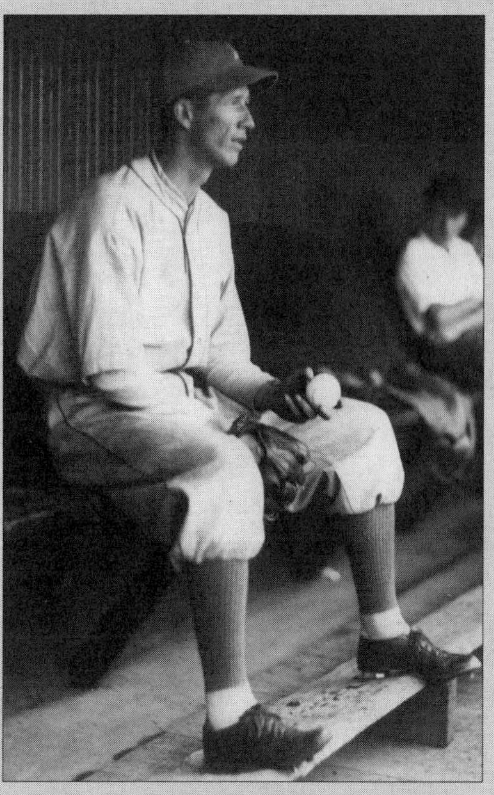

300-game winner Lefty Grove won 195 times as a member of the Athletics.

HISTORY

ATHLETICS YEAR-BY-YEAR

Year	W	L	Place	Games Back	Manager	Leaders: Batting avg.	Hits	Home runs	RBIs	Wins	ERA
1901	74	62	4th	9	Mack	Lajoie, .422	Lajoie, 229	Lajoie, 14	Lajoie, 125	Fraser, 22	Plank, 3.31
1902	83	53	1st	+5	Mack	L. Cross, .342	L. Cross, 191	Seybold, 16	L. Cross, 108	Waddell, 24	Waddell, 2.05
1903	75	60	2nd	14½	Mack	Hartsel, .311	L. Cross, 163	Seybold, 8	L. Cross, 90	Plank, 23	Plank, 2.38
1904	81	70	5th	12½	Mack	Davis, .309	L. Cross, 176	Davis, 10	D. Murphy, 77	Plank, 26	Waddell, 1.62
1905	92	56	1st	+2	Mack	Davis, .285	Davis, 173	Davis, 8	Davis, 83	Waddell, 27	Waddell, 1.48
1906	78	67	4th	12	Mack	Seybold, .316	Davis, 161	Davis, 12	Davis, 96	Plank, 19	Waddell, 2.21
1907	88	57	2nd	1½	Mack	Nicholls, .302	Davis, 155	Davis, 8	Davis, 87	Plank, 24	Bender, 2.05
1908	68	85	6th	22	Mack	D. Murphy, .265	D. Murphy, 139	Davis, 5	D. Murphy, 66	Vickers, 18	Bender, 1.75
1909	95	58	2nd	3½	Mack	E. Collins, .346	E. Collins, 198	D. Murphy, 5	Baker, 85	Plank, 19	Krause, 1.39
1910	102	48	1st	+14½	Mack	E. Collins, .322	E. Collins, 188	D. Murphy, Oldring, 4	E. Collins, 81	Coombs, 31	Coombs, 1.30
1911	101	50	1st	+13½	Mack	E. Collins, .365	Baker, 198	Baker, 11	Baker, 115	Coombs, 28	Plank 2.10
1912	90	62	3rd	15	Mack	E. Collins, .348	Baker, 200	Baker, 10	Baker, 130	Plank, 26	Plank 2.22
1913	96	57	1st	+6½	Mack	E. Collins, .345	Baker, 190	Baker, 12	Baker, 117	Bender, 21	Bender, 2.21
1914	99	53	1st	+8½	Mack	E. Collins, .344	Baker, 182	Baker, 9	McInnis, 95	Bender, Bush, 17	Bressler, 1.77
1915	43	109	8th	58½	Mack	McInnis, .314	Strunk, 144	Oldring, 6	Lajoie, 61	Wyckoff, 10	Knowlson, 3.49
1916	36	117	8th	54½	Mack	Strunk, .316	Strunk, 172	Schang, 7	McInnis, 60	Bush, 15	Bush, 2.57
1917	55	98	8th	44½	Mack	McInnis, .303	McInnis, 172	Bodie, 7	Bodie, 74	Bush, 11	Bush, 2.47
1918	52	76	8th	24	Mack	Burns, .352	Burns, 178	T. Walker, 11	Burns, 70	Perry, 21	Perry, 1.98
1919	36	104	8th	52	Mack	Burns, .296	Burns, 139	T. Walker, 10	T. Walker, 64	J. Johnson, Kinney, 9	Naylor, 3.34
1920	48	106	8th	50	Mack	Dugan, .322	Dugan, 158	T. Walker, 17	T. Walker, 82	Perry, 11	Rommel, 2.85
1921	53	100	8th	45	Mack	Witt, .315	Witt, 198	T. Walker, 23	T. Walker, 101	Rommel, 16	Rommel, 3.94
1922	65	89	7th	29	Mack	B. Miller, .335	Galloway, 185	T. Walker, 37	T. Walker, 99	Rommel, 27	Rommel, 3.28
1923	69	83	6th	29	Mack	Hauser, .307	Hauser, 165	Hauser, 17	Hauser, 94	Rommel, 18	Rommel, 3.27
1924	71	81	5th	20	Mack	B. Miller, .342	Simmons, 183	Hauser, 27	Hauser, 115	Rommel, 18	Rommel, 3.95
1925	88	64	2nd	8½	Mack	Simmons, .387	Simmons, 253	Simmons, 24	Simmons, 129	Rommel, 21	Gray, 3.27
1926	83	67	3rd	6	Mack	Simmons, .341	Simmons, 199	Simmons, 19	Simmons, 109	Grove, 13	Grove, 2.51
1927	91	63	2nd	19	Mack	Simmons, .392	Cobb, 175	Simmons, 15	Simmons, 108	Grove, 20	Grove, 3.19
1928	98	55	2nd	2½	Mack	Simmons, .351	B. Miller, 168	Hauser, 16	Simmons, 107	Grove, 24	Grove, 2.58
1929	104	46	1st	+18	Mack	Simmons, .365	Simmons, 212	Simmons, 34	Simmons, 157	Earnshaw, 24	Grove, 2.81
1930	102	52	1st	+8	Mack	Simmons, .381	Simmons, 211	Foxx, 37	Simmons, 165	Grove, 28	Grove, 2.54
1931	107	45	1st	+13½	Mack	Simmons, .390	Simmons, 200	Foxx, 30	Simmons, 128	Grove, 31	Grove, 2.06
1932	94	60	2nd	13	Mack	Foxx, .364	Simmons, 216	Foxx, 58	Foxx, 169	Grove, 25	Grove, 2.84
1933	79	72	3rd	19½	Mack	Foxx, .356	Foxx, 204	Foxx, 48	Foxx, 163	Grove, 24	Grove, 3.20
1934	68	82	5th	31	Mack	Foxx, .334	Cramer, 202	Foxx, 44	Foxx, 130	Marcum, 14	Cain, 4.41
1935	58	91	8th	34	Mack	Foxx, .346	Cramer, 214	Foxx, 36	Foxx, 115	Marcum, 17	Mahaffey, 3.90
1936	53	100	8th	49	Mack	Moses, .345	Moses, 202	B. Johnson, 25	B. Johnson, 121	Kelley, 15	Kelley, 3.86
1937	54	97	7th	46½	Mack	Moses, .320	Moses, 208	B. Johnson, Moses, 25	B. Johnson, 108	Kelley, 13	E. Smith, 3.94
1938	53	99	8th	46	Mack	B. Johnson, .313	Moses, 181	B. Johnson, 30	B. Johnson, 113	Caster, 16	Caster, 4.35
1939	55	97	7th	51½	Mack	B. Johnson, .338	B. Johnson, 184	B. Johnson, 23	B. Johnson, 114	Nelson, 10	Nelson, 4.78
1940	54	100	8th	36	Mack	Moses, .309	Siebert, 170	B. Johnson, 31	B. Johnson, 103	Babich, 14	Babich, 3.73
1941	64	90	8th	37	Mack	Siebert, .334	Chapman, 178	Chapman, 25	B. Johnson, 107	Knott, 13	Marchildon, 3.57
1942	55	99	8th	48	Mack	B. Johnson, .291	B. Johnson, 160	B. Johnson, 13	B. Johnson, 80	Marchildon, 17	Wolff, 3.32
1943	49	105	8th	49	Mack	Hall, .256	Siebert, 140	Estalella, 11	Siebert, 72	Flores, 12	Flores, 3.11
1944	72	82	*5th	17	Mack	Siebert, .306	Estalella, 151	Hayes, 13	Hayes, 78	Christopher, 14	Berry, 1.94
1945	52	98	8th	34½	Mack	Estalella, .299	Hall, 161	Estalella, 8	Kell, 56	Christopher, 13	Berry, 2.35
1946	49	105	8th	55	Mack	McCosky, .354	Chapman, 142	Chapman, 20	Chapman, 67	Marchildon, 13	Flores, 2.32
1947	78	76	5th	19	Mack	McCosky, .328	McCosky, 179	Chapman, 14	Chapman, 83	Marchildon, 19	Fowler, 2.81
1948	84	70	4th	12½	Mack	McCosky, .326	Majeski, 183	Joost, 16	Majeski, 120	Fowler, 15	Fowler, 3.78
1949	81	73	5th	16	Mack	Valo, .283	Chapman, 164	Chapman, 24	Chapman, 108	Kellner, 20	Shantz, 3.40
1950	52	102	8th	46	Mack	Dillinger, Lehner, .309	Fain, 147	Chapman, 23	Chapman, 95	Hooper, 15	Brissie, 4.02
1951	70	84	6th	28	Dykes	Fain, .344	Joost, 160	Zernial, 33	Zernial, 125	Shantz, 18	Zoldak, 3.16
1952	79	75	4th	16	Dykes	Fain, .327	Fain, 176	Zernial, 29	Zernial, 100	Shantz, 24	Shantz, 2.48
1953	59	95	7th	41½	Dykes	Philley, .303	Philley, 188	Zernial, 42	Zernial, 108	Byrd, Kellner, 11	Fricano, 3.88
1954	51	103	8th	60	Joost	Finigan, .302	Finigan, 147	Wilson, 15	Zernial, 62	Portocarrero, 9	Burtschy, 3.80
							—KANSAS CITY ATHLETICS—				
1955	63	91	6th	33	Boudreau	Power, .319	Power, 190	Zernial, 30	Zernial, 84	Ditmar, 12	Gorman, 3.55
1956	52	102	8th	45	Boudreau	Power, .309	Power, 164	Simpson, 21	Simpson, 105	Ditmar, 12	Burnette, 2.89
1957	59	94	7th	38½	Boudreau, Craft	H. Smith, .303	Power, 121	Zernial, 27	Zernial, 69	Morgan, Trucks, 9	Trucks, 3.03
1958	73	81	7th	19	Craft	Cerv, .305	Cerv, 157	Cerv, 38	Cerv, 104	Garver, 12	Dickson, 3.27
1959	66	88	7th	28	Craft	Tuttle, .300	Tuttle, 139	Cerv, 20	Cerv, 87	B. Daley, 16	B. Daley, 3.16
1960	58	96	8th	39	Elliot	Williams, .288	Lumpe, 156	Siebern, 19	Siebern, 69	B. Daley, 16	Herbert, 3.28
1961	61	100	*9th	47½	Gordon, Bauer	Siebern, .296	Howser, 171	Siebern 18	Siebern, 98	Bass, 11	Archer, 3.20
1962	72	90	9th	24	Bauer	Siebern, .308	Lumpe, 193	Siebern, 25	Siebern, 117	Rakow, 14	Pena, 3.01
1963	73	89	8th	31½	Lopat	Causey, .280	Charles, 161	Siebern, Lumpe, 16	Siebern, 83	Pena, Wickersham, 12	Drabowsky, 3.05
1964	57	105	10th	42	Lopat, McGaha	Causey, .281	Causey, 170	Colavito, 34	Colavito, 102	Pena, 12	Stock, 1.94
1965	59	103	10th	43	McGaha, Sullivan	Campaneris, .270	Campaneris, 156	Harrelson, 23	Harrelson, 66	Sheldon, Talbot, 10	O'Donoghue, Sheldon, 3.95
1966	74	86	7th	23	Dark	Cater, .292	Campaneris, 153	Repoz, 11	Green, 62	Krausse, 14	Aker, 1.99
1967	62	99	10th	29½	Dark, Appling	Donaldson, .276	Campaneris, 149	Monday, 14	Monday, 58	Hunter, 13	Hunter, 2.81
							—OAKLAND ATHLETICS—				
1968	82	80	6th	21	Kennedy	Cater, .290	Campaneris, 177	Jackson, 29	Jackson, 74	Odom, 16	Nash, 2.28
							—WEST DIVISION—				
1969	88	74	2nd	9	Bauer, McNamara	Bando, .281	Bando, 171	Jackson, 47	Jackson, 118	Dobson, Odom, 15	Odom, 2.92
1970	89	73	2nd	9	McNamara	Rudi, .309	Campaneris, 168	Mincher, 27	Bando, 75	Hunter, 18	Segui, 2.56
1971	101	60	†1st	+16	Williams	Jackson, .277	Jackson, 157	Jackson, 32	Bando, 94	Blue, 24	Blue, 1.82
1972	93	62	‡1st	+5½	Williams	Rudi, .305	Rudi, 181	Epstein, 26	Bando, 77	Hunter, 21	Hunter, 2.04
1973	94	68	‡1st	+6	Williams	Jackson, .293	Bando, 170	Jackson, 32	Jackson, 117	Holtzman, Hunter, 21	Fingers, 1.92
1974	90	72	‡1st	+5	Dark	Rudi, .293	Rudi, 174	Jackson, 29	Bando, 103	Hunter, 25	Lindblad, 2.06
1975	98	64	†1st	+7	Dark	Washington, .308	Washington, 182	Jackson, 36	Jackson, 104	Blue, 22	Todd, 2.29
1976	87	74	2nd	2½	Tanner	North, .276	North, 163	Bando, 27	Rudi, 94	Blue, 18	Blue, 2.35
1977	63	98	7th	38½	McKeon, Winkles	Page, .307	Sanguillen, 157	Gross, 22	Page, 75	Blue, 14	Torrealba, 2.62
1978	69	93	6th	23	Winkles, McKeon	Page, .285	Page, 147	Page, 17	Page, 70	Johnson, 11	Sosa, 2.64
1979	54	108	7th	34	Marshall	Revering, .288	Revering, 136	Newman, 22	Revering, 77	Langford, 12	McCatty, 4.22
1980	83	79	2nd	14	Martin	R. Henderson, .303	R. Henderson, 179	Armas, 35	Armas, 109	Norris, 22	Norris, 2.53
1981	64	45	∞†1st/2nd	—	Martin	R. Henderson, .319	R. Henderson, 135	Armas, 22	Armas, 76	McCatty, 14	McCatty, 2.32
1982	68	94	5th	25	Martin	Burroughs, .277	R. Henderson, 143	Armas, 28	Murphy, 94	Keough, Langford, 11	Underwood, 3.29
1983	74	88	4th	25	Boros	Lansford, .308	R. Henderson, 150	Lopes, Murphy, 17	Murphy, 75	Codiroli, 12	Burgmeier, 2.81
1984	77	85	4th	7	Boros, Moore	Lansford, .300	Lansford, 179	Kingman, 35	Kingman, 118	Burris, 13	Caudill, 2.71
1985	77	85	*4th	14	Moore	Bochte, .295	Griffin, 166	Kingman, 30	Kingman, 91	Codiroli, 14	Howell, 2.85
1986	76	86	*3rd	16	Moore, La Russa	Griffin, .285	Griffin, 169	Kingman, 35	Canseco, 117	Young, 13	Haas, 2.74
1987	81	81	3rd	4	La Russa	Lansford, McGwire, .289	Canseco, 162	McGwire, 49	McGwire, 118	Stewart, 20	Eckersley, 3.03
1988	104	58	‡1st	+13	La Russa	Canseco, .307	Canseco, 187	Canseco, 42	Canseco, 124	Stewart, 21	Nelson, 3.06
1989	99	63	‡1st	+7	La Russa	Lansford, .336	Lansford, 185	McGwire, 33	Parker, 97	Stewart, 21	Burns, 2.24
1990	103	59	‡1st	+9	La Russa	R. Henderson, .325	R. Henderson, 159	McGwire, 39	McGwire, 108	Welch, 27	Stewart, 2.56
1991	84	78	4th	11	La Russa	Baines, .295	D. Henderson, 158	Canseco, 44	Canseco, 122	Moore, 17	Moore, 2.96
1992	96	66	†1st	+6	La Russa	Bordick, .300	Bordick, 151	McGwire, 42	McGwire, 104	Moore, 17	Parrett, 3.02
1993	68	94	7th	26	La Russa	R. Henderson, .327	Gates, 155	Sierra, 22	Sierra, 101	Witt, 14	Witt, 4.21
1994	51	63	2nd	1	La Russa	Berroa, .306	Javier, 114	Sierra, 23	Sierra, 92	Darling, 10	Ontiveros, 2.65
1995	67	77	4th	11	La Russa	R. Henderson, .300	Berroa, 152	McGwire, 39	McGwire, 90	Stottlemyre, 14	Ontiveros, 4.3
1996	78	84	3rd	12	Howe	McGwire, .312	Berroa, 170	McGwire, 52	McGwire, 113	Wasdin, 8	Prieto, 4.157
1997	65	97	4th	25	Howe	Stairs, .298	Giambi, 152	McGwire, 34	Giambi, McGwire, 81	Small, 9	Small, 4.28
1998	74	88	4th	14	Howe	Giambi, .295	Grieve, 168	Giambi, 27	Giambi, 110	Rogers, 16	Rogers, 3.17
1999	87	75	2nd	8	Howe	Giambi, .315	Giambi, 181	Stairs, 38	Giambi, 123	Heredia, 13	Hudson, 3.23
2000	91	70	▲1st	½	Howe	Ja. Giambi, .333	Ja. Giambi, 170	Ja. Giambi, 43	Ja. Giambi, 137	Hudson, 20	Zito, 2.72
2001	102	60	▲2nd	14	Howe	Ja. Giambi, .342	Ja. Giambi, Long, 178	Ja. Giambi, 38	Ja. Giambi, 120	Mulder, 21	Hudson, 3.37
2002	103	59	▲1st	+4	Howe	Tejada, .308	Tejada, 204	Chavez, Tejada, 34	Tejada, 131	Zito, 23	Zito, 2.75

* Tied for position. † Lost Championship Series. ‡ Won Championship Series. ∞ First half 37-23; second half 27-22. ▲ Lost Division Series.

Note: Batting average minimum 350 at-bats; ERA minimum 90 innings pitched.

Seattle Mariners

Lefthander Randy Johnson.

FRANCHISE CHRONOLOGY

First season: 1977, as a result of the two-team expansion that increased the American League to 14 teams. The Mariners were shut out by California, 7-0, in their A.L. debut and went on to lose 98 games. They finished their first season in sixth place, 38 games behind A.L. West Division-champion Kansas City.

1978-present: The Mariners have not had much to brag about in their short existence. Before 1995, they had never finished above fourth place and had two winning seasons to show for 18 years. Over that same span, their expansion mate, Toronto, had won five division titles, two pennants and a pair of World Series. But the Mariners' fortunes changed in 1995. That year they earned their first division championship and won the A.L.'s first division playoff series before losing in the Championship Series. The team won division titles in 1997 and 2001, winning a major league record-tying 116 games the latter year. Despite their recent regular-season success, the Mariners are still looking for a league championship.

MARINERS VS. OPPONENTS BY DECADE

	A's	Indians	Orioles	Red Sox	Tigers	Twins	White Sox	Yankees	Angels	Rangers	Brewers	Royals	Blue Jays	Devil Rays	Interleague	Decade Record
1977-79	15-28	9-22	6-26	8-25	13-20	20-23	21-22	15-18	18-25	18-25	11-21	13-30	20-12			187-297
1980-89	46-78	48-72	51-63	54-66	48-66	59-67	52-71	45-68	48-79	65-65	53-59	59-70	45-69			673-893
1990-99	50-71	52-54	57-58	46-71	53-58	65-51	62-59	56-61	64-59	71-54	48-35	55-64	50-54	14-9	21-29	764-787
2000-02	25-26	11-12	19-9	16-12	12-11	21-9	16-14	17-11	33-18	35-17		20-10	20-8	21-9	34-20	300-186
Totals	136-203	120-160	133-156	124-174	126-155	165-150	151-166	133-158	163-181	189-161	112-115	147-174	135-143	35-18	55-49	1924-2163

Interleague results: 7-5 vs. Diamondbacks, 1-2 vs. Cubs, 3-0 vs. Reds, 12-7 vs. Rockies, 2-1 vs. Astros, 8-8 vs. Dodgers, 2-1 vs. Cardinals, 13-16 vs. Padres, 7-9 vs. Giants.

ALL-TIME RECORD OF EXPANSION TEAMS

Team	W	L	Pct.	DT	P	WS
Arizona	440	370	.543	3	1	1
Kansas City	2,675	2,694	.498	6	2	1
Houston	3,229	3,285	.496	7	0	0
Toronto	2,025	2,063	.495	5	2	2
Anaheim	3,243	3,431	.486	3	1	1
Montreal	2,605	2,769	.485	2	0	0
Colorado	740	817	.475	0	0	0
New York	3,091	3,412	.475	4	4	2
Milwaukee	2,545	2,831	.473	2	1	0
Seattle	1,924	2,163	.471	3	0	0
Texas	3,097	3,560	.465	4	0	0
San Diego	2,460	2,921	.457	3	2	0
Florida	706	847	.455	0	1	1
Tampa Bay	318	490	.394	0	0	0

DT—Division Titles. P—Pennants won. WS—World Series won.

MANAGERS

Name	*Years*	*Record*
Darrell Johnson	1977-80	226-362
Maury Wills	1980-81	26-56
Rene Lachemann	1981-83	140-180
Del Crandall	1983-84	93-141

MANAGERS—*cont'd.*

Name	*Years*	*Record*
Chuck Cottier	1984-86	98-119
Marty Martinez	1986	0-1
Dick Williams	1986-88	159-192
Jimmy Snyder	1988	45-60
Jim Lefebvre	1989-91	233-253
Bill Plummer	1992	64-98
Lou Piniella	1993-2002	840-711

WEST DIVISION CHAMPIONS

Year	*Record*	*Manager*	*ALCS Result*
1995	79-66	Piniella	Lost to Indians
1997	90-72	Piniella	Lost Div. Series
2001	116-46	Piniella	Lost to Yankees

WILD-CARD QUALIFIERS

Year	*Record*	*Manager*	*Div. Series Result*	*ALCS Result*
2000	91-71	Piniella	Defeated White Sox	Lost to Yankees

BALLPARK CHRONOLOGY

Safeco Field (1999-present)

Capacity: 47,772.
First game: Padres 3, Mariners 2 (July 15, 1999).
First batter: Quilvio Veras, Padres.
First hit: Eric Owens, Padres (single).
First run: Quilvio Veras, Padres (3rd inning).
First home run: Russ Davis, Mariners (July 17).
First winning pitcher: Will Cunnane, Padres.
First-season attendance: 2,915,908 (includes Kingdome attendance prior to July 15).

The Kingdome (1977-99)

Capacity: 59,856.
First game: California 7, Mariners 0 (April 6, 1977).
First-season attendance: 1,338,511.

ATTENDANCE HIGHS

Total	*Season*	*Park*
3,540,482	2002	Safeco Field
3,507,975	2001	Safeco Field
3,198,995	1997	Kingdome
3,150,034	2000	Safeco Field
2,915,908	1999	Kingdome/Safeco Field

A.L. MVP

Ken Griffey Jr. ,OF, 1997
Ichiro Suzuki, OF, 2001

CY YOUNG WINNER

Randy Johnson, LH, 1995

ROOKIE OF THE YEAR

Alvin Davis, 1B, 1984
Kazuhiro Sasaki, P, 2000
Ichiro Suzuki, OF, 2001

MANAGERS OF THE YEAR

Lou Piniella, 1995, 2001

The powerful bat of center fielder Ken Griffey Jr. thrilled Seattle fans for 11 seasons and helped the Mariners rise out of the A.L. West cellar.

MILESTONE PERFORMANCES

25-plus home runs

56— Ken Griffey Jr. 1997, 1998
49— Ken Griffey Jr. 1996
48— Ken Griffey Jr. 1999
45— Ken Griffey Jr. 1993
44— Jay Buhner 1996
42— Alex Rodriguez 1998
Alex Rodriguez 1999
41— Alex Rodriguez 2000
40— Ken Griffey Jr. 1994
Jay Buhner 1995, 1997
37— Edgar Martinez 2000
Bret Boone 2001
36— Alex Rodriguez 1996
32— Gorman Thomas 1985
31— Tino Martinez 1995
Paul Sorrento 1997
29— Willie Horton 1979
Alvin Davis 1987
Edgar Martinez 1995, 1998
28— Jim Presley 1985
Edgar Martinez 1997
27— Lee Stanton 1977
Alvin Davis 1984
Jim Presley 1986
Ken Phelps 1987
Jay Buhner 1991, 1993
Ken Griffey Jr. 1992
26— Phil Bradley 1985
Jay Buhner 2000
25— Danny Tartabull 1986
Jay Buhner 1992
Mike Cameron 2001, 2002

100-plus RBIs

147— Ken Griffey Jr. 1997
146— Ken Griffey Jr. 1998
145— Edgar Martinez 2000
141— Bret Boone 2001
140— Ken Griffey Jr. 1996
138— Jay Buhner 1996
134— Ken Griffey Jr. 1999
132— Alex Rodriguez 2000
124— Alex Rodriguez 1998
123— Alex Rodriguez 1996
121— Jay Buhner 1995
116— Alvin Davis 1984
Edgar Martinez 2001
113— Edgar Martinez 1995
111— Tino Martinez 1995
Alex Rodriguez 1999
110— Mike Cameron 2001
109— Ken Griffey Jr. 1993
Jay Buhner 1997
108— Edgar Martinez 1997
107— Jim Presley 1986
Bret Boone 2002
106— Willie Horton 1979
103— Ken Griffey Jr. 1992
Edgar Martinez 1996
John Olerud 2000
102— Edgar Martinez 1998
John Olerud 2002
100— Bruce Bochte 1979
Alvin Davis 1987
Ken Griffey Jr. 1991

20-plus victories

1997— Randy Johnson 20-4
2001— Jamie Moyer 20-6

A.L. home run champions

1994— Ken Griffey Jr. 40
1997— Ken Griffey Jr. 56
1998— Ken Griffey Jr. 56
1999— Ken Griffey Jr. 48

A.L. RBI champions

1997— Ken Griffey Jr. 147
2000— Edgar Martinez 145
2001— Bret Boone 141

A.L. batting champions

1992— Edgar Martinez .... .343
1995— Edgar Martinez .... .356
1996— Alex Rodriguez .... .358
2001— Ichiro Suzuki .... .350

A.L. ERA champions

1995— Randy Johnson 2.48
2001— Freddy Garcia 3.05

A.L. strikeout champions

1982— Floyd Bannister 209
1984— Mark Langston 204
1986— Mark Langston 245
1987— Mark Langston 262
1992— Randy Johnson 241
1993— Randy Johnson 308
1994— Randy Johnson 204
1995— Randy Johnson 294

No-hit pitchers
(9 innings or more)

1990— Randy Johnson .... 2-0 vs. Detroit
1993— Chris Bosio .... 7-0 vs. Boston

Longest hitting streaks

24— Joey Cora 1997
23— Ichiro Suzuki 2001
21— Dan Meyer 1979
Richie Zisk 1982
Ichiro Suzuki 2001
20— Alex Rodriguez 1996
19— Phil Bradley 1986
18— Joey Cora 1996
17— Edgar Martinez 1992, 1997
Alex Rodriguez 2000
16— Harold Reynolds 1989
Craig Reynolds 1978
Alex Rodriguez 1997
Joey Cora, 2 1998
Ken Griffey Jr. 1999
15— Willie Horton 1979
Richie Zisk 1981
Jack Perconte 1985
Edgar Martinez 1991
David Segui 1999
Ichiro Suzuki 2001, 2002

Second baseman Harold Reynolds was an offensive and defensive rock while the Mariners struggled through the 1980s.

INDIVIDUAL SEASON, GAME RECORDS

Speedy Julio Cruz, a second baseman during the team's formative years, holds the club record with 290 career stolen bases.

SEASON

Batting

Record		Player	Year
At-bats	692	Ichiro Suzuki	2001
Runs	141	Alex Rodriguez	1996
Hits	242	Ichiro Suzuki	2001
Singles	192	Ichiro Suzuki	2001
Doubles	54	Alex Rodriguez	1996
Triples	11	Harold Reynolds	1988
Home runs	56	Ken Griffey Jr.	1997, 1998
Home runs, rookie	27	Alvin Davis	1984
Grand slams	4	Edgar Martinez	2000
Total bases	393	Ken Griffey Jr..	1997
RBIs	147	Ken Griffey Jr.	1997
Walks	123	Edgar Martinez	1996
Most strikeouts	176	Mike Cameron	2002
Fewest strikeouts	34	Harold Reynolds	1987
Batting average	.358	Alex Rodriguez	1996
Slugging pct.	.674	Ken Griffey Jr.	1994
Stolen bases	60	Harold Reynolds	1987

Pitching

Record		Player	Year
Games	78	Ed Vande Berg	1982
Complete games	14	Mike Moore	1985
		Mark Langston	1987
Innings	272	Mark Langston	1987
Wins	20	Randy Johnson	1997
		Jamie Moyer	2001
Losses	19	Matt Young	1985
		Mike Moore	1987
Winning pct.	.900 (18-2)	Randy Johnson	1995
Walks	152	Randy Johnson	1991
Strikeouts	308	Randy Johnson	1993
Shutouts	4	Dave Fleming	1992
		Randy Johnson	1994
Home runs allowed	35	Scott Bankhead	1987
Lowest ERA	2.28	Randy Johnson	1997
Saves	45	Kazuhiro Sasaki	2001

GAME

Batting

Record		Player	Date
Runs	5	Last by Alex Rodriguez.	4-16-2000
Hits	5	Last by Ruben Sierra	5-16-2002
Doubles	3	Last by David Bell	7-15-99
Triples	2	Last by Ichiro Suzuki	4-21-2002
Home runs	4	Mike Cameron	5-2-2002
RBIs	8	Alvin Davis	5-9-86
		Mike Blowers	5-24-95
		Mike Cameron	8-19-2001
Total bases	16	Mike Cameron	5-2-2002
Stolen bases	4	Last by Mark McLemore	5-30-2001

CAREER LEADERS

BATTING

Games	
Edgar Martinez	1,769
Ken Griffey	1,535
Jay Buhner	1,440
Alvin Davis	1,166
Harold Reynolds	1,155
Dan Wilson	1,041
Dave Valle	846
Jim Presley	799
Alex Rodriguez	790
Julio Cruz	742

At-bats	
Edgar Martinez	6,230
Ken Griffey	5,832
Jay Buhner	4,922
Alvin Davis	4,136
Harold Reynolds	4,090
Dan Wilson	3,423
Alex Rodriguez	3,126
Jim Presley	2,946
Julio Cruz	2,667
Dave Valle	2,502

Runs	
Edgar Martinez	1,102
Ken Griffey	1,063
Jay Buhner	790
Alex Rodriguez	627
Alvin Davis	563
Harold Reynolds	543
Julio Cruz	402
Dan Wilson	376
Joey Cora	354
Jim Presley	351

Hits	
Edgar Martinez	1,973
Ken Griffey	1,742
Jay Buhner	1,255
Alvin Davis	1,163
Harold Reynolds	1,063
Alex Rodriguez	966
Dan Wilson	910
Jim Presley	736
Bruce Bochte	697
Phil Bradley	649
Julio Cruz	649

Doubles	
Edgar Martinez	466
Ken Griffey	320
Jay Buhner	231
Alvin Davis	212
Harold Reynolds	200
Alex Rodriguez	194
Dan Wilson	179
Jim Presley	147
Bruce Bochte	134
Al Cowens	128

Triples	
Harold Reynolds	48
Ken Griffey	30
Phil Bradley	26
Spike Owen	23
Ruppert Jones	20
Jay Buhner	19
Dan Meyer	19
Joey Cora	18
Al Cowens	17
Julio Cruz	16
Leon Roberts	16
Ichiro Suzuki	16

Home runs	
Ken Griffey	398
Jay Buhner	307
Edgar Martinez	273
Alex Rodriguez	189
Alvin Davis	160
Jim Presley	115
Ken Phelps	105
Tino Martinez	88
Dan Wilson	82
Dave Henderson	79

Total bases	
Ken Griffey	3,316
Edgar Martinez	3,288
Jay Buhner	2,445
Alvin Davis	1,875
Alex Rodriguez	1,753
Harold Reynolds	1,410
Dan Wilson	1,357
Jim Presley	1,254
Bruce Bochte	1,031
Phil Bradley	969

Runs batted in	
Ken Griffey	1,152
Edgar Martinez	1,100
Jay Buhner	951
Alvin Davis	667
Alex Rodriguez	595
Dan Wilson	430
Jim Presley	418
Bruce Bochte	329
Dave Valle	318
Dan Meyer	313

Extra-base hits	
Edgar Martinez	754
Ken Griffey	748
Jay Buhner	557
Alex Rodriguez	396
Alvin Davis	382
Jim Presley	275
Dan Wilson	272
Harold Reynolds	265
Bruce Bochte	205
Dave Henderson	205

Batting average
(Minimum 500 games)

Batting average	
Edgar Martinez	.317
Alex Rodriguez	.309
Phil Bradley	.301
Ken Griffey	.299
Joey Cora	.293
Bruce Bochte	.290
Alvin Davis	.281
Rich Amaral	.278
Dan Wilson	.266
Dan Meyer	.265
Tino Martinez	.265

Stolen bases	
Julio Cruz	290
Harold Reynolds	228
Ken Griffey	167
Alex Rodriguez	133
Phil Bradley	107
Henry Cotto	102
Rich Amaral	97
Mike Cameron	89
Mark McLemore	87
Ichiro Suzuki	87

PITCHING

Earned-run average
(Minimum 500 innings)

Earned-run average	
Randy Johnson	3.42
Erik Hanson	3.69
Brian Holman	3.73
Floyd Bannister	3.75
Jamie Moyer	3.80
Freddy Garcia	3.83
Mark Langston	4.01
Matt Young	4.13
Jim Beattie	4.14
Scott Bankhead	4.16

Wins	
Randy Johnson	130
Jamie Moyer	98
Mark Langston	74
Mike Moore	66
Freddy Garcia	60
Erik Hanson	56
Matt Young	45
Glenn Abbott	44
Jim Beattie	43
John Halama	41
Bill Swift	41

Losses	
Mike Moore	96
Randy Johnson	74
Jim Beattie	72
Mark Langston	67
Matt Young	66
Glenn Abbott	62
Erik Hanson	54
Floyd Bannister	50
Bill Swift	49
Jamie Moyer	48

Innings pitched	
Randy Johnson	1,838.1
Mike Moore	1,457.0
Jamie Moyer	1,316.0
Mark Langston	1,197.2
Erik Hanson	967.1
Jim Beattie	944.2
Glenn Abbott	904.0
Bill Swift	903.2
Matt Young	864.1
Freddy Garcia	788.0

Strikeouts	
Randy Johnson	2,162
Mark Langston	1,078
Mike Moore	937
Erik Hanson	801
Jamie Moyer	654
Matt Young	597
Freddy Garcia	593
Floyd Bannister	564
Jim Beattie	563
Jeff Fassero	466

Bases on balls	
Randy Johnson	884
Mark Langston	575
Mike Moore	535
Jim Beattie	369
Matt Young	365
Bill Swift	304
Jamie Moyer	299
Freddy Garcia	286
Erik Hanson	285
Floyd Bannister	250

Games	
Mike Jackson	335
Jeff Nelson	337
Bobby Ayala	292
Bill Swift	282
Randy Johnson	274
Ed Vande Berg	272
Norm Charlton	249
Mike Schooler	243
Mike Moore	227
Arthur Rhodes	209

Shutouts	
Randy Johnson	19
Mark Langston	9
Mike Moore	9
Floyd Bannister	7
Jim Beattie	6
Dave Fleming	5
Brian Holman	5
Jamie Moyer	5
Matt Young	5
Freddy Garcia	4

Saves	
Kazuhiro Sasaki	119
Mike Schooler	98
Norm Charlton	67
Bobby Ayala	56
Bill Caudill	52
Shane Rawley	36
Edwin Nunez	35
Mike Jackson	34
Jose Mesa	34
Enrique Romo	26

TEAM SEASON, GAME RECORDS

SEASON

Batting		
Most at-bats	5,680	2001
Most runs	993	1996
Fewest runs	558	1983
Most hits	1,637	2001
Most singles	1,120	2001
Most doubles	343	1996
Most triples	52	1979
Most home runs	264	1997
Fewest home runs	97	1978
Most grand slams	11	1996, 2000
Most pinch-hit home runs	5	1994, 1996
Most total bases	2,741	1996
Most stolen bases	174	1987, 2001
Highest batting average	.288	2001
Lowest batting average	.240	1983
Highest slugging pct	.485	1997

Pitching		
Lowest ERA	3.69	1990
Highest ERA	5.24	1999
Most complete games	39	1987
Most shutouts	14	2001
Most saves	56	2001
Most walks	684	1999
Most strikeouts	1,156	1998

Fielding		
Most errors	156	1986
Fewest errors	83	2001
Most double plays	191	1986
Highest fielding average	.986	2001

General		
Most games won	116	2001
Most games lost	104	1978
Highest win pct	.716	2001
Lowest win pct	.350	1978

GAME, INNING

Batting		
Most runs, game	22	4-29-99
Most runs, inning	11	4-29-99
Most hits, game	24	6-11-96
Most home runs, game	7	Last: 5-2-2002
Most total bases, game	44	4-16-2000

Outfielder Jay Buhner ranks second on the Mariners' career home run chart.

HISTORY

MARINERS YEAR-BY-YEAR

Year	W	L	Place	Games Back	Manager	Leaders: Batting avg.	Hits	Home runs	RBIs	Wins	ERA
						WEST DIVISION					
1977	64	98	6th	38	Johnson	Stanton, .275	Meyer, 159	Stanton, 27	Meyer, Stanton, 90	Abbott, 12	Romo, 2.83
1978	56	104	7th	35	Johnson	Roberts, .301	Reynolds, 160	Roberts, 22	Roberts, 92	Romo, 11	Romo, 3.69
1979	67	95	6th	21	Johnson	Bochte, .316	Horton, 180	Horton, 29	Horton, 106	Parrott, 14	Parrott, 3.77
1980	59	103	7th	38	Johnson, Wills	Bochte, .300	Bochte, 156	Paciorek, 15	Bochte, 78	Abbott, 12	Rawley, 3.33
1981	44	65	*6th/5th	—	Wills, Lachemann	Paciorek, .326	Paciorek, 132	Zisk, 16	Paciorek, 66	Bannister, 9	Abbott, 3.95
1982	76	86	4th	17	Lachemann	Bochte, .297	Bochte, Cowens, 151	Zisk, 21	Cowens, 78	Bannister, Caudill, 12	Caudill, 2.35
1983	60	102	7th	39	Lachemann, Crandall	S. Henderson, .294	D. Henderson, 136	Putnam, 19	Putnam, 67	Young, 11	Young, 3.27
1984	74	88	†5th	10	Crandall, Cottier	Perconte, .294	Perconte, 180	Davis, 27	Davis, 116	Langston, 17	Langston, 3.40
1985	74	88	6th	17	Cottier	P. Bradley, .300	P. Bradley, 192	G. Thomas, 32	P. Bradley, 88	Moore, 17	Nunez, 3.09
1986	67	95	7th	25	Cottier, Martinez, Williams	P. Bradley, .310	P. Bradley, Presley, 163	Presley, 27	Presley, 107	Langston, 12	Young, 3.82
1987	78	84	4th	7	Williams	Brantley, .302	P. Bradley, 179	Davis, 29	Davis, 100	Langston, 19	Guetterman, 3.81
1988	68	93	7th	35½	Williams, Snyder	Davis, .295	Reynolds, 169	Balboni, 21	Davis, 69	Langston, 15	Jackson, 2.63
1989	73	89	6th	26	Lefebvre	Davis, .305	Reynolds, 184	Leonard, 24	Davis, 95	Bankhead, 14	Jackson, 3.17
1990	77	85	5th	26	Lefebvre	E. Martinez, .302	Griffey Jr., 179	Griffey Jr., 22	Griffey Jr., 80	Hanson, 18	Swift, 2.39
1991	83	79	5th	12	Lefebvre	Griffey Jr., .327	Griffey Jr., 179	Buhner, 27	Griffey Jr., 100	Holman, R. Johnson, 13	Swift, 1.99
1992	64	98	7th	32	Plummer	E. Martinez, .343	E. Martinez, 181	Griffey Jr., 27	Griffey Jr., 103	Fleming, 17	Fleming, 3.39
1993	82	80	4th	12	Piniella	Griffey Jr., .309	Griffey Jr., 180	Griffey Jr., 45	Griffey Jr., 109	R. Johnson, 19	R. Johnson, 3.24
1994	49	63	3rd	2	Piniella	Griffey Jr., .323	Griffey Jr., 140	Griffey Jr., 40	Griffey Jr., 90	R. Johnson, 13	R. Johnson, 3.19
1995	78	66	‡§∞1st	+1	Piniella	E. Martinez, .356	E. Martinez, 182	Buhner, 40	Buhner, 121	Johnson, 18	Johnson, 2.48
1996	85	75	2nd	4½	Piniella	Rodriguez, .358	Rodriguez, 215	Griffey Jr., 49	Griffey Jr., 140	Hitchcock, Moyer, 13	Moyer, 3.98
1997	90	72	▲1st	+6	Piniella	E. Martinez, .330	Griffey Jr., 185	Griffey Jr., 56	Griffey Jr., 147	Johnson, 20	Johnson, 2.28
1998	76	85	3rd	11½	Piniella	E. Martinez, .322	Rodriguez, 213	Griffey Jr., 56	Griffey Jr., 146	Moyer, 15	Moyer, 3.53
1999	79	83	3rd	16	Piniella	E. Martinez, .337	Griffey Jr., 173	Griffey Jr., 48	Griffey Jr., 134	F. Garcia, 17	Moyer, 3.87
2000	91	71	§∞ 2nd	½	Piniella	E. Martinez, .324	E. Martinez, 180	Rodriguez, 41	E. Martinez, 145	Sele, 17	Garcia, 3.91
2001	116	46	§∞1st	+14	Piniella	Suzuki, .350	Suzuki, 242	Boone, 37	Boone, 141	Moyer, 20	Garcia, 3.05
2002	93	69	3rd	10	Piniella	Suzuki, .321	Suzuki, 208	Cameron, 25	Boone, 107	Garcia, 16	Pineiro, 3.24

* First half 21-36; second half 23-29. † Tied for position. ‡ Won division playoff. § Won Division Series. ∞ Lost Championship Series. ▲ Lost Division Series.

Note: Batting average minimum 350 at-bats; ERA minimum 90 innings pitched.

Ruppert Jones

A PARTNERSHIP that included actor Danny Kaye was granted the American League's 13th franchise on February 6, 1976, as part of a two-team expansion that would increase the A.L. roster to 14. The Mariners represented baseball's second attempt to establish a team in Seattle. The Pilots played the 1969 season there before transferring operations to Milwaukee.

The Mariners stocked their roster with 30 players from the November 5, 1976, expansion draft, including first pick Ruppert Jones, an outfielder from the Kansas City organization. The team made its Major League debut on April 6, 1977, losing, 7-0, to the California Angels at Seattle's Kingdome.

Expansion draft (November 5, 1976)

Players

Player	Team	Position
Juan Bernhardt	New York	infield
Steve Braun	Minnesota	outfield
Dave Collins	California	outfield
Julio Cruz	California	second base
Luis Delgado	Boston	outfield
*Ruppert Jones	Kansas City	outfield
Joe Lis	Cleveland	first base
Carlos Lopez	California	outfield
Tom McMillan	Cleveland	shortstop
Dan Meyer	Detroit	first base
Tommie Smith	Cleveland	outfield
Leroy Stanton	California	outfield
Bill Stein	Chicago	third base
Bob Stinson	Kansas City	catcher

Pitchers

Pitcher	Team	Throws
Glenn Abbott	Oakland	righthanded
Steve Barr	Texas	righthanded
Pete Broberg	Milwaukee	righthanded
Steve Burke	Boston	righthanded
Joe Erardi	Milwaukee	righthanded
Bob Galasso	Baltimore	righthanded
Alan Griffin	Oakland	righthanded
Grant Jackson	New York	lefthanded
Rick Jones	Boston	lefthanded
Bill Laxton	Detroit	lefthanded
Frank MacCormack	Detroit	righthanded
Dave Pagan	Baltimore	righthanded
Dick Pole	Boston	righthanded
Roy Thomas	Chicago	righthanded
Stan Thomas	Cleveland	righthanded
Gary Wheelock	California	righthanded

*First pick

Opening day lineup

April 6, 1977

Dave Collins, designated hitter
Jose Baez, second base
Steve Braun, left field
Lee Stanton, right field
Bill Stein, third base
Dan Meyer, first base
Ruppert Jones, center field
Bob Stinson, catcher
Craig Reynolds, shortstop
Diego Segui, pitcher

Craig Reynolds

Mariners firsts

First hit: Jose Baez, April 6, 1977, vs. California
First home run: Juan Bernhardt, April 10, 1977, vs. California
First RBI: Dan Meyer, April 8, 1977 vs. California
First win: Bill Laxton, April 8, 1977, vs. California
First shutout: Dave Pagan, May 19, 1977, 3-0 at Oakland

TAMPA BAY DEVIL RAYS

Third baseman Bobby Smith.

FRANCHISE CHRONOLOGY

The beginnings: Tampa Bay, a longtime home to minor league baseball, the Gulf Coast Rookie League and spring training, pursued a Major League team for about 19 years before the dream was realized. At a March 9, 1995, owner's meeting, the vote was 28-0 to admit two new franchises, a Phoenix-based team that would be known as the Diamondbacks and a Tampa club, awarded to a local group headed by Tampa businessman Vincent J. Naimoli, that would become the Devil Rays. The franchise became the state's second, only two years after the Florida Marlins had begun play as an expansion team in Miami. Both teams were stocked in a November 1997 expansion draft and began play in the 1998 season—Arizona as a member of the N.L. West Division and the Devil Rays in the rugged A.L. East. The Diamondbacks and Devil Rays were the 13th and 14th expansion teams in baseball's long history.
First season: The March 31, 1998, debut on Florida's west coast was long on pageantry and short on success. The Devil Rays fell behind 11-0 and dropped an 11-6 decision to the Detroit Tigers at Tropicana Field. Tampa Bay went on to record a 66-99 first-season finish, 51 games behind the record-setting New York Yankees.
1999-present: Clearly, improvement has been the goal for the Devil Rays, although they've yet to win 70 games in a season while playing in, arguably, baseball's best division.

DEVIL RAYS VS. OPPONENTS BY DECADE

	A's	Indians	Orioles	Red Sox	Tigers	Twins	White Sox	Yankees	Angels	Rangers	Royals	Blue Jays	Mariners	Interleague	Decade Record
1998-99	7-14	7-12	14-10	12-13	11-9	9-12	10-11	5-19	10-13	8-15	11-10	10-15	9-14	9-25	132-192
2000-02	5-22	5-17	23-28	14-36	11-10	14-10	9-15	17-32	9-21	13-17	9-13	22-28	9-21	26-28	186-298
Totals	12-36	12-29	37-38	26-49	22-19	23-22	19-26	22-51	19-34	21-32	20-23	32-43	18-35	35-53	318-490

Interleague results: 3-9 vs. Braves, 0-3 vs. Rockies, 11-17 vs. Marlins, 1-2 vs. Dodgers, 5-7 vs. Expos, 5-7 vs. Mets, 8-4 vs. Phillies, 1-2 vs. Padres, 1-2 vs. Giants.

ALL-TIME RECORD OF EXPANSION TEAMS

Team	W	L	Pct.	DT	P	WS
Arizona	440	370	.543	3	1	1
Kansas City	2,675	2,694	.498	6	2	1
Houston	3,229	3,285	.496	7	0	0
Toronto	2,025	2,063	.495	5	2	2
Anaheim	3,243	3,431	.486	3	1	1
Montreal	2,605	2,769	.485	2	0	0
Colorado	740	817	.475	0	0	0
New York	3,091	3,412	.475	4	4	2
Milwaukee	2,545	2,831	.473	2	1	0
Seattle	1,924	2,163	.471	3	0	0
Texas	3,097	3,560	.465	4	0	0
San Diego	2,460	2,921	.457	3	2	0
Florida	706	847	.455	0	1	1
Tampa Bay	318	490	.394	0	0	0

DT—Division Titles. P—Pennants won. WS—World Series won.

BALLPARK CHRONOLOGY

Tropicana Field (1998-present)

Capacity: 44,445.
First game: Tigers 11, Devil Rays 6 (March 31, 1998).
First batter: Brian Hunter, Tigers.
First hit: Tony Clark, Tigers (single).
First run: Tony Clark, Tigers (2nd inning).
First home run: Luis Gonzalez, Tigers.
First winning pitcher: Justin Thompson, Tigers..
First-season attendance: 2,506,023.

MANAGERS

Name	*Years*	*Record*
Larry Rothschild	1998-2001	205-294
Hal McRae	2001-2002	113-196

ATTENDANCE HIGHS

Total	*Season*	*Park*
2,506,023	1998	Tropicana Field
1,749,567	1999	Tropicana Field
1,549,052	2000	Tropicana Field
1,227,673	2001	Tropicana Field
1,065,762	2002	Tropicana Field

HISTORY

Expansion draft (November 18, 1998)

Players

Bobby Abreu	Houston	outfield
Rich Butler	Toronto	outfield
Miguel Cairo	Cubs	second base
Steve Cox	Oakland	first base
Mike Difelice	St. Louis	catcher
Brooks Kieschnick	Cubs	first base
Aaron Ledesma	Baltimore	shortstop
Quinton McCracken	Colorado	outfield
Carlos Mendoza	N.Y. Mets	outfield
Herbert Perry	Cleveland	first base
Kerry Robinson	St. Louis	outfield
Andy Sheets	Seattle	shortstop
Bobby Smith	Atlanta	third base
Bubba Trammell	Detroit	outfield
Chris Wilcox	N.Y. Yankees	outfield
Randy Winn	Florida	outfield
Dmitri Young	Cincinnati	outfield/1B

Pitchers

Brian Boehringer	N.Y. Yankees	righthanded
Dan Carlson	San Francisco	righthanded
Mike Duvall	Florida	lefthanded
Vaughn Eshelman	Oakland	lefthanded
Rick Gorecki	Los Angeles	righthanded
Santos Hernandez	San Francisco	righthanded
Jason Johnson	Pittsburgh	righthanded
Ryan Karp	Philadelphia	lefthanded
John LeRoy	Atlanta	righthanded
Albie Lopez	Cleveland	lefthanded
Jim Mecir	Boston	righthanded
Jose Paniagua	Montreal	righthanded
Bryan Rekar	Colorado	righthanded
*Tony Saunders	Florida	lefthanded
Dennis Springer	Anaheim	righthanded
Ramon Tatis	Cubs	lefthanded
Terrell Wade	Atlanta	lefthanded
Esteban Yan	Baltimore	righthanded

*First pick

Opening day lineup

March 31, 1998

Quinton McCracken, center field
Miguel Cairo, second base
Wade Boggs, third base
Fred McGriff, first base
Mike Kelly, left field
Paul Sorrento, designated hitter
John Flaherty, catcher
Dave Martinez, right field
Kevin Stocker, shortstop
Wilson Alvarez, pitcher

Tony Saunders

Devil Rays firsts

First hit: Dave Martinez, March 31, 1998, vs. Detroit (single)
First home run: Wade Boggs, March 31, 1998, vs. Detroit
First RBI: Wade Boggs, March 31, 1998, vs. Detroit
First win: Rolando Arrojo, April 1, 1998, vs. Detroit
First shutout: Rolando Arrojo, April 30, 1998, at Minnesota

MILESTONE PERFORMANCES

20-plus home runs

- 34—Jose Canseco 1999
- 32—Fred McGriff 1999
- 28—Greg Vaughn 2000
- 27—Fred McGriff 2000
- 24—Greg Vaughn 2001
- 23—Aubrey Huff 2002
- 21—Gerald Williams 2000

100-plus RBIs

- 106—Fred McGriff 2000
- 104—Fred McGriff 1999

20-plus victories

None

A.L. home run champions

None

A.L. RBI champions

None

A.L. batting champions

None

A.L. ERA champions

None

A.L. strikeout champions

None

No-hit pitchers
(9 innings or more)

None

Longest hitting streaks

- 18—Quinton McCracken 1998
- 17—Aubrey Huff 2002

INDIVIDUAL SEASON, GAME RECORDS

SEASON

Batting

Record	Total	Player	Year
At-bats	632	Gerald Williams	2000
Runs	87	Gerald Williams	2000
Hits	181	Randy Winn	2002
Singles	127	Quinton McCracken	1998
Doubles	39	Randy Winn	2002
Triples	9	Randy Winn	1998, 2000
Home runs	34	Jose Canseco	1999
Home runs, rookie	12	Bubba Trammell	1998
Grand slams	2	Paul Sorrento	1998
		Fred McGriff	2000
		Ben Grieve	2001
		Greg Vaughn	2001
Total bases	292	Fred McGriff	1999
RBIs	106	Fred McGriff	2000
Walks	91	Fred McGriff	2000
Most strikeouts	159	Ben Grieve	2001
Fewest strikeouts	44	Miguel Cairo	1998
Batting average	.310	Fred McGriff	1999
Slugging pct.	.563	Jose Canseco	1999
Stolen bases	31	Jason Tyner	2001

Pitching

Record	Total	Player	Year
Games	72	Roberto Hernandez	1999
Complete games	5	Joe Kennedy	2002
Innings	224	Tanyon Sturtze	2002
Wins	14	Rolando Arrojo	1998
Losses	15	Tony Saunders	1998
		Bobby Witt	1999
Winning pct.	.538 (14-12)	Rolando Arrojo	1998
Walks	111	Tony Saunders	1998
Strikeouts	172	Tony Saunders	1998
Shutouts	2	Rolando Arrojo	1998
		Bobby Witt	1999
Home runs allowed	33	Tanyon Sturtze	2002
Lowest ERA	3.56	Rolando Arrojo	1998
Saves	43	Roberto Hernandez	1999

GAME

Batting

Record	Total	Player	Date
Runs	3	Randy Winn	9-17-2002
Hits	4	Last by Aubrey Huff	8-10-2002
Doubles	3	Last by Fred McGriff	5-19-2001
Triples	2	Last by Jose Guillen	6-7-2000
Home runs	2	Last by Jared Sandberg	8-10-2002
RBIs	6	Paul Sorrento	5-3-98
Total bases	10	Last by Randy Winn	6-9-2002
Stolen bases	3	Brent Abernathy	7-18-2002

CAREER LEADERS

BATTING

Games

Fred McGriff	550
Randy Winn	519
John Flaherty	471
Miguel Cairo	389
Steve Cox	378
Greg Vaughn	332
Ben Grieve	290
Aubrey Huff	263
Dave Martinez	262
Bobby Smith	258

At-bats

Fred McGriff	2,002
Randy Winn	1,836
John Flaherty	1,673
Miguel Cairo	1,355
Steve Cox	1,239
Greg Vaughn	1,197
Ben Grieve	1,024
Aubrey Huff	987
Dave Martinez	927
Gerald Williams	864

Runs

Fred McGriff	270
Randy Winn	264
Greg Vaughn	185
Miguel Cairo	159
John Flaherty	157
Steve Cox	146
Ben Grieve	134
Dave Martinez	122
Aubrey Huff	121
Gerald Williams	117

Hits

Fred McGriff	590
Randy Winn	513
John Flaherty	422
Miguel Cairo	373
Steve Cox	324
Aubrey Huff	279
Greg Vaughn	271
Ben Grieve	264
Dave Martinez	252
Gerald Williams	221

Doubles

Fred McGriff	99
Randy Winn	94
John Flaherty	82
Steve Cox	72
Greg Vaughn	62
Ben Grieve	60
Miguel Cairo	59
Aubrey Huff	57
Bubba Trammell	48
Chris Gomez	47
Gerald Williams	47

Triples

Randy Winn	28
Miguel Cairo	12
Quinton McCracken	8
Dave Martinez	7
Carl Crawford	6
Kevin Stocker	6
Jason Tyner	6
Brent Abernathy	5
Wade Boggs	5
Mike Difelice	5
Jose Guillen	5
Felix Martinez	5

Home runs

Fred McGriff	97
Greg Vaughn	60
Jose Canseco	43
Steve Cox	39
John Flaherty	35
Aubrey Huff	35
Bubba Trammell	33
Ben Grieve	30
Paul Sorrento	28
Gerald Williams	25

Total bases

Fred McGriff	982
Randy Winn	735
John Flaherty	611
Greg Vaughn	519
Steve Cox	517
Miguel Cairo	483
Aubrey Huff	443
Ben Grieve	418
Gerald Williams	347
Bubba Trammell	344

Runs batted in

Fred McGriff	352
John Flaherty	196
Greg Vaughn	185
Randy Winn	182
Steve Cox	158
Ben Grieve	136
Jose Canseco	125
Aubrey Huff	118
Miguel Cairo	116
Bobby Smith	107
Bubba Trammell	107

Extra-base hits

Fred McGriff	197
Randy Winn	146
Greg Vaughn	125
John Flaherty	118
Steve Cox	113
Aubrey Huff	93
Ben Grieve	92
Bubba Trammell	84
Miguel Cairo	80
Jose Canseco	77

Batting average
(Minimum 175 games)

Fred McGriff	.295
Wade Boggs	.289
Bubba Trammell	.285
Aubrey Huff	.283
Randy Winn	.279
Quinton McCracken	.277
Miguel Cairo	.275
Dave Martinez	.272
Russ Johnson	.265
Steve Cox	.262

Stolen bases

Randy Winn	80
Miguel Cairo	69
Jason Tyner	44
Quinton McCracken	25
Dave Martinez	22
Greg Vaughn	22
Gerald Williams	22
Brent Abernathy	18
Ben Grieve	15
Felix Martinez	15
Kevin Stocker	15

PITCHING

Earned-run average
(Minimum 175 innings)

Roberto Hernandez	3.43
Rick White	3.81
Rolando Arrojo	4.23
Albie Lopez	4.27
Joe Kennedy	4.50
Tony Saunders	4.53
Tanyon Sturtze	4.58
Wilson Alvarez	4.62
Paul Wilson	4.66
Esteban Yan	5.01

Wins

Albie Lopez	26
Esteban Yan	26
Ryan Rupe	23
Rolando Arrojo	21
Tanyon Sturtze	19
Bryan Rekar	18
Wilson Alvarez	17
Joe Kennedy	15
Paul Wilson	15
Jim Mecir	14
Victor Zambrano	14

Losses

Bryan Rekar	37
Ryan Rupe	37
Albie Lopez	31
Tanyon Sturtze	30
Esteban Yan	30
Wilson Alvarez	26
Paul Wilson	25
Rolando Arrojo	24
Joe Kennedy	19
Tony Saunders	18

Innings pitched

Bryan Rekar	495.1
Tanyon Sturtze	472.0
Ryan Rupe	466.2
Albie Lopez	453.2
Esteban Yan	418.2
Paul Wilson	396.0
Wilson Alvarez	377.2
Rolando Arrojo	342.2
Joe Kennedy	314.1
Rick White	248.0

Strikeouts

Esteban Yan	351
Ryan Rupe	348
Bryan Rekar	292
Wilson Alvarez	291
Tanyon Sturtze	285
Paul Wilson	270
Albie Lopez	262
Rolando Arrojo	259
Tony Saunders	202
Joe Kennedy	187

Bases on balls

Wilson Alvarez	183
Tanyon Sturtze	182
Albie Lopez	177
Ryan Rupe	161
Esteban Yan	155
Bryan Rekar	146
Tony Saunders	140
Paul Wilson	135
Rolando Arrojo	125
Doug Creek	109

Games

Esteban Yan	266
Roberto Hernandez	207
Albie Lopez	170
Rick White	145
Doug Creek	140
Jim Mecir	123
Bryan Rekar	98
Tanyon Sturtze	91
Scott Aldred	85
Ryan Rupe	85

Shutouts

Rolando Arrojo	2
Albie Lopez	2
Bobby Witt	2
Travis Harper	1
Joe Kennedy	1
Steve Trachsel	1

Saves

Roberto Hernandez	101
Esteban Yan	42
Travis Phelps	5
Albie Lopez	4
Victor Zambrano	3
Lance Carter	2
Rick White	2
Wilson Alvarez	1
Doug Creek	1
Travis Harper	1
Steve Kent	1
Jim Mecir	1
Jeff Sparks	1
Tanyon Sturtze	1

TEAM SEASON, GAME RECORDS

SEASON

Batting		
Most at-bats	5,604	2002
Most runs	772	1999
Fewest runs	620	1998
Most hits	1,531	1999
Most singles	1,085	1999
Most doubles	311	2001
Most triples	43	1998
Most home runs	145	1999
Fewest home runs	162	2000
Most grand slams	4	2000, 2001
Most pinch-hit home runs	3	1998
Most total bases	2,296	1999
Most stolen bases	120	1998
Highest batting average	.274	1999
Lowest batting average	.253	2002
Highest slugging pct.	.411	1999
Pitching		
Lowest ERA	4.35	1998
Highest ERA	5.29	2002
Most complete games	12	2002
Most shutouts	8	1998, 2000
Most saves	45	1999
Most walks	695	1999
Most strikeouts	1,055	1999
Fielding		
Most errors	139	2001
Fewest errors	94	1998
Most double plays	198	1999
Highest fielding average	.985	1998
General		
Most games won	69	1999, 2000
Most games lost	106	2002
Highest win pct.	.429	2000
Lowest win pct.	.342	2002

GAME, INNING

Batting		
Most runs, game	15	5-30-99, 9-19-99
Most runs, inning	11	5-20-2000
Most hits, game	20	5-20-2000
Most home runs, game	6	8-10-2002
Most total bases, game	36	5-30-99, 8-10-2002

Fred McGriff has added 78 home runs and 291 RBIs to his career totals as the first baseman for the Devil Rays.

DEVIL RAYS YEAR-BY-YEAR

				Games		Leaders					
Year	W	L	Place	Back	Manager	Batting avg.	Hits	Home runs	RBIs	Wins	ERA
1998	63	99	5th	51	Rothschild	Ledesma, .324	McCracken, 179	McGriff, 19	McGriff, 81	Arrojo, 14	Arrojo, 3.56
1999	69	93	5th	29	Rothschild	McGriff, .310	McGriff, 164	Canseco, 34	McGriff, 104	Alvarez, 9	White, 4.08
2000	69	92	5th	18	Rothschild	Perry, .302	Williams, 173	Vaughn, 28	McGriff, 106	Lopez, 11	Lopez, 4.13
2001	62	100	5th	34	Rothschild, McRae	McGriff, .318	Grieve, 143	Vaughn, 24	Vaughn, 82	Sturtze, 11	Sturtze, 4.42
2002	55	106	5th	48	McRae	Winn, .298	Winn, 181	Huff, 23	Winn, 75	Kennedy, Zambrano, 8	Kennedy, 4.53

* Tied for position. † Lost Championship Series. ‡ Won Championship Series. ∞ First half 37-23; second half 27-22. ▲ Lost Division Series.

Note: Batting average minimum 350 at-bats; ERA minimum 90 innings pitched.

Texas Rangers

FRANCHISE CHRONOLOGY

First season: 1961, in Washington, as part of baseball's first expansion. The Senators, who were replacing a Washington Senators franchise that was relocating to Minnesota, dropped a 4-3 decision to Chicago in their Major League debut en route to a 61-100 first-season record.

1962-1971: The Senators, upholding the long tradition of their Washington predecessors, lost 100 or more games in each of their first four seasons and never finished above fourth place in their 11-year existence. The highlight of their Washington stay was an 86-76 mark in 1969, the first season of divisional play. That Senators team still finished 23 games behind East Division winner Baltimore.

1972-present: The Senators, relocated to Arlington, Texas, as the Texas Rangers, dropped a 1-0 debut to California and struggled to consecutive 100-loss seasons. The Rangers have fared better than their Washington ancestor, but they still are looking for their first pennant and World Series appearance. Their first West Division title was accompanied by an asterisk—the Rangers finished first in the strike-halted 1994 season with a 52-62 record. Their second, third and fourth titles, in 1996, '98 and '99, were all followed by losses to the New York Yankees in the Division Series.

First baseman Frank Howard.

RANGERS VS. OPPONENTS BY DECADE

	A's	Indians	Orioles	Red Sox	Tigers	Twins	White Sox	Yankees	Angels	Brewers	Royals	Blue Jays	Mariners	Devil Rays	Interleague	Decade Record
1961-69	77-78	73-88	52-110	75-86	68-94	56-99	61-95	55-104	80-76	5-7	5-7					607-844
1970-79	76-78	71-58	50-77	56-72	64-64	76-80	65-90	49-79	79-77	49-67	69-84	18-16	25-18			747-860
1980-89	66-57	57-55	39-72	53-64	47-73	65-64	64-59	54-62	55-68	52-63	54-70	49-67	65-65			720-839
1990-99	63-61	63-50	46-60	61-43	63-54	70-50	59-58	54-54	61-63	46-44	61-56	63-53	54-71	15-8	28-22	807-747
2000-02	23-27	13-15	19-11	8-16	10-18	12-18	11-17	9-17	24-26		14-14	15-13	17-35	17-13	24-30	216-270
Totals	305-301	277-266	206-330	253-281	252-303	279-311	260-319	221-316	299-310	152-181	203-231	145-149	161-189	32-21	52-52	3097-3560

Interleague results: 10-6 vs. Diamondbacks, 0-3 vs. Braves, 2-1 vs. Cubs, 2-1 vs. Reds, 8-8 vs. Rockies, 5-7 vs. Astros, 7-9 vs. Dodgers, 3-0 vs. Pirates, 8-8 vs. Padres, 7-9 vs. Giants.

MANAGERS

(Washington Senators, 1961-71)

Name	*Years*	*Record*
Mickey Vernon	1961-63	135-227
Gil Hodges	1963-67	321-444
Jim Lemon	1968	65-96
Ted Williams	1969-72	273-364
Whitey Herzog	1973	47-91
Del Wilber	1973	1-0
Billy Martin	1973-75	137-141
Frank Lucchesi	1975-77	142-149
Eddie Stanky	1977	1-0
Connie Ryan	1977	2-4
Billy Hunter	1977-78	146-108
Pat Corrales	1978-80	160-164
Don Zimmer	1981-82	95-106
Darrell Johnson	1982	26-40
Doug Rader	1983-85	155-200
Bobby Valentine	1985-92	581-605
Toby Harrah	1992	32-44
Kevin Kennedy	1993-94	138-138
Johnny Oates	1995-2001	506-476
Jerry Narron	2001-2002	134-162

WEST DIVISION CHAMPIONS

Year	*Record*	*Manager*	*Div. Series Result*
1994	52-62	Kennedy	None
1996	90-72	Oates	Lost to Yankees
1998	88-74	Oates	Lost to Yankees
1999	95-67	Oates	Lost to Yankees

ALL-TIME RECORD OF EXPANSION TEAMS

Team	W	L	Pct.	DT	P	WS
Arizona	440	370	.543	3	1	1
Kansas City	2,675	2,694	.498	6	2	1
Houston	3,229	3,285	.496	7	0	0
Toronto	2,025	2,063	.495	5	2	2
Anaheim	3,243	3,431	.486	3	1	1
Montreal	2,605	2,769	.485	2	0	0
Colorado	740	817	.475	0	0	0
New York	3,091	3,412	.475	4	4	2
Milwaukee	2,545	2,831	.473	2	1	0
Seattle	1,924	2,163	.471	3	0	0
Texas	3,097	3,560	.465	4	0	0
San Diego	2,460	2,921	.457	3	2	0
Florida	706	847	.455	0	1	1
Tampa Bay	318	490	.394	0	0	0

DT—Division Titles. P—Pennants won. WS—World Series won.

First baseman Pete O'Brien was Mr. Reliable during seven seasons with the Rangers.

ATTENDANCE HIGHS

Total	*Season*	*Park*
2,945,228	1997	The Ballpark in Ar
2,927,409	1998	The Ballpark in Ar
2,888,920	1996	The Ballpark in Ar
2,831,111	2001	The Ballpark in Ar
2,800,147	2000	The Ballpark in Ar

BALLPARK CHRONOLOGY

The Ballpark in Arlington (1994-present)

Capacity: 49,115.
First game: Milwaukee 4, Rangers 3 (April 11, 1994).
First batter: Pat Listach, Brewers.
First hit: David Hulse, Rangers (single).
First run: Dave Nilsson, Brewers (5th inning).
First home run: Dave Nilsson, Brewers.
First winning pitcher: Jaime Navarro, Brewers.
First-season attendance: 2,503,198.

Griffith Stadium, Washington, D.C. (1961)

Capacity: 27,410.
First game: Chicago 4, Senators 3 (April 10, 1961).
First-season attendance: 597,287.

RFK Stadium, Washington, D.C. (1962-71)

Capacity: 45,016.
First game: Senators 4, Detroit 1 (April 9, 1962).
First-season attendance: 729,775.

Arlington Stadium, Texas (1972-93)

Capacity: 43,521.
First game: Rangers 7, California 6 (April 21, 1972).
First-season attendance: 662,974.

Note: RFK Stadium was originally called D.C. Stadium.

A.L. MVPs

Jeff Burroughs, OF, 1974
Juan Gonzalez, OF, 1996
Juan Gonzalez, OF, 1998
Ivan Rodriguez, C, 1999

ROOKIE OF THE YEAR

Mike Hargrove, 1B, 1974

MANAGER OF THE YEAR

*Johnny Oates, 1996

*Co-winner

RETIRED UNIFORM

No.	*Name*	*Pos.*
34	Nolan Ryan	P

MILESTONE PERFORMANCES

25-plus home runs

57—Alex Rodriguez 2002
52—Alex Rodriguez 2001
48—Frank Howard 1969
47—Juan Gonzalez 1996
Rafael Palmeiro 1999, 2001
46—Juan Gonzalez 1993
45—Juan Gonzalez 1998
44—Frank Howard 1968, 1970
43—Juan Gonzalez 1992
Rafael Palmeiro 2002
42—Juan Gonzalez 1997
39—Juan Gonzalez 1999
Rafael Palmeiro 2000
38—Dean Palmer 1996
37—Rafael Palmeiro 1993
36—Frank Howard 1967
35—Ivan Rodriguez 1999
33—Dean Palmer 1993
32—Larry Parrish 1987
Mickey Tettleton 1995
31—Jose Canseco 1994
30—Mike Epstein 1969
Jeff Burroughs 1973
Pete Incaviglia 1986
Ruben Sierra 1987
29—Jeff Burroughs 1975
Bobby Bonds 1978
Ruben Sierra 1989
28—Don Lock 1964
Larry Parrish 1986
27—Don Lock 1963
Toby Harrah 1977
Pete Incaviglia 1987
Juan Gonzalez 1991, 1995
Ivan Rodriguez 2000
26—Frank Howard 1971
Larry Parrish 1983
Rafael Palmeiro 1991
Dean Palmer 1992
Rusty Greer 1997
25—Jeff Burroughs 1974
Ruben Sierra 1991
Ivan Rodriguez 2001

100-plus RBIs

157—Juan Gonzalez 1998
148—Rafael Palmeiro 1999
144—Juan Gonzalez 1996
142—Alex Rodriguez 2002
135—Alex Rodriguez 2001
131—Juan Gonzalez 1997
128—Juan Gonzalez 1999
126—Frank Howard 1970
123—Rafael Palmeiro 2001
120—Rafael Palmeiro 2000
119—Ruben Sierra 1989
118—Jeff Burroughs 1974
Juan Gonzalez 1993
117—Al Oliver 1980
116—Ruben Sierra 1991
113—Ivan Rodriguez 1999
111—Frank Howard 1969
109—Ruben Sierra 1987
Juan Gonzalez 1992
108—Rusty Greer 1998
107—Dean Palmer 1996
106—Frank Howard 1968
105—Rafael Palmeiro 1993, 2002
102—Juan Gonzalez 1991
Will Clark 1998
101—Buddy Bell 1979
Larry Parrish 1984
Rusty Greer 1999
100—Larry Parrish 1987
Rusty Greer 1996

20-plus victories

1974—Fergie Jenkins 25-12
1992—Kevin Brown 21-11
1998—Rick Helling 20-7

A.L. home run champions

1968—Frank Howard 44
1970—Frank Howard 44
1992—Juan Gonzalez 43
1993—Juan Gonzalez 46
2001—Alex Rodriguez 52
2002—Alex Rodriguez 57

A.L. RBI champions

1970—Frank Howard 126
1974—Jeff Burroughs 118
1989—Ruben Sierra 119
1998—Juan Gonzalez 157
2002—Alex Rodriguez 142

A.L. batting champions

1991—Julio Franco ..... .341

A.L. ERA champions

1961—Dick Donovan 2.40
1969—Dick Bosman 2.19
1983—Rick Honeycutt 2.42

A.L. strikeout champions

1989—Nolan Ryan 301
1990—Nolan Ryan 232

No-hit pitchers

(9 innings or more)

1973—Jim Bibby ..... 6-0 vs. Oakland
1977—Bert Blyleven ..... 6-0 vs. California
1990—Nolan Ryan ..... 5-0 vs. Oakland
1991—Nolan Ryan ..... 3-0 vs. Toronto
1994—Kenny Rogers ....4-0 vs. California (Perfect)

Longest hitting streaks

28—Gabe Kapler 2000
24—Mickey Rivers 1980
22—Jim Sundberg 1978
21—Johnny Grubb 1979
Buddy Bell 1980
Al Oliver 1980
Juan Gonzalez ..... 1996 (2 times)
20—Mickey Rivers 1980
Juan Gonzalez 1998
Ivan Rodriguez 1999
19—Ken McMullen 1967
Billy Sample 1981
Scott Fletcher 1986
Ivan Rodriguez 1996
18—Bill Stein 1981
Billy Sample 1982
Ruben Sierra 1991
17—Gene Woodling 1961
Chuck Hinton 1962
Ken Hamlin 1965
Cesar Tovar 1974
Toby Harrah 1976
Al Oliver 1980
Jim Sundberg 1981
Buddy Bell 1983
Todd Zeile 1999
16—Juan Beniquez 1977
Willie Montanez 1979
Rafael Palmeiro 1993

Venerable righthander Charlie Hough knuckleballed his way to 139 victories with the Rangers, a club career record.

INDIVIDUAL SEASON, GAME RECORDS

Catcher Jim Sundberg (left) and designated hitter Richie Zisk were teammates on the 1978, '79 and '80 Texas teams.

SEASON

Batting			
At-bats	670	Buddy Bell	1979
Runs	133	Alex Rodriguez	2001
Hits	210	Mickey Rivers	1980
Singles	165	Mickey Rivers	1980
Doubles	50	Juan Gonzalez	1998
Triples	14	Ruben Sierra	1989
Home runs	57	Alex Rodriguez	2002
Home runs, rookie	30	Pete Incaviglia	1986
Grand slams	3	3 times	
		Last by Rafael Palmeiro	1999
Total bases	393	Alex Rodriguez	2001
RBIs	157	Juan Gonzalez	1998
Walks	132	Frank Howard	1970
Most strikeouts	185	Pete Incaviglia	1986
Batting average	.341	Julio Franco	1991
Slugging pct.	.643	Juan Gonzalez	1996
Stolen bases	52	Bump Wills	1978
Pitching			
Games	85	Mitch Williams	1987
Complete games	29	Fergie Jenkins	1974
Innings	328.1	Fergie Jenkins	1974
Wins	25	Fergie Jenkins	1974
Losses	22	Denny McLain	1971
Winning pct.	.741 (20-7)	Rick Helling	1998
Walks	143	Bobby Witt	1986
Strikeouts	301	Nolan Ryan	1989
Shutouts	6	Fergie Jenkins	1974
		Bert Blyleven	1976
Home runs allowed	41	Rick Helling	1999
Lowest ERA	2.17	Mike Paul	1972
Saves	43	John Wetteland	1999

GAME

Batting			
Runs	5	Pete O'Brien	5-29-87
Hits	5	Last by Michael Young	6-14-2002
Doubles	3	Last by Alex Rodriguez	4-7-2001
Triples	2	Last by Michael Young	9-3-2002
Home runs	3	Last by Alex Rodriguez	8-17-2002
RBIs	9	Ivan Rodriguez	4-13-99
Total bases	14	Jose Canseco	6-13-94
Stolen bases	5	Scarborough Green	9-28-2000

CAREER LEADERS

BATTING

Games	
Jim Sundberg	1,512
Ivan Rodriguez	1,479
Rafael Palmeiro	1,419
Toby Harrah	1,355
Juan Gonzalez	1,318
Frank Howard	1,172
Ruben Sierra	1,147
Ed Brinkman	1,143
Rusty Greer	1,027
Buddy Bell	958

At-bats	
Ivan Rodriguez	5,656
Rafael Palmeiro	5,269
Juan Gonzalez	5,108
Jim Sundberg	4,684
Toby Harrah	4,572
Ruben Sierra	4,447
Frank Howard	4,120
Ed Brinkman	3,847
Rusty Greer	3,829
Buddy Bell	3,623

Runs	
Rafael Palmeiro	866
Ivan Rodriguez	852
Juan Gonzalez	829
Rusty Greer	643
Toby Harrah	631
Ruben Sierra	631
Frank Howard	544
Jim Sundberg	482
Buddy Bell	471
Dean Palmer	425

Hits	
Ivan Rodriguez	1,723
Rafael Palmeiro	1,546
Juan Gonzalez	1,499
Ruben Sierra	1,246
Jim Sundberg	1,180
Toby Harrah	1,174
Rusty Greer	1,166
Frank Howard	1,141
Buddy Bell	1,060
Pete O'Brien	914

Doubles	
Ivan Rodriguez	344
Juan Gonzalez	303
Rafael Palmeiro	300
Rusty Greer	258
Ruben Sierra	248
Jim Sundberg	200
Buddy Bell	197
Toby Harrah	187
Pete O'Brien	161
Frank Howard	155

Triples	
Ruben Sierra	44
Chuck Hinton	30
Ivan Rodriguez	28
Ed Brinkman	27
Jim Sundberg	27
Rusty Greer	25
Ed Stroud	24
Rafael Palmeiro	23
Toby Harrah	22
Oddibe McDowell	22
Del Unser	22

Home runs	
Juan Gonzalez	348
Rafael Palmeiro	283
Frank Howard	246
Ivan Rodriguez	215
Ruben Sierra	177
Dean Palmer	154
Larry Parrish	149
Toby Harrah	124
Pete Incaviglia	124
Rusty Greer	119

Total bases	
Juan Gonzalez	2,886
Ivan Rodriguez	2,768
Rafael Palmeiro	2,741
Ruben Sierra	2,113
Frank Howard	2,074
Rusty Greer	1,831
Toby Harrah	1,777
Jim Sundberg	1,614
Buddy Bell	1,560
Larry Parrish	1,464

Runs batted in	
Juan Gonzalez	1,110
Rafael Palmeiro	927
Ivan Rodriguez	829
Ruben Sierra	730
Frank Howard	701
Rusty Greer	614
Toby Harrah	568
Larry Parrish	522
Buddy Bell	499
Pete O'Brien	487

Extra-base hits	
Juan Gonzalez	671
Rafael Palmeiro	606
Ivan Rodriguez	587
Ruben Sierra	469
Frank Howard	421
Rusty Greer	402
Toby Harrah	333
Buddy Bell	305
Larry Parrish	305
Dean Palmer	296

Batting average
(Minimum 500 games)

Batting average	
Al Oliver	.319
Will Clark	.308
Julio Franco	.307
Ivan Rodriguez	.305
Rusty Greer	.305
Mickey Rivers	.303
Juan Gonzalez	.293
Rafael Palmeiro	.293
Mike Hargrove	.293
Buddy Bell	.293

Stolen bases	
Bump Wills	161
Toby Harrah	153
Dave Nelson	144
Oddibe McDowell	129
Julio Franco	98
Tom Goodwin	93
Chuck Hinton	92
Bill Sample	92
Cecil Espy	91
Ruben Sierra	89

PITCHING

Earned-run average
(Minimum 500 innings)

Earned-run average	
Gaylord Perry	3.26
Dick Bosman	3.35
Jon Matlack	3.41
Nolan Ryan	3.43
Claude Osteen	3.46
Joe Coleman	3.51
Fergie Jenkins	3.56
Casey Cox	3.67
Charlie Hough	3.68
Danny Darwin	3.72

Wins	
Charlie Hough	139
Bobby Witt	104
Kenny Rogers	101
Fergie Jenkins	93
Kevin Brown	78
Rick Helling	68
Jose Guzman	66
Dick Bosman	59
Danny Darwin	55
Darren Oliver	54

Losses	
Charlie Hough	123
Bobby Witt	104
Kenny Rogers	79
Fergie Jenkins	72
Dick Bosman	64
Kevin Brown	64
Jose Guzman	62
Bennie Daniels	60
Danny Darwin	52
Rick Helling	51

Innings pitched	
Charlie Hough	2,308.0
Bobby Witt	1,680.2
Kenny Rogers	1,502.0
Fergie Jenkins	1,410.1
Kevin Brown	1,278.2
Dick Bosman	1,103.1
Jose Guzman	1,013.2
Rick Helling	1,008.0
Jon Matlack	915.0
Danny Darwin	872.0

Strikeouts	
Charlie Hough	1,452
Bobby Witt	1,405
Kenny Rogers	988
Nolan Ryan	939
Fergie Jenkins	895
Kevin Brown	742
Jose Guzman	715
Rick Helling	687
Gaylord Perry	575
Dick Bosman	573

Bases on balls	
Bobby Witt	1,001
Charlie Hough	965
Kenny Rogers	567
Kevin Brown	428
Jose Guzman	395
Rick Helling	381
Jim Hannan	378
Darren Oliver	376
Nolan Ryan	353
Roger Pavlik	351

Games	
Kenny Rogers	463
Jeff Russell	445
Charlie Hough	344
Casey Cox	302
Bobby Witt	276
Darold Knowles	271
Ron Kline	260
Jim Hannan	248
John Wetteland	248
Mitch Williams	232

Shutouts	
Fergie Jenkins	17
Gaylord Perry	12
Bert Blyleven	11
Charlie Hough	11
Dick Bosman	9
Jim Bibby	8
Tom Cheney	7
Joe Coleman	7
Doc Medich	7
Kevin Brown	6
Phil Ortega	6
Nolan Ryan	6

Saves	
John Wetteland	150
Jeff Russell	134
Ron Kline	83
Darold Knowles	64
Tom Henke	58
Jim Kern	37
Steve Foucault	35
Mitch Williams	32
Jeff Zimmerman	32
Greg Harris	31
Mike Henneman	31

TEAM SEASON, GAME RECORDS

SEASON

Batting		
Most at-bats	5,703	1991
Most runs	945	1999
Fewest runs	461	1972
Most hits	1,653	1999
Most singles	1,202	1980
Most doubles	330	2000
Most triples	46	1989
Most home runs	246	2001
Fewest home runs	56	1972
Most grand slams	8	1999
Most pinch-hit home runs	8	1965, 1966
Most total bases	2,705	1999
Most stolen bases	196	1978
Highest batting average	.293	1980, 1996, 1999
Lowest batting average	.217	1972
Highest slugging pct	.479	1999

Pitching		
Lowest ERA	3.31	1983
Highest ERA	5.71	2001
Most complete games	63	1976
Most shutouts	17	1977
Most saves	47	1999
Most walks	760	1987
Most strikeouts	1,112	1989

Fielding		
Most errors	191	1975
Fewest errors	87	1996
Most double plays	173	1970, 1975
Highest fielding average	.986	1996

General		
Most games won	95	1999
Most games lost	106	1963
Highest win pct.	.586	1999
Lowest win pct.	.346	1963

GAME, INNING

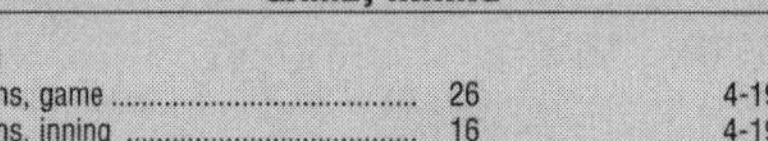

Batting		
Most runs, game	26	4-19-96
Most runs, inning	16	4-19-96
Most hits, game	23	4-2-98
Most home runs, game	7	9-13-86
Most total bases, game	43	9-13-86

Third baseman Toby Harrah ranks high on most Rangers offensive charts.

RANGERS YEAR-BY-YEAR

Year	W	L	Place	Games Back	Manager	Leaders: Batting avg.	Hits	Home runs	RBIs	Wins	ERA
						WASHINGTON SENATORS					
1961	61	100	*9th	47½	Vernon	Green, .280	O'Connell, 128	G. Green, 18	Tasby, 63	Daniels, 12	Donovan, 2.40
1962	60	101	10th	35½	Vernon	Hinton, .310	Hinton, 168	Bright, Hinton, 17	Hinton, 75	Stenhouse, 11	Cheney, 3.17
1963	56	106	10th	48½	Vernon, Hodges	Hinton, .269	Hinton, 152	Lock, 27	Lock, 82	Osteen, 9	Cheney, 2.71
1964	62	100	9th	37	Hodges	Hinton, .274	Hinton, 141	Lock, 28	Lock, 80	Osteen, 15	Ridzik, 2.89
1965	70	92	8th	32	Hodges	Howard, .289	Howard, 149	Howard, 21	Howard, 84	Richert, 15	Richert, 2.60
1966	71	88	8th	25½	Hodges	Howard, .278	Valentine, 140	Howard, 18	Howard, 71	Richert, 14	Kline, 2.39
1967	76	85	*6th	15½	Hodges	Howard, .256	McMullen, 138	Howard, 36	Howard, 89	Pascual, 12	Knowles, 2.70
1968	65	96	10th	37½	Lemon	Howard, .274	Howard, 164	Howard, 44	Howard, 106	Pascual, 13	Pascual, 2.69
						EAST DIVISION					
1969	86	76	4th	23	Williams	Howard, .296	Howard, 175	Howard, 48	Howard, 111	Bosman, 14	Bosman, 2.19
1970	70	92	6th	38	Williams	Howard, .283	Brinkman, 164	Howard, 44	Howard, 126	Bosman, 16	Knowles, 2.04
1971	63	96	5th	38½	Williams	Howard, .279	Howard, 153	Howard, 26	Howard, 83	Bosman, 12	Gogolewski, 2.75
						TEXAS RANGERS					
						WEST DIVISION					
1972	54	100	6th	38½	Williams	Biittner, Harrah, .259	Billings, 119	Ford, 14	Billings, 58	Hand, 10	Paul, 2.17
1973	57	105	6th	37	Herzog, Wilber, Martin	A. Johnson, .287	A. Johnson, 179	Burroughs, 30	Burroughs, 85	Bibby, 9	Bibby, 3.24
1974	84	76	2nd	5	Martin	Hargrove, .323	Burroughs, 167	Burroughs, 25	Burroughs, 118	Jenkins, 25	Foucault, 2.24
1975	79	83	3rd	19	Martin, Lucchesi	Hargrove, .303	Randle, 166	Burroughs, 29	Burroughs, 94	Jenkins, 17	G. Perry, 3.03
1976	76	86	*4th	14	Lucchesi	Hargrove, .287	Hargrove, 155	Grieve, 20	Burroughs, 86	G. Perry, 15	Blyleven, 2.76
1977	94	68	2nd	8	Lucchesi, Stanky, Ryan, Hunter	Hargrove, .305	Hargrove, 160	Harrah, 27	Harrah, 87	Alexander, 17	Blyleven, 2.72
1978	87	75	*2nd	5	Hunter, Corrales	Oliver, .324	Oliver, 170	Bonds, 29	Oliver, 89	Jenkins, 18	Matlack, 2.27
1979	83	79	3rd	5	Corrales	Oliver, .323	Bell, 200	Bell, Putnam, Zisk, 18	Bell, 101	Comer, 17	Kern, 1.57
1980	76	85	4th	20½	Corrales	Rivers, .333	Rivers, 210	Oliver, Zisk, 19	Oliver, 117	Medich, 14	Darwin, 2.63
1981	57	48	†2nd/3rd	—	Zimmer	Oliver, .309	Oliver, 130	Bell, 10	Bell, 64	Honeycutt, 11	Medich, 3.08
1982	64	98	6th	29	Zimmer, Johnson	Bell, .296	Bell, 159	Hostetler, 22	Bell, Hostetler, 67	Hough, 16	Schmidt, 3.20
1983	77	85	3rd	22	Rader	Bell, .277	Wright, 175	Parrish, 26	Parrish, 88	Hough, 15	Honeycutt, 2.42
1984	69	92	7th	14½	Rader	Bell, .315	Parrish, 175	Parrish, 22	Parrish, 101	Hough, 16	Tanana, 3.25
1985	62	99	7th	28½	Rader, Valentine	Ward, .287	Ward, 170	O'Brien, 22	O'Brien, 92	Hough, 14	Harris, 2.47
1986	87	75	2nd	5	Valentine	Ward, .316	O'Brien, 160	Incaviglia, 30	Parrish, 94	Hough, 17	Harris, 2.83
1987	75	87	*6th	10	Valentine	Fletcher, .287	Fletcher, Sierra, 169	Parrish, 32	Sierra, 109	Hough, 18	Mohorcic, 2.99
1988	70	91	6th	33½	Valentine	Petralli, .282	Sierra, 156	Sierra, 23	Sierra, 91	Hough, 15	Hough, 3.32
1989	83	79	4th	16	Valentine	Franco, .316	Sierra, 194	Sierra, 29	Sierra, 119	Ryan, 16	Ryan, 3.20
1990	83	79	3rd	20	Valentine	Palmeiro, .319	Palmeiro, 191	Incaviglia, 24	Sierra, 96	Witt, 17	Rogers, 3.13
1991	85	77	3rd	10	Valentine	Franco, .341	Palmeiro, Sierra, 203	Gonzalez, 27	Sierra, 116	Guzman, 13	Ryan, 2.91
1992	77	85	4th	19	Valentine, Harrah	Sierra, .278	Palmeiro, 163	Gonzalez, 43	Gonzalez, 109	Brown, 21	Brown, 3.32
1993	86	76	2nd	8	Kennedy	Gonzalez, .310	Palmeiro, 176	Gonzalez, 46	Gonzalez, 118	Rogers, 16	Pavlik, 3.41
1994	52	62	1st	+1	Kennedy	Clark, .329	Clark, 128	Canseco, 31	Canseco, 90	Rogers, 11	Rogers, 4.46
1995	74	70	3rd	4	Oates	Rodriguez, .303	Nixon, 174	Tettleton, 32	Clark, 92	Rogers, 17	Rogers, 3.38
1996	90	72	‡1st	+4½	Oates	Greer, .332	Rodriguez, 192	Gonzalez, 47	Gonzalez, 144	Hill, Witt, 16	Hill, 3.63
1997	77	85	3rd	13	Oates	Clark, .326	Greer, 193	Gonzalez, 42	Gonzalez, 131	Oliver, 13	Oliver, 4.20
1998	88	74	‡1st	+3	Oates	Rodriguez, .321	Gonzalez, 193	Gonzalez, 45	Gonzalez, 157	Helling, 20	Sele, 4.23
1999	95	67	‡1st	+8	Oates	Rodriguez, .332	Rodriguez, 199	Palmeiro, 47	Palmeiro, 148	Sele, 18	Loaiza, 4.56
2000	71	91	4th	20½	Oates	Rodriguez, .347	Palmeiro, 163	Palmeiro, 39	Palmeiro, 120	Helling, 16	Helling, 4.48
2001	73	89	4th	43	Oates, Narron	Catalanotto, .330	A. Rodriguez, 201	A. Rodriguez, 52	A. Rodriguez, 135	Helling, 12	Davis, 4.45
2002	72	90	4th	31	Narron	A. Rodriguez, .300	A. Rodriguez, 187	A. Rodriguez, 57	A. Rodriguez, 142	Rogers, 13	Rogers, 3.84

* Tied for position. †First half 33-22; second half 24-26. ‡ Lost Division Series.

Note: Batting average minimum 350 at-bats; ERA minimum 90 innings pitched.

Bobby Shantz

WASHINGTON lost one team and gained another in the two-team 1961 American League expansion that marked the first addition of baseball franchises in more than six decades. The original Senators were granted permission to move to Minneapolis/St. Paul for the 1961 season and the new Senators, under the ownership of Elwood R. Quesada, were admitted to the fold on October 26, 1960, along with the Los Angeles Angels.

The new Senators, who would become the Texas Rangers after 11 Washington seasons, grabbed lefthander Bobby Shantz with their first pick in the December 14, 1960, A.L. expansion draft and 31 players overall. They made their Major League debut on April 10, 1961, dropping a 4-3 decision to the Chicago White Sox.

Expansion draft (December 14, 1960)

Players

Player	Team	Position
Chester Boak	Kansas City	second base
Leo Burke	Baltimore	infield
Pete Daley	Kansas City	catcher
Dutch Dotterer	Kansas City	catcher
Gene Green	Baltimore	catcher
Joe Hicks	Chicago	outfield
Chuck Hinton	Baltimore	outfield
Bob Johnson	Kansas City	infield
Marty Keough	Cleveland	outfield
Jim King	Cleveland	outfield
Billy Klaus	Baltimore	infield
Dale Long	New York	first base
Jim Mahoney	Boston	shortstop
John Schaive	Minnesota	second base
Haywood Sullivan	Boston	catcher
Willie Tasby	Boston	outfield
Coot Veal	Detroit	shortstop
Gene Woodling	Baltimore	outfield
Bud Zipfel	New York	first base

Pitchers

Pitcher	Team	Throws
Pete Burnside	Detroit	lefthanded
Dick Donovan	Chicago	righthanded
Rudy Hernandez	Minnesota	righthanded
Ed Hobaugh	Chicago	righthanded
John Klippstein	Cleveland	righthanded
Hector Maestri	Minnesota	righthanded
Carl Mathias	Cleveland	lefthanded
Joe McClain	Minnesota	righthanded
*Bobby Shantz	New York	lefthanded
Dave Sisler	Detroit	righthanded
Tom Sturdivant	Boston	righthanded
Hal Woodeshick	Minnesota	lefthanded

*First pick

Opening day lineup

April 10, 1961

Coot Veal, shortstop
Billy Klaus, third base
Marty Keough, right field
Dale Long, first base
Gene Woodling, left field
Willie Tasby, center field
Danny O'Connell, second base
Pete Daley, catcher
Dick Donovan, pitcher

Billy Klaus

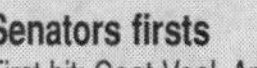

Senators firsts

First hit: Coot Veal, April 10, 1961, vs. Chicago (single)
First home run: Billy Klaus, April 15, 1961, vs. Cleveland
First RBI: Gene Woodling, April 10, 1961, vs. Chicago
First win: Joe McClain, April 14, 1961, vs. Cleveland
First shutout: Tom Sturdivant, May 13, 1969, 4-0 vs. Boston

HISTORY

TORONTO BLUE JAYS

Outfielder George Bell.

FRANCHISE CHRONOLOGY

First season: 1977, as part of a two-team expansion that increased the American League field to 14 teams. The Blue Jays celebrated the debut of A.L. baseball in Canada with a 9-5 victory over Chicago, but they would go on to lose 107 times and finish last in the A.L. East, 45½ games behind the New York Yankees.

1978-present: The Blue Jays struggled for six seasons as they built the foundation for a franchise that would rise to prominence. Building patiently from within, the Jays topped 100 losses in each of their first three seasons and occupied the basement of the A.L. East Division five consecutive years. But the patience was rewarded in 1985 when the young and talented Blue Jays, playing in their ninth season, captured their first East Division title and began a run that would produce consecutive World Series championships in 1992 and '93. The Blue Jays lost three Championship Series before securing 1992 postseason victories over Oakland and Atlanta—and the first World Series triumph for a Canadian-based team.

BLUE JAYS VS. OPPONENTS BY DECADE

	A's	Indians	Orioles	Red Sox	Tigers	Twins	White Sox	Yankees	Angels	Rangers	Brewers	Royals	Mariners	Devil Rays	Interleague	Decade Record
1977-79	15-18	14-27	14-29	11-32	15-28	6-26	14-19	14-29	12-20	16-18	13-30	10-22	12-20			166-318
1980-89	53-67	71-52	61-62	62-59	68-59	64-50	70-50	57-65	63-57	67-49	56-71	56-60	69-45			817-746
1990-99	53-55	65-56	69-54	52-72	70-52	72-38	54-53	57-64	58-53	53-63	45-52	62-55	54-50	15-10	22-27	801-754
2000-02	12-16	11-13	33-18	21-29	19-5	10-13	10-12	24-26	13-17	13-15		13-11	8-20	28-22	26-28	241-245
Totals	133-156	161-148	177-163	146-192	172-144	152-127	148-134	152-184	146-147	149-145	114-153	141-148	143-135	43-32	48-55	2025-2063

Interleague results: 2-1 vs. Diamondbacks, 9-6 vs. Braves, 3-0 vs. Rockies, 4-11 vs. Marlins, 1-2 vs. Dodgers, 18-13 vs. Expos, 3-12 vs. Mets, 7-8 vs. Phillies, 1-2 vs. Giants.

MANAGERS

Name	*Years*	*Record*
Roy Hartsfield	1977-79	166-318
Bobby Mattick	1980-81	104-164
Bobby Cox	1982-85	355-292
Jimy Williams	1986-89	281-241
Cito Gaston	1989-97	702-650
Mel Queen	1997	4-1
Tim Johnson	1998	88-74
Jim Fregosi	1999-2000	167-159
Buck Martinez	2001-2002	100-115
Carlos Tosca	2002	58-51

WORLD SERIES CHAMPIONS

Year	*Loser*	*Length*	*MVP*
1992	Atlanta	6 games	Borders
1993	Philadelphia	6 games	Molitor

Second baseman Roberto Alomar was a key figure for the 1992 and '93 championship teams.

A.L. PENNANT WINNERS

Year	*Record*	*Manager*	*Series Result*
1992	96-66	Gaston	Defeated Braves
1993	95-67	Gaston	Defeated Phillies

EAST DIVISION CHAMPIONS

Year	*Record*	*Manager*	*ALCS Result*
1985	99-62	Cox	Lost to Royals
1989	89-73	Williams, Gaston	Lost to A's
1991	91-71	Gaston	Lost to Twins
1992	96-66	Gaston	Defeated A's
1993	95-67	Gaston	Defeated White Sox

ALL-TIME RECORD OF EXPANSION TEAMS

Team	W	L	Pct.	DT	P	WS
Arizona	440	370	.543	3	1	1
Kansas City	2,675	2,694	.498	6	2	1
Houston	3,229	3,285	.496	7	0	0
Toronto	2,025	2,063	.495	5	2	2
Anaheim	3,243	3,431	.486	3	1	1
Montreal	2,605	2,769	.485	2	0	0
Colorado	740	817	.475	0	0	0
New York	3,091	3,412	.475	4	4	2
Milwaukee	2,545	2,831	.473	2	1	0
Seattle	1,924	2,163	.471	3	0	0
Texas	3,097	3,560	.465	4	0	0
San Diego	2,460	2,921	.457	3	2	0
Florida	706	847	.455	0	1	1
Tampa Bay	318	490	.394	0	0	0

DT—Division Titles. P—Pennants won. WS—World Series won.

ATTENDANCE HIGHS

Total	*Season*	*Park*
4,057,098	1993	SkyDome
4,028,318	1992	SkyDome
4,001,526	1991	SkyDome
3,885,284	1990	SkyDome
3,375,883	1989	SkyDome

BALLPARK CHRONOLOGY

SkyDome (1989-present)

Capacity: 45,100.
First game: Milwaukee 5, Blue Jays 3 (June 5, 1989).
First batter: Paul Molitor, Brewers.
First hit: Paul Molitor, Brewers (double).
First run: Paul Molitor, Brewers (1st inning).
First home run: Fred McGriff, Blue Jays.
First winning pitcher: Don August, Brewers.
First-season attendance: 3,375,883 (SkyDome and Exhibition Stadium).

Exhibition Stadium (1977-89)

Capacity: 43,737.
First game: Blue Jays 9, Chicago 5 (April 7, 1977).
First-season attendance: 1,701,052.

A.L. MVP

George Bell, OF, 1987

CY YOUNG WINNER

Pat Hentgen, RH, 1996
Roger Clemens, RH, 1997
Roger Clemens, RH, 1998

ROOKIE OF THE YEAR

Alfredo Griffin, SS, 1979
Eric Hinske, 3B, 2002

MANAGER OF THE YEAR

Bobby Cox, 1985

MILESTONE PERFORMANCES

25-plus home runs

47—George Bell 1987
46—Jose Canseco 1998
44—Carlos Delgado 1999
42—Shawn Green 1999
41—Carlos Delgado 2000
Tony Batista 2000
40—Jesse Barfield 1986
39—Carlos Delgado 2001
38—Carlos Delgado 1998
36—Fred McGriff 1989
Ed Sprague 1996
35—Fred McGriff 1990
Shawn Green 1998
34—Fred McGriff 1988
Joe Carter 1992
Jose Cruz 2001
33—Joe Carter 1991, 1993
Carlos Delgado 2002
32—Brad Fullmer 2000
31—George Bell 1986
Kelly Gruber 1990
Tony Batista *1999
Jose Cruz 2000
30—John Mayberry 1980
Joe Carter 1996
Carlos Delgado 1997
28—George Bell 1985
Jesse Barfield 1987
27—Willie Upshaw 1983
Jesse Barfield 1983, 1985
Joe Carter 1994
Raul Mondesi 2001
26—George Bell 1984
Lloyd Moseby 1987
Dave Winfield 1992
25—Joe Carter 1995
Carlos Delgado 1996

^26 with Blue Jays, 5 with Diamondbacks.

100-plus RBIs

137—Carlos Delgado 2000
134—George Bell 1987
Carlos Delgado 1999
123—Shawn Green 1999
121—Joe Carter 1993
119—Joe Carter 1992
118—Kelly Gruber 1990
115—Carlos Delgado 1998
114—Tony Batista 2000
111—Paul Molitor 1993
108—Jesse Barfield 1986
George Bell 1986
Joe Carter 1991
Dave Winfield 1992
Carlos Delgado 2002
107—John Olerud 1993
Joe Carter 1996
Jose Canseco 1998
104—Willie Upshaw 1983
George Bell 1989
Brad Fullmer 2000
103—Joe Carter 1994
102—Joe Carter 1997
Carlos Delgado 2001
101—Ed Sprague 1996
100—Shawn Green 1998
Tony Batista *1999
Vernon Wells 2002

*79 with Blue Jays, 21 with Diamondbacks.

20-plus victories

1992—Jack Morris 21-6
1996—Pat Hentgen 20-10
1997—Roger Clemens 21-7
1998—Roger Clemens 20-6
2000—David Wells 20-8

A.L. home run champions

1986—Jesse Barfield 40
1989—Fred McGriff 36

A.L. RBI champions

1987—George Bell 134

A.L. batting champions

1993—John Olerud .... .363

A.L. ERA champions

1985—Dave Stieb 2.48
1987—Jimmy Key 2.76
1996—Juan Guzman 2.93
1997—Roger Clemens 2.05
1998—Roger Clemens 2.65

A.L. strikeout champions

1997—Roger Clemens 292
1998—Roger Clemens 271

No-hit pitchers

(9 innings or more)

1990—Dave Stieb .... 3-0 vs. Cleveland

Longest hitting streaks

28—Shawn Green 1999
26—John Olerud 1993
Shannon Stewart 1999
22—George Bell 1989
Carlos Delgado 2000
21—Damaso Garcia 1983
Lloyd Moseby 1983
Dave Martinez 2000
20—Damaso Garcia 1982
19—Alfredo Griffin 1980
Roberto Alomar 1995
Carlos Delgado 1998
Jose Cruz 2001
18—Damaso Garcia 1986
Tony Fernandez 1987
17—John Mayberry 1980
Damaso Garcia 1982
George Bell 1987
Dave Winfield 1992
Tony Batista 1999
16—Dave McKay 1978
Jesse Barfield 1985
Damaso Garcia 1985
Tony Fernandez 1989
Roberto Alomar 1992
Joe Carter 1992
Ed Sprague 1995
Shannon Stewart 1999, 2001
15—Roy Howell 1977
George Bell 1986
Kelly Gruber 1989
Tony Fernandez 1990
Kelly Gruber 1990
Roberto Alomar 1991
Carlos Delgado 1997
Alex Gonzalez 2000

Eric Hinske's .279 batting average, 24 home runs and 84 RBIs helped the third baseman win A.L. 2002 Rookie of the Year honors.

INDIVIDUAL SEASON, GAME RECORDS

Slick-fielding shortstop Tony Fernandez holds single-season Blue Jays records for at-bats, hits, singles and triples.

SEASON

Batting			
At-bats	687	Tony Fernandez	1986
Runs	134	Shawn Green	1999
Hits	213	Tony Fernandez	1986
Singles	161	Tony Fernandez	1986
Doubles	57	Carlos Delgado	2000
Triples	17	Tony Fernandez	1990
Home runs	47	George Bell	1987
Home runs, rookie	24	Eric Hinske	2002
Grand slams	3	Carlos Delgado	1997
		Darrin Fletcher	2000
Total bases	378	Carlos Delgado	2000
RBIs	137	Carlos Delgado	2000
		Carlos Delgado	1999
Walks	123	Carlos Delgado	2000
Most strikeouts	159	Jose Canseco	1998
Fewest strikeouts	21	Bob Bailor	1978
Batting average	.363	John Olerud	1993
Slugging pct.	.664	Carlos Delgado	2000
Stolen bases	60	Dave Collins	1984
Pitching			
Games	89	Mark Eichorn	1987
Complete games	19	Dave Stieb	1982
Innings	288.1	Dave Stieb	1982
Wins	21	Jack Morris	1992
		Roger Clemens	1997
Losses	18	Jerry Garvin	1977
		Phil Huffman	1979
Winning pct.	.824	Juan Guzman	1993
Walks	128	Jim Clancy	1980
Strikeouts	292	Roger Clemens	1997
Shutouts	5	Dave Stieb	1982
Home runs allowed	36	Woody Williams	1998
Lowest ERA	2.05	Roger Clemens	1997
Saves	45	Duane Ward	1993

GAME

Batting			
Runs	5	Carlos Delgado	5-3-99
Hits	5	Last by Shannon Stewart	9-19-2002
Doubles	4	Last by Shannon Stewart	7-18-2000
Triples	2	Last by Shannon Stewart	9-20-97
Home runs	3	Last by Chris Woodward	8-7-2002
RBIs	9	Roy Howell	9-10-77
Total bases	13	Roy Howell	9-10-77
Stolen bases	4	Last by Otis Nixon	8-14-96

CAREER LEADERS

BATTING

Games	
Tony Fernandez	1,450
Lloyd Moseby	1,392
Ernie Whitt	1,218
George Bell	1,181
Carlos Delgado	1,134
Rance Mulliniks	1,115
Willie Upshaw	1,115
Joe Carter	1,039
Jesse Barfield	1,032
Alfredo Griffin	982

At-bats	
Tony Fernandez	5,335
Lloyd Moseby	5,124
George Bell	4,528
Joe Carter	4,093
Carlos Delgado	3,980
Willie Upshaw	3,710
Damaso Garcia	3,572
Ernie Whitt	3,514
Jesse Barfield	3,463
Alfredo Griffin	3,396

Runs	
Lloyd Moseby	768
Tony Fernandez	704
Carlos Delgado	698
George Bell	641
Joe Carter	578
Willie Upshaw	538
Shannon Stewart	534
Jesse Barfield	530
John Olerud	464
Damaso Garcia	453

Hits	
Tony Fernandez	1,583
Lloyd Moseby	1,319
George Bell	1,294
Carlos Delgado	1,118
Joe Carter	1,051
Damaso Garcia	1,028
Willie Upshaw	982
Shannon Stewart	951
Jesse Barfield	919
John Olerud	910

Doubles	
Tony Fernandez	291
Carlos Delgado	279
Lloyd Moseby	242
George Bell	237
Joe Carter	218
John Olerud	213
Rance Mulliniks	204
Shannon Stewart	196
Willie Upshaw	177
Damaso Garcia	172
Alex Gonzalez	172

Triples	
Tony Fernandez	72
Lloyd Moseby	60
Alfredo Griffin	50
Willie Upshaw	42
Roberto Alomar	36
Devon White	34
George Bell	32
Shannon Stewart	30
Joe Carter	28
Jesse Barfield	27

Home runs	
Carlos Delgado	262
Joe Carter	203
George Bell	202
Jesse Barfield	179
Lloyd Moseby	149
Ernie Whitt	131
Fred McGriff	125
Jose Cruz Jr.	122
Shawn Green	119
Kelly Gruber	114

Total bases	
Carlos Delgado	2,203
George Bell	2,201
Tony Fernandez	2,198
Lloyd Moseby	2,128
Joe Carter	1,934
Jesse Barfield	1,672
Willie Upshaw	1,579
Ernie Whitt	1,475
John Olerud	1,462
Shannon Stewart	1,405

Runs batted in	
Carlos Delgado	814
George Bell	740
Joe Carter	736
Lloyd Moseby	651
Tony Fernandez	613
Jesse Barfield	527
Ernie Whitt	518
Willie Upshaw	478
John Olerud	471
Kelly Gruber	434

Extra-base hits	
Carlos Delgado	551
George Bell	471
Lloyd Moseby	451
Joe Carter	449
Tony Fernandez	423
Jesse Barfield	368
Willie Upshaw	331
John Olerud	328
Ernie Whitt	310
Shawn Green	298

Batting average (Minimum 500 games)	
Roberto Alomar	.307
Shannon Stewart	.302
Tony Fernandez	.297
John Olerud	.293
Damaso Garcia	.288
George Bell	.286
Shawn Green	.286
Carlos Delgado	.281
Rance Mulliniks	.280
Fred McGriff	.278

Stolen bases	
Lloyd Moseby	255
Roberto Alomar	206
Damaso Garcia	194
Tony Fernandez	172
Shannon Stewart	162
Devon White	126
Otis Nixon	101
Dave Collins	91
Jose Cruz Jr.	85
Alex Gonzalez	85

PITCHING

Earned-run average (Minimum 500 innings)	
Tom Henke	2.48
Duane Ward	3.18
Dave Stieb	3.42
Jimmy Key	3.42
Doyle Alexander	3.56
Paul Quantrill	3.67
John Cerutti	3.87
David Wells	4.06
Jim Acker	4.07
Juan Guzman	4.07

Wins	
Dave Stieb	175
Jim Clancy	128
Jimmy Key	116
Pat Hentgen	105
David Wells	84
Juan Guzman	76
Todd Stottlemyre	69
Luis Leal	51
Chris Carpenter	49
Doyle Alexander	46
John Cerutti	46

Losses	
Jim Clancy	140
Dave Stieb	134
Jimmy Key	81
Pat Hentgen	76
Todd Stottlemyre	70
Juan Guzman	62
Luis Leal	58
Jesse Jefferson	56
David Wells	55
Chris Carpenter	50

Innings pitched	
Dave Stieb	2,873.0
Jim Clancy	2,204.2
Jimmy Key	1,695.2
Pat Hentgen	1,555.2
Juan Guzman	1,215.2
David Wells	1,148.2
Todd Stottlemyre	1,139.0
Luis Leal	946.0
Chris Carpenter	870.2
John Cerutti	772.1

Strikeouts	
Dave Stieb	1,658
Jim Clancy	1,237
Juan Guzman	1,030
Pat Hentgen	995
Jimmy Key	944
David Wells	784
Duane Ward	671
Todd Stottlemyre	662
Tom Henke	644
Chris Carpenter	612

Bases on balls	
Dave Stieb	1,020
Jim Clancy	814
Pat Hentgen	557
Juan Guzman	546
Todd Stottlemyre	414
Jimmy Key	404
Chris Carpenter	331
Luis Leal	320
Kelvim Escobar	316
David Wells	294

Games	
Duane Ward	452
Tom Henke	446
Dave Stieb	439
Paul Quantrill	386
Jim Clancy	352
Jimmy Key	317
David Wells	306
Mike Timlin	305
Jim Acker	281
Mark Eichhorn	279

Shutouts	
Dave Stieb	30
Jim Clancy	11
Jimmy Key	10
Pat Hentgen	9
Roger Clemens	6
Chris Carpenter	5
Jesse Jefferson	4
Todd Stottlemyre	4
Doyle Alexander	3
Jim Gott	3
Roy Halladay	3
Luis Leal	3
Dave Lemanczyk	3
Esteban Loaiza	3

Saves	
Tom Henke	217
Duane Ward	121
Billy Koch	100
Kelvim Escobar	54
Mike Timlin	52
Joey McLaughlin	31
Roy Lee Jackson	30
Randy Myers	28
Darren Hall	20
Tony Castillo	16
Bill Caudill	16

TEAM SEASON, GAME RECORDS

SEASON

Batting		
Most at-bats	5,716	1986
Most runs	883	1999
Fewest runs	590	1978
Most hits	1,580	1999
Most singles	1,069	1984
Most doubles	337	1999
Most triples	68	1984
Most home runs	244	2000
Fewest home runs	95	1979
Most grand slams	9	2000
Most pinch-hit home runs	6	1984
Most total bases	2,664	2000
Most stolen bases	193	1984
Highest batting average	.280	1999
Lowest batting average	.244	1997
Highest slugging pct	.469	2000

Pitching		
Lowest ERA	3.29	1985
Highest ERA	5.14	2000
Most complete games	44	1979
Most shutouts	17	1988
Most saves	60	1991
Most walks	635	1980
Most strikeouts	1,154	1998

Fielding		
Most errors	164	1977
Fewest errors	86	1990
Most double plays	206	1980
Highest fielding average	.986	1990

General		
Most games won	99	1985
Most games lost	109	1979
Highest win pct	.615	1985
Lowest win pct	.327	1979

GAME, INNING

Batting		
Most runs, game	24	6-26-78
Most runs, inning	11	7-20-84
Most hits, game	25	8-9-99
Most home runs, game	10	9-14-87
Most total bases, game	53	9-14-87

Righthander Jim Clancy ranks second on Toronto's all-time victory chart with 128.

BLUE JAYS YEAR-BY-YEAR

				Games		Leaders					
Year	W	L	Place	Back	Manager	Batting avg.	Hits	Home runs	RBIs	Wins	ERA
							EAST DIVISION				
1977	54	107	7th	45½	Hartsfield	Howell, .316	Bailor, 154	Fairly, 19	Ault, Fairly, 64	Lemanczyk, 13	Vuckovich, 3.47
1978	59	102	7th	40	Hartsfield	Carty, .284	Bailor, 164	Mayberry, 22	Mayberry, 70	Clancy, 10	Murphy, 3.93
1979	53	109	7th	50½	Hartsfield	Griffin, .287	Griffin, 179	Mayberry, 21	Mayberry, 74	T. Underwood, 9	T. Underwood, 3.69
1980	67	95	7th	36	Mattick	Woods, .300	Griffin, 166	Mayberry, 30	Mayberry, 82	Clancy, 13	Clancy, 3.30
1981	37	69	*7th/7th	—	Mattick	Garcia, .252	Moseby, 88	Mayberry, 17	Mayberry, Moseby, 43	Stieb, 11	Stieb, 3.19
1982	78	84	†6th	17	Cox	Garcia, .310	Garcia, 185	Upshaw, 21	Upshaw, 75	Stieb, 17	Jackson, 3.06
1983	89	73	4th	9	Cox	Bonnell, .318	Upshaw, 177	Barfield, Upshaw, 27	Upshaw, 104	Stieb, 17	Stieb, 3.04
1984	89	73	2nd	15	Cox	Collins, .308	Garcia, 180	Bell, 26	Moseby, 92	Alexander, 17	Stieb, 2.83
1985	99	62	‡1st	+2	Cox	Mulliniks, .295	Bell, 167	Bell, 28	Bell, 95	Alexander, 17	Stieb, 2.48
1986	86	76	4th	9½	J. Williams	Fernandez, .310	Fernandez, 213	Barfield, 40	Barfield, Bell, 108	Clancy, Key, Eichhorn, 14	Eichhorn, 1.72
1987	96	66	2nd	2	J. Williams	Fernandez, .322	Bell, 188	Bell, 47	Bell, 134	Key, 17	Key, 2.76
1988	87	75	†3rd	2	J. Williams	Lee, .291	Fernandez, 186	McGriff, 34	Bell, 97	Stieb, 16	Stieb, 3.04
1989	89	73	‡1st	+2	J. Williams, Gaston	Bell, .297	Bell, 182	McGriff, 36	Bell, 104	Stieb, 17	Cerutti, 3.07
1990	86	76	2nd	2	Gaston	McGriff, .300	Fernandez, 175	McGriff, 35	Gruber, 118	Stieb, 18	Stieb, 2.93
1991	91	71	‡1st	+7	Gaston	Alomar, .295	Alomar, 188	Carter, 33	Carter, 108	Key, 17	Ward, 2.77
1992	96	66	§1st	+4	Gaston	Alomar, .310	Alomar, 177	Carter, 34	Carter, 119	Morris, 21	Ward, 1.95
1993	95	67	§1st	+7	Gaston	Olerud, .363	Molitor, 211	Carter, 33	Carter, 121	Hentgen, 19	Hentgen, 3.87
1994	55	60	3rd	16	Gaston	Molitor, .341	Molitor, 155	Carter, 27	Carter, 103	Hentgen, 13	Hentgen, 3.40
1995	56	88	5th	30	Gaston	Alomar, .300	Alomar, 155	Carter, 25	Carter, 76	Leiter, 11	Leiter, 3.64
1996	74	88	4th	18	Gaston	Nixon, .286	Carter, 158	Sprague, 36	Carter, 107	Hentgen, 20	Guzman, 2.93
1997	76	86	5th	22	Gaston, Queen	Green, .287	Carter, 143	Delgado, 30	Carter, 102	Clemens, 21	Clemens, 2.05
1998	88	74	3rd	26	T. Johnson	Fernandez, .321	Green, 175	Canseco, 46	Delgado, 115	Clemens, 20	Clemens, 2.65
1999	84	78	3rd	14	Fregosi	Fernandez, .328	Green, 190	Delgado, 44	Delgado, 134	Wells, 17	Halladay, 3.92
2000	83	79	3rd	4½	Fregosi	Delgado, .344	Delgado, 196	Delgado, 41	Delgado, 137	Wells, 20	F. Castillo, 3.59
2001	80	82	3rd	16	Martinez	Stewart, .316	Stewart, 202	Delgado, 39	Delgado, 102	Carpenter, Loaiza, Quantrill, 11	Halladay, 3.16
2002	78	84	3rd	25½	Martinez, Tosca	Stewart, .303	Stewart, 175	Delgado, 33	Delgado, 108	Halladay, 19	Halladay, 2.93

* First half 16-42; second half 21-27. † Tied for position. ‡ Lost Championship Series. § Won Championship Series.

Note: Batting average minimum 350 at-bats; ERA minimum 90 innings pitched.

Bob Bailor

TORONTO was welcomed into the American League fold on March 26, 1976, when owners granted ownership approval to Labatt Breweries and Imperial Trust, giving the Blue Jays distinction as the first A.L. team outside the continental United States. The Blue Jays, the A.L.'s 14th franchise, joined the league with the Seattle Mariners.

Infielder Bob Bailor gained distinction as the first of 30 Toronto selections in the November 5, 1976, A.L. expansion draft. American League baseball made a successful Canadian debut on April 7, 1977, when the Blue Jays defeated the Chicago White Sox, 9-5, at Exhibition Stadium.

Expansion draft (November 5, 1976)

Players

Player	From	Position
Doug Ault	Texas	first base
*Bob Bailor	Baltimore	infield
Steve Bowling	Milwaukee	outfield
Rico Carty	Cleveland	outfield
Sam Ewing	Chicago	first base
Garth Iorg	New York	infield
Jim Mason	New York	shortstop
Dave McKay	Minnesota	third base
Steve Staggs	Kansas City	second base
Otto Velez	New York	outfield
Ernie Whitt	Boston	catcher
Mike Weathers	Oakland	infield
Al Woods	Minnesota	outfield
Gary Woods	Oakland	outfield

Pitchers

Pitcher	From	Throws
Larry Anderson	Milwaukee	righthanded
Tom Bruno	Kansas City	righthanded
Jeff Byrd	Texas	righthanded
Jim Clancy	Texas	righthanded
Mike Darr	Baltimore	righthanded
Dennis DeBarr	Detroit	lefthanded
Butch Edge	Milwaukee	righthanded
Al Fitzmorris	Kansas City	righthanded
Jerry Garvin	Minnesota	lefthanded
Steve Hargan	Texas	righthanded
Leon Hooten	Oakland	righthanded
Jesse Jefferson	Chicago	righthanded
Dave Lemanczyk	Detroit	righthanded
Bill Singer	Minnesota	righthanded
Pete Vuckovich	Chicago	righthanded
Mike Willis	Baltimore	lefthanded

*First pick

Opening day lineup

April 7, 1977

John Scott, left field
Hector Torres, shortstop
Doug Ault, first base
Otto Velez, designated hitter
Gary Woods, center field
Steve Bowling, right field
Pedro Garcia, second base
Dave McKay, third base
Rick Cerone, catcher
Bill Singer, pitcher

Doug Ault

Blue Jays firsts

First hit: Doug Ault, April 7, 1977, vs. Chicago
First home run: Doug Ault, April 7, 1977, vs. Chicago
First RBI: Doug Ault, April 7, 1977, vs. Chicago
First win: Jerry Johnson, April 7, 1977, vs. Chicago
First shutout: Pete Vuckovich, June 26, 1977, 2-0 at Baltimore

Arizona Diamondbacks

First baseman Travis Lee.

FRANCHISE CHRONOLOGY

The beginnings: Arizona, a longtime bastion of minor league baseball and spring training, joined the Major League ranks on March 9, 1995, when owners unanimously approved expansion to Phoenix and Tampa. The 13th and 14th expansion cubs in Major League history were also the earliest-formed expansion teams, gaining approval more than three years before they would throw their first pitch against big-league competition. The Diamondbacks were awarded to a group headed by Jerry Colangelo, the man who had built the Phoenix Suns into one of the most admired franchises in the NBA. Both teams were stocked in a November 1997 expansion draft and began play in the 1998 season, Arizona as part of the National League West division.

First season: Major League baseball made its Arizona debut on March 31, 1998, at Bank One Ballpark in Phoenix when the Diamondbacks dropped a 9-2 decision to the Rockies. Arizona went on to compile a 65-97 first-year record, two games better than Tampa Bay in its A.L. debut season. The Diamondbacks finished in the N.L. West basement, 33 games behind San Diego.

1999-present: In only their second season, the Diamondbacks won 100 games and the N.L. West title, thanks to an offseason barrage of high-price veteran free-agent signings. And after struggling to an 85-77 record in 2000, the Diamondbacks finished at 92-70 in 2001 and the four-year-old club became the youngest championship team in baseball history after beating the New York Yankees in a seven-game World Series.

DIAMONDBACKS VS. OPPONENTS BY DECADE

	Braves	Cardinals	Cubs	Dodgers	Giants	Phillies	Pirates	Reds	Astros	Mets	Expos	Padres	Marlins	Rockies	Brewers	Interleague	Decade Record
1998-99	5-13	6-11	12-9	11-14	14-10	10-8	11-5	5-13	9-9	11-7	8-10	14-11	14-3	12-13	11-7	12-16	165-159
2000-02	11-11	9-12	15-9	26-25	24-27	15-8	15-6	13-6	11-8	10-12	11-10	33-18	13-8	34-17	11-10	24-24	275-211
Totals	16-24	15-23	27-18	37-39	38-37	25-16	26-11	18-19	20-17	21-19	19-20	47-29	27-11	46-30	22-17	36-40	440-370

Interleague results: 7-5 vs. Angels, 2-1 vs. Orioles, 3-0 vs. Red Sox, 2-1 vs. Indians, 4-2 vs. Tigers, 2-1 vs. Royals, 1-2 vs. Yankees, 3-9 vs. Athletics, 5-7 vs. Mariners, 6-10 vs. Rangers, 1-2 vs. Blue Jays.

ALL-TIME RECORD OF EXPANSION TEAMS

Team	W	L	Pct.	DT	P	WS
Arizona	440	370	.543	3	1	1
Kansas City	2,675	2,694	.498	6	2	1
Houston	3,229	3,285	.496	7	0	0
Toronto	2,025	2,063	.495	5	2	2
Anaheim	3,243	3,431	.486	3	1	1
Montreal	2,605	2,769	.485	2	0	0
Colorado	740	817	.475	0	0	0
New York	3,091	3,412	.475	4	4	2
Milwaukee	2,545	2,831	.473	2	1	0
Seattle	1,924	2,163	.471	3	0	0
Texas	3,097	3,560	.465	4	0	0
San Diego	2,460	2,921	.457	3	2	0
Florida	706	847	.455	0	1	1
Tampa Bay	318	490	.394	0	0	0

DT—Division Titles. P—Pennants won. WS—World Series won.

BALLPARK CHRONOLOGY

Bank One Ballpark (1998-present)

Capacity: 49,033.
First game: Rockies 9, Diamondbacks 2 (March 31, 1998).
First batter: Mike Lansing, Rockies.
First hit: Mike Lansing, Rockies (single).
First run: Vinny Castilla, Rockies (2nd inning).
First home run: Vinny Castilla, Rockies.
First winning pitcher: Darryl Kile, Rockies.
First-season attendance: 3,602,856.

MANAGERS

Name	*Years*	*Record*
Buck Showalter	1998-2000	250-236
Bob Brenly	2001-02	190-134

WORLD SERIES CHAMPIONS

Year	*Loser*	*Length*	*MVP*
2001	N.Y. Yankees	7 games	Johnson, Schilling

N.L. PENNANT WINNERS

Year	*Record*	*Manager*	*Series Result*
2001	92-70	Brenly	Defeated Yankees

WEST DIVISION CHAMPIONS

Year	*Record*	*Manager*	*NLCS Result*
1999	100-62	Showalter	Lost to Mets
2001	92-70	Brenly	Defeated Braves
2002	98-64	Brenly	Lost in Div. Series

ATTENDANCE HIGHS

Total	*Season*	*Park*
3,602,856	1998	Bank One Ballpark
3,200,725	2002	Bank One Ballpark
3,017,489	1999	Bank One Ballpark
2,912,516	2000	Bank One Ballpark
2,740,554	2001	Bank One Ballpark

CY YOUNG WINNERS

Randy Johnson, LH, 1999, 2000, 2001, 2002

Expansion draft (November 18, 1998)

Players

Player	Team	Position
Gabe Alvarez	San Diego	third base
Tony Batista	Oakland	shortstop
Mike Bell	Anaheim	third base
Yamil Benetez	Kansas City	outfield
Brent Brede	Minnesota	outfield
David Dellucci	Baltimore	outfield
Edwin Diaz	Texas	second base
Jorge Fabregas	White Sox	catcher
Hanley Frias	Texas	shortstop
Karim Garcia	Los Angeles	outfield
Dan Klassen	Milwaukee	shortstop
Damian Miller	Minnesota	catcher
Joe Randa	Pittsburgh	third base
Kelly Stinnett	Milwaukee	catcher

Pitchers

Pitcher	Team	Throws
Joel Adamson	Milwaukee	lefthanded
*Brian Anderson	Cleveland	lefthanded
Jason Boyd	Philadelphia	righthanded
Hector Carrasco	Kansas City	righthanded
Chris Clemons	White Sox	righthanded
Bryan Corey	Detroit	righthanded
Omar Daal	Toronto	lefthanded
Matt Drews	Detroit	righthanded
Todd Erdos	San Diego	righthanded
Ben Ford	N.Y. Yankees	righthanded
Marty Janzen	Toronto	righthanded
Cory Lidle	N.Y. Mets	righthanded
Thomas Martin	Houston	lefthanded
Jesus Martinez	Los Angeles	lefthanded
Chuck McElroy	White Sox	lefthanded
Clint Sodowsky	Pittsburgh	righthanded
Russ Springer	Houston	righthanded
Jeff Suppan	Boston	righthanded
Neil Weber	Montreal	lefthanded
Scott Winchester	Cincinnati	righthanded
Bob Wolcott	Seattle	righthanded

*First pick

Opening day lineup

March 31, 1998

Devon White, center field
Jay Bell, shortstop
Travis Lee, first base
Matt Williams, third base
Brent Brede, left field
Karim Garcia, right field
Jorge Fabregas, catcher
Edwin Diaz, second base
Andy Benes, pitcher

Brian Anderson

Diamondbacks firsts

First hit: Travis Lee, March 31, 1998, vs. Colorado (single)
First home run: Travis Lee, March 31, 1998, vs. Colorado
First RBI: Travis Lee, March 31, 1998, vs. Colorado
First win: Andy Benes, April 5, 1998, vs. San Francisco
First shutout: Omar Daal, July 20, 1998, 4-0 vs. Cubs.

MILESTONE PERFORMANCES

20-plus home runs
- 57—Luis Gonzalez 2001
- 38—Jay Bell 1999
- 35—Matt Williams 1999
- Steve Finley 2000
- 34—Steve Finley 1999
- 33—Reggie Sanders 2001
- 31—Luis Gonzalez 2000
- 28—Luis Gonzalez 2002
- 26—Luis Gonzalez 1999
- 25—Steve Finley 2002
- 22—Travis Lee 1998
- Devon White 1998
- 20—Jay Bell 1998
- Matt Williams 1998

100-plus RBIs
- 142—Matt Williams 1999
- Luis Gonzalez 2001
- 114—Luis Gonzalez 2000
- 112—Jay Bell 1999
- 111—Luis Gonzalez 1999
- 103—Steve Finley 1999
- Luis Gonzalez 2002

20-plus victories
- 2001—Curt Schilling 22-6
- Randy Johnson 21-6
- 2002—Randy Johnson 24-5
- Curt Schilling 23-7

N.L. home run champions
None

N.L. RBI champions
None

N.L. batting champions
None

N.L. ERA champions
- 1999—Randy Johnson 2.48
- 2001—Randy Johnson 2.49
- 2002—Randy Johnson 2.32

N.L. strikeout champions
- 1999—Randy Johnson 364
- 2000—Randy Johnson 347
- 2001—Randy Johnson 372
- 2002—Randy Johnson 334

No-hit pitchers
(9 innings or more)
None

Longest hitting streaks
- 30—Luis Gonzalez 1999
- 24—Tony Womack 2000
- 19—Matt Williams 1999
- 18—Mark Grace 2001
- Junior Spivey 2002
- 16—Luis Gonzalez 1999
- 15—Tony Bautista 2000

INDIVIDUAL SEASON, GAME RECORDS

SEASON

Batting

Category	Record	Player	Year
At-bats	627	Matt Williams	1999
Runs	132	Jay Bell	1999
Hits	206	Luis Gonzalez	1999
Singles	131	Luis Gonzalez	1999
		Tony Womack	1999
Doubles	47	Luis Gonzalez	2000
Triples	14	Tony Womack	2000
Home runs	57	Luis Gonzalez	2001
Home runs, rookie	22	Travis Lee	1998
Grand slams	2	Matt Williams	1998
		Travis Lee	1999
		Matt Williams	1999
		Luis Gonzalez	2001
Total bases	419	Luis Gonzalez	2001
RBIs	142	Matt Williams	1999
		Luis Gonzalez	2001
Walks	100	Luis Gonzalez	2001
Most strikeouts	132	Jay Bell	1999
Fewest strikeouts	36	Mark Grace	2001
Batting average	.336	Luis Gonzalez	1999
Slugging pct.	.688	Luis Gonzalez	2001
Stolen bases	72	Tony Womack	1999

Pitching

Category	Record	Player	Year
Games	78	Byung-Hyun Kim	2001
Complete games	12	Randy Johnson	1999
Innings	271.2	Randy Johnson	1999
Wins	24	Randy Johnson	2002
Losses	15	Willie Blair	1998
Winning pct.	.829 (24-5)	Randy Johnson	2002
Walks	82	Andy Benes	1999
Strikeouts	372	Randy Johnson	2001
Shutouts	4	Randy Johnson	2002
Home runs allowed	39	Brian Anderson	1998
Lowest ERA	2.48	Randy Johnson	1999
Saves	36	Byung-Hyun Kim	2002

GAME

Batting

Category	Record	Player	Date
Runs	4	Last by Greg Colbrunn	9-18-2002
Hits	5	Last by Greg Colbrunn	9-18-2002
Doubles	3	Last by Greg Colbrunn	10-2-2001
Triples	2	Last by Tony Womack	6-21-2000
Home runs	3	Last by Erubiel Durazo	5-17-2002
RBIs	9	Erubiel Durazo	5-17-2002
Total bases	14	Last by Greg Colbrunn	9-18-2002
Stolen bases	4	Tony Womack	8-3-2000

CAREER LEADERS

BATTING

Games

Player	Games
Luis Gonzalez	625
Jay Bell	616
Steve Finley	598
Tony Womack	568
Matt Williams	551
Damian Miller	467
David Dellucci	433
Travis Lee	338
Craig Counsell	320
Greg Colbrunn	314

At-bats

Player	At-bats
Luis Gonzalez	2,365
Tony Womack	2,302
Jay Bell	2,180
Matt Williams	2,131
Steve Finley	2,129
Damian Miller	1,465
Travis Lee	1,161
Craig Counsell	1,046
David Dellucci	1,021
Andy Fox	862

Runs

Player	Runs
Luis Gonzalez	436
Tony Womack	362
Jay Bell	360
Steve Finley	348
Matt Williams	300
Damian Miller	180
Craig Counsell	162
Travis Lee	162
Erubiel Durazo	146
Junior Spivey	136

Hits

Player	Hits
Luis Gonzalez	747
Tony Womack	625
Matt Williams	596
Steve Finley	588
Jay Bell	573
Damian Miller	394
Craig Counsell	297
Travis Lee	292
David Dellucci	282
Greg Colbrunn	232

Doubles

Player	Doubles
Luis Gonzalez	147
Matt Williams	118
Jay Bell	116
Steve Finley	110
Damian Miller	98
Tony Womack	88
Craig Counsell	52
Greg Colbrunn	51
David Dellucci	50
Mark Grace	50

Triples

Player	Triples
Tony Womack	34
Steve Finley	23
Jay Bell	18
David Dellucci	17
Luis Gonzalez	16
Danny Bautista	11
Junior Spivey	9
Andy Fox	8
Karim Garcia	8
Quinton McCracken	8

Home runs

Player	Home runs
Luis Gonzalez	142
Steve Finley	108
Matt Williams	95
Jay Bell	91
Damian Miller	48
Erubiel Durazo	47
Travis Lee	39
Greg Colbrunn	34
Reggie Sanders	33
Kelly Stinnett	33

Total bases

Player	Total bases
Luis Gonzalez	1,352
Steve Finley	1,068
Matt Williams	1,013
Jay Bell	998
Tony Womack	838
Damian Miller	640
Travis Lee	466
David Dellucci	435
Greg Colbrunn	397
Erubiel Durazo	395

Runs batted in

Player	RBIs
Luis Gonzalez	470
Matt Williams	365
Steve Finley	361
Jay Bell	304
Damian Miller	194
Tony Womack	185
Travis Lee	162
Erubiel Durazo	149
David Dellucci	137
Greg Colbrunn	126
Mark Grace	126

Extra-base hits

Player	Extra-base hits
Luis Gonzalez	305
Steve Finley	241
Jay Bell	225
Matt Williams	220
Damian Miller	148
Tony Womack	141
Travis Lee	92
Greg Colbrunn	91
David Dellucci	90
Erubiel Durazo	89

Batting average
(Minimum 175 games)

Player	Average
Greg Colbrunn	.317
Luis Gonzalez	.316
Danny Bautista	.313
Junior Spivey	.291
Craig Counsell	.284
Mark Grace	.280
Matt Williams	.280
Erubiel Durazo	.278
David Dellucci	.276
Steve Finley	.276

Stolen bases

Player	Stolen bases
Tony Womack	174
Steve Finley	47
Travis Lee	30
Devon White	22
Luis Gonzalez	21
Andy Fox	20
Jay Bell	17
Craig Counsell	16
Reggie Sanders	14
Junior Spivey	14

PITCHING

Earned-run average
(Minimum 175 innings)

Player	ERA
Randy Johnson	2.48
Curt Schilling	3.20
Byung-Hyun Kim	3.21
Greg Swindell	3.76
Miguel Batista	3.89
Omar Daal	4.11
Andy Benes	4.36
Brian Anderson	4.52
Todd Stottlemyre	4.77
Armando Reynoso	4.99

Wins

Player	Wins
Randy Johnson	81
Curt Schilling	50
Brian Anderson	41
Andy Benes	27
Omar Daal	26
Armando Reynoso	22
Byung-Hyun Kim	20
Miguel Batista	19
Todd Stottlemyre	15
Gregg Olson	12

Losses

Player	Losses
Brian Anderson	42
Omar Daal	31
Randy Johnson	27
Andy Benes	25
Armando Reynoso	24
Curt Schilling	19
Miguel Batista	17
Byung-Hyun Kim	17
Willie Blair	15
Greg Swindell	14

Innings pitched

Player	Innings
Randy Johnson	1,030.0
Brian Anderson	840.2
Curt Schilling	613.2
Omar Daal	473.1
Andy Benes	429.2
Armando Reynoso	386.0
Miguel Batista	324.0
Byung-Hyun Kim	280.0
Greg Swindell	227.1
Todd Stottlemyre	217.0

Strikeouts

Player	Strikeouts
Randy Johnson	1,417
Curt Schilling	681
Brian Anderson	410
Byung-Hyun Kim	347
Omar Daal	325
Andy Benes	305
Miguel Batista	202
Armando Reynoso	185
Greg Swindell	180
Todd Stottlemyre	162

Bases on balls

Player	Bases on balls
Randy Johnson	288
Omar Daal	172
Andy Benes	156
Brian Anderson	153
Byung-Hyun Kim	136
Armando Reynoso	133
Miguel Batista	130
Curt Schilling	85
Todd Stottlemyre	83
Matt Mantei	70

Games

Player	Games
Byung-Hyun Kim	236
Greg Swindell	225
Brian Anderson	160
Randy Johnson	140
Gregg Olson	125
Mike Morgan	120
Matt Mantei	116
Dan Plesac	96
Russ Springer	96
Omar Daal	85

Shutouts

Player	Shutouts
Randy Johnson	11
Curt Schilling	3
Brian Anderson	2
Omar Daal	2
Albie Lopez	2

Saves

Player	Saves
Byung-Hyun Kim	70
Gregg Olson	44
Matt Mantei	41
Bret Prinz	9
Mike Morgan	5
Felix Rodriguez	5
Mike Myers	4
Greg Swindell	4
Brian Anderson	1
Willie Banks	1
Troy Brohawn	1
Bobby Chouinard	1
Alan Embree	1
Darren Holmes	1
Vladimir Nunez	1
Dan Plesac	1
Russ Springer	1

TEAM SEASON, GAME RECORDS

Luis Gonzalez led the Diamondbacks in home runs (28) and RBIs (103) in 2002.

SEASON

Batting		
Most at-bats	5,658	1999
Most runs	908	1999
Fewest runs	665	1998
Most hits	1,566	1999
Most singles	1,015	1999
Most doubles	289	1999
Most triples	46	1998, 1999
Most home runs	216	1999
Fewest home runs	159	1998
Most grand slams	9	2001
Most pinch-hit home runs	14	2001
Most total bases	2,595	1999
Most stolen bases	137	1999
Highest batting average	.277	1999
Lowest batting average	.246	1998
Highest slugging pct.	.459	1999
Pitching		
Lowest ERA	3.77	1999
Highest ERA	4.64	1998
Most complete games	16	1999, 2000
Most shutouts	13	2001
Most saves	42	1999
Most walks	543	1999
Most strikeouts	1,303	2002
Fielding		
Most errors	107	2000
Fewest errors	84	2001
Most double plays	148	2001
Highest fielding average	.986	2001
General		
Most games won	100	1999
Most games lost	97	1998
Highest win pct.	.617	1999
Lowest win pct.	.401	1998

GAME, INNING

Batting		
Most runs, game	17	Last on 9-18-2002
Most runs, inning	8	Last on 4-25-2002
Most hits, game	20	6-2-99, 5-8-2000
Most home runs, game	5	Last on 9-28-2002
Most total bases, game	40	4-17-01

DIAMONDBACKS YEAR-BY-YEAR

				Games		Leaders					
Year	W	L	Place	Back	Manager	Batting avg.	Hits	Home runs	RBIs	Wins	ERA
						EAST DIVISION					
1998	65	97	5th	33	Showalter	White, .279	White, 157	Lee, White, 22	White, 85	Benes, 14	Daal, 2.88
1999	100	62	*1st	+14	Showalter	Gonzalez, .336	Gonzalez, 206	Bell, 38	Williams, 142	Johnson, 17	Johnson, 2.48
2000	85	77	3rd	12	Showalter	Gonzalez, .311	Gonzalez, 192	Finley, 35	Gonzalez, 114	Johnson, 19	Johnson, 2.64
2001	92	70	†‡1st	+2	Brenly	Gonzalez, .325	Gonzalez, 198	Gonzalez, 57	Gonzalez, 142	Schilling, 22	Johnson, 2.49
2002	98	64	*1st	+2½	Brenly	Spivey, .301	Spivey, 162	Gonzalez, 28	Gonzalez, 103	Johnson, 24	Johnson, 2.32

* Lost Division Series. † Won Division Series. ‡Won Championship Series.

Note: Batting average minimum 350 at-bats; ERA minimum 90 innings pitched.

Atlanta Braves

FRANCHISE CHRONOLOGY

First season: 1876, in Boston, as a member of the new National League. The "Red Stockings" defeated Philadelphia, 6-5, in their franchise debut and went on to finish fourth with a 39-31 first-year record.
1877-1900: Boston's "Beaneaters" were dominant in the pre-1900 era. They won consecutive pennants in 1877 and '78, returned to the top in 1883 and powered their way to five more flags in the 1890s.
1901-1952: Such success did not carry over to the modern era. Over the next 52 seasons, the Braves would win only two more pennants—while finishing sixth, seventh or eighth 33 times. One of the pennants was secured by the Miracle Braves of 1914, who recovered from a 15-game deficit to overtake the Giants with a 68-19 stretch run and then swept past powerful Philadelphia in the World Series. When the financially strapped Braves transferred to Milwaukee after the 1952 season, they broke up a baseball alignment that had existed since 1903.
1953-1965: The Braves were embraced by Milwaukee fans and rewarded them with a 1957 World Series victory and a 1958 pennant. But when the team fell into the second division in the early 1960s, enthusiasm waned and management began another search for greener pastures. After the 1965 season, the Braves made their second franchise shift in 14 years—this time to Atlanta.
1966-present: It took another quarter century for the Braves to regain status as an N.L. power, but they did so with a vengeance. After winning West Division titles in 1969 and 1982 and losing in the NLCS both years, they embarked on a record run that produced 11 straight division titles, five pennants and one World Series win—a six-game triumph over Cleveland in 1995.

Outfielder Hank Aaron.

BRAVES VS. OPPONENTS BY DECADE

	Cardinals	Cubs	Dodgers	Giants	Phillies	Pirates	Reds	Astros	Mets	Expos	Padres	Marlins	Rockies	Brewers	D'backs	Interleague	Decade Record
1900-09	98-111	76-135	95-114	83-125	87-119	58-153	90-120										587-877
1910-19	110-100	87-127	105-103	73-137	90-123	104-109	97-116										666-815
1920-29	85-135	80-139	90-128	82-137	100-118	77-141	89-130										603-928
1930-39	98-121	74-146	117-103	89-127	122-97	92-125	108-110										700-829
1940-49	76-144	111-108	90-129	100-116	132-87	105-112	105-112										719-808
1950-59	119-101	126-94	92-129	126-94	118-102	139-81	134-86										854-687
1960-69	88-94	92-90	89-99	97-91	107-75	88-94	85-103	95-49	89-49	8-4	13-5						851-753
1970-79	51-69	54-66	70-106	84-95	62-58	43-77	60-120	85-91	59-61	60-58	97-82						725-883
1980-89	47-68	57-55	69-105	79-94	64-53	58-53	81-92	78-96	46-68	45-72	88-89						712-845
1990-99	71-43	62-43	68-55	69-53	70-50	62-45	82-49	71-53	69-50	70-50	79-44	51-36	50-26	12-4	13-5	26-23	925-629
2000-02	11-8	12-9	11-11	13-8	29-21	13-6	10-9	11-10	29-22	32-19	14-7	26-24	13-9	14-7	11-11	35-19	284-200
Totals	854-994	831-1012	896-1082	895-1077	981-903	839-996	941-1047	340-299	292-250	215-203	291-227	77-60	63-35	26-11	24-16	61-42	7626-8254

Interleague results: 7-8 vs. Orioles, 20-10 vs. Red Sox, 3-0 vs. White Sox, 3-3 vs. Tigers, 2-1 vs. Twins, 8-8 vs. Yankees, 9-3 vs. Devil Rays, 3-0 vs. Rangers, 6-9 vs. Blue Jays.

MANAGERS

(Boston Braves, 1876-1952)
(Milwaukee Braves, 1953-65)

Name	Years	Record
Harry Wright	1876-81	254-187
John Morrill	1882, 1883-86, 1887-88	335-296
Jack Burdock	1883	30-24
King Kelly	1887	49-43
Jim Hart	1889	83-45
Frank Selee	1890-1901	1004-649
Al Buckenberger	1902-04	186-242
Fred Tenney	1905-07, 1911	202-402
Joe Kelley	1908	63-91
Frank Bowerman	1909	22-54
Harry Smith	1909	23-54
Fred Lake	1910	53-100
Johnny Kling	1912	52-101
George Stallings	1913-20	579-597
Fred Mitchell	1921-23	186-274
Dave Bancroft	1924-27	249-363
Jack Slattery	1928	11-20
Rogers Hornsby	1928	39-83
Emil Fuchs	1929	56-98
Bill McKechnie	1930-37	560-666
Casey Stengel	1938-43	373-491
Bob Coleman	1943, 1944-45	128-165
Del Bissonette	1945	25-34
Billy Southworth	1946-51	424-358
Tommy Holmes	1951-52	61-69
Charlie Grimm	1952-56	341-285
Fred Haney	1956-59	341-231
Chuck Dressen	1960-61	159-124
Birdie Tebbetts	1961-62	98-89
Bobby Bragan	1963-66	310-287
Billy Hitchcock	1966-67	110-100
Ken Silvestri	1967	0-3
Lum Harris	1968-72	379-373
Eddie Mathews	1972-74	149-161
Clyde King	1974-75	96-101
Connie Ryan	1975	9-18
Dave Bristol	1976-77	131-192
Ted Turner	1977	0-1
Bobby Cox	1978-81, 1990-2002	1,450-1,112
Joe Torre	1982-84	257-229
Eddie Haas	1985	50-71
Bobby Wine	1985	16-25
Chuck Tanner	1986-88	153-208
Russ Nixon	1988-90	130-216

WORLD SERIES CHAMPIONS

Year	Loser	Length	MVP
1914	Philadelphia	4 games	None
1957	N.Y. Yankees	7 games	Burdette
1995	Cleveland	6 games	Glavine

N.L. PENNANT WINNERS

Year	Record	Manager	Series Result
1877	42-18	Wright	None
1878	41-19	Wright	None
1883	63-35	Burdock, Morrill	None
1891	87-51	Selee	None
1892	102-48	Selee	None
1893	86-43	Selee	None
1897	93-39	Selee	None
1898	102-47	Selee	None
1914	94-59	Stallings	Defeated A's
1948	91-62	Southworth	Lost to Indians
1957	95-59	Haney	Defeated Yankees
1958	92-62	Haney	Lost to Yankees
1991	94-68	Cox	Lost to Twins
1992	98-64	Cox	Lost to Blue Jays
1995	90-54	Cox	Defeated Indians
1996	96-66	Cox	Lost to Yankees
1999	103-59	Cox	Lost to Yankees

WEST DIVISION CHAMPIONS

Year	Record	Manager	NLCS Result
1969	93-69	Harris	Lost to Mets
1982	89-73	Torre	Lost to Cardinals
1991	94-68	Cox	Defeated Pirates
1992	98-64	Cox	Defeated Pirates
1993	104-58	Cox	Lost to Phillies

EAST DIVISION CHAMPIONS

Year	Record	Manager	NLCS Result
1995	90-54	Cox	Defeated Reds
1996	96-66	Cox	Defeated Cardinals
1997	101-61	Cox	Lost to Marlins
1998	106-56	Cox	Lost to Padres
1999	103-59	Cox	Defeated Mets
2000	95-67	Cox	Lost in Div. Series
2001	88-74	Cox	Lost to D'backs
2002	101-59	Cox	Lost in Div. Series

ATTENDANCE HIGHS

Total	Season	Park
3,884,720	1993	Fulton County Stadium
3,463,988	1997	Turner Field
3,361,350	1998	Turner Field
3,284,901	1999	Turner Field
3,234,301	2000	Turner Field

RETIRED UNIFORMS

No.	Name	Pos.
3	Dale Murphy	OF
21	Warren Spahn	P
35	Phil Niekro	P
41	Ed Mathews	3B
44	Hank Aaron	OF

BALLPARK CHRONOLOGY

Turner Field (1997-present)

Capacity: 50,091.
First game: Braves 5, Cubs 4 (April 4, 1997).
First batter: Brian McRae, Cubs.
First hit: Chipper Jones, Braves (single).
First run: Michael Tucker, Braves (3rd inning).
First home run: Michael Tucker, Braves
First winning pitcher: Brad Clontz, Braves.
First-season attendance: 3,463,988.

South End Grounds I and II, Boston (1876-1914)

First game: Boston 6, Philadelphia 5 (April 22, 1876).

Braves Field, Boston (1915-52)

Capacity: 40,000.
First game: Braves 3, St. Louis 1 (August 18, 1915).
First-season attendance (1916): 313,495.

County Stadium, Milwaukee (1953-65)

Capacity: 43,394.
First game: Braves 3, St. Louis 2, 10 innings (April 14, 1953).
First-season attendance: 1,826,397.

Atlanta-Fulton County Stadium (1966-96)

Capacity: 52,710.
First game: Pittsburgh 3, Braves 2, 13 innings (April 12, 1966).
First-season attendance: 1,539,801.

N.L. MVPs

Bob Elliott, 3B, 1947
Hank Aaron, OF, 1957
Dale Murphy, OF, 1982
Dale Murphy, OF, 1983
Terry Pendleton, 3B, 1991
Chipper Jones, 3B, 1999

CY YOUNG WINNERS

Warren Spahn, LH, 1957
Tom Glavine, LH, 1991
Greg Maddux, RH, 1993
Greg Maddux, RH, 1994
Greg Maddux, RH, 1995
John Smoltz, RH, 1996
Tom Glavine, LH, 1998

ROOKIES OF THE YEAR

Alvin Dark, SS, 1948
Sam Jethroe, OF, 1950
Earl Williams, C, 1971
Bob Horner, 3B, 1978
David Justice, OF, 1990
Rafael Furcal, SS, 2000

MANAGER OF THE YEAR

Bobby Cox, 1991

MILESTONE PERFORMANCES

30-plus home runs

47— Eddie Mathews 1953
Hank Aaron 1971
46— Eddie Mathews 1959
45— Hank Aaron 1962
Chipper Jones 1999
44— Hank Aaron 1957, 1963, 1966, 1969
Dale Murphy 1987
Andres Galarraga 1998
43— Dave Johnson 1973
41— Eddie Mathews 1955
Darrell Evans 1973
Jeff Burroughs 1977
40— Eddie Mathews 1954
Hank Aaron 1960, 1973
Dave Justice 1993
39— Wally Berger 1930
Hank Aaron 1959, 1967
Eddie Mathews 1960
38— Joe Adcock 1956
Hank Aaron 1970
Chipper Jones 2001
37— Eddie Mathews 1956
Dale Murphy 1985
Fred McGriff *1993
36— Joe Torre 1966
Dale Murphy 1982, 1983, 1984
Ron Gant 1993
Chipper Jones 2000
Andruw Jones 2000
35— Joe Adcock 1961
Bob Horner 1980
Andruw Jones 2002
34— Wally Berger 1934, 1935
Hank Aaron 1961, 1972
Orlando Cepeda 1970
Fred McGriff 1994
Ryan Klesko 1996
Chipper Jones 1998
Javier Lopez 1998
Andruw Jones 2001
33— Earl Williams 1971
Bob Horner 1979
Dale Murphy 1980
32— Eddie Mathews 1957, 1961, 1965
Hank Aaron 1965
Bob Horner 1982
Ron Gant 1990, 1991
31— Eddie Mathews 1958
Mack Jones 1965
Felipe Alou 1966
Andruw Jones 1998
30— Hank Aaron 1958
Chipper Jones 1996

*18 with Padres; 19 with Braves.

100-plus RBIs

145— Hugh Duffy 1894
135— Eddie Mathews 1953
132— Hank Aaron 1957
130— Wally Berger 1935
Hank Aaron 1963
128— Hank Aaron 1962
127— Hank Aaron 1966
126— Hank Aaron 1960
124— Eddie Mathews 1960
123— Hank Aaron 1959
121— Wally Berger 1934
Dale Murphy 1983
Andres Galarraga 1998
120— Hank Aaron 1961
Dave Justice 1993
119— Wally Berger 1930
118— Hank Aaron 1970, 1971
117— Tommy Holmes 1945
Ron Gant 1993
115— Brian Jordan 1999
114— Eddie Mathews 1959
Jeff Burroughs 1977
113— Bob Elliott 1947
111— Orlando Cepeda 1970
Dale Murphy 1985
Chipper Jones 1997, 2000
110— Chipper Jones 1996
Chipper Jones 1999
109— Sid Gordon 1951
Joe Torre 1964
Hank Aaron 1967
Dale Murphy 1982
108— Joe Adcock 1961
107— Bob Elliott 1950
Fred McGriff 1996
Chipper Jones 1998
106— Wally Berger 1933
Hank Aaron 1955
105— Dale Murphy 1987
Ron Gant 1991
Terry Pendleton 1992
104— Darrell Evans 1973
Javier Lopez 1998
Andruw Jones 2000, 2001
103— Sid Gordon 1950
Eddie Mathews 1954
Joe Adcock 1956
102— Chipper Jones 2001
101— Eddie Mathews 1955
Joe Torre 1966
Rico Carty 1970
100— Bill Sweeney 1912
Bob Elliott 1948
Dale Murphy 1984
Andres Galarraga 2000
Chipper Jones 2002

20-plus victories

1877— Tommy Bond 40-17
1878— Tommy Bond 40-19
1879— Tommy Bond 43-19
1880— Tommy Bond 26-29
1881— Jim Whitney 31-33
1882— Jim Whitney 24-21
1883— Jim Whitney 37-21
Charlie Buffinton 25-14
1884— Charlie Buffinton 48-16
Jim Whitney 23-14
1885— Charlie Buffinton 22-27
1886— Hoss Radbourn 27-31
Bill Stemmeyer 22-18
1887— Hoss Radbourn 24-23
Michael Madden 21-14
1888— John Clarkson 33-20
1889— John Clarkson 49-19
Hoss Radbourn 20-11
1890— Kid Nichols 27-19
John Clarkson 26-18
Charlie Getzien 23-17
1891— John Clarkson 33-19
Kid Nichols 30-17
Harry Staley *24-13
1892— Kid Nichols 35-16
Jack Stivetts 35-16
Harry Staley 22-10
1893— Kid Nichols 34-14
Jack Stivetts 20-12
1894— Kid Nichols 32-13
Jack Stivetts 26-14
1895— Kid Nichols 26-16
1896— Kid Nichols 30-14
Jack Stivetts 22-14
1897— Kid Nichols 31-11
Fred Klobedanz 26-7
Ted Lewis 21-12
1898— Kid Nichols 31-12
Ted Lewis 26-8
Vic Willis 25-13
1899— Vic Willis 27-8
Kid Nichols 21-19
1900— Bill Dinneen 20-14
1901— Vic Willis 20-17
1902— Togie Pittinger 27-16
Vic Willis 27-20
1905— Irv Young 20-21
1914— Bill James 26-7
Dick Rudolph 26-10
1915— Dick Rudolph 22-19
1921— Joe Oeschger 20-14
1933— Ben Cantwell 20-10
1937— Lou Fette 20-10
Jim Turner 20-11
1946— Johnny Sain 20-14
1947— Warren Spahn 21-10
Johnny Sain 21-12
1948— Johnny Sain 24-15
1949— Warren Spahn 21-14
1950— Warren Spahn 21-17
Johnny Sain 20-13
1951— Warren Spahn 22-14
1953— Warren Spahn 23-7
1954— Warren Spahn 21-12
1956— Warren Spahn 20-11
1957— Warren Spahn 21-11
1958— Warren Spahn 22-11
Lew Burdette 20-10
1959— Lew Burdette 21-15
Warren Spahn 21-15
1960— Warren Spahn 21-10
1961— Warren Spahn 21-13
1963— Warren Spahn 23-7
1965— Tony Cloninger 24-11
1969— Phil Niekro 23-13
1974— Phil Niekro 20-13
1979— Phil Niekro 21-20
1991— Tom Glavine 20-11
1992— Tom Glavine 20-8
1993— Tom Glavine 22-6
Greg Maddux 20-10
1997— Denny Neagle 20-5
1998— Tom Glavine 20-6
2000— Tom Glavine 21-9

* 4-5 with Pittsburgh; 20-8 with Boston.

N.L. home run champions

1879— Charley Jones 9
1880— John O'Rourke *6
1891— Harry Stovey *16
1894— Hugh Duffy 18
1897— Hugh Duffy 11
1898— Jimmy Collins 15
1900— Herman Long 12
1907— Dave Brain 10
1910— Fred Beck *10
1935— Wally Berger 34
1945— Tommy Holmes 28
1953— Eddie Mathews 47
1957— Hank Aaron 44
1959— Eddie Mathews 46
1963— Hank Aaron *44
1966— Hank Aaron 44
1967— Hank Aaron 39
1984— Dale Murphy *36
1985— Dale Murphy 37

* Tied for league lead

INDIVIDUAL SEASON, GAME RECORDS

SEASON

Batting

Category	Record	Player	Year
At-bats	671	Marquis Grissom	1996
Runs	160	Hugh Duffy	1894
Hits	236	Hugh Duffy	1894
Singles	180	Ralph Garr	1971
Doubles	50	Hugh Duffy	1894
Triples	20	Dick Johnston	1887
Home runs	47	Eddie Mathews	1953
		Hank Aaron	1971
Home runs, rookie	38	Wally Berger	1930
Grand slams	4	Sid Gordon	1950
Total bases	400	Hank Aaron	1959
RBIs	145	Hugh Duffy	1894
Walks	131	Bob Elliott	1948
Most strikeouts	146	Andres Galarraga	1998
Fewest strikeouts	9	Tommy Holmes	1945
Batting average	.438	Hugh Duffy	1894
Slugging pct.	.679	Hugh Duffy	1894
Stolen bases	93	Billy Hamilton	1896

Pitching

Category	Record	Player	Year
Games	81	Brad Clontz	1996
Complete games	68	John Clarkson	1889
Innings	620	John Clarkson	1889
Wins	49	John Clarkson	1889
Losses	29	Vic Willis	1905
		Tommy Bond	1880
Winning pct.	.905 (19-2)	Greg Maddux	1995
Walks	164	Phil Niekro	1977
Strikeouts	417	Charlie Buffinton	1884
Shutouts	12	Tommy Bond	1879
Home runs allowed	41	Phil Niekro	1979
Lowest ERA	1.56	Greg Maddux	1994
Saves	55	John Smoltz	2002

GAME

Batting

Category	Record	Player	Date
Runs	6	Frank Torre	9-2-57
Hits	6	Felix Millan	7-6-70
Doubles	4	Last by Rafael Ramirez	5-21-86
Triples	3	Last by Rafael Furcal	4-21-2002
Home runs	4	Last by Bob Horner	7-6-86
RBIs	9	Tony Cloninger	7-3-66
Total bases	18	Joe Adcock	7-31-54
Stolen bases	6	Otis Nixon	6-16-91

N.L. RBI champions

1935— Wally Berger 130
1957— Hank Aaron 132
1960— Hank Aaron 126
1963— Hank Aaron 130
1966— Hank Aaron 127
1982— Dale Murphy *109
1983— Dale Murphy 121

* Tied for league lead

N.L. batting champions

1877— Deacon White .387
1889— Dan Brouthers .373
1893— Hugh Duffy .363
1894— Hugh Duffy .440
1928— Rogers Hornsby .387
1942— Ernie Lombardi .330
1956— Hank Aaron .328
1959— Hank Aaron .355
1970— Rico Carty .366
1974— Ralph Garr .353
1991— Terry Pendleton .319

N.L. ERA champions

1937— Jim Turner 2.38
1947— Warren Spahn 2.33
1951— Chet Nichols 2.88
1953— Warren Spahn 2.10
1956— Lew Burdette 2.70
1961— Warren Spahn 3.02
1967— Phil Niekro 1.87
1974— Buzz Capra 2.28
1993— Greg Maddux 2.36
1994— Greg Maddux 1.56
1995— Greg Maddux 1.63
1997— Greg Maddux 2.22

N.L. strikeout champions

1877— Tommy Bond 170
1878— Tommy Bond 182
1883— Jim Whitney 345
1889— John Clarkson 284
1902— Vic Willis 225
1949— Warren Spahn 151
1950— Warren Spahn 191
1951— Warren Spahn *164
1952— Warren Spahn 183
1977— Phil Niekro 262
1992— John Smoltz 215
1996— John Smoltz 276

* Tied for league lead

No-hit pitchers

(9 innings or more)
1892— Jack Stivetts 11-0 vs. Brooklyn
1907— Frank Pfeffer 6-0 vs. Cincinnati
1914— George Davis 7-0 vs. Philadelphia
1916— Tom Hughes 2-0 vs. Pittsburgh
1944— Jim Tobin 2-0 vs. Brooklyn
1950— Vern Bickford 7-0 vs. Brooklyn
1954— Jim Wilson 2-0 vs. Philadelphia
1960— Lew Burdette 1-0 vs. Philadelphia
1960— Warren Spahn 4-0 vs. Philadelphia
1961— Warren Spahn 1-0 vs. San Francisco
1973— Phil Niekro 9-0 vs. San Diego
1991— Kent Mercker–Mark Wohlers–
Alejandro Pena 1-0 vs. San Diego
1994— Kent Mercker 6-0 vs. Los Angeles

Longest hitting streaks

37— Tommy Holmes 1945
31— Rico Carty 1970
29— Rowland Office 1976
28— Marquis Grissom 1996
27— Hugh Duffy 1893
26— Hugh Duffy 1894, 1895
Germany Long 1897
Bill Sweeney 1911
25— Jimmy Bannon 1894
Hank Aaron 1956, 1962
23— Jimmy Collins 1897
Germany Long 1895
Gene DeMontreville 1901
Alvin Dark 1948
Red Schoendienst 1957
22— Hugh Duffy 1894
Earl Torgeson 1950
Hank Aaron 1959
Felipe Alou 1968
Hank Aaron 1971
Ralph Garr 1971
21— Jimmy Bannon 1895
Chick Stahl 1897
Billy Hamilton 1898
20— Tommy Holmes 1946, 1949
Andy Pafko 1953
Joe Adcock 1959
Bob Horner 1979
Otis Nixon 1991

CAREER LEADERS

BATTING

Games
Player	
Hank Aaron	3,076
Eddie Mathews	2,223
Dale Murphy	1,926
Rabbit Maranville	1,795
Fred Tenney	1,737
Herman Long	1,647
Bobby Lowe	1,411
Del Crandall	1,394
Johnny Logan	1,351
Tommy Holmes	1,289

At-bats
Player	
Hank Aaron	11,628
Eddie Mathews	8,049
Dale Murphy	7,098
Herman Long	6,781
Rabbit Maranville	6,724
Fred Tenney	6,637
Bobby Lowe	5,623
Tommy Holmes	4,956
Johnny Logan	4,931
John Morrill	4,799

Runs
Player	
Hank Aaron	2,107
Eddie Mathews	1,452
Herman Long	1,292
Fred Tenney	1,134
Dale Murphy	1,103
Bobby Lowe	1,000
Hugh Duffy	998
Billy Nash	915
Chipper Jones	863
John Morrill	837

Hits
Player	
Hank Aaron	3,600
Eddie Mathews	2,201
Fred Tenney	1,994
Herman Long	1,902
Dale Murphy	1,901
Rabbit Maranville	1,696
Bobby Lowe	1,608
Hugh Duffy	1,545
Tommy Holmes	1,503
Chipper Jones	1,419

Doubles
Player	
Hank Aaron	600
Eddie Mathews	338
Dale Murphy	306
Herman Long	295
Tommy Holmes	291
Chipper Jones	272
Wally Berger	248
Rabbit Maranville	244
Fred Tenney	242
John Morrill	234

Triples
Player	
Rabbit Maranville	103
Hank Aaron	96
Herman Long	91
John Morrill	80
Bill Bruton	79
Fred Tenney	74
Hugh Duffy	73
Bobby Lowe	71
Sam Wise	71
Eddie Mathews	70

Home runs
Player	
Hank Aaron	733
Eddie Mathews	493
Dale Murphy	371
Chipper Jones	253
Joe Adcock	239
Bob Horner	215
Wally Berger	199
Andruw Jones	185
Javy Lopez	171
Del Crandall	170

Total bases
Player	
Hank Aaron	6,591
Eddie Mathews	4,158
Dale Murphy	3,394
Herman Long	2,643
Chipper Jones	2,498
Fred Tenney	2,435
Rabbit Maranville	2,215
Wally Berger	2,212
Joe Adcock	2,164
Tommy Holmes	2,152

Runs batted in
Player	
Hank Aaron	2,202
Eddie Mathews	1,388
Dale Murphy	1,143
Herman Long	964
Hugh Duffy	927
Bobby Lowe	872
Chipper Jones	837
Billy Nash	811
Joe Adcock	760
Wally Berger	746

Extra-base hits
Player	
Hank Aaron	1,429
Eddie Mathews	901
Dale Murphy	714
Chipper Jones	549
Wally Berger	499
Herman Long	474
Joe Adcock	458
Tommy Holmes	426
Bob Horner	382
Andruw Jones	396

Batting average
(Minimum 500 games)

Player	
Billy Hamilton	.339
Hugh Duffy	.332
Chick Stahl	.327
Rico Carty	.317
Ralph Garr	.317
Lance Richbourg	.311
Hank Aaron	.310
Jimmy Collins	.309
Chipper Jones	.309
Wally Berger	.304

Stolen bases
Player	
Herman Long	434
Hugh Duffy	331
Billy Hamilton	274
Bobby Lowe	260
Fred Tenney	260
Hank Aaron	240
King Kelly	238
Billy Nash	232
Rabbit Maranville	194
Otis Nixon	186

PITCHING

Earned-run average
(Minimum 1,000 innings)

Player	
Tommy Bond	2.21
Jim Whitney	2.49
Greg Maddux	2.51
Dick Rudolph	2.62
John Clarkson	2.82
Vic Willis	2.82
Charlie Buffinton	2.83
Kid Nichols	3.00
Warren Spahn	3.05
Lefty Tyler	3.06

Wins
Player	
Warren Spahn	356
Kid Nichols	329
Phil Niekro	268
Tom Glavine	242
Lew Burdette	179
Greg Maddux	178
John Smoltz	163
Vic Willis	151
Tommy Bond	149
John Clarkson	149

Losses
Player	
Phil Niekro	230
Warren Spahn	229
Kid Nichols	183
Vic Willis	147
Tom Glavine	143
Jim Whitney	121
Lew Burdette	120
Bob Smith	120
Ed Brandt	119
John Smoltz	118

Innings pitched
Player	
Warren Spahn	5,046.0
Phil Niekro	4,622.2
Kid Nichols	4,549.0
Tom Glavine	3,344.2
Lew Burdette	2,638.0
Vic Willis	2,575.0
John Smoltz	2,553.2
Greg Maddux	2,308.1
Jim Whitney	2,263.2
Tommy Bond	2,127.1

Strikeouts
Player	
Phil Niekro	2,912
Warren Spahn	2,493
John Smoltz	2,240
Tom Glavine	2,054
Greg Maddux	1,704
Kid Nichols	1,680
Vic Willis	1,161
Jim Whitney	1,157
Lew Burdette	923
Charlie Buffinton	911

Bases on balls
Player	
Phil Niekro	1,458
Warren Spahn	1,378
Kid Nichols	1,163
Tom Glavine	1,140
Vic Willis	854
John Smoltz	808
Bob Buhl	782
Lefty Tyler	678
John Clarkson	676
Jack Stivetts	651

Games
Player	
Phil Niekro	740
Warren Spahn	714
Gene Garber	557
Kid Nichols	557
Tom Glavine	505
Lew Burdette	468
John Smoltz	467
Rick Camp	414
Mark Wohlers	388
Steve Bedrosian	350

Shutouts
Player	
Warren Spahn	63
Kid Nichols	44
Phil Niekro	43
Lew Burdette	30
Tommy Bond	29
Dick Rudolph	27
Vic Willis	26
Tom Glavine	22
Lefty Tyler	22
Greg Maddux	21

Saves
Player	
Gene Garber	141
Mark Wohlers	112
John Rocker	83
Cecil Upshaw	78
John Smoltz	65
Rick Camp	57
Mike Stanton	55
Don McMahon	50
Kerry Ligtenberg	44
Greg McMichael	44

TEAM SEASON, GAME RECORDS

SEASON

Batting
Record		Year
Most at-bats	5,631	1973
Most runs	1,220	1894
Fewest runs	408	1906
Most hits	1,567	1925
Most singles	1,196	1925
Most doubles	309	1999
Most triples	100	1921
Most home runs	215	1998
Fewest home runs	15	1909
Most grand slams	12	1997
Most pinch-hit home runs	9	1992
Most total bases	2,483	1998
Most stolen bases	189	1902
Highest batting average	.292	1925
Lowest batting average	.223	1909
Highest slugging pct.	.453	1998

Pitching
Record		Year
Lowest ERA	2.19	1916
Highest ERA	5.12	1929
Most complete games	139	1905
Most shutouts	24	1992
Most saves	57	2002
Most walks	701	1977
Most strikeouts	1,245	1996

Fielding
Record		Year
Most errors	361	1903
Fewest errors	91	1998
Most double plays	197	1985
Highest fielding average	.985	1998

General
Record		Year
Most games won	106	1998
Most games lost	115	1935
Highest win pct.	.705	1897
Lowest win pct.	.248	1935

GAME, INNING

Batting
Record		Date
Most runs, game	30	6-9-1883
Most runs, inning	16	6-18-1894
Most hits, game	32	9-3-1896
Most home runs, game	8	8-30-53
Most total bases, game	47	8-30-53

Third baseman Eddie Mathews hit a team-record 47 home runs in 1953.

BRAVES YEAR-BY-YEAR

Year	W	L	Place	Games Back	Manager	Batting avg.	Hits	Home runs	RBIs	Wins	ERA
						BOSTON BRAVES					
1901	69	69	5th	20½	Selee	DeMontreville, .300	DeMontreville, 173	DeMontreville, 5	DeMontreville, 72	Willis, 20	Willis, 2.36
1902	73	64	3rd	29	Buckenberger	Tenney, .315	Cooley, 162	5 Tied, 2	Carney, Gremminger, 65	Pittinger, Willis, 27	Willis, 2.20
1903	58	80	6th	32	Buckenberger	Tenney, .313	Cooley, 160	Moran, 7	Cooley, 70	Pittinger, 18	Willis, 2.98
1904	55	98	7th	51	Buckenberger	J. Delahanty, .285	Abbaticchio, 148	Cooley, 5	Cooley, 70	Willis, 18	Pittinger, 2.66
1905	51	103	7th	54½	Tenney	Tenney, .288	Abbaticchio, 170	J. Delahanty, 5	J. Delahanty, Wolverton, 55	Young, 20	Young, 2.90
1906	49	102	8th	66½	Tenney	Tenney, .283	Tenney, 154	Bates, 6	Bates, Howard, 54	Young, 16	Lindaman, 2.43
1907	58	90	7th	47	Tenney	Beaumont, .322	Beaumont, 187	Brain, 10	Beaumont, 62	Dorner, Flaherty, 12	Flaherty, 2.70
1908	63	91	6th	36	Kelley	Ritchey, 2.73	Beaumont, 127	Dahlen, 3	McGann, 55	Flaherty, Lindaman, Ferguson 12	McCarthy, 1.63
1909	45	108	8th	65½	Bowerman, H. Smith	Beaumont, .263	Becker, 138	Becker, 6	Beaumont, 60	Mattern, 15	Richie, 2.32
1910	53	100	8th	50½	Lake	Miller, .286	Beck, 157	Beck, 10	Beck, 64	Mattern, 16	Brown, 2.67
1911	44	107	8th	54	Tenney	Miller, .333	Miller, 192	Miller, 7	Miller, 91	Brown, 8	Brown, 4.29
1912	52	101	8th	52	Kling	Sweeney, .344	Sweeney, 204	Houser, 8	Sweeney, 100	Perdue, 13	Hess, 3.76
1913	69	82	5th	31½	Stallings	Connolly, .281	Myers, 143	Lord, 6	Connolly, 57	Perdue, Tyler, 16	James, Tyler, 2.79
1914	94	59	1st	+10½	Stallings	Connolly, .306	Schmidt, 153	Connolly, 9	Maranville, 78	Rudolph, James, 26	James, 1.90
1915	83	69	2nd	7	Stallings	Magee, .280	Magee, 160	6 Tied, 2	Magee, 87	Rudolph, 22	Hughes, 2.12
1916	89	63	3rd	4	Stallings	Konetchy, .260	Konetchy, 147	Maranville, 4	Konetchy, 70	Rudolph, 19	Nehf, 2.01
1917	72	81	6th	25½	Stallings	R. Smith, .295	R. Smith, 149	Powell, 4	R. Smith, 62	Nehf, 17	Nehf, 2.16
1918	53	71	7th	28½	Stallings	R. Smith, .298	R. Smith, 128	Wickland, 4	R. Smith, 65	Nehf, 15	Fillingim, 2.23
1919	57	82	6th	38½	Stallings	Holke, .292	Holke, 151	Maranville, 5	Holke, 48	Rudolph, 13	Rudolph, 2.17
1920	62	90	7th	30	Stallings	Holke, .294	Holke, 162	Powell, 6	Holke, 64	Oeschger, 15	Fillingim, 3.11
1921	79	74	4th	15	Mitchell	Boeckel, .313	Powell, 191	Powell, 12	Boeckel, 84	Oeschger, 20	Fillingim, 3.45
1922	53	100	8th	39½	Mitchell	Powell, .296	Powell, 163	Boeckel, Powell, 6	Ford, 60	F. Miller, Marquard, 11	F. Miller, 3.51
1923	54	100	7th	41½	Mitchell	Southworth, .319	Southworth, 195	Boeckel, 7	McInnis, 95	Genewich, 13	Barnes, 2.76
1924	53	100	8th	40	Bancroft	McInnis, .291	McInnis, 169	Tierney, 6	McInnis, 59	Barnes, 15	Cooney, 3.18
1925	70	83	5th	25	Bancroft	Burrus, .340	Burrus, 200	Welsh, 7	Burrus, 87	Benton, Cooney, 14	Benton, 3.09
1926	66	86	7th	22	Bancroft	E. Brown, .328	E. Brown, 201	Burrus, Welsh, 3	E. Brown, 84	Benton, 14	Werts, 3.28
1927	60	94	7th	34	Bancroft, Hornsby	Richbourg, .309	E. Brown, 171	Fournier, 10	E. Brown, 75	Genewich, Greenfield, 11	B. Smith, 3.76
1928	50	103	7th	44½	Slattery	Hornsby, .387	Richbourg, 206	Hornsby, 21	Hornsby, 94	B. Smith, 13	Delaney, 3.79
1929	56	98	8th	43	Fuchs	Sisler, .326	Sisler, 205	Harper, 10	Sisler, 79	Seibold, 12	Cunningham, 4.52
1930	70	84	6th	22	McKechnie	Spohrer, .317	Berger, 172	Berger, 38	Berger, 119	Seibold, 15	Seibold, 4.12
1931	64	90	7th	37	McKechnie	Berger, .323	Berger, 199	Berger, 19	Berger, 84	Brandt, 18	Brandt, 2.92
1932	77	77	5th	13	McKechnie	Berger, .307	Berger, 185	Berger, 17	Berger, 73	Brandt, 16	Betts, 2.80
1933	83	71	4th	9	McKechnie	Berger, .313	Jordan, 168	Berger, 27	Berger, 106	Cantwell, 20	Brandt, 2.60
1934	78	73	4th	16	McKechnie	Jordan, .311	Berger, 183	Berger, 34	Berger, 121	Betts, Frankhouse, 17	Frankhouse, 3.20
1935	38	115	8th	61½	McKechnie	Lee, .303	Berger, 174	Berger, 34	Berger, 130	Frankhouse, 11	B. Smith, 3.94
1936	71	83	6th	21	McKechnie	Jordan, .323	Moore, 185	Berger, 25	Berger, 91	MacFayden, 17	MacFayden, 2.87
1937	79	73	5th	16	McKechnie	Moore, .283	Moore, 159	Moore, 16	Cuccinello, 80	Fette, Turner, 20	Turner, 2.38
1938	77	75	5th	12	Stengel	Garms, .315	Cuccinello, 147	V. DiMaggio, 14	Cuccinello, 76	MacFayden, Turner, 14	Hutchinson, 2.74
1939	63	88	7th	32½	Stengel	Hassett, .308	Hassett, 182	West, 19	West, 82	Posedel, 15	Fette, 2.96
1940	65	87	7th	34½	Stengel	Cooney, .318	E. Miller, 157	Ross, 17	Ross, 89	Errickson, Posedel, 12	Salvo, 3.08
1941	62	92	7th	38	Stengel	Cooney, .319	Cooney, 141	West, 12	E. Miller, West, 68	Tobin, 12	Earley, 2.53
1942	59	89	7th	44	Stengel	Holmes, .278	Holmes, 155	West, 16	West, 56	Javery, Tobin, 12	Javery, Salvo, 3.03
1943	68	85	6th	36½	Stengel	Holmes, .270	Holmes, 170	Workman, 10	Workman, 67	Javery, 17	Andrews, 2.57
1944	65	89	6th	40	Coleman	Holmes, .309	Holmes, 195	Nieman, 16	Holmes, 73	Tobin, 18	Tobin, 3.01
1945	67	85	6th	30	Coleman, Bissonette	Holmes, .352	Holmes, 224	Holmes, 28	Holmes, 117	Tobin, 9	Wright, 2.51
1946	81	72	4th	15½	Southworth	Hopp, .333	Holmes, 176	Litwhiler, 8	Holmes, 79	Sain, 20	Sain, 2.21
1947	86	68	3rd	8	Southworth	Elliott, .317	Holmes, 191	Elliott, 22	Elliott, 113	Sain, Spahn, 21	Spahn, 2.33
1948	91	62	1st	+6½	Southworth	Holmes, .325	Holmes, 190	Elliott, 23	Elliott, 100	Sain, 24	Sain, 2.60
1949	75	79	4th	22	Southworth	Stanky, .285	Dark, 146	Elliott, 17	Elliott, 76	Spahn, 21	Spahn, 3.07
1950	83	71	4th	8	Southworth	Elliott, .305	Torgeson, 167	Gordon, 27	Elliott, 107	Spahn, 21	Spahn, 3.16
1951	76	78	4th	20½	Southworth, Holmes	Gordon, .287	Jethroe, 160	Gordon, 29	Gordon, 109	Spahn, 22	Nichols, 2.88
1952	64	89	7th	32	Holmes, Grimm	Gordon, .289	Gordon, 151	Gordon, Mathews, 25	Gordon, 75	Spahn, 14	Spahn, 2.98
						MILWAUKEE BRAVES					
1953	92	62	2nd	13	Grimm	Mathews, .302	Mathews, 175	Mathews, 47	Mathews, 135	Spahn, 23	Spahn, 2.10
1954	89	65	3rd	8	Grimm	Adcock, .308	Bruton, 161	Mathews, 40	Mathews, 103	Spahn, 21	Jolly, 2.43
1955	85	69	2nd	13½	Grimm	Aaron, .314	Aaron, 189	Mathews, 41	Aaron, 106	Spahn, 17	Buhl, 3.21
1956	92	62	2nd	1	Grimm, Haney	Aaron, .328	Aaron, 200	Adcock, 38	Adcock, 103	Spahn, 20	Burdette, 2.70
1957	95	59	1st	+8	Haney	Aaron, .322	Aaron, 198	Aaron, 44	Aaron, 132	Spahn, 21	Spahn, 2.69
1958	92	62	1st	+8	Haney	Aaron, .326	Aaron, 196	Mathews, 31	Aaron, 95	Spahn, 22	Jay, 2.14
1959	86	70	*2nd	2	Haney	Aaron, .355	Aaron 223	Mathews, 46	Aaron, 123	Burdette, Spahn, 21	Rush, 2.40
1960	88	66	2nd	7	Dressen	Adcock, .298	Bruton, 180	Aaron, 40	Aaron, 126	Spahn, 21	Buhl, 3.09
1961	83	71	4th	10	Dressen, Tebbetts	Aaron, .327	Aaron, 197	Adcock, 35	Aaron, 120	Spahn, 21	McMahon, 2.84
1962	86	76	5th	15½	Tebbetts	Aaron, .323	Aaron, 191	Aaron, 45	Aaron, 128	Spahn, 18	Shaw, 2.80
1963	84	78	6th	15	Bragan	Aaron, .319	Aaron, 201	Aaron, 44	Aaron, 130	Spahn, 23	Spahn, 2.60
1964	88	74	5th	5	Bragan	Carty, .330	Torre, 193	Aaron, 24	Torre, 109	Cloninger, 19	Cloninger, 3.56
1965	86	76	5th	11	Bragan	Aaron, .318	Aaron, 181	Aaron, Mathews, 32	Mathews, 95	Cloninger, 24	O'Dell, 2.18
						ATLANTA BRAVES					
1966	85	77	5th	10	Bragan, Hitchcock	F. Alou, .327	F. Alou, 218	Aaron, 44	Aaron, 127	Cloninger, Johnson, 14	Carroll, 2.37
1967	77	85	7th	24½	Hitchcock, Silvestri	Aaron, .307	Aaron, 184	Aaron, 39	Aaron, 109	Jarvis, 15	Niekro, 1.87
1968	81	81	5th	16	Harris	F. Alou, .317	F. Alou, 210	Aaron, 29	Aaron, 86	Jarvis, 16	Pappas, 2.37
						WEST DIVISION					
1969	93	69	†1st	+3	Harris	Aaron, .300	Millan, 174	Aaron, 44	Aaron, 97	Niekro, 23	Niekro, 2.56
1970	76	86	5th	26	Harris	Carty, .366	Millan, 183	Aaron, 38	Aaron, 118	Jarvis, 16	Jarvis, 3.61
1971	82	80	3rd	8	Harris	Garr, .343	Garr, 219	Aaron, 47	Aaron, 118	Niekro, 15	T. Kelley, 2.96
1972	70	84	4th	25	Harris, Mathews	Garr, .325	Garr, 180	Aaron, 34	Williams, 87	Niekro, 16	Niekro, 3.06
1973	76	85	5th	22½	Mathews	Aaron, .301	Garr, 200	D. Johnson, 43	Evans, 104	Morton, 15	Niekro, 3.31
1974	88	74	3rd	14	Mathews, King	Garr, .353	Garr, 214	Evans, 25	Evans, 79	Niekro, 20	House, 1.93
1975	67	94	5th	40½	King, Ryan	Office, .290	Garr, 174	Evans, 22	Evans, 73	Morton, 17	Niekro, 3.20
1976	70	92	6th	32	Bristol	Montanez, .321	Montanez, 135	Wynn, 17	Wynn, 66	Niekro, 17	Messersmith, 3.04
1977	61	101	6th	37	Bristol , Turner	Bonnell, .300	Burroughs, Matthews, 157	Burroughs, 41	Burroughs, 114	Niekro, 16	Niekro, 4.03
1978	69	93	6th	26	Cox	Burroughs, .301	Burroughs, 147	Burroughs, Horner, 23	Murphy, 79	Niekro, 19	McWilliams, 2.81
1979	66	94	6th	23½	Cox	Horner, .314	Matthews, 192	Horner, 33	Horner, 98	Niekro, 21	Niekro, 3.39
1980	81	80	4th	11	Cox	Chambliss, .282	Chambliss, 170	Horner, 35	Horner, Murphy, 89	Niekro, 15	Camp, 1.91
1981	50	56	‡4th/5th	—	Cox	Washington, .291	Chambliss, 110	Horner, 15	Chambliss, 51	Camp, 9	R. Mahler, 2.80
1982	89	73	†1st	+1	Torre	Murphy, .281	Ramirez, 169	Murphy, 36	Murphy, 109	Niekro, 17	Garber, 2.34
1983	88	74	2nd	3	Torre	Horner, .303	Ramirez, 185	Murphy, 36	Murphy, 121	McMurtry, Perez, 15	McMurtry, 3.08
1984	80	82	§2nd	12	Torre	Murphy, .290	Murphy, 176	Murphy, 36	Murphy, 100	Perez, 14	Garber, 3.06
1985	66	96	5th	29	Haas, Wine	Murphy, .300	Murphy, 185	Murphy, 37	Murphy, 111	R. Mahler, 17	R. Mahler, 3.48
1986	72	89	6th	23½	Tanner	Horner, .273	Murphy, 163	Murphy, 29	Horner, 87	Mahler, 14	Dedmon, 2.98
1987	69	92	5th	20½	Tanner	James, .312	Murphy, 167	Murphy, 44	Murphy, 105	Z. Smith, 15	Dedmon, 3.91
1988	54	106	6th	39½	Tanner, Nixon	Perry, .300	Perry, 164	Murphy, 24	Murphy, 77	Mahler, 9	Alvarez, 2.99
1989	63	97	6th	28	Nixon	L. Smith, .315	L. Smith, 152	L. Smith, 21	Murphy, 84	Glavine, 14	Acker, 2.67
1990	65	97	6th	26	Nixon, Cox	L. Smith, .305	Gant, 174	Gant, 32	Gant, 84	Smoltz, 14	Leibrandt, 3.16
1991	94	68	∞1st	+1	Cox	Pendleton, .319	Pendleton, 187	Gant, 32	Gant, 105	Glavine, 20	Glavine, 2.55
1992	98	64	∞1st	+8	Cox	Pendleton, .311	Pendleton, 199	Justice, Pendleton, 21	Pendleton, 105	Glavine, 20	Glavine, 2.76
1993	104	58	†1st	+1	Cox	Blauser, .305	Blauser, 182	Justice, 40	Justice, 120	Glavine, 22	McMichael, 2.06
						EAST DIVISION					
1994	68	46	2nd	6	Cox	McGriff, .318	McGriff, 135	McGriff, 34	McGriff, 94	Maddux, 16	Maddux, 1.56
1995	90	54	▲∞1st	+21	Cox	McGriff, .280	McGriff, 148	McGriff, 27	McGriff, 93	Maddux, 19	Maddux, 1.63
1996	96	66	▲∞1st	+8	Cox	C. Jones, .309	Grissom, 207	Klesko, 34	C. Jones, 110	Smoltz, 24	Maddux, 2.72
1997	101	61	▲†1st	+9	Cox	Lofton, .333	C. Jones, 176	Klesko, 24	C. Jones, 111	Neagle, 20	Maddux, 2.20
1998	106	56	▲†1st	+18	Cox	C. Jones, .313	C. Jones, 188	Galarraga, 44	Galarraga, 121	Glavine, 20	Maddux, 2.22
1999	103	59	▲∞1st	+6½	Cox	C. Jones, .319	C. Jones, 181	C. Jones, 45	B. Jordan, 115	Maddux, 19	Millwood, 2.68
2000	95	67	◆1st	+1	Cox	C. Jones, .311	A. Jones, 199	C. Jones, A. Jones, 36	C. Jones, 111	Glavine, 21	Maddux, 3.00
2001	88	74	▲†1st	+2	Cox	C. Jones, .330	C. Jones, 189	C. Jones, 38	A. Jones, 104	Maddux, 17	Burkett, 3.04
2002	101	59	◆1st	+19	Cox	C. Jones, .327	C. Jones, 179	A. Jones, 35	C. Jones, 100	Glavine, Millwood, 18	Maddux, 2.62

The column group from Batting avg. through ERA is headed "Leaders".

* Lost pennant playoff. † Lost Championship Series. ‡ First half 25-29; second half 25-27. § Tied for position. ∞ Won Championship Series. ▲ Won Division Series. ◆ Lost Division Series.

Note: Batting average minimum 350 at-bats; ERA minimum 90 innings pitched.

Chicago Cubs

Shortstop Ernie Banks.

FRANCHISE CHRONOLOGY

First season: 1876, as a member of the new National League. The "White Stockings" defeated Louisville, 4-0, in their first N.L. game and went on to win the league's first pennant with a 52-14 record.

1877-1900: Chicago, under the inspired leadership of player/manager Cap Anson, won five pennants as the premier franchise of the 1880s. But after a second-place finish in 1891, the team sank to seventh place and never mounted another pre-1900 challenge.

1901-present: The 1906 Cubs set a Major League record with 116 victories before being upset by the White Sox in the World Series. But that disappointment was followed by consecutive Series victories over Detroit—a success the franchise never would be able to duplicate. Over the next nine decades, the Cubs failed to bring another Series banner to Chicago. Pennants in 1910, 1918, 1929, 1932, 1935, 1938 and 1945 were followed by fall classic defeats, and East Division titles in 1984 and 1989 were followed by Championship Series losses. The Cubs qualified for the playoffs as the N.L. wild-card after the 1998 campaign, but a Division Series loss to Atlanta continued their record streak of consecutive seasons without winning a World Series. Chicago was one of five teams placed in the Central Division when the N.L. adopted its three-division format in 1994.

CUBS VS. OPPONENTS BY DECADE

	Braves	Cardinals	Dodgers	Giants	Phillies	Pirates	Reds	Astros	Mets	Expos	Padres	Marlins	Rockies	Brewers	D'backs	Interleague	Decade Record
1900-09	135-76	144-64	135-74	115-97	119-90	99-112	132-79										879-592
1910-19	127-87	136-78	117-98	99-116	110-101	118-95	119-93										826-668
1920-29	139-80	112-105	115-104	99-121	132-88	95-125	115-105										807-728
1930-39	146-74	111-109	127-89	117-102	147-73	120-100	121-99										889-646
1940-49	108-111	82-138	101-119	110-109	121-99	104-116	110-110										736-802
1950-59	94-126	107-113	85-134	90-130	92-128	114-106	90-129										672-866
1960-69	90-92	73-114	80-102	76-106	93-95	78-110	79-103	66-72	79-65	10-8	11-1						735-868
1970-79	66-54	93-87	52-68	59-61	87-92	66-111	59-61	55-65	86-93	88-89	74-46						785-827
1980-89	55-57	81-89	57-61	57-61	78-95	81-95	54-59	51-64	83-92	77-95	61-53						735-821
1990-99	43-62	71-67	47-61	57-53	60-63	63-76	51-68	51-70	62-57	57-62	59-51	39-36	38-40	12-12	9-12	20-23	739-813
2000-02	9-12	18-30	9-12	10-11	12-9	23-24	22-24	21-27	7-12	10-11	7-13	8-11	11-10	21-26	9-15	23-19	220-266
Totals	1012-831	1028-994	925-922	889-967	1051-933	961-1070	952-930	244-298	317-319	242-265	212-164	47-47	49-50	33-38	18-27	43-42	8023-7897

Interleague results: 14-16 vs. White Sox, 2-6 vs. Indians, 3-5 vs. Tigers, 9-6 vs. Royals, 2-1 vs. Brewers, 10-5 vs. Twins, 2-1 vs. Mariners, 1-2 vs. Rangers.

MANAGERS

Name	*Years*	*Record*
Al Spalding	1876-77	78-47
Bob Ferguson	1878	30-30
Silver Flint	1879	5-12
Cap Anson	1879-97	1283-932
Tom Burns	1898-99	160-138
Tom Loftus	1900-01	118-161
Frank Selee	1902-05	280-213
Frank Chance	1905-12	768-389
Johnny Evers	1913, 1921	129-120
Hank O'Day	1914	78-76
Roger Bresnahan	1915	73-80
Joe Tinker	1916	67-86
Fred Mitchell	1917-20	308-269
Bill Killefer	1921-25	300-293
Rabbit Maranville	1925	23-30
George Gibson	1925	12-14
Joe McCarthy	1926-30	442-321
Rogers Hornsby	1930-32	141-116
Charlie Grimm	1932-38, 1944-49, 1960	946-782
Gabby Hartnett	1938-40	203-176
Jimmie Wilson	1941-44	213-258
Roy Johnson	1944	0-1
Frank Frisch	1949-51	141-196
Phil Cavarretta	1951-53	169-213
Stan Hack	1954-56	196-265
Bob Scheffing	1957-59	208-254
Lou Boudreau	1960	54-83
*Vedie Himsl	1961	10-21
*Harry Craft	1961	7-9
*Elvin Tappe	1961-62	46-70
*Lou Klein	1961-62, 1965	65-82
*Charlie Metro	1962	43-69
Bob Kennedy	1963-65	182-198
Leo Durocher	1966-72	535-526
Whitey Lockman	1972-74	157-162
Jim Marshall	1974-76	175-218
Herman Franks	1977-79	238-241
Joe Amalfitano	1979, 1980-81	66-116
Preston Gomez	1980	38-52
Lee Elia	1982-83	127-158
Charlie Fox	1983	17-22
Jim Frey	1984-86	196-182
John Vukovich	1986	1-1
Gene Michael	1986-87	114-124
Frank Lucchesi	1987	8-17
Don Zimmer	1988-91	265-258
Joe Altobelli	1991	0-1
Jim Essian	1991	59-63
Jim Lefebvre	1992-93	162-162
Tom Trebelhorn	1994	49-64
Jim Riggleman	1995-2000	439-516
Don Baylor	2001-02	122-124
Bruce Kimm	2002	33-45

* Members of College of Coaches.

WORLD SERIES CHAMPIONS

Year	*Loser*	*Length*	*MVP*
1907	Detroit	5 games	None
1908	Detroit	5 games	None

N.L. PENNANT WINNERS

Year	*Record*	*Manager*	*Series Result*
1876	52-14	Spalding	None
1880	67-17	Anson	None
1881	56-28	Anson	None
1882	55-29	Anson	None
1885	87-25	Anson	None
1886	90-34	Anson	None
1906	116-36	Chance	Lost to White Sox
1907	107-45	Chance	Defeated Tigers
1908	99-55	Chance	Defeated Tigers
1910	104-50	Chance	Lost to A's
1918	84-45	Mitchell	Lost to Red Sox
1929	98-54	McCarthy	Lost to A's
1932	90-64	Hornsby, Grimm	Lost to Yankees
1935	100-54	Grimm	Lost to Tigers
1938	89-63	Grimm, Hartnett	Lost to Yankees
1945	98-56	Grimm	Lost to Tigers

EAST DIVISION CHAMPIONS

Year	*Record*	*Manager*	*NLCS Result*
1984	96-65	Frey	Lost to Padres
1989	93-69	Zimmer	Lost to Giants

WILD-CARD QUALIFIERS

Year	*Record*	*Manager*	*Div. Series Result*
1998	90-73	Riggleman	Lost to Braves

ATTENDANCE HIGHS

Total	*Season*	*Park*
2,813,800	1999	Wrigley Field
2,779,456	2001	Wrigley Field
2,734,511	2000	Wrigley Field
2,693,071	2002	Wrigley Field
2,653,763	1993	Wrigley Field

BALLPARK CHRONOLOGY

Wrigley Field (1916-present)

Capacity: 39,241.
First game: Cubs 7, Cincinnati 6, 11 innings (April 20, 1916).
First batter: Red Killefer, Reds.
First hit: Red Killefer (single).
First run: Red Killefer (5th inning).
First home run: Johnny Beall, Reds.
First winning pitcher: Gene Packard, Cubs.
First-season attendance: 453,685.

State Street Grounds (1876-77)

First game: Chicago 6, Cincinnati 0 (May 10, 1876).

Lakefront Park (1878-84)

First game: Indianapolis 5, Chicago 3 (May 14, 1878).

West Side Park (1885-92)

First game: Chicago 9, St. Louis 2 (June 6, 1885).

South Side Park (1891-94)

First game: Chicago 1, Pittsburgh 0 (May 5, 1891).

West Side Grounds (1893-1915)

First game: Cincinnati 13, Chicago 12 (May 14, 1893).

Note: South Side Park shared home games with West Side Park in 1891 and '92 and West Side Grounds in 1893 and '94.

N.L. MVPs

Gabby Hartnett, C, 1935
Phil Cavarretta, 1B, 1945
Hank Sauer, OF, 1952
Ernie Banks, SS, 1958
Ernie Banks, SS, 1959
Ryne Sandberg, 2B, 1984
Andre Dawson, OF, 1987
Sammy Sosa, OF, 1998

CY YOUNG WINNERS

Ferguson Jenkins, RH, 1971
Bruce Sutter, RH, 1979
Rick Sutcliffe, RH, 1984
Greg Maddux, RH, 1992

ROOKIES OF THE YEAR

Billy Williams, OF, 1961
Ken Hubbs, 2B, 1962
Jerome Walton, OF, 1989
Kerry Wood, P, 1998

MANAGERS OF THE YEAR

Jim Frey, 1984
Don Zimmer, 1989

RETIRED UNIFORMS

No.	*Name*	*Pos.*
14	Ernie Banks	SS
23	Ryan Sandberg	2B
26	Billy Williams	OF

HISTORY

MILESTONE PERFORMANCES

30-plus home runs

66— Sammy Sosa 1998
64— Sammy Sosa 2001
63— Sammy Sosa 1999
56— Hack Wilson 1930
50— Sammy Sosa 2000
49— Andre Dawson 1987
Sammy Sosa 2002
48— Dave Kingman 1979
47— Ernie Banks 1958
45— Ernie Banks 1959
44— Ernie Banks 1955
43— Ernie Banks 1957
42— Billy Williams 1970
41— Hank Sauer 1954
Ernie Banks 1960
40— Ryne Sandberg 1990
Sammy Sosa 1996
39— Rogers Hornsby 1929
Hack Wilson 1929
37— Gabby Hartnett 1930
Hank Sauer 1952
Ernie Banks 1962
Billy Williams 1972
36— Andy Pafko 1950
Sammy Sosa 1995, 1997
34— Billy Williams 1965
33— Bill Nicholson 1944
Billy Williams 1964
Ron Santo 1965
Sammy Sosa 1993
32— Hank Sauer 1950
Ernie Banks 1968
Jim Hickman 1970
Rick Monday 1976
31— Hack Wilson 1928
Ron Santo 1967
Andre Dawson 1991
Henry Rodriguez 1998
Fred McGriff *2001
30— Hack Wilson 1927
Hank Sauer 1951
Ron Santo 1964, 1966
Billy Williams 1968
Ryne Sandberg 1989
Rick Wilkins 1993
Fred McGriff 2002

*19 with Devil Rays; 12 with Cubs.

100-plus RBIs

191— Hack Wilson 1930
160— Sammy Sosa 2001
159— Hack Wilson 1929
158— Sammy Sosa 1998
149— Rogers Hornsby 1929
143— Ernie Banks 1959
141— Sammy Sosa 1999
138— Sammy Sosa 2000
137— Andre Dawson 1987
134— Kiki Cuyler 1930
129— Hack Wilson 1927
Ernie Banks 1958
Billy Williams 1970
128— Bill Nicholson 1943
123— Ron Santo 1969
122— Gabby Hartnett 1930
Bill Nicholson 1944
Billy Williams 1972
121— Hank Sauer 1952
120— Hack Wilson 1928
119— Sammy Sosa 1995, 1997
117— Ernie Banks 1955, 1960
115— Frank Demaree 1937
Jim Hickman 1970
Dave Kingman 1979
114— Ron Santo 1964, 1970
110— Riggs Stephenson 1929
Andy Pafko 1945
109— Hack Wilson 1926
108— Billy Williams 1965
Sammy Sosa 2002
107— Frank Schulte 1911
106— Ernie Banks 1965, 1969
Keith Moreland 1985
105— Bill Buckner 1982
104— Ernie Banks 1962
Andre Dawson 1991
103— Hank Sauer 1950, 1954
Fred McGriff 2002
102— Ernie Banks 1957
101— Andy Pafko 1948
Ron Santo 1965
100— Andre Dawson 1990
Ryne Sandberg 1990, 1991
Sammy Sosa 1996

20-plus victories

1876— Al Spalding 47-13
1878— Terry Larkin 29-26
1879— Terry Larkin 30-23
1880— Larry Corcoran 43-14
Fred Goldsmith 22-3
1881— Larry Corcoran 31-14
Fred Goldsmith 25-13
1882— Fred Goldsmith 28-16
Larry Corcoran 27-13
1883— Larry Corcoran 31-21
Fred Goldsmith 28-18
1884— Larry Corcoran 35-23
1885— John Clarkson 53-16
Jim McCormick *21-7
1886— John Clarkson 36-17
Jim McCormick 31-11
John Flynn 23-6
1887— John Clarkson 38-21
1888— Gus Krock 25-14
1890— Bill Hutchinson 42-25
Pat Luby 20-9
1891— Bill Hutchinson 44-19
1892— Bill Hutchinson 36-36
Ad Gumbert 22-19
1894— Clark Griffith 21-14
1895— Clark Griffith 26-14
William Terry 21-14
1896— Clark Griffith 23-11
1897— Clark Griffith 21-18
1898— Clark Griffith 24-10
Jim Callahan 20-10
1899— Clark Griffith 22-14
Jim Callahan 21-12
1902— Jack Taylor 23-11
1903— Jack Taylor 21-14
Jake Weimer 21-9
1904— Jake Weimer 20-14
1906— Mordecai Brown 26-6
Jack Pfiester 20-8
Jack Taylor † 20-12
1907— Orval Overall 23-7
Mordecai Brown 20-6
1908— Mordecai Brown 29-9
Ed Reulbach 24-7
1909— Mordecai Brown 27-9
Orval Overall 20-11
1910— Mordecai Brown 25-13
Leonard Cole 20-4
1911— Mordecai Brown 21-11
1912— Larry Cheney 26-10
1913— Larry Cheney 21-14
1914— Hippo Vaughn 21-13
Larry Cheney 20-18
1915— Hippo Vaughn 20-12
1917— Hippo Vaughn 23-13
1918— Hippo Vaughn 22-10
1919— Hippo Vaughn 21-14
1920— Grover Alexander 27-14
1923— Grover Alexander 22-12
1927— Charlie Root 26-15
1929— Pat Malone 22-10
1930— Pat Malone 20-9
1932— Lon Warneke 22-6
1933— Guy Bush 20-12
1934— Lon Warneke 22-10
1935— Bill Lee 20-6
Lon Warneke 20-13
1938— Bill Lee 22-9
1940— Claude Passeau 20-13
1945— Hank Wyse 22-10
Hank Borowy ‡ 21-7
1963— Dick Ellsworth 22-10
1964— Larry Jackson 24-11
1967— Fergie Jenkins 20-13
1968— Fergie Jenkins 20-15
1969— Fergie Jenkins 21-15
Bill Hands 20-14
1970— Fergie Jenkins 22-16
1971— Fergie Jenkins 24-13
1972— Fergie Jenkins 20-12
1977— Rick Reuschel 20-10
1984— Rick Sutcliffe ∞ 20-6
1992— Greg Maddux 20-11
2001— Jon Lieber 20-6

*1-3 with Providence; 20-4 with Chicago. †8-9 with Cardinals; 12-3 with Cubs. ‡10-5 with Yankees; 11-2 with Cubs. ∞ 4-5 with Indians; 16-1 with Cubs.

N.L. home run champions

1884— Ned Williamson 27
1885— Abner Dalrymple 11
1888— Jimmy Ryan 16
1890— Walt Wilmot *13
1910— Frank Schulte *10
1911— Frank Schulte 21
1912— Heinie Zimmerman 14
1916— Cy Williams *12
1926— Hack Wilson 21
1927— Hack Wilson *30
1928— Hack Wilson *31
1930— Hack Wilson 56
1943— Bill Nicholson 29
1944— Bill Nicholson 33
1952— Hank Sauer *37
1958— Ernie Banks 47
1960— Ernie Banks 41
1979— Dave Kingman 48
1987— Andre Dawson 49
1990— Ryne Sandberg 40
2000— Sammy Sosa 50
2002— Sammy Sosa 49

* Tied for league lead

N.L. RBI champions

1906— Harry Steinfeldt *83
1911— Frank Schulte 121
1929— Hack Wilson 159
1930— Hack Wilson 191
1943— Bill Nicholson 128
1944— Bill Nicholson 122
1952— Hank Sauer 121
1958— Ernie Banks 129
1959— Ernie Banks 143
1987— Andre Dawson 137
1998— Sammy Sosa 158
2001— Sammy Sosa 160

* Tied for league lead

N.L. batting champions

1876— Ross Barnes .429
1880— George Gore .360
1881— Cap Anson .399
1884— King Kelly .354
1886— King Kelly .388
1888— Cap Anson .344
1912— Heinie Zimmerman .372
1945— Phil Cavarretta .355
1972— Billy Williams .333
1975— Bill Madlock .354
1976— Bill Madlock .339
1980— Bill Buckner .324

N.L. ERA champions

1902— Jack Taylor 1.33
1906— Mordecai Brown 1.04
1907— Jack Pfiester 1.15
1918— Jim Vaughn 1.74
1919— Grover Alexander 1.72
1920— Grover Alexander 1.91
1932— Lon Warneke 2.37
1938— Bill Lee 2.66
1945— Hank Borowy 2.13

N.L. strikeout champions

1880— Larry Corcoran 268
1885— John Clarkson 308
1887— John Clarkson 237
1892— Bill Hutchinson 316
1909— Orval Overall 205
1918— Jim Vaughn 148
1919— Jim Vaughn 141
1920— Grover Alexander 173
1929— Pat Malone 166
1938— Clay Bryant 135
1946— Johnny Schmitz 135
1955— Sam Jones 198
1956— Sam Jones 176
1969— Fergie Jenkins 273

No-hit pitchers

(9 innings or more)

1880— Larry Corcoran 6-0 vs. Boston
1882— Larry Corcoran 5-0 vs. Worcester
1884— Larry Corcoran 6-0 vs. Providence
1885— John Clarkson 4-0 vs. Providence
1898— Walter Thornton 2-0 vs. Brooklyn
1915— Jim Lavender 2-0 vs. New York
1955— Sam Jones 4-0 vs. Pittsburgh
1960— Don Cardwell 4-0 vs. St. Louis
1969— Ken Holtzman 3-0 vs. Atlanta
1971— Ken Holtzman 1-0 vs. Cincinnati
1972— Burt Hooton 4-0 vs. Philadelphia
Milt Pappas 8-0 vs. San Diego

Longest hitting streaks

42— Bill Dahlen 1894
30— Jerome Walton 1989
Cal McVey 1876
29— Jimmy Ryan 2002
28— Bill Dahlen 1894
Ron Santo 1966
27— Hack Wilson 1929
Glenn Beckert 1968
26— George Decker 1896
Hack Wilson 1927
Gabby Hartnett 1937
Glenn Beckert 1973
25— Hack Wilson 1926
24— Gabby Hartnett 1937
Stan Hack 1945
23— Heinie Zimmerman 1912
22— Hack Wilson 1930
21— Glenn Beckert 1966
Lenny Randle 1980
20— Billy Herman 1934
Rafael Palmeiro 1988

INDIVIDUAL SEASON, GAME RECORDS

SEASON

Batting			
At-bats	666	Billy Herman	1935
Runs	156	Rogers Hornsby	1929
Hits	229	Rogers Hornsby	1929
Singles	165	Earl Adams	1927
Doubles	57	Billy Herman	1935, 1936
Triples	21	Frank Schulte	1911
		Vic Saier	1913
Home runs	66	Sammy Sosa	1998
Home runs, rookie	25	Billy Williams	1961
Grand slams	5	Ernie Banks	1955
Total bases	425	Sammy Sosa	2001
RBIs	191	Hack Wilson	1930
Walks	147	Jimmy Sheckard	1911
Most strikeouts	174	Sammy Sosa	1997
Fewest strikeouts	5	Charlie Hollocher	1922
Batting average	.388	King Kelly	1886
		Bill Lange	1895
Slugging pct.	.737	Sammy Sosa	2001
Stolen bases	67	Frank Chance	1903
Pitching			
Games	84	Ted Abernathy	1965
		Dick Tidrow	1980
Complete games	33	Jack Taylor	1902, 1903
		Grover Alexander	1920
Innings	363.1	Grover Alexander	1920
Wins	29	Mordecai Brown	1908
Losses	23	Tom Hughes	1901
Winning pct.	.941 (16-1)	Rick Sutcliffe	1984
Walks	185	Sam Jones	1955
Strikeouts	274	Fergie Jenkins	1970
Shutouts	9	6 times	
		Last by Bill Lee	1938
Home runs allowed	38	Warren Hacker	1955
Lowest ERA	1.04	Mordecai Brown	1906
Saves	53	Randy Myers	1993

GAME

Batting			
Runs	6	Cap Anson	8-24-1886
		Jimmy Ryan	7-25-1894
Hits	6	Last by Sammy Sosa	7-2-93
Doubles	4	Last by Billy Williams	4-9-69
Triples	3	Last by Shawon Dunston	7-28-90
Home runs	3	Last by Sammy Sosa	8-10-2002
RBIs	9	Last by Sammy Sosa	8-10-2002
Total bases	14	Last by George Mitterwald	4-17-74
Stolen bases	7	George Gore	6-25-1881

HISTORY

CAREER LEADERS

BATTING

Games

Player	
Ernie Banks	2,528
Cap Anson	2,277
Billy Williams	2,213
Ryne Sandberg	2,151
Ron Santo	2,126
Phil Cavarretta	1,953
Stan Hack	1,938
Gabby Hartnett	1,926
Mark Grace	1,910
Jimmy Ryan	1,662

At-bats

Player	
Ernie Banks	9,421
Cap Anson	9,176
Billy Williams	8,479
Ryne Sandberg	8,379
Ron Santo	7,768
Stan Hack	7,278
Mark Grace	7,156
Jimmy Ryan	6,818
Phil Cavarretta	6,592
Don Kessinger	6,355

Runs

Player	
Cap Anson	1,782
Jimmy Ryan	1,463
Ryne Sandberg	1,316
Billy Williams	1,306
Ernie Banks	1,305
Stan Hack	1,239
Ron Santo	1,109
Sammy Sosa	1,077
Mark Grace	1,057
Phil Cavarretta	968

Hits

Player	
Cap Anson	2,996
Ernie Banks	2,583
Billy Williams	2,510
Ryne Sandberg	2,385
Mark Grace	2,201
Stan Hack	2,193
Ron Santo	2,171
Jimmy Ryan	2,074
Phil Cavarretta	1,927
Gabby Hartnett	1,867

Doubles

Player	
Cap Anson	529
Mark Grace	456
Ernie Banks	407
Ryne Sandberg	403
Billy Williams	402
Gabby Hartnett	391
Stan Hack	363
Jimmy Ryan	362
Ron Santo	353
Billy Herman	346

Triples

Player	
Jimmy Ryan	142
Cap Anson	124
Frank Schulte	117
Bill Dahlen	106
Phil Cavarretta	99
Joe Tinker	93
Ernie Banks	90
Billy Williams	87
Stan Hack	81
Bill Lange	80
Ned Williamson	80
Heinie Zimmerman	80

Home runs

Player	
Ernie Banks	512
Sammy Sosa	470
Billy Williams	392
Ron Santo	337
Ryne Sandberg	282
Gabby Hartnett	231
Bill Nicholson	205
Hank Sauer	198
Hack Wilson	190
Andre Dawson	174

Total bases

Player	
Ernie Banks	4,706
Billy Williams	4,262
Cap Anson	4,064
Ryne Sandberg	3,786
Ron Santo	3,667
Sammy Sosa	3,447
Mark Grace	3,187
Gabby Hartnett	3,079
Jimmy Ryan	3,017
Stan Hack	2,889

Runs batted in

Player	
Cap Anson	1,880
Ernie Banks	1,636
Billy Williams	1,353
Ron Santo	1,290
Sammy Sosa	1,231
Gabby Hartnett	1,153
Ryne Sandberg	1,061
Mark Grace	1,004
Jimmy Ryan	914
Phil Cavarretta	896

Extra-base hits

Player	
Ernie Banks	1,009
Billy Williams	881
Ryne Sandberg	761
Ron Santo	756
Sammy Sosa	755
Cap Anson	750
Gabby Hartnett	686
Mark Grace	647
Jimmy Ryan	603
Phil Cavarretta	532

Batting average

(Minimum 500 games)

Player	
Riggs Stephenson	.336
Bill Lange	.330
Cap Anson	.327
Kiki Cuyler	.325
Bill Everitt	.323
Hack Wilson	.322
King Kelly	.316
George Gore	.315
Frank Demaree	.309
Billy Herman	.309

Stolen bases

Player	
Frank Chance	402
Bill Lange	399
Jimmy Ryan	369
Ryne Sandberg	344
Joe Tinker	304
Walt Wilmot	292
Johnny Evers	291
Bill Dahlen	285
Fred Pfeffer	263
Cap Anson	247

PITCHING

Earned-run average

(Minimum 1,000 innings)

Player	
Mordecai Brown	1.80
Jack Pfiester	1.85
Orval Overall	1.91
Ed Reulbach	2.24
Larry Corcoran	2.26
Hippo Vaughn	2.34
Terry Larkin	2.34
John Clarkson	2.39
Carl Lundgren	2.42
Jack Taylor	2.65

Wins

Player	
Charlie Root	201
Mordecai Brown	188
Bill Hutchison	181
Larry Corcoran	175
Fergie Jenkins	167
Guy Bush	152
Clark Griffith	152
Hippo Vaughn	151
Bill Lee	139
John Clarkson	137

Losses

Player	
Bill Hutchison	158
Charlie Root	156
Bob Rush	140
Fergie Jenkins	132
Rick Reuschel	127
Bill Lee	123
Dick Ellsworth	110
Hippo Vaughn	105
Guy Bush	101
Clark Griffith	96

Innings pitched

Player	
Charlie Root	3,137.1
Bill Hutchison	3,022.1
Fergie Jenkins	2,673.2
Larry Corcoran	2,338.1
Mordecai Brown	2,329.0
Rick Reuschel	2,290.0
Bill Lee	2,271.1
Hippo Vaughn	2,216.1
Guy Bush	2,201.2
Clark Griffith	2,188.2

Strikeouts

Player	
Fergie Jenkins	2,038
Charlie Root	1,432
Rick Reuschel	1,367
Bill Hutchison	1,225
Hippo Vaughn	1,138
Larry Corcoran	1,086
Bob Rush	1,076
Mordecai Brown	1,043
Ken Holtzman	988
John Clarkson	960

Bases on balls

Player	
Bill Hutchison	1,109
Charlie Root	871
Guy Bush	734
Bob Rush	725
Bill Lee	704
Sheriff Blake	661
Ed Reulbach	650
Rick Reuschel	640
Hippo Vaughn	621
Fergie Jenkins	600

Games

Player	
Charlie Root	605
Lee Smith	458
Don Elston	449
Guy Bush	428
Fergie Jenkins	401
Bill Hutchison	368
Bill Lee	364
Rick Reuschel	358
Mordecai Brown	346
Bob Rush	339

Shutouts

Player	
Mordecai Brown	48
Hippo Vaughn	35
Ed Reulbach	31
Fergie Jenkins	29
Orval Overall	28
Bill Lee	25
Grover Alexander	24
Larry Corcoran	22
Claude Passeau	22
Larry French	21
Bill Hutchison	21
Charlie Root	21

Saves

Player	
Lee Smith	180
Bruce Sutter	133
Randy Myers	112
Don Elston	63
Phil Regan	60
Rod Beck	58
Mitch Williams	52
Charlie Root	40
Ted Abernathy	39
Mordecai Brown	39
Lindy McDaniel	39

TEAM SEASON, GAME RECORDS

SEASON

Batting

Record		Year
Most at-bats	5,675	1988
Most runs	998	1930
Fewest runs	454	1919
Most hits	1,722	1930
Most singles	1,226	1921
Most doubles	340	1931
Most triples	101	1911
Most home runs	212	1998
Fewest home runs	6	1902
Most grand slams	9	1929
Most pinch-hit home runs	10	1998
Most total bases	2,684	1930
Most stolen bases	283	1906
Highest batting average	.309	1930
Lowest batting average	.238	1963, 1965
Highest slugging pct	.481	1930

Pitching

Record		Year
Lowest ERA	1.73	1907
Highest ERA	5.27	1999
Most complete games	139	1904
Most shutouts	32	1907, 1909
Most saves	56	1993, 1998
Most walks	628	1987
Most strikeouts	1,344	2001

Fielding

Record		Year
Most errors	418	1900
Fewest errors	100	2000
Most double plays	176	1928
Highest fielding average	.984	1998

General

Record		Year
Most games won	116	1906
Most games lost	103	1962, 1966
Highest win pct	.798	1880
Lowest win pct	.364	1962, 1966

GAME, INNING

Batting

Record		Date
Most runs, game	36	6-29-1897
Most runs, inning	18	9-6-1883
Most hits, game	32	7-3-1883, 6-29-1897
Most home runs, game	7	Last 5-17-77
Most total bases, game	54	8-25-1891

Dependable third baseman Ron Santo hit 337 home runs while wearing a Cubs uniform.

HISTORY

CUBS YEAR-BY-YEAR

Year	W	L	Place	Games Back	Manager	Leaders: Batting avg.	Hits	Home runs	RBIs	Wins	ERA
1901	53	86	6th	37	Loftus	Hartsel, .335	Hartsel, 187	Hartsel, 7	Dexter, 66	Waddell, 14	Waddell, 2.81
1902	68	69	5th	34	Selee	Slagle, .315	Slagle, 143	Dexter, Tinker, 2	Kling, 57	Taylor, 23	Taylor, 1.33
1903	82	56	3rd	8	Selee	Chance, .327	Slagle, 162	Kling, 3	Chance, 81	Taylor, 21	Weimer, 2.30
1904	93	60	2nd	13	Selee	Chance, .310	Casey, 147	Chance, 6	McCarthy, 51	Weimer, 20	M. Brown, 1.86
1905	92	61	3rd	13	Selee, Chance	Chance, .316	Slagle, 153	Chance, Maloney, Tinker, 2	Chance, 70	M. Brown, Reulbach, Weimer, 18	Reulbach, 1.42
1906	116	36	1st	+20	Chance	Steinfeldt, .327	Steinfeldt, 176	Schulte, 7	Steinfeldt, 83	M. Brown, 26	M. Brown, 1.04
1907	107	45	1st	+17	Chance	Chance, .293	Steinfeldt, 144	Evers, Schulte, 2	Steinfeldt, 70	Overall, 23	Pfiester, 1.15
1908	99	55	1st	+1	Chance	Evers, .300	Tinker, 146	Tinker, 6	Tinker, 68	M. Brown, 29	M. Brown, 1.47
1909	104	49	2nd	6½	Chance	Hofman, .285	Hofman, 150	Schulte, Tinker, 4	Schulte, 60	M. Brown, 27	M. Brown, 1.31
1910	104	50	1st	+13	Chance	Hofman, .325	Schulte, 168	Schulte, 10	Hofman, 86	M. Brown, 25	Pfiester, 1.79
1911	92	62	2nd	7½	Chance	Zimmerman, .307	Schulte, 173	Schulte, 21	Schulte, 107	M. Brown, 21	Richie, 2.31
1912	91	59	3rd	11½	Chance	Zimmerman, .372	Zimmerman, 207	Zimmerman, 14	Zimmerman, 99	Cheney, 26	Cheyney, 2.85
1913	88	65	3rd	13½	Evers	Zimmerman, .313	Saier, 149	Saier, 14	Zimmerman, 95	Cheyney, 21	Pearce, 2.31
1914	78	76	4th	16½	O'Day	Zimmerman, .296	Zimmerman, 167	Saier, 18	Zimmerman, 87	Vaughn, 21	Vaughn, 2.05
1915	73	80	4th	17½	Bresnahan	Fisher, .287	Fisher, 163	Williams, 13	Saier, Williams, 64	Vaughn, 20	Humphries, 2.31
1916	67	86	5th	26½	Tinker	Zimmerman, .291	Saier, 126	Williams, 12	Williams, 66	Vaughn, 17	Vaughn, 2.20
1917	74	80	5th	24	Mitchell	Mann, .273	Merkle, 146	Doyle, 6	Doyle, 61	Vaughn, 23	Vaughn, 2.01
1918	84	45	1st	+10½	Mitchell	Hollocher, .316	Hollocher, 161	Flack, 4	Merkle, 65	Vaughn, 22	Vaughn, 1.74
1919	75	65	3rd	21	Mitchell	Flack, .294	Flack, 138	Flack, 6	Merkle, 62	Vaughn, 21	Alexander, 1.72
1920	75	79	*5th	18	Mitchell	Flack, .302	Flack, 157	Robertson, 10	Robertson, 75	Alexander, 27	Alexander, 1.91
1921	64	89	7th	30	Evers, Killefer	Grimes, .321	Flack, 172	Flack, Grimes, 6	Grimes, 79	Alexander, 15	Alexander, 3.39
1922	80	74	5th	13	Killefer	Grimes, .354	Hollocher, 201	Grimes, 14	Grimes, 99	Aldridge, Alexander, 16	Aldridge, 3.52
1923	83	71	4th	12½	Killefer	Statz, O'Farrell, .319	Statz, 209	Miller, 20	Friberg, Miller, 88	Alexander, 22	Keen, 3.00
1924	81	72	5th	12	Killefer	Grantham, .316	Statz, 152	Hartnett, 16	Friberg, 82	Kaufmann, 16	Alexander, 3.03
1925	68	86	8th	27½	Killefer, Maranville, Gibson	Freigau, .307	Adams, 180	Hartnett, 24	Grimm, 76	Alexander, 15	Alexander, 3.39
1926	82	72	4th	7	McCarthy	Wilson, .321	Adams, 193	Wilson, 21	Wilson, 109	Root, 18	Root, 2.82
1927	85	68	4th	8½	McCarthy	Stephenson, .344	Stephenson, 199	Wilson, 30	Wilson, 129	Root, 26	Bush, 3.03
1928	91	63	3rd	4	McCarthy	Stephenson, .324	Stephenson, 166	Wilson, 31	Wilson, 120	Malone, 18	Blake, 2.47
1929	98	54	1st	+10½	McCarthy	Hornsby, .380	Hornsby, 229	Hornsby, Wilson, 39	Wilson, 159	Malone, 22	Root, 3.47
1930	90	64	2nd	2	McCarthy, Hornsby	Wilson, .356	Cuyler, 228	Wilson, 56	Wilson, 191	Malone, 20	Malone, 3.94
1931	84	70	3rd	17	Hornsby	Grimm, Hornsby, .331	Cuyler, English, 202	Hornsby, 16	Hornsby, 90	Root, 17	B. Smith, 3.22
1932	90	64	1st	+4	Hornsby, Grimm	Stephenson, .324	B. Herman, 206	Moore, 13	Stephenson, 85	Warneke, 22	Warneke, 2.37
1933	86	68	3rd	6	Grimm	Herman, .289	B. Herman, 173	Hartnett, B. Herman, 16	B. Herman, 93	Bush, 20	Warneke, 2.00
1934	86	65	3rd	8	Grimm	Cuyler, .338	Cuyler, 189	Hartnett, 22	Hartnett, 90	Warneke, 22	Warneke, 3.21
1935	100	54	1st	+4	Grimm	Hartnett, .344	B. Herman, 227	Klein, 21	Hartnett, 91	Lee, Warneke, 20	French, Lee, 2.96
1936	87	67	*2nd	5	Grimm	Demaree, .350	Demaree, 212	Demaree, 16	Demaree, 96	French, Lee, 18	C. Davis, 3.00
1937	93	61	2nd	3	Grimm	Hartnett, .354	Demaree, 199	Galan, 18	Demaree, 115	Carleton, French, 16	Carleton, 3.15
1938	89	63	1st	+2	Grimm, Hartnett	Hack, .320	Hack, 195	Collins, 13	Galan, 69	Lee, 22	Lee, 2.66
1939	84	70	4th	13	Hartnett	Leiber, .310	Hack, B. Herman, 191	Leiber, 24	Leiber, 88	Lee, 19	Passeau, 3.05
1940	75	79	5th	25½	Hartnett	Hack, .317	Hack, 191	Nicholson, 25	Nicholson, 98	Passeau, 20	Passeau, 2.50
1941	70	84	6th	30	Wilson	Hack, .317	Hack, 186	Nicholson, 26	Nicholson, 98	Passeau, 14	Olsen, 3.15
1942	68	86	6th	38	Wilson	Hack, .Novikoff, .300	Nicholson, 173	Nicholson, 21	Nicholson, 78	Passeau, 19	Warneke, 2.27
1943	74	79	5th	30½	Wilson	Nicholson, .309	Nicholson, 188	Nicholson, 29	Nicholson, 128	Bithorn, 18	Hanyzewski, 2.56
1944	75	79	4th	30	Wilson, Grimm	Cavarretta, .321	Cavarretta, 197	Nicholson, 33	Nicholson, 122	Wyse, 16	Passeau, 2.89
1945	98	56	1st	+3	Grimm	Cavarretta, .355	Hack, 193	Nicholson, 13	Pafko, 110	Wyse, 22	Borowy, 2.13
1946	82	71	3rd	14½	Grimm	Waitkus, .304	Cavarretta, 150	Cavarretta, Nicholson, 8	Cavarretta, 78	Wyse, 14	Erickson, 2.43
1947	69	85	6th	25	Grimm	Cavarretta, .314	Pafko, 155	Nicholson, 26	Nicholson, 75	Schmitz, 13	Schmitz, 3.22
1948	64	90	8th	27½	Grimm	Pafko, .312	Pafko, 171	Pafko, 26	Pafko, 101	Schmitz, 18	Schmitz, 2.64
1949	61	93	8th	36	Grimm, Frisch	Cavarretta, .294	Pafko, 146	Sauer, 27	Sauer, 83	Schmitz, 11	Chapman, 3.98
1950	64	89	7th	26½	Frisch	Pafko, .304	Pafko, 156	Pafko, 36	Sauer, 103	Rush, 13	Hiller, 3.53
1951	62	92	8th	34½	Frisch, Cavarretta	Baumholtz, .284	Baumholtz, 159	Sauer, 30	Sauer, 89	Rush, 11	Leonard, 2.64
1952	77	77	5th	19½	Cavarretta	Baumholtz, .325	Fondy, 166	Sauer, 37	Sauer, 121	Rush, 17	Hacker, 2.58
1953	65	89	7th	40	Cavarretta	Fondy, .309	Fondy, 184	Kiner, 28	Kiner, 87	Hacker, Minner, 12	Pollet, 4.12
1954	64	90	7th	33	Hack	Sauer, .288	Banks, 163	Sauer, 41	Sauer, 103	Rush, 13	Davis, 3.52
1955	72	81	6th	26	Hack	Banks, .295	Banks, 176	Banks, 44	Banks, 117	Jones, 14	Jeffcoat, 2.95
1956	60	94	8th	33	Hack	Banks, .297	Banks, 160	Banks, 28	Banks, 85	Rush, 13	Rush, 3.19
1957	62	92	*7th	33	Scheffing	Long, .305	Banks, 169	Banks, 43	Banks, 102	Drott, 15	Brosnan, 3.38
1958	72	82	*5th	20	Scheffing	Banks, .313	Banks, 193	Banks, 47	Banks, 129	Hobbie, 10	Elston, 2.88
1959	74	80	*5th	13	Scheffing	Banks, .304	Banks, 179	Banks, 45	Banks, 143	Hobbie, 16	Henry, 2.68
1960	60	94	7th	35	Grimm, Boudreau	Ashburn, .291	Banks, 162	Banks, 41	Banks, 117	Hobbie, 16	Elston, 3.40
1961	64	90	7th	29	Himsl, Craft, Tappe, Klein	Altman, .303	Santo, 164	Banks, 29	Altman, 96	Cardwell, 15	Cardwell, 3.82
1962	59	103	9th	42½	Metro, Tappe,Klein	Altman, .318	Williams, 184	Banks, 37	Banks, 104	Buhl, 12	Buhl, 3.69
1963	82	80	7th	17	Kennedy	Santo, .297	Santo, 187	Santo, Williams, 25	Santo, 99	Ellsworth, 22	Ellsworth, 2.11
1964	76	86	8th	17	Kennedy	Santo, .313	Williams, 201	Williams, 33	Santo, 114	Jackson, 24	Jackson, 3.14
1965	72	90	8th	25	Kennedy, Klein	Williams, .315	Williams, 203	Williams, 34	Williams, 108	Ellsworth, Jackson, 14	Abernathy, 2.57
1966	59	103	10th	36	Durocher	Santo, .312	Beckert, 188	Santo, 30	Santo, 94	Holtzman, 11	Jenkins, 3.31
1967	87	74	3rd	14	Durocher	Santo, .300	Santo, Williams, 176	Santo, 31	Santo, 98	Jenkins, 20	Hands, 2.46
1968	84	78	3rd	13	Durocher	Beckert, .294	Beckert, 189	Banks, 32	Santo, Williams, 98	Jenkins, 20	Regan, 2.20
								EAST DIVISION			
1969	92	70	2nd	8	Durocher	Williams, .293	Williams, 188	Santo, 29	Santo, 123	Jenkins, 21	Hands, 2.49
1970	84	78	2nd	5	Durocher	Williams, .322	Williams, 205	Williams, 42	Williams, 129	Jenkins, 22	Pappas, 2.68
1971	83	79	*3rd	14	Durocher	Beckert, .342	Beckert, 181	Williams, 28	Williams, 93	Jenkins, 24	Jenkins, 2.77
1972	85	70	2nd	11	Durocher, Lockman	Williams, .333	Williams, 191	Williams, 37	Williams, 122	Jenkins, 20	Pappas, 2.77
1973	77	84	5th	5	Lockman	Cardenal, .303	Williams, 166	Monday, 26	Williams, 86	Hooton, Jenkins, R. Reuschel, 14	Locker, 2.54
1974	66	96	6th	22	Lockman, Marshall	Madlock, .313	Cardenal, 159	Monday, 20	Morales, 82	R. Reuschel, 13	Bonham, 3.86
1975	75	87	*5th	17½	Marshall	Madlock, .354	Cardenal, Madlock, 182	Thornton, 18	Morales, 91	Burris, 15	R. Reuschel, 3.73
1976	75	87	4th	26	Marshall	Madlock, .339	Madlock, 174	Monday, 32	Madlock, 84	Burris, 15	Burris, 3.11
1977	81	81	4th	20	Franks	Ontiveros, .299	DeJesus, 166	Murcer, 27	Murcer, 89	R. Reuschel, 20	Sutter, 1.34
1978	79	83	3rd	11	Franks	Buckner, .323	DeJesus, 172	Kingman, 28	Kingman, 79	Reuschel, 14	Sutter, 3.18
1979	80	82	5th	18	Franks, Amalfitano	Kingman, .288	DeJesus, 180	Kingman, 48	Kingman, 115	Reuschel, 18	Sutter, 2.22
1980	64	98	6th	27	Gomez, Amalfitano	Buckner, .324	Buckner, 187	Martin, 23	Martin, 73	McGlothen, 12	Caudill, 2.19
1981	38	65	†6th/5th	—	Amalfitano	Buckner, .311	Buckner, 131	Buckner, Durham, 10	Buckner, 75	Krukow, 9	R. Reuschel, 3.47
1982	73	89	5th	19	Elia	Durham, .312	Buckner, 201	Durham, 22	Buckner, 105	Jenkins, 14	L. Smith, 2.69
1983	71	91	5th	19	Elia, Fox	Moreland, .302	Buckner, 175	Cey, J. Davis, 24	Cey, 90	Rainey, 14	L. Smith, 1.65
1984	96	65	‡1st	+6½	Frey	Sandberg, .314	Sandberg, 200	Cey, 25	Cey, 97	Sutcliffe, 16	Sutcliffe, 2.69
1985	77	84	4th	23½	Frey	Moreland, .307	Sandberg, 186	Sandberg, 26	Moreland, 106	Eckersley, 11	L. Smith, 3.04
1986	70	90	5th	37	Frey, Vukovich, Michael	Sandberg, .284	Sandberg, 178	J. Davis, Matthews, 21	Moreland, 79	Sanderson, L. Smith, 9	L. Smith, 3.09
1987	76	85	6th	18½	Michael, Lucchesi	Sandberg, .294	Dawson, 178	Dawson, 49	Dawson, 137	Sutcliffe, 18	Sutcliffe, 3.68
1988	77	85	4th	24	Zimmer	Palmeiro, .307	Dawson, 179	Dawson, 24	Dawson, 79	Maddux, 18	Maddux, 3.18
1989	93	69	‡1st	+6	Zimmer	Grace, .314	Sandberg, 176	Sandberg, 30	Grace, 79	Maddux, 19	Maddux, 2.95
1990	77	85	*4th	18	Zimmer	Dawson, .310	Sandberg, 188	Sandberg, 40	Dawson, Sandberg, 100	Maddux, 15	Assenmacher, 2.80
1991	77	83	4th	20	Zimmer, Altobelli, Essian	Sandberg, .291	Sandberg, 170	Dawson, 31	Dawson, 104	Maddux, 15	McElroy, 1.95
1992	78	84	4th	18	Lefebvre	Grace, .307	Sandberg, 186	Sandberg, 26	Dawson, 90	Maddux, 20	Maddux, 2.18
1993	84	78	4th	13	Lefebvre	Grace, .325	Grace, 193	Sosa, 33	Grace, 98	Hibbard, 15	Bautista, 2.82
								CENTRAL DIVISION			
1994	49	64	5th	16½	Trebelhorn	Sosa, .300	Sosa, 128	Sosa, 25	Sosa, 70	Trachsel, 9	Trachsel, 3.21
1995	73	71	3rd	12	Riggleman	Grace, .326	Grace, 180	Sosa, 36	Sosa, 119	Foster, 12	Castillo, 3.21
1996	76	86	4th	12	Riggleman	Grace, .331	Grace, 181	Sosa, 40	Sosa, 100	Navarro, 15	Adams, 2.94
1997	68	94	5th	16	Riggleman	Grace, .319	Grace, 177	Sosa, 36	Sosa, 119	Gonzalez, 11,	Mulholland, 4.07
1998	90	73	§∞2nd	12½	Riggleman	Grace, Sosa, .307	Sosa, 196	Sosa, 66	Sosa, 158	Tapani, 19	Mulholland, 2.82
1999	67	95	6th	30	Riggleman	Grace, .309	Grace, 183	Sosa, 63	Sosa, 141	Lieber, 10	Lieber, 4.07
2000	65	97	6th	30	Baylor	Sosa, .320	Sosa, 193	Sosa, 50	Sosa, 138	Lieber, 12	Lieber, 4.41
2001	88	74	3rd	5	Baylor	Sosa, .328	Sosa, 189	Sosa, 64	Sosa, 160	Lieber, 20	Wood, 3.36
2002	67	95	5th	30	Baylor, Kimm	Sosa, .288	Sosa, 160	Sosa, 49	Sosa, 108	Clement, Wood, 12	Clement, 3.60

* Tied for position. † First half 15-37; second half 23-28. ‡ Lost Championship Series. § Won wild-card playoff. ∞ Lost Division Series.

Note: Batting average minimum 350 at-bats; ERA minimum 90 innings pitched.

Cincinnati Reds

Infielder/outfielder Pete Rose.

FRANCHISE CHRONOLOGY

First season: 1876, as a member of the new National League. The Red Stockings won their first N.L. game, beating St. Louis, 2-1. That would be one of the few highlights in a 9-56 debut.

1877-1900: The Reds played five seasons in the N.L., sat out a year and returned as a member of the new American Association in 1882. After eight seasons in the A.A., they transferred back to the N.L., where they remain today. The Reds' only pre-1900 pennant came in 1882, the American Association's inaugural season.

1901-present: Through the first 39 years of the century, the Reds' only success was a tainted one: a victory over Chicago in the infamous "Black Sox" World Series of 1919. But four decades of futility ended in 1940 when the Reds punctuated their second straight pennant with a seven-game World Series victory over Detroit. Although usually competitive, Cincinnati's first sustained success did not occur until the 1970s, when the Big Red Machine of Sparky Anderson won six West Division titles, four pennants and two World Series. The Reds won their fifth fall classic in 1990. Cincinnati was one of five teams placed in the Central Division when the N.L. adopted its three-division format in 1994.

REDS VS. OPPONENTS BY DECADE

	Braves	Cardinals	Cubs	Dodgers	Giants	Phillies	Pirates	Astros	Mets	Expos	Padres	Marlins	Rockies	Brewers	D'backs	Interleague	Decade Record
1900-09	120-90	119-91	79-132	114-97	87-123	105-105	81-131										705-769
1910-19	116-97	109-108	93-119	121-93	85-129	91-124	102-109										717-779
1920-29	130-89	105-115	105-115	122-96	86-134	149-68	101-118										798-735
1930-39	110-108	73-147	99-121	108-112	79-139	116-99	79-140										664-866
1940-49	112-105	87-133	110-110	87-133	120-100	136-84	115-104										767-769
1950-59	86-134	96-124	129-90	91-129	92-128	113-107	134-86										741-798
1960-69	103-85	92-90	103-79	94-94	84-103	107-75	90-92	85-59	83-54	8-4	11-7						860-742
1970-79	120-60	74-46	61-59	97-79	99-78	73-47	65-54	105-74	80-40	74-46	105-74						953-657
1980-89	92-81	50-63	59-54	80-98	91-85	60-55	64-50	81-93	55-62	53-64	96-78						781-783
1990-99	49-82	62-51	68-51	57-65	58-66	68-39	64-59	76-63	49-59	57-48	69-61	43-32	41-34	12-11	13-5	23-20	809-746
2000-02	9-10	22-27	24-22	12-9	9-12	7-12	27-21	19-27	11-10	11-10	11-10	12-9	12-12	24-24	6-13	13-29	229-257
Totals	1047-941	889-995	930-952	983-1005	890-1097	1025-815	922-964	366-316	278-225	203-172	292-230	55-41	53-46	36-35	19-18	36-49	8024-7901

Interleague results: 1-2 vs. Angels, 2-9 vs. White Sox, 11-13 vs. Indians, 6-6 vs. Tigers, 5-3 vs. Royals, 3-0 vs. Brewers, 7-8 vs. Twins, 0-3 vs. Athletics, 0-3 vs. Mariners, 1-2 vs. Rangers.

MANAGERS

Name	*Years*	*Record*
Charlie Gould	1876	9-56
Lip Pike	1877	3-11
Bob Addy	1877	5-19
Jack Manning	1877	7-12
Cal McVey	1878, 1879	71-51
Deacon White	1879	9-9
John Clapp	1880	21-59
Pop Snyder	1882-83, 1884	140-76
Will White	1884	44-27
Oliver Caylor	1885-86	128-122
Gus Schmelz	1887-89	237-171
Tom Loftus	1890-91	133-136
Charles Comiskey	1892-94	202-206
Buck Ewing	1895-99	394-297
Bob Allen	1900	62-77
Biddy McPhee	1901-02	79-124
Frank Bancroft	1902	9-7
Joe Kelley	1902-05	275-230
Ned Hanlon	1906-07	130-174
John Ganzel	1908	73-81
Clark Griffith	1909-11	222-238
Hank O'Day	1912	75-78
Joe Tinker	1913	64-89
Buck Herzog	1914-16	165-226
Christy Mathewson	1916-18	164-176
Heinie Groh	1918	7-3
Pat Moran	1919-23	425-329
Jack Hendricks	1924-29	469-450
Dan Howley	1930-32	177-285
Donie Bush	1933	58-94
Bob O'Farrell	1934	30-60
Chuck Dressen	1934-37	214-282
Bobby Wallace	1937	5-20
Bill McKechnie	1938-46	744-631
Hank Gowdy	1946	3-1
Johnny Neun	1947-48	117-137
Bucky Walters	1948-49	81-123
Luke Sewell	1950-52	174-234
Earle Brucker	1952	3-2
Rogers Hornsby	1952-53	91-106
Buster Mills	1953	4-4
Birdie Tebbetts	1954-58	372-357
Jimmie Dykes	1958	24-17
Mayo Smith	1959	35-45
Fred Hutchinson	1959-64	443-372
Dick Sisler	1964-65	121-94
Don Heffner	1966	37-46
Dave Bristol	1966-69	298-265
Sparky Anderson	1970-78	863-586
John McNamara	1979-82	279-244
Russ Nixon	1982-83	101-131

MANAGERS—*cont'd.*

Name	*Years*	*Record*
Vern Rapp	1984	51-70
Pete Rose	1984-89	412-373
Tommy Helms	1988, 1989	28-36
Lou Piniella	1990-92	255-231
Tony Perez	1993	20-24
Dave Johnson	1993-95	204-172
Ray Knight	1996-97	124-137
Jack McKeon	1997-2000	291-259
Bob Boone	2001-02	144-180

WORLD SERIES CHAMPIONS

Year	*Loser*	*Length*	*MVP*
1919	Chicago	8 games	None
1940	Detroit	7 games	None
1975	Boston	7 games	Rose
1976	N.Y. Yankees	4 games	Bench
1990	Oakland	4 games	Rijo

A.A. PENNANT WINNERS

Year	*Record*	*Manager*	*Series Result*
1882	55-25	Snyder	None

N.L. PENNANT WINNERS

Year	*Record*	*Manager*	*Series Result*
1919	96-44	Moran	Defeated White Sox
1939	97-57	McKechnie	Lost to Yankees
1940	100-53	McKechnie	Defeated Tigers
1961	93-61	Hutchinson	Lost to Yankees
1970	102-60	Anderson	Lost to Orioles
1972	95-59	Anderson	Lost to A's
1975	108-54	Anderson	Defeated Red Sox
1976	102-60	Anderson	Defeated Yankees
1990	91-71	Piniella	Defeated A's

WEST DIVISION CHAMPIONS

Year	*Record*	*Manager*	*NLCS Result*
1970	102-60	Anderson	Defeated Pirates
1972	95-59	Anderson	Defeated Pirates
1973	99-63	Anderson	Lost to Mets
1975	108-54	Anderson	Defeated Pirates
1976	102-60	Anderson	Defeated Phillies
1979	90-71	McNamara	Lost to Pirates
1990	91-71	Piniella	Defeated Pirates

CENTRAL DIVISION CHAMPIONS

Year	*Record*	*Manager*	*NLCS Result*
1994	66-48	Johnson	None
1995	85-59	Johnson	Lost to Braves

ATTENDANCE HIGHS

Total	*Season*	*Park*
2,629,708	1976	Riverfront Stadium
2,577,351	2000	Riverfront Stadium
2,532,497	1978	Riverfront Stadium
2,519,670	1977	Riverfront Stadium
2,453,232	1993	Riverfront Stadium

BALLPARK CHRONOLOGY

Great American Ball Park (Opens in 2003)

Capacity: 42,000.

Cinergy Field, formerly Riverfront Stadium (1970-2002)

Capacity: 52,953.
First game: Atlanta 8, Reds 2 (June 30, 1970).
First batter: Sonny Jackson, Braves.
First hit: Felix Millan, Braves (single).
First run: Felix Millan, Braves (1st inning).
First home run: Hank Aaron, Braves.
First winning pitcher: Pat Jarvis, Braves.
First-season attendance (1971): 1,501,122.

Avenue Grounds (1876-79)

First game: Cincinnati 2, St. Louis 1 (April 25, 1876).

Bank Street Grounds (1880)

First game: Chicago 4, Cincinnati 3 (May 1, 1880).

Redland Field I (1882-1901)

Palace of the Fans (1902-11)

First game: Chicago 6, Reds 1 (April 17, 1902).
First-season attendance: 217,300.

Crosley Field (1912-70)

Capacity: 29,603.
First game: Reds 10, Chicago 6 (April 11, 1912).
First-season attendance: 344,000.

N.L. MVPs

Ernie Lombardi, C, 1938
Bucky Walters, P, 1939
Frank McCormick, 1B, 1940
Frank Robinson, OF, 1961
Johnny Bench, C, 1970
Johnny Bench, C, 1972
Pete Rose, OF, 1973
Joe Morgan, 2B, 1975
Joe Morgan, 2B, 1976

N.L. MVPs—*cont'd.*

George Foster, OF, 1977
Barry Larkin, SS, 1995

ROOKIES OF THE YEAR

Frank Robinson, OF, 1956
Pete Rose, 2B, 1963
Tommy Helms, 3B, 1966
Johnny Bench, C, 1968
*Pat Zachry, P, 1976
Chris Sabo, 3B, 1988
Scott Williamson, P, 1999

* Co-winner.

MANAGER OF THE YEAR

Jack McKeon, 1999

RETIRED UNIFORMS

No.	*Name*	*Pos.*
1	Fred Hutchinson	Man.
5	Johnny Bench	C
8	Joe Morgan	2B
18	Ted Kluszewski	OF
20	Frank Robinson	OF

INDIVIDUAL SEASON, GAME RECORDS

SEASON

Batting

At-bats	680	Pete Rose	1973
Runs	134	Frank Robinson	1962
Hits	230	Pete Rose	1973
Singles	181	Pete Rose	1973
Doubles	51	Frank Robinson	1962
		Pete Rose	1978
Triples	25	Bid McPhee	1890
Home runs	52	George Foster	1977
Home runs, rookie	38	Frank Robinson	1956
Grand slams	3	5 times	
		Last by Chris Sabo	1993
Total bases	388	George Foster	1977
RBIs	149	George Foster	1977
Walks	132	Joe Morgan	1975
Most strikeouts	170	Adam Dunn	2002
Fewest strikeouts	13	Frank McCormick	1941
Batting average	.383	Bug Holliday	1894
Slugging pct.	.681	Kevin Mitchell	1994
Stolen bases	93	Arlie Latham	1891

Pitching (since 1900)

Games	90	Wayne Granger	1969
Complete games	41	Noodles Hahn	1901
Innings	375.1	Noodles Hahn	1901
Wins	27	Dolf Luque	1923
		Bucky Walters	1939
Losses	25	Paul Derringer	1933
Winning pct.	.875 (14-2)	Tom Seaver	1981
Walks	162	Johnny Vander Meer	1943
Strikeouts	274	Mario Soto	1982
Shutouts	7	4 times	
		Last by Jack Billingham	1973
Home runs allowed	36	Tom Browning	1988
Lowest ERA	1.57	Fred Toney	1915
Saves	44	Jeff Brantley	1996

GAME

Batting

Runs	5	Last by Jeffrey Hammonds and Sean Casey	5-19-99
Hits	6	Last by Walker Cooper	7-6-49
Doubles	4	Last by Billy Hatcher	8-21-90
Triples	3	Last by Herm Winningham	8-15-90
Home runs	3	Last by Aaron Boone	8-9-2002
RBIs	10	Walker Cooper	7-6-49
Total bases	15	Walker Cooper	7-6-49
Stolen bases	4	Last by Deion Sanders	4-14-97

MILESTONE PERFORMANCES

30-plus home runs

52—George Foster ... 1977
49—Ted Kluszewski ... 1954
47—Ted Kluszewski ... 1955
45—Johnny Bench ... 1970
Greg Vaughn ... 1999
40—Ted Kluszewski ... 1953
Wally Post ... 1955
Tony Perez ... 1970
Johnny Bench ... 1972
George Foster ... 1978
Ken Griffey Jr. ... 2000
39—Frank Robinson ... 1956
Lee May ... 1971
38—Frank Robinson ... 1956
Lee May ... 1969
37—Frank Robinson ... 1961
Tony Perez ... 1969
Eric Davis ... 1987
36—Wally Post ... 1956
Frank Robinson ... 1959
35—Hank Sauer ... 1948
Ted Kluszewski ... 1956
34—Lee May ... 1970
Dave Parker ... 1985
Eric Davis ... 1989
33—Frank Robinson ... 1965
Johnny Bench ... 1974
Barry Larkin ... 1996
32—Deron Johnson ... 1965
31—George Crowe ... 1957
Frank Robinson ... 1958, 1960
Johnny Bench ... 1977
Dave Parker ... 1986
30—Ival Goodman ... 1938
Gus Bell ... 1953
George Foster ... 1979
Kevin Mitchell ... 1994

100-plus RBIs

149—George Foster ... 1977
148—Johnny Bench ... 1970
141—Ted Kluszewski ... 1954
136—Frank Robinson ... 1962
130—Deron Johnson ... 1965
129—Tony Perez ... 1970
Johnny Bench ... 1974
128—Frank McCormick ... 1939
127—Frank McCormick ... 1940
125—Frank Robinson ... 1959
Johnny Bench ... 1972
Dave Parker ... 1985
124—Frank Robinson ... 1961
122—Tony Perez ... 1969
121—Cy Seymour ... 1905
George Foster ... 1976
120—George Foster ... 1978
118—Greg Vaughn ... 1999
Ken Griffey Jr. ... 2000
116—Dave Parker ... 1986
115—Gus Bell ... 1959
113—Ted Kluszewski ... 1955
Frank Robinson ... 1965
111—Ted Kluszewski ... 1950
Joe Morgan ... 1976
110—Lee May ... 1969
Johnny Bench ... 1975
109—Wally Post ... 1955
Tony Perez ... 1975
Johnny Bench ... 1977
108—Ted Kluszewski ... 1953
106—Frank McCormick ... 1938
Vada Pinson ... 1963
105—Gus Bell ... 1953
104—Sam Crawford ... 1901
Gus Bell ... 1955
Johnny Bench ... 1973
103—George Kelly ... 1929
102—Frank McCormick ... 1944
Ted Kluszewski ... 1956
Tony Perez ... 1967
101—Gus Bell ... 1954
Tony Perez ... 1973, 1974
Eric Davis ... 1989
100—Jim Greengrass ... 1953
Vada Pinson ... 1962
Eric Davis ... 1987

20-plus victories

1878—Will White ... 30-21
1879—Will White ... 43-31
1890—Billy Rhines ... 28-17
1891—Tony Mullane ... 23-26
1892—Tony Mullane ... 21-13
Frank Dwyer ... *21-18
1896—Frank Dwyer ... 24-11
1897—Ted Breitenstein ... 23-12
Billy Rhines ... 21-15
1898—Pink Hawley ... 27-11
Ted Breitenstein ... 20-14
1899—Noodles Hahn ... 23-8
1901—Noodles Hahn ... 22-19
1902—Noodles Hahn ... 23-12
1903—Noodles Hahn ... 22-12
1904—Charles Harper ... 23-9
1905—Bob Ewing ... 20-11
1906—Jake Weimer ... 20-14
1910—George Suggs ... 20-12
1917—Fred Toney ... 24-16
Pete Schneider ... 20-19
1919—Slim Sallee ... 21-7
1922—Eppa Rixey ... 25-13
1923—Dolf Luque ... 27-8
Pete Donohue ... 21-15
Eppa Rixey ... 20-15
1924—Carl Mays ... 20-9
1925—Eppa Rixey ... 21-11
Pete Donohue ... 21-14
1926—Pete Donohue ... 20-14
1935—Paul Derringer ... 22-13
1938—Paul Derringer ... 21-14
1939—Bucky Walters ... 27-11
Paul Derringer ... 25-7
1940—Bucky Walters ... 22-10
Paul Derringer ... 20-12
1943—Elmer Riddle ... 21-11
1944—Bucky Walters ... 23-8
1947—Ewell Blackwell ... 22-8
1961—Joey Jay ... 21-10
1962—Bob Purkey ... 23-5
Joey Jay ... 21-14
1963—Jim Maloney ... 23-7
1965—Sammy Ellis ... 22-10
Jim Maloney ... 20-9
1970—Jim Merritt ... 20-12
1977—Tom Seaver ... †21-6
1985—Tom Browning ... 20-9
1988—Danny Jackson ... 23-8

*2-8 with St. Louis; 19-10 with Cincinnati; †7-3 with Mets; 14-3 with Reds.

N.L. home run champions

1877—Lip Pike ... 4
1892—Bug Holliday ... 13
1901—Sam Crawford ... 16
1905—Fred Odwell ... 9
1954—Ted Kluszewski ... 49
1970—Johnny Bench ... 45
1972—Johnny Bench ... 40
1977—George Foster ... 52
1978—George Foster ... 40

N.L. RBI champions

1905—Cy Seymour ... 121
1918—Sherry Magee ... 76
1939—Frank McCormick ... 128
1954—Ted Kluszewski ... 141
1965—Deron Johnson ... 130
1970—Johnny Bench ... 148
1972—Johnny Bench ... 125
1974—Johnny Bench ... 129
1976—George Foster ... 121
1977—George Foster ... 149
1978—George Foster ... 120
1985—Dave Parker ... 125

N.L. batting champions

1905—Cy Seymour ... .377
1916—Hal Chase ... .339
1917—Edd Roush ... .341
1919—Edd Roush ... .321
1926—Bubbles Hargrave ... .353
1938—Ernie Lombardi ... .342
1968—Pete Rose ... .335
1969—Pete Rose ... .348
1973—Pete Rose ... .338

N.L. ERA champions

1923—Dolf Luque ... 1.93
1925—Dolf Luque ... 2.63
1939—Bucky Walters ... 2.29
1940—Bucky Walters ... 2.48
1941—Elmer Riddle ... 2.24
1944—Ed Heusser ... 2.38

N.L. strikeout champions

1899—Noodles Hahn ... 145
1900—Noodles Hahn ... 132
1901—Noodles Hahn ... 239
1939—Bucky Walters ... *137
1941—Johnny Vander Meer ... 202
1942—Johnny Vander Meer ... 186
1943—Johnny Vander Meer ... 174
1947—Ewell Blackwell ... 193
1993—Jose Rijo ... 227

* Tied for league lead

No-hit pitchers

1892—Bumpus Jones ... 7-1 vs. Pittsburgh
1898—Ted Breitenstein ... 11-0 vs. Pittsburgh
1900—Noodles Hahn ... 4-0 vs. Philadelphia
1917—Fred Toney ... 1-0 vs. Chicago (10 innings)
1919—Hod Eller ... 6-0 vs. St. Louis
1938—Johnny Vander Meer ... 3-0 vs. Boston
Johnny Vander Meer ... 6-0 vs. Brooklyn
1944—Clyde Shoun ... 1-0 vs. Boston
1947—Ewell Blackwell ... 6-0 vs. Boston
1965—Jim Maloney ... 1-0 vs. Chicago (10 innings)
1968—George Culver ... 6-1 vs. Philadelphia
1969—Jim Maloney ... 10-0 vs. Houston
1978—Tom Seaver ... 4-0 vs. St. Louis
1988—Tom Browning 1-0 vs. Los Angeles (Perfect)

Longest hitting streaks

44—Pete Rose ... 1978
30—Elmer Smith ... 1898
29—Hal Morris ... 1996
27—Edd Roush ... 1920, 1924
Vada Pinson ... 1965
25—Rube Bressler ... 1927
Pete Rose ... 1967
24—Cy Seymour ... 1903
Hughie Critz ... 1928
Tommy Harper ... 1966
23—Heinie Groh ... 1917
Vada Pinson ... 1965
22—Jake Daubert ... 1922
Pete Rose ... 1968
21—Cy Seymour ... 1905
Ron Oester ... 1984
Barry Larkin ... 1988
Sean Casey ... 2000
20—Al Libke ... 1945
Tony Perez ... 1968
Pete Rose ... 1977 (twice)

CAREER LEADERS

BATTING

Games

Player	Games
Pete Rose	2,722
Dave Concepcion	2,488
Johnny Bench	2,158
Barry Larkin	1,999
Tony Perez	1,948
Vada Pinson	1,565
Frank Robinson	1,502
Dan Driessen	1,480
Edd Roush	1,399
Roy McMillan	1,348

At-bats

Player	At-bats
Pete Rose	10,934
Dave Concepcion	8,723
Johnny Bench	7,658
Barry Larkin	7,350
Tony Perez	6,846
Vada Pinson	6,335
Frank Robinson	5,527
Edd Roush	5,384
Ted Kluszewski	4,961
Tommy Corcoran	4,852

Runs

Player	Runs
Pete Rose	1,741
Barry Larkin	1,235
Johnny Bench	1,091
Frank Robinson	1,043
Dave Concepcion	993
Vada Pinson	978
Tony Perez	936
Bid McPhee	922
Joe Morgan	816
Edd Roush	815

Hits

Player	Hits
Pete Rose	3,358
Dave Concepcion	2,326
Barry Larkin	2,172
Johnny Bench	2,048
Tony Perez	1,934
Vada Pinson	1,881
Edd Roush	1,784
Frank Robinson	1,673
Ted Kluszewski	1,499
Frank McCormick	1,439

Doubles

Player	Doubles
Pete Rose	601
Barry Larkin	410
Dave Concepcion	389
Johnny Bench	381
Vada Pinson	342
Tony Perez	339
Frank Robinson	318
Frank McCormick	285
Edd Roush	260
Ted Kluszewski	244

Triples

Player	Triples
Edd Roush	152
Pete Rose	115
Bid McPhee	113
Vada Pinson	96
Curt Walker	94
Mike Mitchell	88
Ival Goodman	79
Jake Daubert	78
Jake Beckley	77
Heinie Groh	75

Home runs

Player	Home runs
Johnny Bench	389
Frank Robinson	324
Tony Perez	287
Ted Kluszewski	251
George Foster	244
Eric Davis	203
Barry Larkin	188
Vada Pinson	186
Wally Post	172
Gus Bell	160

Total bases

Player	Total bases
Pete Rose	4,645
Johnny Bench	3,644
Barry Larkin	3,290
Tony Perez	3,246
Dave Concepcion	3,114
Frank Robinson	3,063
Vada Pinson	2,973
Ted Kluszewski	2,542
Edd Roush	2,489
George Foster	2,289

Runs batted in

Player	Runs batted in
Johnny Bench	1,376
Tony Perez	1,192
Pete Rose	1,036
Frank Robinson	1,009
Dave Concepcion	950
Barry Larkin	898
Ted Kluszewski	886
George Foster	861
Vada Pinson	814
Frank McCormick	803

Extra-base hits

Player	Extra-base hits
Pete Rose	868
Johnny Bench	794
Frank Robinson	692
Tony Perez	682
Barry Larkin	670
Vada Pinson	624
Dave Concepcion	538
Ted Kluszewski	518
George Foster	488
Edd Roush	459

Batting average

(Minimum 500 games)

Player	Batting average
Cy Seymour	.332
Edd Roush	.331
Jake Beckley	.325
Bubbles Hargrave	.314
Sean Casey	.312
Rube Bressler	.311
Ernie Lombardi	.311
Bug Holliday	.310
Dusty Miller	.308
Pete Rose	.307

Stolen bases

Player	Stolen bases
Joe Morgan	406
Barry Larkin	375
Arlie Latham	340
Dave Concepcion	321
Bob Bescher	320
Bid McPhee	316
Eric Davis	270
Vada Pinson	221
Bug Holliday	206
Edd Roush	199

PITCHING

Earned-run average

(Minimum 1,000 innings)

Player	ERA
Bob Ewing	2.37
Noodles Hahn	2.52
Pete Schneider	2.65
Jose Rijo	2.83
Bucky Walters	2.93
Tony Mullane	2.99
Gary Nolan	3.02
George Suggs	3.03
Don Gullett	3.03
Dolf Luque	3.09

Wins

Player	Wins
Eppa Rixey	179
Paul Derringer	161
Bucky Walters	160
Dolf Luque	154
Jim Maloney	134
Frank Dwyer	133
Joe Nuxhall	130
Pete Donohue	127
Noodles Hahn	127
Tom Browning	123

Losses

Player	Losses
Dolf Luque	152
Paul Derringer	150
Eppa Rixey	148
Johnny Vander Meer	116
Pete Donohue	110
Joe Nuxhall	109
Bucky Walters	107
Bob Ewing	103
Frank Dwyer	100
Red Lucas	99
Ken Raffensberger	99

Innings pitched

Player	Innings pitched
Eppa Rixey	2,890.2
Dolf Luque	2,668.2
Paul Derringer	2,615.1
Bucky Walters	2,355.2
Joe Nuxhall	2,169.1
Johnny Vander Meer	2,028.0
Bob Ewing	2,020.1
Pete Donohue	1,996.1
Frank Dwyer	1,992.2
Noodles Hahn	1,987.1

Strikeouts

Player	Strikeouts
Jim Maloney	1,592
Mario Soto	1,449
Joe Nuxhall	1,289
Jose Rijo	1,251
Johnny Vander Meer	1,251
Paul Derringer	1,062
Gary Nolan	1,035
Jim O'Toole	1,002
Tom Browning	997
Dolf Luque	970

Bases on balls

Player	Bases on balls
Johnny Vander Meer	1,072
Bucky Walters	806
Jim Maloney	786
Dolf Luque	756
Joe Nuxhall	706
Mario Soto	657
Eppa Rixey	603
Herm Wehmeier	591
Ewell Blackwell	532
Fred Norman	531

Games

Player	Games
Pedro Borbon	531
Clay Carroll	486
Joe Nuxhall	484
Tom Hume	457
Scott Sullivan	444
Eppa Rixey	440
Dolf Luque	395
Paul Derringer	393
John Franco	393
Rob Dibble	354

Shutouts

Player	Shutouts
Bucky Walters	32
Jim Maloney	30
Johnny Vander Meer	29
Ken Raffensberger	25
Paul Derringer	24
Noodles Hahn	24
Dolf Luque	24
Eppa Rixey	23
Joe Nuxhall	20
Jack Billingham	18
Red Lucas	18

Saves

Player	Saves
John Franco	148
Danny Graves	129
Clay Carroll	119
Jeff Brantley	88
Rob Dibble	88
Tom Hume	88
Pedro Borbon	76
Wayne Granger	73
Jeff Shaw	69
Bill Henry	64

TEAM SEASON, GAME RECORDS

SEASON

Batting

Record	Total	Year
Most at-bats	5,767	1968
Most runs	865	1999
Fewest runs	488	1908
Most hits	1,599	1976
Most singles	1,191	1922
Most doubles	312	1999
Most triples	120	1926
Most home runs	221	1956
Fewest home runs	14	1908, 1916
Most grand slams	9	2002
Most pinch-hit home runs	12	1957
Most total bases	2,549	1999
Most stolen bases	310	1910
Highest batting average	.296	1922
Lowest batting average	.227	1908
Highest slugging pct	.451	1999

Pitching

Record	Total	Year
Lowest ERA	2.23	1919
Highest ERA	5.08	1930
Most complete games	142	1904
Most shutouts	23	1919
Most saves	60	1970, 1972
Most walks	659	2000
Most strikeouts	1,159	1997

Fielding

Record	Total	Year
Most errors	355	1901
Fewest errors	95	1977
Most double plays	194	1928, 1931, 1954
Highest fielding average	.986	1995

General

Record	Total	Year
Most games won	108	1975
Most games lost	101	1982
Highest win pct	.686	1919
Lowest win pct	.138	1876

GAME, INNING

Batting

Record	Total	Date
Most runs, game	30	6-18-1893
Most runs, inning	14	6-18-1893, 8-3-89
Most hits, game	32	6-18-1893
Most home runs, game	9	9-4-99
Most total bases, game	55	6-18-1893, 5-19-99

George Foster joined an exclusive club in 1977 when he blasted a team-record 52 home runs.

HISTORY

REDS YEAR-BY-YEAR

Year	W	L	Place	Games Back	Manager	Leaders: Batting avg.	Hits	Home runs	RBIs	Wins	ERA
1901	52	87	8th	38	McPhee	Crawford, .330	Beckley, 178	Crawford, 16	Crawford, 104	Hahn, 22	Hahn, 2.71
1902	70	70	4th	33½	McPhee, Bancroft, Kelley	Crawford, .333	Crawford, 185	Beckley, 5	Crawford, 78	Hahn, 23	Hahn, 1.77
1903	74	65	4th	16½	Kelley	Donlin, .351	Seymour, 191	Donlin, Seymour, 7	Steinfeldt, 83	Hahn, 22	Hahn, 2.52
1904	88	65	3rd	18	Kelley	Seymour, .313	Seymour, 166	Dolan, 6	Corcoran, 74	Harper, 23	Hahn, 2.06
1905	79	74	5th	26	Kelley	Seymour, .377	Seymour, 219	Odwell, 9	Seymour, 121	Ewing, 20	Ewing, 2.51
1906	64	87	6th	51½	Hanlon	Huggins, .292	Huggins, 159	Schlei, Seymour, 4	Schlei, 54	Weimer, 20	Weimer, 2.22
1907	66	87	6th	41½	Hanlon	Mitchell, .292	Mitchell, 163	Kane, Mitchell, 3	Ganzel, 64	Coakley, Ewing, 17	Ewing, 1.73
1908	73	81	5th	26	Ganzel	Lobert, .293	Lobert, 167	Lobert, 4	Lobert, 63	Ewing, Spade, 17	Coakley, 1.86
1909	77	76	4th	33½	Griffith	Mitchell, .310	Mitchell, 162	3 Tied, 4	Mitchell, 86	Fromme, 19	Fromme, 1.90
1910	75	79	5th	29	Griffith	Paskert, .300	Hoblitzell, 170	Mitchell, 5,	Mitchell, 88	Suggs, 20	Suggs, 2.40
1911	70	83	6th	29	Griffith	Bates, .292	Hoblitzell, 180	Hoblitzell, 11	Hoblitzell, 91	Suggs, 15	Keefe, 2.69
1912	75	78	4th	29	O'Day	Marsans, .317	Hoblitzell, 164	Bescher, 4, Mitchell, 4	Hoblitzell, 85	Suggs, 19	Fromme, 2.74
1913	64	89	7th	37½	Tinker	Tinker, .317	Hoblitzell, 143	Bates, 6	Hoblitzell, 62	Johnson, 14	Ames, 2.88
1914	60	94	8th	34½	Herzog	Groh, .288	Herzog, 140	Niehoff, 4	Niehoff, 49	Benton, 16	Douglas, 2.56
1915	71	83	7th	20	Herzog	T. Griffith, .307	T. Griffith, 179	T. Griffith, 4	T. Griffith, 85	Dale, 18	Toney, 1.58
1916	60	93	*7th	33½	Herzog, Mathewson	Chase, .339	Chase, 184	Chase, 4	Chase, 82	Toney, 14	Toney, 2.28
1917	78	76	4th	20	Mathewson	Roush, .341	Groh, 182	Chase, Roush, Thorpe, 4	Chase, 86	Toney, 24	Schneider, 2.10
1918	68	60	3rd	15½	Mathewson, Groh	Roush, .333	Groh, 158	Roush, 5	S. Magee, 76	Eller, 16	Eller, 2.36
1919	96	44	1st	+9	Moran	Roush, .321	Roush, 162	Groh, 5	Roush, 71	Sallee, 21	Ruether, 1.82
1920	82	71	3rd	10½	Moran	Roush, .339	Roush, 196	Daubert, Roush, 4	Roush, 90	Ring, 17	Ruether, 2.47
1921	70	83	6th	24	Moran	Roush, .352	Bohne, 175	Roush, 4	Roush, 71	Rixey, 19	Rixey, 2.78
1922	86	68	2nd	7	Moran	Harper, .340	Daubert, 205	Daubert, 12	Duncan, 94	Rixey, 25	Donohue, 3.12
1923	91	63	2nd	4½	Moran	Roush, .351	Duncan, Roush, 185	Hargrave, 10	Roush, 88	Luque, 27	Luque, 1.93
1924	83	70	4th	10	Hendricks	Roush, .348	Roush, 168	4 Tied, 4	Roush, 72	Mays, 20	Rixey, 2.76
1925	80	73	3rd	15	Hendricks	Roush, .339	Roush, 183	Roush, E. Smith, 8	Roush, 83	Donohue, Rixey, 21	Luque, 2.63
1926	87	67	2nd	2	Hendricks	Roush, .323	Roush, 182	Roush, 7	Pipp, 99	Donohue, 20	Mays, 3.14
1927	75	78	5th	18½	Hendricks	Allen, .295	Dressen, 160	Walker, 6	Walker, 80	Lucas, 18	Luque, 3.20
1928	78	74	5th	16	Hendricks	Allen, .305	Critz, 190	Picinich, 7	Walker, 73	Rixey, 19	Kolp, 3.19
1929	66	88	7th	33	Hendricks	Walker, .313	Swanson, 172	Walker, 7	Kelly, 103	Lucas, 19	Lucas, 3.60
1930	59	95	7th	33	Howley	Heilmann, .333	Heilmann, 153	Heilmann, 19	Heilmann, 91	Lucas, 14	Kolp, 4.22
1931	58	96	8th	43	Howley	Stripp, .324	Cuccinello, 181	Cullop, 8	Cuccinello, 93	Lucas, 14	Benton, 3.35
1932	60	94	8th	30	Howley	Herman, .326	Herman, 188	Herman, 16	Herman, 87	Johnson, Lucas, 13	Rixey, 2.66
1933	58	94	8th	33	Bush	Hafey, .303	Hafey, 172	Bottomley, 13	Bottomley, 83	Benton, Lucas, 10	Rixey, 3.15
1934	52	99	8th	42	O'Farrell, Dressen	Pool, .327	Koenig, 172	Hafey, 18	Bottomley, 78	Derringer, 15	Frey, 3.52
1935	68	85	6th	31½	Dressen	Riggs, .278	Goodman, 159	Goodman, Lombardi, 12	Goodman, 72	Derringer, 22	Brennan, 3.15
1936	74	80	5th	18	Dressen	Lombardi, .333	Cuyler, 185	Goodman, 17	Cuyler, 74	Derringer, 19	Davis, 3.58
1937	56	98	8th	40	Dressen, Wallace	Lombardi, .334	Goodman, 150	Kampouris, 17	Kampouris, 71	Grissom, 12	Schott, 2.97
1938	82	68	4th	6	McKechnie	Lombardi, .342	F. McCormick, 209	Goodman, 30	F. McCormick, 106	Derringer, 21	Derringer, 2.93
1939	97	57	1st	+4½	McKechnie	F. McCormick, .332	F. McCormick, 209	Lombardi, 20	F. McCormick, 128	Walters, 27	Walters, 2.29
1940	100	53	1st	+12	McKechnie	Lombardi, .319	F. McCormick, 191	F. McCormick, 19	F. McCormick, 127	Walters, 22	Walters, 2.48
1941	88	66	3rd	12	McKechnie	M. McCormick, .287	F. McCormick, 162	F. McCormick, 17	F. McCormick, 97	Riddle, Walters, 19	Riddle, 2.24
1942	76	76	4th	29	McKechnie	F. McCormick, .277	F. McCormick, 156	F. McCormick, 13	F. McCormick, 89	Vander Meer, 18	Vander Meer, 2.43
1943	87	67	2nd	18	McKechnie	F. McCormick, .303	Frey, 154	Tipton, 9	Miller, 71	Riddle, 21	Beggs, 2.34
1944	89	65	3rd	16	McKechnie	F. McCormick, .305	F. McCormick, 177	F. McCormick, 20	F. McCormick, 102	Walters, 23	Heusser, 2.38
1945	61	93	7th	37	McKechnie	Libke, .283	Clay, 184	Miller, 13	F. McCormick, 81	Bowman, Heusser, 11	Walters, 2.68
1946	67	87	6th	30	McKechnie	Hatton, .271	Haas, 141	Hatton, 14	Hatton, 69	Beggs, 12	Beggs, 2.32
1947	73	81	5th	21	Neun	Galan, .314	Baumholtz, 182	Miller, 19	Miller, 87	Blackwell, 22	Blackwell, 2.47
1948	64	89	7th	27	Neun, Walters	Adams, .298	Wyrostek, 140	Sauer, 35	Sauer, 97	Vander Meer, 17	Vander Meer, 3.41
1949	62	92	7th	35	Walters	Kluszewski, .309	Kluszewski, 164	Cooper, 16	Hatton, 69	Raffensberger, 18	Erautt, 3.36
1950	66	87	6th	24½	Sewell	Kluszewski, .307	Kluszewski, 165	Kluszewski, 25	Kluszewski, 111	Blackwell, 17	Blackwell, 2.97
1951	68	86	6th	28½	Sewell	Wyrostek, .311	Wyrostek, 167	Ryan, 16	Kluszewski, 77	Blackwell, Raffensberger, 16	Perkowski, 2.82
1952	69	85	6th	27½	Sewell, Hornsby	Kluszewski, .320	Adams, 180	Kluszewski, 16	Kluszewski, 86	Raffensberger, 17	Raffensberger, 2.81
1953	68	86	6th	37	Hornsby, Mills	Kluszewski, .316	G. Bell, 183	Kluszewski, 40	Kluszewski, 108	Perkowski, 12	Baczewski, 3.45
1954	74	80	5th	23	Tebbetts	Kluszewski, .326	Kluszewski, 187	Kluszewski, 49	Kluszewski, 141	Fowler, Nuxhall, Valentine, 12	Fowler, 3.83
1955	75	79	5th	23½	Tebbetts	Kluszewski, .314	Kluszewski, 192	Kluszewski, 47	Kluszewski, 113	Nuxhall, 17	Freeman, 2.16
1956	91	63	3rd	2	Tebbetts	Kluszewski, .302	Temple, 180	Robinson, 38	Kluszewski, 102	Lawrence, 19	Freeman, 3.40
1957	80	74	4th	15	Tebbetts	Robinson, .322	Robinson, 197	Crowe, 31	Crowe, 92	Lawrence, 16	Lawrence, 3.52
1958	76	78	4th	16	Tebbetts, Dykes	Lynch, .312	Temple, 166	Robinson, 31	Robinson, 83	Purkey, 17	Haddix, 3.52
1959	74	80	*5th	13	Smith, Hutchinson	Pinson, .316	Pinson, 205	Robinson, 36	Robinson, 125	Newcombe, Purkey, 13	Newcombe, 3.16
1960	67	87	6th	28	Hutchinson	Robinson, .297	Pinson, 187	Robinson, 31	Robinson, 83	Purkey, 17	Brosnan, 2.36
1961	93	61	1st	+4	Hutchinson	Pinson, .343	Pinson, 208	Robinson, 37	Robinson, 124	Jay, 21	O'Toole, 3.10
1962	98	64	3rd	3½	Hutchinson	Robinson, .342	Robinson, 208	Robinson, 39	Robinson, 136	Purkey, 23	Purkey, 2.81
1963	86	76	5th	13	Hutchinson	Pinson, .313	Pinson, 204	Pinson, 22	Pinson, 106	Maloney, 23	Nuxhall, 2.61
1964	92	70	*2nd	1	Hutchinson, Sisler	Robinson, .306	Robinson, 174	Robinson, 29	Robinson, 96	O'Toole, 17	Ellis, 2.57
1965	89	73	4th	8	Sisler	Rose, .312	Rose, 209	Robinson, 33	De. Johnson, 130	Ellis, 22	Maloney, 2.54
1966	76	84	7th	18	Heffner	Rose, .313	Rose, 205	De. Johnson, 24	Cardenas, De. Johnson, 81	Maloney, 16	McCool, 2.48
1967	87	75	4th	14½	Bristol	Rose, .301	Pinson, 187	Perez, 26	Perez, 102	Pappas, 16	Abernathy, 1.27
1968	83	79	4th	14	Bristol	Rose, .335	Rose, 210	May, 22	Perez, 92	Maloney, 16	Carroll, 2.29
								WEST DIVISION			
1969	89	73	3rd	4	Bristol	Rose, .348	Rose, 218	May, 38	Perez, 122	Merritt, 17	Maloney, 2.77
1970	102	60	†1st	+14½	Anderson	Perez, .317	Rose, 205	Bench, 45	Bench, 148	Merritt, 20	Carroll, 2.59
1971	79	83	*4th	11	Anderson	Rose, .304	Rose, 192	May, 39	May, 98	Gullett, 16	Carroll, 2.50
1972	95	59	†1st	+10½	Anderson	Rose, .307	Rose, 198	Bench, 40	Bench, 125	Nolan, 15	Nolan, 1.99
1973	99	63	‡1st	+3½	Anderson	Rose, .338	Rose, 230	Perez, 27	Bench, 104	Billingham, 19	Borbon, 2.16
1974	98	64	2nd	4	Anderson	Morgan, .293	Rose, 185	Bench, 33	Bench, 129	Billingham, 19	Carroll, 2.15
1975	108	54	†1st	+20	Anderson	Morgan, .327	Rose, 210	Bench, 28	Bench, 110	Billingham, Gullett, Nolan, 15	Gullett, 2.42
1976	102	60	†1st	+10	Anderson	Griffey, .336	Rose, 215	Foster, 29	Foster, 121	Nolan, 15	Eastwick, 2.09
1977	88	74	2nd	10	Anderson	Foster, .320	Rose, 204	Foster, 52	Foster, 149	Norman, Seaver, 14	Seaver, 2.34
1978	92	69	2nd	2½	Anderson	Rose, .302	Rose, 198	Foster, 40	Foster, 120	Seaver, 16	Bair, 1.97
1979	90	71	‡1st	+1½	McNamara	Knight, Collins, .318	Knight, 175	Foster, 30	Foster, 98	Seaver, 16	Hume, 2.76
1980	89	73	3rd	3½	McNamara	Collins, .303	Collins, 167	Foster, 25	Foster, 93	Pastore, 13	Hume, 2.56
1981	66	42	§2nd/2nd	–	McNamara	Griffey, .311	Concepcion, 129	Foster, 22	Foster, 90	Seaver, 14	Seaver, 2.54
1982	61	101	6th	28	McNamara, Nixon	Cedeno, .289	Concepcion, 164	Driessen, 17	Cedeno, Driessen, 57	Soto, 14	Soto, 2.79
1983	74	88	6th	17	Nixon	Driessen, .277	Oester, 145	Redus, 17	Oester, 58	Soto, 17	Soto, 2.70
1984	70	92	5th	22	Rapp, Rose	Parker, .285	Parker, 173	Parker, 16	Parker, 94	Soto, 18	Power, 2.82
1985	89	72	2nd	5½	Rose	Parker, .312	Parker, 198	Parker, 34	Parker, 125	Browning, 20	Franco, 2.18
1986	86	76	2nd	10	Rose	B. Bell, .278	Parker, 174	Parker, 31	Parker, 116	Gullickson, 15	Franco, 2.94
1987	84	78	2nd	6	Rose	Daniels, .334	Davis, 139	Davis, 37	Davis, 100	Browning, Gullickson, Power, 10	Williams, 2.30
1988	87	74	2nd	7	Rose	Larkin, .296	Larkin, 174	Davis, 26	Davis, 93	Jackson, 23	Rijo, 2.39
1989	75	87	5th	17	Rose, Helms	Davis, .281	Benzinger, 154	Davis, 34	Davis, 101	Browning, 15	Dibble, 2.09
1990	91	71	†1st	+5	Piniella	Duncan, .306	Larkin, 185	Sabo, 25	Davis, 86	Browning, 15	Dibble, 1.74
1991	74	88	5th	20	Piniella	Morris, .318	Sabo, 175	O'Neill, 28	O'Neill, 91	Rijo, 15	Rijo, 2.51
1992	90	72	2nd	8	Piniella	Roberts, .323	Roberts, 172	O'Neill, 14	Larkin, 78	Belcher, Rijo, 15	Rijo, 2.56
1993	73	89	5th	31	Perez, Johnson	Morris, .317	Sabo, 143	Sabo, 21	Sanders, 83	Rijo, 14	Rijo, 2.48
								CENTRAL DIVISION			
1994	66	48	1st	+½	Johnson	Morris, .335	Morris, 146	Mitchell, 30	Morris, 78	Smiley, 11	Rijo, 3.08
1995	85	59	∞‡1st	+9	Johnson	Larkin, .319	Larkin, 158	Gant, 29	R. Sanders, 99	Schourek, 18	Schourek, 3.22
1996	81	81	3rd	7	Knight	Morris, .313	Morris, 165	Larkin, 33	Larkin, 89	Smiley, 13	Shaw, 2.49
1997	76	86	3rd	8	Knight, McKeon	D. Sanders, .273	D. Sanders, 127	Greene, 26	Greene, 91	Burba, Tomko, 11	Shaw, 2.38
1998	77	85	4th	25	McKeon	Young, .310	Young, Larkin, 166	B. Boone, 24	B. Boone, 95	Harnisch, 14	Harnisch, 3.14
1999	96	67	◆2nd	1½	McKeon	Casey, .332	Casey, 197	Vaughn, 45	Vaughn, 118	Harnisch, 16	Williamson, 2.41
2000	85	77	2nd	10	McKeon	Stynes, .334	D. Young, 166	Griffey Jr., 40	Griffey Jr., 118	Parris, 12	Graves, 2.57
2001	66	96	5th	27	Boone	Casey, .310	Casey, 165	Griffey Jr., 22	Casey, 89	Dessens, 10	Sullivan, 3.31
2002	78	84	3rd	19	Boone	Walker, .299	Walker, 183	A. Boone, Dunn, 26	A. Boone, 87	Haynes, 15	Dessens, 3.03

* Tied for position. † Won Championship Series. ‡ Lost Championship Series. § First half 35-21; second half 31-21. ∞ Won Division Series; ◆ Lost wild-card playoff.

Note: Batting average minimum 350 at-bats; ERA minimum 90 innings pitched.

Colorado Rockies

Outfielder Dante Bichette.

FRANCHISE CHRONOLOGY

First season: 1993, as part of a two-team expansion that increased the National League to 14 teams and the Major Leagues to 28. The Rockies lost their first game at New York, 3-0, and went on to finish sixth in the seven-team N.L. West Division with a 67-95 record, 37 games behind the first-place Braves.

1994-present: The Rockies improved to a 53-64 second-season record and 77-67 in 1995, when they finished one game behind Los Angeles in the realigned West Division. Their second-place record was good enough to earn the N.L.'s first wild-card berth under an expanded playoff format and gave Colorado the distinction of reaching postseason play faster than any previous expansion team. The Rockies' first playoff visit ended with a four-game Division Series loss to the Braves. Colorado made history in its debut season with a Major League-record attendance of 4,483,350 and drew well over 3 million fans in each of the next two strike-shortened campaigns.

ROCKIES VS. OPPONENTS BY DECADE

	Braves	Cardinals	Cubs	Dodgers	Giants	Phillies	Pirates	Reds	Astros	Mets	Expos	Padres	Marlins	Brewers	D'backs	Interleague	Decade Record
1993-99	26-50	40-37	40-38	40-46	34-52	29-36	36-34	34-41	41-33	36-32	37-30	41-45	38-40	10-10	13-12	17-23	512-559
2000-02	9-13	13-10	10-11	19-32	23-28	11-10	13-8	12-12	10-11	10-12	14-8	27-24	13-9	12-9	17-34	15-27	228-258
Totals	35-63	53-47	50-49	59-78	57-80	40-46	49-42	46-53	51-44	46-44	51-38	68-69	51-49	22-19	30-46	32-50	740-817

Interleague results: 4-12 vs. Angels, 1-2 vs. Red Sox, 1-2 vs. Indians, 1-2 vs. Yankees, 7-9 vs. Athletics, 7-12 vs. Mariners, 3-0 vs. Devil Rays, 8-8 vs. Rangers, 0-3 vs. Blue Jays.

MANAGERS

Name	*Years*	*Record*
Don Baylor	1993-98	440-469
Jim Leyland	1999	72-90
Buddy Bell	2000-02	161-185
Clint Hurdle	2002	67-73

WILD-CARD QUALIFIERS

Year	*Record*	*Manager*	*Div. Series Result*
1995	77-67	Baylor	Lost to Braves

ATTENDANCE HIGHS

Total	*Season*	*Park*
4,483,350	1993	Mile High Stadium
3,891,014	1996	Coors Field
3,888,453	1997	Coors Field
3,789,347	1998	Coors Field
3,390,037	1995	Coors Field

Don Baylor guided the Rockies to the postseason and won the N.L. Manager of the Year Award in 1995.

ALL-TIME RECORD OF EXPANSION TEAMS

Team	W	L	Pct.	DT	P	WS
Arizona	440	370	.543	3	1	1
Kansas City	2,675	2,694	.498	6	2	1
Houston	3,229	3,285	.496	7	0	0
Toronto	2,025	2,063	.495	5	2	2
Anaheim	3,243	3,431	.486	3	1	1
Montreal	2,605	2,769	.485	2	0	0
Colorado	740	817	.475	0	0	0
New York	3,091	3,412	.475	4	4	2
Milwaukee	2,545	2,831	.473	2	1	0
Seattle	1,924	2,163	.471	3	0	0
Texas	3,097	3,560	.465	4	0	0
San Diego	2,460	2,921	.457	3	2	0
Florida	706	847	.455	0	1	1
Tampa Bay	318	490	.394	0	0	0

DT—Division Titles. P—Pennants won. WS—World Series won.

BALLPARK CHRONOLOGY

Coors Field (1995-present)

Capacity: 50,449.
First game: Rockies 11, New York 9 (April 26, 1995).
First batter: Brett Butler, Mets.
First hit: Brett Butler, Mets (single).
First run: Walt Weiss, Rockies (1st inning).
First home run: Rico Brogna, Mets.
First winning pitcher: Mark Thompson, Rockies.
First-season attendance: 3,390,037.

Mile High Stadium (1993-94)

Capacity: 76,100.
First game: Rockies 11, Expos 4 (April 9, 1993).
First-season attendance: 4,483,350.

N.L. MVP

Larry Walker, OF, 1997

ROOKIE OF THE YEAR

Jason Jennings, P, 2002

MANAGER OF THE YEAR

Don Baylor, 1995

RETIRED UNIFORMS

None

MILESTONE PERFORMANCES

30-plus home runs
49—Larry Walker 1997
Todd Helton 2001
46—Vinny Castilla 1998
47—Andres Galarraga 1996
42—Todd Helton 2000
41—Andres Galarraga 1997
40—Dante Bichette 1995
Ellis Burks 1996
Vinny Castilla 1996, 1997
38—Larry Walker 2001
37—Larry Walker 1999
36—Larry Walker 1995
35—Todd Helton 1999
34—Dante Bichette 1999
33—Vinny Castilla 1999
32—Vinny Castilla 1995
Ellis Burks 1997
31—Andres Galarraga 1994
Andres Galarraga 1995
Dante Bichette 1996
30—Todd Helton 2002

100-plus RBIs
150—Andres Galarraga 1996
147—Todd Helton 2000
146—Todd Helton 2001
144—Vinny Castilla 1998
141—Dante Bichette 1996
140—Andres Galarraga 1997
133—Dante Bichette 1999
130—Larry Walker 1997
128—Dante Bichette 1995
Ellis Burks 1996
123—Larry Walker 2001
122—Dante Bichette 1998
118—Dante Bichette 1997
115—Larry Walker 1999
Jeff Cirillo 2000
113—Vinny Castilla 1996, 1997
Todd Helton 1999
109—Todd Helton 2002
106—Andres Galarraga 1995
Jeffrey Hammonds 2000
104—Todd Walker 2002
102—Vinny Castilla 1999
101—Larry Walker 1995

20-plus victories
None

N.L. home run champions
1995—Dante Bichette 40
1996—Andres Galarraga 47
1997—Larry Walker 49

N.L. RBI champions
1995—Dante Bichette 128
1996—Andres Galarraga 150
1997—Andres Galarraga 140
2000—Todd Helton 147

N.L. batting champions
1993—Andres Galarraga .... .370
1998—Larry Walker .... .363
1999—Larry Walker .... .379
2000—Todd Helton .... .372
2001—Larry Walker .... .350

N.L. ERA champions
None

N.L. strikeout champions
None

No-hit pitchers
None

Longest hitting streaks
23—Dante Bichette 1995
22—Vinny Castilla 1997
21—Larry Walker 1999
20—Larry Walker 1998
19—Eric Young 1995
Dante Bichette 1995
18—Larry Walker 1999
Jeffrey Hammonds 2000
17—Eric Young 1996
Neifi Perez 2001
Juan Uribe 2002
Larry Walker 2002
16—Dante Bichette 1994
Larry Walker 1997
Juan Pierre 2000
Todd Hollandsworth 2001
15—Andres Galarraga 1993
Neifi Perez 1998
Juan Pierre 2000

Second baseman Eric Young, an original Rockie, enjoyed a breakthrough 1996 season.

INDIVIDUAL SEASON, GAME RECORDS

Right fielder Larry Walker has two N.L. batting titles and one MVP Award during his tenure with the Rockies.

SEASON

Batting			
At-bats	690	Neifi Perez	1999
Runs	143	Larry Walker	1997
Hits	219	Dante Bichette	1998
Singles	163	Juan Pierre	2001
Doubles	59	Todd Helton	2000
Triples	11	Neifi Perez	1999, 2000
		Juan Pierre	2001
		Juan Uribe	2001
Home runs	49	Larry Walker	1997
		Todd Helton	2001
Home runs, rookie	25	Todd Helton	1998
Grand slams	2	8 times	
		Last by Greg Norton	2002
Total bases	409	Larry Walker	1997
RBIs	150	Andres Galarraga	1996
Walks	103	Todd Helton	2000
Most strikeouts	157	Andres Galarraga	1996
Fewest strikeouts	29	Juan Pierre	2001
Batting average	.379	Larry Walker	1999
Slugging pct.	.720	Larry Walker	1997
Stolen bases	53	Eric Young	1996
Pitching			
Games	79	Todd Jones	2002
		Mike Myers	2000
Complete games	7	Pedro Astacio	1999
Innings	232.0	Pedro Astacio	1999
Wins	17	Kevin Ritz	1996
		Pedro Astacio	1999
Losses	17	Darryl Kile	1998
Winning pct.	.846	Gabe White	2000
Walks	109	Darryl Kile	1999
Strikeouts	210	Pedro Astacio	1999
Shutouts	2	Roger Bailey	1997
Home runs allowed	39	Pedro Astacio	1998
Lowest ERA	1.99	Mike Myers	2000
Saves	41	Jose Jimenez	2002

GAME

Batting			
Runs	5	Last by Larry Walker	9-24-2001
Hits	6	Andres Galarraga	7-3-95
Doubles	3	Last by Jay Payton	9-22-2002
Triples	2	Last by Brent Butler	5-28-2002 (12 inn.)
		Last (9 inn.) by Todd Helton	4-19-2002
Home runs	3	Last by Jose Ortiz	8-17-2001
RBIs	8	Last by Larry Walker	4-28-99
Total bases	14	Last by Jeff Cirillo	6-28-2000
Stolen bases	6	Eric Young	6-30-96

CAREER LEADERS

BATTING

Games
Dante Bichette	1,018
Larry Walker	989
Vinny Castilla	935
Todd Helton	821
Andres Galarraga	679
Neifi Perez	668
Eric Young	613
Walt Weiss	523
Ellis Burks	520
John Vander Wal	465

At-bats
Dante Bichette	4,050
Larry Walker	3,514
Vinny Castilla	3,495
Todd Helton	2,921
Neifi Perez	2,728
Andres Galarraga	2,667
Eric Young	2,120
Ellis Burks	1,821
Walt Weiss	1,760
Juan Pierre	1,409

Runs
Larry Walker	784
Dante Bichette	665
Todd Helton	582
Vinny Castilla	516
Andres Galarraga	476
Neifi Perez	395
Eric Young	378
Ellis Burks	361
Walt Weiss	264
Juan Pierre	224

Hits
Dante Bichette	1,278
Larry Walker	1,197
Vinny Castilla	1,044
Todd Helton	973
Andres Galarraga	843
Neifi Perez	769
Eric Young	626
Ellis Burks	558
Walt Weiss	469
Juan Pierre	434

Doubles
Dante Bichette	270
Larry Walker	263
Todd Helton	230
Vinny Castilla	165
Andres Galarraga	155
Neifi Perez	125
Ellis Burks	104
Eric Young	102
Jeff Cirillo	79
Walt Weiss	71

Triples
Neifi Perez	49
Larry Walker	34
Eric Young	28
Ellis Burks	24
Dante Bichette	18
Juan Uribe	18
Vinny Castilla	17
Juan Pierre	16
Terry Shumpert	16
Todd Helton	15

Home runs
Larry Walker	236
Vinny Castilla	203
Dante Bichette	201
Todd Helton	186
Andres Galarraga	172
Ellis Burks	115
Neifi Perez	43
Jeff Reed	36
Charlie Hayes	35
Terry Shumpert	30
Eric Young	30

Total bases
Larry Walker	2,236
Dante Bichette	2,187
Vinny Castilla	1,852
Todd Helton	1,791
Andres Galarraga	1,540
Neifi Perez	1,121
Ellis Burks	1,055
Eric Young	874
Walt Weiss	610
Jeff Cirillo	535

Runs batted in
Dante Bichette	826
Larry Walker	749
Todd Helton	623
Vinny Castilla	610
Andres Galarraga	579
Ellis Burks	337
Neifi Perez	281
Eric Young	227
Jeff Cirillo	198
Charlie Hayes	148

Extra-base hits
Larry Walker	533
Dante Bichette	489
Todd Helton	431
Vinny Castilla	385
Andres Galarraga	340
Ellis Burks	243
Neifi Perez	217
Eric Young	160
Jeff Cirillo	113
Terry Shumpert	110

Batting average
(Minimum 350 games)

Larry Walker	.341
Todd Helton	.333
Andres Galarraga	.316
Dante Bichette	.316
Juan Pierre	.308
Ellis Burks	.306
Vinny Castilla	.299
Eric Young	.295
Jeff Reed	.286
Terry Shumpert	.282

Stolen bases
Eric Young	180
Larry Walker	117
Dante Bichette	105
Juan Pierre	100
Andres Galarraga	55
Ellis Burks	52
Quinton McCracken	45
Walt Weiss	42
Terry Shumpert	40
Tom Goodwin	39

PITCHING

Earned-run average
(Minimum 350 innings)

Steve Reed	3.68
Armando Reynoso	4.65
Roger Bailey	4.90
Curtis Leskanic	4.92
John Thomson	5.01
Kevin Ritz	5.20
Pedro Astacio	5.43
Jamey Wright	5.57
Mike Hampton	5.75
Brian Bohanon	5.82

Wins
Pedro Astacio	53
Kevin Ritz	39
Curtis Leskanic	31
Armando Reynoso	30
Brian Bohanon	29
John Thomson	27
Steve Reed	25
Jamey Wright	25
Darren Holmes	23
Mike Hampton	21
Darryl Kile	21

Losses
Pedro Astacio	48
John Thomson	43
Kevin Ritz	38
Jamey Wright	33
Armando Reynoso	31
Brian Bohanon	30
Darryl Kile	30
Mike Hampton	28
Shawn Chacon	21
Greg Harris	20
Curtis Leskanic	20
Mark Thompson	20

Innings pitched
Pedro Astacio	827.1
John Thomson	611.0
Kevin Ritz	576.1
Jamey Wright	541.2
Armando Reynoso	503.0
Brian Bohanon	471.1
Curtis Leskanic	470.0
Darryl Kile	421.0
Mike Hampton	381.2
Steve Reed	369.2

Strikeouts
Pedro Astacio	749
Curtis Leskanic	415
John Thomson	390
Kevin Ritz	337
Bruce Ruffin	319
Darren Holmes	297
Steve Reed	275
Darryl Kile	274
Armando Reynoso	270
Brian Bohanon	265

Bases on balls
Pedro Astacio	290
Jamey Wright	261
Kevin Ritz	253
Curtis Leskanic	221
Brian Bohanon	218
Darryl Kile	205
John Thomson	188
Mike Hampton	176
Armando Reynoso	170
Bruce Ruffin	165

Games
Curtis Leskanic	356
Steve Reed	329
Mike Munoz	300
Darren Holmes	263
Bruce Ruffin	246
Mike DeJean	224
Jerry Dipoto	222
Jose Jimenez	202
Mike Myers	151
Dave Veres	136
Gabe White	136

Shutouts
Roger Bailey	2
Brian Bohanon	2
John Thomson	2
Pedro Astacio	1
Mark Brownson	1
Mike Hampton	1
Jason Jennings	1
Darryl Kile	1
David Nied	1
Mark Thompson	1

Saves
Jose Jimenez	82
Bruce Ruffin	60
Darren Holmes	46
Dave Veres	39
Jerry Dipoto	36
Curtis Leskanic	20
Steve Reed	15
Mike Munoz	8
Jay Powell	7
Gabe White	5

TEAM SEASON, GAME RECORDS

SEASON

Batting
Most at-bats	5,717	1999
Most runs	968	2000
Fewest runs	758	1993
Most hits	1,664	2000
Most singles	1,130	2000
Most doubles	333	1998
Most triples	61	2001
Most home runs	239	1997
Fewest home runs	142	1993
Most grand slams	5	1994, 1998, 2002
Most pinch-hit home runs	11	1995
Most total bases	2,748	2001
Most stolen bases	201	1996
Highest batting average	.294	2000
Lowest batting average	.273	1993
Highest slugging pct	.483	2001

Pitching
Lowest ERA	4.97	1995
Highest ERA	6.01	1999
Most complete games	12	1999
Most shutouts	8	2001, 2002
Most saves	43	1995, 2002
Most walks	737	1999
Most strikeouts	1,058	2001

Fielding
Most errors	167	1993
Fewest errors	94	2000
Most double plays	202	1997
Highest fielding average	.985	2000

General
Most games won	83	1996, 1997
Most games lost	95	1993
Highest win pct.	.535	1995
Lowest win pct.	.414	1993

GAME, INNING

Batting
Most runs, game	19	6-7-96, 6-18,2000
Most runs, inning	11	7-12-96
Most hits, game	24	5-3-2000
Most home runs, game	7	Last 4-5-97
Most total bases, game	42	6-18-2000

HISTORY

ROCKIES YEAR-BY-YEAR

Year	W	L	Place	Games Back	Manager	Leaders: Batting avg.	Hits	Home runs	RBIs	Wins	ERA
WEST DIVISION											
1993	67	95	6th	37	Baylor	Galarraga, .370	Hayes, 175	Hayes, 25	Galarraga, Hayes, 98	Reynoso, 12	Ruffin, 3.87
1994	53	64	3rd	6½	Baylor	Galarraga, .319	Bichette, 147	Galarraga, 31	Bichette, 95	Freeman, 10	Freeman, 2.80
1995	77	67	*2nd	1	Baylor	Bichette, .340	Bichette, 197	Bichette, 40	Bichette, 128	Ritz, 11	Leskanic, 3.40
1996	83	79	3rd	8	Baylor	Burks, .344	Burks, 211	Galarraga, 47	Galarraga, 150	Ritz, 17	Reynoso, 4.96
1997	83	79	3rd	7	Baylor	Walker, .366	Walker, 208	Walker, 49	Galarraga, 140	Bailey, Holmes, 9	Bailey, 4.29
1998	77	85	4th	21	Baylor	Walker, .363	Bichette, 219	Castilla, 46	Castilla, 144	Kile, Astacio, 13	Thomson, 4.81
1999	72	90	5th	28	Leyland	Walker, .379	Perez, 193	Walker, 37	Bichette, 133	Astacio, 17	Wright, 4.87
2000	82	80	4th	15	Bell	Helton, .372	Helton, 216	Helton, 42	Helton, 147	Bohanon, Astacio, 12	Tavarez, 4.43
2001	73	89	5th	19	Bell	L. Walker, .350	Pierre, 202	Helton, 49	Helton, 146	Hampton, 14	Thomson, 4.04
2002	73	89	4th	25	Bell, Hurdle	L. Walker, .338	Helton, 182	Helton, 30	Helton, 109	Jennings, 16	Jennings, 4.52

* Lost Division Series.

Note: Batting average minimum 350 at-bats; ERA minimum 90 innings pitched.

David Nied

MAJOR LEAGUE Baseball became a Mile High reality on July 5, 1991, when owners tabbed Denver and South Florida for the 13th and 14th franchises in the National League fraternity. With the Colorado Baseball Partnership in place and the proposal for a new stadium approved, the Rockies began preparation for a 1993 season inaugural.

The Rockies selected pitcher David Nied as the first of 36 picks in the November 17, 1992, expansion draft. The team dropped a 3-0 decision in its April 5, 1993, Major League debut at New York, but rebounded for an 11-4 victory over Montreal in its April 9 Mile High Stadium opener.

Expansion draft (November 17, 1992)

Players

Player	Team	Position
Brad Ausmus	N.Y. Yankees	catcher
Freddie Benavides	Cincinnati	infield
Pedro Castellano	Chicago Cubs	infield
Vinny Castilla	Atlanta	infield
Braulio Castillo	Philadelphia	outfield
Jerald Clark	San Diego	outfield
Alex Cole	Pittsburgh	outfield
Joe Girardi	Chicago Cubs	catcher
Charlie Hayes	N.Y. Yankees	third base
Roberto Mejia	Los Angeles	infield
J. Owens	Minnesota	catcher
Jody Reed	Boston	infield
Kevin Reimer	Texas	outfield
Jim Tatum	Milwaukee	infield
Eric Wedge	Boston	catcher
Eric Young	Los Angeles	infield

Pitchers

Pitcher	Team	Throws
Scott Aldred	Detroit	lefthanded
Andy Ashby	Philadelphia	righthanded
Willie Blair	Houston	righthanded
Doug Bochtler	Montreal	righthanded
Denis Boucher	Cleveland	lefthanded
Scott Fredrickson	San Diego	righthanded
Ryan Hawblitzel	Chicago Cubs	righthanded
Butch Henry	Houston	righthanded
Darren Holmes	Milwaukee	righthanded
Calvin Jones	Seattle	righthanded
Curt Leskanic	Minnesota	righthanded
Brett Merriman	California	righthanded
Marcus Moore	Toronto	righthanded
*David Nied	Atlanta	righthanded
Lance Painter	San Diego	lefthanded
Steve Reed	San Francisco	righthanded
Armando Reynoso	Atlanta	righthanded
Kevin Ritz	Detroit	righthanded
Mo Sanford	Cincinnati	righthanded
Keith Shepherd	Philadelphia	righthanded

*First pick

Opening day lineup

April 5, 1993

Eric Young, second base
Alex Cole, center field
Dante Bichette, right field
Andres Galarraga, first base
Jerald Clark, left field
Charlie Hayes, third base
Joe Girardi, catcher
Freddie Benavides, shortstop
David Nied, pitcher

Charlie Hayes

Rockies firsts

First hit: Andres Galarraga, April 5, 1993, at New York (single)
First home run: Dante Bichette, April 7, 1993, at New York
First RBI: Dante Bichette, April 7, 1993, at New York
First win: Bryn Smith, April 9, 1993, vs. Montreal
First shutout: David Nied (7 inn.), Bruce Ruffin (1), Darren Holmes (1), April 14, 1994, 5-0 at Philadelphia
First CG shutout: David Nied, June 21, 1994, 8-0 vs. Houston

FLORIDA MARLINS

FRANCHISE CHRONOLOGY

First season: 1993, as part of a two-team expansion that increased the National League to 14 teams and the Major Leagues to 28. The Marlins collected 14 hits and defeated Los Angeles, 6-3, in their major league debut and went on to post a 64-98 first-year record. That was good for sixth place in the seven-team N.L. East Division, 33 games behind first-place Philadelphia.

1994-present: The Marlins improved to 51-64 in the strike-interrupted 1994 season and climbed to within nine games of .500 in the strike-shortened 1995 campaign. But the real breakthrough came in 1997 when the five-year-old Marlins, buoyed by an offseason spending spree that beefed up their roster, won 92 games, earned a wild-card berth and made a Cinderella run through the playoffs, beating Atlanta in the NLCS to claim the pennant and defeating Cleveland in a seven-game World Series. In the process, they became the youngest championship team in baseball history before the four-year-old Arizona Diamondbacks won the World Series in 2001.

Outfielder Gary Sheffield.

MARLINS VS. OPPONENTS BY DECADE

	Braves	Cardinals	Cubs	Dodgers	Giants	Phillies	Pirates	Reds	Astros	Mets	Expos	Padres	Rockies	Brewers	D'backs	Interleague	Decade Record
1993-99	36-51	29-40	36-39	35-35	25-42	34-52	30-42	32-43	32-39	36-50	38-46	30-34	40-38	5-13	3-14	31-18	472-596
2000-02	24-26	10-11	11-8	7-15	9-13	24-27	13-8	9-12	9-11	21-29	29-22	10-12	9-13	11-8	8-13	30-23	234-251
Totals	60-77	39-51	47-47	42-50	34-55	58-79	43-50	41-55	41-50	57-79	67-68	40-46	49-51	16-21	11-27	61-41	706-847

Interleague results: 11-4 vs. Orioles, 6-9 vs. Red Sox, 3-0 vs. Indians, 4-2 vs. Tigers, 2-1 vs. Royals, 1-2 vs. Twins, 6-8 vs. Yankees, 17-11 vs. Devil Rays, 11-4 vs. Blue Jays.

MANAGERS

Name	*Years*	*Record*
Rene Lachemann	1993-96	221-285
Cookie Rojas	1996	1-0
John Boles	1996, 1999-2001	205-241
Jim Leyland	1997-98	146-178
Tony Perez	2001	54-60
Jeff Torborg	2002	79-83

WORLD SERIES CHAMPION

Year	*Loser*	*Length*	*MVP*
1997	Cleveland	7 games	L. Hernandez

N.L. PENNANT WINNER

Year	*Record*	*Manager*	*Series Result*
1997	92-70	Leyland	Defeated Braves

WILD-CARD QUALIFIER

Year	*Record*	*Manager*	*Div. Series Result*	*NLCS Result*
1997	90-72	Leyland	Defeated Giants	Defeated Braves

ALL-TIME RECORD OF EXPANSION TEAMS

Team	W	L	Pct.	DT	P	WS
Arizona	440	370	.543	3	1	1
Kansas City	2,675	2,694	.498	6	2	1
Houston	3,229	3,285	.496	7	0	0
Toronto	2,025	2,063	.495	5	2	2
Anaheim	3,243	3,431	.486	3	1	1
Montreal	2,605	2,769	.485	2	0	0
Colorado	740	817	.475	0	0	0
New York	3,091	3,412	.475	4	4	2
Milwaukee	2,545	2,831	.473	2	1	0
Seattle	1,924	2,163	.471	3	0	0
Texas	3,097	3,560	.465	4	0	0
San Diego	2,460	2,921	.457	3	2	0
Florida	706	847	.455	0	1	1
Tampa Bay	318	490	.394	0	0	0

DT—Division Titles. P—Pennants won. WS—World Series won.

Despite Jim Leyland's sub-.500 overall record with the team, he guided the Marlins to their World Series title in 1997.

BALLPARK CHRONOLOGY

Pro Player Stadium, formerly Joe Robbie Stadium (1993-present)

Capacity: 36,331.
First game: Marlins 6, Los Angeles 3 (April 5, 1993).
First batter: Jose Offerman, Dodgers.
First hit: Bret Barberie, Marlins (single).
First run: Benito Santiago, Marlins (2nd inning).
First home run: Tim Wallach, Dodgers.
First winning pitcher: Charlie Hough, Marlins.
First-season attendance: 3,064,847.

ATTENDANCE HIGHS

Total	*Season*	*Park*
3,064,847	1993	Joe Robbie Stadium
2,364,387	1997	Joe Robbie Stadium
1,937,467	1994	Joe Robbie Stadium
1,750,395	1998	Joe Robbie Stadium
1,746,767	1996	Joe Robbie Stadium

RETIRED UNIFORMS

None

MILESTONE PERFORMANCES

25-plus home runs
42— Gary Sheffield 1996
31— Preston Wilson 2000
Cliff Floyd 2001
28— Derrek Lee 2000
27— Gary Sheffield 1994
Derrek Lee 2002
26— Jeff Conine 1996
Preston Wilson 1999
25— Jeff Conine 1995

100-plus RBIs
121— Preston Wilson 2000
120— Gary Sheffield 1996
115— Moises Alou 1997
105— Jeff Conine 1995
103— Cliff Floyd 2001
100— Mike Lowell 2001

20-plus victories
None

N.L. home run champions
None

N.L. RBI champions
None

N.L. batting champions
None

N.L. ERA champions
1996— Kevin Brown 1.89

N.L. strikeout champions
None

No-hit pitchers
(9 innings or more)
1996— Al Leiter .... 11-0 vs. Colorado
1997— Kevin Brown .... 9-0 vs. San Francisco
2001— A.J. Burnett .... 3-0 vs. San Diego

Longest hitting streaks
35— Luis Castillo 2002
25— Kevin Millar 2002
22— Edgar Renteria 1996
Luis Castillo 1999
21— Greg Colbrunn 1996
19— Luis Castillo 2000
18— Cliff Floyd 2001
Kevin Millar 2002
17— Greg Colbrunn 1995
16— Mike Lowell 2000, 2002
15— Bret Barberie 1993
Chuck Carr 1993

Outfielder Jeff Conine's steady bat helped the Marlins navigate the rough expansion waters.

INDIVIDUAL SEASON, GAME RECORDS

Second baseman Luis Castillo continues to put up excellent offensive numbers for the Marlins. He compiled a major league-leading 35-game hitting streak in 2002.

SEASON

Batting

At-bats	617	Edgar Renteria	1997
Runs	123	Cliff Floyd	2001
Hits	185	Luis Castillo	2002
Singles	160	Luis Castillo	2002
Doubles	45	Cliff Floyd	1998
Triples	10	Luis Castillo	2001
Home runs	42	Gary Sheffield	1996
Home runs, rookie	26	Preston Wilson	1999
Grand slams	3	Bobby Bonilla	1997
Total bases	324	Gary Sheffield	1996
RBIs	121	Preston Wilson	2000
Walks	142	Gary Sheffield	1996
Most strikeouts	187	Preston Wilson	2000
Fewest strikeouts	46	Mark Kotsay	2000
Batting average	.334	Luis Castillo	2000
Slugging pct.	.624	Gary Sheffield	1996
Stolen bases	62	Luis Castillo	2000

Pitching

Games	78	Braden Looper	2002
Complete games	9	Livan Hernandez	1998
Innings	237.1	Kevin Brown	1997
Wins	17	Kevin Brown	1996
		Alex Fernandez	1997
Losses	17	Jack Armstrong	1993
Winning pct.	.667	Pat Rapp	1995
		Kevin Brown	1997
Walks	119	Al Leiter	1996
Strikeouts	209	Ryan Dempster	2000
Shutouts	5	A.J. Burnett	2002
Home runs allowed	37	Livan Hernandez	1998
Lowest ERA	1.89	Kevin Brown	1996
Saves	45	Bryan Harvey,	1993
		Antonio Alfonseca	2000

GAME

Batting

Runs	4	Last by Derrek Lee	6-10-2002
		Last (9 inn.) by Mike Redmond	5-12-2002
Hits	5	Last by Eric Owens	4-27-2001
Doubles	3	Last by Mike Lowell	4-27-2002
Triples	2	Jesus Tavarez	8-28-95
Home runs	2	Last by Mike Lowell	9-29-2002
RBIs	7	Last by Gary Sheffield	9-18-95
Stolen bases	4	Luis Castillo	5-17-2000

CAREER LEADERS

BATTING

Games

Player	G
Jeff Conine	718
Luis Castillo	704
Derrek Lee	689
Cliff Floyd	637
Preston Wilson	588
Charles Johnson	587
Gary Sheffield	558
Mike Lowell	543
Kevin Millar	500
Mark Kotsay	468

At-bats

Player	AB
Luis Castillo	2,749
Jeff Conine	2,531
Derrek Lee	2,291
Cliff Floyd	2,247
Preston Wilson	2,096
Mike Lowell	1,964
Charles Johnson	1,936
Gary Sheffield	1,870
Alex Gonzalez	1,697
Mark Kotsay	1,655

Runs

Player	R
Luis Castillo	413
Cliff Floyd	392
Gary Sheffield	365
Jeff Conine	337
Derrek Lee	331
Preston Wilson	315
Mike Lowell	258
Edgar Renteria	237
Mark Kotsay	221
Kevin Millar	205

Hits

Player	H
Luis Castillo	790
Jeff Conine	737
Cliff Floyd	661
Derrek Lee	600
Preston Wilson	549
Gary Sheffield	538
Mike Lowell	536
Charles Johnson	467
Mark Kotsay	463
Edgar Renteria	450

Doubles

Player	2B
Cliff Floyd	167
Mike Lowell	134
Derrek Lee	128
Jeff Conine	122
Charles Johnson	111
Kevin Millar	111
Preston Wilson	108
Gary Sheffield	98
Alex Gonzalez	90
Luis Castillo	87

Triples

Player	3B
Luis Castillo	25
Mark Kotsay	22
Kurt Abbott	19
Derrek Lee	16
Jeff Conine	14
Alex Gonzalez	14
Todd Dunwoody	12
Kevin Millar	12
Preston Wilson	11
Cliff Floyd	9

Home runs

Player	HR
Gary Sheffield	122
Cliff Floyd	110
Preston Wilson	104
Jeff Conine	98
Derrek Lee	98
Mike Lowell	76
Charles Johnson	75
Kevin Millar	59
Greg Colbrunn	45
Kurt Abbott	40

Total bases

Player	TB
Jeff Conine	1,181
Cliff Floyd	1,176
Derrek Lee	1,054
Gary Sheffield	1,016
Preston Wilson	991
Luis Castillo	951
Mike Lowell	898
Charles Johnson	809
Kevin Millar	755
Mark Kotsay	680

Runs batted in

Player	RBI
Jeff Conine	422
Cliff Floyd	409
Gary Sheffield	380
Mike Lowell	330
Preston Wilson	329
Derrek Lee	325
Charles Johnson	277
Kevin Millar	251
Greg Colbrunn	189
Mark Kotsay	179

Extra-base hits

Player	XBH
Cliff Floyd	286
Derrek Lee	242
Jeff Conine	234
Gary Sheffield	227
Preston Wilson	223
Mike Lowell	210
Charles Johnson	189
Kevin Millar	182
Alex Gonzalez	139
Mark Kotsay	133

Batting average

(Minimum 350 games)

Player	AVG
Kevin Millar	.296
Cliff Floyd	.294
Jeff Conine	.291
Gary Sheffield	.288
Edgar Renteria	.288
Luis Castillo	.287
Mark Kotsay	.280
Dave Berg	.273
Mike Lowell	.273
Alex Arias	.265

Stolen bases

Player	SB
Luis Castillo	229
Chuck Carr	115
Cliff Floyd	90
Edgar Renteria	89
Preston Wilson	87
Gary Sheffield	74
Quilvio Veras	64
Andy Fox	40
Mark Kotsay	39
Devon White	35

PITCHING

Earned-run average

(Minimum 350 innings)

Player	ERA
Kevin Brown	2.30
Al Leiter	3.51
Alex Fernandez	3.59
A.J. Burnett	3.82
Pat Rapp	4.18
Brad Penny	4.26
Livan Hernandez	4.39
Chris Hammond	4.52
Ryan Dempster	4.64
Jesus Sanchez	5.06

Wins

Player	W
Ryan Dempster	42
Pat Rapp	37
Kevin Brown	33
A.J. Burnett	30
Chris Hammond	29
Alex Fernandez	28
Al Leiter	27
Brad Penny	26
Livan Hernandez	24
Jesus Sanchez	23

Losses

Player	L
Ryan Dempster	43
Pat Rapp	43
Chris Hammond	32
Jesus Sanchez	32
A.J. Burnett	30
Brian Meadows	28
Charlie Hough	25
Antonio Alfonseca	24
John Burkett	24
Alex Fernandez	24
Livan Hernandez	24
Vladimir Nunez	24
Brad Penny	24

Innings pitched

Player	IP
Ryan Dempster	759.2
Pat Rapp	665.2
Chris Hammond	520.0
A.J. Burnett	501.2
Jesus Sanchez	494.0
Kevin Brown	470.1
Livan Hernandez	469.2
Brad Penny	454.0
Alex Fernandez	414.0
Al Leiter	366.2

Strikeouts

Player	SO
Ryan Dempster	628
A.J. Burnett	421
Pat Rapp	384
Jesus Sanchez	368
Kevin Brown	364
Livan Hernandez	333
Chris Hammond	332
Al Leiter	332
Robb Nen	328
Brad Penny	327

Bases on balls

Player	BB
Ryan Dempster	395
Pat Rapp	326
Jesus Sanchez	258
A.J. Burnett	242
Al Leiter	210
Livan Hernandez	199
Chris Hammond	171
Brad Penny	164
David Weathers	152
Vladimir Nunez	135

Games

Player	G
Braden Looper	294
Antonio Alfonseca	274
Vic Darensbourg	271
Robb Nen	269
Armando Almanza	184
Jay Powell	183
Yorkis Perez	177
Vladimir Nunez	163
Jesus Sanchez	142
Terry Mathews	138

Shutouts

Player	ShO
A.J. Burnett	6
Kevin Brown	5
Pat Rapp	4
Chris Hammond	3
Ryan Dempster	2
Brad Penny	2
Jesus Sanchez	2
Dennis Springer	2
Ryan Bowen	1
Alex Fernandez	1
Mark Gardner	1
Charlie Hough	1
Al Leiter	1

Saves

Player	SV
Robb Nen	108
Antonio Alfonseca	102
Bryan Harvey	51
Vladimir Nunez	20
Matt Mantei	19
Braden Looper	18
Jeremy Hernandez	9
Terry Mathews	7
Jay Powell	7
Armando Almanza	2
Vic Darensbourg	2
Felix Heredia	2
Trevor Hoffman	2
Rob Stanifer	2

TEAM SEASON, GAME RECORDS

SEASON

Batting

Record	Value	Year
Most at-bats	5,578	1999
Most runs	742	2001
Fewest runs	581	1993
Most hits	1,465	1999
Most singles	1,034	1993
Most doubles	325	2001
Most triples	44	1999
Most home runs	166	2001
Fewest home runs	94	1993, 1994
Most grand slams	9	1997
Most pinch-hit home runs	8	1999
Most total bases	2,344	2001
Most stolen bases	177	2002
Highest batting average	.266	1994
Lowest batting average	.248	1993
Highest slugging pct.	.423	2001

Pitching

Record	Value	Year
Lowest ERA	3.83	1997
Highest ERA	5.18	1998
Most complete games	12	1995, 1997
Most shutouts	13	1996
Most saves	48	1993, 2000
Most walks	715	1998
Most strikeouts	1,188	1997

Fielding

Record	Value	Year
Most errors	129	1998
Fewest errors	103	2001
Most double plays	187	1996
Highest fielding average	.983	2001, 2002

General

Record	Value	Year
Most games won	92	1997
Most games lost	108	1998
Highest win pct	.568	1997
Lowest win pct	.333	1998

GAME, INNING

Batting

Record	Value	Date
Most runs, game	17	9-17-95
Most runs, inning	8	Last 9-17-2001
Most hits, game	24	7-15-96
Most home runs, game	4	Last 9-24-2002
Most total bases, game	39	9-17-99

HISTORY

MARLINS YEAR-BY-YEAR

Year	W	L	Place	Games Back	Manager	Leaders: Batting avg.	Hits	Home runs	RBIs	Wins	ERA
								EAST DIVISION			
1993	64	98	6th	33	Lachemann	Conine, .292	Conine, 174	Destrade, 20	Destrade, 87	Hammond, 11	Aquino, 3.42
1994	51	64	5th	23½	Lachemann	Conine, .319	Conine, 144	Sheffield, 27	Conine, 82	Weathers, 8	Rapp, 3.85
1995	67	76	4th	22½	Lachemann	Conine, .302	Pendleton, 149	Conine, 25	Conine, 105	Burkett, Rapp, 14	Rapp, 3.44
1996	80	82	3rd	16	R. Lachemann, Boles	Sheffield, .314	Conine, 175	Sheffield, 42	Sheffield, 120	Brown, 17	Brown, 1.89
1997	92	70	*†2nd	9	Leyland	Bonilla, .297	Renteria, 171	Alou, 23	Alou, 115	Fernandez, 17	Brown, 2.69
1998	54	108	5th	52	Leyland	Renteria, .282	Floyd, 166	Floyd, 22	Floyd, 90	Meadows, 11	Ojala, 4.25
1999	64	98	5th	39	Boles	Castillo, .302	Gonzalez, 155	Wilson, 26	Wilson, 71	Meadows, 11	Fernandez, 3.38
2000	79	82	3rd	15½	Boles	Castillo, .334	Castillo, 180	Wilson, 31	Wilson, 121	Dempster, 14	C. Smith, 3.25
2001	76	86	4th	12	Boles, Perez	Floyd, .317	Floyd, 176	Floyd, 31	Floyd, 103	Dempster, 15	Nunez, 2.74
2002	79	83	4th	23	Torborg	Castillo, .305	Castillo, 185	Lee, 27	Lowell, 92	Burnett, 12	Burnett, 3.30

* Won Division Series. † Won Championship Series.

Note: Batting average minimum 350 at-bats; ERA minimum 90 innings pitched.

Nigel Wilson

FLORIDA, long associated with spring training baseball, received its own Major League franchise when National League owners unanimously approved expansion to Denver and Miami. The Marlins, owned by H. Wayne Huizenga, joined the Colorado Rockies as the 13th and 14th N.L. franchises.

The Marlins stocked their roster with 36 selections in the November 17, 1992, expansion draft, grabbing outfielder Nigel Wilson with their first pick. Florida made its April 5, 1993, Major League debut a successful one, beating the Los Angeles Dodgers, 6-3, at Joe Robbie Stadium.

Expansion draft (November 17, 1992)

Players

Player	From	Position
Bret Barberie	Montreal	infield
Chuck Carr	St. Louis	outfield
Jeff Conine	Kansas City	outfield
Steve Decker	San Francisco	catcher
Chris Donnels	N.Y. Mets	infield
Carl Everett	N.Y. Yankees	outfield
Monty Fariss	Texas	outfield
Junior Felix	California	outfield
Eric Helfand	Oakland	catcher
Ramon Martinez	Pittsburgh	infield
Kerwin Moore	Kansas City	outfield
Bob Natal	Montreal	catcher
Jesus Tavarez	Seattle	outfield
*Nigel Wilson	Toronto	outfield
Darrell Whitmore	Cleveland	outfield

Pitchers

Pitcher	From	Throws
Jack Armstrong	Cleveland	righthanded
Scott Baker	St. Louis	lefthanded
Andres Berumen	Kansas City	righthanded
Ryan Bowen	Houston	righthanded
Cris Carpenter	St. Louis	righthanded
Scott Chiamparino	Texas	righthanded
Jim Corsi	Oakland	righthanded
Tom Edens	Minnesota	righthanded
Brian Harvey	California	righthanded
Greg Hibbard	Chicago White Sox	lefthanded
Trevor Hoffman	Cincinnati	righthanded
Danny Jackson	Pittsburgh	lefthanded
John Johnstone	N.Y. Mets	righthanded
Richie Lewis	Baltimore	righthanded
Jose Martinez	N.Y. Mets	righthanded
Jamie McAndrew	Los Angeles	righthanded
Robert Person	Chicago White Sox	righthanded
Pat Rapp	San Francisco	righthanded
Jeff Tabaka	Milwaukee	lefthanded
Dave Weathers	Toronto	righthanded
Kip Yaughn	Baltimore	righthanded

* First pick

Opening day lineup

April 5, 1993

Scott Pose, center field
Bret Barberie, second base
Junior Felix, right field
Orestes Destrade, first base
Dave Magadan, third base
Benito Santiago, catcher
Jeff Conine, left field
Walt Weiss, shortstop
Charlie Hough, pitcher

Jeff Conine

Marlins firsts

First hit: Bret Barberie, April 5, 1993, vs. Los Angeles (single)
First home run: Benito Santiago, April 12, 1993, at San Francisco
First RBI: Walt Weiss, April 5, 1993, vs. Los Angeles
First win: Charlie Hough, April 5, 1993, vs. Los Angeles
First shutout: Ryan Bowen, May 15, 1993, 8-0 at St. Louis

HOUSTON ASTROS

FRANCHISE CHRONOLOGY

First season: 1962, as one of two entries in the National League's first modern-era expansion. The Colt .45s, as they were known for three seasons, pounded the Chicago Cubs, 11-2, in their big-league debut and went on to finish with a 64-96 first-year record, good for eighth place in the 10-team N.L. field.

1963-present: The Astros still are looking for their first pennant, an honor the New York Mets, their expansion mate, has claimed three times. They came excruciatingly close in two N.L. Championship Series: 1980, when they dropped a 10-inning Game 5 thriller to Philadelphia; and 1986, when they lost a 16-inning Game 6 decision in an expansion showdown with the Mets. Those two West Division titles and consecutive Central titles that were followed by Division Series losses in 1997, '98, '99 and 2001 are all the Astros have to show for more than four decades of Major League Baseball, although they have finished second or third 14 times since division play began in 1969. In a historical sense, Houston will be long remembered as the franchise that brought indoor baseball and AstroTurf to the major leagues.

Righthander Mike Scott.

ASTROS VS. OPPONENTS BY DECADE

	Braves	Cardinals	Cubs	Dodgers	Giants	Phillies	Pirates	Reds	Mets	Expos	Padres	Marlins	Rockies	Brewers	D'backs	Interleague	Decade Record
1962-69	49-95	59-79	72-66	57-87	55-89	51-87	45-93	59-85	87-49	11-1	10-8						555-739
1970-79	91-85	56-64	65-55	76-104	90-90	59-61	44-75	74-105	61-59	71-49	106-70						793-817
1980-89	96-78	56-58	64-51	82-93	98-79	57-61	63-51	93-81	61-56	60-55	89-87						819-750
1990-99	53-71	60-62	70-51	65-57	69-57	62-43	67-54	63-76	61-46	57-51	62-67	39-32	33-41	17-7	9-9	26-18	813-742
2000-02	10-11	21-26	27-21	8-13	5-16	11-10	30-17	27-19	9-10	13-8	9-15	11-9	11-10	29-19	8-11	20-22	249-237
Totals	299-340	252-289	298-244	288-354	317-331	240-262	249-290	316-366	279-220	212-164	276-247	50-41	44-51	46-26	17-20	46-40	3229-3285

Interleague results: 5-7 vs. White Sox, 8-7 vs. Indians, 7-2 vs. Tigers, 11-4 vs. Royals, 1-2 vs. Brewers, 6-8 vs. Twins, 0-3 vs. Athletics, 1-2 vs. Mariners, 7-5 vs. Rangers.

MANAGERS

(Houston Colt .45s, 1962-64)

Name	*Years*	*Record*
Harry Craft	1962-64	191-280
Lum Harris	1964-65	70-105
Grady Hatton	1966-68	164-221
Harry Walker	1968-72	355-353
Leo Durocher	1972-73	98-95
Salty Parker	1972	1-0
Preston Gomez	1973-75	128-161
Bill Virdon	1975-82	544-522
Bob Lillis	1982-85	276-261
Hal Lanier	1986-88	254-232
Art Howe	1989-93	392-418
Terry Collins	1994-96	224-197
Larry Dierker	1997-2001	448-362
Jimy Williams	2002	84-78

WEST DIVISION CHAMPIONS

Year	*Record*	*Manager*	*NLCS Result*
1980	93-70	Virdon	Lost to Phillies
1981*	61-49	Virdon	None
1986	96-66	Lanier	Lost to Mets

* Second-half champion; lost division playoff to Dodgers.

CENTRAL DIVISION CHAMPIONS

Year	*Record*	*Manager*	*Div. Series Result*
1997	84-78	Dierker	Lost to Braves
1998	102-60	Dierker	Lost to Padres
1999	97-65	Dierker	Lost to Braves
2001	93-69	Dierker	Lost to Braves

ALL-TIME RECORD OF EXPANSION TEAMS

Team	W	L	Pct.	DT	P	WS
Arizona	440	370	.543	3	1	1
Kansas City	2,675	2,694	.498	6	2	1
Houston	3,229	3,285	.496	7	0	0
Toronto	2,025	2,063	.495	5	2	2
Anaheim	3,243	3,431	.486	3	1	1
Montreal	2,605	2,769	.485	2	0	0
Colorado	740	817	.475	0	0	0
New York	3,091	3,412	.475	4	4	2
Milwaukee	2,545	2,831	.473	2	1	0
Seattle	1,924	2,163	.471	3	0	0
Texas	3,097	3,560	.465	4	0	0
San Diego	2,460	2,921	.457	3	2	0
Florida	706	847	.455	0	1	1
Tampa Bay	318	490	.394	0	0	0

DT—Division Titles. P—Pennants won. WS—World Series won.

ATTENDANCE HIGHS

Total	*Season*	*Park*
3,056,139	2000	Enron Field
2,904,280	2001	Enron Field
2,706,020	1999	Astrodome
2,517,407	2002	Minute Maid Park
2,450,451	1998	Astrodome

BALLPARK CHRONOLOGY

Minute Maid Park, formerly Enron Field (2000-present)

Capacity: 40,950.
First game: Philadelphia 4, Astros 1 (April 7, 2000).
First batter: Doug Glanville, Phillies.
First hit: Doug Glanville, Phillies (single).
First run: Scott Rolen, Phillies (7th inning).
First home run: Scott Rolen, Phillies.
First winning pitcher: Randy Wolf, Phillies.
First-season attendance: 3,056,139.

The Astrodome (1965-present)

Capacity: 54,313.
First game: Philadelphia 2, Astros 0 (April 12, 1965).
First-season attendance: 2,151,470.

Colt Stadium (1962-64)

Capacity: 32,601.
First game: Astros 11, Chicago 2 (April 10, 1962).
First-season attendance: 924,456.

N.L. MVP

Jeff Bagwell, 1B, 1994

CY YOUNG WINNER

Mike Scott, RH, 1986

ROOKIE OF THE YEAR

Jeff Bagwell, 1B, 1991

MANAGERS OF THE YEAR

Hal Lanier, 1986
Larry Dierker, 1998

RETIRED UNIFORMS

No.	*Name*	*Pos.*
25	Jose Cruz	OF
32	Jim Umbricht	P
33	Mike Scott	P
34	Nolan Ryan	P
40	Don Wilson	P

Hard-hitting Jimmy Wynn was Houston's major power source in the late 1960s.

HISTORY

MILESTONE PERFORMANCES

25-plus home runs

47— Jeff Bagwell 2000
44— Richard Hidalgo 2000
43— Jeff Bagwell 1997
42— Jeff Bagwell 1999
Lance Berkman 2002
39— Jeff Bagwell 1994, 2001
38— Moises Alou 1998
37— Jimmy Wynn 1967
34— Glenn Davis 1989
Jeff Bagwell 1998
Lance Berkman 2001
33— Jimmy Wynn 1969
31— Glenn Davis 1986
Jeff Bagwell 1996, 2002
30— Glenn Davis 1988
Moises Alou 2000
29— Lee May 1972
28— Lee May 1973
27— Jimmy Wynn 1970
Glenn Davis 1987
Moises Alou 2001
26— Jimmy Wynn 1968
Cesar Cedeno 1974
25— Doug Rader 1970
Cesar Cedeno 1973
Carl Everett 1999

100-plus RBIs

135— Jeff Bagwell 1997
132— Jeff Bagwell 2000
130— Jeff Bagwell 2001
128— Lance Berkman 2002
126— Jeff Bagwell 1999
Lance Berkman 2001
124— Moises Alou 1998
122— Richard Hidalgo 2000
120— Jeff Bagwell 1996
116— Jeff Bagwell 1994
114— Moises Alou 2000
113— Derek Bell 1996
111— Jeff Bagwell 1998
110— Bob Watson 1977
108— Derek Bell 1998
Carl Everett 1999
Moises Alou 2001
107— Jimmy Wynn 1967
105— Lee May 1973
102— Cesar Cedeno 1974
Bob Watson 1976
101— Glenn Davis 1986

20-plus victories

1969— Larry Dierker 20-13
1976— J.R. Richard 20-15
1979— Joe Niekro 21-11
1980— Joe Niekro 20-12
1989— Mike Scott 20-10
1999— Mike Hampton 22-4
Jose Lima 21-10

N.L. home run champions

None

N.L. RBI champions

1994— Jeff Bagwell 116
2002— Lance Berkman 128

N.L. batting champions

None

N.L. ERA champions

1979— J.R. Richard 2.71
1981— Nolan Ryan 1.69
1986— Mike Scott 2.22
1987— Nolan Ryan 2.76
1990— Danny Darwin 2.21

N.L. strikeout champions

1978— J.R. Richard 303
1979— J.R. Richard 313
1986— Mike Scott 306
1987— Nolan Ryan 270
1988— Nolan Ryan 228

No-hit pitchers

(9 innings or more)

1963— Don Nottebart .... 4-1 vs. Philadelphia
1964— Ken Johnson .... 0-1 vs. Cincinnati
1967— Don Wilson .... 2-0 vs. Atlanta
1969— Don Wilson .... 4-0 at Cincinnati
1976— Larry Dierker .... 6-0 vs. Montreal
1979— Ken Forsch .... 6-0 vs. Atlanta
1981— Nolan Ryan .... 5-0 vs. Los Angeles
1986— Mike Scott .... 2-0 vs. San Francisco
1993— Darryl Kile .... 7-1 vs. New York

Longest hitting streaks

24— Tony Eusebio 2000
23— Art Howe 1981
Luis Gonzalez 1997
Moises Alou 2001
22— Cesar Cedeno 1977
21— Lee May 1973
Dickie Thon 1982
Lance Berkman 2001
20— Rusty Staub 1967
Kevin Bass 1986
19— Bob Watson 1973
Cesar Cedeno 1976
Jose Cruz 1983
18— Terry Puhl 1978
Jeff Bagwell 1994, 2000
Craig Biggio 2001
17— Rusty Staub 1966
Doug Rader 1970
Terry Puhl 1977
Bob Watson 1978
16— Roman Mejias 1962
Jim Wynn 1968
Joe Morgan 1971
Ray Knight 1982
Billy Hatcher 1987
Craig Biggio 2000
15— Sonny Jackson 1966
Enos Cabell 1979
Jose Cruz 1979
Craig Reynolds 1979
Bill Doran 1984
Richard Hidalgo 2000
Jeff Bagwell 2002
Daryle Ward 2002

Center fielder Cesar Cedeno brought a nice blend of power and speed to the Astros' lineup for more than a decade.

INDIVIDUAL SEASON, GAME RECORDS

Righthanded knuckleballer Joe Niekro reached the 20-victory plateau for the Astros in the 1979 and '80 seasons.

SEASON

Batting

At-bats	660	Enos Cabell	1978
Runs	152	Jeff Bagwell	2000
Hits	210	Craig Biggiol	1998
Singles	160	Sonny Jackson	1966
Doubles	56	Craig Biggio	1999
Triples	14	Roger Metzger	1973
Home runs	47	Jeff Bagwell	2000
Home runs, rookie	20	Glenn Davis	1985
Grand slams	2	Last by Jeff Bagwell	2001
Total bases	363	Jeff Bagwell	2000
RBIs	135	Jeff Bagwell	1997
Walks	149	Jeff Bagwell	1999
Most strikeouts	145	Lee May	1972
Fewest strikeouts	13	Nellie Fox	1964
Batting average	.368	Jeff Bagwell	1994
Slugging pct.	.750	Jeff Bagwell	1994
Stolen bases	65	Gerald Young	1988

Pitching

Games	83	Octavio Dotel	2002
Complete games	20	Larry Dierker	1969
Innings	305.1	Larry Dierker	1969
Wins	22	Mike Hampton	1999
Losses	20	Dick Farrell	1962
Winning pct.	.909 (10-1)	Randy Johnson	1998
Walks	151	J.R. Richard	1976
Strikeouts	313	J.R. Richard	1979
Shutouts	6	Dave A. Roberts	1973
Home runs allowed	48	Jose Lima	2000
Lowest ERA	1.69	Nolan Ryan	1981
Saves	39	Billy Wagner	1999, 2001

GAME

Batting

Runs	5	Last by Craig Biggio	6-4-96
Hits	6	Joe Morgan	7-8-65
Doubles	4	Jeff Bagwell	6-14-96
Triples	3	Craig Reynolds	5-16-81
Home runs	3	Last by Lance Berkman	4-16-2002
RBIs	7	Last by Jeff Bagwell	7-7-2001
Total bases	13	Lee May	6-21-73
		Jeff Bagwell	6-24-94
Stolen bases	4	Last by Roger Cedeno	4-22-2000

CAREER LEADERS

BATTING

Games

Player	G
Craig Biggio	2,100
Jose Cruz	1,870
Jeff Bagwell	1,795
Terry Puhl	1,516
Cesar Cedeno	1,512
Jimmy Wynn	1,426
Bob Watson	1,381
Doug Rader	1,178
Craig Reynolds	1,170
Bill Doran	1,165

At-bats

Player	AB
Craig Biggio	7,960
Jose Cruz	6,629
Jeff Bagwell	6,520
Cesar Cedeno	5,732
Jimmy Wynn	5,063
Bob Watson	4,883
Terry Puhl	4,837
Bill Doran	4,264
Doug Rader	4,232
Enos Cabell	4,005

Runs

Player	R
Craig Biggio	1,401
Jeff Bagwell	1,293
Cesar Cedeno	890
Jose Cruz	871
Jimmy Wynn	829
Terry Puhl	676
Bob Watson	640
Bill Doran	611
Joe Morgan	597
Enos Cabell	522

Hits

Player	H
Craig Biggio	2,295
Jose Cruz	1,969
Jeff Bagwell	1,803
Cesar Cedeno	1,659
Bob Watson	1,448
Terry Puhl	1,357
Jimmy Wynn	1,291
Bill Doran	1,139
Enos Cabell	1,124
Doug Rader	1,060

Doubles

Player	2B
Craig Biggio	473
Jeff Bagwell	427
Cesar Cedeno	343
Jose Cruz	335
Bob Watson	241
Jimmy Wynn	228
Terry Puhl	226
Ken Caminiti	204
Doug Rader	197
Kevin Bass	194

Triples

Player	3B
Jose Cruz	80
Joe Morgan	63
Roger Metzger	62
Terry Puhl	56
Cesar Cedeno	55
Craig Reynolds	55
Craig Biggio	49
Enos Cabell	45
Steve Finley	41
Bill Doran	35

Home runs

Player	HR
Jeff Bagwell	380
Jimmy Wynn	223
Craig Biggio	195
Glenn Davis	166
Cesar Cedeno	163
Bob Watson	139
Jose Cruz	138
Doug Rader	128
Ken Caminiti	103
Richard Hidalgo	102

Total bases

Player	TB
Jeff Bagwell	3,592
Craig Biggio	3,451
Jose Cruz	2,846
Cesar Cedeno	2,601
Jimmy Wynn	2,252
Bob Watson	2,166
Terry Puhl	1,881
Doug Rader	1,701
Bill Doran	1,596
Ken Caminiti	1,578

Runs batted in

Player	RBI
Jeff Bagwell	1,321
Jose Cruz	942
Craig Biggio	869
Bob Watson	782
Cesar Cedeno	778
Jimmy Wynn	719
Doug Rader	600
Ken Caminiti	546
Glenn Davis	518
Kevin Bass	468

Extra-base hits

Player	XBH
Jeff Bagwell	835
Craig Biggio	717
Cesar Cedeno	561
Jose Cruz	553
Jimmy Wynn	483
Bob Watson	410
Doug Rader	355
Terry Puhl	344
Glenn Davis	326
Ken Caminiti	321

Batting average

(Minimum 500 games)

Player	Avg.
Jeff Bagwell	.302
Bob Watson	.297
Jose Cruz	.292
Cesar Cedeno	.289
Bill Spiers	.288
Craig Biggio	.288
Derek Bell	.284
Richard Hidalgo	.282
Jesus Alou	.282
Enos Cabell	.281

Stolen bases

Player	SB
Cesar Cedeno	487
Craig Biggio	381
Jose Cruz	288
Joe Morgan	219
Terry Puhl	217
Enos Cabell	191
Bill Doran	191
Jeff Bagwell	185
Jimmy Wynn	180
Gerald Young	153

PITCHING

Earned-run average

(Minimum 1,000 innings)

Player	ERA
Joe Sambito	2.42
Dave Smith	2.53
Mike Cuellar	2.74
Nolan Ryan	3.13
Don Wilson	3.15
J.R. Richard	3.15
Ken Forsch	3.18
Danny Darwin	3.21
Joe Niekro	3.22
Larry Dierker	3.28

Wins

Player	W
Joe Niekro	144
Larry Dierker	137
Mike Scott	110
J.R. Richard	107
Nolan Ryan	106
Don Wilson	104
Shane Reynolds	103
Bob Knepper	93
Ken Forsch	78
Darryl Kile	71

Losses

Player	L
Larry Dierker	117
Joe Niekro	116
Bob Knepper	100
Nolan Ryan	94
Don Wilson	92
Shane Reynolds	86
Ken Forsch	81
Mike Scott	81
J.R. Richard	71
Darryl Kile	65

Innings pitched

(Minimum 500 innings)

Player	IP
Larry Dierker	2,294.1
Joe Niekro	2,270.0
Nolan Ryan	1,854.2
Don Wilson	1,748.1
Bob Knepper	1,738.0
Mike Scott	1,704.0
Shane Reynolds	1,622.1
J.R. Richard	1,606.0
Ken Forsch	1,493.2
Darryl Kile	1,200.0

Strikeouts

Player	SO
Nolan Ryan	1,866
J.R. Richard	1,493
Larry Dierker	1,487
Mike Scott	1,318
Shane Reynolds	1,309
Don Wilson	1,283
Joe Niekro	1,178
Darryl Kile	973
Bob Knepper	946
Ken Forsch	815

Bases on balls

Player	BB
Joe Niekro	818
Nolan Ryan	796
J.R. Richard	770
Larry Dierker	695
Don Wilson	640
Darryl Kile	562
Bob Knepper	521
Mike Scott	505
Tom Griffin	441
Ken Forsch	428

Games

Player	G
Dave Smith	563
Ken Forsch	421
Joe Niekro	397
Billy Wagner	386
Joe Sambito	353
Larry Dierker	345
Bob Knepper	284
Nolan Ryan	282
Jim Ray	280
Shane Reynolds	274

Shutouts

Player	ShO
Larry Dierker	25
Joe Niekro	21
Mike Scott	21
Don Wilson	20
J.R. Richard	19
Bob Knepper	18
Nolan Ryan	13
Dave Roberts	11
Ken Forsch	9
Tom Griffin	9

Saves

Player	SV
Dave Smith	199
Billy Wagner	181
Fred Gladding	76
Joe Sambito	72
Doug Jones	62
Ken Forsch	50
Frank DiPino	43
Todd Jones	39
Hal Woodeshick	36
John Hudek	29

TEAM SEASON, GAME RECORDS

SEASON

Batting

Record	Total	Year
Most at-bats	5,641	1998
Most runs	938	2000
Fewest runs	394	1981
Most hits	1,578	1998
Most singles	1,097	1984
Most doubles	326	1998
Most triples	67	1980, 1984
Most home runs	249	2000
Fewest home runs	45	1981
Most grand slams	7	2001
Most pinch-hit home runs	9	1995
Most total bases	2,655	2000
Most stolen bases	198	1988
Highest batting average	.280	1998
Lowest batting average	.220	1963
Highest slugging pct	.477	2000

Pitching

Record	Total	Year
Lowest ERA	2.66	1981
Highest ERA	5.42	2000
Most complete games	55	1979
Most shutouts	19	1979, 1981, 1986
Most saves	51	1986
Most walks	679	1975
Most strikeouts	1,228	2001

Fielding

Record	Total	Year
Most errors	174	1966
Fewest errors	76	1994
Most double plays	175	1999
Highest fielding average	.986	2002

General

Record	Total	Year
Most games won	102	1998
Most games lost	97	1965, 1975, 1991
Highest win pct	.630	1998
Lowest win pct	.398	1975

GAME, INNING

Batting

Record	Total	Date
Most runs, game	19	6-25-95, 5-11-99
Most runs, inning	12	5-31-75
Most hits, game	25	5-30-76, 7-2-76
Most home runs, game	7	9-9-2000
Most total bases, game	44	9-9-2000

When outfielder Jose Cruz left Houston after the 1987 season, he held many career records.

ASTROS YEAR-BY-YEAR

Year	W	L	Place	Games Back	Manager	Leaders: Batting avg.	Hits	Home runs	RBIs	Wins	ERA
							COLT .45s				
1962	64	96	8th	36½	Craft	Mejias, .286	Mejias, 162	Mejias, 24	Mejias, 76	Bruce, Farrell 10	Farrell, 3.01
1963	66	96	9th	33	Craft	Spangler, .281	Warwick, 134	Bateman, 10	Bateman, 59	Farrell, 14	Woodeshick, 1.97
1964	66	96	9th	27	Craft, Harris	Aspromonte, .280	Aspromonte, 155	Bond, 20	Bond, 85	Bruce, 15	Larsen, 2.26
1965	65	97	9th	32	Harris	Wynn, .275	Morgan, 163	Wynn, 22	Wynn, 73	Farrell, 11	Raymond, 2.90
1966	72	90	8th	23	Hatton	Jackson, .292	Jackson, 174	Wynn, 18	Bateman 70	Giusti, 15	Cuellar, 2.22
1967	69	93	9th	32½	Hatton	Staub, .333	Staub, 182	Wynn, 37	Wynn, 107	Cuellar, 16	Wilson, 2.79
1968	72	90	10th	25	Hatton, Walker	Staub, .291	Staub, 172	Wynn, 26	Staub, 72	Wilson, 13	Cuellar, 2.74
							WEST DIVISION				
1969	81	81	5th	12	Walker	Menke, .Wynn, .269	Menke, 149	Wynn, 33	Menke, 90	Dierker, 20	Dierker, 2.33
1970	79	83	4th	23	Walker	Cedeno, .310	Menke, 171	Wynn, 27	Menke, 92	Dierker, 16	Ray, 3.26
1971	79	83	*4th	11	Walker	Watson, .288	Cedeno, 161	Morgan, 13	Cedeno, 81	Wilson, 16	Ray, 2.12
1972	84	69	2nd	10½	Walker, Durocher, Parker	Cedeno, .320	Cedeno, 179	May, 29	May, 98	Dierker, Wilson 15	Wilson, 2.68
1973	82	80	4th	17	Durocher, Gomez	Cedeno, .320	Watson, 179	May, 28	May, 105	Roberts, 17	Roberts, 2.86
1974	81	81	4th	21	Gomez	Gross, .314	Gross, 185	Cedeno, 26	Cedeno, 102	Griffin, 14	Forsch, 2.79
1975	64	97	6th	43½	Gomez, Virdon	Watson, .324	Watson, 157	C. Johnson, 20	Watson, 85	Dierker, 14	Forsch, 3.22
1976	80	82	3rd	22	Virdon	Watson, .313	Watson, 183	Cedeno, 18	Watson, 102	Richard, 20	Forsch, 2.15
1977	81	81	3rd	17	Virdon	Cruz, .299	Cabell, 176	Watson, 22	Watson, 110	Richard, 18	Richard, 2.97
1978	74	88	5th	21	Virdon	Cruz, .315	Cabell, 195	Watson, 14	Cruz, 83	Richard, 18	Forsch, 2.70
1979	89	73	2nd	1½	Virdon	Leonard, .290	Puhl, 172	Cruz, 9	Cruz, 72	Niekro, 21	Sambito, 1.77
1980	93	70	†‡1st	+1	Virdon	Cedeno, .309	Cruz, 185	Puhl, 13	Cruz, 91	Niekro, 20	Richard, 1.89
1981	61	49	§3rd/1st	—	Virdon	Howe, .296	Cruz, 109	Cruz, 13	Cruz, 55	Ryan, Sutton 11	Ryan, 1.69
1982	77	85	5th	12	Virdon, Lillis	Knight, .294	Knight, 179	Garner, 13	Garner, 83	Niekro, 17	Niekro, 2.47
1983	85	77	3rd	6	Lillis	Cruz, .318	Cruz, 189	Thon, 20	Cruz, 92	Niekro, 15	Ryan, 2.98
1984	80	82	*2nd	12	Lillis	Cruz, .312	Cruz, 187	Cruz, 12	Cruz, 95	Niekro, 16	Dawley, 1.93
1985	83	79	*3rd	12	Lillis	Cruz, .300	Doran, 166	Davis, 20	Cruz, 79	Scott, 18	Scott, 3.29
1986	96	66	‡1st	+10	Lanier	Walling, .312	Bass, 184	Davis, 31	Davis, 101	Scott, 18	Scott, 2.22
1987	76	86	3rd	14	Lanier	Hatcher, .296	Doran, 177	Davis, 27	Davis, 93	Scott, 16	Ryan, 2.76
1988	82	80	5th	12½	Lanier	Ramirez, .276	Ramirez, 156	Davis, 30	Davis, 99	Knepper, Scott 14	Agosto, 2.26
1989	86	76	3rd	6	Howe	Davis, .269	Davis, 156	Davis, 34	Davis, 89	Scott, 20	Darwin, 2.36
1990	75	87	*4th	16	Howe	Biggio, .276	Biggio, 153	Stubbs, 23	Stubbs, 71	Darwin, Portugal 11	Darwin, 2.21
1991	65	97	6th	29	Howe	Biggio, .295	Finley, 170	Bagwell, 15	Bagwell, 82	Harnisch, 12	Harnisch, 2.70
1992	81	81	4th	17	Howe	Caminiti, .294	Finley, 177	Anthony, 19	Bagwell, 96	D. Jones, 11	D. Jones, 1.85
1993	85	77	3rd	19	Howe	Bagwell, .320	Biggio, 175	Biggio, 21	Bagwell, 88	Portugal, 18	Hernandez, 2.61
							CENTRAL DIVISION				
1994	66	49	2nd	½	Collins	Bagwell, .368	Bagwell, 147	Bagwell, 39	Bagwell, 116	Drabek, 12	Drabek, 2.84
1995	76	68	2nd	9	Collins	Bell, .334	Biggio, 167	Biggio, 22	Bagwell, 87	Reynolds, 10	Veres, 2.26
1996	82	80	2nd	6	Collins	Bagwell, .315	Bagwell, 179	Bagwell, 31	Bagwell, 120	Reynolds, 16	Hampton, 3.59
1997	84	78	∞1st	+5	Dierker	Biggio, .309	Biggio, 191	Bagwell, 43	Bagwell, 135	Kile, 19	Kile, 2.57
1998	102	60	∞1st	+12½	Dierker	Biggio, .325	Biggio, 210	Alou, 38	Alou, 124	Reynolds, 19	Hampton, 3.36
1999	97	65	∞1st	+1½	Dierker	Everett, .325	Biggio, 188	Bagwell, 42	Bagwell, 126	Hampton, 22	Hampton, 2.90
2000	72	90	4th	23	Dierker	M. Alou, .355	Bagwell, 183	Bagwell, 47	Bagwell, 132	Elarton, 17	Elarton, 4.83
2001	93	69	*∞1st	0	Dierker	M. Alou, Berkman, .331	Berkman, 191	Bagwell, 39	Bagwell, 130	Miller, 16	Dotel, 2.66
2002	84	78	2nd	13	Williams	Berkman, .292	Berkman, 169	Berkman, 42	Berkman, 128	Oswalt, 19	Oswalt, 3.01

* Tied for position. † Won division playoff. ‡ Lost Championship Series. § First half 28-29; second half 33-20. ∞ Lost Division Series.

Note: Batting average minimum 350 at-bats; ERA minimum 90 innings pitched.

Eddie Bressoud

HOUSTON became part of the National League family in a two-team 1962 expansion that marked the first league structural change since 1900. Houston and New York were granted franchise approval on October 16, 1960, bringing the N.L. membership roster to 10.

The Colt .45s stocked their first roster with 23 selections in the October 10, 1961, expansion draft, leading off with infielder Eddie Bressoud. Houston made its Major League debut a successful one, defeating the Chicago Cubs, 11-2, at Colt Stadium en route to a 64-96 first-year record.

Expansion draft (October 10, 1961)

Players

Player	Team	Position
Joe Amalfitano	San Francisco	infield
Bob Aspromonte	Los Angeles	infield
*Eddie Bressoud	San Francisco	infield
Dick Gernert	Cincinnati	infield
Al Heist	Chicago	outfield
Bob Lillis	St. Louis	infield
Norm Larker	Los Angeles	infield
Roman Mejias	Pittsburgh	outfield
Ed Olivares	St. Louis	infield
Merritt Ranew	Milwaukee	catcher
Hal Smith	Pittsburgh	catcher
Al Spangler	Milwaukee	outfield
Don Taussig	St. Louis	outfield
George Williams	Philadelphia	infield

Pitchers

Pitcher	Team	Throws
Dick Drott	Chicago	righthanded
Dick Farrell	Los Angeles	righthanded
Jim Golden	Los Angeles	righthanded
Jesse Hickman	Philadelphia	righthanded
Ken Johnson	Cincinnati	righthanded
Sam Jones	San Francisco	righthanded
Paul Roof	Milwaukee	righthanded
Bobby Shantz	Pittsburgh	lefthanded
Jim Umbricht	Pittsburgh	righthanded

*First pick

Opening day lineup

April 10, 1962

Bob Aspromonte, third base
Al Spangler, center field
Roman Mejias, right field
Norm Larker, first base
Jim Pendleton, left field
Hal Smith, catcher
Joe Amalfitano, second base
Don Buddin, shortstop
Bobby Shantz, pitcher

Bob Aspromonte

Colt .45s firsts

First hit: Bob Aspromonte, April 10, 1962, vs. Chicago
First home run: Roman Mejias, April 10, 1962, vs. Chicago
First RBI: Al Spangler, April 10, 1962, vs. Chicago
First win: Bobby Shantz, April 10, 1962, vs. Chicago
First shutout: Hal Woodeshick (8 inn.), Dick Farrell (1) April 11, 1962, 2-0 vs. Chicago
First CG shutout: Dean Stone, April 12, 1962, 2-0 vs. Chicago

Los Angeles Dodgers

Manager Walter Alston.

FRANCHISE CHRONOLOGY

First season: 1884, in Brooklyn, as a member of the American Association. The first-year "Bridegrooms" won only 40 games and finished ninth in the league's 13-team field.

1885-1900: Brooklyn celebrated its first A.A. pennant in 1889 by transferring to the more prestigious National League. The Bridegrooms lost their N.L. opener to Boston, 15-9, but went on to claim another pennant with an 86-43 record. Renamed "Superbas," they would close out the century with consecutive pennants under manager Ned Hanlon.

1901-57: The modern-era "Dodgers" might have more aptly been named "Bridesmaids." From 1916 to 1954, they finished second seven times and won seven N.L. pennants, losing every World Series appearance. "Wait til next year" became the rallying cry of frustrated Brooklyn fans, who nevertheless supported their beloved "Bums" with a fervor unmatched in major league baseball. Walter Alston's Dodgers finally broke through with a victory in the 1955 World Series against the hated Yankees, but two years later owner Peter O'Malley moved his franchise to the greener pastures of the West Coast.

1958-present: The Dodgers became less lovable but more efficient in Los Angeles. In 42 seasons, they have claimed nine N.L. pennants, five World Series championships and nine West Division titles while finishing second 14 times. Incredibly, that success has been choreographed by five full-time managers: Alston (1958-76), Tom Lasorda (1976-96), Bill Russell, who replaced the ailing Lasorda midway through the 1996 season, Davey Johnson (1999 and 2000), and current manager Jim Tracy (2001 and 2002).

DODGERS VS. OPPONENTS BY DECADE

	Braves	Cardinals	Cubs	Giants	Phillies	Pirates	Reds	Astros	Mets	Expos	Padres	Marlins	Rockies	Brewers	D'backs	Interleague	Decade Record
1900-09	114-95	115-93	74-135	80-128	93-112	76-132	97-114										649-809
1910-19	103-105	105-104	98-117	88-125	99-110	110-105	93-121										696-787
1920-29	128-90	101-119	104-115	106-113	133-87	97-122	96-122										765-768
1930-39	103-117	91-127	89-127	98-120	128-89	113-105	112-108										734-793
1940-49	129-90	90-132	119-101	137-82	162-58	124-96	133-87										894-646
1950-59	129-92	135-85	134-85	117-106	128-92	141-79	129-91										913-630
1960-69	99-89	91-91	102-80	83-108	106-76	100-82	94-94	87-57	94-44	10-2	12-6						878-729
1970-79	106-70	67-53	68-52	108-72	63-56	65-55	79-97	104-76	68-52	73-47	109-71						910-701
1980-89	105-69	62-56	61-57	95-79	55-59	61-53	98-80	93-82	50-63	67-48	78-95						825-741
1990-99	55-68	52-55	61-47	70-70	61-54	61-50	65-57	57-65	58-53	57-56	68-71	35-35	46-40	12-6	14-11	25-19	797-757
2000-02	11-11	8-13	12-9	26-24	12-10	15-9	9-12	13-8	10-11	12-9	27-24	15-7	32-19	13-6	25-26	24-24	264-222
Totals	1082-896	917-928	922-925	1008-1027	1040-803	963-888	1005-983	354-288	280-223	219-162	294-267	50-42	78-59	25-12	39-37	49-43	8325-7583

Interleague results: 16-16 vs. Angels, 2-1 vs. Orioles, 3-0 vs. Red Sox, 7-9 vs. Athletics, 8-8 vs. Mariners, 2-1 vs. Devil Rays, 9-7 vs. Rangers, 2-1 vs. Blue Jays.

MANAGERS

(Brooklyn Dodgers, 1884-1957)

Name	Years	Record
George Taylor	1884	40-64
Charlie Hackett	1885	15-22
Charlie Byrne	1885-87	174-172
Bill McGunnigle	1888-90	268-138
Monte Ward	1891-92	156-135
Dave Foutz	1893-96	264-257
Billy Barnie	1897-98	76-91
Ned Hanlon	1899-1905	511-488
Patsy Donovan	1906-08	184-270
Harry Lumley	1909	55-98
Bill Dahlen	1910-13	251-355
Wilbert Robinson	1914-31	1375-1341
Max Carey	1932-33	146-161
Casey Stengel	1934-36	208-251
Burleigh Grimes	1937-38	131-171
Leo Durocher	1939-46, 1948	738-565
Clyde Sukeforth	1947	2-0
Burt Shotton	1947, 1948-50	326-215
Chuck Dressen	1951-53	298-166
Walter Alston	1954-76	2040-1613
Tom Lasorda	1976-96	1599-1439
Bill Russell	1996-98	173-149
Glenn Hoffman	1998	47-41
Davey Johnson	1999-2000	163-162
Jim Tracy	2001-02	178-146

WORLD SERIES CHAMPIONS

Year	Loser	Length	MVP
1955	N.Y. Yankees	7 games	Podres
1959	Chicago	6 games	Sherry
1963	N.Y. Yankees	4 games	Koufax
1965	Minnesota	7 games	Koufax
1981	N.Y. Yankees	6 games	Cey, Guerrero, Yeager
1988	Oakland	5 games	Hershiser

A.A. PENNANT WINNERS

Year	Record	Manager	Series Result
1889	93-44	McGunnigle	None

N.L. PENNANT WINNERS

Year	Record	Manager	Series Result
1890	86-43	McGunnigle	None
1899	101-47	Hanlon	None
1900	82-54	Hanlon	None
1916	94-60	Robinson	Lost to Red Sox
1920	93-61	Robinson	Lost to Indians
1941	100-54	Durocher	Lost to Yankees
1947	94-60	Sukeforth, Shotton	Lost to Yankees
1949	97-57	Shotton	Lost to Yankees
1952	96-57	Dressen	Lost to Yankees
1953	105-49	Dressen	Lost to Yankees
1955	98-55	Alston	Defeated Yankees
1956	93-61	Alston	Lost to Yankees
1959	88-68	Alston	Defeated White Sox
1963	99-63	Alston	Defeated Yankees
1965	97-65	Alston	Defeated Twins
1966	95-67	Alston	Lost to Orioles
1974	102-60	Alston	Lost to A's

N.L. PENNANT WINNERS—*cont'd.*

Year	Record	Manager	Series Result
1977	98-64	Lasorda	Lost to Yankees
1978	95-67	Lasorda	Lost to Yankees
1981	63-47	Lasorda	Defeated Yankees
1988	94-67	Lasorda	Defeated A's

WEST DIVISION CHAMPIONS

Year	Record	Manager	NLCS Result
1974	102-60	Alston	Defeated Pirates
1977	98-64	Lasorda	Defeated Phillies
1978	95-67	Lasorda	Defeated Phillies
*1981	63-47	Lasorda	Defeated Expos
1983	91-71	Lasorda	Lost to Phillies
1985	95-67	Lasorda	Lost to Cardinals
1988	94-67	Lasorda	Defeated Mets
1994	58-56	Lasorda	None
1995	78-66	Lasorda	Lost in Division Series

* First-half champion; won division playoff from Astros.

WILD-CARD QUALIFIERS

Year	Record	Manager	Div. Series Result
1996	90-72	Lasorda, Russell	Lost to Braves

ATTENDANCE HIGHS

Total	Season	Park
3,608,881	1982	Dodger Stadium
3,510,313	1983	Dodger Stadium
3,348,170	1991	Dodger Stadium
3,347,845	1978	Dodger Stadium
3,318,886	1997	Dodger Stadium

BALLPARK CHRONOLOGY

Dodger Stadium (1962-present)

Capacity: 56,000.
First game: Cincinnati 6, Dodgers 3 (April 10, 1962).
First batter: Eddie Kasko, Reds.
First hit: Eddie Kasko, Reds (double).
First run: Eddie Kasko, Reds (1st inning).
First home run: Wally Post, Reds.
First winning pitcher: Bob Purkey, Reds.
First-season attendance: 2,755,184.

Washington Park, Brooklyn (1884-90)

First game: Brooklyn (A.A.) 11, Washington 3 (May 5, 1884).

Eastern Park, Brooklyn (1891-97)

First game: New York 6, Brooklyn 5 (April 27, 1891).

Washington Park II, Brooklyn (1898-1912)

First game: Philadelphia 6, Brooklyn 4 (April 30, 1898).

Ebbets Field, Brooklyn (1913-57)

Capacity: 31,497.
First game: Philadelphia 1, Dodgers 0 (April 9, 1913).
First-season attendance: 347,000.

Roosevelt Stadium, Jersey City (1956-57)

(Site of 15 games over two seasons)
Capacity: 24,167.
First game: Dodgers 5, Philadelphia 4, 10 innings (April 19, 1956).

Los Angeles Memorial Coliseum (1958-61)

Capacity: 93,600.
First game: Dodgers 6, San Francisco 5 (April 18, 1958).
First-season attendance: 1,845,556.

N.L. MVPs

Dolph Camilli, 1B, 1941
Jackie Robinson, 2B, 1949
Roy Campanella, C, 1951
Roy Campanella, C, 1953
Roy Campanella, C, 1955
Don Newcombe, P, 1956
Maury Wills, SS, 1962
Sandy Koufax, P, 1963
Steve Garvey, 1B, 1974
Kirk Gibson, OF, 1988

CY YOUNG WINNERS

Don Newcombe, RH, 1956
Don Drysdale, RH, 1962
Sandy Koufax, LH, 1963
Sandy Koufax, LH, 1965
Sandy Koufax, LH, 1966
Mike Marshall, RH, 1974
Fernando Valenzuela, LH, 1981
Orel Hershiser, RH, 1988

ROOKIES OF THE YEAR

Jackie Robinson, 1B, 1947
Don Newcombe, P, 1949
Joe Black, P, 1952
Jim Gilliam, 2B, 1953
Frank Howard, OF, 1960
Jim Lefebvre, 2B, 1965
Ted Sizemore, 2B, 1969
Rick Sutcliffe, P, 1979
Steve Howe, P, 1980
Fernando Valenzuela, P, 1981
Steve Sax, 2B, 1982
Eric Karros, 1B, 1992
Mike Piazza, C, 1993
Raul Mondesi, OF, 1994
Hideo Nomo, P, 1995
Todd Hollandsworth, OF, 1996

MANAGERS OF THE YEAR

Tom Lasorda, 1983
Tom Lasorda, 1988

RETIRED UNIFORMS

No.	Name	Pos.
1	Pee Wee Reese	SS
2	Tommy Lasorda	Man.
4	Duke Snider	OF
19	Jim Gilliam	IF
20	Don Sutton	P
24	Walter Alston	Man.
32	Sandy Koufax	P
39	Roy Campanella	C
42	Jackie Robinson	2B
53	Don Drysdale	P

HISTORY

MILESTONE PERFORMANCES

30-plus home runs

49— Shawn Green 2001
43— Duke Snider 1956
Gary Sheffield 2000
42— Duke Snider 1953, 1955
Gil Hodges 1954
Shawn Green 2002
41— Roy Campanella 1953
40— Gil Hodges 1951
Duke Snider 1954, 1957
Mike Piazza 1997
36— Mike Piazza 1996
Gary Sheffield 2001
35— Babe Herman 1930
Mike Piazza 1993
34— Dolph Camilli 1941
Eric Karros 1996
Eric Karros 1999
Gary Sheffield 1999
33— Roy Campanella 1951
Steve Garvey 1977
Pedro Guerrero 1985
Raul Mondesi 1999
32— Gil Hodges 1950, 1952, 1956
Roy Campanella 1955
Jimmy Wynn 1974
Reggie Smith 1977
Pedro Guerrero 1982, 1983
Eric Karros 1995
Mike Piazza 1995
31— Roy Campanella 1950
Duke Snider 1950
Gil Hodges 1953
Frank Howard 1962
Eric Karros 1997, 2000
Todd Zeile 1997
30— Dusty Baker 1977
Ron Cey 1977
Raul Mondesi 1997, 1998

100-plus RBIs

153— Tommy Davis 1962
142— Roy Campanella 1953
136— Duke Snider 1955
130— Jack Fournier 1925
Babe Herman 1930
Gil Hodges 1954
Duke Snider 1954
126— Glenn Wright 1930
Duke Snider 1953
125— Shawn Green 2001
124— Dixie Walker 1945
Jackie Robinson 1949
Mike Piazza 1997
123— Hack Wilson 1932
122— Gil Hodges 1953
120— Dolph Camilli 1941
119— Frank Howard 1962
116— Jack Fournier 1924
Dixie Walker 1946
115— Gil Hodges 1949
Steve Garvey 1977
114— Shawn Green 2002
113— Babe Herman 1929
Del Bissonette 1930
Gil Hodges 1950
Steve Garvey 1978
112— Zack Wheat 1922
Mike Piazza 1993
Eric Karros 1999
111— Wes Parker 1970
Steve Garvey 1974
Eric Karros 1996
110— Luis Olmo 1945
Ron Cey 1977
Steve Garvey 1979
109— Dolph Camilli 1942
Gary Sheffield 2000
108— Roy Campanella 1951
Jimmy Wynn 1974
107— Duke Snider 1950
Roy Campanella 1955
106— Del Bissonette 1928
Carl Furillo 1949, 1950
Steve Garvey 1980
Eric Karros 2000
105— Eric Karros 1995
Mike Piazza 1996
104— Dolph Camilli 1939
Eric Karros 1997
103— Zack Wheat 1925
Gil Hodges 1951
Pedro Guerrero 1983
102— Jack Fournier 1923
Sam Leslie 1934
Gil Hodges 1952, 1955
101— Duke Snider 1951, 1956
Ron Cey 1975
Gary Sheffield 1999
100— Dolph Camilli 1938
Billy Herman 1943
Pedro Guerrero 1982
Gary Sheffield 2001

20-plus victories

1890— Tom Lovett 30-11
Adonis Terry 26-16
Bob Caruthers 23-11
1891— Tom Lovett 23-19
1892— George Haddock 29-13
Ed Stein 27-16
1893— Brickyard Kennedy 25-20
1894— Ed Stein 26-14
Brickyard Kennedy 24-20
1899— Jim Hughes 28-6
Jack Dunn 23-13
Brickyard Kennedy 22-9
1900— Joseph McGinnity 28-8
Brickyard Kennedy 20-13
1901— William Donovan 25-15
1903— Henry Schmidt 21-13
1911— Nap Rucker 22-18
1914— Jeff Pfeffer 23-12
1916— Jeff Pfeffer 25-11
1920— Burleigh Grimes 23-11
1921— Burleigh Grimes 22-13
1922— Walter Reuther 21-12
1923— Burleigh Grimes 21-18
1924— Dazzy Vance 28-6
Burleigh Grimes 22-13
1925— Dazzy Vance 22-9
1928— Dazzy Vance 22-10
1932— William Clark 20-12
1939— Luke Hamlin 20-13
1941— Kirby Higbe 22-9
Whit Wyatt 22-10
1947— Ralph Branca 21-12
1951— Preacher Roe 22-3
Don Newcombe 20-9
1953— Carl Erskine 20-6
1955— Don Newcombe 20-5
1956— Don Newcombe 27-7
1962— Don Drysdale 25-9
1963— Sandy Koufax 25-5
1965— Sandy Koufax 26-8
Don Drysdale 23-12
1966— Sandy Koufax 27-9
1969— Claude Osteen 20-15
Bill Singer 20-12
1971— Al Downing 20-9
1972— Claude Osteen 20-11
1974— Andy Messersmith 20-6
1976— Don Sutton 21-10
1977— Tommy John 20-7
1986— Fernando Valenzuela 21-11
1988— Orel Hershiser 23-8
1990— Ramon Martinez 20-6

N.L. home run champions

1890— Oyster Burns *13
1903— Jimmy Sheckard 9
1904— Harry Lumley 9
1906— Tim Jordan 12
1908— Tim Jordan 12
1924— Jack Fournier 27
1941— Dolph Camilli 34
1956— Duke Snider 43

* Tied for league lead

N.L. RBI champions

1919— Hy Myers 73
1941— Dolph Camilli 120
1945— Dixie Walker 124
1953— Roy Campanella 142
1955— Duke Snider 136
1962— Tommy Davis 153

N.L. batting champions

1892— Dan Brouthers .335
1913— Jake Daubert .350
1914— Jake Daubert .329
1918— Zack Wheat .335
1932— Lefty O'Doul .368
1941— Pete Reiser .343
1944— Dixie Walker .357
1949— Jackie Robinson .342
1953— Carl Furillo .344
1962— Tommy Davis .346
1963— Tommy Davis .326

N.L. ERA champions

1924— Dazzy Vance 2.16
1928— Dazzy Vance 2.09
1930— Dazzy Vance 2.61
1957— Johnny Podres 2.66
1962— Sandy Koufax 2.54
1963— Sandy Koufax 1.88
1964— Sandy Koufax 1.74
1965— Sandy Koufax 2.04
1966— Sandy Koufax 1.73
1980— Don Sutton 2.20
1984— Alejandro Pena 2.48
2000— Kevin Brown 2.58

N.L. strikeout champions

1921— Burleigh Grimes 136
1922— Dazzy Vance 134
1923— Dazzy Vance 197
1924— Dazzy Vance 262
1925— Dazzy Vance 221
1926— Dazzy Vance 140
1927— Dazzy Vance 184
1928— Dazzy Vance 200
1936— Van Lingle Mungo 238
1951— Don Newcombe 164
1959— Don Drysdale 242
1960— Don Drysdale 246
1961— Sandy Koufax 269
1962— Don Drysdale 232
1963— Sandy Koufax 306
1965— Sandy Koufax 382
1966— Sandy Koufax 317
1981— Fernando Valenzuela 180
1995— Hideo Nomo 236

No-hit pitchers

(9 innings or more)

1891— Thomas Lovett 4-0 vs. New York
1906— Malcolm Eason 2-0 vs. St. Louis
1908— Nap Rucker 6-0 vs. Boston
1925— Dazzy Vance 10-1 vs. Philadelphia
1940— Tex Carleton 3-0 vs. Cincinnati
1946— Edward Head 5-0 vs. Boston
1948— Rex Barney 2-0 vs. New York
1952— Carl Erskine 5-0 vs. Chicago
1956— Carl Erskine 3-0 vs. New York
Sal Maglie 5-0 vs. Philadelphia
1962— Sandy Koufax 5-0 vs. New York
1963— Sandy Koufax 8-0 vs. San Francisco
1964— Sandy Koufax 3-0 vs. Philadelphia
1965— Sandy Koufax 1-0 vs. Chicago (Perfect)
1970— Bill Singer 5-0 vs. Philadelphia
1980— Jerry Reuss 8-0 vs. San Francisco
1990— Fernando Valenzuela 6-0 vs. St. Louis
1992— Kevin Gross 2-0 vs. San Francisco
1995— Ramon Martinez 7-0 vs. Florida
1996— Hideo Nomo 9-0 vs. Colorado

Longest hitting streaks

31— Willie Davis 1969
29— Zack Wheat 1916
27— Joe Medwick 1942
Duke Snider 1953
26— Willie Keeler 1902
Zack Wheat 1918
25— Gink Hendrick 1929
Buzz Boyle 1934
Willie Davis 1971
Steve Sax 1986
24— Willie Keeler 1899
Zack Wheat 1924
John Shelby 1988
23— Hy Myers 1915
Brett Butler 1991
22— Duke Snider 1950
Pee Wee Reese 1951
21— Jackie Robinson 1947
Steve Garvey 1978
20— Jimmy Johnston 1921
Zack Wheat 1923
Johnny Frederick 1933
Tommy Davis 1960, 1964
Maury Wills 1965
Steve Garvey 1978

INDIVIDUAL SEASON, GAME RECORDS

SEASON

Batting

At-bats	695	Maury Wills	1962
Runs	148	Hub Collins	1890
Hits	241	Babe Herman	1930
Singles	187	Willie Keeler	1899
Doubles	52	John Frederick	1929
Triples	26	George Treadway	1894
Home runs	49	Shawn Green	2001
Home runs, rookie	35	Mike Piazza	1993
Grand slams	3	Last by Mike Piazza	1998
Total bases	416	Babe Herman	1930
RBIs	153	Tommy Davis	1962
Walks	148	Eddie Stanky	1945
Most strikeouts	149	Bill Grabarkewitz	1970
Fewest strikeouts	15	Jim Johnston	1923
Batting average	.393	Babe Herman	1930
Slugging pct.	.678	Babe Herman	1930
Stolen bases	104	Maury Wills	1962

Pitching

Games	106	Mike Marshall	1974
Complete games	40	Brickyard Kennedy	1893
Innings	382.2	Brickyard Kennedy	1893
Wins	30	Tom Lovett	1890
Losses	27	George Bell	1910
Winning pct.	.933 (14-1)	Phil Regan	1966
Walks	152	Bill Donovan	1901
Strikeouts	382	Sandy Koufax	1965
Shutouts	11	Sandy Koufax	1963
Home runs allowed	38	Don Sutton	1970
Lowest ERA	1.58	Rube Marquard	1916
Saves	52	Eric Gagne	2002

GAME

Batting

Runs	6	Shawn Green	5-23-2002
Hits	6	Last by Shawn Green	5-23-2002
Doubles	3	Last by Eric Karros	4-9-99
Triples	3	Jimmy Sheckard	4-18-01
Home runs	4	Gil Hodges	8-31-50
		Shawn Green	5-23-2002
RBIs	9	Gil Hodges	8-31-50
		Ron Cey	7-31-74
Total bases	19	Shawn Green	5-23-2002
Stolen bases	5	Davey Lopes	8-24-74

HISTORY

CAREER LEADERS

BATTING

Games
Player	G
Zack Wheat	2,322
Bill Russell	2,181
Pee Wee Reese	2,166
Gil Hodges	2,006
Jim Gilliam	1,956
Willie Davis	1,952
Duke Snider	1,923
Carl Furillo	1,806
Steve Garvey	1,727
Eric Karros	1,601

At-bats
Player	AB
Zack Wheat	8,859
Pee Wee Reese	8,058
Willie Davis	7,495
Bill Russell	7,318
Jim Gilliam	7,119
Gil Hodges	6,881
Duke Snider	6,640
Steve Garvey	6,543
Carl Furillo	6,378
Maury Wills	6,156

Runs
Player	R
Pee Wee Reese	1,338
Zack Wheat	1,255
Duke Snider	1,199
Jim Gilliam	1,163
Gil Hodges	1,088
Willie Davis	1,004
Jackie Robinson	947
Carl Furillo	895
Mike Griffin	882
Maury Wills	876

Hits
Player	H
Zack Wheat	2,804
Pee Wee Reese	2,170
Willie Davis	2,091
Duke Snider	1,995
Steve Garvey	1,968
Bill Russell	1,926
Carl Furillo	1,910
Jim Gilliam	1,889
Gil Hodges	1,884
Maury Wills	1,732

Doubles
Player	2B
Zack Wheat	464
Duke Snider	343
Steve Garvey	333
Pee Wee Reese	330
Carl Furillo	324
Willie Davis	321
Jim Gilliam	304
Eric Karros	302
Gil Hodges	294
Bill Russell	293

Triples
Player	3B
Zack Wheat	171
Willie Davis	110
Hy Myers	97
Jake Daubert	87
John Hummel	82
Duke Snider	82
Pee Wee Reese	80
Tom Daly	76
Jimmy Sheckard	76
Jimmy Johnston	73

Home runs
Player	HR
Duke Snider	389
Gil Hodges	361
Eric Karros	270
Roy Campanella	242
Ron Cey	228
Steve Garvey	211
Carl Furillo	192
Mike Piazza	177
Pedro Guerrero	171
Raul Mondesi	163

Total bases
Player	TB
Zack Wheat	4,003
Duke Snider	3,669
Gil Hodges	3,357
Willie Davis	3,094
Pee Wee Reese	3,038
Steve Garvey	3,004
Carl Furillo	2,922
Eric Karros	2,740
Jim Gilliam	2,530
Bill Russell	2,471

Runs batted in
Player	RBI
Duke Snider	1,271
Gil Hodges	1,254
Zack Wheat	1,210
Carl Furillo	1,058
Steve Garvey	992
Eric Karros	976
Pee Wee Reese	885
Roy Campanella	856
Willie Davis	849
Ron Cey	842

Extra-base hits
Player	XBH
Duke Snider	814
Zack Wheat	766
Gil Hodges	703
Willie Davis	585
Eric Karros	582
Steve Garvey	579
Carl Furillo	572
Pee Wee Reese	536
Ron Cey	469
Jackie Robinson	464

Batting average
(Minimum 500 games)

Player	Avg.
Willie Keeler	.352
Babe Herman	.339
Jack Fournier	.337
Mike Piazza	.331
Zack Wheat	.317
Babe Phelps	.315
Manny Mota	.315
Fielder Jones	.313
Gary Sheffield	.312
Jackie Robinson	.311

Stolen bases
Player	SB
Maury Wills	490
Davey Lopes	418
Willie Davis	335
Tom Daly	298
Steve Sax	290
Mike Griffin	264
Pee Wee Reese	232
Jimmy Sheckard	212
Jim Gilliam	203
Zack Wheat	203

PITCHING

Earned-run average
(Minimum 1,000 innings)

Player	ERA
Jeff Pfeffer	2.31
Nap Rucker	2.42
Sandy Koufax	2.76
George Bell	2.85
Whit Wyatt	2.86
Sherry Smith	2.91
Don Drysdale	2.95
Doc Scanlan	2.96
Tommy John	2.97
Bill Singer	3.03

Wins
Player	W
Don Sutton	233
Don Drysdale	209
Dazzy Vance	190
Brickyard Kennedy	177
Sandy Koufax	165
Burleigh Grimes	158
Claude Osteen	147
Fernando Valenzuela	141
Johnny Podres	136
Orel Hershiser	135

Losses
Player	L
Don Sutton	181
Don Drysdale	166
Brickyard Kennedy	149
Nap Rucker	134
Dazzy Vance	131
Claude Osteen	126
Burleigh Grimes	121
Fernando Valenzuela	116
Orel Hershiser	107
Johnny Podres	104

Innings pitched
Player	IP
Don Sutton	3,816.1
Don Drysdale	3,432.0
Brickyard Kennedy	2,866.0
Dazzy Vance	2,757.2
Burleigh Grimes	2,425.2
Claude Osteen	2,396.2
Nap Rucker	2,375.1
Fernando Valenzuela	2,348.2
Sandy Koufax	2,324.1
Orel Hershiser	2,180.2

Strikeouts
Player	SO
Don Sutton	2,696
Don Drysdale	2,486
Sandy Koufax	2,396
Dazzy Vance	1,918
Fernando Valenzuela	1,759
Orel Hershiser	1,456
Johnny Podres	1,331
Ramon Martinez	1,314
Bob Welch	1,292
Nap Rucker	1,217

Bases on balls
Player	BB
Brickyard Kennedy	1,130
Don Sutton	996
Fernando Valenzuela	915
Don Drysdale	855
Sandy Koufax	817
Dazzy Vance	764
Burleigh Grimes	744
Ramon Martinez	704
Nap Rucker	701
Van Mungo	697

Games
Player	G
Don Sutton	550
Don Drysdale	518
Jim Brewer	474
Ron Perranoski	457
Clem Labine	425
Charlie Hough	401
Sandy Koufax	397
Brickyard Kennedy	382
Dazzy Vance	378
Johnny Podres	366

Shutouts
Player	ShO
Don Sutton	52
Don Drysdale	49
Sandy Koufax	40
Nap Rucker	38
Claude Osteen	34
Fernando Valenzuela	29
Dazzy Vance	29
Jeff Pfeffer	25
Orel Hershiser	24
Johnny Podres	23
Bob Welch	23

Saves
Player	SV
Jeff Shaw	129
Todd Worrell	127
Jim Brewer	125
Ron Perranoski	101
Jay Howell	85
Clem Labine	83
Tom Niedenfuer	64
Charlie Hough	60
Steve Howe	59
Eric Gagne	52

TEAM SEASON, GAME RECORDS

SEASON

Batting
Record	No.	Year
Most at-bats	5,642	1982
Most runs	1,021	1894
Fewest runs	375	1908
Most hits	1,654	1930
Most singles	1,223	1925
Most doubles	303	1930
Most triples	130	1894
Most home runs	211	2000
Fewest home runs	14	1915
Most grand slams	8	1952, 2000
Most pinch-hit home runs	12	2000
Most total bases	2,545	1953
Most stolen bases	409	1892
Highest batting average	.313	1894
Lowest batting average	.213	1908
Highest slugging pct.	.474	1953

Pitching
Record	No.	Year
Lowest ERA	2.12	1916
Highest ERA	4.92	1929
Most complete games	135	1904
Most shutouts	24	1963, 1988
Most saves	56	2002
Most walks	671	1946
Most strikeouts	1,212	1996, 2001

Fielding
Record	No.	Year
Most errors	432	1891
Fewest errors	90	2002
Most double plays	198	1958
Highest fielding average	.985	2002

General
Record	No.	Year
Most games won	105	1953
Most games lost	104	1905
Highest win pct.	.682	1953
Lowest win pct.	.316	1905

GAME, INNING

Batting
Record	No.	Date
Most runs, game	25	5-20-1896, 9-23-01
Most runs, inning	15	5-21-52
Most hits, game	28	6-23-30, 8-22-17
Most home runs, game	8	5-23-2002
Most total bases, game	48	8-20-74

Smooth-fielding first baseman Steve Garvey was a five-time member of the Dodgers' 100-RBI fraternity.

DODGERS YEAR-BY-YEAR

Year	W	L	Place	Games Back	Manager	Leaders: Batting avg.	Hits	Home runs	RBIs	Wins	ERA
						BROOKLYN DODGERS					
1901	79	57	3rd	9½	Hanlon	Sheckard, .354	Keeler, 202	Sheckard, 11	Sheckard, 104	Donovan, 25	Donovan, 2.77
1902	75	63	2nd	27½	Hanlon	Keeler, .333	Keeler, 186	McCreery, Sheckard, 4	Dahlen, 74	Kitson, 19	Newton, 2.42
1903	70	66	5th	19	Hanlon	Sheckard, .332	Sheckard, 171	Sheckard, 9	Doyle, 91	Schmidt, 22	O. Jones, 2.94
1904	56	97	6th	50	Hanlon	Lumley, .279	Lumley, 161	Lumley, 9	Lumley, 78	O. Jones, 17	Garvin, 1.68
1905	48	104	8th	56½	Hanlon	Lumley, .293	Lumley, 148	Lumley, 7	Batch, 49	Scanlan, 14	Scanlan, 2.92
1906	66	86	5th	50	Donovan	Lumley, .324	Lumley, 157	Jordan, 12	Jordan, 78	Scanlan, 18	Stricklett, 2.72
1907	65	83	5th	40	Donovan	Jordan, .274	Jordan, 133	Lumley, 9	Lumley, 66	Pastorius, 16	Rucker, 2.06
1908	53	101	7th	46	Donovan	Jordan, .247	Hummel, 143	Jordan, 12	Jordan, 60	Rucker, 17	Wilhelm, 1.87
1909	55	98	6th	55½	Lumley	Hummel, .280	Burch, 163	Hummel, 4	Hummel, 52	Bell, 16	Rucker, 2.24
1910	64	90	6th	40	Dahlen	Wheat, .284	Wheat, 172	Daubert, 8	Hummel, 74	Rucker, 17	Rucker, 2.58
1911	64	86	7th	33½	Dahlen	Daubert, .307	Daubert, 176	Erwin, 7	Wheat, 76	Rucker, 22	Ragan, 2.11
1912	58	95	7th	46	Dahlen	Daubert, .308	Daubert, 172	Wheat, 8	Daubert, 66	Rucker, 18	Rucker, 2.21
1913	65	84	6th	34½	Dahlen	Daubert, .350	Daubert, 178	Cutshaw, Stengel, Wheat, 7	Cutshaw, 80	Ragan, 15	Reulbach, 2.05
1914	75	79	5th	19½	Robinson	Daubert, .329	Wheat, 170	Wheat, 9	Wheat, 89	Pfeffer, 23	Pfeffer, 1.97
1915	80	72	3rd	10	Robinson	Daubert, .301	Daubert, 164	Wheat, 5	Wheat, 66	Pfeffer, 19	Pfeffer, 2.10
1916	94	60	1st	+2½	Robinson	Daubert, .316	Wheat, 177	Wheat, 9	Wheat, 73	Pfeffer, 25	Marquard, 1.58
1917	70	81	7th	26½	Robinson	Wheat, .312	Olson, 156	Hickman, Stengel, 6	Stengel, 73	Marquard, 19	Pfeffer, 2.23
1918	57	69	5th	25½	Robinson	Wheat, .335	Wheat, 137	Myers, 4	Wheat, 51	Grimes, 19	Grimes, 2.14
1919	69	71	5th	27	Robinson	Myers, .307	Olson, 164	Griffith, 6	Myers, 73	Pfeffer, 17	S. Smith, 2.24
1920	93	61	1st	+7	Robinson	Wheat, .328	Wheat, 191	Wheat, 9	Myers, 80	Grimes, 23	S. Smith, 1.85
1921	77	75	5th	16½	Robinson	Kilduff, .388	J. Johnston, 203	Wheat, 14	Wheat, 85	Grimes, 22	Grimes, 2.83
1922	76	78	6th	17	Robinson	Wheat, .335	Wheat, 201	Wheat, 16	Wheat, 112	Ruether, 21	Shriver, 2.99
1923	76	78	6th	19½	Robinson	Fournier, .351	J. Johnston, 203	Fournier, 22	Fournier, 102	Grimes, 21	Decatur, 2.58
1924	92	62	2nd	1½	Robinson	Wheat, .375	Wheat, 212	Fournier, 27	Fournier, 116	Vance, 28	Vance, 2.16
1925	68	85	*6th	27	Robinson	Wheat, .359	Wheat, 221	Fournier, 22	Fournier, 130	Vance, 22	Vance, 3.53
1926	71	82	6th	17½	Robinson	Herman, .319	Herman, 158	Fournier, Herman, 11	Herman, 81	Petty, 17	Petty, 2.84
1927	65	88	6th	28½	Robinson	Hendrick, .310	Partridge, 149	Herman, 14	Herman, 73	Vance, 16	Vance, 2.70
1928	77	76	6th	17½	Robinson	Herman, .340	Bissonette, 188	Bissonette, 25	Bissonette, 106	Vance, 22	Vance, 2.09
1929	70	83	6th	28½	Robinson	Herman, .381	Herman, 217	Frederick, 24	Herman, 113	Clark, 16	Clark, 3.74
1930	86	68	4th	6	Robinson	Herman, .393	Herman, 241	Herman, 35	Herman, 130	Vance, 17	Vance, 2.61
1931	79	73	4th	21	Robinson	O'Doul, .336	Herman, 191	Herman, 18	Herman, 97	Clark, 14	Clark, 3.20
1932	81	73	3rd	9	Carey	O'Doul, .368	O'Doul, 219	H. Wilson, 23	H. Wilson, 123	Clark, 20	Clark, 3.49
1933	65	88	6th	26½	Carey	Frederick, .308	Frederick, 171	Cuccinello, D. Taylor, H. Wilson, 9	Cuccinello, 65	Mungo, 16	Mungo, 2.72
1934	71	81	6th	23½	Stengel	Leslie, .332	Leslie, 181	Cuccinello, Koenecke, 14	Leslie, 102	Mungo, 18	Leonard, 3.28
1935	70	83	5th	29½	Stengel	Leslie, .308	Leslie, 160	Frey, 11	Leslie, 93	Mungo, 16	Clark, 3.30
1936	67	87	7th	25	Stengel	Stripp, .317	Hassett, 197	Phelps, 5	Hassett, 82	Mungo, 18	Mungo, 3.35
1937	62	91	6th	33½	Grimes	Manush, .333	Hassett, 169	Lavagetto, 8	Manush, 73	Butcher, Hamlin, 11	Mungo, 2.91
1938	69	80	7th	18½	Grimes	Koy, .299	Koy, 156	Camilli, 24	Camilli, 100	Hamlin, Tamulis, 12	Fitzsimmons, 3.02
1939	84	69	3rd	12½	Durocher	Lavagetto, .300	Lavagetto, 176	Camilli, 26	Camilli, 104	Hamlin, 20	Wyatt, 2.31
1940	88	65	2nd	12	Durocher	Walker, .308	Walker, 171	Camilli, 23	Camilli, 96	Fitzsimmons, 16	Fitzsimmons, 2.81
1941	100	54	1st	+2½	Durocher	Reiser, .343	Reiser, 184	Camilli, 34	Camilli, 120	Higbe, Wyatt, 22	Wyatt, 2.34
1942	104	50	2nd	2	Durocher	Reiser, .310	Medwick, 166	Camilli, 26	Camilli, 109	Wyatt, 19	French, 1.83
1943	81	72	3rd	23½	Durocher	Herman, .330	Herman, 193	Galan, 9	Herman, 100	Wyatt, 14	Wyatt, 2.49
1944	63	91	7th	42	Durocher	Walker, .357	Walker, 191	Walker, 13	Galan, 93	C. Davis, 10	C. Davis, 3.34
1945	87	67	3rd	11	Durocher	Rosen, .325	Rosen, 197	Rosen, 12	Walker, 124	Gregg, 18	Branca, 3.03
1946	96	60	†2nd	2	Durocher	Walker, .319	Walker, 184	Reiser, 11	Walker, 116	Higbe, 17	Casey, Melton, 1.99
1947	94	60	1st	+5	Sukeforth, Shotton	Reiser, .309	Robinson, 175	Reese, Robinson, 12	Walker, 94	Branca, 21	Branca, 2.67
1948	84	70	3rd	7½	Durocher, Shotton	Furillo, .297	Robinson, 170	Hermanski, 15	Robinson, 85	Barney, 15	Roe, 2.63
1949	97	57	1st	+1	Shotton	Robinson, .342	Robinson, 203	Hodges, Snider, 23	Robinson, 124	Newcombe, 17	Roe, 2.79
1950	89	65	2nd	2	Shotton	Robinson, .328	Snider, 199	Hodges, 32	Hodges, 113	Newcombe, Roe, 19	Roe, 3.30
1951	97	60	†2nd	1	Dressen	Robinson, .338	Furillo, 197	Hodges, 40	Campanella, 108	Roe, 22	Roe, 3.04
1952	96	57	1st	+4½	Dressen	Robinson, .308	Snider, 162	Hodges, 32	Hodges, 102	Black, 15	Black, 2.15
1953	105	49	1st	+13	Dressen	Furillo, .344	Snider, 198	Snider, 42	Campanella, 142	Erskine, 20	Labine, 2.77
1954	92	62	2nd	5	Alston	Snider, .341	Snider, 199	Hodges, 42	Hodges, Snider, 130	Erskine, 18	Meyer, 3.99
1955	98	55	1st	+13½	Alston	Campanella, .318	Snider, 166	Snider, 42	Snider, 136	Newcombe, 20	Craig, 2.78
1956	93	61	1st	+1	Alston	Gilliam, .300	Gilliam, 178	Snider, 43	Snider, 101	Newcombe, 27	Drysdale, 2.64
1957	84	70	3rd	11	Alston	Furillo, .306	Hodges, 173	Snider, 40	Hodges, 98	Drysdale, 17	Podres, 2.66
						LOS ANGELES DODGERS					
1958	71	83	7th	21	Alston	Furillo, .290	Gilliam, 145	Hodges, Neal, 22	Furillo, 83	Podres, 13	Podres, 3.73
1959	88	68	‡1st	+2	Alston	Snider, .308	Neal, 177	Hodges, 25	Snider, 88	Drysdale, 17	Drysdale, 3.45
1960	82	72	4th	13	Alston	Larker, .323	Wills, 152	Howard, 23	Larker, 78	Drysdale, 15	Drysdale, 2.84
1961	89	65	2nd	4	Alston	Moon, .328	Wills, 173	Roseboro, 18	Moon, 88	Koufax, Podres, 18	Perranoski, 2.65
1962	102	63	†2nd	1	Alston	T. Davis, .346	T. Davis, 230	Howard, 31	T. Davis, 153	Drysdale, 25	Koufax, 2.54
1963	99	63	1st	+6	Alston	T. Davis, .326	T. Davis, 181	Howard, 28	T. Davis, 88	Koufax, 25	Koufax, 1.88
1964	80	82	*6th	13	Alston	W. Davis, .294	W. Davis, 180	Howard, 24	T. Davis, 86	Koufax, 19	Koufax, 1.74
1965	97	65	1st	+2	Alston	Wills, .286	Wills, 186	Johnson, Lefebvre, 12	Fairly, 70	Koufax, 26	Koufax, 2.04
1966	95	67	1st	+1½	Alston	Fairly, .288	W. Davis, 177	Lefebvre, 24	Lefebvre, 74	Koufax, 27	Koufax, 1.73
1967	73	89	8th	28½	Alston	Hunt, .263	W. Davis, 146	Ferrara, 16	Fairly, 55	Osteen, 17	Perranoski, 2.45
1968	76	86	7th	21	Alston	Haller, .285	W. Davis, 161	Gabrielson, 10	Haller, 53	Drysdale, 14	Drysdale, 2.15
						WEST DIVISION					
1969	85	77	4th	8	Alston	W. Davis, .311	Sizemore, 160	Kosco, 19	Kosco, 74	Osteen, Singer, 20	Singer, 2.34
1970	87	74	2nd	14½	Alston	Parker, .319	Parker, 196	Grabarkewitz, 17	Parker, 111	Osteen, 16	Singer, Vance, 3.13
1971	89	73	2nd	1	Alston	W. Davis, .309	W. Davis, 198	Allen, 23	Allen, 90	Downing, 20	Brewer, 1.89
1972	85	70	3rd	10½	Alston	Mota, .323	W. Davis, 178	W. Davis, Robinson, 19	W. Davis, 79	Osteen, 20	Sutton, 2.08
1973	95	66	2nd	3½	Alston	Crawford, .295	W. Davis, 171	Ferguson, 25	Ferguson, 88	Sutton, 18	Sutton, 2.42
1974	102	60	§1st	+4	Alston	Buckner, .314	Garvey, 200	Wynn, 32	Garvey, 111	Messersmith, 20	Marshall, 2.42
1975	88	74	2nd	20	Alston	Garvey, .319	Garvey, 210	Cey, 25	Cey, 101	Messersmith, 19	Messersmith, 2.29
1976	92	70	2nd	10	Alston, Lasorda	Garvey, .317	Garvey, 200	Cey, 23	Cey, Garvey, 80	Sutton, 21	Hough, 2.20
1977	98	64	§1st	+10	Lasorda	R. Smith, .307	Garvey, 192	Garvey, 33	Garvey, 115	John, 20	Hooton, 2.62
1978	95	67	§1st	+2½	Lasorda	Garvey, .316	Garvey, 202	R. Smith, 29	Garvey, 113	Hooton, 19	Welch, 2.03
1979	79	83	3rd	11½	Lasorda	Garvey, .315	Garvey, 204	Cey, Garvey, Lopes, 28	Garvey, 110	Sutcliffe, 17	Hooton, 2.97
1980	92	71	∞2nd	1	Lasorda	Garvey, .304	Garvey, 200	Baker, 29	Garvey, 106	Reuss, 18	Sutton, 2.20
1981	63	47	▲§1st/4th	—	Lasorda	Baker, .320	Baker, 128	Cey, 13	Garvey, 64	Valenzuela, 13	Hooton, 2.28
1982	88	74	2nd	1	Lasorda	Guerrero, .304	Sax, 180	Guerrero, 32	Guerrero, 100	Valenzuela, 19	Howe, 2.08
1983	91	71	◆1st	+3	Lasorda	Guerrero, .298	Sax, 175	Guerrero, 32	Guerrero, 103	Valenzuela, Welch, 15	Niedenfuer, 1.90
1984	79	83	4th	13	Lasorda	Guerrero, .303	Guerrero, 162	Marshall, 21	Guerrero, 72	Welch, 13	Pena, 2.48
1985	95	67	◆1st	+5½	Lasorda	Guerrero, .320	Guerrero, 156	Guerrero, 33	Marshall, 95	Hershiser, 19	Hershiser, 2.03
1986	73	89	5th	23	Lasorda	Sax, .332	Sax, 210	Stubbs, 23	Madlock, 60	Valenzuela, 21	Valenzuela, 3.14
1987	73	89	4th	17	Lasorda	Guerrero, .338	Guerrero, 184	Guerrero, 27	Guerrero, 89	Hershiser, 16	Hershiser, 3.06
1988	94	67	§1st	+7	Lasorda	Gibson, .290	Sax, 175	Gibson, 25	Marshall, 82	Hershiser, 23	Pena, 1.91
1989	77	83	4th	14	Lasorda	Randolph, .282	Randolph, 155	Murray, 20	Murray, 88	Belcher, Hershiser, 15	Hershiser, 2.31
1990	86	76	2nd	5	Lasorda	Murray, .330	Murray, 184	Daniels, 27	Murray, 95	R. Martinez, 20	Crews, 2.77
1991	93	69	2nd	1	Lasorda	Butler, .296	Butler, 182	Strawberry, 28	Strawberry, 99	R. Martinez, 17	Belcher, 2.62
1992	63	99	6th	35	Lasorda	Butler, .309	Butler, 171	Karros, 20	Karros, 88	Candiotti, 11	Astacio, 1.98
1993	81	81	4th	23	Lasorda	Piazza, .318	Butler, 181	Piazza, 35	Piazza, 112	Astacio, 14	P. Martinez, 2.61
1994	58	56	1st	+3½	Lasorda	Piazza, .319	Mondesi, 133	Piazza, 24	Piazza, 92	R. Martinez, 12	Gross, 3.60
1995	78	66	■1st	+1	Lasorda	Piazza, .346	Karros, 164	Karros, Piazza, 32	Karros, 105	Martinez, 17	Nomo, 2.54
1996	90	72	■2nd	1	Lasorda, Russell	Piazza, .336	Mondesi, 188	Piazza, 36	Karros, 111	Nomo, 16	Nomo, 3.19
1997	88	74	2nd	2	Russell	Piazza, .362	Piazza, 201	Piazza, 40	Piazza, 124	Nomo, Park, 14	Valdes, 2.65
1998	83	79	3rd	15	Russell, Hoffman	Sheffield, .302	Mondesi, 162	Mondesi, 30	Mondesi, 90	Perez, Valdes, 11	Bohanon, 2.67
1999	77	85	3rd	23	Johnson	Grudzielanek, .326	Karros, 176	Karros, Sheffield, 34	Karros, 112	Brown, 18	Brown, 3.00
2000	86	76	2nd	11	Johnson	Sheffield, .325	Grudzielanek, 172	Sheffield, 43	Sheffield, 109	Park, 18	Brown, 2.58
2001	86	76	3rd	6	Tracy	LoDuca, .320	Green, 184	Green, 49	Green, 125	Park, 15	Brown, 2.65
2002	92	70	3rd	6	Tracy	Green, Jordan, .285	Green, 166	Green, 42	Green, 114	Nomo, 16	Perez, 3.00

* Tied for position. † Lost pennant playoff. ‡ Won pennant playoff. § Won Championship Series. ∞ Lost division playoff. ▲ First half 36-21; second half 27-26. ◆ Lost Championship Series. ■ Lost Division Series.

Note: Batting average minimum 350 at-bats; ERA minimum 90 innings pitched.

MILWAUKEE BREWERS

FRANCHISE CHRONOLOGY

First season: 1969, in Seattle, as part of a two-team American League expansion. The Pilots defeated California, 4-3, in their Major League debut, but that's about the only thing that went right. By season's end, the Pilots were resting in the cellar of the A.L. West Division with 98 losses and battling serious financial problems. Before the 1970 campaign could get under way, Seattle already held distinction as a here-today-gone-tomorrow Major League city.

1970-present: Baseball, American League-style, returned to Milwaukee after a four-year absence when the Pilots were shifted from Seattle and renamed the Brewers. Milwaukee, former home of the National League Braves, lost its A.L. debut, 12-0, to the Angels and posted only one more victory in its first season than the Pilots had in Seattle. It would take eight years for the Brewers to enjoy a winning season and 11 before they would qualify for postseason play—a one-time division playoff set up because of the 1981 players' strike. Milwaukee's banner season came a year later when the Brewers won their only A.L. pennant and dropped a seven-game World Series heartbreaker to St. Louis. The team made history after the 1997 season when it switched from the American League to the National League—the first ever to make such a crossover.

Shortstop/outfielder Robin Yount.

BREWERS VS. A.L. OPPONENTS BY DECADE

	A's	Indians	Orioles	Red Sox	Tigers	Twins	White Sox	Yankees	Angels	Rangers	Royals	Blue Jays	Mariners	Interleague	Decade Record
1969	5-13	5-7	3-9	6-6	2-10	6-12	8-10	5-7	9-9	7-5	8-10				64-98
1970-79	54-74	78-75	54-100	63-93	66-91	54-75	62-68	74-83	67-61	67-49	48-80	30-13	21-11		738-873
1980-89	50-64	70-56	59-64	67-62	64-66	68-52	58-55	62-61	54-61	63-52	59-58	71-56	59-53		804-760
1990-97	50-35	41-56	45-52	47-50	56-42	52-46	41-56	39-56	37-47	44-46	47-50	52-45	35-48	8-7	594-636
Totals	159-186	194-194	161-225	183-211	188-209	180-185	169-189	180-207	167-178	181-152	162-198	153-114	115-112	8-7	2200-2367

Interleague results: 1-2 vs. Cubs; 0-3 vs. Reds; 2-1 vs. Astros; 2-1 vs. Pirates; 3-0 vs. Cardinals.

BREWERS VS. N.L. OPPONENTS BY DECADE

	Braves	Cardinals	Cubs	Dodgers	Giants	Phillies	Pirates	Reds	Astros	Mets	Expos	Padres	Marlins	Rockies	D'backs	Interleague	Decade Record
1998-99	4-12	10-14	12-12	6-12	9-9	9-9	14-9	11-12	7-17	3-13	11-7	6-11	13-5	10-10	7-11	16-12	148-175
2000-02	7-14	19-27	26-21	6-13	9-15	6-13	17-31	24-24	19-29	6-15	10-11	8-13	8-11	9-12	10-11	13-29	197-289
Totals	11-26	29-41	38-33	12-25	18-24	15-22	31-40	35-36	26-46	9-28	21-18	14-24	21-16	19-22	17-22	29-41	345-464

Interleague results: 0-3 vs. Angels, 4-8 vs. White Sox, 5-7 vs. Indians, 6-6 vs. Tigers, 7-5 vs. Royals, 7-9 vs. Twins, 0-3 vs. Athletics.

MANAGERS

(Seattle Pilots, 1969)

Name	*Years*	*Record*
Joe Schultz	1969	64-98
Dave Bristol	1970-72	144-209
Del Crandall	1972-75	271-338
Alex Grammas	1976-77	133-190
George Bamberger	1978-80, 1985-86	377-351
Buck Rodgers	1980-82	124-102
Harvey Kuenn	1982-83	160-118
Rene Lachemann	1984	67-94
Tom Trebelhorn	1986-91	422-397
Phil Garner	1992-99	563-617

Paul Molitor's journey to 3,000 career hits started in Milwaukee.

MANAGERS—*cont'd.*

Name	*Years*	*Record*
Jim Lefebvre	1999	22-27
Davey Lopes	2000-02	144-195
Jerry Royster	2002	53-94

A.L. PENNANT WINNERS

Year	*Record*	*Manager*	*Series Result*
1982	95-67	Rodgers, Kuenn	Lost to Cardinals

EAST DIVISION CHAMPIONS

Year	*Record*	*Manager*	*ALCS Result*
*1981	62-47	Rodgers	None
1982	95-67	Rodgers, Kuenn	Defeated Angels

* Second-half champion; lost division playoff to Yankees.

ALL-TIME RECORD OF EXPANSION TEAMS

Team	W	L	Pct.	DT	P	WS
Arizona	440	370	.543	3	1	1
Kansas City	2,675	2,694	.498	6	2	1
Houston	3,229	3,285	.496	7	0	0
Toronto	2,025	2,063	.495	5	2	2
Anaheim	3,243	3,431	.486	3	1	1
Montreal	2,605	2,769	.485	2	0	0
Colorado	740	817	.475	0	0	0
New York	3,091	3,412	.475	4	4	2
Milwaukee	2,545	2,831	.473	2	1	0
Seattle	1,924	2,163	.471	3	0	0
Texas	3,097	3,560	.465	4	0	0
San Diego	2,460	2,921	.457	3	2	0
Florida	706	847	.455	0	1	1
Tampa Bay	318	490	.394	0	0	0

DT—Division Titles. P—Pennants won. WS—World Series won.

ATTENDANCE HIGHS

Total	*Season*	*Park*
2,811,041	2001	Miller Park
2,397,131	1983	County Stadium
1,978,896	1982	County Stadium
1,970,735	1989	County Stadium
1,969,693	2002	Miller Park

BALLPARK CHRONOLOGY

Miller Park (2001-present)

Capacity: 41,900.
First game: Brewers 5, Cincinnati 4 (April 6, 2001).
First batter: Barry Larkin, Reds.
First hit: Sean Casey, Reds (single).
First run: Barry Larkin, Reds (4th inning).
First home run: Michael Tucker, Reds (4th inning).
First winning pitcher: David Weathers, Brewers.
First-season attendance: 2,811,041.

County Stadium (1970-2000)

Capacity: 53,192.
First game: California 12, Brewers 0 (April 7, 1970).
First-season attendance: 933,690.

Sick's Stadium, Seattle (1969)

Capacity: 25,420.
First game: Pilots 7, Chicago 0 (April 11, 1969).
First-season attendance: 677,944.

A.L. MVPs

Rollie Fingers, P, 1981
Robin Yount, SS, 1982
Robin Yount, OF, 1989

CY YOUNG WINNERS

Rollie Fingers, RH, 1981
Pete Vuckovich, RH, 1982

ROOKIE OF THE YEAR

Pat Listach, SS, 1992

RETIRED UNIFORMS

No.	*Name*	*Pos.*
4	Paul Molitor	3B-DH
19	Robin Yount	SS-OF
34	Rollie Fingers	P
44	Hank Aaron	OF

MILESTONE PERFORMANCES

25-plus home runs

45— Gorman Thomas 1979
Richie Sexson 2001
41— Ben Oglivie 1980
39— Gorman Thomas 1982
38— Gorman Thomas 1980
Jeromy Burnitz 1998
36— George Scott 1975
34— Larry Hisle 1978
Ben Oglivie 1982
John Jaha 1996
Geoff Jenkins 2000
Jeromy Burnitz 2001
33— Rob Deer 1986
Jeromy Burnitz 1999
32— Gorman Thomas 1978
Cecil Cooper 1982
31— Tommy Harper 1970
Greg Vaughn 1996
Jeromy Burnitz 2000
30— Cecil Cooper 1983
Greg Vaughn 1993
29— Ben Oglivie 1979
Robin Yount 1982
Rob Deer 1987
Richie Sexson 2002
28— Sixto Lezcano 1979
27— Rob Deer 1990
Greg Vaughn 1991
Jeromy Burnitz 1997
26— Rob Deer 1989
25— Don Mincher 1969
Dave May 1973
Don Money 1977
Cecil Cooper 1980
Dale Sveum 1987
Jose Hernandez 2001

100-plus RBIs

126— Cecil Cooper 1983
125— Jeromy Burnitz 1998
Richie Sexson 2001
123— Gorman Thomas 1979
122— Cecil Cooper 1980
121— Cecil Cooper 1982
118— Ben Oglivie 1980
John Jaha 1996
115— Larry Hisle 1978
114— Robin Yount 1982
112— Gorman Thomas 1982
109— George Scott 1975
108— Ted Simmons 1983
107— George Scott 1973
106— Cecil Cooper 1979
105— Gorman Thomas 1980
103— Robin Yount 1987, 1989
Jeromy Burnitz 1999
102— Ben Oglivie 1982
Richie Sexson 2002
101— Sixto Lezcano 1979
100— Jeromy Burnitz 2001

20-plus victories

1973— Jim Colborn 20-12
1978— Mike Caldwell 22-9
1986— Teddy Higuera 20-11

A.L. home run champions

1975— George Scott *36
1979— Gorman Thomas 45
1980— Ben Oglivie *41
1982— Gorman Thomas *39

* Tied for league lead

A.L. RBI champions

1975— George Scott 109
1980— Cecil Cooper 122
1983— Cecil Cooper *126

* Tied for league lead

A.L. batting champions

None

A.L. ERA champions

None

A.L. strikeout champions

None

No-hit pitchers

(9 innings or more)

1987— Juan Nieves .... 7-0 vs. Baltimore

Longest hitting streaks

39— Paul Molitor 1987
24— Dave May 1973
22— Cecil Cooper 1980
19— Robin Yount 1989
Paul Molitor 1989, 1990
Darryl Hamilton 1991
18— Robin Yount 1980
17— Cecil Cooper 1982
Paul Molitor 1982
Pat Listach 1992
16— John Briggs 1974
Robin Yount 1976
Cecil Cooper 1979
Paul Molitor 1979, 1985
Ben Oglivie 1979, 1983
Ted Simmons 1983
Gary Sheffield 1990
Greg Vaughn 1991
Mark Loretta 2001
15— Billy Conigliaro 1972
Don Money 1973
Paul Molitor 1978
Darryl Hamilton 1991, 1992
B.J. Surhoff 1993
Kevin Seitzer 1994
Greg Vaughn 1996

Dependable second baseman Jim Gantner played 1,801 games in a Brewers uniform, third on the team's all-time list.

INDIVIDUAL SEASON, GAME RECORDS

Slugging outfielder Gorman Thomas topped the 30-home run plateau four times in the 1970s and '80s.

SEASON

Batting			
At-bats	666	Paul Molitor	1982
Runs	136	Paul Molitor	1982
Hits	219	Cecil Cooper	1980
Singles	157	Cecil Cooper	1980
Doubles	49	Robin Yount	1980
Triples	16	Paul Molitor	1979
Home runs	45	Gorman Thomas	1979
		Richie Sexson	2001
Home runs, rookie	17	Danny Walton	1970
		Greg Vaughn	1990
Grand slams	3	John Jaha	1995
		Devon White	2001
Total bases	367	Robin Yount	1982
RBIs	126	Cecil Cooper	1983
Walks	99	Jeromy Burnitz	2000
Most strikeouts	188	Jose Hernandez	2002
Fewest strikeouts	35	Fernando Vina	1996
Batting average	.353	Paul Molitor	1987
Slugging pct.	.578	Robin Yount	1982
Stolen bases	73	Tommy Harper	1969
Pitching			
Games	83	Ken Sanders	1971
Complete games	23	Mike Caldwell	1978
Innings	314.1	Jim Colborn	1973
Wins	22	Mike Caldwell	1978
Losses	20	Clyde Wright	1974
Winning pct.	.846 (11-2)	Cal Eldred	1992
Walks	106	Pete Broberg	1975
Strikeouts	240	Teddy Higuera	1987
Shutouts	6	Mike Caldwell	1978
Home runs allowed	35	Mike Caldwell	1983
Lowest ERA	2.36	Mike Caldwell	1978
Saves	37	Bob Wickman	1999

GAME

Batting			
Runs	4	Last by Richie Sexson	5-31-2002
Hits	6	John Briggs	8-4-73
		Kevin Reimer	8-24-93
Doubles	3	Last by Richie Sexson	9-7-2002
Triples	2	Last by Jose Valentin	9-29-99
Home runs	3	Last by Jeromy Burnitz	9-25-2001
RBIs	7	Last by Richie Sexson	4-18-2002
Total bases	13	Paul Molitor	5-12-82
		Fernando Vina	9-12-96
Stolen bases	4	Tommy Harper	6-18-69
		John Jaha	9-11-92

CAREER LEADERS

BATTING

Games

Robin Yount	2,856
Paul Molitor	1,856
Jim Gantner	1,801
Cecil Cooper	1,490
Charlie Moore	1,283
Don Money	1,196
Ben Oglivie	1,149
B.J. Surhoff	1,102
Gorman Thomas	1,102
Greg Vaughn	903

At-bats

Robin Yount	11,008
Paul Molitor	7,520
Jim Gantner	6,189
Cecil Cooper	6,019
Don Money	4,330
Ben Oglivie	4,136
Charlie Moore	3,926
B.J. Surhoff	3,884
Gorman Thomas	3,544
Greg Vaughn	3,244

Runs

Robin Yount	1,632
Paul Molitor	1,275
Cecil Cooper	821
Jim Gantner	726
Don Money	596
Ben Oglivie	567
Greg Vaughn	528
Gorman Thomas	524
B.J. Surhoff	472
Jeromy Burnitz	467

Hits

Robin Yount	3,142
Paul Molitor	2,281
Cecil Cooper	1,815
Jim Gantner	1,696
Don Money	1,168
Ben Oglivie	1,144
B.J. Surhoff	1,064
Charlie Moore	1,029
Jeff Cirillo	864
George Scott	851

Doubles

Robin Yount	583
Paul Molitor	405
Cecil Cooper	345
Jim Gantner	262
Don Money	215
Ben Oglivie	194
B.J. Surhoff	194
Jeff Cirillo	186
Charlie Moore	177
Gorman Thomas	172

Triples

Robin Yount	126
Paul Molitor	86
Charlie Moore	42
Jim Gantner	38
Cecil Cooper	33
Fernando Vina	26
B.J. Surhoff	24
Sixto Lezcano	22
Darryl Hamilton	21
Ben Oglivie	21

Home runs

Robin Yount	251
Gorman Thomas	208
Cecil Cooper	201
Ben Oglivie	176
Greg Vaughn	169
Jeromy Burnitz	165
Paul Molitor	160
Rob Deer	137
Don Money	134
George Scott	115

Total bases

Robin Yount	4,730
Paul Molitor	3,338
Cecil Cooper	2,829
Jim Gantner	2,175
Ben Oglivie	1,908
Don Money	1,825
Gorman Thomas	1,635
Greg Vaughn	1,490
B.J. Surhoff	1,477
Jeromy Burnitz	1,406

Runs batted in

Robin Yount	1,406
Cecil Cooper	944
Paul Molitor	790
Ben Oglivie	685
Gorman Thomas	605
Jim Gantner	568
Greg Vaughn	566
Don Money	529
Jeromy Burnitz	525
B.J. Surhoff	524

Extra-base hits

Robin Yount	960
Paul Molitor	651
Cecil Cooper	579
Gorman Thomas	392
Ben Oglivie	391
Don Money	369
Jim Gantner	347
Jeromy Burnitz	345
Greg Vaughn	340
B.J. Surhoff	275

Batting average
(Minimum 500 games)

Jeff Cirillo	.307
Paul Molitor	.303
Cecil Cooper	.302
Kevin Seitzer	.300
Darryl Hamilton	.290
Mark Loretta	.289
Fernando Vina	.286
Robin Yount	.285
Dave Nilsson	.284
George Scott	.283

Stolen bases

Paul Molitor	412
Robin Yount	271
Jim Gantner	137
Tommy Harper	136
Pat Listach	112
Darryl Hamilton	109
Mike Felder	108
B.J. Surhoff	102
Jose Valentin	78
Cecil Cooper	77

PITCHING

Earned-run average
(Minimum 500 innings)

Dan Plesac	3.21
Chuck Crim	3.47
Teddy Higuera	3.61
Jim Colborn	3.65
Lary Sorensen	3.72
Mike Caldwell	3.74
Skip Lockwood	3.75
Chris Bosio	3.76
Eduardo Rodriguez	3.78
Marty Pattin	3.82

Wins

Jim Slaton	117
Mike Caldwell	102
Teddy Higuera	94
Moose Haas	91
Bill Wegman	81
Chris Bosio	67
Bill Travers	65
Cal Eldred	64
Jaime Navarro	62
Jim Colborn	57

Losses

Jim Slaton	121
Bill Wegman	90
Mike Caldwell	80
Moose Haas	79
Bill Travers	67
Cal Eldred	65
Teddy Higuera	64
Jaime Navarro	64
Chris Bosio	62
Jim Colborn	60

Innings pitched

Jim Slaton	2,025.1
Mike Caldwell	1,604.2
Moose Haas	1,542.0
Bill Wegman	1,482.2
Teddy Higuera	1,380.0
Chris Bosio	1,190.0
Jim Colborn	1,118.0
Cal Eldred	1,078.2
Bill Travers	1,068.1
Jaime Navarro	1,061.2

Strikeouts

Teddy Higuera	1,081
Jim Slaton	929
Moose Haas	800
Chris Bosio	749
Bill Wegman	696
Cal Eldred	686
Mike Caldwell	540
Jaime Navarro	531
Bob McClure	497
Jim Colborn	495

Bases on balls

Jim Slaton	760
Cal Eldred	448
Teddy Higuera	443
Moose Haas	408
Bill Travers	392
Bob McClure	363
Mike Caldwell	353
Bill Wegman	352
Jerry Augustine	340
Jaime Navarro	336

Games

Dan Plesac	365
Jim Slaton	364
Bob McClure	352
Chuck Crim	332
Mike Fetters	289
Jerry Augustine	279
Bob Wickman	272
Bill Wegman	262
Bill Castro	253
Moose Haas	245

Shutouts

Jim Slaton	19
Mike Caldwell	18
Teddy Higuera	12
Bill Travers	10
Chris Bosio	8
Moose Haas	8
Jim Colborn	7
Lary Sorensen	7
Jerry Augustine	6
Jaime Navarro	6
Bill Parsons	6
Marty Pattin	6

Saves

Dan Plesac	133
Rollie Fingers	97
Mike Fetters	79
Bob Wickman	79
Doug Henry	61
Ken Sanders	61
Doug Jones	49
Bill Castro	44
Chuck Crim	42
Tom Murphy	41

TEAM SEASON, GAME RECORDS

SEASON

Batting

Most at-bats	5,733	1982
Most runs	894	1996
Fewest runs	494	1972
Most hits	1,599	1982
Most singles	1,107	1991
Most doubles	304	1996
Most triples	57	1983
Most home runs	216	1982
Fewest home runs	82	1992
Most grand slams	10	1995
Most pinch-hit home runs	8	2002
Most total bases	2,605	1982
Most stolen bases	256	1992
Highest batting average	.280	1979
Lowest batting average	.229	1971
Highest slugging pct	.455	1982

Pitching

Lowest ERA	3.38	1971
Highest ERA	5.14	1996
Most complete games	62	1978
Most shutouts	23	1971
Most saves	51	1988
Most walks	728	2000
Most strikeouts	1,063	1998

Fielding

Most errors	180	1975
Fewest errors	89	1992
Most double plays	189	1980
Highest fielding average	.986	1992

General

Most games won	95	1979, 1982
Most games lost	106	2002
Highest win pct	.590	1979
Lowest win pct	.346	2002

GAME, INNING

Batting

Most runs, game	22	8-28-92
Most runs, inning	13	7-8-90
Most hits, game	31	8-28-92
Most home runs, game	7	4-29-80
Most total bases, game	40	5-15-2001 (10 inn.)
	38	8-28-92, 4-26-2001

The sweet swing of first baseman Cecil Cooper produced 1,815 hits, 201 home runs and 944 RBIs for the Brewers.

BREWERS YEAR-BY-YEAR

Year	W	L	Place	Games Back	Manager	Leaders: Batting avg.	Hits	Home runs	RBIs	Wins	ERA
								SEATTLE PILOTS			
								WEST DIVISION			
1969	64	98	6th	33	Schultz	T. Davis, .271	Harper, 126	Mincher, 25	T. Davis, 80	Brabender, 13	Gelnar, 3.31
								MILWAUKEE BREWERS			
1970	65	97	4th	33	Bristol	Harper, .296	Harper, 179	Harper, 31	Harper, 82	Pattin, 14	Sanders, 1.75
1971	69	92	6th	32	Bristol	May, .277	Harper, 151	Briggs, 21	May, 65	Pattin, 14	Sanders, 1.91
								EAST DIVISION			
1972	65	91	6th	21	Bristol, Crandall	Rodriguez, .285	Scott, 154	Briggs, 21	Scott, 88	Lonborg, 14	Lonborg, 2.83
1973	74	88	5th	23	Crandall	Scott, .306	May, 189	May, 25	Scott, 107	Colborn, 20	Colborn, 3.18
1974	76	86	5th	15	Crandall	Money, .283	Scott, 170	Briggs, Scott, 17	Scott, 82	Slaton, 13	Murphy, 1.90
1975	68	94	5th	28	Crandall	Scott, .285	Scott, 176	Scott, 36	Scott, 109	Broberg, 14	Hausman, 4.10
1976	66	95	6th	32	Grammas	Lezcano, .285	Scott, 166	Scott, 18	Scott, 77	Travers, 15	Travers, 2.81
1977	67	95	6th	33	Grammas	Cooper, .300	Cooper, 193	Money, 25	Money, 83	Augustine, 12	Slaton, 3.58
1978	93	69	3rd	6½	Bamberger	Cooper, .312	Bando, 154	Hisle, 34	Hisle, 115	Caldwell, 22	Caldwell, 2.37
1979	95	66	2nd	8	Bamberger	Molitor, .322	Molitor, 188	G. Thomas, 45	G. Thomas, 123	Caldwell, 16	Caldwell, 3.29
1980	86	76	3rd	17	Bamberger, Rodgers	Cooper, .352	Cooper, 219	Oglivie, 41	Cooper, 122	Haas, 16	McClure, 3.07
1981	62	47	*3rd/1st	—	Rodgers	Cooper, .320	Cooper, 133	G. Thomas, 21	Oglivie, 72	Vuckovich, 14	Vuckovich, 3.55
1982	95	67	†1st	+1	Rodgers, Kuenn	Yount, .331	Yount, 210	G. Thomas, 39	Cooper, 121	Vuckovich, 18	Slaton, 3.29
1983	87	75	5th	11	Kuenn	Simmons, Yount, .308	Cooper, 203	Cooper, 30	Cooper, 126	Slaton, 14	Tellmann, 2.80
1984	67	94	7th	36½	Lachemann	Yount, .298	Yount, 186	Yount, 16	Yount, 80	Sutton, 14	Sutton, 3.77
1985	71	90	6th	28	Bamberger	Molitor, .297	Cooper, 185	Cooper, 16	Cooper, 99	Higuera, 15	Darwin, 3.80
1986	77	84	6th	18	Bamberger, Trebelhorn	Yount, .312	Yount, 163	Deer, 33	Deer, 86	Higuera, 20	Higuera, 2.79
1987	91	71	3rd	7	Trebelhorn	Molitor, .353	Yount, 198	Deer, 28	Yount, 103	Higuera, 18	Crim, 3.67
1988	87	75	‡3rd	2	Trebelhorn	Molitor, .312	Molitor, Yount, 190	Deer, 23	Yount, 91	Higuera, 16	Higuera, 2.45
1989	81	81	4th	8	Trebelhorn	Yount, .318	Yount, 195	Deer, 26	Yount, 103	Bosio, 15	Crim, 2.83
1990	74	88	6th	14	Trebelhorn	Sheffield, .294	Parker, 176	Deer, 27	Parker, 92	Robinson, 12	Robinson, 2.91
1991	83	79	4th	8	Trebelhorn	Randolph, .327	Molitor, 216	Vaughn, 27	Vaughn, 98	Navarro, Wegman, 15	Wegman, 2.84
1992	92	70	2nd	4	Garner	Molitor, .320	Molitor, 195	Vaughn, 23	Molitor, 89	Navarro, 17	Eldred, 1.79
1993	69	93	7th	26	Garner	Hamilton, .310	Hamilton, 161	Vaughn, 30	Vaughn, 97	Eldred, 16	Miranda, 3.30
								CENTRAL DIVISION			
1994	53	62	5th	15	Garner	Seitzer, .314	Nilsson, 109	Vaughn, 19	Nilsson, 69	Eldred, 11	Bones, 3.43
1995	65	79	4th	35	Garner	Surhoff, .320	Seitzer, 153	Jaha, 20	Surhoff, 73	Bones, 10	Karl, 4.14
1996	80	82	3rd	19½	Garner	Nilsson, .331	Cirillo, 184	Jaha, 34	Jaha, 118	Karl, 13	McDonald, 3.90
1997	78	83	3rd	8	Garner	Cirillo, .288	Cirillo, 167	Burnitz, 27	Burnitz, 85	Eldred, 13	Wickman, 2.73
								NATIONAL LEAGUE			
								CENTRAL DIVISION			
1998	74	88	5th	28	Garner	Cirillo, .321	Vina, 198	Burnitz, 38	Burnitz, 125	Woodard, Karl, 10	Woodard, 4.18
1999	74	87	5th	22½	Garner, Lefebvre	Cirillo, .326	Cirillo, 198	Burnitz, 33	Burnitz, 103	Nomo, 12	Woodard, 4.52
2000	73	89	3rd	22	Lopes	Jenkins, .303	Jenkins, 155	Jenkins, 34	Burnitz, 98	D'Amico, Haynes, 12	D'Amico, 2.67
2001	68	94	4th	25	Lopes	Loretta, .289	Sexson, 162	Sexson, 45	Sexson, 125	Sheets, Wright, 11	Sheets, 4.76
2002	56	106	6th	41	Lopes, Royster	Hernandez, .288	Sexson, 159	Sexson, 29	Sexson, 102	Sheets, 11	Sheets, 4.15

* First half 31-25; second half 31-22. † Won Championship Series. ‡ Tied for position.

Note: Batting average minimum 350 at-bats; ERA minimum 90 innings pitched.

Don Mincher

SEATTLE joined Kansas City, San Diego and Montreal in the four-team 1969 expansion that brought baseball's membership roster to a modern-record 24 teams.The franchise, which would last only one season in Seattle before moving to Milwaukee as the Brewers, came to life December 1, 1967, when the bid by Pacific Northwest Sports, Inc., was officially approved and the name "Pilots" was adopted three months later.

The Pilots selected 30 players in the October 15, 1968, expansion draft, leading off with veteran first baseman Don Mincher. The Pilots defeated the California Angels, 4-3, in their April 8, 1969, debut at Anaheim Stadium—one of 64 victories the team would post in its brief history. One year later on April 7, the Brewers lost their American League debut, 12-0, to the same Angels.

Expansion draft (October 15, 1968)

Players

Player	From	Position
Wayne Comer	Detroit	outfield
Tommy Davis	Chicago	outfield
Mike Ferraro	New York	infield
Jim Gosger	Oakland	outfield
Larry Haney	Baltimore	catcher
Tommy Harper	Cleveland	outfield
Steve Hovley	California	outfield
Gerry McNertney	Chicago	catcher
*Don Mincher	California	first base
Ray Oyler	Detroit	shortstop
Lou Piniella	Cleveland	outfield
Rich Rollins	Minnesota	third base
Chico Salmon	Cleveland	second base

Pitchers

Pitcher	From	Throws
Jack Aker	Oakland	righthanded
Dick Baney	Boston	righthanded
Steve Barber	New York	lefthanded
Dick Bates	Washington	righthanded
Gary Bell	Boston	righthanded
Darrell Brandon	Boston	righthanded
Paul Click	California	righthanded
Skip Lockwood	Oakland	righthanded
Mike Marshall	Detroit	righthanded
John Miklos	Washington	lefthanded
John Morris	Baltimore	lefthanded
Marty Pattin	California	righthanded
Bob Richmond	Washington	righthanded
Gerry Schoen	Washington	righthanded
Diego Segui.	Oakland	righthanded
Lou Stephen	Minnesota	righthanded
Gary Timberlake	New York	lefthanded

*First pick

Opening day lineups

April 8, 1969 (Seattle Pilots)

Tommy Harper, second base
Steve Whitaker, right field
Tommy Davis, left field
Don Mincher, first base
Rich Rollins, third base
Jim Gosger, center field
Jerry McNertney, catcher
Ray Oyler, shortstop
Marty Pattin, pitcher

April 7, 1970 (Milwaukee Brewers)

Tommy Harper, second base
Russ Snyder, center field
Mike Hegan, first base
Danny Walton, left field
Jerry McNertney, catcher
Steve Hovley, right field
Max Alvis, third base
Ted Kubiak, shortstop
Lew Krausse, pitcher

Tommy Harper

Pilots firsts

First hit: Tommy Harper, April 8, 1969, at California (double)
First home run: Mike Hegan, April 8, 1969, at California
First RBI: Mike Hegan, April 8, 1969, at California
First win: Marty Pattin, April 8, 1968, at California
First shutout: Gary Bell, April 11, 1969, 7-0 vs. Chicago

MONTREAL EXPOS

FRANCHISE CHRONOLOGY

First season: 1969, as one of two National League expansion teams and baseball's first Canadian franchise. The Expos rallied for an 11-10 opening day victory over New York and posted an 8-7 victory over St. Louis six days later in the first Major League game on foreign soil, but they stumbled to a 52-110 first-season record and finished 48 games behind the Mets in the new N.L. East Division.

1970-present: The Expos, one of baseball's so-called small-market franchises, still are looking for their first N.L. pennant and World Series appearance. They came close in 1981, when they survived a strike-forced divisional playoff before suffering a heartbreaking N.L. Championship Series loss to the Los Angeles Dodgers. And they were sailing along with baseball's best record in 1994 when another players' strike brought a sudden halt to the season—and realistic hopes for a championship. When the strike finally ended in 1995, the Expos began auctioning off high-priced players and entered the new season with a talented, but inexperienced, team. While the Expos continue to grope for success, their Canadian cousins, the Toronto Blue Jays, have won two World Series since entering the American League in 1977.

Center fielder Andre Dawson.

EXPOS VS. OPPONENTS BY DECADE

	Braves	Cardinals	Cubs	Dodgers	Giants	Phillies	Pirates	Reds	Astros	Mets	Padres	Marlins	Rockies	Brewers	D'backs	Interleague	Decade Record
1969	4-8	7-11	8-10	2-10	1-11	11-7	5-13	4-8	1-11	5-13	4-8						52-110
1970-79	58-60	85-93	89-88	47-73	59-61	88-90	73-107	46-74	49-71	94-86	60-59						748-862
1980-89	72-45	95-82	95-77	48-67	59-56	87-86	88-86	64-53	55-60	85-89	63-51						811-752
1990-99	50-70	64-61	62-57	56-57	56-59	65-73	65-61	48-57	51-57	69-68	71-40	46-38	30-37	7-11	10-8	26-23	776-777
2000-02	19-32	7-12	11-10	9-12	9-13	25-25	11-8	10-11	8-13	22-28	9-13	22-29	8-14	11-10	10-11	27-27	218-268
Totals	203-215	258-259	265-242	162-219	184-200	276-281	242-275	172-203	164-212	275-284	207-171	68-67	38-51	18-21	20-19	53-50	2605-2769

Interleague results: 9-6 vs. Orioles, 7-8 vs. Red Sox, 2-1 vs. White Sox, 2-1 vs. Indians, 4-2 vs. Tigers, 3-0 vs. Royals, 6-9 vs. Yankees, 7-5 vs. Devil Rays, 13-18 vs. Blue Jays.

MANAGERS

Name	*Years*	*Record*
Gene Mauch	1969-75	499-627
Karl Kuehl	1976	43-85
Charlie Fox	1976	12-22
Dick Williams	1977-81	380-347
Jim Fanning	1981-82, 1984	116-103
Bill Virdon	1983-84	146-147
Buck Rodgers	1985-91	520-499
Tom Runnells	1991-92	68-81
Felipe Alou	1992-2001	691-717
Jeff Torborg	2001	47-62
Frank Robinson	2002	83-79

EAST DIVISION CHAMPIONS

Year	*Record*	*Manager*	*NLCS Result*
*1981	60-48	Williams, Fanning	Lost to Dodgers
1994	74-40	Alou	None

* Second-half champion; won division playoff over Phillies.

ALL-TIME RECORD OF EXPANSION TEAMS

Team	W	L	Pct.	DT	P	WS
Arizona	440	370	.543	3	1	1
Kansas City	2,675	2,694	.498	6	2	1
Houston	3,229	3,285	.496	7	0	0
Toronto	2,025	2,063	.495	5	2	2
Anaheim	3,243	3,431	.486	3	1	1
Montreal	2,605	2,769	.485	2	0	0
Colorado	740	817	.475	0	0	0
New York	3,091	3,412	.475	4	4	2
Milwaukee	2,545	2,831	.473	2	1	0
Seattle	1,924	2,163	.471	3	0	0
Texas	3,097	3,560	.465	4	0	0
San Diego	2,460	2,921	.457	3	2	0
Florida	706	847	.455	0	1	1
Tampa Bay	318	490	.394	0	0	0

DT—Division Titles. P—Pennants won. WS—World Series won.

BALLPARK CHRONOLOGY

Olympic Stadium (1977-present)

Capacity: 46,620.
First game: Philadelphia 7, Expos 2 (April 15, 1977).
First batter: Jay Johnstone, Phillies.
First hit: Dave Cash, Expos (single).
First run: Greg Luzinski, Phillies (2nd inning).
First home run: Ellis Valentine, Expos.
First winning pitcher: Steve Carlton, Phillies.
First-season attendance: 1,433,757.

Jarry Park (1969-76)

Capacity: 28,000.
First game: Expos 8, St. Louis 7 (April 14, 1969).
First-season attendance: 1,212,608.

ATTENDANCE HIGHS

Total	*Season*	*Park*
2,320,651	1983	Olympic Stadium
2,318,292	1982	Olympic Stadium
2,208,175	1980	Olympic Stadium
2,102,173	1979	Olympic Stadium
1,850,324	1987	Olympic Stadium

CY YOUNG WINNER

Pedro Martinez, RH, 1997

ROOKIES OF THE YEAR

Carl Morton, P, 1970
Andre Dawson, OF, 1977

MANAGERS OF THE YEAR

Buck Rodgers, 1987
Felipe Alou, 1994

RETIRED UNIFORMS

No.	*Name*	*Pos.*
8	Gary Carter	C
10	Rusty Staub	1B-OF
	Andre Dawson	OF

Outfielder/first baseman Rusty Staub was one of the most popular players in Expos history.

HISTORY

MILESTONE PERFORMANCES

25-plus home runs
44—Vladimir Guerrero 2000
42—Vladimir Guerrero 1999
39—Vladimir Guerrero 2002
38—Vladimir Guerrero 1998
36—Henry Rodriguez 1996
34—Vladimir Guerrero 2001
32—Andre Dawson 1983
31—Gary Carter 1977
30—Rusty Staub 1970
Larry Parrish 1979
29—Rusty Staub 1969
Gary Carter 1980, 1982
Andres Galarraga 1988
28—Bob Bailey 1970
Tim Wallach 1982
Rondell White 1997
27—Gary Carter 1984
26—Bob Bailey 1973
Tim Wallach 1987
Henry Rodriguez 1997
25—Ellis Valentine 1977, 1978
Andre Dawson 1978, 1979
Shane Andrews 1998
Lee Stevens 2001

100-plus RBIs
131—Vladimir Guerrero 1999
123—Tim Wallach 1987
Vladimir Guerrero 2000
113—Andre Dawson 1983
111—Vladimir Guerrero 2002
109—Al Oliver 1982
Vladimir Guerrero 1998
108—Vladimir Guerrero 2001
106—Gary Carter 1984
103—Ken Singleton 1973
Henry Rodriguez 1996
101—Gary Carter 1981
100—Hubie Brooks 1985

20-plus victories
1978—Ross Grimsley 20-11

N.L. home run champions
None

N.L. RBI champions
1982—Al Oliver *109
1984—Gary Carter *106
* Tied for league lead

N.L. batting champions
1982—Al Oliver .... .331
1986—Tim Raines .... .334

N.L. ERA champions
1982—Steve Rogers 2.40
1991—Dennis Martinez 2.39
1997—Pedro Martinez 1.90

N.L. strikeout champions
None

No-hit pitchers
(9 innings or more)
1969—Bill Stoneman ....7-0 vs. Philadelphia
1972—Bill Stoneman ....7-0 vs. New York
1981—Charlie Lea ....4-0 vs. San Francisco
1991—Dennis Martinez....2-0 vs. Los Angeles

Longest hitting streaks
31—Vladimir Guerrero 1999
26—Vladimir Guerrero 2002
21—Delino DeShields 1993
Jose Vidro 2002
19—Warren Cromartie 1979
Andre Dawson 1980
Peter Bergeron 2001
18—Pepe Mangual 1975
Warren Cromartie 1980
David Segui 1980
F.P. Santangelo 1997
17—Bob Bailey 1973
Tim Raines 1986
Mark Grudzielanek 1996, 1997
16—Rusty Staub 1971
Tony Perez 1977
Ellis Valentine 1978
Andre Dawson 1981
Henry Rodriguez 1997
Brad Fullmer 1999
Endy Chavez 2002
15—Ken Singleton 1973
Boots Day 1971
Warren Cromartie 1978
Larry Parrish 1978
Al Oliver 1982
Delino DeShields 1990
Mike Lansing 1997

During Gary Carter's successful 11-year Montreal stay, he ranked as one of the best hitting catchers in the game.

INDIVIDUAL SEASON, GAME RECORDS

Steady righthander Steve Rogers set a club record when he pitched more than 300 innings in a workhorse 1977 season.

SEASON

Batting

Record		Player	Year
At-bats	659	Warren Cromartie	1979
Runs	133	Tim Raines	1983
Hits	206	Vladimir Guerrero	2002
Singles	157	Mark Grudzielanek	1996
Doubles	54	Mark Grudzielanek	1997
Triples	13	3 times	
		Last by Mitch Webster	1986
Home runs	44	Vladimir Guerrero	2000
Home runs, rookie	20	Brad Wilkerson	2002
Grand slams	2	14 times	
		Last by Henry Rodriguez	1997
Total bases	369	Vladimir Guerrero	2000
RBIs	131	Vladimir Guerrero	1999
Walks	123	Ken Singleton	1973
Most strikeouts	169	Andres Galarraga	1990
Fewest strikeouts	29	Dave Cash	1978
Batting average	.345	Vladimir Guerrero	2000
Slugging pct.	.664	Vladimir Guerrero	2000
Stolen bases	97	Ron LeFlore	1980

Pitching

Record		Player	Year
Games	92	Mike Marshall	1973
Complete games	20	Bill Stoneman	1971
Innings	301.2	Steve Rogers	1977
Wins	20	Ross Grimsley	1978
Losses	22	Steve Rogers	1974
Winning pct.	.783 (18-5)	Bryn Smith	1985
Walks	146	Bill Stoneman	1971
Strikeouts	305	Pedro Martinez	1997
Shutouts	5	5 times	
		Last by Carlos Perez	1997
Home runs allowed	31	Javier Vazquez	1998
Lowest ERA	1.90	Pedro Martinez	1997
Saves	43	John Wetteland	1993

GAME

Batting

Record		Player	Date
Runs	5	Last by Rondell White	6-11-95
Hits	6	Rondell White	6-11-95
Doubles	3	Last by Lee Stevens	6-27-2000
Triples	2	Last by Orlando Cabrera	7-30-98
Home runs	3	Last by Tim Wallach	5-4-87
RBIs	8	Last by Tim Wallach	5-13-90
Total bases	14	Larry Parrish	5-29-77, 7-30-78
Stolen bases	4	Last by Marquis Grissom	7-21-92

CAREER LEADERS

BATTING

Games

Tim Wallach	1,767
Gary Carter	1,503
Tim Raines	1,452
Andre Dawson	1,443
Warren Cromartie	1,038
Larry Parrish	967
Bob Bailey	951
Andres Galarraga	951
Chris Speier	895
Vladimir Guerrero	892

At-bats

Tim Wallach	6,529
Andre Dawson	5,628
Tim Raines	5,383
Gary Carter	5,303
Warren Cromartie	3,796
Larry Parrish	3,411
Andres Galarraga	3,374
Vladimir Guerrero	3,369
Bob Bailey	2,991
Chris Speier	2,902

Runs

Tim Raines	947
Andre Dawson	828
Tim Wallach	737
Gary Carter	707
Vladimir Guerrero	570
Warren Cromartie	446
Marquis Grissom	430
Andres Galarraga	424
Larry Parrish	421
Rondell White	420

Hits

Tim Wallach	1,694
Tim Raines	1,622
Andre Dawson	1,575
Gary Carter	1,427
Vladimir Guerrero	1,085
Warren Cromartie	1,063
Andres Galarraga	906
Larry Parrish	896
Rondell White	808
Bob Bailey	791

Doubles

Tim Wallach	360
Andre Dawson	295
Tim Raines	281
Gary Carter	274
Warren Cromartie	222
Larry Parrish	208
Vladimir Guerrero	206
Jose Vidro	197
Andres Galarraga	180
Mike Lansing	165
Rondell White	165

Triples

Tim Raines	82
Andre Dawson	67
Vladimir Guerrero	31
Tim Wallach	31
Warren Cromartie	30
Delino DeShields	25
Mitch Webster	25
Gary Carter	24
Larry Parrish	24
Bob Bailey	23
Marquis Grissom	23
Rondell White	23

Home runs

Andre Dawson	225
Gary Carter	220
Vladimir Guerrero	209
Tim Wallach	204
Bob Bailey	118
Andres Galarraga	115
Rondell White	101
Larry Parrish	100
Larry Walker	99
Tim Raines	96

Total bases

Tim Wallach	2,728
Andre Dawson	2,679
Gary Carter	2,409
Tim Raines	2,355
Vladimir Guerrero	1,980
Warren Cromartie	1,525
Andres Galarraga	1,459
Larry Parrish	1,452
Rondell White	1,322
Bob Bailey	1,307

Runs batted in

Tim Wallach	905
Andre Dawson	838
Gary Carter	823
Vladimir Guerrero	623
Tim Raines	556
Andres Galarraga	473
Bob Bailey	466
Larry Parrish	444
Hubie Brooks	390
Larry Walker	384
Rondell White	384

Extra-base hits

Tim Wallach	595
Andre Dawson	587
Gary Carter	518
Tim Raines	459
Vladimir Guerrero	446
Larry Parrish	332
Warren Cromartie	312
Andres Galarraga	309
Rondell White	289
Jose Vidro	278

Batting average

(Minimum 500 games)

Vladimir Guerrero	.322
Jose Vidro	.305
Tim Raines	.301
Rusty Staub	.294
Rondell White	.293
Moises Alou	.292
Ellis Valentine	.288
Larry Walker	.282
Warren Cromartie	.280
Andre Dawson	.280

Stolen bases

Tim Raines	635
Marquis Grissom	266
Andre Dawson	253
Delino DeShields	187
Rodney Scott	139
Otis Nixon	133
Vladimir Guerrero	114
Larry Walker	98
Ron LeFlore	97
Mike Lansing	96
Mitch Webster	96

PITCHING

Earned-run average

(Minimum 500 innings)

Tim Burke	2.61
Jeff Reardon	2.84
Ken Hill	3.04
Pedro Martinez	3.06
Dennis Martinez	3.06
Dan Schatzeder	3.09
Mel Rojas	3.11
Steve Rogers	3.17
Jeff Fassero	3.20
Woodie Fryman	3.24

Wins

Steve Rogers	158
Dennis Martinez	100
Bryn Smith	81
Bill Gullickson	72
Steve Renko	68
Jeff Fassero	58
Scott Sanderson	56
Charlie Lea	55
Pedro Martinez	55
Woodie Fryman	51
Bill Stoneman	51
Javier Vazquez	51

Losses

Steve Rogers	152
Steve Renko	82
Dennis Martinez	72
Bill Stoneman	72
Bryn Smith	71
Bill Gullickson	61
Javier Vazquez	56
Woodie Fryman	52
Ernie McAnally	49
Jeff Fassero	48

Innings pitched

Steve Rogers	2,837.2
Dennis Martinez	1,609.0
Bryn Smith	1,400.1
Steve Renko	1,359.1
Bill Gullickson	1,186.1
Bill Stoneman	1,085.1
Javier Vazquez	998.2
Scott Sanderson	883.0
Jeff Fassero	850.0
Pedro Martinez	797.1

Strikeouts

Steve Rogers	1,621
Dennis Martinez	973
Pedro Martinez	843
Bryn Smith	838
Javier Vazquez	835
Bill Stoneman	831
Steve Renko	810
Jeff Fassero	750
Bill Gullickson	678
Scott Sanderson	603

Bases on balls

Steve Rogers	876
Steve Renko	624
Bill Stoneman	535
Dennis Martinez	407
Bryn Smith	341
Mike Torrez	303
Charlie Lea	291
Bill Gullickson	288
Carl Morton	279
Jeff Fassero	274
Woodie Fryman	274
Javier Vazquez	274

Games

Tim Burke	425
Steve Rogers	399
Mel Rojas	388
Jeff Reardon	359
Woodie Fryman	297
Ugueth Urbina	296
Anthony Telford	293
Bryn Smith	284
Steve Kline	269
Jeff Fassero	262

Shutouts

Steve Rogers	37
Bill Stoneman	15
Dennis Martinez	13
Woodie Fryman	8
Charlie Lea	8
Pedro Martinez	8
Scott Sanderson	8
Bryn Smith	8
Bill Gullickson	6
Ernie McAnally	6
Carlos Perez	6
Steve Renko	6
Floyd Youmans	6

Saves

Jeff Reardon	152
Ugueth Urbina	125
Mel Rojas	109
John Wetteland	105
Tim Burke	101
Mike Marshall	75
Woodie Fryman	52
Dale Murray	33
Elias Sosa	30
Claude Raymond	24

TEAM SEASON, GAME RECORDS

SEASON

Batting

Most at-bats	5,675	1977
Most runs	741	1987, 1996
Fewest runs	513	1972
Most hits	1,482	1983
Most singles	1,042	1983
Most doubles	339	1997
Most triples	61	1980
Most home runs	178	2000
Fewest home runs	86	1974
Most grand slams	9	1996
Most pinch-hit home runs	9	1973, 2002
Most total bases	2,389	2000
Most stolen bases	237	1980
Highest batting average	.266	2000
Lowest batting average	.234	1972
Highest slugging pct	.432	2000

Pitching

Lowest ERA	3.08	1988
Highest ERA	5.13	2000
Most complete games	49	1971
Most shutouts	18	1979
Most saves	61	1993
Most walks	716	1970
Most strikeouts	1,206	1996

Fielding

Most errors	184	1969
Fewest errors	110	1990
Most double plays	193	1970
Highest fielding average	.982	1990

General

Most games won	95	1979
Most games lost	108	2001
Highest win pct	.649	1994
Lowest win pct	.321	1969, 2001

GAME, INNING

Batting

Most runs, game	21	Last 4-28-96
Most runs, inning	13	5-7-97
Most hits, game	28	7-30-78
Most home runs, game	8	7-30-78
Most total bases, game	58	7-30-78

Third baseman Tim Wallach holds numerous team records, including hits (1,694) and RBIs (905).

HISTORY

EXPOS YEAR-BY-YEAR

Year	W	L	Place	Games Back	Manager	Leaders: Batting avg.	Hits	Home runs	RBIs	Wins	ERA
								EAST DIVISION			
1969	52	110	6th	48	Mauch	Staub, .302	Staub, 166	Staub, 29	Laboy, 83	Stoneman, 11	Waslewski, 3.29
1970	73	89	6th	16	Mauch	Fairly, .288	Staub, 156	Staub, 30	Staub, 94	Morton, 18	Morton, 3.60
1971	71	90	5th	25½	Mauch	Staub, .311	Staub, 186	Staub, 19	Staub, 97	Stoneman, 17	Stoneman, 3.15
1972	70	86	5th	26½	Mauch	Fairly, .278	Singleton, 139	Fairly, 17	Fairly, 68	Torrez, 16	Marshall, 1.78
1973	79	83	4th	3½	Mauch	Hunt, .309	Singleton, 169	Bailey, 26	Singleton, 103	Renko, 15	Rogers, 1.54
1974	79	82	4th	8½	Mauch	W. Davis, .295	W. Davis, 180	Bailey, 20	W. Davis, 89	Rogers, Torrez, 15	Taylor, 2.17
1975	75	87	*5th	17½	Mauch	Parrish, .274	Parrish, 146	Jorgensen, 18	Carter, 68	Murray, 15	Warthen, 3.11
1976	55	107	6th	46	Kuehl, Fox	Foli, .264	Foli, 144	Parrish, 11	Parrish, 61	Fryman, 13	Rogers, 3.21
1977	75	87	5th	26	Williams	Valentine, .293	Cash, 188	Carter, 31	Perez, 91	Rogers, 17	Rogers, 3.10
1978	76	86	4th	14	Williams	Cromartie, .297	Cromartie, 180	Dawson, Valentine, 25	Perez, 78	Grimsley, 20	Dues, 2.36
1979	95	65	2nd	2	Williams	Parrish, .307	Cromartie, 181	Parrish, 30	Dawson, 92	Lee, 16	Sosa, 1.96
1980	90	72	2nd	1	Williams	Dawson, .308	Dawson, 178	Carter, 29	Carter, 101	Rogers, Sanderson, 16	Palmer, Rogers, 2.98
1981	60	48	†‡3rd/1st	—	Williams, Fanning	Cromartie, Raines, .304	Dawson, 119	Dawson, 24	Carter, 68	Rogers, 12	Gullickson, 2.80
1982	86	76	3rd	6	Fanning	Oliver, .331	Oliver, 204	Carter, 29	Oliver, 109	Rogers, 19	Reardon, 2.06
1983	82	80	3rd	8	Virdon	Oliver, .300	Dawson, 189	Dawson, 32	Dawson, 113	Gullickson, Rogers, 17	B. Smith, 2.49
1984	78	83	5th	18	Virdon, Fanning	Raines, .309	Raines, 192	Carter, 27	Carter, 106	Lea, 15	Schatzeder, 2.71
1985	84	77	3rd	16½	Rodgers	Raines, .320	Raines, 184	Dawson, 23	Brooks, 100	B. Smith, 18	Burke, 2.39
1986	78	83	4th	29½	Rodgers	Raines, .334	Raines, 194	Dawson, 20	Dawson, 78	Youmans, 13	McGaffigan, 2.65
1987	91	71	3rd	4	Rodgers	Raines, .330	Wallach, 177	Wallach, 26	Wallach, 123	Heaton, 13	Burke, 1.19
1988	81	81	3rd	20	Rodgers	Galarraga, .302	Galarraga, 184	Galarraga, 29	Galarraga, 92	Martinez, 15	P. Perez, 2.44
1989	81	81	4th	12	Rodgers	Raines, .286	Wallach, 159	Galarraga, 23	Galarraga, 85	Martinez, 16	Langston, 2.39
1990	85	77	3rd	10	Rodgers	Wallach, .296	Wallach, 185	Wallach, 21	Wallach, 98	Sampen, 12	Boyd, 2.93
1991	71	90	6th	26½	Rodgers, Runnells	Calderon, .300	Grissom, 149	Calderon, 19	Calderon, 75	Martinez, 14	Martinez, 2.39
1992	87	75	2nd	9	Runnells, F. Alou	Walker, .301	Grissom, 180	Walker, 23	Walker, 93	Hill, Martinez, 16	Rojas, 1.43
1993	94	68	2nd	3	F. Alou	Grissom, .298	Grissom, 188	Walker, 22	Grissom, 95	Martinez, 15	Fassero, 2.29
1994	74	40	1st	+6	F. Alou	M. Alou, .339	M. Alou, 143	M. Alou, 22	Walker, 86	Hill, 16	Henry, 2.43
1995	66	78	5th	24	Alou	Segui, .309	Cordero, 147	Alou, Berry, Tarasco, 14	Segui, 68	Martinez, 14	Henry, 2.84
1996	88	74	2nd	8	Alou	Grudzielanek, .306	Grudzielanek, 201	Rodriguez, 36	Rodriguez, 103	Fassero, 15	Fassero, 3.30
1997	78	84	4th	23	Alou	Segui, .307	Grudzielanek, 177	White, 28	Rodriguez, 83	Martinez, 17	Martinez, 1.90
1998	65	97	4th	41	Alou	V. Guerrero, .324	V. Guerrero, 202	V. iGuerrero, 38	V.Guerrero, 109	Hermanson, 14	Hermanson, 3.13
1999	68	94	4th	35	Alou	V. Guerrero, .316	V .Guerrero, 193	V. Guerrero, 42	V.Guerrero, 131	Hermanson, Vazquez, 9	Telford, 3.94
2000	67	95	4th	28	Alou	V. Guerrero, .345	Vidro, 200	V. Guerrero, 44	V. Guerrero, 123	Hermanson, 12	Pavano, 3.06
2001	68	94	5th	20	Alou, Torborg	Vidro, .319	Guerrero, 184	Guerrero, 34	Guerrero, 108	Vazquez, 16	Vazquez, 3.42
2002	83	79	2nd	19	Robinson	V. Guerrero, .336	V. Guerrero, 206	V. Guerrero, 39	V. Guerrero, 111	Ohka, 13	Ohka, 3.18

* Tied for position. † First half 30-25; second half 30-23. ‡ Lost Championship Series.

Note: Batting average minimum 350 at-bats; ERA minimum 90 innings pitched.

Manny Mota

MONTREAL made history May 27, 1968, when it was awarded an expansion franchise—the first outside the continental United States. Montreal joined San Diego in the National League and Kansas City and Seattle in the American League as part of a four-team expansion that brought baseball's membership roster to 24 teams.

The infant Expos took their first step when they made versatile Manny Mota their first pick of the October 14, 1968, expansion draft—one of 30 overall selections. Montreal made its Major League debut on April 8, 1969, with an 11-10 victory over the Mets at New York's Shea Stadium. The long-awaited home inaugural at Jarry Park took place on April 14, and the Expos celebrated with an 8-7 victory over St. Louis in the first Major League regular-season game on foreign soil.

Expansion draft (October 14, 1968)

Players

Player	From	Position
Jesus Alou	San Francisco	outfield
John Bateman	Houston	catcher
John Boccabella	Chicago	catcher
Ron Brand	Houston	catcher
Donn Clendenon	Pittsburgh	first base
Ty Cline	San Francisco	outfield
Jim Fairey	Los Angeles	outfield
Angel Hermoso	Atlanta	infield
Jose Herrera	Houston	infield
Garry Jestadt	Chicago	infield
Mack Jones	Cincinnati	outfield
Coco Laboy	St. Louis	infield
*Manny Mota	Pittsburgh	infield/outfield
Gary Sutherland	Philadelphia	infield/outfield
Jim Williams	Cincinnati	shortstop
Maury Wills	Pittsburgh	shortstop

Pitchers

Pitcher	From	Throws
Jack Billingham	Los Angeles	righthanded
John Glass	New York	righthanded
Jim (Mudcat) Grant	Los Angeles	righthanded
Skip Guinn	Atlanta	lefthanded
Larry Jackson	Philadelphia	righthanded
Larry Jaster	St. Louis	lefthanded
Ernie McAnally	New York	righthanded
Dan McGinn	Cincinnati	lefthanded
Carl Morton	Atlanta	righthanded
Bob Reynolds	San Francisco	righthanded
Jerry Robertson	St. Louis	righthanded
Don Shaw	New York	lefthanded
Bill Stoneman	Chicago	righthanded
Mike Wegener	Philadelphia	righthanded

*First pick

Opening day lineup

April 8, 1969

Maury Wills, shortstop
Gary Sutherland, second base
Rusty Staub, right field
Mack Jones, left field
Bob Bailey, first base
John Batemen, catcher
Coco Laboy, third base
Don Hahn, center field
Mudcat Grant, pitcher

Rusty Staub

Expos firsts

First hit: Maury Wills, April 8, 1969, at New York (single)
First home run: Dan McGinn, April 8, 1969, at New York
First RBI: Bob Bailey, April 8, 1969, at New York
First win: Don Shaw, April 8, 1969, at New York
First shutout: Bill Stoneman (no-hitter), April 17, 1969, 7-0 at Philadelphia

NEW YORK METS

FRANCHISE CHRONOLOGY

First season: 1962, as one of two new teams in the National League's first modern-era expansion. The Mets dropped an 11-4 opener to St. Louis and stumbled to 120 first-year losses, a 20th-century record.

1963-present: The early year Mets were bumbling and inept—and lovable. New York, devoid of an N.L. franchise since losing the Dodgers and Giants in 1957, fervently embraced the mistake-prone Mets as they struggled to 452 losses in their first four seasons (an average of 113) under irascible manager Casey Stengel. But that feeling changed in 1969, when the upstart New Yorkers, coming off a ninth-place finish, won 100 games and finished first in the newly created East Division. They punctuated their surprising success with a three-game sweep of Atlanta in the first N.L. Championship Series and a shocking five-game victory over powerful Baltimore in the World Series. The Miracle Mets had risen from ineptitude to the top of the baseball world. No longer lovable losers, the Mets remained consistent contenders, winning another pennant in 1973, another Series championship in 1986 and their fourth pennant in 2000 before losing in the World Series to the Yankees.

Manager Gil Hodges (14).

METS VS. OPPONENTS BY DECADE

	Braves	Cardinals	Cubs	Dodgers	Giants	Phillies	Pirates	Reds	Astros	Expos	Padres	Marlins	Rockies	Brewers	D'backs	Interleague	Decade Record
1962-69	49-89	54-90	65-79	44-94	51-87	53-91	51-93	54-83	49-87	13-5	11-1						494-799
1970-79	61-59	85-93	93-86	52-68	62-58	83-97	78-98	40-80	59-61	86-94	64-56						763-850
1980-89	68-46	87-86	92-83	63-50	49-65	90-86	102-69	62-55	56-61	89-85	58-57						816-743
1990-99	50-69	67-55	57-62	53-58	58-56	69-70	58-67	59-49	46-61	68-69	52-63	50-36	32-36	13-3	7-11	28-21	767-786
2000-02	22-29	10-11	12-7	11-10	6-15	26-25	12-8	10-11	10-9	28-22	7-15	29-21	12-10	15-6	12-10	29-25	251-234
Totals	250-292	303-335	319-317	223-280	226-281	321-369	301-335	225-278	220-279	284-275	192-192	79-57	44-46	28-9	19-21	57-46	3091-3412

Interleague results: 11-5 vs. Orioles, 8-7 vs. Red Sox, 1-2 vs. White Sox, 2-1 vs. Indians, 0-3 vs. Tigers, 2-1 vs. Royals, 2-1 vs. Twins, 12-18 vs. Yankees, 7-5 vs. Devil Rays, 12-3 vs. Blue Jays.

MANAGERS

Name	*Years*	*Record*
Casey Stengel	1962-65	175-404
Wes Westrum	1965-67	142-237
Salty Parker	1967	4-7
Gil Hodges	1968-71	339-309
Yogi Berra	1972-75	292-296
Roy McMillan	1975	26-27
Joe Frazier	1976-77	101-106
Joe Torre	1977-81	286-420
George Bamberger	1982-83	81-127
Frank Howard	1983	52-64
Dave Johnson	1984-90	595-417
Bud Harrelson	1990-91	145-129
Mike Cubbage	1991	3-4
Jeff Torborg	1992-93	85-115
Dallas Green	1993-96	229-283
Bobby Valentine	1996-2002	536-467

WORLD SERIES CHAMPIONS

Year	*Loser*	*Length*	*MVP*
1969	Baltimore	5 games	Clendenon
1986	Boston	7 games	Knight

N.L. PENNANT WINNERS

Year	*Record*	*Manager*	*Series Result*
1969	100-62	Hodges	Defeated Orioles
1973	82-79	Berra	Lost to A's
1986	108-54	Johnson	Defeated Red Sox
2000	94-68	Valentine	Lost to Yankees

EAST DIVISION CHAMPIONS

Year	*Record*	*Manager*	*NLCS Result*
1969	100-62	Hodges	Defeated Braves
1973	82-79	Berra	Defeated Reds
1986	108-54	Johnson	Defeated Astros
1988	100-60	Johnson	Lost to Dodgers

WILD-CARD QUALIFIERS

Year	*Record*	*Manager*	*NLCS Result*
1999	97-66	Valentine	Lost to Braves
2000	94-68	Valentine	Defeated Cardinals

ALL-TIME RECORD OF EXPANSION TEAMS

Team	W	L	Pct.	DT	P	WS
Arizona	440	370	.543	3	1	1
Kansas City	2,675	2,694	.498	6	2	1
Houston	3,229	3,285	.496	7	0	0
Toronto	2,025	2,063	.495	5	2	2
Anaheim	3,243	3,431	.486	3	1	1

ALL-TIME RECORD OF EXPANSION TEAMS—*cont'd.*

Team	W	L	Pct.	DT	P	WS
Montreal	2,605	2,769	.485	2	0	0
Colorado	740	817	.475	0	0	0
New York	3,091	3,412	.475	4	4	2
Milwaukee	2,545	2,831	.473	2	1	0
Seattle	1,924	2,163	.471	3	0	0
Texas	3,097	3,560	.465	4	0	0
San Diego	2,460	2,921	.457	3	2	0
Florida	706	847	.455	0	1	1
Tampa Bay	318	490	.394	0	0	0

DT—Division Titles. P—Pennants won. WS—World Series won.

ATTENDANCE HIGHS

Total	*Season*	*Park*
3,047,724	1988	Shea Stadium
3,027,121	1987	Shea Stadium
2,918,710	1989	Shea Stadium
2,804,838	2002	Shea Stadium
2,800,221	2000	Shea Stadium

BALLPARK CHRONOLOGY

Shea Stadium (1964-present)

Capacity: 56,749.
First game: Pittsburgh 4, Mets 3 (April 17, 1964).
First batter: Dick Schofield, Pirates.
First hit: Willie Stargell, Pirates (home run).
First run: Willie Stargell, Pirates (2nd inning).
First home run: Willie Stargell, Pirates.
First winning pitcher: Bob Friend, Pirates.
First-season attendance: 1,732,597.

Polo Grounds (1962-63)

First game: Pittsburgh 4, Mets 3 (April 13, 1962).
First-season attendance: 922,530.

CY YOUNG WINNERS

Tom Seaver, RH, 1969
Tom Seaver, RH, 1973
Tom Seaver, RH, 1975
Dwight Gooden, RH, 1985

ROOKIES OF THE YEAR

Tom Seaver, P, 1967
Jon Matlack, P, 1972
Darryl Strawberry, OF, 1983
Dwight Gooden, P, 1984

RETIRED UNIFORMS

No.	*Name*	*Pos.*
14	Gil Hodges	Man.
37	Casey Stengel	Man.
41	Tom Seaver	P

Manager Casey Stengel and outfielder Ed Kranepool date back to the New York Mets' inaugural season of 1962.

MILESTONE PERFORMANCES

25-plus home runs

41— Todd Hundley 1996
40— Mike Piazza 1999
39— Darryl Strawberry 1987, 1988
38— Howard Johnson 1991
Mike Piazza 2000
37— Dave Kingman 1976, 1982
Darryl Strawberry 1990
36— Dave Kingman 1975
Howard Johnson 1987, 1989
Mike Piazza 2001
34— Frank Thomas 1962
Bobby Bonilla 1993
33— Mike Piazza 2002
32— Gary Carter 1985
Mike Piazza *1998
Robin Ventura 1999
30— Bernard Gilkey 1996
Todd Hundley 1997
29— Darryl Strawberry 1985, 1989
Kevin McReynolds 1987
28— George Foster 1983
27— Darryl Strawberry 1986
Kevin McReynolds 1987
Eddie Murray 1993
Edgardo Alfonzo 1999
26— Tommie Agee 1969
Darryl Strawberry 1983, 1984
Mo Vaughn 2002
25— Edgardo Alfonzo 2000

*9 with Los Angeles; 23 with Mets.

100-plus RBIs

124— Mike Piazza 1999
120— Robin Ventura 1999
117— Howard Johnson 1991
Bernard Gilkey 1996
113— Mike Piazza 2000
112— Todd Hundley 1996
111— Mike Piazza *1998
108— Darryl Strawberry 1990
Edgardo Alfonzo 1999
105— Rusty Staub 1975
Gary Carter 1986
104— Darryl Strawberry 1987
102— John Olerud 1997
101— Darryl Strawberry 1988
Howard Johnson 1989
100— Gary Carter 1985
Eddie Murray 1993

*30 with Los Angeles; 5 with Florida; 76 with Mets.

20-plus victories

1969— Tom Seaver 25-7
1971— Tom Seaver 20-10
1972— Tom Seaver 21-12
1975— Tom Seaver 22-9
1976— Jerry Koosman 21-10
1985— Dwight Gooden 24-4
1988— David Cone 20-3
1990— Frank Viola 20-12

N.L. home run champions

1982— Dave Kingman 37
1988— Darryl Strawberry 39
1991— Howard Johnson 38

N.L. RBI champion

1991— Howard Johnson 117

N.L. batting champions

None

N.L. ERA champions

1970— Tom Seaver 2.81
1971— Tom Seaver 1.76
1973— Tom Seaver 2.08
1978— Craig Swan 2.43
1985— Dwight Gooden 1.53

N.L. strikeout champions

1970— Tom Seaver 283
1971— Tom Seaver 289
1973— Tom Seaver 251
1975— Tom Seaver 243
1976— Tom Seaver 235
1984— Dwight Gooden 276
1985— Dwight Gooden 268
1990— David Cone 233
1991— David Cone 241

No-hit pitchers

(9 innings or more)

None

Longest hitting streaks

24— Hubie Brooks 1984
Mike Piazza 1999
23— Cleon Jones 1970
Mike Vail 1975
John Olerud 1998
21— Mike Piazza 2000
20— Tommie Agee 1970
Butch Huskey 1997
Edgardo Alfonzo 1997
19— Tommie Agee 1970
Lee Mazzilli 1979
Felix Millan 1975
18— Ed Kranepool 1975
Lee Mazzilli 1980
Felix Millan 1973
Darryl Strawberry 1990
Frank Thomas 1962
17— Lance Johnson 1996
16— Joe Torre 1975
John Milner 1976
Jose Vizcaino 1994
15— Rusty Staub 1973
John Stearns 1977
John Stearns 1982
Mookie Wilson 1984
Rico Brogna 1994
Edgardo Alfonzo 2001

First baseman Keith Hernandez (right) brought his golden glove and steady bat to New York midway through the 1983 season.

INDIVIDUAL SEASON, GAME RECORDS

Outfielder Darryl Strawberry hit 252 home runs for the Mets before taking his bat to the Los Angeles Dodgers in 1991.

SEASON

Batting			
At-bats	682	Lance Johnson	1996
Runs	123	Edgardo Alfonzo	1999
Hits	227	Lance Johnson	1996
Singles	166	Lance Johnson	1996
Doubles	44	Bernard Gilkey	1996
Triples	21	Lance Johnson	1996
Home runs	41	Todd Hundley	1996
Home runs, rookie	26	Darryl Strawberry	1983
Grand slams	3	John Milner	1976
		Mike Piazza	2000
		Robin Ventura	1999
Total bases	327	Lance Johnson	1996
RBIs	124	Mike Piazza	1999
Walks	125	John Olerud	1999
Most strikeouts	156	Tommie Agee	1970
		Dave Kingman	1982
Fewest strikeouts	14	Felix Millan	1974
Batting average	.353	John Olerud	1998
Slugging pct.	.614	Mike Piazza	2000
Stolen bases	66	Roger Cedeno	1999
Pitching			
Games	80	Turk Wendell	1999
Complete games	21	Tom Seaver	1971
Innings	290.2	Tom Seaver	1970
Wins	25	Tom Seaver	1969
Losses	24	Roger Craig	1962
		Jack Fisher	1965
Winning pct.	.870 (20-3)	David Cone	1988
Walks	116	Nolan Ryan	1971
Strikeouts	289	Tom Seaver	1971
Shutouts	8	Dwight Gooden	1985
Home runs allowed	35	Roger Craig	1962
Lowest ERA	1.53	Dwight Gooden	1985
Saves	43	Armando Benitez	2001

GAME

Batting			
Runs	6	Edgardo Alfonzo	8-30-99
Hits	6	Edgardo Alfonzo	8-30-99
Doubles	3	Last by Edgardo Alfonzo	4-18-2000
Triples	3	Doug Flynn	8-5-80
Home runs	3	Last by Edgardo Alfonzo	8-30-99
RBIs	8	Dave Kingman	6-4-76
Total bases	16	Edgardo Alfonzo	8-30-99
Stolen bases	4	Last by Roger Cedeno	5-14-99

CAREER LEADERS

BATTING

Games	
Ed Kranepool	1,853
Bud Harrelson	1,322
Jerry Grote	1,235
Cleon Jones	1,201
Howard Johnson	1,154
Mookie Wilson	1,116
Darryl Strawberry	1,109
Edgardo Alfonzo	1,086
Lee Mazzilli	979
Rusty Staub	942

At-bats	
Ed Kranepool	5,436
Bud Harrelson	4,390
Cleon Jones	4,223
Mookie Wilson	4,027
Howard Johnson	3,968
Darryl Strawberry	3,903
Edgardo Alfonzo	3,897
Jerry Grote	3,881
Keith Hernandez	3,164
Lee Mazzilli	3,013

Runs	
Darryl Strawberry	662
Howard Johnson	627
Edgardo Alfonzo	614
Mookie Wilson	592
Cleon Jones	563
Ed Kranepool	536
Bud Harrelson	490
Keith Hernandez	455
Mike Piazza	407
Kevin McReynolds	405

Hits	
Ed Kranepool	1,418
Cleon Jones	1,188
Edgardo Alfonzo	1,136
Mookie Wilson	1,112
Bud Harrelson	1,029
Darryl Strawberry	1,025
Howard Johnson	997
Jerry Grote	994
Keith Hernandez	939
Lee Mazzilli	796

Doubles	
Ed Kranepool	225
Howard Johnson	214
Edgardo Alfonzo	212
Darryl Strawberry	187
Cleon Jones	182
Mookie Wilson	170
Keith Hernandez	159
Kevin McReynolds	153
John Stearns	152
Lee Mazzilli	148

Triples	
Mookie Wilson	62
Bud Harrelson	45
Cleon Jones	33
Steve Henderson	31
Darryl Strawberry	30
Lance Johnson	27
Doug Flynn	26
Ed Kranepool	25
Lee Mazzilli	22
Wayne Garrett	20
Ron Swoboda	20

Home runs	
Darryl Strawberry	252
Howard Johnson	192
Mike Piazza	170
Dave Kingman	154
Todd Hundley	124
Kevin McReynolds	122
Edgardo Alfonzo	120
Ed Kranepool	118
George Foster	99
Bobby Bonilla	95

Total bases	
Ed Kranepool	2,047
Darryl Strawberry	2,028
Howard Johnson	1,823
Edgardo Alfonzo	1,736
Cleon Jones	1,715
Mookie Wilson	1,586
Mike Piazza	1,390
Keith Hernandez	1,358
Kevin McReynolds	1,338
Jerry Grote	1,278

Runs batted in	
Darryl Strawberry	733
Howard Johnson	629
Ed Kranepool	614
Edgardo Alfonzo	538
Cleon Jones	521
Mike Piazza	505
Keith Hernandez	468
Kevin McReynolds	456
Rusty Staub	399
Todd Hundley	397

Extra-base hits	
Darryl Strawberry	469
Howard Johnson	424
Ed Kranepool	368
Edgardo Alfonzo	346
Cleon Jones	308
Mike Piazza	308
Mookie Wilson	292
Kevin McReynolds	289
Keith Hernandez	249
Todd Hundley	249

Batting average
(Minimum 500 games)

Batting average	
Mike Piazza	.310
Keith Hernandez	.297
Edgardo Alfonzo	.292
Dave Magadan	.292
Wally Backman	.283
Cleon Jones	.281
Lenny Dykstra	.278
Felix Millan	.278
Mookie Wilson	.276
Rusty Staub	.276

Stolen bases	
Mookie Wilson	281
Howard Johnson	202
Darryl Strawberry	191
Lee Mazzilli	152
Lenny Dykstra	116
Bud Harrelson	115
Wally Backman	106
Vince Coleman	99
Tommie Agee	92
Roger Cedeno	91
Cleon Jones	91
John Stearns	91

PITCHING

Earned-run average
(Minimum 500 innings)

Earned-run average	
Tom Seaver	2.57
Jesse Orosco	2.73
John Franco	2.96
Jon Matlack	3.03
David Cone	3.08
Jerry Koosman	3.09
Dwight Gooden	3.10
Bob Ojeda	3.12
Sid Fernandez	3.14
Bret Saberhagen	3.16

Wins	
Tom Seaver	198
Dwight Gooden	157
Jerry Koosman	140
Ron Darling	99
Sid Fernandez	98
Jon Matlack	82
David Cone	80
Bobby Jones	74
Al Leiter	70
Rick Reed	59
Craig Swan	59

Losses	
Jerry Koosman	137
Tom Seaver	124
Dwight Gooden	85
Jon Matlack	81
Al Jackson	80
Sid Fernandez	78
Jack Fisher	73
Craig Swan	71
Ron Darling	70
Bobby Jones	56

Innings pitched	
Tom Seaver	3,045.1
Jerry Koosman	2,544.2
Dwight Gooden	2,169.2
Ron Darling	1,620.0
Sid Fernandez	1,584.2
Jon Matlack	1,448.0
Craig Swan	1,230.2
Bobby Jones	1,215.2
David Cone	1,191.1
Al Leiter	1,005.2

Strikeouts	
Tom Seaver	2,541
Dwight Gooden	1,875
Jerry Koosman	1,799
Sid Fernandez	1,449
David Cone	1,159
Ron Darling	1,148
Jon Matlack	1,023
Al Leiter	850
Bobby Jones	714
Craig Swan	671

Bases on balls	
Tom Seaver	847
Jerry Koosman	820
Dwight Gooden	651
Ron Darling	614
Sid Fernandez	596
Jon Matlack	419
David Cone	418
Craig Swan	368
Al Leiter	355
Bobby Jones	353

Games	
John Franco	605
Tom Seaver	401
Jerry Koosman	376
Jesse Orosco	372
Tug McGraw	361
Dwight Gooden	305
Jeff Innis	288
Turk Wendell	285
Roger McDowell	280
Armando Benitez	288

Shutouts	
Tom Seaver	44
Jerry Koosman	26
Jon Matlack	26
Dwight Gooden	23
David Cone	15
Ron Darling	10
Al Jackson	10
Sid Fernandez	9
Bob Ojeda	9
Gary Gentry	8

Saves	
John Franco	274
Armando Benitez	139
Jesse Orosco	107
Tug McGraw	86
Roger McDowell	84
Neil Allen	69
Skip Lockwood	65
Randy Myers	56
Ron Taylor	49
Doug Sisk	33

TEAM SEASON, GAME RECORDS

SEASON

Batting		
Most at-bats	5,618	1996
Most runs	853	1999
Fewest runs	473	1968
Most hits	1,553	1999
Most singles	1,087	1980
Most doubles	297	1999
Most triples	47	1978, 1996
Most home runs	198	2000
Fewest home runs	61	1980
Most grand slams	8	1999, 2000
Most pinch-hit home runs	12	1983
Most total bases	2,430	1987
Most stolen bases	159	1987
Highest batting average	.279	1999
Lowest batting average	.219	1963
Highest slugging pct	.434	1987, 1999

Pitching		
Lowest ERA	2.72	1968
Highest ERA	5.04	1962
Most complete games	53	1976
Most shutouts	28	1969
Most saves	51	1987
Most walks	617	1999
Most strikeouts	1,217	1990

Fielding		
Most errors	210	1962, 1963
Fewest errors	68	1999
Most double plays	171	1966, 1983
Highest fielding average	.989	1999

General		
Most games won	108	1986
Most games lost	120	1962
Highest win pct	.667	1986
Lowest win pct	.250	1962

GAME, INNING

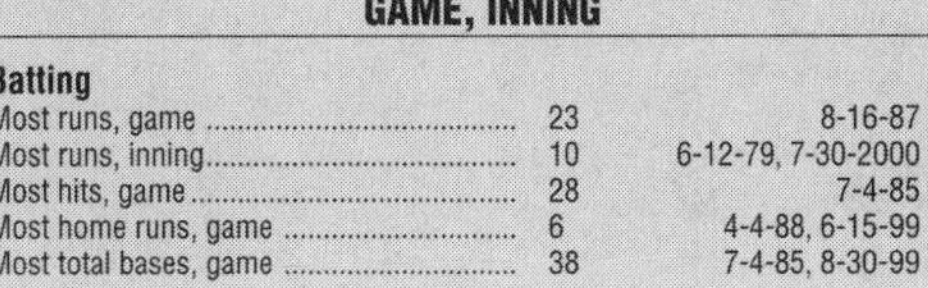

Batting		
Most runs, game	23	8-16-87
Most runs, inning	10	6-12-79, 7-30-2000
Most hits, game	28	7-4-85
Most home runs, game	6	4-4-88, 6-15-99
Most total bases, game	38	7-4-85, 8-30-99

Lefthanded starter Jerry Koosman was a key figure in the Mets' 1969 World Series miracle.

HISTORY

METS YEAR-BY-YEAR

Year	W	L	Place	Games Back	Manager	Leaders: Batting avg.	Hits	Home runs	RBIs	Wins	ERA
1962	40	120	10th	60½	Stengel	Ashburn, .306	Thomas, 152	Thomas, 34	Thomas, 94	Craig, 10	Jackson, 4.40
1963	51	111	10th	48	Stengel	Hunt, .272	Hunt, 145	Hickman, 17	Thomas, 60	Jackson, 13	Willey, 3.10
1964	53	109	10th	40	Stengel	Hunt, .303	Christopher, 163	C. Smith, 20	Christopher, 76	Jackson, 11	Wakefield, 3.61
1965	50	112	10th	47	Stengel, Westrum	Kranepool, .253	Kranepool, 133	Swoboda, 19	C. Smith, 62	Fisher, Jackson, 8	McGraw, 3.32
1966	66	95	9th	28½	Westrum	Hunt, .288	Hunt, 138	Kranepool, 16	Boyer, 61	Fisher, Ribant, B. Shaw, 11	Ribant, 3.20
1967	61	101	10th	40½	Westrum, Parker	T. Davis, .302	T. Davis, 174	T. Davis, 16	T. Davis, 73	Seaver, 16	Seaver, 2.76
1968	73	89	9th	24	Hodges	Jones, .297	Jones, 151	Charles, 15	Swoboda, 59	Koosman, 19	Koosman, 2.08
								EAST DIVISION			
1969	100	62	*1st	+8	Hodges	Jones, .340	Jones, 164	Agee, 26	Agee, 76	Seaver, 25	Seaver, 2.21
1970	83	79	3rd	6	Hodges	Shamsky, .293	Agee, 182	Agee, 24	Clendenon, 97	Seaver, 18	Seaver, 2.82
1971	83	79	†3rd	14	Hodges	Jones, .319	Jones, 161	Agee, Jones, Kranepool, 14	Jones, 69	Seaver, 20	McGraw, 1.70
1972	83	73	3rd	13½	Berra	Jones, .245	Agee, 96	Milner, 17	Jones, 52	Seaver, 21	McGraw, 1.70
1973	82	79	*1st	+1½	Berra	Millan, .290	Millan, 185	Milner, 23	Staub, 76	Seaver, 19	Seaver, 2.08
1974	71	91	5th	17	Berra	Jones, .282	Staub, 145	Milner, 20	Staub, 78	Koosman, 15	Matlack, 2.41
1975	82	80	†3rd	10½	Berra, McMillan	Grote, .295	Millan, 191	Kingman, 36	Staub, 105	Seaver, 22	Seaver, 2.38
1976	86	76	3rd	15	Frazier	Kranepool, .292	Millan, 150	Kingman, 37	Kingman, 86	Koosman, 21	Seaver, 2.59
1977	64	98	6th	37	Frazier, Torre	Randle, .304	Randle, 156	Henderson, Milner, Stearns, 12	Henderson, 65	Espinosa, 10	Seaver, 3.00
1978	66	96	6th	24	Torre	Mazzilli, .273	Henderson, Montanez, 156	Montanez, 17	Montanez, 96	Espinosa, 11	Swan, 2.43
1979	63	99	6th	35	Torre	Henderson, .306	Mazzilli, 181	Youngblood, 16	Hebner, Mazzilli, 79	Swan, 14	Swan, 3.29
1980	67	95	5th	24	Torre	Henderson, .290	Mazzilli, 162	Mazzilli, 16	Mazzilli, 76	Bomback, 10	Reardon, 2.61
1981	41	62	‡5th/4th	—	Torre	Brooks, .307	Brooks, 110	Kingman, 22	Kingman, 59	Allen, Zachry, 7	Falcone, 2.55
1982	65	97	6th	27	Bamberger	Stearns, .293	Wilson, 178	Kingman, 37	Kingman, 99	Swan, 11	Orosco, 2.72
1983	68	94	6th	22	Bamberger, Howard	Wilson, .276	Wilson, 176	Foster, 28	Foster, 90	Orosco, 13	Orosco, 1.47
1984	90	72	2nd	6½	D. Johnson	Hernandez, .311	Hernandez, 171	Strawberry, 26	Strawberry, 97	Gooden, 17	Orosco, 2.59
1985	98	64	2nd	3	D. Johnson	Hernandez, .309	Hernandez, 183	Carter, 32	Carter, 100	Gooden, 24	Gooden, 1.53
1986	108	54	*1st	+21½	D. Johnson	Backman, .320	Hernandez, 171	Strawberry, 27	Carter, 105	Ojeda, 18	Ojeda, 2.57
1987	92	70	2nd	3	D. Johnson	Wilson, .299	Hernandez, 170	Strawberry, 39	Strawberry, 104	Gooden, 15	Gooden, 3.21
1988	100	60	§1st	+15	D. Johnson	Wilson, .296	McReynolds, 159	Strawberry, 39	Strawberry, 101	Cone, 20	Cone, 2.22
1989	87	75	2nd	6	D. Johnson	H. Johnson, .287	H. Johnson, 164	H. Johnson, 36	H. Johnson, 101	Cone, Darling, Fernandez, 14	Fernandez, 2.83
1990	91	71	2nd	4	Johnson, Harrelson	Magadan, .328	Jefferies, 171	Strawberry, 37	Strawberry, 108	Viola, 20	Viola, 2.67
1991	77	84	5th	20½	Harrelson, Cubbage	Jefferies, .272	H. Johnson, 146	H. Johnson, 38	H. Johnson, 117	Cone, 14	Cone, 3.29
1992	72	90	5th	24	Torborg	Murray, .261	Murray, 144	Bonilla, 19	Murray, 93	Fernandez, 14	Fernandez, 2.73
1993	59	103	7th	38	Torborg, Green	Murray, .285	Murray, 174	Bonilla, 34	Murray, 100	Gooden, 12	Fernandez, 2.93
1994	55	58	3rd	18½	Green	Kent, .292	Kent, 121	Bonilla, 20	Kent, 68	Saberhagen, 14	Saberhagen, 2.74
1995	69	75	†2nd	21	Green	Brogna, .289	Vizcaino, 146	Brogna, 22	Brogna, 76	B. Jones, 10	Isringhausen, 2.81
1996	71	91	4th	25	Green, Valentine	Johnson, .333	Johnson, 227	Hundley, 41	Gilkey, 117	Clark, 14	Clark, 3.43
1997	88	74	3rd	13	Valentine	Alfonzo, .315	Alfonzo, 163	Hundley, 30	Olerud, 102	B. Jones, 15	Reed, 2.89
1998	88	74	2nd	18	Valentine	Olerud, .353	Olerud, 197	Piazza, 32	Piazza, 111	Leiter, 17	Leiter, 2.47
1999	97	66	▲§2nd	6½	Valentine	Henderson, .315	Alfonzo, 191	Piazza, 40	Piazza, 124	Leiter, Hershiser, 13	Leiter, 4.23
2000	94	68	▲*2nd	1	Valentine	Alfonzo, .324	Alfonzo, 176	Piazza, 38	Piazza, 113	Leiter, 16	Hampton, 3.15
2001	82	80	3rd	6	Valentine	Relaford, .302	Piazza, 151	Piazza, 36	Piazza, 94	Appier, Leiter, Trachsel, 11	Leiter, 3.31
2002	75	86	5th	26½	Valentine	Alfonzo, .308	Alomar, 157	Piazza, 33	Piazza, 98	Leiter, 13	Trachsel, 3.37

* Won Championship Series. † Tied for position. ‡ First half 17-34; second half 24-28. § Lost Championship Series. ∞ Won wild-card playoff. ▲ Won Division Series.

Note: Batting average minimum 350 at-bats; ERA minimum 90 innings pitched.

Hobie Landrith

NATIONAL LEAGUE baseball returned to the nation's largest metropolitan area on October 16, 1960, when owners approved 1962 expansion to New York and Houston. The arrival of the "Mets" filled the void created by the 1958 departures of the Dodgers and Giants to the West Coast, and it set the stage for the triumphant New York return of former Yankees manager Casey Stengel as the lovable boss of New York's expansion bumblers.

The Mets stocked their roster with 22 players from the October 10, 1961, expansion draft, grabbing catcher Hobie Landrith with their first pick. The franchise debut took place on April 11, 1962, when the Mets dropped an 11-4 decision at St. Louis—the first of 120 losses they would suffer in their inaugural season.

Expansion draft (October 10, 1961)

Players

Player	From	Position
Gus Bell	Cincinnati	outfield
Ed Bouchee	Chicago	first base
Chris Cannizzaro	St. Louis	catcher
Elio Chacon	Cincinnati	second base
Joe Christopher	Pittsburgh	outfield
Clarence Coleman	Philadelphia	catcher
John DeMerit.	Milwaukee	outfield
Sammy Drake	Chicago	infield
Jim Hickman	St. Louis	outfield
Gil Hodges	Los Angeles	first base
*Hobie Landrith	San Francisco	catcher
Felix Mantilla.	Milwaukee	shortstop
Bobby Gene Smith	Philadelphia	outfield
Lee Walls	Philadelphia	outfield
Don Zimmer	Chicago	second base

Pitchers

Pitcher	From	Throws
Craig Anderson	St. Louis	righthanded
Roger Craig	Los Angeles	righthanded
Ray Daviault	San Francisco	righthanded
Jay Hook	Cincinnati	righthanded
Al Jackson	Pittsburgh	lefthanded
Sherman Jones	Cincinnati	righthanded
Bob Miller	St. Louis	righthanded

*First pick

Opening day lineup

April 11, 1962

Richie Ashburn, center field
Felix Mantilla, shortstop
Charlie Neal, second base
Frank Thomas, left field
Gus Bell, right field
Gil Hodges, first base
Don Zimmer, third base
Hobie Landrith, catcher
Roger Craig, pitcher

Roger Craig

Mets firsts

First hit: Gus Bell, April 11, 1962, at St. Louis (single)
First home run: Gil Hodges, April 11, 1962, at St. Louis
First RBI: Charlie Neal, April 11, 1962, at St. Louis
First win: Jay Hook, April 23, 1962, at Pittsburgh
First shutout: Al Jackson, April 29, 1962, 8-0 vs. Philadelphia

PHILADELPHIA PHILLIES

FRANCHISE CHRONOLOGY

First season: 1883, as a member of the National League. The Phillies dropped an opening 4-3 decision to Providence and went on to lose 81 of 98 games. They finished in last place, 46 games behind first-place Boston and 23 games behind seventh-place Detroit.

1884-1900: The Phillies improved from that first-season disaster, but never enough to claim a pennant. They finished second once and third six times before entering the new century.

1901-present: The modern-era Phillies were not much different from their predecessors. They did not claim their first N.L. pennant until 1915, 32 years after their birth, and failed to win a World Series championship until 1980, at the not-so-tender age of 97. Over their long history, the Phillies have finished last in their league or division 31 times, more than once every four years. They went 34 years between their first and second pennants and 30 more between their second and third. Their most successful run came from 1976 to 1983, when they won five East Division titles, two pennants and their only World Series—a six-game 1980 triumph over Kansas City. Philadelphia fans were treated to their fifth pennant in 1993, but they watched their Phillies lose a six-game World Series to Toronto.

Third baseman Mike Schmidt.

PHILLIES VS. OPPONENTS BY DECADE

	Braves	Cardinals	Cubs	Dodgers	Giants	Pirates	Reds	Astros	Mets	Expos	Padres	Marlins	Rockies	Brewers	D'backs	Interleague	Decade Record
1900-09	119-87	121-90	90-119	112-93	87-121	75-137	105-105										709-752
1910-19	123-90	112-98	101-110	110-99	85-124	107-105	124-91										762-717
1920-29	118-100	69-151	88-132	87-133	65-149	71-148	68-149										566-962
1930-39	97-122	61-159	73-147	89-128	72-145	90-126	99-116										581-943
1940-49	87-132	70-150	99-121	58-162	91-129	95-121	84-136										584-951
1950-59	102-118	107-113	128-92	92-128	99-121	132-88	107-113										767-773
1960-69	75-107	79-108	95-93	76-106	77-105	89-98	75-107	87-51	91-53	7-11	8-4						759-843
1970-79	58-62	91-86	92-87	56-63	67-53	79-101	47-73	61-59	97-83	90-88	74-46						812-801
1980-89	53-64	80-95	95-78	59-55	61-54	91-83	55-60	61-57	86-90	86-87	56-57						783-780
1990-99	50-70	57-67	63-60	54-61	44-67	58-66	39-68	43-62	70-69	73-65	53-60	52-34	36-29	9-9	8-10	23-26	732-823
2000-02	21-29	8-13	9-12	10-12	8-13	10-11	12-7	10-11	25-26	25-25	9-11	27-24	10-11	13-6	8-15	26-28	231-254
Totals	903-981	855-1130	933-1051	803-1040	756-1081	897-1084	815-1025	262-240	369-321	281-276	200-178	79-58	46-40	22-15	16-25	49-54	7286-8599

Interleague results: 13-17 vs. Orioles, 9-7 vs. Red Sox, 1-2 vs. White Sox, 2-1 vs. Indians, 4-2 vs. Tigers, 1-2 vs. Twins, 7-8 vs. Yankees, 4-8 vs. Devil Rays, 8-7 vs. Blue Jays.

MANAGERS

Name	*Years*	*Record*
Bob Ferguson	1883	4-13
Blondie Purcell	1883	13-68
Harry Wright	1884-93	636-566
Jack Clements	1890	13-6
Al Reach	1890	4-7
Bob Allen	1890	25-10
Albert Irwin	1894-95	149-110
Billy Nash	1896	62-68
George Stallings	1897-98	74-104
Bill Shettsline	1898-1902	367-303
Chief Zimmer	1903	49-86
Hugh Duffy	1904-06	206-251
Bill Murray	1907-09	240-214
Red Dooin	1910-14	392-370
Pat Moran	1915-18	323-257
Jack Coombs	1919	18-44
Gavvy Cravath	1919-20	91-137
Bill Donovan	1921	25-62
Kaiser Wilhelm	1921-22	83-137
Art Fletcher	1923-26	231-378
Stuffy McInnis	1927	51-103
Burt Shotton	1928-33	370-549
Jimmy Wilson	1934-38	280-477
Hans Lobert	1938, 1942	42-111
Doc Prothro	1939-41	138-320
Bucky Harris	1943	38-52
Fred Fitzsimmons	1943-45	105-181
Ben Chapman	1945-48	196-276
Dusty Cooke	1948	6-6
Eddie Sawyer	1948-52, 1958-60	390-423
Steve O'Neill	1952-54	182-140
Terry Moore	1954	35-42
Mayo Smith	1955-58	264-282
Andy Cohen	1960	1-0
Gene Mauch	1960-68	646-684
George Myatt	1968, 1969	20-35
Bob Skinner	1968-69	92-123
Frank Lucchesi	1970-72	166-233
Paul Owens	1972, 1983-84	161-158
Danny Ozark	1973-79	594-510
Dallas Green	1979-81	169-130
Pat Corrales	1982-83	132-115
John Felske	1985-87	190-194
Lee Elia	1987-88	111-142
John Vukovich	1988	5-4
Nick Leyva	1989-91	148-189
Jim Fregosi	1991-96	431-463
Terry Francona	1997-2000	285-363
Larry Bowa	2001-02	166-157

WORLD SERIES CHAMPIONS

Year	*Loser*	*Length*	*MVP*
1980	Kansas City	6 games	Schmidt

N.L. PENNANT WINNERS

Year	*Record*	*Manager*	*Series Result*
1915	90-62	Moran	Lost to Red Sox
1950	91-63	Sawyer	Lost to Yankees
1980	91-71	Green	Defeated Royals
1983	90-72	Corrales, Owens	Lost to Orioles
1993	97-65	Fregosi	Lost to Blue Jays

EAST DIVISION CHAMPIONS

Year	*Record*	*Manager*	*NLCS Result*
1976	101-61	Ozark	Lost to Reds
1977	101-61	Ozark	Lost to Dodgers
1978	90-72	Ozark	Lost to Dodgers
1980	91-71	Green	Defeated Astros
*1981	59-48	Green	None
1983	90-72	Corrales, Owens	Defeated Dodgers
1993	97-65	Fregosi	Defeated Braves

* First-half champion; lost division series to Expos.

ATTENDANCE HIGHS

Total	*Season*	*Park*
3,137,674	1993	Veterans Stadium
2,775,011	1979	Veterans Stadium
2,700,007	1977	Veterans Stadium
2,651,650	1980	Veterans Stadium
2,583,389	1978	Veterans Stadium

BALLPARK CHRONOLOGY

Veterans Stadium (1971-present)

Capacity: 62,418.
First game: Phillies 4, Montreal 1 (April 10, 1971).
First batter: Boots Day, Expos.
First hit: Larry Bowa, Phillies (single).
First run: Ron Hunt, Expos (6th inning).
First home run: Don Money, Phillies.
First winning pitcher: Jim Bunning, Phillies.
First-season attendance: 1,511,223.

Recreation Park (1883-86)

First game: Providence 4, Philadelphia 3 (May 1, 1883).

Huntington Street Grounds/Baker Bowl (1887-1938)

Capacity: 18,800.
First game: Phillies 19, New York 10 (April 30, 1887).

Shibe Park (1927, 1938-70)

Capacity: 33,608.
First game: St. Louis 2, Phillies 1 (May 16, 1927).
First-season attendance (1939): 277,973.

N.L. MVPs

Chuck Klein, OF, 1932
Jim Konstanty, P, 1950
Mike Schmidt, 3B, 1980
Mike Schmidt, 3B, 1981
Mike Schmidt, 3B, 1986

CY YOUNG WINNERS

Steve Carlton, LH, 1972
Steve Carlton, LH, 1977
Steve Carlton, LH, 1980
Steve Carlton, LH, 1982
John Denny, RH, 1983
Steve Bedrosian, RH, 1987

ROOKIES OF THE YEAR

Jack Sanford, P, 1957
Dick Allen, 3B, 1964
Scott Rolen, 3B, 1997

MANAGER OF THE YEAR

Larry Bowa, 2001

RETIRED UNIFORMS

No.	*Name*	*Pos.*
1	Richie Ashburn	OF
20	Mike Schmidt	3B
32	Steve Carlton	P
36	Robin Roberts	P

MILESTONE PERFORMANCES

30-plus home runs
48— Mike Schmidt ... 1980
45— Mike Schmidt ... 1979
43— Chuck Klein ... 1929
41— Cy Williams ... 1923
40— Chuck Klein ... 1930
Richie Allen ... 1966
Mike Schmidt ... 1983
39— Greg Luzinski ... 1977
38— Chuck Klein ... 1932
Mike Schmidt ... 1975, 1976, 1977
37— Mike Schmidt ... 1986
Pat Burrell ... 2002
36— Mike Schmidt ... 1974, 1984
35— Greg Luzinski ... 1978
Mike Schmidt ... 1982, 1987
34— Deron Johnson ... 1971
Greg Luzinski ... 1975
33— Richie Allen ... 1968
Mike Schmidt ... 1985
32— Lefty O'Doul ... 1929
Stan Lopata ... 1956
Johnny Callison ... 1965
Richie Allen ... 1969
31— Don Hurst ... 1929
Chuck Klein ... 1931
Del Ennis ... 1950
Johnny Callison ... 1964
Mike Schmidt ... 1981
Scott Rolen ... 1998
Mike Lieberthal ... 1999
Bobby Abreu ... 2001
30— Cy Williams ... 1927
Del Ennis ... 1948
Willie Montanez ... 1971
Benito Santiago ... 1996

100-plus RBIs
170— Chuck Klein ... 1930
165— Sam Thompson ... 1895
146— Ed Delahanty ... 1893
145— Chuck Klein ... 1929
143— Don Hurst ... 1932
141— Sam Thompson ... 1894
137— Ed Delahanty ... 1899
Chuck Klein ... 1932
131— Ed Delahanty ... 1894
130— Greg Luzinski ... 1977
128— Gavvy Cravath ... 1913
127— Nap Lajoie ... 1897, 1898
126— Sam Thompson ... 1893
Ed Delahanty ... 1896
Del Ennis ... 1950
125— Lave Cross ... 1894
Don Hurst ... 1929
Del Ennis ... 1953
124— Pinky Whitney ... 1932
123— Sherry Magee ... 1910
122— Lefty O'Doul ... 1929
121— Chuck Klein ... 1931
Mike Schmidt ... 1980
120— Chuck Klein ... 1933
Del Ennis ... 1955
Greg Luzinski ... 1975
119— Del Ennis ... 1954
Mike Schmidt ... 1986
117— Pinky Whitney ... 1930
116— Mike Schmidt ... 1974
Pat Burrell ... 2002
115— Gavvy Cravath ... 1915
Pinky Whitney ... 1929
114— Cy Williams ... 1923
Mike Schmidt ... 1979
113— Mike Schmidt ... 1987
111— Sam Thompson ... 1889
110— Elmer Flick ... 1900
Del Ennis ... 1949
Richie Allen ... 1966
Scott Rolen ... 1998
Bobby Abreu ... 2001
109— Ed Delahanty ... 1900
Mike Schmidt ... 1983
Darren Daulton ... 1992
108— Ed Delahanty ... 1901
107— Del Ennis ... 1952
Don Demeter ... 1962
Mike Schmidt ... 1976
Scott Rolen ... 2001
106— Ed Delahanty ... 1895
Mike Schmidt ... 1984
105— Darren Daulton ... 1993
104— Sam Thompson ... 1892
Ron Northey ... 1944
John Callison ... 1964
Rico Brogna ... 1998
103— Sherry Magee ... 1914
Pinky Whitney ... 1928
Bill White ... 1966
102— Sam Thompson ... 1890
Dolf Camilli ... 1936
Rico Brogna ... 1999
101— Lave Cross ... 1895
John Callison ... 1965
Mike Schmidt ... 1977
Greg Luzinski ... 1978
100— Sam Thompson ... 1896
Gavvy Cravath ... 1914
Juan Samuel ... 1987

20-plus victories
1884— Charlie Ferguson ... 21-25
1885— Charlie Ferguson ... 26-20
Ed Daily ... 26-23
1886— Charlie Ferguson ... 30-9
Dan Casey ... 24-18
1887— Dan Casey ... 28-13
Charlie Ferguson ... 22-10
Charlie Buffinton ... 21-17
1888— Charlie Buffinton ... 28-17
1889— Charlie Buffinton ... 28-16
1890— Kid Gleason ... 38-17
Tom Vickery ... 24-22
1891— Kid Gleason ... 24-22
Charles Esper ... 20-15
1892— Gus Weyhing ... 32-21
1893— Gus Weyhing ... 23-16
1894— Jack Taylor ... 23-13
1895— Jack Taylor ... 26-14
Kid Carsey ... 24-16
1896— Jack Taylor ... 20-21
1898— Wiley Piatt ... 24-14
1899— Wiley Piatt ... 23-15
Red Donahue ... 21-8
Charles Fraser ... 21-12
1901— Al Orth ... 20-12
Red Donahue ... 21-13
1905— Charlie Pittinger ... 23-14
1907— Frank Sparks ... 22-8
1908— George McQuillan ... 23-17
1910— Earl Moore ... 22-15
1911— Grover Alexander ... 28-13
1913— Tom Seaton ... 27-12
Grover Alexander ... 22-8
1914— Grover Alexander ... 27-15
Erskine Mayer ... 21-19
1915— Grover Alexander ... 31-10
Erskine Mayer ... 21-15
1916— Grover Alexander ... 33-12
Eppa Rixey ... 22-10
1917— Grover Alexander ... 30-13
1950— Robin Roberts ... 20-11
1951— Robin Roberts ... 21-15
1952— Robin Roberts ... 28-7
1953— Robin Roberts ... 23-16
1954— Robin Roberts ... 23-15
1955— Robin Roberts ... 23-14
1966— Chris Short ... 20-10
1972— Steve Carlton ... 27-10
1976— Steve Carlton ... 20-7
1977— Steve Carlton ... 23-10
1980— Steve Carlton ... 24-9
1982— Steve Carlton ... 23-11

N.L. home run champions
1876— George Hall ... 5
1889— Sam Thompson ... 20
1893— Ed Delahanty ... 19
1895— Sam Thompson ... 18
1896— Ed Delahanty ... *13
1897— Nap Lajoie ... 10
1913— Gavvy Cravath ... 19
1914— Gavvy Cravath ... 19
1915— Gavvy Cravath ... 24
1917— Gavvy Cravath ... *12
1918— Gavvy Cravath ... 8
1919— Gavvy Cravath ... 12
1920— Cy Williams ... 15
1923— Cy Williams ... 41
1927— Cy Williams ... *30
1929— Chuck Klein ... 43
1931— Chuck Klein ... 31
1932— Chuck Klein ... *38
1933— Chuck Klein ... 28
1974— Mike Schmidt ... 36
1975— Mike Schmidt ... 38
1976— Mike Schmidt ... 38
1980— Mike Schmidt ... 48
1981— Mike Schmidt ... 31
1983— Mike Schmidt ... 40
1984— Mike Schmidt ... *36
1986— Mike Schmidt ... 37

* Tied for league lead

N.L. RBI champions
1907— Sherry Magee ... 85
1910— Sherry Magee ... 123
1913— Gavvy Cravath ... 128
1914— Sherry Magee ... 103
1915— Gavvy Cravath ... 115
1931— Chuck Klein ... 121
1932— Don Hurst ... 143
1933— Chuck Klein ... 120
1950— Del Ennis ... 126
1975— Greg Luzinski ... 120
1980— Mike Schmidt ... 121
1981— Mike Schmidt ... 91
1984— Mike Schmidt ... *106
1986— Mike Schmidt ... 119
1992— Darren Daulton ... 109

* Tied for league lead

N.L. batting champions
1891— Billy Hamilton ... .340
1899— Ed Delahanty ... .410
1910— Sherry Magee ... .331
1929— Lefty O'Doul ... .398
1933— Chuck Klein ... .368
1947— Harry Walker ... *.363
1955— Richie Ashburn ... .338
1958— Richie Ashburn ... .350

*10 games with Cardinals; 130 with Phillies.

N.L. ERA champions
1915— Grover Alexander ... 1.22
1916— Grover Alexander ... 1.55
1917— Grover Alexander ... 1.83
1972— Steve Carlton ... 1.97

N.L. strikeout champions
1910— Earl Moore ... 185
1912— Grover Alexander ... 195
1913— Tom Seaton ... 168
1914— Grover Alexander ... 214
1915— Grover Alexander ... 241
1916— Grover Alexander ... 167
1917— Grover Alexander ... 201
1940— Kirby Higbe ... 137
1953— Robin Roberts ... 198
1954— Robin Roberts ... 185
1957— Jack Sanford ... 188
1967— Jim Bunning ... 253
1972— Steve Carlton ... 310
1974— Steve Carlton ... 240
1980— Steve Carlton ... 286
1982— Steve Carlton ... 286
1983— Steve Carlton ... 275
1997— Curt Schilling ... 319
1998— Curt Schilling ... 300

No-hit pitchers
(9 innings or more)
1885— Charles Ferguson ... 1-0 vs. Providence
1898— Red Donahue ... 5-0 vs. Boston
1903— Charles Fraser ... 10-0 vs. Chicago
1906— John Lush ... 6-0 vs. Brooklyn
1964— Jim Bunning ... 6-0 vs. New York (Perfect)
1971— Rick Wise ... 4-0 vs. Cincinnati
1990— Terry Mulholland ... 6-0 vs. San Francisco
1991— Tommy Greene ... 2-0 vs. Montreal

Longest hitting streaks
36— Billy Hamilton ... 1894
31— Ed Delahanty ... 1899
26— Chuck Klein ... 1930 (twice)
24— Willie Montanez ... 1974
23— Goldie Rapp ... 1921
Johnny Moore ... 1934
Richie Ashburn ... 1948
Pete Rose ... 1979
Lonnie Smith ... 1981
Lenny Dykstra ... 1990
22— Chuck Klein ... 1931
Chick Fullis ... 1933
21— Ed Dalahanty ... 1897
Irish Meusel ... 1920
Danny Litwhiler ... 1940
Pete Rose ... 1982
20— Nap Lajoie ... 1897
Chuck Klein ... 1932
Richie Ashburn ... 1951
Pancho Herrera ... 1960
Garry Maddox ... 1978

INDIVIDUAL SEASON, GAME RECORDS

SEASON

Batting

At-bats	701	Juan Samuel	1984
Runs	196	Billy Hamilton	1894
Hits	254	Lefty O'Doul	1929
Singles	181	Lefty O'Doul	1929
		Richie Ashburn	1951
Doubles	59	Chuck Klein	1930
Triples	26	Sam Thompson	1894
Home runs	48	Mike Schmidt	1980
Home runs, rookie	30	Willie Montanez	1971
Grand slams	4	Vince DiMaggio	1945
Total bases	445	Chuck Klein	1930
RBIs	170	Chuck Klein	1930
Walks	129	Lenny Dykstra	1993
Most strikeouts	180	Mike Schmidt	1975
Fewest strikeouts	8	Emil Verban	1947
Batting average	.408	Ed Delahanty	1899
Slugging pct.	.687	Chuck Klein	1930
Stolen bases	115	Billy Hamilton	1891

Pitching (since 1900)

Games	90	Kent Tekulve	1987
Complete games	38	Grover Alexander	1916
Innings	388.2	Grover Alexander	1916
Wins	33	Grover Alexander	1916
Losses	24	Chick Fraser	1904
Winning pct.	.800 (28-7)	Robin Roberts	1952
	.800 (16-4)	Tommy Greene	1993
Walks	164	Earl Moore	1911
Strikeouts	319	Curt Schilling	1997
Shutouts	16	Grover Alexander	1916
Home runs allowed	46	Robin Roberts	1956
Lowest ERA	1.22	Grover Alexander	1915
Saves	45	Jose Mesa	2002

GAME

Batting

Runs	5	Last by Mariano Duncan	5-3-92
Hits	6	Connie Ryan	4-16-53
Doubles	4	Last by Willie Jones	4-20-49
Triples	3	Harry Wolverton	7-13-1900
Home runs	4	Chuck Klein	7-10-36
		Mike Schmidt	4-17-76
RBIs	8	Last by Mike Schmidt	4-17-76
Total bases	17	Mike Schmidt	4-17-76
Stolen bases	4	Sherry Magee	7-12-06, 8-31-06

HISTORY

CAREER LEADERS

BATTING

Games
Mike Schmidt	2,404
Richie Ashburn	1,794
Larry Bowa	1,739
Tony Taylor	1,669
Del Ennis	1,630
Ed Delahanty	1,557
Sherry Magee	1,521
Willie Jones	1,520
Granny Hamner	1,501
Cy Williams	1,463

At-bats
Mike Schmidt	8,352
Richie Ashburn	7,122
Larry Bowa	6,815
Ed Delahanty	6,365
Del Ennis	6,327
Tony Taylor	5,799
Granny Hamner	5,772
Sherry Magee	5,505
Willie Jones	5,419
Johnny Callison	5,306

Runs
Mike Schmidt	1,506
Ed Delahanty	1,368
Richie Ashburn	1,114
Chuck Klein	963
Sam Thompson	930
Roy Thomas	923
Sherry Magee	898
Del Ennis	891
Billy Hamilton	880
Cy Williams	825

Hits
Mike Schmidt	2,234
Richie Ashburn	2,217
Ed Delahanty	2,214
Del Ennis	1,812
Larry Bowa	1,798
Chuck Klein	1,705
Sherry Magee	1,647
Cy Williams	1,553
Granny Hamner	1,518
Tony Taylor	1,511

Doubles
Ed Delahanty	442
Mike Schmidt	408
Sherry Magee	337
Chuck Klein	336
Del Ennis	310
Richie Ashburn	287
Sam Thompson	275
Granny Hamner	271
Johnny Callison	265
Greg Luzinski	253

Triples
Ed Delahanty	158
Sherry Magee	127
Sam Thompson	107
Richie Ashburn	97
Johnny Callison	84
Larry Bowa	81
Gavvy Cravath	72
Juan Samuel	71
Del Ennis	65
Dick Allen	64
Chuck Klein	64
John Titus	64

Home runs
Mike Schmidt	548
Del Ennis	259
Chuck Klein	243
Greg Luzinski	223
Cy Williams	217
Dick Allen	204
Johnny Callison	185
Willie Jones	180
Scott Rolen	150
Darren Daulton	134

Total bases
Mike Schmidt	4,404
Ed Delahanty	3,233
Del Ennis	3,029
Chuck Klein	2,898
Richie Ashburn	2,764
Cy Williams	2,539
Sherry Magee	2,463
Johnny Callison	2,426
Greg Luzinski	2,263
Sam Thompson	2,252

Runs batted in
Mike Schmidt	1,595
Ed Delahanty	1,288
Del Ennis	1,124
Chuck Klein	983
Sam Thompson	963
Sherry Magee	886
Greg Luzinski	811
Cy Williams	795
Willie Jones	753
Pinky Whitney	734

Extra-base hits
Mike Schmidt	1,015
Ed Delahanty	687
Chuck Klein	643
Del Ennis	634
Sherry Magee	539
Johnny Callison	534
Cy Williams	503
Greg Luzinski	497
Sam Thompson	477
Dick Allen	472

Batting average
(Minimum 500 games)

Billy Hamilton	.361
Ed Delahanty	.348
Elmer Flick	.338
Sam Thompson	.334
Chuck Klein	.326
Spud Davis	.321
Bobby Abreu	.312
Freddy Leach	.312
Richie Ashburn	.311
John Kruk	.309

Stolen bases
Billy Hamilton	510
Ed Delahanty	411
Sherry Magee	387
Jim Fogarty	289
Larry Bowa	288
Juan Samuel	249
Roy Thomas	228
Von Hayes	202
Richie Ashburn	199
Sam Thompson	192

PITCHING

Earned-run average
(Minimum 1,000 innings)

Grover Alexander	2.18
Tully Sparks	2.48
Earl Moore	2.63
Charlie Ferguson	2.67
Erskine Mayer	2.81
Eppa Rixey	2.83
Charlie Buffinton	2.89
Dan Casey	2.91
Jim Bunning	2.93
Steve Carlton	3.09

Wins
Steve Carlton	241
Robin Roberts	234
Grover Alexander	190
Chris Short	132
Curt Simmons	115
Curt Schilling	101
Al Orth	100
Charlie Ferguson	99
Jack Taylor	96
Tully Sparks	95

Losses
Robin Roberts	199
Steve Carlton	161
Chris Short	127
Curt Simmons	110
Eppa Rixey	103
Bill Duggleby	99
Jimmy Ring	98
Tully Sparks	95
Grover Alexander	91
Hugh Mulcahy	89

Innings pitched
Robin Roberts	3,739.1
Steve Carlton	3,697.1
Grover Alexander	2,513.2
Chris Short	2,253.0
Curt Simmons	1,939.2
Tully Sparks	1,698.0
Bill Duggleby	1,684.0
Curt Schilling	1,659.1
Eppa Rixey	1,604.0
Jim Bunning	1,520.2

Strikeouts
Steve Carlton	3,031
Robin Roberts	1,871
Chris Short	1,585
Curt Schilling	1,554
Grover Alexander	1,409
Jim Bunning	1,197
Curt Simmons	1,052
Larry Christenson	781
Charlie Ferguson	728
Kevin Gross	727

Bases on balls
Steve Carlton	1,252
Chris Short	762
Robin Roberts	718
Curt Simmons	718
Jimmy Ring	636
Grover Alexander	561
Kid Carsey	540
Earl Moore	518
Kid Gleason	482
Hugh Mulcahy	480

Games
Robin Roberts	529
Steve Carlton	499
Tug McGraw	463
Chris Short	459
Ron Reed	458
Turk Farrell	359
Grover Alexander	338
Jack Baldschun	333
Ricky Bottalico	330
Curt Simmons	325

Shutouts
Grover Alexander	61
Steve Carlton	39
Robin Roberts	35
Chris Short	24
Jim Bunning	23
Curt Simmons	18
Tully Sparks	18
George McQuillan	17
Earl Moore	17
Bill Duggleby	16

Saves
Steve Bedrosian	103
Mitch Williams	102
Tug McGraw	94
Ron Reed	90
Jose Mesa	87
Ricky Bottalico	78
Turk Farrell	65
Jack Baldschun	59
Al Holland	55
Jim Konstanty	54

TEAM SEASON, GAME RECORDS

SEASON

Batting
Most at-bats	5,685	1993
Most runs	944	1930
Fewest runs	394	1942
Most hits	1,783	1930
Most singles	1,338	1894
Most doubles	345	1930
Most triples	148	1894
Most home runs	186	1977
Fewest home runs	11	1908
Most grand slams	8	1993
Most pinch-hit home runs	11	1958
Most total bases	2,594	1930
Most stolen bases	200	1908
Highest batting average	.343	1894
Lowest batting average	.232	1942
Highest slugging pct.	.467	1929

Pitching
Lowest ERA	2.10	1908
Highest ERA	6.71	1930
Most complete games	131	1904
Most shutouts	24	1916
Most saves	48	1987
Most walks	682	1974
Most strikeouts	1,117	1993

Fielding
Most errors	403	1904
Fewest errors	88	2002
Most double plays	179	1961, 1973
Highest fielding average	.986	2002

General
Most games won	101	1976, 1977
Most games lost	111	1941
Highest win pct	.623	1886, 1976, 1977
Lowest win pct	.173	1883

GAME, INNING

Batting
Most runs, game	29	8-17-1894
Most runs, inning	12	10-2-1897, 7-21-23
Most hits, game	36	8-17-1894
Most home runs, game	7	9-8-98
Most total bases, game	49	8-17-1894

Hard-throwing lefthander Steve Carlton won 241 of his 329 games in 14-plus seasons with the Phillies.

HISTORY

PHILLIES YEAR-BY-YEAR

Year	W	L	Place	Games Back	Manager	Leaders: Batting avg.	Hits	Home runs	RBIs	Wins	ERA
1901	83	57	2nd	7½	Shettsline	Delahanty, .354	Delahanty, 192	Delahanty, Flick, 8	Delahanty, 108	Donahue, 21	Orth, 2.27
1902	56	81	7th	46	Shettsline	S. Barry, .287	S. Barry, 156	S. Barry, 3	S. Barry, 58	White, 16	White, 2.53
1903	49	86	7th	39½	Zimmer	Thomas, .327	Thomas, 156	Keister, 3	Keister, 63	Duggleby, 13	Sparks, 2.72
1904	52	100	8th	53½	Duffy	Titus, .294	Gleason, 161	Dooin, 6	Magee, 57	Fraser, 14	Corridon, 2.19
1905	83	69	4th	21½	Duffy	Thomas, .317	Magee, 180	Magee, 5	Magee, 98	Pittinger, 23	Sparks, 2.18
1906	71	82	4th	45½	Duffy	Magee, .282	Magee, 159	Magee, 6	Magee, 67	Sparks, 19	Sparks, 2.16
1907	83	64	3rd	21½	Murray	Magee, .328	Magee, 165	Magee, 4	Magee, 85	Sparks, 22	Richie, 1.77
1908	83	71	4th	16	Murray	Bransfield, .304	Bransfield, 160	Bransfield, 3	Bransfield, 71	McQuillan, 23	McQuillan, 1.53
1909	74	79	5th	36½	Murray	Bransfield, .292	Grant, 170	Titus, 3	Magee, 66	Moore, 18	Moore, 2.10
1910	78	75	4th	25½	Dooin	Magee, .331	Magee, 172	Magee, 6	Magee, 123	Moore, 22	McQuillan, 1.60
1911	79	73	4th	19½	Dooin	Luderus, .301	Luderus, 166	Luderus, 16	Luderus, 99	Alexander, 28	Alexander, 2.57
1912	73	79	5th	30½	Dooin	Paskert, .315	Paskert, 170	Cravath, 11	Magee, 72	Alexander, 19	Rixey, 2.50
1913	88	63	2nd	12½	Dooin	Cravath, .341	Cravath, 179	Cravath, 19	Cravath, 128	Seaton, 27	Brennan, 2.39
1914	74	80	6th	20½	Dooin	Becker, .325	Magee, 171	Cravath, 19	Magee, 103	Alexander, 27	Alexander, 2.38
1915	90	62	1st	+7	Moran	Luderus, .315	Luderus, 157	Cravath, 24	Cravath, 115	Alexander, 31	Alexander, 1.22
1916	91	62	2nd	2½	Moran	Cravath, .283	Paskert, 155	Cravath, 11	Cravath, 70	Alexander, 33	Alexander, 1.55
1917	87	65	2nd	10	Moran	Cravath, Whitted, .280	Whitted, 155	Cravath, 12	Cravath, 83	Alexander, 30	Bender, 1.67
1918	55	68	6th	26	Moran	Luderus, .288	Luderus, 135	Cravath, 8	Luderus, 67	Hogg, Pendergast, 13	Jacobs, 2.41
1919	47	90	8th	47½	Coombs, Cravath	I. Meusel, .305	I. Meusel, 159	Cravath, 12	I. Meusel, 59	Meadows, 8	Meadows, 2.33
1920	62	91	8th	30½	Cravath	Williams, .325	Williams, 192	Williams, 15	Williams, 72	Meadows, 16	Meadows, 2.84
1921	51	103	8th	43½	Donovan, Wilhelm	Williams, .320	Williams, 180	Williams, 18	Williams, 75	Meadows, 11	Winters, 3.63
1922	57	96	7th	35½	Wilhelm	Walker, .337	Walker, 196	Williams, 26	Williams, 92	Meadows, Ring, 12	Weinert, 3.40
1923	50	104	8th	45½	Fletcher	Lee, .321	Holke, 175	Williams, 41	Williams, 114	Ring, 18	Ring, 3.87
1924	55	96	7th	37	Fletcher	Williams, .328	Williams, 183	Williams, 24	Williams, 93	Hubbell, Ring, 10	Ring, 3.97
1925	68	85	*6th	27	Fletcher	Harper, .349	Harper, 173	Harper, 18	Harper, 97	Ring, 14	Carlson, 4.23
1926	58	93	8th	29½	Fletcher	Leach, .329	Leach, 162	Williams, 18	Leach, 71	Carlson, 17	Carlson, 3.23
1927	51	103	8th	43	McInnis	Leach, Wrightstone, .306	Thompson, 181	Williams, 30	Williams, 98	Scott, 9	Ulrich, 3.17
1928	43	109	8th	51	Shotton	Leach, .304	Thompson, 182	Hurst, 19	Whitney, 103	Benge, 8	Benge, 4.55
1929	71	82	5th	27½	Shotton	O'Doul, .398	O'Doul, 254	Klein, 43	Klein, 145	Willoughby, 15	Willoughby, 4.99
1930	52	102	8th	40	Shotton	Klein, .386	Klein, 250	Klein, 40	Klein, 170	Collins, 16	Collins, 4.78
1931	66	88	6th	35	Shotton	Klein, .337	Klein, 200	Klein, 31	Klein, 121	J. Elliott, 19	Benge, 3.17
1932	78	76	4th	12	Shotton	Klein, .348	Klein, 226	Klein, 38	Hurst, 143	Collins, 14	Hansen, 3.72
1933	60	92	7th	31	Shotton	Klein, .368	Klein, 223	Klein, 28	Klein, 120	Holley, 13	Holley, 3.53
1934	56	93	7th	37	Wilson	Moore, .343	Allen, 192	Camilli, 12	Moore, 93	C. Davis, 19	C. Davis, 2.95
1935	64	89	7th	35½	Wilson	Moore, .323	Allen, 198	Camilli, 25	Camilli, 102	C. Davis, 16	S. Johnson, 3.56
1936	54	100	8th	38	Wilson	Moore, .328	Chiozza, 170	Camilli, 28	Camilli, 102	Passeau, Walters, 11	Passeau, 3.48
1937	61	92	7th	34½	Wilson	Whitney, .341	Whitney, 166	Camilli, 27	Camilli, 80	LeMaster, 15	Passeau, 4.34
1938	45	105	8th	43	Wilson, Lobert	Weintraub, .311	Martin, 139	Klein, 8	Arnovich, 72	Passeau, 11	Butcher, 2.93
1939	45	106	8th	50½	Prothro	Arnovich, .324	Arnovich, 159	Marty, Mueller, 9	Arnovich, 67	Higbe, 10	S. Johnson, 3.81
1940	50	103	8th	50	Prothro	May, .293	May, 147	Rizzo, 20	Rizzo, 53	Higbe, 14	Mulcahy, 3.60
1941	43	111	8th	57	Prothro	Etten, .311	Litwhiler, 180	Litwhiler, 18	Etten, 79	Hughes, Podgajny, 9	Pearson, 3.57
1942	42	109	8th	62½	Lobert	Litwhiler, .271	Litwhiler, 160	Litwhiler, 9	Litwhiler, 56	Hughes, 12	Hughes, 3.06
1943	64	90	7th	41	Harris, Fitzsimmons	Dahlgren, .287	Northey, 163	Northey, 16	Northey, 68	Rowe, 14	Barrett, 2.39
1944	61	92	8th	43½	Fitzsimmons	Northey, .288	Lupien, 169	Northey, 22	Northey, 104	Raffensberger, Schanz, 13	Raffensberger, 3.06
1945	46	108	8th	52	Fitzsimmons, Chapman	Wasdell, .300	Wasdell, 150	V. DiMaggio, 19	V. DiMaggio, 84	Karl, 9	Karl, 2.99
1946	69	85	5th	28	Chapman	Ennis, .313	Ennis, 169	Ennis, 17	Ennis, 73	Judd, Rowe, 11	Rowe, 2.12
1947	62	92	*7th	32	Chapman	Walker, .371	Walker, 181	Seminick, 13	Ennis, 81	Leonard, 17	Leonard, 2.68
1948	66	88	6th	25½	Chapman, Cooke, Sawyer	Ashburn, .333	Ennis, 171	Ennis, 30	Ennis, 95	Leonard, 12	Leonard, 2.51
1949	81	73	3rd	16	Sawyer	Ennis, .302	Ashburn, 188	Ennis, 25	Ennis, 110	Heintzelman, Meyer, 17	Heintzelman, 3.02
1950	91	63	1st	+2	Sawyer	Ennis, .311	Ennis, 180	Ennis, 31	Ennis, 126	Roberts, 20	Konstanty, 2.66
1951	73	81	5th	23½	Sawyer	Ashburn, .344	Ashburn, 221	W. Jones, 22	W. Jones, 81	Roberts, 21	Roberts, 3.03
1952	87	67	4th	9½	Sawyer, O'Neill	Burgess, .296	Ashburn, 173	Ennis, 20	Ennis, 107	Roberts, 28	Roberts, 2.59
1953	83	71	*3rd	22	O'Neill	Ashburn, .330	Ashburn, 205	Ennis, 29	Ennis, 125	Roberts, 23	Roberts, 2.75
1954	75	79	4th	22	O'Neill, Moore	Ashburn, .313	Hamner, 178	Ennis, 25	Ennis, 119	Roberts, 23	Simmons, 2.81
1955	77	77	4th	21½	Smith	Ashburn, .338	Ashburn, 180	Ennis, 29	Ennis, 120	Roberts, 23	B. Miller, 2.41
1956	71	83	5th	22	Smith	Ashburn, .303	Ashburn, 190	Lopata, 32	Ennis, Lopata, 95	Roberts, 19	B. Miller, 3.24
1957	77	77	5th	19	Smith	Ashburn, .297	Ashburn, 186	Repulski, 20	Bouchee, 76	Sanford, 19	Sanford, 3.08
1958	69	85	8th	23	Smith, Sawyer	Ashburn, .350	Ashburn, 215	H. Anderson, 23	H. Anderson, 97	Roberts, 17	Roberts, 3.24
1959	64	90	8th	23	Sawyer	Bouchee, .285	Ashburn, 150	Freese, 23	Post, 94	Roberts, 15	Conley, 3.00
1960	59	95	8th	36	Sawyer, Cohen, Mauch	Taylor, .287	Taylor, 145	Herrera, 17	Herrera, 71	Roberts, 12	Mahaffey, 3.31
1961	47	107	8th	46	Mauch	Gonzalez, .277	Callison, 121	Demeter, 20	Demeter, 68	Mahaffey, 11	Ferrarese, 2.76
1962	81	80	7th	20	Mauch	Demeter, .307	Callison, 181	Demeter, 29	Demeter, 107	Mahaffey, 19	Baldschun, 2.96
1963	87	75	4th	12	Mauch	Gonzalez, .306	Taylor, 180	Callison, 26	Demeter, 83	Culp, 14	Klippstein, 1.93
1964	92	70	*2nd	1	Mauch	Allen, .318	Allen, 201	Callison, 31	Callison, 104	Bunning, 19	Short, 2.20
1965	85	76	6th	11½	Mauch	Rojas, .303	Allen, 187	Callison, 32	Callison, 101	Bunning, 19	Bunning, 2.60
1966	87	75	4th	8	Mauch	Allen, .317	Callison, 169	Allen, 40	Allen, 110	Short, 20	Bunning, 2.41
1967	82	80	5th	19½	Mauch	Gonzalez, .339	Gonzalez, 172	Allen, 23	Allen, 77	Bunning, 17	Farrell, 2.05
1968	76	86	*7th	21	Mauch, Myatt, Skinner	Gonzalez, .264	Rojas, 144	Allen, 33	Allen, 90	Short, 19	L. Jackson, 2.77
								EAST DIVISION			
1969	63	99	5th	37	Skinner, Myatt	Allen, .288	Taylor, 146	Allen, 32	Allen, 89	Wise, 15	Wise, 3.23
1970	73	88	5th	15½	Lucchesi	Taylor, .301	D. Johnson, 147	D. Johnson, 27	D. Johnson, 93	Wise, 13	Selma, 2.75
1971	67	95	6th	30	Lucchesi	McCarver, .278	Bowa, 162	D. Johnson, 34	Montanez, 99	Wise, 17	Wise, 2.88
1972	59	97	6th	37½	Lucchesi, Owens	Luzinski, .281	Luzinski, 158	Luzinski, 18	Luzinski, 68	Carlton, 27	Carlton, 1.97
1973	71	91	6th	11½	Ozark	Unser, .289	Luzinski, 174	Luzinski, 29	Luzinski, 97	Brett, Carlton, Lonborg, Twitchell, 13	Twitchell, 2.50
1974	80	82	3rd	8	Ozark	Montanez, .304	Cash, 206	Schmidt, 36	Schmidt, 116	Lonborg, 17	Lonborg, 3.21
1975	86	76	2nd	6½	Ozark	Johnstone, .329	Cash, 213	Schmidt, 38	Luzinski, 120	Carlton, 15	Hilgendorf, 2.14
1976	101	61	†1st	+9	Ozark	Maddox, .330	Cash, 189	Schmidt, 38	Schmidt, 107	Carlton, 20	McGraw, 2.50
1977	101	61	†1st	+5	Ozark	Luzinski, .309	Bowa, 175	Luzinski, 39	Luzinski, 130	Carlton, 23	Garber, 2.35
1978	90	72	†1st	+1½	Ozark	Bowa, .294	Bowa, 192	Luzinski, 35	Luzinski, 101	Carlton, 16	Reed, 2.24
1979	84	78	4th	14	Ozark, Green	Rose, .331	Rose, 208	Schmidt, 45	Schmidt, 114	Carlton, 18	Carlton, 3.62
1980	91	71	‡1st	+1	Green	McBride, .309	Rose, 185	Schmidt, 48	Schmidt, 121	Carlton, 24	McGraw, 1.46
1981	59	48	§1st/3rd	—	Green	Rose, .325	Rose, 140	Schmidt, 31	Schmidt, 91	Carlton, 13	Carlton, 2.42
1982	89	73	2nd	3	Corrales	Diaz, .288	Matthews, 173	Schmidt, 35	Schmidt, 87	Carlton, 23	Reed, 2.66
1983	90	72	‡1st	+6	Corrales, Owens	Hayes, .265	Schmidt, 136	Schmidt, 40	Schmidt, 109	Denny, 19	Holland, 2.26
1984	81	81	4th	15½	Owens	V. Hayes, .292	Samuel, 191	Schmidt, 36	Schmidt, 106	Koosman, 14	Andersen, 2.38
1985	75	87	5th	26	Felske	Schmidt, .277	Samuel, 175	Schmidt, 33	Wilson, 102	Gross, 15	Rawley, 3.31
1986	86	75	2nd	21½	Felske	V. Hayes, .305	V. Hayes, 187	Schmidt, 37	Schmidt, 119	Gross, 12	Ruffin, 2.46
1987	80	82	*4th	15	Felske, Elia	M. Thompson, .302	Samuel, 178	Schmidt, 35	Schmidt, 113	Rawley, 17	Tekulve, 3.09
1988	65	96	6th	35½	Elia, Vukovich	M. Thompson, .288	Samuel, 153	James, 19	Samuel, 67	Gross, 12	G. Harris, 2.36
1989	67	95	6th	26	Leyva	Herr, .287	Herr, 161	V. Hayes, 26	V. Hayes, 78	Howell, Parrett, 12	Parrett, 2.98
1990	77	85	*4th	18	Leyva	Dykstra, .325	Dykstra, 192	V. Hayes, 17	V. Hayes, 73	Combs, 10	Mulholland, 3.34
1991	78	84	3rd	20	Leyva, Fregosi	Kruk, .294	Kruk, 158	Kruk, 21	Kruk, 92	Mulholland, 16	Greene, 3.38
1992	70	92	6th	26	Fregosi	Kruk, .323	Kruk, 164	Daulton, Hollins, 27	Daulton, 109	Schilling, 14	Schilling, 2.35
1993	97	65	‡1st	+3	Fregosi	Eisenreich, .318	Dykstra, 194	Daulton, Incaviglia, 24	Daulton, 105	Greene, Schilling, 16	Mulholland, 3.25
1994	54	61	4th	20½	Fregosi	Kruk, .302	Duncan, 93	Daulton, 15	Daulton, 56	D. Jackson, 14	Munoz, 2.67
1995	69	75	*2nd	21	Fregosi	Eisenreich, .316	Jefferies, 147	Hayes, Jefferies, Whiten, 11	Hayes, 85	Quantrill, 11	Schilling, 3.57
1996	67	95	5th	29	Fregosi	Jefferies, .292	Morandini, 135	Santiago, 30	Santiago, 85	Schilling, 9	Schilling, 3.19
1997	68	94	5th	33	Francona	Morandini, .295	Morandini, 163	Rolen, 21	Rolen, 92	Schilling, 17	Schilling, 2.97
1998	75	87	3rd	31	Francona	Abreu, .312	Glanville, 189	Rolen, 31	Rolen, 110	Schilling, 15	Schilling, 3.25
1999	77	85	3rd	26	Francona	Abreu, .335	Glanville, 204	Lieberthal, 31	Brogna, 102	Schilling, Byrd, 15	Schilling, 3.54
2000	65	97	5th	30	Francona	Abreu, .316	Abreu, 182	Rolen, 26	Rolen, 89	Wolf, 11	Chen, 3.64
2001	86	76	2nd	2	Bowa	Anderson, .293	Rollins, 180	Abreu, 31	Abreu, 110	Person, 15	Wolf, 3.70
2002	80	81	3rd	21½	Bowa	Abreu, .308	Abreu, 176	Burrell, 37	Burrell, 116	Padilla, 14	Wolf, 3.20

* Tied for position. † Lost Championship Series. ‡ Won Championship Series. § First half 34-21; second half 25-27.

Note: Batting average minimum 350 at-bats; ERA minimum 90 innings pitched.

Pittsburgh Pirates

FRANCHISE CHRONOLOGY

First season: 1882, as a member of the American Association. The Allegheny club finished its first Pittsburgh season 39-39, good for fourth place in the seven-team field.

1883-1900: The Pirates played five A.A. seasons before jumping to the National League in 1887. In their first 14 N.L. seasons, they never finished first. But they did rise to second place in 1900, setting the stage for three consecutive pennants.

1901-present: The Pirates, with the arrival of manager Fred Clarke and shortstop Honus Wagner, became a consistent member of the N.L.'s first-division fraternity—a membership they would keep through most of the century. But strong teams did not translate into many pennants. After losing the first World Series in 1903, the Pirates captured their first championship in 1909 and their second 15 years later. There would be only three more—a memorable 1960 Series victory that ended on Bill Mazeroski's immortal home run and triumphs in 1971 and '79. The Pirates' most successful run came in the 1970s when they won six division titles and finished second three times. Consecutive division titles in 1990, '91 and '92 all resulted in Championship Series losses. Pittsburgh was one of five teams placed in the Central Division when the N.L. adopted its three-division format in 1994.

Shortstop Honus Wagner.

PIRATES VS. OPPONENTS BY DECADE

	Braves	Cardinals	Cubs	Dodgers	Giants	Phillies	Reds	Astros	Mets	Expos	Padres	Marlins	Rockies	Brewers	D'backs	Interleague	Decade Record
1900-09	153-58	158-53	112-99	132-76	115-96	137-75	131-81										938-538
1910-19	109-104	127-83	95-118	105-110	86-127	105-107	109-102										736-751
1920-29	141-77	117-102	125-95	122-97	106-113	148-71	118-101										877-656
1930-39	125-92	121-99	100-120	105-113	95-125	126-90	140-79										812-718
1940-49	112-105	98-122	116-104	96-124	109-111	121-95	104-115										756-776
1950-59	81-139	87-132	106-114	79-141	89-131	88-132	86-134										616-923
1960-69	94-88	81-107	110-78	82-100	82-100	98-89	92-90	93-45	93-51	13-5	10-2						848-755
1970-79	77-43	101-79	111-66	55-65	58-62	101-79	54-65	75-44	98-78	107-73	79-41						916-695
1980-89	53-58	75-98	95-81	53-61	55-63	83-91	50-64	51-63	69-102	86-88	62-56						732-825
1990-99	45-62	76-62	76-63	50-61	55-52	66-58	59-64	54-67	67-58	61-65	55-53	42-30	34-36	9-14	5-11	20-23	774-779
2000-02	6-13	13-33	24-23	9-15	5-15	11-10	21-27	17-30	8-12	8-11	11-10	8-13	8-13	31-17	6-15	17-25	203-282
Totals	996-839	1054-970	1070-961	888-963	855-995	1084-897	964-922	290-249	335-301	275-242	217-162	50-43	42-49	40-31	11-26	37-48	8208-7698

Interleague results: 1-2 vs. Angels, 5-6 vs. White Sox, 8-7 vs. Indians, 7-8 vs. Tigers, 8-9 vs. Royals, 1-2 vs. Brewers, 7-8 vs. Twins, 0-3 vs. Athletics, 0-3 vs. Rangers.

MANAGERS

Name	Years	Record
Al Pratt	1882-83	51-59
Ormond Butler	1883	17-36
Joe Battin	1883, 1884	8-18
Denny McKnight	1884	4-8
Bob Ferguson	1884	11-31
George Creamer	1884	0-8
Horace Phillips	1884-89	294-316
Fred Dunlap	1889	7-10
Ned Hanlon	1889, 1891	57-65
Guy Hecker	1890	23-113
Bill McGunnigle	1891	24-33
Tom Burns	1892	27-32
Al Buckenberger	1892-94	187-144
Connie Mack	1894-96	149-134
Patsy Donovan	1897, 1899	129-129
Bill Watkins	1898-99	79-91
Fred Clarke	1900-15	1422-969
Jimmy Callahan	1916-17	85-129
Honus Wagner	1917	1-4
Hugo Bezdek	1917-19	166-187
George Gibson	1920-22, 1932-34	401-330
Bill McKechnie	1922-26	409-293
Donie Bush	1927-29	246-178
Pie Traynor	1934-39	457-406
Jewel Ens	1929-31	176-167
Frank Frisch	1940-46	539-528
Spud Davis	1946	1-2
Billy Herman	1947	61-92
Bill Burwell	1947	1-0
Billy Meyer	1948-52	317-452
Fred Haney	1953-55	163-299
Bobby Bragan	1956-57	102-155
Danny Murtaugh	1957-64, 1967, 1970-71, 1973-76	1115-950
Harry Walker	1965-67	224-184
Larry Shepard	1968-69	164-155
Alex Grammas	1969	4-1
Bill Virdon	1972-73	163-128
Chuck Tanner	1977-85	711-685
Jim Leyland	1986-96	851-863
Gene Lamont	1997-2000	295-352
Lloyd McClendon	2001-02	134-189

WORLD SERIES CHAMPIONS

Year	Loser	Length	MVP
1909	Detroit	7 games	None
1925	Washington	7 games	None
1960	N.Y. Yankees	7 games	Richardson
1971	Baltimore	7 games	Clemente
1979	Baltimore	7 games	Stargell

N.L. PENNANT WINNERS

Year	Record	Manager	Series Result
1901	90-49	Clarke	None
1902	103-36	Clarke	None
1903	91-49	Clarke	Lost to Red Sox
1909	110-42	Clarke	Defeated Tigers
1925	95-58	McKechnie	Defeated Senators
1927	94-60	Bush	Lost to Yankees
1960	95-59	Murtaugh	Defeated Yankees
1971	97-65	Murtaugh	Defeated Orioles
1979	98-64	Tanner	Defeated Orioles

EAST DIVISION CHAMPIONS

Year	Record	Manager	NLCS Result
1970	89-73	Murtaugh	Lost to Reds
1971	97-65	Murtaugh	Defeated Giants
1972	96-59	Virdon	Lost to Reds
1974	88-74	Murtaugh	Lost to Dodgers
1975	92-69	Murtaugh	Lost to Reds
1979	98-64	Tanner	Defeated Reds
1990	95-67	Leyland	Lost to Reds
1991	98-64	Leyland	Lost to Braves
1992	96-66	Leyland	Lost to Braves

ATTENDANCE HIGHS

Total	Season	Park
2,436,126	2001	PNC Park
2,065,302	1991	Three Rivers Stadium
2,049,908	1990	Three Rivers Stadium
1,866,713	1988	Three Rivers Stadium
1,829,395	1992	Three Rivers Stadium

BALLPARK CHRONOLOGY

PNC Park (2001-present)

Capacity: 37,898.
First game: Cincinnati 8, Pirates 2 (April 9, 2001).
First batter: Barry Larkin, Reds.
First hit: Sean Casey, Reds (home run).
First run: Dmitri Young, Reds (1st inning).
First home run: Sean Casey, Reds (1st inning).
First winning pitcher: Chris Reitsma, Reds.
First-season attendance: 2,436,126.

Three Rivers Stadium (1970-2000)

Capacity: 47,972.
First game: Cincinnati 3, Pirates 2 (July 16, 1970).
First-season attendance: 1,341,947.

Exposition Park (1882-84)

Recreation Park (1887-90)

Exposition Park III (1891-1909)

Capacity: 16,000.
First game: Chicago 7, Pittsburgh 6, 10 innings (April 22, 1891).

Forbes Field (1909-70)

Capacity: 35,000.
First game: Chicago 3, Pirates 2 (June 30, 1909).
First-season attendance (1910): 436,586.

N.L. MVPs

Dick Groat, SS, 1960
Roberto Clemente, OF, 1966
Dave Parker, OF, 1978
*Willie Stargell, 1B, 1979
Barry Bonds, OF, 1990
Barry Bonds, OF, 1992

* Co-winner.

CY YOUNG WINNERS

Vernon Law, RH, 1960
Doug Drabek, RH, 1990

MANAGERS OF THE YEAR

Jim Leyland, 1990
Jim Leyland, 1992

RETIRED UNIFORMS

No.	Name	Pos.
1	Billy Meyer	Man.
4	Ralph Kiner	OF
8	Willie Stargell	1B
9	Bill Mazeroski	2B
20	Pie Traynor	3B
21	Roberto Clemente	OF
33	Honus Wagner	SS
40	Danny Murtaugh	Man.

MILESTONE PERFORMANCES

30-plus home runs

54—Ralph Kiner 1949
51—Ralph Kiner 1947
48—Willie Stargell 1971
47—Ralph Kiner 1950
44—Willie Stargell 1973
42—Ralph Kiner 1951
40—Ralph Kiner 1948
39—Brian Giles 1999
38—Brian Giles 2002
37—Ralph Kiner 1952
Brian Giles 2001
35—Frank Thomas 1958
Dick Stuart 1961
Brian Giles 2000
34—Barry Bonds 1992
Aramis Ramirez 2001
33—Willie Stargell 1966, 1972
Barry Bonds 1990
32—Willie Stargell 1979
Bobby Bonilla 1990
31—Willie Stargell 1970
Jason Thompson 1982
30—Frank Thomas 1953
Dave Parker 1978
Jeff King 1996

100-plus RBIs

131—Paul Waner 1927
127—Ralph Kiner 1947, 1949
126—Honus Wagner 1901
125—Willie Stargell 1971
124—Pie Traynor 1928
123—Ralph Kiner 1948
Brian Giles 2000
121—Glenn Wright 1925
120—Bobby Bonilla 1990
119—Adam Comorosky 1930
Pie Traynor 1930
Roberto Clemente 1966
Willie Stargell 1973
118—Gus Suhr 1936
Ralph Kiner 1950
117—Dick Stuart 1961
Dave Parker 1978
116—Maurice Van Robays 1940
Barry Bonds 1991
115—Brian Giles 1999
114—Clyde Barnhart 1925
Barry Bonds 1990
112—Willie Stargell 1972
Aramis Ramirez 2001
111—Glenn Wright 1924
Johnny Rizzo 1938
Jeff King 1996
110—Roberto Clemente 1967
109—Honus Wagner 1908
Ralph Kiner 1951
Frank Thomas 1958
108—Pie Traynor 1929
Bob Elliott 1944
Bob Elliott 1945
Kevin Young 1998
107—Lou Bierbauer 1894
Owen Wilson 1911
Gus Suhr 1930
Willie Stargell 1965
106—Pie Traynor 1925, 1927
Kevin Young 1999
105—Glenn Wright 1927
104—Elbie Fletcher 1940
Wally Westlake 1949
Bill Robinson 1977
103—Pie Traynor 1931
Gus Suhr 1934
Barry Bonds 1992
Brian Giles 2002
102—Honus Wagner 1912
Kiki Cuyler 1925
Bill Brubaker 1936
Frank Thomas 1953
Willie Stargell 1966
101—Honus Wagner 1903, 1905
Pie Traynor 1923
Bob Elliott 1943
Babe Dahlgren 1944
Dave Parker 1975
Jason Thompson 1982
100—Honus Wagner 1900, 1909
Paul Waner 1929
Vince DiMaggio 1941
Richie Zisk 1974
Bobby Bonilla 1988, 1991
Andy Van Slyke 1988

20-plus victories

1887—Pud Galvin 28-21
1888—Ed Morris 29-23
Pud Galvin 23-25
1889—Pud Galvin 23-16
Harry Staley 21-26
1891—Mark Baldwin 22-28
1892—Mark Baldwin 26-27
1893—Frank Killen 36-14
1895—Pink Hawley 31-22
1896—Frank Killen 30-18
Pink Hawley 22-21
1898—Jesse Tannehill 25-13
1899—Jesse Tannehill 24-14
Sam Leever 21-23
1900—Jesse Tannehill 20-6
Deacon Phillippe 20-13
1901—Deacon Phillippe 22-12
Jack Chesbro 21-10
1902—Jack Chesbro 28-6
Jesse Tannehill 20-6
Deacon Phillippe 20-9
1903—Sam Leever 25-7
Deacon Phillippe 25-9
1905—Sam Leever 20-5
Deacon Phillippe 20-13
1906—Vic Willis 23-13
Sam Leever 22-7
1907—Vic Willis 21-11
Al Leifield 20-16
1908—Nick Maddox 23-8
Vic Willis 23-11
1909—Howard Camnitz 25-6
Vic Willis 22-11
1911—Babe Adams 22-12
Howard Camnitz 20-15
1912—Claude Hendrix 24-9
Howard Camnitz 22-12
1913—Babe Adams 21-10
1915—Al Mamaux 21-8
1916—Al Mamaux 21-15
1920—Wilbur Cooper 24-15
1921—Wilbur Cooper 22-14
1922—Wilbur Cooper 23-14
1923—John Morrison 25-13
1924—Wilbur Cooper 20-14
1926—Remy Kremer 20-6
Lee Meadows 20-9
1927—Carmen Hill 22-11
1928—Burleigh Grimes 25-14
1930—Remy Kremer 20-12
1943—Rip Sewell 21-9
1944—Rip Sewell 21-12
1951—Murry Dickson 20-16
1958—Bob Friend 22-14
1960—Vernon Law 20-9
1977—John Candelaria 20-5
1990—Doug Drabek 22-6
1991—John Smiley 20-8

N.L. home run champions

1902—Tommy Leach 6
1946—Ralph Kiner 23
1947—Ralph Kiner *51
1948—Ralph Kiner *40
1949—Ralph Kiner 54
1950—Ralph Kiner 47
1951—Ralph Kiner 42
1952—Ralph Kiner *37
1971—Willie Stargell 48
1973—Willie Stargell 44

* Tied for league lead

N.L. RBI champions

1901—Honus Wagner 126
1902—Honus Wagner 91
1906—Jim Nealon 83
1908—Honus Wagner 109
1909—Honus Wagner 100
1911—Owen Wilson 107
1912—Honus Wagner 102
1927—Paul Waner 131
1949—Ralph Kiner 127
1973—Willie Stargell 119

N.L. batting champions

1900—Honus Wagner .381
1902—Clarence Beaumont .357
1903—Honus Wagner .355
1904—Honus Wagner .349
1906—Honus Wagner .339
1907—Honus Wagner .350
1908—Honus Wagner .354
1909—Honus Wagner .339
1911—Honus Wagner .334
1927—Paul Waner .380
1934—Paul Waner .362
1935—Arky Vaughan .385
1936—Paul Waner .373
1940—Debs Garms .355
1960—Dick Groat .325
1961—Roberto Clemente .351
1964—Roberto Clemente .339
1965—Roberto Clemente .329
1966—Mateo Alou .342
1967—Roberto Clemente .357
1977—Dave Parker .338
1978—Dave Parker .334
1981—Bill Madlock .341
1983—Bill Madlock .323

N.L. ERA champions

1900—Rube Waddell 2.37
1901—Jesse Tannehill 2.18
1903—Sam Leever 2.06
1926—Ray Kremer 2.61
1927—Ray Kremer 2.47
1935—Cy Blanton 2.59
1955—Bob Friend 2.84
1977—John Candelaria 2.34

N.L. strikeout champions

1900—Rube Waddell 130
1945—Preacher Roe 148
1964—Bob Veale 250

No-hit pitchers

(9 innings or more)

1907—Nick Maddox 2-1 vs. Brooklyn
1951—Cliff Chambers 3-0 vs. Boston
1969—Bob Moose 4-0 vs. New York
1970—Dock Ellis 2-0 vs. San Diego
1976—John Candelaria 2-0 vs. Los Angeles
1997—Francisco Cordova-Ricardo Rincon 3-0 vs. Houston (10 innings)

Longest hitting streaks

27—Jimmy Williams 1899
26—Jimmy Williams 1899
Danny O'Connell 1953
25—Charlie Grimm 1923
Fred Lindstrom 1933
24—Maury Wills 1968
23—Danny Murtaugh 1948
Al Oliver 1974
22—Dave Parker 1977 (twice)
Jay Bell 1992
21—Frank Gustine 1947
Gene Alley 1969
Richie Zisk 1974
Al Oliver 1974
Carlos Garcia 1995
20—Roberto Clemente 1965
Rennie Stennett 1977
Al Martin 1999

Hank Greenberg (left) and Ralph Kiner, two of the game's premier sluggers, joined forces for one Pittsburgh season in 1947.

INDIVIDUAL SEASON, GAME RECORDS

SEASON

Batting

Category	Record	Player	Year
At-bats	698	Matty Alou	1969
Runs	148	Jake Stenzel	1894
Hits	237	Paul Waner	1927
Singles	198	Lloyd Waner	1927
Doubles	62	Paul Waner	1932
Triples	36	Chief Wilson	1912
Home runs	54	Ralph Kiner	1949
Home runs, rookie	23	Johnny Rizzo	1938
		Ralph Kiner	1946
Grand slams	4	Ralph Kiner	1949
Total bases	366	Kiki Cuyler	1925
RBIs	131	Paul Waner	1927
Walks	137	Ralph Kiner	1951
Most strikeouts	163	Donn Clendenon	1969
Fewest strikeouts	7	Pie Traynor	1929
Batting average	.385	Arky Vaughan	1935
Slugging pct.	.658	Ralph Kiner	1949
Stolen bases	96	Omar Moreno	1980

Pitching

Category	Record	Player	Year
Games	94	Kent Tekulve	1979
Complete games	54	Ed Morris	1888
Innings	330.2	Burleigh Grimes	1928
Wins	34	Frank Killen	1893
Losses	21	Murry Dickson	1952
Winning pct.	.947 (18-1)	Elroy Face	1959
Walks	159	Marty O'Toole	1912
Strikeouts	276	Bob Veale	1965
Shutouts	12	Ed Morris	1886
Home runs allowed	32	Murry Dickson	1951
Lowest ERA	1.56	Howie Camnitz	1908
Saves	46	Mike Williams	2002

GAME

Batting

Category	Record	Player	Date
Runs	6	Ginger Beaumont	7-22-1899
Hits	7	Rennie Stennett	9-16-75
Doubles	4	Paul Waner	5-20-32
Triples	3	Last by Roberto Clemente	9-8-58
Home runs	3	Last by Darnell Coles	9-30-87
RBIs	9	Johnny Rizzo	5-30-39
Total bases	15	Willie Stargell	5-22-68
Stolen bases	4	Last by Tony Womack	9-6-97

CAREER LEADERS

BATTING

Games

Player	
Roberto Clemente	2,433
Honus Wagner	2,433
Willie Stargell	2,360
Max Carey	2,178
Bill Mazeroski	2,163
Paul Waner	2,154
Pie Traynor	1,941
Lloyd Waner	1,803
Tommy Leach	1,574
Fred Clarke	1,479

At-bats

Player	
Roberto Clemente	9,454
Honus Wagner	9,034
Paul Waner	8,429
Max Carey	8,406
Willie Stargell	7,927
Bill Mazeroski	7,755
Pie Traynor	7,559
Lloyd Waner	7,256
Tommy Leach	5,910
Fred Clarke	5,472

Runs

Player	
Honus Wagner	1,521
Paul Waner	1,493
Roberto Clemente	1,416
Max Carey	1,414
Willie Stargell	1,195
Pie Traynor	1,183
Lloyd Waner	1,151
Fred Clarke	1,015
Tommy Leach	1,009
Arky Vaughan	936

Hits

Player	
Roberto Clemente	3,000
Honus Wagner	2,967
Paul Waner	2,868
Max Carey	2,416
Pie Traynor	2,416
Lloyd Waner	2,317
Willie Stargell	2,232
Bill Mazeroski	2,016
Arky Vaughan	1,709
Fred Clarke	1,638

Doubles

Player	
Paul Waner	558
Honus Wagner	551
Roberto Clemente	440
Willie Stargell	423
Max Carey	375
Pie Traynor	371
Dave Parker	296
Bill Mazeroski	294
Arky Vaughan	291
Al Oliver	276
Gus Suhr	276

Triples

Player	
Honus Wagner	232
Paul Waner	187
Roberto Clemente	166
Pie Traynor	164
Fred Clarke	156
Max Carey	148
Tommy Leach	139
Arky Vaughan	116
Lloyd Waner	114
Jake Beckley	113

Home runs

Player	
Willie Stargell	475
Ralph Kiner	301
Roberto Clemente	240
Barry Bonds	176
Dave Parker	166
Frank Thomas	163
Brian Giles	149
Bill Mazeroski	138
Al Oliver	135
Kevin Young	134

Total bases

Player	
Roberto Clemente	4,492
Honus Wagner	4,228
Willie Stargell	4,190
Paul Waner	4,127
Pie Traynor	3,289
Max Carey	3,288
Lloyd Waner	2,895
Bill Mazeroski	2,848
Arky Vaughan	2,484
Dave Parker	2,397

Runs batted in

Player	
Willie Stargell	1,540
Honus Wagner	1,475
Roberto Clemente	1,305
Pie Traynor	1,273
Paul Waner	1,177
Bill Mazeroski	853
Ralph Kiner	801
Gus Suhr	789
Arky Vaughan	764
Dave Parker	758

Extra-base hits

Player	
Willie Stargell	953
Honus Wagner	865
Paul Waner	854
Roberto Clemente	846
Pie Traynor	593
Max Carey	590
Dave Parker	524
Bill Mazeroski	494
Arky Vaughan	491
Ralph Kiner	486

Batting average

(Minimum 500 games)

Player	
Paul Waner	.340
Kiki Cuyler	.336
Honus Wagner	.328
Matty Alou	.327
Elmer Smith	.325
Arky Vaughan	.324
Ginger Beaumont	.321
Pie Traynor	.320
Lloyd Waner	.319
Roberto Clemente	.317

Stolen bases

Player	
Max Carey	688
Honus Wagner	639
Omar Moreno	412
Patsy Donovan	312
Tommy Leach	271
Fred Clarke	261
Barry Bonds	251
Frank Taveras	206
Ginger Beaumont	200
Jake Stenzel	188

PITCHING

Earned-run average

(Minimum 1,000 innings)

Player	
Vic Willis	2.08
Lefty Leifield	2.38
Sam Leever	2.47
Deacon Phillippe	2.50
Howie Camnitz	2.63
Kent Tekulve	2.68
Wilbur Cooper	2.74
Babe Adams	2.74
Jesse Tannehill	2.75
Doug Drabek	3.02

Wins

Player	
Wilbur Cooper	202
Babe Adams	194
Sam Leever	194
Bob Friend	191
Deacon Phillippe	168
Vern Law	162
Ray Kremer	143
Rip Sewell	143
John Candelaria	124
Howie Camnitz	116
Jesse Tannehill	116
Bob Veale	116

Losses

Player	
Bob Friend	218
Wilbur Cooper	159
Vern Law	147
Babe Adams	139
Sam Leever	100
Rip Sewell	97
Roy Face	93
Deacon Phillippe	92
Ron Kline	91
Bob Veale	91

Innings pitched

Player	
Bob Friend	3,480.1
Wilbur Cooper	3,199.0
Babe Adams	2,991.1
Vern Law	2,672.0
Sam Leever	2,660.2
Deacon Phillippe	2,286.0
Rip Sewell	2,108.2
Ray Kremer	1,954.2
John Candelaria	1,873.0
Bob Veale	1,868.2

Strikeouts

Player	
Bob Friend	1,682
Bob Veale	1,652
Wilbur Cooper	1,191
John Candelaria	1,159
Vern Law	1,092
Babe Adams	1,036
Steve Blass	896
Dock Ellis	869
Deacon Phillippe	861
Rick Rhoden	852

Bases on balls

Player	
Bob Friend	869
Bob Veale	839
Wilbur Cooper	762
Rip Sewell	740
Steve Blass	597
Vern Law	597
Sam Leever	587
Howie Camnitz	532
Frank Killen	519
Ray Kremer	483

Games

Player	
Roy Face	802
Kent Tekulve	722
Bob Friend	568
Vern Law	483
Babe Adams	481
Wilbur Cooper	469
Dave Giusti	410
Sam Leever	388
Rip Sewell	385
Al McBean	376

Shutouts

Player	
Babe Adams	44
Sam Leever	39
Bob Friend	35
Wilbur Cooper	33
Vern Law	28
Lefty Leifield	28
Deacon Phillippe	25
Vic Willis	23
Rip Sewell	20
Bob Veale	20

Saves

Player	
Roy Face	188
Kent Tekulve	158
Dave Giusti	133
Mike Williams	115
Stan Belinda	61
Al McBean	59
Bill Landrum	56
Jim Gott	50
Rich Loiselle	49
Don Robinson	43

TEAM SEASON, GAME RECORDS

SEASON

Batting

Record		Year
Most at-bats	5,724	1967
Most runs	912	1925
Fewest runs	464	1917
Most hits	1,698	1922
Most singles	1,297	1922
Most doubles	320	2000
Most triples	129	1912
Most home runs	171	1999
Fewest home runs	9	1917
Most grand slams	7	1978, 1996
Most pinch-hit home runs	10	1996, 2001
Most total bases	2,430	1966
Most stolen bases	264	1907
Highest batting average	.309	1928
Lowest batting average	.231	1952
Highest slugging pct	.449	1930

Pitching

Record		Year
Lowest ERA	2.48	1918
Highest ERA	5.24	1930
Most complete games	133	1904
Most shutouts	26	1906
Most saves	52	1979
Most walks	711	2000
Most strikeouts	1,124	1969

Fielding

Record		Year
Most errors	295	1903
Fewest errors	105	1993
Most double plays	215	1966
Highest fielding average	.984	1992

General

Record		Year
Most games won	110	1909
Most games lost	113	1890
Highest win pct	.741	1902
Lowest win pct	.169	1890

GAME, INNING

Batting

Record		Date
Most runs, game	27	6-6-1894
Most runs, inning	12	4-22-1892, 6-6-1894
Most hits, game	27	8-8-22
Most home runs, game	7	6-8-1894, 8-16-47
Most total bases, game	47	8-1-70

Second baseman Bill Mazeroski will always be remembered for his 1960 World Series home run.

PIRATES YEAR-BY-YEAR

Year	W	L	Place	Games Back	Manager	Batting avg.	Hits	Home runs	RBIs	Wins	ERA
1901	90	49	1st	+7½	Clarke	Wagner, .353	Wagner, 194	Beaumont, 8	Wagner, 126	Phillippe, 22	Tannehill, 2.18
1902	103	36	1st	+27½	Clarke	Beaumont, .357	Beaumont, 193	Leach, 6	Wagner, 91	Chesbro, 28	Tannehill, 1.95
1903	91	49	1st	+6½	Clarke	Wagner, .355	Beaumont, 209	Beaumont, Leach, 7	Wagner, 101	Leever, 25	Leever, 2.06
1904	87	66	4th	19	Clarke	Wagner, .349	Beaumont, 185	Wagner, 4	Wagner, 75	Flaherty, 19	Flaherty, 2.05
1905	96	57	2nd	9	Clarke	Wagner, .363	Wagner, 199	Wagner, 6	Wagner, 101	Leever, Phillippe, 20	Phillippe, 2.19
1906	93	60	3rd	23½	Clarke	Wagner, .339	Wagner, 175	Nealon, 3	Nealon, 83	Willis, 23	Willis, 1.73
1907	91	63	2nd	17	Clarke	Wagner, .350	Wagner, 180	Wagner, 6	Abbaticchio, Wagner, 82	Willis, 21	Leever, 1.66
1908	98	56	*2nd	1	Clarke	Wagner, .354	Wagner, 201	Wagner, 10	Wagner, 109	Maddox, Willis, 23	Camnitz, 1.56
1909	110	42	1st	+6½	Clarke	Wagner, .339	Wagner, 168	Leach, 6	Wagner, 100	Camnitz, 25	Adams, 1.11
1910	86	67	3rd	17½	Clarke	Wagner, .320	Byrne, 178	Flynn, 6	Wagner, 81	Adams, 18	Adams, 2.24
1911	85	69	3rd	14½	Clarke	Wagner, .334	Wilson, 163	Wilson, 12	Wilson, 107	Adams, 22	Adams, 2.33
1912	93	58	2nd	10	Clarke	Wagner, .324	Wagner, 181	Wilson, 11	Wagner, 102	Hendrix, 24	Robinson, 2.26
1913	78	71	4th	21½	Clarke	Viox, .317	Carey, 172	Wilson, 10	D. Miller, 90	Adams, 21	Adams, 2.15
1914	69	85	7th	25½	Clarke	Viox, .265	Carey, 144	Konetchy, 4	Viox, 57	Cooper, 16	Cooper, 2.13
1915	73	81	5th	18	Clarke	Hinchman, .307	Hinchman, 177	Wagner, 6	Wagner, 78	Mamaux, 21	Mamaux, 2.04
1916	65	89	6th	29	Callahan	Hinchman, .315	Hinchman, 175	Carey, 7	Hinchman, 76	Mamaux, 21	Cooper, 1.87
1917	51	103	8th	47	Callahan, Wagner, Bezdek	Carey, .296	Carey, 174	Fischer, 3	Carey, 51	Cooper, 17	Cooper, 2.36
1918	65	60	4th	17	Bezdek	Cutshaw, .285	Cutshaw, 132	Cutchaw, 5	Cutshaw, 68	Cooper, 19	Cooper, 2.11
1919	71	68	4th	24½	Bezdek	Southworth, .280	Bigbee, 132	Stengel, 4	Southworth, 61	Cooper, 19	Adams, 1.98
1920	79	75	4th	14	Gibson	Carey, .289	Southworth, 155	Bigbee, Nicholson, 4	Whitted, 74	Cooper, 24	Adams, 2.16
1921	90	63	2nd	4	Gibson	Cutshaw, .340	Bigbee, 204	Carey, Grimm, Whitted, 7	Grimm, 71	Cooper, 22	Adams, 2.64
1922	85	69	*3rd	8	Gibson, McKechnie	Bigbee, .350	Bigbee, 215	Russell, 12	Bigbee, 99	Cooper, 23	Cooper, 3.18
1923	87	67	3rd	8½	McKechnie	Grimm, .345	Traynor, 208	Traynor, 12	Traynor, 101	Morrison, 25	Meadows, 3.01
1924	90	63	3rd	3	McKechnie	Cuyler, .354	Carey, 178	Cuyler, 9	Wright, 111	Cooper, 20	Yde, 2.83
1925	95	58	1st	+8½	McKechnie	Cuyler, .357	Cuyler, 220	Cuyler, Wright, 18	Wright, 121	Meadows, 19	Aldridge, 3.63
1926	84	69	3rd	4½	McKechnie	P. Waner, .336	Cuyler, 197	Cuyler, Grantham, P. Waner, Wright, 8	Cuyler, Traynor, 92	Kremer, Meadows, 20	Kremer, 2.61
1927	94	60	1st	+1½	Bush	P. Waner, .380	P. Waner, 237	P. Waner, Wright, 9	P. Waner, 131	Hill, 22	Kremer, 2.47
1928	85	67	4th	9	Bush	P. Waner, .370	P. Waner, 223	Grantham, 10	Traynor, 124	Grimes, 25	Grimes, 2.99
1929	88	65	2nd	10½	Bush, Ens	Traynor, .356	L. Waner, 234	P. Waner, 15	Traynor, 108	Kremer, 18	Grimes, 3.13
1930	80	74	5th	12	Ens	P. Waner, .368	P. Waner, 217	Grantham, 18	Comorosky, Traynor, 119	Kremer, 20	French, 4.36
1931	75	79	5th	26	Ens	P. Waner, .322	L. Waner, 214	Grantham, 10	Traynor, 103	Meine, 19	Meine, 2.98
1932	86	68	2nd	4	Gibson	P. Waner, .341	P. Waner, 215	Grace, P. Waner, 8	Piet, 85	French, 18	Swetonic, 2.82
1933	87	67	2nd	5	Gibson	Piet, .323	P. Waner, 191	Suhr, 10	Vaughan, 97	French, 18	French, 2.72
1934	74	76	5th	19½	Gibson, Traynor	P. Waner, .362	P. Waner, 217	P. Waner, 14	Suhr, 103	Hoyt, 15	Hoyt, 2.93
1935	86	67	4th	13½	Traynor	Vaughan, .385	Jensen, 203	Vaughan, 19	Vaughan, 99	Blanton, 18	Blanton, 2.58
1936	84	70	4th	8	Traynor	P. Waner, .373	P. Waner, 218	Suhr, 11	Suhr, 118	Swift, 16	Hoyt, 2.70
1937	86	68	3rd	10	Traynor	P. Waner, .354	P. Waner, 219	Young, 9	Suhr, 97	Blanton, 14	Bauers, 2.88
1938	86	64	2nd	2	Traynor	Vaughan, .322	L. Waner, 194	Rizzo, 23	Rizzo, 111	Brown, 15	Klinger, 2.99
1939	68	85	6th	28½	Traynor	P. Waner, .328	Vaughan, 182	Fletcher, 12	Fletcher, 71	Klinger, 14	Brown, 3.37
1940	78	76	4th	22½	Frisch	Garms, .355	Vaughan, 178	V. DiMaggio, 19	Van Robays, 116	Sewell, 16	Sewell, 2.80
1941	81	73	4th	19	Frisch	Vaughan, .316	Fletcher, 150	V. DiMaggio, 21	V. DiMaggio, 100	Butcher, 17	Dietz, 2.33
1942	66	81	5th	36½	Frisch	Elliott, .296	Elliott, 166	V. DiMaggio, 15	Elliott, 89	Sewell, 17	Gornicki, 2.57
1943	80	74	4th	25	Frisch	Elliott, .315	Elliott, 183	V. DiMaggio, 15	Elliott, 101	Sewell, 21	Sewell, 2.54
1944	90	63	2nd	14½	Frisch	Russell, .312	Russell, 181	Dahlgren, 12	Elliott, 108	Sewell, 21	Ostermueller, 2.73
1945	82	72	4th	16	Frisch	Elliott, .290	Elliott, 157	Barrett, Salkeld, 15	Elliott, 108	Strincevich, 16	Roe, 2.87
1946	63	91	7th	34	Frisch, S. Davis	Cox, .290	Russell, 143	Kiner, 23	Kiner, 81	Ostermueller, 13	Bahr, 2.63
1947	62	92	*7th	32	Herman, Burwell	Kiner, .313	Gustine, 183	Kiner, 51	Kiner, 127	Ostermueller, 12	Sewell, 3.57
1948	83	71	4th	8½	Meyer	Walker, .316	Rojek, 186	Kiner, 40	Kiner, 123	Chesnes, 14	Higbe, 3.36
1949	71	83	6th	26	Meyer	Hopp, .318	Kiner, 170	Kiner, 54	Kiner, 127	Chambers, 13	Dickson, 3.29
1950	57	96	8th	33½	Meyer	Murtaugh, .294	Kiner, 149	Kiner, 47	Kiner, 118	Chambers, 12	Dickson, 3.80
1951	64	90	7th	32½	Meyer	Kiner, .309	Bell, 167	Kiner, 42	Kiner, 109	Dickson, 20	Dickson, 4.02
1952	42	112	8th	54½	Meyer	Groat, .284	Kiner, 126	Kiner, 37	Kiner, 87	Dickson, 14	Dickson, 3.57
1953	50	104	8th	55	Haney	O'Connell, .294	O'Connell, 173	Thomas, 30	Thomas, 102	Dickson, 10	Hetki, 3.95
1954	53	101	8th	44	Haney	Gordon, .306	Thomas, 172	Thomas, 23	Thomas, 94	Littlefield, 10	Littlefield, 3.60
1955	60	94	8th	38½	Haney	Long, .291	Groat, 139	Thomas, 25	Long, 79	Friend, 14	Friend, 2.83
1956	66	88	7th	27	Bragan	Virdon, .334	Virdon, 170	Long, 27	Long, 91	Friend, 17	Kline, 3.38
1957	62	92	*7th	33	Bragan, Murtaugh	Groat, .315	Thomas, 172	Thomas, 23	Thomas, 89	Friend, 14	Law, 2.87
1958	84	70	2nd	8	Murtaugh	Skinner, .321	Groat, 175	Thomas, 35	Thomas, 109	Friend, 22	Witt, 1.61
1959	78	76	4th	9	Murtaugh	Burgess, Stuart, .297	Hoak, 166	Stuart, 27	Stuart, 78	Face, Law, 18	Face, 2.70
1960	95	59	1st	+7	Murtaugh	Groat, .325	Groat, 186	Stuart, 23	Clemente, 94	Law, 20	Face, 2.90
1961	75	79	6th	18	Murtaugh	Clemente, .351	Clemente, 201	Stuart, 35	Stuart, 117	Friend, 14	Gibbon, 3.32
1962	93	68	4th	8	Murtaugh	Burgess, .328	Groat, 199	Skinner, 20	Mazeroski, 81	Friend, 18	Face, 1.88
1963	74	88	8th	25	Murtaugh	Clemente, .320	Clemente, 192	Clemente, 17	Clemente, 76	Friend, 17	Friend, 2.34
1964	80	82	*6th	13	Murtaugh	Clemente, .339	Clemente, 211	Stargell, 21	Clemente, 87	Veale, 18	McBean, 1.91
1965	90	72	3rd	7	Walker	Clemente, .329	Clemente, 194	Stargell, 27	Stargell, 107	Law, Veale, 17	Law, 2.15
1966	92	70	3rd	3	Walker	M. Alou, .342	Clemente, 202	Stargell, 33	Clemente, 119	Veale, 16	Veale, 3.02
1967	81	81	6th	20½	Walker, Murtaugh	Clemente, .357	Clemente, 209	Clemente, 23	Clemente, 110	Veale, 16	McBean, 2.54
1968	80	82	6th	17	Shepard	M. Alou, .332	M. Alou, 185	Stargell, 24	Clendenon, 87	Blass, 18	Kline, 1.68
							EAST DIVISION				
1969	88	74	3rd	12	Shepard, Grammas	Clemente, .345	M. Alou, 231	Stargell, 29	Stargell, 92	Blass, 16	Moose, 2.91
1970	89	73	†1st	+5	Murtaugh	Clemente, .352	M. Alou, 201	Stargell, 31	Stargell, 85	Walker, 15	Walker, 3.04
1971	97	65	‡1st	+7	Murtaugh	Clemente, .341	Clemente, 178	Stargell, 48	Stargell, 125	Ellis, 19	Blass, 2.85
1972	96	59	†1st	+11	Virdon	Davalillo, .318	Oliver, 176	Stargell, 33	Stargell, 112	Blass, 19	Blass, 2.49
1973	80	82	3rd	2½	Virdon, Murtaugh	Stargell, .299	Oliver, 191	Stargell, 44	Stargell, 119	Briles, 14	Giusti, 2.37
1974	88	74	†1st	+1½	Murtaugh	Oliver, .321	Oliver, 198	Stargell, 25	Zisk, 100	Reuss, 16	Rooker, 2.78
1975	92	69	†1st	+6½	Murtaugh	Sanguillen, .328	Oliver, Stennett, 176	Parker, 25	Parker, 101	Reuss, 18	Reuss, 2.54
1976	92	70	2nd	9	Murtaugh	Oliver, .323	Cash, 189	B. Robinson, Zisk, 21	Parker, 90	Candelaria, 16	Tekulve, 2.45
1977	96	66	2nd	5	Tanner	Parker, .338	Parker, 215	B. Robinson, 26	B. Robinson, 104	Candelaria, 20	Gossage, 1.62
1978	88	73	2nd	1½	Tanner	Parker, .334	Parker, 194	Parker, 30	Parker, 117	Blyleven, D. Robinson, 14	Tekulve, 2.33
1979	98	64	‡1st	+2	Tanner	Parker, .310	Moreno, 196	Stargell, 32	Parker, 94	Candelaria, 14	Tekulve, 2.75
1980	83	79	3rd	8	Tanner	Easler, .338	Moreno, 168	Easler, 21	Parker, 79	Bibby, 19	Solomon, 2.69
1981	46	56	§4th/6th	—	Tanner	Madlock, .341	Moreno, 120	Thompson, 15	Parker, 48	Rhoden, 9	Tekulve, 2.49
1982	84	78	4th	8	Tanner	Madlock, .319	Ray, 182	Thompson, 31	Thompson, 101	D. Robinson, 15	Scurry, 1.74
1983	84	78	2nd	6	Tanner	Madlock, .323	Pena, Ray, 163	Thompson, 18	Thompson, 76	Candelaria, McWilliams, 15	Tekulve, 1.64
1984	75	87	6th	21½	Tanner	Lacy, .321	Wynne, 174	Thompson, 17	Pena, 78	Rhoden, 14	Candelaria, Rhoden, 2.72
1985	57	104	6th	43½	Tanner	Orsulak, .300	Ray, 163	Thompson, 12	Ray, 70	Reuschel, 14	Reuschel, 2.27
1986	64	98	6th	44	Leyland	Ray, .301	Ray, 174	Morrison, 23	Morrison, 88	Rhoden, 15	Rhoden, 2.84
1987	80	82	*4th	15	Leyland	Bonilla, .300	Van Slyke, 165	Bonds, 25	Van Slyke, 82	Dunne, 13	Reuschel, 2.75
1988	85	75	2nd	15	Leyland	Van Slyke, .288	Van Slyke, 169	Van Slyke, 25	Bonilla, Van Slyke, 100	Drabek, 15	Walk, 2.71
1989	74	88	5th	19	Leyland	Bonilla, .281	Bonilla, 173	Bonilla, 24	Bonilla, 26	Drabek, 14	Drabek, 2.80
1990	95	67	†1st	+4	Leyland	Bonds, .301	Bonilla, 175	Bonds, 33	Bonilla, 120	Drabek, 22	Drabek, 2.76
1991	98	64	†1st	+14	Leyland	Bonilla, .302	Bonilla, 174	Bonds, 25	Bonds, 116	Smiley, 20	Tomlin, 2.98
1992	96	66	†1st	+9	Leyland	Van Slyke, .324	Van Slyke, 199	Bonds, 34	Bonds, 103	Drabek, 15	Wakefield, 2.15
1993	75	87	5th	22	Leyland	Merced, .313	Bell, 187	Martin, 18	King, 98	Walk, 13	Cooke, 3.89
							CENTRAL DIVISION				
1994	53	61	*3rd	13	Leyland	Garcia, .277	Bell, 117	Clark, 10	Merced, 51	Z. Smith, 10	Z. Smith, 3.27
1995	58	86	5th	27	Leyland	Merced, .300	Merced, 146	King, 18	King, 87	Neagle, 13	Neagle, 3.43
1996	73	89	5th	15	Leyland	Martin, .300	Martin, 189	King, 30	King, 111	Lieber, 9	Lieber, 3.99
1997	79	83	2nd	5	Lamont	Randa, .302	Womack, 178	Young, 18	Young, 74	Cordova, Lieber, Loaiza, 11	Cordova, 3.63
1998	69	93	6th	33	Lamont	Kendall, .327	Womack, 185	Young, 27	Young, 108	Cordova, 13	Cordova, 3.31
1999	78	83	3rd	18½	Lamont	Giles, .315	Young, 174	Giles, 39	Giles, 115	Ritchie, 15	Ritchie, 3.49
2000	69	93	5th	26	Lamont	Kendall, .320	Kendall, 185	Giles, 35	Giles, 123	Silva, 11	Benson, 3.86
2001	62	100	6th	31	McClendon	Giles, .309	Ramirez, 181	Giles, 37	Ramirez, 112	Ritchie, 11	Williams, 3.71
2002	72	89	4th	24½	McClendon	Giles, .298	Kendall, 154	Giles, 38	Giles, 103	Fogg, Wells, 12	Wells, 3.58

* Tied for position. † Lost Championship Series. ‡ Won Championship Series. § First half 25-23; second half 21-33.

Note: Batting average minimum 350 at-bats; ERA minimum 90 innings pitched.

St. Louis Cardinals

Outfielder Stan Musial.

FRANCHISE CHRONOLOGY

First season: 1882, as a member of the new American Association. The "Browns" struggled to a 37-43 first-year record and finished fifth in the six-team field.

1883-1900: The Browns captured four consecutive A.A pennants from 1885 through 1888, but their success ended there. When the A.A. folded after the 1891 season, they joined the National League and sank quietly into the second division.

1901-present: The Cardinals trail only the Yankees in World Series championships and only the Yankees and Dodgers in pennants. And all of their success was achieved after 1926, when they captured their first N.L. flag and World Series. The history of Cardinals baseball has been colorful and consistent, spiced by some of the sport's most memorable moments. St. Louis won two pennants in the 1920s, three in the 1930s, four in the 1940s, three in the 1960s and three in the 1980s. Nine of the pennants led to championships, including the Gas House Gang's 1934 fall classic romp past Detroit and Enos Slaughter's 1946 Series-ending Mad Dash. The Cardinals have finished first only seven times since division play began in 1969, but three of them resulted in World Series appearances (a 1982 victory, 1985 and '87 losses). The Cardinals, who lost in the 1996, 2000 and 2002 N.L. Championship Series, were placed in the Central Division when the N.L. adopted the three-division format in 1994.

CARDINALS VS. OPPONENTS BY DECADE

	Braves	Cubs	Dodgers	Giants	Phillies	Pirates	Reds	Astros	Mets	Expos	Padres	Marlins	Rockies	Brewers	D'backs	Interleague	Decade Record
1900-09	111-98	64-144	93-115	78-133	90-121	53-158	91-119										580-888
1910-19	100-110	78-136	104-105	81-131	98-112	83-127	108-109										652-830
1920-29	135-85	105-112	119-101	95-123	151-69	102-117	115-105										822-712
1930-39	121-98	109-111	127-91	107-110	159-61	99-121	147-73										869-665
1940-49	144-76	138-82	132-90	141-77	150-70	122-98	133-87										960-580
1950-59	101-119	113-107	85-135	108-112	113-107	132-87	124-96										776-763
1960-69	94-88	114-73	91-91	92-90	108-79	107-81	90-92	79-59	90-54	11-7	8-4						884-718
1970-79	69-51	87-93	53-67	60-60	86-91	79-101	46-74	64-56	93-85	93-85	70-50						800-813
1980-89	68-47	89-81	56-62	60-53	95-80	98-75	63-50	58-56	86-87	82-95	70-48						825-734
1990-99	43-71	67-71	55-52	58-54	67-57	62-76	51-62	62-60	55-67	61-64	56-51	40-29	37-40	14-10	11-6	19-24	758-794
2000-02	8-11	30-18	13-8	10-11	13-8	33-13	27-22	26-21	11-10	12-7	19-2	11-10	10-13	27-19	12-9	23-19	285-201
Totals	994-854	994-1028	928-917	890-954	1130-855	970-1054	995-889	289-252	335-303	259-258	223-155	51-39	47-53	41-29	23-15	42-43	8211-7698

Interleague results: 2-1 vs. Angels, 10-5 vs. White Sox, 3-8 vs. Indians, 6-8 vs. Tigers, 11-10 vs. Royals, 0-3 vs. Brewers, 9-6 vs. Twins, 1-2 vs. Mariners.

MANAGERS

Name	*Years*	*Record*
Ned Cuthbert	1882	37-43
Ted Sullivan	1883	53-26
Charlie Comiskey	1883, 1884-89, 1891	561-273
Tommy McCarthy	1890	15-12
John Kerins	1890	9-8
Chief Roseman	1890	7-8
Count Campau	1890	27-14
Joe Gerhardt	1890	20-16
Jack Glasscock	1892	1-3
John Stricker	1892	6-17
John Crooks	1892	27-33
George Gore	1892	6-9
Bob Caruthers	1892	16-32
Bill Watkins	1893	57-75
George Miller	1894	56-76
Al Buckenberger	1895	16-34
Chris Von Der Ahe	1895, 1896, 1897	3-14
Joe Quinn	1895	11-28
Lew Phelan	1895	11-30
Harry Diddlebock	1896	7-10
Arlie Latham	1896	0-3
Roger Connor	1896	8-37
Tom Dowd	1896-97	31-60
Hugh Nicol	1897	8-32
Bill Hallman	1897	13-36
Tim Hurst	1898	39-111
Patsy Tebeau	1899-1900	126-117
Patsy Donovan	1901-03	175-236
Kid Nichols	1904-05	80-88
Jimmy Burke	1905	34-56
Stanley Robison	1905	19-31
John McCloskey	1906-08	153-304
Roger Bresnahan	1909-12	255-352
Miller Huggins	1913-17	346-415
Jack Hendricks	1918	51-78
Branch Rickey	1919-25	458-485
Rogers Hornsby	1925-26	153-116
Bob O'Farrell	1927	92-61
Bill McKechnie	1928-29	129-88
Billy Southworth	1929, 1940-45	620-346
Gabby Street	1929, 1930-33	312-242
Frank Frisch	1933-38	458-354
Mike Gonzalez	1938, 1940	9-13
Ray Blades	1939-40	106-85
Eddie Dyer	1946-50	446-325
Marty Marion	1951	81-73
Eddie Stanky	1952-55	260-238
Harry Walker	1955	51-67
Fred Hutchinson	1956-58	232-220
Stan Hack	1958	3-7
Solly Hemus	1959-61	190-192
Johnny Keane	1961-64	317-249
Red Schoendienst	1965-76, 1980, 1990	1041-955
Vern Rapp	1977-78	89-90
Ken Boyer	1978-80	166-190
Whitey Herzog	1980, 1981-90	822-728
Joe Torre	1990-95	351-354
Mike Jorgensen	1995	42-54
Tony La Russa	1996-2002	604-529

WORLD SERIES CHAMPIONS

Year	*Loser*	*Length*	*MVP*
1926	N.Y. Yankees	7 games	None
1931	Philadelphia	7 games	None
1934	Detroit	7 games	None
1942	N.Y. Yankees	5 games	None
1944	St.L. Browns	6 games	None
1946	Boston	7 games	None
1964	N.Y. Yankees	7 games	Gibson
1967	Boston	7 games	Gibson
1982	Milwaukee	7 games	Porter

A.A. PENNANT WINNERS

Year	*Record*	*Manager*	*Series Result*
1885	79-33	Comiskey	None
1886	93-46	Comiskey	None
1887	95-40	Comiskey	None
1888	92-43	Comiskey	None

N.L. PENNANT WINNERS

Year	*Record*	*Manager*	*Series Result*
1926	89-65	Hornsby	Defeated Yankees
1928	95-59	McKechnie	Lost to Yankees
1930	92-62	Street	Lost to A's
1931	101-53	Street	Defeated A's
1934	95-58	Frisch	Defeated Tigers
1942	106-48	Southworth	Defeated Yankees
1943	105-49	Southworth	Lost to Yankees
1944	105-49	Southworth	Defeated Browns
1946	98-58	Dyer	Defeated Red Sox
1964	93-69	Keane	Defeated Yankees
1967	101-60	Schoendienst	Defeated Red Sox
1968	97-65	Schoendiesnt	Lost to Tigers
1982	92-70	Herzog	Defeated Brewers
1985	101-61	Herzog	Lost to Royals
1987	95-67	Herzog	Lost to Twins

EAST DIVISION CHAMPIONS

Year	*Record*	*Manager*	*NLCS Result*
1982	92-70	Herzog	Defeated Braves
1985	101-61	Herzog	Defeated Dodgers
1987	95-67	Herzog	Defeated Giants

CENTRAL DIVISION CHAMPIONS

Year	*Record*	*Manager*	*NLCS Result*
1996	88-74	La Russa	Lost to Braves
2000	95-67	La Russa	Lost to Mets
2002	97-65	La Russa	Lost to Giants

WILD-CARD QUALIFIERS

Year	*Record*	*Manager*	*Div. Series Result*
2001	93-69	La Russa	Lost to D'backs

ATTENDANCE HIGHS

Total	*Season*	*Park*
3,336,493	2000	Busch Stadium
3,236,103	1999	Busch Stadium
3,195,021	1998	Busch Stadium
3,113,091	2001	Busch Stadium
3,080,980	1989	Busch Stadium

BALLPARK CHRONOLOGY

Busch Memorial Stadium (1966-present)

Capacity: 50,354.
First game: Cardinals 4, Atlanta 3, 12 innings (May 12, 1966).
First batter: Felipe Alou, Braves.
First hit: Gary Geiger, Braves (single).
First run: Jerry Buchek, Cardinals (3rd inning).
First home run: Felipe Alou, Braves.
First winning pitcher: Don Dennis, Cardinals.
First-season attendance: 1,712,980.

Sportsman's Park I (1882-91)

Capacity: 6,000.
First game: St. Louis 9, Louisville 7 (May 2, 1882).

Union Park (1892-97)

League Park (1898)

Robison Field (1899-1920)

Capacity: 14,500.

Sportsman's Park II (1920-66)

Capacity: 30,500.
First game: Pittsburgh 6, St. Louis 2, 10 innings (July 1, 1920).
First full-season attendance: 384,773 (1921).

Note: Sportsman's Park was renamed Busch Stadium in 1953.

N.L. MVPs

Frank Frisch, 2B, 1931
Dizzy Dean, P, 1934
Joe Medwick, OF, 1937
Mort Cooper, P, 1942
Stan Musial, OF, 1943
Marty Marion, SS, 1944
Stan Musial, 1B, 1946
Stan Musial OF, 1948
Ken Boyer, 3B, 1964
Orlando Cepeda, 1B, 1967
Bob Gibson, P, 1968
Joe Torre, 3B, 1971
*Keith Hernandez, 1B, 1979
Willie McGee, OF, 1985

* Co-winner.

CY YOUNG WINNERS

Bob Gibson, RH, 1968
Bob Gibson, RH, 1970

ROOKIES OF THE YEAR

Wally Moon, OF, 1954
Bill Virdon, OF, 1955
Bake McBride, OF, 1974
Vince Coleman, OF, 1985
Todd Worrell, P, 1986
Albert Pujols, OF-3B-1B, 2001

MANAGERS OF THE YEAR

Whitey Herzog, 1985
Tony La Russa, 2002

RETIRED UNIFORMS

No.	*Name*	*Pos.*
1	Ozzie Smith	SS
2	Red Schoendienst	2B
6	Stan Musial	OF, 1B
9	Enos Slaughter	OF
14	Ken Boyer	3B
17	Dizzy Dean	P
20	Lou Brock	OF
45	Bob Gibson	P

MILESTONE PERFORMANCES

30-plus home runs

70— Mark McGwire 1998
65— Mark McGwire 1999
43— Johnny Mize 1940
42— Rogers Hornsby 1922
Jim Edmonds 2000
39— Rogers Hornsby 1925
Stan Musial 1948
37— Albert Pujols 2001
36— Stan Musial 1949
35— Rip Collins 1934
Stan Musial 1954
Jack Clark 1987
34— Dick Allen 1970
Fernando Tatis 1999
Albert Pujols 2002
33— Stan Musial 1955
32— Stan Musial 1951
Ken Boyer 1960
Mark McGwire 2000
31— Jim Bottomley 1928
Joe Medwick 1937
Ray Lankford 1997, 1998
Scott Rolen *2002
30— Stan Musial 1953
Ron Gant 1996
Jim Edmonds 2001

*17 with Phillies, 14 with Cardinals.

100-plus RBIs

154— Joe Medwick 1937
152— Rogers Hornsby 1922
147— Mark McGwire 1998
Mark McGwire 1999
143— Rogers Hornsby 1925
138— Joe Medwick 1936
137— Jim Bottomley 1929
Johnny Mize 1940
Joe Torre 1971
136— Jim Bottomley 1928
131— Stan Musial 1948
130— Enos Slaughter 1946
Albert Pujols 2001
128— Jim Bottomley 1925
Rip Collins 1934
127— Albert Pujols 2002
126— Rogers Hornsby 1921
Joe Medwick 1935
Stan Musial 1954
125— Chick Hafey 1929
124— Jim Bottomley 1927
123— Stan Musial 1949
122— Rip Collins 1935
Joe Medwick 1938
120— Jim Bottomley 1926
119— Ken Boyer 1964
117— Joe Medwick 1939
Pedro Guerrero 1989
114— Frank Frisch 1930
113— Johnny Mize 1937
Stan Musial 1953
112— Ray Jablonski 1953
111— Jim Bottomley 1924
Chick Hafey 1928
Ken Boyer 1963
Orlando Cepeda 1967
110— Tom Herr 1985
Jim Edmonds 2001
Scott Rolen ..... †2002
109— Buster Adams *1945
Stan Musial 1950, 1956
Bill White 1963
George Hendrick 1980
108— Johnny Mize 1939
Stan Musial 1951, 1955
Jim Edmonds 2000
107— Chick Hafey 1930
Fernando Tatis 1999
106— Joe Medwick 1934
Jack Clark 1987
105— Del Ennis 1957
Keith Hernandez 1979
Willie McGee 1987
Ray Lankford 1998
104— Whitey Kurowski 1947
Ray Jablonski 1954
George Hendrick 1982
Brian Jordan 1996
103— Stan Musial 1946
Ted Simmons 1974
Todd Zeile 1993
102— Austin McHenry 1921
Johnny Mize 1938
Ray Sanders 1944
Whitey Kurowski 1945
Stan Musial 1957
Bill White 1962, 1964
101— Enos Slaughter 1950, 1952
Joe Torre 1969
Dick Allen 1970
100— Les Bell 1926
Johnny Mize 1941
Joe Torre 1970
Reggie Smith 1974
Ted Simmons 1975

*8 with Phillies, 101 with Cardinals.
†66 with Phillies, 44 with Cardinals.

20-plus victories

1892— Kid Gleason 20-24
1893— Kid Gleason 21-22
1894— Ted Breitenstein 27-23
1899— Cy Young 26-16
Jack Powell 23-19
1901— Jack Harper 23-13
1904— Kid Nichols 21-13
Jack Taylor 20-19
1911— Bob Harmon 23-16
1920— Bill Doak 20-12
1923— Jesse Haines 20-13
1926— Flint Rhem 20-7
1927— Jesse Haines 24-10
Grover Alexander 21-10
1928— Bill Sherdel 21-10
Jesse Haines 20-8
1933— Dizzy Dean 20-18
1934— Dizzy Dean 30-7
1935— Dizzy Dean 28-12
1936— Dizzy Dean 24-13
1939— Curt Davis 22-16
1942— Mort Cooper 22-7
Johnny Beazley 21-6
1943— Mort Cooper 21-8
1944— Mort Cooper 22-7
1945— Red Barrett *23-12
1946— Howie Pollet 21-10
1948— Harry Brecheen 20-7
1949— Howie Pollet 20-9
1953— Harvey Haddix 20-9
1960— Ernie Broglio 21-9
1964— Ray Sadecki 20-11
1965— Bob Gibson 20-12
1966— Bob Gibson 21-12
1968— Bob Gibson 22-9
1969— Bob Gibson 20-13
1970— Bob Gibson 23-7
1971— Steve Carlton 20-9
1977— Bob Forsch 20-7
1984— Joaquin Andujar 20-14
1985— Joaquin Andujar 21-12
John Tudor 21-8
2000— Darryl Kile 20-9
2001— Matt Morris 22-8

*2-3 with Braves, 21-9 with Cardinals.

N.L. home run champions

1922— Rogers Hornsby 42
1925— Rogers Hornsby 39
1928— Jim Bottomley *31
1934— Rip Collins *35
1937— Joe Medwick *31
1939— Johnny Mize 28
1940— Johnny Mize 43
1998— Mark McGwire 70
1999— Mark McGwire 65

*Tied for league lead.

N.L. RBI champions

1920— Rogers Hornsby *94
1921— Rogers Hornsby 126
1922— Rogers Hornsby 152
1925— Rogers Hornsby 143
1926— Jim Bottomley 120
1928— Jim Bottomley 136
1936— Joe Medwick 138
1937— Joe Medwick 154
1938— Joe Medwick 122
1940— Johnny Mize 137
1946— Enos Slaughter 130
1948— Stan Musial 131
1956— Stan Musial 109
1964— Ken Boyer 119
1967— Orlando Cepeda 111
1971— Joe Torre 137
1999— Mark McGwire 147

* Tied for league lead

INDIVIDUAL SEASON, GAME RECORDS

SEASON

Batting

Record		Player	Year
At-bats	689	Lou Brock	1967
Runs	141	Rogers Hornsby	1922
Hits	250	Rogers Hornsby	1922
Singles	181	Jesse Burkett	1901
Doubles	64	Joe Medwick	1936
Triples	33	Perry Werden	1893
Home runs	70	Mark McGwire	1998
Home runs, rookie	37	Albert Pujols	2001
Grand slams	3	3 times	
		Last by Fernando Tatis	1999
Total bases	450	Rogers Hornsby	1922
RBIs	154	Joe Medwick	1937
Walks	162	Mark McGwire	1998
Most strikeouts	167	Jim Edmonds	2000
Fewest strikeouts	10	Frank Frisch	1927
Batting average	.424	Rogers Hornsby	1924
Slugging pct.	.756	Rogers Hornsby	1922
Stolen bases	118	Lou Brock	1974

Pitching (since 1900)

Record		Player	Year
Games	89	Steve Kline	2001
Complete games	39	Jack Taylor	1904
Innings	352.1	Stoney McGlynn	1907
Wins	30	Dizzy Dean	1934
Losses	25	Stoney McGlynn	1907
		Art Raymond	1908
Winning pct.	.833 (10-2)	John Tudor	1987
Walks	181	Bob Harmon	1911
Strikeouts	274	Bob Gibson	1970
Shutouts	13	Bob Gibson	1968
Home runs allowed	39	Murry Dickson	1948
Lowest ERA	1.12	Bob Gibson	1968
Saves	47	Lee Smith	1991

GAME

Batting

Record		Player	Date
Runs	5	Last by J.D. Drew	5-1-99
Hits	6	Last by Terry Moore	9-5-35
Doubles	4	Joe Medwick	8-4-37
Triples	3	Last by Jim Bottomley	6-21-27
Home runs	4	Mark Whiten	9-7-93
RBIs	12	Jim Bottomley	9-16-24
		Mark Whiten	9-7-93
Total bases	16	Mark Whiten	9-7-93
Stolen bases	5	Lonnie Smith	9-4-82

N.L. batting champions

1901— Jesse Burkett ..... .376
1920— Rogers Hornsby ..... .370
1921— Rogers Hornsby ..... .397
1922— Rogers Hornsby ..... .401
1923— Rogers Hornsby ..... .384
1924— Rogers Hornsby ..... .424
1925— Rogers Hornsby ..... .403
1931— Chick Hafey ..... .349
1937— Joe Medwick ..... .374
1939— Johnny Mize ..... .349
1943— Stan Musial ..... .357
1946— Stan Musial ..... .365
1948— Stan Musial ..... .376
1950— Stan Musial ..... .346
1951— Stan Musial ..... .355
1952— Stan Musial ..... .336
1957— Stan Musial ..... .351
1971— Joe Torre ..... .363
1979— Keith Hernandez ..... .344
1985— Willie McGee ..... .353
1990— Willie McGee ..... .335

N.L. ERA champions

1914— Bill Doak 1.72
1921— Bill Doak 2.59
1942— Mort Cooper 1.78
1943— Howie Pollet 1.75
1946— Howie Pollet 2.10
1948— Harry Brecheen 2.24
1968— Bob Gibson 1.12
1976— John Denny 2.52
1988— Joe Magrane 2.18

N.L. strikeout champions

1906— Fred Beebe 171
1930— Bill Hallahan 177
1931— Bill Hallahan 159
1932— Dizzy Dean 191
1933— Dizzy Dean 199
1934— Dizzy Dean 195
1935— Dizzy Dean 182
1948— Harry Brecheen 149
1958— Sam Jones 225
1966— Bob Gibson 268
1989— Jose DeLeon 201

No-hit pitchers

(9 innings or more)
1924— Jesse Haines ..... 5-0 vs. Boston
1934— Paul Dean ..... 3-0 vs. Brooklyn
1941— Lon Warneke ..... 2-0 vs. Cincinnati
1968— Ray Washburn ..... 2-0 vs. San Francisco
1971— Bob Gibson ..... 11-0 vs. Pittsburgh
1978— Bob Forsch ..... 5-0 vs. Philadelphia
1983— Bob Forsch ..... 3-0 vs. Montreal
1999— Jose Jimenez ..... 1-0 vs. Arizona
2001— Bud Smith ..... 4-0 vs. San Diego

Longest hitting streaks

33— Rogers Hornsby 1922
30— Stan Musial 1950
29— Harry Walker 1943
Ken Boyer 1959
28— Joe Medwick 1935
Red Schoendienst 1954
26— Lou Brock 1971
25— Joe McEwing 1999
24— Pepper Martin 1935
Stan Musial 1952
Wally Moon 1957
23— Pepper Martin 1935
Jose Oquendo 1989
22— Taylor Douthit 1930
Johnny Mize 1936
Harry Walker 1943
Stan Musial 1943
Whitey Kurowski 1943
Vada Pinson 1969
Joe Torre 1971
Willie McGee 1990
21— Les Bell 1926
Ernie Orsatti 1932
Joe Medwick 1932
Enos Slaughter 1940
Lou Klein 1943
20— Ed Konetchy 1910
Terry Moore 1942
Stan Musial 1957
Wally Moon 1957
Bill White 1964
Lou Brock 1967
John Mabry 1997
Placido Polanco 2001

CAREER LEADERS

BATTING

Games

Stan Musial	3,026
Lou Brock	2,289
Ozzie Smith	1,990
Enos Slaughter	1,820
Red Schoendienst	1,795
Curt Flood	1,738
Ken Boyer	1,667
Willie McGee	1,661
Rogers Hornsby	1,580
Julian Javier	1,578

At-bats

Stan Musial	10,972
Lou Brock	9,125
Ozzie Smith	7,160
Red Schoendienst	6,841
Enos Slaughter	6,775
Ken Boyer	6,334
Curt Flood	6,318
Rogers Hornsby	5,881
Willie McGee	5,734
Ted Simmons	5,725

Runs

Stan Musial	1,949
Lou Brock	1,427
Rogers Hornsby	1,089
Enos Slaughter	1,071
Red Schoendienst	1,025
Ozzie Smith	991
Ken Boyer	988
Jim Bottomley	921
Ray Lankford	892
Curt Flood	845

Hits

Stan Musial	3,630
Lou Brock	2,713
Rogers Hornsby	2,110
Enos Slaughter	2,064
Red Schoendienst	1,980
Ozzie Smith	1,944
Ken Boyer	1,855
Curt Flood	1,853
Jim Bottomley	1,727
Ted Simmons	1,704

Doubles

Stan Musial	725
Lou Brock	434
Joe Medwick	377
Rogers Hornsby	367
Enos Slaughter	366
Red Schoendienst	352
Jim Bottomley	344
Ozzie Smith	338
Ted Simmons	332
Ray Lankford	325

Triples

Stan Musial	177
Rogers Hornsby	143
Enos Slaughter	135
Lou Brock	121
Jim Bottomley	119
Ed Konetchy	94
Willie McGee	83
Joe Medwick	81
Pepper Martin	75
Garry Templeton	69

Home runs

Stan Musial	475
Ken Boyer	255
Ray Lankford	222
Mark McGwire	220
Rogers Hornsby	193
Jim Bottomley	181
Ted Simmons	172
Johnny Mize	158
Joe Medwick	152
Enos Slaughter	146

Total bases

Stan Musial	6,134
Lou Brock	3,776
Rogers Hornsby	3,342
Enos Slaughter	3,138
Ken Boyer	3,011
Jim Bottomley	2,852
Red Schoendienst	2,657
Ted Simmons	2,626
Joe Medwick	2,585
Ray Lankford	2,521

Runs batted in

Stan Musial	1,951
Enos Slaughter	1,148
Jim Bottomley	1,105
Rogers Hornsby	1,072
Ken Boyer	1,001
Ted Simmons	929
Joe Medwick	923
Lou Brock	814
Ray Lankford	807
Frankie Frisch	720

Extra-base hits

Stan Musial	1,377
Rogers Hornsby	703
Lou Brock	684
Enos Slaughter	647
Jim Bottomley	644
Joe Medwick	610
Ray Lankford	598
Ken Boyer	585
Ted Simmons	541
Red Schoendienst	482

Batting average

(Minimum 500 games)

Rogers Hornsby	.359
Johnny Mize	.336
Joe Medwick	.335
Stan Musial	.331
Chick Hafey	.326
Jim Bottomley	.325
Frankie Frisch	.312
George Watkins	.309
Joe Torre	.308
Rip Collins	.307

Stolen bases

Lou Brock	888
Vince Coleman	549
Ozzie Smith	433
Willie McGee	301
Ray Lankford	248
Jack Smith	203
Frankie Frisch	195
Tommy Dowd	189
Miller Huggins	174
Lonnie Smith	173

PITCHING

Earned-run average

(Minimum 1,000 innings)

Slim Sallee	2.67
Mort Cooper	2.77
Max Lanier	2.84
Harry Brecheen	2.91
Bob Gibson	2.91
Bill Doak	2.93
Dizzy Dean	2.99
Lee Meadows	3.00
Howie Pollet	3.06
Steve Carlton	3.10

Wins

Bob Gibson	251
Jesse Haines	210
Bob Forsch	163
Bill Sherdel	153
Bill Doak	144
Dizzy Dean	134
Harry Brecheen	128
Slim Sallee	106
Mort Cooper	105
Larry Jackson	101
Max Lanier	101

Losses

Bob Gibson	174
Jesse Haines	158
Bill Doak	136
Bill Sherdel	131
Bob Forsch	127
Ted Breitenstein	125
Slim Sallee	107
Larry Jackson	86
Bob Harmon	81
Harry Brecheen	79

Innings pitched

Bob Gibson	3,884.1
Jesse Haines	3,203.2
Bob Forsch	2,658.2
Bill Sherdel	2,450.2
Bill Doak	2,387.0
Ted Breitenstein	1,905.2
Slim Sallee	1,905.1
Harry Brecheen	1,790.1
Dizzy Dean	1,737.1
Larry Jackson	1,672.1

Strikeouts

Bob Gibson	3,117
Dizzy Dean	1,095
Bob Forsch	1,079
Jesse Haines	979
Steve Carlton	951
Bill Doak	938
Larry Jackson	899
Harry Brecheen	857
Vinegar Bemizell	789
Bill Hallahan	784

Bases on balls

Bob Gibson	1,336
Jesse Haines	870
Ted Breitenstein	829
Bob Forsch	780
Bill Doak	740
Bill Hallahan	648
Bill Sherdel	595
Bob Harmon	594
Vinegar Bemizell	568
Max Lanier	524

Games

Jesse Haines	554
Bob Gibson	528
Bill Sherdel	465
Bob Forsch	455
Al Brazle	441
Bill Doak	376
Todd Worrell	348
Lindy McDaniel	336
Larry Jackson	330
Al Hrabosky	329

Shutouts

Bob Gibson	56
Bill Doak	30
Mort Cooper	28
Harry Brecheen	25
Jesse Haines	24
Dizzy Dean	23
Max Lanier	20
Howie Pollet	20
Bob Forsch	19
Ernie Broglio	18

Saves

Lee Smith	160
Todd Worrell	129
Bruce Sutter	127
Dennis Eckersley	66
Lindy McDaniel	64
Al Brazle	60
Joe Hoerner	60
Al Hrabosky	59
Dave Veres	48
Ken Dayley	39

TEAM SEASON, GAME RECORDS

SEASON

Batting

Most at-bats	5,734	1979
Most runs	1,004	1930
Fewest runs	372	1908
Most hits	1,732	1930
Most singles	1,223	1920
Most doubles	373	1939
Most triples	96	1920
Most home runs	235	2000
Fewest home runs	10	1906
Most grand slams	11	2000
Most pinch-hit home runs	10	1998
Most total bases	2,595	1930
Most stolen bases	314	1985
Highest batting average	.314	1930
Lowest batting average	.223	1908
Highest slugging pct	.471	1930

Pitching

Lowest ERA	2.38	1914
Highest ERA	6.21	1897
Most complete games	146	1904
Most shutouts	30	1968
Most saves	54	1993
Most walks	701	1911
Most strikeouts	1,130	1997

Fielding

Most errors	354	1903
Fewest errors	94	1992
Most double plays	192	1974
Highest fielding average	.985	1992

General

Most games won	106	1942
Most games lost	111	1898
Highest win pct	.703	1876
Lowest win pct	.221	1897

GAME, INNING

Batting

Most runs, game	28	7-6-29
Most runs, inning	12	9-16-26
Most hits, game	30	6-1-1895
Most home runs, game	7	5-7-40, 7-12-96
Most total bases, game	49	5-7-40

Intimidating Bob Gibson powered his way to 251 victories and 3,117 strikeouts with the Cardinals.

CARDINALS YEAR-BY-YEAR

				Games		Leaders					
Year	W	L	Place	Back	Manager	Batting avg.	Hits	Home runs	RBIs	Wins	ERA
1901	76	64	4th	14½	Donovan	Burkett, .376	Burkett, 228	Burkett, 10	Wallace, 91	Harper, 23	Sudhoff, 3.52
1902	56	78	6th	44½	Donovan	Donovan, .315	Barclay, 163	Barclay, Smoot, 3	Barclay, 53	O'Neill, 17	Currie, 2.60
1903	43	94	8th	46½	Donovan	Donovan, .327	Smoot, 148	Smoot, 4	Brain, 60	M. Brown, McFarland, 9	M. Brown, 2.60
1904	75	79	5th	31½	Nichols	Beckley, .325	Beckley, 179	Brain, 7	Brain, 72	Nichols, Taylor, 21	Nichols, 2.02
1905	58	96	6th	47½	Nichols, Burke, Robison	Smoot, .311	Smoot, 166	Grady, 4	Smoot, 58	Taylor, Thielman, 15	B. Brown, 2.97
1906	52	98	7th	63	McCloskey	Bennett, .262	Bennett, 156	Grady, 3	Beckley, 44	Beebe, 9	Taylor, 2.15
1907	52	101	8th	55½	McCloskey	Murray, .262	Byrne, 143	Murray, 7	Murray, 46	Karger, 15	Karger, 2.04
1908	49	105	8th	50	McCloskey	Murray, .282	Murray, 167	Murray, 7	Murray, 62	Raymond, 14	Raymond, 2.03
1909	54	98	7th	56	Bresnahan	Konetchy, .286	Konetchy, 165	Konetchy, 4	Konetchy, 80	Beebe, 15	Sallee, 2.42
1910	63	90	7th	40½	Bresnahan	Konetchy, .302	Konetchy, 157	Ellis, 4	Konetchy, 78	Lush, 14	Sallee, 2.97
1911	75	74	5th	22	Bresnahan	Evans, .294	Konetchy, 165	Konetchy, 6	Konetchy, 88	Harmon, 23	Sallee, 2.76
1912	63	90	6th	41	Bresnahan	Konetchy, .314	Konetchy, 169	Konetchy, 8	Konetchy, 82	Harmon, 18	Sallee, 2.60
1913	51	99	8th	49	Huggins	Oakes, .291	Oakes, 156	Konetchy, 7	Konetchy, 68	Sallee, 18	Sallee, 2.71
1914	81	72	3rd	13	Huggins	D, Miller, .290	D, Miller, 166	Wilson, 9	D, Miller, 88	Doak, 20	Doak, 1.72
1915	72	81	6th	18½	Huggins	Snyder, .298	Long, 149	Bescher, 4	D, Miller, 72	Doak, 16	Doak, 2.64
1916	60	93	*7th	33½	Huggins	Hornsby, .313	Hornsby, 155	Bescher, Hornsby, J. Smith, 6	Hornsby, 65	Doak, Meadows, 12	Meadows, 2.58
1917	82	70	3rd	15	Huggins	Hornsby, .327	Hornsby, 171	Hornsby, 8	Hornsby, 66	Doak, 16	Packard, 2.47
1918	51	78	8th	33	Hendricks	Fisher, .317	Paulette, 126	Cruise, 6	Hornsby, 60	Packard, 12	Ames, 2.31
1919	54	83	7th	40½	Rickey	Hornsby, .318	Hornsby, 163	Hornsby, 8	Hornsby, 71	Doak, 13	Goodwin, 2.51
1920	75	79	*5th	18	Rickey	Hornsby, .370	Hornsby, 218	McHenry, 10	Hornsby, 94	Doak, 20	Doak, 2.53
1921	87	66	3rd	7	Rickey	Hornsby, .397	Hornsby, 235	Hornsby, 21	Hornsby, 126	Haines, 18	Doak, 2.59
1922	85	69	*3rd	8	Rickey	Hornsby, .401	Hornsby, 250	Hornsby, 42	Hornsby, 152	Pfeffer, 19	Pfeffer, 3.58
1923	79	74	5th	16	Rickey	Hornsby, .384	Bottomley, 194	Hornsby, 17	Stock, 96	Haines, 20	Haines, 3.11
1924	65	89	6th	28½	Rickey	Hornsby, .424	Hornsby, 227	Hornsby, 25	Bottomley, 111	Sothoron, 10	Dickerman, 2.41
1925	77	76	4th	18	Rickey, Hornsby	Hornsby, .403	Bottomley, 227	Hornsby, 39	Hornsby, 143	Sherdel, 15	Reinhart, 3.05
1926	89	65	1st	+2	Hornsby	Bell, .325	Bell, 189	Bottomley, 19	Bottomley, 120	Rhem, 20	Alexander, 2.91
1927	92	61	2nd	1½	O'Farrell	Frisch, .337	Frisch, 208	Bottomley, 19	Bottomley, 124	Haines, 24	Alexander, 2.52
1928	95	59	1st	+2	McKechnie	Hafey, .337	Douthit, 181	Bottomley, 31	Bottomley, 136	Sherdel, 21	Sherdel, 2.86
1929	78	74	4th	20	McKechnie, Southworth, Street	Hafey, .338	Douthit, 206	Bottomley, Hafey, 29	Bottomley, 137	Haines, Johnson, 13	Johnson, 3.60
1930	92	62	1st	+2	Street	Watkins, .373	Douthit, 201	Hafey, 26	Frisch, 114	Halahan, 15	Grimes, 3.01
1931	101	53	1st	+13	Street	Hafey, .349	Adams, 178	Hafey, 16	Hafey, 95	Hallahan, 19	Johnson, 3.00
1932	72	82	*6th	18	Street	Orsatti, .336	Collins, 153	Collins, 21	Collins, 91	D. Dean, 18	Hallahan, 3.11
1933	82	71	5th	9½	Street, Frisch	Martin, .316	Martin, 189	Medwick, 18	Medwick, 98	D. Dean, 20	Haines, 2.50
1934	95	58	1st	+2	Frisch	Collins, .333	Collins, 200	Collins, 35	Collins, 116	D. Dean, 30	D. Dean, 2.66
1935	96	58	2nd	4	Frisch	Medwick, .353	Medwick, 224	Collins, Medwick, 23	Medwick, 126	D. Dean, 28	Heusser, 2.92
1936	87	67	*2nd	5	Frisch	Medwick, .351	Medwick, 233	Mize, 19	Medwick, 138	D. Dean, 24	D. Dean, 3.17
1937	81	73	4th	15	Frisch	Medwick, .374	Medwick, 237	Medwick, 31	Medwick, 154	Warneke, 18	D. Dean, 2.69
1938	71	80	6th	17½	Frisch, Gonzalez	Mize, .337	Medwick, 190	Mize, 27	Medwick, 122	Weiland, 16	McGee, 3.21
1939	92	61	2nd	4½	Blades	Mize, .349	Medwick, 201	Mize, 28	Medwick, 117	Davis, 22	Bowman, 2.60
1940	84	69	3rd	16	Blades, Gonzalez, Southworth	Mize, .314	Mize, 182	Mize, 43	Mize, 137	McGee, Warneke, 16	Warneke, 3.14
1941	97	56	2nd	2½	Southworth	Mize, .317	J. Brown, 168	Mize, 16	Mize, 100	Warneke, White, 17	White, 2.40
1942	106	48	1st	+2	Southworth	Slaughter, .318	Slaughter, 188	Slaughter, 13	Slaughter, 98	M. Cooper, 22	M. Cooper, 1.78
1943	105	49	1st	+18	Southworth	Musial, .357	Musial, 220	Kurowski, Musial, 13	W. Cooper, Musial, 81	M. Cooper, 21	Pollet, 1.75
1944	105	49	1st	+14½	Southworth	Musial, .347	Musial, 197	Kurowski, 20	Sanders, 102	M. Cooper, 22	Munger, 1.34
1945	95	59	2nd	3	Southworth	Kurowski, .323	Adams, 169	Kurowski, 27	Kurowski, 102	Barrett, 21	Brecheen, 2.52
1946	98	58	†1st	+2	Dyer	Musial, .365	Musial, 228	Slaughter, 18	Slaughter, 130	Pollet, 21	Pollet, 2.10
1947	89	65	2nd	5	Dyer	Musial, .312	Musial, 183	Kurowski, 27	Kurowski, 104	Brecheen, Munger, 16	Brazle, 2.84
1948	85	69	2nd	6½	Dyer	Musial, .376	Musial, 230	Musial, 39	Musial, 131	Brecheen, 20	Brecheen, 2.24
1949	96	58	2nd	1	Dyer	Musial, .338	Musial, 207	Musial, 36	Musial, 123	Pollet, 20	Staley, 2.73
1950	78	75	5th	12½	Dyer	Musial, .346	Musial, 192	Musial, 28	Musial, 109	Pollet, 14	Lanier, 3.13
1951	81	73	3rd	15½	Marion	Musial, .355	Musial, 205	Musial, 32	Musial, 108	Staley, 19	Brazle, 3.09
1952	88	66	3rd	8½	Stanky	Musial, .336	Musial, 194	Musial, 21	Slaughter, 101	Staley, 17	Staley, 3.27
1953	83	71	*3rd	22	Stanky	Schoendienst, .342	Musial, 200	Musial, 30	Musial, 113	Haddix, 20	Haddix, 3.06
1954	72	82	6th	25	Stanky	Musial, .330	Musial, 195	Musial, 35	Musial, 126	Haddix, 18	Poholsky, 3.06
1955	68	86	7th	30½	Stanky, Walker	Musial, .319	Musial, 179	Musial, 33	Musial, 108	Haddix, 12	LaPalme, 2.75
1956	76	78	4th	17	Hutchinson	Musial, .310	Musial, 184	Musial, 27	Musial, 109	Mizell, 14	Dickson, 3.07
1957	87	67	2nd	8	Hutchinson	Musial, .351	Blasingame, Musial, 176	Musial, 29	Ennis, 105	Jackson, McDaniel, 15	Jackson, 3.47
1958	72	82	*5th	20	Hutchinson, Hack	Musial, .337	Boyer, 175	Boyer, 23	Boyer, 90	S. Jones, 14	S. Jones, 2.88
1959	71	83	7th	16	Hemus	Cunningham, .345	Blasingame, 178	Boyer, 28	Boyer, 94	Jackson, McDaniel, 14	Jackson, 3.30
1960	86	68	3rd	9	Hemus	Boyer, .304	Boyer, 168	Boyer, 32	Boyer, 97	Broglio, 21	McDaniel, 2.09
1961	80	74	5th	13	Hemus, Keane	Boyer, .329	Boyer, 194	Boyer, 24	Boyer, 95	Jackson, Sadecki, 14	C. Simmons, 3.13
1962	84	78	6th	17½	Keane	Musial, .330	White, 199	Boyer, 24	White, 102	Jackson, 16	Gibson, 2.85
1963	93	69	2nd	6	Keane	Groat, .319	Groat, 201	White, 27	Boyer, 111	Broglio, Gibson, 18	C. Simmons, 2.48
1964	93	69	1st	+1	Keane	Brock, .348	Flood, 211	Boyer, 24	Boyer, 119	Sadecki, 20	Gibson, 3.01
1965	80	81	7th	16½	Schoendienst	Flood, .310	Flood, 191	White, 24	Flood, 83	Gibson, 20	Gibson, 3.07
1966	83	79	6th	12	Schoendienst	Cepeda, .303	Brock, 183	Cepeda, 17	Flood, 78	Gibson, 21	Gibson, 2.44
1967	101	60	1st	+10½	Schoendienst	Flood, .335	Brock, 206	Cepeda, 25	Cepeda, 111	Hughes, 16	Briles, 2.43
1968	97	65	1st	+9	Schoendienst	Flood, .301	Flood, 186	Cepeda, 16	Shannon, 79	Gibson, 22	Gibson, 1.12
							EAST DIVISION				
1969	87	75	4th	13	Schoendienst	Brock, .298	Brock, 195	Torre, 18	Torre, 101	Gibson, 20	Carlton, 2.17
1970	76	86	4th	13	Schoendienst	Torre, .325	Torre, 203	Allen, 34	Allen, 101	Gibson, 23	Taylor, 3.11
1971	90	72	2nd	7	Schoendienst	Torre, .363	Torre, 230	Torre, 24	Torre, 137	Carlton, 20	Gibson, 3.04
1972	75	81	4th	21½	Schoendienst	M. Alou, .314	Brock, 193	T. Simmons, 16	T. Simmons, 96	Gibson, 19	Gibson, 2.46
1973	81	81	2nd	1½	Schoendienst	T. Simmons, .310	Brock, 193	T. Simmons, Torre, 13	T. Simmons, 91	Wise, 16	Gibson, 2.77
1974	86	75	2nd	1½	Schoendienst	McBride, R. Smith, .309	Brock, 194	R. Smith, 23	T. Simmons, 103	McGlothen, 16	McGlothen, 2.70
1975	82	80	*3rd	10½	Schoendienst	T. Simmons, .332	T. Simmons, 193	R. Smith, 19	T. Simmons, 100	Forsch, McGlothen, 15	Hrabosky, 1.66
1976	72	90	5th	29	Schoendienst	Crawford, .304	T. Simmons, 159	Cruz, 13	T. Simmons, 75	McGlothen, 13	Denny, 2.52
1977	83	79	3rd	18	Rapp	Templeton, .322	Templeton, 200	T. Simmons, 21	T. Simmons, 95	Forsch, 20	Carroll, 2.50
1978	69	93	5th	21	Rapp. Krol. Boyer	Hendrick, .288	Templeton, 181	T. Simmons, 22	T. Simmons, 80	Denny, 14	Vuckovich, 2.55
1979	86	76	3rd	12	Boyer	Hernandez, .344	Templeton, 211	T. Simmons, 26	Hernandez, 105	S. Martinez, Vuckovich, 15	Fulgham, 2.53
1980	74	88	4th	17	Boyer, Krol, Herzog, Schoendienst	Hernandez, .321	Hernandez, 191	Hendrick, 25	Hendrick, 109	Vuckovich, 12	Vuckovich, 3.41
1981	59	43	‡2nd/2nd	—	Herzog	Hernandez, .306	Hernandez, 115	Hendrick, 18	Hendrick, 61	Forsch, 10	Forsch, 3.19
1982	92	70	§1st	+3	Herzog	L. Smith, .307	L. Smith, 182	Hendrick, 19	Hendrick, 104	Andujar, Forsch, 15	Andujar, 2.47
1983	79	83	4th	11	Herzog	L. Smith, .321	McGee, 172	Hendrick 18	Hendrick, 97	LaPoint, Stuper, 12	Stuper, 3.68
1984	84	78	3rd	12½	Herzog	McGee, .291	McGee, 166	Green, 15	Hendrick, 69	Andujar, 20	Sutter, 1.54
1985	101	61	§1st	+3	Herzog	McGee, .353	McGee, 216	Clark, 22	Herr, 110	Andujar, Tudor, 21	Tudor, 1.93
1986	79	82	3rd	28½	Herzog	O. Smith, .280	O. Smith, 144	Van Slyke, 13	Herr, Van Slyke, 61	Forsch, 14	Worrell, 2.08
1987	95	67	§1st	+3	Herzog	O. Smith, .303	O. Smith, 182	Clark, 35	Clark, 106	Cox, Forsch, Mathews, 11	Worrell, 2.66
1988	76	86	5th	25	Herzog	McGee, .292	McGee, 164	Brunansky, 22	Brunansky, 79	DeLeon, 13	Magrane, 2.18
1989	86	76	3rd	7	Herzog	Guerrero, .311	Guerrero, 177	Brunansky, 20	Guerrero, 117	Magrane, 18	Magrane, 2.91
1990	70	92	6th	25	Herzog, Schoendienst, Torre	McGee, .335	McGee, 168	Zeile, 15	Guerrero, 80	Tudor, 12	Tudor, 2.40
1991	84	78	2nd	14	Torre	Jose, .305	Jose, 173	Zeile, 11	Zeile, 81	B. Smith, 12	DeLeon, 2.71
1992	83	79	3rd	13	Torre	Gilkey, .302	Lankford, 175	Lankford, 20	Lankford, 86	Tewksbury, 16	Perez, 1.84
1993	87	75	3rd	10	Torre	Jefferies, .342	Jefferies, 186	Whiten, 25	Zeile, 103	Tewksbury, 17	Osborne, 3.76
							CENTRAL DIVISION				
1994	53	61	*4th	13	Torre	Jefferies, .325	Jefferies, 129	Lankford, Zeile, 19	Zeile, 75	Tewksbury, 12	Palacios, 4.44
1995	62	81	4th	22½	Torre, Jorgensen	Mabry, .307	Jordan, 145	Lankford, 25	Lankford, 82	DeLucia, 8	Morgan, 3.56
1996	88	74	∞▲1st	+6	La Russa	Jordan, .310	Mabry, 161	Gant, 30	Jordan, 104	An. Benes, 18	Osborne, 3.53
1997	73	89	4th	11	La Russa	DeShields, .295	DeShields, 169	Lankford, 31	Lankford, 98	Morris, Stottlemyre, 12	Al. Benes, 2.89
1998	83	79	3rd	19	La Russa	Jordan, .316	Jordan, 178	McGwire, 70	McGwire, 147	Mercker, 11	Morris, 2.53
1999	75	86	4th	21½	La Russa	Lankford, .306	Renteria, 161	McGwire, 65	McGwire, 147	Bottenfield, 18	Bottenfield, 3.97
2000	95	67	∞▲1st	+10	La Russa	Vina, .300	Renteria, 156	Edmonds, 42	Edmonds, 108	Kile, 20	Ankiel, 3.50
2001	93	69	*◆1st	0	La Russa	Pujols, .329	Pujols, 194	Pujols, 37	Pujols, 130	Morris, 22	Kile, 3.09
2002	97	65	∞▲1st	+13	La Russa	Pujols, .314	Pujols, 185	Pujols, 34	Pujols, 127	Morris, 17	Morris, 3.42

*Tied for position. † Won pennant playoff. ‡First half 30-20; second half 29-23. § Won Championship Series. ∞ Won Division Series. ▲ Lost Championship Series. ◆ Lost Division Series.
Note: Batting average minimum 350 at-bats; ERA minimum 90 innings pitched.

San Diego Padres

Outfielder Tony Gwynn.

FRANCHISE CHRONOLOGY

First season: 1969, as part of a two-team expansion that increased the National League field to 12. The Padres defeated Houston, 2-1, in their Major League debut but finished their first season mired deep in the N.L. West Division basement with a 52-110 record—41 games behind first-place Atlanta and 29 behind the fifth-place Houston Astros.

1970-present: The Padres finished last in each of their first six seasons, losing 100 or more games in four of them and at least 95 in the other two. Even when the Padres recorded their first winning record in 1978, their 10th season, they finished fourth, 11 games behind first-place Los Angeles. They have finished higher than third only four times, but they do have three division titles and two N.L. pennants to show for their 34-year existence. Their first excursion into the fall classic came in 1984 after an exciting come-from-behind five-game N.L. Championship Series victory over Chicago. Their second came in 1998, after an equally surprising NLCS victory over Atlanta. Both ended in losses—in '84 to the Detroit Tigers and in '98 to the New York Yankees.

PADRES VS. OPPONENTS BY DECADE

	Braves	Cardinals	Cubs	Dodgers	Giants	Phillies	Pirates	Reds	Astros	Mets	Expos	Marlins	Rockies	Brewers	D'backs	Interleague	Decade Record
969	5-13	4-8	1-11	6-12	6-12	4-8	2-10	7-11	8-10	1-11	8-4						52-110
970-79	82-97	50-70	46-74	71-109	72-104	46-74	41-79	74-105	70-106	56-64	59-60						667-942
980-89	89-88	48-70	53-61	95-78	91-84	57-56	56-62	78-96	87-89	57-58	51-63						762-805
990-99	44-79	51-56	51-59	71-68	71-65	60-53	53-55	61-69	67-62	63-52	40-71	34-30	45-41	11-6	11-14	25-19	758-799
000-02	7-14	2-19	13-7	24-27	15-35	11-9	10-11	10-11	15-9	15-7	13-9	12-10	24-27	13-8	18-33	19-29	221-265
otals	227-291	155-223	164-212	267-294	255-300	178-200	162-217	230-292	247-276	192-192	171-207	46-40	69-68	24-14	29-47	44-48	2460-2921

nterleague results: 9-7 vs. Angels, 1-2 vs. Orioles, 1-2 vs. Red Sox, 1-2 vs. Royals, 1-2 vs. Yankees, 5-11 vs. Athletics, 16-13 vs. Mariners, 2-1 vs. Devil Rays, 8-8 vs. Rangers.

MANAGERS

Name	*Years*	*Record*
Preston Gomez	1969-72	180-316
Don Zimmer	1972-73	114-190
John McNamara	1974-77	224-310
Bob Skinner	1977	1-0
Alvin Dark	1977	48-65
Roger Craig	1978-79	152-171
Jerry Coleman	1980	73-89
Frank Howard	1981	41-69
Dick Williams	1982-85	337-311
Steve Boros	1986	74-88
Larry Bowa	1987-88	81-127
Jack McKeon	1988-90	193-164
Greg Riddoch	1990-92	200-194
Jim Riggleman	1992-94	112-179
Bruce Bochy	1995-2002	630-648

N.L. PENNANT WINNER

Year	*Record*	*Manager*	*Series Result*
1984	92-70	Williams	Lost to Tigers
1998	98-64	Bochy	Lost to Yankees

WEST DIVISION CHAMPIONS

Year	*Record*	*Manager*	*NLCS Result*
1984	92-70	Williams	Defeated Cubs
1996	91-71	Bochy	Lost in Division Series
1998	98-64	Bochy	Defeated Braves

ALL-TIME RECORD OF EXPANSION TEAMS

Team	W	L	Pct.	DT	P	WS
Arizona	440	370	.543	3	1	1
Kansas City	2,675	2,694	.498	6	2	1
Houston	3,229	3,285	.496	7	0	0
Toronto	2,025	2,063	.495	5	2	2
Anaheim	3,243	3,431	.486	3	1	1
Montreal	2,605	2,769	.485	2	0	0
Colorado	740	817	.475	0	0	0
New York	3,091	3,412	.475	4	4	2
Milwaukee	2,545	2,831	.473	2	1	0
Seattle	1,924	2,163	.471	3	0	0
Texas	3,097	3,560	.465	4	0	0
San Diego	2,460	2,921	.457	3	2	0
Florida	706	847	.455	0	1	1
Tampa Bay	318	490	.394	0	0	0

DT—Division Titles. P—Pennants won. WS—World Series won.

BALLPARK CHRONOLOGY

Qualcomm Stadium, formerly San Diego Jack Murphy Stadium (1969-present)

Capacity: 63,890.
First game: Padres 2, Houston 1 (April 8, 1969).
First batter: Jesus Alou, Astros.
First hit: Jesus Alou, Astros (single).
First run: Jesus Alou, Astros (1st inning).
First home run: Ed Spezio, Padres.
First winning pitcher: Dick Selma, Padres.
First-season attendance: 512,970.

ATTENDANCE HIGHS

Total	*Season*	*Park*
2,555,901	1998	Qualcomm Stadium
2,523,538	1999	Qualcomm Stadium
2,423,149	2000	Qualcomm Stadium
2,377,969	2001	Qualcomm Stadium
2,220,416	2002	Qualcomm Stadium

N.L. MVP

Ken Caminiti, 3B, 1996

CY YOUNG WINNERS

Randy Jones, LH, 1976
Gaylord Perry, RH, 1978
Mark Davis, LH, 1989

ROOKIES OF THE YEAR

*Butch Metzger, P, 1976
Benito Santiago, C, 1987

* Co-winner.

MANAGER OF THE YEAR

Bruce Bochy, 1996

RETIRED UNIFORM

No.	*Name*	*Pos.*
6	Steve Garvey	1B
35	Randy Jones	P

Outfielder Cito Gaston (left) and first baseman Nate Colbert were original Padres.

MILESTONE PERFORMANCES

25-plus home runs

50—Greg Vaughn 1998
41—Phil Nevin 2001
40—Ken Caminiti 1996
38—Nate Colbert 1970, 1972
35—Fred McGriff 1992
34—Dave Winfield 1979
Phil Plantier 1993
33—Gary Sheffield 1992
31—Fred McGriff 1991
Phil Nevin 2000
30—Steve Finley 1996
Ryan Klesko 2001
29—Ken Caminiti 1998
Ryan Klesko 2002
28—Steve Finley 1997
27—Nate Colbert 1971
26—Kevin McReynolds 1986
Jack Clark 1989
Ken Caminiti 1995, 1997
Reggie Sanders 1999
Ryan Klesko 2000
25—Dave Winfield 1977
Jack Clark 1989
Bubba Trammell 2001

100-plus RBIs

130—Ken Caminiti 1996
126—Phil Nevin 2001
119—Tony Gwynn 1997
Greg Vaughn 1998
118—Dave Winfield 1979
115—Joe Carter 1990
113—Ryan Klesko 2001
111—Nate Colbert 1972
107—Phil Nevin 2000
106—Fred McGriff 1991
104—Fred McGriff 1992
100—Gary Sheffield 1992
Phil Plantier 1993

20-plus victories

1975—Randy Jones 20-12
1976—Randy Jones 22-14
1978—Gaylord Perry 21-6

N.L. home run champions

1992—Fred McGriff 35

N.L. RBI champions

1979—Dave Winfield 118

N.L. batting champions

1984—Tony Gwynn .351
1987—Tony Gwynn .370
1988—Tony Gwynn .313
1989—Tony Gwynn .336
1992—Gary Sheffield .330
1994—Tony Gwynn .394
1995—Tony Gwynn .368
1996—Tony Gwynn .353
1997—Tony Gwynn .372

N.L. ERA champions

1975—Randy Jones 2.24

N.L. strikeout champions

1994—Andy Benes 189

No-hit pitchers

(9 innings or more)
None

Longest hitting streaks

34—Benito Santiago 1987
27—John Flaherty 1996
25—Tony Gwynn 1983
23—Bip Roberts 1994
21—Bobby Brown 1983
Steve Finley 1996
20—Tony Gwynn 1997
19—Tony Fernandez 1992
Tony Gwynn 1997
18—Tony Gwynn 1988
Chris James 1989
Gary Sheffield 1992
Eric Owens 1999
17—Steve Garvey 1984
Roberto Alomar 1989
16—Dave Winfield 1977
Tony Gwynn 1999
Ryan Klesko 2002
Mark Kotsay 2002
15—Ivan Murrell 1969
Cito Gaston 1972
Nate Colbert 1972
Bobby Tolan 1984
Jerry Mumphrey 1980
Broderick Perkins 1981
Tony Gwynn 1982, 1986, 1991, 1995
Kevin McReynolds 1985
Jeff Gardner 1993
Deivi Cruz 2002

Lefthander Randy Jones, the franchise's first Cy Young winner, recorded two of the Padres' three 20-victory seasons.

INDIVIDUAL SEASON, GAME RECORDS

Switch-hitting shortstop Garry Templeton came to San Diego in the trade that sent Ozzie Smith to St. Louis.

SEASON

Batting

At-bats	655	Steve Finley	1996
Runs	126	Steve Finley	1996
Hits	220	Tony Gwynn	1997
Singles	177	Tony Gwynn	1984
Doubles	49	Tony Gwynn	1997
Triples	13	Tony Gwynn	1987
Home runs	50	Greg Vaughn	1998
Home runs, rookie	18	Benito Santiago	1987
Grand slams	4	Phil Nevin	2001
Total bases	348	Steve Finley	1996
RBIs	130	Ken Caminiti	1996
Walks	132	Jack Clark	1989
Most strikeouts	150	Nate Colbert	1970
Fewest strikeouts	16	Tony Gwynn	1992
Batting average	.394	Tony Gwynn	1994
Slugging pct.	.621	Ken Caminiti	1996
Stolen bases	70	Alan Wiggins	1984

Pitching

Games	83	Craig Lefferts	1986
Complete games	25	Randy Jones	1976
Innings	315.1	Randy Jones	1976
Wins	22	Randy Jones	1976
Losses	22	Randy Jones	1974
Winning pct.	.778 (21-6)	Gaylord Perry	1978
Walks	125	Matt Clement	2000
Strikeouts	257	Kevin Brown	1998
Shutouts	6	Fred Norman	1972
		Randy Jones	1975
Home runs allowed	37	Kevin Jarvis	2001
		Bobby J. Jones	2001
Lowest ERA	2.10	David Roberts	1971
Saves	53	Trevor Hoffman	1998

GAME

Batting

Runs	5	Al Martin	4-16-2000
Hits	5	Last by Tony Gwynn	4-28-98
Doubles	3	Last by Kevin Nicholson	7-9-2000
Triples	2	Last by Mark Sweeney	8-27-98
Home runs	3	Last by Bret Boonei	6-23-2000
RBIs	8	Nate Colbert	8-1-72
		Ken Caminiti	9-19-95
Total bases	13	Steve Finley	6-23-97
Stolen bases	5	Last by Damian Jackson	6-28-99

CAREER LEADERS

BATTING

Games	
Tony Gwynn	2,440
Garry Templeton	1,286
Dave Winfield	1,117
Tim Flannery	972
Gene Richards	939
Nate Colbert	866
Terry Kennedy	835
Benito Santiago	789
Carmelo Martinez	783
Cito Gaston	766

At-bats	
Tony Gwynn	9,288
Garry Templeton	4,512
Dave Winfield	3,997
Gene Richards	3,414
Nate Colbert	3,080
Terry Kennedy	2,987
Benito Santiago	2,872
Cito Gaston	2,615
Tim Flannery	2,473
Steve Finley	2,396

Runs	
Tony Gwynn	1,383
Dave Winfield	599
Gene Richards	484
Nate Colbert	442
Garry Templeton	430
Steve Finley	423
Bip Roberts	378
Ken Caminiti	362
Benito Santiago	312
Terry Kennedy	308

Hits	
Tony Gwynn	3,141
Garry Templeton	1,135
Dave Winfield	1,134
Gene Richards	994
Terry Kennedy	817
Nate Colbert	780
Benito Santiago	758
Bip Roberts	673
Cito Gaston	672
Steve Finley	662

Doubles	
Tony Gwynn	543
Garry Templeton	195
Dave Winfield	179
Terry Kennedy	158
Steve Finley	134
Nate Colbert	130
Ken Caminiti	127
Benito Santiago	124
Gene Richards	123
Carmelo Martinez	111

Triples	
Tony Gwynn	85
Gene Richards	63
Dave Winfield	39
Garry Templeton	36
Cito Gaston	29
Steve Finley	28
Tim Flannery	25
Luis Salazar	24
Nate Colbert	22
Bip Roberts	21

Home runs	
Nate Colbert	163
Dave Winfield	154
Tony Gwynn	135
Ken Caminiti	121
Phil Nevin	108
Ryan Klesko	85
Benito Santiago	85
Fred McGriff	84
Steve Finley	82
Carmelo Martinez	82

Total bases	
Tony Gwynn	4,259
Dave Winfield	1,853
Garry Templeton	1,531
Nate Colbert	1,443
Gene Richards	1,321
Terry Kennedy	1,217
Benito Santiago	1,167
Steve Finley	1,098
Ken Caminiti	1,086
Cito Gaston	1,054

Runs batted in	
Tony Gwynn	1,138
Dave Winfield	626
Nate Colbert	481
Garry Templeton	427
Terry Kennedy	424
Ken Caminiti	396
Phil Nevin	375
Benito Santiago	375
Carmelo Martinez	337
Steve Garvey	316
Cito Gaston	316

Extra-base hits	
Tony Gwynn	763
Dave Winfield	372
Nate Colbert	315
Garry Templeton	274
Ken Caminiti	250
Steve Finley	244
Terry Kennedy	241
Benito Santiago	224
Phil Nevin	217
Gene Richards	212

Batting average (Minimum 500 games)	
Tony Gwynn	.338
Bip Roberts	.298
Ken Caminiti	.295
Phil Nevin	.293
Gene Richards	.291
Johnny Grubb	.286
Dave Winfield	.284
Steve Finley	.276
Steve Garvey	.275
Terry Kennedy	.274

Stolen bases	
Tony Gwynn	319
Gene Richards	242
Alan Wiggins	171
Bip Roberts	148
Ozzie Smith	147
Dave Winfield	133
Enzo Hernandez	129
Garry Templeton	101
Luis Salazar	93
Rickey Henderson	91

PITCHING

Earned-run average (Minimum 500 innings)	
Trevor Hoffman	2.76
Greg Harris	2.95
Dave Roberts	2.99
Dave Dravecky	3.12
Craig Lefferts	3.24
Bruce Hurst	3.27
Randy Jones	3.30
Andy Benes	3.57
Bob Shirley	3.58
Eric Show	3.59

Wins	
Eric Show	100
Randy Jones	92
Ed Whitson	77
Andy Ashby	70
Andy Benes	69
Andy Hawkins	60
Joey Hamilton	55
Bruce Hurst	55
Dave Dravecky	53
Clay Kirby	52

Losses	
Randy Jones	105
Eric Show	87
Clay Kirby	81
Andy Benes	75
Ed Whitson	72
Steve Arlin	62
Andy Ashby	62
Bill Greif	61
Andy Hawkins	58
Bob Shirley	57

Innings pitched	
Randy Jones	1,766.0
Eric Show	1,603.1
Ed Whitson	1,354.1
Andy Benes	1,235.0
Andy Ashby	1,210.0
Clay Kirby	1,128.0
Andy Hawkins	1,102.2
Joey Hamilton	934.2
Bruce Hurst	911.2
Dave Dravecky	900.1

Strikeouts	
Andy Benes	1,036
Eric Show	951
Andy Ashby	827
Clay Kirby	802
Trevor Hoffman	771
Ed Whitson	767
Randy Jones	677
Joey Hamilton	639
Bruce Hurst	616
Sterling Hitchcock	534

Bases on balls	
Eric Show	593
Clay Kirby	505
Randy Jones	414
Andy Hawkins	412
Andy Benes	402
Steve Arlin	351
Ed Whitson	350
Dave Freisleben	346
Joey Hamilton	343
Tim Lollar	328

Games	
Trevor Hoffman	604
Craig Lefferts	375
Eric Show	309
Rollie Fingers	265
Randy Jones	264
Dave Tomlin	239
Mark Davis	230
Gary Lucas	230
Lance McCullers	229
Ed Whitson	227

Shutouts	
Randy Jones	18
Steve Arlin	11
Eric Show	11
Bruce Hurst	10
Andy Benes	8
Andy Hawkins	7
Clay Kirby	7
Andy Ashby	6
Dave Dravecky	6
Dave Freisleben	6
Fred Norman	6
Ed Whitson	6

Saves	
Trevor Hoffman	350
Rollie Fingers	108
Rich Gossage	83
Mark Davis	78
Craig Lefferts	64
Gary Lucas	49
Randy Myers	38
Lance McCullers	36
Luis DeLeon	31
Gene Harris	23

TEAM SEASON, GAME RECORDS

SEASON

Batting		
Most at-bats	5,655	1996
Most runs	795	1997
Fewest runs	468	1969
Most hits	1,519	1997
Most singles	1,105	1980
Most doubles	295	1998
Most triples	53	1979
Most home runs	172	1970
Fewest home runs	64	1976
Most grand slams	10	2001
Most pinch-hit home runs	10	1995
Most total bases	2,282	1997
Most stolen bases	239	1980
Highest batting average	.275	1994
Lowest batting average	.225	1969
Highest slugging pct	.409	1998

Pitching		
Lowest ERA	3.22	1971
Highest ERA	4.98	1997
Most complete games	47	1971,1976
Most shutouts	19	1985
Most saves	55	1978, 1998
Most walks	715	1974
Most strikeouts	1,194	1996

Fielding		
Most errors	189	1977
Fewest errors	104	1998
Most double plays	171	1978
Highest fielding average	.983	1998

General		
Most games won	98	1998
Most games lost	110	1969
Highest win pct	.605	1998
Lowest win pct	.321	1969

GAME, INNING

Batting		
Most runs, game	20	Last 5-19-01
Most runs, inning	13	8-24-93, 5-31-94
Most hits, game	24	4-19-82
Most home runs, game	6	Last 6-17-98
Most total bases, game	39	5-23-70

Former Dodger Steve Garvey led the Padres to their first World Series appearance in 1984.

HISTORY

PADRES YEAR-BY-YEAR

Year	W	L	Place	Games Back	Manager	Leaders: Batting avg.	Hits	Home runs	RBIs	Wins	ERA
								—WEST DIVISION—			
1969	52	110	6th	41	Gomez	O. Brown, .264	O. Brown, 150	Colbert, 24	Colbert, 66	J. Niekro, Santorini, 8	Kelley, 3.57
1970	63	99	6th	39	Gomez	Gaston, .318	Gaston, 186	Colbert, 38	Gaston, 93	Dobson, 12	Coombs, 3.30
1971	61	100	6th	28½	Gomez	O. Brown, .273	Colbert, 149	Colbert, 27	Colbert, 84	Kirby, 15	Roberts, 2.10
1972	58	95	6th	36½	Gomez, Zimmer	Lee, .300	Colbert, 141	Colbert, 38	Colbert, 111	Kirby, 12	Ross, 2.45
1973	60	102	6th	39	Zimmer	Grubb, .311	Colbert, Kendall, 143	Colbert, 22	Colbert, 80	Arlin, 11	R. Jones, 3.16
1974	60	102	6th	42	McNamara	Grubb, .286	Winfield, 132	McCovey, 22	Winfield, 75	Freisleben, Greif, Hardy, Spillner, 9	Freisleben, 3.65
1975	71	91	4th	37	McNamara	Fuentes, .280	Fuentes, 158	McCovey, 23	Winfield, 76	R. Jones, 20	R. Jones, 2.24
1976	73	89	5th	29	McNamara	Ivie, .291	Winfield, 139	Winfield, 13	Ivie, 70	R. Jones, 22	R. Jones, 2.74
1977	69	93	5th	29	McNamara, Skinner, Dark	Hendrick, .311	Winfield, 169	Winfield, 25	Winfield, 92	Shirley, 12	Fingers, 2.99
1978	84	78	4th	11	Craig	Winfield, Richards, .308	Winfield, 181	Winfield, 24	Winfield, 97	G. Perry, 21	D'Acquisto, 2.13
1979	68	93	5th	22	Craig	Winfield, .308	Winfield, 184	Winfield, 34	Winfield, 118	G. Perry, 12	G. Perry, 3.05
1980	73	89	6th	19½	Coleman	Richards, .301	Richards, 193	Winfield, 20	Winfield, 87	Fingers, Shirley, 11	Fingers, 2.80
1981	41	69	*6th/6th	—	Howard	Salazar, .303	Salazar, 121	Lefebvre, 8	Richards, 42	Eichelberger, 8	Lucas, 2.00
1982	81	81	4th	8	Williams	Kennedy, .295	Kennedy, 166	Kennedy, 21	Kennedy, 97	Lollar, 16	DeLeon, 2.03
1983	81	81	4th	10	Williams	Garvey, .294	Kennedy, 156	Kennedy, 17	Kennedy, 98	Show, 15	Thurmond, 2.65
1984	92	70	†1st	+12	Williams	Gwynn, .351	Gwynn, 213	McReynolds, Nettles, 20	Garvey, 86	Show, 15	Lefferts, 2.13
1985	83	79	‡3rd	12	Williams	Gwynn, .317	Gwynn, 197	C. Martinez, 21	Garvey, 81	Hawkins, 18	Dravecky, 2.93
1986	74	88	4th	22	Boros	Gwynn, .329	Gwynn, 211	McReynolds, 26	McReynolds, 96	Hawkins, McCullers, 10	McCullers, 2.78
1987	65	97	6th	25	Bowa	Gwynn, .370	Gwynn, 218	Kruk, 20	Kruk, 91	Whitson, 10	McCullers, 3.72
1988	83	78	3rd	11	Bowa, McKeon	Gwynn, .313	Gwynn, 163	C. Martinez, 18	Gwynn, 70	Show, 16	M. Davis, 2.01
1989	89	73	2nd	3	McKeon	Gwynn, .336	Gwynn, 203	J. Clark, 26	J. Clark, 94	Whitson, 16	M. Davis, 1.85
1990	75	87	‡4th	16	McKeon, Riddoch	Gwynn, B. Roberts, .309	Gwynn, 177	J. Clark, 25	Carter, 115	Whitson, 14	Harris, 2.30
1991	84	78	3rd	10	Riddoch	Gwynn, .317	Gwynn, 168	McGriff, 31	McGriff, 106	Benes, Hurst, 15	Harris, 2.23
1992	82	80	3rd	16	Riddoch, Riggleman	Sheffield, .330	Sheffield, 184	McGriff, 35	McGriff, 104	Hurst, 14	Rodriguez, 2.37
1993	61	101	7th	43	Riggleman	Gwynn, .358	Gwynn, 175	Plantier, 34	Plantier, 100	Benes, 15	Harris, 3.67
1994	47	70	4th	12½	Riggleman	Gwynn, .394	Gwynn, 165	Plantier, 18	Gwynn, 64	Hamilton, 9	Hamilton, 2.98
1995	70	74	3rd	8	Bochy	Gwynn, .368	Gwynn, 197	Caminiti, 26	Caminiti, 94	Ashby, 12	Ashby, 2.94
1996	91	71	∞1st	+1	Bochy	Gwynn, .353	Finley, 195	Caminiti, 40	Caminiti, 130	Hamilton, 15	Worrell, 3.05
1997	76	86	4th	14	Bochy	Gwynn, .372	Gwynn, 220	Finley, 28	Gwynn, 119	Hamilton, 12	Ashby, 4.13
1998	98	64	▲◆1st	+9½	Bochy	Gwynn, .321	Vaughn, 156	Vaughn, 50	Vaughn, 119	Brown, 18	Brown, 2.38
1999	74	88	4th	26	Bochy	Gwynn, .338	Gwynn, 139	Sanders, 26	Nevin, 85	Ashby, 14	Boehringer, 3.24
2000	76	86	5th	21	Bochy	Nevin, .303	Owens, 171	Nevin, 31	Nevin, 107	Clement, 13	Tollberg, 3.58
2001	79	83	4th	13	Bochy	Nevin, .306	Nevin, 167	Nevin, 41	Nevin, 126	Jarvis, 12	Lawrence, 3.45
2002	66	96	5th	32	Bochy	Klesko, .300	Kotsay, 169	Klesko, 29	Klesko, 95	Lawrence, 12	Lawrence, 3.69

* First half 23-33; second half 18-36. † Won Championship Series. ‡ Tied for position. ∞ Lost Division Series. ▲ Won Division Series. ◆ Won Championship Series.

Note: Batting average minimum 350 at-bats; ERA minimum 90 innings pitched.

Ollie Brown

ANSWERING the American League's decision to expand in the 1969 season, the National League approved franchises for San Diego and Montreal, bringing its roster to 12 teams. The "Padres" began operation as the N.L.'s third West Coast team and first since the move of the Dodgers and Giants to Los Angeles and San Francisco.

The Padres began their player-procurement efforts in the October 14, 1968, expansion draft by selecting outfielder Ollie Brown with their first pick and 30 players total. The team opened play April 8, 1969, with a 2-1 victory over Houston at San Diego Stadium.

Expansion draft (October 14, 1968)

Players

Player	From	Position
Jose Arcia	Chicago	infield
*Ollie Brown	San Francisco	outfield
Nate Colbert	Houston	first base
Jerry DaVannon	St. Louis	infield
Al Ferrara	Los Angeles	outfield
Tony Gonzalez	Philadelphia	outfield
Clarence Gaston	Atlanta	outfield
Fred Kendall	Cincinnati	catcher
Jerry Morales	New York	outfield
Ivan Murrell	Houston	outfield
Roberto Pena	Philadelphia	second base
Rafael Robles	San Francisco	shortstop
Ron Slocum	Pittsburgh	catcher/infield
Larry Stahl	New York	outfield
Zoilo Versalles	Los Angeles	shortstop
Jim Williams	Los Angeles	outfield

Pitchers

Pitcher	From	Throws
Steve Arlin	Philadelphia	righthanded
Mike Corkins	San Francisco	righthanded
Tom Dukes	Houston	righthanded
Dave Giusti	St. Louis	righthanded
Dick James	Chicago	righthanded
Fred Katawczik	Cincinnati	lefthanded
Dick Kelley	Atlanta	lefthanded
Clay Kirby	St. Louis	righthanded
Al McBean	Pittsburgh	righthanded
Billy McCool	Cincinnati	lefthanded
Frank Reberger	Chicago	righthanded
Dave Roberts	Pittsburgh	lefthanded
Al Santorini	Atlanta	righthanded
Dick Selma	New York	righthanded

*First pick

Opening day lineup

April 8, 1969

Rafael Robles, shortstop
Roberto Pena, second base
Tony Gonzalez, center field
Ollie Brown, right field
Bill Davis, first base
Larry Stahl, left field
Ed Spiezio, third base
Chris Cannizzaro, catcher
Dick Selma, pitcher

Ed Spiezio

Padres firsts

First hit: Ed Spiezio, April 8, 1969, vs. Houston (home run)
First home run: Ed Spiezio, April 8, 1969, vs. Houston
First RBI: Ed Spiezio, April 8, 1969, vs. Houston
First win: Dick Selma, April 8, 1969, vs. Houston
First shutout: Johnny Podres (7 innings), Tommie Sisk (2), April 9, 1969, 2-0 vs. Houston
First CG shutout: Joe Niekro, June 27, 1969, 5-0 vs. Los Angeles

HISTORY

San Francisco Giants

Center fielder Willie Mays.

FRANCHISE CHRONOLOGY

First season: 1883, in New York, as a member of the National League. The "Gothams" defeated Boston, 7-5, in their debut and completed a respectable first-year showing with a 46-50 record.

1884-1900: The Giants captured consecutive pennants in 1888 and '89, but they would not taste success again until the turn of the century, when John McGraw began his 30-year managerial run.

1901-57: Under McGraw's direction, the Giants ruled the National League for three decades. His teams won 10 pennants, finished second 11 times and captured three World Series, a record unmatched over the period. And when McGraw retired during the 1932 season, first baseman Bill Terry took over and led the Giants to three more pennants and another championship in a 10-year reign. But spoiled Giants fans would enjoy only one more Series winner over the team's final 16 seasons in New York. That startling victory came in 1954, when the Giants swept the powerful Cleveland Indians in the fall classic.

1958-present: It's hard to believe the once-proud Giants have not won a World Series in their 44-year San Francisco stay. They came excruciatingly close in 1962 and 2002 when they lost seven-game battles to the Yankees and Angels, respectively, but West Division titles in 1971 and 1987 were followed by N.L. Championship Series losses and others in 1997 and 2000 were followed by Division Series losses. The Giants also played in the 1989 World Series, but they were swept by Bay Area-rival Oakland in a classic memorable only because it was interrupted by a devastating earthquake.

GIANTS VS. OPPONENTS BY DECADE

	Braves	Cardinals	Cubs	Dodgers	Phillies	Pirates	Reds	Astros	Mets	Expos	Padres	Marlins	Rockies	Brewers	D'backs	Interleague	Decade Record
1900-09	125-83	133-78	97-115	128-80	121-87	96-115	123-87										823-645
1910-19	137-73	131-81	116-99	125-88	124-85	127-86	129-85										889-597
1920-29	137-82	123-95	121-99	113-106	149-65	113-106	134-86										890-639
1930-39	127-89	110-107	102-117	120-98	145-72	125-95	139-79										868-657
1940-49	116-100	77-141	109-110	82-137	129-91	111-109	100-120										724-808
1950-59	94-126	112-108	130-90	106-117	121-99	131-89	128-92										822-721
1960-69	91-97	90-92	106-76	108-83	105-77	100-82	103-84	89-55	87-51	11-1	12-6						902-704
1970-79	95-84	60-60	61-59	72-108	53-67	62-58	78-99	90-90	58-62	61-59	104-72						794-818
1980-89	94-79	53-60	61-57	79-95	54-61	63-55	85-91	79-98	65-49	56-59	84-91						773-795
1990-99	53-69	54-58	53-57	70-70	67-44	52-55	66-58	57-69	56-58	59-56	65-71	42-25	52-34	9-9	10-14	25-19	790-766
2000-02	8-13	11-10	11-10	24-26	13-8	15-5	12-9	16-5	15-6	13-9	35-15	13-9	28-23	15-9	27-24	26-22	282-203
Totals	1077-895	954-890	967-889	1027-1008	1081-756	995-855	1097-890	331-317	281-226	200-184	300-255	55-34	80-57	24-18	37-38	51-41	8557-7353

Interleague results: 11-5 vs. Angels, 1-2 vs. Orioles, 1-2 vs. Yankees, 16-16 vs. Athletics, 9-7 vs. Mariners, 2-1 vs. Devil Rays, 9-7 vs. Rangers, 2-1 vs. Blue Jays.

MANAGERS

(New York Giants, 1883-1957)

Name	*Years*	*Record*
John Clapp	1883	46-50
Jim Price	1884	56-42
Monte Ward	1884, 1893-94	162-116
Jim Mutrie	1885-91	529-345
Pat Powers	1892	71-80
George Davis	1895, 1900-01	107-139
Jack Doyle	1895	32-31
Harvey Watkins	1895	18-17
Arthur Irwin	1896	36-53
Bill Joyce	1896-98	179-122
Cap Anson	1898	9-13
John Day	1899	29-35
Fred Hoey	1899	31-55
Buck Ewing	1900	21-41
Horace Fogel	1902	18-23
Heinie Smith	1902	5-27
John McGraw	1902-32	2604-1801
Bill Terry	1932-41	823-661
Mel Ott	1942-48	464-530
Leo Durocher	1948-55	637-523
Bill Rigney	1956-60, 1976	406-430
Tom Sheehan	1960	46-50
Alvin Dark	1961-64	366-277
Herman Franks	1965-68	367-280
Clyde King	1969-70	109-95
Charlie Fox	1970-74	348-327
Wes Westrum	1974-75	118-129
Joe Altobelli	1977-79	225-239
Dave Bristol	1979-80	85-98
Frank Robinson	1981-84	264-277
Danny Ozark	1984	24-32
Jim Davenport	1985	56-88
Roger Craig	1985-92	586-566
Dusty Baker	1993-2002	840-715

WORLD SERIES CHAMPIONS

Year	*Loser*	*Length*	*MVP*
1905	Philadelphia	5 games	None
1921	N.Y. Yankees	8 games	None
1922	N.Y. Yankees	5 games	None
1933	Washington	5 games	None
1954	Cleveland	4 games	None

N.L. PENNANT WINNERS

Year	*Record*	*Manager*	*Series Result*
1888	84-47	Mutrie	None
1889	83-43	Mutrie	None
1904	106-47	McGraw	None
1905	105-48	McGraw	Defeated A's
1911	99-54	McGraw	Lost to A's
1912	103-48	McGraw	Lost to Red Sox
1913	101-51	McGraw	Lost to A's
1917	98-56	McGraw	Lost to White Sox
1921	94-59	McGraw	Defeated Yankees
1922	93-61	McGraw	Defeated Yankees
1923	95-58	McGraw	Lost to Yankees
1924	93-60	McGraw	Lost to Senators

N.L. PENNANT WINNERS—*cont'd.*

Year	*Record*	*Manager*	*Series Result*
1933	91-61	Terry	Defeated Senators
1936	92-62	Terry	Lost to Yankees
1937	95-57	Terry	Lost to Yankees
1951	98-59	Durocher	Lost to Yankees
1954	97-57	Durocher	Defeated Indians
1962	103-62	Dark	Lost to Yankees
1989	92-70	Craig	Lost to A's
2002	95-66	Baker	Lost to Angels

WEST DIVISION CHAMPIONS

Year	*Record*	*Manager*	*NLCS Result*
1971	90-72	Fox	Lost to Pirates
1987	90-72	Craig	Lost to Cardinals
1989	92-70	Craig	Defeated Cubs
1997	90-72	Baker	Lost Division Series
2000	97-65	Baker	Lost Division Series

WILD-CARD QUALIFIERS

Year	*Record*	*Manager*	*Div. Series Result*
2002	95-66	Baker	Defeated Braves

NLCS Result
Defeated Cardinals

World Series Result
Lost to Angels

ATTENDANCE HIGHS

Total	*Season*	*Park*
3,315,330	2000	Pacific Bell Park
3,277,244	2001	Pacific Bell Park
3,253,205	2002	Pacific Bell Park
2,606,354	1993	Candlestick Park
2,078,095	1999	3Com Park

BALLPARK CHRONOLOGY

Pacific Bell Park (2000-present)

Capacity: 41,341.
First game: Giants 3, St. Louis 1 (April 12, 1960).
First batter: Joe Cunningham, Cardinals.
First hit: Bill White, Cardinals (single).
First run: Don Blasingame, Giants (1st inning).
First home run: Leon Wagner, Cardinals.
First winning pitcher: Sam Jones, Giants.
First-season attendance: 1,795,356.

3Com Park, formerly Candlestick Park (1960-present)

Capacity: 63,000.
First game: Giants 3, St. Louis 1 (April 12, 1960).
First-season attendance: 1,795,356.

Polo Grounds I, New York (1883-88)

First game: Giants 7, Boston 5 (May 1, 1883).

Oakland Park, New York (2 games 1889)

First game: Boston 8, Giants 7 (April 24, 1889).

St. George Grounds, New York (25 games 1889)

First game: Giants 4, Washington 2 (April 29, 1889).

Polo Grounds II, New York (1889-90)

First game: Giants 7, Pittsburgh 5 (July 8, 1889).

Polo Grounds III, New York (1891-1957)

Capacity: 55,987.
First game: Boston 4, Giants 3 (April 22, 1891).

Seals Stadium, San Francisco (1958-59)

Capacity: 22,900.
First game: Giants 8, Los Angeles 0 (April 15, 1958).
First-season attendance: 1,272,625.

N.L. MVPs

Carl Hubbell, P, 1933
Carl Hubbell, P, 1936
Willie Mays, OF, 1954
Willie Mays, OF, 1965
Willie McCovey, 1B, 1969
Kevin Mitchell, OF, 1989
Barry Bonds, OF, 1993, 2001, 2002
Jeff Kent, 2B, 2000

CY YOUNG WINNER

Mike McCormick, LH, 1967

ROOKIES OF THE YEAR

Willie Mays, OF, 1951
Orlando Cepeda, 1B, 1958
Willie McCovey, 1B, 1959
Gary Matthews, OF, 1973
John Montefusco, P, 1975

MANAGER OF THE YEAR

Dusty Baker, 1993, 1997, 2000

RETIRED UNIFORMS

No.	*Name*	*Pos.*
	Christy Mathewson	P
	John McGraw	Man.
3	Bill Terry	1B
4	Mel Ott	OF
11	Carl Hubbell	P
24	Willie Mays	OF
27	Juan Marichal	P
30	Orlando Cepeda	1B
44	Willie McCovey	1B

Longest hitting streaks

33—George Davis 1893
27—Charles Hickman 1900
26—Jack Clark 1978
24—Mike Donlin 1908
Fred Lindstrom 1930
Don Mueller 1955
Willie McCovey 1963
23—Joe Moore 1934
22—Alvin Dark 1952
Willie McCovey 1959
21—Mel Ott 1937
Willie Mays 1954, 1957
Don Mueller 1954
Robby Thompson 1993
20—Mike Tiernan 1891
Joe Moore 1932
Willie Mays 1964

MILESTONE PERFORMANCES

30-plus home runs
73— Barry Bonds ... 2001
52— Willie Mays ... 1965
51— Johnny Mize ... 1947
Willie Mays ... 1955
49— Willie Mays ... 1962
Barry Bonds ... 2000
47— Willie Mays ... 1964
Kevin Mitchell ... 1989
46— Orlando Cepeda ... 1961
Barry Bonds ... 1993, 2002
45— Willie McCovey ... 1969
44— Willie McCovey ... 1963
43— Matt Williams ... 1994
42— Mel Ott ... 1929
Barry Bonds ... 1996
41— Willie Mays ... 1954
40— Johnny Mize ... 1948
Willie Mays ... 1961
Barry Bonds ... 1997
39— Willie McCovey ... 1965, 1970
Bobby Bonds ... 1973
38— Mel Ott ... 1932
Willie Mays ... 1963
Matt Williams ... 1993
37— Willie Mays ... 1966
Barry Bonds ... 1994, 1998
Rich Aurilia ... 2001
Jeff Kent ... 2002
36— Willard Marshall ... 1947
Willie Mays ... 1956
Willie McCovey ... 1966, 1968
35— Mel Ott ... 1934
Walker Cooper ... 1947
Willie Mays ... 1957
Orlando Cepeda ... 1962
Will Clark ... 1987
Kevin Mitchell ... 1990
34— Willie Mays ... 1959
Orlando Cepeda ... 1963
Matt Williams ... 1991
Barry Bonds ... 1999
33— Mel Ott ... 1936
Jim Hart ... 1966
Bobby Bonds ... 1971
Matt Williams ... 1990
Barry Bonds ... 1995
Jeff Kent ... 2000
32— Bobby Thomson ... 1951
Bobby Bonds ... 1969
31— Mel Ott ... 1935, 1937
Orlando Cepeda ... 1964
Jim Hart ... 1964
Willie McCovey ... 1967
Jeff Kent ... 1998
Ellis Burks ... 1999
30— Sid Gordon ... 1948
Darrell Evans ... 1983

100-plus RBIs
151— Mel Ott ... 1929
142— Orlando Cepeda ... 1961
141— Willie Mays ... 1962
138— Johnny Mize ... 1947
137— Barry Bonds ... 2001
136— George Kelly ... 1924
135— Mel Ott ... 1934, 1936
132— Irish Meusel ... 1922
129— Bill Terry ... 1930
Barry Bonds ... 1996
128— Jeff Kent ... 1998
127— Willie Mays ... 1955
126— Willie McCovey ... 1969, 1970
125— Irish Meusel ... 1923
Rogers Hornsby ... 1927
Johnny Mize ... 1948
Kevin Mitchell ... 1989
Jeff Kent ... 2000
123— Mel Ott ... 1932
Willie Mays ... 1961
Barry Bonds ... 1993
122— George Kelly ... 1921
Walker Cooper ... 1947
Matt Williams ... 1990
122— Barry Bonds ... 1998
121— Monte Irvin ... 1951
Bill Terry ... 1927
Jeff Kent ... 1997
119— Mel Ott ... 1930
117— Bill Terry ... 1929, 1932
116— Mel Ott ... 1938
Will Clark ... 1991
115— Mel Ott ... 1931
114— Mel Ott ... 1935
Orlando Cepeda ... 1962
112— Bill Terry ... 1931
Willie Mays ... 1965
111— Irish Meusel ... 1925
Frankie Frisch ... 1929
Willie Mays ... 1964
Will Clark ... 1989
110— Johnny Mize ... 1942
Willie Mays ... 1954
Matt Williams ... 1993
Barry Bonds ... 2002
109— Bobby Thomson ... 1949
Will Clark ... 1988
108— Sam Mertes ... 1905
Bobby Thomson ... 1952
Jeff Kent ... 2002
107— George Kelly ... 1922
Fred Lindstrom ... 1928
Hank Leiber ... 1935
Willard Marshall ... 1947
Sid Gordon ... 1948
Dick Dietz ... 1970
106— Mike Donlin ... 1908
Fred Lindstrom ... 1930
Bobby Thomson ... 1953
Barry Bonds ... 2000
Jeff Kent ... 2001
105— Orlando Cepeda ... 1959
Willie McCovey ... 1968
104— Sam Mertes ... 1903
Norm Young ... 1941
Willie Mays ... 1959
Barry Bonds ... 1995
J.T. Snow ... 1997
103— George Kelly ... 1923
Mel Ott ... 1933
Willie Mays ... 1960, 1963, 1966
Jack Clark ... 1982
102— Henry Zimmerman ... 1917
Ross Youngs ... 1921
Irish Meusel ... 1924
Bobby Bonds ... 1971
Willie McCovey ... 1963
101— Bill Terry ... 1928
Travis Jackson ... 1934
Norm Young ... 1940
Bobby Thomson ... 1951
Barry Bonds ... 1997
Jeff Kent ... 1999
100— Frankie Frisch ... 1921

20-plus victories
1883— Mickey Welch ... 39-21
1884— Mickey Welch ... 39-21
1885— Mickey Welch ... 44-11
Tim Keefe ... 32-13
1886— Tim Keefe ... 42-20
Mickey Welch ... 33-22
1887— Tim Keefe ... 35-19
Mickey Welch ... 22-15
1888— Tim Keefe ... 35-12
1889— Tim Keefe ... 28-13
Mickey Welch ... 27-12
1890— Amos Rusie ... 29-34
1891— Amos Rusie ... 33-20
John Ewing ... 21-8
1892— Amos Rusie ... 31-31
Silver King ... 23-24
1893— Amos Rusie ... 33-21
1894— Amos Rusie ... 36-13
Jouett Meekin ... 33-9
1895— Amos Rusie ... 23-23
1896— Jouett Meekin ... 26-14
1897— Amos Rusie ... 28-10
Jouett Meekin ... 20-11
Cy Seymour ... 20-14
1898— Cy Seymour ... 25-19
Amos Rusie ... 20-11
1901— Christy Mathewson ... 20-17
1903— Joe McGinnity ... 31-20
Christy Mathewson ... 30-13
1904— Joe McGinnity ... 35-8
Christy Mathewson ... 33-12
Luther Taylor ... 21-15
1905— Christy Mathewson ... 31-9
Leon Ames ... 22-8
Joe McGinnity ... 21-15
1906— Joe McGinnity ... 27-12
Christy Mathewson ... 22-12
1907— Christy Mathewson ... 24-12
1908— Christy Mathewson ... 37-11
George Wiltse ... 23-14
1909— Christy Mathewson ... 25-6
George Wiltse ... 20-11
1910— Christy Mathewson ... 27-9
1911— Christy Mathewson ... 26-13
Rube Marquard ... 24-7
1912— Rube Marquard ... 26-11
Christy Mathewson ... 23-12
1913— Christy Mathewson ... 25-11
Rube Marquard ... 23-10
Jeff Tesreau ... 22-13
1914— Jeff Tesreau ... 26-10
Christy Mathewson ... 24-13
1917— Ferdie Schupp ... 21-7
1919— Jess Barnes ... 25-9
1920— Fred Toney ... 21-11
Art Nehf ... 21-12
Jess Barnes ... 20-15
1921— Art Nehf ... 20-10
1928— Larry Benton ... 25-9
Fred Fitzsimmons ... 20-9
1933— Carl Hubbell ... 23-12
1934— Hal Schumacher ... 23-10
Carl Hubbell ... 21-12
1935— Carl Hubbell ... 23-12
1936— Carl Hubbell ... 26-6
1937— Carl Hubbell ... 22-8
Cliff Melton ... 20-9
1944— Bill Voiselle ... 21-16
1947— Larry Jansen ... 21-5
1951— Sal Maglie ... 23-6
Larry Jansen ... 23-11
1954— Johnny Antonelli ... 21-7
1956— Johnny Antonelli ... 20-13
1959— Sam Jones ... 21-15
1962— Jack Sanford ... 24-7
1963— Juan Marichal ... 25-8
1964— Juan Marichal ... 21-8
1965— Juan Marichal ... 22-13
1966— Juan Marichal ... 25-6
Gaylord Perry ... 21-8
1967— Mike McCormick ... 22-10
1968— Juan Marichal ... 26-9
1969— Juan Marichal ... 21-11
1970— Gaylord Perry ... 23-13
1973— Ron Bryant ... 24-12
1986— Mike Krukow ... 20-9
1993— John Burkett ... 22-7
Bill Swift ... 21-8

N.L. home run champions
1883— Buck Ewing ... 10
1890— Mark Tiernan ... *13
1891— Mark Tiernan ... *16
1909— Red Murray ... 7
1916— Dave Robertson ... *12
1917— Dave Robertson ... *12
1921— George Kelly ... 23
1932— Mel Ott ... *38
1934— Mel Ott ... *35
1936— Mel Ott ... 33
1937— Mel Ott ... *31
1938— Mel Ott ... 36
1942— Mel Ott ... 30
1947— Johnny Mize ... *51
1948— Johnny Mize ... *40
1955— Willie Mays ... 51
1961— Orlando Cepeda ... 46
1962— Willie Mays ... 49
1963— Willie McCovey ... *44
1964— Willie Mays ... 47
1965— Willie Mays ... 52
1968— Willie McCovey ... 36
1969— Willie McCovey ... 45
1989— Kevin Mitchell ... 47
1993— Barry Bonds ... 46
1994— Matt Williams ... 43
2001— Barry Bonds ... 73

* Tied for league lead

N.L. RBI champions
1903— Sam Mertes ... 104
1904— Bill Dahlen ... 80
1917— Heinie Zimmerman ... 102
1920— George Kelly ... *94
1923— Irish Meusel ... 125
1924— George Kelly ... 136
1934— Mel Ott ... 135
1942— Johnny Mize ... 110
1947— Johnny Mize ... 138
1951— Monte Irvin ... 121
1961— Orlando Cepeda ... 142
1968— Willie McCovey ... 105
1969— Willie McCovey ... 126
1988— Will Clark ... 109
1989— Kevin Mitchell ... 125
1990— Matt Williams ... 122
1993— Barry Bonds ... 123

* Tied for league lead

N.L. batting champions
1885— Roger Connor ... .371
1890— Jack Glasscock ... .336
1915— Larry Doyle ... .320
1930— Bill Terry ... .401
1954— Willie Mays ... .345
2002— Barry Bonds ... .370

N.L. ERA champions
1904— Joe McGinnity ... 1.61
1905— Christy Mathewson ... 1.28
1908— Christy Mathewson ... 1.43
1909— Christy Mathewson ... 1.14
1911— Christy Mathewson ... 1.99
1912— Jeff Tesreau ... 1.96
1913— Christy Mathewson ... 2.06
1917— Fred Anderson ... 1.44
1922— Phil Douglas ... 2.63
1929— Bill Walker ... 3.09
1931— Bill Walker ... 2.26
1933— Carl Hubbell ... 1.66
1934— Carl Hubbell ... 2.30
1936— Carl Hubbell ... 2.31
1949— Dave Koslo ... 2.50
1950— Sal Maglie ... 2.71
1952— Hoyt Wilhelm ... 2.43
1954— Johnny Antonelli ... 2.30
1958— Stu Miller ... 2.47
1959— Sam Jones ... 2.83
1960— Mike McCormick ... 2.70
1969— Juan Marichal ... 2.10
1983— Atlee Hammaker ... 2.25
1989— Scott Garrelts ... 2.28
1992— Bill Swift ... 2.08

N.L. strikeout champions
1888— Tim Keefe ... 335
1890— Amos Rusie ... 341
1891— Amos Rusie ... 337
1893— Amos Rusie ... 208
1894— Amos Rusie ... 195
1895— Amos Rusie ... 201
1898— Cy Seymour ... 239
1903— Christy Mathewson ... 267
1904— Christy Mathewson ... 212
1905— Christy Mathewson ... 206
1907— Christy Mathewson ... 178
1908— Christy Mathewson ... 259
1911— Rube Marquard ... 237
1937— Carl Hubbell ... 159
1944— Bill Voiselle ... 161

No-hit pitchers
(9 innings or more)
1891— Amos Rusie ... 6-0 vs. Brooklyn
1901— Christy Mathewson ... 5-0 vs. St. Louis
1905— Christy Mathewson ... 1-0 vs. Chicago
1908— George Wiltse ... 1-0 vs. Philadelphia
1912— Jeff Tesreau ... 3-0 vs. Philadelphia
1915— Rube Marquard ... 2-0 vs. Brooklyn
1922— Jesse Barnes ... 6-0 vs. Philadelphia
1929— Carl Hubbell ... 11-0 vs. Pittsburgh
1963— Juan Marichal ... 1-0 vs. Houston
1968— Gaylord Perry ... 1-0 vs. St. Louis
1975— Ed Halicki ... 6-0 vs. New York
1976— John Montefusco ... 9-0 vs. Atlanta

INDIVIDUAL SEASON, GAME RECORDS

SEASON

Batting

At-bats	681	Joe Moore	1935
Runs	146	Mike Tiernan	1893
Hits	254	Bill Terry	1930
Singles	177	Bill Terry	1930
Doubles	49	Jeff Kent	2001
Triples	26	George Davis	1893
Home runs	73	Barry Bonds	2001
Home runs, rookie	31	Jim Hart	1964
Grand slams	3	3 times	
		Last by Jeff Kent	1997
Total bases	411	Barry Bonds	2001
RBIs	151	Mel Ott	1929
Walks	198	Barry Bonds	2002
Most strikeouts	189	Bobby Bonds	1970
Fewest strikeouts	12	Frankie Frisch	1923
Batting average	.401	Bill Terry	1930
Slugging pct.	.863	Barry Bonds	2001
Stolen bases	111	John Ward	1883

Pitching

Games	89	Julian Tavarez	1997
Complete games	44	Joe McGinnity	1903
Innings	434	Joe McGinnity	1903
Wins	37	Christy Mathewson	1908
Losses	27	Luther Taylor	1901
Winning pct.	.833 (15-3)	Hoyt Wilhelm	1952
Walks	128	Jeff Tesreau	1914
Strikeouts	267	Christy Mathewson	1903
Shutouts	12	Christy Mathewson	1908
Home runs allowed	36	Larry Jansen	1949
Lowest ERA	1.14	Christy Mathewson	1909
Saves	48	Rod Beck	1993

GAME

Batting

Runs	6	Last by Mel Ott	4-30-44
Hits	6	Last by Mike Benjamin	6-14-95
Doubles	3	Last by Ramon Martinez	8-16-2002
Triples	4	Bill Joyce	5-18-1897
Home runs	4	Willie Mays	4-30-61
RBIs	11	Phil Weintraub	4-30-44
Total bases	16	Willie Mays	4-30-61
Stolen bases	5	Dan McGann	5-27-04

CAREER LEADERS

BATTING

Games

Player	Games
Willie Mays	2,857
Mel Ott	2,730
Willie McCovey	2,256
Bill Terry	1,721
Travis Jackson	1,656
Larry Doyle	1,622
Jim Davenport	1,501
Whitey Lockman	1,485
Mike Tiernan	1,478
Barry Bonds	1,429

At-bats

Player	At-bats
Willie Mays	10,477
Mel Ott	9,456
Willie McCovey	7,214
Bill Terry	6,428
Travis Jackson	6,086
Larry Doyle	5,995
Mike Tiernan	5,947
Whitey Lockman	5,584
Jo-Jo Moore	5,427
George Burns	5,311

Runs

Player	Runs
Willie Mays	2,011
Mel Ott	1,859
Mike Tiernan	1,348
Barry Bonds	1,158
Bill Terry	1,120
Willie McCovey	1,113
Roger Connor	1,021
George Van Haltren	976
Larry Doyle	906
George Burns	877

Hits

Player	Hits
Willie Mays	3,187
Mel Ott	2,876
Bill Terry	2,193
Willie McCovey	1,974
Mike Tiernan	1,838
Travis Jackson	1,768
Larry Doyle	1,751
Jo-Jo Moore	1,615
George Van Haltren	1,580
Whitey Lockman	1,571

Doubles

Player	Doubles
Willie Mays	504
Mel Ott	488
Bill Terry	373
Willie McCovey	308
Barry Bonds	294
Travis Jackson	291
Larry Doyle	275
George Burns	267
Jo-Jo Moore	258
Mike Tiernan	257

Triples

Player	Triples
Mike Tiernan	162
Willie Mays	139
Roger Connor	131
Larry Doyle	117
Bill Terry	112
Buck Ewing	109
George Davis	98
Ross Youngs	93
George Van Haltren	88
Travis Jackson	86

Home runs

Player	Home runs
Willie Mays	646
Mel Ott	511
Willie McCovey	469
Barry Bonds	437
Matt Williams	247
Orlando Cepeda	226
Bobby Thomson	189
Bobby Bonds	186
Will Clark	176
Jeff Kent	175

Total bases

Player	Total bases
Willie Mays	5,907
Mel Ott	5,041
Willie McCovey	3,779
Bill Terry	3,252
Barry Bonds	3,157
Mike Tiernan	2,737
Travis Jackson	2,636
Larry Doyle	2,461
Orlando Cepeda	2,234
Whitey Lockman	2,216
Jo-Jo Moore	2,216

Runs batted in

Player	RBI
Mel Ott	1,860
Willie Mays	1,859
Willie McCovey	1,388
Barry Bonds	1,096
Bill Terry	1,078
Travis Jackson	929
Mike Tiernan	853
George Davis	819
Roger Connor	786
Orlando Cepeda	767

Extra-base hits

Player	Extra-base hits
Willie Mays	1,289
Mel Ott	1,071
Willie McCovey	822
Barry Bonds	768
Bill Terry	639
Mike Tiernan	525
Travis Jackson	512
Orlando Cepeda	474
Will Clark	462
Larry Doyle	459

Batting average

(Minimum 500 games)

Player	Average
Bill Terry	.341
George Davis	.332
Ross Youngs	.322
Frankie Frisch	.322
George Van Haltren	.321
Freddie Lindstrom	.318
Roger Connor	.314
Irish Meusel	.314
Shanty Hogan	.311
Barry Bonds	.311

Stolen bases

Player	Stolen bases
Mike Tiernan	428
George Davis	357
Willie Mays	336
George Burns	334
John Ward	332
George Van Haltren	320
Larry Doyle	291
Art Devlin	266
Bobby Bonds	263
Jack Doyle	255

PITCHING

Earned-run average

(Minimum 1,000 innings)

Player	ERA
Christy Mathewson	2.12
Joe McGinnity	2.38
Jeff Tesreau	2.43
Red Ames	2.45
Hooks Wiltse	2.48
Tim Keefe	2.53
Mickey Welch	2.69
Dummy Taylor	2.77
Rube Benton	2.79
Juan Marichal	2.84

Wins

Player	Wins
Christy Mathewson	372
Carl Hubbell	253
Juan Marichal	238
Mickey Welch	238
Amos Rusie	234
Tim Keefe	174
Freddie Fitzsimmons	170
Hal Schumacher	158
Joe McGinnity	151
Hooks Wiltse	136

Losses

Player	Losses
Christy Mathewson	188
Amos Rusie	163
Carl Hubbell	154
Mickey Welch	146
Juan Marichal	140
Hal Schumacher	121
Freddie Fitzsimmons	114
Gaylord Perry	109
Dave Koslo	104
Dummy Taylor	103

Innings pitched

Player	Innings
Christy Mathewson	4,779.2
Carl Hubbell	3,590.1
Mickey Welch	3,579.0
Amos Rusie	3,531.2
Juan Marichal	3,444.0
Freddie Fitzsimmons	2,514.1
Hal Schumacher	2,482.1
Gaylord Perry	2,294.2
Tim Keefe	2,265.0
Joe McGinnity	2,151.1

Strikeouts

Player	Strikeouts
Christy Mathewson	2,504
Juan Marichal	2,281
Amos Rusie	1,835
Carl Hubbell	1,677
Gaylord Perry	1,606
Mickey Welch	1,570
Tim Keefe	1,303
Red Ames	1,169
Mike McCormick	1,030
Bobby Bolin	977

Bases on balls

Player	Bases on balls
Amos Rusie	1,588
Mickey Welch	1,077
Hal Schumacher	902
Christy Mathewson	847
Carl Hubbell	725
Juan Marichal	690
Freddie Fitzsimmons	670
Cy Seymour	656
Jouett Meekin	653
Red Ames	620

Games

Player	Games
Gary Lavelle	647
Christy Mathewson	635
Greg Minton	552
Carl Hubbell	535
Randy Moffitt	459
Juan Marichal	458
Amos Rusie	427
Mickey Welch	427
Rod Beck	416
Freddie Fitzsimmons	403

Shutouts

Player	Shutouts
Christy Mathewson	79
Juan Marichal	52
Carl Hubbell	36
Amos Rusie	29
Mickey Welch	28
Jeff Tesreau	27
Hooks Wiltse	27
Joe McGinnity	26
Hal Schumacher	26
Freddie Fitzsimmons	22
Tim Keefe	22

Saves

Player	Saves
Robb Nen	206
Rod Beck	199
Gary Lavelle	127
Greg Minton	125
Randy Moffitt	83
Frank Linzy	78
Marv Grissom	58
Ace Adams	49
Scott Garrelts	48
Stu Miller	47

TEAM SEASON, GAME RECORDS

SEASON

Batting

Record		Year
Most at-bats	5,650	1984
Most runs	959	1930
Fewest runs	540	1956
Most hits	1,769	1930
Most singles	1,279	1930
Most doubles	307	1999
Most triples	105	1911
Most home runs	235	2001
Fewest home runs	15	1906
Most grand slams	7	1951, 1954, 1970, 1998
Most pinch-hit home runs	14	2001
Most total bases	2,628	1930
Most stolen bases	347	1911
Highest batting average	.319	1930
Lowest batting average	.233	1985
Highest slugging pct.	.473	1930

Pitching

Record		Year
Lowest ERA	2.14	1908
Highest ERA	4.86	1995
Most complete games	127	1904
Most shutouts	25	1908
Most saves	50	1993
Most walks	660	1946
Most strikeouts	1,086	1998

Fielding

Record		Year
Most errors	348	1901
Fewest errors	90	2002
Most double plays	183	1987
Highest fielding average	.985	2000

General

Record		Year
Most games won	106	1904
Most games lost	100	1985
Highest win pct	.759	1885
Lowest win pct	.353	1902

GAME, INNING

Batting

Record		Date
Most runs, game	29	6-15-1887
Most runs, inning	13	Last 7-15-97
Most hits, game	31	6-9-01
Most home runs, game	8	4-30-61
Most total bases, game	50	5-13-58

Lefthander Carl Hubbell used his outstanding screwball to post 253 victories for the Giants.

GIANTS YEAR-BY-YEAR

Year	W	L	Place	Games Back	Manager	Leaders: Batting avg.	Hits	Home runs	RBIs	Wins	ERA
							NEW YORK GIANTS				
1901	52	85	7th	37	G. Davis	Van Haltren, .335	Van Haltren, 182	G. Davis, 7	Ganzel, 66	Mathewson, 20	Mathewson, 2.41
1902	48	88	8th	53½	Fogel, H. Smith, McGraw	Brodie, .281	H. Smith, 129	Brodie, 3	Lauder, 44	Mathewson, 14	McGinnity, 2.06
1903	84	55	2nd	6½	McGraw	Bresnahan, .350	Browne, 185	Mertes, 7	Mertes, 104	McGinnity, 31	Mathewson, 2.26
1904	106	47	1st	+13	McGraw	McGann, .286	Browne, 169	McGann, 6	Dahlen, 80	McGinnity, 35	McGinnity, 1.61
1905	105	48	1st	+9	McGraw	Donlin, .356	Donlin, 216	Dahlen, Donlin, 7	Mertes, 108	Mathewson, 31	Mathewson, 1.27
1906	96	56	2nd	20	McGraw	Devlin, .299	Devlin, 149	Seymour, Strang, 4	Devlin, 65	McGinnity, 27	Taylor, 2.20
1907	82	71	4th	25½	McGraw	Seymour, .294	Shannon, 155	Browne, 5	Seymour, 75	Mathewson, 24	Mathewson, 2.00
1908	98	56	*2nd	1	McGraw	Donlin, .334	Donlin, 198	Donlin, 6	Donlin, 106	Mathewson, 37	Mathewson, 1.43
1909	92	61	3rd	18½	McGraw	Doyle, .302	Doyle, 172	Murray, 7	Murray, 91	Mathewson, 25	Mathewson, 1.14
1910	91	63	2nd	13	McGraw	Snodgrass, .321	Doyle, 164	Doyle, 8	Murray, 87	Mathewson, 27	Mathewson, 1.89
1911	99	54	1st	+7½	McGraw	Meyers, .332	Doyle, 163	Doyle, 13	Merkle, 84	Mathewson, 26	Mathewson, 1.99
1912	103	48	1st	+10	McGraw	Meyers, .358	Doyle, 184	Merkle, 11	Murray, 92	Marquard, 26	Tesreau, 1.96
1913	101	51	1st	+12½	McGraw	Meyers, .312	Burns, 173	Doyle, Shafer, 5	Doyle, 73	Mathewson, 25	Mathewson, 2.06
1914	84	70	2nd	10½	McGraw	Burns, .303	Burns, 170	Merkle, 7	Fletcher, 79	Tesreau, 26	Tesreau, 2.37
1915	69	83	8th	21	McGraw	Doyle, .320	Doyle, 189	Doyle, Merkle, 4	Fletcher, 74	Tesreau, 19	Tesreau, 2.29
1916	86	66	4th	7	McGraw	Robertson, .307	Robertson, 180	Robertson, 12	Kauff, 74	Perritt, 18	Schupp, 0.90
1917	98	56	1st	+10	McGraw	Kauff, .308	Burns, 180	Robertson, 12	Zimmerman, 102	Schupp, 21	F. Anderson, 1.44
1918	71	53	2nd	10½	McGraw	Youngs, .302	Youngs, 143	Burns, 4	Zimmerman, 56	Perritt, 18	Sallee, 2.25
1919	87	53	2nd	9	McGraw	Youngs, .311	Burns, 162	Kauff, 10	Kauff, 67	J. Barnes, 25	Nehf, 1.50
1920	86	68	2nd	7	McGraw	Youngs, .351	Youngs, 204	Kelly, 11	Kelly, 94	Nehf, Toney, 21	Barnes, 2.64
1921	94	59	1st	+4	McGraw	Frisch, .341	Frisch, 211	Kelly, 23	Kelly, 122	Nehf, 20	J. Barnes, 3.10
1922	93	61	1st	+7	McGraw	Meusel, Youngs, .331	Bancroft, 209	Kelly, 17	I. Meusel, 132	Nehf, 19	Douglas, 2.63
1923	95	58	1st	+4½	McGraw	Frisch, .348	Frisch, 223	I. Meusel, 19	I. Meusel, 125	Ryan, Scott, 16	Jonnard, 3.28
1924	93	60	1st	+1½	McGraw	Youngs, .356	Frisch, 198	Kelly, 21	Kelly, 136	V. Barnes, Bentley, 16	McQuillan, 2.69
1925	86	66	2nd	8½	McGraw	Frisch, .331	Kelly, 181	I. Meusel, 21	I. Meusel, 111	V. Barnes, 15	Scott, 3.15
1926	74	77	5th	13½	McGraw	Jackson, .327	Frisch, 171	Kelly, 13	Kelly, 80	Fitzsimmons, 14	V. Barnes, 2.87
1927	92	62	3rd	2	McGraw	Hornsby, .361	Hornsby, 205	Hornsby, 26	Hornsby, 125	Grimes, 19	Grimes, 3.54
1928	93	61	2nd	2	McGraw	Lindstrom, .358	Lindstrom, 231	Ott, 18	Lindstrom, 107	Benton, 25	Benton, 2.73
1929	84	67	3rd	13½	McGraw	Terry, .372	Terry, 226	Ott, 42	Ott, 151	Hubbell, 18	Walker, 3.09
1930	87	67	3rd	5	McGraw	Terry, .401	Terry, 254	Ott, 25	Terry, 129	Fitzsimmons, 19	J. Brown, 1.80
1931	87	65	2nd	13	McGraw	Terry, .349	Terry, 213	Ott, 29	Ott, 115	Fitzsimmons, 18	Walker, 2.26
1932	72	82	*6th	18	McGraw, Terry	Terry, .350	Terry, 225	Ott, 38	Ott, 123	Hubbell, 18	Hubbell, 2.50
1933	91	61	1st	+5	Terry	Terry, .322	Ott, 164	Ott, 23	Ott, 103	Hubbell, 23	Hubbell, 1.66
1934	93	60	2nd	2	Terry	Terry, .354	Terry, 213	Ott, 35	Ott, 135	Schumacher, 23	Hubbell, 2.30
1935	91	62	3rd	8½	Terry	Terry, .341	Leiber, Terry, 203	Ott, 31	Ott, 114	Hubbell, 23	Schumacher, 2.89
1936	92	62	1st	+5	Terry	Ott, .328	Moore, 205	Ott, 33	Ott, 135	Hubbell, 26	Hubbell, 2.31
1937	95	57	1st	+3	Terry	Ripple, .317	Moore, 180	Ott, 31	Ott, 95	Hubbell, 22	Melton, 2.61
1938	83	67	3rd	5	Terry	Ott, .311	Ott, 164	Ott, 36	Ott, 116	Gumbert, 15	Hubbell, 3.07
1939	77	74	5th	18½	Terry	Bonura, .321	Demaree, 170	Ott, 27	Bonura, 85	Gumbert, 18	Hubbell, 2.75
1940	72	80	6th	27½	Terry	Demaree, .302	Whitehead, 160	Ott, 19	Young, 101	Schumacher, 13	Schumacher, 3.25
1941	74	79	5th	25½	Terry	Bartell, .303	Rucker, 179	Ott, 27	Young, 104	Schumacher, 12	Melton, 3.01
1942	85	67	3rd	20	Ott	Mize, .305	Mize, 165	Ott, 30	Mize, 110	Lohman, 13	Lohrman, 2.56
1943	55	98	8th	49½	Ott	Witek, .314	Witek, 195	Ott, 18	Gordon, 63	Adams, 11	Adams, 2.82
1944	67	87	5th	38	Ott	Medwick, .337	Medwick, 165	Ott, 26	Medwick, 85	Voiselle, 21	Voiselle, 3.02
1945	78	74	5th	19	Ott	Ott, .308	Hausmann, 174	Ott, 21	Ott, 79	Mungo, Voiselle, 14	Mungo, 3.20
1946	61	93	8th	36	Ott	Mize, .337	Marshall, 144	Mize, 22	Mize, 70	Koslo, 14	Kennedy, 3.42
1947	81	73	4th	13	Ott	Cooper, .305	Mize, 177	Mize, 51	Mize, 138	Jansen, 21	Jansen, 3.16
1948	78	76	5th	13½	Ott, Durocher	Gordon, .299	Lockman, 167	Mize, 40	Mize, 125	Jansen, 18	Hansen, 2.97
1949	73	81	5th	24	Durocher	Thomson, .309	Thomson, 198	Thomson, 27	Thomson, 109	Jansen, Jones, 15	Koslo, 2.50
1950	86	68	3rd	5	Durocher	Stanky, .300	Dark, 164	Thomson, 25	H. Thompson, 91	Jansen, 19	Hearn, 1.94
1951	98	59	†1st	+1	Durocher	Irvin, .312	Dark, 196	Thomson, 32	Irvin, 121	Jansen, Maglie, 23	Maglie, 2.93
1952	92	62	2nd	4½	Durocher	Dark, .301	Dark, 177	Thomson, 24	Thomson, 108	Maglie, 18	Wilhelm, 2.43
1953	70	84	5th	35	Durocher	Mueller, .333	Dark, 194	Thomson, 26	Thomson, 106	Gomez, 13	Wilhelm, 3.04
1954	97	57	1st	+5	Durocher	Mays, .345	Mueller, 212	Mays, 41	Mays, 110	Antonelli, 21	Wilhelm, 2.10
1955	80	74	3rd	18½	Durocher	Mays, .319	Mays, Mueller, 185	Mays, 51	Mays, 127	Antonelli, Hearn, 14	Antonelli, 3.33
1956	67	87	6th	26	Rigney	Brandt, .299	Mays, 171	Mays, 36	Mays, 84	Antonelli, 20	Antonelli, 2.86
1957	69	85	6th	26	Rigney	Mays, .333	Mays, 195	Mays, 35	Mays, 97	Gomez, 15	Barclay, 3.44
							SAN FRANCISCO GIANTS				
1958	80	74	3rd	12	Rigney	Mays, .347	Mays, 208	Mays, 29	Cepeda, Mays, 96	Antonelli, 13	Miller, 2.47
1959	83	71	3rd	4	Rigney	Cepeda, .317	Cepeda, 192	Mays, 34	Cepeda, 105	S. Jones, 21	S. Jones, 2.83
1960	79	75	5th	16	Rigney, Sheehan	Mays, .319	Mays, 199	Mays, 29	Mays, 103	S. Jones, 18	McCormick, 2.70
1961	85	69	3rd	8	Dark	Cepeda, .311	Cepeda, 182	Cepeda, 46	Cepeda, 142	Miller, 14	McCormick, 3.20
1962	103	62	†1st	+1	Dark	F. Alou, .316	Cepeda, 191	Mays, 49	Mays, 141	Sanford, 24	Marichal, 3.36
1963	88	74	3rd	11	Dark	Cepeda, .316	Mays, 187	McCovey, 44	Mays, 103	Marichal, 25	Marichal, 2.41
1964	90	72	4th	3	Dark	Cepeda, .304	Mays, 171	Mays, 47	Mays, 111	Marichal, 21	Marichal, 2.48
1965	95	67	2nd	2	Franks	Mays, .317	Hart, Mays, 177	Mays, 52	Mays, 112	Marichal, 22	Marichal, 2.13
1966	93	68	2nd	1½	Franks	McCovey, .295	Hart, 165	Mays, 37	Mays, 103	Marichal, 25	Marichal, 2.23
1967	91	71	2nd	10½	Franks	J. Alou, .292	Hart, 167	McCovey, 31	Hart, 99	McCormick, 22	Linzy, 1.51
1968	88	74	2nd	9	Franks	McCovey, .293	McCovey, 153	McCovey, 36	McCovey, 105	Marichal, 26	Bolin, 1.99
							WEST DIVISION				
1969	90	72	2nd	3	King	McCovey, .320	Bo. Bonds, 161	McCovey, 45	McCovey, 126	Marichal, 21	Marichal, 2.10
1970	86	76	3rd	16	King, Fox	Bo. Bonds, .302	Bo. Bonds, 200	McCovey, 39	McCovey, 126	Perry, 23	McMahon, 2.96
1971	90	72	‡1st	+1	Fox	Bo. Bonds, .288	Bo. Bonds, 178	Bo. Bonds, 33	Bo. Bonds, 102	Marichal, 18	Perry, 2.76
1972	69	86	5th	26½	Fox	Speier, .269	Bo. Bonds, 162	Kingman, 29	Kingman, 83	Bryant, 14	Barr, 2.87
1973	88	74	3rd	11	Fox	Maddox, .319	Maddox, 187	Bo. Bonds, 39	Bo. Bonds, 96	Bryant, 24	Moffitt, 2.42
1974	72	90	5th	30	Fox, Westrum	Matthews, .287	Matthews, 161	Bo. Bonds, 21	Matthews, 82	Caldwell, 14	Barr, 2.74
1975	80	81	3rd	27½	Westrum	Joshua, .318	Joshua, 161	Matthews, 12	Murcer, 91	Montefusco, 15	Montefusco, 2.88
1976	74	88	4th	28	Rigney	Matthews, .279	Matthews, 164	Murcer, 23	Murcer, 90	Montefusco, 16	Moffitt, 2.27
1977	75	87	4th	23	Altobelli	Madlock, .302	Madlock, 161	McCovey, 28	McCovey, 86	Halicki, 16	Lavelle, 2.05
1978	89	73	3rd	6	Altobelli	Madlock, .309	J. Clark, 181	J. Clark, 25	J. Clark, 98	Blue, 18	Knepper, 2.63
1979	71	91	4th	19½	Altobelli, Bristol	Whitfield, .287	J. Clark, 144	Ivie, 27	Ivie, 89	Blue, 14	Lavelle, 2.51
1980	75	86	5th	17	Bristol	J. Clark, .284	Evans, 147	J. Clark, 22	J. Clark, 82	Blue 14	Minton, 2.46
1981	56	55	§5th/3rd	—	Robinson	Herndon, .288	Herndon, 105	J. Clark, 17	J. Clark, 53	Alexander, 11	Holland, 2.41
1982	87	75	3rd	2	Robinson	Morgan, .289	C. Davis, 167	J. Clark, 27	J. Clark, 103	Laskey, 13	Minton, 1.83
1983	79	83	5th	12	Robinson	Youngblood, .292	Evans, 154	Evans, 30	Leonard, 87	Laskey, 13	Hammaker, 2.25
1984	66	96	6th	26	Robinson, Ozark	C. Davis, .315	C. Davis, 157	C. Davis, Leonard, 21	Leonard, 86	Krukow, 11	Lavelle, 2.76
1985	62	100	6th	33	Davenport, Craig	C. Brown, .271	C. Davis, 130	Brenly, 19	Leonard, 62	Garrelts, 9	Garrelts, 2.30
1986	83	79	3rd	13	Craig	C. Brown, .317	Thompson, 149	Maldonado, 18	Maldonado, 85	Krukow, 20	Krukow, 2.94
1987	90	72	‡1st	+6	Craig	Aldrete, .325	W. Clark, 163	W. Clark, 35	W. Clark, 91	LaCoss, 13	J.Robinson, 2.79
1988	83	79	4th	11½	Craig	Butler, .287	Butler, 163	W. Clark, 29	W. Clark, 109	Reuschel, 19	D. Robinson, 2.45
1989	92	70	∞1st	+3	Craig	W. Clark, .333	W. Clark, 194	Mitchell, 47	Mitchell, 127	Reuschel, 17	Garrelts, 2.28
1990	85	77	3rd	6	Craig	Butler, .309	Butler, 192	Mitchell, 35	M. Williams, 122	Burkett, 14	Burkett, 3.79
1991	75	87	4th	19	Craig	McGee, .312	W. Clark, 170	M. Williams, 34	W. Clark, 116	Wilson, 13	Brantley, 2.45
1992	72	90	5th	26	Craig	W. Clark, .300	W. Clark, 154	M. Williams, 20	W. Clark, 73	Burkett, 13	Beck, 1.76
1993	103	59	2nd	1	Baker	Ba. Bonds, .336	Ba. Bonds, 181	Ba. Bonds, 46	Ba. Bonds, 123	Burkett, 22	Swift, 2.82
1994	55	60	2nd	3½	Baker	Ba. Bonds, .312	Ba. Bonds, 122	M. Williams, 43	M. Williams, 96	Portugal, 10	Swift, 3.38
1995	67	77	4th	11	Baker	Carreon, .301	Ba. Bonds, 149	Ba. Bonds, 33	Ba. Bonds, 104	Leiter, 10	VanLandingham, 3.67
1996	68	94	4th	23	Baker	Ba. Bonds, .308	Ba. Bonds, 159	Ba. Bonds, 42	Ba. Bonds, 129	Gardner, 12	Rueter, 3.97
1997	90	72	▲1st	+2	Baker	Mueller, .292	Ba. Bonds, 155	Ba. Bonds, 40	Kent, 121	Estes, 19	Estes, 3.18
1998	89	74	◆2nd	9½	Baker	Ba. Bonds, .305	Ba. Bonds, 167	Ba. Bonds, 37	Kent, 127	Rueter, 16	Gardner, 4.27
1999	86	76	2nd	14	Baker	Benard, .290	Benard, 163	Ba. Bonds, 34	Kent, 101	Ortiz, 18	Ortiz, 3.81
2000	97	65	▲1st	+11	Baker	Burks, .344	Kent, 196	Ba. Bonds, 49	Kent, 125	L. Hernandez, 17	L. Hernandez, 3.75
2001	90	72	2nd	2	Baker	Ba. Bonds, .328	Aurilia, 206	Ba. Bonds, 73	Ba. Bonds, 137	Ortiz, 17	Ortiz, 3.29
2002	95	66	■∞2nd	2½	Baker	Ba. Bonds, .370	Kent, 195	Ba. Bonds, 46	Ba. Bonds, 110	Ortiz, Rueter, 12	Rueter, 3.23

* Tied for position. † Won pennant playoff. ‡ Lost Championship Series. § First half 27-32, second half 29-23. ∞ Won Championship Series. ▲ Lost Division Series. ◆ Lost wild-card playoff. ■Won Division Series.
Note: Batting average minimum 350 at-bats, ERA minimum 90 innings pitched.

For the Record

The record-setting 1927 New York Yankees featured (from left) Babe Ruth, diminutive manager Miller Huggins and Lou Gehrig.

INTRODUCTION

For the second straight year, San Francisco's Barry Bonds in 2002 set numerous single-season and career records. But he wasn't the only one. Here's a look at some of the major records set and tied in 2002:

■ MAJOR LEAGUE RECORDS SET IN THE AMERICAN LEAGUE

Most runs, career: 2,288, Rickey Henderson*

Most at-bats, no triples, season: 662, Miguel Tejada, Oakland

Most leadoff home runs, career: 80, Rickey Henderson*

Most home runs, shortstop, season: 57, Alex Rodriguez, Texas

Most home runs, two consecutive innings: 3, Nomar Garciaparra, Boston, July 23 (1st game; 3rd & 4th inn)

Most walks, career: 2,179, Rickey Henderson*

Most consecutive games, home run, club: 27, Texas, August 11 - September 9

Most stolen bases, career: 1,403, Rickey Henderson*

Most caught stealing, career: 335, Rickey Henderson*

Most hit batsmen, club, pitchers, season: 94, Tampa Bay

Highest fielding percentage, shortstop, career (min.: 1,000 games): .984, Omar Vizquel*

Highest fielding percentage, shortstop, season (min.: 100 games): .998, Mike Bordick, Baltimore

Most consecutive errorless games, shortstop, season and career: 110, Mike Bordick, Baltimore, April 11 - September 29

Most consecutive errorless chances, shortstop, season and career: 543, Mike Bordick, Baltimore, April 10 - September 29

■ MAJOR LEAGUE RECORDS SET IN THE NATIONAL LEAGUE

Highest on-base percentage, season: .582, Barry Bonds, San Francisco

Most hits, pinch-hitter, career: 173, Lenny Harris*

Most home runs, three consecutive games: 7, Shawn Green, Los Angeles, May 23 (4), 24 (1), 25 (2)

Most total bases, game: 19, Shawn Green, Los Angeles, May 23

Most walks, season: 198, Barry Bonds, San Francisco

Most intentional walks, career: 423, Barry Bonds*

Most intentional walks, season: 68, Barry Bonds, San Francisco

Most seasons, leading league, intentional walks: 8, Barry Bonds*

Most intentional walks, club, season: 103, San Francisco

Highest stolen base percentage, career (min.: 300 att.): .847, Tim Raines, Sr.

Most games pitched, career: 1,187, Jesse Orosco*

Most games, relief pitcher, career: 1,183, Jesse Orosco*

Most pitchers, club, season: 37, San Diego

Most relief appearances, club, season: Colorado, 506

Most pitchers, both clubs, game: 16, Houston (8) vs. San Francisco (8), September 28

Most putouts, pitcher, career: 443, Greg Maddux*

■ MAJOR LEAGUE RECORDS TIED IN THE AMERICAN LEAGUE

Most seasons, outfielder: 24, Rickey Henderson

Most players, club, season: 59, Cleveland

Most doubles, inning: 2, Robert Fick, Detroit, May 29 (7th inn); Bobby Kielty, Minnesota, June 4 (7th inn)

Most home runs, game: 4, Mike Cameron, Seattle, May 2

Most home runs, inning: 2, Bret Boone, Seattle, May 2 (1st inn); Mike Cameron, Seattle, May 2 (1st inn); Jared Sandberg, Tampa Bay, June 11 (5th inn); Nomar Garciaparra, Boston, July 23 (day game; third inn); Carl Everett, Texas, July 26 (7th inn)

Most home runs, two consecutive games: 5, Nomar Garciaparra, Boston, July 21 (2), 23 (day game; 3); Alex Rodriguez, Texas, August 17 (3), 18 (2)

Most home runs, consecutive at-bats: 4, Troy Glaus, Anaheim, September 15 (3), 16 (1)

Most grand slams, consecutive games: 2, David Eckstein, Anaheim, April 27, 28

Most sacrifice flies, game: 3, Edgar Martinez, Seattle, August 3

■ MAJOR LEAGUE RECORDS TIED IN THE NATIONAL LEAGUE

Most home runs, game: 4, Shawn Green, Los Angeles, May 23

Most home runs, inning: 2, Mark Bellhorn, Chicago, August 29 (4th inn); Aaron Boone, Cincinnati, August 9 (1st inn)

Most home runs, two consecutive games: 5, Shawn Green, Los Angeles, May 23 (4), 24 (1)

Most home runs, consecutive at-bats: 4, Shawn Green, Los Angeles, June 14 (2), 15 (2); Andruw Jones, Atlanta, September 7 (2), 8 (2)

Most games, three or more home runs, career: 6, Sammy Sosa, Chicago

Most total bases, two consecutive games: 25, Shawn Green, Los Angeles, May 23 (19), 24 (6)

Most extra-base hits, game: 5, Shawn Green, Los Angeles, May 23

Most grand slams, club, game: 2, Milwaukee vs. Chicago, May 12 (Casanova, Sexson)

Most players, club, season: 59, San Diego

Most players, both clubs, game: 45, Atlanta (24) vs. New York (21), September 29

Most pinch-hitters, club, inning: 6, Los Angeles, September 14 (6th)

Most seasons leading league, games started, pitchers: 6, Tom Glavine

Most seasons, 300 or more strikeouts: 6, Randy Johnson

■ AMERICAN LEAGUE RECORDS SET

Most home runs, second baseman, season: 39, Alfonso Soriano, New York

Most stolen bases, career: 1,270, Rickey Henderson*

Most caught stealing, career: 293, Rickey Henderson*

Most strikeouts, career: 3,909, Roger Clemens*

Most relief appearances, club, season: Texas, 487

Most consecutive errorless chances, outfielder, career: 592, Johnny Damon

■ AMERICAN LEAGUE RECORDS TIED

Most consecutive seasons, 50 or more home runs: 2, Alex Rodriguez

Most home runs, three consecutive games: 6, Alex Rodriguez, Texas, August 16 (1), 17 (3), 19 (2)

Most players four or more hits, game: 4, Minnesota vs. Cleveland, June 4

Most home runs, both teams, game: 12, Detroit (6) vs. Chicago (6)

Most players, both clubs, home run, game: 9, Detroit (5) vs. Chicago (4), July 2

■ NATIONAL LEAGUE RECORDS SET

Highest slugging percentage, career (min.: 5000 AB): .595, Barry Bonds*

Most home runs, catcher, career: 336, Mike Piazza

Most consecutive seasons, 30 or more home runs: 11, Barry Bonds*

Most runs batted in, two consecutive games: 14, Sammy Sosa, Chicago, August 10 (9), 11 (5)

Most seasons leading league, walks: 8, Barry Bonds*

Most consecutive games, walk: 18, Barry Bonds, San Francisco, September 9-28

Most saves, season: 55, John Smoltz, Atlanta

Most consecutive seasons, 300 or more strikeouts: 4, Randy Johnson

■ NATIONAL LEAGUE RECORDS TIED

Most runs scored, game: 6, Shawn Green, Los Angeles, May 23

Most consecutive seasons, 40 or more home runs: 5, Sammy Sosa

Most seasons, 100 or more runs batted in: 11, Barry Bonds

Most consecutive seasons, 100 or more runs batted in: 8, Sammy Sosa

Most seasons, 100 or more walks: 10, Barry Bonds, San Francisco

Most grounded into double plays, season: 30, Brad Ausmus, Houston

Most players, two or more home runs, club, game: 3, San Francisco vs. Colorado, July 2

Most home runs, club, three consecutive games: 15, Chicago, August 10, 11, 12

Most games pitched, rookie, season: 78, Ricky Stone, Houston

*Extended own record

Shawn Green had six hits, six runs, four home runs and 19 total bases in a May 23 game vs. Milwaukee, breaking Joe Adcock's 48-year-old record for total bases in a game.

Career

REGULAR SEASON

SERVICE

YEARS PLAYED

1.	Deacon McGuire	26
2.	Eddie Collins	25
	Bobby Wallace	25
4.	Ty Cobb	24
	Rick Dempsey	24
	Carlton Fisk	24
	Rickey Henderson	24
	Pete Rose	24
9.	Hank Aaron	23
	Rogers Hornsby	23
	Rabbit Maranville	23
	Tony Perez	23
	Tim Raines Sr.	23
	Brooks Robinson	23
	Rusty Staub	23
	Carl Yastrzemski	23
17.	many tied with 22	

YEARS ONE CLUB

1.	Brooks Robinson, Orioles	23
	Carl Yastrzemski, Red Sox	23
3.	Cap Anson, Cubs	22
	Ty Cobb, Tigers	22
	Al Kaline, Tigers	22
	Stan Musial, Cardinals	22
	Mel Ott, Giants	22
8.	Hank Aaron, Braves	21
	George Brett, Royals	21
	Harmon Killebrew, Senators/Twins	21
	Willie Mays, Giants	21
	Cal Ripken Jr., Orioles	21
	Willie Stargell, Pirates	21
14.	Luke Appling, White Sox	20
	Phil Cavarretta, Cubs	20
	Tony Gwynn, Padres	20
	Alan Trammell, Tigers	20
	Robin Yount, Brewers	20
19.	10 tied with 19	

YEARS PITCHED

1.	Nolan Ryan	27
2.	Tommy John	26
3.	Charlie Hough	25
	Jim Kaat	25
5.	Steve Carlton	24
	Dennis Eckersley	24
	Phil Niekro	24
8.	Dennis Martinez	23
	Jesse Orosco	23
	Jack Quinn	23
	Don Sutton	23
	Early Wynn	23
13.	Bert Blyleven	22
	Rich Gossage	22
	Sam Jones	22
	Mike Morgan	22
	Joe Niekro	22
	Herb Pennock	22
	Gaylord Perry	22
	Jerry Reuss	22
	Red Ruffing	22
	Cy Young	22

YEARS PITCHED ONE CLUB

1.	Walter Johnson, Senators	21
	Ted Lyons, White Sox	21
	Phil Niekro, Braves	21
4.	Red Faber, White Sox	20
	Mel Harder, Indians	20
	Warren Spahn, Braves	20
7.	Jim Palmer, Orioles	19
8.	Babe Adams, Pirates	18
	Bob Feller, Indians	18
	Jesse Haines, Cardinals	18
11.	Bob Gibson, Cardinals	17
	Christy Mathewson, Giants	17
13.	Tommy Bridges, Tigers	16
	Whitey Ford, Yankees	16
	Tom Glavine, Braves	16
	Carl Hubbell, Giants	16
	Vern Law, Pirates	16
	Charlie Root, Cubs	16
	Don Sutton, Dodgers	16
20.	many tied with 15	

BATTING

GAMES

1.	Pete Rose	3,562
2.	Carl Yastrzemski	3,308
3.	Hank Aaron	3,298
4.	Rickey Henderson	3,051
5.	Ty Cobb	3,035
6.	Eddie Murray	3,026
	Stan Musial	3,026
8.	Cal Ripken Jr.	3,001
9.	Willie Mays	2,992
10.	Dave Winfield	2,973
11.	Rusty Staub	2,951
12.	Brooks Robinson	2,896
13.	Robin Yount	2,856
14.	Al Kaline	2,834
15.	Harold Baines	2,830
16.	Eddie Collins	2,826
17.	Reggie Jackson	2,820
18.	Frank Robinson	2,808
19.	Honus Wagner	2,794
20.	Tris Speaker	2,789

CONSECUTIVE GAMES PLAYED

1.	Cal Ripken Jr.	2,632
2.	Lou Gehrig	2,130
3.	Everett Scott	1,307
4.	Steve Garvey	1,207
5.	Billy Williams	1,117
6.	Joe Sewell	1,103
7.	Stan Musial	895
8.	Eddie Yost	829
9.	Gus Suhr	822
10.	Nellie Fox	798
11.	Pete Rose	745
12.	Dale Murphy	740
13.	Richie Ashburn	730
14.	Ernie Banks	717
15.	Pete Rose	678
16.	Earl Averill	673
17.	Frank McCormick	652
18.	Sandy Alomar Sr.	648
19.	Eddie Brown	618
20.	Roy McMillan	585

HIGHEST AVERAGE

(Minimum 1,500 hits)

1.	Ty Cobb	.366
2.	Rogers Hornsby	.358
3.	Joe Jackson	.356
4.	Dan Brouthers	.349
	Pete Browning	.349
6.	Ed Delahanty	.346
7.	Tris Speaker	.345
8.	Ted Williams	.344
	Billy Hamilton	.344
10.	Babe Ruth	.342
	Harry Heilmann	.342
12.	Willie Keeler	.341
	Bill Terry	.341
14.	George Sisler	.340
	Lou Gehrig	.340
16.	Tony Gwynn	.338
	Jesse Burkett	.338
	Nap Lajoie	.338
19.	Riggs Stephenson	.336
20.	Sam Thompson	.335

YEARS LEADING LEAGUE IN AVERAGE

1.	Ty Cobb	12
2.	Tony Gwynn	8
	Honus Wagner	8
4.	Rod Carew	7
	Rogers Hornsby	7
	Stan Musial	7
7.	Ted Williams	6
8.	Wade Boggs	5
	Dan Brouthers	5
10.	Cap Anson	4
	Roberto Clemente	4
	Harry Heilmann	4
	Bill Madlock	4
14.	George Brett	3
	Pete Browning	3
	Jesse Burkett	3
	Nap Lajoie	3
	Tony Oliva	3
	Pete Rose	3
	Larry Walker	3
	Paul Waner	3
	Carl Yastrzemski	3

YEARS TOPPING .300

1.	Ty Cobb	23
2.	Cap Anson	19
3.	Tony Gwynn	18
	Tris Speaker	18
5.	Eddie Collins	17
	Stan Musial	17
7.	Babe Ruth	16
	Honus Wagner	16
	Ted Williams	16
10.	Wade Boggs	15
	Dan Brouthers	15
	Rod Carew	15
	Rogers Hornsby	15
	Nap Lajoie	15
	Pete Rose	15
16.	Hank Aaron	14
	Luke Appling	14
	Paul Waner	14
19.	9 tied with 13	

In the early 1960s, Pete Rose was a young player looking for recognition. By the time he retired, he was baseball's all-time career hit leader.

CONSECUTIVE .300 SEASONS

1.	Ty Cobb	23
2.	Tony Gwynn	17
3.	Stan Musial	16
4.	Cap Anson	15
	Rod Carew	15
	Honus Wagner	15
7.	Dan Brouthers	14
8.	Willie Keeler	13
9.	Lou Gehrig	12
	Billy Hamilton	12
	Harry Heilmann	12
	Paul Waner	12
13.	Ed Delahanty	11
	Frank Frisch	11
	Rogers Hornsby	11
	Joe Kelley	11
	Al Simmons	11
18.	Wade Boggs	10
	Jesse Burkett	10
	Nap Lajoie	10
	Joe Medwick	10
	Tris Speaker	10
	Bill Terry	10
	Arky Vaughan	10
	Ted Williams	10

AT-BATS

1.	Pete Rose	14,053
2.	Hank Aaron	12,364
3.	Carl Yastrzemski	11,988
4.	Cal Ripken Jr.	11,551
5.	Ty Cobb	11,434
6.	Eddie Murray	11,336
7.	Robin Yount	11,008
8.	Dave Winfield	11,003
9.	Stan Musial	10,972
10.	Rickey Henderson	10,889
11.	Willie Mays	10,881
12.	Paul Molitor	10,835
13.	Brooks Robinson	10,654
14.	Honus Wagner	10,439
15.	George Brett	10,349
16.	Lou Brock	10,332
17.	Luis Aparicio	10,230
18.	Tris Speaker	10,195
19.	Al Kaline	10,116
20.	Rabbit Maranville	10,078

RUNS SCORED

1.	Rickey Henderson	2,288
2.	Ty Cobb	2,246
3.	Hank Aaron	2,174
	Babe Ruth	2,174
5.	Pete Rose	2,165
6.	Willie Mays	2,062
7.	Stan Musial	1,949
8.	Lou Gehrig	1,888
9.	Tris Speaker	1,882
10.	Mel Ott	1,859
11.	Barry Bonds	1,830
12.	Frank Robinson	1,829
13.	Eddie Collins	1,821

14.	Carl Yastrzemski	1,816
15.	Ted Williams	1,798
16.	Paul Molitor	1,782
17.	Charlie Gehringer	1,774
18.	Jimmie Foxx	1,751
19.	Honus Wagner	1,739
20.	Cap Anson	1,722

YEARS LEADING LEAGUE IN RUNS

1.	Babe Ruth	8
2.	Mickey Mantle	6
	Ted Williams	6
4.	George Burns	5
	Ty Cobb	5
	Rickey Henderson	5
	Rogers Hornsby	5
	Stan Musial	5
9.	Lou Gehrig	4
	Billy Hamilton	4
	Pete Rose	4
	Harry Stovey	4
13.	Hank Aaron	3
	Jeff Bagwell	3
	Eddie Collins	3
	King Kelly	3
	Chuck Klein	3
	Paul Molitor	3
	Frank Robinson	3
	Ryne Sandberg	3
	Duke Snider	3
	Sammy Sosa	3
	Arky Vaughan	3
	Carl Yastrzemski	3

100-RUN SEASONS

1.	Hank Aaron	15
2.	Lou Gehrig	13
	Rickey Henderson	13
4.	Charlie Gehringer	12
	Willie Mays	12
	Babe Ruth	12
7.	Ty Cobb	11
	Jimmie Foxx	11
	Billy Hamilton	11
	Stan Musial	11
	George Van Haltren	11
12.	Barry Bonds	10
	Ed Delahanty	10
	Mike Griffin	10
	Bid McPhee	10
	Pete Rose	10
	Sam Thompson	10
18.	many tied with 9	

HITS

1.	Pete Rose	4,256
2.	Ty Cobb	4,189
3.	Hank Aaron	3,771
4.	Stan Musial	3,630
5.	Tris Speaker	3,514
6.	Honus Wagner	3,420
7.	Carl Yastrzemski	3,419
8.	Paul Molitor	3,319
9.	Eddie Collins	3,315
10.	Willie Mays	3,283
11.	Eddie Murray	3,255
12.	Nap Lajoie	3,242
13.	Cal Ripken Jr.	3,184
14.	George Brett	3,154
15.	Paul Waner	3,152
16.	Robin Yount	3,142
17.	Tony Gwynn	3,141
18.	Dave Winfield	3,110
19.	Cap Anson	3,056
20.	Rod Carew	3,053

YEARS LEADING LEAGUE IN HITS

1.	Ty Cobb	8
2.	Tony Gwynn	7
	Pete Rose	7
4.	Stan Musial	6
5.	Tony Oliva	5
6.	Ginger Beaumont	4
	Dan Brouthers	4
	Nellie Fox	4
	Rogers Hornsby	4
	Harvey Kuenn	4
	Nap Lajoie	4
	Kirby Puckett	4
13.	Richie Ashburn	3
	George Brett	3
	Jesse Burkett	3
	Rod Carew	3
	Willie Keeler	3
	Frank McCormick	3
	Paul Molitor	3
	Johnny Pesky	3

200-HIT SEASONS

1.	Pete Rose	10
2.	Ty Cobb	9
3.	Lou Gehrig	8
	Willie Keeler	8
	Paul Waner	8
6.	Wade Boggs	7
	Charlie Gehringer	7
	Rogers Hornsby	7
9.	Jesse Burkett	6
	Steve Garvey	6
	Stan Musial	6
	Sam Rice	6
	Al Simmons	6
	George Sisler	6
	Bill Terry	6
16.	Tony Gwynn	5
	Chuck Klein	5
	Kirby Puckett	5
19.	many tied with 4	

PINCH HITS

1.	Lenny Harris	173
2.	Manny Mota	150
3.	Smoky Burgess	145
4.	Greg Gross	143
5.	Jose Morales	123
6.	Dave Hansen	120
7.	John Vander Wal	119
8.	Jerry Lynch	116
9.	Red Lucas	114
10.	Steve Braun	113
11.	Terry Crowley	108
	Denny Walling	108
13.	Gates Brown	107
14.	Mike Lum	103
15.	Jim Dwyer	102
16.	Rusty Staub	100
17.	Dave Clark	96
18.	Larry Biittner	95
	Vic Davalillo	95
	Gerald Perry	95

SINGLES

1.	Pete Rose	3,215
2.	Ty Cobb	3,053
3.	Eddie Collins	2,643
4.	Willie Keeler	2,513
5.	Honus Wagner	2,424
6.	Rod Carew	2,404
7.	Tris Speaker	2,383
8.	Tony Gwynn	2,378
9.	Paul Molitor	2,366
10.	Nap Lajoie	2,340
11.	Hank Aaron	2,294
12.	Jesse Burkett	2,273
13.	Sam Rice	2,271
14.	Carl Yastrzemski	2,262
15.	Wade Boggs	2,253
	Stan Musial	2,253
17.	Lou Brock	2,247
18.	Cap Anson	2,246
19.	Paul Waner	2,243
20.	Robin Yount	2,182

DOUBLES

1.	Tris Speaker	792
2.	Pete Rose	746
3.	Stan Musial	725
4.	Ty Cobb	724
5.	George Brett	665
6.	Nap Lajoie	657
7.	Carl Yastrzemski	646
8.	Honus Wagner	643
9.	Hank Aaron	624
10.	Paul Molitor	605
	Paul Waner	605
12.	Cal Ripken Jr.	603
13.	Robin Yount	583
14.	Wade Boggs	578
15.	Charlie Gehringer	574
16.	Eddie Murray	560
17.	Tony Gwynn	543
18.	Harry Heilmann	542
19.	Rogers Hornsby	541
20.	Joe Medwick	540
	Dave Winfield	540

TRIPLES

1.	Sam Crawford	309
2.	Ty Cobb	295
3.	Honus Wagner	252
4.	Jake Beckley	244
5.	Roger Connor	233
6.	Tris Speaker	222
7.	Fred Clarke	220
8.	Dan Brouthers	205
9.	Joe Kelley	194
10.	Paul Waner	191
11.	Bid McPhee	189
12.	Eddie Collins	187
13.	Ed Delahanty	186
14.	Sam Rice	184
15.	Jesse Burkett	182
	Ed Konetchy	182
	Edd Roush	182
18.	Buck Ewing	178
19.	Rabbit Maranville	177
	Stan Musial	177

HOME RUNS

1.	Hank Aaron	755
2.	Babe Ruth	714
3.	Willie Mays	660
4.	Barry Bonds	613
5.	Frank Robinson	586
6.	Mark McGwire	583
7.	Harmon Killebrew	573
8.	Reggie Jackson	563
9.	Mike Schmidt	548
10.	Mickey Mantle	536
11.	Jimmie Foxx	534
12.	Willie McCovey	521
	Ted Williams	521
14.	Ernie Banks	512
	Eddie Mathews	512
16.	Mel Ott	511
17.	Eddie Murray	504
18.	Sammy Sosa	499
19.	Lou Gehrig	493
20.	Rafael Palmeiro	490

HOME RUNS, A.L.

1.	Babe Ruth	708
2.	Harmon Killebrew	573
3.	Reggie Jackson	563
4.	Mickey Mantle	536
5.	Jimmie Foxx	524
6.	Ted Williams	521
7.	Lou Gehrig	493
8.	Rafael Palmeiro	465
9.	Jose Canseco	462
10.	Carl Yastrzemski	452
11.	Cal Ripken Jr.	431
12.	Juan Gonzalez	405
13.	Al Kaline	399
14.	Ken Griffey Jr.	398
15.	Eddie Murray	396
16.	Dwight Evans	385
17.	Harold Baines	384
18.	Jim Rice	382
19.	Albert Belle	381
20.	Norm Cash	377

HOME RUNS, N.L.

1.	Hank Aaron	733
2.	Willie Mays	660
3.	Barry Bonds	613
4.	Mike Schmidt	548
5.	Willie McCovey	521
6.	Ernie Banks	512
7.	Mel Ott	511
8.	Eddie Mathews	503
9.	Stan Musial	475
	Willie Stargell	475
11.	Sammy Sosa	470
12.	Andre Dawson	409
13.	Duke Snider	407
14.	Dale Murphy	398
15.	Billy Williams	392
16.	Johnny Bench	389
17.	Jeff Bagwell	380
18.	Andres Galarraga	376
19.	Gil Hodges	370
20.	Andres Galarraga	367

HOME RUNS, ONE CLUB

1.	Hank Aaron, Braves	733
2.	Babe Ruth, Yankees	659
3.	Willie Mays, Giants	646
4.	Harmon Killebrew, Senators/Twins	559
5.	Mike Schmidt, Phillies	548
6.	Mickey Mantle, Yankees	536
7.	Ted Williams, Red Sox	521
8.	Ernie Banks, Cubs	512
9.	Mel Ott, Giants	511
10.	Lou Gehrig, Yankees	493
	Eddie Mathews, Braves	493
12.	Stan Musial, Cardinals	475
	Willie Stargell, Pirates	475
14.	Sammy Sosa, Cubs	470
15.	Willie McCovey, Giants	469
16.	Carl Yastrzemski, Red Sox	452
17.	Barry Bonds, Giants	437
18.	Cal Ripken Jr., Orioles	431
19.	Al Kaline, Tigers	399
20.	Ken Griffey Jr., Mariners	398

HOME RUNS, RIGHTHANDER

1.	Hank Aaron	755
2.	Willie Mays	660
3.	Frank Robinson	586
4.	Mark McGwire	583
5.	Harmon Killebrew	573
6.	Mike Schmidt	548
7.	Jimmie Foxx	534
8.	Ernie Banks	512
9.	Sammy Sosa	499
10.	Dave Winfield	465
11.	Jose Canseco	462
12.	Dave Kingman	442
13.	Andre Dawson	438
14.	Cal Ripken Jr.	431
15.	Juan Gonzalez	405
16.	Al Kaline	399
17.	Dale Murphy	398
18.	Joe Carter	396
19.	Johnny Bench	389
20.	Andres Galarraga	386

HOME RUNS, LEFTHANDER

1.	Babe Ruth	714
2.	Barry Bonds	613
3.	Reggie Jackson	563
4.	Willie McCovey	521
	Ted Williams	521
6.	Eddie Mathews	512
7.	Mel Ott	511
8.	Lou Gehrig	493
9.	Rafael Palmeiro	490
10.	Fred McGriff	478
11.	Stan Musial	475
	Willie Stargell	475
13.	Ken Griffey Jr.	468
14.	Carl Yastrzemski	452
15.	Billy Williams	426
16.	Darrell Evans	414
17.	Duke Snider	407
18.	Graig Nettles	390
19.	Harold Baines	384
20.	Norm Cash	377

HOME RUNS, SWITCH HITTER

1.	Mickey Mantle	536
2.	Eddie Murray	504
3.	Chili Davis	350
4.	Reggie Smith	314
5.	Bobby Bonilla	287
6.	Ruben Sierra	276
7.	Chipper Jones	253
8.	Ted Simmons	248
9.	Ken Singleton	246
10.	Mickey Tettleton	245
11.	Ken Caminiti	239
12.	Howard Johnson	228
13.	Bernie Williams	226
14.	Devon White	208
15.	Roberto Alomar	201
16.	Todd Hundley	200
17.	Tim Raines Sr.	170
18.	Jose Valentin	168
19.	J.T. Snow	165
20.	Roy Smalley	163

HOME RUNS, FIRST BASEMAN

1.	Mark McGwire	566
2.	Lou Gehrig	493
3.	Jimmie Foxx	480
4.	Willie McCovey	439
5.	Fred McGriff	416
6.	Eddie Murray	409
7.	Rafael Palmeiro	389
8.	Jeff Bagwell	377
9.	Andres Galarraga	370
10.	Norm Cash	367

HOME RUNS, SECOND BASEMAN

1.	Ryne Sandberg	275
2.	Joe Morgan	266
3.	Rogers Hornsby	264
4.	Joe Gordon	246
5.	Lou Whitaker	239
6.	Jeff Kent	231
7.	Bobby Doerr	223
8.	Roberto Alomar	198
9.	Bobby Grich	196
10.	Bret Boone	184

HOME RUNS, THIRD BASEMAN

1.	Mike Schmidt	509
2.	Eddie Mathews	486
3.	Graig Nettles	368
4.	Matt Williams	355
5.	Ron Santo	337
6.	Gary Gaetti	333
7.	Ron Cey	312
8.	Brooks Robinson	266
9.	Robin Ventura	264
10.	Ken Boyer	260

HOME RUNS, SHORTSTOP

1.	Cal Ripken Jr.	345
2.	Alex Rodriguez	298
3.	Ernie Banks	277
4.	Vern Stephens	213
5.	Barry Larkin	186
6.	Alan Trammell	177
7.	Joe Cronin	155
8.	Nomar Garciaparra	145
9.	Eddie Joost	129
	Miguel Tejada	129

HOME RUNS, OUTFIELDER

1.	Babe Ruth	692
2.	Hank Aaron	661
3.	Willie Mays	642

4. Barry Bonds 607
5. Ted Williams 514
6. Sammy Sosa 498
7. Mickey Mantle 490
8. Frank Robinson 463
9. Reggie Jackson 458
10. Mel Ott 457

HOME RUNS, CATCHER

1. Carlton Fisk 351
2. Johnny Bench 327
3. Mike Piazza 336
4. Yogi Berra 306
5. Gary Carter 298
6. Lance Parrish 295
7. Roy Campanella 239
8. Gabby Hartnett 232
9. Ivan Rodriguez 210
10. Bill Dickey 200

HOME RUNS, PITCHER

1. Wes Ferrell 37
2. Bob Lemon 35
Warren Spahn 35
4. Red Ruffing 34
5. Earl Wilson 33
6. Don Drysdale 29
7. John Clarkson 24
Bob Gibson 24
9. Walter Johnson 23
10. Jack Stivetts 20
Dizzy Trout 20

HOME RUNS, DESIGNATED HITTER

1. Don Baylor 219
2. Harold Baines 214
3. Jose Cansco 208
Edgar Martinez 208
5. Chili Davis 200

LEADOFF HOMERS

1. Rickey Henderson 80
2. Brady Anderson 43
3. Bobby Bonds 35
4. Devon White 34
5. Paul Molitor 33
6. Chuck Knoblauch 31
7. Craig Biggio 30
Tony Phillips 30
9. Davey Lopes 28
Eddie Yost 28
11. Brian Downing 25
Kenny Lofton 25
13. Lou Brock 24
14. Tommy Harper 23
Lou Whitaker 23
16. Jimmy Ryan 22
Ray Durham 21
18. Felipe Alou 20
Barry Bonds 20
Lenny Dykstra 20

20-HOME RUN SEASONS

1. Hank Aaron 20
2. Willie Mays 17
Frank Robinson 17
4. Reggie Jackson 16
Eddie Murray 16
Babe Ruth 16
Ted Williams 16
8. Barry Bonds 15
Fred McGriff 15
Mel Ott 15
Willie Stargell 15
Dave Winfield 15
13. Mickey Mantle 14
Eddie Mathews 14
Mike Schmidt 14
Billy Williams 14
17. Ernie Banks 13
Andre Dawson 13
Lou Gehrig 13
Harmon Killebrew 13
Mark McGwire 13

30-HOME RUN SEASONS

1. Hank Aaron 15
2. Babe Ruth 13
Mike Schmidt 13
4. Barry Bonds 12
Jimmie Foxx 12
6. Willie Mays 11
Mark McGwire 11
Frank Robinson 11
9. Lou Gehrig 10
Harmon Killebrew 10
Eddie Mathews 10
Fred McGriff 10
13. Mickey Mantle 9
Rafael Palmeiro 9
Mike Piazza 9
Sammy Sosa 9
17. Jeff Bagwell 8

Albert Belle 8
Jose Canseco 8
Mel Ott 8
Ted Williams 8

PINCH-HIT HOME RUNS

1. Cliff Johnson 20
2. Jerry Lynch 18
3. John Vander Wal 17
4. Gates Brown 16
Smoky Burgess 16
Willie McCovey 16
7. George Crowe 14
Dave Hansen 14
9. Glenallen Hill 13
10. Joe Adcock 12
Bob Cerv 12
Jose Morales 12
Graig Nettles 12
14. Jeff Burroughs 11
Jay Johnstone 11
Candy Maldonado 11
Fred Whitfield 11
Cy Williams 11
19. many tied with 10

GRAND SLAMS

1. Lou Gehrig 23
2. Eddie Murray 19
3. Willie McCovey 18
4. Jimmie Foxx 17
Ted Williams 17
6. Hank Aaron 16
Dave Kingman 16
Babe Ruth 16
Robin Ventura 16
10. Manny Ramirez 15
11. Ken Griffey Jr. 14
Gil Hodges 14
Mark McGwire 14
Mike Piazza 14
15. Harold Baines 13
Albert Belle 13
Joe DiMaggio 13
George Foster 13
Ralph Kiner 13
20. Ernie Banks 12
Don Baylor 12
Rogers Hornsby 12
Joe Rudi 12
Rudy York 12

MULTIPLE-HOME RUN GAMES

1. Babe Ruth 72
2. Mark McGwire 67
3. Willie Mays 63
4. Hank Aaron 62
5. Barry Bonds 61
6. Sammy Sosa 58
7. Jimmie Foxx 55
8. Frank Robinson 54
9. Eddie Mathews 49
Mel Ott 49
11. Ken Griffey Jr. 46
Harmon Killebrew 46
Mickey Mantle 46
14. Willie McCovey 44
Mike Schmidt 44
16. Juan Gonzalez 43
Dave Kingman 43
18. Ernie Banks 42
Lou Gehrig 42
Reggie Jackson 42

MOST HOMERS PER AT-BAT

1. Mark McGwire .094
2. Babe Ruth .085
3. Barry Bonds .074
4. Jim Thome .072
5. Sammy Sosa .071
Ralph Kiner .071
7. Harmon Killebrew .070
Manny Ramirez .070
9. Alex Rodriguez .068
Mike Piazza .068
Ken Griffey Jr. .068
Ted Williams .068
13. Juan Gonzalez .066
Dave Kingman .066
Mickey Mantle .066
Carlos Delgado .066
Jimmie Foxx .066
Mike Schmidt .066
19. Jose Canseco .065
Albert Belle .065

TOTAL BASES

1. Hank Aaron 6,856
2. Stan Musial 6,134
3. Willie Mays 6,066
4. Ty Cobb 5,854
5. Babe Ruth 5,793
6. Pete Rose 5,752
7. Carl Yastrzemski 5,539
8. Eddie Murray 5,397
9. Frank Robinson 5,373
10. Dave Winfield 5,221
11. Cal Ripken Jr. 5,168
12. Tris Speaker 5,101
13. Lou Gehrig 5,060
14. George Brett 5,044
15. Mel Ott 5,041
16. Barry Bonds 4,961
17. Jimmie Foxx 4,956
18. Ted Williams 4,884
19. Honus Wagner 4,870
20. Paul Molitor 4,854

300-TOTAL BASE SEASONS

1. Hank Aaron 15
2. Lou Gehrig 13
Willie Mays 13
Stan Musial 13
5. Babe Ruth 11
6. Jimmie Foxx 10
7. Joe DiMaggio 9
Rafael Palmeiro 9
Billy Williams 9
Ted Williams 9
11. Rogers Hornsby 8
Frank Robinson 8
13. Jeff Bagwell 7
Barry Bonds 7
Juan Gonzalez 7
Hank Greenberg 7
Mel Ott 7
Paul Waner 7
19. many tied with 6

SLUGGING PERCENTAGE

(Minimum 2,000 total bases)

1. Babe Ruth .690
2. Ted Williams .634
3. Lou Gehrig .632
4. Jimmie Foxx .609
5. Hank Greenberg .605
6. Manny Ramirez .599
7. Barry Bonds .595
8. Mark McGwire .588
9. Joe DiMaggio .579
Alex Rodriguez .579
11. Rogers Hornsby .577
12. Mike Piazza .576
13. Larry Walker .574
14. Frank Thomas .568
15. Jim Thome .567
16. Albert Belle .564
17. Juan Gonzalez .563
18. Johnny Mize .562
Ken Griffey Jr. .562
20. Stan Musial .559

EXTRA-BASE HITS

1. Hank Aaron 1,477
2. Stan Musial 1,377
3. Babe Ruth 1,356
4. Willie Mays 1,323
5. Barry Bonds 1,200
6. Lou Gehrig 1,190
7. Frank Robinson 1,186
8. Carl Yastrzemski 1,157
9. Ty Cobb 1,136
10. Tris Speaker 1,131
11. George Brett 1,119
12. Jimmie Foxx 1,117
Ted Williams 1,117
14. Eddie Murray 1,099
15. Dave Winfield 1,093
16. Cal Ripken Jr. 1,078
17. Reggie Jackson 1,075
18. Mel Ott 1,071
19. Rafael Palmeiro 1,048
20. Pete Rose 1,041

RUNS BATTED IN

1. Hank Aaron 2,297
2. Babe Ruth 2,213
3. Lou Gehrig 1,995
4. Stan Musial 1,951
5. Ty Cobb 1,938
6. Jimmie Foxx 1,922
7. Eddie Murray 1,917
8. Willie Mays 1,903
9. Cap Anson 1,880
10. Mel Ott 1,860
11. Carl Yastrzemski 1,844
12. Ted Williams 1,839
13. Dave Winfield 1,833
14. Al Simmons 1,827
15. Frank Robinson 1,812
16. Honus Wagner 1,733
17. Reggie Jackson 1,702
18. Cal Ripken Jr. 1,695
19. Barry Bonds 1,652
Tony Perez 1,652

RBIs, RIGHTHANDER

1. Hank Aaron 2,297
2. Jimmie Foxx 1,922
3. Willie Mays 1,903
4. Cap Anson 1,880
5. Dave Winfield 1,833
6. Al Simmons 1,827
7. Frank Robinson 1,812
8. Honus Wagner 1,733
9. Cal Ripken Jr. 1,695
10. Tony Perez 1,652
11. Ernie Banks 1,636
12. Nap Lajoie 1,599
13. Mike Schmidt 1,595
14. Andre Dawson 1,591
15. Rogers Hornsby 1,584
Harmon Killebrew 1,584
17. Al Kaline 1,583
18. Harry Heilmann 1,539
19. Joe DiMaggio 1,537
20. Ed Delahanty 1,466

RBIs, LEFTHANDER

1. Babe Ruth 2,213
2. Lou Gehrig 1,995
3. Stan Musial 1,951
4. Ty Cobb 1,938
5. Mel Ott 1,860
6. Carl Yastrzemski 1,844
7. Ted Williams 1,839
8. Reggie Jackson 1,702
9. Barry Bonds 1,652
10. Harold Baines 1,628
11. Goose Goslin 1,609
12. George Brett 1,595
13. Jake Beckley 1,577
14. Rafael Palmeiro 1,575
15. Willie McCovey 1,555
16. Willie Stargell 1,540
17. Tris Speaker 1,529
18. Sam Crawford 1,525
19. Fred McGriff 1,503
20. Dave Parker 1,493

RBIs, SWITCH HITTER

1. Eddie Murray 1,917
2. Mickey Mantle 1,509
3. George Davis 1,439
4. Ted Simmons 1,389
5. Chili Davis 1,372
6. Pete Rose 1,314
7. Frankie Frisch 1,244
8. Ruben Sierra 1,181
9. Bobby Bonilla 1,173
10. Reggie Smith 1,092
11. Roberto Alomar 1,071
12. Ken Singleton 1,065
13. Bernie Williams 998
14. Ken Caminiti 983
15. Tim Raines Sr. 980
16. John Anderson 976
17. Terry Pendleton 946
18. Tommy Tucker 932
19. Duke Farrell 916
20. Willie McGee 856

100-RBI SEASONS

1. Jimmie Foxx 13
Lou Gehrig 13
Babe Ruth 13
4. Al Simmons 12
5. Barry Bonds 11
Hank Aaron 11
Goose Goslin 11
8. Joe Carter 10
Willie Mays 10
Stan Musial 10
11. Albert Belle 9
Joe DiMaggio 9
Harmon Killebrew 9
Mel Ott 9
Rafael Palmeiro 9
Mike Schmidt 9
Frank Thomas 9
Honus Wagner 9
Ted Williams 9
20. many tied with 8

WALKS

1. Rickey Henderson 2,179
2. Babe Ruth 2,062
3. Ted Williams 2,019
4. Barry Bonds 1,922
5. Joe Morgan 1,865
6. Carl Yastrzemski 1,845
7. Mickey Mantle 1,733
8. Mel Ott 1,708
9. Eddie Yost 1,614
10. Darrell Evans 1,605
11. Stan Musial 1,599
12. Pete Rose 1,566
13. Harmon Killebrew 1,559
14. Lou Gehrig 1,508
15. Mike Schmidt 1,507

The majority of outfielder Rickey Henderson's 1,403 career stolen bases came during his four stints with the Oakland A's.

16.	Eddie Collins	1,499
17.	Willie Mays	1,464
18.	Jimmie Foxx	1,452
19.	Eddie Mathews	1,444
20.	Frank Robinson	1,420

100-WALK SEASONS

1.	Babe Ruth	13
2.	Lou Gehrig	11
	Ted Williams	11
4.	Barry Bonds	10
	Mickey Mantle	10
	Mel Ott	10
7.	Frank Thomas	9
8.	Joe Morgan	8
	Eddie Yost	8
10.	Jeff Bagwell	7
	Max Bishop	7
	Jimmie Foxx	7
	Rickey Henderson	7
	Harmon Killebrew	7
	Mike Schmidt	7
	Roy Thomas	7
17.	Harlond Clift	6
	Eddie Joost	6
	Ralph Kiner	6
	Eddie Stanky	6
	Gene Tenace	6
	Jim Thome	6
	Jimmy Wynn	6
	Carl Yastrzemski	6

INTENTIONAL WALKS

1.	Barry Bonds	423
2.	Hank Aaron	293
3.	Willie McCovey	260
4.	George Brett	229
5.	Willie Stargell	227
6.	Eddie Murray	222
7.	Frank Robinson	218
8.	Tony Gwynn	203
9.	Mike Schmidt	201
10.	Ken Griffey Jr.	199
11.	Ernie Banks	198
12.	Rusty Staub	193
13.	Willie Mays	192
14.	Carl Yastrzemski	190
15.	Chili Davis	188
	Ted Simmons	188
17.	Harold Baines	187
18.	Billy Williams	182
19.	Wade Boggs	180
20.	Dave Winfield	172

STRIKEOUTS

1.	Reggie Jackson	2,597
2.	Jose Canseco	1,942
3.	Andres Galarraga	1,939
4.	Willie Stargell	1,936
5.	Mike Schmidt	1,883
6.	Tony Perez	1,867
7.	Dwight Evans	1,834
8.	Dave Kingman	1,816
9.	Fred McGriff	1,797
10.	Bobby Bonds	1,757
11.	Dale Murphy	1,748
12.	Lou Brock	1,730
13.	Mickey Mantle	1,710
14.	Harmon Killebrew	1,699
15.	Chili Davis	1,698
16	Sammy Sosa	1,690
17.	Dave Winfield	1,686
18.	Rickey Henderson	1,678
19.	Gary Gaetti	1,602
20.	Mark McGwire	1,596

100-STRIKEOUT SEASONS

1.	Reggie Jackson	18
2.	Dave Kingman	13
	Fred McGriff	13
	Willie Stargell	13
5.	Mike Schmidt	12
6.	Jose Canseco	11
	Ray Lankford	11
	Dale Murphy	11
9.	Dick Allen	10
	Bobby Bonds	10
	Andres Galarraga	10
	Frank Howard	10
	Greg Luzinski	10
	Lee May	10
	Mark McGwire	10
	Tony Perez	10
	Sammy Sosa	10
18.	Lou Brock	9
	Travis Fryman	9
	Tim Salmon	9
	Danny Tartabull	9
	Greg Vaughn	9
	Mo Vaughn	9

HIT BY PITCH

1.	Hughie Jennings	287
2.	Tommy Tucker	272
3.	Don Baylor	267
4.	Ron Hunt	243
5.	Dan McGann	230
6.	Craig Biggio	214
7.	Frank Robinson	198
8.	Minnie Minoso	192
9.	Jake Beckley	183
10.	Andres Galarraga	175
11.	Curt Welch	173
12.	Kid Elberfeld	165
13.	Brady Anderson	154
	Fred Clarke	154
15.	Chet Lemon	151
16.	Carlton Fisk	143
17.	Nellie Fox	142
18.	Art Fletcher	141
	Fernando Vina	141
20.	Bill Dahlen	140

STOLEN BASES

1.	Rickey Henderson	1,403
2.	Lou Brock	938
3.	Billy Hamilton	912
4.	Ty Cobb	892
5.	Tim Raines Sr.	808
6.	Vince Coleman	752
7.	Eddie Collins	745
8.	Arlie Latham	742
9.	Max Carey	738
10.	Honus Wagner	723
11.	Joe Morgan	689
12.	Willie Wilson	668
13.	Tom Brown	657
14.	Bert Campaneris	649
15.	Otis Nixon	620
16.	George Davis	619
17.	Dummy Hoy	596
18.	Maury Wills	586
19.	George Van Haltren	583
20.	Ozzie Smith	580

CAUGHT STEALING

1.	Rickey Henderson	335
2.	Lou Brock	307
3.	Brett Butler	257
4.	Maury Wills	208
5.	Bert Campaneris	199
6.	Rod Carew	187
7.	Otis Nixon	186
8.	Omar Moreno	182
9.	Cesar Cedeno	179
10.	Ty Cobb	178
	Steve Sax	178
12.	Vince Coleman	177
	George Burns	174
14.	Eddie Collins	173
15.	Bobby Bonds	169
16.	Joe Morgan	162
	Billy North	162
18.	Pete Rose	149
19.	Ozzie Smith	148
20.	Delino DeShields	147

STEAL PERCENTAGE

1.	Tim Raines Sr.	84.70
2.	Eric Davis	84.10
3.	Tony Womack	83.62
4.	Willie Wilson	83.29
5.	Davey Lopes	83.01
6.	Barry Larkin	82.96
7.	Stan Javier	82.83
8.	Julio Cruz	81.47
9.	Brian L. Hunter	81.00
10.	Joe Morgan	80.96
11.	Vince Coleman	80.95
12.	Roberto Alomar	80.77
13.	Rickey Henderson	80.72
14.	Andy VanSlyke	80.59
15.	Lenny Dykstra	79.83
16.	Ozzie Smith	79.67
17.	Gary Redus	79.51
18.	Paul Molitor	79.37
19.	Kenny Lofton	79.25
20.	Marquis Grissom	78.86

50-STEAL SEASONS

1.	Rickey Henderson	13
2.	Lou Brock	12
3.	Billy Hamilton	9
	Arlie Latham	9
5.	Ty Cobb	8
	Tim Raines Sr.	8
7.	Bert Campaneris	7
	Vince Coleman	7
9.	Tom Brown	6
	Max Carey	6
	Cesar Cedeno	6
	Eddie Collins	6
	Kenny Lofton	6
	Harry Stovey	6
	Curt Welch	6
16.	Ned Hanlon	5
	Dummy Hoy	5
	King Kelly	5
	Omar Moreno	5
	Joe Morgan	5
	Otis Nixon	5
	Honus Wagner	5
	John Ward	5
	Maury Wills	5

STEALS OF HOME

1.	Ty Cobb	50
2.	Max Carey	33
3.	George J. Burns	28
4.	Honus Wagner	27
5.	Sherry Magee	23
	Frank Schulte	23
7.	Johnny Evers	21
8.	George Sisler	20
9.	Frankie Frisch	19
	Jackie Robinson	19
11.	Jimmy Sheckard	18
	Tris Speaker	18
	Joe Tinker	18
14.	Rod Carew	17
	Eddie Collins	17
	Larry Doyle	17
17.	Tommy Leach	16
18.	Ben Chapman	15
	Fred Clarke	15
	Lou Gehrig	15

PITCHING

GAMES

1.	Jesse Orosco	1,187
2.	Dennis Eckersley	1,071
3.	Hoyt Wilhelm	1,070
4.	Kent Tekulve	1,050
5.	Lee Smith	1,022
6.	Dan Plesac	1,006
7.	Rich Gossage	1,002
8.	John Franco	998
9.	Lindy McDaniel	987
10.	Mike Jackson	960
11.	Rollie Fingers	944
12.	Gene Garber	931
13.	Cy Young	906
14.	Sparky Lyle	899
15.	Jim Kaat	898
16.	Paul Assenmacher	884
17.	Jeff Reardon	880
18.	Don McMahon	874
19.	Phil Niekro	864
20.	Charlie Hough	858

GAMES STARTED

1.	Cy Young	815
2.	Nolan Ryan	773
3.	Don Sutton	756
4.	Phil Niekro	716
5.	Steve Carlton	709
6.	Tommy John	700
7.	Gaylord Perry	690
8.	Bert Blyleven	685
9.	Pud Galvin	681
10.	Walter Johnson	666
11.	Warren Spahn	665
12.	Tom Seaver	647
13.	Jim Kaat	625
14.	Frank Tanana	616
15.	Early Wynn	612
16.	Robin Roberts	609
17.	Grover Alexander	600
18.	Fergie Jenkins	594
	Tim Keefe	594
20.	Roger Clemens	573

COMPLETE GAMES

1.	Cy Young	749
2.	Pud Galvin	639
3.	Tim Keefe	554
4.	Kid Nichols	532
5.	Walter Johnson	531
6.	Mickey Welch	525
7.	Charles Radbourn	489
8.	John Clarkson	485
9.	Tony Mullane	468
10.	Jim McCormick	466
11.	Gus Weyhing	449
12.	Grover Alexander	437
13.	Christy Mathewson	435
14.	Jack Powell	422
15.	Eddie Plank	410
16.	Will White	394
17.	Amos Rusie	393
18.	Vic Willis	388
19.	Warren Spahn	382
20.	Jim Whitney	377

OPENING DAY STARTS

1.	Tom Seaver	16
2.	Steve Carlton	14
	Walter Johnson	14
	Jack Morris	14
5.	Robin Roberts	13
	Cy Young	13
7.	Grover Alexander	12

Rank	Player	No.
	Bert Blyleven	12
9.	Roger Clemens	11
	Ferguson Jenkins	11
	Dennis Martinez	11
12.	Bob Gibson	10
	Juan Marichal	10
	George Mullin	10
	Warren Spahn	10
16.	Randy Johnson	9
	Phil Niekro	9
	Gaylord Perry	9
	Steve Rogers	9
	Nolan Ryan	9
	Rick Sutcliffe	9
	Don Sutton	9

INNINGS PITCHED

Rank	Player	IP
1.	Cy Young	7,356.0
2.	Pud Galvin	5,941.1
3.	Walter Johnson	5,914.2
4.	Phil Niekro	5,404.1
5.	Nolan Ryan	5,386.0
6.	Gaylord Perry	5,350.1
7.	Don Sutton	5,282.1
8.	Warren Spahn	5,243.2
9.	Steve Carlton	5,217.1
10.	Grover Alexander	5,190.0
11.	Kid Nichols	5,066.1
12.	Tim Keefe	5,049.2
13.	Bert Blyleven	4,970.0
14.	Mickey Welch	4,802.0
15.	Christy Mathewson	4,788.2
16.	Tom Seaver	4,782.2
17.	Tommy John	4,710.1
18.	Robin Roberts	4,688.2
19.	Early Wynn	4,564.0
20.	John Clarkson	4,536.1

INNINGS PITCHED, STARTER

Rank	Player	IP
1.	Cy Young	7034.2
2.	Pud Galvin	5872.2
3.	Walter Johnson	5550.1
4.	Nolan Ryan	5326.0
5.	Don Sutton	5248.1
6.	Steve Carlton	5165.0
7.	Gaylord Perry	5161.2
8.	Phil Niekro	5149.1
9.	Warren Spahn	5106.2
10.	Tim Keefe	5021.1
11.	Grover Alexander	4983.1
12.	Bert Blyleven	4957.1
13.	Kid Nichols	4891.1
14.	Tom Seaver	4776.0
15.	Christy Mathewson	4753.1
16.	Mickey Welch	4749.0
17.	Tommy John	4622.0
18.	Robin Roberts	4567.1
19.	John Clarkson	4491.1
20.	Charles Radbourn	4419.0

INNINGS PITCHED, RELIEVER

Rank	Player	IP
1.	Hoyt Wilhelm	1871.0
2.	Lindy McDaniel	1694.0
3.	Rich Gossage	1556.2
4.	Rollie Fingers	1500.1
5.	Gene Garber	1452.2
6.	Kent Tekulve	1436.1
7.	Sparky Lyle	1390.1
8.	Tug McGraw	1301.1
9.	Don McMahon	1297.0
10.	Mike Marshall	1259.1
11.	Lee Smith	1252.1
12.	Tom Burgmeier	1248.2
13.	Jesse Orosco	1243.0
14.	Roy Face	1212.1
15.	Clay Carroll	1204.2
16.	Eddie Fisher	1186.0
17.	Bill Campbell	1177.1
18.	Ron Perranoski	1170.2
19.	Bob Stanley	1157.0
20.	Jeff Reardon	1132.1

200-INNING SEASONS

Rank	Player	No.
1.	Don Sutton	20
2.	Phil Niekro	19
	Cy Young	19
4.	Walter Johnson	18
5.	Gaylord Perry	17
	Warren Spahn	17
7.	Grover Alexander	16
	Bert Blyleven	16
	Steve Carlton	16
	Tom Seaver	16
11.	Eddie Plank	15
	Jack Powell	15
13.	Jim Kaat	14
	Greg Maddux	14
	Christy Mathewson	14
	Robin Roberts	14
	Red Ruffing	14
	Nolan Ryan	14
	Early Wynn	14
20.	9 tied with 13	

Giants manager John McGraw (left) and pitching ace Christy Mathewson, who posted 373 career victories.

300-INNING SEASONS

Rank	Player	No.
1.	Cy Young	16
2.	Kid Nichols	12
3.	Pud Galvin	11
	Christy Mathewson	11
5.	Tim Keefe	10
6.	Grover Alexander	9
	Walter Johnson	9
	Joe McGinnity	9
	Mickey Welch	9
	Gus Weyhing	9
11.	John Clarkson	8
	Jim McCormick	8
	Tony Mullane	8
	Charles Radbourn	8
	Amos Rusie	8
	Jim Whitney	8
	Vic Willis	8
18.	Charlie Buffinton	7
19.	many tied with 6	

LOWEST ERA

(Minimum 1,500 innings)

Rank	Player	ERA
1.	Ed Walsh	1.82
2.	Addie Joss	1.89
3.	Mordecai Brown	2.06
4.	John Ward	2.10
5.	Christy Mathewson	2.13
6.	Rube Waddell	2.16
7.	Walter Johnson	2.17
8.	Orval Overall	2.23
9.	Tommy Bond	2.25
10.	Will White	2.28
	Ed Reulbach	2.28
12.	Jim Scott	2.30
13.	Eddie Plank	2.35
14.	Larry Corcoran	2.36
15.	George McQuillan	2.38
	Ed Killian	2.38
	Eddie Cicotte	2.38
18.	Doc White	2.39
19.	Nap Rucker	2.42
20.	Jeff Tesreau	2.43

VICTORIES

Rank	Player	W
1.	Cy Young	511
2.	Walter Johnson	417
3.	Grover Alexander	373
	Christy Mathewson	373
5.	Warren Spahn	363
6.	Pud Galvin	361
	Kid Nichols	361
8.	Tim Keefe	342
9.	Steve Carlton	329
10.	John Clarkson	328
11.	Eddie Plank	326
12.	Nolan Ryan	324
	Don Sutton	324
14.	Phil Niekro	318
15.	Gaylord Perry	314
16.	Tom Seaver	311
17.	Charles Radbourn	309
18.	Mickey Welch	307
19.	Lefty Grove	300
	Early Wynn	300

VICTORIES, RIGHTHANDER

Rank	Player	W
1.	Cy Young	511
2.	Walter Johnson	417
3.	Grover Alexander	373
	Christy Mathewson	373
5.	Pud Galvin	361
	Kid Nichols	361
7.	Tim Keefe	342
8.	John Clarkson	328
9.	Nolan Ryan	324
	Don Sutton	324
11.	Phil Niekro	318
12.	Gaylord Perry	314
13.	Tom Seaver	311
14.	Charles Radbourn	309
15.	Mickey Welch	307
16.	Early Wynn	300
17.	Roger Clemens	293
18.	Bert Blyleven	287
19.	Robin Roberts	286
20.	Fergie Jenkins	284
	Tony Mullane	284

VICTORIES, LEFTHANDER

Rank	Player	W
1.	Warren Spahn	363
2.	Steve Carlton	329
3.	Eddie Plank	326
4.	Lefty Grove	300
5.	Tommy John	288
6.	Jim Kaat	283
7.	Eppa Rixey	266
8.	Carl Hubbell	253
9.	Tom Glavine	242
10.	Herb Pennock	241
11.	Frank Tanana	240
12.	Whitey Ford	236
13.	Randy Johnson	224
14.	Jerry Koosman	222
15.	Jerry Reuss	220
16.	Earl Whitehill	218
17.	Mickey Lolich	217
18.	Wilbur Cooper	216
19.	Billy Pierce	211
20.	Vida Blue	209

VICTORIES, RELIEVER

Rank	Player	W
1.	Hoyt Wilhelm	124
2.	Lindy McDaniel	119
3.	Rich Gossage	115
4.	Rollie Fingers	107
5.	Sparky Lyle	99
6.	Roy Face	96
7.	Gene Garber	94
	Kent Tekulve	94
9.	Mike Marshall	92
10.	Don McMahon	90
11.	Tug McGraw	89
12.	Clay Carroll	88
13.	John Franco	85
	Bob Stanley	85
15.	Jesse Orosco	84
16.	Bill Campbell	80
	Gary Lavelle	80
18.	Tom Burgmeier	79
	Stu Miller	79
	Ron Perranoski	79

OPENING DAY VICTORIES

Rank	Player	W
1.	Walter Johnson	9
2.	Grover Alexander	8
	Jack Morris	8
4.	Jimmy Key	7
	Tom Seaver	7
6.	John Clarkson	6
	Wes Ferrell	6
	Dwight Gooden	6
	Mickey Lolich	6
	Greg Maddux	6
	Juan Marichal	6
	Kid Nichols	6
13.	Roger Clemens	5
	Don Drysdale	5
	Randy Johnson	5
	George Mullin	5
	Jim Palmer	5
	Robin Roberts	5
	Nolan Ryan	5
	Rick Sutcliffe	5
	Lon Warneke	5
	Cy Young	5

20-VICTORY SEASONS

Rank	Player	No.
1.	Cy Young	15
2.	Christy Mathewson	13
	Warren Spahn	13
4.	Walter Johnson	12
5.	Kid Nichols	11
6.	Jim Galvin	10
7.	Grover Alexander	9
	Charley Radbourn	9
	Mickey Welch	9
10.	John Clarkson	8
	Lefty Grove	8
	Jim McCormick	8
	Joe McGinnity	8

	Tony Mullane	8
	Jim Palmer	8
	Eddie Plank	8
	Amos Rusie	8
	Vic Willis	8
19.	6 tied with 7	

20 VICTORIES, RIGHTHANDER

1.	Cy Young	15
2.	Christy Mathewson	13
3.	Walter Johnson	12
4.	Kid Nichols	11
5.	Jim Galvin	10
6.	Grover Alexander	9
	Charley Radbourn	9
	Mickey Welch	9
9.	John Clarkson	8
	Jim McCormick	8
	Joe McGinnity	8
	Tony Mullane	8
	Jim Palmer	8
	Amos Rusie	8
	Vic Willis	8
16.	Charlie Buffinton	7
	Clark Griffith	7
	Fergie Jenkins	7
	Tim Keefe	7
	Bob Lemon	7
	Gus Weyhing	7

20 VICTORIES, LEFTHANDER

1.	Warren Spahn	13
2.	Lefty Grove	8
	Eddie Plank	8
4.	Steve Carlton	6
	Jesse Tannehill	6
6.	Tom Glavine	5
	Carl Hubbell	5
	Hippo Vaughn	5
9.	Wilbur Cooper	4
	Mike Cuellar	4
	Lefty Gomez	4
	Noodles Hahn	4
	Dave McNally	4
	Ed Morris	4
	Hal Newhouser	4
	Eppa Rixey	4
	Rube Waddell	4
	Wilbur Wood	4
19.	many tied with 3	

CONSECUTIVE 20-VICTORY SEASONS

1.	Christy Mathewson	12
2.	Walter Johnson	10
	Kid Nichols	10
4.	Cy Young	9
5.	John Clarkson	8
	Jim McCormick	8
	Joe McGinnity	8
	Amos Rusie	8
9.	Lefty Grove	7
	Tim Keefe	7
	Charley Radbourn	7
	Mickey Welch	7
	Gus Weyhing	7
14.	Mordecai Brown	6
	Bob Caruthers	6
	Jim Galvin	6
	Clark Griffith	6
	Fergie Jenkins	6
	Tony Mullane	6
	Robin Roberts	6
	Warren Spahn	6

30-VICTORY SEASONS

1.	Kid Nichols	7
2.	John Clarkson	6
	Tim Keefe	6
4.	Tony Mullane	5
	Will White	5
	Cy Young	5
7.	Tommy Bond	4
	Larry Corcoran	4
	Silver King	4
	Christy Mathewson	4
	Jim McCormick	4
	Amos Rusie	4
	Mickey Welch	4
	Gus Weyhing	4
15.	Grover Alexander	3
	Bob Caruthers	3
	Pud Galvin	3
	Bill Hutchison	3
	Bobby Mathews	3
	Ed Morris	3
	Charles Radbourn	3

WINNING PERCENTAGE

(Minimum 75 victories)

1.	Spud Chandler	.717
2.	Pedro Martinez	.707
3.	Dave Foutz	.690
	Whitey Ford	.690
5.	Bob Caruthers	.688
6.	Don Gullett	.686
7.	Lefty Grove	.680
8.	Randy Johnson	.679
9.	Jay Hughes	.675
10.	Joe Wood	.672
11.	Babe Ruth	.671
12.	Bill Hoffer	.667
	Vic Raschi	.667
14.	Larry Corcoran	.665
	Christy Mathewson	.665
16.	Roger Clemens	.660
	Sam Leever	.660
18.	Sal Maglie	.657
19.	Sandy Koufax	.655
20.	Johnny Allen	.654

CONSECUTIVE VICTORIES

1.	Carl Hubbell	24
2.	Roy Face	22
3.	Rube Marquard	20
	Roger Clemens	20
5.	Tim Keefe	19
6.	Charles Radbourn	18
	Pat Luby	18
8.	Mickey Welch	17
	Johnny Allen	17
	Dave McNally	17
11.	Tim Keefe	16
	Jim McCormick	16
	Bill Donovan	16
	Walter Johnson	16
	Joe Wood	16
	Lefty Grove	16
	Alvin Crowder	16
	Schoolboy Rowe	16
	Ewell Blackwell	16
	Jack Sanford	16
	Tom Seaver	16
	Rick Sutcliffe	16
	Randy Johnson	16
	Roger Clemens	16

LOSSES

1.	Cy Young	316
2.	Jim Galvin	308
3.	Nolan Ryan	292
4.	Walter Johnson	279
5.	Phil Niekro	274
6.	Gaylord Perry	265
7.	Don Sutton	256
8.	Jack Powell	254
9.	Eppa Rixey	251
10.	Bert Blyleven	250
11.	Robin Roberts	245
	Warren Spahn	245
13.	Steve Carlton	244
	Early Wynn	244
15.	Jim Kaat	237
16.	Frank Tanana	236
17.	Gus Weyhing	232
18.	Tommy John	231
19.	Bob Friend	230
	Ted Lyons	230

LOSSES, RIGHTHANDER

1.	Cy Young	316
2.	Jim Galvin	308
3.	Nolan Ryan	292
4.	Walter Johnson	279
5.	Phil Niekro	274
6.	Gaylord Perry	265
7.	Don Sutton	256
8.	Jack Powell	254
9.	Bert Blyleven	250
10.	Robin Roberts	245
11.	Early Wynn	244
12.	Gus Weyhing	232
13.	Bob Friend	230
	Ted Lyons	230
15.	Fergie Jenkins	226
16.	Tim Keefe	225
	Red Ruffing	225
18.	Bobo Newsom	222
19.	Tony Mullane	220
20.	Jack Quinn	218

LOSSES, LEFTHANDER

1.	Eppa Rixey	251
2.	Warren Spahn	245
3.	Steve Carlton	244
4.	Jim Kaat	237
5.	Frank Tanana	236
6.	Tommy John	231
7.	Jerry Koosman	209
8.	Claude Osteen	195
9.	Eddie Plank	194
10.	Mickey Lolich	191
	Jerry Reuss	191
	Tom Zachary	191
13.	Earl Whitehill	185
14.	Curt Simmons	183
15.	Wilbur Cooper	178
16.	Rube Marquard	177
17.	Chuck Finley	173
18.	Larry French	171
19.	Ted Breitenstein	170
20.	Billy Pierce	169

SAVES

1.	Lee Smith	478
2.	John Franco	422
3.	Dennis Eckersley	390
4.	Jeff Reardon	367
5.	Trevor Hoffman	352
6.	Randy Myers	347
7.	Rollie Fingers	341
8.	John Wetteland	330
9.	Roberto Hernandez	320
10.	Rick Aguilera	318
11.	Robb Nen	314
12.	Tom Henke	311
13.	Rich Gossage	310
14.	Jeff Montgomery	304
15.	Doug Jones	303
16.	Bruce Sutter	300
17.	Rod Beck	266
18.	Todd Worrell	256
19.	Dave Righetti	252
20.	Troy Percival	250

SHUTOUTS

1.	Walter Johnson	110
2.	Grover Alexander	90
3.	Christy Mathewson	79
4.	Cy Young	76
5.	Eddie Plank	69
6.	Warren Spahn	63
7.	Nolan Ryan	61
	Tom Seaver	61
9.	Bert Blyleven	60
10.	Don Sutton	58
11.	Pud Galvin	57
	Ed Walsh	57
13.	Bob Gibson	56
14.	Mordecai Brown	55
	Steve Carlton	55
16.	Jim Palmer	53
	Gaylord Perry	53
18.	Juan Marichal	52
19.	Rube Waddell	50
	Vic Willis	50

SHUTOUTS, RIGHTHANDER

1.	Walter Johnson	110
2.	Grover Alexander	90
3.	Christy Mathewson	79
4.	Cy Young	76
5.	Nolan Ryan	61
	Tom Seaver	61
7.	Bert Blyleven	60
8.	Don Sutton	58
9.	Pud Galvin	57
	Ed Walsh	57
11.	Bob Gibson	56
12.	Mordecai Brown	55
13.	Jim Palmer	53
	Gaylord Perry	53
15.	Juan Marichal	52
16.	Vic Willis	50
17.	Don Drysdale	49
	Fergie Jenkins	49
	Luis Tiant	49
	Early Wynn	49

SHUTOUTS, LEFTHANDER

1.	Eddie Plank	69
2.	Warren Spahn	63
3.	Steve Carlton	55
4.	Rube Waddell	50
5.	Tommy John	46
6.	Whitey Ford	45
	Doc White	45
8.	Mickey Lolich	41
	Hippo Vaughn	41
10.	Larry French	40
	Sandy Koufax	40
	Claude Osteen	40
13.	Jerry Reuss	39
14.	Billy Pierce	38
	Nap Rucker	38
16.	Vida Blue	37
	Eppa Rixey	37
18.	Mike Cuellar	36
	Carl Hubbell	36
	Curt Simmons	36

1-0 VICTORIES

1.	Walter Johnson	38
2.	Grover Alexander	17
3.	Bert Blyleven	15
4.	Christy Mathewson	14
5.	Dean Chance	13
	Eddie Plank	13
	Ed Walsh	13
	Doc White	13
	Cy Young	13
10.	Steve Carlton	12
	Stan Coveleski	12
	Gaylord Perry	12
13.	Fergie Jenkins	11
	Greg Maddux	11
	Kid Nichols	11
	Nap Rucker	11
	Nolan Ryan	11
18.	9 tied with 10	

NO-HIT GAMES

1.	Nolan Ryan	7
2.	Sandy Koufax	4
3.	Larry Corcoran	3
	Bob Feller	3
	Cy Young	3
6.	Al Atkinson	2
	Ted Breitenstein	2
	Jim Bunning	2
	Steve Busby	2
	Carl Erskine	2
	Bob Forsch	2
	Jim Galvin	2
	Ken Holtzman	2
	Tom L. Hughes	2
	Addie Joss	2
	Dutch Leonard	2
	Jim Maloney	2
	Christy Mathewson	2
	Allie Reynolds	2
	Frank Smith	2
	Warren Spahn	2
	Bill Stoneman	2
	Adonis Terry	2
	Virgil Trucks	2
	Johnny Vander Meer	2
	Don Wilson	2

1-HIT GAMES

(No-hit games in parentheses)

1.	Nolan Ryan (7)	12
	Bob Feller (3)	12
3.	Walter Johnson (1)	7
	Addie Joss (1)	7
	Charles Radbourn (1)	7
6.	Mordecai Brown	6
	Steve Carlton	6
8.	Bert Blyleven (1)	5
	Jim Maloney (2)	5
	Jim Palmer (1)	5
	Tom Seaver (1)	5
	Dave Stieb (1)	5
	Ed Walsh (1)	5
	Grover Alexander	5
	Tim Keefe	5
	Don Sutton	5
	Doc White	5

RUNS ALLOWED

1.	Jim Galvin	3,315
2.	Cy Young	3,167
3.	Gus Weyhing	2,796
4.	Mickey Welch	2,556
5.	Tony Mullane	2,523
6.	Kid Nichols	2,480
7.	Tim Keefe	2,467
8.	John Clarkson	2,384
9.	Phil Niekro	2,337
10.	Adonis Terry	2,303
11.	Charley Radbourn	2,273
12.	Nolan Ryan	2,178
13.	Steve Carlton	2,130
14.	Gaylord Perry	2,128
15.	Red Ruffing	2,115
16.	Don Sutton	2,104
17.	Jim McCormick	2,095
18.	Amos Rusie	2,068
19.	Ted Lyons	2,056
20.	Burleigh Grimes	2,050

HITS ALLOWED

1.	Cy Young	7,092
2.	Jim Galvin	6,352
3.	Phil Niekro	5,044
4.	Gaylord Perry	4,938
5.	Kid Nichols	4,929
6.	Walter Johnson	4,913
7.	Grover Alexander	4,868
8.	Warren Spahn	4,830
9.	Tommy John	4,783
10.	Don Sutton	4,692
11.	Steve Carlton	4,672
12.	Eppa Rixey	4,633
13.	Bert Blyleven	4,632
14.	Jim Kaat	4,620
15.	Mickey Welch	4,588
16.	Robin Roberts	4,582
17.	Gus Weyhing	4,576
18.	Ted Lyons	4,489
19.	Tim Keefe	4,438
20.	Burleigh Grimes	4,412

HOME RUNS ALLOWED

1.	Robin Roberts	505
2.	Fergie Jenkins	484

3.	Phil Niekro	482
4.	Don Sutton	472
5.	Frank Tanana	448
6.	Warren Spahn	434
7.	Bert Blyleven	430
8.	Steve Carlton	414
9.	Gaylord Perry	399
10.	Jim Kaat	395
11.	Jack Morris	389
12.	Charlie Hough	383
13.	Tom Seaver	380
14.	Catfish Hunter	374
15.	Jim Bunning	372
	Dennis Martinez	372
17.	Dennis Eckersley	347
	Mickey Lolich	347
19.	Luis Tiant	346
20.	Early Wynn	338

GRAND SLAMS ALLOWED

1.	Nolan Ryan	10
2.	Ned Garver	9
	Jim Kaat	9
	Milt Pappas	9
	Jerry Reuss	9
	Lee Smith	9
	Frank Viola	9
8.	Willie Blair	8
	Bert Blyleven	8
	Jim Brewer	8
	Roy Face	8
	Bob Feller	8
	Alex Fernandez	8
	Mike Jackson	8
	Johnny Klippstein	8
	Lindy McDaniel	8
	Tug McGraw	8
	Jesse Orosco	8
	Gaylord Perry	8
	Frank Tanana	8
	Early Wynn	8

STRIKEOUTS

1.	Nolan Ryan	5,714
2.	Steve Carlton	4,136
3.	Roger Clemens	3,909
4.	Randy Johnson	3,746
5.	Bert Blyleven	3,701
6.	Tom Seaver	3,640
7.	Don Sutton	3,574
8.	Gaylord Perry	3,534
9.	Walter Johnson	3,509
10.	Phil Niekro	3,342
11.	Fergie Jenkins	3,192
12.	Bob Gibson	3,117
13.	Jim Bunning	2,855
14.	Mickey Lolich	2,832
15.	Cy Young	2,803
16.	Frank Tanana	2,773
17.	David Cone	2,655
18.	Greg Maddux	2,641
19.	Chuck Finley	2,610
20.	Warren Spahn	2,583

STRIKEOUTS, RIGHTHANDER

1.	Nolan Ryan	5,714
2.	Roger Clemens	3,909
3.	Bert Blyleven	3,701
4.	Tom Seaver	3,640
5.	Don Sutton	3,574
6.	Gaylord Perry	3,534
7.	Walter Johnson	3,509
8.	Phil Niekro	3,342
9.	Fergie Jenkins	3,192
10.	Bob Gibson	3,117
11.	Jim Bunning	2,855
12.	Cy Young	2,803
13.	David Cone	2,655
14.	Greg Maddux	2,641
15.	Bob Feller	2,581
16.	Tim Keefe	2,564
17.	Christy Mathewson	2,507
18.	Don Drysdale	2,486
19.	Jack Morris	2,478
20.	Luis Tiant	2,416

STRIKEOUTS, LEFTHANDER

1.	Steve Carlton	4,136
2.	Randy Johnson	3,746
3.	Mickey Lolich	2,832
4.	Frank Tanana	2,773
5.	Chuck Finley	2,610
6.	Warren Spahn	2,583
7.	Jerry Koosman	2,556
8.	Mark Langston	2,464
9.	Jim Kaat	2,461
10.	Sam McDowell	2,453
11.	Sandy Koufax	2,396
12.	Rube Waddell	2,316
13.	Lefty Grove	2,266
14.	Eddie Plank	2,246
15.	Tommy John	2,245
16.	Vida Blue	2,175
17.	Fernando Valenzuela	2,074

18.	Tom Glavine	2,054
19.	Billy Pierce	1,999
20.	Whitey Ford	1,956

WALKS

1.	Nolan Ryan	2,795
2.	Steve Carlton	1,833
3.	Phil Niekro	1,809
4.	Early Wynn	1,775
5.	Bob Feller	1,764
6.	Bobo Newsom	1,732
7.	Amos Rusie	1,707
8.	Charlie Hough	1,665
9.	Gus Weyhing	1,570
10.	Red Ruffing	1,541
11.	Bump Hadley	1,442
12.	Warren Spahn	1,434
13.	Earl Whitehill	1,431
14.	Tony Mullane	1,408
15.	Sam Jones	1,396
16.	Jack Morris	1,390
	Tom Seaver	1,390
18.	Gaylord Perry	1,379
19.	Bobby Witt	1,375
20.	Mike Torrez	1,371

HIT BATSMEN

1.	Gus Weyhing	278
2.	Chick Fraser	219
3.	Pink Hawley	210
4.	Walter Johnson	205
5.	Eddie Plank	190
6.	Tony Mullane	185
7.	Joe McGinnity	179
8.	Charlie Hough	174
9.	Clark Griffith	171
10.	Cy Young	163
11.	Jim Bunning	160
12.	Nolan Ryan	158
13.	Vic Willis	156
14.	Bert Blyleven	155
15.	Don Drysdale	154
16.	Bert Cunningham	148
	Adonis Terry	148
18.	Silver King	146
19.	Win Mercer	144
20.	Frank Foreman	142

WILD PITCHES

1.	Tony Mullane	343
2.	Nolan Ryan	277
3.	Mickey Welch	274
4.	Tim Keefe	240
	Gus Weyhing	240
6.	Phil Niekro	226
7.	Mark Baldwin	221
	Will White	221
9.	Jim Galvin	220
10.	Charley Radbourn	214
	Jim Whitney	214
12.	Jack Morris	206
	Adonis Terry	206
14.	Matt Kilroy	203
15.	Tommy John	187
16.	Steve Carlton	183
17.	John Clarkson	182
18.	Charlie Hough	179
	Toad Ramsey	179
20.	Hardie Henderson	178

FIELDING

GOLD GLOVES, PITCHER

1.	Jim Kaat	16
2.	Greg Maddux	12
3.	Bob Gibson	9
4.	Bobby Shantz	8
5.	Mark Langston	7
6.	Phil Niekro	5
	Ron Guidry	5
	Mike Mussina	5
9.	Jim Palmer	4
10.	Harvey Haddix	3

GOLD GLOVES, CATCHER

1.	Johnny Bench	10
	Ivan Rodriguez	10
3.	Bob Boone	7
4.	Jim Sundberg	6
5.	Bill Freehan	5
6.	Del Crandall	4
	Charles Johnson	4
	Tony Pena	4
9.	Earl Battey	3
	Gary Carter	3
	Sherm Lollar	3
	Thurman Munson	3
	Tom Pagnozzi	3
	Lance Parrish	3
	Benito Santiago	3

GOLD GLOVES, FIRST BASE

1.	Keith Hernandez	11
2.	Don Mattingly	9
3.	George Scott	8
4.	Vic Power	7
	Bill White	7
6.	Wes Parker	6
	J.T. Snow	6
8.	Steve Garvey	4
	Mark Grace	4
10.	Gil Hodges	3
	Eddie Murray	3
	Rafael Palmeiro	3
	Joe Pepitone	3

GOLD GLOVES, SECOND BASE

1.	Roberto Alomar	10
2.	Ryne Sandberg	9
3.	Bill Mazeroski	8
	Frank White	8
5.	Joe Morgan	5
	Bobby Richardson	5
7.	Craig Biggio	4
	Bobby Grich	4
9.	Nellie Fox	3
	Davey Johnson	3
	Bobby Knoop	3
	Harold Reynolds	3
	Manny Trillo	3
	Lou Whitaker	3

GOLD GLOVES, THIRD BASE

1.	Brooks Robinson	16
2.	Mike Schmidt	10
3.	Buddy Bell	6
	Robin Ventura	6
5.	Ken Boyer	5
	Doug Rader	5
	Ron Santo	5
8.	Gary Gaetti	4
	Scott Rolen	4
	Matt Williams	4
11.	Ken Caminiti	3
	Frank Malzone	3
	Terry Pendleton	3
	Tim Wallach	3

GOLD GLOVES, SHORTSTOP

1.	Ozzie Smith	13
2.	Luis Aparicio	9
	Omar Vizquel	9
4.	Mark Belanger	8
5.	Dave Concepcion	5
6.	Tony Fernandez	4
	Alan Trammell	4
8.	Barry Larkin	3
	Roy McMillan	3
	Rey Ordonez	3

GOLD GLOVES, OUTFIELD

1.	Roberto Clemente	12
	Willie Mays	12
3.	Ken Griffey Jr.	10
	Al Kaline	10
5.	Paul Blair	8
	Barry Bonds	8
	Andre Dawson	8
	Dwight Evans	8
	Garry Maddox	8
10.	Curt Flood	7
	Larry Walker	7
	Devon White	7
	Dave Winfield	7
	Carl Yastrzemski	7

UNASSISTED TRIPLE PLAYS

Neal Ball, SS, Indians	7-19-09
*Bill Wambganss, 2B, Indians	10-10-20
George Burns, 1B, Red Sox	9-14-23
Ernie Padgett, SS, Braves	10-6-23
Glenn Wright, SS, Pirates	5-7-25
Jimmy Cooney, SS, Cubs	5-30-27
Johnny Neun, 1B, Tigers	5-31-27
Ron Hansen, SS, Senators	7-30-68
Mickey Morandini, 2B, Phillies	9-20-92
John Valentin, SS, Red Sox	7-8-94
Randy Velarde, 2B, A's	5-29-2000

*World Series game

MANAGERIAL

YEARS AS MANAGER

1.	Connie Mack	53
2.	John McGraw	33
3.	Bucky Harris	29
4.	Sparky Anderson	26
	Gene Mauch	26
6.	Bill McKechnie	25
	Casey Stengel	25
8.	Leo Durocher	24
	Tony La Russa	24
	Joe McCarthy	24
11.	Walter Alston	23
12.	Bobby Cox	21
	Jimmy Dykes	21
	Tom Lasorda	21
	Joe Torre	21
	Dick Williams	21
17.	Cap Anson	20
	Clark Griffith	20
	Ralph Houk	20
20.	Fred Clarke	19
	Charlie Grimm	19
	Ned Hanlon	19
	John McNamara	19
	Wilbert Robinson	19
	Chuck Tanner	19

VICTORIES, MANAGER

1.	Connie Mack	3,731
2.	John McGraw	2,763
3.	Sparky Anderson	2,194
4.	Bucky Harris	2,157
5.	Joe McCarthy	2,125
6.	Walter Alston	2,040
7.	Leo Durocher	2,008
8.	Tony La Russa	1,924
9.	Casey Stengel	1,905
10.	Gene Mauch	1,902
11.	Bill McKechnie	1,896
12.	Bobby Cox	1,805
13.	Ralph Houk	1,619
14.	Fred Clarke	1,602
15.	Tom Lasorda	1,599
16.	Dick Williams	1,571
17.	Joe Torre	1,558
18.	Clark Griffith	1,491
19.	Earl Weaver	1,480
20.	Miller Huggins	1,413

TEAMS MANAGED

1.	Frank Bancroft	7
2.	Jack Chapman	6
	Jimmy Dykes	6
	Bob Ferguson	6
	Rogers Hornsby	6
	Tom Loftus	6
	John McNamara	6
	Dick Williams	6
9.	John Clapp	5
	Patsy Donovan	5
	Chuck Dressen	5
	Ned Hanlon	5
	Bucky Harris	5
	Billy Martin	5
	Bill McKechnie	5
	Gus Schmelz	5
	Bill Watkins	5
	Don Zimmer	5

PENNANTS WON, MANAGER

1.	John McGraw	10
	Casey Stengel	10
3.	Connie Mack	9
	Joe McCarthy	9
5.	Walter Alston	7
6.	Miller Huggins	6
7.	Sparky Anderson	5
	Cap Anson	5
	Fred Clarke	5
	Bobby Cox	5
	Ned Hanlon	5
	Frank Selee	5
	Joe Torre	5
14.	Frank Chance	4
	Charlie Comiskey	4
	Tom Lasorda	4
	Bill McKechnie	4
	Billy Southworth	4
	Earl Weaver	4
	Dick Williams	4

WORLD SERIES WON, MANAGER

1.	Joe McCarthy	7
	Casey Stengel	7
3.	Connie Mack	5
4.	Walter Alston	4
	Joe Torre	4
6.	Sparky Anderson	3
	Miller Huggins	3
	John McGraw	3
9.	Bill Carrigan	2
	Frank Chance	2
	Cito Gaston	2
	Bucky Harris	2
	Ralph Houk	2
	Tom Kelly	2
	Tom Lasorda	2
	Bill McKechnie	2
	Danny Murtaugh	2
	Billy Southworth	2
	Dick Williams	2

LEAGUE CHAMPIONSHIP SERIES

SERVICE

SERIES PLAYED

Rank	Player	Total
1.	Reggie Jackson	11
2.	Tom Glavine	9
	John Smoltz	9
4.	Richie Hebner	8
	David Justice	8
	Greg Maddux	8
	Hal McRae	8
	Bob Welch	8
9.	Don Baylor	7
	Paul Blair	7
	Rickey Henderson	7
	Rick Honeycutt	7
	Tino Martinez	7
	Joe Morgan	7
	Graig Nettles	7
	Jim Palmer	7
	Pete Rose	7
	Mark Wohlers	7
19.	many tied with 6	

SERIES PITCHED

Rank	Player	Total
1.	Tom Glavine	9
	John Smoltz	9
3.	Greg Maddux	8
	Bob Welch	8
5.	Rick Honeycutt	7
	Mark Wohlers	7
7.	Roger Clemens	6
	David Cone	6
	Dennis Eckersley	6
	Don Gullett	6
	Catfish Hunter	6
	Jimmy Key	6
	Tug McGraw	6
	Jeff Nelson	6
	Jim Palmer	6
	Ron Reed	6
	Mike Stanton	6
18.	many tied with 5	

BATTING

GAMES

Rank	Player	Total
1.	David Justice	46
2.	Reggie Jackson	45
3.	Terry Pendleton	38
4.	Tino Martinez	37
5.	Chipper Jones	34
	John Olerud	34
7.	Rickey Henderson	33
8.	Ron Gant	31
	Mark Lemke	31
	Paul O'Neill	31
11.	Jeff Blauser	29
12.	Roberto Alomar	28
	Don Baylor	28
	Fred McGriff	28
	Hal McRae	28
	Pete Rose	28
17.	many tied with 27	

HIGHEST AVERAGE

(Minimum 50 at-bats)

Rank	Player	Avg.
1.	Will Clark	.468
2.	Mickey Rivers	.386
3.	Pete Rose	.381
4.	Dusty Baker	.371
5.	Bernie Williams	.360
6.	Steve Garvey	.356
7.	Brooks Robinson	.348
8.	Devon White	.347
9.	George Brett	.340
10.	Thurman Munson	.339
11.	Tony Fernandez	.338
12.	Bill Russell	.337
13.	Harold Baines	.333
14.	Cal Ripken Jr.	.328
15.	Lenny Dykstra	.323
16.	Paul O'Neill	.321
17.	Darrell Porter	.317
18.	Carney Lansford	.316
	Roberto Alomar	.316
20.	Chipper Jones	.315

AT-BATS

Rank	Player	Total
1.	David Justice	166
2.	Reggie Jackson	163
3.	Tino Martinez	141
4.	Terry Pendleton	135
5.	John Olerud	131
6.	Chipper Jones	127
7.	Rickey Henderson	123
8.	Pete Rose	118
9.	Ron Gant	117
10.	Roberto Alomar	114
11.	Mark Lemke	110
12.	Fred McGriff	109
13.	Derek Jeter	108
14.	Paul O'Neill	106
15.	Chuck Knoblauch	104
16.	George Brett	103
17.	Bernie Williams	100
18.	Kenny Lofton	99
19.	Don Baylor	96
	Joe Morgan	96

RUNS SCORED

Rank	Player	Total
1.	David Justice	24
2.	George Brett	22
	Rickey Henderson	22
	Bernie Williams	22
5.	Chipper Jones	20
6.	Jeff Blauser	18
	Fred McGriff	18
	John Olerud	18
9.	Ron Gant	17
	Derek Jeter	17
	Tino Martinez	17
	Pete Rose	17
13.	Reggie Jackson	16
	Devon White	16
	Barry Bonds	15
16.	Steve Garvey	15
	Andruw Jones	15
	Chuck Knoblauch	15
	Willie McGee	15
20.	5 tied with 14	

HITS

Rank	Player	Total
1.	Pete Rose	45
2.	Chipper Jones	40
3.	David Justice	39
4.	John Olerud	38
5.	Reggie Jackson	37
6.	Roberto Alomar	36
	Bernie Williams	36
8.	George Brett	35
9.	Fred McGriff	34
	Paul O'Neill	34
11.	Devon White	33
12.	Steve Garvey	32
13.	Derek Jeter	31
	Mark Lemke	31
15.	Rickey Henderson	30
	Chuck Knoblauch	30
	Terry Pendleton	30
18.	Will Clark	29
	Tino Martinez	29
20.	Bill Russell	28

SINGLES

Rank	Player	Total
1.	Pete Rose	34
2.	Chipper Jones	30
3.	Roberto Alomar	29
4.	John Olerud	27
5.	David Justice	26
	Devon White	26
7.	Bill Russell	25
8.	Bob Boone	24
	Reggie Jackson	24
	Mark Lemke	24
	Paul O'Neill	24
12.	Chuck Knoblauch	23
	Fred McGriff	23
	Bernie Williams	23
15.	Derek Jeter	22
	Carney Lansford	22
	Terry Pendleton	22
18.	Tony Fernandez	20
	Steve Garvey	20
	Kenny Lofton	20
	Tino Martinez	20

DOUBLES

Rank	Player	Total
1.	Ron Cey	7
	Will Clark	7
	Richie Hebner	7
	Rickey Henderson	7
	Reggie Jackson	7
	Chipper Jones	7
	David Justice	7
	Chuck Knoblauch	7
	Javy Lopez	7
	Fred McGriff	7
	Hal McRae	7
	Pete Rose	7
	Mike Schmidt	7
14.	Doug De Cinces	6
	Tony Fernandez	6
	Mark Lemke	6
	Greg Luzinski	6
	Tino Martinez	6
	John Olerud	6
	Tim Raines Sr.	6
	Brooks Robinson	6
	Andy Van Slyke	6
	Roy White	6
	Bernie Williams	6

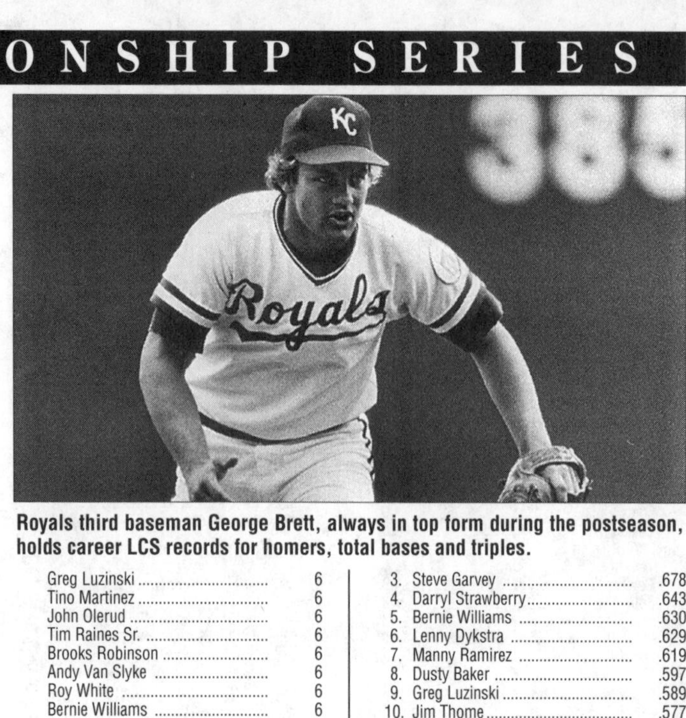

Royals third baseman George Brett, always in top form during the postseason, holds career LCS records for homers, total bases and triples.

TRIPLES

Rank	Player	Total
1.	George Brett	4
2.	Mariano Duncan	3
	Keith Lockhart	3
	Kenny Lofton	3
	Willie McGee	3
6.	Johnny Bench	2
	Jeff Blauser	2
	Rickey Henderson	2
	Jose Lind	2
	Davey Lopes	2
	Terry Pendleton	2
	Luis Salazar	2
	Ozzie Smith	2
	Andy Van Slyke	2
15.	many tied with 1	1

HOME RUNS

Rank	Player	Total
1.	George Brett	9
2.	Steve Garvey	8
3.	Darryl Strawberry	7
	Bernie Williams	7
5.	Reggie Jackson	6
	David Justice	6
	Manny Ramirez	6
	Jim Thome	6
9.	Sal Bando	5
	Johnny Bench	5
	Ron Gant	5
	Javy Lopez	5
	Greg Luzinski	5
	Gary Matthews	5
	Graig Nettles	5
	John Olerud	5
	Paul O'Neill	5
18.	many tied with 4.	

TOTAL BASES

Rank	Player	Total
1.	George Brett	75
2.	David Justice	64
3.	Pete Rose	63
	Bernie Williams	63
5.	Reggie Jackson	62
6.	Steve Garvey	61
7.	John Olerud	59
8.	Chipper Jones	56
9.	Paul O'Neill	54
10.	Fred McGriff	52
11.	Will Clark	50
12.	Roberto Alomar	49
	Derek Jeter	49
	Javy Lopez	49
15.	Rickey Henderson	47
16.	Ron Gant	45
	Darryl Strawberry	45
18.	Johnny Bench	44
	Tino Martinez	44
20.	Greg Luzinski	43
	Devon White	43

SLUGGING PERCENTAGE

(Minimum 50 at-bats)

Rank	Player	Pct.
1.	Will Clark	.806
2.	George Brett	.728
3.	Steve Garvey	.678
4.	Darryl Strawberry	.643
5.	Bernie Williams	.630
6.	Lenny Dykstra	.629
7.	Manny Ramirez	.619
8.	Dusty Baker	.597
9.	Greg Luzinski	.589
10.	Jim Thome	.577
11.	Javy Lopez	.544
12.	Pete Rose	.534
13.	Johnny Bench	.530
14.	Sal Bando	.527
15.	Brooks Robinson	.522
16.	Dave Henderson	.520
17.	Paul O'Neill	.509
18.	Ron Cey	.500
	Thurman Munson	.500
20.	Graig Nettles	.494

EXTRA-BASE HITS

Rank	Player	Total
1.	George Brett	18
2.	Reggie Jackson	13
	David Justice	13
	Bernie Williams	13
5.	Will Clark	12
	Steve Garvey	12
	Javy Lopez	12
	Greg Luzinski	12
9.	Johnny Bench	11
	Ron Cey	11
	Rickey Henderson	11
	Fred McGriff	11
	John Olerud	11
	Pete Rose	11
15.	Lenny Dykstra	10
	Ron Gant	10
	Richie Hebner	10
	Chipper Jones	10
	Paul O'Neill	10
	Darryl Strawberry	10

RUNS BATTED IN

Rank	Player	Total
1.	David Justice	27
2.	Steve Garvey	21
	John Olerud	21
	Bernie Williams	21
5.	Reggie Jackson	20
6.	George Brett	19
	Graig Nettles	19
8.	Fred McGriff	18
	Paul O'Neill	18
10.	Don Baylor	17
	Ron Gant	17
	Darryl Strawberry	17
13.	Roberto Alomar	15
	Chipper Jones	15
	Al Oliver	15
16.	Ron Cey	14
	Javy Lopez	14
	Terry Pendleton	14
19.	9 tied with 13	

WALKS

Rank	Player	Total
1.	Barry Bonds	24
	Chipper Jones	24
	David Justice	24
4.	Joe Morgan	23
5.	Bernie Williams	21
6.	Rickey Henderson	19
7.	Reggie Jackson	17
8.	Darrell Porter	16
	Jorge Posada	16

10. Roberto Alomar 15
Jeff Blauser 15
Ryan Klesko 15
Chuck Knoblauch 15
Mark Lemke 15
Tino Martinez 15
John Olerud 15
Robin Ventura 14
18. Ron Cey 13
Gene Tenace 13
20. Derek Jeter 12
Fred McGriff 12
Eddie Murray 12

STRIKEOUTS

1. Reggie Jackson 41
2. Tino Martinez 30
3. David Justice 28
4. Ron Gant 26
5. Cesar Geronimo 24
Rickey Henderson 24
Kenny Lofton 24
8. Jeff Blauser 23
Chipper Jones 23
Fred McGriff 23
11. Bobby Grich 22
Derek Jeter 22
Devon White 22
14. Marquis Grissom 21
Willie McGee 21
Darryl Strawberry 21
17. Mariano Duncan 20
Javy Lopez 20
Greg Luzinski 20
Bernie Williams 20

STOLEN BASES

1. Rickey Henderson 17
2. Roberto Alomar 11
3. Davey Lopes 9
4. Ron Gant 8
Kenny Lofton 8
Joe Morgan 8
Amos Otis 8
Willie Wilson 8
9. Omar Vizquel 7
10. Barry Bonds 6
Bert Campaneris 6
Vince Coleman 6
Kirk Gibson 6
Derek Jeter 6
Steve Sax 6
Walt Weiss 6
17. Tony Fernandez 5
Ken Griffey Jr. 5
Marquis Grissom 5
Chipper Jones 5
Otis Nixon 5

PITCHING

GAMES

1. Rick Honeycutt 20
2. Mark Wohlers 19
3. Dennis Eckersley 18
Randy Myers 18
5. John Smoltz 17
Mike Stanton 17
7. Mariano Rivera 16
8. Armando Benitez 15
Tom Glavine 15
Greg Maddux 15
Tug McGraw 15
Jeff Nelson 15
13. Jesse Orosco 14
14. Paul Assenmacher 13
Dave Giusti 13
Alejandro Pena 13
Ron Reed 13
18. Tom Henke 12
Mike Jackson 12
John Rocker 12

GAMES STARTED

1. Tom Glavine 15
2. Greg Maddux 14
3. John Smoltz 13
4. Catfish Hunter 10
Dave Stewart 10
6. Roger Clemens 9
7. Steve Carlton 8
David Cone 8
Orel Hershiser 8
10. Steve Avery 7
Doug Drabek 7
Tommy John 7
Jim Palmer 7
Andy Pettitte 7
Jerry Reuss 7
16. 8 tied with 6

GAMES RELIEVED

1. Rick Honeycutt 20
2. Mark Wohlers 19
3. Randy Myers 18
4. Dennis Eckersley 17
Mike Stanton 17
6. Mariano Rivera 16
7. Armando Benitez 15
Tug McGraw 15
Jeff Nelson 15
10. Jesse Orosco 14
11. Paul Assenmacher 13
Dave Giusti 13
Alejandro Pena 13
14. Tom Henke 12
Mike Jackson 12
Ron Reed 12
John Rocker 12
18. Rollie Fingers 11
Jose Mesa 11
Arthur Lee Rhodes 11
Duane Ward 11

COMPLETE GAMES

1. Jim Palmer 5
2. Catfish Hunter 3
Tommy John 3
4. Mike Boddicker 2
Kevin Brown 2
Danny Cox 2
Mike Cuellar 2
Doug Drabek 2
Orel Hershiser 2
Ken Holtzman 2
Bruce Hurst 2
Dennis Leonard 2
Dave McNally 2
Jack Morris 2
Mike Scott 2
Don Sutton 2
Tim Wakefield 2
18. many tied with 1

INNINGS PITCHED

1. John Smoltz 95.1
2. Tom Glavine 92.1
3. Greg Maddux 85.1
4. Dave Stewart 75.1
5. Catfish Hunter 69.1
6. Orel Hershiser 65.1
7. Jim Palmer 59.2
8. Steve Carlton 53.2
9. Roger Clemens 53.1
10. David Cone 51.0
11. Don Sutton 49.0
12. Doug Drabek 48.1
13. Andy Pettitte 48.0
14. Tommy John 47.2
15. Steve Avery 45.1
16. Mike Cuellar 44.0
17. Dwight Gooden 42.1
18. Orlando Hernandez 42.0
19. Nolan Ryan 41.1
20. Don Gullett 40.2
Jack Morris 40.2

LOWEST ERA

(Minimum 30 innings)

1. Orel Hershiser 1.52
2. Randy Johnson 1.72
3. Fernando Valenzuela 1.95
4. Jim Palmer 1.96
5. Don Sutton 2.02
6. Dave Stewart 2.03
7. Doug Drabek 2.05
8. Ken Holtzman 2.06
9. Tommy John 2.08
10. Juan Guzman 2.27
11. Dwight Gooden 2.34
12. Steve Avery 2.38
13. Charles Nagy 2.64
14. Paul Splittorff 2.68
Dave McNally 2.68
16. John Smoltz 2.83
17. Tom Seaver 2.84
18. Danny Jackson 2.94
19. Orlando Hernandez 3.00
John Tudor 3.00

VICTORIES

1. Dave Stewart 8
2. John Smoltz 6
3. Tom Glavine 5
Juan Guzman 5
Andy Pettitte 5
6. Steve Avery 4
Steve Carlton 4
David Cone 4
Orlando Hernandez 4
Orel Hershiser 4
Catfish Hunter 4
Tommy John 4
Bruce Kison 4
Greg Maddux 4
Jim Palmer 4
Don Sutton 4
17. many tied with 3 3

LOSSES

1. Tom Glavine 9
2. Greg Maddux 8
3. Jerry Reuss 7
4. Doug Drabek 5
5. Doyle Alexander 4
Todd Stottlemyre 4
7. Roger Clemens 3
Alex Fernandez 3
Gene Garber 3
Don Gullett 3
Ken Holtzman 3
Catfish Hunter 3
Charlie Leibrandt 3
Dennis Leonard 3
Chad Ogea 3
Aaron Sele 3
Zane Smith 3
Dave Stieb 3
19. many tied with 2

SAVES

1. Dennis Eckersley 11
2. Mariano Rivera 6
3. Tug McGraw 5
Robb Nen 5
5. Ken Dayley 4
Dave Giusti 4
Randy Myers 4
Alejandro Pena 4
9. Rick Aguilera 3
Steve Bedrosian 3
Armando Benitez 3
Pedro Borbon 3
Rich Gossage 3
Tom Henke 3
Jose Mesa 3
Jeff Reardon 3
Duane Ward 3
18. 10 tied with 2

RUNS ALLOWED

1. Greg Maddux 50
2. Tom Glavine 40
3. John Smoltz 33
4. Catfish Hunter 25
Jerry Reuss 25
Todd Stottlemyre 25
7. Doyle Alexander 23
Roger Clemens 23
David Cone 23
10. Steve Carlton 22
Jack Morris 22
12. Andy Pettitte 20
13. Andy Benes 19
Nolan Ryan 19
15. Scott Erickson 18
Don Gullett 18
Bob Welch 18
18. Ed Figueroa 17
Tommy John 17
Dave Stewart 17

HITS ALLOWED

1. Tom Glavine 91
2. Greg Maddux 86
3. John Smoltz 81
4. Catfish Hunter 57
5. Steve Carlton 53
6. Dave Stewart 52
7. Orel Hershiser 49
8. Jim Palmer 46
Andy Pettitte 46
10. David Cone 45
11. Roger Clemens 43
Larry Gura 43
13. Doug Drabek 40
Tommy John 40
15. Jack Morris 39
16. Danny Jackson 38
Todd Stottlemyre 38
18. Jimmy Key 37
Jerry Reuss 37
Don Sutton 37

HOME RUNS ALLOWED

1. Catfish Hunter 12
2. Tom Glavine 8
Andy Pettitte 8
John Smoltz 8
5. Dave McNally 7
Dave Stewart 7
7. Doyle Alexander 6
Steve Blass 6
Scott Erickson 6
Greg Maddux 6
Jim Perry 6
12. Andy Benes 5
Steve Carlton 5
David Cone 5
Bruce Hurst 5
Jim Palmer 5
Tom Seaver 5
Aaron Sele 5
Eric Show 5
Todd Stottlemyre 5
Don Sutton 5
John Tudor 5

TOTAL BASES ALLOWED

1. Tom Glavine 142
2. Greg Maddux 125
John Smoltz 125
4. Catfish Hunter 112
5. Steve Carlton 85
6. Dave Stewart 80
7. Andy Pettitte 77
8. Jim Palmer 75
9. David Cone 69
10. Doyle Alexander 63
Larry Gura 63
Todd Stottlemyre 63
13. Roger Clemens 61
14. Orel Hershiser 60
Jack Morris 60
16. Dave McNally 59
Don Sutton 59
18. Bob Welch 58
19. Scott Erickson 57
Jimmy Key 57
Dennis Leonard 57

STRIKEOUTS

1. John Smoltz 89
2. Greg Maddux 64
3. Tom Glavine 62
4. Roger Clemens 53
5. Orel Hershiser 47
6. Jim Palmer 46
Nolan Ryan 46
8. David Cone 45
9. Orlando Hernandez 40
10. Steve Carlton 39
Dave Stewart 39
12. Steve Avery 37
Catfish Hunter 37
David Wells 37
15. Mike Mussina 34
16. Doug Drabek 33
Dwight Gooden 33
Denny Neagle 33
19. Randy Johnson 32
20. Curt Schilling 31

WALKS

1. Tom Glavine 37
2. John Smoltz 34
3. Steve Carlton 28
4. Greg Maddux 25
Dave Stewart 25
6. David Cone 24
7. Orlando Hernandez 21
8. Roger Clemens 20
Orel Hershiser 20
10. Mike Cuellar 19
Jim Palmer 19
Fernando Valenzuela 19
13. Juan Guzman 18
Catfish Hunter 18
15. Steve Avery 17
Jerry Reuss 17
17. Dwight Gooden 16
Tug McGraw 16
Denny Neagle 16
Dave Stieb 16

WORLD SERIES

SERVICE

SERIES PLAYED

	Player	
1.	Yogi Berra	14
2.	Mickey Mantle	12
3.	Whitey Ford	11
4.	Joe DiMaggio	10
	Elston Howard	10
	Babe Ruth	10
7.	Hank Bauer	9
	Phil Rizzuto	9
9.	Bill Dickey	8
	Frankie Frisch	8
	Gil McDougald	8
	Bill Skowron	8
13.	Joe Collins	7
	Frankie Crosetti	7
	Carl Furillo	7
	Lou Gehrig	7
	Jim Gilliam	7
	Gil Hodges	7
	Waite Hoyt	7
	Tony Lazzeri	7
	Roger Maris	7
	Pee Wee Reese	7
	Bobby Richardson	7
	Red Ruffing	7

SERIES PITCHED

	Player	
1.	Whitey Ford	11
2.	Waite Hoyt	7
	Red Ruffing	7
4.	Catfish Hunter	6
	Johnny Murphy	6
	Jim Palmer	6
	Vic Raschi	6
	Allie Reynolds	6
	Mike Stanton	6
10.	Chief Bender	5
	Joe Bush	5
	David Cone	5
	Don Drysdale	5
	Carl Erskine	5
	Tom Glavine	5
	Lefty Gomez	5
	Don Gullett	5
	Clem Labine	5
	Don Larsen	5
	Ed Lopat	5
	Rube Marquard	5
	Art Nehf	5
	Herb Pennock	5
	Andy Pettitte	5
	Mariano Rivera	5
	Bob Shawkey	5
	John Smoltz	5
	Dave Stewart	5
	Ralph Terry	5
	Bob Turley	5

BATTING

GAMES

	Player	
1.	Yogi Berra	75
2.	Mickey Mantle	65
3.	Elston Howard	54
4.	Hank Bauer	53
	Gil McDougald	53
6.	Phil Rizzuto	52
7.	Joe DiMaggio	51
8.	Frankie Frisch	50
9.	Pee Wee Reese	44
10.	Roger Maris	41
	Babe Ruth	41
12.	Carl Furillo	40
13.	Jim Gilliam	39
	Gil Hodges	39
	Bill Skowron	39
16.	Bill Dickey	38
	Jackie Robinson	38
18.	Tony Kubek	37
19.	Joe Collins	36
	David Justice	36
	Bobby Richardson	36
	Duke Snider	36

HIGHEST AVERAGE

(Minimum 50 at-bats)

	Player	
1.	Pepper Martin	.418
	Paul Molitor	.418
3.	Lou Brock	.391
4.	Marquis Grissom	.390
5.	Thurman Munson	.373
	George Brett	.373
7.	Hank Aaron	.364
8.	Frank Baker	.363
9.	Roberto Clemente	.362
10.	Lou Gehrig	.361
11.	Reggie Jackson	.357
12.	Carl Yastrzemski	.352
13.	Earle Combs	.350
14.	Stan Hack	.348
15.	Joe Jackson	.345
16.	Jimmie Foxx	.344
17.	Rickey Henderson	.339
18.	Julian Javier	.333
	Billy Martin	.333
20.	Al Simmons	.329

AT-BATS

	Player	
1.	Yogi Berra	259
2.	Mickey Mantle	230
3.	Joe DiMaggio	199
4.	Frankie Frisch	197
5.	Gil McDougald	190
6.	Hank Bauer	188
7.	Phil Rizzuto	183
8.	Elston Howard	171
9.	Pee Wee Reese	169
10.	Roger Maris	152
11.	Jim Gilliam	147
12.	Tony Kubek	146
13.	Bill Dickey	145
14.	Jackie Robinson	137
15.	Bill Skowron	133
	Duke Snider	133
17.	Gil Hodges	131
	Bobby Richardson	131
19.	Pete Rose	130
20.	Goose Goslin	129
	Bob Meusel	129
	Babe Ruth	129

RUNS SCORED

	Player	
1.	Mickey Mantle	42
2.	Yogi Berra	41
3.	Babe Ruth	37
4.	Lou Gehrig	30
5.	Joe DiMaggio	27
6.	Roger Maris	26
7.	Elston Howard	25
8.	Gil McDougald	23
9.	Derek Jeter	22
	Jackie Robinson	22
11.	Hank Bauer	21
	Reggie Jackson	21
	Phil Rizzuto	21
	Duke Snider	21
	Gene Woodling	21
16.	Eddie Collins	20
	Pee Wee Reese	20
18.	Bill Dickey	19
	Frank Robinson	19
	Bill Skowron	19

HITS

	Player	
1.	Yogi Berra	71
2.	Mickey Mantle	59
3.	Frankie Frisch	58
4.	Joe DiMaggio	54
5.	Hank Bauer	46
	Pee Wee Reese	46
7.	Gil McDougald	45
	Phil Rizzuto	45
9.	Lou Gehrig	43
10.	Eddie Collins	42
	Elston Howard	42
	Babe Ruth	42
13.	Bobby Richardson	40
14.	Bill Skowron	39
15.	Duke Snider	38
16.	Bill Dickey	37
	Goose Goslin	37
18.	Steve Garvey	36
19.	Gil Hodges	35
	Reggie Jackson	35
	Tony Kubek	35
	Pete Rose	35

SINGLES

	Player	
1.	Yogi Berra	49
2.	Frankie Frisch	45
3.	Joe DiMaggio	40
	Phil Rizzuto	40
5.	Pee Wee Reese	39
6.	Hank Bauer	34
7.	Eddie Collins	33
	Mickey Mantle	33
	Gil McDougald	33
10.	Tony Kubek	31
	Bobby Richardson	31
12.	Bill Dickey	30
13.	Steve Garvey	29
	Elston Howard	29
15.	Red Rolfe	28
16.	Gil Hodges	27
	Pete Rose	27
18.	Bill Skowron	26
19.	Goose Goslin	25
	Marquis Grissom	25

DOUBLES

	Player	
1.	Yogi Berra	10
	Frankie Frisch	10
3.	Jack Barry	9
	Pete Fox	9
	Carl Furillo	9
6.	Lou Gehrig	8
	Lonnie Smith	8
	Duke Snider	8
9.	Frank Baker	7
	Lou Brock	7
	Eddie Collins	7
	Rick Dempsey	7
	Hank Greenberg	7
	Chick Hafey	7
	Elston Howard	7
	Reggie Jackson	7
	Marty Marion	7
	Pepper Martin	7
	Danny Murphy	7
	Stan Musial	7
	Terry Pendleton	7
	Jackie Robinson	7
	Devon White	7

TRIPLES

	Player	
1.	Billy Johnson	4
	Tommy Leach	4
	Tris Speaker	4
4.	Hank Bauer	3
	Bobby Brown	3
	Dave Concepcion	3
	Buck Freeman	3
	Frankie Frisch	3
	Lou Gehrig	3
	Dan Gladden	3
	Mark Lemke	3
	Billy Martin	3
	Tim McCarver	3
	Bob Meusel	3
	Freddy Parent	3
	Chick Stahl	3
	Devon White	3
18.	many tied with 2	

HOME RUNS

	Player	
1.	Mickey Mantle	18
2.	Babe Ruth	15
3.	Yogi Berra	12
4.	Duke Snider	11
5.	Lou Gehrig	10
	Reggie Jackson	10
7.	Joe DiMaggio	8
	Frank Robinson	8
	Bill Skowron	8
10.	Hank Bauer	7
	Goose Goslin	7
	Gil McDougald	7
13.	Lenny Dykstra	6
	Roger Maris	6
	Al Simmons	6
	Reggie Smith	6
17.	Johnny Bench	5
	Bill Dickey	5
	Hank Greenberg	5
	Gil Hodges	5
	Elston Howard	5
	Charlie Keller	5
	Billy Martin	5

TOTAL BASES

	Player	
1.	Mickey Mantle	123
2.	Yogi Berra	117
3.	Babe Ruth	96
4.	Lou Gehrig	87
5.	Joe DiMaggio	84
6.	Duke Snider	79
7.	Hank Bauer	75
8.	Frankie Frisch	74
	Reggie Jackson	74
10.	Gil McDougald	72
11.	Bill Skowron	69
12.	Elston Howard	66
13.	Goose Goslin	63
14.	Pee Wee Reese	59
15.	Lou Brock	57
16.	Roger Maris	56
	Billy Martin	56
18.	Bill Dickey	55
19.	Gil Hodges	54
	Phil Rizzuto	54

SLUGGING PERCENTAGE

(Minimum 50 at-bats)

	Player	
1.	Reggie Jackson	.755
2.	Babe Ruth	.744
3.	Lou Gehrig	.731
4.	Lenny Dykstra	.700
5.	Al Simmons	.658
6.	Lou Brock	.655
7.	Pepper Martin	.636
	Paul Molitor	.636
9.	Hank Greenberg	.624
10.	Charlie Keller	.611
11.	Jimmie Foxx	.609
12.	Rickey Henderson	.607
13.	Dave Henderson	.606
14.	Hank Aaron	.600
15.	Duke Snider	.594
16.	Dwight Evans	.580
17.	Steve Yeager	.579
18.	Willie Stargell	.574
19.	Billy Martin	.566
20.	Carl Yastrzemski	.556

EXTRA-BASE HITS

	Player	
1.	Mickey Mantle	26
2.	Yogi Berra	22
	Babe Ruth	22
4.	Lou Gehrig	21
5.	Duke Snider	19
6.	Reggie Jackson	18
7.	Joe DiMaggio	14
	Hank Greenberg	14
9.	Lou Brock	13
	Frankie Frisch	13
	Elston Howard	13
	Bill Skowron	13
	Lonnie Smith	13
14.	Hank Bauer	12
	Goose Goslin	12
	Gil McDougald	12
	Al Simmons	12
18.	Carl Furillo	11
	Dave Henderson	11
	Roger Maris	11
	Frank Robinson	11
	Devon White	11

RUNS BATTED IN

	Player	
1.	Mickey Mantle	40
2.	Yogi Berra	39
3.	Lou Gehrig	35
4.	Babe Ruth	33
5.	Joe DiMaggio	30
6.	Bill Skowron	29
7.	Duke Snider	26
8.	Hank Bauer	24
	Bill Dickey	24
	Reggie Jackson	24
	Gil McDougald	24
12.	Hank Greenberg	22
13.	Gil Hodges	21
	David Justice	21
15.	Goose Goslin	19
	Elston Howard	19
	Tony Lazzeri	19
	Billy Martin	19
19.	Frank Baker	18
	Charlie Keller	18
	Roger Maris	18

WALKS

1.	Mickey Mantle	43
2.	Babe Ruth	33
3.	Yogi Berra	32
4.	Phil Rizzuto	30
5.	Lou Gehrig	26
	David Justice	26
7.	Mickey Cochrane	25
8.	Jim Gilliam	23
9.	Jackie Robinson	21
10.	Gil McDougald	20
11.	Joe DiMaggio	19
	Gene Woodling	19
13.	Roger Maris	18
	Pee Wee Reese	18
	Bernie Williams	18
16.	Gil Hodges	17
	Gene Tenace	17
	Ross Youngs	17
19.	Paul O'Neill	16
	Pete Rose	16

STRIKEOUTS

1.	Mickey Mantle	54
2.	Elston Howard	37
3.	Duke Snider	33
4.	David Justice	30
	Babe Ruth	30
6.	Gil McDougald	29
7.	Derek Jeter	26
	Bill Skowron	26
9.	Hank Bauer	25
10.	Reggie Jackson	24
	Bob Meusel	24
	Bernie Williams	24
13.	Joe DiMaggio	23
	George Kelly	23
	Tony Kubek	23
	Frank Robinson	23
	Devon White	23
18.	Jim Bottomley	22
	Joe Collins	22
	Gil Hodges	22
	Lonnie Smith	22

STOLEN BASES

1.	Lou Brock	14
	Eddie Collins	14
3.	Frank Chance	10
	Davey Lopes	10
	Phil Rizzuto	10
6.	Frankie Frisch	9
	Honus Wagner	9
8.	Johnny Evers	8
9.	Roberto Alomar	7
	Rickey Henderson	7
	Pepper Martin	7
	Joe Morgan	7
	Joe Tinker	7
14.	Vince Coleman	6
	Chuck Knoblauch	6
	Kenny Lofton	6
	Jackie Robinson	6
	Jimmy Slagle	6
	Bobby Tolan	6
	Omar Vizquel	6
	Maury Wills	6

PITCHING

GAMES

1.	Whitey Ford	22
2.	Mike Stanton	20
3.	Mariano Rivera	18
4.	Rollie Fingers	16
5.	Allie Reynolds	15
	Bob Turley	15
7.	Clay Carroll	14
8.	Clem Labine	13
	Jeff Nelson	13
	Mark Wohlers	13
11.	Waite Hoyt	12
	Catfish Hunter	12
	Art Nehf	12
14.	Paul Derringer	11
	Carl Erskine	11
	Rube Marquard	11
	Christy Mathewson	11
	Vic Raschi	11
19.	8 tied with 10	

GAMES STARTED

1.	Whitey Ford	22
2.	Waite Hoyt	11
	Christy Mathewson	11
4.	Chief Bender	10
	Red Ruffing	10
6.	Bob Gibson	9
	Catfish Hunter	9
	Art Nehf	9
	Allie Reynolds	9
10.	George Earnshaw	8
	Tom Glavine	8
	Rube Marquard	8
	Jim Palmer	8
	Andy Pettitte	8
	Vic Raschi	8
	John Smoltz	8
	Dave Stewart	8
	Don Sutton	8
	Bob Turley	8
20.	many tied with 7	

GAMES RELIEVED

1.	Mike Stanton	20
2.	Mariano Rivera	18
3.	Rollie Fingers	16
4.	Clay Carroll	14
5.	Jeff Nelson	13
	Mark Wohlers	13
7.	Clem Labine	12
8.	Pedro Borbon	10
	Dan Quisenberry	10
10.	Paul Assenmacher	9
	Hugh Casey	9
	Tug McGraw	9
13.	Ken Dayley	8
	Rich Gossage	8
	Don McMahon	8
	Johnny Murphy	8
	Duane Ward	8
18.	many tied with 7	

COMPLETE GAMES

1.	Christy Mathewson	10
2.	Chief Bender	9
3.	Bob Gibson	8
	Red Ruffing	8
5.	Whitey Ford	7
6.	Waite Hoyt	6
	George Mullin	6
	Art Nehf	6
	Eddie Plank	6
10.	Mordecai Brown	5
	Joe Bush	5
	Bill Donovan	5
	George Earnshaw	5
	Walter Johnson	5
	Carl Mays	5
	Deacon Phillippe	5
	Allie Reynolds	5
18.	many tied with 4	

INNINGS PITCHED

1.	Whitey Ford	146.0
2.	Christy Mathewson	101.2
3.	Red Ruffing	85.2
4.	Chief Bender	85.0
5.	Waite Hoyt	83.2
6.	Bob Gibson	81.0
7.	Art Nehf	79.0
8.	Allie Reynolds	77.1
9.	Jim Palmer	64.2
10.	Catfish Hunter	63.0
11.	George Earnshaw	62.2
12.	Joe Bush	60.2
13.	Vic Raschi	60.1
14.	Rube Marquard	58.2
15.	Tom Glavine	58.1
16.	George Mullin	58.0
17.	Mordecai Brown	57.2
18.	Carl Mays	57.1
19.	Sandy Koufax	57.0
	Dave Stewart	57.0

LOWEST ERA

(Minimum 30 innings)

1.	Harry Brecheen	0.83
2.	Babe Ruth	0.87
3.	Sherry Smith	0.89
4.	Sandy Koufax	0.95
5.	Monte Pearson	1.01
6.	Christy Mathewson	1.06
7.	Eddie Plank	1.32
8.	Rollie Fingers	1.35
9.	Bill Hallahan	1.36
10.	Roger Clemens	1.56
11.	George Earnshaw	1.58
12.	Spud Chandler	1.62
13.	Jesse Haines	1.67
14.	Ron Guidry	1.69
15.	Max Lanier	1.71
16.	Stan Coveleski	1.74
17.	Lefty Grove	1.75
	Orval Overall	1.75
19.	Carl Hubbell	1.79
20.	Ernie Shore	1.82

VICTORIES

1.	Whitey Ford	10
2.	Bob Gibson	7
	Allie Reynolds	7
	Red Ruffing	7
5.	Chief Bender	6
	Lefty Gomez	6
	Waite Hoyt	6
8.	Mordecai Brown	5
	Jack Coombs	5
	Catfish Hunter	5
	Christy Mathewson	5
	Herb Pennock	5
	Vic Raschi	5
14.	many tied with 4	

LOSSES

1.	Whitey Ford	8
2.	Joe Bush	5
	Rube Marquard	5
	Christy Mathewson	5
	Eddie Plank	5
	Schoolboy Rowe	5
7.	Chief Bender	4
	Mordecai Brown	4
	Paul Derringer	4
	Bill Donovan	4
	Burleigh Grimes	4
	Waite Hoyt	4
	Charlie Leibrandt	4
	Carl Mays	4
	Art Nehf	4
	Don Newcombe	4
	Bill Sherdel	4
	Dave Stewart	4
	Ed Summers	4
	Ralph Terry	4

SAVES

1.	Mariano Rivera	8
2.	Rollie Fingers	6
3.	Johnny Murphy	4
	Robb Nen	4
	Allie Reynolds	4
	John Wetteland	4
7.	Roy Face	3
	Firpo Marberry	3
	Will McEnaney	3
	Tug McGraw	3
	Herb Pennock	3
	Troy Percival	3
	Kent Tekulve	3
	Todd Worrell	3
15.	many tied with 2	

RUNS ALLOWED

1.	Whitey Ford	51
2.	Red Ruffing	32
	Don Sutton	32
4.	Chief Bender	28
	Carl Erskine	28
	Burleigh Grimes	28
	Waite Hoyt	28
	Rube Marquard	28
9.	Andy Pettitte	27
10.	Mordecai Brown	26
	Paul Derringer	26
12.	Allie Reynolds	25
	Bob Shawkey	25
	Dave Stewart	25
15.	Catfish Hunter	24
16.	Don Gullett	23
	Art Nehf	23
	Jim Palmer	23
	Schoolboy Rowe	23
20.	Tommy Bridges	22
	Christy Mathewson	22
	George Mullin	22

HITS ALLOWED

1.	Whitey Ford	132
2.	Waite Hoyt	81
3.	Christy Mathewson	76
4.	Red Ruffing	74
5.	Chief Bender	64
6.	Allie Reynolds	61
7.	Catfish Hunter	57
8.	Walter Johnson	56
9.	Bob Gibson	55
	Jim Palmer	55
	Don Sutton	55
12.	Andy Pettitte	54
13.	Tommy Bridges	52
	Rube Marquard	52
	Vic Raschi	52
16.	Lefty Gomez	51
	Ed Lopat	51
18.	Mordecai Brown	50
	Art Nehf	50
	Schoolboy Rowe	50

HOME RUNS ALLOWED

1.	Catfish Hunter	9
2.	Don Drysdale	8
	Whitey Ford	8
	Tom Glavine	8
	Burleigh Grimes	8
	Don Newcombe	8
	Gary Nolan	8
	Allie Reynolds	8
	Charlie Root	8
10.	Don Sutton	7
11.	Lew Burdette	6
	Roger Craig	6
	Bob Gibson	6
	Bob Turley	6
15.	many tied with 5	

TOTAL BASES ALLOWED

1.	Whitey Ford	184
2.	Christy Mathewson	105
	Allie Reynolds	105
4.	Red Ruffing	104
5.	Waite Hoyt	102
6.	Catfish Hunter	94
7.	Chief Bender	91
8.	Don Sutton	88
9.	Burleigh Grimes	87
10.	Bob Gibson	86
	Rube Marquard	86
12.	Walter Johnson	85
13.	Jim Palmer	82
14.	Vic Raschi	79
15.	Tommy Bridges	78
16.	Andy Pettitte	75
17.	Schoolboy Rowe	73
	Warren Spahn	73
19.	Jack Morris	70
20.	Ralph Terry	69

STRIKEOUTS

1.	Whitey Ford	94
2.	Bob Gibson	92
3.	Allie Reynolds	62
4.	Sandy Koufax	61
	Red Ruffing	61
6.	Chief Bender	59
7.	George Earnshaw	56
8.	John Smoltz	52
9.	Waite Hoyt	49
10.	Christy Mathewson	48
11.	Bob Turley	46
12.	Jim Palmer	44
13.	Roger Clemens	43
	Vic Raschi	43
15.	Jack Morris	40
16.	Tom Glavine	38
17.	Don Gullett	37
18.	Don Drysdale	36
	Lefty Grove	36
	George Mullin	36

WALKS

1.	Whitey Ford	34
2.	Art Nehf	32
	Allie Reynolds	32
4.	Jim Palmer	31
5.	Bob Turley	29
6.	Paul Derringer	27
	Red Ruffing	27
8.	Burleigh Grimes	26
	Don Gullett	26
10.	Vic Raschi	25
11.	Carl Erskine	24
12.	Bill Hallahan	23
	Dave Stewart	23
14.	Waite Hoyt	22
15.	Chief Bender	21
	Jack Coombs	21
	John Smoltz	21
18.	Joe Bush	20
	David Cone	20
	Tom Glavine	20

SERVICE

GAMES SELECTED, PLAYER

Rank	Player	No.
1.	Hank Aaron	25
2.	Willie Mays	24
	Stan Musial	24
4.	Mickey Mantle	20
5.	Cal Ripken Jr.	19
	Ted Williams	19
7.	Yogi Berra	18
	Rod Carew	18
	Al Kaline	18
	Brooks Robinson	18
	Carl Yastrzemski	18
12.	Pete Rose	17
	Warren Spahn	17
14.	Tony Gwynn	16
15.	Roberto Clemente	15
	Nellie Fox	15
	Ozzie Smith	15
18.	Ernie Banks	14
	Johnny Bench	14
	Reggie Jackson	14
	Frank Robinson	14

GAMES SELECTED, PITCHER

Rank	Player	No.
1.	Warren Spahn	17
2.	Tom Seaver	12
3.	Steve Carlton	10
	Don Drysdale	10
	Whitey Ford	10
	Juan Marichal	10
7.	Jim Bunning	9
	Bob Gibson	9
	Rich Gossage	9
	Carl Hubbell	9
	Early Wynn	9
12.	Roger Clemens	8
	Bob Feller	8
	Catfish Hunter	8
	Randy Johnson	8
	Sandy Koufax	8
	Greg Maddux	8
	Nolan Ryan	8
	Hoyt Wilhelm	8

BATTING

GAMES

Rank	Player	No.
1.	Hank Aaron	24
	Willie Mays	24
	Stan Musial	24
4.	Cal Ripken Jr.	18
	Brooks Robinson	18
	Ted Williams	18
7.	Al Kaline	16
	Mickey Mantle	16
	Pete Rose	16
10.	Yogi Berra	15
	Rod Carew	15
12.	Roberto Clemente	14
	Ozzie Smith	14
	Carl Yastrzemski	14
15.	Ernie Banks	13
	Nellie Fox	13
	Tony Gwynn	13
18.	Roberto Alomar	12
	Johnny Bench	12
	Wade Boggs	12
	Reggie Jackson	12
	Dave Winfield	12

HIGHEST AVERAGE

(Minimum 10 at-bats)

Rank	Player	Avg.
1.	Richie Ashburn	.600
2.	Charlie Gehringer	.500
	Ted Kluszewski	.500
4.	Al Simmons	.462
5.	Joe Carter	.455
	Leon Wagner	.455
7.	Ken Griffey Jr.	.435
8.	Billy Herman	.433
9.	Bill Skowron	.429
10.	Sandy Alomar Jr.	.417
11.	Stan Hack	.400
	Chipper Jones	.400
	Andy Pafko	.400
	Bill Terry	.400
15.	Steve Garvey	.393
16.	Bobby Bonilla	.385
	Will Clark	.385
	Ernie Lombardi	.385
19.	Enos Slaughter	.381
20.	Nellie Fox	.368

AT-BATS

Rank	Player	No.
1.	Willie Mays	75
2.	Hank Aaron	67
3.	Stan Musial	63
4.	Cal Ripken Jr.	49
5.	Ted Williams	46
6.	Brooks Robinson	45
7.	Mickey Mantle	43
8.	Yogi Berra	41
	Rod Carew	41
10.	Joe DiMaggio	40
11.	Nellie Fox	38
12.	Al Kaline	37
13.	Dave Winfield	36
14.	Carl Yastrzemski	34
15.	Ernie Banks	33
	Pete Rose	33
17.	Roberto Clemente	31
18.	Roberto Alomar	30
	Billy Herman	30
20.	Tony Gwynn	29

RUNS SCORED

Rank	Player	No.
1.	Willie Mays	20
2.	Stan Musial	11
3.	Ted Williams	10
4.	Rod Carew	8
5.	Hank Aaron	7
	Joe DiMaggio	7
	Nellie Fox	7
	Steve Garvey	7
	Al Kaline	7
	Joe Morgan	7
	Jackie Robinson	7
12.	Dave Winfield	6
13.	Roberto Alomar	5
	Johnny Bench	5
	Yogi Berra	5
	Barry Bonds	5
	George Brett	5
	Fred Lynn	5
	Mickey Mantle	5
	Brooks Robinson	5
	Arky Vaughan	5

HITS

Rank	Player	No.
1.	Willie Mays	23
2.	Stan Musial	20
3.	Nellie Fox	14
	Ted Williams	14
5.	Hank Aaron	13
	Billy Herman	13
	Cal Ripken Jr.	13
	Brooks Robinson	13
	Dave Winfield	13
10.	Al Kaline	12
11.	Steve Garvey	11
12.	Ernie Banks	10
	Johnny Bench	10
	Rod Carew	10
	Roberto Clemente	10
	Charlie Gehringer	10
	Ken Griffey Jr.	10
	Mickey Mantle	10
	Carl Yastrzemski	10
20.	Wade Boggs	9
	Joe DiMaggio	9

SINGLES

Rank	Player	No.
1.	Willie Mays	15
2.	Nellie Fox	14
3.	Stan Musial	12
4.	Hank Aaron	11
	Billy Herman	11
6.	Al Kaline	9
	Brooks Robinson	9
8.	Wade Boggs	8
	Charlie Gehringer	8
	Mickey Mantle	8
	Cal Ripken Jr.	8
12.	Johnny Bench	7
	Yogi Berra	7
	Rod Carew	7
	Ken Griffey Jr.	7
	Rickey Henderson	7
	Ivan Rodriguez	7
	Ted Williams	7
	Carl Yastrzemski	7
20.	7 tied with 6	

DOUBLES

Rank	Player	No.
1.	Dave Winfield	7
2.	Ernie Banks	3
	Barry Bonds	3
	Joe Cronin	3
	Joe Gordon	3
	Ted Kluszewski	3
	Tony Oliva	3
	Al Oliver	3
	Cal Ripken Jr.	3
	Al Simmons	3
11.	many tied with 2	

TRIPLES

Rank	Player	No.
1.	Willie Mays	3
	Brooks Robinson	3
3.	Rod Carew	2
	Steve Garvey	2
5.	many tied with 1	

HOME RUNS

Rank	Player	No.
1.	Stan Musial	6
2.	Fred Lynn	4
	Ted Williams	4
4.	Johnny Bench	3
	Gary Carter	3
	Rocky Colavito	3
	Harmon Killebrew	3
	Ralph Kiner	3
	Willie Mays	3
10.	Hank Aaron	2
	Roberto Alomar	2
	Barry Bonds	2
	Ken Boyer	2
	Frankie Frisch	2
	Steve Garvey	2
	Lou Gehrig	2
	Al Kaline	2
	Mickey Mantle	2
	Eddie Mathews	2
	Willie McCovey	2
	Mike Piazza	2
	Cal Ripken Jr.	2
	Frank Robinson	2
	Al Rosen	2
	Arky Vaughan	2

TOTAL BASES

Rank	Player	No.
1.	Willie Mays	40
	Stan Musial	40
3.	Ted Williams	30
4.	Steve Garvey	23
5.	Cal Ripken Jr.	22
	Brooks Robinson	22
7.	Dave Winfield	20
8.	Hank Aaron	19
	Johnny Bench	19
	Al Kaline	19
11.	Ernie Banks	18
	Fred Lynn	18
13.	Roberto Clemente	17
	Harmon Killebrew	17
15.	Rocky Colavito	16
	Mickey Mantle	16
17.	Barry Bonds	15
	Rod Carew	15
	Gary Carter	15
	Ken Griffey Jr.	15
	Billy Herman	15
	Arky Vaughan	15
	Carl Yastrzemski	15

SLUGGING PERCENTAGE

(Minimum 10 at-bats)

Rank	Player	Pct.
1.	Ralph Kiner	.933
2.	Ted Kluszewski	.929
3.	Fred Lynn	.900
4.	Steve Garvey	.821
5.	Al Rosen	.818
6.	Gary Carter	.750
7.	George Foster	.727
	Leon Wagner	.727
9.	Richie Ashburn	.700
	Larry Doby	.700
	Chipper Jones	.700
12.	Al Simmons	.692
13.	Arky Vaughan	.682
14.	Johnny Bench	.679
15.	Sandy Alomar Jr.	.667
	Mike Schmidt	.667
17.	Harmon Killebrew	.654
18.	Ken Griffey Jr.	.652
	Ted Williams	.652
20.	Rocky Colavito	.640

EXTRA-BASE HITS

Rank	Player	No.
1.	Willie Mays	8
	Stan Musial	8
3.	Ted Williams	7
	Dave Winfield	7
5.	Steve Garvey	6
6.	Ernie Banks	5
	Barry Bonds	5
	Cal Ripken Jr.	5
9.	George Brett	4
	Roberto Clemente	4
	Rocky Colavito	4
	Ralph Kiner	4
	Ted Kluszewski	4
	Fred Lynn	4
	Brooks Robinson	4
	Mike Schmidt	4
17.	many tied with 3	

Yankees All-Star Lefty Gomez.

RUNS BATTED IN

Rank	Player	No.
1.	Ted Williams	12
2.	Fred Lynn	10
	Stan Musial	10
4.	Willie Mays	9
5.	Hank Aaron	8
	Rocky Colavito	8
	Cal Ripken Jr.	8
8.	Barry Bonds	7
	Steve Garvey	7
10.	Johnny Bench	6
	Joe DiMaggio	6
	Al Kaline	6
	Harmon Killebrew	6
	Joe Medwick	6
15.	George Brett	5
	Gary Carter	5
	George Foster	5
	Nellie Fox	5
	Lou Gehrig	5
	Ken Griffey Jr.	5
	Dick Groat	5
	Mike Piazza	5
	Brooks Robinson	5
	Al Rosen	5
	Dave Winfield	5
	Carl Yastrzemski	5

WALKS

Rank	Player	No.
1.	Ted Williams	11
2.	Charlie Gehringer	9
	Mickey Mantle	9
4.	Rod Carew	7
	Willie Mays	7
	Stan Musial	7
7.	Lou Gehrig	6
8.	Ron Santo	5
9.	Wade Boggs	4
	George Brett	4
	Bill Dickey	4
	Reggie Jackson	4
	Joe Morgan	4
	Enos Slaughter	4
	Carl Yastrzemski	4
16.	many tied with 3	

STRIKEOUTS

Rank	Player	No.
1.	Mickey Mantle	17
2.	Willie Mays	14
3.	Ted Williams	10
4.	Roberto Clemente	9
	Reggie Jackson	9
	Mark McGwire	9
	Ryne Sandberg	9

8.	Hank Aaron	8
	Ernie Banks	8
	Joe Gordon	8
	Jim Rice	8
	Carl Yastrzemski	8
13.	Dick Allen	7
	Carlton Fisk	7
	Jimmie Foxx	7
	Elston Howard	7
	Stan Musial	7
	Frank Robinson	7
	Alex Rodriguez	7
20.	many tied with 6	

STOLEN BASES

1.	Willie Mays	6
2.	Roberto Alomar	5
	Kenny Lofton	5
4.	Rod Carew	3
	Steve Sax	3
6.	Hank Aaron	2
	Lou Brock	2
	Charlie Gehringer	2
	Kelly Gruber	2
	Rickey Henderson	2
	Tim Raines Sr.	2
	Ozzie Smith	2
	Darryl Strawberry	2
14.	many tied with 1	

PITCHING

GAMES

1.	Jim Bunning	8
	Don Drysdale	8
	Juan Marichal	8
	Tom Seaver	8
5.	Roger Clemens	7
	Randy Johnson	7
	Warren Spahn	7
	Dave Stieb	7
	Early Wynn	7
10.	Ewell Blackwell	6
	Dennis Eckersley	6
	Whitey Ford	6
	Bob Gibson	6
	Rich Gossage	6
	Catfish Hunter	6
16.	many tied with 5	

GAMES STARTED

1.	Don Drysdale	5
	Lefty Gomez	5
	Robin Roberts	5
4.	Randy Johnson	4
	Jim Palmer	4
6.	Vida Blue	3
	Jim Bunning	3
	Whitey Ford	3
	Greg Maddux	3
	Jack Morris	3
	Billy Pierce	3
	Warren Spahn	3
13.	Steve Carlton	2
	Dean Chance	2
	Roger Clemens	2
	Mort Cooper	2
	Dizzy Dean	2
	Paul Derringer	2
	Bob Feller	2
	Bob Friend	2
	Tom Glavine	2
	Dwight Gooden	2
	Juan Marichal	2
	Vic Raschi	2
	Red Ruffing	2
	Curt Schilling	2
	Curt Simmons	2
	Dave Stieb	2
	David Wells	2

GAMES RELIEVED

1.	Tom Seaver	7
2.	Rich Gossage	6
	Juan Marichal	6
	Early Wynn	6
5.	Ewell Blackwell	5
	Jim Bunning	5
	Roger Clemens	5
	David Cone	5
	Dennis Eckersley	5
	Rollie Fingers	5
	Bob Gibson	5
	Catfish Hunter	5
	Dave Stieb	5
14.	many tied with 4	

INNINGS PITCHED

1.	Don Drysdale	19.1
2.	Jim Bunning	18.0
	Lefty Gomez	18.0
	Juan Marichal	18.0
5.	Robin Roberts	14.0
	Warren Spahn	14.0
7.	Ewell Blackwell	13.2
8.	Mel Harder	13.0
	Tom Seaver	13.0
10.	Catfish Hunter	12.2
	Jim Palmer	12.2
12.	Bob Feller	12.1
	Early Wynn	12.1
14.	Whitey Ford	12.0
15.	Dave Stieb	11.2
16.	Bob Gibson	11.0
	Randy Johnson	11.0
	Vic Raschi	11.0
19.	Jack Morris	10.2
	Hal Newhouser	10.2
	Billy Pierce	10.2

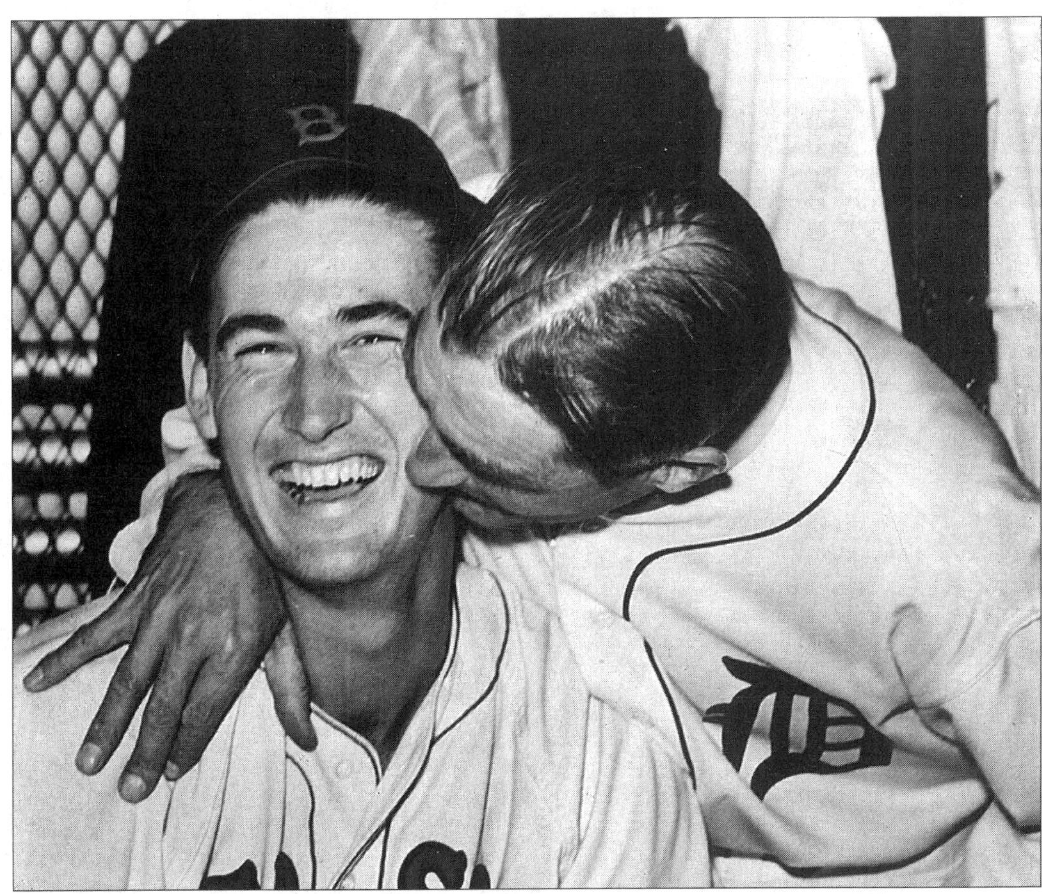

1941 All-Star Game hero Ted Williams (left) gets a victory hug from American League manager Del Baker.

LOWEST ERA

(Minimum 9 innings)

1.	Juan Marichal	0.50
2.	Mel Harder	0.69
3.	Bob Feller	0.73
4.	Dave Stieb	0.77
5.	Randy Johnson	0.82
6.	Jim Bunning	1.00
7.	Ewell Blackwell	1.32
8.	Don Drysdale	1.40
9.	Hal Newhouser	1.69
10.	Bucky Walters	2.00
11.	Vic Raschi	2.45
12.	Lefty Gomez	2.50
13.	Jack Morris	2.53
14.	Roger Clemens	2.70
	Dizzy Dean	2.70
16.	Carl Hubbell	2.79
17.	Early Wynn	2.92
18.	Warren Spahn	3.21
19.	Bob Gibson	3.27
20.	Billy Pierce	3.38

VICTORIES

1.	Lefty Gomez	3
2.	Vida Blue	2
	Don Drysdale	2
	Bob Friend	2
	Juan Marichal	2
	Bruce Sutter	2
7.	many tied with 1	

LOSSES

1.	Mort Cooper	2
	Whitey Ford	2
	Dwight Gooden	2
	Catfish Hunter	2
	Claude Passeau	2
	Luis Tiant	2
7.	many tied with 1	

SAVES

1.	Dennis Eckersley	3
2.	Mel Harder	2
3.	many tied with 1	

RUNS ALLOWED

1.	Whitey Ford	13
2.	Robin Roberts	10
	Warren Spahn	10
4.	Tom Glavine	9
	Catfish Hunter	9
6.	Vida Blue	8
	Jim Palmer	8
	Tom Seaver	8
9.	Mort Cooper	7
	Rich Gossage	7
	Atlee Hammaker	7
	Claude Passeau	7
13.	Roy Face	6
	Lefty Gomez	6
	Tex Hughson	6
	Van Mungo	6
	Gaylord Perry	6
	Red Ruffing	6
19.	8 tied with 5	

HITS ALLOWED

1.	Whitey Ford	19
2.	Robin Roberts	17
	Warren Spahn	17
4.	Tom Glavine	15
	Catfish Hunter	15
6.	Jack Morris	14
	Gaylord Perry	14
	Tom Seaver	14
9.	Red Ruffing	13
10.	Vida Blue	12
11.	Bob Gibson	11
	Lefty Gomez	11
	Jim Palmer	11
14.	Dizzy Dean	10
	Don Drysdale	10
	Lefty Grove	10
	Tex Hughson	10
	Nolan Ryan	10
	Bucky Walters	10
	Lon Warneke	10

HOME RUNS ALLOWED

1.	Vida Blue	4
	Catfish Hunter	4
3.	Steve Carlton	3
	Mort Cooper	3
	Whitey Ford	3
	Jim Palmer	3
	Milt Pappas	3
	Robin Roberts	3
	Tom Seaver	3
10.	many tied with 2	

STRIKEOUTS

1.	Don Drysdale	19
2.	Tom Seaver	16
3.	Jim Palmer	14
4.	Jim Bunning	13
	Bob Feller	13
	Catfish Hunter	13
7.	Ewell Blackwell	12
	Juan Marichal	12
	Sam McDowell	12
	Billy Pierce	12
11.	Carl Hubbell	11
	Randy Johnson	11
	Johnny Vander Meer	11
14.	Dizzy Dean	10
	Bob Gibson	10
	Dick Radatz	10
	Nolan Ryan	10
	Warren Spahn	10
	Dave Stieb	10
20.	5 tied with 9	

WALKS

1.	Jim Palmer	7
2.	Carl Hubbell	6
	Robin Roberts	6
	Dave Stieb	6
	Lon Warneke	6
6.	Ewell Blackwell	5
	Steve Carlton	5
	Dizzy Dean	5
	Bob Gibson	5
	Bill Hallahan	5
	Nolan Ryan	5
	Warren Spahn	5
13.	many tied with 4	

SINGLE SEASON

REGULAR SEASON (1876-1900)

BATTING

*HIGHEST AVERAGE

1.	Tip O'Neill, St. Louis A.A., 1887	.485
2.	Pete Browning, Louisville A.A., 1887	.457
3.	Bob Caruthers, St. Louis A.A., 1887	.456
4.	Hugh Duffy, Boston N.L., 1894	.440
5.	Yank Robinson, St. Louis A.A., 1887	.427
6.	Willie Keeler, Baltimore N.L., 1897	.424
7.	Cap Anson, Chicago N.L., 1887	.421
8.	Dan Brouthers, Detroit N.L., 1887	.420
9.	Denny Lyons, Philadelphia A.A., 1887	.415
	Sam Thompson, Philadelphia N.L., 1894	.415
11.	Fred Dunlap, St. Louis U.A., 1884	.412
12.	Reddy Mack, Louisville A.A., 1887	.410
	Ed Delahanty, Philadelphia N.L., 1899	.410
	Jesse Burkett, Cleveland N.L., 1896	.410
15.	Oyster Burns, Baltimore A.A., 1887	.409
16.	Sam Thompson, Detroit N.L., 1887	.407
17.	Jesse Burkett, Cleveland N.L., 1895	.405
18.	Ed Delahanty, Philadelphia N.L., 1895	.404
	Ed Delahanty, Philadelphia N.L., 1894	.404
	Ross Barnes, Chicago N.L., 1876	.404

*Based on players averaging at least 3.1 at-bats for every game played by their teams.

RUNS SCORED

1.	Billy Hamilton, Philadelphia N.L., 1894	198
2.	Tom Brown, Boston A.A., 1891	177
3.	Tip O'Neill, St. Louis A.A., 1887	167
4.	Billy Hamilton, Philadelphia N.L., 1895	166
5.	Willie Keeler, Baltimore N.L., 1894	165
	Joe Kelley, Baltimore N.L., 1894	165
7.	Arlie Latham, St. Louis A.A., 1887	163
8.	Willie Keeler, Baltimore N.L., 1895	162
9.	Hugh Duffy, Chicago P.L., 1890	161
10.	Jesse Burkett, Cleveland N.L., 1896	160
	Hugh Duffy, Boston N.L., 1894	160
	Fred Dunlap, St. Louis U.A., 1884	160
13.	Hughie Jennings, Baltimore N.L., 1895	159
14.	Bobby Lowe, Boston N.L., 1894	158
15.	John McGraw, Baltimore N.L., 1894	156
16.	King Kelly, Chicago N.L., 1886	155
17.	Dan Brouthers, Detroit N.L., 1887	153
	Jesse Burkett, Cleveland N.L., 1895	153
	Billy Hamilton, Boston N.L., 1896	153
	Willie Keeler, Baltimore N.L., 1896	153

HITS

1.	Pete Browning, Louisville A.A., 1887	275
	Tip O'Neill, St. Louis A.A., 1887	275
3.	Denny Lyons, Philadelphia A.A., 1887	256
4.	Oyster Burns, Baltimore A.A., 1887	251
5.	Arlie Latham, St. Louis A.A., 1887	243
6.	Dan Brouthers, Detroit N.L., 1887	240
	Jesse Burkett, Cleveland N.L., 1896	240
8.	Willie Keeler, Baltimore N.L., 1897	239
9.	Ed Delahanty, Philadelphia N.L., 1899	238
10.	Hugh Duffy, Boston N.L., 1894	237
11.	Paul Radford, New York A.A., 1887	235
	Sam Thompson, Detroit N.L., 1887	235
13.	Reddy Mack, Louisville A.A., 1887	230
14.	Jesse Burkett, Cleveland N.L., 1895	225
	Billy Hamilton, Philadelphia N.L., 1894	225
16.	Cap Anson, Chicago N.L., 1887	224
	Bill McClellan, Brooklyn A.A., 1887	224
18.	Yank Robinson, St. Louis A.A., 1887	223
19.	Frank Fennelly, Cincinnati A.A., 1887	222
	Sam Thompson, Philadelphia N.L., 1893	222

HOME RUNS

1.	Ned Williamson, Chicago N.L., 1884	27
2.	Buck Freeman, Washington N.L., 1899	25
	Fred Pfeffer, Chicago N.L., 1884	25
4.	Abner Dalrymple, Chicago N.L., 1884	22
5.	Cap Anson, Chicago N.L., 1884	21
6.	Sam Thompson, Philadelphia N.L., 1889	20
7.	Ed Delahanty, Philadelphia N.L., 1893	19
	Bug Holliday, Cincinnati A.A., 1889	19
	Billy O'Brien, Washington N.L., 1887	19
	Harry Stovey, Philadelphia A.A., 1889	19
11.	Jerry Denny, Indianapolis N.L., 1889	18
	Hugh Duffy, Boston N.L., 1894	18
	Sam Thompson, Philadelphia N.L., 1895	18
14.	Jack Clements, Philadelphia N.L., 1893	17
	Roger Connor, New York N.L., 1887	17
	Bill Joyce, Washington N.L., 1894	17
	Bill Joyce, Washington N.L., 1895	17
	Bobby Lowe, Boston N.L., 1894	17
	Jimmy Ryan, Chicago N.L., 1889	17
20.	5 tied with 16	

TOTAL BASES

1.	Tip O'Neill, St. Louis A.A., 1887	407
2.	Hugh Duffy, Boston N.L., 1894	374
3.	Pete Browning, Louisville A.A., 1887	354
4.	Dan Brouthers, Detroit N.L., 1887	352
	Sam Thompson, Philadelphia N.L., 1895	352
6.	Oyster Burns, Baltimore A.A., 1887	349
7.	Ed Delahanty, Philadelphia N.L., 1893	347
8.	Denny Lyons, Philadelphia A.A., 1887	345
9.	Sam Thompson, Detroit N.L., 1887	340
10.	Ed Delahanty, Philadelphia N.L., 1899	338
11.	Buck Freeman, Washington N.L., 1899	331
12.	Roger Connor, New York N.L., 1887	330
13.	Jimmy Williams, Pittsburgh N.L., 1899	329
14.	Bobby Lowe, Boston N.L., 1894	319
15.	Sam Thompson, Philadelphia N.L., 1893	318
16.	Jesse Burkett, Cleveland N.L., 1896	317
17.	Ed Delahanty, Philadelphia N.L., 1896	315
18.	Sam Thompson, Philadelphia N.L., 1894	314
19.	Nap Lajoie, Philadelphia N.L., 1897	310
20.	Willie Keeler, Baltimore N.L., 1894	305
	Joe Kelley, Baltimore N.L., 1894	305

EXTRA-BASE HITS

1.	Hugh Duffy, Boston N.L., 1894	85
	Tip O'Neill, St. Louis A.A., 1887	85
3.	Sam Thompson, Philadelphia N.L., 1895	84
4.	Ed Delahanty, Philadelphia N.L., 1896	74
	Joe Kelley, Baltimore N.L., 1894	74
6.	Ed Delahanty, Philadelphia N.L., 1899	73
	Sam Thompson, Philadelphia N.L., 1894	73
8.	Ed Delahanty, Philadelphia N.L., 1893	72
	Nap Lajoie, Philadelphia N.L., 1897	72
	Jake Stenzel, Pittsburgh N.L., 1894	72
11.	Dan Brouthers, Baltimore N.L., 1894	71
	Honus Wagner, Pittsburgh N.L., 1900	71
13.	Ed Delahanty, Philadelphia N.L., 1895	70
	Harry Stovey, Philadelphia A.A., 1889	70
15.	Jake Beckley, Pittsburgh P.L., 1890	69
	Buck Freeman, Washington N.L., 1899	69
17.	Dan Brouthers, Detroit N.L., 1887	68
	Roger Connor, New York-St. Louis N.L., 1894	68
19.	Harry Stovey, Boston N.L., 1891	67
20.	Dan Brouthers, Detroit N.L., 1886	66

RUNS BATTED IN

1.	Sam Thompson, Detroit N.L., 1887	166
2.	Sam Thompson, Philadelphia N.L., 1895	165
3.	Cap Anson, Chicago N.L., 1886	147
	Sam Thompson, Philadelphia N.L., 1894	147
5.	Ed Delahanty, Philadelphia N.L., 1893	146
	Hardy Richardson, Boston P.L., 1890	146
7.	Hugh Duffy, Boston N.L., 1894	145
8.	Ed Delahanty, Philadelphia N.L., 1899	137
9.	George Davis, New York N.L., 1897	136
10.	Steve Brodie, Baltimore N.L., 1895	134
	Joe Kelley, Baltimore N.L., 1895	134
12.	Ed Delahanty, Philadelphia N.L., 1894	133
	Ed McKean, Cleveland N.L., 1893	133
14.	Jimmy Collins, Boston N.L., 1897	132
	Lave Cross, Philadelphia N.L., 1894	132
16.	Roger Connor, New York N.L., 1889	130
	Walt Wilmot, Chicago N.L., 1894	130
18.	Hugh Duffy, Boston N.L., 1897	129
19.	Dan Brouthers, Baltimore N.L., 1894	128
	Oyster Burns, Brooklyn N.L., 1890	128
	Ed McKean, Cleveland N.L., 1894	128

STOLEN BASES

1.	Hugh Nicol, Cincinnati A.A., 1887	138
2.	Arlie Latham, St. Louis A.A., 1887	129
3.	Charlie Comiskey, St. Louis A.A., 1887	117
4.	Billy Hamilton, Kansas City A.A., 1889	111
	Billy Hamilton, Philadelphia N.L., 1891	111
	John Ward, New York N.L., 1887	111
7.	Arlie Latham, St. Louis A.A., 1888	109
8.	Tom Brown, Boston A.A., 1891	106
9.	Pete Browning, Louisville A.A., 1887	103
	Hugh Nicol, Cincinnati A.A., 1888	103
11.	Jim Fogarty, Philadelphia N.L., 1887	102
	Billy Hamilton, Philadelphia N.L., 1890	102
13.	Billy Hamilton, Philadelphia N.L., 1894	100
14.	Jim Fogarty, Philadelphia N.L., 1889	99
15.	Billy Hamilton, Philadelphia N.L., 1895	97
	Harry Stovey, Boston P.L., 1890	97
17.	Bid McPhee, Cincinnati A.A., 1887	95
	Curt Welch, Philadelphia A.A., 1888	95
19.	Mike Griffin, Baltimore A.A., 1887	94
20.	Tommy McCarthy, St. Louis A.A., 1888	93

PITCHING

COMPLETE GAMES

1.	Will White, Cincinnati N.L., 1879	75
2.	Charley Radbourn, Providence N.L., 1884	73
3.	Pud Galvin, Buffalo N.L., 1883	72
	Guy Hecker, Louisville A.A., 1884	72
	Jim McCormick, Cleveland N.L., 1880	72
6.	Pud Galvin, Buffalo N.L., 1884	71
7.	John Clarkson, Chicago N.L., 1885	68
	John Clarkson, Boston N.L., 1889	68
	Tim Keefe, New York A.A., 1883	68
10.	Bill Hutchison, Chicago N.L., 1892	67
11.	Jim Devlin, Louisville N.L., 1876	66
	Matt Kilroy, Baltimore A.A., 1886	66
	Matt Kilroy, Baltimore A.A., 1887	66
	Charles Radbourn, Providence N.L., 1883	66
	Toad Ramsey, Louisville A.A., 1886	66
16.	Pud Galvin, Buffalo N.L., 1879	65
	Bill Hutchison, Chicago N.L., 1890	65
	Jim McCormick, Cleveland N.L., 1882	65
19.	4 tied with 64	

INNINGS PITCHED

1.	Will White, Cincinnati N.L., 1879	680.0
2.	Charles Radbourn, Providence N.L., 1884	678.2
3.	Guy Hecker, Louisville A.A., 1884	670.2
4.	Jim McCormick, Cleveland N.L., 1880	657.2
5.	Pud Galvin, Buffalo N.L., 1883	656.1
6.	Pud Galvin, Buffalo N.L., 1884	636.1
7.	Charley Radbourn, Providence N.L., 1883	632.1
8.	John Clarkson, Chicago N.L., 1885	623.0
9.	Jim Devlin, Louisville N.L., 1876	622.0
	Bill Hutchison, Chicago N.L., 1892	622.0
11.	John Clarkson, Boston N.L., 1889	620.0
12.	Tim Keefe, New York A.A., 1883	619.0
13.	Bill Hutchison, Chicago N.L., 1890	603.0
14.	Jim McCormick, Cleveland N.L., 1882	595.2
	John Ward, Providence N.L., 1880	595.0
16.	Pud Galvin, Buffalo N.L., 1879	593.0
17.	Lee Richmond, Worchester N.L., 1880	590.2
18.	Matt Kilroy, Baltimore A.A., 1887	589.1
19.	Toad Ramsey, Louisville A.A., 1886	588.2
20.	Charlie Buffinton, Boston N.L., 1884	587.0
	John Ward, Providence N.L., 1879	587.0

*LOWEST ERA

1.	Tim Keefe, Troy N.L., 1880	0.86
2.	Denny Driscoll, Pittsburgh A.A., 1882	1.21
3.	George Bradley, St. Louis N.L., 1876	1.23
4.	Guy Hecker, Louisville A.A., 1882	1.30
5.	George Bradley, Providence N.L., 1880	1.38
	Charles Radbourn, Providence N.L., 1884	1.38
7.	John Ward, Providence N.L., 1878	1.51
8.	Harry McCormick, Cincinnati A.A., 1882	1.52
9.	Will White, Cincinnati A.A., 1882	1.54
10.	Jim Devlin, Louisville N.L., 1876	1.56
11.	Tim Keefe, New York N.L., 1885	1.58
12.	Silver King, St. Louis A.A., 1888	1.63
13.	Mickey Welch, New York N.L., 1885	1.66
14.	Candy Cummings, Hartford N.L., 1876	1.67
15.	Tommy Bond, Hartford N.L., 1876	1.68
16.	Jim McCormick, Indianapolis N.L., 1878	1.69
17.	Charlie Sweeney, Prov. N.L.-St.L. U.A., 1884	1.70
18.	John Ward, Providence N.L., 1880	1.74
	Henry Boyle, St. Louis U.A., 1884	1.74
	Tim Keefe, New York N.L., 1888	1.74

*Leaders based on pitchers whose total innings equal or surpass total games played by their teams.

VICTORIES

1.	Charley Radbourn, Providence N.L., 1884	59
2.	John Clarkson, Chicago N.L., 1885	53
3.	Guy Hecker, Louisville A.A., 1884	52
4.	John Clarkson, Boston N.L., 1889	49
5.	Charlie Buffinton, Boston N.L., 1884	48
	Charles Radbourn, Providence N.L., 1883	48
7.	Al Spalding, Chicago N.L., 1876	47
	John Ward, Providence N.L., 1879	47
9.	Pud Galvin, Buffalo N.L., 1883	46
	Pud Galvin, Buffalo N.L., 1884	46
	Matt Kilroy, Baltimore A.A., 1887	46
12.	George Bradley, St. Louis N.L., 1876	45
	Silver King, St. Louis A.A., 1888	45
	Jim McCormick, Cleveland N.L., 1880	45
15.	Bill Hutchison, Chicago N.L., 1891	44
	Mickey Welch, New York N.L., 1885	44
17.	5 tied with 43	

LOSSES

1.	John Coleman, Philadelphia N.L., 1883	48
2.	Will White, Cincinnati N.L., 1880	42
3.	Larry McKeon, Indianapolis A.A., 1884	41
4.	George Bradley, Troy N.L., 1879	40
	Jim McCormick, Cleveland N.L., 1879	40
6.	Kid Carsey, Washington A.A., 1891	37
	George Cobb, Baltimore N.L., 1892	37
	Henry Porter, Kansas City A.A., 1888	37
9.	Bill Hutchison, Chicago N.L., 1892	36
	Stump Wiedman, Kansas City N.L., 1886	36
11.	Jim Devlin, Louisville N.L., 1876	35
	Red Donahue, St. Louis N.L., 1897	35

	Pud Galvin, Buffalo N.L., 1880	35
	Hardie Henderson, Baltimore A.A., 1885	35
	Fleury Sullivan, Pittsburgh A.A., 1884	35
	Adonis Terry, Brooklyn A.A., 1884	35
7.	Mark Baldwin, Colorado A.A., 1889	34
	Bob Barr, Wash.-Ind. A.A., 1884	34
	Matt Kilroy, Baltimore A.A., 1886	34
	Bobby Mathews, New York N.L., 1876	34
	Al Mays, New York, A.A., 1887	34
	Amos Rusie, New York N.L., 1890	34

SHUTOUTS

1.	George Bradley, St. Louis N.L., 1876	16
2.	Pud Galvin, Buffalo N.L., 1884	12
	Ed Morris, Pittsburgh A.A., 1886	12
4.	Tommy Bond, Boston N.L., 1879	11
	Dave Foutz, St. Louis A.A., 1886	11
	Charles Radbourn, Providence N.L., 1884	11
7.	John Clarkson, Chicago N.L., 1885	10
	Jim McCormick, Cle. N.L.-Cin. U.A., 1884	10
9.	Tommy Bond, Boston N.L., 1878	9
	George Derby, Detroit N.L., 1881	9
	Cy Young, Cleveland N.L., 1892	9
12.	Charlie Buffinton, Boston N.L., 1884	8
	John Clarkson, Boston N.L., 1889	8
	Tim Keefe, New York N.L., 1888	8
	Ben Sanders, Philadelphia N.L., 1888	8
	Al Spalding, Chicago N.L., 1876	8
	John Ward, Providence N.L., 1880	8
	Will White, Cincinnati A.A., 1882	8
19.	10 tied with 7	

STRIKEOUTS

1.	Matt Kilroy, Baltimore A.A., 1886	513
2.	Toad Ramsey, Louisville A.A., 1886	499
3.	Hugh Daily, Chi.-Pit.-Wash. U.A., 1884	483
4.	Dupee Shaw, Detroit N.L.-Boston U.A., 1884	451
5.	Charles Radbourn, Providence N.L., 1884	441
6.	Charlie Buffinton, Boston N.L., 1884	417
7.	Guy Hecker, Louisville A.A., 1884	385
8.	Bill Sweeney, Baltimore U.A., 1884	374
9.	Pud Galvin, Buffalo N.L., 1884	369
10.	Mark Baldwin, Colorado A.A., 1889	368
11.	Tim Keefe, New York A.A., 1883	359
12.	Toad Ramsey, Louisville A.A., 1887	355
13.	Hardie Henderson, Baltimore A.A., 1884	346
14.	Mickey Welch, New York N.L., 1884	345
	Jim Whitney, Boston N.L., 1883	345
16.	Jim McCormick, Cle. N.L.-Cin. U.A., 1884	343
17.	Amos Rusie, New York N.L., 1890	341
18.	Amos Rusie, New York N.L., 1891	337
	Charlie Sweeney, Prov. N.L.-St.L. U.A., 1884	337
20.	Tim Keefe, New York N.L., 1888	335

REGULAR SEASON (1901-2002)

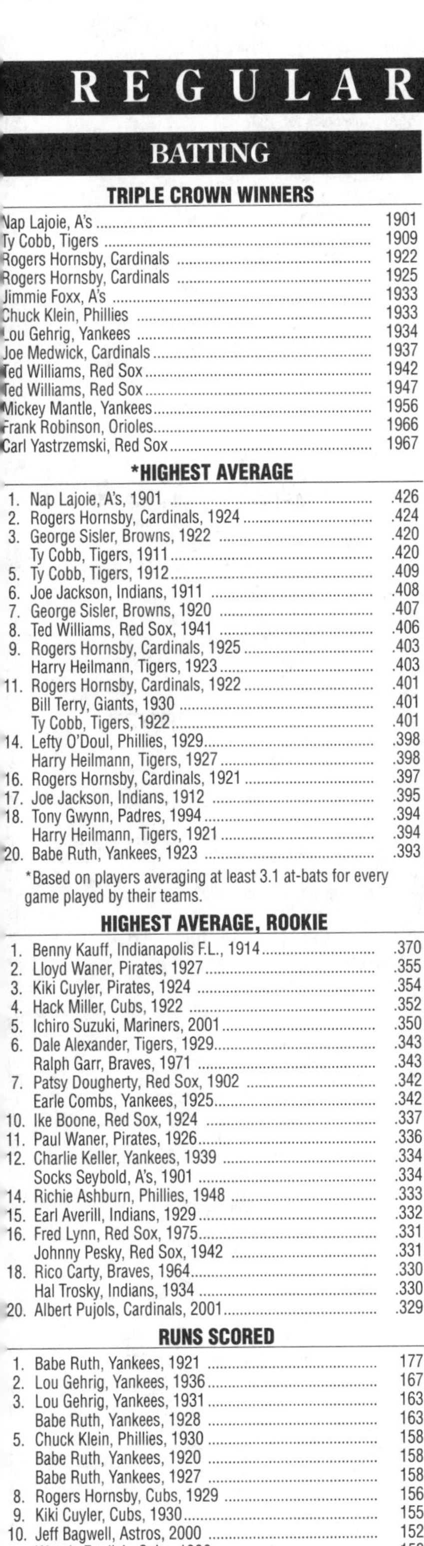

BATTING

TRIPLE CROWN WINNERS

Nap Lajoie, A's	1901
Ty Cobb, Tigers	1909
Rogers Hornsby, Cardinals	1922
Rogers Hornsby, Cardinals	1925
Jimmie Foxx, A's	1933
Chuck Klein, Phillies	1933
Lou Gehrig, Yankees	1934
Joe Medwick, Cardinals	1937
Ted Williams, Red Sox	1942
Ted Williams, Red Sox	1947
Mickey Mantle, Yankees	1956
Frank Robinson, Orioles	1966
Carl Yastrzemski, Red Sox	1967

***HIGHEST AVERAGE**

1.	Nap Lajoie, A's, 1901	.426
2.	Rogers Hornsby, Cardinals, 1924	.424
3.	George Sisler, Browns, 1922	.420
	Ty Cobb, Tigers, 1911	.420
5.	Ty Cobb, Tigers, 1912	.409
6.	Joe Jackson, Indians, 1911	.408
7.	George Sisler, Browns, 1920	.407
8.	Ted Williams, Red Sox, 1941	.406
9.	Rogers Hornsby, Cardinals, 1925	.403
	Harry Heilmann, Tigers, 1923	.403
11.	Rogers Hornsby, Cardinals, 1922	.401
	Bill Terry, Giants, 1930	.401
	Ty Cobb, Tigers, 1922	.401
14.	Lefty O'Doul, Phillies, 1929	.398
	Harry Heilmann, Tigers, 1927	.398
16.	Rogers Hornsby, Cardinals, 1921	.397
17.	Joe Jackson, Indians, 1912	.395
18.	Tony Gwynn, Padres, 1994	.394
	Harry Heilmann, Tigers, 1921	.394
20.	Babe Ruth, Yankees, 1923	.393

*Based on players averaging at least 3.1 at-bats for every game played by their teams.

HIGHEST AVERAGE, ROOKIE

1.	Benny Kauff, Indianapolis F.L., 1914	.370
2.	Lloyd Waner, Pirates, 1927	.355
3.	Kiki Cuyler, Pirates, 1924	.354
4.	Hack Miller, Cubs, 1922	.352
5.	Ichiro Suzuki, Mariners, 2001	.350
6.	Dale Alexander, Tigers, 1929	.343
	Ralph Garr, Braves, 1971	.343
7.	Patsy Dougherty, Red Sox, 1902	.342
	Earle Combs, Yankees, 1925	.342
10.	Ike Boone, Red Sox, 1924	.337
11.	Paul Waner, Pirates, 1926	.336
12.	Charlie Keller, Yankees, 1939	.334
	Socks Seybold, A's, 1901	.334
14.	Richie Ashburn, Phillies, 1948	.333
15.	Earl Averill, Indians, 1929	.332
16.	Fred Lynn, Red Sox, 1975	.331
	Johnny Pesky, Red Sox, 1942	.331
18.	Rico Carty, Braves, 1964	.330
	Hal Trosky, Indians, 1934	.330
20.	Albert Pujols, Cardinals, 2001	.329

RUNS SCORED

1.	Babe Ruth, Yankees, 1921	177
2.	Lou Gehrig, Yankees, 1936	167
3.	Lou Gehrig, Yankees, 1931	163
	Babe Ruth, Yankees, 1928	163
5.	Chuck Klein, Phillies, 1930	158
	Babe Ruth, Yankees, 1920	158
	Babe Ruth, Yankees, 1927	158
8.	Rogers Hornsby, Cubs, 1929	156
9.	Kiki Cuyler, Cubs, 1930	155
10.	Jeff Bagwell, Astros, 2000	152
	Woody English, Cubs, 1930	152
	Chuck Klein, Phillies, 1932	152

Pittsburgh's Waner brothers, Lloyd (left) and Paul, rank high among single-season rookie hitters.

	Lefty O'Doul, Phillies, 1929	152
	Al Simmons, A's, 1930	152
15.	Joe DiMaggio, Yankees, 1937	151
	Jimmie Foxx, A's, 1932	151
	Babe Ruth, Yankees, 1923	151
18.	Babe Ruth, Yankees, 1930	150
	Ted Williams, Red Sox, 1949	150
20.	Lou Gehrig, Yankees, 1927	149
	Babe Ruth, Yankees, 1931	149

HITS

1.	George Sisler, Browns, 1920	257
2.	Lefty O'Doul, Phillies, 1929	254
	Bill Terry, Giants, 1930	254
4.	Al Simmons, A's, 1925	253
5.	Rogers Hornsby, Cardinals, 1922	250
	Chuck Klein, Phillies, 1930	250
7.	Ty Cobb, Tigers, 1911	248
8.	George Sisler, Browns, 1922	246
9.	Ichiro Suzuki, Mariners, 2001	242
10.	Babe Herman, Dodgers, 1930	241
	Heinie Manush, Browns, 1928	241
12.	Wade Boggs, Red Sox, 1985	240
	Darin Erstad, Angels, 2000	240
14.	Rod Carew, Twins, 1977	239
15.	Don Mattingly, Yankees, 1986	238
16.	Harry Heilmann, Tigers, 1921	237
	Joe Medwick, Cardinals, 1937	237
	Paul Waner, Pirates, 1927	237
19.	Jack Tobin, Browns, 1921	236
20.	Rogers Hornsby, Cardinals, 1921	235

HITS, ROOKIE

1.	Ichiro Suzuki, Mariners, 2001	242
2.	Lloyd Waner, Pirates, 1927	223
3.	Ralph Garr, Braves, 1971	219
4.	Tony Oliva, Twins, 1964	217
5.	Dale Alexander, Tigers, 1929	215
6.	Benny Kauff, Indianapolis F.L., 1914	211
7.	Nomar Garciaparra, Red Sox, 1997	209
	Harvey Kuenn, Tigers, 1953	209
9.	Kevin Seitzer, Royals, 1987	207
10.	Joe DiMaggio, Yankees, 1936	206
	Johnny Frederick, Dodgers, 1929	206
	Hal Trosky, Indians, 1934	206
13.	Johnny Pesky, Red Sox, 1942	205
14.	Earle Combs, Yankees, 1925	203
15.	Dick Allen, Phillies, 1964	201
	Roy Johnson, Tigers, 1929	201
17.	Dick Wakefield, Tigers, 1943	200
18.	Earl Averill, Indians, 1929	198
19.	Buddy Hassett, Dodgers, 1936	197
20.	Carlos Beltran, Royals, 1999	194
	Albert Pujols, Cardinals, 2001	194

LONGEST HITTING STREAKS

1.	Joe DiMaggio, Yankees, 1941	56
2.	Pete Rose, Reds, 1978	44
3.	George Sisler, Browns, 1922	41
4.	Ty Cobb, Tigers, 1911	40
5.	Paul Molitor, Brewers, 1987	39
6.	Tommy Holmes, Braves, 1945	37
7.	Ty Cobb, Tigers, 1917	35
	Luis Castillo, Marlins, 2002	35
9.	George Sisler, Browns, 1925	34
	George McQuinn, Browns, 1938	34
	Dom DiMaggio, Red Sox, 1949	34
	Benito Santiago, Padres, 1987	34
13.	Hal Chase, Yankees, 1907	33
	Rogers Hornsby, Cardinals, 1922	33
	Heinie Manush, Senators, 1933	33
16.	Nap Lajoie, Indians, 1906	31
	Sam Rice, Senators, 1924	31
	Willie Davis, Dodgers, 1969	31
	Rico Carty, Braves, 1970	31
	Ken Landreaux, Twins, 1980	31
	Vladimir Guerrero, Expos, 1999	31

LONGEST HITTING STREAKS, ROOKIE

1.	Benito Santiago, Padres, 1987	34
2.	Jerome Walton, Cubs, 1989	30
	Nomar Garciaparra, Red Sox, 1997	30
4.	Jimmy Williams, 1899	27
5.	Guy Curtright, White Sox, 1943	26
6.	Joe McEwing, Cardinals, 1999	25
7.	Chico Carrasquel, White Sox, 1950	24
8.	Richie Ashburn, Phillies, 1948	23
	Al Dark, Braves, 1948	23

	Kent Hrbek, Twins, 1982	23
	Goldie Rapp, Phillies, 1921	23
	Ichiro Suzuki, Mariners, 2001	23
	Mike Vail, Mets, 1975	23
14.	Ralph Garr, Braves, 1971	22
	Willie McCovey, Giants, 1959	22
	Dale Mitchell, Indians, 1947	22
	Johnny Mize, Cardinals, 1936	22
	Edgar Renteria, Marlins, 1996	22
19.	Lou Klein, Cardinals, 1943	21
	Danny Litwhiler, Phillies, 1940	21
	Jackie Robinson, Dodgers, 1947	21
	Dick Wakefield, Tigers, 1943	21
	Taffy Wright, Senators, 1938	21

CONSECUTIVE HITS

1.	Pinky Higgins, Red Sox, 1938	12
	Walt Dropo, Tigers, 1952	12
3.	Tris Speaker, Indians, 1920	11
	Johnny Pesky, Red Sox, 1946	11
5.	Ed Delahanty, Phillies, 1897	10
	Jake Gettman, Senators, 1897	10
	Ed Konetchy, Dodgers, 1919	10
	George Sisler, Browns, 1921	10
	Harry Heilmann, Tigers, 1922	10
	Kiki Cuyler, Pirates, 1925	10
	Harry McCurdy, White Sox, 1926	10
	Chick Hafey, Cardinals, 1929	10
	Joe Medwick, Cardinals, 1936	10
	Rip Radcliff, White Sox, 1938	10
	Buddy Hassett, Braves, 1940	10
	Woody Williams, Reds, 1943	10
	Ken Singleton, Orioles, 1981	10
	Bip Roberts, Reds, 1992	10
	Frank Thomas, White Sox, 1997	10
	Joe Randa, Royals, 1999	10
	Frank Catalanotto, Rangers, 2000	10

PINCH HITS

1.	John Vander Wal, Rockies, 1995	28
2.	Lenny Harris, Rockies-Diamondbacks, 1999	26
3.	Jose Morales, Expos, 1976	25
4.	Dave Philley, Orioles, 1961	24
	Vic Davalillo, Cardinals, 1970	24
	Rusty Staub, Mets, 1983	24
	Gerald Perry, Cardinals, 1993	24
8.	Sam Leslie, Giants, 1932	22
	Peanuts Lowrey, Cardinals, 1953	22
	Red Schoendienst, Cardinals, 1962	22
	Wallace Johnson, Expos, 1988	22
	Mark Sweeney, Cardinals-Padres, 1997	22
	Lenny Harris, Brewers, 2002	22
14.	Doc Miller, Phillies, 1913	21
	Smoky Burgess, White Sox, 1966	21
	Lenny Harris, Mets, 2001	21
	Merv Rettenmund, Padres, 1977	21
18.	Ed Coleman, Browns, 1936	20
	Frenchy Bordagaray, Cardinals, 1938	20
	Joe Frazier, Cardinals, 1954	20
	Smoky Burgess, White Sox, 1965	20
	Ken Boswell, Astros, 1976	20
	Jerry Turner, Padres, 1978	20
	Thad Bosley, Cubs, 1985	20
	Chris Chambliss, Braves, 1986	20
	Dave Clark, Cubs, 1997	20

SINGLES

1.	Lloyd Waner, Pirates, 1927	198
2.	Ichiro Suzuki, Mariners, 2001	192
3.	Wade Boggs, Red Sox, 1985	187
4.	Willie Wilson, Royals, 1980	184
5.	Matty Alou, Pirates, 1969	183
6.	Sam Rice, Senators, 1925	182
7.	Richie Ashburn, Phillies, 1951	181
	Jesse Burkett, Cardinals, 1901	181
	Lefty O'Doul, Phillies, 1929	181
	Pete Rose, Reds, 1973	181
	Lloyd Waner, Pirates, 1929	181
12.	Rod Carew, Twins, 1974	180
	Ralph Garr, Braves, 1971	180
	Lloyd Waner, Pirates, 1928	180
15.	Jack Tobin, Browns, 1921	179
	Maury Wills, Dodgers, 1962	179
17.	Curt Flood, Cardinals, 1964	178
	George Sisler, Browns, 1922	178
	Paul Waner, Pirates, 1937	178
20.	Tony Gwynn, Padres, 1984	177
	Bill Terry, Giants, 1930	177

DOUBLES

1.	Earl Webb, Red Sox, 1931	67
2.	George Burns, Indians, 1926	64
	Joe Medwick, Cardinals, 1936	64
4.	Hank Greenberg, Tigers, 1934	63
5.	Paul Waner, Pirates, 1932	62
6.	Charlie Gehringer, Tigers, 1936	60
7.	Todd Helton, Rockies, 2000	59
	Chuck Klein, Phillies, 1930	59
	Tris Speaker, Indians, 1923	59
10.	Carlos Delgado, Blue Jays, 2000	57
	Billy Herman, Cubs, 1935	57
	Billy Herman, Cubs, 1936	57
13.	Garret Anderson, Angels, 2002	56
	Craig Biggio, Astros, 1999	56
	Nomar Garciaparra, Red Sox, 2002	56
	George Kell, Tigers, 1950	56
	Joe Medwick, Cardinals, 1937	56
18.	Lance Berkman, Astros, 2001	55
	Gee Walker, Tigers, 1936	55
20.	Mark Grudzielanek, Expos, 1997	54
	Todd Helton, Rockies, 2001	54
	Hal McRae, Royals, 1977	54
	John Olerud, Blue Jays, 1993	54
	Alex Rodriguez, Mariners, 1996	54

TRIPLES

1.	Chief Wilson, Pirates, 1912	36
2.	Sam Crawford, Tigers, 1914	26
	Kiki Cuyler, Pirates, 1925	26
	Joe Jackson, Indians, 1912	26
5.	Sam Crawford, Tigers, 1903	25
	Larry Doyle, Giants, 1911	25
	Tom Long, Cardinals, 1915	25
8.	Ty Cobb, Tigers, 1911	24
	Ty Cobb, Tigers, 1917	24
10.	Ty Cobb, Tigers, 1912	23
	Earle Combs, Yankees, 1927	23
	Adam Comorosky, Pirates, 1930	23
	Sam Crawford, Tigers, 1913	23
	Dale Mitchell, Indians, 1949	23
15.	many tied with 22	

HOME RUNS

1.	Barry Bonds, Giants, 2001	73
2.	Mark McGwire, Cardinals, 1998	70
3.	Sammy Sosa, Cubs, 1998	66
4.	Mark McGwire, Cardinals, 1999	65
5.	Sammy Sosa, Cubs, 2001	64
6.	Sammy Sosa, Cubs, 1999	63
7.	Roger Maris, Yankees, 1961	61
8.	Babe Ruth, Yankees, 1927	60
9.	Babe Ruth, Yankees, 1921	59
10.	Jimmie Foxx, A's, 1932	58
	Hank Greenberg, Tigers, 1938	58
	Mark McGwire, A's-Cardinals, 1997	58
13.	Luis Gonzalez, Diamondbacks, 2001	57
	Alex Rodriguez, Rangers, 2002	57
15.	Ken Griffey Jr., Mariners, 1997	56
	Ken Griffey Jr., Mariners, 1998	56
	Hack Wilson, Cubs, 1930	56
18.	Ralph Kiner, Pirates, 1949	54
	Mickey Mantle, Yankees, 1961	54
	Babe Ruth, Yankees, 1920	54
	Babe Ruth, Yankees, 1928	54

HOME RUNS, RIGHTHANDER

1.	Mark McGwire, Cardinals, 1998	70
2.	Sammy Sosa, Cubs, 1998	66
3.	Mark McGwire, Cardinals, 1999	65
4.	Sammy Sosa, Cubs, 2001	64
5.	Sammy Sosa, Cubs, 1999	63
6.	Jimmie Foxx, A's, 1932	58
	Hank Greenberg, Tigers, 1938	58
	Mark McGwire, A's-Cardinals, 1997	58
9.	Alex Rodriguez, Rangers, 2002	57
10.	Hack Wilson, Cubs, 1930	56
11.	Ralph Kiner, Pirates, 1949	54
12.	George Foster, Reds, 1977	52
	Willie Mays, Giants, 1965	52
	Mark McGwire, A's, 1996	52
	Alex Rodriguez, Rangers, 2001	52
16.	Cecil Fielder, Tigers, 1990	51
	Ralph Kiner, Pirates, 1947	51
	Willie Mays, Giants, 1955	51
19.	Albert Belle, Indians, 1995	50
	Jimmie Foxx, Red Sox, 1938	50
	Sammy Sosa, Cubs, 2000	50
	Greg Vaughn, Padres, 1998	50

HOME RUNS, LEFTHANDER

1.	Barry Bonds, Giants, 2001	73
2.	Roger Maris, Yankees, 1961	61
3.	Babe Ruth, Yankees, 1927	60
4.	Babe Ruth, Yankees, 1921	59
5.	Luis Gonzalez, Diamondbacks, 2001	57
6.	Ken Griffey Jr., Mariners, 1997	56
	Ken Griffey Jr., Mariners, 1998	56
8.	Babe Ruth, Yankees, 1920	54
	Babe Ruth, Yankees, 1928	54
10.	Jim Thome, Indians, 2002	52
11.	Johnny Mize, Giants, 1947	51
12.	Brady Anderson, Orioles, 1996	50
13.	Barry Bonds, Giants, 2000	49
	Lou Gehrig, Yankees, 1934	49
	Lou Gehrig, Yankees, 1936	49
	Shawn Green, Dodgers, 2001	49
	Ken Griffey Jr., Mariners, 1996	49
	Todd Helton, Rockies, 2001	49
	Ted Kluszewski, Reds, 1954	49
	Babe Ruth, Yankees, 1930	49
	Jim Thome, Indians, 2001	49
	Larry Walker, Rockies, 1997	49

HOME RUNS, SWITCH HITTER

1.	Mickey Mantle, Yankees, 1961	54
2.	Mickey Mantle, Yankees, 1956	52
3.	Chipper Jones, Braves, 1999	45
4.	Lance Berkman, Astros, 2002	42
	Mickey Mantle, Yankees, 1958	42
6.	Todd Hundley, Mets, 1996	41
7.	Ken Caminiti, Padres, 1996	40
	Mickey Mantle, Yankees, 1960	40
9.	Howard Johnson, Mets, 1991	38
	Chipper Jones, Braves, 2001	38
11.	Mickey Mantle, Yankees, 1955	37
12.	Howard Johnson, Mets, 1987	36
	Howard Johnson, Mets, 1989	36
	Chipper Jones, Braves, 2000	36
15.	Rip Collins, Cardinals, 1934	35
	Mickey Mantle, Yankees, 1964	35
	Ken Singleton, Orioles, 1979	35
18.	Lance Berkman, Astros, 2001	34
19.	Bobby Bonilla, Mets, 1993	34
	Tony Clark, Tigers, 1998	34
	Jose Cruz Jr., Blue Jays, 2001	34
	Carl Everett, Red Sox, 2000	34
	Chipper Jones, Braves, 1998	34
	Mickey Mantle, Yankees, 1957	34

HOME RUNS, FIRST BASEMAN

1.	Mark McGwire, Cardinals, 1998	69
2.	Mark McGwire, Cardinals, 1999	65
3.	Hank Greenberg, Tigers, 1938	58
4.	Mark McGwire, A's-Cardinals, 1997	57
5.	Jimmie Foxx, A's, 1932	51
	Johnny Mize, Giants, 1947	51
7.	Jimmie Foxx, Red Sox, 1938	50
8.	Lou Gehrig, Yankees, 1934	49
	Lou Gehrig, Yankees, 1936	49
	Ted Kluszewski, Reds, 1954	49
	Todd Helton, Rockies, 2001	49

HOME RUNS, SECOND BASEMAN

1.	Rogers Hornsby, Cardinals, 1922	42
	Davey Johnson, Braves, 1973	42
3.	Ryne Sandberg, Cubs, 1990	40
4.	Rogers Hornsby, Cardinals, 1925	39
	Rogers Hornsby, Cubs, 1929	39
	Alfonso Soriano, Yankees, 2002	39
7.	Jay Bell, Diamondbacks, 1999	38
8.	Bret Boone, Mariners, 2001	36
	Jeff Kent, Giants, 2002	36
10.	Joe Gordon, Indians, 1948	32
	Jeff Kent, Giants, 2000	32

HOME RUNS, THIRD BASEMAN

1.	Mike Schmidt, Phillies, 1980	48
2.	Eddie Mathews, Braves, 1953	47
3.	Eddie Mathews, Braves, 1959	46
	Vinny Castilla, Rockies, 1998	46
	Troy Glaus, Angels, 2000	46
6.	Mike Schmidt, Phillies, 1979	45
	Chipper Jones, 1999	45
8.	Al Rosen, Indians, 1953	43
	Matt Williams, Giants, 1994	43
10.	Harmon Killebrew, Senators, 1959	42

HOME RUNS, SHORTSTOP

1.	Alex Rodriguez, Rangers, 2002	57
2.	Alex Rodriguez, Mariners, 2001	52
3.	Ernie Banks, Cubs, 1958	47
4.	Ernie Banks, Cubs, 1959	45
5.	Ernie Banks, Cubs, 1955	44
6.	Alex Rodriguez, Mariners, 1998	42
	Alex Rodriguez, Mariners, 1999	42
8.	Ernie Banks, Cubs, 1960	41
	Alex Rodriguez, Mariners, 2000	41
10.	Rico Petrocelli, Red Sox, 1969	40

HOME RUNS, OUTFIELDER

1.	Barry Bonds, Giants, 2001	71
2.	Sammy Sosa, Cubs, 1998	66
3.	Sammy Sosa, Cubs, 2001	64
4.	Sammy Sosa, Cubs, 1999	63
5.	Roger Maris, Yankees, 1961	61
6.	Babe Ruth, Yankees, 1927	60
7.	Babe Ruth, Yankees, 1921	58
8.	Luis Gonzalez, Diamondbacks, 2001	57
9.	Hack Wilson, Cubs, 1930	56
	Ken Griffey Jr., Mariners, 1998	56
11.	Babe Ruth, Yankees, 1920	54
	Babe Ruth, Yankees, 1928	54
	Ralph Kiner, Pirates, 1949	54
	Mickey Mantle, Yankees, 1961	54
	Ken Griffey Jr., Mariners, 1997	54
16.	Mickey Mantle, Yankees, 1956	52
	Willie Mays, Giants, 1965	52
	George Foster, Reds, 1977	52
19.	Ralph Kiner, Pirates, 1947	51
	Willie Mays, Giants, 1962	51

HOME RUNS, CATCHER

1.	Todd Hundley, Mets, 1996	41
2.	Roy Campanella, Dodgers, 1953	40
	Mike Piazza, Dodgers, 1997	40
	Mike Piazza, Mets, 1999	40
5.	Johnny Bench, Reds, 1970	38
6.	Gabby Hartnett, Cubs, 1930	36
	Mike Piazza, Dodgers, 1996	36
8.	Walker Cooper, Giants, 1947	35
	Mike Piazza, Dodgers, 1993	35
	Mike Piazza, Dodgers, 2000	35

HOME RUNS, PITCHER

1.	Wes Ferrell, Indians, 1931	9
2.	Wes Ferrell, Indians, 1933	7
	Bob Lemon, Indians, 1949	7
	Don Newcombe, Dodgers, 1955	7
	Don Drysdale, Dodgers, 1958	7
	Don Drysdale, Dodgers, 1965	7
	Earl Wilson, Tigers, 1968	7
	Mike Hampton, Rockies, 2001	7

HOME RUNS, DESIGNATED HITTER

1.	Rafael Palmeiro, Rangers, 1999	37
	Edgar Martinez, Mariners, 2000	37
3.	Dave Kingman, A's, 1984	35
	Dave Kingman, A's, 1986	35
	John Jaha, A's, 1999	35
6.	Greg Luzinski, White Sox, 1983	32
	Gorman Thomas, Mariners, 1985	32
	Jose Canseco, Devil Rays, 1999	32
	Brad Fullmer, Blue Jays, 2000	32
	Ellis Burks, Indians, 2002	32

HOME RUNS, ROOKIE

1.	Mark McGwire, A's, 1987	49
2.	Wally Berger, Braves, 1930	38
	Frank Robinson, Reds, 1956	38
4.	Albert Pujols, Cardinals, 2001	37
	Al Rosen, Indians, 1950	37
6.	Ron Kittle, White Sox, 1983	35
	Mike Piazza, Dodgers, 1993	35
	Hal Trosky, Indians, 1934	35
9.	Walt Dropo, Red Sox, 1950	34
10.	Jose Canseco, A's, 1986	33
	Jimmie Hall, Twins, 1963	33
	Earl Williams, Braves, 1971	33
13.	Matt Nokes, Tigers, 1987	32
	Tony Oliva, Twins, 1964	32
15.	Jim Ray Hart, Giants, 1964	31
	Tim Salmon, Angels, 1993	31
	Ted Williams, Red Sox, 1939	31
18.	Bob Allison, Senators, 1959	30
	Nomar Garciaparra, Red Sox, 1997	30
	Pete Incaviglia, Rangers, 1986	30
	Willie Montanez, Phillies, 1971	30

CONSECUTIVE GAMES WITH HOME RUN

1.	Don Mattingly, Yankees, 1987 (10)	8
	Dale Long, Pirates, 1956 (8)	8
	Ken Griffey Jr., Mariners, 1993 (8)	8
	Jim Thome, Indians, 2002 (7)	7
5.	Frank Howard, Senators, 1968 (10)	6
	Barry Bonds, Giants, 2001 (9)	6
	George Kelly, Giants, 1924 (7)	6
	Walker Cooper, Giants, 1947 (7)	6
	Willie Mays, Giants, 1955 (7)	6
	Roger Maris, Yankees, 1961 (7)	6
	Graig Nettles, Padres, 1984 (7)	6
	Ken Williams, Browns, 1922 (6)	6
	Lou Gehrig, Yankees, 1931 (6)	6
	Roy Sievers, Senators, 1957 (6)	6
	Reggie Jackson, Orioles, 1976 (6)	6
	Barry Bonds, Giants, 2001 (6)	6
	Jose Cruz Jr., Blue Jays, 2001 (6)	6
18.	Jim Bottomley, Cardinals (7), 1929	5
	Babe Ruth, Yankees, (7) 1921	5
	Vic Wertz, Tigers, (7) 1950	5
	Johnny Bench, Reds (7), 1972	5
	Mike Schmidt, Phillies (7), 1979	5

Note: Number in ( ) is homer total during streak.

MOST HOMERS PER AT-BAT

1.	Barry Bonds, Giants, 2001	.153
2.	Mark McGwire, Cardinals, 1998	.138
3.	Mark McGwire, Cardinals, 1999	.125
4.	Mark McGwire, Cardinals, 1996	.123
5.	Babe Ruth, Yankees, 1920	.118
6.	Babe Ruth, Yankees, 1927	.111
	Sammy Sosa, Cubs, 2001	.111
8.	Babe Ruth, Yankees, 1921	.109
9.	Mark McGwire, A's-Cardinals, 1997	.107
10.	Mickey Mantle, Yankees, 1961	.105
11.	Hank Greenberg, Tigers, 1938	.104
12.	Roger Maris, Yankees, 1961	.103
	Sammy Sosa, Cubs, 1998	.103
14.	Barry Bonds, Cubs, 2000	.102
15.	Sammy Sosa, Cubs, 1999	.101
	Babe Ruth, Yankees, 1928	.101
17.	Jimmie Foxx, A's, 1932	.099
18.	Ralph Kiner, Pirates, 1949	.098
	Mickey Mantle, Yankees, 1956	.098
20.	Jeff Bagwell, Astros, 1994	.097

PINCH-HIT HOME RUNS

1.	Dave Hansen, Dodgers, 2000	7
	Craig Wilson, Pirates, 2001	7
3.	Johnny Frederick, Dodgers, 1932	6
4.	Joe Cronin, Red Sox, 1943	5
	Butch Nieman, Braves, 1945	5
	Gene Freese, Phillies, 1959	5
	Jerry Lynch, Reds, 1961	5
	Cliff Johnson, Astros, 1974	5
	Lee Lacy, Dodgers, 1978	5
	Jerry Turner, Padres, 1978	5
	Billy Ashley, Dodgers, 1996	5
	David Dellucci, Diamondbacks, 2001	5
	Erubiel Durazo, Diamondbacks, 2001	5

Roger Maris (left), Ted Williams (center) and Mickey Mantle rate high on baseball's all-time slugging charts.

GRAND SLAMS

1.	Don Mattingly, Yankees, 1987	6
2.	Ernie Banks, Cubs, 1955	5
	Jim Gentile, Orioles, 1961	5
4.	Frank Schulte, Cubs, 1911	4
	Babe Ruth, Red Sox, 1919	4
	Lou Gehrig, Yankees, 1934	4
	Rudy York, Tigers, 1938	4
	Vince DiMaggio, Phillies, 1945	4
	Tommy Henrich, Yankees, 1948	4
	Ralph Kiner, Pirates, 1949	4
	Sid Gordon, Braves, 1950	4
	Al Rosen, Indians, 1951	4
	Ray Boone, Indians-Tigers, 1953	4
	Jim Northrup, Tigers, 1968	4
	Albert Belle, White Sox, 1997	4
	Jason Giambi, A's, 2000	4
	Edgar Martinez, Mariners, 2000	4
	Phil Nevin, Padres, 2001	4

TOTAL BASES

1.	Babe Ruth, Yankees, 1921	457
2.	Rogers Hornsby, Cardinals, 1922	450
3.	Lou Gehrig, Yankees, 1927	447
4.	Chuck Klein, Phillies, 1930	445
5.	Jimmie Foxx, A's, 1932	438
6.	Stan Musial, Cardinals, 1948	429
7.	Sammy Sosa, Cubs, 2001	425
8.	Hack Wilson, Cubs, 1930	423
9.	Chuck Klein, Phillies, 1932	420
10.	Lou Gehrig, Yankees, 1930	419
	Luis Gonzalez, Diamondbacks, 2001	419
12.	Joe DiMaggio, Yankees, 1937	418
13.	Babe Ruth, Yankees, 1927	417
14.	Babe Herman, Dodgers, 1930	416
	Sammy Sosa, Cubs, 1998	416
16.	Barry Bonds, Giants, 2001	411
17.	Lou Gehrig, Yankees, 1931	410
18.	Lou Gehrig, Yankees, 1934	409
	Rogers Hornsby, Cubs, 1929	409
	Larry Walker, Rockies, 1997	409

*SLUGGING PERCENTAGE

1.	Barry Bonds, Giants, 2001	.863
2.	Babe Ruth, Yankees, 1920	.847
3.	Babe Ruth, Yankees, 1921	.846
4.	Barry Bonds, Giants, 2002	.799
5.	Babe Ruth, Yankees, 1927	.772
6.	Lou Gehrig, Yankees, 1927	.765
7.	Babe Ruth, Yankees, 1923	.764
8.	Rogers Hornsby, Cardinals, 1925	.756
9.	Mark McGwire, Cardinals, 1998	.752
10.	Jeff Bagwell, Astros, 1994	.750
11.	Jimmie Foxx, A's, 1932	.749
12.	Babe Ruth, Yankees, 1924	.739
13.	Babe Ruth, Yankees, 1926	.737
	Sammy Sosa, Cubs, 2001	.737
15.	Ted Williams, Red Sox, 1941	.735
16.	Babe Ruth, Yankees, 1930	.732
17.	Ted Williams, Red Sox, 1957	.731
18.	Mark McGwire, A's, 1996	.730
19.	Frank Thomas, White Sox, 1994	.729
20.	Hack Wilson, Cubs, 1930	.723

*Based on players averaging at least 3.1 at-bats for every game played by their teams.

EXTRA-BASE HITS

1.	Babe Ruth, Yankees, 1921	119
2.	Lou Gehrig, Yankees, 1927	117
3.	Barry Bonds, Giants, 2001	107
	Chuck Klein, Phillies, 1930	107
5.	Todd Helton, Rockies, 2001	105
6.	Albert Belle, Indians, 1995	103
	Hank Greenberg, Tigers, 1937	103
	Todd Helton, Rockies, 2000	103
	Chuck Klein, Phillies, 1932	103
	Stan Musial, Cardinals, 1948	103
	Sammy Sosa, Cubs, 2001	103
12.	Rogers Hornsby, Cardinals, 1922	102
13.	Jimmie Foxx, A's, 1932	100
	Lou Gehrig, Yankees, 1930	100
	Luis Gonzalez, Diamondbacks, 2001	100
16.	Albert Belle, White Sox, 1998	99
	Carlos Delgado, Blue Jays, 2000	99
	Hank Greenberg, Tigers, 1940	99
	Babe Ruth, Yankees, 1920	99
	Babe Ruth, Yankees, 1923	99
	Larry Walker, Rockies, 1997	99

RUNS BATTED IN

1.	Hack Wilson, Cubs, 1930	191
2.	Lou Gehrig, Yankees, 1931	184
3.	Hank Greenberg, Tigers, 1937	183
4.	Jimmie Foxx, Red Sox, 1938	175
	Lou Gehrig, Yankees, 1927	175
6.	Lou Gehrig, Yankees, 1930	174
7.	Babe Ruth, Yankees, 1921	171
8.	Hank Greenberg, Tigers, 1935	170
	Chuck Klein, Phillies, 1930	170
10.	Jimmie Foxx, A's, 1932	169
11.	Joe DiMaggio, Yankees, 1937	167
12.	Lou Gehrig, Yankees, 1934	165
	Manny Ramirez, Indians, 1999	165
	Al Simmons, A's, 1930	165
15.	Babe Ruth, Yankees, 1927	164
16.	Jimmie Foxx, A's, 1933	163
	Babe Ruth, Yankees, 1931	163
18.	Hal Trosky, Indians, 1936	162
19.	Sammy Sosa, Cubs, 2001	160
20.	4 tied with 159	

RBIs, RIGHTHANDER

1.	Hack Wilson, Cubs, 1930	191
2.	Hank Greenberg, Tigers, 1937	183
3.	Jimmie Foxx, Red Sox, 1938	175
4.	Hank Greenberg, Tigers, 1935	170
5.	Jimmie Foxx, A's, 1932	169
6.	Joe DiMaggio, Yankees, 1937	167
7.	Manny Ramirez, Indians, 1999	165
	Al Simmons, A's, 1930	165
9.	Jimmie Foxx, A's, 1933	163
10.	Sammy Sosa, Cubs, 2001	160
11.	Vern Stephens, Red Sox, 1949	159
	Hack Wilson, Cubs, 1929	159
13.	Sammy Sosa, Cubs, 1998	158
14.	Juan Gonzalez, Rangers, 1998	157

	Al Simmons, A's, 1929	157
16.	Jimmie Foxx, A's, 1930	156
17.	Joe DiMaggio, Yankees, 1948	155
18.	Joe Medwick, Cardinals, 1937	154
19.	Tommy Davis, Dodgers, 1962	153
20.	Albert Belle, White Sox, 1998	152
	Rogers Hornsby, Cardinals, 1922	152

RBIs, LEFTHANDER

1.	Lou Gehrig, Yankees, 1931	184
2.	Lou Gehrig, Yankees, 1927	175
3.	Lou Gehrig, Yankees, 1930	174
4.	Babe Ruth, Yankees, 1921	171
5.	Chuck Klein, Phillies, 1930	170
6.	Lou Gehrig, Yankees, 1934	165
7.	Babe Ruth, Yankees, 1927	164
8.	Babe Ruth, Yankees, 1931	163
9.	Hal Trosky, Indians, 1936	162
10.	Lou Gehrig, Yankees, 1937	159
	Ted Williams, Red Sox, 1949	159
12.	Ken Williams, Browns, 1922	155
13.	Babe Ruth, Yankees, 1929	154
14.	Babe Ruth, Yankees, 1930	153
15.	Lou Gehrig, Yankees, 1936	152
16.	Lou Gehrig, Yankees, 1932	151
	Mel Ott, Giants, 1929	151
18.	Rafael Palmeiro, Rangers, 1999	148
19.	Ken Griffey Jr., Mariners, 1997	147
	Todd Helton, Rockies, 2000	147

RBIs, SWITCH HITTER

1.	Ken Caminiti, Padres, 1996	130
	Mickey Mantle, Yankees, 1956	130
3.	Ripper Collins, Cardinals, 1934	128
	Mickey Mantle, Yankees, 1961	128
	Lance Berkman, Astros, 2002	128
6.	Lance Berkman, Astros, 2001	126
7.	Eddie Murray, Orioles, 1985	124
8.	Ripper Collins, Cardinals, 1935	122
9.	Bernie Williams, Yankees, 2000	121
10.	Roberto Alomar, Indians, 1999	120
	Bobby Bonilla, Pirates, 1990	120
12.	Ruben Sierra, Rangers, 1989	119
13.	Tony Clark, Tigers, 1997	117
	Howard Johnson, Mets, 1991	117
15.	Bobby Bonilla, Orioles, 1996	116
	Eddie Murray, Orioles, 1980	116
	Ruben Sierra, Rangers, 1991	116
18.	Bernie Williams, Yankees, 1999	115
19.	Carlos Baerga, Indians, 1993	114
	Frankie Frisch, Cardinals, 1930	114

RBIs, ROOKIE

1.	Ted Williams, Red Sox, 1939	145
2.	Walt Dropo, Red Sox, 1950	144
3.	Hal Trosky, Indians, 1934	142
4.	Dale Alexander, Tigers, 1929	137
5.	Albert Pujols, Cardinals, 2001	130
6.	Joe DiMaggio, Yankees, 1936	125
7.	Wally Berger, Braves, 1930	119
8.	Mark McGwire, A's, 1987	118
9.	Jose Canseco, A's, 1986	117
	Joe Vosmik, Indians, 1931	117
11.	Alvin Davis, Mariners, 1984	116
	Al Rosen, Indians, 1950	116
13.	Smead Jolley, White Sox, 1930	114
	Tony Lazzeri, Yankees, 1926	114
15.	Ken Keltner, Indians, 1938	113
16.	Ray Jablonski, Cardinals, 1953	112
	Mike Piazza, Dodgers, 1993	112
18.	Johnny Rizzo, Pirates, 1938	111
	Glenn Wright, Pirates, 1924	111
20.	Zeke Bonura, White Sox, 1934	110

WALKS

1.	Barry Bonds, Giants, 2002	198
2.	Barry Bonds, Giants, 2001	177
3.	Babe Ruth, Yankees, 1923	170
4.	Mark McGwire, Cardinals, 1998	162
	Ted Williams, Red Sox, 1947	162
	Ted Williams, Red Sox, 1949	162
7.	Ted Williams, Red Sox, 1946	156
8.	Barry Bonds, Giants, 1996	151
	Eddie Yost, Senators, 1956	151
10.	Jeff Bagwell, Astros, 1999	149
	Eddie Joost, A's, 1949	149
12.	Babe Ruth, Yankees, 1920	148
	Eddie Stanky, Dodgers, 1945	148
	Jimmy Wynn, Astros, 1969	148
15.	Jimmy Sheckard, Cubs, 1911	147
16.	Mickey Mantle, Yankees, 1957	146
17.	Barry Bonds, Giants, 1997	145
	Harmon Killebrew, Twins, 1969	145
	Babe Ruth, Yankees, 1921	145
	Ted Williams, Red Sox, 1941	145
	Ted Williams, Red Sox, 1942	145

INTENTIONAL WALKS

1.	Barry Bonds, Giants, 2002	68
2.	Willie McCovey, Giants, 1969	45
3.	Barry Bonds, Giants, 1993	43
4.	Willie McCovey, Giants, 1970	40
5.	Sammy Sosa, Cubs, 2001	37
6.	Barry Bonds, Giants, 2001	35
7.	Barry Bonds, Giants, 1997	34
8.	John Olerud, Blue Jays, 1993	33
	Ted Williams, Red Sox, 1957	33
10.	Barry Bonds, Pirates, 1992	32
	Kevin Mitchell, Giants, 1989	32
12.	George Brett, Royals, 1985	31
13.	Barry Bonds, Giants, 1996	30
14.	Barry Bonds, Giants, 1998	29
	Frank Howard, Senators, 1970	29
	Dale Murphy, Braves, 1987	29
	Adolfo Phillips, Cubs, 1967	29
	Frank Thomas, White Sox, 1995	29
19.	Ernie Banks, Cubs, 1960	28
	Mark McGwire, Cardinals, 1998	28

STRIKEOUTS

1.	Bobby Bonds, Giants, 1970	189
2.	Jose Hernandez, Brewers, 2002	188
3.	Bobby Bonds, Giants, 1969	187
	Preston Wilson, Marlins, 2000	187
5.	Rob Deer, Brewers, 1987	186
6.	Jose Hernandez, Brewers, 2001	185
	Pete Incaviglia, Rangers, 1986	185
	Jim Thome, Indians, 2001	185
9.	Cecil Fielder, Tigers, 1990	182
10.	Mo Vaughn, Angels, 2000	181
11.	Mike Schmidt, Phillies, 1975	180
12.	Rob Deer, Brewers, 1986	179
13.	Richie Sexson, Brewers, 2001	178
14.	Mike Cameron, Mariners, 2002	176
15.	Jay Buhner, Mariners, 1997	175
	Jose Canseco, A's, 1986	175
	Rob Deer, Tigers, 1991	175
	Dave Nicholson, White Sox, 1963	175
	Gorman Thomas, Brewers, 1979	175
20.	Sammy Sosa, Cubs, 1997	174

STOLEN BASES

1.	Rickey Henderson, A's, 1982	130
2.	Lou Brock, Cardinals, 1974	118
3.	Vince Coleman, Cardinals, 1985	110
4.	Vince Coleman, Cardinals, 1987	109
5.	Rickey Henderson, A's, 1983	108
6.	Vince Coleman, Cardinals, 1986	107
7.	Maury Wills, Dodgers, 1962	104
8.	Rickey Henderson, A's, 1980	100
9.	Ron LeFlore, Expos, 1980	97
10.	Ty Cobb, Tigers, 1915	96
	Omar Moreno, Pirates, 1980	96
12.	Maury Wills, Dodgers, 1965	94
13.	Rickey Henderson, Yankees, 1988	93
14.	Tim Raines Sr., Expos, 1983	90
15.	Clyde Milan, Senators, 1912	88
16.	Rickey Henderson, Yankees, 1986	87
17.	Ty Cobb, Tigers, 1911	83
	Willie Wilson, Royals, 1979	83
19.	Bob Bescher, Reds, 1911	81
	Vince Coleman, Cardinals, 1988	81
	Eddie Collins, A's, 1910	81

PITCHING

GAMES

1.	Mike Marshall, Dodgers, 1974	106
2.	Kent Tekulve, Pirates, 1979	94
3.	Mike Marshall, Expos, 1973	92
4.	Kent Tekulve, Pirates, 1978	91
5.	Wayne Granger, Reds, 1969	90
	Mike Marshall, Twins, 1979	90
	Kent Tekulve, Phillies, 1987	90
8.	Mark Eichhorn, Blue Jays, 1987	89
	Steve Kline, Cardinals, 2001	89
	Julian Tavarez, Giants, 1997	89
11.	Mike Myers, Tigers, 1997	88
	Sean Runyan, Tigers, 1998	88
	Wilbur Wood, White Sox, 1968	88
14.	Rob Murphy, Reds, 1987	87
15.	Paul Quantrill, Dodgers, 2002	86
16.	Kent Tekulve, Pirates, 1982	85
	Frank Williams, Reds, 1987	85
	Mitch Williams, Rangers, 1987	85
19.	Ted Abernathy, Cubs, 1965	84
	Stan Belinda, Reds, 1997	84
	Graeme Lloyd, Expos, 2001	84
	Dan Quisenberry, Royals, 1985	84
	Enrique Romo, Pirates, 1979	84
	Dick Tidrow, Cubs, 1980	84
	Billy Koch, A's, 2002	84

GAMES STARTED

1.	Jack Chesbro, Yankees, 1904	51
2.	Ed Walsh, White Sox, 1908	49
	Wilbur Wood, White Sox, 1972	49
4.	Joe McGinnity, Giants, 1903	48
	Wilbur Wood, White Sox, 1973	48
6.	Dave Davenport, St. Louis F.L., 1915	46
	Christy Mathewson, Giants, 1904	46
	Rube Waddell, A's, 1904	46
	Ed Walsh, White Sox, 1907	46
	Vic Willis, Braves, 1902	46
11.	Grover Alexander, Phillies, 1916	45
	Mickey Lolich, Tigers, 1971	45
	Jack Powell, Yankees, 1904	45
14.	Grover Alexander, Phillies, 1917	44
	Christy Mathewson, Giants, 1908	44
	Joe McGinnity, Giants, 1904	44
	George Mullin, Tigers, 1904	44
	Phil Niekro, Braves, 1979	44
	George Uhle, Indians, 1923	44
20.	9 tied with 43	

COMPLETE GAMES

1.	Jack Chesbro, Yankees, 1904	48
2.	Vic Willis, Braves, 1902	45
3.	Joe McGinnity, Giants, 1903	44
4.	George Mullin, Tigers, 1904	42
	Ed Walsh, White Sox, 1908	42
6.	Noodles Hahn, Reds, 1901	41
	Cy Young, Red Sox, 1902	41
	Irv Young, Braves, 1905	41
9.	Cy Young, Red Sox, 1904	40
10.	Bill Dinneen, Red Sox, 1902	39
	Joe McGinnity, Orioles, 1901	39
	Jack Taylor, Cardinals, 1904	39
	Rube Waddell, A's, 1904	39
	Vic Willis, Braves, 1904	39
15.	Grover Alexander, Phillies, 1916	38
	Walter Johnson, Senators, 1910	38
	Oscar Jones, Dodgers, 1904	38
	Joe McGinnity, Giants, 1904	38
	Jack Powell, Yankees, 1904	38
	Cy Young, Red Sox, 1901	38

INNINGS PITCHED

1.	Ed Walsh, White Sox, 1908	464.0
2.	Jack Chesbro, Yankees, 1904	454.2
3.	Joe McGinnity, Giants, 1903	434.0
4.	Ed Walsh, White Sox, 1907	422.1
5.	Vic Willis, Braves, 1902	410.0
6.	Joe McGinnity, Giants, 1904	408.0
7.	Ed Walsh, White Sox, 1912	393.0
8.	Dave Davenport, St. Louis F.L., 1915	392.2
9.	Christy Mathewson, Giants, 1908	390.2
10.	Jack Powell, Yankees, 1904	390.1
11.	Togie Pittinger, Braves, 1902	389.1
12.	Grover Alexander, Phillies, 1916	389.0
13.	Grover Alexander, Phillies, 1917	388.0
14.	Cy Young, Red Sox, 1902	384.2
15.	Rube Waddell, A's, 1904	383.0
16.	George Mullin, Tigers, 1904	382.1
17.	Joe McGinnity, Orioles, 1901	382.0
18.	Cy Young, Red Sox, 1904	380.0
19.	Irv Young, Braves, 1905	378.0
20.	Cy Falkenberg, Indianapolis F.L., 1914	377.1

CONSECUTIVE SCORELESS INNINGS

1.	Orel Hershiser, Dodgers, 1988	59
2.	Don Drysdale, Dodgers, 1968	58
3.	Walter Johnson, Senators, 1913	55.2
4.	Jack Coombs, A's, 1910	53
5.	Ed Reulbach, Cubs, 1908	*50
6.	Bob Gibson, Cardinals, 1968	47
7.	Carl Hubbell, Giants, 1933	45.1
8.	Cy Young, Red Sox, 1904	45
	Doc White, White Sox, 1904	45
	Sal Maglie, Giants, 1950	45
11.	Rube Waddell, A's, 1905	43.2
12.	Rube Foster, Red Sox, 1914	42
13.	Jack Chesbro, Pirates, 1902	41
	Grover Alexander, Phillies, 1911	41
	Art Nehf, Braves, 1917	41
	Luis Tiant, Indians, 1968	41
17.	Walter Johnson, Senators, 1918	40
	Gaylord Perry, Giants, 1967	40
	Luis Tiant, Red Sox, 1972	40
20.	Mordecai Brown, Cubs, 1908	39.2
	Billy Pierce, White Sox, 1953	39.2

* 44 in 1908; 6 in 1909.

*LOWEST ERA

1.	Dutch Leonard, Red Sox, 1914	0.96
2.	Mordecai Brown, Cubs, 1906	1.04
3.	Bob Gibson, Cardinals, 1968	1.12
4.	Christy Mathewson, Giants, 1909	1.14
	Walter Johnson, Senators, 1913	1.14
6.	Jack Pfiester, Cubs, 1907	1.15

Rank	Pitcher	Total
7.	Addie Joss, Indians, 1908	1.16
8.	Carl Lundgren, Cubs, 1907	1.17
9.	Grover Alexander, Phillies, 1915	1.22
10.	Cy Young, Red Sox, 1908	1.26
11.	Ed Walsh, White Sox, 1910	1.27
	Walter Johnson, Senators, 1918	1.27
13.	Christy Mathewson, Giants, 1905	1.28
14.	Jack Coombs, A's, 1910	1.30
15.	Mordecai Brown, Cubs, 1909	1.31
16.	Jack Taylor, Cubs, 1902	1.33
17.	Walter Johnson, Senators, 1910	1.36
18.	Walter Johnson, Senators, 1912	1.39
	Mordecai Brown, Cubs, 1907	1.39
	Harry Krause, A's, 1909	1.39

*Leaders based on pitchers whose total innings equal total games played by their teams.

VICTORIES

Rank	Pitcher	Total
1.	Jack Chesbro, Yankees, 1904	41
2.	Ed Walsh, White Sox, 1908	40
3.	Christy Mathewson, Giants, 1908	37
4.	Walter Johnson, Senators, 1913	36
5.	Joe McGinnity, Giants, 1904	35
6.	Joe Wood, Red Sox, 1912	34
7.	Grover Alexander, Phillies, 1916	33
	Walter Johnson, Senators, 1912	33
	Christy Mathewson, Giants, 1904	33
	Cy Young, Red Sox, 1901	33
11.	Cy Young, Red Sox, 1902	32
12.	Grover Alexander, Phillies, 1915	31
	Jim Bagby, Indians, 1920	31
	Jack Coombs, A's, 1910	31
	Lefty Grove, A's, 1931	31
	Christy Mathewson, Giants, 1905	31
	Joe McGinnity, Giants, 1903	31
	Denny McLain, Tigers, 1968	31
19.	Grover Alexander, Phillies, 1917	30
	Dizzy Dean, Cardinals, 1934	30
	Christy Mathewson, Giants, 1903	30

WINNING PERCENTAGE

(Minimum 15 victories)

Rank	Pitcher	Total
1.	Roy Face, Pirates, 1959	.947
2.	Johnny Allen, Indians, 1937	.938
3.	Greg Maddux, Braves, 1995	.905
4.	Randy Johnson, Mariners, 1995	.900
5.	Ron Guidry, Yankees, 1978	.893
6.	Freddie Fitzsimmons, Dodgers, 1940	.889
7.	Lefty Grove, A's, 1931	.886
8.	Bob Stanley, Red Sox, 1978	.882
9.	Preacher Roe, Dodgers, 1951	.880
10.	Joe Wood, Red Sox, 1912	.872
11.	Roger Clemens, Yankees, 2001	.870
12.	David Cone, Mets, 1988	.870
13.	Orel Hershiser, Dodgers, 1985	.864
14.	Bill Donovan, Tigers, 1907	.862
	Whitey Ford, Yankees, 1961	.862
16.	Roger Clemens, Red Sox, 1986	.857
	Dwight Gooden, Mets, 1985	.857
18.	Pedro Martinez, Red Sox, 1999	.852
19.	Chief Bender, A's, 1914	.850
	John Smoltz, Braves, 1998	.850

CONSECUTIVE VICTORIES

Rank	Pitcher	Total
1.	Rube Marquard, Giants, 1912	19
2.	Roy Face, Pirates, 1959	17
3.	Walter Johnson, Senators, 1912	16
	Joe Wood, Red Sox, 1912	16
	Lefty Grove, A's, 1931	16
	Schoolboy Rowe, Tigers, 1934	16
	Carl Hubbell, Giants, 1936	16
	Ewell Blackwell, Reds, 1947	16
	Jack Sanford, Giants, 1962	16
	Roger Clemens, Yankees, 2001	16
11.	Dazzy Vance, Dodgers, 1924	15
	Alvin Crowder, Senators, 1932	15
	Johnny Allen, Indians, 1937	15
	Bob Gibson, Cardinals, 1968	15
	Dave McNally, Orioles, 1969	15
	Steve Carlton, Phillies, 1972	15
	Gaylord Perry, Indians, 1974	15
	Roger Clemens, Blue Jays, 1998	15
19.	many tied with 14	

LOSSES

Rank	Pitcher	Total
1.	Vic Willis, Braves, 1905	29
2.	George Bell, Dodgers, 1910	27
	Paul Derringer, Cardinals-Reds, 1933	27
	Dummy Taylor, Giants, 1901	27
5.	Gus Dorner, Reds-Braves, 1906	26
	Bob Groom, Senators, 1909	26
	Happy Townsend, Senators, 1904	26
8.	Ben Cantwell, Braves, 1935	25
	Pete Dowling, Brewers-Indians, 1901	25
	Patsy Flaherty, White Sox, 1903	25
	Fred Glade, Browns, 1905	25
	Walter Johnson, Senators, 1909	25
	Oscar Jones, Dodgers, 1904	25
	Stoney McGlynn, Cardinals, 1907	25
	Harry McIntire, Dodgers, 1905	25
	Scott Perry, A's, 1920	25
	Bugs Raymond, Cardinals, 1908	25
	Red Ruffing, Red Sox, 1928	25
	Vic Willis, Braves, 1904	25
	Irv Young, Braves, 1906	25

SAVES

Rank	Pitcher	Total
1.	Bobby Thigpen, White Sox, 1990	57
2.	John Smoltz, Braves, 2002	55
3.	Trevor Hoffman, Padres, 1998	53
	Randy Myers, Cubs, 1993	53
5.	Eric Gagne, Dodgers, 2002	52
6.	Rod Beck, Cubs, 1998	51
	Dennis Eckersley, A's, 1992	51
8.	Mariano Rivera, Yankees, 2001	50
9.	Rod Beck, Giants, 1993	48
	Dennis Eckersley, A's, 1990	48
	Jeff Shaw, Reds-Dodgers, 1998	48
12.	Lee Smith, Cardinals, 1991	47
13.	Tom Gordon, Red Sox, 1998	46
	Bryan Harvey, Angels, 1991	46
	Jose Mesa, Indians, 1995	46
	Dave Righetti, Yankees, 1986	46
	Lee Smith, Cardinals-Yankees, 1993	46
	Mike Williams, Pirates, 2002	46
19.	Antonio Alfonseca, Marlins, 2000	45
	Dennis Eckersley, A's, 1988	45
	Bryan Harvey, Marlins, 1993	45
	Jeff Montgomery, Royals, 1993	45
	Randy Myers, Orioles, 1997	45
	Robb Nen, Giants, 2001	45
	Dan Quisenberry, Royals, 1983	45
	Mariano Rivera, Yankees, 1999	45
	Kazuhiro Sasaki, Mariners, 2001	45
	Bruce Sutter, Cardinals, 1984	45
	Duane Ward, Blue Jays, 1993	45
	Eddie Guardado, Twins, 2002	45
	Jose Mesa, Phillies, 2002	45

SHUTOUTS

Rank	Pitcher	Total
1.	Grover Alexander, Phillies, 1916	16
2.	Jack Coombs, A's, 1910	13
	Bob Gibson, Cardinals, 1968	13
4.	Grover Alexander, Phillies, 1915	12
5.	Dean Chance, Angels, 1964	11
	Walter Johnson, Senators, 1913	11
	Sandy Koufax, Dodgers, 1963	11
	Christy Mathewson, Giants, 1908	11
	Ed Walsh, White Sox, 1908	11
10.	Mort Cooper, Cardinals, 1942	10
	Dave Davenport, St. Louis F.L., 1915	10
	Bob Feller, Indians, 1946	10
	Carl Hubbell, Giants, 1933	10
	Bob Lemon, Indians, 1948	10
	Juan Marichal, Giants, 1965	10
	Jim Palmer, Orioles, 1975	10
	John Tudor, Cardinals, 1985	10
	Ed Walsh, White Sox, 1906	10
	Joe Wood, Red Sox, 1912	10
	Cy Young, Red Sox, 1904	10

RUNS ALLOWED

Rank	Pitcher	Total
1.	Snake Wiltse, A's-Orioles, 1902	226
2.	Joe McGinnity, Orioles, 1901	219
3.	Chick Fraser, A's, 1901	210
4.	Pete Dowling, Brewers-Indians, 1901	209
5.	Bobo Newsom, Browns, 1938	205
	Togie Pittinger, Braves, 1903	205
7.	Bill Carrick, Senators, 1901	198
8.	Bill Phillips, Reds, 1901	196
9.	Bill Carrick, Senators, 1902	194
10.	Dummy Taylor, Giants, 1901	193
11.	Harry Howell, Orioles, 1901	188
	Harry McIntire, Dodgers, 1905	188
13.	Sam Gray, Browns, 1931	187
14.	Case Patten, Senators, 1902	186
15.	Watty Lee, Senators, 1901	184
16.	Bill Reidy, Brewers, 1901	183
17.	Dickie Kerr, White Sox, 1921	182
18.	Ray Kremer, Pirates, 1930	181
	Al Orth, Senators, 1902	181
20.	Ray Benge, Phillies, 1930	178

HITS ALLOWED

Rank	Pitcher	Total
1.	Joe McGinnity, Orioles, 1901	412
2.	Snake Wiltse, A's-Orioles, 1902	397
3.	Togie Pittinger, Braves, 1903	396
4.	Joe McGinnity, Giants, 1903	391
5.	Oscar Jones, Dodgers, 1904	387
6.	Wilbur Wood, White Sox, 1973	381
7.	George Uhle, Indians, 1923	378
8.	Dummy Taylor, Giants, 1901	377
9.	Vic Willis, Braves, 1902	372
10.	Noodles Hahn, Reds, 1901	370
11.	Bill Carrick, Senators, 1901	367
	Al Orth, Senators, 1902	367
	Case Patten, Senators, 1904	367
14.	Ray Kremer, Pirates, 1930	366
15.	Urban Shocker, Browns, 1922	365
16.	Bill Phillips, Reds, 1901	364
	Bill Reidy, Brewers, 1901	364
18.	Jack Coombs, A's, 1911	360
	Togie Pittinger, Braves, 1902	360
20.	Dickie Kerr, White Sox, 1921	357
	Vic Willis, Braves, 1904	357

STRIKEOUTS

Rank	Pitcher	Total
1.	Nolan Ryan, Angels, 1973	383
2.	Sandy Koufax, Dodgers, 1965	382
3.	Randy Johnson, Diamondbacks, 2001	372
4.	Nolan Ryan, Angels, 1974	367
5.	Randy Johnson, Diamondbacks, 1999	364
6.	Rube Waddell, A's, 1904	349
7.	Bob Feller, Indians, 1946	348
8.	Randy Johnson, Diamondbacks, 2000	347
9.	Nolan Ryan, Angels, 1977	341
10.	Randy Johnson, Diamondbacks, 2002	334
11.	Randy Johnson, Mariners-Astros, 1998	329
	Nolan Ryan, Angels, 1972	329
13.	Nolan Ryan, Angels, 1976	327
14.	Sam McDowell, Indians, 1965	325
15.	Curt Schilling, Phillies, 1997	319
16.	Sandy Koufax, Dodgers, 1966	317
17.	Curt Schilling, Diamondbacks, 2002	316
18.	Walter Johnson, Senators, 1910	313
	Pedro Martinez, Red Sox, 1999	313
	J.R. Richard, Astros, 1979	313

WALKS

Rank	Pitcher	Total
1.	Bob Feller, Indians, 1938	208
2.	Nolan Ryan, Angels, 1977	204
3.	Nolan Ryan, Angels, 1974	202
4.	Bob Feller, Indians, 1941	194
5.	Bobo Newsom, Browns, 1938	192
6.	Sam Jones, Cubs, 1955	185
7.	Nolan Ryan, Angels, 1976	183
8.	Bob Harmon, Cardinals, 1911	181
	Bob Turley, Orioles, 1954	181
10.	Tommy Byrne, Yankees, 1949	179
11.	Bob Turley, Yankees, 1955	177
12.	Bump Hadley, White Sox-Browns, 1932	171
13.	Elmer Myers, A's, 1916	168
14.	Bobo Newsom, Senators-Red Sox, 1937	167
15.	Weldon Wyckoff, A's, 1915	165
16.	Earl Moore, Phillies, 1911	164
	Phil Niekro, Braves, 1977	164
18.	Nolan Ryan, Angels, 1973	162
	Johnny Vander Meer, Reds, 1943	162
20.	Tommy Byrne, Yankees, 1950	160

HIT BATSMEN

Rank	Pitcher	Total
1.	Chick Fraser, A's, 1901	32
2.	Jack Warhop, Yankees, 1909	26
3.	Chief Bender, A's, 1903	25
4.	Otto Hess, Indians, 1906	24
	Eddie Plank, A's, 1905	24
6.	Howard Ehmke, Tigers, 1922	23
	Eddie Plank, A's, 1903	23
	Jake Weimer, Reds, 1907	23
9.	Cy Morgan, Red Sox-A's, 1909	22
10.	Jack Chesbro, Pirates, 1902	21
	Joe McGinnity, Orioles, 1901	21
	Harry McIntire, Dodgers, 1909	21
	Cy Morgan, A's, 1911	21
	Tom Murphy, Angels, 1969	21
	Doc Newton, Reds-Dodgers, 1901	21
	Henry Schmidt, Dodgers, 1903	21
17.	many tied with 20	

WILD PITCHES

Rank	Pitcher	Total
1.	Red Ames, Giants, 1905	30
2.	Tony Cloninger, Braves, 1966	27
3.	Larry Cheney, Cubs, 1914	26
	Juan Guzman, Blue Jays, 1993	26
5.	Jack Morris, Tigers, 1987	24
6.	Matt Clement, Padres, 2000	23
	Tim Leary, Yankees, 1990	23
	Christy Mathewson, Giants, 1901	23
9.	Tony Cloninger, Braves, 1965	22
	Jack Hamilton, Phillies, 1962	22
	Mike Moore, A's, 1992	22
	Bobby Witt, Rangers, 1986	22
13.	Ken Howell, Phillies, 1989	21
	Walter Johnson, Senators, 1910	21
	Joe Niekro, Astros-Yankees, 1985	21
	Nolan Ryan, Angels, 1977	21
	Scott Williamson, Reds, 2000	21
	Earl Wilson, Red Sox, 1963	21
19.	6 tied with 20	

BATTING

3-GAME SERIES

HIGHEST AVERAGE

(Minimum 9 at-bats)

	Player	Avg.
1.	Jay Johnstone, Phillies, 1976	.778
2.	Brooks Robinson, Orioles, 1970	.583
3.	Darrell Porter, Cardinals, 1982	.556
	Ozzie Smith, Cardinals, 1982	.556
5.	Frank White, Royals, 1980	.545
6.	Art Shamsky, Mets, 1969	.538
7.	Sal Bando, A's, 1975	.500
	Jerry Mumphrey, Yankees, 1981	.500
	Graig Nettles, Yankees, 1981	.500
	Tony Oliva, Twins, 1970	.500
	Brooks Robinson, Orioles, 1969	.500
	Willie Stargell, Pirates, 1970	.500
	Bob Watson, Yankees, 1980	.500
	Richie Zisk, Pirates, 1975	.500

RUNS

	Player	No.
1.	Mark Belanger, Orioles, 1970	5
2.	Tommie Agee, Mets, 1969	4
	Mark Belanger, Orioles, 1969	4
	Ken Boswell, Mets, 1969	4
	Rico Carty, Braves, 1969	4
	Dave Concepcion, Reds, 1976	4
	Carlton Fisk, Red Sox, 1975	4
	Phil Garner, Pirates, 1979	4
	Tony Gonzalez, Braves, 1969	4
	Davey Johnson, Orioles, 1970	4
	Cleon Jones, Mets, 1969	4
	Willie McGee, Cardinals, 1982	4
	Larry Milbourne, Yankees, 1981	4
	Boog Powell, Orioles, 1971	4
	Carl Yastrzemski, Red Sox, 1975	4

HITS

	Player	No.
1.	Jay Johnstone, Phillies, 1976	7
	Brooks Robinson, Orioles, 1969	7
	Brooks Robinson, Orioles, 1970	7
	Art Shamsky, Mets, 1969	7
5.	Sal Bando, A's, 1975	6
	Paul Blair, Orioles, 1969	6
	Dave Concepcion, Reds, 1979	6
	Cleon Jones, Mets, 1969	6
	Larry Milbourne, Yankees, 1981	6
	Jerry Mumphrey, Yankees, 1981	6
	Graig Nettles, Yankees, 1981	6
	Tony Oliva, Twins, 1970	6
	Boog Powell, Orioles, 1970	6
	Pete Rose, Reds, 1976	6
	Willie Stargell, Pirates, 1970	6
	Bob Watson, Yankees, 1980	6
	Frank White, Royals, 1980	6

HOME RUNS

	Player	No.
1.	Hank Aaron, Braves, 1969	3
2.	Tommie Agee, Mets, 1969	2
	Ken Boswell, Mets, 1969	2
	George Brett, Royals, 1980	2
	George Foster, Reds, 1976	2
	Reggie Jackson, A's, 1971	2
	Davey Johnson, Orioles, 1970	2
	Harmon Killebrew, Twins, 1970	2
	Boog Powell, Orioles, 1971	2
	Willie Stargell, Pirates, 1979	2

TOTAL BASES

	Player	No.
1.	Hank Aaron, Braves, 1969	16
2.	Willie Stargell, Pirates, 1979	13
3.	Tommie Agee, Mets, 1969	12
4.	Paul Blair, Orioles, 1969	11
	Reggie Jackson, A's, 1971	11
	Cleon Jones, Mets, 1969	11
	Willie McGee, Cardinals, 1982	11
	Graig Nettles, Yankees, 1981	11
	Tony Oliva, Twins, 1970	11
	Boog Powell, Orioles, 1970	11
	Bob Watson, Yankees, 1980	11

RUNS BATTED IN

	Player	No.
1.	Graig Nettles, Yankees, 1981	9
2.	Hank Aaron, Braves, 1969	7
3.	Paul Blair, Orioles, 1969	6
	Boog Powell, Orioles, 1970	6
	Willie Stargell, Pirates, 1979	6
6.	Ken Boswell, Mets, 1969	5
	Willie McGee, Cardinals, 1982	5
8.	Tommie Agee, Mets, 1969	4
	George Brett, Royals, 1980	4
	Mike Cuellar, Orioles, 1970	4
	George Foster, Reds, 1976	4
	Ken Griffey Sr., Reds, 1975	4
	Davey Johnson, Orioles, 1970	4
	Cleon Jones, Mets, 1969	4
	Harmon Killebrew, Twins, 1970	4
	Tony Perez, Reds, 1975	4
	Willie Wilson, Royals, 1980	4

STOLEN BASES

	Player	No.
1.	Joe Morgan, Reds, 1975	4
2.	Ken Griffey Sr., Reds, 1975	3
3.	Tommie Agee, Mets, 1969	2
	Juan Beniquez, Red Sox, 1975	2
	Dave Collins, Reds, 1979	2
	Dave Concepcion, Reds, 1975	2
	Ken Griffey Sr., Reds, 1976	2
	Rickey Henderson, A's, 1981	2
	Cleon Jones, Mets, 1969	2
	Bill Madlock, Pirates, 1979	2
	Joe Morgan, Reds, 1976	2
	Amos Otis, Royals, 1980	2

4-GAME SERIES

HIGHEST AVERAGE

(Minimum 12 at-bats)

	Player	Avg.
1.	Dusty Baker, Dodgers, 1978	.467
	Mike Schmidt, Phillies, 1983	.467
3.	Reggie Jackson, Yankees, 1978	.462
4.	Wade Boggs, Red Sox, 1990	.438
	Chipper Jones, Braves, 1995	.438
	Carney Lansford, A's, 1990	.438
	Fred McGriff, Braves, 1995	.438
	Bob Robertson, Pirates, 1971	.438
9.	Gary Matthews, Phillies, 1983	.429
	Willie McCovey, Giants, 1971	.429
	Amos Otis, Royals, 1978	.429

RUNS

	Player	No.
1.	George Brett, Royals, 1978	7
2.	Steve Garvey, Dodgers, 1978	6
3.	Al Bumbry, Orioles, 1979	5
	Dave Cash, Pirates, 1971	5
	Reggie Jackson, Yankees, 1978	5
	Fred McGriff, Braves, 1995	5
	Eddie Murray, Orioles, 1983	5
	Cal Ripken Jr., Orioles, 1983	5
	Bob Robertson, Pirates, 1971	5
	Mike Schmidt, Phillies, 1983	5
	Roy White, Yankees, 1978	5

HITS

	Player	No.
1.	Dave Cash, Pirates, 1971	8
2.	Dusty Baker, Dodgers, 1978	7
	Wade Boggs, Red Sox, 1990	7
	George Brett, Royals, 1978	7
	Rod Carew, Angels, 1979	7
	Steve Garvey, Dodgers, 1974	7
	Steve Garvey, Dodgers, 1978	7
	Chipper Jones, Braves, 1995	7
	Carney Lansford, A's, 1990	7
	Barry Larkin, Reds, 1995	7
	Rudy Law, White Sox, 1983	7
	Davey Lopes, Dodgers, 1978	7
	Fred McGriff, Braves, 1995	7
	Bob Robertson, Pirates, 1971	7
	Bill Russell, Dodgers, 1974	7
	Bill Russell, Dodgers, 1978	7
	Mike Schmidt, Phillies, 1983	7

HOME RUNS

	Player	No.
1.	Steve Garvey, Dodgers, 1978	4
	Bob Robertson, Pirates, 1971	4
3.	George Brett, Royals, 1978	3
	Jose Canseco, A's, 1988	3
	Gary Matthews, Phillies, 1983	3
6.	Dusty Baker, Dodgers, 1977	2
	Sal Bando, A's, 1974	2
	Dan Ford, Angels, 1979	2
	Steve Garvey, Dodgers, 1974	2
	Richie Hebner, Pirates, 1971	2
	Reggie Jackson, Yankees, 1978	2
	Davey Lopes, Dodgers, 1978	2
	Greg Luzinski, Phillies, 1978	2
	Willie McCovey, Giants, 1971	2
	Willie Stargell, Pirates, 1974	2

TOTAL BASES

	Player	No.
1.	Steve Garvey, Dodgers, 1978	22
2.	Bob Robertson, Pirates, 1971	20
3.	George Brett, Royals, 1978	19
4.	Davey Lopes, Dodgers, 1978	16
5.	Jose Canseco, A's, 1988	15
	Gary Matthews, Phillies, 1983	15
7.	Steve Garvey, Dodgers, 1974	14
	Greg Luzinski, Phillies, 1978	14
9.	Reggie Jackson, Yankees, 1978	13
10.	Dusty Baker, Dodgers, 1977	12
	Dan Ford, Angels, 1979	12
	Richie Hebner, Pirates, 1971	12
	Willie McCovey, Giants, 1971	12
	Mike Schmidt, Phillies, 1983	12
	Willie Stargell, Pirates, 1974	12

RUNS BATTED IN

	Player	No.
1.	Dusty Baker, Dodgers, 1977	8
	Gary Matthews, Phillies, 1983	8
3.	Steve Garvey, Dodgers, 1978	7
4.	Reggie Jackson, Yankees, 1978	6
	Willie McCovey, Giants, 1971	6
	Bob Robertson, Pirates, 1971	6
7.	Mike Devereaux, Braves, 1995	5
	Steve Garvey, Dodgers, 1974	5
	Davey Lopes, Dodgers, 1978	5
	Eddie Murray, Orioles, 1979	5
	Al Oliver, Pirates, 1971	5

STOLEN BASES

	Player	No.
1.	Amos Otis, Royals, 1978	4
2.	Davey Lopes, Dodgers, 1974	3
3.	Al Bumbry, Orioles, 1979	2
	Jose Canseco, A's, 1990	2
	Julio Cruz, White Sox, 1983	2
	Rickey Henderson, A's, 1990	2
	Pat Kelly, Orioles, 1979	2
	Rudy Law, White Sox, 1983	2
	Willie McGee, A's, 1990	2
10.	many tied with 1	

5-GAME SERIES

HIGHEST AVERAGE

(Minimum 15 at-bats)

	Player	Avg.
1.	Will Clark, Giants, 1989	.650
2.	Mark Grace, Cubs, 1989	.647
3.	Fred Lynn, Angels, 1982	.611
4.	Terry Puhl, Astros, 1980	.526
5.	Chris Chambliss, Yankees, 1976	.524
6.	Roberto Alomar, Blue Jays, 1991	.474
	Bernie Williams, Yankees, 1996	.474
8.	Jose Offerman, Red Sox, 1999	.458
9.	Pete Rose, Reds, 1972	.450
10.	Edgardo Alfonzo, Mets, 2000	.444
	George Brett, Royals, 1976	.444
	Hal McRae, Royals, 1977	.444

RUNS

	Player	No.
1.	Will Clark, Giants, 1989	8
	Rickey Henderson, A's, 1989	8
	Timo Perez, Mets, 2000	8
4.	Mike Pizaaz, Mets, 2000	7
5.	Brett Butler, Giants, 1989	6
	Tony Fernandez, Blue Jays, 1989	6
	Tony Gwynn, Padres, 1984	6
	Hal McRae, Royals, 1977	6
	Ryne Sandberg, Cubs, 1989	6
	Bernie Williams, Yankees, 1996	6

HITS

	Player	No.
1.	Will Clark, Giants, 1989	13
2.	Chris Chambliss, Yankees, 1976	11
	Mark Grace, Cubs, 1989	11
	Fred Lynn, Angels, 1982	11
	Jose Offerman, Red Sox, 1999	11
6.	Derek Jeter, Yankees, 1996	10
	Thurman Munson, Yankees, 1976	10
	Terry Puhl, Astros, 1980	10
9.	Roberto Alomar, Blue Jays, 1991	9
	Kirby Puckett, Twins, 1991	9
	Mickey Rivers, Yankees, 1977	9
	Pete Rose, Reds, 1972	9
	Bernie Williams, Yankees, 1996	9

HOME RUNS

	Player	No.
1.	Rusty Staub, Mets, 1973	3
	Darryl Strawberry, Yankees, 1996	3
	Todd Zeile, Orioles, 1996	3
	Bernie Williams, Yankees, 2001	3
	Adam Kennedy, Angels, 2002	3
6.	Sal Bando, A's, 1973	2
	Bret Boone, Mariners, 2001	2
	Scott Brosius, Yankees, 1999	2
	Tom Brunansky, Twins, 1987	2
	Bert Campaneris, A's, 1973	2
	Chris Chambliss, Yankees, 1976	2
	Will Clark, Giants, 1989	2
	Jody Davis, Cubs, 1984	2
	Leon Durham, Cubs, 1984	2
	Cecil Fielder, Yankees, 1996	2
	Gary Gaetti, Twins, 1987	2
	Greg Gagne, Twins, 1987	2
	Nomar Garciaparra, Red Sox, 1999	2
	Rickey Henderson, A's, 1989	2
	Chet Lemon, Tigers, 1987	2
	Gary Matthews, Cubs, 1984	2
	Kevin Mitchell, Giants, 1989	2
	Paul Molitor, Brewers, 1982	2
	Joe Morgan, Reds, 1972	2
	Graig Nettles, Yankees, 1976	2
	Paul O'Neill, Yankees, 2001	2
	Rafael Palmeiro, Orioles, 1996	2
	Dave Parker, A's, 1989	2
	Mike Piazza, Mets, 2000	2
	Kirby Puckett, Twins, 1991	2
	Pete Rose, Reds, 1973	2
	Robby Thompson, Giants, 1989	2
	Bernie Williams, Yankees, 1996	2

	Matt Williams, Giants, 1989	2
	Rich Aurilia, Giants, 2002	2
	Benito Santiago, Giants, 2002	2

TOTAL BASES

1.	Will Clark, Giants, 1989	24
2.	Chris Chambliss, Yankees, 1976	20
3.	Mark Grace, Cubs, 1989	19
4.	Bernie Williams, Yankees, 1996	18
5.	Tom Brunansky, Twins, 1987	17
	Todd Zeile, Orioles, 1996	17
7.	Nomar Garciaparra, Red Sox, 1999	16
	Fred Lynn, Angels, 1982	16
	Mike Piazza, Mets, 2000	16
	Kirby Puckett, Twins, 1991	16
	Ryne Sandberg, Cubs, 1989	16

RUNS BATTED IN

1.	Don Baylor, Angels, 1982	10
2.	Tom Brunansky, Twins, 1987	9
	Matt Williams, Giants, 1989	9
4.	Chris Chambliss, Yankees, 1976	8
	Will Clark, Giants, 1989	8
	Cecil Fielder, Yankees, 1996	8
	Mark Grace, Cubs, 1989	8
	Todd Zeile, Mets, 2000	8
9.	Steve Garvey, Padres, 1984	7
	Kevin Mitchell, Giants, 1989	7

STOLEN BASES

1.	Rickey Henderson, A's, 1989	8
2.	Tony Fernandez, Blue Jays, 1989	5
	Davey Lopes, Dodgers, 1981	5
4.	Randy Bush, Twins, 1987	3
	Bert Campaneris, A's, 1973	3
	Kirk Gibson, Tigers, 1987	3
	Dan Gladden, Twins, 1991	3
	Nelson Liriano, Blue Jays, 1989	3
	Edgar Renteria, Cardinals, 2000	3
	Ryne Sandberg, Cubs, 1984	3
	Devon White, Blue Jays, 1991	3

6-GAME SERIES

HIGHEST AVERAGE

(Minimum 18 at-bats)

1.	Eddie Perez, Braves, 1999	.500
2.	Kenny Lofton, Indians, 1995	.458
3.	Tim Raines Sr., White Sox, 1993	.444
	Devon White, Blue Jays, 1993	.444
5.	Harold Baines, A's, 1992	.440
	Omar Vizquel, Indians, 1998	.440
7.	Fred McGriff, Braves, 1993	.435
	Ozzie Smith, Cardinals, 1985	.435
	Bernie Williams, Yankees, 2000	.435
10.	Roberto Alomar, Blue Jays, 1992	.423

RUNS

1.	Paul Molitor, Blue Jays, 1993	7
	Dave Winfield, Blue Jays, 1992	7
3.	Harold Baines, A's, 1992	6
	Derek Jeter, Yankees, 2000	6
	Willie McGee, Cardinals, 1985	6
	Fred McGriff, Braves, 1993	6
	Paul O'Neill, Yankees, 1998	6
	Gary Sheffield, Marlins, 1997	6
9.	Brady Anderson, Orioles, 1997	5
	Wally Backman, Mets, 1986	5
	Jeff Blauser, Braves, 1993	5
	Jeff Blauser, Braves, 1997	5
	Jay Buhner, Mariners, 1995	5
	Lenny Dykstra, Phillies, 1993	5
	Rickey Henderson, A's, 1992	5
	Andruw Jones, Braves, 1999	5
	Chipper Jones, Braves, 1997	5
	Barry Larkin, Reds, 1990	5
	Bill Madlock, Dodgers, 1985	5
	Tino Martinez, Yankees, 2000	5
	John Olerud, Blue Jays, 1993	5
	Tim Raines Sr., White Sox, 1993	5
	Bernie Williams, Yankees, 2000	5

HITS

1.	Tim Raines Sr., White Sox, 1993	12
	Devon White, Blue Jays, 1993	12
3.	Roberto Alomar, Blue Jays, 1992	11
	Harold Baines, A's, 1992	11
	Kenny Lofton, Indians, 1995	11
	Omar Vizquel, Indians, 1998	11
7.	Carlos Baerga, Indians, 1995	10
	Fred McGriff, Braves, 1993	10
	Eddie Perez, Braves, 1999	10
	Ozzie Smith, Cardinals, 1985	10
	Bernie Williams, Yankees, 2000	10

HOME RUNS

1.	Jim Thome, Indians, 1998	4
2.	Jay Buhner, Mariners, 1995	3
	Bill Madlock, Dodgers, 1985	3
4.	Roberto Alomar, Blue Jays, 1992	2
	Brady Anderson, Orioles, 1997	2
	Jeff Blauser, Braves, 1993	2
	Ken Caminiti, Padres, 1998	2
	Lenny Dykstra, Phillies, 1993	2
	Dave Hollins, Phillies, 1993	2
	Derek Jeter, Yankees, 2000	2
	Chipper Jones, Braves, 1997	2
	Brian Jordan, Braves, 1999	2
	David Justice, Yankees, 2000	2
	Ryan Klesko, Braves, 1997	2
	Candy Maldonado, Blue Jays, 1992	2
	John Olerud, Mets, 1999	2
	Eddie Perez, Braves, 1999	2
	Manny Ramirez, Indians, 1995	2
	Manny Ramirez, Indians, 1997	2
	Manny Ramirez, Indians, 1998	2
	Alex Rodriguez, Mariners, 2000	2
	Darryl Strawberry, Mets, 1986	2
	Jim Thome, Indians, 1995	2
	Dave Winfield, Blue Jays, 1992	2

TOTAL BASES

1.	Jim Thome, Indians, 1998	19
2.	Roberto Alomar, Blue Jays, 1992	18
	Jay Buhner, Mariners, 1995	18
	Bill Madlock, Dodgers, 1985	18
	Eddie Perez, Braves, 1999	18
	Devon White, Blue Jays, 1993	18
7.	Brady Anderson, Orioles, 1997	17
	Alex Rodriguez, Mariners, 2000	17
9.	Harold Baines, A's, 1992	16
	Paul Molitor, Blue Jays, 1993	16
	Ozzie Smith, Cardinals, 1985	16

RUNS BATTED IN

1.	David Justice, Yankees, 2000	8
	Jim Thome, Indians, 1998	8
3.	Bill Madlock, Dodgers, 1985	7
	Ruben Sierra, A's, 1992	7
5.	Scott Brosius, Yankees, 1998	6
	Tom Herr, Cardinals, 1985	6
	Lance Johnson, White Sox, 1993	6
	Candy Maldonado, Blue Jays, 1992	6
	John Olerud, Mets, 1999	6
10.	Moises Alou, Marlins, 1997	5
	Jay Buhner, Mariners, 1995	5
	Chili Davis, Yankees, 1998	5
	Derek Jeter, Yankees, 2000	5
	Charles Johnson, Marlins, 1997	5
	Brian Jordan, Braves, 1999	5
	John Kruk, Phillies, 1993	5
	Paul Molitor, Blue Jays, 1993	5
	Paul O'Neill, Yankees, 2000	5
	Terry Pendleton, Braves, 1993	5
	Eddie Perez, Braves, 1999	5
	Alex Rodriguez, Mariners, 2000	5
	Terry Steinbach, A's, 1992	5
	Darryl Strawberry, Mets, 1986	5
	Jim Thome, Indians, 1995	5
	Michael Tucker, Braves, 1998	5
	Robin Ventura, White Sox, 1993	5
	Bernie Williams, Yankees, 1998	5

STOLEN BASES

1.	Willie Wilson, A's, 1992	7
2.	Roberto Alomar, Blue Jays, 1992	5
	Kenny Lofton, Indians, 1995	5
4.	Roberto Alomar, Blue Jays, 1993	4
	Vince Coleman, Mariners, 1995	4
	Omar Vizquel, Indians, 1998	4
7.	Marquis Grissom, Indians, 1997	3
	Billy Hatcher, Astros, 1986	3
	Derek Jeter, Yankees, 1998	3
	Chipper Jones, Braves, 1999	3
	Barry Larkin, Reds, 1990	3
	Omar Vizquel, Indians, 1995	3
	Gerald Williams, Braves, 1999	3

7-GAME SERIES

HIGHEST AVERAGE

(Minimum 21 at-bats)

1.	Javy Lopez, Braves, 1996	.542
2.	Bob Boone, Angels, 1986	.455
3.	Mark Lemke, Braves, 1996	.444
4.	Chipper Jones, Braves, 1996	.440
5.	Spike Owen, Red Sox, 1986	.429
6.	Jeffrey Leonard, Giants, 1987	.417
7.	Jay Bell, Pirates, 1991	.414
8.	Tony Pena, Cardinals, 1987	.381
9.	Marty Barrett, Red Sox, 1986	.367
10.	Mike Scioscia, Dodgers, 1988	.364

RUNS

1.	Javy Lopez, Braves, 1996	8
	Jim Rice, Red Sox, 1986	8
3.	Marquis Grissom, Braves, 1996	7
	Steve Sax, Dodgers, 1988	7
5.	Don Baylor, Red Sox, 1986	6
	George Brett, Royals, 1985	6
	Lenny Dykstra, Mets, 1988	6
	Chipper Jones, Braves, 1996	6
	Fred McGriff, Braves, 1996	6
10.	many tied with 5	

HITS

1.	Javy Lopez, Braves, 1996	13
2.	Jay Bell, Pirates, 1991	12
	Mark Lemke, Braves, 1996	12
4.	Marty Barrett, Red Sox, 1986	11
	Chipper Jones, Braves, 1996	11
6.	Bob Boone, Angels, 1986	10
	Rich Gedman, Red Sox, 1986	10
	Marquis Grissom, Braves, 1996	10
	Jeffrey Leonard, Giants, 1987	10
10.	Don Baylor, Red Sox, 1986	9
	George Bell, Blue Jays, 1985	9
	Will Clark, Giants, 1987	9
	Doug DeCinces, Angels, 1986	9
	Gregg Jefferies, Mets, 1988	9
	Spike Owen, Red Sox, 1986	9
	Gary Pettis, Angels, 1986	9
	Dick Schofield, Angeles, 1986	9
	Darryl Strawberry, Mets, 1988	9
	Willie Wilson, Royals, 1985	9

HOME RUNS

1.	Jeffrey Leonard, Giants, 1987	4
2.	George Brett, Royals, 1985	3
3.	Ron Gant, Braves, 1992	2
	Ron Gant, Cardinals, 1996	2
	Kirk Gibson, Dodgers, 1988	2
	David Justice, Braves, 1992	2
	Javy Lopez, Braves, 1996	2
	Fred McGriff, Braves, 1996	2
	Kevin McReynolds, Mets, 1988	2
	Jim Rice, Red Sox, 1986	2
	Pat Sheridan, Royals, 1985	2

TOTAL BASES

1.	Javy Lopez, Braves, 1996	24
2.	Jeffrey Leonard, Giants, 1987	22
3.	George Brett, Royals, 1985	19
4.	Jay Bell, Pirates, 1991	17
	Mark Lemke, Braves, 1996	17
6.	Don Baylor, Red Sox, 1986	15
	Doug DeCinces, Angels, 1986	15
	Fred McGriff, Braves, 1996	15
	Kevin McReynolds, Mets, 1988	15
10.	Will Clark, Giants, 1987	14
	Rich Gedman, Red Sox, 1986	14
	Marquis Grissom, Braves, 1996	14
	David Justice, Braves, 1992	14
	Darryl Strawberry, Mets, 1988	14

RUNS BATTED IN

1.	Brian Downing, Angels, 1986	7
	Fred McGriff, Braves, 1996	7
3.	Ron Gant, Braves, 1992	6
	Rich Gedman, Red Sox, 1986	6
	Kirk Gibson, Dodgers, 1988	6
	David Justice, Braves, 1992	6
	Javy Lopez, Braves, 1996	6
	Jim Rice, Red Sox, 1986	6
	Darryl Strawberry, Mets, 1988	6
	Jim Sundberg, Royals, 1985	6

STOLEN BASES

1.	Ron Gant, Braves, 1991	7
2.	Steve Sax, Dodgers, 1988	5
3.	Barry Bonds, Pirates, 1991	3
	Otis Nixon, Braves, 1992	3
5.	Kirk Gibson, Dodgers, 1988	2
	Marquis Grissom, Braves, 1996	2
	Kevin McReynolds, Mets, 1988	2
	Gary Redus, Pirates, 1991	2
	John Shelby, Dodgers, 1988	2
	Robby Thompson, Giants, 1987	2

PITCHING

3-GAME SERIES

INNINGS PITCHED

1.	Ken Holtzman, A's, 1975	11.0
	Dave McNally, Orioles, 1969	11.0
3.	Dave Boswell, Twins, 1969	10.2
4.	Dock Ellis, Pirates, 1970	9.2
5.	Bert Blyleven, Pirates, 1979	9.0
	Mike Cuellar, Orioles, 1971	9.0
	Bob Forsch, Cardinals, 1982	9.0
	Don Gullett, Reds, 1975	9.0
	Larry Gura, Royals, 1980	9.0
	Dave McNally, Orioles, 1970	9.0
	Gary Nolan, Reds, 1970	9.0
	Jim Palmer, Orioles, 1969	9.0
	Jim Palmer, Orioles, 1970	9.0
	Jim Palmer, Orioles, 1971	9.0
	Luis Tiant, Red Sox, 1975	9.0

LOWEST ERA

(Minimum 9 innings)

1.	Bob Forsch, Cardinals, 1982	0.00
	Dave McNally, Orioles, 1969	0.00

Gary Nolan, Reds, 1970 ... 0.00
Luis Tiant, Red Sox, 1975 ... 0.00
5. Dave Boswell, Twins, 1969 ... 0.84
6. Bert Blyleven, Pirates, 1979 ... 1.00
Mike Cuellar, Orioles, 1971 ... 1.00
Jim Palmer, Orioles, 1970 ... 1.00
9. Larry Gura, Royals, 1980 ... 2.00
Jim Palmer, Orioles, 1969 ... 2.00

VICTORIES

1. Joaquin Andujar, Cardinals, 1982 ... 1
Bert Blyleven, Pirates, 1979 ... 1
Mike Cuellar, Orioles, 1971 ... 1
Rawly Eastwick, Reds, 1975 ... 1
Rawly Eastwick, Reds, 1976 ... 1
Bob Forsch, Cardinals, 1982 ... 1
George Frazier, Yankees, 1981 ... 1
Don Gullett, Reds, 1975 ... 1
Don Gullett, Reds, 1976 ... 1
Larry Gura, Royals, 1980 ... 1
Dick Hall, Orioles, 1969 ... 1
Dick Hall, Orioles, 1970 ... 1
Grant Jackson, Pirates, 1979 ... 1
Tommy John, Yankees, 1981 ... 1
Dennis Leonard, Royals, 1980 ... 1
Aurelio Lopez, Tigers, 1984 ... 1
Dave McNally, Orioles, 1969 ... 1
Dave McNally, Orioles, 1970 ... 1
Dave McNally, Orioles, 1971 ... 1
Jim Merritt, Reds, 1970 ... 1
Roger Moret, Red Sox, 1975 ... 1
Jack Morris, Tigers, 1984 ... 1
Gary Nolan, Reds, 1970 ... 1
Fred Norman, Reds, 1975 ... 1
Jim Palmer, Orioles, 1969 ... 1
Jim Palmer, Orioles, 1970 ... 1
Jim Palmer, Orioles, 1971 ... 1
Dan Quisenberry, Royals, 1980 ... 1
Dave Righetti, Yankees, 1981 ... 1
Don Robinson, Pirates, 1979 ... 1
Nolan Ryan, Mets, 1969 ... 1
Tom Seaver, Mets, 1969 ... 1
Bruce Sutter, Cardinals, 1982 ... 1
Ron Taylor, Mets, 1969 ... 1
Luis Tiant, Red Sox, 1975 ... 1
Milt Wilcox, Reds, 1970 ... 1
Milt Wilcox, Tigers, 1984 ... 1
Rick Wise, Red Sox, 1975 ... 1
Pat Zachry, Reds, 1976 ... 1

SAVES

1. Dick Drago, Red Sox, 1975 ... 2
Don Gullett, Reds, 1970 ... 2
3. Pedro Borbon, Reds, 1975 ... 1
Pedro Borbon, Reds, 1976 ... 1
Clay Carroll, Reds, 1970 ... 1
Rawly Eastwick, Reds, 1975 ... 1
Rich Gossage, Yankees, 1981 ... 1
Willie Hernandez, Tigers, 1984 ... 1
Tug McGraw, Mets, 1969 ... 1
Dan Quisenberry, Royals, 1980 ... 1
Don Robinson, Pirates, 1979 ... 1
Bruce Sutter, Cardinals, 1982 ... 1
Ron Taylor, Mets, 1969 ... 1
Eddie Watt, Orioles, 1971 ... 1

4-GAME SERIES

INNINGS PITCHED

1. Don Sutton, Dodgers, 1974 ... 17.0
2. Dave Stewart, A's, 1990 ... 16.0
3. Gaylord Perry, Giants, 1971 ... 14.2
4. Pete Schourek, Reds, 1995 ... 14.1
5. Steve Carlton, Phillies, 1983 ... 13.2
Tommy John, Dodgers, 1977 ... 13.2
7. Dave Stewart, A's, 1988 ... 13.1
8. Bruce Hurst, Red Sox, 1988 ... 13.0
9. Mike Cuellar, Orioles, 1974 ... 12.2
10. Dennis Leonard, Royals, 1978 ... 12.0
Jerry Reuss, Dodgers, 1983 ... 12.0

LOWEST ERA

(Minimum 9 innings)

1. Vida Blue, A's, 1974 ... 0.00
Mike Boddicker, Orioles, 1983 ... 0.00
Ken Holtzman, A's, 1974 ... 0.00
Tommy John, Dodgers, 1978 ... 0.00
Scott McGregor, Orioles, 1979 ... 0.00
6. Don Sutton, Dodgers, 1974 ... 0.53
7. Steve Carlton, Phillies, 1983 ... 0.66
Tommy John, Dodgers, 1977 ... 0.66
9. Britt Burns, White Sox, 1983 ... 0.96
10. 3 tied with 1.00

VICTORIES

1. Steve Carlton, Phillies, 1983 ... 2
Gene Nelson, A's, 1988 ... 2
Dave Stewart, A's, 1990 ... 2
Don Sutton, Dodgers, 1974 ... 2
5. many tied with 1

SAVES

1. Dennis Eckersley, A's, 1988 ... 4
2. Dave Giusti, Pirates, 1971 ... 3
3. Dennis Eckersley, A's, 1990 ... 2
4. Ken Clay, Yankees, 1978 ... 1
Rollie Fingers, A's, 1974 ... 1
Mike Garman, Dodgers, 1977 ... 1
Rich Gossage, Yankees, 1978 ... 1
Al Holland, Phillies, 1983 ... 1
Rick Honeycutt, A's, 1990 ... 1
Tug McGraw, Phillies, 1977 ... 1
Greg McMichael, Braves, 1995 ... 1
Tom Niedenfuer, Dodgers, 1983 ... 1
Sammy Stewart, Orioles, 1983 ... 1

5-GAME SERIES

INNINGS PITCHED

1. Mickey Lolich, Tigers, 1972 ... 19.0
2. Ray Burris, Expos, 1981 ... 17.0
3. Tom Seaver, Mets, 1973 ... 16.2
4. Catfish Hunter, A's, 1973 ... 16.1
5. Mike Hampton, Mets, 2000 ... 16.0
Dave Stewart, A's, 1989 ... 16.0
Randy Johnson, Diamondbacks, 2001 ... 16.0
7. Steve Blass, Pirates, 1972 ... 15.2
8. Catfish Hunter, A's, 1972 ... 15.1
9. Orlando Hernandez, Yankees, 1999 ... 15.0
Andy Pettitte, Yankees, 1996 ... 15.0
Paul Splittorff, Royals, 1977 ... 15.0

LOWEST ERA

(Minimum 9 innings)

1. Joe Coleman, Tigers, 1972 ... 0.00
Mike Hampton, Mets, 2000 ... 0.00
Burt Hooton, Dodgers, 1981 ... 0.00
Jon Matlack, Mets, 1973 ... 0.00
Joe Niekro, Astros, 1980 ... 0.00
Blue Moon Odom, A's, 1972 ... 0.00
7. Ray Burris, Expos, 1981 ... 0.53
8. Ken Holtzman, A's, 1973 ... 0.82
9. Sparky Lyle, Yankees, 1977 ... 0.96
10. Ross Grimsley, Reds, 1972 ... 1.00
Curt Schilling, Diamondbacks, 2001 ... 1.00

VICTORIES

1. Bert Blyleven, Twins, 1987 ... 2
Mike Hampton, Mets, 2000 ... 2
Burt Hooton, Dodgers, 1981 ... 2
Catfish Hunter, A's, 1973 ... 2
Craig Lefferts, Padres, 1984 ... 2
Sparky Lyle, Yankees, 1977 ... 2
Jack Morris, Twins, 1991 ... 2
Blue Moon Odom, A's, 1972 ... 2
Andy Pettitte, Yankees, 2001 ... 2
Dave Stewart, A's, 1989 ... 2
Randy Johnson, Diamondbacks, 2001 ... 2
Francisco Rodriguez, Angels, 2002 ... 2
Tim Worrell, Giants, 2002 ... 2

SAVES

1. Rick Aguilera, Twins, 1991 ... 3
Steve Bedrosian, Giants, 1989 ... 3
Dennis Eckersley, A's, 1989 ... 3
4. Pete Ladd, Brewers, 1982 ... 2
Tug McGraw, Phillies, 1980 ... 2
Jeff Reardon, Twins, 1987 ... 2
Mariano Rivera, Yankees, 1999 ... 2
Mariano Rivera, Yankees, 2001 ... 2
Byung-Hyun Kim, Diamondbacks, 2001 ... 2
Robb Nen, Giants, 2002 ... 2
Troy Percival, Angels, 2002 ... 2

6-GAME SERIES

INNINGS PITCHED

1. Mike Scott, Astros, 1986 ... 18.0
2. Dwight Gooden, Mets, 1986 ... 17.0
3. Dave Stewart, A's, 1992 ... 16.2
4. Doug Drabek, Pirates, 1990 ... 16.1
5. Randy Johnson, Diamondbacks, 2001 ... 16.0
Curt Schilling, Phillies, 1993 ... 16.0
7. David Wells, Yankees, 1998 ... 15.2
8. Orel Hershiser, Dodgers, 1985 ... 15.1
Randy Johnson, Mariners, 1995 ... 15.1
Bob Knepper, Astros, 1986 ... 15.1

LOWEST ERA

(Minimum 9 innings)

1. Roger Clemens, Yankees, 2000 ... 0.00
Denny Neagle, Braves, 1997 ... 0.00
3. Mike Scott, Astros, 1986 ... 0.50
4. Mike Mussina, Orioles, 1997 ... 0.60
5. Livan Hernandez, Marlins, 1997 ... 0.84
6. Sterling Hitchcock, Padres, 1998 ... 0.90
7. Wilson Alvarez, White Sox, 1993 ... 1.00
Bartolo Colon, Indians, 1998 ... 1.00
Curt Schilling, Diamondbacks, 2001 ... 1.00
10. Dwight Gooden, Mets, 1986 ... 1.06

VICTORIES

1. Jesse Orosco, Mets, 1986 ... 3
2. Kevin Brown, Marlins, 1997 ... 2
Freddy Garcia, Mariners, 2000 ... 2
Juan Guzman, Blue Jays, 1992 ... 2
Juan Guzman, Blue Jays, 1993 ... 2
Livan Hernandez, Marlins, 1997 ... 2
Orlando Hernandez, Mariners, 2000 ... 2
Orel Hershiser, Indians, 1995 ... 2
Sterling Hitchcock, Padres, 1998 ... 2
Randy Johnson, Diamondbacks, 2001 ... 2
Mike Scott, Astros, 1986 ... 2
Dave Stewart, Blue Jays, 1993 ... 2
David Wells, Yankees, 1998 ... 2
Mitch Williams, Phillies, 1993 ... 2

SAVES

1. Tom Henke, Blue Jays, 1992 ... 3
Randy Myers, Reds, 1990 ... 3
3. Ken Dayley, Cardinals, 1985 ... 2
Byung-Hyun Kim, Diamondbacks, 2001 ... 2
Jose Mesa, Indians, 1997 ... 2
Robb Nen, Marlins, 1997 ... 2
Duane Ward, Blue Jays, 1993 ... 2
Mitch Williams, Phillies, 1993 ... 2
8. many tied with 1

7-GAME SERIES

INNINGS PITCHED

1. Orel Hershiser, Dodgers, 1988 ... 24.2
2. Roger Clemens, Red Sox, 1986 ... 22.2
3. John Smoltz, Braves, 1992 ... 20.1
Dave Stieb, Blue Jays, 1985 ... 20.1
5. Dwight Gooden, Mets, 1988 ... 18.1
6. Tim Wakefield, Pirates, 1992 ... 18.0
7. Mike Witt, Angels, 1986 ... 17.2
8. Danny Cox, Cardinals, 1987 ... 17.0
Doug Drabek, Pirates, 1992 ... 17.0
10. Steve Avery, Braves, 1991 ... 16.1

LOWEST ERA

(Minimum 9 innings)

1. Steve Avery, Braves, 1991 ... 0.00
Danny Jackson, Royals, 1985 ... 0.00
Dennis Lamp, Blue Jays, 1985 ... 0.00
4. Doug Drabek, Pirates, 1991 ... 0.60
Dave Dravecky, Giants, 1987 ... 0.60
6. Zane Smith, Pirates, 1991 ... 0.61
7. John Candelaria, Angels, 1986 ... 0.84
8. Orel Hershiser, Dodgers, 1988 ... 1.09
9. John Smoltz, Braves, 1996 ... 1.20
10. Bud Black, Royals, 1985 ... 1.69

VICTORIES

1. Steve Avery, Braves, 1991 ... 2
Tim Belcher, Dodgers, 1988 ... 2
Tom Henke, Blue Jays, 1985 ... 2
Randy Myers, Mets, 1988 ... 2
John Smoltz, Braves, 1991 ... 2
John Smoltz, Braves, 1992 ... 2
John Smoltz, Braves, 1996 ... 2
Tim Wakefield, Pirates, 1992 ... 2
9. many tied with 1

SAVES

1. Alejandro Pena, Braves, 1991 ... 3
2. Ken Dayley, Cardinals, 1987 ... 2
Mark Wohlers, Braves, 1996 ... 2
4. Dennis Eckersley, Cardinals, 1996 ... 1
Orel Hershiser, Dodgers, 1988 ... 1
Brian Holton, Dodgers, 1988 ... 1
Roger Mason, Pirates, 1991 ... 1
Donnie Moore, Angels, 1986 ... 1
Alejandro Pena, Dodgers, 1988 ... 1
Dan Quisenberry, Royals, 1985 ... 1
Jeff Reardon, Braves, 1992 ... 1
Calvin Schiraldi, Red Sox, 1986 ... 1
Bob Walk, Pirates, 1991 ... 1
Todd Worrell, Cardinals, 1987 ... 1

BATTING

4-GAME SERIES

HIGHEST AVERAGE

(Minimum 12 at-bats)

1. Billy Hatcher, Reds, 1990 .750
2. Babe Ruth, Yankees, 1928 .625
3. Chris Sabo, Reds, 1990 .563
4. Bret Boone, Braves, 1999 .538
5. Johnny Bench, Reds, 1976 .533
6. Lou Gehrig, Yankees, 1932 .529
   Thurman Munson, Yankees, 1976 .529
8. Tony Gwynn, Padres, 1998 .500
   Mark Koenig, Yankees, 1927 .500
   Joe Marty, Cubs, 1938 .500
   Vic Wertz, Indians, 1954 .500

RUNS

1. Lou Gehrig, Yankees, 1932 9
   Babe Ruth, Yankees, 1928 9
3. Earle Combs, Yankees, 1932 8
   Charlie Keller, Yankees, 1939 8
5. Earle Combs, Yankees, 1927 6
   Billy Hatcher, Reds, 1990 6
   Dave Henderson, A's, 1989 6
   Babe Ruth, Yankees, 1932 6
   Hank Thompson, Giants, 1954 6
10. 8 tied with 5

HITS

1. Babe Ruth, Yankees, 1928 10
2. Lou Gehrig, Yankees, 1932 9
   Billy Hatcher, Reds, 1990 9
   Rickey Henderson, A's, 1989 9
   Mark Koenig, Yankees, 1927 9
   Thurman Munson, Yankees, 1976 9
   Chris Sabo, Reds, 1990 9
8. Johnny Bench, Reds, 1976 8
   Scott Brosius, Yankees, 1998 8
   Tony Gwynn, Padres, 1998 8
   Stan Hack, Cubs, 1938 8
   Riggs Stephenson, Cubs, 1932 8
   Vic Wertz, Indians, 1954 8

HOME RUNS

1. Lou Gehrig, Yankees, 1928 4
2. Lou Gehrig, Yankees, 1932 3
   Charlie Keller, Yankees, 1939 3
   Babe Ruth, Yankees, 1928 3
5. Johnny Bench, Reds, 1976 2
   Scott Brosius, Yankees, 1998 2
   Bill Dickey, Yankees, 1939 2
   Dave Henderson, A's, 1989 2
   Tony Lazzeri, Yankees, 1932 2
   Dusty Rhodes, Giants, 1954 2
   Frank Robinson, Orioles, 1966 2
   Babe Ruth, Yankees, 1927 2
   Babe Ruth, Yankees, 1932 2
   Chris Sabo, Reds, 1990 2
   Greg Vaughn, Padres, 1998 2

TOTAL BASES

1. Babe Ruth, Yankees, 1928 22
2. Lou Gehrig, Yankees, 1928 19
   Lou Gehrig, Yankees, 1932 19
   Charlie Keller, Yankees, 1939 19
5. Johnny Bench, Reds, 1976 17
   Rickey Henderson, A's, 1989 17
7. Chris Sabo, Reds, 1990 16
8. Billy Hatcher, Reds, 1990 15
   Vic Wertz, Indians, 1954 15
10. Scott Brosius, Yankees, 1998 14
   Hank Gowdy, Braves, 1914 14

RUNS BATTED IN

1. Lou Gehrig, Yankees, 1928 9
2. Lou Gehrig, Yankees, 1932 8
3. Dusty Rhodes, Giants, 1954 7
   Babe Ruth, Yankees, 1927 7
   Terry Steinbach, A's, 1989 7
6. Johnny Bench, Reds, 1976 6
   Scott Brosius, Yankees, 1998 6
   Ben Chapman, Yankees, 1932 6
   Frankie Crosetti, Yankees, 1938 6
   Joe Gordon, Yankees, 1938 6
   Charlie Keller, Yankees, 1939 6
   Babe Ruth, Yankees, 1932 6

STOLEN BASES

1. Rickey Henderson, A's, 1989 3
   Rickey Henderson, A's, 1990 3
   Derek Jeter, Yankees, 1999 3
4. Brett Butler, Giants, 1989 2
   Charlie Deal, Braves, 1914 2
   Frankie Frisch, Cardinals, 1928 2
   Cesar Geronimo, Reds, 1976 2
   Billy Jurges, Cubs, 1932 2
   Tony Lazzeri, Yankees, 1928 2
   Rabbit Maranville, Braves, 1914 2
   Bob Meusel, Yankees, 1928 2
   Joe Morgan, Reds, 1976 2

5-GAME SERIES

HIGHEST AVERAGE

(Minimum 15 at-bats)

1. Paul Blair, Orioles, 1970 .474
   Heinie Groh, Giants, 1922 .474
   Paul O'Neill, Yankees, 2000 .474
4. Frankie Frisch, Giants, 1922 .471
   Harry Steinfeldt, Cubs, 1907 .471
   Hack Wilson, Cubs, 1929 .471
7. Frank Baker, A's, 1913 .450
   Alan Trammell, Tigers, 1984 .450
9. Duffy Lewis, Red Sox, 1915 .444
10. Fred Luderus, Phillies, 1915 .438

RUNS

1. Frank Baker, A's, 1910 6
   Harry Hooper, Red Sox, 1916 6
   Derek Jeter, Yankees, 2000 6
   Lee May, Reds, 1970 6
   Danny Murphy, A's, 1910 6
   Boog Powell, Orioles, 1970 6
   Al Simmons, A's, 1929 6
   Lou Whitaker, Tigers, 1984 6
9. many tied with 5

HITS

1. Frank Baker, A's, 1910 9
   Frank Baker, A's, 1913 9
   Paul Blair, Orioles, 1970 9
   Eddie Collins, A's, 1910 9
   Heinie Groh, Giants, 1922 9
   Derek Jeter, Yankees, 2000 9
   Jo-Jo Moore, Giants, 1937 9
   Paul O'Neill, Yankees, 2000 9
   Bobby Richardson, Yankees, 1961 9
   Brooks Robinson, Orioles, 1970 9
   Alan Trammell, Tigers, 1984 9

HOME RUNS

1. Donn Clendenon, Mets, 1969 3
2. Kurt Bevacqua, Padres, 1984 2
   Johnny Blanchard, Yankees, 1961 2
   Jimmie Foxx, A's, 1929 2
   Larry Gardner, Red Sox, 1916 2
   Kirk Gibson, Tigers, 1984 2
   Mule Haas, A's, 1929 2
   Mickey Hatcher, Dodgers, 1988 2
   Harry Hooper, Red Sox, 1915 2
   Derek Jeter, Yankees, 2000 2
   Charlie Keller, Yankees, 1942 2
   Lee May, Reds, 1970 2
   Joe Morgan, Phillies, 1983 2
   Eddie Murray, Orioles, 1983 2
   Mel Ott, Giants, 1933 2
   Mike Piazza, Mets, 2000 2
   Boog Powell, Orioles, 1970 2
   Brooks Robinson, Orioles, 1970 2
   Frank Robinson, Orioles, 1970 2
   Al Simmons, A's, 1929 2
   Alan Trammell, Tigers, 1984 2
   Aaron Ward, Yankees, 1922 2

TOTAL BASES

1. Derek Jeter, Yankees, 2000 19
2. Brooks Robinson, Orioles, 1970 17
3. Alan Trammell, Tigers, 1984 16
4. Kurt Bevacqua, Padres, 1984 15
   Donn Clendenon, Mets, 1969 15
   Lee May, Reds, 1970 15
   Paul O'Neill, Yankees, 2000 15
8. Jimmie Foxx, A's, 1929 14
   Mickey Hatcher, Dodgers, 1988 14
   Mike Piazza, Mets, 2000 14

RUNS BATTED IN

1. Danny Murphy, A's, 1910 9
2. Lee May, Reds, 1970 8
3. Frank Baker, A's, 1913 7
   Kirk Gibson, Tigers, 1984 7
   Hector Lopez, Yankees, 1961 7
   Irish Meusel, Giants, 1922 7
   Wally Schang, A's, 1913 7
8. 6 tied with 6

STOLEN BASES

1. Jimmy Slagle, Cubs, 1907 6
2. Frank Chance, Cubs, 1908 5
3. Eddie Collins, A's, 1910 4
4. Frank Chance, Cubs, 1907 3
   Eddie Collins, A's, 1913 3
   Bill Dahlen, Giants, 1905 3
   Art Devlin, Giants, 1905 3
   Johnny Evers, Cubs, 1907 3
   Kirk Gibson, Tigers, 1984 3
   Davy Jones, Tigers, 1907 3

6-GAME SERIES

HIGHEST AVERAGE

(Minimum 18 at-bats)

1. Billy Martin, Yankees, 1953 .500
   Paul Molitor, Blue Jays, 1993 .500
   Dave Robertson, Giants, 1917 .500
4. Roberto Alomar, Blue Jays, 1993 .480
5. Amos Otis, Royals, 1980 .478
6. Monte Irvin, Giants, 1951 .458
7. Jake Powell, Yankees, 1936 .455
8. Pat Borders, Blue Jays, 1992 .450
   Reggie Jackson, Yankees, 1977 .450
10. Marquis Grissom, Braves, 1996 .444

RUNS

1. Reggie Jackson, Yankees, 1977 10
   Paul Molitor, Blue Jays, 1993 10
3. Lenny Dykstra, Phillies, 1993 9
   Roy White, Yankees, 1978 9
5. Jake Powell, Yankees, 1936 8
   Babe Ruth, Yankees, 1923 8
   Devon White, Blue Jays, 1993 8
8. Frank Baker, A's, 1911 7
   Davey Lopes, Dodgers, 1978 7
   Reggie Smith, Dodgers, 1977 7

HITS

1. Roberto Alomar, Blue Jays, 1993 12
   Marquis Grissom, Braves, 1996 12
   Billy Martin, Yankees, 1953 12
   Paul Molitor, Blue Jays, 1993 12
5. Monte Irvin, Giants, 1951 11
   Amos Otis, Royals, 1980 11
   Dave Robertson, Giants, 1917 11
   Bill Russell, Dodgers, 1978 11
9. 10 tied with 10

HOME RUNS

1. Reggie Jackson, Yankees, 1977 5
2. Willie Aikens, Royals, 1980 4
   Lenny Dykstra, Phillies, 1993 4
4. Ryan Klesko, Braves, 1995 3
   Ted Kluszewski, White Sox, 1959 3
   Davey Lopes, Dodgers, 1978 3
   Amos Otis, Royals, 1980 3
   Babe Ruth, Yankees, 1923 3
   Reggie Smith, Dodgers, 1977 3
10. many tied with 2

TOTAL BASES

1. Reggie Jackson, Yankees, 1977 25
2. Paul Molitor, Blue Jays, 1993 24
3. Billy Martin, Yankees, 1953 23
4. Willie Aikens, Royals, 1980 22
   Amos Otis, Royals, 1980 22
6. Lenny Dykstra, Phillies, 1993 21
7. Ted Kluszewski, White Sox, 1959 19
   Babe Ruth, Yankees, 1923 19
9. Charlie Neal, Dodgers, 1959 18
10. Frank Baker, A's, 1911 17
   Jim Gilliam, Dodgers, 1953 17
   Davey Lopes, Dodgers, 1978 17
   Devon White, Blue Jays, 1993 17

RUNS BATTED IN

1. Ted Kluszewski, White Sox, 1959 10
2. Tony Fernandez, Blue Jays, 1993 9
3. Willie Aikens, Royals, 1980 8
   Joe Carter, Blue Jays, 1993 8
   Lenny Dykstra, Phillies, 1993 8
   Reggie Jackson, Yankees, 1977 8
   Reggie Jackson, Yankees, 1978 8
   Billy Martin, Yankees, 1953 8
   Bob Meusel, Yankees, 1923 8
   Paul Molitor, Blue Jays, 1993 8

STOLEN BASES

1. Kenny Lofton, Indians, 1995 6
2. Otis Nixon, Braves, 1992 5
   Deion Sanders, Braves, 1992 5
4. Roberto Alomar, Blue Jays, 1993 4
   Lenny Dykstra, Phillies, 1993 4
   Davey Lopes, Dodgers, 1981 4
7. Roberto Alomar, 1992 3
   Larry Bowa, Phillies, 1980 3
   Eddie Collins, White Sox, 1917 3
   Mariano Duncan, Phillies, 1993 3
   Marquis Grissom, Braves, 1995 3
   Joe Tinker, Cubs, 1906 3

7-Game Series

HIGHEST AVERAGE

(Minimum 21 at-bats)

1.	Phil Garner, Pirates, 1979	.500
	Pepper Martin, Cardinals, 1931	.500
3.	Tim McCarver, Cardinals, 1964	.478
4.	Lou Brock, Cardinals, 1968	.464
5.	Max Carey, Pirates, 1925	.458
6.	Joe Harris, Senators, 1925	.440
7.	Tony Perez, Reds, 1972	.435
8.	Marty Barrett, Red Sox, 1986	.433
9.	Phil Cavarretta, Cubs, 1945	.423
	Rusty Staub, Mets, 1973	.423

RUNS

1.	Lou Brock, Cardinals, 1967	8
	Billy Johnson, Yankees, 1947	8
	Tommy Leach, Pirates, 1909	8
	Mickey Mantle, Yankees, 1960	8
	Mickey Mantle, Yankees, 1964	8
	Pepper Martin, Cardinals, 1934	8
	Freddy Parent, Red Sox, 1903	8
	Bobby Richardson, Yankees, 1960	8
	Jim Thome, Indians, 1997	8
	Matt Williams, Indians, 1997	8
	Barry Bonds, Giants, 2002	8

HITS

1.	Marty Barrett, Red Sox, 1986	13
	Lou Brock, Cardinals, 1968	13
	Bobby Richardson, Yankees, 1964	13
4.	Lou Brock, Cardinals, 1967	12
	Roberto Clemente, Pirates, 1971	12
	Phil Garner, Pirates, 1979	12
	Buck Herzog, Giants, 1912	12
	Joe Jackson, White Sox, 1919	12
	Pepper Martin, Cardinals, 1931	12
	Sam Rice, Senators, 1925	12
	Bill Skowron, Yankees, 1960	12
	Willie Stargell, Pirates, 1979	12
	Robin Yount, Brewers, 1982	12

HOME RUNS

1.	Hank Bauer, Yankees, 1958	4
	Babe Ruth, Yankees, 1926	4
	Duke Snider, Dodgers, 1952	4
	Duke Snider, Dodgers, 1955	4
	Gene Tenace, A's, 1972	4
	Barry Bonds, Giants, 2002	4
6.	many tied with 3	

TOTAL BASES

1.	Willie Stargell, Pirates, 1979	25
2.	Lou Brock, Cardinals, 1968	24
	Duke Snider, Dodgers, 1952	24
4.	Hank Aaron, Braves, 1957	22
	Hank Bauer, Yankees, 1958	22
	Roberto Clemente, Pirates, 1971	22
	Joe Harris, Senators, 1925	22
	Barry Bonds, Giants, 2002	22
	Troy Glaus, Angels, 2002	22
10.	Goose Goslin, Senators, 1924	21
	Duke Snider, Dodgers, 1955	21
	Gene Tenace, A's, 1972	21
	Carl Yastrzemski, Red Sox, 1967	21

RUNS BATTED IN

1.	Bobby Richardson, Yankees, 1960	12
2.	Mickey Mantle, Yankees, 1960	11
3.	Sandy Alomar Jr., Indians, 1997	10
	Yogi Berra, Yankees, 1956	10
5.	Moises Alou, Marlins, 1997	9
	Gary Carter, Mets, 1986	9
	Dwight Evans, Red Sox, 1986	9
	Gene Tenace, A's, 1972	9
9.	many tied with 8	

STOLEN BASES

1.	Lou Brock, Cardinals, 1967	7
	Lou Brock, Cardinals, 1968	7
3.	Vince Coleman, Cardinals, 1987	6
	Honus Wagner, Pirates, 1909	6
5.	Pepper Martin, Cardinals, 1931	5
	Bobby Tolan, Reds, 1972	5
	Omar Vizquel, Indians, 1997	5
8.	Josh Devore, Giants, 1912	4
	Chuck Knoblauch, Twins, 1991	4
10.	many tied with 3	

PITCHING

4-Game Series

INNINGS PITCHED

1.	Waite Hoyt, Yankees, 1928	18.0
	Sandy Koufax, Dodgers, 1963	18.0
	Dick Rudolph, Braves, 1914	18.0
	Red Ruffing, Yankees, 1938	18.0
5.	Dave Stewart, A's, 1989	16.0
6.	Paul Derringer, Reds, 1939	15.1
	Jose Rijo, Reds, 1990	15.1
8.	Jim Konstanty, Phillies, 1950	15.0
9.	Kevin Brown, Padres, 1998	14.1
10.	Bob Lemon, Indians, 1954	13.1
	Bill Sherdel, Cardinals, 1928	13.1

LOWEST ERA

(Minimum 9 innings)

1.	Wally Bunker, Orioles, 1966	0.00
	Don Drysdale, Dodgers, 1963	0.00
	Bill James, Braves, 1914	0.00
	Jim Palmer, Orioles, 1966	0.00
	Monte Pearson, Yankees, 1939	0.00
	Vic Raschi, Yankees, 1950	0.00
7.	Dick Rudolph, Braves, 1914	0.50
8.	Jose Rijo, Reds, 1990	0.59
9.	Johnny Antonelli, Giants, 1954	0.84
	Wilcy Moore, Yankees, 1927	0.84

VICTORIES

1.	Waite Hoyt, Yankees, 1928	2
	Bill James, Braves, 1914	2
	Sandy Koufax, Dodgers, 1963	2
	Mike Moore, A's, 1989	2
	Jose Rijo, Reds, 1990	2
	Dick Rudolph, Braves, 1914	2
	Red Ruffing, Yankees, 1938	2
	Dave Stewart, A's, 1989	2
9.	many tied with 1	

SAVES

1.	Mariano Rivera, Yankees, 1998	3
2.	Will McEnaney, Reds, 1976	2
	Herb Pennock, Yankees, 1932	2
	Mariano Rivera, Yankees, 1999	2
5.	Johnny Antonelli, Giants, 1954	1
	Dennis Eckersley, A's, 1989	1
	Wilcy Moore, Yankees, 1927	1
	Johnny Murphy, Yankees, 1938	1
	Randy Myers, Reds, 1990	1
	Ron Perranoski, Dodgers, 1963	1
	Allie Reynolds, Yankees, 1950	1
	Hoyt Wilhelm, Giants, 1954	1

5-Game Series

INNINGS PITCHED

1.	Jack Coombs, A's, 1910	27.0
	Christy Mathewson, Giants, 1905	27.0
3.	Bill Donovan, Tigers, 1907	21.0
4.	Carl Hubbell, Giants, 1933	20.0
5.	Christy Mathewson, Giants, 1913	19.0
	Eddie Plank, A's, 1913	19.0
7.	Chief Bender, A's, 1910	18.2
8.	Orval Overall, Cubs, 1908	18.1
9.	10 tied with 18.0	

LOWEST ERA

(Minimum 9 innings)

1.	Mike Boddicker, Orioles, 1983	0.00
	Mordecai Brown, Cubs, 1907	0.00
	Mordecai Brown, Cubs, 1908	0.00
	Clay Carroll, Reds, 1970	0.00
	Whitey Ford, Yankees, 1961	0.00
	Carl Hubbell, Giants, 1933	0.00
	Christy Mathewson, Giants, 1905	0.00
	Joe McGinnity, Giants, 1905	0.00
	George Mullin, Tigers, 1908	0.00
	Allie Reynolds, Yankees, 1949	0.00
	Preacher Roe, Dodgers, 1949	0.00
	Marius Russo, Yankees, 1943	0.00
	Jack Scott, Giants, 1922	0.00
	Ernie White, Cardinals, 1942	0.00
	Earl Whitehill, Senators, 1933	0.00

VICTORIES

1.	Jack Coombs, A's, 1910	3
	Christy Mathewson, Giants, 1905	3
3.	Johnny Beazley, Cardinals, 1942	2
	Chief Bender, A's, 1913	2
	Mordecai Brown, Cubs, 1908	2
	Spud Chandler, Yankees, 1943	2
	Whitey Ford, Yankees, 1961	2
	Rube Foster, Red Sox, 1915	2
	Lefty Gomez, Yankees, 1937	2
	Orel Hershiser, Dodgers, 1988	2
	Carl Hubbell, Giants, 1933	2
	Jerry Koosman, Mets, 1969	2
	Jack Morris, Tigers, 1984	2
	Orval Overall, Cubs, 1908	2
	Ernie Shore, Red Sox, 1916	2
	Mike Stanton, Yankees, 2000	2

SAVES

1.	Rollie Fingers, A's, 1974	2
	Lefty Grove, A's, 1929	2
	Willie Hernandez, Tigers, 1984	2
	Tippy Martinez, Orioles, 1983	2
	Mariano Rivera, Yankees, 2000	2
6.	many tied with 1	

6-Game Series

INNINGS PITCHED

1.	Red Faber, White Sox, 1917	27.0
	Christy Mathewson, Giants, 1911	27.0
	Hippo Vaughn, Cubs, 1918	27.0
4.	Chief Bender, A's, 1911	26.0
5.	George Earnshaw, A's, 1930	25.0
6.	Eddie Cicotte, White Sox, 1917	23.0
	Lefty Tyler, Cubs, 1918	23.0
8.	Schoolboy Rowe, Tigers, 1935	21.0
9.	Jack Coombs, A's, 1911	20.0
10.	Mordecai Brown, Cubs, 1906	19.2

LOWEST ERA

(Minimum 9 innings)

1.	Gene Bearden, Indians, 1948	0.00
	Rube Benton, Giants, 1917	0.00
	Jack Kramer, Browns, 1944	0.00
4.	Ed Lopat, Yankees, 1951	0.50
5.	Lon Warneke, Cubs, 1935	0.54
6.	John Smoltz, Braves, 1996	0.64
7.	Tommy John, Yankees, 1981	0.69
8.	Larry Sherry, Dodgers, 1959	0.71
9.	George Earnshaw, A's, 1930	0.72
10.	Vic Raschi, Yankees, 1951	0.87

VICTORIES

1.	Red Faber, White Sox, 1917	3
2.	Chief Bender, A's, 1911	2
	Tommy Bridges, Tigers, 1935	2
	Steve Carlton, Phillies, 1980	2
	George Earnshaw, A's, 1930	2
	Tom Glavine, Braves, 1995	2
	Lefty Gomez, Yankees, 1936	2
	Lefty Grove, A's, 1930	2
	Jimmy Key, Blue Jays, 1992	2
	Bob Lemon, Indians, 1948	2
	Ed Lopat, Yankees, 1951	2
	Carl Mays, Red Sox, 1918	2
	Herb Pennock, Yankees, 1923	2
	Babe Ruth, Red Sox, 1918	2
	Larry Sherry, Dodgers, 1959	2
	Mike Torrez, Yankees, 1977	2
	Ed Walsh, White Sox, 1906	2
	Duane Ward, Blue Jays, 1992	2
	Lon Warneke, Cubs, 1935	2

SAVES

1.	John Wetteland, Yankees, 1996	4
2.	Rich Gossage, Yankees, 1981	2
	Tom Henke, Blue Jays, 1992	2
	Tug McGraw, Phillies, 1980	2
	Larry Sherry, Dodgers, 1959	2
	Duane Ward, Blue Jays, 1993	2
	Mark Wohlers, Braves, 1995	2
8.	many tied with 1	

7-Game Series

INNINGS PITCHED

1.	Deacon Phillippe, Pirates, 1903	44.0
2.	Bill Dinneen, Red Sox, 1903	35.0
3.	Cy Young, Red Sox, 1903	34.0
4.	George Mullin, Tigers, 1909	32.0
5.	Christy Mathewson, Giants, 1912	28.2
	Warren Spahn, Braves, 1958	28.2
7.	8 tied with 27.0	

LOWEST ERA

(Minimum 9 innings)

1.	Jack Billingham, Reds, 1972	0.00
	Nelson Briles, Pirates, 1971	0.00
	Joe Dobson, Red Sox, 1946	0.00
	Whitey Ford, Yankees, 1960	0.00
	Waite Hoyt, Yankees, 1921	0.00
	Clem Labine, Dodgers, 1956	0.00
	Don Larsen, Yankees, 1956	0.00
	Duster Mails, Indians, 1920	0.00
9.	Sandy Koufax, Dodgers, 1965	0.38
10.	Harry Brecheen, Cardinals, 1946	0.45

VICTORIES

1.	Babe Adams, Pirates, 1909	3
	Harry Brecheen, Cardinals, 1946	3
	Lew Burdette, Braves, 1957	3
	Stan Coveleski, Indians, 1920	3
	Bill Dinneen, Red Sox, 1903	3
	Bob Gibson, Cardinals, 1967	3
	Randy Johnson, Diamondbacks, 2001	3
	Mickey Lolich, Tigers, 1968	3
	Deacon Phillippe, Pirates, 1903	3
	Joe Wood, Red Sox, 1912	3
10.	many tied with 2	

SAVES

1.	Roy Face, Pirates, 1960	3
	Kent Tekulve, Pirates, 1979	3
	Troy Percival, Angels, 2002	3
4.	Rick Aguilera, Twins, 1991	2
	Rollie Fingers, A's, 1972	2
	Rollie Fingers, A's, 1973	2
	Darold Knowles, A's, 1973	2
	Firpo Marberry, Senators, 1924	2
	Bob McClure, Brewers, 1982	2
	Robb Nen, Marlins, 1997	2
	Jesse Orosco, Mets, 1986	2
	Bruce Sutter, Cardinals, 1982	2
	Todd Worrell, Cardinals, 1987	2
	Robb Nen, Giants, 2002	2

SINGLE GAME

REGULAR SEASON (1901-2002)

BATTING

FOUR-HOMER GAMES

	Player	No.
1.	Lou Gehrig, Yankees, June 3, 1932	1
	Chuck Klein, Phillies, July 10, 1936 (10 inn.)	1
	Pat Seerey, White Sox, July 18, 1948 (11 inn.)	1
	Gil Hodges, Dodgers, Aug. 31, 1950	1
	Joe Adcock, Braves, July 31, 1954	1
	Rocky Colavito, Indians, June 10, 1959	1
	Willie Mays, Giants, April 30, 1961	1
	Mike Schmidt, Phillies, April 17, 1976 (10 inn.)	1
	Bob Horner, Braves, July 6, 1986	1
	Mark Whiten, Cardinals, Sept. 7, 1993	1
	Mike Cameron, Mariners, May 2, 2002	1
	Shawn Green, Dodgers, May 23, 2002	1

HITS, A.L.

	Player	No.
1.	Johnny Burnett, Indians, July 10, 1932 (18 inn.)	9
2.	Rocky Colavito, Tigers, June 24, 1962 (22 inn.)	7
	Cesar Gutierrez, Tigers, June 21, 1970 (12 inn.)	7
4.	Mike Donlin, Orioles, June 24, 1901	6
	Doc Nance, Tigers, July 13, 1901	6
	Ervin Harvey, Indians, April 25, 1902	6
	Danny Murphy, A's, July 8, 1902	6
	Jimmy Williams, Orioles, Aug. 25, 1902	6
	Bobby Veach, Tigers, Sept. 17, 1920 (12 inn.)	6
	George Sisler, Browns, Aug. 9, 1921 (19 inn.)	6
	Frank Brower, Indians, Aug. 7, 1923	6
	George H. Burns, Indians., June 19, 1924	6
	Ty Cobb, Tigers, May 5, 1925	6
	Jimmie Foxx, A's, May 30, 1930 (13 inn.)	6
	Doc Cramer, A's, June 20, 1932	6
	Jimmie Foxx, A's, July 10, 1932 (18 inn.)	6
	Sam West, Browns, April 13, 1933 (11 inn.)	6
	Myril Hoag, Yankees, June 6, 1934	6
	Bob Johnson, A's, June 16, 1934 (11 inn.)	6
	Doc Cramer, A's, July 13, 1935	6
	Bruce Campbell, Indians, July 2, 1936	6
	Rip Radcliff, White Sox, July 18, 1936	6
	Hank Steinbacher, White Sox, June 22, 1938	6
	George Myatt, Senators, May 1, 1944	6
	Stan Spence, Senators, June 1, 1944	6
	George Kell, Tigers, Sept. 20, 1946	6
	Jim Fridley, Indians, April 29, 1952	6
	Jimmy Piersall, Red Sox, June 10, 1953	6
	Joe DeMaestri, A's, July 8, 1955	6
	Pete Runnels, Red Sox, Aug. 30, 1960 (15 inn.)	6
	Floyd Robinson, White Sox, July 22, 1962	6
	Bob Oliver, Royals, May 4, 1969	6
	Jim Northrup, Tigers, Aug. 28, 1969 (13 inn.)	6
	John Briggs, Brewers, Aug. 4, 1973	6
	Jorge Orta, Indians, June 15, 1980	6
	Jerry Remy, Red Sox, Sept. 3, 1981 (20 inn.)	6
	Kevin Seitzer, Royals, Aug. 2, 1987	6
	Kirby Puckett, Twins, Aug. 30, 1987	6
	Kirby Puckett, Twins, May 23, 1991 (11 inn.)	6
	Carlos Baerga, Indians, April 11, 1992 (18 inn.)	6
	Kevin Reimer, Brewers, Aug. 24, 1993 (13 inn.)	6
	Lance Johnson, White Sox, Sept. 23, 1995	6
	Gerald Williams, Yankees, May 1, 1996 (15 inn.)	6
	Garret Anderson, Angels, Sept. 27, 1996 (15 inn.)	6
	Damion Easley, Tigers, Aug. 8, 2001	6

HITS, N.L.

	Player	No.
1.	Rennie Stennett, Pirates, Sept. 16, 1975	7
2.	Kip Selbach, Giants, June 9, 1901	6
	George Cutshaw, Dodgers, Aug. 9, 1915	6
	Carson Bigbee, Pirates, Aug. 22, 1917 (22 inn.)	6
	Dave Bancroft, Giants, June 28, 1920	6
	Johnny Gooch, Pirates, July 7, 1922 (18 inn.)	6
	Max Carey, Pirates, July 7, 1922 (18 inn.)	6
	Jack Fournier, Dodgers, June 29, 1923	6
	Kiki Cuyler, Pirates, Aug. 9, 1924	6
	Frankie Frisch, Giants, Sept. 10, 1924	6
	Jim Bottomley, Cardinals, Sept. 16, 1924	6
	Paul Waner, Pirates, Aug. 26, 1926	6
	Lloyd Waner, Pirates, June 15, 1929 (14 inn.)	6
	Hank DeBerry, Dodgers, June 23, 1929 (14 inn.)	6
	Wally Gilbert, Dodgers, May 30, 1931	6
	Jim Bottomley, Cardinals, Aug. 5, 1931	6
	Tony Cuccinello, Reds, Aug. 13, 1931	6
	Terry Moore, Cardinals, Sept. 5, 1935	6
	Ernie Lombardi, Reds, May 9, 1937	6
	Frank Demaree, Cubs, July 5, 1937 (14 inn.)	6
	Cookie Lavagetto, Dodgers, Sept. 23, 1939	6
	Walker Cooper, Reds, July 6, 1949	6
	Johnny Hopp, Pirates, May 14, 1950	6
	Connie Ryan, Phillies, April 16, 1953	6
	Dick Groat, Pirates, May 13, 1960	6
	Jesus Alou, Giants, July 10, 1964	6
	Joe Morgan, Astros, July 8, 1965 (12 inn.)	6
	Felix Millan, Braves, July 6, 1970	6
	Don Kessinger, Cubs, July 17, 1971 (10 inn.)	6
	Willie Davis, Dodgers, May 24, 1973 (19 inn.)	6
	Bill Madlock, Cubs, July 26, 1975 (10 inn.)	6
	Jose Cardenal, Cubs, May 2, 1976 (14 inn.)	6
	Gene Richards, Padres, July 26, 1977 (15 inn.)	6
	Jim Lefebvre, Padres, Sept. 13, 1982 (16 inn.)	6
	Wally Backman, Pirates, April 27, 1990	6
	Sammy Sosa, Cubs, July 2, 1993	6
	Tony Gwynn, Padres, Aug. 4, 1993 (12 inn.)	6
	Rondell White, Expos, June 11, 1995 (13 inn.)	6
	Mike Benjamin, Giants, June 14, 1995 (13 inn.)	6
	Andres Galarraga, Rockies, July 3, 1995	6
	Edgardo Alfonzo, Mets, August 30, 1999	6
	Paul Lo Duca, Dodgers, May 28, 2001 (11 inn.)	6
	Shawn Green, Dodgers, May 23, 2002	6

RUNS

	Player	No.
1.	Mel Ott, Giants, Aug. 4, 1934	6
	Mel Ott, Giants, April 30, 1944	6
	Johnny Pesky, Red Sox, May 8, 1946	6
	Frank Torre, Braves, Sept. 2, 1957	6
	Spike Owen, Red Sox, Aug. 21, 1986	6
	Edgardo Alfonzo, Mets, August 30, 1999	6
	Shawn Green, Dodgers, May 23, 2002	6
8.	many tied with 5	

DOUBLES

	Player	No.
1.	Pop Dillon, Tigers, April 25, 1901	4
	Gavvy Cravath, Phillies, Aug. 8, 1915	4
	Denny Sothern, Phillies, June 6, 1930	4
	Paul Waner, Pirates, May 20, 1932	4
	Dick Bartell, Phillies, April 15, 1933	4
	Ernie Lombardi, Reds, May 8, 1935	4
	Billy Werber, Red Sox, July 17, 1935	4
	Frankie Hayes, A's, July 25, 1936	4
	Mike Kreevich, White Sox, Sept. 4, 1937	4
	Joe Medwick, Cardinals, Aug. 4, 1937	4
	Marv Owen, White Sox, April 23, 1939	4
	Billy Werber, Reds, May 13, 1940 (14 inn.)	4
	Johnny Lindell, Yankees, Aug. 17, 1944	4
	Lou Boudreau, Indians, July 14, 1946	4
	Willie Jones, Phillies, April 20, 1949	4
	Al Zarilla, Red Sox, June 8, 1950	4
	Jim Greengrass, Reds, April 13, 1954	4
	Vic Wertz, Indians, Sept. 26, 1956	4
	Charlie Lau, Orioles, July 13, 1962	4
	Billy Bruton, Tigers, May 19, 1963	4
	Billy Williams, Cubs, April 9, 1969	4
	Orlando Cepeda, Red Sox, Aug. 8, 1973	4
	Jim Mason, Yankees, July 8, 1974	4
	Dave Duncan, Orioles, June 30, 1975	4
	Rick Miller, Red Sox, May 11, 1981	4
	Rafael Ramirez, Braves, May 21, 1986 (13 inn.)	4
	Damaso Garcia, Blue Jays, June 27, 1986	4
	Kirby Puckett, Twins, May 13, 1989	4
	Billy Hatcher, Reds, Aug. 21, 1990	4
	Jeff Bagwell, Astros, June 14, 1996	4
	Sandy Alomar Jr., Indians, June 6, 1997	4
	Albert Belle, Orioles, August 29, 1999	4
	Albert Belle, Orioles, September 23, 1999	4
	Johnny Damon, Royals, July 18, 2000	4
	Shannon Stewart, Blue Jays, July 18, 2000	4

3-HOME RUN GAMES

	Player	No.
1.	Sammy Sosa, Cubs, 2001	3
2.	Johnny Mize, Cardinals, 1938	2
	Johnny Mize, Cardinals, 1939	2
	Ralph Kiner, Pirates, 1947	2
	Ted Williams, Red Sox, 1957	2
	Willie Mays, Giants., 1961	2
	Willie Stargell, Pirates, 1971	2
	Dave Kingman, Cubs, 1979	2
	Doug DeCinces, Angels, 1982	2
	Joe Carter, Indians, 1989	2
	Cecil Fielder, Tigers, 1990	2
	German Berroa, A's, 1996	2
	Steve Finley, Padres, 1997	2
	Mark McGwire, Cardinals, 1998	2
	Barry Bonds, Giants, 2001	2
	Jeromy Burnitz, Brewers, 2001	2
	Carlos Delgado, Blue Jays, 2001	2

2-HOME RUN GAMES

	Player	No.
1.	Hank Greenberg, Tigers, 1938	11
	Sammy Sosa, Cubs, 1998	11
3.	Jimmie Foxx, Red Sox, 1938	10
	Ralph Kiner, Pirates, 1947	10
	Mark McGwire, Cardinals, 1998	10
	Barry Bonds, Giants, 2001	10
	Sammy Sosa, Cubs, 2001	10
	Alex Rodriguez, Rangers, 2002	10
9.	Willie Mays, Giants, 1955	9
	George Bell, Blue Jays, 1987	9
	Mark McGwire, Cardinals, 1999	9
12.	many tied with 8.	

HOME RUNS FIRST AT-BAT, A.L.

Player	Date
Luke Stuart, Browns	Aug. 8, 1921
Earl Averill, Indians	April 16, 1929
Ace Parker, A's	April 30, 1937
Gene Hasson, A's	Sept. 9, 1937
Bill Lefebvre, Red Sox	June 10, 1938
Hack Miller, Tigers	April 23, 1944
Eddie Pellagrini, Red Sox	April 22, 1946
George Vico, Tigers	April 20, 1948
Bob Nieman, Browns	Sept. 14, 1951
Bob Tillman, Red Sox	May 19, 1962
John Kennedy, Senators	Sept. 5, 1962
Buster Narum, Orioles	May 3, 1963
Gates Brown, Tigers	June 19, 1963
Bert Campaneris, A's	July 23, 1964
Bill Roman, Tigers	Sept. 30, 1964
Brant Alyea, Senators	Sept. 12, 1965
John Miller, Yankees	Sept. 11, 1966
Rick Renick, Twins	July 11, 1968
Joe Keough, A's	Aug. 7, 1968
Gene Lamont, Tigers	Sept. 2, 1970
Don Rose, Angels	May 24, 1972
Reggie J. Sanders, Tigers	Sept. 1, 1974
Dave McKay, Twins	Aug. 22, 1975
Al Woods, Blue Jays	April 7, 1977
Dave Machemer, Angels	June 21, 1978
Gary Gaetti, Twins	Sept. 20, 1981
Andre David, Twins	June 29, 1984
Terry Steinbach, A's	Sept. 12, 1986
Jay Bell, Indians	Sept. 29, 1986
Junior Felix, Blue Jays	May 4, 1989
Jon Nunnally, Royals	April 29, 1995
Carlos Lee, White Sox	May 7, 1999
Esteban Yan, Devil Rays	June 4, 2000
Marcus Thames, Yankees	June 10, 2002
Miguel Olivo, White Sox	Sept. 15, 2002

HOME RUNS FIRST AT-BAT, N.L.

Player	Date
Johnny Bates, Braves	April 12, 1906
Walter Mueller, Pirates	May 7, 1922
Clise Dudley, Dodgers	April 27, 1929
Gordon Slade, Dodgers	May 24, 1930
Eddie Morgan, Cardinals	April 14, 1936
Ernie Koy, Dodgers	April 19, 1938
Emmett Mueller, Phillies	April 19, 1938
Clyde Vollmer, Reds	May 31, 1942
Paul Gillespie, Cubs	Sept. 11, 1942
Buddy Kerr, Giants	Sept. 8, 1943
Whitey Lockman, Giants	July 5, 1945
Dan Bankhead, Dodgers	Aug. 26, 1947
Les Layton, Giants	May 21, 1948
Ed Sanicki, Phillies	Sept. 14, 1949
Ted Tappe, Reds	Sept. 14, 1950
Hoyt Wilhelm, Giants	April 23, 1952
Wally Moon, Cardinals	April 13, 1954
Chuck Tanner, Braves	April 12, 1955
Bill White, Giants	May 7, 1956
Frank Ernaga, Cubs	May 24, 1957
Don Leppert, Pirates	June 18, 1961
Cuno Barragan, Cubs	Sept. 1, 1961
Benny Ayala, Mets	Aug. 27, 1974
John Montefusco, Giants	Sept. 3, 1974
Jose Sosa, Astros	July 30, 1975
Johnnie Lemaster, Giants	Sept. 2, 1975
Tim Wallach, Expos	Sept. 6, 1980
Carmelo Martinez, Cubs	Aug. 22, 1983
Mike Fitzgerald, Mets	Sept. 13, 1983
Will Clark, Giants	April 8, 1986
Ricky Jordan, Phillies	July 17, 1988
Jose Offerman, Dodgers	Aug. 19, 1990
Dave Eiland, Padres	April 10, 1992
Jim Bullinger, Cubs	June 8, 1992
Jay Gainer, Rockies	May 14, 1993
Mitch Lyden, Marlins	June 16, 1993
Garey Ingram, Dodgers	May 19, 1994
Jermaine Dye, Braves	May 17, 1996
Dustin Hermanson, Expos	April 16, 1997
Brad Fullmer, Expos	Sept. 2, 1997
Marlon Anderson, Phillies	Sept. 8, 1998
Guillermo Mota, Expos	June 9, 1999
Alex Cabrera, Diamondbacks	June 26, 2000
Keith McDonald, Cardinals	July 4, 2000
Chris Richard, Cardinals	July 17, 2000
Gene Stechschulte, Cardinals	April 17, 2001

GRAND SLAMS

	Player	No.
1.	Tony Lazzeri, Yankees, May 24, 1936	2
	Jim Tabor, Red Sox, July 4, 1939	2
	Rudy York, Red Sox, July 27, 1946	2
	Jim Gentile, Orioles, May 9, 1961	2
	Tony Cloninger, Braves, July 3, 1966	2
	Jim Northrup, Tigers, June 24, 1968	2
	Frank Robinson, Orioles, June 26, 1970	2

Robin Ventura, White Sox, Sept. 4, 1995 — 2
Chris Hoiles, Orioles, August 14, 1998 — 2
Fernando Tatis, Cardinals, April 23, 1999 — 2
Nomar Garciaparra, Red Sox, May 10, 1999 — 2

TOTAL BASES

1.	Shawn Green, Dodgers, May 23, 2002	19
2.	Joe Adcock, Braves, July 31, 1954	18
3.	Gil Hodges, Dodgers, Aug. 31, 1950	17
	Mike Schmidt, Phillies, April 17, 1976 (10 inn.)	17
5.	Ty Cobb, Tigers, May 5, 1925	16
	Lou Gehrig, Yankees, June 3, 1932	16
	Jimmie Foxx, A's, July 10, 1932 (18 inn.)	16
	Chuck Klein, Phillies, July 10, 1936 (10 inn.)	16
	Pat Seerey, White Sox, July 18, 1948 (11 inn.)	16
	Rocky Colavito, Indians, June 10, 1959	16
	Willie Mays, Giants, April 30, 1961	16
	Fred Lynn, Red Sox, June 18, 1975	16
	Bob Horner, Braves, July 6, 1986	16
	Mark Whiten, Cardinals, Sept. 7, 1993	16
	Edgardo Alfonzo, Mets, August 30, 1999	16
	Mike Cameron, Mariners, May 2, 2002	16

RUNS BATTED IN

1.	Jim Bottomley, Cardinals, Sept. 16, 1924	12
	Mark Whiten, Cardinals, Sept. 7, 1993	12
3.	Tony Lazzeri, Yankees, May 24, 1936	11
	Phil Weintraub, Giants, April 30, 1944	11
5.	Rudy York, Red Sox, May 27, 1946	10
	Walker Cooper, Reds, July 6, 1949	10
	Norm Zauchin, Red Sox, May 27, 1955	10
	Reggie Jackson, A's, June 14, 1969	10
	Fred Lynn, Red Sox, June 18, 1975	10
	Nomar Garciaparra, Red Sox, May 10, 1999	10

STOLEN BASES

1.	Eddie Collins, A's, Sept. 11, 1912	6
	Eddie Collins, A's, Sept. 22, 1912	6
	Otis Nixon, Braves, June 16, 1991	6
	Eric Young, Rockies, June 30, 1996	6
5.	Dan McGann, Giants, May 27, 1904	5
	Clyde Milan, Senators, June 14, 1912	5
	Johnny Neun, Tigers, July 9, 1927	5
	Amos Otis, Royals, Sept. 7, 1971	5
	Davey Lopes, Dodgers, Aug. 24, 1974	5
	Bert Campaneris, A's, April 24, 1976	5
	Lonnie Smith, Cardinals, Sept. 4, 1982	5
	Alan Wiggins, Padres, May 17, 1984	5
	Tony Gwynn, Padres, Sept. 20, 1986	5
	Rickey Henderson, A's, July 29, 1989	5
	Alex Cole, Indians, Aug. 1, 1990	5
	Alex Cole, Indians, May 3, 1992	5
	Damian Jackson, Padres, June 28, 1999	5
	Kenny Lofton, Indians, Sept. 3, 2000	5

STEALING HOME

1.	Honus Wagner, Pirates, June 20, 1901	2
	Ed Konetchy, Cardinals, Sept. 30, 1907	2
	Joe Tinker, Cubs, June 28, 1910	2
	Larry Doyle, Giants, Sept. 18, 1911	2
	Sherry Magee, Phillies, July 20, 1912	2
	Joe Jackson, Indians, Aug. 11, 1912	2
	Guy Zinn, Yankees, Aug. 15, 1912	2
	Eddie Collins, A's, Sept. 6, 1913	2
	Bill Barrett, White Sox, May 1, 1924	2
	Doc Gautreau, Braves, Sept. 3, 1927	2
	Vic Power, Indians, Aug. 14, 1958 (10 inn.)	2

PITCHING

WALKS

1.	Bruno Haas, A's, June 23, 1915	16
	Tommy Byrne, Yankees, Aug. 22, 1951 (13 inn.)	16
3.	Carroll Brown, A's, July 12, 1913	15
4.	Henry Mathewson, Giants, Oct. 5, 1906	14
	Skipper Friday, Senators, June 17, 1923	14
6.	Mal Eason, Braves, Sept. 3, 1902	13
	Pete Schneider, Reds, July 6, 1918	13
	George Turbeville, A's, Aug. 24, 1935 (15 inn.)	13
	Tommy Byrne, Yankees, June 8, 1949	13
	Dick Weik, Senators, Sept. 1, 1949	13
	Bud Podbielan, Reds, May 18, 1953 (11 inn.)	13

STRIKEOUTS

1.	Tom Cheney, Senators, Sept. 12, 1962 (16 inn.)	21
2.	Roger Clemens, Red Sox, April 29, 1986	20
	Roger Clemens, Red Sox, Sept. 18, 1996	20
	Kerry Wood, Cubs, May 6, 1998	20
	Randy Johnson, Diamondbacks, May 8, 2001 (11 inn.)	20
5.	Luis Tiant, Indians, July 3, 1968 (10 inn.)	19
	Steve Carlton, Cardinals, Sept. 15, 1969	19
	Tom Seaver, Mets, April 22, 1970	19
	Nolan Ryan, Angels, June 14, 1974 (12 inn.)	19
	Nolan Ryan, Angels, Aug. 12, 1974	19
	Nolan Ryan, Angels, Aug. 20, 1974 (11 inn.)	19
	Nolan Ryan, Angels, June 8, 1977 (10 inn.)	19
	David Cone, Mets, Oct. 6, 1991	19
	Randy Johnson, Mariners, June 24, 1997	19
	Randy Johnson, Mariners, Aug. 8, 1997	19

LEAGUE CHAMPIONSHIP SERIES

BATTING

RUNS

1.	Bob Robertson, Pirates, Oct. 3, 1971	4
	Steve Garvey, Dodgers, Oct. 9, 1974	4
	Mark Brouhard, Brewers, Oct. 9, 1982	4
	Eddie Murray, Orioles, Oct. 7, 1983	4
	George Brett, Royals, Oct. 11, 1985	4
	Will Clark, Giants, Oct. 4, 1989	4
	Fred McGriff, Braves, Oct. 17, 1996	4
	Javy Lopez, Braves, Oct. 14, 1996	4
9.	many tied with 3	

HITS

1.	Paul Blair, Orioles, Oct. 6, 1969	5
2.	Brooks Robinson, Orioles, Oct. 4, 1969	4
	Don Buford, Orioles, Oct. 6, 1969	4
	Bob Robertson, Pirates, Oct. 3, 1971	4
	Ron Cey, Dodgers, Oct. 6, 1974	4
	Steve Garvey, Dodgers, Oct. 9, 1974	4
	Sal Bando, A's, Oct. 5, 1975	4
	Mickey Rivers, Yankees, Oct. 14, 1976	4
	Mickey Rivers, Yankees, Oct. 8, 1977	4
	Chris Chambliss, Yankees, Oct. 4, 1978	4
	Dusty Baker, Dodgers, Oct. 7, 1978 (10 inn.)	4
	Terry Puhl, Astros, Oct. 12, 1980 (10 inn.)	4
	Jerry Mumphrey, Yankees, Oct. 14, 1981	4
	Graig Nettles, Yankees, Oct. 14, 1981	4
	Steve Garvey, Padres, Oct. 6, 1984	4
	George Brett, Royals, Oct. 11, 1985	4
	Tito Landrum, Cardinals, Oct. 13, 1985	4
	Rich Gedman, Red Sox, Oct. 12, 1986 (11 inn.)	4
	Spike Owen, Red Sox, Oct. 14, 1986	4
	Kevin McReynolds, Mets, Oct. 11, 1988	4
	Will Clark, Giants, Oct. 4, 1989	4
	Kelly Gruber, Blue Jays, Oct. 7, 1989	4
	Otis Nixon, Braves, Oct. 10, 1992	4
	Roberto Alomar, Blue Jays, Oct. 11, 1992	4
	John Olerud, Blue Jays, Oct. 11, 1992 (11 inn.)	4
	Jerry Browne, A's, Oct. 12, 1992	4
	Paul Molitor, Blue Jays, Oct. 5, 1993	4
	Ed Sprague, Blue Jays, Oct. 5, 1993	4
	Tim Raines Sr., White Sox, Oct. 8, 1993	4
	Manny Ramirez, Indians, Oct. 11, 1995	4
	Derek Jeter, Yankees, Oct. 9, 1996	4
	Chipper Jones, Braves, Oct. 9, 1996	4
	Mark Lemke, Braves, Oct. 14, 1996	4
	Javy Lopez, Braves, Oct. 14, 1996	4
	Keith Lockhart, Braves, Oct. 14, 1997	4
	Nomar Garciaparra, Red Sox, Oct. 16, 1999	4
	Alex Rodriguez, Mariners, Oct. 17, 2000	4
	Adam Kennedy, Angels, Oct. 13, 2002	4

HOME RUNS

1.	Bob Robertson, Pirates, Oct. 3, 1971	3
	George Brett, Royals, Oct. 6, 1978	3
	Adam Kennedy, Angels, Oct. 13, 2002	3
4.	Boog Powell, Orioles, Oct. 4, 1971	2
	Reggie Jackson, A's, Oct. 5, 1971	2
	Sal Bando, A's, Oct. 7, 1973	2
	Rusty Staub, Mets, Oct. 8, 1973	2
	Steve Garvey, Dodgers, Oct. 9, 1974	2
	Graig Nettles, Yankees, Oct. 13, 1976	2
	Steve Garvey, Dodgers, Oct. 4, 1978	2
	Gary Matthews, Cubs, Oct. 2, 1984	2
	George Brett, Royals, Oct. 11, 1985	2
	Gary Gaetti, Twins, Oct. 7, 1987	2
	Rickey Henderson, A's, Oct. 7, 1989	2
	Will Clark, Giants, Oct. 4, 1989	2
	David Justice, Braves, Oct. 13, 1992	2
	Manny Ramirez, Indians, Oct. 11, 1995	2
	Jay Buhner, Mariners, Oct. 13, 1995	2
	Ron Gant, Cardinals, Oct. 12, 1996	2
	Darryl Strawberry, Yankees, Oct. 12, 1996	2
	Jim Thome, Indians, Oct. 9, 1998	2
	Rich Aurilia, Giants, Oct. 10, 2002	2

RUNS BATTED IN

1.	Will Clark, Giants, Oct. 4, 1989	6
2.	Paul Blair, Orioles, Oct. 6, 1969	5
	Bob Robertson, Pirates, Oct. 3, 1971	5
	Don Baylor, Angels, Oct. 5, 1982	5
	Steve Garvey, Padres, Oct. 6, 1984	5
	Michael Tucker, Braves, Oct. 12, 1998	5
	John Valentin, Red Sox, Oct. 16, 1999	5
	Bret Boone, Mariners, Oct. 20, 2001	5
	Adam Kennedy, Angels, Oct. 13, 2002	5
8.	many tied with 4	

TOTAL BASES

1.	Bob Robertson, Pirates, Oct. 3, 1971	14
2.	Adam Kennedy, Angels, Oct. 13, 2002	13
3.	George Brett, Royals, Oct. 6, 1978	12
4.	Steve Garvey, Dodgers, Oct. 4, 1978	11
	George Brett, Royals, Oct. 11, 1985	11
	Will Clark, Giants, Oct. 4, 1989	11
7.	Paul Blair, Orioles, Oct. 6, 1969	10
	Steve Garvey, Dodgers, Oct. 9, 1974	10
	Manny Ramirez, Indians, Oct. 11, 1995	10
10.	Reggie Jackson, A's, Oct. 5, 1971	9
	Ron Cey, Dodgers, Oct. 6, 1974	9
	David Justice, Braves, Oct. 13, 1992	9
	Darryl Strawberry, Yankees, Oct. 12, 1996	9
	Javy Lopez, Braves, Oct. 14, 1996	9

STOLEN BASES

1.	Rickey Henderson, A's, Oct. 4, 1989	4
2.	Joe Morgan, Reds, Oct. 4, 1975	3
	Ken Griffey Sr., Reds, Oct. 5, 1975	3
	Steve Sax, Dodgers, Oct. 9, 1988 (12 inn.)	3
	Ron Gant, Braves, Oct. 10, 1991	3
	Willie Wilson, A's, Oct. 8, 1992	3
	Roberto Alomar, Blue Jays, Oct. 10, 1993	3

PITCHING

RUNS ALLOWED

1.	Phil Niekro, Braves, Oct. 4, 1969	9
2.	Jim Perry, Twins, Oct. 3, 1970	8
	Roger Clemens, Red Sox, Oct. 7, 1986	8
	Greg A. Harris, Padres, Oct. 2, 1984	8
	Greg Maddux, Cubs, Oct. 4, 1989	8
	Tom Glavine, Braves, Oct. 13, 1992	8
	Greg Maddux, Braves, Oct. 10, 1996	8
	Hideki Irabu, Yankees, Oct. 16, 1999	8
9.	many tied with 7	

HITS ALLOWED

1.	Jack McDowell, White Sox, Oct. 5, 1993	13
	Hideki Irabu, Yankees, Oct. 16, 1999	13
3.	Larry Gura, Royals, Oct. 9, 1986	12
4.	Bruce Hurst, Red Sox, Oct. 8, 1986	11
	Roger Erickson, Orioles, Oct. 12, 1997	11
	Kevin Brown, Marlins, Oct. 14, 1997	11
7.	Pat Jarvis, Braves, Oct. 6, 1969	10
	Jim Palmer, Orioles, Oct. 6, 1969	10
	Mike Cuellar, Orioles, Oct. 3, 1970	10
	Gaylord Perry, Giants, Oct. 6, 1971	10
	Burt Hooton, Dodgers, Oct. 4, 1978	10
	Larry Gura, Royals, Oct. 8, 1980	10
	Roger Clemens, Red Sox, Oct. 7, 1986	10
	Kirk McCaskill, Angels, Oct. 8, 1986	10
	Bob Ojeda, Mets, Oct. 9, 1986	10
	John Tudor, Cardinals, Oct. 7, 1987	10
	Al Leiter, Marlins, Oct. 11, 1997	10
	Tom Glavine, Braves, Oct. 14, 1997	10
	Ramon Ortiz, Giants, Oct. 9, 2002	10
	Matt Morris, Cardinals, Oct. 10, 2002	10

STRIKEOUTS

1.	Mike Mussina, Orioles, Oct. 11, 1997	15
	Livan Hernandez, Marlins, Oct. 12, 1997	15
	Roger Clemens, Yankees, Oct. 14, 2000	15
4.	Joe Coleman, Tigers, Oct. 10, 1972	14
	John Candelaria, Pirates, Oct. 7, 1975	14
	Mike Boddicker, Orioles, Oct. 6, 1983	14
	Mike Scott, Astros, Oct. 8, 1986	14
8.	Tom Seaver, Mets, Oct. 6, 1973	13
9.	Jim Palmer, Orioles, Oct. 5, 1970	12
	Jim Palmer, Orioles, Oct. 6, 1973	12
	Nolan Ryan, Astros, Oct. 14, 1986	12
	Pedro Martinez, Red Sox, Oct. 16, 1999	12
	Curt Schilling, Diamondbacks, Oct. 19, 2001	12

WALKS

1.	Mike Cuellar, Orioles, Oct. 9, 1974	9
2.	Fernando Valenzuela, Dodgers, Oct. 14, 1985	8
	Juan Guzman, Blue Jays, Oct. 5, 1993	8
	Paul Abbott, Mariners, Oct. 21, 2001	8
5.	Dave Boswell, Twins, Oct. 5, 1969	7
	Dave Stieb, Blue Jays, Oct. 12, 1985	7
	Tom Glavine, Braves, Oct. 14, 1997	7
8.	Diego Segui, A's, Oct. 5, 1971	6
	Bruce Kison, Pirates, Oct. 8, 1974	6
	Matt Keough, A's, Oct. 15, 1981	6
	Bob Welch, Dodgers, Oct. 12, 1985	6
	Tom Glavine, Braves, Oct. 8, 1998	6

WORLD SERIES

BATTING

RUNS

1.	Babe Ruth, Yankees, Oct. 6, 1926	4
	Earle Combs, Yankees, Oct. 2, 1932	4
	Frankie Crosetti, Yankees, Oct. 2, 1936	4
	Enos Slaughter, Cardinals, Oct. 10, 1946	4
	Reggie Jackson, Yankees, Oct. 18, 1977	4
	Kirby Puckett, Twins, Oct. 24, 1987	4
	Carney Lansford, A's, Oct. 17, 1989	4
	Lenny Dykstra, Phillies, Oct. 20, 1993	4
	Jeff Kent, Giants, Oct. 24, 2002	4

HITS

1.	Paul Molitor, Brewers, Oct. 12, 1982	5
2.	Tommy Leach, Pirates, Oct. 1, 1903	4
	Ginger Beaumont, Pirates, Oct. 8, 1903	4
	Frank Isbell, White Sox, Oct. 13, 1906	4
	Ed Hahn, White Sox, Oct. 14, 1906	4
	Ty Cobb, Tigers, Oct. 12, 1908	4
	Larry Doyle, Giants, Oct. 25, 1911	4
	Danny Murphy, A's, Oct. 26, 1911	4
	Frankie Frisch, Giants, Oct. 5, 1921	4
	George J. Burns, Giants, Oct. 7, 1921	4
	Frank Snyder, Giants, Oct. 7, 1921	4
	Ross Youngs, Giants, Oct. 13, 1923	4
	Joe Dugan, Yankees, Oct. 14, 1923	4
	Goose Goslin, Senators, Oct. 7, 1924	4
	Fred Lindstrom, Giants, Oct. 8, 1924	4
	Max Carey, Pirates, Oct. 15, 1925	4
	Mel Ott, Giants, Oct. 3, 1933	4
	Joe Medwick, Cardinals, Oct. 3, 1934	4
	Hank Greenberg, Tigers, Oct. 6, 1934	4
	Ripper Collins, Cardinals, Oct. 9, 1934	4
	Bill Dickey, Yankees, Oct. 5, 1938	4
	Charlie Keller, Yankees, Oct. 5, 1941	4
	Stan Hack, Cubs, Oct. 8, 1945	4
	Joe Garagiola, Cardinals, Oct. 10, 1946	4
	Whitey Kurowski, Cardinals, Oct. 10, 1946	4
	Wally Moses, Red Sox, Oct. 10, 1946	4
	Enos Slaughter, Cardinals, Oct. 10, 1946	4
	Monte Irvin, Giants, Oct. 4, 1951	4
	Vic Wertz, Indians, Sept. 29, 1954	4
	Jim Gilliam, Dodgers, Oct. 6, 1959	4
	Mickey Mantle, Yankees, Oct. 8, 1960	4
	Maury Wills, Dodgers, Oct. 11, 1965	4
	Lou Brock, Cardinals, Oct. 4, 1967	4
	Brooks Robinson, Orioles, Oct. 14, 1970	4
	Reggie Jackson, A's, Oct. 14, 1973 (12 inn.)	4
	Rusty Staub, Mets, Oct. 17, 1973	4
	Thurman Munson, Yankees, Oct. 21, 1976	4
	Dave Parker, Pirates, Oct. 10, 1979	4
	Kiko Garcia, Orioles, Oct. 12, 1979	4
	Bill Madlock, Pirates, Oct. 14, 1979	4
	Willie Stargell, Pirates, Oct. 17, 1979	4
	Robin Yount, Brewers, Oct. 12, 1982	4
	Robin Yount, Brewers, Oct. 17, 1982	4
	George Brett, Royals, Oct. 27, 1985	4
	Lenny Dykstra, Mets, Oct. 21, 1986	4
	Kirby Puckett, Twins, Oct. 24, 1987	4
	Dave Henderson, A's, Oct. 19, 1988	4
	Billy Hatcher, Reds, Oct. 17, 1990 (10 inn.)	4
	Terry Pendleton, Braves, Oct. 26, 1991 (11 inn.)	4
	Roberto Alomar, Blue Jays, Oct. 19, 1993	4
	Bret Boone, Braves, Oct. 26, 1999	4
	Reggie Sanders, Diamondbacks, Nov. 3, 2001	4
	Tim Salmon, Angels, Oct. 20, 2002	4

HOME RUNS

1.	Babe Ruth, Yankees, Oct. 6, 1926	3
	Babe Ruth, Yankees, Oct. 9, 1928	3
	Reggie Jackson, Yankees, Oct. 18, 1977	3
4.	Patsy Dougherty, Red Sox, Oct. 2, 1903	2
	Harry Hooper, Red Sox, Oct. 13, 1915	2
	Benny Kauff, Giants, Oct. 11, 1917	2
	Babe Ruth, Yankees, Oct. 11, 1923	2
	Lou Gehrig, Yankees, Oct. 7, 1928	2
	Lou Gehrig, Yankees, Oct. 1, 1932	2
	Babe Ruth, Yankees, Oct. 1, 1932	2
	Tony Lazzeri, Yankees, Oct. 2, 1932	2
	Charlie Keller, Yankees, Oct. 7, 1939	2
	Bob Elliott, Braves, Oct. 10, 1948	2
	Duke Snider, Dodgers, Oct. 6, 1952	2
	Joe Collins, Yankees, Sept. 28, 1955	2
	Duke Snider, Dodgers, Oct. 2, 1955	2
	Yogi Berra, Yankees, Oct. 10, 1956	2
	Tony Kubek, Yankees, Oct. 5, 1957	2
	Mickey Mantle, Yankees, Oct. 2, 1958	2
	Ted Kluszewski, White Sox, Oct. 1, 1959	2
	Charlie Neal, Dodgers, Oct. 2, 1959	2
	Mickey Mantle, Yankees, Oct. 6, 1960	2
	Carl Yastrzemski, Red Sox, Oct. 5, 1967	2
	Rico Petrocelli, Red Sox, Oct. 11, 1967	2
	Gene Tenace, A's, Oct. 14, 1972	2
	Tony Perez, Reds, Oct. 16, 1975	2
	Johnny Bench, Reds, Oct. 21, 1976	2
	Davey Lopes, Dodgers, Oct. 10, 1978	2
	Willie Aikens, Royals, Oct. 14, 1980	2
	Willie Aikens, Royals, Oct. 18, 1980	2
	Willie McGee, Cardinals, Oct. 15. 1982	2
	Eddie Murray, Orioles, Oct. 16, 1983	2
	Alan Trammell, Tigers, Oct. 13, 1984	2
	Kirk Gibson, Tigers, Oct. 14, 1984	2
	Gary Carter, Mets, Oct. 22, 1986	2
	Dave Henderson, A's, Oct. 27, 1989	2
	Chris Sabo, Reds, Oct. 19, 1990	2
	Andruw Jones, Braves, Oct. 20, 1996	2
	Greg Vaughn, Padres, Oct. 17, 1998	2
	Scott Brosius, Yankees, Oct. 20, 1998	2
	Chad Curtis, Yankees, Oct. 26, 1999	2
	Troy Glaus, Angels, Oct. 19, 2002	2
	Tim Salmon, Angels, Oct. 20, 2002	2
	Jeff Kent, Giants, Oct. 24, 2002	2

TOTAL BASES

1.	Babe Ruth, Yankees, Oct. 6, 1926	12
	Babe Ruth, Yankees, Oct. 9, 1928	12
	Reggie Jackson, Yankees, Oct. 18, 1977	12
4.	Duke Snider, Dodgers, Oct. 2, 1955	10
	Gary Carter, Mets, Oct. 22, 1986	10
	Dave Henderson, A's, Oct. 27, 1989	10
	Lenny Dykstra, Phillies, Oct. 20, 1993	10
	Tim Salmon, Angels, Oct. 20, 2002	10
	Jeff Kent, Giants, Oct. 24, 2002	10
10.	many tied with 9	

RUNS BATTED IN

1.	Bobby Richardson, Yankees, Oct. 8, 1960	6
2.	Bill Dickey, Yankees, Oct. 2, 1936	5
	Tony Lazzeri, Yankees, Oct. 2, 1936	5
	Ted Kluszewski, White Sox, Oct. 1, 1959	5
	Mickey Mantle, Yankees, Oct. 6, 1960	5
	Hector Lopez, Yankees, Oct. 9, 1961	5
	Rusty Staub, Mets, Oct. 17, 1973	5
	Johnny Bench, Reds, Oct. 21, 1976	5
	Reggie Jackson, Yankees, Oct. 18, 1977	5
	Davey Lopes, Dodgers, Oct. 10, 1978	5
	Thurman Munson, Yankees, Oct. 15, 1978	5
	Pedro Guerrero, Dodgers, Oct. 28, 1981	5
	Kirk Gibson, Tigers, Oct. 14, 1984	5
	Dan Gladden, Twins, Oct. 17, 1987	5
	David Justice, Braves, Oct. 24, 1991	5
	Milt Thompson, Phillies, Oct. 20, 1993	5
	Tony Fernandez, Blue Jays, Oct. 20, 1993	5
	Andruw Jones, Braves, Oct. 20, 1996	5
	Gary Sheffield, Marlins, Oct. 12, 1997	5
	Danny Bautista, Diamondbacks, Nov. 3, 2001	5

STOLEN BASES

1.	Honus Wagner, Pirates, Oct. 11, 1909	3
	Willie Davis, Dodgers, Oct. 11, 1965	3
	Lou Brock, Cardinals, Oct. 12, 1967	3
	Lou Brock, Cardinals, Oct. 5, 1968	3

PITCHING

RUNS ALLOWED

1.	Bill Kennedy, Pirates, Oct. 7, 1903	10
2.	Andy Coakley, A's, Oct. 12, 1905	9
	Mordecai Brown, Cubs, Oct. 18, 1910	9
	Walter Johnson, Senators, Oct. 15, 1925	9
	Jay Witasick, Yankees, Nov. 3, 2001	9
6.	Jack Pfiester, Cubs, Oct. 12, 1908	8
	Ed Summers, Tigers, Oct. 13, 1909	8
	Hooks Wiltse, Giants, Oct. 26, 1911	8
	Slim Sallee, Giants, Oct. 13, 1917	8
	Grover Alexander, Cardinals, Oct. 5, 1928	8
	Guy Bush, Cubs, Sept. 28, 1932	8

HITS ALLOWED

1.	Walter Johnson, Senators, Oct. 15, 1925	15
2.	Walter Johnson, Senators, Oct. 4, 1924	14
	Waite Hoyt, Yankees, Oct. 6, 1926	14
	Mike Caldwell, Brewers, Oct. 17, 1982	14
5.	Mordecai Brown, Cubs, Oct. 18, 1910	13
	Slim Sallee, Giants, Oct. 13, 1917	13
	Jim Bagby Sr., Indians, Oct. 10, 1920	13
	Walter Johnson, Senators, Oct. 8, 1924	13
	Bob Turley, Yankees, Oct. 6, 1960	13
10.	7 tied with 12	

STRIKEOUTS

1.	Bob Gibson, Cardinals, Oct. 2, 1968	17
2.	Sandy Koufax, Dodgers, Oct. 2, 1963	15
3.	Carl Erskine, Dodgers, Oct. 2, 1953	14
4.	Howard Ehmke, A's, Oct. 8, 1929	13
	Bob Gibson, Cardinals, Oct. 12, 1964 (10 inn.)	13
6.	Ed Walsh, White Sox, Oct. 11, 1906	12
	Bill Donovan, Tigers, Oct. 8, 1907 (12 inn.)	12
	Walter Johnson, Senators, Oct. 24, 1924 (12 inn.)	12
	Mort Cooper, Cardinals, Oct. 8, 1944	12
	Tom Seaver, Mets, Oct. 16, 1973	12
	Orlando Hernandez, Yankees, Oct. 24, 2000	12

WALKS

1.	Bill Bevens, Yankees, Oct. 3, 1947	10
2.	Jack Coombs, A's, Oct. 18, 1910	9
	Rex Barney, Dodgers, Oct. 4, 1947	9
4.	Jim Hearn, Giants, Oct. 6, 1951	8
	Bob Turley, Yankees, Oct. 9, 1956 (10 inn.)	8
	Jim Palmer, Orioles, Oct. 11, 1971	8
7.	Art Nehf, Giants, Oct. 6, 1921	7
	Tex Carleton, Cubs, Oct. 5, 1935	7
	Lefty Gomez, Yankees, Oct. 2, 1936	7
	Allie Reynolds, Yankees, Oct. 4, 1951	7
	Ron Guidry, Yankees, Oct. 13, 1978	7
	Fernando Valenzuela, Dodgers, Oct. 23, 1981	7

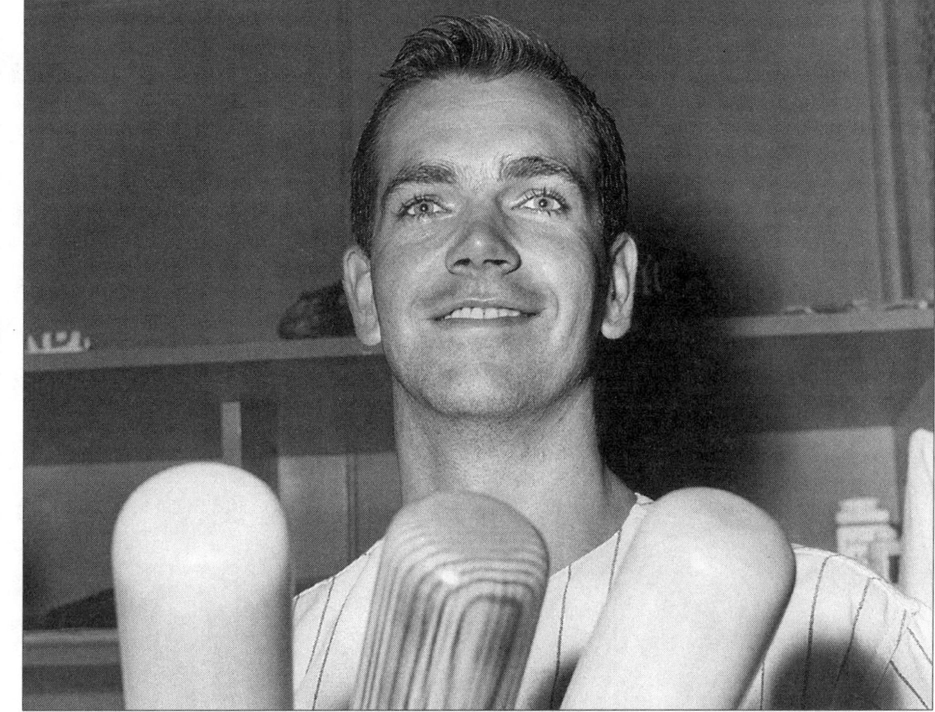

Yankees second baseman Bobby Richardson had six RBIs in a 1960 Series game against Pittsburgh.

HIGHEST AVERAGE

(Minimum 4 at-bats)

1. Ted Williams, Red Sox, 1946 ...... 1.000
2. Joe Medwick, Cardinals, 1937 ...... .800
3. Roberto Alomar, Orioles, 1998 ...... .750
Rickey Henderson, A's, 1982 ...... .750
Lance Johnson, Mets, 1996 ...... .750
Harmon Killebrew, Twins, 1964 ...... .750
Willie Mays, Giants, 1960 (1st game) ...... .750
Willie Mays, Giants, 1960 (2nd game) ...... .750
Stan Musial, Cardinals, 1949 ...... .750
Brooks Robinson, Orioles, 1966 ...... .750
Ivan Rodriguez, Rangers, 1998 ...... .750
Al Rosen, Indians, 1954 ...... .750
Duke Snider, Dodgers, 1954 ...... .750
Arky Vaughan, Pirates, 1941 ...... .750
Leon Wagner, Angels, 1962 (2nd game) ...... .750
Carl Yastrzemski, Red Sox, 1967 ...... .750

RUNS

1. Ted Williams, Red Sox, 1946 4
2. Joe DiMaggio, Yankees, 1941 3
Frankie Frisch, Cardinals, 1934 3
Jackie Robinson, Dodgers, 1949 3
Al Simmons, White Sox, 1934 3
6. many tied with 2

HITS

1. Joe Medwick, Cardinals, 1937 4
Ted Williams, Red Sox, 1946 4
Carl Yastrzemski, Red Sox, 1970 4
4. many tied with 3

DOUBLES

1. Ernie Banks, Cubs, 1959 (1st game) 2
Barry Bonds, Giants, 1993 2
Ted Kluszewski, Reds, 1956 2
Joe Medwick, Cardinals, 1937 2
Al Simmons, White Sox, 1934 2
Paul Konerko, White Sox, 2002 2
Damian Miller, Diamondbacks, 2002 2
8. many tied with 1

HOME RUNS

1. Gary Carter, Expos, 1981 2
Willie McCovey, Giants, 1969 2
Al Rosen, Indians, 1954 2
Arky Vaughan, Pirates, 1941 2
Ted Williams, Red Sox, 1946 2
6. many tied with 1

HOME RUN, FIRST AT-BAT

Max West, Braves, 1940
Hoot Evers, Tigers, 1948
Jim Gilliam, Dodgers, 1959 (2nd game)
George Altman, Cubs, 1961 (1st game)
Johnny Bench, Reds, 1969
Dick Dietz, Giants, 1970
Lee Mazzilli, Mets, 1979
Terry Steinbach, A's, 1988
Bo Jackson, Royals, 1989
Jeff Conine, Marlins, 1995
Javy Lopez, Braves, 1997

TOTAL BASES

1. Ted Williams, Red Sox, 1946 10
2. Al Rosen, Indians, 1954 9
Arky Vaughan, Pirates, 1941 9
4. Gary Carter, Expos, 1981 8
Vince DiMaggio, Pirates, 1943 8
Willie McCovey, Giants, 1969 8
7. Ken Griffey Jr., Mariners, 1992 7
8. many tied with 6

RUNS BATTED IN

1. Al Rosen, Indians, 1954 5
Ted Williams, Red Sox, 1946 5
3. Rocky Colavito, Tigers, 1962 (2nd game) 4
Lou Gehrig, Yankees, 1937 4
Fred Lynn, Angels, 1983 4
Arky Vaughan, Pirates, 1941 4
Ted Williams, Red Sox, 1941 4
8. many tied with 3

STOLEN BASES

1. Roberto Alomar, Blue Jays, 1992 2
Kelly Gruber, Blue Jays, 1990 2
Kenny Lofton, Indians, 1996 2
Willie Mays, Giants, 1963 2
5. many tied with 1

Giants All-Star Willie McCovey hit two home runs for the National League in 1969.

PITCHING

RUNS ALLOWED

1. Atlee Hammaker, Giants, 1983 7
2. Sandy Consuegra, White Sox, 1954 5
Whitey Ford, Yankees, 1955 5
Tom Glavine, Braves, 1992 5
Jim Maloney, Reds, 1965 5
Blue Moon Odom, A's, 1969 5
Jim Palmer, Orioles, 1977 5
Claude Passeau, Cubs, 1941 5
9. many tied with 4

HITS ALLOWED

1. Tom Glavine, Braves, 1992 9
2. Tommy Bridges, Tigers, 1937 7
3. Atlee Hammaker, Giants, 1983 6
Claude Passeau, Cubs, 1941 6
Lon Warneke, Cubs, 1933 6
6. many tied with 5

STRIKEOUTS

1. Carl Hubbell, Giants, 1934 6
Larry Jansen, Giants, 1950 6
Fergie Jenkins, Cubs, 1967 6
Johnny Vander Meer, Reds, 1943 6
5. Don Drysdale, Dodgers, 1959 (2nd game) 5
Pedro Martinez, Red Sox, 1999 5
Stu Miller, Giants, 1961 (2nd game) 5
Joe Nuxhall, Reds, 1955 5
Billy Pierce, White Sox, 1956 5
Dick Radatz, Red Sox, 1963 5
Dick Radatz, Red Sox, 1964 5
Robin Roberts, Phillies, 1954 5
Hal Schumacher, Giants, 1935 5
Tom Seaver, Mets, 1968 5
Fernando Valenzuela, Dodgers, 1986 5

WALKS

1. Bill Hallahan, Cardinals, 1933 5
2. Jim Palmer, Orioles, 1978 4
3. Ewell Blackwell, Reds, 1948 3
Ralph Branca, Dodgers, 1948 3
Kevin Brown, Dodgers, 2000 3
Don Drysdale, Dodgers, 1959 (2nd game) 3
Tom Glavine, Braves, 1998 3
Jim Kern, Rangers, 1979 3
Bill Lee, Cubs, 1939 3
Mike McCormick, Giants, 1960 (1st game) 3
Sam McDowell, Indians, 1970 3
Andy Messersmith, Dodgers, 1974 3
Joe Nuxhall, Reds, 1955 3
Dan Petry, Tigers, 1985 3
Johnny Podres, Dodgers, 1960 (2nd game) 3
Vic Raschi, Yankees, 1949 3
Lon Warneke, Cubs, 1934 3
Lon Warneke, Cubs, 1936 3
Early Wynn, White Sox, 1959 (2nd game) 3

TEAM

HIGHS AND LOWS (1901-2002)

PENNANTS, A.L.
1. Yankees 38
2. Athletics 15
3. Red Sox 10
4. Tigers 9
5. Orioles/Browns 7
6. Twins/Senators 6
7. White Sox 5
Indians 5
9. Royals 2
Blue Jays 2

PENNANTS, N.L.
1. Dodgers 18
Giants 18
3. Cardinals 15
4. Cubs 10
5. Pirates 9
Reds 9
Braves 9
8. Phillies 5
9. Mets 4
10. Padres 2

LCS WINNERS, A.L.
1. Yankees 9
2. Athletics 6
3. Orioles 5
4. Royals 2
Red Sox 2
Twins 2
Blue Jays 2
Indians 2
9. Brewers 1
Tigers 1

LCS WINNERS, N.L.
1. Dodgers 5
Reds 5
Braves 5
4. Mets 4
5. Phillies 3
Cardinals 3
7. Giants 2
Pirates 2
Padres 2
10. Marlins 1
Diamondbacks 1

WORLD SERIES WINNERS
1. Yankees 26
2. Cardinals 9
Athletics 9
4. Dodgers 6
5. Giants 5
Pirates 5
Reds 5
Red Sox 5
9. Tigers 4
10. Braves 3
Orioles 3
Twins 3

ALL-STAR GAME WINNERS
1. National League 40
2. American League 31
3. games tied 2

VICTORIES, SEASON
1. Cubs, 1906 116
Mariners, 2001 116
3. Yankees, 1998 114
4. Indians, 1954 111
5. Pirates, 1909 110
Yankees, 1927 110
7. Yankees, 1961 109
Orioles, 1969 109
9. Orioles, 1970 108
Reds, 1975 108
Mets, 1986 108

LOSSES, SEASON
1. Mets, 1962 120
2. Athletics, 1916 117
3. Braves, 1935 115
4. Senators, 1904 113
5. Pirates, 1952 112
Mets, 1965 112
7. Red Sox, 1932 111
Browns, 1939 111
Phillies, 1941 111
Mets, 1963 111

LARGEST 1ST/2ND-PLACE MARGIN
1. Indians, 1995 30.0
2. Pirates, 1902 27.5
3. Yankees, 1998 22.0
4. Mets, 1986 21.5
Indians, 1999 21.5
6. Braves, 1995 21.0
7. Cubs, 1906 20.0
Reds, 1975 20.0
White Sox, 1983 20.0
10. Yankees, 1936 19.5

LARGEST 1ST/LAST-PLACE MARGIN
1. Cubs, 1906 66.5
2. Pirates, 1909 65.5
3. Yankees, 1939 64.5
4. Yankees, 1932 64.0
5. Cardinals, 1942 62.5
6. Cubs, 1935 61.5
7. Giants, 1962 60.5
8. Indians, 1954 60.0
9. Yankees, 1927 59.0
10. Red Sox, 1915 58.5

MOST DAYS IN 1ST PLACE
1. Mariners, 2001 (184) 184
2. Orioles, 1997 (182) 182
3. Tigers, 1984 (182) 181
Phillies, 1993 (182) 181
Indians, 1998 (181) 181
6. Indians, 1999 (182) 179
Cardinals, 2000 (182) 179
8. Reds, 1970 (179) 178
Reds, 1990 (178) 178
Rangers, 1999 (182) 178

LONGEST WINNING STREAKS
1. Giants, 1916 26
2. Cubs, 1935 21
3. Athletics, 2002 20
4. White Sox, 1906 19
Yankees, 1947 19
6. Giants, 1904 18
Yankees, 1953 18
8. Giants, 1907 17
Giants, 1916 17
Senators, 1912 17
Athletics, 1931 17

LONGEST LOSING STREAKS
1. Phillies, 1961 23
2. Orioles, 1988 21
3. Red Sox, 1906 20
Athletics, 1916 20
Athletics, 1943 20
Expos, 1969 20
7. Braves, 1906 19
Reds, 1914 19
Tigers, 1975 19
10. Athletics, 1920 18
Senators, 1948 18
Senators, 1959 18

HIGHEST TEAM AVERAGE
1. Giants, 1930 .319
2. Tigers, 1921 .316
3. Phillies, 1930 .315
4. Cardinals, 1930 .314
5. Browns, 1922 .313
6. Yankees, 1930 .309
Pirates, 1928 .309
Phillies, 1929 .309
Cubs, 1930 .309
10. Browns, 1920 .308

RUNS SCORED, SEASON
1. Yankees, 1931 1,067
2. Yankees, 1936 1,065
3. Yankees, 1930 1,062
4. Red Sox, 1950 1,027
5. Indians, 1999 1,009
6. Cardinals, 1930 1,004
7. Yankees, 1932 1,002
8. Cubs, 1930 998
9. Mariners, 1996 993
10. Cubs, 1929 982

FEWEST RUNS, SEASON
(Minimum 140 games)
1. Cardinals, 1908 371
2. Dodgers, 1908 377
3. Senators, 1909 380
4. Phillies, 1942 394
5. Braves, 1906 408
6. Cardinals, 1907 419
7. Braves, 1909 435
8. Senators, 1903 437
Senators, 1904 437
10. Browns, 1909 441

HOME RUNS, GAME
1. Blue Jays, Sept. 14, 1987 10
2. Reds, Sept. 4, 1999 9
3. Yankees, June 28, 1939 8
Braves, Aug. 30, 1953 8
Reds, Aug. 18, 1956 8
Giants, April 30, 1961 8
Twins, Aug. 29, 1963 8
Red Sox, July 4, 1977 8
Expos, July 30, 1978 8
Athletics, June 27, 1996 8
Indians, April 25, 1997 8
Tigers, June 20, 2000 8
Dodgers, May 23, 2002 8

HOME RUNS, SEASON
1. Mariners, 1997 264
2. Orioles, 1996 257
3. Astros, 2000 249
4. Rangers, 2001 246
5. Mariners, 1996 245
6. Mariners, 1999 244
Blue Jays, 2000 244
8. Athletics, 1996 243
9. Yankees, 1961 240
10. Rockies, 1997 239
Athletics, 2000 239

FEWEST HOME RUNS, SEASON
(Minimum 140 games)
1. White Sox, 1908 3
2. White Sox, 1909 4
Senators, 1917 4
Senators, 1918 4
5. Phillies, 1902 5
White Sox, 1907 5
Cardinals, 1918 5
8. Cubs, 1902 6
Giants, 1902 6
10. White Sox, 1906 7
White Sox, 1910 7

STOLEN BASES, SEASON
1. Giants, 1911 347
2. A's, 1976 341
3. Giants, 1912 319
4. Cardinals, 1985 314
5. Reds, 1910 310
6. Giants, 1913 296
7. Giants, 1905 291
8. Reds, 1911 289
9. Giants, 1906 288
Yankees, 1910 288

LOWEST ERA, SEASON
1. Cubs, 1907 1.73
2. Cubs, 1909 1.75
Cubs, 1906 1.75
4. A's, 1910 1.79
5. A's, 1909 1.93
6. White Sox, 1905 1.99
7. Indians, 1908 2.02
8. White Sox, 1910 2.03
9. Cubs, 1905 2.04
10. White Sox, 1909 2.05

HIGHEST ERA, SEASON
1. Phillies, 1930 6.72
2. Tigers, 1996 6.38
3. Browns, 1936 6.24
4. Phillies, 1929 6.13
5. Athletics, 1936 6.08
6. Rockies, 1999 6.01
Browns, 1939 6.01
8. Browns, 1937 6.00
9. Browns, 1938 5.81
10. Athletics, 1939 5.79

FRANCHISE RECORDS

Franchise	Years	Games	Won	Lost	Pct.
Yankees	1901 - 2002	15827	8895	6840	.565
Diamondbacks	1998 - 2002	810	440	370	.543
Giants	1901 - 2002	15862	8497	7275	.539
Dodgers	1901 - 2002	15861	8243	7529	.523
Cardinals	1901 - 2002	15873	8146	7623	.517
Pirates	1901 - 2002	15861	8129	7638	.516
Red Sox	1901 - 2002	15839	8070	7686	.512
Indians	1901 - 2002	15853	8061	7701	.511
Tigers	1901 - 2002	15878	8035	7750	.509
White Sox	1901 - 2002	15847	7942	7802	.504
Reds	1901 - 2002	15875	7962	7824	.504
Cubs	1901 - 2002	15880	7958	7822	.504
Royals	1969 - 2002	5371	2675	2694	.498
Astros/Colt .45s	1962 - 2002	6518	3229	3285	.496
Blue Jays	1977 - 2002	4091	2025	2063	.495
Angels	1965 - 2002	6677	3243	3431	.486
Expos	1969 - 2002	5378	2605	2769	.485
Athletics	1901 - 2002	15814	7595	8132	.483
Braves	1901 - 2002	15849	7560	8182	.480
Twins/Senators	1901 - 2002	15859	7523	8227	.478
Orioles/Browns/Brewers	1901 - 2002	15852	7519	8224	.478
Mets	1962 - 2002	6511	3091	3412	.475
Rockies	1993 - 2002	1557	740	817	.475
Brewers/Pilots	1969 - 2002	5380	2545	2831	.473
Mariners	1977 - 2002	4089	1924	2163	.471
Rangers/Senators	1961 - 2002	6663	3097	3560	.465
Phillies	1901 - 2002	15821	7211	8536	.458
Padres	1969 - 2002	5383	2460	2921	.457
Marlins	1993 - 2002	1553	706	847	.455
Devil Rays	1998 - 2002	808	318	490	.394

LONGEST GAMES, INNINGS
1. Dodgers 1 at Braves 1, May 1, 1920 26
2. Cardinals 4 at Mets 3, Sept. 11, 1974 25
White Sox 7 vs. Brewers 6, May 8, 1984 25
4. A's 4 at Red Sox 1, Sept. 1, 1906 24
Tigers 1 at Athletics 1, July 21, 1945 24
Astros 1 vs. Mets 0, April 25, 1968 24
7. Dodgers 2 at Braves 2, June 27, 1939 23
Giants 8 at Mets 6, May 31, 1964 23
9. 8 tied at 22

RUNS SCORED, GAME
1. Red Sox vs. Browns, June 8, 1950 29
White Sox vs. A's, April 23, 1955 29
3. Cardinals vs. Phillies, July 6, 1929 28
4. Indians vs. Red Sox, July 7, 1923 27
5. Cubs vs. Phillies, Aug. 25, 1922 26
Giants vs. Dodgers, April 30, 1944 26
Indians vs. Browns, Aug. 12, 1948 26
Phillies vs. Mets, April 11, 1985 26
Cubs vs. Rockies, Aug. 18, 1995 26
Rangers vs. Orioles, April 19, 1996 26

RUNS SCORED, INNING
1. Red Sox vs. Tigers, June 18, 1953 (7th) 17
2. Rangers vs. Orioles, April 19, 1996 (8th) 16
3. Dodgers vs. Reds, May 21, 1952 (1st) 15
4. Yankees vs. Senators, July 6, 1920 (5th) 14
Cubs vs. Phillies, Aug. 25, 1922 (4th) 14
Indians vs. A's, June 18, 1950 (1st) 14
Reds vs. Astros, Aug. 3, 1989 (1st) 14
8. many tied with 13

BASEBALL CLASSICS

MEMORABLE MOMENTS

MERKLE'S BONER

September 23, 1908, at the Polo Grounds

New York Giants first baseman Fred Merkle claimed status as baseball's biggest goat when he failed to touch second base on an apparent game-ending hit against the Chicago Cubs, a mistake that would cost his team a pennant. With two out and runners on first and third in the bottom of the ninth of a 1-1 tie, Al Bridwell singled to center and Moose McCormick scored the winning run. But when Merkle failed to touch second, Cubs second baseman Johnny Evers appealed for the forceout and umpire Hank O'Day concurred, disallowing the run. League officials later declared the game a tie and the teams went on to finish the season with identical records. The Cubs won a makeup game—and the pennant.

Chicago	AB	R	H	PO	A	E
Hayden,rf	4	0	0	1	0	0
Evers,2b	4	0	1	3	7	0
Schulte,lf	4	0	0	1	0	0
Chance,1b	4	0	1	11	1	0
Steinfeldt,3b	2	0	0	0	1	1
Hofman,cf	3	0	1	2	0	0
Tinker,ss	3	1	1	8	6	2
Kling,c	3	0	1	0	1	0
Pfiester,p	3	0	0	1	0	0
Totals	30	1	5	27	16	3

New York	AB	R	H	PO	A	E
Herzog,2b	3	1	1	1	1	0
Bresnahan,c	3	0	0	10	0	0
Donlin,rf	4	0	1	2	0	0
Seymour,cf	4	0	1	1	0	0
Devlin,3b	4	0	2	0	2	0
McCormick,lf	3	0	0	1	0	0
Merkle,1b	3	0	1	10	1	0
Bridwell,ss	4	0	0	2	8	0
Mathewson,p	3	0	0	0	2	0
Totals	31	1	6	27	14	0

Chicago ....000 100 000—1
New York ....000 010 000—1

Runs batted in: Tinker, Donlin.
Home run: Tinker.
Sacrifice hits: Steinfeldt, Bresnahan.
Double plays: Tinker and Chance 2; Evers and Chance; Mathewson, Bridwell and Merkle.
Left on bases: Chicago 3, New York 7.

Chicago	IP	H	R	ER	BB	SO
Pfiester	9	6	1	0	2	0

New York	IP	H	R	ER	BB	SO
Mathewson	9	5	1	1	0	9

Hit by pitcher: McCormick (by Pfiester).
Umpires: O'Day, Emslie.
Time: 1:30. **Attendance:** 20,000.

A GIANT MISPLAY

October 16, 1912, at Fenway Park

The Boston Red Sox, given life by New York Giants center fielder Fred Snodgrass' 10th-inning error, scored two runs and claimed a 3-2 victory in the decisive eighth game of the World Series. After Snodgrass dropped a routine fly ball to open the inning, the Giants also failed to catch a foul pop by Tris Speaker, who then singled home the tying run. Larry Gardner produced the winner with a sacrifice fly.

New York	AB	R	H	PO	A	E
Devore,rf	3	1	1	3	1	0
Doyle,2b	5	0	0	1	5	1
Snodgrass,cf	4	0	1	4	1	1
Murray,lf	5	1	2	3	0	0
Merkle,1b	5	0	1	10	0	0
Herzog,3b	5	0	2	2	1	0
Meyers,c	3	0	0	4	1	0
Fletcher,ss	3	0	1	2	3	0
bMcCormick	1	0	0	0	0	0
Shafer,ss	0	0	0	0	0	0
Mathewson,p	4	0	1	0	3	0
Totals	38	2	9	29	15	2

Boston	AB	R	H	PO	A	E
Hooper,rf	5	0	0	3	0	0
Yerkes,2b	4	1	1	0	3	0
Speaker,cf	4	0	2	2	0	1
Lewis,lf	4	0	0	1	0	0
Gardner,3b	3	0	1	1	4	2
Stahl,1b	4	1	2	15	0	1
Wagner,ss	3	0	1	3	5	1
Cady,c	4	0	0	5	3	0
Bedient,p	2	0	0	0	1	0
aHenriksen	1	0	1	0	0	0
Wood,p	0	0	0	0	2	0
cEngle	1	1	0	0	0	0
Totals	35	3	8	30	18	5

New York ....001 000 000 1—2
Boston ....000 000 100 2—3

a Doubled for Bedient in seventh.
b Flied out for Fletcher in ninth.
c Reached second on Snodgrass' error in 10th.
d Two out when winning run scored.

Runs batted in: Murray, Merkle, Speaker, Gardner, Henriksen.
Doubles: Murray 2, Herzog, Gardner, Stahl, Henriksen.
Sacrifice hit: Meyers.
Sacrifice fly: Gardner.
Stolen bases: Devore.
Left on bases: New York 11, Boston 9.

New York	IP	H	R	ER	BB	SO
Mathewson (L)	9⅔	8	3	2	5	4

Boston	IP	H	R	ER	BB	SO
Bedient	7	6	1	1	3	2
Wood (W)	3	3	1	1	1	2

Umpires: O'Loughlin, Rigler, Klem, Evans.
Time: 2:39. **Attendance:** 17,034.

A DOUBLE NO-NO

May 2, 1917, at Wrigley Field

Cincinnati lefthander Fred Toney and Chicago righthander Hippo Vaughn hooked up in the most efficient pitching duel in baseball history—the game's only double nine-inning no-hitter. Vaughn allowed two 10th-inning hits and the Cubs broke through for an unearned run that Toney made stand up in the bottom of the inning, completing his no-hit gem. Vaughn had to settle for a tough-luck loss.

Cincinnati	AB	R	H	PO	A	E
Groh,3b	1	0	0	2	2	0
Getz,3b	1	0	0	2	1	0
Kopf,ss	4	1	1	1	4	0
Neale,cf	4	0	0	1	0	0
Chase,1b	4	0	0	12	0	0
Thorpe,rf	4	0	1	1	0	0
Shean,2b	3	0	0	3	2	0
Cueto,lf	3	0	0	5	0	0
Huhn,c	3	0	0	3	0	0
Toney,p	3	0	0	0	1	0
Totals	30	1	2	30	10	0

Chicago	AB	R	H	PO	A	E
Zeider,ss	4	0	0	1	0	0
Wolter,rf	4	0	0	0	0	0
Doyle,2b	4	0	0	5	4	0
Merkle,1b	4	0	0	7	1	0
Williams,cf	2	0	0	2	0	1
Mann,lf	3	0	0	0	0	0
Wilson,c	3	0	0	14	1	0
Deal,3b	3	0	0	1	0	0
Vaughn,p	3	0	0	0	3	0
Totals	30	0	0	30	9	1

Cincinnati ....000 000 000 1—1
Chicago ....000 000 000 0—0

Runs batted in: Thorpe.
Stolen bases: Chase.
Double plays: Doyle, Merkle and Zeider; Doyle and Merkle.
Left on bases: Cincinnati 1, Chicago 2.

Cincinnati	IP	H	R	ER	BB	SO
Toney (W)	10	0	0	0	2	3

Chicago	IP	H	R	ER	BB	SO
Vaughn (L)	10	2	1	0	2	10

Umpires: Orth, Rigler.
Time: 1:50. **Attendance:** 3,500.

A 26-INNING STANDOFF

May 1, 1920, at Braves Field

Brooklyn's Leon Cadore and Boston's Joe Oeschger matched zeroes in the longest pitching duel in baseball history—a 26-inning, 1-1 marathon that was called because of darkness. Cadore allowed 15 hits and Oeschger nine, but neither pitcher surrendered a run over the last 20 innings. Brooklyn scored in the fifth and Boston tied the game an inning later.

Brooklyn	AB	R	H	PO	A	E
Olson,2b	10	0	1	6	9	1
Neis,rf	10	0	1	9	0	0
Johnston,3b	10	0	2	2	1	0
Wheat,lf	9	0	2	3	0	0
Myers,cf	2	0	1	2	0	0
Hood,cf	6	0	1	8	1	0
Konetchy,1b	9	0	1	30	1	0
Ward,ss	10	0	0	6	3	1
Krueger,c	2	1	0	4	3	0
Elliott,c	7	0	0	7	3	0
Cadore,p	10	0	0	1	12	0
Totals	85	1	9	78	33	2

Boston	AB	R	H	PO	A	E
Powell,cf	8	0	1	8	0	0
Pick,2b	11	0	0	5	10	2
Mann,lf	10	0	2	6	0	0
Cruise,rf	9	1	1	4	0	0
Holke,1b	10	0	2	43	1	0
Boeckel,3b	11	0	3	1	7	0
Maranville,ss	10	0	3	1	9	0
O'Neil,c	2	0	0	4	3	0
aChristenbury	1	0	1	0	0	0
Gowdy,c	6	0	1	6	0	0
Oeschger,p	9	0	1	0	11	0
Totals	87	1	15	78	41	2

a Singled for O'Neil in ninth.

Brk. 000 010 000 000 000
Bos. 000 001 000 000 000

Brk. ....000 000 000 00—1
Bos. ....000 000 000 00—1

Runs batted in: Olson, Boeckel.
Doubles: Oeschger, Maranville.
Triple: Cruise.
Sacrifice hits: Powell, O'Neil, Cruise, Hood, Holke.
Stolen bases: Myers, Hood.
Double plays: Olson and Konetchy; Oeschger, Gowdy, Holke and Gowdy.
Left on bases: Brooklyn 11, Boston 17.

Brooklyn	IP	H	R	ER	BB	SO
Cadore	26	15	1	1	5	7

Boston	IP	H	R	ER	BB	SO
Oeschger	26	9	1	1	4	7

Wild pitch: Oeschger.

Umpires: McCormick, Hart.
Time: 3:50. **Attendance:** 2,500.

SENATORIAL SPLENDOR

October 10, 1924, at Griffith Stadium

The Washington Senators, long the doormat of the American League, captured their first World Series when two routine Game 7 ground balls inexplicably hopped over the head of New York Giants third baseman Fred Lindstrom, producing three runs. The Senators tied the game, 3-3, on manager Bucky Harris' two-run, bad-hop single in the eighth inning and won in the 12th, 4-3, on Earl McNeely's bad-hop bouncer.

New York	AB	R	H	PO	A	E
Lindstrom,3b	5	0	1	0	3	0
Frisch,2b	5	0	2	3	4	0
Youngs,rf-lf	2	1	0	2	0	0
Kelly,cf-1b	6	1	1	8	1	0
Terry,1b	2	0	0	6	1	0
aMeusel,lf-rf	3	0	1	1	0	0
Wilson,lf-cf	5	1	1	4	0	0
Jackson,ss	6	0	0	1	4	2
Gowdy,c	6	0	1	8	0	1
Barnes,p	4	0	0	1	2	0
Nehf,p	0	0	0	0	0	0
McQuillan,p	0	0	0	0	0	0
eGroh	1	0	1	0	0	0
fSouthworth	0	0	0	0	0	0
Bentley,p	0	0	0	0	0	0
Totals	45	3	8	34	15	3

New York Giants first baseman Fred Merkle is usually blamed for his team's failure to win the 1908 National League pennant.

Washington	AB	R	H	PO	A	E
McNeely,cf	6	0	1	0	0	0
Harris,2b	5	1	3	4	1	0
Rice,rf	5	0	0	2	0	0
Goslin,lf	5	0	2	3	0	0
Judge,1b	4	0	1	11	1	1
Bluege,ss	5	0	0	1	7	2
Taylor,3b	2	0	0	0	3	1
bLeibold	1	1	1	0	0	0
Miller,3b	2	0	0	1	1	0
Ruel,c	5	2	2	13	0	0
Odgen,p	0	0	0	0	0	0
Mogridge,p	1	0	0	0	0	0
Marberry,p	1	0	0	1	0	0
cTate	0	0	0	0	0	0
dShirley	0	0	0	0	0	0
Johnson,p	2	0	0	0	1	0
Totals	44	4	10	36	14	4

New York..........000 003 000 000—3
Washington......000 100 020 001—4

a Flied out for Terry in sixth.
b Doubled for Taylor in eighth.
c Walked for Marberry in eighth.
d Ran for Tate in eighth.
e Singled for McQuillan in 11th.
f Ran for Groh in 11th.
g One out when winning run scored.

Runs batted in: Harris 3, McNeely, Meusel.
Doubles: Lindstrom, Leibold, Ruel, Goslin, McNeely.
Triple: Frisch.
Home run: Harris.
Sacrifice hit: Lindstrom.
Sacrifice fly: Meusel.
Stolen bases: Youngs.
Double plays: Kelly and Jackson; Jackson, Frisch and Kelly; Johnson, Bluege and Judge.
Left on bases: New York 14, Washington 8.

New York	IP	H	R	ER	BB	SO
Barnes	7⅔	6	3	3	1	6
Nehf	⅓	1	0	0	0	0
McQuillan	1⅔	0	0	0	0	1
Bentley (L)	1⅓	3	1	1	1	0

Washington	IP	H	R	ER	BB	SO
Odgen	⅓	0	0	0	1	1
Mogridge	4⅔	4	2	1	1	3
Marberry	3	1	1	0	1	3
Johnson (W)	4	3	0	0	3	5

Mogridge pitched to two batters in sixth.

Umpires: Dinneen, Quigley, Connolly, Klem.
Time: 3:00. **Attendance:** 31,667.

A'S VAULT PAST CUBS

October 12, 1929, at Shibe Park

Down 8-0 after six innings of World Series Game 4, the Philadelphia Athletics rocked the Chicago Cubs with a 10-run seventh-inning explosion that produced a 10-8 victory and a three-games-to-one advantage in the fall classic. The key blow in the biggest inning in Series history was a three-run, inside-the-park home run by Philadelphia's Mule Haas.

Chicago	AB	R	H	PO	A	E
McMillan,3b	4	0	0	1	3	0
English,ss	4	0	0	2	1	0
Hornsby,2b	5	2	2	1	1	0
Wilson,cf	3	1	2	3	0	1
Cuyler,rf	4	2	3	0	0	1
Stephenson,lf	4	1	1	2	1	0
Grimm,1b	4	2	2	7	0	0
Taylor,c	3	0	0	8	1	0
Root,p	3	0	0	0	0	0
Nehf,p	0	0	0	0	0	0
Blake,p	0	0	0	0	0	0
Malone,p	0	0	0	0	0	0
bHartnett	1	0	0	0	0	0
Carlson,p	0	0	0	0	1	0
Totals	35	8	10	24	8	2

Philadelphia	AB	R	H	PO	A	E
Bishop,2b	5	1	2	2	3	0
Haas,cf	4	1	1	2	0	0
Cochrane,c	4	1	2	9	0	0
Simmons,lf	5	2	2	0	0	0
Foxx,1b	4	2	2	10	0	0
Miller,rf	3	1	2	3	0	1
Dykes,3b	4	1	3	0	2	0
Boley,ss	3	1	1	1	5	0
Quinn,p	2	0	0	0	0	0
Walberg,p	0	0	0	0	0	1
Rommel,p	0	0	0	0	0	0
aBurns	2	0	0	0	0	0
Grove,p	0	0	0	0	0	0
Totals	36	10	15	27	10	2

Chicago ....000 205 100—8
Philadelphia ....000 000 100x—10

a Popped out and struck out for Rommel in seventh.
b Struck out for Malone in eighth.

Runs batted in: Cuyler 2, Stephenson, Grimm 2, Taylor, Bishop, Haas 3, Simmons, Foxx, Dykes 3, Boley.
Doubles: Cochrane, Dykes.
Triple: Hornsby.
Home runs: Grimm, Haas, Simmons.
Sacrifice hits: Taylor, Haas, Boley.
Double play: Dykes, Bishop and Foxx.
Left on bases: Philadelphia 10, Chicago 6.

Chicago	IP	H	R	ER	BB	SO
Root	6⅓	9	6	6	0	3
Nehf	0	1	2	2	1	0
Blake (L)	0	2	2	2	0	0
Malone	⅔	1	0	0	0	2
Carlson	1	2	0	0	0	1

Philadelphia	IP	H	R	ER	BB	SO
Quinn	5	7	6	5	2	2
Walberg	1	1	1	0	0	2
Rommel (W)	1	2	1	1	1	0
Grove (S)	2	0	0	0	0	4

Nehf pitched to two batters in seventh.
Blake pitched to two batters in seventh.
Quinn pitched to four batters in sixth.
Hit by pitcher: Miller (by Malone).

Umpires: Van Graflan, Klem, Dinneen, Moran.
Time: 2:12. **Attendance:** 29,921.

RUTH'S CALLED SHOT

October 1, 1932, at Wrigley Field

New York slugger Babe Ruth, ever the showman, livened up Game 3 of the World Series with his dramatic called-shot home run, breaking a 4-4 tie and sparking the Yankees to a 7-5 victory. Responding to the taunting of Cubs players and fans, Ruth made a sweeping gesture toward the center-field stands and then deposited Charlie Root's 2-2 pitch precisely where he had pointed. The home run, his second of the game, helped the Yankees to a Series-controlling 3-0 lead.

New York	AB	R	H	PO	A	E
Combs,cf	5	1	0	1	0	0
Sewell,3b	2	1	0	2	2	0
Ruth,lf	4	2	2	2	0	0
Gehrig,1b	5	2	2	13	1	0
Lazzeri,2b	4	1	0	3	4	1
Dickey,c	4	0	1	2	1	0
Chapman,rf	4	0	2	0	0	0
Crosetti,ss	4	0	1	4	4	0
Pipgras,p	5	0	0	0	0	0
Pennock,p	0	0	0	0	1	0
Totals	37	7	8	27	13	1

Chicago	AB	R	H	PO	A	E
Herman,2b	4	1	0	1	2	1
English,3b	4	0	0	0	3	0
Cuyler,rf	4	1	3	1	0	0
Stephenson,lf	4	0	1	1	0	0
Moore,cf	3	1	0	3	0	0
Grimm,1b	4	0	1	8	0	0
Hartnett,c	4	1	1	10	1	1
Jurges,ss	4	1	3	3	3	2
Root,p	2	0	0	0	0	0
Malone,p	0	0	0	0	0	0
aGudat	1	0	0	0	0	0
May,p	0	0	0	0	0	0
Tinning,p	0	0	0	0	0	0
bKoenig	0	0	0	0	0	0
cHemlsey	1	0	0	0	0	0
Totals	35	5	9	27	9	4

New York ....301 020 001—7
Chicago ....102 100 001—5

a Popped out for Malone in seventh.
b Announced for Tinning in ninth.
c Struck out for Koenig in ninth.

Runs batted in: Ruth 4, Gehrig 2, Cuyler 2, Grimm, Chapman, Hartnett.
Doubles: Chapman, Cuyler, Jurges, Grimm.
Home runs: Ruth 2, Gehrig 2, Hartnett.
Stolen bases: Jurges.
Double plays: Sewell, Lazzeri and Gehrig; Herman, Jurges and Grimm.
Left on bases: New York 11, Chicago 6.

New York	IP	H	R	ER	BB	SO
Pipgras (W)	8	9	5	4	3	1
Pennock (S)	1	0	0	0	0	1

Chicago	IP	H	R	ER	BB	SO
Root (L)	4⅓	6	6	5	3	4
Malone	2⅔	1	0	0	4	4
May	1⅓	1	1	0	0	1
Tinning	⅔	0	0	0	0	1

Pipgras pitched to two batters in ninth.
Hit by pitcher: Sewell (by May).

Umpires: Van Graflan, Magerkurth, Dinneen, Klem.
Time: 2:11. **Attendance:** 49,986.

VANDER MEER'S DOUBLE

June 15, 1938, at Ebbets Field

Cincinnati lefthander Johnny Vander Meer pitched an historic 6-0 no-hitter against the Brooklyn Dodgers—his unprecedented second straight hitless game and the first night contest at Brooklyn's Ebbets Field. Vander Meer's victory came four days after he had no-hit Boston, 3-0.

Cincinnati	AB	R	H	PO	A	E
Frey,2b	5	0	1	2	2	0
Berger,lf	5	1	3	1	0	0
Goodman,rf	3	2	1	3	0	0
McCormick,1b	5	1	1	9	1	0
Lombardi,c	3	1	0	9	0	0
Craft,cf	5	0	3	1	0	0
Riggs,3b	4	0	1	0	3	0
Myers,ss	4	0	0	0	1	0
Vander Meer,p	4	1	1	2	4	0
Totals	38	6	11	27	11	0

Brooklyn	AB	R	H	PO	A	E
Cuyler,rf	2	0	0	1	0	0
Coscarart,2b	2	0	0	1	2	0
aBrack	1	0	0	0	0	0
Hudson,2b	1	0	0	1	0	0
Hassett,lf	4	0	0	3	0	0
Phelps,c	3	0	0	9	0	0
cRosen	0	0	0	0	0	0
Lavagetto,3b	2	0	0	0	2	2
Camilli,1b	1	0	0	7	0	0
Koy,cf	4	0	0	4	0	0
Durocher,ss	4	0	0	1	2	0
Butcher,p	0	0	0	0	1	0
Presnell,p	2	0	0	0	0	0
Hamlin,p	0	0	0	0	1	0
bEnglish	1	0	0	0	0	0
Tamulis,p	0	0	0	0	0	0
Totals	27	0	0	27	8	2

Cincinnati ....004 000 110—6
Brooklyn......................000 000 000—0

a Batted for Coscarart in sixth.
b Struck out for Hamlin in eighth.
c Ran for Phelps in ninth.

Runs batted in: McCormick 3, Riggs, Craft, Berger.
Double: Berger.
Triple: Berger.
Home run: McCormick.
Stolen bases: Goodman.
Left on bases: Cincinnati 9, Brooklyn 8.

Cincinnati	IP	H	R	ER	BB	SO
Vander Meer (W)	9	0	0	0	8	7

Brooklyn	IP	H	R	ER	BB	SO
Butcher (L)	2⅔	5	4	4	3	1
Pressnell	3⅔	4	1	1	0	3
Hamlin	1⅔	2	1	1	1	3
Tamulis	1	0	0	0	0	0

Umpires: Stewart, Stark, Barr.
Time: 2:22. **Attendance:** 38,748.

WILLIAMS' STAR RISES

July 8, 1941, at Briggs Stadium

Young Boston slugger Ted Williams carved his first niche in baseball lore with a two-out, three-run, ninth-inning homer that gave the American League a dramatic 7-5 victory over the National League in baseball's ninth All-Star Game. Williams capped the four-run A.L. ninth with a monster drive off Chicago's Claude Passeau that bounced off the upper right-field parapet of Detroit's Briggs Stadium.

National League	AB	R	H	PO	A	E
Hack,3b	2	0	1	3	0	0
fLavagetto,3b	1	0	0	0	0	0
Moore,lf	5	0	0	0	0	0
Reiser,cf	4	0	0	6	0	2
Mize,1b	4	1	1	5	0	0
McCormick,1b	0	0	0	0	0	0
Nicholson,rf	1	0	0	1	0	0
Elliott,rf	1	0	0	0	0	0
Slaughter,rf	2	1	1	0	0	0
Vaughan,ss	4	2	3	1	2	0
Miller,ss	0	0	0	0	1	0
Frey,3b	1	0	1	1	3	0
cHerman,2b	3	0	2	3	0	0
Owen,c	1	0	0	0	0	0
Lopez,c	1	0	0	3	0	0
Danning,c	1	0	0	3	0	0
Wyatt,p	0	0	0	0	0	0
aOtt	1	0	0	0	0	0
Derringer,p	0	0	0	0	1	0
Walters,p	1	1	1	0	0	0
dMedwick	1	0	0	0	0	0
Passeau,p	1	0	0	0	0	0
Totals	35	5	10	26	7	2

American League	AB	R	H	PO	A	E
Doerr,2b	3	0	0	0	0	0
Gordon,2b	2	1	1	2	0	0
Travis,3b	4	1	1	1	2	0
J.DiMaggio,cf	4	3	1	1	0	0
Williams,lf	4	1	2	3	0	1
Heath,rf	2	0	0	1	0	1
D.DiMaggio,rf	1	0	1	1	0	0
Cronin,ss	2	0	0	3	0	0
Boudreau,ss	2	0	2	0	1	0
York,1b	3	0	1	6	2	0
Foxx,1b	1	0	0	2	2	0
Dickey,c	3	0	1	4	2	0
Hayes,c	1	0	0	2	0	0
Feller,p	0	0	0	0	1	0
bCullenbine	1	0	0	0	0	0
Lee,p	1	0	0	0	1	0
Hudson,p	0	0	0	0	0	0
eKeller	1	0	0	0	0	0
Smith,p	0	0	0	1	0	1
gKeltner	1	1	1	0	0	0
Totals	36	7	11	27	11	3

National League ....000 001 220—5
American League ......000 101 014—7

a Struck out for Wyatt in third.
b Grounded out for Feller in third.
c Singled for Frey in fifth.
d Grounded out for Walters in seventh.
e Struck out for Hudson in seventh.
f Grounded out for Hack in ninth.
g Singled for Smith in ninth.
h Two out when winning run scored.

Runs batted in: Williams 4, Moore, Boudreau, Vaughan 4, D.DiMaggio, J.DiMaggio.
Doubles: Travis, Williams, Walters, Herman, Mize, J.DiMaggio.
Home runs: Vaughan 2, Williams.
Sacrifice hits: Hack, Lopez.
Double plays: Frey, Vaughan and Mize; York and Cronin.
Left on bases: National League 6, American League 7.

National League	IP	H	R	ER	BB	SO
Wyatt	2	0	0	0	1	0
Derringer	2	2	1	1	0	1
Walters	2	3	1	1	2	2
Passeau (L)	2⅔	6	5	5	1	3

American League	IP	H	R	ER	BB	SO
Feller	3	1	0	0	0	4
Lee	3	4	1	1	0	0
Hudson	1	3	2	2	1	1
Smith (W)	2	2	2	2	0	2

Umpires: Summers, Grieve, Jorda, Pinelli.
Time: 2:23. **Attendance:** 54,674.

DiMAGGIO'S STREAK ENDS

July 17, 1941, at Municipal Stadium

Cleveland pitchers Al Smith and Jim Bagby Jr. retired New York's Joe DiMaggio three times and ended the Yankees center fielder's record hitting streak at 56 games. DiMaggio, who had not gone hitless in more than two months, grounded out to third base twice, walked and bounced into an eighth-inning double play during the Yankees' 4-3 victory.

New York	AB	R	H	PO	A	E
Sturm,1b	4	0	1	10	2	0
Rolfe,3b	4	1	2	2	3	0
Henrich,rf	3	0	1	4	0	0
DiMaggio,cf	3	0	0	2	0	0
Gordon,2b	4	1	2	0	1	0
Rosar,c	4	0	0	5	1	0
Keller,lf	3	1	1	0	0	0
Rizzuto,ss	4	0	0	2	1	0
Gomez,p	4	1	1	2	1	0
Murphy,p	0	0	0	0	1	0
Totals	33	4	8	27	10	0

Cleveland	AB	R	H	PO	A	E
Weatherly,cf	5	0	1	4	0	0
Keltner,3b	3	0	1	1	4	0
Boudreau,ss	3	0	0	0	2	0
Heath,rf	4	0	0	0	0	0
Walker,lf	3	2	2	1	0	0
Grimes,1b	3	1	1	12	0	0
Mack,2b	3	0	0	4	7	0
aRosenthal	1	0	1	0	0	0
Hemsley,c	3	0	1	5	1	0
bTrosky	1	0	0	0	0	0
Smith,p	3	0	0	0	0	0
Bagby,p	0	0	0	0	0	0
cCampbell	1	0	0	0	0	0
Totals	33	3	7	27	14	0

New York ....100 000 120—4
Cleveland ....000 100 002—3

a Tripled for Mack in ninth.
b Grounded out for Hemsley in ninth.
c Hit into fielders choice for Bagby in ninth.

Runs batted in: Henrich, Walker, Gomez, Gordon, Rolfe, Rosenthal 2.
Doubles: Henrich, Rolfe.
Triples: Keller, Rosenthal.
Home runs: Walker, Gordon.
Sacrifice hit: Boudreau.
Double play: Boudreau, Mack and Grimes.
Passed ball: Hemsley.
Left on bases: New York 5, Cleveland 7.

New York	IP	H	R	ER	BB	SO
Gomez (W)	8	6	3	3	3	5
Murphy (S)	1	1	0	0	0	0

Cleveland	IP	H	R	ER	BB	SO
Smith (L)	7⅓	7	4	4	2	4
Bagby	1⅔	1	0	0	1	1

Gomez pitched to two batters in ninth.

Umpires: Summers, Rue, Stewart.
Time: 2:03. **Attendance:** 67,468.

OWEN'S PASSED BALL

October 5, 1941, at Ebbets Field

With his Dodgers leading the New York Yankees, 4-3, and one out away from evening the World Series at two games apiece, Brooklyn catcher Mickey Owen missed connections on a third strike, allowing Tommy Henrich to reach first base. Given new life, the Yankees exploded for four ninth-inning runs, recorded a 7-4 victory and set the stage for a Series-clinching victory the next day.

New York	AB	R	H	PO	A	E
Sturm,1b	5	0	2	9	1	0
Rolfe,3b	5	1	2	0	2	0
Henrich,rf	4	1	0	3	0	0
DiMaggio,cf	4	1	2	2	0	0
Keller,lf	5	1	4	1	0	0
Dickey,c	2	2	0	7	0	0
Gordon,2b	5	1	2	2	3	0
Rizzuto,ss	4	0	0	2	3	0
Donald,p	2	0	0	0	1	0
Breuer,p	1	0	0	0	1	0
bSelkirk	1	0	0	0	0	0
Murphy,p	1	0	0	1	0	0
Totals	39	7	12	27	11	0

Brooklyn	AB	R	H	PO	A	E
Reese,ss	5	0	0	2	4	0
Walker,rf	5	1	2	5	0	0
Reiser,cf	5	1	2	1	0	0
Camilli,1b	4	0	2	10	1	0
Riggs,3b	3	0	0	0	2	0
Medwick,lf	2	0	0	1	0	0
Allen,p	0	0	0	0	0	0
Casey,p	2	0	1	0	3	0
Owen,c	2	1	0	2	1	1
Coscarart,2b	3	1	0	4	2	0
Higbe,p	1	0	1	0	1	0
French,p	0	0	0	0	0	0
aWasdell,lf	3	0	1	2	0	0
Totals	35	4	9	27	14	1

New York ....1 0 0 2 0 0 0 0 4—7
Brooklyn.....................0 0 0 2 2 0 0 0 0—4

a Doubled for French in fourth.
b Grounded out for Breuer in eighth.

Runs batted in: Keller 3, Sturm 2, Gordon 2, Wasdell 2, Reiser 2.
Doubles: Keller 2, Walker, Camilli, Wasdell, Gordon.
Home run: Reiser.
Double play: Gordon, Rizzuto and Sturm.
Left on bases: New York 11, Brooklyn 8.

New York	IP	H	R	ER	BB	SO
Donald	4	6	4	4	3	2
Breuer	3	3	0	0	1	2
Murphy (W)	2	0	0	0	0	1

Brooklyn	IP	H	R	ER	BB	SO
Higbe	3⅔	6	3	3	2	1
French	⅓	0	0	0	0	0
Allen	⅔	1	0	0	1	0
Casey (L)	4⅓	5	4	0	2	1

Donald pitched to two batters in fifth.
Hit by pitcher: Henrich (by Allen).

Umpires: Goetz, McGowan, Pinelli, Grieve.
Time: 2:54. **Attendance:** 33,813

SLAUGHTER'S MAD DASH

October 15, 1946, at Sportsman's Park

St. Louis Cardinals outfielder Enos Slaughter decided the World Series with his daring Game 7 dash around the bases on a hit to left-center field by Harry Walker. Slaughter's eighth-inning heroics were successful because Boston shortstop Johnny Pesky, obviously surprised that Slaughter didn't stop at third, hesitated before making a weak relay throw to the plate.

Boston	AB	R	H	PO	A	E
Moses,rf	4	1	1	1	0	0
Pesky,ss	4	0	1	2	1	0
DiMaggio,cf	3	0	1	0	0	0
cCulberson,cf	0	0	0	0	0	0
Williams,lf	4	0	0	3	1	0
York,1b	4	0	1	10	1	0
dCampbell	0	0	0	0	0	0
Doerr,2b	4	0	2	3	7	0
Higgins,3b	4	0	0	0	1	0
H.Wagner,c	2	0	0	4	0	0
aRussell	1	1	1	0	0	0
Partee,c	1	0	0	0	0	0
Ferriss,p	2	0	0	0	0	0
Dobson,p	0	0	0	0	1	0
bMetkovich	1	1	1	0	0	0
Klinger,p	0	0	0	1	0	0
Johnson,p	0	0	0	0	0	0
eMcBride	1	0	0	0	0	0
Totals	35	3	8	24	12	0

St. Louis	AB	R	H	PO	A	E
Schoendienst,2b	4	0	2	2	3	0
Moore,cf	4	0	1	3	0	0
Musial,1b	3	0	1	6	0	0
Slaughter,rf	3	1	1	4	0	0
Kurowski,3b	4	1	1	3	1	1
Garigiola,c	3	0	0	4	0	0
Rice,c	1	0	0	0	0	0
Walker,lf	3	1	2	3	0	0
Marion,ss	2	0	0	2	1	0
Dickson,p	3	1	1	0	1	0
Brecheen,p	1	0	0	0	0	0
Totals	31	4	9	27	6	1

Boston ....1 0 0 0 0 0 0 2 0—3
St. Louis....................0 1 0 0 2 0 0 1 x—4

a Singled for H.Wagner in eighth.
b Doubled for Dobson in eighth.
c Ran for DiMaggio in eighth.
d Ran for York in ninth.
e Rolled out for Johnson in ninth.

Runs batted in: DiMaggio 3, Walker 2, Dickson, Schoendienst.
Doubles: Musial, Kurowski, Dickson, DiMaggio, Metkovich, Walker.
Sacrifice hit: Marion.
Left on bases: Boston 6, St. Louis 8.

Boston	IP	H	R	ER	BB	SO
Ferris	4⅓	7	3	3	1	1
Dobson	2⅔	0	0	0	2	2
Klinger (L)	⅔	2	1	1	1	0
Johnson	⅓	0	0	0	0	0

St. Louis	IP	H	R	ER	BB	SO
Dickson	7	5	3	3	1	3
Brecheen (W)	2	3	0	0	0	1

Dickson pitched to two batters in eighth.

Umpires: Barlick, Berry, Ballanfant, Hubbard.
Time: 2:17. **Attendance:** 36,143

ROBINSON BREAKS BARRIER

April 15, 1947, at Ebbets Field

Jackie Robinson made his long-awaited debut as baseball's first black Major League player in more than six decades when he started at first base in Brooklyn's season-opening 5-3 victory over Boston. The 28-year-old Robinson, a former college football and track star, went 0-for-3 but reached base on a seventh-inning error and came around to score the winning run.

Boston	AB	R	H	PO	A	E
Culler,ss	3	0	0	0	2	0
eHolmes	1	0	0	0	0	0
Sisti,ss	0	0	0	0	0	0
Hopp,cf	5	0	1	2	0	0
McCormick,rf	4	0	3	2	0	0
Elliott,3b	2	0	1	0	2	0
Litwhiler,lf	3	1	0	1	0	0
Rowell,lf	1	0	0	0	0	0
Torgeson,1b	4	1	0	10	1	1
Masi,c	3	0	0	4	0	0
Ryan,2b	4	1	3	4	7	0
Sain,p	1	0	0	0	1	0
Cooper,p	0	0	0	1	0	0
dNeill	0	0	0	0	0	0
Lanfranconi,p	0	0	0	0	0	0
Totals	31	3	8	24	13	1

Brooklyn	AB	R	H	PO	A	E
Stanky,2b	3	1	0	0	3	0
Robinson,1b	3	1	0	11	0	0
Schultz,1b	0	0	0	1	0	0
Reiser,cf	2	3	2	2	0	0
Walker,rf	3	0	1	0	0	0
Tatum,rf	0	0	0	0	0	0
cVaughan	1	0	0	0	0	0
Furillo,rf	0	0	0	0	0	0
Hermanski,lf	4	0	1	3	0	0
Edwards,c	2	0	0	2	0	1
aRackley	0	0	0	0	0	0
Bragan,c	1	0	0	3	0	0
Jorgensen,3b	3	0	0	0	4	0
Reese,ss	3	0	1	3	2	0
Hatten,p	2	0	1	1	1	0
bStevens	1	0	0	0	0	0
Gregg,p	1	0	0	1	0	0
Casey,p	0	0	0	0	0	0
Totals	29	5	6	27	10	1

Boston ....0 0 0 0 1 2 0 0 0—3
Brooklyn......................0 0 0 1 0 1 3 0 x—5

a Ran for Edwards in sixth.
b Struck out for Hatten in sixth.
c Grounded out for Tatum in seventh.
d Hit by pitch for Cooper in eighth.
e Flied out for Culler in eighth.

Runs batted in: Edwards, Hopp, Ryan 2, Jorgensen, Reiser 2, Hermanski.
Doubles: Reese, Reiser.
Sacrifice hits: Masi, Culler, Sain 2, Robinson.

Brooklyn's Cookie Lavagetto (right) is mobbed after his Game 4-winning hit in the 1947 World Series ended Bill Bevens' hope for a no-hitter.

Double plays: Stanky, Reese and Robinson; Culler, Ryan and Torgeson.
Left on bases: Boston 12, Brooklyn 7.

Boston	IP	H	R	ER	BB	SO
Sain (L)	6	6	5	4	5	1
Cooper	1	0	0	0	0	0
Lanfranconi	1	0	0	0	0	2

Brooklyn	IP	H	R	ER	BB	SO
Hatten	6	6	3	2	3	2
Gregg (W)	2⅓	2	0	0	2	2
Casey (S)	⅔	0	0	0	0	0

Sain pitched to three batters in seventh.
Hit by pitcher: Litwhiler (by Hatten), Edwards (by Sain), Neill (by Gregg).
Wild pitch: Hatten.

Umpires: Pinelli, Barlick, Gore.
Time: 2:26. **Attendance:** 25,623.

BEVENS' NEAR-MISS

October 3, 1947, at Ebbets Field

New York Yankees pitcher Bill Bevens, one out away from the first no-hitter in World Series history, surrendered a two-run double to Brooklyn pinch hitter Cookie Lavagetto and dropped a heart-breaking 3-2 decision to the Dodgers. After Bevens walked two Dodgers in the ninth inning of the Game 4 classic, his ninth and 10th free passes, Lavagetto lined an opposite-field drive off the right-field wall, allowing Brooklyn to tie the Series at two games apiece.

New York	AB	R	H	PO	A	E
Stirnweiss,2b	4	1	2	2	1	0
Henrich,rf	5	0	1	2	0	0
Berra,c	4	0	0	6	1	1
DiMaggio,cf	2	0	0	2	0	0
McQuinn,1b	4	0	1	7	0	0
Johnson,3b	4	1	1	3	2	0
Lindell,lf	3	0	2	3	0	0
Rizzuto,ss	4	0	1	1	2	0
Bevens,p	3	0	0	0	1	0
Totals	33	2	8	26	7	1

Brooklyn	AB	R	H	PO	A	E
Stanky,2b	1	0	0	2	3	0
aLavagetto	1	0	1	0	0	0
Reese,ss	4	0	0	3	5	1
Robinson,1b	4	0	0	11	1	0
Walker,rf	2	0	0	0	1	0
Hermanski,lf	4	0	0	2	0	0
Edwards,c	4	0	0	7	1	1
Furillo,cf	3	0	0	2	0	0
bGionfriddo	0	1	0	0	0	0
Jorgensen,3b	2	1	0	0	1	1
Taylor,p	0	0	0	0	0	0
Gregg,p	1	0	0	0	1	0
aVaughan	0	0	0	0	0	0
Behrman,p	0	0	0	0	1	0
Casey,p	0	0	0	0	1	0
cReiser	0	0	0	0	0	0
dMiksis	0	1	0	0	0	0
Totals	26	3	1	27	15	3

New York ....1 0 0 1 0 0 0 0 0—2
Brooklyn.....................0 0 0 0 1 0 0 0 2—3

a Walked for Gregg in seventh.
b Ran for Furillo in ninth.
c Walked for Casey in ninth.
d Ran for Reiser in ninth.
e Doubled for Stanky in ninth.
f Two out when winning run scored.

Runs batted in: DiMaggio, Lindell, Reese, Lavagetto 2.
Doubles: Lindell, Lavagetto.
Triple: Johnson.
Sacrifice hits: Stanky, Bevens.
Stolen bases: Rizzuto, Reese, Gionfriddo.
Double plays: Reese, Stanky and Robinson; Gregg, Reese and Robinson; Edwards and Robinson.
Left on bases: New York 9, Brooklyn 8.

New York	IP	H	R	ER	BB	SO
Bevens (L)	8⅔	1	3	3	10	5

Brooklyn	IP	H	R	ER	BB	SO
Taylor	0	2	1	0	1	0
Gregg	7	4	1	1	3	5
Behrman	1⅓	2	0	0	0	0
Casey (W)	⅔	0	0	0	0	0

Taylor pitched to four batters in first.
Wild pitch: Bevens.

Umpires: Goetz, McGowan, Pinelli, Rommel, Boyer, Magerkurth.
Time: 2:20. **Attendance:** 33,443

GIONFRIDDO SAVES THE DAY

October 5, 1947, at Yankee Stadium

Defensive replacement Al Gionfriddo jumped into the World Series spotlight when he made a spectacular sixth-inning catch of Yankees slugger Joe DiMaggio's bid for a home run, preserving an 8-6 victory that forced a decisive seventh game. With the Dodgers leading 8-5 and two New York runners on base, DiMaggio hit a monster drive that a twisting Gionfriddo speared at the 415-foot sign, just as it appeared the ball would drop into the bullpen for a game-tying homer. The Yankees rebounded to win the Series the next day.

Brooklyn	AB	R	H	PO	A	E
Stanky,2b	5	2	2	4	2	0
Reese,ss	4	2	3	2	1	0
J.Robinson,1b	5	1	2	7	1	0
Walker,rf	5	0	1	3	0	0
Hermanski,lf	1	0	0	0	0	0
bMiksis,lf	1	0	0	0	0	0
Gionfriddo,lf	2	0	0	1	0	0
Edwards,c	4	1	1	5	0	0
Furillo,cf	4	1	2	4	1	0
Jorgensen,3b	2	0	0	1	1	1
cLavagetto,3b	2	0	0	0	1	0
Lombardi,p	1	0	0	0	0	0
Branca,p	1	0	0	0	1	0
dBragan	1	0	1	0	0	0
eBankhead	0	1	0	0	0	0
Hatten,p	1	0	0	0	0	0
Casey,p	0	0	0	0	1	0
Totals	39	8	12	27	9	1

New York	AB	R	H	PO	A	E
Stirnweiss,2b	5	0	0	1	6	0
Henrich,rf-lf	5	1	2	1	0	0
Lindell,lf	2	1	2	0	0	0
Berra,rf	3	0	2	1	0	0
DiMaggio,cf	5	1	1	5	0	0
Johnson,3b	5	1	2	1	5	0
Phillips,1b	1	0	0	4	0	0
aBrown	1	0	1	0	0	0
McQuinn,1b	1	0	0	6	0	1
Rizzuto,ss	4	0	1	6	1	0
Lollar,c	1	1	1	0	0	0
A.Robinson,c	4	1	2	2	0	1
Reynolds,p	0	0	0	0	0	0
Drews,p	2	0	0	0	1	0
Page,p	0	0	0	0	0	0
Newsom,p	0	0	0	0	0	0
fClark	1	0	0	0	0	0
Raschi,p	0	0	0	0	0	0
gHouk	1	0	1	0	0	0
Wensloff,p	0	0	0	0	1	0
hFrey	1	0	0	0	0	0
Totals	42	6	15	27	14	2

Brooklyn....................2 0 2 0 0 4 0 0 0—8
New York ....0 0 4 1 0 0 0 0 1—6

a Singled for Phillips in third.
b Popped out for Hermanski in fifth.
c Flied out for Jorgensen in sixth.
d Doubled for Branca in sixth.
e Ran for Bragan in sixth.
f Lined out for Newsom in sixth.
g Singled for Raschi in seventh.
h Forced A.Robinson for Wensloff in ninth.

Runs batted in: J.Robinson, Walker, Stirnweiss, Lindell, Johnson, Brown, Berra, Lavagetto, Reese 2, Frey, Bragan.
Doubles: Reese, J.Robinson, Walker, Lollar, Furillo, Bragan.
Double play: Rizzuto and Phillips.
Passed ball: Lollar.
Left on bases: New York 13, Brooklyn 6.

Brooklyn	IP	H	R	ER	BB	SO
Lombardi	2⅔	5	4	4	0	2
Branca (W)	2⅓	6	1	1	0	2
Hatten	3	3	1	1	4	0
Casey (S)	1	1	0	0	0	0

New York	IP	H	R	ER	BB	SO
Reynolds	2⅓	6	4	3	1	0
Drews	2	1	0	0	1	0
Page (L)	1	4	4	4	0	1
Newsom	⅔	1	0	0	0	0
Raschi	1	0	0	0	0	1
Wensloff	2	0	0	0	0	0

Hatten pitched to two batters in ninth.
Wild pitch: Lombardi.

Umpires: Pinelli, Rommel, Goetz, McGowman, Boyer, Magerkurth.
Time: 3:19. **Attendance:** 74,065.

Bobby Thomson poses with Giants owner Horace Stoneham (left) and manager Leo Durocher after his pennant-deciding homer.

THE SHOT HEARD 'ROUND THE WORLD

October 3, 1951, at the Polo Grounds

Bobby Thomson's three-run, ninth-inning home run, considered by many historians the most dramatic in baseball history, gave the New York Giants a 5-4 victory over Brooklyn and settled a wild N.L. pennant race. Thomson connected off Dodgers righthander Ralph Branca with two out and the Giants trailing, 4-2, in Game 3 of a pennant playoff series. Thomson's dramatics were preceded by Al Dark and Don Mueller singles and Whitey Lockman's run-scoring double.

Brooklyn	AB	R	H	PO	A	E
Furillo,rf	5	0	0	0	0	0
Reese,ss	4	2	1	2	5	0
Snider,cf	3	1	2	1	0	0
Robinson,2b	2	1	1	3	2	0
Pafko,lf	4	0	1	4	1	0
Hodges,1b	4	0	0	11	1	0
Cox,3b	4	0	2	1	3	0
Walker,c	4	0	1	2	0	0
Newcombe,p	4	0	0	1	1	0
Branca,p	0	0	0	0	0	0
Totals	34	4	8	25	13	0

New York	AB	R	H	PO	A	E
Stanky,2b	4	0	0	0	4	0
Dark,ss	4	1	1	2	2	0
Mueller,rf	4	0	1	0	0	0
cHartung	0	1	0	0	0	0
Irvin,lf	4	1	1	1	0	0
Lockman,1b	3	1	2	11	1	0
Thomson,3b	4	1	3	4	1	0
Mays,cf	3	0	0	1	0	0
Westrum,c	0	0	0	7	1	0
aRigney	1	0	0	0	0	0
Noble,c	0	0	0	0	0	0
Maglie,p	2	0	0	1	2	0
bThompson	1	0	0	0	0	0
Jansen,p	0	0	0	0	0	0
Totals	30	5	8	27	11	0

Brooklyn....................1 0 0 0 0 0 0 3 0—4
New York ....0 0 0 0 0 0 1 0 4—5

a Struck out for Westrum in eighth.
b Grounded out for Maglie in eighth.
c Ran for Mueller in ninth.
d One out when winning run scored.

Runs batted in: Robinson, Thomson 4, Pafko, Cox, Lockman
Doubles: Thomson, Irvin, Lockman.
Home run: Thomson.
Sacrifice hit: Lockman.
Double plays: Cox, Robinson and Hodges; Reese, Robinson and Hodges.
Left on bases: Brooklyn 7, New York 3.

Brooklyn	IP	H	R	ER	BB	SO
Newcombe	8⅓	7	4	4	2	2
Branca (L)	0	1	1	1	0	0

New York	IP	H	R	ER	BB	SO
Maglie	8	8	4	4	4	6
Jansen (W)	1	0	0	0	0	2

Branca pitched to one batter in ninth.
Wild pitch: Maglie.

Umpires: Jorda, Conlan, Stewart, Goetz.
Time: 2:28. **Attendance:** 34,320.

MAYS STUNS INDIANS

September 29, 1954, at the Polo Grounds

Willie Mays took his place in baseball lore when he made a dramatic eighth-inning, over-the-shoulder catch on a 460-foot drive by Cleveland's Vic Wertz, saving the New York Giants in Game 1 of the World Series. Mays made his remarkable catch with the score tied 2-2 and Indians positioned on first and second base. The Giants went on to win the Series opener, 5-2, on Dusty Rhodes' 10th-inning homer, keying a stunning fall classic sweep.

Cleveland	AB	R	H	PO	A	E
Smith,lf	4	1	1	1	0	0
Avila,2b	5	1	1	2	3	0
Doby,cf	3	0	1	3	0	0
Rosen,3b	5	0	1	1	3	0
Wertz,1b	5	0	4	11	1	0
dRegalado	0	0	0	0	0	0
Grasso,c	0	0	0	1	0	0
Philley,rf	3	0	0	0	0	0
aMajeski	0	0	0	0	0	0
bMitchell	0	0	0	0	0	0
Dente,ss	0	0	0	0	0	0
Strickland,ss	3	0	0	2	3	0
cPope,rf	1	0	0	0	0	0
Hegan,c	4	0	0	6	1	0
eGlynn,1b	1	0	0	0	0	0
Lemon,p	4	0	0	1	1	0
Totals	38	2	8	28	12	0

New York	AB	R	H	PO	A	E
Lockman,1b	5	1	1	9	0	0
Dark,ss	4	0	2	3	2	0
Mueller,rf	5	1	2	2	0	2
Mays,cf	3	1	0	2	0	0
Thompson,3b	3	1	1	3	3	0
Irvin,lf	3	0	0	5	0	1
fRhodes	1	1	1	0	0	0
Williams,2b	4	0	0	1	1	0
Westrum,c	4	0	2	5	0	0
Maglie,p	3	0	0	0	2	0
Liddle,p	0	0	0	0	0	0
Grissom,p	1	0	0	0	0	0
Totals	36	5	9	30	8	3

Cleveland ....2 0 0 0 0 0 0 0 0 0—2
New York ....0 0 2 0 0 0 0 0 0 3—5

a Announced for Philley in eighth.
b Walked for Majeski in eighth.
c Called out on strikes for Strickland in eighth.
d Ran for Wertz in 10th.
e Struck out for Hegan in 10th.
f Hit home run for Irvin in 10th.
i One out when winning run scored.

Runs batted in: Wertz 2, Mueller, Thompson, Rhodes 3.
Double: Wertz.
Triple: Wertz.
Home run: Rhodes.
Sacrifice hits: Irvin, Dente.
Stolen bases: Mays.
Left on bases: Cleveland 13, New York 9.

Cleveland	IP	H	R	ER	BB	SO
Lemon (L)	9⅓	9	5	5	5	6

New York	IP	H	R	ER	BB	SO
Maglie	7	7	2	2	2	2
Liddle	⅓	0	0	0	0	0
Grissom (W)	2⅔	1	0	0	3	2

Maglie pitched to two batters in eighth.
Hit by pitcher: Smith (by Maglie).
Wild pitch: Lemon.

Umpires: Barlick, Berry, Conlan, Stevens, Warneke, Napp.
Time: 3:11. **Attendance:** 52,751.

AMOROS TO THE RESCUE

October 4, 1955, at Yankee Stadium

With his team leading 2-0 in the sixth inning of World Series Game 7, Brooklyn left fielder Sandy Amoros streaked into the left-field corner and made a spectacular, Series-saving catch of Yogi Berra's line drive. Amoros made the dramatic play with two Yankees on base, wheeled around and doubled Gil McDougald off first, securing Johnny Podres' shutout.

Brooklyn	AB	R	H	PO	A	E
Gilliam,lf-2b	4	0	1	2	0	0
Reese,ss	4	1	1	2	6	0
Snider,cf	3	0	0	2	0	0
Campanella,c	3	1	1	5	0	0
Furillo,rf	3	0	0	3	0	0
Hodges,1b	2	0	1	10	0	0
Hoak,3b	3	0	1	1	1	0
Zimmer,2b	2	0	0	0	2	0
aShuba	1	0	0	0	0	0
Amoros,lf	0	0	0	2	1	0
Podres,p	4	0	0	0	1	0
Totals	29	2	5	27	11	0

New York	AB	R	H	PO	A	E
Rizzuto,ss	3	0	1	1	3	0
Martin,2b	3	0	1	1	6	0
McDougald,3b	4	0	3	1	1	0
Berra,c	4	0	1	4	1	0
Bauer,rf	4	0	0	1	0	0
Skowron,1b	4	0	1	11	1	1
Cerv,cf	4	0	0	5	0	0
Howard,lf	4	0	1	2	0	0
Byrne,p	2	0	0	0	2	0
Grim,p	0	0	0	1	0	0
bMantle	1	0	0	0	0	0
Turley,p	0	0	0	0	0	0
Totals	33	0	8	27	14	1

FOR THE RECORD

Don Larsen celebrates with Yankees owners Dan Topping (left) and Dell Webb in a perfect World Series moment.

Brooklyn	000	101	000—2
New York	000	000	000—0

a Grounded out for Zimmer in sixth.
b Popped out for Grim in seventh.

Runs batted in: Hodges 2.
Doubles: Skowron, Campanella, Berra.
Sacrifice hits: Snider, Campanella.
Sacrifice fly: Hodges.
Double play: Amoros, Reese and Hodges.
Left on bases: Brooklyn 8, New York 8.

Brooklyn	IP	H	R	ER	BB	SO
Podres (W)	9	8	0	0	2	4

New York	IP	H	R	ER	BB	SO
Byrne (L)	5⅓	3	2	1	3	2
Grim	1⅔	1	0	0	1	1
Turley	2	1	0	0	1	1

Wild pitch: Grim.

Umpires: Honochick, Dascoli, Summers, Ballanfant, Flaherty, Donatelli.
Time: 2:44. **Attendance:** 62,465.

WORLD SERIES PERFECTION

October 8, 1956, at Yankee Stadium

Yankees righthander Don Larsen retired all 27 Brooklyn Dodgers he faced in a perfect 2-0 World Series victory—the only no-hitter ever pitched in postseason play. Larsen, who went to ball three on only one batter, outdueled Dodgers starter Sal Maglie in the Game 5 classic and received all the run support he needed on Mickey Mantle's fourth-inning homer.

Brooklyn	AB	R	H	PO	A	E
Gilliam,2b	3	0	0	2	0	0
Reese,ss	3	0	0	4	2	0
Snider,cf	3	0	0	1	0	0
Robinson,3b	3	0	0	2	4	0
Hodges,1b	3	0	0	5	1	0
Amoros,lf	3	0	0	3	0	0
Furillo,rf	3	0	0	0	0	0
Campanella,c	3	0	0	7	2	0
Maglie,p	2	0	0	0	1	0
aMitchell	1	0	0	0	0	0
Totals	27	0	0	24	10	0

New York	AB	R	H	PO	A	E
Bauer,rf	4	0	1	4	0	0
Collins,1b	4	0	1	7	0	0
Mantle,cf	3	1	1	4	0	0
Berra,c	3	0	0	7	0	0
Slaughter,lf	2	0	0	1	0	0
Martin,2b	3	0	1	3	4	0
McDougald,ss	2	0	0	0	2	0
Carey,3b	3	1	1	1	1	0
Larsen,p	2	0	0	0	1	0
Totals	26	2	5	27	8	0

Brooklyn	000	000	000—0
New York	000	101	00x—2

a Called out on strikes for Maglie in ninth.

Runs batted in: Mantle, Bauer.
Home run: Mantle.
Sacrifice hit: Larsen.
Double plays: Reese and Hodges; Hodges, Campanella, Robinson, Campanella and Robinson.
Left on bases: Brooklyn 0, New York 3.

Brooklyn	IP	H	R	ER	BB	SO
Maglie (L)	8	5	2	2	2	5

New York	IP	H	R	ER	BB	SO
Larsen (W)	9	0	0	0	0	7

Umpires: Pinelli, Soar, Boggess, Napp, Gorman, Runge.
Time: 2:06. **Attendance:** 64,519.

AN IMPERFECT ENDING

May 26, 1959, at County Stadium

Pittsburgh lefthander Harvey Haddix retired 36 consecutive Milwaukee batters over 12 perfect innings, but he ended up losing the game on a 13th-inning error, walk and double. Milwaukee starter Lew Burdette shut out the Pirates on 12 hits and Joe Adcock broke Haddix's hitless string with his one-out blow—an apparent home run that was ruled a double because Adcock passed teammate Hank Aaron while circling the bases.

Pittsburgh	AB	R	H	PO	A	E
Schofield,ss	6	0	3	2	4	0
Virdon,cf	6	0	1	8	0	0
Burgess,c	5	0	0	8	0	0
Nelson,1b	5	0	2	14	0	0
Skinner,lf	5	0	1	4	0	0
Mazeroski,2b	5	0	1	1	1	0
Hoak,3b	5	0	2	0	6	1
Mejias,rf	3	0	1	1	0	0
aStuart	1	0	0	0	0	0
Christopher,rf	1	0	0	0	0	0
Haddix,p	5	0	1	0	2	0
Totals	47	0	12	38	13	1

Milwaukee	AB	R	H	PO	A	E
O'Brien,2b	3	0	0	2	5	0
bRice	1	0	0	0	0	0
Mantilla,2b	1	1	0	1	2	0
Mathews,3b	4	0	0	2	3	0
Aaron,rf	4	0	0	1	0	0
Adcock,1b	5	0	1	17	3	0
Covington,lf	4	0	0	4	0	0
Crandall,c	4	0	0	2	1	0
Pafko,cf	4	0	0	6	0	0
Logan,ss	4	0	0	3	5	0
Burdette,p	4	0	0	1	3	0
Totals	38	1	1	39	22	0

Pittsburgh	000	000	000	000	0—0
Milwaukee	000	000	000	000	1—1

a Flied out for Mejias in 10th.
b Flied out for O'Brien in 10th.
c Two out when winning run scored.

Run batted in: Adcock.
Double: Adcock.
Sacrifice hit: Mathews.
Double plays: Logan and Adcock; Mathews, O'Brien and Adcock; Adcock and Logan.
Left on bases: Pittsburgh 8, Milwaukee 1.

Pittsburgh	IP	H	R	ER	BB	SO
Haddix (L)	12⅔	1	1	1	1	8

Milwaukee	IP	H	R	ER	BB	SO
Burdette (W)	13	12	0	0	0	2

Umpires: Smith, Dascoli, Secory, Dixon.
Time: 2:54. **Attendance:** 19,194.

MAZEROSKI STUNS YANKEES

October 13, 1960, at Forbes Field

Second baseman Bill Mazeroski ended Pittsburgh's 35-year title drought when he hammered a stunning bottom-of-the-ninth-inning home run over the left-field fence against the New York Yankees, breaking a 9-9 tie in Game 7 of the World Series. Mazeroski, leading off the ninth after the Yankees had rallied for two runs in the top of the inning, became the first player to end a Series with a home run.

New York	AB	R	H	PO	A	E
Richardson,2b	5	2	2	2	5	0
Kubek,ss	3	1	0	3	2	0
DeMaestri,ss	0	0	0	0	0	0
dLong	1	0	1	0	0	0
eMcDougald,3b	0	1	0	0	0	0
Maris,rf	5	0	0	2	0	1
Mantle,cf	5	1	3	0	0	0
Berra,lf	4	2	1	3	0	0
Skowron,1b	5	2	2	10	2	0
Blanchard,c	4	0	1	1	1	0
Boyer,3b-ss	4	0	1	0	3	0
Turley,p	0	0	0	0	0	0
Stafford,p	0	0	0	0	1	0
aLopez	1	0	1	0	0	0
Shantz,p	3	0	1	3	1	0
Coates,p	0	0	0	0	0	0
Terry,p	0	0	0	0	0	0
Totals	40	9	13	24	15	1

Pittsburgh	AB	R	H	PO	A	E
Virdon,cf	4	1	2	3	0	0
Groat,ss	4	1	1	3	2	0
Skinner,lf	2	1	0	1	0	0
Nelson,1b	3	1	1	7	0	0
Clemente,rf	4	1	1	4	0	0
Burgess,c	3	0	2	0	0	0
bChristopher	0	0	0	0	0	0
Smith,c	1	1	1	1	0	0
Hoak,3b	3	1	0	3	2	0
Mazeroski,2b	4	2	2	5	0	0
Law,p	2	0	0	0	1	0
Face,p	0	0	0	0	1	0
cCimoli	1	1	1	0	0	0
Friend,p	0	0	0	0	0	0
Haddix,p	0	0	0	0	0	0
Totals	31	10	11	27	6	0

New York	000	014	022—9
Pittsburgh	220	000	051—10

a Singled for Stafford in third.
b Ran for Burgess in seventh.
c Singled for Face in eighth.
d Singled for DeMaestri in ninth.
e Ran for Long in ninth.
f None out when winning run scored.

Runs batted in: Mantle 2, Berra 4, Skowron, Blanchard, Boyer, Virdon 2, Groat, Nelson 2, Clemente, Smith 3, Mazeroski.
Double: Boyer.
Home runs: Nelson, Skowron, Berra, Smith, Mazeroski.
Sacrifice hit: Skinner.
Double plays: Stafford, Blanchard and Skowron; Richardson, Kubek and Skowron; Kubek, Richardson and Skowron.
Left on bases: New York 6, Pittsburgh 1.

New York	IP	H	R	ER	BB	SO
Turley	1	2	3	3	1	0
Stafford	1	2	1	1	1	0
Shantz	5	4	3	3	1	0
Coates	⅔	2	2	2	0	0
Terry (L)	⅓	1	1	1	0	0

Pittsburgh	IP	H	R	ER	BB	SO
Law	5	4	3	3	1	0
Face	3	6	4	4	1	0
Friend	0	2	2	2	0	0
Haddix (W)	1	1	0	0	0	0

Turley pitched to one batter in second.
Shantz pitched to three batters in eighth.
Terry pitched to one batter in ninth.
Law pitched to two batters in sixth.
Friend pitched to two batters in ninth.

Umpires: Jackowski, Chylak, Boggess, Stevens, Landes, Honochick.
Time: 2:36. **Attendance:** 36,683.

MARIS HITS 61ST

October 1, 1961, at Yankee Stadium

New York outfielder Roger Maris claimed baseball's single-season home run record when he drove a fourth-inning pitch from Boston righthander Tracy Stallard into the right-field seats on the final day of the regular season. Maris' 61st home run broke the 1927 record of Yankee predecessor Babe Ruth and provided the only run in a 1-0 victory.

Boston	AB	R	H	PO	A	E
Schilling,2b	4	0	1	3	2	0
Geiger,cf	4	0	0	1	0	0
Yastrzemski,lf	4	0	1	1	0	0
Malzone,3b	4	0	0	0	0	0
Clinton,rf	4	0	0	4	0	0
Runnels,1b	3	0	0	7	0	0
Gile,1b	0	0	0	1	0	0
Nixon,c	3	0	2	5	0	0
Green,ss	2	0	0	1	2	0
Stallard,p	1	0	0	0	1	0
bJensen	1	0	0	0	0	0
Nichols,p	0	0	0	1	0	0
Totals	30	0	4	24	5	0

New York	AB	R	H	PO	A	E
Richardson,2b	4	0	0	1	1	0
Kubek,ss	4	0	2	3	4	0
Maris,cf	4	1	1	3	0	0
Berra,lf	2	0	0	0	0	0
Lopez,lf-rf	1	0	0	2	0	0
Blanchard,rf-c	3	0	0	3	0	0
Howard,c	2	0	0	7	2	0
Reed,lf	1	0	1	1	0	0
Skowron,1b	2	0	0	4	0	0
Hale,1b	1	0	1	2	1	0
Boyer,3b	2	0	0	1	0	0
Stafford,p	2	0	0	0	0	0
Reniff,p	0	0	0	0	0	0
aTresh	1	0	0	0	0	0
Arroyo,p	0	0	0	0	0	0
Totals	29	1	5	27	8	0

Boston	000	000	000—0
New York	000	100	00x—1

a Popped out for Reniff in seventh.
b Popped out for Stallard in eighth.

Run batted in: Maris.
Triple: Nixon.
Home run: Maris.
Sacrifice hit: Stallard.
Stolen bases: Geiger.
Passed ball: Nixon.
Left on bases: Boston 5, New York 5.

Boston	IP	H	R	ER	BB	SO
Stallard (L)	7	5	1	1	1	5
Nichols	1	0	0	0	0	0

New York	IP	H	R	ER	BB	SO
Stafford (W)	6	3	0	0	1	7
Reniff	1	0	0	0	0	1
Arroyo (S)	2	1	0	0	0	1

Wild pitch: Stallard.

Umpires: Kinnamon, Flaherty, Honochick, Salerno.
Time: 1:57. **Attendance:** 23,154.

McLAIN WINS 30TH

September 14, 1968, at Tiger Stadium

Denny McLain became the first 30-game winner in 34 years when Detroit rallied for two ninth-inning runs and a 5-4 victory over Oakland. McLain, who struck out 10 and yielded two home runs to Reggie Jackson, joined a select circle when Willie Horton's single drove in Mickey Stanley with the winner. McLain became the first 30-win man since St. Louis star Dizzy Dean in 1934.

Oakland	AB	R	H	PO	A	E
Campaneris,ss	4	0	1	2	1	0
Monday,cf	4	0	1	2	0	0
Cater,1b	4	1	2	6	3	1
Bando,3b	3	0	0	1	0	1
Jackson,rf	4	2	2	3	1	0
Green,2b	4	0	0	2	1	0
Keough,lf	3	0	0	0	0	0
Gosger,lf	0	0	0	0	0	0
Duncan,c	2	1	0	7	0	0
Dobson,p	1	0	0	0	0	0
Aker,p	0	0	0	0	0	0
Lindblad,p	0	0	0	0	0	0
aDonaldson	0	0	0	0	0	0
Segui,p	1	0	0	2	1	0
Totals	30	4	6	25	7	2

Detroit	AB	R	H	PO	A	E
McAuliffe,2b	5	0	1	2	1	0
Stanley,cf	5	1	2	1	0	0
Northrup,rf	4	1	0	4	1	0
Horton,lf	5	1	2	0	0	0
Cash,1b	4	1	2	6	0	0
Freehan,c	3	0	1	10	2	0
Matchick,ss	4	0	1	2	0	1
Wert,3b	2	0	0	1	1	0
bBrown	1	0	0	0	0	0
Tracewski,3b	0	0	0	0	1	0
McLain,p	1	0	0	1	0	0
cKaline	0	1	0	0	0	0
Totals	34	5	9	27	6	1

Oakland ....000 211 000—4
Detroit ....000 300 002—5

a Sacrificed for Lindblad in fifth.
b Grounded out for Wert in eighth.
c Walked for McLain in ninth.
d One out when winning run scored.

Runs batted in: Campaneris, Jackson 3, Horton, Cash 3.
Home runs: Jackson 2, Cash.
Double plays: Northrup and Cash.
Sacrifice hits: Bando, Donaldson, McLain.
Left on bases: Oakland 2, Detroit 10.

Oakland	IP	H	R	ER	BB	SO
Dobson	3⅔	4	3	3	2	4
Aker	0	0	0	0	1	0
Lindblad	⅓	0	0	0	0	1
Segui (L)	4⅓	5	2	1	2	1

Detroit	IP	H	R	ER	BB	SO
McLain (W)	9	6	4	4	1	10

Aker pitched to one batter in fourth.
Wild pitch: Aker.

Umpires: Napp, Umont, Haller, Neudecker.
Time: 3:00. **Attendance:** 33,688.

AARON HITS 715TH

April 8, 1974, at Atlanta Stadium

Braves outfielder Hank Aaron unseated all-time home run king Babe Ruth when he connected for career home run No. 715 in the fourth inning of a game against Los Angeles. The three-run blast off Dodgers lefthander Al Downing helped the Braves secure a 7-4 victory.

Los Angeles	AB	R	H	PO	A	E
Lopes,2b	2	1	0	2	2	1
cLacy,2b	1	0	0	0	0	0
Buckner,lf	3	0	1	1	1	1
Wynn,cf	4	0	1	2	0	0
Ferguson,c	4	0	0	4	0	1
Crawford,rf	4	1	1	1	0	0
Cey,3b	4	0	1	2	3	1
Garvey,1b	4	1	1	11	0	0
Russell,ss	4	0	1	1	4	2
Downing,p	1	1	1	0	3	0
Marshall,p	1	0	0	0	1	0
dJoshua	1	0	0	0	0	0
Hough,p	0	0	0	0	1	0
eMota	1	0	0	0	0	0
Totals	34	4	7	24	15	6

Atlanta	AB	R	H	PO	A	E
Garr,rf-lf	3	0	0	0	0	0
Lum,1b	5	0	0	10	0	0
Evans,3b	4	1	0	1	4	0
Aaron,lf	3	2	1	0	0	0
Office,cf	0	0	0	0	0	0
Baker,cf-rf	2	1	1	2	0	0
Johnson,2b	3	1	1	2	2	0
Foster,2b	0	0	0	0	0	0
Correll,c	4	1	0	11	0	0
Robinson,ss	0	0	0	0	1	0
aTepedino	0	0	0	0	0	0
Perez,ss	2	1	1	1	2	0
Reed,p	2	0	0	0	1	0
bOates	1	0	0	0	0	0
Capra,p	0	0	0	0	0	0
Totals	29	7	4	27	10	0

Los Angeles ....003 001 000—4
Atlanta ....010 402 00x—7

a Walked for Robinson in fourth.
b Reached on fielder's choice for Reed in sixth.
c Struck out for Lopes in seventh.
d Struck out for Marshall in seventh.
e Lined out for Hough in ninth.

Runs batted in: Wynn 2, Cey, Downing, Garr, Lum, Aaron 2, Tepedino, Oates.
Doubles: Baker, Russell, Wynn.
Home run: Aaron.
Sacrifice hit: Garr.
Sacrifice fly: Garr.
Passed ball: Ferguson.
Left on bases: Los Angeles 5, Atlanta 7.

Los Angeles	IP	H	R	ER	BB	SO
Downing (L)	3	2	5	2	4	2
Marshall	3	2	2	1	1	1
Hough	2	0	0	0	2	1

Atlanta	IP	H	R	ER	BB	SO
Reed (W)	6	7	4	4	1	4
Capra (S)	3	0	0	0	1	6

Downing pitched to four batters in fourth.
Wild pitch: Reed.

Umpires: Davidson, Pulli, Weyer, Sudol.
Time: 2:27. **Attendance:** 53,775.

FISK'S INSTANT WINNER

October 21, 1975, at Fenway Park

Boston catcher Carlton Fisk, leading off the bottom of the 12th inning of World Series Game 6, hit a high drive off the left-field foul pole at Fenway Park, giving the Red Sox a 7-6 victory over Cincinnati in one of the most dramatic games in fall classic history. Fisk's blast ended a see-saw battle and forced a decisive seventh game.

Cincinnati	AB	R	H	PO	A	E
Rose,3b	5	1	2	0	2	0
Griffey,rf	5	2	2	0	0	0
Morgan,2b	6	1	1	4	4	0
Bench,c	6	0	1	8	0	0
Perez,1b	6	0	2	11	2	0
Foster,lf	6	0	2	4	1	0
Concepcion,ss	6	0	1	3	4	0
Geronimo,cf	6	1	2	2	0	0
Nolan,p	0	0	0	1	0	0
aChaney	1	0	0	0	0	0
Norman,p	0	0	0	0	0	0
Billingham,p	0	0	0	0	0	0
bArmbrister	0	1	0	0	0	0
Carroll,p	0	0	0	0	0	0
cCrowley	1	0	1	0	0	0
Borbon,p	1	0	0	0	0	0
Eastwick,p	0	0	0	0	0	0
McEnaney,p	0	0	0	0	0	0
eDriessen	1	0	0	0	0	0
Darcy,p	0	0	0	0	1	0
Totals	50	6	14	33	14	0

Boston	AB	R	H	PO	A	E
Cooper,1b	5	0	0	8	0	0
Drago,p	0	0	0	0	0	0
fMiller	1	0	0	0	0	0
Wise,p	0	0	0	0	0	0
Doyle,2b	5	0	1	0	2	0
Yastrzemski,lf-lb	6	1	3	7	1	0
Fisk,c	4	2	2	9	1	0
Lynn,cf	4	2	2	2	0	0
Petrocelli,3b	4	1	0	1	1	0
Evans,rf	5	0	1	5	1	0
Burleson,ss	3	0	0	3	2	1
Tiant,p	2	0	0	0	2	0
Moret,p	0	0	0	0	1	0
dCarbo,lf	2	1	1	1	0	0
Totals	41	7	10	36	11	1

Cincinnati ......000 030 210 000—6
Boston ....300 000 030 001—7

a Flied out for Nolan in third.
b Walked for Billingham in fifth.
c Singled for Carroll in sixth.
d Homered for Moret in eighth.
e Flied out for McEnaney in 10th.
f Flied out for Drago in 11th.

Runs batted in: Griffey 2, Bench, Foster 2, Geronimo, Lynn 3, Carbo 3, Fisk.
Doubles: Doyle, Evans, Foster.
Triple: Griffey.
Home runs: Lynn, Geronimo, Carbo, Fisk.
Stolen bases: Concepcion.
Sacrifice hit: Tiant.
Double plays: Foster and Bench; Evans, Yastrzemski and Burleson.
Left on bases: Boston 11, Boston 9.

Cincinnati	IP	H	R	ER	BB	SO
Nolan	2	3	3	3	0	2
Norman	⅔	1	0	0	2	0
Billingham	1⅓	1	0	0	1	1
Carroll	1	1	0	0	0	0
Borbon	2	1	2	2	2	1
Eastwick	1	2	1	1	1	2
McEnaney	1	0	0	0	1	0
Darcy (L)	2	1	1	1	0	1

Boston	IP	H	R	ER	BB	SO
Tiant	7	11	6	6	2	5
Moret	1	0	0	0	0	0
Drago	3	1	0	0	0	1
Wise (W)	1	2	0	0	0	1

Borbon pitched to two batters in eighth.
Eastwick pitched to two batters in ninth.
Darcy pitched to one batter in 12th.
Tiant pitched to one batter in eighth.
Hit by pitcher: Rose (by Drago).

Umpires: Davidson, Frantz, Colosi, Barnett, Stello, Maloney.
Time: 4:01. **Attendance:** 35,205.

JACKSON SLUGS DODGERS

October 18, 1977, at Yankee Stadium

Reggie Jackson blasted the Los Angeles Dodgers into oblivion with three dramatic Game 6 home runs that gave the New York Yankees a World Series-clinching 8-4 victory and their first championship since 1962. Jackson hit two-run homers off Burt Hooton and Elias Sosa and a solo eighth-inning shot off Charlie Hough, capping the first five-homer Series in fall classic history.

Pirates 1960 World Series hero Bill Mazeroski heads for home after his championship-deciding home run.

Los Angeles	AB	R	H	PO	A	E
Lopes,2b	4	0	1	0	4	0
Russell,ss	3	0	0	1	4	0
Smith,rf	4	2	1	1	0	0
Cey,3b	3	1	1	0	1	0
Garvey,1b	4	1	2	13	0	0
Baker,lf	4	0	1	2	0	0
Monday,cf	4	0	1	3	0	0
Yeager,c	3	0	1	4	2	0
bDavalillo	1	0	1	0	0	0
Hooton,p	2	0	0	0	0	0
Sosa,p	0	0	0	0	0	0
Rau,p	0	0	0	0	0	0
aGoodson	1	0	0	0	0	0
Hough,p	0	0	0	0	0	0
cLacy	1	0	0	0	0	0
Totals	34	4	9	24	11	0

New York	AB	R	H	PO	A	E
Rivers,cf	4	0	2	1	0	0
Randolph,2b	4	1	0	2	3	0
Munson,c	4	1	1	6	0	0
Jackson,rf	3	4	3	5	0	0
Chambliss,1b	4	2	2	9	1	0
Nettles,3b	4	0	0	0	0	0
Piniella,lf	3	0	0	2	1	0
Dent,ss	2	0	0	1	4	1
Torrez,p	3	0	0	1	2	0
Totals	31	8	8	27	11	1

Los Angeles ....2 0 1 000 0 0 1—4
New York ....0 2 0 3 2 0 0 1 x—8

a Struck out for Rau in seventh.
b Bunted safely for Yeager in ninth.
c Popped out for Hough in ninth.

Runs batted in: Garvey 2, Smith, Davalillo, Chambliss 2, Jackson 5, Piniella.
Double: Chambliss.
Triple: Garvey.
Home runs: Chambliss, Smith, Jackson 3.
Sacrifice fly: Piniella.
Double plays: Dent, Randolph and Chambliss; Dent and Chambliss.
Passed ball: Munson.
Left on bases: New York 5, Los Angeles 2.

Los Angeles	IP	H	R	ER	BB	SO
Hooton (L)	3	3	4	4	1	1
Sosa	1⅔	3	3	3	1	0
Rau	1⅓	0	0	0	0	1
Hough	2	2	1	1	0	3

New York	IP	H	R	ER	BB	SO
Torrez (W)	9	9	4	2	2	6

Hooton pitched to three batters in fourth.

Umpires: McSherry, Chylak, Sudol, McCoy, Dale, Evans.
Time: 2:18. **Attendance:** 56,407.

ROSE PASSES COBB

September 11, 1985, at Riverfront Stadium

Pete Rose lined a 2-1 pitch from San Diego righthander Eric Show into left-center field for career hit No. 4,192, ending his long chase of Ty Cobb and securing his status as baseball's all-time top hit man. The first-inning drive touched off a wild celebration that included player congratulations, presentations and several long ovations before play resumed in the Reds' eventual 2-0 victory.

San Diego	AB	R	H	PO	A	E
Templeton,ss	4	0	0	3	3	0
Royster,2b	4	0	1	2	3	0
Gwynn,rf	4	0	1	2	0	0
Garvey,1b	4	0	0	6	0	0
Martinez,lf	3	0	0	4	0	0
McReynolds,cf	3	0	1	2	0	0
Bochy,c	3	0	1	3	1	0
Bevacqua,3b	3	0	1	2	1	0
Show,p	2	0	0	0	1	1
aDavis	1	0	0	0	0	0
Jackson,p	0	0	0	0	0	0
Walter,p	0	0	0	0	0	0
Totals	31	0	5	24	9	1

Cincinnati	AB	R	H	PO	A	E
Milner,cf	5	0	0	5	0	0
Rose,1b	3	2	2	6	1	0
Parker,rf	1	0	1	3	0	0
Esasky,lf	3	0	0	0	0	0
Venable,lf	0	0	0	0	0	0
Bell,3b	4	0	1	0	3	0
Concepcion,ss	4	0	1	1	2	0
Diaz,c	3	0	1	7	0	0
bRedus	0	0	0	0	0	0
Van Gorder,c	0	0	0	0	0	0
Oester,2b	3	0	1	4	3	0
Browning,p	4	0	1	0	0	0
Franco,p	0	0	0	0	0	0
Power,p	0	0	0	1	0	0
Totals	30	2	8	27	9	0

San Diego ....0 0 0 000 0 0 0—0
Cincinnati ....0 0 1 000 1 0 x—2

a Grounded into double play for Show in eighth.
b Ran for Diaz in eighth.

Runs batted in: Esasky 2.
Doubles: Browning, Diaz, Bell.
Triple: Rose.
Sacrifice fly: Esasky.
Stolen base: Gwynn.
Double plays: Templeton, Royster and Garvey; Concepcion, Oester and Rose.
Left on bases: San Diego 4, Cincinnati 11.

San Diego	IP	H	R	ER	BB	SO
Show (L)	7	7	2	2	5	1
Jackson	⅓	1	0	0	1	0
Walter	⅔	0	0	0	0	2

Cincinnati	IP	H	R	ER	BB	SO
Browning (W)	8⅓	5	0	0	0	6
Franco	⅓	0	0	0	0	0
Power (S)	⅓	0	0	0	0	0

Umpires: Weyer, Montague, Brocklander, Rennert.
Time: 2:17. **Attendance:** 47,237.

CLEMENS STRIKES OUT 20

April 29, 1986, at Fenway Park

Boston fireballer Roger Clemens claimed baseball's nine-inning strikeout record when he fanned 20 Seattle Mariners during a 3-1 victory. The Red Sox's "Rocket Man" struck out the side in three innings and fanned an A.L. record-tying eight straight batters from the fourth to the sixth. Clemens broke the record of 19 strikeouts shared by Steve Carlton, Tom Seaver and Nolan Ryan.

Seattle	AB	R	H	PO	A	E
Owen,ss	4	0	1	1	5	0
Bradley,lf	4	0	0	2	0	0
Phelps,1b	4	0	0	6	0	0
Thomas,dh	3	1	1	0	0	0
Presley,3b	3	0	0	1	1	0
Calderon,rf	3	0	0	1	1	0
Tartabull,2b	3	0	1	3	1	1
Henderson,cf	3	0	0	5	0	0
Yeager,c	2	0	0	4	2	0
bCowens	1	0	0	0	0	0
Kearney,c	0	0	0	1	0	0
Moore,p	0	0	0	0	0	0
Young,p	0	0	0	0	0	0
Best,p	0	0	0	0	0	0
Totals	30	1	3	24	10	1

Boston	AB	R	H	PO	A	E
Evans,rf	4	1	2	0	0	0
Boggs,3b	3	0	0	0	0	0
Buckner,dh	4	0	2	0	0	0
Rice,lf	4	0	1	1	0	0
Baylor,1b	3	0	1	1	1	1
Stapleton,1b	0	0	0	1	0	0
Gedman,c	4	0	1	20	0	0
Barrett,2b	3	0	0	0	1	0
Lyons,cf	3	1	1	3	0	0
Hoffman,ss	2	0	0	0	1	0
aRomero,ss	0	1	0	0	0	0
Clemens,p	0	0	0	1	0	0
Totals	30	3	8	27	3	1

Seattle ....0 0 0 000 1 0 0—1
Boston ....0 0 0 000 3 0 x—3

a Ran for Hoffman in seventh.
b Flied out for Yeager in eighth.

Runs batted in: Thomas, Evans 3.
Double: Buckner.
Home runs: Thomas, Evans.
Double play: Yeager and Tartabull.
Left on bases: Seattle 2, Boston 7.

Seattle	IP	H	R	ER	BB	SO
Moore (L)	7⅓	8	3	3	4	4
Young	⅓	0	0	0	0	0
Best	⅓	0	0	0	0	1

Boston	IP	H	R	ER	BB	SO
Clemens (W)	9	3	1	1	0	20

Umpires: Voltaggio, Welke, Phillips, McCoy.
Time: 2:39. **Attendance:** 13,414.

HERSHISER PASSES DRYSDALE

September 28, 1988, at Jack Murphy Stadium

Los Angeles ace Orel Hershiser completed the greatest run of pitching perfection in baseball history when he worked 10 shutout innings against San Diego on the final day of the regular season and extended his record scoreless-innings streak to 59. Hershiser, who recorded six straight shutouts, broke the 20-year-old scoreless-innings mark of former Dodger Don Drysdale, who ran off 58 in 1968.

Los Angeles	AB	R	H	PO	A	E
Sax,2b	5	0	0	3	7	0
Sharperson,2b	2	0	0	0	1	0
Stubbs,1b	5	0	0	21	0	1
gHatcher,1b	1	1	1	0	0	0
Gibson,lf	5	0	1	2	0	0
Orosco,p	0	0	0	0	0	0
Woodson,3b	2	0	1	1	1	0
Shelby,cf	5	0	1	2	0	0
C.Gywnn,lf	1	0	0	0	0	0
Mi.Davis,rf	4	0	0	4	0	0
Gonzalez,rf-lf-cf	3	0	0	2	0	0
Scioscia,c	4	0	0	2	0	0
Dempsey,c	3	0	0	5	2	0
Hamilton,3b	5	0	0	0	2	0
Crews,p	0	0	0	0	0	0
dHeep	1	0	0	0	0	0
K.Howell,p	0	0	0	0	0	0
Horton,p	0	0	0	0	0	0
Griffin,ss	5	0	1	4	5	0
Hershiser,p	3	0	1	0	5	0
Devereaux,rf	2	0	0	1	0	0
Totals	56	1	6	47	23	1

San Diego	AB	R	H	PO	A	E
R.Alomar,2b	7	0	1	0	5	0
Flannery,3b	4	0	1	1	0	0
bRoberts,3b	1	0	0	0	0	1
T.Gwynn,cf	5	0	0	10	0	0
Jefferson,cf	1	0	0	0	0	0
Martinez,1b	5	1	0	11	0	0
Wynne,rf	5	0	2	8	0	0
hParent	1	1	1	0	0	0
Santiago,c	5	0	0	13	0	0
Ready,lf	6	0	0	1	0	0
Templeton,ss	5	0	0	4	3	1
Hawkins,p	3	0	0	0	1	0
aMoreland	1	0	0	0	0	0
Ma.Davis,p	0	0	0	0	0	0
cNelson	1	0	0	0	0	0
McCullers,p	0	0	0	0	0	0
eBrown	0	0	0	0	0	0
fThon	0	0	0	0	0	0
Leiper,p	0	0	0	0	0	0
Totals	50	2	5	48	9	2

L.A. ....0 0 0 000 000 000 000 1—1
S Diego ..0 0 0 000 000 000 000 2—2

a Flied out for Hawkins in 10th.
b Ran for T.Gwynn in 11th.
c Struck out for Ma.Davis in 12th.
d Flied out for Crews in 14th.
e Walked for McCullers in 15th.
f Ran for Brown in 15th.
g Singled for Stubbs in 16th.
h Homered for Wynne in 16th.
i Two out when winning run scored.

Runs batted in: Parent 2.
Double: Griffin.
Triple: Woodson.
Home run: Parent.
Sacrifice hits: Hershiser, Santiago.
Stolen bases: T.Gwynn, Thon, Gonzalez.
Double play: Dempsey and Griffin.
Passed ball: Santiago.
Left on bases: Los Angeles 11, San Diego 10.

Los Angeles	IP	H	R	ER	BB	SO
Hershiser	10	4	0	0	1	3
Orosco	1	0	0	0	4	0
Crews	2	0	0	0	0	2
K.Howell	2⅔	0	1	1	3	3
Horton (L)	0	1	1	1	0	0

San Diego	IP	H	R	ER	BB	SO
Hawkins	10	4	0	0	2	6
Ma.Davis	2	0	0	0	0	4
McCullers	3	1	0	0	0	4
Leiper (W)	1	1	1	0	0	0

Horton pitched to one batter in 16th.
Hit by pitcher: Griffin (by Hawkins).

Umpires: West, Runge, Engel, Williams.
Time: 4:24. **Attendance:** 22,596.

GIBSON SHOCKS A'S

October 15, 1988, at Dodger Stadium

Los Angeles pinch hitter Kirk Gibson, limping badly on his injured leg and wincing with every painful swing, blasted a pitch from Oakland relief ace Dennis Eckersley over the right-field fence with two out in the ninth inning, giving the Dodgers a 5-4 victory in a storybook conclusion to Game 1 of the World Series. With the Dodgers trailing 4-3 and a runner on base, Gibson looked overmatched as he worked the count to 3-2. That's when he connected for the first come-from-behind game-winning homer in Series history.

Oakland	AB	R	H	PO	A	E
Lansford,3b	4	1	0	2	2	0
Henderson,cf	5	0	2	4	0	0
Canseco,rf	4	1	1	3	0	0
Parker,lf	2	0	0	1	0	0
cJavier,lf	1	0	1	0	0	0
McGwire,1b	3	0	0	6	0	0
Steinbach,c	4	0	1	5	0	0
Hassey,c	0	0	0	1	0	0
Hubbard,2b	4	1	2	2	0	0
Weiss,ss	4	0	0	2	3	0
Stewart,p	3	1	0	0	0	0
Eckersley,p	0	0	0	0	0	0
Totals	34	4	7	26	5	0

Los Angeles	AB	R	H	PO	A	E
Sax,2b	3	1	1	3	1	0
Stubbs,1b	4	0	0	7	0	0
Hatcher,lf	3	1	1	1	0	0
Marshall,rf	4	1	1	2	0	0
Shelby,cf	4	0	1	3	0	0
Scioscia,c	4	0	1	9	0	0
Hamilton,3b	4	0	0	1	1	0
Griffin,ss	2	0	1	1	4	0
eM.Davis	0	1	0	0	0	0
Belcher,p	0	0	0	0	0	0
aHeep	1	0	0	0	0	0
Leary,p	0	0	0	0	1	0
bWoodson	1	0	0	0	0	0
Holton,p	0	0	0	0	1	0
dGonzalez	1	0	0	0	0	0
Pena,p	0	0	0	0	0	0
fGibson	1	1	1	0	0	0
Totals	32	5	7	27	8	0

Oakland ....0 4 0 000 0 0 0—4
Los Angeles ....2 0 0 001 0 0 2—5

a Grounded out for Belcher in second.
b Forced Griffin for Leary in fifth.
c Ran for Parker in seventh.
d Struck out for Holton in seventh.
e Walked for Griffin in ninth.
f Hit two run homer for Pena in ninth.

Runs batted in: Canseco 4, Hatcher 2, Scioscia, Gibson 2.
Double: Henderson.
Home runs: Hatcher, Canseco, Gibson.
Stolen bases: Canseco, Sax, M. Davis.
Double play: Lansford and McGwire.
Left on bases: Oakland 10, Los Angeles 5.

Oakland	IP	H	R	ER	BB	SO
Stewart	8	6	3	3	2	5
Eckersley (L)	⅔	1	2	2	1	1

Los Angeles	IP	H	R	ER	BB	SO
Belcher	2	3	4	4	4	3
Leary	3	3	0	0	1	3
Holton	2	0	0	0	1	0
Pena (W)	2	1	0	0	0	3

Hit by pitcher: Canseco (by Belcher), Sax (by Stewart).
Wild pitch: Stewart.
Balk: Stewart.

Umpires: Harvey, Merrill, Froemming, Cousins, Crawford, McCoy.
Time: 3:04. **Attendance:** 55,983.

CARTER'S HAPPY ENDING

October 23, 1993, at SkyDome

Toronto outfielder Joe Carter hit a three-run, ninth-inning home run off Philadelphia reliever Mitch Williams, giving the Blue Jays a dramatic 8-6 victory over Philadelphia and their second straight World Series championship. The seesaw Game 6 battle ended suddenly when Carter drove a one-out Williams pitch into the left-field seats at SkyDome and danced euphorically around the bases. It marked the first time a team trailing in the ninth had won a World Series on a home run.

Philadelphia	AB	R	H	PO	A	E
Dykstra,cf	3	1	1	5	0	0
Duncan,dh	5	1	1	0	0	0
Kruk,1b	3	0	0	6	0	0
Hollins,3b	5	1	1	0	1	0
Batiste,3b	0	0	0	0	0	0
Daulton,c	4	1	1	3	0	0
Eisenreich,rf	5	0	2	2	0	0
Thompson,lf	3	0	0	4	0	0
aIncaviglia,lf	0	0	0	3	0	0
Stocker,ss	3	1	0	0	1	0
Morandini,2b	4	1	1	2	0	0
Mulholland,p	0	0	0	0	1	0
Mason,p	0	0	0	0	0	0
West,p	0	0	0	0	0	0
Andersen,p	0	0	0	0	0	0
M.Williams,p	0	0	0	0	0	0
Totals	35	6	7	25	3	0

Toronto	AB	R	H	PO	A	E
Henderson,lf	4	1	0	2	0	0
White,cf	4	1	0	6	0	0
Molitor,dh	5	3	3	0	0	0
Carter,rf	4	1	1	3	0	0
Olerud,1b	3	1	1	6	0	0
bGriffin,3b	0	0	0	0	0	0
Alomar,2b	4	1	3	1	3	1
Fernandez,ss	3	0	0	1	0	0
Sprague,3b-1b	2	0	0	3	2	1
Borders,c	4	0	2	5	0	0
Stewart,p	0	0	0	0	1	0
Cox,p	0	0	0	0	0	0
Leiter,p	0	0	0	0	0	0
D.Ward,p	0	0	0	0	0	0
Totals	33	8	10	27	6	2

Philadelphia ....0 0 0 1 0 0 5 0 0—6
Toronto ....3 0 0 1 1 0 0 0 3—8

a Hit sacrifice fly for Thompson in seventh.
b Ran for Olerud in eighth.

Runs batted in: Dykstra 3, Hollins, Eisenreich, Incaviglia, Molitor 2, Carter 4, Alomar, Sprague.
Doubles: Daulton, Olerud, Alomar.
Triple: Molitor.
Home runs: Molitor, Dykstra, Carter.
Sacrifice flies: Incaviglia, Carter, Sprague.
Stolen bases: Dykstra, Duncan.
Left on bases: Philadelphia 9, Toronto 7.

Philadelphia	IP	H	R	ER	BB	SO
Mulholland	5	7	5	5	1	1
Mason	2⅓	1	0	0	0	2
West	0	0	0	0	1	0
Andersen	⅔	0	0	0	1	0
M.Williams (L)	⅓	2	3	3	1	0

Toronto	IP	H	R	ER	BB	SO
Stewart	6	4	4	4	4	2
Cox	⅓	3	2	2	1	1
Leiter	1⅔	0	0	0	1	2
D.Ward (W)	1	0	0	0	0	0

West pitched to one batter in eighth.
Stewart pitched to three batters in seventh.
Hit by pitcher: Fernandez (by Andersen).

Umpires: DeMuth, Phillips, Runge, Johnson, Williams, McClelland.
Time: 3:27. **Attendance:** 52,195.

RIPKEN PLAYS ON

September 6, 1995, at Camden Yards

Baltimore shortstop Cal Ripken played in his 2,131st consecutive game, passing Lou Gehrig on the all-time iron-man list. Ripken punctuated his record-setter with a fourth-inning home run and the celebration began an inning later when California batted to make the game official. After Ripken was honored in a memorable, nationally televised showcase, the Orioles went on to record a 4-2 victory.

California	AB	R	H	PO	A	E
Phillips,3b	4	0	0	0	3	1
Edmonds,cf	3	1	1	1	0	0
Salmon,rf	4	1	3	1	0	0
Davis,dh	3	0	0	0	0	0
Snow,1b	4	0	1	6	0	0
G.Anderson,lf	4	0	0	4	0	0
Hudler,2b	2	0	0	2	1	0
aOwen,2b	2	0	0	0	0	0
Fabregas,c	3	0	0	9	0	0
Easley,ss	2	0	1	1	0	0
bO.Palmeiro	1	0	0	0	0	0
Correia,ss	0	0	0	0	0	0
Boskie,p	0	0	0	0	0	0
Bielecki,p	0	0	0	0	0	0
Patterson,p	0	0	0	0	0	0
James,p	0	0	0	0	0	0
Totals	32	2	6	24	4	1

Baltimore	AB	R	H	PO	A	E
B.Anderson,cf	4	0	1	2	0	0
Alexander,2b	4	0	0	2	1	0
R.Palmeiro,1b	4	2	3	7	0	0
Bonilla,rf	4	1	1	1	0	0
J.Brown,rf	0	0	0	0	0	0
Ripken,ss	4	1	2	1	4	0
Baines,dh	4	0	1	0	0	0
Hoiles,c	4	0	1	8	1	0
Huson,3b	4	0	0	1	1	0
Smith,lf	2	0	0	5	0	0
Mussina,p	0	0	0	0	0	0
Clark,p	0	0	0	0	0	0
Orosco,p	0	0	0	0	0	0
Totals	34	4	9	27	7	0

California ....1 0 0 0 0 0 0 1 0—2
Baltimore ....1 0 0 2 0 0 1 0 x—4

a Grounded out for Hudler in seventh.
b Grounded out for Easley in eighth.

Runs batted in: Salmon 2, R.Palmeiro 2, Bonilla, Ripken.
Doubles: Easley, Salmon, Baines.
Triple: Edmonds.
Home runs: Salmon, R.Palmeiro 2, Bonilla, Ripken.
Double play: Ripken and R.Palmeiro.
Left on bases: California 5, Baltimore 7.

California	IP	H	R	ER	BB	SO
Boskie (L)	5	6	3	3	1	4
Bielecki	1	1	0	0	0	2
Patterson	⅔	1	1	1	0	1
James	1⅓	1	0	0	0	1

Baltimore	IP	H	R	ER	BB	SO
Mussina (W)	7⅔	5	2	2	2	7
Clark	0	1	0	0	0	0
Orosco (S)	1⅓	0	0	0	0	2

Clark pitched to one batter in eighth.

Umpires: Barron, Kosc, Morrison, Clark.
Time: 3:35, **Attendance:** 46,272.

FOUR-HOMER GAMES

BOBBY LOWE

May 30, 1894, at Boston

Boston second baseman Lowe, baseball's first four-homer man, connected twice in the third inning of a 20-11 victory over Cincinnati.

Cincinnati	AB	R	H	PO	A	E
Hoy,cf	6	1	1	3	0	1
McCarthy,1b	5	2	2	9	1	0
Latham,3b	4	3	2	0	3	2
Holliday,lf	4	3	2	1	0	0
McPhee,2b	5	0	2	4	3	0
Vaughn,c	5	1	2	3	5	1
Canavan,rf	5	1	1	2	0	0
Smith,ss	5	0	1	1	5	1
Chamberlain,p	5	0	1	1	1	0
Totals	44	11	14	24	18	5

Boston	AB	R	H	PO	A	E
Lowe,2b	6	4	5	2	2	1
Long,ss	3	5	2	2	4	2
Duffy,cf	5	0	1	1	0	0
McCarthy,lf	6	2	3	3	0	0
Nash,3b	4	3	3	1	1	0
Tucker,1b	2	1	0	10	2	0
Bannon,rf	4	2	2	1	0	0
Ryan,c	5	2	2	5	0	0
Nichols,p	5	1	1	2	3	0
Totals	40	20	19	27	12	3

Cincinnati ....2 0 0 0 4 0 0 0 5—11
Boston ....2 0 9 0 1 5 2 1 x—20

Runs batted in: Lowe 6, Nichols 4, Bannon 2, McCarthy 2, Ryan 2, Duffy, Long, Nash, Holliday 5, Vaughn 4, Canavan, Latham.
Doubles: Latham 2, Smith, Chamberlain, Long, McCarthy.
Home runs: Holliday 2, Vaughn, Canavan, Lowe 4, Long.
Stolen bases: Nash 2, Long, Duffy, Hoy, Latham.
Passed ball: Vaughn.
Left on bases: Cincinnati 7, Boston 10.

Cincinnati	IP	H	R	ER	BB	SO
Chamberlain (L)	8	19	20	18	8	3

Boston	IP	H	R	ER	BB	SO
Nichols (W)	9	14	11	11	2	3

Hit by pitcher: Long (by Chamberlain), Tucker (by Chamberlain).
Wild pitches: Chamberlain, Nichols.

Umpire: Swartwood.
Time: 2:15. **Attendance:** 8,000.

ED DELAHANTY

July 13, 1896, at Chicago

All four of Delahanty's homers were inside-the-park shots and the Philadelphia outfielder added a single for a record 17 total bases.

Philadelphia	AB	R	H	PO	A	E
Cooley,lf	3	1	1	1	0	0
Hulen,ss	4	1	1	1	4	0
Mertes,cf	5	1	0	1	0	0
Delahanty,1b	5	4	5	9	0	0
Thompson,rf	5	0	1	2	0	0
Hallman,2b	4	1	1	5	3	0
Clements,c	2	0	0	5	3	0
Nash,3b	4	0	0	0	3	1
Garvin,p	4	0	0	0	1	0
Totals	36	8	9	24	14	1

Chicago	AB	R	H	PO	A	E
Everitt,3b	3	1	2	1	3	0
Dahlen,ss	2	2	0	0	0	0
Lange,cf	4	2	2	4	0	0
Anson,1b	3	0	1	12	2	0
Ryan,rf	4	1	1	2	0	1
Decker,lf	4	1	1	0	0	1
Pfeffer,2b	4	0	2	1	4	0
Terry,p	4	1	2	2	3	0
Donohue,c	3	1	0	5	0	0
Totals	31	9	11	27	12	2

Philadelphia ....1 2 0 0 3 0 1 0 1—8
Chicago ....1 0 4 0 1 0 0 3 x—9

Runs batted in: Delahanty 7, Garvin 1, Lange 5, Pfeffer 2, Anson.
Doubles: Thompson, Lange, Decker, Terry.
Triples: Lange, Pfeffer.
Home runs: Delahanty 4.
Double play: Hulen, Hallman and Delahanty.
Left on bases: Philadelphia 6, Chicago 4.

Philadelphia	IP	H	R	ER	BB	SO
Garvin (L)	8	11	9	8	4	4

Chicago	IP	H	R	ER	BB	SO
Terry (W)	9	9	8	7	3	4

Wild pitch: Garvin.

Umpire: Emslie.
Time: 2:15. **Attendance:** 1,100.

LOU GEHRIG

June 3, 1932, at Philadelphia

Yankees first baseman Gehrig became the first modern and A.L. player to hit four homers in a game and he narrowly missed a fifth in the ninth inning, when he flew out deep to center.

New York	AB	R	H	PO	A	E
Combs,cf	5	2	3	3	0	0
Saltzgaver,2b	4	1	1	3	2	0
Ruth,lf	5	2	2	3	0	1
Hoag,lf	0	1	0	1	0	0
Gehrig,1b	6	4	4	7	0	1
Chapman,rf	5	3	2	4	0	0
Dickey,c	4	2	2	5	0	0
Lazzeri,3b	6	3	5	0	1	0
Crosetti,ss	6	1	2	0	5	2
Allen,p	2	0	0	1	0	1
Rhodes,p	1	0	1	0	0	0
Brown,p	1	0	0	0	1	0
Gomez,p	1	1	1	0	0	0
Totals	46	20	23	27	9	5

Philadelphia	AB	R	H	PO	A	E
Bishop,2b	4	2	2	3	2	0
Cramer,cf	5	1	1	1	0	0
cRoettger	1	0	0	0	0	0
Miller,lf	0	0	0	0	0	0
Cochrane,c	5	1	1	10	2	0
dWilliams	1	0	0	0	0	0
Simmons,lf-cf	4	2	0	2	0	0
Foxx,1b	3	3	2	8	0	0
Coleman,rf	6	2	2	2	1	0
McNair,ss	5	1	3	1	2	0
Dykes,3b	4	1	1	0	1	0
Earnshaw,p	2	0	0	0	2	1
aHaas	1	0	1	0	0	0
Mahaffey,p	0	0	0	0	0	0
Walberg,p	0	0	0	0	0	0
Krausse,p	0	0	0	0	0	0
bMadjeski	1	0	0	0	0	0
Rommel,p	0	0	0	0	1	0
Totals	42	13	13	27	11	1

New York ....2 0 0 2 3 2 3 2 6—20
Philadelphia ....2 0 0 6 0 2 0 2 1—13

a Singled for Earnshaw in fifth.
b Reached on error for Krausse in eighth.
c Flied out for Cramer in eighth.
d Batted for Cochrane in ninth.

Runs batted in: Combs, Saltzgaver, Ruth, Gehrig 6, Chapman, Dickey, Lazzeri 6, Crosetti 2, Cramer 3, Cochrane 2, Foxx, Coleman 3, McNair 2.
Doubles: Ruth, Lazzeri, Coleman, McNair.
Triples: Chapman, Lazzeri, Bishop, Cramer, Foxx.
Home runs: Combs, Ruth, Gehrig 4, Lazzeri, Cochrane, Foxx.
Stolen bases: Lazzeri.
Double plays: Cochrane and McNair; Bishop and Foxx; Coleman and Cochrane.
Left on bases: New York 6, Philadelphia 11.

New York	IP	H	R	ER	BB	SO
Allen	3⅔	7	8	4	5	2
Rhodes	1⅓	1	2	2	2	0
Brown (W)	2	3	2	1	1	0
Gomez	2	2	1	1	0	1

Philadelphia	IP	H	R	ER	BB	SO
Earnshaw	5	8	7	6	2	8
Mahaffey (L)	1	6	4	4	0	0
Walberg	1	2	1	1	1	1
Krausse	1	4	2	2	0	0
Rommel	1	3	6	6	3	0

Wild pitch: Rhodes.

Umpires: Geisel, McGowan, Van Graflan.
Time: 2:55. **Attendance:** 7,300.

CHUCK KLEIN

July 10, 1936, at Pittsburgh

Philadelphia outfielder Klein needed a 10th inning to get his fourth homer and it proved to be the game-winner in a 9-6 Phillies victory over the Pirates.

Philadelphia	AB	R	H	PO	A	E
Sulik,cf	5	1	1	5	0	0
Moore,lf	5	1	1	1	0	0
Klein,rf	5	4	4	5	0	0
Camilli,1b	4	2	1	10	1	0
Atwood,c	4	0	1	2	0	0
Wilson,c	0	1	0	0	0	0
Chiozza,3b	5	0	2	1	1	0
Norris,ss	4	0	1	3	4	2
Gomez,2b	5	0	0	3	2	0
Passeau,p	4	0	1	0	0	0
Walters,p	0	0	0	0	1	0
Totals	41	9	12	30	9	2

Pittsburgh	AB	R	H	PO	A	E
Jensen,lf	4	1	1	3	0	0
L.Waner,cf	4	1	1	4	0	1
P.Waner,rf	4	2	2	1	0	0
Vaughan,ss	5	0	1	2	2	2
Suhr,1b	4	0	2	13	1	0
Brubaker,3b	5	0	0	1	1	0
Young,2b	3	0	1	1	5	0
Lavagetto,2b	1	1	0	1	1	1
Todd,c	2	0	0	3	0	0
Padden,c	2	1	0	1	0	0
Weaver,p	1	0	0	0	2	0
aLucas	1	0	0	0	0	0
Brown,p	1	0	0	0	2	0
bSchulte	1	0	1	0	0	0
cFinney	0	0	0	0	0	0
Swift,p	0	0	0	0	0	0
Totals	38	6	9	30	14	4

Philadelphia ....4 0 0 0 1 0 1 0 0 3— 9
Pittsburgh ....0 0 0 1 0 3 0 0 2 0— 6

a Batted for Weaver in fifth.
b Singled for Brown in ninth.
c Ran for Schulte in ninth.

Runs batted in: Klein 6, Chiozza, Norris 2, L.Waner, P.Waner, Vaughan, Suhr, Schulte.
Double: Camilli.
Triple: Suhr.
Home runs: Klein 4.
Double plays: Chiozza, Gomez and Camilli; Camilli, Norris and Camilli; Walters, Gomez and Camilli; Vaughan, Lavagetto and Suhr.
Left on bases: Philadelphia 5, Pittsburgh 7.

Philadelphia	IP	H	R	ER	BB	SO
Passeau	8⅔	8	6	4	2	1
Walters (W)	1⅓	1	0	0	2	0

Pittsburgh	IP	H	R	ER	BB	SO
Weaver	5	6	5	4	1	2
Brown	4	2	1	1	0	1
Swift (L)	1	4	3	2	0	0

Umpires: Sears, Klem, Ballanfant.
Time: 2:25. **Attendance:** 2,500.

PAT SEEREY

July 18, 1948, at Philadelphia

Seerey, like Klein, needed extra innings to tie the record and he also made his fourth homer a game-winner—an 11th-inning blast in Chicago's 12-11 victory over the Athletics.

Chicago	AB	R	H	PO	A	E
Kolloway,2b	7	2	5	5	2	0
Lupien,1b	7	1	1	8	2	0
Appling,3b	7	1	3	2	5	0
Seerey,lf	6	4	4	3	0	0
Robinson,c	6	0	3	4	1	0
Wright,rf	6	0	2	0	0	0
Philley,cf	6	1	2	5	0	0
Michaels,ss	6	3	4	6	3	1
Papish,p	0	0	0	0	1	0
Moulder,p	1	0	0	0	0	0
aHodgin	1	0	0	0	0	0
Caldwell,p	0	0	0	0	0	0
bBaker	1	0	0	0	0	0
Judson,p	3	0	0	0	0	0
Pieretti,p	0	0	0	0	0	0
Totals	57	12	24	33	14	1

FOR THE RECORD

Philadelphia	AB	R	H	PO	A	E
Joost,ss	7	4	4	1	2	0
McCosky,lf	2	2	1	3	1	0
White,cf	4	1	2	2	0	0
Brissie,p	0	0	0	0	0	0
dChapman	0	0	0	0	0	0
eDeMars	0	0	0	0	0	0
Fain,1b	5	0	0	13	0	0
Majeski,3b	5	0	1	0	3	0
Valo,rf	3	0	1	4	0	0
Rosar,c	3	0	0	5	0	0
Guerra,c	3	0	0	3	0	0
Suder,2b	5	2	1	2	1	0
Scheib,p	1	1	0	0	4	0
Savage,p	1	0	0	0	0	0
Harris,p	1	1	1	0	0	1
J.Coleman,p	0	0	0	0	0	0
cR.Coleman,cf	2	0	1	0	0	0
Totals	42	11	12	33	11	1

Chicago ....001 125 200 01—12
Philadelphia ......140 110 400 00—11

a Flied out for Moulder in fourth.
b Flied out for Caldwell in sixth.
c Grounded out for J.Coleman in ninth.
d Walked for Brissie in 11th.
e Ran for Chapman in 11th.

Runs batted in: Kolloway 3, Appling, Seerey 7, Baker, Joost 5, McCosky, Fain 2, Majeski.
Doubles: Robinson, Wright, Kolloway, Philley, Joost 2, Majeski.
Triple: Kolloway.
Home runs: Seerey 4, Joost.
Sacrifice hits: McCosky, White 2.
Stolen base: Appling.
Double plays: McCosky and Rosar; Kolloway, Michaels and Lupien.
Left on bases: Chicago 15, Philadelphia 14.

Chicago	IP	H	R	ER	BB	SO
Papish	1	3	5	4	4	0
Moulder	2	0	0	0	0	1
Caldwell	2	4	2	2	1	1
Judson (W)	5⅔	5	4	4	7	2
Pieretti (S)	⅓	0	0	0	0	0

Philadelphia	IP	H	R	ER	BB	SO
Scheib	4⅔	9	4	4	1	2
Savage	1	5	5	5	1	0
Harris	1⅔	4	2	1	0	0
J.Coleman	1⅔	2	0	0	1	1
Brissie (L)	2	4	1	1	0	1

Papish pitched to four batters in second.
Hit by pitcher: Valo (by Papish).
Wild pitches: Papish, Moulder, Savage.
Balk: Judson.

Umpires: Hurley, Berry, Grieve.
Time: 3:44. **Attendance:** 17,296.

GIL HODGES

August 31, 1950, at Brooklyn

Hodges, the Dodgers' big first baseman, connected off four different Boston pitchers and finished the game with nine RBIs.

Boston	AB	R	H	PO	A	E
Hartsfield,2b	5	0	1	4	1	3
Jethroe,cf	5	0	0	1	0	0
Torgeson,1b	4	1	1	7	0	0
Elliott,3b	3	0	1	1	4	0
Cooper,c	3	0	0	3	0	0
Crandall,c	1	1	0	2	0	1
Gordon,lf	4	1	3	4	0	0
Marshall,rf	4	0	2	1	0	0
Kerr,ss	3	0	0	1	4	0
Spahn,p	1	0	0	0	0	0
Roy,p	0	0	0	0	1	0
Haefner,p	0	0	0	0	0	0
aReiser	1	0	0	0	0	0
Hall,p	0	0	0	0	1	0
Antonelli,p	1	0	0	0	0	0
bHolmes	1	0	0	0	0	0
Totals	36	3	8	24	11	4

Brooklyn	AB	R	H	PO	A	E
Brown,lf	5	0	1	1	0	0
Reese,ss	5	1	2	1	4	1
Snider,cf	5	1	1	4	0	0
Robinson,2b	5	1	1	2	1	0
Morgan,3b	0	0	0	0	1	0
Furillo,rf	5	4	2	1	0	0
Hodges,1b	6	5	5	7	1	0
Campanella,c	4	2	2	4	0	0
Edwards,c	1	1	1	2	0	0
Cox,3b-2b	5	3	2	3	3	0
Erskine,p	5	1	4	2	0	0
Totals	46	19	21	27	10	1

Boston ....010 000 020—3
Brooklyn...................037 004 32x—19

a Struck out for Haefner in fifth.
b Lined out for Antonelli in ninth.

Runs batted in: Hodges 9, Reese 3, Gordon 2, Snider 3, Brown 2, Marshall.
Doubles: Reese, Edwards, Marshall 2.
Home runs: Hodges 4, Gordon, Snider.
Sacrifice hit: Cox.
Left on bases: Boston 9, Brooklyn 12.

Boston	IP	H	R	ER	BB	SO
Spahn (L)	2	7	5	5	1	2
Roy	⅓	3	3	3	0	0
Haefner	1⅔	1	2	2	1	0
Hall	1⅔	6	4	4	3	1
Antonelli	2⅓	4	5	4	2	2

Brooklyn	IP	H	R	ER	BB	SO
Erskine (W)	9	8	3	3	2	6

Spahn pitched to two batters in third.
Hit by pitcher: Erskine (by Antonelli).

Umpires: Conlan, Gore, Stewart.
Time: 3:03. **Attendance:** 14,226.

JOE ADCOCK

July 31, 1954, at Brooklyn

Milwaukee first baseman Adcock homered off four different Dodgers pitchers and punctuated his big game with a double and 18 total bases.

Milwaukee	AB	R	H	PO	A	E
Bruton,cf	6	0	4	4	0	0
O'Connell,2b	5	0	0	4	4	0
Mathews,3b	4	3	2	3	2	0
Aaron,lf	5	2	2	0	0	0
Adcock,1b	5	5	5	11	0	0
Pafko,rf	4	2	3	0	0	0
Pendleton,rf	1	1	0	0	0	0
Logan,ss	2	1	1	1	1	0
Smalley,ss	2	1	1	0	1	0
Crandall,c	4	0	0	2	1	0
Calderone,c	1	0	1	2	0	0
Wilson,p	1	0	0	0	0	0
Burdette,p	3	0	0	0	4	0
Buhl,p	0	0	0	0	0	0
Jolly,p	1	0	0	0	0	0
Totals	44	15	19	27	13	0

Brooklyn	AB	R	H	PO	A	E
Gilliam,2b	4	1	4	3	1	0
Reese,ss	3	0	1	1	2	0
Zimmer,ss	1	0	0	1	1	0
Snider,cf	4	0	1	0	0	0
Shuba,lf	1	0	0	0	0	0
Hodges,1b	5	1	1	7	0	0
Amoros,lf-cf	5	2	3	6	0	0
Robinson,3b	0	0	0	0	0	0
Hoak,3b	2	1	1	0	1	1
Furillo,rf	5	1	2	3	0	0
Walker,c	5	1	1	6	1	0
Newcombe,p	0	0	0	0	0	0
Labine,p	0	0	0	0	0	0
aMoryn	1	0	0	0	0	0
Palica,p	0	0	0	0	0	1
Wojey,p	1	0	0	0	1	0
bPodres,p	2	0	2	0	1	0
Totals	39	7	16	27	8	1

Milwaukee ....132 030 303—15
Brooklyn...................100 001 041—7

a Grounded into double play for Labine in second.
b Singled for Wojey in seventh.

Runs batted in: Mathews 2, Snider, Adcock 7, Logan, Bruton, Pafko 2, Hoak 2, Hodges, Furillo, Walker 2.
Doubles: Gilliam, Pafko, Bruton 3, Amoros, Adcock, Aaron.
Triple: Amoros.
Home runs: Mathews 2, Adcock 4, Hoak, Pafko, Hodges, Walker.
Sacrifice hit: O'Connell.
Sacrifice fly: Hoak.
Double plays: Mathews, O'Connell and Adcock; O'Connell, Logan and Adcock; Zimmer, Gilliam and Hodges.
Left on bases: Milwaukee 5, Brooklyn 10.

Milwaukee	IP	H	R	ER	BB	SO
Wilson	1	5	1	1	0	0
Burdette (W)	6⅓	8	5	5	2	3
Buhl	0	2	0	0	0	0
Jolly	1⅔	1	1	1	1	1

Brooklyn	IP	H	R	ER	BB	SO
Newcombe (L)	1	4	4	4	0	0
Labine	1	1	0	0	0	0
Palica	2⅓	5	5	5	2	1
Wojey	2⅔	4	3	3	0	3
Podres	2	5	3	2	0	1

Hit by pitcher: Robinson (by Wilson).
Wild pitch: Podres.

Umpires: Boggess, Engeln, Stewart, Barlick.
Time: 2:53. **Attendance:** 12,263.

ROCKY COLAVITO

June 10, 1959, at Baltimore

Cleveland outfielder Colavito rocked the Orioles and joined Lowe and Gehrig as the only players to hit their four homers consecutively.

Cleveland	AB	R	H	PO	A	E
Held,ss	5	1	1	5	1	0
Power,1b	4	1	0	4	1	0
Francona,cf	5	2	2	2	0	0
Colavito,rf	4	5	4	3	0	0
Minoso,lf	5	1	3	1	0	0
Jones,3b	3	0	0	1	1	0
Strickland,3b	2	0	1	1	1	0
Brown,c	4	0	1	7	1	0
Martin,2b	3	1	1	3	0	0
aWebster,2b	1	0	0	0	0	0
Bell,p	3	0	0	0	1	0
Garcia,p	1	0	0	0	0	0
Totals	40	11	13	27	6	0

Baltimore	AB	R	H	PO	A	E
Pearson,cf	3	1	2	5	0	0
Pilarcik,rf	5	1	1	2	0	0
Woodling,lf	5	1	3	3	0	0
Triandos,c	2	0	1	5	0	0
Ginsberg,c	1	1	0	0	0	0
Hale,1b	3	0	0	4	0	0
Zuverink,p	0	0	0	0	0	0
bBoyd	1	0	0	0	0	0
Johnson,p	0	0	0	0	0	0
cNieman	1	1	1	0	0	0
Klaus,3b	5	0	2	0	1	0
Carrasquel,ss	5	0	0	2	3	0
Gardner,2b	4	1	1	1	5	0
Walker,p	1	1	1	0	0	0
Portocarrero,p	1	0	0	0	0	0
Lockman,1b	1	1	0	5	0	0
Totals	38	8	12	27	9	0

Cleveland ....312 013 001—11
Baltimore ....120 000 401—8

a Popped out for Martin in seventh.
b Flied out for Zuverink in seventh.
c Doubled for Johnson in ninth.

Runs batted in: Francona, Colavito 6, Minoso 3, Martin, Pilarcik 2, Woodling, Triandos, Klaus 4.
Doubles: Brown, Held, Francona, Klaus, Nieman.
Home runs: Minoso, Martin, Colavito 4.
Sacrifice fly: Triandos.
Stolen bases: Minoso.
Left on bases: Cleveland 0, Baltimore 8.

Cleveland	IP	H	R	ER	BB	SO
Bell (W)	6⅓	8	7	7	4	3
Garcia	2⅔	4	1	1	0	3

Baltimore	IP	H	R	ER	BB	SO
Walker (L)	2⅓	4	6	6	2	1
Portocarrero	3⅔	7	4	4	1	3
Zuverink	1⅓	0	0	0	0	0
Johnson	2	2	1	1	0	0

Umpires: Summers, McKinley, Soar, Chylak.
Time: 2:54. **Attendance:** 15,883.

WILLIE MAYS

April 30, 1961, at Milwaukee

New York Giants center fielder Mays connected in the first, third, sixth and eighth innings, driving in eight of his team's 14 runs against the Braves.

San Francisco	AB	R	H	PO	A	E
Hiller,2b	6	2	3	3	2	0
Davenport,3b	4	3	1	1	4	0
Mays,cf	5	4	4	3	0	0
McCovey,1b	3	0	0	5	0	0
Marshall,1b	0	0	0	3	0	0
Cepeda,lf	5	1	1	3	0	0
M.Alou,lf	0	0	0	1	0	0
F.Alou,rf	4	1	1	3	0	0
Bailey,c	4	0	0	3	0	0
Pagan,ss	5	3	4	2	1	0
Loes,p	3	0	0	0	2	0
Totals	39	14	14	27	9	0

Milwaukee	AB	R	H	PO	A	E
McMillan,ss	4	1	1	2	3	0
Bolling,2b	4	1	2	4	4	0
Mathews,3b	4	0	1	0	4	1
Aaron,cf	4	2	2	2	0	0
Roach,lf	4	0	1	2	0	0
Adcock,1b	4	0	0	13	1	0
Lau,c	3	0	1	2	0	0
McMahon,p	0	0	0	0	1	0
Brunet,p	0	0	0	0	1	0
cMaye	0	0	0	0	0	0
DeMerit,rf	4	0	0	0	0	0
Burdette,p	1	0	0	1	1	0
Willey,p	0	0	0	1	0	0
Drabowsky,p	0	0	0	0	0	0
aMartin	1	0	0	0	0	0
Morehead,p	0	0	0	0	0	0
MacKenzie,p	0	0	0	0	0	0
bLogan	1	0	0	0	0	0
Taylor,c	0	0	0	0	0	0
Totals	34	4	8	27	15	1

San Francisco............103 304 030—14
Milwaukee ....300 001 000— 4

a Flied out for Drabowsky in fifth.
b Struck out for MacKenzie in seventh.
c Walked for Brunet in ninth.

Runs batted in: Hiller, Davenport, Mays 8, Cepeda, F.Alou, Pagan 2, Aaron 4.
Doubles: Hiller 2.
Triple: Davenport.
Home runs: Mays 4, Pagan 2, Cepeda, F.Alou, Aaron 2.
Sacrifice hits: Loes 2.
Double plays: Davenport, Hiller and Marshall; Burdette, McMillan and Adcock; Bolling, McMillan and Adcock.
Left on bases: San Francisco 6, Milwaukee 4.

San Francisco	IP	H	R	ER	BB	SO
Loes (W)	9	8	4	4	1	3

Milwaukee	IP	H	R	ER	BB	SO
Burdette (L)	3	5	5	5	0	0
Willey	1	3	2	2	0	0
Drabowsky	1	0	0	0	1	0
Morehead	1	2	4	4	1	1
MacKenzie	1	0	0	0	0	1
McMahon	1	3	3	3	2	0
Brunet	1	1	0	0	0	0

Burdette pitched to one batter in fourth.
Hit by pitcher: Davenport (by Burdette), Bailey (by Mackenzie).

Umpires: Pelekoudas, Forman, Conlan, Donatelli, Burkhart.
Time: 2:40. **Attendance:** 13,114.

MIKE SCHMIDT

April 17, 1976, at Chicago

Philadelphia third baseman Schmidt hit a two-run shot in the 10th inning—his fourth consecutive homer in the Phillies' 18-16 victory.

Philadelphia	AB	R	H	PO	A	E
Cash,2b	6	1	2	4	3	0
Bowa,ss	6	3	3	2	0	0
Johnstone,rf	5	2	4	5	0	0
Luzinski,lf	5	0	1	0	0	0
Brown,lf	0	0	0	0	0	0
Allen,1b	5	2	1	5	0	0
Schmidt,3b	6	4	5	2	3	0
Maddox,rf	5	2	2	4	0	0
McGraw,p	0	0	0	0	0	0
eMcCarver	1	1	1	0	0	0
Underwood,p	0	0	0	0	0	0
Lonborg,p	0	0	0	0	0	0
Boone,c	6	1	3	8	0	0
Carlton,p	1	0	0	0	0	0
Schueler,p	0	0	0	0	0	0
Garber,p	0	0	0	0	0	0
aHutton	0	0	0	0	0	0
Reed,p	0	0	0	0	0	0
bMartin	1	0	0	0	0	0
Twitchell,p	0	0	0	0	0	0
cTolan,cf	3	2	2	0	0	0
Totals	50	18	24	30	6	0

Chicago	AB	R	H	PO	A	E
Monday,cf	6	3	4	4	0	0
Cardenal,lf	5	1	1	1	0	0
Summers,lf	0	0	0	3	0	0
dMitterwald	1	0	0	0	0	0
Wallis,lf	1	0	0	0	0	0
Madlock,3b	7	2	3	0	0	0
Morales,rf	5	2	1	1	0	0
Thornton,1b	4	3	1	10	1	0
Trillo,2b	5	0	2	2	3	0
Swisher,c	6	1	3	5	0	0
Rosello,ss	4	1	2	2	3	0
Kelleher,ss	2	0	1	1	1	0
R.Reuschel,p	1	2	0	1	3	0
Garman,p	0	0	0	0	0	0
Knowles,p	0	0	0	0	1	0
P.Reuschel,p	0	0	0	0	0	0
Schultz,p	0	0	0	0	2	0
fAdams	1	1	1	0	0	0
Totals	48	16	19	30	14	0

Philadelphia ....010 120 353 3—18
Chicago ....075 100 002 1—16

a Walked for Garber in fourth.
b Grounded out for Reed in sixth.

c Singled for Twitchell in eighth.
d Struck out for Summers in eighth.
e Singled for McGraw in 10th.
f Doubled for Schultz in 10th.

Runs batted in: Cash 2, Bowa, Johnstone 2, Luzinski, Allen 2, Schmidt 8, Maddox, Monday 4, Madlock 3, Thornton, Trillo 3, Swisher 4, Rosello.
Doubles: Cardenal, Madlock, Thornton, Boone, Adams.
Triples: Johnstone, Bowa.
Home runs: Maddox, Swisher, Monday 2, Schmidt 4, Boone.
Sacrifice hits: R.Reuschel, Johnstone.
Sacrifice flies: Luzinski, Cash.
Double plays: Trillo, Rosello and Thornton; Schmidt, Cash and Allen.
Left on bases: Philadelphia 8, Chicago 12.

Philadelphia	IP	H	R	ER	BB	SO
Carlton	1 2/3	7	7	7	2	1
Schueler	2/3	3	3	3	0	0
Garber	2/3	2	2	2	1	1
Reed	2	1	1	1	1	1
Twitchell	2	0	0	0	1	1
McGraw (W)	2	4	2	2	1	2
Underwood	2/3	2	1	1	0	1
Lonborg (S)	1/3	0	0	0	0	0

Chicago	IP	H	R	ER	BB	SO
R.Reuschel	7	14	7	7	1	4
Garman	2/3	4	5	5	1	1
Knowles (L)	1 1/3	3	4	4	1	0
P.Reuschel	0	3	2	2	0	0
Schultz	1	0	0	0	0	0

Knowles pitched to one batter in 10th.
P.Reuschel pitched to two batters in 10th.
Hit by pitcher: R. Reuschel (by Schueler), Thornton (by Garber), Monday (by Twitchell).
Balk: Schultz.

Umpires: Vargo, Olsen, Davidson, Rennert.
Time: 3:42. **Attendance:** 28,287.

BOB HORNER

July 6, 1986, at Atlanta

Atlanta first baseman Horner became the first four-homer man in 10 years and the first to accomplish the feat during a loss. The Expos defeated the Braves, 11-8.

Montreal	AB	R	H	PO	A	E
Webster,lf	6	2	5	1	0	0
Wright,cf	6	1	2	4	0	0
Dawson,rf	6	1	2	2	0	0
Brooks,ss	5	1	2	1	3	0
Wallach,3b	2	1	0	1	3	1
Galarraga,1b	2	0	0	4	1	0
Krenchicki,1b	1	0	1	3	0	0
Reardon,p	0	0	0	0	0	0
Fitzgerald,c	3	2	1	4	0	0
Newman,2b	4	3	2	5	3	0
McGaffigan,p	2	0	1	1	0	0
Burke,p	1	0	0	0	0	0
Law,1b	1	0	0	1	0	0
Totals	39	11	16	27	10	1

Atlanta	AB	R	H	PO	A	E
Moreno,rf	4	0	1	2	0	0
dSimmons,3b	1	0	0	0	0	0
Oberkfell,3b-2b	5	1	4	2	4	0
Murphy,cf	5	0	0	2	0	0
Horner,1b	5	4	4	8	1	1
Griffey,lf	5	0	2	0	0	0
Thomas,ss	4	0	1	0	4	0
Virgil,c	4	1	1	6	1	0
Hubbard,2b	3	1	1	6	2	0
bChambliss	0	0	0	0	0	0
Garber,p	0	0	0	0	0	0
Smith,p	1	0	0	0	1	0
Dedmon,p	0	1	0	0	0	0
aSample	1	0	0	0	0	0
Assenmacher,p	0	0	0	0	0	0
cRamirez,rf	1	0	0	1	0	0
Totals	39	8	14	27	13	1

Montreal....................0 0 1 3 6 0 1 0 0—11
Atlanta ....0 1 0 1 5 0 0 0 1— 8

a Grounded out for Dedmon in sixth.
b Walked for Hubbard in eighth.
c Struck out for Assenmacher in eighth.
d Grounded out for Moreno in eighth.

Runs batted in: Webster 3, Wright, Dawson 2, Fitzgerald 2, Newman 2, McGaffigan, Oberkfell, Horner 6, Hubbard.
Doubles: Dawson, Webster, Fitzgerald, Wright, Brooks, Virgil, Hubbard, Krenchicki.
Home runs: Horner 4, Newman, Webster, Dawson.
Sacrifice hits: McGaffigan, Dedmon, Krenchicki.
Stolen bases: Webster, Griffey.
Passed ball: Virgil.
Double plays: Brooks, Newman and Galarraga; Oberkfell and Horner; Wallach, Newman and Law.
Left on bases: Montreal 10, Atlanta 6.

Montreal	IP	H	R	ER	BB	SO
McGaffigan	4 2/3	8	7	4	0	2
Burke (W)	2 2/3	4	0	0	1	1
Reardon (S)	1 2/3	2	1	1	0	1

Atlanta	IP	H	R	ER	BB	SO
Smith (L)	4	9	8	8	2	3
Dedmon	2	4	2	2	1	2
Assenmacher	2	2	1	1	2	1
Garber	1	1	0	0	0	0

Smith pitched to four batters in fifth.
Hit by pitcher: Galarraga (by Dedmon), Fitzgerald (by Dedmon).

Umpires: Poncino, Gregg, Davis, Harvey.
Time: 3:06. **Attendance:** 18,153.

MARK WHITEN

September 7, 1993, at Cincinnati

St. Louis outfielder Whiten doubled his pleasure by matching the Major League single-game records for homers and RBIs (12). His outburst came in the second game of a doubleheader after he had gone hitless in the opener.

St. Louis	AB	R	H	PO	A	E
Pena,2b	3	1	1	2	3	0
Maclin,lf	4	1	0	2	0	0
Gilkey,rf	5	1	1	3	0	0
Zeile,3b	2	3	1	0	0	1
Royer,3b	1	0	0	0	1	0
Perry,1b	4	4	3	8	0	0
Whiten,cf	5	4	4	5	0	0
Pagnozzi,c	5	0	1	4	0	1
Cromer,ss	5	0	0	2	4	0
Tewksbury,p	2	1	0	1	2	0
Totals	36	15	11	27	10	2

Cincinnati	AB	R	H	PO	A	E
Howard,lf	3	1	0	2	0	0
Dibble,p	0	0	0	0	0	0
Brumfield,cf	4	1	2	4	0	0
Morris,1b	2	0	1	5	0	0
Daugherty,rf	1	0	1	0	0	0
Sabo,3b	3	0	0	2	2	0
Varsho,lf	1	0	0	0	0	0
Costo,rf-3b	4	0	1	2	0	0
Samuel,2b	4	0	0	1	1	0
Wilson,c	4	0	0	10	1	0
Branson,ss	4	0	1	0	2	0
Luebbers,p	1	0	0	0	1	0
aTubbs	1	0	0	0	0	0
Anderson,p	0	0	0	0	0	0
Bushing,p	0	0	0	0	0	0
bDorsett,1b	2	0	1	1	0	0
Totals	34	2	7	27	7	0

St. Louis....................4 0 0 0 1 3 4 1 2—15
Cincinnati...................2 0 0 0 0 0 0 0 0— 2

a Grounded out for Luebbers in fifth.
b Singled for Bushing in seventh.

Runs batted in: Pena, Maclin, Perry, Whiten 12, Morris.
Double: Brumfield.
Home runs: Pena, Whiten 4.
Sacrifice hit: Pena.
Sacrifice flies: Maclin, Morris.
Stolen base: Maclin, Brumfield.
Left on bases: St. Louis 2, Cincinnati 7.

St. Louis	IP	H	R	ER	BB	SO
Tewksbury (W)	9	7	2	2	1	4

Cincinnati	IP	H	R	ER	BB	SO
Luebbers (L)	5	2	5	5	4	3
Anderson	1 2/3	6	7	7	2	2
Bushing	1/3	0	0	0	0	0
Dibble	2	3	3	3	0	5

Wild pitch: Luebbers.

Umpires: Marsh, Kellog, Vanover, Wendelstedt.
Time: 2:17. **Attendance:** 22,606.

MIKE CAMERON

May 2, 2002, at Chicago

Seattle outfielder Cameron began his night by hitting back-to-back home runs with Bret Boone twice in the first inning—the first time the same teammates ever belted consecutive homers twice in one inning.

Seattle	AB	R	H	RBI	BB	SO
Suzuki, rf	4	3	1	1	0	0
Relaford, rf	0	0	0	0	1	0
Boone, 2b	4	2	2	4	2	2
Cameron, cf	5	4	4	4	0	0
Olerud, 1b	5	2	2	1	0	0
Sierra, dh	6	1	2	1	0	2
Guillen, ss	3	1	1	1	1	0
Ugueto, ss	1	0	0	0	0	0
McLemore, lf	2	1	1	0	0	0
Gipson, lf	3	0	1	0	0	0
Davis, c	5	0	1	1	0	1
Cirillo, 3b	4	1	1	2	0	0
Totals	42	15	16	15	4	5

Chicago	AB	R	H	RBI	BB	SO
Lofton, cf	2	0	0	0	1	0
Rowand, cf	2	0	0	0	0	1
Durham, 2b	4	1	0	0	1	1
Thomas, dh	4	0	1	0	1	0
Ordonez, rf	2	0	0	0	1	0
Graffanino, ss	1	0	1	2	1	0
Konerko, 1b	5	0	0	0	0	0
Valentin, 3b	4	0	2	0	0	0
Lee, lf	4	1	2	1	0	1
Johnson, c	4	0	0	0	0	1
Clayton, ss	2	1	2	1	0	0
Liefer, rf	1	1	1	0	1	0
Totals	35	4	9	4	6	4

Seattle ....10 0 2 0 1 0 1 0 1—15
Chicago ....0 0 0 1 1 0 2 0 0— 4

Doubles: Olerud, Sierra 2, Thomas, Graffanino.
Home runs: Boone 2, Cameron 4, Cirillo, Lee, Clayton.
Sacrifice flies: Cirillo, Olerud.
Error: Durham.
Double play: Olerud and Ugueto.
Left on bases: Seattle 8, Chicago 10.

Seattle	IP	H	R	ER	BB	SO
Baldwin (W)	7	7	4	4	4	3
Halama	2	2	0	0	2	1

Chicago	IP	H	R	ER	BB	SO
Rauch (L)	1/3	6	8	5	0	0
Parque	6	9	6	6	1	3
Porzio	2 2/3	1	1	1	3	2

Hit by pitcher: Suzuki (by Rauch), Cameron (by Porzio).

Umpires: Randazzo, Froemming, Rapuano, Poncino.
Time: 3:00. **Attendance:** 12,891.

SHAWN GREEN

May 23, 2002, at Milwaukee

Los Angeles outfielder Green collected six hits, six runs, seven RBIs and a Major League-record 19 total bases in his big game.

Los Angeles	AB	R	H	RBI	BB	SO
Izturis, ss	4	2	2	0	0	0
Reboulet, ph-ss	2	0	0	0	0	1
Beltre, 3b	5	1	1	2	0	1
Green, rf	6	6	6	7	0	0
Karros, 1b	3	2	1	0	1	1
Hansen, 1b	2	1	1	1	0	0
Jordan, lf	3	1	3	3	0	0
Bocachica, ph-lf	3	1	1	2	0	0
Grissom, cf	2	0	0	1	2	0
Grudzielanek, 2b	3	0	1	0	0	1
Cora, ph-2b	2	0	0	0	0	0
Kreuter, c	4	1	3	0	1	0
Ishii, p	3	1	0	0	0	1
Mota, p	1	0	0	0	0	1
Williams, p	1	0	0	0	0	1
Totals	44	16	19	16	4	7

Milwaukee	AB	R	H	RBI	BB	SO
Belliard, 2b	4	1	2	0	1	0
Loretta, 3b	5	0	2	0	0	1
Hammonds, cf-rf	4	0	1	0	0	1
Jensen, ph	1	0	0	0	0	0
Sexson, 1b	3	1	1	0	2	0
Ochoa, rf-lf	4	1	2	3	1	1
Jenkins, lf	3	0	0	0	0	1
Sanchez, cf	2	0	0	0	0	0
Hernandez, ss	2	0	1	0	0	1
Mallette, p	0	0	0	0	0	0
Young, ph	1	0	0	0	0	0
Buddie, p	0	0	0	0	0	0
Harris, ph	1	0	0	0	0	1
Cabrera, p	0	0	0	0	0	0
Vizcaino, p	0	0	0	0	0	0
Bako, c	4	0	1	0	0	2
Rusch, p	0	0	0	0	0	0
De Los Santos, p	0	0	0	0	1	0
Lopez, ss	2	0	0	0	1	0
Totals	36	3	10	3	6	8

Los Angeles ....3 5 0 1 1 0 0 2 4—16
Milwaukee ....1 0 0 0 1 0 0 0 1— 3

Doubles: Green, Karros, Kreuter.
Home runs: Green 4, Jordan, Bocachica, Beltre, Hansen, Ochoa.
Sacrifice hit: Beltre.
Sacrifice fly: Grissom.
Error: Reboulet.
Double plays: Grudzielanek, Izturis and Karros; Izturis, Cora and Karros.
Left on bases: Los Angeles 7, Milwaukee 12.

Los Angeles	IP	H	R	ER	BB	SO
Ishii (W)	5 1/3	8	2	2	6	6
Mota	1 2/3	0	0	0	0	1
Williams	2	2	1	1	0	1

Milwaukee	IP	H	R	ER	BB	SO
Rusch (L)	1 2/3	9	8	8	2	0
De Los Santos	1 1/3	0	0	0	0	1
Mallette	2	3	2	2	2	3
Buddie	2	1	0	0	0	2
Cabrera	1 2/3	6	6	6	0	1
Vizcaino	1/3	0	0	0	0	0

Wild pitches: Ishii 2, Mallette.

Umpires: Gorman, Cuzzi, Crawford, West.
Time: 3:00. **Attendance:** 12,891.

Atlanta third baseman Bob Horner became the first modern big-league player to hit four home runs in a game his team lost.

BABE RUTH'S 60 HOME RUNS—1927

HR No.	Team game No.	Date	Opposing pitcher, Club	Place	Inn.	On base
1.	4	April 15	Howard Ehmke (righthander), Philadelphia	H	1	0
2.	11	April 23	Rube Walberg (lefthander), Philadelphia	A	1	0
3.	12	April 24	Sloppy Thurston (righthander), Washington	A	6	0
4.	14	April 29	Slim Harriss (righthander), Boston	A	5	0
5.	16	May 1	Jack Quinn (righthander), Philadelphia	H	1	1
6.	16	May 1	Rube Walberg (lefthander), Philadelphia	H	8	0
7.	24	May 10	Milt Gaston (righthander), St. Louis	A	1	2
8.	25	May 11	Ernie Nevers (righthander), St. Louis	A	1	1
9.	29	May 17	Rip H. Collins (righthander), Detroit	A	8	0
10.	33	May 22	Benn Karr (righthander), Cleveland	A	6	1
11.	34	May 23	Sloppy Thurston (righthander), Washington	A	1	0
12.	37	May *28	Sloppy Thurston (righthander), Washington	H	7	2
13.	39	May 29	Danny MacFayden (righthander), Boston	H	8	0
14.	41	May ‡30	Rube Walberg (lefthander), Philadelphia	A	11	0
15.	42	May *31	Jack Quinn (righthander), Philadelphia	A	1	1
16.	43	May †31	Howard Ehmke (righthander), Philadelphia	A	5	1
17.	47	June 5	Earl Whitehill (lefthander), Detroit	H	6	0
18.	48	June 7	Tommy Thomas (righthander), Chicago	H	4	0
19.	52	June 11	Garland Buckeye (lefthander), Cleveland	H	3	1
20.	52	June 11	Garland Buckeye (lefthander), Cleveland	H	5	0
21.	53	June 12	George Uhle (righthander), Cleveland	H	7	0
22.	55	June 16	Tom Zachary (lefthander), St. Louis	H	1	1
23.	60	June *22	Hal Wiltse (lefthander), Boston	A	5	0
24.	60	June *22	Hal Wiltse (lefthander), Boston	A	7	1
25.	70	June 30	Slim Harriss (righthander), Boston	H	4	1
26.	73	July 3	Hod Lisenbee (righthander), Washington	A	1	0
27.	78	July †8	Don Hankins (righthander), Detroit	A	2	2
28.	79	July *9	Ken Holloway (righthander), Detroit	A	1	1
29.	79	July *9	Ken Holloway (righthander), Detroit	A	4	2
30.	83	July 12	Joe Shaute (lefthander), Cleveland	A	9	1
31.	94	July 24	Tommy Thomas (righthander), Chicago	A	3	0
32.	95	July *26	Milt Gaston (righthander), St. Louis	H	1	1
33.	95	July *26	Milt Gaston (righthander), St. Louis	H	6	0
34.	98	July 28	Lefty Stewart (lefthander), St. Louis	H	8	1
35.	106	Aug. 5	George S. Smith (righthander), Detroit	H	8	0
36.	110	Aug. 10	Tom Zachary (lefthander), Washington	A	3	2
37.	114	Aug. 16	Tommy Thomas (righthander), Chicago	A	5	0
38.	115	Aug. 17	Sarge Connally (righthander), Chicago	A	11	0
39.	118	Aug. 20	Jake Miller (lefthander), Cleveland	A	1	1
40.	120	Aug. 22	Joe Shaute (lefthander), Cleveland	A	6	0
41.	124	Aug. 27	Ernie Nevers (righthander), St. Louis	A	8	1
42.	125	Aug. 28	Ernie Wingard (lefthander), St. Louis	A	1	1
43.	127	Aug. 31	Tony Welzer (righthander), Boston	H	8	0
44.	128	Sept. 2	Rube Walberg (lefthander), Philadelphia	A	1	0
45.	132	Sept. *6	Tony Welzer (righthander), Boston	A	6	2
46.	132	Sept. *6	Tony Welzer (righthander), Boston	A	7	1
47.	133	Sept. †6	Jack Russell (righthander), Boston	A	9	0
48.	134	Sept. 7	Danny MacFayden (righthander), Boston	A	1	0
49.	134	Sept. 7	Slim Harriss (righthander), Boston	A	8	1
50.	138	Sept. 11	Milt Gaston (righthander), St. Louis	H	4	0
51.	139	Sept. *13	Willis Hudlin (righthander), Cleveland	H	7	1
52.	140	Sept. †13	Joe Shaute (lefthander), Cleveland	H	4	0
53.	143	Sept. 16	Ted Blankenship (righthander), Chicago	H	3	0
54.	147	Sept. †18	Ted Lyons (righthander), Chicago	H	5	1
55.	148	Sept. 21	Sam Gibson (righthander), Detroit	H	9	0
56.	149	Sept. 22	Ken Holloway (righthander), Detroit	H	9	1
57.	152	Sept. 27	Lefty Grove (lefthander), Philadelphia	H	6	3
58.	153	Sept. 29	Hod Lisenbee (righthander), Washington	H	1	0
59.	153	Sept. 29	Paul Hopkins (righthander), Washington	H	5	3
60.	154	Sept. 30	Tom Zachary (lefthander), Washington	H	8	1

*First game of doubleheader. †Second game of doubleheader. ‡Afternoon game of split doubleheader. New York A.L. played 155 games in 1927 (one tie on April 14), with Ruth participating in 151 games. (No home run for Ruth in game No. 155 on October 1.)

ROGER MARIS' 61 HOME RUNS—1961

HR No.	Team game No.	Date	Opposing pitcher, Club	Place	Inn.	On base
1.	11	April 26	Paul Foytack (righthander), Detroit	A	5	0
2.	17	May 3	Pedro Ramos (righthander), Minnesota	A	7	2
3.	20	May 6	Eli Grba (righthander), Los Angeles	A	5	0
4.	29	May 17	Pete Burnside (lefthander), Washington	H	8	1
5.	30	May 19	Jim Perry (righthander), Cleveland	A	1	1
6.	31	May 20	Gary Bell (righthander), Cleveland	A	3	0
7.	32	May *21	Chuck Estrada (righthander), Baltimore	H	1	0
8.	35	May 24	Gene Conley (righthander), Boston	H	4	1
9.	38	May *28	Cal McLish (righthander), Chicago	H	2	1
10.	40	May 30	Gene Conley (righthander), Boston	A	3	0
11.	40	May 30	Mike Fornieles (righthander), Boston	A	8	2
12.	41	May 31	Billy Muffett (righthander), Boston	A	3	0
13.	43	June 2	Cal McLish (righthander), Chicago	A	3	2
14.	44	June 3	Bob Shaw (righthander), Chicago	A	8	2
15.	45	June 4	Russ Kemmerer (righthander), Chicago	A	3	0
16.	48	June 6	Ed Palmquist (righthander), Minnesota	H	6	2
17.	49	June 7	Pedro Ramos (righthander), Minnesota	H	3	2
18.	52	June 9	Ray Herbert (righthander), Kansas City	H	7	1
19.	55	June †11	Eli Grba (righthander), Los Angeles	H	3	0
20.	55	June †11	Johnny James (righthander), Los Angeles	H	7	0
21.	57	June 13	Jim Perry (righthander), Cleveland	A	6	0
22.	58	June 14	Gary Bell (righthander), Cleveland	A	4	1
23.	61	June 17	Don Mossi (lefthander), Detroit	A	4	0
24.	62	June 18	Jerry Casale (righthander), Detroit	A	8	1
25.	63	June 19	Jim Archer (lefthander), Kansas City	A	9	0
26.	64	June 20	Joe Nuxhall (lefthander), Kansas City	A	1	0
27.	66	June 22	Norm Bass (righthander), Kansas City	A	2	1
28.	74	July 1	Dave Sisler (righthander), Washington	H	9	1
29.	75	July 2	Pete Burnside (lefthander), Washington	H	3	2
30.	75	July 2	Johnny Klippstein (righthander), Washington	H	7	1
31.	77	July †4	Frank Lary (righthander), Detroit	H	8	1
32.	78	July 5	Frank Funk (righthander), Cleveland	H	7	0
33.	82	July *9	Bill Monbouquette (righthander), Boston	H	7	0
34.	84	July 13	Early Wynn (righthander), Chicago	A	1	1
35.	86	July 15	Ray Herbert (righthander), Chicago	A	3	0
36.	92	July 21	Bill Monbouquette (righthander), Boston	A	1	0
37.	95	July *25	Frank Baumann (lefthander), Chicago	H	4	1
38.	95	July *25	Don Larsen (righthander), Chicago	H	8	0
39.	96	July †25	Russ Kemmerer (righthander), Chicago	H	4	0
40.	96	July †25	Warren Hacker (righthander), Chicago	H	6	2
41.	106	Aug. 4	Camilo Pascual (righthander), Minnesota	H	1	2
42.	114	Aug. 11	Pete Burnside (lefthander), Washington	A	5	0
43.	115	Aug. 12	Dick Donovan (righthander), Washington	A	4	0
44.	116	Aug. *13	Bennie Daniels (righthander), Washington	A	4	0
45.	117	Aug. †13	Marty Kutyna (righthander), Washington	A	1	1
46.	118	Aug. 15	Juan Pizarro (lefthander), Chicago	H	4	0
47.	119	Aug. 16	Billy Pierce (lefthander), Chicago	H	1	1
48.	119	Aug. 16	Billy Pierce (lefthander), Chicago	H	3	1
49.	124	Aug. *20	Jim Perry (righthander), Cleveland	A	3	1
50.	125	Aug. 22	Ken McBride (righthander), Los Angeles	A	6	1
51.	129	Aug. 26	Jerry Walker (righthander), Kansas City	A	6	0
52.	135	Sept. 2	Frank Lary (righthander), Detroit	H	6	0
53.	135	Sept. 2	Hank Aguirre (lefthander), Detroit	H	8	1
54.	140	Sept. 6	Tom Cheney (righthander), Washington	H	4	0
55.	141	Sept. 7	Dick Stigman (lefthander), Cleveland	H	3	0
56.	143	Sept. 9	Mudcat Grant (righthander), Cleveland	H	7	0
57.	151	Sept. 16	Frank Lary (righthander), Detroit	A	3	1
58.	152	Sept. 17	Terry Fox (righthander), Detroit	A	12	1
59.	155	Sept. 20	Milt Pappas (righthander), Baltimore	A	3	0
60.	159	Sept. 26	Jack Fisher (righthander), Baltimore	H	3	0
61.	163	Oct. 1	Tracy Stallard (righthander), Boston	H	4	0

*First game of doubleheader. †Second game of doubleheader. New York played 163 games in 1961 (one tie on April 22). Maris did not hit a home run in this game. Maris played in 161 games.

MARK McGWIRE'S 70 HOME RUNS—1998

HR No.	Team game No.	Date	Opposing pitcher, Club	Place	Inn.	On base
1.	1	March 31	Ramon Martinez (righthander), Los Angeles	H	5	3
2.	2	April 2	Frank Lankford (righthander), Los Angeles	H	12	2
3.	3	April 3	Mark Langston (lefthander), San Diego	H	5	1
4.	4	April 4	Don Wengert (righthander), San Diego	H	6	2
5.	13	April 14	Jeff Suppan (righthander), Arizona	H	3	1
6.	13	April 14	Jeff Suppan (righthander), Arizona	H	5	0
7.	13	April 14	Barry Manuel (righthander), Arizona	H	8	1
8.	15	April 17	Matt Whiteside (righthander), Philadelphia	H	4	1
9.	19	April 21	Trey Moore (lefthander), Montreal	A	3	1
10.	23	April 25	Jerry Spradlin (righthander), Philadelphia	A	7	1
11.	27	April 30	Marc Pisciotta (righthander), Chicago	A	8	1
12.	28	May 1	Rod Beck (righthander), Chicago	A	9	1
13.	34	May 8	Rick Reed (righthander), New York	A	3	1
14.	36	May 12	Paul Wagner (righthander), Milwaukee	H	5	2
15.	38	May 14	Kevin Millwood (righthander), Atlanta	H	4	0
16.	40	May 16	Livan Hernandez (righthander), Florida	H	4	0
17.	42	May 18	Jesus Sanchez (lefthander), Florida	H	4	0
18.	43	May 19	Tyler Green (righthander), Philadelphia	A	3	1
19.	43	May 19	Tyler Green (righthander), Philadelphia	A	5	1
20.	43	May 19	Wayne Gomes (righthander), Philadelphia	A	8	1
21.	46	May 22	Mark Gardner (righthander), San Francisco	H	6	1
22.	47	May 23	Rich Rodriguez (lefthander), San Francisco	H	4	0
23.	47	May 23	John Johnstone (righthander), San Francisco	H	5	2
24.	48	May 24	Robb Nen (righthander), San Francisco	H	12	1
25.	49	May 25	John Thomson (righthander), Colorado	H	1	0
26.	52	May 29	Dan Miceli (righthander), San Diego	A	9	1
27.	53	May 30	Andy Ashby (righthander), San Diego	A	1	0
28.	59	June 5	Orel Hershiser (righthander), San Fran.	A	1	1
29.	62	June 8	Jason Bere (righthander), Chicago AL	A	4	1
30.	64	June 10	Jim Parque (lefthander), Chicago AL	A	3	2
31.	65	June 12	Andy Benes (righthander), Arizona	A	3	3
32.	69	June 17	Jose Lima (righthander), Houston	A	3	0
33.	70	June 18	Shane Reynolds (righthander), Houston	A	5	0
34.	76	June 24	Jaret Wright (righthander), Cleveland AL	A	4	0
35.	77	June 25	Dave Burba (righthander), Cleveland AL	A	1	0
36.	79	June 27	Mike Trombley (righthander), Minnesota AL	A	7	1
37.	81	June 30	Glendon Rusch (lefthander), Kansas City AL	H	7	0
38.	89	July 11	Billy Wagner (lefthander), Houston	H	11	1
39.	90	July 12	Sean Bergman (righthander), Houston	H	1	0
40.	90	July 12	Scott Elarton (righthander), Houston	H	7	0
41.	95	July 17	Brian Bohanon (lefthander), Los Angeles	H	1	0
42.	95	July 17	Antonio Osuna (righthander), Los Angeles	H	8	0
43.	98	July 20	Brian Boehringer (righthander), San Diego	A	5	1
44.	104	July 26	John Thomson (righthander), Colorado	A	4	0
45.	105	July 28	Mike Myers (lefthander), Milwaukee	H	8	0
46.	115	Aug. 8	Mark Clark (righthander), Chicago	H	4	0
47.	118	Aug. 11	Bobby Jones (righthander), New York	H	4	0
48.	124	Aug. 19	Matt Karchner (righthander), Chicago	A	8	0
49.	124	Aug. 19	Terry Mulholland (righthander), Chicago	A	10	0
50.	125	Aug. *20	Willie Blair (righthander), New York	A	7	0

HR No.	Team game No.	Date		Opposing pitcher, Club	Place	Inn.	On base
51.	126	Aug.	†20	Rick Reed (righthander), New York	A	1	0
52.	129	Aug.	22	Francisco Cordova (righthander), Pitt.	A	1	0
53.	130	Aug.	23	Ricardo Rincon (lefthander), Pittsburgh	A	8	0
54.	133	Aug.	26	Justin Speier (righthander), Florida	H	8	1
55.	137	Aug.	30	Dennis Martinez (righthander), Atlanta	H	7	2
56.	139	Sept.	1	Livan Hernandez (righthander), Florida	A	7	0
57.	139	Sept.	1	Donn Pall (righthander), Florida	A	9	0
58.	140	Sept.	2	Brian Edmondson (righthander), Florida	A	7	1
59.	140	Sept.	2	Rob Stanifer (righthander), Florida	A	8	1
60.	142	Sept.	5	Dennis Reyes (lefthander), Cincinnati	H	1	1
61.	144	Sept.	7	Mike Morgan (righthander), Chicago	H	1	0
62.	145	Sept.	8	Steve Trachsel (righthander), Chicago	H	4	0
63.	152	Sept.	*15	Jason Christiansen (lefthander), Pitt.	H	9	0
64.	155	Sept.	18	Rafael Roque (lefthander), Milwaukee	A	4	1
65.	157	Sept.	20	Scott Karl (lefthander), Milwaukee	A	1	1
66.	161	Sept.	25	Shayne Bennett (righthander), Montreal	H	5	1
67.	162	Sept.	26	Dustin Hermanson (righthander), Montreal	H	4	0
68.	162	Sept.	26	Kirk Bullinger (righthander), Montreal	H	7	1
69.	163	Sept.	27	Mike Thurman (righthander), Montreal	H	3	0
70.	163	Sept.	27	Carl Pavano (righthander), Montreal	H	7	2

*First game of doubleheader. †Second game of doubleheader. St. Louis played 163 games in 1998 (one tie on Aug. 24). McGwire played in 155 games.

SAMMY SOSA'S 66 HOME RUNS—1998

HR No.	Team game No.	Date		Opposing pitcher, Club	Place	Inn.	On base
1.	5	April	4	Marc Valdes (righthander), Montreal	H	3	0
2.	11	April	11	Anthony Telford (righthander), Montreal	A	7	0
3.	14	April	15	Dennis Cook (lefthander), New York	A	8	0
4.	21	April	23	Dan Miceli (righthander), San Diego	H	9	0
5.	22	April	24	Ismael Valdes (righthander), Los Angeles	A	1	0
6.	25	April	27	Joe Hamilton (righthander), San Diego	A	1	1
7.	30	May	3	Cliff Politte (righthander), St. Louis	H	1	0
8.	42	May	16	Scott Sullivan (righthander), Cincinnati	A	3	2
9.	47	May	22	Greg Maddux (righthander), Atlanta	A	1	0
10.	50	May	25	Kevin Millwood (righthander), Atlanta	A	4	0
11.	50	May	25	Mike Cather (righthander), Atlanta	A	8	2
12.	51	May	27	Darrin Winston (lefthander), Phil.	H	8	0
13.	51	May	27	Wayne Gomes (righthander), Philadelphia	H	9	1
14.	56	June	1	Ryan Dempster (righthander), Florida	H	1	1
15.	56	June	1	Oscar Henriquez (righthander), Florida	H	8	2
16.	58	June	3	Livan Hernandez (righthander), Florida	H	5	1
17.	59	June	5	Jim Parque (lefthander), Chicago AL	H	5	1
18.	60	June	6	Carlos Castillo (righthander), Chi. AL	H	7	0
19.	61	June	7	James Baldwin (righthander), Chicago AL	H	5	2
20.	62	June	8	LaTroy Hawkins (righthander), Minn. AL	A	3	0
21.	66	June	13	Mark Portugal (righthander), Phil.	A	6	1
22.	68	June	15	Cal Eldred (righthander), Milwaukee	H	1	0
23.	68	June	15	Cal Eldred (righthander), Milwaukee	H	3	0
24.	68	June	15	Cal Eldred (righthander), Milwaukee	H	7	0
25.	70	June	17	Bronswell Patrick (righthander), Milw.	H	4	0
26.	72	June	19	Carlton Loewer (righthander), Phil.	H	1	0
27.	72	June	19	Carlton Loewer (righthander), Phil.	H	5	1
28.	73	June	20	Matt Beech (lefthander), Philadelphia	H	3	1
29.	73	June	20	Toby Borland (righthander), Philadelphia	H	6	2
30.	74	June	21	Tyler Green (righthander), Philadelphia	H	4	0
31.	77	June	24	Seth Greisinger (righthander), Det. AL	A	1	0
32.	78	June	25	Brian Moehler (righthander), Detroit AL	A	7	0
33.	82	June	30	Alan Embree (lefthander), Arizona	H	8	0
34.	88	July	9	Jeff Juden (righthander), Milwaukee	A	2	1
35.	89	July	10	Scott Karl (lefthander), Milwaukee	A	2	0
36.	95	July	17	Kirt Ojala (lefthander), Florida	A	6	1
37.	100	July	22	Miguel Batista (righthander), Montreal	H	8	2
38.	105	July	26	Rick Reed (righthander), New York	H	6	1
39.	106	July	27	Willie Blair (righthander), Arizona	A	6	1
40.	106	July	27	Alan Embree (lefthander), Arizona	A	8	3
41.	107	July	28	Bob Wolcott (righthander), Arizona	A	5	3
42.	110	July	31	Jamey Wright (righthander), Colorado	H	1	0
43.	115	Aug.	5	Andy Benes (righthander), Arizona	H	3	1
44.	117	Aug.	8	Rich Croushore (righthander), St. Louis	A	9	1
45.	119	Aug.	10	Russ Ortiz (righthander), San Francisco	A	5	0
46.	119	Aug.	10	Chris Brock (righthander), San Francisco	A	7	0
47.	124	Aug.	16	Sean Bergman (righthander), Houston	A	4	0
48.	126	Aug.	19	Kent Bottenfield (righthander), St.L.	H	5	1
49.	128	Aug.	21	Orel Hershiser (righthander), San Fran.	H	5	1
50.	130	Aug.	23	Jose Lima (righthander), Houston	H	5	0
51.	130	Aug.	23	Jose Lima (righthander), Houston	H	8	0
52.	133	Aug.	26	Brett Tomko (righthander), Cincinnati	A	3	0
53.	135	Aug.	28	John Thomson (righthander), Colorado	A	1	0
54.	137	Aug.	30	Darryl Kile (righthander), Colorado	A	1	1
55.	138	Aug.	31	Brett Tomko (righthander), Cincinnati	H	3	1
56.	140	Sept.	2	Jason Bere (righthander), Cincinnati	H	6	0
57.	141	Sept.	4	Jason Schmidt (righthander), Pittsburgh	A	1	0
58.	142	Sept.	5	Sean Lawrence (lefthander), Pittsburgh	A	6	0
59.	148	Sept.	11	Bill Pulphiser (lefthander), Milwaukee	H	5	0
60.	149	Sept.	12	Valerio de los Santos (lefthander), Mil.	H	7	2
61.	150	Sept.	13	Bronswell Patrick (righthander), Milw.	H	5	1
62.	150	Sept.	13	Eric Plunk (righthander), Milwaukee	H	9	0
63.	153	Sept.	16	Brian Boehringer (righthander), S.D.	A	8	3
64.	159	Sept.	23	Rafael Roque (lefthander), Milwaukee	A	5	0
65.	159	Sept.	23	Rod Henderson (righthander), Milwaukee	A	6	0
66.	160	Sept.	25	Jose Lima (righthander), Houston	A	4	0

*First game of doubleheader. †Second game of doubleheader. Chicago played 163 games in 1998 (playoff game on Sept. 28). Sosa played in 159 games.

BARRY BONDS' 73 HOME RUNS—2001

HR No.	Team game No.	Date		Opposing pitcher, Club	Place	Inn.	On base
1.	1	April	2	Woody Williams (righthander), San Diego	H	5	0
2.	9	April	12	Adam Eaton (righthander), San Diego	A	4	0
3.	10	April	13	Jamey Wright (righthander), Milwaukee	A	1	1
4.	11	April	14	Jimmy Haynes (righthander), Milwaukee	A	5	2
5.	12	April	15	Dave Weathers (righthander), Milwaukee	A	8	0
6.	13	April	17	Terry Adams (righthander), Los Angeles	H	8	1
7.	14	April	18	Chan Ho Park (righthander), Los Angeles	H	7	0
8.	16	April	20	Jimmy Haynes (righthander), Milwaukee	H	4	1
9.	19	April	24	Jim Brower (righthander), Cincinnati	H	3	1
10.	21	April	26	Scott Sullivan (righthander), Cincinnati	H	8	1
11.	24	April	29	Manny Aybar (righthander), Chicago N.L.	H	4	0
12.	26	May	2	Todd Ritchie (righthander), Pittsburgh	A	5	1
13.	27	May	3	Jimmy Anderson (lefthander), Pittsburgh	A	1	1
14.	28	May	4	Bruce Chen (lefthander), Philadelphia	A	6	1
15.	35	May	11	Steve Trachsel (righthander), New York N.L.	H	4	0
16.	40	May	17	Chuck Smith (righthander), Florida	A	3	1
17.	41	May	18	Mike Remlinger (lefthander), Atlanta	A	8	0
18.	42	May	19	Odalis Perez (lefthander), Atlanta	A	3	0
19.	42	May	19	Jose Cabrera (righthander), Atlanta	A	7	0
20.	42	May	19	Jason Marquis (righthander), Atlanta	A	8	0
21.	43	May	20	John Burkett (righthander), Atlanta	A	1	0
22.	43	May	20	Mike Remlinger (lefthander), Atlanta	A	7	0
23.	44	May	21	Curt Schilling (righthander), Arizona	A	4	0
24.	45	May	22	Russ Springer (righthander), Arizona	A	9	1
25.	47	May	24	John Thomson (righthander), Colorado	H	3	0
26.	50	May	27	Denny Neagle (lefthander), Colorado	H	1	1
27.	53	May	30	Robert Ellis (righthander), Arizona	H	2	0
28.	53	May	30	Robert Ellis (righthander), Arizona	H	6	1
29.	54	June	1	Shawn Chacon (righthander), Colorado	A	3	1
30.	57	June	4	Bobby J. Jones (righthander), San Diego	H	4	0
31.	58	June	5	Wascar Serrano (righthander), San Diego	H	3	1
32.	60	June	7	Brian Lawrence (righthander), San Diego	H	7	1
33.	64	June	12	Pat Rapp (righthander), Anaheim	H	1	0
34.	66	June	14	Lou Pote (righthander), Anaheim	H	6	0
35.	67	June	15	Mark Mulder (lefthander), Oakland	H	1	0
36.	67	June	15	Mark Mulder (lefthander), Oakland	H	6	0
37.	70	June	19	Adam Eaton (righthander), San Diego	A	5	0
38.	71	June	20	Rodney Myers (righthander), San Diego	A	8	1
39.	74	June	23	Darryl Kile (righthander), St. Louis	A	1	1
40.	89	July	12	Paul Abbott (righthander), Seattle	A	1	0
41.	95	July	18	Mike Hampton (lefthander), Colorado	H	4	0
42.	95	July	18	Mike Hampton (lefthander), Colorado	H	5	1
43.	103	July	26	Curt Schilling (righthander), Arizona	A	4	0
44.	103	July	26	Curt Schilling (righthander), Arizona	A	5	3
45.	104	July	27	Brian Anderson (lefthander), Arizona	A	4	0
46.	108	Aug.	1	Joe Beimel (lefthander), Pittsburgh	H	1	0
47.	111	Aug.	4	Nelson Figueroa (righthander), Philadelphia	H	6	1
48.	113	Aug.	7	Danny Graves (righthander), Cincinnati	A	11	0
49.	115	Aug.	9	Scott Winchester (righthander), Cincinnati	A	3	0
50.	117	Aug.	11	Joe Borowski (righthander), Chicago N.L.	A	2	2
51.	119	Aug.	14	Ricky Bones (righthander), Florida	H	6	3
52.	121	Aug.	16	A.J. Burnett (righthander), Florida	H	4	0
53.	121	Aug.	16	Vic Darensbourg (lefthander), Florida	H	8	2
54.	123	Aug.	18	Jason Marquis (righthander), Atlanta	H	8	0
55.	127	Aug.	23	Graeme Lloyd (lefthander), Montreal	A	9	0
56.	131	Aug.	27	Kevin Appier (righthander), New York N.L.	A	5	0
57.	135	Aug.	31	John Thomson (righthander), Colorado	H	8	1
58.	138	Sept.	3	Jason Jennings (righthander), Colorado	H	4	0
59.	139	Sept.	4	Miguel Batista (righthander), Arizona	H	7	0
60.	141	Sept.	6	Albie Lopez (righthander), Arizona	H	2	0
61.	144	Sept.	9	Scott Elarton (righthander), Colorado	A	1	0
62.	144	Sept.	9	Scott Elarton (righthander), Colorado	A	5	0
63.	144	Sept.	9	Todd Belitz (lefthander), Colorado	A	11	2
64.	147	Sept.	20	Wade Miller (righthander), Houston	H	5	1
65.	150	Sept.	23	Jason Middlebrook (righthander), San Diego	A	2	0
66.	150	Sept.	23	Jason Middlebrook (righthander), San Diego	A	4	0
67.	151	Sept.	24	James Baldwin (righthander), Los Angeles	A	7	0
68.	154	Sept.	28	Jason Middlebrook (righthander), San Diego	H	2	0
69.	155	Sept.	29	Chuck McElroy (lefthander), San Diego	H	6	0
70.	159	Oct.	4	Wilfredo Rodriguez (lefthander), Houston	A	9	0
71.	160	Oct.	5	Chan Ho Park (righthander), Los Angeles	H	1	0
72.	160	Oct.	5	Chan Ho Park (righthander), Los Angeles	H	3	0
73.	162	Oct.	7	Dennis Springer (righthander), Los Angeles	H	1	0

Bonds played in 153 games.

HACK WILSON'S 191 RBIs, 56 HOME RUNS—1930

Date		Result	Site	AB	H	HR	RBI	HR Total	RBI Total
April	15	Cubs 9, Cardinals 8	A	4	1	0	1	0	1
	21	Cubs 9, Reds 1	A	5	1	1	3	1	4
	22	Cardinals 8, Cubs 3	H	4	1	1	3	2	7
	25*	Cubs 6, Reds 5	H	5	3	1	2	3	9
	28	Cubs 7, Pirates 4	H	2	1	0	1	3	10
	30	Cubs 5, Pirates 2	H	4	1	1	1	4	11
May	4	Cubs 8, Phillies 7	H	3	3	0	2	4	13
	6	Cubs 3, Dodgers 1	H	3	1	1	2	5	15
	7	Cubs 9, Dodgers 5	H	4	2	0	4	5	19
	8	Cubs 7, Dodgers 4	H	4	2	1	1	6	20
	9	Cubs 6, Giants 5	H	4	3	0	2	6	22
	10	Giants 9, Cubs 4	H	3	2	1	3	7	25
	12	Giants 14, Cubs 12	H	2	1	1	1	8	26
	13	Cubs 9, Braves 8	H	2	1	1	3	9	29
	15	Braves 10, Cubs 8	H	5	2	0	2	9	31
	18†	Cubs 9, Cardinals 6	A	3	2	2	3	11	34

Date	Result	Site	AB	H	HR	RBI	HR Total	RBI Total
20	Cardinals 16, Cubs 3	A	4	1	1	1	12	35
22	Cubs 12, Pirates 5	A	4	2	0	1	12	36
24	Cubs 5, Pirates 3	A	4	1	0	1	12	37
26	Reds 8, Cubs 2	H	4	1	1	2	13	39
28	Cubs 6, Reds 5	H	3	1	0	2	13	41
30‡	Cubs 9, Cardinals 8	H	3	1	1	1	14	42
31	Cubs 6, Cardinals 5	H	5	1	0	2	14	44
June 1	Cubs 16, Pirates 4	H	5	4	2	5	16	49
3	Cubs 15, Braves 2	A	4	1	0	1	16	50
4	Cubs 18, Braves 10	A	5	2	0	1	16	51
5	Cubs 10, Braves 7	A	6	2	1	1	17	52
6	Cubs 13, Dodgers 0	A	5	2	0	1	17	53
7	Dodgers 12, Cubs 9	A	4	1	1	2	18	55
10	Phillies 6, Cubs 2	A	2	1	0	1	18	56
12	Phillies 5, Cubs 3	A	2	1	0	2	18	58
14	Cubs 8, Giants 5	A	3	1	0	2	18	60
16	Cubs 8, Giants 5	A	4	1	0	1	18	61
19	Cubs 10, Braves 4	H	4	1	1	3	19	64
21*†	Cubs 5, Braves 4	H	5	3	1	2	20	66
22	Braves 3, Cubs 2	H	4	1	1	1	21	67
23	Cubs 21, Phillies 8	H	6	5	1	5	22	72
24	Cubs 6, Phillies 1	H	5	2	0	1	22	73
July 1	Giants 7, Cubs 5	H	3	2	1	1	23	74
2	Giants 9, Cubs 8	H	5	2	0	2	23	76
4‡	Pirates 5, Cubs 1	A	3	0	0	1	23	77
5	Cubs 12, Pirates 3	A	4	3	0	3	23	80
6†	Reds 5, Cubs 4	A	3	2	1	1	24	81
6‡	Reds 8, Cubs 7	A	4	2	0	1	24	82
16†	Cubs 6, Dodgers 4	A	3	1	0	2	24	84
18	Cubs 6, Dodgers 2	A	5	3	1	1	25	85
19	Cubs 5, Dodgers 4	A	3	1	1	2	26	87
20	Giants 13, Cubs 5	A	4	1	1	1	27	88
21	Cubs 6, Giants 0	A	5	2	2	3	29	91
24	Cubs 19, Phillies 15	A	5	2	0	1	29	92
25	Cubs 9, Phillies 5	A	3	1	0	1	29	93
26	Cubs 16, Phillies 2	A	5	3	3	5	32	98
27	Reds 6, Cubs 5	A	2	1	0	1	32	99
28†	Cubs 3, Reds 2	H	4	1	0	2	32	101
28‡	Cubs 5, Reds 3	H	4	1	0	1	32	102
29	Reds 4, Cubs 3	H	3	1	1	2	33	104
Aug. 1	Cubs 10, Pirates 7	H	3	1	0	2	33	106
2	Pirates 14, Cubs 8	H	5	2	1	1	34	107
3	Pirates 12, Cubs 8	H	4	2	1	2	35	109
5	Cubs 5, Cardinals 4	A	3	1	1	2	36	112
7	Cubs 6, Cardinals 5	A	3	2	0	3	36	114
10†	Cubs 6, Braves 0	H	4	2	2	4	38	118
10‡	Cubs 17, Braves 1	H	4	2	1	3	39	121
13	Dodgers 15, Cubs 5	H	4	2	1	2	40	123
14	Cubs 5, Dodgers 1	H	3	2	0	2	40	125
15§	Cubs 4, Dodgers 3	H	4	1	0	1	40	126
16†	Cubs 10, Phillies 9	H	5	2	1	3	41	129
17	Cubs 5, Phillies 4	H	3	1	0	2	41	131
18	Cubs 17, Phillies 3	H	5	4	1	4	42	135
19†	Phillies 9, Cubs 8	H	4	3	1	1	43	136
20	Phillies 10, Cubs 8	H	2	0	0	2	43	138
21	Giants 13, Cubs 6	H	5	1	0	2	43	140
22	Cubs 12, Giants 4	H	3	1	0	1	43	141
23	Cubs 4, Giants 2	H	3	1	0	3	43	144
26	Cubs 7, Pirates 5	H	3	2	1	4	44	148
27	Pirates 10, Cubs 8	H	5	2	0	3	44	151
30	Cubs 16, Cardinals 4	H	3	3	2	6	46	156
Sept. 3	Pirates 9, Cubs 6	A	5	3	0	1	46	158
4§	Cubs 10, Pirates 7	A	5	2	0	1	46	159
5	Pirates 8, Cubs 7	A	5	0	0	1	46	160
6	Cubs 19, Pirates 14	A	6	3	1	4	47	164
11	Dodgers 2, Cubs 1	A	4	1	1	1	48	165
12	Cubs 17, Phillies 4	A	5	5	1	6	49	171
15†	Phillies 12, Cubs 11	A	5	2	0	1	49	172
15‡	Cubs 6, Phillies 4	A	3	1	1	1	50	173
17	Cubs 5, Giants 2	A	4	3	2	4	52	177
19	Cubs 5, Braves 4	A	4	1	0	1	52	178
20	Braves 3, Cubs 2	A	3	1	0	1	52	179
22	Cubs 6, Braves 2	A	4	2	1	3	53	182
26	Cubs 7, Reds 5	H	4	2	1	3	54	185
27	Cubs 13, Reds 8	H	4	2	2	4	56	189
28	Cubs 13, Reds 11	H	3	2	0	2	56	191

* 12 innings. †First game of doubleheader. ‡ Second game of doubleheader. § 10 innings.

JOE DiMAGGIO'S 56-GAME HITTING STREAK—1941

Date	Opposing pitcher, Club	AB	R	H	2B	3B	HR	RBI
May 15	Eddie Smith, Chicago	4	0	1	0	0	0	1
16	Thornton Lee, Chicago	4	2	2	0	1	1	1
17	Johnny Rigney, Chicago	3	1	1	0	0	0	0
18	Bob Harris (2), Johnny Niggeling (1), St. Louis	3	3	3	1	0	0	1
19	Denny Galehouse, St. Louis	3	0	1	1	0	0	0
20	Eldon Auker, St. Louis	5	1	1	0	0	0	1
21	Schoolboy Rowe (1), Al Benton (1), Detroit	5	0	2	0	0	0	1
22	Archie McKain, Detroit	4	0	1	0	0	0	1
23	Dick Newsome, Boston	5	0	1	0	0	0	2
24	Earl Johnson, Boston	4	2	1	0	0	0	2
25	Lefty Grove, Boston	4	0	1	0	0	0	0
27	Ken Chase (1), Red Anderson (2), Alex Carrasquel (1), Washington	5	3	4	0	0	1	3
28	Sid Hudson, Washington	4	1	1	0	1	0	0
29	Steve Sundra, Washington	3	1	1	0	0	0	0
30	Earl Johnson, Boston	2	1	1	0	0	0	0
30	Mickey Harris, Boston	3	0	1	1	0	0	0
June 1	Al Milnar, Cleveland	4	1	1	0	0	0	0
1	Mel Harder, Cleveland	4	0	1	0	0	0	0
2	Bob Feller, Cleveland	4	2	2	1	0	0	0
3	Dizzy Trout, Detroit	4	1	1	0	0	1	1
5	Hal Newhouser, Detroit	5	1	1	0	1	0	1
7	Bob Muncrief (1), Johnny Allen (1), George Caster (1), St. Louis	5	2	3	0	0	0	1
8	Eldon Auker, St. Louis	4	3	2	0	0	2	4
8	George Caster (1), Jack Kramer (1), St. Louis	4	1	2	1	0	1	3
10	Johnny Rigney, Chicago	5	1	1	0	0	0	0
12	Thornton Lee, Chicago	4	1	2	0	0	1	1
14	Bob Feller, Cleveland	2	0	1	1	0	0	1
15	Jim Bagby, Cleveland	3	1	1	0	0	1	1
16	Al Milnar, Cleveland	5	0	1	1	0	0	0
17	Johnny Rigney, Chicago	4	1	1	0	0	0	0
18	Thornton Lee, Chicago	3	0	1	0	0	0	0
19	Eddie Smith (1), Buck Ross (2), Chicago	3	2	3	0	0	1	2
20	Bobo Newsom (2), Archie McKain (2), Detroit	5	3	4	1	0	0	1
21	Dizzy Trout, Detroit	4	0	1	0	0	0	1
22	Hal Newhouser (1), Bobo Newsom (1), Detroit	5	1	2	1	0	1	2
24	Bob Muncrief, St. Louis	4	1	1	0	0	0	0
25	Denny Galehouse, St. Louis	4	1	1	0	0	1	3
26	Eldon Auker, St. Louis	4	0	1	1	0	0	1
27	Chubby Dean, Philadelphia	3	1	2	0	0	1	2
28	Johnny Babich (1), Lum Harris (1), Philadelphia	5	1	2	1	0	0	0
29	Dutch E. Leonard, Washington	4	1	1	1	0	0	0
29	Red Anderson, Washington	5	1	1	0	0	0	1
July 1	Mickey Harris (1), Mike Ryba (1), Boston	4	0	2	0	0	0	1
1	Jack Wilson, Boston	3	1	1	0	0	0	1
2	Dick Newsome, Boston	5	1	1	0	0	1	3
5	Phil Marchildon, Philadelphia	4	2	1	0	0	1	2
6	Johnny Babich (1), Bump Hadley (3), Phi.	5	2	4	1	0	0	2
6	Jack Knott, Philadelphia	4	0	2	0	1	0	2
10	Johnny Niggeling, St. Louis	2	0	1	0	0	0	0
11	Bob Harris (3), Jack Kramer (1), St. Louis	5	1	4	0	0	1	2
12	Eldon Auker (1), Bob Muncrief (1), St. Louis	5	1	2	1	0	0	1
13	Ted Lyons (2), Jack Hallett (1), Chicago	4	2	3	0	0	0	0
13	Thornton Lee, Chicago	4	0	1	0	0	0	0
14	Johnny Rigney, Chicago	3	0	1	0	0	0	0
15	Eddie Smith, Chicago	4	1	2	1	0	0	2
16	Al Milnar (2), Joe Krakauskas (1), Cleveland	4	3	3	1	0	0	0
Totals for 56 games		223	56	91	16	4	15	55

Note: Numbers in parentheses refer to hits off each pitcher. Streak stopped July 17 at Cleveland, New York won, 4-3. First inning, Al Smith pitching, thrown out by Ken Keltner; fourth inning, Smith pitching, received base on balls; seventh inning, Smith pitching, thrown out by Keltner; eighth inning, Jim Bagby Jr., pitching, grounded into double play.

RICKEY HENDERSON'S 130-STEAL SEASON—1982

SB No.	Team Game	Date	Opposing pitcher, Club	Base	Inning
1	3	April 8	Mike Witt, California	2	1
2	3	April 8	Luis Sanchez, California	2	14
3	4	April 9	Gaylord Perry, Seattle	2	7
4	5	April*11	Floyd Bannister, Seattle	2	5
5	5	April*11	Ed Vande Berg, Seattle	2	12
6	7	April 13	Terry Felton, Minnesota	2	8
7	8	April 14	Brad Havens, Minnesota	2	1
8	8	April 14	Terry Felton, Minnesota	3	4
9	9	April 15	Al Williams, Minnesota	2	4
10	10	April 16	Floyd Bannister, Seattle	2	1
11	11	April 17	Mike Moore, Seattle	2‡	2
12	11	April 17	Larry Andersen, Seattle	2	4
13	12	April 18	Ed Nunez, Seattle	2	6
14	14	April 20	Al Williams, Minnesota	2	5
15	15	April 21	Darrell Jackson, Minnesota	3	1
16	16	April 23	Ken Forsch, California	3	1
17	16	April 23	Ken Forsch, California	2	3
18	19	April*28	Mike Flanagan, Baltimore	3‡	2
19	20	April†28	Scott McGregor, Baltimore	3	3
20	21	April 29	Dennis Martinez, Baltimore	2	1
21	21	April 29	Dennis Martinez, Baltimore	2	2
22	22	April 30	John Denny, Cleveland	2	5
23	23	May 1	Ed Whitson, Cleveland	2	9
24	23	May 1	Ed Whitson, Cleveland	3	9
25	24	May 2	Rick Waits, Cleveland	2	3
26	25	May 3	Tommy John, New York	2	5
27	27	May 6	John Denny, Cleveland	2	1
28	27	May 6	John Denny, Cleveland	3	1
29	29	May 8	Len Barker, Cleveland	2	1
30	29	May 8	Len Barker, Cleveland	3	1
31	29	May 8	Dan Spillner, Cleveland	2	9
32	30	May 9	Lary Sorensen, Cleveland	2	9
33	31	May 10	Tim Stoddard, Baltimore	3	9
34	32	May 11	Scott McGregor, Baltimore	2	1
35	32	May 11	Scott McGregor, Baltimore	2	3
36	36	May 15	George Frazier, New York	3‡	7
37	37	May 16	George Frazier, New York	2	5
38	37	May 16	George Frazier, New York	3	5
39	39	May 19	Dan Petry, Detroit	2	1
40	42	May 22	Bob Ojeda, Boston	2	1
41	42	May 22	Bob Ojeda, Boston	3	1
42	43	May 23	Dennis Eckersley, Boston	2‡	3
43	45	May 26	Bob McClure, Milwaukee	2	7
44	45	May 26	Dwight Bernard, Milwaukee	2	9
45	45	May 26	Dwight Bernard, Milwaukee	3	9
46	49	May 30*	Pat Underwood, Detroit	2	1
47	49	May 30*	Pat Underwood, Detroit	3	1
48	49	May 30*	Pat Underwood, Detroit	2	3
49	49	May 30*	Pat Underwood, Detroit	3	3
50	51	June 1	Chuck Rainey, Boston	2	1

SB No.	Team Game	Date	Opposing pitcher, Club	Base	Inning
51	51	June 1	Chuck Rainey, Boston	2	3
52	53	June 4	Moose Haas, Milwaukee	2	3
53	55	June 6	Pete Vuckovich, Milwaukee	3	1
54	55	June 6	Pete Vuckovich, Milwaukee	2	3
55	57	June 8	Dennis Lamp, Chicago	2‡	5
56	57	June 8	Jerry Koosman, Chicago	2	7
57	57	June 8	Jerry Koosman, Chicago	3	7
58	58	June 9	LaMarr Hoyt, Chicago	2	3
59	61	June 13	Luis Leal, Toronto	2	2
60	61	June 13	Roy Jackson, Toronto	2	7
61	61	June 13	Roy Jackson, Toronto	3	7
62	61	June 13	Dale Murray, Toronto	2	8
63	62	June 14	Jerry Garvin, Toronto	2	7
64	63	June 15	LaMarr Hoyt, Chicago	2	1
65	66	June 18	Jerry Garvin, Toronto	2	1
66	66	June 18	Roy Jackson, Toronto	2	7
67	70	June 22	Dan Quisenberry, Kansas City	2	8
68	70	June 22	Dan Quisenberry, Kansas City	3	8
69	73	June 25	Frank Tanana, Texas	2	1
70	73	June 25	Frank Tanana, Texas	2	3
71	74	June 26	Steve Comer, Texas	2	8
72	77	June 29	Don Hood, Kansas City	3	5
73	78	June 30	Paul Splittorff, Kansas City	2	1
74	79	July 2	Charlie Hough, Texas	2	3
75	79	July 2	Charlie Hough, Texas	3	9
76	80	July 3	Rick Honeycutt, Texas	2	5
77	81	July 4	Doc Medich, Texas	2	2
78	83	July 6	Len Barker, Cleveland	2	1
79	83	July 6	Len Barber, Cleveland	2	5
80	85	July 8	Doyle Alexander, New York	2	1
81	85	July 8	Doyle Alexander, New York	3‡	1
82	86	July 9	Scott McGregor, Baltimore	3	1
83	87	July 10	Dennis Martinez, Baltimore	3	1
84	88	July 11	Storm Davis, Baltimore	2	3
85	89	July 15	Mike Morgan, New York	2	5
86	90	July 16	Roger Erickson, New York	2	1
87	93	July 19	Lary Sorensen, Cleveland	2	3
88	94	July 20	Ed Whitson, Cleveland	2	7
89	94	July 20	Ed Whitson, Cleveland	3‡	7
90	97	July 24	Scott McGregor, Baltimore	2	6
91	97	July 24	Scott McGregor, Baltimore	3	6
92	98	July 25	Dennis Martinez, Baltimore	2	7
93	99	July 26	Ken Forsch, California	2	1
94	99	July 26	Andy Hassler, California	H‡	8
95	100	July 27	Dave Goltz, California	2	9
96	102	July 29	Brad Havens, Minnesota	3‡	1
97	103	July 30	Al Williams, Minnesota	2	1
98	103	July 30	Al Williams, Minnesota	3	1
99	103	July 30	Ron Davis, Minnesota	2	8
100	106	Aug. 2	Mike Stanton, Seattle	2	7
101	108	Aug. 4†	Jim Beattie, Seattle	2	1
102	109	Aug. 4*	Rich Bordi, Seattle	2	1
103	109	Aug. 4*	Rich Bordi, Seattle	3	1
104	110	Aug. 6	Frank Viola, Minnesota	2	6
105	112	Aug. 8	Brad Havens, Minnesota	2	3
106	115	Aug. 11	Floyd Bannister, Seattle	2	5
107	115	Aug. 11	Floyd Bannister, Seattle	3	5
108	117	Aug. 14	Steve Renko, California	2	5
109	118	Aug. 15	Ken Forsch, California	2	3
110	120	Aug. 17	Moose Haas, Milwaukee	2	1
111	122	Aug. 19	Jim Slaton, Milwaukee	2	7
112	124	Aug. 21	Chuck Rainey, Boston	2	1
113	124	Aug. 21	Chuck Rainey, Boston	2	3
114	124	Aug. 21	Luis Aponte, Boston	2	8
115	126	Aug. 23	Dan Petry, Detroit	2	3
116	127	Aug. 24	Jerry Ujdur, Detroit	2	1
117	127	Aug. 24	Jerry Ujdur, Detroit	3‡	1
118	128	Aug. 26	Mike Caldwell, Milwaukee	2	1
119	129	Aug. 27	Doc Medich, Milwaukee	2	3
120	129	Aug. 27	Doc Medich, Milwaukee	2	6
121	129	Aug. 27	Doc Medich, Milwaukee	2	8
122	129	Aug. 27	Doc Medich, Milwaukee	3	8
123	132	Aug. 30	Mark Clear, Boston	3	8
124	135	Sept. 3	Jerry Ujdur, Detroit	2	1
125	154	Sept. 25	Dennis Leonard, Kansas City	2	4
126	158	Sept. 28	Jim Farr, Texas	2	6
127	161	Oct. 1	Bill Castro, Kansas City	2	3
128	162	Oct. 2	Vida Blue, Kansas City	2	2
129	162	Oct. 2	Vida Blue, Kansas City	2	4
130	162	Oct. 2	Vida Blue, Kansas City	3	4

*Second game of doubleheader. †First game of doubleheader. ‡Part of double steal.
Note: Oakland played 162 games and Henderson played in 149.

On the covers

Front (above)

Alex Rodriguez (Photo by Robert Seale/Sporting News).

Back

Photos by (clockwise from top left): Dilip Vishwanat/Sporting News, Dilip Vishwanat/Sporting News, Robert Seale/Sporting News, Dilip Vishwanat/Sporting News, John Cordes for the Sporting News.

Contributing Photographers

Albert Dickson/Sporting News—Pages 9, 79, 135, 168, 169, 241R.

Robert Seale/Sporting News—Pages 10, 118, 119, 140, 245.

Major League Baseball Photos—Page 11L, R.

Dilip Vishwanat/Sporting News—Pages 73, 80, 131, 132, 133, 134, 136, 137, 141, 324, 328.

Tom Hauck for the Sporting News—Page 74.

John Cordes for the Sporting News—Pages 138, 167, 378.

Doug Devoe for the Sporting News—Pages 241L, 243.

Steve Russell for the Sporting News—Page 249.

Bob Leverone/Sporting News—Page 327B.

Sporting News Archives—Pages 143-160, 162-166, 247, 257-417.